MOTOR
IMPORTED CAR REPAIR MANUAL

3rd Edition

Editor
Louis C. Forier, SAE

Managing Editor
Larry Solnik, SAE

Associate Editors
Michael Kromida, SAE · Dan Irizarry, SAE · Warren Schildknecht, SAE

Editorial Assistants
Bob Noskowicz · Katherine Keen

Published by
MOTOR

1790 Broadway, New York, N. Y. 10019

The Automotive Business Magazine

Printed in the U.S.A. © Copyright 1978 by The Hearst Corporation
Library of Congress Catalog Number: 77-95231

ISBN 0-910992-91-6

INDEX

This Edition Covers Mechanical Specifications and Service Procedures on 1972-77 Popular Models & 1978 Fiesta

AUSTIN MARINA

INDEX OF SERVICE OPERATIONS

AUSTIN MARINA

GENERAL ENGINE SPECIFICATIONS

Year	Engine	Carburetor	Bore & Stroke	Piston Displacement Cubic Inches	Compression Ratio	Maximum Brake H.P. @ R.P.M.	Maximum Torque Lbs. Ft. @ R.P.M.	Normal Oil Pressure
1973-75	4—109.7	1 Barrel	3.160 x 3.50	109.7	8.0	77 @ —	87 @ 2750	50—70

TUNE UP SPECIFICATIONS

The following specifications are published from the latest information available. This date should be used only in the absence of a decal affixed in the engine compartment.

▲Before removing wires from distributor cap, determine location of the No. 1 wire in cap, as distributor position may have been altered from that shown at the end of this chart.

Year	Sparkplug		Distributor		Ignition Timing			Carb. Adjustment			
								Hot Idle Speed		Idle "CO"%	
	Type	Gap Inch	Point Gap Inch	Dwell Angle Deg.	Firing Order Fig.	Timing BTDC ①	Mark Location	Std. Trans.	Auto. Trans.	Std. Trans.	Auto. Trans.
1973-75	N9Y	.035	.014—.016	57—63	②	③	④	850	850	2	2

①—BTDC: Before top dead center.
②—Firing order 1,3,4,2. Timed at No. 1 cylinder located at front of engine.
③—Exc. 1975, 12° BTDC; 1975, 10° BTDC. Timed at 1500 R.P.M. with vacuum line at distributor disconnected & plugged.
④—Mark located on pulley.

STARTING MOTOR SPECIFICATIONS

Year	Model	Brush Spring Tension Oz.	Minimum Brush Length In.	Resistance Test			Lock Torque Test	
				Amps.	Torque Ft. Lbs.	R.P.M.	Amps.	Torque Ft. Lbs.
1973-75	Lucas 2M100	36	⅜	300	7.3	1000	463	14.4

VALVE SPECIFICATIONS

Year	Valve Lash		Valve Angles		Valve Spring Installed Height	Stem Clearance		Stem Diameter	
	Int.	Exh.	Seat	Face		Intake	Exhaust	Intake	Exhaust
1973-75	.013H	.013H	45½	—	1.44	.0008—.0018	.0014—.0024	.3429—.3434	.3423—.3428

ALTERNATOR & REGULATOR SPECIFICATIONS

Year	Alternator		Regulator
	Model	Rated Output @ 14 Volts 6000 R.P.M.	Model
1973-75	Lucas 17ACR	36	14TR

BRAKE SPECIFICATIONS

Year	Brake Drum Inside Diameter	Wheel Cylinder Bore		Master Cylinder Bore Diameter
		Front Disc	Rear Drum	
1973-75	8	—	①	.75

①—Early models, .625"; Late models, .70".

AUSTIN MARINA

ENGINE TIGHTENING SPECIFICATIONS*

*Torque specifications are for clean and lightly lubricated threads only. Dry or dirty threads increase friction which prevents accurate measurement of tightness.

Year	Cylinder Head Bolts Ft. Lbs.	Manifold to Cylinder Head Ft. Lbs.	Rocker shaft Nuts Ft. Lbs.	Rocker Arm Cover Ft. Lbs.	Connecting Rod Cap Bolts Ft. Lbs.	Main Bearing Cap Bolts Ft. Lbs.	Flywheel to Crankshaft Ft. Lbs.	Vibration Damper or Pulley Ft. Lbs.
1973-75	45—50	15	25	4	33	70	40	70—80

COOLING SYSTEM & CAPACITY DATA

Year	Cooling Capacity, Pts. Less A/C	Cooling Capacity, Pts. With A/C	Radiator Cap Relief Pressure Lbs.	Thermo. Opening Temp.	Fuel Tank Gals.	Engine Oil Refill Qts.	Transmission Oil Manual Trans. Pints	Transmission Oil Auto. Trans. Pints	Rear Axle Oil Pints
1973-75	10¾	10¾	15	180	13	4①	1¾	11½②	1½

①—Includes filter.
②—13 with oil cooler.

PISTONS, PINS, RINGS, CRANKSHAFT & BEARING

Year	Piston Clearance Top Of Skirt	Ring End Gap① Comp	Ring End Gap① Oil	Wrist Pin Diameter	Rod Bearings Shaft Diameter	Rod Bearings Bearing Clearance	Main Bearings Shaft Diameter	Main Bearings Bearing Clearance	Main Bearings Thrust on Bearing No.	Main Bearings Shaft End Play
1973-75	.0021—.0037	.012	.015	.8126	1.8759—1.8764	.0015—.0032	2.1262—2.127	.0010—.0027	3	.002—.003

①—Fit rings in tapered bore for clearance listed in tightest portion of ring travel.

WHEEL ALIGNMENT SPECIFICATIONS

Year	Caster Angle, Degrees Limits	Caster Angle, Degrees Desired	Camber Angle, Degrees Limits	Camber Angle, Degrees Desired	Kingpin Inclination Degrees	Toe-In Inch.
1973-75	+½ to +2½	+2	−1¹/₆ to +1¹/₁₂	+⁸/₆	7½	¹/₁₆

Electrical Section

NOTE: All work should be done with the battery disconnected.

DISTRIBUTOR, REPLACE
Removal

1. Rotate crankshaft until groove in crankshaft pulley lines up with static ignition pointer on timing indicator. The distributor rotor should point to that part of the distributor cap that is connected to No. 1 spark plug, Fig. 1.
2. Remove distributor cap and disconnect primary lead from distributor.
3. Disconnect vacuum line from vacuum advance and remove two screws holding distributor clamp flange to cylinder block.
4. Remove distributor.

Installation

1. Reverse removal procedure to the point of attaching the distributor cap.

NOTE: Do not tighten flange retaining screws.

2. With crankshaft and rotor positioned as above, rotate distributor within limits of slotted holes in flange until breaker points just open.
3. Tighten retaining screws to 8 to 10 ft. lbs. and complete installation.

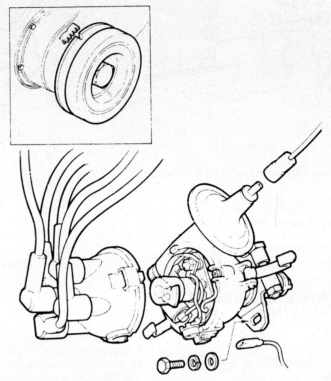

Fig. 1 Distributor removal & installation

ALTERNATOR, REPLACE
Removal

1. Loosen adjusting link retaining nut.
2. Remove connector from its socket in the alternator end cover.
3. Remove hardware from each mounting.
4. Remove adjusting link retaining bolt and washer.
5. Remove drive belt.
6. Remove alternator.

Installation

1. Reverse procedure to install, leaving bolts loose.

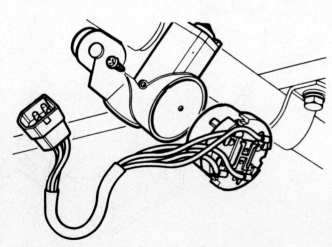

Fig. 2 Ignition switch removal & installation

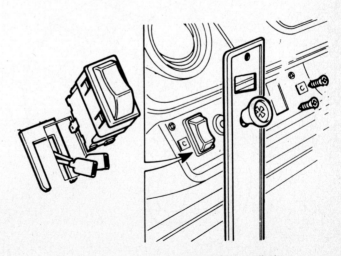

Fig. 3 Headlight switch removal & installation

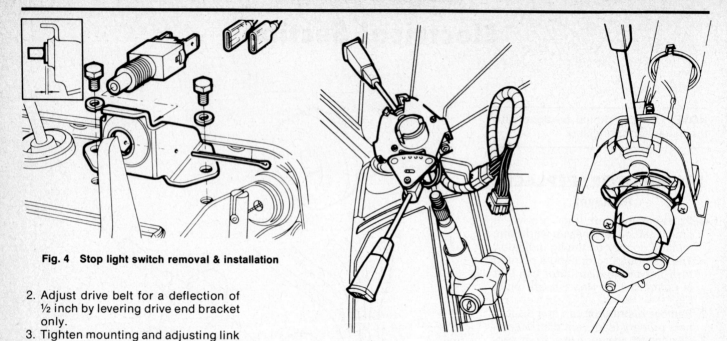

Fig. 4   Stop light switch removal & installation

2. Adjust drive belt for a deflection of ½ inch by levering drive end bracket only.
3. Tighten mounting and adjusting link hardware.

Fig. 5   Combination switch removal & installation

ALTERNATOR ON VEHICLE TESTING

1. Remove cable connector from alternator.
2. Connect ground side of a voltmeter to ground.
3. Switch on ignition switch.
4. Connect positive side of voltmeter to each of the alternator cable connectors in turn. Battery voltage must be reaching the alternator before you proceed.

5. Reconnect cable connector to alternator. Disconnect brown cable with eyelet from terminal on starter motor solenoid. Connect an ammeter between brown cable and terminal. Connect a voltmeter across battery. Run engine at 6,000 rpm. If a zero ammeter reading shows, remove and overhaul alternator. If ammeter reads below 10 amps and

voltmeter reads between 13.6-14.4 volts, check the alternator on a bench. Alternator output should be 36 amps at 14 volts at 6,000 rpm. If ammeter reads below 10 amps and voltmeter reads below 13.6 volts, replace voltage regulator. If ammeter reads above 10 amps and voltmeter reads above 14.4 volts, replace voltage regulator.

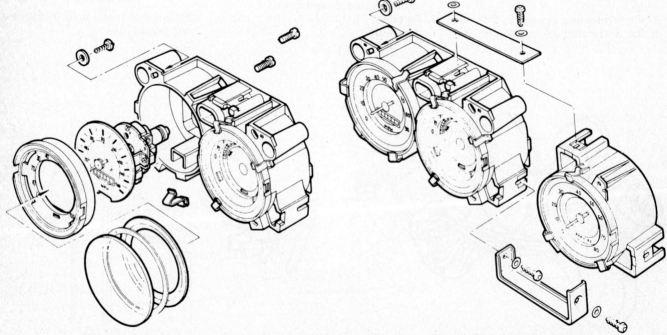

Fig. 6   Instrument clutcher

Fig. 7   Tachometer removal

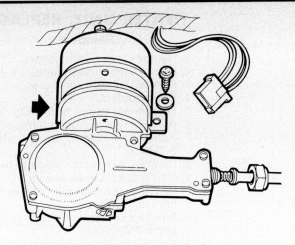

Fig. 8   W/S wiper motor removal

STARTER MOTOR, REPLACE

1. Detach all leads from terminals on starter solenoid switch.
2. Remove hardware holding starter to engine.
3. Remove starter.

IGNITION/STARTER/ STEERING LOCK SWITCH, REPLACE

1. Remove four screws holding switch cowls.
2. Remove switch cowls.
3. Disconnect electric leads at harness connections, Fig. 2.
4. Remove screw retaining switch in lock housing.
5. Remove switch.
6. Follow a reverse procedure to install switch, but notice that locating cam on switch sets in groove in lock housing.

LIGHT SWITCH, REPLACE

1. Pull choke control knob out as far as possible.
2. Remove two screws holding cover plate.
3. Lift back cover plate and disconnect wires from terminal on rear of light switch, Fig. 3.
4. Remove switch using tool 18G1201.

STOPLIGHT SWITCH, REPLACE

1. Disconnect all wiring from switch, Fig. 4.
2. Remove screws holding switch mounting bracket, and remove the

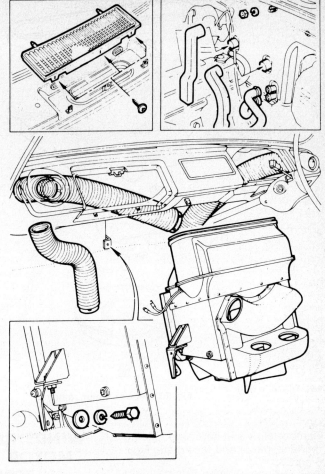

Fig. 9   Heater unit removal

bracket and switch assembly.
3. Remove the cotter pin holding the switch, and unscrew the switch from the bracket.
4. To replace, screw the switch into the bracket until one complete thread of the switch housing can be seen on the pedal side of the bracket.

DIMMER/FLASHER, DIRECTIONAL SIGNAL, HORN SWITCH, REPLACE

Removal

1. Remove steering column cowl.
2. Remove cover from center of the steering wheel.
3. Remove steering wheel retainer nut.
4. Mark relation of the steering wheel to inner steering column.
5. Remove steering wheel using tools 18G2 and 18G2E.
6. Disconnect switch wires at connector under the dash.
7. Loosen switch clamp screw and lift switch from steering column, Fig. 5.

Installation

Reverse procedure to install, but note the following:
1. The lug on the inner diameter of the switch fits into the slot in the outer steering column.
2. The striker cam on the nylon switch center is in line with and toward the switch handle.

INSTRUMENT CLUSTER, REPLACE

1. Remove four screws holding instrument panel. Note that the two longest screws are on top.
2. Press release lever on speedometer cable to disconnect cable.
3. Disconnect electric multi-connector from rear of the panel.
4. Disconnect lead at rear of tachometer.
5. Remove instrument panel.
6. Remove four screws holding instrument pack to instrument panel.
7. Remove hardware from rear of gauges.

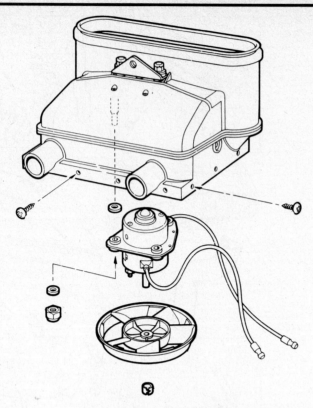

Fig. 10 Blower motor removal

HEATER UNIT, REPLACE
Removal

1. Remove lower dash panel.
2. Remove instrument panel.
3. Remove tubes from heater.
4. Drain coolant.
5. Disconnect heater hoses, Fig. 9.
6. Remove two plenum drain tubes.
7. Remove nut holding top of heater to bulkhead.
8. Remove two bolts holding heater side brackets to bulkhead.
9. Disconnect heater motor leads from harness connector.
10. Pull top of heater to rear to clear upper fixing stud.
11. Pull lower part of the heater to rear until heater is tipped and can be removed under panel support rail on passenger side.

Installation

1. Remove three screws holding air intake grille.
2. Remove grille.
3. Position heater on top stud and fit nut and washer loosely.
4. Through air intake grille, fit seal over grille housing panel.
5. Complete installation by reversing procedures used in removal.

BLOWER MOTOR, REPLACE

1. Remove the heater unit as outlined under Heater Unit, Replace.
2. Remove heater plenum chamber attaching screws.
3. Lift plenum chamber clear of heater body.
4. Remove three nuts holding blower motor, Fig. 10.
5. Remove clip holding fan and remove fan.

8. Remove clips and hardware holding the lens, panel and face plate, Figs. 6 and 7.
9. Remove fuel and temperature gauges.
10. Remove two screws holding speedometer and three clips holding lens and bezel.
11. Remove speedometer.

WINDSHIELD WIPER MOTOR & DRIVE, REPLACE

1. Remove wiper arms and blades.
2. Remove screw holding wiper motor clamp band, Fig. 8.
3. Disconnect wiper drive cable tube securing nut.
4. Disconnect electric connector from motor.
5. Press motor clamp band into release slot and lift motor clear.
6. Pull drive cable from tube.

Engine Section

ENGINE, REPLACE
Removal

1. Remove hood.
2. Drain cooling system.
3. Remove radiator and battery.
4. Remove air cleaner assembly and temperature control valve.
5. Remove hot and cold air intake hoses.
6. Remove carburetor assembly.
7. Remove all lines, hoses and cables

that would interfere with removal of engine.
8. Support engine using a lifting sling. The center of lift should be at a point above oil dipstick.
9. Raise the front of the vehicle.

NOTE: Fit suitable safety supports.

10. Disconnect exhaust pipe from exhaust manifold. Support exhaust system.

11. Remove starter motor.
12. Remove bolts holding oil pan connecting plate to flywheel housing.
13. Remove lower bolts holding flywheel housing and support transmission.
14. Remove upper bolts holding flywheel housing.

NOTE: The bolt next to the oil pressure switches support the battery ground.

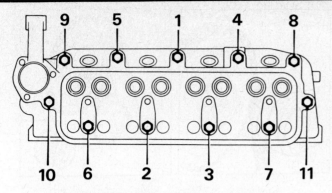

Fig. 1 Cylinder head tightening sequence

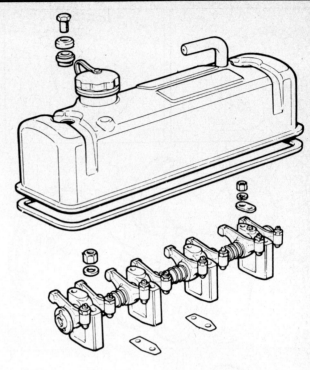

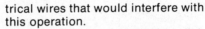

Fig. 2 Rocker shaft assembly

15. Remove nut holding each mount rubber to engine bracket.
16. Remove bolts and nuts holding each engine mount to chassis.
17. Remove engine mounts.
18. Move engine assembly forward until clutch cover is clear of input shaft.
19. Lift engine from the car.

Installation

1. Lubricate bore of input shaft bushing with a high melting point grease.
2. Lower engine into vehicle.
3. Move engine to rear, engaging splines on input shaft with splines of clutch driven plate.
4. Position engine mounts and loosely attach engine bracket.
5. Fit and tighten engine mount bolts, flywheel housing and oil pan connecting plate bolts.
6. Remove transmission support and engine lift and complete installation.

CYLINDER HEAD, REPLACE
Removal

1. Drain cooling system.
2. Disconnect all hoses, lines and electrical wires that would interfere with this operation.
3. Loosen air pump adjusting link bolts and remove air pump.
4. Remove outer heat shield.
5. Remove air cleaner assembly.
6. Remove intake and exhaust manifolds and carburetor.
7. Remove air temperature control inner heat shield.
8. Remove rocker shaft and pushrods.

NOTE: Keep pushrods in order.

9. Remove air injection system air rail.
10. Remove cylinder head nuts.

NOTE: Before removing, note the position of the special nut fitted to retain the air rail.

11. Remove cylinder head.

Installation

Reverse procedure to install. Fit a new cylinder head gasket so end marked "Front" faces water pump and side marked "Top" faces upward. Tighten cylinder head nuts gradually in the sequence shown in Fig. 1.

ROCKER SHAFT, REPLACE

1. Drain cooling system.
2. Remove vacuum line from manifold.
3. Loosen two cap nuts and remove rocker cover.

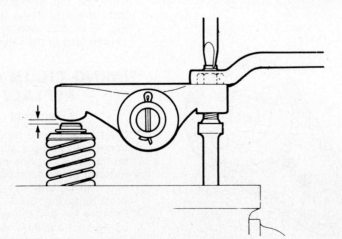

Fig. 3 Adjusting valve clearance

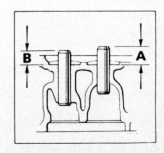

Fig. 4 Valve guide installation

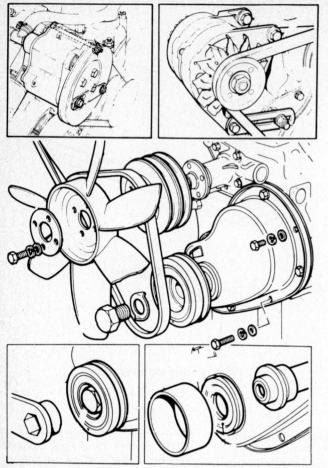

Fig. 5   Timing chain cover replacement

Fig. 6   Timing chain removal & installation

4. Evenly loosen and remove eight nuts holding rocker shaft brackets to cylinder head.
5. Remove lockwasher from rear rocker shaft bracket.
6. Remove rocker shaft, Fig. 2.

NOTE: Retrieve shims below two center brackets.

VALVES, ADJUST

1. Remove rocker cover.
2. Check clearance between valve rocker arms and valve stems in the following order:
    Check No. 1 valve with No. 8 fully open
    Check No. 3 valve with No. 6 fully open
    Check No. 5 valve with No. 4 fully open
    Check No. 2 valve with No. 7 fully open
    Check No. 8 valve with No. 1 fully open
    Check No. 6 valve with No. 3 fully open

    Check No. 4 valve with No. 5 fully open
    Check No. 7 valve with No. 2 fully open
3. Loosen locknut and rotate screw clockwise to decrease clearance or counterclockwise to increase clearance, Fig. 3.
4. Retighten locknut, holding screw against rotation.

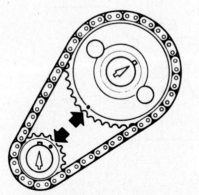

Fig. 7   Valve timing marks

VALVE GUIDE SERVICE

1. Press out worn valve guides.
2. Press in new intake valve guides from top of cylinder head until top of guide at "A," Fig. 4, is .75 inch above the machined face of the valve spring seat.
3. Press in new exhaust valve guides from the top of the cylinder head until the top of the guide at "B," Fig. 4, is .625 inch above the machined face of the valve spring seat.

TIMING CHAIN COVER, REPLACE

Removal

1. Drain coolant and remove radiator.
2. Loosen air pump attaching bolt, air pump adjusting link pivot bolts, alternator attachment bolts and alternator pivot link nut, and remove drive belts, Fig. 5.
3. Remove fan and pulley.
4. Using tool 18G98A, remove crankshaft pulley retaining bolt.
5. Remove crankshaft pulley.

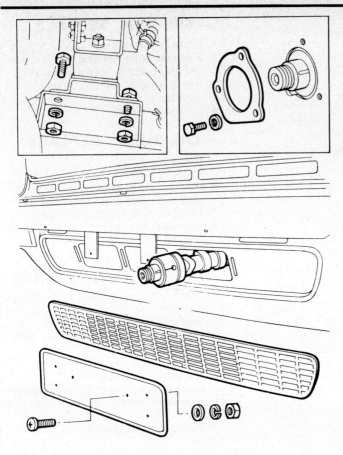

Fig. 8 Camshaft replacement

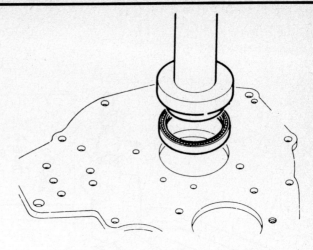

Fig. 9 Crankshaft rear oil seal installation

6. Remove hardware from timing gear cover and remove cover.
7. Remove oil seal from cover.

Installation

1. Dip a new oil seal in oil and fit the new seal to the cover using tools 18G134 and 18G134BD.

NOTE: The lip of the seal must face inward.

2. Replace front cover gasket if damaged.
3. Using tool 18G1046, center oil seal on crankshaft as you position the cover.
4. Complete reassembly, adjusting alternator and air pump belt tension.

TIMING CHAIN & GEARS, REPLACE

Removal

1. Remove timing chain cover.
2. Remove oil slinger.
3. Remove two screws holding chain tensioner, Fig. 6.
4. Remove chain tensioner and gasket.

5. Remove camshaft nut lock.
6. Using tool 18G98A, remove camshaft nut.
7. Remove timing chain and gears.

Installation

1. Rotate crankshaft so keyways are at TDC.
2. Rotate camshaft so keyway is at 2 o'clock.
3. Fit gears, checking alignment and gap with a straightedge.
4. Remove crankshaft drive keys, and select and fit shims as needed to properly refit the drive keys.
5. Assemble timing chain and gears with timing mark on each gear facing each other, Fig. 7.
6. Complete installation.

CAMSHAFT, REPLACE

Removal

1. Drain cooling system.
2. Remove radiator, rocker shaft, distributor drive shaft, tappets, fuel pump, timing chain cover, timing chain and gears, and hardware holding the camshaft lockplate.

3. Remove number plate and drill out the rivets holding the air intake grille.
4. Support engine.
5. Remove bolts holding engine mounts to chassis.
6. Lower engine until camshaft aligns with air intake grille opening.
7. Remove camshaft, Fig. 8.

Installation

1. Assemble camshaft lockplate and gear to camshaft.
2. Check camshaft end play. Specification: .003 to .007 inch.
3. Replace lockplate if end play is excessive.
4. Remove lockplate and gear.
5. Reverse procedure to install.

CRANKSHAFT REAR OIL SEAL, REPLACE

Removal

1. Remove transmission, clutch, flywheel and transmission adaptor plate.
2. Remove crankshaft rear oil seal from transmission adaptor plate using tool Nos. 18G134 and 18G134CQ.

Installation

1. Lubricate a new oil seal with SAE 90 EP oil.
2. Press new seal into transmission adaptor plate using tool Nos. 18G134 and 18G134CQ, Fig. 9.

NOTE: The lips of the seal face the front of the engine and must be flush with front face of transmission adaptor plate.

3. Complete installation.

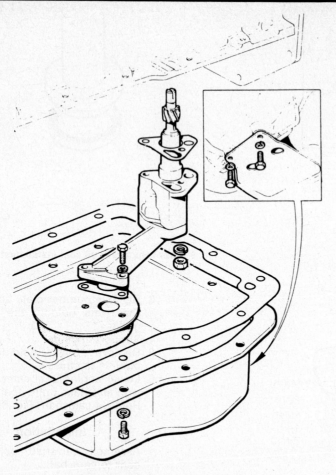

Fig. 10   Oil pump replacement

OIL PAN, REPLACE

1. Drain crankcase.
2. Remove bolts holding oil pan connecting plate to flywheel housing.
3. Remove bolts holding oil pan to engine block.
4. Remove oil pan.

OIL PUMP, REPLACE

1. Drain crankcase.
2. Remove oil pan.
3. Remove bolts holding oil strainer.
4. Remove oil strainer and gasket.
5. Remove nuts holding oil pump.
6. Remove oil pump and gasket, Fig. 10.

WATER PUMP, REPLACE

1. Drain cooling system and remove radiator.
2. Remove fan and drive pulley.
3. Remove screws holding air pump adjusting link.
4. Remove top mounting screw and nut holding alternator.
5. Disconnect hose from water pump.
6. Remove water pump attaching bolts.
7. Remove water pump.

FUEL PUMP, REPLACE

1. Disconnect fuel lines.
2. Remove two nuts holding pump.
3. Remove fuel pump.

Carburetor Section

CARBURETOR ADJUSTMENT

1. Remove air cleaner.
2. Check throttle for sticking.
3. Unscrew throttle adjusting screw (3), Fig. 2, until it is just clear of throttle lever. Be sure throttle is closed. Turn screw clockwise one and one-half full turns.
4. Raise piston, (4) Fig. 2, of carburetor with lifting pin and check to see that it falls freely on to the bridge when the pin is released. If the piston sticks at all, the carburetor should be overhauled.
5. Lift and support the piston clear of the bridge so the jet is visible. If this isn't possible to do because of the way in which the carburetor is installed, remove the suction piston chamber to get at the jet.
6. Turn the jet adjusting screw, (6) Fig. 2, counterclockwise until the jet is flush with the bridge or is as high as possible without exceeding the height of the bridge.
7. Check that needle shank is flush with bottom of piston, (7) Fig. 2.
8. Turn jet adjusting screw, (8) Fig. 2, two turns clockwise.
9. Turn fast idle adjusting screw, (9) Fig. 2, counterclockwise until it is clear of cam.
10. Reinstall suction piston chamber if it was removed, (10) Fig. 2. Using the lifting pin, check to see that the piston falls freely onto the bridge.
11. Fill piston damper reservoir with oil until the level is ½ inch above the top of the hollow piston rod.
12. Connect a tachometer.
13. Run engine at fast idle speed until it reaches normal operating temperature.
14. Increase engine speed to 2,500 rpm.

for 30 seconds.
15. Connect an exhaust gas analyzer.

NOTE: During the adjustment procedure, if the correct setting cannot be obtained within three minutes, increase engine speed to 2,500 rpm for 30 seconds.

16. Adjust the throttle adjusting screw, (16) Fig. 3, to get the specified idling speed.

NOTE: During the following procedure, just before taking readings on the tachometer and exhaust gas analyzer, tap the neck of the suction chamber with a light non-metallic instrument such as the handle of a screwdriver.

17. Turn the jet adjusting screw, (17) Fig. 3, clockwise (to enrich) or

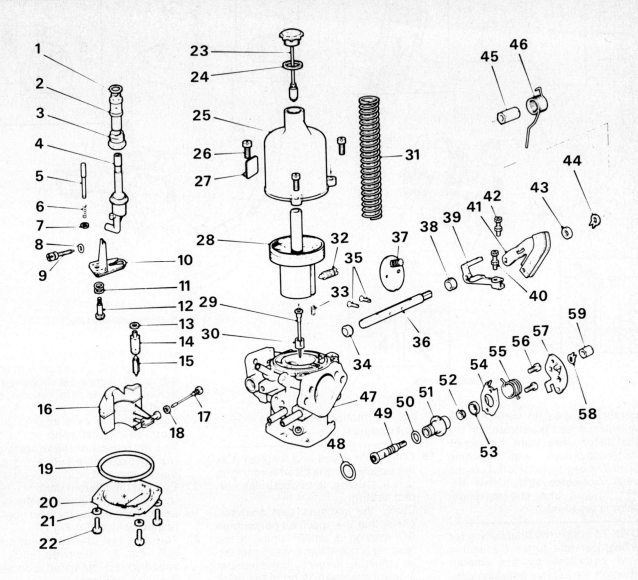

1. Jet bearing washer
2. Jet bearing
3. Jet bearing nut
4. Jet and head assembly
5. Lifting pin
6. Lifting pin spring
7. Circlip
8. Adjusting screw seal
9. Jet adjusting screw
10. Bi-metal jet lever
11. Jet lever spring
12. Jet lever screw
13. Needle seat washer (if required)
14. Float needle seat
15. Float needle
16. Float
17. Float pivot
18. Pivot seal
19. Float chamber cover seal
20. Float chamber cover

21. Spring washer
22. Cover screw
23. Piston damper
24. Damper washer
25. Suction chamber
26. Chamber screw
27. Identity tag
28. Piston
29. Jet needle
30. Needle guide
31. Piston spring
32. Needle retaining screw
33. Needle spring
34. Throttle spindle seal
35. Throttle disc screws
36. Throttle spindle
37. Throttle disc
38. Throttle spindle seal
39. Throttle actuating lever

40. Fast idle screw
41. Throttle lever
42. Throttle adjusting screw
43. Plain washer
44. Tab washer
45. Retaining nut
46. Throttle spring
47. Body
48. Cold start seal
49. Cold start spindle
50. 'O' ring
51. Cold start body
52. Spindle seal
53. End cover
54. Retaining plate
55. Cold start spring
56. Retaining screw
57. Fast idle cam
58. Tab washer
59. Retaining nut

Fig. 1 Disassembled view of type HIF carburetor

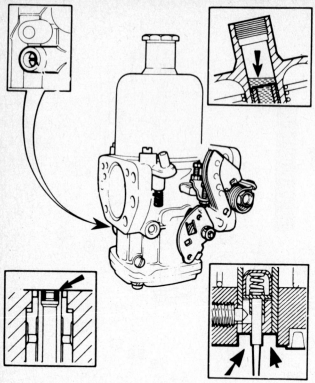

Fig. 2 Carburetor adjustments

Fig. 3 Carburetor adjustments

counterclockwise (to weaken) until the fastest speed is indicated on the tachometer. Now, turn the screw counterclockwise until engine speed just begins to fall off. Turn the screw clockwise very slowly the least amount until the maximum speed is regained.

NOTE: To obtain the final setting for the best lean idle, turn the adjusting screw clockwise by the amount shown on the vehicle emission control information label in the engine compartment.

18. Check idle speed and readjust it as necessary with the throttle adjusting screw, (18) Fig. 3, to obtain the correct setting.
19. Using the exhaust gas analyzer, check that the specified percentage CO reading is within limits. If the reading is not within limits, reset the jet adjusting screw by the minimum amount necessary to bring the read-

ing just within limits. If an adjustment exceeding one-half turn of the adjusting screw is required to achieve this, the carburetor must be overhauled.
20. With fast idle cam against return stop, check that there is $1/16$ inch free movement of the mixture control (choke) cable before the cable moves the cam.
21. Pull out the mixture control (choke) until the arrow marked on the cam is positioned under the fast idle adjusting screw, (21) Fig. 3.
22. Turn the fast idle adjusting screw, (22) Fig. 3, clockwise until the specified fast idle speed is obtained.
23. Refit the air cleaner.

Emission Controls Section

EGR VALVE
Testing

To check the operation of the EGR valve, warm up the engine, and open and close the throttle several times. Observe or feel the EGR valve, which should open and close with changes in engine speed. The EGR valve should close at once when the throttle is closed.

Service
1. Remove the EGR valve from the exhaust manifold.
2. Clean valve seat with a wire brush.
3. Insert valve opening into a standard spark plug machine and lift the diaphragm.
4. Blast the valve for 30 seconds.
5. Use compressed air and a brush to remove all traces of carbon.

FUEL ABSORPTION CANISTER, REPLACE

1. Disconnect all lines at the canister, Fig. 1.
2. Remove the bracket nut and bolt.
3. Remove the canister.
4. Transfer the restrictor in the old canister to the new canister.
5. Install the new canister.

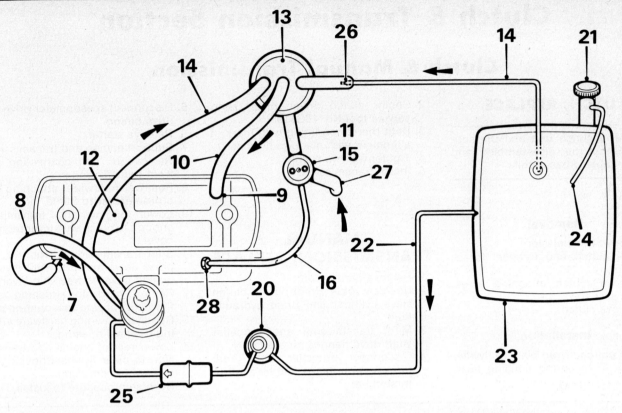

7. Oil separator/flame trap
8. Breather pipe
9. Restricted connection
10. Purge line
11. Running-on control hose
12. Sealed oil filler cap
13. Charcoal adsorption canister

14. Vapour lines
15. Running-on control valve
16. Running-on control pipe
20. Fuel pump
21. Sealed fuel filler cap
22. Fuel pipe

23. Fuel tank
24. Capacity limiting pipe
25. Fuel line filter
26. Restrictor
27. Air vent pipe
28. Inlet manifold connection

Fig. 1 Evaporative emission control system

CATALYTIC CONVERTER, REPLACE

1. Remove the catalytic converter support bracket.
2. Release the catalytic converter from the tailpipe.

NOTE: It may now be necessary to remove the carburetor.

3. Remove the nuts holding the catalytic converter and front pipe to the exhaust manifold.
4. Remove the catalytic converter and front pipe, and exhaust manifold gasket.
5. Fit a new catalytic converter.
6. Reset the catalytic converter warning indicator to zero.

AIR PUMP BELT TENSION, ADJUST

1. Loosen the securing bolt and two adjusting link bolts.
2. Move the air pump to get a belt deflection of ½ in.
3. Tighten the bolts.

Clutch & Transmission Section

Clutch & Manual Transmission

CLUTCH, REPLACE

NOTE: The clutch unit and pressure plate cannot be disassembled and must be replaced as a unit.

Removal

1. Remove transmission.
2. Mark clutch and flywheel for assembly.
3. Remove clutch attaching screws and washers.
4. Remove clutch.

Installation

1. Refit clutch driven plate to flywheel with clutch spring housing facing out.
2. Center clutch driven plate using service tool No. 18G1195.
3. Refit the clutch lining with mark in alignment with mark on flywheel.
4. Tighten screws evenly.
5. Install transmission.

MANUAL TRANSMISSION, REPLACE

1. Remove carburetor.
2. Unscrew pipe union from clutch slave cylinder and drain hydraulic fluid.
3. Mark transmission and propeller shaft drive flanges for assembly.
4. Disconnect propeller shaft from transmission flange and tie shaft to torsion bar.
5. Disconnect speedometer drive from drive pinion.
6. Remove starter.
7. Support engine and transmission.
8. Remove oil pan connecting plate from transmission.
9. Remove hardware attaching rear crossmember to frame.
10. Lower engine and transmission enough to reach shift lever retaining cover.
11. Shift transmission to Neutral, then press down and turn shift lever retaining cover to free shift lever.
12. Remove hardware attaching top of flywheel housing to mounting plate.
13. Remove remaining hardware attaching flywheel housing.
14. Lower rear of engine and transmission to clear flywheel housing and remove transmission.
15. Reverse procedure to install.

Automatic Transmission

TROUBLE SHOOTING

Road test the car as outlined in Fig. 1, Parts 1 and 2. Use the numbers under "Repair Procedure" and the accompanying list to solve the condition.

ADJUSTMENTS

Downshift Cable, Adjust

1. Warm transmission to normal operating temperature.
2. Shut off engine.
3. Remove plug from line pressure take-off point and connect tool No. 18G6772. Switch tool to "4 cylinder" and to "X 100" scale.
4. Chock wheels, apply parking brake, select "N" on shift quadrant and let engine idle.
5. Disconnect kickdown cable at throttle.
6. Apply foot brake, select "D" on shift quadrant and note pressure which should be 50 to 60 psi.
7. Reconnect kickdown cable and repeat test. Pressure readings should be the same. If not, adjust cable.
8. Increase engine speed by 500 rpm and note the increase in pressure, which should be 20 psi.
9. Stop engine and make adjustments as follows:
   a. If pressure increase is less than 20 psi, increase length of cable, Fig. 2.
   b. If pressure increase is more than 20 psi, decrease length of cable.
10. Recheck pressure and repeat procedure until pressure increase is set properly.

Manual Linkage, Adjust

1. Apply parking brake and set shift lever in "N."
2. Select "Park," release parking brake and rock car back and forth. The pawl should hold car.
3. To adjust, disconnect shift lever at transmission, Fig. 3.
4. Undo the turnbuckle locknut and

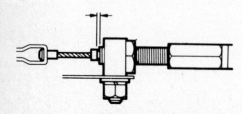

Fig. 2 Shift linkage adjustment

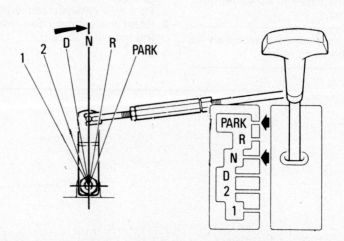

Fig. 3 Downshift cable adjustment

set it ¼-⁵/₁₆ inch from end of short shift-change rod.

5. Adjust turnbuckle to locknut (note right-hand thread). Tighten locknut.
6. Move lever at the transmission fully forward, then move back three detents to "N" position.
7. With shift lever in "N" position, the end of the selector rod should freely enter the hole in the transmission lever.
8. Adjust length of shift lever by turning short rod and turnbuckle on the long rod.
9. Reconnect rod and lock retaining clip.

TRANSMISSION, REPLACE

1. Disconnect downshift cable from throttle linkage.
2. Remove filler tube and dipstick assembly from transmission.
3. Disconnect exhaust pipe from exhaust manifold and from retaining bracket.
4. Drain transmission.
5. Disconnect transmission shift lever and leads from neutral safety switch and backup light switch and oil cooler lines.
6. Mark propeller shaft and transmission flanges, then remove propeller shaft from output shaft flange. Securing shaft to torsion bar.
7. Disconnect speedometer cable.
8. Support torque converter and remove hardware holding rear engine mount crossmember to frame.
9. Lower transmission, supporting it with a suitable jack.
10. Remove hardware holding transmission to torque converter housing and move transmission to the rear.

CAUTION: Do not put weight on the input shaft.

11. Reverse procedure to install, but note the following:
   a. The converter and front drive pump have to be aligned.
   b. Carefully align transmission and torque securing nuts to 8-13 ft. lbs.

Test	Problem	Solution
1. Check that starter will operate only with selector lever in 'P' and 'N' and that reverse lights (when fitted) operate only in 'R'.	Starter will not operate in 'P' or 'N' Starter operates in all selector positions	19 20
2. Apply parking and service brakes and with engine idling select 'N-D,' 'N-2,' 'N-1' and 'N-R.' Transmission engagement should be felt in each position.	Harsh engagement of 'D,' '2,' '1' or 'R'	4.3

3. Check stall speed in '1' and 'R.'
 	
Do not stall for more than 10 seconds
	High stall speed:
	   a. With slip and squawk in '1'
	   b. With slip and squawk in 'R' ....
	Low stall speed: more than 600 rev/min below normal ....
	Low stall speed: less than 600 rev/min below normal ....
		2, 3, 13*a*, *c*, *f*, 11
		1, 2, 3, 13*a*, *c*, *f*, *e*, 12
		21
		23

4. Transmission at normal temperature, select 'D'; release brakes and accelerate with minimum throttle. Check for 1-2 and 2-3 shifts. Confirm that third gear has been obtained by selecting '2' when a 3-2 shift should be felt. **NOTE:** A feature of this transmission is that a slight increase in throttle depression between 15 and 30 mph may produce a 3-2 down-shift (part throttle down-shift).	No drive in 'D' '2' or '1' .... No drive in 'D,' drive in '1' .... No drive in 'D,' '2,' '1' or 'R' .... Delayed or no 1-2 shift .... Slip on 1-2 shift .... Delayed or no 2-3 shift (if normal drive in 'R,' omit 12) .... Slip or engine run-up on 2-3 shift .... Harsh gear-shifts .... Drag in 'D' and '2' .... Drag or binding on 2-3 shift	1, 2, 3, 13*a*, 11, 16 1, 2, 3, 16 1, 2, 3, 13*a*, 11, 16, 17 3, 14, 13*a*, 5, 6 2, 3, 5, 6, 7, 13*c*, *f* 3, 14, 13, *g*, *h*, *c*, *d*, 5, 6, 12 2, 3, 5, 13*a*, *c*, 12 3 8 5, 6
5. From a standing start, accelerate using 'kick-down.' Check for 1-2 and 2-3 shifts.	Slip on full throttle take-off in 'D' ...... Loss of performance and overheating in third gear .... Other possible faults are as given in test No. 4	1, 2, 3, 13*a*, *c*, 11 21 Continue as in Test 4

Fig. 1   Automatic transmission trouble shooting chart (Part 1 of 2)

Test	Problem	Solution
6. *a.* At 40 mph (65 km/h) in top gear release accelerator and select '2.' Check for 3-2 shift and engine braking. Check for 2-1 roll out.	No 3-2 down-shift or engine braking	1, 5, 6, 7, 12
b. At 15 mph (25 km/h) in second gear release accelerator and select '1.' Check for 2-1 shift.	No 2-1 down-shift and engine braking	8, 9, 10
7. *a.* At 40 mph (65 km/h) in top gear, depress accelerator to kick-down, when the gearbox should down-shift to second gear.	Transmission will not down-shift	3, 13*f, g,* 14
b. At 20 mph (30 km/h) in second gear, depress accelerator to kick-down when gearbox should down-shift to first gear.	Transmission will not down-shift	3, 13*f, g,* 14
8. *a.* Stop, engage '1' and accelerate to 20 mph (30 km/h). Check for clutch slip or break-away noise (squawk) and that no up-shift occurs.	Slip, squawk or shudder on take-off in '1' Transmission up-shifts	1, 2, 3, 13, 11 1
b. Stop, engage 'R' and reverse the vehicle using full throttle if possible. Check for clutch or break-away noise (squawk).	Slip, squawk or shudder on take-off in 'R' As above, with engine braking available in '1' .... Slip but no shudder on take-off in 'R.' No engine braking available in '1' .... Drag in 'R' .... No drive in 'R,' no engine braking in '1' ..... As above, with engine braking in '1'	1,2,3,13*b,c,e,f,g*,12 1, 2, 3 1, 2, 3, 8, 9, 10 5 1,2,3,8,13*e,f,g*,9, 10,12 1,2,3,13*e*,12
9. Stop vehicle facing downhill, apply the brakes and select 'P.' Release the brakes and check that pawl holds. Re-apply the brakes before disengaging 'P.'' Repeat facing uphill.	Parking pawl inoperative .... Miscellaneous: Screech or whine increasing with engine speed .... Grinding or grating noise from gearbox Knocking noise from torque converter area .... At high speeds in 'D' transmission down-shifts to second ratio and immediately up-shifts back to third ratio	1, 15 17 18 22 12

SOLUTIONS

1. Recheck fluid level.
2. Check manual linkage adjustment.
3. Check adjustment of down-shift valve cable.
4. Reduce engine idle speed.
5. Check adjustment of front band.
6. Check front servo seals and fit of tubes.
7. Check front band for wear.
8. Check adjustment of rear band.
9. Check rear servo seal and fit of tubes.
10. Check rear band for wear.
11. Examine front clutch, check ball valve and seals, also forward sun gear shaft sealing rings. Verify that cup plug in driven shaft is not leaking or dislodged.

12. Examine rear clutch, check ball valve and seals. Verify that rear clutch spring seat inner lip is not proud. Check fit of tubes.
13. Strip valve bodies and clean, checking:
   a. Primary regulator valve sticking.
   b. Secondary regulator valve sticking.
   c. Throttle valve sticking.
   d. Modulator valve sticking.
   e. Servo orifice control valve sticking.
   f. 1 to 2 shift valve sticking.
   g. 2 to 3 shift valve sticking.
   h. 2 to 3 shift valve plunger sticking.
14. Strip governor valve and clean.
15. Examine parking pawl, gear, and

internal linkage.
16. Examine one-way clutch.
17. Strip and examine pump and drive tangs.
18. Strip and examine gear train.
19. Adjust starter inhibitor switch inwards.
20. Adjust starter inhibitor switch outwards.
21. Replace torque converter.
22. Examine torque converter plate for cracks or fracture.
23. Check engine performance.

Fig. 2 Automatic transmission trouble shooting chart (Part 2 of 2)

Rear Axle & Brakes Section

AXLE SHAFT, BEARING & OIL SEAL

Removal

1. Raise vehicle and remove wheel, axle shaft nut, and brake drum, Fig. 1.
2. Remove rear hub from axle shaft with tool No. 18G304 or 18G304Z.
3. Remove clevis pin and disconnect parking brake cable from wheel cylinder.
4. Disconnect brake line.
5. Remove hardware holding brake backing plate.
6. Remove oil retainer.

IMPORTANT: Note the fitted position of lip in relation to brake cylinder.

7. Remove backing plate assembly.
8. Remove oil seal from housing using tool No. 18G1087.
9. Remove axle shaft key.

NOTE: Place a container under the end of the axle case to catch oil when axle shaft and oil seal are removed.

10. Remove axle shaft using tool No. 18G284.
11. Remove inner oil seal using tool No. 18G1087.
12. Press bearing from axle shaft.

Installation

1. Pack bearing with lithium-based grease and dip a new oil seal in light oil before reassembly.

2. Fit new oil seal using tool No. 18G1200.

NOTE: The lip of the seal must face inward.

3. Press bearing onto axle shaft until a space of 2.84 inches exists from bearing to threaded end of axle shaft.

4. Complete reassembly noting the following:
   a. That the hub seal is refitted properly. Use tool No. 18G1200.
   b. That you use a new rear hub joint washer.
   c. That backing plate securing nuts are torqued to 22 ft. lbs.
   d. That axle shaft threads and nuts are clean.
   e. That three drops of Loctite LT270 are applied to threads of the axle shaft nut and nut is torqued to 105 ft. lbs.
   f. That brake system is bled.

DISC BRAKE REPAIRS

Pads, Replace

1. Remove wheel, spring clips, retaining pins, and brake pads and anti-squeak shims, Fig. 2.
2. Clean exposed end of piston, making sure that recesses in caliper are free of rust and grit.
3. Push piston to the base of the cylinder, using tool No. 18G590.

NOTE: The level of the fluid in the master cylinder will rise, and it may be necessary to siphon off some to keep it from overflowing.

4. Tighten bleed screw and complete installation by noting the following:
   a. Pads are interchangeable from side to side.
   b. Anti-squeak shims are installed with the arrow pointing upwards.

Caliper, Remove

1. Raise vehicle and remove wheel.
2. Disconnect brake line from flexible hose and plug flexible hose.
3. Disconnect brake line from caliper.
4. Remove caliper attaching bolts and lift caliper off disc, Fig. 3.
5. Reverse procedure to install. Torque bolts to 50 ft. lbs.

PARKING BRAKE, ADJUST

1. Set parking brake lever on fourth ratchet tooth and check for braking effect.
2. If braking effect is not adequate, loosen adjusting locknut.
3. Turn adjusting nut clockwise, holding outer cable against rotation, until desired adjustment is obtained, Fig. 4.
4. Tighten locknut, then release brake and check to ensure rear wheels rotate freely.

MASTER CYLINDER, REPLACE

1. Remove fluid lines from master cylinder, plugging outlet ports to pre-

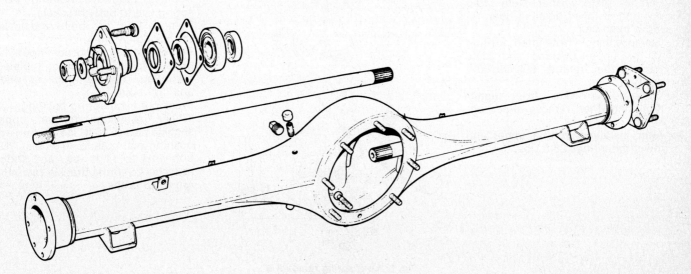

Fig. 1 Rear axle assembly

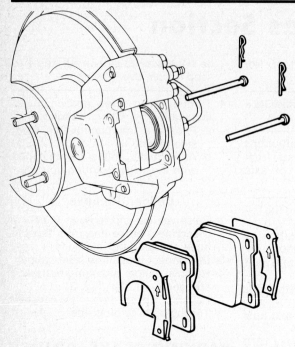

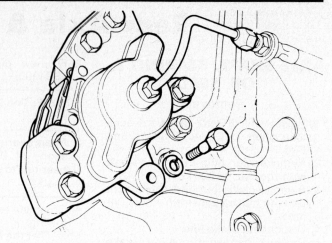

Fig. 3 Caliper mounting bolt locations

Fig. 2 Brake pad removal & installation

vent loss of brake fluid.
2. Remove master cylinder retaining nuts.
3. Remove master cylinder.
4. Reverse procedure to install. Torque retaining nuts to 15.5-19.5 ft. lbs.

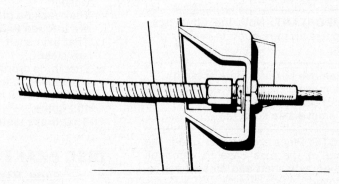

Fig. 4 Parking brake cable adjustment

Rear Suspension Section

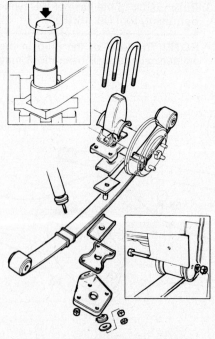

Fig. 1 Leaf spring removal & installation

SHOCK ABSORBERS, REPLACE

1. Remove shock absorber lower locknut and retaining nut.
2. Remove plate washer. Note fitted position of lower bushing, then remove bushing.
3. Collapse shock. Note fitted position of the upper bushing and plate washer, then remove bushing and washer.
4. Remove hardware from upper mounting, then remove shock absorber.
5. After installing, torque upper and lower mountings 28 ft. lbs.

LEAF SPRINGS, REPLACE

1. Remove spring shackle plate, Fig. 1.
2. Support rear axle.
3. Remove shock absorber.
4. Remove hardware holding front spring eye to body brackets.
5. Remove four "U" bolts and lower the spring and mountings.
6. Remove shock absorber mounting plate, spring mounting plates, mounting rubbers, packing plate and "U" bolts.
7. Press out each spring bushing.
8. When installing, torque upper shackle nuts to 28 ft. lbs., spring eye bushing bolt nuts to 40 ft. lbs., "U" bolt nuts to 14 ft. lbs., and shock absorber to spring bracket retaining nut to 28 ft. lbs.

Front Suspension & Steering Section

FRONT WHEEL ALIGNMENT

Checking

1. If using a basebar-type gauge, take measurements behind wheel center at rim edge, then move car ahead half a wheel revolution. Take another measurement at same points on wheel rim.
2. If an optical gauge is used, take three readings, each at 120 degrees of wheel rim movement and calculate average.

Adjusting

1. Loosen locknut on both tie rods.

2. Loosen clip holding rack seal to tie rod.
3. Rotate each tie rod in the required direction by an equal amount to correct the misalignment.

NOTE: Both are right-hand threaded.

---

4. Tighten locknut 35-40 ft. lbs.

WHEEL BEARINGS, ADJUST

1. Remove wheel and grease cap.
2. Remove cotter pin and retainer.
3. Loosen adjusting nut, spin the hub, and while it is spinning tighten nut to 5 ft. lbs.
4. Stop the hub spinning and loosen the nut.
5. Tighten nut finger.
6. Position nut retainer so half cotter pin hole is covered by one of the prongs of the retainer.
7. Loosen nut and retainer until cotter pin hole is totally uncovered.
8. Insert cotter pin and lock it in place.

NOTE: At minimum end play figure cited above, a considerable amount of movement will be felt from the wheel. However, do not reduce end play below 0.001 inch. Bearings must not be preloaded.

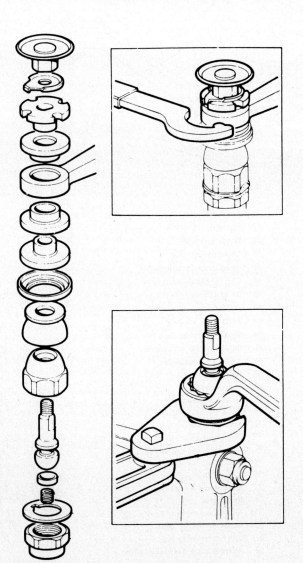

Fig. 1   Replace ball joint
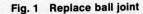

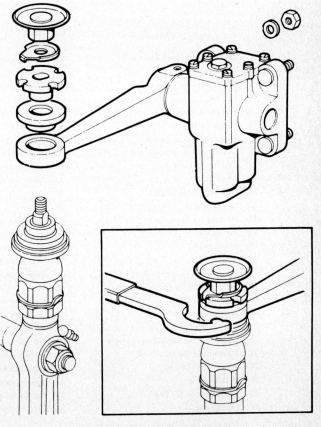

Fig. 2   Replace shock absorber

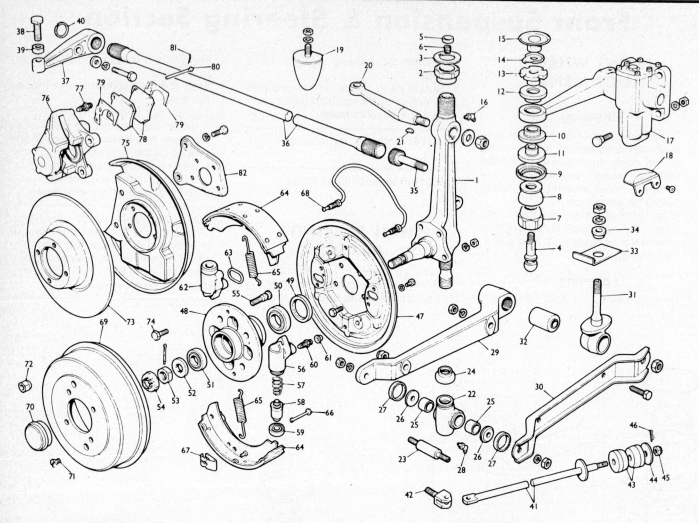

1.	Swivel pin and stub axle—R.H.
2.	Locknut for ball pin
3.	Tab washer for ball pin
4.	Ball pin
5.	Seat for ball pin
6.	Spring for ball pin
7.	Retaining nut for ball pin
8.	Dust cover for retaining nut
9.	Clip for dust cover
10.	Lower bush
11.	Housing for lower bush
12.	Upper bush
13.	Housing for upper bush
14.	Tab washer
15.	Reaction pad
16.	Grease nipple
17.	Front shock absorber—R.H.
18.	Bump rubber for shock absorber
19.	Rebound rubber
20.	Steering lever—R.H.
21.	Key for lever
22.	Lower link for swivel pin—R.H.
23.	Fulcrum pin for link
24.	Rubber seal for link
25.	Bush for link
26.	Thrust washer for link
27.	Sealing ring
28.	Grease nipple for lower link
29.	Lower arm—rear
30.	Lower arm—front
31.	Eyebolt
32.	Bush for eyebolt
33.	Reinforcement plate
34.	Bush for plate
35.	Serrated bolt
36.	Torsion bar
37.	Lever for torsion bar
38.	Adjusting screw
39.	Locknut
40.	Circlip for torsion bar
41.	Tie-rod
42.	Fork for tie-rod
43.	Pad for tie-rod
44.	Plain washer
45.	Nut
46.	Retaining clip for tie-rod
47.	Brake backplate
48.	Wheel hub
49.	Oil seal for hub
50.	Inner bearing
51.	Outer bearing.
52.	Splined washer
53.	Nut for stub axle
54.	Retainer for nut
55.	Wheel stud
56.	Brake cylinder—R.H.
57.	Spring
58.	Piston assembly
59.	Cover for cylinder
60.	Bleed screw for cylinder
61.	Cap for bleed screw
62.	Brake cylinder—L.H.
63.	Sealing ring for cylinder
64.	Brake-shoe assembly
65.	Spring for brake-shoe
66.	Steady-pin for brake-shoe
67.	Spring for steady-pin
68.	Bridge pipe
69.	Brake-drum
70.	Grease retaining cap
71.	Screw for brake-drum
72.	Wheel nut
73.	Front brake disc—R.H.
74.	Bolt for brake disc to hub
75.	Mud shield for disc
76.	Brake calliper—R.H.
77.	Bleed screw for calliper
78.	Brake pads
79.	Anti-squeal shims
80.	Retaining pin for pads
81.	Clip for retaining pin
82.	Adaptor plate for brake calliper

Front suspension assembly

BALL JOINTS, REPLACE
Removal

1. Release shock absorber arm.
2. Remove dust cover and retaining clip, Fig. 1.
3. Unlock washer.
4. Using tool No. 18G1192 to hold locknut, remove ball pin retainer.
5. Remove ball pin.
6. Remove ball seat and spring.
7. Remove washer and locknut.

Installation

1. Do all operations up to fitting ball pin retainer.
2. Loosen locknut fully.
3. Tighten ball retainer until torque needed to produce articulation of ball pin is 32-52 in. lbs.
4. Hold ball retainer against rotation and torque locknut to 70-80 ft. lbs. using tool No. 18G1202 and a torque wrench.
5. Complete installation.

FRONT SHOCKS, REPLACE

1. Place a jack under lower suspension arm, then raise vehicle and position supports.
2. Remove wheel.
3. Loosen reaction pad nut, hold upper bushing nut with tool No. 18G202 and remove nut, Fig. 2.
4. Remove lock washer, upper bushing housing and upper bushing.
5. Raise shock absorber arm.
6. Remove four nuts holding shock absorber and remove shock absorber.
7. When installing shock absorber, torque reaction pad nut to 35-40 ft. lbs. and shock retaining nuts to 26-28 ft. lbs.

STEERING RACK, REPLACE

1. Remove instrument panel.

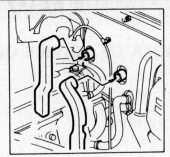
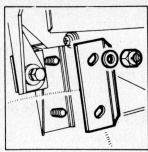
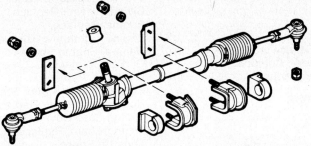
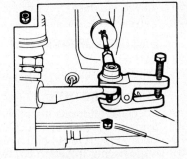

Fig. 3   Removing rack & pinion steering gear

2. Disconnect steering column and ignition switch connections at harness connectors.
3. Remove hardware holding column to upper and lower supports.
4. Remove bolt and nut holding flexible joint to rack pinion.
5. Lift out steering column assembly.
6. Remove two heater drain tubes.
7. Lift and support the front of vehicle.
8. Release tie rod ball pin ends.
9. Using tool No. 18G1063, disconnect tie rod ball pin ends from steering levers.
10. Remove hardware holding each rack clamp bracket to bulkhead.
11. Remove clamp brackets, Fig. 3.
12. Remove rack through wheel housing.
13. Remove pinion seal.
14. When installing, torque rack clamp nuts to 20-22 ft. lbs., tie rod ball pin nuts to 20-24 ft. lbs. and lower flexible joint bolt to 17-20 ft. lbs.

BMW

INDEX OF SERVICE OPERATIONS

BMW

GENERAL ENGINE SPECIFICATIONS

Year	Engine	Carburetor	Bore and Stroke	Piston Displacement Cubic Inches	Compression Ratio	Maximum Brake H.P. @ R.P.M.	Maximum Torque Ft. Lbs. @ R.P.M.	Normal Oil Pressure Pounds
1972-74	2002	1 Barrel	3.504 x 3.150	121.4	8.3	100 @ 5500	116 @ 3500	57
	2002Tii	Fuel Inj.	3.504 x 3.150	121.4	9.0	130 @ 5800	131 @ 3500	57
	3.0 CS	2 Barrel	3.504 x 3.150	182.1	9.0	180 @ 5500	188 @ 4300	71
1975-76	2002	1 Barrel	3.504 x 3.150	121.4	8.3	100 @ 5500	116 @ 3500	57
	530	Fuel Inj.	3.504 x 3.150	182.1	8.1	175 @ 5500	188 @ 4500	71
	3.0Si	Fuel Inj.	3.504 x 3.150	182.1	9.5	200 @ 5500	200 @ 4300	71
1977	530i	Fuel Inj.	3.504 x 3.150	182.1	8.1	175 @ 5500	188 @ 4500	71
	320i	Fuel Inj.	3.504 x 3.150	121.4	8.1	①	②	57
	3.0i	Fuel Inj.	3.504 x 3.150	182.1	9.5	200 @ 5500	200 @ 4300	71

①—Exc. Calif., 110 @ 5800; Calif., 105 @ 5800.   ②—Exc. Calif., 112 @ 3750; Calif., 108 @ 3750.

TUNE UP SPECIFICATIONS

The following specifications are published from the latest information available. This data should be used only in the absence of a decal affixed in the engine compartment.

★When using a timing light, disconnect vacuum hose or tube at distributor and plug opening in hose or tube so idle speed will not be affected.

▲Before removing wires from distributor cap, determine location of the No. 1 wire in cap, as distributor position may have been altered from that shown at the end of this chart.

Year	Spark Plug Type	Gap Inch	Point Gap Inch	Dwell Angle Deg.	Firing Order Fig. ▲	Timing BTDC	Mark Fig.	Hot Idle Speed Std. Trans.	Hot Idle Speed Auto. Trans.	Idle Co% Std. Trans.	Idle Co% Auto. Trans.
1972-73											
2002	W145T30	.024	.014	58—64	⑦	25°①	⑨	900	900	3.0—4.0	—
2002Tii	W175T30	.024	.014	59—61	⑦	25°②	⑨	925	—	2.0—3.0	—
3.0	W145T30	.024	.014	35—41	⑧	22°③	⑨	900	—	3.0—4.0	—
1974											
2002	W145T30	.024	.014	58—64	⑦	25°①	⑨	900	900	0.8—1.2	.8—1.2
2002Tii	W175T30	.024	.014	59—61	⑦	25°②	⑨	900	—	0.8—1.2	—
3.0	W145T30	.024	.014	35—41	⑧	22°③	⑨	900	900	3.0—4.0	3.0—4.0
1975											
2002	W145T30	.024	.014	58—64	⑦	25°①	⑨	900	900	1.5—3.0	1.5—3.0
530	N9Y	.023	.014	35—41	⑧	22°③	⑨	925	925	1.5—3.0	1.5—3.0
3.0	W145T30	.024	.014	35—41	⑧	22°④	⑨	925	925	3.0—4.0	3.0—4.0
1976											
2002	W145T30	.024	.014	59—65	⑦	25°①	⑨	900	900	3.0—4.0	3.0—4.0
530	N9Y	.023	.014	35—41	⑧	22°③	⑨	925	925	1.5—3.0	1.5—3.0
3.0	W145T30	.023	.014	35—41	⑧	22°④	⑨	925	925	3.0—4.0	3.0—4.0
1977											
530	N9Y	.023	.014	35—41	⑧	22°③	⑨	925	925	—	—
320i	W145T30	.024	.014	59—65	⑦	25°⑤	⑨	925	925	⑥	⑥
320iA	N10Y	.024	.014	59—65	⑦	25°⑤	⑨	925	925	⑥	⑥
3.0	W145T30	.024	.015	35—41	⑧	22°④	⑨	925	925	3.0—4.0	3.0—4.0

—Not Available
①—At 1400 RPM.
②—At 2700 RPM.
③—At 1700 RPM.
④—At 2500 RPM.
⑤—Exc. Calif., at 2400 RPM; Calif., at 2200 RPM.
⑥—Exc. Calif., 2.0; Calif., 3.5.
⑦—Firing Order 1342.
⑧—Firing Order 153624.
⑨—Timed at No. 1 cyl., front of engine. Disconnect vacuum hose & align ball on flywheel with the pointer.

DISTRIBUTOR SPECIFICATIONS

If unit is checked on vehicle, double the RPM and degrees to get crankshaft figures.

Distributor Part No.	Centrifugal Advance Degrees @ RPM of Distributor		Vacuum Advance	
	Advance Starts	Full Advance	Inches of Vacuum To Start Plunger	Max. Adv. Dist. Deg. @ Vacuum
231180003	0 @ 400	21.6 @ 2000	4.72—5.91	7.68 @ 8.27
231305059	0 @ 500	7.5 @ 1100	3.15—4.72	7.68 @ 9.45
231170214	0 @ 500	16 @ 2000	2.75—3.93	8.30 @ 8.28
231162002	0 @ 400	14 @ 1500	6.30—9.07	7.0 @ 12.63
231169007	0 @ 350	14 @ 1500	3.15—5.52	8.0 @ 12.63
231306001	0 @ 600	11 @ 1750	6.71—8.28	10.6 @ 11.84
231180005	0 @ 400	16 @ 1300	4.72—5.92	6.0 @ 8.68
231151008	0 @ 600	16 @ 1750	4.72—5.92	6.0 @ 12.63
231151009	0 @ 500	21.6 @ 1600	—	—

—Not Available

ALTERNATOR SPECIFICATIONS

Year	Model	Rated Hot Output Amps.	Output @ 14 Volts	
			2000 RPM Amps.	6000 RPM Amps
1972-74	All	45	30	45
1975	KI-14V45A	45	30	45
	14V55A	55	37	55
1976	KI-14V	55	37	55
	14V55A	55	37	55
	KI-14V45A24	45	35	45
1977	All	55	37	55

STARTING MOTOR SPECIFICATIONS

Year	Model	Resistance Test	
		Amps	Volts
1972-7	2002	210	9.6
1972-77	3.0	270	9.1
1975-77	530	270	9.1
1977	320	210	9.6

COOLING SYSTEM & CAPACITY DATA

Year	Model	Cooling Capacity Qts.	Radiator Cap Relief Pressure, Lbs.	Thermo Opening Temp.	Fuel Tank Gal.	Engine Oil Refill Qts. ①	Transmission Oil		Rear Axle Oil Pints
							Man. Trans. Pints.	Auto. Trans. Qts.	
1972-76	2002	7.4	14.2	176	13.2	4.20	2.2	5.3	2
1972-77	3.0	12.6	14.2	②	③	5.30	2.1	8	3.4
1975-77	530	12.6	14.2	②	18.5	5.25	2.3	8	3.4
1977	320	7.4	14	175	18	4.25	2	5.5	2.3

①—Not including filter.
②—Exc. Auto. trans., 184°; Auto. trans., 176°.
③—3.0S, 19.8 gals.; 3.0CS, 18.5 gals.

BMW

VALVE SPECIFICATIONS

Year	Model	Valve Lash	Valve Angles		Valve Spring Pressure Lbs. @ In.	Stem Clearance		Stem Diameter	
			Seat	Face		Intake	Exhaust	Intake	Exhaust
1972-76	2002	.0059—.0079	45	45½	154 @ 1.122	.0008	.0008	.3150	.3150
1972-77	3.0	.012—.014	45	45½	154 @ 1.1	.0008	.0008	.3150	.3150
1975-77	530	.012—.014	45	45½	154 @ 1.121	.0008	.0008	.3149	.3149
1977	320	.008—.010	45	45½	154 @ 1.122	.0010—.0020	.0015—.0030	.3149	.3149

PISTON PINS, RINGS, CRANKSHAFT & BEARINGS

Year	Model	Piston Clearance Top of Skirt	Ring End Gap ①		Wristpin Diameter	Rod Bearings		Main Bearings		
			Comp.	Oil		Shaft Diameter	Bearing Clearance	Shaft Diameter	Bearing Clearance	Shaft End Play
1972-76	2002	.0018	.012	.010	.8861	1.8898	.0009—.0027	2.1654	.0012—.0027	.003—.006
1972-77	3.0	.0018	.012	.010	.8661	1.8898	.0009—.0027	2.3622	.0012—.0028	.003—.006
1975-77	530	.0018	.012	.010	.8661	1.8897	.0009—.0027	2.3622	.0012—.0028	.003—.006
1977	320	.0018	.012	.010	.8661	1.8898	.0009—.0031	2.1653	.0012—.0027	.003—.006

①—Fit rings in tapered bores for clearance listed in tightest portion of ring travel.

ENGINE TIGHTENING SPECIFICATIONS

Year	Model	Spark Plugs Ft. Lbs.	Exhaust Manifold Ft. Lbs.	Camshaft Sprocket Ft. Lbs.	Cam Cover Ft. Lbs.	Connecting Rod Cap Bolts Ft. Lbs.	Main Bearing Cap Bolts Ft. Lbs.	Flywheel to Crankshaft Ft. Lbs.	Vibration Damper or Pulley Ft. Lbs.
1972-76	2002	18—22	22—24	—	6.5—8	38—41	42—46	72—83	101—108
1972-77	3.0	18—22	22—24	101—108	6.5—8	38—41	42—46	72—83	174—188
1975-77	530	18—22	22—24	101—116	—	38—41	42—46	72—83	320—330
1977	320	18—22	22—24	—	6.5—8	38—41	42—46	72—83	101—108

—Not Available

BRAKE SPECIFICATIONS

Year	Model	Brake Drum Inside Diameter	Wheel Cylinder Bore Diameter			Master Cylinder Bore Diameter
			Front Disc Brake	Rear Disc Brake	Rear Drum Brake	
1972-76	2002	9.06	1.34	—	.625	.8125
1972-74	2002Tii	9.06	1.574	—	.6875	.9375
1972-74	3.0	—	1.574	1.654	—	.9375
1975-77	530	—	1.574	1.654	—	.9360
1975-77	3.0	—	1.574	1.654	—	.8740
1977	320	9.842	1.890	—	.7500	.8125

—Not Available

REAR AXLE SPECIFICATIONS

Year	Model	Carrier Type	Ring Gear & Pinion Backlash		Pinion Bearing Preload		Differential Bearing Preload	
			Method	Adjustment	Method	New Bearing Inch-Lbs.	Method	New Bearing Inch-Lbs.
1972-76	2002	Removable	①	.0028—.0047	Bushing	1.4—1.8②	Shim	17—24
1972-77	3.0	Removable	Shim	.0024—.0043	Bushing	32③	Shim	—
1975-77	530	Removable	Shim	.0020—.0040	Sleeve	28③	Shim	12—14
1977	320	Removable	Shim	.0020—.0040	Bushing	28③	Shim	17—24②

—Not Available
① —Compensation rings.
② —W/O shaft seal.
③ —With shaft seal.

WHEEL ALIGNMENT SPECIFICATIONS

Year	Model	Caster Angle, Degrees		Camber Angle, Degrees		Toe-In, Inch	Toe-out on Turns, Degrees	
		Limits	Desired	Limits	Desired		Outer Wheel	Inner Wheel
1972-76	2002	+3½ to +4½	+4	0 to +1	+½	.059	19	20
1972-74	3.0	+9 to +10	+9½	0 to +1	+½	.04	18½	20
1975-77	530	+7¹/₆ to +8¹/₆	+7²/₃	−½ to +½	0	.059	18¹/₆	20
1975-77	3.0	+9¹/₆ to +10¹/₆	+9²/₃	0 to +1	+½	.04	18¹/₃	20
1977	320	+7⁵/₆ to +8⁵/₆	+8¹/₃	−½ to +½	0	.059	19¼	20

Electrical Section

DISTRIBUTOR, REPLACE

1. Remove cap and cable from terminal No. 1.
2. Remove vacuum hose and rotate engine so that cylinder No. 1 is at TDC, rotor notch and distributor body notch will line up.
3. Loosen clamp or screw and remove distributor.
4. To install distributor, turn rotor about 1⅜" counter-clockwise, then engage distributor drive until notches line up.

DISTRIBUTOR SERVICE

1. Remove distributor.
2. Remove vacuum advance unit and contact breaker plate.
3. Wedge cam up with two screwdrivers until retaining snap ring comes

Fig. 1 Distributor body, shaft & gear disassembled

Fig. 2 Distributor shaft, cam & centrifugal weights

Fig. 3 Alternator test connections. 2002, 3.0 & 530 models

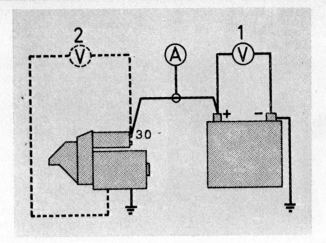

Fig. 4 Starter test connections

out of groove. Leave lubricating felt in place.
4. With a ⅛″ drill, drill out tapered pin and remove gear.
5. Pull out shaft, weights and cam, Fig. 1.
6. Replace, if necessary, bushes, springs, washers, shaft, clips and ignition parts, Fig. 2.
7. When reassembling, apply lubricant where needed.
8. Bench test reassembled unit, then install unit and adjust timing.

ALTERNATOR, REPLACE

1. Disconnect battery ground cable. On 320 models, disconnect positive cable as well. On 530 models, loosen charcoal canister. On 530, 3.0 and 2002, pull off multiple plug, then disconnect red and brown wires at alternator. On 320 models, disconnect black/red B+, blue D+ and brown ground wires.
2. On 2002 Tii models, remove front stabilizer bar.
3. Release belt and remove mounting

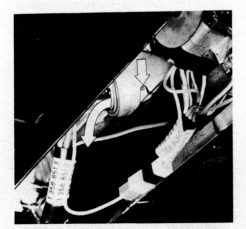

Fig. 5 Removing ignition switch set screw

bolts to lift out alternator.
4. Reverse procedure to install.

ALTERNATOR IN-VEHICLE TESTS

2002, 3.0 & 530 Models

NOTE: This procedure is only done if indicator light will not go out and battery connections and belt tension are correct.

1. Disconnect electrical plug at regulator.
2. Bridge between flat male of D+/61 blue wire and flat male of DF black wire. Connect test lamp as shown in Fig. 3. Start engine and run it at 1000 R.P.M. Immediate loss of indicator light means a defective regulator. If light fails to go out, alternator is defective.

STARTER, REPLACE

Disconnect battery ground cable at battery and wires at starter solenoid. On 320 models, disconnect intake cowl off mixture control unit and support bracket. Remove flange bolts and starter. Reverse procedure to install.

STARTER IN-VEHICLE TESTS

2002, 3.0 & 530 Models

In-vehicle starter tests are applicable only to models with standard transmissions. Models equipped with automatics must have their starters bench tested.

The in-vehicle test requires engaging car in fourth gear, depressing starter for 2-3 seconds. With two voltmeters and an ammeter hooked up as in Fig. 4, voltmeters should read not less that 8

volts under load, with both voltmeters reading equally. Check load current against specifications. Unequal voltmeter readings indicate faulty ground cable connections.

IGNITION SWITCH, REPLACE

1. Disconnect battery ground cable.
2. Remove lower casing under steering column, Fig. 5.
3. Some models require lower left center instrument panel trim be removed.
4. With key set at "halt" on 2002 models, and at the "0" position on 320 models, loosen set screw and pull switch away.
5. Disconnect switch from horn wires, multiple connectors and harness straps.
6. Remove switch.
7. Reverse procedure to install.

LIGHT SWITCH, REPLACE

1. Unscrew light switch knob, while holding shaft with an appropriate

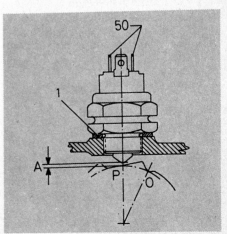

Fig. 6 Neutral safety switch adjustment. 2002 models

Fig. 7 Neutral safety switch installation. 320 models

screws you loosened so that selector lever shows correctly in all positions.

W/ZF Borg Warner Transmission

1. Pull off multi-connector.
2. Remove cable clamps, selector arm retaining nut and selector arm.
3. Pull out cable and switch.
4. Install switch temporarily, at position "0".
5. Rotate control valve shaft clockwise to "stop" position, then counterclockwise two notches to "0" position.
6. Lock switch into place and check indexing by going through various transmission gear positions, noting light indications.

Fig. 8 Neutral safety switch removal. 530 models

punch inserted through hole in shaft.
2. Remove any panels which restrict access.
3. Loosen collar or escutcheon.
4. Pull switch through hole and disconnect from multiple plug.
5. Reverse procedure to install.

STOP LIGHT SWITCH, REPLACE

1. Remove necessary trim on certain series.
2. Pull off electrical connections to switch.
3. Loosen locknut and unscrew switch.
4. To replace, screw in switch and lock it so that a quarter inch of black contact button is visible.
5. Reinstall connectors and install trim.

NEUTRAL SAFETY SWITCH, REPLACE

2002A Models

1. Neutral safety switch is located at right rear side of transmission. Disconnect wire connector and remove switch.
2. Reverse procedure to install. Adjust switch as shown in Fig. 6.

3.0 Models

W/3HP-20 Transmission

1. At selector arm, disconnect multi-connector, then unscrew retaining plate and pull cable away from clips.
2. Disconnect linkage rod from arm and loosen screw at lower end of selector arm.
3. Loosen second screw and pull away reversing light cable.
4. Replace switch and adjust with two

320 Models

1. Remove selector lever and base, then drive out pin and separate lower section from this assembly.
2. Remove central gate screw, then switch.
3. When installing switch, make sure that bosses or pins of switch fit into appropriate gate holes, Fig. 7.
4. Reassemble selector group.

530 Models

1. Disconnect multi-plug, located by steering column flanges.
2. Loosen nut, selector lever and remove switch, Fig. 8.
3. Reverse procedure to install.

TURN SIGNAL SWITCH, REPLACE

1. In all cases, remove necessary trim panels and steering wheel.
2. Disconnect battery ground cable.
3. Disconnect multi-pin plug from signal harness.

Fig. 9 Turn signal switch canceling cam adjustment

4. Disconnect all harness clips in area.
5. On 530 models, disconnect plug. On all models, remove switch.
6. Make sure wheels are pointing straight ahead before reassembling switch.
7. When installing switch, make sure that there is a gap of .012 inch between switch cam and reset dog, Fig. 9. On 320 models, be sure to secure ground wire on left side assembly screw.

INSTRUMENT CLUSTER, REPLACE

1. Disconnect battery ground cable.
2. On 320 models, remove steering wheel.
3. On 320, 530 and 2002 models, remove center instrument panel trim.
4. On 530 models, remove or loosen upper steering column jacket attaching screws. On 2002 models, remove or loosen lower section of steering column jacket. On 3.0 models, remove instrument hood and speaker grille.
5. On 3.0 models, remove screw under speaker grille.
6. Disconnect speedometer cable. On 2002 models, remove cluster hood attaching screws.
7. After removing knurled nut where required, pull instrument carrier.
8. Separate main plugs, tachometer wires and fog lamp indicator light wire, if equipped.
9. On some models equipped with automatic transmission, it may be necessary to disconnect wires at gearshift diagram and resistor.
10. On 530 models, when installing cluster, be sure that speedometer cable fits into guide.

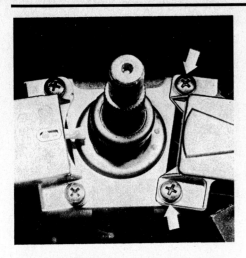

Fig. 10 W/S wiper switch removal. 2002 models

WINDSHIELD WIPER SWITCH, REPLACE

2002 Models

1. Disconnect battery ground cable.
2. Detach upper steering column trim and lower center facial trim, then lower steering column trim and push out of way.
3. Disconnect plug and cable strap from column.
4. Remove wheel, then remove screws and pull out complete with plug, Fig. 10.

3.0 Models

1. Remove bottom middle left dash cover and loosen switch collar, then remove and disconnect cables.

320 Models

1. Disconnect battery ground cable.
2. Remove lower trim and steering wheel.
3. Loosen screws, wire straps and disconnect plug.
4. Remove switch.

530 Models

1. Disconnect battery ground cable.
2. Remove lower trim and steering wheel.
3. Loosen screws, clips and disconnect plug.
4. Remove switch.

WINDSHIELD WIPER MOTOR, REPLACE

2002 Models

1. Remove nut and drive crank, then remove screws, unscrew ground and disconnect cable from contact strip and remove motor.

3.0 Models

1. From engine compartment, remove cover of heater unit.
2. Detach drive crank, then unscrew motor and tilt down to remove.
3. Remove motor harness multi-pin plug from board.

530 Models

1. Remove firewall top section.
2. Disconnect crank and drive arm, then loosen mounting screws.
3. Disconnect plug and remove motor.

RADIO, REPLACE

2002 Models

1. Disconnect antenna, ground and hot lead from hazard wiring.
2. Remove radio, speaker and storage compartment.
3. Remove speaker and receiver from storage compartment.

3.0 Models

1. Remove speaker grille at top of dash.

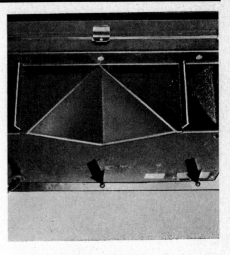

Fig. 11 Removing heater case rivets. 2002 models

2. Remove speaker and disconnect speaker wires.
3. Disconnect antenna, hot lead and ground.
4. Dismount receiver from shelf below fresh air grille by removing two countersunk screws from each sidewall.

BLOWER MOTOR, REPLACE

2002 Models

1. After removing heater, break rivets, Fig. 11, then remove all clamps, Fig. 12, and hose clamps and rubber sleeves.
2. Loosen control valve cable lock nut and remove all screws on mounting bracket, then pull cable out.
3. Disconnect heater valve bowden cable.
4. Disconnect electrical cable from housing.
5. Open grille mounting clamps and remove motor and fan as a unit

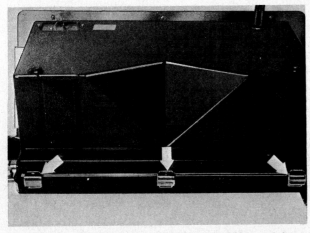

Fig. 12 Removing heater case clips. 2002 models

Fig. 13 Removing heater cover plate. 3.0 models

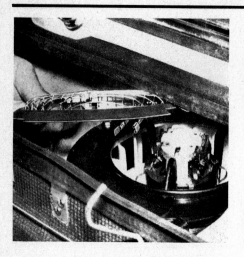

Fig. 14   Removing blower motor cover. 3.0 models

Fig. 15   Removing heater cover plate. 530 models

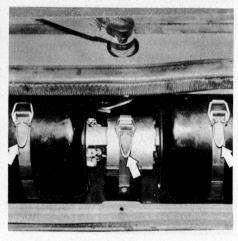

Fig. 16   Removing blower motor. 530 models

through the bottom. Fan and motor are balanced together.

3.0 Models

1. Remove heater cover plate from engine compartment side, Fig. 13.
2. Remove protective grid and disconnect cables, Fig. 14.
3. Remove motor mounting screws and slip motor out at an upward angle.
4. When replacing heater cover, use caulking.

530 Models

1. From engine compartment, open heater cover plate mounting clips, Fig. 15, and remove upper housing and outer intake ducting.
2. Disconnect wires and remove motor, Fig. 16.
3. When reinstalling, flat surfaces of duct face downward and web connecting two squirrel cages must be properly engaged in housing.

HEATER CORE, REPLACE

2002 Models

1. Disconnect battery ground cable, drain coolant and remove hoses and checking valve.

2. Remove storage tray, outer tube casing, lower center trim panel, outer left hand trim panel and upper casing.
3. Pull off control knobs, and panel through which levers protrude.
4. On right side, remove ash tray and knob and screws holding plate through which knob lever protrudes.
5. Remove screws on plate behind this.
6. Pull electrical connection apart, then remove left hand air hose near steering post and turn casing bracket.
7. Remove heater retaining nuts.
8. Remove panel below glove compartment, then pull right hand air hose and lift out heater.

3.0 Models

1. Drain coolant, remove hose, coverplate and fresh air grille. On coupe models, remove heater control cover, fresh air nozzle hoses and intermediate section.
2. Pull defroster nozzle hoses off heater and press left hand air hose manifolds together to remove.
3. Remove control levers and threaded knobs for left instrument panel trim.
4. Unscrew front and rear switch

plates, then unscrew heater.
5. Tilt heater and switch inward and remove.
6. On replacement, install switch first temporarily.
7. Apply foam sealant to cover plate of step 1.

530 Models

1. Disconnect battery ground, then drain coolant.
2. Remove glove compartment and center tray, hoses and frame with foam seal.
3. Detach center lower instrument panel trim and heater controls.
4. Depress lock projection and pull off control shafts from joints, then disconnect electrical plugs at heater.
5. Pull white plugs from underneath and remove connector.
6. Remove top center dash cover and remove connector.
7. Disconnect wire plug and pull out No. 7 wire.
8. Loosen cap screw and remove holder.
9. Remove upper heater wall from engine compartment.
10. In this trough, remove the nuts, washers and rubber seals near both corners of the blower cages.
11. Remove heater from driver's compartment by turning it to the right.

Engine Section

ENGINE, REPLACE

2002 Models

1. Drain coolant, then disconnect battery ground cable. Disconnect plug and B+ lead from alternator and starter cable.
2. Remove air cleaner and breather tube. On 2002A models, disconnect

cable from choke and auto. start valve, then disconnect plug connection from starter lock and cable harness from transmission retainer.
3. Remove radiator, heater hoses, dash panel connections and carburetor linkage.
4. Disconnect drive shaft at rear of transmission and clutch slave cylin-

der from housing, then exhaust pipe from manifold. On 2002A models, remove selector and detach selector rod from lever. Drop center drive shaft bearing support.
5. Attach hoist to front and rear engine fixtures, then remove crossmenber, front engine mounts, speedometer shaft and lead from back-up light

Fig. 1 Cylinder head tightening sequence. 320 and 2002 models

Fig. 2 Cylinder head tightening sequence. 3.0 and 530 models

switch. On 2002A models, remove back-up light lead from back-up light/starter lock switch. Remove windshield washer bottle.

6. With transmission dropped down, hoist out engine and transmission.

7. Reverse procedure to install, being careful to set front motor mount stops to ⅛ in.

2002 Tii Fuel Injected Models

1. Remove battery ground cable, and multiple plug from alternator.

2. Drain coolant, then remove transmission and air filter.

3. Remove fuel hose from pump and fuel filter from panel.

4. Disconnect thermo-time switch cable, vacuum hose from air container, and start valve cable.

5. Disconnect accelerator linkage, starter cable, heater hoses and fuel reflow hose. Remove cap, rotor and ignition cables.

6. Attach hoist, then remove windshield washer bottle, front motor mounts and lift out engine. Cable harness at left front motor mount must be cleared.

7. Reverse procedure to install.

3.0 Models

Less Fuel Injection

1. Remove hood, negative cable, air filters, windshield washer bottle, then drain coolant and remove radiator and hoses.

2. Remove fan, then disconnect wires from heat sender, and fuel and vacuum hoses.

3. Disconnect cables from starter, oil pressure switch, starter solenoid and alternator.

4. Disconnect accelerator linkage.

5. Remove power steering pump on cars so equipped.

6. Attach hoist to front and rear engine positions.

7. Remove transmission, clutch slave cylinder, clutch release arm and bearing, then disconnect back-up light lead.

8. Loosen mounts and remove engine.

9. Reverse procedure to install.

With Fuel Injection

1. Remove hood, negative cable, air filter, windshield washer bottle, then drain coolant and remove radiator and hoses.

2. Disconnect coil wires and white wire from pre-resistor. Remove harness from supports or disconnect at plug in some cases.

3. Remove vacuum hoses from collector and water hose from reservoir.

4. Disconnect throttle linkage, then disconnect plug from pressure sensor and cable from oil pressure switch. Remove plugs from main and time switch-over relays, cables from starter, plug and cable from alternator and cable from heat sender.

5. Remove fuel hoses from pressure regulator and circular pipes.

6. Remove fan, then loosen engine mounts and power steering pump.

7. Attach hoist, remove clutch release and lift out.

8. On 3.0 automatic transmission models, remove transmission first.

9. Reverse procedure to install.

320 Models

1. Drain radiator and coolant, then remove transmission, radiator, intake cowl, fuel lines and hoses and vacuum hoses.

2. Remove battery, heater hoses, pressure converter hoses and accelerator cable holder.

3. Disconnect wires and cables from ignition coil, alternator, starter and injection controls.

4. Attach hoist and remove top engine damper, engine mounts and lift engine.

5. When installing engine do not mix up the hoses. Code them where necessary.

530 Models

1. Drain radiator and engine coolant, then remove transmission. Dismount power steering pump from engine leaving hoses intact, then remove hood and radiator.

2. Remove air cleaner and volume control. Disconnect distributor vacuum hose, battery ground cable, fuel feed hose at filter, hose at charcoal canister, vacuum hoses at brake booster and EGR valve. Remove adaptor, vacuum control valve, blowoff valve. Disconnect fuel return hose at fuel pressure governor and heater hoses.

3. Disconnect accelerator linkage.

4. Disconnect wiring to coil, starter, alternator, equipment carrier, governor, relays and injection controls.

5. Install hoist, remove engine mounts and lift engine.

6. Reverse procedure to install, taking care to install colored hoses in their proper locations.

CYLINDER HEAD, REPLACE

2002 Models

1. Drain coolant and disconnect battery ground cable.

2. Remove valve cover, breather tube, connector, air filter. Disconnect carburetor and choke linkage, heater and other water hoses and fuel hose from pump. In the case of the

Fig. 3 Adjusting valve clearance

Tii models, remove hoses and electrical connections from injection unit.

3. Disconnect wires from coil and sending switches.
4. Place piston No. 1 at TDC, rotor and body notches aligned. Remove upper timing case cover. Note that indicator points to second notch on pulley when turning clockwise.
5. Remove chain tensioner, sprocket bolt safeties and sprocket.
6. Disconnect exhaust pipe.
7. Remove cylinder head bolts and cylinder head.
8. When replacing head, tighten cylinder head bolts in sequence shown in Fig. 1. with engine cold.
9. When installing cam sprocket, notch in camshaft flange must be aligned with boss on head above it and dowel pin hole facing downward.

3.0 Models

Less Fuel Injection

1. Drain coolant and remove negative

Fig. 5 Removing distributor flange. 320 and 2002 models

cable, vacuum hose from brake booster, dipstick support and fuel and water hoses. Remove cylinder head cover.
2. Position piston No. 1 to TDC, rotor and distributor body notches aligned. Remove upper timing case cover.
3. Remove chain tensioner, cam sprocket safeties, bolts and cam sprocket.
4. Disconnect exhaust pipe.
5. Remove cylinder head bolts and cylinder head.
6. When replacing, align sprocket so that dowel pin is at 7:30 and bore hole threaded hole and projection are aligned.
7. Tighten cylinder head bolts in sequence shown in Fig. 2.

With Fuel Injection

1. Drain coolant and disconnect battery ground cable. Remove intake filter, windshield washer bottle, distributor cap, water hoses, vacuum hoses, fuel hoses and ignition and oil pressure switch wires and remove cylinder head cover.
2. Remove upper timing case cover, tensioner, safety bolts and sprocket with No. 1 piston at TDC.
3. Remove engine exhaust pipe, then disconnect throttle linkage and air intake preheat water hose.
4. Loosen cylinder head bolts and remove cylinder head.
5. When replacing, follow 3.0 carbureted sprocket installation and head bolt tightening sequence as shown in Fig. 2.

320 Models

1. Drain coolant, then disconnect battery ground cable and remove cylinder head cover and intake cowl.
2. Disconnect vacuum hoses, accelerator cable, injection valve wires, temperature sensor and temperature timing wires. Disconnect water hoses at head, hoses at thermo valve, throttle housing and EGR valve.
3. Remove distributor cap, oil dipstick clamp and exhaust pipe.
4. Disconnect wire plugs at cold start valve, auxiliary air valve and timing valve, distributor and oil pressure sending switch.
5. As before set piston No. 1 at TDC, then remove upper timing case cover, tensioner and sprocket.
6. Loosen cylinder head bolts and remove head.
7. When installing, align cam sprocket as on 2002 models.
8. Again, tighten cylinder head bolts down in sequence shown in Fig. 1.

Fig. 4 Removing rocker shaft snap ring

530 Models

1. Drain coolant and disconnect battery ground cable. Remove cylinder head cover, upper timing case cover, tensioner, sprocket and exhaust pipe.
2. Disconnect water and vacuum hoses, ignition wires, oil pressure sending switch wires, plugs at injection valves, temperature timing switch and coolant temperature sensor.
3. Disconnect water hoses at throttle housing and holder and auxiliary air valve.
4. Disconnect throttle linkage, hoses at thermostat housing, charcoal filter and fuel filter. Clear electrical harness through intake manifold.
5. Disconnect tubes at EGR filter.
6. Loosen cylinder head bolts and remove head.
7. When installing, replace cam sprocket.
8. Tighten cylinder head bolts in sequence shown in Fig. 2.

Fig. 6 Rocker shaft assembly

Fig. 7 Upper timing case cover bolt tightening sequence. 320 and 2002 models

Fig. 8 Lower timing case cover. 3.0 and 530 models

VALVES, ADJUST

1. The valves should be adjusted in firing order at TOC, i.e. 1-3-4-2 or 1-5-3-6-2-4.
2. Loosen eccentric nut and rotate eccentric with adjusting tool to clearances shown in specifications, Fig. 3.

ROCKER ARM SHAFT, REPLACE

1. Remove camshaft, slide thrust rings aside and remove snap rings, Fig. 4.
2. On 2002 and 320 models, remove distributor flange, Fig. 5.
3. Drive shafts out with special punch No. 6012 for 2002 models, No. 11 3 040 for 320 models.
4. On 3.0 and 530 models, remove plugs from forward end of both shafts. Remove locating pins, then thread in special slide hammer puller No. 7004 for 3.0 models, or No.

11 3 060 for 530 models and remove front shafts. Remove rear shaft cover and remove rear shafts.
5. Replace any worn rockers at this time.
6. Replace shafts in reverse order being careful to align them so head bolts move freely through recesses in shafts, Fig. 6.
7. Note that on 2002 and 320 models, rear end of rocker shaft on inlet side is open and on exhaust side is closed. Plug if necessary.

TIMING CASE COVER, REPLACE

2002 Models

1. Drain coolant and disconnect battery ground cable. Remove water pump, upper timing case cover and tensioner, Fig. 7.
2. Disconnect cable from alternator.
3. Remove lower flywheel cover plate and lock flywheel.

4. Remove pulley nut and pulley.
5. Unbolt lower timing case cover at front engine face and at front of oil pan and remove, Fig. 8.

3.0 & 530 Models

1. Drain coolant and remove thermostat housing cover, thermostat, distributor cap and ignition lead. Set piston No. 1 to TDC.
2. Disconnect vacuum hoses and remove upper timing case cover, Fig. 9.
3. Remove timing case cover with worm wheel. Note that when reinstalling it must point to distributor body notch.
4. Remove tensioner, then loosen alternator and remove belt.
5. Remove lower cover plate at flywheel and lock flywheel.
6. Remove nut and vibration damper.
7. Remove lower timing case cover bolts from engine face and oil pan area, then remove cover, Fig. 8.

Fig. 9 Upper timing case cover bolt tightening sequence. 3.0 and 530 models

Fig. 10 Remove timing chain tension piston

1-35

Fig. 11 Aligning camshaft flange. 320 and 2002 models

320 Models

1. Disconnect battery ground cable and drain coolant, then remove cylinder head cover and disconnect exhaust pipe.
2. Remove upper timing cover, Fig. 7.
3. Remove water pump, alternator, chain tensioner, air pump and tension strut with bracket.
4. Remove lower cover, then lock flywheel.
5. Remove nut and vibration damper.
6. Unbolt lower timing cover and remove, Fig. 8.

TIMING CHAIN, REPLACE

1. Remove upper and lower timing case covers.
2. Set No. 1 piston at TDC position.
3. Remove tensioner, Fig. 10, safeties, bolts and cam sprocket.
4. On 2002 and 320 models, remove snap ring at lower end of chain guide rail and unscrew pivot pin at top end until front edge of guide touches inside edge of head gasket extension that protrudes out in that area. Remove upper end of chain from cam sprocket, pull guide outward and to right, then remove chain from guide.
5. On 3.0 and 530 models, remove chain from lower sprocket and swing chain out of guide to right. On 320 models, remove guide rail, if necessary.

6. When replacing chain, reverse procedure, but align cam flange with notch facing up in line with projection above it and with bore hole facing down on 2002 and 320 models, Fig. 11. On 3.0 and 530 models, dowel pin should be at 7:30 on clock and sprocket bore must be in line with threaded bore in flange and projection, Fig. 12.

CAMSHAFT, REPLACE

1. On 530 models, disconnect pipe at EGR and intake manifold, then disconnect water hose.
2. Remove cylinder head. On 2002 and 320 models, remove distributor. On 3.0 and 530 models, remove fuel pump and push rod. On 320 models, remove cold start valve. BMW fixtures should be used to hold heads in these operations: No. 11 1 040 for 320 models, No. 11 1 060 for 530 models, No. 7003 for 3.0 models, No. 6025-2 for 2002 injected models, and No. 6025-1 for 2002 carbureted models.
3. On 320 models, remove both metal tubes at exhaust manifold flange as well as cold start valve.
4. Remove oil pipe.
5. On 2002, remove fuel pump, pull tappets out a little.
6. On all series, adjust tappet clearance at maximum to prevent damage and apply special pressure frame and apply pressure to rockers.
7. Remove guide plate just behind camshaft flange and remove camshaft in all models except 530. On 530 models, remove bolts behind notches in camshaft flange, along flange's horizontal centerline, and remove camshaft.

REAR OIL SEAL, REPLACE

1. Drain oil from pan, then remove transmission and flywheel.
2. Loosen oil pan and carefully pull down while separating oil pan gasket with a knife.
3. Remove clutch end cover bolts around perimeter of crankshaft flange exercising care where it meets extension of oil pan gasket.
4. Remove and replace sealing ring with appropriate driver.
5. Reverse procedure to install.

Fig. 12 Aligning camshaft sprocket. 3.0 and 530 models

OIL PAN, REPLACE

1. Drain oil.
2. On 2002 models, attach a hoist to engine, loosen motor mounts, place piston No. 4 at TDC, lift slightly and remove pan in a forward motion.
3. On 3.0 models, remove lower apron, stabilizer bar, power steering pump from its mountings, brackets bolts. On 3.0 and 530 models, turn engine to place piston No. 6 at TDC, and remove pan.
4. On 530 models remove stabilizer and pan.
5. On 320 models, remove steering from front axle beam and remove pan.

OIL PUMP, REPLACE

1. Drain pan, then remove pan.
2. Remove oil pump sprocket, Fig. 73.
3. Remove pump.
4. Upon reassembly, adjust chain to yield under slight pressure.

WATER PUMP, REPLACE

1. Drain coolant, remove fan, belt, in some cases, bracket.
2. Disconnect hose, then remove pump.

FUEL PUMP, REPLACE

1. Disconnect electric plug at pump, then hoses.
2. Remove pump. Those pumps with expansion tanks must be removed with the expansion tanks.

Carburetor Section

Refer to Figs. 1 and 2 for exploded views of Solex 36-40 PDSI and 40 PDSIT carburetors.

ADJUSTMENTS

2002 & 2002A Models

Idle Speed Adjust

1. With ignition timing, dwell and valve lash correctly adjusted, adjust idle speed screw to obtain 800 ± 100 rpm.
2. Reset idle mixture screw to get maximum, smooth rpm, and then reset idle speed and CO percentage to specifications.
3. To check fuel level in bowl, run engine, shut it off and remove the carburetor fuel hose, cover and gasket. Insert a depth gauge and read 0.7-0.75 in. Fig. 3. Corrections are made with seal beneath float check valve.
4. To adjust hand choke, you must set both cable, housing and butterfly valve as follows:
   a. With air cleaner off, push choke lever against stop and see that cable housing does not protrude past its final clamp more than 0.6 in., Fig. 4. With this setting, inner choke cable should be 0.08 in. from dashboard stop, adjusted by inner cable.
   b. With choke lever set at second step, gap between butterfly and air horn inner surface should be 0.21 in., Fig. 5. Check with an appropriate machine drill bit and adjust by means of hex-head screw in arc slot.
5. To adjust automatic choke, first make sure that butterfly valve remains closed at ambient temperatures of 68 degrees F. or less. Spring housing notch must align with casting peg, Fig. 6.

Remove automatic choke cover, press choke rod down as far as it will go, Fig. 7, and insert a 0.260 bit in gap between valve and inside surface of air horn, Fig. 8. Adjustment is accomplished by loosening the nut at bottom of choke housing and turning threaded bolt, Fig. 9.

7. Accelerator pump—The jet must spray parallel to the venturi wall for carburetors with one vacuum line and onto the horizontal land at the top of the venturi for carburetors with two vacuum lines. Changes in the amount of fuel pumped in can be done by adjusting the length of the stroke with the nuts on the end of the pump rod: Clockwise for more and counter-clockwise for less.

3.0 Models With Twin Carburetors

Idle Speed Adjustment, Units Without By-pass

1. With correct ignition timing, dwell, valve lash and temperature, the carburetors must be synchronized. There are two types, with and without bypass. The non-bypass type is covered first.
2. Remove air cleaner, disconnect rear carburetor rod and connect up special tool air cleaner simulator No. 13 00 000.
3. Turn in both mixture screws (top of

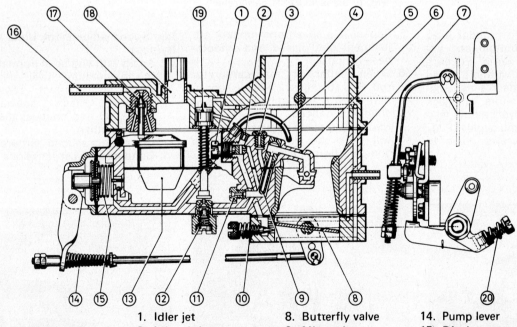

1. Idler jet	8. Butterfly valve	14. Pump lever
2. Idler air jet	9. Mixer pipe	15. Diaphragm spring
3. Air regulating jet	10. Idling mixture	16. Pump diaphragm
4. Starter valve	regulating screw	17. Float needle valve
5. Injection pipe	11. Main jet	18. Float chamber bleed
6. Outlet pipe	12. Enrichment valve	19. Vacuum plunger
7. Venturi tube	13. Float	20. Idling speed adjusting screw

Fig. 1 Solex 36-40 PDSI carburetor

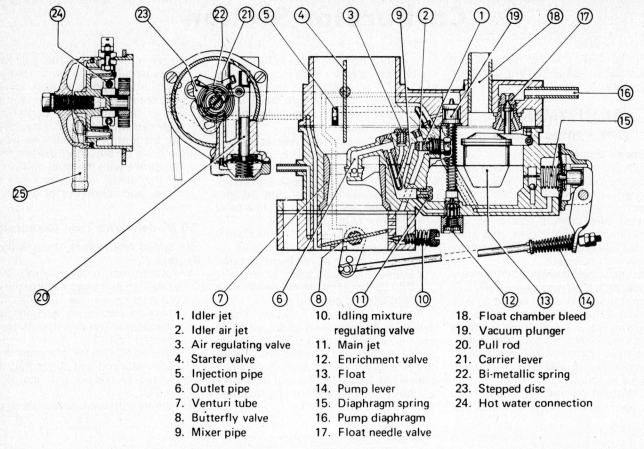

1. Idler jet
2. Idler air jet
3. Air regulating valve
4. Starter valve
5. Injection pipe
6. Outlet pipe
7. Venturi tube
8. Butterfly valve
9. Mixer pipe
10. Idling mixture regulating valve
11. Main jet
12. Enrichment valve
13. Float
14. Pump lever
15. Diaphragm spring
16. Pump diaphragm
17. Float needle valve
18. Float chamber bleed
19. Vacuum plunger
20. Pull rod
21. Carrier lever
22. Bi-metallic spring
23. Stepped disc
24. Hot water connection

Fig. 2   Solex 40 PDSIT carburetor

air horn opposite to cylinder head cover) until they bottom and unscrew them 1½-2 turns. Equalize both throttle valves with idle speed adjusting screws. Attach a manometer to both carburetors to check equalization and advance both mixture screws to maximum idle R.P.M.
4. Back idle speedscrews down to achieve 900 R.P.M.

5. Repeat idle speed and mixture adjustment until speed and smoothness is correct.
6. When reattaching rear carburetor rod, Fig. 10, adjust it if necessary so that when it is attached, no speed change is noticed.
7. Naturally, replacement of air cleaner will drop the R.P.M. slightly, so compensate accordingly.

Idle Speed Adjustment, Units With By-pass
1. Again with engine at normal operating temperature, dwell, timing and valve lash correct, remove air cleaner, attach special tool 13 00 000 and connect the secondary breather.
2. Disconnect second carburetor rod.
3. Connect exhaust emissions test unit

Fig. 3   Checking float lever

Fig. 4   Checking choke cable adjustment

Fig. 5   Checking choke valve clearance

Fig. 6 Automatic choke adjustment

Fig. 7 Pressing down choke rod

Fig. 8 Checking choke valve to air horn clearance

Fig. 9 Choke valve adjustment

and manometer.

4. Using the idle mixture adjusting screws in the carburetor bases, synchronize both carburetors until 900-1000 R.P.M. is reached.
5. Using the idle mixture screws just to the right of those turned in step 4, adjust the CO percentage.
6. In the event of an R.P.M. change, repeat steps 4, 5.
7. Again, replace the carburetor rod, adjusting its length if necessary to compensate for any R.P.M. change.

Fig. 10 Rear carburetor rod

Fuel Injection Section

1 Fuel tank
2 Fuel delivery pump
3 Pressure reservoir
4 Fuel filter
5 Fuel distributor
6 System pressure regulator
7 Warm-up regulator
8 Safety switch
9 Sensor plate
10 Throttle valve
11 Idle adjusting screw
12 Auxiliary air regulator
13 Start valve
14 Thermo timing valve
15 Injection valves
16 Air inlet
17 Vacuum regulator
18 Auxiliary air valve

Injection press.
System pressure
Return
Control pressure

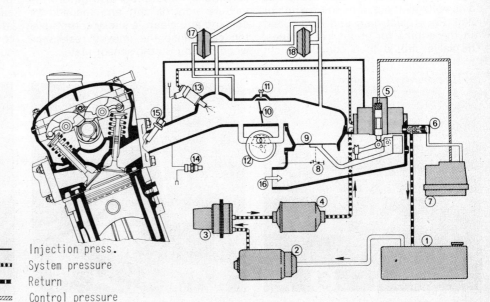

Fig. 1 CIS fuel injection system. 320 models

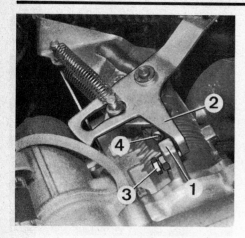

Fig. 2 Basic throttle setting.

Fig. 3 Auxiliary air regulator

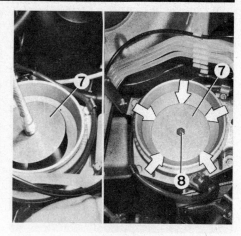

Fig. 4 Sensor plate

BOSCH CONTINUOUS INJECTION SYSTEM

320i & 320iA Models

This model uses the Bosch CIS (Continuous Injection System), Fig. 1, thus eliminating the electronic control unit.

Basic Throttle Setting

After disconnecting the accelerator cable from the operating lever, adjust the stop screw 3 so there is 0.040 inches between the stop boss, and the lever 2. Loosen the butterfly, Fig. 2, valve clamping screw and adjust the valve to zero play and retighten the screw. Run screw 3 in one more turn and lock. Match up the accelerator cable to the operating lever and reconnect.

Auxiliary Air Regulator

Disconnect plug 5 at auxiliary air regulator and pull off both hoses, Fig. 3. Turn on ignition and check that 5 has some voltage. If not, look to fuse and/or relay. Reconnect plug and hoses, and run the engine for about five minutes. The valve should then completely cut

off the air hole or it needs replacement. When the engine is cold, at about 69 degrees F. the cut off should be about half open.

Mixture Control Unit/Sensor Plate

Remove the intake cowl from throttle housing and mixture control unit, turn ignition on for about 5 seconds, during which time you should raise up the sensor plate slowly with a magnet. The resistance to the upward pull should be constant and when allowed to return to its down position, there should be no binding. Adjust with centering screw if necessary to prevent scraping or binding on the walls, Fig. 4. Note the seated position of the sensor plate in, Fig. 5. If it seats too high, you get engine run on. If it seats too low, you can get poor hot and cold starts.

If the control piston, Fig. 6, (which prevents fluctuation in the air flow sensor) sticks, remove fuel distributor from mixture control unit and inspect for damage and clean. A sticky control piston can cause the uneven resistance when pulling up the sensor plate.

Pressure Testing

Insert a 2-way valve, tee, and pressure gauge as shown, Fig. 7, between the control pressure line and the fuel distributor. If vehicle is experiencing cold start or warm up problems, disconnect the plug (5) at the auxiliary air regulator, Fig. 3. The previous procedure should have already been performed so sensor plate has free movement. Disconnect plug (15) at the mixture control unit, Fig. 8. Turn on ignition to start pump. Set the two-way valve to open so fuel can flow straight through. Use the chart, Fig. 9, to determine any problem in cold engine control pressure due to defective controls. If the pressure is low for a given coolant temperature, the warm up regulator is bad and if the pressure at a given coolant temperature is too high, return fuel flow is restricted or the warm up regulator is bad. Turn ignition off.

Now, test the warm engine control pressure. Leave the two way valve at the same position and remove the plug 15 at mixture control. Turn the ignition on to actuate the pump and see if the pressure goes up to 48-54 p.s.i. in 3 minutes

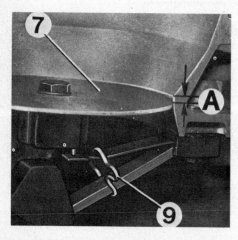

Fig. 5 Sensor plate adjustment

Fig. 6 Control piston (10)

Fig. 7 Connecting test gauge

Fig. 8 Testing pressure control unit

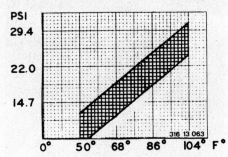

Fig. 9 Pressure control chart

Fig. 10 Control pressure electrical connector

for an engine which had been running at operating temperature and was turned off just before this test was begun. If pressure is proper, then the warm up regulator is good.

If the pressure does not come up to the standard, check wire No. 1, Fig. 10, for no voltage and correct if necessary. Check heating coil for defect, and finally replace warm up regulator.

To test control pressure on warm, running engine, install the intake cowl, connect plug 5 to auxiliary air regulator and plug 15 to mixture control unit. Run the engine at idle speed and check pressure at 48-54 p.s.i.

To check cold or warm *system* pressure, shut the two way valve with engine stopped, disconnect plug 15 at mixture control, start pump by turning on the ignition and measure 64-74 p.s.i. Turn the ignition off. Several possibilities exist. If System pressure is low:
a. Leaks in lines, connections
b. Clogged filter
c. Engine run on
d. Weak pump
e. Incorrect pressure adjustment

Correct by shims 17 as in Figs. 11 and 12.
If System pressure is high:
a. Fuel return flow restricted
b. Pressure regulator setting wrong
c. Control Piston stuck
Hot starting troubles can be caused by transfer valve not opening at 50-57 p.s.i.

Cut off pressure and leaks are found by opening the two way valve, turning on the ignition, disconnecting plug 15 at mixture control unit and reconnecting it, turning off ignition. Cutoff pressure must not drop below 24 p.s.i. for several minutes. If it does, look for:
a. O-ring 20 in, Fig. 12.
b. Warm up regulator or line leaks.
c. Fuel pump check valve leak.
d. Pressure reservoir leak.
e. O-ring 21 on transfer valve leaks.
Now, remove the pressure tester.

Vacuum Regulator, Check

On coasting, the throttle valve will be closed, and air must be supplied past the throttle valve by the bypass hole. To test this, disconnect vacuum hose 2, Fig. 13, plug connector on header. Rev the engine to 3000 R.P.M. momentarily and the speed should drop suddenly. When the hose is connected the same procedure should let the engine R.P.M.'s drop slowly.

Auxiliary Air Valve, Check

To match the extra fuel during the cold start and warm up period, air is supplied by the auxiliary air valve, Fig. 14. Therefore after starting and for a brief period afterwards, the engine R.P.M. is higher than specifications if the auxiliary air valve is working properly.

Temperature Timing Switch

The function of the temperature timing switch, Fig. 15, is to keep the cold start valve injecting extra fuel according to the coolant temperature. At -4 degrees F. the maximum time for the cold start valve is 8 seconds and the cut off is zero second at 95 degrees F. To test, disconnect plug 19 from the temperature timing switch and connect a test lamp from battery positive (hot) to connection W on the switch. The light must go on at temperatures below 95 degrees F and go off at above 95 degrees F.

Cold Start Valve, Check

Again, disconnect plug 19 at temperature timing switch, Fig. 16 ground contact W in plug, disconnect terminal 50 at solenoid, Fig. 17 remove cold start valve, connect relay terminal 87, Fig. 18, to battery positive (hot) and the valve should eject fuel. If not replace it.

Mixture Control, Replace

Remove the intake cowl 1, the three slotted screws 2, bend open the clips 3

Fig. 11 Pressure regulator valve

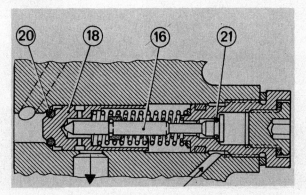

Fig. 12 Pressure regulator valve crossectional view

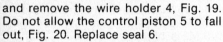

Fig. 13   Vacuum regulator (1)

Fig. 14   Auxiliary air valve

Fig. 15   Temperature timing switch

and remove the wire holder 4, Fig. 19. Do not allow the control piston 5 to fall out, Fig. 20. Replace seal 6.

Disconnect plug 7 and hoses 8, Fig. 21. Loosen nuts 9 and lift out the mixture control unit, Fig. 22.

Separate upper housing 10, replace gasket 11 and separate lower housing section from air cleaner housing, Fig. 23. Note that venturis are different so for 49 state version use air flow sensor 0 438 120 030 and for California cars, use air flow sensor 0 438 120 039.

Fuel Distributor, Replace

Again, there is a California version and a 49 state version:
0 438 040 019 for 49 states
0 438 040 027 for California
Disconnect the following fuel lines:
a. 1-4 to valves
b. 5 to warm up regulator
c. 6 to fuel filter outlet
d. 7 to warm up regulator
e. 8 to start valve
f. 9 to fuel tank
Remove the slot head mounting screws.

Lift distributor off mixture control unit, Fig. 24, replace seal, check piston for damage.

Injection Valves, Replace

Remove intake cowl and intake pipes 2,3.

Pry up injection valves from intake with a screwdriver, Fig. 25 and 26. Disconnect them from the lines and mark. To install, first place rubber ring seal into intake groove and guide valve insulators back into intake.

Warm Up Regulator, Replace

To replace, remove control line 1, return line 2 and disconnect plug 3. Remove, Fig. 27.

Auxiliary Air Regulator, Replace

Disconnect plug 1, hoses 2,3. Remove, Fig. 28.

BOSCH ELECTRONIC FUEL INJECTION (EFI) SYSTEM

Fuel Pressure Regulator Service

3.0Si & 3.0SiA

1. Insert a pressure gauge in line be-

tween the ring line and fuel filter.
2. Run engine at idle speed. Fuel pressure should be 25.56 to 31.24 PSI.
3. If fuel pressure is not within specifications, loosen the locknut and turn the adjusting screw to obtain proper fuel pressure, Fig. 29.
4. To replace the regulator:
   a. Disconnect the three hoses, Fig. 29.
   b. Remove the lock nut.
   c. Remove fuel pressure regulator bracket.

530i & 530iA

1. Insert a pressure gauge between cold start valve and fuel line.
2. Disconnect air volume control electrical connector and connect a jumper wire between terminals 36 and 39, Fig. 30.
3. Turn ignition "On" to activate fuel pump.
4. Clamp fuel return hose closed until pressure builds to approximately 60 PSI, then release the clamp. Fuel pressure should drop to 32-38 PSI. If not, replace fuel pressure regulator.

Fig. 16   Temperature timing switch

Fig. 17   Cold start solenoid

Fig. 18 Cold start solenoid relay

Fig. 19 Component locations

5. To replace the regulator:
   a. Remove No. 4 cylinder intake pipe.
   b. Disconnect fuel hoses from regulator, Fig. 31.
   c. Disconnect vacuum hose from collector.
   d. Remove fuel pressure regulator.

Fuel Lines, Replace

3.0Si & 3.0SiA
1. Remove intake pipes.
2. With tool 6068, remove hoses from front and rear circular pipes.
3. Remove front and rear circular pipes.

530i & 530iA
1. Remove intake air collector.
2. To replace front fuel line:
   a. Disconnect line (1) from fuel pressure regulator (2), Fig. 32.
   b. Disconnect line (3) from line (1), Fig. 32.
   c. Disconnect fuel line from injectors.
   d. Remove front fuel line.
3. To remove rear fuel line:
   a. Disconnect line (4) from fuel pressure regulator (2), Fig. 33.
   b. Disconnect line (5) from line (4), Fig. 33.
   c. Disconnect fuel line from injectors.
   d. Remove rear fuel line.

Throttle Valve Manifold, Replace

3.0Si & 3.0SiA
1. Remove air filter.
2. Drain coolant.
3. Disconnect electrical connector from throttle valve switch.
4. Disconnect throttle linkage and hoses from manifold.
5. Remove cylinder head cover, then the throttle valve manifold from the air collector.

Throttle Operating Lever, Replace

1. Remove air filter.
2. Disconnect throttle return springs, pull rod, retainer, washers and operating lever.
3. Loosen the clamp nut and remove throttle lever.
4. Install throttle lever and operating lever.

5. Loosen lock nut and back off screw.
6. Close throttle valve, then rotate screw inward to obtain .039 inch play between roller and end of throttle valve gate.
7. Tighten clamp nut.
8. Adjust throttle valve switch and idle speed.

Control Unit, Replace

3.0Si & 3.0SiA
1. Remove rear seat.
2. Open harness clamp, then pull cover slide and disconnect harness plug.
3. Remove control unit from floor.

530i & 530iA
1. Position clamp rearward.
2. Pull electrical connect outward toward the right.
3. Remove control unit from vehicle.

Air Volume Control, Replace

530i & 530iA
1. Disconnect electrical connector (1), Fig. 30.
2. Loosen clamps (2 and 3), Fig. 30.

Fig. 20 Retaining control piston in position

Fig. 21 Disconnecting mixture control unit hoses and wires

Fig. 22 Removing mixture control unit

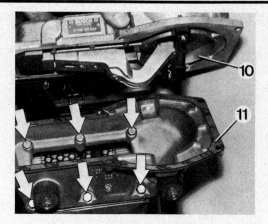

Fig. 23 Replacing mixture control unit

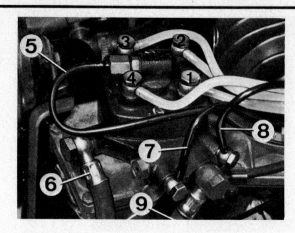

Fig. 24 Replacing fuel distributor

3. Remove air cleaner (4) and the ai volume control (5), Fig. 30.
4. Remove carrier (6), Fig. 30.

Temperature Timing Switch, Replace

530i & 530iA
1. Drain coolant.
2. Disconnect wiring connectors.
3. Remove temperature timing switch, Fig. 33.

Coolant Temperature Sensor, Replace

All
1. Drain coolant.
2. Disconnect electrical connector.
3. Remove coolant temperature sensor.

Intake Air Temperature Sensor, Replace

3.0Si & 3.0SiA
1. Disconnect electrical connector.
2. Remove intake air temperature sensor from air collector.

530i & 530iA
The intake air temperature sensor is an integral component of the air volume control. If the sensor is defective, the air volume control must be replaced.

Pressure Sensor, Replace

3.0Si & 3.0SiA
1. Disconnect electrical connector and vacuum hose.
2. Remove carrier plate from bearing block.

NOTE: On automatic transmission models, disconnect electrical connector for starter locking relay.

3. Remove pressure sensor from carrier plate.

Starter Valve, Replace

3.0Si & 3.0SiA
1. Disconnect electrical connector.
2. Disconnect fuel hose from valve.
3. Remove starter valve from air collector.

Throttle Switch, Check

530i & 530iA
1. Disconnect electrical connectors from switch.
2. Connect a jumper wire between terminal 18, Fig. 34 and the 30 terminal on the cold start relay.
3. Connect a test lamp between terminal 2 and the ground, Fig. 34. The test lamp should light when the switch is in the idle (Off) position.
4. Connect the test lamp between terminal 3 and the ground, Fig. 34. The test lamp should light when the switch is in the full throttle position.
5. The switch may be adjusted by loosening the switch and moving it. If the switch cannot be adjusted properly, replace the switch.

Start Valve, Check

530i & 530iA
1. Remove start valve from air collector.
2. Disconnect the electrical connectors from the air volume control.

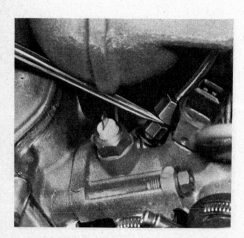

Fig. 25 Removing injection valves

Fig. 26 Injection valve

Fig. 27 Removing warm-up regulator

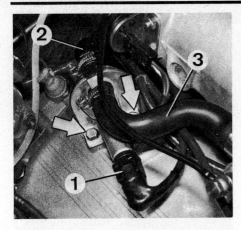

Fig. 28 Removing auxiliary air valve

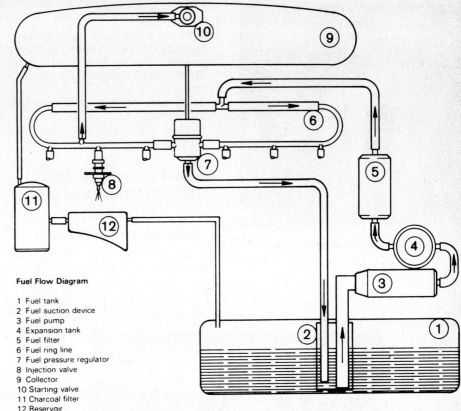

Fuel Flow Diagram

1 Fuel tank
2 Fuel suction device
3 Fuel pump
4 Expansion tank
5 Fuel filter
6 Fuel ring line
7 Fuel pressure regulator
8 Injection valve
9 Collector
10 Starting valve
11 Charcoal filter
12 Reservoir

Fig. 29 Bosch electronic fuel injection
system. 530 models

3. Connect a jumper wire between terminals 36 and 39, Fig. 35.
4. Disconnect electrical connectors from cold start relay.
5. Connect terminal 87 on cold start relay and the 30 terminal on the cold start relay with a jumper wire.
6. Turn ignition "On" to activate fuel pump. Fuel should be ejected from the starting valve.

Temperature Timing Switch, Check

530i & 530iA

1. Disconnect electrical connectors from cold start relay.
2. Connect an ohmmeter between relay terminal 86, Fig. 36, and the ground. The ohmmeter reading should be 40-70 ohms.
3. Connect an ohmmeter between terminal 86c (connection W on temperature timing switch) and the ground.

4. Connect terminal 86 with terminal 30 on the cold start relay with a jumper wire. The ohmmeter should indicate infinity at temperatures above 59° F. or zero ohms at −4° F. for 8 seconds.

Cold Start Relay Check

530i & 530iA

1. Disconnect electrical connectors and remove relay.
2. Connect a jumper wire between

terminal 85 and the ground.
3. Using jumper wires, connect terminals 30 and 86 with the battery positive terminal.
4. Connect a test lamp between either terminal 86 or 87 and the ground. The test lamp should light, Fig. 37.

Injector Valves Check

530i & 530iA

1. Disconnect electrical connectors

Fig. 30 Air volume control electrical
connector

Fig. 31 Replacing regulator

Fig. 32 Replacing intake air collector

Fig. 33 Temperature timing switch

from injector valves.
2. Turn ignition "On."
3. Connect a test lamp between both connector connections and the ground. The test lamp should light. Check each injector valve connector.
4. Reconnect injector valve electrical connectors.
5. Remove distributor cap and open the closed points.

KUGELFISCHER FUEL INJECTION SYSTEM (2002tii)

Injection Pump, Replace

1. Drain coolant and remove air cleaner housing and breather hose.

Fig. 34 Checking throttle switch

Fig. 35 Checking start valve

Fig. 36 Checking temperature timing switch

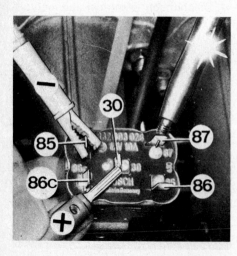

Fig. 37 Checking cold start relay

Fig. 38 Water return hose (4), oil return hose (5) and screw (7)

Fig. 39 Notch in u-belt aligned with lower section of dust cap

Fig. 40 Removing intermediate shaft

Fig. 41 Replacing warm-up regulator

2. Disconnect injection lines and ring fitting. Cover pressure valve ports.
3. Disconnect fuel return hose, oil feed and return hoses, water inlet and return hoses, auxiliary air hose and the oil dipstick bracket.
4. Remove screw 7, Fig. 38, and disconnect linkage from pump lever. Remove dust cap from front side of pump.
5. Place No. 1 cylinder at top dead center, aligning pulley mark with mark on lower dust cap, Fig. 39. Loosen sprocket nut, then with tool No. 6078, remove sprocket and belt.
6. Remove pump retaining bolts.
7. Lift pump from cover and remove intermediate shaft from warm-up sensor pivot, Fig. 40.
8. Remove pump.
9. Reverse procedure to install.

Warm-up Sensor, Replace

1. Drain coolant and remove air cleaner housing.
2. Disconnect water inlet and return hoses and auxiliary hose, then the return spring.
3. Remove sensor mounting screws and, using a screwdriver, force sensor toward rear and remove sensor. Disconnect accelerator linkage.
4. Reverse procedure to install.

Adjustment

1. Remove air regulating cone and insert retainer No. 6063 into cone groove, Fig. 41.
2. Adjust clearance "A," Fig. 5, with plate nut to .102 inch. This is the engine cold setting.
3. With engine at normal operating temperature, check clearances "A" and "B," Fig. 42. Clearance "A" should be .35-.39 inch and clearance "B" should be .157 inch.
4. If the clearance in step 3 cannot be obtained, replace the sensor.

Suction Valve, Replace

The suction valve is replaced with tool No. 6076, Fig. 43.

Pressure Valve, Replace

1. Disconnect injection pipe from pump.
2. Remove pressure valve, Fig. 44.
3. Reverse procedure to install.

Pressure Relief Valve, Replace

If the fuel pressure exceeds 28.4 PSI, relief valve replacement is required. To replace valve, disconnect fuel return hose and remove valve, Fig. 45.

Injection Valves, Replace

1. Remove fuel line from valve.
2. On some models, it may be necessary to disconnect the induction pipe.
3. Remove injection valve.
4. Reverse procedure to install. Replace the sealing ring when installing valve.

Injection Pipe, Replace

1. Remove the necessary filter components and resonator pipes.

Fig. 42 Adjusting warm-up sensor

Fig. 43 Replacing suction valve

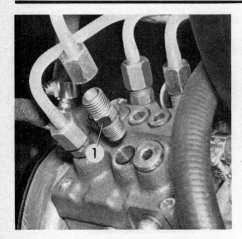

Fig. 44 Replacing pressure valve

Fig. 45 Replacing pressure regulating valve.

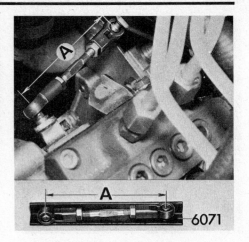

Fig. 46 Adjusting connecting rod

2. Disconnect pipe from pump and cylinder.
3. Reverse procedure to install.

Synchronizing Throttle Valve With Injection Pump

1. Connect turnbuckle and adjust length "A" to 3.346 inch with gauge No. 6071, Fig. 46.
2. Remove throttle valve cover and back out adjusting screw 1, Fig. 47, until it no longer contacts eccentric, then loosen clamping screws 2, Fig. 47.
3. Using pull hook No. 6075, lock regulating lever to bore in pump housing through last notch in lever, Fig. 48.
4. Insert gauge pin No. 6077 into throttle valve housing bore, Fig. 49, press eccentric against pin and tighten clamp screws.
5. Remove hook and gauge pin.
6. Rotate the adjusting screw until the eccentric covers approximately one-third of the bore hole, Fig. 50.

7. Remove No. 1 resonator pipe and insert the pull hook through first notch in regulating lever and into pump housing bore, Fig. 51.
8. Adjust stop screw 3, Fig. 51, to contact the pump lever.

Air Temperature Sensor Check

Connect a test lamp between the battery positive terminal and the tag on the sensor, Fig. 52. The lamp should light if the temperature is below 63°F. If not, replace the sensor.

Coolant Temperature Sensor Check

Disconnect electrical lead at sensor, then connect a test lamp between battery terminal and sensor terminal. If lamp does not light above 113° F, replace sensor, Fig. 53.

Start Valve Check

1. Remove start valve from throttle valve.

2. Turn ignition "On."
3. Connect SV wire from time switch to battery positive terminal, Fig. 54. Fuel should be ejected from feed pipe.
4. Disconnect SV wire from battery. Fuel flow should stop and the valve should not drip fuel.

Thermo-Time Switch Check

1. Disconnect electrical connector from switch.
2. Connect a test lamp between battery positive terminal and the "W" terminal on the switch, Fig. 55.
3. The test lamp should light if coolant temperature is below 95° F.
4. With the test lamp still connected, connect a jumper wire between switch terminal "G" and the battery positive terminal, Fig. 55. This will heat the bimetal contact and the lamp will remain lit, then will go out when the contact opens.

Fig. 47 Eccentric adjusting screw (7)

Fig. 48 Securing regulating lever in pump housing bore through upper slotted hole

Fig. 49 Installing setting pin 6077

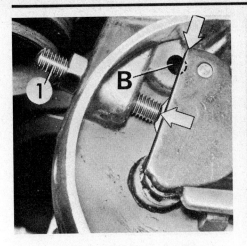

Fig. 50 Checking synchronization

Fig. 51 Adjusting full loading

Fig. 52 Checking air temperature sensor

Time Switch Check

1. Remove time switch from firewall.
2. Connect a test lamp between the "SV" terminal and the ground, Fig. 56.
3. Disconnect cable "4" from ignition coil.
4. Operate starter. The test lamp should go out after 9-15 seconds at 4°F, 4-10 seconds at 32°F. or 1 second at 95° F.
5. Disconnect electrical connector from switch and operate starter. The lamp should light for 1 second then go out.
6. Connect the test lamp between the "TH" terminal and the ground, Fig. 57, and operate starter. The lamp should remain lit when starter is operating.

Start Valve, Replace

1. Disconnect cable plug (1), Fig. 58, and fuel hose (2).
2. Remove start valve (3), Fig. 58.

Trouble-Shooting

Engine Will Not Start When Cold, Fuel Pump Operable

1. Low fuel pump pressure.
2. Starting valve injects improper fuel quantity.
3. No fuel.
4. Dirty spark plugs.

Engine Will Not Start When Warm, Fuel Pump Operable

1. Improper fuel pump pressure.
2. Starting valve not cutting out.
3. No fuel.

Fuel Pump Inoperable

1. Fuse No. 11 blown.
2. Incomplete electrical circuit to fuel pump.

Engine Hunts At Idle Speed

1. Lean idle mixture.
2. Centrifugal advance starts early.
3. Leaking intake air pipe.
4. Injection pump adjusted improperly.
5. Sticking throttle valve.

Engine Does Not Idle At Proper Speed After Cold Start

1. Air regulation cone dirty.
2. Warm-up system maladjusted.
3. Binding warm-up unit.

High Engine Idle Speed

1. Idle speed maladjusted.
2. Pre-ignition.
3. Accelerator linkage bars misaligned.
4. Injection pump maladjusted.
5. Binding throttle valve.

Low Engine Idle Speed

1. Idle speed maladjusted.
2. Binding warm-up unit.
3. Injection pump maladjusted.

Engine Stops Running & Sputters

1. Throttle valve not synchronized with injection pump.
2. Defective injection valve.
3. Binding pump plunger.
4. Leaking pressure valves.
5. Defective suction valves.

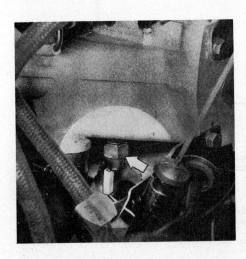

Fig. 53 Checking coolant temperature sensor

Fig. 54 Checking start valve

Fig. 55 Checking thermo time switch

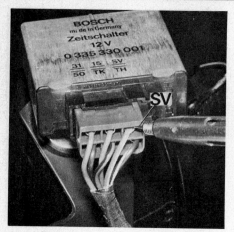

Fig. 56 Checking time switch

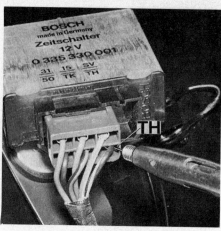

Fig. 57 Checking time switch

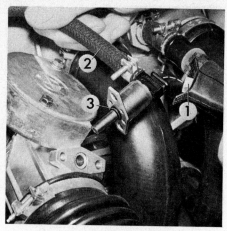

Fig. 58 Replacing start valve

6. Fluctuating fuel pressure.

Engine Backfires On Coast
1. Throttle valve not synchronized with injection pump.
2. Throttle valve does not return to idle position.
3. Idle speed maladjusted.
4. Idle speed stop bolt turned in too far.

Engine Does Not Develop Full Power
1. Low fuel pump pressure.
2. Defective injection valve.

3. Throttle valve not synchronized with injection pump.
4. Throttle valve travel inadequate.

Engine Runs Rough Under Partial Load
1. Binding throttle valve.
2. Improper throttle valve opening.
3. Spherical shell for intermediate shaft in warm-up unit housing loose or improperly positioned.
4. Connecting rod between injection pump and intermediate shaft too

long.
5. Insufficient amount of fuel injected per stroke.

Excessive Fuel Consumption
1. Warm-up unit does not deactivate.
2. Leaking starter valve.
3. Throttle valve not synchronized with injection pump.
4. Injection pump maladjusted.
5. Defective temperature retard switch.

Emission Controls Section

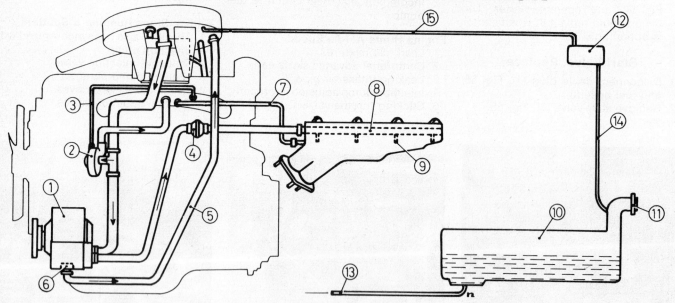

1 air pump	6 pressure regulating unit	11 fuel tank filler cap (not vented)
2 control valve	7 exhaust gas recirculation pipe	12 vapour storage line
3 control pipe	8 air distributor pipe	13 fuel pipe
4 check valve	9 blow-in pipe	14 vapour purge line
5 return pipe for excess air	10 fuel tank	15 purification pipe

Fig. 1 Emission control system with air pump. 2002 models

Fig. 2   Control valve. 2002 models

Fig. 3   Check valve. 2002 models

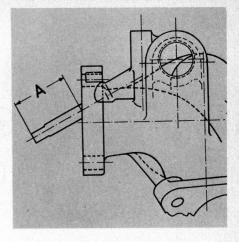

Fig. 4   Blow-in pipe. 2002 models

SYSTEM SERVICING
2002

For models equipped with air pump, Fig. 1:

a. Replace control valve, Fig. 2, if carburetor adjustment is difficult and compression, ignition and valve lash are correct or if car backfires upon release of accelerator from high RPM.

b. Check valve, Fig. 3, should be checked for one way operation and replaced if faulty.

c. Remove blow-in pipe, Fig. 4, and check for closure to 113°F.

d. Pressure regulator, Fig. 5, can be checked as follows:
   1. Remove return pipe and place palm of hand on unit. Run engine between 1500 and 2100 RPM.
   2. If the excess pressure valve opens before 1700 RPM, replace pressure regulator. If it opens later than 2000 RPM, replace air pump.

For models without air pump, Figs. 6 and 7:

a. With ignition, compression and valve lash correct, adjust dashpot by first disconnecting dashpot vacuum hoses and plugging. Set engine at 1600 RPM with dashpot, then open hose and connect to dashpot, Fig. 8. When you remove hose from dashpot, engine should pick up several hundred RPM showing correct retard action.

b. If dashpot does not move at engine speeds of less than 1650±100 RPM, pull hose and check for vacuum in it. If there is, replace dashpot. If not, remove magnetic valve electric plug, Fig. 9, and check that it shows 12 volts or more at 1900 RPM or more. If it does, replace valve. If not, check brown and red/white cable of engine speed switch (3) with voltmeter. No reading at RPM greater than 1900 means a defective speedswitch, Fig. 10. Some reading means you have to change relay (4), Fig. 11.

Exhaust Gas Recirculation

To check diaphragm valve, set engine at 950 RPM and pull vacuum control

Fig. 5   Pressure regulator. 2002 models

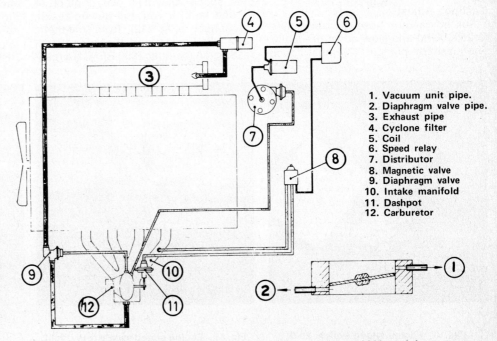

1. Vacuum unit pipe.
2. Diaphragm valve pipe.
3. Exhaust pipe
4. Cyclone filter
5. Coil
6. Speed relay
7. Distributor
8. Magnetic valve
9. Diaphragm valve
10. Intake manifold
11. Dashpot
12. Carburetor

Fig. 6   Emission control system without air pump. 2002 models

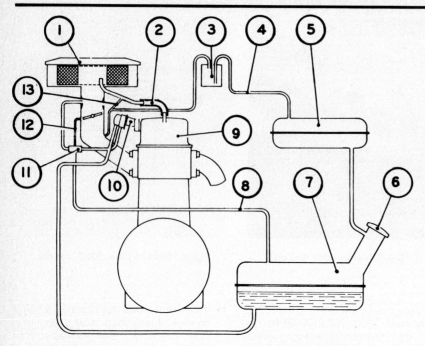

1. air cleaner
2. primary crankcase vent
3. activated carbon filter
4. vapour purge line
5. vapour storage tank
6. sealed fuel filler cap
7. fuel tank
8. excess fuel pipe
9. cylinder head cover
10. fuel pump
11. fuel return control valve
12. vacuum hose
13. secondary crankcase vacuum control

Fig. 7   Evaporative emission control system. 2002 models

Fig. 8   Dashpot adjustment. 2002 models

Fig. 9   Magnetic valve. 2002 models

hose to valve from carburetor and connect it to vacuum hose for secondary crankcase vacuum control, Fig. 12. If engine speed drops to 500-600 RPM, valve is functioning correctly. If drop is only slight, clean recirculation pipes from exhaust manifold to intake pipe. If this doesn't help, change valve.

3.0
Dashpot, Adjust

Pull off vacuum hose (6), run engine at 2500 RPM and slow down gradually. The dashpot plunger (7) must touch carburetor linkage (8), Fig. 13. Adjust by turning dashpot (9) and locking with nut (10), then reconnect hose.

If dashpot does not lose contact with linkage at speeds less than 1800 RPM, pull vacuum hose and check for suction. If there is suction, replace pot. If there is no suction in hose, check engine speed relay (11) for contact or ground fault. If you still get no result, disconnect plug (12) from magnetic valve (13), Fig. 14, and check for 12 volt reading on meter at 2000 RPM. No read-

ing means replace speed sensitive relay (14). To check ignition timing switch-over which controls retard up to 2500 RPM and advance above that, remove vacuum hose (1) and check suction, Fig. 15. If there is no suction, disconnect plug from magnetic valve (17) and apply voltmeter with engine at 2200 RPM. A zero reading means speed sen-

Fig. 10   Engine speed switch. 2002 models

Fig. 11   Engine speed switch relay. 2002 models

Fig. 12   EGR vacuum control hose connected to secondary crankcase vacuum control. 2002 models

BMW

Fig. 13 Dashpot adjustment. 3.0 models

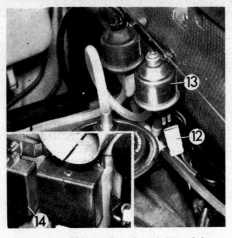

Fig. 14 Magnetic valve. 3.0 models

Fig. 15 Ignition timing switch-over

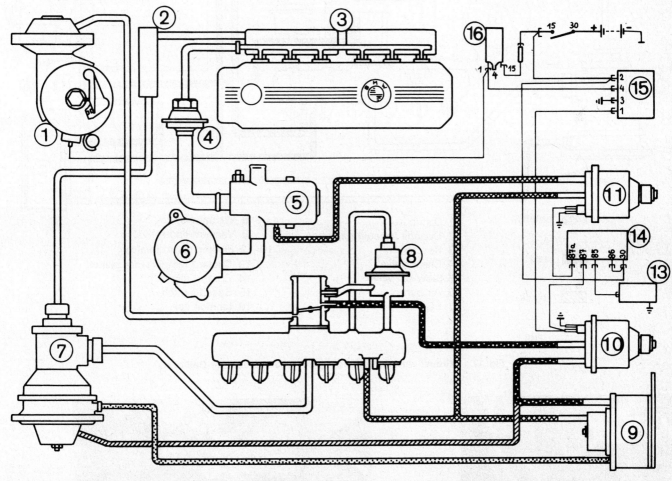

white	1 Distributor	8 Vacuum limiter
blue	2 Cyclone exhaust gas filter	9 Vacuum control valve
	3 Reactor	10-11 Electric control valve
	4 Check valve	13 Coolant temperature switch
black	5 Blow-off valve	14 Control relay
	6 Air pump	15 Speed switch
red	7 EGR valve	16 Ignition coil

Fig. 16 Exhaust emission control system. 530 models except California

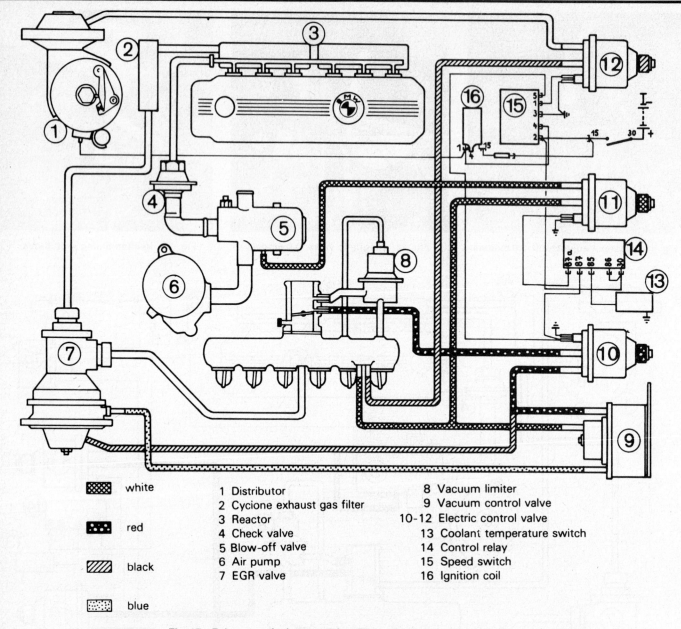

	white	1	Distributor	8	Vacuum limiter
	red	2	Cycione exhaust gas filter	9	Vacuum control valve
	black	3	Reactor	10-12	Electric control valve
	blue	4	Check valve	13	Coolant temperature switch
		5	Blow-off valve	14	Control relay
		6	Air pump	15	Speed switch
		7	EGR valve	16	Ignition coil

Fig. 17   Exhaust emission control system. 530 models for California

Fig. 18   Disconnecting hose (1)

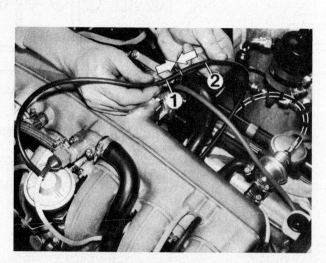

Fig. 19   Connecting hose (1) to hose (2)

Fig. 20 Connecting hose (2) to hose (3)

Fig. 21 Checking blow-off valve. 530 models

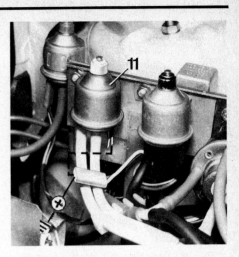

Fig. 22 Control valve. 530 models

sitive relay (16) must be replaced. If reading is 12 volts, change magnetic valve (17).

Exhaust Gas Recirculation

To check diaphragm valve, set engine at 900 RPM. Reconnect hoses as in this test for 2002 model and you should notice engine dropping off to about 750 RPM. That indicates correct functioning of valve. If drop off is only slight, clean pipes. If this doesn't work, change valve.

530, Figs. 16 & 17

Exhaust Gas Recirculation

To test EGR valve with engine at idle, disconnect black hose (1) at adaptor, Fig. 18, before vacuum control valve. Disconnect hose (2) at vacuum limiter and connect to hose (1), Fig. 19. Engine should drop about 100 RPM.

Connect hose (1) to adaptor again. Disconnect hose (3) and connect it to hose (2), Fig. 20. Engine should drop about 200 RPM. Connect hoses (2, 3) back in their original places.

Blow-off Valves

Air should be blown through hose (4), Fig. 21, for a second or two when coolant temperature goes above 113 degrees F. If not, disconnect control valve (11), plug, Fig. 22, and check with test lamp. Lamp should go on above 113 degrees F. and off below that. If these tests show power supply is good, replace control valve.

Vacuum Control Valve

To test closing at idle, disconnect red hose (1) at adaptor to solenoid, Fig. 23. Disconnect red hose (2) at solenoid and connect it to adaptor. Disconnect black hose at EGR valve and plug. Engine RPM should not drop.

To test opening at idle, disconnect white hose (3) at vacuum control valve, Fig. 24. Disconnect red hose (1) at adaptor to solenoid and leave open. Connect white hose (3) to adaptor. Engine should drop about 200-300 RPM.

Air Pump

To test, disconnect air hose (1),

Fig. 25, and increase engine speed. Pump output should increase with engine speed. If not, check belt. If this doesn't help, change the pump.

Vacuum Limiter (HC Control)

With engine at normal temperature, disconnect hose at pump and vacuum hose at distributor. Adjust CO to 1.5-3.0 per cent. Accelerate engine (rear wheels on roller set up as on a dynomometer) and allow to slow down as if coasting down to idle. HC should remain within 350 rpm. Above this usually means engine wear.

Check Valve

Check for one way action or exhaust residue on control valve, in hoses of air pump.

Red Control Valve

Disconnect hoses (A,B) from red electric control valve (10), Fig. 26, with engine off at coolant temperature below 113 degrees F. Connect hose (A) to center of throttle housing and hose (B) at

Fig. 23 Checking closing of vacuum control valve. 530 models

Fig. 24 Checking opening of vacuum control valve. 530 models

Fig. 25 Checking air pump operation. 530 models

Fig. 26 Checking red electric control valve. 530 models

Fig. 27 Checking coolant temperature switch. 530 models

Fig. 28 Speed switch. 530 models

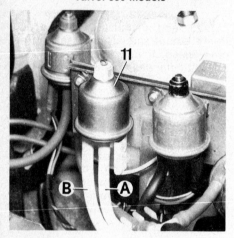

Fig. 29 Checking white control valve. 530 models

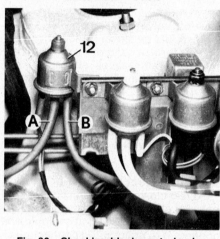

Fig. 30 Checking black control valve. 530 models

Fig. 31 Checking speed switch. 530 models

side of vacuum control adaptor. Also connect one hose to center connection and blow in air. The valve works if air flow with ignition off or no air flows with ignition on. Note coolant temperature switch (13), control switch (14), speed switch (15).

Coolant Temperature Switch and Control Relay

With coolant temperature below 113 degrees F., turn ignition on, disconnect plug at red valve (10), connect test lamp. If test lamp is on when coolant is below specified temperature, coolant temperature switch (13) and control relay (14) are working correctly.

If light doesn't go on, ground test lamp. If light goes on now, red valve (10), is improperly grounded, Fig. 26.

Second test: if light is not on, disconnect wire at temperature switch (13), connect to ground. If light does not go on, replace control valve (14) after checking terminal 30 for current.

Coolant Temperature Switch (13), Speed Switch (15), Control Relay (14)

With control temperature above 113 degrees F., turn ignition on, disconnect plug at red valve (10), and connect test lamp, Fig. 27. Okay if lamp is off. If lamp

Fig. 32 Checking air pump. 320 models

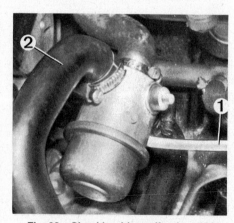

Fig. 33 Checking blow-off valve. 320 models

Fig. 34 Checking check valve. 320 models

Fig. 35 Checking thermo valve. 320 models

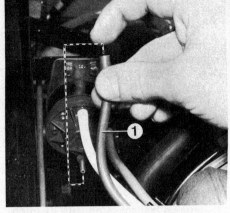

Fig. 36 Checking pressure connector. 320 models

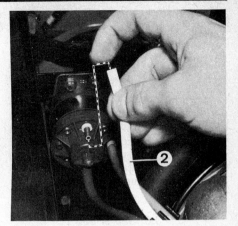

Fig. 37 Checking intake manifold vacuum. 320 models

is on, coolant temperature switch (13) or control relay (14) is defective.

Now, with engine running at normal operating temperature, if test lamp goes on above 3000 RPM function is normal. If test lamp is out, change speed switch (15), Fig. 28.

White Control Valve (11)

This valve, Fig. 29, initiates blow-off valve. Blow-off valve is open below 113 degrees F. and white control valve is open below this temperature. With both hoses (A,B) disconnected at valve (11), ignition on, temperature of coolant above 113 degrees F., connect a hose at center connection and blow in air. Valve (11) is operating properly if no air flows with ignition on and air flows with ignition off.

Now disconnect plug at valve (11) and connect test lamp. The light must be on with engine coolant temperature above 113 degrees F. If not, connect test lamp to ground to check for faulty ground (lamp lights). Disconnect coolant temperature switch (13) plug; light should go on. If not, control relay (14) is faulty.

Black Valve (12) Calif. Only

This valve cuts out retarded ignition

vacuum control above 3000 RPM. Disconnect hoses (A,B) at valve (12) with ignition off. Blow air into hose connected to center connector. Air should flow at RPM lower than 3000 but not above. If this is not the case, check feed and ground of speed switch (15). Idle engine, then disconnect plug at valve (12) and connect test lamp. Test lamp should not light, Fig. 30. If it does, change speed switch (15), Fig. 31. Increase speed slowly to over 3000 RPM. Test lamp should light. If not, ground lamp, and if lamp lights, there is faulty ground. If lamp still doesn't light, change speed switch (15).

320

Air Pump

To check air pump, detach hose (1) at pump, Fig. 32, start engine, and pump output should increase as engine speed is increased. If not, check belt. If there is no improvement, change pump.

Blow-Off Valve

Disconnect vacuum hose (1) with engine running, Fig. 33. You should be able to feel suction at vacuum hose, and when you reattach it air should be felt rushing through hose (2).

Check Valve

Disconnect hose (3) at blow-off valve and introduce air, Fig. 34. Flow should be toward exhaust manifold. With suction applied to hose (3), valve should close.

Thermo Valve

Disconnect hoses (1,2) at their other ends, Fig. 35, (throttle housing and EGR valve respectively) and blow in air. Thermo valve (PE20 276) should be closed up to 91 degrees F. and open above 109 degrees Fl.

Pressure Converter

With engine running, check for proper exhaust gas counter pressure/control pressure by removing red hose (1) at converter and feel pressure, Fig. 36.

Reconnect red hose and disconnect white hose (2) and feel vacuum, Fig. 37. Replace white hose then disconnect red and blue hoses (1,3) and feel blue hose connector on converter for vacuum, Fig. 38. If no vacuum, replace converter.

EGR Valve

Disconnect blue hose at EGR, Fig. 39. RPM shouldn't change. If it does, throttle valve gap is excessive at idle or EGR is not closing. Now, with blue hose disconnected at EGR and black hose disconnected at header, disconnect red hose at throttle housing and connect to header. Speed should drop. If it doesn't, change EGR valve.

Start fresh, and disconnect black hose from header, red hose at thermo valve and connect red hose to header. There should be no drop in R.P.M. If there is, either EGR won't close or pressure converter is bad.

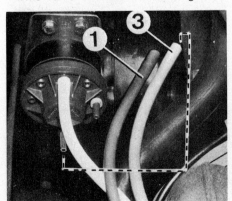

Fig. 38 Checking regulating pressure. 320 models

Fig. 39 Checking EGR valve. 320 models

Clutch & Transmission Section

CLUTCH PEDAL, ADJUST

2002

These models have both mechanical and hydraulic types of clutch release mechanisms. In either case adjustment occurs on threaded rod connected clutch release arm. To adjust, loosen locknut, then rotate rod until .67-.75 inch play is obtained and tighten locknut.

3.0, 320 & 530

The clutch release mechanisms on these models are all hydraulically operated. The adjustments are on turnbuckled rod which is connected to foot pedal arm. To adjust, loosen locknut, then rotate turnbuckle until .67-.75 inch play is obtained and tighten locknut.

CLUTCH, REPLACE

2002

1. Remove transmission.
2. Lock flywheel with an appropriate device and unbolt clutch cover and driven plate.
3. Reverse procedure to install, using centering tool to align clutch, Fig. 1. Lubricate clutch main drive gear pilot bearing and gradually tighten cover.
4. Adjust clutch pedal lash.

3.0

There are two types of clutch release arms, inside and outside.
1. For models with outside arm, remove transmission first, then remove clutch slave cylinder snap ring retainer, Fig. 2, and move cylinder forward. Remove attaching bolts and clutch housing.
2. For models with inside arm, remove slave cylinder first, Fig. 3, then transmission, followed by clutch housing.
3. Remove clutch cover and driven plate.
4. Reverse procedure to install, using centering tool to align clutch, Fig. 1.

320

1. Remove transmission with its integral clutch housing.
2. Remove clutch cover and driven plate. Check clutch main drive gear needle bearing in crankshaft hub.
3. Replace as described under 2002 model procedure.
4. Adjust lash.

MANUAL TRANSMISSION, REPLACE

2002 & 320

1. Remove upper mounting bolts, then all brackets at flange and disconnect exhaust pipe at manifold.
2. Disconnect drive shaft, leaving special coupling on shaft. Disconnect center bearing and position drive shaft aside.
3. Disconnect back-up light switch wire, speedometer cable, harness from holders, and remove cover plate to gain access to driver's compartment. On 2002 models, remove snap ring at ball fulcrum of shift lever as well.
4. Remove snap ring retainer, washer and disconnect selector linkage, then remove slave cylinder and lower cover of clutch housing.

5. Remove crossmember, then remove transmission to rear.
6. When reinstalling transmission, pre-load drive shaft center bearing by 0.078 inches and replace coupling stop nuts.

3.0 & 530

1. Remove complete exhaust system selector lever, driveshaft at rear of transmission, support at center bearing, speedometer cable, back-up light switch, heat guard for 320 models and position driveshaft aside.
2. Support engine between front axle carrier and oil pan.
3. With inside clutch mechanism, remove slave cylinder and unbolt transmission. Remove crossmember and rubber bearing. With transmission pulled out slightly, lift steel wire spring over spherical pin collar of clutch release assembly, and remove transmission. When installing, align clutch release bearing and arm. Then, slide guide sleeve into bearing, through driven plate and push transmission into position.

AUTOMATIC TRANSMISSION, REPLACE

1. Drain transmission oil, then remove negative cable, oil filler tube and bracket, accelerator connections, electrical plugs and connections, speedometer and disconnect engine pipe at manifold in the 2002, 320, complete exhaust system removal on 3.0 and 530.
2. Remove oil coolers where neces-

Fig. 1 Aligning clutch disc

Fig. 2 Slave cylinder retaining ring (1) and circlip (2)

Fig. 3 Slave cylinder retaining nuts

sary, disconnect drive shaft at rear of transmission, remove center bearing support and push drive shaft aside. Remove guard covers, unbolt four torque converter bolts from drive plate. Disconnect selector rod.

3. Support transmission on a suitable jack, remove crossmember, unbolt transmission and remove with converter.

4. When installing, make sure that torque converter is correctly mated to primary pump.

AUTOMATIC TRANSMISSION ADJUSTMENTS

Shift Selector, Adjust

1. Set lever arm at transmission in "O" (Neutral). Disconnect selector rod at bottom end of selector lever and adjust it so that stop lug contacts gear shift gate. Then, shorten it as follows: Three turns on the 2002 and 3.0 models, Two and a half on 530 models and One turn on the 320 models.

Following this, on 3.0, you must adjust auxiliary rod to switch quadrant.

Accelerator Linkage & Cable, Adjust

2002

1. Adjust accelerator linkage with air cleaner and accelerator cable disconnected. Press pedal down to kickdown position where throttle valve must be fully open. Throttle valve must not extend beyond its vertical position. Bend stop to adjust. The accelerator linkage length can be adjusted with the turnbuckle.

2. Adjust the accelerator cable with the cable disconnected from the throttle bellcrank at the carburetors. Check alignment of pin and hole with both throttles and pedal in full throttle position.

3.0 & 530

1. With tension rod disconnected, synchronize idle speed and disconnect accelerator cable from bellcrank.

2. Adjust tension rod so that when connected, bellcrank will be against

its stop. Do not allow tension rod to move to its kickdown position.

3. With a clearance of .0098-.0197 inches between nipple and cable sleeve, clevis hole of throttle rod must line up with hole in bellcrank with no slack in accelerator cable.

4. Press pedal down on kickdown stop and adjust thrust rod so that space between nipple and cable sleeve end is 1.4567 inches.

320

1. Adjust accelerator cable with basic idle setting correct, by moving locknuts at bracket so that there is 0.008-0.012 inches slack at cable eye.

2. Now, depress pedal to full throttle stop screw and adjust screw so that there is 0.020 inch play between operating lever and its stop.

3. With transmission in neutral, adjust play A near end of transmission cable housing to 0.010-0.030 inches with clevis locknut. With pedal depressed to kickdown stop, play A should be 1.712-2.027 inches, again adjusted with stop screw.

AUTOMATIC TRANSMISSION TROUBLESHOOTING
2002A (3 HP-12 Transmission)

Condition	Cause	Correction
Shift points too high	a) Accelerator cable incorrectly adjusted b) Governor bush jammed c) Excessive axial clearance at governor piston rings d) Shift control valve not working correctly	a) Adjust accelerator cable b) Free both governor bush and piston c) Renew piston rings d) Exchange control unit
Shift points too low	a) Accelerator cable incorrectly adjusted b) Governor bush jammed c) Shift control valve not working correctly	a) Adjust accelerator cable b) Free both governor bush and piston c) Exchange control unit
No kickdown reaction	a) Accelerator cable incorrectly adjusted b) Shift control valve stuck	a) Adjust accelerator cable b) Exchange control unit
Selector lever cannot be placed in position P	a) Control linkage incorrectly adjusted b) Locking mechanism defective	a) Adjust control linkage b) Overhaul locking mechanism
Selector lever cannot be placed in position R	a) Control linkage incorrectly adjusted	a) Adjust control linkage
No forward or reverse movement	a) Oil quantity too small b) Drive lug on converter broken c) Oil pressure too low	a) Correct oil level b) Renew converter c) Dismantle transmission
Only 1st gear in position A	a) Control valve and control pistons 1 and 2 jammed b) Governor bush jammed	a) Exchange control unit b) Free both governor bush and piston

(continued)

Condition	Cause	Correction
Only 1st and 2nd gear in position A	a) Control valve and control pistons 2 and 3 jammed	a) Exchange control unit
	b) Excessive axial clearance at rectangular rings for clutch B	b) Renew rectangular rings
	c) Clutch valve and clutch damper B not working	c) Renew control unit
	d) Centering plate bush warped	d) Renew bush and/or centering plate
Moves only in 2nd gear	a) Control valves and control pistons 1, 2 and 3 jammed	a) Exchange control unit
Moves only in 3rd gear	a) Control valves and control pistons 1, 2 and 3 jammed	a) Exchange control unit
	b) Governor bush jammed	b) Free both governor bush and pistons
No movement in reverse	a) Control linkage incorrectly adjusted	a) Adjust control linkage
	b) Clutch valve and clutch damper B not working	b) Dismantle transmission
	c) Excessive axial clearance at rectangular rings for clutch B	c) Renew rectangular rings
Transmission slipping	a) Accelerator cable disconnected	a) Attach accelerator cable
	b) Oil quantity too low	b) Correct oil level
	c) Shift control valve jammed	c) Exchange control unit
Transmission shift from 1st to 2nd gear slipping	a) Clutches C and C' slipping	a) Dismantle transmission
	b) Clutch valve and clutch damper C not working	b) Dismantle transmission
	c) Accelerator cable disconnected	c) Attach accelerator cable
	d) Oil quantity too low	d) Correct oil level
	e) Shift control valve jammed	e) Exchange control unit
Transmission slipping during shift from 2nd to 3rd gear	a) Clutch B slipping	a) Dismantle transmission
	b) Excessive axial clearance at rectangular rings for clutch B	b) Renew rectangular rings
	c) Centering plate bush warped	c) Renew bush and/or centering plate
	d) Accelerator cable disconnected	d) Attach accelerator cable
	e) Oil quantity too low	e) Correct oil level
	f) Oil pressure too low	f) Dismantle transmission
	g) Shift control valve jammed	g) Exchange control unit
3rd gear slipping	a) Clutch B slipping	a) Dismantle transmission
	b) Excessive axial clearance at rectangular rings	b) Renew rectangular rings
	c) Accelerator cable disconnected	c) Attach accelerator cable
	d) Oil quantity too low	d) Correct oil level
	e) Oil pressure too low	e) Dismantle transmission
	f) Shift control valve jammed	f) Exchange control unit
No power transmitted in 1st gear in position A when kickdown used	a) 1st gear freewheel defective	a) Renew freewheel
In position 2 change from 2nd to 1st very rough	a) Clutch valve and clutch damper D not working	a) Exchange control unit
No brake effect in 1st gear in positions 2 and 1	a) Clutch valve and clutch damper D defective	a) Exchange control unit
	b) Clutch D defective	b) Renew clutch D
No brake effect in 2nd gear in positions 2 and 1	a) Clutch C' defective	a) Renew clutch C'

(continued)

Condition	Cause	Correction
High pitched whine depending on speed and load cycle	a) Propeller shaft center bearing defective	a) Renew center bearing
Rattling noise when idling	a) Drive plate broken b) Welded lugs broken away from converter	a) Renew drive plate b) Renew converter
Buzzing noise when idling. Disappears with acceleration in position O	a) Valve vibrating in control unit	a) Correct oil level
Whistling noise depending on gear	a) Planetary gear set noisy	a) Renew planetary gear
Converter dome oiling up	a) Shaft seal defective b) O-ring defective at primary pump housing c) Converter leaking at weld seams d) Plugs leaking	a) Renew shaft seal b) Renew O-ring c) Renew converter d) Renew seal
Output flange oiling up	a) Shaft seal defective	a) Renew shaft seal
Filler pipe losing oil	a) O-ring defective or missing	a) Renew O-ring
Loss of oil at vent	a) Oil level incorrect	a) Correct oil level
Speedometer drive oiling up	a) O-ring defective	a) Renew speedometer bushing

320 (3 HP-22 Transmission)

Condition	Cause	Correction
Shift points too high	a) Accelerator cable setting wrong b) Governor bushing seized c) Governor piston rings defective or worn d) Throttle pressure valve malfunctions e) Shift valves jammed	a) Adjust accelerator cable b) Clean or replace governor c) Replace piston rings d) Replace control unit e) Replace control unit
Shift points too low	a) Accelerator cable setting wrong b) Governor bushing seized c) Throttle pressure valve malfunctions d) Plastic balls in transfer plate leak	a) Adjust accelerator cable b) Clean or replace governor c) Replace control unit d) Replace control unit
Shift points too high or too low and shift movements too long and too soft	a) Clutch C + C' damaged by 1-2 gear shifts b) Clutch B damaged by 2-3 gear shifts	a) Replace clutches C and C' b) Replace clutch B
No kickdown shifts	a) Accelerator cable setting wrong b) Control unit setting wrong c) Throttle pressure valve sticks d) Plastic balls in transfer plate leak	a) Adjust accelerator cable b) Adjust control unit c) Replace control unit d) Replace control unit
Selector lever cannot be moved to P	a) Selector linkage setting wrong b) Locking device defective	a) Adjust selector linkage b) Repair locking device
Parking position will not disengage	a) Parking lock pawl caught in teeth of output shell b) Excessive friction in parking lock device	a) Replace parking lock pawl b) Repair parking lock device
Parking position does not hold (slips)	a) Selector rod setting wrong	a) Adjust selector rod
No forward or reverse drive	a) Oil level insufficient b) Pump drive defective c) Drive plate broken d) Parking lock pawl stuck e) Clutches A and B defective	a) Correct oil level b) Replace converter and pump c) Replace drive plate d) Replace pawl e) Disassemble transmission

(continued)

Condition	Cause	Correction
No drive in reverse and 2nd gear	a) Shift valve stuck in 3rd gear position	a) Replace control unit Disassemble transmission if metal particles or abrasion are found in oil sump
Hard engagement jolt or definite double knock when engaging reverse gear	a) Damper B defective or wrong cover parts	a) Replace control unit
Car cannot be started in O	a) Transmission switch defective	a) Replace transmission switch
Car creeps or runs in O	a) Selector rod setting wrong b) Clutch A aired too slowly c) Clutch A defective (bonded)	a) Adjust selector rod b) Disassemble transmission c) Disassemble transmission
Drive in 1st gear only when in A	a) 1st-2nd shift valve stuck b) Governor bushing seized	a) Replace control unit b) Clean or replace governor
Drive in 1st and 2nd gear only when in A	a) 2nd-3rd shift valve stuck	a) Replace control unit
Drive in 2nd gear only	a) 1st-2nd and 2nd-3rd shift valves stuck	a) Replace control unit
Drive in 3rd gear only	a) 1st-2nd and 2nd-3rd shift valves stuck b) Governor bushing seized	a) Replace control unit b) Clean or replace governor
Grinding shifts	a) Accelerator cable disengaged or maladjusted b) Oil level too low c) Throttle pressure valve stuck d) Clutch A defective	a) Connect or adjust accelerator cable b) Correct oil level c) Replace control unit d) Disassemble transmission
Grinding shifts from 1st to 2nd gear	a) Clutches C and C' slip b) Clutch valve and damper C malfunction c) Accelerator cable disengaged or maladjusted d) Oil level too low e) Throttle pressure valve stuck f) One-way clutch F defective	a) Disassemble transmission b) Disassemble transmission c) Connect or adjust accelerator cable d) Correct oil level e) Replace control unit f) Disassemble transmission
Grinding shifts from 2nd to 3rd gear	a) Clutch B slips b) Accelerator cable disengaged or maladjusted c) Oil level too low d) Oil pressure too low e) Throttle pressure valve stuck f) One-way clutch E defective	a) Replace clutch B b) Connect or adjust accelerator cable c) Correct oil level d) Disassemble transmission e) Replace control unit f) Disassemble transmission
3rd gear slips	a) Clutch B slips b) Accelerator cable disengaged or maladjusted c) Oil level too low d) Oil pressure too low e) Throttle pressure valve stuck	a) Disassemble transmission b) Connect or adjust accelerator cable c) Correct oil level d) Disassemble transmission e) Replace control unit
No forward drive	a) Selector linkage setting wrong b) Clutch A defective or oil lost through leak in supply line	a) Adjust selector linkage b) Replace clutch A

(continued)

Condition	Cause	Correction
No reverse drive	a) Selector linkage setting wrong b) Clutch B or D defective c) Clutch valve and damper B malfunctioning d) Oil level too low, pump cannot draw in oil	a) Adjust selector linkage b) Disassemble transmission c) Replace control unit d) Correct oil level
Slipping or shaking in reverse gear	a) Clutch B or D damaged b) Serious loss of oil in supply line to B or D	a) Disassemble transmission b) Disassemble transmission
Stall speed too high	a) Oil level too low b) Engaged clutch slips c) One-way clutch (F or G) slips	a) Correct oil level b) Disassemble transmission c) Disassemble transmission
Stall speed too low	a) Torque converter defective b) Engine output insufficient	a) Replace torque converter b) Test engine
Transmission vibrates at fast move-offs	a) Clutch A defective b) Propeller shaft center bearing defective c) One-way clutch F or G defective	a) Replace clutch A b) Replace center bearing c) Disassemble transmission
Transmission shifts hard or down	a) Accelerator cable setting wrong b) Clutch A defective	a) Adjust accelerator cable
Drive in O	a) Selector linkage setting wrong b) Clutch A (forward) bonded c) Clutch B (reverse) bonded	a) Adjust selector linkage b) Disassemble transmission c) Disassemble transmission
No braking effect from 1st gear when in 2 and 1	a) Clutch valve and damper D defective b) Clutch D defective	a) Replace control unit b) Replace clutch D
No braking effect from 2nd gear when in 2 and 1	a) Clutch C' defective	a) Replace clutch C'
Transmission shifts too early when downshifting from 2nd to 1st gear manually	a) Locking valve pressure too high b) Loss of pressure in governor supply line between governor and shift valves	a) Replace control unit b) Disassemble transmission
Transmission shifts too late when downshifting from 2nd to 1st gear manually	a) Locking valve pressure too low b) Governor pressure too high	a) Replace control unit b) Disassemble transmission
Stall speed in forward too high	a) Clutch A or 1st gear one-way clutch slips	a) Disassemble transmission
Stall speed in forward too low	a) Engine output not sufficient b) Converter one-way clutch defective	a) Check engine tuning b) Replace converter
Whining depending on speed and load	a) Center bearing of propeller shaft defective	a) Replace center bearing
Rattling noise in neutral	a) Drive plate broken b) Welded drive dogs on converter damaged	a) Replace drive plate b) Replace converter
Growling noise in neutral, eliminated when accelerating in O	a) Valve chatter in control unit b) Oil pump draws in air	a) Correct oil level b) Tighten valve body mounting screws, check gasket

(continued)

Condition	Cause	Correction
Oil on torque converter bell housing	a) Shaft seal leaking b) Primary pump body O-ring shot c) Converter leaks at welded seams d) Plug leaks	a) Replace shaft seal b) Replace O-ring c) Replace converter d) Replace seal
Oil on output flange	a) Shaft seal leaking	a) Replace shaft seal
Oil on speedometer drive	a) O-ring leaking b) Shaft seal in speedometer bushing leaking	a) Replace O-ring b) Replace speedometer bushing

3.0 & 530 (ZF-BW65 Transmission)

Condition	Cause/Correction
Starter not working in P or O Starter working in all selector positions Backup light not burning	Check transmission switch, connections and wires; replacing defective parts
Erratic movement when engaging positions A, 1 and R	Adjust engine idle speed Adjust accelerator cable Clean or replace valve body
Car moves in position O	Check selector lever adjustment, front clutch, stator support shaft bearing and front gaskets of sun gear shafts, replacing damaged parts
Stall speed higher than specified and transmission pulls in positions 1 and R	Adjust accelerator cable. Check main pressure—clean valve body if pressure too low. Check air cleaner, pump and intake manifold seal.
Transmission pulls in position 1 only	Check front clutch, stator support shaft bearing and front gaskets on sun gear shaft, replacing damaged parts.
Transmission pulls in position R only	Adjust rear brake band. Check rear power gaskets, pipe tightness, rear clutch, seals and rear brake band, replacing damaged parts.
Stall speed lower than 1150 rpm	Replace torque converter.
Positions, except P, difficult to engage	Check selector lever adjustment.
Parking lock does not hold car	Check selector lever adjustment, parking lock, linkage and lock, replacing damaged parts.
No drive in positions A, 2, 1 or R, however P functions correctly	Correct oil level, selector lever and accelerator cable adjustments.
No drive in A, 2 or 1	Check drive pinion seals, tightness of governor pressure tube, front clutch, stator support shaft bearing and front gaskets on sun gear-shaft, replacing damaged parts.
No drive in position A 1st gear	Replace one-way clutch.
No drive in position A 1st gear, however connection in position 1	Check one-way clutch—perhaps installed backwards.

(continued)

Condition	Cause/Correction
No 2nd gear in position A or 2	Adjust front brake band. Check front power seals and tightness of pipes. Clean or replace valve body.
No 3rd gear in position A, however reverse normal	Clean or replace valve body and governor.
2nd gear slips in position A	Adjust front brake band.
1st gear slips in position A or 1, reverse gear slips	Adjust rear brake band.
No engine braking effect in position 1, no drive in reverse	Adjust rear brake band, or check for wear. Check rear power seals and tightness of pipes.
Improper or hesitant kickdown Improper partial throttle points	Adjust accelerator cable. Check main pressure. Clean valve body if pressure too low. Check pump and seal on intake manifold. Clean governor, check drive pinion seals and tightness of governor tube.
Improper shift from 1st to 2nd	Clean or replace valve body.
Improper shift from 2nd to 3rd	Clean or replace valve body.
Transmission will not upshift	Clean governor. Check drive pinion seals and tightness of governor tube.
No 3rd gear in position A, reverse not working	Clean valve body, check rear clutch feed pipes and piston rings in hub of intermediate shaft.
Top speeds not possible in all gears, especially in position A 3rd gear	Replace torque converter.
Erratic and hesitant shifts	Adjust accelerator cable. Check main pressure, clean valve body if pressure too low. Check air cleaner, pump and seal on intake manifold.
Engine whines when shifting in and out of 2nd	Adjust front brake band. Check front power seals and tightness of pipes. Check front brake band for wear. Clean or replace valve body.
Engine whines when shifting in and out of 3rd	Check rear clutch feed pipe, rear clutch and seals. Clean or replace valve body.
Whining noise with engine running	Check pump gears and bearing sleeve at face of converter.
Irregular transmission noise, but not in position A 3rd gear	Check set of planetary gears.
Engine whines for a little while after starting, if engine was off for at least 12 hours	Converter pressure valve defective, but not detrimental for operation.

Rear Axle & Brakes Section

Fig. 1 Driving out stub axle. 2002 & 320 models

Fig. 2 Removing seal, bearing shim & spacer. 2002 & 320 models

Fig. 3 Measuring spacer sleeve. 2002 & 320 models

AXLE SHAFT, SEALS & BEARINGS, REPLACE

2002 & 320 Models

1. Raise and support rear of vehicle, then remove road wheel, cotter pin, axle nut and drum. On 320 models, remove small screw and two wheel bolts.
2. Using appropriate puller, remove drive flange, then disconnect outboard end of output shaft from inside stub axle flange and position aside.
3. Replace axle nut on stub axle backwards and drive out with a soft faced or plastic faced hammer.
4. Drive out seal and bearing, Fig. 1, then remove shim or locating ring and spacer from hub, Fig. 2.
5. Inner bearing and seal can be driven out at this time.

6. When replacing, install inner seal and bearing first, then measure spacer length, Fig. 3, and inside hub distance from outer bearing race land to outer race of inner bearing, Fig. 4. Subtract second number from first, subtract .004 in. for clearance to obtain shim or ring thickness required to fit bearings.

3.0 & 530 Models

1. Raise and support rear of vehicle and remove road wheel, then disconnect outboard end of output shaft from rear stub axle flange.
2. Unlock flange nut and pull flange off. Place nut on axle threads backwards.
3. Remove caliper and disc, then drive out stub axle to outside with a soft faced mallet.
4. Drive out bearings and seals, per-

form same measurements as before to calculate shim.
5. Reverse procedure to install.

PARKING BRAKE, ADJUST

2002 & 320 Models

1. Raise and support rear of vehicle with parking brake off.
2. Tighten up rear brakes by turning right eccentric clockwise and left eccentric counterclockwise on each rear wheel, just barely allowing free rotation.
3. In driver's compartment, unlock locknut on parking brake cable and tighten adjusting nut until parking brake locks at less than five notches.

3.0 & 530 Models

1. Raise and support rear of vehicle

Fig. 4 Measuring distance between inner & outer bearing race contact surfaces. 2002 & 320 models

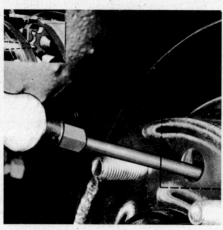

Fig. 5 Adjusting rear brake

Fig. 6 Adjusting parking brake lever

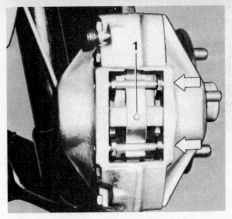

Fig. 7 Caliper retaining pins & spring

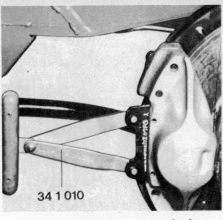

Fig. 8 Using tool to remove brake shoes

Fig. 9 Using tool to press piston against stop

with parking brake off.

2. Remove wheels, then insert a screwdriver through drum hole, Fig. 5. Models with rear discs brakes, have a drum brake in addition to disc brake for parking brake.

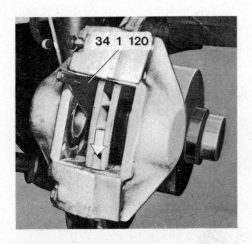

Fig. 10 Positioning piston in caliper

Turn star wheel adjustor on parking brake.

3. Adjust parking brake cable until less than five notches are used in applying brake, then tighten locknut, Fig. 6.

MASTER CYLINDER, REPLACE

1. On 2002 models, remove air cleaner. On 320 models, remove mixture control unit.
2. Siphon fluid from reservoir, then disconnect and position various hydraulic output tubes out of way.
3. Unbolt master cylinder from booster.
4. Fill and pre-bleed master cylinder.
5. Reverse procedure to install, then bleed brake system.

FRONT & REAR DISC BRAKES

Brake Pads, Replace

1. Remove wheel, then drive out re-

taining pins and remove cross-spring, Fig. 7.
2. Remove pads with two hook extractor No. 34 1-010, or a two hook extractor with slide hammer, No. 34 1000. The hooks fit into ear holes of pads, Fig. 8.
3. Replace with same type and color. Remove some master cylinder fluid. Brush out pad area and check disc.
4. Squeeze back pistons with an appropriate tool, then slide pads into place, Fig. 9. Make sure to set pads at 20 degree position with tool No. 34 1 120, Fig. 10.
5. Install cross-spring and pins, then bleed brake system.

Caliper, Replace

1. Remove wheel, then siphon some fluid from master cylinder.
2. Remove two mounting bolts and disconnect hydraulic line, Fig. 11.
3. Reverse procedure to install, observing proper torque and sequence, Fig. 16, then bleed brake system.
4. Caliper mounting bolt torques:

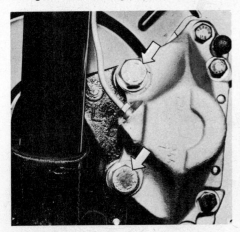

Fig. 11 Caliper mounting bolts

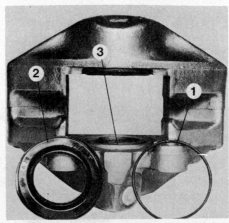

Fig. 12 Removing piston boot & snap ring

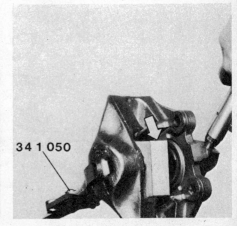

Fig. 13 Using compressed air to remove piston

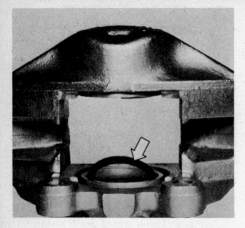

Fig. 14 Removing seal from piston bore

Fig. 15 Caliper seal locations

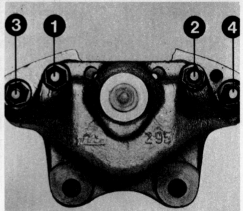

Fig. 16 Stretch bolts tightening sequence

Front (All series) 58-69 ft. lbs. Rear (3.0,530) 44-48 ft. lbs.

Caliper Overhaul

1. Remove brake pads, then snap out retaining ring and protective rubber, Fig. 12.
2. With special pliers, lock in one piston, insert a .30 in. thick piece of wood into caliper gap and force piston out by injecting compressed air into hydraulic connection, Fig. 13. Always protect any piston from damage.
3. Remove rubber sealing rings with a plastic tipped tool, Fig. 14.
4. Clean all surfaces with brake fluid.

NOTE: Never machine or hone any of these parts.

5. Only if a leak is evident at joint should you split caliper halves. Install seal(s) and assemble halves with new expansion bolts, Fig. 15.
6. When reinstalling pistons, use special 20 degree piston rotational alignment tool. The 20 degree portion must face incoming pad.

Rear Suspension Section

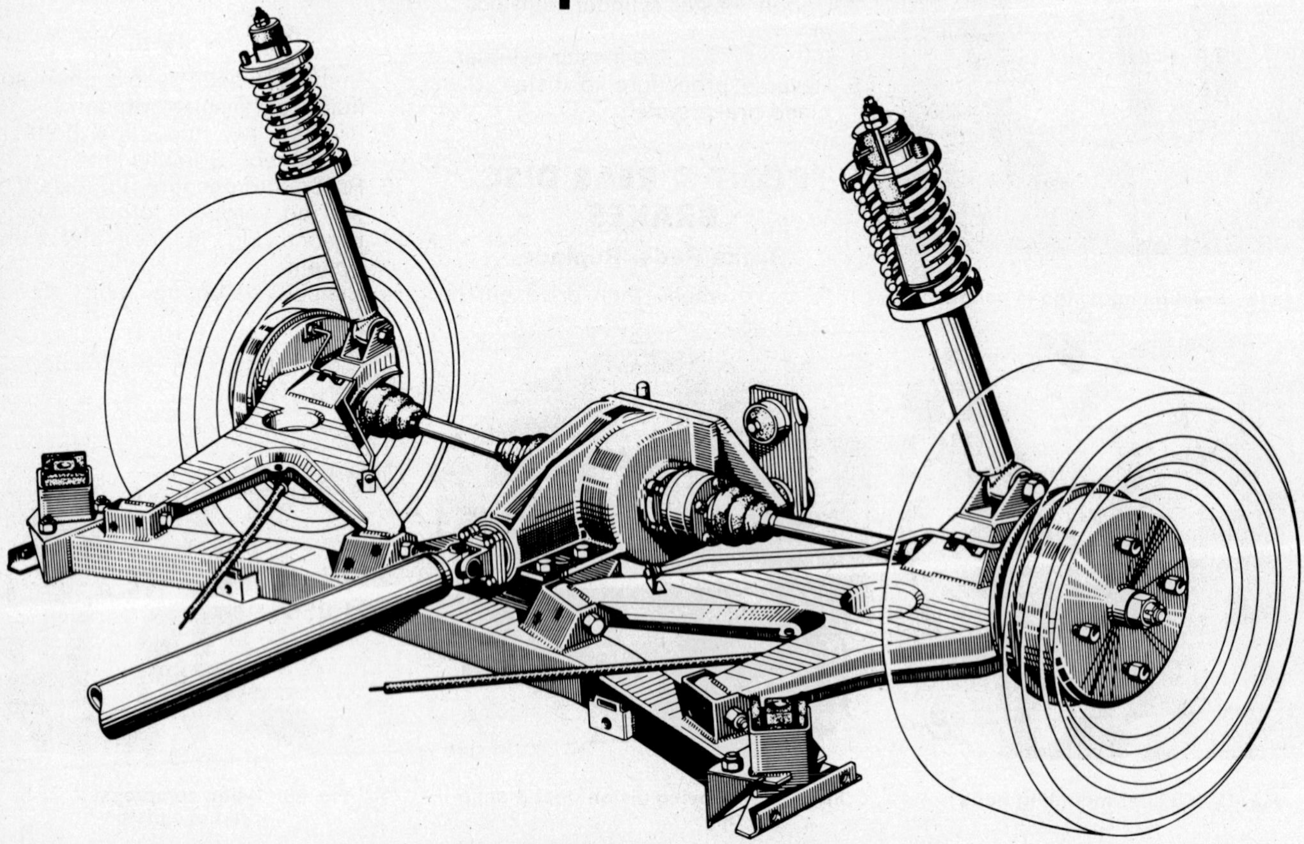

Fig. 1 Sectional view of rear suspension. 320 models

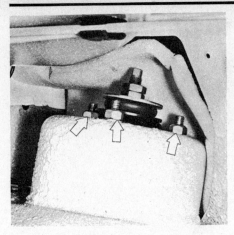

Fig. 2 Suspension unit attaching bolts. 3.0, 320 & 530 models

REAR COIL SPRING, REPLACE

2002 Models

1. After removing shock, remove rear wheel and disconnect stabilizer end from trailing arm.
2. Disconnect output shaft from stub axle flange and tie out of way.
3. Slowly lower trailing arm on a hydraulic jack and remove spring.
4. Replace only in pairs to avoid tilting of car.
5. Index lower damper ring recess with bulge on mounting plate and rotate spring so that spring end hits stop in damping ring.

Fig. 3 Compressing coil spring. 3.0, 320 & 530 models

REAR SHOCK ABSORBER, REPLACE

2002 Models

1. Raise and support rear of vehicle and control arm using a suitable jack.
2. Remove locknut, nut washer and bushing.
3. Disconnect lower shock end, compress and remove shock.

REAR COIL SPRING/SHOCK ABSORBER, REPLACE

3.0, 320 & 530 Models

1. Raise and support rear of vehicle and trailing using a suitable jack. Remove lower shock end mounting bolt at arm.
2. Remove centering plate or bushing on the 3.0 early versions from upper end in wheelhousing area, Fig. 2.
3. Remove assembly.
4. Compress coil spring in a safe fixture 33 3 110 for 320 models, 6035

for the 530 and 3.0 models, Fig. 3, disassemble components, Fig. 4.
5. When assembling, make sure of alignment of spring ends and damper ring, Fig. 5.
6. On certain 3.0 models without spring damper rings, rings can be added later. To do this with shock spring assemblies out of vehicle, remove sleeve, fit longer knurl head bolts to centering bush and install new sleeve with recesses for those bolts. Then, enlarge upper mounting holes in wheelhouse from 0.534 to 0.629 inches.
7. Install assembly with damping ring on top end.

Fig. 4 Coil spring & shock absorber. 3.0, 320 & 530 models

Fig. 5 Coil spring & damper end alignment. 3.0, 320 & 530 models

Front Suspension & Steering Section

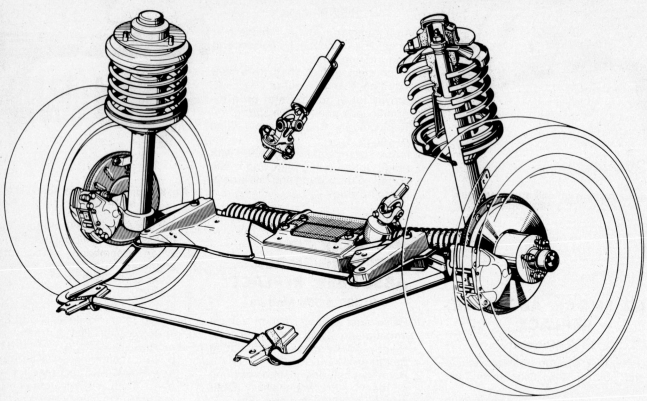

Fig. 1   Front suspension. 320 models (Typical)

WHEEL ALIGNMENT

Alignment is limited to checking and toe-in due to the built-in front end geometry. The toe-in is adjusted by means of threaded sleeves on tie rods. Should there be a misalignment in castor, camber or toe-out, there is a bent member, such as wishbone, trailing arm, steering arm or tie-rod.

WHEEL BEARINGS, ADJUST

1. Remove front wheel, end cap and cotter pin.
2. On 2002 models, apply 22-24 ft. lbs. torque on castellated nut while rotating hub. Then give complete bearing assembly two more turns without disturbing castellated nut.

Loosen nut until you see slight end play and hub and nut rotate together. Retighten castellated nut to 2.2 ft. lbs. and back off to nearest hole and insert pin.
3. On 3.0 models, tighten castellated nut to 7.25 ft. lbs. while rotating hub. Back nut off about ¼ turn to get end play. Attach dial indicator support to wheel and attach indicator so that it

Fig. 2   Pressing guide joint from steering arm. 3.0 models

Fig. 3   Disconnecting tie rod end from steering arm. 2002 models

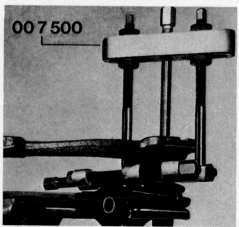

Fig. 4   Disconnecting track rod from guide joint. 2002 & 530 models

Fig. 5 Ball joint end play check. 2002 models

contacts axle end. Adjust end play to .0008-.0024 in.

4. On 530 models, tighten nut to 7 ft. lbs. while rotating hub. Back off 1/3 turn, then attach dial indicator and adjust play for .0008-.0024 inches.

5. On 320 models, tighten castellated nut to 22-24 ft. lbs. while rotating hub. Screw on bearing cap two turns without disturbing nut. Back off nut until end play occurs and re-tighten to 2 ft. lbs.

CONTROL ARM, REPLACE

1. Remove wheel, then remove safety wire from three bolts on 3.0, 2002, and 530 models.
2. Disconnect stabilizer or trailing arm. On 3.0 models, press ball joint out of steering arm, Fig. 2.

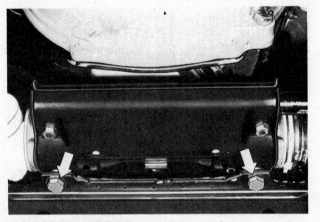

Fig. 7 Removing steering gear from front axle support. 320 models

3. Remove control arm from axle.
4. On 2002 models, press tie rod end from steering arm using tool No. 322050, Fig. 3.
5. Disconnect three bolts which were safety wired from 3.0, 530 and 2002 models, and remove arm. On 2002, and 530 models, press track rod from ball joint, Fig. 4. On 320 models, press out control arm from steering knuckle with tool No. 311 100.
6. Replace rubber bushings with press.
7. On 2002 models, check ball joint end play, Fig. 5. End play should be .094 in., if not replace ball joint. To replace ball joint, drill rivet heads, then punch rivets, and replace with SHR M 8 x 20 bolts and M 8 hex nuts.
8. Rubber bushings in axle are replaced in a like manner to step 6.
9. When reassembling, replace all self-locking nuts.

FRONT COIL SPRING/SHOCK ABSORBER, REPLACE

1. Remove wheel and disconnect brakeline neat shock.
2. Remove caliper and tie it back. Remove safety wire from three bolts at lower end of strut on 2002, 3.0 and 530 models.
3. On 320 models, press tie rod from steering arm using tool No. 32 2050,

Fig. 6 Disconnecting tie rods from steering knuckles. 320 models

then control arm from steering knuckle. On 2002 models, remove wishbone from axle.
4. On 2002, 3.0 and 530 models, remove three nuts which had been safety wired and separate joint.
5. Detach upper ends at wheelhousing.
6. Separate components in a special compressor for spring as in rear spring and shock section.

STEERING GEAR, REPLACE

2002 & 3.0 Models W/Manual Steering

1. Loosen universal or flange and slide up.
2. Press off necessary track rods and rods from box sector arm.
3. Unbolt steering box from axle and remove.

3.0 Models W/Power Steering & 530 Models

1. Turn steering wheel full left and drain fluid.
2. Press track rod from sector arm. Loosen flange or universal and slide up.
3. Disconnect hoses and remove steering box from axle.

320 Models

1. Remove front wheels and press tie rods off steering knuckles, Fig. 6.
2. Unbolt steering from front axle, Fig. 7. Loosen coupling.
3. Pull steering gear off.

CAPRI

INDEX OF SERVICE OPERATIONS

GENERAL ENGINE SPECIFICATIONS

Year	Engine	Carburetor	Bore and Stroke inches	Piston Displacement, Cubic Inches (CC)	Compression Ratio	Maximum Brake H.P. @ R.P.M.	Maximum Torque Lbs. Ft. @ R.P.M.	Normal Oil Pressure Pounds
1972	4-1600 cc	1 Barrel	3.188 x 3.056	98 (1600)	7.5	—	—	35—60
	4-2000 cc	2 Barrel	3.575 x 3.029	122 (2000)	8.2	—	—	35—60
	V6-2600 cc	2 Barrell	3.545 x 2.630	159 (2600)	8.2	—	—	40—55
1973	4-2000 cc	2 Barrel	3.575 x 3.029	122 (2000)	8.2	—	—	45—65
	V6-2600 cc	2 Barrel	3.545 x 2.630	159 (2600)	8.2	—	—	40—55
1974	4-2000 cc	2 Barrel	3.575 x 3.029	122 (2000)	8.2	80 @ 5400	98 @ 3000	45—65
	V6-2800 cc	2 Barrel	3.66 x 2.70	171 (2800)	8.2	105 @ 4600	140 @ 3200	40 Min
1976-77	4-2300	2 Barrel	3.78 x 3.126	140 (2300)	9.0	92 @ 5000	121 @ 3000	40—60
	V6-2800 cc ①	2 Barrel	3.66 x 2.70	171 (2800)	8.4	110 @ 4800	148 @ 3000	40—55
	V6-2800 cc ②	2 Barrel	3.66 x 2.70	171 (2800)	8.4	③	147 @ 3000	40—55

—Not Available
① —Man. trans.
② —Auto. trans.
③ —Except Calif., 111 @ 4800; Calif., 109 @ 4800.

TUNE UP SPECIFICATIONS

The following specifications are published from the latest information available. This
data should be used only in the absence of a decal affixed in the engine compartment.

★When using a timing light, disconnect vacuum hose or tube at distributor and plug opening in tube or hose so idle speed will not be affected.

●When checking compression, lowest cylinder must be within 75 percent of highest.

▲Before removing wires from distributor cap, determine location of the No. 1 wire in cap, as distributor position may have been altered from that shown at the end of this chart.

Year	Spark Plug		Distributor		Ignition Timing★			Carb. Adjustments					
								Hot Idle Speed ②		Air Fuel Ratio		Idle CO%	
	Type	Gap Inch	Point Gap Inch	Dwell Angle Deg.	Firing Order Fig. ▲	Timing BTDC ①	Mark Fig.	Std. Trans.	Auto. Trans.	Std. Trans.	Auto. Trans.	Std. Trans.	Auto. Trans.
1972													
1600 cc	AGR-22	.030	.025	36—40	A	12°	B	900/500 ③		—	—	1.5—2.5	—
2000 cc	BRF-32D	.034	.025	36—40	⑨	④	⑩	750/500 ⑤	650/550D ⑤	—	—	1.5—2.5	1.5—2.5
2600 cc	AGR-32	.035	.025	37—40	F	12°	G	750	650D	—	—	1.0—2.0	1.0—2.0
1973													
2000 cc	BRF-42	.030	.025	37—41	⑨	④	⑩	750	825N	—	—	1.5—2.5	1.5—2.5
2600 cc	AGR-32	.035	.025	37—41	F	⑥	G	750	650D	—	—	1.0 ⑦	1.0 ⑦
1974													
2000 cc	BSF-32	.030	.025	37—41	⑨	④	⑩	750	825N	—	—	—	—
2800 cc	AGR-42	.034	.025	37—41	F	12°	G	750	650D	—	—	—	—

TUNE UP SPECIFICATIONS—Continued

The following specifications are published from the latest information available. This data should be used only in the absence of a decal affixed in the engine compartment.

★When using a timing light, disconnect vacuum hose or tube at distributor and plug opening in tube or hose so idle speed will not be affected.

●When checking compression, lowest cylinder must be within 75 percent of highest.

▲Before removing wires from distributor cap, determine location of the No. 1 wire in cap, as distributor position may have been altered from that shown at the end of this chart.

| Year | Spark Plug | | Distributor | | Ignition Timing★ | | | Carb. Adjustments | | | | | |
| | Type | Gap Inch | Point Gap Inch | Dwell Angle Deg. | Firing Order Fig. ▲ | Timing BTDC ① | Mark Fig. | Hot Idle Speed ② | | Air Fuel Ratio | | Idle CO% | |
								Std. Trans.	Auto. Trans.	Std. Trans.	Auto. Trans.	Std. Trans.	Auto. Trans.
1976-77													
2300 cc	AGRF-52	.034	—	—	H	10°	D	850	700D	—	—	—	—
2800 cc	AGR-42	.034	—	—	F	⑧	G	950	800D	—	—	—	—

① —BTDC — Before Top Dead Center.
② —D: Drive. N: Neutral.
③ —Headlights on high beam, A/C off; lower idle speed with solenoid disconnected.
④ —Man. trans., 6° BTDC; auto. trans., 10° BTDC.
⑤ —Headlight on high beam, A/C on; lower idle speed with solenoid disconnected.
⑥ —Man. trans., 12° BTDC; auto. trans., 8° BTDC.
⑦ —Maximum.
⑧ —Man. trans. 8° BTDC; auto. trans., 10° BTDC.
⑨ —Since there are two alternate ignition wiring possibilities, be sure that the ignition wires are reinstalled in their proper locations referring to Fig. C.
⑩ —Refer to Figs. D & E to determine pulley used.

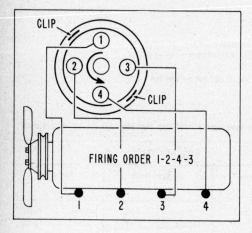

Fig. A

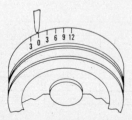

Fig. D

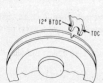

Fig. B

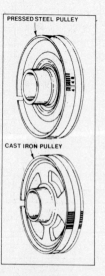

Fig. E

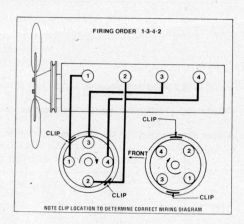

Fig. C

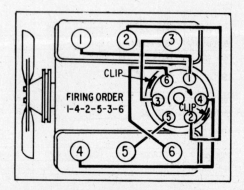

Fig. F

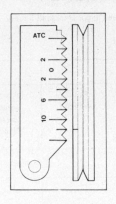

Fig. G

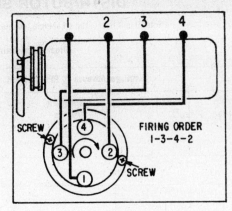

Fig. H

ALTERNATOR & REGULATOR SPECIFICATIONS

Year	Make or Model	Current Rating		Field Current @ 75°F.		Voltage Regulator				Field Relay	
		Amperes	Volts	Amperes	Volts	Make or Model	Voltage @ 75°F.	Contact Gap	Armature Air Gap	Armature Air Gap	Closing Voltage @ 75°F.
1972	17ACR ①	35	14	—	—	—	14.1—14.4	—	—	—	—
1972-73	K-1 ②	35	14	—	—	—	14.1—14.4	—	—	—	—
1974-77	K-2 ② ③	35	14	—	—	—	13.7—14.4	—	—	—	—
1976-77	K-1 ② ④	55	14	—	—	—	13.7—14.4	—	—	—	—

—Not Available
① —Lucas alternator.
② —Bosch alternator.
③ —1974 all & 1976-77 models less A/C.
④ —1976-77 models with A/C.

STARTING MOTOR SPECIFICATIONS

Year	Engine Model	Ident. No.	Brush Spring Tension, Ounces	No Load Test			Torque Test		
				Amperes	Volts	R.P.M.	Amperes	Volts	Torque Lbs. Ft.
1972	1600	25183 ①	28	—	—	—	—	—	—
	1600	1208049 ②	42.3	—	—	—	—	—	—
	2000	25183 ①	28	—	—	—	—	—	—
	2000	25203 ①	28	—	—	—	—	—	—
	2000	25204 ①	28	—	—	—	—	—	—
	2000	1211989 ②	42.3	—	—	—	—	—	—
	2000	1311038 ②	42.3	—	—	—	—	—	—
	26000	1311033 ②	42.3	—	—	—	—	—	—
1973	2000	25204 ①	28	—	—	—	—	—	—
	2000	1211989 ②	42.3	—	—	—	—	—	—
	2000	1311038 ②	42.3	—	—	—	—	—	—
	2600	1311033 ②	42.3	—	—	—	—	—	—
1974	2000	1211206 ②	42.3	—	—	—	—	—	—
	2000	1311038 ②	42.3	—	—	—	—	—	—
	2800	1311033 ②	42.3	—	—	—	—	—	—
	2800	1311046 ②	42.3	—	—	—	—	—	—
1976-77	2300	1311107 ②	42.3	54	—	—	—	—	—
	2300	1311121 ②	42.3	54	—	—	—	—	—
	2800	1311049 ②	42.3	56	—	—	—	—	—

—Not Available
① —Lucas.
② —Bosch.

DISTRIBUTOR SPECIFICATIONS

★Note: If unit is checked on vehicle, double RPM and degrees to get crankshaft figures.

Breaker arm spring tension 17-21.

Distributor Ident. No.	Centrifugal Advance @ RPM of Distributor				Full Advance	Vacuum Advance		Distributor Retard
	Advance Starts	Intermediate Advance				Inches of Vacuum to Start Plunger	Max. Adv. Dist. Deg. @ Vacuum	Max. Retard Dist. Deg. @ Vacuum
1972								
71BB-BEA	—	—	—	—	—	—	—	—
72BB-LA	—	—	—	—	—	—	—	—
72HF-EA	—	—	—	—	—	—	—	—
72HF-GA	—	—	—	—	—	—	—	—
A73SX-AGA	—	—	—	—	—	—	—	—
A73SX-FA	—	—	—	—	—	—	—	—
1972-73								
72TF-AB	0-½ @ 500	1-3 @ 750	3½-5½ @ 1000	7-9 @ 1500	12 @ 2000	5	7½ @ 20	7 @ 20
72TF-ADB	0-½ @ 500	1-3 @ 750	3½-5½ @ 1000	7-9 @ 1500	12 @ 2000	5	7½ @ 20	4 @ 20
73HF-CA	—	—	—	—	—	—	—	—
73TF-AA	½-¾ @ 500	1-3 @ 750	3½-5½ @ 1000	7-9 @ 1500	10 @ 2000	5	4 @ 20	7 @ 20
73TF-BA	½-¾ @ 500	1-3 @ 750	3½-5½ @ 1000	7-9 @ 1500	10 @ 2000	5	4 @ 20	4 @ 20
1973								
73HF-DA	—	—	—	—	—	—	—	—
1974								
A73SX-ACA	—	—	—	—	—	—	—	—
A73SX-AEA	—	—	—	—	—	—	—	—
74HF-CA	0-2 @ 500	3½-5½ @ 750	5½-7½ @ 1000	7½-9½ @ 1500	12 @ 2000	5	3½ @ 20	4 @ 20
74HF-DA	—	—	—	—	—	—	—	—
74HF-JA	0-½ @ 500	0-1 @ 750	3-5 @ 1000	6-8 @ 1500	10 @ 2000	5	5½ @ 20	4 @ 20
74HF-MA	—	—	—	—	—	—	—	—
74TF-NA	0-½ @ 500	1-3 @ 750	3½-5½ @ 1000	7½-9½ @ 1500	10 @ 2000	5	4 @ 20	7 @ 20
74TF-RA	0-½ @ 500	1-3 @ 750	3½-5½ @ 1000	7½-9½ @ 1500	10 @ 2000	5	4 @ 20	4 @ 20
74TF-TA	0-½ @ 500	1-3 @ 750	3½-5½ @ 1000	7½-9½ @ 1500	10 @ 2000	5	4 @ 20	—
1976-77								
75TF-BA	—	—	—	—	—	—	—	—
75TF-HA	—	—	—	—	—	—	—	—
75TF-JA	—	—	—	—	—	—	—	—
D58E-FA	—	—	—	—	—	—	—	—
D58E-GA	—	—	—	—	—	—	—	—
D6EE-BA	−¾ to ¾ @ 500	−1¼ to ¾ @ 700	—	—	1¾ @ 1000	5	13¼ @ 15	—
77TF-AA	—	—	—	—	—	—	—	—
77TF-CA	—	—	—	—	—	—	—	—
77TF-DA	—	—	—	—	—	—	—	—

—Not Available

PISTONS, RINGS, PINS, CRANKSHAFT & BEARING SPECIFICATIONS

Year	Model or Engine	Piston Clearance, Inch	Ring End Gap, Inch		Piston Pin Diameter, Inch	Rod Bearings, Inch		Main Bearings Inch		Thrust on Bearing No.	Crankshaft End Play, Inch
			Comp.	Oil		Shaft Diameter	Bearing Clearance	Shaft Diameter	Bearing Clearance		
1972-73	1600	.0013—.0019	.009	.009	.81	1.936—1.937	.0004—.0024	2.1253—2.1261	.0005—.0016	3	.003—.011
	2000	.001—.002	.002	.015	.944	2.046—2.047	.0006—.0026	2.2432—2.2440	.0005—.0015	3	.003—.011
	2600	.001—.003	.015	.015	.945	2.125—2.126	.0005—.002	2.243—2.244	.0005—.002	3	.004—.008
1974	2000	.001—.002	.015	.016	.944	2.046—2.047	.0006—.0026	2.2432—2.2440	.0006—.0016	3	.003—.011
	2800	.001—.0025	.015	.015	.945	2.125—2.126	.0006—.0021	2.243—2.244	.0006—.0019	3	.004—.008
1976-77	2300	.0014—.0022	.010	.015	.912	2.046—2.047	.0008—.0015	2.3982—2.3990	.0008—.0026	3	.004—.008
	2800	.0011—.0019	.015	.015	.945	2.125—2.126	.0005—.0022	2.243—2.244	.0005—.0019	3	.004—.008

VALVE SPECIFICATIONS

Year	Engine	Valve Lash		Valve Angles		Valve Spring Installed Height	Valve Spring Pressure Lbs. @ In.	Stem Clearance		Stem Diameter, Standard	
		Int.	Exh.	Seat	Face			Intake	Exhaust	Intake	Exhaust
1972-73	1600	.010H	.017	45	45	1.263	122 @ .95	.0008—.0027	.0017—.0036	.3098—.3105	.3089—.3096
	2000	.008C	.010C	44	45	1.417	68 @ 1.418	.0008—.0027	.0018—.0035	.3159—.3167	.3149—.3156
	2600	.014C	.016C	45	—	—	—	—	—	.316	.315
1974	2000	.008C	.010C	45	44	1.417	176 @ 1.02	.0008—.0025	.0018—.0035	.3159—.3167	.3149—.3156
	2800	.014H	.016H	45	44	—	150 @ 1.222	.0008—.0025	.0018—.0035	.3159—.3166	.3149—.3157
1976-77	2300	.008C	.010C	45	44	1.5313	189 @ 1.16	.0010—.0027	.0015—.0032	.3416—.3423	.3411—.3418
	2800	.014H	.016H	45	44	1.5938	105 @ 1.222	.0008—.0025	.0018—.0035	.3158—.3167	.3149—.3156

ENGINE TIGHTENING SPECIFICATIONS

★Torque specifications are for clean and lightly lubricated threads only. Dry or dirty threads produce increased friction which prevents accurate measurement of tightness.

Year	Engine	Spark Plugs Ft. Lbs.	Cylinder Head Bolts Ft. Lbs.	Intake Manifold Ft. Lbs.	Exhaust Manifold Ft. Lbs.	Rocker Arm Shaft Bracket Ft. Lbs.	Rocker Arm Cover Ft. Lbs.	Connecting Rod Cap Bolts Ft. Lbs.	Main Bearing Cap Bolts Ft. Lbs.	Flywheel to Crankshaft Ft. Lbs.	Vibration Damper or Pulley Ft. Lbs.
1972-73	1600	22—28	65—70	12—15	15—18	25—30	2.5—3.5	30—35	65—70	50—55	24—28
	2000	14—20	65—80	12—15	①	32—36	4—6	29—34	65—75	47—51	39—43
	2600	22—28	65—80	15—18	—	32—36	5—8	22—26	65—75	45—50	32—36
1974	2000	14—20	65—80	12—15	15—18	32—36	4—6	29—34	65—75	47—51	39—43
	2800	15—22	65—80	15—18	—	43—49	5—8	21—25	65—75	47—52	92—104
1976-77	2300	10—15	80—90	14—21	16—23	—	4—7	30—36	80—90	54—64	80—114
	2800	15—20	65—80	15—18	16—23	43—49	3—5	21—25	65—75	47—51	93—103

①—1972, 12-15 Ft. lbs.; 1973, 15-18 ft. lbs.

CAPRI

BRAKE SPECIFICATIONS

Year	Model	Rear Drum I.D.	Wheel Cyl. Bore		Disc Brake Rotor					Master Cyl. I.D.
			Front Disc	Rear Drum	Nominal Thickness	Minimum Thickness	Thickness Variation (Parallelism)	Run Out (TIR)	Finish (microinch)	
1972	All	9	2.125	.75	.50	.45	.0004	.0020	30—45	.813
1973	All	9	2.125	.75	.50	.45	.0004	.0020	30—45	.813
1974	All	9	2.125	.75	.50	—	—	.0035	—	.813
1976-77	All	9	2.125	.70	.50	—	—	.0035	—	.813

REAR AXLE SPECIFICATIONS

Year	Model	Carrier Type	Ring Gear & Pinion Backlash		Pinion Bearing Preload			Differential Bearing Preload		
			Method	Adjustment	Method	New Bearings Inch—Lbs.	Used Bearings Inch—Lbs.	Method	New Bearings Inch—Lbs.	Used Bearings Inch—Lbs.
1972	All	Intergral	Shims	.047—.086	Spacer	13—19	—	Shims	.0012—.0031	—
1973	All	Integral	Shims	.047—.086	Spacer	13—19	—	Shims	.0012—.0031	—
1974	All	Integral	Shims	.047—.086	Spacer	13—19	—	Shims	.0012—.0031	—
1976-77	All	Integral	Shims	.047—.086	Spacer	13—19	—	Shims	.0012—.0031	—

WHEEL ALIGNMENT SPECIFICATIONS

Year	Model	Caster Angle, Degrees		Camber Angle, Degrees				Toe-in Inch.	Kingpin Inclination
		Limits	Desired	Limits		Desired			
				Left	Right	Left	Right		
1972-74	All	+½ to +2½	+1½	+¼ to +1¾	+¼ to +1¾	+1	+1	¼—⅜	7½—8½
1976-77	All	+1 to +2¼	+1½	+¾ to +2¼	+¾ to +2¼	+1½	+1½	¼—⅜	7½—8½

COOLING SYSTEM & CAPACITY DATA

Year	Model or Engine	Cooling Capacity, Qts.			Radiator Cap Relief Pressure, Lbs.		Thermo. Opening Temp.	Fuel Tank Gals.	Engine Oil Refill Qts.	Transmission Oil		Rear Axle Oil Pints
		No Heater	With Heater	With A/C	With A/C	No A/C				4 Speed Pints	Auto Trans. Pints	
1972	1600	—	6½	6½	13	13	185—192	12	3 ②	2.87	16	2.3
	2000	—	8	8	13	13	185—192	12	3½ ②	2.8	16	2.3
	2600	—	8.25	8.25	13	13	185—192	12	4¼ ①	2.8	16	2.3
1973	2000	—	8	8	13	13	185—192	12	4 ①	2.8	16	2.3
	2600	—	8.25	8.25	13	13	185—192	12	4¼ ①	2.8	16	2.3
1974	2000	—	8.1	8.1	13	13	185—192	12	4 ①	2.8	16	2.32
	2800	—	10.8	10.8	13	13	183—190	12	4¼ ①	2.8	16	2.32
1976-77	2300	—	8.5	8.5	13	13	185—192	11.8	4¼ ①	2.8	16	2.32
	2800	—	8.5	8.5	13	13	183—190	11.8	4¼ ①	2.8	16	2.32

① —Add 1 qt. with filter change.
② —Add ½ qt. with filter change.

Electrical Section

DISTRIBUTOR, REPLACE

1600 cc Engine

1. Remove distributor cap and disconnect vacuum lines from distributor.
2. Scribe a mark on distributor body and engine block indicating position of body in block, then scribe another mark on distributor body showing position of rotor.
3. Remove hold down bolt and remove distributor.
4. When installing distributor, align marks previously made on distributor body, engine and rotor, then install distributor and hold down bolt.
5. Check engine timing and adjust as necessary.

1972-74 2000, V6-2600 & 2800 cc Engines

NOTE: On some 2000 cc engines, it may be necessary to position air pump aside to gain access to distributor.

1. On V6-2600 and 2800cc engines, remove air cleaner.
2. On 1972-73 models, rotate engine until timing notch on crankshaft pulley is aligned with specified BTDC mark. Ensure No. 1 cylinder is on compression stroke by removing oil filler cap. On 2000 cc engines, cam lobe visible through opening. On all models, distributor rotor should be pointing to No. 1 cylinder mark on distributor body. On 1974 models ensure rotor is aligned with index mark on top of distributor body.
3. Remove distributor hold down bolt and remove distributor.

NOTE: Hex shaft that drives oil pump may stick in distributor and be withdrawn with pump.

4. When installing distributor, ensure alignment marks are properly aligned, then install distributor and hold down bolt.
5. Check engine timing and adjust as necessary.

1976-77 2300 & V6-2800 cc Engines

1. Remove air cleaner, then disconnect distributor wire connector from vehicle wiring harness.
2. Disconnect vacuum lines from distributor, then remove distributor cap and position aside.
3. Scribe a mark on distributor body

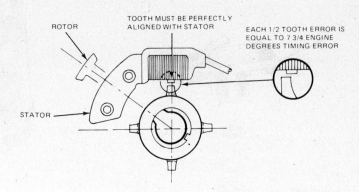

Fig. 1   Distributor stator and armature segment alignment. Bosch breakerless distributor

and cylinder block indicating position of rotor in distributor and distributor in block.
4. When installing distributor, align rotor with mark on distributor housing and mark on distributor housing with mark on engine.

NOTE: If engine was cranked while distributor was removed, crank engine until No. 1 cylinder is at TDC compression stroke, then align initial timing mark on timing pointer with timing mark on crankshaft damper. Install distributor with one of the armature segments aligned as shown in Fig. 1, and rotor as No. 1 firing position. Ensure oil pump intermediate shaft properly engages distributor shaft.

5. Install distributor cap, then connect distributor wire connector to vehicle wiring harness.
6. Adjust timing as necessary, then connect vacuum line to distributor.

1972-74 DISTRIBUTOR, REPAIRS

Autolite Distributor

1600 cc Engine

If distributor has been disassembled, refer to Fig. 2 at reassembly.
1. Install thrust washers onto shaft, slide shaft into housing and install thrust washer, wave washer and drive gear. Install tension pin.
2. Install cam assembly making sure advance stop is in correct slot and install snap ring. Replace felt wick.
3. Install vacuum advance unit.
4. Install advance springs to posts from which they were removed, lubricate governor weight pivots and install governor weights with flat edge adjacent to cam spindle and install spring clips.
5. Install grommet in lower plate leaving sufficient wire to reach contact point connection. Connect ground spring to pivot post and place upper plate on lower plate, engaging the hold down spindle in keyhole slot and install the two spring washers, flat washer and large snap ring.
6. Check clearance between upper and lower plates, beneath nylon bearing nearest to the hold down pin. Maximum clearance is .010 inch. If clearance is excessive, thread nut further onto hold down screw.
7. Install contact points and condenser onto breaker plate assembly and install the assembly and secure with two screws.

Bosch Distributor

2000 cc Engine

NOTE: On 1972-74 units, replacement parts for servicing the distributor shaft, drive gear, bushing and cam are not available. In addition on 1974 units, the advance weights, advance springs and breaker plate are not serviceable since the breaker plate is permanently staked into the housing.

If distributor has been disassembled, refer to Fig. 3 at reassembly.
1. Lubricate pivot pins and install advance weights. Lubricate shaft and

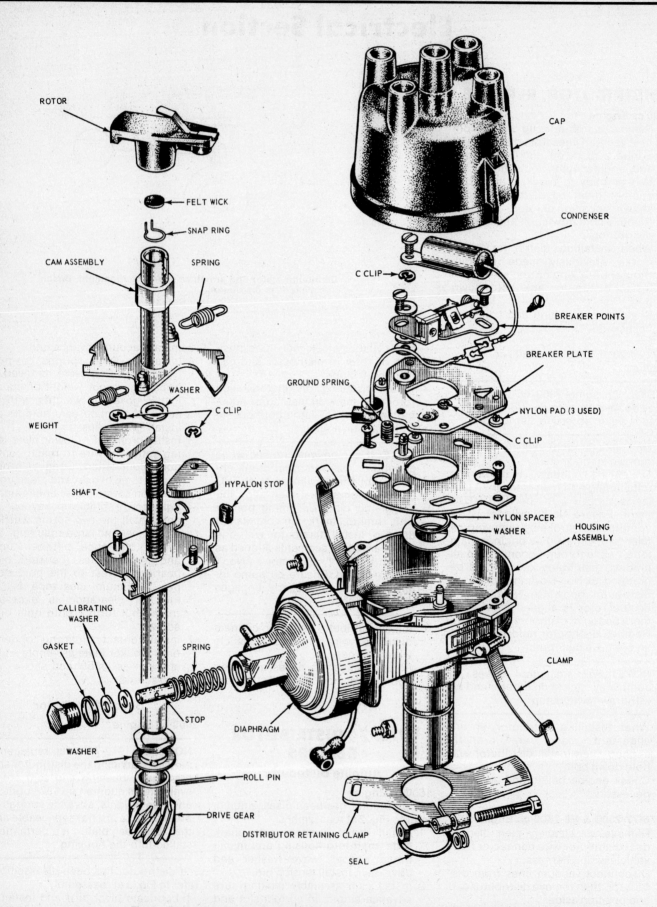

Fig. 2 Exploded view of Autolite/Motorcraft 1600cc dual advance distributor

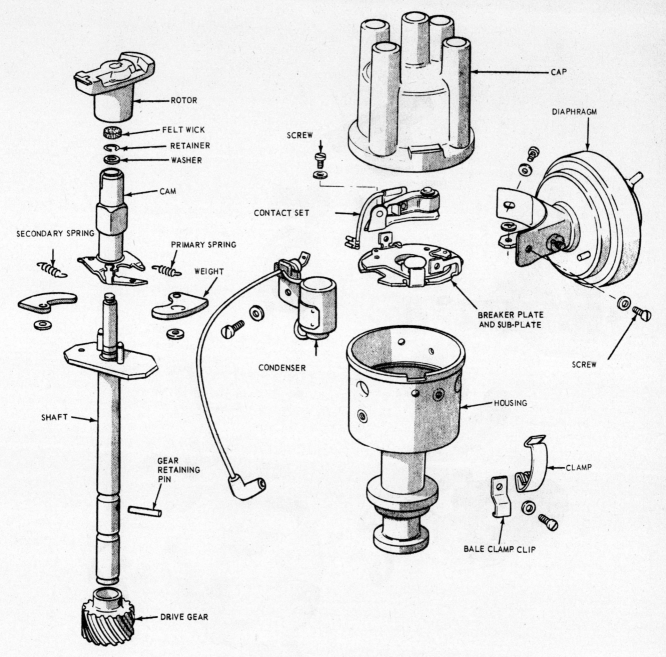

Fig. 3 Exploded view of Bosch 2000cc distributor

install cam assembly.

2. Install advance springs and advance plate, securing plate with clip and screws.

3. Insert grommet and condenser wire through hole in housing and install condenser and contact points.

4. Install vacuum advance unit. Hook vacuum advance rod over pin in advance plate and install snap ring.

1972-74 V6-2600 & 2800 cc Engine

If distributor has been disassembled, refer to Fig. 4 at reassembly.

1. Lubricate top of distributor shaft

and install cam assembly, then retaining ring and felt wick.

2. Lubricate pivot pins and install advance weights, "C" clips and advance springs.

3. Place breaker plate into housing, ensuring mounting holes are aligned. It may be necessary to lightly tap breaker plate to seat plate on wedged perches in housing.

4. Install vacuum advance unit, breaker points and cam wiper.

5. Place terminal and grommet into slot on side of housing and install condenser.

6. Connect breaker point lead to terminal, then install rotor.

1976-77 BOSCH BREAKERLESS IGNITION SYSTEM DIAGNOSIS
Description

The (B/L) ignition system, Fig. 5, does not use ignition points and is controlled by an electronic module, also a new oil filled coil is incorporated. Total diagnosis of system requires only a volt-ohmmeter tester.

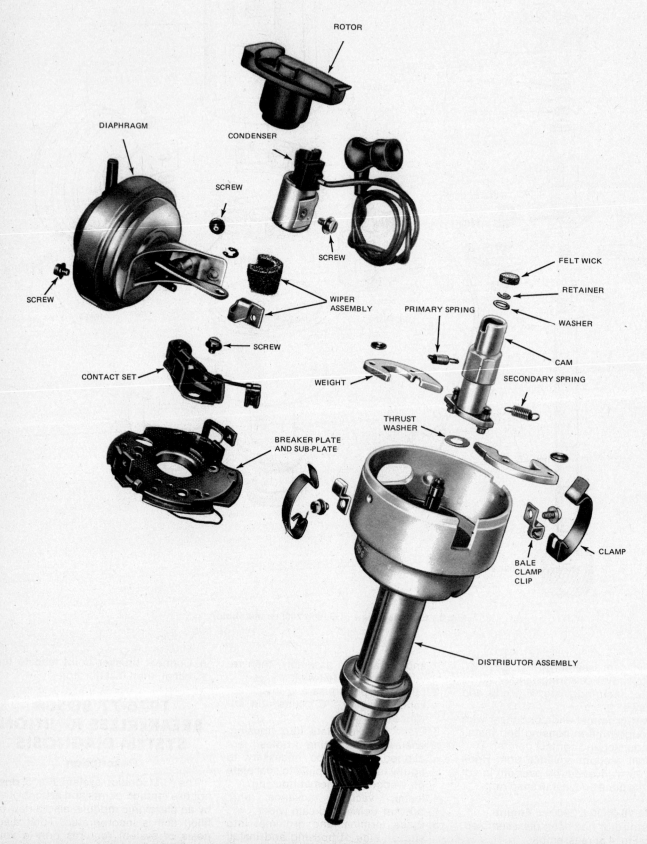

ROTOR

DIAPHRAGM

CONDENSER

SCREW

SCREW

SCREW

FELT WICK

RETAINER

WASHER

WIPER ASSEMBLY

PRIMARY SPRING

CAM

SCREW

SECONDARY SPRING

CONTACT SET

WEIGHT

BREAKER PLATE AND SUB-PLATE

THRUST WASHER

CLAMP

BALE CLAMP CLIP

DISTRIBUTOR ASSEMBLY

Fig. 4 Exploded view of Bosch dual advance distributor. 1972-74 V6-2600 & 2800cc engine

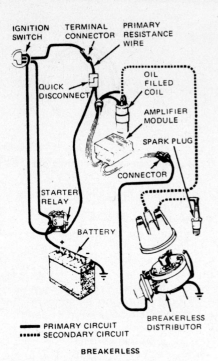

Fig. 5 Bosch breakerless ignition system

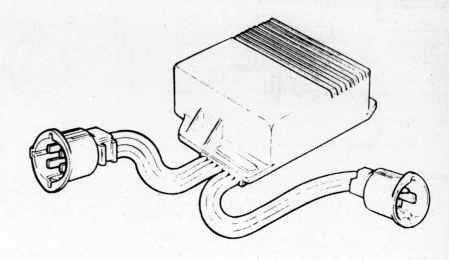

Fig. 6 Bosch breakerless ignition system module

The electronic module, Fig. 6, is the brain of this system and is well protected from outside elements such as heat and shock. This module can not be disassembled and must be replaced if malfunctioning.

The conventional ignition coils are not to be used with this system. The proper coil is easily identified as it is all blue and terminals are labeled differently from conventional ignition coils "BAT" (battery) and "DEC" (Distributor Electronic Control).

The ignition switch energizes the module through the white wire while engine is cranking and through the red wire when engine is running.

The distributor shaft and armature rotation, Fig. 7, causes the armature poles to pass by the core of the magnetic pick-up assembly. In turn cutting the magnetic field and signaling the electronic module, Figs. 8, through the orange and purple wires to break the primary ignition current, thus inducing secondary voltage in the coil to fire the spark plugs. The coil is then energized again by the primary circuit and ready for the next spark cycle. This primary circuit is controlled by a timing circuit in the module.

The B/L ignition system is protected against electrical current produced during normal vehicle operation and against reverse polarity or high voltage accidentally applied if vehicle is jump started.

Trouble Isolation

Before start tests, ensure battery is fully charged. Disconnect coil high tension lead from distributor cap, then turn ignition switch on. Hold high tension lead approximately 3/16 inch from cylinder head, then using a remote starter switch crank engine and observe spark intensity. If spark is observed, trouble lies in secondary ignition circuit. If no spark is observed, check to ensure coil high tension lead is in good condition.

Disconnect three and four way connector at electronic module. Using a sensitive volt-ohmmeter perform test refering to Figs. 8, 9 and 10.

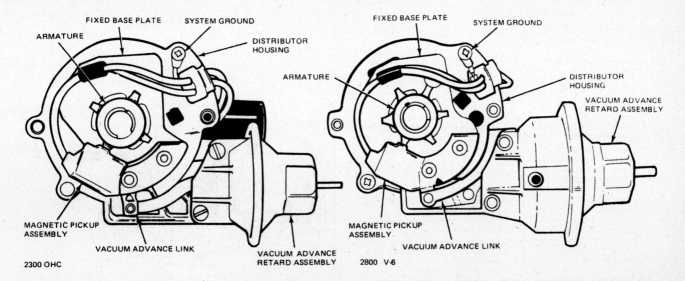

Fig. 7 Bosch breakerless ignition system distributor

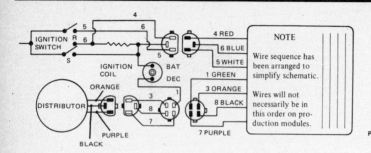

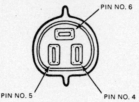

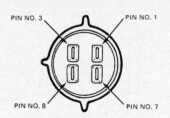

Fig. 8 Bosch breakerless ignition primary circuit

Fig. 9 Bosch breakerless ignition system connectors

Module Bias Test

With ignition switch in on position, measure voltage between pin 3 and engine ground. If reading is less than battery voltage, repair voltage feed to module for running conditions (red wire).

Battery Source Test

1. Connect voltmeter between coil battery terminal and engine ground.
2. Connect a jumper wire between coil "DEC" terminal and engine ground.
3. Turn ignition switch on, ensure all lights and accessories are off.
4. Voltmeter should read between 4.9 and 7.9 volts.
5. If voltmeter reading is less then 4.9 volts, check primary wiring for worn insulation, broken strands and loose or corroded terminals. Also check resistance wiring for defects.
6. If voltmeter reading is above 7.9 volts, check resistance wire and replace if necessary.

Cranking Test

While cranking engine measure voltage between pin 1 and engine ground. If voltmeter reading is not 8 to 12 volts, repair voltage feed to module for starting conditions (white wire).

Starting Circuit Test

If voltmeter reading is not between 8 and 12 volts, ignition by-pass circuit is opened or grounded from either starter solenoid or ignition switch to pin 5. Check primary wire connections at coils.

Distributor Test

1. Disconnect three wire connector at distributor pigtail.
2. Set voltmeter to 2.5 volt scale, then connect leads to the two parallel blades on connector.
3. Remove distributor cap and visually inspect distributor for improperly installed or damaged components. Check to ensure armature is tight on

sleeve and that roll pin is properly installed.
4. If distributor is properly assembled and not damaged, but voltmeter does not oscillate, replace magnetic pick-up assembly.

Amplifier Module Test

1. Without removing existing module from vehicle, disconnect electrical connectors and connect a known good module. Substitute module does not have to be installed on vehicle to operate properly.
2. If engine starts and operates properly, proceed to step 3. If engine fails to start, defect is in wiring or other vehicle system. Inspect and repair as necessary.
3. Reconnect original module and attempt to start and run engine. If engine fails to start, replace module.
4. With engine operating, check ignition primary wiring for proper connections.

Ignition Coil Test

1. Connect ohmmeter between coil "BAT" or "DEC" terminals. Primary resistance must be 1.0 to 2.0 ohms.
2. Connect ohmmeter between "BAT" or "DEC" terminal and coil tower. Secondary resistance must be 7000 to 13000 ohms.

Short Test

Connect ohmmeter between pin 5 and engine ground. If ohmmeter read-

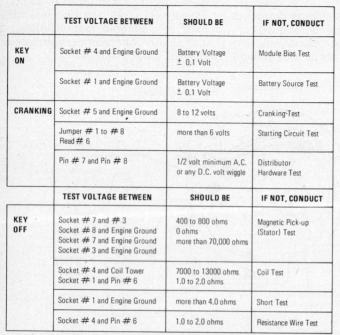

	TEST VOLTAGE BETWEEN	SHOULD BE	IF NOT, CONDUCT
KEY ON	Socket # 4 and Engine Ground	Battery Voltage ± 0.1 Volt	Module Bias Test
	Socket # 1 and Engine Ground	Battery Voltage ± 0.1 Volt	Battery Source Test
CRANKING	Socket # 5 and Engine Ground	8 to 12 volts	Cranking Test
	Jumper # 1 to # 8 Read # 6	more than 6 volts	Starting Circuit Test
	Pin # 7 and Pin # 8	1/2 volt minimum A.C. or any D.C. volt wiggle	Distributor Hardware Test

	TEST VOLTAGE BETWEEN	SHOULD BE	IF NOT, CONDUCT
KEY OFF	Socket # 7 and # 3 Socket # 8 and Engine Ground Socket # 7 and Engine Ground Socket # 3 and Engine Ground	400 to 800 ohms 0 ohms more than 70,000 ohms	Magnetic Pick-up (Stator) Test
	Socket # 4 and Coil Tower Socket # 1 and Pin # 6	7000 to 13000 ohms 1.0 to 2.0 ohms	Coil Test
	Socket # 1 and Engine Ground	more than 4.0 ohms	Short Test
	Socket # 4 and Pin # 6	1.0 to 2.0 ohms	Resistance Wire Test

Fig. 10 Bosch breakerless ignition system trouble isolation chart

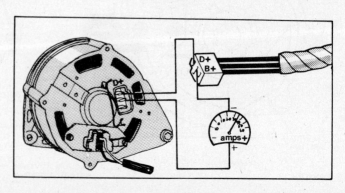

Fig. 11 Alternator output test. Bosch

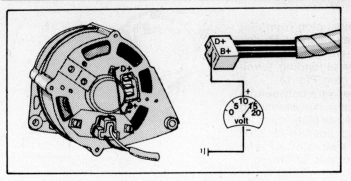

Fig. 12 Alternator wiring continuity check. Bosch

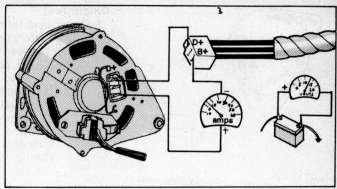

Fig. 13 Voltage regulator voltage setting check. Bosch

ing is less than 4 ohms, check for ground at "DEC" terminal of coil or in primary wiring to coil.

BOSCH ALTERNATORS

Alternator, Replace

4 Cylinder Engine
1. Disconnect battery cable.
2. Disconnect retaining clip securing wiring plug to rear of alternator and disconnect wiring plug.
3. Disconnect regulator to alternator wiring connector at alternator.
4. Disconnect heater hose bracket at alternator.
5. Loosen alternator mounting bolts and tilt alternator towards engine and remove fan belt.
6. Remove mounting bolts and remove alternator.

V6 Engine
1. Disconnect battery ground cable.
2. Disconnect two multiple connectors at rear of alternator.
3. Remove carburetor air cleaner and exhaust manifold heat duct to gain access for alternator removal.
4. Remove adjusting bolt from rear side of alternator.
5. Remove two alternator to bracket attaching bolts. Then slide alternator back and away from mounting bracket and lift it out between battery tray and exhaust manifold.

In-Vehicle Tests

Output Test
1. Disconnect connector plug from rear of alternator, then connect an ammeter between alternator center terminal and corresponding terminal of connector plug, Fig. 11.

2. Connect a jumper wire between "D" plus terminal and corresponding terminal of connector plug.
3. Turn on headlamps for approximately 5 minutes, then start engine and operate at 3000 RPM. Ammeter reading should be approximately 35 amps, at normal operating temperature. On 1976-77 models equipped with A/C, ammeter reading should be approximately 55 amps at operating temperature.
4. If the above readings cannot be obtained, remove alternator and bench test.

Alternator Wiring Continuity Test
1. Disconnector connector plug from rear of alternator
2. Connect voltmeter negative lead to ground, then place ignition switch in on position and contact each of the connector terminals with positive lead of voltmeter. Each terminal should read battery voltage, if not check wiring for defects, Fig. 12.

Voltage Drop Test Ground Side
1. Connect voltmeter between battery ground terminal and alternator casing.
2. Start engine and operate at 3000 RPM. If voltmeter reading exceeds .25 volts, high resistance is indicated in negative side of charging system.
3. If high resistance is indicated, check for loose, dirty or corroded connections.

Voltage Regulator Voltage Setting Check
1. Connect voltmeter between battery main terminals.
2. Connect ammeter in series between alternator B plus terminal and corresponding terminal of connector plug, Fig. 13.
3. Connect a jumper wire between D positive terminal and corresponding terminal of connector plug.
4. On 1972-74 models start engine and

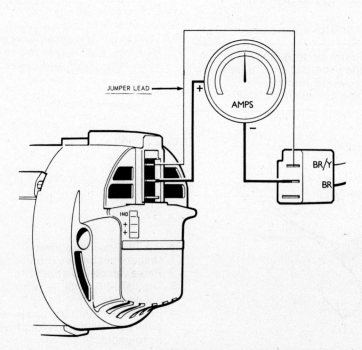

Fig. 14 Alternator output test. Lucas

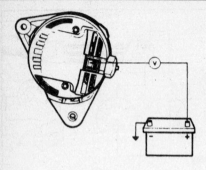

Fig. 15 Alternator voltage drop test. Lucas

operate at 3000 RPM until charging rate falls below 10 amps. On 1972 models, voltmeter should read 14.1 to 14.4 volts. On 1973-74 models, voltmeter should read 13.7 to 14.4 volts.

5. On 1976-77 models, start engine and operate at 2000 RPM until charging rate falls 3 and 5 amps. Voltmeter should read 13.6 to 14.5 volts.

6. If the above reading cannot be obtained, the regulator should be replaced.

LUCAS ALTERNATOR

Alternator, Replace

1. Disconnect battery ground cable and unplug leads on rear of alternator.
2. Loosen three mounting bolts and tilt alternator towards engine.
3. Remove fan belt and alternator mounting bolts and remove alternator.

In-Vehicle Tests

NOTE: Do not run alternator with wires disconnected, otherwise damage to regulator may occur.

Output Test

1. Disconnect terminal plug from rear of alternator, then connect an ammeter between alternator positive terminal and corresponding terminal of connector plug, Fig. 14.
2. Connect a jumper wire between indicator terminal and corresponding terminal of connector plug.
3. Start engine and operate at 3100 RPM, note that alternator warning lamp should go out at approximately 600 RPM.
4. Turn on all vehicle lighting, with headlamps on low beam for approximately 5 minutes.
5. Ammeter reading should indicate rated output at normal operating temperature. If ammeter reading falls below 34 amps., the alternator should be removed for bench testing.

Voltage Drop Test

Connect a voltmeter set at low range scalebetween battery positive terminal and positive terminal of alternator, Fig. 15. Start engine and turn headlamps on high beam. Operate engine at approximately 3000 RPM and note voltmeter reading. A voltmeter reading exceeding .5 volts, indicates high resistance in positive side of charging circuit.

Connect voltmeter between battery negative terminal and alternator casing, Fig. 16, then perform test as described above. A voltmeter reading exceeding .25 volts indicates high resistance in negative side of charging circuit.

If a high resistance is indicated check for loose, dirty or corroded connectors.

Voltage Regulator Setting Check

NOTE: Before performing this check, the Voltage Drop test should be made to ensure wiring and connections in the charging circuit are satisfactory.

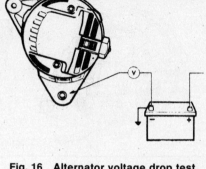

Fig. 16 Alternator voltage drop test. Lucas

1. Connect a voltmeter between main terminals of battery.
2. Connect a 0 to 60 amp. scale ammeter in series between alternator main output positive cable and its connection with the starter solenoid.
3. Start and operate engine at 2660 RPM until ammeter shows an output current not exceeding 7.5 amps. Voltmeter reading should be 14.1 to 14.5 volts.
4. If readings obtained are unstable or not within specified limits, the voltage regulator is faulty and should be replaced.

STARTER, REPLACE

1600 cc Engine

1. Disconnect battery ground cable.
2. Remove starter motor leads from starter.
3. Remove the two solenoid attaching nuts, washers and connecting wire and remove the solenoid.
4. With parking brake applied, jack up front of car and install work stands.
5. Remove the lower two securing bolts and loosen the upper mounting bolt.
6. Support the motor, remove the bolt and remove the motor.

2000 & 2300 cc Engine

1. Disconnect battery ground cable.
2. Disconnect wires at solenoid switch.
3. Remove three starter motor attaching screws and remove the starter assembly.

2600 & 2800 cc V6 Engines

1. Disconnect battery ground cable.
2. Raise vehicle on a hoist.
3. On 1976-77 units, remove the heat shield.
4. Disconnect battery cable and two push-on wire connectors from starter solenoid.
5. Remove two starter attaching bolts and remove the starter.

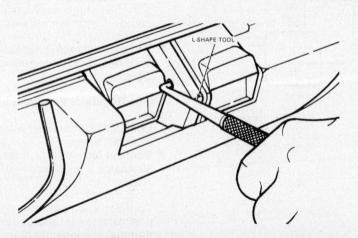

Fig. 17 Headlight and front W/S wiper switch removal

IGNITION SWITCH, REPLACE

1972

1. Disconnect battery ground cable.
2. Unfasten and remove steering column shroud.
3. Be sure ignition key is in "0" position and disconnect wires from switch, noting their respective positions.
4. Remove screws securing switch to lock and withdraw the switch.

1973-74

1. Disconnect battery ground cable.
2. Remove screws securing steering column shroud. Remove lower half of shroud and release shroud upper half retaining lug from its spring clip on steering column by pulling sharply upward.
3. Be sure ignition is in "0" position.
4. Remove ashtray and withdraw hazard flasher switch and disconnect wiring at connector.
5. Remove screws holding turn signal switch. Release the switch and leave it hanging on wiring harness.
6. Remove screws holding lower dash trim panel. Pull trim panel forward and down to gain access to cigar lighter and clock cable connectors. Disconnect cables and remove trim panel from dash.
7. Pull of instrument light control knob. Remove lower screws securing instrument cluster bezel, release bezel from its upper location by pulling downward, and disconnect seat belt warning light wire at connector.
8. Disconnect oil pressure line union.
9. Remove screws securing instrument cluster assembly to instrument panel. Disconnect speedometer cable and multi-plug connector from rear of cluster and remove cluster assembly.
10. Remove multi-plug from ignition switch.
11. Remove screws securing switch to lock and remove switch.

1976-77

1. Disconnect battery ground cable.
2. Remove screws securing steering column shroud. Remove lower half of shroud and release upper half retaining lug from its spring clip on column by pulling sharply upward.
3. Be sure ignition key is in "0" position.
4. Remove screws holding lower left dash trim panel. Pull trim panel forward and down and remove connector from hazard warning flasher switch. Remove trim panel.
5. Disconnect ignition wires at connector.
6. Remove screws securing switch to lock and withdraw switch.

STEERING LOCK

After removal of ignition switch as noted previously, the steering lock may be removed by drilling out the shear bolts or by the use of a screw extractor.

HEADLIGHT SWITCH, REPLACE

1972

1. Disconnect battery ground cable.
2. Reach under instrument panel and disconnect multi-pin connector from rear of switch.
3. Depress two switch retaining clips and push switch out of panel.

1973-77

1. Disconnect battery ground cable.
2. Loosen screws securing lower dash panel.
3. Depress switch and insert a suitable L-shaped tool and pull assembly from dash, Fig. 17.

STOP LIGHT SWITCH, REPLACE

1. Disconnect battery ground cable.
2. Note position of wires on switch, then disconnect wires.
3. Unscrew locknut and remove the switch

NEUTRAL SAFETY SWITCH, REPLACE

1972-74

C4 Transmission

1. Remove downshift cable from transmission downshift lever.
2. Remove transmission downshift outer lever retaining nut and lever.
3. Remove two switch attaching bolts, disconnect multiple wire connector and remove switch.

Borg Warner Transmission

1. Place transmission selector lever in "D" position.
2. Raise vehicle and disconnect four leads from switch.
3. Using an $^{11}/_{16}$" crowsfoot wrench, loosen locknut and unscrew switch from transmission noting number of turns required to remove it.

1976-77

1. Raise car on a hoist and disconnect cable connector from switch.
2. Using a thin wall socket, remove the switch and "O" ring.

TURN SIGNAL, HEADLIGHT DIMMER & HORN SWITCH, REPLACE

1. Disconnect battery ground cable.
2. Remove bolts securing column to underside of instrument panel and lower the column.
3. Remove two screws securing steering column shrouds and remove the shrouds.
4. Remove two screws securing switch to column.
5. Disconnect multi-pin plug and remove switch.

INSTRUMENT CLUSTER SERVICE

1972

Standard Cluster

1. Disconnect battery ground cable.
2. Remove two bolts attaching column to underside of dash and lower column.
3. Remove five phillips screws attaching cluster and pad assembly to panel, Fig. 18.
4. Carefully pull the cluster and pad assembly rearward to gain access to connections at rear of panel.
5. Disconnect speedometer cable and wires noting positions of wires.
6. Carefully remove the cluster and pad assembly from car.
7. Remove four screws attaching cluster to pad.

GT Cluster

1. Disconnect battery ground cable.
2. Remove two heater control knobs.
3. Remove four screws attaching access cover at right of panel and remove the cover.
4. Remove three screws and loosen (do not remove) one nut retaining cluster and pad to the panel, Fig. 19.
5. Remove two fuse panel attaching screws and lower fuse panel.
6. Carefully pull cluster and pad assembly rearward to gain access to connections at back of panel.
7. Disconnect speedometer cable and wires noting position of wires.
8. Disconnect oil pressure gauge tube at gauge being careful not to bend or twist the tube.
9. Carefully remove cluster and pad assembly from car.

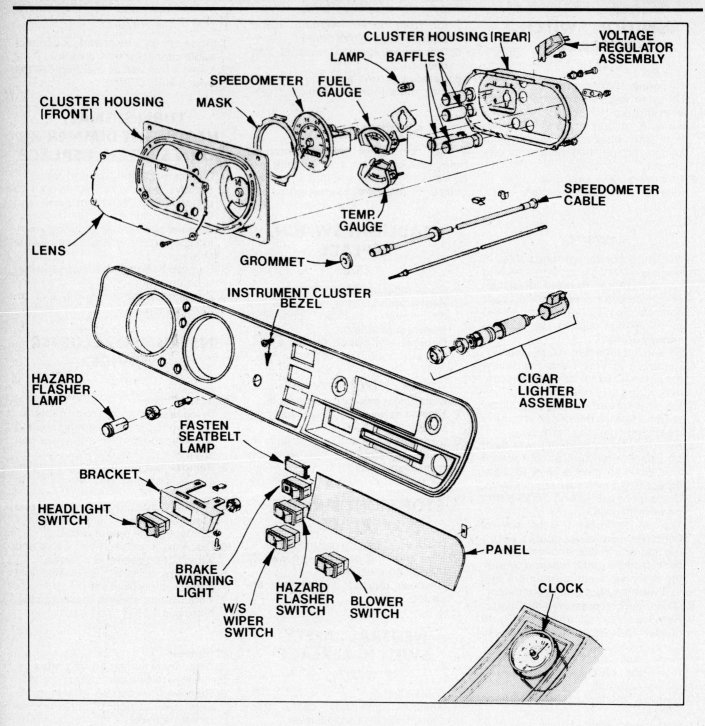

Fig. 18 Standard instrument cluster. 1972 models

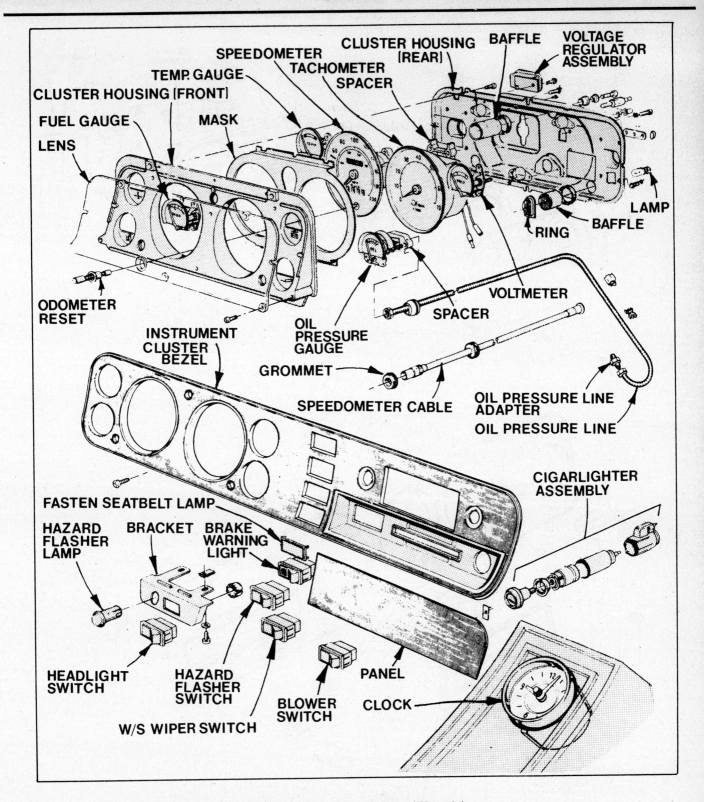

Fig. 19   GT instrument cluster. 1972 models

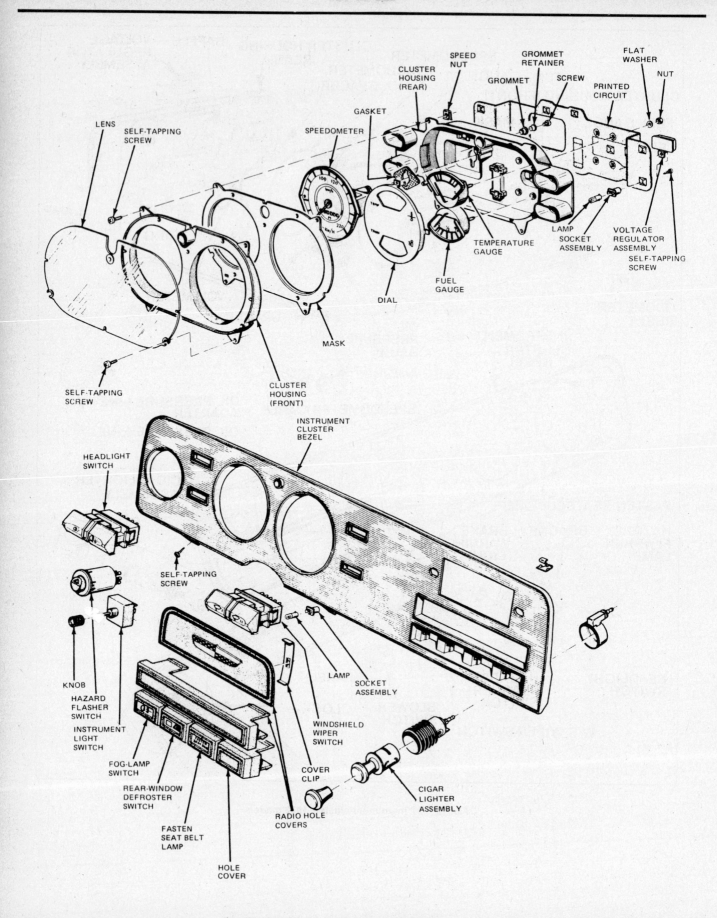

Fig. 20 Standard instrument cluster. 1973-74 models

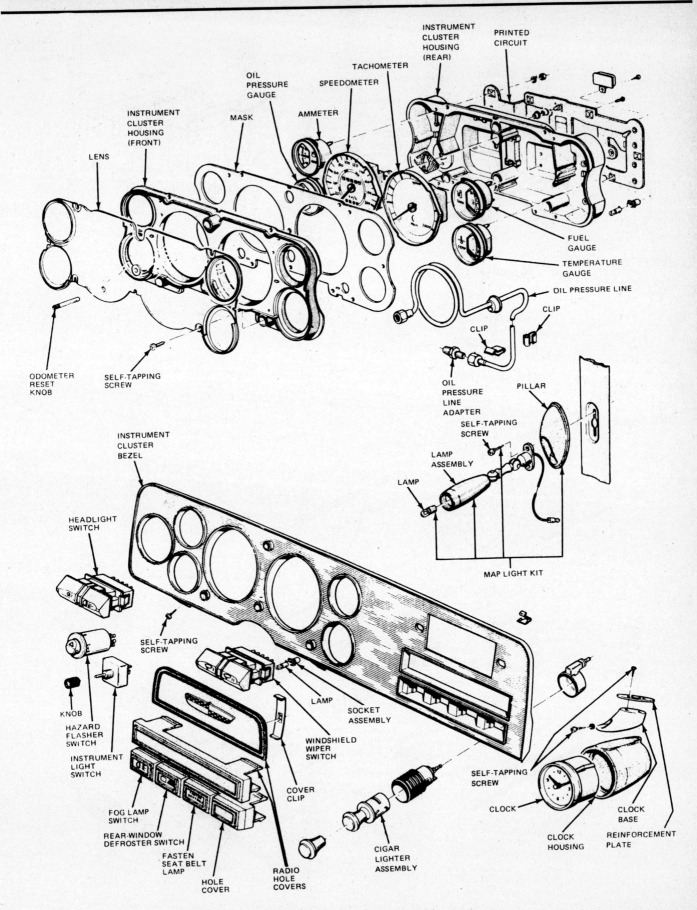

Fig. 21 GT instrument cluster. 1973-74 models

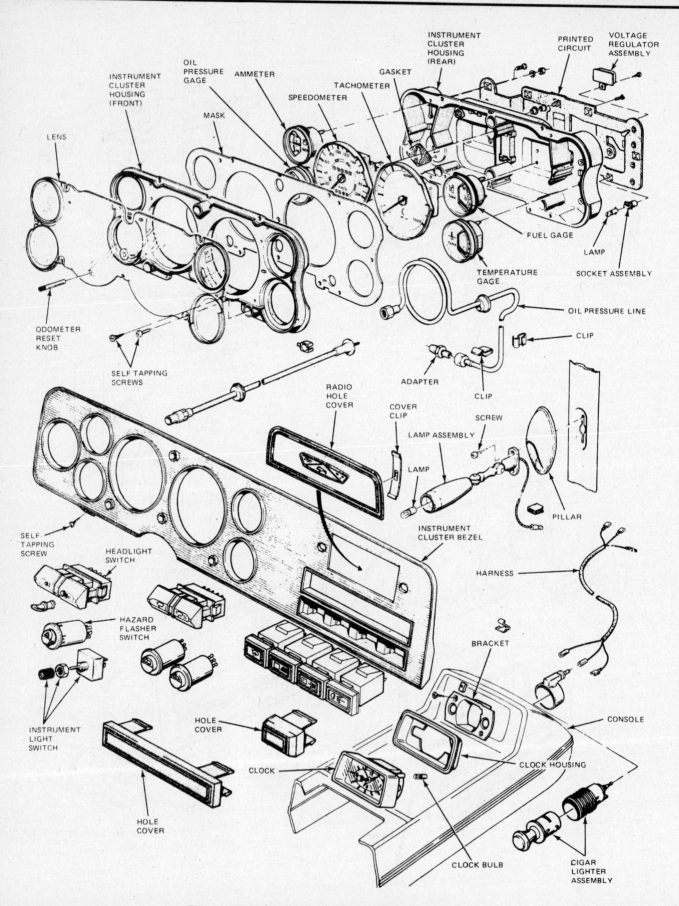

Fig. 22 Instrument cluster. 1976-77 models less A/C

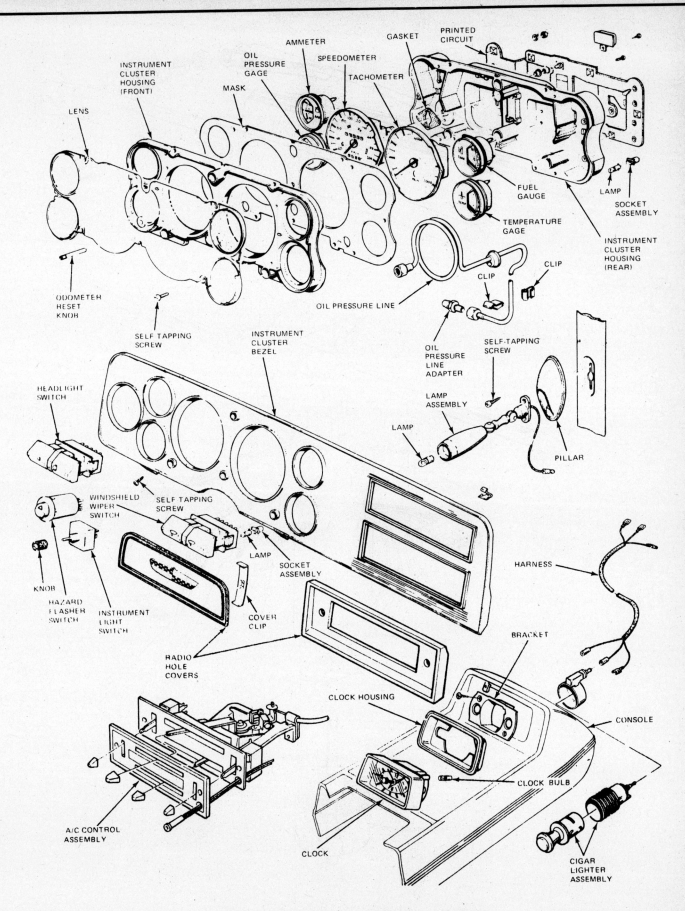

Fig. 23 Instrument cluster. 1976-77 models with A/C

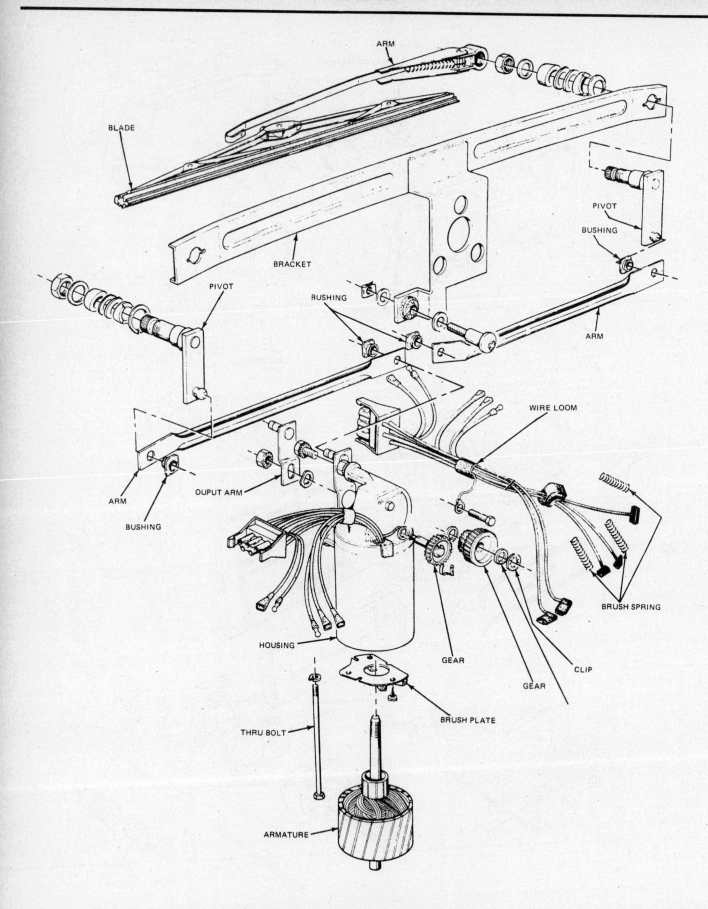

Fig. 24   W/S wiper system. 1972-74 models

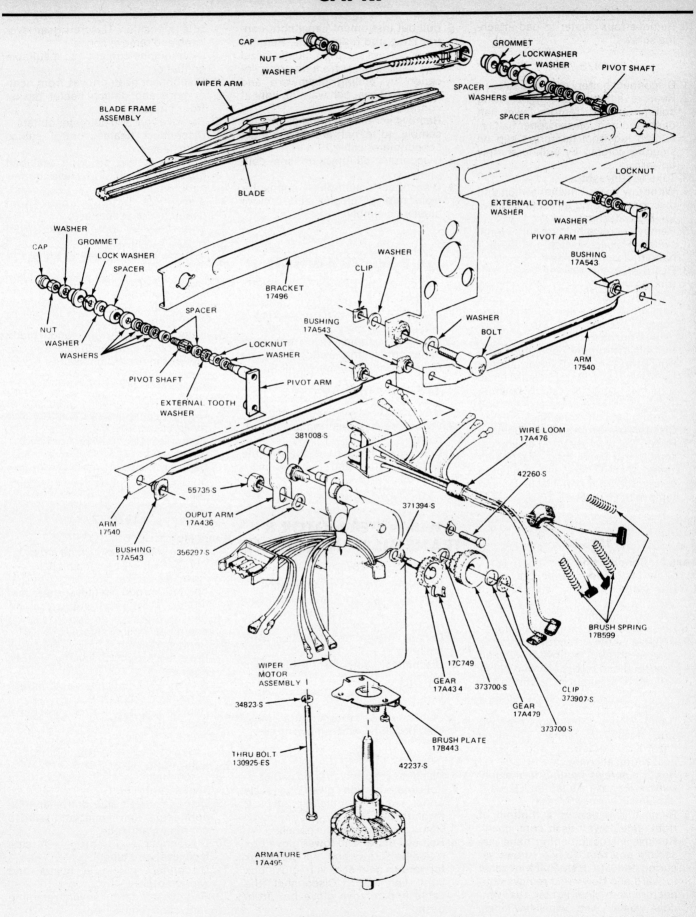

Fig. 25 Front W/S wiper system. 1976-77 models

10. Remove four cluster to pad attaching screws.

1973-74

1. Disconnect battery ground cable.
2. Remove screws securing steering column shroud; remove lower half of shroud and release upper half retaining lug from its spring clip on steering column by pulling sharply upward.
3. Take out the ashtray.
4. Withdraw hazard flasher switch and disconnect wiring at cable connector, Figs. 20 and 21.
5. Remove screws holding turn signal switch. Release switch and leave it hanging in wire harness.
6. Remove screws holding lower dash trim panel. Pull trim panel forward and down to gain access to cigar and clock cable connectors. Disconnect cables and remove trim panel from dash.
7. Pull off instrument panel light control knob. Remove lower screws securing cluster bezel, release bezel from its upper location by pulling downward and disconnect seat belt warning light at connector.
8. Disconnect oil pressure line union.
9. Remove screws securing cluster assembly to panel and disconnect speedometer cable and multi-plug connector from rear of cluster and remove the cluster.

1976-77

Less Air Conditioning

Follow instructions given previously for 1974 models and refer to Fig. 22.

With Air Conditioning

1. Disconnect battery ground cable.
2. Remove screws securing steering column shroud; remove lower half of shroud and release shroud upper half retaining lug from its spring clip on the column by pulling sharply upward.
3. Remove screws holding lower left side dash trim panel. Withdraw hazard flasher switch and disconnect wiring at connector, Fig. 23.
4. Remove screws holding turn signal switch. Release switch and leave it hanging in wiring harness.
5. Remove two screws at bottom of right side lower dash trim panel. Remove air conditioning panel assembly and remove two screws securing panel to dash. Pull trim panel forward and down and remove connectors from cigar lighter, rear window washer and wiper switches. Remove trim panel from dash.

6. Pull out instrument panel light control knob and radio knobs. Remove lower screws securing cluster bezel and release bezel from its upper location by pulling downward and disconnect seat belt warning light at connector.
7. Remove screws securing cluster assembly to panel and disconnect speedometer cable.
8. Disconnect oil pressure line coupling.
9. Disconnect multi-plug connector from rear of cluster and remove cluster assembly.

W/S WIPER SWITCH

1972

1. Remove lower dash trim panel as described previously for instrument cluster.
2. Working behind the instrument panel, push the switch from its housing and disconnect multi-plug.

1973-77

1. Disconnect battery ground cable.
2. Loosen screws securing lower dash panel.
3. Depress switch and insert a suitable L-shaped tool and pull assembly from dash, Fig. 17.

W/S WIPER MOTOR & TRANSMISSION, REPLACE

1972

1. Disconnect battery ground cable.
2. Remove wiper arms and nuts securing pivots to the body, Fig. 24.
3. Remove front parcel tray.
4. Detach heater to defroster vent hose.
5. Disconnect two control cables from heater.
6. Remove screws attaching wiper motor to bracket.
7. Disconnect wires from motor noting their positions, and remove motor.

1973-74

1. Disconnect battery ground cable.
2. Follow instructions given previously under instrument cluster (steps 2 through 6).
3. Remove foot pedal trim panel.
4. Remove upper and lower glove box retaining screws and pull glove box forward to gain access to glove box light connector. Disconnect the cable and remove glove box from dash.
5. Remove screws holding center con-

sole in position. Unscrew gear lever knob and remove console.
6. Drain engine coolant into a suitable container.
7. Disconnect heater hoses from heater core and detach heater gasket from bulkhead.
8. Remove vent and defroster outlets.
9. Disconnect heater control cables from heater.
10. Remove screws securing seat belt buzzer to dash and leave buzzer hanging on harness.
11. Disconnect wiring harness from heater motor at connector.
12. Remove wiper motor bracket from bulkhead, Fig. 24.
13. Remove heater retaining bolts and lift heater from car.
14. Remove screws securing left defroster to dash panel.
15. Disconnect harness connections from wiper motor.
16. Remove wiper arm and blade assemblies from spindles and remove spindles from cowl top panel. Remove sleeves and sealing washers.
17. Remove wiper motor complete with linkage, simultaneously lifting out the left defroster.
18. Remove wiper linkage from motor driveshaft.
19. Separate motor from mounting bracket.

1976-77

Front Motor

1. Disconnect battery ground cable.
2. Remove wiper arms and blades.
3. Remove screws securing steering column shroud. Remove lower half of shroud and release upper half retaining lug from its spring clip on column by pulling sharply upward.
4. Remove retaining screws and pull lower dash panel assembly clear of dash panel.
5. Disconnect cigar lighter and remove panel from car.
6. Remove instrument cluster bezel and cluster.
7. Remove glovebox catch striker and glovebox. Disconnect glovebox light wiring.
8. Disconnect heater cables from heater controls.
9. Disconnect left side defroster tube connector from heater and remove connector and tube.
10. Disconnect and remove left side face level vent tube.
11. Disconnect wiring at heater and wiper motor.
12. Remove left defroster vent retaining screw and remove vent.
13. Remove wiper spindle retaining

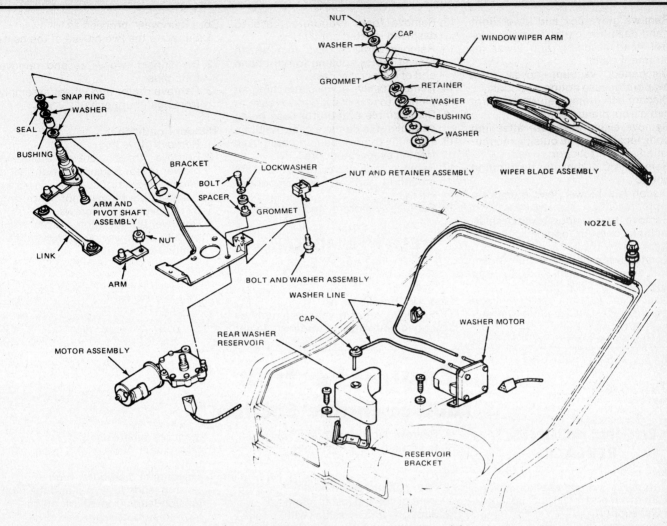

Fig. 26   Rear W/S wiper system. 1976-77 models

nuts and motor bracket retaining screw and remove motor and linkage assembly from vehicle, Fig. 25.

14. Separate motor from linkage.

Rear Motor

1. Disconnect battery ground cable.
2. Remove wiper arm and blade.
3. Open tailgate and remove tailgate trim panel.
4. Disconnect wiring at wiper motor.
5. Remove wiper spindle retaining nut, three motor bracket retaining screws and remove motor and linkage assembly from tailgate, Fig. 26.
6. Remove drive spindle nut and three retaining bolts and remove motor from bracket.
7. Remove linkage from bracket and remove snap ring at wiper spindle end.

HEATER CORE REMOVAL

1972

1. Disconnect battery ground cable and drain cooling system.

2. Disconnect heater hoses from heater core tubes.
3. Remove cover plate and gasket from around core tubes at dash.
4. Inside car, remove parcel tray.
5. If equipped with a console, it must be removed as follows:
   a. Remove two screws at forward end (console to floor).
   b. Lift up gear shift lever boot and remove two screws at rear end.
   c. Pry up rear panel and remove two screws.
   d. Gently pry up clock panel and disconnect two wires and one bulb.
   e. Remove main screw at rear end of the area under clock panel.
   f. Slide plastic brace below hand brake lever forward and remove it. Then lift console out of car.
6. Remove control cable retaining clips and disconnect cables from control levers.
7. Disconnect three wire connectors from terminals on heater and disconnect bullet connector on other wire.

8. Disconnect left and right vent ducts and left and right defroster ducts from heater.
9. For access to one mounting screw at left side of heater, remove the wiper motor as previously described.
10. Remove four heater to dash mounting screws and remove heater from car.
11. Separate two halves of the heater.
12 Slide core out of heater lower half.

1973-77

Less Air Conditioner

Follow the procedure for 1972 models and note that the seat belt buzzer will have to be removed from the dash and allowed to hang on the harness.

With Air Conditioner

1. Discharge the A/C system and drain coolant.
2. Disconnect A/C refrigerant lines from evaporator core in engine compartment and disconnect heater hoses from core.

3. Remove glove box and lower right hand dash trim panel. Remove control head assembly and lower instrument panel.
4. Disconnect vacuum hoses from evaporator case noting positions.
5. Disconnect temperature control cable from blend door lever.
6. Remove evaporator case attaching bolts located beside outside recirculation air control door.
7. Remove A/C and heater distribution ducts.
8. Disconnect blower lead plug from motor resistor.
9. Remove three evaporator to dash attaching nuts in engine compartment.
10. Rotate evaporator assembly down and away from dash and out from under instrument panel.
11. Disconnect vacuum motor linkage for the A/C-Heat and the Defrost/Heat doors.

12. Remove foam evaporator case to dash pad located core tubes.
13. Remove three screws that attach blower motor housing to right hand end of evaporator case.
14. Remove twelve screws attaching air plenum to rear of evaporator case.
15. Disassemble evaporator case being careful not to damage case molding.
16. Carefully remove de-icing bulb from front of evaporator core.
17. Remove evaporator case to core mounting screws from evaporator case front.
18. Remove evaporator and heater core.

BLOWER MOTOR, REMOVE

1972-77

Less Air Conditioner

After removal of heater assembly as described previously under "Heater Core Removal," proceed as follows:
1. Separate the two halves of the heater.
2. Disconnect two wires and remove four clips.
3. Remove motor and wheel assembly from heater upper half.

With Air Conditioner
1. Remove glove box.
2. Remove three screws attaching blower motor housing to right hand end of evaporator case.
3. Disassemble blower motor housing by removing three screws.
4. Remove blower motor from front portion of blower motor housing by removing three nuts.

Engine Section
1600 cc Engine Section

ENGINE MOUNTS, REPLACE

Front
1. With parking brake applied, jack up front of car and install jack stands to lower support.
2. Support the engine on a jack and remove the engine oil pan shield, if equipped.
3. Remove the engine right mounting, Fig. 1.
4. Replace engine right mounting.
5. Remove engine left mounting.
6. Replace engine left mounting.
7. Remove jack from under engine and replace oil pan shield.

8. Remove jack stands and lower car to ground.

Rear
1. With parking brake applied, jack up front of car and install stands.
2. Support transmission with a suitable jack.
3. Disconnect crossmember from body floor pan.
4. Remove engine rear mounting center bolt and remove crossmember, Fig. 2.
5. Remove engine mounting and retainer from crossmember.

ENGINE, REPLACE

1. Remove the hood.
2. Disconnect battery lead and ground cable.
3. Drain cooling system into suitable container.
4. Disconnect radiator hoses from engine and remove radiator.
5. Disconnect hot air pipe at air cleaner and remove air cleaner.
6. Disconnect heater hoses, one from water pump and one from intake manifold.
7. Disconnect accelerator linkage from carburetor.
8. Disconnect temperature gauge and oil pressure gauge sender unit leads and alternator leads.
9. Disconnect exhaust pipe from manifold and remove hot air pipes from manifold, where used.
10. Disconnect fuel intake pipe from fuel pump.
11. Disconnect distributor high and low tension leads from coil and the high tension leads from spark plugs. Remove distributor cap.
12. Jack up front of car and install jack stands.
13. Disconnect starter motor lead and remove starter motor.
14. Remove clutch housing lower bolts and remove the cover.
15. Remove stands and jack from beneath car.
16. Remove clutch housing to engine bolts.

Fig. 1 Engine front mount

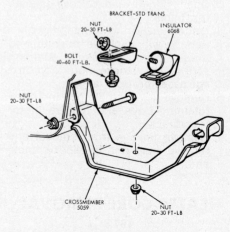

Fig. 2 Engine rear mount

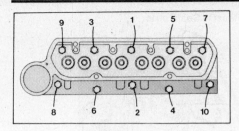

Fig. 3 Cylinder head tightening sequence

VALVE LIFT SPECS.

Engine	Year	Intake	Exhaust
1600 cc	1972	.2967	.3199

VALVE TIMING

Intake Opens Before TDC

Engine	Year	Degrees
1600 cc	1972	17

1600 cc Engine—Set Hot

Valve Depressed	Valves to Adjust to .010	.017
no. 1	no. 3	no. 8
no. 2	no. 7	no. 5
no. 3	no. 6	no. 1
no. 5	no. 2	no. 4

Fig. 4 Valve adjustment table

VALVES, ADJUST

1. Start engine and allow it to idle for 20 minutes.
2. Turn engine off and remove air cleaner and wires from spark plugs.
3. Disconnect wires and linkage necessary to remove rocker arm cover noting position of all parts disconnected.
4. Remove rocker arm cover.
5. Rotate crankshaft clockwise by hand until number 1 and 6 valves are completely depressed and adjust valves 3 and 8. Valves are numbered from 1 to 8 (front to rear). Continue through sequence given in Fig. 4 until all valves are adjusted.

VALVE GUIDES

Valve guides consist of holes bored in the cylinder head. For service, the guides can be reamed oversize to accommodate valves with oversize stems. Valves with oversize stems are available in .003″, .015″ and .030″ oversizes.

ROCKER ARM SERVICE

1. Remove air cleaner from carburetor.
2. Disconnect spark plug leads, remove them from clips on rocker cover and position aside.
3. Remove rocker cover attaching screws, remove the rocker cover and discard the gasket.
4. Remove rocker shaft attaching bolts

evenly and lift off the rocker arm shaft assembly.
5. Remove cotter pin from one end of shaft and slip the flat washer, crimped washer and second flat washer off the shaft. The rocker arm shaft supports, rocker arms and springs can now be removed from shaft.
6. Remove plugs from rocker shaft ends by drilling a hole in one plug. Insert a long rod through the drilled plug and knock the opposite plug out of the shaft. Remove the drilled plug in the same manner.
7. Clean all parts in a suitable degreaser.
8. When assembling shaft, refit new plugs to rocker shaft ends. Assemble the shaft noting the bolt hole in rocker arm shaft support must be on same side as adjusting screw in rocker arm. The rocker arms are right and left hand, the rocker pads being inclined towards the shaft support.

VALVE LIFTERS, REPLACE

The chilled cast iron tappets can only be removed from the engine after the camshaft has been removed. See "Camshaft, Replace" further on in this section.

TIMING CASE COVER

1. Drain engine coolant into a suitable container.
2. Disconnect radiator hoses at engine.
3. Remove radiator assembly.
4. Remove fan belt and then remove fan and water pump pulley.
5. Remove the water pump.
6. Using a suitable puller, remove crankshaft pulley.
7. Unfasten and remove front cover.
8. When replacing cover, install a new oil seal as this seal can only be replaced when the cover is removed.

TIMING CHAIN

1. Remove the timing cover as described previously.

17. Install and support the engine on a suitable lifting device.
18. Disconnect engine mountings from front crossmember.
19. Suitably support the transmission.
20. Pull engine forward off main drive gear and lift out of engine compartment.

CYLINDER HEAD, REPLACE

1. Disconnect hot air and crankcase ventilation hoses at air cleaner and remove air cleaner.
2. Disconnect fuel line at pump and carburetor.
3. Drain cooling system into suitable container.
4. Disconnect spark plug wires and position out of way.
5. Disconnect heater and vacuum hoses at intake manifold and the hoses at choke housing.
6. Disconnect exhaust pipe from manifold.
7. Disconnect throttle linkage and vacuum advance line from carburetor, then disconnect lead from temperature sending unit.
8. Remove thermostat housing, pull to one side and remove thermostat.
9. Remove rocker arm cover and gasket.
10. Remove rocker arm shaft bolts evenly and lift off the rocker arm shaft assembly.
11. Lift out the push rods from their locations and keep them in their correct order.
12. Remove cylinder head bolts and lift off the head and gasket.

NOTE: Do not lay the head flat on its face as damage to the spark plugs or gasket surface can occur.

13. Reverse procedure to install and tighten cylinder head bolts in sequence shown in Fig. 3.

VALVE ARRANGEMENT

Front to Rear

1600 cc Engine . . . . E-I-I-E-E-I-I-E

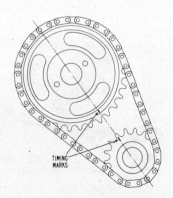

Fig. 5 Valve timing marks

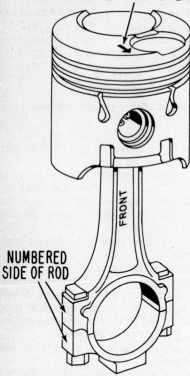

ARROW TOWARD FRONT OF ENGINE

NUMBERED SIDE OF ROD

FRONT

Fig. 6   Piston and rod assembly

2. Remove crankshaft oil slinger. Remove camshaft sprocket retainer and bolts.
3. Remove camshaft sprocket and disconnect timing chain. Remove chain tensioner and bolts. When replacing chain, be sure to align marks when sprocket is fitted, Fig. 5.

CAMSHAFT, REPLACE

1. Remove engine as previously described.
2. With engine mounted on a stand, disconnect fuel line at the pump.
3. Loosen alternator and remove the belt.
4. Remove the fan and water pump pulley.
5. Remove the oil and fuel pumps from cylinder block.
6. Unfasten and remove the rocker arm cover.
7. Remove the distributor from the cylinder block.
8. Remove rocker arm shaft support bolts evenly and lift off the rocker arm shaft.
9. Withdraw push rods from their locations taking care to keep them in their correct order.
10. Invert engine on stand and remove oil pan and gaskets.
11. Remove dipstick, crankshaft pulley, front cover and oil slinger.

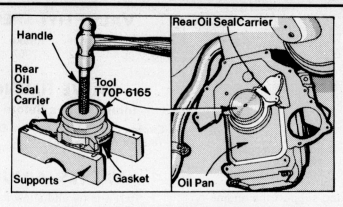

Fig. 7   Installing crankshaft rear oil seal

12. Remove timing chain tensioner assembly.
13. Remove crankshaft sprocket and timing chain.
14. With engine inverted, remove camshaft thrust plate and withdraw the camshaft.
15. If necessary, remove tappets from their locations in block.

PISTON & ROD, ASSEMBLE

Assemble the rod to the piston with the Front mark on the rod on the same side of the assembly as the arrow in the piston crown, Fig. 6.

PISTONS, PINS & RINGS

Oversize pistons and rings are available in .0015, .0025 and .0030". Oversize pins are not available.

MAIN & ROD BEARINGS

Undersize main bearings are available in .010, .020 and .030". Rod bearing undersizes are available in .010, .020, .030 and .040".

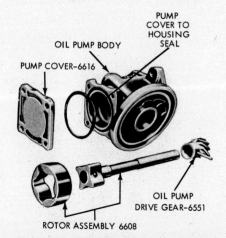

PUMP COVER TO HOUSING SEAL

OIL PUMP BODY

PUMP COVER-6616

OIL PUMP DRIVE GEAR-6551

ROTOR ASSEMBLY 6608

Fig. 8   Eccentric Bi-rotor type oil pump

CRANKSHAFT OIL SEAL

With the engine removed and mounted on a work stand, proceed as follows:

1. Remove the clutch pressure plate bolts evenly and remove the pressure plate and clutch disc.
2. Remove the flywheel.
3. Remove the oil pan and gaskets.
4. Remove the rear oil seal carrier.
5. Install new seal using tool No. T70P-61651, Fig. 7.

OIL PAN, REPLACE

1. Drain engine oil into suitable container.
2. Remove oil level dipstick and disconnect battery ground cable.
3. Disconnect throttle linkage from carburetor.
4. Disconnect steering cable from rack and pinion.
5. Disconnect rack and pinion from crossmember and move it forward to provide clearance for oil pan.
6. Unfasten and remove starter motor.
7. Remove left bottom bolt from lower rear cover and remove cover.
8. Unfasten and remove the oil pan and gasket.
9. Remove oil pump and inlet tube as an assembly.

OIL PUMP, REPLACE

The oil pump may be one of two different types, an eccentric bi-rotor or a sliding vane type. The pumps are directly interchangeable, differing only in internal design. The oil pump and filter assembly is bolted to the right side of the block and can be removed with the engine in place.

OIL PUMP REPAIRS

Bi-rotor type pump

1. Remove filter body and element and extract sealing ring from groove.

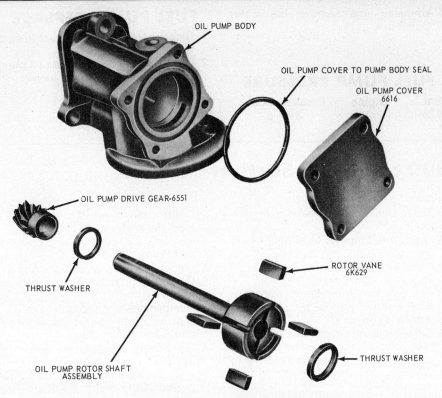

Fig. 9   Sliding vane type oil pump

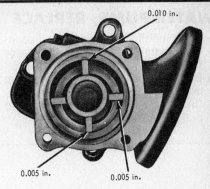

Fig. 10   Checking vane and rotor clearances

2. Remove end plate and withdraw "O" ring from groove in pump body, Fig. 8.
3. Check clearance between lobes of inner and outer rotors. This should not exceed .006". The rotors are supplied in a matched set only so if clearance is excessive a new rotor must be fitted.
4. Check clearance between outer rotor and housing. This should not exceed .010". If excessive a new rotor set and/or pump body should be fitted.
5. Place a straight edge across face of pump body and check clearance between face of rotors and straight edge. This should not exceed .005". If excessive the face of the pump body can be carefully lapped on a flat surface.
6. If necessary to replace rotor or drive shaft, remove outer rotor, then drive out retaining pin securing gear to shaft and pull off the gear.
7. Withdraw inner rotor and drive shaft.

Vane type pump
1. Remove filter body and element and extract sealing ring from groove.
2. Remove end plate, keeping pump shaft vertical. Withdraw "O" ring from groove in pump body, Fig. 9.
3. Place a straight edge across face of pump body and check clearance be-

tween face of vanes and rotor and straight edge. This should not exceed .005". If excessive, the face of the pump body can be carefully lapped on a flat surface.
4. Turn oil pump until one of the vanes is in the center of the cam form. Check clearance between rotor and pump body at closest point. If clear-

ance exceeds .005" the body is worn and a new pump should be installed, Fig. 10.
5. With rotor in same position, centralize the locating ring and check clearance between the diametrically opposite vane and pump body. If clearance exceeds .010" the vanes are worn and should be replaced, Fig. 10.
6. Check van clearance in locating grooves. If it exceeds .005" the vanes and/or rotor are worn and should be replaced, Fig. 10.
7. If necessary to replace rotor or drive shaft, lift out the vanes and the outer locating ring. Drive out retaining pin securing the gear and pull off the gear.
8. Remove the drive shaft and rotor arm assembly together with the vane locating inner ring from pump housing.

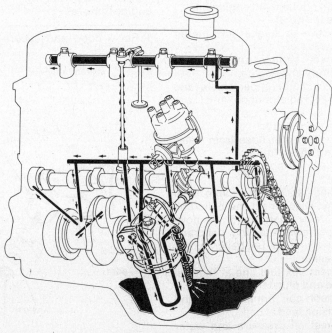

Engine oiling system

WATER PUMP, REPLACE

1. Drain cooling system and disconnect heater hose and lower radiator hose from the pump.
2. Loosen alternator and remove drive belt.
3. Unfasten and remove the fan and pulley.
4. Unfasten and remove the water pump and gasket.

FUEL PUMP PRESSURE

Year	Engine	Pressure, Lbs.
1972	1600 cc	3½ - 5

FUEL PUMP, REPLACE

1. Disconnect inlet and outlet lines at the pump.
2. Unfasten and remove the fuel pump and gasket. Discard the gasket.

2000 cc Engine Section

ENGINE MOUNTS, REPLACE

Front

1. Remove insulator pump and lower attaching nut, Fig. 1.
2. Raise engine just high enough to remove the insulator.
3. Remove support bracket attaching screws and remove the bracket.

Rear

1. Place a jack or support under transmission.
2. Remove insulator to extension housing retaining screw.
3. Remove four rear engine support bracket to body screws and remove rear support assembly.
4. Remove two screws retaining insulator to support bracket.

ENGINE, REPLACE

1972-73

1. Remove radiator lower splash shield and drain coolant and engine oil.
2. Remove the hood.
3. Remove the air cleaner and the air cleaner adapter.
4. Disconnect battery ground cable from battery and engine.
5. Remove radiator upper shield and disconnect radiator upper and lower hoses.
6. Remove the radiator.
7. Disconnect heater hose from water pump and choke fitting.
8. Disconnect wiring plug from alternator.
9. Disconnect accelerator cable from bellcrank. Disconnect the bellcrank to carburetor shaft swivel. Remove two capscrews retaining bellcrank to intake manifold. Set bellcrank assembly aside.
10. Disconnect flex fuel line at the fuel tank line and plug tank line.
11. Disconnect coil primary wire and high tension lead at coil.
12. Disconnect oil pressure and water temperature wires at sending units.
13. Raise the vehicle and remove starter.
14. Disconnect muffler inlet pipe at exhaust manifold.
15. Remove flywheel or converter housing lower front cover.
16. On vehicle with manual transmission, remove flywheel housing lower attaching bolts.
17. On vehicle with automatic transmission, disconnect converter from flex plate. Remove converter housing to cylinder block lower attaching capscrews.
18. Disconnect engine mounts at underbody bracket.
19. Lower vehicle. Support transmission and flywheel, or converter housing, with a suitable jack.
20. Attach engine lift and raise engine from chassis.

1974

NOTE: If engine is equipped with Thermactor air pump, remove or disconnect parts that will interfere with engine removal.

1. Raise hood and secure in vertical position.

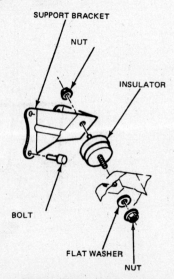

Fig. 1   Engine front mount

2. Drain cooling system and the oil from the engine.
3. Remove air cleaner and exhaust manifold shroud.
4. Disconnect battery ground cable.
5. Remove upper and lower radiator hoses.
6. Remove radiator and fan.
7. Disconnect heater hose from water pump and choke fitting.
8. Disconnect alternator wires from alternator, starter cable from starter and accelerator cable from carburetor. Disconnect kickdown cable if equipped with automatic transmission. On a vehicle with air conditioner, remove compressor from mounting bracket and position out of way, leaving refrigerant lines attached.
9. Disconnect flex fuel line at fuel tank line and plug tank line.
10. Disconnect: coil primary wire at coil, oil pressure gauge tubing, warning light and water temperature wires at sending units.
11. Remove starter.
12. Raise vehicle and remove flywheel or converter housing upper attaching bolts.
13. Disconnect muffler inlet pipe at exhaust manifold and disconnect engine mounts at underbody bracket. Remove flywheel or converter housing cover.
14. On vehicle with manual transmission, remove flywheel housing lower attaching bolts.
15. On vehicle with automatic transmission, disconnect converter from flex plate. Remove converter housing lower bolts.
16. Lower vehicle and support transmission and flywheel or converter housing with suitable jack.
17. Attach engine lift and raise engine out of vehicle.

CYLINDER HEAD, REPLACE

1. Drain cooling system and remove air cleaner and rocker arm cover.
2. Remove exhaust manifold and re-

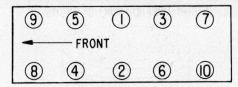

Fig. 2 Cylinder head tightening sequence

move intake manifold, carburetor and decel valve as an assembly.

3. Remove camshaft drive belt cover.
4. Loosen drive belt tensioner and remove drive belt.
5. Remove water outlet elbow from head.
6. Remove cylinder head attaching bolts.

NOTE: The cylinder head retaining bolts have 12 point heads.

7. Lift head and camshaft assembly from engine.
8. Reverse procedure to install. Tighten bolts in sequence shown in cylinder head Fig. 2 and intake manifold bolts in sequence shown in Fig. 3.

NOTE: Do not overtighten the valve cover retaining screws, also make certain the valve cover gasket is aligned properly. It is possible to block the oil return hole on the right side of the front camshaft bearing support if the above cautions are not adhered to. If the oil return hole becomes blocked, sufficient oil pressure can build up in the front camshaft bearing area and push the oil seal out of position.

VALVE ARRANGEMENT
Front to Rear

2000 cc Engine .... E-I-E-I-E-I-E-I

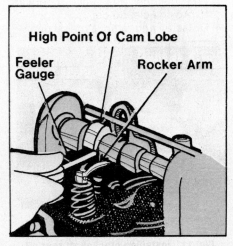

Fig. 5 Checking valve clearance

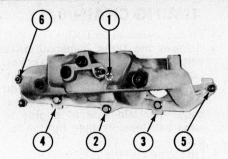

Fig. 3 Intake manifold tightening sequence

VALVE LIFT SPECS.

Engine	Year	Intake	Exhaust
2000 cc	1972-74	.3993	.3993

VALVE TIMING
Intake Opens Before TDC

Engine	Year	Degrees
2000 cc	1972-74	24

VALVES, ADJUST

1. If there is a clamp between heat shroud pipe and air cleaner duct and valve assembly, loosen the clamp.
2. Disconnect crankcase ventilation hose and carbon cannister hose at air cleaner.
3. Remove wing nuts and unsnap wire clips on air cleaner cover and lift air cleaner off carburetor.
4. Remove screws (11 mm) from rocker cover.
5. Remove spark plug wires from retainer and move out of way.
6. Remove rocker cover.
7. Rotate the crankshaft clockwise by hand until the high point of the number 1 cam lobe is pointing down. Check clearances on valves 6

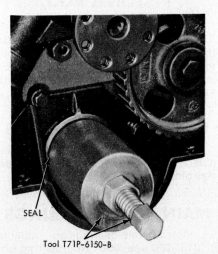

Fig. 6 Removing crankshaft oil seal

2000 cc Engine—Set at Any Temperature

Valve Depressed	Valves to Adjust to .008	.010
no. 1	no. 6	no. 7
no. 2	no. 8	no. 3
no. 3	no. 2	no. 5
no. 6	no. 4	no. 1

Fig. 4 Valve adjustment table

and 7. Consult Fig. 4 and continue on through sequence until all valves are adjusted, Fig. 5.

VALVE GUIDES

Valve guides consist of holes bored in the cylinder head. For service, the guides can be reamed oversize to accommodate valves with oversize stems. Valves with oversize stems are available in .003", .015" and .030" oversizes on all engines except the 1974 2000 cc engine. Valves with oversize stems for the 1974 2000 cc engine are available in oversizes of .008", .016" and .032".

ROCKER ARM SERVICE

1. Remove air cleaner.
2. Remove rocker arm cover.
3. Rotate crankshaft as required to place the low side of the camshaft lobe next to the rocker arm that is being replaced.
4. Remove the rocker arm retaining spring.
5. Depress the valve spring with Tool T71P6565-A just enough to remove the rocker arm.

NOTE: Refer to "NOTE" under "Cylinder Head, Replace" before installing valve cover.

Fig. 7 Installing crankshaft oil seal

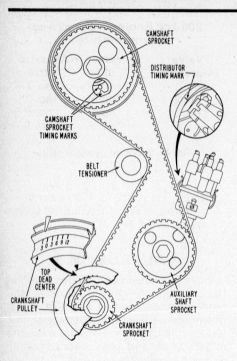

Fig. 8 Timing marks

TIMING CASE COVER

It is not necessary to remove the front cover to replace the crankshaft oil seal. Proceed as follows:
1. Remove alternator belt.
2. Remove crankshaft pulley bolt and slide pulley off shaft.
3. Remove camshaft drive belt and slide sprocket and belt guide off the crankshaft. If sprocket cannot be slid off shaft use a puller.
4. Install tool T71P-6150A over end of crankshaft and remove seal, Fig. 6.
5. Install a new seal with tool T71P-6150B, Fig. 7.

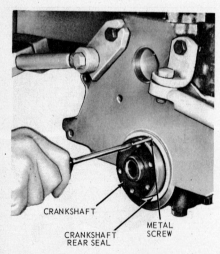

Fig. 10 Removing crankshaft rear oil seal

TIMING CHAIN/BELT

1. Place crankshaft on TDC.
2. Remove the three camshaft drive belt cover screws and remove cover.
3. Loosen camshaft drive belt tensioner adjustment bolt, Fig. 8 and force the tensioner toward the exhaust manifold side of engine to relax belt tension, then tighten the bolt.
4. Lift the belt off the sprockets.

NOTE: Do not rotate the crankshaft or the camshaft after the belt is removed. Rotating either one will impair valve timing.

5. To install, make sure timing marks are aligned as in Fig. 8 and place the belt over the sprockets.
6. Loosen the tensioner adjustment bolt to place tension on the belt.
7. Rotate the crankshaft two complete turns to place the timing marks in the proper position and to remove all slack from the belt. Torque the adjustment bolt and the pivot bolt.
8. Position camshaft drive belt cover and install screws.
9. Start engine and check ignition timing and adjust as required.

CAMSHAFT, REPLACE

After removal of cylinder head, proceed as follows:
1. Remove rocker arms.
2. Remove camshaft gear bolt and washer, and slide the gear and the belt guide plate off the shaft.
3. Remove camshaft thrust plate from rear of head and carefully slide camshaft from the rear of the head.

PISTON & ROD, ASSEMBLE

Assemble the piston to the rod with the oil squirt hole in the rod positioned to the right side of the engine. The arrow on the piston must face forward, Fig. 9.

PISTONS, PINS & RINGS

Oversize pistons and rings are available in .003, .020, .030 and .040". Oversize pins are not available.

MAIN & ROD BEARINGS

Undersize main bearings are available in .010, .020 and .030". Rod bearing undersizes are available in .010 and .020".

ARROW TOWARD FRONT OF ENGINE

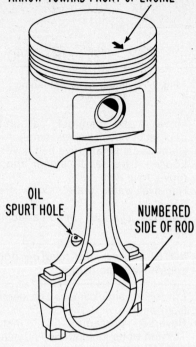

Fig. 9 Piston and rod assembly

CRANKSHAFT OIL SEAL

1. Remove transmission, clutch and flywheel or the automatic transmission, converter and flywheel.
2. Remove crankshaft rear seal with a sheet metal screw as shown in Fig. 10.
3. Install new seal with tool T71P-6701A as shown in Fig. 11.

OIL PAN, REPLACE

1. Drain crankcase and remove oil dipstick and flywheel inspection cover.
2. Disconnect steering cable from rack and pinion.
3. Disconnect rack and pinion from crossmember and move it forward to provide clearance.
4. Unfasten and remove the oil pan.

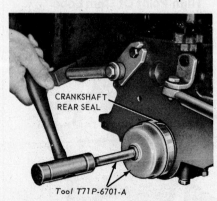

Fig. 11 Installing crankshaft rear oil seal

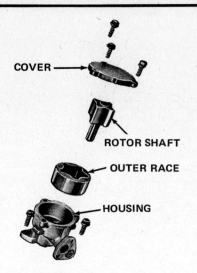

Fig. 12 Oil pump assembly

OIL PUMP, REPLACE

The oil pump is easily removed after removal of the oil pan.

OIL PUMP REPAIRS

1. Remove end plate and withdraw "O" ring from groove in body, Fig. 12.
2. Check clearance between lobes of inner and outer rotors. This should not exceed .006". Rotors are supplied only in a matched pair.
3. Check clearance between outer rotor and the housing. This should not exceed .010".
4. Place a straight edge across face of pump body. Clearance between face of rotors and straight edge should

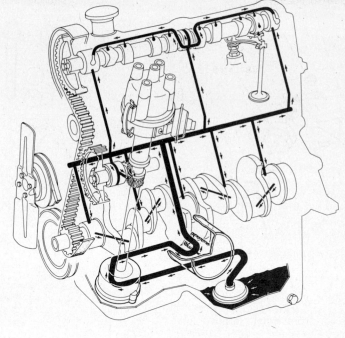

Engine oiling system

not exceed .005".
5. If necessary to replace rotor or drive shaft, remove outer rotor and then drive out retaining pin securing gear to shaft and pull off the gear.
6. Withdraw inner rotor and drive shaft.

WATER PUMP, REPLACE

1. Drain cooling system and disconnect heater hose and radiator lower hose from pump.
2. Loosen alternator and remove belt.
3. Remove fan, spacer and pulley.

4. Remove camshaft drive belt cover.
5. Unfasten and remove the pump.

FUEL PUMP PRESSURE

Year	Engine	Pressure, Lbs.
1972-74	4-cyl.	3½ - 4½

FUEL PUMP, REPLACE

1. Disconnect inlet and outlet lines at pump.
2. Unfasten and remove pump.
3. On 1972-73 models, remove actuator rod.

2300 cc Engine Section

ENGINE MOUNTS, REPLACE

Front
1. Remove insulator upper and lower attaching nut, Fig. 1.
2. Raise engine just high enough to remove the insulator.
3. Remove support bracket attaching screws and remove the bracket.

Rear
1. Place a jack or support under transmission.
2. Remove insulator to extension housing retaining screw.
3. Remove four rear engine support bracket to body screws and remove rear support assembly.

4. Remove two screws retaining insulator to support bracket.

ENGINE, REPLACE

1. Disconnect battery cables.
2. Remove air cleaner noting location of disconnected hoses and components.
3. Remove hood.
4. Raise car on a hoist and remove engine shield.
5. Remove lower radiator and drain coolant.
6. Remove starter and converter bolt access plug.
7. Remove three converter-to-flywheel bolts.

8. Remove flywheel or converter housing cover. With manual shift transmission, remove flywheel housing lower attaching bolts. With automatic transmission, disconnect converter from flywheel and remove converter housing lower attaching bolts.
9. Remove exhaust from manifold.
10. Remove transmission cooler lines from radiator.
11. Remove engine mount nuts.
12. Drain engine oil and disconnect fuel lines at pump and plug lines.
13. Remove power steering pump pulley.
14. Remove lower power steering-to-bracket bolt. Upper bolts will be removed later.

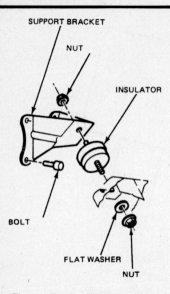

Fig. 1 Engine front mounting

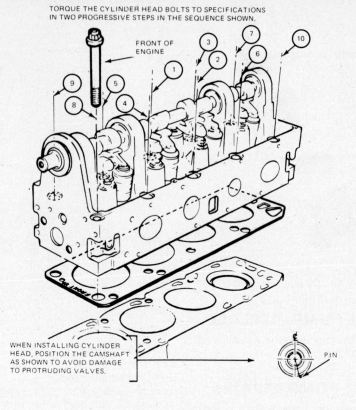

TORQUE THE CYLINDER HEAD BOLTS TO SPECIFICATIONS IN TWO PROGRESSIVE STEPS IN THE SEQUENCE SHOWN.

WHEN INSTALLING CYLINDER HEAD, POSITION THE CAMSHAFT AS SHOWN TO AVOID DAMAGE TO PROTRUDING VALVES.

Fig. 2 Cylinder head tightening sequence

15. Lower car from hoist, remove fan shroud and disconnect upper radiator hose.
16. Remove radiator and disconnect heater and vacuum hoses at engine noting location.
17. Disconnect: power brake hose, oil pressure line, kickdown cable.
18. Disconnect accelerator cable clip at ball stud. Pull slightly on cable while depressing tangs one at a time on bracket clip and remove throttle cable.
19. Disconnect: idle solenoid, water temperature wire, vacuum amplifier, vacuum hose and coil wire from distributor, alternator wires and ground wires noting locations.
20. Remove alternator adjusting arm bolt.
21. Remove power steering pump-to-bracket bolts and remove pump.

22. Disconnect choke wire.
23. Support transmission and flywheel or converter housing with suitable jack.
24. Attach engine lift and raise engine out of vehicle.

CYLINDER HEAD, REPLACE

1. Drain cooling system and remove air cleaner and rocker arm cover.

2. Remove intake and exhaust manifolds and carburetor.
3. Remove timing case cover and drive belt.
4. Remove water outlet elbow from head.
5. Remove cylinder head bolts, then remove cylinder head.

NOTE: The cylinder head retaining bolts have 12 point heads.

6. Reverse procedure to install. Torque cylinder head bolts in sequence shown in Fig. 2 and intake manifold bolts in sequence shown in Fig. 3.

CAUTION: When installing cylinder head, position camshaft at 5 o'clock position, Fig. 2, allowing minimal protrusion of the valves from the cylinder head.

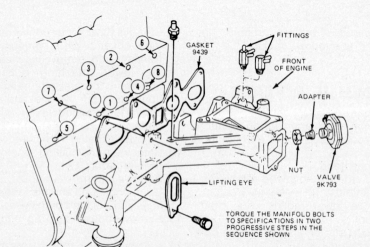

TORQUE THE MANIFOLD BOLTS TO SPECIFICATIONS IN TWO PROGRESSIVE STEPS IN THE SEQUENCE SHOWN

Fig. 3 Intake manifold tightening sequence

VALVE ARRANGEMENT
Front to Rear

2300 cc Engine . . . . E-I-E-I-E-I-E-I

VALVE LIFT SPECS.

Engine	Year	Intake	Exhaust
2300 cc	1976	.400	.400

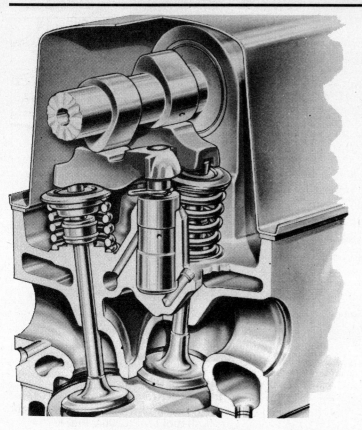

Fig. 4 Valve train installation

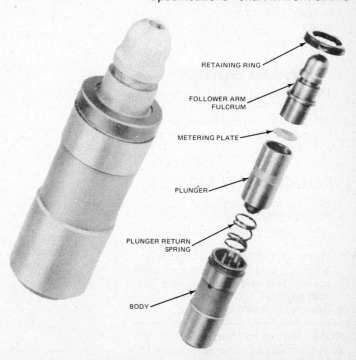

Fig. 5 Checking valve clearance

1. Crank engine to position camshaft with flat section of lobe facing rocker arm of valve being checked.
2. Remove rocker arm retaining spring.

NOTE: Late models do not incorporate the retaining spring.

3. Collapse lash adjuster with tool T74P-6565B and insert correct size feeler gauge between rocker arm and camshaft lobe, Fig. 5. If clearance is not as listed in the "Valve Specifications" chart in front of this

VALVE TIMING

Intake Opens Before TDC

Engine	Year	Degrees
2300 cc	1976	22

VALVES, ADJUST

The valve lash on this engine cannot be adjusted due to the use of hydraulic valve lash adjusters, Fig. 4. However, the valve train can be checked for wear as follows:

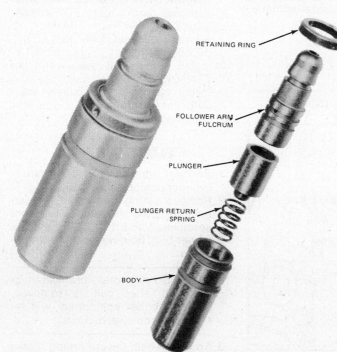

Fig. 6 Valve lash adjuster, Type I

Fig. 7 Valve lash adjuster, Type II

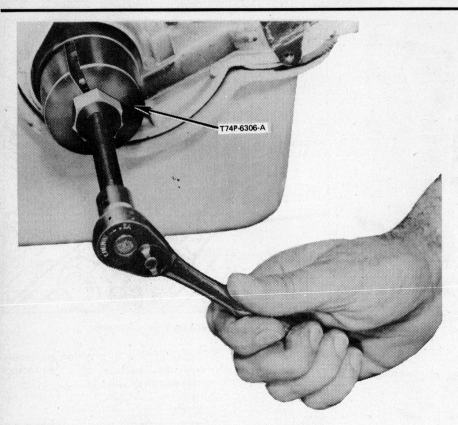

Fig. 8 Crankshaft sprocket removal

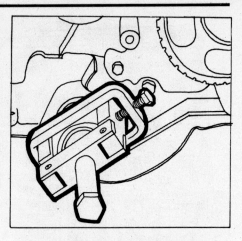

Fig. 9 Crankshaft front oil seal removal

chapter, remove rocker arm and check for wear and replace as necessary. If rocker arm is found satisfactory, check valve spring assembled height and adjust as needed. If valve spring assembled height is within specifications listed in the front of this chapter, remove lash adjuster and clean or replace as necessary.

VALVE GUIDES

Valve guides consist of holes bored in the cylinder head. For service the guides can be reamed oversize to accommodate valves with oversize stems of .008, .016 and .032″.

ROCKER ARM SERVICE

1. Remove rocker arm cover.
2. Rotate camshaft until flat section of lobe faces rocker arm being removed.
3. With tool T74P-6565B, collapse lash adjuster and, if necessary, valve spring and slide rocker arm over lash adjuster.
4. Reverse procedure to install.

NOTE: Before rotating camshaft, ensure that lash adjuster is collapsed to prevent valve train damage.

LASH ADJUSTER, REPLACE

The hydraulic valve lash adjusters can be removed after rocker arm removal. There are two types of lash adjusters available, Type I, being the standard lash adjuster, Fig. 6, and Type II, having a .020 inch oversize outside diameter, Fig. 7.

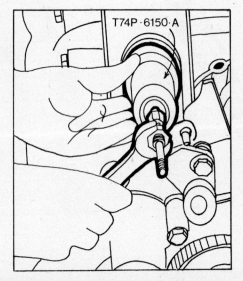

Fig. 10 Engine front seal installation

FRONT ENGINE SEALS, REPLACE

To gain access to the front engine seals, remove the timing belt cover and proceed as follows:

Crankshaft Oil Seal
1. Without removing cylinder front cover, remove crankshaft sprocket with tool T74P-6306A, Fig. 8.
2. Remove crankshaft oil seal with tool T74P-6700B, Fig. 9.
3. Install a new crankshaft oil seal with tool T74P-6150A, Fig. 10.
4. Install crankshaft sprocket with recess facing engine block, Fig. 11.

Camshaft & Auxiliary Shaft Oil Seals
1. Remove camshaft or auxiliary shaft sprocket with tool T74P-6256A, Fig. 12.
2. Remove oil seal with tool T74P-6700B, Fig. 13.
3. Install a new oil seal with tool T74P-6150A, Fig. 10.
4. Install camshaft or auxiliary shaft sprocket with tool T74P-6256A with center arbor removed.

TIMING BELT

1. Position crankshaft at TDC, No. 1 cylinder compression stroke.
2. Remove timing belt cover, loosen belt tensioner, and remove belt from sprockets, Fig. 11. Tighten tensioner bolt, holding tensioner in position.

NOTE: Do not rotate crankshaft or camshaft after belt is removed. Rotating either component will result in improper valve timing.

3. To install belt, ensure timing marks are aligned, Fig. 14, and place belt over sprockets.

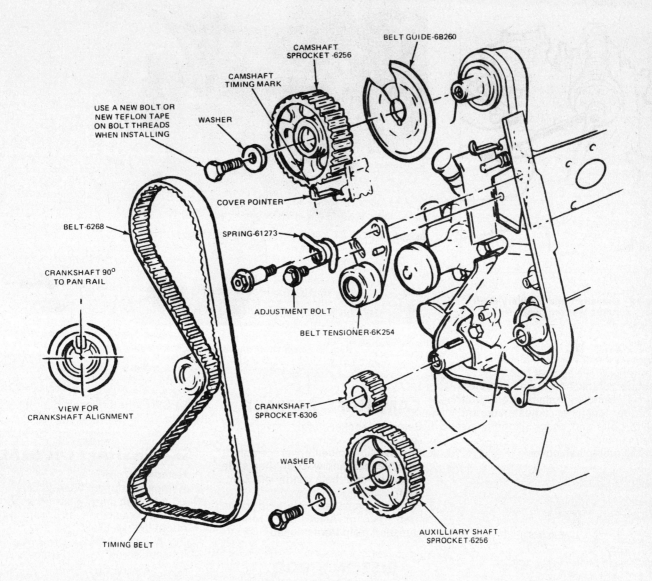

USE A NEW BOLT OR NEW TEFLON TAPE ON BOLT THREADS WHEN INSTALLING

WASHER

CAMSHAFT TIMING MARK

CAMSHAFT SPROCKET -6256

BELT GUIDE-6B260

COVER POINTER

BELT-6268

CRANKSHAFT 90° TO PAN RAIL

VIEW FOR CRANKSHAFT ALIGNMENT

SPRING-61273

ADJUSTMENT BOLT

BELT TENSIONER-6K254

CRANKSHAFT SPROCKET-6306

WASHER

TIMING BELT

AUXILLIARY SHAFT SPROCKET-6256

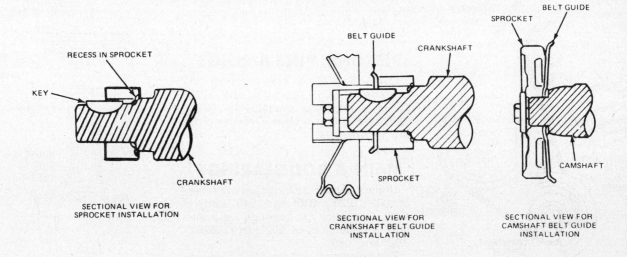

RECESS IN SPROCKET

KEY

CRANKSHAFT

SECTIONAL VIEW FOR SPROCKET INSTALLATION

BELT GUIDE

CRANKSHAFT

SPROCKET

SECTIONAL VIEW FOR CRANKSHAFT BELT GUIDE INSTALLATION

SPROCKET

BELT GUIDE

CAMSHAFT

SECTIONAL VIEW FOR CAMSHAFT BELT GUIDE INSTALLATION

Fig. 11 Drive belt and sprocket installation

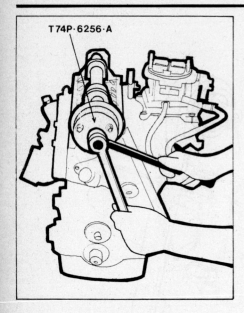

Fig. 12 Camshaft and auxiliary shaft sprocket removal

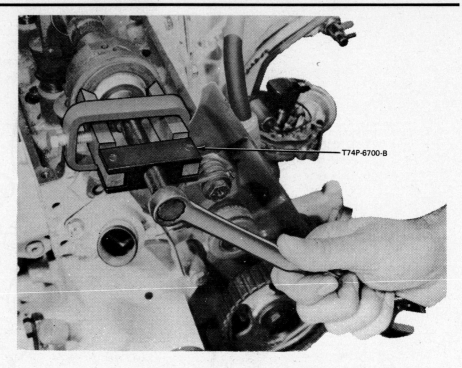

Fig. 13 Camshaft and auxiliary shaft seals removal

4. Loosen tensioner bolt, allowing tensioner to move against belt.
5. Rotate crankshaft two complete turns, removing slack from belt. Torque tensioner adjustment and pivot bolts and check alignment of timing marks, Fig. 15.
6. Install timing belt cover.

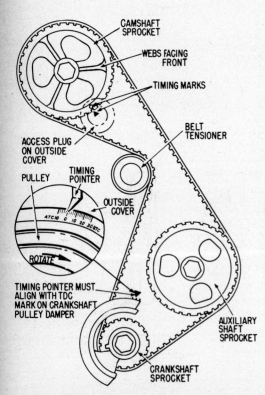

Fig. 14 Valve timing marks

CAMSHAFT, REPLACE

1. Remove rocker arm cover and rocker arms.
2. Remove timing belt cover, camshaft sprocket bolt and washer, then slide sprocket and belt guide off camshaft.
3. Remove camshaft retaining plate from rear of head, then remove camshaft from front of head.

PISTON & ROD, ASSEMBLE

Assemble the rod to the piston with the arrow on top of piston facing front of engine, Fig. 15.

PISTONS, PINS & RINGS

Oversize pistons are available in oversizes of .003″, .020″, .030″ and .040″. Oversize rings are available in .020″, .030″ and .040″ oversizes. Oversize pins are not available.

MAIN & ROD BEARINGS

Undersize main bearings are available in .002″, .020″, .030″ and .040″ undersizes. Undersize rod bearings are available in undersizes of .002″, .010″, .020″, .030″ and .040″.

The crankshaft and main bearings are installed with arrows on main bearing caps facing front of engine, Fig. 16. Install PCV baffle between bearing journals No. 3 and 4.

CRANKSHAFT OIL SEAL

1. Remove oil pan.
2. Remove rear main bearing cap.
3. Loosen remaining bearing caps, allowing crankshaft to drop down about $1/32″$.
4. Install a sheet metal screw into seal and pull screw to remove seal.

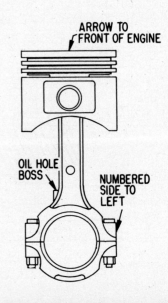

Fig. 15 Piston and rod assembly

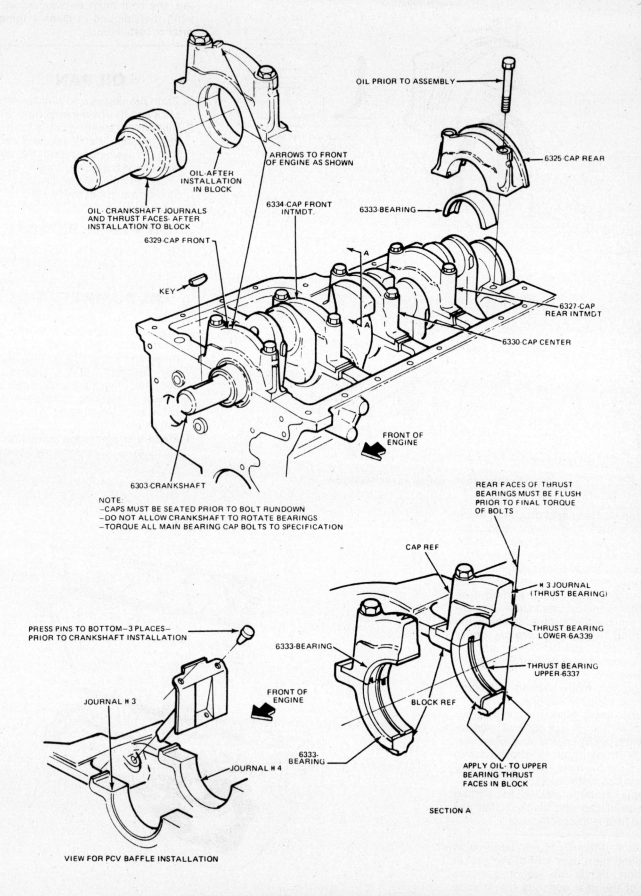

Fig. 16 Crankshaft and main bearing installation

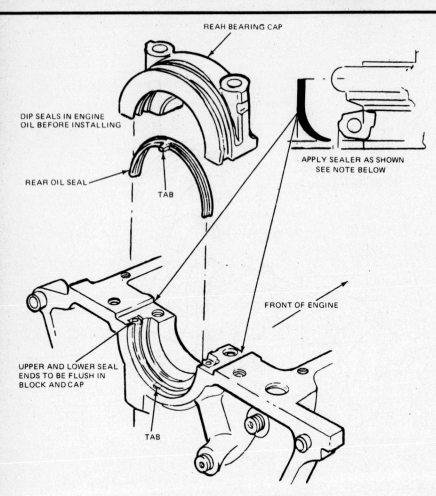

Fig. 17 Crankshaft rear oil seal installation

ing, the seal must be washed in solvent, then dipped in clean engine oil prior to installation.

OIL PAN

1. Drain crankcase and remove oil dipstick and flywheel inspection cover.
2. Disconnect steering cable from rack and pinion, then rack and pinion from crossmember and move forward to provide clearance.
3. Unfasten and remove oil pan. To install oil pan, refer to Fig. 18.

OIL PUMP, REPLACE

The oil pump, Fig. 19, can be removed after oil pan removal, Fig. 20.

OIL PUMP REPAIRS

1. Remove end plate and withdraw O ring from groove in body.
2. Check clearance between lobes of inner and outer rotors. This should not exceed .006″. Rotors are supplied only in a matched pair.
3. Check clearance between outer rotor and the housing. This should not exceed .010″.
4. Place a straightedge across face of pump body. Clearance between face

5. Carefully clean seal groove in block with a brush and solvent. Also clean seal groove in bearing cap.
6. Dip seal halves in clean engine oil.
7. Carefully install upper seal half in its groove with locating tab toward rear of engine, Fig. 17, by rotating it on shaft journal of crankshaft until approximately ⅜″ protrudes below the parting surface. *Be sure no rubber has been shaved from outside diameter of seal by bottom edge of groove.*
8. Retighten main bearing caps and torque to specifications.
9. Install lower seal in main bearing cap with undercut side of seal toward front of engine, and allow seal to protrude about ⅜″ above parting surface to mate with upper seal upon cap installation.
10. Apply suitable sealer to parting faces of cap and block. Install cap and torque to specifications.

NOTE: If difficulty is encountered in installing the upper half of the seal in position, lightly lap (sandpaper) the side of the seal opposite the lip side using a medium grit paper. After sand-

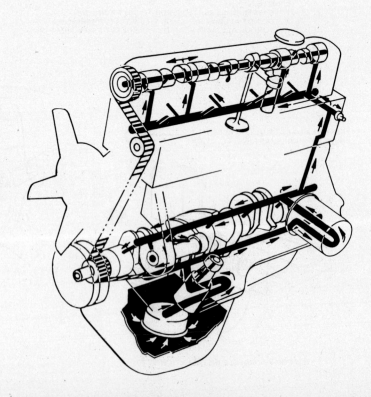

Engine oiling system

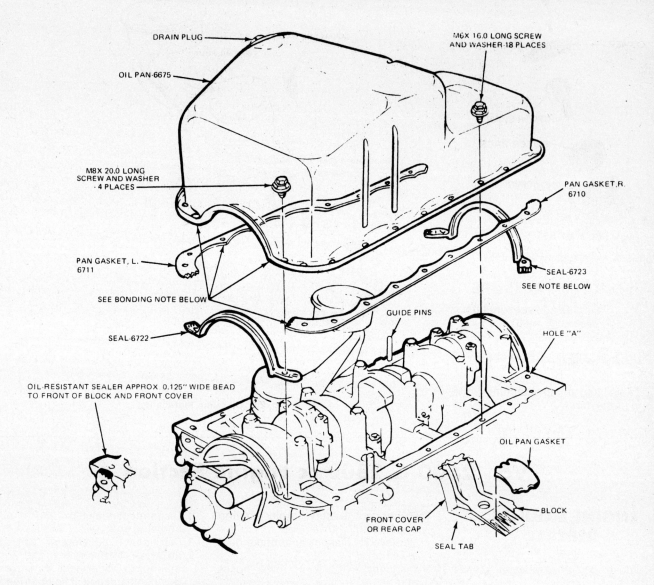

DRAIN PLUG

OIL PAN-6675

M6X 16.0 LONG SCREW
AND WASHER-18 PLACES

M8X 20.0 LONG
SCREW AND WASHER
- 4 PLACES

PAN GASKET, L.
6711

SEE BONDING NOTE BELOW

SEAL-6722

OIL-RESISTANT SEALER APPROX 0.125" WIDE BEAD
TO FRONT OF BLOCK AND FRONT COVER

PAN GASKET, R.
6710

SEAL-6723
SEE NOTE BELOW

GUIDE PINS

HOLE "A"

OIL PAN GASKET

BLOCK

FRONT COVER
OR REAR CAP

SEAL TAB

1. APPLY GASKET ADHESIVE EVENLY TO OIL PAN FLANGE AND TO PAN SIDE GASKETS. ALLOW ADHESIVE TO DRY PAST WET STAGE, THEN INSTALL GASKETS TO OIL PAN.
2. APPLY SEALER TO JOINT OF BLOCK AND FRONT COVER. INSTALL SEALS TO FRONT COVER AND REAR BEARING CAP AND PRESS SEAL TABS FIRMLY INTO BLOCK. BE SURE TO INSTALL THE REAR SEAL BEFORE THE REAR MAIN BEARING CAP SEALER HAS CURED.
3. POSITION 2 GUIDE PINS AND INSTALL THE OIL PAN. SECURE THE PAN WITH THE FOUR M8 BOLTS SHOWN ABOVE.
4. REMOVE THE GUIDE PINS AND INSTALL AND TORQUE THE EIGHTEEN M6 BOLTS, BEGINNING AT HOLE A AND WORKING CLOCKWISE AROUND THE PAN.

Fig. 18   Oil pan installation

of rotors and straightedge should not exceed .005".

5. If necessary to replace rotor or drive shaft, remove outer rotor and then drive out retaining pin securing the skew gear to drive shaft and pull off the gear.

6. Withdraw inner rotor and drive shaft.

WATER PUMP, REPLACE

1. Drain cooling system and discon-

nect hoses from pump.
2. Loosen alternator and remove drive belt.
3. Remove fan, spacer and pulley.
4. Remove water pump attaching bolts and water pump.

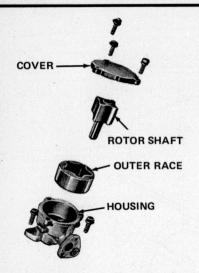

Fig. 19   Oil pump assembly

FUEL PUMP PRESSURE

Year	Engine	Pressure Lbs.
1976-77	2300 cc	3½ - 4½

FUEL PUMP, REPLACE

1. Disconnect fuel lines from pump.
2. Remove fuel pump attaching bolts and fuel pump.

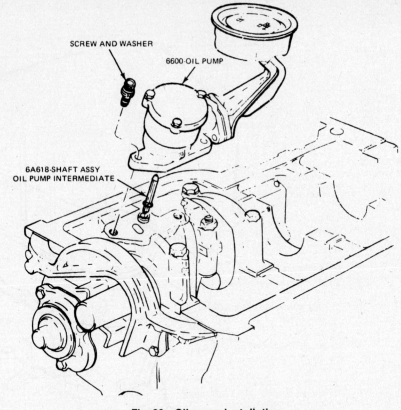

Fig. 20   Oil pump installation

V6 - 2600 & 2800 cc Engine Section

ENGINE MOUNTS, REPLACE

Front

1. Remove insulator upper and lower attaching nuts, Fig. 1.
2. Raise engine just high enough to remove insulator.
3. Remove support bracket attaching screws and remove the bracket.

Rear

1. Place a jack or support under transmission.
2. Remove insulator to extension housing retaining bolt, Fig. 2.
3. Remove four rear engine support bracket to body bolts. Remove rear support assembly.
4. Remove two bolts retaining insulator to support bracket.

ENGINE, REPLACE

1972-74

If engine is equipped with Thermactor air pump, remove or disconnect parts that will interfere with removal of engine.

1. Disconnect battery, drain cooling system and remove hood.
2. Remove air cleaner and intake duct assembly.
3. Disconnect upper and lower hoses at radiator.
4. Unfasten fan shroud and remove radiator and shroud.
5. Remove alternator and bracket and position out of way. Disconnect alternator ground wire from block.
6. Disconnect heater hoses at block and water pump.
7. Remove ground wires from block.
8. Disconnect fuel tank line at pump and plug end.
9. Disconnect accelerator cable or linkage at carburetor and intake manifold. Disconnect transmission downshift linkage, if so equipped.
10. Disconnect wire loom at coil. Disconnect brake booster line.
11. Raise vehicle and support with safety stands.
12. Disconnect muffler inlet pipes at exhaust manifolds.
13. Disconnect starter cable and remove starter.

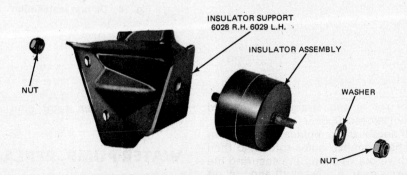

Fig. 1   Engine front mount. V6-2600 & 2800cc

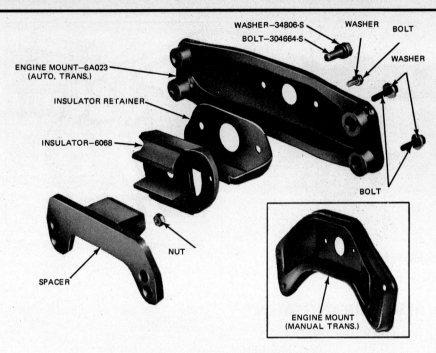

Fig. 2 Engine rear mount. V6-2600 & 2800cc

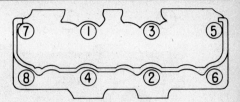

Fig. 3 Cylinder head tightening sequence. 1972-73 V6-2600cc

16. Disconnect oil pressure line and drain crankcase.
17. Lower car from hoist.
18. Remove downshift rod. On vehicles with manual transmission, remove the clutch linkage.
19. Disconnect upper radiator hose.
20. Remove fan shroud and radiator.
21. Disconnect heater hoses at engine as required; remove hose retainer at rocker cover and position hoses aside.
22. Disconnect distributor vacuum line, distributor connector and coil wire.
23. Disconnect transmission vacuum line at intake manifold.
24. Disconnect accelerator cable retaining clip at ball stud. Pull on cable and depress tangs one at a time on bracket clip and remove throttle cable.
25. Disconnect rear ground wire.
26. Disconnect alternator connectors.
27. Position a jack under transmission.
28. Attach engine lift and raise engine slightly and carefully pull it from transmission and out of vehicle.

CYLINDER HEAD, REPLACE

1. Remove air cleaner. Disconnect battery ground cable. Disconnect linkage and drain cooling system.
2. Remove distributor cap with plug wires as an assembly. Remove distributor vacuum line, distributor,

14. Remove engine front support through bolts.
15. If equipped with automatic transmission, remove converter inspection cover and disconnect flywheel from converter. Remove downshift rod, converter housing-to-engine block bolts and the adapter plate-to-converter housing bolts. If equipped with manual transmission, remove clutch linkage and bell housing-to-engine block bolts.
16. Lower the vehicle.
17. Support transmission using a suitable jack, raise engine slightly and pull from transmission, then lift engine from engine compartment.

1976-77

1. Disconnect battery cables.
2. Remove air cleaner assembly noting location of hoses and components.
3. Remove hood.
4. Raise car on a hoist.
5. Remove lower radiator and drain cooling system.
6. Remove the starter.
7. Remove converter bolt access plug

and remove the three converter-to-flywheel bolts.
8. Disconnect exhaust pipes from manifold.
9. Remove lower four bolts retaining converter housing to engine.
10. Remove upper two converter housing bolts retaining converter housing to engine block.
11. Remove nuts retaining engine supports to chassis brackets.
12. Disconnect transmission oil cooler lines at radiator, if so equipped.
13. Disconnect fuel tank line at pump and plug line.
14. Loosen power steering pump idler.
15. Remove power steering pump-to-bracket bolts and remove pump from bracket.

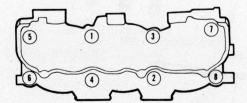

Fig. 4 Cylinder head tightening sequence. 1974 & 1976 V6-2800cc

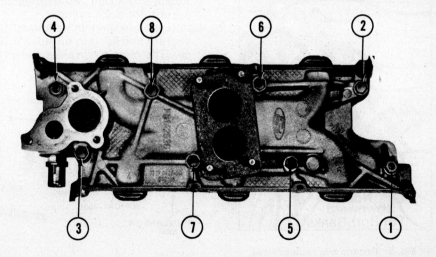

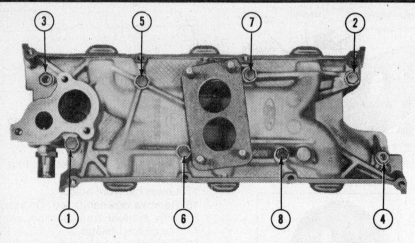

Fig. 6 Intake manifold tightening sequence. 1974 & 1976 V6-2800cc

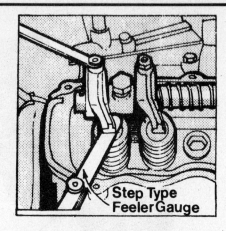

Fig. 7 Adjusting valve lash. V6-2600 & 2800cc

coolant outlet hose, hose from pump to water outlet, rocker arm covers, fuel line and filter, carburetor and intake manifold.
3. Remove rocker arm shaft (by loosening bolts two turns at a time, in sequence) and oil baffles. Remove push rods keeping them in order for proper assembly.
4. Remove exhaust manifold.
5. Unbolt and remove cylinder head and gaskets.

NOTE: On reassembly, gaskets are marked "Front" and "Top" and the right and left sides are not interchangeable.

6. Reverse procedure to install. Torque cylinder head bolts in sequence shown in Figs. 3 and 4 and intake manifold bolts in sequence shown in Figs. 5 and 6.

VALVE ARRANGEMENT
Front to Rear

Right .... I-E-I-E-E-I
Left .... I-E-E-I-E-I

VALVE LIFT SPECS.

Engine	Year	Intake	Exhaust
2600, 2800 cc	1972-77	.3730	.3730

VALVE TIMING
Intake Opens Before TDC

Engine	Year	Degrees
2600, 2800 cc	1972-77	20

VALVES, ADJUST
Cold Setting

1. Remove rocker arm covers.
2. Rotate crankshaft until No. 1 cylinder is at TDC compression stroke and set valve lash on No. 1 cylinder.
3. Rotate crankshaft 120 degrees and set lash for No. 4 cylinder.
4. Rotate crankshaft an additional 120 degrees and set lash on No. 2 cylinder. The remaining valves are set in

the same manner following the firing order.

Hot Setting

With engine at operating temparature and idling, set valve lash with a step type (Go-NoGo) feeler gauge, Fig. 7.

VALVE GUIDES

Valve guides consist of holes bored in the cylinder head. For service the guides can be reamed oversize to accommodate valves with oversize stems of .008, .016 and .032".

ROCKER ARM SERVICE

Remove emission control equipment as necessary to remove cover.
1. Remove spark plug wires from plugs and rocker arm cover.
2. Disconnect throttle rod to carburetor.
3. Remove rocker cover attaching screws. Tap cover with a plastic mallet to break gasket seal and remove cover.
4. Remove rocker arm shaft stand retaining bolts by loosening the bolts two turns at a time in sequence. Lift

Fig. 8 Rocker arm replacement. V6-2600 & 2800cc

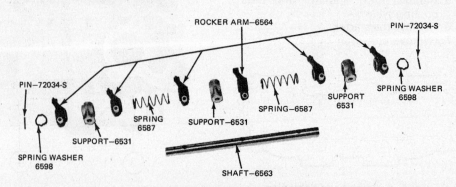

Fig. 9 Rocker arm and shaft assembly. V6-2600 & 2800cc

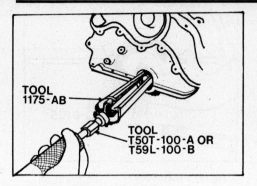

Fig. 10   Removing crankshaft front oil seal. V6-2600 & 2800cc

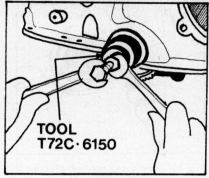

Fig. 11   Installing crankshaft front oil seal. V6-2600 & 2800cc

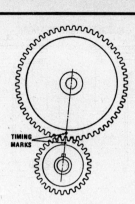

Fig. 12   Valve timing marks. V6-2600 & 2800cc

off rocker shaft assembly and oil baffle, Fig. 8.

5. Remove spring washer and pin from each end of rocker arm shaft.

6. Slide rocker arms, springs and shaft supports off the shafts being sure to mark parts for assembly in same locations, Fig. 9.

7. If necessary, remove plugs from each end of shaft. Drill the plug on one end. Use a rod to knock out the plug on the opposite end. Working from the open end, knock out the remaining plug.

NOTE: Upon installation, the oil holes in the rocker shaft must point down when the shaft is installed.

VALVE LIFTERS, REPLACE

1. Remove cylinder head and related parts as previously described.

2. Remove valve lifters with a magnet placing them in a rack in proper sequence.

TIMING CASE COVER

1. Remove oil pan as described further on in this chapter.

2. Drain cooling system and remove radiator and any other parts to provide necessary clearance.

3. Remove alternator and drive belts. Remove water pump and hoses.

4. Remove fan.

5. Remove drive pulley from crankshaft. If necessary, remove guide sleeves from cylinder block.

6. Remove front cover bolts. Tap cover lightly with a plastic mallet to break gasket seal and remove cover. If front cover plate gasket must be replaced, remove two screws and remove plate.

CRANKSHAFT FRONT OIL SEAL

The crankshaft front oil seal may be serviced without removing the cylinder front cover as follows:

1. Drain coolant and remove radiator, crankshaft pulley and water pump drive belt.

2. Pull oil seal from front cover, Fig. 10.

3. Install new oil seal with tool T72C-6150, Fig. 11.

4. Install crankshaft pulley, water pump drive belt, radiator, then refill cooling system.

TIMING GEARS

1. Drain cooling system and crankcase, then remove radiator and oil pan.

2. Remove cylinder front cover and water pump.

3. Align timing marks, Fig. 12.

4. Using a suitable gear puller, remove crankshaft gear and key.

5. Remove camshaft gear with a suitable gear puller

NOTE: Do not rotate crankshaft or camshaft with gears removed as rotation of either component can result in improper valve timing.

6. Install key in camshaft, then press camshaft gear onto camshaft.

7. Install key in crankshaft, then press crankshaft gear onto crankshaft with tool T72C-6150, Fig. 13, and make sure timing marks are aligned, Fig. 12.

8. Install cylinder front cover, water pump, radiator and oil pan.

9. Refill cooling system and oil pan. Start engine and adjust ignition timing, if necessary.

Fig. 13   Installing crankshaft gear. V6-2600 & 2800cc

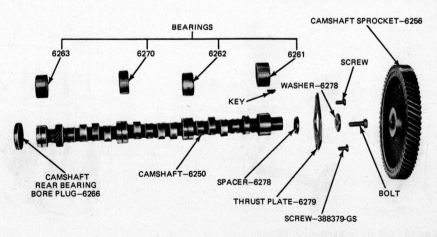

Fig. 14   Camshaft components. V6-2600 & 2800cc

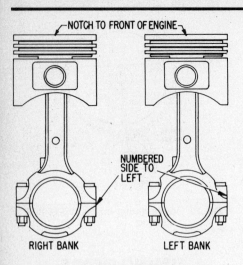

Fig. 15 Piston and rod assembly. V6-2600 & 2800cc

CAMSHAFT, REPLACE

1. Drain coolant and remove radiator, fan, spacer, water pump pulley and drive belt.
2. Remove distributor cap with plug wires as an assembly. Remove distributor vacuum line, distributor, alternator, rocker covers, fuel line and filter, carburetor and intake manifold.
3. Remove rocker arm and shaft assemblies. Lift out the push rods and place them in a marked rack so they can be installed in same locations.
4. Drain crankcase and remove oil pan.
5. Remove drive sprocket bolt and slide sprocket off shaft.
6. Remove front cover and water pump as an assembly.
7. Remove camshaft gear retaining bolt and slide gear off camshaft.
8. Remove camshaft thrust plate and screws.
9. Using a magnet, remove valve lifters placing them in a marked rack for proper assembly.
10. Carefully pull camshaft from block avoiding damage to camshaft bear-

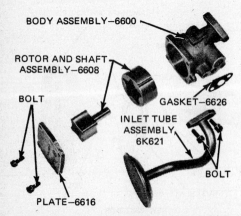

Fig. 18 Oil pump assembly. V6-2600 & 2800cc

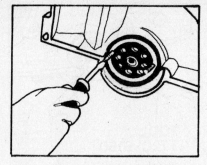

Fig. 16 Removing crankshaft rear oil seal. V6-2600 & 2800cc

ings. Remove camshaft gear key and spacer ring.

PISTON & ROD ASSEMBLY

Assemble piston to the rod with the notches facing front of engine and the numbered side of the rod facing toward left side of engine, Fig. 15.

PISTONS, PINS & RINGS

Oversize pistons and rings are available in .020" and .040" oversizes. Oversize pins are not available.

CRANKSHAFT REAR OIL SEAL

1. Remove transmission. Remove clutch pressure plate and disc if so equipped.

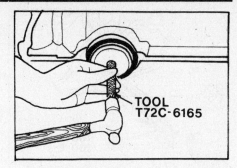

Fig. 17 Installing crankshaft rear oil seal. V6-2600 & 2800cc

2. Remove flywheel, flywheel housing and rear plate.
3. Use an awl to punch two holes in the rear oil seal. Punch holes on opposite sides of crankshaft and just above the bearing cap to block split line then install a sheet metal screw in each hole, Fig. 16. Use two large screwdrivers or small pry bars and pry against both screws at the same time to remove the seal. It may be necessary to place small blocks of wood against the block to provide a fulcrum point for the pry bars. Use caution throughout this operation to avoid scratching or otherwise damaging the crankshaft oil seal surface.
4. Clean oil seal recess in cylinder block and main bearing cap.
5. Install new seal using tool No. T72C-6165-A, Fig. 17.

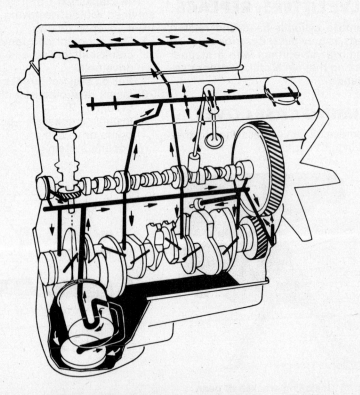

Engine oiling system. V6-2600 & 2800cc

OIL PAN, REPLACE

1. Remove oil level dipstick. Remove bolts attaching fan shroud to radiator. Position shroud over fan. Disconnect battery ground cable. Loosen alternator bracket and adjusting bolts.
2. Raise the vehicle and drain crankcase.
3. Remove splash shield and the starter.
4. Remove engine front support nuts.
5. Raise the engine and place wood blocks between engine front supports and chassis brackets.
6. Remove clutch or converter housing cover.
7. Unfasten and remove the oil pan.

OIL PUMP, REPLACE

The oil pump can be removed after the oil pan has been removed.

OIL PUMP REPAIRS

1. Remove end plate and withdraw ''0'' ring from groove in body, Fig. 18.
2. Check clearance between lobes of inner and outer rotors. This should not exceed .006". Rotors are supplied only in a matched pair.
3. Check clearance between outer rotor and the housing. This should not exceed .010".
4. Place a straight edge across face of pump body. Clearance between face of rotors and straight edge should not exceed .005".
5. If necessaary to replace rotor or drive shaft, remove outer rotor and then drive out retaining pin securing gear to shaft and pull off the gear.
6. Withdraw inner rotor and drive shaft.

WATER PUMP, REPLACE

1. Drain coolant. Detach radiator lower hose and the heater return hose from water inlet housing.
2. Loosen alternator mounting bolts and remove belt. Remove fan shroud bolts and position shroud behind fan. Remove the fan and pulley and remove the shroud.
3. Remove water pump bolts and remove pump assembly, water inlet housing and thermostat from the front cover. Note the location of the different length bolts.

FUEL PUMP PRESSURE

Year	Engine	Pressure, Lbs.
1972-77	All	3½-5½

FUEL PUMP, REPLACE

1. Disconnect inlet and outlet lines at fuel pump.
2. Unfasten and remove fuel pump.

Carburetor Section

MODEL 1250-1V CARB. ADJUSTMENT SPECIFICATIONS

Year	Carb. Model ①	Idle Mixture Turns Open	Float Setting	Pump Stroke	Fast Idle Speed	Choke Pull down	Dechoke Clearance	Choke Link Position	Choke Setting
1972	72IF-KEA	—	—	—	1700	—	—	—	Index
	721F-KEB	—	—	—	1700	—	—	—	Index

—Not Available

① —Stamped on side of carburetor fuel bowl or tag attached to bowl cover.

MODEL 2150-2V CARB. ADJUSTMENT SPECIFICATIONS

Year	Carb. Model ①	Idle Mixture Turns Open	Float Level (Dry)	Float Level (Wet)	Pump Setting Hole No. ②	Choke Plate Clearance (Pull down)	Fast Idle Cam Linkage Clearance	Fast Idle Speed (Hot Engine)	Dechoke Clearance ③	Dashpot Setting	Choke Setting
1976-77	75TF-AA	—	—	—	—	—	—	—	—	—	—
	75TF-BA	—	—	—	—	—	—	—	—	—	—
	75TF-CA	—	—	—	—	—	—	—	—	—	—
	75TF-DA	—	—	—	—	—	—	—	—	—	—
	D5PE-BRA	—	—	—	—	—	—	—	—	—	—
	D5PE-BPA	—	—	—	—	—	—	—	—	—	—
	T67F-AA	—	⅜	¾	No. 2	.100	.120	1700	—	—	3 Rich
	T67F-BA	—	⅜	¾	No. 2	.100	.120	1600	—	—	3 Rich
	T67F-CA	—	⅜	¾	No. 2	.110	.130	1700	—	—	3 Rich
	T67F-DA	—	⅜	¾	No. 2	.110	.130	1600	—	—	3 Rich

—Not Available

① —Stamped on left side of fuel bowl or on tag attached to bowl cover.

② —With link in inboard hole in pump lever.

③ —Minimum clearance between choke plate and air horn wall with throttle plates wide open.

MODEL 5200 ADJUSTMENT SPECIFICATIONS

Year	Carb. Model ①	Idle Mixture Turns Open	Float Level	Pump Setting (Hole)	Choke Pull down	Dechoke Clearance	Fast Idle Speed	Fast Idle Cam Clearance	Choke Setting
1972	D2RF-AA	—	—	—	—	—	—	—	—
	D2RF-BA	—	—	—	—	—	—	—	—
	72HF-DA	—	—	—	—	—	—	—	—
	72HF-EA	—	—	—	—	—	—	—	—
	72TF-BEA	—	.420	No. 2	.236	.256	1800	.118	1 Lean
	72TF-BFA	—	.420	No. 3	.236	.256	1600	.156	Index
1973	72HF-DA	—	—	—	—	—	—	—	—
	72HF-EA	—	—	—	—	—	—	—	—
	73HF-AA	—	—	—	—	—	—	—	—
	73HF-BA	—	—	—	—	—	—	—	—
	73HF-LA	—	—	—	—	—	—	—	—
	73HF-BB	—	—	—	—	—	—	—	—
	73HF-MB	—	—	—	—	—	—	—	—
	73TF-AA	—	.420	No. 2	.237	.256	1600	.118	1 Lean
	73TF-BA	—	.420	No. 2	.237	.256	1800	.118	Index
1974	D4PE-ASA	—	—	—	—	—	—	—	—
	D4PE-ALA	—	—	—	—	—	—	—	—
	D4PE-ALB	—	—	—	—	—	—	—	—
	D42E-EA	—	—	—	—	—	—	—	—
	D42E-FA	—	—	—	—	—	—	—	—
	D42E-HA	—	—	—	—	—	—	—	—
	D42E-JA	—	—	—	—	—	—	—	—
	D42E-EB	—	—	—	—	—	—	—	—
	74HF-AA	—	—	—	—	—	—	—	—
	74HF-BA	—	—	—	—	—	—	—	—
	74HF-EA	—	—	—	—	—	—	—	—
	74HF-FA	—	—	—	—	—	—	—	—
	74TF-AA	—	—	—	—	—	—	—	—
	74TF-AB	—	—	—	—	—	—	—	—
	74TF-BA	—	—	—	—	—	—	—	—
	74TF-BB	—	—	—	—	—	—	—	—
	74TF-CA	—	—	—	—	—	—	—	—
	74TF-DA	—	—	—	—	—	—	—	—
	74TF-DB	—	—	—	—	—	—	—	—
1976-77	D58E-EA	—	—	—	—	—	—	—	—
	D58E-FA	—	—	—	—	—	—	—	—
	D58E-GA	—	—	—	—	—	—	—	—
	D58E-HA	—	—	—	—	—	—	—	—
	T67F-AB	—	.460	No. 2	①	6.5③	—	4③	1 Lean
	T67F-BB	—	.460	No. 2	②	6.5③	—	3③	Index
	T67F-CB	—	.460	No. 2	①	6.5③	—	4③	1 Lean
	T67F-DB	—	.460	No. 2	②	6.5③	Idle Speed	3③	Index
	757F-AA	—	—	—	—	—	—	—	—
	757F-BA	—	—	—	—	—	—	—	—
	757F-CA	—	—	—	—	—	—	—	—
	757F-DA	—	—	—	—	—	—	—	—
	767F-AB	—	—	—	—	—	—	—	—
	767F-AC	—	—	—	—	—	—	—	—
	767F-AE	—	—	—	—	—	—	—	—
	767F-BA	—	—	—	—	—	—	—	—
	767F-BB	—	—	—	—	—	—	—	—
	767F-BC	—	—	—	—	—	—	—	—
	767F-CB	—	—	—	—	—	—	—	—
	767F-CE	—	—	—	—	—	—	—	—

—Not Available
①—Tag attached to carburetor.

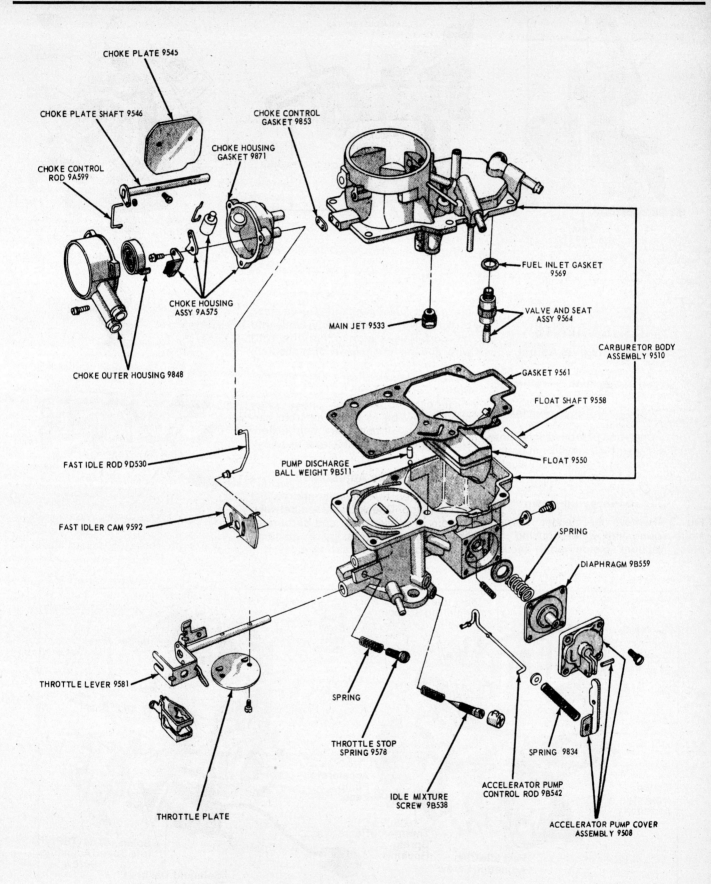

Fig. 1 Exploded view of Model 1250 one barrel carburetor

CHOKE PLATE 9545

CHOKE PLATE SHAFT 9546

CHOKE CONTROL GASKET 9853

CHOKE HOUSING GASKET 9871

CHOKE CONTROL ROD 9A599

CHOKE HOUSING ASSY 9A575

CHOKE OUTER HOUSING 9848

FUEL INLET GASKET 9569

MAIN JET 9533

VALVE AND SEAT ASSY 9564

CARBURETOR BODY ASSEMBLY 9510

GASKET 9561

FLOAT SHAFT 9558

FLOAT 9550

FAST IDLE ROD 9D530

PUMP DISCHARGE BALL WEIGHT 9B511

FAST IDLER CAM 9592

SPRING

DIAPHRAGM 9B559

THROTTLE LEVER 9581

SPRING

THROTTLE STOP SPRING 9578

IDLE MIXTURE SCREW 9B538

SPRING 9834

ACCELERATOR PUMP CONTROL ROD 9B542

ACCELERATOR PUMP COVER ASSEMBLY 9508

THROTTLE PLATE

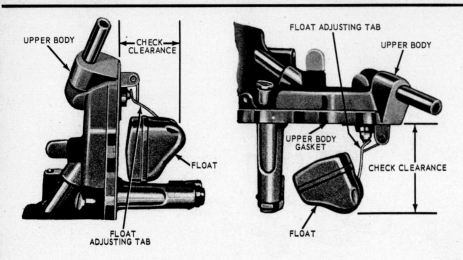

Fig. 2 Fuel and Float level settings. Model 1250

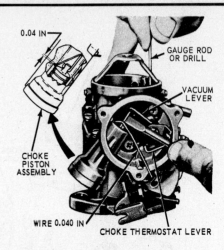

Fig. 3 Choke plate pull down clearance. Model 1250

MODEL 1250 ADJUSTMENTS

Fuel & Float Level Adjust

Fig. 2—With carburetor upper body held in vertical position, measure distance between upper body gasket and bottom of float (left view in illustration). Bend tab to adjust.

Turn upper body to horizontal position and measure distance from bottom of float to gasket (right view in illustration). Bend tab to adjust.

Choke Plate Pull-Down

Fig. 3—Remove air cleaner, thermostatic spring and water housing. Depress vacuum piston until vacuum bleed port is revealed and insert a piece of wire .040″ thick, suitably bent, into this port. Raise piston to trap wire. With wire and piston held in this position, close the choke plate until its movement is stopped through the linkage. Partially open throttle for fast idle tab to clear cam. Bottom of choke plate should now be as specified from carburetor body. If necessary, bend extension of choke thermostat lever to adjust.

Dechoke Adjustment

Fig. 4—Open throttle fully and hold it against stop. Check clearance between bottom of choke plate and carburetor body. Adjust if necessary, by bending the projection on the fast idle cam.

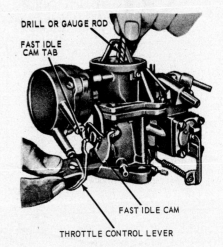

Fig. 4 De-choke adjustment. Model 1250

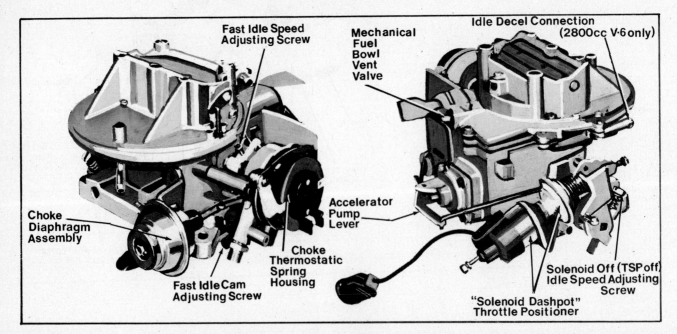

Fig. 5 Motorcraft 2150 carburetor (typical)

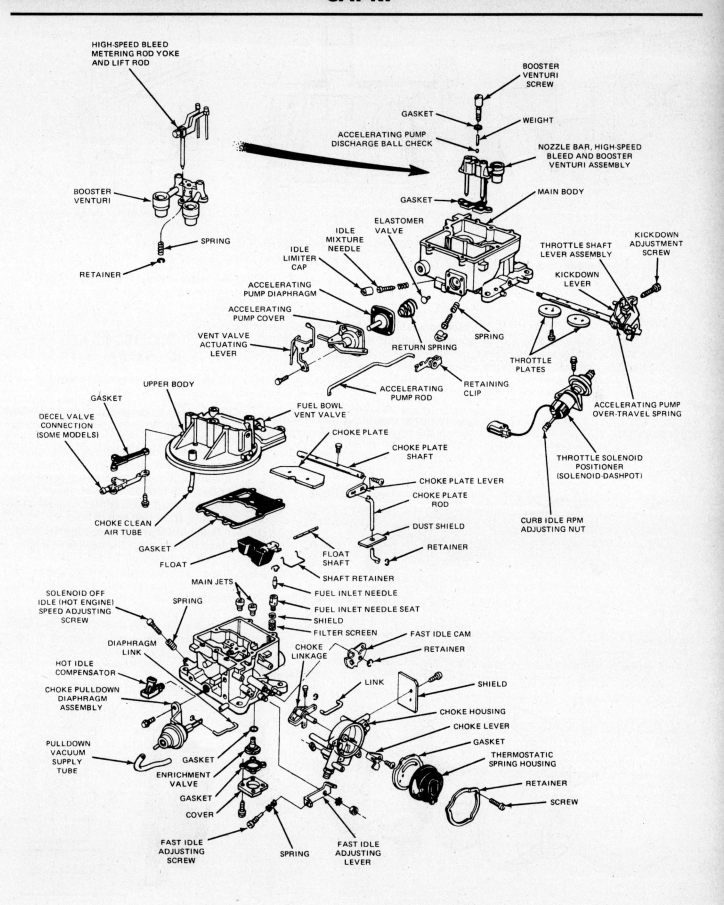

Fig. 6 Exploded view of Model 2150 two barrel carburetor

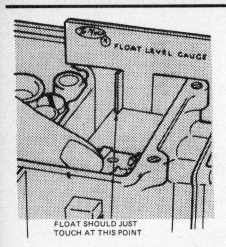

FLOAT SHOULD JUST
TOUCH AT THIS POINT

Fig. 7 Float level adjustment. Model
2150

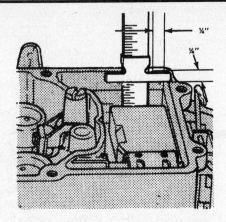

Fig. 8 Fuel level adjustment. Model
2150

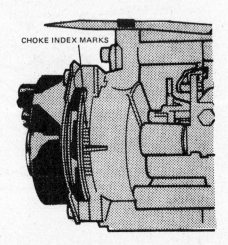

Fig. 9 Accelerator pump stroke
adjustment. Model 2150

Accelerator Pump Adjustment

Unscrew the throttle stop screw until the throttle plate is fully closed. Depress the accelerator pump diaphragm plunger and check the clearance between the operating lever and the plunger. Refer to *Specifications Chart*. Adjust by bending the gooseneck of the pump push rod.

Fast Idle Adjustment

With the choke plate pulldown correctly adjusted and held in the pulldown position, check that the throttle lever fast idle tab is on the second step of the fast idle cam at the arrow on the fast idle cam. If necessary, bend the fast idle rod at its existing bend. Install thermostatic spring and water housing.

At normal operating temperature position the throttle lever fast idle tab on the second step of the cam and check the engine speed. Adjust if necessary by bending the tab contacting the fast idle cam.

MODEL 2150 ADJUSTMENTS
Float Level Adjustment

Fig. 7—This is a preliminary adjustment; the final adjustment must be made after the carburetor is mounted on the engine.

With air horn removed, float raised and fuel inlet needle seated, measure distance between top surface of throttle body and top surface of float. Take measurement near center of float at a point ⅛" from free end of float.

If a cardboard float gauge is used, place the gauge in the corner of the enlarged end section of the fuel bowl as shown. The gauge should touch the float near the end but not on the end radius.

Depress the float tab to seat the fuel inlet needle. The float height is measured from the gasket surface of the

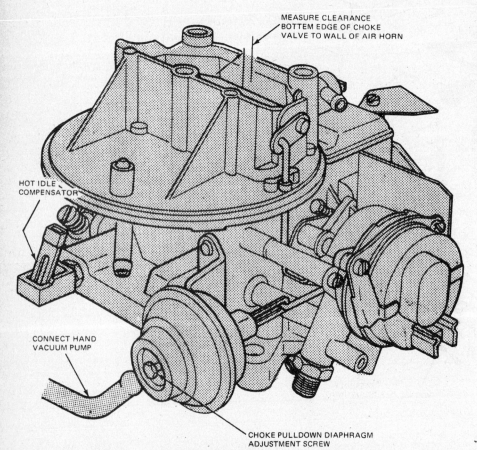

MEASURE CLEARANCE
BOTTOM EDGE OF CHOKE
VALVE TO WALL OF AIR HORN

HOT IDLE
COMPENSATOR

CONNECT HAND
VACUUM PUMP

CHOKE PULLDOWN DIAPHRAGM
ADJUSTMENT SCREW

Fig. 10 Choke plate pulldown adjustment. Model 2150

CHOKE INDEX MARKS

Fig. 11 Automatic choke adjustment. Model 2150

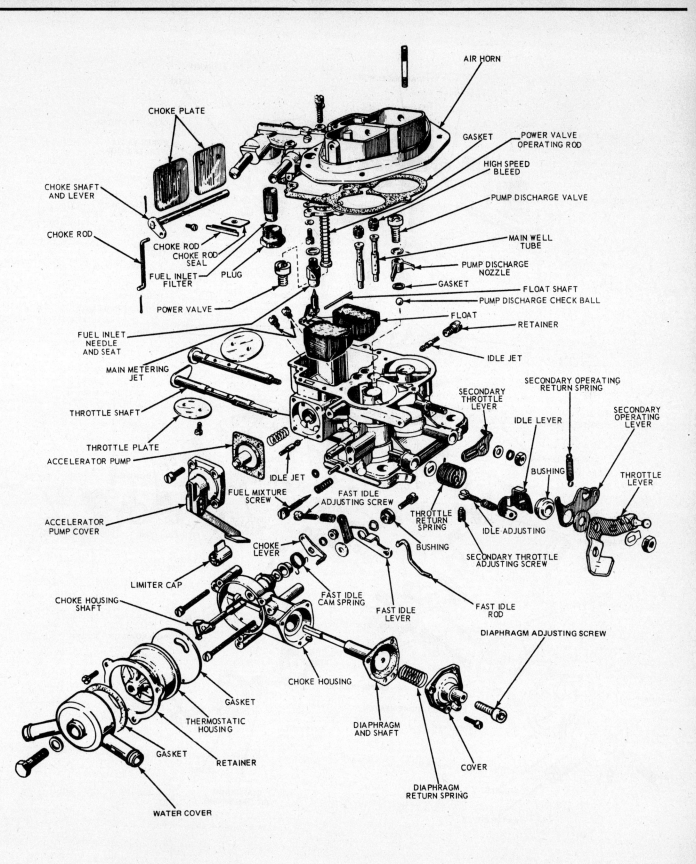

Fig. 13   Exploded view of Model 5200 two barrel carburetor. 1972-73 models

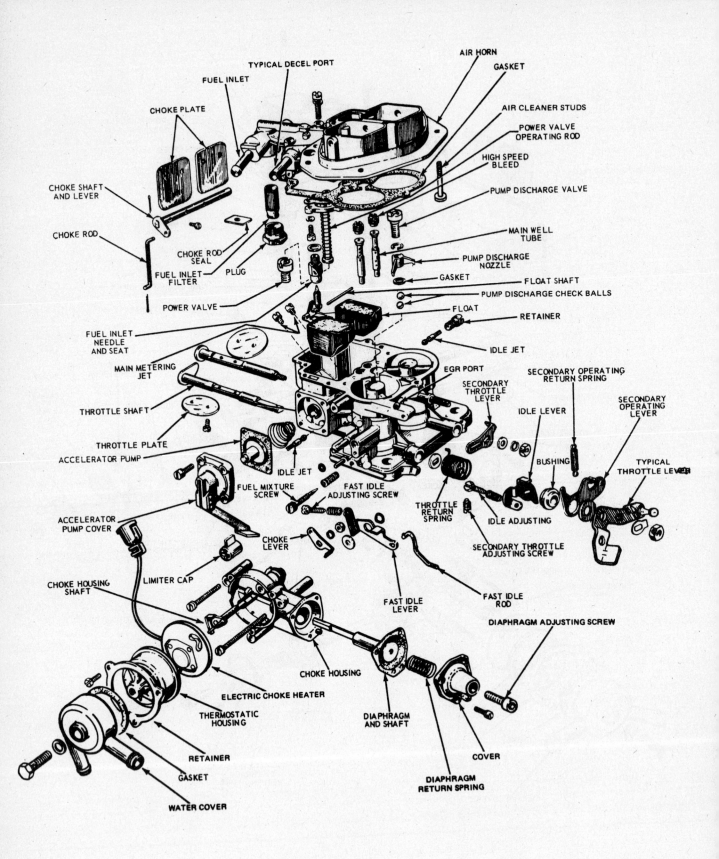

Fig. 14 Exploded view of Model 5200 two barrel carburetor. 1974 models

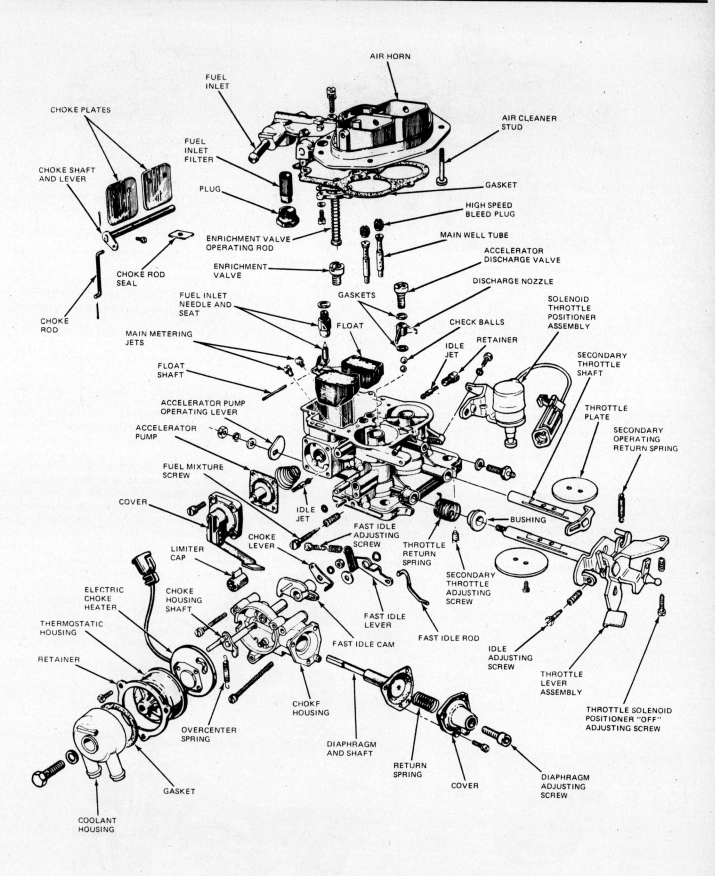

Fig. 15 Exploded view of Model 5200 two barrel carburetor. 1976-77 models

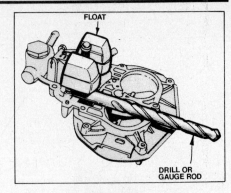

Fig. 16 Dry float setting. Model 5200

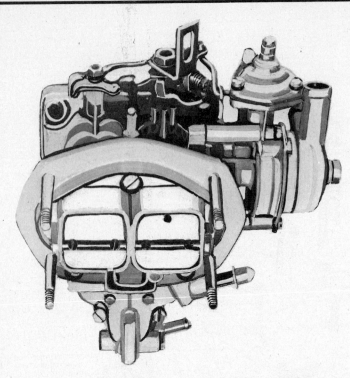

Fig. 12   Model 5200 two barrel carburetor (typical)

throttle body with gasket removed. If the float height is not as listed in the *Specifications Chart,* bend tab on float as required to achieve the desired setting.

Fuel Level Adjustment

Fig. 8—With vehicle on a level surface, operate engine until normal temperature is reached, then stop engine and check fuel level as follows:

1. Remove carburetor air cleaner.
2. Remove air horn retaining screws and carburetor identification tag.
3. Temporarily leave air horn and gasket in position on throttle body and start engine.
4. Allow engine to idle for several minutes, then rotate air horn and remove air horn gasket to gain access to float or floats.
5. While engine is idling, use a standard depth gauge to measure vertical distance from top machined surface of throttle body to level of fuel in bowl. The measurement must be made at least ¼" away from any vertical surface to assure an accurate reading.
6. If the fuel level is not as listed in the *Specifications Chart,* stop the engine to avoid any fire hazard due to fuel spray when float setting is disturbed.
7. To adjust fuel level, bend float tab (contacting fuel inlet needle) upward in relation to original position to raise the fuel level, and downward to lower it.
8. Each time an adjustment is made to the float tab to alter the fuel level, the engine must be started and permitted to idle for at least three minutes to stabilize the fuel level. Check fuel level after each adjust-

Fig. 17   Float adjusting point and bumper spring adjustment. Model 5200

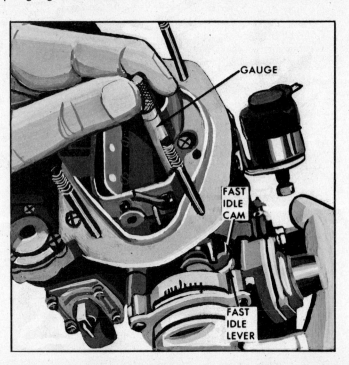

Fig. 18   De-choke adjustment. Model 5200

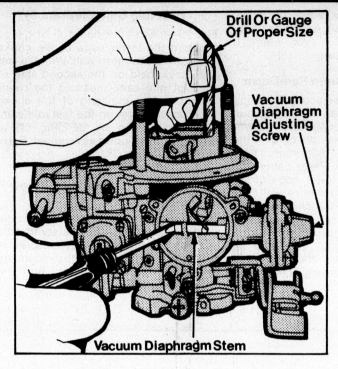

Fig. 19 Choke plate pulldown adjustment. Model 5200

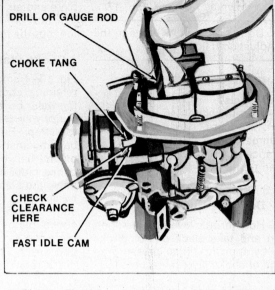

Fig. 20 Fast idle cam clearance. Model 5200

ment until the specified level is achieved.

9. Assemble carburetor with a new air horn gasket. Then adjust idle speed and mixture, and anti-stall dashpot, if so equipped.

Accelerating Pump Adjustment

Fig. 9—The primary throttle shaft lever (overtravel lever) has 4 holes and the accelerating pump link has 2 or 4 holes to control the pump stroke for various atmospheric temperatures, operating conditions and specific engine applications.

NOTE: The stroke should not be changed from the specified setting.

1. To release rod from retainer clip, press tab end of clip toward rod. Then, at the same time, press rod away from clip until it is disengaged.

2. Position clip over specified hole in overtravel lever. Press ends of clip together and insert operating rod through clip and lever. Release clip to engage rod.

Choke Plate Clearance (Pulldown) Adjustment

1. Set throttle on fast idle cam top step, then loosen choke thermostatic housing retaining screws and set housing 90° in rich direction.

2. Activate pulldown motor by manually forcing pulldown control diaphragm link in direction of applied vacuum or by applying vacuum to external vacuum tube.

3. Check clearance between lower edge of choke plate and center of carburetor air horn wall nearest fuel bowl Fig. 10. Refer to *Specifications Chart*. If clearance is not as specified, reset by adjusting diaphragm stop on end of choke pulldown diaphragm.

Automatic Choke Valve Tension

Turn thermostatic spring cover against spring tension until index mark on cover is aligned with mark specified in the *Specifications Chart* on choke housing, Fig. 11.

MODEL 5200 ADJUSTMENTS
Dry Float Setting

Fig. 16—With the bowl cover held in an inverted position and the float tang resting lightly on the spring loaded fuel inlet needle, measure the clearance between the edge of the float and the bowl cover.

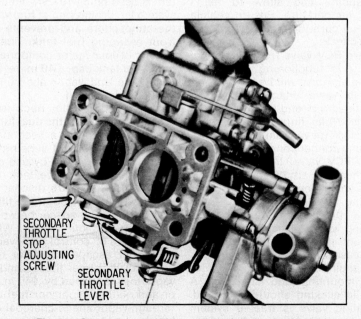

Fig. 21 Secondary throttle stop adjustment. Model 5200

Adjust clearance by bending the float tang up or down as required, Fig. 17.

NOTE: Do not scratch or damage the tang. Adjust both floats equally.

Float Bumper Spring

1972-74 Models

Fig. 17—With bowl held in the inverted position, measure distance between float bumper spring and float drop tang. If clearance is not within specification, bend tang until proper clearance is obtained.

Dechoke Clearance

Fig. 18—Hold throttle lever in wide open position and take slack out of choke linkage by applying finger pressure on top edge of choke plate. Measure clearance between lower edge of choke plate and air horn wall. Adjust by bending tab on fast idle lever where it touches the fast idle cam.

Choke Plate Vacuum Pull-Down

Fig. 19—Remove three screws and ring retaining choke spring cover and pull the water cover and choke spring cover out of way. Set the fast idle cam on the top step. Push the diaphragm stem back against its stop. Place gauge rod or drill between the lower edge of the choke plate and the air horn wall. Remove the slack from the choke linkage by applying finger pressure to the top edge of the choke plate. Adjust the choke plate-to-air horn clearance by removing the plug from the diaphragm and turning the adjusting screw in or out as required.

Fast Idle Cam Clearance

Fig. 20—Insert specified drill or gauge between the lower edge of the choke plate and the air horn wall. With the fast idle screw held on the second step of the fast idle cam, measure the clearance between the tang of the choke lever and the arm on the fast idle cam. Adjust clearance by bending choke lever tang up or down as required. Refer to *Specifications Chart*.

Secondary Throttle Stop Screw Adjustment

Fig. 21—Back off the secondary throttle stop screw until the secondary throttle plate seats in its bore. Turn the screw in until it touches the tab on the secondary throttle lever. On all units, turn the screw inward an additional ¼ turn.

Emission Controls Section

POSITIVE CRANKCASE VENTILATION (PCV) SYSTEM

Description

All engines produce small amounts of blowby gases which seep past the piston rings and into the crankcase. These blowby gases are the result of the high pressures developed within the combustion chamber during the combustion process, and contain undesirable pollutants. To prevent blowby gases from entering the atmosphere while allowing proper crankcase ventilation, all engines use a PCV system.

The PCV system prevents blowby gases from escaping by routing them through a vacuum controlled ventilating valve and a hose into the intake manifold. The blowby gases mix with the air/fuel mixture and are burned in the combustion chambers. When the engine is running, fresh air is drawn into the crankcase through a tube or hose connected to the air cleaner housing.

The PCV valve consists of a needle valve, spring and housing. When the engine is off, the spring holds the needle valve closed to stop vapors from entering the intake manifold. When the engine is running, manifold vacuum unseats the valve allowing crankcase vapors to enter the intake manifold. In case of a backfire in the intake manifold, the valve closes, stopping the backflow and preventing ignition of fumes in the crankcase. During certain engine conditions, more blowby gases are created than the ventilator valve can handle. The excess is returned through the air intake tube to the air cleaner and carburetor where it is burned in the engine.

Testing

Start engine and allow to reach operating temperature. Ensure vehicle is at normal curb idle and perform the following check:

1. Remove PCV valve from mounting, if valve is functioning properly a hissing air noise will be heard as air through valve. Place finger over valve inlet, a strong vacuum should be felt. While finger is over valve inlet check for vacuum leaks in hose lines and connections.
2. Install PCV valve, then remove air inlet hose at air cleaner. Loosely hold a small piece of stiff paper over opening at end of hose. Paper should be sucked against hose opening with noticeable force after suffcent time has elapsed for crankcase pressures to lower.
3. Stop engine and remove PCV valve from mounting and shake it. A metallic clicking should be heard, indicating valve is free. If system passes both engine running and engine stopped test, system is functioning properly. If system has failed either test, replace appropriate component and repeat test. If system still does not pass test, clean system.

EVAPORATIVE EMISSION CONTROL SYSTEM

The evaporative emission control system is used on all 1972-77 models. This system limits emission of fuel vapor into the atmosphere and prevents raw fuel from escaping fuel tank. The system consist of four major components, fuel tank, fuel tank cap, .040 in. restrictor in vapor line and vapor absorbing charcoal canister, Fig. 1.

The fuel tank filler neck is double sealed and provides the dual function of venting air through a secondary concentric chamber and sensing fuel fill level. This is achieved by use of a twin tube neck. As level of fuel tank rises during filling, vapors are discharged into the atmosphere through the fill control tube and annular spacer between inner filler tube and outer neck. When fuel level covers fill control tube, vapors can no longer escape and filler tube will begin to fill. Under these conditions, a vapor lock is formed by .040 in. restrictor and neither vapor nor fuel can flow through vapor line to charcoal canister. Level in fuel tank is therefore controlled

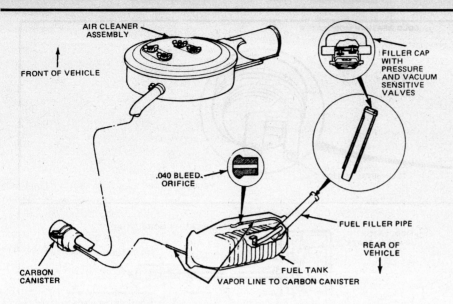

Fig. 1 Fuel evaporative emissions control system. V6 engine

decreases, the vacuum produced opens vacuum valve in tank cap. This allows air to enter from atmosphere until pressure balance is restored and valve closes.

THERMOSTATIC CONTROLLED AIR CLEANER
Description

Temperature Controlled 1972-74 Models

Carburetor air temperature is thermostatically controlled by the air duct and valve assembly, Fig. 2. Air from engine compartment or heated air from the shrouded exhaust manifold is supplied to the engine.

The air cleaner and heat stove as-

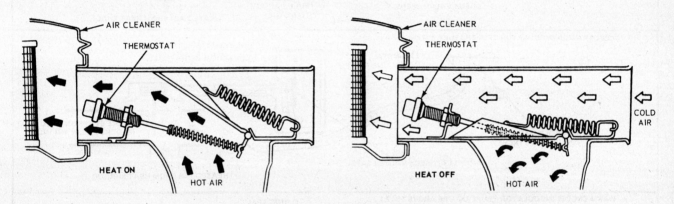

Fig. 2 Temperature operated duct and valve assembly. 1972-74 models

by the fill control tube which is positioned to maintain an expansion volume of 10 percent tank capacity at top of tank.

The fuel filler cap incorporates two valves, one to release excess pressure from inside tank should vapor tube become plugged, and a vacuum relief valve to admit air into tank as fuel is consumed.

When conditions of thermal expansion in fuel tank promote a vapor flow, vapor is forced through the .040 in. restrictor. This allows vapor to pass through system and be absorbed by charcoal canister. The canister is opened to the atmosphere on one side and connected to the air cleaner by a length of hose on the other side. Vapors absorbed by the canister when vehicle is stationary are extracted by flow of air through canister into air filter when vehicle is started.

Should a restriction develop in vapor line between tank and charcoal canister

causing vapor pressure in system to reach .7 to 1.5 psi., the pressure relief on tank cap opens, allowing vapor to discharge into the atmosphere.

As fuel is consumed or temperature

sembly is designed to provide carburetor with air at a temperature of approximately 90 to 100° F. During engine warm up, air is drawn from the exhaust manifold shroud over thermostatic bulb

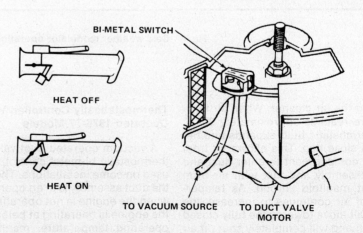

Fig. 3 Vacuum operated duct and valve assembly. 1976-77 models

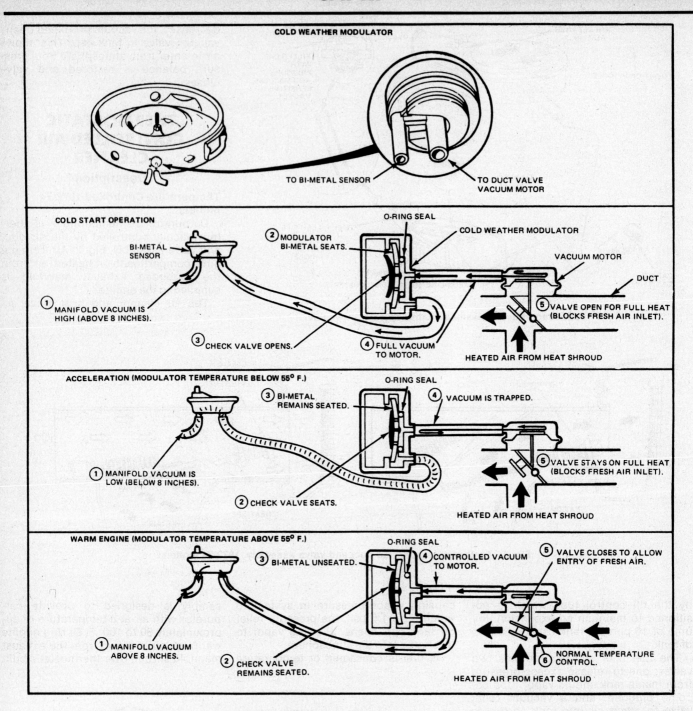

Fig. 4 Cold weather modulator operation. 1976-77 models

and into the air cleaner. When air temperature reaches approximately 90° F, the thermostatic bulb expands and begins to close flap. This allows air from engine compartment to enter duct and valve assembly and mix with air from exhaust manifold shroud. As temperature of air continues to increase, the valve will move towards the fully closed position and will completely shut off air from exhaust manifold shroud.

Thermostatically Controlled Vacuum Operated 1976-77 Models

A vacuum operated duct valve with a thermostatic bi-metal control, Fig. 3, is used on some installations. The valve in the duct assembly is in an open position when the engine is not operating. When the engine is operating at below normal operating temperature, manifold vacuum is routed through the bi-metal switch to the vacuum motor to close the duct valve allowing only heated air to enter the air cleaner. When the engine reaches normal operating temperature the bi-metal switch opens an air bleed which eliminates the vacuum and the duct valve opens allowing only cold air to enter the air cleaner. During periods of acceleration the duct valve will open regardless of temperature due to the loss of manifold vacuum.

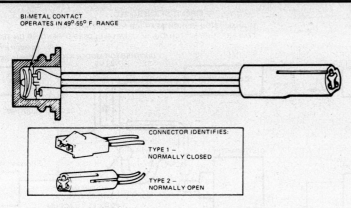

Fig. 5 Air cleaner temperature switch. 1976-77 models

4. Raise water temperature to 100° F, then allow 5 minutes for temperature to stabilize and observe valve plate position. Valve plate should be in the heat on position.
5. Raise water temperature to 135° F, then allow 5 minutes for temperature stabilize and observe valve plate position. Valve plate should be in the heat off position. If valve plate does not operate in this manner and no interference between plate and duct is observed, replace duct and valve assembly.

Cold Weather Modulator 1976-77 Models

This modulator, Fig. 4, located in the air cleaner housing of some 1976-77 models, prevents the air cleaner door from opening to non-heated outside air at ambient temperatures below 55° F. At ambient temperatures above 55° F., the modulator is inoperative. During acceleration at ambient temperatures below 55° F., the modulator located in-line between the bi-metal sensor and vacuum duct motor, will close off vacuum to the motor and hold the duct open.

Air Cleaner Temperature Switch 1976-77 Models

1976-77 vehicles with CTAV systems and those with Thermactor systems used with catalytic converters, are equipped with a bi-metallic temperature switch mounted in the air cleaner housing. The two type switches used may be identified by the connector, Fig. 5. The first type has normally closed contacts, while the second type has normally open contacts. Refer to "Cold Engine Lockout" under "Air Pump Systems," for operation of these switches.

Testing

1972 1600 cc Engine & 1972-74 2000 cc Engine

1. With duct and valve assembly in position, engine cold and ambient temperature in engine compartment 85° F or below, flap valve should be in the open position closing off cold air intake. If valve is not opened, check for wear or breakage of valve in duct and replace duct and valve assembly as necessary.
2. Remove assembly from vehicle and immerse in water so that thermostatic bulb is completely covered. Raise temperature of water to 85° F, then allow 5 minutes for temperature to stabilize and observe valve position.

Flap valve should be in the open position.
3. Increase water temperature to 110° F, then allow 5 minutes for temperature to stabilize and observe valve position. Flap valve should be in closed position shutting off hot air from exhaust manifold shroud. If flap valve does not operate in this manner and no binding or mechanical damage is present, replace thermostatic bulb.

1972-74 V6-2600 & 2800 cc Engines

1. With duct assembly installed on vehicle, engine cold and ambient temperature in engine compartment less than 100° F, valve plate should be in heat on position.
2. If plate is not in heat on position, check for interference between plate and duct and realign plate if necessary.
3. Remove duct and valve assembly from vehicle, then immerse duct assembly in water so that thermostat capsule in completely cover.

Duct & Valve Assembly Test 1976-77 Models

NOTE: Do not immerse any part of duct and valve assembly in water, otherwise temperature sensor switch may become damaged.

1. By pass cold weather modulator or vacuum delay valve by connecting 3/16 in. diameter vacuum line from sensor directly to 1/4 in. diameter vacuum motor line using a reducer.
2. Remove necessary items so that duct door can be viewed, also remove air cleaner cover.
3. Check to ensure that duct door is in open position. If duct door is closed, check for binding and repair as necessary.
4. Position magnetic temperature indicator T75L-9601-A as near as possible to temperature sensor on air inlet side.
5. Start engine, with engine cold and ambient temperature below 75° F, duct and valve door should be in closed or full heat position. If duct valve door is not closed, turn off engine and cool temperature sensor to a temperature below 75° F by spray-

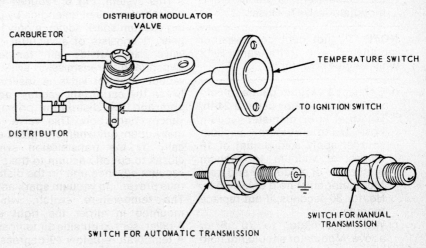

Fig. 6 Transmission spark control system

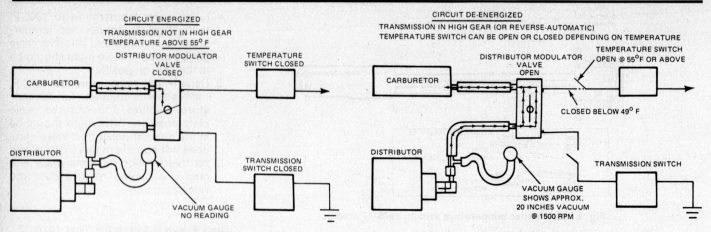

Fig. 7   TRS system energized   **Fig. 8   TRS system de-energized**

ing with R-12 refrigerant from a 14 oz. can. Start engine, if duct valve door is closed proceed to next step. If valve door is opened during idle, refer to Vacuum Motor Test as outlined below.

NOTE: Do not cool temperature sensor with R-12 refrigerant while engine is running.

6. Position air cleaner cover on air cleaner, but do not install wing nuts.
7. Start engine and observe duct valve door. When door starts to open to heat off position, remove air cleaner cover and note temperature indicator reading. Temperature reading should not exceed 120° F. If door does not open, replace temperature sensor. After completing test, turn off engine, install air cleaner cover and connect cold weather modulator.
8. On models with cold weather modulator, proceed as follows:
   a. Cool cold weather modulator to 40° F or less by spraying with R-12 refrigerant. Allow sufficient time for temperature to stabilize and modulator valve to close.

NOTE: Do not cool cold weather modulator with refrigerant R-12 while engine is running.

   b. Connect a vacuum gauge to cold weather modulator using a 24 in. length of ¼ in. diameter vacuum hose. Using an external vacuum source, apply a minimum of 16 inches of vacuum to vacuum motor side of modulator and trap. Modulator must hold at least 5 in. Hg. for 30 seconds, if not replace modulator.
   c. Warm modulator to 70° F or above. Modulator should not hold vacuum at or above this temper-

ature. If modulator does not operate in this manner, it should be replaced.

Vacuum Motor Test 1976-77 Models
1. Check duct valve door valve for binding and correct if necessary before performing test.
2. Disconnect vacuum hose from vacuum motor connector tube.
3. Connect an external vacuum source of 16 in. Hg. to vacuum motor. If duct door remains opened, replace vacuum motor.
4. Using external source of vacuum, apply a minimum of 16 in. Hg. vacuum and trap. Vacuum motor should remain closed for 60 seconds, if not replace motor.

T.R.S. SYSTEM
Transmission Regulated Spark Control System

NOTE: This system is used on all 1972 California models with 1600 cc engine.

This system, Fig. 6, reduces the exhaust emissions of an engine by providing vacuum spark advance only in high gear. It consists of a vacuum control valve, an outside air temperature switch, and a transmission switch. The vacuum control valve is inserted between the carburetor vacuum advance port and the distributor primary advance connection. This valve is normally open, but when energized electrically by the transmission switch it closes to cut off vacuum to the primary vacuum advance unit on the distributor thus preventing vacuum spark advance. The temperature switch, which is mounted in either the right or left A-pillar, senses outside air temperature. A temperature below 49 degrees F will cause the switch contacts to open,

thereby de-energizing the vacuum valve and allowing normal vacuum advance in all gears. A temperature of 60 degrees F causes the contacts to close, thereby cutting off vacuum to the advance side of the distributor in all but high gear.

Testing
Manual Transmission
With a vacuum gauge connected to the T.R.S. system, Figs. 7, 8 and 9, between the vacuum control valve and the distributor advance unit, and the temperature switch known to be above 65 degrees F, proceed as follows:
1. Start the engine in Neutral. No vacuum should be indicated on the gauge (circuit energized).
2. Disengage the clutch and increase engine speed to 1000 to 1500 rpm. The vacuum indication should still remain at zero.
3. Disengage the clutch then place the transmission in high gear. With the engine running between 1000-1500 rpm and the clutch disengaged, a vacuum of at least 6 inches of mercury should be indicated on the gauge. Make sure the engine is stopped before engaging the clutch.
4. To test transmission switch, proceed as follows: Disconnect both wires from the vacuum control valve. Connnect the transmission switch lead from the valve blade terminal in series with a test light to the positive terminal of the battery, Fig. 10. With the engine and ignition off, move the gear selector through all positions. The light should stay on in all but high gear. If the light stays on in high gear, the circuit is grounded or the switch is inoperative. If the light does not go on in any gear, the circuit is open or again the switch is inoperative.
5. To test the temperature switch, proceed as follows: Disconnect both

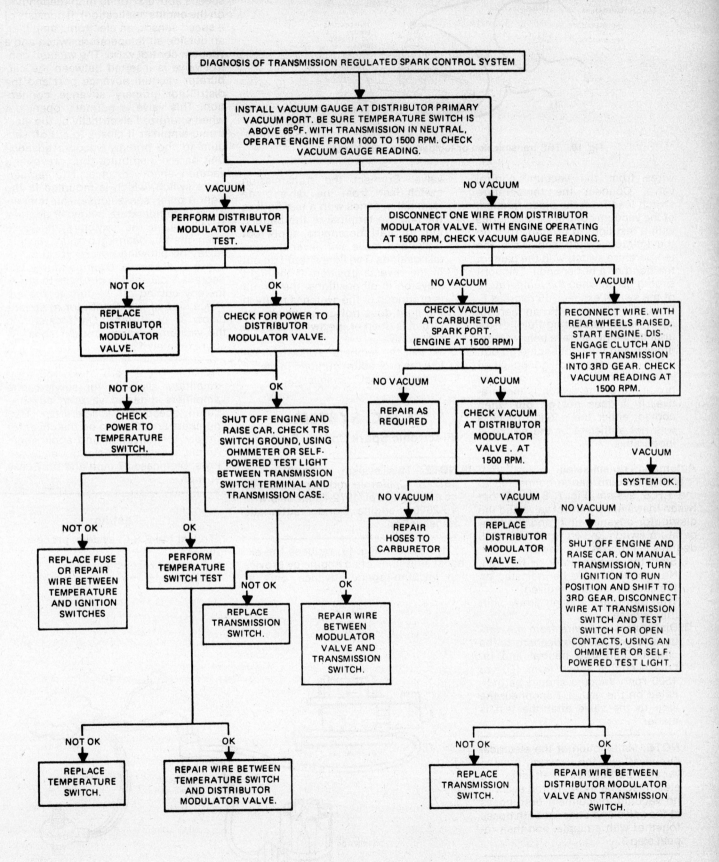

Fig. 9 TRS system diagnosis

DIAGNOSIS OF TRANSMISSION REGULATED SPARK CONTROL SYSTEM

INSTALL VACUUM GAUGE AT DISTRIBUTOR PRIMARY VACUUM PORT. BE SURE TEMPERATURE SWITCH IS ABOVE 65°F. WITH TRANSMISSION IN NEUTRAL, OPERATE ENGINE FROM 1000 TO 1500 RPM. CHECK VACUUM GAUGE READING.

VACUUM

PERFORM DISTRIBUTOR MODULATOR VALVE TEST.

NOT OK

REPLACE DISTRIBUTOR MODULATOR VALVE.

OK

CHECK FOR POWER TO DISTRIBUTOR MODULATOR VALVE.

NOT OK

CHECK POWER TO TEMPERATURE SWITCH.

OK

SHUT OFF ENGINE AND RAISE CAR. CHECK TRS SWITCH GROUND, USING OHMMETER OR SELF-POWERED TEST LIGHT BETWEEN TRANSMISSION SWITCH TERMINAL AND TRANSMISSION CASE.

NOT OK

REPLACE FUSE OR REPAIR WIRE BETWEEN TEMPERATURE AND IGNITION SWITCHES

OK

PERFORM TEMPERATURE SWITCH TEST

NOT OK

REPLACE TRANSMISSION SWITCH.

OK

REPAIR WIRE BETWEEN MODULATOR VALVE AND TRANSMISSION SWITCH.

NOT OK

REPLACE TEMPERATURE SWITCH.

OK

REPAIR WIRE BETWEEN TEMPERATURE SWITCH AND DISTRIBUTOR MODULATOR VALVE.

NO VACUUM

DISCONNECT ONE WIRE FROM DISTRIBUTOR MODULATOR VALVE. WITH ENGINE OPERATING AT 1500 RPM, CHECK VACUUM GAUGE READING.

NO VACUUM

CHECK VACUUM AT CARBURETOR SPARK PORT. (ENGINE AT 1500 RPM)

NO VACUUM

REPAIR AS REQUIRED

VACUUM

CHECK VACUUM AT DISTRIBUTOR MODULATOR VALVE. AT 1500 RPM.

NO VACUUM

REPAIR HOSES TO CARBURETOR

VACUUM

REPLACE DISTRIBUTOR MODULATOR VALVE.

VACUUM

RECONNECT WIRE. WITH REAR WHEELS RAISED, START ENGINE. DISENGAGE CLUTCH AND SHIFT TRANSMISSION INTO 3RD GEAR. CHECK VACUUM READING AT 1500 RPM.

VACUUM

SYSTEM OK.

NO VACUUM

SHUT OFF ENGINE AND RAISE CAR. ON MANUAL TRANSMISSION, TURN IGNITION TO RUN POSITION AND SHIFT TO 3RD GEAR. DISCONNECT WIRE AT TRANSMISSION SWITCH AND TEST SWITCH FOR OPEN CONTACTS, USING AN OHMMETER OR SELF-POWERED TEST LIGHT.

NOT OK

REPLACE TRANSMISSION SWITCH.

OK

REPAIR WIRE BETWEEN DISTRIBUTOR MODULATOR VALVE AND TRANSMISSION SWITCH.

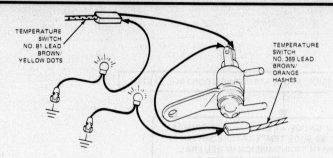

Fig. 10   TRS transmission or temperature switch test

wires from the vacuum control valve. Connect the temperature switch lead from the blade terminal of the vacuum control valve in series with a test light to ground. Turn on the ignition switch and warm the temperature switch with the palm of the hand or a hot sponge. The light should go on when the temperature of the switch exceeds 65 degrees F. Cool the switch with an aerosol spray (such as starting fluid) or ice until its temperature is below 49 degrees F and the light should go out. If the light does not go on when warmed, the circuit is open or grounded or the switch is inoperative. If it does not go out when cooled, either the cooling process was not sufficient or the switch is inoperative.

Automatic Transmission

With a vacuum gauge connected to the T.R.S. system, Fig. 7, 8 and 9, between the vacuum control valve and the distributor advance unit, and the temperature switch known to be above 65 degrees F, proceed as follows:
1. Start the engine (Park or Neutral). No vacuum should be indicated on the gauge (circuit energized).
2. With foot brake applied firmly, shift into reverse.
3. Disconnect one wire from the vacuum control valve to deenergize the circuit. Shift into neutral and increase engine speed from 1000 to 1500 rpm. Vacuum should be indicated on the gauge. Reconnect the wire to the valve after the test is made.

NOTE: Malfunction of the electrical circuit affects the vacuum, but the vacuum portion has no effect on the electrical. Therefore, in the event of no vacuum, disconnect both hoses at the valve and connect both hoses together with a nipple, and then repeat step 3.

4. To test transmission switch, proceed as follows: Disconnect both wires from the vacuum control valve. Connect the transmission switch lead from the valve blade terminal in series with a test light to the positive terminal of the battery, Fig. 10. Start the engine, apply foot brake and move shift lever through all positions. The light should go out in the reverse position. If the light stays on in all positions, the circuit is grounded or the switch is faulty. If the light does not go on at all, the circuit is open or the switch is again inoperative.
5. To test the temperature switch, follow the procedure outlined in step 5 under "Manual Transmission."

E.S.C. SYSTEM
Electronic Spark Control System

NOTE: This system is used on all 1972-73 California models with 2000 cc engine and all 1972-73 models with V6-2600 engine and automatic transmission.

This system, Fig. 11, reduces the exhaust emissions of an engine by providing vacuum spark advance only at speeds above 37 or 40 mph (depending on the engine application). It consists of a speed sensor, an electronic amplifier, an outside air temperature switch and a vacuum control valve. The vacuum control valve is inserted between the carburetor vacuum advance port and the distributor primary advance connection. This valve is normally open, but when energized electrically by the electronic amplifier it closes to cut off vacuum to the primary vacuum advance unit on the distributor thus preventing vacuum spark advance. The temperature switch, which is mounted in the right A pillar, senses ouside air temperature. A temperature below 49 degrees F will cause the switch contacts to open, thereby deenergizing the vacuum valve and allowing normal vacuum advance at all speeds. A temperature of 65 degrees F causes the contacts to close, thereby cutting off vacuum to the advance side of the distributor at speeds below 37 or 40 mph. On deceleration the vacuum advance cut-out speed is approximately 18 mph.

NOTE: There are two different amplifiers available for service. The amplifiers differ in vacuum advance cut-in speed on acceleration. Part numbers are stamped on the cover for proper identification and application. Amplifier cases are color coded as follows; blue case 37 mph and gray case 40 mph.

Testing

To test the E.S.C. system, proceed as follows:
1. Raise the rear wheels.
2. Disconnect the vacuum hose at the

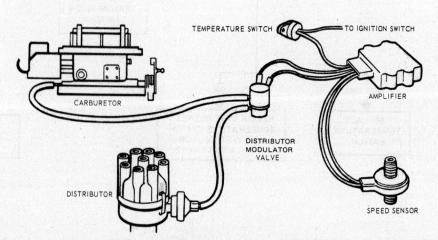

Fig. 11   Electronic spark control system

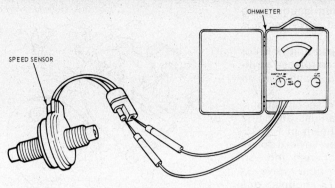

Fig. 12   ECS speed sensor continuity test

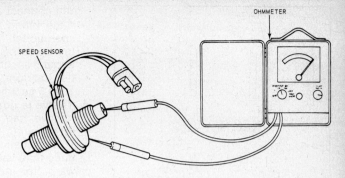

Fig. 13   ECS speed sensor ground check

distributor primary advance diaphragm and connect it to a vacuum gauge.

3. Ensure that the temperature switch is above 65 degrees F by warming it with the hand or a hot sponge.
4. Start the engine and put the transmission in drive.
5. The vacuum gauge should register zero until the appropriate 37 or 40 mph speed is attained, at which point it should register at least 6" Hg.
6. If there is no vacuum in any case at over 37 mph, there are three possible causes:
   a. No vacuum at the carburetor vacuum advance port. With the transmission in Park or Neutral, block open the throttle to about 1500 rpm and determine if there is vacuum at carburetor vacuum advance port. Repair as necessary.
   b. Pinched, blocked, misrouted or disconnected hoses. Follow vacuum hose from carburetor to the ESC vacuum control valve.
   c. Inoperative ESC control system. Disconnect one or both electrical leads at ESC vacuum control valve and follow vacuum to the

gauge at the distributor.
   d. Throttle down the engine.
   e. If there is no vacuum in step c, reconnect the ESC vacuum control valve.
7. If there is vacuum below the cut in speeds, trouble exists in the ESC system which prevents the valve from being energized. Therefore, it is necessary to test the individual system components:
   a. Temperature Switch Test: This test can be made in the vehicle or on the bench. Disconnect the multiple plug and connect an ohmmeter to both wire terminals from the switch. Place the switch in the palm of the hand and allow sufficient time to warm it. If the ohmmeter registers a reading with the switch at 65 degrees F or higher, the switch is good.

   To test the switch at low temperature, chill it with ice or water which is below 49 degrees F. At this temperature the switch should be open and no reading should register on the ohmmeter. If the switch is good, check the power supply.
   b. Power Supply Test: Ground the

lead on a test lamp and check for voltage at the temperature switch connector of the instrument panel wiring. With ignition on, the lamp should light. If no voltage is present at the terminal, replace or repair the wiring to the ignition switch or replace the ignition switch. If the previous steps have not located the problem, replace the electronic amplifier.
   c. Speed Sensor Test: Disconnect the speed sensor at the multiple plug and check the sensor for continuity using an ohmmeter, Fig. 12. Resistance of the speed sensor at room temperature is 40-60 ohms.

   Also, check the resistance of the speed sensor to ground, Fig. 13. There should be no continuity between the black wire and the case. Replace the speed sensor if the resistance readings are incorrect.

DECEL VALVE

This valve, Fig. 14, used on the 1600 cc, 2000 cc, 2600 cc and 1974 2800 cc engines, is mounted on the intake manifold adjacent to the carburetor and meters an additional amount of fuel and air during engine deceleration periods. This additional fuel and air, together with engine modifications, permits more complete combustion with the re-

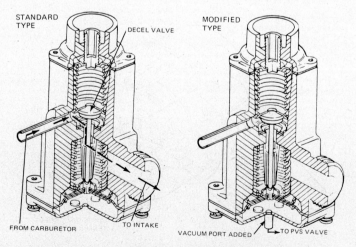

Fig. 14   Standard and modified type decel valves

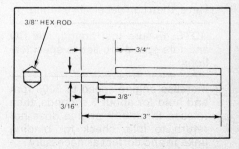

Fig. 15   Decel valve adjusting tool

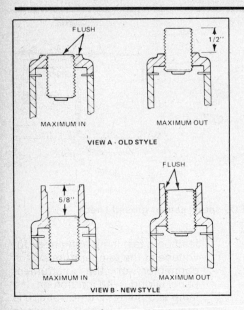

Fig. 16 Decel valve adjustment limits

sultant being lower levels of exhaust emissions. During engine deceleration, manifold vacuum forces the diaphragm assembly against the spring in the decel valve, which in turn raises the decel valve (open position). With the valve open, existing manifold vacuum pulls a metered amount of fuel and air from the carburetor, which travels through the decel valve body assembly into the intake manifold. The decel valve remains open and continues to feed additional air and fuel for a specified time.

Testing & Adjustment

High Idle Speed

NOTE: On 1972 models with 1600 cc engine, it is important to determine which carburetor model is used due to specification differences. The 28mm venturi carburetor used on early models is stamped 701W-9510-EA; the 25mm venturi carburetor used on later models is stamped 701W-9510-EB.

1. Connect tachometer to engine, then operate engine and allow to reach operating temperature.
2. Disconnect rubber hose between decel valve and carburetor at decel valve, then cap decel valve fitting.

NOTE: Ensure that timing, idle CO and idle speed are set to specifications.

3. Increase engine speed to 3000 rpm and hold for about 5 seconds, then release throttle. If engine does not return to idle, check for binding linkage and correct as necessary.
4. Remove cap from decel valve fitting

and connect a vacuum gauge using a tee fitting so that valve remains operational.

5. Increase engine speed and hold for about 5 seconds, then release throttle. Vacuum should reach zero in 1.5-3.5 seconds.
6. If valve is not within specifications, remove cap and adjust adjusting screw using tool shown in Fig. 15. Turn adjusting screw inward to reduce time valve is opened and outward to increase time valve is opened. On 1972-73 models, one turn of adjusting screw in either direction will increase or decrease valve timing approximately ½ second. On all models, if valve timing cannot be adjusted within limit of adjusting screw travel, Fig. 16, replace decel valve.

Rough Idle

1. Rough idle or excessively lean fuel air mixture can be caused by a ruptured or leaking decel valve diaphragm.
   a. On models with standard decel valve, check to ensure four diaphragm cover attaching screws are tight. If screws are tight, remove decel valve and install plug in manifold bore. If idle quality improves, replace decel valve.
   b. On models with modified decel valve, place finger over small hole in bottom valve. If idle quality or speed improve, diaphragm is leaking and should be replaced.

ELECTRIC ASSIST CHOKE

The electric assist choke is used on 1974 and 1976-77 models, Fig. 17 & 18. The electric choke system consists of a choke cap, thermostatic spring, a bimetal temperature sensing disc

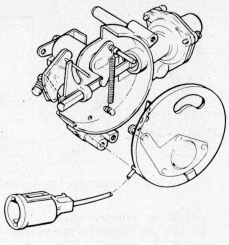

Fig. 17 Electric assisted choke. Model 5200 2V carburetor

(switch), and a ceramic positive temperature coefficient (PTC) heater. The choke is powered from terminal or tap of the alternator. Current is constantly supplied to the ambient temperature switch. The system is grounded through a ground strap connected to the carburetor body. At temperatures below approximately 60 degrees, the switch opens and no current is supplied to the ceramic heater located within the thermostatic spring. Normal thermostatic spring choking action then occurs. At temperatures above approximately 60-65 degrees, the temperature sensing switch closes and current is supplied to the ceramic heater. As the heater warms, it causes the thermostatic spring to pull the choke plates open within 1-1½ minutes.

Testing

1. Remove air cleaner and make certain that it was not interfering with

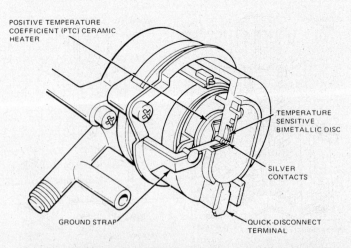

Fig. 18 Electric assisted choke. Model 2150 2V carburetor

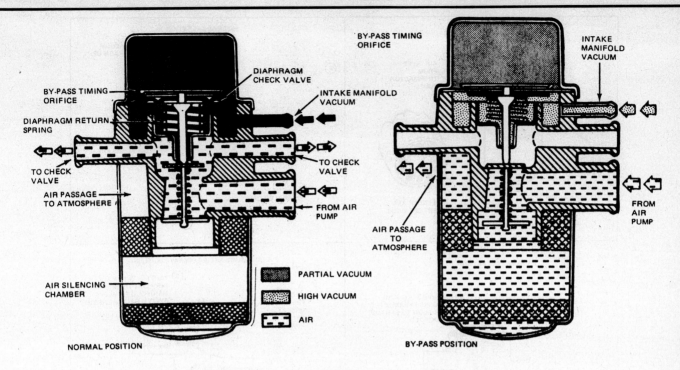

Fig. 19   Air by-pass valve. 1974 models

the choke plate, then check linkages and fast idle cam for freedom of operation.

NOTE: If delay valve is used, make certain it is operating properly.

2. On 1976-77 models with 2800 cc engine, disconnect hot air supply tube from choke housing, then using Choke Tester LRE-34618 or equivalent, check for correct operation of choke.

3. On all models, disconnect stator lead and connect a 0-3 amp ammeter between choke lead connector and stator lead, then start engine and observe reading.

4. On 1976-77 models with 2800 cc engine, cool choke until temperature is less than 55 F. If current flow is noted, cap is defective.

5. On all models, after about 5 minutes of engine operation, a current read-

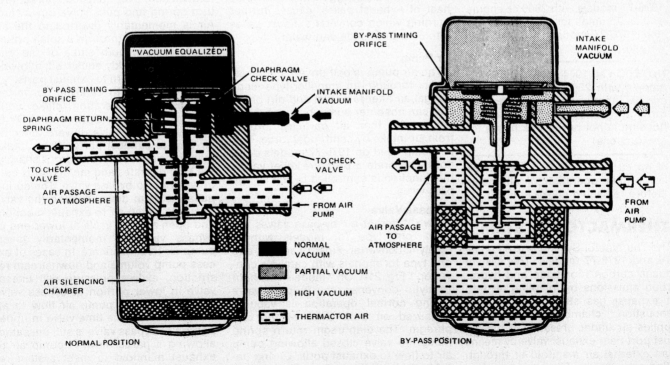

Fig. 20   Air by-pass valve. 1976-77 models less catalytic converter

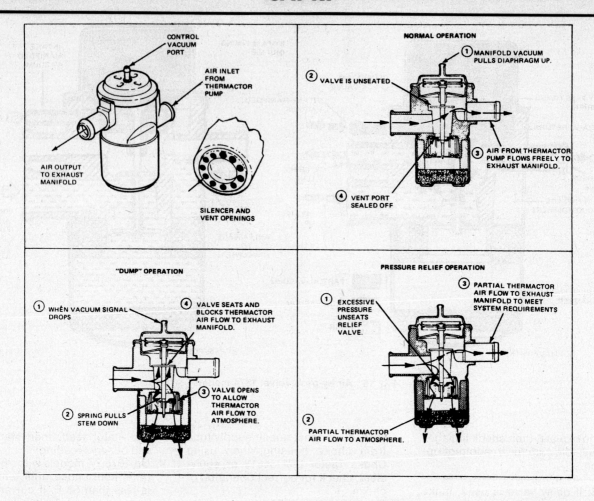

Fig. 21 Air by-pass valve. 1976-77 models w/catalytic converter

ing of .3-1 amps should be noted for 1976-77 models with 2800 cc engine and .3-.75 amps for all 1974 models and 1976-77 models with 2300 cc engine.

NOTE: On all 1974 models and 1976 models with 2300 cc engine, make certain that coolant is flowing through choke housing. If choke housing is not hot, check hoses for obstructions.

6. If no current draw is noted, check for proper operation of alternator before replacing choke housing.

THERMACTOR SYSTEM

The Thermactor System is used on all 1974 and 1976-77 models. This system reduces carbon monoxide and hydrocarbon emissions by injecting air into hot exhaust gas stream as it leaves combustion chamber. The pump supplies air under pressure to the exhaust port near exhaust valve by means of an external air manifold or through drilled passages in cylinder head or ex-

haust manifold. Oxygen in the air plus heat of exhaust gases, causes further burning which converts exhaust gases into carbon dioxide and water.

Air Pump

The air pump is belt driven and takes air in through an impeller-type centrifugal air filter fan. Dust and dirt particles can not enter pump, because these are heavier than air particles thrown from air intake by centrifugal force. The air pump used on 1976-77 models does not incorporate a pressure relief valve, this function is controlled by the air by-pass valve.

By-pass Valve

Two different air by-pass valves are used, one type for models without catalytic converter, Figs. 19 and 20, and one type for models with catalytic converter, Fig. 21. On models without catalytic converter, the by-pass valve during normal operation is vacuum equalized on both sides of the diaphragm. The diaphragm return spring holds the valve closed allowing pump air to flow to exhaust ports. During deceleration, a sudden rise in intake mani-

fold vacuum over comes diaphragm return spring and pulls valve downward. Air is momentarily diverted to the atmosphere, then through a small orifice in diaphragm, both sides of the diaphragm are quickly equalized, allowing air to flow to return to exhaust ports.

On models with catalytic converter, during normal operation intake manifold vacuum is applied through VDV to by-pass to hold valve upward allowing air flow to exhaust ports. When intake manifold vacuum rises or drops sharply, the VDV operates and momentarily cuts off vacuum to bypass valve. The spring pulls the stem down, seating the valve to cut off pump air to exhaust manifold and open a dump valve at lower end of bypass valve to momentarily divert pump air to atmosphere. In cases of excess pump volume and downstream restriction, excess pressure will unseat valve in lower portion of bypass valve and allow partial pump air flow to atmosphere. At same time valve in upper portion of bypass valve is still unseated, allowing a partial flow of pump air to exhaust manifold to meet system requirements.

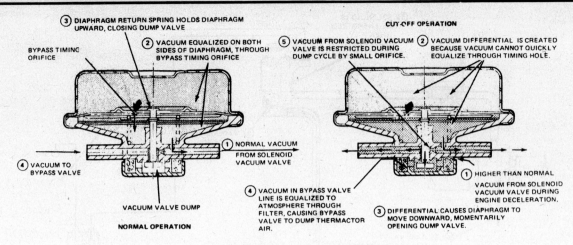

Fig. 22 Vacuum differential valve

Vacuum Differential Valve (VDV)

On 1976-77 models with 2800 cc engine, Thermactor system and catalytic converters, a (VDV) Fig. 22, is used to control the operation of the air bypass valve. Under normal operation, vacuum applied through the VDV holds the valve upward, blocking the vent port and allowing Thermactor air flow. During acceleration of deceleration or in case of system failure, the VDV momentarily cuts off vacuum flow to the bypass valve, diverting the Thermactor air flow to atmosphere. In case of excessive pressure of system restriction, the excess pressure will unseat the valve in the lower part of the bypass valve, allowing a partial flow of air to atmosphere. At the same time, the valve in the upper part of the valve remains unseated allowing a partial flow of air to the exhaust manifold.

Exhaust Check Valve

This valve, used on 1974 and 1976-77 models, allows thermactor air to enter exhaust port drillings, but prevents reverse flow of exhaust gases in event of improper operation of system components. This valve is located between by-pass valve and exhaust port drillings, either on air manifold or engine.

Cold Engine Lockout System

This system is used on 1976-77 models with the Thermactor system and catalytic converters. It consists of an electrically operated vacuum solenoid in the vacuum circuit to the by-pass

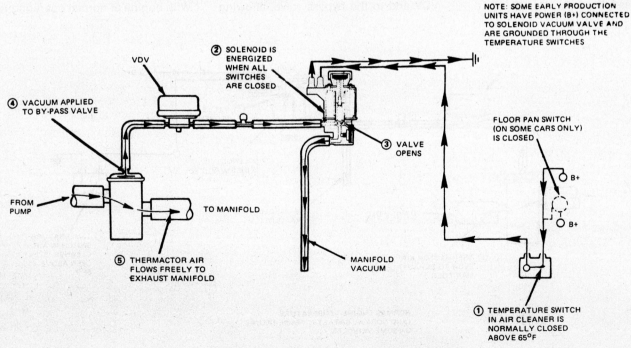

Fig. 23 Cold engine lockout system. Normally closed switches

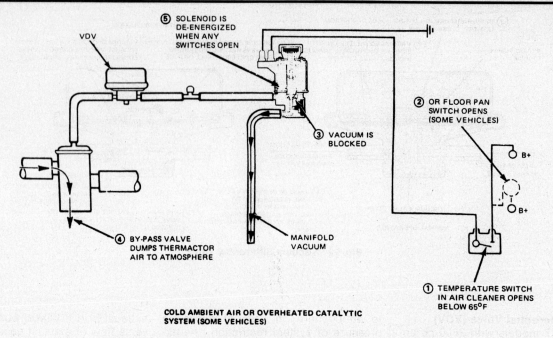

Fig. 24 Cold engine lockout system. Normally closed switches

valve and temperature sensors in the air cleaner housing and floor pan (on some models).

Two different type systems are used. The first type consists of normally closed switches that provide current to the solenoid only when the engine is warm. The second type consists of normally open switches that provide current to the solenoid only when the engine is cold. Operation of both systems is as follows:

Normally Closed Switches, Type 1, Figs. 23 & 24

With engine at normal operating temperature and all components operating properly, electrical path is provided through the solenoid vacuum valve, air cleaner sensor, floor pan temperature sensor (on some models) and to ground. This provides vacuum flow through the vacuum solenoid valve, VDV and to the bypass valve, allowing

Thermactor air flow.

If any of the switches should operate due to low intake air temperature or over-heated floor pan (on some models), the vacuum solenoid will stop vacuum flow, causing the bypass valve to divert Thermactor air to atmosphere.

Normally Open Switches, Type 2, Figs. 25 & 26

With engine at normal operating tem-

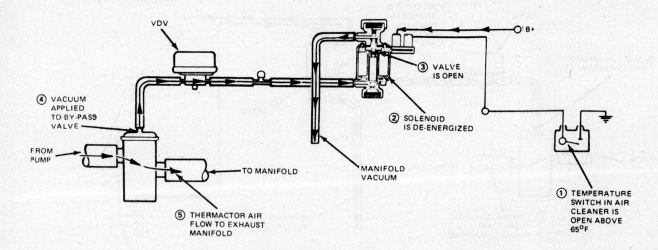

Fig. 25 Cold engine lockout system. Normally opened switches

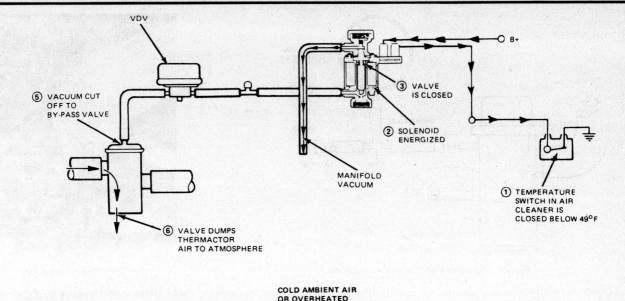

Fig. 26 Cold engine lockout system. Normally opened switches

perature and all components operating properly, the solenoid vacuum valve is inoperative, thereby providing vacuum flow through the solenoid vacuum valve, VDV and to the bypass valve, allowing Thermactor air flow. With the engine cold, the air cleaner sensor operates, providing current flow through the solenoid vacuum to ground. If the floor pan sensor operates (on some models), it will provide current flow through the solenoid to ground.

If the solenoid vacuum valve operates, it stops the vacuum flow to the bypass valve, causing the Thermactor air flow to be diverted to atmosphere.

Testing
AIR PUMP SUPPLY TEST
1. Remove air cleaner and inspect all hoses and hose connections in system, then check air pump belt tension.
2. Start engine and allow to reach operating temperature. If a noise complaint can isolated to air pump, replace pump.
3. Stop engine and disconnect air pump to bypass valve air supply hose at bypass valve.
4. Insert Thermactor pump test gauge T75L-9486-A in end of hose disconnected from bypass valve, then clamp hose securely to tester.

NOTE: Position gauge so that air blast emitted will be harmlessly dissipated.

5. Connect a tachometer to engine, then start engine.
6. Slowly increase engine speed to 1000 rpm and observe pressure reading on test gauge. On 1974 models, air pump pressure must be a minimum of 1 psi. On 1976-77 models, air pump pressure must be a minimum of 2.25 psi. If pump air supply is not within specifications, replace pump.
7. If test gauge is not available, increase engine speed to 1500 rpm and place hand over hose opening. Air flow should be heard and felt, if not replace pump.
8. Stop engine and remove test equipment. Connect air supply hose to bypass valve and install air cleaner.

AIR BYPASS VALVE TEST
1974 Models
1. Remove bypass valve pass to check valve hose at bypass valve.
2. With engine operating at normal idle speed, ensure air is flowing from bypass valve hose connection port to exhaust ports.
3. Pinch off vacuum hose to bypass valve for approximately 5 to 8 seconds to simulate air bypass cycle.
4. Release hose, air flow through bypass valve should diminish or stop for a short time, then return to normal.
5. Disconnect vacuum hose at bypass valve, then tee in vacuum gauge and short piece hose approximately 3 inches in length with a plug, Fig. 27.

6. Start engine and note vacuum reading.
7. Remove plug and connect hose to bypass valve and note reading. If vacuum reading does not correspond with reading obtained in step above within 60 seconds, replace bypass valve.

1976-77 Models
1. Remove bypass valve to check valve hose at bypass valve, then connect tachometer to engine.
2. Operate engine at 1500 rpm and check to ensure that air is flowing from bypass valve hose connection.
3. On models without catalytic converter, operate engine at 1500 rpm, place hand over bypass valve hose connection and pinch off vacuum hose for approximately 5 to 8 seconds, then release hose. Air flow should diminish or stop, then return to normal. If valve does not operate in this manner replace valve.
4. On models with catalytic converter, remove vacuum hose from top of bypass valve and plug. Operate engine 1500 rpm and place hand over bypass valve hose connection, there should be virtually no air flow from valve. Air flow will be discharged through exhaust ports in end of valve silencer cover. Remove plug from vacuum hose and connect hose to bypass valve.
5. On all models, install tool T75P-9486-A or equivalent to bypass valve outlet using a short length of hose. Increase engine speed to 1000 rpm

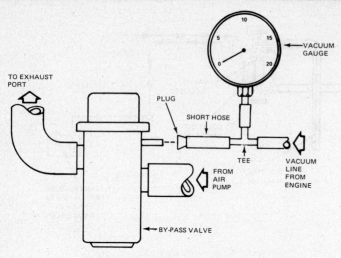

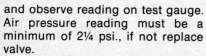

Fig. 27 By-pass valve test connections

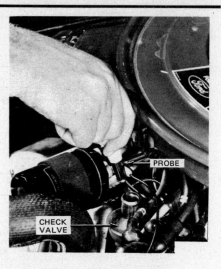

Fig. 28 Check valve test

and observe reading on test gauge. Air pressure reading must be a minimum of 2¼ psi., if not replace valve.

6. Remove test equipment, then connect bypass valve air supply hose.

CHECK VALVE TEST
1974 Models

1. Start engine and allow to reach operating temperature. Inspect hoses and connections for leaks.
2. Disconnect air supply hose at check valve.
3. Check to ensure valve plate is lightly seated against valve away from air manifold.
4. Insert probe into hose connection and depress valve plate. Valve plate should return freely to original position when released, Fig. 28.
5. If two check valves are used, check both for free operation.
6. With hoses disconnected, start engine, then slowly increase speed to 1500 rpm and check for exhaust gas leaks at check valve. If valve is leaking or stuck closed, replace valve.

NOTE: Flutter and vibration of valve at idle speed is normal due to exhaust pulsations in manifold.

1976-77 Models

1. Check condition and connection of hoses and correct as necessary.
2. Disconnect bypass valve to check valve hose at bypass valve.
3. Connect tester T75L-9487-A or equivalent to check valve hose and install clamp.
4. Squeeze bulb on tester to force as much air from bulb as possible. Quickly release bulb, bulb should remain collapsed for at least 15 seconds.

5. If bulb does not remain collapsed for at least 15 seconds, remove check valve hose and install a new piece of same diameter hose, then repeat test. If bulb now remains collapsed for at least 15 seconds, check valve hose is defective and should be replaced. If bulb does not remain collapsed for at least 15 seconds, check valve is defective and should be replaced.

CHECK VALVE PRESSURE TEST
1976-77 Models with Catalytic Converter

1. Connect tachometer to engine, then disconnect air hose at check valve.
2. Remove check valve from engine, then connect air hose to valve and tighten clamp.
3. Connect adapter to tester T75L-9487-A or equivalent. With engine operating at 1000 rpm, hold tester adapter against check valve air discharge hole. Pressure should be equal to or a maximum of ½ psi, below reading obtained in Air Bypass Valve Test step 5. If reading is more than ½ psi. below reading obtained previously, check valve should be replaced.
4. During test exhaust gas should be emitted from check valve mounting connection, if not, check external manifold or crossover pipe and internal drilled heads for restriction.
5. Install check valve, then connect hose and tighten clamp.
6. Start engine and operate at idle speed. Between idle speed and 1000 rpm, bypass valve should not dump air to atmosphere. If air is bypassed and Thermactor components check to be satisfactory, check external manifold or crossover pipe and drilled head passages for restriction.

VACUUM RESERVOIR CHECK
1976-77 Models with Catalytic Converter (If Equipped)

1. Disconnect vacuum hose from reservoir and connect vacuum hose of same diameter fitted with a tee.
2. Connect a vacuum gauge to one side of tee and an external vacuum source to other side of tee.
3. Charge reservoir to 14 in. Hg. of vacuum and trap. Vacuum reading on gauge should not drop more than 1 in. Hg. in one minute. If reservoir drops more than one in. Hg., it should be replaced.
4. Remove test equipment, then connect hose and tighten clamp.

SPARK CONTROL SYSTEMS

Non-Thermal Control System

1. Remove air cleaner and SDV, then check SDV as described under Spark Delay Valve Testing.
2. Connect tee fitting and vacuum gauge at distributor.
3. Observe vacuum gauge for a quick rise and fall as throttle is opened and closed. If vacuum is observed, system is operating properly. If vacuum is not observed, check for plugged vacuum lines and carburetor port.
4. If equipped with cooling PVS, with engine at operating temperature and idle speed, check vacuum at distributor. If vacuum reading is 2 in. Hg. or less, PVS is operating properly. If vacuum reading is more than 2 in. Hg., remove carburetor to PVS vacuum line at PVS. If vacuum reading is still greater than 2 in. Hg., PVS is leaking and should be replaced.
5. Remove vacuum gauge and tee, then install SDV and air cleaner and connect vacuum lines.

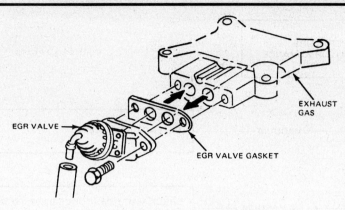

Fig. 29 Spacer entry EGR system

Cold Lock Out Spark System

1. Remove air cleaner and spark delay valve, then test spark delay valve as described under Spark Delay Valve Testing.
2. Connect tee fitting and vacuum gauge to primary side of distributor.
3. Observe vacuum gauge for a quick rise and fall as throttle is opened and closed. If vacuum is observed, system is operating properly. If vacuum is not observed, check for plugged vacuum lines for carburetor port.
4. Remove vacuum gauge and tee, then connect vacuum line and install SDV and air cleaner.

SOLENOID VACUUM VALVE

1976-77 Models With Catalytic Converter

NOTE: This normally closed vacuum solenoid is used in conjunction with type 1 air cleaner switch.

---

1. Start engine and allow to reach operating temperature.
2. With engine idling, disconnect vacuum hose to bypass valve. Air should be dumped to atmosphere through exhaust ports in end of valve silencer cover. Re-connect vacuum hose. If air is dumped to atmosphere, solenoid hoses are connected correctly.
3. Disconnect vacuum supply hose from solenoid valve and check to ensure vacuum is present. If vacuum is not present, check vacuum sources and repair as necessary.

NOTE: Vacuum supply hose always goes to bottom fitting of solenoid vacuum valve.

---

4. Wire connector from solenoid valve and determine which wire has B+ voltage when ignition switch is in the run position. Connect wire to solenoid valve.
5. With engine idling, ground other exposed terminal on solenoid valve. Thermactor air should not be dumped to atmosphere. If solenoid valve does not operate in this manner it should be replaced.

EGR SYSTEM

The Exhaust Gas Recirculation (EGR) System is used on 1974 and 1976-77 models. This system is designed to re-introduce small amounts of exhaust gas into combustion cycle, thus reducing combustion temperatures and generation of nitrous oxides. Amount of gas re-introduced and timing of cycle are controlled by engine vacuum, temperature and on some models vehicle speed.

The EGR valve is a vacuum operated unit that is attached to a spacer which is installed under the carburetor, Fig. 29. When valve is opened, exhaust gases are permitted to enter intake manifold passages. When valve is closed, exhaust gases are prevented from entering intake manifold passages. This valve can only be cleaned by sand blasting equipment or replaced.

The venturi vacuum amplifier is used on all 1974 models and 1976-77 models with 2300 cc engine, Figs. 30 and 31. This component uses a relatively weak venturi signal from throat of carburetor to shape a strong intake manifold signal to operate the EGR valve. Intake manifold vacuum operates EGR valve, under control of carburetor venturi vacuum. This makes it possible to achieve an accurate, repeatable and almost exact proportion of venturi airflow and EGR flow. The amplifier features a vacuum reservoir and check valve to maintain an adequate vacuum supply regardless of variations in engine manifold vacuum.

A relief valve is also used to cancel

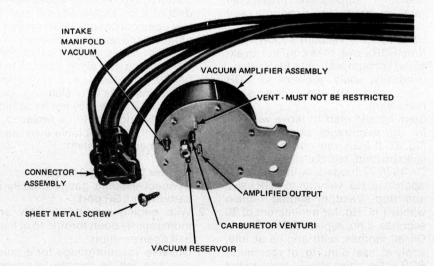

Fig. 30 Venturi vacuum amplifier. 1974 models

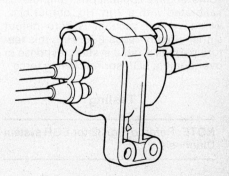

Fig. 31 Venturi vacuum amplifier. 1976-77 2300cc models

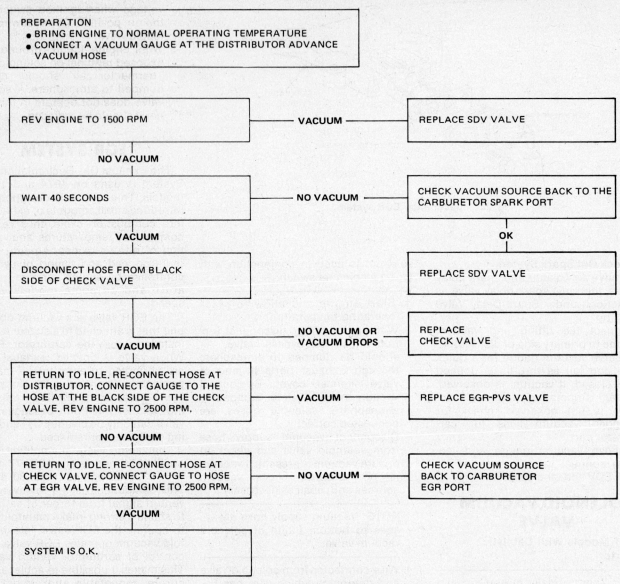

Fig. 32 EGR system diagnosis

output EGR signal whenever venturi vacuum signal is equal to or greater than intake manifold vacuum. This allows EGR valve to close at or near wide-open throttle, when maximum power is required from engine. On some engine applications, amplifier is calibrated with a 2 in. Hg. output bias. When venturi vacuum is zero output signal already reads 2 in. Hg., this feature permits a rapid system response in over-coming EGR spring closing force.

Testing

NOTE: Refer to Fig. 32 for EGR system Diagnosis.

EGR Valve In Vehicle Test
1. Start engine and allow to reach operating temperature. Inspect all vacuum hoses for condition and connections in system.
2. Remove EGR vacuum supply hose from EGR valve, then connect an external vacuum source to EGR valve.
3. Gradually apply vacuum to EGR valve and observe valve stem movement.
4. Stem should start to move within 1 in. Hg. diaphragm signal vacuum, Fig. 33. If EGR valve does not meet specification, replace valve.
5. On 1976-77 models, with engine off apply 8 in. Hg. vacuum to EGR valve and trap. Vacuum should remain within 1 in. Hg. for a minimum of 30 seconds, if not replace EGR valve.
6. On all models, with engine at idle, apply at least 8 in. Hg. of vacuum to EGR valve. Valve should move to full extent of travel and engine should start to run rough, idle speed should decrease or engine should stall. If idle does not change, EGR system is plugged and should be cleaned.
7. Connect hoses to EGR valve, then start engine and allow time for temperatures to stabilize. If engine idle is unacceptable after cleaning operation, EGR valve may not be sealing properly and should be replaced. If idle is still unacceptable problem is in other engine system.

Carburetor EGR Port(s) Check
1. Connect vacuum gauge directly to carburetor EGR port.
2. With engine running, quickly and momentarily open throttle to at least half open position.
3. Observe vacuum gauge for a quick rise and fall as throttle is opened and closed. If no vacuum reading is

Basic No. 9D475	Type	Start-to-Open Inches HG
75TF-AA D4TE-AA	P	2.9
75TF-GA D4UE-AA	P	2.9
75TF-MA D4TE-FA	TS	2.5
75TF-FA D4TE-JA	TS	3.0

P – Poppet   TS – Tapered Stem

Fig. 33   EGR start to open specifications

observed, carburetor EGR port is plugged and should be cleaned.

EGR PVS Functional Check (Two Connector Type)

NOTE: Ensure EGR valve, external vacuum passages and solenoid valve, if equipped are functional.

1. Disconnect both vacuum hoses at PVS valve, then connect vacuum gauge to either port. Connect an external vacuum source to other PVS port.
2. Start engine and allow to reach operating temperature, a vacuum reading should be noted on vacuum gauge. If no reading is noted, PVS has failed and should be replaced.

EGR PVS Functional Check (Three Connector Type)

NOTE: Ensure EGR valve, external vacuum passages and solenoid valve, if equipped are functional.

1. Disconnect EGR valve vacuum hose at carburetor and connect an external vacuum source to hose.
2. Disconnect EGR valve hose at EGR valve and connect a vacuum gauge.
3. Start engine and allow to reach operating temperature, a vacuum reading should be noted on vacuum gauge. If no vacuum reading is noted, PVS should be replaced.

EGR Venturi Amplifier Check

NOTE: Before checking amplifier, inspect all other components in system and vacuum hoses for condition and routing.

1. Operate engine until normal operating temperature is obtained.
2. Disconnect amplifier vacuum hose at EGR valve and connect a vacuum gauge to hose.
3. On 1974 models, disconnect vacuum hose at carburetor venturi.
4. On 1976-77 models, disconnect reservoir vacuum hose and tee hose with vacuum source line, then connect vacuum source line to manifold vacuum.
5. On 1974 models, with engine idling vacuum gauge reading should be within .3 in. Hg. of specified bias valve. If reading is not within specifications, replace amplifier.
6. On 1976-77 models, depress accelerator and release after engine has reached 1500 to 2000 rpm. After engine has reached idle speed disconnect vacuum hose at carburetor venturi and note vacuum gauge reading. Vacuum gauge reading should be within .3 in. Hg. of specified bias value shown in Fig. 34. If reading is not within specifications, replace amplifier.
7. On all models, depress accelerator and release after engine has reached 1500 to 2000 rpm. If vacuum gauge shows an increase of greater than 1 in. Hg. during acceleration period, replace amplifier.
8. Connect vacuum hose to carburetor venturi port. If vacuum gauge reading increases more than .5 in. Hg., check idle speed and adjust as necessary.
9. On 1974 models, disconnect external reservoir vacuum hose at amplifier and cap. Increase engine speed to 1500 to 2000 rpm, vacuum reading should increase to 4 in. Hg. or more. If not replace amplifier.
10. On 1976-77 models, increase engine speed to 1500 to 2000 rpm, vacuum should increase to 4 in. Hg. or more and return to bias vacuum after engine returns to idle speed. If readings are not within specifications, replace amplifier.

11. On 1976-77 models, connect "R" nipple to manifold vacuum, "S" nipple to spark port vacuum, "V" nipple to venturi vacuum and "C" nipple to vacuum gauge. Depress accelerator and release after engine has reached 1500 to 2000 rpm. After engine has returned to idle speed, remove vacuum hose at venturi. Check spark port vacuum, a vacuum reading of greater than 2 in. Hg. could cause amplifier vacuum output to increase. Vacuum gauge reading should be less than .5 in. Hg., if not replace amplifier.
12. On 1976-77 models, to check external amplifier vacuum reservoir proceed as follows:
   a. If reservoir does not have an external check valve, disconnect reservoir to amplifier hose. Charge reservoir with external vacuum source to 14 in. Hg. and trap. Vacuum should remain within 1 in. Hg. for 1 minute, if not replace reservoir.
   b. If reservoir is equipped with an external check valve, using an external vacuum source apply 15 in. Hg. at tee between check and reservoir on amplifier side of tee and trap. Vacuum should remain within 1 in. Hg. for 1 minute, if not proceed to step c.
   c. Remove hose to reservoir at tee and charge reservoir to 15 in. Hg. and trap. Vacuum must remain within 1 in. Hg. for 1 minute, if not replace reservoir. If reservoir is within specifications proceed to step d.
   d. Remove vacuum hose to check valve at tee and apply 15 in. Hg. of vacuum and trap. Vacuum reading should remain within 1 in. Hg. for one minute, if not replace check valve.

Cold Start Cycle (CSC)

NOTE: This system is used on all 1974 and 1976-77 models.

Part Number Prefix & Suffix (Basic No. 9E451)	Code Number on Unit	Amplification Ratio of Unit	Bias Rating of Unit (In. Hg.)	Service Bias Specification
Stamped in "Yellow"				
75EB - B1A, -2A, -3A	10-0	10:1	0	0-5
75EB - C1A, -2A, -3A	10-5	10:1	.5	.2 - .8
75EB - A1A, -2A, -3A	10-1	10:1	1.0	.7 - 1.3

Note: The different numerals in the suffix denote alternate vendor sources "1" for Frame, "2" for Marvel Scheblor, "3" for Ranco

Fig. 34   Vacuum bias specifications

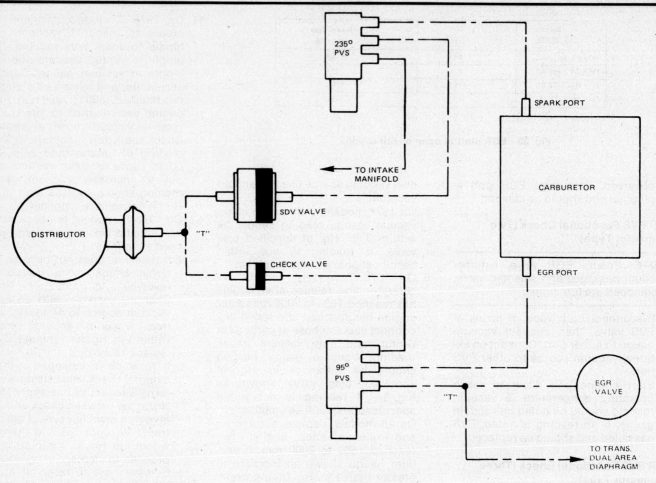

Fig. 35 EGR/CSC System

The EGR/CSC System regulates both distributor advance and EGR valve operation according to coolant temperature by sequentially switching vacuum signals. The major system components are a 95° F EGR-PVS (Ported Vacuum Switch) valve, a SDV (Spark Delay Valve) and a vacuum check valve, Fig. 35.

When engine coolant temperature is below 82° F, The EGR-PVS valve admits carburetor EGR port vacuum (at about 2500 RPM) directly to the distributor advance diaphragm, through the one way check valve. At the same time, the EGR-PVS valve shuts off carburetor EGR vacuum to the EGR valve and transmission diaphragm.

When engine coolant temperature is 95° F and above, the EGR-PVS valve is actuated and directs carburetor EGR vacuum to the EGR valve and transmission diaphragm instead of the distributor. At temperatures between 82° and 95° F, the EGR-PVS valve may be open, closed or in mid position.

The Spark Delay Valve (SDV) delays carburetor vacuum to the distributor advance by restricting the vacuum signal through the SDV for a predeter-

mined time. During normal acceleration, little or no vacuum is admitted to the distributor advance diaphragm until acceleration is completed and engine coolant temperature is 95° F or higher.

The check valve blocks off vacuum signal from the SDV to the EGR-PVS valve so that carburetor spark vacuum will not be dissipated when the EGR-PVS valve is actuated above 95° F.

The 235° F PVS valve which is not part of the EGR-CSC system is connected to the distributor vacuum advance to prevent engine overheating while idling.

SPARK DELAY VALVE
Description

NOTE: The spark delay valve is used on 1974 and 1976-77 models.

This unit is used in conjunction with some of the other Ford systems. Its purpose is to further reduce emissions by delaying the spark advance during rapid acceleration and by cutting off advance immediately upon deceleration.

This plastic disc-shaped valve is installed in the carburetor vacuum line at the distributor advance diaphragm. It is a one way valve and will not operate if installed backwards. The black side of the valve must be toward the carburetor. This valve cannot be repaired.

NOTE: On all systems which employ the dual diaphragm distributor the line which has high vacuum at idle (normal operating temperature) is connected to the secondary (retard) side of the distributor vacuum advance unit. This is the connection closest to the distributor cap.

Testing

NOTE: To perform the following procedure, an external vacuum source capable of maintaining a minimum constant 10 inches Hg. is required.

Mono Delay Valve
1. Set external vacuum source to 10 inches Hg. and connect black side of delay valve to vacuum source.

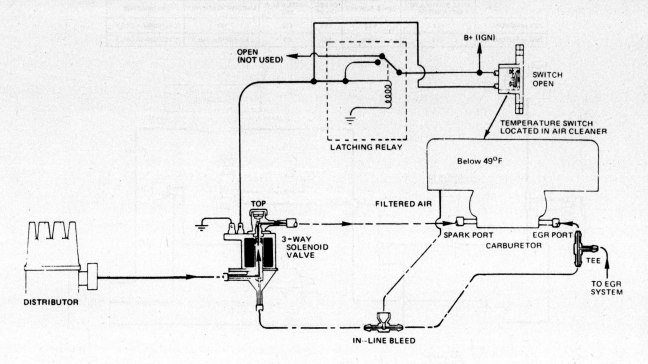

Fig. 36 CTAV system below 49°F

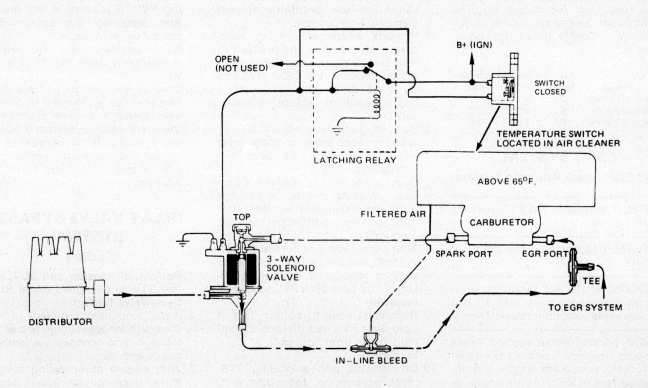

Fig. 37 CTAV system above 65°F

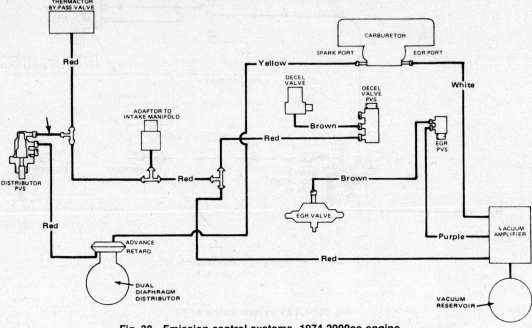

	DUAL DIAPHRAGM DISTRIBUTOR	EGR & EGR PVS	DECEL VALVE	DECEL VALVE PVS	VACUUM RESERVOIR	THERMACTOR
2000 cc MANUAL	YES	YES	YES	YES	NO	CALIFORNIA ONLY
2000 cc AUTOMATIC	YES	YES	NO	NO	CALIFORNIA ONLY	CALIFORNIA ONLY

EMISSION CONTROL SYSTEM COMPONENT APPLICATION

Fig. 38 Emission control systems. 1974 2000cc engine

2. Connect a vacuum gauge with a 24 inch hose to colored side of delay valve.

3. Apply 10 inches Hg. vacuum and observe time in seconds for gauge to read from 0-8 inches Hg. The minimum and maximum time for gauge to read 8 inches Hg. should be as follows:

Color	I.D. No.	Time in Seconds Min.	Max.
Black and Brown	2	2	5
Black and White	5	4	12
Black and Yellow	10	5.8	14

CSSA SYSTEM

Cold Start Spark Advance System

NOTE: If engine is pinging, perform steps 1 thru 4.

1. Connect tachometer and start engine.

CAUTION: Do not leave transmission in drive for more than 15 seconds while performing steps 2 and 4.

2. With parking brake applied, brake pedal depressed and transmission in drive, accelerate engine and observe rpm at which spark knock or pinging occurs.

3. Place transmission in neutral and accelerate engine to 1500 rpm to allow transmission to cool. Repeat this step three times.

4. Disconnect and plug vacuum advance line from distributor. Repeat step 2 to recorded rpm.

5. If spark knock or pinging reoccurred, stop engine and proceed to next step. If spark knock or pinging did not reoccur, the CSSA PVS and or retard delay valve (if used) is faulty. Repair or replace as necessary.

6. Remove spark delay valve (SDV), or vacuum check valve, or spark delay valve and check as described further on.

7. Using a tee fitting, connect a vacuum gauge to distributor advance hose and disconnect and plug vacuum hose from bottom port of Cold Start PVS.

8. With engine idling at normal operating temperature, there should be no vacuum reading. If vacuum is obtained, the Cold Start PVS should be replaced.

9. Reconnect hose to bottom port of Cold Start PVS and disconnect and plug hose from top port of Cold Start PVS.

10. On vehicles with a cooling PVS, check vacuum at distributor with engine at normal idle. If reading is 2 inches Hg. or less, the cooling PVS is operating properly. If vacuum reading is greater than specified, disconnect and plug the top vacuum line from the carburetor to the cooling PVS. If reading is still greater than specified, the cooling PVS should be replaced.

11. With engine idling in neutral, momentarily open the throttle half way.

12. Observe vacuum gauge for a quick rise and fall as throttle is opened and closed. If vacuum is obtained, the spark advance system is operating properly. If no vacuum is obtained, check vacuum line for leakage or obstruction and correct as necessary.

DELAY VALVE BYPASS SYSTEM

Testing

1. Remove air cleaner and SDV, then test STV as described under Spark Delay Valve Testing.

2. Install a connector in place of SDV, then disconnect vacuum line at distributor and connect a vacuum gauge and tee.

3. With engine at operating temperature, momentarily open throttle and observe vacuum gauge reading

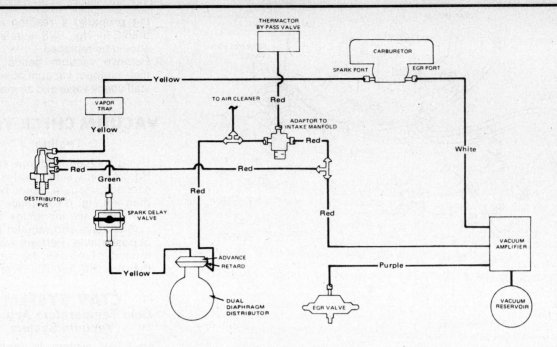

Fig. 39 Emission control systems. 1974 V6-2800cc engine

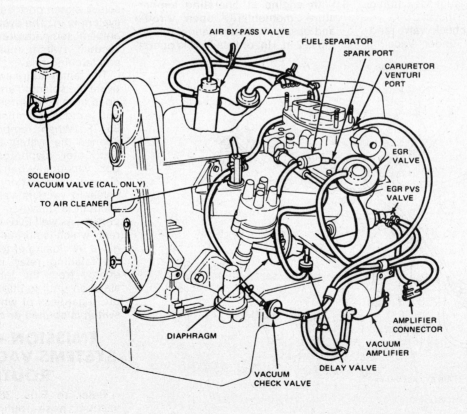

Fig. 40 Emission control systems. 1976-77 2300cc engine

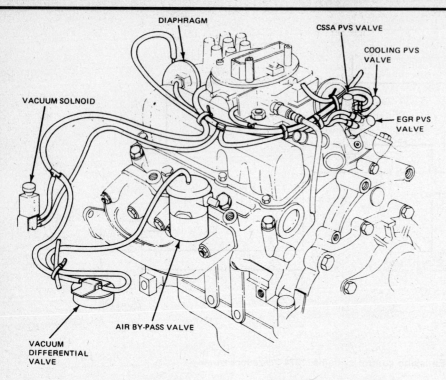

Fig. 41 Emission control systems. 1976-77 V6-2800cc engine except Calif.

for a quick rise and fall as throttle is opened and closed. If vacuum is observed, system is operating properly. If no vacuum is observed check for plugged vacuum line or carburetor port.
4. Remove vacuum gauge, tee fitting and connector, then install SDV.
5. Remove vacuum check valve and test as described under Vacuum

Check Valve Test.
6. Install check valve in hose to distributor.
7. Connect vacuum gauge and tee in vacuum line from PVS to check valve.
8. With engine at operating temperature, momentarily open throttle and observe vacuum gauge. If reading is 2 in. Hg. or less PVS is operat-

ing properly. If reading is greater than 2 in. Hg., PVS is defective and should be replaced.
9. Remove vacuum gauge and tee, then connect vacuum hoses and install check valve and air cleaner.

VACUUM CHECK VALVE
Testing

1. Using a vacuum source, apply 5 in. Hg. to check side of valve. After 30 seconds, vacuum should not be less than 4 in. Hg., if so replace valve.
2. Connect vacuum gauge to check side of valve and vacuum source to opposite side. Perform test as performed in step one, if vacuum is less than 4 in. Hg., replace valve.

CTAV SYSTEM
Cold Temperature Actuated Vacuum System

The CTAV system is used on all 1976-77 models. This system is used to more accurately match spark advance to engine requirements under cold weather conditions. If ambient air temperature is below 49° F, system will select spark port vacuum for distributor modulation, Fig. 36, and if temperature is above 65° F, system will select EGR vacuum, Fig. 37. If temperature is between 49° F and 65° F, system may select either port depending on cycle system is in. The system consists of an ambient temperature switch, three way vacuum switch, inline vacuum bleed and latching relay.

The temperature switch is used to activate the solenoid and it is calibrated to open at temperatures at or below 49° F and to close at temperatures at or above 65° F. When temperature switch is opened the system is inoperative and distributor diaphragm receives spark port vacuum. When switch is closed, current from battery energizes 3 way solenoid vacuum valve and EGR port vacuum is delivered to distributor diaphragm as well EGR valve. The latching relay which is normally off, is also energized by closing of temperature switch. On latching relay is on, it receives energy from the ignition switch and stays on until ignition switch is turned off, regardless of whether temperature switch is opened or closed.

EMISSION CONTROL SYSTEMS VACUUM HOSE ROUTING

Refer to Figs. 38 through 42 for vacuum hose routing for 1974 and 1976-77 models.

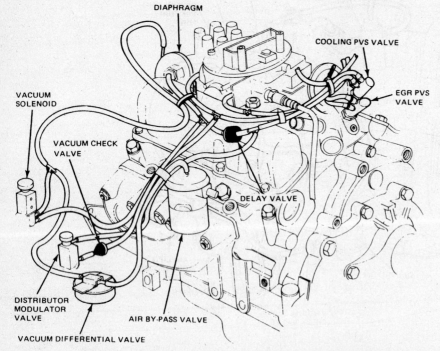

Fig. 42 Emission control systems. 1976-77 V6-2800cc engine California

Clutch & Transmission Section
Clutch & Manual Transmission

CLUTCH PEDAL, ADJUST

1. Remove release lever boot and daub ball joint lubricant on ball end of cable, then replace boot.
2. Pull clutch pedal back against stop and place wooden block under pedal, then raise vehicle.
3. On models with 1600, 2000 or 2300 cc engine, loosen adjusting nut locknut, then pull clutch cable forward to remove slack from system. While holding cable, turn adjusting nut to obtain specified clearance between clutch housing cable bushing and adjusting nut. Clearance should be .138 to .144 in. on 1972 models, .120 to .140 in. on 1973 models and 3.15 to 3.65 mm. on 1974 and 1976-77 models. Tighten locknut and lower vehicle, Fig. 1.
4. On models with 2600 and 2800 cc engines, pull clutch cable forward until adjusting nut is pulled out of recess in clutch housing cable bushing. It may be necessary to remove boot from side of clutch housing and manually pull release lever forward to assist in freeing adjusting nut from recess. With adjusting nut out recess, pull clutch cable forward until release lever free play is eliminated, then turn adjusting nut until it just comes in contact with cable bushing, Fig. 1. Align adjusting nut and bushing flats, then release cable and allow nut to enter recess.
5. Remove wooden block from under clutch pedal, then full depress clutch two times before measuring clutch pedal free play.
6. With clutch pedal against stop, measure distance from lower edge of pedal to floor board, Fig. 1. Depress pedal until a slight pressure is felt, then measure distance to floor board. On models with 1600, 2000 and 2300 clutch pedal free play should be ½ to ¾ in. for 1972 models, .780 to .930 in. for 1973 models, ¾ to $^{15}/_{16}$ in. for 1974 models and .866 to 1.023 in. for 1976-77 models. On models with 2600 and 2800 cc engine, clutch pedal free play should be .940 to 1.080 for 1972-73 models, $^{15}/_{16}$ to $1^{1}/_{16}$ for 1974 models and 1.063 to 1.220 in. for 1976-77 models.
7. If clutch pedal free play is not within

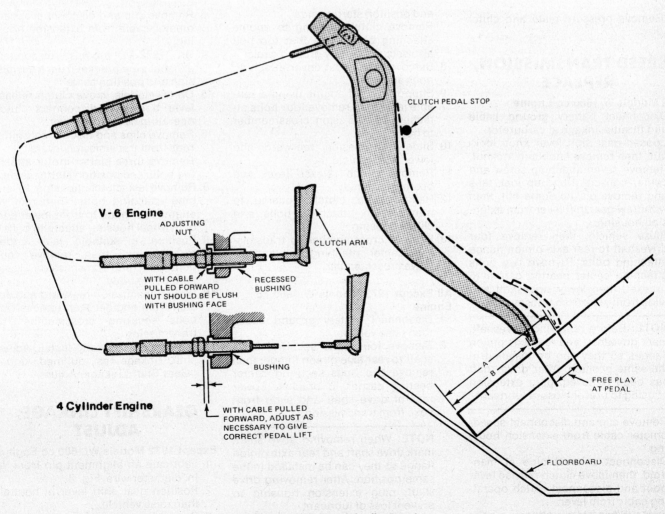

Fig. 1 Clutch pedal adjustment

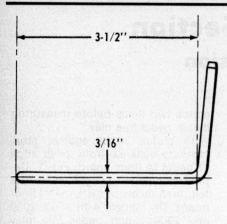

Fig. 2   Alignment pin

limits, readjust cable as described above. Also ensure clutch release lever boot is properly installed.

CLUTCH, REPLACE

1. Remove transmission and clutch housing as an assembly as outlined under "Transmission Replace."
2. Loosen pressure plate attaching evenly, working diagonally across clutch.
3. Remove pressure plate and clutch disc.

4 SPEED TRANSMISSION, REPLACE

1972 Models W/1600 cc Engine

1. Disconnect battery ground cable and throttle linkage at carburetor.
2. Loosen gear shift lever knob locknut, then remove knob and locknut. Remove seven attaching screw and center console. Bend up lock tabs and remove plastic dome nut, then withdraw gearshift lever from extension housing.
3. Raise vehicle, then remove four driveshaft to rear axle pinion flange attaching bolts. Remove two bolts attaching center bearing carrier to bracket, then lower driveshaft and slide front yoke from transmission.

NOTE: Before removing driveshaft, mark driveshaft and rear axle pinion flanges so they can be installed in the same position. After drive shaft has been removed, plug extension housing to prevent loss of lubricant.

4. Remove clip and disconnect speedometer cable from extension housing.
5. Disconnect exhaust pipe at manifold, then move clutch release lever boot and disconnect clutch operating cable from lever.
6. Remove two starter attaching bolts

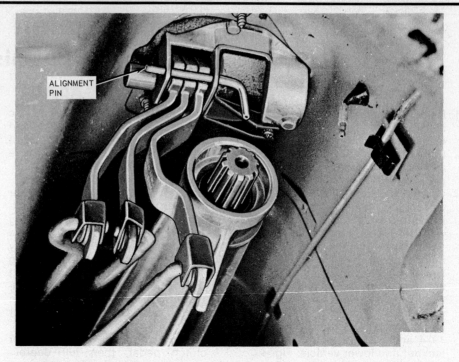

Fig. 3   Gear shift linkage adjustment. Except 1972 models w/1600cc engine

and position starter aside.
7. Remove clutch housing to engine attaching bolts, note that top bolt also secures battery ground cable.
8. Remove lower dust cover attaching bolts and cover.
9. Support rear of engine using a suitable jack, then remove four bolts attaching transmission crossmember to body.
10. Slide transmission rearward and lower from vehicle.
11. Remove clutch release lever and bearing assembly.
12. Remove four clutch housing to transmission attaching bolts and clutch housing.
13. Remove crossmember to transmission center attaching bolt and remove crossmember.

All Except 1972 Models W/1600 cc Engine

1. Disconnect battery ground cable, then raise vehicle.
2. Remove four bolts securing drive shaft to rear axle pinion flange, then remove two bolts securing center bearing carrier to bracket. Lower rear of drive shaft and slide front yoke from transmission.

NOTE: When removing drive shaft, mark drive shaft and rear axle pinion flange so they can be installed in the same position. After removing drive shaft, plug extension housing to prevent loss of lubricant.

3. Remove clip and disconnect speedometer cable from extension housing.
4. On 1972-74 models, disconnect exhaust pipe bracket from transmission and position aside.
5. On all models, move clutch release lever boot and disconnect clutch operating cable from lever.
6. Remove clips and disconnect shifter rods from transmission levers.
7. Remove three starter motor attaching bolts and position starter aside.
8. Remove six clutch housing to engine attaching bolts, then remove engine rear plate to front lower part of flywheel housing attaching bolts.
9. Position a suitable jack under transmission, then remove four bolts attaching transmission crossmember to body.
10. Slide transmission rearward and detach from engine, then remove two bolts securing crossmember to transmission.
11. Reverse procedure to install. Adjust shift linkage as outlined under "Gear Shift Linkage, Adjust."

GEARSHIFT LINKAGE, ADJUST

Except 1972 Models W/1600 cc Engine

1. Fabricate an alignment pin from 3/16 in. diameter wire, Fig. 2.
2. Position gear shift lever in neutral, then raise vehicle.
3. Remove retainers and disconnect

shifter rods from transmission levers.

4. Insert alignment pin through gear shift body, ensure shifter levers are

correctly positioned, Fig. 3.

5. Position transmission levers in neutral, then adjust length of shifter rods so that they can be inserted into transmission shift levers.

6. Install shifter rods and retainers, then remove alignment pin.

7. Lower vehicle and check shifter operation.

Automatic Transmission

TROUBLE SHOOTING

Refer to Figs. 4 through 4F for trouble shooting procedures.

PROBLEM DIAGNOSIS — AUTOMATIC TRANSMISSION

PROBLEM	POSSIBLE CAUSE	CORRECTION
• No drive, slips or chatters in first gear in D. All other gears normal.	• Faulty one-way clutch.	• Repair or replace one-way clutch.
• No drive, slips or chatters in second gear.	• Improper fluid level.	• Perform fluid level check.
	• Damaged or improperly adjusted linkage.	• Repair or adjust linkage.
	• Intermediate band out of adjustment.	• Adjust intermediate band.
	• Faulty band or clutch application, or oil pressure control system.	• Perform control pressure test.
	• Faulty servo and/or internal leaks.	• Perform air pressure test.
	• Dirty or sticking valve body.	• Clean, repair or replace valve body.
	• Polished, glazed intermediate band or drum.	• Replace or repair as required.
• Starts in high — in D drag or lockup at 1 2 shift point or in 2 or 1.	• Improper fluid level.	• Perform fluid level check.
	• Damaged or improperly adjusted linkage.	• Repair or adjust linkage.
	• Faulty governor.	• Repair or replace governor, clean screen.
	• Faulty clutches and/or internal leaks.	• Perform air pressure test.
	• Valve body loose.	• Tighten to specifications.
	• Dirty, sticking valve body.	• Clean, repair or replace valve body.
	• Poor mating of valve body to case mounting surfaces.	• Replace valve body or case.
• Starts up in 2nd or 3rd but no lockup at 1-2 shift points.	• Improper fluid level.	• Perform fluid level check.
	• Damaged or improperly adjusted linkage.	• Repair or adjust linkage.
	• Improper band and/or clutch application, or oil pressure control system.	• Perform control pressure test.
	• Faulty governor.	• Perform governor check. Replace or repair governor, clean screen.
	• Valve body loose.	• Tighten to specification.
	• Dirty or sticking valve body.	• Clean, repair or replace valve body.
	• Cross leaks between valve body and case mating surface.	• Replace valve body and/or case as required.

Fig. 4   Automatic transmission trouble shooting guide. Part 1 of 7

PROBLEM DIAGNOSIS – AUTOMATIC TRANSMISSION

PROBLEM	POSSIBLE CAUSE	CORRECTION
• Slow initial engagement.	• Improper fluid level. • Damaged or improperly adjusted linkage. • Contaminated fluid. • Faulty clutch and band application, or oil control pressure system.	• Add fluid as required. • Repair or adjust linkage. • Perform fluid level check. • Perform control pressure test.
• Rough initial engagement in either forward or reverse.	• Improper fluid level. • High engine idle. • Looseness in the driveshaft, U-joints or engine mounts. • Incorrect linkage adjustment. • Faulty clutch or band application, or oil control pressure system. • Sticking or dirty valve body.	• Perform fluid level check. • Adjust idle to specifications. • Repair as required. • Repair or adjust linkage. • Perform control pressure test. • Clean, repair or replace valve body.
• No drive in any gear.	• Improper fluid level. • Damaged or improperly adjusted linkage. • Faulty clutch or band application, or oil control pressure system. • Internal leakage. • Valve body loose. • Faulty clutches. • Sticking or dirty valve body.	• Perform fluid level check. • Repair or adjust linkage. • Perform control pressure test. • Check and repair as required. • Tighten to specification. • Perform air pressure test. • Clean, repair or replace valve body.
• No drive forward – reverse OK.	• Improper fluid level. • Damaged or improperly adjusted linkage. • Faulty clutch or band application, or oil pressure control system. • Faulty forward clutch or governor. • Valve body loose • Dirty or sticking valve body.	• Perform fluid level check. • Repair or adjust linkage. • Perform control pressure test. • Perform air pressure test. • Tighten to specification. • Clean, repair or replace valve body.
• No drive, slips or chatters in reverse – forward OK.	• Improper fluid level. • Damaged or improperly adjusted linkage. • Looseness in the driveshaft, U-joints or engine mounts. • Bands or clutches out of adjustment. • Faulty oil pressure control system. • Faulty reverse clutch or servo. • Valve body loose. • Dirty or sticking valve body.	• Perform fluid level check. • Repair or adjust linkage. • Repair as required. • **Adjust reverse band.** • Perform control pressure test. • Perform air pressure test. • Tighten to specifications. • Clean, repair or replace valve body.

Fig. 4A   Automatic transmission trouble shooting guide. Part 2 of 7

PROBLEM DIAGNOSIS – AUTOMATIC TRANSMISSION

PROBLEM	POSSIBLE CAUSE	CORRECTION
• Shift points incorrect.	• Improper fluid level. • Improper vacuum hose routing or leaks. • Improper operation of EGR system. • Linkage out of adjustment. • Improper speedometer gear installed. • Improper clutch or band application, or oil pressure control system. • Faulty governor. • Dirty or sticking valve body.	• Perform fluid level check. • Correct hose routing. • Repair or replace as required. • Repair or adjust linkage. • Replace gear. • Perform shift test and control pressure test. • Repair or replace governor – clean screen. • Clean, repair or replace valve body.
• No upshift at any speed in D.	• Improper fluid level. • Vacuum leak to diaphragm unit. • Linkage out of adjustment. • Improper band or clutch application, or oil pressure control system. • Faulty governor. • Dirty or sticking valve body.	• Perform fluid level check. • Repair vacuum line or hose. • Repair or adjust linkage. • Perform control pressure test. • Repair or replace governor, clean screen. • Clean, repair or replace valve body.
• Shifts 1-3 in D.	• Improper fluid level. • Intermediate band out of adjustment. • Faulty front servo and/or internal leaks. • Polished, glazed band or drum. • Improper band or clutch application, or oil pressure control system. • Dirty or sticking valve body.	• Perform fluid level check. • Adjust band. • Perform air pressure test. Repair front servo and/or internal leaks. • Repair or replace band or drum. • Perform control pressure test. • Clean, repair or replace valve body.
• Engine over-speeds on 2-3 shift.	• Improper fluid level. • Linkage out of adjustment. • Improper band or clutch application, or oil pressure control system. • Faulty high clutch and/or intermediate servo. • Dirty or sticking valve body.	• Perform fluid level check. • Repair or adjust linkage. • Perform control pressure test. • Perform air pressure test. Repair as required. • Clean repair or replace valve body.

Fig. 4B Automatic transmission trouble shooting guide. Part 3 of 7

PROBLEM DIAGNOSIS – AUTOMATIC TRANSMISSION

PROBLEM	POSSIBLE CAUSE	CORRECTION
• Mushy 1-2 shift.	• Improper fluid level • Incorrect engine idle and/or performance. • Improper linkage adjustment. • Intermediate band out of adjustment. • Improper band or clutch application, or oil pressure control system. • Faulty high clutch and/or intermediate servo release. • Polished, glazed band or drum. • Dirty or sticking valve body.	• Perform fluid level check. • Tune adjust engine idle as required • Repair or adjust linkage. • Adjust intermediate band. • Perform control pressure test. • Perform air pressure test. Repair as required. • Repair or replace as required. • Clean, repair or replace valve body.
• Rough 1-2 shift.	• Improper fluid level. • Incorrect engine idle or performance. • Intermediate band out of adjustment. • Improper band or clutch application, or oil pressure control system. • Faulty intermediate servo. • Dirty or sticking valve body.	• Perform fluid level check. • Tune, and adjust engine idle. • Adjust intermediate band. • Perform control pressure test. • Air pressure check intermediate servo. • Clean, repair or replace valve body.
• Rough 2-3 shift.	• Improper fluid level. • Incorrect engine idle or performance. • Improper band or clutch application, or oil control pressure system. • Faulty intermediate servo apply and release and high clutch piston check ball. • Dirty or sticking valve body.	• Perform fluid level check. • Tune and adjust engine idle. • Perform control pressure test. • Air pressure test the intermediate servo apply and release and the high clutch piston check ball. Repair as required. • Clean, repair or replace valve body.
• Rough 3-1 shift at closed throttle in D.	• Improper fluid level. • Incorrect engine idle or performance. • Improper linkage adjustment. • Improper clutch or band application, or oil pressure control system. • Faulty governor operation. • Dirty or sticking valve body.	• Perform fluid level check. • Tune, and adjust engine idle. • Repair or adjust linkage. • Perform control pressure test. • Perform governor test. Repair as required. • Clean, repair or replace valve body

Fig. 4C Automatic transmission trouble shooting guide. Part 4 of 7

PROBLEM DIAGNOSIS — AUTOMATIC TRANSMISSION

PROBLEM	POSSIBLE CAUSE	CORRECTION
• No forced downshifts.	• Improper fluid level. • Linkage out of adjustment. • Improper clutch or band application, or oil pressure control system. • Faulty internal kickdown linkage. • Dirty or sticking valve body.	• Perform fluid level check. • Repair or adjust linkage. • Perform control pressure test. • Repair internal kickdown linkage. • Clean, repair or replace valve body.
• No 3-1 shift in D.	• Improper fluid level. • Incorrect engine idle, or performance. • Faulty governor. • Dirty or sticking valve body.	• Perform fluid level check. • Tune, and adjust engine idle. • Perform governor check. Repair as required. • Clean, repair or replace valve body.
• Runaway engine on 3-2 downshift.	• Improper fluid level. • Linkage out of adjustment. • Intermediate band out of adjustment. • Improper band or clutch application, or oil pressure control system. • Faulty intermediate servo. • Polished, glazed band or drum. • Dirty or sticking valve body.	• Perform fluid level check. • Repair or adjust linkage. • Adjust intermediate band. • Perform control pressure test. • Air pressure test check the intermediate servo. Repair servo and/or seals. • Repair or replace as required. • Clean, repair or replace valve body.
• No engine braking in manual first gear.	• Improper fluid level. • Linkage out of adjustment. • Bands or clutches out of adjustment. • Faulty oil pressure control system. • Faulty reverse servo. • Polished, glazed band or drum.	• Perform fluid level check. • Repair or adjust linkage. • **Adjust reverse band.** • Perform control pressure test. • Perform air pressure test of reverse servo. Repair reverse clutch or rear servo as required. • Repair or replace as required.

Fig. 4D Automatic transmission trouble shooting guide. Part 5 of 7

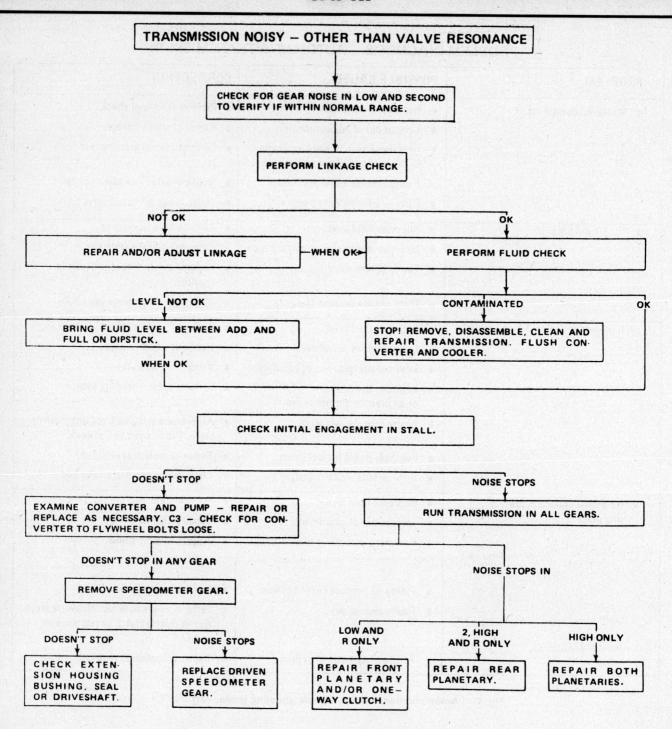

Fig. 4E   Automatic transmission trouble shooting guide. Part 6 of 7

PROBLEM DIAGNOSIS — AUTOMATIC TRANSMISSION

PROBLEM	POSSIBLE CAUSE	CORRECTION
• No engine braking in manual second gear.	• Improper fluid level. • Linkage out of adjustment • Intermediate band out of adjustment. • Improper band or clutch application, or oil pressure control system. • Intermediate servo leaking. • Polished or glazed band or drum.	• Perform fluid level check. • Repair or adjust linkage. • Adjust intermediate band. • Perform control pressure test • Perform air pressure test of intermediate servo for leakage. Repair as required. • Repair or replace as required.
• Transmission noisy — valve resonance.	• Improper fluid level. • Linkage out of adjustment. • Improper band or clutch application, or oil pressure control system. • Cooler lines grounding. • Dirty sticking valve body. • Internal leakage or pump cavitation.	• Perform fluid level check. • Repair or adjust linkage. • Perform control pressure test. • Free up cooler lines. • Clean, repair or replace valve body. • Repair as required.
• Transmission overheats.	• Improper fluid level. • Incorrect engine idle, or performance. • Improper clutch or band application, or oil pressure control system • Restriction in cooler or lines. • Seized one-way clutch. • Dirty or sticking valve body.	• Perform fluid level check. • Tune, or adjust engine idle. • Perform control pressure test. • Repair restriction. • Replace one-way clutch. • Clean, repair or replace valve body.
• Transmission fluid leaks.	• Improper fluid level. • Leakage at gasket, seals, etc. • Vacuum diaphragm unit leaking.	• Perform fluid level check. • Remove all traces of lube on exposed surfaces of transmission. Check the vent for free breathing. Operate transmission at normal temperatures and inspect for leakage. Repair as required. • Replace diaphragm.

Fig. 4F   Automatic transmission trouble shooting guide. Part 7 of 7

CONTROL PRESSURE CHECK

Borg Warner

1. Connect tachometer to engine and pressure gauge to control pressure outlet at rear of transmission, Fig. 5.
2. Firmly apply parking brake, then start engine and allow engine and transmission to reach operating temperature.
3. Adjust engine idle speed to 630-680 rpm in drive position, then note pressure gauge reading. Pressure should be 50-65 psi.
4. Increase engine speed to 1130-1180 rpm and note pressure gauge read-ing. Pressure should be 15-20 psi. above pressure reading recorded at idle speed.

Fig. 5   Control pressure test connection. Borg Warner

NOTE: Do not hold engine at this speed for longer than 20 seconds in drive, otherwise damage to transmission may result. If during test engine speed exceeds specified rpm, allow engine to return to idle, then note pressure and restart test.

5. If pressures are not within limits, adjust downshift valve control cable as described further on in this section then recheck pressures.

C3 & C4

ENGINE IDLE

With the transmission in neutral and engine at correct idle speed, vacuum

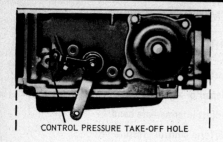

CONTROL PRESSURE TAKE-OFF HOLE

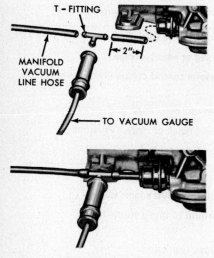

T - FITTING

MANIFOLD VACUUM LINE HOSE

← 2" →

← TO VACUUM GAUGE

Fig. 7   Vacuum line test connection. C3 & C4 (Typical)

Application	Throttle Position	Vacuum In. H.G.	Range	Control Pressure P.S.I.
C3 Transmission				
1976	Closed	15 & Above	P, N, D, 2, 1	50—60
	Closed	15 & Above	R	66—77
	As Required	10①	D, 2, 1	65—85
C4 Transmission				
1972	Closed	Above 15	P, N, D	52—85
	Closed	Above 15	2, 1	52—115
	Closed	Above 15	R	52—180
	As Required	10	P, N, D	96—110
	As Required	Below 1	D, 2, 1	143—160
	As Required	Below 1	R	230—260
1973	Closed	Above 12	P, N, D	55—86
	Closed	Above 12	2, 1	55—122
	Closed	Above 12	R	55—197
	As Required	10	D	98—110
	As Required	Below 1	R	239—272
	As Required	Below 1	D, 2, 1	143—164
1974	Closed	15 & Above	P, N, D	55—86
	Closed	15 & Above	2, 1	55—122
	Closed	15 & Above	R	55—197
	As Required	10①	D	98—110
	As Required	10①	2, 1	90—115

①—On models with dual diaphragm type EGR valve, disconnect front port hose and plug.

Fig. 8   Control pressure at zero governor rpm. C3 & C4

gauge should show a minimum of 18 inches, Figs. 6 and 7. If vacuum reading is lower than 18 inches, an engine problem is indicated or there is leakage in the vacuum line. Make necessary repairs to obtain a minimum vacuum of 18 inches.

NOTE: At different altitudes above sea level, it may not be possible to obtain 18 inches of vacuum at engine idle.

Depress accelerator pedal quickly and observe the vacuum gauge. The amount of vacuum should decrease and increase with the changes in throttle openings. If the vacuum response to changes in throttle opening is too slow the vacuum line to the diaphragm unit could be restricted. Make necessary repairs before completing the test.

At engine idle, check transmission control pressure gauge at all selector lever positions. Control pressures should agree with the specifications listed in Fig. 8.

PRESSURE INCREASE TEST

The control pressure increase should be checked in all ranges except Park and Neutral. Shift the transmission into D1, D2, L and R, then check control pressure increase in each range.

With the correct control pressure at engine idle, advance the throttle until the engine vacuum reading falls to approximately 17 inches. As the vacuum gauge reading decreases into these specifications, the control pressure should start to increase.

Control pressure increase may be noted immediately when the throttle is opened due to increased pump output, resulting from increased engine rpm. When this happens, the pressure increase point can be checked by using a distributor vacuum tester. Install the distributor tester vacuum line on the diaphragm assembly. Adjust the tester to provide 18 inches of vacuum. Increase engine speed to 600-700 rpm. Reduce the tester vacuum reading to approximately 17 inches and observe the transmission pressure gauge for the pressure decrease.

PRESSURE TEST AT 10" VACUUM

This test should be made in the forward driving ranges. Advance the throttle until engine vacuum reading is 10 inches and check the control pressure regulation. Control pressure should be as given in Fig. 8.

PRESSURE TEST AT 3" VACUUM

This test should be made in forward driving ranges. The pressure obtained

should be as listed in Fig. 8.

Between each test move the selector lever to neutral and run the engine at 1000 rpm for 15 seconds to cool the converter.

If the vacuum and pressure gauge readings are within specifications, the diaphragm unit and transmission control pressure regulating system are operating properly.

If transmission control pressure is too low, too high, fails to increase with throttle opening, or is extremely erratic, use the procedure given under the following appropriate heading to resolve the problem.

Pressure Low at Engine Idle

If control pressure at engine idle is too low in all selector lever positions, trouble other than the diaphragm unit is indicated. When pressure is low in all ranges, check for excessive leakage in front pump, case and control valve body, or a sticking control pressure regulator valve.

Pressure High at Engine Idle

If pressure is too high in all ranges the trouble may be in the diaphragm unit or its connecting vacuum tubes and hoses, throttle valve or control rod.

With the engine idling, disconnect the hose from the diaphragm unit and check engine manifold vacuum. Hold a thumb over the end of the hose and

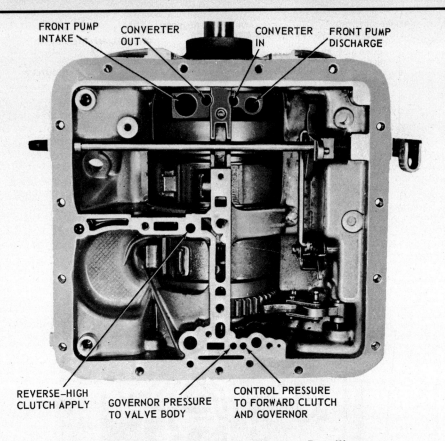

FRONT PUMP INTAKE CONVERTER OUT CONVERTER IN FRONT PUMP DISCHARGE

REVERSE–HIGH CLUTCH APPLY GOVERNOR PRESSURE TO VALVE BODY CONTROL PRESSURE TO FORWARD CLUTCH AND GOVERNOR

Fig. 9 Case fluid passage hole identification. Borg Warner

clutches or bands. The inoperative units can be located through a series of checks by substituting air pressure for the fluid pressure to determine the location of the malfunction.

When the selector lever is at Drive Left a "NO DRIVE" condition may be caused by an inoperative forward clutch. A "NO DRIVE" condition at Drive Right or 1 may be caused by an inoperative forward clutch or one-way clutch. When there is no drive in L, the difficulty could be caused by improper functioning of the forward clutch or low-reverse band and the one way clutch. The low-reverse band cannot be checked in L or 1. If the low-reverse band fails, the one-way clutch will hold the gear train and operation will be normal. Failure to drive in reverse range could be caused by a malfunction of the reverse-high clutch or low-reverse band. Erratic shifts could be caused by a stuck governor valve.

To make the air pressure checks, drain the transmission fluid, and then remove the oil pan and the control valve body assembly. The inoperative units can be located by introducing air pressure into the transmission case passages leading to the clutches, servos, and governor.

check for vacuum. If engine speeds up when hose is disconnected and slows down as the thumb is held against end of hose, the vacuum source is satisfactory.

Stop the engine and remove the diaphragm unit and its control rod. Inspect control rod for a bent condition and for corrosion. Check diaphragm unit for leakage with the distributor tester.

Pressure Does Not Increase at 17″ Vacuum

When the control pressure is within specification at engine idle, but does not increase, as the vacuum is decreased to the specified limits, first check the control rod between the vacuum unit and throttle valve for proper engagement. If the control rod is not assembled into the end of the throttle valve or vacuum unit, the valve cannot regulate throttle pressure to increase control pressure. Next, check for a stuck secondary or primary throttle valve, pressure booster valve, or a stuck control pressure regulator valve.

If control pressure increases before or after vacuum is decreased to approximately 17 inches, check for a leaking diaphragm assembly, bent diaphragm can, or worn or bent control rod to the throttle valve.

Pressure Not Within 10″ or 3″ of Vacuum

If idle pressure and pressure point increase are within specifications, but pressures at 10 or 3 inches of vacuum are not within specification in all ranges, excessive leakage, low pump capacity, or a restricted oil pan screen is indicated.

If pressures are not within specifications for specific selector lever positions only, this indicates excessive leakage in the clutch or servo circuits used in those ranges.

When the control pressure is within specifications at engine idle, *but not within specifications* at the pressure rise point of 17 inches of vacuum, at 10 inches of vacuum, or at 3 inches of vacuum, the vacuum diaphragm unit may need adjustment.

The vacuum diaphragm assembly has an adjusting screw in the vacuum hose connecting tube. The inner end of the screw bears against a plate which in turn bears against the vacuum diaphragm spring.

AIR PRESSURE TESTS

A "NO DRIVE" condition can exist, even with correct transmission fluid pressure, because of inoperative

Forward Clutch

Apply air pressure to the transmission case forward clutch passage, Fig. 9, 10 or 11. A dull thud can be heard when the clutch piston is applied. If no noise is heard, place the finger tips on the input shell and again apply air pressure to the forward clutch passage. Movement of piston can be felt as clutch is applied.

Apply air pressure to the control pressure to governor passage and listen for a sharp clicking or whistling noise. The noise indicates secondary governor valve movement.

Reverse-High Clutch

Apply air pressure to the reverse-high clutch passage, Fig. 9, 10 or 11. A dull thud indicates that the reverse-high clutch piston has moved to the applied position. If no noise is heard, place the finger tips on the clutch drum and again apply air pressure to detect movement of the piston.

Hold the air nozzle in the intermediate servo apply passage, Fig. 11. Operation of the servo is indicated by a tightening of the intermediate band around the drum. Continue to apply air pressure into the intermediate servo apply passage, and introduce air pressure into the intermediate servo release passage. The intermediate servo should release the band against the apply pressure.

Low-Reverse Servo

Apply air pressure to the low reverse apply passage, Fig. 9, 10 or 11. The low-reverse band should tighten around the drum if the servo is operating properly.

If the servos do not operate, disassemble, clean and inspect them to locate the source of the trouble.

If air pressure applied to either of the clutch passages fails to operate a clutch or operates both clutches at once, remove and, with air pressure, check the fluid passages in the case and front pump to detect obstructions.

If the passages are clear, remove the clutch assemblies, and clean and inspect the malfunctioning clutch to locate the trouble.

STALL TEST

Start the engine and allow it to react its normal operating temperature. Apply both the parking brake and service brakes while making tests.

The stall test is made in D2, D1, L or R at full throttle to check engine performance, converter clutch operation or installation, and the holding ability of the forward clutch, reverse-high clutch, low-reverse band and the gear train one-way clutch. *While making this test, do not hold the throttle open for more than five seconds at a time.* Then move the selector lever to neutral and run the engine at 1000 rpm for about 15 seconds to cool the converter before making the next test. If the engine speed recorded by the tachometer exceeds the maximum limits specified in Fig. 12, release the accelerator immediately because clutch or band slippage is indicated.

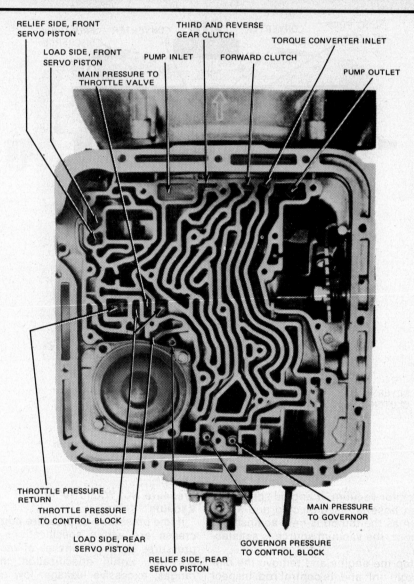

Fig. 10 Case fluid passage hole identification. C3

Stall Speed Too High

If stall speed exceeds specifications, band or clutch slippage is indicated depending on transmission selector lever position.

Excessive engine rpm only in D1, D2, and L indicates either reverse-high clutch or low-reverse band slippage. Excessive engine rpm only in D1 indicates gear train one way clutch slippage.

Stall Speed Too Low

When stall speed tests are low and the engine is properly tuned, converter stator clutch problems are indicated. A road test must be performed to determine the exact cause of the trouble.

If the stall test speeds are 300 to 400 rpm below specifications in above table and the car cruises properly but has very poor acceleration, the converter stator clutch is slipping.

If the stall test speeds are 300 to 400 rpm below specifications, and the car drags at cruising speeds but acceleration is poor, the stator clutch could be installed backwards.

When the stall test shows normal speeds with good acceleration but the car drags at cruising speeds, the difficulty is due to a seized stator assembly.

INITIAL ENGAGEMENT TESTS

Initial engagement tests are made to determine if initial band and clutch engagements are smooth.

Run the engine until its normal operating temperature is reached. With the engine at correct idle speed, shift selector lever from N to D2, D1, L and R.

Observe the initial band and clutch engagements. Band and clutch engagements should be smooth in all positions.

Rough initial engagements in D1, D2, L and R are caused by high engine idle speed or high control pressures.

VACUUM UNIT, ADJUST

All readings slightly high or all readings slightly low may indicate the vacuum unit needs adjustment to correct a particular shift condition.

For example, if the pressure at 10 inches of vacuum was 120 psi and the pressure at 3 inches of vacuum was 170 psi, and upshifts and downshifts were harsh, a diaphragm adjustment to reduce the diaphragm assembly spring force would be required.

If the pressure readings are low, and

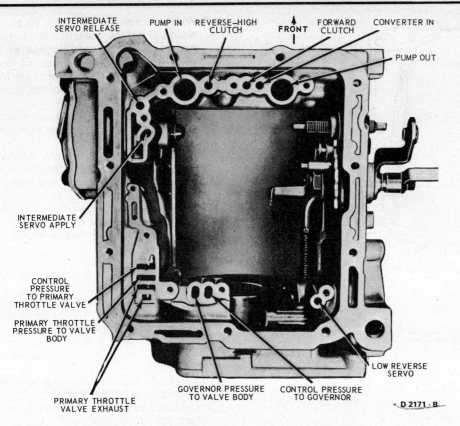

Fig. 11 Case fluid passage hole identification. C4

Labels on figure: INTERMEDIATE SERVO RELEASE, PUMP IN, REVERSE–HIGH CLUTCH, FRONT, FORWARD CLUTCH, CONVERTER IN, PUMP OUT, INTERMEDIATE SERVO APPLY, CONTROL PRESSURE TO PRIMARY THROTTLE VALVE, PRIMARY THROTTLE PRESSURE TO VALVE BODY, PRIMARY THROTTLE VALVE EXHAUST, GOVERNOR PRESSURE TO VALVE BODY, CONTROL PRESSURE TO GOVERNOR, LOW REVERSE SERVO, D 2171-B

Year	Engine	R.P.M.
1976-77	2300 cc	2250-2500
	2800 cc	1800-2200

Fig. 12 Stall speed limits

1. Refering to Transmission Control Pressure Checks, adjust downshift control valve cable to obtain required pressures.

1972-73 C4

1. Place throttle in wide open position.
2. Position downshift cable so that tang just contacts throttle shaft.
3. Loosen two downshift cable adjusting nuts at bracket and move cable as required, then tighten locknut.

1974 C4 & 1976-77 C3

1. Hold accelerator pedal in full throttle position using a suitable weight.
2. Place transmission lever in full kickdown position.
3. Loosen locknut A, Fig. 15, and adjust nut B to obtain a clearance of .20 to .50 inch on 1974 models and .020 to .080 inch on 1976-77 models, between carburetor linkage downshift lever and throttle operating shaft, then tighten locknut.
4. Remove weight from accelerator and check adjustment.

BANDS, ADJUST

Intermediate Band

1972-73 Borg Warner

1. Raise vehicle and drain fluid from transmission.
2. Remove transmission oil pan, then remove servo rear mounting bolt, two fluid transfer tubes and cam plate, Fig. 16.
3. Pull out on servo actuating lever and insert a ¼ inch spacer between adjusting screw and servo piston stem, then using tool No. T71P-77225-A, torque adjusting screw to 10 in. lbs., Fig. 17.
4. Hold adjusting screw stationary and position one-way clutch spring two threads away from actuating with long leg of spring facing rearward, Fig. 18. Once positioned, install cam plate engaging leg of spring in cam plate slot.
5. Install two fluid transfer tubes and transmission oil pan and gasket.
6. Lower vehicle and fill transmission to proper level with specified fluid.

1972-74 C4 & 1976-77 C3

1. On C3 units, remove downshift rod from transmission downshift lever.

---

control pressure does not start to build up until vacuum drops to 15 inches, an adjustment to increase diaphragm spring force is required.

To increase control pressure, turn the adjusting screw in clockwise. To reduce control pressure, back the adjusting screw out by turning it counterclockwise. *One complete turn* of the adjusting screw (360°) will change idle line control pressure approximately 2-3 psi. After the adjustment is made, install the vacuum line and make all the pressure checks as outlined in the Control Pressure Limits Table.

NOTE: The diaphragm should not be adjusted to provide pressures below the ranges in the Control Pressure Limits Table, in order to change shift feel. To do so could result in soft or slipping shift points and damage to the transmission.

MANUAL LINKAGE, ADJUST

1972-74 Models

1. Place selector lever in "D" position.
2. Raise vehicle, then remove clevis pin and disconnect cable and bushing from transmission, Fig. 13.
3. Place transmission manual lever in "D" position, third detent from rear of transmission.
4. Adjust length of cable until clevis pin holes in manual lever and end of cable are aligned.
5. Connect cable, then lower vehicle and check operation of transmission in each selector position.

1976-77 Models

1. Place transmission selector lever in D position.
2. Raise car and loosen shift rod retaining nut, Fig. 14.
3. Move transmission manual lever to D position.
4. Tighten attaching nut to 10-20 ft. lbs.

DOWNSHIFT LINKAGE, ADJUST

1972-73 Borg Warner Transmission

NOTE: Downshift valve control cable governs transmission control pressure, which in turn determines shift points. It also manually downshifts transmisssion at wide open throttle.

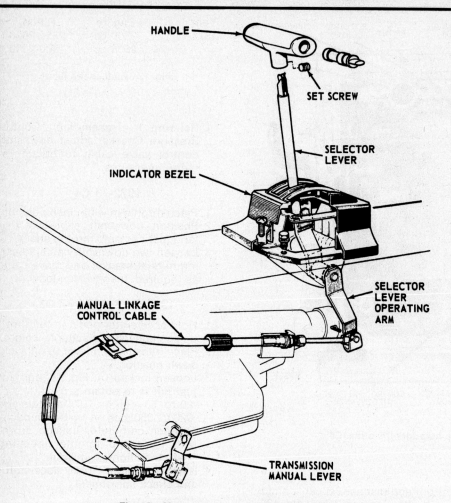

HANDLE

SET SCREW

SELECTOR LEVER

INDICATOR BEZEL

MANUAL LINKAGE CONTROL CABLE

SELECTOR LEVER OPERATING ARM

TRANSMISSION MANUAL LEVER

Fig. 13 Manual linkage. 1972-74 models

2. With transmission manual lever in Neutral, rotate switch and insert gauge pin (No. 43 drill shank end) into the gauge pin holes of the switch. The gauge pin must be inserted to a full $^{31}/_{64}$" into the three holes of the switch.
3. Tighten the two switch attaching bolts and remove the gauge pin from the switch.
4. Check operation of switch. Engine should start only with transmission selector lever in Neutral and Park.

Borg Warner Transmission
1. Place selector lever in "D" position.
2. Raise vehicle and disconnect four leads from switch.
3. Loosen the locknut using an $^{11}/_{16}$" crowsfoot wrench and unscrew the switch a couple of turns.
4. Connect a self powered test light across the two larger terminals (back-up light terminals).
5. Screw the switch in until test light goes out. Mark switch position at this point.
6. Move test light to the two smaller terminals (starter terminals).
7. Continue to screw in the switch until test light comes on. Mark the new position on the case.
8. Unscrew the switch until it is midway between the two positions marked on the case.
9. Tighten the locknut to secure the switch to the case. Connect the four leads to proper terminals.
10. Lower vehicle and check operation of switch in all selector lever positions.

2. On all models, clean dirt from adjusting screw area, then remove and discard locknut.
3. Install new locknut on adjusting screw, then using tool, Fig. 19 and 20, tighten adjusting screw until tool handle clicks. The tool is a preset torque wrench which clicks and overruns when torque on adjusting screw reaches 10 ft. lbs.
4. Back off adjusting screw exactly 1½ turns on C3 units and 1¾ turns on C4 units.
5. Hold adjusting screw from turning and torque locknut to 35 to 45 ft. lbs.
6. On C3 units, connect downshift linkage to downshift lever.

Low-Reverse Band
1972-73 Borg Warner
1. Remove console, then roll back carpet on right side of tunnel.
2. If vehicle is not equipped with an access hole follow procedure as outlined in Fig. 21.
3. Adjust low-reverse band using tool No. 7195-C, then back off one complete turn and install plug.

4. Place carpet over tunnel and install console.

1972-74 C4
1. Clean dirt from band adjusting screw area, then remove and discard locknut.
2. Install new lock nut on adjusting screw, then using tool, Fig. 22, tighten adjusting until tool handle clicks. The tool is a pre-set torque wrench which clicks and overruns when torque on adjusting screws reaches 10 ft. lbs.
3. Back off adjusting screw exactly 3 complete turns.
4. Hold adjusting screw from turning and torque lock nut to 35 to 45 ft. lbs.

NEUTRAL SAFETY SWITCH, ADJUST
1972-74

C4 Transmission
1. With manual lever properly adjusted, loosen the two switch attaching bolts.

TRANSMISSION, REPLACE
1972-73 Borg Warner
1. Remove transmission dipstick, then disconnect downshift control valve cable.
2. Raise vehicle and drain fluid from transmission.
3. Mark driveshaft and pinion flange, then remove four bolts and washers.
4. Remove two bolts attaching center bearing to body, then lower drive shaft and withdraw from transmission.
5. Disconnect exhaust pipe bracket from transmission bracket, then loosen bracket and position exhaust pipe aside.
6. Disconnect speedometer cable from extension housing.
7. Remove starter and converter housing front cover.
8. Remove four flywheel to converter attaching bolts, then disconnect manual linkage control cable.

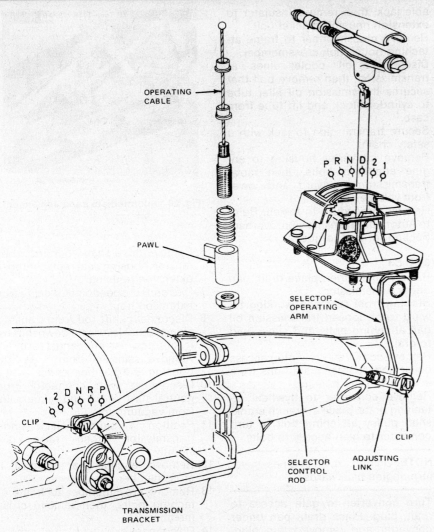

Fig. 14 Manual linkage. 1976-77 models

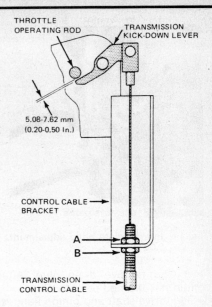

Fig. 15 Downshift linkage adjustment. 1974 & 1976-77 models

sembly is moved rearward.

14. Lower transmission and converter as an assembly from vehicle.
15. Reverse procedure to install. Refer to Automatic Transmission Overhaul Section for bolt torque specifications.

1972-74 C4

1. Raise vehicle, then place drain pan under transmission.
2. Starting from rear and working toward front, loosen transmission oil pan attaching bolts and allow fluid to drain.
3. Remove starter, then remove access cover from lower converter housing.
4. Remove converter to flywheel attaching nuts, place a wrench on crankshaft pulley attaching bolt to turn converter to gain access to nuts.
5. On models with V6 engine, turn converter to gain access to drain plug. Place drain pan under conver-

9. Disconnect neutral safety switch wire connector.
10. Position suitable jack under transmission and secure transmission to jack using a safety chain.
11. Remove four support to body attaching bolts.

12. Remove six converter housing to engine attaching bolts, then remove fluid filler tube.
13. Using a pry bar, exert pressure between flywheel and converter to prevent converter from being disengaged from transmission when as-

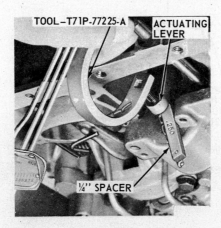

Fig. 16 Cam plate removal and installation. Borg Warner

Fig. 17 Intermediate band adjustment. Borg Warner

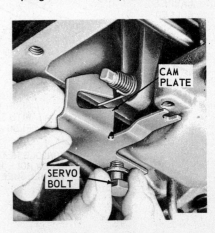

Fig. 18 Positioning one-way clutch spring. Borg Warner

Fig. 19 Intermediate band adjustment. C3

Fig. 20 Intermediate band adjustment. C4

ter and remove drain plug. After fluid has drained replace plug.

6. Mark drive shaft and pinion flanges, then remove four bolts and washers.
7. Remove two bolts securing center bearing to body, then lower drive shaft assembly and withdraw from transmission.
8. Disconnect speedometer cable from extension housing.
9. Disconnect shift cable from manual lever, then remove two bolts securing cable bracket to converter housing and position cable and bracket aside.
10. Disconnect downshift cable from transmission downshift lever.
11. Disconnect neutral start switch wires from retaining clamps and connectors.
12. Disconnect vacuum line from vacuum unit.
13. Support transmission using a suit-

able jack, then remove insulator to extension housing bracket bolt.
14. Remove crossmember to frame attaching bolts, then crossmember.
15. Disconnect oil cooler lines at transmission, then remove bolt that secures transmission oil filler tube to cylinder block and lift tube from case.
16. Secure transmission to jack with a safety chain.
17. Remove converter housing to engine attaching bolts, then move transmission rearward and lower from vehicle.
18. Reverse procedure to install. Refer to Automatic Transmission Overhaul Section for bolt torques.

1976-77 C3

1. Raise vehicle, then place drain pan under transmission.
2. Starting from rear and working toward front, loosen transmission oil pan attaching bolts and allow fluid to drain.
3. Remove converter drain plug access cover and adapter plate bolts from lower converter housing.
4. Remove converter to flywheel attaching bolts, place a wrench crankshaft pulley attaching bolt to turn converter to gain access to bolts.

NOTE: On belt driven engines, never turn engine backwards.

5. Turn converter to gain access to drain plug. Place drain pan under converter and remove drain plug. After fluid has drained replace drain plug.

6. Remove drive shaft, then install extension housing seal replacer tool in extension housing.
7. Disconnect speedometer cable from extension housing.
8. Disconnect shift rod from transmission manual lever and downshift rod from transmission manual lever.
9. Remove starter from converter housing and position aside.
10. Disconnect wire connector from neutral start switch and vacuum line from vacuum unit.
11. Position a suitable jack under transmission, then raise jack slightly.
12. Remove engine rear support to crossmember nut.
13. Remove crossmember to frame attaching bolts, then remove crossmember.
14. Disconnect exhaust pipe at exhaust manifold.
15. Lower jack under transmission and allow transmission to hang.
16. Position jack under front of engine and raise engine to gain access to two upper converter housing to engine attaching bolts.
17. Disconnect oil cooler lines at transmission and cap lines and fitting.

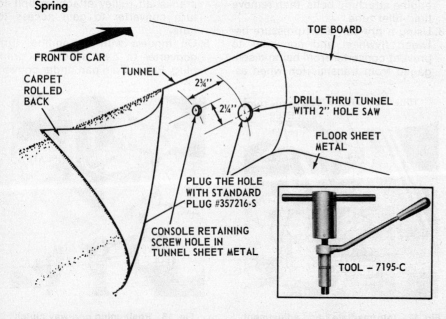

Fig. 21 Low-reverse band adjustment. Borg Warner

Fig. 22 Low-reverse band adjustment. C4

18. Remove two lower converter housing to engine attaching bolts.
19. Remove transmission filler tube.
20. Secure jack to transmission with a safety chain.
21. Remove two upper converter housing to engine attaching bolts, then move transmission rearward and lower from vehicle.
22. Reverse procedure to install. Position converter to transmission ensuring converter hub is fully en-

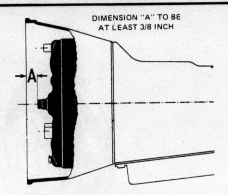

DIMENSION "A" TO BE AT LEAST 3/8 INCH

Fig. 23 Converter hub to housing flange position. C3

gaged in pump gears, Fig. 23. Prior to installing transmission on engine, flywheel must be indexed with pilot hole in six o'clock position. When assembling flywheel to converter, first install attaching bolt through pilot hole and torque to 27 to 37 ft. lbs., then install remaining two bolts. Refer to Automatic Transmission Overhaul Section for bolt torque specifications.

Rear Axle & Brakes Section

AXLE SHAFT/SEAL & BEARING, REPLACE

1. Raise rear of vehicle and remove rear wheel and brake drum.
2. Remove bearing retainer to axle housing attaching bolts. These bolts are accessible through holes in axle shaft flange.
3. Using a suitable puller, remove axle shaft and bearing from housing, Fig. 1.
4. Using a chisle, nick inner bearing retainer in several places, then slide retainer off axle shaft, Fig. 2.
5. Press bearing and seal from axle shaft using tool No. T69P-4621-A, Fig. 3.
6. Lightly coat axle bearing bores with rear axle lubricant.
7. Position bearing retainer on axle shaft, then press on bearing using tool T69P-4621-A.
8. Using tool, press on bearing inner retainer until seated firmly against bearing, Fig. 4.

NOTE: Before installing retainer, axle shaft and inside diameter of retainer should be wiped with a clean dry cloth. Do not lubricate or degrease inner bearing retainer.

9. Position axle shaft in housing and engage splines in differential side gear, then tap shaft into position.
10. Install bearing retainer attaching bolts and washers, then torque bolts to 15 to 18 ft. lbs.
11. Install brake drum and wheel, then lower vehicle.

BRAKE ADJUSTMENTS

Front brakes are fixed caliper discs. The friction pads can be replaced without removing the calipers. There are shims behind the pads and these should be refitted exactly as removed.

Rear brakes, Figs. 5 and 6, are drum-type that automatically adjust whenever the parking brake is applied.

After relining rear brakes, adjust by slowly and carefully actuate the parking brake and releasing several times (until the clicking of the rear brakes' star wheel adjuster stops). Unless care is taken, it is possible for the parking brake lever to override the star wheel

when it is in the fully released position, which is where it normally is left to insure ease of drum reinstallation.

PARKING BRAKE, ADJUST

1972-74
1. Release parking brake, then raise vehicle.

NOTE: Before adjusting, ensure cable is properly routed and all cable guides are well greased, Fig. 7.

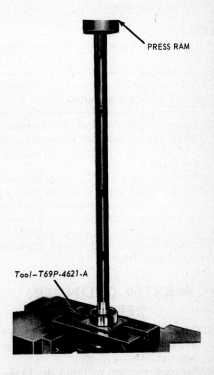

PRESS RAM

Tool-T69P-4621-A

Fig. 3 Pressing bearing from axle shaft

Tool-T50T-100-A
Tool-T66L-4234-A

Fig. 1 Removing rear axle shaft

Fig. 2 Splitting bearing inner retainer for bearing removal

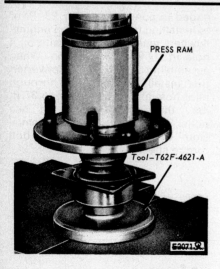

Fig. 4 Pressing inner bearing retainer on axle shaft

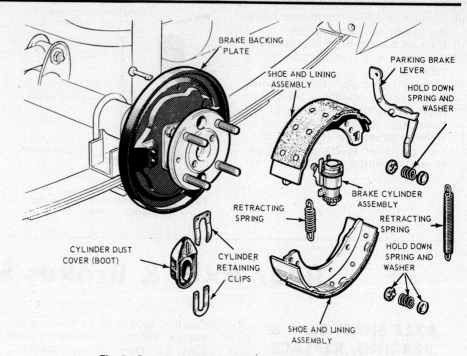

Fig. 5 Rear brake disassembled. 1972-74 models

2. Loosen lock nut on primary cable end adjacent to relay lever on axle housing. Adjust cable until all slack is removed and relay lever is just clear of stop, then tighten lock nut, Fig. 8.
3. Loosen lock nut on transverse cable end near right rear brake. Adjust cable until all slack is removed, then tighten lock nut.

NOTE: After adjusting transverse cable, ensure operating levers are against stops.

4. Lower vehicle and check parking brake operation.

1976-77
1. Release parking brake, then raise vehicle.

NOTE: Before adjusting, ensure cable is properly routed.

2. Engage keyed sleeve A into abutment slot B, then turn adjuster nut C until all slack is removed from cable, Fig. 9.
3. Parking brake cable is properly adjusted, when there is a clearance of .039 to .059 inch between parking brake lever stop and brake backing plate.
4. Lower vehicle and check parking brake operation.

MASTER CYLINDER, REPLACE

1. Siphon fluid from reservoir, then disconnect brake lines from master cylinder.
2. Remove master cylinder to brake booster attaching nuts, then using

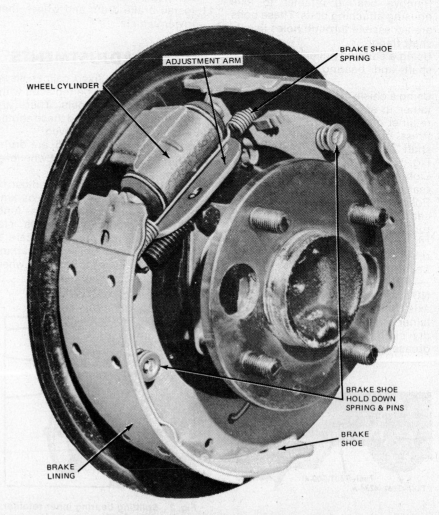

Fig. 6 Rear brake assembly. 1976-77 models

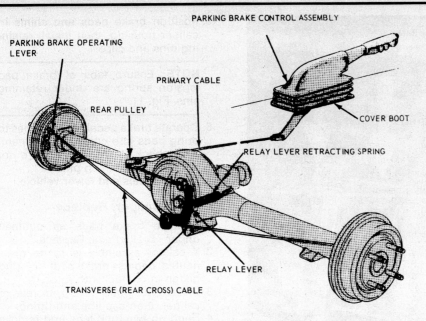

Fig. 7 Parking brake installation. 1972-74 models

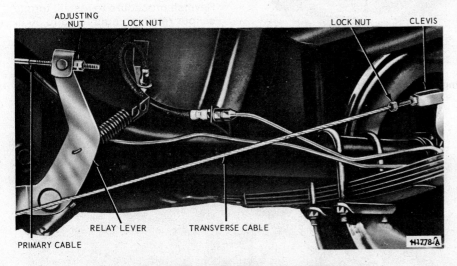

Fig. 8 Parking linkage adjusting points. 1972-74 models

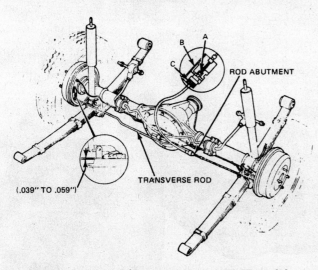

Fig. 9 Parking brake adjustment. 1976-77 models

care not to damage vacuum seal lift master cylinder from booster.
3. Place master and fluid seal on push rod, and hold in this position.
4. Connect brake lines and tighten fittings finger tight.
5. Install master cylinder on brake booster, then tighten brake line fittings.
6. Fill reservoir with brake fluid, then bleed entire brake system and check brake operation.

NOTE: When Bleeding system on 1972-74 models, piston in pressure differential valve and switch assembly must be held in central position. Remove cap from base of pressure differential valve, then insert screwdriver with blade modified to dimensions given in Fig. 10, through boss in base of valve to centeralize piston. If this is not done, brake warning light will come on and be difficult to turn off. On 1976-77 models, piston in pressure differential valve is self centering and does not need to be held in central position.

POWER BRAKE UNIT, REPLACE

1. Remove clevis pin, then disconnect push rod from brake pedal.
2. Remove master cylinder attaching nuts, then position master cylinder away from brake booster. Use care not to damage fluid seal.
3. Disconnect vacuum line from booster, then remove booster to dash panel attaching screws and booster assembly.
4. Remove mounting bracket and gasket from booster.
5. Install bracket and gasket on brake booster.

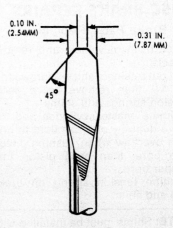

Fig. 10 Valve and switch assembly piston centralizing tool

Fig. 11 Brake pad retaining pins and clips

5. Position brake pads and shims in caliper housing, then install retaining pins and clips.

NOTE: Ensure tabs of brake pad tension spring are under retaining pins, Fig. 11.

6. Operate brake pedal several times to bring pads into correct adjustment, then check to ensure pads are not binding on retaining pins.
7. Install wheels and lower vehicle.

Caliper, Replace

1. Remove brake pads as outlined under "Brake Pads, Replace."
2. If caliper assembly is to be overhauled, depress brake pedal to bring piston in contact with rotor.
3. Disconnect brake line from rear of caliper, then cap line and fitting.
4. Bend up two lock tabs and remove caliper attaching bolts and caliper, Fig. 13.
5. Reverse procedure to install, torque caliper retaining nuts to 45 to 50 ft. lbs. After installation, bleed brake system.

NOTE: When Bleeding system on 1972-74 models, piston in pressure

6. Position booster assembly on dash panel, then connect push rod to brake pedal and install clevis pin.
7. Install and tighten booster to dash panel attaching screws, then connect vacuum line.
8. Position master cylinder on brake booster, then install and tighten attaching nuts.

DISC BRAKE REPAIRS
Brake Pads, Replace

1. Raise front of vehicle and remove wheels.
2. Pull out retainers and withdraw pins, Fig. 11, then remove brake pads, tension springs and shims.
3. Examine master cylinder and remove quantity of brake fluid to prevent overflow when pushing piston into bore, then push piston into caliper bore.
4. Position tension spring on brake pad and shim.

NOTE: Shims must be installed with arrows facing upward, Fig. 12.

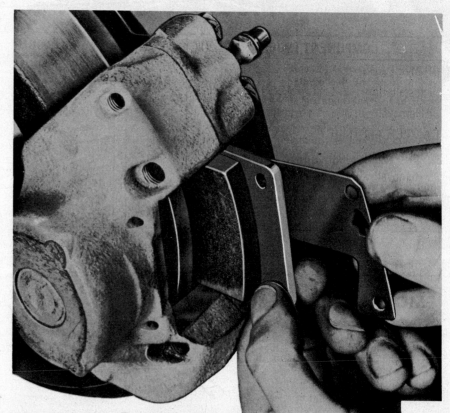

Fig. 12 Installing brake pads and shims

Fig. 13 Caliper mounting bolt location

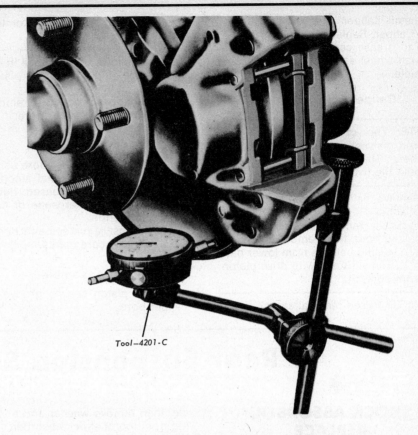

Tool—4201-C

Fig. 14 Checking disc brake rotor runout

differential valve and switch assembly must be held in central position. Remove cap from base of pressure differential valve, then insert screwdriver with blade modified to dimensions given in Fig. 10, through boss in base of valve to centralize piston. If this is not done, brake warning light will come on and be difficult to turn off. On 1976-77 models, piston in pressure differential valve is self centering and does not need to be held in central position.

Hub & Rotor Assembly, Replace

1. Remove caliper as outlined under "Caliper, Replace."
2. Remove cotter pin and spindle nut, then remove thrust washer and outer bearing.
3. Remove hub and rotor assembly from spindle.
4. Bend up lock tabs and remove hub to rotor attaching bolts, then separate rotor from hub.
5. Clean mating surfaces of hub and rotor, then position rotor on hub aligning mating marks.
6. Install new locking plates and bolts. Torque bolts to 30 to 34 ft. lbs., then bend up locking tabs.
7. Install hub and rotor on spindle, then install outer bearing, thrust washer and adjusting nut.
8. Adjust wheel bearing as outlined in Front End and Steering Section under Wheel Bearing, Adjust, then install adjusting nut retainer and cotter pin.
9. Check rotor run out as follows:
   a. Remove cotter pin and castellated nut from ball joint, then seperate connect-rod from steering arm outer end.
   b. Attach dial indicator to steering arm, then check rotor run out, Fig. 14. Run out must be within .0035 inch, total indicator reading. If excessive run out is indicated check for worn or distorted rotor, dirt between rotor and hub faces or misaligned hub bearings and correct as necessary.
   c. Remove dial indicator and connect connecting rod end to steering arm. Torque castellated nut to 18 to 22 ft. lbs., then install cotter pin.

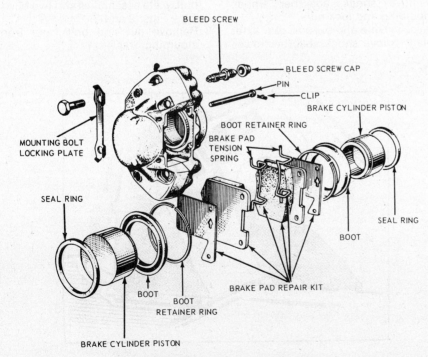

BLEED SCREW

BLEED SCREW CAP

PIN

CLIP

BRAKE CYLINDER PISTON

BOOT RETAINER RING

BRAKE PAD TENSION SPRING

MOUNTING BOLT LOCKING PLATE

SEAL RING

SEAL RING

BOOT

BOOT

BOOT RETAINER RING

BRAKE PAD REPAIR KIT

BRAKE CYLINDER PISTON

Fig. 15 Caliper assembly disassembled

10. Install caliper as described under "Caliper, Replace."
11. Tap grease cap onto hub, then install wheel assembly and lower vehicle.

Caliper Disassemble

NOTE: The caliper consist of two paired halves which are bolted together. Under no circumstances should the two halves be seperated.

1. Remove caliper as outlined under "Caliper, Replace."
2. Partically remove one piston from caliper bore, then remove snap ring and sealing bellows from lower part of piston skirt and with draw piston from bore, Fig. 15.

NOTE: Piston removal can be facili-tated by using air pressure or low hydraulic pressure.

3. Remove bellows from groove in cylinder bore, then withdraw piston sealing ring.
4. Using the above procedure, remove piston from other caliper bore.

Cleaning & Inspection

1. Clean piston and caliper bore using brake fluid or commercial alcohol. Do not use mineral based fluids such as gasoline, kerosene or carbon tetrachloride.
2. Check to ensure pistons and bores are free from score marks.

Caliper Assemble

1. Assemble piston seal to groove in caliper bore.

2. Install bellows into bore with lip that is turned outward installed in bore groove, Fig. 15.
3. Lubricate piston with clean brake fluid, then place piston, crown first through bellows and into caliper bore.

NOTE: When installing piston use care not to damage bellow.

4. Install inner edge of bellows into groove provided in piston skirt, then push piston into caliper as far as possible.
5. Install snap ring securing bellows to caliper.
6. Using above procedure, install other piston in caliper bore.
7. Install caliper as outlined under "Caliper, Replace."

Rear Suspension Section

SHOCK ABSORBER, REPLACE

1972-74 Models
1. Raise vehicle, then from inside trunk remove upper shock attaching nuts, washer and bushing.
2. Remove lower shock absorber attaching bolt, nut and lock washer from axle housing bracket, then remove shock absorber from vehicle.
3. Remove bushing and steel washer from top of shock absorber.
4. When installing shock absorber, torque lower attaching bolt to 40 to 45 ft. lbs. and upper attaching nut to 15 to 20 ft. lbs.

Early 1976 Models
1. Remove two rear seat attaching bolts and rear seat.
2. Remove seat belt attaching bolt from upper end of door post, then remove seat belt.
3. Remove post and upper quarter window trim.
4. Remove two screws from rear rocker panel, then remove door weatherstrip and side trim area.
5. Remove side trim panel and luggage compartment carpet, then tilt rear seat back rest forward and remove rear trim and side panel.
6. Remove shock absorber upper attaching nuts, washer and bushing.
7. Raise vehicle and remove shock absorber lower attaching bolt, nut and washer.
8. Remove shock absorber from vehi-

cle, then remove washer and bushing from top of shock absorber.
9. When installing shock absorber, torque lower attaching bolt to 40 to 45 ft. lbs. and upper attaching nut to 15 to 20 ft. lbs.

Late 1976-77 Models
1. Fold rear seat back forward, then remove load space trim panel plug, Fig. 1.
2. Remove shock absorber upper mounting and lock nuts.
3. Raise vehicle and support rear axle, then remove shock absorber lower

attaching bolts and shock absorber.
4. Reverse procedure to install. Torque lower attaching bolts to 39 to 47 ft. lbs. and upper attaching nuts to 21 to 25 ft. lbs.

REAR SPRING, REPLACE

1. Raise vehicle and support rear axle.
2. Remove rear shackle nuts, washers, bolt, plate assemblies and two bushings, Figs. 2 and 3.
3. Remove nut and bolt from front mounting bracket.

Fig. 1 Upper shock absorber mounting access plug. Late 1976-77 models

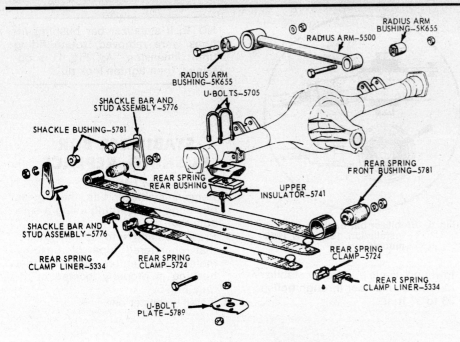

Fig. 2 Rear suspension. 1972 models

assembly. Install nuts and washers, but do not tighten.

12. Remove support from rear axle and lower vehicle.
13. Torque spring front eye bolt to 27 to 32 ft. lbs., rear shackle nuts to 8 to 10 ft. lbs. and U bolts to 18 to 26 ft. lbs.

RADIUS ARM, REPLACE

1972 Models

1. Remove through bolt and disconnect radius arm from axle housing, Fig. 2.

NOTE: It maybe necessary to use a "C" clamp and screwdriver to relieve tension when removing through bolt.

2. Disconnect radius arm from body mounting and remove from vehicle.

4. Remove U bolts and attachment plate, then remove spring assembly.
5. Remove insulator sleeve and retainer plate from spring.
6. Remove spring eye bushings using tool T70P-5029, if necessary.
7. Install spring front and rear eye bushings using tool T70P-5029, if removed.
8. Position front of spring in body mounting bracket, then loosely in-

stall through bolt, nut and washer.
9. Position rubber insulator sleeve around spring, then place retainer plate over insulator.
10. Position spring to axle housing, then install plate, U bolts and nuts. Tighten nuts to approximately 5 ft. lbs.
11. Install rear shackle bushings in body holes, then locate spring in position and assemble rear shackle and plate

10.24 + .01 in (262 + 2.5 mm)

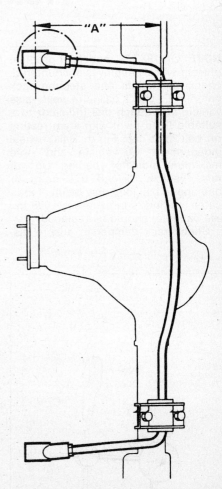

Fig. 4 Stabilizer bar bushing fitting to axle housing dimensions. 1973-74 & 1976-77 models

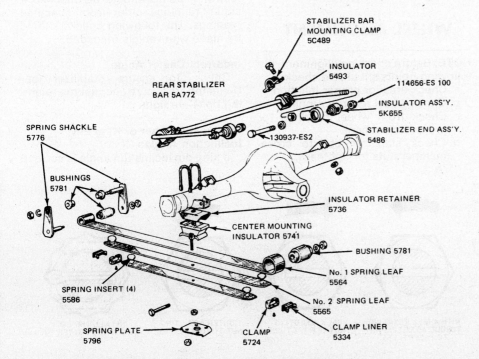

Fig. 3 Rear suspension. 1973-77 & 1976-77 models

3. Reverse procedure to install. Lower vehicle and torque through bolts to 25 to 30 ft. lbs.

STABILIZER BAR, REPLACE

1973-74 & 1976-77 Models

1. Raise vehicle, then on 1973-74 models, disconnect primary parking brake cable from relay lever on rear axle housing.
2. On all models, using a suitable tool, push stabilizer bar rearward to relieve tension from clamp bolts, then remove retaining clamps from rear axle housing, Fig. 3.
3. Remove stabilizer bar to side member through bolts, then remove stabilizer bar.
4. Reverse procedure to install. Torque stabilizer clamp to axle housing attaching bolts to 29 to 37 ft. lbs. After

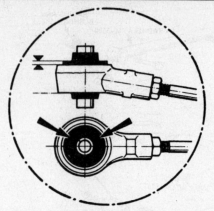

Fig. 5 Stabilizer bar bushing installation. 1973-74 & 1976 models

lowering vehicle, torque stabilizer bar to side member through bolts to 33 to 37 ft. lbs.

NOTE: If stabilizer bar bushing fittings were removed, rotate fitting until dimension "A," Fig. 4, is obtained, then tighten lock nuts.

STABILIZER BAR BUSHING, REPLACE

1973-74 & 1976-77 Models

1. Remove stabilizer bar, then press bushings out of fitting using a suitable tool.
2. Press bushing into fitting, ensure that chamfered side of bushing metal sleeve enters first and that bushing is properly located in fitting, Fig. 5.
3. Install stabilizer bar.

Front Suspension Section

NOTE: On 1972-74 models, if problem of front wheel shimmy is encountered, check ball joints and steering rack damper. To check ball joint wear, raise vehicle and attach dial indicator to a suitable fixed pivot with stem resting on ball joint cap, Fig. 1. Raise wheel independent of vehicle and note maximum indicator reading. Do not raise vehicle beyond this point or damage to ball joint may result. If indicator reading is in excess of .098 in., the ball joint should be replaced.

Check rack damper to ensure distance between underside cover plate and top of slipper is .0035 in. before adding shims and adjust if necessary. Check pinion preload and reset to 18 in. lbs. if necessary. When steering is removed, check movement of tie rods and adjust to 5 lb. pull if necessary.

WHEEL ALIGNMENT

NOTE: Before checking alignment, the following points should be checked:
 a. Check tires for proper inflation.
 b. Check wheel for true running.
 c. Check front wheel bearings for proper adjustment.
 d. Check stabilizer bar to crossmember nuts for tightness.
 e. Check ball joints for excessive play.
 f. Check front springs for proper seating.

Caster, camber and king pin inclination angles are not adjustable, but the following points should be checked if actual readings differ from specified readings. The following checks should be made with vehicle unloaded.

Incorrect Caster Angle

Check to ensure stabilizer bar U-clamps are secure and that the retaining bolts are tight.

Incorrect Camber or King Pin Inclination Angles

If king pin inclination angle is correct,

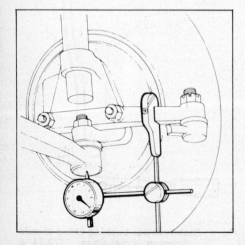

Fig. 1 Checking ball joints for wear

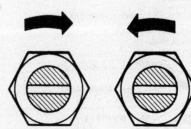

WITH WHEEL ROTATING, TORQUE ADJUSTING NUT, TO 17-25 FT. LBS.

BACK ADJUSTING NUT OFF 1/2 TURN

TIGHTEN ADJUSTING NUT TO 10-15 IN.-LBS.

INSTALL THE LOCK AND A NEW COTTER PIN

Fig. 2 Wheel bearing adjustment

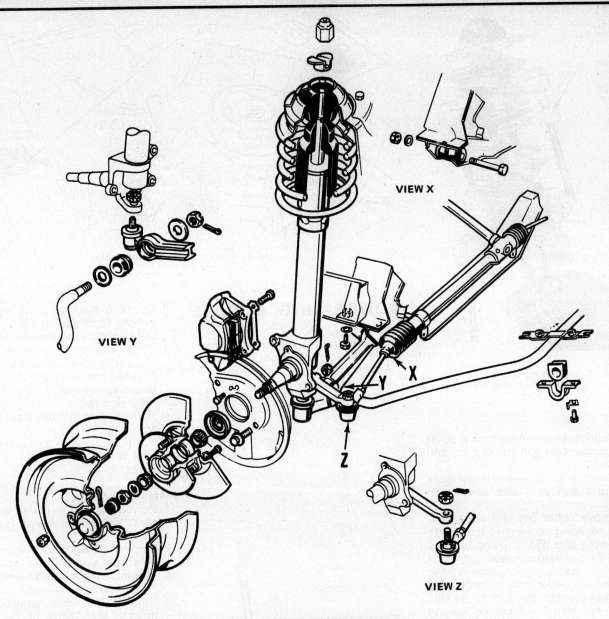

VIEW X

VIEW Y

Y

X

Z

VIEW Z

Fig. 3 Front suspension (typical)

but camber angle is incorrect, check wheel spindle for distortion. If king pin inclination and camber angles are both incorrect, check lower control arm for distortion and lower ball joint for looseness and wear. Also check lower control arm to crossmember mounting for wear and distortion.

Incorrect Wheel Lock Angles

If wheel lock angles are incorrect or uneven, check toe-in. If toe-in is correct, check connecting rods which should be approximately the same length. If there is an appreciable difference, in excess of ¼ in., wheel lock angles will be adversely effected. Minor differences in track rod length are acceptable.

If toe-in and connecting rod lengths are satisfactory, check steering arms and track rods for distortion. Also check ball joints for excessive play and wear.

WHEEL BEARINGS, ADJUST

1. Raise vehicle, then remove wheel and dust cap from hub.
2. Wipe excess grease from end of spindle, then remove cotter pin and nut lock.
3. Loosen adjusting nut three turns, then rock hub and rotor assembly to push brake pads away from rotor.
4. While rotating hub and rotor assembly, torque adjusting nut to 17 to 25 ft. lbs. to seat bearings, Fig. 2.
5. Back adjusting nut off ½ turn, then

retighten nut to 10 to 15 in. lbs.
6. Position nut lock on adjusting nut so that castellations align with cotter pin hole, then install cotter pin.
7. Check rotation of hub and rotor assembly, if hub rotates properly install dust cap and wheel. If hub rotates roughly or noisely, clean or replace bearings and races as necessary.
8. Before driving vehicle, pump brake pedal several times to obtain normal brake pad to rotor clearance.

FRONT SUSPENSION ASSEMBLY, REPLACE

Removal
1. Raise vehicle and remove wheel.

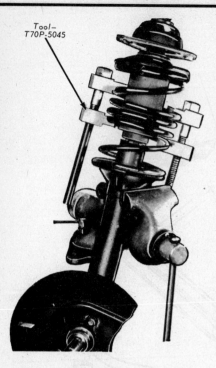

Fig. 4 Compressing spring with adjustable spring retainers

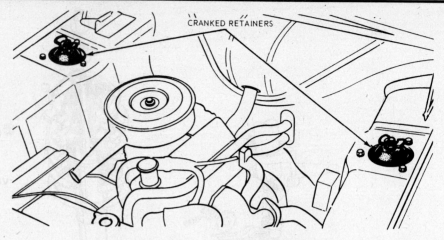

Fig. 5 Cranked retainer positioning

2. Disconnect brake hose from bracket on suspension unit and cap line and fitting.
3. Position a suitable jack under track control arm and raise suspension unit.
4. Remove cotter pin and castellated nut securing connecting rod end to steering arm, Fig. 3. Using tool No. 3290C, separate connecting rod ball joint from steering arm, then remove jack from under track control arm.
5. Remove cotter pin and castellated nut securing track control arm to base of suspension unit, then disconnect track control arm.
6. Remove three bolts securing top mount assembly to fender apron, then remove suspension unit from vehicle.

Installation
1. Position suspension assembly in vehicle, then install three attaching bolts and torque to 15 to 18 ft. lbs.
2. Assemble track control arm ball stud to base of suspension unit. Torque stud nut to 30 to 35 ft. lbs. and install cotter pin.
3. Attach connecting rod end to steering arm. Torque attaching nut to 18 to 22 ft. lbs. and install cotter pin.
4. Remove caps from brake line and fitting, then connect brake line to suspension unit bracket.
5. Bleed brake system, then install wheel and lower vehicle.

FRONT SPRING, REPLACE
Removal
1. Remove front suspension assembly as outlined under Front Suspension Assembly, Replace.
2. Install adjustable spring retainer on spring, Fig. 4.

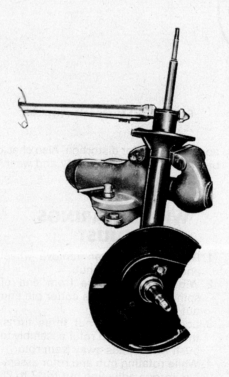

Fig. 6 Removing bump stop platform

3. On 1976 models, using a suitable punch, force piston rod nut collar out of piston rod keyway.
4. On all models, remove piston rod nut and cranked retainer.
5. Remove top mount assembly and upper spring seat, then pull bumper off piston rod.
6. Remove spring from front suspension unit.
7. Position spring in a vise, then carefully remove adjustable spring retainer.

Installation
1. Position spring in a vise and compress with adjustable spring retainers.
2. Remove spring from vise and install on suspension unit.
3. Assemble top mount assembly, then install cranked retainer.
4. On 1972-74 models, apply Loctite to threads, then install piston rod nut and torque to 5 to 10 ft. lbs.
5. On 1976-77 models, install new collared piston rod nut and torque to 5 to 10 ft. lbs. Do not bend nut collar into piston rod keyway at this time.
6. On all models, remove adjustable spring retainer from spring.
7. Install suspension assembly in vehicle.
8. Lower vehicle, then loosen piston rod nut and retighten to 28 to 32 ft. lbs.

NOTE: When tightening piston rod nut, wheels must be in the straight ahead position and cranked retainer must face inward, toward engine, Fig. 5.

9. On 1976-77 models, after tightening piston rod nut, force nut collar into piston rod keyway using a suitable punch.

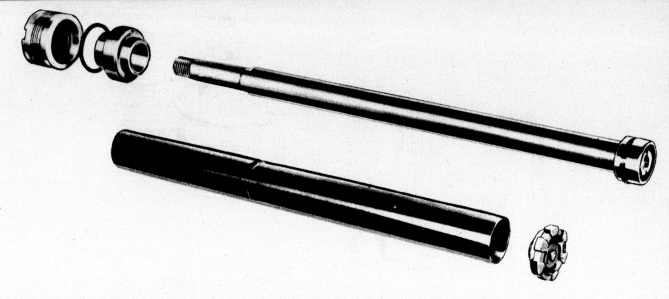

Fig. 7 Front suspension unit. 1972-74 models

PISTON ROD & CYLINDER ASSEMBLY, REPLACE
1972-74 Models

1. Remove suspension assembly as outlined under Front Suspension Assembly, Replace.
2. Remove front spring as outlined under "Front Spring, Replace."
3. Using a suitable wrench, remove bump stop platform, Fig. 6.
4. Remove any burrs from top edge of machined area of piston rod using a suitable stone. If this is not done, coated bearing surface of bushing may become damaged when removing or installing gland and bushing assembly.
5. Lift piston upward until gland and bushing assembly is clear of outer casing, then slide gland assembly off rod and empty fluid into a suitable waste container.
6. Push compression valve out of base of cylinder, then push piston rod downward and withdraw from cylinder, Fig. 7.
7. Remove piston ring from piston, if necessary.
8. Wash all components in a suitable solvent, then check for wear and damage.

NOTE: Do not remove piston from piston rod as these components are serviced as an assembly.

9. Install piston ring, if removed.
10. Insert piston rod into cylinder, then push compression valve into base of cylinder, Fig. 7.

11. Carefully push cylinder and piston rod assembly into outer casing, then fill unit with 326 cc of specified fluid.
12. Position bushing guide on piston rod end, Fig. 8, then install gland and bushing assembly. Push gland and bushing assembly down until they are below top of outer casing.

Tool –
T65P-3A537-B

Fig. 8 Replacing gland and bushing assembly

13. Position "O" ring on top of gland and bushing assembly, then install bump stop platform on top of outer casing. Using a suitable wrench, torque bump stop to 55 to 60 ft. lbs., Fig. 6.
14. Install front spring as outlined under "Front Spring, Replace."
15. Install suspension assembly as outlined under Front Suspension Assembly, Replace.

SHOCK CARTRIDGE, REPLACE
1976-77 Models

1. Remove suspension assembly as outlined under Front Suspension Assembly, Replace.
2. Remove front spring as outlined under Front Spring, Replace.
3. Using a suitable wrench, Fig. 6, remove shock cartridge, Fig. 9.
4. Install shock into top of outer casing, then using a suitable, torque cartridge to 55 to 60 ft. lbs.
5. Install front as outlined under Front Spring, Replace.
6. Install suspension assembly as outlined under Front Suspension Assembly, Replace.

STABILIZER BAR, REPLACE

1. Raise vehicle, then bend back lock tabs and remove two mounting clamps from front of stabilizer bar, Fig. 10.
2. Remove cotter pins and castellated nuts that secure stabilizer bar to

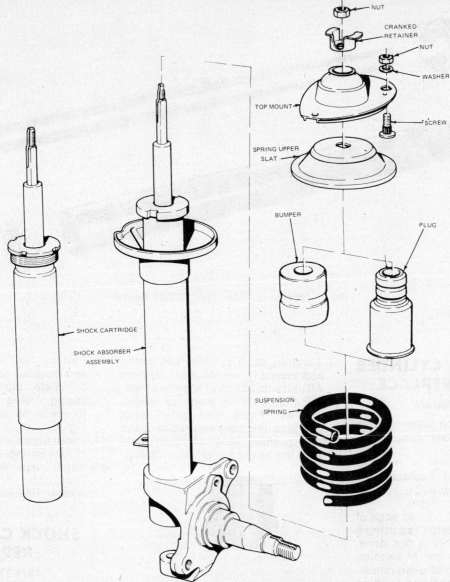

NUT
CRANKED RETAINER
NUT
WASHER
TOP MOUNT
SCREW
SPRING UPPER SLAT
BUMPER
PLUG
SHOCK CARTRIDGE
SHOCK ABSORBER ASSEMBLY
SUSPENSION SPRING

Fig. 9 Front Suspension unit. 1976-77 models

track control arms, then remove dished washers.

3. Pull stabilizer forward and remove from vehicle.

4. Remove sleeve and large washer from each end of stabilizer bar, then remove mounting bushings.

5. Position mounting bushings on stabilizer bar, then install large washers and sleeves.

6. Insert stabilizer bar through bores in track control arm, then install dished washers. Ensure washers are properly positioned.

7. Install castellated nut attaching stabilizer to track control arm. Do not tighten nuts until after vehicle has been lowered.

8. Position mounting clamps on stabilizer bar, then secure clamps to mounting points with new self locking washers.

9. Lower vehicle, then torque stabilizer

bar to track control arm castellated nuts to 15 to 45 ft. lbs. and install cotter pin. Torque stabilizer bar mounting clamp attaching bolts to 15 to 18 ft. lbs. and bend up tabs on locking washers.

TRACK CONTROL ARM ASSEMBLY, REPLACE

1. Raise vehicle and remove cotter pin and castellated nut securing track control arm to stabilizer bar, then pull off large dished washer, Fig. 10.

2. Remove self locking nut and flat washer from track control arm pivot bolt and release inner end of track control arm.

3. Remove cotter pin and nut securing track control arm ball joint to base of suspension unit and separate joint.

4. Assemble track control arm ball joint stud to base of suspension unit, then torque castellated nut to 30 to 35 ft. lbs. and install cotter pin.

5. Position track control arm so that it locates over stabilizer bar.

6. Install pivot bolt, flat washer and self locking nut. Do not torque nut until after vehicle is lowered.

7. Assemble dished washer to end of stabilizer bar. Ensure washer is properly positioned.

8. Lower vehicle and torque pivot nut to 22 to 27 ft. lbs., then torque stabilizer bar castellated nut to 15 to 45 ft. lbs. and install cotter pin.

MANUAL STEERING GEAR, REPLACE

1. Set steering wheel in straight ahead position.

2. Raise and support vehicle on hoist.
3. Bend back lock tabs and remove screws retaining steering gear to mounting brackets on crossmember, then remove screws, locking plates and U-clamps.
4. Separate connecting rods from spindle arms and remove steering gear from vehicle.

NOTE: Turn one wheel to its stop to allow steering gear assembly to be moved sideways, allowing other end to clear stabilizer bar.

---

5. Remove connecting rods and locknuts, noting number of turns required to remove them.
6. Reverse procedure to install.

POWER STEERING GEAR, REPLACE

1. Disconnect battery ground cable.
2. Remove engine splash shield, if used.
3. Disconnect lines from rack and allow fluid to drain.

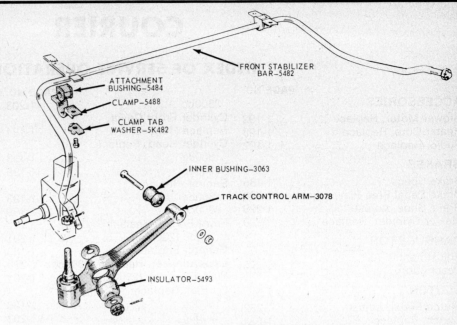

ATTACHMENT BUSHING—5484
CLAMP—5488
CLAMP TAB WASHER—5K482
FRONT STABILIZER BAR—5482
INNER BUSHING—3063
TRACK CONTROL ARM—3078
INSULATOR—5493

Fig. 10 Stabilizer bar and track control arm

4. Remove steering coupling lower clamp bolt, then separate tie rod ends from steering arm.

5. Remove steering rack retaining bolts and remove rack from vehicle.
6. Reverse procedure to install.

COURIER

INDEX OF SERVICE OPERATIONS

COURIER

MODEL INDEX & ENGINE APPLICATION

Model	Year	Engine Make	Standard Engine Model	Crankcase Refill Capacity, Qts.	Cooling System Capacity, Qts.
Courier	1972-77	Toyo Kogyo	4-109	4①	7½
Courier	1977	Isuzu	4-140	4①	7½

①—Add quart with filter replacement.

WHEEL ALIGNMENT SPECIFICATIONS

Model	Year	Caster, Deg.	Camber, Deg.	Toe-In, In.
Courier	1972	+1	+1⅜	⁵⁄₆₄—⅛
Courier	1973-76	+1	+1⅔	0—¼
Courier	1977	+1	+⅞	0—¼

GENERAL ENGINE SPECIFICATIONS

Year	Engine Model	Carb. Type	Bore & Stroke	Comp. Ratio	Horsepower @ R.P.M.	Torque Lbs. Ft. @ R.P.M.	Normal Oil Pressure Lbs.
1972-75	4-109.6	2 Bore	3.07 x 3.70	8.6	74 @ 5000	92 @ 3500	50—64
1976-77	4-109.6	2 Bore	3.07 x 3.70	8.6	—	—	50—64
1977	4-140	2 Barrel	3.78 x 3.126	—	—	—	40—60

TUNE UP SPECIFICATIONS

The following specifications are published from the latest information available. This data should be used only in the absence of a decal affixed in the engine compartment.

▲Before removing wires from distributor cap, determine location of No. 1 wire in cap, as distributor position may have been altered from that shown at the end of this chart.

Year	Engine	Spark Plug Type	Spark Plug Gap Inch	Distributor Point Gap Inch	Distributor Dwell Angle Deg.	Firing Order Fig. ▲	Ignition Timing BTDC ①	Ignition Timing Mark Locations Fig.	Hot Idle Speed	Comp. Press. P.S.I.	Fuel Pump Press., Lbs.
1972-73	4-109	AG32A	.031	.020	49—55	A	5°	B	725	②	2.8—3.6
1974	4-109	AG32A	.031	.020	49—55	A	3°	B	—	②	2.8—3.6
1975	4-109	AG32A	.031	.020	49—55	A	5°	B	—	②	2.8—3.6

①—Before top dead center. ②—When checking compression, lowest cylinder must be within 75 percent of highest.

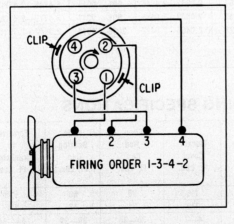

Fig. A

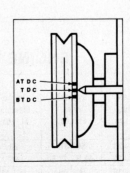

Fig. B

COURIER

DISTRIBUTOR SPECIFICATIONS

Year	Engine	Distributor Number	Breaker Gap, In.	Dwell Angle, Deg.	Breaker Arm Spring Tension Oz.	Centrifugal Advance Deg. @ Dist. R.P.M.		Vacuum Advance Deg. @ In. of Mercury		
						Advance Starts	Maximum Advance	Advance Starts	Maximum Advance	Retard
1972-73	4-109②	—	.020	49—55	17—20	0 @ 550	10.5 @ 2600	—	—	5 ATDC③
	4-109①	—	.020	49—55	17—20	0 @ 600	14 @ 2200	0 @ 12.6	7.5 @ 21.7	—
1974	4-109④	—	.020	49—55	17—20	0 @ 600	14 @ 2200	0 @ 8.7	7.5 @ 17.7	—
	4-109⑤	—	.020	49—55	17—20	0 @ 660	14 @ 2200	0 @ 10.6	7.5 @ 19.7	—

①—California.
②—Except California.
③—After top dead center.
④—Manual trans.
⑤—Auto. trans.

VALVE SPECIFICATIONS

Year	Engine	Valve Lash (Hot)		Valve Angles		Valve Springs		Valve Stem Clearance		Stem Diameter	
		Int.	Exh.	Seat	Face	Installed Height	Pressure Lbs. @ In.	Intake	Exhaust	Intake	Exhaust
1972	4-109	.012①	.012②	45	45	—	31½ @ 1¹¹/₃₂	.0007—.0023	.0007—.0023	.3150—.3168	.3150—.3168
1973	4-109	.012H	.013H	45	45	—	31½ @ 1¹¹/₃₂	.0007—.0021	.0007—.0023	.3161—.3167	.3159—.3161
1974-77	4-109	.012H	.012H	45	45	—	26.8 @ 1²³/₆₄	.0007—.0021	.0007—.0023	.3161—.3167	.3159—.3167
1977	4-140	③	③	45	44	1¹⁹/₃₂	75 @ 1.56	.0010—.0027	.0015—.0032	.3416—.3423	.3411—.3418

①—Exc. Calif.; Calif., .014.
②—Exc. Calif.; Calif., .016.
③—Collapsed tappet gap, .040—.050″.

PISTON, PIN, RING, CRANKSHAFT & BEARING SPECIFICATIONS

Year	Engine	Piston Clearance	Ring End Gap In. (Minimum)		Piston Pin Diam.	Rod Bearing		Main Bearing		Shaft End Play
			Comp.	Oil		Shaft Diameter	Bearing Clearance	Shaft Diameter	Bearing Clearance	
1972	4-109	.0022—.0028	.008—.016	.008—.016	.8659	2.0842—2.0866	.001—.0011	2.4784—2.4804	.0005—.0015	.003—.012
1973	4-109	.0022—.0028	.008—.016	.008—.016	.8657	2.0842—2.0846	.001—.0011	2.4746—2.4780	.0005—.0015	.003—.01
1974-77	4-109	.0022—.0028	.008—.016	.008—.016	.8657	2.0842—2.0848	.001—.0011	2.4779—2.4785	.0005—.0015	.003—.01
1977	4-140	.0014—.0022	.010	.015	.9122	2.0464—2.0472	.0008—.0015	2.3982—2.3990	.0008—.0015	.004—.008

ENGINE TIGHTENING SPECIFICATIONS

Year	Engine	Spark Plug Ft. Lbs.	Cylinder Head Ft. Lbs.	Intake Manifold Ft. Lbs.	Exhaust Manifold Ft. Lbs.	Rocker Cover Ft. Lbs.	Conn. Rod Cap. Ft. Lbs.	Main Bearing Cap. Ft. Lbs.	Flywheel to Crankshaft Ft. Lbs.	Oil Pump Sprocket Ft. Lbs.	Damper or Pulley Ft. Lbs.
1972-74	4-109	20—25	60—70	20	20	1½	30	60	115	25	—
1975-77	4-109	20—25	62.5—72.5	16	19	1½	31	63	115	23.5	—
1977	4-140	5—10	80—90	14—21	16—23	4—7	30—36	80—90	54—64	—	—

ALTERNATOR & REGULATOR SPECIFICATIONS

Year	Model	Alternator Cold Output @ 15 Volts Amperes @ 2000 R.P.M.	Regulator Voltage Regulator	
			Volts	Volts @ R.P.M.
1972-77	35 Amp.	35	14—15	1800

STARTING MOTOR SPECIFICATIONS

Year	Brush Spring Tension Oz.	Free Speed Test		
		Amperes	Volts	R.P.M.
1972-77	38	50①	11	5000②

①—Maximum.
②—Minimum.

COOLING SYSTEM & CAPACITY DATA

Year	Model or Engine	Cooling Capacity, Qts.		Radiator Cap Relief Pressure, Lbs.		Thermo. Opening Temp. ①	Fuel Tank Gals.	Engine Oil Refill Qts. ②	Transmission Oil			Rear Axle Oil Pints
		With Heater	With A/C	With A/C	No A/C				4 Speed Pints	5 Speed Pints	Auto. Trans. Qts. ③	
1972-73	4-109	7½	—	—	13	180	11.7	4	3	—	—	2.7
1974-76	4-109	7½	—	—	13	180	11.7	4	3	—	6.6④	3.2
1977	All	7½	—	—	13	180	⑤	4.1	3	3.6	6.6④	2.8

①—For permanent type anti-freeze.
②—Add one quart with filter change.
③—Approximate. Make final check with dipstick.
④—Total capacity; refill capacity, 3 quarts.
⑤—107" Wheel base, 15 gals; 113" Wheel base 17.5 gals.

REAR AXLE SPECIFICATIONS

Year	Model	Carrier Type	Ring Gear & Pinion Backlash		Pinion Bearing Preload			Differential Bearing Preload		
			Method	Adjustment	Method	New Bearings Inch—Lbs.	Used Bearings Inch—Lbs.	Method	New Bearing Inch—Lbs.	Used Bearing Inch—Lbs.
1972-74	All	Removable	①	.0075—.0083	Shims	11—15	—	①	.0045	—
1975-77	All	Removable	①	.0075—.0083	②	11.3—15.6	—	①	.0045	—

①—Threaded adjusters.
②—Collapsable spacer.

BRAKE SPECIFICATIONS

Year	Model	Drum I.D.	Wheel Cyl. Bore			Disc Brake Rotor					Master Cyl. I.D.
			Rear Drum	Front Drum	Front Disc	Nominal Thickness	Minimum Thickness	Thickness Variation (Parallelism)	Run Out (TIR)	Finish (micro in.)	
1972-76	All	10.236	¹³/₁₆	1	—	—	—	—	—	—	¾
1977	All	10.236	¾	—	2⅛	.4724	.4331	—	.0039	—	⅞

Electrical Section

DISTRIBUTOR, REPLACE

1800 cc Engine

Removal

1. Remove distributor cap and disconnect vacuum hose from vacuum advance unit.
2. Scribe a mark on distributor body and on cylinder head to indicate position of distributor. Then, scribe a mark on distributor body indicating position of distributor rotor.
3. Disconnect primary wires from distributor.
4. Remove distributor hold-down nut, lock washer and flat washer.
5. Remove distributor from engine.

Installation

1. If engine has been cranked, it is necessary to properly position the crankshaft for distributor installation. Rotate crankshaft until No. 1 piston is on compression stroke, then align TDC mark on pulley with the pointer.

2. If the engine has been cranked, slide distributor into cylinder head with the distributor rotor facing the No. 1 firing position.
3. If the engine has not been cranked, slide distributor into cylinder head, ensuring all index marks made during removal are aligned.
4. Loosely install the distributor hold-down flat washer, lock washer and nut.
5. Install distributor cap and connect primary wires.
6. Plug vacuum advance vacuum hose and time the engine to specifications. Tighten distributor hold-down nut.
7. Connect vacuum advance vacuum hose.

2300 cc Engine

Removal

1. Remove distributor cap and disconnect vacuum hose from vacuum advance unit.

2. Remove rubber plug from timing chain cover.
3. Scribe a mark between distributor housing and cylinder block. Then, scribe a mark on the housing indicating position of rotor.
4. Scribe a mark between cam gear and the inside of the timing chain cover.
5. The marks made in steps 3 and 4 should be used to install the distributor if the engine is not cranked after the distributor is removed.
6. Disconnect primary wires from distributor.
7. Remove distributor attaching bolt and lock plate.
8. Remove distributor from engine.

Installation

1. If the engine was cranked after the distributor was removed, it will be necessary to place No. 1 piston at top dead center, compression stroke. Crank engine until No. 1 cyl-

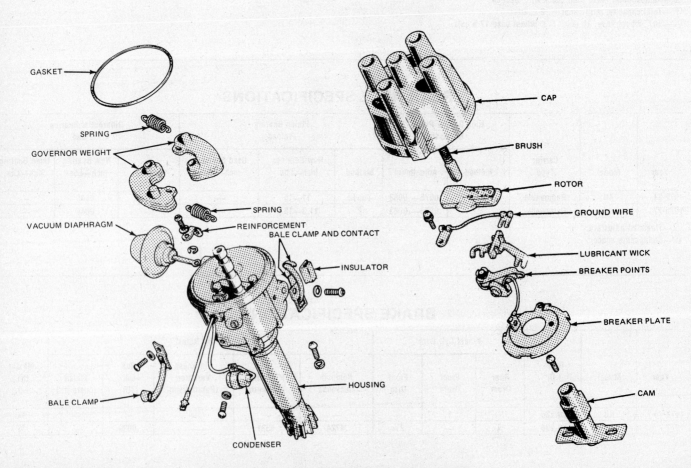

Fig. 1 Single breaker point distributor, disassembled

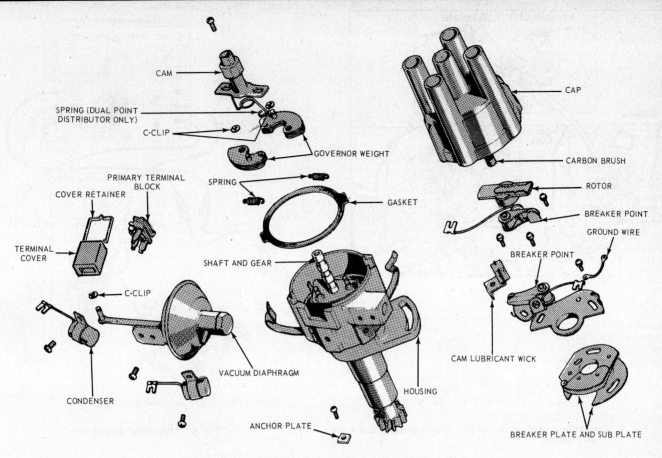

Fig. 2 Dual breaker point distributor, disassembled

inder is on compression stroke. Continue to rotate engine until the TDC mark on pulley aligns with pointer. The mark on the cam gear should align with the cam gear indicator. Install distributor into engine with rotor facing the No. 1 firing position.

2. If engine was not cranked after distributor was removed, install distributor into engine, ensuring all index marks made during removal are aligned.
3. Install lock plate and attaching bolt.
4. Install primary wires and distributor cap.
5. Adjust ignition timing and connect vacuum hose.

DISTRIBUTOR SERVICE
1800 cc Engine
Disassembly

1. Remove distributor cap and rotor, Figs. 1 and 2.
2. Loosen condenser lead attaching nuts and remove the condenser.
3. Disconnect breaker point lead from terminal and remove primary terminal block from distributor housing.

4. Remove "C" clip securing vacuum advance diaphragm link to breaker plate.
5. Remove breaker point attaching screw, then the points and cam lubricant felt retainer from breaker plate.
6. Remove cam attaching screws and the vacuum advance diaphragm attaching screws.

NOTE: Single point distributors are equipped with a reinforcement plate.

7. On dual point distributors, remove breaker plate subplate attaching screws and anchor plates.
8. On single point distributors, remove bale clamp attaching screws, then the bale clamps, ground terminal and the insulator.
9. On dual point distributors, rotate subplate counter-clockwise with a small screwdriver until the terminal block recess in the subplate is located below the vacuum advance diaphragm link, Fig. 3.
10. On all distributors, disconnect vacuum advance diaphragm link from breaker plate and remove diaphragm.

11. Remove breaker plate and subplate from distributor housing.
12. Lift cam and spring from centrifugal advance weights and from housing.

NOTE: The cam spring is used on the dual point distributor only.

13. Remove centrifugal advance springs and weights.

Assembly

1. Lubricate centrifugal weight pivot pins with distributor cam lubricant and position centrifugal weights on pins, then connect springs to the posts. On dual point distributors, the springs are retained with "C" clips.
2. Lubricate upper surface of shaft with distributor cam lubricant.
3. On dual point distributors, position the cam spring, Fig. 4, to interference with the centrifugal weight drive pin.
4. On all distributors, position cam on distributor shaft, ensuring each drive pin enters slot. Secure cam to the shaft with attaching screw. On dual point distributors, press end of cam spring to release spring to the normal operating position, Fig. 43.

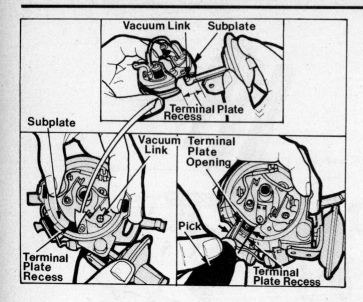

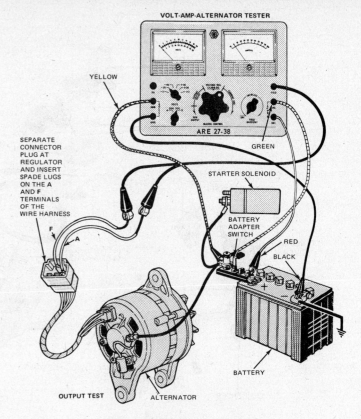

Fig. 4 Positioning cam return spring, dual breaker point distributor

Fig. 5 Alternator output test

5. On single point distributors, place breaker plate into housing and install insulator, ground terminal and bale clamps. Ensure the breaker plate ground wire is placed between the housing and plate and secured with a bale clamp attaching screw. Install vacuum advance diaphragm,

reinforcing plate and the attaching screws. Secure vacuum advance diaphragm link with a "C" clip.
6. On dual point distributors, install vacuum advance diaphragm, breaker plate and subplate. Ensure the terminal block recess in the subplate is aligned with the vacuum ad-

vance diaphragm link, Fig. 3. Hold subplate in position, rotate the breaker plate and insert the vacuum advance diaphragm link into breaker plate, then secure link with a "C" clip and the unit with two attaching screws. Rotate subplate clockwise with a screwdriver to align terminal

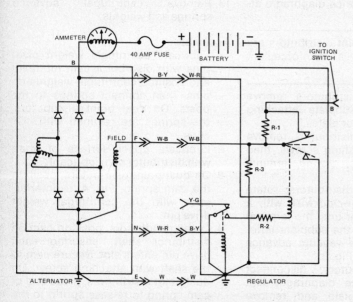

Fig. 6 Alternator charging circuit

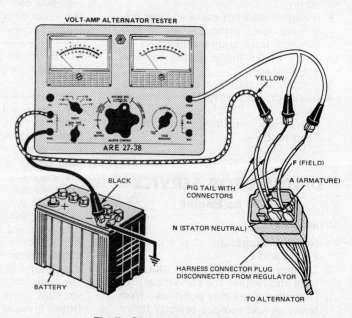

Fig. 7 Stator neutral voltage test

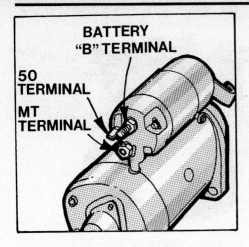

Fig. 8   Starter solenoid terminals

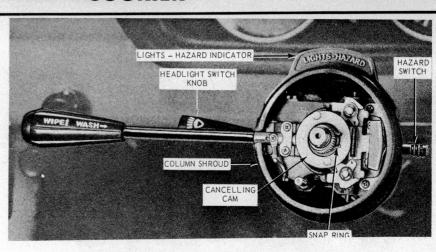

Fig. 9   Combination switch installation

block recess in subplate with terminal block opening in housing. Install subplate anchor plates, attaching screws and breaker point ground wire.

7. On all distributors, install breaker points and the cam lubricant wick and retainers.
8. Install condenser.
9. Install terminal block into housing. If equipped, and connect leads to terminals.

ALTERNATOR, REPLACE

1. Disconnect battery ground cable.
2. Remove nut retaining wire to alternator terminal, then pull multiple connector from rear of alternator.
3. Remove alternator adjusting arm bolt.
4. Remove distributor cap and rotor.
5. Remove alternator pivot bolt.
6. Remove alternator from vehicle.
7. Reverse procedure to install.

ALTERNATOR IN-TRUCK TESTING
Alternator Output Test

1. Make the connections and tester knob adjustments, Fig. 5 (Output Test). Be sure that the field rheostat knob is at the OFF position at the start of this test.
2. Close the battery adapter switch. Start the engine, then open the battery adapter switch.
3. Increase the engine speed to approximately 2000 rpm (use a tachometer following the manufacturers instructions). Turn off all lights and electrical accessories.
4. Turn the field rheostat clockwise until 15 volts is indicated on the voltmeter upper scale. Turn the master control clockwise until the voltmeter indicates between 11 and 12 volts. Holding the master control in this position, turn the field rheostat clockwise to its maximum rotation. Turn the master control counter clockwise until the voltmeter indicates 15 volts. Observe the ammeter reading. Add 2 amperes to this reading to obtain alternator output. If rated output cannot be obtained, increase the engine speed to 2900 rpm and repeat this step.

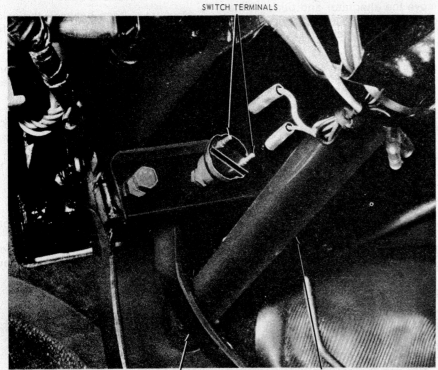

Fig. 10   Stop light switch installation

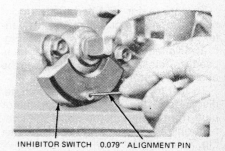

Fig. 11   Neutral start switch adjustment

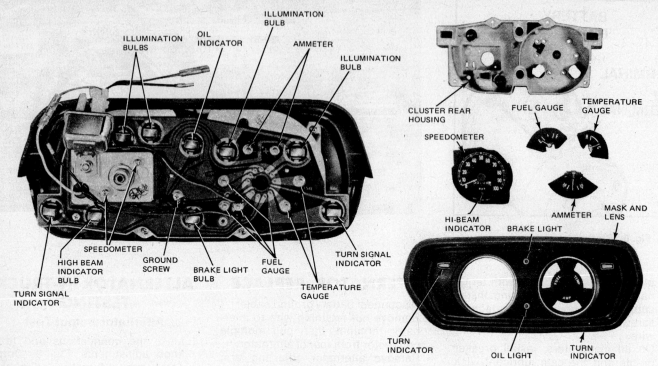

Fig. 12   Instrument cluster (Typical)

5. Return the field rheostat knob to OFF, release the master control knob, and stop the engine. Disconnect the test equipment, if no further tests are to be made.

If the alternator output is not O.K. it will be necessary to remove the alternator from the vehicle and perform the necessary bench tests to locate the defect.

An output of approximately 2 to 5 amperes below specification usually indicates an open alternator diode. An output of approximately 10 amperes below specification usually indicates a shorted alternator diode. An alternator with a shorted diode will usually whine, which will be most noticeable at idle speeds.

Stator Neutral Voltage Test

The alternator STA terminal is connected to the stator coil neutral or center point of the alternator windings. Fig. 6. The voltage generated at this point is used to close the field relay in the charge indicator light system.

To test for the stator neutral voltage, disconnect the regulator connector plug from the regulator. Make the connections and tester knob adjustments, Fig. 7

Start the engine and run it at 1000 rpm (use a tachometer). Turn off all lights and accessories. Rotate the field rheostat clockwise until at least 6 volts is indicated on the voltmeter upper scale. If 6 volts or more is not obtained, remove the alternator and perform the diode and stator tests to determine which part of the alternator is damaged.

Regulator Test

1. Connect tachometer to engine, then connect voltmeter positive lead to alternator B terminal and negative lead to regulator body (ground).
2. Start and operate engine at 1800 RPM and note voltmeter reading.
3. Voltmeter reading should be 14 to 15 volts. If reading is not within limits the regulator must be replaced.

STARTER, REPLACE

1. Disconnect battery ground cable.
2. Remove air cleaner and air intake tube.
3. Disconnect battery cable from starter solenoid battery terminal and pull the ignition switch wire from solenoid 50 terminal.
4. Remove the two starter attaching bolts, washers and nuts.
5. Tilt the drive end of the starter downward and remove from vehicle.
6. Reverse procedure to install.

STARTER IN-TRUCK TESTING

Solenoid Test

1. Measure voltage between the solenoid "50" terminal, Fig. 8, and the ground with the ignition switch in the "Start" position.
2. If the voltage in step 1 is 8 or more volts, remove starter and bench test the solenoid.
3. If voltage in step 1 is less than 8 volts, check complete starting system circuit.

IGNITION SWITCH, REPLACE

1. Disconnect battery ground cable.
2. Disconnect wiring connector from rear of ignition switch.
3. Remove switch retaining nut, then the switch from rear of instrument panel.
4. Reverse procedure to install.

COMBINATION SWITCH, REPLACE

1. Disconnect battery ground cable.
2. Remove steering wheel.
3. Remove plastic lights, hazard indicator and steering column shroud.

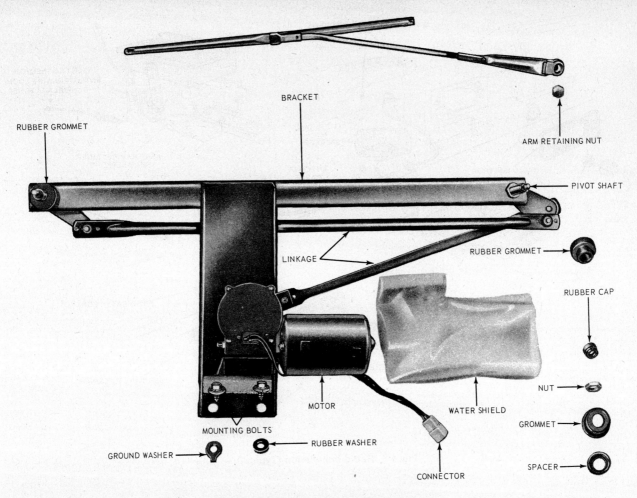

RUBBER GROMMET

BRACKET

ARM RETAINING NUT

PIVOT SHAFT

RUBBER GROMMET

RUBBER CAP

LINKAGE

NUT

MOTOR

WATER SHIELD

GROMMET

MOUNTING BOLTS

RUBBER WASHER

SPACER

GROUND WASHER

CONNECTOR

Fig. 13   Windshield wiper motor & linkage

4. Disconnect multiple connectors at base of steering column.
5. Pull headlamp switch knob from shaft, Fig. 9.
6. Remove switch snap ring retainer and pull turn signal indicator cancelling cam from shaft.
7. Remove retaining bolt near bottom of switch and pull combination switch from column.
8. Reverse procedure to install.

STOP LIGHT SWITCH, REPLACE

1. Disconnect electrical leads from switch, Fig. 10.
2. Remove switch retaining nut and the switch.
3. Reverse procedure to install.

NEUTRAL START SWITCH
Replace

1. Place transmission selector lever in the Neutral position.
2. Raise and remove transmission

manual lever retaining nut and the lever.
3. Disconnect electrical connector from switch.
4. Remove switch retaining bolts and the switch.
5. Reverse procedure to install.

Adjust

1. With manual linkage properly adjusted, place transmission manual lever in neutral, then remove transmission manual lever.
2. Loosen switch retaining bolts, Fig. 11, and remove alignment pin hole screw at switch bottom.
3. Rotate switch and insert a .079 inch diameter pin through alignment pin hole and into internal rotor hole, then tighten the switch retaining bolts and remove alignment pin.
4. Install alignment pin hole screw and the transmission manual lever.
5. Check switch for proper operation. The engine should start only when the transmission selector lever is in the neutral or park positions.

INSTRUMENT CLUSTER, REPLACE

1. Disconnect battery ground cable.
2. Remove screws securing cluster to instrument panel and pull cluster outward.
3. Disconnect speedometer cable, printed circuit multiple connector and the ammeter leads, Fig. 12. Note position of ammeter leads before disconnecting.
4. Remove screw attaching ground lead to rear of cluster.
5. On vehicles equipped with an air pump, remove the two connectors at the speedometer sensor switch.
6. On all vehicles, remove cluster from vehicle.
7. Reverse procedure to install.

W/S WIPER MOTOR & TRANSMISSION, REPLACE

1. Disconnect battery ground cable.
2. Remove wiper arm retaining nuts

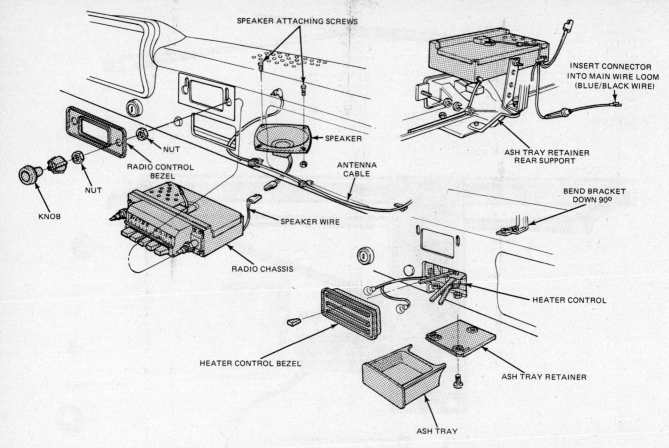

Fig. 14 Radio installation (Typical)

and the arm and blade assemblies, Fig. 13.

3. Remove rubber cap, nut, tapered spacer and rubber grommet from both pivot shafts.

4. Remove wiper motor and bracket assembly retaining bolts and washers.

5. Disconnect wiper motor electrical connector and remove motor and bracket assembly from vehicle. Note position of the rubber and ground washers at the bracket mounting holes. Remove plastic water shield.

6. Remove transmission to motor output arm retaining clip and position linkage aside.

7. Remove wiper motor to bracket retaining bolts and the motor.

8. Reverse procedure to install.

RADIO, REPLACE

1. Disconnect battery ground cable.

2. Remove ash tray, retainer and rear retainer support, Fig. 14.

3. Remove heater control knobs, bezel and right hand defroster hose.

4. Remove heater control and position toward the left.

5. Remove radio rear support bracket.

6. Bend bracket on dash panel downward 90°.

7. Remove radio knobs, attaching nuts and bezel.

8. Remove radio from rear of instru-

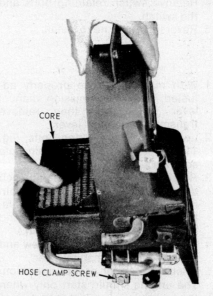

Fig. 16 Heater core, replace

ment panel and disconnect wiring from radio.

9. Remove radio from vehicle.

10. Reverse procedure to install.

BLOWER MOTOR, REPLACE

1. Disconnect battery ground cable and drain cooling system.

2. Remove water valve shield from left side of heater assembly.

3. Disconnect heater hoses and plug core openings.

4. Disconnect control cables from water valve and the heat-defrost and outside-recirc. doors.

5. Disconnect blower motor electrical connector, Fig. 15.

6. Remove glove box.

7. From engine compartment, remove heater assembly to dash panel retaining bolt and two nuts.

8. Disconnect defroster ducts from heater assembly and remove assembly from vehicle.

9. Remove screws securing heater assembly halves and separate assembly halves, Fig. 15.

VIEW A

FAN

RETAINING NUT

VIEW B

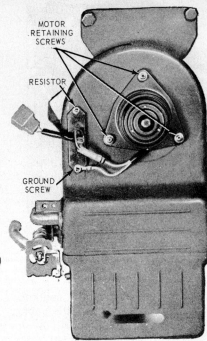
MOTOR RETAINING SCREWS

RESISTOR

GROUND SCREW

VIEW C

RETAINING SCREWS

Fig. 15 Blower motor, replace

10. Loosen fan retaining nut and lightly tap on nut to loosen fan, then remove nut and fan from motor shaft.
11. Remove motor to case retaining screws and disconnect resistor wiring and the motor ground wire.

12. Rotate motor and remove from case.
13. Reverse procedure to install.

HEATER CORE, REPLACE

1. Perform steps 1 through 9 as out-

lined under "Blower Motor, Replace" procedure.
2. Slide heater core from case, Fig. 16.
3. Reverse procedure to install.

Engine Section
1800cc Engine Section

ENGINE, REPLACE

1. Remove the hood and drain cooling system.
2. Remove air cleaner, disconnect radiator hoses at radiator and remove the radiator.
3. Disconnect accelerator linkage and fuel line at carburetor.
4. Unfasten linkage from intake manifold and remove linkage.
5. Disconnect cable at air by-pass valve on California models.
6. Disconnect choke cable, battery wires, coil wire at distributor and coil lead wire.
7. Remove the fan. Loosen alternator and remove belt.
8. If so equipped, remove Thermactor bolts and remove belt.
9. Remove alternator bracket and adjusting arm bolts and position alternator out of way. Disconnect Thermactor hoses at pump and remove Thermactor bracket and ad-

justing arm bolts and position pump out of way.
10. Remove heater hoses from front and rear of intake manifold and disconnect Thermactor air filter hose at by-pass valve.
11. Disconnect oil pressure gauge wire and boot from sending unit.
12. Remove bolt attaching battery cable to block and remove wires from starter solenoid.
13. Raise vehicle on hoist and drain crankcase. Remove engine front lower shield.
14. Disconnect exhaust pipe from manifold.
15. Remove flywheel housing bolts, lower starter nuts and one lower bolt. Remove lower exhaust pipe bolt and let pipe hang.
16. Lower vehicle and remove starter upper bolts and remove starter.
17. Support transmission with suitable jack and attach a sling to engine hanger brackets.

18. Remove nuts and bolts from engine mounts and using a lifting device attached to the sling, pull the engine forward until it clears the transmission shaft.
19. Reverse procedure to install.

CYLINDER HEAD, REPLACE

1. Drain cooling system, remove hood and air cleaner.
2. Disconnect lead wire and vacuum line from distributor.
3. Rotate crankshaft to place #1 cylinder on top dead center of compression stroke.
4. Remove plug wires and distributor cap as an assembly and remove distributor outlined under "Distributor, Replace" procedure in the Electrical Section.
5. Remove rocker arm cover.
6. Raise vehicle and disconnect exhaust pipe from manifold.
7. Lower vehicle and remove ac-

Fig. 1 Lower front head bolt. 1800cc engine

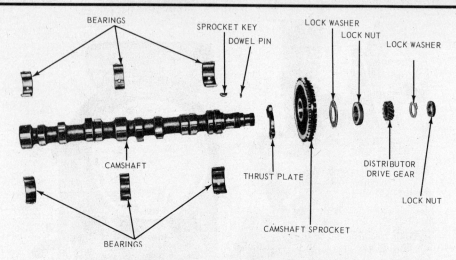

Fig. 2 Camshaft assembly. 1800cc engine

celerator linkage.
8. Disconnect temperature sending unit wire. Disconnect throttle cable at air by-pass valve, if so equipped. Disconnect choke cable at carburetor and fuel line at carburetor.
9. Disconnect Thermactor, if so equipped, and disconnect heater return hose at intake manifold. Disconnect by-pass hose and water pump hose.
10. Disconnect upper radiator hose at engine. Disconnect lead wire from air cut valve and remove intake manifold bracket.
11. Remove lower front head bolt, Fig. 1.
12. Remove nut, washer and distributor gear from camshaft and then remove nut, washer and camshaft gear, Fig. 2.
13. Remove cylinder head bolts.

14. Remove rocker arm assembly and camshaft.
15. Remove tension from timing chain as described further on.
16. Reverse procedure to install head and torque bolts, Fig. 3.

TIMING CHAIN TENSION

1. Remove crankshaft pulley and water pump and remove cover from tensioner.
2. Rotate crankshaft slightly in direction of rotation. Lift release on tensioner and compress snubber spring fully. Wedge a screwdriver in tensioner so it will not release, Fig. 4.
3. Remove two blind plugs and aluminum washers from holes in

chain cover and cylinder head. Loosen guide strip attaching screws.
4. Press top of chain guide strip with a lever through adjusting hole in head.
5. Tighten guide strip attaching screws with a screwdriver inserted through holes in chain cover.
6. Remove screwdriver from tensioner allowing snubber to take up slack.
7. Install blind plugs and washers in their holes in cover and head.
8. Install chain tensioner cover and gasket.
9. Install water pump and crankshaft pulley. Replace belts and adjust tension.

CYLINDER FRONT COVER

1. Remove hood and drain cooling system.
2. Disconnect hoses at radiator and remove radiator.
3. Remove belts, crankshaft pulley and water pump.

Fig. 3 Cylinder head tightening sequence. 1800cc engine

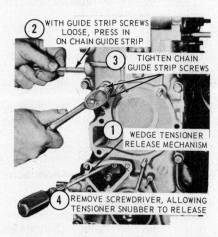

Fig. 4 Adjusting timing chain tension. 1800cc engine

Fig. 5 Checking valve clearance at valve. 1800cc engine

Fig. 6 Checking valve clearance at camshaft. 1800cc engine

Fig. 7 Valve guide removal. 1800cc engine

4. Remove cylinder head to front cover bolt.
5. Raise vehicle on hoist and remove engine front shield.
6. Disconnect emission line from oil pan.
7. Remove oil pan after draining.
8. Lower vehicle and remove alternator bracket and position alternator out of way. Position Thermactor pump aside, if so equipped. Remove steel tube bolts from front of engine.
9. Unfasten and remove front cover.

VALVES, ADJUST

1. Run engine until normal operating temperature is reached.
2. Shut off engine and remove rocker arm cover. Torque head bolts to proper torque.
3. Rotate crankshaft so #1 piston is at top dead center of compression stroke.
4. Check valve clearance with a feeler gauge at the valve or the camshaft, Figs. 5 and 6.
5. If clearance is incorrect, loosen adjusting screw locknut and turn adjusting screw until proper clearance is obtained. Hold screw in this position and tighten locknut.
6. Continue rotating crankshaft, adjusting valves for each cylinder at

top dead center of compression stroke in firing order sequence.

VALVE GUIDES

Valve guides in these engines are replaceable, therefore if inspection reveals need for replacement, drive out old guides with proper tool, Fig. 7.

When installing new guides, press in each guide squarely until the ring on the guide touches the head, Fig. 8. Note

that intake and exhaust valve guides are different.

ROCKER ARM COVER & SHAFT ASSEMBLY

1. Disconnect choke cable and position out of way. If so equipped, disconnect air by-pass valve cable and move out of way.

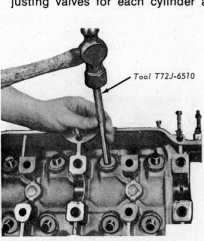

Fig. 8 Valve guide installation. 1800cc engine

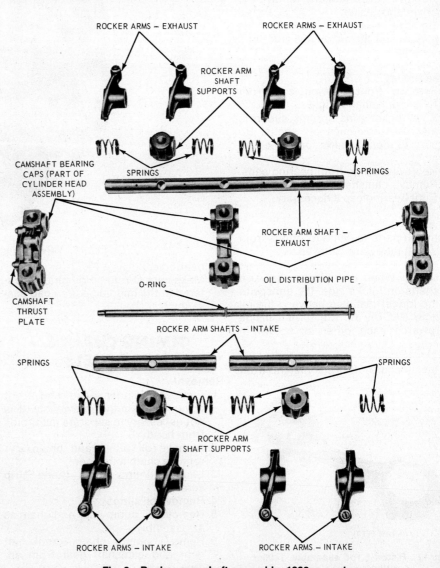

Fig. 9 Rocker arm shaft assembly. 1800cc engine

Fig. 10 Crankshaft gear & timing chain installation. 1800cc engine

2. Disconnect spark plug leads, remove from clip on rocker cover and move out of way.
3. Remove cover nuts and remove the cover and gasket.
4. Remove rocker arm shaft bolts evenly and lift off rocker arm shaft assembly.

Disassembly

1. Remove front bearing cap from rocker arm shafts, Fig. 9.
2. Slide rocker arms, springs, supports and bearings caps off shafts. Be sure to identify parts for proper assembly.
3. Remove oil pipe from bearing caps. Remove camshaft thrust plate from front bearing cap if necessary.

Assembly

1. Install parts to same locations from which they were removed.

NOTE: When installing rocker arm shafts on intake side, the ends with the longer distance between the oil hole and the tip are turned inside towards each other as shown in Fig. 9.

---

2. Install camshaft thrust plate to front

Fig. 12 Piston & rod assembly. 1800cc engine

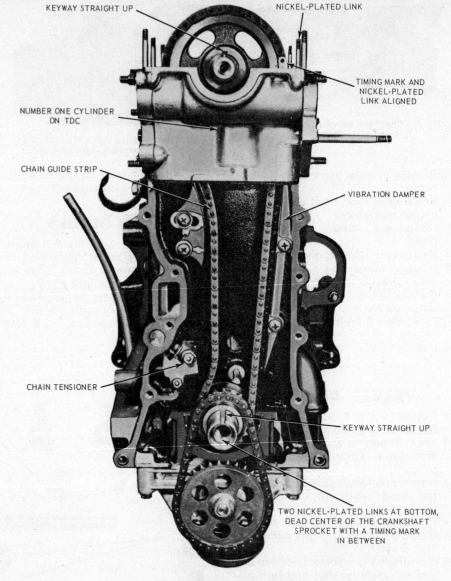

Fig. 11 Valve timing marks. 1800cc engine

bearing cap.
3. Make sure O-ring on oil pipe is centered in the middle bearing cap passage.

TIMING CHAIN & SPROCKETS

Removal

1. Remove cylinder head and front cover as described previously. It is not necessary to separate manifolds from head.
2. Remove oil pump and chain and remove chain tensioner.
3. Loosen timing chain guide strip screws.
4. Remove oil slinger.
5. Remove oil pump gear and chain as an assembly.
6. Remove timing chain, crankshaft gear and camshaft gear from engine.

Installation

1. Position crankshaft gear to chain and position gear and chain to crankshaft, Fig. 10.
2. Position oil pump chain and gear to crankshaft and oil pump.
3. Install oil slinger.

Fig. 13 Crankshaft rear oil seal removal. 1800cc engine

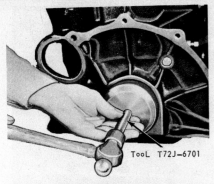

Fig. 14 Crankshaft rear oil seal installation. 1800cc engine

4. Install oil pump washer and nut. Bend washer over the nut.
5. Install timing chain tensioner. Do not release snubber spring tension.
6. Remove tensioner cover and remove blind plugs and washers from cover.
7. Replace cylinder head and camshaft. Before replacing rocker arm shaft assembly and camshaft bearing caps, obtain correct valve timing, Fig. 11, by rotating crankshaft to top dead center of #1 cylinder on compression stroke. It may be necessary to move camshaft gear one or more teeth in the chain to obtain correct timing.
8. Install rocker shaft and camshaft bearing caps and install and torque cylinder head bolts.
9. Adjust chain tension and release snubber.
10. Replace front cover.
11. Adjust valve clearance cold. Run engine and torque head bolts and adjust valve clearance hot.

CAMSHAFT

1. Remove hood and water pump.
2. Disconnect wire and vacuum line

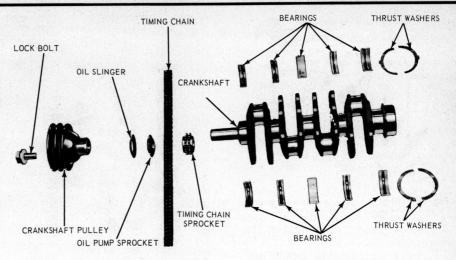

Fig. 15 Crankshaft assembly. 1800cc engine

from distributor.
3. Rotate crankshaft to place #1 cylinder at top dead center of compression stroke.
4. Remove plug wires and distributor cap as an assembly and remove distributor.
5. Remove rocker arm cover.
6. Relieve tension on timing chain.
7. Remove cylinder head bolts and rocker arm assembly.
8. Remove nut, washer and distributor gear from camshaft and remove nut and washer holding camshaft gear, Fig. 2.
9. Remove camshaft.

NOTE: Do not remove camshaft gear from chain. Use care to insure that gear teeth and chain relationship is not disturbed.

PISTON & ROD, ASSEMBLE

Lubricate all parts with light engine oil. Position the rod in the piston and push the pin into place, Fig. 12. When the pin is centered in the piston replace the retaining clips.

CRANKSHAFT OIL SEAL

If the rear oil seal is the only operation being performed, it can be done in the car. If the oil seal is being replaced in conjunction with rear main bearing replacement, the engine must be removed.

To replace seal only in car, proceed as follows:
1. Remove transmission, clutch disc, plate and flywheel.
2. Use an awl to punch two holes in the oil seal. Punch holes in seal on opposite sides of crankshaft and just

above the bearing cap to cylinder block split line.
3. Install a sheet metal screw in each hole, Fig. 13. Using two large screwdrivers pry against both screws at same time to remove the seal. It may be necessary to place small blocks of wood against the block to provide a fulcrum point for prying. Use caution to avoid scratching crankshaft seal surface.
4. Clean recesses in block and main bearing cap.

Installation
1. Coat the seal to block surface of the seal with oil and coat the seal contact surface of the seal and crankshaft with Lubriplate. Start seal in recess and install with tool shown in Fig. 14.

CRANKSHAFT OIL SEAL

If the rear oil seal is the only operation being performed, it can be done in the car. If the oil seal is being replaced in conjunction with rear main bearing replacement, the engine must be removed.

Fig. 17 Oil pump installation. 1800cc engine

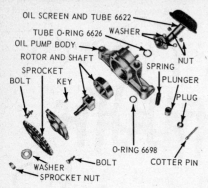

Fig. 18 Oil pump disassembled. 1800cc engine

To replace seal only in vehicle, proceed as follows:

1. Remove transmission, clutch disc, plate and flywheel.
2. Use an awl to punch two holes in the oil seal. Punch holes in seal on opposite sides of crankshaft and just above the bearing cap to cylinder block split line.
3. Install a sheet metal screw in each hole, Fig. 13. Using two large screwdrivers pry against both screws at same time to remove the seal. It may be necessary to place small blocks of wood against the block to provide a fulcrum point for prying. Use caution to avoid scratching crankshaft seal surface.
4. Clean recesses in block and main bearing cap.

Installation

1. Coat the seal to block surface of the seal with oil and coat the seal contact surface of the seal and crankshaft with Lubriplate. Start seal in recess and install with tool shown in Fig. 14.

CRANKSHAFT END PLAY

End play is controlled by the use of thrust washers, Fig. 15. To check, take up the end play in one direction. Insert a feeler between crankshaft and thrust washer. Install correct thickness of thrust washers to establish specified end play.

OIL PAN, REPLACE

1. Raise vehicle on hoist, drain crankcase and remove engine front lower shield.
2. Remove clutch release cylinder attaching nuts and let cylinder hang.
3. Remove engine rear brace bolts and loosen bolts on left side.
4. Disconnect emission line from oil pan.
5. Remove oil pan nuts and bolts and lower pan onto crossmember.

6. Remove oil pump pick up tube from pump and remove oil pan.

OIL PUMP, REPLACE

Removal

1. Remove oil pan as described previously.
2. Remove oil pump gear attaching nut.
3. Remove oil pump to block bolts. Loosen gear on pump.
4. Remove the oil pump and remove the gear.

Installation

1. Position pump gear to the chain.
2. Position pump to the gear and block, Figs. 16 and 17.
3. Install pump to block bolts.
4. Install washer and gear and nut and bend lock tab on washer.
5. Install oil pan.

OIL PUMP REPAIRS

Disassembly

1. Remove oil inlet tube, then the cover attaching screws and the cover, Fig. 18.
2. Remove inner rotor and shaft assembly, then the outer race.
3. Remove cotter pin from body. Pull cap from chamber and remove spring and plunger.

Assembly

1. Install the plunger, spring and cap.
2. Install new cotter pin.

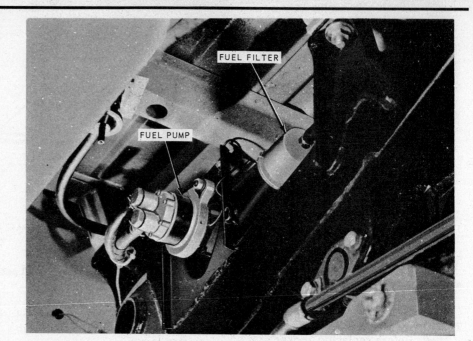

Fig. 19 Fuel pump installation. 1800cc engine

3. Install outer race and the inner rotor and shaft assembly. The inner rotor and shaft and the outer race is serviced as an assembly. Any component should not be replaced individually.
4. Install cover and tighten attaching screws.
5. Install new oil inlet tube gasket on pump, then the oil inlet tube.

WATER PUMP, REPLACE

1. Drain cooling system and remove the hood.
2. Remove lower hose from the pump.
3. Disconnect upper hose at engine and lower hole at radiator.
4. Slacken alternator and Thermactor pump, if so equipped, and remove drive belts.
5. Remove the fan and pulley and the crankshaft pulley.
6. Unfasten and remove water pump.

FUEL PUMP

An external electric fuel pump mounted on the left frame side rail adjacent to the fuel tank is used, Fig. 19. Current is provided to the pump through the ignition circuit when the key is in the run position.

1. Remove fuel pump shield from the frame.
2. Disconnect fuel inlet and outlet hoses at pump.
3. Remove bolts attaching pump to the mounting bracket and remove the pump.
4. Reverse procedure to install.

Engine Section
2300cc Engine Section

ENGINE, REPLACE

1. Disconnect battery cables.
2. Scribe hood hinge locations and remove hood.
3. Drain cooling system.
4. Remove air cleaner and heat stove assembly.
5. Remove radiator hoses.
6. Remove radiator shroud and radiator.
7. Disconnnect air pump hoses from pump.
8. Disconnect heater hoses from intake manifold and dash panel.
9. Disconnect choke cable and accelerator linkage from carburetor.
10. Disconnect vacuum brake booster hose.
11. Disconnect vacuum lines from vacuum amplifier.
12. Disconnect coil wire from distributor and the coil wiring.
13. Remove alternator drive belt and bracket, then position alternator aside.
14. Disconnect fuel line from carburetor.
15. Disconnect battery ground cable from cylinder block.
16. Raise and support vehicle and drain oil pan.

17. Disconnect exhaust pipe from exhaust manifold.
18. Remove exhaust pipe hanger from transmission.
19. Remove engine support attaching bolts and the right engine mount bracket from engine.
20. Remove the lower transmission to engine attaching bolts.
21. Lower vehicle.
22. Support transmission with a suitable jack and remove the remaining transmission to engine attaching bolts.
23. Attach suitable engine lifting equipment to engine.
24. Remove clutch slave cylinder from transmission.
25. Pull engine forward to clear transmission shaft, then remove engine from vehicle.
26. Reverse procedure to install.

CYLINDER HEAD, REPLACE

1. Drain cooling system and remove air cleaner and rocker arm cover.
2. Remove intake and exhaust manifolds and carburetor.
3. Remove timing case cover and drive belt.

4. Remove water outlet elbow from head.
5. Remove cylinder head bolts, then remove cylinder head.

NOTE: The cylinder head retaining bolts have 12 point heads.

---

6. Reverse procedure to install. Torque cylinder head bolts in sequence shown in Fig. 1 and intake manifold bolts in sequence shown in Fig. 2.

CAUTION: When installing cylinder head, position camshaft at 5 o'clock position, Fig. 1, allowing minimal protrusion of the valves from the cylinder head.

VALVE ARRANGEMENT
Front to Rear

2300 cc Engine . . . . .E-I-E-I-E-I-E-I

VALVE LIFT SPECS.

Engine	Year	Intake	Exhaust
2300 cc	1977	.400	.400

VALVE TIMING
Intake Opens Before TDC

Engine	Year	Degrees
2300 cc	1977	22

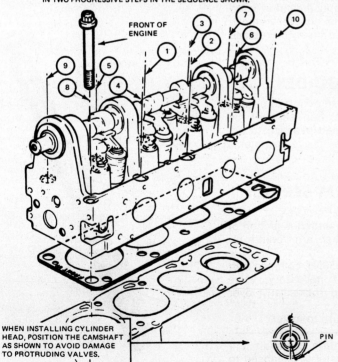

TORQUE THE CYLINDER HEAD BOLTS TO SPECIFICATIONS IN TWO PROGRESSIVE STEPS IN THE SEQUENCE SHOWN.

FRONT OF ENGINE

WHEN INSTALLING CYLINDER HEAD, POSITION THE CAMSHAFT AS SHOWN TO AVOID DAMAGE TO PROTRUDING VALVES.

PIN

Fig. 1 Cylinder head installation. 2300cc engine

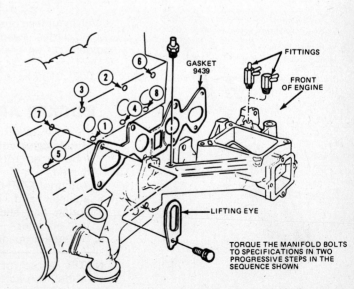

GASKET 9439

FITTINGS

FRONT OF ENGINE

LIFTING EYE

TORQUE THE MANIFOLD BOLTS TO SPECIFICATIONS IN TWO PROGRESSIVE STEPS IN THE SEQUENCE SHOWN

Fig. 2 Intake manifold installation. 2300cc engine

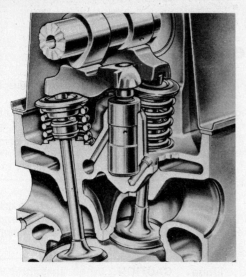

Fig. 3 Valve train installation. 2300cc engine

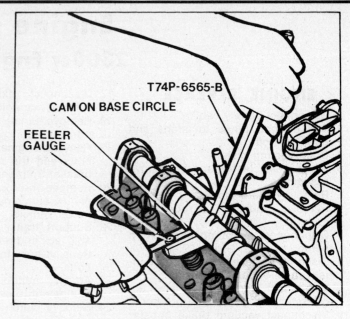

T74P-6565-B
CAM ON BASE CIRCLE
FEELER GAUGE

Fig. 4 Checking valve clearance. 2300cc engine

VALVES, ADJUST

The valve lash on this engine cannot be adjusted due to the use of hydraulic valve lash adjusters. Fig. 3. However, the valve train can be checked for wear as follows:

1. Crank engine to position camshaft with flat section of lobe facing rocker arm of valve being checked.

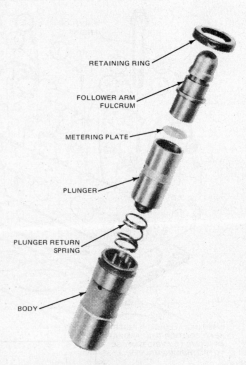

RETAINING RING

FOLLOWER ARM FULCRUM

PLUNGER

PLUNGER RETURN SPRING

BODY

Fig. 5 Valve lash adjuster, Type I. 2300cc engine

2. Collapse lash adjuster with tool T74P-6565B and insert correct size feeler gauge between rocker arm and cam shaft lobe, Fig. 4. If clearance is not as listed in the "Valve Specifications" chart in front of this chapter, remove rocker arm and check for wear and replace as necessary. If rocker arm is found satisfactory, check valve spring assembled height and adjust as needed. If valve spring assembled height is within specifications listed in the front of this chapter, remove lash adjuster and clean or replace as necessary.

VALVE GUIDES

Valve guides consist of holes bored in the cylinder head. For service the guides can be reamed oversize to accommodate valves with oversize stems of .003, .015 and .030".

ROCKER ARM SERVICE

1. Remove rocker arm cover.
2. Rotate camshaft until flat section of lobe faces rocker arm being removed.
3. With tool T74P-6565B, collapse lash adjuster and, if necessary, valve spring and slide rocker arm over lash adjuster.
4. Reverse procedure to install.

NOTE: Before rotating camshaft, ensure that lash adjuster is collapsed to prevent valve train damage.

LASH ADJUSTER, REPLACE

The hydraulic valve lash adjusters can be removed after rocker arm removal. There are two types of lash adjusters available, Type I, being the standard lash adjuster, Fig. 5, and Type II, having a .020 inch oversize outside diameter, Fig. 6.

RETAINING RING

FOLLOWER ARM FULCRUM

METERING PLATE

PLUNGER

PLUNGER RETURN SPRING

BODY

Fig. 6 Valve lash adjuster, Type II. 2300cc engine

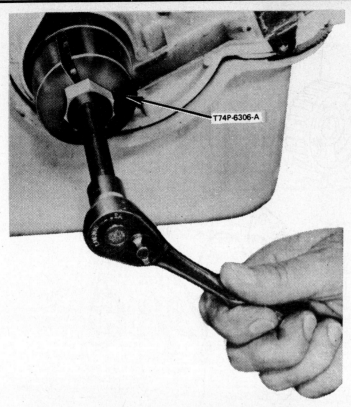

Fig. 7 Crankshaft sprocket removal. 2300cc engine

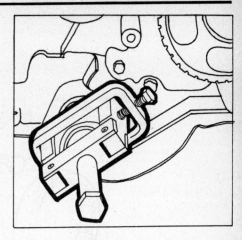

Fig. 8 Crankshaft front oil seal removal. 2300cc engine

FRONT ENGINE SEALS, REPLACE

To gain access to the front engine seals, remove the timing belt cover and proceed as follows:

Crankshaft Oil Seal
1. Without removing cylinder front cover, remove crankshaft sprocket with tool T74P-6306A, Fig. 7.
2. Remove crankshaft oil seal with tool T74P-6700B, Fig. 8.
3. Install a new crankshaft oil seal with tool T74P-6150A, Fig. 9.
4. Install crankshaft sprocket with recess facing engine block, Fig. 10.

Camshaft & Auxiliary Shaft Oil Seals
1. Remove camshaft or auxiliary shaft sprocket with tool T74P-6256A, Fig. 11.
2. Remove oil seal with tool T74P-6700B, Fig. 12.
3. Install a new oil seal with tool T74P-6150A, Fig. 9.
4. Install camshaft or auxiliary shaft sprocket with tool T74P-6256A with center arbor removed.

TIMING BELT
1. Position crankshaft at TDC, No. 1 cylinder compression stroke.
2. Remove timing belt cover, loosen belt tensioner, and remove belt from sprockets, Fig. 10. Tighten tensioner bolt, holding tensioner in position.

NOTE: Do not rotate crankshaft or camshaft after belt is removed. Rotating either component will result in improper valve timing.

3. To install belt, ensure timing marks are aligned, Fig. 13, and place belt over sprockets.

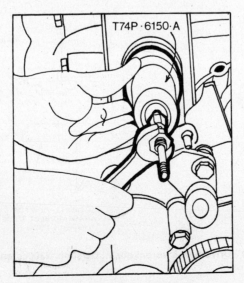

Fig. 9 Crankshaft front oil seal installation. 2300cc engine

4. Loosen tensioner bolt, allowing tensioner to move against belt.
5. Rotate crankshaft two complete turns, removing slack from belt. Torque tensioner adjustment and pivot bolts and check alignment of timing marks, Fig. 13.
6. Install timing belt cover.

CAMSHAFT, REPLACE
1. Remove rocker arm cover and rocker arms.
2. Remove timing belt cover, camshaft sprocket bolt and washer, then slide sprocket and belt guide off camshaft.
3. Remove camshaft retaining plate from rear of head, then remove camshaft from front of head.

PISTON & ROD, ASSEMBLE

Assemble the rod to the piston with the arrow on top of piston facing front of engine, Fig. 14.

PISTONS, PINS & RINGS

Oversize pistons are available in oversizes of .003″, .020″, .030″ and .040″. Oversize rings are available in .020″, .030″ and .040″ oversizes. Oversize pins are not available.

MAIN & ROD BEARINGS

Undersize main bearings are available in .002″, .020″, .030″ and .040″ undersizes. Undersize rod bearings are available in undersizes of .002″, .010″, .020″, .030″ and .040″.

The crankshaft and main bearings are installed with arrows on main bearing caps facing front of engine, Fig. 15. Install PCV baffle between bearing journals No. 3 and 4.

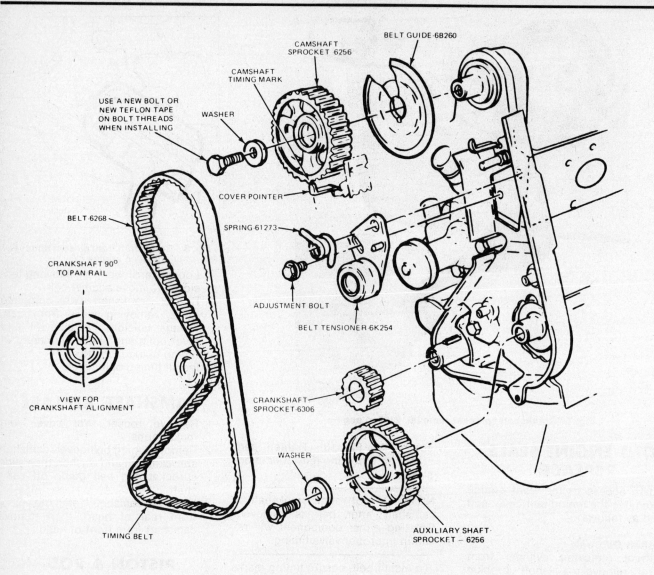

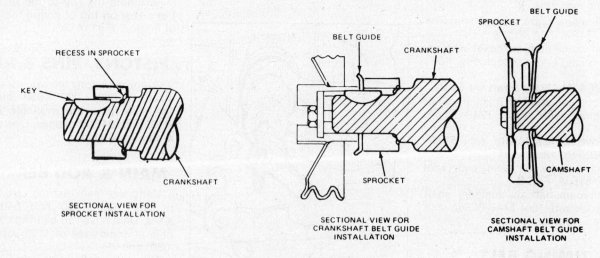

RECESS IN SPROCKET

KEY

CRANKSHAFT

SECTIONAL VIEW FOR
SPROCKET INSTALLATION

BELT GUIDE

CRANKSHAFT

SPROCKET

SECTIONAL VIEW FOR
CRANKSHAFT BELT GUIDE
INSTALLATION

SPROCKET

BELT GUIDE

CAMSHAFT

SECTIONAL VIEW FOR
CAMSHAFT BELT GUIDE
INSTALLATION

Fig. 10 Drive belt & sprockets installation. 2300cc engine

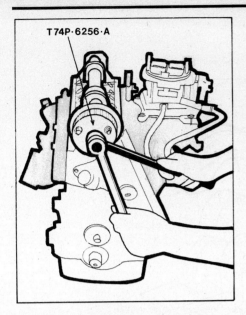

Fig. 11 Camshaft & auxiliary shaft sprockets removal. 2300cc engine

T74P·6256·A

T74P-6700-B

OIL PAN

1. Drain crankcase and remove oil dipstick and flywheel inspection cover.
2. Disconnect steering cable from rack and pinion, then rack and pinion from crossmember and move forward to provide clearance.
3. Unfasten and remove oil pan. To install oil pan, refer to Fig. 16.

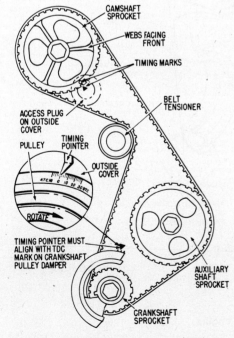

Fig. 13 Valve timing marks. 2300cc engine

CAMSHAFT SPROCKET
WEBS FACING FRONT
TIMING MARKS
BELT TENSIONER
ACCESS PLUG ON OUTSIDE COVER
PULLEY
TIMING POINTER
OUTSIDE COVER
ROTATE
TIMING POINTER MUST ALIGN WITH TDC MARK ON CRANKSHAFT PULLEY DAMPER
AUXILIARY SHAFT SPROCKET
CRANKSHAFT SPROCKET

CRANKSHAFT OIL SEAL

1. Remove oil pan.
2. Remove rear main bearing cap.
3. Loosen remaining bearing caps, allowing crankshaft to drop down about $1/32''$.
4. Install a sheet metal screw into seal and pull screw to remove seal.
5. Carefully clean seal groove in block with a brush and solvent. Also clean seal groove in bearing cap.
6. Dip seal halves in clean engine oil.
7. Carefully install upper seal half in its groove with locating tab toward rear of engine, Fig. 17, by rotating it on shaft journal of crankshaft until approximately $3/8''$ protrudes below the parting surface. *Be sure no rubber has been shaved from outside diameter of seal by bottom edge of groove.*
8. Retighten main bearing caps and torque to specifications.
9. Install lower seal in main bearing cap with undercut side of seal toward front of engine, and allow seal to protrude about $3/8''$ above parting surface to mate with upper seal upon cap installation.
10. Apply suitable sealer to parting faces of cap and block. Install cap and torque to specifications.

NOTE: If difficulty is encountered in installing the upper half of the seal in position, lightly lap (sandpaper) the side of the seal opposite the lip side using a medium grit paper. After sanding, the seal must be washed in solvent, then dipped in clean engine oil prior to installation.

OIL PUMP, REPLACE

The oil pump, Fig. 18, can be removed after oil pan removal, Fig. 19.

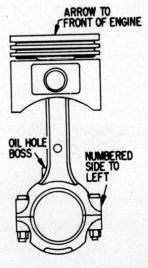

ARROW TO FRONT OF ENGINE
OIL HOLE BOSS
NUMBERED SIDE TO LEFT

Fig. 14 Piston & rod assembly. 2300cc engine

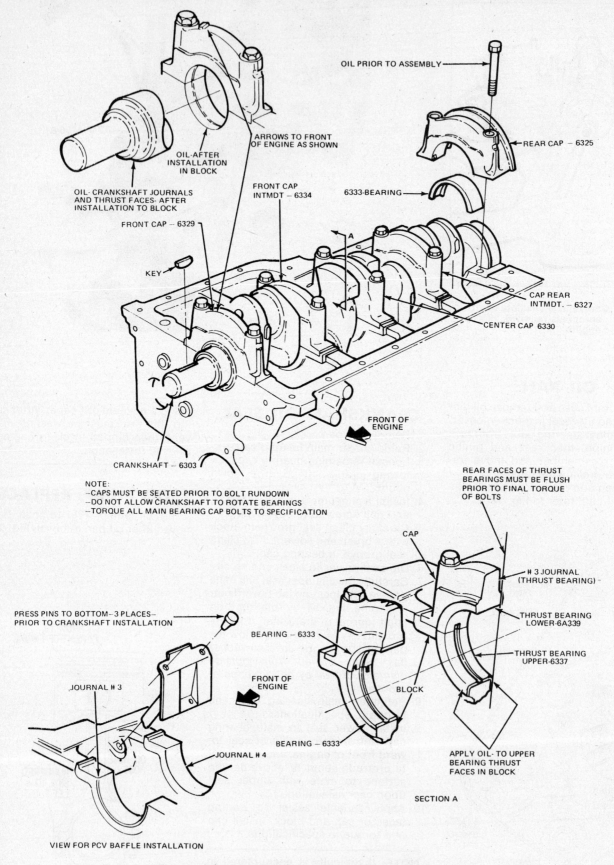

OIL PRIOR TO ASSEMBLY

ARROWS TO FRONT OF ENGINE AS SHOWN

OIL-AFTER INSTALLATION IN BLOCK

REAR CAP — 6325

OIL- CRANKSHAFT JOURNALS AND THRUST FACES- AFTER INSTALLATION TO BLOCK

FRONT CAP INTMDT — 6334

6333-BEARING

FRONT CAP — 6329

KEY

A

A

CAP REAR INTMDT. — 6327

CENTER CAP 6330

FRONT OF ENGINE

CRANKSHAFT — 6303

NOTE:
—CAPS MUST BE SEATED PRIOR TO BOLT RUNDOWN
—DO NOT ALLOW CRANKSHAFT TO ROTATE BEARINGS
—TORQUE ALL MAIN BEARING CAP BOLTS TO SPECIFICATION

REAR FACES OF THRUST BEARINGS MUST BE FLUSH PRIOR TO FINAL TORQUE OF BOLTS

CAP

3 JOURNAL (THRUST BEARING)

THRUST BEARING LOWER-6A339

THRUST BEARING UPPER-6337

PRESS PINS TO BOTTOM- 3 PLACES- PRIOR TO CRANKSHAFT INSTALLATION

BEARING — 6333

FRONT OF ENGINE

BLOCK

JOURNAL # 3

JOURNAL # 4

BEARING — 6333

APPLY OIL- TO UPPER BEARING THRUST FACES IN BLOCK

SECTION A

VIEW FOR PCV BAFFLE INSTALLATION

Fig. 15 Crankshaft & main bearing installation. 2300cc engine

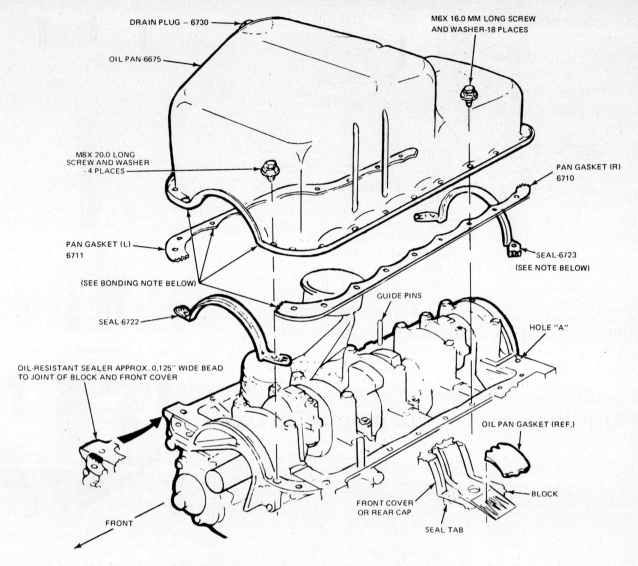

DRAIN PLUG – 6730

OIL PAN-6675

M6X 16.0 MM LONG SCREW
AND WASHER-18 PLACES

M8X 20.0 LONG
SCREW AND WASHER
- 4 PLACES

PAN GASKET (R)
6710

PAN GASKET (L)
6711

SEAL-6723
(SEE NOTE BELOW)

(SEE BONDING NOTE BELOW)

SEAL-6722

GUIDE PINS

HOLE "A"

OIL-RESISTANT SEALER APPROX. 0.125" WIDE BEAD
TO JOINT OF BLOCK AND FRONT COVER

OIL PAN GASKET (REF.)

FRONT

FRONT COVER
OR REAR CAP

SEAL TAB

BLOCK

1. APPLY GASKET ADHESIVE EVENLY TO OIL PAN FLANGE AND TO PAN SIDE
   GASKETS. ALLOW ADHESIVE TO DRY PAST WET STAGE, THEN INSTALL
   GASKETS TO OIL PAN.
2. APPLY SEALER TO JOINT OF BLOCK AND FRONT COVER. INSTALL SEALS TO
   FRONT COVER AND REAR BEARING CAP AND PRESS SEAL TABS FIRMLY INTO
   BLOCK. BE SURE TO INSTALL THE REAR SEAL BEFORE THE REAR MAIN
   BEARING CAP SEALER HAS CURED.
3. POSITION 2 GUIDE PINS AND INSTALL THE OIL PAN. SECURE THE PAN WITH
   THE FOUR M8 BOLTS SHOWN ABOVE.
4. REMOVE THE GUIDE PINS AND INSTALL AND TORQUE THE EIGHTEEN M6 BOLTS,
   BEGINNING AT HOLE "A" AND WORKING CLOCKWISE AROUND THE PAN.

Fig. 16 Crankshaft rear oil seal installation. 2300cc engine

OIL PUMP REPAIRS

1. Remove end plate and withdraw O ring from groove in body.
2. Check clearance between lobes of inner and outer rotors. This should not exceed .006". Rotors are supplied only in a matched pair.
3. Check clearance between outer rotor and the housing, Fig. 20. This should not exceed .010".
4. Place a straightedge across face of pump body, Fig. 21. Clearance between face of rotors and straightedge should not exceed .005".
5. If necessary to replace rotor or drive shaft, remove outer rotor and then drive out retaining pin securing the skew gear to drive shaft and pull off the gear.
6. Withdraw inner rotor and drive shaft.

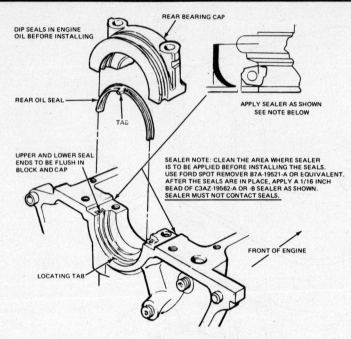

Fig. 17 Oil pan installation. 2300cc engine

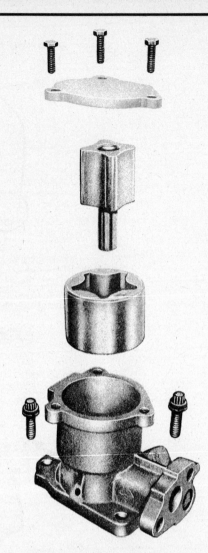

Fig. 18 Oil pump disassembled. 2300cc engine

BELT TENSION DATA

	New Ft. Lbs.	Used Ft. Lbs.
1977 All	140	110

WATER PUMP, REPLACE

1. Drain cooling system and disconnect hoses from pump.
2. Loosen alternator and remove drive belt.

3. Remove fan, spacer and pulley.
4. Remove water pump attaching bolts and water pump after removing drive belt cover, Fig. 22.

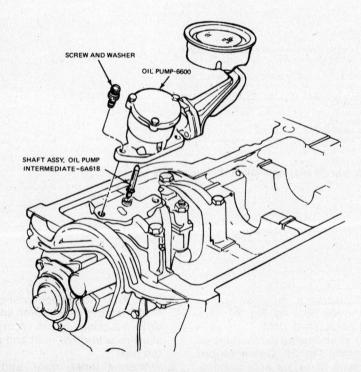

Fig. 19 Oil pump installation. 2300cc engine

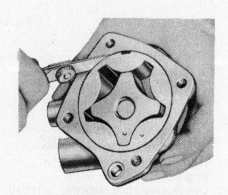

Fig. 20 Checking oil pump outer rotor to housing clearance. 2300cc engine

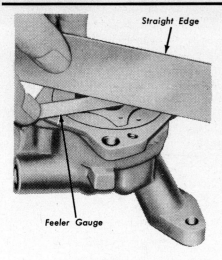

Fig. 21 Checking oil pump rotor end play. 2300cc engine

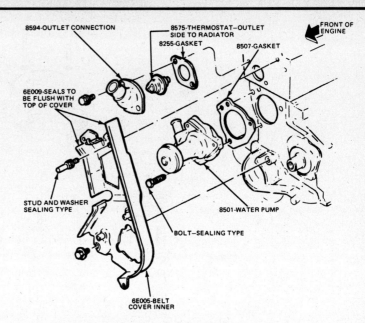

Fig. 22 Water pump installation. 2300cc engine

FUEL PUMP PRESSURE

Year	Engine	Pressure Lbs.
1977	2300 cc	5-7

FUEL PUMP, REPLACE

An external electric fuel pump mounted on the left frame side rail adjacent to the fuel tank is used. Current is provided to the pump through the ignition circuit when the key is in the run position.

1. Remove fuel pump shield from the frame.
2. Disconnect fuel inlet and outlet hoses at pump.
3. Remove bolts attaching pump to the mounting bracket and remove the pump.
4. Reverse procedure to install.

Carburetor Section

DESCRIPTION

A Zenith-Stromberg two-stage, two venturi downdraft carburetor, Figs. 1, 2 and 3.

The primary stage includes a curb idle system, accelerator pump system, idle transfer system, main metering system and power enrichment system.

The secondary stage includes an idle transfer system, main metering system and a power enrichment system.

Choking action is accomplished by a cable operated manual choke.

ADJUSTMENTS

Idle Speed & Fuel Mixture

1. Set transmission in neutral.
2. Start engine and allow it to run until at operating temperature.
3. Connect a tachometer to engine and set curb idle speed to specification, Fig. 4.
4. Connect an exhaust emission analyzer to vehicle and turn mixture

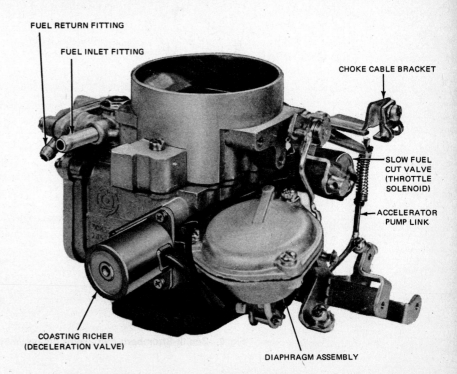

Fig. 1 Zenith-Stromberg carburetor

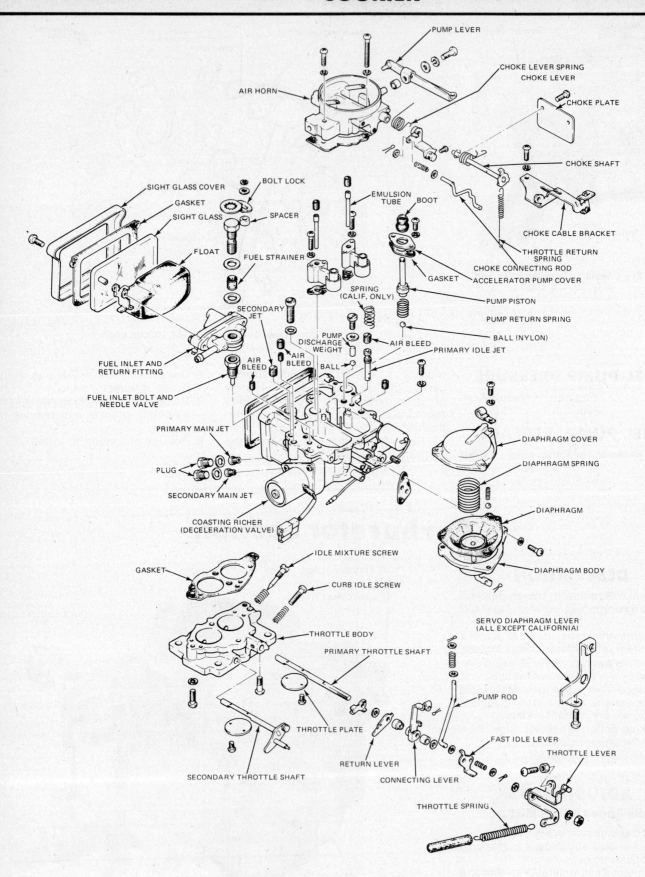

Fig. 2 Zenith-Stromberg carburetor disassembled, 1972-74

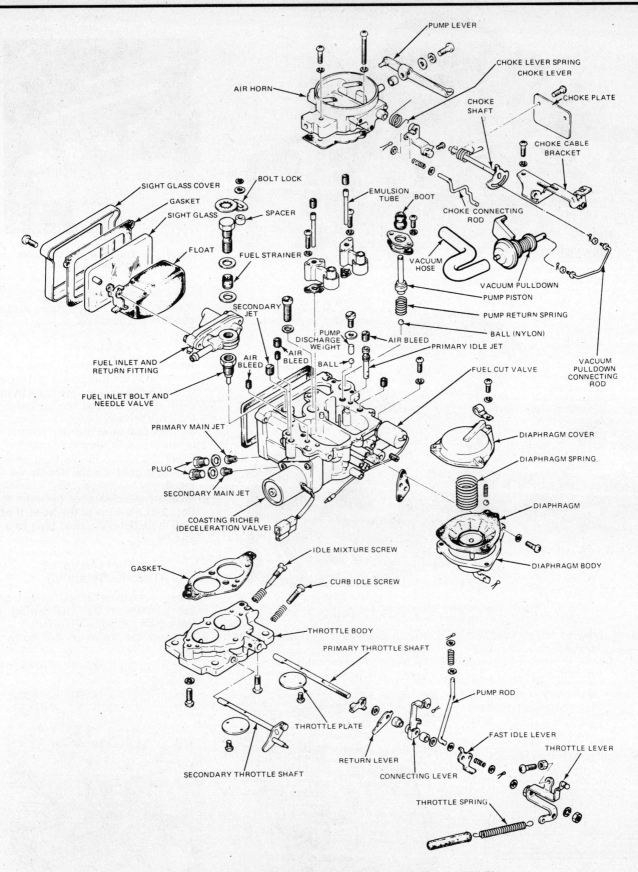

Fig. 3 Zenith-Stromberg carburetor disassembled, 1975-76

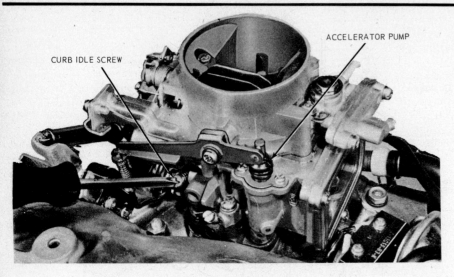

CURB IDLE SCREW

ACCELERATOR PUMP

Fig. 4 Curb idle speed adjustment

ACCELERATING PUMP

IDLE FUEL MIXTURE ADJUSTING SCREW

Fig. 5 Idle mixture adjustment

adjusting screw to obtain specified idle CO%, Fig. 5.

Fast Idle

1. With choke plate fully closed, measure clearance between primary

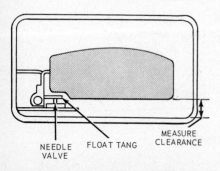

NEEDLE VALVE FLOAT TANG MEASURE CLEARANCE

Fig. 6 Float adjustment

throttle plate and the wall of the throttle bore.
2. If not within specification, bend the

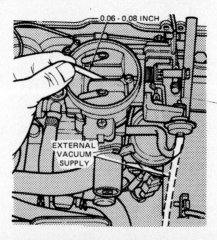

0.06 - 0.08 INCH

EXTERNAL VACUUM SUPPLY

Fig. 8 Choke plate clearance

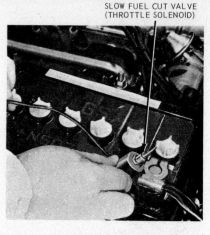

SLOW FUEL CUT VALVE (THROTTLE SOLENOID)

Fig. 7 Testing slow fuel cut valve (Throttle solenoid)

fast idle lever where it contacts the throttle lever tang until proper clearance is obtained.

Float Level

1. With engine operating, check the fuel level in the fuel bowl sight glass. If level is not to specified mark in the sight glass, remove the carburetor from the vehicle.
2. Remove fuel bowl center.
3. Invert the carburetor on a stand and lower the float until the tang on the float just contacts the needle valve, Fig. 6.
4. Measure the clearance between the float and the edge of the bowl. If not .256 inch, bend the float tang to adjust.

Slow Fuel Cut Valve (Throttle Solenoid)

1. Remove the slow fuel cut valve from the carburetor by unscrewing it from the main body.
2. Connect the valve to the battery, Fig. 7.
3. When current is applied to the valve,

Fig. 9 Vacuum pulldown adjustment

the valve stem should be pulled into the valve body. If it does not operate properly, replace the valve.

Vacuum Pulldown

1. Place choke in fully closed position.

2. Disconnect vacuum line from pull-down.
3. With external vacuum source connected pulldown should start to operate at 5.9 to 7.5 in. Hg.
4. Increase vacuum to 9.8 to 12 in. Hg.

and check clearance between air horn and choke plate, Fig. 8. Clearance should be .06-.08 inch.
5. If adjustment is necessary, bend pulldown connecting rod, Fig. 9, to obtain specified clearance.

Emission Controls Section

POSITIVE CRANKCASE VENTILATION (PCV) SYSTEM

This system diverts blow-by gasses into the intake manifold to be burned by the engine. The system consists of a positive crankcase ventilation (PCV) valve, an oil separator and the hoses needed to connect these components. Ventilating air is routed into the rocker cover from the air cleaner, then through the oil separator and to the PCV valve. The PCV valve is operated by the difference in pressure between the intake manifold and the rocker cover. When there is no difference in pressure or the pressure of the intake manifold is greater than the rocker cover, the PCV valve is pulled toward the rocker cover by the tension of the valve spring, Fig. 1. If there is a large difference in pressure, the high vacuum of the intake manifold overcomes the tension of the valve spring and the valve is pulled toward the intake manifold side by the manifold vacuum, Fig. 1. The air then passes

through the restricted passage in the valve. If the difference in pressure is small, the valve is balanced by the tension of the valve spring and intake manifold vacuum, Fig. 1. This valve position increases the flow of ventilating air.

PCV Valve Test

1. Remove hose from PCV valve.
2. Start and run engine at 700-1000 RPM.
3. Hold a finger over end of PCV valve. A distinct vacuum should be felt. If not, replace PCV valve.

THERMACTOR AIR INJECTION SYSTEM

The Thermactor air injection system reduces the level of hydrocarbon, carbon monoxide and NOx emissions by oxidizing the hydrocarbon and carbon monoxide contaminants in the exhaust ports of the cylinder head. Air under pressure is injected into the exhaust ports near each exhaust valve. The oxygen in the air plus the heat of the exhaust gasses induces further combustion of the exhaust gasses.

The system incorporates an air pump,

check valve, air injection nozzles, air injection manifold, Fig. 2, air by-pass valve on 1972-74 models, air control valve on 1975-77 models, a vacuum delay valve on 1977 2300 cc California models and the hoses necessary to connect the components.

Air under pressure flows through a hose to the air manifold which distributes the air to the injection nozzles in each exhaust port. The air oxidizes the unburned portion of the exhaust gasses, in turn reducing the level of harmful emissions. A relief valve, located on the air pump, relieves excess pressure in the pump, protecting the pump and reducing excessive power loss. A check valve, located in the inlet air side of the air manifold, prevents backflow of exhaust gasses when the air pressure from the pump is lower than that of the exhaust gas. The difference in pressure opens the valve and air from the pump may flow into the air injection manifold. If the exhaust gas pressure exceeds the air pressure because of engine speed increases or air pressure decreases, the check valve will close immediately to prevent hot exhaust gas from entering into and damaging the air pump or the connecting rubber hoses.

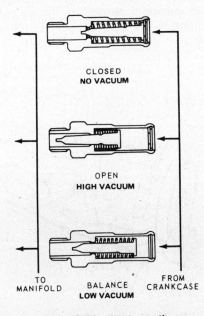

Fig. 1   PCV valve operation

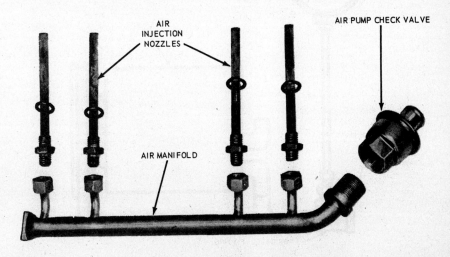

Fig. 2   Air manifold assembly, 1800cc engine

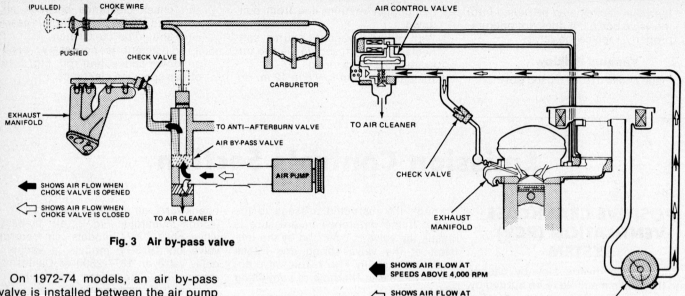

Fig. 3   Air by-pass valve

SHOWS AIR FLOW WHEN CHOKE VALVE IS OPENED

SHOWS AIR FLOW WHEN CHOKE VALVE IS CLOSED

SHOWS AIR FLOW AT SPEEDS ABOVE 4,000 RPM

SHOWS AIR FLOW AT SPEEDS BELOW 4,000 RPM

Fig. 4   Air control valve. 1975-76 1800cc engine

On 1972-74 models, an air by-pass valve is installed between the air pump and check valve, Fig. 3. All air from the pump passes through this by-pass valve and is directed to the check valve and manifold. However, when the manual choke cable is pulled, the air by-pass cable which is interlocked with the choke cable, pulls the by-pass valve plunger up, in turn cutting off air flow to the check valve and injection manifold. The air is then pumped to the atmosphere. This action prevents exhaust system overheating during choking action.

On 1975-76 models, an air control valve is installed between the air pump and check valve, Fig. 4. This valve consists of two relief valve, activated by the control unit, the engine RPM speed switch, and intake manifold vacuum for the distributor vacuum advance. At engine speeds below 4000 RPM on manual transmission models or 4300 RPM on automatic transmission models, the No.1 relief valve is closed and air from the pump is directed to the check valve, into the air injection manifold. By injecting air during low speed driving, exhaust system overheating is prevented. At engines speeds over 4000 RPM on manual transmission models, or 4300 RPM on automatic transmission models, the No. 1 relief valve is opened and air from the pump is directly vented to the atmosphere. The No. 2 relief valve opens when intake manifold vacuum exceeds 6.3 in. Hg. During periods of low engine load, a small amount of air for injection is needed since there is a decreased volume of exhaust gasses. When the No. 2 relief valve is open, the air to the injection manifold is reduced.

On 1977 models, an air control valve is installed between the air pump and check valve on California models. On the 1800 cc engine and the 2300 cc engine equipped with automatic transmission, the air control valve has one relief valve and is activated by intake manifold vacuum. On 2300 cc engine equipped with manual transmission, the air control valve has two relief valves, No. 1

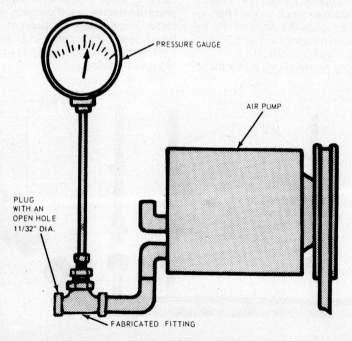

Fig. 5   Air pump test

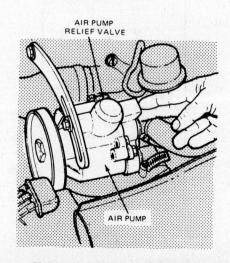

Fig. 6   Air pump relief valve test

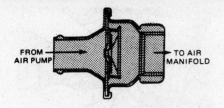

Fig. 7   Air manifold check valve test

FROM AIR PUMP — TO AIR MANIFOLD

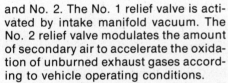

OUTLET HOSE

Fig. 8   Air control valve test. Exc. 1977 models

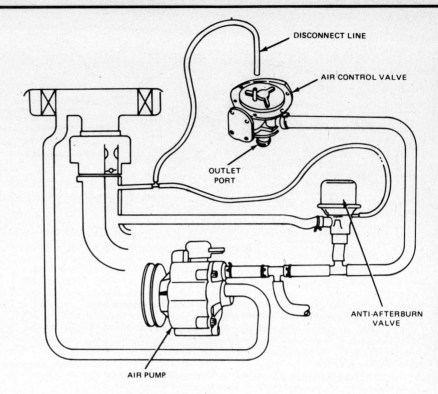

DISCONNECT LINE

AIR CONTROL VALVE

OUTLET PORT

ANTI-AFTERBURN VALVE

AIR PUMP

Fig. 8A   Air control valve test. 1977 1800cc engine

and No. 2. The No. 1 relief valve is activated by intake manifold vacuum. The No. 2 relief valve modulates the amount of secondary air to accelerate the oxidation of unburned exhaust gases according to vehicle operating conditions.

At low engine speeds, the No. 1 relief valve is closed on all California models and air from the pump is directed to the check valve and into the air injection nozzles. This prevents the exhaust system from overheating at low speeds. At higher speeds, the No. 1 relief valve opens, venting the air pump air to the atmosphere.

The No. 2 relief valve opens to reduce air flow to the injection manifold during low engine load when only a small volume of air for injection is necessary due to the decreased volume of exhaust gases. When engine load increases, the valve closes and increases air flow to the injection manifold.

Testing

Air Pump Test

1. Disconnect air pump outlet hose from by-pass valve or air control valve.
2. Connect a tee fitting in the outlet hose and connect a pressure gauge to the tee fitting. Also, insert a plug with a $^{11}/_{32}$ inch hole in the remaining port of the tee fitting, Fig. 5.
3. Start and run engine at 1250-1500 RPM. Ensure the choke is fully open.
4. Check pressure reading. If below 1 PSI, replace the air pump.

Air Pump Relief Valve Test

1. With engine operating at idle speed, check relief valve for air flow, Fig. 6. If air flow is noted, replace the relief valve and air pump assembly.
2. Increase engine speed to 3000 RPM. If air flows from the valve, the valve is satisfactory. If air does not flow from the valve or if the valve is excessively noisy, replace the relief valve and air pump assembly.

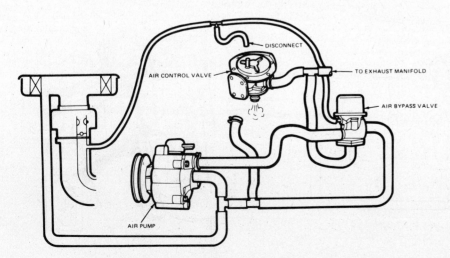

DISCONNECT

AIR CONTROL VALVE

TO EXHAUST MANIFOLD

AIR BYPASS VALVE

AIR PUMP

Fig. 8B   Air control valve test. 1977 2300cc engine with automatic transmission

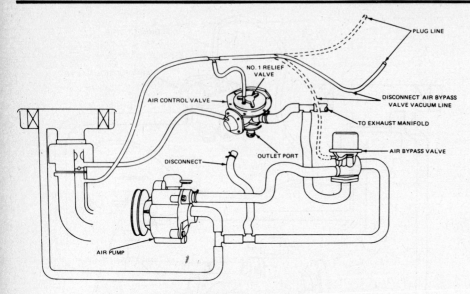

Fig. 8C   Air control valve test. 1977 2300cc engine with manual transmission

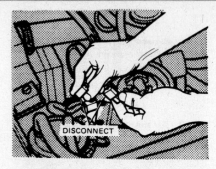

Fig. 9   Air control valve solenoid test

When engine speed falls below 4000 or 4300 RPM, as determined by model, the air discharge should stop.
4. If valve does not test satisfactory, replace valve.

Air Manifold Check Valve

1. Remove check valve from air injection manifold.
2. Blow through the intake side of the valve, then the outlet side, Fig. 7.
3. Air should pass through the valve from the intake side only. If air passes from the outlet side, replace the check valve.

Air By-Pass Valve Test

1. Disconnect air hose at the check valve.
2. Open the choke and start and run engine at 1500 RPM. Air should flow from the hose.
3. Close choke. No air should flow from the hose at full choke. Replace by-pass valve if air flow is noted.

Air Control Valve Test Exc. 1977 Models

1. Start and run engine at idle speed. Check if air is not discharged from outlet of air control valve, Fig. 8.
2. Disconnect electrical lead from air control valve solenoid, Fig. 9. Check for air discharge from valve outlet.
3. Reconnect electrical lead to valve solenoid and increase engine above 4000 RPM on manual transmission models or 4300 RPM on automatic transmission vehicles. Air should be discharged from the valve outlet.

Air Control Valve Test 1977 Exc. 2300 cc Manual Transmission

1. Disconnect air hose at bottom of air control valve, Figs. 8A and 8B.
2. Start and run engine at idle speed.
3. Air should not be discharged from air control valve outlet port.
4. Disconnect intake manifold vacuum line from top of air control valve. Air should now be discharged from the outlet port.
5. If valve does not operate properly, replace air control valve, if necessary.

Air Control Valve Test, 1977 2300 cc Manual Transmission

1. Disconnect air hose from bottom of air control valve, Fig. 8C.
2. Start and run engine at idle speed.

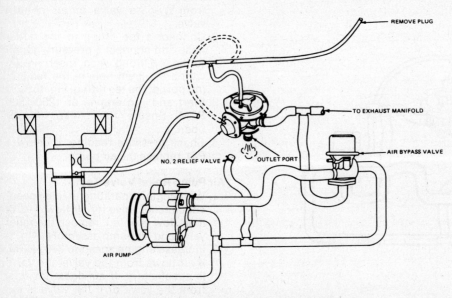

Fig. 8D   Air control valve test. 1977 2300cc engine with manual transmission (No. 2 relief valve)

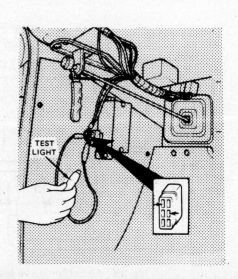

Fig. 10   Control unit test

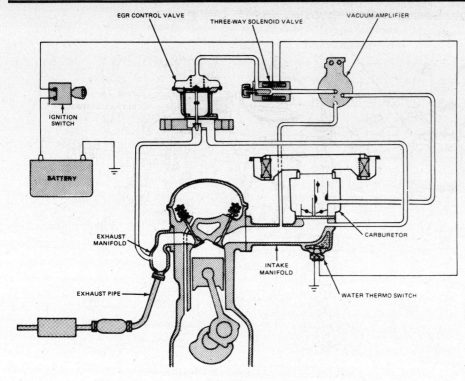

Fig. 11 EGR system (Typical)

turn reducing the generation of nitrous oxides (NOx). The amount of exhaust gas recirculated and the timing of the cycle are controlled by various parameters such as engine vacuum and temperature.

The EGR valve is a vacuum operated, cone type unit. When the valve is open, exhaust gas enters the intake manifold. A three-way solenoid valve is used to control the vacuum supply to the EGR valve. Power to the three-way solenoid is controlled by a water thermo switch. When the water temperature is below 131° F., the switch is closed, in turn energizing the three-way solenoid valve. The solenoid valve then closes the vacuum passage within the valve and cutting vacuum to the EGR valve. When water temperature is above 131° F., the water thermo switch is open, de-energizing the three-way solenoid valve. The vacuum passage within the valve is open, permitting intake manifold vacuum to control the EGR valve diaphragm. A vacuum amplifier is used to supply varying amounts of vacuum to the EGR valve diaphragm to actuate the valve during acceleration or at various engine speeds.

An EGR warning lamp on the instrument panel is activated after every 12,500 miles. The warning lamp glows whenever the ignition switch is placed in the "On" position. When the warning lamp is lit, the EGR valve should be tested and the switch reset.

3. Disconnect vacuum line from air bypass valve. Air should be discharged from air control valve outlet port.
4. Plug the disconnected air bypass valve vacuum line. No air should be discharged from the outlet port.
5. Disconnect intake manifold vacuum line from the No. 2 relief valve. Remove plug from disconnect air bypass valve vacuum line and connect line to the No. 2 relief valve, Fig. 8D. Air should be discharged from the air control valve outlet port.
6. If valve does not operate properly, check vacuum lines and replace air control valve, if necessary.

Control Unit (Engine RPM Speed Switch) Test, 1975 1800 cc Engine
1. Connect a test lamp to the control unit connector, Fig. 10.
2. Start engine. The test lamp should illuminate with the engine idling.
3. Increase engine speed. The test lamp should go out at approximately 4000 RPM on manual transmission models or 4300 RPM on automatic transmission models.
4. If the test lamp does not go off at the specified RPM or the test lamp is off during engine idling, replace control unit.

EXHAUST GAS RECIRCULATION (EGR) SYSTEM

This system, Fig. 11, used on 1976 California vehicles equipped with a manual transmission and all 1977 models, introduces small amounts of exhaust gas into the combustion cycle, reducing combustion temperatures, in

Testing
EGR Control Valve Test
1. Run engine at idle speed and disconnect vacuum hose from EGR valve.
2. Disconnect intake manifold vacuum

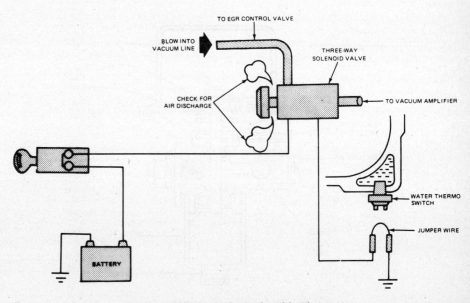

Fig. 12 EGR three-way solenoid valve test

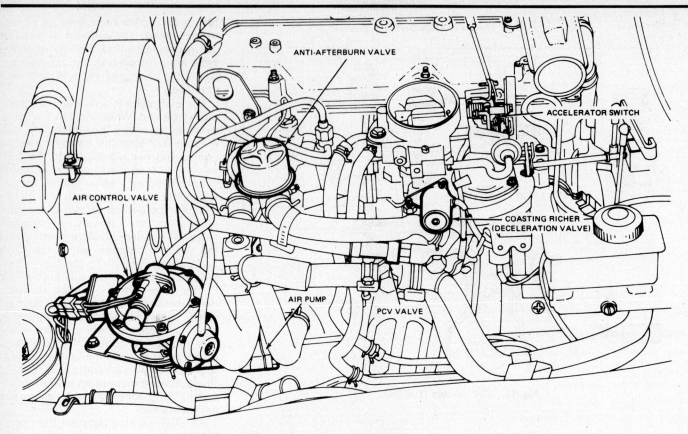

Fig. 13 Deceleration control system, 1972 California & all 1973-76 models

line from vacuum amplifier and connect to EGR valve. The engine should then stall or idle roughly. If not, stop engine and remove the EGR valve.

3. Clean passages of EGR valve and pipe with a brush and a wire.

4. Install EGR valve and repeat test. If engine still does not stall or run roughly, replace the EGR valve and repeat test.

CHECK VALVE

VACUUM SENSING TUBE

AIR OUTLET

CHECK VALVE

AIR CHAMBER

METERING ORIFICE

DIAPHRAGM

AIR VALVE

AIR INLET

Fig. 14 Anti-afterburn valve

5. If test is satisfactory, reconnect vacuum lines to original positions.

Three-way Solenoid Valve Test
1. Disconnect electrical connectors from water thermo switch and connect a jumper wire between the connectors.
2. Turn ignition switch to "On" position.
3. Disconnect vacuum hose from EGR

valve and blow into the hose, Fig. 12. Check for air discharge at the three-way solenoid valve relief port. If air does not discharge, replace the three-way solenoid valve.
4. Turn ignition switch to "Off" position.
5. Remove jumper wire from the water thermo switch connectors and disconnect vacuum amplifier vacuum line from the three-way solenoid valve, Fig. 12.
6. Turn ignition switch to "On" position.
7. Blow into EGR valve hose. Check for air discharge at the vacuum amplifier port of the three-way control valve. If air does not discharge, replace the three-way solenoid valve.
8. If valve tests satisfactory, reconnect all vacuum hoses and electrical connections in original positions.

Vaccum Amplifier Test
1. With engine at operating temperature, disconnect vacuum amplifier vacuum hose from the three-way solenoid valve and connect a vacuum gauge to the hose.
2. Disconnect vacuum amplifier hose from the carburetor.
3. Depress accelerator several times and allow engine to run at idle speed. The vacuum gauge should

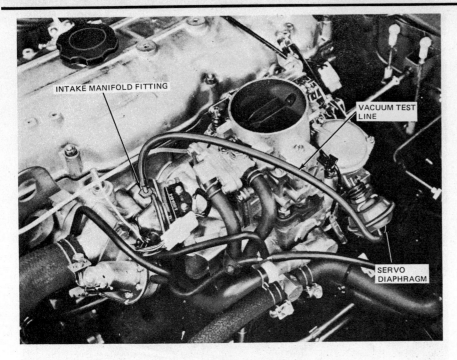

Fig. 15 Servo diaphragm test, 1972 exc. California

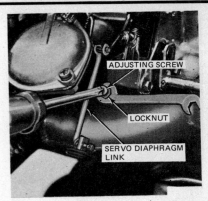

Fig. 16 Servo diaphragm adjustment, 1972 exc. California

indicate 2.0+.04 inch Hg. (50+ 10mm Hg.).

4. Reconnect vacuum amplifier vacuum hose to carburetor and increase engine speed to 3500 RPM. The vacuum gauge should now indicate 3.54 inch Hg. (90mm Hg.). If not, replace vacuum amplifier.

5. Reconnect all vacuum hoses to original positions.

EGR Warning Switch Reset

After performing the necessary EGR system maintenance, the EGR warning lamp switch can be reset. The switch is installed behind the speedometer and is reset as follows:

1. Remove cover from switch.

2. Slide the switch knob to the opposite position and the warning lamp will go out.

DECELERATION CONTROL SYSTEM
Description

1972 Exc. California

The deceleration control system on these models is a three part system. One part controls throttle opening during deceleration, another part acts to retard spark during deceleration and a third part retards the spark during engine idle.

A vacuum control valve is the compo-

nent which controls both the spark retard and the throttle opening during deceleration. The vacuum control valve senses the higher intake manifold vacuum and activates both systems. The throttle opening system uses a servo diaphragm assembly connected to the primary throttle shaft. During deceleration, the vacuum control valve opens to allow vacuum to be applied to the servo diaphragm. The diaphragm then moves to open the primary throttle plate slightly and feed additional fuel to enrich the mixture.

The spark retard system uses a dual point distributor and a vacuum switch. During deceleration, the vacuum control valve opens to allow vacuum to be applied to the vacuum switch. The vacuum switch then closes and activates the retard breaker points in the distributor to retard the spark. During acceleration and normal operation, the spark is controlled by the standard breaker point set. During deceleration, the standard breaker points are bypassed and the spark is controlled by the retard set. This retard circuit retards spark advance 7-10 degrees, decreasing engine speed.

During engine idle, the accelerator switch controls the retard points in the distributor. When the engine is running

Fig. 17 Vacuum control valve test, 1972 exc. California

Altitude (Feet)	Vacuum Reading (In. Hg.)
+ 10,000	13.80
+ 9,000	14.55
+ 8,000	15.30
+ 7,000	16.05
+ 6,000	16.80
+ 5,000	17.55
+ 4,000	18.30
+ 3,000	19.05
+ 2,000	19.80
+ 1,000	20.55
Sea Level	21.30
– 1,000	22.05

Fig. 18 Vacuum control valve altitude compensation valve, 1972 exc. California

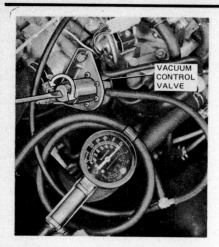

Fig. 19 Vacuum control valve adjustment, 1972 exc. California

Fig. 20 Vacuum switch test, 1972 exc. California

above idle, the accelerator switch is open and the distributor operates on the standard breaker point set. When the accelerator pedal is released, the switch is closed and the retard breaker point set is activated, retarding spark advance.

1972 California & All 1973-77

This deceleration control system, Fig. 13, maintains a balanced air-fuel mixture during deceleration. An anti-afterburn valve, Fig. 14, is used to prevent fuel detonation in the exhaust manifold and a deceleration (coasting richer) valve is used to prevent overly lean air-fuel mixtures. The deceleration valve is controlled by a speedometer switch, accelerator switch and on 1972-74 models, a clutch switch.

The anti-afterburn valve prevents an abnormal combustion (afterburning) in the exhaust system. At the start of sudden deceleration, a rich air-fuel mixture is present in the intake manifold and is supplied to each cylinder. This rich mixture does not burn completely and is discharged into the exhaust system. The air supplied from the air pump dilutes the unburned rich mixture into a combustible state, causing an abnormal combustion or afterburning in the exhaust system. To prevent this condition, the anti-afterburn valve allows air from the pump to flow into the intake manifold in accordance with engine load, diluting the overly rich mixture to be supplied to each cylinder to a proper ratio so the mixture may be burned normally in the cylinder.

The anti-afterburn valve is controlled and operated by intake manifold vacuum. The valve is activated when intake manifold vacuum suddenly increases and is kept open in proportion to the amount of pressure change sensed by the diaphragm of the valve system. The diaphragm is installed with the check valve and the metering orifice. The check valve permits air flow only from the vacuum sensing chamber to the air chamber. Therefore, if the air in the vacuum sensing tube decreases, the check valve opens and allows air flow into the air chamber to equalize the vacuum of both chambers. If the vacuum increases, the check valve closes and the diaphragm moves downward until the air flow through the metering orifice equalizes the vacuum. When the diaphragm is pushed downward, the air valve opens to allow air flow to the intake manifold. However, as the pressure is equalized, the spring returns the diaphragm and air valve to the closed position. The time required to equalize the vacuum is in proportion to the amount of vacuum change applied to the diaphragm.

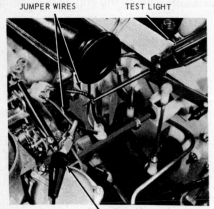

Fig. 21 Accelerator switch test

Fig. 22 Accelerator switch adjustment

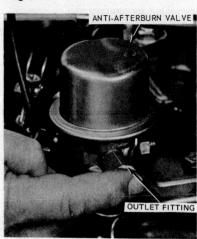

Fig. 23 Anti-afterburn valve test

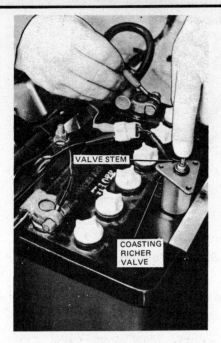

Fig. 24 Deceleration valve test, 1972-74

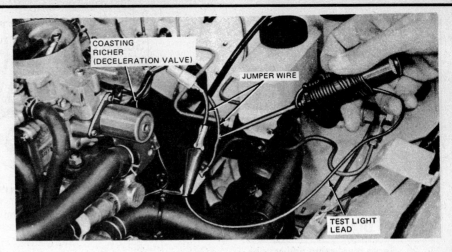

Fig. 25 Deceleration valve test, 1972-77

As the anti-afterburn valve completes its operation, the deceleration valve adds additional fuel to enrichen the lean mixture created in the intake manifold by the deceleration action. This additional fuel permits more complete combustion and reduced emission contaminates.

The deceleration valve operates when all its controlling switches are closed. The accelerator switch closes the circuit when the accelerator pedal is released. The speedometer switch closes the circuit at speeds above 17-23 MPH. On 1972-74 models, the clutch switch closes the circuit when the clutch pedal is released.

On 1976 models, California vehicles equipped with manual transmission has a Throttle Opener system to protect the catalytic converter against abnormally high temperatures by maintaining an optimum air-fuel mixture to the engine during deceleration. This system incorporates a servo diaphragm and throttle lever which opens the primary throttle valve in the carburetor. A vacuum control valve is used to detect intake manifold vacuum and actuates the servo diaphragm during deceleration.

System Testing, 1972 Exc. California

Servo Diaphragm

1. Disconnect the vacuum lines from servo diaphragm, vacuum control valve at intake manifold and the distributor vacuum advance unit.
2. Connect a vacuum line from the intake manifold to the servo diaphragm, Fig. 15.
3. Start engine. The engine RPM should be 1300-1500 RPM. If engine speed is not within specification but is within the 750-1700 RPM range, adjust the speed with the servo diaphragm adjusting screw, Fig. 16. If the specified RPM cannot be ob-

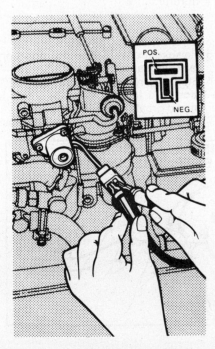

Fig. 26 Deceleration valve test, 1975-77

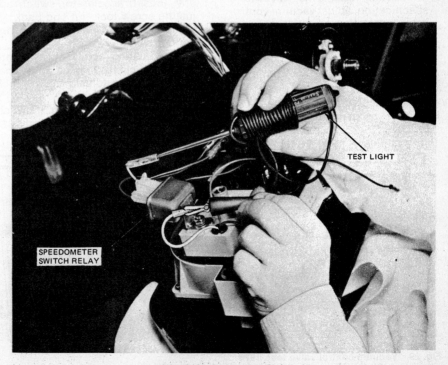

Fig. 27 Speedometer switch test

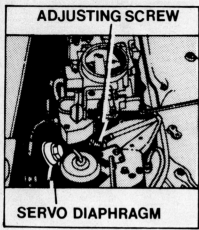

Fig. 28 Servo diaphragm adjustment, 1976 with throttle opener system

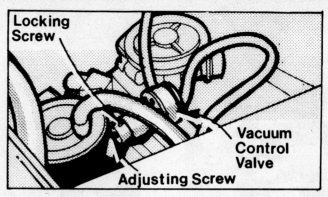

Fig. 30 Vacuum control valve adjustment, 1976 with throttle opener system

tained with the adjusting screw, replace the servo diaphragm.

Vacuum Control Valve

1. Connect a vacuum gauge with a tee fitting in the vacuum line between the vacuum control valve and the intake manifold, Fig. 17.
2. Start and run engine at 3000 RPM, then suddenly release accelerator and observe vacuum gauge. The vacuum reading should rise above 21.3 inch Hg., drop to approximately 21.3 inch Hg. and hesitate at this point for 1-2 seconds. The vacuum should then drop to the normal idle reading of 16-18 inch Hg. Refer to Fig. 18 for altitude compensation.
3. If vacuum reading is not within specification, adjust vacuum control valve by rotating adjusting screw at top of valve, Fig. 19. If specified readings cannot be obtained by the adjusting screw, replace the vacuum control valve.

Vacuum Switch

1. Connect a vacuum gauge with a tee

fitting in the vacuum line between the vacuum switch and vacuum control valve, Fig. 20.
2. Connect an external vacuum source to the tee fitting and apply more than 8 inch Hg. of vacuum, Fig. 20. Then, allow the vacuum to drop. At approximately 6 inch Hg, the vacuum switch should produce an audible click. If no click is heard or if the click is heard above 6½-7 inch Hg., replace the vacuum switch.

Accelerator Switch

1. Connect jumper wires and a test lamp at the accelerator switch electrical connector, Fig. 21.
2. Start and idle engine. The test lamp should be "On."
3. Depress the accelerator and the test lamp should go "Out."
4. If the switch does not operate properly, loosen accelerator switch adjusting screw lock nut and back off adjusting screw until it does not contact switch, Fig. 22.
5. Turn adjusting screw inward until the switch clicks, then an additional ¾ turn. Tighten adjusting screw lock nut.
6. Recheck switch operation. If switch still does not function properly, replace the switch.

System Testing, 1972 California & All 1973-77

Anti-Afterburn Valve

1. Remove outlet hose from anti-afterburn valve.
2. Hold finger over outlet fitting, Fig. 23, and increase engine RPM, then release accelerator. Air should flow for approximately 3 seconds. If valve passes air for more than 3 seconds or does not pass air, replace the valve.

Deceleration Valve, 1972-74

1. Remove deceleration valve from carburetor.
2. Using jumper wires connect deceleration valve electrical connectors to battery, Fig. 24. When power is applied to the valve, the solenoid stem should be pulled into the body.
3. Install deceleration valve on carburetor.
4. Connect a test lamp and jumper wire on the deceleration valve electrical connector, Fig. 25.
5. Raise rear of vehicle and support on jack stands.
6. Start and run engine with transmission in a forward gear to obtain a speed greater than 30 MPH.
7. Release accelerator and the test

Fig. 29 Vacuum control valve test, 1976 with throttle opener system

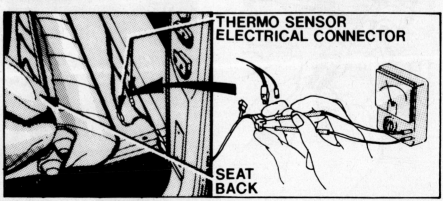

Fig. 31 Catalyst warning system test

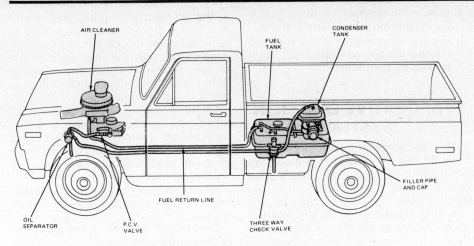

Fig. 32 Evaporative emission control system, 1972

lamp should illuminate until the speed falls below 17-23 MPH.

8. If the system is functioning properly, no further testing is required. If the system is unsatisfactory, test the clutch switch, accelerator switch and speedometer switch to determine faulty component of system.

Deceleration Valve, 1975-77

1. Start and run engine at idle speed.
2. Disconnect deceleration valve electrical connector from carburetor and, using jumper wires, connect electrical connector directly to battery, Fig. 26. Engine speed should rise to 950-1200 RPM. This increase in engine speed indicates proper operation of the deceleration valve.
3. Connect a test lamp and jumper wire on the deceleration valve electrical connector, Fig. 25.
4. Raise rear of vehicle and support on jack stands.
5. Start and run engine with transmission in a forward gear to obtain a speed greater than 30 MPH.
6. Release accelerator and the test lamp should illuminate until the speed falls below 17-23 MPH.
7. If the system is functioning properly, no further testing is required. If the system is unsatisfactory, test the accelerator switch and speedometer switch.

Clutch Switch, 1972-74

The clutch is activated by the clutch pedal. When checking the switch with a circuit tester, the test lamp should illuminate when the clutch pedal is released and should be "Off" with the clutch pedal depressed.

Accelerator Switch, 1972-77

The accelerator switch is actuated by a throttle lever link on the carburetor.

When checking the switch with a circuit tester, the test lamp should illuminate when the accelerator pedal is released and should be "Off" with the accelerator pedal depressed.

Speedometer Switch, 1972-77

1. If the accelerator switch and on 1972-74 models, the clutch switch, tests satisfactory, remove instrument cluster and connect a test lamp to speedometer switch relay, Fig. 27.
2. Reconnect speedometer cable and ground wire.
3. Raise rear of vehicle and support on jack stands.
4. Start engine and place transmission in a forward gear.
5. Accelerate engine. Test lamp should illuminate at 17-23 MPH and remain "On."

Servo Diaphragm, Throttle Opener System

1. Disconnect the vacuum control valve intake manifold vacuum sens-

ing hose from tee fitting near the air control valve.
2. Disconnect vacuum line from vacuum control valve and connect line to tee fitting so intake manifold vacuum can be applied directly to the servo diaphragm.
3. Disconnect vacuum hose from distributor vacuum advance unit.
4. Start engine. The engine speed should raise to 1300-1500 RPM. If engine speed is not within specifications, adjust by turning adjusting screw on servo diaphragm throttle lever, Fig. 28.

Vacuum Control Valve, Throttle Opener System

1. Disconnect and plug intake manifold vacuum hose from anti-afterburn valve at the tee fitting. Connect a vacuum gauge to the tee fitting, Fig. 29.
2. Start engine and raise speed to 3000 RPM, then release accelerator and observe vacuum gauge. The vacuum reading should drop to 22.4 inch Hg. momentarily before dropping to the normal idle vacuum reading.
3. If the vacuum reading is not within specifications, loosen locking screw and rotate adjusting screw on vacuum control valve until the proper reading is obtained.

NOTE: The vacuum level at which the vacuum control valve operates was set at an atmospheric pressure of 22.9 inch Hg. If the atmospheric pressure at time of testing is different than 22.9 inch Hg., change the desired reading by adding or subtracting the amount equivalent to the difference between 22.9 inch Hg. and the actual atmospheric reading.

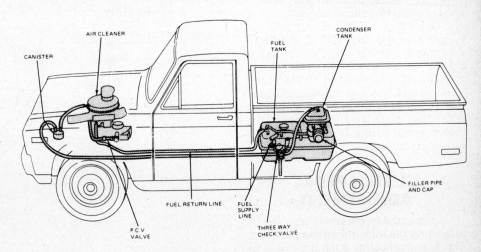

Fig. 33 Evaporative emission control system, 1973-76

CATALYTIC CONVERTER

1976-77 California vehicles equipped with a manual transmission use a catalytic converter to reduce hydrocarbon and carbon monoxide exhaust emission levels. These vehicles are also equipped with a catalyst warning system. This system is comprised of a thermo sensor on the catalytic converter, monitoring converter temperature, and a warning lamp on the instrument panel which illuminates when the thermo sensor detects converter temperatures over 1742° F.

Warning System Test

1. Turn ignition switch to "On" position. The warning lamp should illuminate, indicating that the bulb and electrical wiring are satisfactory. If lamp does not light, check bulb.
2. Start engine and if the system is satisfactory, the warning lamp should go out. If not, stop engine and tilt the seatback forward.
3. Disconnect the catalytic converter thermo sensor electrical connectors, Fig. 31.
4. With an ohmmeter, check the circuit on the thermo sensor side of the wiring for continuity, Fig. 31. Replace the thermo sensor if the reading indicates no continuity.

EVAPORATIVE EMISSION SYSTEM

The evaporative emission system, Figs. 32 and 33, is used to prevent the emission of gasoline vapors, generated by the ambient temperature, into the atmosphere. The system consists of a fuel tank, condenser tank, check valve, an oil separator on 1972 models and a carbon canister on 1973-77 models.

When the engine is not running, the fuel vapor in the fuel tank is channeled to the condenser tank. The fuel returns to the tank as the ambient temperature changes and the fuel vapor is condensed. During engine operation, the fuel vapor that has not condensed is routed to the oil separator on 1972 models or the carbon canister on 1973-77 models. On 1972 models, the fuel vapor is then passed into the PCV system. On 1973-76 models, the fuel vapor in the canister is absorbed by the carbon and is stored. The stored vapor is removed from the carbon by fresh air passing through the inlet hole in the bottom of the canister. The vapor is then passed into the air cleaner and to the combustion chamber.

On 1972 models, the check valve, located between the condenser tank and oil separator, permits fuel vapor to flow to the oil separator during normal operation. If the vapor line becomes restricted or the PCV valve is inoperative, built up pressure will open the check valve and vent the pressure to the atmosphere.

On 1973-77 models, the check valve or fuel vapor valve, located between the condenser tank and the carbon canister, permits fuel vapor and ventilation to flow during normal operation. If the vapor line between the check valve and canister become clogged, ventilation of the fuel system does not occur and fuel supply to the engine is cut off. When the fuel vapor in the fuel tank is expanded due to intense heat, the pressure in the tank increases. To prevent this increase in pressure, the check valve opens to release the pressure to the atmosphere.

Clutch & Transmission Section
Clutch

HYDRAULIC CLUTCH RELEASE

The hydraulic clutch linkage consists of a dash mounted master cylinder operated by a pedal. The master cylinder is connected to a clutch release slave cylinder by means of rigid and flexible lines. To control clutch engagement, a one-way valve on the master cylinder decelerates the fluid return flow from the release cylinder when foot pressure on the pedal is released. The release slave cylinder is mounted on the clutch housing and operates the clutch release lever by means of an adjustable push rod. The push rod connecting the clutch pedal to the master cylinder is also adjustable.

CLUTCH PEDAL ADJUSTMENT

Clutch pedal free travel is adjusted by loosening the lock nut on the push rod, Fig. 1, and adjusting push rod length by rotating the rod until the pedal has a

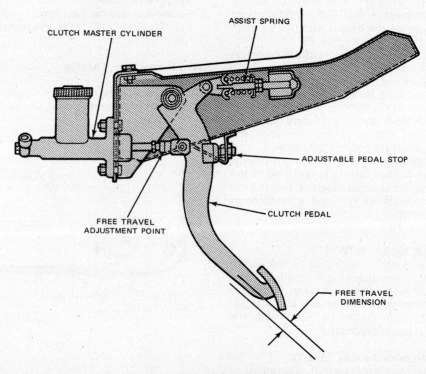

Fig. 1 Clutch pedal adjustment

free travel of $^{13}/_{16}$" to $1^{3}/_{16}$" when measured at pedal pad as shown. Tighten lock nut when adjustment is complete.

RELEASE LEVER ADJUSTMENT
1972-75

NOTE: This adjustment must be maintained to specification to prevent release bearing and clutch damage.

1. Raise vehicle and disconnect release lever return spring at the lever, Fig. 2.
2. Loosen lock nut and rotate the adjusting nut until a clearance of $^{1}/_{8}$" to $^{9}/_{64}$" is obtained between bullet nosed end of adjusting nut and the release lever. Tighten lock nut.

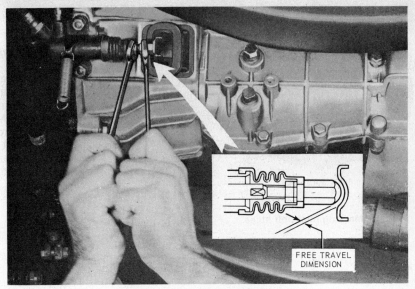

Fig. 2   Release lever adjustment

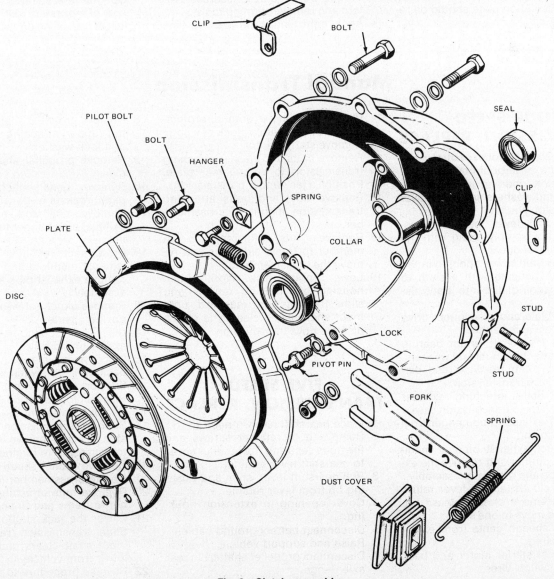

Fig. 3   Clutch assembly

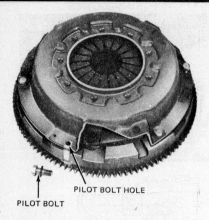

PILOT BOLT HOLE

PILOT BOLT

Fig. 4 Marking pilot bolt holes

1976-77

These vehicles do not incorporate a release lever adjustment. However, measure clearance between push rod and clutch fork. If clearance is less than $^{13}/_{64}$ inch, the clutch plate should be replaced.

CLUTCH, REPLACE
Removal

1. Remove transmission as described further on.
2. Remove the 4 standard bolts and 2 pilot bolts holding clutch cover assembly to flywheel and remove clutch cover and disc, Fig. 3. Mark the flywheel and cover if it is to be reused, to show location of pilot bolt holes, Fig. 4. Note that two opposite holes in the cover are reamed for exact fit with the pilot bolts.

Installation

1. Position clutch disc to flywheel, Fig. 5.
2. Position clutch cover to flywheel and install the 4 standard and 2 pilot bolts finger tight. To avoid distortion tighten the bolts a few turns at a time until they are tight.
3. Torque bolts using crisscross pattern and remove aligning tool.
4. Apply light film of lubricant to face

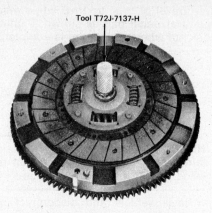

Tool T72J-7137-H

Fig. 5 Clutch disc installation

of release bearing, release lever contact area of release bearing hub and the input shaft bearing retainer. Operate release lever to check freedom of movement of linkage.
5. Install transmission.

Manual Transmission

FOUR SPEED TRANSMISSION, REPLACE

1. Place gearshift lever in neutral.
2. Lift up the large boot covering shift lever floor opening and remove screws and washers securing tower to extension housing.
3. Remove shift lever, tower and gasket as an assembly along with the two shift lever boots.
4. Cover the shift tower opening in the extension housing with a cloth to avoid dropping dirt into transmission.
5. Raise vehicle and disconnect drive shaft at rear axle flange.
6. Remove drive shaft center bearing support attaching nuts and washers.
7. Pull drive shaft rearward and disconnect from transmission.
8. Remove bolts attaching exhaust pipe brackets to transmission case.
9. Unfasten exhaust pipe hanger from clutch housing.
10. Disconnect exhaust pipe at manifold and muffler and remove the exhaust pipe and resonator assembly.
11. Unhook clutch release lever return spring. Remove clutch release cylinder and move to one side.
12. Remove speedo cable from extension housing.
13. Disconnect starter motor and back up lamp switch wires.

14. Place a jack under engine, protecting the oil pan with a block of wood.
15. Remove starter motor.
16. Remove bolts and washer attaching transmission to engine rear plate. Position a jack under transmission.
17. Remove nuts and bolts attaching transmission mount to crossmember.
18. Remove nuts attaching crossmember to frame side rails and remove the crossmember.
19. Lower engine jack. Work clutch housing off locating dowels and slide transmission rearward until input shaft spline clears the clutch disc. Remove transmission.

FIVE SPEED TRANSMISSION, REPLACE

1. Place gearshift lever in neutral.
2. Remove boot retainer screws and the bolts securing the retainer cover to gearshift lever retainer.
3. Pull gearshift lever, shim and bushing up from lever retainer.
4. Cover opening in extension housing.
5. Disconnect battery ground cable.
6. Raise and support vehicle.
7. Disconnect propeller shaft from rear axle flange.

8. Remove propeller shaft center bearing support attaching nuts, washers and lock washers.
9. Remove propeller shaft from vehicle.
10. Remove bolts attaching exhaust pipe brackets to transmission case.
11. Remove bolt and nut attaching exhaust pipe hanger to clutch housing.
12. Disconnect exhaust pipe from exhaust manifold and muffler, then remove exhaust pipe and resonator assembly.
13. Remove clutch release cylinder and position aside.
14. Disconnect speedometer cable from extension housing.
15. Disconnect starter motor and back-up lamp switch wiring.
16. Support engine with a suitable jack. Place a block of wood under oil pan.
17. Remove starter motor.
18. Support transmission with a suitable jack and remove bolts securing transmission to engine rear plate.
19. Remove bolts securing transmission to crossmember mount.
20. Remove nuts attaching crossmember to frame and the crossmember.
21. Lower the jack supporting engine. Slide transmission rearward until input shaft clears clutch disc and lower from vehicle.
22. Reverse procedure to install.

Automatic Transmission

JATCO
Testing

Control Pressure Check

If shifts do not occur within limits or the transmission slips during the shift point, the line pressure and governor pressure must be checked.
Line Pressure Test

NOTE: Transmission must be at normal operating temperature.

1. Connect pressure gauge to proper port, Fig. 6. Gauge should be visible from driver's seat.
2. Chock wheels and apply parking brake.
3. With transmission in the range being checked, run engine at idle speed and note pressure reading.
4. Apply service brakes and depress accelerator pedal slowly until the wide open position is reached. Observe pressure gauge and check for a smooth rise in pressure. Also, note pressure reading at stall speed, 1750-2000 RPM. Refer to Control Pressure Chart, Figs. 7 and 8.

NOTE: Total time for this test must not exceed five seconds.

5. Check line pressure in each range. Operate engine at 1200 RPM in Park or Neutral for at least one minute, allowing transmission to cool.

Governor Pressure Test

The governor pressure should be tested when shift points are not within specifications.
1. Connect pressure gauge to governor pressure outlet port, Fig. 6.
2. Check pressure with vehicle operating at speeds specified in the Governor Pressure Chart, Figs. 9 and 10. If pressures are not within specifications, disassemble and check governor valve.

Stall Test

The stall test is used to determine engine performance, converter clutch op-

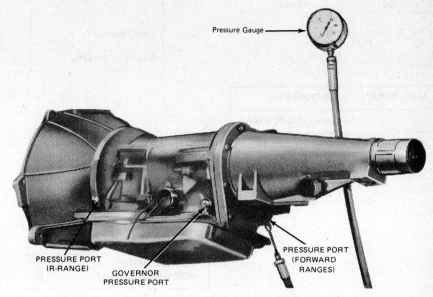

Fig. 6 Pressure test port locations

eration or installation and the holding ability of the clutches, band, low-reverse brake and the one-way clutch.

With engine and transmission at operating temperatures, apply service and parking brakes. Depress accelerator to wide open position and note engine RPM. Stall speed is 1750-2000 RPM. Perform test in each driving range. Do not hold throttle in wide open position longer than five seconds at a time. Also, run engine at 1200 RPM in Park or Neutral for about one minute between tests to allow converter to cool.

NOTE: If engine speed exceeds 2000 RPM, release accelerator immediately since clutch, brake or band slippage is indicated.

Shift Point Checks

Check minimum throttle upshift in "D". Transmission should start in first gear. Shift to second and then to third gear within the shift points specified in the Shift Speed Chart, Figs. 11 and 12.

While transmission is in third gear, depress accelerator through detent (to floor) and transmission should downshift to second or first gear depending on vehicle speed.

Check closed throttle downshift from third to first by coasting down from thirty MPH in third gear. Downshift should occur within limits specified in the Shift Speed Chart, Fig. 9.

When the selector lever is in "2," the transmission should operate only in second gear.

With transmission in third gear and road speed over thirty MPH, the transmission should shift to second gear when selector lever is placed in "2" or "1" from "D" position. The transmission should downshift from second or third gears to first gear when the same manual shift is made below approximately 25 MPH.

Air Pressure Checks

A "No Drive" condition can exist with correct fluid pressure due to inoperative

RANGE	PRESSURE P.S.I.
R	220-270
D	135-156
2	142-170
1	135-156

Fig. 7 Control pressure chart. 1974-76

RANGE	IDLE 18" VACUUM	10" VACUUM	WIDE OPEN THROTTLE THROUGH DETENT
P	42-73		
R	66-97	164-194	266-296
N	42-73		
D	42-73	99-129	164-194
2nd	146-189①	146-189	164-194
1st	42-73	99-129	164-194

Fig. 8 Control pressure chart. 1977 (governor pressure at zero and transmission at operating temperature)

SPEED M.P.H.	PRESSURE P.S.I.
20	14-20
35	29-36
50	50-61

Fig. 9   Governor pressure chart. 1974-76

SPEED M.P.H.	PRESSURE P.S.I.	
	2.47 Axle	2.79 Axle
20	19-25	21-27
35	32-39	37-44
50	52-60	63-71

Fig. 10   Governor pressure chart. 1977

THROTTLE POSITION	RANGE	SHIFT SPEED M.P.H.
Kickdown	D1-D2	28-41
	D2-D3	51-68
	D3-D2	44-57
	D2-D1	19-29
Half Throttle	D1-D2	7-17
	D2-D3	14-36
Minimum Throttle	D2-D1	22-30

Fig. 11   Shift speed chart. 1974-76

THROTTLE POSITION	RANGE	SHIFT	2.47:1 AXLE	2.79:1 AXLE
CLOSED	D	1-2	9-14	8-13
15" VACUUM	D	2-3	16-29	14-27
	1	2-1	28-40	25-37
TO DETENT (TORQUE DEMAND)	D	1-2	9-20	8-19
	D	2-3	18-30	16-28
THROUGH DETENT WIDE OPEN THROTTLE	D	1-2	39-51	34-46
	D	2-3	71-83	63-75

Fig. 12   Shift speed chart. 1977

clutches or bands. The inoperative units may be located through a series of checks by substituting air pressure for fluid pressure.

To perform these checks, remove oil pan and valve body assembly. The inoperative units can be located by applying air pressure to the various transmission case passages, Fig. 13.

Adjustments

Manual Linkage, Adjust

1. Place transmission selector lever in neutral position, raise vehicle and disconnect clevis from selector lever operating arm lower end, Fig. 14.

2. Place transmission manual lever in neutral position, third detent from rear of transmission.
3. Loosen two clevis retaining nuts and adjust clevis to freely enter hole in lever, then tighten the retaining nuts.
4. Lower vehicle and check for proper operation.

Kickdown Switch, Adjust

1. Place ignition switch in "On" position, loosen kick-down switch re-

taining nut, Fig. 15, and adjust switch to actuate when accelerator pedal is within 7/8-15/16 inch of full pedal travel.
2. Tighten retaining nut and check switch for proper operation.

Brake Band, Adjust

1. Raise vehicle, drain transmission and remove oil pan.
2. Loosen the brake band adjusting screw lock nut and torque adjusting screw to 9-11 ft-lbs, then back off adjusting screw two turns, Fig. 16. Torque adjusting screw lock nut to 22-29 ft-lbs.
3. Install oil pan, lower vehicle and refill transmission.

In-Truck Repairs

Control Valve Body

1. Raise vehicle, drain transmission and remove oil pan.
2. Remove downshift solenoid, vacuum diaphragm, vacuum diaphragm rod and O-rings.
3. Remove seven valve body to case attaching bolts. Hold manual valve to keep it from sliding out of the valve body, then remove valve body from the case.

NOTE: Failure to hold the manual valve while removing control assembly may result in valve damage.

4. Reverse procedure to install.

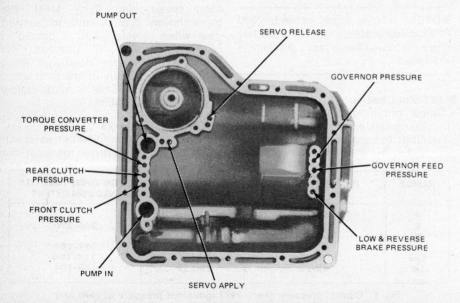

Fig. 13   Fluid passage identification for air pressure checks

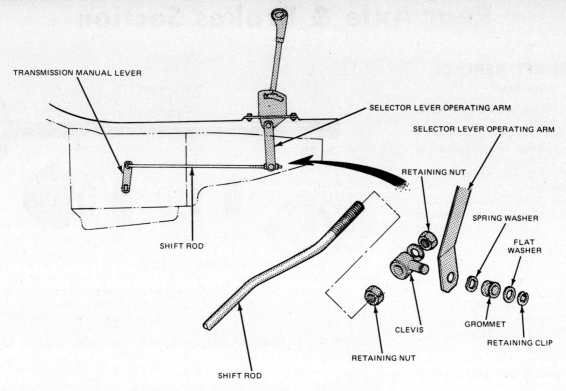

Fig. 14 Manual linkage adjustment

Servo

1. Raise vehicle, drain transmission and remove oil pan.
2. Remove servo retainer to case bolts, then the retainer and servo piston as an assembly and the return spring from the case.
3. Reverse procedure to install.

Extension Housing Seal

1. Raise vehicle and disconnect drive shaft.
2. Using a sharp chisel, remove seal from extension housing.
3. Install seal with a suitable tool.
4. Connect drive shaft.

Extension Housing

1. Raise vehicle and disconnect drive shaft from rear axle.
2. Remove drive shaft center bearing support nuts, lower drive shaft assembly and withdraw from transmission.

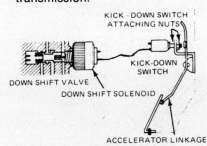

Fig. 15 Kickdown switch adjustment

3. Disconnect speedometer cable from extension housing.
4. Remove transmission rear support to crossmember bolts, raise transmission slightly with a suitable jack and loosen extension housing bolts to drain transmission fluid.
5. Remove extension housing to case bolts, then the extension housing.
6. Reverse procedure to install.

Governor

1. Remove the extension housing as outlined previously.
2. Remove governor housing to oil distributor bolts, then the governor housing from distributor.
3. Reverse procedure to install.

Transmission, Replace

1. Disconnect battery ground cable, then raise vehicle.
2. Drain transmission.
3. Remove exhaust pipe bracket to right side converter housing bolt and exhaust pipe flange bolts at rear of resonator, then disconnect pipe.
4. Disconnect drive shaft and remove center bearing support nuts, then lower drive shaft assembly from vehicle.
5. Disconnect speedometer cable, shift linkage, vacuum hose, oil cooler lines and electrical wiring from transmission.

6. Remove converter housing access cover.
7. Mark relationship between drive plate and torque converter for alignment during reassembly, then remove torque converter to drive plate bolts.
8. Remove transmission rear support to crossmember bolts.
9. Support transmission with a suitable jack and remove crossmember.
10. Secure transmission to the jack with safety chain.
11. Lower transmission and remove starter motor. Then, remove converter housing to engine bolts. Remove transmission fluid filler tube.
12. With a suitable tool, exert pressure between flex plate and converter, preventing the converter from disengaging from transmission as the assembly is moved rearward.
13. Lower transmission and converter as an assembly and remove from vehicle.
14. Reverse procedure to install.

Fig. 16 Brake band adjustment

Rear Axle & Brakes Section

AXLE SHAFT, REPLACE

Removal

1. Raise vehicle and remove rear wheel and brake drum.
2. Remove the brake shoe assembly.
3. Remove parking brake cable retainer.
4. Disconnect hydraulic brake lines at wheel cylinders.

NOTE: Rear wheels each contain an upper and a lower dual piston wheel cylinder.

5. Remove nuts holding the backing plate and bearing housing to the axle housing, Fig. 1.
6. Slide complete axle shaft assembly from the housing. Remove the oil seal from the housing if necessary.

Installation

1. Install a new oil seal in axle housing, if necessary.
2. Install rear axle shaft assembly.
3. Using two bolts and nuts, temporarily assemble the bearing housing and backing plate to axle housing flange.
4. Mount a dial indicator to backing plate to check end play. If only one axle shaft has been removed, the end play should be .002"-.004" on 1972 models and .002"-.006" on 1973-76 models. If both shafts have been removed, check the end play immediately after first shaft has been installed. End play for first shaft should be .026"-.033". The second shaft should then be .002"-.004" on 1972 models and .002"-.006" on 1973-76 models. Use adjusting shims to bring this result.
5. After adjusting end play, install and tighten all bolts and nuts.
6. Install brake shoe assembly.
7. Install brake drum and wheel, connect brake lines and bleed brakes.
8. Lower vehicle and check brakes.

CARRIER, REPLACE

Removal

1. Raise vehicle, drain lubricant, clean magnetic drain plug and reinstall it.
2. Remove axle shafts as outlined previously.
3. Mark drive shaft and companion flange for correct reassembly and then disconnect the drive shaft.

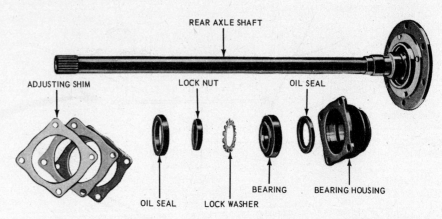

Fig. 1   Axle shaft components

4. Remove carrier retaining nuts and remove carrier.

Installation

1. Clean sealing surfaces of the carrier and the housing. No gasket is required.
2. Apply oil resistant sealer to the surfaces.
3. Position carrier to case install and torque retaining nuts to 15 ft. lbs.
4. Connect drive shaft following markings closely to prevent an out of balance condition.

5. Install axle shafts, wheels and drums.
6. Fill axle with proper grade and amount of lubricant.
7. Lower vehicle.

BRAKE PEDAL FREE PLAY ADJUSTMENT

1. Loosen the lock nut on the master cylinder push rod at the clevis which attaches the push rod to the pedal, Fig. 2.

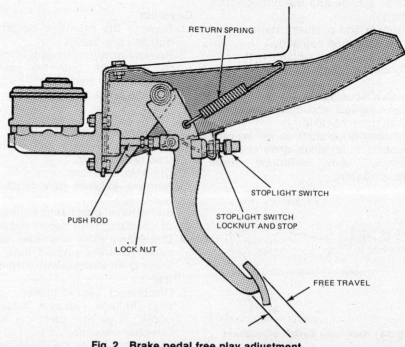

Fig. 2   Brake pedal free play adjustment

2. Turn the master cylinder push rod either in or out to obtain the dimension of free play 5/8" to 1" on 1972-74 models and 1/8" to 11/32" on 1975-76 models.
3. Tighten the lock nut to 13 ft. lbs.

BRAKE SHOE ADJUSTMENT

When making a brake shoe adjustment on the rear wheels, be sure that the parking brake is fully released by disconnecting the equalizer clevis pin. Then adjust brakes as follows:
1. Raise vehicle until tires are free of ground.
2. Remove adjusting slot covers from backing plate.
3. Turn lower wheel cylinder adjusting wheel inside hole to expand the brake shoe until it locks against the drum.
4. Back off the adjusting screw 6 to 8 notches on 1972-74 models and 5 notches on 1975-76 models, so that drum rotates freely.
5. If vehicle is equipped with dual brake cylinders, repeat the above operation on the upper wheel cylinder.
6. Connect parking brake equalizer clevis pin and recheck operation.

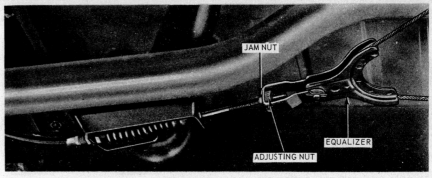

Fig. 3   Parking brake cable adjustment

Replace hole covers and lower vehicle.

Parking Brake Cable Adjustment

Before adjusting the parking brake, be sure the service brakes are properly adjusted. Adjust the parking brake as follows:
1. Adjust length of front cable with the adjusting nut on the end of the cable, Fig. 3, so that the rear brakes are locked when the parking brake lever is pulled out 5 to 10 notches.
2. After adjustment, apply parking brake several times; then, release and make sure that the rear wheels rotate freely without drag.

MASTER CYLINDER, REPLACE

1. Disconnect brake hydraulic lines from master cylinder outlet ports.
2. Remove nuts and lockwashers securing master cylinder to dash panel and lift master cylinder and boot assembly away from dash panel and push rod.
3. Position master cylinder and boot assembly on the dash panel while guiding the push rod to contact the master cylinder piston. Install and torque master cylinder lockwashers and nuts to 11.4-17 ft. lbs.
4. Connect brake hydraulic lines to master cylinder outlet ports.
5. Bleed the brake system and check brake pedal free travel.

Rear Suspension Section

SHOCK ABSORBER, REPLACE

1. With rear axle properly supported, remove nuts, washers and rubber bushings from the shock absorber upper and lower mountings, Fig. 1.
2. Remove shock absorber from vehicle.
3. Reverse procedure to install.

LEAF SPRINGS, REPLACE

1. Raise and support vehicle at frame and rear axle.
2. Disconnect shock absorber from lower mounting, Fig. 1.
3. Remove spring clip nuts and plate.
4. Remove spring pin nut, then the two bolts and nuts securing spring pin to frame.
5. Remove spring and lower front end of spring.
6. Remove shackle plate nuts and the shackle plate, then the spring from vehicle.
7. Reverse procedure to install.

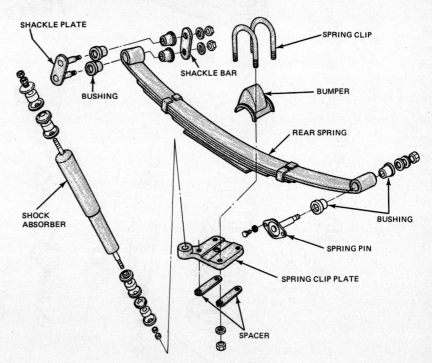

Fig. 1   Rear suspension

Front Suspension & Steering Section

FRONT WHEEL BEARINGS, ADJUST

1. Raise vehicle until wheel and tire clear floor.
2. Pry off hub cap or wheel cover and remove the grease cap.
3. Wipe excess grease from end of spindle and remove cotter pin and nut lock.
4. While rotating wheel, hub and drum assembly, torque adjusting nut to 17-25 ft. lbs. to seat the bearings, Fig. 1.
5. Back off the adjusting nut one half turn. Retighten the adjusting nut to 10-15 in. lbs. on 1972 models and 6-8 ft. lbs. on 1973-76 models with a torque wrench.
6. Position the nut lock on the adjust-

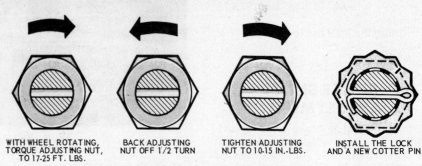

WITH WHEEL ROTATING, TORQUE ADJUSTING NUT, TO 17-25 FT. LBS.

BACK ADJUSTING NUT OFF 1/2 TURN

TIGHTEN ADJUSTING NUT TO 10-15 IN.-LBS.

INSTALL THE LOCK AND A NEW COTTER PIN

Fig. 1   Front wheel bearing adjustment

ing nut so castellations on the lock are aligned with the cotter pin hole in the spindle. Install a new cotter pin and bend the ends around the castellated flange of the nut lock.

WHEEL ALIGNMENT
Caster

Caster is the forward or rearward tilt of the upper ball joint. The standard

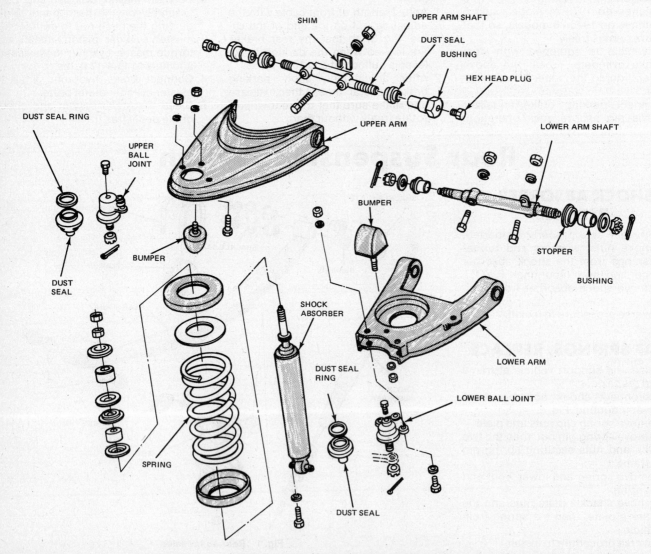

Fig. 2   Front suspension disassembled

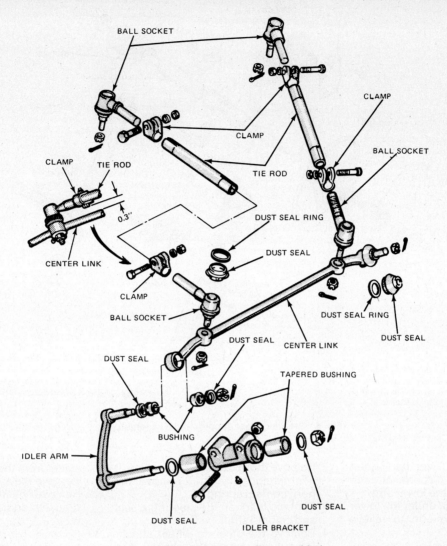

Fig. 3   Steering linkage disassembled

caster angle is plus ¾ to plus 1¼. If incorrect, adjust the shims between the upper arm shaft and the frame or turn the upper arm shaft until the correct angle is obtained, Fig. 2.

Camber

Camber is the outward tilting of the front wheels at the top from the vertical. The standard camber angle is plus 1 to plus 1¾. If incorrect, adjust by adding or subtracting the shim between the upper arm shaft and the frame. The shim is available in thicknesses of .040, .064, .080 and .128″.

Toe-In

Toe-in is the inward pointing of both front wheels and is necessary to offset the effect of camber. Toe-in should be ⁵/₆₄″ to ⅛″ on 1972 models and 0 to ¼″ on 1973-76 models. Adjust by turning the tie rod to provide equal adjustments at both wheels, Fig. 3.

NOTE: It is important to tighten the clamps with the bolts horizontal and below the rod to prevent interference with the steering link.

FRONT SHOCK ABSORBER, REPLACE

1. Remove nuts attaching the upper end of the shock to the crossmember.
2. Remove rubber bushings and washers.
3. Remove bolts that attach lower end of shock to the lower arm.
4. Remove the shock from under the lower arm.

UPPER CONTROL ARM, REPLACE

1. Raise vehicle on a hoist and place stands under the lower arm.

2. Lower the vehicle on the stands until upper arm is off the bumper stop.
3. Remove wheel cover and the wheel.
4. Remove cotter pin and nut retaining upper ball joint. Break the tapered fit loose by striking with a hammer and separate the ball joint from the spindle.
5. From under the hood, remove the two upper arm retaining bolts and remove the arm from the vehicle. At this point, the ball joint can be removed from the arm, if required.

LOWER CONTROL ARM, REPLACE

1. Raise front of vehicle and position stands under both sides of the frame just back of the lower arms.
2. Remove the wheel cover and wheel.
3. Remove two lower shock absorber retaining bolts and push shock up into spring.

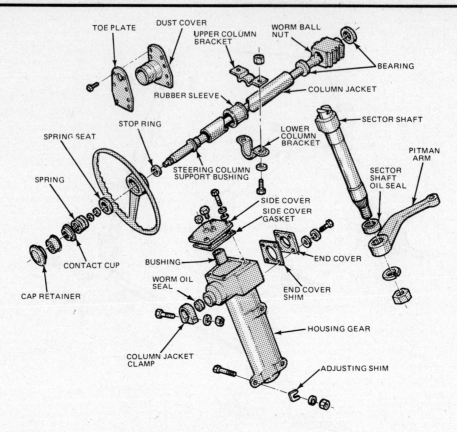

Fig. 4 Steering gear & column disassembled

4. Remove front stabilizer bar retaining bolt and disconnect the stabilizer bar from the lower arm.
5. Position a floor jack under the lower arm and raise the arm to relieve spring pressure.
6. Remove the three lower arm to ball joint retaining bolts and pull the spindle and ball joint away from lower arm.
7. Lower the lower arm on the jack and remove the spring from the vehicle.
8. Remove the three lower arm retaining bolts and remove the lower arm from the vehicle.

STEERING GEAR, REPLACE

The steering gear, Fig. 3, is the recirculating ball type and is replaced as follows:
1. Disconnect battery ground cable.

2. Remove horn button by turning it counterclockwise and remove the horn contact spring.
3. Scribe a mark on the steering wheel and column shaft.
4. Remove the steering wheel attaching nut and remove the wheel.
5. Remove cancelling cam snap ring and cam from top of steering shaft.
6. Remove the dimmer and self-cancelling switch wires at connectors.
7. Remove steering column support bracket.
8. Position floor covering and insulator pad away from bottom of steering column.
9. Remove four screws and two bolts retaining the toe plate and boot to the dash panel.
10. Loosen the bolt securing the bottom of the column jacket and remove the

jacket from the shaft.
11. Remove the air cleaner assembly.
12. Remove heater hoses from their brackets and position hoses out of way.
13. Remove hydraulic lines from the brake and clutch master cylinders and plug the ports on both cylinders.
14. Remove nuts securing brake and clutch master cylinders to dash and lift the cylinders out of the vehicle.
15. Raise vehicle and disconnect the pitman arm from the steering gear sector shaft.
16. Remove the bolts retaining the gear to the frame and at this point check for the possible presence of an aligning shim between the gear and the frame.
17. Lower vehicle and remove the gear and shaft assembly.

DATSUN

INDEX OF SERVICE OPERATIONS

DATSUN

GENERAL ENGINE SPECIFICATIONS

Year	Engine	Car-buretor	Bore & Stroke	Piston Displacement, Cubic Inches	Compression Ratio	Maximum H.P. @ R.P.M.	Maximum Torque @ R.P.M.	Normal Oil Pressure
1972	68 Horsepower....A12	2 Bore	2.874 x 2.756	71.5	9.0	68 @ 6000	70.1 @ 3600	45
	96 Horsepower....L16	2 Bore	3.267 x 2.902	62.8	8.5	96 @ 5600	99.8 @ 3600	57
	151 Horsepower....L24	①	3.27 x 2.90	146	8.8	151 @ 5600	145.7 @ 4400	52
1973	Horsepower....A12	2 Bore	2.874 x 2.756	71.5	8.5	—	—	47
	Horsepower....L16	2 Bore	3.267 x 2.902	62.8	8.5	—	—	54
	Horsepower....L18	2 Bore	3.35 x 3.07	108	8.5	—	—	54
	Horsepower....L24	①	3.27 x 2.90	146	8.8	—	—	54
1974	Horsepower....A13	2 Bore	2.87 x 3.03	78.6	8.5	—	—	47
	Horsepower....L18	2 Bore	3.35 x 3.07	108	8.5	—	—	54
	Horsepower....L20B	2 Bore	3.35 x 3.39	119	8.5	—	—	54
	Horsepower....L26	①	3.27 x 3.11	156.5	8.8	—	—	54
1975	Horsepower....A14	2 Bore	2.99 x 3.03	85.2	8.5	—	—	64
	Horsepower....L20B	2 Bore	3.35 x 3.39	119	8.5	—	—	54
	Horsepower....L28	Fuel Inj.	3.39 x 3.11	168	8.3	—	—	54
1976	Horsepower....A14	2 Bore	2.992 x 3.031	85.2	8.5	—	—	64
	Horsepower....L20B	2 Bore	3.35 x 3.39	119	8.5	—	—	54
	Horsepower....L28	Fuel Inj.	3.39 x 3.11	168	8.3	—	—	54
1977	Horsepower....A14	2 Bore	2.992 x 3.031	85.2	8.5	—	—	64
	Horsepower....L20B	2 Bore	3.35 x 3.39	119	8.5	—	—	54
	Horsepower....L24	Fuel Inj.	3.27 x 2.90	146	8.6	—	—	55
	Horsepower....L28	Fuel Inj.	3.39 x 3.11	168	8.3	—	—	55

—Not Available.
①—Two one bore carburetors.

TUNE UP SPECIFICATIONS

The following specifications are published from the latest information available. This data should be used only in the absence of a decal affixed in the engine compartment.

★When using a timing light, disconnect vacuum hose or tube at distributor and plug opening in tube or hose so idle speed will not be affected.

▲Before removing wires from distributor cap, determine location of the No. 1 wire in cap, as distributor position may have been altered from that shown at the end of this chart.

Year	Spark Plug		Distributor		Ignition Timing			Carb. Adjustments			
	Type	Gap Inch	Point Gap Inch	Dwell Angle Degree	Firing Order Fig.	Timing BTDC	Mark Fig.	Hot Idle Speed		Idle CO%	
								Std. Trans.	Auto. Trans.	Std. Trans.	Auto. Trans.
1972											
A12	BP-6E	.033	.020	49—55	A	5°	D	700	600	2.0—3.0	2.0—3.0
L16	BP5-ES	.034	.020	49—55	B	7°	D	550	550	2.0	2.0
L24	BP6-ES	.033	.020	35—41	C	17°	E	750	600	6.0	6.0
1973											
A12	BP5-ES	.033	.020	49—55	A	5°	D	800	650	1.5	1.5
L16	B6-ES	.030	.020	49—55	B	5°	D	800	650	1.5	1.5
L18	B6-ES	.030	.020	49—55	B	5°	D	800	650	1.5	1.5
L24	BP6-ES	.033	.020	①	C	②	E	750	600	1.3	.9
1974											
A13	BP5-ES	.033	.020	49—55	A	5°	D	800	650	1.5	1.5
L18	B6-ES	.030	.020	49—55	B	12°	D	800	650	1.5	1.5
L20B	B6-ES	.030	.020	49—55	B	12°	D	750	650	3.0	3.0
L26	BP6-ES	.033	—	—	C	③	E	750	600	1.3	.9

Continued

TUNE UP SPECIFICATIONS—Continued

Year	Spark Plug Type	Gap Inch	Point Gap Inch	Dwell Angle Degree	Firing Order Fig.	Timing BTDC	Mark Fig.	Hot Idle Speed Std. Trans.	Hot Idle Speed Auto. Trans.	Idle CO% Std. Trans.	Idle CO% Auto. Trans.
1975											
A14④	BP5-ES	.033	.020	49—55	A	10°	D	700	650	2.0	2.0
A14⑤	BP5-ES	.033	—	—	A	⑥	D	700	650	2.0	2.0
L20B④⑦	BP6-ES	.034	.020	49—55	B	12°	D	750	650	2.0	2.0
L20B⑤⑦	BP6-ES	.034	—	—	B	12°	D	750	650	2.0	2.0
L20B④⑧	BP6-ES	.034	.020	49—55	B	12°	D	750	650	2.0	2.0
L20B⑤⑧	BP6-ES	.034	.020	49—55	B	10°	D	750	650	2.0	2.0
L28④	B6-ES	.030	—	—	C	13°	E	800	700	—	—
L28⑤	B6-ES	.030	—	—	C	10°	E	800	700	—	—
1976											
A14④⑨	BP5-ES	.033	.020	49—55	A	10°	D	700	—	2.0	—
A14⑤⑨	BP5-ES	.033	—	—	A	10°	D	700	—	2.0	—
A14④⑩	BP5-ES	.033	.020	49—55	A	10°	D	—	650	—	2.0
A14⑤⑩	BP5-ES	.033	—	—	A	8°	D	—	650	—	2.0
L20B④⑦	BP6-ES	.033	.020	49—55	B	12°	D	750	650	2.0	2.0
L20B⑤⑦	BP6-ES-11	.041	—	—	B	12°	D	750	650	2.0	2.0
L20B④⑧	BP6-ES	.033	.020	49—55	B	12°	D	750	650	2.0	2.0
L20B⑤⑧	BP6-ES-11	.041	—	—	B	⑫	D	750	650	2.0	2.0
L28④	B6-ES	.030	—	—	C	13°	E	800	700	—	—
L28⑤	B6-ES	.030	—	—	C	10°	E	800	700	—	—
1977											
A14④⑨	BP5-ES-11	.041	.020	49—55	A	10°	D	700	—	2.0	—
A14⑤⑨	BP5-ES-11	.041	—	—	A	10°	D	700	—	2.0	—
A14④⑩	BP5-ES-11	.041	.020	49—55	A	8°	D	—	650	—	2.0
A14⑤⑩	BP5-ES-11	.041	—	—	A	10°	D	—	650	—	2.0
L20B④⑨⑬	BP6-ES-11	.041	.020	49—55	B	10°	D	600	—	1.0	—
L20B⑤⑨⑬	BP6-ES-11	.041	—	—	B	12°	D	600	—	1.0	—
L20B④⑩⑬	BP6-ES-11	.041	.020	49—55	B	12°	D	—	600	—	1.0
L20B⑤⑩⑬	BP6-ES-11	.041	—	—	B	12°	D	—	750	—	1.0
L20B④⑨⑭	BP6-ES-11	.041	.020	49—55	B	12°	D	600	—	1.0	—
L20B⑤⑨⑭	BP6-ES-11	.041	—	—	B	12°	D	600	—	1.0	—
L20B④⑩⑭	BP6-ES-11	.041	.020	49—55	B	12°	D	—	600	—	1.0
L20B⑤⑩⑭	BP6-ES-11	.041	—	—	B	12°	D	—	600	—	1.0
L20B④⑧⑨	BP6-ES	.033	.020	49—55	B	12°	D	750	—	2.0	—
L20B⑤⑧⑨	BP6-ES-11	.041	—	—	B	10°	D	750	—	2.0	—
L20B④⑧⑩	BP6-ES	.033	.020	49—55	B	12°	D	—	650	—	2.0
L20B⑤⑧⑩	BP6-ES-11	.041	—	—	B	12°	D	—	650	—	2.0
L24	BP6-ES-11	.041	—	—	C	10°	E	700	600	⑮	⑮
L28	BP6-ES-11	.041	—	—	C	10°	E	800	700	⑮	⑮

—Not Available
① —Manual trans. 35—41; auto. trans., 33—39.
② —Manual trans., 7° BTDC; auto. trans., 5° BTDC.
③ —Manual trans., 8° BTDC; auto. trans., 15° BTDC.
④ —Exc. California.
⑤ —California.
⑥ —Manual trans., 10° BTDC; auto. trans., 8° BTDC.
⑦ —610 & 710.
⑧ —Pick-up.
⑨ —Manual trans.
⑩ —Auto. trans.
⑪ —Exc. Calif., 12° BTDC; Calif., 10° BTDC.
⑫ —Manual trans., 10° BTDC; auto. trans., 12° BTDC.
⑬ —200 SX.
⑭ —710.
⑮ —Exc. Calif., 1.0; Calif., 0.5.

TUNE UP NOTES—Continued

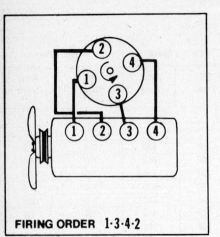

FIRING ORDER 1·3·4·2

Fig. A

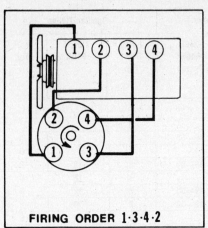

FIRING ORDER 1·3·4·2

Fig. B

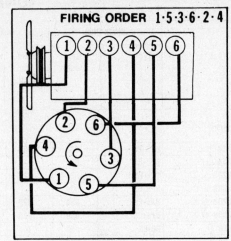

FIRING ORDER 1·5·3·6·2·4

Fig. C

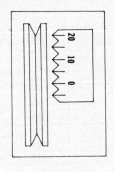

Fig. D

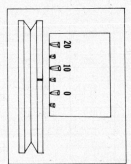

Fig. E

DISTRIBUTOR SPECIFICATIONS

★Note: If unit is checked on the vehicle, double the RPM and degrees to get crankshaft figures.

Distributor Part No.	Centrifugal Advance Degrees @ Distributor RPM				Vacuum Advance	
	Advance Starts	Intermediate Advance		Full Advance	Inches of Vacuum to Start Plunger	Max. Advance Dist. Deg. @ Vacuum
1972						
D412-63	0 @ 650	4.8 @1000	8 @ 1500	13 @ 2000	13.5 @ 2100	6	6½ @ 13.8
D410-58	0 @ 550	5.1 @ 900	6 @ 1000	8 @ 1300	11 @ 1500	5	9 @ 12
D606-52	0 @ 550	—	—	—	6 @ 1000	3.9	7½ @ 13
1973						
D412-80	0 @ 650	2 @ 800	5.8 @ 1200	12 @ 2000	13.5 @ 2100	6.5	7½ @ 10
D412-89	0 @ 650	2 @ 800	5 @ 1200	11 @ 2000	13.5 @ 2100	13	7 @ 18
D410-66A	0 @ 950	4.9 @ 1500	7 @ 1800	8.5 @ 2000	11 @ 2350	6.2	7½ @ 11.8
D410-67	0 @ 960	6 @ 1500	9 @ 1800	10.7 @ 2000	11 @ 2015	6.2	7½ @ 11.8
D611-54	0 @ 580	5 @ 800	7 @ 1000	10 @ 1200	12 @ 1400	11.3	7 @ 17.7
D612-54	0 @ 580	4.5 @ 800	7 @ 1000	9.5 @ 1200	13 @ 1480	9¾	10 @ 17.7
1974						
D4A2-02	0 @ 550	—	—	—	13.5 @ 1975	5.9	6½ @ 9½
D4A2-01	0 @ 550	—	—	—	10 @ 2150	5.9	3½ @ 9.8
D6F3-01	0 @ 500	—	—	—	13 @ 1600	11.8	6 @ 18.7
D6F3-02	0 @ 500	—	—	—	13 @ 1600	11.8	6 @ 18.7

Continued

DISTRIBUTOR SPECIFICATIONS—Continued

| Distributor Part No. | Centrifugal Advance Degrees @ Distributor RPM | | | | Vacuum Advance | |
	Advance Starts	Intermediate Advance		Full Advance	Inches of Vacuum to Start Plunger	Max. Advance Dist. Deg. @ Vacuum
1975						
D4A4-02	0 @ 550	—	—	—	14 @ 2150	4.1	9 @ 8.9
D4A4-03	0 @ 550	—	—	—	14 @ 2150	6.7	6½ @ 11.8
D4A4-04	0 @ 600	—	—	—	11 @ 1950	5.9	5 @ 9.8
D4A4-05	—	—	—	—	—	—	—
D4A4-06	0 @ 550	—	—	—	11 @ 2300	5.9	3 @ 9.8
D4A4-07	0 @ 600	—	—	—	11 @ 1950	6.7	6½ @ 11.8
D4F4-03	0 @ 600	—	—	—	11 @ 1950	5.9	3 @ 9.8
D6F4-01	0 @ 600	—	—	—	10 @ 1360	7.9	7½ @ 13.8
D6F4-02	0 @ 600	—	—	—	10 @ 1360	9.8	5½ @ 13.8
D6F4-03	0 @ 600	—	—	—	8.5 @ 1250	7.9	7½ @ 13.8
1976						
D4A5-04	0 @ 550	—	—	—	14 @ 2300	4.1	9 @ 9.8
D4A5-05	0 @ 550	—	—	—	14 @ 2300	6.7	6½ @ 11.8
D4F5-01	0 @ 550	—	—	—	14 @ 2300	4.1	9 @ 9.8
D4F4-02	0 @ 550	—	—	—	14 @ 2150	6.7	6½ @ 11.8
D4A4-04	0 @ 600	—	—	—	11 @ 1950	5.9	5 @ 9.8
D4A4-06	0 @ 550	—	—	—	11 @ 2300	5.9	3 @ 9.8
D4F4-03	0 @ 600	—	—	—	11 @ 1950	5.9	3 @ 9.8
D4F4-04	0 @ 550	—	—	—	11 @ 2300	5.9	3 @ 9.8
D6F4-01	0 @ 600	—	—	—	10 @ 1360	7.9	7½ @ 13.8
D6F4-02	0 @ 600	—	—	—	10 @ 1360	9.8	5½ @ 13.8
D6F4-03	0 @ 600	—	—	—	8.5 @ 1250	7.9	7½ @ 13.8
1977						
D4A5-05	0 @ 550	—	—	—	14 @ 2300	6.7	6½ @ 11.8
D4A5-13	0 @ 550	—	—	—	14 @ 2300	4.1	15 @ 15.5
D4F5-03	0 @ 550	—	—	—	14 @ 2300	4.1	15 @ 15.5
D4F5-04	0 @ 550	—	—	—	14 @ 2300	4.1	15 @ 15.4
D4F5-05	0 @ 550	—	—	—	14 @ 2150	6.7	9 @ 11.8
D4A4-06	0 @ 550	—	—	—	12 @ 2300	5.9	3 @ 9.8
D4A4-07	0 @ 600	—	—	—	11 @ 1950	6.7	6½ @ 11.8
D4A6-03	0 @ 600	—	—	—	11 @ 1950	3.5	4 @ 6.3
D4A5-14	0 @ 600	—	—	—	11 @ 1950	2.8	10 @ 7.7
D4F4-03	0 @ 600	—	—	—	11 @ 1950	5.9	3 @ 9.8
D4F4-04	0 @ 550	—	—	—	11 @ 2300	5.9	3 @ 9.8
D4F4-07	0 @ 600	—	—	—	11 @ 1950	3.5	3 @ 5.5
D4F5-06	0 @ 600	—	—	—	11 @ 1950	2.8	10 @ 7.7
D6F4-03	0 @ 600	—	—	—	8.5 @ 1250	7.9	7½ @ 13.8
D6F5-02	0 @ 600	—	—	—	8.5 @ 1250	5.9	9 @ 11.6
D6F6-01	0 @ 600	—	—	—	8.5 @ 1250	2.8	12½ @ 9.5
D6F5-03	0 @ 600	—	—	—	8.5 @ 1250	5.9	5 @ 9.8

—Not Available

DATSUN

VALVE SPECIFICATIONS

Year	Engine	Valve Lash		Valve Angles		Valve Spring Installed Height	Valve Spring Pressure Lbs. @ In.	Stem Clearance		Stem Diameter	
		Int.	Exh.	Seat	Face			Intake	Exhaust	Intake	Exhaust
1972	A12	.014 H	.014 H	45	—	1.52	129 @ 1.19	.0006—.0018	.0016—.0028	.3138—.3144	.3128—.3134
	L16	.011 H	.011 H	45	—	1.53	105 @ 1.21	.0006—.0018	.0016—.0028	.31	.31
	L24	.010 H	.012 H	45	—	1.57	108 @ 1.16	.0008—.0021	.0016—.0029	.31	.31
1973	A12	.014 H	.014 H	45	—	1.52	129 @ 1.19	.0006—.0018	.0016—.0028	.3138—.3144	.3128—.3134
	L16	.010 H	.012 H	45	—	①	108 @ 1.16	.0008—.0021	.0016—.0029	.3136—.3142	.3128—.3134
	L18	.010 H	.012 H	45	—	①	108 @ 1.16	.0008—.0021	.0016—.0029	.3136—.3142	.3128—.3134
	L24	.010 H	.012 H	45	—	1.57	108 @ 1.16	.0008—.0021	.0016—.0029	.3114—.3138	.3128—.3134
1974	A13	.014 H	.014 H	45	—	1.52	129 @ 1.19	.0006—.0018	.0016—.0028	.3128—.3134	.3128—.3134
	L18	.010 H	.012 H	45.5	—	1.57	108 @ 1.16	.0008—.0021	.0002—.0003	.3136—.3142	.3128—.3134
	L20B	.010 H	.012 H	44.5	—	1.57	108 @ 1.16	.0008—.0021	.0016—.0029	.3136—.3142	.3128—.3134
	L26	.010 H	.012 H	45	—	1.57	108 @ 1.16	.0008—.0021	.0016—.0029	.3136—.3142	.3128—.3134
1975	A14	.014 H	.014 H	45	—	—	129 @ 1.19	.0006—.0018	.0016—.0028	.3138—.3144	.3128—.3134
	L20B	.010 H	.012 H	45.5	—	1.57	108 @ 1.16	.0008—.0021	.0016—.0029	.3136—.3142	.3128—.3134
	L28	.010 H	.012 H	45	—	1.57	108 @ 1.16	.0008—.0021	.0016—.0029	.3136—.3142	.3128—.3134
1976	A14	.014 H	.014 H	45	—	—	129 @ 1.19	.0006—.0018	.0016—.0028	.3138—.3144	.3128—.3134
	L20B	.010 H	.012 H	45	—	1.57	108 @ 1.16	.0008—.0021	.0016—.0029	.3136—.3142	.3128—.3134
	L28	.010 H	.012 H	45	—	1.57	108 @ 1.16	.0008—.0021	.0016—.0029	.3136—.3142	.3128—.3134
1977	A14	.014 H	.014 H	45	—	—	129 @ 1.19	.0006—.0018	.0016—.0028	.3138—.3144	.3128—.3134
	L20B	.010 H	.012 H	45	—	1.57	108 @ 1.16	.0008—.0021	.0016—.0029	.3136—.3142	.3128—.3134
	L24	.010 H	.012 H	45	—	1.57	②	.0008—.0021	.0016—.0029	.3136—.3142	.3128—.3134
	L28	.010 H	.012 H	45	—	1.57	108 @ 1.16	.0008—.0021	.0016—.0029	.3136—.3142	.3128—.3134

—Not Available
① —Intake, 1.56; exhaust, 1.38.
② —Intake, 105 @ 1.18; exhaust, 108 @ 1.16.

PISTONS, PINS, RINGS, CRANKSHAFT & BEARINGS

Year	Engine	Piston Clearance	Ring End Gap		Wristpin Diameter	Rod Bearings		Main Bearings		
			Comp.	Oil		Shaft Diameter	Bearing Clearance	Shaft Diameter	Bearing Clearance	Shaft End Play
1972	A12	.0009—.0017	.0079	.0118	.6870	1.7701—1.7706	.0008—.0020	1.9666—1.9671	.0008—.0024	.002—.006
	L16	.0010—.0018	①	.0059	.8267	1.967—1.9675	.0006—.0026	2.1631—2.1636	.0008—.0028	.002—.006
	L24	.0010—.0018	①	.0059	.8267	1.967—1.9675	.0006—.0026	2.1631—2.1636	.0008—.0028	.002—.007
1973	A12	.0009—.0017	.0079	.0118	.6870	1.7701—1.7706	.0008—.0020	1.9666—1.9671	.0008—.0024	.002—.006
	L16	.0010—.0018	②	.0118	.8265	1.967—1.9675	.0010—.0022	2.1631—2.1636	.0008—.0024	.002—.007
	L18	.0010—.0018	②	.0118	.8265	1.967—1.9675	.0010—.0022	2.1631—2.1636	.0008—.0024	.002—.007
	L24	.0010—.0018	①	.0059	.8267	1.967—1.9675	.0010—.0022	2.1631—2.1636	.0008—.0028	.002—.007
1974	A13	.0009—.0017	.0079	.0118	.6870	1.7701—1.7706	.0008—.0020	1.9666—1.9671	.0008—.0024	.002—.006
	L18	.0010—.0018	③	.0118	.8266	1.967—1.9675	.0010—.0022	2.3599—2.360	.0008—.0024	.002—.007
	L20B	.0010—.0018	③	.0118	.8266	1.966—1.9667	.0010—.0022	2.633—2.630	.0008—.0024	.002—.007
	L26	.0010—.0018	①	.0059	.8266	1.967—1.9675	.0010—.0022	2.1631—2.1636	.0008—.0028	.002—.007
1975	A14	.0009—.0017	④	.0118	.7479	1.7701—1.7706	.0008—.0020	1.9666—1.9671	.0008—.0024	.002—.006
	L20B	.0010—.0018	③	.0118	.8266	1.966—1.967	.0010—.0022	2.633—2.630	.0008—.0024	.002—.007
	L28	.0010—.0018	①	.0059	.8266	1.967—1.9675	.0010—.0022	2.1631—2.1636	.0008—.0028	.002—.007
1976	A14	.0009—.0017	④	.0118	.7479	1.7701—1.7706	.0008—.0020	1.9666—1.9671	.0008—.0024	.002—.006
	L20B	.0010—.0018	③	.0118	.8266	1.967—1.9675	.0010—.0022	2.3599—2.3604	.0008—.0024	.002—.007
	L28	.0010—.0018	①	.059	.8266	1.967—1.9675	.0010—.0022	2.1631—2.1636	.0008—.0028	.002—.007
1977	A14	.0009—.0017	④	.0118	.7479	1.7701—1.7706	.0008—.0020	1.9666—1.9671	.0008—.0024	.002—.006
	L20B	.0010—.0018	③	.0118	.8266	1.967—1.9675	.0010—.0022	2.3599—2.3604	.0008—.0024	.002—.007
	L24	.0010—.0018	②	.0118	.8266	1.967—1.9675	.0010—.0022	2.1631—2.1636	.0008—.0028	.002—.007
	L28	.0010—.0018	③	.0118	.8266	1.967—1.9675	.0010—.0022	2.1631—2.1636	.0008—.0028	.002—.007

① —Top ring, .0091; second ring, .0059.
② —Top ring, .0098; second ring, .0059.
③ —Top ring, .0098; second ring, .0018.
④ —Top ring, .0079; second ring, .0059.

DATSUN

ENGINE TIGHTENING SPECIFICATIONS

★Torque specifications listed are in Ft. Lbs. and are for clean and lightly lubricated threads only. Dry or dirty threads produce increased friction which prevents accurate measurement of tightness.

Year	Engine	Spark Plugs	Cylinder Head Bolts	Manifold Nuts or Bolts	Rocker Shaft Bracket Bolts	Camshaft Sprocket Bolt(s)	Oil Pan Bolts	Connecting Rod Cap Bolts	Main Bearing Cap Bolts	Flywheel to Crankshaft	Vibration Damper or Pulley
1972	A12	18	35	8.2	16.5	32	3.5	25	39	50	112
	L16	13	39.8	—	—	102	4	21	36	72	122
	L24	13	54	—	—	41	4.3	21	36	101	122
1973	A12	13	42	8.2	16.5	32	3.5	25	39	50	112
	L16	13	43	10	—	102	5.5	25	37	108	100
	L18	13	54	10	—	102	5.5	37	37	108	100
	L24	13	52	6½	—	102	5.5	37	37	108	100
1974	A13	13	53	8.2	16	32	3.5	25	39	57	125
	L18	14	54	10.2	—	102	5.5	37	37	108	100
	L20B	15	54	10.2	—	102	5.5	37	37	108	100
	L26	13	57	7.2	—	101	6	29	37	100	100
1975	A14	13	53	12.5	16	32	3.5	25	39	57	125
	L20B	13	54	10.2	—	102	5.5	37	37	108	100
	L28	15	57	①	—	101	6	37	37	101	101
1976	A14	13	53	12.5	16	32	3.5	25	39	57	126
	L20B	13	54	10.2	—	102	5.5	37	37	108	100
	L28	13	57	①	—	101	6	37	37	101	101
1977	A14	13	53	12.5	16	32	3.5	25	39	57	126
	L20B	15	54	10.5	—	102	5.5	37	37	108	100
	L24	13	56	①	—	101	5.5	37	37	101	100
	L28	13	56	①	—	101	5.5	37	37	101	100

—Not Available
①—Size 8M, 11.5; Size 10M, 32.

ALTERNATOR & REGULATOR SPECIFICATIONS

Year	Alternator			Regulator				Charge Relay	
	Model	Rated Hot Output Amps.	Cold Output Amps. @ 2500 RPM	Model	Regulated Voltage	Core Gap	Point Gap	Core Gap	Point Gap
1972	LT133-05	33	24	TL12-37	14.3—15.3	.315	.013	.354	.018
	LT130-41	30	22	TL12-17	14—15	.393	①	.206	②
	LT150-05	50	37.5	TL12-57	14.3—15.3	.315	.013	.353	.019
1973	LT135-133	35	28	TL12-57	14.3—15.3	.315	.013	.353	.019
	LT135-13B	50	37.5	TL12-57	14.3—15.3	.315	.013	.353	.019
	LT135-13B	35	28	TL12-57	14.3—15.3	.315	.013	.353	.019
	LT150-10	50	37.5	TL12-57	14.3—15.3	.315	.013	.353	.019
1974	LT135-13B	35	28	TL12-79	14.3—15.3	.031	.014	.035	.020
	LT150-05	50	28	TL12-79	14.3—15.3	.031	.014	.035	.020
	LT150-13	50	37.5	TL12-79	14.3—15.3	.031	.014	.035	.020
	LT150-05B	50	37.5	TL12-58	14.3—15.3	.031	.014	.035	.020
	LT150-10	50	37.5	TL12-79	14.3—15.3	.031	.014	.035	.020
1975	LT150-19	50	37.5	TL12-82	14.3—15.3	.031	.014	.035	.020
	LT150-13	50	37.5	TL12-82	14.3—15.3	.031	.014	.035	.020
	LT150-13B	35	28	TL12-85	14.3—15.3	.031	.014	.035	.020
	LT160-23	60	42	TL12-85	14.3—15.3	.031	.014	.035	.020
1976	LT150-19	50	37.5	TL12-82B	14.3—15.3	.031	.014	.035	.020
	LT150-26	50	37.5	TL12-85B	14.3—15.3	.031	.014	.035	.020
	LT150-13	50	37.5	TL12-82B	14.3—15.3	.031	.016	.035	.014
	LT135-13B	35	28	TL12-85B	14.3—15.3	.031	.014	.035	.020
	LT160-23	60	45	TL12-85B	14.3—15.3	.031	.016	.035	.014

Continued
1-239

DATSUN

ALTERNATOR & REGULATION SPECIFICATIONS—Continued

Year	Alternator			Regulator				Charge Relay	
	Model	Rated Hot Output Amps.	Cold Output Amps. @ 2500 RPM	Model	Regulated Voltage	Core Gap	Point Gap	Core Gap	Point Gap
1977	LT150-26	50	37.5	TL12-82C	14.3—15.3	.031	.016	.035	.020
	LT150-26	50	37.5	TL12-85C	14.3—15.3	.031	.016	.035	.014
	LT135-36B	35	28	TL12-85C	14.3—15.3	.031	.016	.035	.014
	LT138-01B	38	30	TL12-85C	14.3—15.3	.031	.016	.035	.014
	LT150-25	50	37.5	TL12-82B	14.3—15.3	.031	.014	.035	.020
	LT160-39	60	45	TL12-82C	14.3—15.3	.031	.016	.035	.020
	LT160-23C	60	45	TL12-85C	14.3—15.3	.031	.016	.035	.014

①—Primary point gap, .037; Secondary point gap, .177.
②—Primary point gap, .0079; Secondary point gap, .177.

STARTER MOTOR SPECIFICATIONS

Year	Engine	Starter Number	Brush Spring Tension Oz.	Free Speed Test		
				Amps. ①	Volts.	R.P.M. ②
1972	A12	S114-87L	28	60	12	7000
	A16	S114-103	28	60	12	7000
	L24	S114-122N	56	60	12	7000
1973	A12③	S114-87M	56	60	12	7000
	A12④	S114-156	28	60	12	6000
	L16③	S114-103P	56	60	12	7000
	L16④	S114-126M	56	60	12	6000
	L18③	S114-103P	56	60	12	7000
	L18④	S114-126M	56	60	12	6000
	L24③	S114-122N	56	60	12	5000
	L24④	S114-182	56	60	12	6000
1974	A13③	S114-87M	56	60	12	7000
	A13④	S114-156	28	60	12	6000
	L18③	S114-103P	56	60	12	7000
	L18④	S114-126M	56	60	12	6000
	L20B③	S114-103P	56	60	12	7000
	L20B④	S114-126M	56	60	12	6000
	L26③	S114-122N	56	60	12	5000
	L26④	S114-182	56	60	12	6000
1975	A14③	S114-160	56	60	12	7000
	A14④	S114-163	56	60	12	7000
	L20B③	S114-170	56	60	12	7000
	L20B④	S114-180	56	60	12	6000
	L28③	S114-122N	56	60	12	5000
	L28④	S114-182	56	60	12	6000
1976	A14③⑤	S114-160	56	60	12	7000
	A14③⑥	S114-161B	56	60	12	7000
	A14④⑤	S114-163	56	60	12	7000
	A14⑥	S114-208B	56	60	12	7000
	L20B③	S114-170	56	60	12	7000
	L20B④	S114-180	56	60	12	6000
	L28③	S114-122N	56	60	12	5000
	L28④	S114-182	56	60	12	6000
1977	A14③⑤	S114-160B	56	60	12	7000
	A14③⑥	S114-161B	56	60	12	7000
	A14④⑤	S114-163B	56	60	12	7000
	A14⑥	S114-208B	56	60	12	7000
	L20B③	S114-170B	56	60	12	7000
	L20B④	S114-180B	56	60	12	6000
	L24③	S114-173B	56	60	12	5000
	L24④	S114-182B	56	60	12	6000
	L28③	S114-173B	56	60	12	5000
	L28④	S114-182B	56	60	12	6000

①—Maximum. ②—Minimum. ③—Manual trans. ④—Auto. trans. ⑤—B210. ⑥—F10.

DATSUN

BRAKE SPECIFICATIONS

Year	Model	Brake Drum Inside Diameter	Wheel Cylinder Bore Diameter			Master Cylinder Bore Diameter	Disc Brake Rotor Specifications			
			Disc Brake	Front Drum Brake	Rear Drum Brake		Nominal Thickness	Minimum Refinish Thickness	Thickness Variation Parallelism	Lateral Run-out (T.I.R.)
1972	B110	8	1.894	—	11/16	11/16	.3740	.3307	—	.0012
	510	9	2.000	—	13/16	¾	.3940	.3310	—	.0024
	240Z	9	2.125	—	7/8	7/8	.4920	.4130	.0012	.0059
	521	10	—	13/16	13/16	¾	—	—	—	—
	620	10	—	¾	¾	①	—	—	—	—
1973	B110	8	1.894	—	11/16	11/16	.3740	.3307	—	.0012
	510	9	2.000	—	13/16	¾	.3940	.3310	—	.0048
	240Z	9	2.125	—	7/8	7/8	.4920	.4130	.0012	.0059
	610	9	2.000	—	7/8	¾	.3940	.3310	.0012	.0048
	620	10	—	¾	③	①	—	—	—	—
1974	B210	8	2.012	—	13/16	¾	.3740	.3310	—	.0047
	610	9	2.000	—	7/8	¾	.3940	.3310	.0012	.0048
	710	9	2.000	—	13/16	¾	.3940	.3310	.0012	.0024
	260Z	9	2.125	—	7/8	7/8	.4920	.4130	.0012	.0059
	620	10	—	¾	③	②	—	—	—	—
1975	B210	8	2.012	—	13/16	¾	.3740	.331	—	.0047
	610	9	2.012	—	7/8	¾	.3940	.331	—	.0048
	710	9	2.000	—	13/16	¾	.3940	.331	.0012	.0024
	280Z	9	2.125	—	7/8	7/8	.4920	.4130	.0012	.0039
	620	10	—	¾	11/16	¾	—	—	—	—
1976	B210	8	2.012	—	13/16	¾	.3740	.3310	—	.0047
	610	9	2.012	—	13/16	¾	.3940	.3310	—	.0048
	710	9	2.012	—	13/16	¾	.3940	.3310	—	.0047
	F10	8	1.894	—	11/16	¾	—	.3310	—	.0059
	280Z	9	2.125	—	7/8	7/8	.4920	.4130	.0012	.0039
	620	10	—	¾	¾	¾	—	—	—	—
1977	B210	8	2.012	—	13/16	¾	.3740	.3310	.0012	.0047
	710	9	2.012	—	13/16	¾	.3940	.3310	—	.0047
	810	9	2.125	—	13/16	13/16	.4920	.4130	—	.0059
	280Z	9	2.125	—	7/8	7/8	.4920	.4130	.0012	.0039
	F10	8	1.894	—	11/16	¾	—	.3390	—	.0059
	200SX	9	2.012	—	13/16	¾	—	.3310	.0012	.0047
	620	10	—	¾	¾	¾	—	—	—	—

—Not Available
① —Single, 11/16"; Tandem, ¾".
② —Without master-vac, 11/16"; with master-vac, ¾".
③ —With auto. trans., ¾"; without auto. trans., 11/16".

WHEEL ALIGNMENT SPECIFICATIONS

Year	Model	Caster Angle, Degrees		Camber Angle, Degrees		Toe-In, Inch	King Pin Inclination
		Limits	Desired	Limits	Desired		
1972	B110①	+1 1/6 to +2 1/6	+1 2/3	+7/12 to +1 7/12	+1 1/12	.16 to .24	+7 11/12
	B110②	+1 1/12 to +2 1/12	+1 7/12	+¾ to +1¾	+1¼	.20 to .28	+7¾
	510①	—	+1 7/12	—	+5/12	.12 to .24	—
	510②	—	+1 2/3	—	+7/12	.18 to .20	—
	240Z	+2 5/12 to +3 5/12	+2 11/12	+1 to +1 1/3	+5/6	.08 to .20	+12 1/6
	521③	—	+1 5/6	—	+1¼	.08 to .12	+6¼
	521④	—	+1 11/12	—	+1 1/3	.08 to .12	+6 1/6
	620⑤	—	+1 5/6	—	+1¼	.08 to .12	+6¼
	620⑥	—	+1 5/6	—	+1½	.08 to .12	+6

WHEEL ALIGNMENT SPECIFICATIONS—Continued

Year	Model	Caster Angle, Degrees		Camber Angle, Degrees		Toe-In, Inch	King Pin Inclination
		Limits	Desired	Limits	Desired		
1973	B110	$+\frac{1}{3}$ to $+1\frac{5}{6}$	$+1\frac{1}{12}$	$+2\frac{1}{12}$ to $+5$	$+3\frac{1}{2}$	.08 to .32	$+7\frac{11}{12}$
	510①	—	$+1\frac{7}{12}$	—	$+\frac{5}{12}$	.12 to .24	—
	510②	—	$+1\frac{2}{3}$	—	$+\frac{7}{12}$	.12 to .24	—
	240Z	$+2\frac{1}{6}$ to $+3\frac{2}{3}$	$+2\frac{11}{12}$	$+\frac{1}{12}$ to $+1\frac{7}{12}$	$+\frac{5}{6}$	.06 to .22	$+12\frac{1}{6}$
	610①	$+\frac{3}{4}$ to $+2\frac{1}{4}$	$+1\frac{1}{2}$	$+1$ to $+2\frac{1}{2}$	$+1\frac{3}{4}$	.24 to .35	$+7\frac{1}{6}$
	610②	$+1\frac{11}{12}$ to $+2\frac{5}{12}$	$+2$	$+1\frac{1}{6}$ to $+2\frac{2}{3}$	$+1\frac{11}{12}$	.32 to .43	$+6\frac{11}{12}$
	620⑤	$+1\frac{1}{12}$ to $+2\frac{7}{12}$	$+1\frac{5}{6}$	$+\frac{1}{4}$ to $+2\frac{1}{4}$	$+1\frac{1}{4}$	.04 to .20	$+6\frac{1}{4}$
	620⑥	$+1\frac{1}{12}$ to $2\frac{7}{12}$	$+1\frac{5}{6}$	$+\frac{1}{2}$ to $+2\frac{1}{2}$	$+1\frac{1}{2}$	.08 to .12	$+6$
1974	B210	$+1\frac{1}{4}$ to $2\frac{1}{4}$	$+1\frac{3}{4}$	$+\frac{2}{3}$ to $+1\frac{2}{3}$	$+1\frac{1}{6}$	.08 to .16	$+8\frac{2}{3}$
	610	$+1\frac{1}{4}$ to $+2\frac{3}{4}$	$+2$	⑦	⑧	.43 to .55	⑨
	710	$+1\frac{1}{6}$ to $+2\frac{1}{3}$	$+1\frac{11}{12}$	$+1\frac{5}{12}$ to $+2\frac{11}{12}$	$+2\frac{1}{6}$	.31 to .43	$+6\frac{5}{12}$
	260Z	$+2\frac{1}{6}$ to $+3\frac{2}{3}$	$+2\frac{11}{12}$	0 to $+1\frac{1}{2}$	$+\frac{3}{4}$	.08 to .20	$+12\frac{1}{6}$
	620⑤	$+1\frac{1}{12}$ to $+2\frac{7}{12}$	$+1\frac{5}{6}$	$+\frac{1}{4}$ to $+2\frac{1}{4}$	$+1\frac{1}{4}$	.04 to .20	$+6\frac{1}{4}$
	620⑥	$+1\frac{1}{12}$ to $+2\frac{7}{12}$	$+1\frac{5}{6}$	$+\frac{1}{2}$ to $+2\frac{1}{2}$	$+1\frac{1}{2}$	.08 to .12	$+6$
1975	B210	$+1$ to $+2\frac{1}{2}$	$+1\frac{3}{4}$	$+\frac{5}{12}$ to $+1\frac{11}{12}$	$+1\frac{1}{6}$	.08 to .16	$+8\frac{1}{4}$
	610	$+1\frac{1}{4}$ to $+2\frac{3}{4}$	$+2$	⑦	⑧	.43 to .55	⑨
	710	$+1\frac{1}{6}$ to $+2\frac{1}{3}$	$+1\frac{11}{12}$	$+1\frac{5}{12}$ to $+2\frac{11}{12}$	$+2\frac{1}{6}$	.32 to .43	$+6\frac{5}{12}$
	280Z	$+2\frac{1}{2}$ to $+3\frac{1}{2}$	$+3$	$+\frac{1}{3}$ to $+1\frac{5}{6}$	$+1\frac{1}{12}$	0 to .12	$+12$
	620	$+1\frac{1}{12}$ to $+2\frac{7}{12}$	$+1\frac{5}{6}$	$+\frac{1}{4}$ to $+2\frac{1}{4}$	$+1\frac{1}{4}$	.04 to.20	$+6\frac{1}{4}$
1976	B210	$+1$ to $+2\frac{1}{2}$	$+1\frac{3}{4}$	$+\frac{5}{12}$ to $+1\frac{11}{12}$	$+1\frac{1}{6}$	.08 to .16	$+8\frac{1}{4}$
	610	$+1\frac{1}{12}$ to $2\frac{7}{12}$	$+1\frac{5}{6}$	$+1\frac{1}{4}$ to $+2\frac{3}{4}$	$+2$	⑩	$+7$
	710	$+1\frac{1}{12}$ to $+2\frac{7}{12}$	$+1\frac{5}{6}$	$+1\frac{1}{4}$ to $2\frac{3}{4}$	$+2$	⑩	$+7$
	F10	$+\frac{1}{3}$ to $+1\frac{5}{6}$	$+1\frac{1}{12}$	$+\frac{5}{6}$ to $+2\frac{1}{3}$	$+1\frac{7}{12}$	⑪	$+10$
	280Z	$+2\frac{1}{2}$ to $+3\frac{1}{2}$	$+3$	$+\frac{1}{3}$ to $+1\frac{5}{6}$	$+1\frac{1}{12}$	0 to .12	$+12$
	620	$+1\frac{1}{12}$ to $2\frac{7}{12}$	$+1\frac{5}{6}$	$+\frac{1}{4}$ to $+2\frac{1}{4}$	$+1\frac{1}{4}$	.04 to .20	$+6\frac{1}{4}$
1977	B210	$+1$ to $+2\frac{1}{2}$	$+1\frac{3}{4}$	$+\frac{5}{12}$ to $+1\frac{11}{12}$	$+1\frac{1}{6}$	.08 to .16	$+8\frac{1}{4}$
	710	$+1\frac{1}{12}$ to $+2\frac{7}{12}$	$+1\frac{5}{6}$	$+1\frac{1}{4}$ to $+2\frac{3}{4}$	$+2$	⑩	$+7$
	810	$+1\frac{1}{6}$ to $+2\frac{2}{3}$	$+1\frac{11}{12}$	0 to $+1\frac{1}{2}$	$+\frac{3}{4}$	0 to .08	$+7\frac{11}{12}$
	F10	$+\frac{1}{3}$ to $+1\frac{5}{6}$	$+1\frac{1}{12}$	$+\frac{5}{6}$ to $+2\frac{1}{3}$	$+1\frac{7}{12}$	⑪	$+10$
	200SX	$+1\frac{1}{12}$ to $2\frac{7}{12}$	$+1\frac{5}{6}$	$+\frac{1}{3}$ to $+1\frac{5}{6}$	$+1\frac{1}{12}$	.08 to .16	$+7\frac{5}{6}$
	280Z	$+2\frac{1}{2}$ to $+3\frac{1}{2}$	$+3$	$+\frac{1}{3}$ to $+1\frac{5}{6}$	$+1\frac{1}{12}$	0 to .20	$+12$
	620	$+1\frac{1}{12}$ to $+2\frac{7}{12}$	$+1\frac{5}{6}$	$+\frac{1}{4}$ to $+2\frac{1}{4}$	$+1\frac{1}{4}$	.08 to .12	$+6\frac{1}{4}$

—**Not Available.**
①—Sedan & Coupe.
②—Wagon.
③—Exc. Double Cabin.
④—Double Cabin.
⑤—Exc. Double Pick-up.
⑥—Double Pick-up.
⑦—Sedan & Hardtop +1¼ to +2¾; Wagon, +1½ to +3.
⑧—Sedan & Hardtop +2; Wagon, +2¼.
⑨—Sedan & Hardtop, +6²/3; Wagon +6½.
⑩—Without Radial tires; .24 to .31; with Radial tires, .16 to .24.
⑪—Without Radial tires, .20 to .28, with Radial tires 0 to .08.

DATSUN

COOLING SYSTEM & CAPACITY DATA

Year	Model	Cooling Cap. Qts.	Radiator Cap Relief Pressure, Lbs.	Thermo. Opening Temp.	Fuel Tank Gals.	Engine Oil Refill Qts. ③	Transmission Oil		Rear Axle Oil Pints
							Manual Trans. Pt.	Auto. Trans. Qts.	
1972	B110	$5^{3}/_{16}$	12.8	180	①	4	2½	5⅞	1⅝
	510	—	13	180	—	5	3⅜	5⅞	④
	240Z	8½	13	180	15⅞	5¼	3⅛	5⅞	2⅛
	521	7	13	180	10.8	5	4	—	1⅝
	620	6½	13	180	10.8	5	3⅝	—	2⅛
1973	B110	$5^{3}/_{16}$	13	180	①	4	2½	5⅞	1⅝
	510	—	—	—	—	—	—	—	—
	240Z	10¼	13	18	15⅞	5⅛	3⅛	5⅞	2⅛
	610	7	13	180	⑤	4½	4¼	5⅞	④
	620	5¾	13	180	11⅞	4½	3⅝	6	2⅛
1974	B210	5⅜	13	180	11½	3⅜	2½	5⅞	1⅞
	610	6⅞	13	180	⑤	4½	4¼	5⅞	⑥
	710	6⅞	13	180	13¼	4⅜	4¼	5⅞	2¾
	260Z	10	13	180	15⅞	5	3⅛	5⅞	2⅛
	620	6⅜	13	180	11⅞	5⅛	3½	5⅞	2⅛
1975	B210	6¼	13	180	11½	4⅛	2¾	5⅝	1⅞
	610	7¼	13	180	⑦	4½	4¼	5⅞	④
	710	7¼	13	180	⑧	4½	4¼	5⅞	2¾
	280Z	10	13	180	17¼	5	3⅛	5⅞	2¾
	620	6⅜	13	180	11⅞	5⅛	3½	5⅞	2⅛
1976	B210	6¼	13	180	11½	3⅞	2¾	5⅞	1⅞
	610	7¼	13	180	⑦	4½	4¼	5⅞	④
	710	7¼	13	180	⑧	4⅛	4¼	5⅞	2¾
	F10	7	13	180	⑨	3⅝	4⅛	—	—
	280Z	11	13	180	17⅛	5	3⅛	5⅞	2¾
	620	8½	13	180	11⅞	4½	3½	5⅞	2⅛
1977	B210	6¼	13	180	11½	3⅞	⑩	5⅝	1⅞
	710	7¼	13	180	⑧	4½	3⅝	5⅞	2¾
	810	11	13	180	⑪	4½	3⅝	5⅞	2⅛
	280Z	10⅞	13	180	17⅛	5	②	5⅞	2¾
	F10	7	13	180	10⅝	3⅝	4⅞	—	—
	200SX	7⅞	13	180	15⅞	4½	3⅝	5⅞	2¾
	620	8½	13	180	11⅞	4½	②	5⅞	2⅛

—Not Available.
① —Exc. two door sedan, 10 gals.; two door sedan, 10½ gals.
② —4 speed, 3⅝ pts.; 5 speed, 4¼ pts.
③ —Includes filter.
④ —Sedan, 1¾ pts.; wagons, 2⅛ pts.
⑤ —Sedan, 14½ gals.; wagons, 13¾ gals.
⑥ —Sedan, 1¾ pts.; wagon w/auto trans., 2¾ pts.; wagon w/man. trans., 2⅛ pts.
⑦ —Sedan & hardtop, 14½ gals.; wagons, exc. Calif., 13¾ gals., Calif., 13 gals.
⑧ —Sedan & hardtop, 13¼ gals.; wagons, exc. Calif., 11⅞ gals., Calif., 13¼ gals.
⑨ —Sedan & hatchback, 10⅝ gals.; wagons, 9¼ gals.
⑩ —4 speed, 2¾ pts.; 5 speed, 3⅝ pts.
⑪ —Exc. Wagon, 15⅞ gals.; wagons, 14½ gals.

Electrical Section

DISTRIBUTOR, REPLACE

Removal

1. Mark position of No. 1 tower of distributor cap on distributor housing.
2. Remove distributor cap.
3. Crank engine to align rotor with No. 1 mark on housing.
4. Place a mark between distributor housing and engine.
5. Remove distributor retaining bolt and the distributor.

NOTE: Do not crank engine when distributor is removed from engine.

Installation

1. Align rotor with No. 1 mark on housing.
2. If engine was cranked when distributor was removed from engine, crank engine until No. 1 cylinder is on compression stroke and the timing marks align on the pulley and front cover.
3. Install distributor into engine, aligning all index marks made during removal.
4. Loosely install distributor retaining bolt.
5. Adjust ignition timing and tighten distributor retaining bolt.

DISTRIBUTOR SERVICE

Point Type Distributor

Fig. 1
1. Remove distributor cap and rotor.
2. Remove vacuum advance assembly.
3. Remove breaker points.
4. Remove breaker plate assembly.
5. Drive out roll pin and disconnect collar from rotating assembly.

6. When cam is being removed, remove set screw since the shaft head is secured by the screw. Place a mark across cam and shaft to aid reassembly in original position.
7. Disconnect governor weights and springs.
8. Reverse procedure to assemble.

Breakerless Type Distributor

Fig. 2
1. Remove distributor cap and rotor.
2. Remove vacuum advance unit.
3. Remove pick-up coil assembly.
4. Remove reluctor from shaft using two screwdrivers to pry upward on both side of reluctor.

NOTE: On 2602 and 2802 distributors, the reluctor cannot be removed.

---

5. Remove breaker plate assembly.
6. Drive out roll pin and remove gear.
7. Remove shaft assembly.
8. Mark relationship between rotor shaft and drive shaft. Remove rotor shaft set screw and the rotor shaft.
9. Remove governor springs and weights.
10. Reverse procedure to assemble, noting the following:
    a. If the contactor was removed from the breaker plate assembly, adjust cam to contactor clearance to .012 inch (.3mm)
    b. Ensure that reluctor is properly positioned on shaft. Drive in roll pin with slit facing toward outer end of shaft.
    c. When installing gear on shaft, align punch mark in gear with mark on distributor housing so the rotor points to the No. 1 firing position.

ALTERNATOR, REPLACE

1. Disconnect battery ground cable.

2. Disconnect wiring from alternator.
3. Loosen adjusting bolt.
4. Remove drive belt.
5. Remove alternator bracket and the alternator.
6. Reverse procedure to install.

ALTERNATOR TESTING

Alternator Test

1. Disconnect electrical connectors from alternator.
2. With a jumper wire, connect terminal "A" to terminal "F," Fig. 3.
3. Connect one probe from voltmeter positive terminal to terminal "A" and the other test probe to ground. The voltmeter should indicate battery voltage.
4. Turn headlamps on to "High Beam" and start engine.
5. Run engine at approximately 1100 RPM and note voltmeter reading.
6. If voltmeter indicates over 12.5 volts, the alternator is satisfactory. If not, remove alternator and bench test.

Regulator Test & Adjustments

1. Connect test equipment, Fig. 4.
2. Start and run engine at 2500 RPM.
3. Note ammeter reading after several minutes.
4. If ammeter reading is below 5 amps, proceed to step 6.
5. If ammeter reading is above 5 amps, replace battery with a fully charged battery, if available and repeat steps 1 through 3 and note ammeter reading. If ammeter reading is below 5 amps, proceed to next step. If a fully charged battery is not available connect a ¼ ohm resistor in series, Fig. 4. Note ammeter reading. If ammeter reading is below 5 amps, proceed to next step. If ammeter reading is not below 5 amps, recharge battery and repeat steps 1 through 3 and note ammeter read-

1 Cap assembly
2 Rotor head assembly
3 Condenser assembly
4 Ground wire assembly
5 Lead wire assembly
6 Contact set
7 Breaker plate assembly
8 Packing
9 Cam assembly
10 Governor spring
11 Governor weight
12 Shaft assembly
13 Vacuum controller
14 Terminal assembly
15 Housing
16 Fixing plate
17 O-ring
18 Collar

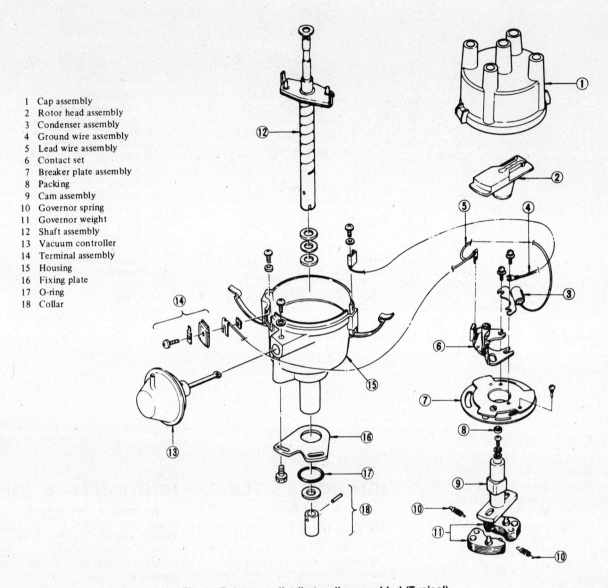

Fig. 1 Point type distributor disassembled (Typical)

ing. Then, proceed to next step.

6. Run engine at 2500 RPM and note voltmeter reading.
7. If voltmeter reading is 14.15-15.15 at 86° F., the regulator is satisfactory. If not, replace regulator.

Core Gap Adjustment

Loosen screw securing contact set on yoke and move contact to obtain specified gap, Fig. 5. Refer to the "Alternator and Regulator Specifications" at the front of this chapter.

Point Gap Adjustment

Loosen screw securing upper contact and move upper contact to obtain specified gap, Fig. 6. Refer to the "Alternator and Regulator Specifications" at the front of this chapter.

Voltage Adjustment

Loosen adjusting screw lock nut. Rotate adjusting screw clockwise to increase voltage setting or counterclockwise to decrease voltage setting, Fig. 7.

Charge Relay Test & Adjustment

1. Connect positive probe of voltmeter to regulator lead connector "N" and the negative probe to ground, Fig. 8.
2. Start and run engine at idle and note voltmeter reading.
3. If no voltage is noted, check continuity between the "N" terminals of regulator and alternator.
4. If charge warning lamp is "On" and the voltmeter reading is below 5.2

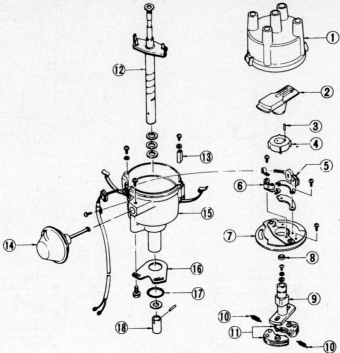

1 Cap assembly
2 Rotor head assembly
3 Roll pin
4 Reluctor
5 Pick-up coil
6 Contactor
7 Breaker plate assembly
8 Packing
9 Rotor shaft
10 Governor spring
11 Governor weight
12 Shaft assembly
13 Cap setter
14 Vacuum controller
15 Housing
16 Fixing plate
17 O-ring
18 Collar

Fig. 2 Breakerless type distributor disassembled (Typical)

volts, check alternator drive belt tension and if correct, adjust regulator.

5. If the charge warning lamp is "On" and the voltmeter reading is above 5.2 volts, adjust charge relay contact points or, if satisfactory, replace regulator.

6. If the charge warning lamp is "Off" and the voltage reading is over 5.2 volts, the charge relay is satisfactory.

Core Gap & Point Gap Adjustments

The charge relay core gap and point gap adjustments are performed in the same manner as the regulator core gap and point gap adjustments.

STARTER, REPLACE

1. Disconnect battery ground cable.
2. Disconnect starter wiring from starter.
3. Remove starter retaining bolts and the starter.
4. Reverse procedure to install.

IGNITION SWITCH, REPLACE

1972 Pick-Up & 1972-73 B110

1. Disconnect the electrical connector from switch.
2. Loosen the ring nut and remove switch from bracket.
3. Reverse procedure to install.

1972-73 510

1. Disconnect electrical connector from switch.
2. Remove switch retaining screw and the switch.
3. Reverse procedure to install.

All Exc. 1972 Pick-Up & 1972-73 B110 & 510

1. Remove the four upper and lower shell cover retaining screws, then the shell covers.
2. Disconnect electrical connectors from switch.
3. Remove switch retaining screw from steering lock, Fig. 9.
4. Remove switch.
5. Reverse procedure to install.

IGNITION LOCK, REPLACE

The ignition lock is retaining by two shear type screws, Fig. 10. It is necessary to drill out these screws to remove ignition lock from steering tube. When installing, ensure that the shear type screws are used.

NEUTRAL SAFETY (INHIBITOR) SWITCH, ADJUST

1. With manual linkage properly adjusted, place transmission manual lever in neutral, then remove the transmission lever.
2. Loosen inhibitor switch retaining bolts, Fig. 11, and remove alignment pin hole screw at bottom of switch.
3. Rotate switch and insert a .059 inch diameter pin through alignment pin hole and into internal rotor hole, then tighten switch retaining bolts and remove alignment pin.
4. Install alignment pin hole screw and the transmission manual lever.
5. Check switch for proper operation.

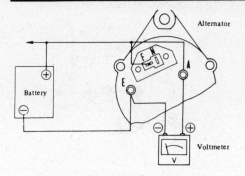

Fig. 3   Alternator test connections

STOPLIGHT SWITCH, REPLACE

NOTE: The stop light switch is located on the brake pedal support.

1. Disconnect the switch electrical connectors.
2. Loosen switch retaining lock nut and remove switch.
3. Reverse procedure to install.

LIGHT SWITCH, REPLACE

B110, B210, 200SX, 710 & Pick-up

1. Disconnect battery ground cable.
2. Depress the switch knob and turn counter-clockwise and remove knob.
3. Remove ring nut or escutcheon securing switch assembly to instrument panel, Fig. 12.
4. Disconnect the switch electrical connector.
5. On 710 & 1977 B210, disconnect illumination fiberscope at illumination lamp.
6. Remove light switch.
7. Reverse procedure to install.

F10

1. Disconnect battery ground cable.

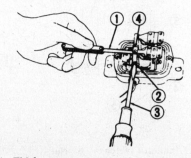

1 Thickness gauge
2 3 mm (0.118 in) dia. screw
3 Crosshead screwdriver
4 Upper contact

Fig. 6   Regulator point gap adjustment

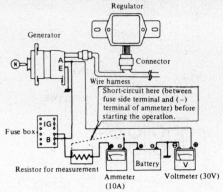

Fig. 4   Regulator test connections

2. Remove steering column cover.
3. Disconnect the harness connector.
4. Remove the switch retaining screws, Fig. 13.
5. Remove switch.
6. Reverse procedure to install.

510

1. Remove knob by pushing inward and turning counter-clockwise.
2. Remove washer.
3. Disconnect speedometer cable and all electrical connectors from cluster.
4. Remove instrument panel upper garnish and package tray.
5. Remove heater control knobs and the control.
6. Remove steering column shell cover and disconnect side ventilator duct and nozzle.
7. Remove instrument panel to bracket retaining nuts, located on the side of the panel.
8. Remove instrument panel upper retaining screws, then the instrument panel.
9. Disconnect wiring from light switch connector.
10. Loosen switch nut and remove switch.
11. Reverse procedure to install.

610

1. Disconnect battery ground cable.
2. Remove upper and lower shell covers from steering column.
3. Remove cluster lid.
4. Remove five screws from front of cluster lid "A," Fig. 14, and one screw from behind the cluster, then the cluster lid.
5. Remove switch knob by depressing and turning counter-clockwise.
6. Remove light switch.
7. Reverse procedure to install.

810

NOTE: The light switch and turn signal

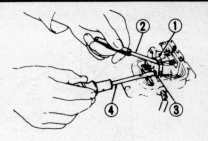

1 Contact set
2 Thickness gauge
3 4 mm (0.157 in) dia. screw
4 Crosshead screwdriver

Fig. 5   Regulator core gap adjustment

switch is incorporated into one assembly.

1. Disconnect battery ground cable.
2. Remove horn ring and steering wheel.
3. Remove steering column shell covers.
4. Disconnect combination switch electrical connectors.
5. Remove combination switch retaining screws and the switch, Fig. 15.
6. Reverse procedure to install.

240Z, 260Z & 280Z

NOTE: The light switch, W/S wiper switch and the turn signal switch are incorporated into one assembly.

1. Disconnect battery ground cable.
2. Remove steering column shell covers.
3. Disconnect lead wires from combination switch. Note there are six connectors.
4. Remove two screws securing the combination switch to steering column jacket, Fig. 16. The switch will then separate into two pieces and can be removed.
5. Reverse procedure to install.

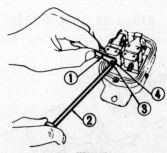

1 Wrench
2 Crosshead screwdriver
3 Adjusting screw
4 Lock nut

Fig. 7   Voltage adjustment

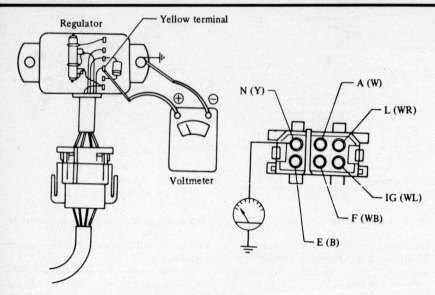

Fig. 8   Charge relay test

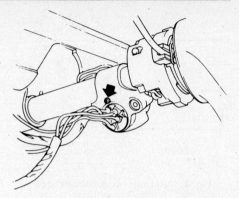

Fig. 9   Ignition switch replacement. All exc. 1972 Pick-Up & 1972-73 B110 & 510

9. Disconnect wiring connector from wiper switch.
10. Loosen switch nut and remove switch.
11. Reverse procedure to install.

TURN SIGNAL SWITCH, REPLACE

B110, B210, 200SX, 610, 710, F10 & Pick-Up

1. Disconnect battery ground cable.
2. Remove steering wheel.
3. Remove the four upper and lower shell cover retaining screws, then the shell covers.
4. Disconnect the switch electrical connectors.
5. Loosen the switch retaining screws and remove switch from column.
6. Reverse procedure to install.

510

1. Disconnect battery ground cable.
2. Remove horn ring and steering wheel.
3. Remove steering column shell cover.
4. Remove the locating screw and retaining screw from switch assembly and the switch.
5. Reverse procedure to install.

810, 240Z, 260Z & 280Z

Refer to the "Light Switch, Replace"

procedure since the light switch and turn signal switch are incorporated into one assembly.

W/S WIPER SWITCH, REPLACE

B110, B210, 200SX & F10

1. Disconnect battery ground cable.
2. Disconnect electrical connector from switch.
3. On all except 1972-73 models, disconnect illumination fiberscope at illumination lamp.
4. On all models, depress switch knob and turn counter-clockwise and remove knob.
5. Remove switch retaining nut or escutcheon.
6. Remove switch from instrument cluster.
7. Reverse procedure to install.

510

1. Remove knob by pushing inward and turning counter-clockwise.
2. Remove washer.
3. Disconnect speedometer cable and all electrical connectors from cluster.
4. Remove instrument panel upper garnish and package tray.
5. Remove heater control knobs and the control.
6. Remove steering column shell cover and disconnect side ventilator duct and nozzle.
7. Remove instrument panel to bracket retaining nuts, located on side of panel.
8. Remove instrument panel upper retaining screws, then the instrument panel.

610

1. Disconnect battery ground cable.
2. Remove upper and lower shell covers from steering column.
3. Remove cluster lid.
4. Remove five screws from front of lower left hand cluster and one screw from behind the cluster, then the cluster lid, Fig. 14.
5. Remove switch knob be depressing and turning counter-clockwise.
6. Remove wiper switch.
7. Reverse procedure to install.

710

1. Disconnect battery ground cable.
2. Disconnect electrical connector and fiberscope from switch.
3. Remove switch knob by depressing twisting.
4. Remove switch retaining ring nut.
5. Remove cluster lid "C" as outlined

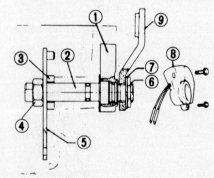

1	Inhibitor switch	6	Nut
2	Manual shaft	7	Washer
3	Washer	8	Inhibitor switch
4	Nut	9	Range select lever
5	Manual plate		

Fig. 11   Neutral safety (Inhibitor) switch adjustment

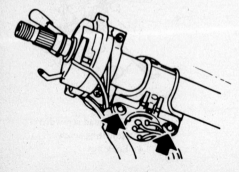

Fig. 10   Ignition lock replacement

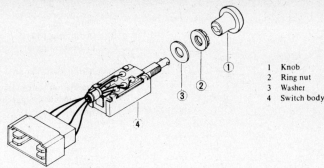

Fig. 12   Light switch. B110, B210, 200SX, 710 & Pick-up (Typical)

1   Knob
2   Ring nut
3   Washer
4   Switch body

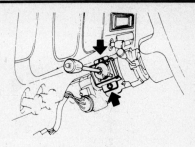

Fig. 13   Light switch. F10

under "Instrument Cluster, Replace" procedure for 710 models.

6. Remove the metal retaining nut from cluster lid "A" and cluster lid "A."
7. Remove switch from cluster lid.
8. Reverse procedure to install.

810

1. Disconnect battery ground cable.
2. Remove steering column shell covers.
3. Remove wiper switch to combination switch retaining screws and the wiper switch.
4. Reverse procedure to install.

Rear Wiper Switch

1. Disconnect battery ground cable.
2. Remove cluster lid as outlined under "Instrument Cluster, Replace" procedure for 810 models.
3. Disconnect electrical connector from switch.
4. Remove switch knob by depressing and twisting.
5. Remove switch retaining ring nut and switch.
6. Reverse procedure to install.

240Z, 260Z & 280Z

Refer to the "Light Switch, Replace" procedure for wiper switch replacement.

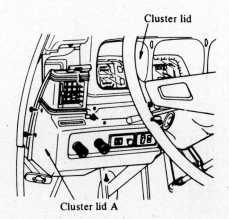

Cluster lid

Cluster lid A

Fig. 14   Removing cluster lid "A". 610

Pick-Up

1972
1. Disconnect battery ground cable.
2. Disconnect electrical connector from switch.
3. Loosen switch knob set screw and remove switch knob.
4. Remove nut washer and spacer retaining switch.
5. Remove switch from rear of instrument panel.
6. Reverse procedure to install.

1973-77
1. Disconnect battery ground cable.
2. Depress switch knob and rotate counter-clockwise, then pull from switch.
3. Remove switch escutcheon and spacer.
4. Disconnect electrical connector from switch.
5. Remove spacer and switch.
6. Reverse procedure to install.

INSTRUMENT CLUSTER, REPLACE

B110

1. Disconnect battery ground cable.
2. Remove knobs from W/S wiper switch, light switch and choke lever.
3. Disconnect electrical connector from cigar lighter, then remove the lighter outer case.
4. Remove radio and heater control knobs.
5. Remove shell cover from steering tube.
6. Remove screws securing meter housing to instrument panel.

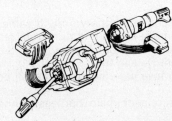

Fig. 15   Light switch & turn signal switch assembly. 810

7. Pull cluster lid slightly rearward.
8. Disconnect speedometer cable.
9. Remove cluster lid from instrument panel.
10. Remove the four screws securing the combination meter from the cluster lid.
11. Remove combination meter.
12. Reverse procedure to install.

B210 & 200SX

1. Disconnect battery ground cable.
2. Remove shell cover attaching screws and the covers.
3. Remove ash tray and cover.
4. Remove knobs from wiper switch, light switch and illumination switch, then the retaining ring nuts from each switch.
5. Remove radio knobs and retaining nuts, if equipped.
6. Remove the nine screws securing the cluster lid to instrument panel, Fig. 17.
7. Pull the cluster lid from panel slightly and disconnect electrical connectors.
8. Remove cluster lid.
9. Remove combination meter retaining screws.
10. Disconnect speedometer cable and electrical connectors from combination meter.
11. Remove combination meter.
12. Reverse procedure to install.

510

1. Disconnect battery ground cable.
2. Disconnect speedometer cable and all electrical connectors from cluster.

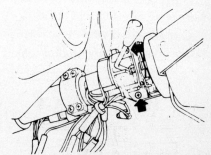

Fig. 16   Light switch, W/S wiper switch & turn signal switch. 240Z, 260Z & 280Z

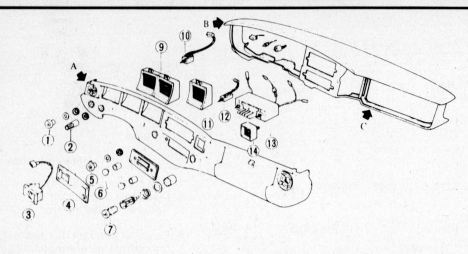

A: Cluster lid
B: Instrument pad
C: Instrument panel

1   Lighting switch knob
2   Illumination control knob
3   Rear window defogger switch (Option)
4   Escutcheon
5   Wiper switch knob
6   Knob for radio
7   Cigarette lighter
8   Combination meter
9   Lighting switch
10 Tachometer (Option)
11 Wiper switch
12 Radio (Option)
13 Clock (Option)

Fig. 17 Instrument cluster. B210 & 200SX

3. Remove combination meter cover retaining screws and the cover.
4. Remove the combination meter retaining screws and the combination meter.
5. Reverse procedure to install.

610

1. Disconnect battery ground cable.
2. Remove steering column shell covers.
3. Remove two cluster lid retaining screws and the cluster lid cover, Fig. 18.
4. Remove two retaining screws in the top of the instrument openings outboard and inboard.
5. Pull instrument panel rearward and disconnect electrical connector from printed circuit housing.
6. Disconnect speedometer cable and the remaining wiring from cluster.
7. Remove cluster lid from instrument panel.
8. To remove speedometer:
   a. Remove odometer knob, if equipped.
   b. Remove the printed circuit housing retaining screws and the printed circuit housing with speedometer, water temperature and fuel gauges.
   c. Remove speedometer retaining screws and the speedometer, Fig. 19.
9. Reverse procedure to install.

710

1. Disconnect battery ground cable.

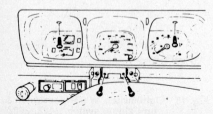

Fig. 18 Cluster lid removal. 610

2. Remove screws securing steering column shell covers and the covers.
3. Remove wiper switch knob and the illumination control switch. Remove ring nuts from switches. On 1976-77 models, remove cluster lid "C," Fig. 20.
4. On 1974-75 models, remove two screws securing cluster lid "C" to instrument panel, then the cluster lid, Fig. 20.
5. On all models, remove ash tray.
6. Disconnect the four electrical connectors for instrument harness.
7. Remove ten screws from around cluster lid "A," Fig. 20.

NOTE: Five screws are located on the upper side and three screws are located on the lower side. Remove two screws at ash tray cover and one behind cluster lid "C."

---

8. Disconnect speedometer cable and electrical leads from radio.
9. Disconnect the knob illumination fiber-scopes and the tachometer electrical connector.
10. Remove cluster lid "A," Fig. 20.
11. Disconnect electrical connector from lower housing of combination meter and remove odometer knob.
12. Remove six screws securing combination meter to housing and the combination meter.
13. Reverse procedure to install.

810

1. Disconnect battery ground cable.
2. Remove knobs and nuts from radio and choke control wire.
3. Remove ash tray.
4. Remove steering column shell covers.
5. Disconnect main harness connectors.
6. Remove cluster lid retaining screws and the cluster lid, Fig. 21.

7. Disconnect electrical connectors from combination meter.
8. Disconnect speedometer cable.
9. Remove combination meter retaining screws and the combination meter, Fig. 22.
10. Reverse procedure to install.

F10

1. Disconnect battery ground cable.
2. Remove knobs and ring nuts from all switches on instrument panel.
3. Remove the four screws securing the panel cover to the panel.
4. Remove the ash tray.
5. Pull the panel cover from the panel and disconnect cigar lighter electrical connector.
6. Remove the panel cover, Fig. 23.
7. Remove the combination meter retaining screws, Fig. 24.
8. Pull the combination meter slightly from panel and disconnect the speedometer cable and the electrical connectors.
9. Remove combination meter.
10. Reverse procedure to install.

240Z

1. Disconnect battery ground cable.

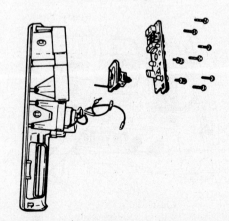

Fig. 19 Speedometer removal. 610

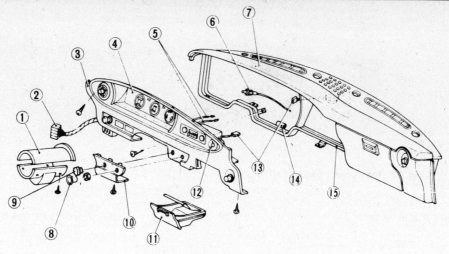

1	Shell covers	6	Speedometer cable	11	Ash tray (inner case)
2	Instrument harness	7	Instrument upper pad	12	Clock
3	Cluster lid-A	8	Wiper and washer switch knob	13	Speaker harness
4	Combination meter	9	Illumination control switch	14	Illumination bulb
5	Illumination fiber scope	10	Cluster lid-C	15	Instrument panel

Fig. 20   Instrument cluster. 710

2. Remove heater air duct.
3. Disconnect speedometer cable.
4. Loosen wing nuts from speedometer and tachometer mounting brackets.
5. Disconnect electrical connectors from clusters.
6. Remove speedometer or tachometer from instrument panel.
7. Reverse procedure to install.

260Z & 280Z

Tachometer Cluster

1. Disconnect battery ground cable.
2. Remove screw retaining tachometer at upper side of instrument panel, Fig. 25.
3. Remove screw retaining tachometer to instrument panel bracket from beneath panel.
4. Pull tachometer from instrument panel slightly and disconnect electrical connector.
5. Remove tachometer from vehicle.

6. Reverse procedure to install.

Speedometer Cluster

1. Remove tachometer cluster as outlined previously.
2. Disconnect speedometer cable.
3. Disconnect trip meter reset cable.
4. Remove screw retaining speedometer at upper side of instrument panel, Fig. 25.
5. Remove screw retaining speedometer to instrument panel bracket from beneath panel. Also, disconnect lead wire for resistor at connector.
6. Pull speedometer from instrument panel slightly and disconnect electrical connector.
7. Remove speedometer from vehicle.
8. Reverse procedure to install.

Pick-Up

1972

1. Disconnect battery ground cable.

2. Remove two set screws from lower part of combination meter.
3. Disconnect electrical connector from combination meter.
4. Disconnect speedometer cable.
5. Remove combination meter.
6. Reverse procedure to install.

1973-77

1. Disconnect battery ground cable.
2. Remove three screws retaining cluster lid to instrument panel.
3. Remove one screw retaining combination meter to instrument panel from beneath panel.
4. Pull cluster lid from instrument panel slightly.
5. Disconnect speedometer cable.
6. Disconnect electrical connectors from combination meter. If equipped with clock, disconnect electrical connectors from clock.
7. Remove four screws retaining combination meter to cluster lid.

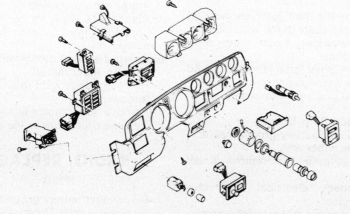

Fig. 21   Instrument cluster. 810

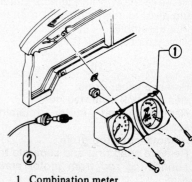

1 Combination meter
2 Speedometer cable

Fig. 22   Combination meter removal. 810

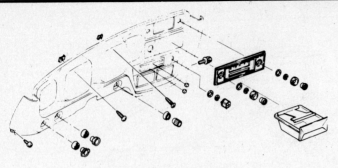

Fig. 23 Instrument panel. F10

Fig. 24 Combination meter removal. F10

8. Remove combination meter assembly, Fig. 26.
9. Reverse procedure to install.

W/S WIPER MOTOR & LINKAGE, REPLACE

B110

1. Disconnect electrical connector from motor.
2. From inside passenger compartment, remove nut securing motor worm wheel shaft to the connecting rod.
3. Remove the three motor mounting bolts and the motor.
4. Reverse procedure to install.

B210, 200SX, 610 & 810

1. Remove wiper arms.
2. Disconnect electrical connector from motor.
3. Remove top grille retaining screws and top grille.
4. Remove the three motor mounting bolts.
5. Pull the motor away from the firewall slightly and disconnect the motor shaft from linkage.
6. Remove the motor.
7. Remove the two flange nuts attaching pivot to cowl top panel, then the link assembly.
8. Reverse procedure to install.

510

1. Remove wiper arms.
2. Remove link retaining nut.
3. Remove wiper motor retaining screws.
4. Remove cowl top grille.
5. Remove snap ring and separate the connecting rod from motor crank arm.
6. Remove nut retaining cowl to pivot section.
7. Remove motor and linkage assembly.

710

1. Remove wiper arms.
2. Disconnect electrical connector from motor.
3. Remove cowl top grille retaining screws and the cowl top grille.
4. Remove two flange nuts retaining pivot to cowl top panel.
5. Disconnect linkage from wiper motor connecting arm.
6. Remove wiper motor and linkage.
7. Reverse procedure to install.

810

Rear Motor

1. Disconnect battery ground cable.
2. Remove wiper arm.
3. Remove tailgate trim and sealed screen.
4. Disconnect wiper motor electrical connector.
5. Remove wiper motor retaining bolts and the wiper motor.
6. Reverse procedure to install.

F10

Front Motor

1. Disconnect battery ground cable.
2. Remove the instrument panel cover.
3. Remove glove box.
4. Remove wiper arm from pivot shaft.
5. Disconnect electrical connector from motor.
6. Remove wiper motor attaching screws.
7. Remove the ball joint connecting the motor shaft to the wiper link.
8. Remove wiper motor from cowl dash panel.
9. Remove pivot attaching bolts and the link assembly.
10. Reverse procedure to install.

Sport Wagon Rear Motor

1. Disconnect battery ground cable.
2. Remove wiper arm.
3. Open tailgate and remove finish panel.
4. Disconnect electrical connector from motor.
5. Remove wiper motor bracket retaining screws.

6. Remove nut attaching motor pivot, then the wiper motor.
7. Reverse procedure to install.

240Z, 260Z & 280Z

1. Remove wiper arms.
2. Disconnect electrical connector from motor.
3. Remove cowl top grille retaining screws and the cowl top grille.
4. Remove four wiper motor bracket retaining screws.
5. Remove wiper motor.
6. Remove three screws retaining pivot, then the linkage assembly.
7. Reverse procedure to install.

Pick-Up

1972

1. Remove wiper arms.
2. Disconnect electrical connector from wiper motor.
3. Separate wiper motor drive shaft arm from connecting rod.
4. Remove wiper motor retaining bolts and the wiper motor.
5. Loosen set screws securing pivot shafts, then the pivot shafts and connecting rod assembly.
6. Reverse procedure to install.

1973-77

1. Remove wiper arms.
2. Remove cowl top grille.
3. Remove stop ring connecting wiper motor arm to connecting rod.
4. Disconnect wiper motor electrical connector from beneath instrument panel.
5. Remove wiper motor retaining bolts and the wiper motor.
6. Remove flange nuts retaining pivot to cowl top.
7. Remove wiper motor linkage.
8. Reverse procedure to install.

RADIO, REPLACE

B110

1. Disconnect battery ground cable.
2. Remove knobs from W/S wiper switch, light switch and choke lever.

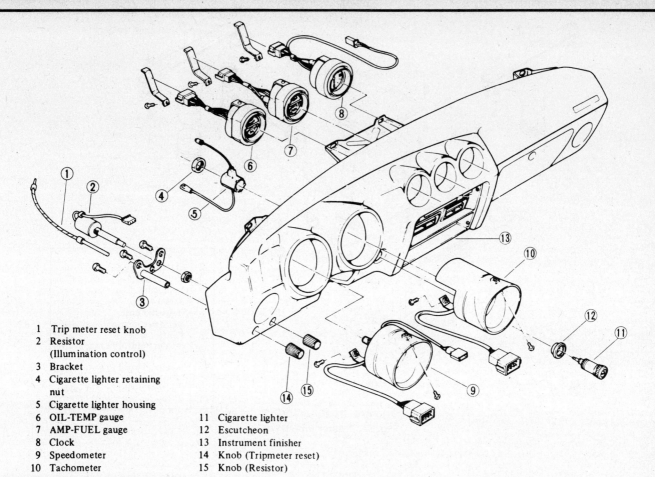

1. Trip meter reset knob
2. Resistor (Illumination control)
3. Bracket
4. Cigarette lighter retaining nut
5. Cigarette lighter housing
6. OIL-TEMP gauge
7. AMP-FUEL gauge
8. Clock
9. Speedometer
10. Tachometer
11. Cigarette lighter
12. Escutcheon
13. Instrument finisher
14. Knob (Tripmeter reset)
15. Knob (Resistor)

Fig. 25 Instrument cluster. 260Z & 280Z

3. Disconnect electrical connector from cigar lighter, then remove the lighter outer case.
4. Remove radio and heater control knobs.
5. Remove shell cover from steering tube.
6. Remove screws securing meter housing to instrument panel.
7. Pull cluster lid slightly rearward and disconnect speedometer cable.
8. Remove cluster lid from instrument panel.
9. Disconnect electrical connectors from radio.
10. Remove radio attaching nuts from front of radio.
11. Remove screws securing radio to mounting bracket, then the radio from instrument panel.
12. Reverse procedure to install.

B210 & 200 SX

1. Disconnect battery ground cable.
2. Remove shell cover attaching screws and the covers.
3. Remove ash tray and cover.
4. Remove knobs from wiper switch, light switch and illumination switch,

then the retaining ring nuts from each switch.
5. Remove radio knobs and retaining nuts.
6. Remove the nine screws securing the cluster lid to instrument panel.
7. Pull cluster lid from panel slightly and disconnect speedometer cable and electrical connectors.
8. Remove cluster lid.
9. Disconnect electrical connectors from radio.
10. Remove screws securing radio to mounting bracket and the radio.
11. Reverse procedure to install.

510

1. Disconnect battery ground cable.

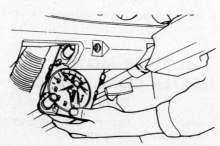

Fig. 26 Combination meter removal. 1973-77 Pick-up

2. Disconnect all electrical connections from radio.
3. Remove knobs from radio control shafts.
4. Remove the four cluster lid retaining screws.
5. Remove cluster lid and radio assembly.
6. Remove lock nuts securing radio to cluster lid.
7. Reverse procedure to install.

610

1. Disconnect battery ground cable.
2. Remove radio control knobs.
3. Remove instrument panel.
4. Disconnect electrical connectors from radio.
5. Remove radio attaching screws and the radio.
6. Reverse procedure to install.

710

1. Disconnect battery ground cable.
2. Remove cluster lid "C" and cluster lid "A" as outlined under "Instrument Cluster, Replace" procedure for 710 models.
3. Remove four radio retaining screws and the radio.
4. Reverse procedure to install.

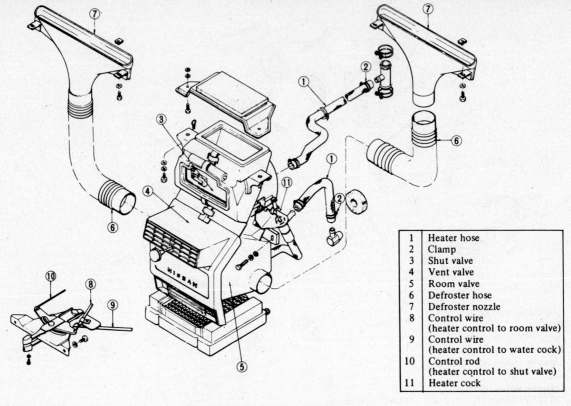

1	Heater hose
2	Clamp
3	Shut valve
4	Vent valve
5	Room valve
6	Defroster hose
7	Defroster nozzle
8	Control wire (heater control to room valve)
9	Control wire (heater control to water cock)
10	Control rod (heater control to shut valve)
11	Heater cock

Fig. 27 Heater unit. B110

810

1. Disconnect battery ground cable.
2. Remove cluster lid as outlined under "Instrument Cluster, Replace" procedure for 810 models.
3. Remove radio bracket to instrument panel attaching screw.
4. Disconnect electrical leads from radio.
5. Remove radio from vehicle.
6. Reverse procedure to install.

F10

1. Disconnect battery ground cable.
2. Remove instrument panel cover.
3. Remove radio bracket to instrument panel attaching screw.
4. Disconnect electrical connectors from radio.
5. Remove radio from instrument panel.
6. Reverse procedure to install.

240Z, 260Z & 280Z

1. Disconnect battery ground cable.
2. Remove console box.
3. Disconnect electrical connectors from radio.
4. Remove radio knobs and two nuts retaining escutcheon to radio.
5. Remove two screws retaining radio to console box and the radio.
6. Reverse procedure to install.

Pick-Up

1972

1. Disconnect battery ground cable.
2. Remove radio knobs, nuts, plain washers and spring washers from radio shafts.
3. Remove screw securing radio mounting bracket to instrument panel.
4. Disconnect electrical leads from radio.
5. Remove radio from vehicle.
6. Reverse procedure to install.

1973-77

1. Disconnect battery ground cable.
2. Remove radio knobs, nuts and washers from shafts.
3. Remove bezel from front of radio.
4. Disconnect electrical leads from radio.
5. Remove radio from vehicle.
6. Reverse procedure to install.

BLOWER MOTOR & HEATER CORE, REPLACE

B110

1. Disconnect battery ground cable and drain cooling system.
2. Remove package tray and ash tray.
3. Disconnect heater hose from core.
4. Disconnect electrical connectors from heater unit, heater control and main harness.
5. Remove wire clamps and disconnect the two control wires between water cock and heater control, and room valve and heater control at heater unit side.
6. Disconnect control rod from shut valve.
7. Remove left and right hand defroster hoses.
8. Remove heater unit retaining screws and the heater unit, Fig. 27.
9. Remove blower motor and heater core from heater unit.
10. Reverse procedure to install.

B210

1. Disconnect battery ground cable and drain cooling system.
2. Remove heater control.
3. Disconnect heater hose from heater cock.
4. Remove clips retaining the right and left side heater box, then separate heater box halves.
5. Remove heater core and heat valve, Fig. 28.
6. Disconnect electrical connector from blower motor.
7. Remove nut retaining fan to motor, then the fan.
8. Remove screws securing blower

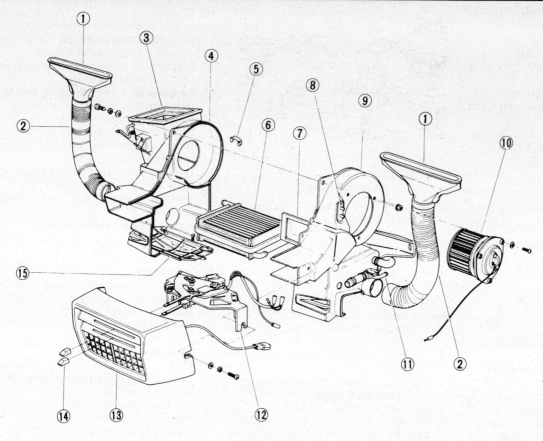

1	Defroster nozzle
2	Defroster hose
3	Air intake box
4	Heater box (L.H.)
5	Clip
6	Heater core
7	Ventilator valve
8	Resistor
9	Heater box (R.H.)
10	Fan and fan motor
11	Heater cock
12	Heater control
13	Center ventilator
14	Knob
15	Heat valve

Fig. 28   Heater unit. B210 & 200SX (Typical)

motor to heater box and the motor, Fig. 28.
9. Reverse procedure to install.

200 SX

1. Disconnect battery ground cable and drain cooling system.
2. Remove heater control.
3. Disconnect heater hose from heater cock.
4. Remove connecting rod from air mix door.
5. Remove clips retaining the left and right side heater box, then separate heater box halves.
6. Remove heater core, air mix door, vent door, and room door.
7. Disconnect electrical connector from blower motor.
8. Remove blower motor attaching screws.
9. Remove blower motor from heater box, Fig. 28.
10. Reverse procedure to install.

510

1. Disconnect battery ground cable and drain cooling system.
2. Disconnect heater to engine hot water pipe.
3. Remove defroster hoses.

4. Disconnect electrical connector from blower motor.
5. Disconnect the two heater control wires from heater unit.
6. Remove ventilator retaining bolts and the ventilator.
7. Remove the four heater unit retaining bolts and the heater unit.
8. Remove heater core and blower motor from heater unit.
9. Reverse procedure to install.

610

Blower Motor Less A/C

1. Disconnect battery ground cable.
2. Drain cooling system.
3. Disconnect heater hoses from core.
4. Remove center ventilator and center console box, if equipped.
5. Remove heater duct hose.
6. Remove defroster hoses.
7. Disconnect control cables from air mix door, mode door and defroster door.
8. Disconnect electrical connectors from heater unit.
9. Remove heater unit retaining bolts and the heater unit.
10. Remove blower motor from heater unit.
11. Reverse procedure to install.

Heater Core Less A/C

1. Disconnect battery ground cable and drain cooling system.
2. Disconnect heater hoses from heater core.
3. Disconnect control cables from the side of the heater unit.
4. Remove clips and the grille heater box.
5. Pull heater core from heater unit, Fig. 29.
6. Reverse procedure to install.

Blower Motor & Heater Core With A/C

1. Disconnect battery ground cable and drain cooling system.
2. Disconnect heater hoses from heater core.
3. Remove grommet cover and grommet from dash panel.
4. Discharge A/C refrigerant system.
5. Disconnect refrigerant lines from evaporator and plug lines and core openings immediately.
6. Remove center console box and the center ventilator grille.
7. Remove cluster lids.
8. Remove air duct.
9. Disconnect control cables from all air doors and thermostat.
10. Disconnect electrical connectors from heater unit, control assembly and thermostat.

DATSUN

11. Remove control assembly from instrument panel.
12. Remove defroster hoses.
13. Remove air intake housing.
14. Disconnect evaporator housing drain hose.
15. Remove evaporator housing.
16. Remove heater unit attaching bolts and the heater unit.
17. Remove heater core and blower motor from heater unit, Fig. 30.
18. Reverse procedure to install.

710

Blower Motor Less A/C

1. Disconnect battery ground cable.
2. Remove three blower motor retaining screws.
3. Remove screw retaining blower motor electrical connector.
4. Remove blower motor from heater unit, Fig. 31.
5. Reverse procedure to install.

Blower Motor With A/C

1. Disconnect battery ground cable.
2. Remove defroster duct.
3. Disconnect blower motor electrical connector from A/C sub-harness.
4. Remove screw retaining blower motor electrical connector.
5. Remove three screws retaining blower motor to heater unit and the blower motor, Fig. 30.
6. Reverse procedure to install.

Heater Core Less A/C

1. Disconnect battery ground cable and drain cooling system.
2. Remove clamps from heater core and disconnect heater hoses from heater core.

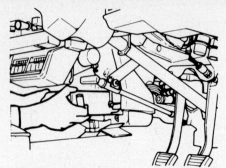

Fig. 29 Heater core removal. 610 less air conditioning

3. Remove console box, if equipped.
4. Loosen defroster room door cable clips.
5. Remove two clips and four screws; heat unit grille, then the heater unit.
6. Pull heater core from heater unit, Fig. 31.
7. Reverse procedure to install.

Heater Core With A/C

1. Disconnect battery ground cable and drain cooling system.
2. Disconnect heater hoses in engine compartment.
3. Remove grommet cover and grommet from dash panel.
4. Discharge refrigerant system.
5. Loosen flare nuts at each connection of inlet and outlet pipes of evaporator. Plug all open fittings and connections.
6. Remove package tray and center console, if equipped.
7. Remove cluster lid.
8. Remove air duct.
9. Remove wiring harness from clips on air intake housing and evaporator housing.

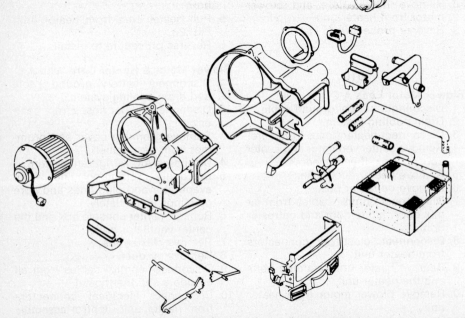

Fig. 30 Heater unit. 610 & 710 with air conditioning

10. Disconnect control cables from air intake door and thermostat.
11. Disconnect thermostat electrical connector from A/C harness.
12. Disconnect drain hose from bottom of evaporator housing.
13. Remove air intake housing and the evaporator housing.
14. Remove defroster ducts.
15. Disconnect A/C harness connectors from main harness and A/C engine room harness.
16. Remove three heater unit attaching bolts and the heater unit.
17. Remove heater core from heater unit, Fig. 30.
18. Reverse procedure to install.

810

Blower Motor

1. Disconnect battery ground cable.
2. Remove package tray.
3. Remove cluster lid.
4. If equipped with A/C, disconnect vacuum hoses from air intake door actuator.
5. On all models, remove screws securing blower housing, then the blower housing.
6. Remove blower motor from housing, Fig. 32.
7. Reverse procedure to install.

Heater Core

1. Disconnect battery ground cable and drain cooling system.
2. Remove console box and bracket.
3. Remove front floor mat.
4. Remove rear heater duct.
5. Disconnect heater hoses from heater core.
6. Remove heater duct.
7. Remove defroster hoses from each side of heater unit.
8. Remove intake door control cable from air intake box.
9. Disconnect harness connectors from heater unit. If equipped with A/C, disconnect vacuum hoses from vacuum switch.
10. Remove heater unit retaining bolts and the heater unit.
11. Remove center ventilation cover and heater control assembly.
12. Remove screws securing door shafts.
13. Remove clips securing heater unit halves.
14. Separate heater unit halves and remove heater core, Fig. 33.
15. Reverse procedure to install.

F10

1. Disconnect battery ground cable.
2. Drain cooling system.
3. Disconnect heater hoses from heater core.
4. Remove the defroster hoses from

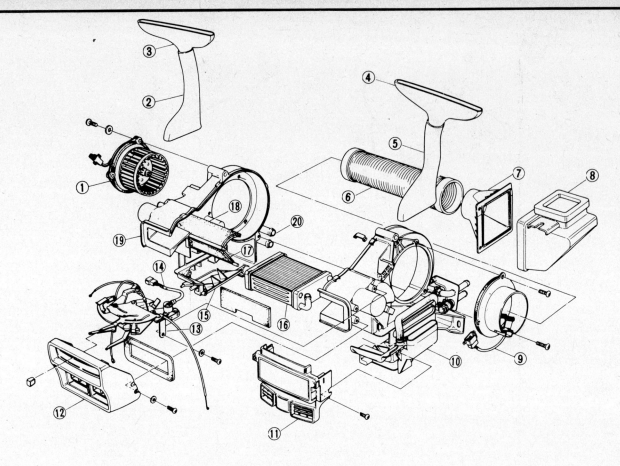

1	Fan and fan motor	8	Air intake housing	15	Defroster room door
2	Defroster duct (L.H.)	9	Resistor	16	Heater core
3	Defroster nozzle (L.H.)	10	Heater box (R.H.)	17	Air mix door
4	Defroster nozzle (R.H.)	11	Heating unit grille	18	Mode door
5	Defroster duct (R.H.)	12	Center ventilator	19	Heater box (L.H.)
6	Intake duct hose	13	Heater control	20	Heater cock
7	Air intake duct	14	Fan switch		

Fig. 31   Heater unit. 710 less air conditioning

both sides of heater unit.
5. Remove the cable retaining clamps for the heater cock, floor door and intake door.
6. Disconnect electrical connectors from heater unit.
7. Remove the heater unit retaining screws, then the heater unit.
8. Remove heater core and blower

motor from heater unit, Fig. 34.
9. Reverse procedure to install.

240Z, 260Z & 280Z
Blower Motor Less A/C
1. Disconnect battery ground cable.
2. Disconnect control cable for air intake box.
3. Disconnect blower motor wiring.

4. Remove blower motor retaining screws and the blower motor, Fig. 35.
5. Reverse procedure to install.

Blower Motor With A/C
1. Disconnect battery ground cable.
2. Remove glove box.
3. Remove defroster duct from right side of heater unit.
4. Disconnect blower motor wiring.
5. Remove blower motor retaining screws and the blower motor.
6. Reverse procedure to install.

Heater Core Less A/C
1. Disconnect battery ground cable and drain cooling system.
2. Remove console box.
3. Remove four screws retaining finisher and disconnect lead wires, then remove finisher.
4. Remove six screws retaining three-way ventilation duct to instrument panel. Disconnect ven-

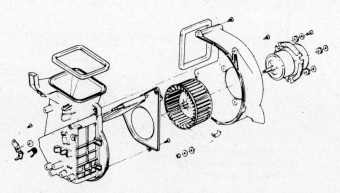

Fig. 32   Blower motor installation. 810

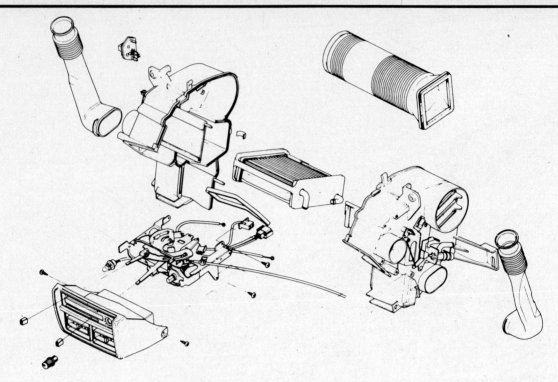

Fig. 33   Heater core installation. 810

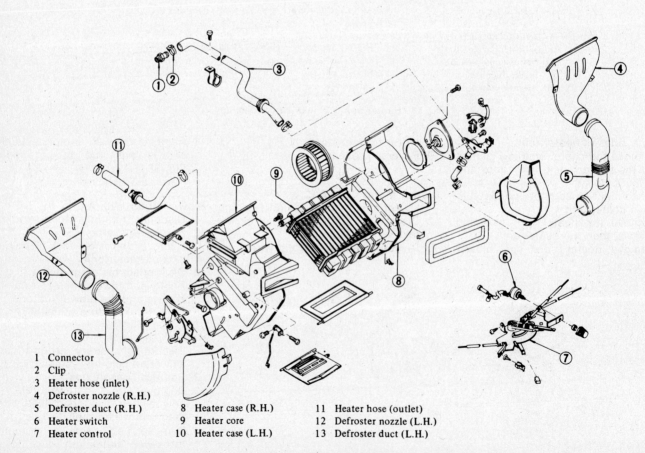

1 Connector		
2 Clip		
3 Heater hose (inlet)		
4 Defroster nozzle (R.H.)		
5 Defroster duct (R.H.)	8 Heater case (R.H.)	11 Heater hose (outlet)
6 Heater switch	9 Heater core	12 Defroster nozzle (L.H.)
7 Heater control	10 Heater case (L.H.)	13 Defroster duct (L.H.)

Fig. 34   Heater unit. F10

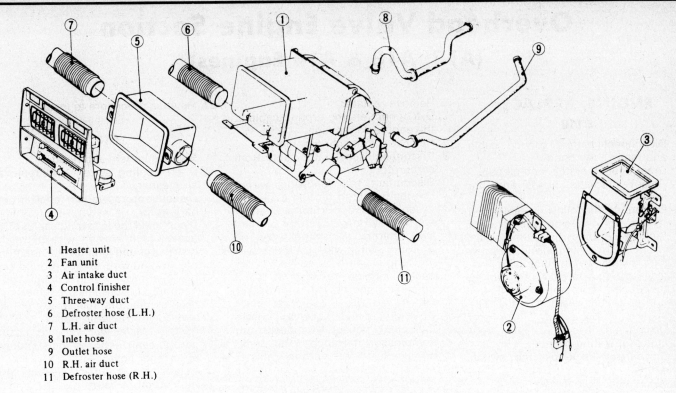

1 Heater unit
2 Fan unit
3 Air intake duct
4 Control finisher
5 Three-way duct
6 Defroster hose (L.H.)
7 L.H. air duct
8 Inlet hose
9 Outlet hose
10 R.H. air duct
11 Defroster hose (R.H.)

Fig. 35 Heater unit. 240Z, 260Z & 280Z less air conditioning

tilator duct hose from three-way ventilation duct and remove three-way ventilation duct.
5. Remove heater control.
6. Disconnect defroster ducts from heater unit and the two heater hoses on right side of unit.
7. Remove three screws retaining heater control and ventilation duct to heater unit.
8. Remove two nuts and four screws retaining heater unit to body panel. The nuts and two screws are located on the engine compartment side of the dash panel. The remaining two screws are located under the heater control location.
9. Move heater unit toward right side and remove from vehicle.
10. Loosen hose clamp on heater cock side.
11. Remove heater cock retaining screws and the heater cock.
12. Remove "E" ring from floor door operating rod.
13. Remove five screws and the side cover.
14. Pull heater core from heater unit, Fig. 35.
15. Reverse procedure to install.

Heater Core With A/C
1. Disconnect battery ground cable and drain cooling system.
2. Disconnect heater hoses from heater core tubes.
3. Remove glove box.

4. Disconnect vacuum hose from air intake door actuator.
5. Remove defroster duct from right side.
6. Remove wiring connectors for blower motor and resistor.
7. Remove three bolts mounting blower housing assembly.
8. Remove blower housing and air intake housing assembly.
9. Disconnect hoses from vacuum water cock.
10. Remove vacuum water cock mounting screws.
11. Remove vacuum hose from vacuum water cock, then the vacuum water cock from heater unit.
12. Remove control cable from water cock.
13. Remove control cable from heater door, then disconnect heater door rod from heater door.
14. Remove heater core cover retaining screws and pull heater core from heater unit.
15. Reverse procedure to install.

Pick-Up
Heater Core & Blower Motor, 1972
1. Disconnect battery ground cable and drain cooling system.
2. Remove instrument panel.
3. Disconnect control cables and electrical wiring from heater unit.
4. Disconnect heater hoses from core.
5. Remove air intake duct from dash panel and heater unit.

6. Remove defroster nozzle from rear of instrument panel.
7. Remove bolts retaining heater unit to dash panel, then the heater unit.
8. Remove heater core and blower motor from heater unit.
9. Reverse procedure to install.

Blower Motor, 1973-77
1. Disconnect battery ground cable and drain cooling system.
2. Remove defroster hoses.
3. Disconnect control cables from valves and water cock.
4. Disconnect blower motor electrical leads.
5. Disconnect heater hoses from core and water cock.
6. Remove heater housing retaining bolts and the heater housing.
7. Remove nine spring clips and disassemble the heater housing.
8. Remove blower motor retaining screws and the blower motor.
9. Reverse procedure to install.

Heater Core, 1973-77
1. Disconnect battery ground cable and drain cooling system.
2. Remove defroster hoses.
3. Disconnect heater hoses from core tubes.
4. Remove four clips and front cover.
5. Remove heater core from heater housing.
6. Reverse procedure to install.

Overhead Valve Engine Section
(A12, A13 & A14 Engines)

ENGINE, REPLACE
B110

1. Disconnect battery ground cable and remove the hood.
2. Drain cooling system and oil pan.
3. Remove radiator hoses and the radiator.
4. Disconnect the following cables and hoses: high ten--sion wire between ignition coil and distributor, water temperature switch wiring, oil pressure switch wiring, distributor primary wiring, starter motor wiring, fuel hoses, alternator wiring, heater hoses, and accelerator and choke cables.
5. Disconnect hydraulic line from clutch operating cylinder.
6. Disconnect back-up lamp switch wiring.
7. Disconnect speedometer cable.
8. Remove propeller shaft.
9. Remove shift lever.
10. If equipped with automatic transmission, disconnect shift rods.
11. On all models, attach suitable engine lifting equipment to engine.
12. Remove front engine mount nuts.
13. Support transmission with a suitable jack and remove rear engine mount nuts.
14. Remove engine and transmission assembly from vehicle.
15. Reverse procedure to install.

B210

1. Disconnect battery ground cable from battery terminal and fusible link at connector.
2. Scribe hood hinge locations and remove hood.
3. Remove under cover.
4. Drain cooling system and oil pan.
5. Disconnect radiator hoses from radiator and the transmission oil cooler lines, if equipped.

6. Remove radiator.
7. Disconnect engine ground cable at the engine connection.
8. Remove air cleaner assembly.
9. Disconnect accelerator cable from carburetor.
10. Disconnect the following wiring connectors: high tension cable between coil and distributor, battery cable to starter, distributor primary wire, thermal transmitter wire, oil pressure switch wire, alternator wiring, engine harness at No. 1 connector, engine harness at No. 2 connector and the A/C compressor clutch lead wire, if equipped.
11. Disconnect the following hoses: fuel pump hoses, A/C hoses from compressor, if equipped, air pump air cleaner hose, carbon canister hoses, altitude compensator hoses, emergency air relief valve hoses, heater hoses, Master-Vac vacuum hose from intake manifold.
12. On manual transmission models, remove clutch operating cylinder from clutch housing.
13. On all models, disconnect speedometer cable from transmission.
14. Remove transmission control linkage.
15. Disconnect exhaust pipe from exhaust manifold.
16. Remove catalytic converter sensor harness protector and two front tube clamps, if equipped. Support the front tube end.
17. Remove propeller shaft.
18. Support transmission with a suitable jack.
19. Remove bolts securing rear engine crossmember to body.
20. Attach suitable engine lifting equipment to engine.
21. Raise engine slightly and remove bolts securing front engine mount brackets to front mount insulators.
22. Remove engine and transmission from vehicle.

23. Reverse procedure to install.

F10

1. Remove battery and hood.
2. Drain cooling system and remove air cleaner.
3. Disconnect accelerator cable from carburetor.
4. Disconnect the following cables and hoses: high tension wire between distributor and ignition coil, ignition coil ground wire, engine ground cable, distributor wiring at block connections, fusible links, engine harness connectors, fuel hoses, upper and lower radiator hoses, heater hoses, Master-Vac vacuum hose, carbon canister hoses and air pump air cleaner hose.
5. Remove air pump air cleaner and the carbon canister.
6. Remove auxiliary fan.
7. Remove W/S washer tank.
8. Remove radiator and fan motor assembly.
9. Remove clutch operating cylinder from clutch housing.
10. Remove right and left buffer rods.
11. Disconnect speedometer cable.
12. Disconnect shift rods from transmission.
13. Attach suitable engine lifting equipment to engine.
14. Disconnect exhaust pipe from exhaust manifold.
15. Disconnect exhaust pipe from rear engine mounting and exhaust tube clamp.
16. Disconnect drive shafts from differential side flanges.
17. Remove radius link support attaching bolt and lower the transmission shift rods.
18. Remove mounting insulator bolts and nuts.
19. Remove engine and transmission assembly from vehicle.
20. Reverse procedure to install.

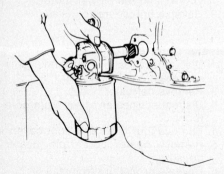

Fig. 1 Oil pump replacement

Fig. 2 Manifolds replacement

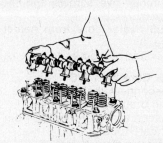

Fig. 3 Rocker shaft assembly replacement

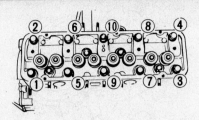

Fig. 4 Cylinder head bolt loosening sequence

ENGINE DISASSEMBLY

1. Remove clutch assembly.
2. Remove accessories from engine and the mounting brackets.
3. Remove fan, fan spacer and pulley.
4. Remove oil level gauge.
5. Remove distributor cap and high tension cables as an assembly.
6. Disconnect distributor vacuum line from distributor and remove distributor.
7. Disconnect fuel line from carburetor.
8. Remove fuel pump and fuel line.
9. Remove thermostat housing and thermostat.
10. Remove engine mounting brackets.
11. Remove oil pump and filter assembly, Fig. 1.
12. Remove spark plugs.
13. Remove air cleaner and air cleaner brackets.
14. Remove vacuum control valve assembly and bracket as a unit.
15. Remove carburetor and baffle plate.
16. Remove E.G.R. control valve, if equipped.
17. Remove intake and exhaust manifold assemblies, Fig. 2.
18. Remove P.C.V. hose.
19. Remove rocker cover.
20. Loosen valve rocker adjusting nuts and turn adjusting screws out to disengage push rods. Then evenly loosen rocker shaft bolts.
21. Remove rocker shaft assembly, Fig. 3.
22. Remove push rods, and keep them in correct order.
23. Loosen and remove cylinder head bolts in the sequence, Fig. 4, then the cylinder head, Fig. 5.

Fig. 5 Cylinder head replacement

24. Invert engine.
25. Remove oil pan and oil strainer.
26. Invert engine.
27. Remove water pump.
28. Remove crank pulley and timing chain cover, Fig. 6.
29. Remove oil thrower and chain tensioner.
30. Loosen camshaft sprocket bolt and remove both sprockets and timing chain as an assembly.
31. Remove connecting rod caps and push piston and connecting rod assemblies, Fig. 7.
    Remove connecting rod bearings and keep them in order.
32. Remove flywheel and rear plate.
33. Gradually loosen and remove main bearing cap bolts in sequence, Fig. 8, and the caps.
34. Remove rear oil seal, Fig. 9.
35. Remove crankshaft.
36. Remove main bearings from block and bearing caps.
37. Remove baffle plate and steel net, Fig. 10.
38. Remove camshaft plate, Fig. 11. Carefully remove camshaft by pulling it toward the front of engine.

Piston & Rod Disassembly

1. Remove piston rings with a ring remover, Fig. 12.
2. Press out piston pin.
3. Keep disassembled parts in order.

Cylinder Head Disassembly

1. Compress valve spring and remove valve collet.

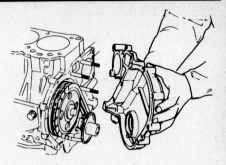

Fig. 6 Timing chain cover replacement

2. Release Valve Lifter and remove spring retainer, spring, oil seal, spring seat and valve, Fig. 13.
3. Place valve train components in order.

ASSEMBLY

Cylinder Head Assembly

1. Insert valve into valve guide.
2. Insert valve spring seat into valve guide. Install valve lip seal by lightly tapping head with a plastic hammer, Fig. 14.
3. Install valve spring and valve spring retainer. Compress valve spring and install valve collets in place, Fig. 13.

Piston & Rod Assembly

1. Assemble pistons, piston pins and connecting rods to designated cylinder. Assemble so oil jet hole of connecting rod big end is directed toward right side of cylinder block. Be sure to install piston in cylinders with stamped number of piston head facing toward front of engine, Fig. 15.
2. Install piston rings. Install top and second rings in right position, with marked side up, Fig. 16.
3. Install bearings on connecting rod and connecting rod cap.

Rocker Shaft Assembly

Refer to Fig. 17 to assemble rocker shaft.

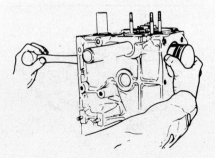

Fig. 7 Piston & rod removal

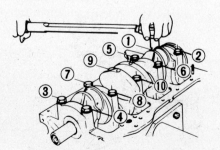

Fig. 8 Main bearing cap loosening sequence

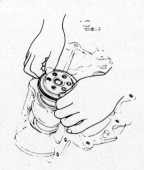

Fig. 9 Rear oil seal removal

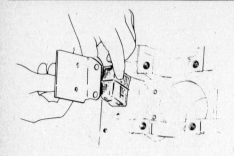

Fig. 10   Baffle plate & steel net replacement

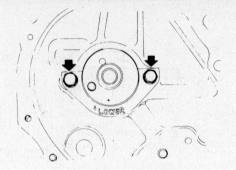

Fig. 11   Camshaft plate

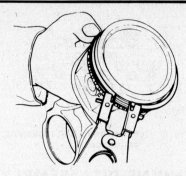

Fig. 12   Piston ring removal

Fig. 13   Valve components

Engine Assembly

1. Apply a light coat of engine oil to sliding surfaces of valve lifters; insert lifters in holes in cylinder block.
2. To install camshaft, be sure to coat sliding surfaces of camshaft bushings with a light coat of engine oil. Insert camshaft in cylinder block from front side of engine, exercising care not to damage camshaft bushings.
3. Install camshaft locating plate, Fig. 11.

NOTE: Set locating plate so the "Lower" mark comes to engine bottom side.

4. Install baffle plate and steel net, Fig. 10.
5. Set main bearings at proper portion of cylinder block and caps.
6. Apply engine oil to main bearing surfaces on both sides of cylinder block and cap. Install crankshaft.
7. Install main bearing cap and torque bolts in sequence, Fig. 18, to specifications. Arrow mark on bearing cap should face front of engine.
8. Make sure there is proper end play at crankshaft.

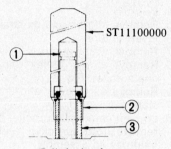

ST11100000

Cylinder head

1 Valve   3 Valve guide
2 Lip seal

Fig. 14   Valve lip seal installation

9. Install rear oil seal using suitable drift, Fig. 19. Apply lithium grease to sealing lip of oil seal.
10. Install rear plate.
11. Install flywheel securely, and torque bolts to specifications.
12. Rotate engine quarter turn and install piston and rod assembly. Install pistons so number stamped on piston head faces toward front of engine.
13. Apply engine oil to bearing surfaces. Install connecting rod caps.
14. Insert crank sprocket keys in keyways of crankshaft. Install camshaft and crankshaft sprockets temporarily for adjustment of tooth height by using adjusting washers.
15. Install timing chain and camshaft sprocket with their markings properly aligned, Fig. 20. Oil sprocket

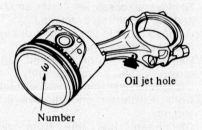

Oil jet hole

Number

Fig. 15   Piston & rod assembly

teeth and chain with engine oil.

NOTE: Make sure camshaft sprocket dowel hole and crankshaft sprocket key are in line and both dowel hole and key are located downward, Fig. 20.

16. Torque camshaft sprocket bolt to specifications.
17. Install chain tensioner and torque tensioner attaching bolts to 4.3-5.8 ft. lbs., Fig. 21.
18. Check projection "L" of tensioner spindle, Fig. 22.
    Correct projection "L" is below .591 inch. If not, replace spindle.
19. Install oil thrower in front of camshaft sprocket.
20. Press new oil seal in timing chain cover.
21. Install timing chain cover with gasket in place, Fig. 6.

NOTE: Apply lithium grease to sealing lip of oil seal.

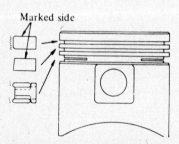

Marked side

Fig. 16   Piston ring installation

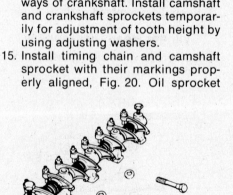

Fig. 17   Rocker shaft assembly

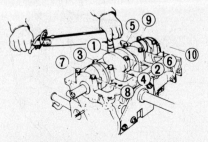

Fig. 18   Main bearing cap tightening sequence

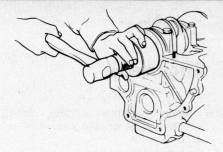

Fig. 19   Rear oil seal installation

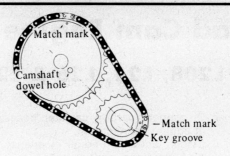

Match mark

Camshaft
dowel hole

—Match mark
Key groove

Fig. 20   Timing mark alignment

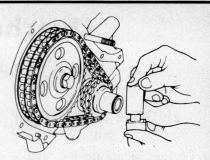

**Fig. 21   Timing chain tensioner
installation**

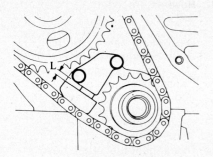

L

**Fig. 22   Checking projection of
tensioner spindle**

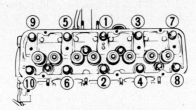

**Fig. 23   Cylinder head tightening
sequence**

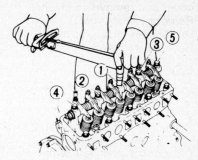

**Fig. 24   Rocker shaft tightening
sequence**

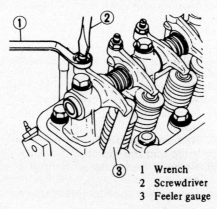

1   Wrench
2   Screwdriver
3   Feeler gauge

Fig. 25   Valve adjustment

22. Install water pump with gasket in place.
23. Install crank pulley, then set No. 1 piston at T.D.C. on compression stroke.
24. Invert engine. Install oil strainer and oil pan using new gasket and oil seal.
25. Install gasket and cylinder head. Torque cylinder head bolts in sequence, Fig. 23, to specifications.
26. Apply engine oil to both ends of push rods and insert to proper sequence.
27. Apply engine oil to valve stem end and rocker arm contact surfaces. Position rocker shaft assembly on cylinder head. Torque bolts to specifications in sequence, Fig. 24.
28. Adjust valve clearance to specifications, Fig. 25.
29. Install rocker cover.
30. Install intake and exhaust manifold assemblies, Fig. 2.

31. Install E.G.R. control valve, if equipped.
32. Install baffle plate and carburetor.
33. Install vacuum control valve assembly and bracket.
34. Install air cleaner bracket and air cleaner.

35. Connect air, vacuum and blow-by hoses to air cleaner.
36. Install pipe connector to control valve hose and engine mounting brackets.
37. Install distributor.
38. Install spark plugs.
39. Install oil pump and filter assembly, Fig. 1.
40. Install thermostat and thermostat housing.
41. Install gasket and spacer, then fuel pump and fuel lines.
42. Install distributor vacuum line.
43. Install distributor cap and high tension cables as an assembly. Connect high tension cables.
44. Insert oil level gauge.
45. Install fan, fan pulley and fan spacer. Lock bolts by bending lock washers.
46. Install accessories and mounting brackets.
47. Install clutch and cover assembly.

Overhead Cam Engine Section

(L16, L18, L20B, L24, L26 & L28 Engines)

ENGINE, REPLACE

510

1. Remove battery and the hood.
2. Drain cooling system and oil pan.
3. Disconnect PCV hose from rocker cover and remove air cleaner.
4. Remove radiator grille.
5. Disconnect oil cooler pipes.
6. Remove radiator hoses and the radiator.
7. Remove engine fan and pulley.
8. Disconnect fuel pump hoses.
9. Disconnect heater hoses from engine.
10. Disconnect accelerator and choke cables from carburetor.
11. Disconnect the following wiring: starter, alternator, ignition coil, oil pressure switch and water temperature switch.
12. Disconnect speedometer cable.
13. Disconnect back-up lamp switch wiring.
14. Disconnect shift rods and remove cross shaft and bracket from side member.
15. Disconnect exhaust pipe from exhaust manifold.
16. Disconnect center exhaust pipe from rear pipe, then remove front exhaust pipe, pre-muffler and center exhaust pipe.
17. Remove propeller shaft.
18. Support and raise transmission with a suitable jack.
19. Remove rear engine mounting crossmember by removing engine mounting insulator bolts, crossmember bolts and parking brake cable clamp.
20. Remove front engine mount bolts.
21. Attach suitable engine lifting equipment to engine.
22. Remove engine and transmission assembly from vehicle.
23. Reverse procedure to install.

610 & 710

1. Disconnect battery ground cable.
2. Drain cooling system and oil pan.
3. On models equipped with automatic transmission, remove splash board and disconnect transmission oil cooler hoses.
4. On all models, scribe hood hinge locations and remove hood.
5. Remove air cleaner assembly.
6. Disconnect fuel pump hoses and fuel return hose at engine side.

7. Disconnect carbon canister hoses at engine connection.
8. Disconnect air pump air cleaner to air pump hose at air cleaner.
9. Disconnect the following wiring connectors: distributor terminal wires at top of radiator, high tension cable between coil and distributor, battery ground cable at engine connection, starter motor wiring, electrical connector positioned above the right front engine mounting bracket and the electrical connector positioned under the ignition coil.
10. Disconnect Master-Vac vacuum line at intake manifold.
11. Disconnect A/C vacuum hose from intake manifold.
12. If equipped with A/C, remove fast idle control device actuator from bracket.
13. On all models, disconnect accelerator linkage from carburetor.
14. Disconnect heater hoses.
15. Disconnect refrigerant hoses from A/C compressor, if equipped.
16. Remove upper and lower radiator hoses.
17. Remove radiator shrouds, radiator grille and the radiator.
18. Remove transmission control linkage.
19. Disconnect speedometer cable from transmission.
20. On manual transmission models, remove clutch operating cylinder from clutch housing.
21. Remove heat shield insulators from front exhaust pipe and catalytic converter and disconnect front exhaust pipe from catalytic converter, if equipped.
22. On models without catalytic converter, disconnect exhaust pipe from rear pipe.
23. On all models, remove front exhaust pipe mounting and disconnect front exhaust pipe from exhaust manifold.
24. Remove propeller shaft.
25. Support transmission with a suitable jack.
26. Remove damper attaching bolts and the damper from rear engine mounting support.
27. Remove rear engine mount insulator to rear engine support attaching bolts.
28. Remove rear engine mount support to body attaching bolts and the support.

29. Attach suitable engine lifting equipment to engine and raise engine slightly.
30. Remove front engine mount bracket to insulator attaching bolts.
31. Remove engine from vehicle.
32. Reverse procedure to install.

200SX

1. Disconnect battery ground cable.
2. Drain cooling system and oil pan.
3. On models equipped with automatic transmission, remove splash board and disconnect transmission oil cooler pipes from radiator.
4. On all models, remove hood.
5. Remove air cleaner.
6. Disconnect fuel pump hoses.
7. Disconnect carbon canister hoses.
8. Disconnect air pump cleaner to air pump hose at air cleaner.
9. Disconnect the following wiring connections: distributor terminal, high tension cable between ignition coil and distributor, battery ground cable at engine connection, starter motor wiring, electrical connector located above right hand engine mount bracket and electrical connector near ignition coil.
10. Disconnect Master-Vac vacuum hose at intake manifold.
11. Disconnect vacuum hose from FICD actuator, then remove actuator from bracket.
12. Disconnect accelerator cable from carburetor.
13. Disconnect heater hoses.
14. If equipped with A/C, remove A/C compressor and position aside. Do not disconnect refrigerant lines.
15. Remove upper and lower radiator hoses.
16. Remove radiator shroud, grille and the radiator.
17. Remove transmission control linkage.
18. Disconnect speedometer cable from extension housing.
19. Remove clutch operating cylinder, if equipped.
20. If equipped with catalytic converter, remove heat shield insulator from front exhaust pipe and catalytic converter. Then, disconnect exhaust pipe from converter.
21. On models not equipped with catalytic converter, disconnect front exhaust pipe from rear pipe.
22. On all models, remove front exhaust pipe mounting.

23. Disconnect exhaust pipe from exhaust manifold.
24. Remove propeller shaft center bearing bracket and the propeller shaft.
25. Support transmission with a suitable jack.
26. Remove damper attaching bolts and the damper from rear engine mount support, if equipped.
27. Remove rear engine insulator to support attaching bolts.
28. Attaching suitable engine lifting equipment to engine, raise engine slightly.
29. Remove rear engine crossmember to body attaching bolts.
30. Remove engine front mount bolts.
31. Remove engine and transmission from vehicle.
32. Reverse procedure to install.

240Z & 260Z

1. Disconnect battery ground cable and remove the hood.
2. Remove air cleaner.
3. Drain cooling system and oil pan.
4. Disconnect radiator upper and lower hoses.
5. Disconnect transmission oil cooler lines from radiator, if equipped.
6. Remove radiator and shroud.
7. If equipped with automatic transmission, remove splash board and disconnect vacuum hose.
8. Disconnect accelerator linkage.
9. Disconnect the following cables and hoses: engine ground cable, starter motor wiring, high tension cable between ignition coil and distributor, distributor wiring at connector, thermal transmitter wiring, oil pressure switch wiring, water temperature, temperature switch wiring, alternator wiring, choke wires, throttle opener solenoid, if equipped, choke heater wiring, EGR solenoid valve wiring, if equipped, vacuum cutting solenoid, if equipped, carbon canister hoses, fuel hoses, heater hoses, Master-Vac vacuum hose, back-up lamp switch wiring, neutral switch wiring, top switch wiring, inhibitor switch wiring and downshift solenoid wiring.
10. Remove clutch operating cylinder.
11. Disconnect speedometer cable.
12. Disconnect transmission control linkage.
13. Disconnect exhaust pipe from exhaust manifold.
14. Remove propeller shaft.
15. Support transmission with a suitable jack.
16. Remove bolts attaching rear engine crossmember to body.
17. Attach suitable engine lifting equipment to engine.
18. Remove front engine mount bolts.

19. Remove engine and transmission assembly from vehicle.
20. Reverse procedure to install.

280Z

1. Disconnect battery ground cable.
2. Disconnect ground wire from fuel pump.
3. Disconnect starter wiring.
4. Remove two screws securing cold start valve to intake manifold, then the cold start valve. Place cold start valve in a container and turn ignition switch to "Start" position. This relieves fuel pressure.
5. Scribe hood hinge locations and remove hood.
6. Drain cooling system and oil pan.
7. Disconnect radiator hoses from radiator.
8. Remove air flow meter.
9. Remove air duct clamps.
10. Remove air cleaner.
11. Disconnect hoses from carbon canister and remove canister.
12. If equipped with automatic transmission, remove splash board and disconnect transmission oil cooler hoses from radiator and the vacuum hose.
13. On all models, remove radiator and shroud.
14. Disconnect accelerator linkage.
15. Disconnect the following wiring connectors: engine ground cable at engine connection, EGR solenoid valve, fuel injectors, throttle valve switch, boost control deceleration device solenoid valve, high tension cable between coil and distributor, wire to block terminal distributor harness, wire to thermostat housing, wire to vacuum cutting solenoid, wire to air regulator, alternator wiring, oil pressure switch wire, back-up lamp switch wire, neutral safety switch wire, top detecting switch wire and downshift solenoid wire, if equipped.
16. Disconnect the following hoses: fuel return hose, fuel charge hose, heater hoses and Master-Vac vacuum at intake manifold.
17. On manual transmission models, remove clutch operating cylinder from clutch housing.
18. On all models, disconnect speedometer cable from transmission.
19. On manual transmission models, remove center console and the "C" ring and control lever pin from transmission striking rod guide, then the control lever.
20. On automatic transmission models, disconnect selector lever.
21. On all models, disconnect exhaust pipe from exhaust manifold.

22. Remove front exhaust pipe bracket from extension housing.
23. Remove bolts securing underbody insulator and hang on exhaust pipe.
24. Remove propeller shaft.
25. Support transmission with a suitable jack.
26. Remove bolts securing engine rear crossmember to body.
27. Attach suitable engine lifting equipment to engine and raise engine slightly.
28. Remove bolts securing engine support to front mount insulators.
29. Remove engine from vehicle.
30. Reverse procedure to install.

810

1. Disconnect battery ground cable.
2. Disconnect fuel pump ground wire.
3. Disconnect wire from starter motor "S" terminal.
4. Remove screws securing cold start valve to intake manifold, then the cold start valve. Place cold start valve in a container and turn ignition switch to "Start" position. This relieves the fuel pressure.
5. Remove hood.
6. Drain cooling system and oil pan.
7. Remove air cleaner ducts.
8. Disconnect radiator upper and lower hoses.
9. Remove air cleaner and air flow meter assembly.
10. Disconnect carbon canister hoses.
11. Remove radiator and shroud.
12. On models equipped with automatic transmission:
    a. Remove splash board.
    b. Disconnect oil cooler lines from radiator.
    c. Disconnect vacuum hose.
13. On models equipped with A/C and power steering:
    a. Remove power steering pump and bracket.
    b. Remove A/C compressor and bracket.
14. Disconnect accelerator cable from car.
15. Disconnect the following cables and hoses: engine ground cable, starter motor wiring, EGR solenoid wire, fuel injector wiring, throttle valve switch wiring, BCDD wiring, high tension wire between ignition coil and distributor, wire to block terminal distributor harness, wire to thermostat housing, vacuum cutting solenoid wiring, cold start valve wiring, air regulator wiring, fuel hoses, heater hoses, Master-Vac vacuum hose, alternator wiring, oil pressure switch wiring, back-up lamp switch wiring, neutral switch wiring, top switch wiring, inhibitor switch housing and downshift solenoid wiring.

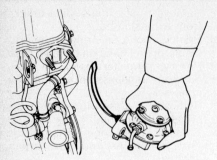

Fig. 1 Fuel pump replacement

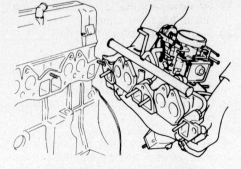

Fig. 2 Manifolds replacement

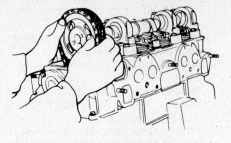

Fig. 3 Camshaft sprocket removal

16. Disconnect speedometer cable.
17. If equipped with manual transmission, remove "C" ring and shift lever pin from transmission striking rod, then the shift lever.
18. If equipped with automatic transmission disconnect range lever.
19. On all models, disconnect exhaust pipe from exhaust manifold.
20. Remove exhaust pipe bracket from rear mounting insulator.
21. Remove propeller shaft center bearing bracket and the propeller shaft.
22. Support transmission with a suitable jack.
23. Remove bolts securing rear engine crossmember to body.
24. Attach suitable engine lifting equipment to engine and raise engine slightly.
25. Remove front engine mount bolts.
26. Remove engine and transmission assembly from vehicle.
27. Reverse procedure to install.

Pick-Up

1. Disconnect battery ground cable.
2. Scribe hood hinge locations and remove hood.
3. Remove air cleaner.
4. Disconnect carbon canister hoses.
5. Remove air hose between air pump and air pump cleaner.
6. Drain cooling system and oil pan.
7. Disconnect radiator upper and lower hoses from engine.
8. On automatic transmission models, disconnect transmission oil cooler hoses from radiator.

9. On all models, disconnect the following wiring connectors: engine ground cable at engine connection, high tension cable between coil and distributor, distributor primary wire, oil pressure switch wire, thermal transmitter wire, wire to choke heater, vacuum control solenoid wire, anti-diesel solenoid wire, alternator wiring, starter wiring, and back-up lamp switch wiring.
10. Disconnect accelerator cable from carburetor.
11. Disconnect heater hoses.
12. Disconnect Master-Vac vacuum hose at intake manifold.
13. Disconnect speedometer cable and transmission control linkage from transmission.
14. Remove shift lever.
15. On manual transmission models, remove clutch operating cylinder and flexible hose from clutch housing.
16. On all models, disconnect exhaust pipe from exhaust manifold.
17. Remove propeller shaft.
18. Attach suitable engine lifting equipment to engine and raise engine slightly.
19. Remove engine front mount bolts at front support.
20. Support transmission with a suitable jack.
21. Loosen the two rear engine mounting bolts.

22. Remove the four bolts securing engine mount rear support to side member, then the rear support.
23. Remove engine from vehicle.
24. Reverse procedure to install.

ENGINE DISASSEMBLY

1. Remove clutch assembly from flywheel.
2. Drain engine oil and coolant.
3. Remove accessories and mounting brackets.
4. Remove cooling fan.
5. Remove engine mounting brackets.
6. Remove oil filter.
7. Remove oil pressure switch.
8. Remove oil level gauge.
9. Remove carburetor from intake manifold.
10. Disconnect distributor high tension cables from spark plugs.
11. Disconnect vacuum hose from distributor and remove distributor assembly.
12. Disconnect fuel hose from fuel pump and remove fuel and vacuum hoses (combined) from cylinder head, if equipped.
13. Remove fuel pump assembly from cylinder head, if equipped, Fig. 1.
14. If equipped with fuel injection, remove fuel injection components.
15. Remove intake and exhaust manifold assembly from cylinder head, Fig. 2.

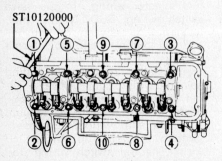

ST10120000

Fig. 4 Cylinder head loosening sequence

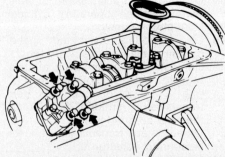

Fig. 5 Oil pump replacement

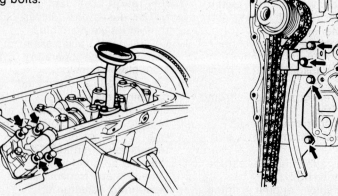

Fig. 6 Timing chain & tensioner removal

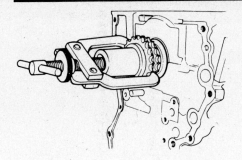

Fig. 7 Crankshaft sprocket removal

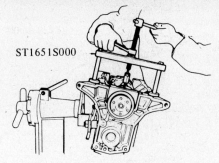

ST1651S000

Fig. 8 Rear main bearing cap removal

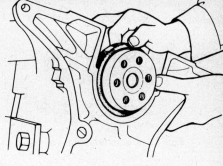

Fig. 9 Rear oil seal removal

16. Remove crankshaft pulley bolt and washer, then the pulley with a suitable puller.
17. Remove water pump assembly.
18. Remove rocker cover.
19. Remove spark plugs.
20. Remove fuel pump drive cam.
21. Remove camshaft sprocket, Fig. 3.
22. Remove cylinder head assembly. Loosen and remove cylinder head bolts in sequence, Fig. 4.
23. Invert engine.
24. Remove oil pan and oil strainer, Fig. 5.
25. Remove oil pump and its drive spindle.
26. Remove front cover.
27. Remove chain tensioner and chain slack side guide, Fig. 6.
28. Remove timing chain.
29. Remove oil thrower, crankshaft worm gear and chain drive sprocket, Fig. 7.
30. Remove piston and connecting rod assembly. Remove connecting rod bearings, keeping them in order.
31. Remove flywheel and rear plate.
32. Remove main bearing caps. Remove center and rear bearing caps with a puller, Fig. 8. Keep caps in order.
33. Remove two side seals from rear main bearing cap.
34. Remove rear oil seal, Fig. 9.
35. Remove crankshaft.
36. Remove baffle plate and cylinder block net, Fig. 10.

Piston & Rod Disassembly

1. Remove piston rings with a ring remover, Fig. 11.
2. Press piston pin.

Cylinder Head Disassembly

1. Remove valve rocker springs. Loosen valve rocker pivot lock nut and remove rocker arm by pressing valve spring downward, Fig. 12.
2. Remove locating plate, and the camshaft, Fig. 13.

NOTE: Be careful not to damage camshaft bearings and cam lobes.

3. Remove valves, Figs. 14 and 15.

ASSEMBLY
Cylinder Head Assembly

1. Valve assembly and valve spring:
   a. Place valve spring seat in position and install valve guide with oil seal, Fig. 14.
   b. Assemble valve as follows: valve, inner and outer valve springs, spring retainer, valve collet and valve rocker guide, Fig. 15.
2. Valve rocker pivot assembly:
   a. Screw valve rocker pivots joined with lock nuts into pivot bushing.
3. Camshaft assembly:
   a. Install locating plate and carefully install camshaft in cylinder head. Do not damage the bearing inside. Oblong groove of locating plate must be directed toward front side of engine.
4. Install camshaft sprocket on camshaft, Fig. 16, and torque with fuel pump drive cam to specifications.
5. Install rocker arms by pressing valve springs down with a screwdriver, Fig. 12.
6. Install valve rocker springs.
7. Rotate camshaft so both valves for #1 cylinder are closed.

Piston & Rod Assembly

1. Assemble pistons, piston pins and connecting rods on the designated cylinder. Assemble so that oil jet of connecting rod big end is directed toward right side of cylinder block. Be sure to install piston in cylinders with notch mark of piston head toward front of engine, Fig. 17.
2. Install piston rings. Install top and second rings in right position, with marked side up, Fig. 18.
3. Install bearings on connecting rod and connecting rod cap.

Engine Assembly

1. Set main bearings at the proper portion of cylinder block.
2. Install baffle plate and cylinder block net.
3. Apply engine oil to main bearing surfaces on both sides of cylinder block and cap and then install crankshaft.
4. Install main bearing cap and torque

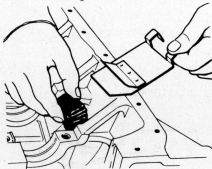

Fig. 10 Baffle plate & steel net replacement

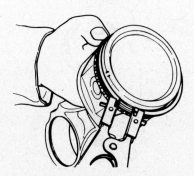

Fig. 11 Piston ring removal

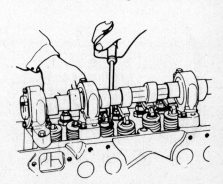

Fig. 12 Rocker arm removal

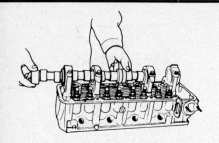

Fig. 13 Camshaft removal

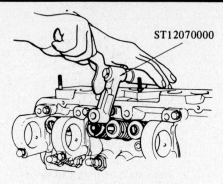

ST12070000

Fig. 14 Valve removal

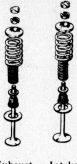

Exhaust Intake

Fig. 15 Valve components

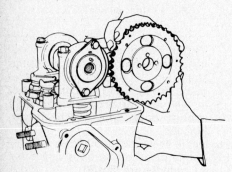

Fig. 16 Camshaft sprocket installation

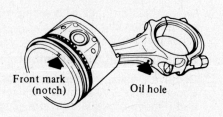

Front mark (notch)   Oil hole

Fig. 17 Piston & rod assembly

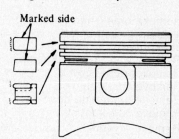

Marked side

Fig. 18 Piston ring installation

bolts to specifications, in sequence, Fig. 19.
5. Make sure that crankshaft has proper end play.
6. Install side oil seals into rear main bearing cap, Fig. 20. Prior to installing, apply sealant to seals.
7. Install rear oil seal, Fig. 21.
8. Install rear end plate.
9. Install flywheel securely, and tighten bolts to specified torque.
10. Insert pistons in corresponding cylinder. Install so that notch mark on piston head faces to front of engine, Fig. 17.
11. Install and torque connecting rod caps.
12. Install cylinder head assembly.
13. Install crankshaft sprocket and oil pump drive gear, and the oil thrower.
14. Install timing chain, noting the following:
   a. Make sure that crankshaft and camshaft keys point upwards, Fig. 22.
   b. Install timing chain by aligning mating marks with marks of crankshaft sprocket and camshaft sprocket at the right hand side. There are forty-four chain links between two mating marks of timing chain.
15. Install chain slack side guide to cylinder block.
16. Install chain tensioner, Fig. 23.
17. Press new oil seal in front cover.
18. Install front cover with gasket in place, Fig. 24.
19. Install crankshaft pulley and water pump assembly, then set No. 1 piston at T.D.C. on compression stroke.
20. Torque cylinder head bolts in sequence, Fig. 25, to specifications.

21. Install oil pump and distributor driving spindle in front cover, Fig. 26.
22. Install fuel pump, water inlet elbow.

NOTE: Install fuel pump spacer and packing between spacer and block, spacer and fuel pump.

23. Install oil strainer, oil pan gasket and oil pan.
24. Adjust valve clearance to specifications, Fig. 27.
25. Install rocker cover to cylinder head.
26. Install intake manifold to exhaust manifold.
27. Install heatshield plate on manifold assembly.
28. Install air gallery pipe on exhaust manifold, if equipped.
29. Install manifold gasket and manifold assembly on cylinder head, Fig. 2.
30. If equipped with fuel injection, install fuel injection components.

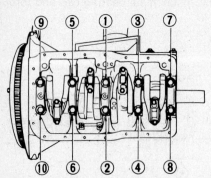

Fig. 19 Main bearing cap tightening sequence

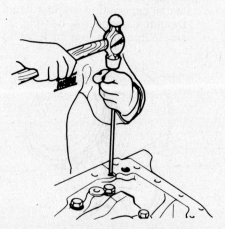

Fig. 20 Side oil seal installation

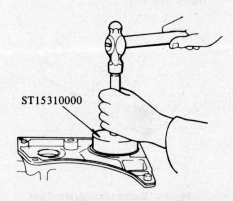

ST15310000

Fig. 21 Rear oil seal installation

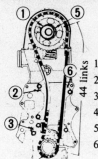

1 Fuel pump drive cam
2 Chain guide
3 Chain tensioner
4 Crank sprocket
5 Cam sprocket
6 Chain guide

44 links

Fig. 22 Timing chain installation

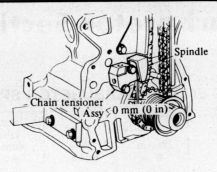

Spindle

Chain tensioner Assy

0 mm (0 in)

Fig. 23 Timing chain tensioner installation

Fig. 24 Front cover installation

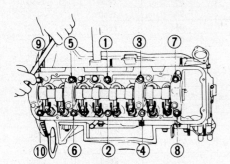

Fig. 25 Cylinder head tightening sequence

Fig. 26 Oil pump installation

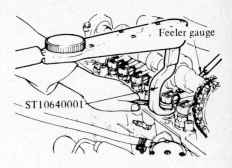

Feeler gauge

ST10640001

Fig. 27 Valve adjustment

31. Install blow-by gas pipe on cylinder block and tighten with rear engine slinger.
32. Install thermostat housing gasket, thermostat housing and thermostat.
33. Install thermal vacuum valve on thermostat housing, if equipped.
34. Install E.G.R. passage and E.G.R. valve on intake manifold, if equipped.
35. Connect E.G.R. tube to E.G.R. tube and exhaust manifold, if equipped.
36. Install check valve on air gallery pipe, if equipped.
37. Install air cleaner bracket on intake manifold.
38. Install air control valve on air cleaner bracket, if equipped.

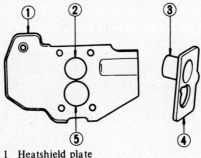

1 Heatshield plate
2 Primary hole
3 Duct
4 Joint seat
5 Secondary hole

Fig. 28 Carburetor joint seat

39. Install vacuum and fuel tubes (combined) on cylinder head.
40. Install distributor assembly.
41. Install heatshield plate, joint seat and carburetor, Fig. 29.
42. Install dash pot bracket and dash pot to intake manifold, if equipped.
43. Connect all air, vacuum and fuel hoses and then secure with clamps.
44. Install carburetor air cleaner on carburetor and connect air and vacuum hoses.
45. Install spark plugs.
46. Connect distributor high tension cables to spark plugs.
47. Install accessories and mounting brackets.
48. Install engine mounting brackets.
49. Install clutch assembly on flywheel.

Carburetor Section

A12, A13 & A14 ENGINE CARBURETOR SPECIFICATIONS

Year	Carb. No.	Float Level "H"	Float Level "h"	Vacuum Break "B"	Choke Unloader "C"	Throttle Valve Interlock Opening "G1"	Fast Idle Off-Car "A"	Fast Idle On-Car RPM	Dashpot RPM
1972	DCG306	.472	.059	—	—	.480	—	—	—
1973	DCH306-4	.748	.059	.047	.079	.228	.030	1950	—
	DCH306-5	.748	.059	.050	.079	.228	.044	2800	1950
1974	DCH306-6	.748	.059	.055	.079	.230	.030	1950	—
	DCH306-7	.748	.059	.059	.079	.230	.044	2800	1950
1975	DCH306-10	.748	.059	.056	.079	.230	.033	2550	2350
	DCH306-11	.748	.063	.059	.079	.230	.044	2550	1950
	DCH306-14	.748	.059	.056	.079	.230	.033	2800	1950
	DCH306-15	.748	.063	.059	.079	.230	.044	2800	1950
1976	DCH306-10A	.748	.059	.056	.079	.230	.033	2550	2350
	DCH306-11A	.748	.063	.056	.079	.230	.033	2550	1950
	DCH306-14A	.748	.059	.059	.079	.230	.044	2800	1950
	DCH306-15A	.748	.063	.059	.079	.230	.044	2800	1950
	DCH306-16	.748	.059	.059	.079	.230	.033	2550	2350
	DCH306-17	.748	.059	.059	.079	.230	.033	2550	1950
1977	DCH306-10B	.748	.059	.056	.079	.230	.031	2300	2350
	DCH306-11B	.748	.063	.056	.079	.230	.031	2300	1950
	DCH306-14B	.748	.059	.059	.079	.230	.042	2800	1950
	DCH306-15B	.748	.063	.059	.079	.230	.042	2800	1950
	DCH306-16A	.748	.059	.059	.079	.230	.031	2300	2350
	DCH306-17A	.748	.059	.059	.079	.230	.031	2300	1950

L16, L18 & L20B ENGINE CARBURETOR SPECIFICATIONS

Year	Carb. No.	Float Level "H"	Float Level "h"	Vacuum Break "B"	Choke Unloader "C"	Throttle Valve Interlock Opening "G1"	Fast Idle Off-Car "A"	Fast Idle On-Car RPM	Dashpot RPM
1972	DAF328	—	.006	—	—	.051	.030	—	1900
1973	DCH340-1	—	.059	.067	.173	.291	.046	2400	1700
	DCH340-2	—	.059	.067	.173	.291	.037	2000	1700
	DCH340-5	—	.059	.067	.173	.291	.046	2400	1700
	DCH340-7	—	.059	.067	.173	.291	.037	2000	1700
	DCH340-8	—	.059	.067	.173	.291	.046	2400	1700
	DCH340-9	—	.059	.067	.173	.291	.037	2000	1700
1974	DCH340-10	—	.059	.067	.173	.291	.037	2000	1700
	DCH340-11	—	.059	.067	.173	.291	.046	2400	1700
	DCH340-12	—	.059	.067	.173	.291	.037	2000	1700
	DCH340-13	—	.059	.067	.173	.291	.046	2400	1700
	DCH340-14	—	.059	.067	.173	.291	.046	2400	1700
	DCH340-15	—	.059	.067	.173	.291	.037	2000	1700
1975	DCH340-41	.283	.059	.065	.096	.291	.044	2000	2000
	DCH340-42	.283	.059	.065	.096	.291	.050	2400	1750
	DCH340-43	.283	.059	.065	.096	.291	.044	2000	2000
	DCH340-44	.283	.059	.065	.096	.291	.050	2400	1750
	DCH340-47	.283	.059	.065	.096	.291	.044	2000	2000
	DCH340-48	.283	.059	.065	.096	.291	.050	2400	1750

Continued

L16, L18 & L20B ENGINE CARBURETOR SPECIFICATIONS—Continued

Year	Carb. No.	Float Level		Vacuum Break "B"	Choke Unloader "C"	Throttle Valve Interlock Opening "G1"	Fast Idle		Dashpot RPM
		"H"	"h"				Off-Car "A"	On-Car RPM	
1976	DCH340-41A	.283	.059	.059	.096	.291	.044	2000	2000
	DCH340-42B	.283	.059	.059	.096	.291	.050	2400	1750
	DCH340-43A	.283	.059	.056	.096	.291	.044	2000	2000
	DCH340-44A	.283	.059	.056	.096	.291	.050	2400	1750
	DCH340-45A	.283	.059	.056	.096	.291	.044	2000	2000
	DCH340-46	.283	.059	.059	.096	.291	.050	2400	1750
	DCH340-47	.283	.059	.056	.096	.291	.044	2000	2000
	DCH340-48	.283	.059	.056	.096	.291	.050	2400	1750
1977	DCH340-41B	.283	.059	.059	.097	.291	.055	2350	2000
	DCH340-42C	.283	.059	.059	.097	.291	.065	2700	1750
	DCH340-45B	.283	.059	.056	.096	.291	.055	2350	2000
	DCH340-46A	.283	.059	.059	.096	.291	.064	2700	1750
	DCH340-47A	.283	.059	.056	.096	.291	.055	2350	2000
	DCH340-48A	.283	.059	.056	.096	.291	.064	2700	1750
	DCH340-49A	.283	.059	.059	.096	.291	.055	2300	2000
	DCH340-50A	.283	.059	.059	.097	.291	.065	2700	1750
	DCH340-51A	.283	.059	.069	.097	.291	.055	2300	2000
	DCH340-52A	.283	.059	.069	.097	.291	.065	2700	1750
	DCH340-53A	.283	.059	.069	.097	.291	.055	2300	2000
	DCH340-54B	.283	.059	.069	.097	.291	.065	2700	1750

A12, A13 & A14 ENGINE

Float & Fuel Level, Adjust

1. Invert float chamber to allow float to come into contact with needle valve, and measure clearance "H", Fig. 1. Clearance should be as listed in the specifications chart.

   The top float position can be adjusted by bending float seat.

   Upon completion of the adjustment, check fuel level with attached level gauge.

2. Adjust bottom float position so that clearance "h" between float seat and needle valve stem is as listed in the specifications chart when float is fully raised. Bend float stopper as required.

3. On 1975-77 models, after adjustments in steps 1 and 2 above have been made, make sure that when fuel is delivered to the float chamber, the fuel level is maintained at .75 inch, Fig. 2.

Vacuum Break, Adjust

1. Close choke valve completely.
2. Hold choke valve by stretching rubber band between choke shaft lever and stationary part of carburetor.
3. Pull vacuum break stem and check and adjust gap "B", Fig. 3, between choke valve and carburetor body.

Choke Unloader, Adjust

1. Close choke valve completely.
2. Hold choke valve by stretching a rubber band between choke shaft lever and stationary part of carburetor.
3. Pull throttle lever until it completely opens.
4. Check clearance "C", Fig. 4, between choke valve and carburetor body. Adjust by bending unloader tang.

Primary & Secondary Throttle Valve Interlock Opening, Adjust

1. Open primary side throttle valve 48° from fully closed position, and measure clearance "G1" between throttle valve and throttle chamber inside wall, Fig. 5.
2. Then, bend connecting rod as necessary so that secondary throttle valve is about to open.

Fast Idle Speed, Adjust

1. Off-engine:
   a. Remove bi-metal cover.

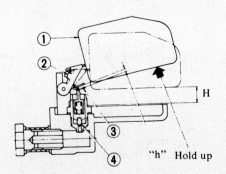

1 Float 3 Float seat
2 Float stopper 4 Needle valve

Fig. 1 Float level adjustment. A12, A13 & A14 engine

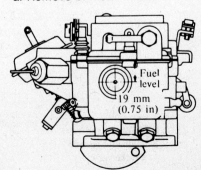

Fuel level
19 mm (0.75 in)

Fig. 2 Fuel level adjustment. A12, A13 & A14 engine

b. Place fast idle arm on second step of first idle cam. Then adjust fast idle adjusting screw as shown at "A," Fig. 6. The clearance "A" should be as listed in the specifications chart.

2. On-engine:

a. Warm up engine sufficiently. Set fast idle cam at 2nd step, and read engine speed.

b. Fast idle cam is properly set if engine speed is within range as listed in the specifications chart.

Dashpot, Adjust

1. Idling speed of engine and mixture must be well tuned up and engine sufficiently warm.

2. Turn throttle valve by hand, and read engine speed when dashpot just touches stopper lever.

3. Adjust position of dashpot by turning nut, Fig. 7, until engine speed is as listed in the specifications chart.

L16, L18 & L20B ENGINE

Float & Fuel Level, Adjust

1. On 1975-77 models, invert float chamber to allow float to come into contact with needle valve, and measure clearance "H," Fig. 8. Clearance should be as listed in the specifications chart. The top float position can be adjusted by bending float seat.

2. Adjust bottom float position so that

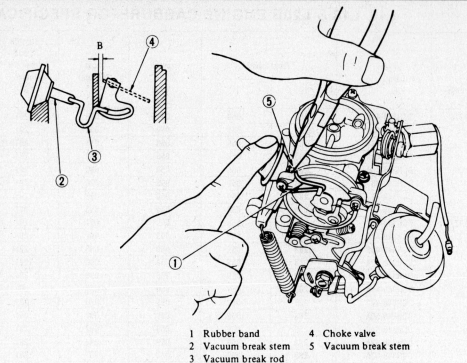

1	Rubber band	4	Choke valve
2	Vacuum break stem	5	Vacuum break stem
3	Vacuum break rod		

Fig. 3 Vacuum break adjustment. A12, A13 & A14 engine

clearance "h" between float seat and needle valve stem, Fig. 8, is as listed in the specifications chart when float is fully raised. Bend float stopper as required.

3. After adjustments in steps 1 and 2 have been made, make sure that when fuel is delivered to the float chamber, the fuel level is maintained at .91 inch, Fig. 9.

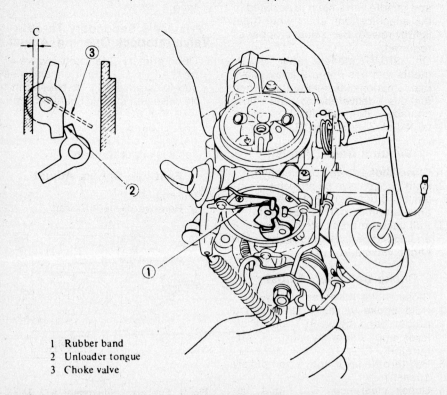

1	Rubber band
2	Unloader tongue
3	Choke valve

Fig. 4 Choke unloader adjustment. A12, A13 & A14 engine

1	Connecting rod
2	Secondary connecting lever
3	Throttle lever
4	Secondary throttle valve
5	Primary throttle valve
6	Throttle chamber

Fig. 5 Interlock opening adjustment. A12, A13 & A14 engine

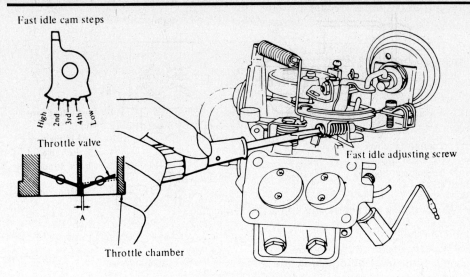

Fast idle cam steps

High | 2nd | 3rd | 4th | Low

Throttle valve

Fast idle adjusting screw

Throttle chamber

A

Fig. 6 Fast idle adjustment. A12, A13 & A14 engine

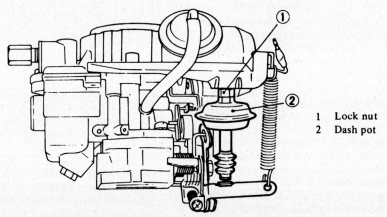

1 Lock nut
2 Dash pot

Fig. 7 Dashpot adjustment. A12, A13 & A14 engine

Vacuum Break, Adjust

1. Close choke valve completely.
2. Hold choke valve by stretching a rubber band between choke piston lever and stationary part of carburetor.

3. Pull vacuum break rod with pliers and adjust the clearance between choke valve and carburetor body, "B," Fig. 10. Clearance should be as listed in the specifications chart. Adjust by bending vacuum break rod.

Choke Unloader, Adjust

1. Close choke valve completely.
2. Hold choke valve by stretching a rubber band between choke piston lever and stationary part of carburetor.

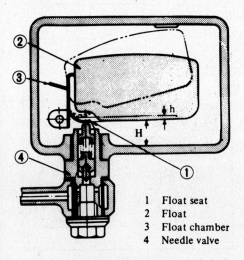

1 Float seat
2 Float
3 Float chamber
4 Needle valve

Fig. 8 Float level adjustment. L16, L18 & L20B engine

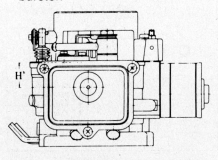

Fig. 9 Fuel level adjustment. L16, L18 & L20B engine

3. Pull throttle lever until fully open.
4. Adjust clearance between choke valve and carburetor body to specifications by bending unloader tang.

Primary & Secondary Throttle Valve Interlock Opening, Adjust

When primary throttle valve is opened 50° the adjust plate integrated with throttle valve is in contact with return plate at "A," Fig. 11.

When throttle valve is opened further, locking arm is detached from secondary throttle arm, permitting secondary system to start operation.

Linkage between primary and secondary throttles will function properly if distance between throttle valve and inner wall of throttle chamber is as listed in the specifications chart.

Adjustment is made by bending connecting link, Fig. 4.

Choke Coil, Adjust

1. Align bi-metal cover index mark with center of choke housing index mark, Fig. 12.

Fast Idle Speed, Adjust

1. With carburetor assembly removed from engine, measure throttle valve clearance, "A," Fig. 13, with a wire gauge, placing the upper side of fast idling screw on the second step of the fast idling cam.
2. Install carburetor on engine.
3. Start engine and measure speed. Fast idle speed should be as listed in the specifications chart.
4. To adjust fast idle rpm, turn fast idling screw counterclockwise to increase rpm, or clockwise to decrease.
5. Reverse procedure to install.

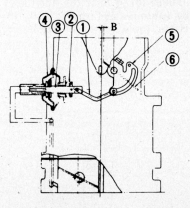

1 Choke piston rod
2 Choke spring
3 Choke piston
4 Diaphragm cover
5 Choke piston lever
6 Choke valve

Fig. 10 Vacuum break adjustment. L16, L18 & L20B engine

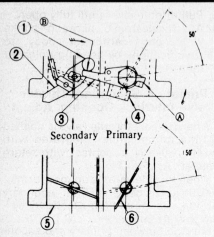

Secondary Primary

1 Roller	4 Adjust plate
2 Connecting lever	5 Throttle chamber
3 Return plate	6 Throttle valve

Fig. 11   Interlock opening adjustment. L16, L18 & L20B engine

Dashpot, Adjust

1. Idling speed of engine and mixture must be well tuned up and engine sufficiently warm.
2. Accelerate engine and read engine speed when dash pot just touches stopper lever.
3. Adjust position of dash pot by turning nut until engine speed is as listed in the specifications chart.
4. Tighten lock nuts.
5. Make sure that engine speed drops smoothly from 2,000 to 1,000 rpm in about three seconds.

L24 ENGINE

Float Level, Adjust

1. Check the position of float lever.
2. Adjust the float level by bending the stopper of the float lever, Fig. 14.
   a. Lower the stopper by 0.23 mm (0.0091 in) to raise the float level by 1 mm (0.0394 in).
   b. Raise the stopper by 0.23 mm (0.0091 in) to lower the float level by 1 mm (0.0394 in).
3. After adjusting the stopper of the float lever, install the cover to the carburetor float chamber and install

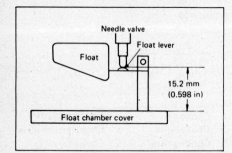

Fig. 14   Float level adjustment. L24 engine

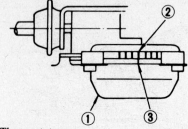

| 1 Thermostat cover (Bi-metal chamber) |
| 2 Thermostat housing |
| 3 Groove |

Fig. 12   Choke coil adjustment. L16, L18 & L20B engine

the carburetor to the engine. Check the float level by cranking the engine.

Fast Idle Speed, Adjust

Choke valve at fully closed position automatically opens throttle valve at an optimum angle for starting engine through a link mechanism.

1. Place upper side of fast idling screw on the first step of fast idle cam. Then adjust fast idle adjusting screw so that the clearance of throttle valve, "G," Fig. 15, will be 0.59 to 0.64 mm (0.023 to 0.025 in). If not correct, adjust by turning fast idling screw in or out as necessary.
2. If necessary, adjust choke valve opening by bending the connecting rod between choke valve shaft and first idle cam, Fig. 16.

L26 ENGINE

Float Level, Adjust

1. Remove float chamber cover from carburetor.
2. Invert carburetor to check the position of float lever. Ensure that both floats touch the inner wall of car-

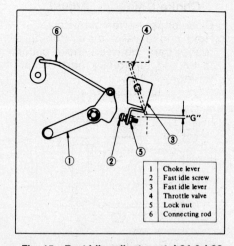

1	Choke lever
2	Fast idle screw
3	Fast idle lever
4	Throttle valve
5	Lock nut
6	Connecting rod

Fig. 15   Fast idle adjustment. L24 & L26 engine

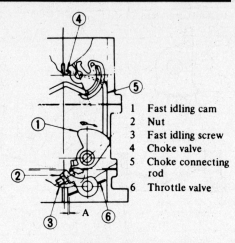

1	Fast idling cam
2	Nut
3	Fast idling screw
4	Choke valve
5	Choke connecting rod
6	Throttle valve

Fig. 13   Fast idle adjustment. L16, L18 & L20B engine

buretor when carburetor is turned upside down on a float surface.
3. Measure the dimension "H" between the end face of the float chamber and float lever tongue which make contact with needle valve, Fig. 17. Dimension "H" should be .472-.512 inch.
4. Measure the "H" dimension at point "A" of float lever, Fig. 18. If it is not held within the specified value, Fig. 18, adjust the tongue by bending the end as required.
5. Measure the gap "G" between the power valve nozzle and float, Fig. 19. Gap should be .020-.079 inch. If the gap is not held within the specified range, adjust by bending the stopper as required. The above adjustment is particularly necessary to prevent mutual interference between the float and power valve.

NOTE: Whenever the stopper is bent for adjustment, check the dimension "H" to ensure that it is held within the specified range.

6. After adjusting the tongue of float

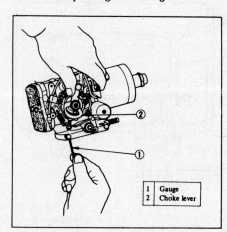

| 1 | Gauge |
| 2 | Choke lever |

Fig. 16   Measuring fast idle opening. L24 & L26 engine

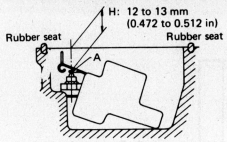

Fig. 17 Float level adjustment. L26 engine

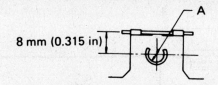

Fig. 18 Measuring "H" at point "A." L26 engine

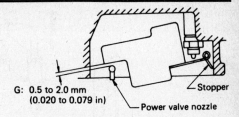

Fig. 19 "G" dimension of float. L26 engine

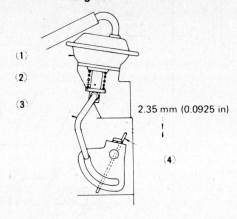

1 Choke piston   3 Choke piston rod
2 Diaphragm rod   4 Choke valve

Fig. 20 Choke piston adjustment. L26 engine

lever, install float chamber cover on carburetor float chamber and install carburetor on engine. The normal fuel level is even with the center line of the float level window.

Fast Idle Speed, Adjust

Choke valve at fully closed position automatically opens throttle through a link mechanism.

Place upper side of fast idle screw on the first step of choke lever. Then adjust fast idle adjusting screw so that the clearance of throttle valve, "G," Fig. 15, is .023-.025 inch. Adjust by turning fast idle screw in or out as necessary.

Choke Piston, Adjust

1. Completely close choke valve.
2. Close choke valve by stretching a suitable rubber band between choke lever which is connected to choke wire, and stationary part of carburetor.
3. Pull diaphragm rod with pliers and adjust the gap between choke valve and carburetor body to .0925 by bending choke piston rod, Fig. 20.

Fuel Injection Section

BOSCH L-JETRONIC SYSTEM

This electronic fuel injection system, Fig. 1 uses various sensors to convert engine operating conditions into electronic signals. These signals are sent to the control unit where the optimum injector open-valve time period is computed.

Fuel System

Fuel Flow

Fuel is drawn from the fuel tank into the fuel pump. As fuel flows through the mechanical fuel damper, pulsation in the fuel flow is dampened.

The fuel is then filtered in the fuel filter, flows through the fuel line, and is injected into the intake manifold cylinder branch from the injector.

Excess fuel is fed through the pressure regulator and is returned to the fuel tank. The pressure regulator controls the fuel pressure so the pressure difference between the fuel pressure and the intake manifold vacuum is a constant 36.3 psi. During starting when the coolant temperature is below specifications, the cold start valve is actuated by the thermotime switch to increase the quantity of fuel.

Injection System

The fuel injection system provides simultaneous injection of fuel into the intake manifold for all cylinders. Injection of fuel occurs at each revolution of the engine, and the injected amount of fuel injected is half the quantity required for one cycle operation of the engine. The ignition signal of the ignition coil is utilized for correct injection of fuel. However, the signal from the ignition coil does not specify the timing for injection. It specifies the frequency of injections since the injection timing is constant.

Air Flow System

Intake air from the air cleaner is metered at the air flow meter, flows through the throttle chamber and into the intake manifold, then flows through each intake manifold branch into the cylinder. Air flow is controlled by the throttle valve located in the throttle chamber. During idling, the throttle valve is almost closed and the air is fed through the bypass port mounted to the throttle chamber. The quantity of suction air is adjusted by the idle speed adjusting screw. During warm-up, the air flow is bypassed through the air regulator to increase engine rpm.

Fuel Cut

Fuel cut is accomplished during deceleration when the engine does not require fuel.

Exc. California Models

When engine speed is above 3,200 rpm and throttle valve idle switch contacts are closed, fuel injection does not take place. When engine speed drops below 2,800 rpm, fuel cut is released and fuel injection is resumed.

The injection of fuel provides smooth engine idling without stopping the engine.

Fuel cut is not accomplished during deceleration when engine rpm is below 3,200 rpm.

California Models

Fuel shut-off is accomplished when engine speed reaches about 1,800 rpm or higher and throttle valve is closed. The fuel shut-off is released when engine rpm drops to 1,300 rpm even if the throttle valve is kept closed.

When the engine is running at between 1,800 and 1,300 rpm, the fuel shut-off occurs when the throttle valve returns to the closed position from open position. It does not occur if the throttle valve is kept closed even when the en-

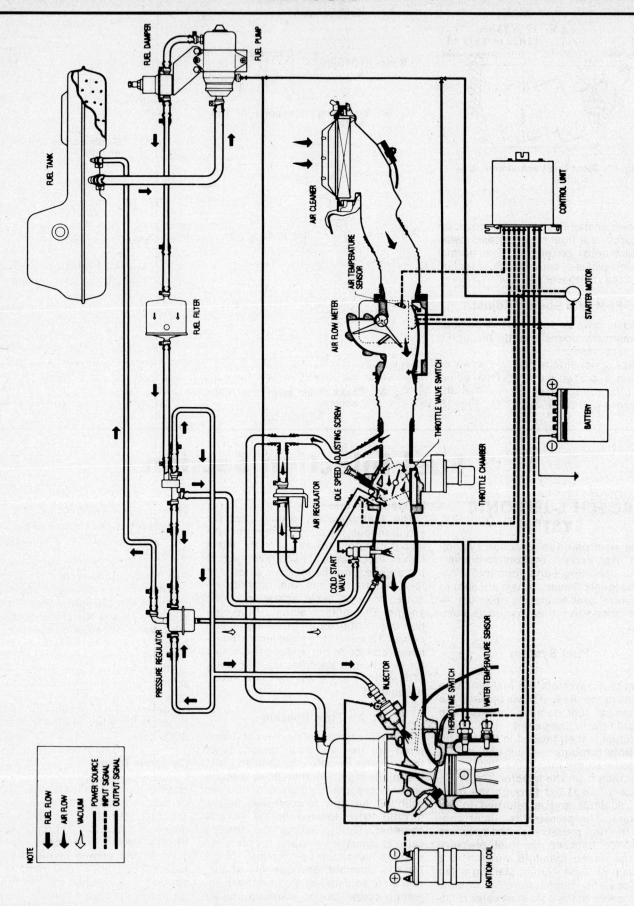

Fig. 1 Bosch L-Jetronic fuel injection system

gine rpm is increased to the specified range.

Altitude Compensation

Altitude compensation prevents deterioration of exhaust emissions caused by an enriched air-fuel mixture.

Atmospheric pressure varies according to the altitude. The higher the altitude, the lower the atmospheric pressure. At an atmospheric pressure of 26 inHg or below, corresponding to an altitude of 3,675 ft. or higher, the altitude switch transmits an "ON" signal to the control unit, decreasing fuel by 6% and providing an appropriate air-fuel mixture ratio.

System Components

Control Unit

The control unit, Fig. 2, is mounted on a bracket on the driver seat side dash panel. The control unit is connected to the electronic fuel injection harness by a multi-connector and the electronic fuel injection harness is connected to the other sensors.

The purpose of the control unit is to generate a pulse signal. Upon receiving an electrical signal from each sensor, the control unit generates a pulse signal and the duration, injector open-valve time period, is controlled to provide an optimum quantity of fuel according to the engine demands.

The control unit consists of three integrated circuits formed on the printed circuit board.

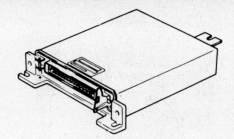

Fig. 2   Control unit

Air Flow Meter

The air flow meter, Fig. 3, measures the quantity of intake air, and sends a signal to the control unit so the base pulse width can be determined for correct fuel injection.

The air flow meter is provided with a flap in the air passage. As the air flows through the passage, the flap rotates and the angle of rotation is electronically monitored to measure air flow rate.

The flap is able to rotate to an angle where an equilibrium can be maintained between the air flow pressure and the return torque of the coil spring. The damper chamber and compensating plate are provided as a damper for the flap so the flap will not be disturbed by pulsation in manifold vacuum during operation.

The compensating plate is interlinked with the flap, and as the flap rotates, the compensating plate rotates in the damper chamber providing a small

clearance between the chamber wall.

During idling, when the amount of intake air is small, the air flows parallel with the flap through the bypass port so the specified intake air flow can be provided correctly.

The bypass port has been factory adjusted, but can be adjusted further, if necessary, by turning the air bypass screw.

The fuel pump relay contact is provided in the potentiometer section of the air flow meter. This contact remains in the "OFF" position when the flap is not actuated. The relay turns "ON" when the flap turns 8°, and electric current flows through the fuel pump relay to the fuel pump.

Air Temperature Sensor

The air temperature sensor, incorporated into the air flow meter, Fig. 4, monitors change in the intake air temperature and transmits a signal to control fuel injection in response to the varying pulse duration.

The temperature sensing unit utilizes a thermister which is sensitive in the low temperature range.

The electrical resistance of the thermister decreases in response to the rise in air temperature.

Water Temperature Sensor

The water temperature sensor, incorporated into the thermostat housing, Fig. 5, monitors change in cooling water temperature and transmits a sig-

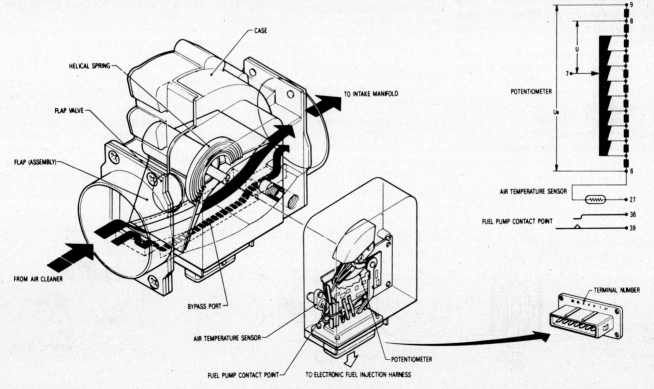

Fig. 3   Air flow meter

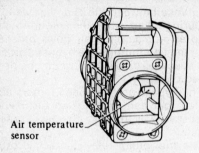

Fig. 4 Air temperature sensor

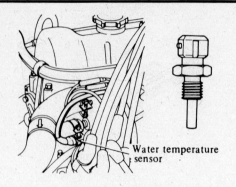

Fig. 5 Water temperature switch

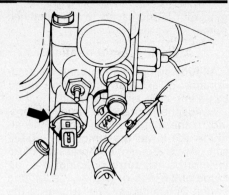

Fig. 6 Thermotime switch

nal for the fuel enrichment to change the pulse duration during warm-up.

The temperature sensing unit employs a thermister which is very sensitive in the low temperature range.

The electrical resistance of the thermister decreases in response to the rise in water temperature.

Thermotime Switch

The thermotime switch is incorporated into the thermostat housing, Fig. 6.

A harness is connected to the cold start valve from the thermotime switch. The bimetal contact in the thermotime switch opens or closes depending on the cooling water temperature, and sends a signal to the cold start valve so an additional amount of fuel can be injected for cranking operation of the engine when the cooling water temperature is below 57-72° F.

The thermotime switch is "ON" when the cooling water temperature is below 57-72° F. However, repeated operation of the ignition switch may result in excessively rich mixture. To prevent the rich mixture the bimetal is equipped with a heater. Electric current flows through the heater when the ignition switch is in the start position, and heats the bimetal. Through repeated operation of the ignition switch, then, the bimetal is sufficiently heated to open the thermotime switch, stopping excessive injection of fuel from the cold start valve.

The temperature at which the bimetal contact turns "ON" or "OFF" can be changed within the range of 57-72° F.

Cold Start Valve

The cold start valve operates on the electromagnetic principle. The valve injects fuel into the intake manifold independently of the injector operation so the engine can be cranked smoothly during cold weather.

To improve fuel-air mixing at lower temperatures, the cold start valve incorporates a swirl type nozzle which has a turn chamber at the end, Fig. 7. With this construction, fuel is injected at an angle of 90° and better atomization of fuel can be obtained.

EFI Relay

The relay is located in front of the battery, Fig. 8. It is made in two sections; the main relay section and the fuel pump relay section. The main relay section actuates the electronic fuel injection system through the ignition switch, and the fuel pump relay section actuates the fuel pump and air regulator. These two relays are incorporated into one case.

Throttle Valve Switch

The throttle valve switch is attached to the throttle chamber, Fig. 9, and actuates in response to accelerator pedal movement. This switch has two sets of

contact points. One set monitors the idle position and the other set monitors full throttle position.

The idle contacts close when the throttle valve is positioned at idle and open when at any other throttle position.

The full throttle contacts close only when the throttle valve is positioned at full throttle or more than 34 degree opening of the throttle valve. The contacts are open when the throttle valve is at any other position.

The idle switch compensates for enrichment during idle and after idle, and sends fuel cut signal. The full throttle switch compensates for enrichment in full throttle.

Dropping Resistor

The dropping resistor is mounted on the air cleaner bracket below the air cleaner, Fig. 10.

The dropping resistor is provided to reduce electric current flowing through the injector and control unit.

Altitude Switch

This switch, used on some models, is attached on the left side of the instrument panel in the driver's compartment. This switch consists of a bellows and a microswitch. The switch transmits an "ON" or "OFF" signal to the control unit according to change in atmospher-

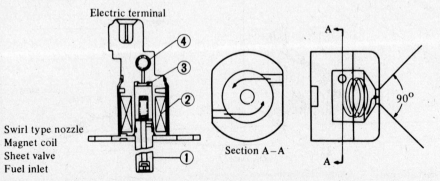

1 Swirl type nozzle
2 Magnet coil
3 Sheet valve
4 Fuel inlet

Fig. 7 Cold start valve

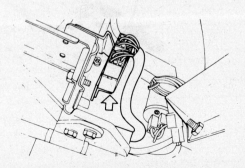

Fig. 8 EFI relay

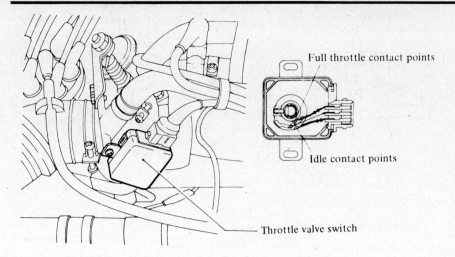

Full throttle contact points

Idle contact points

Throttle valve switch

Fig. 9 Throttle valve switch

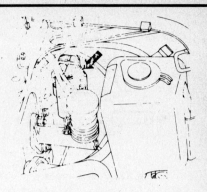

Fig. 10 Dropping resistor

ic pressure. When the atmospheric pressure drops below 26 inHg, an "ON" signal is transmitted to decrease fuel by 6%.

Fuel Pump

The fuel pump is mounted near the fuel tank and right rear wheel. The pump utilizes a wet type construction where a vane pump with roller is directly coupled to a motor filled with fuel.

The relief valve, Fig. 11, in the pump opens when the pressure in the fuel line rises over 43 to 64 psi due to a problem in the pressure system.

The check valve prevents abrupt drop of pressure in the fuel pipe when stopping the engine.

When the ignition switch is turned to the "START" position, the fuel pump is actuated irrespective of the position of the air flow meter contact point. After starting the engine, the air flow meter contact turns "ON" through rotation of the engine, thereby actuating the fuel pump. If engine stalls, the air flow meter contact is turned "OFF," and the fuel pump is stopped, though the ignition switch remains in the "ON" position. The fuel supply is cut off for safety purposes when the engine accidentally stops during driving.

Fuel Damper

The fuel damper is provided to suppress pulsation in fuel flow discharged from the fuel pump, Fig. 12. No adjust-

ment is allowed on this damper.

Pressure Regulator

The pressure regulator controls the pressure of fuel so a pressure difference of 36.3 psi can be maintained between the fuel pressure and intake vacuum. This constant differential pressure provides optimum fuel injection in every mode of engine operation.

When the intake manifold vacuum becomes great enough to overcome the diaphragm spring force as combined with the fuel pressure at the pressure line, the diaphragm becomes empty on the intake-side, Fig. 13. This opens the return-side port to allow fuel to flow to the tank for reducing fuel pressure.

If fuel pressure is higher than the intake manifold vacuum by 36.3 psi, the diaphragm returns to the original position by spring force and closes the return port.

The pressure regulator maintains the

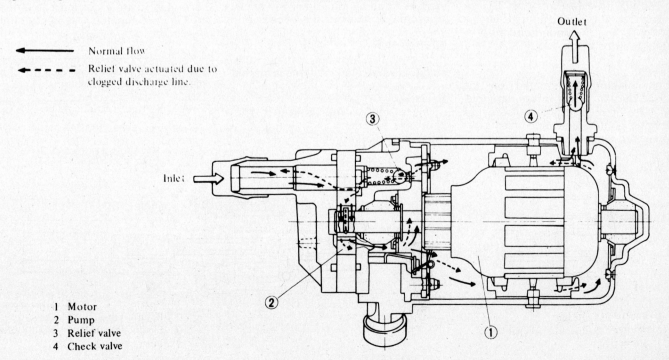

→ Normal flow

--→ Relief valve actuated due to clogged discharge line.

Inlet

Outlet

1 Motor
2 Pump
3 Relief valve
4 Check valve

Fig. 11 Fuel pump

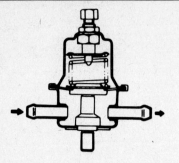

Fig. 12   Fuel damper

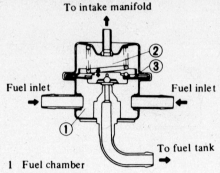

To intake manifold

Fuel inlet   Fuel inlet

To fuel tank

1 Fuel chamber
2 Spring chamber
3 Diaphragm

Fig. 13   Pressure regulator

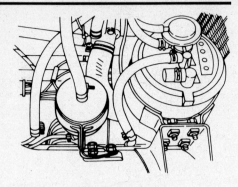

Fig. 14   Fuel filter

fuel pressure in the fuel line 36.3 psi higher than the pressure in the intake manifold.

Fuel Filter

The fuel filter is mounted on the right hand side of the engine compartment, Fig. 14.

The filter paper type element is replaced with the filter body as an assembly.

Air Regulator

The air regulator, Fig. 15, bypasses the throttle valve to control the quantity of air for increasing the engine idling speed when starting the engine at an underhood temperature of below 176° F.

A bimetal and a heater are incorporated into the air regulator. When the ignition switch is turned to the "START" position or when the engine is running, electric current flows through the heater, and the bimetal, as it is heated by the heater, begins to move and closes the air passage in a few minutes. The air passage remains closed until the engine is stopped and the underhood air temperature drops below 176° F.

Injector

The injector is mounted on the branch portion of the intake manifold. The injector receives the pulse signal from the control unit, and injects the fuel toward the intake valve in the cylinder head.

The injector operates on the solenoid valve principle. When a driving pulse is applied to the coil incorporated into the injector, the plunger is pulled into the solenoid, thereby opening the needle valve for fuel injection, Fig. 16. The quantity of injected fuel is in proportion to the duration of the pulse applied from the control unit.

Throttle Chamber

The throttle chamber, located between the intake manifold and air flow meter, is equipped with a valve, Fig. 17. This valve controls the intake air flow in response to accelerator pedal movement. The rotary shaft of this valve is connected to the throttle valve switch.

This valve remains closed during engine idling, and the air required for idling passes through the bypass port into the intake manifold. Idle adjustment is made by the idle speed adjusting screw located in the bypass port. There is another bypass line in this throttle chamber to pass sufficient air through the air regulator into the intake manifold when a cold engine is started.

Harness

One wiring harness is used to connect lines between the control unit and the related major units.

The harness from the 35-pin connector connected to the control unit is combined with the main harness at the side dash on the driver's side, and runs to the engine compartment.

From the engine compartment, the harness is connected to various units; the air flow meter, air temperature sensor, throttle valve switch, air regulator, injector, cold start valve, dropping resistor, E.F.I. relay.

Connectors in the engine compartment are used only in the line between the 35-pin connector and water temperature sensor, and between the cold start valve and thermotime switch.

TROUBLE-SHOOTING

Refer to the "Trouble-Shooting Chart, Fig. 18, and the wiring diagram, Fig. 19, to determine the procedure to be used. Disconnect battery ground cable, then the 35 pin connector from control unit.

Procedure I

NOTE: This procedure uses an ohmmeter to check continuity.

1. Throttle valve switch (Idle Switch):
   a. Make sure that throttle valve

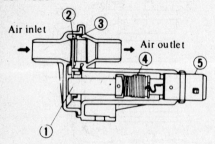

Air inlet

Air outlet

1 Bimetal   4 Heater
2 Shutter   5 Electric terminal
3 Sleeve

Fig. 15   Air regulator

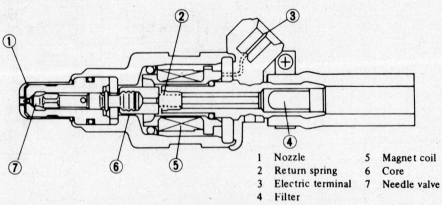

1 Nozzle   5 Magnet coil
2 Return spring   6 Core
3 Electric terminal 7 Needle valve
4 Filter

Fig. 16   Injector

switch connector is securely connected in place.

b. Check continuity between terminals 2 and 18.

c. If no continuity exists, check wiring between throttle valve switch and control unit connector.

2. Throttle valve switch (Full Throttle Switch):

a. Make sure that throttle valve switch connector is securely connected in place.

b. With accelerator pedal fully depressed, check continuity, between terminals 3 and 18.

c. If no continuity exists, check wiring between throttle valve switch and control unit connector.

3. Air flow meter:

a. Make sure that air flow meter connector is securely connected in place.

b. Check continuity between terminals 6 and 8.

c. Check continuity between terminals 7 and 8.

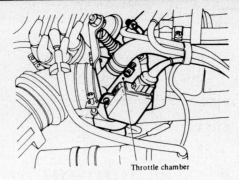

Throttle chamber

Fig. 17   Throttle chamber

d. Check continuity between terminals 8 and 9.

e. If no continuity exists in any step, check wiring between air flow meter and control unit connector.

4. Air temperature sensor:

a. Make sure that air flow meter connector is securely connected in place.

b. Check continuity between terminals 6 and 27.

c. If no continuity exists, check wiring between air temperature sensor and control unit connector.

5. Fuel pump contact points:

a. Remove air cleaner cover and air cleaner element.

b. Make sure that air flow meter connector is securely connected in place.

c. Depress air flow meter flap, and check continuity between terminals 10 and 20.

d. If no continuity exists, check wiring between fuel pump contacts and control unit connector.

6. Water temperature sensor:

a. Make sure that water temperature sensor connector is securely connected in place.

b. Make sure that ground lead wire is properly grounded.

c. Check continuity between terminal 13 and body metal.

d. If no continuity exists, check wiring between water temperature sensor and control unit connector.

7. Fuel injection relay:

a. Make sure that relay connector is securely connected in place.

b. Check continuity between terminal 20 and body metal.

c. If no continuity exists, check wiring between fuel injection relay and control unit connector.

8. Air regulator and fuel pump:

a. Make sure that air regulator and relay connectors are securely connected in place.

b. Make sure that fuel pump harness is securely connected to fuel pump terminal.

c. Check continuity between terminal 34 and body metal.

d. If no continuity exists, check wiring between air regulator and control unit connector.

9. Ground circuit:

a. Make sure that ground connector is securely connected in place.

b. Check all ground lines to ensure that they are properly grounded.

c. Check continuity between terminal 5 and body metal.

d. Check continuity between terminal 16 and body metal.

e. Check continuity between terminal 17 and body metal.

f. Check continuity between terminal 35 and body metal.

g. If no continuity exists in any step, check wiring between the terminal and control unit connector.

10. Altitude switch:

a. Make sure that the altitude switch is securely connected.

b. Check continuity between terminals 9 and 12.

Condition	Procedure	Step
Engine will not start	I	3, 5, 6, 7, 8, 9
	II	1, 2, 3
	III	1, 3
Engine stalls	I	3, 5, 6, 7, 8, 9
	II	1, 2, 3
Engine lacks power	I	1, 2, 3, 4, 6, 8, 10
	II	1, 2, 3
Engine breathes	I	1, 2, 3, 4, 5, 6, 8, 9, 10
	II	1, 2, 3
Rough idle during warm-up	I	1, 3, 4, 5, 6, 8, 9
	II	1, 2, 3
	III	2
Rough idle after warm-up	I	1, 3, 4, 5, 6, 8, 9, 10
	II	1, 2, 3
High idle speed	I	1, 2, 4, 6, 8
	III	2
Engine backfires	I	1, 2, 3, 4, 6, 10
	II	1, 2, 3
Engine afterfires	I	1, 2, 3, 4, 6
	II	3
	III	1
Excessive fuel consumption	I	1, 2, 3, 4, 6, 8
	II	3
	III	2

Fig. 18   Trouble-shooting chart

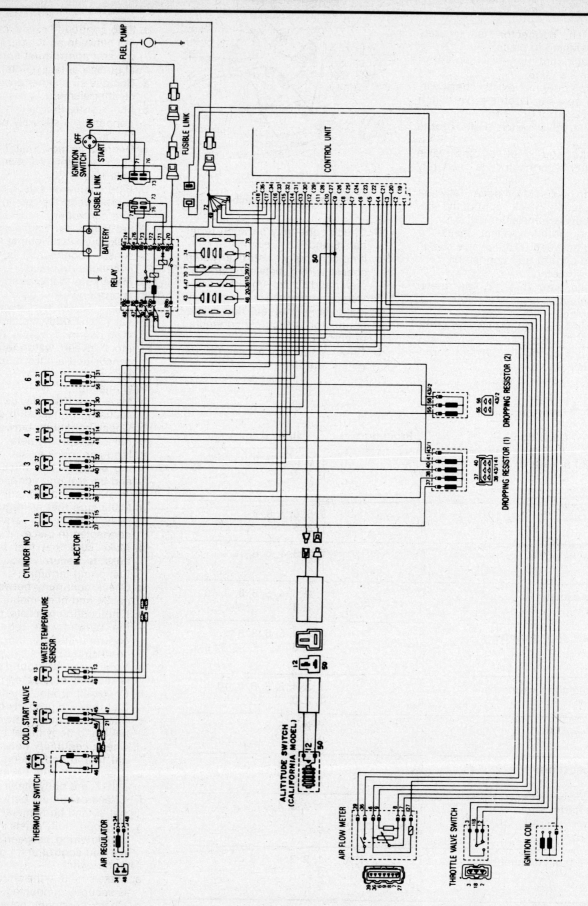

Fig. 19 System wiring diagram

Procedure II

NOTE: This procedure uses a voltmeter to check continuity.

NOTE:
a. Set circuit tester in the DC VOLT (DC ''V'') range.
b. Connect negative terminal of voltmeter to body metal with a lead wire.
c. If tests check unsatisfactory, be sure to turn off the ignition switch and to disconnect battery ground cable before tracing the circuit.

1. Revolution trigger wheel:
   a. Make sure that ignition coil connector is securely connected in place.
   b. Turn ignition switch to the ''ON'' position.
   d. Contact terminal 1 with positive lead wire of voltmeter.
   d. If no voltage is indicated, check wiring between revolution trigger wheel and control unit connector.

2. Power line circuit:
   a. Make sure that relay connector and 4-pin connector are securely connected in place.
   b. Turn ignition switch to the ''ON'' position.
   c. Contact terminal 10 with positive lead of voltmeter.
   d. If no voltage is indicated, check wiring between terminal 10 and control unit connector.

3. Injector and dropping resistors:
   a. Make sure that injector, dropping resistor and relay, and 4-pin connector are securely connected in place.
   b. Turn ignition switch to the ''ON'' position.
   c. Contact terminal 14 cylinder no. 4, with positive lead wire of voltmeter.
   d. Use the same procedure as in step c and take voltmeter reading between terminal 15, cylinder no. 1, and ground.
   e. Use the same procedure as in step c, and take voltmeter reading between terminal 30, cylinder no. 5, and ground.
   f. Use the same procedure as in step c, and take voltmeter reading between terminal 31, cylinder no. 6, and ground.
   g. Use the same procedure as in step c, and take voltmeter reading between terminal 32, cylinder no. 3, and ground.
   h. Use the same procedure as in

step c, and take voltmeter reading between terminal 33, cylinder no. 2, and ground.
   i. If no voltage is indicated in any step, check wiring between the injector and the dropping resistors.

NOTE: This procedure uses a voltmeter to check continuity.

NOTE:
a. Set circuit tester in the DC VOLT (DC ''V'') range.
b. Connect negative terminal of circuit tester to body metal with a lead wire.
c. If tests check unsatisfactory, be sure to turn off the ignition switch and to disconnect battery ground cable before tracing the circuit.
d. Disconnect lead wire from terminal ''S'' of starter motor.
e. Disconnect cold start valve harness connector.

1. Starter signal:
   a. Make sure that relay connector and 4-pin connector are securely connected in place.
   b. Turn ignition switch to the ''START'' position.
   c. Contact terminal 4 with positive lead wire of voltmeter.
   d. If no voltage is indicated, check wiring between terminal 4 and control unit connector.

2. Air regulator:
   a. Make sure that air regulator, relay and 4-pin connector are securely connected in place.
   b. Turn ignition switch to the ''START'' position.
   c. Contact terminal 34 with positive lead wire of voltmeter.
   d. If no voltage is indicated, check wiring between air regulator and control unit connector.

3. Cold start valve and thermotime switch:
   a. Disconnect thermotime switch connector.
   b. Short circuit two pins of thermotime switch harness connector.
   c. Make sure that relay connector is securely connected in place.
   d. Turn ignition switch to the ''START'' position.
   e. Contact terminal 21 with positive lead wire of voltmeter.
   f. If no voltage is indicated, check wiring between cold start valve and thermotime switch and the control unit connector.

COMPONENT TESTING
Control Unit

This procedure uses a miniature lamp to check if the open-valve pulse for cranking the engine is applied to the injector when the engine fails to start. To check, connect a miniature lamp to the harness-side connector of the injector, and crank the engine. If the lamp flashes due to pulse voltage applied to the injector, the control unit is normal. Since two different power transistors are used (one is for No. 1, 2, and 3 cylinders, and the other is for No. 4, 5, and 6 cylinders), the procedure must be performed on both the No. 1 and No. 4 cylinders.

For confirmation purposes, remove the harness connector of the cooling water temperature sensor. If the lamp flashes more brightly, then it is positive indication that the control unit is functioning normally. This procedure may be limited to the No. 1 or No. 4 cylinder only.

Test Conditions
1. The engine must be cranked at a speed of more than 80 rpm.
2. The control unit may fail to generate a correct pulse signal at an excessively low battery voltage. It is recommended that a battery voltage of more than 9 volts be applied during the cranking operation.

Testing No. 1 Cylinder
1. Turn ignition switch to the ''OFF'' position.
2. Disconnect harness connector of injector.
3. Disconnect cold start valve harness connector.
4. Connect a miniature lamp to the injector harness connector of the No. 1 cylinder.
5. Turn ignition starter switch on to crank engine and observe lamp.
6. Disconnect cooling water temperature sensor harness connector and observe if the lamp becomes brighter.

Testing No. 4 Cylinder
1. Connect lamp to the injector harness connector of the No. 4 cylinder.
2. Turn ignition switch on to crank engine, and observe lamp.

Test Results
The lamp should flash when the engine is cranked. In the No. 1 cylinder, if the lamp is brighter when the cooling water temperature sensor connector has been disconnected, it indicates that the control unit is normal. If the lamp

does not flash, or if the lamp does not become brighter when the cooling water temperature sensor harness connector is removed, it indicates that the control unit is faulty. Replace the control unit, and repeat procedure.

If the lamp flashes when the engine is cranked, but does not become brighter when the water temperature sensor connector is disconnected, it is an indication that the water temperature sensor is faulty. Check the water temperature sensor.

Air Flow Meter

This procedure can be performed without removing air flow meter. When testing air flow meter, remove air cleaner cover and air cleaner element.

CAUTION: Before testing air flow meter, remove battery ground cable.

Potentiometer Test
1. Measure the resistance between terminals 8 and 6, Fig. 19. Resistance should be approximately 180 ohms.
2. Measure the resistance between terminals 9 and 8, Fig. 19. Resistance is approximately 100 ohms.
3. Connect a 12-volt dc across terminal 9 (positive) and terminal 6 (negative), Fig. 19.
4. Connect the positive lead of a voltmeter to terminal 8 and negative lead to terminal 7, Fig. 19.
5. Gradually open the flap to ensure that the voltmeter indication decreases proportionately. If the indication varies abruptly, the potentiometer may be faulty.

Insulation Test
Check insulation resistance between the air flow meter body and any one of terminals 6, 7, 8 and 9, Fig. 19. If continuity exists, the air flow meter is faulty.

Flap Test
Fully open the flap to check freedom of movement.

Fuel Pump Contact Point Test
Continuity should exist between terminals 36 and 39 of the air flow meter when the flap is opened approximately 8 degrees, Fig. 19. Continuity should not exist when the flap is fully closed. If continuity does not exist when the flap is opened or continuity exists at a different position, replace air flow meter.

Air Temperature Sensor
This procedure can be performed without removing air flow meter. When

Air or Water Temperature	Resistance
−22°F.	20.3-33
−14°F.	7.6-10.8
50°F.	3.25-4.15
68°F.	2.25-2.75
122°F.	0.74-0.94
176°F.	0.29-0.36

Fig. 20 Air & coolant temperature sensors specification chart

testing air temperature sensor, remove air cleaner cover and air cleaner element.

Insulation Resistance Test
Check insulation resistance between terminal 27, Fig. 19, and air flow meter body. If continuity exists, the air temperature sensor is faulty. The air temperature sensor and air flow meter should be replaced as an assembly.

Continuity Test
1. Disconnect battery ground cable.
2. Measure the outside air temperature.
3. Measure resistance between terminals 27 and 6 of the air flow meter connector.
4. If resistance is not within specifications, Fig. 20, replace air temperature sensor.

Water Temperature Sensor

This test can be performed with the sensor either on or off the vehicle.

ON Engine Test
Check the resistance of the water temperature sensor before and after engine warm-up.
1. Disconnect battery ground cable.
2. Disconnect the water temperature sensor harness connector.
3. Place a thermometer in the radiator coolant when the engine is cold, and measure the coolant temperature (which is used as a reference sensor temperature) and sensor resistance.

NOTE: When measuring cooling temperature, insert a rod type thermometer into the radiator.

4. Connect the water temperature sensor harness connector.
5. Connect battery ground cable.
6. Warm up the engine sufficiently.

7. Disconnect battery ground cable.
8. Disconnect the water temperature sensor harness connector.
9. Measure the sensor resistance.
10. If resistance is not within specifications, Fig. 20, replace water temperature sensor.

OFF Engine Test
1. Immerse the sensor into water maintained at a temperature of 68° F. and measure sensor resistance which should be 2.25-2.75 ohms.
2. Then, dip the sensor into water maintained at a temperature of 176° F. and measure sensor resistance which should be .29-.36 ohms.

Insulation Resistance Test
This test is performed on the engine.
1. Disconnect battery ground cable.
2. Disconnect the sensor harness connector.
3. Check continuity between the engine block and one of the terminals at sensor, Fig. 19.
4. If continuity exists, the sensor is faulty.

Thermotime Switch
Static Test
1. Disconnect ground cable from battery.
2. Disconnect electric connector of thermotime switch.
3. Measure the resistance between terminal 46, Fig. 19, and switch body.
4. The resistance is zero when the cooling water temperature is less than 57° F.
5. The resistance is zero or infinite when the cooling water temperature is between 57-72° F.
6. The resistance is infinite when the cooling water temperature is more than 72° F.
7. Measure the resistance between terminal 45, Fig. 19, and switch body. Resistance should be 70-86 ohms.

Dynamic Test
1. Disconnect ground cable from battery.
2. Disconnect electric connector of thermotime switch.
3. Remove thermotime switch from thermostat housing.
4. Immerse heat-sensing portion of thermotime switch into cooling water maintained at 50° F.
5. When the thermotime switch temperature is just about the same as the cooling water temperature, measure the resistance between terminal 45 and 46. The resistance should be about 78 ohms.

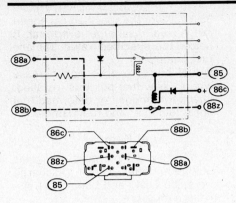

Fig. 21 Checking main relay

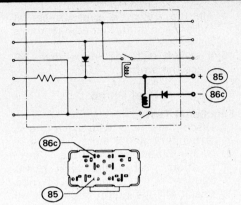

Fig. 22 Checking main relay

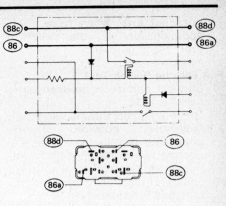

Fig. 23 Checking fuel pump relay

6. Increase cooling water temperature at a rate of 1.8° F. per second until it is more than 77° F, then check continuity between terminal 45 and 46.
7. If the ohmmeter reading increases from about 78 ohms to infinite, circuit is satisfactory.

Cold Start Valve

1. Disconnect lead wire from the S terminal of starter motor.
2. Turn ignition switch to the "Start" position, and make sure that fuel pump is operating properly. Operating sound should be heard.
3. Disconnect ground cable from battery.
4. Remove two screws securing cold start valve to intake manifold and the cold start valve.
5. Disconnect electric connector of cold start valve.
6. Place cold start valve into a transparent glass container of a minimum 1.22 cu in capacity, plug the transparent glass container opening with a clean rag.
7. Connect ground cable to battery.
8. Turn ignition switch to the "Start" position. Cold start valve should not inject fuel.

9. Turn ignition switch to the "Off" position, and connect a jumper wire between cold start valve and battery terminals.
10. Cold start valve should inject fuel. If not, proceed to step 11.
11. With ignition switch in the "Start" position and cold start valve set as outlined in step 9, fuel should be injected.

Electronic Fuel Injection Relay

1. Disconnect ground cable from battery.
2. Remove relay from vehicle.

Main Relay Test

> **NOTE:**
> a. Before applying test voltage to relay, connect a fuse in series with lead wire to prevent damage to the circuit.
> b. If available, use a 7-volt dc in place of 12-volt to test relay operation.

1. Connect 12-volt dc between positive terminal 86c and negative terminal 85, Fig. 21.
   "Clicks" should be heard and continuity should exist between terminals 88Z and 88A, and between 88Z and 88B, Fig. 21.
2. Connect 12-volt dc between positive terminal 85 and negative terminal 86C, Fig. 22. No clicks should be heard.
3. If steps 1 and 2 are not satisfactory, the relay is faulty.

Fuel Pump Relay Test

> **NOTE:**
> a. Before applying test voltage to relay, connect a fuse in series with lead wire to prevent damage to the circuit.

b. If available, use a 7-volt dc in place of 12-volt to test relay operation.

1. Make sure continuity exists between terminals 88D and 88C, and between 86A and 86, Fig. 23.
2. Connect 12-volt dc to positive terminal 86A and negative terminal 85. "Clicks" should be heard and continuity should exist between terminals 88Y and 88D, Fig. 24.
3. Connect 12-volt dc to positive terminal 85 and negative terminal 86A, Fig. 25. No "clicks" should be heard.
4. If steps 1 through 3 are not satisfactory, the relay is faulty.

Throttle Valve Switch

1. Disconnect ground cable from battery.
2. Remove throttle valve switch connector.

Idle Switch Test

1. Connect ohmmeter between terminals 2 and 18, Fig. 19.
2. If continuity exists when throttle valve is in the idle position, and

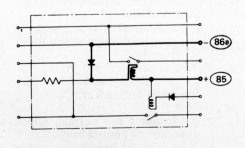
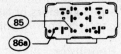

Fig. 24 Checking fuel pump relay

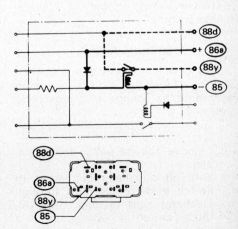

Fig. 25 Checking fuel pump relay

does not exist when valve open, approximately 4°, idle switch is functioning properly.

Full Throttle Switch Test

1. Connect ohmmeter between terminals 3 and 18.
2. Gradually open throttle valve from fully-closed position. Observe ohmmeter reading when valve is opened approximately 34°. If ohmmeter reading at all other valve positions is greater than that at 34°, full switch is functioning properly.

Insulation Test

Connect ohmmeter between body metal and terminals 2, 3 and 18, Fig. 19. Ohmmeter reading should be infinite.

Dropping Resistors

1. Disconnect ground cable from battery.
2. Disconnect 4-pin and 6-pin connectors of dropping resistors from electronic fuel injection harness connectors.
3. Perform resistance checks on dropping resistor (6-pin connector side) between the following points, Fig. 19:
   a. 43/1 and terminal 41 (Number four cylinder resistor)
   b. 43/1 and terminal 40 (Number three cylinder resistor)
   c. 43/1 and terminal 38 (Number two cylinder resistor)
   d. 43/1 and terminal 37 (Number one cylinder resistor)
   The resistance should be approximately 6 ohms.
4. Perform resistance checks on dropping resistor (4-pin connector side) between the following points, Fig. 19:
   a. 43/2 and terminal 56 (Number six cylinder resistor)
   b. 43/2 and terminal 55 (Number five cylinder resistor)
   The resistance should be approximately 6 ohms.

Altitude Switch

This switch contains a microswitch which performs the "On-Off" operation according to change in atmospheric pressure.

1. Disconnect ground cable from battery.
2. Remove altitude switch from vehicle.
3. With an ohmmeter connected to switch leads, orally blow through discharge port or suck back. Altitude switch is satisfactory if a "click" is heard and continuity exists on ohmmeter scale.

4. Altitude switch is pressure-set at factory and no further adjustment is necessary.
5. If switch is found inoperative, replace the switch.

Fuel Pump

Functional Test

1. Disconnect lead wire from the S terminal of starter motor.
2. With ignition switch to the "Start" position, ensure that fuel pump sounds while operating. If not, check all fuel pump circuits. If all circuits are satisfactory, replace fuel pump.

Discharge Pressure Test

1. Disconnect ground cable from battery.
2. Disconnect cold start valve harness connector.
3. Connect two jumper wires to battery positive and negative terminals.
4. Release pressure in fuel system by connecting other terminals of jumper wires to cold start valve connector for two or three seconds.

NOTE: Be careful to keep both terminals separate to avoid short circuit.

5. Connect a fuel pressure gauge between fuel tube and fuel hose of fuel filter.
6. Disconnect lead wire from S terminal of starter motor.
7. Disconnect electric connector from cold start valve.
8. Connect ground cable to battery.
9. Turn ignition switch to the "Start" position to operate fuel pump. Fuel pressure should be 36.3 psi.
10. If fuel pressure is not as specified, replace fuel pressure regulator, and repeat pressure discharge tests.
    If fuel pressure is below the specified value, check for clogged or deformed fuel lines, and if necessary, replace fuel pump.

Fuel Discharge Test

1. Connect a fuel pressure gauge as outlined under Fuel Discharge Pressure Check.
2. Check fuel pressure, observing the full-load requirements described below.

Full Load Test

1. Check fuel pressure with the engine at full throttle, starting with 13 mph up to 38 mph. The shift gear should be in 2nd position.
   If fuel pressure is approximately

36.3 psi over the specified car speed range, fuel discharge is normal. If below the specified value, replace fuel pump.
2. If fuel pressure does not increase when a new fuel pump is installed, check for clogged or deformed fuel lines, fuel filter and fuel damper.

Fuel Damper

1. Connect a fuel pressure gauge as outlined under "Fuel Discharge Pressure Test" and check fuel discharge pressure.
   If fuel discharge pressure reading fluctuates excessively, replace fuel damper.

Pressure Regulator

1. Connect a fuel pressure gauge as outlined under Fuel Discharge Pressure Check, and check fuel discharge pressure. If a fuel discharge of 36.3 psi is not obtained, replace pressure regulator.

Injector

Continuity Test

1. Disconnect ground cable from battery.
2. Disconnect electric connectors from injectors.
3. Check continuity between the two terminals. Continuity should exist. If not, the injector is faulty.

Testing For Sound

1. If engine can run:
   a. Start the engine and run idle. Attach the tip of a screwdriver to each injector to ensure that it sounds while operating.
   b. If a low sound is produced from any particular injector, that injector is faulty.
2. If engine cannot run:
   a. Disconnect electric connector of cold start valve to protect catalytic converter.
   b. Crank the engine and check that injectors produce sounds to indicate operation.
   c. If a low sound is produced from any particular injector, the injector is faulty.
   d. If no sound is heard from all injectors, check harness for continuity as outlined in "Continuity Test."
   e. If harnesses are normal, check operation of control unit.
   f. If sounds are heard from either Nos. 1, 2 and 3 injectors or Nos. 4, 5 and 6, replace control unit.

Air Regulator

1. Hold rubber hose in the line be-

Fig. 26   Air flow meter installation. 810

Fig. 27   Air flow meter installation. 280Z

tween throttle chamber and air regulator with fingers.
2. Engine speed should be reduced. If not, proceed as follows:
   a. Disconnect air hoses from both ends of air regulator, and visually check to see if air regulator valve opens.
   b. Disconnect electric connector of air regulator, and check continuity. Continuity should exist. If not, air regulator is faulty.
   c. Pry air regulator valve to open with a flat-bladed screwdriver, then close.

Throttle Chamber

1. Remove throttle chamber.
2. Make sure that throttle valve moves smoothly when throttle lever is moved.
3. Make sure that bypass port is free from obstructions and is clean.
4. Make sure that idle adjust screw moves smoothly.

5. Adjust throttle valve for fully-close position.
6. Push dash pot rod with finger to ensure that it moves smoothly.

EGR Vacuum Port Screw

The E.G.R. vacuum port screw attached to the throttle chamber is designed to change the amount of exhaust gas recirculated.

This screw is properly preset at the factory and further adjustment should not be made.

SYSTEM SERVICE

Control Unit, Replace

1. Turn ignition switch to the "OFF" position.
2. Remove bolt securing resin control unit cover to the left dash side panel, and the cover.
3. Disconnect 35-pin coupler from control unit.
4. Remove two bolts securing control unit to dash side panel, and the control unit.

5. Reverse procedure to install.

Air Flow Meter, Replace

810

1. Disconnect battery ground cable.
2. Disconnect harness connector from air flow meter.
3. Disconnect clamp securing air duct between air flow meter and throttle chamber, and disengage air duct at air flow meter, Fig. 26.
4. Remove air cleaner cover and air cleaner element.
5. Remove bolts securing air flow meter and the air flow meter.
6. Reverse procedure to install.

280Z

1. Disconnect battery ground cable.
2. Disconnect rubber hose from each side of air flow meter.
3. Disconnect air flow meter ground cable.
4. Remove three bolts securing air flow meter bracket, Fig. 27.
5. Move air flow meter upward, disconnect harness connector, and remove air flow meter.
6. Reverse procedure to install.

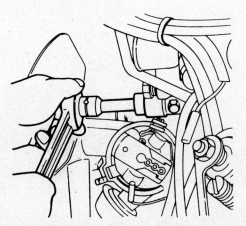

Fig. 28   Water temperature sensor replacement

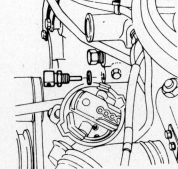

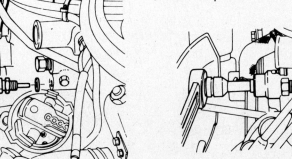

Fig. 29   Thermotime switch replacement

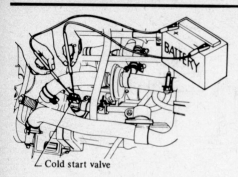

Cold start valve

Fig. 30 Relieving fuel pressure. 810 & 1977 280Z

Air Temperature Sensor, Replace

The air temperature sensor is incorporated into the air flow meter and cannot be replaced as a single unit. When replacement of air temperature sensor is necessary, the air flow meter assembly should be replaced.

Water Temperature Sensor, Replace

1. Disconnect battery ground cable.
2. Remove radiator cap.
3. Remove drain plug from radiator to drain approximately 2 qts. of coolant.
4. Disconnect radiator upper hose.
5. Disconnect water temperature sensor harness connector.
6. Remove water temperature sensor, Fig. 28.
7. Reverse procedure to install.

CAUTION: When connecting water temperature sensor harness, keep it away from high tension wire.

Thermotime Switch, Replace

1. Remove radiator filler cap. Drain cooling water by opening drain valve located on the lower side of radiator.
2. Disconnect water hose at thermostat housing.
3. Disconnect battery ground cable.
4. Disconnect lead wires from thermal transmitter, and remove thermal transmitter.
5. Disconnect electric connector from thermotime switch.
6. Remove thermotime switch by turning counterclockwise, Fig. 29.
7. Reverse procedure to install.

Cold Start Valve, Replace

810 & 1977 280Z

1. Disconnect battery ground cable.
2. Disconnect cold start valve harness connector.
3. Using two jumper wires, Fig. 30, connect each terminal to battery positive and negative terminals.
4. Release pressure in fuel system by connecting other terminals of jumper wires to cold start valve connector for two or three seconds.

NOTE: Be careful to keep both terminals separate in order to avoid short circuit.

5. Remove two screws securing cold start valve to intake manifold.
6. Disconnect clip and disengage cold start valve from fuel hose.
7. Reverse procedure to install.

1975-76 280Z

1. Disconnect battery ground cable.
2. Disconnect ground lead wire from fuel pump.
3. Disconnect lead wire from the "S" terminal of starter motor.
4. Remove two screws securing cold start valve to intake manifold, and the cold start valve.

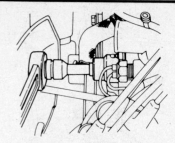

Fig. 31 Relieving fuel pressure. 1975-76 280Z

5. Connect ground cable to battery.
6. Place cold start valve in a container. Turn the ignition switch to the "Start" position, and release fuel line pressure, Fig. 31.
7. Disconnect clip and disengage cold start valve from fuel hose.

NOTE: Place a container to receive fuel left in fuel hose.

8. Reverse procedure to install.

Relay, Replace

1. Disconnect battery cables and remove battery.
2. Remove two screws securing relay to radiator core support, Fig. 32.
3. Disconnect harness connector.
4. Reverse procedure to install.

Throttle Valve Switch, Replace

1. Disconnect battery ground cable.
2. Disconnect throttle valve switch harness connector.
3. Remove two screws securing throttle valve switch to throttle chamber, Fig. 33.
4. Slowly pull throttle valve switch forward.
5. Reverse procedure to install.
6. After installation, adjust the position

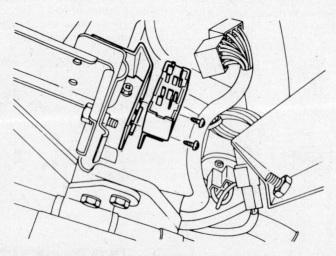

Fig. 32 Relay installation

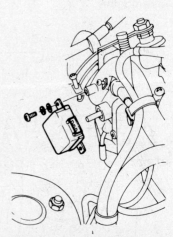

Fig. 33 Throttle valve switch replacement

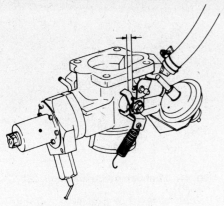

Fig. 34   Throttle valve switch adjustment

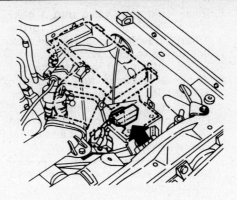

Fig. 35   Dropping resistors installation. 810

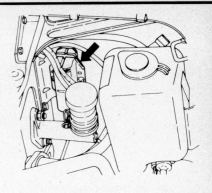

Fig. 36   Dropping resistors installation. 280Z

of throttle valve switch so that idle switch may be changed from "On" to "Off" when engine speed is 1,400 rpm under no load (throttle valve stopper screw-to-throttle valve shaft lever clearance is .047 inch on 810 or .051 inch on 280Z, Fig. 34).

Dropping Resistors, Replace

810
1. Disconnect battery ground cable.
2. Disconnect harness connector from air flow meter.
3. Disconnect rubber hose from air flow meter.
4. Remove bolts securing air cleaner to bracket. Remove air and air flow meter as an assembly.
5. Disconnect two electric connectors from dropping resistor.
6. Remove two screws securing resistors to air cleaner bracket, Fig. 35.
7. Reverse procedure to install.

280Z
1. Disconnect ground cable from battery.
2. Disconnect two electric connectors from dropping resistor.
3. Remove two screws securing dropping resistor to dashboard, Fig. 36.
4. Reverse procedure to install.

Altitude Switch, Replace
1. Disconnect battery ground cable.
2. Disconnect electric connector from altitude switch.

3. Remove bolts securing altitude switch bracket and the altitude switch, Fig. 37.
4. Reverse procedure to install.

Fuel Pump, Replace

810 & 1977 280Z
1. Disconnect battery ground cable.
2. Disconnect cold start valve harness connector.
3. Using two jumper wires, Fig. 30, connect each terminal to battery positive and negative terminals.
4. Release pressure in fuel system by connecting other terminals of jumper wires to cold start valve connector for two or three seconds.
5. Raise and support rear of vehicle.
6. Remove fuel pump cover.
7. Temporarily clamp hose at a suitable location between fuel tank and fuel pump.

NOTE: Be sure to receive fuel into a suitable container.

8. Disconnect clamps at the suction and outlet sides of fuel pump, and the fuel hoses.
9. Remove two screws securing fuel pump bracket, and bracket. The fuel pump can then be removed, Fig. 38.
10. Reverse procedure to install.

1975-76 280Z
1. Disconnect ground cable from battery.
2. Disconnect lead wires from fuel pump.
3. Disconnect lead wire from the "S" terminal of starter motor.
4. Remove two screws securing cold start valve to intake manifold, and remove cold start valve.
5. Connect ground cable to battery.
6. Place cold start valve into a container. Turn ignition switch to the "Start" position, and release fuel line pressure, Fig. 31.
7. Raise and support rear of vehicle.
8. Temporarily clamp hose at a suitable location between fuel tank and fuel pump.

NOTE: Be sure to receive fuel into a suitable container.

9. Disconnect clamps at the suction and outlet sides of fuel pump, and the fuel hoses.
10. Remove two screws securing fuel pump bracket, and bracket. The fuel pump can then be removed, Fig. 39.
11. Reverse procedure to install.

Fuel Damper

810 & 1977 280Z
1. Disconnect battery ground cable.
2. Disconnect cold start valve harness connector.

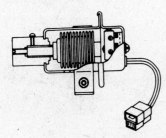

Fig. 37   Altitude switch installation. 810 & 1977 280Z, California models

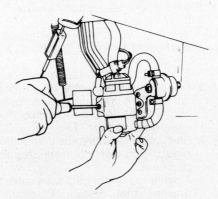

Fig. 38   Fuel pump installation. 810

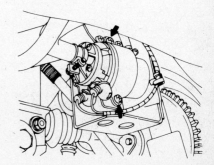

Fig. 39   Fuel pump installation. 280Z

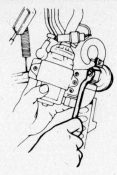

Fig. 40 Fuel damper replacement. 810

3. Using two jumper wires, Fig. 30, connect each terminal to battery positive and negative terminals.
4. Release pressure in fuel system by connecting other terminals of jumper wires to cold start valve connector for two or three seconds.

NOTE: Be careful to keep both terminals separate to avoid a short circuit.

5. Raise and support rear of vehicle.
6. Remove fuel pump cover.
7. Temporarily clamp fuel hose at a suitable location between fuel tank and suction side of fuel pump.
8. Disconnect fuel hose clamps, and the fuel hoses at the inlet and outlet of fuel damper.

NOTE: Be sure to receive fuel into a suitable container.

9. Remove nuts securing fuel damper to bracket, Fig. 40.
10. Reverse procedure to install.

1975-76 280Z
1. Disconnect battery ground cable.
2. Disconnect ground wire from fuel pump.
3. Disconnect lead wire from the "S" terminal of starter motor.
4. Remove two screws securing cold start valve to intake manifold.
5. Connect ground cable to battery.

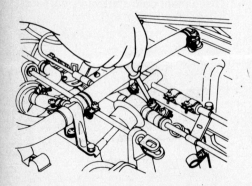

Fig. 42 Pressure regulator replacement

6. Place cold start valve into a container. Turn ignition switch to the "Start" position, and release fuel line pressure, Fig. 31.
7. Raise and support rear of vehicle.
8. Temporarily clamp fuel hose at a suitable location between fuel tank and suction side of fuel pump.
9. Disconnect fuel hose clamps and the fuel hoses at the inlet and outlet of fuel damper.

NOTE: Be sure to receive fuel into a suitable container.

10. Remove nuts securing fuel damper to bracket, Fig. 41.
11. Reverse procedure to install.

Pressure Regulator, Replace

810 & 1977 280Z
1. Disconnect battery ground cable.
2. Disconnect cold start valve harness connector.
3. Using two jumper wires, Fig. 30, connect each terminal to battery positive and negative terminals.
4. Release pressure in fuel system by connecting other terminals of jumper wires to cold start valve connector for two or three seconds.

NOTE: Be careful to keep both terminals separate to avoid a short circuit.

5. Disengage vacuum tube connecting regulator to manifold from pressure regulator.
6. Place a rag under pressure regulator to prevent fuel splash. Disconnect three hose clamps, and disengage fuel hose from pressure regulator, Fig. 42.
7. Reverse procedure to install.

1975-76 280Z
1. Disconnect ground cable from battery.
2. Disconnect ground lead wire from fuel pump.
3. Disconnect lead wire from the "S" terminal of starter motor.
4. Remove two screws securing cold start valve to intake manifold, and the cold start valve.
5. Connect ground cable to battery.
6. Place cold start valve into a container. Turn ignition switch to the "Start" position, and release fuel line pressure, Fig. 31.
7. Disengage vacuum tube connecting regulator to manifold from pressure regulator.
8. Place a rag under cold start valve to prevent fuel splash. Disconnect three hose clamps, and disengage

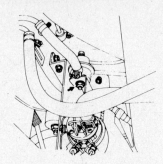

Fig. 41 Fuel damper installation. 280Z

fuel hose from pressure regulator, Fig. 42.
9. Reverse procedure to install.

Fuel Filter, Replace

810 & 1977 280Z
1. Disconnect battery ground cable.
2. Disconnect cold start valve harness connector.
3. Using two jumper wires, Fig. 30, connect each terminal to battery positive and negative terminals.
4. Release pressure in fuel system by connecting other terminals of jumper wires to cold start valve connector for two or three seconds.

NOTE: Be careful to keep both terminals separate to avoid a short circuit.

5. Disconnect clamps securing fuel hoses to the outlet and inlet sides of fuel filter, and the fuel hoses.
6. Remove bolt securing fuel filter to bracket, and fuel filter, Fig. 43.
7. Reverse procedure to install.

1975-76 280Z
1. Disconnect battery ground cable.
2. Disconnect ground lead wire from fuel pump.
3. Disconnect lead wire from the "S" terminal of starter motor.
4. Remove two screws securing cold start valve to intake manifold, and the cold start valve.
5. Connect battery ground cable.
6. Place cold start valve into a con-

Fig. 43 Fuel filter installation (Typical)

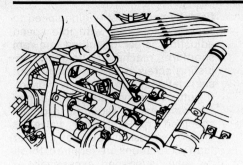

Fig. 44 Removing front fuel pipe attaching screws

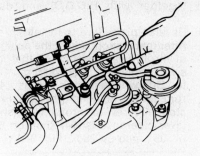

Fig. 45 Removing rear fuel pipe attaching screws

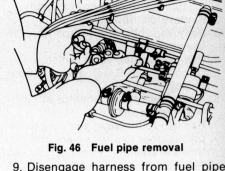

Fig. 46 Fuel pipe removal

tainer. Turn ignition switch to the "Start" position, and release fuel line pressure, Fig. 31.

7. Disconnect clamps securing fuel hoses to the outlet and inlet sides of fuel filter, and the fuel hoses.

8. Remove three bolts securing fuel filter to bracket, and remove fuel filter, Fig. 43.

9. Reverse procedure to install.

Injector, Replace

810 & 1977 280Z

1. Disconnect battery ground cable.
2. Disconnect cold start valve harness connector.
3. Using two jumper wires, Fig. 30, connect each terminal to battery positive and negative terminals.
4. Release pressure in fuel system by connecting other terminals of jumper wires to cold start valve connector for two or three seconds.

NOTE: Be careful to keep both terminals separate to avoid a short circuit.

5. Disconnect battery ground cable.
6. Disconnect electric connector from injector.
7. Disengage harness from fuel pipe "B" wire clamp.
8. To remove the front three injectors, remove screws securing fuel pipe, Fig. 44.
9. To remove the rear three injectors, remove bolts securing fuel pipe "C" to intake manifold. These bolts are located on bracket, Fig. 45.
10. Remove injector hose clamps.

11. Pull fuel pipe forward, and disengage injector and fuel pipe, Fig. 46.
12. On injector rubber hose, measure a point approximately .787 inch from socket end. Using a 150 watt soldering iron, cut hose into braided reinforcement from mark to socket end, Fig. 47. Do not feed soldering iron until it touches injector tail piece.

Then pull rubber hose out with hand.

13. Install injector fuel rubber hose as follows:
   a. Clean exterior of injector tail piece.
   b. Wet inside of new rubber hose with fuel.
   c. Push end of rubber hose with hose socket onto injector tail piece by hand as far as they will go.
   d. Clamp is not necessary at this connection.

1975-76 280Z

1. Disconnect battery ground cable.
2. Disconnect ground lead wire from fuel pump.
3. Disconnect lead wire from the "S" terminal of starter motor.
4. Remove two screws securing cold start valve to intake manifold, and the cold start valve.
5. Connect ground cable to battery.
6. Place cold start valve into a container. Turn ignition switch to the "Start" position, and release fuel line pressure, Fig. 31.
7. Disconnect battery ground cable.
8. Disconnect electric connector from injector.

9. Disengage harness from fuel pipe "B" wire clamp.
10. To remove the front three injectors, remove screws securing fuel pipe, Fig. 44.
11. To remove the rear three injectors, remove bolts securing fuel pipe "C" to intake manifold. These bolts are located on bracket, Fig. 45.
12. Remove injector hose clamps.
13. Pull fuel pipe forward, and disengage injector and fuel pipe, Fig. 46.
14. On injector rubber hose, measure a point approximately .787 inch from socket end using a 150 watt soldering iron, cut hose into braided reinforcement from mark to socket end, Fig. 47. Do not feed soldering iron until it touches injector tail piece.

Then pull rubber hose out with hand.

15. Install injector fuel rubber hose as follows:
   Clean exterior of injector tail piece.
   Wet inside of new rubber hose with fuel.
   Push end of rubber hose with hose socket onto injector tail piece by hand as far as they will go.
   Clamp is not necessary at this connection.

Air Regulator, Replace

1. Disconnect battery ground cable.
2. Disconnect electric connector from regulator.
3. Disconnect clamp on each side of air hose, and disengage hose.
4. Remove two setscrews, Fig. 48.

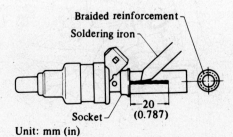

Braided reinforcement
Soldering iron
Socket
20 (0.787)
Unit: mm (in)

Fig. 47 Melting injector hose

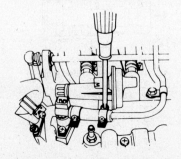

Fig. 48 Air regulator replacement

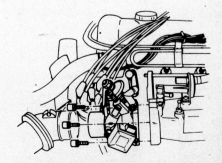

Fig. 49 Throttle chamber installation

Throttle Chamber, Replace

1. Disconnect battery ground cable.
2. Remove distributor cap.
3. Remove rubber hoses from throttle chamber, Fig. 49.
4. Remove throttle valve switch.
5. Disconnect B.C.D.D. harness connector.
6. Disconnect rod connector at auxiliary throttle shaft.
7. Remove four screws securing throttle chamber to intake manifold. The throttle chamber can be removed together with B.C.D.D. and dash pot.
8. Reverse procedure to install.
9. After installation, adjust the position of throttle valve switch so that idle switch may be changed from "On" to "Off" when engine speed is 1,400 rpm under no load (throttle valve stopper screw-to-throttle valve shaft lever clearance is .047 inch on 810 or .051 inch on 280Z, Fig. 34.)

NOTE: After throttle chamber has been installed, warm up engine sufficiently and adjust engine speed to specified idle rpm with idle speed adjusting screw. Specified idle rpm should be reached if idle speed adjusting screw is turned back about six rotations from the "fully closed" (throttle valve) position. If more than six rotations are required to obtain specified rpm, throttle valve is closed excessively at idle; if fewer than six rotations are required, throttle valve is opened excessively or working parts are faulty.

Emission Controls Section

POSITIVE CRANKCASE VENTILATION SYSTEM

This system returns blow-by gas to both the intake manifold and carburetor air cleaner, Fig. 1.

The positive crankcase ventilation (P.C.V.) valve is provided to conduct crankcase blow-by gas to the intake manifold.

During partial throttle operation of the engine, the intake manifold sucks the blow-by gas through the P.C.V. valve.

Normally, the capacity of the valve is sufficient to handle any blow-by and a small amount of ventilating air.

The ventilating air is then drawn from the dust side of the carburetor air cleaner, through the tube connecting carburetor air cleaner to rocker cover, into the crankcase.

Under full-throttle condition, the manifold vacuum is insufficient to draw the blow-by flow through the valve, and its flow goes through the tube connection in the reverse direction.

On engines with an excessively high blow-by some of the flow will go through the tube connection to carburetor air cleaner under all conditions.

Testing

With engine running at idle, remove the ventilator hose from P.C.V. valve; if the valve is working, a hissing noise will be heard as air passes through the valve and a strong vacuum should be felt immediately when a finger is placed over valve inlet, Fig. 2.

AIR INJECTION SYSTEM

The Air Injection System (A.I.S.) injects compressed air (secondary air) coming from the air pump into the exhaust manifold to reduce hydrocarbons and carbon monoxide in exhaust gas through re-combustion.

Air Pump

The air pump is a two-vane type, Fig. 3. It has two positive displacement vanes which require no lubrication.

The die-cast aluminum air pump assembly attached to the front of the engine is driven by an air pump drive belt. A rotor shaft, drive hub, inlet and outlet tubes are visible on the pump exterior. A rotor, vanes, carbon shoes, and shoe springs make up the rotating unit of the pump. The rotor located in the center of the pump is belt-driven. The vanes rotate freely around the off-center pivot pin, and follow the circular-shaped pump bore. In the two-vane type, the vanes form two chambers in the housing. Each vane completes a pumping cycle in every revolution of the rotor. Air is drawn into the inlet cavity through a

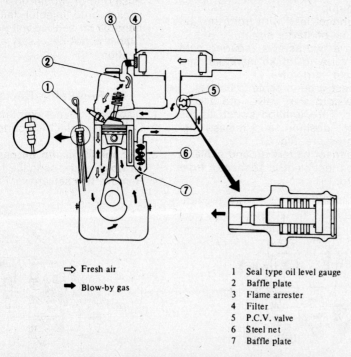

⇨ Fresh air

➡ Blow-by gas

1 Seal type oil level gauge
2 Baffle plate
3 Flame arrester
4 Filter
5 P.C.V. valve
6 Steel net
7 Baffle plate

Fig. 1 Positive crankcase ventilation system (Typical)

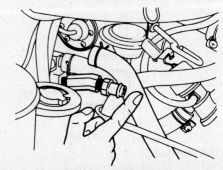

Fig. 2 Testing PCV valve

DATSUN

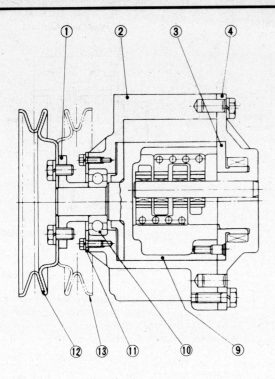

1	Air pump drive hub	5	Vane	10	Ball bearing
2	Housing	6	Carbon shoe	11	Front bearing cover
3	Rotor ring	7	Shoe spring	12	Pulley
4	End cover	8	Stripper	13	Pulley
	(with needle bearing)	9	Rotor shaft		(for air conditioner)

Fig. 3 Air injection pump

tube connected to the air pump air cleaner. Air is sealed between the vanes and moved into a smaller cavity (the compression area).

After compression, a vane passes the outlet cavity. Subsequently it passes the stripper and a section of the housing that separates the outlet and inlet cavities and again reaches the inlet cavity to repeat the pumping cycle.

Carbon shoes (in the slots of the rotor) support the vanes. They are designed to permit sliding of the vanes and to seal the rotor interior from the air cavities. Leaf springs which are behind the leading-side of the shoes compensate for shoe abrasion.

The rotor ring is steel bolted to the rotor end. It positions the rotor and holds the carbon shoes.

The vane uses needle bearings. All bearings have been greased.

There are two types of bearing which support the rotor. Ball bearing is used for the front one and the needle bearing is used for the rear.

Air Control Valve

The air control valve, Fig. 4, controls the quantity of secondary air fed from the air pump according to engine speed and load condition.

The intake manifold vacuum and air pump discharge pressure applied to the diaphragm chamber actuate the valve which is coupled to the diaphragm and control the quantity of secondary air to be fed into the exhaust manifold in response to the engine condition.

Combined Air Control (C.A.C.) Valve

The C.A.C. valve, Fig. 5, controls the quantity of secondary air fed from the air pump according to the load condi-

tion, and it discharges the secondary air into the atmosphere to prevent overheating of the catalytic converter.

This valve is operated by intake manifold vacuum and air pump discharge pressure. When intake manifold vacuum is small or in the high-load range, the No. 2 valve opens; when it is great or in the low-load range, the No. 1 valve opens. If air pump discharge pressure is large or the engine is running at a high speed, the No. 3 valve opens, admitting the air pump discharge pressure to the No. 2 diaphragm chamber of the C.A.C.

Fig. 4 Air control valve

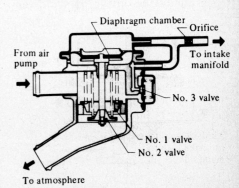

Fig. 5 Combined air control (CAC) valve

1-293

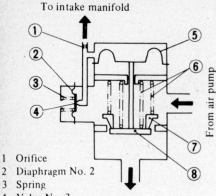

1 Orifice
2 Diaphragm No. 2
3 Spring
4 Valve No. 3
5 Diaphragm No. 1
6 Spring
7 Valve No. 1
8 Valve No. 2

Fig. 6   CAC valve operation

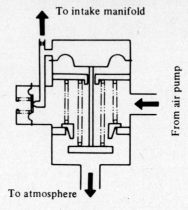

Fig. 7   CAC valve operation

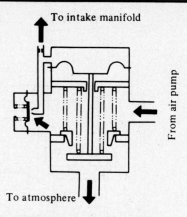

Fig. 8   CAC valve operation

valve and opening the No. 2 valve. At this point, the No. 2 valve serves as a relief valve.

The C.A.C. valve operates as follows:

1. Engine in "low speed" and "light load."

When the engine is operating under these conditions, intake vacuum is high. The No. 2 valve (unitized with the No. 1 diaphragm) is lifted by the intake manifold vacuum, pushing up the No. 1 valve, Fig. 6. These valves will then stop at a position where a balanced condition exists between air pump discharge pressure and spring tension acting on the No. 1 and No. 2 valves. The No. 2 diaphragm, however, does not move due to low engine speed, low air pump discharge pressure and spring tension acting on the No. 3 valve. For this reason, these valves are brought to a balanced condition.

2. Engine in "low speed" and "heavy load".

When the engine is operating under these conditions, intake manifold vacuum is low, and all valves are balanced, Fig. 7.

3. Engine in "high speed" and "light load."

When the engine is operating under these conditions, intake manifold vac-

uum is low. The No. 3 valve moves to the left because of high air pump discharge pressure. All valves are balanced, Fig. 8.

Anti-Backfire Valve

This valve, Fig. 9, is controlled by intake manifold vacuum to prevent backfire in the exhaust system at the initial period of deceleration.

At this period, the mixture in the intake manifold becomes too rich to ignite and burn in the combustion chamber and burns easily in the exhaust system with injected air in the exhaust manifold.

The anti-backfire valve provides air to the intake manifold to make the air-fuel mixture leaner and prevents backfire.

The anti-backfire valve inlet is connected to the air cleaner and the outlet to the intake manifold.

The correct function of this valve reduces hydrocarbon emission during deceleration.

If the valve does not work properly, unburned mixture will be emitted from the combustion chambers and burns with the aid of high-temperature and injected air which causes backfire.

Check Valve

A check valve, Fig. 10, is located in the air pump discharge lines. The valve prevents the backflow of exhaust gas which occurs in the following cases.

1. When the air pump drive belt fails.
2. When relief valve spring fails.

Air Pump Relief Valve

The air pump relief valve, Fig. 11, controls the injection of secondary air into the exhaust system when the engine is running at high speed under a heavily loaded condition. It accomplishes the following functions without affecting the effectiveness of the exhaust emission control system.

1. Minimizes exhaust gas temperature rise.
2. Minimizes horsepower losses resulting from air injection into the exhaust system.
3. Protects pump from excessive back pressure.

The secondary air is discharged from the air pump relief valve to the dust side of the carburetor air cleaner.

Testing

Air Pump

1. Operate engine until it reaches normal operating temperature.

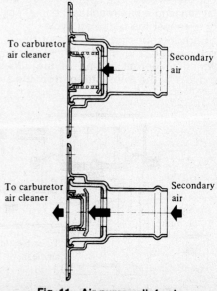

Fig. 11   Air pump relief valve

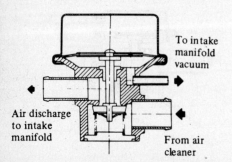

Fig. 9   Anti-backfire valve

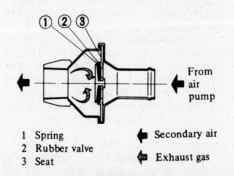

1 Spring
2 Rubber valve
3 Seat

← Secondary air

← Exhaust gas

Fig. 10   Check valve

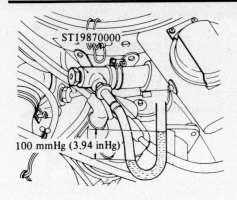

100 mmHg (3.94 inHg)

Fig. 12 Testing air pump

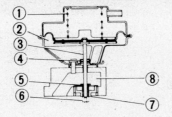

1	Diaphragm spring	5	Valve (open)
2	Diaphragm	6	Valve (close)
3	Valve shaft	7	Valve seat
4	Seal	8	Valve chamber

Fig. 13 EGR valve. 1974

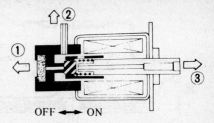

OFF ⟷ ON

1 To atmosphere
2 To E.G.R. control valve
3 To carburetor

Fig. 14 EGR solenoid valve. 1974

2. Inspect all hoses and hose connections for leaks and correct them, if necessary, before checking air injection pump.
3. Check air injection pump belt tension and adjust to specifications if necessary.
4. Disconnect air supply hose at check valve or air control valve or plug C.A.C. valve discharge hose, depending upon application.
5. Disconnect vacuum hose from air control valve for California type only.
6. Insert open pipe end of Air Pump Test Gauge Adapter ST19870000 in air supply hose, Fig. 12. Clamp hose securely to adapter to prevent it from blowing out. Position adapter and test gauge so that air blast emitted through drilled pipe plug will be harmlessly dissipated.
7. Install a tachometer on engine. With engine speed at 1500 rpm for six cylinder engines or 2600 rpm for four cylinder engines, observe pressure produced at test gauge.
   Air pressure should be 100 mmHg (3.94 inHg) or more.
8. If air pressure does not meet specifications, proceed as follows:
   a. Repeat steps 2 and 3.
   b. Disconnect air supply hose at anti-backfire valve. Plug air hose opening, and screw with a clamp. Repeat pressure test.
   c. With engine speed at 1,500 rpm, close hole of test gauge with finger. If a leaking sound is heard or leaking air is felt at relief valve, relief valve is malfunctioning. Re-

lief valve should be replaced.
   d. If air injection pump does not meet minimum requirement of pressure test, it should be replaced.

Check Valve
1. Warm up engine thoroughly.
2. Disconnect hose from check valve.
3. Run the engine at 1500 rpm for six cylinder engines, or 2000 rpm for four cylinder engines, and then return it to idling. Visually check check valve for any signs of leaks before the engine returns to idling speed. If leaks are detected, replace check valve.

Air Pump Relief Valve
1. Disconnect hoses leading to check valve and air control valve from air hose connector, and install blind cap to the connector.
2. With engine running at about 3,000 rpm under no load, check for discharge air at the air outlet of air pump relief valve. If no air is felt, replace the air pump relief valve.

Anti-Backfire Valve
1. Warm up engine thoroughly.
2. Disconnect hose from air cleaner, and place a finger near the outlet.
3. Run engine at about 3,000 rpm under no load, then quickly return it to idling. If a pull or suction force is felt the anti-backfire valve is functioning normally. If no suction is felt, replace the anti-backfire valve.

Air Control Valve
1. Warm up engine thoroughly.
2. Before checking air control valve, check all hoses for loose connection, leaks, etc., and repair or correct if necessary.
3. With engine idling, disconnect the outlet side hose of the air control valve and place hand on the air hose outlet to check for air. If no air is felt, replace the air control valve.
4. Pull vacuum hose off from air control valve. If discharge of air from air

hose stops, the air control valve is normal. If discharge is still felt, replace valve.

Combined Air Control (C.A.C.) Valve
1. Make sure that C.A.C. valve vacuum hose and air hose are not cracked.
2. Warm up engine thoroughly.
3. With engine at idle, place finger over relief air opening in the air cleaner to check for presence of air.
4. Disconnect vacuum hoses at C.A.C. valve. Then make sure that air is discharged from C.A.C. valve at engine idling.
5. Connect an external vacuum source and apply a vacuum of 7.87-9.84 inch Hg. to C.A.C. valve. Then, increase engine speed to 3,000 rpm and confirm that no air leaks from C.A.C. valve.
6. With the above condition, disconnect air hose at check valve and plug it up. At this point, confirm the air leaks from C.A.C. valve.
7. If test results in steps 3, 4, 5 and 6 are satisfactory, the C.A.C. valve is properly functioning.

EXHAUST GAS RECIRCULATION (EGR) SYSTEM
1974

The exhaust gas recirculation system lets exhaust gases recirculate into the

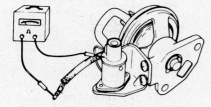

Fig. 15 Testing EGR solenoid valve. 1974

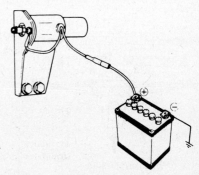

Fig. 16 Testing EGR solenoid valve. 1974

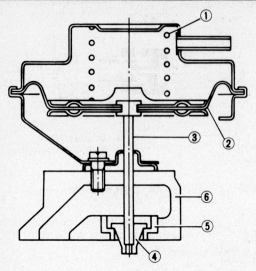

1 Diaphragm spring
2 Diaphragm
3 Valve shaft
4 Valve
5 Valve seat
6 Valve chamber

Fig. 17 EGR valve. 1975-77

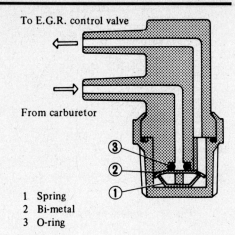

1 Spring
2 Bi-metal
3 O-ring

Fig. 18 Thermal vacuum valve. 1975-77

combustion chamber and reduces the combustion temperature so as to reduce NOx produced in combustion process.

This system comprises the E.G.R. control valve, solenoid valve, water temperature switch, relay, E.G.R. tube and vacuum tube. When the E.G.R. control valve opens, exhaust gases from the exhaust manifold is admitted in the chamber of the adapter equipped with the E.G.R. control valve through the E.G.R. tube, which is measured by the E.G.R. control valve and is drawn into the intake manifold.

EGR Valve

This valve, Fig. 13, is operated by vacuum pressure produced in the intake manifold, and opens and closes the exhaust gas passage.

At idling, the control valve does not operate and the exhaust gases do not recirculate.

When the throttle valve of the carburetor opens to increase the vacuum pressure in the intake manifold, this valve starts to operate and the exhaust gases recirculate.

However, when the throttle valve is fully open and the vacuum pressure is decreased below 50 mmHg (2.0 inHg), this valve will close again.

EGR Solenoid Valve

This improves the starting ability and durability of the engine in the cold condition. The water temperature switch detects the cooling water temperature and operates the E.G.R. solenoid valve fitted to the intake manifold. The E.G.R. solenoid valve, Fig. 14, intermittently shuts off the vacuum passage which leads from the carburetor to the E.G.R. control valve. When the cooling water temperature is below operating temperature, the current flows through the solenoid and so actuates the E.G.R. solenoid valve to shut off the vacuum passage. This prevents the exhaust gases from recirculating.

Water Temperature Switch

The water temperature switch turns the line to solenoid valve on or off at the operating temperature of engine coolant in order to control the E.G.R. system.

TESTING
EGR Valve

1. Remove E.G.R. vacuum hose and check to be certain that vacuum hose is not deformed excessively. If it is, the probability is that E.G.R. control valve is not operating properly due to leakage of vacuum signals. To remedy this condition, replace vacuum hose.
2. Remove E.G.R. control valve from intake manifold.
3. Apply a vacuum of 4.72-5.12 inch Hg. The E.G.R. control valve should stay in the open position for more

than 30 seconds after vacuum is stopped.
4. Visually inspect E.G.R. control valve for sign of damage, wrinkle or other deformation.
5. Clean the E.G.R. control valve seat with brush and compressed air.

EGR Solenoid Valve

1. Check E.G.R. solenoid valve for continuity, Fig. 15.
2. If ohmmeter indicates continuity in step 1, check E.G.R. solenoid valve to ensure that it clicks intermittently when activated, Fig. 16.
   If a click is heard, E.G.R. solenoid valve is satisfactory.

Water Temperature Switch

1. A thermometer and ohmmeter are needed for checking water temperature switch.
2. Checking "OFF" of water temperature switch:
   Starting from water temperature at 25°C (77°F) and below, check continuity of water temperature switch and ensure that a reading is infinite, that is, switch is open.

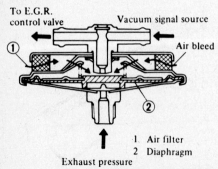

To E.G.R. control valve
Vacuum signal source
1
Air bleed
2
1 Air filter
2 Diaphragm
Exhaust pressure

Fig. 19 Back pressure transducer (BPT) valve. 1975-77

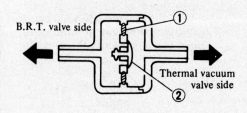

B.R.T. valve side
1
Thermal vacuum valve side
2

1 Sintered metric disc.
2 One-way umbrella valve

Fig. 20 Vacuum delay valve. 1975-77

3. Checking "ON" of water temperature switch:

Increasing water temperature from about 25°C (77°F), make continuity check of water temperature switch. Operation is normal if an ohmmeter reading drops to zero, at water temperature somewhere between 31 to 41°C (88 to 106°F) and remains zero at above 41°C (106°F).

4. If test results in steps 2 and 3 are satisfactory, switch is satisfactory.

1975-77

In the exhaust gas recirculation system, a part of the exhaust gas is returned to the combustion chamber to lower the spark flame temperature during combustion. This results in a reduction of the nitrogen oxide content in the exhaust gas.

The exhaust gas recirculation system consists of an E.G.R. passage, B.P.T. valve, E.G.R. control valve, thermal vacuum valve, E.G.R. tube and hose.

When the E.G.R. control valve is open, some of the exhaust gas is led from the exhaust manifold to the E.G.R. chamber through the E.G.R. passage. The exhaust gas is then controlled in quantity by the E.G.R. valve, and is introduced into the intake manifold.

EGR Valve

The E.G.R. control valve, Fig. 17 controls the quantity of exhaust gas to be led to the intake manifold through vertical movement of the taper valve connected to the diaphragm, to which vacuum is applied in response to the opening of the carburetor throttle valve. The E.G.R. control valve is installed on the E.G.R. passage through a gasket.

E.G.R. control valve construction and type vary with transmission type and car destination. For identification purposes, the part number is stamped on the recessed portion at the top of the valve.

Thermal Vacuum Valve

The thermal vacuum valve, Fig. 18, is mounted on the engine thermostat housing. It detects engine coolant temperature by means of a built-in bi-metal, and opens and closes the vacuum passage in the thermal vacuum valve. When the vacuum passage is open, the carburetor suction vacuum is applied to the diaphragm of the E.G.R. control valve to actuate the taper valve connected to the diaphragm.

Back Pressure Transducer (BPT)

The B.P.T. valve, Fig. 19, monitors exhaust pressure to activate the diaphragm, controlling intake manifold vacuum applied to the E.G.R. control valve. The recirculated exhaust gas is controlled in response to positioning of the E.G.R. control valve or to engine operation.

Vacuum Delay Valve

The vacuum delay valve, Fig. 20, prevents a rapid vacuum drop of the E.G.R. control line. The valve is designed for one-way operation and consists of a one-way umbrella valve and a sintered steel fluidic restrictor.

TESTING
System Test

1. Make a thorough visual check of E.G.R. control system. If necessary, wipe away oil to facilitate inspection. If any hoses are cracked or broken, replace.
2. With engine stopped, inspect E.G.R. control valve for any indication of binding or sticking by moving diaphragm of control valve upwards with a finger.
3. With engine running, inspect E.G.R. control valve and thermal vacuum valve for normal operation.
   a. When engine coolant temperature is low:
   Make sure that EG.R. control valve does not operate when engine speed is increased from idling to 3,000 to 3,500 rpm.
   Place a finger on the diaphragm of E.G.R. control valve to check for valve operation.
   b. When engine coolant temperature is high:
   Make sure that E.G.R. control valve operates when engine speed is increased from idling to 3,000 to 3,500 rpm. Place fingers on the diaphragm of E.G.R. control valve to check for valve operation.
4. If E.G.R. control valve does not operate, check as follows:
   a. Disconnect one end (E.G.R. control valve side) of vacuum hose connecting thermal vacuum valve to E.G.R. control valve.
   b. Increase engine speed from idling to 3,000 to 3,500 rpm.
   c. Make sure that thermal vacuum valve is open, and that carburetor vacuum is present at the end (E.G.R. control valve side) of vacuum hose.
   If vacuum is weak or not present at all, replace thermal vacuum valve. If vacuum is present, replace E.G.R. control valve.

EGR Valve

1. Apply vacuum to E.G.R. control valve. If the valve moves to full position, it is normal.

E.G.R. control valve will remain open for more than 30 seconds after vacuum has cut off.

2. Visually check E.G.R. control valve for damage, wrinkle or deformation.
3. Clean the seating surface of E.G.R. control valve with a brush and compressed air, and remove foreign matter from around the valve and port.

Thermal Vacuum Valve

Apply vacuum to thermal vacuum valve and check to be sure that thermal vacuum valve opens or closes in response to engine coolant temperature as specified.

Thermal vacuum valve should open at a temperature of 40° to 57°C (104° to 135°F) completing the vacuum passage.

Back Pressure Transducer (BPT)

1. Disconnect tow vacuum hose on B.P.T. valve.
2. Plug one of two ports of B.P.T. valve.
3. Apply a pressure above 50 mmH_2O (2 mH_2O) to B.P.T. valve and suck back other port of B.P.T valve to check for leakage. If a leak is noted, replace valve.

Vacuum Delay Valve

1. Remove vacuum delay valve.
2. Blow air from the port of the E.G.R. control valve side. The vacuum delay valve is in good condition if the air flows through the valve.
3. Try again from the opposite side of the valve. The valve is in satisfactory condition if the air flow resistance is greater than that in step 2.
4. If the condition of spark delay valve is unknown, dip port into a cup filled with water. Blow air from brown face side. Small air bubbles should appear.

SPARK TIMING CONTROL SYSTEM
Exc. 1977 A14 Engine

The spark timing control system serves to control the distributor vacuum advance under varying travelling conditions to reduce HC and NOx emissions.

This system provides vacuum advance when the gear is in the top (4th) and neutral position and retarded spark timing at the other positions.

When electric current flows through the vacuum switching valve, the valve opens and introduces air into the vacuum controller of the distributor through a vacuum hose, and vacuum advance is eliminated. When the vacuum switching valve is de-energized, the valve closes and vacuum created by the carburetor is introduced into the vacuum controller of the distributor to provide usual vacuum advance.

The top detecting switch and neutral detecting switch, located on the transmission case, operate so as to interrupt the flow of electric current when the gear is placed into "TOP" and "NEUTRAL", but allows it to flow in the other gear positions.

Testing

1. Ensure that wiring connectors are tightly in place.
2. Ensure that vacuum hoses are properly connected to their positions.
3. Ensure that distributor vacuum controller properly functions.
4. Connect a timing light.
5. Run engine at approximately 1,800 rpm.
6. Disengage clutch. Shift gears in top, 3rd, then neutral positions. Read spark timing in respective shift positions.

   The system is properly functioning if spark timing in both top and neutral positions is approximately 5° greater than that in 3rd position.
7. If correct spark timing is not obtained in step 6, replace top detecting switch or neutral detecting switch as required.

NOTE: Engage the parking brake while the above check is being made. To protect against accidental forward movement, depress brake pedal while clutch pedal is being depressed. When installing switches, apply lock agent to threads.

8. If spark timing does not vary in test described in step 6, proceed as follows:
   a. Disconnect vacuum switching valve green wire connector.
   b. Connect a timing light.
   c. Run engine at approximately 1,800 rpm. Read spark timing.
   d. Connect vacuum switching valve green wire connector directly to battery positive terminal and read spark timing.
   e. Vacuum switching valve is normal if spark timing advances by 5° when connector does not contact battery positive terminal. Replace neutral and top detecting switches. If spark timing does not vary in test above replace vacuum switching valve.
9. Check for voltage in electrical wiring.

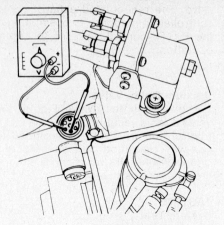
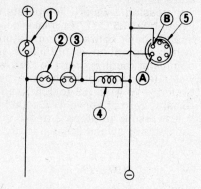

1 Ignition switch
2 Neutral detecting switch
3 Top detecting switch
4 Vacuum switching valve
5 Function test connector

Fig. 21   Testing spark timing control system. Exc. 1977 A14 engine

Turn ignition switch on, but do not run engine. Check for voltage across terminals A and B, Fig. 21. The system is satisfactory if voltage readings below are obtained:

Gear Position	Voltmeter Indication
Neutral	0V
3rd	12V
4th (Top)	0V

1977 A14 Engine

The spark timing control system controls the distributor vacuum advance under varying traveling conditions to reduce HC and Nox emissions.

Operation

1. On manual transmission models except California and California automatic transmission models, spark timing fully advances under all of the following four conditions:
   a. Thermal vacuum valve in "closed" state or cooling water temperature below 12°C (53°F) or above 60°C (140°F).
   b. Vacuum switching valve in "ON" position.
   c. Top detecting switch in "ON" or transmission gear in "TOP" position.
   d. Carburetor vacuum port positioned below throttle valve (with engine operated at other than full throttle).

NOTE: Except under the above conditions, spark timing advances very slightly because of intake manifold vacuum discharged into the atmosphere.

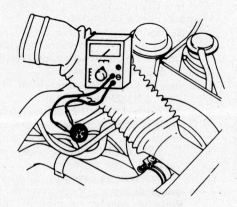
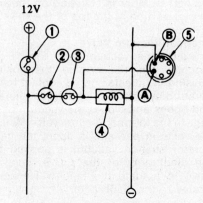

1 Ignition switch
2 Neutral detecting switch
3 Top detecting switch
4 Vacuum switching valve
5 Function test connector

Fig. 22   Testing spark timing control system. 1977 A14 engine

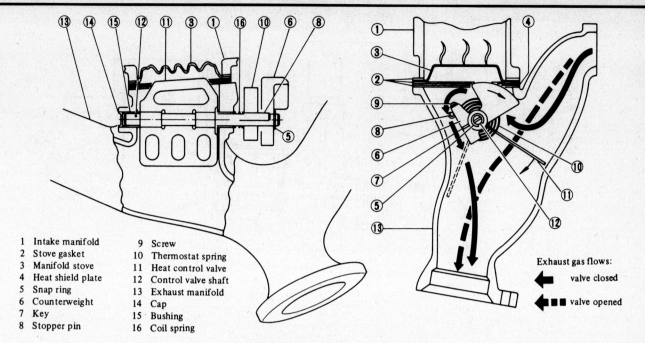

1	Intake manifold	9	Screw
2	Stove gasket	10	Thermostat spring
3	Manifold stove	11	Heat control valve
4	Heat shield plate	12	Control valve shaft
5	Snap ring	13	Exhaust manifold
6	Counterweight	14	Cap
7	Key	15	Bushing
8	Stopper pin	16	Coil spring

Exhaust gas flows:

⬅ valve closed

⬅▪▪ valve opened

Fig. 23 Early fuel evaporative system

2. On automatic transmission models except California, the spark timing advances fully under the following two conditions:
   a. Thermal vacuum valve-T.C.S. in "closed" state or cooling water temperature below 12°C (53°F) or above 60°C (140°F).
   b. Carburetor vacuum port positioned below throttle valve (with engine operated at other than full throttle).

NOTE: Except under the above conditions, the spark timing advances very slightly due to discharge of intake manifold vacuum into the atmosphere.

Testing

1. Ensure that wiring connectors are tightly in place.
2. Ensure that vacuum hoses are properly connected to their positions.
3. Ensure that distributor vacuum controller properly functions.
4. Connect a timing light.
5. Run engine at approximately 1,600 rpm.
6. Disengage clutch. Shift gears in top, 3rd, then neutral positions. Read spark timing in respective shift positions.

   The system is properly functioning if spark timing in top position is approximately 5° greater than that in other positions.

NOTE: Ensure that thermal vacuum valve-T.C.S. is closed or that cooling water is below 12°C (53°F) or above 60°C (140°F).

7. If spark timing does not vary in tests described in step 6, use a voltmeter and check as follows:
8. Check for continuity in electrical wiring with a voltmeter.

   Turn ignition switch on, but do not run engine. Check for voltage across terminals A and B, Fig. 22.

   Electrical wiring circuit is normal if voltmeter readings are as shown in chart below.

Gear Position	Voltmeter Indication
Other	0V
4th (Top)	12V

9. To check each part, proceed as follows:
   a. Vacuum switching valve-T.C.S.
      1. Check vacuum switching valve for proper continuity.
      2. If ohmmeter indicates continuity, check vacuum switching valve to ensure that it clicks when intermittently activated.

         If a click is heard, vacuum switching valve is normal.
      3. Vacuum switching valve is sticking and must be replaced when it does not click in above.
   b. Top detecting switch
      1. To check top detecting switch for proper "ON-OFF" operation, contact leads of an ohmmeter with switch lead wires and shift transmission from "TOP" to other forward gear. If switch does not operate properly, replace.
      2. Install new top detecting switch.
   c. Thermal vacuum valve-T.C.S.
      1. Disconnect, at air cleaner, vacuum hose between thermal vacuum valve and air cleaner.
      2. Disconnect, at vacuum switching valve, vacuum hose between carburetor and vacuum switching valve, then plug valve opening.
      3. Run engine at 2,000 to 2,500 rpm when cooling water temperature is below 12°C (53°F), 15 to 57°C (59 to 134°F), and above 60°C (140°F), respectively, and place finger at vacuum hose opening at each temperature range to check for presence of vacuum.

Cooling Water Temperature	Vacuum Presence
Below 12°C (53°F)	No
15 to 57°C (59 to 134°F)	Yes
Above 60°C (140°F)	No

EARLY FUEL EVAPORATIVE (EFE) SYSTEM

A control valve welded to the valve shaft is installed on the exhaust manifold through bushing. This control valve is called "heat control valve". The heat control valve is actuated by the coil spring, thermostat spring and counterweight, which are assembled on the

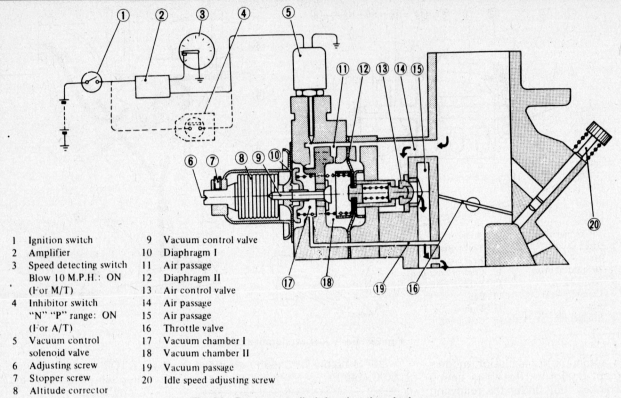

1	Ignition switch	9	Vacuum control valve
2	Amplifier	10	Diaphragm I
3	Speed detecting switch	11	Air passage
	Blow 10 M.P.H.: ON	12	Diaphragm II
	(For M/T)	13	Air control valve
4	Inhibitor switch	14	Air passage
	"N" "P" range: ON	15	Air passage
	(For A/T)	16	Throttle valve
5	Vacuum control	17	Vacuum chamber I
	solenoid valve	18	Vacuum chamber II
6	Adjusting screw	19	Vacuum passage
7	Stopper screw	20	Idle speed adjusting screw
8	Altitude corrector		

Fig. 24 Boost controlled deceleration device

valve shaft projecting to the rear outside of the exhaust manifold. The counterweight is secured to the valve shaft with key, bolt and snap ring.

The early fuel evaporative system is provided with a chamber above a manifold stove mounted between the intake and exhaust manifolds. During engine warm-up, air-fuel mixture in the carburetor is heated in the chamber by exhaust gas. This results in improved evaporation of atomized fuel droplets in the mixture and in smaller content of hydrocarbons (HC) in the exhaust gas especially in cold weather operation.

The exhaust gas flow from the engine is obstructed by the heat control valve in the exhaust manifold, and is changed in direction as shown by the solid lines in Fig. 23. The exhaust gas heats the manifold stove.

Open-close operation of the heat control valve is controlled by the counterweight and thermostat spring which is sensitive to the ambient temperature around the exhaust manifold.

The counterweight rotates counterclockwise and stops at the stopper pin mounted on the exhaust manifold while the engine temperature is low. With this condition, the heat control valve is in the fully closed position, obstructing the flow of exhaust gas. As engine temperature goes up and the ambient temperature becomes high enough to ac-

tuate the thermostat spring, the counterweight begins to rotate clockwise, and again comes into contact with the stopper pin. With this condition, the heat control valve is in the full open position, and exhaust gas passes through the exhaust manifold as shown by the dotted lines in Fig. 23, without heating the manifold stove.

CATALYTIC CONVERTER

The catalytic converter accelerates the chemical reaction of hydrocarbons (HC) and carbon monoxide (CO) in the exhaust gas, and changes them into harmless carbon dioxide (CO_2) and water (H_2O).

The chemical reaction process requires the proper amount of air.

By means of a chemical reaction process as it passes through the catalytic converter, the excess air in the air-fuel mixture (which has not been burned during the combustion process) is utilized to minimize HC and CO emissions.

The exhaust gas which is left unburned during combustion process is gradually oxidized with excess oxygen, and is converted into harmless carbon dioxide (CO_2) and water (H_2O). The catalytic converter, located in the exhaust line, further cleans exhaust gases through catalytic action, and

changes residual hydrocarbons (HC) and carbon monoxide (CO) contained in the exhaust gas into carbon dioxide (CO_2) and water (H_2O) before the exhaust gas is discharged to the atmosphere.

Floor Temperature Warning System

The floor temperature warning system consists of a floor sensor installed on the car's floor, floor sensor relay installed on passenger seat bracket and a floor temperature warning lamp on the instrument panel and wires that connect these parts.

When the floor temperature rises to an abnormal level, the warning lamp will light to call the attention of the driver.

Floor temperature will exceed normal level when temperature rise in the exhaust system succeeding the catalytic converter is caused by either an engine problem or severe driving conditions. Under this condition the floor sensor turns off, causing the starting switch line of the floor sensor relay to turn off and the ignition switch line to turn on; as a result, the floor temperature warning lamp comes on.

When the floor temperature drops below the specified level, the floor sensor relay contacts close.

As the contacts close, the ignition line of the floor sensor relay turns off, while the starting switch side comes on. Thus, the floor temperature warning lamp goes out.

The lamp is functioning satisfactorily if it remains on while the starting motor is in operation. The lamp goes out when the ignition switch is in "IG" position.

BOOST CONTROLLED DECELERATION DEVICE

The Boost Controlled Deceleration Device (B.C.D.D.), Fig. 24, is used to reduce HC emissions emitted during coasting. The B.C.D.D., installed under the throttle chamber as a part of it, supplies additional air to the intake manifold during coasting to maintain the manifold vacuum at the proper operating pressure [470 mmHg (18.5 inHg)].

There are two diaphragms in the device unit. Diaphragm I detects the manifold vacuum and makes the Vacuum Control Valve open when the vacuum exceeds the operating pressure. Diaphragm II operates the Air Control Valve according to the vacuum transmitted through the Vacuum Control Valve. The Air Control Valve regulates the amount of additional air so that the manifold vacuum can be kept at the proper operating pressure. The operating pressure changes depending on altitude; thus, diaphragm II and control valve operations are adjusted automatically in coincidence with the altitude at which the vehicle is driven.

On manual transmission models, this system consists of B.C.D.D., vacuum control solenoid valve, speed-detecting switch and amplifier.

On automatic transmission models, it consists of B.C.D.D., vacuum control solenoid valve and inhibitor switch.

Diaphragm I "10", Fig. 24, monitors the manifold vacuum; when the vacuum exceeds a pre-determined value, it acts

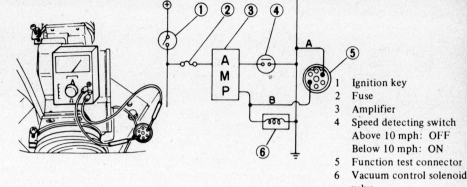

Fig. 25 Testing BCDD circuit. Manual transmission

1 Ignition key
2 Fuse
3 Amplifier
4 Speed detecting switch
  Above 10 mph: OFF
  Below 10 mph: ON
5 Function test connector
6 Vacuum control solenoid valve

so as to open the vacuum control valve "9." This causes the manifold vacuum to be introduced into vacuum chamber II "18" and actuates diaphragm II "12."

When diaphragm II operates, the air control valve "13" opens the passage and introduces the additional air into the manifold.

The amount of air is controlled by the servo-action of the air control valve "13" and vacuum control valve "9" so that the manifold vacuum may be kept at the pre-determined value.

The B.C.D.D. operates when engine speed is in the range of 1,800 to 2,000 rpm.

Manual transmission models:
The vacuum control solenoid valve is controlled by a speed detecting switch that is actuated by the speedometer needle.

As the speed falls below 10 M.P.H., this switch is actuated, producing a signal. This signal actuates the amplifier to open the vacuum control solenoid valve.

Automatic transmission models:
When the shift lever is in the "N" or "P" position, the inhibitor switch mounted on the transmission turns on to open the vacuum control solenoid valve.

Testing
Manual Transmission
1. Check for continuity between A and B when car is brought to a complete stop, Fig. 25.
   B.C.D.D. circuit is functioning properly if continuity exists and voltmeter reading is 0 volts (d-c) in step 2 below.
   If continuity does not exist, check for disconnected connector and/or faulty amplifier, speed detecting switch or B.C.D.D. solenoid valve.
2. Check for presence of voltage across A and B [at a speed of more than 16 km/h (10 MPH)], Fig. 25.
   a. If voltmeter reading is 0 volts at a speed of more than 16 km/h (10 MPH), circuit is functioning properly.
   b. If voltmeter reading is not 0 volts, check for disconnected connector, burned fuse, faulty amplifier, B.C.D.D. solenoid valve or speed detecting switch.
3. If, by above checks, faulty part or unit is located, it should be removed and tested again. If necessary, replace.

Automatic Transmission
1. Turn ignition key to "ON" position.
2. With inhibitor switch "ON" ("N" or

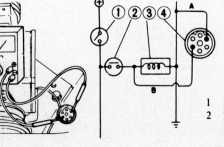

1 Ignition key
2 Inhibitor switch
  N.P. range: ON
  1, 2, D, R, range: OFF
3 Vacuum control solenoid valve
4 Function test connector

Fig. 26 Testing BCDD circuit. Automatic transmission

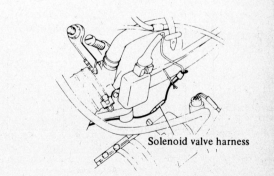

Solenoid valve harness

Fig. 27 Testing solenoid valve

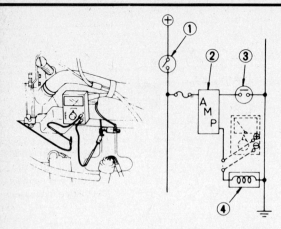

Fig. 28 Testing amplifier

1 Ignition key
2 Amplifire
3 Speed detecting switch
   Above 10 mph : OFF
   Below 10 mph : ON
4 B.C.D.D. solenoid valve

"P" position), check for presence of voltage across A and B, Fig. 26.

a. If voltmeter reading is 12 volts (d-c), B.C.D.D. circuit is functioning properly.

b. If voltmeter reading is zero, check for disconnected connector, faulty solenoid valve or inhibitor switch.

3. With inhibitor switch "OFF" ("1", "2", "D" or "R" position), check for resistance between A and B, Fig. 26.

a. If ohmmeter reading is 15 to 28 ohms, circuit is functioning properly.

b. If ohmmeter reading is not within specifications, check for poor connection of connector, faulty

B.C.D.D. solenoid valve or inhibitor switch.

4. If, by above checks, faulty part or unit is located, it should be removed and tested again. If necessary, replace.

B.C.D.D. Solenoid Valve

1. Turn on engine key. (Do not start engine.)

2. Ensure that solenoid valve clicks when intermittently activated, Fig. 27.

3. If a click is heard, solenoid valve is normal.

4. If a click is not heard, check for continuity with a circuit tester. If discontinuity is detected, replace solenoid valve.

Amplifier

1. Set circuit tester in D-C ampere range (1A min, full scale), connect test probes of tester, Fig. 28.

2. Turn ignition key to "ON" position.

3. Ensure that tester pointer deflects when ignition key is turned on.

4. If tester pointer does not deflect when solenoid valve and speed detecting switch circuits are functioning properly, amplifier is faulty.

B.C.D.D. Adjustment

1. Remove the harness of solenoid valve.

2. Connect rubber hose between vacuum gauge and intake manifold.

3. Warm up the engine until it is heated to operating temperature.
   Then adjust the engine to normal idling setting.

4. Run the engine under no load. Increase engine speed to 3,000 to 3,500 rpm, then quickly close throttle valve.

5. At that time, the manifold vacuum pressure increases abruptly to 23.6 inHg or above and then gradually decreases to the level set at idling.

6. Check that the B.C.D.D. set pressure is within the specified pressure.
   Specified pressure (0 m, sea level and 760 mmHg (29.9 inHg), atmospheric pressure) is 18.1-18.9 inch Hg.

NOTE:

a. When atmospheric pressure is known, operating pressure will be found by tracing the arrow line "A," Fig. 29. When altitude is known, operating pressure will be found by tracing the arrow line "B," Fig. 29.

b. When checking the set pressure of B.C.D.D., find the specified set

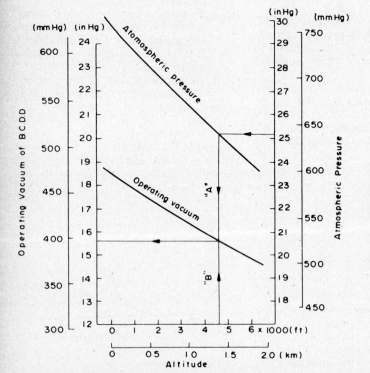

Fig. 29 BCDD operating pressure & altitude chart

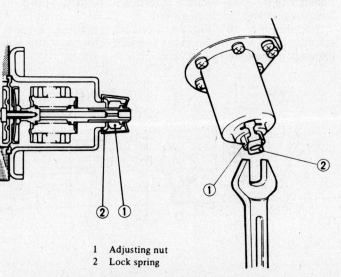

1 Adjusting nut
2 Lock spring

Fig. 30 Adjusting BCDD operating pressure

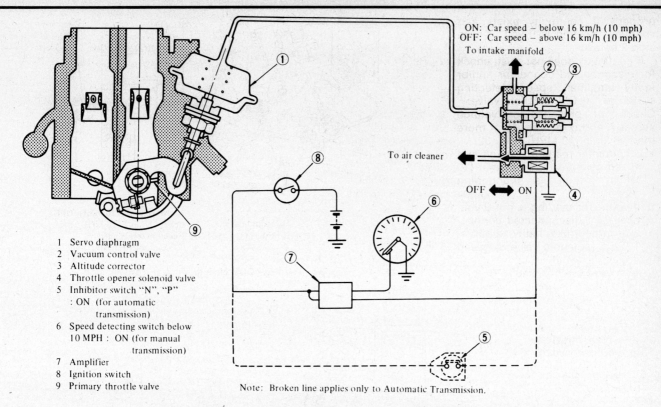

ON: Car speed – below 16 km/h (10 mph)
OFF: Car speed – above 16 km/h (10 mph)
To intake manifold

To air cleaner

OFF ←→ ON

1 Servo diaphragm
2 Vacuum control valve
3 Altitude corrector
4 Throttle opener solenoid valve
5 Inhibitor switch "N", "P"
     : ON (for automatic
                 transmission)
6 Speed detecting switch below
     10 MPH : ON (for manual
                        transmission)
7 Amplifier
8 Ignition switch
9 Primary throttle valve

Note: Broken line applies only to Automatic Transmission.

Fig. 31 Throttle opener control system (Typical)

pressure in Fig. 29, from the atmospheric pressure and altitude of the given location.

7. If it is higher than the set level, turn the adjusting nut clockwise until correct adjustment is made, Fig. 30.
8. Accelerate the engine and check for adjustment.
9. If it is lower than the set level, turn the adjusting screw counterclockwise until correct adjustment is made.
10. Race the engine and check for adjustment.

If engine speed cannot be decreased to idling when checking B.C.D.D. set pressure, proceed as follows:

When the engine speed does not fall to idling speed, it is necessary to reduce the negative idling pressure of the manifold to lower than the set pressure of the B.C.D.D. (The engine speed will not drop to idling speed when the negative idling pressure is higher than the set pressure of the B.C.D.D.).

THROTTLE OPENER CONTROL SYSTEM (T.O.C.S.)

The function of the throttle opener, Fig. 31, is to open the throttle valve of the carburetor slightly while the car is in deceleration. During deceleration, the manifold vacuum rises and the quantity of mixture in the engine is not sufficient for normal combustion to continue; consequently, a great amount of unburned H.C. is emitted.

Carburetors equipped with the throttle opener supply the engine with an adequate charge of combustible mixture to maintain proper combustion during deceleration, resulting in a dramatic reduction in H.C. emission.

The system for the manual transmission model consists of servo diaphragm, vacuum control valve, throttle opener solenoid valve, speed detecting switch and amplifier. On the automatic transmission model, an inhibitor switch and inhibitor relay are used in place of speed detecting switch and amplifier on the manual transmission model. An altitude corrector fitted to vacuum control valve serves to automatically regulate the operating pressure in the system with variation of atmospheric pressure.

At the moment when the manifold vacuum increases, as occurs upon deceleration, the vacuum control valve opens to transfer the manifold vacuum to the servo diaphragm chamber, and the throttle valve of the carburetor opens slightly.

Under this condition, a proper amount of fresh air is sucked into the combustion chamber. As the result, complete combustion of fuel is assisted by this additional air, and the amount of H.C. contained in exhaust gases is dramatically reduced.

Manual Transmission Models

The throttle opener solenoid valve is controlled by a speed detecting switch which is actuated by the speedometer needle.

As the car speed falls below 16 km/h (10 MPH), this switch is activated, producing a signal.

The signal is led to the amplifier so that the signal can be amplified to a degree large enough to actuate the throttle opener solenoid valve.

The throttle opener solenoid valve is actuated and the servo-diaphragm chamber is opened to the atmosphere.

In this case the servo-diaphragm does not operate.

Automatic Transmission Models

As long as the shift lever is in the "N" or "P" position, the inhibitor switch on the transmission is turned on, and the throttle opener solenoid valve is actuated. Under this condition, the servo-diaphragm does not operate, because of the same reason as mentioned for the manual transmission model.

Testing

Manual Transmission

1. Check for continuity between A and B when car is brought to a complete stop.

     T.O.C.S. circuit is functioning

properly if continuity exists and voltmeter reading is 0 volt (d-c) in step 2 below.

If continuity does not exist, check for disconnected connector and/or faulty amplifier, speed detecting switch or T.O.C.S. solenoid valve.

2. Check for presence of voltage across A and B [at a speed of more than 16 km/h (10 MPH)], Fig. 32.

   a. If voltmeter reading is 0 volt at a speed of more than 16 km/h (10 MPH), circuit is functioning properly.

   b. If voltmeter reading is not 0 volt, check for disconnected connector, burned fuse, faulty amplifier, T.O.C.S. solenoid valve or speed detecting switch.

3. If, by above checks, faulty part or unit is located, it should be removed and tested again. If necessary, replace.

Automatic Transmission

1. With inhibitor switch "ON" ("N" or "P" position), check for presence of voltage across A and B, Fig. 33.

   a. If voltmeter reading is 12 volts, T.O.C.S. circuit is functioning properly.

   b. If voltmeter reading is zero, check for disconnected connector, faulty solenoid valve or inhibitor switch.

2. With inhibitor switch "OFF" ("1," "2," "D" or "R" position), check for resistance between A and B, Fig. 33.

   a. If ohmmeter reading is 25 ohms or below, circuit is functioning properly.

   b. If ohmmeter reading is 32 ohms or above, check for poor connection of connector, faulty T.O.C.S. solenoid valve or inhibitor relay.

3. If, by above checks, faulty part or unit is located, it should be removed

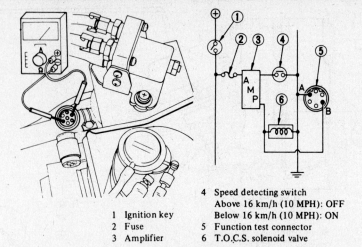

1 Ignition key
2 Fuse
3 Amplifier
4 Speed detecting switch
   Above 16 km/h (10 MPH): OFF
   Below 16 km/h (10 MPH): ON
5 Function test connector
6 T.O.C.S. solenoid valve

Fig. 32 Testing TOCS circuit. Manual transmission

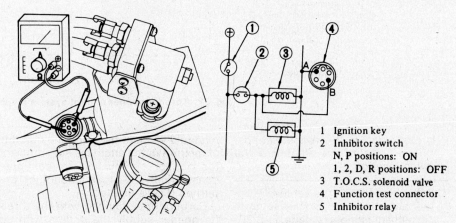

1 Ignition key
2 Inhibitor switch
   N, P positions: ON
   1, 2, D, R positions: OFF
3 T.O.C.S. solenoid valve
4 Function test connector
5 Inhibitor relay

Fig. 33 Testing TOCS circuit. Automatic transmission

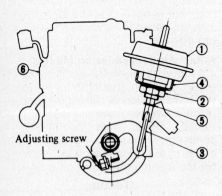

Adjusting screw

1 Servo diaphragm
2 Lock nut
3 Link
4 Bracket
5 Stopper
6 Carburetor

Fig. 34 Adjusting servo diaphragm

1-304

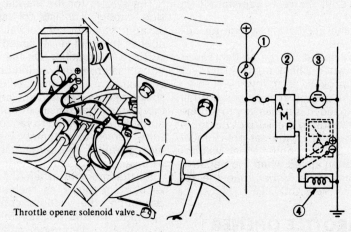

Throttle opener solenoid valve

1 Ignition key
2 Amplifier
3 Speed detecting switch
   Above 16 km/h (10 MPH): OFF
   Below 16 km/h (10 MPH): ON
4 Throttle opener solenoid valve

Fig. 35 Testing amplifier

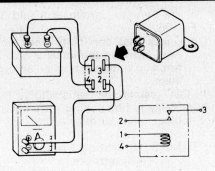

Fig. 36   Testing inhibitor relay

and tested again. If necessary, replace.

Servo Diaphragm

1. Connect engine tachometer.
2. Warm up the engine until it has reached operating temperature.
3. Disconnect rubber hose between servo-diaphragm and vacuum control valve. Then, connect rubber hose to intake manifold.
4. The servo-diaphragm is functioning properly, if engine speed is 1650-1850 rpm on models except California or 1900-2100 on California models.

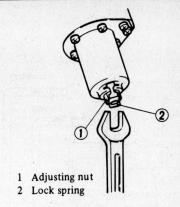

1   Adjusting nut
2   Lock spring

Fig. 37   Adjusting TOCS operating pressure

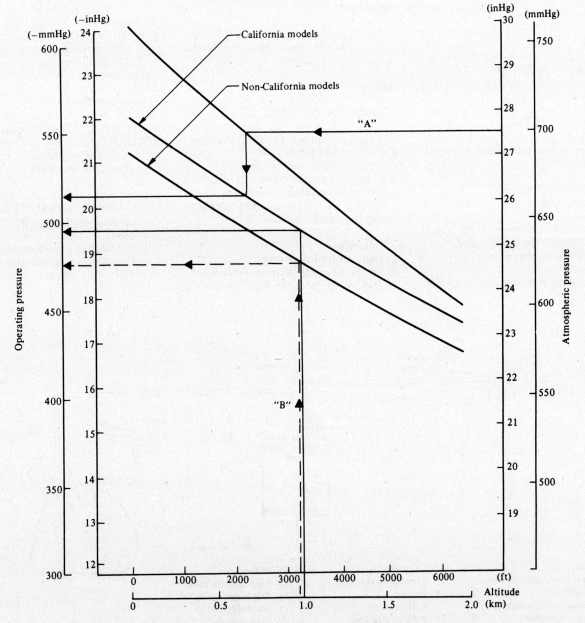

Note: This diagram is applicable both to Manual and Automatic transmission models.

Fig. 38   TOCS operating pressure & altitude chart

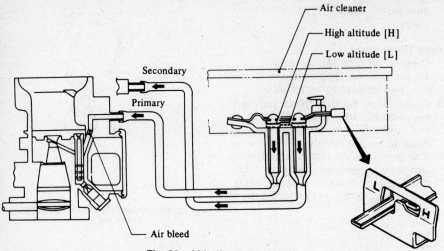

Fig. 39 Altitude compensator

5. If necessary, adjust the engine speed until it is in the specified range, using servo-diaphragm adjusting screw, Fig. 34.

When engine speed is lower than the prescribed range:

Turn adjusting screw clockwise.

When engine speed is higher than the prescribed range:

Turn adjusting screw counterclockwise.

T.O.C.S. Solenoid Valve

1. Turn on engine key. (Do not start engine.)
2. Ensure that solenoid valve clicks when intermittently activated.
3. If a click is heard, solenoid valve is normal.
4. If a click is not heard, check for con-

tinuity with a circuit tester. If discontinuity is detected, replace solenoid valve.

Amplifier

1. Set circuit tester in DC ampere range (1A, full scale), connect test probes of tester, Fig. 35.
2. Turn ignition key to "ON" position.
3. Ensure that tester pointer occillates when ignition key is turned on.
4. If tester pointer does not occillate when solenoid valve and speed detecting switch circuits are functioning properly, amplifier is faulty.

Inhibitor Relay

1. Remove inhibitor relay.
2. Apply 12 volts across terminals 1 and 4 to ensure that continuity

exists between terminals 2 and 3, Fig. 36.
a. Check that continuity does not exist between terminals 2 and 3 when no voltage is applied across them.

If test results are satisfactory, inhibitor relay is functioning properly. If not, replace inhibitor relay.

T.O.C.S. Operating Pressure Adjustment

1. Remove the harness of solenoid valve.
2. Connect rubber hose between vacuum gauge and intake manifold.
3. Warm up the engine until it is heated to operating temperature.

Then adjust the engine at normal idling setting.
4. Run the engine under no load. Increase engine speed to 3,000 to 3,500 rpm, then quickly close throttle valve.
5. At the time, the manifold vacuum pressure increases abruptly to 23.6 inHg. or above and then gradually decreases to the level set at idling.
6. Check that the T.O.C.S. set pressure is within specified pressure.

Specified pressure [0 m, sea level and 760 mmHg (30 in Hg), atmospheric pressure]: 20.5-22 inch Hg. on models except California and 21.3-22.8 inch Hg. for California models.
7. If it is higher than the set level, turn the adjusting screw counterclockwise until correct adjustment is made, Fig. 37

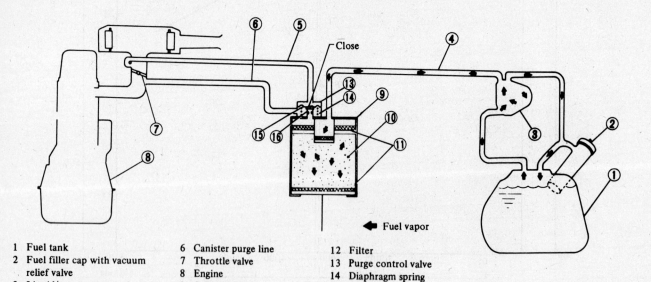

1 Fuel tank	6 Canister purge line	12 Filter
2 Fuel filler cap with vacuum relief valve	7 Throttle valve	13 Purge control valve
3 Liquid/vapor separator	8 Engine	14 Diaphragm spring
4 Vapor vent line	9 Carbon canist	15 Diaphragm
5 Vacuum signal line	10 Activated carbon	16 Fixed orifice
	11 Screen	

Fig. 40 Evaporative emission system (Typical)

a. When atmospheric pressure known, operating pressure will be found by tracing the arrow line "A," Fig. 38. When altitude is known, operating pressure will be found by tracing the arrow line "B," Fig. 38.

b. When checking T.O.C.S. operating pressure, note atmospheric pressure and above sea level in which check is to be made, and determine set pressure by the information furnished in Fig. 38.

8. Accelerate the engine and check the adjustment.

9. If it is lower than the set level, turn the adjusting screw counterclockwise until correct adjustment is made.

10. Accelerate the engine and check the adjustment.

If engine speed can not be decreased to idling when checking T.O.C.S. operating pressure, proceed as follows:

When the engine speed does not fall to idling speed, it is necessary to reduce the negative idling pressure of the manifold to lower than the operating pressure of the T.O.C.S.

ALTITUDE COMPENSATOR

The higher the altitude, the richer the air-fuel mixture ratio and therefore, the higher exhaust gas emissions, even though the engine is properly adjusted for low altitude driving.

The altitude compensator, Fig. 39 is designed to meet emission standards for driving in both low and high altitudes. At high altitudes, additional air is supplied to the carburetor by the altitude compensator. When the altitude compensator lever is set at "H," air is conducted through an air passage to the carburetor. The air passage is closed when the lever is set at "L."

EVAPORATIVE EMISSION SYSTEM

The evaporative emission control system, Fig. 40 is used to reduce hydrocarbons emitted to the atmosphere from the fuel system. This reduction of hydrocarbons is accomplished by activated charcoals in the carbon canister.

This system is made up of the following:

1. Fuel tank with positive sealing filler cap.
2. Vapor-liquid separator.
3. Check valve.
4. Vapor vent line
5. Carbon canister.
6. Vacuum signal line.
7. Canister purge line.

Fuel vapors from the sealed fuel tank are led into the carbon canister.

The canister is filled with activated charcoals to absorb the fuel vapors when the engine is at rest or at idling.

As the throttle valve opens and car speed increases, vacuum pressure in the vacuum signal line forces the purge control valve to open, and admits an orifice to intake manifold and fuel vapor is then drawn into the intake manifold through the canister purge line. See Figure EC-50.

Clutch & Transmission Section

Clutch & Manual Transmission Section

CLUTCH PEDAL FREE PLAY ADJUSTMENT
Exc. F10

1. Adjust clutch pedal free play by adjusting the length of the push rod to the clearance between the clevis pin and clutch pedal, Fig. 1, to .04-.12 inch on B110, B210 and 200SX models or .04-.20 inch on all other models.

F10

1. Adjust stopper bolt to contact clutch pedal lever and secure with locknut, Fig. 2.
2. Clutch pedal free play should be .235-.551 inch.

CLUTCH, REPLACE
Exc. F10

1. Remove transmission as outlined elsewhere in this section.
2. Insert a dummy shaft into the clutch disc hub.

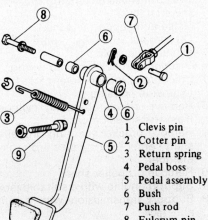

1 Clevis pin
2 Cotter pin
3 Return spring
4 Pedal boss
5 Pedal assembly
6 Bush
7 Push rod
8 Fulcrum pin
9 Pedal stopper

Fig. 1 Clutch pedal adjustment. Exc. F10

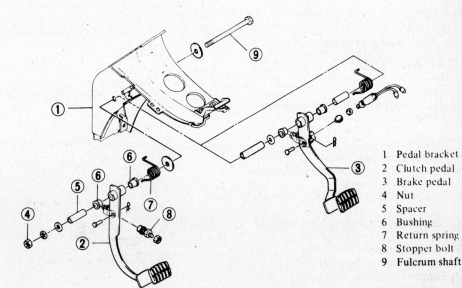

1 Pedal bracket
2 Clutch pedal
3 Brake pedal
4 Nut
5 Spacer
6 Bushing
7 Return spring
8 Stopper bolt
9 Fulcrum shaft

Fig. 2 Clutch pedal adjustment. F10

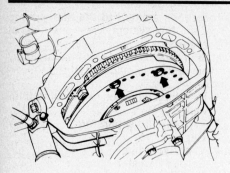

Fig. 3 Clutch cover bolt location. F10

3. Loosen bolts attaching clutch cover, to flywheel alternately.
4. Remove clutch disc and cover assembly.
5. Remove release bearing.
6. Reverse procedure to install.

F10

1. Disconnect battery ground cable.
2. Disconnect the following: fresh air duct, engine harness connector on clutch housing, high tension wire between ignition coil and distributor and carbon canister hoses.
3. Remove inspection cover from upper section of clutch housing, Fig. 3. Remove clutch cover bolts.
4. Turn steering wheel fully to the right.
5. Remove inspection cover from right side wheel house.
6. Remove release lever and the six bolts on bearing housing.
7. Remove primary drive gear through inspection opening, Fig. 4.
8. Remove clutch cover and disc assembly through inspection opening in upper section of clutch housing, Fig. 5. Remove diaphragm.
9. Reverse procedure to install.

MANUAL TRANSMISSION, REPLACE
B110

1. Disconnect battery ground cable.
2. Raise and support vehicle.
3. Disconnect exhaust pipe from exhaust manifold.
4. Remove propeller shaft.
5. Disconnect speedometer cable from extension housing.
6. Disconnect back-up light switch wiring.
7. Disconnect shift rods from shift levers.
8. Remove clutch operating cylinder from transmission case.
9. Support engine with a suitable jack.
10. Support transmission with a suitable jack.

11. Remove nuts attaching transmission to crossmember and the crossmember mounting bolts.
12. Remove starter motor.
13. Lower and remove transmission from vehicle.
14. Reverse procedure to install.

B210 & 200SX

1. Disconnect battery ground cable.
2. Remove console box and floor hole cover attaching screws. Remove rubber boots and cover.
3. Place shift lever in "Neutral."
4. Remove nut and shift lever pin from transmission striking rod guide and the shift lever.
5. Raise and support vehicle.
6. Disconnect front exhaust pipe.
7. Disconnect back-up lamp switch, top switch and neutral switch wiring.
8. Disconnect speedometer cable from extension housing.
9. Remove propeller shaft.
10. Remove clutch operating cylinder from transmission case.
11. Support engine with a suitable jack.
12. Support transmission with a suitable jack.
13. Remove rear engine mount bolts and the crossmember mount bolts.
14. Remove starter motor.
15. Remove bolts securing transmission to engine and gusset.
16. Slide transmission rearward and lower from vehicle.
17. Reverse procedure to install.

510, 610 & 710

1. Disconnect battery ground cable.
2. If equipped with catalytic converter, disconnect catalytic converter sensor harness and remove harness connector.
3. On all models, raise and support vehicle.
4. Loosen shift lever nut and remove lever.
5. If equipped with catalytic converter, disconnect front exhaust pipe from catalytic converter.
6. On models not equipped with

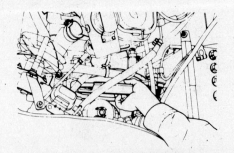

Fig. 5 Clutch cover removal. F10

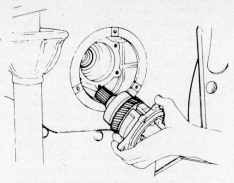

Fig. 4 Primary drive gear assembly removal. F10

catalytic converter, disconnect exhaust pipe from exhaust manifold.
7. On all models, disconnect back-up lamp switch, top switch and neutral switch wiring.
8. Remove clutch operating cylinder from transmission case.
9. Disconnect speedometer cable from extension housing.
10. Remove propeller shaft.
11. Support engine with a suitable jack.
12. Support transmission with a suitable jack.
13. Remove crossmember mounting bolts and rear transmission mount bolts.
14. Remove starter motor.
15. Remove engine to gusset bolts.
16. Remove bolts securing gussets to rear engine plate and transmission case, then separate gussets from engine and transmission.
17. Remove engine to transmission bolts. Lower and remove transmission from vehicle.
18. Reverse procedure to install.

810 & Pick-Up

1. Disconnect battery ground cable.
2. Place shift lever in "Neutral."
3. Remove "C" ring and shift lever pin from transmission striking rod, then the shift lever.
4. Raise and support vehicle.
5. Disconnect exhaust pipe from exhaust manifold.
6. Disconnect back-up lamp wiring.
7. Disconnect speedometer cable from extension housing.
8. Remove clutch operating cylinder from transmission case.
9. Remove bracket securing propeller shaft center bearing on third crossmember.
10. Remove propeller shaft.
11. Support engine with a suitable jack.
12. Support transmission with a suitable jack.
13. Remove rear engine mounting insulator bolts and the rear mounting member bolts.
14. Remove starter motor.

15. Remove engine to transmission bolts. Lower and remove transmission from vehicle.
16. Reverse procedure to install.

F10

1. Disconnect battery ground cable.
2. Remove engine and transmission assembly from vehicle.
3. Remove bolts securing transmission to engine and separate engine from transmission.
4. Reverse procedure to install.

240Z, 260Z & 280Z

1. Disconnect battery ground cable.
2. Disconnect accelerator linkage.
3. Remove center console.
4. Place shift lever in "Neutral" position.
5. Remove "C" ring and shift lever pin from transmission striking rod, then the shift lever.
6. Raise and support vehicle.
7. Disconnect exhaust pipe from exhaust manifold.
8. Remove exhaust pipe bracket from extension housing.
9. Disconnect back-up lamp switch and neutral switch wiring.
10. Remove clutch operating cylinder from transmission case.
11. Disconnect speedometer cable from extension housing.
12. Remove insulator attaching bolts and position insulator on exhaust pipe.
13. Remove propeller shaft.
14. Support engine with a suitable jack.
15. Support transmission with a suitable jack.
16. Remove nut attaching mounting member to rear mounting insulator. Remove mounting member attaching bolts, then the mounting member.
17. Remove starter motor.
18. Remove engine to transmission bolts.
19. Lower and remove transmission from vehicle.
20. Reverse procedure to install.

Jatco Automatic Transmission Section

TROUBLE-SHOOTING

Engine Does Not Start In "N" or "P"

1. Faulty ignition switch or starter motor.
2. Maladjusted manual linkage.
3. Defective inhibitor switch or wiring.

Engine Starts In Ranges Other Than "N" or "P"

1. Maladjusted manual linkage.
2. Defective inhibitor switch or wiring.

Harsh Shift Between "N" & "D"

1. High idle speed.
2. Defective vacuum diaphragm.
3. Throttle oil pressure incorrect.
4. Defective manual valve.
5. Defective rear clutch.

No Drive In "D," But In "2," "1" & "R"

1. Maladjusted manual linkage.
2. Throttle oil pressure incorrect.
3. Defective manual valve.
4. Defective one-way clutch.

No Drive In "D," "2" & "1," But In "R"
(Clutch Slips, Poor Acceleration)

1. Low oil level.
2. Maladjusted manual linkage.
3. Defective governor valve.
4. Throttle oil pressure incorrect.
5. Defective manual valve.
6. Defective rear clutch.
7. Leaking oil passages.

No Drive In "R," But In "D," "2" & "1"
(Clutch Slips, Poor Acceleration)

1. Check oil level.
2. Maladjusted manual linkage.
3. Throttle oil pressure incorrect.
4. Defective manual valve.
5. Defective low-reverse brake.
6. Defective front clutch.
7. Defective rear clutch.
8. Leaking oil passages.
9. Missing or stuck front clutch check ball.

No Drive In Any Range

1. Check oil level.
2. Maladjusted manual linkage.
3. Throttle oil pressure incorrect.
4. Defective manual valve.
5. Defective low-reverse brake.
6. Defective oil pump.
7. Parking linkage does not disengage.

Slipping Clutches or Brake

1. Check oil level.
2. Maladjusted manual linkage.
3. Throttle oil pressure incorrect.
4. Defective manual valve.
5. Defective vacuum diaphragm.
6. Defective oil pump.
7. Leaking oil passages.

Drive In "N"

1. Maladjusted manual linkage.
2. Defective manual valve.
3. Defective rear clutch.

Vehicle Cannot Attain Maximum Speed

1. Check oil level.
2. Maladjusted manual linkage.
3. Throttle oil pressure incorrect.
4. Defective torque converter.
5. Defective band servo.
6. Defective manual valve.
7. Defective brake band.
8. Defective low-reverse brake.
9. Defective rear clutch
10. Defective front clutch.
11. Defective oil pump.

Excessive Creep At Idle

1. High idle speed.

No "2-3" Upshift

1. Maladjusted manual linkage.
2. Defective vacuum diaphragm.
3. Defective manual valve.
4. Defective governor valve.
5. Defective band servo.
6. Defective brake band.
7. Leaking oil passages.

No "1-2" Upshift

1. Maladjusted manual linkage.
2. Defective vacuum diaphragm.
3. Defective kickdown switch or downshift solenoid.
4. Defective manual valve.
5. Defective governor valve.
6. Defective band servo.
7. Defective front clutch.
8. Leaking oil passages.
9. Missing or stuck front clutch check ball.

Delayed Upshifts

1. Defective vacuum diaphragm.
2. Defective downshift solenoid or downshift switch.
3. Throttle oil pressure incorrect.
4. Defective manual valve.
5. Defective governor valve.
6. Leaking oil passages.

Upshift From "1 Directly to 3"

1. Defective manual valve.
2. Defective governor valve.
3. Defective brake band.
4. Leaking oil passages.

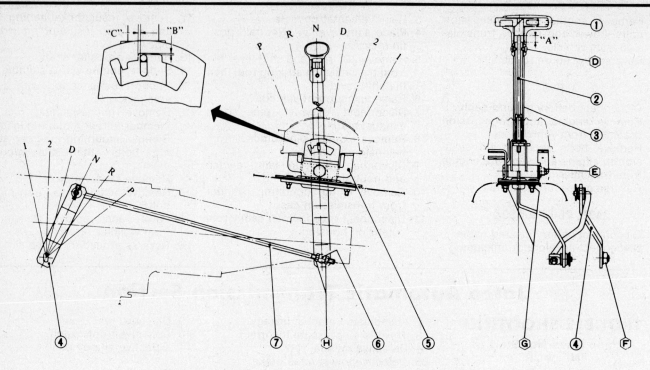

1 Control lever knob
2 Pusher
3 Control lever assembly
4 Selector range lever
5 Control lever bracket
6 Joint trunnion
7 Selector rod

Tightening torque (T) of
nuts and screws   kg-m (ft-lb)
Ⓓ T : 0.07 to 0.13 (0.51 to 0.94)
Ⓔ T : 1.6 to 2.2 (12 to 16)
Ⓕ T : 3 to 4 (22 to 29)
Ⓖ T : 0.35 to 0.45 (2.5 to 3.3)
Ⓗ T : 0.8 to 1.1 (5.8 to 8.0)

Fig. 1   Manual linkage adjustment

Harsh "1-2" Upshift

1. Defective vacuum diaphragm.
2. Defective manual valve.
3. Defective band servo.
4. Defective brake band.

Harsh "2-3" Upshift

1. Defective vacuum diaphragm.
2. Defective downshift solenoid or kickdown switch.
3. Throttle pressure incorrect.
4. Defective manual valve.
5. Defective band servo.
6. Defective front clutch.

Slipping "1-2" Shift

1. Check oil level.
2. Maladjusted manual linkage.
3. Defective vacuum diaphragm.
4. Throttle oil pressure incorrect.
5. Defective manual valve.
6. Defective band servo.
7. Defective brake band.
8. Leaking oil passages.

Slipping "2-3" Shift

1. Check oil level.
2. Maladjusted manual linkage.
3. Defective vacuum diaphragm.

4. Throttle oil pressure incorrect.
5. Defective manual valve.
6. Defective band servo.
7. Defective front clutch.
8. Leaking oil passages.
9. Missing or stuck front clutch check ball.

No "3-2" Downshift

1. Defective vacuum diaphragm.
2. Defective manual valve.
3. Defective governor valve.
4. Defective band servo.
5. Defective front clutch.
6. Defective brake band.
7. Leaking oil passages.

No "2-1" or "3-1" Downshift

1. Defective vacuum diaphragm.
2. Defective manual valve.
3. Defective governor valve.
4. Defective band servo.
5. Defective brake band.
6. Defective one-way clutch.

High Downshift Point Between "3-2" & "2-1"

1. Maladjusted manual linkage.
2. Defective vacuum diaphragm.

3. Defective downshift solenoid or kickdown switch.
4. Throttle oil pressure incorrect.
5. Defective manual valve.
6. Defective governor valve.
7. Leaking oil passages.

No Kickdown

1. Defective downshift solenoid or downshift switch.
2. Defective vacuum diaphragm.
3. Defective manual valve.
4. Defective governor valve.
5. Defective low-reverse brake.
6. Leaking oil passages.

Slipping "3-2" Downshift

1. Defective vacuum diaphragm.
2. Throttle oil pressure incorrect.
3. Defective manual valve.
4. Defective band servo.
5. Defective front clutch.
6. Defective brake band.
7. Leaking oil passages.
8. Missing or stuck front clutch check ball.

Engine Flares On "1-2" Upshift

1. Check oil level.
2. Maladjusted manual linkage.

3. Defective vacuum diaphragm.
4. High idle speed.
5. Defective manual valve.
6. Defective brake band.
7. Defective oil pump.

Noise In "P" or "N"

1. Check oil level.
2. Throttle oil pressure incorrect.
3. Defective oil pump.

Noise In "D," "2," "1" & "R"

1. Check oil level.
2. Throttle oil pressure incorrect.
3. Defective oil pump.
4. Defective one-way clutch.
5. Defective planetary gear.

MANUAL LINKAGE, ADJUST

1. Remove control knob and adjust dimension "A," Fig. 1, to .43-.47 inch.
2. Install control knob, then check and adjust dimension "B," Fig. 1, to .004-.043 by rotating pusher, "2," Fig. 1.
3. Loosen adjusting nuts "H" and place control lever "3" and selector lever "4" in "N" position, Fig. 1. Adjust clearance "C," Fig. 1, by rotating adjusting nuts at trunnion "6," Fig. 1.
4. Check for proper operation.

TRANS., REPLACE
B110, B210 & 200SX

1. Disconnect battery ground cable.
2. Raise and support vehicle.
3. Remove propeller shaft.
4. Disconnect front exhaust pipe.
5. Disconnect selector lever from manual shaft.
6. Disconnect inhibitor switch wiring.
7. Disconnect vacuum tube from vacuum diaphragm and the downshift solenoid wiring.

8. Disconnect speedometer cable from extension housing.
9. Disconnect oil charging pipe.
10. Disconnect oil cooler pipes from transmission case.
11. Support engine with a suitable jack.
12. Support transmission with a suitable jack.
13. Remove starter motor.
14. Remove converter housing cover and the torque converter to flywheel bolts.
15. Remove rear engine mount bolts and crossmember bolts, then disconnect engine and hand brake bracket.
16. Remove engine to transmission bolts.
17. Lower transmission from vehicle.
18. Reverse procedure to install.

510, 610, 710 & 810

1. Disconnect battery ground cable.
2. Disconnect torsion shaft from accelerator linkage.
3. If equipped with catalytic converter, disconnect catalytic converter sensor harness and remove harness protector.
4. On all models, raise and support vehicle.
5. If equipped with catalytic converter, disconnect exhaust pipe from catalytic converter.
6. On models not equipped with catalytic converter, disconnect exhaust pipe from exhaust manifold.
7. Remove propeller shaft.
8. Disconnect selector lever from manual shaft.
9. Disconnect inhibitor switch wiring.
10. Disconnect vacuum tube from diaphragm and the wiring from the downshift solenoid.
11. Disconnect speedometer cable from extension housing.
12. Disconnect oil charging pipe.
13. Disconnect oil cooler pipes from transmission case.

14. Support engine with a suitable jack.
15. Support transmission with a suitable jack.
16. Remove engine rear plate rubber plug.
17. Remove torque converter to flywheel bolts.
18. Remove rear engine mount bolts and the crossmember mounting bolts.
19. Remove starter motor.
20. Remove engine to transmission bolts. Lower and remove transmission from vehicle.
21. Reverse procedure to install.

240Z, 260Z, 280Z & Pick-Up

1. Disconnect battery ground cable.
2. Disconnect torsion shaft from accelerator linkage.
3. Raise and support vehicle.
4. Remove propeller shaft.
5. Disconnect exhaust pipe from exhaust manifold.
6. Remove selector lever from manual shaft.
7. Disconnect inhibitor switch wiring.
8. Disconnect vacuum tube from diaphragm and the downshift switch wiring.
9. Disconnect speedometer cable from extension housing.
10. Disconnect oil charging pipe.
11. Disconnect oil cooler pipes from transmission case.
12. Support engine with a suitable jack.
13. Support transmission with a suitable jack.
14. Remove converter housing cover.
15. Remove torque converter to flywheel bolts.
16. Remove rear engine mount bolts and the crossmember mounting bolts.
17. Remove starter motor.
18. Remove engine to transmission bolts. Lower and remove transmission from vehicle.
19. Reverse procedure to install.

Rear Axle & Brakes Section

WHEEL BEARINGS, ADJUST
F10 Models

1. Raise and support rear of vehicle and remove wheel.
2. Torque wheel lock nut to 18-22 ft. lbs. while rotating drum.
3. Loosen lock nut, then hand tighten the nut, using a socket.

4. Align cotter pin hole in spindle with slit in lock nut. If holes do not align, tighten lock nut slightly.
5. Measuring wheel bearing torque required to start rotation. Using a spring scale hooked on a hub bolt, starting torque should be as follows:
   a. With new grease seal, 1.1-2.6 lbs.
   b. With used grease seal, 1.5 lbs. maximum.

AXLE SHAFT, REPLACE
Exc. Models With Independent Suspension

1. Raise and support rear of vehicle.
2. Disconnect parking brake cable from rear of brake drum.
3. Disconnect brake tube from rear of brake drum.
4. Remove brake drum.
5. Remove nuts retaining brake sup-

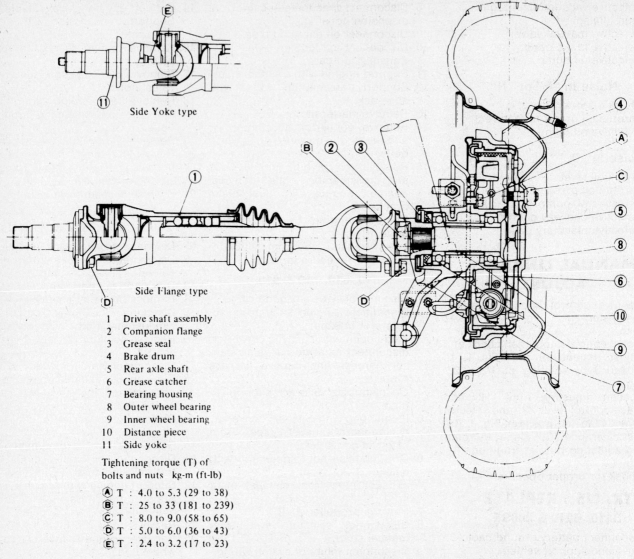

Side Yoke type

Side Flange type

1   Drive shaft assembly
2   Companion flange
3   Grease seal
4   Brake drum
5   Rear axle shaft
6   Grease catcher
7   Bearing housing
8   Outer wheel bearing
9   Inner wheel bearing
10 Distance piece
11 Side yoke

Tightening torque (T) of
bolts and nuts   kg-m (ft-lb)

Ⓐ T : 4.0 to 5.3 (29 to 38)
Ⓑ T : 25 to 33 (181 to 239)
Ⓒ T : 8.0 to 9.0 (58 to 65)
Ⓓ T : 5.0 to 6.0 (36 to 43)
Ⓔ T : 2.4 to 3.2 (17 to 23)

Fig. 1   Rear axle cross-section. Models with independent rear suspension (Typical)

port plate to axle.
6. With a suitable puller, pull axle shaft and brake support plate from axle assembly.
7. Replace oil seal in axle tube.
8. Cut a notch in bearing collar with a chisel.
9. Press bearing from axle shaft.
10. Reverse procedure to install.

With Independent Suspension, Figs. 1 & 2

1. Raise and support rear of vehicle and remove wheel.
2. Remove axle shaft bolts at wheel attachment.
3. Remove rear wheel bearing lock nut.
4. Remove rear axle shaft with a suitable puller.
5. Remove companion flange and bearing washer.
6. Remove inner rear wheel bearing and oil seal.

7. Press rear wheel bearing from axle shaft.
8. Reverse procedure to install.

REAR DRIVE SHAFT, REPLACE
240Z, 260Z & 280Z Models

1. Raise and support rear of vehicle.
2. Disconnect drive shaft at wheel attachment and axle carrier attachment.
3. Remove drive shaft from vehicle, Fig. 2.
4. Reverse procedure to install.

REAR AXLE, REPLACE
F10 Models

1. Raise and support vehicle. Support axle tube with a suitable jack.

2. Remove wheels.
3. Disconnect brake lines and parking brake cables at brakes.
4. Disconnect brake hoses from junction block.
5. Remove parking brake cable bracket and disconnect cable from axle tube.
6. Remove brake drum and brake assembly.
7. Disconnect shock absorber from lower mounting.
8. Remove "U" bolts, rubber bumper and spring seat.
9. Remove axle from vehicle, Fig. 3.
10. Reverse procedure to install.

Exc. F10 Models

1. Raise and support rear of vehicle.
2. Disconnect propeller shaft from differential companion flange.
3. Remove propeller shaft from vehicle.

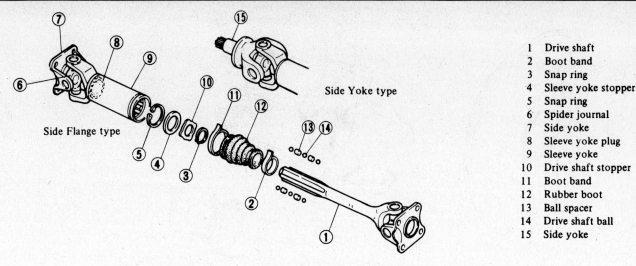

Fig. 2 Rear driveshaft disassembled. Models with independent rear suspension (Typical)

1	Drive shaft
2	Boot band
3	Snap ring
4	Sleeve yoke stopper
5	Snap ring
6	Spider journal
7	Side yoke
8	Sleeve yoke plug
9	Sleeve yoke
10	Drive shaft stopper
11	Boot band
12	Rubber boot
13	Ball spacer
14	Drive shaft ball
15	Side yoke

4. Disconnect parking brake cable from turnbuckle.
5. Disconnect brake pipe at body side.
6. Disconnect shock absorbers at lower mountings.
7. Lower jack under differential case and remove "U" bolts from springs.
8. Move axle assembly rearward and lower from vehicle. When removing the assembly, tilt the assembly to pass under the springs.
9. Reverse procedure to install.

DISC BRAKE, SERVICE
Annette Type

Brake Shoes, Replace
1. Raise and support front of vehicle and remove wheel.
2. Remove clips and pins, then coil spring and shoe springs.
3. Remove brake shoes from caliper, Fig. 3.
4. Reverse procedure to install. Push pistons into caliper when installing.

Caliper, Replace
1. Remove brake shoes as outlined previously.
2. Disconnect brake tube from caliper.
3. Remove bolts securing caliper to steering knuckle.
4. Remove caliper assembly, Fig. 3.
5. Reverse procedure to install.
6. Bleed brake system.

Caliper Overhaul
1. Remove bleeder valve.
2. Push pistons into caliper.

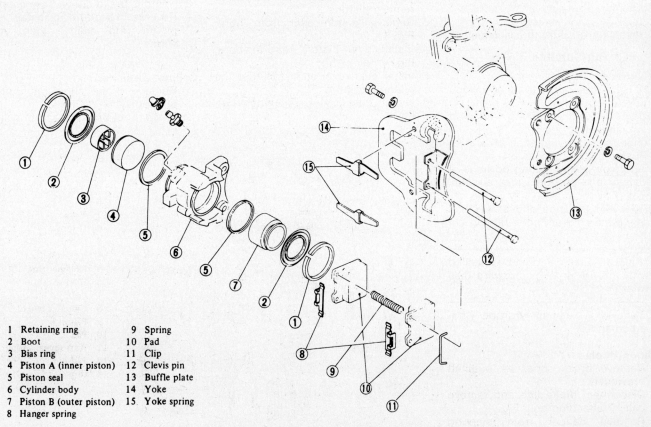

1	Retaining ring	9	Spring
2	Boot	10	Pad
3	Bias ring	11	Clip
4	Piston A (inner piston)	12	Clevis pin
5	Piston seal	13	Buffle plate
6	Cylinder body	14	Yoke
7	Piston B (outer piston)	15	Yoke spring
8	Hanger spring		

Fig. 3 Annette type disc brake disassembled

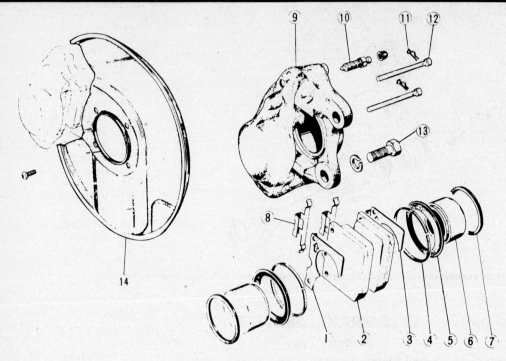

1	Anti-squeal shim R.H.
2	Pad
3	Anti-squeal shim L.H.
4	Retaining ring
5	Dust cover
6	Piston
7	Piston seal
8	Anti-squeal spring
9	Caliper assembly
10	Bleeder
11	Clip
12	Retaining pin
13	Caliper fixing bolt
14	Baffle plate

Fig. 4 Girling-Sumitomo type disc brake disassembled

3. With yoke clamped in a vise, tap top of yoke with a hammer and the caliper will separate from yoke.
4. Remove bias ring from piston "A".
5. Remove retaining rings and boots from both pistons, Fig. 3.
6. Push pistons from caliper in same direction.
7. Remove piston seals.
8. Reverse procedure to assemble.

Girling-Sumitomo S-16

Brake Shoes, Replace
1. Raise and support front of vehicle and remove wheel.
2. Remove clip, retaining pin and anti-squeal spring, then the brake shoe and shim, Fig. 4.
3. Push piston into cylinder.
4. Apply grease to sliding portions of caliper and on both sides of shim, Fig. 4.
5. Install brake shoe and anti-squeal shim, then the spring, retaining pin and clip.

NOTE: The shim should be installed with the arrow facing forward disc rotation.

6. Depress brake pedal to properly position shoes.

Caliper, Replace
1. Remove brake shoes as outlined previously.
2. Disconnect brake line and remove caliper attaching bolt, Fig. 4.
3. Remove caliper from steering knuckle.

4. Reverse procedure to install. Bleed brake system.

Caliper Overhaul
1. Remove retaining ring and dust cover.
2. Apply compressed air to fluid port to remove pistons.
3. Remove piston seal from bore, Fig. 4.
4. Install new piston seal in bore, Fig. 4.
5. Install dust cover on piston, then the piston into bore, Fig. 4.
6. Install dust cover retaining ring, Fig. 4.

N32 Type

Brake Shoes, Replace
1. Raise and support front of vehicle and remove wheel.
2. Remove clip, then the pad pins securing anti-squeal springs, Fig. 5.
3. Remove brake shoes from caliper.
4. Reverse procedure to install. Push piston into caliper then install shoes.

Caliper, Replace
1. Remove brake shoes as outlined previously.
2. Disconnect brake line from caliper.

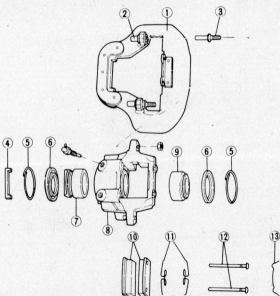

1	Yoke
2	Gripper
3	Gripper pin
4	Yoke holder
5	Retainer ring
6	Dust seal
7	Piston A
8	Cylinder body
9	Piston B
10	Pad
11	Anti-squeal spring
12	Pad pin
13	Clip

Fig. 5 N32 type disc brake disassembled

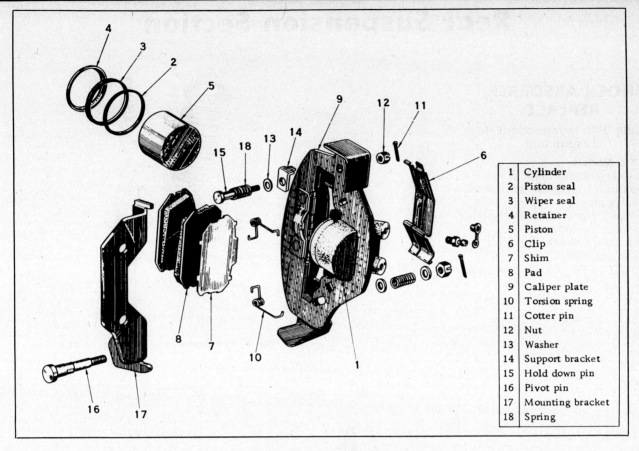

1	Cylinder
2	Piston seal
3	Wiper seal
4	Retainer
5	Piston
6	Clip
7	Shim
8	Pad
9	Caliper plate
10	Torsion spring
11	Cotter pin
12	Nut
13	Washer
14	Support bracket
15	Hold down pin
16	Pivot pin
17	Mounting bracket
18	Spring

Fig. 6 SC type disc brake disassembled

3. Remove caliper attachments, Fig. 5.
4. Remove caliper from vehicle.
5. Reverse procedure to install.

Caliper Overhaul
1. Remove gripper pin attaching nuts.
2. Separate yoke and caliper body.
3. Remove yoke holder from piston.
4. Remove retaining rings and dust seals from both pistons, Fig. 5.
5. To remove pistons, apply compressed air to fluid port.
6. Remove piston seals, Fig. 5.
7. Remove gripper, Fig. 2, if necessary.
8. Reverse procedure to assemble.

SC Type
Brake Shoes, Replace
1. Raise and support front of vehicle and remove wheel.

2. Remove anti-rattle clip from caliper plate, Fig. 6.
3. Loosen bleeder screw and pull caliper plate outboard. Push piston into caliper.
4. Remove the outer brake shoe, Fig. 6.
5. Push caliper plate inboard and remove inner shoe. Push piston into bore.
6. Reverse procedure to install.

Caliper, Replace
1. Raise and support front of vehicle and remove wheel.
2. Disconnect brake hose from brake tube.
3. Remove caliper mounting bolts and the caliper from vehicle, Fig. 6.
4. Reverse procedure to install.

Caliper Overhaul
1. Remove anti-rattle clip from caliper plate, then the brake shoes, Fig. 6.
2. Remove tension springs and the cylinder from caliper plate, Fig. 6.
3. Apply compressed air to fluid port to remove piston, Fig. 6.
4. Remove piston seal from groove in cylinder, Fig. 6, then, the retainer and wiper seal, Fig. 6.
5. Reverse procedure to assemble.

MASTER CYLINDER, REPLACE
1. Disconnect brake lines from master cylinder. Plug lines and master cylinder ports.
2. Remove master cylinder retaining nut and the master cylinder.
3. Reverse procedure to install.

Rear Suspension Section

SHOCK ABSORBER, REPLACE

Models With Independent Rear Suspension

510 & 610 Models

1. Raise and support rear of vehicle.
2. Support suspension arm with a suitable jack.
3. Remove trunk finisher assembly from inside trunk.
4. Disconnect shock absorber from upper mounting.
5. Disconnect shock absorber from mounting on suspension arm.
6. Remove shock absorber from vehicle.
7. Reverse procedure to install.

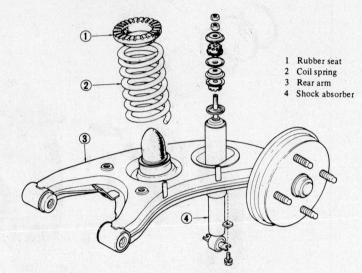

1 Rubber seat
2 Coil spring
3 Rear arm
4 Shock absorber

Fig. 1   Rear suspension. F10 exc. Sport Wagon

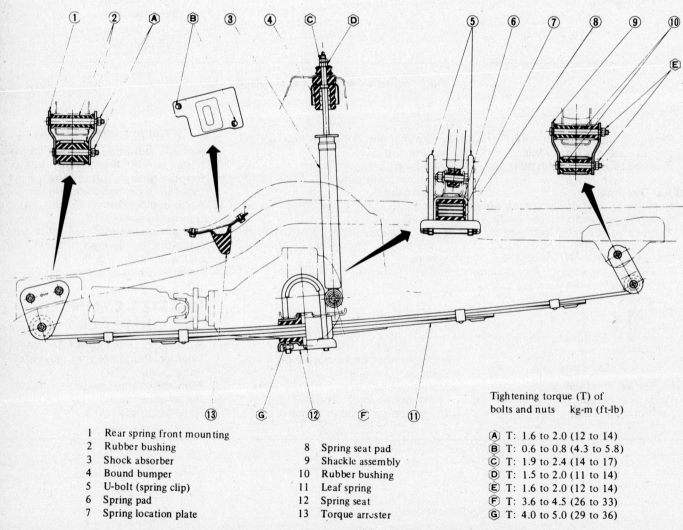

1	Rear spring front mounting	
2	Rubber bushing	
3	Shock absorber	
4	Bound bumper	8 Spring seat pad
5	U-bolt (spring clip)	9 Shackle assembly
6	Spring pad	10 Rubber bushing
7	Spring location plate	11 Leaf spring
		12 Spring seat
		13 Torque arrester

Tightening torque (T) of
bolts and nuts   kg-m (ft-lb)

Ⓐ T: 1.6 to 2.0 (12 to 14)
Ⓑ T: 0.6 to 0.8 (4.3 to 5.8)
Ⓒ T: 1.9 to 2.4 (14 to 17)
Ⓓ T: 1.5 to 2.0 (11 to 14)
Ⓔ T: 1.6 to 2.0 (12 to 14)
Ⓕ T: 3.6 to 4.5 (26 to 33)
Ⓖ T: 4.0 to 5.0 (29 to 36)

Fig. 2   Rear suspension. Models less independent rear suspension (Typical)

F10 Models

1. Raise and support rear of vehicle.
2. Remove wheel.
3. Support rear arm with a suitable jack.
4. Disconnect shock absorber at upper and lower mountings, Fig. 1.
5. Lower jack and remove shock absorber from vehicle.
6. Reverse procedure to install.

Models Less Independent Rear Suspension

1. Raise and support rear of vehicle at rear axle.
2. Disconnect shock absorber at lower mounting, Fig. 2.
3. Disconnect shock absorber at upper mounting, Fig. 2.
4. Remove shock absorber from vehicle.
5. Reverse procedure to install.

COIL SPRING, REPLACE

510 Exc. Sta. Wagon

1. Raise and support rear of vehicle.
2. Remove wheels.
3. Disconnect parking brake cable and return spring.
4. Disconnect driveshaft at wheel attachment.
5. Remove nuts securing rebound bumpers.
6. Support arm with a suitable jack.
7. Disconnect shock absorber from lower mounting.
8. Lower jack slowly and remove coil spring.
9. Reverse procedure to install.

610 Exc. Sta. Wagon

1. Raise and support rear of vehicle and support at chassis.
2. Remove rear wheel.
3. Remove drive shaft at wheel attachment.
4. Disconnect rear brake hose at suspension arm.
5. Support suspension arm with a suitable jack and disconnect shock absorber at lower mounting.
6. Lower jack and remove coil spring.
7. Reverse procedure to install.

F10 Exc. Sport Wagon

1. Raise and support rear of vehicle.
2. Remove wheel.
3. Support rear arm with a suitable jack.
4. Disconnect shock absorber from upper and lower mountings.
5. Slowly lower jack and remove spring from vehicle.
6. Reverse procedure to install.

COIL SPRING & SHOCK ABSORBER, REPLACE

810 Sedan

1. Raise and support rear of vehicle.
2. Remove shock upper attachments from inside trunk, Fig. 3.
3. Disconnect shock absorber from lower mounting, Fig. 3.
4. Remove shock absorber and coil spring assembly from vehicle, Fig. 3.
5. Reverse procedure to install.

STRUT & COIL SPRING, REPLACE

240Z, 260Z, & 280

1. Raise and support rear of vehicle and remove rear wheels.
2. Disconnect brake line connector at body and side brake linkage.
3. Disconnect stabilizer bar from transverse link, Fig. 4.
4. Remove transverse link nuts and bolt from rear transverse spindle at lower end of bearing housing.
5. Remove spindle and separate transverse link from strut assembly, Fig. 4.
6. Disconnect drive shaft from wheel attachment, Fig. 4.
7. Remove strut attachments at upper mounting from passenger compartment.
8. Remove strut from vehicle.
9. Reverse procedure to install.

LEAF SPRING, REPLACE

Exc. F10 Sport Wagon

1. Raise and support rear of vehicle at chassis. Support rear axle to relieve tension from spring.
2. Disconnect shock absorber at lower mounting and remove "U" bolts and spring plates.
3. Disconnect spring from rear shackle, Fig. 2.
4. Disconnect spring from the front body attachment.
5. Remove spring from vehicle.
6. Reverse procedure to install.

F10 Sport Wagon

1. Raise and support vehicle. Support axle tube with a suitable jack.
2. Remove wheel.
3. Disconnect shock absorber from lower mounting.
4. Remove "U" bolt nuts and the rubber bumper and spring seat, Fig. 5.
5. Raise axle tube slightly.
6. Disconnect parking brake cable clamp from spring.
7. Disconnect left spring from rear shackle and front pin, Fig. 5.
8. Remove leaf spring from vehicle.
9. Reverse procedure to install.

REAR ARM, REPLACE

510 & 610 Exc. Sta. Wagon

1. Raise and support rear of vehicle.
2. Remove rear wheel and brake drum.
3. Disconnect drive shaft from axle shaft.
4. Disconnect brake cable from lever.
5. Disconnect brake cable from tube.
6. Remove rear wheel bearing lock nut and the rear axle shaft, wheel bearings and oil seal.
7. Remove brake support plate from suspension arm.
8. Support suspension arm with a suitable jack.
9. Disconnect shock absorber from lower mounting.
10. Lower jack and remove coil spring.
11. Disconnect suspension arm from crossmember.
12. Remove suspension arm from vehicle.
13. Reverse procedure to install.

F10 Exc. Sport Wagon

1. Raise and support rear of vehicle.
2. Remove wheel.
3. Disconnect brake tube.
4. Disconnect parking brake cable.
5. Remove brake drum.
6. Remove brake assembly.
7. Support rear arm with a suitable jack.
8. Disconnect shock absorber from upper and lower mountings.
9. Slowly lower jack and remove shock absorber and coil spring, Fig. 4.
10. Remove rear arm attaching bolts and the rear arm from vehicle.
11. Reverse procedure to install.

TRANSVERSE LINK, REPLACE

240Z, 260Z & 280Z

1. Raise and support rear of vehicle at chassis and remove wheels.
2. Disconnect stabilizer bar from transverse link.
3. Separate transverse link from strut.
4. Support gear carrier with a suitable jack.
5. Remove transverse link inner bolts and damper plate bolts.
6. Remove differential mount front insulator nut.
7. Remove differential mount crossmember.
8. Remove transverse link rear bracket.

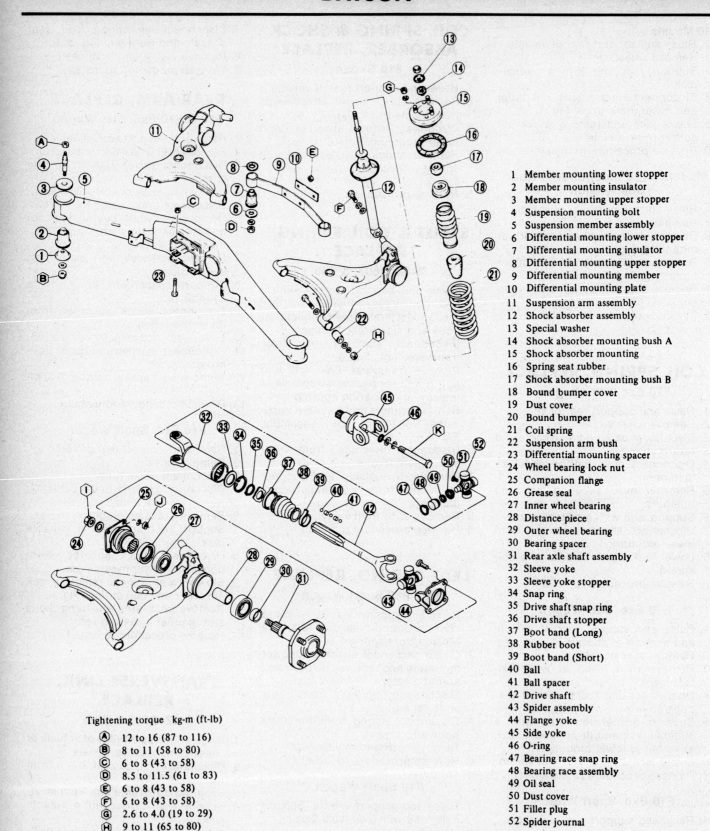

1 Member mounting lower stopper
2 Member mounting insulator
3 Member mounting upper stopper
4 Suspension mounting bolt
5 Suspension member assembly
6 Differential mounting lower stopper
7 Differential mounting insulator
8 Differential mounting upper stopper
9 Differential mounting member
10 Differential mounting plate
11 Suspension arm assembly
12 Shock absorber assembly
13 Special washer
14 Shock absorber mounting bush A
15 Shock absorber mounting
16 Spring seat rubber
17 Shock absorber mounting bush B
18 Bound bumper cover
19 Dust cover
20 Bound bumper
21 Coil spring
22 Suspension arm bush
23 Differential mounting spacer
24 Wheel bearing lock nut
25 Companion flange
26 Grease seal
27 Inner wheel bearing
28 Distance piece
29 Outer wheel bearing
30 Bearing spacer
31 Rear axle shaft assembly
32 Sleeve yoke
33 Sleeve yoke stopper
34 Snap ring
35 Drive shaft snap ring
36 Drive shaft stopper
37 Boot band (Long)
38 Rubber boot
39 Boot band (Short)
40 Ball
41 Ball spacer
42 Drive shaft
43 Spider assembly
44 Flange yoke
45 Side yoke
46 O-ring
47 Bearing race snap ring
48 Bearing race assembly
49 Oil seal
50 Dust cover
51 Filler plug
52 Spider journal

Tightening torque kg-m (ft-lb)

Ⓐ 12 to 16 (87 to 116)
Ⓑ 8 to 11 (58 to 80)
Ⓒ 6 to 8 (43 to 58)
Ⓓ 8.5 to 11.5 (61 to 83)
Ⓔ 6 to 8 (43 to 58)
Ⓕ 6 to 8 (43 to 58)
Ⓖ 2.6 to 4.0 (19 to 29)
Ⓗ 9 to 11 (65 to 80)
Ⓘ 25 to 33 (181 to 239)
Ⓙ 5 to 6 (36 to 43)
Ⓚ 3.2 to 4.3 (23 to 31)

Fig. 3 Rear suspension. 810 sedan

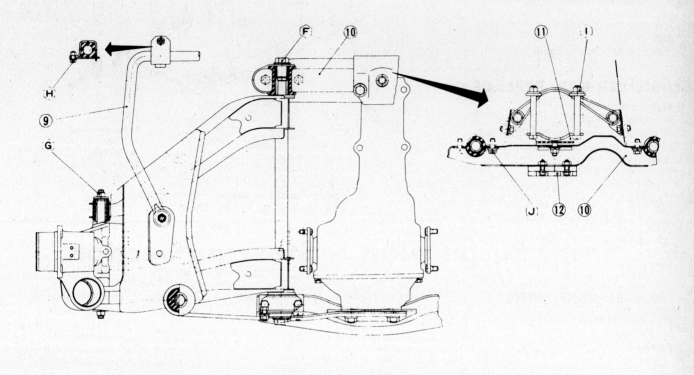

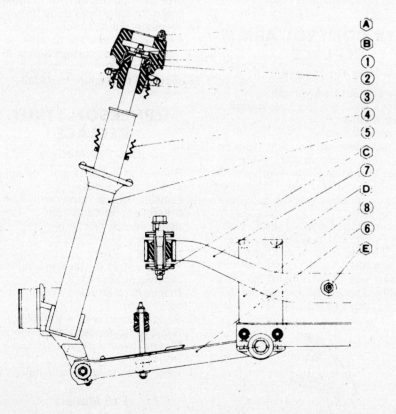

1 Rear strut mounting
   insulator
2 Spacer
3 Bound bumper rubber
4 Dust cover
5 Strut assembly
6 Transverse link
7 Differential case mounting
   member
8 Link mounting brace
9 Stabilizer bar
10 Differential case mounting
   front member
11 Differential case mounting
   front insulator
12 Damper plate

Tightening torque (T) of
bolts and nuts   kg-m (ft-lb)

Ⓐ T : 2.5 to 3.5 (18 to 25)
Ⓑ T : 7.5 to 9.5 (54 to 69)
Ⓒ T : 7.5 to 9.5 (54 to 69)
Ⓓ T : 4.6 to 6.1 (33 to 44)
Ⓔ T : 7.5 to 9.5 (54 to 69)
Ⓕ T : 14 to 16 (101 to 116)
Ⓖ T : 7.5 to 9.5 (54 to 69)
Ⓗ T : 1.0 to 1.2 (7 to 9)
Ⓘ T : 6.0 to 8.0 (43 to 58)
Ⓙ T : 4.6 to 6.1 (33 to 44)

Fig. 4   Rear suspension. 240Z, 260Z & 280Z

9. Remove transverse link from vehicle.
10. Reverse procedure to install.

STABILIZER BAR, REPLACE

1. Raise and support vehicle.
2. Remove muffler.
3. Disconnect stabilizer bar from side member and remove stabilizer bar.
4. Reverse procedure to install.

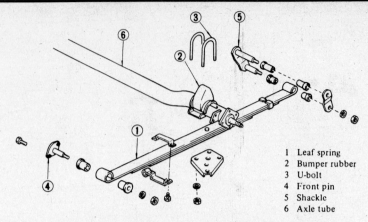

1	Leaf spring
2	Bumper rubber
3	U-bolt
4	Front pin
5	Shackle
6	Axle tube

Fig. 5   Rear suspension. F10 Sport Wagon

Front Suspension & Steering Section

WHEEL ALIGNMENT
Caster & Camber

Exc. Pick-Up Models

Caster and camber cannot be adjusted on these models.

Pick-Up Models

Caster and camber are adjusted by increasing or decreasing the thickness of shims installed between the upper control arm spindle and the mounting bracket.

Toe-In

To adjust toe-in, loosen side rod lock nut and adjust length of side rod as required.

WHEEL BEARINGS, ADJUST

1. Raise and support front of vehicle.
2. Remove brake shoes as outlined elsewhere in this chapter.
3. While rotating disc, torque wheel bearing lock nut to 18-22 ft. lbs.
4. Loosen lock nut approximately 60 degrees. Install adjusting cap and align groove of nut with hole in spindle. If alignment cannot be obtained, change position of adjusting cap. Also, if alignment cannot be obtained, loosen lock nut slightly, but not more than 15 degrees.
5. Install brake shoes.

SHOCK ABSORBER, REPLACE
Pick-Up Models

1. Raise and support vehicle.
2. Remove wheel.

3. Disconnect shock absorber from upper mounting, Fig. 1.
4. Disconnect shock absorber from lower mounting, Fig. 1.
5. Remove shock absorber from vehicle.
6. Reverse procedure to install.

LOWER CONTROL ARMS, REPLACE
Pick-Up Models

1. Raise and support vehicle.
2. Remove wheels and brake drums.
3. Remove wheel hub.
4. Remove brake disc.
5. Remove steering knuckle, torsion bar spring, stabilizer bar, shock absorber and torsion bar, Fig. 2.
6. Remove upper bolt securing knuckle spindle support to upper control arm.
7. Remove upper control arm bushings from knuckle spindle support.
8. Remove bushings from lower control arm pin.
9. Loosen nut at bottom of knuckle spindle support and remove the cotter pin securing the pin.

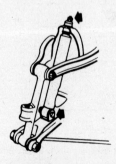

Fig. 1   Shock absorber installation. Pick-up

10. Drive out pin with a suitable drift and remove knuckle spindle support and knuckle spindle from lower control arm. Disconnect dust cover.
11. Remove bolts securing upper control arm spindle and the upper control arm spindle with the camber adjusting shims from body bracket.
12. Remove nut securing lower control arm spindle and the spindle.
13. Remove lower control arm with the torque arm from mounting bracket.
14. Reverse procedure to install.

McPHERSON STRUT, REPLACE
Exc. F10 Models

1. Raise and support front of vehicle and remove wheel.
2. Loosen brake tube and remove brake hose locking spring. Remove plate and brake hose from strut bracket.
3. Remove caliper.
4. Remove strut to steering knuckle attaching bolts, Fig. 3.
5. Disconnect knuckle arm from bottom of strut.
6. Support strut with a suitable jack.
7. Remove upper strut attachments.
8. Slowly lower jack and remove strut from vehicle.
9. Reverse procedure to install.

F10 Models

1. Raise and support vehicle.
2. Remove wheel.
3. Remove cap with a suitable tool and partially loosen the lock nut securing piston rod.
4. Disconnect brake tube.
5. Disconnect side rod.

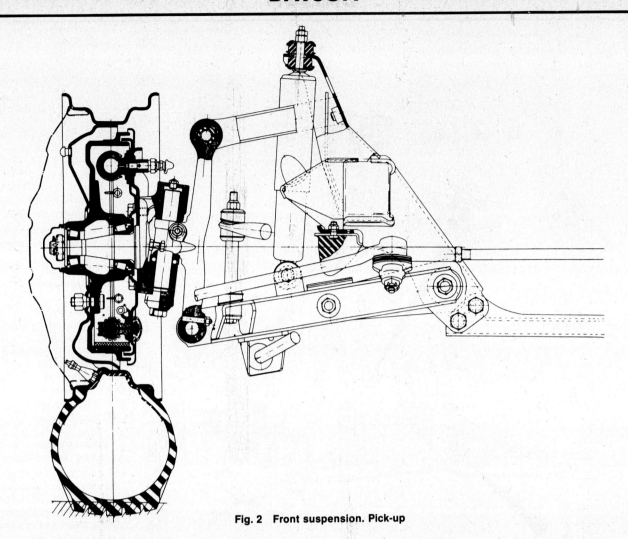

Fig. 2 Front suspension. Pick-up

6. Support transverse link with a suitable jack.
7. Remove bolts securing strut to steering knuckle and separate strut from knuckle, Fig. 4.
8. Remove nuts securing strut to hood ledge and the strut assembly from vehicle.
9. Reverse procedure to install.

TRANSVERSE LINK, REPLACE
F10 Models

1. Raise and support front of vehicle.
2. Remove wheel.
3. Remove transverse link to ball joint bolts.
4. Remove stabilizer bar attaching nut from transverse link.
5. Remove bolts securing transverse link to sub-frame and the transverse link.
6. Reverse procedure to install.

BALL JOINT, REPLACE
F10 Models

1. Raise and support front of vehicle.
2. Remove wheel.
3. Remove ball joint stud nut and separate ball joint stud from steering knuckle.
4. Remove bolts securing ball joint to transverse link and the ball joint.
5. Reverse procedure to install.

TRANSVERSE LINK & BALL JOINT, REPLACE
Exc. 810 Models

1. Raise and support vehicle and remove wheels.
2. Disconnect side rod stud from steering knuckle.
3. Remove steering knuckle attaching bolts and disconnect knuckle arm from bottom of strut.
4. Remove compression rod and stabilizer bar.
5. Loosen transverse link mounting bar and separate link from crossmember.
6. Remove transverse link with ball joint and knuckle arm, Fig. 5.
7. Place transverse link in a vise and remove bolt securing ball joint to transverse arm and the ball joint from the arm.
8. Reverse procedure to install.

810 Models

1. Raise and support front of vehicle.
2. Remove wheels.
3. Remove splashboard.
4. Disconnect side rod from steering knuckle.
5. Disconnect strut from steering knuckle.
6. Remove tension rod and stabilizer bar.
7. Disconnect transverse link from crossmember.
8. To remove left hand transverse link, separate pitman arm from sector shaft and lower the steering linkage. To remove right hand transverse link, disconnect idle arm assembly

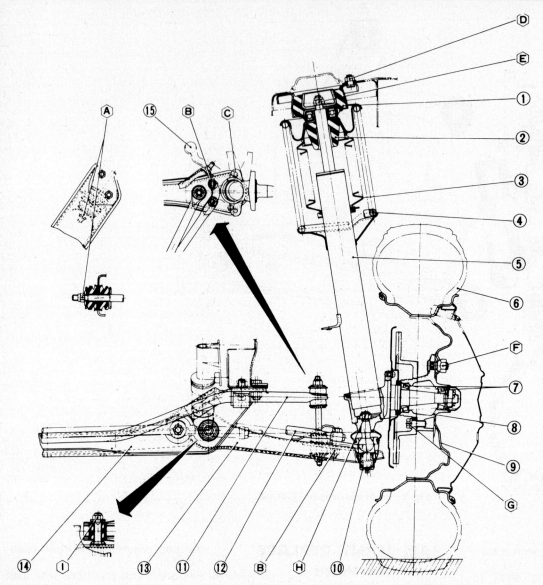

1 Strut mounting insulator
2 Bound bumper rubber
3 Dust cover
4 Coil spring
5 Strut assembly
6 Tire
7 Wheel bearing
8 Wheel hub
9 Road wheel
10 Suspention ball joint
11 Stabilizer bar
12 Tension rod
13 Transverse link
14 Side member
15 Knuckle arm

Tightening torque of bolts
and nuts   kg-m (ft-lb)

Ⓐ 5.0 to 5.5 (36 to 40)
Ⓑ 4.9 to 6.3 (35 to 46)
Ⓒ 1.9 to 2.5 (14 to 18)
Ⓓ 2.5 to 3.5 (18 to 25)
Ⓔ 6.0 to 7.5 (43 to 54)
Ⓕ 8 to 9 (58 to 65)
Ⓖ 3.9 to 5.3 (28 to 38)
Ⓗ 5.5 to 7.6 (40 to 55)
Ⓘ 9.0 to 10.0 (65 to 72)

Fig. 3 Front suspension. Exc. F10 & Pick-up

from frame and lower the steering linkage.
9. Remove transverse link with the ball joint and steering knuckle.
10. Remove ball joint retaining bolts and the ball joint from the transverse link.
11. Reverse procedure to install.

TORSION BAR, REPLACE
Pick-Up Models

1. Raise and support vehicle.
2. Remove wheel.
3. Remove torsion bar nuts.
4. Remove bracket bolt from front of bar, then the torsion bar with the bracket.
5. Reverse procedure to install.

MANUAL STEERING GEAR, REPLACE
B110 Models

1. Disconnect battery ground cable and remove steering wheel.
2. Remove steering column shell covers.
3. Remove turn signal and light switch.
4. Remove hand lever assembly from control rod assembly.
5. Remove steering column to instrument panel attaching bolts.
6. Remove steering column grommet to dash panel bolts.
7. Disconnect shift rod and selector rod from change lever and selector lever.
8. Disconnect gear arm from cross rod.

9. Remove steering gear attaching bolts.
10. Remove steering gear and transmission control from engine compartment.
11. Remove transmission control from steering gear assembly.
12. Reverse procedure to install.

200SX Models

1. Disconnect exhaust pipe from exhaust manifold.
2. Remove bolt securing exhaust pipe to transmission mounting insulator.
3. Remove bolt securing worm shaft to rubber coupling.
4. Remove nut securing pitman arm to sector shaft, then the pitman arm.
5. Remove steering gear attaching

bolts and the steering gear from vehicle.

6. Reverse procedure to install.

B210 Models

1. Remove bolt securing rubber coupling to worm shaft.
2. Remove nut and washer securing pitman arm to sector shaft, then the pitman arm.
3. Remove steering gear attaching bolts and the steering gear from vehicle.
4. Reverse procedure to install.

240Z, 260Z & 280Z Models

1. Raise and support front of vehicle and remove wheels.
2. Disconnect lower joint from steering column at rubber coupling.
3. Loosen bolt securing lower joint assembly to pinion, then the lower joint assembly.
4. Remove splash board.
5. Disconnect side rod studs from steering knuckles.
6. Remove gear housing to crossmember bolts and the gear assembly from vehicle.
7. Reverse procedure to install.

710 Models

1. Remove shield plate to side member screws and the plate.
2. Remove worm shaft to rubber coupling bolt.
3. Remove nut and lick washer securing gear arm to sector shaft, then the gear arm.
4. Remove steering gear attaching bolts and the steering gear from vehicle.
5. Reverse procedure to install.

F10 Models

1. Raise and support front of vehicle.
2. Remove front wheels.
3. Disconnect side rod studs from steering knuckle.
4. Loosen bolt securing lower joint assembly to pinion, then the bolt from lower joint assembly.
5. Remove steering gear attaching bolts and the steering gear from vehicle.
6. Reverse procedure to install.

Pick-Up

1. Disconnect battery ground cable.
2. Remove steering wheel.
3. Remove upper and lower steering column covers.
4. Remove turn signal switch.
5. Remove steering column clamp attaching bolts.
6. Remove bolts securing column

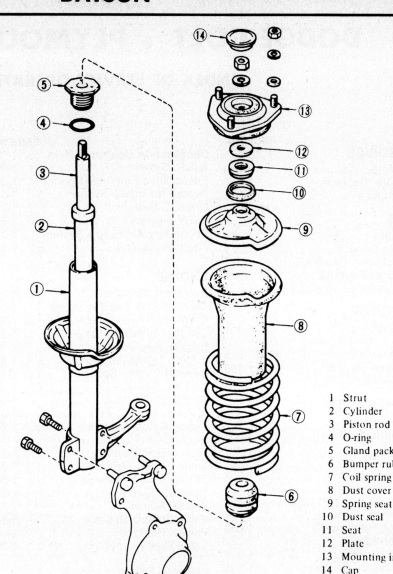

1 Strut
2 Cylinder
3 Piston rod
4 O-ring
5 Gland packing
6 Bumper rubber
7 Coil spring
8 Dust cover
9 Spring seat
10 Dust seal
11 Seat
12 Plate
13 Mounting insulator
14 Cap

Fig. 4   McPherson strut assembly. F10

grommet to dash panel.

7. Remove nut securing pitman arm to sector shaft, then the pitman arm from sector.
8. Remove steering gear attaching

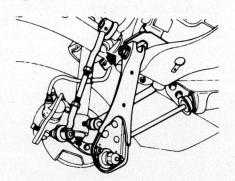

Fig. 5   Transverse link installation

bolts and the steering gear and column assembly from vehicle.

9. Reverse procedure to install.

POWER STEERING GEAR, REPLACE

810 Models

1. Remove air cleaner.
2. Remove bolt securing universal joint to worm shaft.
3. Disconnect hoses from power steering gear. Cap hoses and ports.
4. Remove nut securing pitman arm to sector shaft, then the pitman arm from sector shaft.
5. Remove steering attaching bolts and the steering gear from vehicle.
6. Reverse procedure to install.

DODGE COLT • PLYMOUTH ARROW

INDEX OF SERVICE OPERATIONS

GENERAL ENGINE SPECIFICATIONS

Year	Engine	Car-buretor	Bore & Stroke	Piston Dis-place-ment Cubic Inches (cc)	Com-pres-sion Ratio	Maximum Brake H.P. @ R.P.M.	Maximum Torque Lbs. Ft. @ R.P.M.	Normal Oil Pressure Pounds
1972	4-1600	2 Barrel	3.03 x 3.39 (76 x 83mm)	97.5 (1600)	8.5	85 @ 5600	90 @ 3600	11①
1973	4-1600	2 Barrel	3.03 x 3.39 (76 x 83mm)	97.5 (1600)	8.5	83 @ 5600	89 @ 3600	11①
1974	4-1600	2 Barrel	3.03 x 3.39 (76 x 83mm)	97.5 (1600)	8.5	85 @ 5600	90 @ 3600	11①
	4-2000	2 Barrel	3.31 x 3.54 (84 x 89mm)	121.7 (2000)	8.5	95 @ 5500	110 @ 3600	11①
1975	4-1600	2 Barrel	3.03 x 3.39 (76 x 83mm)	97.5 (1600)	8.5	79 @ 5300	86 @ 3000	11①
	4-2000	2 Barrel	3.31 x 3.54 (84 x 89mm)	121.7 (2000)	8.5	89 @ 5200	105 @ 3000	11①
1976-77	4-1600	2 Barrel	3.03 x 3.39 (76 x 03mm)	97.5 (1600)	8.5	②	③	11①
	4-2000	2 Barrel	3.31 x 3.54 (84 x 89mm)	121.7 (2000)	8.5	④	⑤	11①

①—Minimum at idle.
②—Exc. Calif., 83 @ 5500; Calif., w/ auto. trans., 78 @ 5500, w/ man. trans. 80 @ 5500.
③—Exc. Calif., 89 @ 3500; Calif., w/ auto. trans., 83 @ 3500, w/ man. trans 87 @ 3500.
④—Exc. Calif., 96 @ 5500; Calif., 93 @ 5500.
⑤—Exc. Calif., 109 @ 3500; Calif., 106 @ 3500.

TUNE UP SPECIFICATIONS

The following specifications are published from the latest information available. This data should be used only in the absence of a decal affixed in the engine compartment.

• When checking compression, lowest cylinder must be within 90% of highest.
▲ Before removing wires from distributor cap, determine location of No. 1 wire in cap, as distributor position may have been altered from that shown at the end of this chart.

Year	Engine	Spark Plug Type	Spark Plug Gap Inch	Distributor Point Gap Inch	Distributor Dwell Angle Deg.	Ignition Timing Firing Order Fig. ▲	Ignition Timing Timing BTDC ①	Mark Fig.	Carb. Adjustments Hot Idle Speed Std. Trans.	Carb. Adjustments Hot Idle Speed Auto. Trans.	Idle "CO"% Std. Trans.	Idle "CO"% Auto. Trans.
1972	1600	N-9Y	.030	.020	49—55	A	TDC	B	700	700	—	—
1973	1600	N-9Y	.030	.020	49—55	A	TDC	B	800	800	3.0—5.0	3.0—5.0
1974	1600	N-9Y	.030	.020	49—55	A	②	B	800	800	3.0—4.5	3.0—4.5
	2000	N-9Y	.030	.020	49—55	A	③	C	800	800	3.0—4.5	3.0—4.5
1975	1600	N-9Y	.030	.020	49—55	A	③	D	900	800	1.5—3.0	1.5—3.0
	2000	N-9Y	.030	.020	49—55	A	④	E	900	800	1.5—3.0	1.5—3.0
1976	1600	RN-9Y	.030	.020	49—55	A	③	D	950	850	1.0—2.5	1.0—2.5
	2000	RN-9Y	.030	.020	49—55	F	④	D	950	850	1.0—2.5	1.0—2.5
1977	1600⑤	RN-9Y	.030	.020	49—55	⑩	5°	D	950	850	0.5—2.0	0.5—2.0
	1600⑥	RN-9Y	.030	.020	49—55	⑩	⑧	D	950	850	0.5—2.0	0.5—2.0
	1600⑦	RN-9Y	.030	.020	49—55	⑩	⑨	D	950	850	0.5—2.0	0.5—2.0
	2000⑤	RN-9Y	.030	.020	49—55	F	5°	D	950	850	0.5—2.0	0.5—2.0
	2000⑥	RN-9Y	.030	.020	49—55	F	⑧	D	950	850	0.5—2.0	0.5—2.0
	2000⑦	RN-9Y	.030	.020	49—55	F	⑨	D	950	850	0.5—2.0	0.5—2.0

①—BTDC: Before top dead center.
②—Exc. Auto trans. w/o EGR, TDC; Auto. trans. w/o EGR 3° BTDC.
③—With rubber plug at distributor vacuum removed, TDC; With rubber plug installed, 5° ATDC.
④—With rubber plug at distributor vacuum removed, 3 BTDC; With rubber plug installed, 5° ATDC.

Continued

TUNE UP NOTES — Continued

⑤ —Exc. Calif., and high altitude.
⑥ —High altitude.
⑦ —Calif.
⑧ —With rubber plug at distributor vacuum removed, 10° BTDC, with plug installed, TDC.
⑨ —With rubber plug at distributor vacuum removed, 5° BTDC, with plug installed, 5° ATDC.
⑩ —Less Silent-Shaft, Fig. A; With Silent-Shaft, Fig. F. Silent-Shaft engines can be identified by the distributor being mounted horizontally into the cylinder head.

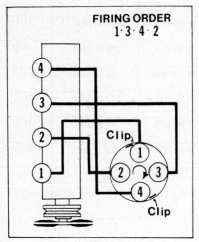

Fig. A

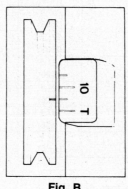

Fig. B

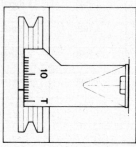

Fig. C

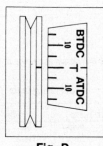

Fig. D

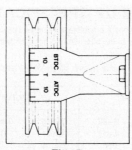

Fig. E

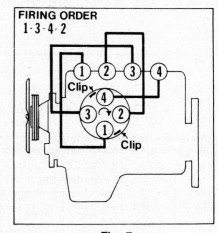

Fig. F

ALTERNATOR & REGULATOR SPECIFICATIONS

| Year | | Alternator | | | | | Regulator | | | | | | |
| | | | | Output @ 14 Volts | | | | Pilot Lamp Relay | | | Constant-Voltage Relay | | |
Year	Model	Rated Hot Output Amps.	Field Current 12 Volts @ 80° F	2500 R.P.M. Amps.	5000 R.P.M. Amps.	Model	Air Gap In.	Point Gap In.	Closing Voltage	Air Gap In.	Point Gap In.	Voltage @ 68° F
1972-73	AG2040K	40	—	33	—	RQB2220D	.041	.036	4.2—5.2	.040	.014	14.3—15.8
1974	AH2040K	40	—	—	—	RWB2220D	.041	.036	4.2—5.2	.040	.014	14.3—15.8
1975-76	AH2045K	45	—	37	—	RQB2220D	.041	.036	4.2—5.2	.040	.014	14.3—15.8
1976	AH2045G	45	—	37	—	RQB2220D	—	—	4.2—5.2	—	—	14.2—15.3
1977	AH2045K	45	—	34	42	RQB—2D	—	—	4.2—5.2	—	—	14.5—15.3
	AH2045G	45	—	34	42	RQB—2D	—	—	4.2—5.2	—	—	14.5—15.3
	021000—6420	45	—	34	42	026000—1764	—	—	4—5.8	—	—	14.5—15.3

DISTRIBUTOR SPECIFICATIONS

If unit is checked on vehicle double the RPM and degrees to get crankshaft figures

Distributor Part No.	Centrifugal Advance Degrees @ RPM of Distributor			Vacuum Advance		Distributor Retard
	Advance Starts	Intermediate Advance	Full Advance	Inches of Vacuum to Start Plunger	Max. Adv. Dist. Deg. @ Vacuum	Max Ref. Dist. Deg. @ Vacuum
1972						
TVG4DR	0 @ 500	6.5 @ 1000	14 @ 3050	6	8.5 @ 11.75	—
1973						
T3T03471	−0.3 @ 500	6.2 @ 1000	14 @ 3050	6.69	8.5 @ 15.75	—
1974						
T3T03871	−0.3 @ 500	6.2 @ 1000	14 @ 3050	6.69	8.5 @ 15.75	—
T3T13671	0 @ 500	7 @ 1400	10 @ 2500	8.66	8.5 @ 17.72	—
1975						
T3T04271	0 @ 500	—	10 @ 2200	4.72	8.5 @ 9.06	−7.5 @ 11.81
T3T13971	0 @ 500	—	10 @ 2500	5.12	8.5 @ 14.17	−4 @ 10.63
T3T13972	0 @ 500	—	10 @ 2500	7.09	8.5 @ 16.14	−4 @ 10.63
1976						
T3T04274	−0.3 @ 500	6.2 @ 1000	14 @ 3050	4.74	8.5 @ 13.78	2.5 @ 10.63
T3T04275	−0.3 @ 500	6.2 @ 1000	14 @ 3050	6.69	8.5 @ 15.75	2.5 @ 10.63
T3T04872	0 @ 500	7 @ 1400	10 @ 2500	5.12	8.5 @ 14.17	4 @ 10.63
T3T04873	0 @ 500	7 @ 1400	10 @ 2500	7.09	8.5 @ 16.14	4 @ 10.63
1977						
T3T03875	0 @ 500	—	10 @ 2200	3.15	11.5 @ 11.02	—
T3T03876	0 @ 500	—	10 @ 2200	2.36	14 @ 9.45	—
T3T04278	0 @ 500	—	10 @ 2200	3.15	10 @ 14.17	5 @ 10.63
T3T04575	0 @ 600	—	10 @ 3000	3.15	10 @ 14.17	—
T3T04874	0 @ 600	—	10 @ 3000	3.15	10 @ 14.17	5 @ 12.20
T3T05672	0 @ 500	—	10 @ 2200	3.15	10 @ 14.17	5 @ 10.63
T3T05771	0 @ 500	—	10 @ 2200	3.15	11.5 @ 11.02	—

STARTING MOTOR SPECIFICATIONS

Year	Part No.	Rotation ①	Brush Spring Tension Ounces	No Load Test			Torque Test		
				Amperes	Volts	R.P.M.	Amperes	Volts	Torque, Ft. Lbs.
1972	MED03	C	56	—	—	—	—	—	—
1973	MED03—1	C	56	55	11	5500	500	6	11.6
1974-75	MEA03—1	C	56	53	10.5	5000	400	6	7
	MED03—4	C	56	55	11	6500	560	6	11
	M4T14572	C	56	62	11	4500	730	6	18
1976-77	M3T12572	C	②	53	10.5	5000	400	6	6.73
	M3T15772	C	②	55	11	6500	560	6	10.85
	M4T14771	C	②	62	11	4500	730	6	18.08

①—Turning direction as viewed from pinion side.
②—1976, 38.4 oz.; 1977 53 oz.

DODGE COLT • PLYMOUTH ARROW

VALVE SPECIFICATIONS

Year	Model	Valve Lash		Valve Angles		Valve Spring Installed Height	Valve Spring Pressure Lbs. @ In.	Stem Clearance		Stem Diameter	
		Int.	Exh.	Seat	Face			Intake	Exhaust	Intake	Exhaust
1972	1600	.006	.010	45	45	1.469	—	.0010—.0022	.0020—.0033	.3149	.3149
1973	1600	.006	.010	45	45	1.469	136.7 @ 1.094	.0010—.0022	.0020—.0033	.315	.315
1974-77	1600	.006	.010	45	45	1.469	61.7 @ 1.469	.0010—.0022	.0020—.0033	.315	.315
	2000	.006	.010	45	45	1.59	①	.0010—.0022	.0020—.0033	.315	.315

①—1974-75, 62.6 lbs. @ 1.59 inch; 1976-77, 61 lbs. @ 1.59 inch.

PISTONS, PINS, RINGS, CRANKSHAFT & BEARINGS

Year	Model	Piston Clearance Top of Skirt	Ring End Gap		Wrist Pin Diameter	Rod Bearings		Main Bearings		Thrust on Bear. No.	Shaft End Play
			Comp.	Oil		Shaft Diameter	Bearing Clearance	Shaft Diameter	Bearing Clearance		
1972-75	1600	.0008—.0016	.006	.006	.748	1.7717	.0004—.0028	2.2441	.0006—.0031	3	.002—.007
1974-75	2000	.0008—.0016	①	.0098	.866	2.0866	.0006—.0025	2.5984	.0010—.0028	3	.002—.007
1976	1600	.0008—.0016	.008	.008	.748	1.7717	.0004—.0028	2.2441	.0006—.0031	3	.002—.007
1976	2000	.0008—.0016	.0098	.0098	.866	2.0866	.0006—.0025	2.5984	②	3	.002—.007
1977	1600	.0008—.0016	.008	.008	.748	1.7717	.0004—.0028	2.2441	.0008—.0028	3	.002—.007
1977	2000	.0008—.0016	.0098	.0078	.866	2.0866	.0008—.0028	2.5984	②	3	.002—.007

①—Top ring, .0118; Center ring, .0098.
②—Exc. #3 bearing, .0008—.0028; #3 bearing .0010—.0030.

ENGINE TIGHTENING SPECIFICATIONS

*Torque specifications are for clean and lightly lubricated threads only. Dry or dirty threads produce increased friction which prevent accurate measurement of tightness.

Engine	Spark Plugs Ft. Lbs.	Cylinder Head Bolts Ft. Lbs.	Camshaft Bearing Caps Ft. Lbs.	Rocker Arm Nuts Ft. Lbs.	Camshaft Sprocket Bolts Ft. Lbs.	Intake Manifold Ft. Lbs.	Exhaust Manifold Ft. Lbs.	Rocker Arm Cover Ft. Lbs.	Connecting Rod Cap Bolts Ft. Lbs.	Main Bearing Cap Bolts Ft. Lbs.	Flywheel To Crank-shaft Ft. Lbs.	Vibration Damper or Pulley Ft. Lbs.
1600	15—21	①	13—14	7—9	②	11—14	11—14	4—5	23—25	36—39	③	④
2000	15—21	⑤	13—14	7—9	36—43	11—14	11—14	4—5	33—35	54—61	⑥	80—93

①—51—54 cold; 58—61 hot.
②—Exc. silent shaft, 36—43; silent shaft, 44—57.
③—1972-76 all, 83—90; 1977, auto. trans., 84—90, man. trans 94—101.
④—Exc. silent shaft, 44—50; silent shaft, 7.5—8.5.
⑤—65—72 cold; 72—79 hot.
⑥—1974-75, 83—90; 1976, 94—101; 1977 auto. trans., 84—90, man. trans., 94—101.

DODGE COLT ● PLYMOUTH ARROW

BRAKE SPECIFICATIONS

Year	Model	Drum Brake I.D.	Wheel Cylinder Bore		Master Cylinder Bore		Disc Brake Rotor				
			Front Disc	Rear Drum	Manual	Power	Nominal Thickness	Minimum Thickness	Thickness Variation Parallelism	Runout (T.I.R.)	Finish (Micro-inch)
1972	All	9.0	1.89	.750	.6875	—	—	—	—	—	—
1973	All	9.0	1.89	.750	.6875	—	0.39	0.33	—	.006	—
1974-76	All	9.0	2.012	.750	①	.8125	0.51	0.45	—	.006	—
1977	All	9.0	2.012	.750	—	.8125	0.51	0.45	—	.006	—

① —With 1600 engine, .6875 inch; with 2000 engine, .8125 inch.

—Not Available

REAR AXLE SPECIFICATIONS

Year	Model	Carrier Type	Ring Gear & Pinion Backlash		Pinion Bearing Preload			Differential Bearing Preload	
			Method	Adjustment	Method	With Seal Inch—Lbs.	Less Seal Inch—Lbs.	Method	Adjustment
1972-73	All	Removable	Shim	.005—.007	Shim	8.7—11.3	6.1—8.7	Shim	①
1974-77	All	Removable	Shim	.005—.007	Shim	9—11	6—9	Shim	①

① —Install .002 inch shims on both sides to obtain zero inch clearance.

WHEEL ALIGNMENT SPECIFICATIONS

Year	Model	Caster Angle, Degrees		Camber Angle, Degrees				Toe-In. Inch	Toe-Out on Turns Degrees	
				Limits		Desired				
		Limits	Desired	Left	Right	Left	Right		Outer Wheel	Inner Wheel
1972	All	1¼ to 1½	1⅜	½ to 1½	½ to 1½	1	1	.08 to .23	32	43
1973	All	½ to 1¼	⅞	½ to 1½	½ to 1½	1	1	.08 to .23	32	43
1974-75	All	¾ to 1¾	1¼	⅓ to 1⅓	⅓ to 1⅓	⅚	⅚	.08 to .23	30½	39
1976	Arrow	1⁷/₁₂ to 2⁷/₁₂	2¹/₁₂	½ to 1½	½ to 1½	1	1	.08 to .23	30	35
	Colt	¾ to 1¾	1¼	⅓ to 1⅓	⅓ to 1⅓	⅚	⅚	.08 to .23	30½	39
1977	①	③	④	¼ to 1¾	¼ to 1¾	1	1	.08 to .23	30	35
	②	⅔ to 1⅔	1¹/₆	⅓ to 1⅓	⅓ to 1⅓	⅚	⅚	.08 to .23	30½	39

① —Arrow & Colt coupe & sedan.
② —Colt hardtop & sta. wagon
③ —Exc. Calif., 1⁷/₁₂° to 2⁷/₁₂°; Calif., 1¼° to 2¼°.
④ —Exc. Calif., 2¹/₁₂°; Calif., 1¾°.

COOLING SYSTEM & CAPACITY DATA

Year	Model or Engine	Cooling Capacity Qts.		Radiator Cap Relief Pressure, Lbs.		Thermo. Opening Temp.	Fuel Tank Gals.	Engine Oil Refill Qts.	Transmission Oil			Rear Axle Oil Pints
		With Heater	With A/C	With A/C	No A/C				4 Speed Qts.	5 Speed Qts.	Auto. Trans. Qts.	
1972-73	1600	7.2	7.2	13	13	180	①	4.2	—	—	5.8	—
1974	1600	6.4	6.4	13	13	180	①	4.2	1.8	—	②	1.2
	2000	8.0	8.0	13	13	180	①	5	1.8	—	②	1.2
1975	1600	6.4	6.4	13	13	180	①	4.2	1.8	2.4	6.8	1.2
	2000	8.0	8.0	13	13	180	①	5	1.8	2.4	6.8	1.2
1976	1600	7.7	7.7	13	13	180	①	4.2	1.8	③	6.8	1.2
	2000	9.5	9.5	13	13	180	①	4.5	1.8	③	6.8	1.2
1977	1600	7.7	7.7	13	13	180	④	4.2	1.8	③	6.8	1.2
	2000	9.5	9.5	13	13	180	④	4.5	1.8	③	6.8	1.2

①—Colt exc. station wagon, 13; Colt station wagon, 11; Arrow 11.9
②—Borg Warner, 5.8; Torqueflite, 6.8.
③—With 1600 engine, 2.1; With 2000 engine 2.4.
④—Arrow & Colt coupe & sedan, 13.2; Colt hardtop, 13.5; Colt station wagon, 11.1.

Electrical Section

DISTRIBUTOR, REPLACE
Removal

1. Disconnect spark plug cables and high tension cable from distributor. Hold and pull the cable caps to remove the cables.
2. Disconnect primary lead at coil.
3. Disconnect vacuum hose.
4. Remove distributor mounting nuts and the distributor.

Installation
1600 cc & 2000 cc Engine Less Silent Shaft

1. Turn crankshaft until No. 1 piston is at top dead center on compression stroke and set the notch in crankshaft pulley to timing mark "T."
2. Turn oil pump drive shaft until groove is in position shown in Figs. 1 and 2. This shaft on 1600 cc engine can be turned with a long-shank screwdriver. On 2000 cc engine, rotate crankshaft to turn shaft.
3. Install the distributor so the lug of distributor shaft enters the oil pump drive shaft groove. Align mating mark on lower end of distributor body with mark spacer. If lug on shaft does not enter groove, rotate crankshaft slightly to aid installation.
4. Adjust breaker point gap to specifications.

5. Install the distributor cap.
6. Connect primary lead at coil.
7. Install high-tension cable and spark plug cables.
8. Connect vacuum hose or hoses.

1600 cc & 2000 cc Engine With Silent Shaft

1. Turn crankshaft until No. 1 piston is at top dead center on compression stroke and align notch on the crankshaft pulley with timing mark, "T."
2. Align mating mark (line) of distributor housing with mating mark (punch) of distributor driven gear, Fig. 3. Insert distributor into cylinder head so the mating marks will be in the uppermost position, Fig. 3.

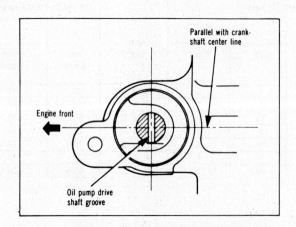

Fig. 1 Oil pump shaft groove positioning for distributor installation. 1600 cc engine less silent shaft

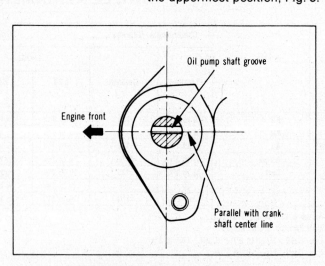

Fig. 2 Oil pump shaft groove positioning for distributor installation. 2000 cc engine less silent shaft

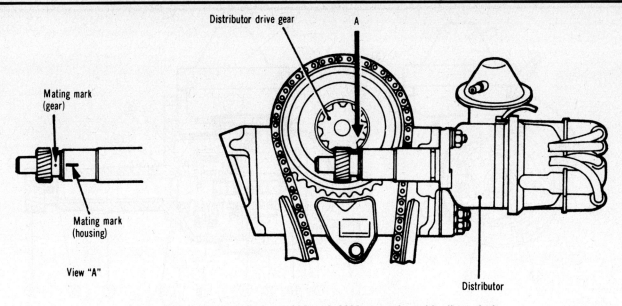

Fig. 3   Distributor installation. 1600 cc & 2000 cc engine with silent shaft

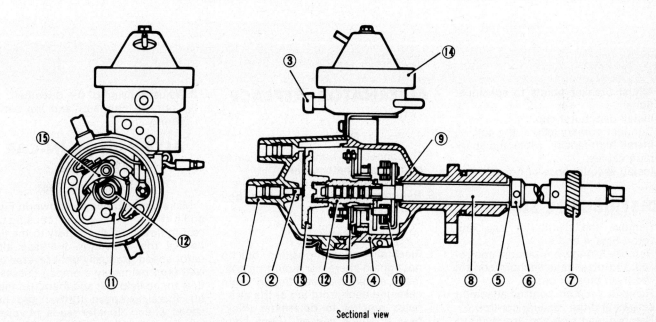

(1) Cap	(5) Washer	(9) Spacer	(13) Rotor
(2) Contactor	(6) Space collar	(10) Governor	(14) Vacuum controller
(3) Rubber cap	(7) Gear	(11) Breaker assembly	(15) Arm support
(4) Housing	(8) Shaft	(12) Cam	

Fig. 4   1600 cc engine distributor, sectional view

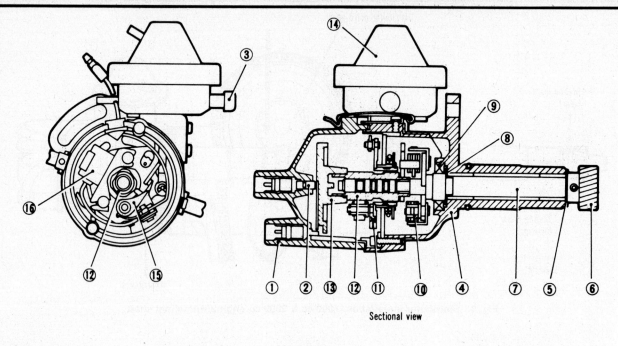

(1) Cap
(2) Contractor
(3) Rubber cap
(4) Housing
(5) Washer
(6) Gear
(7) Shaft
(8) Washer
(9) Oil seal
(10) Governor
(11) Breaker assembly
(12) Cam
(13) Rotor
(14) Vacuum controller
(15) Arm support
(16) Condensor

Fig. 5 2000 cc engine distributor, sectional view (Typical)

3. Adjust breaker points to specifications.
4. Install distributor cap.
5. Connect primary lead at the coil.
6. Install high-tension cable and spark plug cables.
7. Install vacuum hose or hoses.

DISTRIBUTOR SERVICE

1. Remove the distributor cap and rotor, Figs. 4 and 5.
2. Remove E-ring from vacuum control rod and disengage vacuum control rod from breaker base.
3. Remove vacuum control attaching screws and the vacuum control.
4. Remove lead wire and arm support assembly.
5. Remove breaker base.
6. Remove gear, then drive out spring pin.
7. Remove collar and washer.
8. Withdraw governor and shaft assembly from housing.
9. Reverse procedure to assemble.
10. After reassembly, apply multipurpose grease to cam surface and spindle sections.

ALTERNATOR, REPLACE

Removal

1. Disconnect the battery ground cable and the alternator wires.
2. Remove alternator brace bolts.
3. Remove alternator mounting bolt and alternator.

Installation

1. Place alternator in position, but do not tighten alternator mounting bolt. Insert a shim between timing chain case and each front leg of the alternator bracket to determine thickness of shims needed. (Each shim should not fall when released.) Then insert shims as required and install bolts and nuts.

NOTE: The alternator mounting bolt has an offset head to prevent bolt rotation. The nuts should be tightened after making sure that the bolts are in proper position in bolt holes of front bracket legs.

2. Adjust tension of the drive belt.
3. Connect alternator and the battery wiring.

ALTERNATOR IN-CAR TESTING

Performance Test

Make connections as shown in Fig. 6 and turn ignition key "on," causing current to flow from the battery to the field coil of the alternator. Increase alternator speed gradually until reverse current (approximately 2 amps.) ceases to flow to the field coil and then turn the KI off. Increase speed further and note speed when voltmeter reads 14 volts. If reading is 1,100 to 1,200 rpm, the performance of the alternator is satisfactory.

STARTER, REPLACE

Removal

1. Disconnect battery ground cable.
2. Disconnect starter cables.
3. Remove starter mounting bolts and the starter.

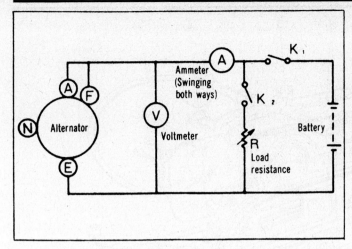

Fig. 6   Alternator performance test connections

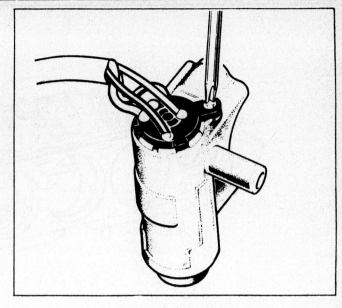

Fig. 7   Ignition switch replacement

Installation

1. Before mounting starter, clean the mating surfaces of starter and the engine.
2. Install starter and tighten mounting bolts so the starter motor shaft is perfectly parallel with the central axis of the engine in all directions. Torque the mounting bolts to 14 to 21 ft. lbs.
3. Connect starter cables and battery ground cable.

IGNITION SWITCH, REPLACE

The ignition switch is of a steering wheel lock type. When the key is turned to "LOCK" position and pulled out, the lock pin automatically ejects from the cylinder and enters a groove in the steering shaft, locking the steering wheel. The ignition switch also incorporates a warning switch circuit which turns on when the key is inserted in the ignition switch.

Removal

When replacing the ignition switch only, remove the column cover, loosen the bolt holding the switch, Fig. 7, and pull out the switch.

Installation

When installing the ignition switch to the column tube, attach it temporarily first and insert the key to check for proper operation. Then tighten the bolt.

LIGHT SWITCH, REPLACE

The light switch is serviced with the instrument cluster. Refer to the "Instrument Cluster, Replace" procedure.

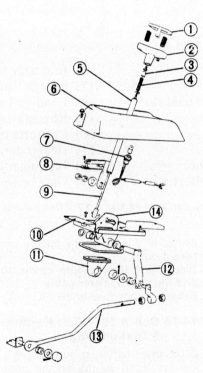

(1) Push button
(2) Shift handle
(3) Rod adjusting nut
(4) Rod return spring
(5) Selector lever assembly
(6) Position indicator assembly
(7) Indicator lamp socket assembly
(8) Inhibitor switch
(9) Shift lever rod
(10) Shift lever bracket assembly
(11) Lever bracket cover
(12) Transmission control arm
(13) Transmission control rod
(14) Selector lever position plate

Fig. 8   Neutral safety switch location

STOP LIGHT SWITCH, REPLACE

The stop light switch also serves as a brake pedal stopper and is located under the instrument panel, behind the brake pedal.

Removal

Disconnect the wire, then remove retaining nut from bracket and the switch.

Installation

Reverse removal procedure. Adjust pedal height by turning the adjusting screw. The measurement should be from the top face of the brake pedal to the floor carpeting. This dimension should be 6.4 to 6.6 inches for 1976-77 models and 6.9 to 7.1 inches for all others.

NEUTRAL SAFETY SWITCH, REPLACE

1. Remove shift lever bracket assembly, Fig. 8.
2. Remove retaining screw and neutral safety switch.
3. Reverse procedure to install.

TURN SIGNAL SWITCH, REPLACE

1. Remove steering wheel with tilt handle in lowest position.
2. Remove instrument cluster and column cover.

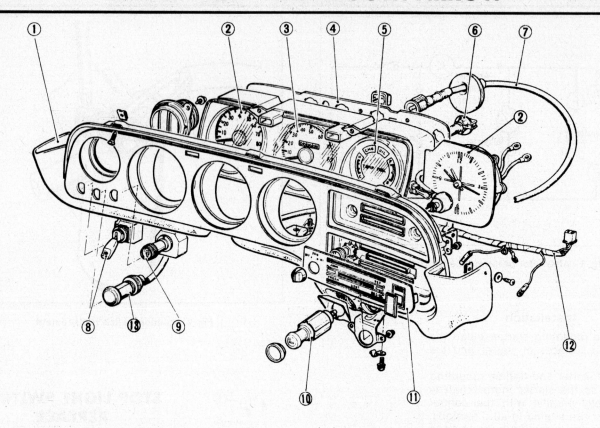

(1) Instrument cluster panel
(2) Tachometer (P-line)
    Clock (Station wagon-Decor package)
(3) Speedometer
(4) Printed board
(5) Combination gauge
    (fuel gauge, temperature gauge,
    oil pressure and charging indicator)
(6) Indicator bulb socket
(7) Speedometer cable
(8) Headlight switch
(9) Rheostat
(10) Cigarette lighter
(11) Heater control panel
(12) Instrument cluster harness
(13) Gate open warning light (Station wagon)

Fig. 9 Instrument cluster. 1974-76 Colt & 1977 Colt hardtop & station wagon

3. Disconnect connectors from switch and remove the switch from column tube.
4. Reverse procedure to install.

NOTE: When installing the switch, observe the following:
a. Install switch in complete alignment with the steering shaft center.
b. Place switch wiring harness along column tube as close as possible to the center line. Clip the wiring securely to prevent it from contacting other parts.

INSTRUMENT CLUSTER SERVICE

1972-1973 Colt

1. Remove the attaching screws at the bottom of the cluster.

2. Unclip at the top of the cluster and take it out.
3. Disconnect the multiple connector and the speedometer cable.
4. Reverse procedure to install.

1974-76 Colt & 1977 Colt Hardtop & Station Wagon

1. Disconnect battery ground cable.
2. Loosen three screws on the upper section of cluster and two screws on the lower section, Fig. 9.
3. Loosen screws securing heater control knob, ash tray and cigar lighter to the mounting brackets.
4. Remove blind cover located at right side of glove box, then the attaching screws on side of cluster.
5. Remove harness cover at bottom of instrument panel and disconnect light switch.
6. Pull cluster outward slightly and disconnect electrical connectors and speedometer cable.

7. Reverse procedure to install.

1976-77 Arrow & 1977 Colt Coupe & Sedan

1. Disconnect battery ground cable.
2. Remove air intake control knob, heater control knob, radio knobs and ring nuts, and the ash tray, Figs. 10 and 11.
3. Remove three upper screws and one lower screw from panel.
4. Remove one screw located behind the blind cover above the air intake control panel.
5. Remove three screws located behind and in the upper inside part of the ash tray opening.
6. Pull instrument cluster outward slightly and disconnect electrical connectors and speedometer cable.

NOTE: Ensure the grounding cable is disconnected.

(1) Instrument cluster panel
(2) Speedometer
(3) Tachometer (P-line)
    Combination gauge (fuel gauge and
    temperature gauge) (H-line and L-line)
(4) Water temperature gauge (P-line)
    Charging indicator (H-line and L-line)

(5) Fuel gauge (P-line)
    Oil pressure indicator (H-line and L-line)
(6) Oil pressure gauge (P-line)
(7) Ammeter (P-line)
(8) Cigarette lighter
(9) Heater control panel
(10) Lighting switch

Fig. 10 Instrument cluster. 1976-77 Arrow

7. Remove cluster from vehicle.
8. Reverse procedure to install.

WINDSHIELD WIPER SWITCH, REPLACE

The wiper switch is incorporated in the turn signal switch. See Turn Signal Switch section.

WINDSHIELD WIPER MOTOR, REPLACE

1972-73

1. Remove motor bracket and body attaching bolts at four places.

2. Remove nut at top of wiper arm on left side and remove wiper arm and blade.
3. Loosen wiper arm shaft lock nut and remove wiper motor assembly.
4. Reverse procedure to install.

1974-1977

NOTE: Uncover wiper removing hole located on the left hand side of the front deck.

1. Remove wiper arm, then the arm shaft lock nut and push shaft inward.

2. Remove bolts securing motor bracket to body and remove the wiper motor assembly.
3. Reverse procedure to install.

WINDSHIELD WIPER TRANSMISSION, REPLACE

1972-73

1. Remove wiper arm.
2. Remove wiper arm shaft attaching nuts and push shaft inward.
3. Remove wiper motor and bracket assembly.
4. Disconnect left side blade shaft from link.

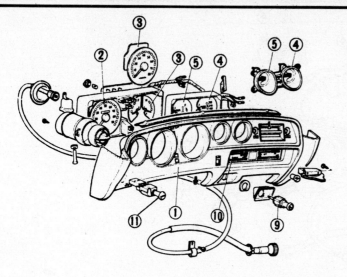

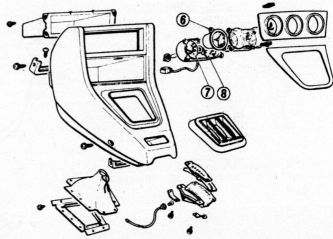

(1) Instrument cluster panel
(2) Speedometer
(3) Tachometer (Sedan – Freeway cruise package)
Combination gauge (fuel gauge and water temperature gauge) (Coupe and Sedan, except Sedan – Freeway cruise package)
(4) Water temperature gauge (Sedan – Freeway cruise package) Charging indicator (Coupe and Sedan, except Sedan – Freeway cruise package)
(5) Fuel gauge (Sedan – Freeway cruise package)
Oil pressure indicator (Coupe and Sedan, except Sedan – Freeway cruise package)
(6) Clock (Sedan – Freeway cruise package)
(7) Oil pressure gauge (Sedan – Freeway cruise package)
(8) Ammeter (Sedan – Freeway cruise package)
(9) Cigarette lighter
(10) Heater control panel
(11) Lighting switch

Fig. 11 Instrument cluster. 1977 Colt coupe & sedan

5. Remove wiper linkage from left side of vehicle.
6. Reverse procedure to install and observe the following:
 a. Ensure the shaft bracket positioning boss is properly positioned in the body hole.
 b. After installation, adjust the wiper blade stop position to .8-1.0 inch above bottom of windshield.

1974-77

1. Remove wiper motor and linkage assembly as outlined under "Windshield Wiper Motor, Replace" 1974-77 procedure.

2. Position wiper motor shaft at right angles to the linkage and remove linkage while holding shaft.
3. Reverse procedure to install and observe the following:
 a. Ensure the shaft bracket positioning boss is properly located in the body hole.
 b. After installation, adjust the wiper blade stop position to .6-.8 inch above bottom of windshield.

RADIO, REPLACE
1972-1973 Colt

1. Disconnect battery ground cable.

2. Remove control padding on top of radio by loosening attaching screws at bottom of radio. After screws have been loosened, push padding downward slightly and slide out.
3. Remove radio switches and knobs and loosen radio and console cover attaching nuts.
4. Remove heater control knobs.
5. Remove wing nut on right side of radio.
6. Remove attaching screws at bottom of console cover.
7. Pull out radio and console cover assembly.
8. Disconnect electrical wiring from radio and remove radio.
9. Reverse procedure to install.

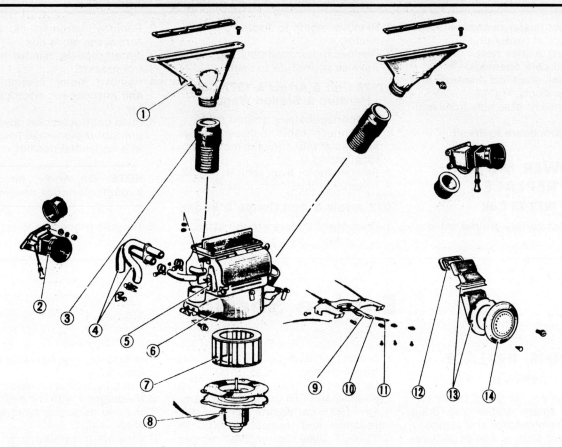

(1) Defroster nozzle
(2) Ventilator duct assembly
(3) Air duct
(4) Water hose
(5) Water valve assembly
(6) Heater assembly
(7) Turbo fan
(8) Motor
(9) Heater-defroster lever
(10) Water valve lever
(11) Air control lever
(12) Valve (sedan, hardtop, and coupe)
(13) Duct assembly (sedan, hardtop, and coupe)
(14) Ventilator garnish (sedan, hardtop, and coupe)

Fig. 12 Heater & blower motor (Typical)

1974-76 Colt & 1977 Colt Hardtop & Station Wagon

1. Disconnect battery ground cable.
2. Remove glove box.
3. Remove knobs and attaching nuts from front of radio.
4. Disconnect electrical wiring from radio.
5. On AM radio, remove radio attaching bracket and the radio.
6. On AM/FM radio, remove bolts from instrument panel reinforcement and the radio.
7. Reverse procedure to install.

1976-77 Arrow & 1977 Colt Coupe & Sedan

1. Disconnect battery ground cable.
2. Remove instrument cluster as outlined under "Instrument Cluster, Replace" procedure.
3. Remove radio knobs and nuts.

4. Remove bolts or screws from radio mounting bracket and disconnect electrical wiring from radio.
5. Remove radio from vehicle.
6. Reverse procedure to install.

HEATER CORE, REPLACE
1972-73 Colt

1. Disconnect battery ground cable and drain radiator.
2. Unfasten center console and pull outward.
3. Remove heater control wires at heater unit.
4. Remove heater control assembly, Fig. 12.
5. Disconnect heater hoses and plug hoses and core openings.
6. Remove heater ducts and the heater unit.
7. Reverse procedure to install.

1976 Colt & Arrow & 1977 Colt Hardtop & Station Wagon

1. Disconnect battery ground cable and drain radiator.
2. Remove glove box, instrument cluster and console box.
3. Disconnect heater control wires at heater unit.
4. Disconnect heater hoses and plug hoses and core openings.
5. Disconnect heater ducts and remove heater unit, Fig. 12.
6. Reverse procedure to install.

1977 Arrow & Colt Coupe & Sedan

1. Disconnect battery ground cable and drain radiator.
2. Place water valve lever in "Off" position.
3. Remove undertray, defroster nozzle and console box.

4. Disconnect heater control wire and connectors at heater unit.
5. Disconnect heater hoses and plug hoses and core openings.
6. Disconnect electrical harness and the heater ducts, Fig. 12.
7. Remove heater assembly from vehicle.
8. Reverse procedure to install.

BLOWER MOTOR, REPLACE

1972-73 Colt

1. Disconnect battery ground cable.

2. Remove motor to heater unit connector.
3. Remove motor assembly, Fig. 12.
4. Reverse procedure to install.

1976 Colt & Arrow & 1977 Colt Hardtop & Station Wagon

1. Disconnect battery ground cable.
2. Disconnect cable between motor and heater unit, then the motor electrical wiring.
3. Remove motor from vehicle, Fig. 12.
4. Reverse procedure to install.

1977 Arrow & Colt Coupe & Sedan

1. Disconnect battery ground cable.

2. Remove instrument cluster and on Arrow, the glove box.
3. On all models, remove heater control bracket.
4. Remove motor assembly, Fig. 12, and disconnect electrical connector.
5. Push control bracket downward and pull out motor while holding motor in a horizontal position.

NOTE: On Arrow, remove motor through glove box opening.

6. Reverse procedure to install.

Engine Section

ENGINE, REPLACE

Removal

Operations In Engine Compartment

1. Remove splash shield and drain coolant from radiator and engine.
2. Disconnect battery cables and remove battery.
3. Disconnect ground strap and wiring of ignition coil, vacuum control solenoid valve, alternator, starting motor, transmission switch, backup light switch, water temperature gauge unit and oil pressure switch.
4. Disconnect air cleaner breather hose. Remove air cleaner and disconnect hot air duct and vacuum hose.
5. Disconnect accelerator rod and heater hoses.
6. Disconnect exhaust pipe from exhaust manifold. The muffler pipe

bracket should be removed from transmission.
7. Disconnect hose between fuel strainer and fuel pump return pipe.
8. On 1600 cc engine remove the radiator and radiator cowl. On 1976-77 2000 cc engine, remove radiator shroud. If equipped with automatic transmission, disconnect cooler lines at radiator.

Operations Inside Car

1. Remove console box, then detach control lever assembly from transmission.

Operations Outside Engine Compartment

1. Remove hood.
2. Disconnect speedometer cable and backup lamp switch wiring from transmission.
3. Disconnect clutch cable from clutch

shift lever, then the cable from cable bracket.
4. Drain transmission fluid.
5. If equipped with dynamic dampers, remove dampers, remove propeller shaft.
6. Support transmission on transmission jack. Remove front and rear insulator locking bolts and nuts, then the rear engine support bracket.
7. Attach cables to engine front and rear hangers, then remove the engine-transmission unit at an angle, moving upward and forward.

CAUTIONS:

a. Use a short cable at the front engine hanger so when the engine-transmission unit if lifted, the transmission is lower than the engine.

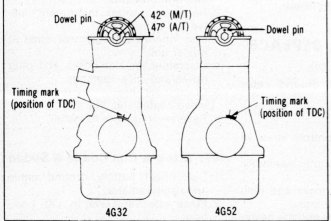

Fig. 1 Positioning camshaft sprocket. 1600 cc Engine less silent shaft & all 2000 cc engines

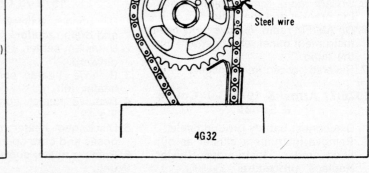

Fig. 2 Securing timing chain. 1600 cc engine less silent shaft

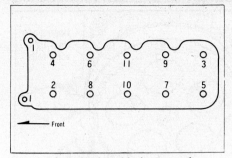

Fig. 3 Cylinder head bolt removal sequence. 1600 cc engine less silent shaft & all 2000 cc engines

b. If the engine-transmission unit cannot be removed because the lower part of the bell housing interferes with relay rod, raise rear end of the transmission until the bell housing is above the relay rod and then pull out the unit.

Installation

Reverse the removal procedure and observe the following items.

1. When installing the engine-transmission unit, place rags at rear of cylinder head to avoid damage to firewall.
2. Lift the engine-transmission unit slightly higher than the mounting position, install the front insulators, then the rear insulators and related parts.

CAUTION: When installing the insulator, use caution not to twist the rubber or smear the rubber with gasoline or oil.

3. When installing a rolling stopper (a stop to restrict engine movement on the mountings), to the front insulator, use care to provide clearance between the stopper and the side of the insulator.
4. To install the rear engine support bracket to the floor stringer of the car body, first tighten bolts to 7 ft.-lbs. torque and see if the tongue of

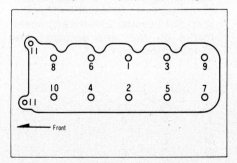

Fig. 5 Cylinder head bolt tightening sequence. 1600 cc engine less silent shaft & all 2000 cc engine

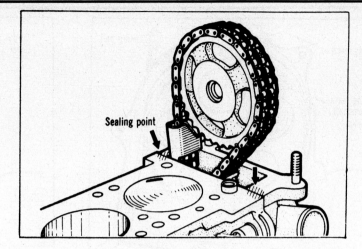

Fig. 4 Cylinder head sealing points. 1600 cc engine less silent shaft & all 2000 cc engines

each lock washer is aligned properly with a flat of the bolt head. If these parts are in alignment, tighten the bolts to 10-12 ft.-lbs. on the 1600 cc engine or 10-14 ft.-lbs. on the 2000 cc engine. Then, bend the tongue of the lock washer. Be sure there is at least .75 in. clearance between the rear support bracket and the exhaust pipe.
5. Securely tighten all engine mounting nuts and bolts.
6. Add the adequate amount of antifreeze and water to the cooling system.
7. Fill the engine crankcase and the transmission with the specified amounts of the proper lubricants. Refer to "Cooling System & Capacity Data" chart.

CYLINDER HEAD, REPLACE
1600 cc Less Silent Shaft & All 2000 cc Engines

Removal

1. Turn crankshaft until No. 1 piston is at top dead center, compression stroke.

NOTE: If dowel pin at forward end of camshaft is in position shown in Fig. 1, when crankshaft pulley notch is aligned with timing mark, "T," at front of the timing chain case, the No. 1 piston is at TDC.

2. Draw a mating mark in white paint on the timing chain, in line with the timing mark on the camshaft

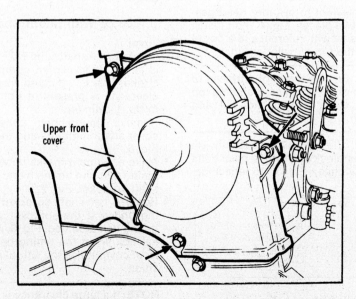

Fig. 6 Timing belt upper front cover removal. 1600 cc engine with silent shaft

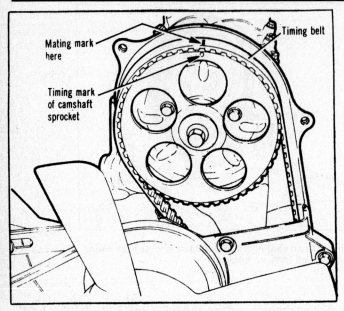

Fig. 7   Timing belt & camshaft sprocket alignment marks. 1600 cc engine with silent shaft

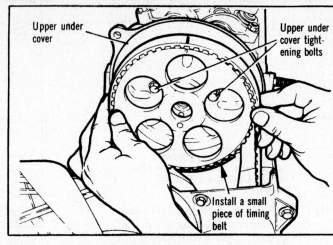

Fig. 8   Camshaft sprocket removal. 1600 cc engine with silent shaft

sprocket. On 1600 cc engine, the chain may be locked against rotation with a steel wire, Fig. 2.

3. Remove camshaft sprocket and on 2000 cc engine with silent shaft, the distributor drive gear.

4. Remove cylinder head bolts and nuts in sequence, Fig. 3. Head bolts should be loosened in two or three stages to prevent cylinder head from warping.

5. The cylinder head is positioned to the cylinder block with two dowel pins, front and rear. When removing the head, be careful not to slide it or twist the sprocket and chain.

Installation

1. Apply sealant to cylinder head gasket in two places, Fig. 4, then install the gasket with reference to a dowel pin in the top of cylinder block.

NOTE: Ensure the joint surfaces of the top of the chain case and the top of the cylinder block are flat and smooth.

2. Install cylinder head assembly on cylinder block and torque head bolts in sequence, Fig. 5, to specifications.

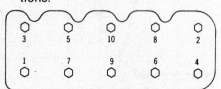

Fig. 9   Cylinder head bolt removal sequence. 1600 cc engine with silent shaft

3. Install the camshaft sprocket on the camshaft while pulling it upward and temporarily tighten the locking bolt. If it is difficult to install the sprocket, slacken the timing chain by loosening the tensioner holder to the left of the chain case and sprocket installation can be done with ease.

4. Turn the crankshaft 90 degrees back.

5. Torque camshaft sprocket locking bolt to specifications.

6. Adjust valves as outlined under "Valves, Adjust" procedure.

7. Run the engine until it reaches normal operating temperature, then retorque head bolts.

1600 cc With Silent Shaft

Removal

1. Rotate crankshaft until No. 1 piston is at top dead center, compression stroke. This is indicated when valve clearance is present at both valves in No. 1 cylinder.

2. Remove timing belt upper front cover attaching bolts and the cover, Fig. 6.

3. Make alignment marks between the timing belt and timing mark on camshaft sprocket, Fig. 7.

4. Remove camshaft sprocket attaching bolt and the sprocket with the timing belt attached, Fig. 8. A sprocket holder on the timing belt lower front cover holds the sprocket in position.

NOTE: If a large clearance is present between the camshaft sprocket and sprocket holder, insert a small piece

of timing belt or other material into this clearance, Fig. 8. This prevents the sprocket from being pulled downward and the timing belt disengaging from the crankshaft or oil pump sprockets.

5. Remove timing belt upper under cover bolts and the cover.

6. Remove cylinder head bolts in sequence, Fig. 9. Loosen the bolts in stages to prevent cylinder head warpage.

7. Remove cylinder head.

Installation

1. Clean cylinder head and block mating surfaces. Ensure all old gasket material is removed.

2. Place cylinder head on block and install and torque head bolts in sequence, Fig. 10, to specifications.

3. Install timing belt upper under cover and tighten attaching bolts, Fig. 11.

4. Pull camshaft sprocket upward and install on camshaft. If the camshaft sprocket is difficult to lift and cannot be easily fitted into the spacers, insert a screwdriver into the sprocket top hole, place the end of the screwdriver under the ridge portion of the upper under cover and pry the sprocket upward. Ensure alignment marks on belt and sprocket are aligned properly, Fig. 7.

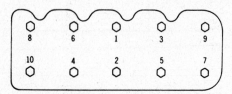

Fig. 10   Cylinder head bolt tightening sequence. 1600 cc engine with silent shaft

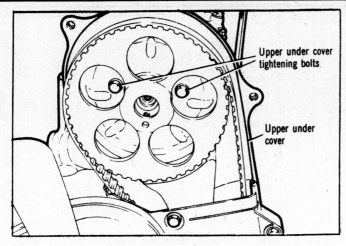

Fig. 11 Timing belt upper under cover installation. 1600 cc engine with silent shaft

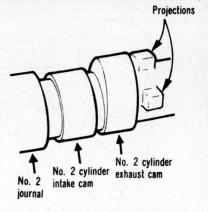

Fig. 12 Camshaft projections for rotation. 1600 cc engine with silent shaft

NOTE: If the dowel pin hole of the camshaft sprocket cannot be aligned with the dowel pin at the end of the spacer, turn the camshaft by striking the two projections located at the rear of the No. 2 cylinder exhaust lobe on the camshaft, Fig. 12. Also, ensure the crankshaft remains stationary.

5. Tighten camshaft sprocket attaching bolt.
6. Install timing belt upper front cover.

VALVES, ADJUST

1. With engine at normal operating temperature, remove rocker cover.
2. Disconnect coil high tension lead at coil.
3. Observe the No. 1 cylinder rocker arms and rotate engine until the No. 1 cylinder exhaust valve starts to close and the intake valve starts to open. This places the No. 4 cylinder at top dead center, compression stroke.
4. Check valve clearance of both valves on No. 4 cylinder. Adjust, if necessary, by loosening the adjusting screw locknut and turning the adjusting screw to obtain proper clearance, Fig. 13. Retighten locknut.
5. Rotate engine while observing the rocker arms on No. 2 cylinder. Stop rotation when the exhaust valve starts to close and the intake valve starts to open.
6. Check and adjust both valves on No. 3 cylinder.
7. Onserve the No. 3 cylinder rocker arms and rotate engine until the exhaust valve starts to close and the intake valve starts to open. Check and adjust valves on No. 2 cylinder.
8. Rotate engine while observing the No. 4 cylinder rocker arms. Stop rotation when the exhaust valve starts to close and the intake valve starts to open.
9. Check and adjust both valves on No. 1 cylinder.
10. Install rocker cover and connect high tension lead at coil.

CAMSHAFT, ROCKER ARMS & SHAFTS, & VALVES, REPLACE
Removal

1. Remove spark plugs.
2. Remove camshaft bearing cap bolts.
3. Holding the front and rear caps, remove rocker arm shaft assembly.
4. Separate assembly into the caps, the rocker arm, springs, rocker arm shafts and the waved washer. The rocker arms should be placed in order and marked to indicate the proper cylinders. The camshaft bearing caps are located with dowel pins in the head. Be careful not to lose them.
5. Remove camshaft.
6. Using a valve spring compressor, remove the retainer locks, then the

Fig. 13 Adjusting valves

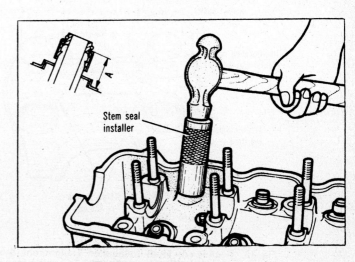

Fig. 14 Installing valve stem seals

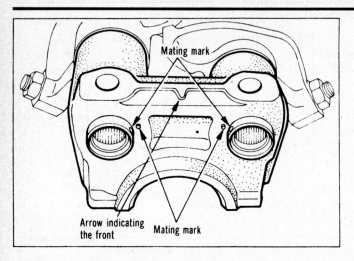

Fig. 15 Rocker arm shaft installation & alignment. 1972-76 1600 cc engine & 1974-76 2000 cc engine

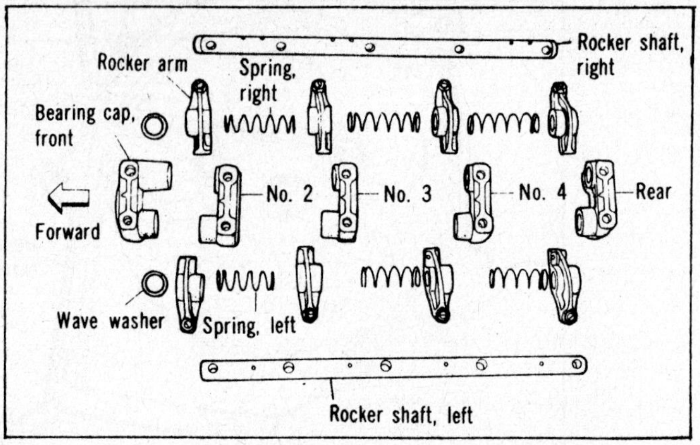

Fig. 16 Rocker arm shaft assembly. 1972-76 1600 cc engine & 1974-76 2000 cc engine (Typical)

spring retainers, springs, spring seats and valves.

NOTE: Keep the valves in proper order.

7. Pry off valve stem seals with a screwdriver and discard.

Installation

Apply new engine oil to all sliding and rotating parts.

1. After installing the spring seat, fit the stem seal on the valve guide. To install, fit the seal in by lightly hammering the special tool, Valve Stem Seal Installer, Fig. 14. Dimension "A," Fig. 14, should be .579—.595 inch.
2. Apply engine oil to each valve and insert valves into the valve guides.
3. Install spring and spring retainers.
4. Using a valve spring compressor, compress the spring and install the retainer lock. When compressing the spring with the spring compressor, check that the valve stem seal is not pressed by the bottom of the retainer. Then install the retainer lock. Ensure the retainer locks are positively installed.
5. Install camshaft in cylinder head. Check camshaft end play. On 1600 cc engine, end play should be .002—.006 inch. On 2000 cc engine, end play should be .004—.008 inch.
6. Assemble the rocker arm shaft assemblies. On 1972-76 1600 cc engines and 1974-76 2000 cc engines, the front bearing cap has an embossed mating mark on the front face, Fig. 15. The rocker arm shaft has an indented mark near the front end. When assembling the rocker shaft with the front bearing cap, align the mating marks, Fig. 15. Also, note that the left rocker shaft has four oil holes and the right shaft has eight oil holes, Fig. 16. These oil holes should face downward when

the shaft is installed. The left springs have a free length of 2.57 inch and the right springs have a free length of 2.10 inch. The bearing caps have an arrow mark indicating the direction of installation, facing toward front of engine. The wave washer should be installed with the convex side facing toward front of engine.

On all 1977 engines, refer to Figs. 17 through 22, to assemble rocker arm shaft assemblies.

7. Install the assembled rocker arm shaft assembly on the cylinder head. The camshaft should be positioned so that the dowel pin on the front end is in the position shown in Figs. 23 through 25, when viewed from the front. Install the dowel bushings of the caps on the stud bolts. Do not twist or do not try to install the caps forcibly. Torque bolts in two or three stages to specifications.

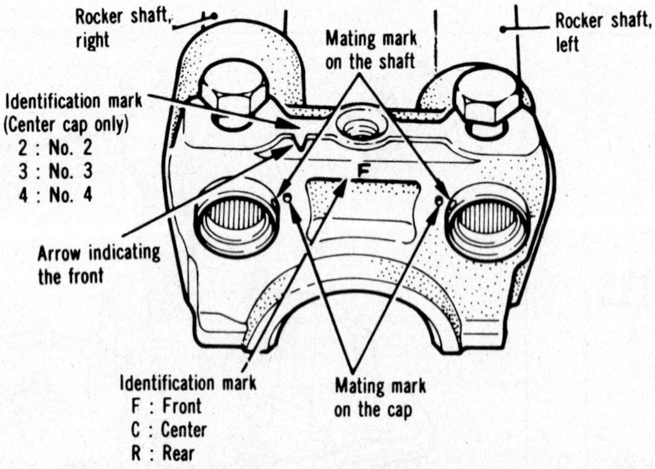

VALVE GUIDES, REPLACE

1. Press or hammer out each old valve guide toward the cylinder block. This should be done with cylinder head heated to about 480 deg. F.
2. Ream each guide hole in the cylinder head to the specified size at normal temperature.
3. After re-heating the cylinder head to about 480 deg., insert the guides. Then using valve guide installer, Fig. 26, press or hammer the intake and exhaust valve guides to the correct position. The tool automatically stops the guides at the proper depth.
4. After installing the valve guides, measure the inside diameter of the guide. Ream out the guide inside diameter, if necessary.

Fig. 17 Rocker arm shaft installation & alignment, & bearing cap identification. 1977 1600 cc engine less silent shaft

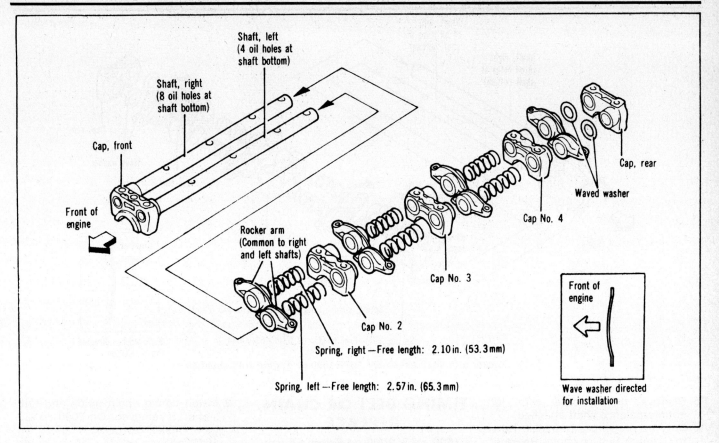

Fig. 18 Rocker arm shaft assembly. 1977 1600 cc engine less silent shaft

TIMING CASE, REPLACE

1600 cc & 2000 cc Engines Less Silent Shaft

1. Remove the oil pressure gauge or oil pressure gauge unit.
2. Remove the oil pan.
3. Remove oil screen and on 2000 cc engine, the oil pump.
4. Remove crankshaft pulley.
5. Remove flywheel.

NOTE: If no other work is to be done on the engine, it is not necessary to remove the flywheel.

6. Remove the tensioner holder on the right side of the timing case and remove the spring and plunger.
7. Remove the timing case.
8. Reverse procedure to install.

1600 cc Engine With Silent Shaft

1. Remove crankshaft pulley.
2. Remove timing belt upper front and lower front covers.

3. Remove crankshaft sprocket bolt.
4. Slightly loosen tensioner mounting bolt and nut, then press tensioner fully in the direction of arrow and tighten nut, Fig. 27. Remove timing belt.
5. Remove camshaft sprocket, crankshaft sprocket and flange.
6. Remove timing belt tensioner.
7. Remove oil pump sprocket. When the oil pump sprocket nut is removed, first remove plug at bottom of left side of cylinder block and insert a suitable screwdriver to keep the left counter-balance shaft in position, Fig. 28.
8. Loosen counterbalance shaft sprocket mounting bolt and remove tensioner "B," Fig. 29, and timing belt "B."
9. Remove crankshaft sprocket "B," Fig. 29, and the counterbalance shaft sprocket.
10. Remove timing belt upper under and lower under covers.
11. Remove water pump.
12. Remove cylinder head assembly.
13. Remove oil pan, oil screen and oil pump cover.
14. Insert a screwdriver through plug hole in left side of cylinder block to hold counterbalance shaft in position, then loosen oil pump driven gear mounting bolt, Fig. 30.

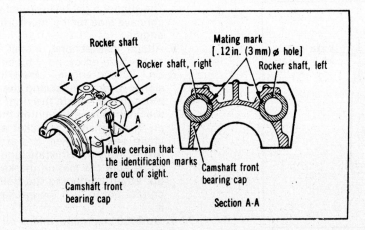

Fig. 19 Rocker arm shaft installation & alignment. 1977 1600 cc engine with silent shaft

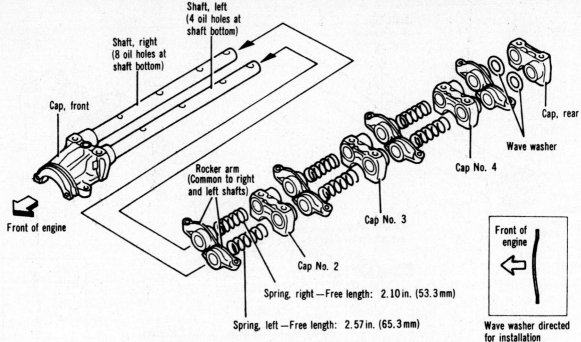

Fig. 20   Rocker arm shaft assembly. 1977 1600 cc engine with silent shaft

15. Remove timing case with left counterbalance shaft attached.
16. Reverse procedure to install. Refer to "Timing Belt or chain, Replace" procedure for timing belt installation.

2000 cc Engine With Silent Shaft

1. Remove oil pressure gauge or oil pressure gauge unit.
2. Remove oil pan and oil screen.
3. Remove crankshaft pulley.
4. Remove flywheel.
5. Remove timing chain case.
6. Reverse procedure to install.

TIMING BELT OR CHAIN, REPLACE

1600 cc & 2000 cc Engine Less Silent Shaft

Removal
1. Remove timing case as described previously.
2. Remove oil slinger and crankshaft gear from crankshaft.
3. Remove crankshaft sprocket, camshaft sprocket and timing chain.

Installation
1. Rotate the crankshaft to place No. 1 piston at top dead center.

2. Install timing chain guide and tensioner, if removed. On 2000 cc engine, install sprocket holder. On 1600 cc engine, the chain guide must be installed so the jet is directed toward the meshing point of the chain and sprocket.
3. With mating punch marks of the crankshaft sprocket and camshaft sprocket aligned with the chrome-plated links of the chain, install the sprocket on the crankshaft with the chain fitted in the guide groove and against the tensioner lever, Fig. 31.
4. Install the key and then install the crankshaft gear and the oil slinger. The crankshaft gear must be installed with the "F" mark on 1600 cc engine and "C" or "A" mark on 2000 cc engine facing front of engine. The slinger must be installed with its concave side facing the front of the engine.
5. Attach gasket and install timing chain case on cylinder block.
6. On 1600 cc engine, insert the tensioner lever plunger and the spring through the hole in the right side of the chain case and tighten the holder. The camshaft sprocket and the chain are supported and stretched respectively with the tensioner lever, so be sure the mating marks match up. When tightening the holder, be careful not to turn the packing with it.
7. On 2000 cc engine, install oil pump.
8. Install oil screen.
9. Install oil pan with a new gasket. The oil pan gasket should be coated with

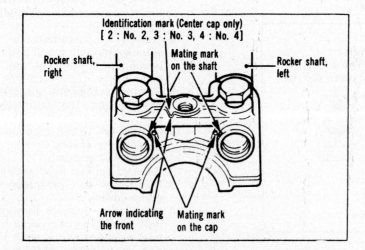

Fig. 21   Rocker arm shaft installation & alignment, & bearing cap identification. 1977 2000 cc engine

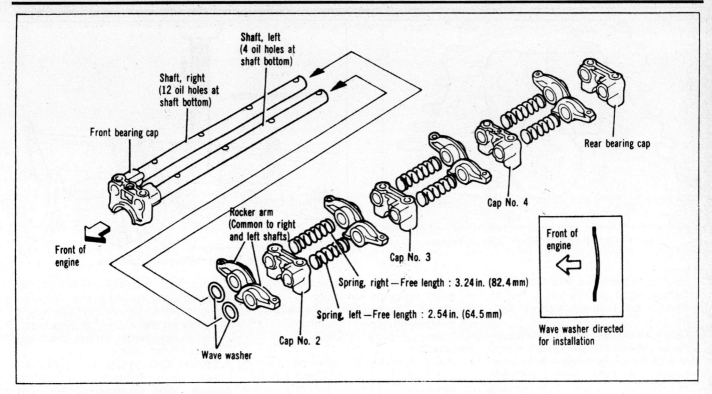

Fig. 22   Rocker arm shaft installation. 1977 2000 cc engine

sealant on the oil pan side. The mating surfaces of the block and chain case and the block to rear oil seal joint faces should be coated with sealant. Tighten oil pan bolts in criss-cross fashion, starting with the one located farthest from the center. Torque bolts to 4.3 to 5.8 ft. lbs.

10. Install oil pressure switch.
11. Install crankshaft pulley. Lock the crankshaft against rotation. Install the camshaft sprocket on the camshaft and install the flywheel before torquing the crankshaft pulley bolts to 43-50 ft. lbs.

12. Turn the engine upright. Do not turn the crankshaft. Install the cylinder head and attach the camshaft sprocket on the camshaft.

1600 cc Engine With Silent Shaft

Removal
1. Perform steps 1 through 4 outlined under "Timing Case, Replace" 1600 cc engine with silent shaft procedure.

Installation
1. Install timing belt. Place belt on crankshaft sprocket, then the oil

pump sprocket and camshaft sprocket. Ensure timing marks are properly aligned, Fig. 32. Also, install crankshaft pulley.
2. Loosen tensioner bolt or nut. Push the tensioner upward to ensure the belt is in complete mesh with the sprocket, then tighten the tensioner mounting nut and bolt.

NOTE: Tighten the nut, then the bolt.

3. Rotate the crankshaft through one revolution. Loosen the tensioner mounting nut and bolt. This applies

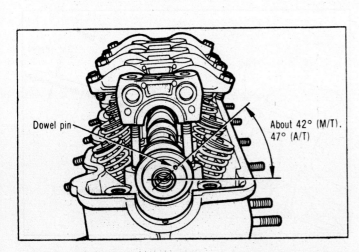

Fig. 23   Camshaft installation. 1600 cc engine less silent shaft

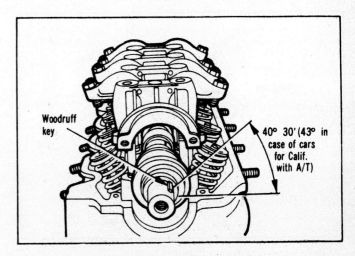

Fig. 24   Camshaft installation. 1600 cc engine with silent shaft

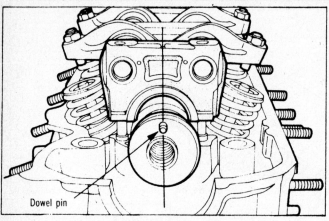

Fig. 25 Camshaft installation. 2000 cc engine

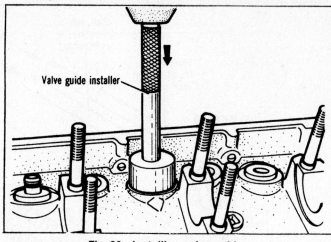

Fig. 26 Installing valve guides

tension to the loose side of the belt. Torque tensioner mounting nut to 13-15 ft. lbs., then tighten the mounting bolt.

4. Check to ensure that when the center of the tension side and the seal line of the under cover are held between the thumb and forefinger, Fig. 33, the clearance between the belt and seal line is .47 inch. Readjust, if necessary.

5. Install timing belt lower and upper front covers.

2000 cc Engine With Silent Shaft

Removal

1. Remove timing chain case as outlined under "Timing Case, Replace" 2000 cc engine with silent shaft procedure.
2. Remove chain guides "A," "B" and "C," Fig. 34.
3. Remove sprocket "B" locking bolts, Fig. 34.
4. Remove crankshaft sprocket "B," counterbalance shaft sprocket "B" and chain "B," Fig. 34.

5. Remove crankshaft sprocket, camshaft sprocket and timing chain, Fig. 35. Depress tensioner as chain is removed.

Installation

1. Rotate crankshaft to place No. 1 piston at top dead center, compression stroke.
2. Install camshaft sprocket and crankshaft sprocket on timing chain. When the sprockets are installed, ensure the mating marks of the chain and sprockets are properly aligned. The mating marks on the sprockets are punched marks on the corresponding teeth. The marks on the chain are two plated links, Fig. 35.
3. Install camshaft sprocket on camshaft and align the keyway of the crankshaft sprocket with the key of the crankshaft and install sprocket on crankshaft. Ensure timing marks are properly aligned, Fig. 35.
4. Install crankshaft sprocket "B," Fig. 35, on the crankshaft.
5. Install two counterbalance shaft

sprockets "B" on chain "B," Fig. 36, aligning the mating marks. The mating marks on sprockets are punched marks on the corresponding teeth. The mating marks on the chain are three plated links.

6. Install chain "B" on crankshaft sprocket, then the two counterbalance shaft sprockets "B" and tighten the lock bolts.
7. Install chain guides "A," "B" and "C," Fig. 36, and loosely install mounting bolts.
8. Tighten chain guides "A" and "C" mounting bolts.
9. Shake right and left sprockets "B" to collect chain slack at point "P," Fig. 36. Adjust position of chain guide "B" so when the chain is pulled in direction of arrow "Y," Fig. 36, the clearance between chain guide "B" and the links of chain "B" will be .04-.14 inch. Tighten chain guide "B" mounting bolts.
10. Install timing case gasket and case.
11. Install oil screen and oil pan.
12. Install crankshaft pulley.

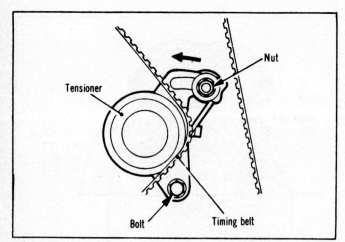

Fig. 27 Removing timing belt. 1600 cc engine with silent shaft

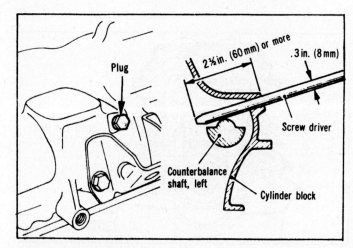

Fig. 28 Removing oil pump sprocket mounting bolt. 1600 cc engine with silent shaft

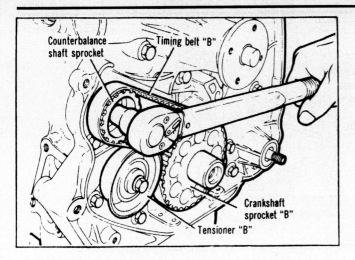

Fig. 29   Removing timing belt & related parts. 1600 cc engine with silent shaft

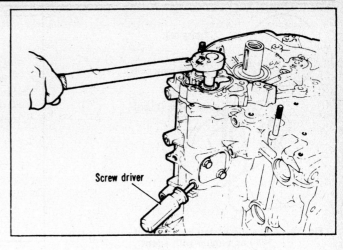

Fig. 30   Removing oil pump driven gear bolt. 1600 cc engine with silent shaft

PISTON & ROD ASSEMBLY

This piston and rod is assembled with the indented arrow on the piston and the embossed numeral on the rod facing toward front of engine. Refer to Figs. 37 through 40 for piston identification.

REAR OIL SEAL, REPLACE

Removal

1. Remove rear oil seal case and separate into three parts: oil seal, separator and case, Fig. 41.

Installation

1. Drive in oil seal from inside case, using the special tool, Fig. 42. Ensure the oil seal plate fits properly in the inner contact surface of the seal case.

2. Install separator with the oil hole facing the bottom of the case.
3. Apply engine oil to oil seal lips.
4. Install the oil seal case in the cylinder block.

OIL PAN, REPLACE

Removal

1. Remove the oil pressure gauge or sender unit.
2. Drain oil pan.
3. Remove the oil pan bolts and oil pan.
4. Reverse procedure to install

OIL PUMP, REPLACE

1600 cc Engine Less Silent Shaft

1. Remove splash shield from beneath vehicle.

2. Remove oil filter.
3. Remove oil pump cover bolts, then the pump rotor assembly with the cover.
4. Reverse procedure to install. Before installing pump, clean mating surfaces of pump cover and timing case.

2000 cc Engine Less Silent Shaft

1. Drain oil pan.
2. Remove oil pan and gasket.
3. Remove oil pump attaching bolts and the oil pump.
4. Rotate engine clockwise to place No. 1 piston at top dead center, compression stroke.
5. Remove distributor cap and set distributor rotor at the No. 1 firing position.

NOTE: Ensure distributor shaft pawl is properly positioned, Fig. 43.

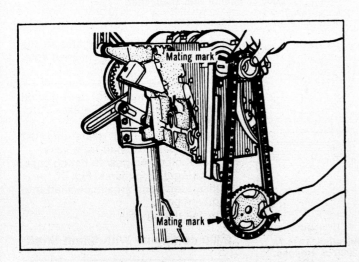

Fig. 31   Installing timing chain & sprockets. 1600 cc & 2000 cc engines less silent shaft

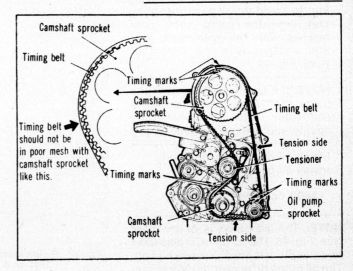

Fig. 32   Timing belt installation. 1600 cc engine with silent shaft

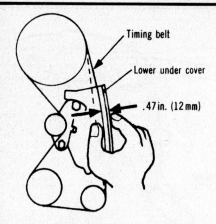

Fig. 33 Adjusting timing belt tension. 1600 cc engine with silent shaft

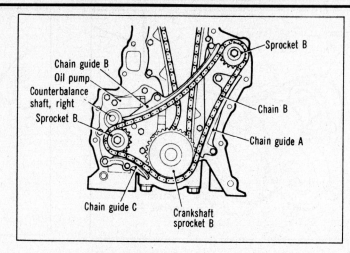

Fig. 34 Counterbalance shaft drive system. 2000 cc engine with silent shaft

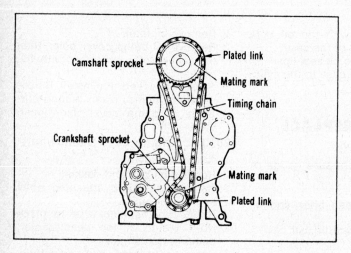

Fig. 35 Timing chain installation. 2000 cc engine with silent shaft

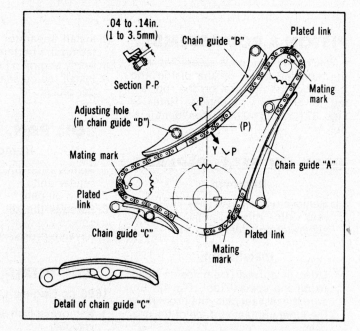

Fig. 36 Adjusting counterbalance shaft drive chain tension. 2000 cc engine with silent shaft

6. With mating mark on oil pump body aligned with marks on the gear, Fig. 44, insert the oil pump into position until the pump shaft gear meshes with the crankshaft gear and engages with the distributor pawl, Fig. 45.

NOTE: If it is difficult to engage the pump shaft driven gear, rotate the distributor rotor clockwise and counter-clockwise to engage gear.

7. Install oil pump attaching bolts.
8. Install oil pan.

1600 cc With Silent Shaft

NOTE: The oil pump is of the gear type, Fig. 46. The oil pump is also used to drive the left counterbalance shaft. The oil pump drive gear has a sprocket driven by a timing belt. The counterbalance shaft is mounted to the oil

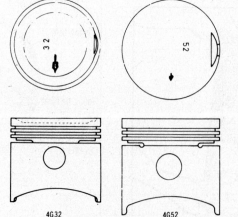

Fig. 37 Piston identification. 1974-75 1600 cc & 2000 cc engines. Note: Designation 4G32 is 1600 cc engine & 4G52 is 2000 cc engine

pump driven gear and rotates in the opposite direction of crankshaft rotation.

1. Remove timing case as outlined under "Timing Case, Replace" procedure.
2. Remove oil pump gears and left counterbalance shaft from case.
3. Install oil pump gear in timing case, aligning timing marks, Fig. 47.
4. Insert left counterbalance shaft into driven gear.
5. Install timing case.

2000 cc Engine With Silent Shaft

NOTE: The oil pump is of the gear type, Fig. 48. The oil pump is also used

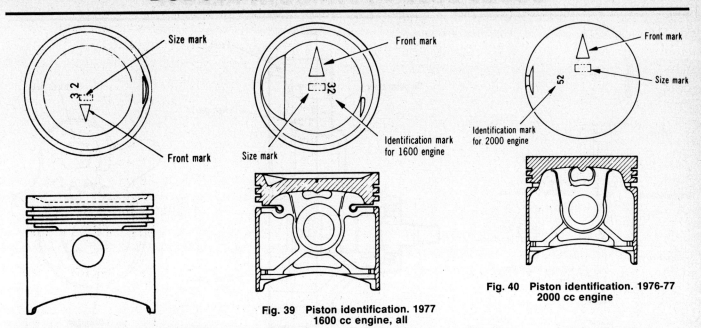

Fig. 38 Piston identification. 1976 1600 cc engine

Fig. 39 Piston identification. 1977 1600 cc engine, all

Fig. 40 Piston identification. 1976-77 2000 cc engine

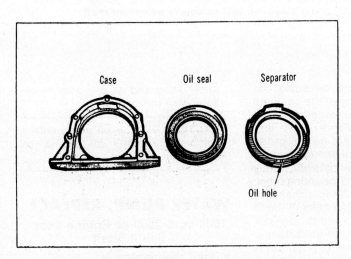

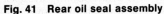

Fig. 41 Rear oil seal assembly

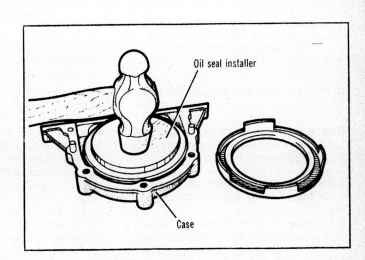

Fig. 42 Installing rear oil seal

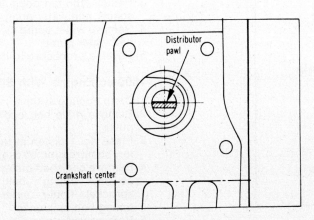

Fig. 43 Distributor pawl alignment. 2000 cc engine less silent shaft

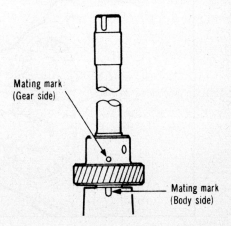

Fig. 44 Oil pump mating marks. 2000 cc engine less silent shaft

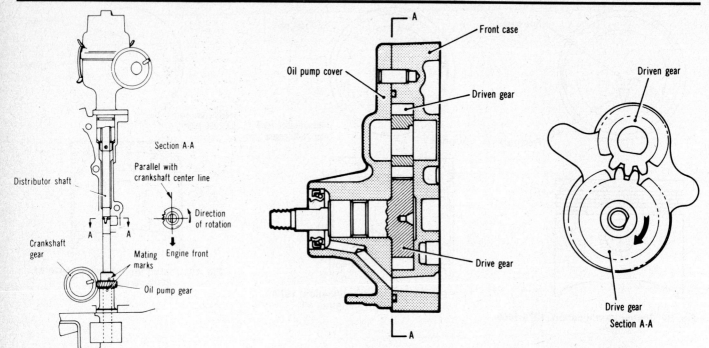

Fig. 45   Oil pump installation. 2000 cc engine less silent shaft

Fig. 46   Oil pump assembly. 1600 cc engine with silent shaft

to drive the right counterbalance shaft. The oil pump drive gear has a sprocket driven by a chain. The counterbalance shaft is mounted to the oil pump driven gear and rotates in the opposite direction of crankshaft rotation.

1. Remove timing chain as outlined under "Timing Belt or Chain, Replace" procedure.
2. Remove bolt locking oil pump driven gear to right balancer shaft, then the oil pump mounting bolts.
3. Remove the oil pump assembly.

4. When installing the oil pump, be sure that the keyway of the oil pump driven gear fits the woodruff key at the end of the balancer shaft and that the key does not go out of the keyway. After the oil pump assembly has been correctly installed, firmly tighten the oil pump mounting bolts. Next, tighten the balancer shaft and driven gear mounting bolts. If the fit of the woodruff key and driven gear is too tight, first insert the balancer shaft into the oil pump, temporarily tighten the bolt and insert the bal-

ancer shaft and oil pump as an assembly in the cylinder block.

CAUTION: Fill the oil pump with a sufficient amount of engine oil (more than .6 cu. in.).

WATER PUMP, REPLACE
1600 cc & 2000 cc Engine Less Silent Shaft

1. Drain cooling system.
2. Loosen alternator support bolt and alternator brace bolt, push alternator toward engine and remove fan belt.
3. Remove the fan bolts, then the fan, spacer and water pump pulley.
4. Remove water pump mounting bolts and water pump.
5. Reverse procedure to install.

1600 cc Engine With Silent Shaft

1. Drain cooling system.
2. Remove drive belt cooling fan and pulley.
3. Place No. 1 piston at top dead center, compression stroke.
4. Remove camshaft pulley, timing belt covers, timing belt, camshaft sprocket, upper under cover and timing belt tensioner.
5. Remove water pump mounting bolts and the water pump.
6. Reverse procedure to install.

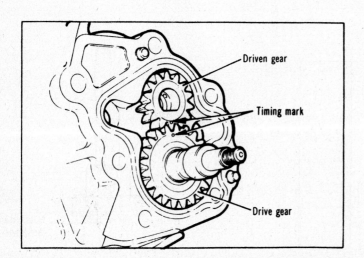

Fig. 47   Oil pump gear alignment. 1600 cc engine with silent shaft

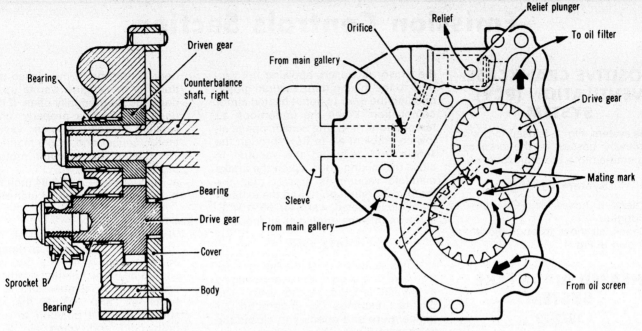

Fig. 48 Oil pump assembly. 2000 cc engine with silent shaft

2000 cc Engine With Silent Shaft

1. Drain cooling system.
2. Remove drive belt, cooling fan and pulley.
3. Remove water pump mounting bolts and the water pump.
4. Reverse procedure to install.

FUEL PUMP, REPLACE
Removal

1. Remove the fuel hoses from the fuel pump.

2. On 1600 cc engine less silent shaft, remove the fuel pump protector.
3. Remove pump attaching bolts and the fuel pump assembly. Remove the insulator and gasket from the cylinder block.

Installation

1. Use two new gaskets and apply sealant to both sides.
2. Install the pump assembly on the cylinder block.
3. Connect the inlet and outlet hoses

to the pump, install and securely tighten the clamps.
4. On 1600 cc engine less silent shaft install the fuel pump protector.
5. Start the engine and check for leaks.

Carburetor Section

FUEL LEVEL ADJUSTMENT

A sight glass is attached to the float chamber. Check to see if fuel level is nearly in the middle. Normal fuel level is within the center mark (1/8-in. diameter) on the sight glass.

To adjust float level, increase or decrease the number of needle valve packings, Fig. 1. A sheet of needle valve packing is .039 in. thick. Adding or removing a sheet of packing will change the float level by .118 in.

AUTOMATIC CHOKE ADJUSTMENT

Loosen bolt securing choke cover to housing and align the center projection on the choke housing with the yellow punch mark on the cover, Fig. 2.

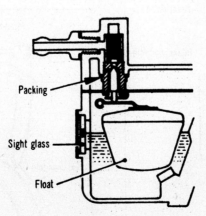

Fig. 1 Fuel level adjustment

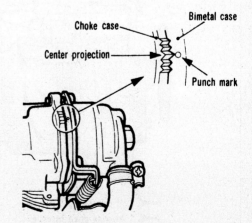

Fig. 2 Automatic choke adjustment

Emission Controls Section

POSITIVE CRANKCASE VENTILATION (PCV) SYSTEM

This system, Fig. 1, is used to prevent the blowby gasses in the crankcase being emitted into the atmosphere.

System Testing

1. Check if hoses or PCV valve is clogged.
2. Check air flow through hoses as shown in Fig. 1.

HEATED AIR INTAKE SYSTEM

1972-73

The heated air intake system, Fig. 2, supplies warm air for combustion. The incoming air is heated to 95°-104° F. to insure smooth driveability during cold engine operation.

The air mixing door is installed in the air cleaner snorkle and is used to mix the incoming cold air with heated air. The sensor, located at the bottom of the air cleaner, opens and closes the vacuum passage between the mixing door vacuum motor and the intake manifold, depending upon underhood air temperature. When the air temperature is low, the sensor is closed, applying full vacuum to the mixing door vacuum motor, opening the door to admit heated air for combustion. When the underhood air temperature rises, the sensor opens allowing ambient air to flow through the sensor and reducing the vacuum to close the mixing door. When the intake manifold vacuum is greater than the motor calibration point and the exhaust manifold is heated, warm air, 95°-104° F. is drawn into the engine at all times.

1974-77

In this system, Fig. 3, the hot air control valve or mixing door is controlled by a bimetal located at the valve. The bimetal responds to underhood air temperature and opens and closes the valve accordingly. When underhood air temperature is below 41° F, the valve permits heated air to enter the air cleaner for combustion. If underhood air temperature is between 41° and 108° F, air flow will occur through both the hot and cold air circuits. When air temperature is above 108° F, air flow for combustion will be through the cold air circuit only.

System Tests

1972-73

1. When the engine is cold, the mixing door should be in the closed position. As the engine warms up the door should gradually open. If door does not operate properly, check vacuum hoses between vacuum motor, sensor and intake manifold.
2. The mixing door vacuum motor is preset as follows:
   a. Fully closed—2.36-3.94 inch Hg.
   b. Wide open—5.91-8.23 inch Hg.

1974-77

1. Visually check position of air control valve. If underhood air temperature is below 41° F, the valve should be in the full heat position. If underhood air temperature is between 41° and 108° F, the valve should be in a position to admit both cold and warm air. If the underhood air temperature is above 108° F, the valve should be in the full cold position.

AIR INJECTION SYSTEM

The air injection system, Fig. 4, is used on 1975 vehicles only. This system supplies secondary air for combustion of the unburned exhaust gasses in the exhaust manifold or thermal reactor. The system consists of an air pump, air control valve, check valve and the necessary connecting hoses or piping.

The air pump, Fig. 5, is a vane type rotary pump driven by a belt. An air cleaner is mounted on the pump to filter the incoming air.

The air control valve, Fig. 6, consists of a relief valve, air shut-off valve, air

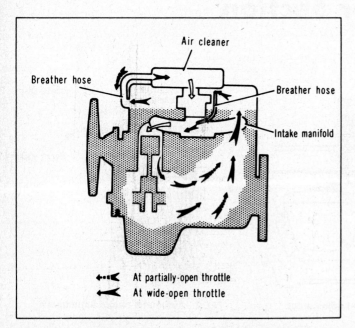

At partially-open throttle
At wide-open throttle

Fig. 1 Positive crankcase ventilation (PCV) system

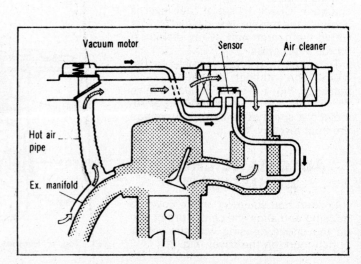

Fig. 2 Heated air intake system. 1972-73

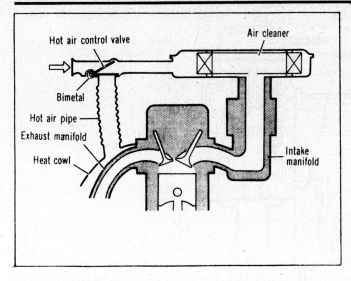

Fig. 3 Heated air intake system. 1974-77 (Typical)

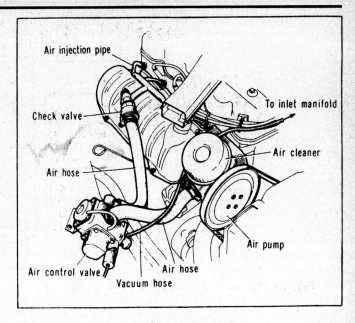

Fig. 4 Air injection system

shut-off solenoid and an orifice. The air control valve automatically controls the quantity of air supplied to the exhaust ports of thermal reactor. The relief valve operates when the spring force is overcome by manifold pressure on California models and air pump discharge pressure on all models. The air shut-off valve diverts the secondary air to the relief side when a vacuum differential exists between vacuum chambers "A" and "B", Fig. 6, or when air pump discharge pressure has acted on chamber "B". The air shut-off valve incorporates a speed sensor on California models or a thermo sensor on all models except California. When either sensor opens the electrical circuit, the air shut-off solenoid admits air pump discharge pressure into vacuum chamber "B". When manifold vacuum suddenly increases, the orifice controls the vacuum acting on Chamber "B" to decrease the pressure below the value of the manifold pressure acting on chamber "A."

The air control valve has three functions in supplying secondary air during vehicle operation as follows:

1. To supply the proper quantity of secondary air to the exhaust manifold at all times to lower exhaust emissions. The relief valve is opened and closed relative to manifold pressure on California models and air pump discharge pressure on all models. Valve position and the subsequent amount of air flow is dependent upon various engine operating conditions.

2. To cut-off the secondary air supply to the thermal reactor during high speed operation on California or to prevent excessive temperatures around the thermal reactor and under the hood or floor. During high speed operation or when underhood or underfloor temperatures have risen above specified values, the speed sensor senses vehicle speed and the thermo sensor senses the excessive temperature, breaks the predetermined electrical circuits. The air shut-off solenoid closes the manifold vacuum passageway and diverts the air pump discharge pressure into vacuum chamber "B." When this air pump pressure is applied to chamber "B," the air shut-off valve is then pushed upward until the valve closes the secondary air passageway and directs the secondary air to the relief side. When the secondary air supply is cut-off, no further combustion of the exhaust gasses takes place. The excessive temperatures will then decrease.

3. To prevent afterburn on deceleration. The air-fuel mixture becomes enriched during deceleration, resulting in an increased amount of unburned gasses. If secondary air is supplied at this time, afterburn will occur. To prevent this afterburn, the secondary air is cut-off during deceleration. When the vehicle is operated at a constant speed, manifold vacuum applied to vacuum chamber "A" is balanced with the pressure applied to chamber "B." Therefore, the air shut-off valve passageway to

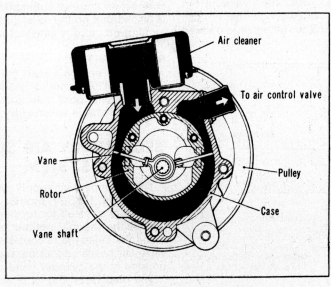

Fig. 5 Air pump section view

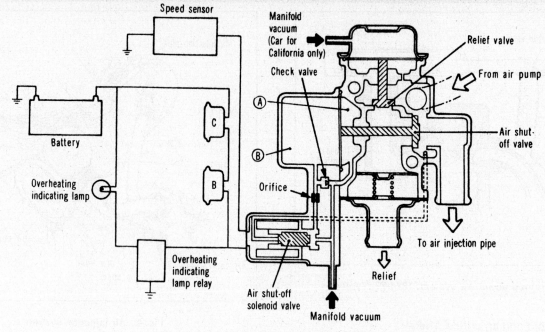

Fig. 6 Air control valve & electrical system

the thermal reactor and exhaust manifold is wide open. When the engine decelerates, manifold vacuum suddenly increases. The increased manifold vacuum is applied to vacuum chamber "A." Vacuum applied to vacuum chamber "B" passes through the orifice and is lowered to a value lower than that applied to chamber "A." This vacuum differential causes the air shut-off valve to temporarily close the air passageway to the thermal reactor or exhaust manifold, diverting the secondary air to the relief side. When engine RPM stabilizes, the vacuum in chamber "A" is equalized with the vacuum in chamber "B" through the orifices and the air shut-off valve is opened

by spring pressure, resupplying secondary air to the thermal reactor or exhaust manifold.

SYSTEM TESTING

Air Discharge Test

With the engine idling, disconnect air hose from check valve. Air should be discharged through the air hose.

Air Shut-Off Valve Test

Ensure the air shut-off solenoid is energized when the ignition switch is turned to the "On" position. Disconnect the air hose on the discharge side. With the engine running at 3,000 RPM, disconnect air shut-off solenoid lead. If air is discharged on the relief side only, the air shut-off valve is satisfactory.

Relief Valve Test

Increase engine speed from idle to 3,500 RPM. Air should be discharged from the relief port. If air is discharged, the relief valve is satisfactory.

SECONDARY AIR SUPPLY SYSTEM

The secondary air supply system, Fig. 7, used on 1976-77 models, supplies secondary air need for further combustion in the thermal reactor or exhaust manifold. This system consists of a reed valve, air hoses and air passages incorporated in the cylinder head.

The reed valve, Fig. 8, is actuated by the exhaust port vacuum generated by

pulsations in the exhaust manifold. The secondary air is drawn from the air cleaner and supplied to the exhaust ports. The reed valve is mounted on the front of the cylinder head on 1600 cc engines and on top of the timing chain case on 2000 cc engines.

Testing

1. Start and run engine at idle.
2. Disconnect air hose from reed valve.
3. Place hand on reed valve intake port. Suction should be felt. If not, the reed valve is defective, requiring replacement.
4. Also, check to ensure that no exhaust is emitted through the valve

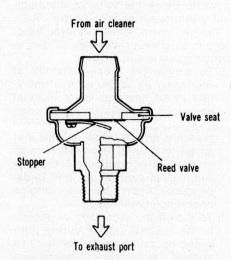

Fig. 8 Secondary air supply system reed valve

Fig. 7 Secondary air supply system

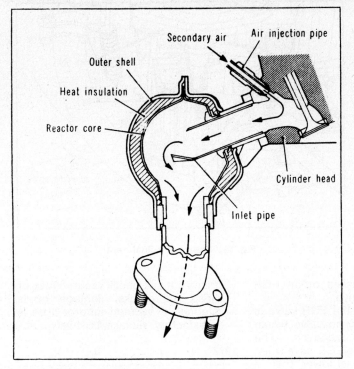

Fig. 9   Thermal reactor

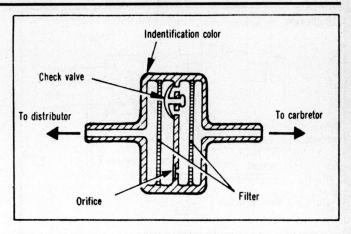

Fig. 10   OSAC valve

intake port. If blow back occurs, replace reed valve.

THERMAL REACTOR

The thermal reactor, Fig. 9, is used on 1975-77 California and 1977 high altitude vehicles. The thermal reactor consists of a shell and a core with heat insulation placed between the shell and the core. Exhaust gas from the cylinder head exhaust port and air from the pump or secondary air supply system are mixed in the reactor. Further combustion of the exhaust gasses then occurs.

Testing

The only test of the thermal reactor is a visual inspection. If any cracks, damage, flange distortion or exhaust gas leakage is present, replace the thermal reactor.

ORIFICE SPARK ADVANCE CONTROL (OSAC) SYSTEM

The OSAC valve, Fig. 10, used on 1977 models, is located in the vacuum line between the distributor and the carburetor and is used to control oxides of nitrogen and hydrocarbon emissions. The OSAC valve delays vacuum spark advance during acceleration by restricting the vacuum flow between the carburetor vacuum port and distributor vacuum advance unit. This restriction is in one direction only. During closed throttle deceleration or wide open throttle acceleration, the carburetor port vacuum drops below the level of vacuum in the distributor vacuum advance unit and there is no delay in retarding the spark timing. The OSAC valve permits the distributor vacuum advance unit to respond to lower vacuum instantaneously.

On California and high altitude models, the OSAC valve is deactivated by a thermo valve when coolant temperature is 104° F or less.

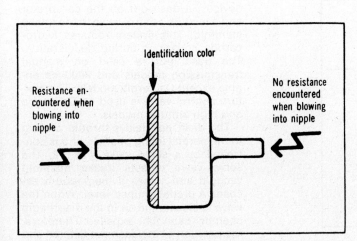

Fig. 11   OSAC valve test

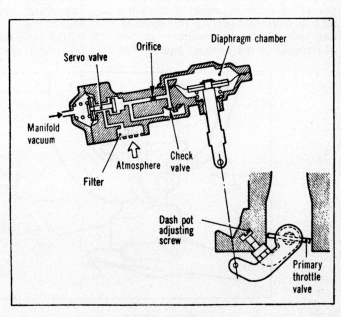

Fig. 12   Dash Pot

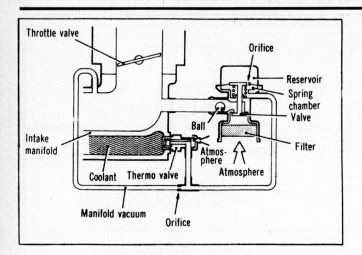

Fig. 13 Mixture control valve

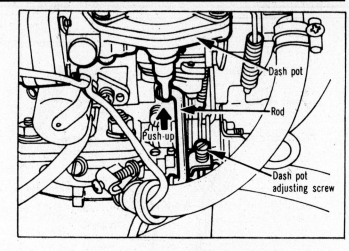

Fig. 14 Dash pot adjustment

Testing

The only test for the OSAC valve is to check if the valve is not clogged and to ensure the valve permits passage of vacuum in one direction only. To check valve, first blow into the nipple on the side having the identification color, Fig. 11. There should be resistance when blowing into this nipple. Then, blow into the nipple on the opposite side. No resistance should be encountered when blowing into this nipple. If resistance is encountered in both directions, the orifice or filter is clogged, requiring OSAC valve replacement.

EXHAUST GAS RECIRCULATION (EGR) SYSTEM

The EGR system recirculates a portion of the exhaust gasses to dilute the air-fuel mixture, lowering the combustion temperature and reducing oxides of nitrogen in the exhaust gasses. The system basically consists of an EGR valve and a thermo valve.

Vacuum applied to the EGR valve is controlled by the thermo valve which senses coolant temperature. The thermo valve closes the EGR valve when coolant temperature is lower than a pre-set value to aid initial start-up and driveability. The EGR valve is also closed at idle since engine vacuum is low.

System Testing

1974-76
1. With engine at normal operating temperature, set engine speed at 3,000-3,200 RPM.
2. Disconnect and connect EGR valve vacuum hose and observe the EGR valve diaphragm.
3. When the vacuum hose is disconnected, the EGR valve diaphragm should lower. When the hose is reconnected, the valve diaphragm should rise.
4. If EGR valve diaphragm operates as outlined in step 3, the valve is satis-

factory. If not, check vacuum tube or hose for cracks, damage or is clogged. If vacuum tube or hose is satisfactory, replace EGR valve.

1977

NOTE: The engine should be cold at the start of this test.

1. Start and run engine at 2,500 Rpm.
2. The EGR valve diaphragm should be stationary. If the diaphragm is activated, check for clogged vacuum hose between EGR control valve and thermo valve.
3. Warm up the engine to normal operating temperature. The EGR valve diaphragm should be activated. If not, check for cracked or clogged vacuum hose, defective thermo valve or EGR valve.

DECELERATION CONTROL SYSTEM

The deceleration control system used on 1977 vehicles is comprised of two devices, a dash pot on the carburetor and a mixture control valve in the intake manifold. This system reduces hydrocarbon emissions during deceleration. The dash pot is used on manual transmission models and 2000 cc engine except California models. The mixture control valve is used on California and high altitude models.

The dash pot delays throttle closing to the normal idling position and is controlled by a servo valve, Fig. 12. The servo valve detects intake manifold vacuum and closes if the vacuum exceeds a predetermined level. When the valve is closed, the air in the diaphragm chamber cannot be expelled. Therefore, the position of the dash pot is fixed and the throttle valve opening is retained

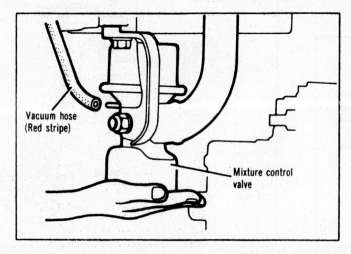

Fig. 15 Mixture control valve test

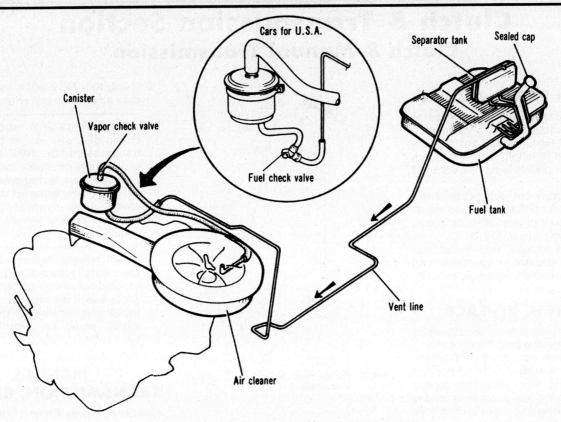

Fig. 16 Evaporative emission system (Typical)

through the carburetor linkage. If intake manifold vacuum falls below a pre-determined value, the servo valve opens and dash pot operates normally.

The mixture control valve, Fig. 13, permits additional air to enter the intake manifold during deceleration and is activated by intake manifold vacuum. When the vehicle is operated at a constant speed, the orifice in the diaphragm of the mixture control valve maintains balanced vacuum in the spring chamber and the reservoir. The valve is then closed by spring pressure. When the throttle valve is suddenly closed, high vacuum from the intake manifold in the spring chamber forces the diaphragm to move the valve to the open position, causing air flow into the intake manifold. The valve will then close slowly, according to the pressure equalization between the spring chamber and the reservoir through the orifice. When the coolant temperature is lower than a preset value, a thermo valve, incorporated in the system, opens and permits ambient air and the intake manifold vacuum acting on the spring chamber to mix, causing the mixture control valve to deactivate. This aids

vehicle performance during cold start conditions. When the coolant temperature rises above the predetermined value, the thermo valve closes and activates the mixture control valve.

System Testing
Dash Pot
1. Connect a tachometer to the engine.
2. With engine at idle speed, push the dash pot rod upward through entire stroke and note engine RPM. On 1600 cc engine, RPM should be 1,900 RPM and on 2000 cc engine, RPM should be 1,500 RPM. Adjust by turning dash pot adjusting screw, Fig. 14.
3. Release dash pot rod and note time required for engine speed to decrease to 1,000 RPM. The time should not exceed six seconds.

Mixture Control Valve
1. With engine idling, remove vacuum hose from mixture control valve.
2. Place hand under mixture control valve and reinstall vacuum hose, Fig. 15. A strong suction should be

felt. If not, the mixture control valve or thermo valve is defective.

EVAPORATIVE EMISSION SYSTEM

The evaporative emission system, Fig. 16, consists of a vapor separator tank, vent line, vapor check valve, charcoal canister and on 1976-77 models, a fuel check valve. The charcoal canister is located between the fuel tank and air cleaner. The fuel vapors are temporarily stored in the canister until the engine is started. When the engine is running, outside air is drawn through the canister, purging the fuel vapor from the charcoal. This air-fuel vapor mixture is then routed to the air cleaner and on to the combustion chambers.

The vapor check valve is closed during engine idling to prevent the purge air entering the canister and carrying the fuel vapor to the air cleaner. This prevents enrichening of the idle mixture causing high idle carbon monoxide emissions.

A fuel check valve is used on 1976-77 models to prevent fuel leakage in event of vehicle roll-over during an accident.

Clutch & Transmission Section
Clutch & Manual Transmission

CLUTCH PEDAL, ADJUST

1. Adjust distance from toe board to top of clutch pedal to dimension shown in Figs. 1 and 2 and be sure difference in height between clutch and brake pedals is no more than .4 in.
2. Slightly draw out outer cable from cable holder of toe board and adjust its free travel to .2 to .24 in. by means of adjusting wheel, Fig. 3.
3. Check to ensure that pedal has specified amount of free travel and proper distance from pedal to floor.

CLUTCH, REPLACE

1. Remove transmission as described under Transmission, Replace.
2. With clutch disc guide MD998017 inserted in center hole to prevent clutch disc from dropping, loosen bolts holding clutch cover assembly one at a time diagonally and remove clutch cover assembly.
3. Remove clutch disc.
4. Remove return clip on transmission side, then remove release bearing carrier and bearing.
5. Using a suitable punch, remove shift arm spring pin and control lever shaft assembly, then remove clutch shaft arm, two felts and return springs.
6. Insert clutch control lever and shaft assembly into transmission case from left side, then install clutch shift arm, two felt packings and two return springs onto shaft.

NOTE: Apply grease to inside sur-

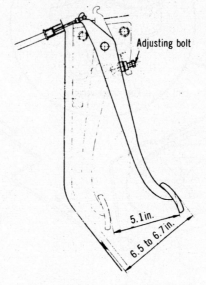

Fig. 1 Clutch pedal adjustment. 1972-76 models

face of bushing and oil seal lips. Apply engine oil to felt packings.

---

7. Align lock pin holes of shift arm and control shaft, then drive in two spring pins using lock pin installer MD998245.

NOTE: On 1977 models, when driving in spring pins, ensure spring pin slot direction is at right angles to centerline of control shaft, Fig. 4.

---

8. Apply suitable grease to clutch disc spline and main drive gear spline.

9. Using tool MD998017, install clutch disc and clutch cover on flywheel.

NOTE: On 1972-76 models, install clutch disc with longer boss facing transmission. On 1977 Models, install clutch disc with manufactures stamped mark facing pressure plate. On all models, when installing clutch cover, align flywheel and clutch cover notches to ensure proper balance.

---

10. Install release bearing and carrier, then install return clip. Apply grease to inside diameter of carrier and fill groove with grease.
11. Install transmission, then adjust clutch pedal as described under Clutch Pedal, Adjust.

MANUAL TRANSMISSION, REPLACE

Operation Inside Engine Compartment
1. Remove air cleaner.
2. Disconnect battery cable from starting motor, then remove starting motor.
3. Remove two bolts from top of the transmission.

Operation Inside Passenger Compartment
1. Remove lock screws, then lift console box upward and remove it. If car does not have a console, lift carpet upward over center tunnel.
2. Remove lock screws, then lift dust cover retaining plate upward and remove it.
3. Turning up dust cover upward, re-

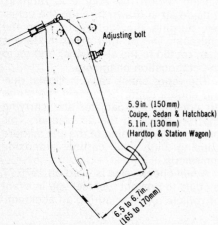

Fig. 2 Clutch pedal adjustment. 1977 models

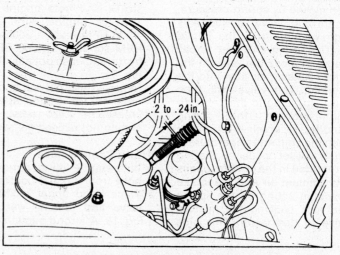

Fig. 3 Clutch pedal free play adjustment

move four attaching bolts at lower part of extension housing and remove gearshift lever assembly.

CAUTION: Remove gearshift lever with lever placed in second speed on four-speed transmission models or first speed on five-speed transmission models.

Operation Outside Engine Compartment
1. With vehicle elevated and supported by safety stands, drain transmission fluid.
2. Remove speedometer cable, then disconnect transmission switch and backup light switch wiring from transmission.
3. Remove bolts from rear of propeller shaft, then draw propeller shaft out of transmission.
4. Disconnect muffler pipe from its bracket.

5. Disconnect clutch cables.
6. With transmission supported on a transmission jack, remove insulators from body members by removing attaching bolts.

CAUTION: The transmission jack should be placed under the under cover. See that the under cover supporting area is as wide as possible.

7. Detach each member from frame and pull it off sideways.
8. Remove bell housing cover.
9. Remove retaining bolts from transmission and draw transmission rearward from engine.

CAUTION: Be careful not to twist front end of the main drive gear.

10. Reverse procedure to install and observe the following items.
    a. When installing control lever assembly, place shift lever in

second-speed position on four-speed transmission models or in first-speed position on five-speed transmission models, so that nylon bushing hole is vertical.

CAUTION: During this operation, use care to prevent dirt from entering transmission at control housing mounting section.

    b. When assembling bell housing cover, check to see that it is not bent. A bent cover will not be attached in firm contact with cylinder block and transmission, resulting in entry of mud into transmission.
    c. Install gear shift lever dust cover snugly into hole in tunnel and attach retaining plate with screws.
11. Adjust clutch pedal as described under Clutch Pedal, Adjust.
12. Fill transmission with specified amount of fluid.

Automatic Transmission

The Borg-Warner automatic transmission was used in 1972, 1973 and some 1974 models. During the 1974 model run, this transmission was replaced by the TorqueFlite, which has been used ever since.

TROUBLE SHOOTING
Borg Warner Units

1. Check to see that only when selector lever is in "P" or "N" position starting motor operates and that in "R" position only, backup lamps are lit.

Trouble and Possible Cause	Remedy
In "P" or "N" position, starting motor does not operate.	a. Adjust inhibitor switch.
In all selector lever positions, starting motor operates.	a. Adjust inhibitor switch.
2. Run engine at normal idling speed and depress brake pedal. Shift selector lever from "N" to "D", from "N" to "L"	and from "N" to "R". Each time of a shift, transmission should be felt.
When "D," "L" or "R" is selected, abnormal shock takes place.	a. Lower engine idling speed. b. Check to see if vacuum diaphragm has been properly adjusted. c. Check vacuum piping for leak.
3. Place selector lever in "L" or "R" position and check stall speed. Also check clutchs for slipping.	**NOTE:** Stall test should not be continued for more than 10 seconds. Otherwise, transmission overheating will result.

Trouble and Possible Cause	Remedy
Stalling speed is a little higher than specified rate. In "L" position, clutch slips or squeaks.	a. Check to see if manual linkage has been properly adjusted. b. Check oil level. c. Check adjustment of vacuum diaphragm. d. Disassemble and clean valve body. e. Check front clutch, front clutch seal and forward sun gear shaft sealing ring. Also make sure that output shaft cup plug does not leak and plug is not loose.
Stalling speed is a little higher than specified rate. In "R" position, clutch slips and squeaks.	a. Check to see if manual linkage is properly adjusted. b. Check oil level. c. Check to see if vacuum diaphragm is properly adjusted. d. Disassemble and wash valve body. e. Check rear clutch, check valve and seal. Also check each tube for fitted condition.
Stalling speed is a little higher than specified rate.	a. Check engine performance.
Stalling speed is more than 600 rpm lower than specified rate.	a. Replace torque converter.
4. Select "D" position with transmission at operating temperature. Subsequently release brake, depress accelerator pedal and check to see if transmission shifts from first to second and from second to third smoothly.	NOTE: When accelerator pedal is depressed lightly, shift is hardly felt. To make sure that transmission is in the third gear, select "L" position. If transmission is in third gear, it immediately shifts down to second. This can be felt with ease.
In "D" position, car won't move. If car operates properly with selector lever in "L" position, items d. and e. may be omitted. If car does not start with selector in "D" "L" or "R" position, add item g.	a. Check to see if manual linkage is properly adjusted. b. Check oil level. c. Check to see if vacuum diaphragm is properly adjusted. d. Disassemble and clean valve body. e. Check front clutch, front clutch seal and forward sun gear shaft sealing ring. Also check driven shaft cup plug for leakage and plugs for looseness. f. Check one-way clutch. g. Disassemble oil pump and check pump and drive tag.

Trouble and Possible Cause	Remedy
1-2 upshift delays or no upshift to 2nd is made.	a. Check to see if vacuum diaphragm is properly adjusted. b. Check vacuum diaphragm for leak. c. Disassemble and clean governor valve. d. Disassemble and clean valve body. e. Check front servo seal and tubes for condition of installation.
In 1-2 upshift, bands slip	a. Check oil level. b. Check to see if vacuum diaphragm is properly adjusted. c. Check to see if front band is properly adjusted. d. Check front servo seal and tubes for condition of installation. e. Check front band for wear. f. Disassemble and clean valve body.
2-3 upshift delays or no upshift to 3rd. is made. (If upshift is made properly in "R", h. may be omitted.)	a. Check to see if vacuum diaphragm is properly adjusted. b. Check vacuum piping for leak. c. Check kickdown solenoid. d. Disassemble and clean governor valve. e. Disassemble and clean valve body. f. Check to see if front band is properly adjusted g. Check front servo seal and tubes for condition of installation. h. Check rear clutch check valve seal for condition. Check tubes for looseness.
In 2-3 upshift, bands and clutches slip and engine runs idle.	a. Check oil level. b. Check to see if vacuum diaphragm is properly adjusted. c. Check to see if front band is properly adjusted. d. Disassemble and clean valve body. e. Check rear clutch check valve seal for condition. Check tubes for looseness.
Shift is accompanied by a shock.	a. Check to see if vacuum diaphragm is properly adjusted. b. Check vacuum piping for leak.
In 2nd or 3rd. speed in "D" position, band drags.	a. Check rear band for adjusted condition.
In 2-3 upshift, band drags or hard shift is felt.	a. Check to see if front band is properly adjusted. b. Check front servo seal and tube for condition of installation.

Trouble and Possible Cause	Remedy
5. Depress accelerator pedal fully (kickdown switch "OFF") to start the car from its stationary	state and check 1-2 and 2-3 upshifts in accordance with Shifting Characteristic Curves.
Fully depress accelerator pedal with selector lever in "D" position (kickdown switch "OFF") and start car. In this case, clutch slips or squeaks, or shudder takes place, or the shift does not meet the specifications.	a. Check to see if manual linkage is properly adjusted. b. Check oil level. c. Check to see if vacuum diaphragm is properly adjusted. d. Check kickdown switch for adjustment and operation and also check connections. e. Check kickdown solenoid. f. Disassemble and clean valve body. g. Check front clutch, front clutch seal and forward sun gear shaft sealing ring. Also check to see if driven shaft cup plug is leaking or loose.
In 3rd. speed "D" position, poor converter performance or overheating takes place.	a. Replace torque converter.
6. At about 24 mph with transmission in the third gear, depress accelerator pedal fully (kickdown switch "OFF"). In	this case, car picks up speeds up to third and no downshift to second speed is made.
Transmission shifts down	a. Check vacuum diaphragm for proper adjustment. b. Check kickdown switch for adjustment. c. Check kickdown solenoid.
7. At car speed of about 30 mph with transmission in third gear, depress accelerator pedal full stroke (kickdown	switch "ON"). In this case, transmission shifts down to second gear.
Transmission won't shift down	a. Check kickdown switch for adjustment, operation, and connection. b. Check kickdown solenoid. c. Disassemble and clean valve body. d. Disassemble and clean governor valve.
8. During travel at car speed of about 15 mph with transmission in third gear, depress accelerator pedal full stroke (kickdown	switch "ON). In this case, transmission shifts down to first gear.

Trouble and Possible Cause	Remedy
Transmission won't shift down	a. Check kickdown switch for adjustment, operation, and connection. b. Check kickdown solenoid. c. Disassemble and clean valve body. d. Disassemble and clean governor valve.
9. Depress accelerator pedal full stroke (kickdown switch "ON") and start car from stationary state. Check 1-2 and	2-3 upshifts in accordance with table of Shifting Characteristic Curves.
Fully depress accelerator pedal with selector lever in "D" position (kickdown switch "OFF") and start car. In this case, clutch slips or squeaks, or shudder takes place, or the shift point does not meet the specifications.	a. Check to see if manual linkage is properly adjusted. b. Check oil level. c. Check to see if vacuum diaphragm is properly adjusted. d. Check the kickdown switch for adjustment and operation and also check up connections. e. Check kickdown solenoid. f. Disassemble and clean valve body. g. Check front clutch, front clutch seal and forward sun gear shaft sealing ring. Also check to see if driven shaft cup plug is not leaking and plug is loose.
10. During travel at car speed of about 40 mph with transmission in third gear, release accelerator pedal and shift selector lever to "L" position. Then	check a downshift to second gear and engine brake. Also, with car running with force of inertia, check 2-1 downshift and engine brake.
3-2 downshift is not made and no engine brake can be applied.	a. Check manual linkage for proper adjustment. b. Check front band for proper adjustment. c. Check front servo seal and tubes for looseness. d. Check front band for wear. e. Check rear clutch check valve seal for condition. Also check tubes for looseness.
2-1 downshift is not made and no engine brake can be applied.	a. Check rear band for proper adjustment. b. Check rear servo seal and tubes for condition of installation. c. Check rear band for wear.
11. With car kept stationary, shift lever to "L" lease brake and depress accelerator pedal full stroke (full throttle) to accelerate to a car speed of about 20 mph. Then check to make certain that bands and clutches are not slipping.	At the same time, make certain that transmission does not shift up.

Trouble and Possible Cause	Remedy
When car is started with selector in "L" position, clutch slips or squeaks and shudder takes place.	a. Check to see if manual linkage is properly adjusted. b. Check oil level. c. Check to see if vacuum diaphragm is properly adjusted. d. Disassemble and clean valve body. e. Check front clutch, front clutch seal and forward sun gear shaft sealing rings for condition. Also check output shaft cup plug for leakage and plug for looseness.
With selector lever in "L" position, transmission shifts up.	a. Check to see if manual linkage is properly adjusted.
12. Stop car and shift selector lever to "R." Release brake. If possible, depress accelerator pedal fully (full throttle) to	reverse car. Check to see if the clutch slips.
On starting car with selector lever in "R," clutch slips or squeaks, or shudder takes place.	a. Check to see if manual linkage is properly adjusted. b. Check oil level. c. Check to see if vacuum diaphragm is properly adjusted. d. Disassemble and clean valve body. e. Check rear clutch check valve seal for condition. Also check tubes for condition of installation.
In "R" position, clutch slips on starting car but no shudder takes place. (If engine brake is applied with selector lever in "L" position and in first gear, items e., f. and g. may be omitted.)	a. Check manual linkage for proper adjustment. b. Check oil level. c. Check vacuum diaphragm for proper adjustment. d. Check rear band for proper adjustment. e. Check rear servo seal and tubes for condition of installation. f. Check rear band for wear.
In "R" position, drag is felt	a. Check front band for adjustment.
In "R" position, car does not move. (If engine brake is applied with the selector lever in "L" position and in the first gear, items d., f. and g. may be omitted.)	a. Check manual linkage for proper adjustment. b. Check oil level. c. Check vacuum diaphragm for proper adjustment. d. Check rear band for adjustment. e. Disassemble and clean valve body. f. Check rear servo seal and tubes for condition of installation. g. Check rear band for wear. h. Check rear clutch check valve seal for condition. Also check tubes for condition of installation.

Trouble and Possible Cause	Remedy
13. Stop car on a down grade by applying brake and select "P" position. Subsequently release brake and make that parking pawl is positively locking up car. Before realeasing parking pawl, that is, before	moving the selector lever off from "P") position, depress brake pedal. Carry out similar test on an upgrade. In this case, make certain that selector lever is in "P" position.
Parking brake does not work	a. Check manual linkage for proper adjustment. b. Check parking pawl, ring gear and inside linkage for condition.
14. Others	
With increase in engine speed, groaning (squeaking) sound is produced.	a. Disassemble oil pump and check pump and drive tag.
Gear box makes noise.	a. Remove and check gear train.
Sound like knocks is heard from around torque converter.	a. Check torque converter drive plate for crack or distortion. Also check to see if drive plate locking bolts are tightened to a specified torque.
During high-speed travel with selector lever in "D" position., transmission shifts down to second gear but shifts up immediately.	a. Check rear clutch check valve seal for condition. Also check tubes for condition of installation. b. Check governor operation.

Torqueflite Units

Refer to Figs. 4 through 7, for trouble shooting and diagnosis.

DIAGNOSIS & TESTING
Borg Warner Units

OIL PRESSURE TEST

1. Remove pipe plug from left rear side of transmission case and install a transmission pressure gauge, Fig. 8.
2. Connect a vacuum gauge to vacuum line midway between vacuum line ends.
3. Start engine and allow to reach operating tempreature.
4. Place selector lever in reverse position and note pressure gauge reading. Pressure gauge should indicate values shown in Fig. 9.
5. If line pressure is below specified valve, remove vacuum diaphragm hose and turn vacuum diaphragm adjusting screw clockwise, Fig. 8. If line pressure is above specified value, turn adjusting counter clockwise. A turn of adjusting screw will change line pressure approximately 10 psi.
6. If line pressure cannot be obtained by this adjustment, inspect vacuum diaphragm.
7. If line pressure is normal in reverse position, check pressure in drive and low ranges with engine manifold vacuum at 12 in. Hg.
8. If oil pressure is low in drive or low positions, but normal line pressure is obtained in reverse, check for governor valve sticking in open position or loose governor valve screw.
9. If oil pressure is normal in all selector lever positions, but no upshifting takes place in drive range, check to ensure governor valve is not stuck in closed position.

VACUUM DIAPHRAGM CHECK

1. If correct line pressure cannot be obtained by adjustment of vacuum diaphragm, check unit for dent or bend and replace as necessary.
2. Remove vacuum hose from diaphragm check hose for presence of oil. If oil is present, diaphragm is leaking and should be replaced.
3. Connect a controllable vacuum source and vacuum gauge to vacuum diaphragm. Install rod into vacuum unit.
4. Gradually increase vacuum pressure on diaphragm and observe movement of rod.
5. Rod must be completely retracted at 18 in. Hg.
7. Clamp hose to confine vacuum pressure within diaphragm, rod must remain in retracted position. If rod moves, diaphragm is leaking and should be replaced.

STALL TEST

With transmission at operating temperature, connect a tachometer to engine. With service and parking brakes applied, place transmission selector lever in L or D, then fully depress accelerator pedal and note stall speed.

NOTE: Do not hold throttle wide opened for more than 10 seconds at a time. Stall speed should be 1650-1950 RPM. If poor acceleration is noted or if

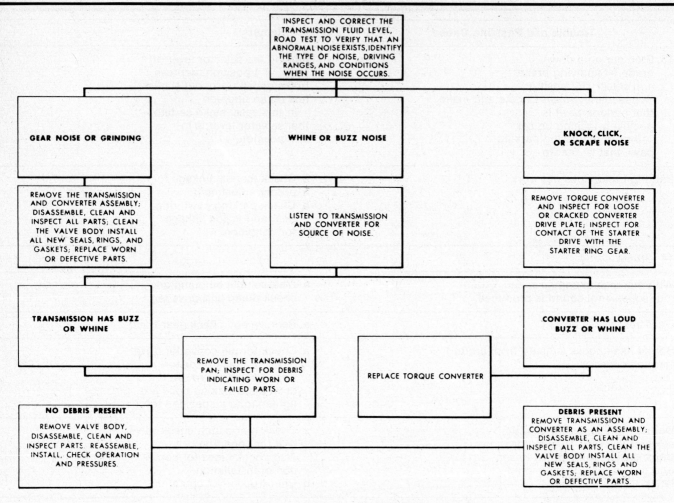

Fig. 4   Diagnosis chart (Abnormal Noise). Torqueflite units

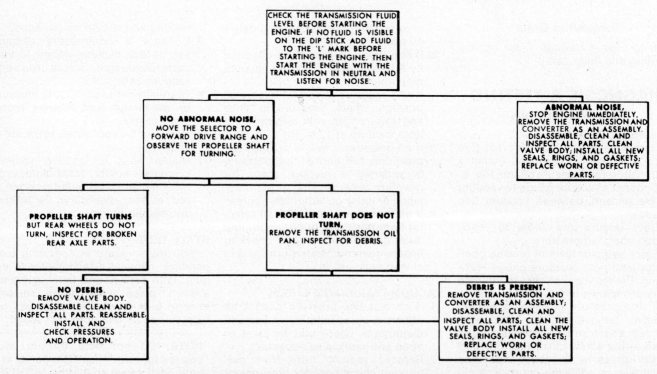

Fig. 5   Diagnosis chart (Vehicle Will Not Move). Torqueflite units

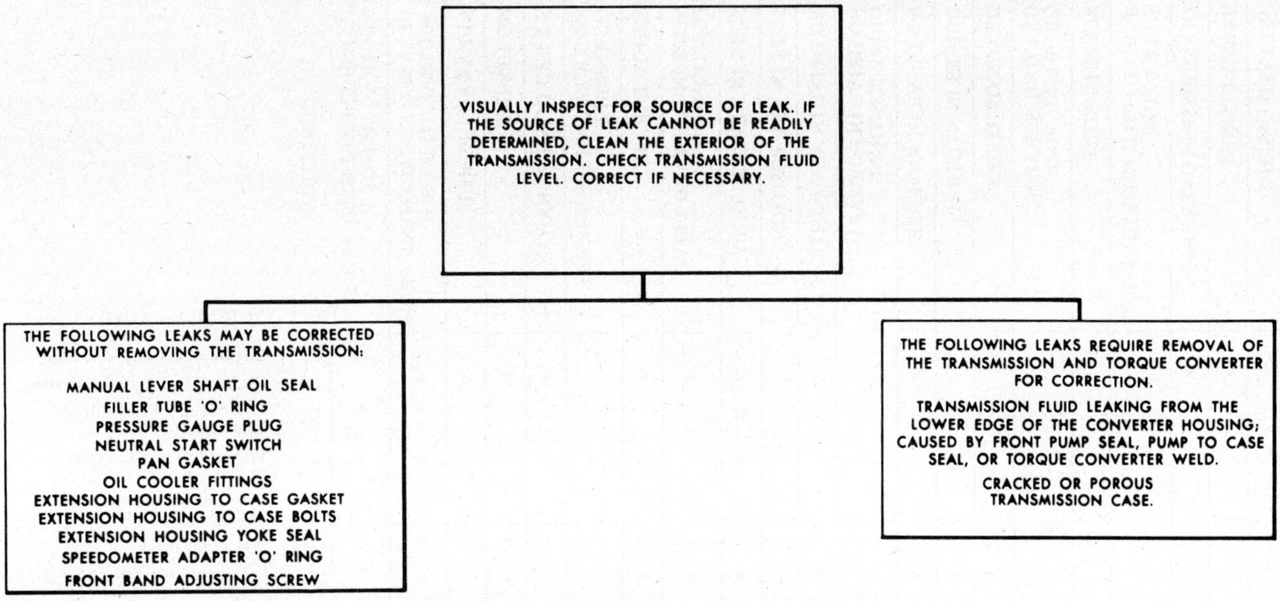

```
┌─────────────────────────────────────────┐
│ VISUALLY INSPECT FOR SOURCE OF LEAK. IF  │
│ THE SOURCE OF LEAK CANNOT BE READILY     │
│ DETERMINED, CLEAN THE EXTERIOR OF THE    │
│ TRANSMISSION. CHECK TRANSMISSION FLUID   │
│ LEVEL. CORRECT IF NECESSARY.             │
└─────────────────────────────────────────┘
```

```
┌──────────────────────────────────────┐       ┌──────────────────────────────────────┐
│ THE FOLLOWING LEAKS MAY BE CORRECTED  │       │ THE FOLLOWING LEAKS REQUIRE REMOVAL OF │
│ WITHOUT REMOVING THE TRANSMISSION:    │       │ THE TRANSMISSION AND TORQUE CONVERTER  │
│                                       │       │ FOR CORRECTION.                        │
│       MANUAL LEVER SHAFT OIL SEAL     │       │ TRANSMISSION FLUID LEAKING FROM THE    │
│         FILLER TUBE 'O' RING          │       │ LOWER EDGE OF THE CONVERTER HOUSING;   │
│        PRESSURE GAUGE PLUG            │       │ CAUSED BY FRONT PUMP SEAL, PUMP TO CASE│
│        NEUTRAL START SWITCH           │       │ SEAL, OR TORQUE CONVERTER WELD.        │
│            PAN GASKET                 │       │       CRACKED OR POROUS                │
│        OIL COOLER FITTINGS            │       │       TRANSMISSION CASE.               │
│  EXTENSION HOUSING TO CASE GASKET     │       └──────────────────────────────────────┘
│  EXTENSION HOUSING TO CASE BOLTS      │
│   EXTENSION HOUSING YOKE SEAL         │
│    SPEEDOMETER ADAPTER 'O' RING       │
│     FRONT BAND ADJUSTING SCREW        │
└──────────────────────────────────────┘
```

Fig. 6   Diagnosis chart (Fluid Leaks). Torqueflite units

vehicle fails to start on a sharp upgrade, converter one-way clutch is slipping or stator support is broken. If stall speed is below 1350 RPM, the torque converter assembly should be replaced. If poor acceleration is noted at speeds above 30 MPH with transmission in third speed gear and in addition no maximum speed is obtainable, stator one-way clutch is locked in operating state and converter assembly should be replaced even if stall speeds are within limits. If stall speed is higher than specified, either gear box clutch is slipping or converter fluid is insufficient.

Torqueflite Units
OIL PRESSURE CHECKS

NOTE: Before performing tests, check fluid level and manual linkage adjustment. Transmission fluid should be at operating temperature.

1. Install a tachometer to engine, then raise vehicle using a hoist that will allow rear wheels to turn. Position tachometer so it can be read from under vehicle.
2. Disconnect throttle and shift rods so that transmission levers can be controlled from under vehicle.

Test 1 (Selector in L)
1. Attach 100 psi. pressure gauges to line and rear servo ports, Fig. 10.
2. Operate engine at 1000 RPM, then move transmission selector lever all the way rearward to L position.
3. Read pressures on both gauges as throttle lever is moved from full rearward position to full forward position.
4. Line pressure should be 54-60 psi. with throttle lever in rearward position and should gradually increase as lever is moved forward to 90-96 psi.
5. Rear servo pressure should read within 3 psi. of line pressure.

Test 2 (Selector in 2)
1. Attach 100 psi. pressure gauges to line pressure port, Fig. 10, and tee into rear cooler line fitting, Fig. 11, to read lubrication pressure.
2. Operate engine at 1000 RPM, then move selector lever one detent forward from full rearward position (2 position).
3. Read pressures on both gauges as throttle lever on transmission is moved from full rearward to full forward position.
4. Line pressure should be 54-60 psi. with throttle lever in rearward position and gradually increase as throttle lever is moved forward to 90-96 psi.
5. Lubrication pressure should be 5-15 psi. with lever rearward and 10-30 psi. with lever forward.

Test 3 (Selector In D)
1. Attach 100 psi, gauges to line and front servo release ports, Fig. 10.
2. Operate engine at 1600 rpm., then move transmission selector lever two detents forward from full rearward position to D position.
3. Note pressure readings on both pressure gauges, with throttle lever rearward a reading of 54-60 psi. should be obtained. As throttle lever is moved forward, pressure reading should gradually increase.
4. Front servo release is pressurized on in direct drive and should be within 3 psi. of line pressure up to downshift point.

Test 4 (Selector In R)
1. Attach a 300 psi. pressure gauge to rear servo apply port, Fig. 10.
2. Operate engine at 1600 rpm., then move transmission selector lever four detents forward from full rearward position to R position.
3. Rear servo pressure should be 230-260 psi.
4. Move selector lever to drive position, pressure reading should drop to zero.

Test Results
1. If correct line pressure is obtained in any one of the above test, pump and pressure regulator are operating properly.
2. Low pressure in D, L and 2, but normal pressure in R indicates leakage in rear clutch circuit.
3. Low pressure in D and R, but normal pressure in L, indicates leakage in front clutch circuit.
4. Low pressure in R and L, but normal pressure in 2 indicates leakage in rear servo circuit.
5. Low line pressure in all positions indicates defective pump, clogged filter or stuck pressure regulator valve.

DELAYED UPSHIFT	HARSH UPSHIFT	TRANSMISSION OVERHEATS	HARD TO FILL, OIL BLOWS OUT FILLER TUBE	BUZZING NOISE	GRATING, SCRAPING GROWLING NOISE	DRAGS OR LOCKS	DRIVES IN NEUTRAL	NO DRIVE IN REVERSE	NO DRIVE IN FORWARD DRIVE POSITIONS	NO DRIVE IN ANY POSITION	SLIPS IN ALL POSITIONS	SLIPS IN REVERSE ONLY	SLIPS IN FORWARD DRIVE POSITIONS	SHIFTS ERRATIC	NO KICKDOWN OR NORMAL DOWNSHIFT	3-2 KICKDOWN RUNAWAY	NO UPSHIFT	RUNAWAY UPSHIFT	DELAYED ENGAGEMENT FROM NEUTRAL TO D OR R	HARSH ENGAGEMENT FROM NEUTRAL TO D OR R	CONDITION	POSSIBLE CAUSE
		×																		×	1	Engine idle speed too high.
	×	×						×	×	×	×	×	×			×	×	×	×		2	Hydraulic pressures too low.
					×	×		×	×												3	Low-reverse band out of adjustment.
				×			×	×	×	×	×	×			×		×		×	×	4	Valve body malfunction or leakage.
					×			×	×		×								×		5	Low-reverse servo, band or linkage malfunction.
		×		×					×	×	×	×	×			×	×	×	×		6	Low fluid level.
		×					×	×	×		×	×	×			×	×		×		7	Incorrect gearshift control linkage adjustment.
			×								×	×	×								8	Oil filter clogged.
		×								×	×	×	×			×	×		×		9	Faulty oil pump.
									×		×	×	×						×		10	Worn or broken input shaft seal rings.
				×							×	×	×	×		×		×	×	×	11	Aerated fluid.
				×																×	12	Engine idle speed too low.
×	×												×		×	×	×				13	Incorrect throttle linkage adjustment.
×	×						×								×	×	×				14	Kickdown band out of adjustment.
									×				×								15	Overrunning clutch not holding.
					×																16	Output shaft bearing and/or bushing damaged.
×													×		×	×	×				17	Governor support seal rings broken or worn.
×	×							×					×		×	×	×		×		18	Worn or broken reaction shaft support seal rings.
×	×												×	×	×	×	×				19	Governor malfunction.
×													×	×	×	×	×		×		20	Kickdown servo band or linkage malfunction.
×									×					×	×	×	×		×	×	21	Worn or faulty front clutch.
																				×	22	High fluid level.
																				×	23	Breather clogged.
			×																	×	24	Hydraulic pressure too high.
		×	×																		25	Kickdown band adjustment too tight.
	×		×																		26	Faulty cooling system.
		×					×														27	Insufficient clutch plate clearance.
		×						×	×	×			×						×	×	28, 29	Worn or faulty rear clutch. Rear clutch dragging.
					×	×		×	×	×											30	Planetary gear sets broken or seized.
					×	×		×		×			×								31	Overrunning clutch worn, broken or seized.
				×																	32	Overrunning clutch inner race damaged.

Fig. 7 General Diagnosis chart. Torqueflite units

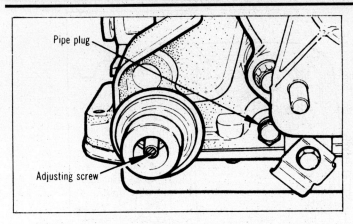

Fig. 8 Oil pressure plug & vacuum diaphragm adjusting screw location. Borg Warner units

Item	Engine manifold vacuum	Control pressure	
		R	D, L
*	12 in.Hg	92 to 98 psi	←
Idling pressure (Check up after sufficient engine warm-up)	17.7 in.Hg	55 to 68 psi	←
Stalling pressure	2 in.Hg	160 to 195 psi	←

Fig. 9 Oil pressure test chart. Borg Warner units

Governor Pressure

NOTE: Perform this test only if transmission shifts at wrong vehicle speeds when throttle linkage is properly adjusted.

1. Connect a 100 psi, pressure gauge to governor pressure tap, Fig. 11.
2. Operate transmission in third gear and note governor pressure reading and vehicle speed, Fig. 12.
3. If governor pressures are within limits, governor valve or weights are probably sticking. Governor pressures should respond smoothly to changes in rpm. and should return to 0-1½ psi. when vehicle has stopped. A pressure above 2 psi. with vehicle stopped will prevent transmission from downshifting.

Throttle Pressure

No pressure tap is provided for throttle pressure. If part throttle upshifts are either early or delayed in relation to vehicle speed, incorrect throttle pressure may be indicated. Engine runaway on either upshifts or downshifts may indicate low throttle pressure setting. Under no circumstances should throttle pressure be adjusted until after transmission throttle linkage has been checked for proper adjustment.

STALL TEST

This test is used to check torque converter stator clutch operation and holding ability of transmission clutches. Transmission fluid level should be checked and engine brought to operating temperature before performing test. When performing test, both service and parking brakes should be applied and front wheels blocked. Do not hold throttle open any longer than necessary to obtain stall speed and never longer than five seconds at a time. If more than one stall test is necessary, operate engine at 1000 RPM in neutral to cool transmission fluid between tests. If engine speed exceeds the maximum limit, release accelerator immediately since transmission clutch slippage is indicated. Stall speed should be between 2200 to 2650 RPM.

If stall speed exceeds 2600 RPM by more than 200 RPM, transmission clutch slippage is indicated.

If low stall speeds are obtained, torque converter stator clutch problems are indicated. If stall speed is 250 to 350 RPM below 2300 RPM and vehicle operates properly at highway speed, but through gear acceleration is poor, stator overrunning clutch is slipping. If stall speed and acceleration are normal, but excessive throttle opening is required to maintain highway speed, stator clutch is seized. If any of the the above problems are encountered, replace torque converter.

NOTE: A whinning or siren like sound due to fluid flow is normal during stall test operation with some converters. Loud metallic noises from loose parts or interference within the assembly indicates a defective torque converter. To confirm source of noise, raise vehicle and operate engine at light throttle in neutral or drive. Listen for noise in area of transmission converter housing.

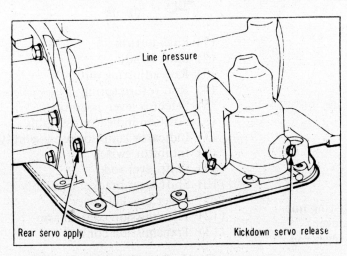

Fig. 10 Oil pressure test connections (right side of case). Torqueflite units

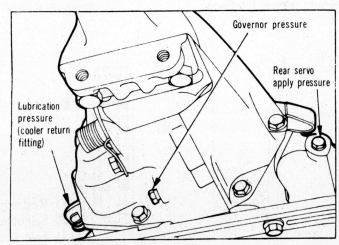

Fig. 11 Oil pressure test connections (rear side of case). Torqueflite units

Year	Engine	MPH	Psi.
1974-75	All	20-21	15
		35-40	40
		52-57	60
1976-77	1600	18-19	15
		32-36	40
		47-52	60
1976-77	2000	20-21	15
		35-40	40
		52-57	60

Fig. 12 Governor pressure specifications. Torqueflite units

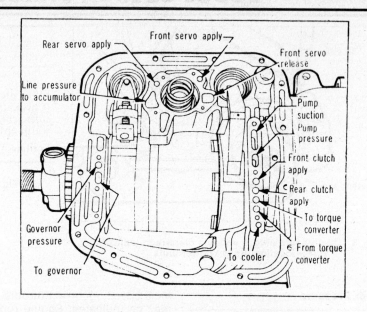

Fig. 13 Air pressure check points. Torqueflite units

AIR PRESSURE CHECKS

The front clutch, rear clutch, kickdown servo, and low and reverse servo may be checked by applying air pressure to their respective passage after the valve body is removed, Fig. 13. To make the checks, proceed as follows, *being sure the compressed air is free of all dirt and moisture.*

Front and Rear Clutches

Apply air pressure to the clutch passages (one at a time) and listen for a dull "thud" which indicates that the clutch is operating. Hold the air pressure on for a few seconds and check system for excessive oil leaks.

If a dull "thud" cannot be heard in the clutches, place the finger tips on clutch housing and again apply air pressure Movement of the piston can be felt as the clutch is applied.

Kickdown Servo

Direct air pressure into kickdown servo "apply" passage. Operation of servo is indicated by a tightening of the front band. Spring tension on the servo should release the band.

Low and Reverse Servo

Direct air pressure into the low and reserve servo "apply" passage. Operation of the servo is indicated by a tightening of the rear band. Spring tension on servo piston should release band.

Service Note

If the clutches and servos operate properly but erratic shift or no upshift conditions are present it indicates that the malfunction exists in the control valve body.

ADJUSTMENTS
Borg Warner Units

Gearshift Linkage, Adjust

Rod adjusting nut at top end of selector lever assembly should be adjusted so that nut will be flush with bottom of lever slot when selector lever is in "N" position, Fig. 14.

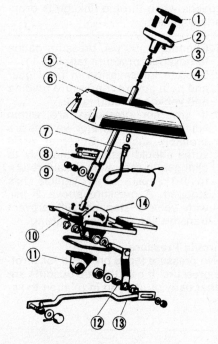

(1) Push button
(2) Shift handle
(3) Rod adjusting nut
(4) Rod return spring
(5) Selector lever assembly
(6) Position indicator assembly
(7) Indicator lamp socket assembly
(8) Inhibitor switch
(9) Shift lever rod
(10) Shift lever bracket assembly
(11) Lever bracket cover
(12) Transmission control arm
(13) Transmission control rod

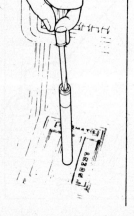

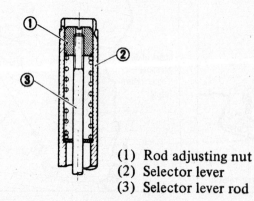

(1) Rod adjusting nut
(2) Selector lever
(3) Selector lever rod

Fig. 14 Adjustment of rod adjusting nut

Fig. 15 Gearshift linkage. Borg Warner units (Typical)

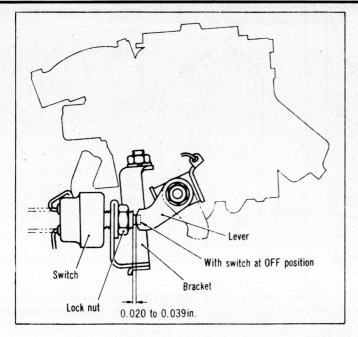

Fig. 16 Kickdown switch adjustment. Borg Warner units

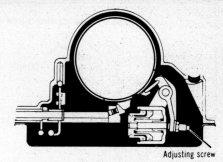

Fig. 17 Front band adjustment. Borg Warner units

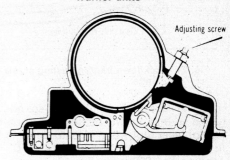

Fig. 18 Rear band adjustment. Borg Warner units

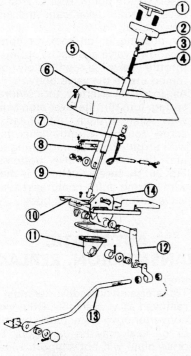

(1) Push button
(2) Shift handle
(3) Rod adjusting nut
(4) Rod return spring
(5) Selector lever assembly
(6) Position indicator assembly
(7) Indicator lamp socket assembly } Except P-line
(8) Inhibitor switch
(9) Shift lever rod
(10) Shift lever bracket assembly
(11) Lever bracket cover
(12) Transmission control arm
(13) Transmission control rod
(14) Selector lever position plate

Fig. 19 Gearshift linkage. Torqueflite units (Typical)

With selector lever in N position, raise vehicle and loosen control rod adjusting nut, Fig. 15. Move control rod three detents from L position to place transmission in N, then tighten adjusting nut.

Kickdown Switch, Adjust
Adjust switch as shown in Fig. 16.

Front Band, Adjust
Remove transmission oil pan, then loosen lock nut, Fig. 17. With servo lever pressed outward, insert special tool, .025 in. block gauge, between adjusting screw and servo piston pin.

Using special tools, adapter and spin torque screwdriver tighten servo adjusting screw to 10 in.-lbs., then tighten lock nut to 20-25 ft.-lbs., and remove gauge.

Rear Band, Adjust
First loosen lock nut, then using special tool, socket, tighten the adjusting screw to 100 ft.-lbs. torque, Fig. 18. From this position, back off adjusting screw ¾ turn and tighten lock nut.

Torqueflite Units
Gearshift Linkage, Adjust
Rod adjusting nut at top end of selec-

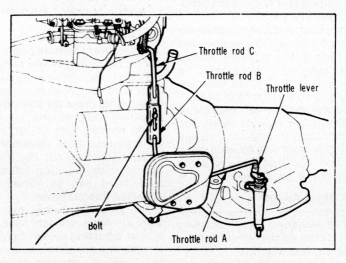

Fig. 20 Throttle rod adjustment. Torqueflite units

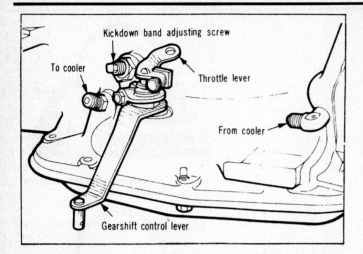

Fig. 21 Kickdown band adjusting screw location. Torqueflite units

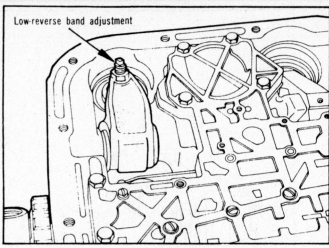

Fig. 22 Low-reverse band adjustment. Torqueflite units

tor lever assembly should be so adjusted so that nut will be flush with bottom of lever slot when selector lever is in "N" position on 1974-76 units or "D" position on 1977 units, Fig. 14.

On 1974-76 models, place selector lever in N position. On 1977 models, place selector lever in D position. Raise vehicle and loosen control arm lock nut, Fig. 19. On 1974-76 models, move transmission lever two detents from L position to place transmission in N. On 1977 models, move transmission lever two detents from L position to place transmission in D. While holding selector lever in position, adjust control rod length, then tighten lock nut to 13 to 17 ft. lbs.

Throttle Linkage, Adjust

1. Warm up engine until it reaches normal operating temperature. With automatic choke off fast idle cam, adjust engine idle speed to specifications. Then adjust throttle rod by the following procedure.
   a. Install each link. Loosen bolts so that rods B and C can slide properly. See Fig. 20.
   b. Lightly push rod A or throttle lever and rod C toward idle stopper and set rods to idle position. At this time, automatic choke must be fully released. Tighten bolt securely to connect rods B and C.
   c. Be sure that when carburetor throttle valve is wide open, the transmission throttle lever moves smoothly from idle to wide open position and that there is some room in the lever stroke.

Kickdown Band, Adjust

NOTE: The kickdown band adjusting screw is located on the left side of the transmission case, Fig. 21.

1. Loosen lock nut and back off approximately five turns. Test adjusting screw for free turning in the transmission case.
2. Using a wrench, Tool C-3380-A with adapter C-3705, tighten band adjusting screw to 47 to 50 in.-lbs. If adapter C-3705 is not used, tighten adjusting screw to 72-in.-lbs., which is the true torque.
3. Back off adjusting screw three turns from 72 in.-lbs. Hold adjusting screw in this position and tighten lock nut to 35 ft.-lbs.

Low & Reverse Band, Adjust

1. Raise vehicle, drain transmission fluid and remove oil pan.
2. This transmission has an Allen socket adjustment screw at servo end of lever, Fig. 22. After removing lock nut, tighten screw to 41 in.-lbs., then back off 7½ turns. Install and tighten lock nut to 30 ft.-lbs.
3. Install oil pan, using a new gasket. Tighten oil pan bolts to 150 in.-lbs.
4. Fill transmission with "DEXRON" type automatic transmission fluid.

Line Pressure Adjustment

An incorrect throttle pressure setting will cause incorrect line pressure readings even though the pressure adjustment is correct. Always inspect and correct throttle pressure adjustment before adjusting line pressure.

The approximate adjustment is $1^5/_{16}$ in., measured from valve body to inner edge of adjusting nut, Fig. 23. However, due to manufacturing tolerances, the adjustment can be varied to obtain specified line pressure.

The adjusting screw may be turned with an Allen wrench. One complete turn of adjusting screw changes closed throttle line pressure approximately $1^2/_3$ psi. Turning adjusting screw counter-

clockwise increases pressure and a clockwise turn decreases pressure.

Throttle Pressure Adjustment

Throttle pressure cannot be tested accurately, therefore adjustment should be measured if a malfunction is evident.

1. Insert gauge pin of Tool C-3763 between throttle lever cam and kickdown lever.
2. By pushing in on tool, compress kickdown valve against its spring so throttle valve is completely bottomed inside the valve body.
3. As force is exerted to compress spring, turn throttle lever stop screw with Allen wrench until head of screw touches throttle lever tang with throttle lever cam touching tool and the throttle valve bottomed, Fig. 24. Be sure adjustment is made with spring fully compressed and valve bottomed in valve body.

AUTOMATIC TRANSMISSION, REPLACE

Removal

1. Transmission and converter must be removed as an assembly. Otherwise, converter drive plate, pump bushing or oil seal may be damaged. The drive plate will not support a load; therefore, none of the weight of the transmission should be allowed to rest on the plate during removal.
2. Disconnect ground cable from battery.
3. Remove cooler lines at transmission.
4. Remove starter motor and cooler line bracket.
5. Loosen pan to drain transmission.
6. Rotate engine clockwise with socket wrench on crankshaft pulley bolt to

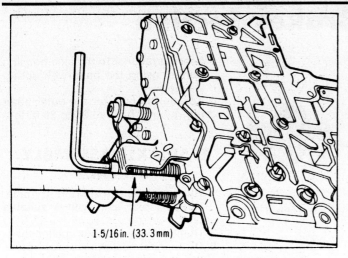

Fig. 23 Line pressure adjustment. Torqueflite units

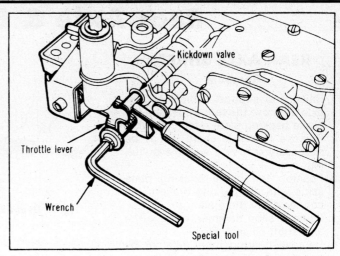

Fig. 24 Throttle pressure adjustment. Torqueflite units

position bolts attaching torque converter to drive plate and remove them.

7. Mark parts for reassembly, then disconnect propeller shaft at rear universal joint. Carefully pull shaft assembly out of the extension housing.

8. Disconnect the gearshift rod and torque shaft assembly from transmission.

9. Disconnect throttle rod from lever at left side of transmission. Remove linkage bellcrank from transmission if so equipped.

10. Remove oil filler tube and speedometer cable.

11. Support rear of the engine using a suitable jack.

12. Raise transmission slightly with service jack to relieve load on the supports.

13. Remove bolts attaching transmission mount to crossmember and crossmember to frame, then remove crossmember.

14. Remove all bell housing attaching bolts.

15. Carefully work transmission and converter assembly rearward off engine block dowels, then disengage converter hub from end of crankshaft. Attach a small C-clamp to edge of bell housing to hold converter in place during transmission removal.

16. Lower transmission and remove assembly from vehicle.

17. To remove converter assembly, remove C-clamp from edge of bell housing, then carefully slide assembly out of transmission.

Installation

NOTE: Transmission and converter must be installed as an assembly. Otherwise, converter drive plate, pump bushing and oil seal will be damaged. The drive plate will not support a load; therefore, none of the weight of the transmission should be allowed to rest on the plate during installation.

1. Rotate pump rotors with Tool C-3756 until two small bolts in handle are vertical.

2. Carefully slide converter assembly over input shaft and reaction shaft. Be sure converter hub slots are also vertical and fully engage pump inner rotor lugs.

NOTE: Test for full engagement by placing a straight edge on face of case. The surface of converter front cover lug should be at least ½ in. to rear of straight edge when converter is pushed all the way into transmission.

3. Attach a small C-clamp to edge of the converter housing to hold converter in place during transmission installation.

4. Inspect converter drive plate for distortion or cracks and replace if necessary. Torque drive plate to crankshaft bolts to 83 to 90 ft.-lbs. If drive plate replacement has been necessary, be sure both transmission dowel pins are in engine block and they are protruding far enough to hold transmission in alignment.

5. Coat converter hub hole in crankshaft with multi-purpose grease. Place transmission and converter assembly on a service jack and position assembly under vehicle for installation. Raise or tilt as necessary until transmission is aligned with engine.

6. Carefully work transmission assembly forward over engine block dowels with converter hub entering the crankshaft opening.

7. After transmission is in position, install converter housing bolts and tighten to 22 to 30 ft.-lbs.

8. Install crossmember to frame and lower transmission to install mount on extension to crossmember.

9. Install oil filler tube and speedometer cable.

10. Connect throttle rod to transmission lever.

11. Connect gearshift rod and torque shaft assembly to transmission lever and frame.

12. Carefully slide sliding yoke into extension housing and on output shaft splines. Align marks made at removal, then connect propeller shaft to rear axle pinion shaft yoke.

13. Rotate engine clockwise with socket wrench on crankshaft pulley bolt, as needed to install converter to drive plate bolts. Tighten to 25 to 30 ft.-lbs.

14. Install starter motor and cooler line bracket.

15. Tighten cooler lines to transmission fittings.

16. Adjust shift and throttle linkage.

17. Refill transmission with "DEXRON" type automatic transmission fluid.

Rear Axle & Brakes Section

REAR AXLE SHAFT

Removal

1. Raise and support vehicle at rear axle. Remove the rear wheel and the brake backing plate retaining nuts.
2. Remove rear axle shaft. It may be necessary to use a suitable puller, Fig. 1.
3. Position the brake backing plate aside with the parking brake cable connected to the plate.
4. Using a slide hammer, remove the axle shaft oil seal, Fig. 2.
5. Remove bearing inner retainer by grinding down a portion of the retainer to a thickness of .04 to .06 inch. Cut the bearing retainer at the ground portion to remove.
6. Press bearing and outer retainer from axle shaft.

Installation

1. Install the outer bearing retainer with flat side facing toward the splined end of the axle shaft, then the bearing and inner bearing retainer.
2. Press in the bearing retainer with the smaller chamfered side facing toward the bearing side.
3. Clean the oil seal seat and apply a thin coat of chassis grease.
4. Using the oil seal installer, force the axle shaft oil seal into the axle housing. Apply a coat of bearing grease over the oil seal lip. Also, apply grease to the surface which the oil seal lip contacts when the axle shaft is installed. When driving in the oil seal, be careful not to distort or damage it.
5. Clearance between the bearing retainer and the bearing is controlled

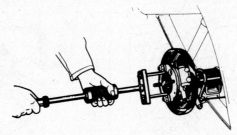

Fig. 1   Rear axle shaft removal

by shims and packings, Fig. 3. To determine the number of packings and shims needed, subtract the sum of dimensions A and B from dimension C. If the resulting figure is less than .0098 in., no packings or shims are needed. If the figure is .0098 to .0197 in., use 1 packing and no shims. When the figure is from .0197 to .0295 in., use two packings and no shims. With a measurement of .0295 to .0394 in., use two packings and one shim. From .0394 to .04192 in., use two packings and two shims.
6. Install the brake backing plate on the rear axle shaft assembly, insert the axle shaft assembly in the axle housing, using care not to damage the oil seal. Then fit the splines of the axle shaft into the differential side pinion.
7. Align the oil escape holes of the packing and the outer bearing retainer and temporarily tighten the

bearing retainer to the axle housing flange, using the bolts with spring washers.
8. Torque the nuts for the outer bearing retainer bolts to 25 to 29 ft. lbs.

REAR AXLE ASSEMBLY, REPLACE

1. Raise vehicle and support at frame. Support rear axle with a suitable jack.
2. Remove wheels and propeller shaft.
3. Disconnect brake hose from brake line.
4. Disconnect parking brake cable from both wheels and remove the parking brake cable lever on axle housing.
5. Remove shock absorbers.
6. Remove leaf springs as outlined under "Leaf Springs, Replace" procedure in the Rear Suspension Section.
7. Lower rear axle assembly and remove from vehicle.
8. Reverse procedure to install.

DISC BRAKE SERVICE
1972-73

Caliper & Brake Shoe Removal
1. Remove the wheel.
2. Disconnect the brake pipe from the brake hose and remove the connector bolt of the flexible hose connected to the caliper.

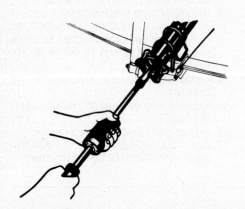

Fig. 2   Rear axle shaft oil seal removal

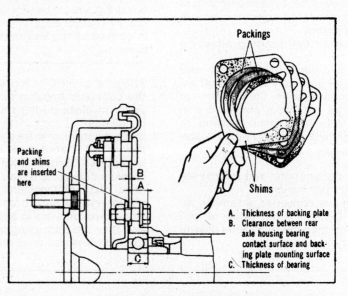

Packings

Packing and shims are inserted here

B
A

Shims

A. Thickness of backing plate
B. Clearance between rear axle housing bearing contact surface and backing plate mounting surface
C. Thickness of bearing

Fig. 3   Rear axle bearing shims

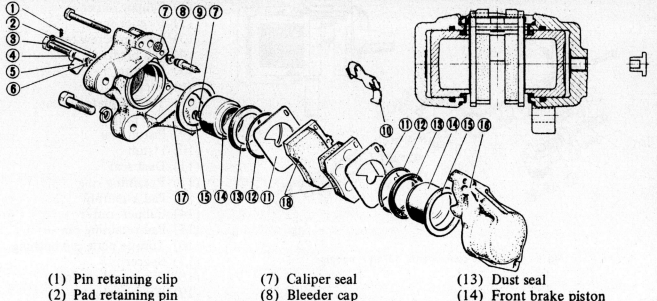

(1) Pin retaining clip
(2) Pad retaining pin
(3) Connector bolt
(4) Gasket
(5) Connector
(6) Gasket

(7) Caliper seal
(8) Bleeder cap
(9) Bleeder screw
(10) Cross spring
(11) Pad shim
(12) Retaining ring

(13) Dust seal
(14) Front brake piston
(15) Piston seal
(16) Caliper (outer)
(17) Caliper (inner)
(18) Pad assembly

Fig. 4   Disc brake components. 1972-73 models

3. Pull out the clip and remove the retaining pin and cross spring, Fig. 4.
4. Hold the backing plate of the pad with pliers and remove the pad assembly and shim.
5. Remove the caliper assembly from vehicle.

Caliper Service
1. Remove retaining ring and dust seal then the piston on the outer side while holding the inner piston carefully with a screwdriver.

NOTE: If the piston on one side is not held down, both pistons may jump out simultaneously and cause personal injury.

2. Remove the inner piston through the union bolt joint cavity by tapping it with a drift.
3. Remove the piston seal, being careful not to damage the cylinder seal groove.
4. Clean all parts with brake fluid.

NOTE: Do not separate caliper halves.

5. Install the piston seal and dust seal.
6. Apply rubber lubricant to the entire surface of the piston seal and to the inner side of the dust seal.
7. Apply rust preventive oil to the piston and cylinder wall, then insert the piston into the cylinder, being careful not to twist the piston.

Caliper & Brake Shoe Installation
1. Install the caliper assembly on the caliper adapter and torque mount bolts to 29-36 ft. lbs.
2. Spread the pistons, using special tool, Piston Expander (C-3992) and insert the pad with the shim. Insert the shim between the pad and the piston with the arrow on the shim facing forward.
3. To install the cross spring, insert the pin into the caliper with the "A" part of the cross spring hooked on the retaining pin and fasten it in position with a clip, Fig. 5. After inserting the lower retaining pin and clipping it, be sure the pad is in between the cross spring flanges "B", Fig. 5. Then firmly press the "C" part of the spring onto the retaining pin by hand.
4. Attach the brake hose to the caliper with a connector bolt through a copper gasket.
5. Torque the connector bolt to 14.5-18 ft. lbs.

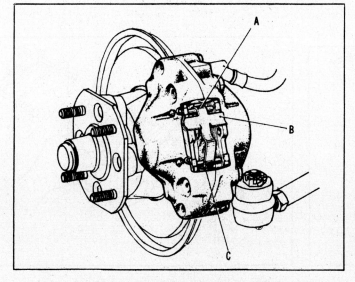

Fig. 5   Shim & cross spring installation. 1972-73 models

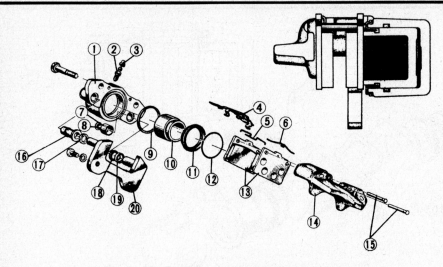

(1) Caliper, inner
(2) Bleeder screw
(3) Bleeder screw cap
(4) Pad protector
(5) K-spring
(6) M-clip
(7) Torque plate pin cap
(8) Cap plug
(9) Piston seal
(10) Piston
(11) Dust seal
(12) Retaining ring
(13) Pad assembly
(14) Caliper, outer
(15) Pad retaining pin
(16) Torque plate pin bushing
(17) Spacer
(18) Wiper seal retainer
(19) Wiper seal
(20) Torque plate

Fig. 6   Disc brake components. 1974-77 models

1974-77

Brake Shoe Removal

1. Remove the wheel.
2. Remove the protector, Fig. 6, by prying up the edge of the clip at the center of the pad protector with a screwdriver.
3. Holding the center of the "M" clip with fingers, detach the "M" clip from the shoe and the ends from the retaining pins.
4. Pull the retaining pins from the caliper assembly and remove the "K" spring.
5. Remove the brake shoe assembly by holding the backing plate area of the pad with pliers.

Caliper Removal

1. Remove the brake shoes as outlined previously.

2. Remove the brake hose clip from the strut area, then disconnect the brake hose from the caliper.
3. Remove the caliper assembly by loosening torque plate and adapter mounting bolts.

Caliper Service

1. Loosen caliper attaching bridge bolts and separate the outer caliper from the inner caliper.
2. After the removal of the dust seal, remove the piston by applying compressed air at the brake hose fitting.

CAUTION: Do not apply high pressure suddenly since the piston may cause personal injury.

---

3. Remove the piston seal, using care not to damage the cylinder.

4. Clean all parts using clean brake fluid.
5. Apply rubber grease to the piston seal and apply brake fluid to the cylinder bore. Insert the piston seal into the piston carefully to prevent distortion.
6. Whenever the torque plate has been removed from the inner caliper, it is necessary to clean the torque plate shaft and the shaft bore of the caliper and apply suitable grease to the rubber bushing, wiper seal inner surface and torque plate shaft before assembly. Apply sufficient grease to the threaded portion of the torque plate shaft.
7. Tighten the inner and outer caliper bridge bolts to 58 to 69 ft. lbs.

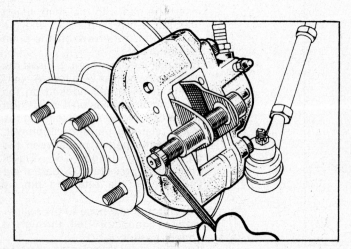

Fig. 7   Brake shoe installation. 1974-77 models

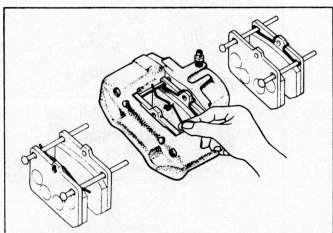

Fig. 8   Installing "K" spring & "M" clip. 1974-77 models

Caliper Installation

1. Install caliper on adapter.
2. Torque the caliper assembly (torque plate) to the adapter bolts to 58 to 72 ft. lbs.
3. Torque the brake hose to 9 to 12 ft. lbs.

Brake Shoe Installation

1. Spread the piston, using the special tool, Piston Spreader (C-3992) and insert the brake shoe through the shim, Fig. 7.
2. Install the K-spring and M-clip, Fig. 8.
3. Install the pad protector.

PARKING BRAKE ADJUSTMENT

1. Release parking brake.
2. Loosen cable attaching bolt and adjusting nut, then move the cable lever toward the right.
3. Set the left cable and torque the cable lever to 11-14 ft. lbs.
4. Tighten the adjusting nut to obtain 0-.04 inch clearance between extension lever and backing plate on all except 1976-77 Arrow and 1977 Colt coupe and sedan. On 1976-77 Arrow and 1977 Colt coupe and sedan, the clearance should be .008-.08 inch.
5. Set the right cable and adjust the extension lever and backing plate clearance as outlined previously.
6. Check parking brake lever travel. On 1972-73 models travel should be less than seven notches. On 1974-77 models, the travel should be approximately eight notches.

MASTER CYLINDER, REPLACE

1. Disconnect the brake tube from the master cylinder.
2. Remove clevis pin connecting the push rod with the pedal, except on a car with power brakes.
3. Remove the attaching bolts from the toeboard or power brake assembly.
4. Reverse procedure to install. Torque attaching bolts to 6 to 9 ft. lbs. Torque brake tube flare nut to 9.5 to 12 ft. lbs. If the car is equipped with power brakes, check clearance between the back of the master cylinder piston and the power brake push rod. It should be 0 to .03 in. If clearance is not correct, adjust the length of the push rod.

POWER BRAKE UNIT, REPLACE

1. Remove master cylinder as outlined previously.
2. Disconnect vacuum hose from power brake unit.
3. Remove pin connecting power brake rod with brake pedal.
4. Remove power brake unit attaching nuts and the power brake unit.
5. Reverse procedure to install.

Front Suspension & Steering Section

WHEEL ALIGNMENT

Camber

The specified camber is built into the steering knuckle, which is part of the strut assembly, and no adjustment is provided.

Caster

1972-1976 Colt & 1977 Colt hardtop & station wagon

Although caster normally requires no adjustment, fine adjustment can be made that will eliminate sideways free play of the bolt retaining the lower arm to the crossmember may be made.

1976-1977 Arrow & 1977 Colt coupe & sedan

As on the other models, caster normally requires no adjustment. However, slight adjustments can be made by moving the strut bar nut by the amount of A in Fig. 1. If caster is adjusted, be sure the wheelbase on both sides is within the range of 92.1 in. ± .4 in.

Toe-in

Toe-in is adjusted by rotating the turnbuckle of the tie rod. The amount of toe-in of the left front wheel is reduced by turning the tie rod turnbuckle toward the front of the car and the amount of toe-in on the right front wheel is reduced by turning it toward the rear of the the car. Both turnbuckles should always be tightened or loosened the same amount. After adjustment, the difference in length between the two tie rods should not exceed .2 in.

WHEEL BEARING ADJUSTMENT

After installing the bearings and wheel hub, tighten the nut to 14.5 ft.-lbs. to seat all parts then loosen the nut. Tighten the nut to 3.6 ft.-lbs. and after installing the cap, install the cotter pin. If, the holes do not align after shifting the position of the installed cap, loosen the nut until a flute on the nut aligns with cotter pin hole in the spindle. Do not back off the nut more than 15°.

LOWER CONTROL ARM, REPLACE

1972-76 Colt & 1977 Colt Hardtop & Station Wagon

1. Disconnect the stabilizer ring from

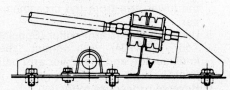

Fig. 1   Caster adjustment. 1976-77 Arrow & 1977 Colt coupe & sedan

the lower arm and remove strut assembly, Fig. 2.
2. Using the tie rod end puller (Special Tool CT-1116), disconnect the steering knuckle arm and the tie rod ball joint.
3. Using a knuckle arm puller (Special Tool CT-1104), disconnect the knuckle arm and the lower arm ball joint.
4. Remove the bolts securing the lower arm to the sub-frame, then the lower arm assembly.
5. Reverse procedure to install.
6. When connecting the strut assembly and the knuckle arm, apply sealer to the flange surface.
7. To install the lower arm shaft, tighten the lower arm shaft nut temporarily and tighten the shaft flange nut to the specified torque. Then lower the wheels to the ground and tighten the shaft nut to the specified torque.

The torque specifications are given below:

Item	Ft. Lbs.
Knuckle arm to ball joint	29-43
Strut assembly to knuckle arm	39
Lower arm flange attaching bolt	7-11
Lower arm shaft attaching nut	43-51
Stabilizer bar link attaching bolt	22-25

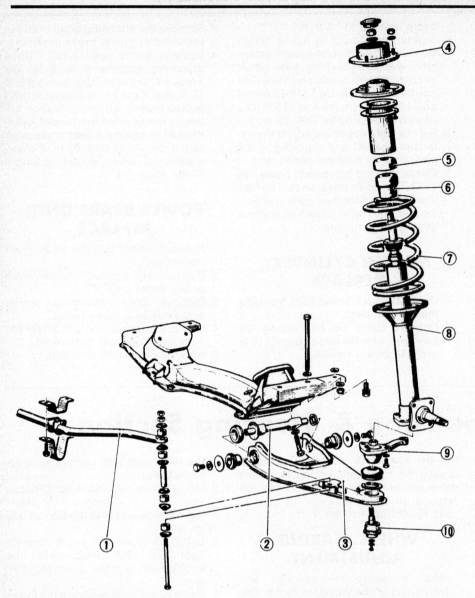

(1) Stabilizer
(2) Lower arm shaft
(3) Lower arm
(4) Strut insulator
(5) Spacer

(6) Bumper rubber
(7) Front spring
(8) Strut assembly
(9) Knuckle arm
(10) Lower ball joint

Fig. 2 Front suspension. 1972-76 Colt & 1977 Colt hardtop & sta. wag.

Item	Ft. Lbs.
Knuckle arm to tie rod end	29-36
Strut bar to lower arm	36-43
Caliper to adapter	51-65
Knuckle to brake caliper and dust cover	29-36

1976-77 Arrow & 1977 Colt Coupe & Sedan

1. Disconnect the stabilizer link and the strut bar from the lower arm and remove the strut assembly, Fig. 3.
2. Using the tie rod end puller (Special Tool CT-1116), disconnect the steering knuckle arm and the tie rod ball joint.

3. Remove bolt securing the strut and knuckle arm and separate the assembly.
4. Turn the steering wheel to pull out the lower arm shaft. Then, remove the lower arm shaft and disconnect the lower arm from the crossmember.
5. Using a knuckle arm puller (Special Tool CT-1104), disconnect the knuckle arm and the lower arm ball joint.
6. Reverse procedure to install.
7. When connecting the strut assembly and the knuckle arm, apply some

sealer to the flange surface.

8. To install the lower arm shaft, tighten the lower arm shaft nut temporarily and tighten the shaft flange nut to the specified torque. Then lower the wheels to the ground and tighten the shaft nut to the specified torque.

   The torque specifications are given below:

Item	Ft. Lbs.
Knuckle arm to ball joint	29-43
Strut assembly to knuckle arm	36-43
Lower arm shaft flange attaching bolt	7-10
Lower arm shaft attaching nut	43-51
Stabilizer bar link attaching bolt	22-25
Knuckle arm to tie rod end	29-36
Strut bar to lower arm	36-43
Caliper to adapter	51-65
Knuckle to brake adapter and dust cover	29-36

LOWER BALL JOINT, REPLACE

1. Remove the lower arm ball joint dust seal by prying up the dust seal ring evenly with a screwdriver.
2. Remove the snap ring.
3. Using special tool, Ball Joint Remover and Installer CT-1131, press ball joint from control arm.

Installation

1. Press the ball joint into the burred hole, by using the special tool, Ball Joint Remover and Installer CT-1131.

NOTE: Replace the lower arm or the ball joint if standard installation pressure is not obtained. Initial pressure must be over 1,550 lbs. Installed depth must be .118 to .236 in. Final pressure must be 11,000 lbs.

2. Install snap ring into the snap ring groove in the ball joint case. Do not open the snap ring any wider than necessary. Insert the snap ring fully into the groove by tapping it through the special tool, Ball Joint Remover and Installer CT-1131. If snap ring is loose in groove, discard it and install new snap ring.
3. Apply suitable packing sealer to the inside of the dust seal metal ring, then press the metal ring into the snap ring surface with a hammer or a press through the special tool, CT-1131.

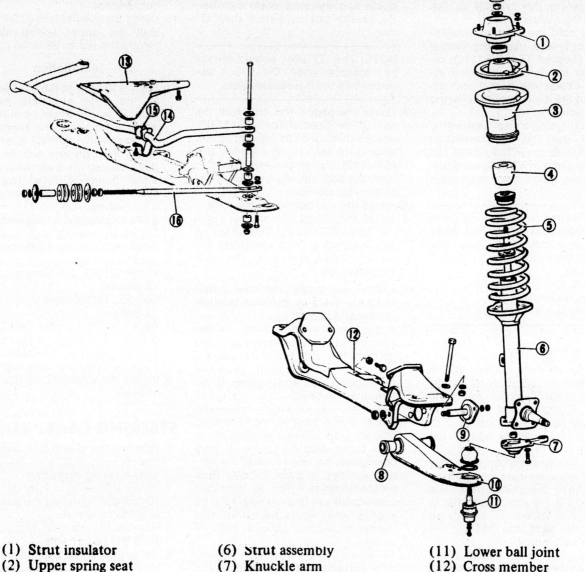

(1) Strut insulator
(2) Upper spring seat
(3) Dust cover
(4) Bumper rubber
(5) Front spring

(6) Strut assembly
(7) Knuckle arm
(8) Lower arm bushing
(9) Lower arm shaft
(10) Lower arm

(11) Lower ball joint
(12) Cross member
(13) Strut bar bracket
(14) Stabilizer
(15) Stabilizer bar bushing
(16) Strut bar

Fig. 3 Front suspension. 1976-77 Arrow & 1977 Colt coupe & sedan

MACPHERSON STRUT SERVICE

Removal

1. Remove front wheel, caliper assembly and the front hub with disc rotor and dust cover.
2. Disconnect the stabilizer link, strut bar and the lower arm. Remove the strut assembly, knuckle arm and strut insulator retaining bolts, Figs. 2 and 3.
3. Remove assembly from vehicle.

Disassembly

1. Securely hold the strut assembly in a vise and remove the upper dust cover. Remove the nuts attaching the insulator to the strut sub-assembly, then the insulator and the spring.

NOTE: Use the spring compressor (Special Tool CT-1105) before removing the nuts so the nut threads will not be damaged while the nuts are being removed. Also, note that the steering knuckle is welded to the strut sub-assembly and cannot be separated.

2. When removing the piston rod insulator retaining nuts, lock each nut using the special wrench (Special Tool CT-1112).
3. Check all disassembled parts for loss of tension, cracks, fractures, etc., and replace any defective parts.

NOTE: Since the insulator ball bearing is built into the insulator assembly, if the ball bearing is defective, the complete insulator assembly should be replaced.

4. If a check of strut sub-assembly (shock absorber) indicates oil leakage, further disassembly is required.
5. Before disassembly, remove all dirt from the outside walls of the sub-as-

sembly, and use care to prevent dirt from entering the cylinder or the fluid during disassembly.

6. Securely hold the strut sub-assembly vertically and, using the special wrench (Special Tool CT-1112), remove the shock absorber seal assembly. Lower the piston rod assembly to the lowest position during this operation.

7. Drain fluid. Using a small screwdriver, pull out the square-section O-ring. Slowly draw the piston rod assembly and guide out upward and remove the guide from the piston rod.

NOTE: The following service parts are available and if any part other than these is found to be defective, the whole strut sub-assembly should be replaced:
  a. Shock absorber assembly
  b. Seal assembly
  c. O-ring (square section)

Assembly

1. Apply fluid to each surface of the shock absorber cylinder and piston.
2. Carefully insert the piston rod in the cylinder. Compress the piston ring as it slides into the cylinder.
3. Assemble the cylinder and piston assembly with the strut outer shell.
4. Fill the shock absorber with new fluid. To expel air from the cylinder, slowly move the piston rod. The capacity of a dry shock absorber is 18.3 cu. in. If some fluid remains on the cylinder walls, the unit will not accept a full charge.
5. With the guide flange placed at the top, insert the piston rod until the guide flange contacts the end of the shock absorber cylinder.

6. Install the "O" ring between the guide and the strut outer cylinder. Be careful not to distort the "O" ring.

NOTE: The "O" ring should always be replaced when the shock absorber has been disassembled.

7. Cover the piston rod end with the seal guide (Special Tool CT-1111B), apply sufficient oil to the seal lip and slide in the seal. Using a special tool (CT-1112), tighten the seal assembly until the seal nut edge contacts the strut outer cylinder.
8. Install the coil spring on the strut.
9. Install the spring compressor (Special Tool CT-1105) on the coil spring to compress it, and compress the spring. Install spring on the strut sub-assembly.
10. Extend the shock absorber piston rod fully out and attach a bumper rubber and spacer.
11. Align the D-shaped hole in the spring seat upper assembly with the dent on the piston rod and install the insulator assembly. Then, install the self-locking nut and tighten it for temporary assembly.

NOTE: Since front springs installed on cars with 2000 cc engines differ from those used on cars with 1600 cc engines, be sure to install the correct springs in each model. Blue paint at location A, Fig. 95, identifies a spring for use in a car with 1600 cc engine, while white paint indicates the spring is for a car with 2000 cc engine.

12. After correctly seating the upper and lower ends of the coil spring on the grooves of the upper and lower spring seats, loosen the spring compressor.
13. Using the special tool (CT-1112), install the upper spring seat and torque the nut to 29 to 36 ft.-lbs.

Installation

1. Secure the key of the strut assembly to the strut assembly mounting bracket on the wheel housing. Then apply adhesive to the lower end of the assembly, connect it with bolts to the knuckle arm with the dowel pins located in their holes in the arms' flange surface. The torque specifications are given below:

Items	Ft. Lbs.
Bolts retaining strut assembly to wheel housing	7-11
Bolts retaining strut assembly to knuckle arm:	
Arrow & 1977 Colt Coupe & Sedan	39
Colt Ex. 1977 Coupe & Sedan	29-36

2. Pack the strut upper bearing with grease and install the dust cap. The proper grease is SAE J310a Multi-purpose Grease or equivalent.
3. Install the stabilizer, hub assembly and wheel.

STEERING GEAR, REPLACE

1. Remove the clamp bolt connecting the steering shaft with the steering gear housing mainshaft.
2. Using Pitman and idler arm puller (C-3894), disconnect the pitman arm and the relay rod.
3. Remove the steering gear assembly from the body frame.
4. Using the pitman arm puller (Special Tool CT-1106), remove the pitman arm from the cross shaft.
5. Reverse procedure to install.

Rear Suspension Section

LEAF SPRING & SHOCK ABSORBER, REPLACE

1. Raise and support vehicle at frame. Support rear axle with a suitable jack. Remove rear wheels.
2. Disconnect shock absorber from upper and lower attachments, Fig. 1, then remove shock absorber from vehicle.

NOTE: If shock absorber is not to be

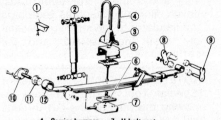

1. Carrier bumper
2. Shock absorber
3. Rubber cushion
4. Spring U-bolt
5. Pad bracket
6. Pad
7. U-bolt seat
8. Shackle plate
9. Spring shackle
10. Spring pin
11. Front eye bushing
12. Leaf spring

Fig. 1. Rear Suspension (Typical)

replaced, do not disconnect shock absorber from spring "U" bolt seat.

3. Loosen "U" bolt nut and raise axle clear of spring seat. Remove spring pad and seat.
4. Disconnect leaf spring at front attachment and rear shackle.
5. Remove leaf spring from vehicle.
6. Reverse procedure to install.

FIAT

INDEX OF SERVICE OPERATIONS

FIAT

GENERAL ENGINE SPECIFICATIONS

Model	Engine No.	Carburetor	Bore & Stroke	Piston Displacement Cubic Inches (cc)	Compression Ratio	Maximum Brake H.P. @ R.P.M.	Maximum Torque Lbs. Ft. @ R.P.M.
850	100G 000	1 Barrel	2.559 x 2.500	51.5 (843)	8.0	34 @ 4800	40 @ 3000
850	100G 002	1 Barrel	2.559 x 2.500	51.5 (843)	8.8	37 @ 5000	41 @ 3400
850	100GBS 040	1 Barrel	2.559 x 2.677	55 (903)	9.5	53 @ 4000	48 @ 4000
128	128A 000	1 Barrel	3.149 x 2.185	68 (1116)	8.5	55 @ 6000	57 @ 3000
128	128AR 000	1 Barrel	3.385 x 2.185	78.7 (1290)	8.9	67 @ 6400	65 @ 4000
128	128A 040	1 Barrel	3.149 x 2.185	68 (1116)	8.5	52 @ 6000	65 @ 4000
128	128A1 040	1 Barrel	3.390 x 2.190	78.7 (1290)	8.5	62 @ 6000	67 @ 4000
128	128A1 031	1 Barrel	3.390 x 2.190	78.7 (1290)	8.5	61 @ 5800	67 @ 4000
X1/9	128AS 040	2 Barrel	3.390 x 2.190	78.7 (1290)	8.5	66.5 @ 6000	67 @ 4000
X1/9	128AS 031	2 Barrel	3.390 x 2.190	78.7 (1290)	8.5	61 @ 5800	67 @ 4000
124	124BC 040	2 Barrel	3.150 x 3.150	98.1 (1608)	8.5	94 @ 6600	94 @ 4000
124	124B2 040	2 Barrel	3.156 x 2.814	87.8 (1438)	8.9	90 @ 6500	80 @ 3600
124	124AC 3.000	2 Barrel	3.150 x 2.815	87.8 (1438)	8.9	80 @ 5800	81 @ 4000
124	132A1 031	2 Barrel	3.310 x 3.120	107.2 (1756)	8.0	83 @ 5800	89 @ 2800
131	132A1 031	2 Barrel	3.310 x 3.120	107.2 (1756)	8.0	83 @ 5800	89 @ 2800
131	132A1 040	2 Barrel	3.310 x 3.120	107.2 (1756)	8.0	86 @ 6200	90 @ 2800

TUNE UP SPECIFICATIONS

Model	Engine No.	Spark Plug Type	Spark Plug Gap	Distributor Point Gap Inch	Distributor Dwell Angle Deg.	Ignition Timing Firing Order Fig.	Ignition Timing Timing BTDC	Ignition Timing Mark Fig.	Carb. Adjustments Hot Idle Speed Std. Trans.	Carb. Adjustments Hot Idle Speed Auto. Trans.
850	100G 000	N9Y	.026	.018	48—54	A	10	②	800	—
850	100G 002	N9Y	.026	.018	48—54	A	11	②	800	—
850	100GBS 040	N7Y	.022	.018	52—58	B	TDC	②	850	—
128	128A 000	N9Y	.024	.015	52—58	C	TDC	③	850	—
128	128A 040	N9Y	.022	.015	52—58	C	TDC	③	850	—
128	128AR 000	N8Y	.026	.015	52—58	C	5	③	850	—
X1/9	All	N9Y	.022	.016	52—58	D	TDC	③	850	—
124	124BC 040	N6Y	.022	.015	52—58	F	5	④	900	—
124	124B2 040	N6Y	.020	.017	52—56	E	10	④	800	—
124	124AC 3.000	N6Y	.022	.017	57—63	E	10	④	800	—
124	132A1 031	N7Y	.025	①	52—58	I	TDC	④	800	—
131	132A1 031	N7Y	.025	①	52—58	I	TDC	④	800	700
131	132A1 040	N7Y	.025	①	52—58	I	TDC	④	850	700

①—Starting points, .012-.019; Running points, .014-.017.
②—Mark located on pulley. Timed at No. 1 cyl., rear of engine.
③—Mark located on pulley. Timed at No. 1 cyl., right side of vehicle.
④—Mark located on pulley. Timed at No. 1 cyl., front of engine.

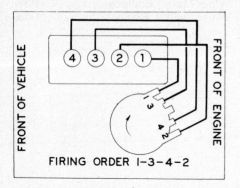

Fig. A

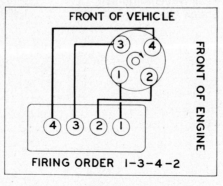

Fig. B

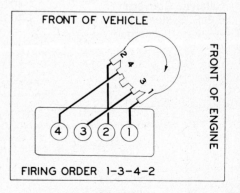

Fig. C

FIAT

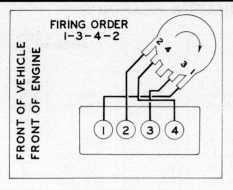

Fig. D

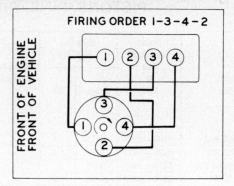

Fig. E

DISTRIBUTOR SPECIFICATIONS

If unit is checked on vehicle, double RPM and degrees to get crankshaft figures.

Model	Advance Starts	Centrifugal Advance Degrees @ RPM of Distributor				Full Advance
			Intermediate Advance			
850 ①	0 @ 500	7 @ 1000	10¼ @ 1500	13½ @ 2000		14 @ 2500
850 ②	0 @ 450	7 @ 1000	9½ @ 1500	12¼ @ 2000		12½ @ 2500
850 ③	0 @ 450	7 @ 1000	9½ @ 1500	12¼ @ 2000		14 @ 2500
128 ④	0 @ 450	5½ @ 750	9½ @ 1500	12 @ 2000		14½ @ 2350
128 ⑤	0 @ 500	6½ @ 1000	8¾ @ 1500	11½ @ 2000		14 @ 2500
X1/9	0 @ 450	6¾ @ 1000	9½ @ 1500	12 @ 2000		14 @ 2350
124 ⑥	0 @ 500	3¾ @ 1000	7½ @ 1500	—		10 @ 1800
124 ⑦	0 @ 500	10½ @ 1000	15 @ 1500	—		17 @ 1700
131	0 @ 500	10½ @ 1000	15 @ 1500	—		17 @ 1700

① —Except Super.
② —Super, up to engine serial no. 515048.
③ —Super, from engine serial no. 515049.
④ —Distributor no. S135B.
⑤ —Exc. distributor no. S135B
⑥ —Exc. engine no. 132A1031.
⑦ —Engine no. 132A1031.

ALTERNATOR & REGULATOR SPECIFICATIONS

Model	Alternator		Regulator						
	Model	Rated Hot Output, Amps	Model	Field Relay			Voltage Regulator		
				Air Gap In.	Point Gap In.	Closing Voltage	Air Gap In.	Point Gap In.	Voltage @ 125°F
850	D90/12/16/3CS ①	230 ②	GN2/12/6	.014	.018	12.6	.042	—	14.2
128	D90/12/16/3E ①	230 ②	GN2/12/16	.014	.018	12.6	.042	—	14.2
128	G114V33	30	AD1/14V	—	—	—	—	—	—
124	A12M124/12/42M	42	RC2/12B	—	—	—	③	—	—
124	D90/12/16/3C5 ①	230 ②	GN2/12/16	.014	.018	12.6	.042	—	14.2
X1/9	A124-14V-44A	53	AD1/14V	—	—	—	—	—	—
131	A124-14V-44A	53	RC2/12D	—	—	—	③	—	—
131	A124-14V-60A	70	RC2/12E	—	—	—	③	—	—

—Not Available
① —Generator.
② —Watts.
③ —Armature to core, .059"; Second stage contact gap, .018".

FIAT

PISTONS, PINS, RINGS, CRANKSHAFT & BEARINGS

Model	Engine No.	Piston Clearance Top of Skirt	Ring End Gap ①		Wristpin Diameter	Rod Bearings		Main Bearings			
			Comp.	Oil		Shaft Diameter	Bearing Clearance	Shaft Diameter	Bearing Clearance	Thrust on Bearing No.	Shaft End Play
850	100G 000	.0008—.0016	.0079	②	—	1.5742—1.5750	.0010—.0028	1.9994—2.0002	.0008—.0024	2	.0024—.0104
850	100G 002	.0020—.0031	.0079	②	—	1.5742—1.5750	.0010—.0028	1.9994—2.0002	.0008—.0024	2	.0024—.0104
850	100GBS 040	.0024—.0032	.0079	②	—	1.5742—1.5750	.0010—.0028	1.9994—2.0002	.0008—.0024	2	.0024—.0102
128	③	.0020—.0028	.0118	.0079	—	1.7913—1.7920	.0014—.0034	1.9990—1.9998	.0019—.0037	5	.0021—.0104
128	④	.0020—.0028	.0118	⑤	—	1.7913—1.7920	.0014—.0034	2.1459—2.1465	.0014—.0034	5	.0021—.0104
X1/9	All	.0020—.0028	.0118	⑤	—	1.7913—1.7920	.0014—.0034	2.1459—2.1465	.0014—.0034	5	.0021—.0104
124	124BC 040	.0025—.0033	.0118	.0079	—	1.8990—1.8994	.0018—.0032	1.9990—1.9998	.0019—.0039	5	.0021—.0104
124	124B2 040	.0031—.0039	.0118	.0079	—	1.7910—1.7920	.0010—.0030	1.9990—1.9998	.0019—.0037	5	.0021—.0102
124	124AC 3.000	.0035—.0043	.0118	.0079	—	1.7916—1.7924	.0010—.0029	1.9990—1.9998	.0019—.0037	5	.0021—.0104
124	132A1 031	.0016—.0024	.0118	.0078	—	2.2329—2.2334	.0019—.0032	2.0860—2.0868	.0020—.0037	5	.0021—.0120
131	All	.0016—.0024	.0118	.0078	—	2.2329—2.2334	.0019—.0032	2.0860—2.0868	.0020—.0037	5	.0021—.0120

—Not Available
① —Fit rings in tapered bores for clearance listed in tightest portion of ring travel.
② —Upper ring, .0079"; lower ring, touch fit.
③ —1972-75.
④ —1976-77.
⑤ —Upper ring, .0118"; lower ring, .0098".

ENGINE TIGHTENING SPECIFICATIONS

Torque specification are for clean and dry threads only. Dirty threads produce increased friction which prevents accurate measurement.

Model	Engine No.	Spark Plugs Ft. Lbs.	Cylinder Head Bolts Ft. Lbs.	Intake Manifold Ft. Lbs.	Exhaust Manifold Ft. Lbs.	Connecting Rod Cap Bolts Ft. Lbs.	Main Bearing Cap Bolts Ft. Lbs.	Flywheel to Crankshaft Ft. Lbs.
850	100G 000	18	29	22	22	25.3	44.8	25.3
850	100G 002	18	29	22	22	25.3	44.8	25.3
850	100GBS 040	18	36	—	18	29	51	36
128	128A 000	29	①	22	22	36	58	61
128	128A 040	29	②	22	22	40	61	61
128	128AR 040	29	②	22	22	40	66	61
128	128AS 040	29	①	22	22	36	58	61.5
X1/9	All	—	①	22	22	36	58	61.5
124	124BC 040	29	58	18	18	40	58	62
124	124B2 040	29	56	18	18	38	59	59
124	124AC 3.000	29	54	18	18	36	58	62
124	132A1 031	29	54	18	18	47	③	61.5
131	All	29	54	18	18	47	③	61.5

—Not Available
① —Exc. upper head, 69 ft. lbs.; Upper head, 14.5 ft. lbs.
② —Exc. upper head, 61 ft. lbs.; Upper head, 14.5 ft. lbs.
③ —Exc. self lock nut, 57.8 ft. lbs.; Self lock nut, 83 ft. lbs.

REAR AXLE SPECIFICATIONS

Year	Model	Ring Gear & Pinion Backlash		Pinion Bearing Preload		Differential Bearing Preload	
		Method	Adjustment Inch	Method	Adjustment In.—Lbs.	Method	Adjustment Inch
1972-75	124	Shim	.0031—.0051	Spacer	14—17	①	—
1975-77	131	Shim	.0031—.0051	Spacer	12—14	Shim	.004

—Not Available
① —Threaded rings.

FIAT

STARTING MOTOR SPECIFICATIONS

Model	Engine No.	Brush Spring Tension, Ounces	Free Speed Test		
			Amps.	Volts	R.P.M.
850	All	40	30	12	8500
128	All	40	30	12	7000
X1/9	All	40	30	11.9	7000
124	124BC 040	18	32	12	5100
124	124B2 040	18	25	12	5100
124	124AC 3.000	35	25	12	5100
124	132A1 031	35.2	28	12	5200
131	All	35.2	28	12	5200

BRAKE SPECIFICATIONS

Year	Model	Brake Drum Inside Diameter	Wheel Cylinder Bore Diamter				Master Cylinder Bore Diameter Diameter
			Drum Brakes		Disc Brakes		
			Front	Rear	Front	Rear	
1972-73	850	7.283	.875	.750	1.772	1.338	.750
1972-77	128	7.294	—	.750	1.890	—	.750
1972-77	124	—	—	—	1.875	1.375	.750
1974-77	X1/9	—	—	—	1.772	1.338	.750
1975-77	131	8.9882	—	.875	1.875	—	.750

—Not Available

WHEEL ALIGNMENT SPECIFICATIONS

Year	Model	Caster Angle, Degrees		Camber Angle, Degrees				Toe-In Inch	Toe-Out on Turns, Degrees	
				Limits		Desired				
		Limits	Desired	Left	Right	Left	Right		Outer Wheel	Inner Wheel
1972-73	850	+8 to +10	+9	+½ to +1¹/₆	+½ to +1¹/₆	+⁵/₆	+⁵/₆	.433—.511 ①	26	32
1972-77	128	+1⁵/₁₂ to +1⁵/₆	+1²/₃	+1¹/₃ to +2	+1¹/₃ to +2	+1²/₃	+1²/₃	0	31¾	35
1972-75	124	+2¹/₁₂ to +2¾	+2¼	−¼ to +⁵/₁₂	−¼ to +⁵/₁₂	+¹/₁₂	+¹/₁₂	.275	—	—
1976-77	124 ②	+3 to +4	+3½	0 to +1	0 to +1	+½	+½	.12	—	—
1974-77	X1/9	+6½ to +7½	+7	−1 to 0	−1 to 0	−½	−½	—	—	—
1975-76	131 ②	+4 to +5	+4½	0 to +1	0 to +1	+½	+½	.08—.16	—	—

—Not Available
① —Rear, +¹/₁₀° to +³/₁₀°.
② —With fully loaded vehicle.

VALVE SPECIFICATIONS

Model	Engine No.	Valve Lash		Valve Angles		Valve Spring Installed Height	Valve Spring Pressure Lbs. @ In.	Stem Clearance		Stem Diameter	
		Int.	Exh.	Seat	Face			Intake	Exhaust	Intake	Exhaust
850	All	.006	.008	45	46	1.339	51.6 @ 1.339	.0009—.0022	.0009—.0022	.2750—.2756	.2750—.2756
124	124BC 040	.018	.020	45	46	①	75.5 @ 1.417 ②	.0012—.0026	.0012—.0026	.3139—.3146	.3139—.3146
124	124B2 040	.017	.019	45	46	①	85.6 @ 1.417 ②	.0013—.0026	.0015—.0028	.3140—.3146	.3137—.3143
124	124AC 3.000	.018	.020	45	46	①	75.5 @ 1.417 ②	.0013—.0026	.0011—.0024	.3140—.3146	.3142—.3148
124	132A1 030	.018	.020	45	46	①	85 @ 1.417 ②	.0012—.0026	.0012—.0026	.3139—.3146	.3139—.3146
131	All	.018	.020	45	46	①	85 @ 1.417 ②	.0012—.0026	.0012—.0026	.3139—.3146	.3139—.3146

① —Outer spring, 1.417"; Inner spring, 1.220".
② —Outer spring.

Electrical Section

DISTRIBUTOR, REPLACE

1. Remove the spark plug wires.
2. Remove the low tension leads.
3. Remove the vacuum lines, if equipped, and the starting points switch wire to manifold.
4. Set the number one piston to TDC, compression stroke with the crankshaft timing marks aligned and the distributor rotor aligned with the number one tower of the distributor. Be sure these marks are still aligned properly when replacing the distributor. Mark the distributor base to engine alignment to facilitate installation.
5. Remove clamp bolt at base of distributor, then the distributor carefully.
6. Reverse procedure to install and set the timing.

DISTRIBUTOR SERVICE

850 and some 124 distributors have the advance mechanism attached to the top of the distributor shaft. Some models have a breakerless distributor which is serviced the same as point type distributors, except magnetic sensors and a trigger wheel are used instead of breaker points and the cams on the shaft. There are two detectors, the main detector and an auxiliary which is switched on in place of the main one when engine water temperature is below 59°+/−5°, to effect a 10° cold-start spark advance. Other distributors use a dual-point system, one set of which is for cold starting. The dwell angle of the starting points may be checked after the wires to the switch in the bottom of the intake manifold are disconnected from the switch and attached together.

Distributors are disassembled by removing cap, rotor, points, condensers, breaker plates and centrifugal advance assemblies on applicable models, Fig. 1. Apply lubricant where needed during reassembly.

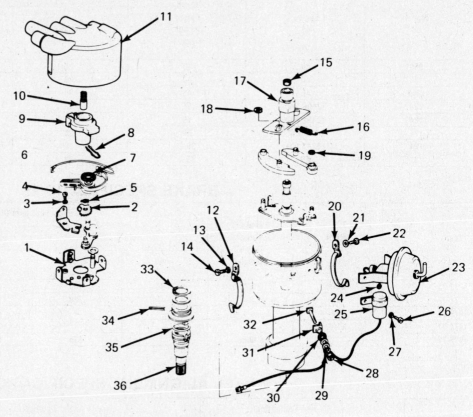

EXPLODED VIEW OF IGNITION DISTRIBUTOR

1. Contact breaker plate	13. Washer	25. Condenser
2. Star gear	14. Screw	26. Screw
3. Washer	15. Rubber ring	27. Washer
4. Screw	16. Spring	28. Nut
5. Clip	17. Cam	29. Lockwasher
6. Contact breaker points	18. Clip	30. Fiber washer
7. Washer	19. Washer	31. Terminal
8. Clip	20. Clip	32. Bolt
9. Rotor	21. Washer	33. Washer
10. Spring contact	22. Screw	34. Pin
11. Cap	23. Vacuum valve	35. Seal
12. Clip	24. Washer	36. Gear

Fig. 1 Exploded view of single point distributor (typical)

ALTERNATOR, REPLACE

Early models have a generator, which has been replaced by an alternator.
1. Disconnect battery ground cable.
2. Disconnect electrical leads to alternator and carefully position aside.
3. Remove nut from upper bracket and, if necessary, the screw holding the bracket to the engine. Remove the lower bracket nuts and drive belt.
4. Remove alternator.
5. Reverse procedure to install.

ALTERNATOR IN-VEHICLE TESTING

1. Turn off all electrical accessories.
2. Connect leads of voltmeter across battery terminals.
3. Set meter to 50V D.C.
4. Start and run engine at 2500rpm for a few minutes.
5. Check that battery indicator light is off.
6. Voltmeter reading should be 14V.

STARTER, REPLACE

124, 128 & 131

1. Raise vehicle and support with jackstands.
2. Disconnect battery ground cable.
3. Remove the exhaust manifold and muffler, if necessary, to provide access to starter.
4. Mark and disconnect starter motor wires.
5. Remove starter mounting bolts and starter.
6. Reverse procedure to install.

IGNITION SWITCH, REPLACE

1. Disconnect battery ground cable.
2. Remove steering column cover or any panels to provide access.
3. Remove wires, then the switch.

TURN SIGNAL & LIGHT SWITCH, REPLACE

850

1. Pry off the horn button, then remove steering wheel.
2. Disconnect the wiring.
3. Loosen the clamp securing the switch to the steering column, then slide switch from column.
4. Reverse procedure to install.

124

1. Remove horn ring mounting and the steering wheel.
2. Remove the two half-collars for the direction switch.
3. Disconnect the wiring.
4. Loosen the clamp holding switch to steering column and slide the switch off column.
5. Reverse procedure to install.

128

1. Remove two steering wheel cover attaching screws.
2. Remove horn button return spring.
3. Remove steering wheel to column attaching nut and the steering wheel.
4. Remove the two housing halves of the assembly.
5. Loosen the clamp securing the assembly to the steering column.
6. Disconnect the electric wiring and slide out the switch assembly.
7. Reverse procedure to install.

X1/9

The outer lighting switch is on the lower left dashboard panel. It is of the toggle type and may be reached from behind.

131

The toggle switch is on the left of the dashboard in a separate small panel which may be pulled out for access.

STOP LIGHT SWITCH, REPLACE

The stop light switch is attached to the brake pedal bracket.
1. Disconnect electrical connector.
2. Remove switch attaching nut and the switch.
3. Reverse procedure to install.

NEUTRAL SAFETY SWITCH, REPLACE

From inside the passenger compartment, remove the center console, disconnect the wires for the switch and remove the switch.

INSTRUMENT CLUSTER SERVICE

850 Sedan

1. Disengage the retaining spring clips and pry the panel up.
2. Disconnect speedometer cable and electrical connections.
3. Remove the panel and cluster.
4. Reverse procedure to install.

850 Coupe

1. Disconnect steering column bracket from instrument panel and rest steering wheel on seat.
2. Remove the panel pad screws and the panel pad.
3. Disconnect speedometer cable and electrical connections.
4. Remove panel attaching nuts, then slide cluster outward.
5. Reverse procedure to install.

850 Spider

1. Disconnect the steering column mounting bracket.
2. Remove the nuts securing the toggle switches and the trip odometer.
3. Disconnect speedometer cable.
4. Remove panel attaching nuts and the cluster.
5. Reverse procedure to install.

124 Spider

1. Remove the four screws attaching the cluster to instrument panel.
2. Disconnect speedometer cable.
3. Disconnect the five cluster connectors.
4. Remove the cluster.
5. Reverse procedure to install.

124 Special

1. Depress the spring from the front of the panel.
2. Remove speedometer cable.
3. Disconnect electrical connectors.
4. Remove cluster.
5. Reverse procedure to install.

128

1. Remove spare wheel from the engine compartment.
2. Remove the speedometer cable retainer plate screw and cable.
3. From inside passenger compartment, remove cluster attaching screws, then the cluster.
4. Reverse procedure to install.

X1/9

1. Remove the five screws securing instrument cluster to instrument panel.
2. Slide cluster out and disconnect the electrical connectors and speedometer cable.
3. Remove the cluster.
4. Reverse procedure to install.

131

1. Remove the panel below the radio and the radio.
2. Loosen the steering column adjusting knob and lower the wheel fully, then remove the knob.
3. Pry out the "Slow Down" indicator, if equipped, in the EGR panel at the lower left of the dashboard. Through the hole in the panel, remove screw holding the panel to the instrument panel.
4. Loosen the screws holding the bottom half of the steering column cover, then move the cover to gain access to the two screws located on both sides of the column on the lower dash panel.
5. Remove the screw through front side of the EGR and instrument panel.
6. Remove the screw through the bottom of the instrument panel on the passenger side.
7. Pull out the small switch panels on both sides of the cluster.
8. Remove the two screws, one on each side of the cluster, which are revealed when the two switch panels are removed.
9. Reach through the control panel opening and disconnect the speedometer cable.
10. Disconnect the electrical connectors, then remove the cluster.
11. Reverse procedure to install.

W/S WIPER SWITCH, REPLACE

850 Coupe & Sedan

The switch is mounted to the left on the dashboard in a small panel. Remove the bezel and the wiring, then the switch.

850 Roadster

The toggle-switch is located to the left on the instrument cluster panel. Remove the panel, the switch bezel and wire, then the switch.

124

On the 124, the switch is located in a small panel on the lower left portion of the dashboard; pull out and remove. On the 124 Special, the switch is mounted on the right side of the steering column. Follow the procedure to remove the steering column cover, then remove the wires and the clamp and switch.

128, 131 & X1/9

The windshield wiper switch is mounted on the right hand side of the steering column and is attached to the turn signal switch underneath the column cover. Refer to switch procedure.

W/S WIPER MOTOR, REPLACE

850 Sedan & Coupe

The wiper motor is removed through an opening in the instrument panel.
1. Remove the instrument cluster.
2. Remove the locking rings on the control switches and the ornamental plate.
3. Remove the instrument panel pad, which is secured by clips.
4. Remove wiper assembly-to-mount attaching screws and the electrical connector, then the motor assembly through the opening.
5. Reverse procedure to install.

850 Spider & Racer

Open the luggage compartment to gain access, then disconnect the linkage, electrical wire, attaching bolts and motor.

124

Access to the motor is from the engine compartment.
1. Remove the left side spacer nut and the left side wiper arm and blade.
2. Remove retaining nuts from bracket, then move the motor back slightly.
3. Remove clip connecting the right half-link to the motor, then the motor.
4. Reverse procedure to install.

128

1. Open the engine compartment lid and remove the spare wheel.
2. Remove the wiper arm and blade assemblies.
3. Remove attaching nuts and wiper blade pivot spacers.
4. Remove the speedometer cable retaining clip from the body.
5. Remove wiper assembly mounting screws and the electrical connector, then remove the assembly.
6. Reverse procedure to install.

131

1. Open the engine compartment hood

and remove the panel on the upper firewall.
2. Disconnect the linkage, wiring and mounting bolts, then remove the motor.
3. Reverse procedure to install.

RADIO, REPLACE

850 Sedan & Coupe

1. Disconnect antenna lead and electrical leads from radio.
2. Remove the radio knobs and attaching nuts, then remove the radio.
3. Reverse procedure to install.

850 Roadster

1. Remove radio knobs and attaching nuts.
2. Remove the right side decorative panel from the dashboard.
3. Remove the antenna lead and electrical leads, then the radio.
4. Reverse procedure to install.

128 & 131

1. Disconnect antenna lead and electrical leads.
2. Remove radio attaching bolts.
3. Remove radio.
4. Reverse procedure to install.

Engine Section

ENGINE, REPLACE
850

1. Raise rear of the car and support on stands.
2. Disconnect battery ground cable.
3. Remove screws and floor covering behind seats.
4. Remove starter and two upper transmission-to-engine bolts.
5. Remove apron below engine.
6. Disconnect fuel line at pump.
7. Disconnect oil pressure indicator wire from sending unit.
8. Disconnect temperature sending unit, ignition coil, generator, and license plate electrical connectors.
9. Drain oil and water and disconnect hoses.
10. Unbolt flywheel housing from transmission.
11. Disconnect exhaust pipe at manifold (and muffler if not using special tool A. 60534).
12. Remove air cleaner and disconnect

choke and accelerator linkage.
13. Attach a chain hoist for support and remove two lower transmission-to-engine bolts.
14. Remove the rear central engine support unit.
15. Remove the two rear bumper support bracket nuts and the two screws and four nuts retaining the lower body panel in order to remove these two units, then remove engine.
16. Reverse procedure to install.

128

NOTE: Engine, clutch, transmission and differential are removed as a unit.

1. Raise and support vehicle.
2. Raise hood and unhook stay rod.
3. Remove spare wheel.
4. Remove lower guards.
5. Drain water from the radiator, supply tank, cylinder block, and pas-

senger compartment heater unit using the following procedure:
   a. completely lower the heater lever inside the car,
   b. open the cock at the bottom of the radiator and remove the radiator cap,
   c. open the cock on the inner side of the cylinder block and remove cap from supply tank.
6. Disconnect battery cables.
7. Disconnect coil-to-distributor wires.
8. Disconnect generator, starter, oil pressure sending unit, and temperature sending unit electrical connectors.
9. Disconnect air cleaner and housing.
10. Disconnect choke and accelerator linkage.
11. Disconnect fuel inlet hose from fuel pump.
12. Disconnect exhaust pipe from manifold.
13. Remove rubber hoses from thermostat-to-radiator union.

14. Disconnect heater hoses to passenger compartment unit.
15. Disconnect speedometer drive cable at engine.
16. Unscrew locknut and nut and remove adjustable rod of flexible cable from clutch release control lever.
17. Disconnect anti-roll bar by removing screws, clamping brackets and body insulators and unscrewing nuts holding ends to control arms.
18. Remove exhaust pipe bracket from transmission.
19. Disconnect rod from the gearshift control lever by removing screw and nut.
20. Remove the ground plate from the transmission housing.
21. Remove left wheel, unscrew left tie rod-to-steering arm attaching nut and disconnect ball joint.
22. Remove shock absorber from inside pillar.
23. Working from engine compartment, remove the reaction strut.
24. Attach a chain hoist for support, then unscrew engine-to-body clamping bolt and, from below, remove the crossmember from the underbody.
25. Loosen constant speed joint nuts, work the shaft of each constant-speed joint out of its seat in the pillars and secure the axle shafts with wire to prevent them from getting out of their seats in the differential.
26. Reverse procedure to install.

124

1. Remove radiator, then place car on jackstands and drain using this procedure: move heater lever to far right, open radiator drain cock and remove plug on right hand side of block, and radiator and auxiliary tank caps.
2. Disconnect battery cables, then ignition coil, generator, starter, oil pressure indicator and temperature indicator wires.
3. Disconnect accelerator rod and slide it out of the lever ball joint toward the dash.
4. Remove air filter and disconnect choke cable.
5. Disconnect line from fuel pump.
6. Disconnect exhaust pipe from manifold.
7. Disconnect radiator and heater hoses and remove two radiator attaching bolts, then slide radiator up and out.
8. Remove gearshift lever by pressing down upper part of sleeve using a screwdriver to release spring from the seat in lower part of lever.
9. Remove transmission cover.

10. From under vehicle, disconnect driveshaft spider and transmission mainshaft from universal. Use a clamp to hold universal together while removing screws.
11. Disconnect speedometer cable at transmission.
12. Disconnect flexible cable at clutch fork.
13. Remove flywheel cover, ground cable and exhaust pipe bracket clip.
14. Remove heat shield from exhaust manifold and three starter motor bolts.
15. Use a hydraulic jack under transmission for support, then remove the four bolts holding transmission to crankcase.
16. Remove transmission support crossmember.
17. Remove transmission by moving rearward, down and out.
18. Remove starter.
19. Remove engine using hoist.
20. Reverse procedure to install.

X1/9 Engine

1. Disconnect battery ground cables.
2. Drain cooling system (removing cap from expansion tank to facilitate).
3. Disconnect heater hose from pump.
4. Disconnect wires from alternator.
5. Remove two bolts holding louvered protection panel below carbon trap in rear firewall.
6. Disconnect choke linkage at carburetor.
7. Disconnect vacuum hoses from carburetor base.
8. Disconnect electrical leads from solenoid and carburetor vent hose at carburetor.
9. Disconnect coil wire at distributor, and wires from starter and oil pressure and temperature sending units.
10. Remove clamp holding fuel lines to firewall and disconnect fuel lines from firewall.
11. Remove stop bolt from accelerator cable, slide off seal, remove retainer clip from cable sheath and remove cable from support.
12. Remove expansion tank retaining bolts (upper and lower), lift tank so water drains into engine, disconnect hoses from tank and thermostat and remove tank. Remove hoses from thermostat.
13. Remove cotter pin holding slave cylinder pushrod to clutch shaft. Loosen two bolts holding slave cylinder to transmission, open bleeder screw of cylinder in order to retract pushrod, then move slave cylinder aside.
14. From underneath, remove the remaining bolt holding louvered panel

and remove panel, then heat shield behind alternator and three panels from bottom of engine compartment and the panel inboard of each rear wheel.
15. Drain transmission/differential.
16. Disconnect electric wires for seat-belt interlock system and back-up lights, remove clamps in order to facilitate removal of wires from engine compartment together with engine.
17. Disconnect speedometer cable from differential and secure out of the way.
18. Remove bolts holding gearshift linkage to the shifting tube.
19. Loosen bolt at transmission end of flexible link and swing out of the way.
20. Remove bolts holding ground strap to body.
21. Remove the four nuts and lock tabs from exhaust manifold flange and the two bolts from the upper bracket at the left end of the muffler, then remove the two nuts retaining the center support of the muffler to the crossmember and remove the muffler assembly. Remove the two nuts and bolt retaining the upper bracket to the differential case and remove bracket.
22. Remove the three bolts holding the axle boot retaining ring on the right and left sides and slide the boots away from the differential (excess oil will drain).
23. Remove handbrake cable bracket at forward end of each suspension control arm.
24. Record the number of shims at each suspension control arm mounting point, then remove the four nuts and bolts and the shims holding the control arms to the body and swing the control arms downward out of their brackets. Move control arms away from differential until the axles are free of the differential, then secure the axle assemblies to control arms.
25. Loosen bolts on each end of lower crossmember and with a jack positioned so as not to damage oil pan or aluminum parts, lower vehicle so that the engine is supported.
26. Remove bolts from the lower crossmember.
27. From engine compartment, disconnect the engine torque rod from its bracket on the engine.
28. Remove bolt from engine mount, then raise the car slightly and rock the engine/transmission assembly in order to clear front engine mount.
29. Carefully raise vehicle and lower the engine to remove.
30. Reverse procedure to install.

131

1. Disconnect battery cables and remove starter.
2. Remove transmission, following this procedure:
   a. Disconnect ground cable.
   b. Remove clamp holding exhaust pipe to exhaust manifold.
   c. Working inside passenger compartment, remove three screws holding transmission cover and remove it.
   d. Push gearshift lever down and pry snap ring out of seat on lever, then remove boot.
   e. Disconnect connector for fast idle switch on transmission, remove grommet and push connector through tunnel.
   f. Place car on jackstands.
   g. Install clamp on universal joint, then remove three bolts and nuts holding front shaft to flexible universal joint.
   h. Remove two bolts holding protection bracket to body and secure driveshaft out of the way.
   i. Disconnect two wires from switch on transmission.
   j. Support transmission (being careful not to damage it) with jack.
   k. Remove starter.
   l. Remove return spring from forked lever, disconnect clutch cable from forked lever, slide cable out of transmission casing. Disconnect wires from switch and speedometer cable from transmission.
   m. Remove bolts holding flywheel cover to transmission.
   n. Remove bolts and washer holding exhaust pipe support to transmission, loosen bolt holding support to pipe and move support out of the way.
   o. Remove two bolts holding transmission crossmember to body and remove crossmember.
   p. Remove bolts holding transmission to engine.
   q. Remove transmission to rear and down.
3. Disconnect wires from oil pressure sending unit and from two thermostat switches in intake manifold.
4. Remove nut holding ground strap to engine mount.
5. Remove nut and washers holding isolator to crossmember.
6. Remove heat shield from alternator, disconnect wires from alternator and remove nut holding isolator to crossmember.
7. Disconnect upper water hose (air conditioned cars: disconnect hose from compressor). Disconnect hose

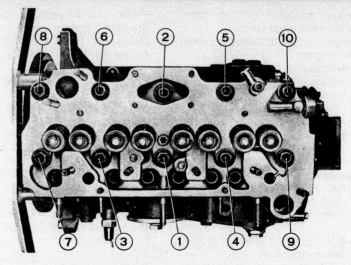

Fig. 1 Cylinder head tightening sequence. 850 models

from drier and clamp holding hoses to radiator.
8. Disconnect wires from thermostat switch and cooling fan.
9. Remove nuts holding radiator and remove radiator.
10. Disconnect vacuum hoses from fittings on intake manifold.
11. Disconnect electrical wires from carburetor and coil.
12. Disconnect fuel inlet and return hoses from carburetor.
13. Disconnect vacuum hose, carburetor vent hose and fast idle vacuum hose from carburetor. Remove two nuts holding linkage on cam housing cover.
14. Remove air cleaner. Cars with air conditioning—open bleed fittings and allow to bleed completely, disconnect compressor and condensor hoses.
15. On right side, disconnect wire to water temperature sending unit. Remove clamp holding exhaust pipe to manifold.
16. Disconnect air hose from pump.
17. Disconnect distributor wires.
18. Lift out engine with hoist.
19. Reverse procedure to install.

CYLINDER HEAD, REPLACE
850

1. Drain cooling system, remove air cleaner, carburetor, distributor (set engine at top dead center on compression stroke to facilitate reinstallation), rocker assembly cover.
2. Disconnect coolant inlet and outlet hoses.
3. Disconnect exhaust pipes from manifold and exhaust manifold from the head.

4. Disconnect spark plug wires from plugs.
5. Disconnect heat sensing unit wire from unit.
6. Unscrew rocker shaft assembly bolts and remove assembly from head. Turn bolts out one turn at a time to avoid warping rocker shaft.
7. Remove pushrods.
8. Remove cylinder head attaching bolts and lift off cylinder head.
9. Reverse procedure to install. Torque bolts in two steps to specifications and in sequence shown in Fig. 1.

128

1. Drain cooling system, remove spare tire from engine compartment, remove air cleaner, disconnect spark plug cables.
2. Disconnect throttle linkage from carburetor.
3. Disconnect fuel line and choke cable from carburetor.
4. Disconnect temperature sending unit electrical lead.
5. Disconnect upper and lower radiator hoses, heater inlet hose, coolant pump delivery hose from thermostat housing.
6. Disconnect exhaust pipe from manifold, remove bracket.
7. Remove belt guard cover (lower screw is removed from below). Set engine at top dead center on appropriate cylinder to facilitate reinstallation of head.
8. Loosen belt tensioner pulley nut and remove belt only from camshaft pulley.
9. Unscrew the belt guard lower screw.
10. Remove the shroud by unscrewing the set screws.
11. Disconnect the reaction rod from the cylinder head bracket.

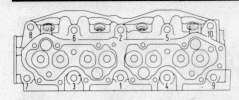

Fig. 2 Cylinder head tightening sequence. 128 & X1/9 models

12. Remove the cylinder head (without a special wrench to reach head bolts, camshaft housing may be removed first). Intake and exhaust manifolds as well as carburetor will remove with head. These parts may be removed best with cylinder head on bench.
13. Install with manifolds, etc., attached, following proper torque specifications and sequence, Fig. 2.

124 W/DOHC

1. Drain cooling system, disconnect upper radiator hose, remove air cleaner and all linkage and hoses connected to carburetor and cylinder head.
2. Remove carburetor and intake manifold as a unit.
3. Disconnect exhaust manifold at head.
4. Remove timing belt cover. Set engine at top dead center to facilitate reassembly.
5. Loosen timing belt tensioner and remove timing belt from camshaft pulleys.
6. Remove spark plug cables.
7. Remove cylinder head attaching bolts and lift head straight up.
8. To reinstall head, be sure pistons 1 and 4 are at TDC, piston #1 is on compression stroke and that camshaft timing marks (on pulleys) are in near proper position.
9. Lower cylinder head straight down and avoid damage to valves from improper contact.
10. Install cylinder head bolts in proper sequence, Fig. 3, and to torque specifications.
11. Refit camshaft drive belt, being careful to have all timing marks in proper position.
12. Tighten idler pulley. Use spring scale to attain sixty pound (60 lbs.) tension on camshaft belt.
13. Check belt tension after turning crankshaft several times and recheck camshaft timing.
14. Reverse rest of procedures in order to complete reassembly.

124 W/OHV

1. Drain radiator and cylinder block, disconnect temperature sending unit wire, spark plug cables, and ac-

celerator rods from cylinder head cover.
2. Remove cylinder head cover.
3. Disconnect all hoses.
4. Disconnect fuel line.
5. Disconnect starter relay cable.
6. Disconnect exhaust pipe from manifold.
7. Remove starter motor heat shield.
8. Remove the rocker shaft assembly with supports and rockers. Leave exhaust, intake manifolds and carburetor on head; they are best removed on bench.
9. Remove pushrods and cylinder head bolts.
10. Remove head. Remove various parts from head to facilitate machining work.
11. Reverse procedure to install, taking care to follow proper torque sequences, Fig. 4, and specifications.

X1/9

1. Drain cooling system and remove air cleaner.
2. Disconnect fuel hoses from carburetor and pull hoses out of their bracket on top of cam cover.
3. Disconnect throttle rod by sliding spring clip down.
4. Disconnect spark plug cables.
5. Disconnect distributor vacuum hose from head.
6. Remove stop bolt from accelerator cable, slide seal off cable, remove clip holding cable on valve cover and remove cable.
7. Remove three water hoses from union at side of block.
8. Disconnect hose from exhaust shroud.
9. Disconnect wires to thermostatic switch on carburetor.
10. Disconnect evaporative hose from carburetor.
11. Disconnect two hoses from air pump.
12. Remove bolts and washers holding timing cover.
13. Remove right lower guard from under engine.
14. Remove lower bolt holding cover, then cover.
15. Remove alternator and water pump drive belt.

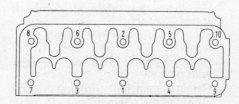

Fig. 4 Cylinder head tightening sequence. 124 models with overhead valve engine

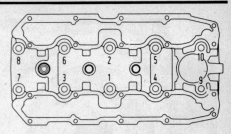

Fig. 3 Cylinder head tightening sequence. 124 & 131 models with dual overhead cam engine

16. Remove two bolts through rear of air pump and support brackets. Loosen bolt through top of pump, move pump and remove drive belt.
17. Loosen nut on tensioner pulley and remove timing belt.
18. Remove lower bolt through belt guard.
19. Remove bolts and nuts holding cylinder head and carefully remove cylinder head. Intake and exhaust manifolds and carburetor will remove with head and are best removed from head on bench.
20. To reassemble, reverse procedure making sure that camshaft, crankshaft and distributor are properly timed and head is put carefully in place to avoid any damage. Follow proper torque sequences, Fig. 2, and specifications.

131

1. Disconnect battery and remove air cleaner; drain cooling system and disconnect hoses. On air-conditioned cars, loosen compressor mount bolts and remove drive belts.
2. Disconnect air hose from air pump and from air manifold.
3. Disconnect two wires to distributor and distributor wire from coil.
4. Remove clamp holding exhaust pipe to manifold.
5. Disconnect heater hoses from cylinder head and tube below exhaust manifold. Remove nut holding water tube clamp to exhaust manifold.
6. Remove three bolts and nut holding timing belt cover and remove it.
7. Remove air pump belt and loosen alternator/water pump belt.
8. Loosen nut on timing belt tensioner and remove belt from pulley.
9. Disconnect accelerator rod from carburetor, remove nuts holding support and move out of the way.
10. Disconnect wires from switches at intake manifold and disconnect vacuum hoses.
11. Disconnect fuel, vapor and vacuum hoses from carburetor.
12. Disconnect wire from temperature sending unit.
13. Disconnect tube from EGR valve

Fig. 5 Timing marks. 850 models

Fig. 6 Timing marks. 124 models with overhead valve engine

tube and remove bolt and nut holding EGR valve tube to support.

14. Disconnect fitting on air manifold from cylinder head and disconnect hose from EGR valve.
15. Remove two bolts holding tube to camshaft covers.
16. Remove bolt holding each camshaft cover. Remove cover and drain oil.
17. Remove two bolts holding dipstick support to cam housing.
18. Remove ten bolts holding cylinder head to crankcase.
19. Remove head.
20. To install head, be sure that crankshaft, camshaft and distributor are in time and that proper torque sequences, Fig. 3, and specifications are followed. Install head carefully in order to avoid damage. Reverse rest of procedure to complete assembly.

ROCKER SHAFT, REPLACE

850 and 124 OHV

Follow procedures outlined in cylinder head section.

TIMING GEAR COVER, REPLACE

850

1. Remove crankshaft/centrifugal oil filter drive belt.
2. Remove oil filter cover and gasket.
3. Remove crankshaft pulley nut while keeping crankshaft from rotating.
4. Remove pulley.
5. Remove timing cover retaining nuts, then cover.
6. Reverse procedure to install.

124 OHV

1. Remove generator and fan drive belt.
2. Remove crankshaft pulley retaining nut, then pulley.
3. Remove timing gear cover retaining screws, then cover.
4. Reverse procedure to install.

124 OHC, 128, X1/9

1. Remove retaining screws and lift cover from engine.
2. Reverse procedure to install.

131

1. Drain cooling system and remove hoses blocking access.
2. Disconnect union from water extension on cylinder head.
3. Remove three bolts holding timing belt cover and remove it.

TIMING CHAIN OR BELT, REPLACE

850

1. Remove timing gear cover as outlined above.
2. Turn engine to align timing marks, Fig. 5.
3. Remove nuts retaining camshaft drive sprocket, then remove sprocket together with chain using a puller.
4. Remove timing chain and replace with new one.
5. Reinstall camshaft sprocket making sure timing chain is around both sprockets and timing marks are aligned, Fig. 5. It may be necessary to rotate camshaft slightly to ac-

complish alignment. Make sure chain stretchers on timing chain face toward the camshaft side of the engine at the top of camshaft sprocket.
6. Install lockplate and screw on camshaft sprocket retaining nut, tightening to 36 ft. lbs. while keeping camshaft from rotating.
7. Install timing gear cover.

124 OHV

1. Remove timing gear cover as outlined above.
2. Align timing marks on sprockets, Fig. 6.
3. Remove camshaft sprocket retaining bolt, then sprocket along with timing chain.
4. Remove timing chain and replace with new one.
5. Install sprocket on camshaft together with timing chain, making sure timing marks are aligned, Fig. 6.
6. Tighten retaining bolt to 35 ft. lbs. while keeping camshaft from turning.
7. Replace cover.

124 DOHC

1. Drain cooling system.
2. Remove upper radiator hose and top section of air duct.
3. Place crankshaft pulley timing mark on TDC, then remove cover.
4. Remove lower protection plate from engine.
5. Loosen generator mounting bolts and remove the drive belt.
6. Slacken timing belt idler pulley, then remove the timing belt.

7. Install new belt over camshaft gears and the idler pulley.
8. Position the spring balance to the hole in the upper right arm of the idler pulley.
9. Adjust belt tension to 60 lbs. between the two runs of the belt where it passes around the idler pulley.
10. Check the valve timing, Fig. 7.
11. Reinstall the timing gear cover and the radiator air duct, then refill the cooling system to the proper level.

128

1. Remove the timing gear cover as outlined above. Lower cover retaining screw from below after removing right side guard.
2. Time valves by aligning timing mark (2) on camshaft sprocket (1) with fixed mark on engine, (3), Fig. 8. Timing mark (7) on crankshaft sprocket (6) must also be aligned with its fixed index mark, Fig. 8.
3. Remove water pump and generator drive belt.
4. Loosen tensioner pulley nut and relieve spring tension in order to remove timing belt.
5. Remove old timing belt and replace with new one.
6. Be sure new belt engages teeth properly and that timing marks are aligned, Fig. 8.
7. Reverse rest of procedure to complete installation.

X1/9

1. Turn crankshaft so that no. 4 piston is at TDC on compression stroke, timing mark on front crankshaft pulley is at TDC and camshaft pulley mark is aligned with the cast finger of the support visible through the hole in the camshaft cover.

CAUTION: Avoid turning camshaft during this procedure in order not to damage valves.

2. Remove the bolts attaching timing cover, then remove right guard from under engine and lower timing cover retaining bolt; cover may be removed.
3. Loosen alternator and remove alternator/water pump drive belt, then remove drive pulley from crankshaft.
4. Loosen air pump and remove drive belt.
5. Remove camshaft cover and check that cam lobes of no. 4 cylinder are facing up.
6. Remove distributor (note position).

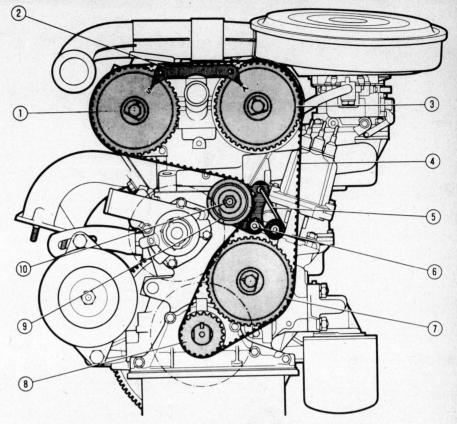

1. CAMSHAFT SPROCKET
2. CAMSHAFT TIMING BRACKET
3. CAMSHAFT SPROCKET
4. TIMING BELT
5. TENSIONER SPRING
6. BRACKET SCREW
7. SPROCKET
8. SPROCKET
9. PULLEY
10. DRIVESHAFT
11. LOCKNUT

Fig. 7   Timing marks. 124 models with dual overhead valve engine

7. Loosen idler pulley locknut, then push it on support and tighten locknut. Remove timing belt (first from idler pulley).
8. Install new timing belt (begin at crankshaft). Twist belt gently to facilitate, but be careful not to kink belt.
9. Install belt over camshaft pulley, moving pulley very slightly to align the slots with the belt cogs.
10. Install belt over idler pulley last, then loosen idler pulley locknut so that pulley may return to tension position. Turn engine only in direction of normal rotation either by putting car in gear or by bumping starter. Do not reverse direction of engine rotation at any time or timing belt will slacken and jump timing.
11. Release idler pulley tension and reset so that all slack is out of belt.
12. Position belt cover on the engine and recheck timing mark alignment. Tighten tensioner pulley nut to 32 ft. lbs.
13. Install pulley on crankshaft.
14. Install drive belt on air pump and adjust tension.

15. Install water pump/alternator drive belt and adjust belt tension.
16. Install timing gear cover, lower right guard and camshaft cover.
17. Install distributor (rotor should point toward no. 4 cylinder tower of cap).

131

1. Remove spark plugs and set engine at TDC of compression stroke of no. 4 cylinder.
2. Check that crankshaft pulley timing mark is in line with TDC mark (longest mark) on timing belt cover. Marks on camshaft pulleys should be aligned with cast finger on support.
3. Place car in fourth gear and apply handbrake.
4. On air conditioned cars, remove compressor drive belts.
5. Partially drain cooling system, then disconnect top hose from radiator and remove union, then timing belt cover.
6. Remove drive belt for air pump and alternator.
7. Loosen nut on tensioner and bolt

FIAT

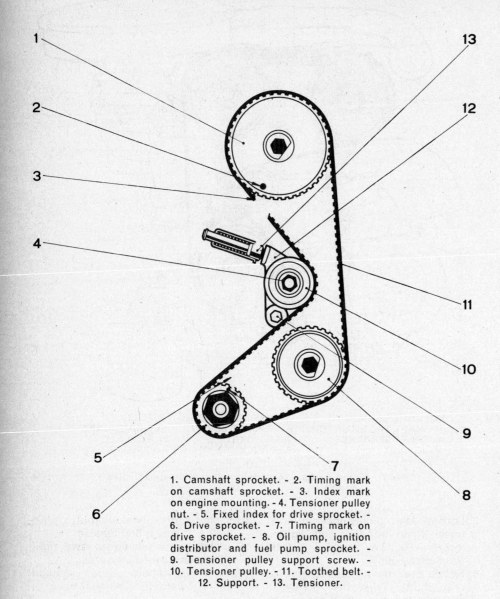

1. Camshaft sprocket. - 2. Timing mark on camshaft sprocket. - 3. Index mark on engine mounting. - 4. Tensioner pulley nut. - 5. Fixed index for drive sprocket. - 6. Drive sprocket. - 7. Timing mark on drive sprocket. - 8. Oil pump, ignition distributor and fuel pump sprocket. - 9. Tensioner pulley support screw. - 10. Tensioner pulley. - 11. Toothed belt. - 12. Support. - 13. Tensioner.

Fig. 8   Timing marks. 128 models

for spring support. Pry tensioner to relieve tension on timing belt, then tighten nut.
8. Remove timing belt. Belt *must* be replaced any time tension is removed.
9. Check that marks on camshaft pulleys are aligned with cast fingers on support and that hole on auxiliary shaft is about in line with bolt for auxiliary shaft pulley and tensioner spring mounting bolt.
10. Loosely install timing belt cover with two bolts and check that mark on crankshaft pulley is in line with TDC mark on cover.
11. Put new belt over crankshaft pulley and auxiliary shaft pulley. Put belt over intake camshaft pulley and exhaust camshaft pulley. Be

sure that all play is between exhaust camshaft pulley and tensioner.
12. Place belt over tensioner, then loosen and refit pulley to take out all slack. Rotate crankshaft two full turns only in direction of normal rotation to remove slack and tighten tensioner bolt and nut.
13. Check that timing marks on camshaft pulleys, auxiliary shaft pulley and crankshaft pulley are aligned properly.
14. Install air pump belt, and alternator/water pump belt. Check and adjust tension.
15. Install timing belt cover and union on cylinder head, fill cooling system, install spark plugs (on air-conditioned cars install and tension compressor drive belts).

CAMSHAFT REMOVAL, REPLACE

850

1. Remove engine from vehicle.
2. Remove the rocker cover, rocker shaft assembly and pushrods.
3. Remove timing chain cover, camshaft timing chain sprocket and timing chain.
4. Remove flywheel.
5. Turn engine upside down and remove valve tappets away from cam lobes (tap on block).
6. Remove camshaft retaining plate from rear of the engine block, then slide camshaft out, being especially careful not to damage camshaft bearings with camshaft lobes.
7. Install camshaft in reverse order. Coat shaft with oil before installation and be sure to align timing marks, Fig. 5 when installing timing chain. Install distributor with rotor facing no. 1 tower when piston no. 1 is in TDC position on compression stroke.

128

1. Remove camshaft drive belt following procedure outlined in camshaft timing belt removal section.
2. Remove camshaft carrier attaching bolts, then camshaft carrier assembly.
3. Remove camshaft drive sprocket.
4. Remove camshaft thrust plate from end of camshaft carrier (opposite belt end).
5. Slide camshaft out of carrier using care to avoid damaging bearings with camshaft lobes.
6. Install camshaft by reversing procedure. Be sure to align timing marks properly when installing belt, Fig. 8. (Refer to belt removal section).

124 DOHC

1. Camshafts in this engine are removed *as per* 128 SOHC engine outlined above; also refer to belt removal section for 124 DOHC engine.

124 OHV

1. Camshaft may be removed without removing engine, providing that radiator and body parts which obstruct the removal are taken off first.
2. Remove fuel pump distributor, cylinder head and valve lifters as described in the section on cylinder head removal. Replace as described in that section.
3. Remove timing chain cover, then camshaft sprocket together with timing chain.

4. Remove two bolts attaching camshaft retainer plate and remove plate.
5. Slide camshaft out of block being especially careful not to damage bearings with the camshaft lobes.
6. Oil camshaft and reverse procedure to reassemble. Make sure to align timing marks, Fig.6.

X1/9

1. Camshaft in this engine is removed *as per* 128 SOHC engine outline above. Also refer to belt removal section for X1/9 engine.

131

1. Remove head as described in that section.
2. Remove four nuts holding carburetor, then remove it along with gasket.
3. Remove nut and clamp holding retaining distributor.
4. Remove nut, bolt and insulator holding air pump to support, then remove two bolts holding air pump support to water extension.
5. Remove two front camhousing bolts and install tool A.60446 using these bolts. Remove pulley retaining bolt. If special tool is not available, hold pulley firmly while removing retaining nut; be careful not to damage pulley. Repeat for other camshaft.
6. Remove camshaft end covers and remove camshafts very carefully.
7. Remove bolts holding cam housings, then remove housings and gaskets.
8. Reverse procedure to install. Oil camshafts and use proper torque sequences and specifications. Refer to belt removal section for timing marks.

VALVES REMOVE, REPLACE

All Engines

1. Remove head as described in head removal section.
2. Remove rocker arm assembly, or camshaft(s).
3. Depress springs with proper tool and remove collets and poppet valves (tappets on engines so fitted).
4. Check sealing at time of replacement.

VALVES AND SEATS, REFACE

1. Lap machined valves into the ground seats (45°30' +/−5').
2. With valves out, check seat faces for

proper cut: 20°, 45°, 70°. Minimum valve edge thickness is: 0.02in. (0.5mm).

VALVE GUIDES, REPLACE

1. Drive out guide with special tool and press fit new guide (available in standard size and 0.008in. (0.2mm) oversize). Interference should be 0.0025 to 0.0043in. (0.063 to 0.08mm).
2. Check inside diameter and ream if necessary. Clean any rough spots caused by installation.

OIL PAN REMOVE, REPLACE

All Engines

1. On 850 models the oil pan may be removed if the rear of the car is jacked up; follow those procedures in the engine removal section which will provide access. On the 128 and X1/9, jack up the car and support the engine with a hoist so that the engine mount crossmember and the splash shields can be removed. On the 124 and 131, a hoist must be used and the engine mounts unbolted to allow the engine to be raised for access to the oil pan.

OIL PUMP REMOVE, REPLACE

All Engines

1. Remove the oil pan.
2. Remove oil pump attaching bolts and then pump.
3. Reverse procedure to install.

ROCKER ARM SHAFTS, REPLACE

850 and 124 OHV

1. Remove or move out of the way those assemblies affixed to rocker assembly cover.
2. Remove rocker arm assembly attaching bolts and lift off rocker assembly.
3. Remove rocker studs from head when necessary by double-nutting them. Stake new studs in place after torqueing properly.

VALVES, ADJUST

850 and 124 OHV (engine cold)

1. The valves should be adjusted in firing order at TDC.
2. Loosen nut and adjust valve accord-

ing to specifications. Tighten nut and recheck adjustment.

OHC & DOHC Engines

1. These engines use a tappet plate (shim) between camshaft and valve. In order to adjust the clearance, this tappet plate must be replaced with one of correct thickness.
2. Remove the camshaft cover(s).
3. Turn engine until maximum clearance is obtained between camshaft and tappet (cam lobe will be facing directly away from tappet).
4. If feeler gauge measurement indicates that adjustment is required, tappet plate must be replaced with one of proper thickness. Tappet plates are available in 0.002 in. increments and *must* be installed with hardened side up (this side marked with punchmark).
5. Remove the old tappet plate by first depressing the tappet with a special tool for this purpose; then remove the tappet plate either with needle-nose pliers or, more conveniently, with a stream of compressed air directed beneath the tappet plate through the slot in the tappet holder itself (which may be rotated into position before the special tool is used).
6. Install a new tappet; determine its thickness by adding to the thickness of the old tappet to arrive at a figure which will bring the clearance to within tolerance.
7. Replace valve cover.

REAR OIL SEAL

850

1. Remove engine and place on stand.
2. Remove clutch assembly, mark relative position of clutch and flywheel for correct reinstallation.
3. Remove flywheel and crankshaft rear seal cover and seal.
4. Reverse procedure to install. Make sure to seat all parts properly.

124 (All) and 131

1. Remove clutch and flywheel, marking them for reinstallation.
2. Remove old seal and seat new one carefully.
3. Reverse procedure to reinstall components.

128 and X1/9

1. Seals are part of transmission/axle unit and are replaced following procedures for this unit.

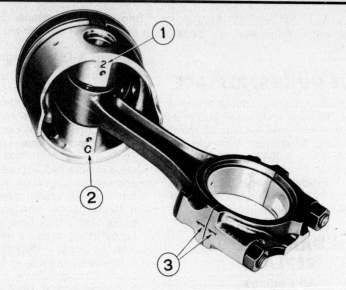

1. Piston pin class number   2. Piston class   3. Connecting rod matching

Fig. 9 Piston and connecting rod assembly

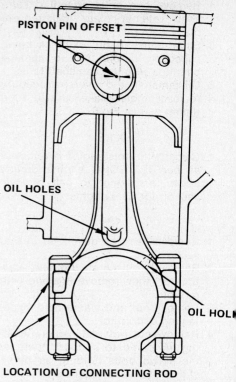

PISTON PIN OFFSET

OIL HOLES

OIL HOL

LOCATION OF CONNECTING ROD TO CYLINDER MATCHING NUMBER

Fig. 10 Piston and connecting rod installation

PISTONS & RODS

1. While it is possible to remove the pistons and rods from some engines by following the procedures for in-vehicle removal of heads and oil pans, this method is sufficiently time consuming and requires enough minor adjustment of hoist and engine position to warrant removing the engine. Follow engine removal procedure appropriate to vehicle and place engine on stand.
2. Remove head and oil pan (drain coolant and oil).
3. Remove oil pump where it impedes access.
4. Remove cap and press piston and connecting rod up and out. Take note of direction rod number faces.
5. Note that cap and rod are matched by number and that these numbers must be adjacent to each other when rod and cap are reassembled, Fig. 9. (If piston and rod are disassembled, see note about markings and assembly in wrist pin section, below. For assembly to crankshaft, see note (#4) in ring installation section.)
6. Torque nuts to proper specifications.

WRIST PINS

1. With piston and connecting rod removed from block, remove wrist pin from piston.
2. A new wrist pin and connecting rod may be installed, or the old ones reinstalled providing that they are in serviceable condition. Since these parts are available from various suppliers, proper code numbers should be checked and the new parts measured and weighed to be sure that they are within tolerances.
3. Connecting rod and piston may be heated in an oven (608°F [320°C]) to facilitate insertion of wrist pin to its seat.
4. Check wrist pin for slide resistance.
5. Note that piston is not a symmetrical design. Therefore, the connecting rod number must be on the side opposite to the piston skirt class letter and the boss division number (stamped on piston boss base), Fig. 10. For reassembly to crankshaft, see note in piston ring section.

PISTON RINGS

NOTE: Replacement parts are supplied by various manufacturers and may vary in weight. Therefore, they should be checked carefully to be sure they are correct.

1. Starting with cleaned pistons, checked with a micrometer and with any burrs or misspacing of ring grooves corrected, install the rings in the normal manner (bottom one first), making sure that the ring gaps are staggered evenly. Check side play and gap.
2. Assemble piston to rod if they have

been separated and replace.
3. Make sure that markings are placed as noted in Pistons and Rods and Wrist Pin sections, above.
4. For final assembly of rods to crankshaft note the following positioning:
   a. *850*—rod and bearing cap numbers face away from the camshaft; the oil hole in the connecting rod will then face toward the camshaft. The piston identification *letter* faces timing chain end of engine.
   b. *124 DOHC*—bearing cap number (and rod number matched to it and adjacent to it) will face away from the auxiliary shaft.
   c. *124 OHV*—the piston identification *letter* faces the front of the engine. The bearing cap number (and rod number matched to it and adjacent to it) face away from the camshaft.
   d. *128 and X1/9*—the piston identification *letter* faces toward the timing belt end of the engine. The cap number (and rod number matched to it and adjacent to it) face away from the auxiliary shaft.
   e. *131*—the cap number (and rod number matched to it and adjacent to it) faces toward auxiliary

shaft. Piston class letter and boss division number are on opposite connecting rod and cap numbers.

WATER PUMP, REPLACE

850

1. Remove apron from right side of the engine and drain engine coolant.
2. Remove drive belt, then disconnect cylinder head and radiator hoses.
3. Detach the air conveyor-to-radiator lockring.
4. Remove water pump attaching bolts and water pump.
5. Reverse procedure to install.

124

1. Some water pumps may be removed without removing the radiator, but it is often faster as well as more convenient to remove the radiator after detaching hoses and bolts.
2. Remove the fan from the water pump flange.
3. Remove the water pump.
4. Reverse procedure to install.

128

1. Remove spare wheel and drain coolant.
2. Disconnect hot air hose and accelerator rod from shroud, then remove shroud.
3. Disconnect passenger compartment heater water delivery and return hoses.
4. Remove upper generator bracket and loosen the two lower bracket

nuts.
5. Remove the water pump attaching bolts and water pump.
6. Reverse the procedure to install.

X1/9

1. Drain engine coolant.
2. Remove panels at lower right side of engine.
3. Remove alternator and drive belt.
4. Disconnect hoses from water pump, including heater hose pipe which is held by three nuts.
5. Remove bolt holding air pump support to water pump.
6. Remove water pump attaching bolts, then pump.
7. Reverse procedure to install.

131

1. Drain engine coolant.
2. Remove alternator and drive belt.
3. Remove two bolts holding heater tube to pump.
4. Remove three bolts holding water pump, then pulley.
5. Remove four bolts holding water pump, then pump.
6. Reverse procedure to install.

FUEL PUMP, REPLACE

Earlier models have a mechanical fuel pump, while some later models, beginning in 1973, have electrical fuel pumps; on some 1973 124 Sport, sedan and station wagon models, the electric fuel pump is located in the luggage campartment and the procedure for the *128* will apply. The X1/9 has a mechanical

pump mounted on the engine near the distributor.

Mechanical Fuel Pump

1. Remove and plug fuel lines from pump, then remove nuts attaching it and pump.
2. On pushrod equipped pumps, remove pushrod, then gasket and insulator.
3. On the 850, the pushrod height should be 0.0394-0.0591 in. Adjust this height using a gasket of appropriate thickness (height is measured from top of gasket).
4. Either replace or disassemble and clean (or rebuild) the old unit.
5. Reverse procedure to install.

Electric Fuel Pump

The 124 fuel pump is located in the luggage compartment; the 128 pump is mounted to the floor boards near the fuel tank (it is activated by a relay in the engine compartment); on the 131 sedan, remove back seat, backrest and top shelf to reach unit; on 131 station wagon, fuel tank must be lowered for access to pump as follows: a) drain tank, b) lift up floor deck, disconnect four hoses (mark them for reinstallation), c) remove screws holding cover over filler hose and remove the clamp holding the hose to the tank, d) remove the four nuts holding tank and lower it.

1. Detach and plug fuel lines.
2. Disconnect electrical leads.
3. Remove pump.
4. Reverse procedure to install. Be sure electrical contacts are clean, especially ground.

Carburetor Section

DESCRIPTION

All engines use Weber, Holley or Solex carburetors. Emissions standards vary by state and should be checked locally. All carburetor adjustment instructions assume correct ignition timing, dwell, valve lash and engine temperature (fully warmed up). All engines are set for smoothest idle, except where idle speed is indicated on a specification tag in late model vehicles, in which case these specifications must be adhered to. Note that the cable throttle linkage can be adjusted after loosening the cable eye hold-down screw and the cable should be checked for proper mounting.

CARBURETOR, REPLACE

1. Disconnect the accelerator rod.
2. Remove air filter and disconnect choke cable and all lines, noting the routing.
3. Remove carburetor mounting bolts, then carburetor and gasket. Cover manifold to prevent dirt from entering.
4. Reverse procedure to install.

FAST IDLE SPEED, ADJUST

1. Press the emission control button, then adjust the fast idle speed to 1550-1650 rpm.
2. Pump the accelerator several times

and check that the regular idle speed is proper.

FLOAT LEVEL, ADJUST

Solex

1. Position float on the gauge, Fig. 2.
2. Bend the float arm so the float is positioned on the three offset support stands of the gauge.

Holley or Weber

1. Hold the carburetor cover vertically so the float arm lightly contacts the ball of the needle.
2. The distance from the float to the

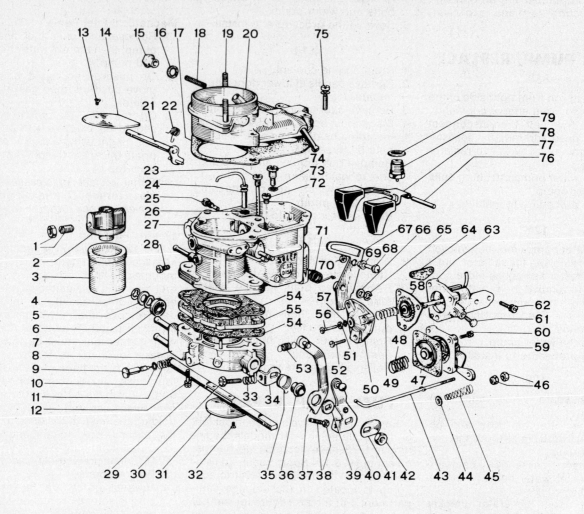

1. Screw and nut for attaching auxiliary venturi.
2. Auxiliary venturi.
3. Main venturi.
4. Spring washer.
5. Spacer.
6. Washer.
7. Disk valve for oil fumes recirculation device.
8. Lower housing.
9. Idle mixture adjustment screw.
10. Grommet.
11. Spring.
12. Screw and washer attaching lower to upper housing.
13. Screw.
14. Cold starting throttle.
15. Filter plug.
16. Filter plug gasket.
17. Gasket.
18. Fuel filter.
19. Stud.
20. Cover.
21. Starting choke throttle shaft.
22. Spring.
23. Emulsion tube.
24. Accelerator pump nozzle and jet.
25. Idle jet.
26. Gasket for nozzle 24.

27. Upper housing.
28. Main venturi attachment screw.
29. Throttle shaft.
30. Idle speed adjustment screw.
31. Throttle.
32. Screw attaching throttle to shaft 29.
33. Spring.
34. Throttle stop lever.
35. Spring.
36. Bushing.
37. Throttle control lever.
38. Throttle opening adjustment screw and nut.
39. Bushing for lever 37.
40. Throttle control lever.
41. Washer.
42. Nut locking throttle linkage to throttle shaft.
43. Rod.
44. Washer.
45. Spring.
46. Accelerator pump delivery adjustment nut and lock nut.
47. Accelerator pump diaphragm.
48. Diaphragm spring.
49. Lean mixture device spring.
50. Lean mixture device cover.
51. Nut.
52. Screw attaching cover 50.
53. Spring returning lever 37.

54. Gaskets.
55. Thermal spacer.
56. Starting throttle opening adjustment screw.
57. Washer.
58. Lean mixture device diaphragm.
59. Accelerator pump cover.
60. Accelerator pump cover attachment screw.
61. Cold starting device control sheath attachment screw.
62. Screw and washer.
63. Lean mixture device housing.
64. Gasket.
65. Spring washer.
66. Shoulder washer.
67. Cold starting control wire lever.
68. Cold starting device control wire locking screw.
69. Bushing for screw 68.
70. Nut for screw 68.
71. Return spring for lever 67.
72. Main jet.
73. Gasket.
74. Accelerator pump valve.
75. Screw attaching cover to upper housing.
76. Float hinge pin.
77. Float.
78. Needle valve.
79. Needle valve gasket.

Fig. 1 Exploded view of Solex C32 DISA carburetor

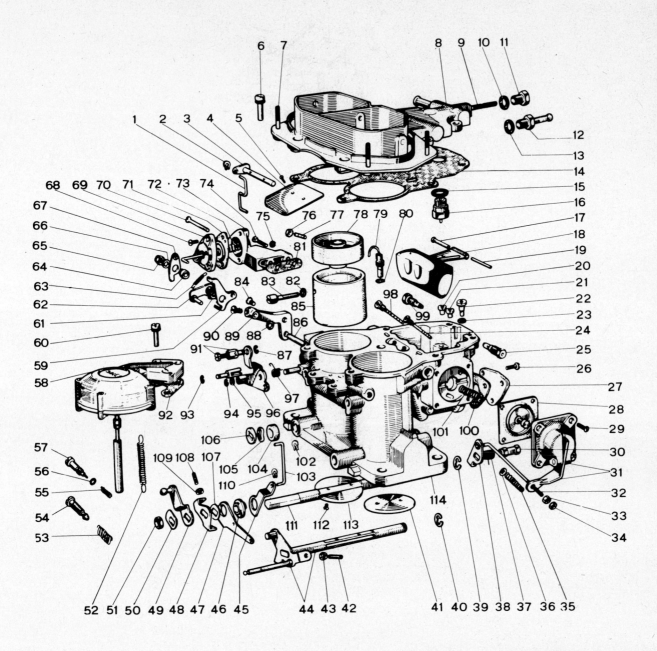

1. Choke throttle control rod. - 2. Rod spring washer. - 3. Choke throttle shaft. - 4. Choke throttle. - 5. Choke throttle mounting screw. -
6. Screw, securing carburetor cover to body. - 7. Stud. - 8. Body cover. - 9. Fuel filter. - 10. Gasket. - 11. Plug. - 12. Connector, fuel return to tank (C 32 EIES 4 only). - 13. Gasket. - 14. Cover gasket. - 15. Gasket. - 16. Needle valve. - 17. Float shaft bushing. - 18. Float. - 19. Float shaft. - 20. Main jet. - 21. Main jet. - 22. Pump jet. - 23. Gasket. - 24. Mixture tube. - 25. Idling jet. - 26. Screw. - 27. Plate. - 28. Pump diaphragm. - 29. Screw. - 30. Intermediate lever mounting nut. - 31. Pump cover. - 32. Pump control rod. - 33. Pump adjusting nut. - 34. Lock nut. - 35. Spring. - 36. Lock washer. - 37. Spring. - 38. Pump actuating idler lever. - 39. Spring washer. - 40. Spring washer. - 41. Secondary throttle valve. - 42. Secondary throttle adjusting screw. - 43. Nut. - 44. Secondary throttle shaft. - 45. Lever, controlling throttle opening. - 46. Bushing. - 47. Idler lever, secondary throttle return. - 48. Throttle stop lever. - 49. Primary throttle actuating lever. - 50. Lock washer. - 51. Nut. - 52. Spring. - 53. Cushion spring. - 54. By-pass idle mixture metering screw. - 55. Cushion screw. - 56. Gasket. - 57. Idle mixture metering screw. - 58. Vacuum device, controlling secondary throttle. - 59. Choke actuating cranked lever. - 60. Screw. - 61. Guide bushing. - 62. Choke actuating idler lever. - 63. Spring. - 64. Spacing bushing. - 65. Nut. - 66. Washer. - 67. Lever for automatic opening of choke throttle. - 68. Screw. - 69. Valve cover. - 70. Screw. - 71. Leaner valve diaphragm. - 72. Spring. - 73. Valve carrier. - 74. Screw. - 75. Spring washer. - 76. Nut. - 77. Screw. - 78. Venturi. - 79. Pump nozzle. - 80. Seal ring. - 81. Gasket. - 82. Spring washer. - 83. Primary Venturi fixing screw. - 84. Screw. - 85. Primary Venturi. - 86. Stud. - 87. Snap ring. - 88. Backing washer. - 89. Support. - 90. Screw. - 91. Adjustable pin and screw. - 92. Gasket. - 93. Snap ring. - 94. Snap ring. - 95. Backing washer. - 96. Choke throttle cable mounting. - 97. Spring. - 98. Mixture tube. - 99. Idling jet. - 100. Gasket. - 101. Spring. - 102. Spring washer. - 103. Link. - 104. Blow-by disk. - 105. Spring washer. - 106. Backing washer. - 107. Spacing washer. - 108. Idle throttle adjusting screw. - 109. Nut. - 110. Spring washer. - 111. Primary throttle shaft. - 112. Primary throttle adjusting screw. - 113. Primary throttle valve. - 114. Main body, carburetor.

Fig. 2   Exploded view of Solex C32 EIES 4/5 carburetor

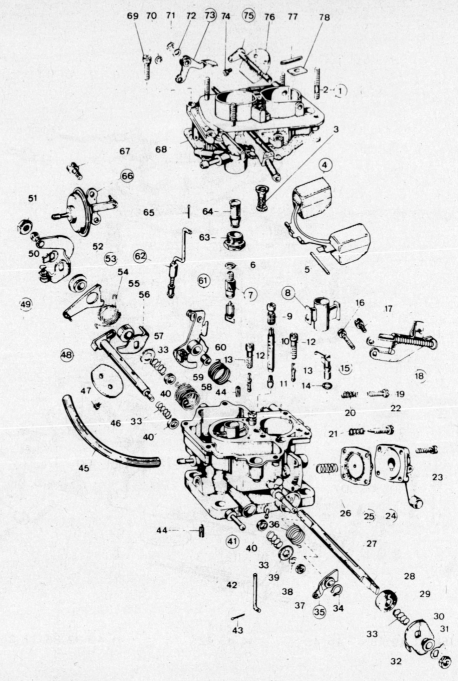

1. Carburetor cover
2. Stud
3. Bowel vent valve
4. Float
5. Pin
6. Gasket
7. Needle valve
8. Venturi
9. Air metering jet
10. Emulsion tube
11. Main Jet
12. Idle jet holder
13. Idle jet
14. Gasket
15. Acceleration pump nozzle
16. Screw

17. Screw
18. Support
19. Idle screw
20. Spring
21. Spring
22. Idle mixture screw
23. Screw
24. Accelerator pump cover
25. Diaphragm
26. Spring
27. Throttle shaft, primary
28. Bushing
29. Lever
30. Bushing
31. Lockwasher
32. Nut
33. Spring

34. Ring
35. Rod
36. Spring
37. Nut
38. Lockwasher
39. Washer
40. Bushing
41. Carburetor body
42. Lever
43. Cotter pin
44. Secondary throttle stop screw
45. Hose
46. Throttle
47. Screw
48. Secondary throttle shaft

49. Lever
50. Lockwasher
51. Nut
52. Bushing
53. Lever
54. Spring
55. Bushing
56. Primary shaft lever
57. Washer
58. Spring
59. Bushing
60. Spring
61. Lever
62. Rod
63. Lifter plug
64. Lifter

65. Cotter pin
66. Choke override
67. Screw
68. Cover gasket
69. Screw
70. Ring
71. Ring
72. Washer
73. Choke override control
74. Screw
75. Choke throttle shaft
76. Choke throttle
77. Plug
78. Dust cover

Fig. 3   Exploded view of Weber 32DMTRA200 carburetor

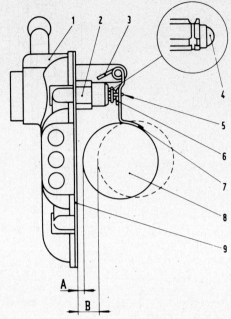

1. Carburetor cover. - 2. Valve seat. - 3. Lever end. - 4. Moving ball. - 5. Needle valve return hook. - 6. Tongue. - 7. Tongues, adjustable to correct float level. - 8. Float. - 9. Gasket.

$$A = .118'' \ (3 \ mm) \qquad B = .452'' \ (11.5 \ mm).$$

Fig. 4 Float level adjustment. 124 models with Weber carburetor

cover should be:
a. On 850, 7mm.
b. On 124, 3mm.
c. On 131, 6mm (to cover gasket face) +/− 1mm.
d. On 128, metal float: 11mm, plastic float: 36mm.

e. On X1/9, 6mm (to cover gasket face).

NOTE: On models equipped with catalytic converter, the distance between float and cover should be 7mm +/− .25mm.

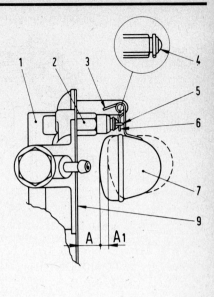

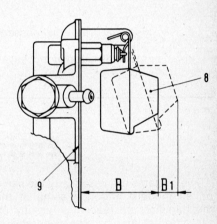

1. Carburetor cover.
2. Needle valve.
3. Lug.
4. Movable ball of needle valve.
5. Recall hook.
6. Tongue.
7. Metal float.
8. Plastic float.
9. Gasket.

Fig. 5 Float level adjustment. 128 models with Weber carburetor

CHOKE, ADJUST

Some models use a hand operated manual choke which can be adjusted where the cable is held to the choke throttle-plate (butterfly) arm by a set screw. On automatic choke/pollution models, observe operation of choke with engine cold and free up if sticking or set for proper closure.

IDLE SPEED & MIXTURE, ADJUST

NOTE: On vehicles equipped with catalytic converter, disconnect air hose from valve on air manifold. On vehicles equipped with automatic transmission, set parking brake and place transmission in Drive.

1. Set idle on models without specifications tag to a smooth rate. On models with specification tag, set to designated idle rpm using tachometer.

2. Insert sample probe of CO/HC tester in the pipe.
3. Use idle mixture screw adjustment to set CO to specifications.
4. If idle changes, reset idle speed screw—move back and forth between idle speed and mixture screws as necessary.
5. If CO percentage is low, check:
a. Air leaks and vacuum leaks.
b. Exhaust leak.
c. Fuel filter.
d. Fuel pump.

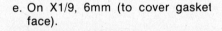

1. Carburetor cover   2. Needle valve   3. Lug
4. Valve needle   5. Movable ball   6. Return hook   7. Tang
8. Float arm   9. Float   10. Gasket

Fig. 6 Float level adjustment. 131 models with Weber carburetor

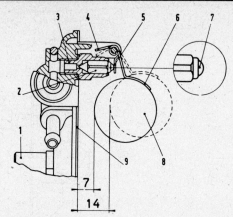

1. Body cover. - 2. Valve needle. - 3. Needle valve. - 4. Lug. - 5-6. Float arms. - 7. Needle valve ball. - 8. Float. - 9. Body cover gasket.
7 = .276'' - 14 = .551''

Fig. 7   Float level adjustment. 850 models with Weber carburetor

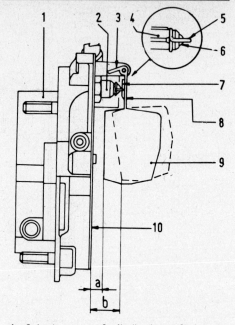

1. Carburetor cover.   2.   Needle valve.   3. Lug.
4. Valve needle.   5.   Return hook.   6. Movable ball.
7. Tang.   8.   Float arm.   9. Float.   10. Gasket.

Fig. 8   Float level adjustment. X1/9 models with Weber carburetor.

e. EGR leak.
f. Clogged carburetor fuel passage and float level.
6. If CO percentage is too high, check:

a. Loose dipstick.
b. Excessive oil in pan.
c. Intake or exhaust valve leak.
d. Float level.

Emission Controls Section

The systems are essentially the same on all models, although some of the mechanisms are placed differently on the different models. The general procedure described below applies to all. Illustrations of typical units are included. 1977 models have the same systems as earlier models, but do not use a catalytic converter.

The exhaust emission control units include the following: Air Injection System, Catalytic Converter, Catalyst Protection System, Exhaust Gas Recirculation system, Carburetor and ignition system modifications.

AIR INJECTION SYSTEM

The function of this system is to convey air to the exhaust manifold so that the oxygen in the air reacts with the hot gasses, causing further combustion in the exhaust system. The air injector will be cut out during cold temperature starts by means of the proper circuit being interlocked by engine water temperature and by a transmission contact which acts on the diverter valve. The function of the air cut off is to maintain the temperature in the exhaust system within safe limits.

The system components are as follows:
1. Air pump, belt-driven from the engine to supply the air.
2. Diverter valve, energized by the vacuum taken from the intake manifold to prevent backfiring during deceleration, shutting off air injected to the exhaust manifold. Through an electrovalve, the diverter valve is also controlled by a thermoswitch and by the transmission in neutral.
3. Check valve, to protect the system from hot gasses.
4. Air injection manifold.
5. Air injectors adjacent to the back of the exhaust valves.

CATALYTIC CONVERTER

The catalytic converter system consists of pellets coated with a catalyst (activated material) such as platinum or palladium and is enclosed in a heat resistant steel case.

When the mixture of exhaust gasses passes through the catalytic converter, the hydrocarbon (HC) and carbon monoxide (CO) content of the exhaust gasses is oxidized and converted into water (H_2O) and carbon dioxide (CO_2). Since large amounts of unburned fuel gasses will cause the temperature of the catalytic converter to rise, a high temperature system is provided. To avoid excessive increase of catalyst temperature during long decelerations, the carburetor idle stop solenoid is governed as follows:
1. When the carburetor throttle is closed in the idle position and the engine speed is higher than 2650 ± 50RPM.
2. Fuel shutoff through an electric contact on the idle speed adjusting screw and through a switch.
3. Through these mechanisms, the fuel shutoff takes place during all decelerations when the throttle is in the closed position and the engine speed is higher than 2650 ± 50RPM.

Warning system for excessive catalyst temperature:
1. If there is a malfunction which causes excessive catalyst temperature, a warning switch activates a "slow down" light on the dashboard.
2. This system consists of a thermocouple located inside the catalytic converter and of a control unit.

3. When the temperature of the substrate reaches 982°C±50°C (1800°F±50°F), a signal light is activated intermittently, increasing in frequency as temperature rises.
4. The operation of the control unit is reversible and the hysteresis of the switching levels is 50°C±10°C (122°F±18°F).
5. Failure of the thermocouple is indicated by continuous activation of the dashboard light.
6. To check the operational condition of the system: put the ignition switch in the "on" position and activate the "Slow Down" signal light.

EXHAUST GAS RECIRCULATION (EGR) SYSTEM

The purpose of the EGR system is to reduce the formation of nitrous oxide (NOx) emission from the exhaust gas. The system injects exhaust gases into the intake manifold in order to reduce peak combustion temperature and thereby to limit the emission of NOx. The components of this system are as follows:
1. Check and flow control valve of recirculated exhaust gasses, actuated by a vacuum signal taken from the carburetor.
2. EGR valve control vacuum control signal check thermovalve, actuated by engine water temperature.
3. Suitable gas intake on exhaust manifold.
4. Connection on intake manifold for introducing exhaust gasses.
5. A warning system connected to the gear box which every 25,000 miles illuminates a warning on the dashboard, "EGR," to signal required EGR system maintainance.

Clutch and Transmission Section

CLUTCH, ADJUST
850
1. Check that the pedal grommet on the dashboard wall does not interfere with the cable action.
2. The clutch is adjusted by means of the adjustable clutch throwout yoke rod to the right of the clutch pedal inside the passenger compartment. Clutch pedal travel should be 1 inch.

128
1. The adjustment nut and locknut are located under the hood in the engine compartment where the clutch cable joins the clutch throwout arm. Adjust pedal free play to 1 inch.

124
1. Raise and support vehicle.
2. The adjustment is located at the clutch cable to clutch throwout rod connection on the clutch cover.
3. Check the cable grommet at the bellhousing.
4. Adjust pedal travel to 0.98 in.

131 & X1/9
1. The adjustment is located on the clutch pedal bracket beneath the dashboard.
2. Clutch pedal free travel should be 1 inch.

CLUTCH, REPLACE
1. Remove transmission or transmission-axle unit.
2. Mark the position of the clutch on the flywheel for reinstallation in the same position.
3. Alternately loosen and remove the bolts holding the clutch cover to the flywheel.
4. Remove the pressure plate and the disc.
5. Check the flywheel face and the pilot bushing and replace if necessary.
6. Reverse procedure to install. Ensure the protrusion of the disc hub faces the transmission unit and the bolts are alternately tightened. Align the disc center with a suitable alignment tool so the transmission shaft can be inserted properly.

MANUAL TRANSMISSION, REPLACE
850

NOTE: The 850 uses a transaxle which is removed as a unit.

1. Disconnect the battery ground cable and remove engine compartment lid, upper headlining, generator and starter.
2. Raise rear of vehicle and support on jackstands.
3. Disconnect the lower shock absorber mountings.
4. Disconnect the gearshift rod and the clutch and speedometer cables.
5. Support transaxle unit with a suitable jack, then remove the transaxle mounting screws from the engine.
6. Remove the flywheel cover, then the screws holding the transaxle support bracket to the body.
7. Disengage the clutch shaft from the plate, then remove the transaxle.
8. Reverse procedure to install.

128
1. Disconnect the battery ground cable and remove spare tire, speedometer cable, clutch return spring and disconnect the clutch adjusting rod at the clutch lever.
2. Remove guard to body nut.
3. Remove transmission-to-engine screws and nuts from above.
4. Attach engine support crosspiece, tool A. 70526.
5. Remove front hubcaps.
6. Remove constant-speed joint-to-wheel hub nuts.
7. Remove left front wheel.
8. Disconnect left tie rod from steering arm.
9. Remove stabilizer bar.
10. Remove two lower left shock absorber-to-pillar attaching screws and nuts.
11. Remove the two lower guards.
12. Remove nuts securing exhaust clamp bracket to transmission.
13. Disconnect gearshift connection lever control rod.
14. Remove the starter motor-to-transmission assembly bolts.
15. Remove engine support crossmember.
16. Remove flywheel cover.
17. Remove the transmission-to-engine attaching bolts from beneath vehicle.
18. Disconnect the ground cable from the transaxle assembly.
19. Secure the axle shafts/constant speed joints to the transmission.
20. Remove the transaxle unit.
21. Reverse procedure to install.

124
1. Inside the passenger compartment, remove the cover plate and the gearshift lever.
2. Raise vehicle and support on jackstands.
3. Remove the flexible coupling from the spider on the mainshaft.
4. Remove speedometer drive from the support on transmission.

5. Remove clutch return spring, then the locknut on the cable and separate the fork from the clutch cable.
6. Remove flywheel cover from bell housing.
7. Remove bolt securing the exhaust pipe bracket to the transmission, then disconnect the exhaust pipe.
8. Remove starter motor heat shield, then the starter motor.
9. Support transmission with a suitable jack, then remove the four transmission to engine bolts.
10. Move the transmission back and down carefully.
11. Reverse procedure to install.

X1/9

1. Remove the air cleaner and the carburetor cooling duct.
2. Disconnect battery ground cable.
3. Disconnect clutch slave operating rod from the clutch operating arm, then remove spring, slave cylinder attaching bolts and position the slave cylinder aside, Fig. 4.
4. Support the engine, then remove the nuts and bolts accessible from top securing the transmission to engine.
5. Raise vehicle and support on jackstands, then remove the rear wheels.
6. Remove the three lower guards on the left side.
7. Mark the position of the gearshift tube in relation to the gearshift flexible link.
8. Remove the two bolts retaining the flexible link to the tube and loosen the bolt at the transmission end of the link, then move the link aside.
9. Disconnect back-up light connector and clamp holding the wiring to the body, then the connector for the seat belt system located inboard and forward of the transmission, near the engine water hoses.
10. Remove starter from transmission.
11. Disconnect the ground strap.
12. Remove the exhaust pipe.
13. Remove the hub nuts attaching the constant speed joints to the wheel hubs.
14. Remove the two bolts and nuts attaching the suspension control arm to the supports, then pull the hub off the constant speed joints and secure the axle shafts to the transmission.
15. Remove the flywheel cover.
16. Remove the crossmember supporting the engine while properly supporting the engine.
17. Remove the remaining nuts and bolts attaching the transmission to the engine.
18. Use a suitable jack to remove the

transmission/differential assembly.
19. Reverse procedure to install.

131

1. Disconnect battery ground cable.
2. Remove the clamp attaching exhaust pipe to exhaust manifold.
3. From inside the passenger compartment, remove the three screws retaining the transmission cover, then the cover.
4. Push the gearshift lever down and pry the snap ring out of the seat on the lever and remove the boot.
5. Disconnect the fast idle switch connector on the transmission, then remove the grommet and push the connector through the tunnel.
6. Raise vehicle and support on jackstands.
7. Install a clamp or tool A. 70025 on the flexible joint between the transmission shaft and the driveshaft and remove the three nuts and bolts.
8. Remove driveshaft protection bracket and position the driveshaft aside.
9. Disconnect the two wires from the switch on the transmission.
10. Support the engine and install a suitable jack under the transmission.
11. Remove starter bolts.
12. Remove the return spring from the clutch lever, disconnect the clutch cable from the lever and slide the cable from transmission housing.
13. Disconnect the wires from the switch above the lever on the clutch housing, then the speedometer cable from the support on the transmission.
14. Remove the bolts attaching the flywheel cover to the transmission.
15. Disconnect the exhaust pipe support from the transmission, then loosen the bolt attaching the support to the pipe and move the support aside.
16. Remove the two bolts attaching the transmission support to the body.
17. Remove the transmission to the engine bolts.
18. Remove transmission.
19. Reverse procedure to install.

AUTOMATIC
TRANSMISSION, REPLACE
850

The Idroconvert unit and transmission are removed as one assembly; follow the procedure for the manual transmission. Since the torque converter is both dynamically and statically

balanced, it is not necessary to remark its position in relation to the flywheel.

131

1. From inside the engine compartment, disconnect the battery, remove the transmission dipstick from its tube and disconnect the tube from the engine bracket.
2. From inside the passenger compartment, remove the center console, disconnect the transmission electrical connector, then push the connector through the floor opening.
3. Raise the vehicle and support it.
4. Remove the transmission drain plug and drain it.
5. Remove the three bolts holding the starter and wire it out of the way.
6. Remove the bolt holding the speedometer cable clamp to the transmission, then remove the speedometer cable out of the way (replace safety wiring on reinstallation).
7. Remove the clamp holding the cooling lines.
8. Remove the two bolts holding the exhaust pipe bracket.
9. Disconnect the vacuum hose from the modulator valve at the rear corner of the oil pan.
10. Disconnect the vacuum tube from the spring clip on the transmission just above the modulator valve.
11. Remove the bolt holding the bracket for the kick-down cable to the transmission (upper right front corner of transmission), then remove the bracket and disconnect the cable from the kick-down valve.
12. Remove the four bolts holding the cover plate at the lower front of the flywheel housing, then the plate.
13. Rotate the flywheel to gain access to the three bolts holding the flywheel to the torque converter and remove the three bolts carefully.
14. Remove the four bolts holding the transmission to the engine.
15. Tilt the rear of the transmission down and slide the transmission rearward, down and out.
16. Reverse the procedure to install, taking care to slide the connector for the switch on the transmission through the floor opening before positioning the transmission, and making sure to position the filler tube up from the bottom.
17. Transmission oil: Use Dextron type oil only. After installation is complete and drain plug installed, add about 5.28 pints of transmission oil. Start the engine and place the lever in D. Warm the engine up. Gradually add two pints of transmission oil.

FIAT

When engine reaches normal operating temperature, check the oil level with the car on level ground, the engine idling the selector in P or N. Do not overfill.

131 AUTOMATIC TRANSMISSION TROUBLE-SHOOTING

Low Oil Level

1. Oil coming out of filler tube.
2. External oil leak.
3. Failed vacuum modulator diaphragm.

Oil Coming Out Of Filler Tube

1. Oil level too high.
2. Water in oil.
3. External vent clogged.
4. Leak in pump suction circuit.

External Oil Leaks

1. Converter housing area:
   a. Leaking converter.
   b. Front converter housing seal.
   c. Sealing washers under converter housing-to-case bolts.
   d. Sealing washers under converter housing-to-pump bolts.
   e. Converter housing-to-case seal.
2. Case and extension area:
   a. Shifter shaft seal.
   b. Extension seal.
   c. Oil pan gasket.
   d. Filler tube O-ring at bottom of tube.
   e. Extension to case gasket.
   f. Vacuum modulator gasket.
   g. Drain plug gasket.
   h. Cooler line fittings.
   i. Speedometer drive housing gasket.

No Drive In Any Position

1. Low oil level.
2. Clogged suction screen.
3. Inner manual valve linkage disconnected.
4. External linkage disconnected.
5. Input shaft broken.
6. Pressure regulator stuck in open position.
7. Failed pump.

No Forward Drive

1. Band worn, will not engage.
2. Band servo piston stuck.
3. Band servo seal ring cracked.

No Drive In D Or 2 But Drive In 1 & R

1. Input sprag installed backwards.
2. Input sprag failure.

No Drive In R, But In All Other Positions

1. Reverse clutch failure.

Drive In N

1. Selector lever linkage improperly adjusted.
2. Planetary carrier broken or locked up.
3. Band adjusted too tight.

Low Oil Pressure

1. Low oil level.
2. Clogged suction screen.
3. Leak in pump suction circuit.
4. Internal leak in pressure circuit.
5. Priming valve stuck.
6. Pressure regulator malfunction.

High Oil Pressure

1. Broken or disconnected vacuum line to the transmission.
2. Failed vacuum modulator.
3. Leak in any part of engine or accessory vacuum system.
4. Pressure regulator malfunction.

No 1-2 Shift

1. Governor valves stuck.
2. 1-2 shift valve stuck in downshifted position.
3. Large leak in governor pressure passage.

Upshifts Only At Part Throttle

1. Detent pressure regulator valve stuck.
2. Detent cable broken or adjusted improperly.

No Part Throttle 3-2 Downshift At Lower Vehicle Speeds

1. 3-2 downshift control valve stuck.

Only Upshifts From 1 To 2

1. 2-3 shift valve stuck.

Sudden Engagement After Increase In RPM

1. Band servo piston binding.

Slipping 1-2 Shift

1. Low oil pressure.
2. 1-2 accumulator valve stuck.
3. Second clutch piston seals leaking.
4. Second clutch piston centrifugal ball stuck open.
5. Second clutch piston cracked or broken.

Slipping 2-3 Shift

1. Low oil pressure.

2. Band adjustment loose.
3. Third clutch piston seals leaking.
4. Third clutch piston centrifugal ball stuck open.
5. Third clutch piston cracked or broken.
6. Input shaft bushing worn.

Harsh 1-2 Shift

1. High oil pressure.
2. 1-2 accumulator valve stuck.

Harsh 2-3 Shift

1. High oil pressure.

Harsh 3-2 Forced Downshift At High Vehicle Speed

1. High speed downshift timing valve stuck open.

Harsh 3-2 Coast Downshift

1. Low speed downshift timing valve stuck open.

131 AUTOMATIC TRANSMISSION OIL PRESSURE CHECK

1. Connect pressure gauge (tool 5907) to transmission.
2. Connect a vacuum gauge to the modulator so that the gauge is visible inside the passenger compartment. Run the engine until it and the transmission are at proper operating temperature. Be sure the engine is running properly.
3. With selector in D and engine idling 750-850rpm, check for an oil pressure of 61-70psi.
4. Drive the vehicle in D with the pedal down past the kick-down position. The transmission should shift up when the oil pressure is between 108-119psi. The vacuum gauge should read 0.86 in./Hg.
5. Put selector at 1 with the car stopped. The oil pressure should be approximately 98-109psi and the vacuum about 12in./Hg.
6. Put selector in 1 or R, apply the brakes and run the engine briefly with the pedal pressed all the way down to the maximum speed that the engine will attain. Oil pressure should be 156-160psi. Do not run the engine this way for more than a few seconds or the transmission could be overheated and serious damage could result.

Brakes, Rear Axle & Suspension Section

REAR SUSPENSION, REPLACE

850

1. Raise and support vehicle.
2. From each side, remove wheel, disconnect the shock absorber, tie off the axle shaft from the wheel shaft joint. (Unlock plates at differential and remove axle if suspension is not removed.)
3. Disconnect handbrake control cable from brake shoe actuating lever.
4. Plug the brake fluid reservoir outlet and remove hydraulic brake line from hose.
5. Disconnect the sway bar at control arm and transmission mounting bracket.

6. Remove control arm-to-body attaching screws at front and rear. Note the number of shims (to be replaced in the same location).
7. Using a hydraulic jack, remove control arm assembly, then coil spring.
8. Control arm bushings may be pressed in and out. Shims are used to take up clearance.
9. Back out shaft-to-flexible joint screws, move back sleeve on axle shaft and remove inner spring. Remove cotter pin and turn out nut four turns. Work the wheel hub part way out, remove the nut completely and replace the flexible joint.
10. Remove backing plate and hub. Unlock the retainer and remove bearing (either tapered or straight).
11. Reverse procedure to install.

128

Removal
1. Raise and support vehicle.
2. Remove rear wheels.
3. Plug outlet hole of the brake fluid reservoir, then detach flexible hose from the pipe.
4. Release hand brake relay lever and detach cable from shoe control levers on brake backing plate.
5. On vehicles so equipped, disconnect braking regulator torsion bar from left control arm.
6. Place a suitable jack under control arm and raise suspension, then detach shock absorbers from the luggage compartment and remove jack.
7. Detach rubber pads which attach leaf spring to control arms.

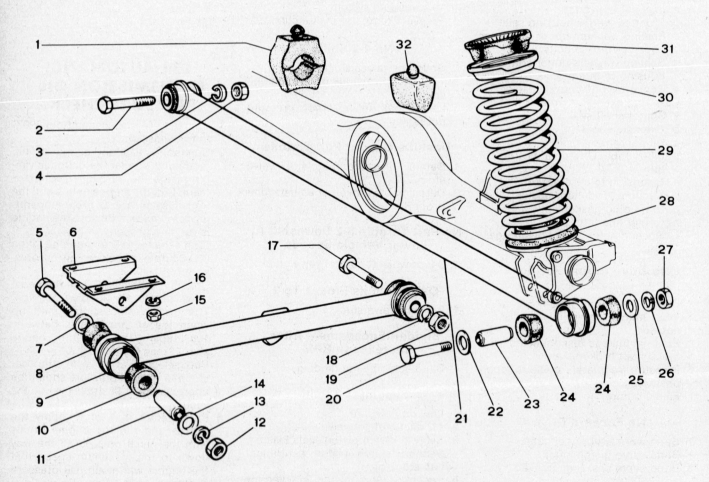

1. Rubber pad. - 2. Bolt anchoring cross rod to body. - 3. Lock washer. - 4. Nut. - 5. Bolt anchoring lower side rod to bracket 6. - 6. Bracket. - 7. Flat washer. - 8. Rubber bushing. - 9. Lower side rod. - 10. Rubber bushing. - 11. Spacer. - 12. Nut. - 13. Lock washer. - 14. Flat washer. - 15. Nut. - 16. Lock washer. - 17. Bolt anchoring lower side rod to axle housing. - 18. Lock washer. - 19. Nut. - 20. Bolt anchoring cross rod to axle housing. - 21. Cross rod. - 22. Flat washer. - 23. Spacer. - 24. Rubber bushings. - 25. Flat washer. - 26. Lock washer. - 27. Nut. - 28. Lower ring-pad. - 29. Coil spring. - 30. Upper seating ring. - 31. Upper rubber ring-pad. - 32. Rubber buffer.

Fig. 1   Rear suspension exploded view. 124 models

8. Remove nuts which attach the swivels of control arms to the large screws that pass through the plate by which suspension is mounted to body.

9. Slide off the control arms (with shocks), noting number of shims between control arm swivels and plate which attaches the suspension to the body.

Installation

1. Attach control arm to body, then lightly tighten the two bolts which pass through the plate.

2. Re-attach the rubber pads which anchor the leaf spring.

3. On vehicles so equipped, attach the braking regulator torsion bar to left control arm.

4. Place bottom rubber bushing on top stud of shock absorber, place a hydraulic jack under suspension and raise entire assembly so that top stud of shock absorber can be inserted in luggage compartment hole.

5. Mount the rubber bushing, retainer cap and self-locking nut on top stud.

6. Re-attach handbrake cable to lever on brake backing plate, then connect brake fluid hose, metal pipe, and reservoir. Bleed the system.

7. Remount the wheels, lower vehicle to ground level.

8. Torque the following nuts with car loaded (4 persons plus 88 lbs. of luggage):
   a. Upper nut of shock to spindle, 43.5 ft. lbs.
   b. Top of bracket to spindle, 43.5 ft. lbs.
   c. Nuts attaching control arm to spindle, 58 ft. lbs.
   d. Nut attaching control arm spindle to body, 36 ft. lbs.
   e. Self-locking nut attaching bushings to swivel connecting control arm to body, 32.5 ft. lbs.

124

Removal, Fig. 1

1. Raise and support vehicle.
2. Remove rear wheels, disconnect driveshaft, brake lines and handbrake cables.
3. Remove the cables from clips on body.
4. Disconnect shock absorbers from inside luggage compartment.
5. Disconnect two stabilizer bar links.
6. Disconnect brake regulator link.
7. Support axle with a suitable jack.
8. Disconnect anchor rods and sway bar.
9. Remove assembly by lowering jack.

10. Remove brackets for stabilizer bar, then the bar.
11. Remove shocks at spring mounts.
12. Remove anchor rods and sway bar from axle.

Installation, Fig. 1

1. Connect anchor rods and sway bar to housing.
2. Bolt shocks to spring seats.
3. Bolt stabilizer bar and links.
4. Set springs and pads in axle plates.
5. Position the jack.
6. Connect axle to body, but do not fully tighten the anchor-rod-to-bracket.
7. Connect stabilizer bar links to housing; do not fully tighten.
8. Connect brake regulator rod to housing.
9. Tighten shock absorbers in luggage compartment.
10. Install driveshaft.
11. Install brake lines and handbrake cables, then bleed system.
12. Install wheels and lower the vehicle to level ground.
13. Torque the following bolts in sequence:
    a. Anchor rod to housing, 72 ft. lbs.
    b. Sway bar to axle, 72 ft. lbs.
    c. Stabilizer bar links to axle, 25 ft. lbs.

X1/9

1. Raise rear of vehicle and support on jackstands, then remove wheels.
2. Disconnect flexible brake tube if caliper is to be removed, if not, remove caliper from assembly and wire it aside.
3. Disconnect parking brake cable from caliper, if the caliper is to be removed.
4. Remove exhaust pipe.
5. Remove nut and bolt holding control arm to bracket at front of suspension. Note number of shims for proper installation and leave them between arm and bracket.
6. Remove nut and bolt holding control arm to bracket at rear of the suspension, noting the shims as at the front of the suspension.
7. Remove hub nut and washer.
8. Remove the three nuts and washers holding top of shock absorber.
9. Slide suspension assembly from constant-speed joint shaft and position the axle shaft so it will not come loose from the differential.
10. To install, first ensure that the correct number of shims are properly positioned.
11. Fully tighten control arm nuts and the upper shock absorber nuts when car is on level ground again.
12. Attach control arm to the brackets.

13. Raise assembly and mount hub to constant-speed joint.
14. Place the upper shock studs through the body holes and install nuts and washers.
15. Install a washer and a new hub nut on shaft and torque to 101 ft. lbs. Stake the nut.
16. Install exhaust pipe and wheels and lower the vehicle.
17. The vehicle must be loaded before torquing the nuts (two persons inside the passenger compartment).
    a. Three shock absorber nuts, 43 ft. lbs.
    b. Control arm nuts, 72 ft. lbs.

131

Removal, Fig. 2

1. Raise rear of vehicle and support on jackstands.
2. Ensure handbrake is off.
3. Disconnect drive shaft from rear axle and remove wheels.
4. Disconnect handbrake cable tension spring from bracket and support, then pull the cable housings back and remove the cable from the bracket. Slide cable out of the support.
5. Remove bolt holding the transverse strut to support, then the strut from the support.
6. Place a suitable jack under the rear axle housing, then remove nuts, bolts and washers holding lower reaction struts to support.
7. Remove brake regulator rod from the bracket.
8. Disconnect brake hose from the "T" fitting on rear axle.
9. Remove nuts, bolts and washers holding upper reaction struts to supports.
10. On sedan models, remove nut and washer from top of shock absorber, then three nuts and washers holding shock absorber to body. Then remove the upper spacer, rubber bushing and support. On station wagon, remove shock absorber upper and lower mounting bolts, then the shock absorber.
11. Lower the axle with the suspension from the car.

Installation, Fig. 2

1. Install the rear axle with the suspension in the car and raise the shock absorbers through the mounts.
2. Install the support, the rubber bushing and spacer on the shock absorber and attach the center shock nuts and the three mounting nuts and washers. Torque shock nut to 18 ft. lbs. and three mount nuts to 11 ft. lbs.
3. Install the upper reaction struts in

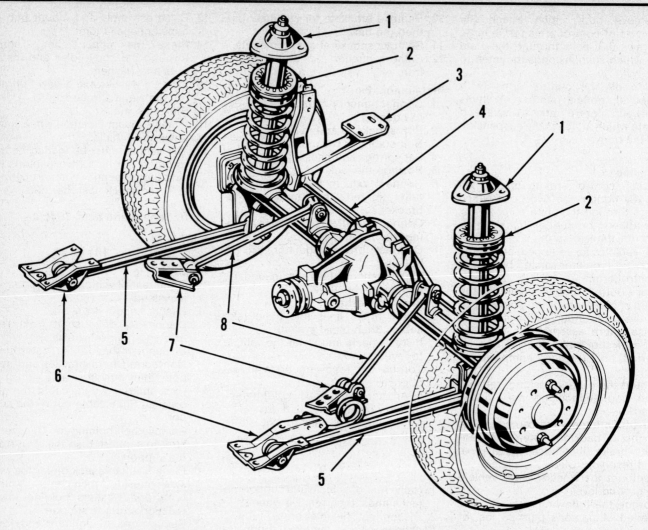

1. Shock absorber
2. Coil spring
3. Transverse strut support
4. Transverse strut
5. Lower reaction strut
6. Lower reaction strut support
7. Upper reaction strut support
8. Upper reaction strut

Fig. 2   Rear suspension assembly. 131 models

the supports, and bolts in place.
4. Install the lower reaction struts in supports and bolts in place.
5. Install brake regulator rod to bracket and connect brake hose to the "T" fitting on axle.
6. Install the hand brake cable in the bracket.
7. Install transverse strut in support and bolt in place.
8. Install drive shaft and the rear wheels.
9. Lower the car to level ground and torque the bolts for upper and lower reaction struts and transverse strut to 58 ft. lbs.

REAR AXLE, REPLACE
124

1. Remove rear hubcaps, loosen studs, raise and support rear of vehicle

and remove wheels.
2. Plug brake fluid reservoir opening and remove brake hose from pipe.
3. Remove drive shaft as follows:
   a. Disconnect flexible joint (tool A. 70025 or a hose clamp which will fit around the circumference of coupling).
   b. Remove guard plate and supporting crossmember.
4. Disconnect handbrake cable from brake caliper actuating levers.
5. Remove brake pressure regulator control rod from axle housing.
6. Place a suitable jack under axle housing.
7. Remove upper shock absorber attaching nuts.
8. Remove the two lower and two upper side rods from axle housing.
9. Remove nut and bolt attaching cross rod to axle housing, then the

cross rod.
10. Lower the axle assembly from vehicle, Fig. 1.
11. Reverse procedure to install.

AXLE SHAFT, REPLACE
124

1. Raise and support rear of vehicle, remove the wheels and the caliper support bracket assembly; the brake lines need not be removed.
2. Remove the snap ring retaining the dust cover.
3. Remove the axle shaft with a slide hammer. The snap ring, dust cover, bearing and collar will be removed also.
4. Remove the oil seal and O-ring. Bearing collar will require a hydraulic press.
5. Reverse procedure to install.

6. Replace seals and O-ring, if they are removed, and bearing.

X1/9

1. Raise rear of vehicle and support on jackstands and remove wheel.
2. Remove the two nuts and bolts attaching shock absorber to pillar.
3. Remove nut holding the ball joint of the control arm in the pillar, then the ball joint from the pillar.
4. Remove nut holding strut ball joint to the pillar, then remove ball joint from pillar.
5. Partially drain transmission; be sure to refill.
6. Remove the three bolts and washers holding the oil seal boot to the differential.
7. Remove axle shaft and wheel hub from the differential.
8. Remove brake caliper and support bracket from pillar.
9. Remove bolts holding the retaining plate and brake rotor to hub, then remove plate and rotor.
10. Remove clamp retaining boot to the constant-speed joint and pull the boot back to uncover the joint. Clean grease from joints.
11. Remove lock ring from constant-speed joints.
12. Remove axle shaft from the constant-speed joint.
13. Reverse procedure to install. Lubricate constant-speed joints to move the axle shafts in and out to check seating of snap-ring in the groove.

131

1. Raise vehicle and support on jackstands and remove the wheel and drum.
2. Remove four bolts and washers holding axle shaft retaining plate.
3. Pull shaft from housing with a slide puller.
4. Remove brake shoe support from shaft.
5. Remove and replace oil seal in the axle housing.
6. Press the bearing retainer, then bearing from the shaft and replace. Heat retainer to 578°F. to install on shaft.
7. Reverse procedure to install.

REAR SPRING, REPLACE

128

1. Raise rear of vehicle and support on jackstands.
2. Remove rear wheels.
3. On vehicles so equipped, remove cotter pin and rod which links the spring to braking regulator.
4. Remove rubber pad anchoring leaf

spring to control arm. Release load from the spring with a suitable jack.
5. After procedure has been followed on both sides, remove the two guides which hold spring to the body, then remove the spring.
6. Check for broken or cracked leaves, smooth contact surfaces, shims and pads between leaves and tension of spring.
7. Reverse procedure to install.

X1/9

1. Remove shock absorber.
2. Use a suitable spring compressor to compress spring.
3. Remove spring seat and slowly release spring.
4. Reverse procedure to install.

SHOCK ABSORBER, REPLACE

850

1. Remove shock absorber upper mounting bolt and lower mounting nut.
2. Remove shock absorber from vehicle.
3. Reverse procedure to install.

124

1. Raise vehicle and support on jackstands.
2. Remove wheels.
3. Disconnect driveshaft from drive pinion sleeve.
4. From inside luggage compartment, remove nuts holding shock absorbers to floor of body, then those retaining lower shock absorber brackets to spring seating plates.
5. Disconnect brake pressure regulator link from axle housing.
6. Place a suitable jack to support rear axle.
7. Disconnect upper and lower side rods and cross rod from body, then lower axle and remove shock absorbers from inside the springs.
8. Reverse procedure to install, however, attach the lower shock to the seat first. Also do not fully tighten reaction rods until vehicle is on level ground. Refer to the "Rear Suspension, Replace" procedure for torque and sequence.

128 & X1/9

1. Remove three nuts and washers attaching shock absorbers at top and the two bolts holding the shock absorbers at the bottom to the pillar.
2. Remove shock absorber from vehicle.
3. Reverse procedure to install.

131

1. Removal of shock absorbers on sedan models, requires removal of suspension. Refer to "Rear Suspension, Replace" procedure.
2. On station wagon models:
   a. Remove bolt holding top of shock absorber to body and the bolt and washers mounting shock absorber to the lower bracket.
   b. Remove shock absorber from vehicle.
   c. Reverse procedure to install.

REAR WHEEL ALIGNMENT

850

1. The toe-in angle is set by moving the plate which holds the rear of the control arm to the body.
2. Raise vehicle, compress springs and position wheels vertical to the ground.
3. The toe-in angle is 0°12' ±6' parallel to the car centerline.

128

1. Camber angle is:
   a. With vehicle loaded: −2°40' to −3°20'.
   b. With vehicle unloaded: 0° to +0°10'.
2. Since toe-in is corrected at the same time as camber, check toe-in. The procedure is the same as that for the front suspension. The values are:
   a. Loaded: .197+/−.079in.
   b. Unloaded: .177+/−.079in.
3. To adjust:
   a. Raise and support vehicle.
   b. Compress one end of leaf spring so that it can be shifted from the flexible guide that anchors it to control arm.
   c. Remove guide.
   d. Slowly release spring.
   e. Remove nuts holding pivot to body.
   f. Partially remove screw in order to free the shims, then adjust the number of shims.
   g. Torque attachment nuts for the two flexible guides to 22 ft. lbs.
4. a. To increase negative camber angle, add an equal number of shims to each screw.
   b. To decrease negative camber angle, remove an equal number of shims from each screw.
   c. To increase toe-in, add shims to rear screw or remove them from the front one.
   d. To decrease toe-in, add shims to front screw or remove them from rear one.

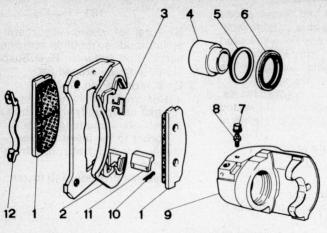

1. Shoe and lining
2. Cliper support bracket
3. Spring
4. Piston
5. Seal
6. Piston dust boot
7. Dust cap
8. Bleeder screw
9. Caliper body
10. Cotter pin
11. Block
12. Lining spring

Fig. 3 Exploded view of front brake caliper. Exc. X1/9 models

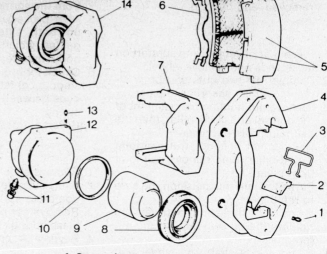

1. Cotter pin
2. Caliper locking block
3. Spring
4. Caliper support bracket
5. Lining pad
6. Lining retainer spring
7. Cylinder housing
8. Dust boot
9. Piston
10. Seal
11. Bleeder screw and dust cap
12. Cylinder
13. Spring and dowel
14. Complete caliper

Fig. 4 Exploded view of front brake caliper. X1/9 models

X1/9

Adjust the toe-in by lengthening or shortening the reaction rod. Toe-in specifications for an unloaded car are +0.360 to +0.510in. Camber for an unloaded car is −1°10′ to −2°10′.

PARKING BRAKE, ADJUST

1. Pull parking brake lever up three notches from full down position.
2. Loosen locknut on tensioner for cable, then turn the cable until wheels are locked. Check if this occurs at the third notch up on lever.
3. Tighten locknut.
4. Ensure that the wheels turn freely when lever is fully released.

DISC BRAKE SERVICE

Brake Pads, Replace

1. Raise the vehicle, support on jackstands and remove wheels.
2. Remove cotter pins from locking blocks and drive blocks out. A dab of grease on the block sliding surfaces when reassembling will facilitate the next removal.
3. Pull brake caliper out, then remove pads and springs.
4. Check that caliper and rotor are in proper condition.
5. Depress piston into bottom of caliper cylinder, making sure that mark on piston faces bleeder screw. On rear units, screw in the piston (clockwise).
6. Reverse procedure to install.

Caliper, Replace

The front and rear brake calipers are similar. When removing rear calipers, disconnect handbrake cable from lever on rear of caliper.

1. Raise vehicle and support on jackstands, then remove wheel.
2. Plug outlet port of brake fluid reservoir, then disconnect brake hose from caliper.
3. Remove cotter pins from locking blocks, then the locking blocks.
4. Pull calipers out and remove springs (flat springs on the 850 and 124) and the brake pads.
5. Reverse procedure to install. Bleed the system and bottom the pistons.

Front Caliper Overhaul

Exc. X1/9, Fig. 3

1. Remove caliper and dust cover.
2. Taking care not to damage any parts, apply compressed air through fluid inlet to push piston out of caliper cylinder.
3. Remove seal.
4. Wash all parts in hot water or a proper solvent and dry (if air hose is used, take care that surfaces are not scratched by minute particles).
5. Install the new piston seal, then the piston until fully bottomed.
6. Install dust cover carefully into caliper body.

X1/9, Fig. 4

1. Remove dust cover, then press down on dowel holding caliper cylinder to caliper support bracket by using a thin rod.
2. Separate cylinder from support bracket, making sure not to lose dowel and spring (be sure to replace).
3. Taking care not to damage any parts, apply compressed air through fluid inlet port.
4. Remove seal and inspect parts.
5. Reverse procedure to assemble.

Rear Caliper Overhaul

When removing piston, be sure to install new seal and dust cap.

NOTE: The brakes cannot be bled properly if the mark on the piston is not facing toward the bleeder, Fig. 5.

1. Remove dust cap.
2. Unscrew piston using a large screwdriver.

NOTE: The piston will come out of hand brake plunger, so be sure to note order of plunger sealing ring, disc springs and, on 124, disc spring thrust washer.

3. Remove seal (replace with a new seal).

1. Cotter pin
2. Caliper locking block
3. Spring
4. Lining pads
5. Lining retainer spring
6. Rubber boot
7. Locking ring
8. Spacer

9. Hand brake shaft
10. Pawl
11. Plunger
12. Spring washers
13. Spring washers
14. Seal
15. Caliper cylinder

16. Piston
17. Seal
18. Dust boot
19. Complete caliper
20. Bleeder screw
21. Bleeder boot
22. Support bracket

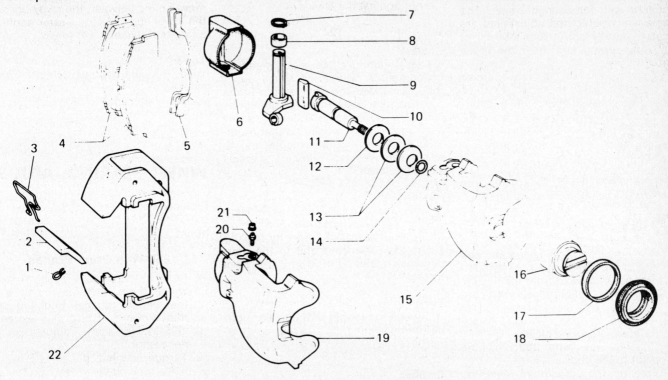

Fig. 5 Exploded view of rear brake caliper (typical)

4. Remove hand brake lever boot.
5. Remove snap-ring and bushing from hand brake cam lever pivot pin, then remove lever along with self-adjusting plunger, plunger seal, the two or three disc springs and spring thrust washer.
6. Clean and inspect parts.
7. Reverse procedure to assemble.

MASTER CYLINDER, REPLACE

124 & 850

1. Remove reservoir cover and plug fluid outlet port.
2. Disconnect pipe between reservoir and master cylinder.
3. Remove the three-way union from master cylinder.
4. Remove master cylinder from the firewall or master vac unit.
5. Remove hoses from master cylinder and switch assembly.
6. Remove master cylinder.

7. Reverse procedure to install. Bleed the system.

131

1. Remove air cleaner.
2. Disconnect vacuum hoses and the three brake fluid tubes from master cylinder.
3. Remove the two nuts and washers attaching master cylinder to power assist.
4. Pull cylinder out and then down to remove from the bracket.
5. Reverse procedure to install. Bleed the system.

128

1. Remove spare wheel from engine compartment.
2. Remove fluid reservoir cover and plug outlet.
3. Disconnect tubes from reservoir to master cylinder.
4. Disconnect fluid delivery tubing to the front and rear brakes.

5. Remove both nuts and washers which hold the master cylinder to body, then remove master cylinder.
6. Reverse procedure to install.

X1/9

1. Remove the steering column:
   a. Disconnect battery cables.
   b. Remove five screws which hold steering column cover halves, then the covers.
   c. Disconnect the three electrical connectors and single wire.
   d. Remove nuts, bolts and washers which hold column to dashboard.
   e. Slide shaft off steering box shaft, then remove column from vehicle.
2. Disconnect hoses from master cylinder reservoir.
3. Remove nuts and washers which hold master cylinder to support.
4. Pull master cylinder from actuating rod.
5. Reverse procedure to install.

Front Suspension & Steering Section

WHEEL ALIGNMENT & TOE-IN, ADJUST

850

Caster & Camber

The caster and camber adjustment requires loading the spring; camber adjustment will not change caster. The shims which affect the adjustment are located slightly above and inboard of the upper swing arm, near the brake hydraulic line.

1. To increase caster: move shims from the rear to the front.
2. To decrease caster: move shims from the front to the rear.
3. To increase camber: add an equal number of shims to both studs

Toe-In

Toe-in is adjusted by turning the threaded sleeves on the tie-rods.

128

Camber

1. The vehicle must be raised and one end of the leaf spring must be compressed to move it from the flexible guide which anchors it to the control arm. Then the guide should be removed.
2. Release the spring slowly.
3. Unscrew the nuts attaching the pivot to the body.
4. Free up the adjustment shims by backing off screw.
5. Adjust the number of shims as required and replace their screw.
6. Repeat operation on the other control-arm-to-body screw, and on the other wheel if required.
7. Reverse procedure, torquing attachment nuts to 22 ft. lbs.
8. Negative camber angle is increased by adding an equal number of shims to the screws and decreased by removing shims.

Caster

Each shim will alter caster angle by 15 minutes. The shims are inserted between the end of the anti-roll bar and the rubber pad of the control arm.

1. Raise vehicle.
2. Remove the anti-roll bar to control arm anchoring nut.
3. Separate the control arm from the body, then withdraw the end of the anti-roll bar from the control arm.
4. Adjust the number of shims as required.
5. Reverse the procedure to reassemble. Lower the vehicle and rock vehicle to settle the suspension before torquing the two attachment nuts.

Toe-In

To obtain the proper degree of toe-in without moving the wheel spokes:

1. Loosen the nut and screw or the hexagon on the ball pin to attain the proper degree of toe-in.
2. Hold the pin in position and lock the nut against the sleeve.

124

Camber

Alter camber angle adjustment by changing the number of shims under the two lower control arm-to-frame crossmember bolts. Increase camber by removing an equal number of shims from each bolt; decrease camber by adding an equal number (neglecting to add or remove equal numbers of shims will affect caster).

Caster

Caster angle is affected by moving shims from the front to the rear bolt of the reverse. Increase caster by moving shims from the front bolt to the rear; decrease caster by moving shims from the rear to the front.

Toe-In

Change the length of the left or right tie rod by turning the sleeves.

X1/9

Camber

NOTE: Camber on these models is not adjustable; it is built-in at 0°—1°. If a reading is obtained outside this measurement, replace the appropriate suspension part(s).

Caster

Caster can be adjusted. Add or remove the shims between the front reaction struts and body and supports. Unloaded vehicle angles are: +6°30′ to +7°30′.

Toe-In

1. Set the wheels straight ahead with the steering wheel spokes properly positioned.
2. Without changing the position of the steering wheel spokes, loosen the locknut on the tie-rod end and turn the ball joint in or out to achieve the proper toe-in (+0.08 to +0.24in.).

131

Camber

The camber is not adjustable and is built-in to 0°—1°. If the measurement obtained is outside this angle, replace the appropriate suspension components.

Caster

Caster can be adjusted. Add or remove shims between the sway bar and the lower support arm. Caster angle on a loaded vehicle is −4° to −5°.

Toe-In

Toe-in is adjusted by turning threaded sleeves on the tie rods to obtain the proper dimensions: 0.08 to 0.16 inch (2 to 4mm).

WHEEL BEARING, ADJUST

A staked hub nut is used and must be replaced if it is necessary to remove the nut. The X1/9 hub nut is located inboard.

850 With Drum Brakes

1. Remove hubcap and push drum inwards, then attach dial indicator so that needle touches hub and pull hub outward. If end play exceeds .0051in. (0.13mm), adjustment is necessary.
2. Torque new hub nut to 14.5 ft. lbs. while rocking the wheel hub four or five times to insure proper seating of bearings.
3. Back off the nut and retorque to 5.1 ft. lbs.
4. Back out the nut 30° (one half of one flat on the nut).
5. Stake the collar of the nut in the groove.
6. End play should be .0010 to .0039in. (0.025 to 0.100mm).

124 & 131

1. Torque the new hub nut to 14.5 ft. lbs. while turning the hub in both directions four or five times to insure proper seating.
2. Back the nut off fully, then retorque to 5 ft. lbs.
3. Then back off the nut 30° (one half of one flat on the nut).
4. Stake the nut into the groove.

WHEEL BEARING, REPLACE

124 & 128

1. Raise and support front of vehicle.
2. Remove hub nut.
3. Remove caliper and brake rotor.

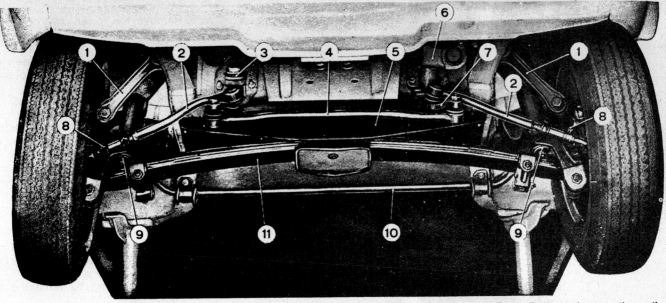

Upper control arms. - 2. Side tie rods. - 3. Idler arm bracket. - 4. Intermediate track rod. - 5. Semi-elliptic spring mouting rail. 6. Steering gear. - 7. Pitman arm. - 8. Tie rod clamps. - 9. Shock absorbers. - 10. Sway eliminator. - 11. Semi-elliptic spring.

Fig. 1 Front suspension assembly. 850 models

4. Remove shock absorber from pillar.
5. Remove tie-rod from steering arm.
6. Remove anti-roll bar from control arm, note number and placement of shims.
7. Remove the control arm from pillar by removing the ball joint nut and freeing the ball joint.
8. Remove pillar and hub from shaft of constant-speed joint.
9. Remove the hub from the pillar on a press.
10. Remove the hub bearing ring nut; on those vehicles with a snap ring, remove the snap ring, then the bearing.
11. Reverse procedure to install.

128 Drive Axle R & R

1. Drain the transmission oil, then unscrew the oil seal boot at the transmission.
2. Remove boot outer clamps at constant-speed joint, then pull back the boots to expose both joints.
3. Open the sealing ring on constant-speed joints and remove shaft ends from the seats in the joints. The wheels should be turned so the shafts can be removed completely from the differential. On earlier vehicles with twin axle shafts, replacement can be made with a later shaft.
4. Reverse procedure to install. Lubricate the constant-speed joints and move the axle shafts in and out to check the seating of the snap-ring in groove.

X1/9

1. Raise vehicle and support on jackstands.
2. Remove wheel.
3. Disconnect brake caliper and support bracket.
4. Remove bolt and centering stud securing the disc and plate.
5. Remove nut holding the tie rod to the pillar.
6. Remove ball joint from pillar.
7. Remove nut holding the control arm to the pillar.
8. Remove two nuts and bolts holding the shock absorber to the pillar.
9. Remove the pillar.
10. Remove the nut and washers holding the hub to the pillar and press hub from the pillar.
11. Remove the ring nut holding the bearing and pull the bearing out.
12. Install a new bearing and ring nut. Torque to 43.4 ft. lbs.
13. Press in the hub, install two washers and torque the nut to 101 ft. lbs., then stake the nut.
14. Reverse the procedure to install.

FRONT SUSPENSION, REPLACE

850

The 850 requires special tools, punches and drivers and a special tool to set the static load for the leaf spring, Fig. 1.

1. Raise and support vehicle, then remove wheels and shock absorbers.

2. Disconnect tie rods from knuckle arms (Fiat tool A. 47035 or equivalent).
3. Separate the sway bar from the semi-elliptic spring.
4. Plug the brake fluid reservoir outlet and disconnect hydraulic brake lines.
5. Support the suspension assembly with a suitable jack and slide out the pin at end of semi-elliptic spring.
6. Remove the screws holding the center of the semi-elliptic spring, then the spring.
7. Remove upper control arm nuts from body shell, then the suspension assembly.
8. Pull the wheel hub cap (tool A. 47014).
9. Drive out the upper bushing from the kingpin housing (tool A. 74042).
10. Remove kingpin and housing bushings (tool A. 74016).
11. Pull off the upper control arm bushings (tool A. 74116).

Kingpin and housing bushing clearance is no more than .008in. New parts clearance is .0006 to .0021in. (0.016 to 0.054mm).

128, Fig. 2

1. Partially back out front wheel stud bolts and hub nuts, then raise front of car and support on jackstands. Then remove the wheels.
2. Remove nuts attaching brake caliper to the pillar and secure the caliper to the body.
3. Remove nuts securing tie-rod ball

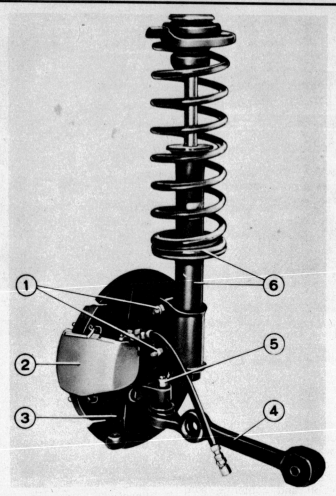

1. Shock absorber bolts   2. Brake caliper   3. Pillar
4. Lower support arm   5. Nut   6. Shock absorber coil spring
assembly

Fig. 2 Front suspension assembly. 128, 131 & X1/9 models

joint to the steering arm, then use a suitable puller to remove the swivel.
4. Remove the nut holding the end of the anti-roll bar to the control arm, then disconnect the control arm from the body.
5. Remove the hub nut.
6. Remove the three nuts in the engine compartment which attach the top of the shock absorber and slide the suspension assembly from the constant-speed joint shaft. Secure the axle shaft so it will not slide out of the differential.
7. To remove the anti-roll bar, remove the bottom guards and the four screws holding the supports and rubber pads to the body.
8. To reinstall, attach the anti-roll bar and mount the hub of the completely reassembled control arm on the constant-speed joint shaft while sliding the upper shock absorber back into the holes. Attach upper shock with three nuts and washers.

Replace the flat washer and nut on the shaft of the constant-speed joint, lubricate the anti-roll bar-to-control arm joint rubber bushings, replace the shims, attach the end of the anti-roll bar and pads to the control arm and attach to the body. Then attach the tie-rod to the steering arm (torque to 58 ft. lbs.). Install the brake caliper.

124, Fig. 3

1. Partially back off front wheel nuts, then raise vehicle and support on jackstands, then remove wheels.
2. Remove shock absorber.
3. Compress the spring with a spring compressor to release pressure on the control arm.
4. Disconnect the stabilizer bar at the lower control arm, then the brake hoses and the tie-rod at the steering knuckle arm.
5. Remove the lock nut and the pivot bolt to separate the control arm

from the body.
6. Remove the lower control arm to crossmember nuts. Observe and mark the shims from each nut for proper reinstallation (between the body and the control arm pivot bar).
7. Install the stabilizer bar.
8. Insert the shims and install the complete wishbone assembly without tightening the nuts completely; bolt the lower control arm to the crossmember.
9. Insert the spring with the compressor attached and seat it compressed enough to allow the upper control arm to be attached, but do not tighten it completely.
10. Attach the stabilizer bar to the control arm, the tie-rod to the steering arm, connect the brake lines and bleed the brake system.
11. Seat the spring by removing the compressor.
12. Install the shock absorber, then the tire.
13. Lower the vehicle onto a level surface and torque the nuts as follows: upper control arm to body, 65 ft. lbs.; lower control arm to crossmember, 43 ft. lbs.; lower control arm to pivot bar, 72 ft. lbs.

X1/9, Fig. 2

The brake calipers need not be removed with the suspension; detach them and wire aside. If calipers are to be removed, disconnect the brake fluid hose from the caliper and plug.

1. Raise and support vehicle on jackstands, then remove the wheel.
2. Remove the bolts and plate holding the strut to the pillar, then the bolt attaching the control arm to the bracket.
3. Remove the nut holding the tie-rod ball joint to the steering arm, then the ball joint.
4. Disconnect the three shock absorber attaching nuts in the engine compartment and lower the suspension assembly. If the springs are to be replaced, match the color coding (a red or yellow stripe).
5. Reverse procedure to install. Lower car to level ground before torquing suspension nuts as follows: upper pillar to tie-rod attaching nut, 58 ft. lbs.; control arm to lower pillar attaching nut, 51 ft. lbs.; secondary strut bar lockplate attaching bolt and control arm to body attaching bolt, 29 ft. lbs.

131, Fig. 2

1. Loosen wheel, raise vehicle and support on jackstands, then remove wheel.

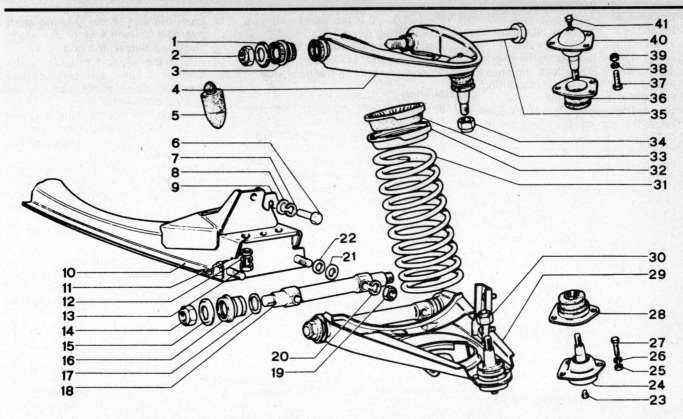

1. Cup. - 2. Nut fixing upper control arm to body. - 3. Resilient bushing. - 4. Upper control arm. - 5. Buffer. - 6. Bolt. - 7. Spring washer. - 8. Flat washer. - 9. Tab strip. - 10. Crossmember. - 11. Flat washer. - 12. Spring washer. - 13. Nut. - 14. Nut fixing pivot bar 18 to lower control arm. - 15. Cup. - 16. Resilient bushing. - 17. Flat washer. - 18. Pivot bar. - 19. Nut fixing lower control arm to crossmember 10. - 20. Spring washer. - 21. Flat washer. - 22. Tab strip. - 23. Plug. - 24. Lower ball joint. - 25. Nut. - 26. Spring washer. - 27. Seal. - 28. Seal. - 29. Lower control arm. - 30. Self-locking nut fixing steering knuckle to lower control arm. - 31. Spring. - 32. Spring seat. - 33. Rubber pad. - 34. Self-locking nut fixing steering knuckle to upper control arm. - 35. Bolt. - 36. Seal. - 37. Bolt. - 38. Spring washer. - 39. Nut. - 40. Upper ball joint. - 41. Plug.

Fig. 3 Exploded view of front suspension. 124 models

2. Disconnect brake hose from tube in clip.
3. Remove the nut holding the ball joint, then the ball joint.
4. Remove the nut holding the sway bar to the lower support arm, then pry the rubber bushing off of the threaded end of the sway bar.
5. Remove the nut and bolt holding the support arm to the bracket on the frame, then the arm from the bracket and push the arm to the rear to remove from sway bar.
6. Remove the three nuts holding the shock absorber inside the engine compartment and lower the suspension assembly.
7. Reverse procedure to install, but do not tighten bolts completely. Lower car to level ground and torque nuts and bolts as follows:
   a. nut holding lower support arm to bracket, 65 ft. lbs.
   b. nut holding sway bar to lower support arm, 43 ft. lbs.
   c. nut holding lower support arm to pillar, 58 ft. lbs.
   d. bolts holding shock absorber to pillar, 36 ft. lbs.

e. nut holding tie-rod to pillar, 58 ft. lbs.

CONTROL ARM SERVICE
850

The 850 has a semi-elliptical front suspension assembly. Refer to "Front Assembly, Replace" procedure.

128, Fig. 2

If the control arm rubber bushing is worn, press out and press fit a new bushing (tool A. 74221). Use a press to install the two-row ball bearing in the knuckle pillar; install snap ring to position bearing. On vehicles using a ring nut, torque to 43.5. If ball joints are worn or damaged, the complete control arm assembly must be replaced.

124, Fig. 3

Remove the arm on the steering knuckle to which the tie-rod is coupled by removing the four nuts and their tabs, thus releasing the brake caliper bracket and the brake disc guard. Then dismantle the steering knuckle and separate it from the ball joints. Bush-

ings in wishbones are pressed out and in, as is the control arm pin.

X1/9, Fig. 2

Remove the nut and washer holding the ball joint in the pillar. If the ball joint is worn or damaged, the control arm must be replaced. The rubber bushing may be pressed out and a new one pressed in after the spacer has been drilled out.

131, Fig. 2

Remove ball joint from pillar. If it is worn or damaged, the control arm must be replaced. The rubber bushing may be removed by pressing out.

COIL SPRING & SHOCK ABSORBER, REPLACE
850

Refer to the "Front Suspension, Replace" procedure.

128, 131 & X1/9

1. Raise vehicle and support on

jackstands.

2. Disconnect the shock absorber at lower mounting.
3. Remove the three nuts in the engine compartment that attach the shock absorber at the upper mounting, then the shock and spring, Fig. 2.
4. Use a spring compressor to compress the spring, then remove the pad mounting nut and the spring, then the shock assembly, which is usually replaced with a complete insert unit.
5. Reverse procedure to install.

124

For coil spring replacement, refer to the "Front Suspension, Replace" procedure. To replace shock absorber proceed as follows:
1. From inside engine compartment, remove the upper end of the shock. A special tool or a wrench may be used to keep the shank from turning.
2. Remove the nut and bolt securing the lower part of the shock absorber to the lower control arm.
3. Remove shock absorber from vehicle.
4. Reverse procedure to install.

STEERING GEAR, REPLACE

850

1. Pry off the horn button, then disconnect the horn.
2. Remove the steering wheel with a suitable puller.
3. From inside the luggage compartment, loosen the steering column-to-worm screw.
4. Raise vehicle and support on jackstands.
5. Disconnect the steering rods from the pitman arm.
6. Remove the mounting nuts, then the steering gear.
7. Reverse procedure to install.

128

Removal
1. Disconnect the battery leads.
2. Raise car and support on jackstands.
3. Remove front wheels.
4. Remove spare wheel.
5. From inside the passenger compartment, disconnect the drive pinion from the lower section of the steering column at the universal joint.
6. Using a suitable puller, remove the tie rods from the steering arms.
7. Remove the screws and nut holding

the top guard to facilitate removal of the steering gear.
8. Remove the steering gear to body mounting bracket screws, then the steering gear from the right side.

Installation
1. Install the steering gear from the right side of the vehicle.
2. Position the steering wheel straight ahead and connect the drive pinion to the lower section of the steering column with universal joints.
3. Attach the steering gear to the bracket, inserting the rubber cushions between them.
4. Connect the tie-rods to the steering arms and torque to 58 ft. lbs.
5. Bolt the top guard to the body.
6. Replace the front wheels and the spare.

124

1. Disconnect battery leads.
2. Remove the horn button and emblem cover.
3. Remove the nut holding the steering wheel to the steering column, then remove the wheel with a suitable puller, if necessary.
4. Remove the four screws holding the directional signal switch half covers, then remove the half covers.
5. Loosen the retaining collar of the directional signal switch on the bracket holding the steering column to the body, then disconnect the wiring and remove the switch.
6. Remove the steering column bracket.
7. Remove the screw that clamps the steering column to the worm shaft, then the steering column from inside the passenger compartment.
8. Remove the nuts holding the left hand steering arm and intermediate arm pins, then the pins with a puller.
9. Remove the three screws holding the steering box to the body, then remove the box.
To avoid any abnormal stress to the steering box, column and support bracket, shims can be placed on the steering box bolts. If this has been done, replace them; otherwise, check to see if shims are necessary. Reinstall the steering box using the following procedure:
10. Install the steering column from inside the passenger compartment through the dashboard.
11. From the engine compartment, install the end of the worm shaft of the steering box to the steering column.
12. Install any shims in original position and bolt the steering box to the body but do not tighten completely.

13. Lock the end of the steering shaft over the splined end of the worm shaft and tighten the bolt.
14. Attach the support bracket to the steering column, and connect it to the instrument panel, but do not tighten completely.
15. Connect the intermediate and left hand ball pins to the pitman arm and torque the self-locking nuts to 22 ft. lbs.
16. Temporarily install the steering wheel to turn the steering column back and forth several times in order to settle the steering assembly, box and bracket.
17. Torque the nuts which hold the steering box in place to 29 ft. lbs.
18. Install the directional signal switch to the steering column and bracket in proper position.
19. Attach the steering column bracket to the instrument panel at 11 ft. lbs.
20. Install the steering wheel with the spokes horizontal and the front wheels straight. Torque the steering wheel nut to 36 ft. lbs. Stake the nut to lock.
21. Connect the electrical connections and secure the ignition switch to the steering column bracket.
22. Install the directional signal switch half covers.
23. Install the horn button cover/emblem.

X1/9

1. Remove the nuts and bolts securing the universal joint on the bottom of the steering column to the steering box pinion shaft.
2. Remove the three screws attaching the gasket cover to the steering box on the floor boards.
3. Raise front of vehicle and support on jackstands, then remove the front wheels.
4. Remove the nuts holding the ball joints in both steering pillars, then the tie-rods from the pillars.
5. Remove the four bolts holding the steering box to the body, then the steering box.
6. Reverse procedure to install.

131

1. Remove the nut holding the tie rod in the steering knuckle on both sides, then the ball joints.
2. Remove the nut and bolt holding the universal joint to the steering box.
3. Remove the four bolts holding the steering box mounts to the crossmember and remove the steering box.
4. Reverse procedure to install.

FIESTA

INDEX OF SERVICE OPERATIONS

FIESTA

GENERAL ENGINE SPECIFICATIONS

Year	Engine	Car-buretor	Bore and Stroke	Piston Displace-ment Cubic Inches	Com-pres-sion Ratio	Maximum Brake H.P. @ R.P.M.	Maximum Torque Ft. Lbs. @ R.P.M.	Normal Oil Pressure Pounds
1978	4—94 (1600cc)	2 Barrel	3.188 x 3.056	94	8.6	—	—	25—45

TUNE UP SPECIFICATIONS

The following specifications are published from the latest information available. This data should be used only in the absence of a decal affixed in the engine compartment.

★When using a timing light, disconnect vacuum hose or tube at distributor and plug opening in hose or tube so idle speed will not be affected.
●When checking compression, lowest cylinder must be within 75 percent of highest.
▲Before removing wires from distributor cap, determine location of the No. 1 wire in cap, as distributor position may have been altered from that shown at the end of this chart.

Year	Engine	Spark Plug		Ignition Timing			Carburetor Adjustment Hot Idle Speed
		Type	Gap Inch	Firing Order Fig.	Timing BTDC ①	Mark Fig.	
1978	4—94	②	②	A	②	B	②

① —BTDC: Before top dead center.
② —Refer to engine decal affixed in the engine compartment.

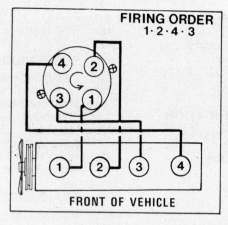

Fig. A

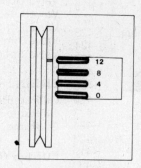

Fig. B

VALVE SPECIFICATIONS

Year	Valve Lash		Valve Angles		Valve Spring Installed Height	Valve Spring Pressure Lbs. @ In.	Stem Clearance		Stem Diameter	
	Int.	Exh.	Seat	Face			Intake	Exhaust	Intake	Exhaust
1978	.010C	.021C	45	45	1.263	122.5 @ .953	.0008—.0027	.0017—.0036	.3098—.3105	.3089—.3096

Continued

PISTONS, PINS, RINGS, CRANKSHAFT & BEARINGS

Year	Piston Clearance	Ring End Gap ①		Wrist-pin Diameter	Rod Bearings		Main Bearings			
		Comp.	Oil		Shaft Diameter	Bearing Clearance	Shaft Diameter	Bearing Clearance	Thrust on Bear. No.	Shaft End Play
1978	.0009—.0017	.009	.009	.8121	1.9368—1.9376	.0004—.0015	2.1253—2.1261	.0005—.0015	3	.003—.011

①—Fit rings in tapered bores for clearance listed in tightest portion of ring travel.

ALTERNATOR & REGULATOR SPECIFICATIONS

Year	Make	Alternator Rated Output, Amperes	Regulator	
			Voltage	R.P.M. ①
1978	Motorcraft	60	13.7—14.4	5000—6000
1978	Bosch	55	13.7—14.4	5000—6000

①—Alternator R.P.M.

STARTING MOTOR SPECIFICATIONS

Year	Make	Brush Spring Tension, Pounds	Maximum Torque, Ft. Lbs.	Volts	Maximum Current, Amps.
1978	Bosch	2.0—2.7	6.9	12	350

ENGINE TIGHTENING SPECIFICATIONS

Torque specifications are for clean and lightly lubricated threads only. Dry or dirty threads produce increased friction which prevents accurate measurement of tightness.

Year	Spark Plug Ft. Lbs.	Cylinder Head Bolts Ft. Lbs.	Intake Manifold Ft. Lbs.	Exhaust Manifold Ft. Lbs.	Rocker Arm Shaft Bracket Ft. Lbs.	Rocker Arm Cover Ft. Lbs.	Connecting Rod Cap Bolt Ft. Lbs.	Main Bearing Cap Bolts Ft. Lbs.	Flywheel to Crankshaft Ft. Lbs.	Vibration Damper or Pulley Ft. Lbs.
1978	10—15	65—70	①	②	25—30	2.5—3.5	30—35	55—60	50—55	24—28

①—Bolts, 12—15 Ft. Lbs.; Nuts, 12—15 Ft. Lbs.; Studs, 9-12 Ft. Lbs.

②—Nuts, 15—18 Ft. Lbs.; Studs, 9—12 Ft. lbs.

WHEEL ALIGNMENT SPECIFICATIONS

Year	Caster Angle, Degrees		Camber Angle, Degrees		Toe-Out Inch
	Limits	Desired	Limits	Desired	
1978	−¾ to +1	+⅓	+1¼ to +3¼	+2¼	+¹⁄₁₀

BRAKE SPECIFICATIONS

Year	Brake Drum Inside Diameter	Wheel Cylinder Bore Diameter		Master Cylinder Bore Diameter	Disc Brake Rotor		
		Front Disc	Rear Drum		Nominal Thickness	Minimum Thickness	Runout (T.I.R.)
1978	7.0	1.89	.59	—	.39	.34	.006

COOLING SYSTEM & CAPACITY DATA

Year	Cooling Capacity Qts.		Radiator Cap Relief Pressure, Lbs.	Thermo. Opening Temp.	Fuel Tank, Gals.	Engine Oil Refill Qts.	Transmission Oil Refill, Pts.
	Less A/C	With A/C					
1978	6.6	6.6	14.5	185°	10	3.5①	5

①—Includes filter.

Electrical Section

IGNITION SYSTEM

The Fiesta ignition system uses a new high-energy rotor, distributor cap, ignition secondary cables, and wide-gap spark plugs to take advantage of the higher energy produced by the Dura-Spark II ignition system, Fig. 1.

System operation is controlled by a solid-state amplifier module mounted on the engine compartment dash panel and connected into the vehicle wiring by multiple connectors, Fig. 2.

NOTE: The Dura-Spark II amplifier module and the ignition coil are "On" when the ignition switch is "On." The ignition system will therefore generate a spark when the ignition switch is turned "Off." This feature may be used to verify circuit continuity and proper

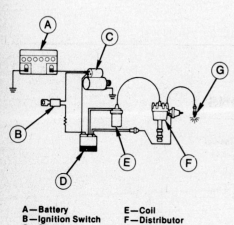

A—Battery E—Coil
B—Ignition Switch F—Distributor
C—Starter G—Spark Plug
D—Module

Fig. 1 Dura-Spark II ignition system

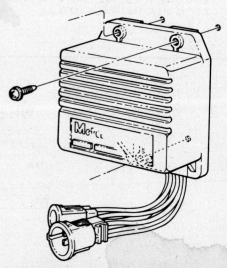

Fig. 2 Dura-Spark II amplifier module

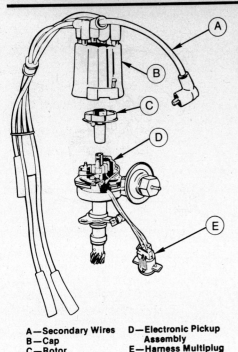

A—Secondary Wires   D—Electronic Pickup
B—Cap   Assembly
C—Rotor   E—Harness Multiplug

Fig. 3 Distributor disassembled

operation of the coil and the ignition switch. However, with the ignition switch "On," the system may be unintentionally triggered and the engine kicked over by removing the distributor cap or otherwise opening the circuit. During any underhood operations, the ignition switch must be "Off," unless the engine is to be started or a specific test which requires the ignition switch to be "On" is to be performed.

Distributor

The distributor assembly consists of the secondary cables (A) which connect the distributor cap (B) to the ignition coil and the spark plugs, Fig. 3, a rotor (C), which mounts to the top of the distributor shaft; an electronic pickup assembly (D), and a three-wire harness multi-plug (E), which provides power to the magnetic pick-up assembly.

The distributor has both a fixed and movable base plate, Fig. 4, and a four-

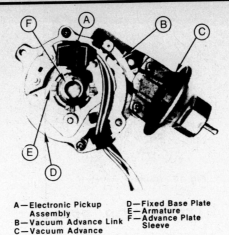

A—Electronic Pickup   D—Fixed Base Plate
     Assembly   E—Armature
B—Vacuum Advance Link   F—Advance Plate
C—Vacuum Advance   Sleeve
     Retard Assembly

Fig. 4 Distributor components

spoke armature which turns with the distributor shaft. It is also equipped with both vacuum and centrifugal spark advance to maintain engine timing under varying engine load and speed conditions. The vacuum advance maintains engine timing under varying engine load conditions, while the centrifugal advance located below the fixed base plate, compensates for changes in engine speed.

As the armature turns with the distributor shaft, a pulse is generated in the magnetic field produced by the pick-up coil assembly whenever an armature spoke passes it. These pulses cause the amplifier module to turn the ignition coil primary current "Off" and "On", producing the high voltage necessary to fire the spark plugs.

Distributor Advance

The distributor advance units operate independently. The vacuum advance unit operates the base plate assembly. The centrifugal advance controls the position of the armature relative to the distributor shaft.

Centrifugal Advance

The centrifugal advance assembly, located below the base plate, has centrifugal weights that move inward or

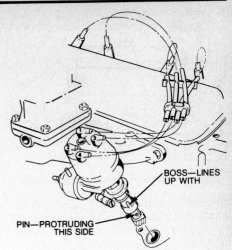

Fig. 5 Distributor alignment for installation

outward with changes in engine speed. As engine speed increases, the weights move the sleeve and plate assembly ahead of the distributor shaft, in turn, advancing the position of the armature. The rate of advance is controlled by calibrated springs.

Vacuum Advance

The diaphragm in the vacuum advance unit operates from carburetor venturi vacuum to advance the timing during normal off-idle driving conditions. The vacuum diaphragm is connected to the base plate on which the magnetic pick-up coil assembly is mounted by the vacuum advance link.

System Operation

When the ignition switch is turned "On," current flows through the primary circuit and the ignition coil is energized. Primary current flow through the coil produces a strong magnetic field around it. When an armature spoke passes the magnetic pick-up assembly, a pulse of voltage is induced which tells the amplifier module to turn the ignition coil primary current "Off." When primary current flow stops, the magnetic field sustained by the current collapses and induces a high voltage pulse in the coil secondary which fires the spark plug. A timing circuit in the amplifier

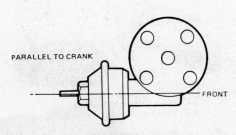

Fig. 6 Distributor installation

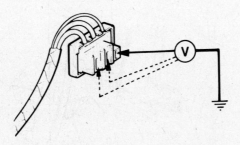

Fig. 7 Alternator wiring continuity test

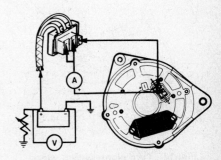

Fig. 8 Alternator output test

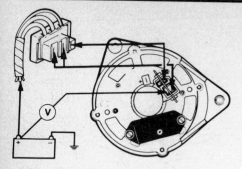

Fig. 9   Regulator control voltage check

module turns the primary current "On" again after the magnetic field around the ignition coil has collapsed. When primary current is "On," if flows from the battery through the ignition switch, the ignition coil primary winding, and the amplifier module circuits to ground.

Distributor Installation

NOTE: With a "Dura Spark" ignition system, if any high tension ignition wire was detached from a spark plug, the distributor cap, or the coil to perform any maintenance operation, silicone grease (Ford #D7AE-19A331-AA) must be applied to the boot before reconnection. Using a small clean screwdriver, apply a thin layer of silicone grease on entire interior surface of the boot.

1. With the No. 1 piston approaching top dead center, the crankshaft is rotated clockwise until the notch on the crankshaft pulley aligns with the 12 degree timing mark on the engine front cover.
2. Make sure that a new "O" ring is installed on the distributor body. Align the projecting side of the pin securing the drive gear to the distributor shaft with the boss in the distributor body, Fig. 5.
3. Install the distributor into the engine block while holding the distributor so that the vacuum advance unit is about parallel to the engine centerline, Fig. 6.

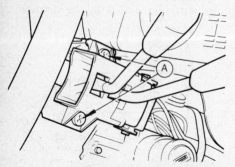

Fig. 12   Turn signal & W/S wiper switches installation

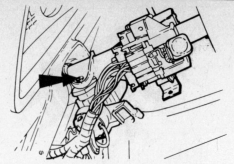

Fig. 10   Ignition switch installation

ALTERNATOR, REPLACE

1. Disconnect battery ground cable.
2. Remove retaining clip securing the wiring plug connector at rear of alternator, and disconnect the wiring plug.
3. Disconnect the alternator wiring connector in the alternator.
4. Disconnect the heater hose bracket at the alternator.
5. Loosen three alternator mounting bolts and tilt the alternator toward the engine. Remove the drive belt.
6. Remove the mounting bolts and the alternator.
7. Reverse procedure to install.

ALTERNATOR TESTING

Alternator Wiring Continuity Test

1. Disconnect the terminal plug from rear of alternator.
2. Connect a voltmeter negative terminal to ground. With the ignition switch turned "On," connect the positive lead to each of the connector wires in turn, Fig. 7.
3. The voltmeter should read battery voltage for each connector. If the battery voltage is not available at the connectors, check wiring circuit.

Voltage Drop Test Ground Side

1. Connect the voltmeter between negative terminal of the battery and the alternator housing.
2. Start engine, switch on the head-

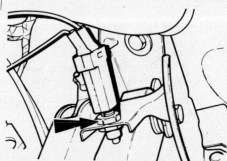

Fig. 13   Stop light switch installation

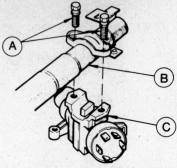

A—Shear-Off Bolts   C—Steering Column
B—Steering Column   Lock Assembly
    Tube

Fig. 11   Ignition lock installation

lights and run engine at approximately 3000 rpm. If voltmeter reading exceeds 0.25 volts, a high resistance in the negative side of the charging circuit is indicated.

If a high resistance is indicated, check for loose, dirty or corroded connections.

Alternator Output Test

1. Disconnect the terminal plug from the rear of the alternator, and connect the ammeter in series between the alternator center terminal and the corresponding socket in the terminal plug, Fig. 8.
2. Connect a jumper lead between the D plus terminal and corresponding socket in the terminal plug.
3. Switch on the headlamps and leave on for five minutes.
4. Start the engine and increase speed to 3000 rpm. The ammeter should read 55 amps at normal operating temperature.

Regulator Control Voltage Check

1. Connect a voltmeter between the main terminals of the battery, Fig. 9.
2. Connect an ammeter in series between the B plus terminal of the connector plug. Connect a jumper

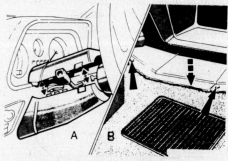

A—Steering Column Upper Shroud
B—Lower Panel

Fig. 14   Panel removal for instrument cluster removal

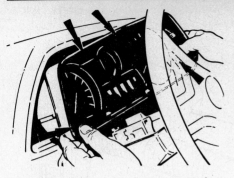

Fig. 15 Instrument cluster removal

lead between the alternator D plus terminal and the corresponding terminal of the connector plug, Fig. 9.

3. Start the engine and increase speed to 2000 rpm.
4. Run the engine until the charging rate falls between 3 and 5 amps. The voltmeter should then read 13.6-14.5 volts.

STARTER, REPLACE

1. Disconnect battery ground cable.
2. Raise and support front of vehicle.
3. Disconnect main battery cable and two wires from solenoid.
4. Remove the two rubber insulators which hold the exhaust connector to the body and engine crossmember. Remove two exhaust clamp bolts securing exhaust down pipe to manifold and carefully lower exhaust system and allow to rest in a position that will allow removal of starter motor. Make sure that the two new exhaust supports and brackets are not excessively strained.
5. Remove starter motor securing bolts and guide starter motor clear of bell housing.
6. Reverse procedure to install.

IGNITION SWITCH, REPLACE

1. Disconnect battery ground cable.
2. Remove steering column upper and lower shrouds.
3. Punch and drill out two lock retaining bolts, Fig. 10.
4. Remove ignition switch.
5. Reverse procedure to install.

IGNITION LOCK, REPLACE

1. Disconnect battery ground cable.
2. Remove crosshead screw from steering column upper shroud. Remove shroud. Remove three screws from lower steering column shroud.

Ease carefully over choke control and remove lower shroud.
3. Turn key to position I (accessories position).
4. Insert a small screwdriver through cutout in underside of ignition housing. Push upwards against retaining spring clip and pull out ignition lock assembly, Fig. 11.
5. Reverse procedure to install.

TURN SIGNAL & W/S WIPER SWITCHES, REPLACE

1. Disconnect battery ground cable.
2. Remove steering column upper shroud.
3. Remove steering column lower shroud.
4. Remove lower dash insulation panel.
5. Remove multi-function lever and other levers retaining screws, Fig. 12, and retaining strap holding wiring to column.
6. Disconnect wiring form switches and remove switches.
7. Reverse procedure to install.

STOP LIGHT SWITCH, REPLACE

1. Disconnect battery ground cable.
2. Disconnect connections at switch on brake pedal. Remove switch locking nut and the switch.
3. Reverse procedure to install.

NOTE: Adjust switch so it does not operate for the first .2 inch of brake pedal travel, but does operate within .8 inch of pedal travel. Pedal travel is to be measured on center line of foot pad.

BACK-UP LAMP SWITCH, REPLACE

1. Disconnect battery ground cable.
2. From engine compartment, discon-

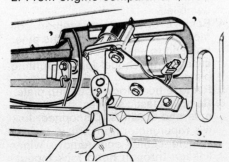

Fig. 17 Rear W/S wiper motor installation

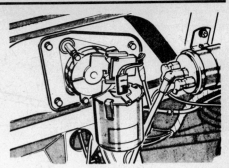

Fig. 16 Front W/S wiper motor installation

nect wiring and remove switch from left hand side of gearbox housing.
3. Reverse procedure to install.

LIGHT SWITCH, REPLACE

1. Disconnect battery ground cable.
2. Ease off or remove crosshead screw. Detach steering column upper shroud. Remove three screws from lower shroud. Ease carefully over choke control and remove lower shroud.
3. Disconnect electrical connectors from switch. Remove two screws and the switch.
4. Reverse procedure to install.

INSTRUMENT CLUSTER, REPLACE

1. Disconnect battery ground cable.
2. Remove steering column top shroud, "A," Fig. 14.
3. Remove two screws from below lower dashboard storage space and drop lower panel, "B," Fig. 14.
4. From behind cluster, hold speedometer cable with fingers. Press grooved section on cable locking catch and remove cable from cluster.
5. Remove the bezel.
6. Remove four crossmember screws from cluster front. Pull cluster assembly from panel. Disconnect multiplug and direction indicator warning light and brake failure warning light and remove cluster from vehicle, Fig. 15.
7. Reverse procedure to install.

W/S WIPER MOTOR, REPLACE

Front Motor

1. Disconnect battery ground cable.
2. Disconnect electrical connectors from wiper motor.
3. Remove three bolts and pull out windshield wiper motor and bracket

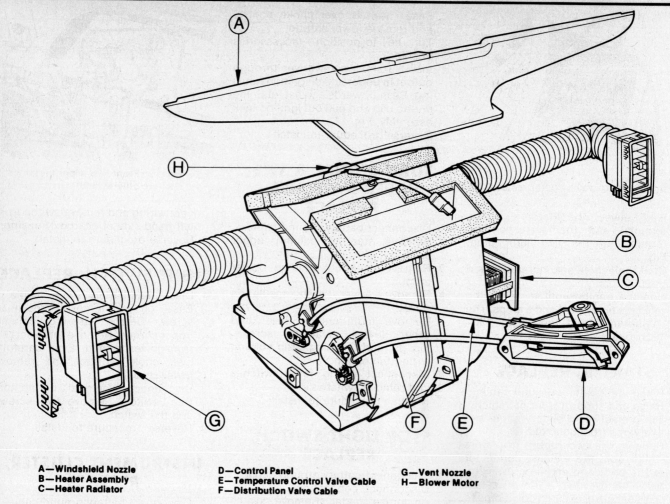

A—Windshield Nozzle
B—Heater Assembly
C—Heater Radiator

D—Control Panel
E—Temperature Control Valve Cable
F—Distribution Valve Cable

G—Vent Nozzle
H—Blower Motor

Fig. 18   Heater unit

assembly so the linkage is accessible.

4. Disconnect wiper motor from linkage and remove motor and bracket assembly.
5. Remove operating arm from motor. Ensure torque reaction is taken by operating arm. If torque is applied to output shaft the internal gear could be damaged. Remove three bolts and separate motor from mounting bracket, Fig. 16.
6. Reverse procedure to install.

Rear Motor

1. Disconnect battery ground cable.
2. Remove rear wiper arm and blade assembly.
3. Remove plastic cup, nut, metal washer, spacer and rubber washer securing pivot shaft.
4. Open rear door. Carefully pry out door trim panel clips and remove panel.
5. Remove two bolts securing bracket to rear door, Fig. 17. Remove screw securing ground lead. Disconnect

multiplug. Remove motor and linkage assembly.
6. Reverse procedure to install.

W/S WIPER TRANSMISSION, REPLACE
Front

1. Disconnect battery ground cable.
2. Disconnect wiper motor electrical connectors and remove three bolts.
3. Remove wiper arm and blade assemblies.
4. Remove one bolt on ignition coil mounting bracket. Loosen the other bolt and to enable coil to be rotated clear of the hood lock mounting plate.
5. Remove hood lock mounting plate.
6. Remove plastic sleeves, spindle arm nuts and washers. Disconnect link w/s wiper motor from arm w/s wiper spindle center and remove wiper linkage through hood lock mounting plate opening.
7. Remove motor and disconnect link

w/s wiper motor from motor operating arm.
8. Reverse procedure to install.

RADIO, REPLACE

1. Disconnect battery ground cable.
2. Remove radio shaft knobs and retaining nuts.
3. Disconnect antenna and electrical leads from radio.
4. Remove the radio to mounting bracket retaining screw from rear of radio.
5. Remove radio from vehicle.
6. Reverse procedure to install.

BLOWER MOTOR & HEATER CORE, REPLACE

1. Disconnect battery ground cable.
2. Loosen retaining clamps on water hoses at heater core. First, remove lower hose and drain coolant into suitable container. Then, remove upper hose. Secure hoses in engine compartment with open ends facing upwards.

Fig. 19 Heater core removal

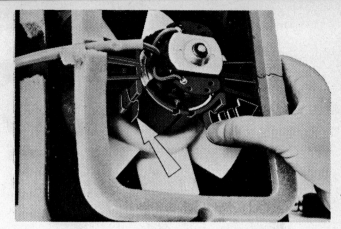

Fig. 20 Blower motor retainer clamps removal

3. Remove cover plate with heater core tube gasket. Seal heater radiator tubes with tape to prevent remaining coolant from spilling.
4. Remove right-hand and left-hand dash lower trim panels.
5. Remove ashtray and ashtray bracket.
6. Remove 2 vent hoses from heater assembly adaptors, if equipped.
7. Remove instrument panel to heater assembly bracket.

8. Remove heater assembly from cowl top panel.
   Pull heater assembly inward until heater core necks clear bulkhead openings. Disconnect wiring connector from blower motor. Remove heater assembly, Fig. 18, complete with cables and control panel to the right side. Drain remaining coolant from heater core.
9. Remove heater core from heater unit, Fig. 19.

10. Using a knife, cut 2 foam gaskets at heater assembly joint.
11. Press out 2 retaining clamps from blower motor mounting, Fig. 20.
12. Separate heater assembly halves using a suitable screwdriver. Carefully separate clips, starting at the defrost outlet. Position heater assembly with control valves facing downwards and remove blower motor.
13. Reverse procedure to install.

Engine Section

ENGINE, REPLACE

NOTE: With a "Dura Spark" ignition system, if any high tension ignition wire was detached from a spark plug, the distributor cap, or the coil to perform any maintenance operation, silicone grease (Ford #D7AE-19A331-AA) must be applied to the boot before reconnection. Using a small clean screwdriver, apply a thin layer of silicone grease on the entire interior surface of the boot.

NOTE: Prior to removal of engine and transmission, engage 4th gear to ensure subsequent gearshift assembly adjustment.

1. Disconnect battery cables and remove battery from tray.
2. Drain coolant. Disconnect radiator hose from lower radiator neck and upper radiator hoses from thermostat upper water neck. Remove heater hoses from side water pipe and intake manifold connector.
3. Remove air cleaner bolts and disconnect breather hose below air cleaner.
4. Disconnect accelerator cable at carburetor and remove cable complete with bracket from intake manifold.
5. Press accelerator cable retaining clip out of carburetor and remove.
6. Remove carburetor to fuel pump fuel line.
7. Disconnect fuel vent hoses from carburetor.
8. Disconnect and remove emission

vacuum hoses and servo vacuum hose.
9. Disconnect leads from temperature sending unit, oil pressure switch, distributor, ignition coil, choke, fan switch (if equipped). Disconnect and remove the engine ground strap.
10. Disconnect the speedometer cable at the speedometer drive.
11. Briefly depress and release cable between lever and bracket and unhook clutch cable from release lever.
12. Remove exhaust manifold heat stove.
13. Disconnect exhaust manifold pipe.

Fig. 1 Left hand drive shaft

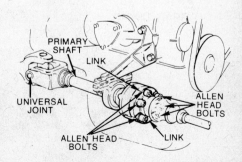

Fig. 2 Right hand drive shaft

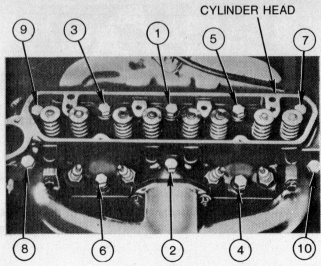

CYLINDER HEAD

Fig. 3   Cylinder head tightening sequence

Valves Open	Adjust Valves
1 & 6	3 & 8
2 & 4	5 & 7
3 & 8	1 & 6
5 & 7	2 & 4

Fig. 4   Valve adjustment chart

   d. Remove bottom engine mounting strap.

25. Lower floor jack and withdraw engine and transmission assembly from underneath vehicle.
26. Reverse procedure to install.

CYLINDER HEAD, REPLACE

1. Disconnect hot air and ventilation hoses at air cleaner and remove air cleaner assembly.
2. Remove fuel line between fuel pump and the carburetor.
3. Drain cooling system.
4. Disconnect the spark plug wires from the plugs and position aside. Disconnect the fan switch.
5. Disconnect the heater and vacuum hoses at the intake manifold. Disconnect the hoses at the choke housing.
6. Disconnect the wire from the temperature sending unit.
7. Disconnect the exhaust inlet pipe and position aside.
8. Disconnect the throttle linkage and

14. Disconnect ground wire at air pump.
15. Raise vehicle on hoist.
16. Release gear selector rod clamp bolt and remove gear selector rod. Unhook spring between selector rod and longitudinal member.
17. Back off mounting nuts on stabilizer rubber insulators and engine mounts. Loosen stud locknut and remove stud from transmission with Allen wrench.
18. Disconnect mounting rubbers and remove complete exhaust system as an assembly.
19. Remove shift tower from floor pan. Rotate gear selector rod with stabilizer halfway around and suspend on wire.
20. Disconnect starter motor and alternator leads.
21. Disconnect left axle driveshaft, Fig. 1, at coupling with stubshaft by removing 6 allen head bolts.

22. Disconnect right hand driveshaft, Fig. 2, at inner constant velocity joint by removing 6 allen head bolts.
23. Support engine and transmission assembly on floor jack.
24. Remove engine mountings as follows:
   a. Remove right front upper engine mounting rubber insulator.
   b. Remove engine-to-body bracket in engine compartment.
   c. Remove left engine mounting.

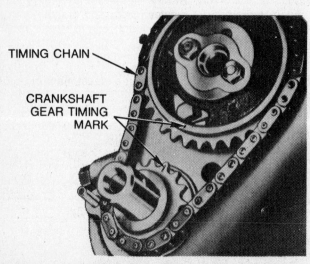

TIMING CHAIN

CRANKSHAFT GEAR TIMING MARK

Fig. 5   Valve timing marks

TIMING CHAIN TENSIONER

TIMING CHAIN TENSIONER PAD

TIMING CHAIN

Fig. 6   Timing chain tensioner installation

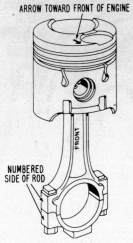

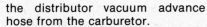

Fig. 7 Piston & rod assembly

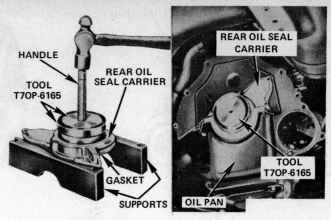

Fig. 8 Crankshaft rear oil seal installation

the distributor vacuum advance hose from the carburetor.

9. Remove the air pump mounting bracket from the cylinder head.
10. Remove the thermostat housing, pull to one side, and remove the thermostat.
11. Remove the rocker arm cover and gasket.
12. Remove the rocker arm shaft assembly.
13. Remove the push-rods.
14. Remove the cylinder head bolts and the cylinder head and gasket.
15. Reverse procedure to install. Torque cylinder head bolts, in sequence, Fig. 3, to specifications.

VALVES, ADJUST

1. With parking brake applied and transmission in Neutral, start the engine, bring to normal operating temperature, and turn off.
2. Reposition or remove components, as necessary, to allow removal of the rocker arm cover.
3. Remove the air cleaner assembly by disconnecting the #3 and #4 spark plug wires at the retaining clip under the air cleaner inlet duct, then loosen the three support bolts at the air cleaner tray.

NOTE: Do not loosen the bolts at the EGR valve or at the intake manifold.

4. Remove rocker arm cover.
5. Torque rocker arm shaft attaching bolts to 25-30 ft. lbs.
6. Check valve clearance as follows: Crank engine until valves No. 1 and No. 6 are fully opened. Now check and adjust valve clearance of valve No. 3 and No. 8. Consult Fig. 4 and continue through the sequence until all valves are adjusted.
7. Reinstall rocker arm cover using a

new gasket and torque attaching screws to 2.5-3.5 ft. lbs.
8. Return all components that were removed or repositioned to their original location.

VALVE LIFT SPECS.

Engine	Intake	Exhaust
1600cc	.2309	.2320

VALVE TIMING

Intake Opens Before TDC

Engine	Degrees
1600cc	29°

VALVE ARRANGEMENT

1600cc Engine . . . . E-I-I-E-E-I-I-E

VALVE GUIDES

Valve guides consist of holes bored in the cylinder head. For service, the guides can be reamed oversize to accommodate valves with oversize stems. Valves are available in standard sizes or .015 inch oversize.

ROCKER ARM SERVICE

1. Remove rocker arm cover.
2. Remove rocker shaft attaching bolts and lift off rocker shaft assembly.
3. Remove cotter pin from one end of shaft and slip flat washer, crimped washer and second flat washer off the shaft. The rocker arm shaft supports, rocker arms and springs can now be removed.
4. Remove plugs from shaft ends by drilling a hole in one plug. Insert a long rod through the drill plug and knock the opposite plug out of the shaft. Remove drilled plug in same manner.

5. To assemble, refit new plugs in ends of shaft. The bolt hole in the rocker arm shaft support must be on the same side as the adjusting screw in the rocker arm. The rocker arms are right and left handed, the rocker pads being inclined towards the supports. Install cotter pins with heads upwards and bend over the legs to secure.

VALVE LIFTERS, REPLACE

The chilled cast iron tappets can only be removed from the engine after the camshaft has been removed. Refer to "Camshaft, Replace" procedure.

FRONT COVER & TIMING CHAIN, REPLACE

1. Remove engine as outlined previously.
2. Remove the air pump drive belt, and then the alternator and water pump drive belt.
3. Remove the water pump.
4. Remove the crankshaft pulley with a suitable puller, then the front cover.
5. Remove the crankshaft oil slinger, camshaft sprocket retainer and bolts.
6. Remove the timing chain tensioner and bolts. Remove the camshaft sprocket and the timing chain.
7. Place the timing chain over the camshaft sprockets so that the timing marks are aligned when the sprocket is installed, Fig. 5. Tighten the bolts and bend up the locking tabs.
8. Install the crankshaft oil slinger camshaft sprocket retainer and bolts. Install the timing chain tensioner, Fig. 6.
9. Place the gasket, portions of oil pan gasket, if necessary, and the end seal on the front cover, with an oil-

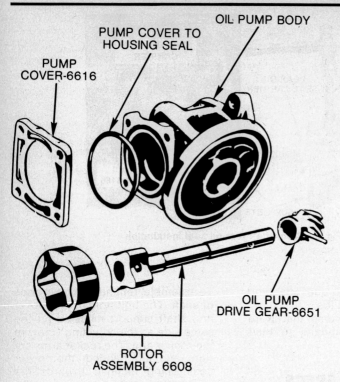

PUMP COVER-6616

PUMP COVER TO HOUSING SEAL

OIL PUMP BODY

OIL PUMP DRIVE GEAR-6651

ROTOR ASSEMBLY 6608

Fig. 9 Oil pump

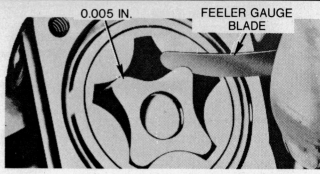

0.005 IN.

FEELER GAUGE BLADE

Fig. 10 Checking clearance between inner & outer rotors

resistant sealer at the ends. The cover will be properly positioned by the centralizing lug and the pulley. Tighten the attaching bolts, then the oil pan bolts.

10. Place the crankshaft pulley on the crankshaft with crankshaft key aligned with the pulley keyway. Tighten the attaching bolt.
11. Install the water pump.
12. Install the water pump and alternator drive belt, then the air pump drive belt.
13. Install the engine assembly.

CAMSHAFT, REPLACE

1. Remove engine as previously described.
2. With engine mounted on a stand, disconnect fuel line at pump.
3. Loosen alternator belt and remove belt.
4. Remove fan and water pump pulley.
5. Remove oil and fuel pumps from cylinder block.
6. Remove distributor.
7. Remove rocker arm cover and remove rocker arm shaft assembly.
8. Withdraw push rods from block and keep them in order for installation.
9. Invert engine on stand and remove the oil pan.
10. Remove dipstick, crankshaft pulley, front cover and oil slinger.
11. Remove timing chain tensioner and remove camshaft sprocket and chain.

12. With engine inverted, remove camshaft thrust plate and withdraw camshaft.

PISTON & ROD ASSEMBLE

Assemble the rod to the piston with the Front mark on the rod on the same side of the assembly as the arrow in the piston crown, Fig. 7.

PISTONS, PINS & RINGS

Oversize pistons and rings are available in .0025 and .030″. Oversize pins are not available.

MAIN & ROD BEARINGS

Undersize main bearings are available in .002, .010, .020 and .030 inch undersizes. Rod bearings are available in undersizes of .001, .002, .010, .020, .030 and .040 inch.

CRANKSHAFT OIL SEAL

With the engine removed and mounted on a work stand, proceed as follows:

1. Remove the pressure plate bolts evenly and remove the pressure plate and clutch disc.
2. Remove the flywheel.
3. Remove the oil pan and gaskets.
4. Remove the rear oil seal carrier and use tool T70P-6165 to remove and install a new seal, Fig. 8.

OIL PAN, REPLACE

1. Drain crankcase and remove oil dipstick.
2. Disconnect battery ground cable.
3. Disconnect throttle linkage from carburetor.
4. Disconnect steering cable from rack and pinion.
5. Disconnect rack and pinion from crossmember and move it forward to provide clearance for oil pan.
6. Remove three bolts and remove starter motor.
7. Remove left bottom bolt from lower rear cover and the cover.
8. Remove engine rear plate.
9. Remove oil pan attaching bolts and the oil pan.
10. Remove oil pump inlet tube.
11. Reverse procedure to install.

OIL PUMP, REPLACE

1. Remove bolts attaching oil pump and filter assembly and the assembly.
2. Remove filter from oil pump.
3. Reverse procedure to install.

OIL PUMP REPAIRS

1. Remove filter body and element and extract sealing ring from the groove.
2. Remove end plate and withdraw O ring from groove in body.
3. Check clearance between lobes of inner and outer rotors. This should not exceed .005″, Fig.10. Rotors are supplied only in a matched pair.
4. Check clearance between outer rotor and the housing. This should not exceed .010″.
5. Place a straightedge across face of pump body. Clearance between face of rotors and straightedge should not exceed .0025″, Fig. 11.
6. If necessary to replace rotor or drive shaft, remove outer rotor and then drive out retaining pin securing the skew gear to drive shaft and pull off the gear.
7. Withdraw inner rotor and drive shaft.

WATER PUMP, REPLACE

Drain the cooling system.

Loosen the clamps and remove the lower hose from the water pump.

Disconnect the heater hose from the water pump.

Loosen the air pump adjusting bolt and move the air pump toward the engine. Remove the air pump drive belt from the water pump pulley.

Loosen the alternator adjusting and mounting bolts. Move the alternator toward the engine and remove the drive belt.

Remove the water pump pulley attaching bolts. Remove the pulley.

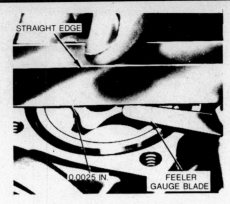

Fig. 11 Checking end play

Remove the water pump-to-cylinder block bolts and lift out water pump and gasket.

FUEL PUMP PRESSURE

Year	Engine	Pressure Lbs.
1976	1600cc	3½

FUEL PUMP, REPLACE

1. Disconnect battery ground cable.
2. Disconnect fuel lines from pump.
3. Remove fuel pump attaching bolts and the fuel pump.
4. Reverse procedure to install.

Carburetor Section

WEBER 740-2V CARB. ADJUSTMENT SPECIFICATIONS

For Idle Speeds, Refer to Engine Decal Affixed In the Engine Compartment.

Year	Carb Model (9510)	Float Setting	Choke Pulldown	Dechoke Clearance	Fast Idle Cam	Choke Setting
1978	771F9510GC, GD ①	.276 ③	.197	.157	.079	Index
	771F9510HA, HB ②	.276 ③	.197	.157	.079	Index

①—Exc. Calif.
②—Calif.
③—In vertical position.

The Weber Model 740 carburetor, Figs. 1 and 2, has five basic metering systems: choke system, idle system, main metering system, acceleration system and power enrichment system.

The choke system is used for cold starting of the engine. It incorporates a bi-metallic spring and an electric heater.

A—Vent Solenoid
B—Vent Connection (External)
C—Fuel Filter
D—Electric Choke
E—Choke Pulldown Diaphragm
F—Dash Pot
G—Fuel Shutoff Solenoid
J—Primary Venturi
K—Secondary Venturi
L—Accelerator Pump

Fig. 1 Weber model 740 carburetor

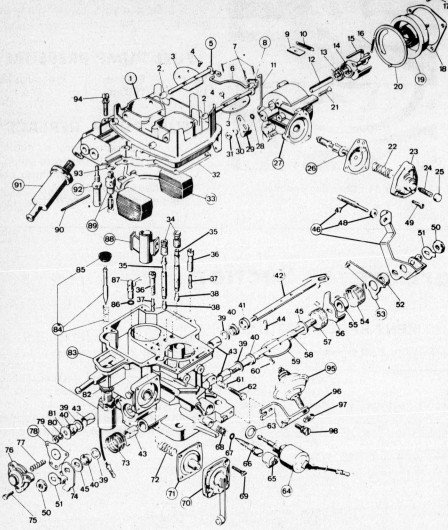

48. FAST IDLE SPEED ADJUSTING SCREW LOCK NUT
49. CHOKE PULL DOWN DIAPHRAGM COVER SCREW
50. PRIMARY THROTTLE SHAFT NUT
51. PRIMARY THROTTLE SHAFT NUT LOCKING TAB
52. SECONDARY THROTTLE OPERATING LEVER BUSHING
53. SECONDARY THROTTLE OPERATING LEVER
54. SECONDARY THROTTLE RETURN SPRING
55. SECONDARY THROTTLE RETURN SPRING SPACER
56. PRIMARY THROTTLE IDLE STOP LEVER
57. PRIMARY THROTTLE RETURN SPRING "A"
58. PRIMARY THROTTLE SHAFT
59. THROTTLE PLATES
60. THROTTLE PLATES SCREWS
61. IDLE SPEED SCREW SPRING
62. IDLE SPEED SCREW
63. IDLE FUEL SHUT OFF SOLENOID WASHER
64. IDLE FUEL SHUT OFF SOLENOID
65. IDLE MIXTURE SCREW LIMITER CAP (BLUE)
66. IDLE MIXTURE SCREW
67. IDLE MIXTURE SCREW "O" RING
68. IDLE MIXTURE SCREW SPRING
69. ACCELERATOR PUMP COVER SCREW
70. ACCELERATOR PUMP COVER (ASSY.)
71. ACCELERATOR PUMP DIAPHRAGM
72. ACCELERATOR PUMP SPRING
73. PRIMARY THROTTLE RETURN SPRING "B"
74. ACCELERATOR PUMP CAM
75. POWER VALVE COVER SCREW
76. POWER VALVE COVER
77. POWER VALVE SPRING
78. POWER VALVE DIAPHRAGM
79. SECONDARY THROTTLE SHAFT NUT
80. SECONDARY THROTTLE SHAFT LOCK WASHER
81. SECONDARY THROTTLE SHAFT WASHER
82. FUEL BOWL VENT SOLENOID WASHER
83. MAIN BODY (ASSY.)
84. FUEL BOWL VENT SOLENOID (ASSY.)
    1. BOWL VENT SPRING
    2. BOWL VENT ARM
85. VITON BOWL VENT SEAL
86. "O" RING SEAL FOR PUMP NOZZLE
87. PUMP SHOOTER
88. FUEL DISCHARGE NOZZLES
89. FUEL INLET SEAT & NEEDLE
90. FLOAT HINGE PIN
91. FUEL FILTER
92. FUEL RETURN LINE CHECK VALVE AND FITTING
93. FUEL INLET SEAT GASKET
94. COVER HOLD DOWN SCREWS
95. DASH POT
96. DASH POT MOUNTING BRACKET
97. DASH POT ADJUSTING LOCK NUT
98. DASH POT MOUNTING BRACKET SCREW

1. COVER (ASSY.)
2. CHOKE SHAFT BUSHINGS
3. CHOKE PLATE
4. CHOKE PLATE SCREWS
5. SECONDARY CHOKE SHAFT
6. SECONDARY CHOKE LINK
7. CHOKE LINKAGE RETAINING CLIPS
8. PRIMARY CHOKE SHAFT
9. PRIMARY CHOKE LINK DIRT SEAL
10. DIRT SEAL RETAINER
11. PRIMARY CHOKE LINK
12. CHOKE BIMETAL SHAFT BUSHING
13. FAST IDLE CAM SPRING
14. CHOKE BIMETAL LEVER
15. CHOKE BIMETAL SHAFT
16. CHOKE ASSIST SPRING
17. ELECTRIC CHOKE RETAINING SCREWS
18. ELECTRIC CHOKE RETAINING RING
19. ELECTRIC CHOKE UNIT
20. CHOKE HOUSING DIRT SHIELD
21. CHOKE HOUSING SCREWS
22. CHOKE PULLDOWN SPRING
23. COVER
24. CHOKE PULLDOWN ADJUSTING SCREW

25. CHOKE PULLDOWN ADJUSTING SCREW SEAL
26. CHOKE PULLDOWN DIAPHRAGM ASSEMBLY
27. CHOKE HOUSING (ASSY.)
28. CHOKE HOUSING VACUUM SEAL (O RING)
29. CHOKE LEVER
30. CHOKE BIMETAL SHAFT LOCK WASHER
31. CHOKE BIMETAL SHAFT NUT
32. COVER GASKET
33. FUEL BOWL FLOAT
34. HIGH SPEED AIR BLEEDS
35. WELL TUBES
36. IDLE JET HOLDER
37. IDLE JET
38. MAIN JET
39. TEFLON SHAFT SEAL
40. TEFLON SHAFT SEAL
41. SECONDARY THROTTLE SHAFT SPACER
42. SECONDARY THROTTLE SHAFT
43. THROTTLE SHAFT BUSHINGS
44. SECONDARY THROTTLE STOP SCREW
45. PRIMARY SHAFT LOCATOR WASHERS
46. THROTTLE LEVER
47. FAST IDLE SPEED ADJUSTING SCREW

Fig. 2   Weber model 740 carburetor disassembled

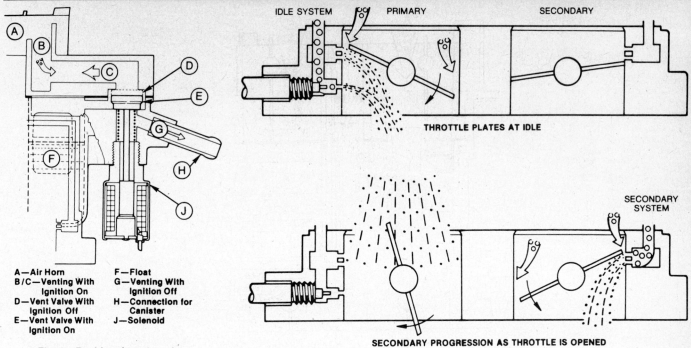

A—Air Horn
B/C—Venting With Ignition On
D—Vent Valve With Ignition Off
E—Vent Valve With Ignition On
F—Float
G—Venting With Ignition Off
H—Connection for Canister
J—Solenoid

Fig. 3 Fuel bowl vent system

IDLE SYSTEM   PRIMARY   SECONDARY

THROTTLE PLATES AT IDLE

SECONDARY SYSTEM

SECONDARY PROGRESSION AS THROTTLE IS OPENED

Fig. 4 Secondary progression

The idle system is a separate and adjustable system for the correct air/fuel mixture for both idle and low speed performance.

The main metering system provides the correct air/fuel mixture for normal cruising speeds. A main metering system is provided for both primary and secondary stage operation.

The acceleration system is mechanically operated from the primary throttle linkage and provides fuel to the primary stage during acceleration. Fuel is provided by a diaphragm-type pump.

The power enrichment system consists of a vacuum-operated power valve and an airflow-regulated pullover system in the secondary. This system is used with the main metering system to provide satisfactory performance during moderate to heavy acceleration.

The distributor and EGR vacuum ports are located in the primary venturi area of the carburetor.

Fuel Inlet System

The fuel inlet system maintains a specified fuel level in the fuel bowl, permitting the basic fuel metering systems to deliver the proper mixture to the engine. Fuel under pressure enters the bowl through the fuel filter in the air horn.

The fuel inlet needle position is controlled by a float and lever assembly which is hinged on the float pin. The amount of fuel entering the bowl is regulated by the distance the inlet needle is moved off its seat. When the float drops,

it causes the inlet needle to drop and additional fuel enters the bowl. As the fuel reaches a specified level, the inlet needle is raised to a position that allows only enough fuel to enter to replace that being used by the metering systems. The float bowl has a dual venting system through a solenoid valve, Fig. 3. When the ignition is "On," the bowl is vented internally to the air cleaner. This balances the bowl with carburetor inlet air.

When the ignition is "Off," the bowl is vented externally, with the vapors stored in the carbon canister and retrieved when the engine is started again.

Idle System

Fuel for idle and off-idle operation flows from the bowl through the primary main metering jet into the main well. Fuel then flows through an idle fuel restriction and is mixed with air entering through the primary idle air bleed.

This air/fuel mixture travels through passages past the idle transfer holes. These holes serve as additional air bleeds during curb idle. Then, the air/fuel mixture moves past the idle mixture screw tip, which controls the amount of discharge. This air/fuel mixture is discharged below the throttle plate.

At speeds slightly above idle, the idle transfer holes begin discharging additional air/fuel mixture. This occurs when the increased opening of the throttle plates exposes the idle transfer holes to intake manifold vacuum.

As the throttle opening and engine speed are increased, airflow through the carburetor also is increased. This creates a vacuum in the venturi, causing the main metering system to begin operation as the idle system tapers off.

Fuel Shut-Off System

When the ignition switch is "On," the fuel shut-off system solenoid is in the operated position, allowing fuel to flow in the idle system of the carburetor. When the ignition switch is turned "Off," the solenoid releases, shutting off the flow of fuel to the carburetor idle system.

Main Metering System

As engine speed increases, air velocity through booster venturi causes a vacuum in the venturi. Fuel then begins to flow through the main metering system due to the high pressure in the bowl and a low pressure at the main discharge nozzle. Fuel flows from the fuel bowl through the main jet, and into the main well. The fuel then moves up the main well tube where it is mixed with air. Air, supplied through the high speed air bleed, mixes with the fuel through small holes in the sides of the main well tubes. The high speed bleed meters an increasing amount of air whenever venturi vacuum increases, to maintain the proper air-fuel ratio.

As the air-fuel mixture moves from the main well tube to the discharge port, it is discharged into the booster venturi.

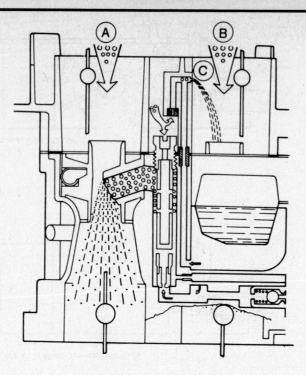

A—Primary Air Flow   B—Secondary Air Flow   C—Secondary Power Enrichment

Fig. 5   Secondary power enrichment system

Secondary Progression

When the primary throttle plate opening reaches approximately 45 degrees, the secondary throttle plate starts to open, Fig. 4. The air-fuel mixture then starts to flow from the secondary transfer holes as they are exposed to manifold vacuum. Further opening of the throttle plates starts the operation of the secondary main metering system, which is similar to the primary system.

Accelerator Pump System

When the throttle plates are opened quickly, airflow through the carburetor responds almost immediately. However, since fuel is heavier than air, there is a brief time lag before fuel flow can gain enough speed to maintain the proper air-fuel ratio. During this lag, the accelerating pump system supplies this required fuel, until the proper air-fuel ratio can be established by the other metering systems.

The moment the throttle plates are opened, the diaphragm rod is pushed upward, forcing fuel from the pump chamber into the discharge passage. Fuel under pressure unseats the discharge check ball and is forced through the pump discharge valve where it sprays into the primary venturi through the pump discharge nozzle.

Excess fuel and pump chamber vapors flow back into the fuel bowl through a restriction.

Pirmary Power Enrichment System

During heavy load conditions of high speed operation, the air-fuel ratio must be increased for higher engine output. The power enrichment system, which is controlled by intake manifold vacuum, supplies this extra fuel during these conditions. Manifold vacuum is applied to the power valve diaphragm from an opening in the carburetor base where it is connected by passages in the main body to the diaphragm. During idle and light load conditions, manifold vacuum is high enough to overcome the opposing power valve spring tension, thus holding the power valve closed. When higher engine output is required, the increased throttle opening results in decreased manifold vacuum. As the manifold vacuum decreases, the valve opens and fuel then flows from the bowl through the power valve to the primary main well. In the primary main well, this extra fuel is added to the main system fuel to enrich the mixture.

Secondary Power Enrichment System

The secondary system is provided with an air velocity operated power system for fuel enrichment, Fig. 5. As the secondary throttle plate approaches wide open position, air velocity through the secondary venturi creates a low pressure at the discharge opening in the air horn. Fuel flows from the bowl through a vertical channel. As this occurs, air enters through a calibrated air bleed and mixes with the fuel, discharging this mixture through the discharge opening.

ADJUSTMENTS

Choke Plate Vacuum Pulldown

1. Remove the three choke retaining screws, retaining ring choke housing and heat shield.
2. Set the fast idle cam on the first step by opening throttle and closing choke plate by hand. Close throttle. The fast idle cam should then be on the first step. Visually check to make certain.
3. Using a hand vacuum pump, set hand pump vacuum to 17 inch Hg. The vacuum pump should be hooked into vacuum channel on pump bore under base of carburetor. Check clearance by using vacuum pressure and light thumb pressure closing choke plates. Measure downstream choke-plate-to-bore clearance.

NOTE: Modulator spring should not be compressed.

4. To adjust the choke-plate-to-air-horn clearance, turn vacuum diaphragm adjusting screw in or out as necessary.

Fast Idle Speed

1. Remove the electric choke cap unit, making note of the setting and the proper bi-metal to choke lever relationship. With the engine running at normal operating temperature with transmission in neutral, set the choke linkage on the kickdown step of the choke cam. The fast idle screw should be against the shoulder of the high step of the cam.
2. Check the fast idle speed. Correct as required.
3. Run engine at approximately 2500 RPM for 15 seconds.
4. Recheck fast idle speed.

Emission Controls Section

COMPONENT LOCATION

Refer to Figs. 1 and 2 for component locations.

THERMACTOR SYSTEM

The Thermactor Exhaust Control System reduces carbon monoxide and hydrocarbon content of combustion by-product gases, by injecting fresh air into the hot exhaust gas stream as it leaves the combustion chamber. A pump supplies air under pressure to the exhaust port near the exhaust valve, by either an external air manifold, or through internal drilled-passages in the cylinder head or exhaust manifold. The oxygen in the fresh air, plus the heat of the exhaust gases, causes further oxidation, which converts the exhaust gases into carbon dioxide and water.

Air Supply Pump
The belt driven air supply pump takes in air through the clean side of the air cleaner.

The air supply pump does not have a pressure relief valve. This function is controlled by the air bypass valve.

Air Bypass Valve
An air bypass valve is used in catalytic converter equipped systems, Fig. 3.

The timed bypass valve operates as follows: During normal operation, vacuum is equalized on both sides of the diaphragm. The diaphragm return

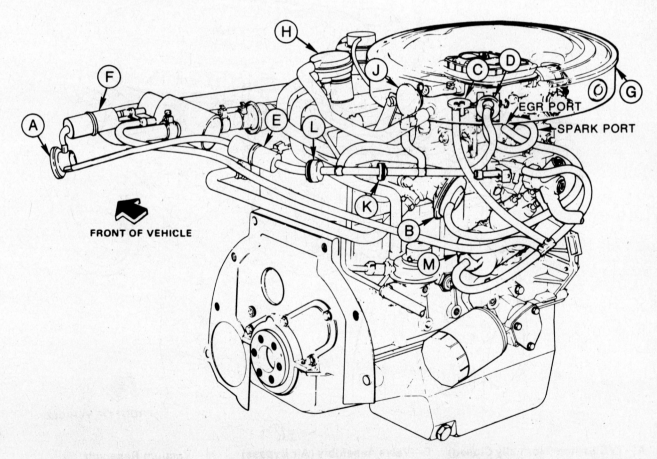

FRONT OF VEHICLE

EGR PORT
SPARK PORT

A—Thermactor Idle Vacuum Valve (TIV)
B—Exhaust Gas Recirculation (EGR) Valve
C—Bimetal Sensor
D—TVS Switch (Normally Open)
E—Vacuum Reservoir
F—Valve Assembly (Air Bypass)
G—Air Cleaner Assembly
H—Oil Filler Cap Assembly
J—Valve Assembly (Vacuum Vent)
K—Check Valve
L—Delay Valve
M—Distributor

Fig. 1 Emission control systems component location. Exc. California

spring holds the valve closed, allowing thermactor pump air to flow to the exhaust ports.

During deceleration, the sudden rise of intake manifold vacuum under the diaphragm overcomes return spring pressure and pulls the valve downward. Air is then diverted to the atmosphere momentarily, because vacuum is quickly equalized on both sides of the diaphragm through a small orifice in the diaphragm.

The normally-closed timed bypass valve used with catalytic systems operates as follows: During normal operation, engine intake manifold vacuum holds the normally-closed valve upward, allowing thermactor air to flow to the cylinder head(s) and blocking vent port.

When engine intake manifold rises or drops sharply (such as during acceleration or deceleration, or system blockage or failure), the Thermactor Idle Vacuum

Valve (TIV) operates and momentarily cuts off the vacuum to the bypass valve. The spring pulls the stem down, seating the valve to cut off pump air to the exhaust manifold, and opening the dump valve at the lower end of the bypass valve to mementarily divert the pump air to the atmosphere. In the case of excess pump volume or a downstream restriction, the excess pressure will unseat the valve in the lower portion of the bypass valve and allow a partial flow of pump air to the atmosphere. At the same time, the valve in the upper part of the bypass is still unseated allowing a partial flow of pump air to the exhaust manifold to meet system requirements.

A timed air by-pass valve is used with some thermactor systems, Fig. 4.

This bypass valve contains an integral vacuum differential function and a vacuum vent. When the vent is blocked, the valve functions as a timed bypass valve.

When the vent is open to atmospheric pressure, however, and a vacuum of 4 inches of Hg or more is applied to the source port, the valve goes immediately to the dump mode.

Vacuum Vent Valve

The Thermactor vacuum vent valve, Fig. 5, provides the make-up air for the thermactor retard delay valve and air bypass valve during idle modes to deactivate the thermactor system after a controlled period of time, Fig. 6.

Application of vacuum from the carburetor to both ports of the thermactor vacuum vent causes the diaphragm to initially move toward the left and the dump valve to seat. With the dump valve seated, the vacuum is applied to the rest of the system.

The removal of the vacuum during idle modes results in the diaphragm moving toward the right. The dump valve leaves the seat, opening the vent

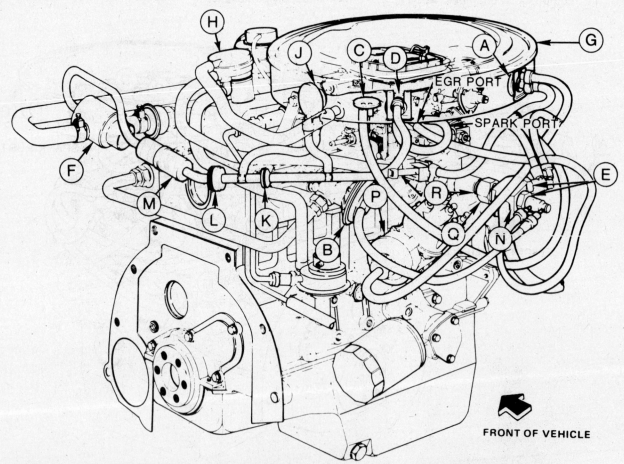

FRONT OF VEHICLE

A—TVS Switch (Normally Closed)
B—EGR Valve
C—Air Cleaner Bimetal Sensor
D—TVS Switch (Normally Open)
E—Ported Vacuum Switch (PVS)
    (2 Required)
F—Valve Assembly (Air Bypass)
G—Air Cleaner Assembly
H—Oil Filler Cap Assembly
J—Valve Assembly (Vacuum Vent)
K—Check Valve
L—Delay Valve
M—Vacuum Reservoir
N—Fitting (PVS Valve)
P—Distributor
Q—Adapter (PVS Fitting)
R—Adapter (PVS Fitting)

Fig. 2 Emission control systems component location. California

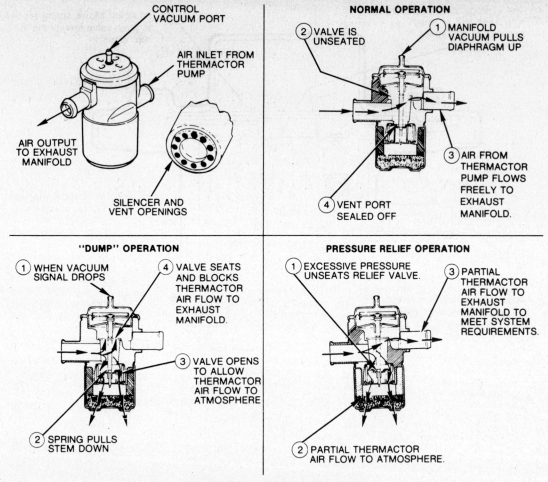

Fig. 3   Air bypass valve operation

CONTROL VACUUM PORT

AIR INLET FROM THERMACTOR PUMP

AIR OUTPUT TO EXHAUST MANIFOLD

SILENCER AND VENT OPENINGS

NORMAL OPERATION

② VALVE IS UNSEATED

① MANIFOLD VACUUM PULLS DIAPHRAGM UP

③ AIR FROM THERMACTOR PUMP FLOWS FREELY TO EXHAUST MANIFOLD.

④ VENT PORT SEALED OFF

"DUMP" OPERATION

① WHEN VACUUM SIGNAL DROPS

④ VALVE SEATS AND BLOCKS THERMACTOR AIR FLOW TO EXHAUST MANIFOLD.

③ VALVE OPENS TO ALLOW THERMACTOR AIR FLOW TO ATMOSPHERE

② SPRING PULLS STEM DOWN

PRESSURE RELIEF OPERATION

① EXCESSIVE PRESSURE UNSEATS RELIEF VALVE.

③ PARTIAL THERMACTOR AIR FLOW TO EXHAUST MANIFOLD TO MEET SYSTEM REQUIREMENTS.

② PARTIAL THERMACTOR AIR FLOW TO ATMOSPHERE.

and allowing air to enter the system to reduce the vacuum previously applied to the retard delay valve.

Exhaust Check Valve

The exhaust gas check valve, Fig. 7, allows thermactor air to enter the exhaust port drillings, but prevents the reverse flow of exhaust gases in the event of improper operation of system components. The valve is located between the bypass valve and the exhaust port drillings, either mounted on the external air manifold or directly on the engine.

Thermactor System With Idle Vacuum Valve & Vacuum Delay Valves

The Timed Air Bypass Valve, Fig. 4, is also used in some applications without a solenoid, vacuum valve and related

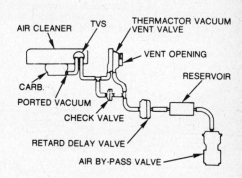

Fig. 6   Vacuum vent valve installation

AIR CLEANER   TVS   THERMACTOR VACUUM VENT VALVE

VENT OPENING

CARB.   RESERVOIR

PORTED VACUUM

CHECK VALVE

RETARD DELAY VALVE

AIR BY-PASS VALVE

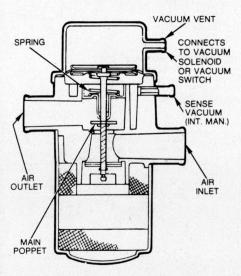

Fig. 4   Timed air bypass valve

VACUUM VENT

SPRING

CONNECTS TO VACUUM SOLENOID OR VACUUM SWITCH

SENSE VACUUM (INT. MAN.)

AIR OUTLET

AIR INLET

MAIN POPPET

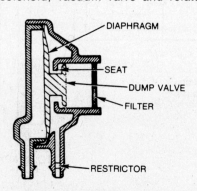

Fig. 5   Vacuum vent valve

DIAPHRAGM

SEAT

DUMP VALVE

FILTER

RESTRICTOR

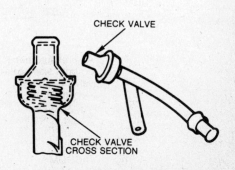

Fig. 7   Exhaust check valve

CHECK VALVE

CHECK VALVE CROSS SECTION

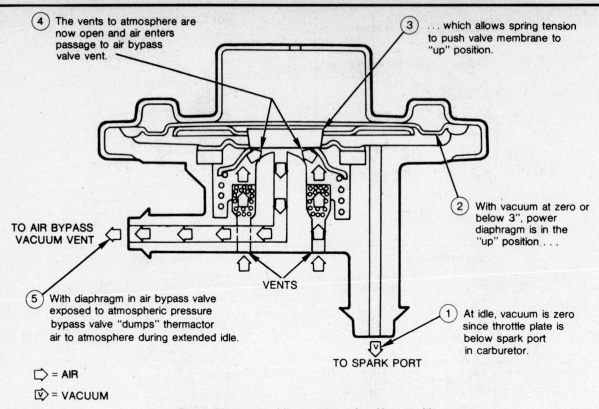

④ The vents to atmosphere are now open and air enters passage to air bypass valve vent.

③ ... which allows spring tension to push valve membrane to "up" position.

② With vacuum at zero or below 3", power diaphragm is in the "up" position ...

TO AIR BYPASS VACUUM VENT

① At idle, vacuum is zero since throttle plate is below spark port in carburetor.

⑤ With diaphragm in air bypass valve exposed to atmospheric pressure bypass valve "dumps" thermactor air to atmosphere during extended idle.

VENTS

TO SPARK PORT

▷ = AIR

Ⓥ = VACUUM

Fig. 8   Thermactor idle vacuum valve. Vent position

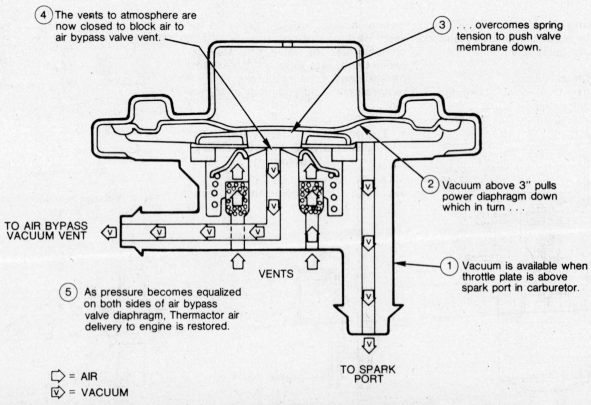

④ The vents to atmosphere are now closed to block air to air bypass valve vent.

③ ... overcomes spring tension to push valve membrane down.

② Vacuum above 3" pulls power diaphragm down which in turn ...

TO AIR BYPASS VACUUM VENT

① Vacuum is available when throttle plate is above spark port in carburetor.

⑤ As pressure becomes equalized on both sides of air bypass valve diaphragm, Thermactor air delivery to engine is restored.

VENTS

TO SPARK PORT

▷ = AIR

Ⓥ = VACUUM

Fig. 9   Thermactor idle vacuum valve. Non-vent position

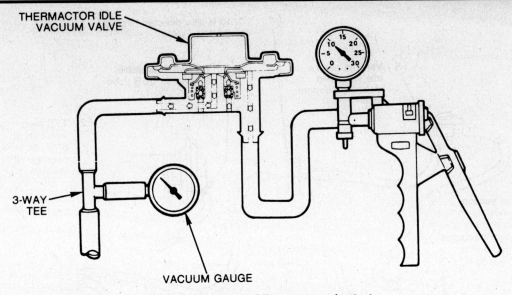

Fig. 10 Thermactor idle vacuum valve test

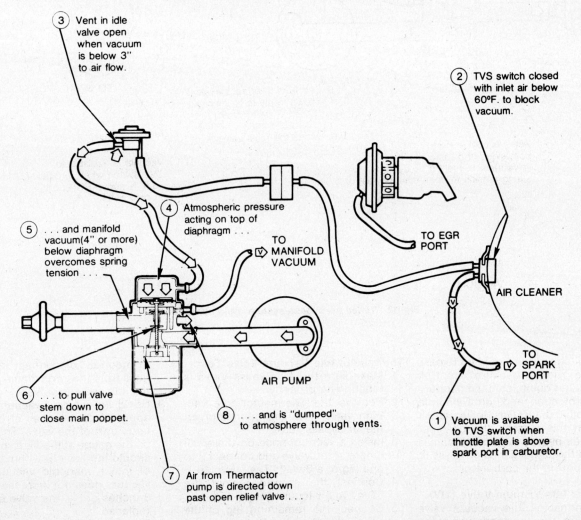

③ Vent in idle valve open when vacuum is below 3" to air flow.

② TVS switch closed with inlet air below 60°F. to block vacuum.

④ Atmospheric pressure acting on top of diaphragm . . .

⑤ . . . and manifold vacuum(4" or more) below diaphragm overcomes spring tension . . .

TO MANIFOLD VACUUM

TO EGR PORT

AIR CLEANER

⑥ . . . to pull valve stem down to close main poppet.

AIR PUMP

⑧ . . . and is "dumped" to atmosphere through vents.

① Vacuum is available to TVS switch when throttle plate is above spark port in carburetor.

TO SPARK PORT

⑦ Air from Thermactor pump is directed down past open relief valve . . .

⇨ = AIR

ᵥ = VACUUM

Fig. 11 Timed air bypass system. Warm or normal operation

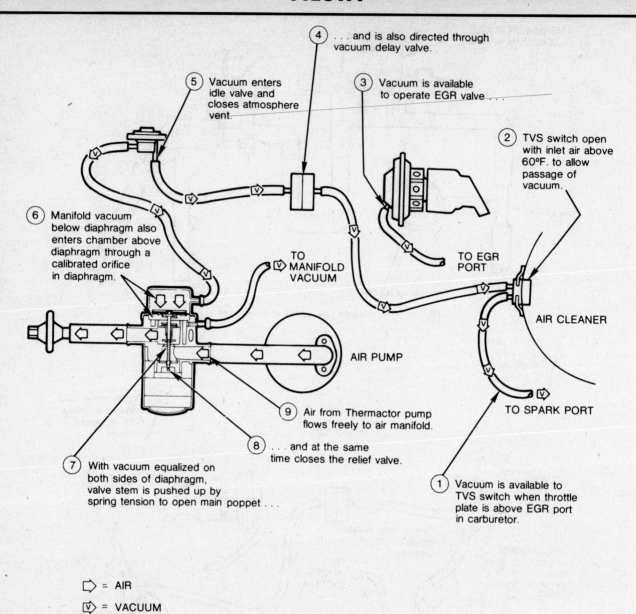

④ . . . and is also directed through vacuum delay valve.

⑤ Vacuum enters idle valve and closes atmosphere vent.

③ Vacuum is available to operate EGR valve . . .

② TVS switch open with inlet air above 60°F. to allow passage of vacuum.

⑥ Manifold vacuum below diaphragm also enters chamber above diaphragm through a calibrated orifice in diaphragm.

TO MANIFOLD VACUUM

TO EGR PORT

AIR CLEANER

AIR PUMP

⑨ Air from Thermactor pump flows freely to air manifold.

⑧ . . . and at the same time closes the relief valve.

TO SPARK PORT

⑦ With vacuum equalized on both sides of diaphragm, valve stem is pushed up by spring tension to open main poppet . . .

① Vacuum is available to TVS switch when throttle plate is above EGR port in carburetor.

⇨ = AIR

Ⅴ = VACUUM

Fig. 12   Timed air bypass system. Cold operation

electric switches. This Timed Air Bypass System provides backfire control, fulltime idle air dump, cold temperature catalyst protection and, on California models, cold Exhaust Gas Recirculation lockout. In this system, the chamber above the air bypass valve diaphragm is connected through a series of valves to the spark port in the carburetor.

Thermactor Idle Vacuum Valve (TIV)

The Thermactor idle vacuum valve uses vacuum from the spark port in the carburetor to control the vacuum vent in the Air Bypass Valve. The specific purpose of this valve is to provide dumping of air during idle periods of approximately ½-to-1 minute or more, Figs. 8 and 9.

Thermactor Idle Vacuum Valve Test

1. Make sure the Air Bypass Valve is functioning properly.
2. Remove the Thermactor idle vacuum valve from the connector on the air bypass valve.
3. Install a vacuum hose on the small nipple of the valve and connect it to one leg of a 3-way "Tee," Fig. 10.
4. Connect the second leg of the "Tee" to a vacuum gauge, Fig. 10.
5. Connect the remaining leg of the "Tee" to the Air Bypass Valve, Fig. 10.
6. Connect a vacuum gauge to the intake manifold, Fig. 10.
7. Warm up the engine to normal operating temperature.
8. With engine at idle and transmission in neutral, disconnect the large hose from the large diameter port of the idle vacuum valve.
9. Using an external vacuum source, apply 3½-to 4 inches of Hg to the large port of the valve. The vacuum on the gauge at the Air Bypass Valve should increase to within 3 inch Hg of intake manifold vacuum. If the vacuum does not increase to within 3 inches of Hg, the valve should be replaced.
10. Remove the vacuum source from the port of the valve. The vacuum gauge reading should drop to 1 in. Hg or less. If not, the valve should be replaced.

Warm Engine Or Normal Operation

Refer to Fig. 11.

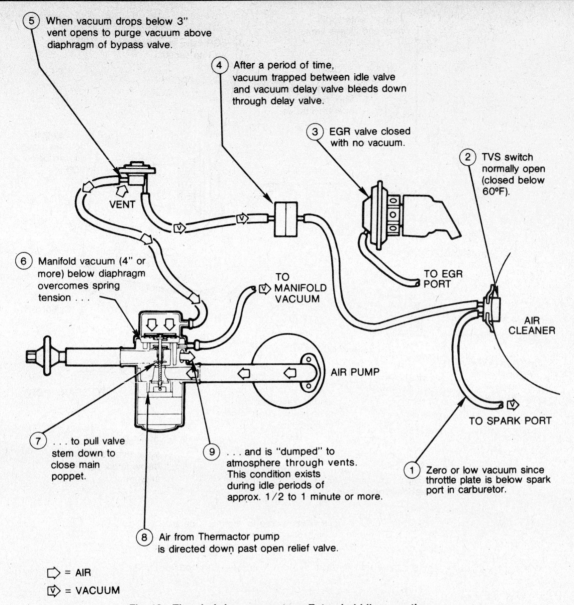

⑤ When vacuum drops below 3" vent opens to purge vacuum above diaphragm of bypass valve.

④ After a period of time, vacuum trapped between idle valve and vacuum delay valve bleeds down through delay valve.

③ EGR valve closed with no vacuum.

② TVS switch normally open (closed below 60°F).

VENT

⑥ Manifold vacuum (4" or more) below diaphragm overcomes spring tension . . .

TO MANIFOLD VACUUM

TO EGR PORT

AIR CLEANER

AIR PUMP

⑦ . . . to pull valve stem down to close main poppet.

⑨ . . . and is "dumped" to atmosphere through vents. This condition exists during idle periods of approx. 1/2 to 1 minute or more.

TO SPARK PORT

① Zero or low vacuum since throttle plate is below spark port in carburetor.

⑧ Air from Thermactor pump is directed down past open relief valve.

▷ = AIR

▽ = VACUUM

Fig. 13 Timed air bypass system. Extended idle operation

Cold Engine Operation

When inlet air temperature is below 60 degrees F, the temperature vacuum switch (TVS) in the air cleaner shuts off carburetor vacuum. This causes the idle vacuum valve to open and vent the chamber above the air bypass valve diaphragm, Fig. 12. Air is dumped to atmosphere to protect the catalytic converter from overheating during warmup. Shutting off vacuum to the EGR valve provides cold engine EGR lockout on California models.

Operation During Extended Idle

At engine idle speeds the throttle plate closes off carburetor vacuum. However, closing the throttle does not immediately vent the Air Bypass Valve and cause the Thermactor air to be dumped since it takes about one minute for the vacuum trapped between the idle vacuum valve and the vacuum delay valve to bleed down and open the idle vacuum valve to atmosphere, Fig. 13. The purpose of the idle vacuum valve is to reduce underbody temperatures by dumping air during extended periods of idling.

Operation During Deceleration

Operation during deceleration is similar to prolonged idle operation except the air is dumped immediately without waiting for vacuum to bleed through the vacuum delay valve since, when the throttle is suddenly closed at highway speeds, manifold vacuum is greatly increased. Vacuum below the air bypass valve diaphragm is much higher than the vacuum trapped above it. This closes the main poppet and opens the relief poppet of the air bypass valve. The air bypass valve returns to normal operation as soon as manifold bleeds through the orifice in the diaphragm, Fig. 14.

Pressure Relief Operation

Pressure relief operation is essentially the same for all three air bypass valves. Pressure from excess pump volume acting on the larger area of the relief poppet tends to partially open it and to partially close the main poppet. This causes the air bypass valve to function as a pressure regulating valve.

Vacuum Delay Valve Test

Refer to Fig. 15 for testing procedure.

Temperature Switch Test

Refer to Fig. 16 for testing procedure.

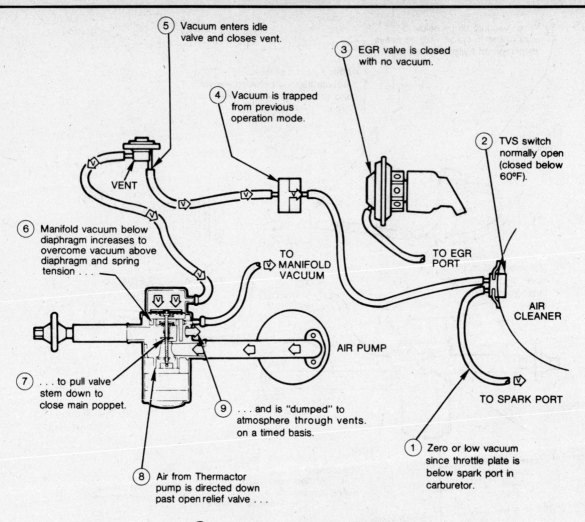

(5) Vacuum enters idle valve and closes vent.

(3) EGR valve is closed with no vacuum.

(4) Vacuum is trapped from previous operation mode.

(2) TVS switch normally open (closed below 60°F).

VENT

(6) Manifold vacuum below diaphragm increases to overcome vacuum above diaphragm and spring tension . . .

TO MANIFOLD VACUUM

TO EGR PORT

AIR CLEANER

(7) . . . to pull valve stem down to close main poppet.

AIR PUMP

(9) . . . and is "dumped" to atmosphere through vents on a timed basis.

(1) Zero or low vacuum since throttle plate is below spark port in carburetor.

TO SPARK PORT

(8) Air from Thermactor pump is directed down past open relief valve . . .

▷ = AIR

▽ = VACUUM

(10) Air bypass valve returns to "normal" operation when vacuum bleeds through orifice in diaphragm to equalize vacuum on both sides of diaphragm.

Fig. 14 Timed air bypass system. Deceleration operation

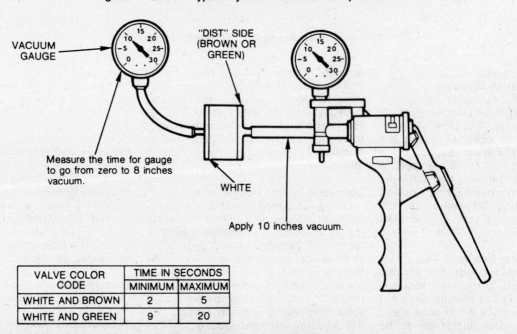

VACUUM GAUGE

"DIST" SIDE (BROWN OR GREEN)

Measure the time for gauge to go from zero to 8 inches vacuum.

WHITE

Apply 10 inches vacuum.

VALVE COLOR CODE	TIME IN SECONDS	
	MINIMUM	MAXIMUM
WHITE AND BROWN	2	5
WHITE AND GREEN	9	20

Fig. 15 Vacuum delay valve test

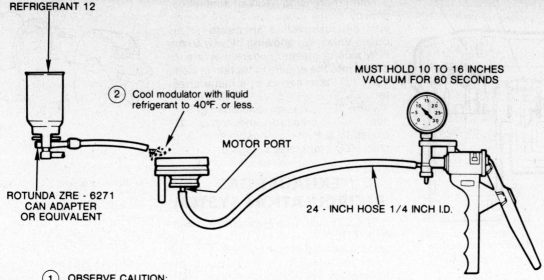

REFRIGERANT 12

② Cool modulator with liquid refrigerant to 40°F. or less.

MUST HOLD 10 TO 16 INCHES
VACUUM FOR 60 SECONDS

MOTOR PORT

ROTUNDA ZRE - 6271
CAN ADAPTER
OR EQUIVALENT

24 - INCH HOSE 1/4 INCH I.D.

① OBSERVE CAUTION:

- Check vacuum pump is leakfree. If not use distributor tester.
- Do not cool with engine running.

- Area must be well ventilated.
- Wear safety goggles.
- Do not spill refrigerant on skin.

Fig. 16 Temperature switch test

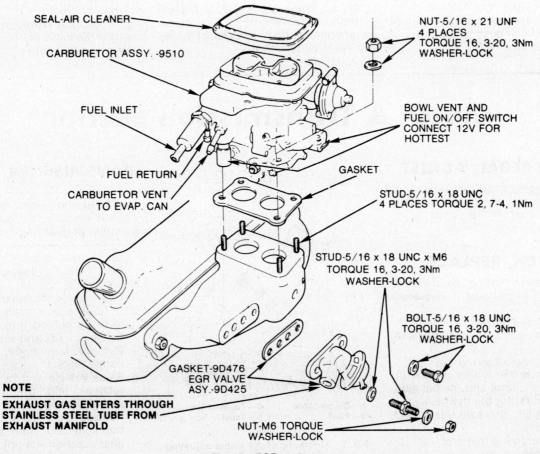

SEAL-AIR CLEANER

CARBURETOR ASSY. -9510

FUEL INLET

FUEL RETURN

CARBURETOR VENT
TO EVAP. CAN

NUT-5/16 x 21 UNF
4 PLACES
TORQUE 16, 3-20, 3Nm
WASHER-LOCK

BOWL VENT AND
FUEL ON/OFF SWITCH
CONNECT 12V FOR
HOTTEST

GASKET

STUD-5/16 x 18 UNC
4 PLACES TORQUE 2, 7-4, 1Nm

STUD-5/16 x 18 UNC x M6
TORQUE 16, 3-20, 3Nm
WASHER-LOCK

BOLT-5/16 x 18 UNC
TORQUE 16, 3-20, 3Nm
WASHER-LOCK

GASKET-9D476
EGR VALVE
ASY.-9D425

NUT-M6 TORQUE
WASHER-LOCK

NOTE

**EXHAUST GAS ENTERS THROUGH
STAINLESS STEEL TUBE FROM
EXHAUST MANIFOLD**

Fig. 18 EGR system

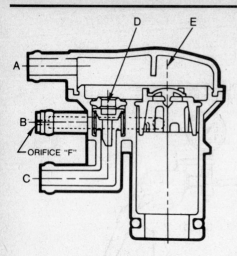

Fig. 17 Oil filler cap assembly

When there is no fresh air ventilation, blowby gases close Valve "D" to prevent oil pushover to air cleaner. This opens Valve "E" allowing blowby to the dirty side of cleaner, where they are induced into the engine induction system. Valve "D" also serves as a flame arrestor.

Valve "E" is designed to open at 3 inches. H_2O pressure and Valve "D" closes to prevent oil pushover at 2 inches H_2O crankcase pressure.

EXHAUST GAS RECIRCULATION SYSTEM

The Exhaust Gas Recirculation System (EGR) is designed to reintroduce small amounts of exhaust gas into the combustion cycle, thus reducing the generation of nitrous oxides. The amount of exhaust gas reintroduced and the timing of the cycle are controlled by various factors such as engine vacuum and temperature.

EGR Valve

The EGR valve is a vacuum-operated unit attached to the intake manifold, Fig. 18.

When the valve is open, exhaust gas is permitted to enter the intake manifold passages. When the valve is closed, internal or external sealing takes place, preventing the flow of exhaust gases into the intake passages.

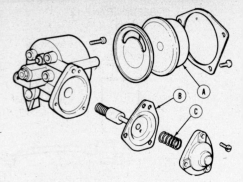

A—Heating Element C—Spring
B—Pulldown Diaphragm

Fig. 19 Electric choke assembly

Spacer Entry EGR System

Exhaust gases are routed directly from the exhaust manifold through a stainless steel tube.

ELECTRIC CHOKE

The electric choke, located in the choke housing, has a bimetal thermostatic coil which is mounted directly onto a heat conduction post. The fully-electric heating element heats the bimetal coil and controls the choke plate opening. The electric choke is connected to the wiring harness by plugging the female connector from the alternator harness into the choke housing. A vacuum diaphragm and spring controls the initial opening of the choke plate after the engine is started.

CRANKCASE VENTILATION SYSTEM

Fresh air is drawn from the engine air cleaner through Tube "A," through Valve "D" into the crankcase, Fig. 17. After mixing with blowby gases, the combined gases are drawn from the crankcase, up into the rocker cover into the engine intake manifold through Tube "B," where they are reburned in the process of combustion. Metering is achieved by Orifice "F."

Clutch & Transmission Section

CLUTCH PEDAL, ADJUST

No adjustment of the clutch pedal is necessary since an automatic adjusting device is installed on the clutch cable, Fig. 1.

CLUTCH, REPLACE

1. Remove transmission as outlined under "Transmission, Replace" procedure.
2. Remove clutch pressure plate bolts from flywheel and the pressure plate and disc.
3. Replace release bearing.
4. Place clutch disc on flywheel with centering mandrel and the flat side of the disc facing the flywheel.
5. Attach clutch pressure plate and tighten bolts.
6. Remove centering mandrel.
7. Install transmission.

A—Clutch Cable C—Toothed Segment
B—Pawl D—Tension Spring

Fig. 1 Automatic clutch cable adjusting device

TRANSMISSION, REPLACE

NOTE: Before removing transmission engage 4th gear to ensure correct adjustment of gear engagement.

1. Disconnect battery ground cable. Install engine support bar, Fig. 3, and clamp.
2. Remove speedometer driven gear.
3. Unhook clutch cable from release lever by pulling through the cable between lever and support.
4. Remove four upper transmission flange bolts.
5. Raise vehicle and remove plunger-retainer and drain oil through plunger-retainer-hole.
6. Remove shift rod bias spring and the shift rod from selector shaft gear. Loosen clamping screw and remove shift rod. Unhook spring be-

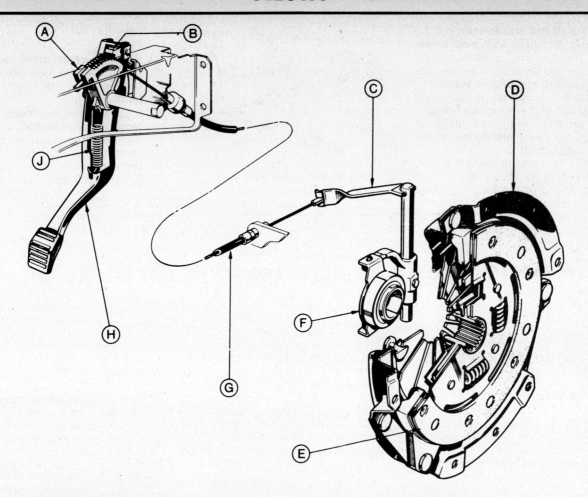

A—Automatic Adjusting Device
    Toothed Segment
B—Automatic Adjusting Device
    Pawl

C—Release Plate Release Shaft
    And Lever
D—Pressure Plate
E—Clutch Disc

F—Release Bearing With Fork
G—Clutch Cable
H—Clutch Pedal
J—Toothed Segment Tension Spring

Fig. 2 Clutch assembly

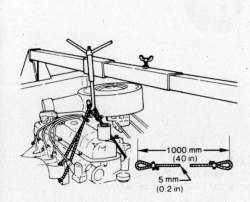

Fig. 3 Engine support bar installation

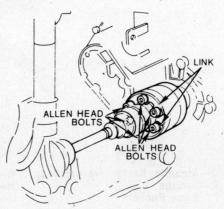

Fig. 4 Left hand drive shaft

Fig. 5 Left hand drive shaft coupling

1-443

tween shift rod and selector rail.

7. Remove stabilizer shift mechanism from transmission. Loosen and reposition two inner nuts on the rubber coupling and engine support.

Unscrew lock nut on stud and screw out of transmission housing with an Allen key. Allow stabilizer and screw to be suspended on engine support bar.

8. Remove left hand driveshaft, Fig. 4, by removing six allen head bolts at the coupling of the inner constant

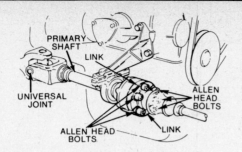

Fig. 6 Right hand drive shaft

velocity joint and the stubshaft, Fig. 5.

9. Remove right front axle shaft, Fig. 6, by removing six allen head bolts at the inner constant velocity joint.

10. Disconnect starter motor cable and remove starter motor.

11. Remove lower flange bolts from transmission and engine mounting.

12. Remove transmission from vehicle.

13. Reverse procedure to install.

Rear Axle, Rear Suspension & Brakes Section

REAR AXLE & SUSPENSION, REPLACE
Fig. 1

1. Raise and support vehicle.
2. Disconnect handbrake cable from the adjuster, Fig. 2.
3. Remove panhard rod bolt retaining rod to body, Fig. 3.
4. Remove bolt retaining panhard rod

to axle and the panhard rod.
5. Disconnect flexible brake lines. Plug ends to prevent loss of fluid.
6. Disconnect exhaust pipe from manifold.
7. Disconnect exhaust pipe from both rear supports and remove the exhaust pipe assembly.
8. Support rear axle with a suitable jack.

9. Remove bolts retaining lower arms to body.
10. Remove two stabilizer bar to body nuts.
11. Raise tailgate, raise parcel tray and remove plastic caps and shock absorber upper attachments.
12. Lower axle assembly and remove from vehicle, Fig. 1.
13. Reverse procedure to install.

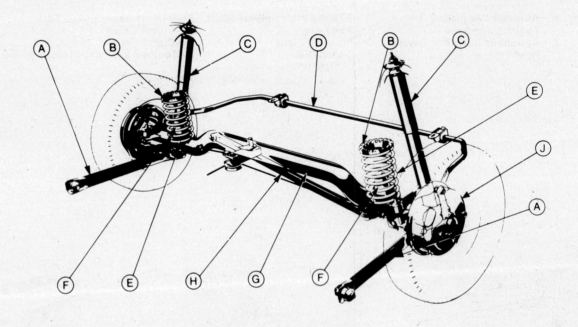

A—Lower Arms
B—Spring Insulator Pads
C—Shock Absorbers
D—Stabilizer Bar (Where Installed)
E—Springs
F—Bump Rubbers
G—Axle
H—Panhard Rod (Transverse)
J—Integral Hub And Brake Drum

Fig. 1 Rear axle & suspension assembly

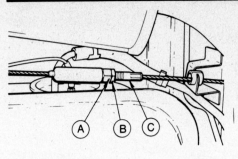

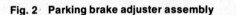

A—Adjuster   C—Handbrake Cable
B—Locknut

Fig. 2   Parking brake adjuster assembly

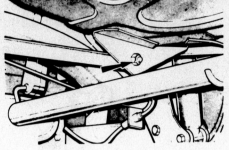

Fig. 3   Panhard rod to body bolt location

Fig. 4   Coil spring insulator

REAR AXLE, REPLACE
Fig. 1

1. Raise and support vehicle.
2. Remove rear wheels.
3. Slacken exhaust pipe from manifold.
4. Release exhaust pipe from rear end supports. Lower the exhaust pipe.
5. Remove bolt and disconnect panhard rod from axle, Fig. 3.
6. Disconnect handbrake cable at adjuster, Fig. 2.
7. Disconnect flexible brake lines from their axle locations. Install plugs to prevent fluid loss.
8. Support rear axle with a suitable jack.
9. Remove two bolts and disconnect shock absorber and stabilizer bar links lower mounts, if equipped, from axle.
10. Remove two bolts and the lower arms from axle.
11. Lower the axle and remove from vehicle.
12. Reverse procedure to install.

REAR WHEEL BEARINGS, ADJUST

1. Raise and support rear of vehicle.
2. Remove rear wheels.

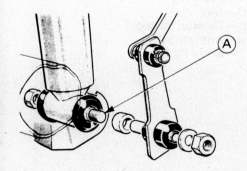

A—Shock Absorber Bolt

Fig. 5   Stabilizer bar attachment

3. Remove grease cup cotter pin and nut retainer.
4. Torque adjuster nut to 27 ft. lbs. while rotating hub. Back off adjusting nut 90°.
5. Install nut retainer, new cotter pin, and grease cup.

COIL SPRINGS, REPLACE

1. Raise and support vehicle.
2. Remove rear wheels.
3. Support rear axle with a suitable jack.
4. Raise tailgate, raise parcel tray and remove plastic cap and shock absorber upper attachment.
5. Remove lower arm bolt from axle.
6. Remove two stabilizer bar to body retaining nuts.
7. Lower the jack and remove spring and insulator, Fig. 4.
8. Reverse procedure to install.

LOWER ARMS, REPLACE

1. Raise and support vehicle.
2. Remove bolt retaining lower arm to body.
3. Remove bolt retaining lower arm to axle and the lower arm.
4. Reverse procedure to install.

STABILIZER BAR, REPLACE

1. Remove two bolts and nuts on each side of shock absorber bottom mounting and remove stabilizer bar, Fig. 5.

NOTE: The bolts also retain the shock absorber lower mountings and need not be removed.

---

2. Reverse procedure to install.

PANHARD ROD, REPLACE

1. Raise and support vehicle.
2. Remove bolt retaining rod to body, Fig. 6.
3. Remove bolt retaining rod to axle and the panhard rod, Fig. 6.

SHOCK ABSORBERS, REPLACE

1. Raise and support vehicle.
2. Remove rear wheels.
3. Support rear axle with a suitable jack.
4. Raise tailgate. Raise parcel tray and disconnect shock absorber upper attachments.
5. Remove locknut and bolt from shock absorber lower axle mounting.
6. Using a lever, remove shock absorber from locating peg.
7. Reverse procedure to install.

DISC BRAKE SERVICE
Brake Shoes, Replace, Fig. 7

Removal

1. Raise and support front of vehicle and remove wheel.
2. Remove retaining pins. Apply slight pressure to piston housing against caliper tension springs and slide out keys.
3. Remove caliper and suspend caliper using a suitable length of wire.
4. Remove brake shoes and anti-rattle clips.

Installation

1. Push piston into its bore, by applying pressure to the face of the pis-

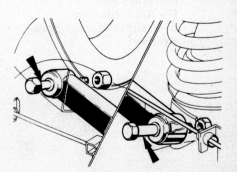

Fig. 6   Panhard rod bolt locations (Attachments)

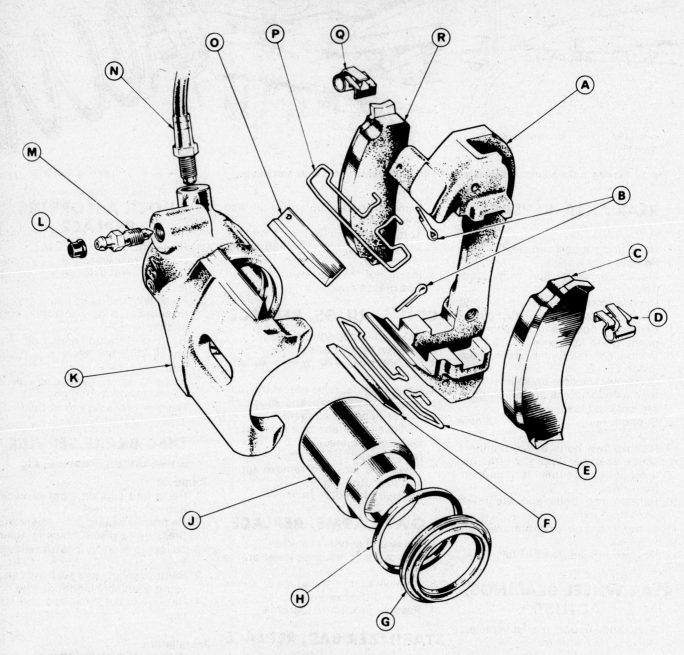

A—Pad Housing (Anchor Bracket)
B—Retaining Pins
C—Brake Pad
D—Antirattle Clip
E—Caliper Tension Spring
F—Key

G—Rubber Bellows
H—Piston Seal
J—Piston
K—Piston Housing
L—Dust Cap
M—Bleed Screw

N—Fluid Hose
O—Key
P—Tension Spring
Q—Antirattle Clip
R—Brake Pad

Fig. 7 Disc brake assembly

ton, making sure that the face of the piston is not damaged.

2. Install new brake shoes and new anti-rattle clips, ensuring that both are correctly placed. Anti-rattle clips must be installed on the top of brake pad.
3. Install caliper.
4. Apply pressure to caliper against caliper tension springs and slide in new keys. Be sure that retaining pin holes in key and piston housing are aligned.
5. Insert new retaining pins from disc side and secure in place.
6. Operate brake several times to bring shoes into correct adjustment.

Caliper, Replace, Fig. 7

Removal

1. Raise and support front of vehicle and remove wheel.
2. Detach brake fluid flexible hose from caliper and install line plug. Remove caliper retaining bolts and the caliper.

Installation

1. Replace caliper assembly and torque two retaining bolts to 37-45 ft. lbs.
2. Remove brake line plug, connect the flexible hose, and torque to 8-11 ft. lbs.
3. Bleed brake circuit.

Caliper Overhaul, Fig. 7

1. Remove piston rubber bellows.
2. Apply air pressure or low hydraulic pressure to the piston through the brake fluid inlet part to remove piston.

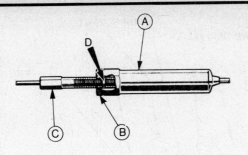

A—Adjuster   C—Handbrake Cable
B—Locknut   D—Machined Section

Fig. 8   Parking brake adjuster

3. Remove piston from annular groove in the piston housing.
4. Install piston seal in annular groove in piston housing.
5. Lubricate piston with clean brake fluid and push piston into bore as far as possible.
6. Install piston rubber bellows between piston housing and piston.

PARKING BRAKE, ADJUST

1. Raise and support vehicle.
2. Loosen adjuster locknut 'B' and rotate cable adjuster 'A' to slacken cable 'C', Fig. 8.
3. Be sure handbrake is in "Off" position. Tighten cable by rotating adjuster until the slack is removed from cable. A noticeable change in cable tension will be apparent when slack is removed and handbrake levers just begin to move off the back stops.
4. After handbrake levers have just

begun to move, rotate adjuster three complete turns and secure locknut.

NOTE: When adjustment is completed, machined groove 'D' must not protrude past locknut 'B', Fig. 8.

MASTER CYLINDER, REPLACE

1. Disconnect battery ground cable.
2. Siphon brake fluid out from reservoir and disconnect brake lines, then install plugs. Disconnect wires from switch in differential valve.
3. Remove spring clip, clevis pin and bushing from pedal and master cylinder pushrod.
4. Remove two nuts and spring washers securing master cylinder to the bulkhead and the master cylinder.
5. Reverse procedure to install.

POWER BRAKE UNIT, REPLACE

1. Remove spring clip and clevis pin securing actuating rod to brake pedal.
2. Disconnect hose from clip and the vacuum hose from check valve.
3. Disconnect brake lines and install line plugs.
4. Remove two nuts and washers securing master cylinder to power brake unit. Remove master cylinder.
5. Remove four nuts and washers securing power brake unit to mounting brackets and the power brake unit.
6. Reverse procedure to install.

Front Suspension & Steering Section

LEFT-HAND DRIVESHAFT, REPLACE

Removal

Fig. 1

1. Remove wheel center cap and the hub retaining nut and washer.
2. Raise and support vehicle and remove wheel.
3. Remove six allen head bolts and linked washers that secure inner C.V. joint to stubshaft flange, Fig. 2.
4. Remove brake caliper retaining bolts and hang caliper with wire.
5. Remove disc and hub assembly. If hub is tight fit on driveshaft, pull hub and disc assembly, using suitable puller.
6. Remove cotter pin and castellated

nut from tie rod ball joint.
7. Using Tool T77F-3290-A, tie-rod end remover adapter with main tool: Tool 3290-C, separate ball joint.
8. Remove lower arm to body mounting retaining bolt and the inner end of arm from mountpoint. Also, remove ball joint to carrier clinch bolt and disconnect outer end of lower arm assembly. Take care not to strain tie bar forward mounting by pushing rear end of bar downwards.
9. Remove driveshaft assembly from spindle carrier and vehicle.

Installation

Fig. 1

1. Clean inner C.V. joint removing all old grease. Repack joint with ap-

proximately 1.5 oz. of grease (Ford Specification: ESA-M1C75-B).
2. Insert outer end of driveshaft through spindle carrier.
3. Loosely connect six allen head bolts securing inner C.V. joint to stubshaft, Fig. 3.
4. Connect lower arm.
   Reconnect ball joint to spindle carrier and install clinch bolt. Position inner end of lower arm in body mounting and retaining bolt and nut.
5. Reconnect tie-rod ball joint to steering arm, install castellated nut and cotter pin.
6. Push hub and disc assembly onto splined end of driveshaft as far as possible. Assemble front hub in-

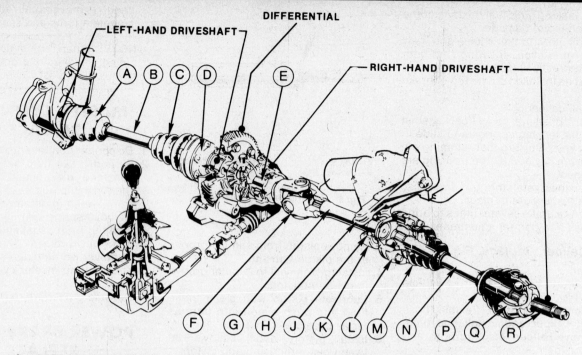

A— LEFT HAND OUTER C.V. JOINT
B— LEFT HAND INTERMEDIATE DRIVESHAFT
C— LEFT HAND INNER C.V. JOINT
D— LEFT HAND STUBSHAFT
E— RIGHT HAND STUBSHAFT
F— UNIVERSAL JOINT
G— PRIMARY SHAFT
H— PRIMARY SHAFT
    BEARING SUPPORT BRACKET

J— PRIMARY SHAFT SUPPORT BEARING
K— PRIMARY SHAFT SUPPORT
    BEARING HOUSING
L— RIGHT-HAND INNER C.V. JOINT
M— BELLOWS
N— RIGHT-HAND INTERMEDIATE
    DRIVESHAFT
P— BELLOWS
Q— RIGHT-HAND OUTER C.V. JOINT
R— SPINDLE SHAFT

Fig. 1 Drive shaft assembly

staller to driveshaft. Pull hub and disc assembly onto driveshaft and remove tool.

NOTE: Do not attempt to drive hub onto driveshaft as this will damage the constant velocity joint.

7. Loosely install plain washer and new hub retaining nut.
8. Install brake caliper and secure with two retaining bolts.
9. Torque six allen head bolts to 28-32 ft. lbs.
10. Install wheel and lower vehicle.
11. Torque hub retaining nut to 180-200 ft. lbs.
12. Stake nut into slot in driveshaft with pin pinch.
13. Install wheel center cap.

RIGHT-HAND DRIVESHAFT, REPLACE
Removal
Fig. 1
1. Remove wheel center cap and the hub retaining nut and washer.
2. Raise and support vehicle.

3. Remove six allen head bolts and linked washers that secure inner C.V. joint to primary shaft flange, Fig. 4.
4. Remove wheel and reinstall two wheel bolts.

NOTE: Bolts should be reinstalled to prevent any strain being placed on the disc retaining screw caused by the tendency for the disc to turn relative to the hub when releasing or tightening the hub nut.

5. Apply foot brake to hold hub and remove hub retaining nut and plain washer.
6. Release foot brake and remove wheel bolts.
7. Remove two bolts securing primary shaft bearing housing to bracket. Allow primary shaft and bearing assembly to rest clear of its location.
8. Remove driveshaft assembly from spindle carrier and vehicle.

Installation
Fig. 1
1. Clean inner C.V. joint removing all old grease. Repack joint with ap-

proximately 1.5 oz. of grease (Ford Specification ESA-M1C75-B).
2. Insert outer end of driveshaft through spindle carrier.
3. Loosely install six allen head bolts securing inner C.V. joint to primary shaft, Fig. 3.
4. Align primary shaft bearing housing to support bracket and secure with two bolts.
5. Loosely install plain washer and new hub retaining nut.
6. Torque six allen head bolts to 28-32 ft. lbs.
7. Install road wheel and lower vehicle.
8. Torque hub retaining nut to 180-200 ft. lbs.
9. Stake nut into slot in driveshaft with pin punch.
10. Install wheel center cap.

PRIMARY SHAFT, REPLACE
Removal
Fig. 1
1. Raise and support vehicle.
2. Remove six allen head bolts and linked washers that secure inner

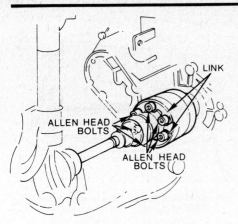

Fig. 2　Left hand drive shaft

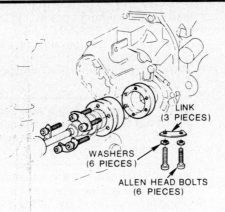

Fig. 3　Allen head bolts installation

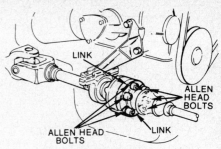

Fig. 4　Right hand drive shaft

constant velocity to primary shaft flange.

NOTE: To avoid strain being applied to the constant velocity joints, the driveshaft should be supported, using a length of wire, to the vehicle underbody.

3. Remove two bolts, securing primary shaft bearing housing to bracket. Guide primary shaft and universal joint from stubshaft.
4. Loosen bearing support bracket at engine block.

NOTE: It is necessary to loosen this bracket to ensure that bearing is not subjected to any stress of misalignment upon reassembly.

5. Clean inner constant velocity joint removing all old grease. Repack joint with approximately 1.5 oz. of grease (Ford Specification ESA-M1C75-B).

Installation
Fig. 1

1. Align primary shaft and universal

joint assembly to stubshaft and slide into position. Secure primary shaft by aligning bearing housing to support bracket and securing with two bolts.
2. Align inner constant velocity joint to primary shaft flange and secure with six allen head bolts. Torque bolts to 28-32 ft. lbs.
3. Tighten bearing support bracket at engine block.
4. Lower vehicle.

WHEEL BEARINGS, REPLACE
Removal

1. Raise and support vehicle.
2. Remove wheel and reinstall two wheel bolts.

NOTE: The wheel bolts should be reinstalled to prevent any strain being placed on the disc retaining screw, caused by the tendency for the disc to turn relative to the hub when releasing or tightening the hub nut.

3. Apply foot brake to hold driveshaft and remove front hub retaining nut and plain washer.
4. Release foot brake and remove wheel bolts.
5. Remove brake caliper retaining bolts and hang caliper free of brake disc.
6. Remove hub and disc assembly. If hub is tight, pull hub and disc assembly using a suitable legged puller, Fig. 5.
7. Remove cotter pin and castellated nut from tie rod ball joint.
8. Separate tie-rod ball joint from tie-rod.
9. Remove lower arm to body mounting retaining bolt and pull down inner end of arm.
10. Remove ball joint to spindle carrier clinch bolt, and separate ball joint from knuckle.
11. Remove top mount to apron panel retaining bolts, Fig. 6.
12. Support driveshaft at outer constant velocity and pull knuckle clear of driveshaft.
13. Remove knuckle and suspension assembly from vehicle.
14. Mount suspension assembly in a soft jawed vise.
15. Using suitable pliers, carefully pull out dust shield from groove in knuckle.

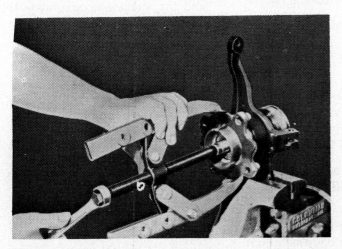

Fig. 5　Hub removal

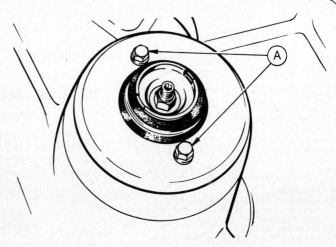

Fig. 6　Top mount

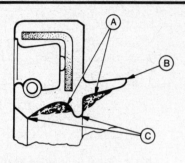

A—Apply Grease Here On Assembly, Half To Fully Filled
B—Axial Sealing Lip
C—Radial Sealing Lips

Fig. 7 Grease retainer installation

16. Using seal remove Tool No. T77F-6700-A and slide hammer T50T-100-A remove inner and outer grease retainers.
17. Remove bearings.
18. Carefully drive out bearing cups, using a flat ended punch. Make sure punch is in good condition and take care not to raise burrs on cups seats as this may prevent new cups from seating properly.
19. Clean knuckle, removing all old grease.

Installation

1. Drive new bearing cup into knuckle.
2. Check that bearing cup is correctly seated by turning over knuckle and viewing cup seating face from rear.
3. Repeat installation operations for remaining bearing cup.
4. Pack new bearings with suitable grease, ensuring that the cavities between rollers are filled.

NOTE: Grease must not be placed in the cavities between the inner and outer bearings and between the grease retainers and bearings.

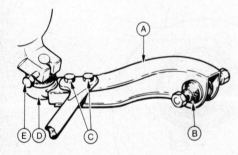

A—Lower Arm
B—Lower Arm To Body Mounting Bolt
C—Ball Joint And Tie Bar To Lower Arm Retaining Bolts
D—Lower Arm Ball Joint
E—Ball Joint To Spindle Carrier Clinch Joint

Fig. 9 Lower arm & ball joint assembly

Use high melting point lithium grease such as ESA-M1C75-B.
5. Insert bearing in one side of axle shaft carrier.
6. Drive grease retainer into knuckle, Fig. 7.

NOTE: Before installing a new seal, grease the cavities between the sealing lips, to provide a lubricant reservoir for the lips, Fig. 8.

7. Repeat steps 5 and 6 for remaining bearing and grease retainer.
8. Using block of wood, gently tap dust shield into position in groove in inner face of knuckle. Be sure cut out in shield is at bottom, and aligned with ball joint location.
9. Lightly lubricate driveshaft splines with grease.
10. Position knuckle and suspension assembly in vehicle, passing knuckle over end of driveshaft.
11. Install top mount in apron panel reinforcement and secure with two bolts.
12. Connect lower arm ball joint to knuckle and install clinch bolt, Fig. 9.
13. Install lower arm inner pivot bolt.
14. Connect tie rod to steering arm on knuckle. Secure with castellated nut and new cotter pin.
15. Push hub and disc assembly onto splined end of driveshaft as far as possible. Install plain washer and new nut to draw hub onto splines.
16. Loosely install plain washer and new hub retaining nut.
17. Install brake caliper and secure with two retaining bolts.
18. Install two wheel bolts to brake disc and hub assembly.
19. Apply foot brake.
20. Torque hub retaining nut to 180-200 ft. lbs.
21. Stake retaining nut into slot in driveshaft with pin punch, Fig. 10.
22. Release brakes.
23. Remove wheel bolts and install wheel.
24. Lower vehicle.

BALL JOINT, REPLACE
Removal

1. Raise and support vehicle.
2. Remove ball joint to axle shaft carrier clinch bolt.
3. Remove the two ball joint to lower arm retaining nuts, and the ball joint, Fig. 9.

Installation

1. Position ball joint on lower arm retaining bolts and secure loosely.

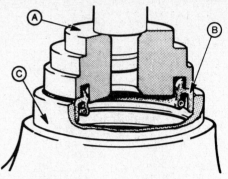

A—Tool Number T77F—1217—B
B—Grease Retainer
C—Knuckle

Fig. 8 Grease retainer

2. Engage stud of ball joint in axle shaft carrier and secure, using clinch bolt and nut.
3. Fully tighten ball joint to lower arm retaining nuts.
4. Lower vehicle.

McPHERSON STRUT, REPLACE
Removal

1. Raise and support vehicle and remove wheel.
2. Remove two bolts retaining suspension strut to knuckle, Fig. 11.
3. Remove two top-mount-to-apron-panel retaining bolts, Fig. 6, and remove suspension strut and spring assembly from vehicle.

Installation

1. Position suspension unit and spring assembly in vehicle and secure with top-mount-to-apron-panel retaining bolts.
2. Connect lower end of suspension strut to knuckle.

NOTE: In production, the relationship between the suspension strut and the knuckle is accurately set

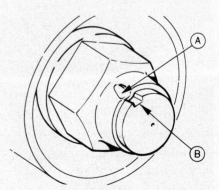

A—Stake In Using Pin Punch
B—Slot In Driveshaft

Fig. 10 Staking hub retaining nut

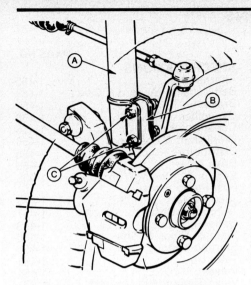

A—Suspension Strut C—Strut To Spindle
B—Knuckle   Carrier Retaining Nuts

Fig. 11 McPhereson strut attachment

using a jig. As this jig is not available in service, the relationship between the strut and knuckle can only be restored if new precision ground bolts are installed in place of standard production bolts. It is therefore essential to check the type of bolts used. If necessary, install new bolts: Part No. E800622-S72.

3. Install wheel and lower vehicle.
4. Check toe-in.

Overhaul

1. Assemble spring compressor to spring and compress spring to release tension from top mount assembly.
2. Remove top mount retaining nut with offset box end wrench. Metric Allen wrench is inserted through hole in tool while strut top nut is turned.
3. Disassemble top mount assembly.
4. Separate spring from strut.
5. Assemble spring and new strut.
6. Assemble top mount components to strut. Ensure correct assembly sequence, Fig. 12.
7. Install top mount retaining nut.
8. Release spring compressors, ensuring spring ends seat correctly in shaped part of spring.

STEERING GEAR, REPLACE
Removal

1. Set steering gear in straight ahead position.
2. Raise and support vehicle.
3. Remove clinch bolt securing steering gear pinion to lower steering shaft.
4. Remove cotter pins and slacken castellated nuts securing tie-rod outer ball joints to steering arms on spindle carriers.
5. Using Adapter, Tool No. T77F-3290-A, separate ball joints from steering arms and remove castellated nuts.
6. Bend back lock tabs. Remove steering gear retaining bolts and clamps and the steering gear from vehicle.
7. Remove tie-rod ends and locknuts, noting number of turns required and disconnect mounting clamp rubber insulators from rack tube.

Installation

1. Mount locknuts and tie-rod ends, screwing them on the same number of turns required to remove them. Install rack tube mounting insulators.
2. Check steering wheel for straight-ahead position.

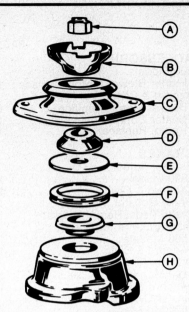

A—Nut   E—Thrust Washer
B—Retainer   F—Rubber Seal
C—Top Mount   G—Phenolic Resin Bearing
D—Spacer   H—Upper Spring Seat

Fig. 12 Top mount assembly

3. Set steering gear in straight-ahead position.
4. Locate steering gear in vehicle and engage steering gear pinion in steering shaft.
5. Secure steering gear with retaining clamps, new lock tabs and bolts. Bend up lock tabs.
6. Assemble tie-rod ends to steering arms. Install castellated nuts and tighten. Install new cotter pins.
7. Tighten steering shaft lower to steering gear pinion with clamp and clamp bolt.
8. Lower vehicle.
9. Check toe-in.
10. Check position of steering wheel.

HONDA

GENERAL ENGINE SPECIFICATIONS

Year	Model	Engine	Carburetor	Bore and Stroke	Piston Displacement, Cubic Inches	Compression Ratio	Maximum Brake H.P. @ R.P.M.	Maximum Torque H.P. @ R.P.M.	Normal Oil Pressure Pounds
1972	600	2—36.5 (598cc)	—	2.91 x 2.74 (74 x 69.6mm)	36.5 (0.60 Ltr.)	8.3	36 @ 6000	31.8 @ 4000	①
1973-74	Civic	4—71.4 (1170cc)	2 Barrel	2.76 x 2.99 70 x 76mm	71.4	8.3	—	—	50-58
1975	Civic	4—76 (1236cc)	2 Barrel	2.83 x 2.99 (72 x 76mm)	75.5 (1.2 Ltr.)	8.1	52 @ 5000	—	48-58③
1975-76	Civic CVCC	4—91 (1487cc)	3 Barrel	2.91 x 3.41 (74 x 86.5mm)	90.8 (1.5 Ltr.)	②	53 @ 5000	68 @ 3000	48-58③
1976-77	Accord	4—98 (1600cc)	3 Barrel	2.91 x 3.66 (74 x 93mm)	97.6 (1.6 Ltr.)	8.0	—	—	54-60③
1977	Civic CVCC	4—90.8 (1487cc)	3 Barrel	2.91 x 3.41 (74 x 86.5mm)	90.8 (1.5 Ltr.)	7.9	60 @ 5000	77 @ 3000	48-58③

—Not Available
① —Oil pump delivery; Manual trans., 3.28 qts./min., Auto. trans., 5.8 qts./min.
② —Sedan, 8.1; Station Wagons, 7.7.
③ —At 3000 R.P.M.

TUNE UP SPECIFICATIONS

The following specifications are published from the latest information available. This data should be used only in the absence of a decal affixed in the engine compartment.

▲Before removing wires from distributor cap, determine location of the No. 1 wire in cap, as distributor position may have been altered from that shown at the end of this chart.

Year	Model	Spark Plug Type	Spark Plug Gap	Distributor Point Gap Inch	Distributor Dwell Angle Deg.	Firing Order Fig.	Ignition Timing Timing BTDC	Ignition Timing Mark Fig.	Carburetor Adjustments Hot Idle Speed Std. Trans.	Carburetor Adjustments Hot Idle Speed Auto. Trans.	Carburetor Adjustments Idle "CO"% Std. Trans.	Carburetor Adjustments Idle "CO"% Auto. Trans.
1972	600	NGK B8ES	.030	.014	90	—	10°	A	1150	950D	—	—
1973-74	Civic	NGK B6ES	.030	.020	49—55	H	①	B	800	750	—	—
1975	CVCC	NGK B6ES	.030	.020	49—55	I	④	⑨	850③	750③	.1—.4	.1—.4
	Civic	NGK B6ES	.030	.020	49—55	H	7°	—	—	—	—	—
1976	CVCC	NGK B6EB	.030	.020	49—55	I	⑤	⑩	800②	700③	.4	.4
	Civic	—	.030	.020	49—55	H	7°	—	—	—	—	—
	Accord	NGK B6EB	.030	.020	49—55	I	⑥	⑪	800②	700③	.4	.4
1977	Civic CVCC	NGK B6EB	.030	.020	49—55	I	⑦	⑩	800②	700③	.4	.4
	Accord	NGK B6EB	.030	.020	49—55	I	⑥	⑪	800②	700③	.4	.4
1978	Civic 1200	—	.030	.020	49—55	H	2°	—	—	—	—	—
	Civic CVCC	—	.030	.020	49—55	I	⑧	—	—	—	—	—
	Accord	—	.030	.020	49—55	I	⑧	—	—	—	—	—

—Not Available
① —With idle retard disconnected, 5° BTDC; with idle retard connected, TDC.
② —With cooling fan on.
③ —With headlights on.
④ —Manual trans., TDC; Auto. trans., 3°ATDC.
⑤ —All manual trans. & sedans with auto. trans., 2 BTDC; Wagons with auto. trans., TDC.
⑥ —Manual trans., 2° BTDC; Auto. trans., TDC.
⑦ —Exc. Calif. & High altitude, 6° BTDC: Calif. exc. wagons with auto. trans., 2° BTDC; Wagons with auto. trans., TDC; High altitude exc. auto. trans., 2 BTDC; Auto. trans., TDC.
⑧ —Exc. Calif., 6° BTDC; Calif., 2° BTDC.
⑨ —Auto. trans., Fig. D; Manual trans., Fig. C.
⑩ —Manual trans., Fig. E; Auto. trans. exc. wagons, Fig. F; Wagons, Fig. G.
⑪ —Auto. trans. Fig. E; Manual trans., Fig. G.

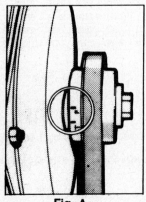

Fig. A

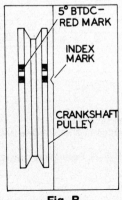

5° BTDC— RED MARK
INDEX MARK
CRANKSHAFT PULLEY

Fig. B

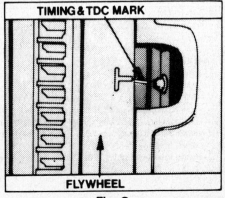

TIMING & TDC MARK
FLYWHEEL

Fig. C

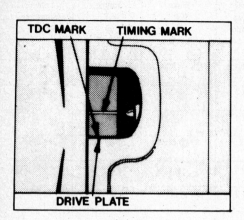

Fig. D

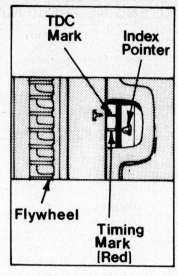

Fig. E

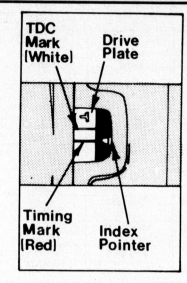

Fig. F

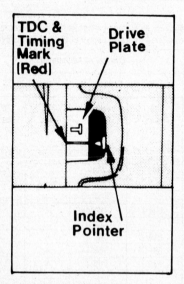

Fig. G

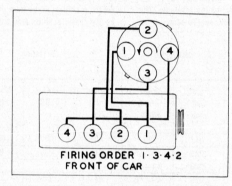

Fig. H

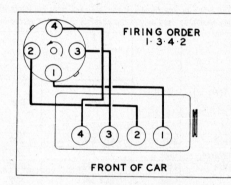

Fig. I

VALVE SPECIFICATIONS

Year	Model	Valve Lash			Valve Angles		Valve Spring Installed Height	Valve Spring Pressure Lbs. @ In.	Stem Clearance			Stem Diameter		
		Int.	Exh.	Aux.	Seat	Face			Intake	Exhaust	Auxiliary	Intake	Exhaust	Auxiliary
1972	600	.004	.004	—	①	45	②	③	.0004—.0016	.0016—.0028	—	.2591—.2594	.2579—.2583	—
1973-75	Civic	.006	.006	—	45	45	④	—	.0004—.0016	.0021—.0031	—	.2591—.2594	.2579—.2583	—
1975-77	Civic CVCC	.006	.006	.006	45	45	⑤	⑥	.0004—.0016	.0020—.0031	.0008—.0020	.2592—.2596	.2580—.2584	.2162—.2166
1976-77	Accord	.006	.006	.006	45	45	⑤	⑦	.0008—.0020	.0020—.0032	.0008—.0020	.2591—.2594	.2579—.2583	.2157—.2161

—Not Available
① —Intake, 58; Exhaust, 48.
② —Inner spring, 1.36; Outer spring, 1.44.
③ —Inner spring, 25.5 @ 1.36; Outer spring, 53.5 @ 1.44.
④ —Free length; Inner spring, 1.6535: Outer spring, 1.5728.
⑤ —Exc. auxiliary valve, Inner spring, 1.358: Outer spring, 1.437: Auxiliary valve, 0.906.
⑥ —Intake valve inner spring, 1.358 @ 20: Intake valve outer spring, 1.437 @ 16.8: Exhaust valve inner spring, 1.358 @ 27.5: Exhaust valve outer spring, 1.437 @ 57: Auxiliary valve, 0.906 @ 15.6.
⑦ —Intake valve inner spring, 1.024 @ 64: Intake valve outer spring, 1.094 @ 78: Exhaust valve inner spring, 1.024 @ 44: Exhaust valve outer spring, 1.108 @ 85: Auxiliary valve, 0.787 @ 23.

HONDA

DISTRIBUTOR SPECIFICATIONS

NOTE: If unit is checked on vehicle, double the RPM and degrees to get crankshaft figures.

Year	Model	Advance Starts	Intermediate Advance			Final Advance	Inches of Vacuum to Start Plunger	Max. Adv. Dist. Deg. @ Vacuum
			Centrifugal Advance @ R.P.M. of Distributor				Vacuum Advance	
1973-74	Civic	0 @ 550	5 @ 800	10 @ 1250	12.5 @ 1650	14.5 @ 2000	5.9	7.5 @ 12
1975	Civic ①	0 @ 700	5 @ 1000	10 @ 1600	15 @ 2000	17 @ 2250	5.9	9.5 @ 12.6
	Civic ②	0 @ 750	3 @ 1000	8 @ 1500	10 @ 1750	12 @ 2000	3.2	5 @ 5.3
	Civic CVCC ①	0 @ 600	5 @ 1100	7 @ 1200	10 @ 1600	14.5 @ 2000	10	4 @ 17
	Civic CVCC ②	0 @ 600	5 @ 1250	7 @ 1500	10 @ 1800	12.5 @ 2400	3.5 ⑤	5 @ 6 ⑤
1976	Civic CVCC ① ③	0 @ 600	5 @ 800	10 @ 1400	11 @ 1600	13 @ 1800	8	10 @ 15.8
	Civic CVCC ① ④	0 @ 600	5 @ 1100	7 @ 1500	10 @ 2000	12 @ 2400	8	10 @ 15.8
	Civic CVCC ②	0 @ 750	3 @ 1100	6 @ 1500	8 @ 1800	11 @ 2100	⑥	⑦
1976-77	Accord ①	0 @ 625	5.5 @ 900	7.5 @ 1125	10 @ 1500	13 @ 1940	7.8	10 @ 15.3
	Accord ②	0 @ 700	5 @ 1400	7.5 @ 1750	—	10.5 @ 2100	⑥	⑦
1977	Civic CVCC ① ③ ⑧	0 @ 700	5 @ 800	7 @ 1100	9 @ 1400	11 @ 1600	4.75	7.5 @ 8.25
	Civic CVCC ① ③ ⑨	0 @ 700	5 @ 800	7 @ 1200	10 @ 1500	12.5 @ 1800	7.8	7.5 @ 13
	Civic CVCC ① ④ ⑨	0 @ 700	5 @ 1100	7.5 @ 1500	10 @ 2000	12 @ 2400	7.8	7.5 @ 13
	Civic CVCC ② ⑨	0 @ 750	2.5 @ 1000	5 @ 1300	7 @ 1700	9 @ 1900	⑥	⑦
	Civic CVCC ⑧ ⑩	0 @ 700	5 @ 800	7 @ 1100	9 @ 1400	11 @ 1600	7.8	7.5 @ 13

—Not Available
① —Manual trans.
② —Auto. trans.
③ —Sedan.
④ —Station wagon.
⑤ —Vacuum retard.
⑥ —Vacuum advance, 6″; Vacuum retard, 3.2″.
⑦ —Vacuum advance, 6 @ 13.5; Vacuum retard, 3.5 @ 4.25.
⑧ —Exc. Calif. & high altitude.
⑨ —Calif. & high altitude.
⑩ —All station wagons & sedans with auto. trans. only.

ALTERNATOR & REGULATOR SPECIFICATIONS

Year	Model	Rated Hot Output	Field Current 12 Volts @ 80°F	Output @ 14 Volts		Model	Field Relay			Voltage Regulator		
				2000 RPM	5000 RPM		Air Gap In.	Point Gap In.	Closing Voltage	Air Gap In.	Point Gap In.	Voltage @ 125°F
1972	600	35	—	25	38	All	.020—.024	.016—.020	—	.032—.047	.016—.020	13.5—14.5
1973-74	Civic ①	35	—	22	37	All	—	—	—	.020	.016—.047	13.5—14.5
1973-74	Civic ②	40	—	32	43	All	—	—	—	.020	.016—.047	13.5—14.5
1975-77	Civic ③	35	2.5	25	35	All	—	—	—	.020	.016—.047	13.5—14.5
1975-77	Civic ④	45	2.5	35	45	All	—	—	—	.020	.016—.047	13.5—14.5
1976-77	Accord	53	—	42	57	All	—	—	—	.020	.016—.047	13.5—14.5

—Not Available
① —Up to chassis No. 1011758.
② —From chassis No. 1011759.
③ —Less A/C.
④ —With A/C.

STARTING MOTOR SPECIFICATIONS

Year	Model	Brush Spring Tension Lbs.	No Load Test			Torque Test		
			Amperes	Volts	R.P.M.	Amperes	Volts	Torque Ft. Lbs.
1972	600	—	50	10.6	6000	—	—	—
1973-75	Civic	3.52	70	12	7000	380	4.9	5.42
1975-76	Civic CVCC	3.18	90	11.5	3000	300	2.5	5.0
1976	Accord	3.18	90	11.5	3000	300	2.5	5.0
1977	Accord	3.18	90	11.5	5000	400	2.4	5.6
1977	Civic CVCC	—	—	—	—	—	—	—

—Not Available

Continued

HONDA

COOLING SYSTEM & CAPACITY DATA

Year	Model	Cooling Capacity Qts.		Radiator Cap Relief Pressure, Lbs.	Thermo. Opening Temp.	Fuel Tank Gals.	Engine Oil Refill Qts.	Transmission Oil			Diff. Oil Pts.
		Less A/C	With A/C					4 Speed Pts.	5 Speed Pts.	Auto. Trans. Pts.	
1972	600	—	—	—	—	6.86	2.6①	④	—	3.4	④
1973-77	Civic	4.2②	4.2②	11—15	203	10.6⑤	3.2	5.2	5.6	5.2	④
1976-77	Accord	6.0③	6.0③	11—14	203	13.2	3.2	—	5.6	5.2	④

—Not Available
①—With manual trans. 3.2 pts.
②—Including reserve tank.
③—Not including reserve tank.
④—Lubricated by engine oil.
⑤—Station wagon, 11 gals.

PISTON, PINS, RINGS, CRANKSHAFT & BEARINGS

Year	Model	Piston Clearance	Ring End Gap ①		Wrist-pin Diameter	Rod Bearings		Main Bearings			
			Comp.	Oil		Shaft Diameter	Bearing Clearance	Shaft Diameter	Bearing Clearance	Thrust on Bear. No.	Shaft End Play
1972	600	.0018—.0024	.0080	.0080	.6692	—	.0002—.0004	—	—	—	—
1973	Civic	.0012	.0079	.0079	—	1.5736—1.5748	.0008—.0015	1.9673—1.9685	.0009—.0017	4	.0039—.0138
1974-75	Civic	.0012	.0079	.0079	—	1.5748—1.5760	.0008—.0015	1.9688—1.9700	.0009—.0017	4	.0039—.0138
1975-77	Civic CVCC	.0012	.0079	.0079	.6693	1.6525—1.6535	.0008—.0015	1.9687—1.9697	.0010—.0021	4	.0039—.0138
1976-77	Accord	.0012	.0079	.0118		1.6526—1.6535	.0008—.0015	1.9687—1.9697	.0010—.0017	4	.0040—.0138

—Not Available
①—Fit rings in tappered bores for clearance listed in tightest portion of ring travel.

ENGINE TIGHTENING SPECIFICATIONS

★ Torque specifications are for clean and lightly lubricated threads only. Dry or dirty
threads produce increased friction which prevents accurate measurement of tightness.

Year	Model	Spark Plugs Ft. Lbs.	Cylinder Head Bolts Ft. Lbs.	Intake Manifold Ft. Lbs.	Exhaust Manifold Ft. Lbs.	Camshaft Carrier Bolts Ft. Lbs.	Connecting Rod Cap Bolts Ft. Lbs.	Main Bearing Cap Bolts Ft. Lbs.	Flywheel to Crankshaft Ft. Lbs.
1972	600	—	①	—	—	—	—	27	—
1973-74	Civic	9—12	②	13—17	13—17	13—16	18—21	27—31	34—38
1975-77	Civic CVCC	11—18	40—47	15—17	15—17	③	18—21	30—35	34—38
1976-77	Accord	11—18	40—47	15—17	15—17	③	18—21	30—35	34—38

—Not Available
①—10mm nut 20—23 ft. lbs., 6mm nut,
   6mm nut 6.5—8.7 ft. lbs.
②—Up to engine # EB1-1019949, 30-35 ft. lbs., from engine # EB1-1019950, 37-42 ft. lbs.
③—M6x1.0 Bolts 7—10 ft. lbs.;
   M8x1.0 Bolts 15—17 ft. lbs.

DRIVE AXLE SPECIFICATIONS

Year	Model	Carrier Type	Ring Gear & Pinion Backlash		Pinion Bearing Preload			Differential Bearing Preload		
			Method	Adjustment	Method	New Bearing Inch.-Lbs.	Used Bearings Inch-Lbs.	Method	New Bearings Inch-Lbs.	Used Bearings Inch-Lbs.
1972	600	①	—	.0039—.0158	—	④	④	—	—	—
1973-77	Civic	①	②	.003—.006	③	—	—	③	—	—
1976-77	Accord	①	②	.003—.006	③	—	—	③	—	—

—Not Available
①—Integral with transmission.
②—Thrust washers.
③—Snap ring.
④—Pinion gear side clearance, .0039"—.0079". Pinion to pinion shaft side clearance, .0012"—.0035".

Continued

BRAKE SPECIFICATIONS

Year	Model	Brake Drum Inside Diameter	Wheel Cylinder Bore Diameter			Master Cylinder Bore Diameter	Disc Brake Rotor Specifications				
			Disc Brakes	Front Drum Brakes	Rear Drum Brakes		Nominal Thickness	Minimum Thickness	Thickness Variation Parallelism	Run Out (T.I.R.)	Finish Micro-Inch
1972	600	7.087	1.688	1.0	.6248	①	.374	.299	—	—	—
1973	Civic	7.08	—	—	—	—	.378	.3543	.0028	.0064	—
1974	Civic	7.08	—	—	—	—	.378	.3543	.0028	.0064	—
1975-77	Civic	②	—	—	—	—	.378 ③	.354 ④	.0028	.0059	—
1976-77	Accord	7.08	—	—	—	—	.473	.449	.0006	.0059	—

—Not Available
①—Single, .748, Dual parallel, .551; Dual tandem, .750.
②—Exc. station wagon, 7.08; Station wagon, 7.87.
③—1976 Station Wagon .473".
④—1976 Station wagon .449".

WHEEL ALIGNMENT SPECIFICATIONS

Year	Model	Caster Angle, Degrees		Camber Angle, Degrees		King Pin Inclination	Toe-Out, Inch
		Limits	Desired	Limits	Desired		
1972	600	—	+1	—	+½	14.5°	.08
1973-75	Civic	—	+1¾	—	+½	8⁵⁵/₆₀	.04
1975	Civic CVCC ①	+1¼ to +2¼	+1¾	−½ to +½	0	8⁵⁵/₆₀	.04
	Civic CVCC ②	+1½ to +2½	+2	−½ to +½	0	8⁵⁵/₆₀	.04
1976	Civic CVCC ①	+1½ to +2½	+2	0 to +1	+½	9¹/₃	.04
1976-77	Civic CVCC ②	+½ to +1½	+1	0 to +1	+½	9¹/₃	.04
1976-77	Accord	+⁵/₆ to +2⁵/₆	+1⁵/₆	−¹/₃ to +1²/₃	+²/₃	12¹/₆	.04
1977	Civic CVCC ①	+1 to +2	+1½	0 to +1	+½	9¹/₃	.04

—Not Available
①—Sedan.
②—Station Wagon.

Electrical Section
Civic & Accord

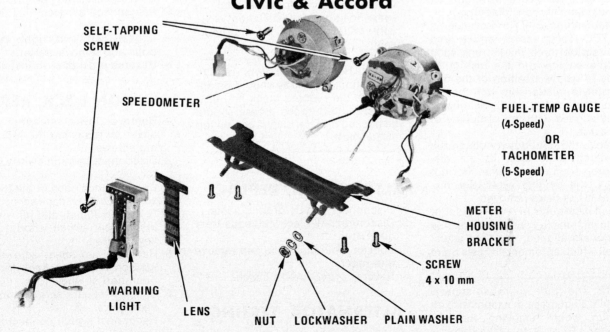

SELF-TAPPING SCREW

SPEEDOMETER

FUEL-TEMP GAUGE (4-Speed) OR TACHOMETER (5-Speed)

METER HOUSING BRACKET

SCREW 4 x 10 mm

WARNING LIGHT

LENS

NUT   LOCKWASHER   PLAIN WASHER

Fig. 1 Instrument cluster assembly. Civic

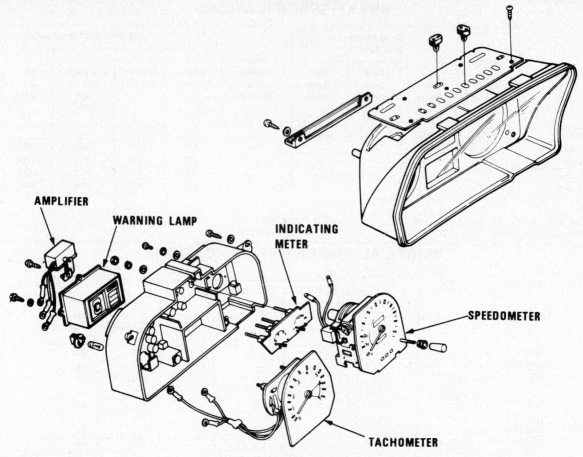

AMPLIFIER

WARNING LAMP

INDICATING METER

SPEEDOMETER

TACHOMETER

Fig. 2 Instrument cluster assembly. Accord

DISTRIBUTOR, REPLACE

1. Disconnect wiring from the distributor cap.
2. Disconnect vacuum hose from vacuum advance (advance/retard on Hondamatic models) diaphragm.
3. Rotate engine until No. 1 cylinder is at TDC compression stroke and then scribe three marks; one each on the engine and the distributor body to fix the position of the distributor in relationship with the engine, and another on the distributor body aligned with the centerline of the rotor.
4. Remove the hold-down nuts on the attaching plate and lift the distributor from the engine. Do not crank the engine after the distributor has been removed.
5. Install distributor in reverse order of removal, make sure that scribe marks are aligned, and then adjust dwell which automatically sets point gap.

NOTE: The rotor will rotate approximately 30 degrees in a clockwise direction when removing the distributor. Thus, if the distributor is disassembled or the rotor otherwise disturbed prior to installation, set it to the same 30 degrees away from the scribed mark and it will return to the scribed position when the drive and driven gears mesh. Further note that accurate scribing is vital, as rotor position for installation varies with model, equipment and point of sale.

NOTE: Honda distributors require lubrication. Cam lube should be applied to the rubbing block and cam lobes; multi-purpose grease should be packed into the plastic cap on top of the shaft.

ALTERNATOR, REPLACE

1. Disconnect battery ground cable.
2. Disconnect all electrical leads from alternator.
3. Loosen mounting bolts and remove alternator.
4. Reverse procedure to install.

ALTERNATOR, TESTING

Check continuity in the output (white) wire between the alternator and the 55 Amp main fuse. If there is continuity, the alternator is malfunctioning.

STARTER, REPLACE

1. Disconnect battery ground cable.
2. Disconnect all electrical leads at starter.
3. Loosen left and right mounting bolts and remove starter.
4. Reverse procedure to install.

IGNITION LOCK, REPLACE

1. Remove lower steering column cover by removing the four attaching screws.
2. Disconnect ignition switch connector.
3. Center punch each of the two shear screws. Drill out each screw, using a ¼-inch (6.35mm) drill bit.
4. Install new switch without ignition key inserted.
5. Hand tighten shear screws, insert ignition key, and check for proper operation of wheel lock.
6. Tighten shear screws until hex heads twist off.
7. Reconnect switch connector.
8. Position switch wiring and install lower steering column cover.

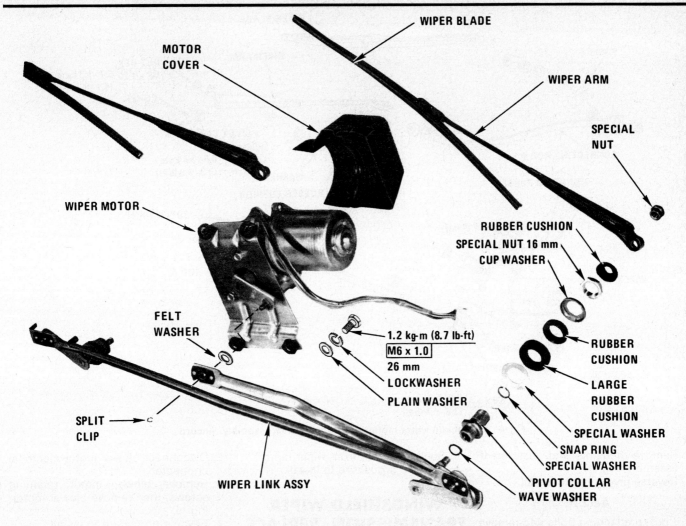

Fig. 3 Windshield wiper motor and transmission assembly. Civic

Labels in figure:
- MOTOR COVER
- WIPER BLADE
- WIPER ARM
- SPECIAL NUT
- WIPER MOTOR
- RUBBER CUSHION
- SPECIAL NUT 16 mm
- CUP WASHER
- FELT WASHER
- 1.2 kg-m (8.7 lb-ft)
- M6 x 1.0
- 26 mm
- LOCKWASHER
- PLAIN WASHER
- RUBBER CUSHION
- LARGE RUBBER CUSHION
- SPECIAL WASHER
- SNAP RING
- SPECIAL WASHER
- PIVOT COLLAR
- WAVE WASHER
- SPLIT CLIP
- WIPER LINK ASSY

COMBINATION SWITCH, REPLACE

1. Remove steering wheel upper cover, exposing the three horn wire connections, and set it aside without disconnecting the hazard warning switch and knob.
2. Disconnect the three horn leads at the column.
3. Remove emblem from center of steering wheel pad, exposing the steering wheel hub attaching bolt.
4. Loosen attaching bolt and remove steering wheel assembly and hub from steering shaft.
5. Remove turn signal cancel key and steering column washer, and remove the combination switch from the shaft. Then disconnect the combination switch connector.
6. Reverse procedure to install. Torque attaching bolt to 29 ft. lbs. (4.0 kg-m).

STOP LIGHT SWITCH, REPLACE

1. Disconnect wiring at switch.
2. Loosen locknut and remove switch.
3. Reverse procedure to install, allowing 0.039-0.196 in. (1-5mm) brake pedal free play.

NEUTRAL SAFETY SWITCH, REPLACE

1. Remove floor console cover.
2. Disconnect electrical connector.
3. Place shift lever in neutral.
4. Remove the two bolts holding switch to selector lever control assembly, and remove switch.
5. To install, position switch slider to neutral position.
6. Check that gear selector lever is in neutral.
7. Position switch with selector lever actuator rod inserted in its slot in switch slider.

8. Hook forward end of switch bracket over forward end of selector lever control assembly and tighten attaching bolts.
9. Plug in electrical connector.
10. Install console cover.

WIPER/WASHER SWITCH, REPLACE

1. Remove steering column upper cover.
2. Disconnect electrical connector.
3. Remove wiper/washer switch.
4. Reverse procedure to install.

INSTRUMENT CLUSTER, REPLACE

Civic

1. Loosen the three nuts on top and to the rear of main cluster housing.
2. Disconnect speedometer cable and electrical connectors.

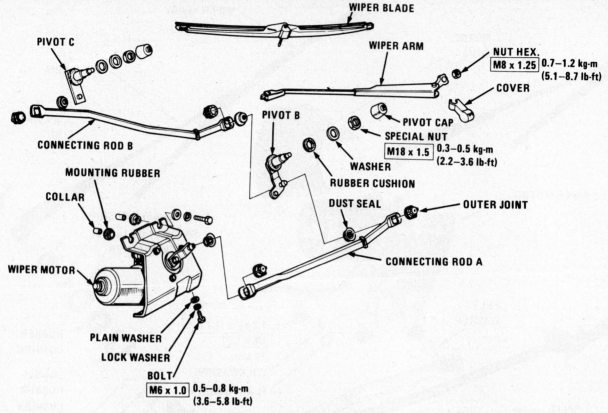

Fig. 4 Windshield wiper motor and transmission assembly. Accord

3. Remove housing and instrument assembly, Fig. 1.
4. Reverse procedure to install.

Accord

1. Loosen attaching bolts and remove steering column lower cover.
2. Remove the two nuts attaching steering column support bracket and allow the column to hang free.
3. Disconnect speedometer cable at instrument end, and remove instrument wire harness from body wire harness couplers.
4. Remove the two screws under dash and just above steering column support.
5. Pull instrument cluster out, squeeze lock tabs, and disconnect wire harness coupler from instrument assembly, Fig. 2.
6. Reverse procedure to install.

WINDSHIELD WIPER MOTOR, REPLACE

1. Unsnap clips carefully with a screwdriver and remove air scoop complete with hood sealing rubber.
2. Remove lower connecting rod from wiper motor pivot arm.
3. Disconnect wiring harness at motor.
4. Loosen the four attaching bolts and remove wiper motor together with its cover from cowl.

5. Separate cover from wiper motor.
6. Reverse procedure to install.

WINDSHIELD WIPER TRANSMISSION, REPLACE

Refer to Figs. 3 and 4, and replace all or part of the linkage in the sequence indicated.

RADIO, REPLACE
Accord

1. Remove the plate immediately under radio by loosening the two attaching screws.
2. Remove the three radio attaching screws.
3. Remove knobs from face plate of radio.
4. Remove heater fan switch knob.
5. Remove two heater lever knobs.
6. Remove heater control bezel.
7. Loosen the three center panel attaching screws and remove panel.
8. Disconnect lighter electrical leads.
9. Disconnect antenna, speaker and power leads, then remove radio.
10. Reverse procedure to install.

BLOWER MOTOR
Civic

1. Disconnect battery ground cable.

2. Disconnect blower motor electrical connector.
3. Remove blower motor retaining screws, then remove blower motor, Fig. 5.
4. Reverse procedure to install.

Accord

1. Disconnect battery ground cable.
2. Remove glove box by loosening three screws holding lower end of the box in position. Then carefully push down on box until it is free of the panel.
3. Remove fresh air control cable from its clamp, and disconnect wiring to the blower motor.
4. Loosen the three attaching bolts and remove blower assembly.
5. Remove blower motor from blower assembly by detaching the holding clip on left side of unit, Fig. 5.
6. Reverse procedure to install.

HEATER CORE
Civic

1. Disconnect battery ground cable and then drain coolant.
2. Disconnect inlet and outlet hoses at the water valve located on the left rear of the heater/blower unit, using rags to absorb coolant residue.
3. Disconnect the two defroster ducts.

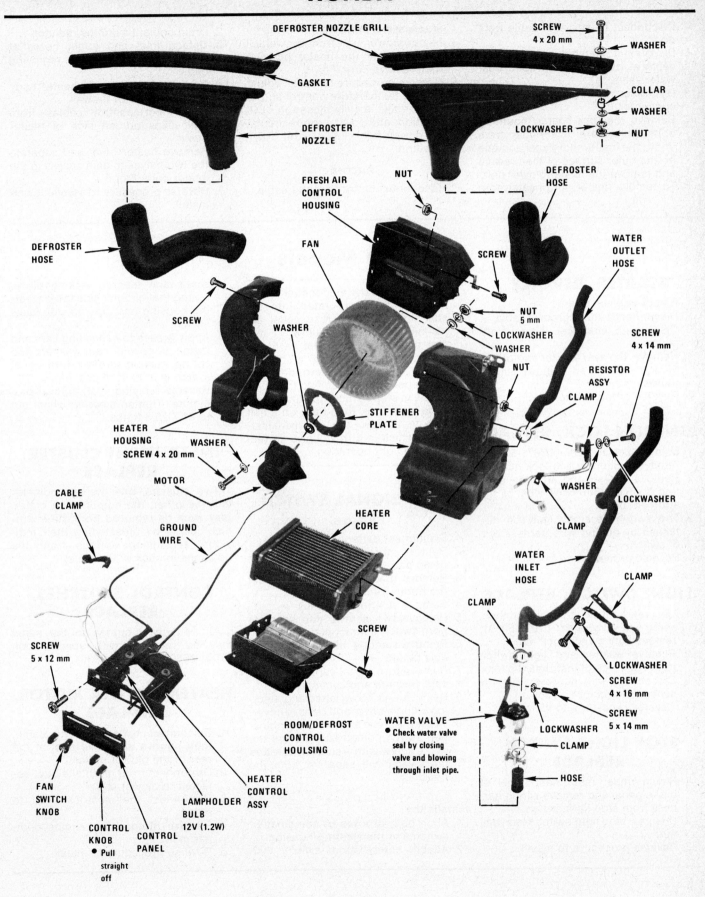

DEFROSTER NOZZLE GRILL

SCREW
4 x 20 mm

WASHER

COLLAR

WASHER

GASKET

LOCKWASHER — NUT

DEFROSTER
NOZZLE

DEFROSTER
HOSE

FRESH AIR
CONTROL
HOUSING

NUT

FAN

SCREW

WATER
OUTLET
HOSE

DEFROSTER
HOSE

SCREW

NUT
5 mm

LOCKWASHER

WASHER

SCREW
4 x 14 mm

WASHER

RESISTOR
ASSY

CLAMP

NUT

HEATER
HOUSING
SCREW 4 x 20 mm

STIFFENER
PLATE

WASHER

LOCKWASHER

MOTOR

WASHER

CABLE
CLAMP

GROUND
WIRE

HEATER
CORE

CLAMP

WATER
INLET
HOSE

CLAMP

CLAMP

LOCKWASHER
SCREW
4 x 16 mm

SCREW

SCREW
5 x 12 mm

ROOM/DEFROST
CONTROL
HOULSING

WATER VALVE
● Check water valve
seal by closing
valve and blowing
through inlet pipe.

LOCKWASHER
SCREW
5 x 14 mm

CLAMP

HOSE

FAN
SWITCH
KNOB

CONTROL
KNOB
● Pull
straight
off

CONTROL
PANEL

LAMPHOLDER
BULB
12V (1.2W)

HEATER
CONTROL
ASSY

Fig. 5   Heater assembly

1-461

4. Disconnect heater door cable from door.
5. Disconnect temperature control cable at its adjustment point near water valve.
6. Disconnect blower motor electrical connector.
7. Remove the four heater mounting bolts (three are accessible from under the instrument panel and one on the outer surface of the firewall) and remove the heater/blower unit.
8. To remove heater core heater core is accessible only after removing the heater/blower unit from the vehicle and separate the heater housing, then remove core, Fig. 5.
9. Reverse procedure to install, adjusting the temperature control so that water valve is fully closed in "LO" position, and so that the recirculating door is fully closed in the "REC" position.

Accord

1. Disconnect battery ground cable.
2. Drain coolant from the radiator.
3. Detach inlet and outlet hoses at their firewall junction by removing clips.
4. Remove nut attaching heater body at the exterior of firewall.
5. Disconnect control cables from their clips on left side of heater body.
6. Remove heater body and separate the two halves to gain access to the heater core, Fig. 5.
7. Reverse procedure to assemble and install.

600 Models

STARTER, REPLACE

1. Remove splash guard.
2. Disconnect battery ground cable.
3. Disconnect electrical wiring from starter.
4. Remove the two starter motor retaining bolts then remove starter motor.
5. Reverse procedure to install.

IGNITION LOCK, REPLACE

1. Using special tool, 07071-56801, remove ignition switch lock nut.
2. Remove washer and also the ignition switch from back side of instrument panel.
3. The switch assembly may be detached by pulling wire harness out of switch.
4. Reverse procedure to install.

LIGHT SWITCH, REPLACE

1. Unscrew light switch knob and then, using special tool No. 07076-59301, remove light switch lock nut.
2. Remove washer and light switch from back side of instrument panel.
3. Disconnect wire harness from the switch and remove switch.
4. Reverse procedure to install.

STOP LIGHT SWITCH, REPLACE

1. Reach under instrument panel at brake pedal and remove wiring harness from stop light switch.
2. Unscrew stop light switch from lock nut.
3. Reverse procedure to install.

NOTE: The brake malfunction warning light is incorporated into the stop light circuit. Brake pedal adjustment height must allow 2-3 mm free play and there must be 5 mm clearance between the stop light switch and the master cylinder push rod to permit the specified free play. Screw in stop light switch until there is no clearance, then back off a half turn to achieve the desired clearance, which in turn will give correct warning light operation.

TURN SIGNAL SWITCH
Removal

1. Disconnect battery ground cable
2. Remove three screws attaching crash pad.
3. Remove the screw and disconnect the horn switch lead.
4. Remove steering shaft nut.
5. Remove two screws and separate horn switch contact plate.
6. Remove steering wheel, using suitable puller.
7. Remove turn signal cancelling cam, cam washers and cam spring.
8. Remove one screw attaching steering column cover and remove cover.
9. Loosen screw attaching combination switch completely, tap the top of the screw with a screwdriver, and the switch will separate from the housing.

Installation

1. Align both grooves of combination switch and the steering housing.
2. Attach combination switch with screw and tapered locking piece, noting that circular side faces steering housing and tapered side faces switch.
3. Apply grease to cancelling cam and install along with cam washers and spring, making sure that turn signal switch is in neutral position.
4. Reverse remainder of removal procedure. Tighten steering wheel nut to 21.7-25.3 ft.-lbs.

INSTRUMENT CLUSTER, REPLACE

Two clusters, one the speedometer and the other, the combination meter, may each be removed from the instrument panel by unfastening their individual tensioning springs from the housings in back of the panel.

CONTROL SWITCHES, REPLACE

All switches mounted in the panel may be removed with special tool, 07071-56801 or 07076-59301.

HEATER BLOWER MOTOR, REPLACE

1. Disconnect battery ground cable, then remove air intake duct at the rear of the blower motor.
2. Disconnect front air intake duct adjacent to blower motor.
3. Disconnect the electrical lead to motor.
4. Remove motor from engine compartment.
5. Reverse procedure to install.

Engine Section

Accord & Civic

ENGINE, REPLACE

Civic

1. Disconnect battery ground cable, then raise and support vehicle and remove both front wheels.
2. Remove both headlight rims and turn signal and parking lights.
3. Remove grille moulding, windshield washer hose and hood.
4. On vehicles with automatic transmission, remove the cooler line bolts.
5. Drain coolant, then disconnect the four coolant hoses.
6. Disconnect connectors from fan motor and temperature sensor, then remove hose from radiator to overflow tank and remove radiator.
7. Disconnect all hoses, wires, cables, lines and hoses as necessary from engine and transmission.
8. Disconnect battery ground cable from transmission bracket, then remove cable.
9. Remove starter motor and distributor.
10. On vehicles with automatic transmission, remove console and disconnect control cable.
11. Remove the upper torque arm.
12. Remove fender well shield from under right fender, then remove speedometer cable retaining bolt and disconnect speedometer cable.
13. Remove pin, collar and drive gear from the speedometer cable assembly.
14. Disconnect stabilizer bar on both sides.
15. Remove bolt holding lower control arm to sub-frame on both sides.
16. Remove the forward mounting nut on the radius rod on both sides.
17. Pry the constant velocity joint out approximately 0.5 in. (12.7mm) and pull the sub-axle out of transmission case, then repeat on opposite side.
18. Remove the center beam support by loosening six bolts.
19. On vehicles with manual transmission, drive out pin securing the shift linkage.
20. Disconnect the lower torque arm from the transmission.
21. On vehicles with automatic transmission, remove the bolt securing the control cable stay, then loosen the two U-bolt nuts and pull control cable out of its housing.

22. Disconnect exhaust pipe from manifold.
23. Remove rear engine mount.
24. Attach a suitable hoist to engine, then raise hoist just enough to put tension on engine.
25. Remove the nut securing the front engine mount.
26. Remove the three bolts and push the left engine support into the shock mount bracket as far as it will go.
27. Lift engine slowly, remove the forward engine mount, and then lift engine clear of car.
28. Reverse procedure to install, noting the following torque values:
    a. Upper torque arm bolts — 55 ft. lbs. (7.5 kg-m).
    b. ATF cooler line bolts — 18 ft. lbs. (1.5 kg-m).
    c. Engine heat shield bolts — 7 ft. lbs. (1.0 kg-m).
    d. Speedometer drive cable bolt — 10 ft. lbs. (1.2 kg-m).

NOTE: During reinstallation, align hole in holder with transmission case hole.

    e. Torque arm to transmission — 7 ft. lbs. (1.0 kg-m).
    f. Hondamatic control cable U-bolt nuts — 7 ft. lbs. (1.0 kg-m).
    g. Rear engine mount nut — 29 ft. lbs. (4.0 kg-m).
    h. Front engine mount to engine bolts — 29 ft. lbs. (4.0 kg-m); front engine mount to frame bolts — 16 ft. lbs. (2.2 kg-m).
    i. Left engine support to engine bolts — 16 ft. lbs. (2.2 kg-m); left engine support to shock bracket bolt — 29 ft. lbs. (4.0 kg-m).

NOTE: When installing, make sure that the constant velocity joint sub-axle bottoms and that the spring clip holds the sub-axle securely in the transmission.

Accord

1. Disconnect battery ground cable, then raise and support vehicle and remove front wheels.
2. Drain engine oil transmission oil and cooling system.
3. Remove air cleaner, preheater control tubes and breather chamber.

4. Disconnect all wires, hoses, cables, lines and tubes from engine and transmission.
5. On vehicles with manual transmission, remove the clutch slave cylinder with hydraulic line attached by loosening the two attaching bolts.
6. Remove the speedometer cable at the transmission and set it aside.
7. Attach a suitable hoist to engine block and raise hoist just enough to remove slack and tension the chain slightly.
8. Remove lower control arm inner bolts, and then the radius rods from the lower control arms, leaving ball joints connected.
9. Before withdrawing the drive shaft from the transmission case, pry snap ring off the groove in the end of the shaft. Then, pull out the shaft by holding the knuckle.
10. Loosen the center beam attaching bolts and remove center beam.
11. On vehicle with manual transmission, remove the shift rod positioner from the transmission case.
12. On vehicles with manual transmission, drive out pin from the shift rod using tool 07944-6110200 and then remove rod.
13. On vehicles with automatic transmission, remove control cable from the transmission.
14. Remove splash guard.
15. Disconnect exhaust pipe by removing manifold attaching nuts and stay attaching bolts.
16. Remove three bolts and push left engine mount into the shock mount bracket.
17. Remove front and rear engine mounts.
18. Raise engine slowly with hoist and remove it from vehicle.
19. Reverse procedure to install.

CYLINDER HEAD, REPLACE

1. Disconnect battery ground cable, then drain cooling system.
2. Disconnect upper radiator hose from thermostat housing.
3. Remove distributor cap, ignition wires and primary wire.
4. Loosen alternator bracket and remove upper bolt from cylinder head.
5. Remove head cover.
6. Disconnect exhaust from manifold.
7. Remove air cleaner.
8. Loosen timing belt pivot and adjust-

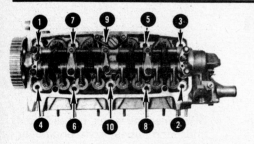

CYLINDER HEAD BOLT REMOVAL SEQUENCE

Fig. 1 Cylinder head bolt removal sequence

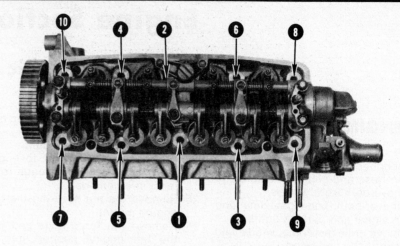

Fig. 2 Cylinder head bolt tightening sequence

ing bolts and then remove timing belt upper cover.

9. Remove timing belt from timing gear.

NOTE: It is not necessary to remove timing belt if only valve or head service is to be performed.

10. Disconnect fuel line, choke cable and throttle cable.
11. Disconnect electrical wires to thermosensor, temperature gauge sending unit, idle cut-off solenoid valve and primary/main cut-off solenoid valve.
12. Disconnect vacuum booster hose at the manifold.
13. Disconnect vacuum hoses from charcoal cannister and related emission hoses from emission control box.

14. Remove cylinder head bolts in sequence shown in Fig. 1, turning each only 30 degrees at a time until loose.

NOTE: Exhaust manifold and heat shield assembly may be left attached to cylinder head or removed at this time.

15. Remove cylinder head.
16. Reverse procedure to install, torquing cylinder head bolts in sequence shown in Fig. 2 to 40-47 ft. lbs. (5.5-6.5 kg-m). Always install a new cylinder head gasket when the cylinder head is removed.

ROCKER ARMS, REPLACE
CVCC Engine

1. Remove cylinder head (camshaft) cover.
2. Compress serrated, two-piece retaining spring pin with pliers and pry spring pin pieces up a little at a time, Fig. 3.

NOTE: Removing either spring pin releases rocker arms and springs.

3. Disassemble one or all parts of rocker arm assembly as necessary as shown in Fig. 3. Identify parts as they are removed to ensure reinstal-

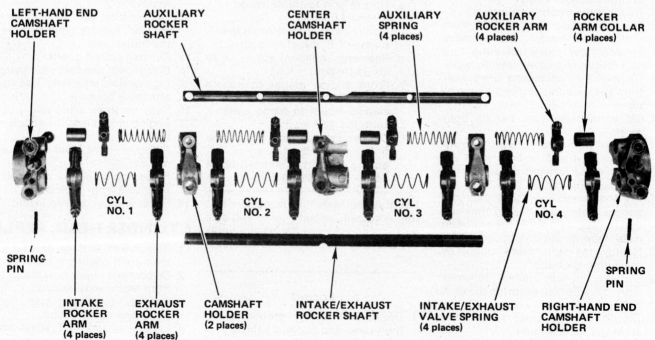

LEFT-HAND END CAMSHAFT HOLDER   AUXILIARY ROCKER SHAFT   CENTER CAMSHAFT HOLDER   AUXILIARY SPRING (4 places)   AUXILIARY ROCKER ARM (4 places)   ROCKER ARM COLLAR (4 places)

CYL NO. 1   CYL NO. 2   CYL NO. 3   CYL NO. 4

SPRING PIN   SPRING PIN

INTAKE ROCKER ARM (4 places)   EXHAUST ROCKER ARM (4 places)   CAMSHAFT HOLDER (2 places)   INTAKE/EXHAUST ROCKER SHAFT   INTAKE/EXHAUST VALVE SPRING (4 places)   RIGHT-HAND END CAMSHAFT HOLDER

● *Identify parts as they are removed to ensure reinstallation in original locations.*

Fig. 3 Rocker arm assembly exploded view. CVCC engine

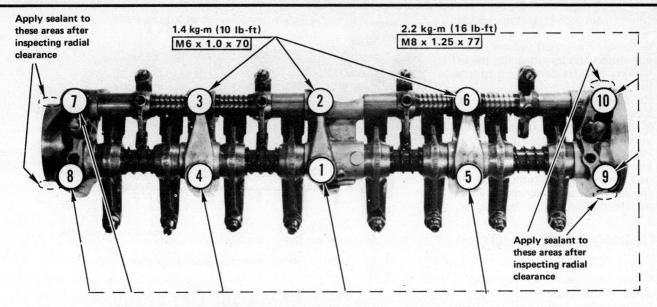

Apply sealant to these areas after inspecting radial clearance

1.4 kg-m (10 lb-ft)
M6 x 1.0 x 70

2.2 kg-m (16 lb-ft)
M8 x 1.25 x 77

Apply sealant to these areas after inspecting radial clearance

Fig. 4 Rocker arm bolts tightening sequence. CVCC engine

lation in original position.

4. Measure outside diameter of intake/exhaust rocker shaft and auxiliary rocker shaft at each arm location, and then measure inside diameter of rocker arm. Difference between diameters should not exceed 0.003 in. (0.08mm). If over limit, replace both the rocker shaft and the applicable rocker arm.
5. Loosen valve adjusting nuts and back off adjusting screws before installing rocker arms.
6. Rotate crankshaft until keyway ("UP" mark at top) is facing up.
7. Lubricate camshaft surfaces.
8. Assemble rocker arms and torque shaft bolts to specifications and in sequence shown in Fig. 4. Then apply sealant as indicated.
9. Install cylinder head cover.

Except CVCC Engine

1. To disassemble cam holders, start with No. 4 cylinder by pulling out retaining pin.
2. Remove holders, rocker collars, rocker arms and springs, Fig. 5.
3. If necessary to separate from holder, remove the remaining pin.
4. Reverse procedure to assemble.

NOTE: The intake rocker arm shaft must be installed with notch facing towards rear of vehicle and oil holes facing down. The exhaust rocker arm shaft must be installed with oil holes facing down and oil hole for dowel pin towards the left side of engine.

VALVE GUIDES, REPLACE

1. For best results, heat cylinder head to 300 degrees F. (150 degrees C.) before removing or installing valve guides.

2. Using tool 07942-6110000, drive valve guide out bottom of cylinder head.
3. Refer to specifications and inspect clearances. If excessive, replace valve and guide as a set.
4. Reheat cylinder head if necessary.
5. Using tool 07943-6710000 as an attachment to tool cited in (2) above, drive valve guide in until driver bottoms.

CAM DRIVE GEARS & TIMING BELT, REPLACE

1. Loosen alternator and remove alternator drive belt.
2. Remove cylinder head cover.
3. Remove upper timing belt cover.
4. Rotate crankshaft until "UP" mark on camshaft driven gear is at the top.

NOTE: Crankshaft may be rotated with engine installed in vehicle using a socket wrench inserted through access hole in the front of left fender well.

5. Loosen timing belt adjustment and pivot bolts.
6. Mark direction of rotation on timing belt and draw it carefully off the driven or camshaft sprocket.

NOTE: Avoid crimping or bending timing belt and avoid letting it contact oil or gasoline. If belt is oil soaked, it must be replaced.

7. Remove driven gear from camshaft by loosening attaching bolt. Be

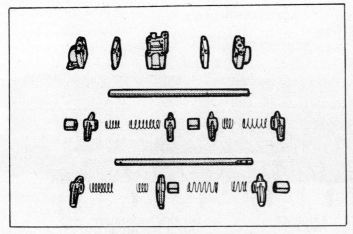

Fig. 5 Rocker arm assembly exploded view. Except CVCC engine

careful not to lose the special washer and key.

8. Remove crankshaft pulley from crankshaft end by loosening the attaching bolt. Be careful not to lose the key.
9. Remove lower cover but leave the loosened adjustment and pivot bolts in place, and then remove timing belt.
10. Remove water pump pulley, spacers, timing belt tensioner and timing belt driving gear on the crankshaft.
11. Reverse procedure to install. Refer to "Timing Belt, Adjust" procedure.

TIMING BELT, ADJUST
CVCC Engine

1. Rotate engine until No. 1 cylinder is at TDC compression stroke.
2. Perform steps 1 thru 3 under "Cam Drive Gears & Timing Belt, Replace," then loosen but do not remove the adjustment and pivot bolts.
3. Rotate crankshaft counterclockwise about ¼ turn to place tension on timing belt.
4. Torque adjustment and then the pivot bolt to 29-33 ft. lbs.
5. Re-torque crankshaft pulley bolt to 58-65 ft. lbs.

NOTE: The spring loaded tensioner will automatically apply the proper tension when the above steps are performed.

Except CVCC Engine

1. Loosen the tensioner pivot bolt and the adjusting bolt.
2. Rotate engine ¼ turn in normal direction of rotation.
3. Retighten the adjusting bolt and then the pivot bolt.

NOTE: The tensioner will automatically apply the proper tension when the above steps are performed.

CAMSHAFT, REPLACE

1. Remove camshaft driven sprocket as described under "Cam Drive Gears and Timing Belt, Replace" procedure.
2. Remove oil pump gear cover, gear shaft and gear.
3. Remove rocker arm assembly.
4. Lift camshaft from cylinder head.
5. Reverse procedure to install, using tool 07947-6340000 to drive new oil seal.

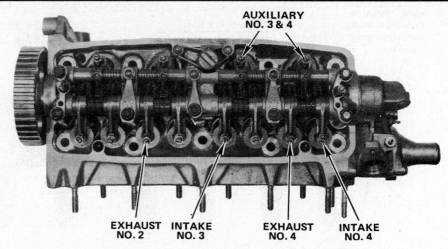

Fig. 6   Valve adjustment sequence. CVCC engine

CAM LOBE LIFT SPECS.

Year	Intake	Aux. Intake	Exhaust
All	1.486-1.495 in. (37.735-37.975mm)	1.732-1.741 in. (43.982-44.222mm)	1.486-1.495 in. 37.735-37.975mm)

VALVES, ADJUST
CVCC Engine

1. Rotate engine until No. 1 cylinder is at TDC compression stroke and mark on crankshaft pulley is aligned with index mark on timing belt cover.
2. Adjust valve clearance to specifications on the following valves, Fig. 6:
No. 1 Intake	No. 1 Exhaust
No. 2 Intake	No. 3 Exhaust
Nos. 1 and 2 Auxiliary Valves	
3. Rotate engine one complete revolution and adjust valve clearance to specifications on the following valves, Fig. 7:
No. 3 Intake	No. 2 Exhaust
No. 4 Intake	No. 4 Exhaust
Nos. 3 and 4 Auxiliary Valves	

NOTE: Tighten intake and exhaust valve locknuts to 13-16 ft. lbs. and auxiliary valve locknuts to 9-12 ft. lbs.

4. Tighten locknut and check clearance again. Repeat adjustment if necessary.

Except CVCC Engine

1. Rotate engine until No. 1 cylinder is at TDC compression stroke and mark on crankshaft pulley is aligned with index mark on timing belt cover.
2. Adjust valve clearance to specifications on the following valves:
No. 1 Intake	No. 1 Exhaust
No. 2 Intake	No. 3 Exhaust

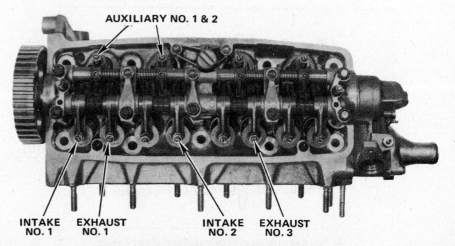

Fig. 7   Valve adjustment sequence. CVCC engine

3. Rotate engine one complete revolution and adjust valve clearance to specifications on the following valves:

   No. 3 Intake   No. 2 Exhaust
   No. 4 Intake   No. 4 Exhaust

4. Check clearance after final adjustment, and repeat adjustment if necessary.

PISTONS & RINGS

On CVCC engines, pistons and rings are available in standard and oversizes of 2.9213-2.9224.

On all except CVCC engines, pistons and rings are available in standard and oversizes of .010, .020, .030 and .040 inch (.25, .50, .75 and 1.00 mm). On 1974 engines, pistons and rings are available in standard and oversizes of .25 mm and .55 mm.

On all engines, when assembling connecting rod onto piston, the oil hole on the connecting rod must be on the same side as the notch on piston head, Fig. 8. When installing piston and connecting rod assembly into engine, the notch on piston head and oil hole on connecting rod must be facing towards the intake manifold.

MAIN & ROD BEARINGS

Main bearings are color coded on their edge according to the following table of tolerances:

COLOR	TOLERANCE
Red	−0.0001 to −0.0002 in.
	(−0.002 to 0.005mm)
Pink	+0.00004 to −0.0001 in.
	(+0.001 to −0.002mm)
Yellow	+0.0002 to +0.00004 in.
	(+0.004 to +0.001mm)
Green	+0.0003 to +0.0002 in.
	(+0.007 to +0.004mm)
Brown	+0.00004 to +0.0003 in.
	(+0.010 to +0.007mm)
Black	+0.0005 to +0.0004 in.
	+0.013 to +0.010mm)
Blue	+0.0006 to +0.0005 in.
	(+0.016 to +0.013mm)

Connecting rod bearings are color coded on their edge according to the following table of tolerances:

COLOR	TOLERANCE
Red	−0.0002 to −0.0003 in.
	(−0.005 to −0.008mm)
Pink	−0.0001 to −0.0002 in.
	(−0.002 to −0.005mm)
Yellow	+0.00004 to −0.0001 in.
	(+0.001 to −0.002mm)
Green	+0.0002 to +0.00004 in.
	(+0.004 to +0.001mm)
Brown	+0.0003 to +0.0002 in.
	(+0.007 to +0.004mm)
Black	+0.0004 to +0.0003 in.
	(+0.010 to +0.007mm)

Install piston with this mark on same side as oil hole in connecting rod.

*During installation, marking points must be toward intake manifold

Fig. 8 Piston and connecting rod assembly

Blue   +0.0005 to +0.0004 in.
              (+0.013 to +0.010mm)

OIL PAN, REMOVAL
CVCC Engine

1. Remove flywheel cover (manual) or drive plate cover (Hondamatic).
2. Loosen attaching bolts and remove oil pan.
3. To install, tighten attaching bolts alternately on each side, moving out alternately from the center, to 12-14 ft. lbs. (1.6-2.0 kg-m).

Except CVCC Engine

1. Raise and support front of vehicle.
2. Attach a chain hoist to clutch cable bracket and lift engine just enough to remove load from center support.
3. Drain engine oil.
4. Remove center beam and engine lower mount rubber.
5. Remove clutch housing dust cover, then remove oil pan attaching bolts and remove oil pan.
6. Reverse procedure to install.

OIL PUMP, REPLACE
CVCC Engine

1. Remove camshaft/valve cover.
2. Remove oil pump gear cover.
3. Raise vehicle and remove oil pan.
4. Loosen attaching bolts and remove oil pump cover, oil pressure relief valve, valve spring, pin and collar.
5. Drive lock pin from oil pump shaft and remove inner and outer pump rotors, Fig. 8.
6. Lower vehicle and lift oil pump gear and shaft from the cylinder head.
7. Reverse procedure to install.

Except CVCC Engine

1. Remove oil pan.
2. Remove oil passage block and oil pump.
3. Reverse procedure to install.

CRANKSHAFT REAR OIL SEAL

1. Remove engine and transmission from vehicle and place on stand.
2. Remove transmission, and then remove flywheel housing and flywheel.
3. Remove oil pan.
4. Remove oil seal, using tool 07949-6110000.
5. Clean seal seating surfaces thoroughly, apply a light coat of oil to the crankshaft and the lip of the seal and position seal with the part number side facing out.
6. Drive seal until it bottoms on flywheel housing, using tool cited in (4) above with attachment 07947-6570100.
7. Install oil pan and then install engine and transmission assembly in vehicle.
8. Fill crankcase and check for leaks.

TIMING BELT GEAR OIL SEAL

1. Follow all procedures in "Cam Drive Gears and Timing Belt, Replace" above.
2. Pry seal from its seat in the crankcase.
3. Clean seal seating surfaces thoroughly, apply a light coat of oil to crankshaft and lip of seal and position seal with part number side facing out.
4. Drive seal until it bottoms in the crankcase, using tool 07947-634000.
5. Install cam drive gears, timing belt, and adjust timing belt. Refer to "Timing Adjust" procedure.
6. Refer to "Cam Drive Gears & Timing Belt, Replace" to install and adjust the remaining components.

FUEL PUMP PRESSURE

YEAR	ENGINE	PRESSURE
All	All	2-3 psi
		(0.13-0.18 kg/cm²)

FUEL PUMP, REMOVAL

NOTE: The fuel pump is located adjacent to the fuel tank under the left rear of the vehicle.

HONDA

1. Disconnect battery ground (−) cable.
2. Raise vehicle.
3. Disconnect electrical leads to the fuel pump.
4. Disconnect inlet and outlet fuel lines, using rags to absorb spillage.
5. Loosen four bracket attaching screws and remove the pump together with bracket.
6. Reverse procedure to install.

BELT TENSION DATA

YEAR	BELT	DEFLECTION	TENSION
All	Air Condition	(Dealer installed. See Mfrs. specs)	
	Timing Belt	(Self-Adjusting)	
	Alternator	0.47-0.67 in.	10.85-24.26 lbs.
		(12-17mm)	(9-11 kg)

WATER PUMP, REPLACE

1. Loosen alternator adjustment bracket and remove alternator belt.
2. Loosen clamps and remove upper coolant hose at pump, along with bracket.
3. Loosen three attaching bolts and remove the water pump pulley.
4. Loosen attaching bolts and remove water pump, along with O-ring.
5. Reverse procedure to install, replacing the O-ring with a new one.

---

600 Models

ENGINE, REPLACE

1. Drain engine oil.
2. Remove battery cable at negative terminal.
3. Remove heater blower motor as described in electrical section above.
4. Disconnect all electrical wiring and control cables lines and hoses from engine.
5. Separate vacuum unit tube from the vacuum unit and the breather tube from the camshaft housing cover.
6. Loosen clamp and separate bellows from air cleaner case.
7. Separate fuel feed line from carburetor.
8. Remove the two insulator mounting bolts and remove insulator, carburetor and bellows from camshaft housing as a unit, being careful not to drop O-ring between the camshaft housing and insulator.
9. Drive out the gear shift joint pin with special tool No. 07047-55101 and separate the gear shift column from the gear shift rod.
10. Push the gear shift rod in towards the engine.
11. Disconnect wiring from both turn signals at lamp housings.
12. Remove turn signal light lenses and bolts mounting the grille on both sides, and the three screws at the top. Then remove grille.
13. Loosen exhaust pipe clamp retaining nut and remove it and clamp from engine mount.
14. Separate exhaust pipes from the cylinder heads.

NOTE: It is unnecessary to remove the exhaust pipe from the engine compartment as it will dismount with the engine.

15. Loosen but do not remove the front wheel nuts and wheel bearing nuts.
16. Place a floor jack under engine crankcase and raise vehicle to a height of 29 inches or more between floor and bottom of front bumper. Leave jack in place and support vehicle with suitable stands at normal jacking points on body side rails.
17. Remove both front wheels and wheel bearing nuts, and then remove the front brake drums, using a suitable puller.
18. Separate backing plates from steering knuckles by removing the four mounting bolts. Do not disconnect the hydraulic hose.

NOTE: An alternate method to step 18 is to disconnect front shock absorbers from body shell, then disconnect the hydraulic hose at both front wheels and remove power unit, sub-frame and front suspension as a unit.

19. Remove steering knuckle clamp bolt and separate knuckle from shock absorber. Insert a screwdriver into knuckle opening to assist if necessary.
20. Remove front and rear sub-frame mounting bolts.
21. Remove the two bolts retaining muffler to vehicle body and remove the rubber insulator.
22. Slowly lower the power unit, sub-frame, exhaust pipe and muffler by means of the floor jack, checking to see that no wiring or other connections remain attached to the vehicle.
23. Remove starter and exhaust assembly from engine.
24. Remove drive shaft from differential.
25. Remove front engine mounting beam and rear mounting bolt, then separate engine and sub-frame.
26. Remove front engine mounting beam bolts and separate beam from engine.
27. Reverse procedure to install.

CAMSHAFT AND ROCKER ARMS, REPLACE

1. Remove carburetor together with intake manifold from the engine.
2. Remove cooling fan housing from engine.
3. Disconnect fan belt from pulley.
4. Remove hydraulic cam chain tensioner.

NOTE: Use correct size socket wrench only. Gently tap the top of tensioner with a plastic hammer if necessary.

5. Remove camshaft housing cover and separate right camshaft holder.
6. Remove right rocker arm shaft and rocker arm.

NOTE: Some engines have a spring installed on both inlet and exhaust rocker arm shafts while others use a rubber spacer on exhaust side. If springs are installed on both sides, replace in their original positions to avoid oil leakage through cylinder stud bolts.

7. Remove left camshaft holder, rocker arm shaft and rocker arm in same manner, observing the precaution in the note above.
8. Remove camshaft chain from its sprocket and pull to the left to remove camshaft.
9. Remove shrouds from both sides and separate camshaft housing from cylinder head, first unscrewing the bolt at the bottom of the intake manifold and then nuts and bolts at top in sequence shown in Fig. 1.

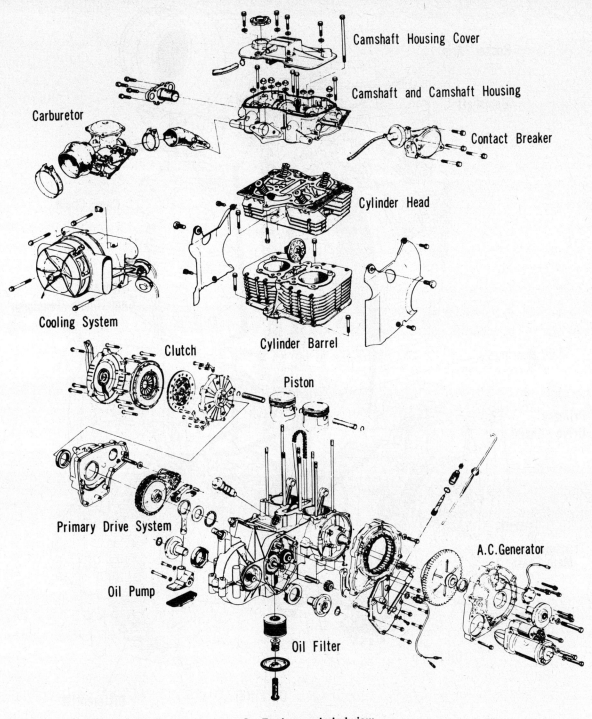

Camshaft Housing Cover

Camshaft and Camshaft Housing

Carburetor

Contact Breaker

Cylinder Head

Cooling System

Cylinder Barrel

Clutch

Piston

Primary Drive System

A.C. Generator

Oil Pump

Oil Filter

Ⓐ **Engine exploded view**

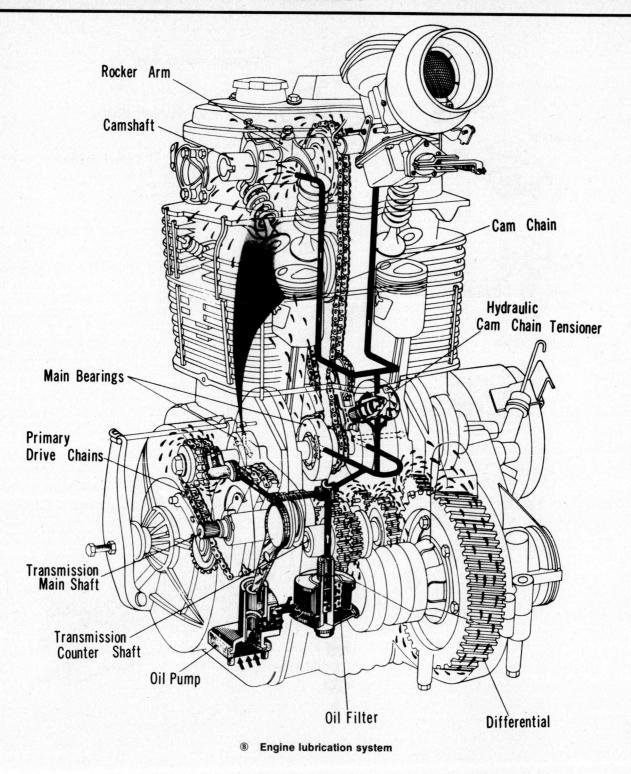

Rocker Arm

Camshaft

Cam Chain

Hydraulic
Cam Chain Tensioner

Main Bearings

Primary
Drive Chains

Transmission
Main Shaft

Transmission
Counter Shaft

Oil Pump

Oil Filter

Differential

Ⓑ Engine lubrication system

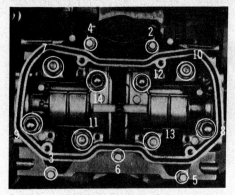

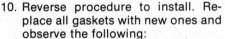

Fig. 1 Cylinder head bolts removal sequence

Fig. 2 Replacing driven sprocket C-clip

10. Reverse procedure to install. Replace all gaskets with new ones and observe the following:
   a. When installing camshaft housing, install nuts and bolts in their original locations in reverse order of removal, Fig. 1. Tighten 10mm nut to (20.3-23.1 ft. lbs.) 2.8-3.2 kg-m, 6mm nuts to 0.9-1.2 kg-m (6.5-8.7 ft. lbs.).
   b. When installing camshaft and chain, turn crankshaft in the normal direction of rotation to align the "T" on the crankshaft pulley with the index mark, then align camshaft so that horizontal mark on sprocket is at the top and parallel to flange surface of camshaft housing. Pull both ends of chain to remove slack and mount chain on sprocket.
   c. Rocker arms are marked "R" and "L" as viewed from direction of travel and must be installed accordingly.
   d. Install right rocker arm and camshaft holder first, making sure that punch mark on rocker arm is toward the top to provide maximum tappet clearance.
   e. Position camshaft by turning engine to TDC, compression stroke, and hold camshaft in that position.

   f. Inspect oil seal in right camshaft holder and replace if necessary, using suitable tool.
   g. After right side installation is completed, rotate crankshaft one complete revolution and realign the "T" mark.
   h. Temporarily install the left camshaft holder off-set 90 degrees from its normally installed position, then install the left rocker arms and rocker arm shafts, and rotate the camshaft holder to its proper position and tighten.
   i. Adjust valve tappet clearance to complete the installation.

VALVES, ADJUST

Normal cold tappet clearance, both intake and exhaust, is 0.08-0.12mm (0.003-0.005 in.). Always set valve clearances when both the left and right valves are lifted to prevent inclination of the camshaft. Rocker arm tightening bolt torque is 28.9 ft. lbs., 4.0 kg-m.

ALLOWABLE CAM LOBE DIMENSIONS

INTAKE	EXHAUST
41.21-41.37mm	40.73-40.89mm
(1.622-1.629 ins.)	(1.604-1.610 ins.)

VALVE TIMING, DEGREES

INTAKE	EXHAUST
5 BTDC Open	40 BBDC Open
20 ABDC Close	10 ATDC Close

CYLINDER HEAD & VALVE TRAIN, REPLACE

1. Disassemble camshaft housing as described previously, then remove the front grille and screen, and remove exhaust pipe from cylinder head.
2. Remove bolt below intake manifold and lift cylinder head off block.
3. Reverse procedure to install, always using new gaskets and making sure that the two hollow pins are installed in their correct locations.

NOTE: Temporarily wiring the cam chain to a convenient point will keep it from dropping into crankcase.

VALVE GUIDES, REPLACE

Valve guides may be removed if necessary by using special tool # 07046-55101. Clearance between intake valve stems and guides should be 0.01-0.04mm (0.0004-0.0016 in.); exhaust

Fig. 3 Damper rubbers

Drive Sprocket Hub

Damper Rubber

Drive Sprocket

Fig. 4 Installing drive sprocket hub onto sprocket

Marking

Rubber

Hub

Fig. 5 Installing damper rubbers

Fig. 6 Aligning inner and outer sprocket

Correct installation

Fig. 7 Checking alignment between inner and outer sprocket

valve stems and guides, 0.04-0.07mm (0.0016-0.0028 in.).

PISTONS AND CYLINDERS, REPLACE

1. Remove cam chain guide roller from cylinder.
2. Remove one forward and two rear cylinder mounting bolts.
3. Gently raise cylinder barrels and separate them from crankcase, tapping gently around the barrels if necessary to free the unit.
4. Place clean rags at base of each piston to prevent foreign objects from entering the crankcase, remove circlip from piston pin, then push piston pin out, and separate piston from connecting rod.
5. Remove rings from pistons by using a spreader or thumb pressure.
6. Reverse procedure to install, making sure that lettered side of piston rings faces upward and that "IN" mark on the piston head faces the air inlet side. When installing the cylinder barrel assembly, use piston seat tool #07033-55101 and ring compressor #07032-56801. Open ends of top ring and oil ring should face asymetrically forward and that

of the second ring should face to the rear. Two of each special tool cited are required to facilitate the installation.

PRIMARY DRIVE, REPLACE

1. Remove clutch assembly and crankcase left side cover.

NOTE: When removing the left side cover with the engine mounted in the vehicle, removal of the lower bolts is facilitated by raising the engine slightly, the lifting point being the engine lower crankcase.

---

2. Remove driven sprocket c-clip and remove the washer from the main shaft, Fig. 2.
3. Remove two oil pump retaining bolts and special washers.
4. Draw out oil pump with drive and driven sprockets as an assembly by holding the two sprockets manually.

5. Remove driven sprocket with oil pump to avoid deforming the oil pump rod.

OIL PUMP

1. Refer to "Primary Drive, Replace" for removal and replacement of oil pump. It may be removed with engine installed in vehicle.
2. To disassemble oil pump, remove pump rod and plunger from pump body, the two being connected by a pin as shown in Fig. 12.
3. At this stage, the strainer, needle thrust bearing and thrust plate may be removed for inspection and cleaning.
4. To install, first insert needle bearing and thrust plate onto transmission main shaft bearing.
5. Insert assembled oil pump into primary driven sprocket with grooved side of pump rod facing driven sprocket.

PRIMARY DRIVE DATA

Primary chain tensioner spring tension	5.07-6.39 lbs. (2.3-2.9kg)
Drive sprocket side clearance	0-0.0078 in. (0-0.2mm)
Thrust plate thickness	0.1157-0.1204 in. (2.94-3.06mm)
Primary driven sprocket side clearance	0.0039-0.0118 in. (0.1-0.3mm)
Driven sprocket eccentricity	0.118 in. (0-0.3mm)

Fig. 8 Installing set plate onto sprocket hub

Fig. 9 Checking fit of chains on sprockets

Fig. 10 Installing primary driven sprocket, drive chains, oil pump and thrust plate

Fig. 11 Installing primary chain tensioner

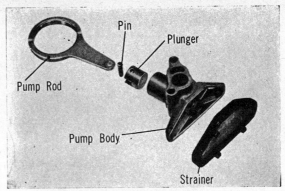

Fig. 12 Oil pump exploded view

6. Install oil pump together with primary drive and left side cover on engine, as above.

NOTE: The oil pump attaching bolts require special iron washers. Do not substitute aluminum washers. Also, when installing left side cover, replace packing in the two knock pins.

FUEL PUMP, REPLACE

1. Remove the electrical leads and disconnect the rubber hose from the fuel inlet and outlet.
2. Remove the two mounting bolts from the fuel pump and separate the pump from the body.
3. Reverse procedure to install.

FUEL PUMP PRESSURE

Pressure should be 2.1 psi with inside diameter of outlet reduced to .005 inch. Drive sprocket eccentricity, limit 0.005 in. (0.15mm).

6. Assemble drive sprocket by applying grease to the damper rubbers, installing the rubbers as shown in Fig. 3.
7. Install the drive sprocket hub on the sprocket, Fig. 4. Use a vise and more grease on the damper rubbers if necessary.
8. Install one of the interchangeable driven sprockets on the sprocket hub and plug in the damper rubbers with the arrow or letter "Y" (late models) upward, Fig. 5. Apply grease to the rubbers if necessary.
9. Install the second or outer sprocket to hub so that aligning marks on each sprocket are aligned, Fig. 6, and that teeth of one sprocket are shifted about one-half pitch from teeth of the other, Fig. 7.
10. Install set plate with chamfered side facing sprocket hub, Fig. 8.
11. Loop the chains over both the drive and driven sprockets, checking the seating of the chain on the teeth by holding as in Fig. 9.
12. Install thrust plate with grooved face outward.
13. Install primary driven sprocket assembly with drive sprocket, primary drive chains, oil pump and thrust plate as a unit, Fig. 10.
14. Secure oil pump with the two mounting bolts.
15. Assemble tongued thrust plate on driven sprocket and secure with circlip.
16. Tighten drive sprocket to a torque of 18 ft. lbs. (2.5 kg-m).
17. Install primary chain tensioner, Fig. 11.

Carburetor Section
Accord & Civic

KEIHIN CARBURETOR ADJUSTMENTS
Float Level, Adjust

1. Remove caps from the auxiliary and primary/secondary jets.
2. Install float level gauge with catch tray and drain bottle (tool 07501-7570001), Fig. 2.
3. Start engine.
4. If float level does not maintain at the line on gauge, raise or lower as necessary with adjustment screws, allowing sufficient time between each adjustment for level to stabilize.
5. Paint tops of the screws after adjustment.

Throttle Cable Adjustment

1. Check cable for freedom of motion and correct as necessary.
2. Check cable free-play at throttle linkage, proper deflection being 0.16-0.40 in. (4-10mm).
3. If deflection is not within specs, turn adjusting nut until cable has no deflection, Fig. 3.
4. Loosen adjusting nut until cable deflects within specifications, then tighten locknut.
5. After adjusting the throttle cable, have someone press down on the accelerator pedal inside the car while checking for full throttle condition at the carburetor.
6. Readjust as necessary, staying within deflection specifications.

Choke Cable Adjustment

NOTE: The hand choke knob serves only to actuate a vacuum-operated choke from two basic settings.

1. Check choke control for binding and correct as necessary.
2. Push choke knob in and check that the choke butterfly valve is fully open.
3. Pull choke knob to second detent position and check that the valve is just at the point of closing.
4. Pull the knob all the way out and

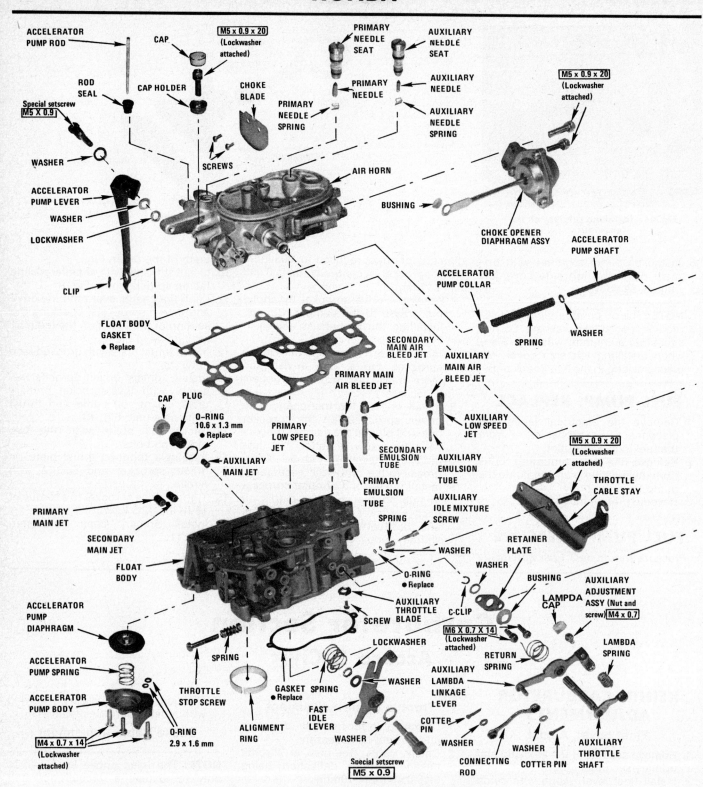

Fig. 1 (Part 1) Keihin carburetor exploded view

ACCELERATOR PUMP ROD

CAP

M5 x 0.9 x 20 (Lockwasher attached)

PRIMARY NEEDLE SEAT

AUXILIARY NEEDLE SEAT

ROD SEAL

CAP HOLDER

CHOKE BLADE

PRIMARY NEEDLE

AUXILIARY NEEDLE

M5 x 0.9 x 20 (Lockwasher attached)

Special setscrew M5 X 0.9

PRIMARY NEEDLE SPRING

AUXILIARY NEEDLE SPRING

WASHER

ACCELERATOR PUMP LEVER

AIR HORN

WASHER

BUSHING

LOCKWASHER

CHOKE OPENER DIAPHRAGM ASSY

ACCELERATOR PUMP SHAFT

CLIP

ACCELERATOR PUMP COLLAR

WASHER

FLOAT BODY GASKET
● Replace

SPRING

SECONDARY MAIN AIR BLEED JET

AUXILIARY MAIN AIR BLEED JET

CAP

PLUG

PRIMARY MAIN AIR BLEED JET

O-RING 10.6 x 1.3 mm
● Replace

PRIMARY LOW SPEED JET

AUXILIARY LOW SPEED JET

M5 x 0.9 x 20 (Lockwasher attached)

AUXILIARY MAIN JET

SECONDARY EMULSION TUBE

AUXILIARY EMULSION TUBE

THROTTLE CABLE STAY

PRIMARY EMULSION TUBE

PRIMARY MAIN JET

AUXILIARY IDLE MIXTURE SCREW

SPRING

SECONDARY MAIN JET

RETAINER PLATE

FLOAT BODY

WASHER

BUSHING

AUXILIARY ADJUSTMENT ASSY (Nut and screw) M4 x 0.7

O-RING
● Replace

WASHER

LAMPDA CAP

ACCELERATOR PUMP DIAPHRAGM

AUXILIARY THROTTLE BLADE

C-CLIP

LAMBDA SPRING

ACCELERATOR PUMP SPRING

SPRING

SCREW

M6 X 0.7 X 14 (Lockwasher attached)

RETURN SPRING

ACCELERATOR PUMP BODY

THROTTLE STOP SCREW

GASKET
● Replace

SPRING

LOCKWASHER

WASHER

AUXILIARY LAMBDA LINKAGE LEVER

M4 x 0.7 x 14 (Lockwasher attached)

O-RING 2.9 x 1.6 mm

ALIGNMENT RING

FAST IDLE LEVER

COTTER PIN

AUXILIARY THROTTLE SHAFT

WASHER

WASHER

WASHER

Special setscrew M5 x 0.9

CONNECTING ROD

COTTER PIN

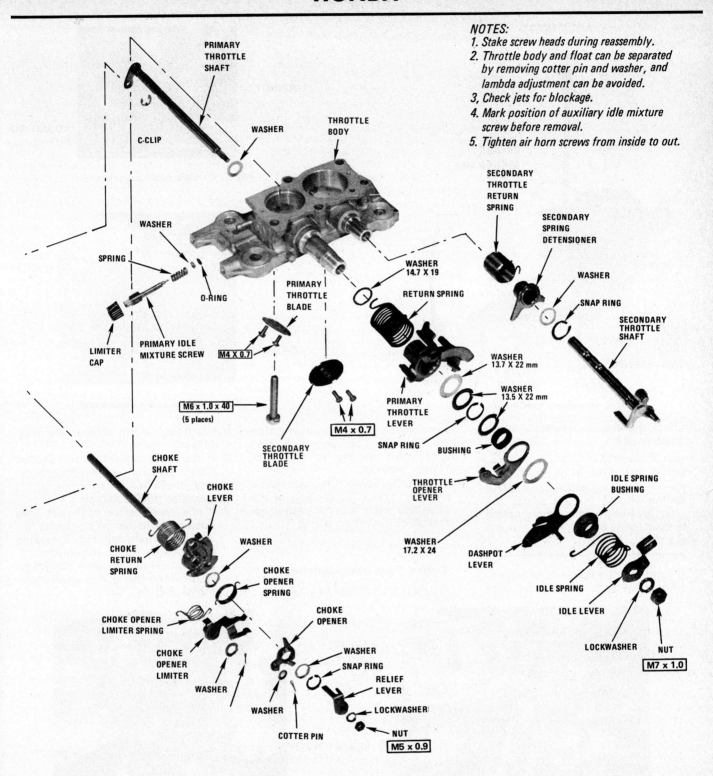

NOTES:
1. Stake screw heads during reassembly.
2. Throttle body and float can be separated by removing cotter pin and washer, and lambda adjustment can be avoided.
3. Check jets for blockage.
4. Mark position of auxiliary idle mixture screw before removal.
5. Tighten air horn screws from inside to out.

Fig. 1 (Part 2) Keihin carburetor exploded view

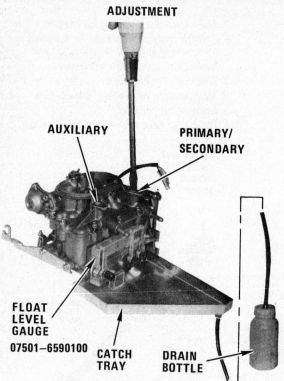

ADJUSTMENT

AUXILIARY

PRIMARY/
SECONDARY

FLOAT
LEVEL
GAUGE
07501—6590100

CATCH
TRAY

DRAIN
BOTTLE

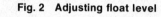

Fig. 2 Adjusting float level

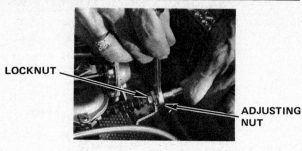

LOCKNUT

ADJUSTING
NUT

Fig. 3 Throttle cable adjustment

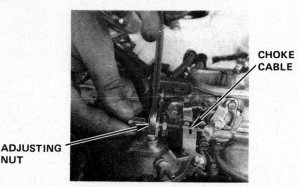

CHOKE
CABLE

ADJUSTING
NUT

Fig. 4 Choke cable adjustment

check that the valve remains in the same position.

NOTE: The position of the valve in the "out" setting and second detent setting should be the same. The "out" position applies more spring tension to the butterfly valve for cold starts.

5. If butterfly valve does not fully open, turn adjusting nut, Fig. 4, "in" until

valve moves off the positioning stop tab. Then turn adjusting nut "out" until valve returns to stop tab. Tighten locknut.
6. If butterfly valve does not close properly, check for binding of the valve and shaft, and for proper operation of the return spring.

Choke Fast Idle Adjustment

1. Connect tachometer to engine.

2. Start engine and allow to warm up fully.
3. Place choke control knob in second detent position, allow 30 seconds, and check if idle speed is within specified 2500-3500 rpm.
4. If idle speed is too high, use long nose pliers to narrow slot in the fast idle adjustment link Fig. 5, making adjustment in small increments.
5. If speed is too low, use a screwdriver to widen the slot in small increments, Fig. 5.

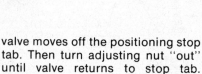

FAST IDLE
ADJUSTING
LINK

SCREWDRIVER

LONG
NOSE
PLIERS

Fig. 5 Choke fast idle adjustment

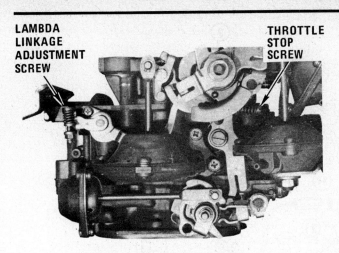

Fig. 6 Throttle stop screw and Lambda linkage adjustment screw

Lambda Linkage, Adjust

1. Back off throttle stop screw, then remove lambda cap, Fig. 6.
2. Loosen locknut, then tighten adjustment screw, Fig. 7 until primary throttle blade opens, Fig. 8.
3. Loosen adjustment screw until primary throttle blade closes.
4. Loosen adjustment screw 2¼ turns after primary throttle blades closes.
5. While holding adjustment screw, tighten locknut.
6. Readjust throttle stop screw after carburetor has been installed.

Accelerator Pump Linkage Adjustment

1. Accelerator pump lever must be in contact with pump shaft.
2. Measure with a vernier caliper the

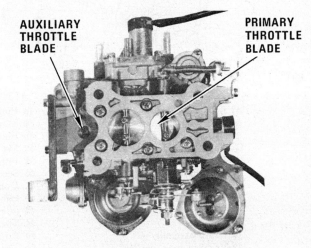

Fig. 7 Throttle adjustment screw

Fig. 8 Primary throttle blade and auxiliary throttle blade

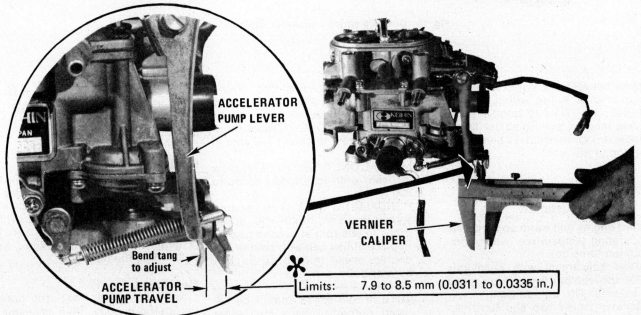

Limits: 7.9 to 8.5 mm (0.0311 to 0.0335 in.)

Fig. 9 Accelerator pump linkage adjustment

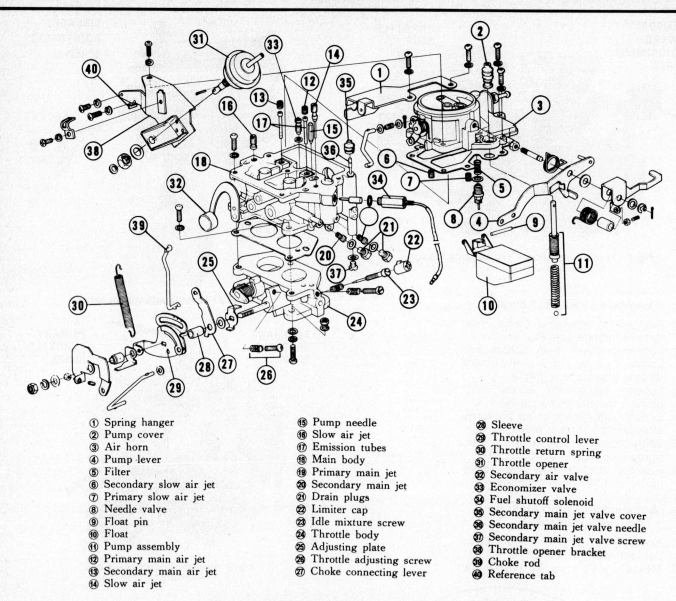

① Spring hanger
② Pump cover
③ Air horn
④ Pump lever
⑤ Filter
⑥ Secondary slow air jet
⑦ Primary slow air jet
⑧ Needle valve
⑨ Float pin
⑩ Float
⑪ Pump assembly
⑫ Primary main air jet
⑬ Secondary main air jet
⑭ Slow air jet

⑮ Pump needle
⑯ Slow air jet
⑰ Emission tubes
⑱ Main body
⑲ Primary main jet
⑳ Secondary main jet
㉑ Drain plugs
㉒ Limiter cap
㉓ Idle mixture screw
㉔ Throttle body
㉕ Adjusting plate
㉖ Throttle adjusting screw
㉗ Choke connecting lever

㉘ Sleeve
㉙ Throttle control lever
㉚ Throttle return spring
㉛ Throttle opener
㉜ Secondary air valve
㉝ Economizer valve
㉞ Fuel shutoff solenoid
㉟ Secondary main jet valve cover
㊱ Secondary main jet valve needle
㊲ Secondary main jet valve screw
㊳ Throttle opener bracket
㊴ Choke rod
㊵ Reference tab

Fig. 10 DCG-306 series carburetor exploded view

travel between the pump lever and stop, Fig. 9. If not within 0.4609-0.4843 in. (11.7-12.3mm), bend lower tang on lever to adjust. Don't under any circumstances bend tang on top of the lever.

Idle Speed and Mixture Adjustment

1. Start engine and warm up to normal operating temperature (when cooling fan turns on).
2. Make adjustment with headlights ON and cooling fan or high-speed heater fan ON, but not both.
3. Remove limiter cap and turn mixture screw out (rich) until highest rpm is obtained.

4. MANUAL ONLY: Adjust throttle stop screw to obtain 880 rpm, removing limiter cap if necessary.
5. HONDAMATIC ONLY: Adjust throttle stop screw to obtain 730 rpm in second gear.
6. MANUAL ONLY: Turn mixture screw in (lean) until idle speed drops to 800 rpm.
7. HONDAMATIC ONLY: Turn mixture screw in (lean) until idle speed drops to 680 rpm in second gear.
8. Replace limiter cap with pointer 180 degrees away from boss on carburetor body.

NOTE: If idle speed cannot be adjusted properly, check for proper throttle cable adjustment.

DCG306-45, 45A, 46 & 46A CARBURETOR ADJUSTMENTS
Float, Adjust

Float Drop, Fig. 11
Invert air horn and raise float, then lower float until it just touches the needle valve stem. Measure distance between float and air horn flange (without gasket) which should be .44 inch (11mm). If not to specifications, adjust by bending the tang.

Float Level, Fig. 11
Raise float until float stop contacts the air horn body, then measure distance between float tang and valve stem which should be .040-.042 inch (1.3-

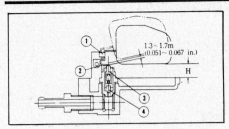

Fig. 11 Adjusting float drop and float level

1.7mm). If not to specifications, adjust by bending float stop tang.

NOTE: Recheck float level when carburetor is installed. Level should be within the range of the dot on the sight glass.

Choke, Adjust

Using a wire gauge, check primary throttle valve opening (G1), Fig. 12 when choke valve is fully closed. If opening is not within .050-.066 inch (1.28-1.68mm) adjust by bending choke rod. Recheck adjustment when carburetor is installed. Fast idle speed should be 2500-2800 rpm.

NOTE: When adjusting fast idle speed, make sure that throttle adjusting screw does not contact stop.

Throttle Valve, Adjust

Check that throttle valve opens completely when throttle lever is moved to the full open position, and that throttle valve closes completely when throttle lever is released. Check clearance (G2), Fig. 13 between primary throttle valve and chamber wall at position where connecting rod starts to open the secondary throttle valve. If not within .221-.237 inch (5.63-6.03mm), adjust by bending connecting rod.

NOTE: After adjusting, operate throttle lever to check for freedom of operation.

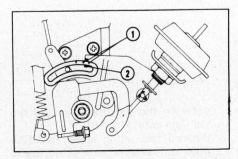

Fig. 14 Carburetor linkage adjustment

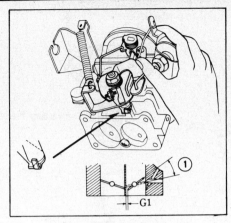

Fig. 12 Choke adjustment

Carburetor Linkage, Adjust

DCG306-45A & 46A

Open primary throttle plate and insert a .032 inch (.8mm) diameter drill bit between plate and bore. If reference tab is not halfway between the two scribed lines on the throttle control lever, bend reference tab to adjust, Fig. 14.

Choke Cable, Adjust

DCG306-45A & 46A

Make sure that carburetor linkage is properly adjusted, and check that with choke knob in, the choke valve is completely open, then slowly pull out choke knob and check for slack in cable. Eliminate any excessive freeplay and recheck for full open when knob is pushed in. Check link rod adjustment by pulling choke knob to first detent. The two scribed lines on the throttle control lever should align on either side of the reference tab, Fig. 15. If not, adjust by bending the choke link rod.

N6D2 CARBURETOR ADJUSTMENTS

NOTE: Do not disassemble the throttle valve, choke valve, main air jets and the check valve collar of the accelerator pump, Fig. 16.

Float Level, Adjust

NOTE: Be certain in assembly that the float valve seat retainer spring is installed with the bent (downward) portion toward the chamber wall.

1. Set carburetor on end as shown in Fig. 17 and move the float back and forth to locate the point where there is a clearance of 0-0.1mm between

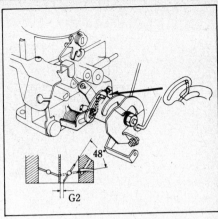

Fig. 13 Throttle valve adjustment

the tip of the float valve and the float arm.

2. With the float positioned as in (2) above, measure the distance "h", Fig. 17. Adjust to 15.0-17.0mm (0.59-0.67 in.) if necessary, making sure that the tip of the float valve hasn't entered the float valve spring to cause a false measurement.

High Altitude, Adjust

1. For normal operation, one 0.4mm shim is positioned at the top of the jet needle flange and another at the bottom of the flange.
2. To adjust for high altitude or extreme cold weather, locate both shims at the bottom of the flange.
3. When installing the vacuum piston assembly containing the jet needle in the carburetor, be sure the protruding section of the upper diaphragm is aligned with its groove in the carburetor body.

Slow Idle, Adjust (Hot)

1. Back-off pilot screw 2⅛ turns.
2. Bring engine speed back to idle with the throttle stop screw.
3. Turn the pilot screw 180 degrees and set it for smoothest operation.
4. Back off the throttle screw and set it for normal idling speed of 1100-1300 rpm.

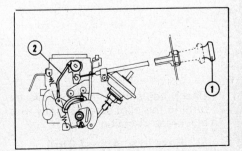

Fig. 15 Choke cable

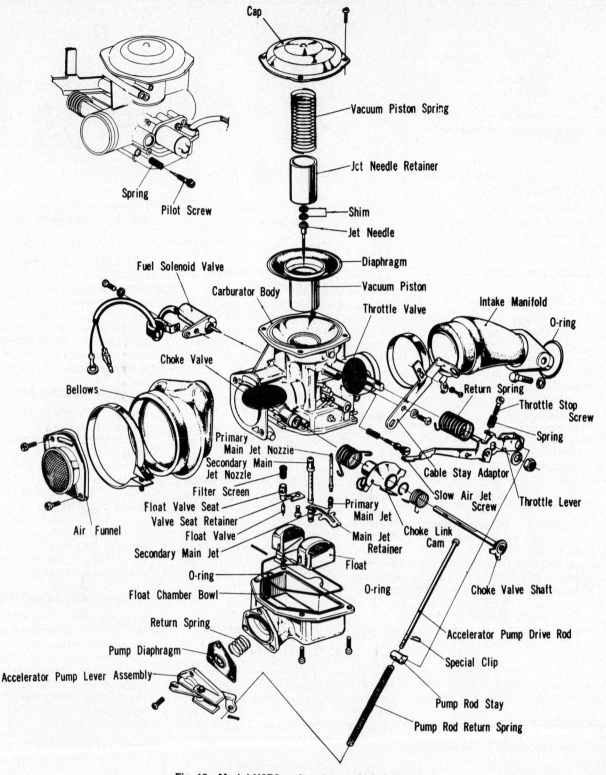

Cap

Vacuum Piston Spring

Jct Needle Retainer

Shim

Jet Needle

Diaphragm

Vacuum Piston

Intake Manifold

O-ring

Spring

Pilot Screw

Fuel Solenoid Valve

Carburator Body

Throttle Valve

Return Spring

Throttle Stop Screw

Spring

Choke Valve

Cable Stay Adaptor

Throttle Lever

Bellows

Slow Air Jet Screw

Primary Main Jet Nozzle

Secondary Main Jet Nozzle

Filter Screen

Float Valve Seat

Valve Seat Retainer

Float Valve

Secondary Main Jet

Primary Main Jet

Main Jet Retainer

Choke Link Cam

Air Funnel

Float

O-ring

O-ring

Float Chamber Bowl

Choke Valve Shaft

Return Spring

Pump Diaphragm

Accelerator Pump Drive Rod

Special Clip

Accelerator Pump Lever Assembly

Pump Rod Stay

Pump Rod Return Spring

Fig. 16 Model N6D2 carburetor exploded view

5. Check adjustment in (4) above by turning the pilot screw slightly in a clockwise direction.

Fast Idle, Adjust (Hot)

1. Open the choke valve fully.

2. Fully close the throttle valve by backing off the throttle stop screw.
3. Bend the tip of the throttle lever so that there is 0.5-1.0mm clearance

between the throttle lever and the fast idle cam, Fig. 18.
4. Desired fast idling speed is 3500-4000 rpm choked to highest speed obtainable.

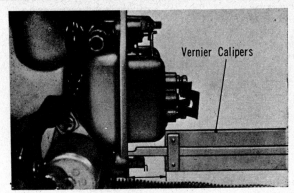

Fig. 17   Float adjustment

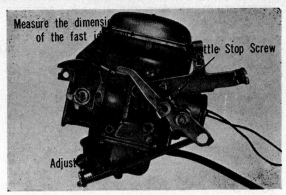

Fig. 18   Fast idle adjustment

Accelerator Pump Adjustment

1. Referring to the diagram Fig. 19, set the stroke to 1.8-2.8mm to obtain fuel volume per stroke of 0.15-0.25cc.

Solenoid Valve Operation

Operation of the solenoid valve may be checked by turning on the ignition switch and listening for the sound of the valve opening. A defective solenoid valve may be replaced as a unit, and properly functioning valves may be re-used when the carburetor is replaced. The carburetor/engine may be made to operate with a defective valve by affixing the valve plunger in the depressed (open) position or by removing the valve assembly and sealing the port.

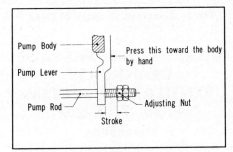

Fig. 19   Accelerator pump adjustment

Emission Controls Section

CVCC ENGINE
Description

This engine, Fig. 1, is designed to reduce the amount of hydrocarbons (HC), carbon monoxide (CO) and nitrogen oxides (NOx) present in the exhaust gases by modifications to the combustion chambers, carburetor and valve train.

The basic principle of the CVCC is progressive ignition of a stratified charge in two chambers which are the main combustion chamber and auxiliary combustion chamber or pre-chamber. These chambers are joined together by a small opening. The auxiliary combustion chamber uses a single small intake valve, and the main combustion chamber uses conventional intake and exhaust valves. All valves are actuated by a single overhead camshaft.

To provide proper intake mixture control under varying operating conditions, the intake air fuel mixture for each cylinder is controlled by three throttle valves in the carburetor, to provide the charge stratification which ensures stable and slow combustion under all operating conditions. This stable and slow combustion provides a low peak temperature which minimizes the formation of NOx and a high average temperature which reduces HC emissions.

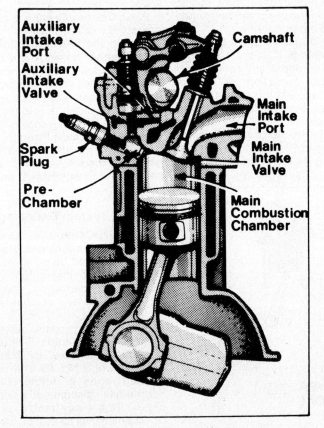

Fig. 1   Cross-sectional view of CVCC engine

Fig. 2 Intake stroke of CVCC engine

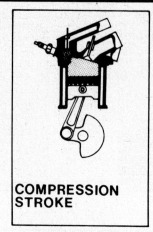

Fig. 3 Compression stroke of CVCC engine

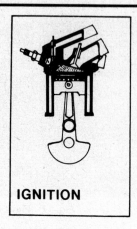

Fig. 4 Ignition stroke of CVCC engine

Operation

During the intake stroke, Fig. 2, a lean mixture is drawn through the main intake valve and into the combustion chamber. At the same time, a rich mixture is drawn through the auxiliary intake valve and into the pre-chamber.

At the end of the compression stroke, Fig. 3, a rich mixture is present in the pre-chamber, a moderate mixture is formed in the main chamber near the pre-chamber outlet, and a very lean mixture is present in the remainder of the main combustion chamber.

During ignition, Fig. 4, the rich mixture in the pre-chamber ignites easily. The flame from the pre-chamber ignites the moderate mixture.

During the power stroke, Fig. 5, the flame area extends further to burn the lean mixture in the main combustion chamber. The formation of CO is minimized because of this lean mixture.

After bottom dead center and during the exhaust stroke, Fig. 6, the air fuel mixture continues to burn. The hot exhaust gases exit through the exhaust valve and the oxidation process continues in the exhaust system.

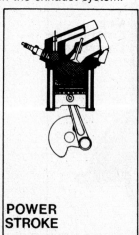

Fig. 5 Power stroke of CVCC engine

DUAL RETURN PASSAGE CRANKCASE VENTILATION SYSTEM FIGS. 7, 8 & 9
Description

Blowby vapor is returned to the combustion chamber through the carburetor and intake manifold. Vapors are separated in the condensation chamber and directed into the carburetor venturi or beneath the throttle plate depending on the amount of manifold vacuum. On some a drain tube is used to collect vapor that has condensed.

When the throttle valve is closed (idle) or partially open, blow-by vapor is returned to the intake manifold through both breather hoses A and B and passage one (fixed orifice). When the throttle valve is wide open, vacuum pressure in the air cleaner case rises and vacuum pressure at passage one (fixed orifice) decreases. Blowby vapor is drawn into the air cleaner case through vapor passage two, from the condensation and breather hose A. A small amount of vapor is returned through passage one (fixed orifice).

System Servicing

1. On 1973-74 models, squeeze lower end of drain tube and drain it of any accumulated oil or water. On 1975-76 models, disconnect drain tube from condensation chamber and drain it of any accumulated oil or water.
2. On 1973-74 models, make sure that intake manifold T-fitting (fixed orifice) is clear by inserting the shank of a No. 65 drill bit through both ends of fitting. On 1975-77 models, disconnect breather hose (B) from 4-way joint, then insert the shank of No. 59 drill bit into fitting to make sure it is clear.

3. On 1975-77 models, remove condensation chamber from air cleaner. Remove any sludge or varnish build-up from chamber, then reinstall it.
4. Inspect all hoses. Tighten loose connections and replace deteriorated hoses.

EVAPORATIVE EMISSION CONTROL SYSTEM
Description

Escape of fuel vapor into the atmosphere is prevented by fuel tank venting and fuel vapor purging, Figs. 10 and 11. A two-way valve in the filler cap regulates the fuel tank pressure or vacuum. Pressure relief allows fuel vapor pressure to be relieved when temperature increases and vacuum relief allows fuel tank vacuum to be relieved when temperature decreases or as the fuel supply is used. Vapor is converted to liquid fuel by a separator and returned to the tank. The portion not convertible is carried through a vent line to a charcoal cannister where it is purged or stored, depend-

Fig. 6 Exhaust stroke of CVCC engine

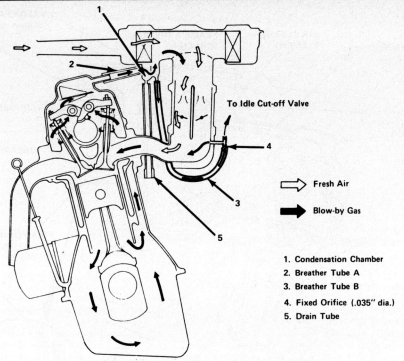

1. Condensation Chamber
2. Breather Tube A
3. Breather Tube B
4. Fixed Orifice (.035" dia.)
5. Drain Tube

⇨ Fresh Air

⬛ Blow-by Gas

To Idle Cut-off Valve

Fig. 7 Dual return passage crankcase ventilation system. 1973-74

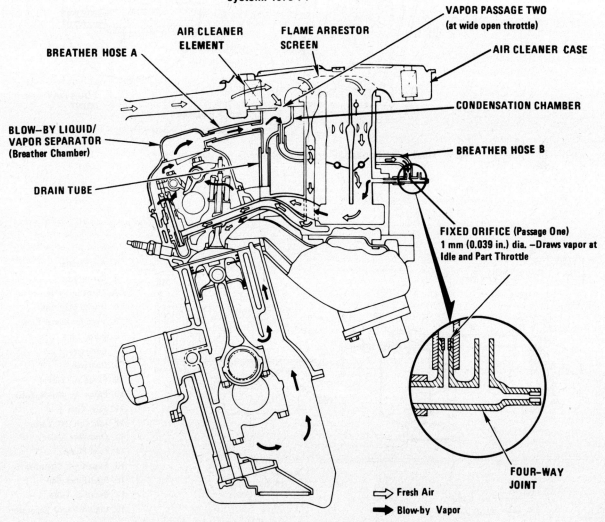

VAPOR PASSAGE TWO (at wide open throttle)

AIR CLEANER CASE

AIR CLEANER ELEMENT

FLAME ARRESTOR SCREEN

BREATHER HOSE A

CONDENSATION CHAMBER

BREATHER HOSE B

BLOW–BY LIQUID/ VAPOR SEPARATOR (Breather Chamber)

DRAIN TUBE

FIXED ORIFICE (Passage One) 1 mm (0.039 in.) dia. –Draws vapor at Idle and Part Throttle

FOUR–WAY JOINT

⇨ Fresh Air

⬛ Blow-by Vapor

Fig. 8 Dual return passage crankcase ventilation system. 1975-76

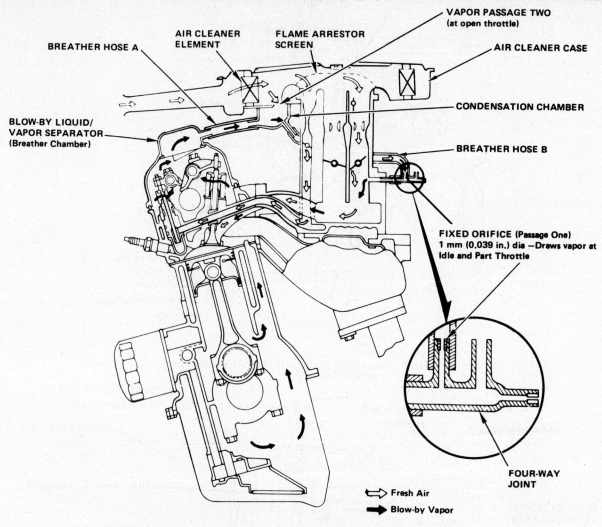

BREATHER HOSE A

AIR CLEANER ELEMENT

FLAME ARRESTOR SCREEN

VAPOR PASSAGE TWO (at open throttle)

AIR CLEANER CASE

BLOW-BY LIQUID/ VAPOR SEPARATOR (Breather Chamber)

CONDENSATION CHAMBER

BREATHER HOSE B

FIXED ORIFICE (Passage One) 1 mm (0.039 in.) dia —Draws vapor at Idle and Part Throttle

FOUR-WAY JOINT

⇨ Fresh Air
➡ Blow-by Vapor

Fig. 9 Dual return passage crankcase ventilation system. 1977

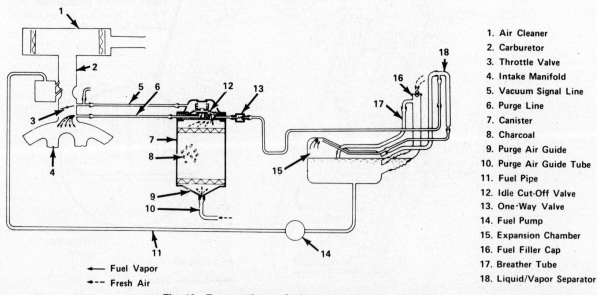

1. Air Cleaner
2. Carburetor
3. Throttle Valve
4. Intake Manifold
5. Vacuum Signal Line
6. Purge Line
7. Canister
8. Charcoal
9. Purge Air Guide
10. Purge Air Guide Tube
11. Fuel Pipe
12. Idle Cut-Off Valve
13. One-Way Valve
14. Fuel Pump
15. Expansion Chamber
16. Fuel Filler Cap
17. Breather Tube
18. Liquid/Vapor Separator

← Fuel Vapor
--→ Fresh Air

Fig. 10 Evaporative emission control system. 1973-74

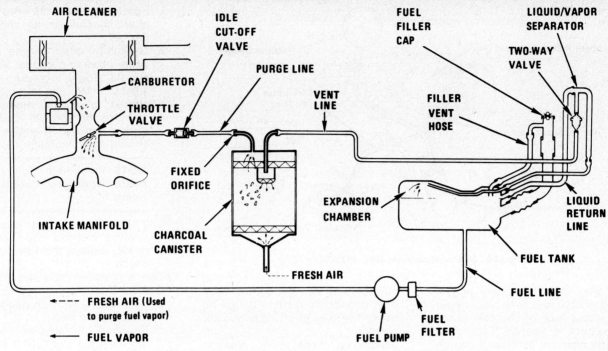

Fig. 11 Evaporative emission control system. 1975-77

ing on the position of the idle cut-off valve. The valve opens and purges the cannister only at part throttle. It is closed whenever the throttle valve is fully closed or wide open. Note that the filler cap vents only when the two-way valve becomes blocked.

System Diagnosis

1973 Charcoal Canister Test

1. Check for loose, disconnected or deteriorated hoses. Tighten loose connections, reconnect disconnected hoses, and replace deteriorated hoses.
2. Pull free end of purge air guide tube and plug it securely, Fig. 12.
3. Disconnect fuel vapor line from charcoal canister and connect a vacuum gauge to fuel vapor inlet, Fig. 12.
4. Start engine and allow to idle. The vacuum gauge should register no vacuum. If vacuum gauge shows vacuum, replace the charcoal canister.
5. Accelerate engine to 2000 rpm. Vacuum gauge should not show a reading. If gauge shows a reading, disconnect purge air guide tube, then accelerate engine and check for vacuum by placing finger over end of tube. If vacuum is available, the system is operating normally. If no vacuum is available, replace charcoal canister and recheck system.
6. If no vacuum reading was obtained with engine at 2000 rpm in step 5, disconnect vacuum signal line and connect vacuum gauge as shown in Fig. 13. Vacuum reading with engine at 2000 rpm should be greater than 3 inches Hg. If vacuum is available, replace charcoal canister and recheck system. If vacuum is not available, or is less than 3 inches Hg., proceed to step 7.
7. If there is no vacuum, or if vacuum is less than 3 inches Hg. with engine at 2000 rpm, check for an obstructed T-fitting or carburetor port. If vacuum is now available, recheck the

system. If vacuum is still not available, proceed to step 8.
8. If vacuum is still not available, or is less than 3 inches Hg, plug the solenoid valve vacuum line, Fig. 14, and check for vacuum. If vacuum is now available, repair or replace the advance-retard solenoid and recheck the system.

1975-77 Charcoal Canister Test

1. Inspect charcoal canister if damaged or leaking.

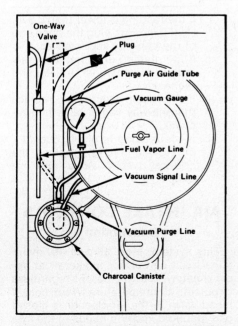

Fig. 12 Charcoal canister test. 1973-74

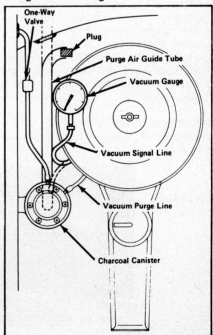

Fig. 13 Charcoal canister test. 1973-74

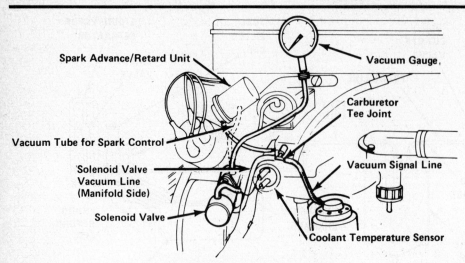

Fig. 14 Charcoal canister test. 1973-74

2. Start engine and increase engine speed to 2000 rpm, then place finger over intake tube of charcoal canister to check for suction. If suction is felt, the charcoal canister is operating properly. If no suction is felt, replace canister and recheck it.

1975-77 Two-Way Valve Test

1. Remove two-way valve from vehicle.
2. Connect a hand vacuum pump to valve with a vacuum gauge "teed" in-line between the pump and valve. Slowly increase vacuum while observing gauge reading. The two-way valve should open at .6 to 1.2 inches Hg. (usually with an audible sound). If valve does not open within the specified vacuum range, install a new valve.
3. Reverse the two-way valve and increase the vacuum while observing the gauge reading. The two-way valve should open at .2 to .6 inches Hg. (usually with an audible sound). If valve does not open within the specified vacuum range, install a new valve.

1975-77 Idle Cut-off Valve

1. Disconnect vacuum hose from carburetor side of idle cut-off valve, then connect a vacuum gauge between the idle cut-off valve and carburetor.
2. Disconnect hose from charcoal canister, Fig. 15.
3. Start engine and gradually increase its speed. As the engine speed is increased, the idle cut-off valve should open (usually with an audible sound). Vacuum gauge reading should momentarily stabilize at 1.5-3.1 inches Hg. If idle cut-off valve opening is not within the range of the vacuum reading, install a new valve and re-check the system.

1974 Idle Cut-off, One Way Valve & Charcoal Canister Test

1. Idle Cut-Off Valve:
   a. Remove the vacuum line at the idle cut-off valve leading to the vacuum advance solenoid and plug the port on the valve (4-speed only).
   b. Install a vacuum gauge between the idle cut-off valve and the carburetor vacuum port as shown in Fig. 16.
   c. Remove the vacuum line leading

from the idle cut-off valve to the charcoal canister as shown in Fig. 16.
   d. Gradually raise engine speed while observing gauge. Vacuum should slowly increase, and at 1.5-3.0 in/Hg, the cut-off valve should open and momentarily stabilize the vacuum reading. A further increase in engine speed should again increase vacuum.

NOTE: An audible sound may be heard when the cut-off valve opens.

   e. If the valve opens at a vacuum reading outside the specified range, replace the valve and recheck.
2. One-Way Vapor Valve and Charcoal Canister:
   a. Remove the vacuum gauge from the previous step.
   b. Reconnect the vacuum line leading from the idle cut-off valve to the charcoal canister.
   c. Install a vacuum gauge in the vacuum line leading from the charcoal canister to the one-way vapor valve as shown in Fig. 17.
   d. Plug the purge air guide tube.
   e. Gradually raise engine speed while observing vacuum gauge. As the vacuum increases the one-way vapor valve should open* and stabilize vacuum at 0.8-1.7 in. Hg. (20-43 mmHg). If the reading is outside this range, see items f and i below.

NOTE: An audible sound may be heard when the valve opens.

   f. If the reading is lower than 0.8 in. Hg (20 mmHg), plug the open end of the one-way vapor valve.
   g. If the reading does not increase, replace the charcoal canister and recheck.
   h. If the reading increases, replace the one-way vapor valve and recheck.
   i. If the reading is higher than 1.7 in. Hg (43 mmHg), replace the one-way vapor valve and recheck.

AIR INTAKE CONTROLS
Description

This system, Figs. 18 and 19, maintains fresh carburetor intake air at approximately 100 degrees F. regardless of outside air temperature. When cold, a bleed valve in the air cleaner is closed and manifold vacuum builds in the system, opening a diaphragm acutated

Fig. 15 Disconnecting vacuum hose from charcoal canister

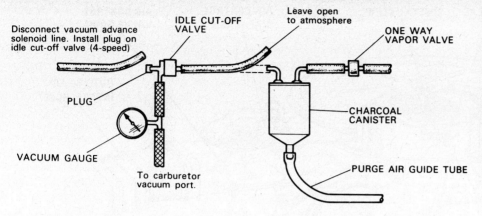

Fig. 16 Checking idle cut-off valve

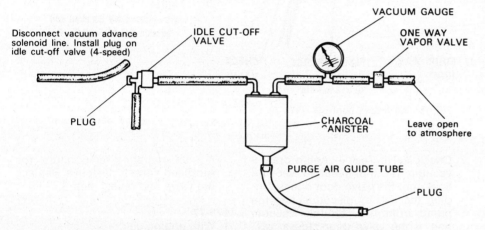

Fig. 17 Checking one-way vapor valve and charcoal canister

door which allows preheated air to enter and blocks outside air. When hot (above 100 degrees F.), the bleed valve opens and manifold vacuum escapes, repositioning the door so that ambient air enters and preheated air is blocked. A check valve prevents vacuum pressure loss to the intake manifold at wide-open throttle. A fixed orifice prevents rapid pressure changes and allows smooth operation of the valve door as well as maintaining the proper fuel-air ratio.

System Diagnosis

1973-74

NOTE: The following tests must be performed with engine cold.

1. Inspect for loose, disconnected or deteriorated vacuum hoses and replace as necessary.
2. Remove the air cleaner cover and element.
3. With the transmission in neutral, and the blue distributor wire disconnected, engage the starter motor for approximately two seconds. Manifold vacuum to the vacuum motor should completely raise the air Control valve door. Once opened, the valve door should stay open unless there is a leak in the system.
4. If the valve door functions properly, proceed to step 8. If the valve door

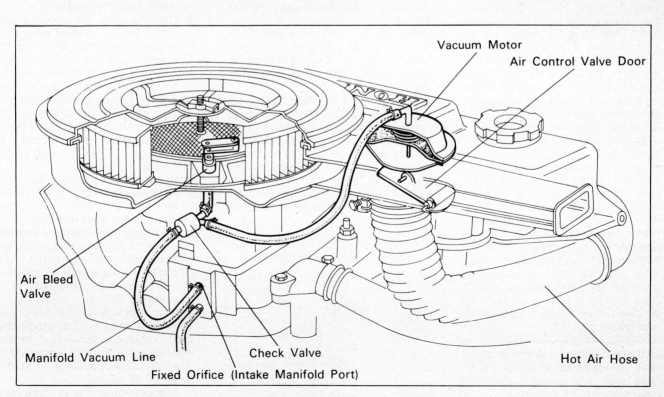

Fig. 18 Air intake controls. 1973-74

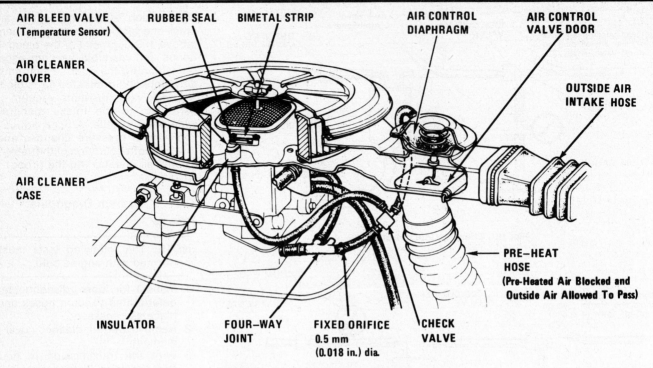

AIR BLEED VALVE (Temperature Sensor)   RUBBER SEAL   BIMETAL STRIP   AIR CONTROL DIAPHRAGM   AIR CONTROL VALVE DOOR

AIR CLEANER COVER

OUTSIDE AIR INTAKE HOSE

AIR CLEANER CASE

PRE–HEAT HOSE
(Pre-Heated Air Blocked and Outside Air Allowed To Pass)

INSULATOR   FOUR–WAY JOINT   FIXED ORIFICE 0.5 mm (0.018 in.) dia.   CHECK VALVE

Fig. 19 Air intake controls. 1975-77

does not open, check the intake manifold port by passing a No. 78 (0.016″ dia.) drill or compressed air through the orifice in the manifold. If the valve door still does not open or will not remain open, proceed to steps 5, 6 and 7.

5. Vacuum Motor Test — Disconnect the vacuum line from the vacuum motor inlet pipe. Fully open the air control valve door, block the vacuum motor inlet pipe, then release the door, Fig. 20. If the door does not remain open, the vacuum motor is defective. Replace if necessary and repeat step 3.

6. Air Bleed Valve Test — Unblock the inlet pipe and make sure that the valve door closes fully, without sticking or binding. Reconnect the vacuum line to the vacuum motor inlet pipe. Connect a vacuum source (hand vacuum pump) to the manifold vacuum line (disconnect at the intake manifold) and draw enough vacuum to fully open the valve door. If the valve door closes, with the manifold vacuum line plugged (by the vacuum pump), then vacuum is leaking through the air bleed valve. Replace if necessary and repeat step 3.

CAUTION: Never force the air bleed valve (bi-metal strip) on or off its valve seat. The bi-metal strip and valve seat may be damaged.

7. Check Valve Test — Again draw a vacuum (at the manifold vacuum line) until the valve door opens. Unplug the line by disconnecting the pump from the manifold vacuum line. If the valve door closes, vacuum is leaking past the check valve. Replace if necessary and repeat step 3.

8. With the air cleaner element in place, and the cover on, fit a vacuum gauge into the line leading to the vacuum motor as shown in Fig. 21.

9. Start the engine and raise the idle to 1500 to 2000 rpm. As the engine warms, the vacuum gauge reading should drop to zero. (Allow sufficient time for the engine to reach normal operating temperature — cooling fan cycles on and off). If the vacuum gauge does not drop to zero before the engine reaches

Vacuum Motor Inlet Pipe (Blocked)

Air Control Valve Door (Fully Open)

Fig. 20 Checking vacuum motor

normal operating temperature, the Air Bleed Valve is defective. Replace the valve and repeat step 3.

1975-77
1. With engine cold:
   a. Remove air cleaner housing cover and filter element.
   b. Crank engine for about 5 seconds. The air control valve door should rise while cranking the engine, and should remain fully open for at least 3 seconds after stopping the engine. If door does not rise, make sure that four way joint port is clear by passing the shank end of a No. 77 drill bit, or by blowing compressed air through the fixed orifice in the four way joint.
2. With engine hot (cooling fan on):
   a. Remove air cleaner cover and filter element and immediately check valve door position.
   b. Valve door should have dropped down to fully closed preheat position. As the air bleed valve cools, the valve door will begin to rise allowing preheated air to enter air cleaner.
3. If air control valve fails to rise or fails to remain open for 3 seconds after cold cranking test in step 1, or if air control valve door fails to drop to the fully closed position in step 2, proceed as follows:
   a. Disconnect and plug hose leading to air bleed valve.

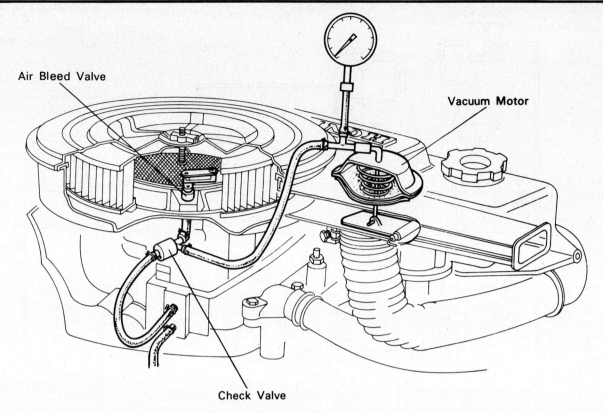

Air Bleed Valve

Vacuum Motor

Check Valve

Fig. 21 Check valve test

b. Crank engine for about 5 seconds. Air control valve door should rise and remain up for at least 3 seconds. If it does not, replace air bleed valve and retest.

c. If door does not rise or remain open for at least 3 seconds, disconnect vacuum hose from air control diaphragm. Raise air control valve door manually and while blocking the inlet pipe, release the valve door.

d. If valve door remains up, replace check valve and retest it. If valve door drops to closed position, replace the air control diaphragm and retest it.

AIR INJECTION SYSTEM

Description

This system, Fig. 22, is used to control hydrocarbon (HC) and carbon monoxide (CO) emissions by adding a metered amount of fresh air into the exhaust ports to extend the combustion process into the exhaust system.

Operation

Pressurized air from the air pump flows through the check valve to the air injection manifold which distributes the air to the air injection nozzles in each exhaust port near the exhaust valves.

The oxygen in the injected air plus the heat of the exhaust gases induce combustion of the unburned hydrocarbons (HC) in the exhaust system.

The check valve at the air injection manifold prevents back flow of exhaust gases. Normally, the air is directed through the check valve and into the air manifold. During deceleration, air is delivered to the intake manifold through the anti-afterburn valve to prevent exhaust afterburning or popping. When manifold vacuum is above the preset vacuum of the air control valve and/or below that of the air by-pass valve, the pressurized air is routed to the air cleaner.

Check Valve, Fig. 23

A check valve is used to prevent exhaust gases from flowing back into the air pump. When air pressure of the pump is greater than that of the exhaust gases, it opens the valve and air passes into the injection manifold. However, when pressure of the exhaust gases exceeds the air pump air pressure, the check will close to prevent gases from entering the air pump, which could damage the air supply hoses and/or air pump.

Air By-Pass Valve, Fig. 24

When manifold vacuum acting on the diaphragm of the air by-pass valve is

below the preset vacuum of the air by-pass valve, the valve opens and by-passes the air from the pump to reduce the amount of injected air. The air control valve of the air by-pass valve assembly controls the amount of injected air by returning air under pressure from the pump to the air cleaner in response to manifold vacuum. The relief valve protects the pump from excess pressure.

Delay Valve, Fig. 25

When intake manifold vacuum drops due to acceleration, this valve delays the operation of the air by-pass valve by allowing the pressure to equalize through the jet within the delay valve.

Anti-Afterburn Valve, Fig. 26

At the start of a sudden deceleration, a rich air-fuel mixture is present in the intake manifold and is supplied to the cylinders. This excessively rich mixture does not burn completely in the combustion chambers. To prevent this partial combustion, the anti-afterburn valve adds fresh air into the intake manifold during these periods of high vacuum to reduce the overrich mixture to a combustion mixture. The valve remains open in proportion to the amount of pressure change sensed by the diaphragm of the anti-afterburn valve.

Check valve "A" and the metering

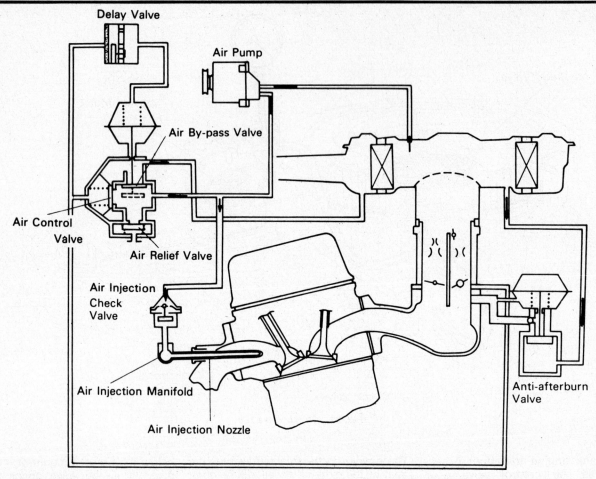

Fig. 22 Air injection system

orifice are built into the diaphragm and allow air to flow only from the sensing chamber to the air chamber. If vacuum in the sensing chamber, which is connected to the intake manifold, decreases, the check valve opens to allow air into the air chamber until the pressures in both chambers equalize. In the event of a sudden increase in manifold vacuum, the entire diaphragm unit is pulled downward. This condition lasts for a few seconds until the pressure in both chambers is equalized by air entering through the metering orifice.

System Diagnosis

System Check
1. Disconnect hose from check valve.
2. Start engine and allow to idle. Check that air is being drawn into the valve by placing a finger over the inlet. A slight vacuum should be felt.
3. If there is no vacuum or if exhaust gases are being forced out of the inlet, replace the valve and recheck.

Air Pump & Relief Valve
1. Check air pump drive belt condition and tension. Replace or adjust as necessary.

2. Check for loose, disconnected or deteriorated hoses. Repair or replace as necessary.
3. Disconnect hose from air pump to check valve at check valve and plug hose, then disconnect air return hose from air cleaner housing and connect a pressure gauge to it.
4. Start engine and raise speed to 3500 rpm. The air pressure gauge should read more than 5.7 psi. If not, replace air pump. At idle, the gauge should read 3.5-5.7 psi. If not, replace the by-pass valve assembly.

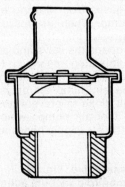

Fig. 23 Check valve

Replace pump if excessively noisy.
5. Remove pressure gauge and reconnect hoses.

Air Control Valve, Delay Valve & By-Pass Valve
1. Disconnect hose from air cleaner housing and check for a small amount of air coming out of hose with engine idling. If there is no air coming out, replace the air by-pass valve and recheck. Check if air flow stops when air control valve is disconnected and plugged at the tube end. If not, replace assembly and recheck.
2. Disconnect air control valve tube. Air flow should resume after 6-14 seconds. If not, proceed to step 3.
3. Disconnect and plug by-pass valve tube. Flow should stop when air control valve tube is connected to air by-pass valve joint. If air flow from return hose stops, replace delay valve and recheck as in step 2. If air flow does not stop, replace air by-pass valve assembly and recheck as in step 2.
4. Reconnect all hoses to proper position.

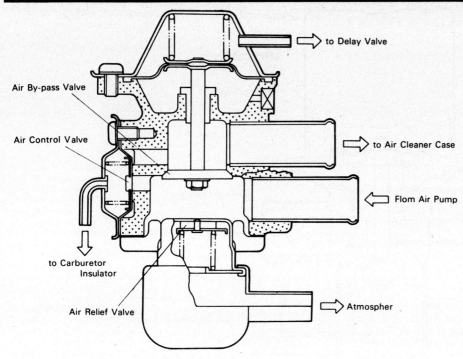

Fig. 24 Air by-pass valve

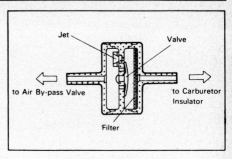

Fig. 25 Delay valve

Anti-Afterburn Valve

1. Check for looseness or deterioration of hoses.
2. Remove air cleaner housing and start engine.
3. With engine idling, there should be no vacuum at valve inlet. There should be vacuum when engine speed is raised to 3500 rpm and then throttle is closed suddenly. If system is not as specified, replace valve and recheck.

IGNITION TIMING RETARD SYSTEM

1975 With Hondamatic Trans.

This system is designed to reduce nitrogen oxides (NOx) during normal vehicle operation by retarding the ignition timing when the intake manifold vacuum becomes high enough.

System Diagnosis

1. Connect a timing light and tachometer to engine.
2. Start engine and allow to idle.
3. Check that ignition timing is advanced by disconnecting the vacuum line to vacuum controller.
4. If timing is not advanced, check for loose, disconnected, deteriorated or clogged vacuum line. Repair or replace as necessary.
5. If timing is still not advanced, replace vacuum controller and recheck.

IGNITION TIMING CONTROL SYSTEM

Description

This system is used in conjunction with the centrifugal advance of the distributor to regulate the ignition timing under certain conditions to reduce the amount of the exhaust emissions. The ignition timing is controlled according to engine speed, load and coolant temperature.

System Operation

1976 With Manual Trans. & 1977 Exc. Calif. & Hi Alt. with Hondamatic Trans. Figs. 27 & 28

When engine coolant temperature is below 149°F, thermosensor (A) energizes the ignition solenoid valve, allowing manifold vacuum to enter the distributor vacuum advance diaphragm through the ignition check valve. The check valve is provided to retain some vacuum at the distributor vacuum advance unit during periods of low manifold vacuum, such as wide open throttle. When coolant temperature is above 149°F, the thermosensor de-energizes the ignition solenoid valve, allowing vacuum to enter the distributor advance unit through the delay valve. The amount of vacuum supplied depends on the position of the throttle and the load on the engine (ported vacuum at the carburetor). This vacuum is applied gradually to the distributor advance unit

according to the characteristics of the delay valve.

1976 With Hondamatic Trans. & 1977 Calif. & Hi Alt. with Hondamatic Trans. Figs. 29 & 30

When engine coolant temperature is above 149°F, thermosensor "A" de-energizes the ignition solenoid valve(s) allowing manifold vacuum to the advance/retard diaphragm on the retard side until vacuum bleeding through the delay valve trips the vacuum switch, and relieves the vacuum.

On 1976 models, when coolant temperature is below 149°F, there is no retard. On 1977 models when coolant temperature is below 149°F, there is no retard and manifold vacuum is supplied to the advance side through solenoid valve "B" and the ignition check valve.

Regardless of engine coolant temperature, the ignition timing is advanced or retarded according to the vacuum created in the carburetor vacuum ports and the delay characteristics of the delay valve.

System Diagnosis

1976 With Manual Trans.

1. With engine cold:
   a. Disconnect vacuum hose from distributor advance unit, then connect a hand vacuum pump to engine and turn ignition key ON.
   b. Draw a vacuum with pump. Vacuum should not drop more than .8 inches Hg in 20 seconds. If vacuum loss is specified, refer to step 1 under "System Troubleshooting."
   c. Turn ignition key OFF. The vacuum should drop to zero.
   d. Start engine. Vacuum gauge should indicate a reading. If not, check port in carburetor manifold.
2. With engine hot:
   a. Allow engine to reach normal operating temperature. With engine warm, there should be no vacuum at idle. If there is vacuum, refer to "System Troubleshooting."

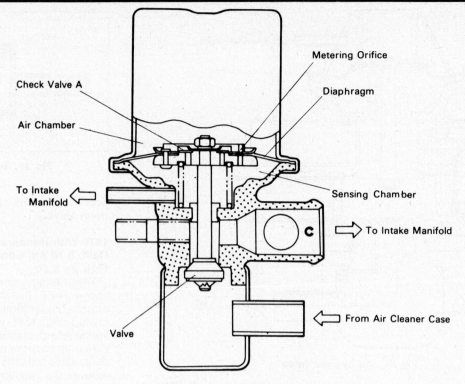

Fig. 26 Anti-afterburn valve

Labels: Check Valve A, Air Chamber, To Intake Manifold, Valve, Metering Orifice, Diaphragm, Sensing Chamber, To Intake Manifold, From Air Cleaner Case

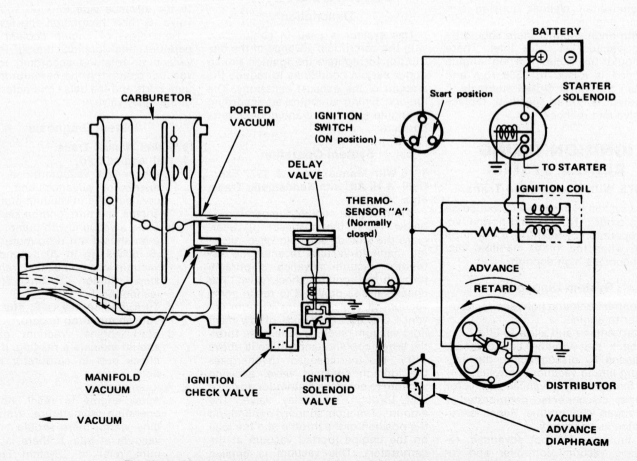

Fig. 27 Ignition timing control system. 1976 models with manual transmission

Labels: CARBURETOR, PORTED VACUUM, DELAY VALVE, IGNITION SWITCH (ON position), Start position, BATTERY, STARTER SOLENOID, TO STARTER, IGNITION COIL, THERMO-SENSOR "A" (Normally closed), ADVANCE, RETARD, MANIFOLD VACUUM, IGNITION CHECK VALVE, IGNITION SOLENOID VALVE, DISTRIBUTOR, VACUUM, VACUUM ADVANCE DIAPHRAGM

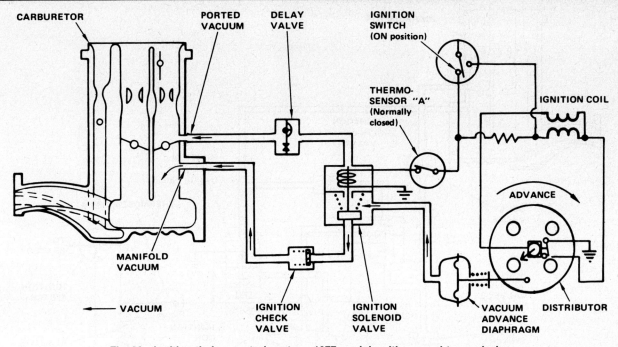

Fig. 28   Ignition timing control system. 1977 models with manual transmission

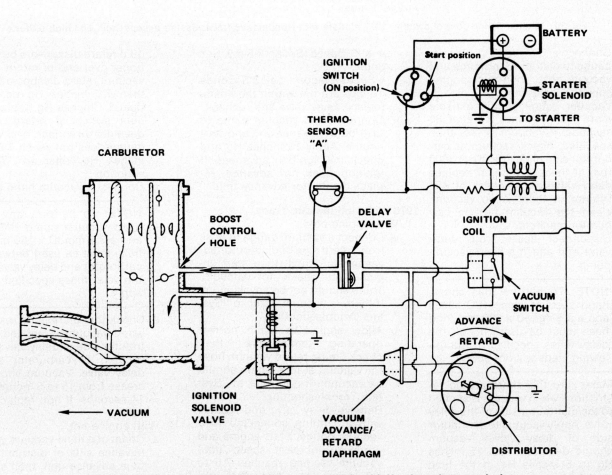

Fig. 29   Ignition timing control system. 1976 models with Hondamatic transmission

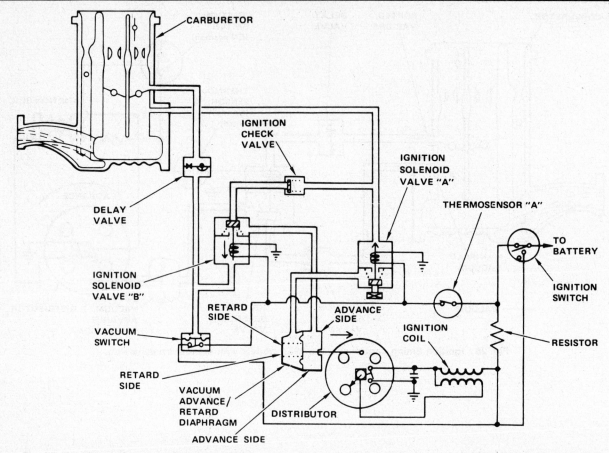

Fig. 30 Ignition timing control system. 1977 models with Hondamatic transmission except Calif. and high altitude

b. Connect a 0-4 inch Hg vacuum gauge to distributor advance unit vacuum hose, then raise engine speed to 3000 rpm.

c. Vacuum gauge should indicate more than 2 inches Hg after 30 seconds. If vacuum is less than specified, check vacuum at carburetor side of delay valve at 3000 rpm. If there is vacuum, replace delay valve and recheck at distributor. If there is no vacuum, clean the vacuum port in carburetor manifold.

d. Disconnect hoses from delay valve and attach a hand vacuum pump.

NOTE: To perform this check, hand vacuum pump H/C 58369 and a 3.5 mm ID x 280 mm long hose must be used. If not, the delay times specified in the following steps will not apply.

e. Make sure that there are no restrictions when vacuum is applied to the distributor side of the delay valve. Apply vacuum to distributor side of delay valve. Vacuum should decrease from 15 inches Hg to 5 inches Hg in the time specified:

4 & 5 Speed Sedan 2.5-9.5 Seconds
4 Speed Wagon   4-13 Seconds
If times are not within the limits, replace delay valve and recheck.

f. Connect hand vacuum pump to distributor advance unit and start engine. Apply 15 inches Hg and check that ignition advances. If ignition does not advance, replace distributor advance unit.

1976 With Hondamatic Trans.

1. With engine cold:
   a. Connect a vacuum gauge to hose from retard side of distributor advance/retard unit, then start engine and check for vacuum. There should not be any vacuum. If there is vacuum, refer to "System Troubleshooting."
   b. Allow engine to reach normal operating temperature, then check timing retard vacuum hose for vacuum at idle. There should be vacuum. If not, refer to "System Troubleshooting."
   c. Remove delay valve and replace with a T-fitting connected to a vacuum gauge. Start engine and gradually increase speed until vacuum reading reaches 7.5 to 8.7 inches Hg. Check that vac-

uum retard disappears by placing finger over end of retard hose. If vacuum retard disappears at less than 7.5 inches Hg or greater than 8.7 inches Hg, replace vacuum switch. If retard vacuum does not disappear, or if vacuum gauge does not reach 7.5 to 8.7 inches Hg, refer to "Troubleshooting."

d. Connect a vacuum hand pump.

NOTE: To perform this check, hand vacuum pump H/C 58369 and a 3.5 mm ID x 280 mm long hose must be used. If not, the delay times specified will not apply.

e. Check that there is no restriction when vacuum is applied to distributor side of delay valve. Apply vacuum to carburetor side of delay valve. Vacuum should decrease from 15 to 5 inches Hg 6 - 14 seconds. If not, replace delay valve.

2. With engine hot:
   a. Connect a hand vacuum pump to advance side of distributor vacuum advance unit, then start engine. Make sure that timing ad-

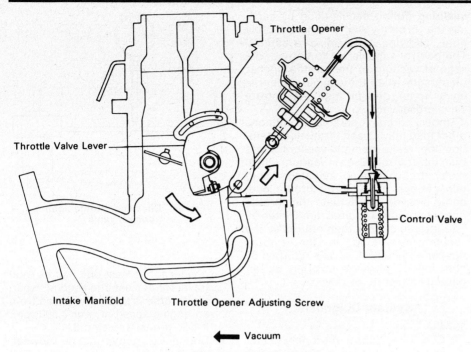

Fig. 31 Throttle opener system

vances when vacuum is applied. If not, replace vacuum advance unit.

b. Connect a hand vacuum pump to retard side of distributor vacuum advance unit, then start engine. Make sure that timing retards when vacuum is applied. If not, replace vacuum advance unit.

1977 Hondamatic Exc. Calif. & High Altitude & All With Manual Trans.

1. Check if vacuum line from distributor vacuum advance unit will hold vacuum. If it does not hold vacuum, check for 12 volts at ignition solenoid. If there is not voltage, check electrical connections.
2. If voltage is present, remove and plug vacuum line to delay valve (distributor side), then turn ignition switch to ON and apply a vacuum to line. If vacuum drop is less than .8 inches in 20 seconds, replace ignition solenoid valve and recheck. If vacuum still drops, replace ignition check valve and replace.
3. Check if there is vacuum at idle with engine at normal operating temperature, check thermosensor continuity. If there is continuity, replace thermosensor and recheck. If there is no continuity, replace ignition valve and recheck.

1977 Hondamatic Calif. & High Altitude

1. With engine cold, check if there is vacuum to the retard side of the dis-tributor vacuum advance unit. If there is vacuum, check voltage at ignition solenoid valve "A" with ignition switch ON. If there is battery voltage, replace ignition solenoid valve "A" and recheck.
2. With coolant temperature below 15°F, disconnect leads from thermosensor "A" and check continuity between thermosensor connectors. If there is no continuity, replace thermosensor and recheck.
3. Check for vacuum at the advance side of distributor vacuum advance unit with engine cold. If there is no vacuum, check hose connections. If there is still no vacuum, test voltage at ignition solenoid valve "B." If there is no voltage, check for vacuum at ignition check valve. If there is no vacuum to solenoid valve, check valve may be blocked or damaged. If there is vacuum, replace ignition solenoid valve "B" and recheck. If there is voltage, refer to step 2 above.
4. If there is no vacuum at the retard side or if there is vacuum to the advance side of the vacuum advance unit when engine is idling at normal operating temperature, disconnect wires from thermosensor "A" and check thermosensor for continuity. If there is continuity, replace thermosensor and recheck. If there is no continuity, reconnect wires to thermosensor and check for battery voltage at snap connector yellow wire. If there is battery voltage, replace vacuum switch and recheck. If there is no voltage and no vacuum retard, check for blocked vacuum port or blocked solenoid valve "A." Repair as necessary and recheck. If there is no voltage and there is vacuum advance, replace solenoid valve "B" and recheck.

System Troubleshooting

1976 With Manual Trans.

1. If vacuum line at distributor will not hold vacuum, check ignition solenoid valve. Disconnect and plug vacuum line to delay valve (distributor side), then turn ignition switch "ON" and draw a vacuum on line to distributor. If vacuum drop is less than .8 inches Hg in 20 seconds, replace ignition solenoid valve and recheck. If vacuum still drops immediately, replace ignition check valve and recheck.
2. Reconnect vacuum line and check for vacuum with engine idling at normal operating temperature. If there is vacuum, test thermosensor "A" for electrical continuity. If there is continuity, replace thermosensor

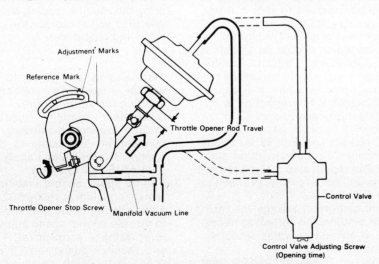

Fig. 32 By-passing throttle opener control valve.

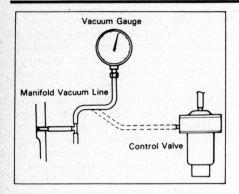

Fig. 33 Checking vacuum source

and recheck. If there is no continuity, replace ignition solenoid valve and recheck.

1976 With Hondamatic Trans.

1. If there is vacuum to retard side of distributor with engine cold while idling:
   a. Check voltage at ignition solenoid valve with ignition switch "ON." If there is battery voltage, repair or replace ignition solenoid valve and recheck.
   b. If there is no voltage in step a, test thermosensor "A" for continuity with coolant less than 150°F. If there is no continuity, replace thermosensor "A" and recheck. If there is continuity, check for a bad connection of fuse. Repair or replace as necessary and recheck.
2. With engine hot, if there is no vacuum at retard side of advance/retard diaphragm with engine idling, disconnect wires from thermosensor "A" and check for continuity:
   a. If there is continuity, replace thermosensor "A" and recheck.
   b. If there is no continuity, reconnect wires to thermosensor and check for battery voltage at black-yellow wire at snap connector. If there is battery voltage, replace vacuum switch and recheck. If there is no voltage, check for a blocked vacuum line or blocked ignition solenoid valve. Repair as necessary and recheck.

THROTTLE OPENER

Description

This system, Fig. 31, is used to control hydrocarbon emissions caused by non-combustible mixtures when the throttle is closed at high engine speed.

Operation

This system is designed to prevent

misfiring during deceleration by causing the throttle valve to remain slightly open, allowing better mixture control. The control valve is set to permit passage of vacuum to the throttle opener diaphragm when the engine coolant is equal to or greater than the control valve preset vacuum.

Under normal operating conditions other than fully closed throttle deceleration, the intake manifold vacuum is less than the control valve set vacuum. Thus, the control valve is not actuated. A sudden change in vacuum (throttle suddenly closed) will actuate the throttle opener for the required time interval. The throttle opener then returns as the vacuum remaining in the throttle opener and control valve is returned by atmospheric pressure entering the air passage at center of valve.

System Diagnosis

1974

1. Check for loose, disconnected or deteriorated vacuum hoses. Repair or replace as necessary.
2. Start engine and allow to reach normal operating temperature, then check idle speed with headlights "ON" and cooling fan "OFF." Vehicles with four speed transmission: idle speed should be 800±50 rpm. Vehicles with Hondamatic transmission: idle speed should be 750±50 rpm with transmission in first gear. Adjust as necessary.
3. To check for proper operation of system, bypass control valve by connecting manifold vacuum directly to throttle opener, Fig. 32. The throttle opener rod should retract with a resultant increase in engine speed. Check that reference mark on throttle opener bracket is between adjustment marks on throttle lever. If operation of system is as specified, proceed to step 7. If not, proceed to step 4.
4. Check throttle opener rod for full retraction which should be .2 inch. If fully retracted, adjust throttle opener stop screw to center the reference mark between the adjustment marks. If full retraction is not available, proceed to step 5.
5. Connect a vacuum gauge to manifold vacuum line, Fig. 33. If there is no vacuum, clear port in intake manifold and repeat step 3. If full retraction is still not available, proceed to step 6.
6. Check carburetor linkage for sticking or binding and correct as necessary. If linkage operates smoothly, repeat step 3.
7. Reconnect hoses and check that control valve will retract throttle

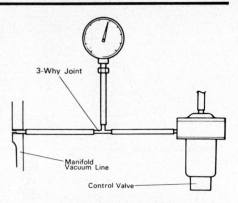

Fig. 34 Checking throttle opener control valve

opener for at least one half its total travel for at least one second, when the throttle is suddenly closed from an engine speed of over 3,500 rpm. If not, proceed to step 8.
8. Connect a vacuum gauge between manifold vacuum line and control valve using a 3-way fitting, Fig. 34. Note vacuum reading as throttle opener is actuated by the control valve when the throttle is suddenly closed from an engine speed of over 3,500 rpm. The vacuum reading should be 21±1.2 inches Hg. If not, adjust control valve adjusting screw.

NOTE: When increasing engine speed to over 3,500 rpm, vacuum should gradually increase. When the throttle is suddenly closed, the vacuum will momentarily increase and stabilize at a higher value, and then gradually decrease. At this point of stabilization, the vacuum reading should be taken.

9. If control valve adjustment does not bring the vacuum reading within the specified value, replace the control valve and repeat step 7.

1975

1. Start engine and allow to reach normal operating temperature (cooling fan starts to run).
1. Disconnect vacuum hose from throttle opener diaphragm, then connect vacuum pump to throttle opener diaphragm and apply a vacuum of 15-20 inches Hg.
3. Engine speed should stabilize and remain constant at 1500-2500 rpm. If engine speed is too low, widen slot in throttle opener speed adjustment lever using a screwdriver, Fig. 35, and recheck adjustment. If engine speed is too high, narrow the slot using needle nose pliers, Fig. 36,

Fig. 35 Increasing throttle opener regulating speed

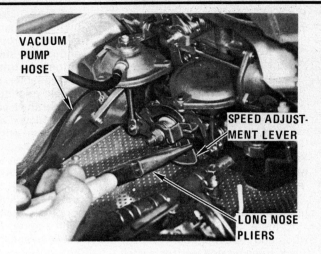

Fig. 36 Decreasing throttle opener regulating speed

and recheck adjustment.

4. Disconnect vacuum hose from dashpot diaphragm, then using a jumper wire, apply 12 volts to yellow-black wire terminal at control box connector, Fig. 37. Slowly open throttle until engine speed is about 4000 rpm, then release throttle.

5. Throttle should return to idle in 3-5 seconds. If not, proceed as follows:
   a. Remove control box cover and throttle opener control valve cover.
   b. Loosen locknut on control valve.
   c. Turn adjusting nut clockwise to decrease return time, or counterclockwise to increase return time.

   NOTE: If return time cannot be adjusted to specifications, refer to "Troubleshooting."

   d. Tighten lock nut and recheck adjustment.

6. Raise and support front of vehicle and apply parking brake.

7. Connect voltmeter positive probe to yellow-black wire terminal at control box connector, Fig. 37. Connect negative probe to black wire terminal.

8. Start engine, then place transmission in second gear and slowly accelerate engine while observing tachometer. As the voltmeter indicates 12 volts, the speedometer should indicate 5-15 mph.

9. Slowly decelerate engine while observing voltmeter. Voltmeter should deflect to zero when speedometer indication drops to between 5 and 15 mph. If there are no voltmeter indications, refer to "Troubleshooting." If voltmeter deflections do not correspond with the specified mph,

install a new speedometer and speed sensor and recheck.

Troubleshooting

1. If throttle does not close with ignition switch in "ON" position or takes longer than 4 seconds to close, replace dashpot solenoid valve and recheck.

2. If throttle closes in less than 1 second, test dashpot solenoid valve for voltage as follows:
   a. Turn ignition switch to "ON" position and measure voltage at dashpot solenoid valve.
   b. If there are about 12 volts, replace dashpot solenoid valve and recheck.
   c. If there is no voltage, check for bad electrical connections or fuse. Inspect wiring and repair or replace as necessary.

3. If throttle opener time cannot be increased, check throttle opener solenoid voltage as follows:
   a. If there are about 12 volts, it indicates either a defective throttle opener solenoid valve or defective throttle control valve. Repair or replace the defective components and recheck.

   NOTE: The throttle control valve can be checked by disconnecting vacuum line to throttle opener and checking for vacuum. The presence of vacuum indicates a failed throttle control valve.

4. If there is no voltage to throttle opener solenoid valve during speed sensor test, check for defective electrical connections, speed sensor or fuse. Repair or replace as necessary and recheck.

TEMPERATURE CONTROLLED SPARK ADVANCE
Description
1973-74 With Hondamatic Trans.

This system is designed to reduce nitrous oxide (NOx) emissions during normal vehicle operation. When engine coolant temperature is about 120° F or higher, the solenoid valve is energized and cuts off vacuum to the vacuum advance unit.

TRANSMISSION & TEMPERATURE CONTROLLED SPARK ADVANCE
Description
1973 With Manual Trans.

This system is designed to reduce nitrous oxide (NOx) emissions during normal vehicle operation by controlling the vacuum advance. When engine coolant temperature is 120° F or higher, and transmission is in first, second or third gear, the solenoid valve cuts off vacuum to the spark advace unit, resulting in lowered NOx emissions. When transmission is in fourth gear, normal vacuum advance is restored.

System Diagnosis

1. Check for loose, disconnected or deteriorated hoses, and replace as necessary.

2. Check coolant temperature sensor switch, Fig. 38, for correct operation using an ohmmeter or continuity light. The switch should normally be open (no continuity across switch terminals) when cool-

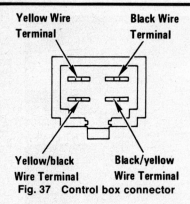

Fig. 37 Control box connector

Yellow Wire Terminal

Black Wire Terminal

Yellow/black Wire Terminal

Black/yellow Wire Terminal

ant temperature is below about 120° F. If there is continuity, replace switch and repeat check.

3. Check transmission sensor switch, Fig. 38. The switch should be open (no continuity across connections) in fourth gear, and closed (continuity across connections) in all other gears. Replace if necessary and repeat check.

4. Connect a vacuum gauge as shown in Fig. 14, then start engine and raise speed to 2000 rpm. With a cold engine, the vacuum gauge reading should be about 3 inches Hg or more. As engine coolant temperature reaches 120° F., (and before that fan starts), the vacuum reading should drop to zero. When transmission is shifted into fourth gear, the vacuum reading should return. If these conditions prevail, the system is operating normally. If vacuum is not initially available, proceed to step 5. If vacuum is initially available, proceed to step 7.

NOTE: If engine is still warm from the previous tests, disconnect the coolant temperature sensor switch before proceding further.

5. Disconnect vacuum signal line from charcoal canister and plug open end to prevent any vacuum leakage into the idle cut-off valve. With line plugged, again check for vacuum with engine running at 2000 rpm. If vacuum is now available, reconnect vacuum signal line and check idle cut-off valve for vacuum leaks. Refer to "Evaporative Emission Control System" for idle cut-off diagnosis. If vacuum is still not available, reconnect vacuum signal line and proceed to step 6.

6. Stop engine and disconnect vacuum line from solenoid valve (line between solenoid valve and T-joint) and connect a vacuum gauge to it. If vacuum is not available, the vacuum port is blocked. Clear the port with compressed air

and repeat step 4. On vehicles with manual transmission, if vacuum is available, replace solenoid valve and repeat step 4. On vehicles with automatic transmission, if vacuum is available, refer to step 8 and check continuity between coolant temperature sensor terminals.

7. On vehicles with manual transmission, run engine at fast idle and check vacuum while shifting transmission into first, second and third gear. If there is vacuum, stop engine and check continuity between coolant temperature sensor terminals. Refer to step 8.

8. With engine warm, check continuity between sensor terminals. If there is no continuity, replace temperature sensor switch, then recheck continuity and repeat step 4. If there is continuity, turn ignition switch on and check for battery voltage to vacuum solenoid. If there is no voltage, check wiring, fuses and connections. When voltage is obtained, repeat step 4. If there is voltage, and temperature sensor switch is operating normally, check connections and/or replace the solenoid valve, then repeat step 4.

TRANSMISSION CONTROLLED SPARK ADVANCE

Description

1974-75 With Manual Trans.

This system is designed to reduce nitrous oxide (NOx) emissions during normal vehicle operation by controlling the vacuum advance. When the transmission is in first, second or third gear, the solenoid valve lets off vacuum to the spark advance unit, resulting in lower NOx levels. When the transmission is in fourth gear, normal vacuum advance is restored.

System Diagnosis

1. Check for loose, disconnected or

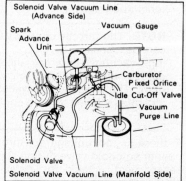

Fig. 39 Checking transmission controlled spark

Solenoid Valve Vacuum Line (Advance Side)

Spark Advance Unit

Vacuum Gauge

Carburetor Fixed Orifice

Idle Cut-Off Valve

Vacuum Purge Line

Solenoid Valve

Solenoid Valve Vacuum Line (Manifold Side)

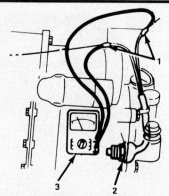

Fig. 38 Checking coolant temperature sensor switch

deteriorated vacuum hoses and replace as necessary.

2. Connect a vacuum gauge as shown in Fig. 14, then start engine and raise speed to 2000 rpm. The vacuum gauge reading should be zero with transmission in neutral. If there is a vacuum reading, proceed to step 4.

3. Shift transmission into fourth gear. The vacuum gauge reading should be 3 inches of vacuum or more at 2000 rpm, and reading should increase as engine speed is increased. If there is no vacuum, proceed to step 5. If there is vacuum, but less than specified, proceed to step 6.

4. Check for battery voltage at solenoid valve with ignition switch on and transmission in neutral. If voltage is available at the solenoid valve and there is vacuum, replace the solenoid valve and repeat step 2. If no voltage is available at the solenoid valve, check transmission switch yellow wire for voltage. If voltage is available, refer to step 5 and check switch operation. If there is no voltage to the switch, check wiring, fuses and connections. When voltage is obtained, repeat step 2.

5. Check transmission sensor switch continuity. The switch should be open (no continuity between connections) when transmission is in fourth gear, and should be closed (continuity across connections) in all other gear positions. Replace switch if defective, and repeat step 2.

6. Disconnect vacuum line from solenoid valve and connect a vacuum gauge to line. With engine running at 2000 rpm, if vacuum is 3 inches Hg or more, replace solenoid valve. If vacuum is less than 3 inches Hg, plug vacuum line to charcoal canister from idle cut-off valve and repeat step 6. If vacuum is still less than 3 inches Hg, check engine condition.

Clutch & Transmission Section
Accord & Civic

CLUTCH, ADJUST
Release Fork, Adjust

1. Loosen slave cylinder pushrod locknut.
2. Hold pushrod end nut stationary and with a screwdriver, turn the slotted pushrod counterclockwise to increase play, clockwise to decrease play. Remove freeplay entirely, then back out 1¾ to 2 turns to achieve the specified freeplay of 0.08-0.1 in. (2.0-2.6mm).
3. Tighten locknut to secure adjustment.

Clutch Pedal, Adjust

1. Turn pedal stopper bolt in or out until pedal height of 7.24 in. (184mm) without floor mat in place is obtained.
2. Loosen lock nut on clutch pedal pushrod and turn rod in or out until the clearance between the clutch pedal pushrod and master cylinder piston is 0.04-0.12 in. (1-3mm).
3. Tighten lock nut.

CLUTCH, REPLACE

1. Raise vehicle and remove engine and transmission assembly as described under "Engine, Replace" procedure.
2. Remove transmission as outlined in "Transmission, Replace" procedure.
3. Remove release fork and bearing by withdrawing pushrod from slave cylinder, removing the boot and set clips on the release fork, withdrawing the fork from the inside, and then removing the releasing bearing in its holder.

NOTE: Removal of release bearing from holder or installation requires driver 07949-6110000 and attachment 07947-6340300.

4. Insert ring gear holder 07924-6570000 into the two holes in the engine block adjacent to the left side of the ring gear, and engage tooth on ring gear holder with teeth on flywheel.
5. Separate clutch diaphragm spring from pressure plate by removing spring stoppers.
6. Loosen eight bolts and remove pressure plate.
7. Slide the clutch friction disc off the shaft.
8. Reverse procedure to install, using ring gear holder cited above and torquing pressure plate bolts to 34-38 ft. lbs. (4.7-5.3 kg-m) in a criss-cross pattern. Be sure mark on pressure plate is aligned with mark on flywheel if pressure plate is re-used. New pressure plates have no marks. Also, use clutch disc alignment tool 07944-6340000 to align clutch disc with crankshaft before tightening pressure plate bolts.

MANUAL TRANSMISSION, REPLACE

1. Raise vehicle and remove engine and transmission assembly as described under "Engine, Replace" procedure.
2. Separate transmission from clutch housing.
3. Reverse procedure to install.

600 Models

CLUTCH, ADJUST
Clutch Pedal Height Adjustment

1. Loosen lock nut on adjusting bolt.
2. Turn adjusting bolt as necessary for clutch pedal height to be the same as the brake pedal.
3. Tighten the lock nut.

NOTE: Pedal height adjustment must be made before lash adjustment.

Clutch Pedal Lash Adjustment

1. Specified pedal lash is 3mm (0.12 in.) at the tip of the clutch release lever.
2. Turn adjusting bolt near base of lever as necessary to obtain specified adjustment.
3. If proper adjustment cannot be obtained, check clutch cable for looseness and/or damage at the release lever and pedal ends.

CLUTCH, REPLACE

1. Loosen release lever lock nut and the adjusting bolt until maximum release lever play is obtained.
2. Hold clutch cable in one hand and remove the rubber cushion from the release lever while pushing in on it with the other hand.
3. Separate clutch cable and release lever.
4. Separate cable from the clutch cover by pulling on the engine side.
5. Remove clutch housing cover by removing bolts.
6. Remove clutch pressure disc by removing bolts.
7. Pull friction plate from splined shaft.
8. Remove clutch drum, being careful not to damage the oil seal.
9. Remove retracting springs, diaphragm setting plate, pressure disc and diaphragm spring.
10. Remove cotter pin and detach release bearing shaft and spring from housing.
11. Remove circlip and push out the release bearing shaft bushing from the housing.
12. Remove release bearing by supporting it in a jig and tapping the shaft lightly with a hammer.
13. Reverse procedure to install.

HONDAMATIC A600 AUTOMATIC TRANSMISSION
Description

The Honda A600 transmission is fully automatic and consists of a three-element torque converter and a 3-speed compound planetary gear set. The transmission is an integral unit with the engine (although separately lubricated) and is contained within the crankcase. However, the crankcase and the hydraulic components may be removed from either the left or right side of the vehicle without disturbing the cylinder head or the upper and lower crankcases. Major repairs to the gear train require removing the entire unit from the vehicle.

HONDA

HONDAMATIC A600 TROUBLE SHOOTING GUIDE

Trouble	Probable Cause (Refer to "Items to Check")

Range Selector Defects
1. Harsh shifting from Neutral to Drive. — E T K
2. Harsh shifting from Neutral to Reverse — E T j k
3. Operation is slow when shifted from Neutral to Drive — B E S a g i
4. Operation is slow when shifted from Neutral to Reverse. — F E s a g i m

Drive Defects
1. No drive in any range
  a. Torque converter not rotating — I
  b. Torque converter rotating — B S a b f g i m
  c. Pressure stalls in all drive ranges. — v w
  d. Torque converter does not rotate unless engine speed is increased — h
2. No forward drive — m u
3. No drive in Drive or Drive 1 — r m
4. No reverse drive.
  a. Engine overspeeds — c m t
  b. Pressure stalls — c s
5. Moves forward in Neutral when engine speed is increased — c j

Shifting Defects
1. No up-shift from Drive 1 — r
  a. No drive in Drive 1 or 2 — u
  b. No drive in Drive 2 only. — Y n q
  c. Normal drive in Drive 2. — Z

No Upshift From Second to Third
1. Second gear engages with third gear. — V
2. Drive speed does not respond to engine speed — n q
3. Engine overspeeds on up-shift from second to third. — n q
4. Normal drive in second and third. — Z
5. Up-shifts from first to third. — V
6. Up-shifts occur at low drive speed. — D U V W
7. Delayed shift spacing. — T U V

Harsh Shifting
1. Harsh shifting from first to second and from third to second. — X p
2. Harsh shifting from second to third. — p
3. Braking occurs when shifted from second to third. — o
4. Severe braking occurs when shifted from third to second. — o
5. Excessive engine noise when shifted from third to second. — Y n q

Stall Speed Defects
1. High stall speed. — B S a e g i m
2. Low stall speed. — F G c

Miscellaneous
1. Parking does not hold — C x
2. Transmission overheats — A c d

Poor Drive Acceleration
1. Poor acceleration at slow speed — c n q
2. Poor acceleration at high speed — A F d n q
3. Poor acceleration in all drive ranges — B D G S a e g i

Items to Check
Preliminary Adjustment Faults

A. Improper engine oil level.

B. Improper automatic transmission fluid level.

C. Improper installation or adjustment of selector cables (A and B).

D. Improper installation or adjustment of throttle secondary cable.

E. Improper engine idle speed.

F. Improper installation or adjustment of throttle cable.

G. Improper adjustment of ignition timing, valve timing, carburetor or improper compression pressure.

Hydraulic Control Faults

S. Stuck regulator valve, foreign particle on valve seat, weak or damaged spring.

T. Stuck regulator spring cap.

U. Stuck 1-2 shift valve, foreign particle on valve seat, weak or damaged spring.

V. Stuck 2-3 shift valve, foreign particle on valve seat, weak or damaged spring.

W. Stuck throttle valve, foreign particle on valve seat, weak or damaged spring or worn throttle drive arm.

X. Stuck timing valve, foreign particle on valve seat, weak or damaged spring.

Y. Clogged 0.8mm orifice in separator plate or defective accumulator valve.

Z. Worn oil seal on end of countershaft, worn or malfunctioning governor valve. Damaged governor weight, or weak or damaged weight spring; clogged 1.2mm orifice in the main valve body separator plate.

Mechanical Faults

a Excessively worn teeth or side face of the pressure pump gears.

b Defective pump impeller shaft or drive mechanism.

c Slipping one-way clutch in torque converter stator.

d Seized one-way clutch in the torque converter stator.

e Insufficient torque converter fluid due to defective torque converter housing oil seal.

f Defective torque converter housing spline or defective primary drive chain.

g Clogged oil strainer screen or air sucked in from strainer.

h Clutch malfunction due to drop off of internal circlip on the primary clutch drum.

i Worn or slipping primary clutch driven plates. Worn primary clutch piston O ring, worn oil seal on the crankcase left side cover (mainshaft end) or oil leak from relief valve.

j Seized primary clutch, distorted drive plates, drop out of the wave spring, malfunction of the relief valve.

k Weak or broken primary clutch wave spring.

l Broken or damaged pump impeller shaft, drive coupling or crankshaft drive mechanism.

m Worn or damaged servo piston O ring; stuck servo valve due to foreign particle. Servo malfunction due to freeze-up of reverse select gear and reverse gear hub.

n Worn or slipping 2nd (3rd) clutch driven plates; worn or damaged piston O ring.

o Seized 2nd (3rd) clutch; distorted drive plates; drop-out of wave spring, weak or broken release spring.

p Weak or broken 2nd (3rd) clutch wave spring.

q Worn or damaged oil sealing ring.

r Slipping one-way clutch on low gear.

s Seized one-way clutch on low gear.

t Defective mainshaft reverse gear.

u Seized countershaft reverse gear.

v Seized mainshaft ball/needle bearings; seized reverse idle gear.

w Seized differential shaft ball bearings.

x Defective parking pawl.

Maintenance

Check fluid level with the dipstick located in the engine compartment on the left side of vehicle. Engine should be running at idle speed and the fluid should be warm to the touch. The gear selector lever should be in 3 position. Fluid level should be between the upper and lower marks on the dipstick. When adding, bring fluid level to the upper mark. Do not overfill. To bring fluid level from the low to high marks requires 0.6 pints (0.25 liters).

If additional fluid is required, use only SAE standard ATF Type A transmission fluid.

NOTE: An accurate check of fluid level cannot be made when the fluid is at normal operating temperature or very cold, as in either case, the reading will be outside the marks.

An accurate check may be made in Manual 1,2,3, D or R selector positions but 3 is recommended because vehicle creep will be minimal with parking brake applied. Do not make the check in N or P because the primary clutch will be disengaged, causing fluid agitation and consequent inaccurate readings.

Fluid should be changed every 12,000 miles (20,000 km) under normal operating conditions. Wrench 07053-58043 or equivalent is required to remove the drain plug. 3.6 US pints (1.7 liters) is required to bring fluid level to the upper mark on the dipstick after a routine drain. Full capacity is 6.8 pints (3.2 liters), the difference accounting for fluid normally retained in the torque converter and fluid control passages.

CAUTION: Do not use Dexron-type fluids in Honda transmissions, except for temporary operation when Type A fluid is unobtainable.

Manual Linkage, Adjust

1. Place selector lever in N position on the quadrant.
2. Disconnect the two selector cables, "A" and "A" in Fig. 1, at their control lever or engine ends, and also at their quadrant ends, Fig. 1.
3. Assuming maladjustment, remove the control lever and cam, Fig. 1, from the driver arm shaft and reposition the assembly so that the punch marks on the lever and shaft are aligned with the cam faced forward. The transmission is now set in N range.
4. Reconnect the cables to the control lever, applying grease to the cable end balls and the sockets on the lever.
5. Connect the upper ends of the cables to the hooks on the selector strap of the selector lever.
6. Set the adjusting nuts so there is no slack in the cables. Complete the adjustment by backing off ½ turn on the adjuster nuts, then tighten the lock nuts.
7. Check for proper cable tension with the selector lever in 1 and P positions. Readjust cable tension (in N position) if necessary so that tension is correct when the indicator plate is exactly centered in its window in 1 and P.
8. Move the selector lever to all positions right and left of N to make sure gear selection is smooth.
9. With the selector lever in P, release the parking brake and rock the vehicle to make sure the front (driving) wheels are locked.
10. Repeat step 8 above with the engine running and on the road.

NOTE: When the cables are properly adjusted, all gear selections made toward the left on the quadrant should be complete when the indicator has moved into the first third of the window; shifts to the right on the quadrant should be complete when the indicator has moved into two-thirds of the window.

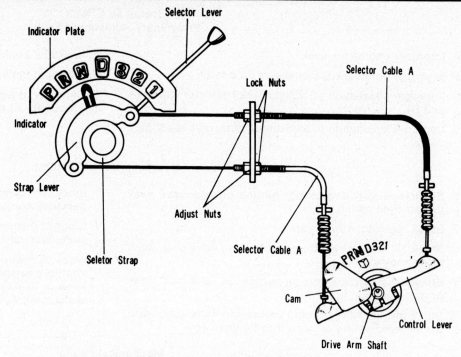

Fig. 1   Manual linkage adjustment

HONDAMATIC 2-SPEED AUTOMATIC TRANSMISSION
Trouble Shooting Guide

Transmission Will Not Move In All Gears
1. Check manual linkage adjustment.
2. Check fluid level.
3. Check oil pressure.
4. Defective servo valve piston.
5. Defective reverse gear selector spline.
6. Slippage of press fitted portion of converter pump inner hub.
7. Damaged pump drive gear spline.
8. Axles not engaged in differential assembly.

Transmission Slips In All Gears
1. Check manual linkage adjustment.
2. Check fluid level.
3. Check oil pressure.
4. Torque converter pump inoperative.
5. Clogged pump strainer.
6. Defective or sticking regulator in valve body.

No D Or R — Engine Stalls On Acceleration
1. Check manual linkage adjustment.
2. Check fluid level.
3. Check stall rpm.
4. Throttle control cable not adjusted properly.
5. Sticking or defective reverse/idler gear.
6. Defective torque converter one-way clutch.

Transmission Slips In D Or R
1. Check manual linkage adjustment.
2. Check fluid level.
3. Check oil pressure.
4. Defective drive clutch.

No L Or Slippage In L
1. Check manual linkage adjustment.
2. Check fluid level.
3. Check oil pressure.
4. Defective low clutch.

Transmission Stalls In R On Acceleration
1. Check manual linkage adjustment.
2. Check fluid level.
3. Check stall rpm.
4. Loose countershaft locknut.

Transmission Slips In R
1. Check manual linkage adjustment.
2. Check fluid level.
3. Check oil pressure.
4. Defective servo valve piston.
5. Defective reverse gear selector spline.
6. Defective drive clutch.

D & L Stall Is Too High
1. Check manual linkage adjustment.
2. Check fluid level.
3. Check stall rpm.
4. Damaged pump drive gear spline.
5. Torque converter pump inoperative.
6. Clogged pump strainer.
7. Defective torque converter one-way clutch.
8. Sticking or breakage of regulator spring cap and/or spring.

D Stall Speed Is Too High
1. Check manual linkage adjustment.
2. Check fluid level.
3. Check stall rpm.
4. Defective servo valve piston.
5. Defective drive clutch.
6. Defective low clutch.

L Stall Speed Is Too High
1. Check manual linkage adjustment.
2. Check fluid level.
3. Check stall rpm.
4. Defective low clutch.
5. Loose countershaft locknut.

D & L Stall Speed Is Too High
1. Check manual linkage adjustment.
2. Check fluid level.
3. Check stall rpm.
4. Throttle control cable not adjusted properly.
5. Slippage of press fitted portion of converter pump inner hub.
6. Defective torque converter one-way clutch.

Poor Acceleration
1. Check manual linkage adjustment.
2. Check fluid level.
3. Defective drive clutch.
4. Defective low clutch.
5. Defective torque converter one-way clutch.

Grinds In Reverse
1. Check manual linkage adjustment.
2. Check fluid level.
3. Defective servo valve piston.
4. Sticking or defective reverse/idler gear.
5. Servo piston sticking in transmission housing recess.

Speedometer Not Operative — Slippage In Low
1. Loose countershaft locknut.

Buzzing Noise In L Or D
1. Torque converter pump inoperative.
2. Loose countershaft locknut.

Engine Cannot Be Turned Over By Hand
1. Oil pump driven gear seized to separator plate.
2. Engine failure.

Loud Noise In All Gears & Neutral & Park
1. Oil pump gear installed upside down.

Car Moves In L But Hesitates In D
1. Thrust washer in low gear assembled incorrectly.
2. Burrs on mainshaft.

Car Will Not Move In Any Gear
1. Countershaft low gear installed backwards.
2. Reverse gear hub installed upside down.

Car Will Accelerate Only To 30 MPH
1. Stator assembled backwards in torque converter.

Vibration In All Gears
1. Torque converter not fully installed causing deformation of flex plate.

Maintenance

To check fluid, drive vehicle for at least 15 minutes to bring fluid to operating temperature and then park on a level surface. Shut off engine and within one minute, loosen dipstick, check fluid and if necessary, add G.M. Dexron to upper level. Transmission fluid should be replaced at the first 15,000 miles and every 30,000 miles thereafter. Replacement requires 2.6 quarts (2.5 lit.). Fill through dipstick opening.

Control Cable, Adjust

1. Start engine. Place selector in reverse and check that engagement is felt.
2. With engine off, remove center console by loosening the attaching screws at each end.
3. Place shift lever in reverse, then remove lock pin and control rod pin.
4. Check that the hole in the cable end is perfectly aligned with the holes in the selector cable bracket.
5. If not aligned, loosen locknuts on control cable and adjust the adjuster as required.
6. Tighten locknuts and replace center console.

Selector Lever Position, Adjust

1. Apply parking brake and run engine while depressing the brake pedal.
2. Move selector lever slowly back and forth from N position, making sure that distance between N and points

where "D" clutch is engaged toward both R and 2 positions are the same. "D" clutch engaging point in either direction is just before slight response is felt. Toward R, reverse gears will be heard.

3. Check that selector lever cannot be moved from N to R unless button on left end of the selector lever knob is depressed.
4. Check that engine does not start in any position other than N or P.
5. Check that back-up lights come on in R positon.
6. Place selector lever in P on a downgrade and check for proper braking action.
7. If necessary, length of control cable may be adjusted by turning adjuster located at the front bottom of the selector lever assembly.

Transmission, Replace

1. Support transmission with a jack, attach hangar plate to transmission, and pull chain tight with hoist.
2. Remove the center beam.
3. Remove the wind control bracket.
4. Remove splash guard.
5. Detach control cable.
6. Remove drive shaft.
7. Turn the crankshaft pulley and remove the eight drive plate attaching bolts.
8. Disconnect the exhaust pipe, all hoses, and the speedometer and shift control cables.
9. Remove attaching bolts to the flywheel cover and engine mount brackets, and lower the transmission and torque converter assembly until it slides away from the engine.
10. Reverse procedure to install, torquing transmission attaching bolts to 29-36 ft. lbs. (4-5 kg-m).

MANUAL TRANSMISSION

The 4-speed constant mesh manual transmission is an integral unit with the engine and is lubricated by the engine oil supply. The only routine service required is to ensure that the engine crankcase contains an adequate supply of engine oil.

Differential, Drive Shaft & Brakes
Civic & Accord

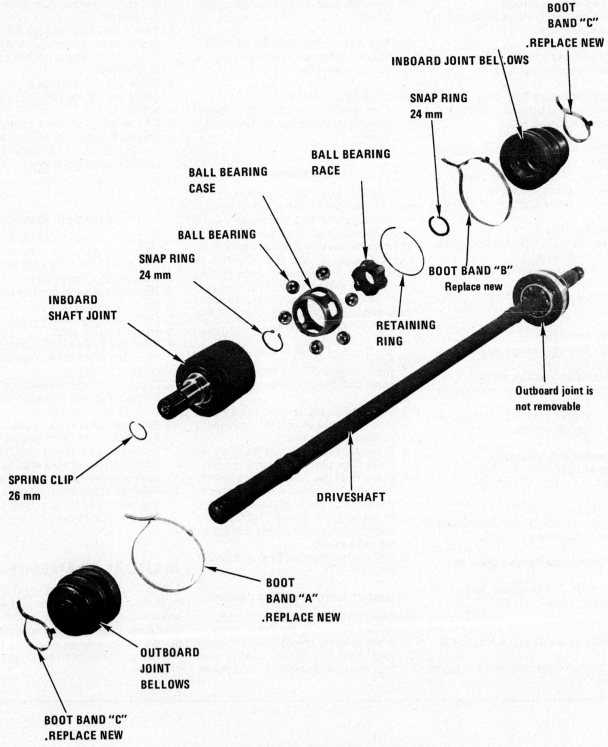

BOOT BAND "C" .REPLACE NEW

INBOARD JOINT BELLOWS

SNAP RING 24 mm

BALL BEARING RACE

BALL BEARING CASE

BALL BEARING

SNAP RING 24 mm

BOOT BAND "B" Replace new

RETAINING RING

INBOARD SHAFT JOINT

Outboard joint is not removable

SPRING CLIP 26 mm

DRIVESHAFT

BOOT BAND "A" .REPLACE NEW

OUTBOARD JOINT BELLOWS

BOOT BAND "C" .REPLACE NEW

Fig. 1 Driveshaft assembly. Civic and Accord

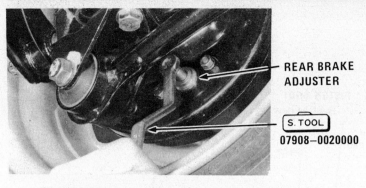

Fig. 2 Adjusting drum brakes. Civic and Accord

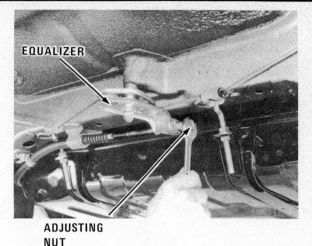

Fig. 3 Adjusting parking brake. Civic and Accord

DIFFERENTIAL

Description

NOTE: The differential is integral with the transmission and either the transmission, or the transmission and engine assembly, must be removed from the vehicle for access to the differential.

Replace

1. Remove either the transmission or the transmission and engine assembly from the vehicle.
2. Referring to "Unit Repair Section" disassemble transmission (following separate procedure for manul and Hondamatic transmission) as required for access to the differential assembly.
3. Remove differential assembly using driver 07965-6340100

NOTE: If the oil seals in either the transmission or clutch housings are removed, they must be replaced with new seals. See Unit Repair Section below for procedures.

NOTE: If replacing the transmission housing, clutch housing or differential side bearings, differential side clearance must checked. Refer to Unit Repair Section below for procedures.

4. Reverse procedure to install.

DRIVE SHAFT, REPLACE

NOTE: Replacement procedures for left and right drive shafts are the same.

1. Drain transmission.
2. Remove cotter pin and loosen spindle nut with socket 07907-6010200 and handle 07907-6010300.

3. Raise car and remove front wheel and spindle nut.
4. Remove cotter pin and nut securing suspension arm ball nut on both sides.
5. Free ball joint from knuckle using driver 07941-6710200 and collar 07941-6710100.
6. Remove ball joint from knuckle.
7. Pry CV joint out approximately 0.5 in. (12.7mm) and pull sub-axle out of transmission case, Fig. 1.
8. Reverse procedure to install, making sure that the CV joint sub-axle bottoms and that the spring clip holds the sub-axle securely in the transmission.

BRAKE PEDAL HEIGHT, ADJUST

1. Back off stop light switch until it no longer interferes with brake pedal adjustment.
2. Loosen lock nut and turn push rod in or out until pedal height of 7.24 inches (184mm) for Accord Models, or 5.32 inches (135mm) for Civic models is obtained, and then tighten lock nut securely.
3. Loosen stop light switch lock nut and turn in switch until its threaded end touches the pedal stopper bracket. Continue turning in stop switch until pedal play is zero, then back off switch ¼-½ turn. Tighten lock nut securely.
4. With pedal free play adjusted, check to see if stop light is off. Readjust if necessary.

BRAKES, ADJUST

1. Raise rear wheels off ground.

2. Depress brake pedal two or three times and release.
3. Turn brake adjuster 07908-0020000 clockwise until wheel will no longer turn, Fig. 2.
4. Back off adjuster 2 clicks (¼ turn = 1 click).
5. Turn wheel and check for dragging. If wheel drags, back off one more click.

PARKING BRAKE, ADJUST

1. Raise rear wheels off ground.
2. Loosen equalizer adjusting nut, Fig. 3.
3. Pull parking brake lever up one notch.
4. Tighten equalizer adjusting nut until rear wheels drag slightly when turned.
5. Release brake lever and check that rear wheels do not drag when turned. Readjust if necessary.

MASTER CYLINDER, REPLACE

1. Disconnect primary and secondary brake lines.
2. Disconnect wires to fluid level sensors.
3. Remove two attaching bolts holding master cylinder to the vacuum booster unit, and remove master cylinder.

NOTE: Booster rod to master cylinder clearance is 0.004-0.0236 in. (0.1-0.6mm). Use tool 07975-6570000 to measure.

4. Reverse procedure to install, bleeding brakes as necessary.

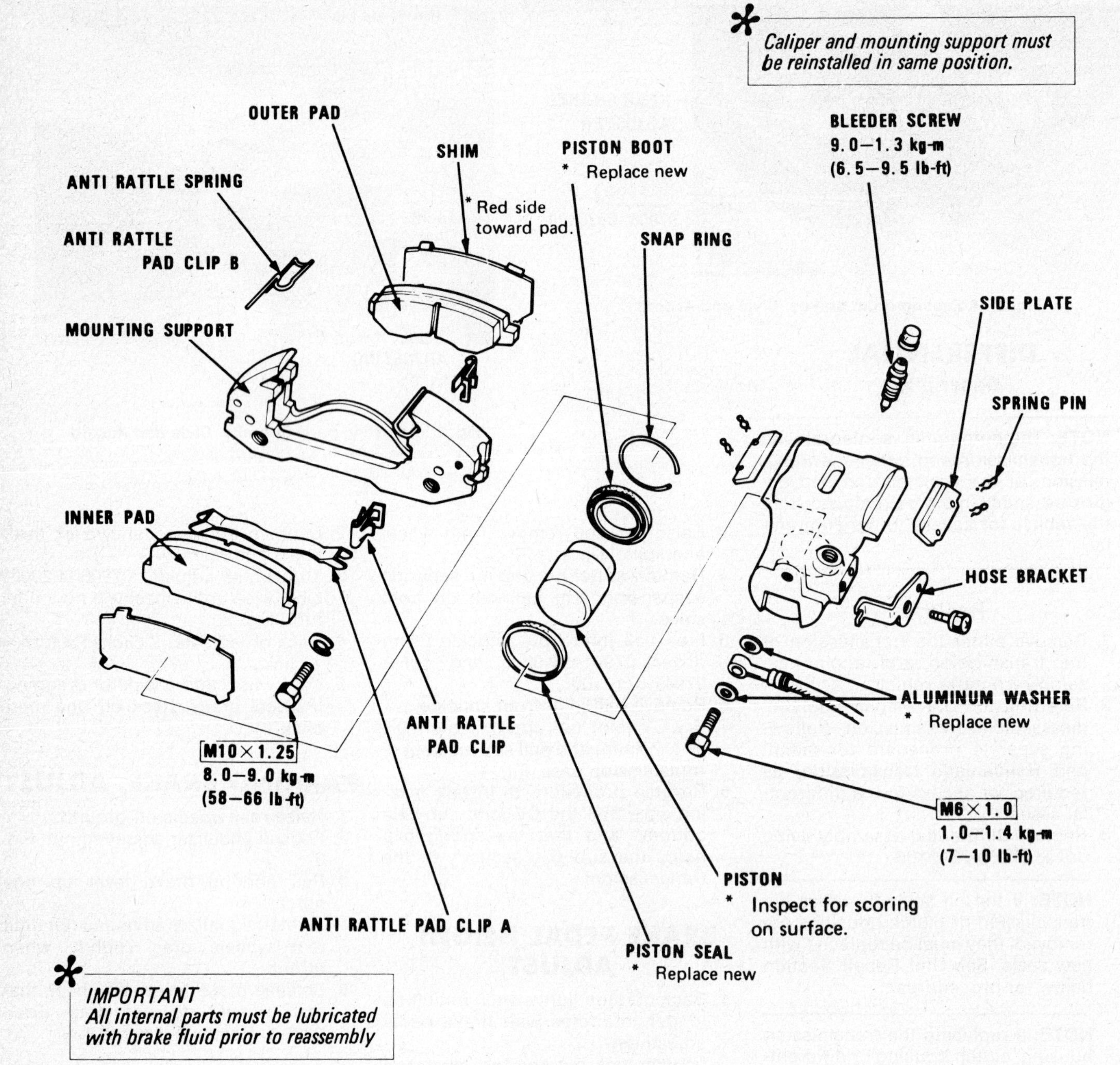

✱ *Caliper and mounting support must be reinstalled in same position.*

OUTER PAD

SHIM
* Red side toward pad.

PISTON BOOT
* Replace new

BLEEDER SCREW
9.0–1.3 kg-m
(6.5–9.5 lb-ft)

ANTI RATTLE SPRING

ANTI RATTLE PAD CLIP B

SNAP RING

SIDE PLATE

MOUNTING SUPPORT

SPRING PIN

INNER PAD

HOSE BRACKET

M10 × 1.25
8.0–9.0 kg-m
(58–66 lb-ft)

ANTI RATTLE PAD CLIP

ALUMINUM WASHER
* Replace new

M6 × 1.0
1.0–1.4 kg-m
(7–10 lb-ft)

PISTON
* Inspect for scoring on surface.

ANTI RATTLE PAD CLIP A

PISTON SEAL
* Replace new

✱ *IMPORTANT*
All internal parts must be lubricated with brake fluid prior to reassembly

Fig. 4   Disc brake assembly exploded view. Civic and Accord

DISC BRAKE SERVICE

Brake Pads, Replace

1. Raise vehicle and remove both front wheels.
2. Remove the four spring pins from the caliper, Fig. 4.
3. Remove side plate, Fig. 4.
4. Remove caliper body, Fig. 4.
5. Remove pads, Fig. 4.
6. Clean all parts thoroughly with alcohol.

7. Reverse procedure to install new pads.

CALIPER, REPLACE

1. Perform procedures 1-5 in "Brake Pads, Replace" above.
2. Remove the two anti-rattle pad clips, Fig. 4.
3. Remove mounting support, Fig. 4.
4. Remove snap ring and then remove piston boot, Fig. 4.
5. Carefully remove piston from

caliper by applying air pressure through brake fluid hole.
6. Remove piston seal and discard, taking care not to damage the cylinder bore.
7. Clean piston and cylinder bore with brake fluid and inspect for scoring, wear or damage.
8. Install new piston seal, Fig. 4.
9. Press piston into caliper, taking care not to damage either surface.
10. Reverse procedure for remainder of assembly.

HONDA

DISC BRAKE ROTOR SPECIFICATIONS
Disc Thickness

Standard (new)	Refinishing Limit	Absolute Wear Limit
0.473 in. (12.0mm)	0.449 in. (11.4mm)	0.437 in. (11.1mm)

NOTE: Measure disc thickness at eight points approximately 45 degrees apart and ¾ in. (19mm) from outer edge of disc. The difference between any measurement should not exceed 0.0006 in. (0.015mm).

600 Models

DIFFERENTIAL
Description

The differential is driven by the final drive gear which is an integral part of the transmission countershaft. The differential is enclosed in the crankcase together with the transmission and crankshaft, and is lubricated by the engine oil. The principle gears in the differential gear are of the helical type.

Removal

To remove the differential, the entire Power Unit must be removed as an assembly as described in the "Engine Section."

DRIVE SHAFT

Description: The front drive shaft assembly consists of an axle shaft and a drive shaft connected by two constant-velocity ball joints which are factory-packed with special grease and enclosed in sealed rubber boots. The outer constant velocity ball joint cannot be disassembled except for removal of the rubber boot. Drive shaft repairs may be made with the power unit installed in the vehicle.

Maintenance

1. Check the rubber boots for damage or deterioration and replace if necessary. (See drive shaft, assembly, for procedure.)
2. Raise the front wheels and check the drive shaft for excessive axial and rotational play. If excessive, check the outboard joint for wear or noise and replace if necessary.
3. Check the front wheel hub nuts and torque to 14-20 kg-m (101-145 ft. lbs.) if necessary.

NOTE: To align the hub nut slot with the cotter key hole in the spindle, always turn the nut in the direction of increased torque. To avoid tightening excessively, first torque to 14 kg-m (101 ft. lbs.) and then align. If alignment happens at 14 kg-m, turn 30 degrees in the direction of increased torque to the next slot.

4. Check the drive shaft mounting bolts for looseness.
5. Check drive shaft splines for excessive wear.

Drive Shaft, Replace

1. Raise vehicle and remove the front wheels and disc brake hubs.
2. Remove the dust seal cover from the knuckle, but not the brake line.
3. Disconnect the drive shaft from the differential joint flange by removing the six bolts.

4. Mount drive shaft replacer 07045-56810 on the knuckle as shown in Fig. 5.
5. Attach drive shaft replacer 07045-56805 on the flange as shown in Fig. 6, thread the retainer of the tool on the drive shaft, oil the center bolt threads and tighten the center bolt with a socket wrench while tapping with a hammer.
6. When the axle shaft has been pushed out about two-thirds of its length, remove the knuckle from the front damper by tapping downward with a soft hammer.
7. Unscrew the center bolt fully and separate the drive shaft from the knuckle.

Inner Universal Joint, Inspection

1. Remove the bellows band by peeling off the end and then tapping with a screwdriver.
2. Move the bellows to expose the flange, remove the circlip, and separate the flange and the drive shaft.
3. Remove the inner ring set circlip, withdraw the steel ball and retainer from the drive shaft and clean both after removal.
4. To assemble, insert the bellows neck band, bellows band and bellows into the drive shaft.
5. Fill the flange approximately two-thirds full with grease.

Fig. 5 Installing tool on driveshaft knuckle. 600 models

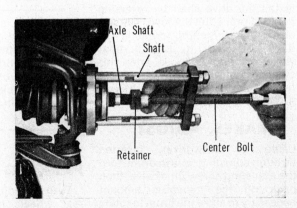

Fig. 6 Installing tool on driveshaft flange. 600 models

Fig. 7 Parking brake adjusting nut. 600 models

6. Set the steel ball in the inner ring and retainer by tapping with a soft hammer.
7. Insert the retainer into the drive shaft and secure with the circlip.
8. Raise the drive shaft with the flange side down, and insert the drive shaft into the flange until a small amount of grease squeezes out.
8. Fill the remaining one-third of the flange with grease.
9. Mount the bellows on the flange by aligning it with the flange's peripheral groove and tighten the bellows band with fastener 07043-55101.
10. Lock the bellows band end with a punch.
11. After locking, remove the special tool and cut the band end so that approximately 10mm (0.4 in.) is left and bend this end.
12. Carefully check the bellows neck band position. Adjustment is made by allowing ambient air pressure inside the bellows after assembly which may be done by gently prying the small (drive shaft) end with a screwdriver.

Drive Shaft, Install

1. Install the inner and outer front wheel bearings using tool 07048-55110.
2. Install the drive shaft by reversing removal procedures above. Knuckle clamp bolt tightening torque is 4.5-5.0 kg-m (33-37 ft. lbs.). If outer wheel bearing is loose after this step, correct with tool 07048-55110.
3. Install the dust seal with tool 07048-55101.

BRAKES, ADJUST

1. Using a screwdriver, inserted through adjusting hole in drum, turn the adjusting screw clockwise, then back off the minimum amount necessary to allow the drum to rotate freely.

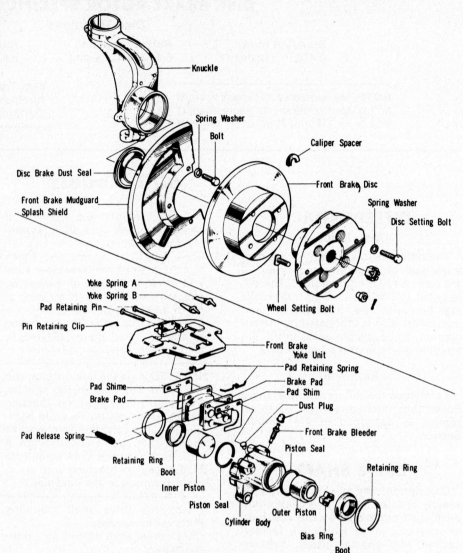

Fig. 8 Disc brake assembly exploded view. 600 models

2. Press the brake pedal several times to centralize the shoes before determining if further adjustment is necessary.

NOTE: It is recommended that the wheel and drum be removed before the adjustment is made for inspection of lining thickness (replace shoes if worn to 1.4mm (0.055 in.) or less in thickness and also so that the wheel cylinder assembly may be lubricated.

PARKING BRAKE, ADJUST

Turn the adjusting nut, Fig. 7, so that rear wheels lock when the parking brake lever is applied 2-3 notches.

MASTER CYLINDER, REPLACE

1. Disconnect the brake pedal and master cylinder push rod by removing the lock pin.
2. Disconnect the electrical wiring and remove the fluid lines to the wheels and the reservoir at the master cylinder.
3. Remove the mounting bolts and remove the master cylinder.
4. Reverse procedure to install.

BRAKE BOOSTER, REPLACE

1. Disconnect the vacuum tube leading from the intake manifold at the booster unit end.

2. Disconnect the master cylinder line and wheel cylinder hose at the booster.

NOTE: Do not depress brake pedal after hydraulic lines to the booster have been disconnected.

3. Dismount the vacuum booster from the upper dash board by removing three bolts and washers.
4. Reverse procedure to install.

DISC BRAKE SERVICE

Brake Pads, Replace

1. Raise the vehicle and remove both front wheels.
2. Remove the pin retaining clip Fig. 8, from its hole in the pad retaining pin.
3. Remove the two pad retaining pins and the two pad retaining springs, releasing the assembly slowly to prevent injury from the springs.
4. Each of the two pads and two shims per brake assembly may now be removed by hand.

NOTE: If the pads are difficult to remove, open the bleeder valve and move the yoke in the direction of the piston.

NOTE: Do not touch the brake pedal once the pads have been removed.

5. Clean exposed areas such as the guide grooves, piston head and yoke sliding surface with alcohol.
6. With the bleeder valve loose, push the inner piston back into the cylinder so that the piston is butted against the boot retaining ring.
7. Push the outer piston back by applying pressure on the yoke so that the piston butts against the retaining ring.
8. Close the bleeder valve and place the new pads together with their shims in position.

NOTE: The shims are interchangeable but must be installed with the arrow "up." Incorrect installation can cause squeaking brakes.

9. First install one of the pins and hook one end of the pad retaining spring on this pin, then clip the center loop

over the top of the pad and hold down the opposite end of the spring while pushing the pin through to align with the inside pad and mounting hole.
10. Insert the pin retaining clip into the hole under the head of the pin. The coil spring, installed only on the leading pin, helps the pads release fully.
11. Apply brake pedal to position the pads against the disc, and then check for proper pedal travel. If travel is excessive, the brake system should be bled.
12. Install the wheels and check for freedom of motion. Approximately 4.5 lbs. force should be required to spin the wheel at its outer circumference. If more force is required, check for worn wheel bearings or misaligned discs. Alignment should be within 0.10mm (0.004 in.).

Caliper Service

Remove, Fig. 8

1. Raise the vehicle and remove the front wheels.
2. Remove the 10mm bolts holding the caliper housing to the knuckle from the bottom side, using a universal socket wrench.

NOTE: It is not necessary to remove the hydraulic hose at this time.

NOTE: Do not lose the two adjusting shims between the caliper and the knuckle.

3. Remove the spindle nut and extract the hub, using a wheel puller.
4. Remove the splash shield from the knuckle.
5. Remove disc brake pads from the caliper assembly as described in the sub-section "Brake Pads, Replace", immediately above.
6. Unfasten the hydraulic hose and remove the caliper assembly.

Disassemble, Fig. 8

1. Lightly tap cylinder body with a plastic hammer to remove body from caliper assembly.
2. Remove the bias ring and the double yoke spring from the caliper.
3. Carefully pry loose the piston boot retainer rings at both ends of the cylinder.

4. Push both inner and outer pistons from the cylinder body with a wooden dowel.
5. Pry loose the piston seals inside the cylinder at both ends.

Assemble, Fig. 8

1. Clean all parts with solvent and dry with compressed air.
2. Apply brake grease on the grooves and sliding surfaces and install the yoke springs with the tongue positioned toward the disc.
4. Apply rubber grease to *new* piston seals and to the seal grooves and install the seals as shown in the insert.

CAUTION: Incorrectly installed seals will result in hydraulic fluid leaks.

5. Apply rubber lubricant sparingly to the inside surface of the cylinder and insert the pistons into the cylinder until the end of the piston skirt is even with the end of the cylinder. The outer and inner pistons are not interchangeable.
6. Insert a *new* bias ring into the outer piston. Install to full depth with the round brim toward the bottom.
7. Install the boots over both pistons and fix in place with retaining rings.
8. Apply grease to the sliding surfaces of the caliper and cylinder body. Then align the bias ring in the outer piston so that the slot in the ring will fit on the cylinder support tongue of the caliper.

Installation

1. Install the splash shield plate on the knuckle and install the dust seal.
2. Install the disc together with the hub on the spindle and tighten the hub nut to 14-20 kg-m (101-145 ft. lbs.), and lock the nut using a new cotter key.
3. Check the run-out of the disc to the spindle. Runout greater than 0.10mm (0.004 in.) near the circumference should be corrected or the disc replaced.
4. Install adjusting shims if necessary (brake pads difficult to fit) between the knuckle and the cylinder body. 0.4 and 0.6mm (0.016 and 0.024 in.) shims are available.
5. Tighten the two bolts which fasten the caliper on the knuckle to a torque of 37-44 ft. lbs. (5-6 kg-m).

DISC BRAKE ROTOR SPECIFICATIONS

Nominal Thickness	Serviceable Limit	Runout (T.I.R.)	Finish Scoring Limit
0.378 (9.6mm)	0.299 (7.6mm)	0.004 (0.10mm)	0.015 (0.4mm)

Rear Suspension Section

Accord & Civic

SEDAN MODELS

Shock Absorber, Replace

1. Raise rear of vehicle and place on safety stands.
2. Remove the rear wheel.
3. Remove brake hoses and pipes.
4. Remove parking brake cable.
5. Compress strut spring evenly using three screw-type compressors.
6. Loosen the lock nut and center nut at the top of the strut.
7. Remove the two mounting nuts at the top of the strut.
8. Remove the steering knuckle bolt at the bottom of the strut, Figs. 1 and 2.
9. Remove the cotter pin and castle nut at the rear edge of the lower arm.
10. Remove the shock absorber (strut).
11. Reverse procedure to install.

Lower Arm & Radius Rod, Replace

1. Raise rear of vehicle and place on safety stand.
2. Remove rear wheel.
3. Remove brake drum.
4. Remove brake hose and pipe.
5. Remove parking brake cable.
6. Remove four attaching bolts and remove backing plate assembly.
7. Remove bolt attaching radius rod to rear wheel hub carrier, Fig. 3.
8. Remove steering knuckle bolt and separate shock absorber from rear wheel hub carrier.
9. Remove cotter pin and then remove castle nut and pivot bolt with bushings and washers from the lower arm and separate the lower arm from the rear wheel hub carrier.
10. Check all bushings for deterioration or wear and check the radius rod for bending or damage.
11. Reverse procedure to assemble, making sure that the dowel on the lower end of the shock absorber seats properly and that a new locking tab is used when attaching the lower arm pivot bolt.

Torque Specifications

Forward radius arm pivot bolt: 43-54 ft. lbs. (6.0-7.5 kg-m)
Inner lower arm pivot bolt: 25.3-36.2 ft. lbs. (3.5-5.0 kg-m)
Rear radius arm pivot bolt: 33-40 ft. lbs. (4.5-5.5 kg-m)
Outer lower arm pivot bolt: 54-65 ft. lbs. (7.5-9.0 kg-m)

12. Place jack under knuckle and raise until car just lifts off the safety stand, then tighten all attaching bolts to specifications above.

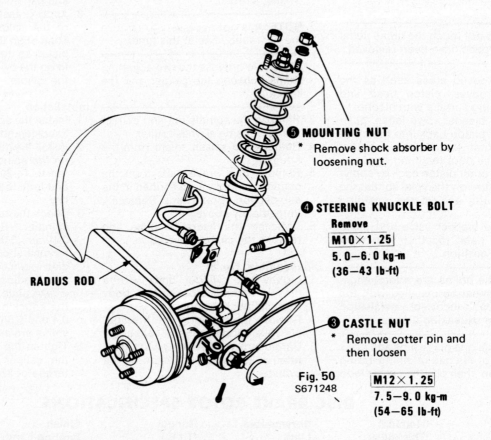

⑤ MOUNTING NUT
* Remove shock absorber by loosening nut.

④ STEERING KNUCKLE BOLT
Remove
M10×1.25
5.0−6.0 kg-m
(36−43 lb-ft)

③ CASTLE NUT
* Remove cotter pin and then loosen

RADIUS ROD

Fig. 50
S671248

M12×1.25
7.5−9.0 kg-m
(54−65 lb-ft)

Fig. 1   Shock absorber attachments. Accord and Civic sedan models

13. Loosen lock nut on the rear radius arm pivot bolt and then turn the adjusting bolt on the outer side until rear wheel toe-out is 0.039 plus or minus 0.078 in. (1mm plus or minus 2 mm).

NOTE: Movement of radius rod is 0.078 in. (2mm) per notch on adjusting cam plate. Change in toe-out is 0.197 in. (5mm) per notch on cam plate.

14. Retighten lock nut to torque specifications above.
15. Check rear spring (strut) height by measuring distance from bottom of rear side marker light to ground. Standard (new) — 26.0 in. (660mm); service limit — 25.4 in. (645mm).

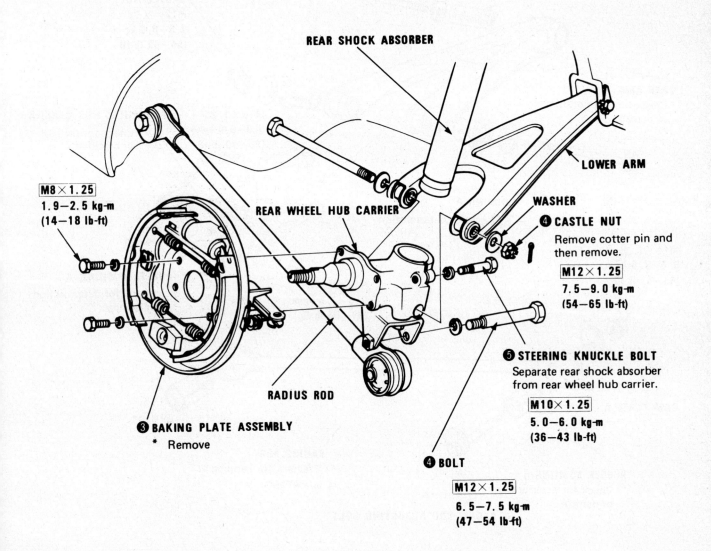

REAR SHOCK ABSORBER

LOWER ARM

M8×1.25
1.9—2.5 kg-m
(14—18 lb-ft)

REAR WHEEL HUB CARRIER

WASHER

❹ CASTLE NUT
Remove cotter pin and then remove.

M12×1.25
7.5—9.0 kg-m
(54—65 lb-ft)

❺ STEERING KNUCKLE BOLT
Separate rear shock absorber from rear wheel hub carrier.

M10×1.25
5.0—6.0 kg-m
(36—43 lb-ft)

RADIUS ROD

❸ BAKING PLATE ASSEMBLY
* Remove

❹ BOLT

M12×1.25
6.5—7.5 kg-m
(47—54 lb-ft)

Fig. 2 Rear suspension exploded view. Accord and Civic sedan models

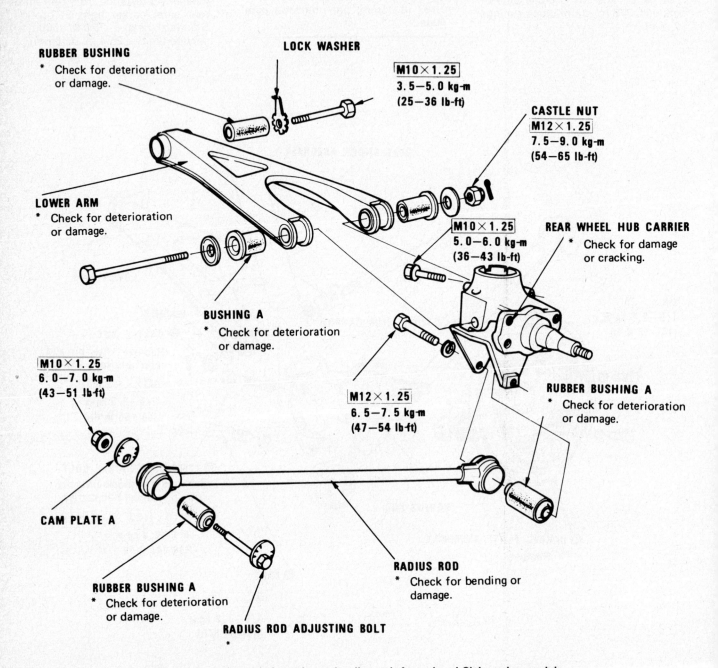

RUBBER BUSHING
* Check for deterioration or damage.

LOCK WASHER

M10×1.25
3.5—5.0 kg-m
(25—36 lb-ft)

CASTLE NUT
M12×1.25
7.5—9.0 kg-m
(54—65 lb-ft)

LOWER ARM
* Check for deterioration or damage.

BUSHING A
* Check for deterioration or damage.

M10×1.25
5.0—6.0 kg-m
(36—43 lb-ft)

REAR WHEEL HUB CARRIER
* Check for damage or cracking.

M10×1.25
6.0—7.0 kg-m
(43—51 lb-ft)

CAM PLATE A

M12×1.25
6.5—7.5 kg-m
(47—54 lb-ft)

RUBBER BUSHING A
* Check for deterioration or damage.

RUBBER BUSHING A
* Check for deterioration or damage.

RADIUS ROD ADJUSTING BOLT
*

RADIUS ROD
* Check for bending or damage.

Fig. 3 Control arm, hub carrier and radius rod. Accord and Civic sedan models

Civic Station Wagon

Refer to Fig. 4 for service procedures.

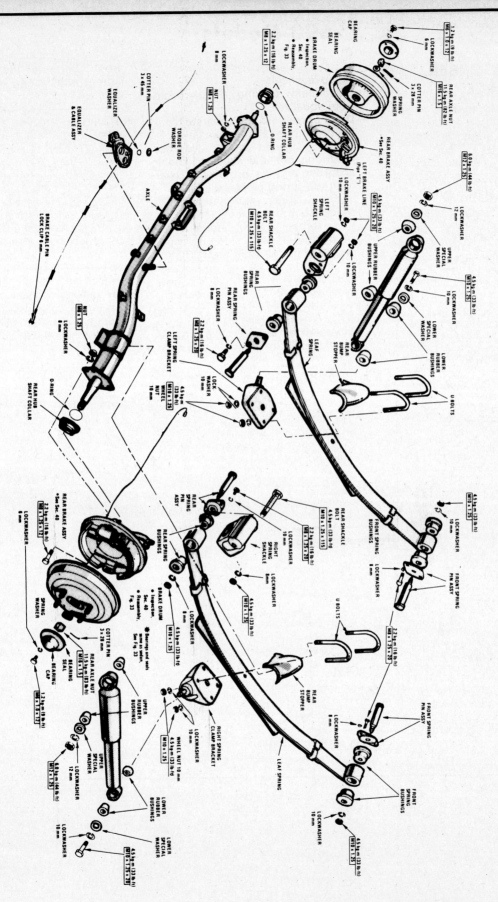

Fig. 4   Rear suspension exploded view. Civic station wagon models

600 Models

SHOCK ABSORBER, REPLACE

1. Remove the shock absorber lower mounting nut and separate the shock absorber from the spring plate, Fig. 5.
2. Remove the rear seat and unscrew the upper shock absorber mounting nut.
3. Reverse procedure to install.

NOTE: The protective cover for the lower mount should be installed facing forward.

COMPONENT REPLACEMENT

1. Raise vehicle and place supports under rear crossmember.

2. Remove wheels.
3. Disconnect parking brake cable from equalizer.
4. Drain brake fluid and separate flexible brake hose from brake line.
5. Remove lower shock absorber mounting nut and separate shock absorber and its protective cover from the spring plate.
6. Remove upper rear (body side) shackle bolt on each side.
7. Remove bolt at spring hanger (forward) end on each side and separate the springs from spring hangers. The axle shaft, brake assemblies and leaf springs may now be removed as a unit.

NOTE: When installing a factory replacement leaf spring, make sure the marked end is positioned toward the front. Be sure the mark (code) agrees with the opposite spring, new or used.

8. Reverse procedure to install. Shackle bolt and hanger bolt tightening torque is 4.0-4.8 kg-m (28.9-34.7 ft. lbs.).

NOTE: If after rear suspension installation, the vehicle appears to ride low on one side, loosen the two spring bolts on the higher side and retighten them with the weight of a man on the higher side.

9. Check rear suspension alignment by wetting a section of pavement, drive the car beyond that to a dry section and examine the tire prints of the four wheels. Rear prints should be an equal distance slightly inside the front tracks.

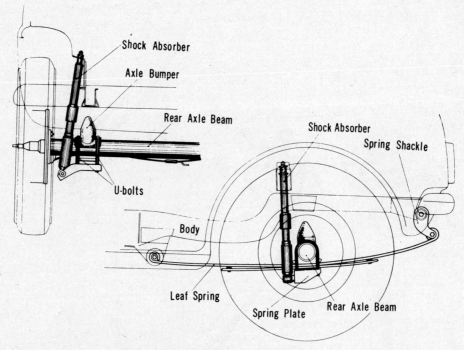

Fig. 5   Rear suspension. 600 models

Front Suspension & Steering

Accord & Civic

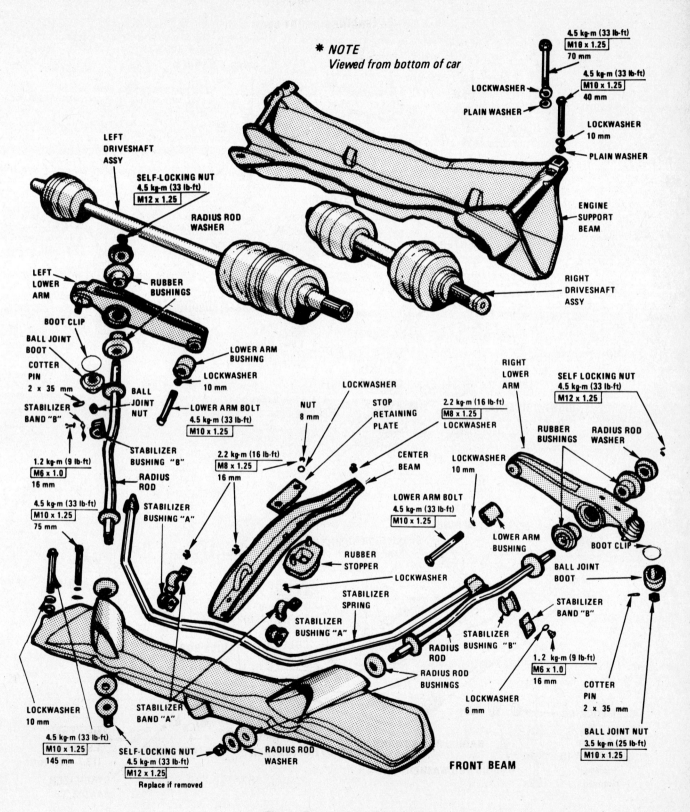

Fig. 1 Front suspension. Civic

HONDA

DESCRIPTION

This front suspension consists of MacPherson struts independently supporting the driving axles, controlled by forward-mounted stabilizer and torque rods, Figs. 1 and 2.

WHEEL ALIGNMENT

Caster & Camber

Caster and camber are not adjustable. If out of specification (camber ½ degree plus or minus 1 degree; caster 2 degrees plus or minus 1 degree), check

suspension for damage and replace components as necessary.

Toe-Out

1. Center the steering wheel, loosen tie-rod locknuts, turn both tie rods in the same direction until both

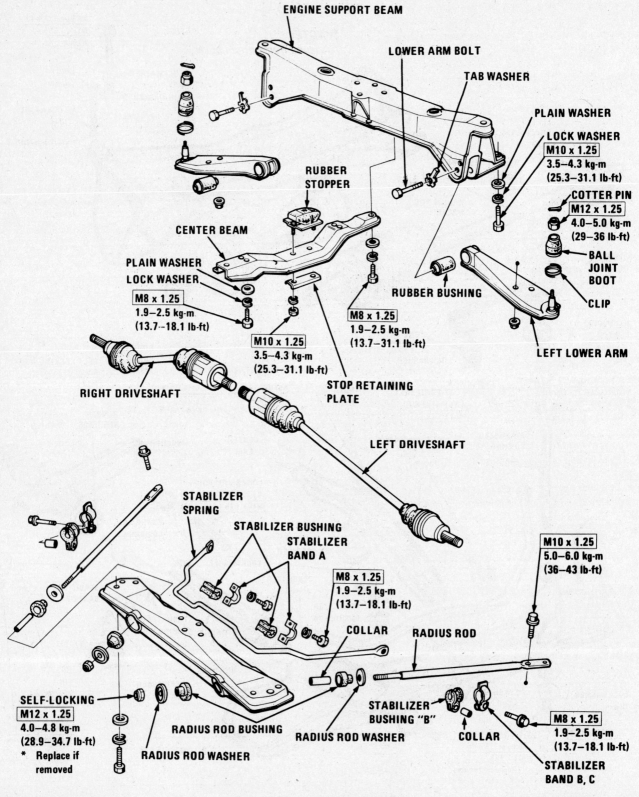

Fig. 2 Front suspension. Accord

front wheels are positioned straight ahead.

2. Adjust toe by turning tie-rod until 1mm plus or minus 3 mm is obtained.

3. Tighten tie-rod locknuts.

SHOCK ABSORBER, REPLACE

1. Remove brake hose clamp bolt and separate clamp and line from mounting bracket on strut.

2. Remove steering knuckle bolt, then separate knuckle from shock absorber.

3. Remove three upper mounting rubber nuts, and remove shock absorber.

4. Reverse procedure to install.

KNUCKLE, WHEEL HUB AND BEARING, REPLACE

1. Raise vehicle and place on safety stands.

2. Remove front wheel.

3. Pry off spindle nut cotter pin and using socket 07907-6010200 and handle 07907-6010300, remove spindle nut.

4. Loosen the two mounting bolts and remove the front brake caliper as an assembly.

5. If knuckle is to remain on vehicle, use special slide hammer (consisting of shaft 07936-5120000, slide 07936-5790000 and attachment 07934-6340100) and remove wheel hub.

6. Detach bolt at lower arm and using tool 07941-6710000, remove tie rod ball joint.

7. Remove bolt securing front knuckle.

8. Using hammer, tap knuckle off shock absorber.

9. Slide drive shaft out of hub.

10. Remove knuckle, hub, backing plate and front brake disc as an assembly.

11. Loosen attaching bolts and remove hub.

12. Loosen attaching bolts and remove front brake disc.

13. Loosen attaching bolts and remove backing plate.

14. Loosen attaching screws and remove front bearing retainer.

15. Using a hydraulic press and special tool set consisting of base 07965-6340300, attachment 07949-6110000 and driver 07947-6340400, press inner and outer front wheel bearings and dust seals from knuckle.

16. Install new bearings with part numbers on both facing inward, using a hydraulic press and special tool set consisting of handle 07949-6110000, attachment 07949-6340200, base 07965-6340400, base 07965-6340300 and pin 07965-6340200.

17. Reverse procedure above for remainder of assembly, making sure that aligning dowel at the bottom of the shock absorber seats properly and that the lower arm pivot bolt is tightened only when car is raised slightly off safety stand by a jack placed under the knuckle. Tighten lower arm pivot bolt to 25-36 ft. lbs. (3.5-5.0 kg-m) and use a new lock tab to secure.

STEERING GEAR, REPLACE

1. Using a suitable hoist, raise engine just enough to remove weight from engine mounts.

2. Disconnect tie rods from knuckles.

3. Disconnect exhaust pipe from manifold.

4. On vehicles with Hondamatic transmission, disconnect control cable from transmission.

5. Remove center beam and heat insulator, then turn steering wheel to full right position.

6. Remove steering shaft connector bolt and spring washer.

7. Remove steering gearbox mounting brackets.

8. Bend left tie-rod upward, then rotate steering gear box until steering pinion faces down and remove from left side of car.

9. Reverse procedure to install.

600 Models

DESCRIPTION

This front suspension system is of the MacPherson strut type with a deep coil spring surrounding the inner shock absorber section, Fig. 3. A stabilizer rod is also used.

WHEEL ALIGNMENT

Caster & Camber

Caster and camber are preset at the factory and cannot be adjusted. Checks, however, may be made with any of a variety of alignment equipment. Standard caster is 1 degree; standard camber is 0.5 degrees. King pin inclination angle, also preset, is 14.5 degrees.

Toe-In, Adjust

To adjust toe-in, loosen the lock nuts on the tie rods. To increase toe-in, turn the right tie rod in the direction of forward wheel rotation and turn the left tie rod in the opposite direction, both in equal amounts until toe-in becomes −2mm (−0.08 in) OUT. Then tighten the lock nuts.

WHEEL BEARINGS, ADJUST

Grasp the free wheel and shake up and down to see if play exists. If there is movement, tighten front hub nuts to 16-18 kg-m (116-123 ft. lbs.). If play still exists, replace bearing.

WHEEL BEARINGS, REPLACE

Removal of the wheel bearings requires removal of the knuckle and lower arm assemblies, described below in this section.

SHOCK ABSORBER & SPRING, REPLACE

1. Raise the front end of the vehicle.

2. Remove tie rod from the knuckle arm with suitable tool.

3. Remove clamp bolt retaining the lower end of the strut and separate the strut from the knuckle.

4. At this time, loosen strut rod nuts as they are too tight to remove after removal of the strut assembly.

5. Remove the three nuts and spring washers and separate the strut assembly from the car body.

6. Remove the strut rod nuts, washers and mounting bracket.

7. Install front strut spring compressor (tools 07034-55110 and 55115) and align with three adjusting screws.

8. Turn handle slowly until the spring is compressed to a level where the ring stopper can be removed.

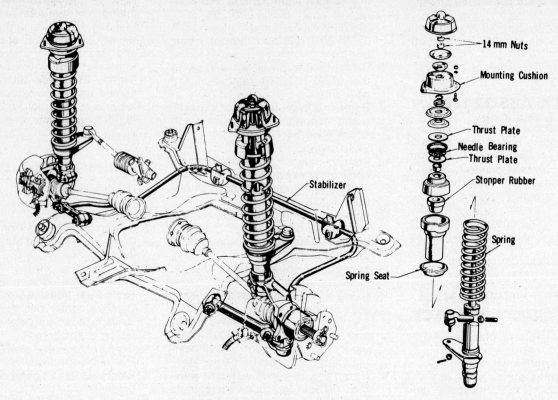

Fig. 3   Front suspension. 600 models

14 mm Nuts
Mounting Cushion
Thrust Plate
Needle Bearing
Thrust Plate
Stopper Rubber
Stabilizer
Spring
Spring Seat

9. Release spring compression slowly and remove the spring.

NOTE: The front struts must be replaced as complete assemblies.

10. Reverse procedure to install.

STABILIZER, REPLACE

1. Raise vehicle so that lower suspension arms hang free.
2. Remove castle nuts at both ends and two bolts at the front to disconnect the stabilizer.
3. Reverse procedure to install, noting that the longer support bracket should be installed on the left side.

STEERING KNUCKLE & CONTROL ARM, REPLACE

1. Remove both front disc brake assemblies as described in Brake Section earlier in this chapter.
2. Extract drive axle shafts from the knuckles as described later in this chapter.
3. Pull out the lower ball joint cotter pin, remove the nut, and separate the lower arm from the knuckle. Tap the knuckle if necessary.
4. Disconnect the lower arm from the sub frame.
5. Loosen the knuckle clamp bolt and separate the knuckle from the front strut.
6. Remove bearing cover.
7. Lightly tap the two wheel bearings and their spacer from the inside of the knuckle, being careful not to

apply force to the inner races.
8. Reverse procedure to install.

NOTE: Installation of bearings will be facilitated by use of tool 07048-55101. The dust seal may be installed with tool 07048-55101.

STEERING GEAR, REPLACE

1. Loosen clamp bolt at steering shaft and pinion gear connection.
2. Disconnect electrical wiring and remove the four bolts retaining the steering column to the instrument panel.
3. Remove the tie rods from the knuckle arms with tool 07092-55103.
4. Remove the four bolts and separate the steering gear box from the firewall.
5. Reverse procedure to install.

JAGUAR XJ-S

INDEX OF SERVICE OPERATIONS

GENERAL ENGINE SPECIFICATIONS

Year	Engine	Fuel System	Bore & Stroke Inch	Piston Displacement Cubic Inches	Compression Ratio	Maximum Net H.P. @ RPM	Maximum Torque Ft. Lbs. @ RPM	Normal Oil Pressure Pounds
1976-77	V12	Fuel Injection	3.54 x 2.76	326	8.0	244 @ 5250	269 @ 4500	—

—Not Available.

TUNE UP SPECIFICATIONS

The following specifications are published from the latest information available. This data should be used only in the absence of a decal affixed in the engine compartment.

▲Before removing wires from distributor cap, determine location of the No. 1 wire in cap, as distributor position may have been altered from that shown at the end of this chart.

Year	Engine	Spark Plug Type	Spark Plug Gap	Distributor Points Gap Inch	Distributor Dwell Angle Deg.	Ignition Timing Firing order	Ignition Timing Timing B.T.D.C. ②	Ignition Timing Mark Location	Hot Idle Speed	Idle CO% @ R.P.M.
1976-77	V-12	N10Y	.035	—	—	①	10	Pulley	750	4.5 @ 750

—Not Available
①—Firing order, 1,7,5,11,3,9,6,12,2,8,4,10.
②—No. 1 cyl., right front of engine

DISTRIBUTOR SPECIFICATIONS

If unit is checked on vehicle, double the R.P.M. & degrees to get crankshaft figures

Distributor Part No.	Centrifugal Advance Degrees @ R.P.M. of Distributor ① Advance Starts	Intermediate Advance			Full Advance	Vacuum Advance Inches of Vacuum to start plunger	Maximum Dist. Deg. @ Vacuum
41675	0 @ 400	½—2½ @ 600	6—8 @ 1000	8—10 @ 1300	11—13 @ 2600 → 14 @ 3500	6	4° @ 10″

①—With vacuum line disconnected from vacuum unit.

ALTERNATOR & REGULATOR SPECIFICATIONS

Year	Alternator Make	Alternator Model	Alternator Field Winding Resistance ohm (68°F)	Alternator Maximum Output	Regulator Model	Regulator Cut in Voltage @ R.P.M.
1976-77	Lucas	20 ACR	3.6	66	Lucas 11 TR	13.5 @ 1500

STARTING MOTOR SPECIFICATIONS

Year	Part No.	Brush Spring Tension (ounces)	No Load Test			Torque Test	
			Amperes	Ft. Lbs.	R.P.M.	Amperes	Ft. Lbs.
1976-77	①	—	540	11	1000	940	25

①—Lucas M45 pre-engaged
—Not Available.

VALVE SPECIFICATIONS

Year	Valve Lash		Valve Angles		Stem to Valve Clearance		Stem Diameter	
	Intake	Exhaust	Seat	Face	Intake	Exhaust	Intake	Exhaust
1976-77	.013	.013	—	44.5	.0020—.0023	.0020—.0023	.3092—.3093	.3092—.3093

—Not Available

PISTONS, PINS, RINGS, CRANKSHAFT & BEARINGS

Year	Piston Clearance Bottom of Skirt ①	Ring End Gap			Wrist Pin Diameter	Rod Bearings		Main Bearing	
		No. 1 Comp.	No. 2 Comp.	Oil		Shaft Diameter	Bearing Clearance	Shaft Diameter	Shaft End Play
1976-77	.0012—.0017	.014—.020	.010—.015	.015—.045	.9375	2.441	.0015—.0034	3.0007—3.0012	.004—.006

①—Measured midway down the bore.

ENGINE TIGHTENING SPECIFICATIONS

*Torque specifications are for clean & lightly lubricated threads only. Dry dirty threads produce increased friction which prevents accurate measurement of tightness

Year	Engine	Spark Plug Ft. Lbs.	Cylinder Head Bolts Ft. Lbs.	Intake Manifold Ft. Lbs.	Camshaft Cap Bolts Ft. Lbs.	Camshaft Cover Bolts Ft. Lbs.	Connecting Rod Cap Bolts Ft. Lbs.	Main Bearing Cap Bolts Ft. Lbs.	Flywheel to Crankshaft Ft. Lbs.
1976-77	V 12	—	①	—	9	8.3	40—41	②	66.7

①—7/16" bolts, 52; 3/8" bolts, 28
②—1/2" bolts, 65; 3/8" bolts, 28
—Not available

BRAKE SPECIFICATIONS

Year	Model	Disc Brake Rotor Nominal Thickness		Master Cylinder Bore Diameter
		Front	Rear	
1976-77	X-J-S V-12	.95	①	.938

① —Standard, .5"; Optional with Overdrive, .95"

WHEEL ALIGNMENT SPECIFICATIONS

Year	Front & Rear Wheel Alignment	Caster Angle, Degrees		Camber Angle, Degrees				Toe-In Inch	Toe-Out on Turns Deg.	
		Limits	Desired	Limits		Desired			Outer Wheel	Inner Wheel
				Left	Right	Left	Right			
1976-77	Front	+3¼ to +3¾	3½	+¼ to +¾	+¼ to +¾	+½	+½	¹⁄₁₆ to ⅛	—	—
	Rear	—	—	−½ to −1	−½ to −1	−¾	−¾	—	—	—

— Not Available.

COOLING SYSTEM CAPACITY DATA

Year	Cooling Capacity Qts.		Radiator Cap Relief Pressure, Lbs.		Thermo Opening Temp.	Fuel Tank Gals.	Engine Oil Refill Qts.	Transmission Oil			Axle Oil Pints
	Without Heater	With A/C	With A/C	No A/C				4 Speed Pints	Overdrive Pints	Auto. trans. Qts.	
1976-77	11.1	11.1	15	15	178	24	11	—	—	—	—

—Not Available

Electrical Section

DISTRIBUTOR, REPLACE

1. Remove three holddown screws securing distributor cap, and remove cap.
2. Rotate engine until No. 1 cylinder mark on timing rotor is aligned with mark scribed on pick-up module.
3. Disconnect cable assembly at connector plug.
4. Disconnect vacuum line from vacuum advance chamber.
5. Remove three Allen screws holding distributor.

NOTE: The screws are accessible through slots in the micro plate housing.

6. Withdraw the distributor.

CAUTION: Do not rotate the engine.

7. Perform steps 3, 4, 5, and 6, above, in reverse order.
8. Check to make sure that No. 1 cylinder mark on timing rotor is in alignment with mark scribed on pick-up module.
9. Replace distributor.
10. Check ignition timing with vacuum line disconnected from vacuum advance chamber by loosening locknut of micro adjustment control and setting vernier at zero.
11. Set engine idle speed at 500-600 rpm and check timing with a timing light. Adjust vernier until timing is at 10° BTDC.
12. Tighten micro adjustment control locknut, then install vacuum line and set engine idle speed at 650-750 rpm.

DISTRIBUTOR, REPAIRS

1. Distributor cap:
   a. Properly identify all spark plug leads and coil lead.
   b. Detach leads from distributor cap, Fig. 1.
   c. Remove three holddown screws and remove distributor cap.
2. High tension rotor:
   a. Remove three holddown screws and remove distributor cap.
   b. Remove high tension rotor.
   c. Put two or three drops of clean engine oil on rotor carrier shaft oil pad.

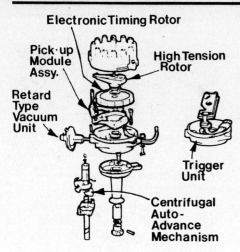

Fig. 1 Exploded view of distributor

Electronic Timing Rotor

Pick-up Module Assy.

High Tension Rotor

Retard Type Vacuum Unit

Trigger Unit

Centrifugal Auto-Advance Mechanism

d. Replace high tension rotor, making sure that keyway is engaged and rotor is fully engaged.
e. Reattach distributor cap.
3. Electronic timing rotor:
 a. Remove distributor cap and high tension rotor.
 b. Disconnect trigger unit cable from main harness at in-line connector.
 c. Remove four nylon screws holding trigger unit to platform.
 d. Remove nylon clamp from right-hand side of trigger unit and remove a trigger unit by releasing rubber seal from distributor housing.
 e. Remove snap clip and washer, then slide electronic timing rotor off rotor carrier shaft.
 f. Reverse procedure to assemble.
4. Pick-up module:
 a. Remove distributor, high tension rotor and electronic timing rotor.
 b. Remove two screws holding pick-up module to pick-up arm. Make sure that you recover two spring washers and two plain washers in addition to the two screws.

c. Pry up cable grommet inwards from distributor housing, and feed cable and cable connector through hole.
d. Lift pick-up module clear of housing.
e. To replace pick-up module, feed cable connector out through hole in distributor housing, and fit grommet into hole, wide end first.
f. Place pick-up module on pick-up arm, with core of module facing inward toward distributor. Secure pick-up module loosely with two screws, plain washers and spring washers.
g. Replace electronic timing rotor.
h. Set distance between pick-up module "E" core face and the outer edge of the timing rotor to 0.020-0.022 in. (0.50-0.55 mm).
i. Tighten pick-up module attaching screws.
j. The remainder of the reassembly is done in reverse of disassembly.

ALTERNATOR, REPLACE

1. Disconnect battery ground cable.
2. Remove air cleaner cover and element.
3. Remove outer nut from pulley adjusting link.
4. Slacken pulley mounting securing bolt.
5. Loosen inner nut on pulley adjusting link.
6. Remove outer drive belt from pulley and Torquatrol unit.
7. Remove bolts holding pulley to engine and remove pulley.
8. Loosen alternator mounting bolts.
9. Loosen inner bolt of alternator drive belt adjustment link, which is on the lower part of the engine beneath all pulleys and belts.
10. Loosen bolt attaching belt adjustment link to alternator.
11. Loosen nut attaching trunnion to timing chain cover.
12. Pivot alternator and remove alternator drive belt.

Fig. 2 Alternator output test connections

13. Disconnect cable harness from alternator.
14. Remove alternator mounting bolt and maneuver the alternator from the engine compartment.
15. Reverse procedure to install.

ALTERNATOR, IN-VEHICLE TESTS
Output Test

1. Run the engine at 3000 rpm for 4 minutes to warm up alternator.
2. Disconnect battery ground cable.
3. Connect an ammeter in series with alternator main output cable and starter solenoid, Fig. 2.
4. Remove connectors from alternator, then remove end cover and reattach connectors.
5. Hook a jumper lead to short out "F" and heg ("-") terminals of control unit.
6. Reattach battery ground cable, turn on all lights and place headlights on high beam.
7. Switch on ignition, seeing that the alternator warning light is "on." Start engine.
8. Slowly increase engine speed to 3000 rpm. The ammeter should read 66 amps, which is maximum rated output of alternator.

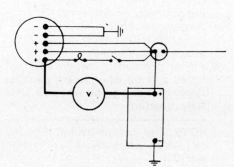

Fig. 3 Alternator voltage drop test connections

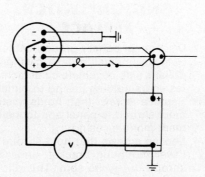

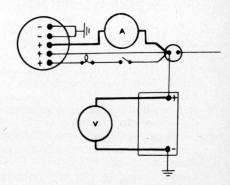

Fig. 4 Alternator regulator test connections

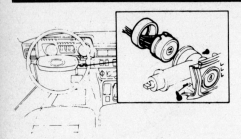

Fig. 5 Ignition switch removal

Voltage Drop Test

1. Connect a voltmeter between battery positive terminal and alternator main output terminal, Fig. 3.
2. Switch on all lights, with headlights on high beam.
3. Start engine, running it at 3000 rpm, and note voltmeter reading. Turn off engine.
4. Transfer voltmeter connections to battery ground terminal and alternator negative terminal, Fig. 3.
5. With all lights on, headlights on high beam, run engine at 3000 rpm and note voltmeter reading.
6. A difference of more than 0.5 volt on positive side indicates high resistance.

Regulator Test

1. To perform this test accurately, all connections must be clean and tight, circuit wiring must be sound and battery must be in a fully charged state.
2. Connect an ammeter in series with starter solenoid and alternator main output cable, Fig. 4.
3. Connect a voltmeter between two battery terminals, Fig. 4.
4. Run engine at 3000 rpm until ammeter shows a reading of less than 10 amps. The voltmeter should read 13.6-14.4 volts. An unstable reading or one outside specified limits indicates a faulty regulator.

STARTER, REPLACE

1. Disconnect battery ground cable.
2. Drain power steering system.
3. Remove bolts securing lower column universal joint to its respective columns on both ends.
4. Remove the heat shield protecting rubber boot which covers inner tie rod joint.
5. Remove bolt that holds lower steering column to steering gear.
6. In the car, disengage lower column upper universal joint from bottom of steering column.
7. Loosen securing clip still holding upper universal joint and remove joint from lower column.

8. Disengage lower column from steering gear and ease it out through the bulkhead.
9. Release clip holding power steering feed and return lines to bridge piece and rack tube assembly.
10. Disconnect feed and return lines from steering gear. Plug lines and nipples on steering gear, and position lines clear of bridge piece and rack tube assembly.
11. Remove bolts holding exhaust pipe to intermediate pipe, then disengage the two pipes.
12. Remove screws attaching front exhaust heat shield to underbody and remove heat shield.
13. Loosen bottom screws that secure steering rack assembly to front suspension, remove bolt that holds rack and heat shield mounting bracket to suspension, and lower rack carefully. Be sure to retrieve pack washers from top mounting joint of steering rack.
14. Remove exhaust pipe.
15. Remove nuts that holds heat shield over starter motor and clip that retains cable. Remove heat shield.
16. Remove nut which holds alternator-to-starter motor cable at starter. Disconnect cable.
17. Disconnect starter solenoid-to-terminal post connector at terminal post. Tie solenoid cable using cord to a suitable support and disconnect cable at bulkhead fitting. Make sure cord is long enough to be pulled up through engine compartment.
18. Remove bolts that hold starter motor to bell housing.
19. Detach string holding solenoid cable and pull entire assembly up through engine compartment.
20. Remove string from cable and remove heat shield bracket and support piece from starter motor.
21. Reverse procedure to install. Be sure to fill and bleed the power steering system.

IGNITION SWITCH, REPLACE

1. Disconnect battery ground cable.
2. Remove underside dash casing on driver's side of vehicle by detaching fasteners holding casing to panel.
3. Remove screw that holds instrument shroud to panel and to instrument module casing.
4. Loosen screws that hold shroud to lower mounting bracket, and ease shroud out of its spot. This allows access to screw holding ignition switch.

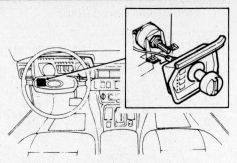

Fig. 6 Headlight switch removal

5. Loosen this screw, and ease the switch and harness out of mount, Fig. 5.
6. Remove rubber retainer and disconnect harness connector to release ignition switch.

HEADLIGHT SWITCH, REPLACE

1. Disconnect battery ground cable.
2. Remove underside dash casing on driver's side of vehicle by detaching fasteners holding casing to panel.
3. Remove screw that holds instrument shroud to panel and to instrument module casing.
4. Loosen screws that hold shroud to lower mounting bracket and ease the shroud clear to gain access to the spring-loaded pin retaining knob.
5. Depress pin and remove knob, which permits removal of shroud, Fig. 6.
6. Remove nut holding headlight switch to mounting bracket.
7. Remove switch from bracket and disconnect wiring harness at connector to free switch.

STOPLIGHT SWITCH, REPLACE

1. Disconnect battery ground cable.
2. Disconnect electrical connectors from switch terminals.
3. Remove switch attaching bolt holding nut.
4. Remove switch.
5. After replacing switch, leave switch attaching bolt loose.
6. Adjust position of switch so stoplights operate when brake pedal is depressed and go off when pedal is fully released.

NOTE: The ignition switch must be on while adjustments are being made.

7. Tighten switch attaching bolt.

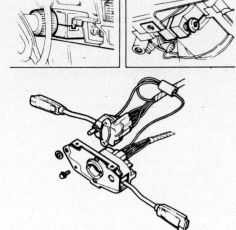

Fig. 7 Combination switch removal

COMBINATION TURN SIGNAL—HIGH BEAM—HAZARD FLASHER—WINDSHIELD WIPER/WASHER SWITCH, REPLACE

1. Disconnect battery ground cable.
2. Loosen steering wheel adjustment ring and extend it to its maximum travel.
3. Remove screws attaching steering column lower shroud. Then remove shroud.
4. Remove steering wheel as follows:
   a. Remove steering wheel horn pad.
   b. Adjust wheels to straight ahead position, then remove ignition key and lock steering wheel.
   c. Remove horn contact rod from upper column.
   d. Remove nut attaching steering wheel to upper column and gently tap steering wheel loose.
5. Remove screw that holds upper shroud to bracket on steering column.
6. Loosen screw holding switch assembly to steering column and withdraw switch assembly and upper shroud. Separate shroud and switch assembly, Fig. 7.
7. Disconnect wiring harness at connectors.
8. Remove nuts and screws holding switch mounting plate and disconnect ground cable at snap connector.
9. Remove windshield wiper-washer switch from assembly.

CAUTION: Do not try to separate the turn signal-high beam-hazard flasher switch from mounting bracket. If switch is faulty, a new switch and bracket assembly will have to be installed.

NEUTRAL SAFETY SWITCH, REPLACE

1. Disconnect battery ground cable.
2. Remove transmission selector lever knob.
3. Remove screws holding transmission selector indicator and remove indicator.
4. Carefully move electric window switch panel until it clears center console. Do not disconnect window switches.
5. Remove screws holding control escutcheon.
6. Lift up on escutcheon slightly to gain access to cigar lighter and doorlock switch terminals. Notice position of terminals before detaching them and removing escutcheon.
7. Detach cable from neutral safety switch.
8. Loosen locknuts holding switch, then remove switch.

INSTRUMENT CLUSTER, REPLACE

1. Disconnect battery ground cable.
2. Remove underside dash casing on driver's side of vehicle by detaching fasteners holding casing to panel.
3. Remove center securing strip and screw from instrument cluster trim.
4. Remove screws holding side trim pieces, then remove trim.
5. Pry off covers from instrument cluster securing screw.
6. Remove screws holding instrument cluster to panel.
7. Disconnect speedometer cable from angle drive at rear of speedometer.
8. Pull cluster forward and disconnect cable harness at connectors.
9. Loosen steering wheel adjustment ring and extend to maximum travel.
10. Maneuver instrument cluster clear of housing.

W/S WIPER MOTOR, REPLACE

1. Disconnect battery ground cable.
2. Remove windshield wiper arms.
3. Remove air inlet grille retaining nuts, bolts and washers, Fig. 8.
4. Raise grille which is attached to windshield wiper assembly.
5. Disconnect washer tube at jet and disconnect multiplug connector at bulkhead.
6. Remove grille and wiper assembly.
7. Remove nuts that secure motor

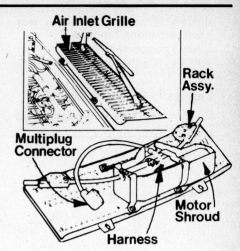

Fig. 8 W/S wiper motor & grille assembly

mounting bracket to grille, then remove bolts that hold bracket to motor. Remove bracket.
8. Turn over grille-motor assembly and remove gearbox spindle nuts.
9. Invert grille-motor assembly again, then remove motor and drive rack assembly.
10. Remove rack cover plate retaining bolts. Lift off cover and remove rack assembly.
11. Take off motor shroud and disconnect harness at gearbox connector. The motor is now free.
12. Reverse procedure to install.

BLOWER MOTOR, REPLACE

There are two blower motors, which are heavy duty motors with attached impellers. Varied speed is obtained by controlled switching of resistances in series with the motors. The right-hand blower assembly has the ambient temperature sensor mounted in the inlet duct. The air flow control flaps are operated by a vacuum actuator situated in the side of the inlet duct.

Right Hand Blower Assembly

1. Disconnect battery ground cable and remove dash liner and console side casing.
2. Remove glove box liner and take out nuts holding mounting plate to blower assembly and lower plate. Pull the plate clear.
3. Disconnect sensor hose from blower assembly duct, the pliable duct from side of air conditioner, the blower harness at block connector and the vacuum line from valve on blower assembly.
4. Wedge open recirculation valve in base of blower assembly and re-

move bolts securing blower assembly to mounting brackets.

5. Ease blower assembly from position and detach the duct by removing tape.

Left Hand Blower Assembly

1. Disconnect battery ground cable and remove dash liner and console side casing.

2. Remove nuts holding bottom of fuse box mounting plate to blower assembly. Loosen nuts holding top of fuse box mounting plate.

3. Ease fuse box clear of blower assembly.

4. Disconnect pliable duct side of air conditioner, blower harness at block connector, and vacuum line from valve servo on blower.

5. The remainder of the procedure is the same as that outlined in steps 4 and 5, Right Hand Blower Assembly, Replace.

Engine Section

ENGINE, REPLACE

1. Remove hood and lower grille.
2. Disconnect battery cables, drain coolant and depressurize fuel system.
3. Discharge air conditioning system and disconnect hoses; immediately seal all connections.
4. Remove engine compartment stays.
5. Disconnect cables from temperature sensors.
6. Disconnect cold-start relay harness, throttle switch-and-trigger unit cable and kickdown switch cable.
7. Remove ground lead to a right-hand intake manifold and main harness. Withdraw the harness.
8. Disconnect cables at cold start injection relay and right-hand water rail feed pipe from heater valve.
9. Disconnect brake vacuum hoses, heater vacuum hose, throttle cable and cables to starter solenoid and starter motor.
10. Remove air cleaners.
11. Remove fuel pipes and plug connections.
12. Disconnect cooling system hoses.
13. On models with automatic transmission, remove transmission oil cooler hoses and plug connections.
14. Disconnect and remove alternator harness.
15. Detach radiator fittings and disconnect A/C receiver-dryer outlet line.
16. Remove fan cowl.

17. Remove radiator top rail together with evaporator and receiver-dryer.
18. Attach engine support tool MS. 53A.
19. Disconnect coolant sensor.
20. Remove radiator and fan.
21. Disconnect exhaust pipes and remove left and right front heat shields.
22. Remove intermediate and rear heat shields.
23. Raise engine at rear engine mounting plate so you can remove collision plate at transmission and rear engine mounting stud.
24. Remove rear engine mounting plate and lower jack.
25. Withdraw propeller shaft from output flange.
26. On models with manual transmission, remove gear shift knob and console retainer. Place gear shift into first gear position and disconnect clutch slave cylinder hose and plug connections.
27. On models with automatic transmission, remove selector cable and selector lever from shaft.
28. Disconnect speedometer cable and unhook ground strap from side of torque converter/bell housing.
29. Remove steering heat shields and left-side exhaust manifold heat shield.
30. Disconnect EGR lines from exhaust manifold and exhaust pipes.
31. Detach and swing power steering oil cooler away from engine.
32. Detach power steering pump.
33. Support transmission.
34. Attach lifting chains to engine front and rear lifting eyes.

NOTE: Removing engine will be facilitated if rear lifting chains are approximately 6 inches (154 mm) longer than front chains.

---

35. Remove the engine.

CYLINDER HEAD, REPLACE
Left Side (B Bank)

1. Disconnect battery.
2. Remove left and right-side camshaft covers.

3. Detach and move thermostat housing out of way.
4. Remove bolts securing fan and Torquatrol unit to spindle.
5. Rotate engine until valve timing gauge C.3993 can be fitted in the slot in the right-side ("A" bank) camshaft front flange, Fig. 1.
6. Remove rubber grommet from timing gear cover.
7. Insert blade of timing chain tensioner retractor and release tool JD.50 through hole to release locking catch on timing chain tensioner.
8. Using timing chain tensioner retractor and release tool JD.50, retract timing chain tensioner. The locking catch will engage when tensioner is properly retracted, Fig. 2.
9. Disconnect camshaft sprocket from camshaft and fit sprocket retaining tool JD.40, Fig. 3.
10. Remove steering linkage heat shield.
11. Remove front heat shield, exhaust pipe heat shield, and exhaust pipe to exhaust manifold.
12. Disconnect EGR line and remove exhaust manifold heat shield.
13. Remove rear exhaust manifold.
14. On models with automatic transmission, disconnect transmission dipstick tube.
15. Disconnect fuel hoses from cooler and plug connections.
16. Detach and move amplifier away from cylinder head.

Valve Timing Gauge C 3993

Fig. 1   Valve timing gauge installed

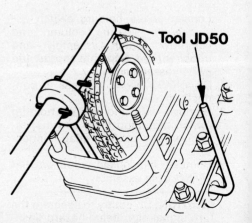

Fig. 2   Retracting timing chain

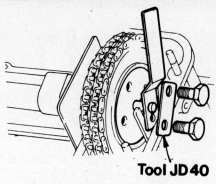

Fig. 3 Retaining tool installation

17. Remove camshaft oil feed bolt.
18. Remove three nuts holding cylinder head to timing cover and progressively loosen cylinder head nuts working from center out.
19. Lift off cylinder head and place it on blocks of wood to avoid damage to valves, which protrude below cylinder head face when open.

CAUTION: Do not remove valve timing gauge from "A" bank camshaft.

20. Rotate camshaft until timing gauge C.3993 can be fitted in slot in left side camshaft.

CAUTION: The mating surface of cylinder head and block must be cleaned before proceeding.

21. Fit cylinder head gasket, making sure that side marked "TOP" is in topmost position.

CAUTION: Do *not* use jointing compound or grease.

22. Fit cylinder head, tightening retaining bolts in order shown in Fig. 4 to a torque of:
    27.5 ft. lbs. (3.7 kg/m) for ⅜ inch nuts.
    52 ft. lbs. (7.2 kg/m) for ⁷/₁₆ inch nuts.
23. Tighten cylinder head to timing cover nuts to a torque of 9 ft. lbs. (1.2 kg/m).

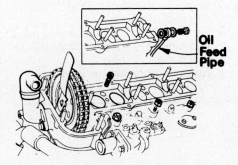

Fig. 5 Removing oil feed pipe

24. Remove sprocket retaining tool JD.40 and check alignment of retaining bolt holes. Be sure camshaft and sprocket holes are aligned.
25. Rotate coupling to line up bolt holes, and bolt coupling to camshaft.
26. Refit retaining clip and remove gauge C.3993 from left side camshaft and rotate engine until remaining camshaft sprocket retaining bolts can be fitted.
27. Continue by reversing operations above not already performed, completing reassembly by adjusting fan belt tension, checking ignition timing and assuring that engine meets emission control standards.

Right Side (A Bank)

The procedure is similar to that explained above for the left side (B bank) cylinder head except as follows:

1. The air conditioner compressor must be disengaged and swung clear of cylinder head.
2. It is not necessary to remove left hand camshaft cover.
3. The starter motor and starter motor heat shield have to be removed.

CAUTION: Do not rotate the engine until cylinder liner retaining tool JD.41 has been fitted to the cylinder head studs.

4. If crankshaft or camshaft are moved, or cylinder head overhauled and/or piston decarbonization has been carried out, you will have to perform the following steps before refitting the cylinder head and completing reassembly as outlined above:
   a. Remove distributor cover and attach a clock gauge to the cylinder head stud.
   b. Rotate the engine using clock gauge to set No. 1 piston at TDC, then remove gauge.
   c. Turn camshaft until valve timing gauge C.3993 can be fitted into slot in camshaft front flange.
   d. Remove cylinder liner retaining tool JD.41 and continue as above.

ROCKER ARM, SERVICE

1. Remove camshaft.
2. Remove oil feed pipe to rocker arm bolt, disconnect breather pipe and progressively loosen retaining nuts and cap screws, working from center out, Fig. 5.
3. Lift off rocker arm.

Timing Cover

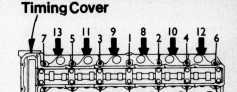

Fig. 4 Cylinder head bolt tightening sequence

CAUTION: Record from order in which tappets and pads are removed to facilitate valve adjustment.

4. Clean rocker arm and cylinder head mating surfaces and smear surfaces with a suitable lubricant.
5. Refit rocker arm, tightening retaining nuts and cap screws from center out.
6. Lubricate tappets and adjusting pads with clean engine oil.
7. Complete reassembly.

VALVES, ADJUST

1. Tighten bearing caps evenly to a torque of 9 ft. lbs. (1.2 kg/m).
2. Check and record clearance between each tappet and heel of each cam. Correct clearance is .012 to .014 in. (.305 to .355 mm) for both intake and exhaust, Fig. 6.
3. Subtract correct valve clearance from dimension you obtain and select adjusting pads that equal the new dimension.

NOTE: Adjusting pads are available in 0.001 inch (0.03 mm) increments from 0.085 inch to 0.110 inch (2.16 to 2.79 mm).

4. Remove camshaft and tappets, and fit adjusting pads.

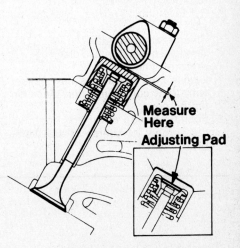

Fig. 6 Valve adjustment

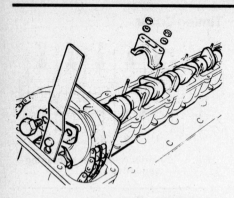

Fig. 7 Camshaft removal

VALVE GUIDES

Valve guides are available in two oversize dimensions. The first, having two identification grooves, has a 0.507 in to 0.506 inch (12.88 mm to 12.85 mm) diameter. The second, having three grooves, has a 0.512 inch to 0.511 inch (13.00 mm to 12.98 mm) diameter.

When new guides are fitted, they should be one size larger than the old guides. Cylinder head bores will require reaming as follows:

a. First oversize (two grooves)—.505 inch + .0005 inch − .0002 inch (12.83 mm + .012 mm − .005 mm).
b. Second oversize (three grooves)—.510 inch + .0005 inch − .0002 inch (12.95 mm + .012 mm − .0005 mm).

TIMING COVER, REPLACE

1. Remove engine and transmission assembly from vehicle, then remove cylinder heads, oil pan assembly, alternator, power steering pump, emission control air pump, air conditioning compressor and water pump.
2. Remove brackets attached to area of disassembly.
3. Remove bolts holding timing cover to block.
4. Remove timing cover. Discard oil seal.
5. Clean mating surfaces.
6. Saturate new oil seal in clean oil and press into timing cover.
7. Smear both sides of a new gasket with joint compound and place on timing cover.
8. Position timing cover and continue reassembly in reverse of disassembly.

TIMING CHAIN, REPLACE

1. Remove timing cover.
2. Fit retaining tool JD.39 in position on pulley shaft and disconnect timing chain from camshaft and pulley shaft sprockets.
3. Remove crankshaft sprocket and chain.

CAUTION: Do not rotate the engine.

CAMSHAFT, REPLACE

1. Remove camshaft cover.
2. Insert timing chain tensioner retractor tool JD.50 through hole in timing cover and retract timing chain tensioner until locking catch engages on step, Fig. 7.
3. Remove camshaft sprocket retaining bolts.
4. Rotate engine until timing gauge C.3993 can be inserted in camshaft slot.
5. Remove two remaining bolts in camshaft sprocket and attach retaining tool JD.40.

CAUTION: Do not rotate engine while the camshaft is disconnected.

6. Remove retainers and lift off camshaft.
7. Oil camshaft journals and tappets.
8. Position camshaft, using gauge C.3993 to position it properly.
9. Reengage retainers, torquing them to 9.0 ft. lbs. (1.2 kg/m).
10. Complete reassembly by reversing above procedure.

PISTONS, PINS & RINGS

Pistons and rings are available in standard size only. If cylinder wear is excessive, replace the cylinder bore liners.

Pistons and wrist pins are a matched assembly. Parts should not be interchanged.

OIL PAN, REPLACE

1. Drain oil.
2. Remove set screws and serrated washers holding oil pan, then lower pan.

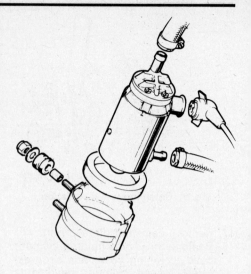

Fig. 8 Fuel pump removal

OIL PUMP, REPLACE

Removing oil pump is an extensive task, requiring almost complete disassembly of engine. It is therefore recommended that oil pump be inspected for wear and damage whenever it is accessible for other reasons.

WATER PUMP, REPLACE

1. Remove drive belt.
2. Remove fan, Torquatrol unit, adjuster assembly and idler pulley housing.
3. Remove power steering, air pump and air conditioner compressor belts.
4. Remove thermostatic switch housing and bottom hose.
5. Remove water pump retaining hardware and water pump.

FUEL PUMP, REPLACE

1. Depressurize the fuel system as described in Fuel Injection Section, then disconnect battery.
2. Remove spare tire.
3. Remove fuel pump cover, Fig. 8.
4. Clamp off intake and outlet hoses.
5. Remove fuel pump retaining band from mounting.
6. Remove electrical connector.
7. Place a receptacle to catch spilled fuel and release hoses.
8. Separate fuel pump retaining band and remove two foam rubber insulation bands.
9. Reverse procedure to install.

Fuel Injection Section

IDLE SPEED ADJUSTMENT

1. Allow engine to reach operating temperature. If engine is warm, but has not been running, start and allow to run for two or three minutes.
2. Set the idle speed adjustment screw to achieve 750 rpm, Fig. 1. If correct idle speed cannot be attained, proceed to steps 3 through 8.
3. Check all lines and hoses to inlet manifolds for tightness and condition.
4. Check tightness of all injectors.
5. See that all joints are tight and that intake manifold-to-cylinder head fasteners are tight.
6. Assure that throttle butterfly valves are adjusted properly.
7. Assure that overrun valves are operating properly.
8. Finally, check operation of auxiliary air valves.

THROTTLE BUTTERFLY VALVES, ADJUST

NOTE: Both butterfly valves must be adjusted.

1. Remove both air cleaners.
2. Loosen locknut on throttle butterfly stop screw and turn back screw, making sure that throttle butterfly valve closes fully.
3. Insert a .004 in. (.105 mm) feeler gauge between top of valve and housing to hold valve open, Fig. 2.
4. Adjust stop screw so it just touches stop arm and tighten locknut keeping feeler gauge in place.
5. Withdraw feeler gauge.

OVERRUN VALVES TEST

1. Remove both air cleaners.
2. Block overrun valve inlet pipes and start engine, Fig. 3.
3. If idle speed now attains 750 rpm, stop engine and unblock one valve only.
4. Start engine and check idle speed. If still to specification, stop engine and unblock other valve.
5. Replace relevant valve that creates an unspecified engine idle.

AUXILIARY AIR VALVE TEST

1. Allow engine to reach operating temperature.
2. Remove left-hand air cleaner.
3. Close idle speed adjustment screw fully.
4. Start engine. If blocking auxiliary air valve inlet doesn't affect idling speed, reset idling speed and replace air cleaner. If blocking auxiliary air valve inlet does affect idling speed, replace auxiliary air valve.

THROTTLE SWITCH, ADJUST

1. Disconnect battery.
2. Remove throttle cross-rods from throttle pulley and pull electrical connector from throttle switch.
3. Remove four nuts and spring washers securing throttle pulley platform to pedestal and lift pulley platform clear.
4. Insert a .050 in. (1.27 mm) feeler gauge between pulley and closed throttle stop, Fig. 4.
5. Connect an ohmmeter between

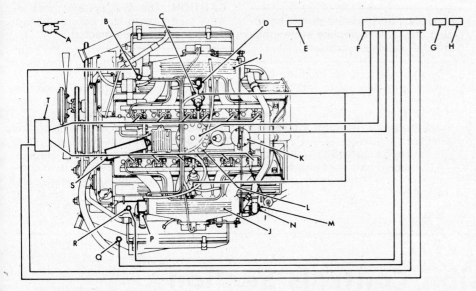

A	Manifold pressure sensor.	K	Throttle switch
B	Thermotime switch	L	Trigger unit
C	Fuel pressure regulator	M	Auxiliary air valve
D	Cold start injector	N	Idle speed regulating screw
E	Cold start relay	P	Overrun valve
F	Electronic control unit (ECU)	Q	Air temperature sensor
G	Fuel pump relay	R	Coolant temperature sensor
H	Main relay	S	Fuel cooler
J	Induction manifolds	T	Power amplifier

Fig. 1   Fuel injection system

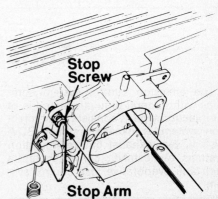

Stop Screw

Stop Arm

Fig. 2   Adjusting throttle valve

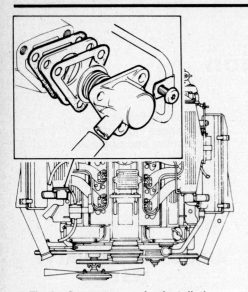

Fig. 3 Overrun run valve installation

terminals 12 and 17 of throttle switch.

6. Turn throttle switch slowly until ohmmeter needle flicks to very high resistance. Tighten two throttle switch screws.
7. Remove feeler gauge. The ohmmeter should now show very low resistance when pulley is against closed stop.
8. Disconnect ohmmeter and fit throttle pulley platform on pedestal. Secure with four nuts and spring washers.
9. Refit throttle cross-rods to throttle pulley. The ball connectors should fit without moving throttle bellcranks. Adjust length of rods, if necessary.

CAUTION: When tightening locknuts, make sure that ball joints remain free.

10. Reconnect electrical connector to throttle switch.
11. Connect battery cable.

FUEL PRESSURE REGULATORS TEST

1. Depressurize fuel system.
2. Loosen clip that secures left-hand cold start injector supply pipe to fuel rail and pull pipe from rail.
3. Connect a pressure gauge to fuel rail.

CAUTION: The pressure gauge must be one that has been tested against an approved standard.

4. Pull negative lead from ignition coil and switch on ignition.
5. Connect terminal 85 of pump relay to ground and check pressure gauge reading. It must be between 28.5—30.8 psi (2.0—2.2 kgf/cm²).

CAUTION: The pressure reading may drop slowly. A rapid drop is not permissible and its cause must be determined.

If a satisfactory result has been obtained, you may reassemble the system. If satisfactory results have not been obtained, the system should be adjusted.

FUEL PRESSURE REGULATORS, ADJUST

CAUTION: Fuel pressure should be adjusted only after complete system has been checked (see above).

1. Remove set screws holding both pressure regulators to intake manifolds.
2. Clamp fuel line between "B" (left) bank pressure regulator intake and fuel rail.
3. Be sure negative lead to ignition coil is connected and start engine.
4. Loosen locknuts at both pressure regulators.

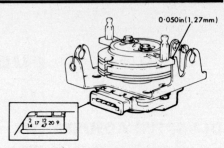

0·050in (1.27mm)

Fig. 4 Throttle switch adjustment

5. Set adjuster bolt on "A" (right) bank regulator to get a pressure gauge reading of 30 psi. (2.1 kgf/cm²).
6. Release clamp at "B" bank regulator and transfer it to "A" bank pressure regulator intake.
7. Set adjuster bolt on "B" bank regulator to get a pressure gauge reading of 30 psi. (2.1 kgf/cm²).
8. Release clamp and assure an overall pressure gauge reading of 28.5-30 psi. (2.0-2.2 kgf/cm²).
9. Secure adjuster bolts on each regulator and tighten locknuts. Turn off ignition.
10. Depressurize fuel system and reassemble system.

DEPRESSURIZING FUEL SYSTEM

CAUTION: The fuel system must always be depressurized before any fuel component is disconnected.

1. Take off right-hand luggage compartment trim panel.
2. Pull cable from terminal 85 of fuel pump relay, and disconnect high tension lead from ignition coil.
3. Switch on ignition and crank engine for several seconds. The fuel system will now be depressurized. Repressurization of the system is accomplished by connecting leads and starting engine.

Emission Controls Section

The emission control system complies with Federal regulations and is of air injection type. It consists of air injection system, crankcase breather (PCV) system, two exhaust gas recirculation systems, two catalytic converters and a fuel tank evaporative loss control system.

NOTE: CO content must not exceed 2

percent or be less than 1 percent, with the air injection system disconnected by removing the blanking plug from the diverter valve diaphragm housing.

An infra-red CO Exhaust gas analyzer, engine and ignition diagnostic equipment and Lucas "EPITEST" fuel injection diagnostic equipment are needed for servicing this system.

ENGINE BREATHER FILTER, REPLACE

1. Remove hose clip securing the rubber cover to breather housing, Fig. 1.
2. Disconnect breather pipe.
3. Remove rubber cover.
4. Lift out filter.

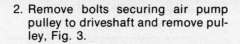

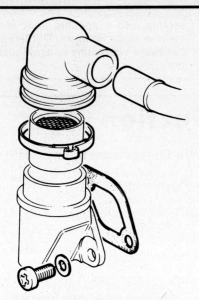

Fig. 1 Engine breather removal

FUEL ABSORPTION CANISTER, REPLACE

1. Remove left-front wheel.
2. Remove screws holding access cover to spoiler, release three studs and remove cover.
3. Note position of and remove hoses from canister, Fig. 2.
4. Release canister clamp and remove canister.

AIR DELIVERY PUMP & DIVERTER VALVE, REPLACE

NOTE: The air pump cannot be serviced or overhauled. In the event of failure, the pump has to be replaced.

1. Remove right-hand air cleaner cover.

2. Remove bolts securing air pump pulley to driveshaft and remove pulley, Fig. 3.

CAUTION: Do not use a screwdriver or wedge to pry off pulley as extensive damage may result.

3. Loosen bolt holding adjuster rod trunnion to pump and remove locknut from adjuster rod.
4. Loosen nut holding air pump mounting bolt and pivot pump away from engine.
5. Support the pump, then remove mounting nut and associated hardware.
6. Disconnect vacuum hose from diverter valve.
7. Release secondary air pipe from diverter valve and discard sealing ring.
8. Remove air pump.
9. Remove bolts holding diverter valve elbow to air pump, then remove elbow and diverter valve.
10. Discard gasket.
11. Reverse procedure to install, using a new gasket and sealing ring.
12. Be sure air pump/compressor drive belt is adjusted to deflect 0.22 in. (5.6 mm) when a load of 6.4 lb. (2.9 kg) is applied midway between two pulleys.

CHECK VALVE, REPLACE

1. Release clips holding air delivery rail hoses to check valve outlets and slide hoses off, Fig. 4.
2. Remove clip holding hose to check valve intake pipe.
3. Remove check valve.

NOTE: Use new hose clips when reinstalling valve.

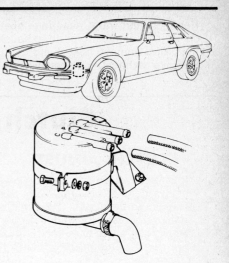

Fig. 2 Fuel absorbtion canister removal

EXHAUST GAS RECIRCULATION VALVE, REPLACE

1. Remove air cleaner cover.
2. Disconnect EGR valve transfer pipe at take-off pipe.
3. Remove electrical connectors from rear of EGR valve, Fig. 5.
4. Remove bolts holding EGR to the elbow.
5. Remove and discard EGR valve-to-elbow gasket.
6. Disconnect transfer pipe from EGR valve.

NOTE: When installing EGR valve, use a new gasket and valve transfer pipe.

CATALYTIC CONVERTERS, REPLACE

1. Remove air cleaner element.
2. Disconnect EGR valve transfer pipe from take-off pipe.
3. From beneath vehicle, remove power steering bellows heat shield.
4. Disconnect exhaust and intermediate pipes. Be sure intermediate pipe is adequately supported.

Diverter Valve

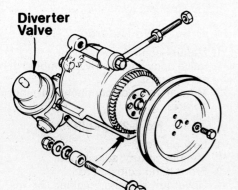

Fig. 3 Air pump and diverter valve assembly removal

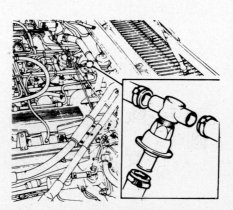

Fig. 4 Check valve removal

Fig. 5 EGR valve

5. Remove hardware securing heat shield and exhaust pipe to exhaust manifold. Remove heat shield.
6. Remove exhaust pipe/catalyst assembly. This procedure can be facilitated if steering is turned.

NOTE: When installing catalyst assembly, use a suitable joint sealer such as Holts Firegum. Tighten pipe hardware alternately to avoid distortion.

Clutch & Transmission Section

CLUTCH, ADJUST

1. Move clutch slave cylinder push rod backwards and forwards. Total free play should be .125 in. (3.2 mm).
2. To adjust, loosen locknut, Fig. 1.
3. Screw push rod in or out of trunnion until correct amount of free play is obtained.
4. Tighten locknut.
5. Operate clutch pedal several times and recheck amount of free travel.

CLUTCH, REPLACE

1. Remove engine and transmission from vehicle.
2. Remove flywheel cover.
3. Remove starter motor.
4. Disconnect transmission breather pipe and detach bell housing and transmission.
5. Mark relative positions of clutch cover to flywheel and balance weights to clutch cover.
6. Remove clutch cover and clutch plates.
7. Remove and replace throwout bearing.
8. Place clutch plates and cover on flywheel, seeing that reference marks made during disassembly are aligned.
9. Refit balance weights, bolts and washers, but do not tighten bolts.
10. Using a dummy shaft, align clutch plates, assuring that clutch cover is properly located on its dowels.
11. Tighten bolts in a diagonal manner to avoid distortion.
12. Complete reassembly by reversing steps 1 through 4 above.

MANUAL TRANSMISSION, REPLACE

1. Remove engine and transmission from vehicle.
2. Remove clutch.
3. Remove clutch fork assembly.
4. Remove and discard locking wire.
5. Knock back locking tabs and remove screws holding bell-housing to transmission. Discard tabs.
6. Remove bell-housing, discarding gasket and oil seal.
7. Coat a new oil seal with clean engine oil.

8. Push oil seal into bell-housing so lip of seal is toward transmission.
9. Coat a new gasket with grease. Place gasket on front of transmission.
10. Cover splines of input shaft with adhesive tape to keep shaft from damaging oil seal and slide bell-housing over shaft.
11. Install new lock plates and tighten screws diagonally to prevent distortion.
12. Turn up tabs of lock plates and wire lock the screws.
13. Complete reassembly by reversing steps 1 through 3 above.

AUTOMATIC TRANSMISSION TROUBLESHOOTING

Harsh Engagement

1. Vacuum control adjustment.
2. Engine idle speed adjustment.
3. Front and/or rear band adjustment.
4. Vacuum leak.
5. Valve body improperly assembled or screws missing.
6. Primary or secondary valve sticking.
7. Throttle valve sticking.

Soft Or Delayed Engagement

1. Low oil level.
2. Manual control adjustment.
3. Engine idle speed adjustment.
4. Front and/or rear band adjustment.
5. Valve body improperly assembled or screws missing.
6. Primary and/or secondary valve sticking.
7. Cutback valve sticking.

Push Rod   Locknut

Fig. 1 Clutch adjustment

No Engagement In Any Position

1. Manual valve disconnected from shift control.
2. Low oil level.
3. Manual control adjustment.
4. Primary valve sticking.
5. Broken converter drive plate.

No Forward Drive

1. In any and all positions:
   a. Manual valve disconnected from shift control.
   b. Low oil level.
   c. Manual control adjustment.
   d. Valve body improperly assembled or screws missing.
   e. Primary valve sticking.
2. In 2 position:
   All of the above plus rear band locked in place, missing or broken oil tubes, and servo regulator valve sticking.
3. In D position:
   All of the above plus rear band adjustment.

No Reverse Drive

1. Manual valve disconnected from shift control.
2. Low oil level.
3. Manual control adjustment.
4. Rear band adjustment.
5. Front band locked in place.
6. Rear band slipping due to:
   a. Faulty servo.
   b. Broken band.
   c. Worn band.
7. Valve body improperly assembled or screws missing.
8. 1-2 shift valve sticking.
9. 2-3 shift valve sticking.

No Neutral

1. Manual control adjustment.
2. Valve body improperly assembled or screws missing.
3. Manual valve disconnected at shift control.

No 1-2 Upshift

1. Low oil level.
2. Manual control adjustment.
3. Front band adjustment.
4. Governor sticking, leaking or improperly assembled.
5. Front band slipping due to:
   a. Faulty servo.

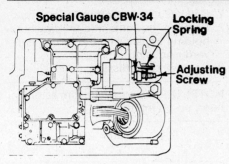

Special Gauge CBW·34 Locking Spring Adjusting Screw

Fig. 2 Front band adjustment

b. Broken band.
c. Worn band.
6. Oil tubes missing or broken.
7. Rear band locked in the applied position.
8. Valve body improperly assembled or screws missing.
9. Primary valve sticking.
10. Throttle valve sticking.
11. 1-2 shift valve sticking.

No 2-3 Upshift

1. Low oil level.
2. Manual control adjustment.
3. Governor sticking, leaking or incorrectly assembled.
4. Oil tubes missing or broken.
5. Valve body improperly assembled or screws missing.
6. Primary valve sticking.
7. 1-2 shift valve sticking.
8. 2-3 shift valve sticking.
9. Governor modulator valve sticking.

Slips 1-2 Shift

1. Low oil level.
2. Vacuum control adjustment.
3. Manual control adjustment.
4. Governor sticking, leaking or incorrectly assembled.
5. Vacuum line restricted.
6. Valve body improperly assembled or screws missing.
7. Primary valve sticking.
8. Throttle valve sticking.
9. Oil tubes missing or broken.
10. Cutback valve sticking.
11. Servo regulator valve sticking.
12. 1-2 shift valve sticking.

Slips 2-3 Shift

1. Low oil level.
2. Vacuum control adjustment.
3. Manual control adjustment.
4. Front band adjustment.
5. Vacuum line restricted.
6. Governor sticking, leaking or incorrectly assembled.
7. Oil tubes missing or broken.
8. Valve body improperly assembled or screws missing.
9. Primary valve sticking.
10. Throttle valve sticking.

11. 1-2 shift valve sticking.
12. 2-3 shift valve sticking.
13. Servo regulator valve sticking.
14. Orifice control valve sticking.
15. 2-3 shift valve plug sticking.

Harsh 1-2 Shift

1. Vacuum control adjustment.
2. Manual control adjustment.
3. Front band adjustment.
4. Rear band adjustment.
5. Vacuum leak.
6. Valve body improperly assembled or screws missing.
7. Primary valve sticking.
8. Secondary valve sticking.
9. Throttle valve sticking.
10. 1-2 shift valve sticking.
11. Cutback valve sticking.

Harsh 2-3 Shift

1. Vacuum control adjustment.
2. Manual control adjustment.
3. Front band adjustment.
4. Vacuum leak.
5. Valve body improperly assembled or screws missing.
6. Primary valve sticking.
7. Throttle valve sticking.
8. Cutback valve sticking.

Low or High Shift Points

1. Vacuum control adjustment.
2. Manual control adjustment.
3. Vacuum leak.
4. Vacuum line restricted.
5. Broken kickdown wire or blown fuse.
6. Governor sticking, leaking or incorrectly assembled.
7. Valve body improperly assembled or screws missing.
8. Primary valve sticking.
9. Throttle valve sticking.
10. 1-2 shift valve sticking.
11. 2-3 shift valve sticking.
12. Throttle modulator valve sticking.
13. 2-3 shift valve plug sticking.
14. Defective solenoid

Low Idle Line Pressure

1. Low oil level.
2. Vacuum control adjustment.
3. Manual control adjustment.
4. Engine idle speed adjustment.
5. Oil tubes missing or broken.
6. Valve body improperly assembled or screws missing.
7. Primary valve sticking.
8. Governor sticking, leaking or incorrectly assembled.

High Idle Line Pressure

1. Valve body improperly assembled or screws missing.
2. Vacuum leak.

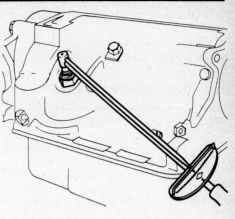

Fig. 3 Rear band adjustment

3. Vacuum control adjustment.
4. Primary valve sticking.
5. Secondary valve sticking.
6. Throttle valve sticking.

Noisy In Neutral

Regulator valve buzz.

Noisy In Park

1. Regulator valve buzz.
2. Dirty oil filter.

Noisy In All Gears

1. Regulator valve buzz.
2. Broken converter plate.
3. Dirty oil filter.

Oil Coming Out Breather Or Filler Tube

1. High oil level.
2. Governor sticking, leaking or incorrectly assembled.
3. Oil tubes missing or broken.
4. Breather plugged.
5. Valve body improperly assembled or screws missing.

AUTOMATIC TRANSMISSION, ADJUSTMENTS

Front Band Adjustment

1. Remove transmission oil pan.
2. Loosen adjusting screw until it no longer is touching contact pin.

NOTE: The adjusting screw has a left-hand thread.

3. Pull front servo operating lever back and insert special gauge CBW.34 between adjusting screw and piston pin, Fig. 2.
4. Using torque screwdriver CBW.548 and adapters, tighten adjusting screw to 10 in. lbs. (0.12 kg-m).

5. Make sure locking spring is located in retaining slot.
6. Remove gauge block.
7. Replace oil pan.

Rear Band Adjustment

NOTE: This adjustment is made outside the transmission.

1. Loosen adjusting screw locknut.
2. Loosen adjusting screw two full turns.
3. Tighten adjusting screw to a torque of 10 ft. lbs. (1.4 kg-m), Fig. 3.
4. Loosen adjusting screw 1¼ turns and tighten locknut.

CAUTION: Make sure adjusting screw does not turn as you tighten locknut. Severe transmission damage can result if you have failed to back off adjusting screw exactly 1¼ turns.

AUTOMATIC TRANSMISSION, REPLACE

1. Remove engine and transmission.
2. Disconnect and plug oil cooler lines.
3. Pull breather pipe off stub pipe.
4. Withdraw dipstick.
5. Disconnect oil filler tube at oil pan.
6. Drain and discard fluid.
7. Pull vacuum line off vacuum unit.
8. Remove four nuts and lockwashers holding transmission to torque converter housing.
9. Remove transmission.

NOTE: Do not allow transmission to hang up on input shaft.

10. To install, reverse steps 1 to 8 above.

NOTE: Make sure that torque converter and transmission input splines are correctly aligned.

11. Replace engine and transmission.
12. Check fluid level.

Rear Axle & Brakes Section

REAR AXLE, DESCRIPTION

The standard rear axle unit is a Salisbury 4 HU final drive incorporating a "Powr Lok" differential. The unit is rigidly attached to a fabricated sheet steel crossbeam which is flexibly mounted to the body structure by four rubber and metal sandwich mounts.

AXLE SHAFT, OIL SEAL & BEARINGS, REPLACE

1. Remove output shaft assembly. Clean assembly and clamp caliper mounting bracket in a vise.
2. Using special spanner SL.15 or SL.15A, turn down tabs of lock washer and remove nut from shaft.
3. Separate shaft and caliper mounting bracket, collecting inner bearing and cone. Mark bearing and cone to facilitate reassembly.
4. Discard spacer and pry oil seal from caliper mounting bracket. Discard oil seal and retrieve outer bearing and cone.
5. Thoroughly clean caliper mounting bracket and inspect axle shaft bearings. Replace bearings if they are damaged.
6. Apply grease to outer bearing assembly and place it in position.
7. Press on a new oil seal, making sure that spring-loaded sealing edge is adjacent to bearing and that sealing edges are loaded with grease.
8. With caliper mounting bracket held in a vise, check to ensure that four brake disc bolts are in position on axle shaft flange. Place shaft through seal and outer bearing assembly.
9. Install a spacer, inner bearing assembly (greased) and lock washer.
10. Place shaft nut in place and tighten by hand.
11. Check torque needed to turn shaft in caliper mounting bracket. Set torque screwdriver initially to a setting of 4 in. lbs. (0.05 kgf/m). The setting should be increased progressively until the torque requirement is established at the point when the shaft starts to turn.
12. Using spanner SL.15 and a pry bar at disc attachment bolts to oppose torque, tighten shaft nut just enough to almost eliminate play from the bearings and remeasure torque as measured in step 11.

NOTE: The torque needed to turn the shaft should be unchanged. If it has increased, loosen the nut slightly and recheck.

13. Tighten shaft nut just slightly, but not more than 3/16 in. (5 mm) and test torque needed to turn shaft. If torque exceeds 2.5 to 3 in. lbs. (0.03-0.035 kgf/m) the torque recorded before in step 11, correct bearing pre-load has been established. If this figure has not been attained, continue to tighten axle shaft nut in small increments, measuring torque after each increment, until desired specification has been reached.

NOTE: If torque required to turn shaft is 4 in. lbs. (0.045 kgf/m) more than that attained in initial tightening sequence in step 11, you will have to disassemble unit, discard spacer and reassemble using a new spacer.

14. Complete reassembly, which is done in reverse of disassembly.

BRAKE SYSTEM, DESCRIPTION

The brake system consists of four disc brake assemblies, tandem master cylinder, power unit and a pressure differential warning actuator (PDWA) that monitors front and rear brake line pressures, providing visual warning to the driver if there is a drop in brake line pressure. The front and rear caliper assemblies are completely independent of each other.

FRONT BRAKE PADS, REPLACE

1. Remove wheel assembly.
2. Remove clips holding pad retaining pins.
3. Remove upper pin only and then the anti-chatter springs.
4. Remove lower pin.
5. Pull pads from caliper.

REAR BRAKE PADS, REPLACE

1. Remove wheel assembly.
2. Remove clips holding pad retaining pins.
3. Remove mounting pins and pull pads from caliper.

NOTE: If thickness of pads, front or rear, is less than 0.125 inch (3.17 mm) new pads should be installed.

FRONT CALIPER, REPLACE

1. Disconnect and plug brake line.
2. Remove lock wire from caliper mounting bolts.
3. Remove caliper mounting bolts, noting position of shims located between steering arm and caliper.
4. Remove caliper.
5. When reassembling, torque caliper mounting bolts to 55 ft. lbs. (7.5 kg/m).

REAR CALIPER, REPLACE

1. Remove handbrake caliper.
2. Loosen brake line connection at three-way connector, then disconnect brake line at caliper and swing line clear of caliper. Be sure to plug brake lines.
3. Remove lock wire holding caliper mounting bolts.
4. Remove caliper mounting bolts.
5. Slide caliper around disc and remove through gap left by removing bracket.
6. When reassembling, torque caliper mounting bolts to 55 ft. lbs. (7.5 kg/m).

FRONT & REAR CALIPER, OVERHAUL

1. Remove pads.
2. Remove spring clips holding piston dust covers.
3. Remove piston dust covers.
4. Fit piston clamp 18G672 to any half of caliper and carefully feed compressed oil into caliper fluid inlet port.
5. Remove pistons from caliper.
6. Carefully pry seals from recesses in caliper cylinder bore.

NOTE: Under no circumstances must the two halves of the caliper be separated. Use extreme caution not to damage the cylinder bore when removing seals.

7. Coat new seals with brake lubricant.
8. Using your fingers only, fit new seals into recesses in caliper cylinder bore.
9. Coat pistons with brake lubricant and reinsert them into caliper cylinder bores.
10. Fit rear dust covers and push pistons in.
11. Position dust covers over caliper rim and secure with spring clips.
12. Complete reassembly in reverse of disassembly.

PARKING BRAKE, ADJUST

1. Raise carpeting to rear of the driver's seat to gain access to adjusting nuts.
2. Loosen cable locknut.
3. Tighten adjusting nut so that when parking brake is released there is a slight amount of cable play.

NOTE: If all play is removed, parking brake caliper may bind.

4. Tighten cable locknut.

MASTER CYLINDER, REPLACE

1. Remove cover from brake fluid reservoir cap and disconnect wires from brake fluid level indicator.
2. Remove reservoir cap and filter.
3. With a syringe, draw lines from master cylinder and plug them.
4. Disconnect brake lines from master cylinder and plug them.
5. Remove master cylinder from power booster.

Rear Suspension Section

COIL SPRING & SHOCK ABSORBER, REPLACE

1. Remove rear wheel.
2. Remove washers and nuts holding bottom of shock absorber to wishbone.
3. Remove shock absorber lower mounting pin, spacer and retaining bracket.
4. Remove fasteners holding upper part of shock absorber to cross member.
5. Remove shock absorber and coil spring assembly.
6. Separate the two using hand press SL.14 and adapter JD.11B.

Front Suspension & Steering Section

WHEEL ALIGNMENT

Caster

Caster angle is adjusted by loosening the four upper wishbone-to-ball joint nuts and refitting shims from one side of the ball joint to the opposite side. Placing the front shims to the rear position decreases caster angle, while placing rear shims to the front position increases caster angle. The rate of alteration is approximately ¼ degree for each 1/16 inch (1.6 mm) shim.

Camber

Camber angle is adjusted by loosening the two nuts holding the end of the upper wishbone away from the ball joint at the trunnion. Add or remove an equal number of shims from both spots. Removing shims decreases camber angle, while adding shims increases camber angle. The rate of alteration is approximately ¼ degree for 1/16 inch (1.6 mm) shim.

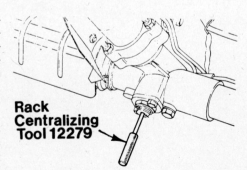

Rack Centralizing Tool 12279

Fig. 1 Toe-in adjustment

Toe-In

1. With tires inflated properly and wheels in a straight-ahead position, remove the grease fitting from the steering rack adjuster nut and insert rack centralizing tool 12279 into the hole.
2. Slowly turn the steering wheel until the tool locates itself in the recess in the rear of the rack.
3. Check toe-in.
4. If adjustment is necessary, loosen the locknuts at the outer ends of the tie rods and loosen the clips holding the tie rod retaining bracket.
5. Turn tie rods equally to attain correct alignment (1/16 to ⅛ inch—1.6 to 3 mm).

WHEEL BEARINGS, ADJUST

Wheel bearings are adjusted by tightening the adjusting nut to eliminate all play and then backing the nut off slightly to provide play of .002 to .005 inch (.05 to .15 mm).

UPPER BALL JOINT, REPLACE

1. Remove the wheel and turn the steering wheel to full lock position.
2. Reinforce brake hose to relieve strain.
3. Remove upper ball joint hardware.
4. Release ball joint from axle carrier with taper separator tool JD.24.
5. Hold the ball joint against taper fit washer and tighten retaining nut to 35-50 ft. lbs. (4.84-6.91 kgf/m).

NOTE: The bolts holding the ball joint to the wishbone must be replaced with heads facing forward.

6. Reassemble in reverse of disassembly, tightening fasteners to 26-32 ft. lbs. (3.60-4.42 kgf/m).

LOWER BALL JOINT, ADJUST

1. Raise the car, remove wheel and place a jack under front spring seat, and lift to relieve pressure on axle carrier.
2. Remove tie rod ball joint fasteners, and separate tie rod from steering arm using steering joint taper separator tool JD.24.
3. Remove all other hardware, leaving ball joint free.

NOTE: Shims are added to obtain correct adjustment. However, excessive wear must not be compensated for by shims. Worn parts must be replaced.

4. Remove shims one by one until ball pin is tight in socket with screws tightened to 15-20 ft. lbs (2.10-2.75 kgf/m).

NOTE: Shims are available in .002 and .004 inch (0.5 and 0.10 mm).

5. Remove screws, ball pin cap, shims and socket. Add shims to value of .004-.006 inch (0.10-0.15 mm).
6. Grease ball pin and socket lightly. Refit the socket ball pin cap and washers.
7. Torque to 15-20 ft. lbs. (2.1-2.75 kgf/m). When correctly adjusted, hub and axle carrier may be pivoted with very slight drag.
8. Apply grease to ball joint and replace tie rod.
9. Tighten tie rod nut to 35-50 ft. lbs. (4.84-6.91 kgf/m).

COIL SPRING, REPLACE

1. Raise vehicle and remove wheel.
2. Fit spring compressor tool JD.6D with adapter JD.6D-1 to spring and compress sufficiently to relieve load on seat fastener.
3. Remove hardware and spring plate.
4. Loosen spring compressor tool and remove spring.
5. When installing, tighten hardware to 27-32 ft. lbs. (3.74-4.42 kgf/m).

SHOCK ABSORBER, REPLACE

1. From beneath hood, remove hardware from shock absorber front mounting.
2. Raise vehicle.
3. Remove locking nut and bolt from bottom of shock.
4. Remove shock absorber from vehicle.
5. Install shock absorber and torque lower mounting bolt to 32-36 ft. lbs. (4.42-4.98 kgf/m) and upper mounting bolt to 27-32 ft. lbs. (3.73-4.42 kgf/m).

POWER STEERING GEAR, REPLACE

1. Remove lower steering column.
2. Draw fluid from steering pump.
3. Release all feed lines and plug.
4. Using ball joint separator JD.24, separate left and right tie rods.
5. Release steering gear from suspension and withdraw from vehicle.
6. Refitting is done in reverse of disassembly, but following points require emphasis:
7. Shims are placed between gear and mounting bracket to obtain a 0.05 inch gap (1.25 mm) on either side of gear and bracket.
8. The gear is aligned using steering alignment tool JD.36A.

LUV

INDEX OF SERVICE OPERATIONS

LUV

GENERAL ENGINE SPECIFICATIONS

Year	Engine Model	Carb. Type	Bore & Stroke	Comp. Ratio	Horsepower @ R.P.M.	Torque Lbs. Ft. @ R.P.M.	Normal Oil Pressure Lbs.
1972-75	4-110	2 Bore	3.31 x 3.23	8.2	75 @ 5000	88 @ 3000	57
1976-77	4-110	2 Bore	3.31 x 3.23	8.5	80 @ 4800	95 @ 3000	57

TUNE UP SPECIFICATIONS

The following specifications are published from the latest information available. This data should be used only in the absence of a decal affixed in the engine compartment.

★When using a timing light, disconnect vacuum hose or tube at distributor and plug opening in hose or tube so idle speed will not be affected.

▲Before removing wires from distributor cap, determine location of No. 1 wire in cap, as distributor position may have been altered from that shown at the end of this chart.

Year	Engine	Spark Plug		Distributor		Firing Order ▲	Ignition Timing★		Hot Idle Speed	Comp. Press. Lbs.	Fuel Pump Press. Lbs.
		Type	Gap Inch	Point Gap Inch	Dwell Angle Deg.		BTDC①	Mark Location			
1972-73	4-110	NGK BP-6ES	③	.020	49-55	Fig. A	8°	Fig. C	700	163②	3¾
1974	4-110	NGK BP-6ES	.035	.020	49-55	Fig. A	12°	Fig. C	700	163②	3¾
1975	4-110	NGK BP-6ES	.030	.020	49-55	Fig. A	12°	Fig. C	700	163②	4½
1976-77	4-110	NGK BPR-6ES	.030	.018	47-57	Fig. B	6°	Fig. D	900	171②	—

—Not available
① —Before Top Dead Center.
② —Variance per cylinder not to exceed 8.5 lbs.
③ —1972 .030; 1973 .035.

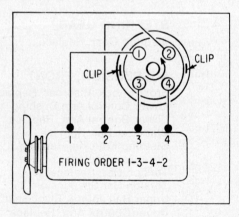

Fig. A

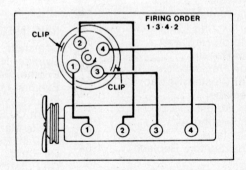

Fig. B

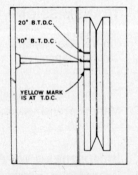

Fig. C

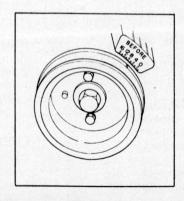

Fig. D

LUV

DISTRIBUTOR SPECIFICATIONS

Year	Model	Distributor Number	Rotation ①	Breaker Gap	Dwell Angle Deg.	Breaker Arm Spring Tension	Centrifugal Advance Deg. @ R.P.M. of Distributor		Vacuum Advance	
							Advance Starts	Full Advance	Inches of Vacuum To Start Plunger	Max. Adv. Dist. Deg. @ Vacuum
1972-73	4-110	D414-62	CC	.020	49-55	1.1-1.43	—	—	—	—
1974	4-110	D417-62	CC	.020	49-55	1.1-1.43	—	—	—	—
1975②	4-110	D417-64	CC	.020	49-55	1.1-1.43	—	—	—	—
1975③	4-110	D417-62	CC	.020	49-55	1.1-1.43	—	—	—	—
1976	4-110	0291003280	CC	.018	47-57	.83-1.27	—	—	—	—
1977	4-110	0291003281	CC	.018	47-57	.83-1.21	—	—	—	—

—Not available
①—As viewed from top.
②—Exc. California.
③—California

ALTERNATOR & REGULATOR SPECIFICATIONS

		Alternator					Regulator						
					Rated Output				Field Relay			Voltage Regulator	
Year	Model	Rotor Resistance (At 68° F)	Stator Resistance (At 68° F)	Amperes @ 1350 R.P.M.	Amperes @ 2500 R.P.M.	Amperes @ 5000 R.P.M.	Model	Air Gap	Point Gap	Closing Voltage	Air Gap	Point Gap	Volts @ 2500 R.P.M.
1972-74	LT 130-83	4.3	.13	8	22	30	TL1Z-66	.035	.020	5	.032	.014	13.5-14.5
1975	LT 135-26	4.3	.13	—	28	35	TL1Z-87	.035	.020	5	.032	.014	13.8-14.8
1976-77	LT 135-30	4.3	.13	—	28	35	TL1Z-87	.035	.020	5	.032	.014	13.8-14.8

—Not Available

STARTING MOTOR SPECIFICATIONS

Year	Starter Model	Brush Spring Tension	Free Speed Test			Resistance Test	
			Amperes	Volts	R.P.M.	Amperes	Volts
1972	S114-118	1.76	60	12	6000①	330	5.1
1973-75	S114-136	1.76	60	12	6000①	330	5.1
1976-77	S114-202	—	60	12	6000①	330	5

—Not Available
①—Minimum.

VALVE SPECIFICATIONS

Year	Engine	Valve Lash	Valve Angles		Valve Springs		Valve Stem Clearance		Valve Stem Diameter	
			Seat	Face	Installed Height	Pressure Lbs. @ In.	Intake	Exhaust	Intake	Exhaust
1972-75	4-110	①	45	45	②	③	.0016-.0079	.0020-.0098	.3102-.3150	.3091-.3150
1976-77	4-110	④	45	45	⑤	⑥	.0009-.0022	.0015-.0031	.3102-.3150	.3091-.3150

①—Intake, .004 inch; exhaust, .006 inch set cold.
②—Outer, 1.58 inch; inner, 1.5 inch.
③—Outer, 47.4 lbs. @ 1.58 inch; inner, 17.8 lbs. @ 1.5 inch.
④—Intake, .006"; exhaust, .010" set cold.
⑤—Outer, 1.614", inner, 1.516".
⑥—Outer, 34.6 lbs. @ 1.614"; inner, 20.1 lbs. @ 1.516".

PISTON, PIN, RING, CRANKSHAFT & BEARING SPECIFICATIONS

Year	Engine	Piston Clearance	Ring End Gap ①		Piston Pin Diam.	Rod Bearing		Main Bearing			
			Comp.	Oil		Shaft Diam.	Bearing Clearance	Shaft Diam.	Bearing Clearance	Thrust Bearing No.	Shaft End Play
1972-75	4-110	.0018-.0026	.008-.016	.012-.039	.8700	1.927-1.929	.00197-.0047	2.203-2.205	.00158-.0047	3	.0059
1976-77	4-110	.0018-.0026	.008-.016	.008-.035	—	1.927-1.929	.0007-.0030	2.203-2.205	.0008-.0025	3	.0059

—Not Available

①—Fit ring at right angles all the way to the skirt using piston head.

ENGINE TIGHTENING SPECIFICATIONS★

★Torque specifications are for clean and lightly lubricated threads only. Dry or dirty threads produce increased friction which prevents accurate measurement of tightness.

Year	Engine	Spark Plug Ft. Lbs.	Cylinder Head Bolts Ft. Lbs.	Connecting Rod Cap Bolts Ft. Lbs.	Main Bearing Cap Bolts Ft. Lbs.	Flywheel to Crankshaft Ft. Lbs.	Vibration Damper or Pulley Ft. Lbs.	Oil Pan Bolts In. Lbs.	Layshaft & Camshaft Timing Sprocket Ft. Lbs.	Flywheel Nut Ft. Lbs.
1972-75	4-110	18-25	①	43	72	36②	—	50	33	36②
1976-77	4-110	18-25	72	33	72	69	—	3.6③	58	69

—Not Available

①—1972-73 All 58 ft. lbs.; 1974-75, 1,2,3 & 6 at 70 ft. lbs.; all others at 60 ft. lbs.

②—1973-75, 69 ft. lbs.

③—Ft. lbs.

COOLING SYSTEM & CAPACITY DATA

Year	Model of Engine	Cooling Capacity, Qts.		Radiator Cap Relief Pressure, Lbs.		Thermo. Opening Temp. ①	Fuel Tank Gals.	Engine Oil Refill Qts. ②	Transmission Oil		Rear Axle Oil Pints
		With Heater	With A/C	With A/C	No A/C				4 Speed Pints	Auto. Trans. Qts.	
1972-73	All	6	6	15	15	177-182	10	4.2	2.6	—	2.7
1974-75	All	6	6	15	15	177-182	13.2	4.2	2.6	—	2.7
1976-77	All	6.4	6.4	15	15	177-182	13.2	5.3	2.7	③	2.7

—Not Available

①—Use permanent type anti-freeze.

②—Includes 1 qt. for filter.

③—Refill, 6 pts.; Overhaul 13 pts.

REAR AXLE SPECIFICATIONS

Year	Model	Carrier Type	Ring Gear & Pinion Backlash		Pinion Bearing Preload			Differential Bearing Preload		
			Method	Adjustment	Method	New Bearings Inch-Lbs.	Used Bearings Inch-Lbs.	Method	New Bearings Inch-Lbs.	Used Bearings Inch-Lbs.
1972-77	All	Removable	Shim	.005-.007	Spacer	17	7-9	Shims	①	①

①—Refer to procedure under "Rear Axle Carrier."

BRAKE SPECIFICATIONS

Year	Model	Drum I.D.	Wheel Cyl. Bore			Disc Brake Rotor					Master Cyl. I.D.
			Rear Drum	Front Drum	Front Disc.	Nominal Thickness	Minimum Thickness	Thickness Variation (Parallelism)	Run Out TIR	Finish (microinch)	
1972-75	All	10	.75	1.06	—	—	—	—	—	—	.875
1976-77	All	10	.75	—	—	.709	.653	.0005	.005	20-60	.875

—Not Available

WHEEL ALIGNMENT SPECIFICATIONS

Year	Caster, Deg.	Camber, Deg.	Toe-In, In.	Kingpin Inclination, Deg.
1972-75	+1/3°	+1°	+1/8	7°
1976	−1/6°	+1/2°	0	7°
1977	−1/6°	+1/2°	0	7½°

Electrical Section

DISTRIBUTOR, REPLACE

1. Disconnect battery ground cable.
2. Remove distributor cap with spark plug wires attached.
3. Disconnect primary lead from coil terminal and vacuum hose from vacuum advance unit.
4. Scribe an alignment mark on distributor housing and engine in line with rotor segment, then remove hold down bolt and remove distributor.
5. Reverse procedure to install. Make sure that rotor segment is aligned with scribed mark on distributor housing and that mark on distributor housing is aligned with mark on engine. Install hold down bolt.
6. Start engine. Check dwell and timing and adjust as necessary.

DISTRIBUTOR REPAIRS
Hitachi Units

1. Remove vacuum controller, Figs. 1 and 2.
2. Disconnect leads and remove breaker points. On dual point distributors, do not disturb the setting of the adjuster plate retaining retarded breaker points.
3. Disconnect primary side terminal and remove breaker plate.
4. Drive roll pin from coupling and shaft, then remove coupling from shaft.

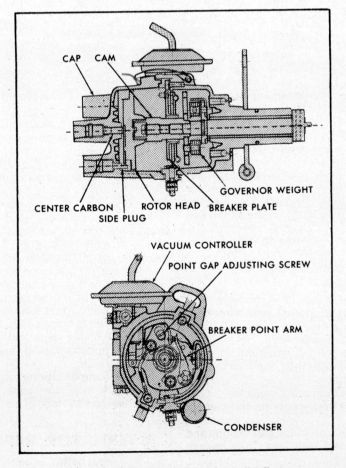

Fig. 1 Hitachi single breaker point distributor

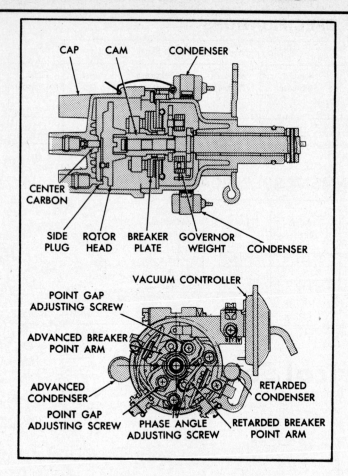

CAP   CAM   CONDENSER

CENTER CARBON

SIDE PLUG   ROTOR HEAD   BREAKER PLATE   GOVERNOR WEIGHT   CONDENSER

VACUUM CONTROLLER

POINT GAP ADJUSTING SCREW

ADVANCED BREAKER POINT ARM

ADVANCED CONDENSER

POINT GAP ADJUSTING SCREW

PHASE ANGLE ADJUSTING SCREW

RETARDED CONDENSER

RETARDED BREAKER POINT ARM

Fig. 2 Hitachi dual breaker point distributor

5. Remove cam retaining screw and disconnect timing lever.
6. Remove centrifugal advance springs and weights.
7. Reverse procedure to assemble. When installing the centrifugal advance springs, ensure the proper spring is installed on the proper side. The primary spring is identified by the round hook on the spring and the secondary spring is identified by a sharp hook on the spring.

Nippon Denso Units

Disassembly
1. Remove dust cover, terminal bolt lock nut and terminal and insulator assembly, Fig. 3.
2. Remove condenser.
3. Remove circlip retaining vacuum advance rod, then the vacuum advance unit.
4. Remove dust-proof gaskets.
5. Remove breaker points and damper spring.
6. Remove distributor cap clamps and disconnect lead wire, then remove breaker plate.
7. Remove screw from end of cam as-

sembly, then the governor springs and cam.
8. Remove circlips retaining governor weights, then the governor weights.
9. Remove caulking from collar set pin and drive pin from collar.
10. Remove collar and distributor shaft.

Assembly
Reverse disassembly procedure to assemble and note the following:
1. Lightly lubricate the distributor shaft, cam, damper spring and breaker arm prior to installation.
2. Position governor springs, Fig. 4, and install cam drive plate with the rear face is turned toward the stop pin on the governor plate.
3. Install the cap clips with the projected portion facing toward the terminal side.
4. Install damper spring to provide .002-.004 inch clearance between the heel and flat face of cam, Fig. 5.

ALTERNATOR, REPLACE

1. Disconnect battery ground cable.
2. Remove air pump.

3. Disconnect alternator connector and cable from terminal A.
4. Remove mounting bolt and fan belt adjusting bolt and remove alternator.
5. Reverse procedure to install.

ALTERNATOR TESTING

NOTE: Alternator must be removed from vehicle for testing.

1. Connect an ohmmeter between E and F terminals, Figs. 6 and 7.
2. If resistance is higher than 4 ohms on 1972-74 models or 5 ohms on 1975-77 models, poor continuity exist between brushes and commutator.
3. If no continuity exist between E and F terminals, check for open in rotor coil circuit, sticking brush or broken lead wire.
4. If resistance is lower than 4 ohms on 1972-74 models or 5 ohms on 1975-77 models, this maybe an indication of rotor coil layer short or circuit being grounded.
5. Connect positive lead of ohmmeter to N terminal and negative lead to A terminal, Figs. 8 and 9. If continuity exist between terminals, one or more of the three positive diodes are shorted.
6. Connect positive lead of ohmmeter to E terminal and negative lead to N terminal, Figs. 10 and 11. If continuity exist, between terminals, than one or more of the three negative diodes are shorted.

REGULATOR TESTING

NOTE: Battery must be fully charged to perform the following test.

1. Connect ammeter and voltmeter as shown in Fig. 12.
2. Operate engine at 2500 RPM and note ammeter reading. Reading should be 5 amps or below. If reading is above 5 amps, battery is not fully charged.
3. Lower engine speed to idle, than gradually increase speed to 2500 RPM. Volt meter reading should be between 13.5-14.5 volts on 1972-74 models and 13.8-14.8 volts on 1975-77 models. If voltmeter reading is not within limits, adjust regulator as outlined under "Regulator Adjustment."

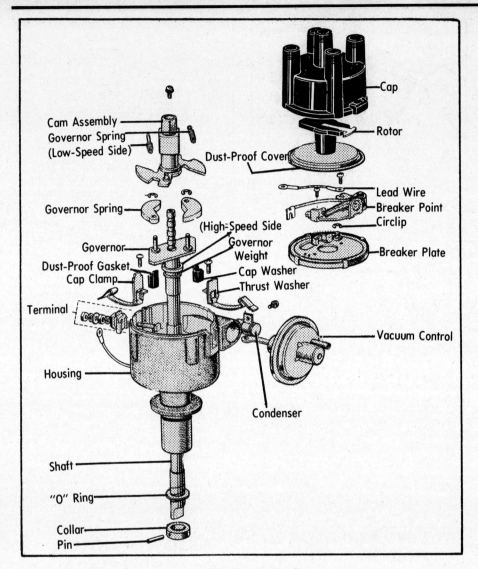

Fig. 3 Nippon Denso distributor

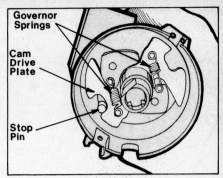

Fig. 4 Governor spring installation. Nippon Denso distributor

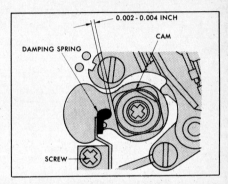

Fig. 5 Damper spring to cam clearance. Nippon Denso distributor

REGULATOR ADJUSTMENT

1. Remove regulator cover and disconnect wire connector.
2. Inspect contacts for roughness and dress as required with #500-600 sand paper.
3. Adjust core gap by loosening contact to yoke attaching screw, then move contacts up or down as required to obtain core gap of .024-.039 inch and tighten attaching screw, Fig. 13.
4. Adjust contact point gap by loosening upper contact attaching screw, then move upper contact up and down as required to obtain a point gap of .012-.016 inch and tighten attaching screw, Fig. 14.
5. Adjust regulated voltage by means of adjusting screw. Loosen lock nut, then turn adjusting screw in to increase voltage and out to decrease voltage, Fig. 15. After correct setting is obtained tighten lock nut.
6. Install cover and connect wire connector, then recheck voltage setting.

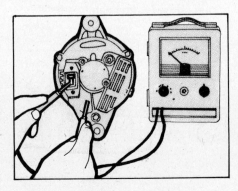

Fig. 6 Testing rotor coil resistance. 1972-74

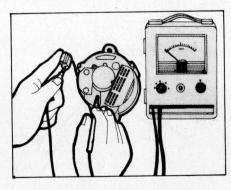

Fig. 7 Testing rotor coil resistance. 1975-77

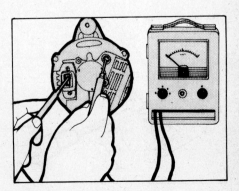

Fig. 8 Positive diode test. 1972-74

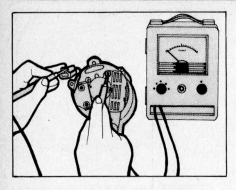

Fig. 9 Positive diode test. 1975-77

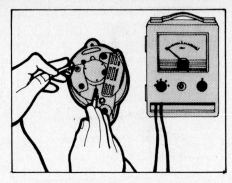

Fig. 11 Negative diode test. 1975-77

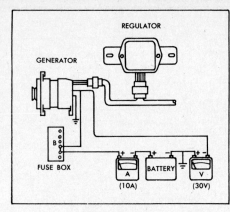

Fig. 12 Regulator test equipment connections

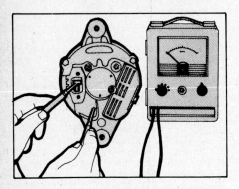

Fig. 10 Negative diode test. 1972-74

STARTER, REPLACE

1. Disconnect battery ground cable.
2. On 1976-77 vehicles, remove EGR pipe.
3. Disconnect wiring from solenoid, then remove bolts and nuts and remove starter assembly.
4. Reverse procedure to install.

TURN SIGNAL SWITCH, REPLACE

1. Disconnect battery ground cable.
2. Remove horn sounder and steering wheel.

3. Remove steering column cowling retaining screws and wire connectors from combination switch to harness.
4. Remove switch clamp to steering column mast jacket screws and remove switch.
5. Reverse procedure to install.

INSTRUMENT CLUSTER, REPLACE

1. Disconnect battery ground cable.
2. Remove wing nuts from rear side of instrument cluster and pull cluster part way out.
3. Disconnect electrical harness at connector and remove cluster.
4. Reverse procedure to install.

W/S WIPER MOTOR & TRANSMISSION

1. Remove wiper blades and arms.
2. Remove pivot retaining bolts, then remove wiper motor mounting bolts and remove motor and transmission.

3. To remove motor from transmission, remove motor shaft nut and 3 bolts, then disconnect connector and grounding wire.
4. Reverse procedure to install.

RADIO, REPLACE

1. Disconnect battery ground cable.
2. Remove ash tray and plate.
3. Remove knobs, jam nuts, washers and face panel from radio.
4. Remove front and rear mounting bracket screws.
5. Disconnect electrical connector and antenna lead, then remove radio.
6. Reverse procedure to install.

BLOWER MOTOR, REPLACE

1. Disconnect battery ground cable.
2. Disconnect electrical wires, then remove retaining screws and remove blower motor.
3. Reverse procedure to install.

HEATER CORE, REPLACE

1. Disconnect battery ground cable.
2. Drain cooling system and disconnect hoses from heater core.

Fig. 13 Adjusting regulator core gap

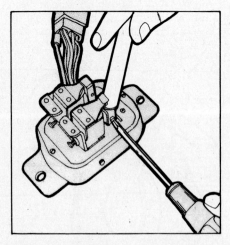

Fig. 14 Adjusting regulator contact point cap

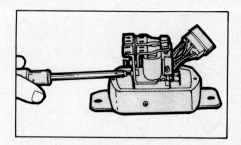

Fig. 15 Adjusting regulator voltage setting

NOTE: Plug core tubes to prevent spilling coolant into vehicle.

3. Remove parcel shelf, then loosen air diverter and defroster door bowden cable clamps and disconnect cables from doors.
4. Disconnect resistor and blower leads, then remove control assembly to instrument panel screws and swing control to left and place on floor.

CAUTION: Use care to avoid damaging water valve bowden cable.

5. Remove heater to dash retaining screws, then pull heater rearward until heater core tubes clear dash opening and remove heater by moving it to the right and down.
6. Remove core clamp tube, then remove the seven retaining screws and separate heater case halves.
7. Remove heater core from case.
8. Reverse procedure to install.

Engine Section
1972-75

ENGINE REPLACE

1. Scribe a reference mark in the area of hinges and remove hood.
2. Disconnect battery ground cable.
3. Drain cooling system and disconnect hoses at radiator. Disconnect heater hose at dashboard and disconnect vacuum hoses. Remove radiator assembly.
4. Drain engine oil.
5. Remove air cleaner and carburetor control linkage rod assemblies. Remove the choke control cable and disconnect carburetor fuel lines.
6. Disconnect exhaust pipe at manifold flange.
7. Disconnect electrical leads at: Generator, starter and the two engine wiring connectors.
8. Disconnect oil pressure and thermometer unit cords. Remove cable from clips on engine body.
9. Disconnect the fuel hose and the two hoses from the check and relief valve.
10. Disconnect propeller shaft and remove from transmission.
11. Disconnect clutch slave cylinder.
12. Disconnect speedometer drive cable from transmission and remove the exhaust pipe bracket from clutch housing.
13. Remove gearshaft lever assembly.
14. Install suitable engine lifting equipment and lift engine slightly to take weight from engine mounts, with engine properly supported remove front and rear engine mountings.

NOTE: Before removing engine from vehicle be sure that auxiliary parts and connections are separated from chassis frame.

15. Remove engine with front end of engine elevated slightly above the rear of engine to gain sufficient clearance from deflector.
16. Reverse procedure to install engine into position in vehicle.

ENGINE DISASSEMBLY

NOTE: Before any major disassembly of engine, remove the following, as necessary; Hoses and cables, fuel pipe and oil feed pipe at joint bolt, fuel pump, distributor, air pump and bracket, generator and carburetor.

Camshaft Timing Sprocket

1. Remove front cover, Fig. 1.
2. Remove oil line from secondary chain tensioner plug and remove chain tensioner together with tension spring.
3. Remove bolt and plate washer retaining timing sprocket, Fig. 2.
4. Remove upper left hand secondary timing chain two dampener bolts, located in front of cylinder head.
5. Separate timing sprocket from camshaft together with chain. Carefully remove timing sprocket from chain to prevent the timing sprocket pin from falling out.

NOTE: Mark position of pin on the timing sprocket before disassembly.

6. Hold chain in position with wire or cord while removing sprocket.

Camshaft Carrier

1. Remove joint bolt from the air injection nozzle and separate the air injection nozzle from the air manifold, Fig. 3. Loosen sleeve nut on air in-

Fig. 1   Camshaft front cover removal

Fig. 2   Timing sprocket removal

Fig. 3   Air injection nozzle separation

Fig. 4 Camshaft carrier locating dowel removal

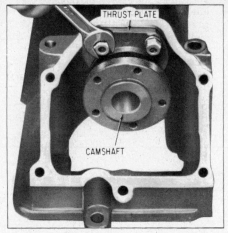

Fig. 5 Camshaft thrust plate removal

Fig. 6 Air injection nozzle removal

jection nozzle, remove the two bolts retaining air manifold bracket and remove air manifold.

NOTE: The camshaft carrier is under valve spring tension. Loosen all bolts alternately, preventing valve spring tension from action on one bolt.

2. Remove camshaft carrier bolts and remove camshaft carrier assembly simultaneously with camshaft.
3. Remove camshaft carrier locating dowels from cylinder head, Fig. 4.

Camshaft

1. Remove two bolts retaining the thrust plate, Fig. 5, remove thrust plate and withdraw camshaft toward front of engine.

Air Injection Nozzle

1. Loosen air injection nozzle sleeve nut, turn nozzle 180 degrees and remove, Fig. 6.

Secondary Timing Sprocket

1. Remove timing gear case access cover.

2. Remove timing sprocket retaining bolt.
3. Remove timing sprocket by using two bolts as a puller, Fig. 7.
4. Remove timing sprocket from chain and remove chain from the top.

Cylinder Head

1. Remove the three bolts retaining timing gear case to cylinder head.
2. Disconnect radiator inlet hose at water pump.
3. Loosen cylinder bolts in progression and remove head.

Timing Gear Case

1. Remove bolts retaining timing gear case cover, Fig. 8.
2. Remove access plug and remove bolt on inner face of gear case.
3. Pry off the gear case with screwdriver inserted into the cutaway portion on outer rim of timing gear case.

NOTE: Remove water pump if necessary.

Crankcase

1. Remove crankcase bolts and insert suitable tool into cutaway portions on both sides of crankcase. Pry off crankcase simultaneously with oil pan, Fig. 9.

Oil Pump

1. Remove oil pump sleeve nut from cylinder body, Fig. 10.
2. Loosen oil pump bolts and remove oil pump.

Primary Timing Sprocket

1. Remove primary chain tensioner retaining nuts, Fig. 11.

NOTE: Remove chain tensioner carefully prohibiting shoe from jumping out of position since shoe is spring loaded.

2. Remove timing sprockets together with chain, using bolts or screw

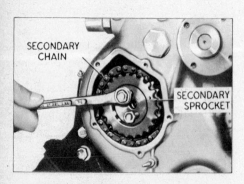

Fig. 7 Secondary timing sprocket removal

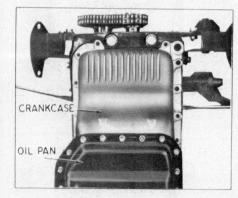

Fig. 8 Timing gear case removal

Fig. 9 Crankcase and oil pan removal

Fig. 10   Oil pump removal

Fig. 11   Primary chain tensioner removal

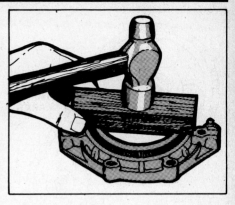

Fig. 12   Installing rear oil seal. 1973-75

rods as puller and inserting them alternately and evenly into threaded holes in the layshaft sprocket.

Layshaft

NOTE: Do not disturb the layshaft bearings when removing layshaft from cylinder body.

1. Remove layshaft thrust plate and remove layshaft.

Piston and Connecting Rod

1. Remove carbon from upper part of cylinder walls and remove pistons with connecting rod parallel to the cylinder wall.

NOTE: Remove pistons in following sequence; No. 1, 4, 2 and 3.

Piston Oversizes

Pistons are available in oversizes of .005, .010, .020, .030, .040, .050 and .060 inches.

ENGINE REASSEMBLY
Crankshaft Rear Oil Seal

1973-75
1. Install oil seal into seal retainer, Fig. 12.

NOTE: Fill oil seal lips with grease before installation.

2. Using cement place gasket against joining surface on the engine.
3. Align dowels into the dowel holes and mount oil seal retainer.

1972
1. Press rear oil seal evenly into the

cylinder body and rear bearing cap, Fig. 13. Portion A, Fig. 14, should be free from depressions or protrusions.
2. Seal must be flush with the side face of bearing cap and cylinder body, cut off excess portions B and C, Fig. 14.

NOTE: Crankshaft can be turned with a torque of 15 to 22 ft. lbs. after proper installation of oil seal. If greater torque is required oil seal is not installed properly.

Crankshaft

1. Install crankshaft in position.
2. Install thrust bearings on both sides of No. 3 journal with smooth face turned toward the crankcase, Fig. 15.

NOTE: Install bearing caps with the rear face cylinder number pointing to

Fig. 13   Installing rear oil seal. 1972

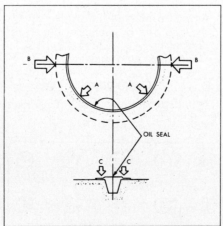

Fig. 14   Fitting rear oil seal. 1972

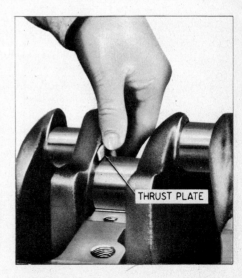

Fig. 15   Installing crankshaft thrust bearings

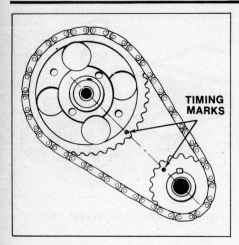

Fig. 16   Layshaft timing mark alignment

the front of engine. Alternately tighten the bearing caps starting with No. 3 bearing cap.

NOTE: Apply liquid gasket to No. 1 and No. 5 bearings before assembly.

Piston and Connecting Rod

1. Rotate No. 1 compression ring to bring gap to side of piston marked "Front." Set the remaining rings with gaps 120 degrees apart.

NOTE: Install pistons in following sequence; No. 1, 4, 2 and 3. The side of connecting rod with mark must be turned toward layshaft side. The connecting rod bearing caps should be tightened in two steps.

2. Install rear plate.
3. Install gasket and front plate.

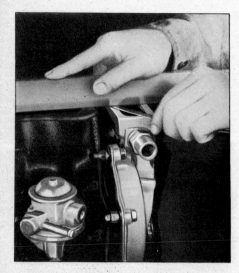

Fig. 19   Checking cylinder body and gear case distortion

Fig. 17   Oil pump rotor slot location

Primary Timing Sprocket

1. Bring No. 1 and 4 pistons to top dead center.
2. Install layshaft and thrust plate on top of layshaft.
3. With primary chain attached, position the crankshaft timing sprocket and layshaft primary timing sprocket into position.

NOTE: Align the timing mark on the layshaft with the timing mark on the crankshaft sprocket, Fig. 16.

4. Align keyway of layshaft with the key in sprocket by turning layshaft, then install both sprockets simultaneously.

NOTE: Hold layshaft through the fuel pump opening while driving sprockets into position.

Oil Pump

1. With No. 4 piston at top dead center, install oil pump in position, with groove in end of pump drive pinion at right angle to the layshaft and the slot in the oil pump rotor toward the rear of the engine, Fig. 17. Position oil pump making sure drive pinion meshes with helical gear on layshaft.
2. Connect oil pipe to cylinder body.

Crankcase

1. Install rubber gaskets into groove

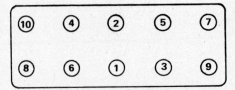

Fig. 20   Cylinder head tightening sequence. 1973-75

Fig. 18   Main bearing rubber gasket installation

on No. 1 and No. 5 main bearing caps, Fig. 18.

NOTE: Install rubber gaskets without providing any clearance at the end of the gaskets.

2. Install crankcase.

Timing Gear Case

1. Install primary gear chain tensioner.
2. Install water pump.
3. Install timing gear case oil seal.

NOTE: Before installation, the clearance between the lips of the oil seal should be filled with grease.

4. Align indexing pin holes with pins and install gear case.
5. Install engine mounts and the water suction hose and clip.

Flywheel

1. Align flywheel pin hole with the pin on crankshaft and install flywheel.

Fig. 21   Air injection nozzle installation

Fig. 22 Secondary sprocket timing mark location

Cylinder Head

NOTE: The upper face of cylinder body must be parallel to the gear case, Fig. 19. If distortion is .0079 inch or more, correct or replace gear case.

1. Install secondary chain tensioner with thicker shoe turned up.
2. Position cylinder head gasket, insert "O" rings into oil ports and install cylinder head.

NOTE: Tighten head bolts equally starting at center bolts and progressing outward. Tighten head bolts to 43 ft. lbs., loosen bolts completely and retighten all head bolts, Fig. 20. *Refer to Engine Tightening Specifications Chart.*

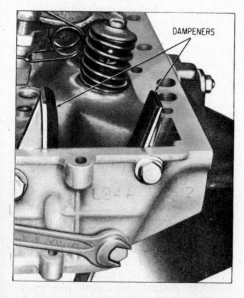

Fig. 24 Chain dampeners removal

3. Tighten the three bolts retaining timing gear case.

NOTE: Install and hand tighten the air injection nozzles, Fig. 21. The air injection nozzles should not be tightened securely until they are connected to the air manifold, after the installation of the camshaft carrier.

Camshaft Carrier

1. Install locating dowels in cylinder head.
2. Align camshaft and camshaft thrust plate setting marks.
3. Position "O" rings into camshaft carrier.

NOTE: Install longest bolt in position of the dowel.

NOTE: Install camshaft carrier and hand tighten the bolts retaining dowels. The bolts securing the dowels should be tightened together with the air manifold bracket.

4. Install and tighten the camshaft carrier bolts in progression to 15 ft. lbs. compressing valve springs evenly.

NOTE: The camshaft carrier bolts also retain two portions of the air manifold bracket.

Secondary Timing Sprocket
Camshaft and Thrust Plate Setting Mark Alignment

Attach camshaft sprocket to camshaft and insert pin into a hole in the camshaft timing sprocket and turn flywheel until marks line up. Remove the camshaft timing sprocket to bring camshaft into a free state and set No. 4 piston to top dead center on compression stroke.

NOTE: If engine has been turned in reverse direction during adjustment, make final adjustment by turning engine in normal rotation, marks must be lined up with chain tensioned properly.

NOTE: Before installing camshaft timing sprocket onto camshaft, clean mating surfaces thoroughly, since drive torque is relayed to the timing sprocket from camshaft by means of frictional contact.

1. With No. 4 piston at top dead center on the compression stroke the setting marks on the camshaft and thrust plate must be aligned.

Fig. 23 Adjusting valve clearance

2. Insert timing chain into gear case through upper opening and hold in position.
3. Install sprocket together with chain in position, with punched mark on sprocket pointing to the key on the layshaft. The punched mark is located approximately at 2 o'clock position, if sprocket is installed properly, Fig. 22.
4. Install camshaft timing sprocket together with timing chain onto the camshaft, with punched mark on sprocket located at 12 o'clock position.
5. Adjust camshaft timing sprocket relative position to the camshaft. The punched mark on the camshaft timing sprocket must be turned up when the drive side of the timing chain is tensioned, by pushing chain tensioner shoe through the access plug hole in the timing gear case cover.

NOTE: If camshaft timing sprocket is correctly installed the punched mark on sprocket should have moved to

Fig. 25 Rocker arm spring removal

Fig. 26 Piston pin removal

be 6⅓ degree from top in the rotative direction.

6. Hold parts in their relative position. Check through each of the five holes in the camshaft timing sprocket to find a hole in alignment with hole in the camshaft flange and insert pin into hole.
7. Tighten layshaft timing sprocket. Install plate washer and tighten camshaft timing sprocket. *Refer to Engine Tightening Specification Chart.*
8. Recheck setting marks for proper alignment.
9. Install gear case front cover and camshaft carrier front cover.

VALVES ADJUST

1. With either No. 1 or No. 4 piston at top dead center, engine timing mark lined up with pointer, hold crankshaft in position and adjust valve clearance to specifications. Loosen lock nut and adjust clearance between rocker arm and cam, by turning the adjusting bolt. Secure adjustment by tightening the lock nut, Fig. 23.

CYLINDER HEAD DISASSEMBLE

1. Remove chain dampeners, Fig. 24.
2. Remove rocker spring from rocker arm, Fig. 25, and remove rocker arm.
3. Remove rocker guide.
4. Remove valve springs, retainer and valve spring seat.

NOTE: Do not remove pivot unless replacement is necessary. Tighten pivot to 90 ft. lbs.

Valve Guides

1. Drive valve guide out toward the valve spring side, using a valve guide remover (if available use J-24237 tool).

NOTE: The valve guides can not be removed downward toward the valve seat, since the valve guides are secured in position with a snap ring.

2. Before installing valve guide in position, lubricate the circumference with oil.
3. Press valve guide into position until it is brought into contact with snap ring.

NOTE: Allowable interference between valve guide and cylinder head is .0016 inch.

Valve Seat Inserts

1. Arc-weld at several points to the inner face of the valve seat insert, rods which are strong enough to pull out the valve seat insert.

NOTE: Exercise care to keep aluminum alloy portion intact.

2. Allow cylinder head to cool two to five minutes after welding rods to valve inserts. After the valve seat insert contracts, supply shock to the rod and remove valve seat insert with rod.
3. After thorough cleaning of the valve seat insert bore, heat bore with steam until thermal expansion takes place. Cool valve insert with dry ice, or other suitable means. After volumetric contraction takes place press valve insert into the valve seat insert bore.

NOTE: The fitting interference is .0032-.0472 inch.

Fig. 28 Checking rotor, vane and pump body clearance

Fig. 27 Checking oil pump rotor clearance

4. Standard contact valve seat width can be obtained, by using seat cutters of 15°, 45°, and 75°.

Reassembly

1. Insert oil seal into upper face of valve guides.
2. Lubricate valve stem and insert into valve guide.
3. Assemble valve lower seat, inner and outer valve spring and spring retainer into cylinder head. Intall unit and valve keys (split collars) in position.

NOTE: Install valve springs with the close pitched end down.

4. Install rocker arms and rocker spring.
5. Install chain dampeners, tighten bolts and align dampener spring with slit in bolt.

PISTONS & CONNECTING RODS DISASSEMBLE

1. Remove piston pin snap rings.
2. Drive out piston pin, Fig. 26.

NOTE: Piston pins, rods and pistons must be assembled into original positions.

Reassembly

NOTE: the side of connecting rod with the cylinder number mark must be on the right side of the groove located on the front part of the piston head.

1. Heat piston to 158° to 212° F., using proper heater. Insert snap ring into groove at one end. Align the connecting rod and piston pin hole. Insert piston pin and install the second snap ring into groove.
2. Install piston rings with the mark NPR or TOP facing up.

OIL PUMP, REPLACE

1. Drain and remove engine crank-case.
2. Disconnect oil feed pipe.
3. Remove oil pump bolts and oil pump.

OIL PUMP SERVICE

1. Flatten out tab.
2. Remove the bolts, strainer case and the pump body cover.
3. Remove vane, do not scratch vane since it could cause loss of oil pressure.
4. Remove pin from pinion and remove pinion from rotor shaft.
5. Remove pin from rotor and remove rotor from rotor shaft.
6. Measure tip clearance with feeler gauge, Fig. 27. If clearance is not within .0012 to .0059 inch or if teeth have considerable damage replace rotor or vane as necessary.
7. Measure clearance between vane and inner wall of pump body with feeler gauge. If clearance is beyond .008 to .011 inch, service pump as necessary.
8. Measure the clearance between rotor, vane and pump body, Fig. 28. If clearance is not within .0016 to .0035 inch, replace the rotor, vane or pump body.
9. Measure outside diameter of rotor shaft and the inside diameter of rotor shaft hole inside pump body with micrometer. If clearance is beyond .008 inch, replace rotor shaft or pump body as necessary.

WATER PUMP REPLACE

1973-75

1. Disconnect battery ground cable.
2. Drain cooling system and remove radiator hoses.
3. Remove radiator and shroud.

Fig. 29   Loosening bolt behind timing gear case. 1973-75

4. Remove generator and air pump belts.
5. Remove fan, pulley and spacer.

NOTE: Loosen but do not remove bolt behind timing case cover, Fig. 29.

---

6. Remove pump and gasket.

1972

1. Disconnect battery positive cable.
2. Drain cooling system and remove grille.
3. Remove radiator and shroud.
4. Remove generator and air pump belts.
5. Remove fan, pulley, spacer and camshaft access cover.
6. With No. 4 piston at top dead center on compression stroke, remove crankshaft pulley.
7. Remove layshaft access cover and the primary oil tensioner.
8. Remove upper chain dampener bolts.
9. Remove camshaft gear and the lay-shaft secondary sprocket.
10. Remove secondary timing chain.
11. Remove left chain dampener.
12. Remove timing case cover and the water pump assembly.

FUEL PUMP, REPLACE

1. Disconnect rubber hose, then remove joint bolt and disconnect pipe from side of fuel pump.

NOTE: Use care to avoid losing joint bolt gaskets when removing joint bolt.

---

2. Remove the two retaining nuts and remove pump.
3. Reverse procedure to install.

Engine Section
1976-77

ENGINE, REPLACE

1. Raise hood and disconnect battery cables.
2. Drain cooling system and oil pan.
3. Remove air cleaner.
4. Disconnect CCS hot air hose and remove manifold cover.
5. Disconnect generator wiring at connector.
6. Disconnect cables grounding cylinder block to frame.
7. Remove nuts connecting the exhaust pipe to exhaust manifold and separate pipe from manifold.
8. Disconnect heater hoses from firewall.
9. Disconnect fuel hoses from carburetor.
10. Disconnect high-tension cable from coil.
11. Disconnect vacuum hose from connector at rear of intake manifold.
12. Disconnect accelerator cable from carburetor.
13. Disconnect the water temperature switch, oil pressure switch and distributor wiring.

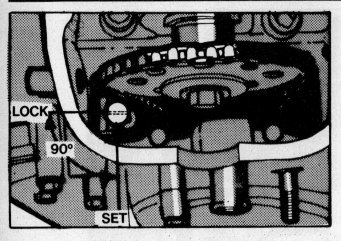

Fig. 1 Locking timing chain adjuster

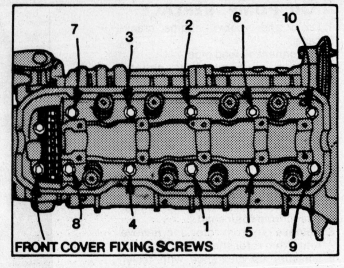

FRONT COVER FIXING SCREWS

Fig. 2 Cylinder head hold-down bolt torque sequence

14. Disconnect carburetor solenoid valve lead and automatic choke wiring.
15. Disconnect back-up lamp switch and high gear switch or neutral switch on California models wiring at connector on rear of engine.
16. Disconnect ECS hose from the oil pan.
17. Remove radiator hoses, radiator and fan.
18. Raise vehicle.
19. On manual transmission models, remove clutch return spring. Remove slave cylinder attaching bolts and fasten to the frame with a piece of wire.
20. Remove starting motor and position aside.
21. Remove flywheel cover and the bell housing bolts.
22. Lower vehicle and support transmission with suitable jack.
23. Lift engine slightly with suitable lifting equipment.
24. Remove engine mount nuts.
25. Raise engine from vehicle.
26. Reverse procedure to install.

INTAKE MANIFOLD, REPLACE

1. Disconnect battery ground cable and remove air cleaner assembly.
2. Remove EGR pipe clamp bolt at rear of cylinder head.
3. Raise vehicle.
4. Remove ERG pipe from intake and exhaust manifolds.
5. Remove ERG valve and bracket assembly from lower side of intake manifold.
6. Lower vehicle and drain cooling system.
7. Disconnect upper radiator hose at water outlet and the heater hose at upper side of manifold.
8. Disconnect fuel line, accelerator linkage, vacuum lines and electrical connections at carburetor.
9. Remove manifold attaching nuts and pull manifold assembly from studs. Support assembly on cam cover and disconnect lower heater hose, then remove manifold assembly.
10. Remove carburetor, water outlet and thermostat from manifold.
11. Remove vacuum fittings, studs and temperature sending switch from manifold.

EXHAUST MANIFOLD, REPLACE

1. Disconnect battery ground cable.
2. Remove ERG pipe clamp bolt at rear of cylinder head.
3. Raise vehicle and remove ERG pipe from intake and exhaust manifolds.
4. Remove exhaust pipe to bell housing and manifold and separate exhaust pipe from manifold.
5. Lower vehicle.
6. Remove manifold shield bolts and shield. Disconnect heat stove hose at air cleaner and remove heat stove.
7. Remove exhaust manifold to cylinder head nuts and the manifold.

CYLINDER HEAD, REPLACE

1. Disconnect battery ground cable.
2. Remove cam cover and the EGR pipe clamp bolt from rear of cylinder head.
3. Raise vehicle and disconnect exhaust pipe from manifold.
4. Lower vehicle and drain cooling system.
5. Disconnect heater hoses from intake manifold and rear of cylinder head.
6. Disconnect accelerator linkage, fuel lines, electrical wiring and vacuum hoses from engine.
7. Remove distributor.
8. Lock timing chain adjuster by depressing and rotating automatic adjuster slide pin 90° clockwise, Fig. 1.
9. Remove camshaft sprocket, however, do not remove the sprocket from the chain.
10. Disconnect AIR hose and check valve from exhaust manifold.
11. Remove cylinder head to timing cover bolts, then the cylinder head holddown bolts.
12. Remove cylinder head from engine.
13. Reverse procedure to install. Torque cylinder head hold-down bolts to specifications in sequence, Fig. 2.

VALVES, ADJUST

1. Remove cam cover.
2. Torque rocker arm shaft bracket nuts to 16 ft. lbs.
3. Position No. 1 piston at top dead center, compression stroke. In this position, adjust the following valves: No. 1 cyl., intake and exhaust; No. 2 cyl., intake; No. 3 cyl., exhaust.
4. Rotate crankshaft 360° and adjust the following valves: No. 2 cyl., exhaust; No. 3 cyl., intake; No. 4 cyl., intake and exhaust.
5. Install cam cover.

ROCKER ARMS & SHAFTS
Removal

1. Remove cam cover.
2. Alternately loosen rocker arm shaft

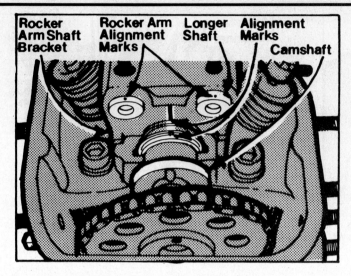

Fig. 3 Rocker arm shaft installation

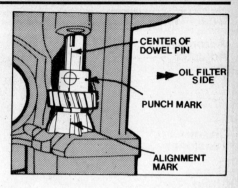

Fig. 4 Oil pump alignment

bracket nuts and remove nuts from brackets.
3. Remove spring from rocker arm shaft, then the rocker arm brackets and arms.

Installation

1. Lubricate rocker arms, shafts and valve stems with engine oil.
2. Install the longer rocker shaft on the exhaust valve side and the shorter rocker shaft on the intake valve side, Fig. 3, with the aligning marks facing front.
3. Install rocker arm shaft brackets and rocker arms on the rocker arm shafts with the cylinder number on the upper face of the brackets are facing toward front of engine.
4. Align the mark on the No. 1 rocker arm shaft bracket with the mark on the rocker arm shafts.
5. The exhaust side rocker arm shaft should project a greater distance from the face of the No. 1 rocker shaft bracket outer face than the intake side rocker arm shaft when the

rocker arm shaft stud holes are aligned with the rocker arm shaft bracket stud holes.
6. Position rocker arm shaft springs between rocker arm shaft bracket and rocker arm.
7. Ensure punch mark on rocker arm shaft is facing upward. Install rocker arm shaft bracket assembly onto cylinder head studs. Align mark on camshaft with mark on No. 1 rocker arm shaft bracket.
8. Torque rocker arm shaft stud nuts to 16 ft. lbs.

NOTE: Hold the rocker arm springs in position while torquing the stud nuts to prevent spring damage.

9. Adjust valves and install cam cover.

FRONT OIL SEAL, REPLACE

1. Disconnect battery ground cable and drain cooling system.
2. Disconenct radiator hoses and remove radiator assembly.
3. Remove drive belts and engine fan.
4. Remove crankshaft pulley center bolt and the pulley and balancer assembly.
5. Pry seal from timing cover with a suitable screwdriver.
6. Install new seal with tool J-26587.

FRONT COVER, REPLACE
Removal

1. Remove cylinder head and oil pan.
2. Remove oil pickup tube from oil pump.
3. Remove harmonic balancer and the AIR pump drive belt.
4. On air conditioned vehicles, remove A/C compressor and position aside.

Remove compressor mounting brackets.
5. Remove distributor assembly.
6. Remove front cover attaching bolts and the front cover.

Installation

1. Install new gasket onto cylinder block.
2. Align oil pump drive gear punch mark with oil filter side of cover, Fig. 4, then align the center of dowel pin with alignment mark on oil pump case.
3. Rotate crankshaft until Nos. 1 and 4 cylinders are at top dead center.
4. Install front cover by engaging pinion gear with oil pump drive gear on crankshaft.
5. Check that punch mark on oil pump drive gear is turned to the rear, viewed through the clearance between front cover and cylinder block, Fig. 5.
6. Check that slit at the end of oil pump shaft is parallel with front face of cylinder block and is offset forward, Fig. 6.
7. Install front cover and tighten front cover bolts.
8. Reverse steps 1 thru. 5 of "Removal" procedure.
9. Check engine timing.
10. Check for leaks.

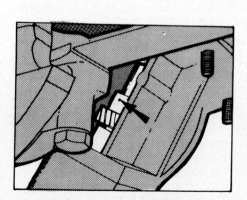

Fig. 5 Checking alignment

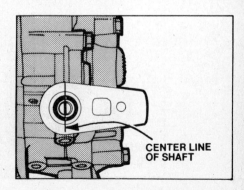

Fig. 6 Oil pump shaft alignment

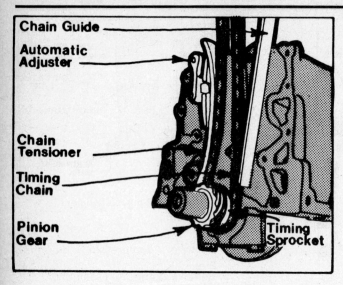

Fig. 7 Timing chain removal

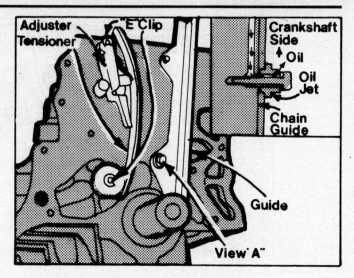

Fig. 8 Timing chain guide, tensioner & adjuster

TIMING CHAIN

1. Remove front cover assembly.
2. Remove timing chain from crankshaft sprocket, Fig. 7.
3. Remove "E" clip and the chain adjuster and tensioner, Fig. 8. Inspect components for wear or damage. Also, inspect chain guide and oil jet. View "A", Fig. 8.
4. Install timing sprocket and pinion gear with groove side toward front cover. Align key grooves with key on crankshaft, then drive into position with tool J-26587.

5. Turn crankshaft so key is turned toward cylinder head side with Nos. 1 and 4 pistons at top dead center.
6. Install timing chain by aligning mark plate on chain with the mark on crankshaft timing sprocket. The side of the chain with mark plate is located on the front side and the side of chain with the most links between mark plates is located on the chain guide side, Fig. 9.
7. Install the camshaft timing sprocket so marked side of sprocket faces forward and the triangular mark aligns with the chain mark plate.

NOTE: Keep the timing chain engaged with camshaft timing sprocket until the camshaft timing sprocket is installed on camshaft.

8. Install front cover assembly as outlined previously.

CAMSHAFT, REPLACE
Removal

1. Remove cam cover.
2. Rotate camshaft until No. 1 cylinder is in firing position. Remove distributor and mark rotor to housing position.
3. Lock timing chain adjuster by depressing and turning the automatic adjuster slide pin 90 degrees in the clockwise direction, Fig. 1.

NOTE: After locking the chain adjuster, ensure the chain is free.

4. Remove timing sprocket to camshaft bolt and the sprocket from the camshaft. Retain timing sprocket on chain damper and tensioner assembly without removing chain from sprocket.
5. Remove rocker arm, shaft and bracket assembly.
6. Remove camshaft assembly.

Installation

1. Lubricate camshaft and journals of cylinder head with engine oil.
2. Install camshaft assembly.
3. Install the rocker arm, shaft and bracket assembly.
4. Align mark on the No. 1 rocker arm shaft bracket with the mark on the camshaft. Also, ensure that the

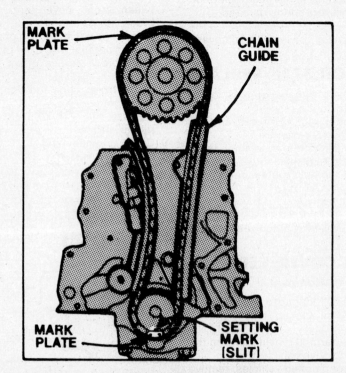

Fig. 9 Timing chain alignment

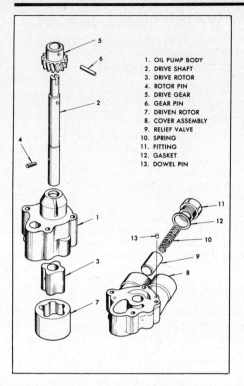

1. OIL PUMP BODY
2. DRIVE SHAFT
3. DRIVE ROTOR
4. ROTOR PIN
5. DRIVE GEAR
6. GEAR PIN
7. DRIVEN ROTOR
8. COVER ASSEMBLY
9. RELIEF VALVE
10. SPRING
11. FITTING
12. GASKET
13. DOWEL PIN

Fig. 10 Oil pump assembly

crankshaft pulley groove is aligned with the TDC mark on front cover.

5. Assemble timing sprocket to the camshaft by aligning sprocket with pin on camshaft, use caution not to remove chain from sprocket.
6. Install sprocket retaining bolt and washer. Remove the half-moon seal at front of head, then torque retaining bolt to 58 ft. lbs. Then replace the half-moon seal in cylinder head.
7. Set automatic adjuster by rotating adjuster slide pin 90 degrees counter-clockwise with a screwdriver, Fig. 1.

NOTE: When the automatic adjuster is set, ensure timing chain is properly tensioned.

8. Check that distributor rotor and mark on distributor housing are aligned with No. 1 piston in the firing position. Timing mark on crank pulley should also align with TDC Mark on front cover.
9. Install distributor cap and cam cover.

REAR MAIN SEAL
Removal

1. Remove oil pan.
2. Remove transmission assembly.
3. On manual transmission models, remove clutch cover and pressure plate assembly.

4. Remove starter and position aside.
5. Remove flywheel and flywheel cover.
6. Remove four rear main seal retainer bolts and the retainer and seal assembly.
7. Pry seal from retainer.

Installation

1. Place new seal in position in retainer. Fill clearance between lips of seal with grease and lubricate seal lip with engine oil.
2. Place retainer on a flat surface and drive seal into place using tool J-22345.
3. Reverse removal Steps 1-6.

NOTE: When installing flywheel, install bolt locks, then torque bolts to 69 ft. lbs. Bend down lock tabs to lock bolts in position.

PISTONS & RODS

Assemble piston to rod with the mark on the piston is facing toward front of engine and the face of the connecting rod with the cylinder number mark is facing toward the starter side of the engine.

Pistons are available in oversizes of .020 and .030 inch.

OIL PAN

1. Disconnect battery ground cable and raise vehicle.
2. Drain oil pan.
3. Remove front splash shield and front crossmember.
4. Disconnect relay rod at idler arm and lower the relay rod.
5. Remove left hand bell housing brace.

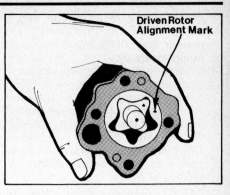

Fig. 11 Aligning drive and driven rotors

6. Disconnect vacuum line at oil pan.
7. Remove oil pan bolts and oil pan.
8. Reverse procedure to install.

OIL PUMP
Removal

1. Remove cam cover, distributor assembly and oil pan.
2. Remove bolt securing oil pick-up tube to engine block and the tube from the oil pump.
3. Remove pump mounting bolts and the oil pump.
4. Remove rubber hose and relief valve assembly from the pump.

Service

1. Measure clearance between drive rotor and driven rotor with a feeler gauge, Fig. 10. If clearance is greater than .0079 inch, replace oil pump assembly.
2. Measure clearance between driven rotor and inner wall of pump body, Fig. 10. If clearance is greater than .0098 inch, replace oil pump assembly.
3. Measure clearance between drive rotor, driven rotor and oil pump

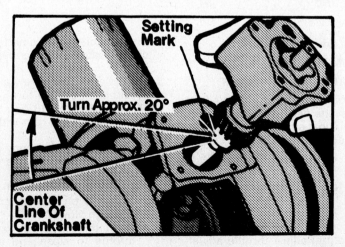

Fig. 12 Oil pump installation

cover with a feeler gauge and a straight edge, Fig. 10. If clearance is greater than .0079 inch, replace oil pump assembly.

4. Determine clearance between drive shaft and drive shaft hole in pump cover. Measure the inside diameter of the shaft hole in the cover and the diameter of the drive shaft. Subtract the drive shaft diameter from the inside diameter of the shaft hole. If the clearance is greater than .0098 inch, replace oil pump.

5. Inspect components for wear or damage.

Installation

1. Align mark on camshaft with mark on No. 1 rocker arm shaft bracket. Align notch on crankshaft pulley with "O" mark on front cover. When these two sets of marks are properly aligned, No. 4 piston is at top dead center, compression stroke.

2. Install driven rotor with alignment mark aligned with mark on drive rotor, Fig. 11.

3. Engage oil pump drive gear with pinion gear on crankshaft so alignment mark on drive gear is turned rearward and approximately 20° from the crankshaft in a clockwise direction, Fig. 12.

4. Ensure oil pump drive gear is turned rearward as viewed from clearance between front cover and cylinder block and the slit at the end of the oil pump drive shaft is parallel with the front face of the cylinder block and is offset forward as viewed through the distributor fitting hole, Fig. 6.

5. Install oil pump cover and mounting bolts.

6. Install relief valve assembly and rubber hose on cover.

7. Connect oil pick-up tube to rubber hose and secure tube to cylinder block.

8. Install oil pan and cam cover.

9. Install distributor so boss on shaft is fitted into slit at end of oil pump drive shaft.

10. Refill engine oil and check for leaks.

WATER PUMP, REPLACE

1. Disconnect battery ground cable.
2. Remove lower cover.
3. Drain cooling system.
4. On models less A/C, remove engine fan.
5. On models with A/C:
   a. Remove air pump and alternator mounting bolts and the fan and air pump drive belt.
   b. Remove engine fan and pulley assembly.
   c. Remove bolts attaching fan set plate and fan pulley.
6. On all models, remove water pump attaching bolts and the water pump.
7. Reverse procedure to install.

FUEL PUMP, REPLACE

1. Disconnect electrical lead and rubber hoses from fuel pump.
2. Remove the mounting bolts and nuts and remove pump.
3. Reverse procedure to install.

Carburetor Section

CARBURETOR ADJUSTMENTS

Year	Carb. Model	Float Level (Wet)	Needle Valve Stroke	Throttle Valve	Secondary Valve Throttle Opening	Idle Mix Screws Turns Open	Throttle Valve Opening Angle ②	Throttle Valve Closing Angle	
								Primary	Secondary
1972	DRJ340	①	.059	.05—.06	.26—.32	3½	17°	10°	20°
1973	DRJ340	①	.059	.06—.07	.26—.32	3½	18½°	10°	20°
1974	DRJ340AC	①	.059	.057—.065	.26—.32	3½	17½°	10°	20°
1975-77	DCP-340	①	.059	.047—.051	.24—.30	—	17°	10°	20°

—Not Available   ①—With line on window glass of float chamber with engine stationary.   ②—With choke valve closed.

CARBURETOR ADJUSTMENTS

Float Level Adjustment

Adjust float level by bending the float seat. Adjust the needle valve stroke by bending the float stopper. *Refer to Carburetor Specifications Chart.*

Idle Adjustment

1972-75
1. With engine at normal operating temperature, adjust throttle adjusting screw to 700 rpm.
2. Disconnect vacuum line to hot idle compensator and plug inlet at manifold.
3. Turn idle mixture screw all the way in and back out 3½ turns for 1972-74, or 2½ turns for 1975.
4. Reset idle to 700 rpm with throttle adjusting screw.
5. Adjust idle mixture screw until fastest and smoothest idle is obtained, then repeat step 4.
6. If equipped with air conditioning,
   a. Turn A/C on the maximum cold and high blower.
   b. Open throttle about ⅓ to allow throttle to close and speed up solenoid to reach full travel.
   c. Adjust speed up controller adjusting screw to set idle at 900 rpm.
   d. Open throttle ⅓ and allow throttle to close. Readjust speed up controller if idle speed is not 900 rpm.
7. Reconnect hot idle compensator.

1976-77
1. Allow engine to reach normal operating temperature, then disconnect and plug distributor vacuum line and hot idle compensator vacuum line.
2. Turn idle mixture screw until seated and back out 3 turns.
3. Adjust throttle adjusting screw to 900 rpm.

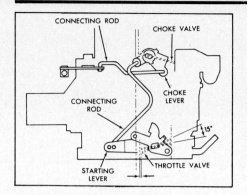

Fig. 1 Primary throttle adjustment. 1972

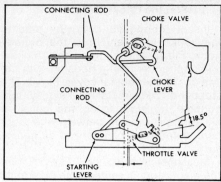

Fig. 2 Primary throttle adjustment. 1973

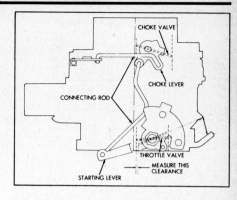

Fig. 3 Primary throttle adjustment. 1974

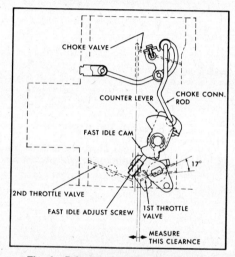

Fig. 4 Primary throttle adjustment. 1975-77

4. Adjust idle mixture adjusting screw to obtain highest rpm, then repeat step 3.
5. Turn idle mixture screw clockwise until engine speed is down to 850 rpm, then turn idle mixture screw ½ turn counterclockwise and repeat step 3.

6. If equipped with air conditioning, refer to step 6 under "1972-75."

Carburetor Linkage Adjustment

Primary Throttle Valve Opening Adjustment

When the choke valve is completely closed, the choke connecting rod should open the primary throttle valve to the specified angle, Figs. 1 to 4. With choke valve tightly closed measure the clearance between the throttle valve and wall of the throttle valve chamber at the center part of the throttle valve. Adjust throttle valve opening angle by bending the connecting rod. *Refer to Carburetor Specifications Chart.*

NOTE: Turn the throttle stop screw all the way in before measuring throttle valve opening clearance.

Secondary Throttle Valve Opening Adjustment

Measure clearance between primary throttle valve and wall of throttle

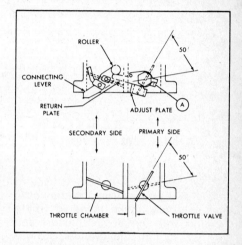

Fig. 5 Secondary throttle valve adjustment. 1972-74

chamber, at center of throttle valve when the adjust plate is brought into contact with point A, Figs. 5 and 6, of the return plate. If necessary, make adjustment by bending the portion A, of the return plate. *Refer to Carburetor Specifications Chart.*

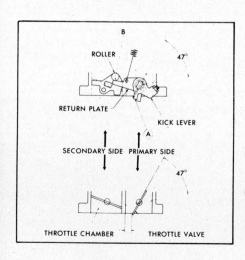

Fig. 6 Secondary throttle valve adjustment. 1975-77

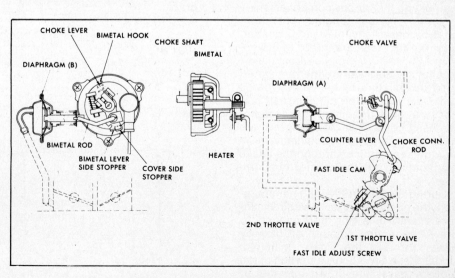

Fig. 7 Electric choke assembly

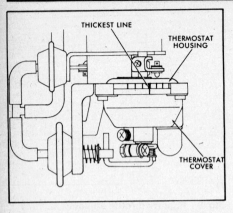

Fig. 8 Thermostat cover adjustment

Electric Choke Adjustment

Install thermostat cover by placing the choke lever end into the bimetal hook, Fig. 7, and aligning the thickest line on the thermostat housing with the line on the thermostat cover, Fig. 8. The stopper on the bimetal lever side should contact the stopper on the cover. If clearance is present between the stoppers, extend the bimetal rod as necessary.

Measure clearance "L," Fig. 9, when the diaphragm is seated. The clearance should be .028-.029 inch. If not, adjust by rotating adjusting screw, Fig. 9.

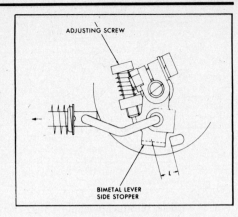

Fig. 9 Stopper clearance

Emission Controls Section

POSITIVE CRANKCASE VENTILATION (PCV) SYSTEM

This system, Figs. 1 and 2, is used to draw blow-by gases from the crankcase back into the intake manifold where they mix with the air fuel mixture and then drawn into the cylinders. These blow-by gases which contain undesirable pollutants, are the result of high pressures developed within the combustion chamber during the combustion process.

This system is of a closed type and consists of a baffle plate for separating oil particles from the blow-by gases, a regulating valve or regulating orifice for controlling suction of blow-by gases, a hose for directing fresh air from the air cleaner into the system, and hoses for connecting the various components.

During normal engine operation, blow-by gases and fuel vapor emitted from the fuel tank are mixed in the engine with fresh air supplied from the air cleaner. Oil particles are then separated from this mixture by the baffle type oil separator located on the camshaft carrier side cover, or built into the center of the head cover. The blow-by gases are then drawn through the regulating valve or regulating orifice, through the intake manifold and into the engine for reburning.

During wide throttle engine operation, the negative pressure within the intake manifold is not high enough to draw the entire amount of blow-by gases through the intake manifold. Under these conditions, a portion of the blow-by gases are drawn into the air cleaner side cover.

The flow control orifice or regulating valve (PCV), regulates the flow of blow-by gases in response to negative pressures developed in the intake manifold under varying engine operating conditions.

System Testing

Clean internal part of hoses and regulating orifice in detergent oil and blow

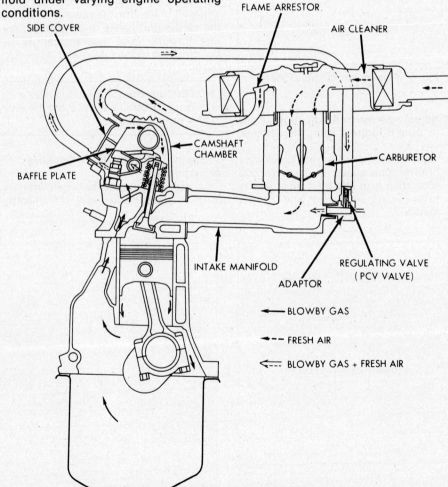

Fig. 1 Positive Crankcase Ventilation (PCV) System. 1972-75

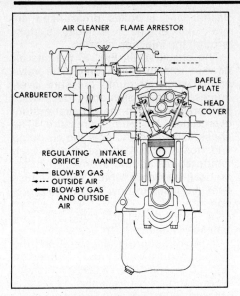

Fig. 2 Positive Crankcase Ventilation (PCV) System. 1976-77

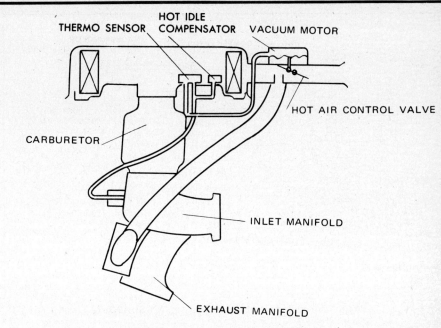

Fig. 3 Thermostatically Controlled Air Cleaner System. 1972-73

away foreign matter with compressed air. If equipped with a regulating valve (PCV), disassemble valve and wash parts in detergent oil and inspect parts for damage. Replace assembly if any parts are found defective.

Inspect hoses for cracks, fatigue or swelling. Replace hoses if defective.

1972-73 THERMOSTATICALLY CONTROLLED AIR CLEANER SYSTEM, 1974-77 CONTROLLED COMBUSTION SYSTEM (CCS)

These systems consist primarily of a thermo sensor, vacuum motor, hot air valve and hot idle compensator. These components are mounted on the air cleaner body and snorkel, Figs. 3, 4 and 5.

When the engine is off, no vacuum is present at the sensor or vacuum motor. The force of the vacuum motor spring closes off the "heated air" passage from the exhaust manifold heat stove.

When the engine is started cold, the thermo sensor is cool allowing maximum vacuum to the vacuum motor, completely opening the hot air control valve, closing off the ambient air passage through the snorkel and opening the air passage from the manifold heat stove. Should the engine be heav-

ily accelerated, the vacuum level in the system will drop to a level low enough so that the diaphragm spring will overcome vacuum and push the hot air control bleed closed.

As the engine warms up and the air past the thermo sensor reaches about 110-111° F (38-44° C), then thermo sensor comes into operation and begins to bleed off the supply of vacuum from the manifold.

At about 111° F (44° C), the thermo sensor completely bleeds off all vacuum to the vacuum motor so that the diaphragm spring closes the hot air control valve to the heat stove passage and opens the ambient air passage through the snorkel.

The hot idle compensator installed in the air cleaner is used to prevent excessive fuel vapors from entering the intake manifold, should an excessive increase in engine temperature occur. As the engine heats up and the air passing over the hot idle compensator reaches a specified temperature, the compensator opens to allow ambient air into the intake manifold to lean out the temporarily rich mixture.

System Testing

Vacuum Motor & Hot Air Switching Valve

1. Using a suitable size hose, connect vacuum motor to intake manifold.
2. Look through air intake side of air cleaner and make sure that hot air switching valve is completely closed.
3. Start and allow engine to run at idle. Air switching valve should work im-

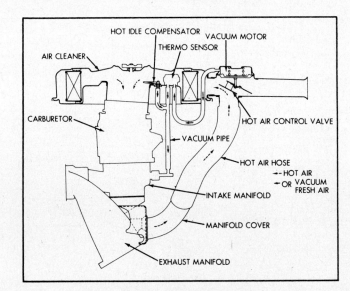

Fig. 4 Controlled Combustion System (CCS). 1974-75

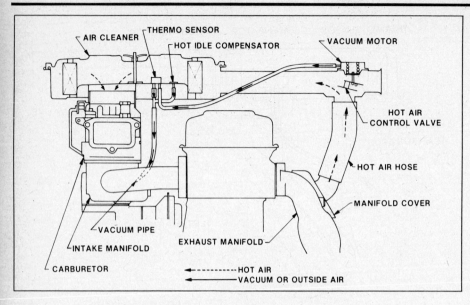

Fig. 5   Controlled Combustion System. (CCS). 1976-77

mediately, closing off fresh air intake side completely. Also, make sure that valve operates smoothly.

Thermo Sensor

1. Remove air cleaner cover, then place a thermocouple type thermometer over sensor and replace cover.
2. Allow engine to cool, then start engine.
3. Look through air intake and make sure that hot air switching valve starts to move in toward fresh air intake side when engine is started.
4. Take temperature reading when valve starts to open, and repeat several times to obtain a mean average reading. If temperature reading is not within 86-115° F for 1972-74, 100-118° F for 1975, or 100-111° F for 1976-77, replace thermo sensor assembly.

Hot Idle Compensator

1. Remove air cleaner cover and place a thermocouple type thermometer over sensor.
2. Start and allow engine to run at idle. Observe thermometer reading when hot idle compensator starts to operate. Its operation is accompanied by a sound outside of air intake.
3. The hot idle compensator is functioning properly if actuating temperature is between 122-149° F for 1972-75, or 115-126° F for 1976-77.

AIR INJECTOR REACTOR (AIR) SYSTEM

This system is used to reduce the hydrocarbon and carbon monoxide con-

tent in the exhaust gases by adding a controlled amount of pressurized air into the exhaust ports, causing oxidation of the gases. The exhaust gases will self ignite when brought into contact with the additional oxygen because of the high temperatures in the exhaust system.

This system consists of an air pump, air injection nozzles, a check valve, a mixture control valve or air bypass valve and hoses necessary to connect the various components, Figs. 6, 7, and 8.

The belt driven air pump, Fig. 9, draws in ambient air from the air

cleaner and supplies pressurized air into the engine's exhaust system through the injection nozzles.

The check valve, Fig. 10 permits air flow in one direction only. The valve opens when air pump pressure overcomes spring tension and closes when backpressure from the exhaust system overcomes air pump pressure. The check valve also protects the air pump and hoses from damage due to high temperatures should a drivebelt break or backfire occur which would cause exhaust gases to flow in reverse direction.

To prevent afterburning in the exhaust system due to an overrich air fuel mixture during deceleration, the mixture control valve, Fig. 11, is used on 1972-75 all and 1976-77 California models and the air bypass valve, Fig. 12, is used on 1976-77 except California models. The mixture control valve prevents afterburning in the exhaust system by supplying additional air into the intake manifold to dilute the air-fuel mixture. The air bypass valve prevents afterburning in the exhaust system by diverting the air pump air to atmosphere, thus avoiding the overrich air fuel mixture from mixing with secondary air from the air pump.

System Testing
Relief Valve

Check for air flowing out of relief valve while slowly accelerating engine. If air begins to flow out before engine speed reaches 2000 rpm, replace valve.

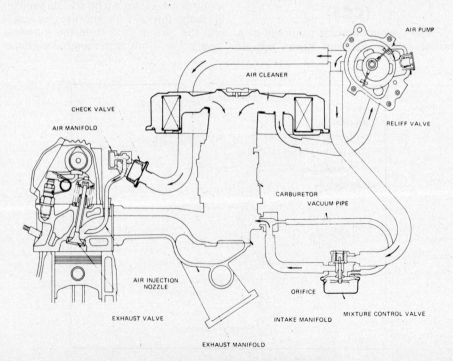

Fig. 6   Air Injector Reactor (AIR) System. 1972-75

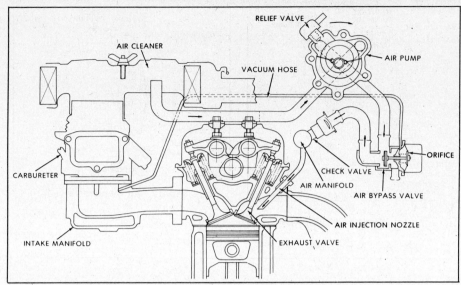

Fig. 7   Air Injector Reactor (AIR) System. 1976-77 except California

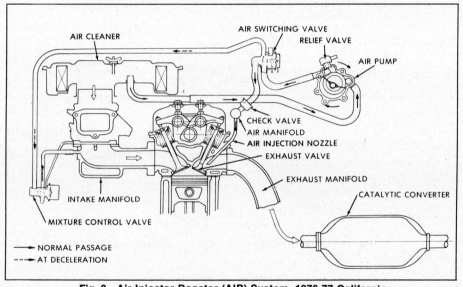

Fig. 8   Air Injector Reactor (AIR) System. 1976-77 California

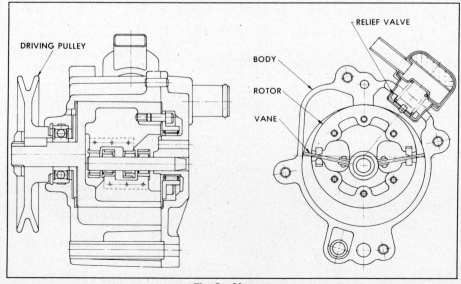

Fig. 9   Air pump

Air Bypass Valve

With engine idling, open throttle completely and release quickly. If valve is operating properly, air will flow out for a few seconds. If air continues to flow out for more than 5 seconds, replace valve.

Check Valve

Remove check valve and test for leakage by first blowing air into valve through pump side and then through air manifold side. Air should flow through air pump side only. If air flows through air manifold side, replace valve. Note that a small amount of air flow through the manifold side is acceptable.

Mixture Control Valve

Disconnect and plug vacuum line from valve. With engine idling, open throttle completely and release quickly. If valve is operating properly, air will flow out for a few seconds. If air continues to flow out for more than 5 seconds, replace valve.

Air Pump

The air pump is not serviceable. The only service procedures is to check for any abnormal noise and replace if found to be defective.

FUEL EVAPORATIVE EMISSION CONTROL SYSTEM

This system is designed to draw the fuel vapor emitted from the fuel tank into the engine crankcase, where it is mixed with blow-by gases and then drawn into the intake manifold for combustion. This system consists of a vapor separator tank, check valve and relief valve and hoses necessary to connect these components, Fig. 13.

The vapor separator tank separates the fuel from the vapor given off by the fuel tank, then returns the fuel to the fuel tank and carriers the vapor into the engine crankcase.

When the engine is off, fuel vapor from the separator flow to the check and relief valve. When the fuel vapor pressure becomes as high as 1 to 1.4 in. Hg., the check valve opens allowing the fuel vapor into the crankcase. When the check valve is open, the valve at the air cleaner side remains closed preventing the flow of vapor into the air cleaner.

When engine is running, negative pressure is developed in the fuel tank or in the engine crankcase. When the differential pressure between the relief side and fuel tank or crankcase becomes 2.06 in. Hg., the relief valve

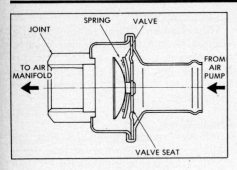

Fig. 10   Check valve

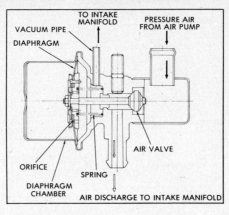

Fig. 11   Mixture control valve

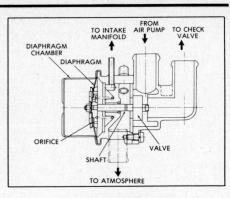

Fig. 12   Air by-pass valve

opens permitting ambient air from the air cleaner into the fuel tank or engine crankcase. This ambient air displaces the vapor within the fuel tank or crankcase to bring the fuel tank or crankcase back into the atmospheric pressure conditions.

System, Testing

Vapor Separator

Check vapor separator for fuel leaks, distortion or dents. Replace if any of the above conditions are found.

Check & Relief Valve

Remove check valve and check for leakage by blowing air into the ports. Air should flow through the check side (crankcase side) but not through the relief side (air cleaner side). Replace valve if not functioning properly.

EXHAUST GAS RECIRCULATION (EGR) SYSTEM

This system, Figs. 14 and 15, is used to reduce oxides of nitrogen emissions by lowering the peak combustion temperature in the engine. This is accomplished by introducing a metered amount of exhaust gases into the intake manifold at throttle positions other than idle.

The EGR valve, Fig. 16, mounted on the intake manifold is used to control the amount of recirculated gas. The recirculated gases are drawn into the bottom of the intake manifold riser, through the exhaust manifold heat stove and to the EGR valve. The EGR vacuum diaphragm is connected to a timed signal port at the carburetor flange.

As the carburetor throttle valve is opened, vacuum is applied to the EGR valve diaphragm. When vacuum reaches about 3.5 in. Hg., the EGR diaphragm starts to open and exhaust gas recirculation starts. At about 8 in. Hg. the EGR valve is fully open.

A thermal vacuum valve, Fig. 17, used on 1976-77 models, senses engine

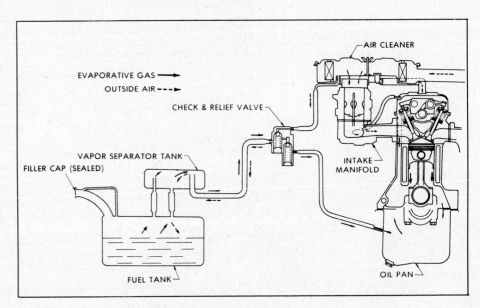

Fig. 13   Evaporative Emission Control System (typical)

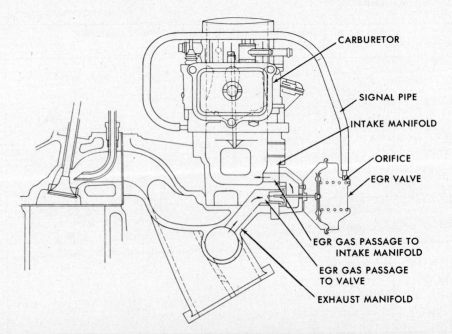

Fig. 14   Exhaust Gas Recirculation (EGR) System. 1974-75

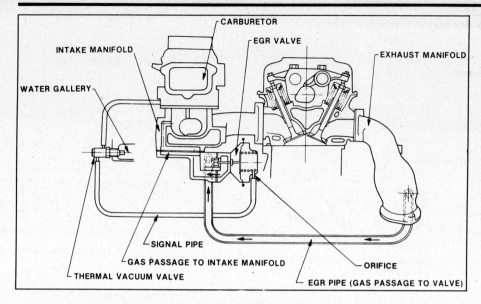

Fig. 15 Exhaust Gas Recirculation (EGR) System. 1976-77

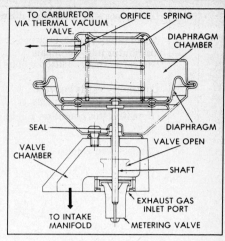

Fig. 16 EGR valve

coolant temperature to regulate the EGR system. When the coolant temperature is below 118-126° F (48-52° C), the EGR system does not operate. When the coolant temperature is above 118°-126° F (48-52° C), the EGR system operates.

System Testing

EGR Valve

1. On 1974-75, check valve shaft for movement by accelerating engine to 2000-2500 rpm. The shaft should move upward at these engine speeds and should move downward when engine speed is reduced to idle.
2. On all models, apply an external vacuum source to EGR valve. The diaphragm should not leak down and should move to the fully up position at about 8 inches Hg.

Thermal Vacuum Valve

Immerse thermo sensing portion of valve into hot water of 118-126° F (48-52° C). Check valve operation by blowing air through the ports. If air does not pass, replace valve.

DUAL BREAKER POINT DISTRIBUTOR SYSTEM

The dual breaker points distributor, Fig. 18, uses two sets of breaker points which permit automatic selection of ignition timing. The retarded breaker points are used when the engine is accelerated or decelerated. The advanced breaker points are for normal engine operation.

The two sets of breaker points are positioned with a relative phase angle of 4 degrees apart, and are connected in parallel in the primary side of the ignition circuit. A distributor relay is in-

serted in the retarded breaker point circuit and accelerator and transmission relays, throttle and ignition relays are connected in parallel with the distributor relay.

When the distributor relay is energized and any of the following conditions are met; transmission is in other than 3rd or 4th gear, carburetor throttle valve opening is less than 7 degrees or greater than 35°, clutch pedal is depressed, or when ignition switch is turned on, the advance breaker points come into operation.

The retarded breaker points come into operation when any of the above conditions do not apply.

The throttle switch is controlled by the cam interlocked with the primary side of the throttle valve, and is activated when the throttle valve is opened beyond 35 degrees.

The distributor relay is energized by the operation ignition switch, accelerator relay, transmission relay, throttle switch or clutch relay. Under any one of these conditions, the dis-

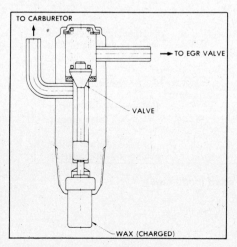

Fig. 17 Thermal vacuum valve

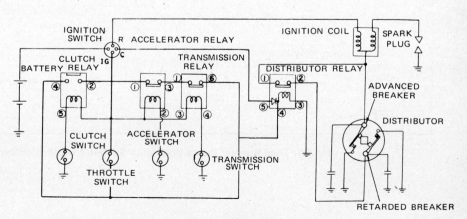

Fig. 18 Dual Breaker Points Distributor System

8.(a) Disconnect lead wires from distributor relay at terminals (4) and (5).

No continuity exists between
distributor relay terminals . . . . Replace distributor relay
(Hereafter this condition will be referred to as "OFF")

Continuity exists between
distributor relay terminals . . . . .Follow step outlined in
(Hereafter this condition will be referred to as "ON")   paragraph (b) below

(b) Connect lead wire to distributor relay terminal (5).

OFF . . . . .Replace ignition switch
           or distributor relay circuit.

ON . . . . Follow step outlined
           in paragraph (c) below.

(c) Connect lead wire to distributor relay terminal (4) and disconnect
lead wire from either one of the throttle switch terminals.

ON . . . . .Replace throttle switch
           or check distributor
           relay circuit.

OFF . . . . .Follow step outlined in
           paragraph (d) below.

(d) Disconnect lead wire from transmission relay terminal (6).

ON . . . . .Follow step outlined
           (i) and (ii) below, after
           connecting lead wire to
           relay terminal (6)

OFF . . . . Following step outlined in
           paragraph (e) below.

(i) Disconnect lead wire from transmission relay terminal (4).

OFF . . . . .Replace transmission
           relay or check relay
           circuit.

ON . . . . .Replace transmission switch
           or check switch circuit.

(ii) Disconnect lead wire from accelerator relay terminal (2).

OFF . . . . Replace accelerator
           relay or check relay
           switch.

ON . . . . Replace accelerator
           switch or check switch
           circuit.

(e) Connect clutch relay terminal (5) to ground.

ON . . . . Replace clutch relay
           or check relay circuit.

OFF . . . . Replace clutch switch
           or check switch circuit.

Fig. 20 Dual Breaker Points Distributor System trouble shooting chart (continued)

Checking Order	Starter Switch	Transmission	Throttle	Clutch	Distributor Relay Normal Condition	Distributor Relay Abnormal Condition	Defective Part or Check Point
1.	ON	*	*	*	OFF	ON	Ignition Switch
2.	OFF	1st, 2nd, Neutral	When opening angle is 7° or less	*	OFF	ON	Transmission and accelerator switch
3.	OFF	*	*	Disengaged	OFF	ON	Clutch Switch
4.	OFF	*	When opening angle is 35° or more	*	OFF	ON	Throttle Switch
5.	OFF	4th, 3rd	When opening angle is 7° or less	Engaged	ON	OFF	Check fuse then refer to checking order No. 8 if still not operating properly
6.	OFF	1st, 2nd or Neutral	When opening angle is 7 − 35°	Engaged	ON	OFF	
7.	OFF	4th or 3rd	When opening angle is 7 − 35°	Engaged	ON	OFF	

Fig. 19 Dual Breaker Points Distributor System trouble shooting chart

tributor circuit it switched from the retarded breaker point circuit to the advanced breaker point circuit.

When the distributor relay is de-energized, the distributor circuit is switched from the advanced breaker point circuit to the retarded breaker point circuit.

System Testing

Testing of this system is accomplished by performing a continuity test on the distributor relay. Disconnect lead wire from distributor relay terminal (retarded contact breaker points) and connect tester to terminal and ground. Turn ignition switch on (engine off) and follow procedure shown in Figs. 19 and 20.

COASTING RICHER SYSTEM

This system, Figs. 21 thru 24, uses a separate fuel system which momentarily enriches the air fuel mixture while the engine is coasting to obtain complete combustion of the exhaust gases. It consists of a solenoid valve in the carburetor connected in series with switches which detect engine coasting conditions.

The solenoid valve is installed in the secondary side of the carburetor and supplies additional fuel into the engine when the valve is opened, Fig. 25. When it opens, the additional fuel drawn out from the float chamber by engine vacuum is metered through the coasting jet and mixed with air supplied through the coasting bleed. The air fuel mixture is then supplied through the coasting valve and into the lower part of the secondary throttle valve. As a result, the air fuel mixture becomes momentarily enriched to promote efficient recombustion of the exhaust gases in the exhaust manifold, thus reducing the hydrocarbon and carbon monoxide content in the exhaust gases. When the mode of engine operation changes from coasting to normal driving, the coasting richer circuit opens and the solenoid valve is deactivated.

Actuation of the solenoid valve is determined by the following switches when they turn on:

a. 1972-75 all and 1976-77 except California models—Accelerator switch, clutch switch (1976-77), clutch relay switch (1972-75, turns on when clutch pedal is depressed) and 3rd-4th gear switch.

b. 1976-77 California models with manual transmission—Accelerator switch, clutch switch, transmission neutral switch and engine speed sensor.

c. 1976-77 California models with automatic transmission—Accelerator switch, inhibitor switch and engine speed sensor.

Accelerator Switch

This switch connected to the linkage, is turned ON when the accelerator pedal is not depressed and is turned OFF and opens the circuit when the accelerator pedal is depressed.

Clutch Switch

This switch, installed near the clutch pedal, is turned OFF when the clutch pedal is depressed and de-energizes the coasting richer circuit.

Transmission Switch

This switch, installed on the transmission gear box turns on when the transmission is shifted into 3rd or 4th gear. When this switch turns ON, the coasting richer circuit is energized.

Transmission Neutral Switch

The switch, installed on the shift quadrant, turns ON when the transmission is shifted into any gear and turns OFF when shifted into neutral. When this switch turns ON, the coasting richer circuit is energized.

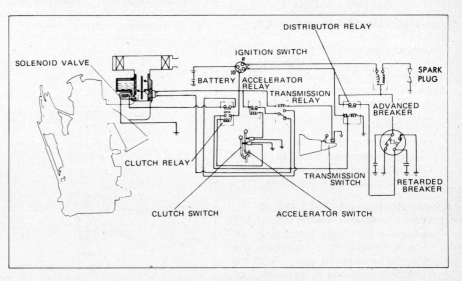

Fig. 21 Coasting Richer System. 1972-73

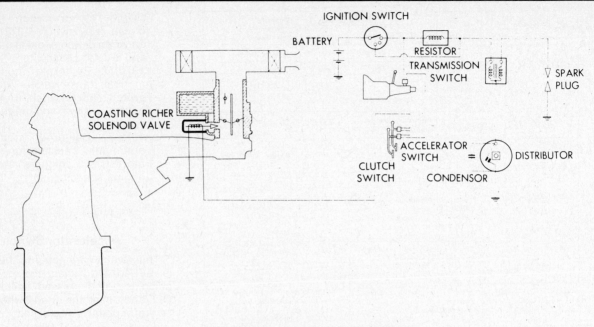

Fig. 22 Coasting Richer System. 1974-75

Inhibitor Switch

This switch, installed on the automatic transmission shift lever, turns ON when the transmission is shifted into drive, low or second. When this switch turns ON, the coasting richer circuit is energized.

Engine Speed Sensor

This sensor senses ignition pulses from the ignition coil to detect engine speed. When engine speed reaches about 1600 rpm, the engine speed sensor turns ON and the coasting richer circuit becomes energized.

System Testing

Accelerator Switch & Clutch Switch, 1972-77

1. Check clearance between pedals, Figs. 26 thru 29. If clearance is not as specified, adjust switch.
2. To check switches, disconnect connector from switch and connect a test light between terminals of switch. If functioning properly, the test light should go ON when the pedals are depressed and should go OFF when the pedals are released. Replace switch(es) if defective.

Accelerator Relay, 1972-73, Fig. 30

1. With accelerator switch off, check voltage at terminals 1 and 3. If voltage is equal at both terminals, the relay is functioning properly. If no voltage is supplied to terminal 3, or voltage is abnormally low, the con-

tact breaker points are defective and should be corrected or replaced.
2. The accelerator relay is functioning properly if voltage to terminal 3 drops to zero when accelerator pedal is depressed. If not, replace relay.

Clutch Relay, 1972-73, Fig. 31

1. Check for voltage between relay terminals 2 and 3, with accelerator pedal released and transmission in either 3rd of 4th gear. If voltage is available at these terminals, the clutch switch is functioning properly.
2. Check for voltage at relay terminal 3 and no voltage at terminal 4 when clutch pedal is released. With clutch pedal released, if there is no voltage

at terminal 3 or if voltage is low, clean or replace breaker points.
3. Check for voltage at terminal 4 and no voltage at terminal 3 when clutch pedal is depressed. With clutch pedal depressed, if there is no voltage at terminal 4, or if voltage to terminal 3 does not drop to zero, the relay coil is defective. Repair or replace relay.

Transmission Switch, 1972-77

1. Disconnect switch wiring and connect test light between switch terminals.
2. Shift gear shift lever through all ranges.
3. Test light should go on only when shift lever is in either 3rd or 4th gear. If not, replace switch.

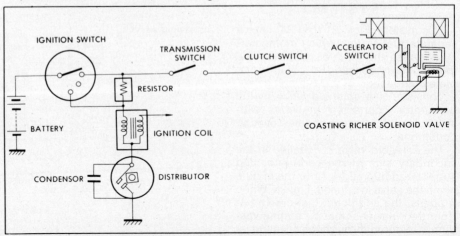

Fig. 23 Coasting Richer System. 1976-77 except California

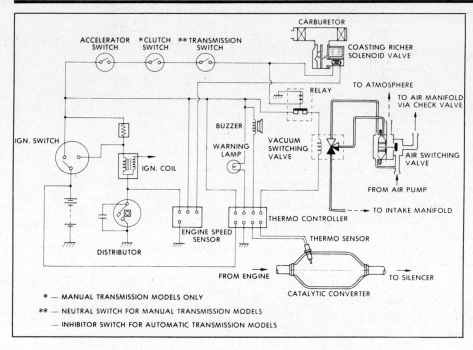

Fig. 24   Coasting Richer System & Over Temperature Control System. 1976-77 California

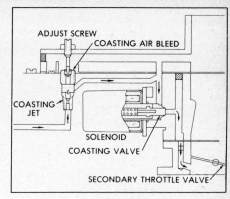

Fig. 25   Coasting Richer System solenoid valve

stalled in the exhaust system to control hydrocarbon and carbon monoxide emissions through a chemical reaction. The chemical reaction involved is the combining of hydrocarbons (HC) and carbon monoxide (CO) with oxygen to form water (H_2O) and carbon dioxide (CO). The catalytic converter allows a faster chemical reaction to occur, and although it enters into the chemical reaction, remains unchanged and ready to repeat the process.

OVER TEMPERATURE CONTROL SYSTEM

This system, Fig. 24, protects the catalytic converter from overheating when the vehicle is coasting. This overheating condition occurs when the catalytic converter tries to oxidize the increased amount of unburned hydrocarbons during coasting.

When the vehicle is coasting, the Coasting Richer System and AIR System are both in operation to prevent overheating of the catalytic converter due to poor combustion. When the catalytic converter temperature reaches 1350° F. due to high temperature and increased load driving conditions, the AIR system air is diverted to atmosphere

Third Gear Relay, 1972-73, Fig. 32

1. With accelerator pedal released, check for voltage at terminals 1 and 4. If voltage is not available, replace transmission switch.
2. Check for voltage at terminals 5 and 6. Relay is functioning properly if voltage at terminal 5 drops to zero and terminal 6 is supplied with voltage when transmission is shifted into neutral position. If no voltage is obtained at terminal 6 or if voltage is abnormally low than voltage at terminal when transmission is shifted in neutral position, the contact points should be cleaned or replaced.
3. If voltage conditions at terminals 5 and 6 are not reversed when the transmission is shifted to 3rd or 4th gear, the relay coil should be replaced.

Inhibitor Switch, 1976-77

NOTE: Adjust inhibitor switch, if engine can be started in any gear shift lever position other than PARK or NEUTRAL.

1. Loosen switch retaining screws and adjust switch so that center of moving piece of switch aligns with neutral position indicator line on steel case when shift lever is set in NEUTRAL position.
2. Check adjustment by performing a continuity test on switch with shift lever in each position

CATALYTIC CONVERTER

Used on 1976-77 California vehicles, the catalytic converter, Fig. 6, is in-

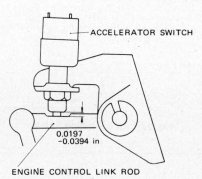

Fig. 26   Accelerator switch adjustment. 1972

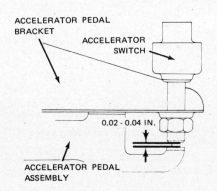

Fig. 27   Accelerator switch adjustment. 1973

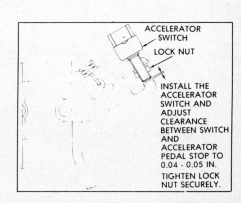

Fig. 28   Accelerator switch adjustment. 1974-77

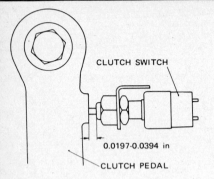

Fig. 29 Clutch switch adjustment. 1972-77

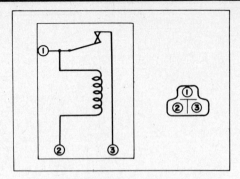

Fig. 30 Accelerator relay terminals

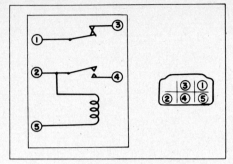

Fig. 31 Clutch relay terminals

in order to reduce the chemical reaction. When catalytic converter temperature exceeds about 1830° F., due to a malfunction such as an ignition failure, a warning light and buzzer indicate an overtemperature condition.

The vacuum switching valve, Fig. 33, used in this system, has an electrically controlled solenoid plunger. When the catalytic converter temperature is over about 1350° F., the solenoid plunger is energized and the vacuum switching valve connects the diaphragm chamber "B" of the air switching valve, Fig. 34, to intake manifold allowing manifold vacuum to be applied to chamber "B." When the solenoid plunger is de-energized, the port is closed, so diaphragm chamber "B" of air switching valve is connected to diaphragm chamber "A."

The air switching valve, Fig. 34, is used to switch air flow from the air pump and is controlled by manifold vacuum and air pump pressure which are switched by the air switching valve. When air pump pressure is applied to diaphragm chamber "B" through the vacuum switching valve, the air from

the air pump flows to the check valve. When manifold vacuum is applied to diaphragm chamber "B," the valve closes air flow to the check valve and diverts it to atmosphere.

A thermo sensor is installed on the front side of the converter and is covered with a stainless steel sheath. Sensing electrical resistance of the thermo sensor, a thermo controller sends ON and OFF signals to the vacuum switching valve, warning lamp and buzzer. When the catalyst temperature reaches about 1350° F., the controller sends an ON signal to the vacuum switching valve, and temperature exceeds about 1830° F, it sends an ON signal to the warning lamp and buzzer.

System Testing

Vacuum Switching Valve

Operation of this valve can be checked by listening for noise from the valve when it is electrically actuated. The valve can be electrically actuated by connecting the connector terminals directly to battery with jumper wires.

Air Switching Valve

With switching valve electrically actuated and engine running, air should

blow out of valve continuously. If not, replace valve.

Thermo Sensor

Run engine at idle for a few minutes, then disconnect sensor connector and check for continuity between connector terminals using a tester. If there is no continuity, replace thermo sensor.

Thermo Controller

If thermo controller is functioning properly, the warning light and buzzer should go on when the ignition switch is turned ON, and then go out automatically a few seconds later.

Engine Speed Sensor

Disconnect speed sensor wiring connector and connect "B," "BR" and "BY" color coded wiring terminals to each other with jumper wires. With engine running at about 1500-1700 rpm, check for continuity between "LgB" color coded wiring terminals. If continuity exists, the engine speed sensor is operating properly.

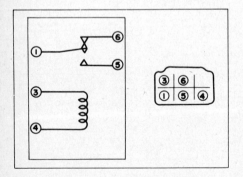

Fig. 32 Third gear relay terminals

Fig. 33 Vacuum switching valve

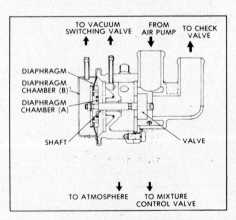

Fig. 34 Air switching valve

Clutch & Transmission Section
Clutch

HYDRAULIC CONTROLS

A single clutch master cylinder is used in conjunction with a slave cylinder, Fig. 1. When the clutch pedal is depressed, brake fluid is forced from the master cylinder into the slave cylinder and the slave cylinder push rod moves the clutch release fork. When the clutch pedal is released, fluid from the slave cylinder feeds back into the master cylinder.

Bleeder fittings are provided on the master and slave cylinders. The procedure for bleeding the system is similar to that used on the brake system.

NOTE: Bleed clutch master cylinder before bleeding the clutch slave cylinder.

Fig. 1 Slave cylinder location

CLUTCH PEDAL ADJUST
Clutch Pedal Free Play

1. Remove the clutch pedal return spring and disconnect the clutch pedal arm from the master cylinder push rod, Fig. 2.
2. Loosen the clutch switch lock nut at the clutch pedal bracket and adjust the height of the clutch pedal until flush with brake pedal. Then retighten lock nut.
3. Adjust the push rod end play by rotating the push rod clevis, a $^{25}/_{32}$ inch pedal free play should be obtained then connect push rod clevis to the clutch pedal arm and tighten the through bolt nut to 25 ft. lbs. Tighten the joint nut and install the clutch pedal return spring.

Shift Fork Free Play

1. Remove clutch shift fork return spring and move shift fork slightly rearward.

Fig. 2 Disconnecting master cylinder push rod

2. Loosen the adjusting nut, Fig. 3, and adjust push-rod until it contacts shift fork.
3. Back-off push-rod approximately 1¾ turns and tighten lock nut.

NOTE: Excessive clearance between the release bearing and diaphragm spring fingers will cause a dragging clutch while too little clearance can cause clutch slipping.

Clutch, Replace

1. Raise vehicle and remove transmission.
2. Mark relationship between clutch assembly and flywheel to aid assembly.
3. Gradually loosen the six clutch cover to flywheel attaching bolts until spring pressure is released.
4. Support clutch pressure plate and cover assembly with a dummy shaft, then remove the attaching bolts and clutch assembly.
5. Reverse procedure to install. Torque clutch attaching bolts to 13 ft. lbs.

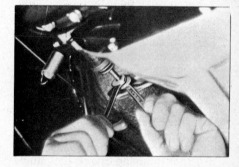

Fig. 3 Adjusting shift fork push rod

Manual Transmission

TRANSMISSION, REPLACE
1972-75

1. Disconnect battery negative cable.
2. Remove air cleaner assembly and disconnect accelerator linkage.
3. Remove gearshift lever, Fig. 4.
4. Remove starter bolts and move starter away from transmission.

5. Disconnect exhaust pipe at flange and hanger at transmission.
6. Disconnect speedometer cable and remove propeller shaft.

NOTE: Insert powerglide transmission plug or yoke into rear extension.

7. Disconnect clutch slave cylinder and push rod from transmission case.
8. Remove flywheel shield and frame to fear mount attaching bolts, Fig. 5.
9. Remove crossmember to frame bolts, lower engine and transmission and support rear of engine.
10. Disconnect the TCS and the back-up lamp connectors.

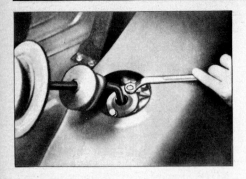

Fig. 4 Gearshift lever removal

11. Remove transmission.
12. Reverse procedure to install.

1976-77
1. Disconnect battery ground cable.
2. Slide gearshift lever boot upward and remove lever, Fig. 4.

3. Remove starter and position aside.
4. Raise vehicle and disconnect exhaust pipe hanger from transmission. Drain transmission.
5. Disconnect speedometer cable.
6. Remove propeller shaft.
7. Remove return spring, clutch slave cylinder and push rod from transmission case. Secure slave cylinder to frame with wire.
8. Remove bolts securing the flywheel cover.
9. Remove frame bracket to transmission rear mount bolts.
10. Raise engine and transmission slightly to remove the crossmember to frame bracket bolts.
11. Remove rear mount bolts from transmission rear cover.
12. Lower the engine and transmission assembly and support rear of engine.

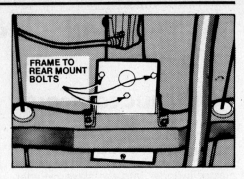

Fig. 5 Frame to rear mount attaching bolt location

13. Disconnect electrical connectors from CRS and back-up lamp switches.
14. Remove transmission to engine attaching bolts and lower transmission from vehicle.
15. Reverse procedure to install.

Automatic Transmission

TROUBLE SHOOTING GUIDE

No Drive in Drive Range

1. Low oil level.
2. Manual linkage maladjusted.
3. Low oil pressure due to:
   a. Restricted or plugged oil screen.
   b. Oil screen gasket improperly installed.
   c. Oil pump pressure regulator.
   d. Pump drive gear tangs damaged by converter.
   e. Case porosity in intake bore.
4. Forward clutch malfunction due to:
   a. Forward clutch not applying due to cracked piston, damaged or missing seals, burned clutch plates, snap ring not in groove.
   b. Forward clutch seal rings damaged or missing on turbine shaft, leaking feed circuits due to damaged or mispositioned gasket.
   c. Clutch housing check ball stuck or missing.
   d. Cup plug leaking or missing from rear of turbine shaft in clutch apply passage.
   e. Incorrect forward clutch piston assembly or incorrect number of clutch plates.
5. Roller clutch malfunction due to missing rollers or springs or possibly galled rollers.

Oil Pressure High Or Low

1. Throttle valve cable maladjusted, binding, disconnected or broken.

2. Throttle lever and bracket improperly installed, disconnected or binding.
3. Throttle valve shift valve, throttle valve or plunger binding.
4. Pressure regulator valve and spring malfunctioning due to:
   a. Binding valve.
   b. Incorrect spring.
   c. Oil pressure control orifice in pump cover plugged, causing high oil pressure.
   d. Pressure regulator bore plug leaking.
5. Manual valve disconnected.
6. Intermediate boost valve binding, causing oil pressures to be incorrect in 2nd and low ranges.
7. Orifice in spacer plate at end of intermediate boost valve plugged.
8. Reserve boost valve binding, causing pressure to be incorrect in reverse only.
9. Orifice in spacer plate at end of reverse boost valve plugged.

1-2 Shift At Full Throttle Only

1. Throttle valve cable maladjusted, binding, disconnected or broken.
2. Throttle lever and bracket assembly binding or disconnected.
3. Throttle valve exhaust ball lifter or number 5 check ball binding, mispositioned or disconnected.

NOTE: If number 5 ball is fully seated, it will cause full throttle valve pressure regardless of throttle valve position.

4. Throttle valve and plunger binding.
5. Valve body gaskets leaking, damaged or incorrectly installed.
6. Porous control valve assembly.

First Speed Only, No 1-2 Shift

1. Due to governor and governor feed passages:
   a. Plugged governor oil feed orifice in spacer plate.
   b. Plugged orifice in spacer plate that feeds governor oil to the shift valves.
   c. Balls missing in governor assembly.
   d. Governor cover O-ring missing or leaking. If governor cover O-ring leaks, an external oil leak will be present and there will be no upshift.
   e. Governor shaft seal missing or damaged.
   f. Governor driven gear stripped.
   g. Governor weights binding.
   h. Governor assembly missing.
2. Control valve assembly 1-2 shift valve or 1-2 throttle valve stuck in downshift position.
3. Porosity in case channels or undrilled 2nd speed feed holes.
4. Excessive leakage between case bore and intermediate band apply ring.
5. Intermediate band anchor pin missing or disconnected from band.
6. Missing or broken intermediate band.
7. Due to intermediate servo assembly:
   a. Servo to cover oil seal ring damage or missing.

b. Porous servo cover or piston.
c. Incorrect intermediate band apply pin.
d. Incorrect cover and piston.

1st & 2nd Only, No 2-3, Shift

1. 2-3 shift valve or 2-3 throttle valve stuck in downshift position.
2. Direct clutch feed orifice in spacer plate plugged.
3. Valve body gaskets leaking, damaged or incorrectly installed.
4. Porosity between case passages.
5. Pump passages plugged or leaking.
6. Pump gasket incorrectly installed.
7. Rear seal on pump cover leaking or missing.
8. Direct clutch oil seals missing or damaged.
9. Direct clutch piston or housing cracked.
10. Direct clutch plates damaged or missing.
11. Direct clutch backing plate snap ring out of groove.
12. Intermediate servo to case oil seal broken or missing on intermediate servo piston.
13. Intermediate servo exhaust hole in case between servo piston seals plugged or undrilled.

Moves Forward in Neutral

1. Manual linkage maladjusted.
2. Forward clutch does not release.
3. Cross leakage between pump passages.
4. Cross leakage to forward clutch through clutch passages.

No Drive in Reverse or Slips in Reverse

1. Throttle valve cable binding or maladjusted.
2. Manual linkage maladjusted.
3. Throttle valve binding.
4. Reverse boost valve binding in bore.
5. Low overrun clutch valve binding in bore.
6. Reverse clutch piston cracked, broken or has missing seals.
7. Reverse clutch plates burned.
8. Reverse clutch has incorrect selective spacer ring.
9. Porosity in passages to direct clutch.
10. Pump to case gasket improperly installed or missing.
11. Pump passages cross leaking or restricted.
12. Pump cover seals damaged or missing.
13. Direct clutch piston or housing cracked.

14. Direct clutch piston seals cut or missing.
15. Direct clutch housing ball check, stuck, leaking or missing.
16. Direct clutch plates burned.
17. Incorrect direct clutch piston.
18. Direct clutch orifices plugged in spacer plate.
19. Intermediate servo to case seal cut or missing.

Slips 1-2 Shift

1. Aerated oil due to low level.
2. 2nd speed feed orifice in spacer plate partially blocked.
3. Improperly installed or missing spacer plate gasket.
4. 1-2 accumulator valve stuck, causing low 1-2 accumulator pressure.
5. Weak or missing 1-2 accumulator valve spring.
6. 1-2 accumulator piston seal leaking or spring missing or broken.
7. Leakage between 1-2 accumulator piston and pin.
8. Incorrect intermediate band apply pin.
9. Excessive leakage between intermediate band apply pin and case.
10. Porous intermediate servo piston.
11. Servo cover to servo seal damaged or missing.
12. Incorrect servo and cover.
13. Throttle valve cable improperly adjusted.
14. Shift throttle valve or throttle valve binding.
15. Intermediate band worn or burned.
16. Case porosity in 2nd clutch passages.

Rough 1-2 Shift

1. Throttle valve cable improperly adjusted or binding.
2. Throttle valve or plunger binding.
3. Shift throttle or 1-2 accumulator valve binding.
4. Incorrect intermediate servo pin.
5. Intermediate servo plan to case seal damaged or missing.
6. 1-2 accumulator oil ring damaged piston stuck, bore damaged or spring broken or missing.

Slips 2-3 Shift

1. Low oil level.
2. Throttle valve cable improperly adjusted.
3. Throttle valve binding.
4. Direct clutch orifice in spacer plate partially blocked.
5. Spacer plate gaskets improperly installed or missing.
6. Intermediate servo to case seal damaged.
7. Porous direct clutch feed passages in case.

8. Pump to case gasket improperly installed or missing.
9. Pump passages cross feeding, leaking or restricted.
10. Pump cover oil seal rings damaged or missing.
11. Direct clutch piston or housing cracked.
12. Direct clutch piston seals cut or missing.
13. Direct clutch plates burned.

Rough 2-3 Shift

1. Throttle valve cable improperly installed or missing.
2. Throttle valve or throttle valve plunger binding.
3. Shift throttle valve binding.
4. Intermediate servo exhaust hole undrilled or plugged between intermediate servo piston seals.
5. Direct clutch exhaust valve number 4 check ball missing or improperly installed.

No Engine Braking In 2nd Speed

1. Intermediate boost valve binding in valve body.
2. Intermediate-Reverse number 3 check ball improperly installed or missing.
3. Shift throttle valve number 3 check ball improperly installed or missing.
4. Intermediate servo to cover seal missing or damaged.
5. Intermediate band off anchor pin, broken or burned.

No Engine Braking In 1st Speed

1. Low overrun clutch valve binding in valve body.

NOTE: The following conditions will also cause no reverse.

2. Low-reverse clutch piston seals broken or missing.
3. Porosity in low-reverse piston or housing.
4. Low-reverse clutch housing snap ring out of case.
5. Cup plug or rubber seal missing or damaged between case and low-reverse clutch housing.

No Part Throttle Downshift

1. Throttle plunger bushing passages obstructed.
2. 2-3 throttle valve bushing passages obstructed.
3. Valve body gaskets improperly installed or damaged.
4. Spacer plate hole obstructed or undrilled.
5. Throttle valve cable maladjusted.
6. Throttle valve or shift throttle valve binding.

Low or High Shift Points

1. Throttle valve cable binding or disconnected.
2. Throttle valve or shift throttle valve binding.
3. Number 1 throttle shift check ball improperly installed or missing.
4. Throttle valve plunger, 1-2 or 2-3 throttle valves binding.
5. Valve body gaskets improperly installed or missing.
6. Pressure regulator valve binding.
7. Throttle valve exhaust number 5 check ball and lifter, improperly installed, disconnected or missing.
8. Throttle lever binding, disconnected or loose at valve body mounting bolt or not positioned at the throttle valve plunger bushing pin locator.
9. Governor shaft to cover seal broken or missing.
10. Governor cover O-rings broken or missing.

NOTE: Outer ring will leak externally and the inner ring will leak internally.

11. Case porosity.

Will Not Hold In Park

1. Manual linkage maladjusted.
2. Parking pawl binding in case.
3. Actuator rod or plunger damaged.
4. Parking pawl damaged.
5. Parking bracket loose or damaged.
6. Detent lever nut loose.
7. Detent lever hole worn or damaged.
8. Detent roller to valve body bolt loose.
9. Detent roller or pin damaged, incorrectly installed or missing.

OIL PRESSURE CHECK

Install oil pressure gauge to transmission. With vehicle stationary and engine running at 1000 rpm, oil pressures should be approximately the same as those shown in Fig. 6.

MAINTENANCE

To check fluid, drive vehicle for at least 15 minutes to bring fluid to operating temperature (200° F). With vehicle on a level surface and engine idling in Park and parking brake applied, the level on the dipstick should be at the "F" mark. To bring the fluid level from the ADD mark to the FULL mark requires 1 pint of fluid. If vehicle cannot be driven sufficiently to bring fluid to operating temperature, the level on the dipstick should be between the two dimples on the dipstick with fluid temperature at 70° F.

If additional fluid is required, use only

RANGE	NORMAL OIL PRESSURES		
	kPa	MODELS	P.S.I.
PARK AT 1000 RPM	275-345	CU	40-50
	345-415	CN CX BR	50-60
	415-480	CH CQ CS BH BZ OZ	60-70
REVERSE AT 1000 RPM	620-725	CU	90-105
	690-795	CN CX BR	100-115
	760-860	CH CQ CS BH BZ OZ	110-125
NEUTRAL AT 1000 RPM	310-345	CU	45-50
	380-420	CN CX BR	55-60
	420-480	CH CQ CS BH BZ OZ	60-70
DRIVE AT 1200 RPM	345-450	CU	50-65
	420-515	CN CX BR	60-75
	480-585	CH CQ CS BH BZ OZ	70-85
INT. AT 1000 RPM	515-620	CU CN	75-90
	585-690	CX BR	85-100
	900-1035	CH CQ CS BH BZ OZ	130-150
LO AT 1000 RPM	515-620	CU CN	75-90
	585-690	CX BR	85-100
	900-1035	CH CQ CS BH BZ OZ	130-150

CAUTION: Total Running Time For This Combination Not To Exceed 2 Minutes.

Fig. 6   Oil pressure chart

Dexron or Dexron II automatic transmission fluid.

NOTE: An early change to a darker color from the usual red color and or a strong odor that is usually associated with over-heated fluid is normal and should not be considered as a positive sign of required maintenance or unit failure.

CAUTION: When adding fluid, do not overfill, as foaming and loss of fluid through the vent may occur as the fluid heats up. Also, if fluid level is too low, complete loss of drive may occur especially when cold, which can cause transmission failure.

Every 60,000 miles, the oil should be drained, the oil pan removed, the screen cleaned and fresh fluid added. For vehicles subjected to more severe use such as heavy city traffic especially in hot weather, prolonged periods of idling or towing, this maintenance should be performed every 15,000 miles.

Draining Bottom Pan

1. Remove front and side oil pan attaching bolts, then loosen the rear oil pan attaching bolts.
2. Carefully pry oil pan loose and allow fluid to drain into a suitable container.
3. Remove the oil pan and gasket, then remove the screen attaching bolts and remove screen.
4. Thoroughly clean oil screen and oil pan with solvent.
5. Install oil screen using a new gasket and torque attaching bolts to 6-10 ft. lbs., then install oil pan using a new

gasket and torque attaching bolts to 10-13 bolts.
6. Add 3 quarts of fluid, then with engine idling and parking brake applied, move selector lever through each range and return selector lever to PARK.
7. Check fluid level and add fluid as required to bring level between the two dimples on the dipstick.

Adding Fluid to Dry Transmission and Converter

1. Add 4½ quarts of fluid.
2. With transmission in PARK and parking brake applied, start the engine and place carburetor on fast idle cam.
3. Move shifter lever through each range, then with transmission in PARK, add additional fluid as required to bring the level between the two dimples on the dipstick.

Manual Linkage, Adjust

1. Loosen control rod locknut. If shift lever swivel is threaded, remove cotter and washers and disconnect rod from shift control lever, Fig. 7.
2. Rotate shift lever to stop in counter-clockwise direction as viewed from left side of transmission, then back off lever three stops to "Neutral" position.
3. While holding shift lever in position, move shift control lever in driver's compartment to "Neutral" position.
4. Push control lever rearward to remove play and tighten control rod locknut. If shift lever swivel is threaded, adjust length of rod so that end of rod aligns with shift lever hole, then insert control rod into

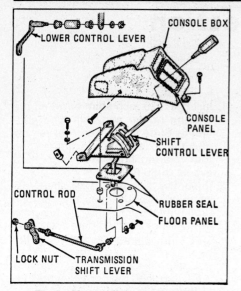

Fig. 7 Manual linkage adjustment

shift lever and install cotter pin and washers and tighten locknut.

5. Check for proper operation of transmission and shift lever and readjust as necessary.

Detent Downshift Cable, Adjust

1. Loosen cable adjustment nuts Fig. 8, then with throttle lever at wide open position, adjust inner cable by turning lower adjusting nut on outer cable so that inner cable is provided with a play of about .04 inch.
2. Tighten upper locknut.
3. Check that stroke of inner cable with throttle at wide open position to closed position is with 1.37-1.41 inches.

IN VEHICLE REPAIRS

Valve Body Assembly

1. Drain transmission fluid, then remove oil pan and screen.
2. Remove detent cable retaining bolt and disconnect cable.
3. Remove throttle lever and bracket assembly. Use care to avoid bending throttle lever link.
4. Remove detent roller and spring assembly.
5. Support valve body and remove retaining bolts, then while holding manual valve, remove valve assembly, spacer plate and gaskets as an assembly to prevent dropping the five check balls.

NOTE: After removing valve body assembly, the intermediate band anchor band pin, and reverse cup plug may be removed.

6. To install control valve reverse re-

moval procedure and torque all valve body bolts to 8 ft. lbs.

CAUTION: Assure that intermediate band anchor pin is located on intermediate band prior to installation of valve body, as damage will result.

Governor

1. Disconnect battery ground cable and remove cleaner.
2. On vehicles with air conditioning, remove the five heater core cover screws, then disconnect the electrical connectors and position heater core aside.
3. Disconnect exhaust pipe and allow to hang down.
4. Support transmission, then remove transmission rear support bolts and propeller shaft and lower transmission until enough clearance is obtained to remove governor.
5. Remove governor retainer ring and cover, then remove governor and washer.

NOTE: If governor to case washer falls into transmission, use a small magnet to remove it. If it cannot be easily removed, replace the washer with a new one.

6. To install governor, reverse removal procedure.

CAUTION: Do not attempt to hammer governor assembly into case, as damage to governor, case or cover may result.

Pressure Regulator Valve

1. Drain transmission fluid, then remove oil pan and screen.
2. Using a small screwdriver or tool J-24684, Fig. 9, compress regulator spring.
3. Remove retaining ring and slowly release spring tension.
4. Remove pressure regulator bore plug, valve, spring and guide.

Fig. 9 Removing or installing pressure regulator

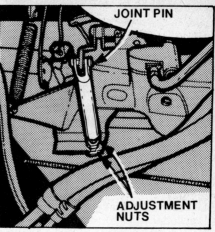

Fig. 8 Detent downshift cable adjustment

5. To assemble, install pressure regulator spring, guide and valve with stem end first and bore plug with hole side out.
6. Using a small screwdriver or tool J-24684, Fig. 9, compress regulator spring and install retaining ring.

TRANSMISSION, REPLACE

1. Disconnect battery ground cable.
2. Disconnect detent cable from carburetor and remove dipstick.
3. Raise and support vehicle, then remove converter housing cover, starter and propeller shaft.

NOTE: Install plug on rear end of transmission to prevent oil leakage.

4. Remove exhaust pipe bracket and disconnect shift linkage and speedometer cable.
5. Loosen nuts retaining oil cooler lines to transmission, then remove clips retaining lines and move lines away to prevent damage when transmission is removed.
6. Remove the three nuts and bolts retaining converter to flex plate and the three nuts and bolts retaining frame bracket to transmission mount.
7. Using a suitable jack, raise engine and transmission, then remove the four bolts retaining frame bracket to crossmember and remove transmission mount.
8. Remove transmission to engine bolts, then lower and remove transmission.

CAUTION: Use care to avoid dropping converter.

9. Reverse procedure to install, making sure that converter rotates freely before torquing nuts and bolts in 30 ft. lbs.

Rear Axle & Brakes Section
Rear Axle

AXLE SHAFT, SEALS & BEARING REPLACE

1. Raise vehicle on hoist.
2. Remove rear wheel and brake drum.
3. Remove brake shoes and disconnect parking brake inner cable, Fig. 1.
4. Disconnect brake line from wheel cylinder.
5. From inboard side of brake backing plate, remove the four nuts from bearing holder through bolts.
6. Pull out axle shaft assembly.

NOTE: Do not strike backing plate in an attempt to remove axle shaft. Use tool J-5748 if necessary.

7. Flatten locking tab on lock washer, then mount axle shaft in vise, clamping vise jaws around lock nut.

NOTE: Do not tighten vise excessively.

8. Place tool J-24246 onto studs and secure with two wheel nuts, then turn axle shaft from lock nut.
9. Remove lock nut, washer, bearing and holder, then using a press, remove brake backing plate from axle shaft.

NOTE: Only a small amount of force is required to remove bearing from shaft. Make sure to support backing plate solidly and hold onto axle shaft to prevent it from falling.

10. Remove oil seal from bearing holder

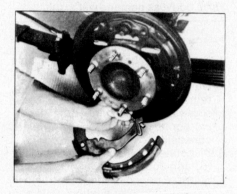

Fig. 1 Disconnecting parking brake inner cable

and drive out bearing outer race using a drift.
11. Reverse steps 7 thru 10 to reassemble shaft. Torque lock nut to 190 ft. lbs.

Installation

NOTE: If both axle shafts have been serviced, the following steps should be used for installation. If only one shaft has been serviced, skip step #1.

1. Insert a .079 inch shim between the bearing holder and axle tube end-flange. Slide the axle shaft assembly into the axle tube and tighten the four bearing holder-to-flange bolts evenly to 55 ft. lbs.
2. Push the opposite axle shaft, assembled without shims, into the axle tube until it comes into contact with thrust block in the differential. Measure the clearance between the bearing holder and flange, Fig. 2, and add .004 inch to this measurement to obtain the correct shim size.
3. Withdraw the axle shaft, and install correct thickness shims between bearing holder and flange face. Torque to 55 ft. lbs.
4. Connect the brake and pipes and bleed brake system.

CARRIER REMOVAL

1. Remove wheels and brake drums.
2. Disconnect brake pipes at both rear wheel cylinder.

NOTE: Cover ends of brake pipes to prevent foreign material into system.

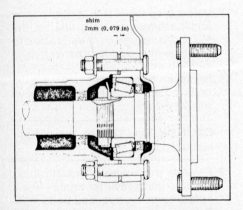

Fig. 2 Measuring axle shaft clearance

shim
2mm (0.079 in)

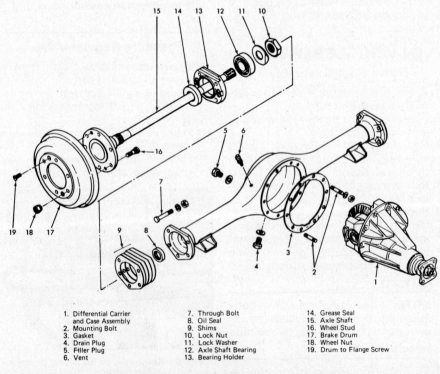

1. Differential Carrier and Case Assembly	7. Through Bolt	14. Grease Seal
2. Mounting Bolt	8. Oil Seal	15. Axle Shaft
3. Gasket	9. Shims	16. Wheel Stud
4. Drain Plug	10. Lock Nut	17. Brake Drum
5. Filler Plug	11. Lock Washer	18. Wheel Nut
6. Vent	12. Axle Shaft Bearing	19. Drum to Flange Screw
	13. Bearing Holder	

Fig. 3 Differential case and carrier assembly

3. Disconnect emergency brake cable brackets at rear spring.
4. Remove bolts from each end flange.
5. Disengage axle shafts from carrier assembly and partially withdraw shafts from axle tube.

NOTE: It is not necessary to remove axle shaft.

6. Disconnect the propeller shaft at the companion flange and remove propeller shaft.
7. Remove the nuts mounting the differential carrier assembly to the axle housing and remove the carrier, Fig. 3.

Installation
1. Clean the faces of the rear axle case

and differential carrier and install gasket.
2. Mount the carrier assembly to the rear axle case and torque nuts to 35 ft. lbs.
3. Install the axle shaft assemblies.
4. Install propeller shaft and torque companion flange bolts to 18 ft. lbs.
5. Fill the rear axle case with hypoid gear lubricant, slightly below the filler hole.

Brakes

BRAKE PEDAL FREE PLAY ADJUSTMENT

When the brake pedal is fully released, the pedal bumper bottoms on the stop lamp switch housing. Brake pedal height adjustment should be performed as follows:
1. Disconnect the battery ground cable.
2. Remove the cotter pin and the push rod clevis pin. Make sure the return spring is connected to the brake pedal.

3. With the pedal at fully release position, measure the distance from the surface of the pedal foot pad to the toe pan, Fig. 4. This distance should be 6.3 to 6.7 inches for 1972 and 5.9 to 6.3 inches for 1973-77.
4. To adjust free play disconnect the stop lamp switch wiring harness. Loosen the stop lamp switch locknut and rotate the switch in bracket until the correct pedal height is obtained and tighten switch locknut.
5. Loosen push rod clevis locknut and rotate clevis on push rod until clevis pin can be installed through clevis and pedal with no binding. Install clevis pin and cotter pin and tighten clevis locknut.

NOTE: Do not force the pin into the pin holes while depressing the pedal.

6. On 1976-77 models, install stop lamp switch. Adjust clearance between switch housing, not the switch actuating pin, and the brake pedal tab to .02-.04 inch. Tighten switch locknut.
7. On all models, connect stop lamp switch wiring harness and battery ground cable.

BRAKE SHOE ADJUSTMENT

1. Raise vehicle and remove adjusting slot covers.

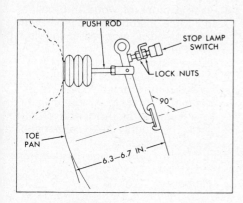

Fig. 4 Adjusting brake pedal free play

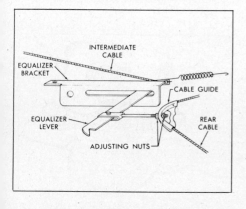

Fig. 5 Adjusting parking brake

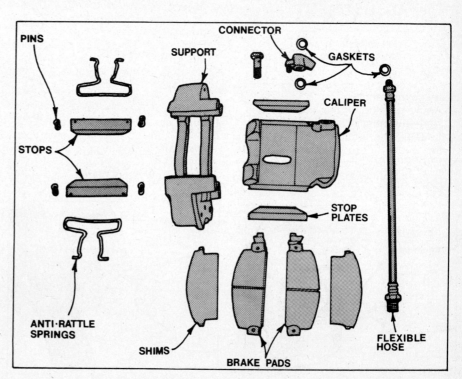

Fig. 6 Disc brake assembly

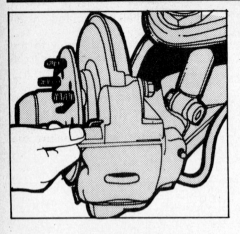

Fig. 7   Removing caliper stops

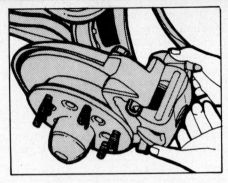

Fig. 8   Removing caliper

Fig. 9   Removing brake shoe and lining assembly

2. Adjust the upper and lower shoes an equal number of notches on front brakes and turn star wheel on rear brakes, until the drum slides over the brake shoes with a slight drag.
3. Retract upper and lower shoes two notches on front brakes and turn star wheel 1¼ turns on rear brakes to retract the shoes. This will allow sufficient lining to drum clearance.
4. Replace slot covers and lower vehicle.
5. Final adjustment is by numerous forward and reverse stops, applying brakes with a firm pedal effort until a satisfactory brake pedal height results.

PARKING BRAKE CABLE ADJUSTMENT

NOTE: The service brake must be properly adjusted before adjusting the parking brake.

1. Raise the vehicle.
2. Apply parking brake two notches, from fully release position.
3. Loosen the equalizer check nut, Fig. 5, adjust the front jam nut until a drag is felt when rear wheels are rotated frontward.

4. Tighten nuts securely.
5. With the parking brake released, no drag should be felt when rotating the rear wheels.
6. Lower vehicle.

DISC BRAKE SERVICE

This floating caliper disc brake, Fig. 6, incorporates a single piston that actuates the inner and outer brake shoe and lining assemblies.

Brake Shoe & Lining, Replace
Removal
1. Raise vehicle and remove wheel assembly.
2. Remove pins from caliper stops, then the stops, Fig. 7.
3. Remove caliper from support, Fig. 8, and the stop plates from the caliper. Secure caliper to frame with wire. Do not allow caliper to hang from brake hose.
4. Remove shoe and lining assemblies and the shims, Fig. 9.
5. Remove anti-rattle springs from support.

Installation
1. Lubricate shims and stop plates.
2. Install anti-rattle springs, shims, and shoe and lining assemblies on the support.
3. Install new stop plates on caliper,

then the caliper, stops and new stop pins.
4. Install wheel assembly and lower vehicle.

Caliper Replace & Overhaul
Removal
1. Perform steps 1, 2 and 3 outlined under "Brake Shoe & Lining, Replace," Removal procedure. However, disconnect brake hose from caliper and cap openings in hose and caliper.
2. Remove caliper from vehicle.

Overhaul
1. Remove dust seal from caliper with a suitable tool, Fig. 10.
2. Place a block of wood into caliper and force piston from caliper with compressed air applied to the fluid port, Fig. 11.
3. Remove piston square seal ring.
4. Inspect cylinder bore and piston for wear, scuffing or corrosion. Stains and minor corrosion in the cylinder bore may be removed with crocus cloth. Thoroughly clean caliper after using crocus cloth.
5. Lubricate cylinder bore and piston square seal, then install piston seal into bore.
6. Install piston into caliper, Fig. 12.
7. Lubricate piston and install dust seal onto piston and caliper.

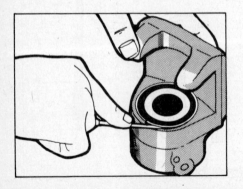

Fig. 10   Removing dust seal

Fig. 11   Removing piston from caliper

Fig. 12   Installing piston

Installation

1. Perform steps 1 and 3 outlined under "Brake Shoe & Lining, Replace" Installation procedure.
2. Connect brake hose to caliper.
3. Install wheel assembly and lower vehicle.

MASTER CYLINDER, REPLACE

1. Disconnect battery ground cable.
2. Disconnect lines from master cylinder. Plug opened lines to prevent entry of dirt.
3. Remove master cylinder bracket bolt, then remove master cylinder to power cylinder nuts and washers and remove master cylinder.

CAUTION: Use care to avoid spilling fluid onto painted surfaces.

4. Reverse procedure to install.

Rear Suspension Section

SHOCK ABSORBER, REPLACE

1. Raise vehicle and support with jack stands placed under frame near rear end of spring brackets.
2. Remove upper and lower shock absorber retaining nuts and remove shock absorber.
3. Reverse procedure to install.

LEAF SPRING REPLACE

1. Remove the shock absorbers, Fig. 1.
2. Remove the parking brake cable clips.
3. Remove the "U" bolts, Fig. 2.
4. Jack up the rear axle case slightly to separate it from the leaf spring assemblies.
5. Remove the front and rear shackle bolt nuts and drive bolt out of shackles, Figs. 3 and 4.
6. Drive out the front shackle bolt and remove the leaf spring assembly rearward.
7. Remove the shackle bolt from the rear springs bracket and remove the shackle.
8. Reverse procedure to install. Torque "U" bolt until to 40 ft. lbs. and shackle bolt nuts to 130 ft. lbs. for 1972-75 or 95 ft. lbs. for 1976-77.

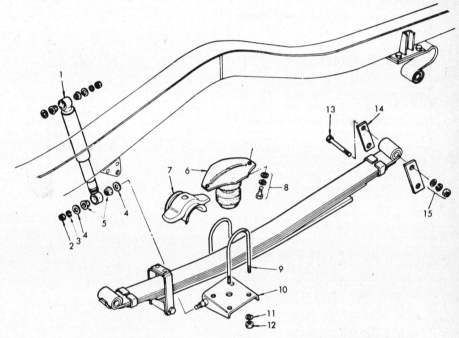

1. Shock Absorber	6. Jounce Bumper	11. Lock Washer
2. Nut	7. Seat	12. Nut
3. Lock Washer	8. Bolt and Washers	13. Shackle Bolt
4. Plain Washer	9. U-Bolt	14. Shackle
5. Bushing	10. Clamp Plate	15. Nut and Washers

Fig. 1   Rear suspension components part arrangement

Fig. 2   U-bolt replacement

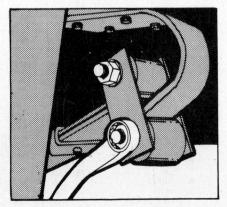

Fig. 3   Rear shackle replacement

Fig. 4   Front shackle replacement

Front Suspension & Steering Section

WHEEL ALIGNMENT
Caster and Camber

Caster and camber adjustments are made by inserting, subtracting or transfering shims between the upper control arm pivot shaft and the frame, Fig. 1. *Refer to Wheel Alignment Specifications Chart.*

Toe-In

The toe-in angle can be adjusted by turning the intermediate rod after loosening the lock nuts on the intermediate rod. *Refer to Wheel Alignment Specification Chart.*

WHEEL BEARINGS ADJUST

1. Tighten spindle nut to 22 lbs. ft. torque while rotating wheel.
2. Turn the hub 2-3 turns and adjust nut to be finger tight, the hub should have no free play.
3. Tighten spindle nut and measure the starting torque by pulling one of the wheel hub studs with an accurate pull scale. The preload torque is 1.1 to 2.6 lbs., when hub begins to rotate.

NOTE: The brake linings must not be in contact with the brake drum when measuring the starting torque.

UPPER CONTROL ARM, BALL JOINT & PIVOT SHAFT REPLACE

1. Support chassis under the lower control arm.
2. Remove the wheel and tire assembly.
3. Disconnect the upper control arm from the knuckle.

NOTE: Wire the knuckle assembly to the frame or other support, to prevent assembly from hanging by the brake flexible line.

4. Remove the two bolts fixing the upper pivot shaft from the engine compartment side and remove the upper control arm. Note the position and number of the shims used for adjusting camber and caster angles, providing for reinstallation of the shims in their original position.

Pivot Shaft Replace

1. Remove the pivot shaft and bushing nuts from the upper control arm.
2. Fill the internal part of the bushings with molybdenum disulfide grease and screw the bushings into the pivot shaft. Follow proper assembly sequence, Fig. 3. Be sure to screw in bushings alternately into the pivot shafts. Avoid grease contact with outer face of the bushings. Use tool J-24258 as other suitable spacer, Fig. 4, and torque bushings to 250 ft. lbs. for 1972 and 220 ft. lbs. for 1973-77.

Fig. 1   Caster and camber adjusting shims

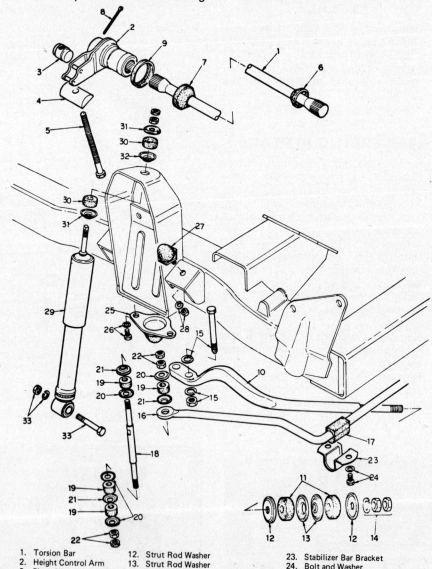

1. Torsion Bar	12. Strut Rod Washer	23. Stabilizer Bar Bracket
2. Height Control Arm	13. Strut Rod Washer	24. Bolt and Washer
3. Pivot Nut	14. Nut, Lock Washer	25. Lower Control Arm Bumper
4. Height Control Seat	15. Bolt, Washer, Nut	26. Bolt, Washer
5. Height Control Bolt	16. Stabilizer Bar	27. Upper Control Arm Bumpers(2)
6. Boot	17. Stabilizer Bushings	28. Nut, Washer
7. Boot	18. Link Stud	29. Shock Absorber
8. Cotter Pin	19. Link Stud Bushings	30. Bushing
9. Seal	20. Stabilizer Link Stud Washers	31. Retainer
10. Strut Rod Assy.	21. Stabilizer Link Stud Washers	32. Retainer
11. Strut Rod Bushings	22. Nuts	33. Bolt, Lock Washer, Nut

Fig. 2   Front suspension component part arrangement

NOTE: Be sure the control arm and bushings are centered properly and the control arm does not bind on the pivot shaft when torqued to specification.

Upper Ball Joint Replace

1. Remove staked nut, retaining ball joint and remove ball joint.
2. Install ball joint in sequence, Fig. 3, tighten securely retaining nut.

NOTE: After installing control arm and inserting alignment shims in proper positions, torque pivot shafts to 55 ft. lbs. for 1972 and 50 ft. lbs. for 1973-77.

LOWER CONTROL ARM REPLACE

1. Remove the wheel and tire assembly.
2. Remove the strut bar and withdraw the stabilizer from the rod.
3. Remove the torsion bar.
4. Remove the lower shock absorber bolt.
5. Take out the two bolts retaining the lower ball joint and disconnect the lower ball joint from the lower control arm.
6. Remove the retaining bolts and the lower control arm, Fig. 5.

Installation

1. Fasten the lower ball joint to the lower control arm and torque retaining bolts to 45 ft. lbs.
2. Mount the lower control arm to the chassis frame. Drive the bolt into position and torque to 135 ft. lbs. for 1972 or 130 ft. lbs. for 1973-77.
3. Install torsion bar.
4. Install the strut bars in position after removing jack.

NOTE: Leave the strut bar to frame nuts finger tight until the vehicle height is adjusted.

Lower Ball Joint Replace

1. Remove ball joint from the steering knuckle.
2. Remove bolts retaining lower ball joint and strut rod.
3. Remove the retaining bolts and the ball joint.

Installation

1. Mount the lower ball joint to the lower control arm. Torque bolts to 45 ft. lbs.
2. Install the ball joint stud into the steering knuckle. Install castellated nut and torque to 80 ft. lbs. for 1972 and 75 ft. lbs. for 1973-77, plus enough to align cotter pin.

FRONT SHOCK ABSORBER

1. With an open end wrench hold the shock absorber upper stem from turning, and then remove the upper stem retaining nut, retainer and rubber grommet.
2. Remove bolt retaining the lower shock absorber to the lower control arm and remove shock absorber assembly.
3. Reverse procedure for installation. Refer to, Fig. 2, for bushing position.

TORSION BAR SUSPENSION

All models are equipped with the short and long arm independent type front suspension, utilizing height control arms. The control arms are attached to the chassis with bolts and bushings at their inner pivot points and to the steering knuckles, at their outer points, Figs. 2 and 3. The fore and aft movement of the front suspension is controlled by strut bars.

Torsion Bar Adjustment

1. With vehicle on a level surface, rock

1. Upper Control Arm	16. Lower Control Arm Link	31. Bolt
2. Pivot Shaft	17. Bolt	32. Nut, Lock Washer
3. Bushing(2)	18. Nut, Lock Washer	33. Hub
4. Cover	19. Bolt	34. Wheel Stud
5. Grease Fitting	20. Nut, Lock Washer	35. Drum
6. Upper Ball Joint	21. Lower Ball Joint	36. Screw
7. Grease Fitting	22. Grease Fitting	37. Outer Wheel Bearing
8. Boot	23. Boot	38. Inner Wheel Bearing
9. Shim	24. Lock Washer	39. Grease Seal
10. Nut, Cotter Pin	25. Nut, Cotter Pin	40. Washer
11. Washer	26. Bolt, Nut, Lock Washer	41. Nut
12. Staked Nut	27. Knuckle	42. Nut Retainer
13. Bolt, Washer	28. Bearing Shoulder Piece	43. Cotter Pin
14. Shims	29. Tie Rod Link	44. Dust Cap
15. Lower Control Arm	30. Bolt	45. Wheel Stud Nut

Fig. 3 Front suspension component part arrangement

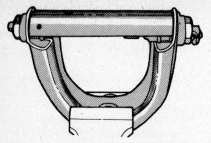

Fig. 4 Installing upper control arm bushing

vehicle up and down to settle suspension.
2. Loosen nuts at front strut bar.
3. Measure clearance between rubber bumper and the lower control arm. The proper clearance should be (⅞) inch.
4. To adjust height, turn adjusting bolt inward to raise height or outward to decrease height.
5. Tighten strut bar nuts.

TORSION BAR REPLACE

1. Remove the height control arm adjusting bolt.
2. Scribe location and remove the height control arm from the torsion bar and third crossmember.
3. Scribe location and withdraw the torsion bar from the lower control arm.
4. Grease torsion bar ends and height control arm. Reverse removal procedure to install the torsion bar, Fig. 1.

STRUT BAR REPLACE

1. Remove the frame side bracket by removing the strut bar nuts, washer and rubber bushings.
2. Remove the two bolts fastening the strut bar to the lower control arm and remove the strut bar.
3. Reverse procedure for installation of strut bar. Refer to Fig. 2 for proper bushing positions and tighten to specification. Strut bar to lower control arm, torque 45 ft. lbs. Strut bar to frame torque, nut 175 ft. lbs.; locknut 50 ft. lbs.

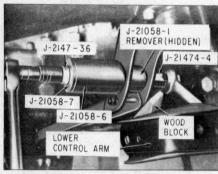

Fig. 6 Removing control arm bushing

LOWER CONTROL ARM BUSHING REPLACE

1972

1. Remove wheel and tire assembly.

NOTE: Removal of the lower control arm bushings necessitates use of special tools.

2. Remove torsion bar.
3. Remove bolts retaining lower control arm link and crossmember to lower control arm.
4. Move lower control arm away from crossmember.
5. Assemble tools and press out bushing and remove tools, Fig. 6.

NOTE: Never use impact tools for removal or installation of bushings or distortion of the crossmember will result.

Installation

1. Assemble the tools and press in the new bushing until it is centered in the bracket, Fig. 7.
2. Remove the tools and reinstall the lower control arm to crossmember, torque to 135 ft. lbs.
3. Install lower control arm link and the torsion bar to control arm.

STEERING KNUCKLE REPLACE

1. Remove the wheel assembly.
2. Disconnect the brake flexible hose from the wheel cylinder.
3. Remove the spindle nut.
4. Remove hub together with brake drum.

NOTE: Replace oil seal if necessary.

5. Remove the two bolts retaining the tie rod end link and shift the link out of way. Remove remaining two bolts and remove the brake backing plate assembly.
6. Disconnect knuckle from the ball joints and remove knuckle.

Installation

1. Reverse procedure to install steering knuckle and adjust wheel bearings, bleed brakes. Torque backing plate bolts and ball joint castellated nuts to specifications.

STEERING GEAR REPLACE

1. Raise vehicle.
2. Remove pitman arm nut and

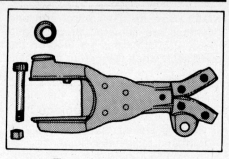

Fig. 5 Lower control arm

washer, mark relationship of shaft to arm. Using a puller remove pitman arm from pitman shaft.
3. Remove engine stone shield.
4. Remove lower clamp to flexible coupling bolts.
5. Remove steering gear to frame bolts and remove steering gear from vehicle.

Installation

1. Place gear in position and install mounting bolts finger tight.
2. Install steering gear flexible coupling bolts and torque to 18 ft. lbs.
3. Tighten steering column mounting bolts.
4. Torque steering gear mounting bolts. Long bolts to 70 ft. lbs. for 1972 and 55 ft. lbs. for 1973-77 and all short bolts to 30 ft. lbs. for 1972 and 20 ft. lbs. for 1973-77.
5. Install pitman arm to shaft, lining up marks made during removal. Install washer and torque nut to 165 ft. lbs. for 1972-73 and 160 ft. lbs. for 1974-77.
6. Install engine stone shield.
7. Lower vehicle.

STABILIZER BAR REPLACE

1. Raise and support vehicle.
2. Disconnect stabilizer bar from lower control arms.
3. Remove stabilizer bar brackets and remove stabilizer.
4. Reverse procedure to install.

Fig. 7 Installing control arm bushing

MAZDA

INDEX OF SERVICE OPERATIONS

MAZDA

GENERAL ENGINE SPECIFICATIONS

Year	Engine	Car-buretor	Bore & Stroke (Inch)	Piston Displacement Cubic Inches	Compression Ratio	Maximum Brake H.P. @ R.P.M.	Maximum Torque Ft. Lbs. @ R.P.M.	Normal Oil Pressure Pounds
1972	4-1196cc ①	2 Barrel	2.756 x 2.992	71.3	8.6	73 @ 6000	72 @ 3500	54
	4-1272cc ①	2 Barrel	2.87 x 3.00	77.6	9.2	—	—	50—64
	4-1586cc ①	2 Barrel	3.07 x 3.27	96.8	8.6	104 @ 6000	106 @ 3500	50—64
	4-1796cc ①	2 Barrel	3.07 x 3.70	109.6	8.6	—	—	—
	R100 ②	4 Barrel	—	59.9	9.4	110 @ 7000	100 @ 4000	43—71
	RX-2 ②	4 Barrel	—	70	9.4			36—71
1973-77	4-1272cc ①	2 Barrel	2.87 x 3.00	77.6	9.2	—	—	50—64
	4-1586cc ①	2 Barrel	3.07 x 3.27	96.8	8.6	—	—	50—64
	4-1796cc ①	2 Barrel	3.07 x 3.70	109.6	8.6	—	—	—
	RX-2 & RX-3 ②	4 Barrel	—	70	9.4	—	—	36—71
1974-77	RX-4, Cosmo & Rotary Pickup ②	4 Barrel	—	80	9.2	—	—	71

—Not Available   ①—Piston Engine.   ②—Rotary Engine.

TUNE UP SPECIFICATIONS—PISTON ENGINE

The following specifications are published from the latest information available. This data should be used only in the absence of a decal affixed in the engine compartment.

▲Before removing wires from distributor cap, determine location of the No. 1 wire in cap, as distributor position may have been altered from that shown at the end of this chart.

Year & Model	Spark Plug Type	Gap Inch	Distributor Point Gap Inch	Dwell Angle Deg.	Ignition Timing Firing Order Fig.	Timing BTDC	Mark Fig.	Carburetor Adjustments Hot Idle Speed Std. Trans.	Auto. Trans.	Idle CO% Std. Trans.	Auto. Trans.
1972											
1800	BP-6ES	.032	.020	49—55	⑲	5°	F	725	725	2.5—4.0	—
1200	BP-6ES	.032	.018	55—61	⑲	8°	A	725	—	2.5—4.5	—
618	BP-6ES	.031	.018	49—55	⑲	5°	⑳	725	725	⑥	⑥
808	BP-6ES	.031	.020	49—55	⑲	8°	⑱	750	—	1.5—3.5	—
1973											
618	BP-6ES	.031	.018	49—55	⑲	①	⑳	725	725	.8—1.5	.8—1.5
808	BP-6ES	.031	.020	49—55	⑲	②	⑱	825	825	1.5—2.5	1.5—2.5
B1600	BP-6ES	.031	.020	49—55	⑲	5°	⑱	825	825	1.5—2.5	—
1974											
808	BP-6ES	.031	.020	49—55	⑲	③	⑱	825	825	1.5—2.5	1.5—2.5
B1600	BP-6ES	.031	.020	49—55	⑲	5°	⑱	825		1.5—2.5	
1975											
808	BP-6ES	.031	.020	49—55	⑲	5°	⑱	800	800	⑦	⑦
B1600	BP-6ES	.031	.020	49—55	⑲	5°	⑱	800		1.5	—
1976											
808 (1300)	BP-6ES	.031	.020	49—55	⑲	④	C	800	—	⑨	⑨
808 (1600)	BP-6ES	.031	.020	49—55	⑲	⑤	⑯	700	700	⑩	⑩
B1600	BP-6ES	.031	.020	49—55	⑲	⑤	⑱	800	—	⑩	⑩
1977											
GLC	BP-6ES	.031	⑪	49—55 ⑫	⑲	11°	C	700	600D	1.5—2.5	1.5—2.5
808 (1300)	BP-6ES	.031	⑪	49—55 ⑫	⑲	⑬	C	700	700	1.5—2.5	1.5—2.5
808 (1600)	BP-6ES	.031	.020	49—55	⑲	⑭	⑰	800	650D	⑮	⑮
B1800	BP-6ES	.031	.020	49—55	⑲	8°	A	700	700	1.5—2.5	1.5—2.5

     Continued

TUNE UP SPECIFICATIONS—PISTON ENGINE—Continued

The following specifications are published from the latest information available. This data should be used only in the absence of a decal affixed in the engine compartment.

▲Before removing wires from distributor cap, determine location of the No. 1 wire in cap, as distributor position may have been altered from that shown at the end of this chart.

Year & Model	Spark Plug		Distributor		Ignition Timing			Carburetor Adjustments			
	Type	Gap Inch	Point Gap Inch	Dwell Angle Deg.	Firing Order Fig.	Timing BTDC	Mark Fig.	Hot Idle Speed		Idle CO%	
								Std. Trans.	Auto. Trans.	Std. Trans.	Auto. Trans.
1978											
GLC	—	.031	—	49—55⑫	⑲	㉑		700	600D	2.0	2.0
B1800	—	.031	—	49—55	⑲	8°		700	—	2.0	2.0

—Not Available

①—Auto. trans., 3° BTDC; Manual trans. 5° BTDC.
②—Manual trans., 5° BTDC; Auto trans. exc. wagon, 5° BTDC, Wagon, 8° BTDC.
③—Auto. trans., 8° BTDC; Manual trans., 5° BTDC.
④—Exc. Calif., 7° BTDC; Calif., 11° BTDC.
⑤—Exc. Calif., 5° BTDC; Calif., 8° BTDC.
⑥—Exc. Calif., 2.5—4.0%; Calif., 1.0—1.5%.
⑦—Exc. Calif., Less than 1.5%; Calif., 1.5—2.5%.
⑨—Exc. Calif., .5%; Calif., 1.5—2.5%.
⑩—Exc. Calif., Less than 1.5%; Calif. 1.0—2.0%.
⑪—Exc. Calif., air gap .012″; Calif., point gap, .020
⑫—Calif. only.

⑬—Calif. & high altitude 11° BTDC; Exc. Calif. & high altitude, 7° BTDC. With coupler at accelerator switch disconnected, 11° BTDC.
⑭—Calif., 8° BTDC; Exc. Calif. 5° BTDC, with coupler at accelerator switch disconnected 13° BTDC.
⑮—Exc. Calif., Less than 1.0%; Calif., 1.0—2.0%.
⑯—Exc. Calif., Fig. D; Calif., Fig. B.
⑰—Exc. Calif., Fig. E; Calif., Fig. A.
⑱—Timing mark located on pulley.
⑲—Firing order, 1342; No. 1 cyl. front of engine.
⑳—Exc. Calif., Fig. B; Calif., Fig. F.
㉑—Exc. Calif., Manual trans., 7° BTDC; Calif., & all Auto. trans., 11° BTDC.

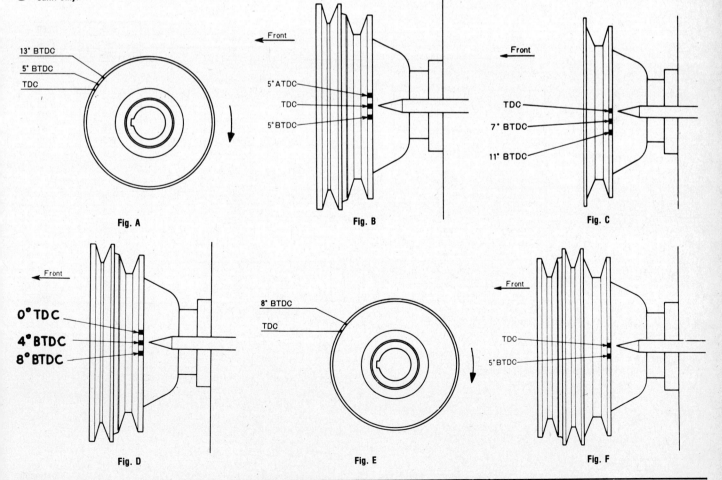

Fig. A   Fig. B   Fig. C

Fig. D   Fig. E   Fig. F

MAZDA

TUNE UP SPECIFICATIONS—ROTARY ENGINE

The following specifications are published from the latest information available. This
data should be used only in the absence of a decal affixed in the engine compartment.

▲Before removing wires from distributor cap, determine location of the No. 1 wire in cap,
as distributor position may have been altered from that shown at the end of this chart.

Year & Model	Spark Plug Type	Gap Inch	Point Gap Inch	Dwell Angle Deg.	Firing Order Fig.	Timing ATDC Leading Dist. Normal	Leading Dist. Retarded	Trailing Dist.	Mark Fig.	Hot Idle Speed Std. Trans.	Auto. Trans.
1972											
R100	B-8EE	.028	.018	55—61		TDC	20°	10°	A	935	—
RX-2	—	.028	.108	55—61		TDC	10°	10°	A	935	—
1973											
RX-2	B-7EM	.028	.018	55—61		TDC	10°	10°	A	900	750D
RX-3	B-7EM	.028	.018	55—61		TDC	10°	10°	A	900	750D
1974											
RX-2	B-7EM	.026	.018	55—61		5°	—	10°	B	900	750D
RX-3	B-7EM	.026	.018	55—61		5°	—	10°	B	900	750D
RX-4	B-7EM	.026	.018	55—61		5°	—	15°	B	900	750D
Pickup	B-7EM	.026	.018	55—61		5°	—	15°	B	900	750D
1975											
RX-3	B-7EM	.026	.018	55—61		TDC	20°	15°	C	800	750D
RX-4	B-7EM	.026	.018	55—61		TDC	20°	15°	C	800	750D
Pickup	B-7EM	.026	.018	55—61		TDC	—	15°	C	800	750D
1976											
RX-3	B-7ET	.041	.018	③		TDC	20°	15°	C	700	700D
RX-4	B-7ET	.041	.018	③		5°	20°	20°	D	700	700D
Cosmo	B-7ET	.041	.018	③		5°	20°	20°	D	700	700D
Pickup ①	B-7EM	.026	.018	③		TDC	20°	15°	C	800	750D
Pickup ②	B-7EM	.026	.018	55—61		TDC	—	15°	C	800	750D
1977											
RX-3	B-7ET	.041	.018	55—61		TDC	—	20°	A	750	750D
RX-4	B-6ET	.041	.018	55—61		5°	—	25°	A	750	750D
Cosmo	B-6ET	.041	.018	55—61		5°	—	25°	A	750	750D
1978											
RX-3	—	.041	—	55—61		TDC	—	20°	—	750	750D
RX-4	—	.041	—	55—61		5°	—	25°	—	750	750D
Cosmo	—	.041	—	55—61		5°	—	25°	—	750	750D

—Not Available
① —Calif.
② —Exc. Calif.
③ —Trailing 55—61°: Leading (normal), 55—61°; Leading (Retard), 50—56°.

Continued

TUNE UP SPECIFICATIONS—ROTARY ENGINE—NOTES—Continued

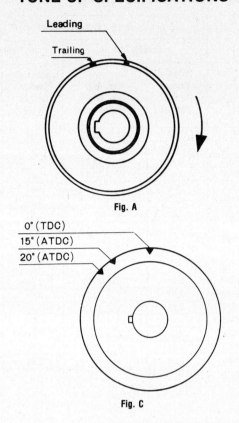

Fig. A

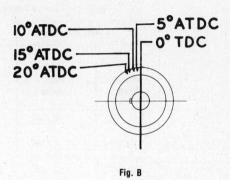

Fig. B

Fig. C

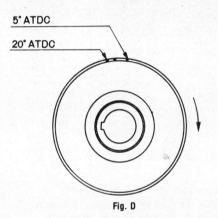

Fig. D

DISTRIBUTOR SPECIFICATIONS—PISTON ENGINE

If unit is checked on vehicle, double the RPM and degrees to get crankshaft figures.

Year	Model	Centrifugal Advance Degrees @ RPM of Distributor		Vacuum Advance	
		Advance Starts	Full Advance	Inches of Vacuum To Start Plunger	Max. Advance Distributor Degrees @ Vacuum
1972	1200	0 @ 600	14 @ 2250	5.12	8.5 @ 11.02
	1800	0 @ 600	9 @ 2600	3.94	8 @ 11.81
	618	0 @ 600	14 @ 2200	①	②
	808	0 @ 550	11 @ 2000	12.6	7.5 @ 21.65
1973-74	618	0 @ 600	14 @ 2200	①	②
	808	0 @ 550	11 @ 2000	12.6	7.5 @ 21.65
	B1600	0 @ 550	11 @ 2000	12.6	7.5 @ 21.65
1975	808	0 @ 550	11 @ 2000	③	④
	B1600	0 @ 550	11 @ 2000	10.63	7.5 @ 19.69
1976	808 (1300)	0 @ 600	12.5 @ 2750	4.72	⑤
	808 (1600)	0 @ 550	11 @ 2000	⑥	⑦
	B1600	—	—	—	—
1977	GLC	0 @ 600	12.5 @ 2750	8.66	6 @ 15.35
	808 (1300)	0 @ 600	12.5 @ 2750	4.72	⑤
	808 (1600)	0 @ 550	11 @ 2000	⑥	⑦
	B1800	0 @ 600	10 @ 1950	—	9 @ 11.81

—Not Available
① —Manual trans., 10.63''; Auto. trans., 12.6''.
② —Manual trans., 7.5° @ 19.69''; Auto. trans., 7.5° @ 21.65''.
③ —Exc. Calif., 10.63''; Calif. 8.66''.
④ —Exc. Calif., 7.5° @ 19.69''; Calif. 7.5° @ 17.72''.
⑤ —Exc. Calif., 11° @ 13.8''; Calif., 11° @ 14.2''.
⑥ —Exc. Calif., 10.63''; Calif., auto. trans., 6.3''; Manual trans., 4.72''.
⑦ —Exc. Calif., 7.5 @ 19.69; Calif., auto. trans., 9° @ 11.02''; Manual trans., 9° @ 9.45''.

Continued

MAZDA

DISTRIBUTOR SPECIFICATIONS—ROTARY ENGINE

Year	Model	Centrifugal Advance Degrees @ RPM of Distributor				Vacuum Advance			
		Leading Dist.		Trailing Dist.		Leading Dist.		Trailing Dist.	
		Advance Starts	Full Advance	Advance Starts	Full Advance	Inches of Vacuum To Start Plunger	Max. Adv. Dist. Deg. @ Vacuum	Inches of Vacuum To Start Plunger	Max. Adv. Dist. Deg. @ Vacuum
1972	R100	0 @ 500	5 @ 1500	—	—	3.94	11 @ 15.75	3.94	5 @ 13.78
	RX-2	—	—	—	—	—	—	—	—
1973	RX-2	0 @ 500	10 @ 1500	0 @ 500	7.5 @ 2000	3.94	11 @ 15.75	5.9	13 @ 15.75
	RX-3	0 @ 500	10 @ 1500	0 @ 500	7.5 @ 2000	3.94	11 @ 15.75	5.9	13 @ 15.75
1974	RX-2	0 @ 500	7.5 @ 1500	0 @ 500	7.5 @ 1500	—	—	3.94	8.5 @ 15.75
	RX-3	0 @ 500	7.5 @ 1500	0 @ 500	7.5 @ 1500	—	—	3.94	8.5 @ 15.75
	RX-4	0 @ 500	10 @ 2000	0 @ 500	10 @ 2000	—	—	3.94	①
	RE-Pickup	0 @ 500	10 @ 2000	0 @ 500	②	—	—	3.94	①
1975	RX-3	0 @ 500	7.5 @ 1250	0 @ 500	7.5 @ 1250	—	—	—	—
	RX-4	0 @ 500	10 @ 1750	0 @ 500	10 @ 1750	—	—	—	—
	RE-Pickup	0 @ 500	10 @ 1750	0 @ 500	10 @ 1750	—	—	—	—
1976	RX-3	0 @ 500	10 @ 1500	0 @ 500	10 @ 1500	3.94	7.5 @ 15.75	3.94	15 @ 15.75
	RX-4	0 @ 500	12.5 @ 2000	0 @ 500	12.5 @ 2000	3.94	5 @ 15.75	3.94	17.5 @ 15.75
	Cosmo	0 @ 500	12.5 @ 2000	0 @ 500	12.5 @ 2000	3.94	5 @ 15.75	3.94	17.5 @ 15.75
	RE-Pickup	0 @ 500	10 @ 1750	0 @ 500	10 @ 1750	—	—	—	—
1977	RX-3	0 @ 500	10 @ 1500	0 @ 500	10 @ 1500	3.94	7.5 @ 15.75	7.87③	15 @ 15.75③
	RX-4	0 @ 500	12.5 @ 2000	0 @ 500	12.5 @ 2000	3.94	5 @ 15.75	3.94	17.5 @ 15.75
	Cosmo	0 @ 500	12.5 @ 2000	0 @ 500	12.5 @ 2000	3.94	5 @ 15.75	3.94	17.5 @ 15.75

—Not Available
①—Manual trans., 15° @ 15.75″; Auto. trans., 13° @ 15.75″.
②—Manual trans., 10° @ 1500; Auto. trans. 10 @ 2000.
③—Manual trans. only.

ALTERNATOR & REGULATOR SPECIFICATIONS

Year	Model	Alternator		Regulator							
		Rated Output Amps.	Output @ 14V, 2500 RPM Amps	Constant Voltage Relay			Pilot Lamp Relay			Regulated Voltage @ 2000 R.P.M.
				Air Gap	Point Gap	Back Gap	Air Gap	Point Gap	Back Gap	
1972	1200	—	20	.027—.043	.012—.016	.027—.043	.035—.047	.027—.043	.027—.043	14—15
1972	1800	—	32	.028—.043	.012—.016	.030—.043	—	—	—	13.5—14.5
1972	R100	—	26.5	.028—.043	.012—.016	.030—.043	—	—	—	13.5—14.5
1972-73	618	—	32	.028—.043	.012—.016	.028—.043	.035—.047	.028—.043	.028—.043	14—15
1972-74	808	—	①	.028—.043	.012—.016	.028—.043	—	—	—	13.5—14.5
1972	RX-2	—	—	—	—	—	—	—	—	—
1973—74	B1600	—	28	.028—.043	.012—.016	.028—.043	.035—.047	.028—.043	.028—.043	14—15
1973	RX-2	—	32	.028—.043	.012—.016	.028—.043	—	—	—	13.5—14.5
1973	RX-3	—	32	.028—.043	.012—.016	.028—.043	—	—	—	13.5—14.5
1974	RX-2	63	56	.028—.043	.012—.016	.028—.043	.035—.047	.028—.043	.028—.043	13.5—14.5
1974	RX-3	50	40	.028—.043	.012—.016	.028—.043	.035—.047	.028—.043	.028—.043	13.5—14.5
1974	RX-4	63	56	.028—.043	.012—.016	.028—.043	.035—.047	.028—.043	.028—.043	13.5—14.5
1974-76	RE-Pickup	50	40	.028—.051	.012—.018	.028—.059	.035—.055	.028—.043	.028—.059	14—15
1975-77	808	—	40	.028—.051	.012—.018	.028—.059	.035—.055	.028—.043	.028—.059	14—15
1975-76	B1600	—	28	.028—.051	.012—.018	.028—.059	.035—.055	.028—.043	.028—.059	14—15
1975-77	RX-3	50	40	.028—.051	.012—.018	.028—.059	.035—.055	.028—.043	.028—.059	14—15
1975-77	RX-4	63	56	.028—.051	.012—.018	.028—.059	.035—.055	.028—.043	.028—.059	14—15
1976-77	Cosmo	63	56	.028—.051	.012—.018	.028—.059	.035—.055	.028—.043	.028—.059	14—15
1977	GLC	—	30	.028—.051	.012—.018	.028—.059	.039—.059	.020—.035	.028—.059	14—15
1977	B1800	—	30	.028—.051	.012—.018	.028—.059	.039—.059	.020—.035	.028—.059	14—15

—Not Available
①—With 1300cc engine, 28 amp; with 1600cc engine, 32 amp.

Continued

MAZDA

STARTER MOTOR SPECIFICATIONS

Year	Model	No Load Test			Torque Test			Min. Brush Length in.	Brush Spring Tension ounces
		Amps	Volts	RPM	Amps	Volts	Torque Ft. Lbs.		
1972-73	RX2 & RX3 ①	70	12	3,600	600	6	19.5	—	56.3
	RX2 & RX3 ②	100	12	1,700	1,200	4	43.4	—	56.3
1974-76	RX2 & RX3 ①	75	11.5	4,900	780	5	8	.45	49—63
1974-76	RX2 & RX3 ②	100	11.5	7,800	1,100	5	17.4	.45	49—63
1974-76	RX4 & Rotary Pick-up ①	75	11.5	4,900	780	5	8	.45	49—63
1974-76	RX4 & Rotary Pick-up ②	100	11.5	7,800	1,100	5	17.4	.45	49—63
1977	RX3SP & RX4 ①	50	11.5	5,600	600	5	6.9	.45	49—63
1977	RX3SP & RX4 ②	100	11.5	6,600	1,050	5	15.9	.45	49—63
1976	Cosmo ①	75	11.5	4,900	780	5	8	.45	49—63
1976	Cosmo ②	100	11.5	7,800	1,100	5	17.4	.45	49—63
1977	Cosmo ①	50	11.5	5,600	600	5	6.9	.45	49—63
1977	Cosmo ②	100	11.5	6,600	1,050	5	15.9	.45	49—63
1972-74	808 (1300)	53	10.5	5,000	400	6	6.7	.45	49—63
1972-74	808 (1600)	60	11.5	6,000	560	7.5	9.4	.45	49—63
1975-77	808	53	10.5	5,000	400	6	6.7	.45	49—63
1977	GLC	53	11.5	6,800	310	5	5.4	.45	46—60
1972-73	B1600	60	11.5	6,000	560	7.5	9.4	.16	35—56
1974	B1600	—	—	—	—	—	—	—	—
1975	B1600	53	10.5	5,000	400	6	6.7	.45	49—63
1972	1800	50	11	5,000	470	7.7	9.4	.45	41.6
1977	B1800	53	11.5	6,800	310	5	5.4	.45	49—63

—Not Available
① —Manual trans.
② —Automatic trans.

VALVE SPECIFICATIONS—PISTON ENGINE

	Valve Lash		Valve Angles		Valve Spring Pressure Lbs. @ inches		Stem Clearance		Stem Diameter	
	Int.	Ext.	Seat	Face	Inner	Outer	Intake	Exhaust	Intake	Exhaust
1200	.010	.010	45	45	—	46.3 @ 1.378	.0008—.0026	.0016—.0034	.2756	.2756
1300	.010	.012	45	45	17.9 @ 1.260	36.6 @ 1.319	.0007—.0021	.0007—.0023	.3142	.3142
1600	.012	.012	45	45	17.9 @ 1.260	26.7 @ 1.339	.0007—.0021	.0007—.0023	.3142	.3140
1800	.012	.012	45	45	19.84 @ 1.1811	37.04 @ 1.2402	.0010—.0028	.0020—.0037	.3142	.3140

—Not Available

PISTONS, PINS, RINGS, CRANKSHAFT & BEARINGS—PISTON ENGINE

Engine	Piston Clearance Top of Skirt	Ring End Gap ①		Wrist Pin Diameter	Rod Bearing		Main Bearing		
		Comp.	Oil		Shaft Diameter	Bearing Clearance	Shaft Diameter	Bearing Clearance	Shaft End Play
1200	.0017—.0022	.008	.008	.7874	1.7717	.0011—.0029	2.2048	.0010—.0020	.0043—.0108
1300	.0021—.0026	.008	.008	.7874	1.7717	.0011—.0029	2.4804	.0012—.0024	.003—.009
1600	.0022—.0028	.008	.008	.8662	2.0866	.0011—.0030	2.4804	.0012—.0024	.003—.009
1800	.0022—.0028	.008	.012	.8662	2.0866	.0011—.0030	2.4804	.0012—.0024	.003—.009

① —Fit rings in tapered bores for clearance listed in tightest portion of ring travel.

Continued

MAZDA

SEAL SPECIFICATIONS—ROTARY ENGINE

Year	Model	Corner Seal Outside Diameter	Side Seal		Oil Seal Contact Width of Lip		Apex Seal	
			Thickness	Width	Desired	Max.	Normal Height	Height Limit
1972-73	All	.4331	.0394	.1378	.008	.0315	.3937	.315
1974-77	All	.433	.039	.138	.008	.031	.335	.276

ROTOR AND HOUSING SPECIFICATIONS—ROTARY ENGINE

Model	Housing						Rotor		
	Rotor		Intermediate		Front & Rear		Side Clearance	Min. Protrusion of land	Max. Protrusion of land
	Width	Distortion Max.	Distortion Max.	Wear Max.	Distortion Max.	Wear Max.			
R100	2.3622	.0020	.0020	.0040	.0020	.0040	—	.004	.006
RX2 & RX3	2.7559	.0020	.0020	.0040	.0020	.0040	①	.003	.008
All Others	3.1438	.0024	.0016	.0039	.0016	.0039	.0039—.0083	.003	.008

—Not Available
①—1972-73, .0051—.0067; 1974-77, .0039—.0083.

SEAL CLEARANCES—ROTARY ENGINE

	Model	Corner Seal		Side Seal						Apex Seals			
		To Rotor Groove		To Rotor Groove		To Corner Seal				To Side Housing		To Rotor Groove	
		Desired	Max.	Desired	Max.	Desired	Max.			Desired	Max.	Desired	Max.
1972	R100	.0013—.0024	.003	.0016—.0028	.004	.0051—.0098	.016			.0004—.0020	.0059	.0014—.0028	.004
1972-73	RX2 & RX3	.0008—.0019	.0031	.001—.003	.004	.002—.006	.016			.0020—.0028	.0039	.0014—.0028	.004
1974-77	All Others	.0008—.0019	.0031	.0012—.0028	.004	.002—.006	.016			.0051—.0067	.012	.0020—.0035	.006

ECCENTRIC SHAFT SPECIFICATIONS—ROTARY ENGINE

Model	Eccentric Shaft End-Play		Max. Shaft Runout	Journal Diameter		Oil Clearance	
	Desired	Maximum		Main Bearing	Rotor Bearing	Main Bearing	Rotor Bearing
R100	.0016—.0028	.0035	.0012	1.6923—1.6929	2.9134	.0016—.0024	.0016—.0031
Exc. R100	.0016—.0028	.0035	.0024 ①	1.6917—1.6935	2.9134	.0016—.0039	.0016—.0039

①—1972-73 RX2 & 3, Less than .0008.

CAMSHAFT SPECIFICATIONS

Year	Engine	Lobe Lift		Bearing Clearance			Journal Diameter			Basic cam Circle @ Inches	Max. Run-out @ Inches	End Play @ Inches	
		Intake @ Inches	Exhaust @ Inches	Front @ Inches	Center @ Inches	Rear @ Inches	Front @ Inches	Center @ Inches	Rear @ Inches			New	Used
1972-77	4-1300	1.7369③	1.7369③	.0014-.0030	.0026-.0042	.0014-.0030	1.6536	1.6536	1.6536	1.4961	.0012	.001-.007	.008
1972-77	4-1600, 1800	1.7731①	1.7784②	.0007-.0027	.0011-.0031	.0007-.0027	1.7717	1.7717	1.7717	1.4961	.0012	.001-.007	.008

①—Wear limit, 1.7653.
②—Wear limit, 1.7640.
③—Wear limit, 1.7290.

TIGHTENING SPECIFICATIONS—PISTON ENGINE

★Torque specifications are for clean and lightly lubricated threads only. Dry or dirty threads produce increased friction which prevents accurate measurement of tightness.

Year	Engine model	Spark Plugs Ft. Lbs.	Cylinder Head Bolts Ft. Lbs.	Intake Manifold Ft. Lbs.	Exhaust Manifold Ft. Lbs.	Rocker Arm Shaft Bracket Ft. Lbs.	Rocker Arm Cover Ft. Lbs.	Connecting Rod Cap Bolts Ft. Lbs.	Main Bearing Cap Bolts Ft. Lbs.	Flywheel to crankshaft Ft. Lbs.	Vibration Damper or Pulley Ft. Lbs.
1972	1200	15	50	16	16	50	6.5	28	45	63	65
1972-74	1300	15	⑥	20	15	⑥	2.2	25.5	47	60	80
1975-77	1300	11—15	①	14—19	②	①	1.1—1.4	36—40	61—65	112—118	101—108
1972-77	1600	11—15	①	14—19	③	①	1.1—1.4	36—40	61—65	112—118	101—108
1972-77	1800	11—15	①	14—19	12—17	①	1.1—1.4	④	61—65	112—118	⑤

①—Cold, 56—60 ft. lbs., Warm, 69—72 ft. lbs.
②—1975-76, 16—21 ft. lbs.; 1977, 12—17 ft. lbs.
③—1972-74, 12—17 ft. lbs.; 1975-77, 16—21 ft. lbs.
④—1972-73, 30-33 ft. lbs.; 1974-77, 36—40 ft. lbs.
⑤—1972-73, 80—94 ft. lbs; 1977, 101—108 ft. lbs.
⑥—Cold, 50 ft. lbs.; Warm, 54 ft. lbs.

TIGHTENING SPECIFICATIONS—ROTARY ENGINE

★Torque specifications are for clean and lightly lubricated threads only. Dry or dirty threads produce increased friction which prevents accurate measurement of tightness.

Engine Model	Spark Plug	Tension Bolts	Eccentric Shaft Pulley Bolt	Intake Manifold	Exhaust Manifold	Flywheel Lock Nut
R100	14	18	50	—	—	350
RX2 & RX3①	10—14	18—20	45—50	15	30	350
RX2 & RX3②	9—13	23—27	③	12—17	23	289—362
RX4	9—13	23—27	③	12—17	—	289—362
Pick-up	9—13	23—27	72—87	12—17	—	289—362
Cosmo	9—13	23—27	③	12—17	—	289—362

—Not Available
①—1972-73.
②—1974-76.
③—1974-76, 54—69 ft. lbs.; 1977, 72—87 ft. lbs.

WHEEL ALIGNMENT SPECIFICATIONS

Year	Model	Caster Angle, Degrees		Camber Angle, Degrees		Toe-In	King Pin Inclination
		Limits	Desired	Limits	Desired	Inch	
1972	1200	—	+2½	—	+5/6	0 to .24	+8 1/6
	1800	+1/6 to +5/6	+½	+2/3 to +1 1/3	+1	0 to .20	+8
	618	0 to +1½	+¾	−¼ to +1¾	+¾	0 to .24	+8¾
	808	+¾ to +1¼	+1	−2/3 to +2/3	0	0 to .24	+8 4/5
	R100	—	+2	—	+59/60	.04 to .12	+8 1/60
	RX-2	+¼ to +1¾	+1 1/20	−¼ to +1 2/3	+¾	0 to .24	+8¾
1973	618	0 to +1½	+¾	−¼ to +¾	+¾	0 to .24	+8¾
	808	+¾ to +1¼	+1	−2/3 to +2/3	0	0 to .24	+8 4/5
	B1600	+2/3 to +1 1/3	+1	+1 2/30 to +1 21/30	+1 11/30	0 to .24	+7 3/5
	RX-2	+¼ to +1¾	+1 1/20	−¼ to +1¾	+¾	0 to .24	+8¾
	RX-3	—	+1¼	—	+2/3	0 to .24	+8 4/5
1974	808	+¾ to 1¼	+1	−2/3 to +2/3	0	0 to .24	+8 4/5
	B1600	+2/3 to +1 1/3	+1	+1 to +1 21/30	+1 11/30	0 to .24	+7 3/5
	RX-2	+¼ to +1¾	+1 1/20	−¼ to +1¾	+¾	0 to .24	+8¾
	RX-3	—	+1¼	—	+2/3	0 to .24	+8 4/5
	RX-4	+1¼ to +2¾	+2	0 to +2	+1	0 to .24	+9¾
	RE-Pickup	+1 9/15 to +2 4/15	+1 14/15	−1/12 to +7/12	+¼	0 to .24	+8 2/3
1975	808	+1 1/12 to +2 7/12	+1 5/6	−¼ to +1¾	+¾	0 to .24	+8¾
	B1600	+2/3 to +1 1/3	+1	+1 1/15 to +1 21/30	+1 11/30	0 to .24	+7 3/5
	RX-3	+1 1/6 to +2 2/3	+1 11/12	−1/12 to +1 11/12	+11/12	0 to .24	+8 7/12
	RX-4	+1¼ to +2¾	+2	0 to +2	+1	0 to .24	+9¾
	RE-Pickup	+13/15 to +1 8/15	+1 1/5	−1/12 to +7/12	+¼	0 to .24	+8¾
1976	808 (1300)	①	②	−1/6 to +1 5/6	+5/6	0 to .24	③
	808 (1600)	④	⑤	0 to +2	+1	0 to .24	+8½
	B1600	—	+1	—	+1 1/3	0 to .24	—
	RX-3	⑥	⑦	⑧	⑨	0 to .24	⑩
	RX-4	+1 1/12 to +2 7/12	+1 5/6	⑪	⑫	0 to .24	⑬
	Cosmo	⑭	⑮	−1 to +2	+1	0 to .24	+9¾
	RE-Pickup	+1 9/15 to +2 4/15	+1 14/15	−1/12 to +7/12	+¼	0	+8¾
1977	GLC	+¾ to +2¼	+1 35/60	−1/3 to +1 2/3	+2/3	0 to .24	+8 5/6
	808 (1300)	⑯	⑰	⑱	⑲	0 to .24	⑳
	808 (1600)	㉑	㉒	㉓	㉔	0 to .24	㉕
	B1800	+2/3 to +1 1/3	+1	+½ to +1¼	+¾	0 to .24	+8¼
	RX-3	—	—	—	—	0 to .24	—
	RX-4	+1 1/12 to +2¾	+1 5/6	⑪	⑫	0 to .24	⑬
	Cosmo	⑭	⑮	−1 to +2	+1	0 to .24	+9¾

—Not Available
①—Sedan, +1 1/12 to +2 7/12 ; Coupe & wagon +11/12 to +2 5/12
②—Sedan, +1 5/6; Coupe & wagon, +1 2/3
③—Sedan & coupe, +8 2/3; wagon, +8 7/12
④—Sedan, +5/6 to +2 1/3; coupe, +¾ to +2¼; Wagon +11/12 to +2 5/12
⑤—Sedan, 1 7/12; Coupe, +1½; Wagon, +1 2/3
⑥—Sedan, +11/12 to +2 5/12; Coupe, +1 2/12 to 2¾; Wagon, +5/6 to +2¼
⑦—Sedan, 1 2/3; Coupe, 1 11/12; Wagon, 1 7/12
⑧—Sedan & coupe, −2/12 to +1 5/6; Wagon, −1/12 to +1 11/12
⑨—Sedan & coupe, +5/6; Wagon, +11/12
⑩—Sedan & coupe, +8 2/3; Wagon, +8½
⑪—Sedan, +1/30 to +2 1/30; Hardtop, 0 to +2; Wagon, +¼ to +2¼
⑫—Sedan, +1 1/30; Hardtop, +1; Wagon, +1¼
⑬—Sedan, +9 2/3; Hardtop, +9¾; Wagon, +9½
⑭—Power steering, +1.5 to +3; Manual steering +¾ to +2¼
⑮—Power steering, +2¼; Manual steering, +1½
⑯—Sedan & wagon, +1 1/12 to +2 7/12; Coupe +1 to +2½
⑰—Sedan & wagon +1 5/6; Coupe, +1¾
⑱—Sedan −1/6 to +1 5/6; Coupe, −1/12 to +1 11/12; Wagon, +0 to +2
⑲—Sedan +5/6; Coupe, +11/12; Wagon, +1
⑳—Sedan, +8 2/3; Coupe, +8 7/12; Wagon, +8½
㉑—Sedan & wagon, +1 1/12 to +2 7/12; Coupe, +1 1/3 to +2 5/6
㉒—Sedan & wagon, +2 5/6; Coupe, +2 1/12
㉓—Sedan & coupe, +1/12 to +2 1/12; Wagon, +1¼
㉔—Sedan & coupe, +1 1/12; Wagon, +1¼
㉕—Sedan & coupe, +8 5/12; Wagon, 8¼

MAZDA

BRAKE SPECIFICATIONS

Year	Model	Brake Drum Inside Diameter	Wheel Cylinder Bore Diameter			Master Cylinder Bore Diameter	Disc Brake Rotor Specifications				
			Disc Brake	Front Drum Brake	Rear Drum Brake		Nominal Thickness	Minimum Refinish Thickness	Thickness Variation Parallelism	Lateral Run-out (T.I.R.)	Finish (Micro-Inch)
1972	1800	7.874	—	—	¾	⅞	.4724	—	—	.0020	—
	1200	7.87	1.894	⅞	¾	①	.3940	—	—	.0012	—
	618	7.874	2.1248	—	11/16	⅞	.4724	.4331	—	.0030	—
	808	7.874	—	—	11/16	¾	.4330	.3940	—	.0030	—
	R100	—	—	—	—	11/16	.3937	—	—	.0059	—
	RX-2	7.874	2.1248	—	11/16	⅞	.4724	.4331	—	.0030	—
1973	618	7.874	2.1248	—	11/16	⅞	.4724	.4331	—	.0030	—
	808	7.874	—	—	11/16	¾	.4330	.3940	—	.0030	—
	B1600	10.236	—	1	13/16	¾	—	—	—	—	—
	RX-2	7.874	2.1248	—	11/16	⅞	.4724	.4331	—	.0030	—
	RX-3	7.874	—	—	¾	⅞	.4330	.3940	—	.0030	—
1974	808	7.874	—	—	11/16	¾	.4330	.3940	—	.0030	—
	B1600	—	—	—	—	—	—	—	—	—	—
	RX-2	7.874	2.1248	—	11/16	⅞	.4724	.4331	—	.0030	—
	RX-3	7.874	—	—	¾	⅞	.4330	.3940	—	.0030	—
	RX-4	9	2.1248	—	11/16	⅞	.4724	.4331	—	.0039	—
	RE-Pickup	10.236	2.1248	—	¾	⅞	.4724	.4331	—	.0039	—
1975	808	7.874	2.0118	—	11/16	13/16	.4331	.3937	—	.0039	—
	B1600	10.236	—	1	13/16	¾	—	—	—	—	—
	RX-3	7.874	2.0118	—	⅝	13/16	.4331	.3937	—	.0039	—
	RX-4	9	2.1248	—	11/16	⅞	.4724	.4331	—	.0039	—
	RE-Pickup	10.236	2.1248	—	¾	⅞	.4724	.4331	—	.0039	—
1976	808	7.874	2.0118	—	11/16	13/16	4.331	.3937	—	.0039	—
	B1600	—	—	—	—	—	—	—	—	—	—
	RX-3	7.874	2.0118	—	⅝	13/16	.4331	.3937	—	.0029	—
	RX-4	9	2.1248	—	11/16	⅞	4.724	.4331	—	.0039	—
	Cosmo	—	②	—	—	⅞	③	④	—	.0039	—
	RE-Pickup	10.236	2.1248	—	¾	⅞	.4724	.4331	—	.0039	—
1977	GLC	7.874	2.0	—	¾	13/16	.5118	.4724	—	.0024	—
	808	7.874	2.0118	—	¾	13/16	.4331	.3937	—	.0039	—
	B1800	10.236	2.1248	—	¾	⅞	.4724	.4331	—	.0039	—
	RX-3	7.874	—	—	—	—	—	.3940	—	.0039	—
	RX-4	9	2.1248	—	11/16	⅞	.4724	.4331	—	.0039	—
	Cosmo	—	②	—	—	⅞	③	④	—	⑤	—

—Not Available
①—Without disc brakes, ¾"; with disc brakes, 11/16".
②—Front, 2.0"; Rear, 1.3752".
③—Front, .7087"; Rear, .3937".
④—Front, .6693"; Rear, .3543".
⑤—Front, .0024"; Rear, .0039".

COOLING SYSTEM & CAPACITY DATA

Year	Model	Cooling Capacity Pts.		Radiator Cap Relief Pressure, Lbs.	Thermo. Opening Temp. F.	Fuel Tank Gals.	Engine Oil Refill Pints	Transmission Oil			Rear Axle Oil Pints
		No Heater	With Heater					3 & 4 Speed Pints	5 Speed Pints	Auto. Trans. Qts.	
1972	1200	8.7	9.7	13	190	①	6.34	2.7	—	—	1.7
1972	1800	14.8	16.1	13	180	13.2	7.6	2.8	—	8	2.5
1972-73	618	—	16	13	180	13	8.2	3	—	—	2.6
1972-77	808 (1300)	10.6	11.6	13	180	②	6.4	2.8	—	—	2.2
1972-77	808 (1600)	—	15.8	13	180	③	7.6	3.2	—	5.8	3
1972	R100	13	15	12.8	170	16	—	2.7	—	—	2.5
1972-74	RX-2	14.8	16.9	12.8	180	16.9	11.6	5.3	—	—	2.5
1973-76	B1600	—	13.6	13	180	11.7	7.6	3	—	—	2.8
1973	RX-3	14.8	16.9	12.8	180	④	11	—	—	—	—
1974	RX-3	—	20.5	13	180	④	11	—	—	—	—
1974	RX-4	—	21	13	180	⑤	13.5	3.6	4.6	6.6	3
1974-76	RE-Pick-up	—	20.5	13	190	21	13.5	3.6	4.6	6.6	2.8

COOLING SYSTEM & CAPACITY DATA—Continued

Year	Model	Cooling Capacity Pts.		Radiator Cap Relief Pressure, Lbs.	Thermo. Opening Temp. F.	Fuel Tank Gals.	Engine Oil Refill Pints	Transmission Oil			Rear Axle Oil Pints
		No Heater	With Heater					3 & 4 Speed Pints	5 Speed Pints	Auto. Trans. Qts.	
1975	RX-3	—	19.2	13	180	⑥	11	3.6	—	6.6	3
1975	RX-4	—	20	13	180	⑦	13.5	3.6	4.6	6.6	2.8
1976-77	RX-3	17.6	19.6	13	190	④	11	3.6	4.6	6.6	3
1976	RX-4	—	20	13	190	⑤	13.5	3.6	4.6	6.6	2.8
1976-77	Cosmo	—	20	13	180	⑧	13.5	—	3.6	6.6	2.6
1977	GLC	10.6	11.6	13	180	10.6	6.4	2.8	3.6	6	1.6
1977	B1800	14	15.2	13	180	⑨	8.2	3	3.6	—	2.8
1977	RX-4	—	20	13	180	⑦	13.5	3	3.6	6.6	2.6

—Not Available

①—Sedan, 10.6 gals.; Estate, 9.2 gals.
②—Sedan & coupe, 11.7 gals.; Wagon 10.4 gals.
③—1975-76 Sedan & coupe, 11.9 gals.; Wagons, 10.4 gals.; 1977 Sedan & coupe 11.1 gals.; Wagons, 10.6 gals.
④—Sedan & coupe, 15.6 gals.; Wagon, 14.3 gals.

⑤—Sedan & hardtop, 16.9 gals.; Wagons, 17.4 gals.
⑥—Sedan & coupe, 15.9 gals.; Wagon, 14.5 gals.
⑦—Sedan & coupe, 17.2 gals.; Wagon, 17.7 gals.
⑧—1976, 16.9 gals.; 1977, 17.2 gals.
⑨—Short body, 14.8 gals.; Long body, 17.4 gals.

Electrical Section

DISTRIBUTOR, REPLACE
Except Rotary Engine

Removal

1. Rotate crankshaft in direction of rotation until the ignition timing mark (No. 1 piston should be in compression stroke) on crankshaft pulley is in line with indicator pin on timing chain cover.
2. Remove distributor cap and disconnect vacuum tube from distributor.
3. Disconnect primary wire at distributor.
4. Remove distributor lock bolt.
5. Slide distributor out of cylinder head.

NOTE: Do not crank engine after dis-

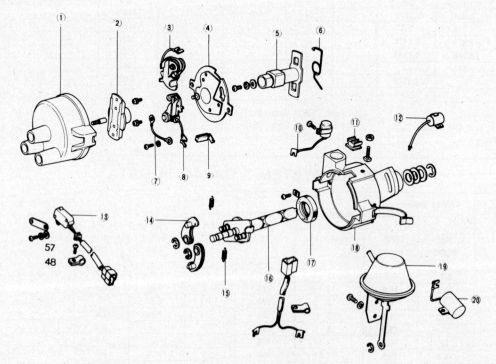

1. Cap
2. Rotor
3. Contact point
4. Breaker base
5. Cam
6. Hair pin spring
7. Earth wire
8. Contact point
9. Felt
10. Condenser
11. Terminal
12. Condenser
13. Vacuum switch (Trailing)
14. Governor
15. Governor spring
16. Shaft
17. Oil seal
18. Housing
19. Vacuum control unit
20. Condenser

Fig. 1 Disassembled view of distributor. Rotary engine models

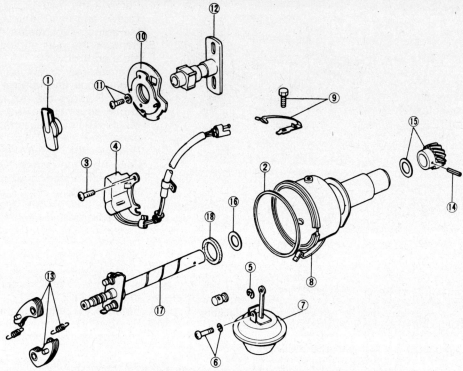

1. Rotor
2. Rubber seal
3. Screw
4. Pick-up coil
5. Clip
6. Screw/washer
7. Vacuum control unit
8. Retaining clip/screw
9. Retaining clip/screw
10. Pick-up coil plate
11. Screw/washer
12. Cam
13. Governor/spring
14. Retaining pin
15. Driven gear/washer
16. Thrust washer
17. Shaft
18. Oil seal

Fig. 2 Disassembled view of distributor. Breakerless type distributor

tributor has been removed.

Installation

1. Align marks on distributor housing and driven gear.
2. Install distributor and lock bolt.
3. Rotate distributor housing to clockwise until contact points close, then, turn it counterclockwise and stop it when contact points just start to separate. Tighten lock bolt.
4. Install distributor rotor and cap.
5. Install high tension leads and connect primary wire.
6. Connect vacuum sensing tube to vacuum control unit.
7. Adjust ignition timing.

Rotary Engine

Removal

1. Disconnect the high tension leads and vacuum tubes from distributor.
2. Disconnect couplers of primary wire and condenser lead from distributor.
3. Remove distributor lock nut.
4. Disconnect vacuum tubes from vacuum control unit of distributor.
5. Pull distributor out of front cover.

Installation

1. Turn eccentric shaft until leading timing mark on eccentric shaft pulley aligns with indicator pin on front cover.

2. Align timing marks on distributor housing and driven gear.
3. Insert distributor so that distributor lock bolt is located in center of slit, and engage gears.
4. Rotate distributor clockwise until leading contact point starts to separate, and tighten distributor lock nut.
5. Install high tension leads and connect primary wire coupler.
6. Adjust ignition timing.
7. Connect vacuum tubes to vacuum control units.

DISTRIBUTOR SERVICE

Breaker Point Type

Except Rotary Engine

Refer to Ford Courier Distributor Service Section for service procedures.

Rotary Engine

1. Remove distributor cap and rotor, Fig. 1.
2. Disconnect primary wires from leading and trailing contact points.
3. Disconnect couplers from condenser leads.
4. Remove primary wires (rubber block) from distributor housing.
5. Remove screws attaching vacuum control units to distributor housing. Remove clips holding vacuum diaphragm links. Remove vacuum control units.
6. Remove bearing stopper set screws

and remove breaker base plate and bearing assembly.
7. Remove snap ring and cam from drive shaft.
8. Drive lock pin out of driven gear with a small drift and remove gear and washers.
9. Remove shaft through top of distributor housing.
10. Remove governors by removing springs.
11. Remove condensers from distributor housing.
12. Reverse procedure to assemble.

Breakerless Type

1. Remove distributor cap and rotor, Fig. 2.
2. Remove screws that attach pick-up coil to pick-up coil plate and remove pick-up coil with wiring.
3. Remove screws that attach vacuum control unit to distributor housing and remove vacuum control unit.
4. Drive lock pin out of driven gear with a small drift and remove gear and washer.
5. Remove screws that attach pick-up coil plate to housing. Push shaft up and remove through top of housing with pick-up coil plate.
6. The reluctor can be removed by removing attaching screw to distributor shaft.
7. The governor weights can be removed by removing governor spring.
8. Reverse procedure to assemble.

ALTERNATOR, REPLACE

1. Open the hood and disconnect the negative cable at battery.
2. Remove the air cleaner, if necessary.
3. Disconnect the wires at the alternator "B" terminal by removing the nut. Pull the multiple connector from the rear of the alternator.
4. Remove the alternator strap bolt.
5. Remove the alternator mounting bolt, and remove the alternator from the vehicle.

ALTERNATOR ON VEHICLE TESTING

1. Disconnect the wire from "B" terminal of the alternator and connect the ammeter with the negative lead of the ammeter to the wire and the positive lead to the "B" terminal, Fig. 3.
2. Disconnect the coupler from the regulator. Connect the disconnected couplers with the suitable wires.
3. Start the engine and take a reading of the ammeter, holding the engine speed to 2,000 rpm.
4. Disconnect the wire from the "F" terminal and short-circuit the wire to the "A" terminal for a moment.
5. If the meter reading increases remarkably, the trouble is in the regulator and if there is no change in current, it is in the alternator.

INSTRUMENT CLUSTER, REPLACE

1974-77 RX4

1. Pull center cap out from steering wheel.
2. Remove steering wheel attaching nut and remove steering wheel.
3. Remove nut attaching ventilator knob and move knob away from the panel.
4. Remove screw attaching choke knob and remove choke knob. Remove nut attaching choke and move choke away from panel.
5. Remove screws attaching column cover and remove column cover.
6. Disconnect wirings from panel light resister by loosening attaching screws.
7. Disconnect wirings to exhaust system over heat warning light.
8. Loosen but do not remove two

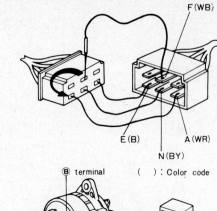

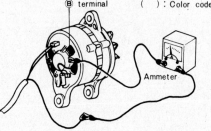

Fig. 3 Alternator test connections

screws and pull column cover out from instrument panel.
   Note that attaching clips give a little resistance when pulling column cover out.
9. Remove meter cover attaching nuts and pull cover out from combination meter.
10. Disconnect wiring connectors from combination meter.
11. Reach under instrument panel and disconnect speedometer cable by pressing on flat surface of plastic connector and pulling cable away from head.
12. Remove nuts attaching combination meter and pull meter top away from dashboard to expose instrument panel.
13. Remove screws attaching cover and remove cover from combination meter.
14. Remove nuts attaching fuel and water temperature gauge assembly and remove gauge assembly from combination meter.
15. Reverse procedure to install.

1976-77 Cosmo

1. Pull the center cap out from the steering wheel.
2. Remove the steering wheel attaching nut and remove the steering wheel.
3. Remove the screws attaching the column cover and remove the column cover.

4. Remove the meter cover attaching screws and pull the cover out from the combination meter.
5. Remove the nuts attaching the remote control.
6. Remove the screw attaching the choke knob and remove the choke knob. Remove the nut holding the choke assembly to the panel, and remove the cable assembly from the panel.
7. Remove the panel light resistor knob from the resistor. Remove the nut attaching the panel light resistor to the panel.
8. Remove the screws attaching the switch panel and remove the switch panel.
9. Remove the screws attaching the ashtray and remove the ashtray.
10. Remove the heater control knobs and radio control knobs by pulling the knob.
11. Remove the radio attaching nuts.
12. Remove the screws attaching the center panel and remove the center panel.
13. Disconnect the wiring connectors from the combination meter.
14. Reach under the instrument panel and disconnect the speedometer cable by pressing on the flat surface of the plastic connector and pulling the cable away from the head.
15. Remove the nuts attaching the combination meter and pull the meter top away from the dashboard to expose the instrument panel.
16. Remove the screws attaching cover and remove the cover from the combination meter.
17. Remove the nuts attaching the fuel and water temperature gauge assembly and remove the gauge assembly from the combination meter.
18. Reverse procedure to install.

W/S WIPER MOTOR, REPLACE

1. Remove the wiper arm attaching screw and remove the wiper arms.
2. Remove the screws attaching the cowl plate and move the front side of the cowl plate up and disconnect the hose for the washer at the nozzle. Then remove the cowl plate.
3. Disconnect the wiring at the wiper motor.
4. Remove bolts attaching the wiper motor and remove the wiper motor.
5. Reverse procedure to install.

Piston Engine Service Section
1300 Engine

ENGINE REPLACE

1. Disconnect the negative cable at the battery.
2. Disconnect the hoses from the air cleaner body, and remove the air cleaner assembly.
3. Drain the cooling system by opening the drain plugs.
4. Drain the engine oil.
5. Disconnect the wire for pick-up coil of the distributor at the igniter, if used.
6. Disconnect the connectors from the water temperature gauge unit and the oil pressure switch.
7. Disconnect the bullet connectors from the water thermo switch.
8. Disconnect the coupler of the reverse lamp switch at the rear side of the engine.
9. Disconnect the wire at the "B" terminal and pull the coupler from the rear of the alternator.
10. Disconnect the positive cable from the "B" terminal and ignition switch wire from the "S" terminal on the starting motor.
11. Disconnect the heater hoses from the inlet manifold and water pump inlet.
12. Disconnect the vacuum sensing tubes (carburetor-three way solenoid valve, EGR control valve-three way solenoid valve) from the three way solenoid valve.
13. Disconnect the vacuum sensing tubes and air hose at the air control valve, if used.
14. Disconnect the vacuum sensing pipe for power brake unit from the inlet manifold.
15. Disconnect the fuel hoses from the carburetor and fuel pump.
16. Disconnect the choke cable and accelerator cable from the carburetor.
17. Disconnect the air conditioning compressor, if equipped.
18. Remove the upper and lower radiator hoses from the radiator.
19. Remove the radiator cowling from the radiator.
20. Remove the radiator attaching bolts and remove the radiator.
21. Remove the exhaust pipe hanger from the bracket on the transmission.
22. Disconnect the exhaust pipe from the exhaust manifold. Remove the gasket.
23. Remove the under cover from the clutch housing.
24. Remove the starting motor.
25. Remove the bolt supporting the transmission to the engine.
26. Support the transmission with a suitable jack.
27. Remove the nuts from the right and left engine mountings.
28. Install a suitable lifting sling onto the engine hanger brackets.
    Attach the sling to a hoist or other lifting device and take up all slack.
29. Pull the engine forward until it clears the clutch shaft.
    Then, lift the engine from the vehicle.
30. Disconnect the EGR pipes from the exhaust manifold and inlet manifold, then, remove the EGR control valve assembly from the inlet manifold.
31. Disconnect the vacuum sensing tube for the vacuum control valve from the inlet manifold.
32. Remove the servo diaphragm and vacuum control valve from the inlet manifold.
33. Disconnect the vacuum sensing tube and air hose for the anti-afterburn valve and remove the anti-afterburn valve from the inlet manifold, if used.
34. Remove the air pump mounting and strap bolts, then, remove the air pump, if used.
35. Remove the engine mounting brackets from the cylinder block.
36. Remove the heat insulator, then, remove the exhaust manifold from the cylinder block.

Fig. 1 Cylinder head to timing chain cover bolt

DISASSEMBLY
Preliminary Components

1. Remove alternator.
2. Remove distributor.
3. Remove thermostat.
4. Remove oil filter.
5. Remove fan and pulley.

Inlet Manifold & Carburetor Assembly

1. Disconnect the vacuum tube (distributor—carburetor) at the carburetor.
2. Loosen the hose band and disconnect the water bypass hose (water pump inlet—inlet manifold) from the inlet manifold.
3. Disconnect the water bypass hose (water bypass pipe—thermostat housing) from the thermostat housing.
4. Disconnect the fuel hose (fuel pump-carburetor) from the carburetor.
5. Disconnect the ventilation hose from the rocker arm cover.
6. Remove the nuts attaching the inlet mainfold to the cylinder head and remove the inlet manifold and carburetor assembly.
7. Remove the nuts attaching the carburetor to the inlet manifold and remove the carburetor.

Fuel Pump

1. Remove the bolts attaching the fuel pump to the cylinder block.
2. Remove the fuel pump, insulator and gaskets.
3. Loosen and remove the plug, and then remove the fuel pump push rod from the cylinder block.

Water Pump

1. Remove the nuts that attach the water pump to the timing chain cover.
2. Remove the alternator strap.
3. Remove the water pump and gasket.

Cylinder Head

1. Remove the attaching bolts and remove the rocker arm cover and gasket.
2. Remove two semicircular oil seals.
3. Install the brake (49 0221 030A) to the flywheel.

Fig. 2 Timing chain tensioner

4. Remove the lock nut and washer and slide the distributor drive gear and spacer off the camshaft.
5. Remove the bolt that attaches the cylinder head to the timing chain cover, Fig. 1.
6. Remove the blind cover from the timing chain cover and install the chain adjuster guide (49 1975 260) to prevent the slipper head of the tensioner from popping out, Fig. 2.
7. Loosen the cylinder head bolts in the reverse order of tightening, Fig. 3.

NOTE: To avoid cylinder head distortion, loosen the bolts a few turns at a time until they are all loose.

8. Remove the rocker arm assembly.
9. Pull the camshaft rearward and remove the camshaft from the camshaft sprocket. Remove the camshaft sprocket.
10. Remove the cylinder head and gasket.

NOTE: When removing only the camshaft or the cylinder head, the timing chain should be lifted upward to prevent the slipper head of the

chain tensioner from popping out and causing a difficulty in adjusting the timing chain.

Valve & Valve Spring

1. Remove the carbon inside the combustion chamber.
2. Using a suitable compressor, compress valve spring.
3. Remove the taper sleeves, upper spring seat, valve springs and lower spring seat.
4. Remove the valve.

NOTE: Place the taper sleeves, upper spring seats, valve springs, lower spring seats and valves in order in a suitable case for reassembling.

Crankshaft Pulley

1. Install the brake (49 0221 030A) to the flywheel.
2. Remove the pulley bolt and pull the pulley off the front end of the crankshaft.

Clutch Assembly

1. Install the brake (49 0221 030A).
2. Remove the bolts attaching the clutch cover to the flywheel and remove the clutch cover and pressure plate assembly and clutch disc.
3. Remove the bolts attaching the flywheel to the rear end of the crankshaft.
4. Remove the ring gear brake and flywheel.

Oil Pan

1. Rotate the cylinder block to an upside down position.
2. Remove the bolts that attach the oil pan to the cylinder block.
3. Remove the oil pan and gasket.

Fig. 3 Cylinder head bolt tightening sequence

Timing Chain Cover

1. Remove the bolts that attach the timing chain cover to the cylinder block.
2. Remove the chain cover and gaskets.
3. Remove the oil baffle plate from the crankshaft.

Timing Chain, Oil Pump Drive Chain & Sprockets

1. Remove the lock nut and washer attaching the oil pump sprocket.
2. Remove the crankshaft sprocket, oil pump drive chain and oil pump sprocket.
3. Remove the spacer from the crankshaft.
4. Remove the timing chain and crankshaft sprocket.
5. Remove the key and spacer from the crankshaft.

Chain Adjuster, Chain Guide Strip & Vibration Damper

Remove the bolts and screws, and then remove the chain adjuster, chain guide strip and vibration damper.

Fig. 4 Removing rear main bearing cap

Fig. 5 Checking for cylinder head distortion

Fig. 6   Removing valve guide

Oil Pump and Oil Strainer

1. Remove the connection bolt attaching the oil outlet pipe to the cylinder block.
2. Remove bolts attaching oil strainer to oil pump and remove the oil strainer and gasket.
3. Remove the bolts that attach the pump cover to the cylinder block and remove the pump cover.
4. Remove the pump shaft and rotors from the cylinder block.

Piston & Connecting Rod

1. Remove the bolts from each connecting rod and remove the bearing caps.
2. Push the piston and connecting rod assembly out of the cylinder block with the handle end of a hammer until the piston rings are free from the cylinder bore. Remove the piston and connecting rod assembly from the top of the block.
3. To separate the piston and connecting rod assembly, remove the clips and remove the piston pin with the installer (49 0221 061A). If tight, heat the piston with a piston heater.

Crankshaft

1. Remove the bolts that attach the main bearing caps to the cylinder block.
2. Remove the main bearing caps and thrust washers. When removing the rear main bearing cap, use the puller (49 0221 270B), Fig. 4.
3. Take out the oil seal from the crankshaft rear end.
4. Remove the crankshaft from the cylinder block.

ENGINE INSPECTION AND REPAIR

Cylinder Head Inspection

Remove all carbon in the combustion chamber and exhaust port.

Be sure that the water passages are open. Inspect the tapped openings. Repair or replace any damaged threads or broken studs.

Check for cylinder head distortion by placing a straight edge on the cylinder head surface. Measure the clearance between the straight edge and the cylinder head surface with a feeler gauge as shown in Fig. 5. If the distortion exceeds 0.15 mm (0.006 in.), grind with a surface grinder.

Manifold Inspection

Check the intake and exhaust manifold for distortion. To check, place the manifold on a surface plate and check the clearance between the manifold and surface plate with a feeler gauge. If excessive distortion is found, correct it by grinding.

Valve Spring Inspection

Examine the springs for corrosion or any damage. If it is severe, replace with new ones.

Measure the free length and the fitting pressure. Replace with new springs if the free length is decreased under 39.1 mm (1.539 in.) on the outer spring and 35.7 mm (1.406 in.) on the inner spring, or if the fitting load is reduced under 16.6 kg (36.6 lb.) on the outer spring and 8.1 kg (17.9 lb.) on the inner spring. Refer to specifications.

Valve Inspection

Remove all carbon from the valves. Visually inspect all valves for warpage, cracks or excessive burning and replace if any of these conditions is found.

Replace any worn, pitted or corroded valves that cannot be cleaned or refaced.

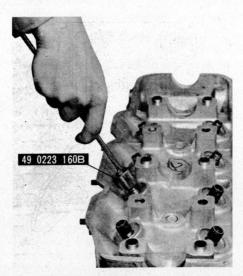

Fig. 8   Installing valve seal

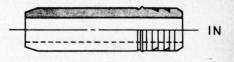

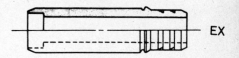

Fig. 7   Intake and exhaust valve guide identification

Measure the diameter of the valve stem at two or three places along the length of the stem with a micrometer. Replace if the stem diameter is less than 7.980 mm (0.3142 in.) on the inlet valve and 7.975 mm (0.3140 in.) on the exhaust valve.

Checking Valve Stem to Guide Clearance

The standard clearance between the valve stem and guide is, under the condition of the guide being fitted with the cylinder head, 0.018-0.053 mm (0.0007-0.0021 in.) on the inlet side and 0.018-0.058 mm (0.0007-0.0023 in.) on the exhaust side. To check this clearance, place the valve in each guide. Check the clearance with a suitably mounted dial indicator, or feel the clearance by moving the stem back and forth. If the clearance is 0.20 mm (0.008 in.) or more, replace the valve guide and valve.

Replacing Valve Guide

1. Press out the old guide with the puller & installer (49 0221 251A), as shown in Fig. 6.
2. Press in the new guide squarely with the same tool until the ring on the guide touches the cylinder head.

NOTE: Intake and exhaust valve guides are different as shown in Fig. 7.

3. Install the new valve seal onto the valve guide with the pusher (49 0223 160B), as shown in Fig. 8.

Refacing Valve

Reface the valves with a valve refacer, following the instructions of the valve refacer manufacturer.

The intake and exhaust valve face has a 90 degree angle.

Take off only the minimum of metal required to clean the valve faces.

NOTE: If the outer edge of the valve (valve margin) becomes less than 1.0

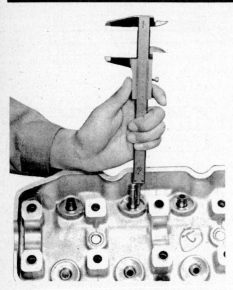

Fig. 9 Checking valve seat sinking

mm (0.039 in.) from excessive grinding, the valve must be replaced.

Inspecting and Refacing Valve Seat

Inspect the valve seats for cracks, burrs, ridges or improper angle and width. If necessary to reface the valve seats, use a valve seat grinder or valve seat cutter and grind to a 90 degree angle. Do not grind any more than is necessary to clean up the valve seat.

NOTE: If the valve guides are to be replaced, this must be done before refac-

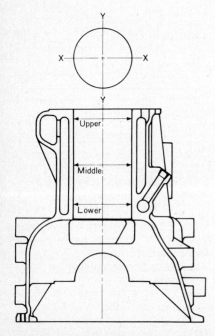

Fig. 11 Checking cylinder bore

ing the valve seat. The valve seat ring is shrinkage-fitted in the cylinder head. However, the seat ring cannot be replaced in view of maintaining strength.

Checking Valve Face & Valve Seat Contact

After the valve or valve seat is ground, check the contact between the valve and valve seat as follows:

1. Apply a thin coat of Prussian Blue on the valve face and insert the valve into the valve seat.
2. Move the valve up and down with hand pressure, rotating the valve.
3. Remove the valve and observe the transfer of Prussian Blue to the valve seat. An even transfer indicates accurate valve and valve seat refacing. If uneven, the valve must be lapped into the valve seat, using a suitable lapping compound.
4. Check the valve seat width with a scale.

   The valve seat width is 1.4 mm (0.055 in.) on both the intake and exhaust valve seats. If the valve seat width is too wide, it can be reduced from inside with a 30° seat cutter and from outside with a 150° seat cutter.

Valve Seat Sinking

When the valve and the valve seat have been refaced several times or when they must be cut deeply for adequate reconditioning, the position of the valve sinks below the standard position. Accordingly, the spring pressure under the fitting condition falls.

Check the sinking of the valve seat by using a vernier calipers as shown in Fig. 9. If the sinking exceeds 0.5 mm (0.020 in.), washers of sufficient thickness to compensate the sinking must be placed under the springs so as to maintain the specified spring pressure. If it is more than 1.5 mm (0.059 in.), replace the valve.

Inspection of Rocker Arm & Shaft

The standard clearance between the rocker arm bore and shaft is 0.020-0.074 mm (0.0008-0.0029 in.). Inspect the clearance and if it is more than 0.10 mm (0.004 in.), replace the rocker·arm or shaft.

Cylinder Block Inspection

Clean the cylinder block with a suitable solvent. Special care must be taken when cleaning the oil passages, coolant passages and cylinder bore to remove all sludge, dirt and carbon deposit. After cleaning, use compressed air to dry the block thoroughly.

Fig. 10 Cylinder bore gauge

Examine the cylinder block for crack and any damage. Examine all machined surfaces of the block for burrs and scores. Check the cylinder block for distortion in the same way, as checking cylinder head for distortion.

Inspecting Cylinder Bore

Check the cylinder bores for wear, scratching and waviness.

Measure the diameter of the cylinder bore by using a cylinder gauge as shown in Fig. 10.

This measurement should be taken in the X-X direction and the Y-Y direction at each of the 3 sections, upper, middle and lower, of one cylinder, as shown in Fig. 11.

The difference between the minimum and maximum values out of the 6 measured values is regarded as the amount of wear.

If the wear of cylinder bore is 0.15 mm (0.0059 in.) or more, it should be honed or rebored. Honing and reboring should be made to correspond to piston and rings oversize and to the recommended piston clearance of 0.053-0.066 mm (0.0021-0.0026 in.)

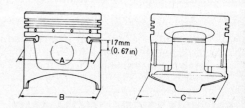

A: 72.952 ± 0.01 mm (2.8722 ± 0.0004 in)
B: 72.963 ± 0.01 mm (2.8726 ± 0.0004 in)
C: 72.653 ± 0.01 mm (2.8594 ± 0.0004 in)

Fig. 12 Piston dimensions

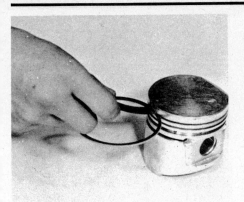

Fig. 13 Checking ring side clearance

NOTE: If any one of the cylinder bores requires reboring, the remaining ones also require reboring. Reboring must not go beyond 1.00 mm (0.040 in.).

The following oversize pistons and rings are available:

0.25 mm (0.010 in.) 0.75 mm (0.030 in.)
0.50 mm (0.020 in.) 1.00 mm (0.040 in.)

Piston Inspection

Carefully inspect the piston and replace if it is severely scored, scratched or burned.

Measure the diameter fo the piston without the piston pin fitted by means of a micrometer. The standard diameter is as shown in Fig. 12. If the wear is severe, replace the piston.

Piston Clearance

Check the clearance between each piston and cylinder by measuring the diameter of the piston and cylinder. Measure the piston diameter at right angle to the piston pin and 17 mm (0.67 in.) below the ring groove. The standard clearance is 0.053-0.066 mm (0.0021-0.0026 in.). If the clearance exceeds 0.15 mm (0.006 in.), rebore the cylinders and use the oversize pistons and rings, referred to under "Inspecting Cylinder Bore."

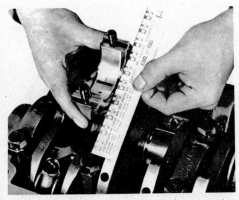

Fig. 15 Checking bearing clearance

Piston Ring Groove Inspection

Remove the carbon from the piston ring grooves by using a ring groove cleaner or a broken piece of piston ring. With a feeler gauge, check the side clearance of the piston rings at several places, as shown in Fig. 13. If it is improper, replace the piston rings. Refer to specifications.

Checking Piston Ring End Gap

Place the piston ring in the cylinder bore below the ring travel, using a piston head to push the ring in squarely. Check the piston ring end gap with a feeler gauge as shown in Fig. 14. The end gap should be 0.20-0.40 mm (0.008-0.016 in.)

Checking Piston Pin Fit

Check that the fit of the piston pin and the connecting rod small end bushing is 0.01-0.03 mm (0.0004-0.0012 in.). Replace if they are worn heavily.

Replacing Small End Bushing

1. Press out the old bush with a suitable mandrel.
2. Press fit the new bush, being sure to align the holes of the bush and connecting rod.
3. Finish the bush with a reamer or a pin hole grinder to the correct fit.

NOTE: The fit is correct when the piston pin slides through the bush with some pressure but without any noticeable looseness.

Connecting Rod Bearing

The connecting rod bearings are aluminum-lined and of the interchangeable type.

When properly installed, the bearings provide proper clearance without filing, scraping or shimming.

Each bearing consists of two halves and should be replaced as a set. The connecting rod bearing sets are available in the standard size and undersize of 0.25, 0.50 and 0.75 mm (0.010, 0.020 and 0.030 in). Inspect the bearing carefully and replace if it is worn, scored or flaked.

Checking Connecting Rod Bearing Clearance

The connecting rod bearing clearance should be 0.027-0.073 mm (0.0011-0.0029 in).

Check the bearing clearance by using a "Plastigauge" as follows:

Fig. 14 Checking ring end gap

1. Clean the surfaces of the bearing and crankpin.
2. Place the "Plastigauge" on the crankpin.
3. Install the bearing cap and tighten the bolts to 4.0-4.5 m-kg (29-33 ft. lbs.). That will flatten the "Plastigauge" to a width which indicates the bearing clearance.
4. Remove the cap and measure the width of the "Plastigauge," using the scale printed on the envelope, Fig. 15.

Checking Connecting Rod Side Play

Check the connecting rod side play with a feeler gauge as shown in Fig. 16. The side play should be between 0.11-0.21 mm (0.004-0.008 in).

Checking Connecting Rod Alignment

Check the connecting rod for bend or twist by using a suitable alignment fixture. Follow the instructions of the fixture manufacturer. If the bend or twist exceeds 0.02 mm in 50 mm (0.002 inch in 5 inches), the connecting rod must be straightened or replaced.

Checking Main Journal and Crankpin

Clean the crankshaft thoroughly with

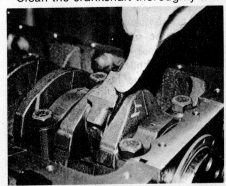

Fig. 16 Checking connecting rod side clearance

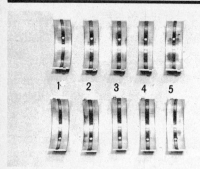

Fig. 17   Main bearings identification

a suitable solvent and blow out the oil passages with compressed air. Inspect the crankshaft for crack, scratch and the oil passages for clog. Measure the diameter of each crankpin and main journal with a micrometer. If the wear is more than 0.05 mm (0.0020 in), the crankshaft should be ground to the undersize of 0.25, 0.50 and 0.75 mm (0.010, 0.020 and 0.030 in). Refer to specifications.

Checking Crankshaft Alignment

To check alignment, mount the crankshaft on the "V" blocks and apply a dial indicator. Slowly rotate the crankshaft and note the reading on the dial indicator. The maximum allowable run-out is 0.03 mm (0.0012 in). If necessary, correct with a press.

Main Bearing

The main bearings are aluminum-lined and interchangeable type. They are classified into 2 types according to the shape as shown in Fig. 17.

When correctly installed, it is provided proper clearance without filing, scraping or shimming.

Each bearing consists of two halves and should be replaced as a set. The main bearings are available in the standard size and undersize of 0.25, 0.50 and 0.75 mm (0.010, 0.020 and 0.030 in).

Inspect the bearings carefully for wear, scoring, flaking or any damage. If any of these conditions exists, replace with new bearings.

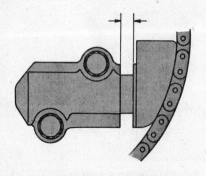

Fig. 19   Checking timing chain stretch

Checking Main Bearing Clearance

Check the main bearing clearance by using a "Plastigauge" in the same manner for the connecting rod bearing clearance.

Note the following differences:
1. The main bearing clearance is 0.031-0.061 mm (0.0012-0.0024 in).
2. The tightening torque of the bearing cap bolts is 6.0-6.5 m-kg (43-47 ft. lbs.).

Checking Crankshaft End Play

The end thrust of the crankshaft is taken by the thrust washers at the rear of the crankshaft.

The standard end play of the crankshaft is 0.08-0.24 mm (0.003-0.009 in).

Check the end play with a dial indicator or a feeler gauge. Correct if the end play exceeds 0.3 mm (0.012 in). The end play can be adjusted by the thrust washer. Thrust washers are available in the oversize of 0.25, 0.50 and 0.75 mm (0.010, 0.020 and 0.030 in).

Camshaft Inspection

Check to see that the cam faces and journals are smooth and are not scored or worn.

Measure the cam height with a micrometer and replace the camshaft if it is less than 43.916 mm (1.7290 in).

The standard cam height is 44.116 mm (1.7369 in) on both inlet and exhaust.

Measure the diameter of the camshaft journals. When they are worn more than 0.05 mm (0.0020 in), replace the camshaft. Refer to specifications for standard diameters of camshaft.

Checking Camshaft Run-Out

Check the camshaft run-out with a dial indicator. The maximum permissible run-out is 0.03 mm (0.0012 in). If necessary, replace the camshaft with a new one.

Checking Camshaft Bearing Clearance

Check the camshaft bearing clearance by using a "Plastigauge" in the same manner for the connecting rod bearing clearance.

Note the following differences:
1. The standard camshaft bearing clearance is 0.019-0.069 mm (0.0007-0.0027 in) for the front and rear, and 0.029-0.079 mm (0.0011-0.0031 in) for the center.
2. The tightening torque of the bolts is 7.7-8.3 m-kg (56-60 ft. lbs.).

   If the clearance exceeds 0.15 mm (0.0059 in), replace the camshaft or cylinder head.

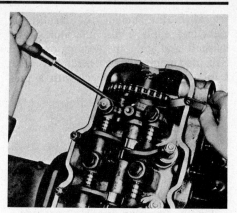

Fig. 18   Checking camshaft end play

Checking Camshaft End Play

The end play of the camshaft is determined by the clearance between the sprocket surface and the thrust plate surface.

Measure this clearance with a feeler gauge as shown in Fig. 18. This clearance should be 0.02-0.18 mm (0.001-0.007 in). If the end play is excessive, replace with a new thrust plate.

Checking Timing Chain For Stretch

Before disassembling the engine, check the stretch of the chain. To check the stretch of the chain, first readjust the tension of the chain as explained under "Adjusting Timing Chain," and then check the protrusion amount of the slipper head, as shown in Fig. 19. If it exceeds 8.0 mm (0.315 in), the chain must be replaced.

Checking Timing Chain, Oil Pump Drive Chain & Sprockets

Check each chain for broken links. Check the sprockets for cracks and worn or damaged teeth. If any defects are found, replace with new parts.

Checking Chain Tensioner

Check the rubber pad on the chain tensioner for wear or damage and the

Fig. 20   Piston and connnecting rod

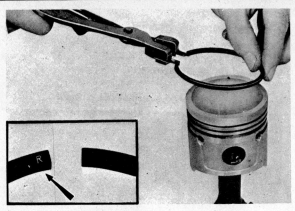

Fig. 21   Installing piston ring

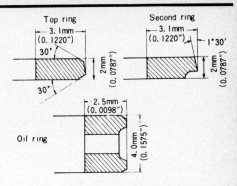

Fig. 22   Piston ring

tensioner spring for loss of tension. If they are defective, replace with a new tensioner assembly.

Checking Chain Guide Strip & Vibration Damper

Check the chain guide strip and chain vibration damper for wear or any damage and replace if they are defective.

ENGINE ASSEMBLY

The procedures for assembling the engine when the engine is to be completely overhauled are as follows:

Assembling Piston & Connecting Rod

1. Install the piston pin clip in the groove on one side of the piston.
2. Place the connecting rod in the piston and align the hole of the connecting rod with the hole of the piston.

NOTE: Care must be taken during the installation that relative positions of the oil hole on the connecting rod big end

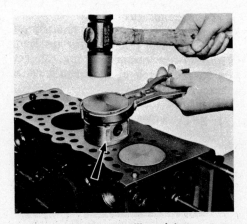

Fig. 23   Installing piston

and the "F" mark on the piston are in accordance with Fig. 20.

3. Insert the piston pin with the installer (49 0221 061A) until the piston pin clip can be fitted.
   Preheat the piston if tight.
4. Fit the piston pin clip in the groove.

Installing Piston Ring

1. Fit the expander in the bottom ring groove and install the oil ring on it with an installer as shown in Fig. 21.
2. Install the second ring and then the top ring.

NOTE: Be sure to install the rings with the inscription mark upward as the faces of the top and second rings are tapered as shown in Fig. 22. Do not expand the rings more than necessary to install, also be careful not to burr the piston with the end of the rings.

Installing Piston and Connecting Rod Assembly

1. Place the piston rings at about 120° apart so that the gap is not located on the thrust side and the piston pin side.
2. Lubricate the entire assembly with engine oil.
3. Using a suitable piston installer, insert the piston and connecting rod assembly from the top of the cylinder block by tapping the piston lightly with a plastic hammer.

NOTE: Insert the piston in the cylinder so that "F" mark on the piston is directed to the front of the engine as shown in Fig. 23.

4. Rotate the cylinder block upside down.
5. Fit the connecting rod bearing halves into their respective locations.

Installing Crankshaft

1. Clean the contact surfaces of the cylinder block, main bearings and crankshaft.
2. Fit the five sets of main bearings properly to the cylinder block and the bearing caps respectively.
3. Fit the half of the thrust washers to the cylinder block with oil grooved surface facing the crankshaft thrust side, Fig. 24.
4. Lubricate the main bearing surfaces with engine oil.
5. Place the crankshaft in the cylinder block, being careful not to drop the thrust washers.
6. Fit the oil seal to the rear end of the crankshaft after applying grease to the seal lip.
7. Insert the rod-shaped oil seals (side seals) into the grooves on both sides of the rear main bearing cap.

NOTE: The side seals should be installed as shown in Fig. 25.

8. Fit the half of the thrust washers to the rear main bearing cap with the grooves toward the crankshaft thrust side, Fig. 26.
9. Install the main bearing caps.
10. Tighten the bolts to 6.0-6.5 m-kg (43-47 ft. lbs.).

NOTE: The main bearing caps are

Fig. 24   Installing thrust washer into block

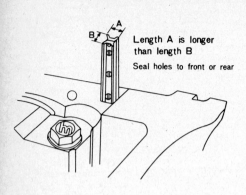

Length A is longer than length B

Seal holes to front or rear

Fig. 25 Installing side seal

marked with a number which shows the order of their arrangement.

Installing Connecting Rod Bearing Cap

1. Fit the connecting rod bearing halves into their respective caps.
2. Lubricate the connecting rod bearing surfaces with engine oil.
3. Install the caps to the connecting rods, ensuring that the identification numbers are matched.
4. Torque the bolts 4.0-4.5 m-kg (24-33 ft. lbs.).
5. Turn the crankshaft and make sure that the rotation is light and smooth.

Installing Oil Pump & Strainer

1. Install the oil pump shaft, inner rotor and outer rotor into the cylinder block bore so that the tally marks on the rotors go outward.
2. Install the pump cover to the cylinder block and tighten the attaching bolts.
3. Install the gasket and oil strainer to the pump cover and connect the oil outlet pipe to the cylinder block with the connection bolt.
4. Prime the oil pump with engine oil.

Fig. 27 Installing chain guide strip and vibration damper

Installing Chain Guide Strip & Vibration Damper

1. Place a new gasket on the cylinder block.
2. Install the chain guide strip. Do not tighten the attaching screws as the tension is adjusted by the chain guide strip, which is explained under "Adjusting Timing Chain."
3. Install the chain vibration damper to the cylinder block and tighten the attaching bolts, Fig. 27.

Installing Timing Chain, Oil Pump Drive Chain and Sprockets

1. Install the spacer onto the crankshaft.
2. Place the timing chain on the crankshaft sprocket and camshaft sprocket with the timing mark and nickel-plated link aligned, Fig. 28.
3. Being careful not to change the relations of timing chain, camshaft sprocket and crankshaft sprocket, fit the crankshaft sprocket onto the crankshaft.
4. Align the keyways of the crankshaft and sprocket, and then install the key.
5. Install the spacer onto the crankshaft.
6. Fit the key on the oil pump shaft.
7. Fit the oil pump drive chain onto the oil pump sprocket and crankshaft sprocket, and install them to the crankshaft and oil pump shaft, aligning the key and keyway.
8. Tighten the nut for the oil pump sprocket to 3.0-3.5 m-kg (22-25 ft. lbs.) and bend the tab of the lockwasher.
9. Fit the spacer and oil baffle plate onto the crankshaft.

Installing Chain Adjuster

1. With the snubber spring compressed fully, install the chain adjuster guide (49 1975 260) to the adjuster as shown in Fig. 29.

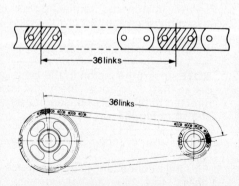

Fig. 28 Aligning timing marks

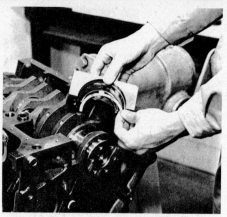

Fig. 26 Installing thrust washer into main bearing cap

2. Without removing the guide, install the adjuster to the cylinder block.
3. Install and tighten the attaching bolts, holding the guide in place. Do not remove the guide until the timing chain is adjusted.

Installing Timing Chain Cover

1. Fit the oil seal into the timing chain cover. Then, fill the oil seal lip with engine oil.
2. Place the gasket on the cylinder block and install the chain cover, aligning the dowel pins. Tighten the bolts.
3. Cut off the excess gaskets along the mounting surfaces of the oil pan and cylinder head.

Installing Oil Pan

1. Before installing the oil pan, make a final internal inspection.
2. Apply a thin coat of gasket paste on the oil pan.
3. Place a new gasket on the cylinder block.
4. Install the oil pan and tighten the bolts little by little in turn until the torque becomes 0.65-0.95 m-kg (5-7 ft. lbs.).

Fig. 29 Installing chain tensioner

Installing Flywheel and Clutch

Install the flywheel and clutch, as described.

Installing Crankshaft Pulley

1. Lock the flywheel with the brake (49 0221 030A).
2. Install the crankshaft pulley to the crankshaft so that the key groove of the pulley aligns with the key on the crankshaft.
3. Tighten the pulley bolt to 11.0-12.0 m-kg (80-87 ft. lbs.).

Installing Cylinder Head

1. Hold the camshaft sprocket and chain securely with a hand and rotate the cylinder block upside down.
2. Place the sprocket and the chain on top of the chain guide strip and the vibration damper.

NOTE: Ensure that the tally marks of both the camshaft sprocket and the chain are engaged properly.

3. Place a new gasket on the cylinder block.
4. Position the cylinder head on the cylinder block, aligning the dowels.

Installing Camshaft

1. Lubricate the camshaft support bores of the cylinder head with engine oil.
2. Install the camshaft to the sprocket, aligning the key and fit the camshaft journals onto the respective support bores, Fig. 30.

Installing Rocker Arm Assembly

1. Assemble the rocker arms, shaft, supporters and bearing caps in the

Fig. 30   Installing camshaft

formation shown in Fig. 31.

NOTE: The center bearing cap is installed with the oil hole facing toward the intake side.

2. Aligning the dowels, position the rocker arm assembly on the cylinder head.
3. Tighten the cylinder head bolts temporarily.
4. Move the rocker arm supporters and offset each of the rocker arms 1 mm (0.04 in) from the valve stem center as shown in Fig. 32.
5. Tighten the cylinder head bolts evenly to 6.5-7.0 m-kg (47-51 ft. lbs.) in the sequence shown in Fig. 3.
6. Tighten the bolt attaching the cylinder head to the timing chain cover.
7. Lock the flywheel with the brake (49 0221 030A).
8. Aligning the key groove with the pin, install the spacer and distributor drive gear to the camshaft. Tighten the lock nut to 7.0-8.0 m-kg (51-58 ft. lbs.) and bend the tab of the lock washer.

Adjusting Timing Chain

1. Slightly rotate the crankshaft in the direction of revolution.
2. Press the top of the chain guide strip with a lever through the opening of the cylinder head (Do not press too hard.) and tighten the guide strip attaching screws with a screwdriver inserted through two holes on the timing chain cover, Fig. 33.
3. Remove the guide which was installed previously. The timing chain now has the proper tension and no further manual adjustment is required.
4. Install the blind plugs and aluminum washers to the two holes on the timing chain cover and cylinder head.
5. Install the cover and gasket for the chain tensioner to the chain cover and tighten the nuts.

Installing Inlet Manifold and Carburetor

1. Place the gasket on the cylinder head and install the inlet manifold to the cylinder head. Tighten the attaching nuts.
2. Place the gasket, insulator, gasket and carburetor in sequence. Tighten the attaching nuts.
3. Connect the vacuum tube (distributor-carburetor) to the carburetor.
4. Connect the water hose (water pump inlet-inlet manifold) to the inlet manifold.
5. Connect the water bypass hose (water bypass pipe-thermostat housing) to the thermostat housing.
6. Connect the fuel hose (fuel pump-carburetor) to the carburetor.

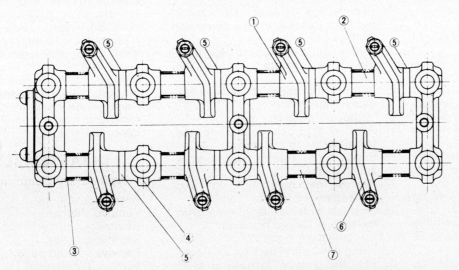

1. Inlet rocker arm
2. Inlet rocker arm shaft
3. Spring
4. Supporter
5. Spacer
6. Exhaust rocker arm
7. Exhaust rocker arm shaft

Fig. 31   Rocker arms and shafts assembly

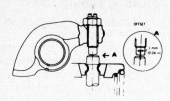

Fig. 32 Rocker arms offset

Installing Distributor

1. Rotate the crankshaft in the direction of revolution until the No. 1 piston is coming up on compression stroke and the ignition timing mark on the crankshaft pulley is in line with the top indicator pin on the timing chain cover.
2. Align the tally marks on the distributor housing and the driven gear, and install the distributor and lock nut.
3. Turn the distributor housing to the

right until the contact points close. Then, turn it to the left and stop it when the contact points just start to separate. Tighten the lock nut.

Adjusting Valve Clearance

To adjust the valve clearance, loosen the lock nut and insert the specified feeler gauge between the rocker arm and the valve stem or between the rocker arm and the cam. Then, turn the adjusting screw until the proper clearance is obtained. Refer to specifications. After adjustment, tighten the lock nut securely and recheck the clearance.

1. Whenever the engine is overhauled, warm up the engine and readjust the valve clearance after tightening the cylinder head bolts to the specified torque.
2. Install rocker arm cover.

Final Assembly

1. Install water pump.
2. Install fan and pulley.

Fig. 33 Adjusting timing chain

3. Install oil filter.
4. Install fuel pump.
5. Install thermostat.
6. Install alternator.
7. Install exhaust manifold.

1600 & 1800 Engine

ENGINE REPLACE

1. Disconnect the negative cable at the battery.
2. Disconnect the hoses from the air cleaner body, and remove the air cleaner assembly.
3. Drain the cooling system by opening the drain plugs.
4. Drain the engine oil.
5. Disconnect the wire for pick-up coil of the distributor at the igniter, if used.
6. Disconnect the connectors from the water temperature gauge unit and the oil pressure switch.
7. Disconnect the bullet connectors from the water thermo switch.
8. Disconnect the coupler of the reverse lamp switch at the rear side of the engine.
9. Disconnect the wire at the "B" terminal and pull the coupler from the rear of the alternator.
10. Disconnect the positive cable from the "B" terminal and ignition switch wire from the "S" terminal on the starting motor.
11. Disconnect the heater hoses from the inlet manifold and water pump inlet.
12. Disconnect the vacuum sensing tubes (carburetor-three way solenoid valve, EGR control valve-three way solenoid valve) from the three way solenoid valve.
13. Disconnect the vacuum sensing tubes and air hose at the air control

valve, if used.
14. Disconnect the vacuum sensing pipe for power brake unit from the inlet manifold.
15. Disconnect the fuel hoses from the carburetor and fuel pump.
16. Disconnect the choke cable and accelerator cable from the carburetor.
17. Disconnect the air conditioning compressor, if equipped.
18. Remove the upper and lower radiator hoses from the radiator.
19. Remove the radiator cowling from the radiator.
20. Remove the radiator attaching bolts and remove the radiator.
21. Remove the exhaust pipe hanger from the bracket on the transmission.
22. Disconnect the exhaust pipe from the exhaust manifold. Remove the gasket.
23. Remove the under cover from the clutch housing.
24. Remove the starting motor.
25. Remove the bolt supporting the transmission to the engine.
26. Support the transmission with a suitable jack.
27. Remove the nuts from the right and left engine mountings.
28. Install a suitable lifting sling onto the engine hanger brackets.
   Attach the sling to a hoist or other lifting device and take up all slack.
29. Pull the engine forward until it clears the clutch shaft.

Then, lift the engine from the vehicle.
30. Disconnect the EGR pipes from the exhaust manifold and inlet manifold, then, remove the EGR control valve assembly from the inlet manifold.
31. Disconnect the vacuum sensing tube for the vacuum control valve from the inlet manifold.
32. Remove the servo diaphragm and vacuum control valve from the inlet manifold.
33. Disconnect the vacuum sensing tube and air hose for the anti-afterburn valve and remove the anti-afterburn valve from the inlet manifold, if used.
34. Remove the air pump mounting and strap bolts, then, remove the air pump, if used.
35. Remove the engine mounting brackets from the cylinder block.
36. Remove the heat insulator, then, remove the exhaust manifold from the cylinder block.

DISASSEMBLY
Preliminary Components

1. Remove distributor.
2. Remove alternator.
3. Remove air pump.
4. Remove oil filter.
5. Remove fan and pulley.
6. Remove water pump.
7. Remove thermostat.

Fig. 1 Cylinder head bolt tightening sequence

Fig. 2 Removing rear main bearing cap

Manifold & Carburetor Assembly

1. Disconnect the vacuum sensing tube (distributor-carburetor) at the carburetor.
2. Disconnect the ventilation hose from the ventilation valve at the inlet manifold.
3. Remove the bolts attaching the inlet manifold to the cylinder head and remove the inlet manifold and carburetor assembly.

Removing Cylinder Head

1. Remove the attaching nuts and remove the rocker arm cover and gasket.
2. Remove two semicircular oil seals.
3. Install the brake (49 0221 030A) or other suitable tool to the flywheel.
4. Remove the lock nut and washer and slide the distributor drive gear off the camshaft.
5. With the spanner (49 0164 631A) or other suitable tool, loosen the locknut holding the camshaft sprocket.
6. Remove the bolt that attaches the cylinder head to the timing chain.
7. Loosen the cylinder head bolts in the reverse order of tightening. Fig. 1.

NOTE: To avoid cylinder head distortion, loosen the bolts a few turns at a time until they are all loose.

8. Remove the rocker arm assembly.
9. Pull the camshaft rearward and remove the camshaft from the camshaft sprocket. Remove the camshaft sprocket.
10. Remove the camshaft bearing halves from the cylinder head.
11. Remove the cylinder head and gasket.

NOTE: When removing only the camshaft or the cylinder head, the timing chain should be lifted upward to prevent the slipper head of the chain adjuster from flying out and causing a difficulty in adjusting the timing chain.

Valve & Valve Spring

1. Remove the carbon inside the combustion chamber.
2. Using suitable spring compressor, compress valve springs.
3. Remove the taper sleeves, upper spring seat, valve springs and lower spring seat.
4. Remove the valve.

NOTE: Place the taper sleeves, upper spring seats, valve springs, lower spring seats and valves in order in a suitable case for reassembling.

Crankshaft Pulley

1. Install the brake (49 0221 030A) or other suitable tool to the flywheel.
2. Remove the pulley bolt and pull the pulley off the front end of the crankshaft.

Clutch Assembly

1. Install the brake (49 0221 030A) or other suitable tool to the flywheel.
2. Remove the bolts holding the clutch cover to the flywheel and remove the clutch cover and pressure plate assembly and clutch disc.
3. Remove the bolts attaching the flywheel to the rear end of the crankshaft.
4. Remove the brake and flywheel.

Oil Pan

1. Rotate the cylinder block to an upside down position.
2. Remove the nuts and bolts that attach the oil pan to the cylinder block.
3. Remove the oil pan and gasket.

Chain Cover

1. Remove the bolts and nuts that attach the timing chain cover to the cylinder block.
2. Remove the chain cover and gaskets.
3. Remove the oil thrower from the crankshaft.

Chain Adjuster, Chain Guide Strip & Vibration Damper

Remove the screws and bolts, and then remove the chain adjuster, chain guide strip and vibration damper.

Timing Chains & Sprockets

1. Remove the lock nut and lock washer attaching the oil pump sprocket.
2. Remove the crankshaft sprocket, oil pump drive chain and oil pump sprocket.
3. Remove the timing chain and crankshaft sprocket.
4. Remove the key from the crankshaft.

Oil Pump & Oil Strainer

1. Remove the nuts attaching the oil strainer to the oil pump and remove the oil strainer and "O" ring.
2. Remove the bolts and remove the oil pump, "O" ring and adjusting washers from the cylinder block.

Piston & Connecting Rod

1. Remove the bolts from each connecting rod and remove the bearing caps.
2. Push the piston and connecting rod assembly out of the cylinder block with the handle end of a hammer until the piston rings are free from the cylinder bore. Remove the piston and connecting rod assembly from the top of the block.
3. To separate the piston and connect-

Fig. 3 Checking for cylinder head distortion

ing rod assembly, remove the clips and remove the piston pin with the installer (49 0223 061). If tight, heat the piston with a piston heater.

Crankshaft

1. Remove the bolts that attach the main bearing caps to the cylinder block.
2. Remove the main bearing caps and thrust washers. When removing the rear main bearing cap, use the puller (49 0221 270B), Fig. 2.
3. Take out the oil seal from the crankshaft rear end.
4. Remove the crankshaft from the cylinder block.

INSPECTION & REPAIR

Cylinder Head Inspection

Remove all carbon in the combustion chamber and exhaust port. Be sure that the water passages are open. Inspect the tapped openings. Repair or replace any damaged threads or broken studs.

Check for cylinder head distortion by placing a straight edge on the cylinder head surface. Measure the clearance between the straight edge and the cylinder head surface with a feeler gauge as shown in Fig. 3. If the distortion exceeds 0.15 mm (0.006 in), grind with a surface grinder.

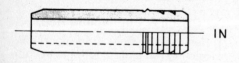

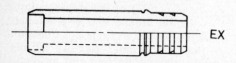

Fig. 5 Intake and exhaust valve guide identification

Manifold Inspection

Check the intake and exhaust manifold for distortion. To check, place the manifold on a surface plate and check the clearance between the manifold and surface plate with a feeler gauge. If excessive distortion is found, correct it by grinding.

Valve Spring Inspection

Examine the springs for corrosion or any damage. If it is severe, replace with new ones. Measure the free length and the fitting pressure. Replace with new springs if the free length is decreased under 36.2 mm (1.425 in) on the outer spring and 35.7 mm (1.406 in) on the inner spring, or if the fitting load is reduced under 12.1 kg (26.7 lbs.) on the outer spring and 8.1 kg (17.9 lbs.) on the inner spring. Refer to specifications.

Valve Inspection

Remove all carbon from the valves. Visually inspect all valves for warpage, cracks or excessive burning and replace if any of these conditions is found.

Replace any worn, pitted or corroded valves that cannot be cleaned or refaced.

Measure the diameter of the valve stem at two or three places along the length of the stem with a micrometer. Replace if the stem diameter is less than 7.980 mm (0.3142 in) on the inlet valve and 7.975 mm (0.3140 in) on the exhaust valve.

Checking Valve Stem to Guide Clearance

The standard clearance between the valve stem and guide is, under the condition of the guide being fitted with the cylinder head, 0.018-0.053 mm (0.0007-0.0021 in) on the inlet side and 0.018-0.058 mm (0.0007-0.0023 in) on the exhaust side.

To check this clearance, place the valve in each guide. Check the clearance with a suitably mounted dial indicator, or feel the clearance by moving the stem back and forth. If the clearance is 0.20 mm (0.008 in) or more, replace the valve guide and valve.

Replacing Valve Guide

1. Press out the old guide with the puller & installer (49 0221 251A), as shown in Fig. 4.
2. Press in the new guide squarely with the same tool until the ring on the guide touches the cylinder head.

NOTE: Intake and exhaust valve

Fig. 4 Removing valve guide

guides are different as shown in Fig. 5.

3. Install the new valve seal onto the valve guide with the pusher (49 0223 160B), as shown in Fig. 6.

Refacing Valve

Reface the valves with a valve refacer, following the instructions of the valve refacer manufacturer.

The intake and exhaust valve face has a 90 degree angle. Take off only the minimum of metal required to clean the valve faces.

NOTE: If the outer edge of the valve (valve margin) becomes less than 1.0 mm (0.039 in) from excessive grinding, the valve must be replaced.

Inspecting & Refacing Valve Seat

Inspect the valve seats for cracks, burrs, ridges or improper angle and

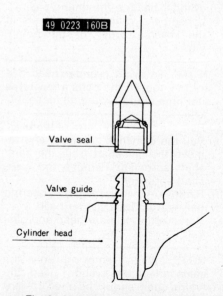

Fig. 6 Installing valve guide seal

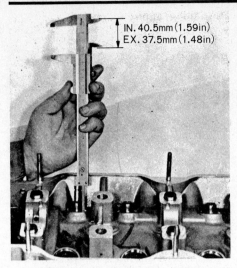

Fig. 7 Checking valve sinking

width. If necessary to reface the valve seats, use a valve seat grinder or valve seat cutter and grind to a 90 degree angle. Do not grind any more than is necessary to clean up the valve seat.

NOTE: If the valve guides are to be replaced, this must be done before refacing the valve seat. The valve seat ring is shrinkage-fitted in the cylinder head. However, the seat ring cannot be replaced in view of maintaining strength.

Checking Valve Face & Valve Seat Contact

After the valve or valve seat is ground, check the contact between the valve and valve seat as follows:
1. Apply a thin coat of Prussian Blue on the valve face and insert the valve into the valve seat.
2. Move the valve up and down with hand pressure, rotating the valve.
3. Remove the valve and observe the transfer of Prussian Blue to the valve seat. An even transfer indicates accurate valve and valve seat

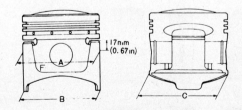

Fig. 1—17 Piston
A: 77.945 ± 0.01 mm (3.0687 ± 0.0004 in)
B: 78.0   ± 0.01 mm (3.0709 ± 0.0004 in)
C: 77.69 ± 0.01 mm (3.0587 ± 0.0004 in)

Fig. 9 Piston dimensions

refacing. If uneven, the valve must be lapped into the valve seat, using a suitable lapping compound.
4. Check the valve seat width with a scale.

The valve seat width is 1.4 mm (0.055 in) on the both intake and exhaust valve seats. If the valve seat width is too wide, it can be reduced from inside with a 30° seat cutter, and from outside with a 150° seat cutter.

Checking Valve Seat Sinking

When the valve and the valve seat have been refaced several times or they must be cut deeply for adequate reconditioning, the position of the valve sinks below the standard position. Accordingly, the spring pressure under the fitting condition falls. Check the sinking of the valve seat by using a vernier calipers as shown in Fig. 7. If the sinking exceeds 0.5 mm (0.020 in), washers of sufficient thickness to compensate the sinking must be placed under the springs so as to maintain the specified spring pressure. If it is more than 1.5 mm (0.059 in), replace the valve.

Inspection of Rocker Arm and Shaft

The standard clearance between the rocker arm bore and shaft is 0.027-0.081 mm (0.0011-0.0032 in). Inspect the clearance and if it is more than 0.10 mm (0.004 in), replace the rocker arm or shaft.

Cylinder Block Inspection

Clean the cylinder block with a suitable solvent. Special care must be taken when cleaning the oil passages, coolant passages and cylinder bore to remove all sludge, dirt and carbon deposit. After cleaning, use compressed air to dry the block thoroughly.

Examine the cylinder block for crack and any damage. Examine all machined surfaces of the block for burrs and scores. Check the cylinder block for distortion in the same way, as described under "Cylinder Head Inspection."

Inspecting Cylinder Bore

Check the cylinder bores for wear, scratching and waviness. Measure the diameter of the cylinder bore by using a cylinder gauge.

This measurement should be taken in the X-X direction and the Y-Y direction at each of the 3 sections, upper, middle and lower, of one cylinder, as shown in Fig. 8. The difference between the minimum and maximum values out of

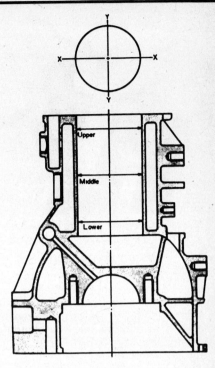

Fig. 8 Cylinder bore checking locations

the 6 measured values is regarded as the amount of wear. If the wear of cylinder bore is 0.15 mm (0.0059 in) or more, it should be honed or rebored. Honing and reboring should be made to correspond to piston and rings oversize and to the recommended piston clearance of 0.057-0.072 mm (0.0022-0.0028 in).

NOTE: If any one of the cylinder bores requires reboring, the remaining ones also require reboring. Reboring must not go beyond 1.00 mm (0.040 in).

The following oversize pistons and rings are available:

0.25 mm (0.010 in)	0.75 mm (0.030 in)
0.50 mm (0.020 in)	1.00 mm (0.040 in)

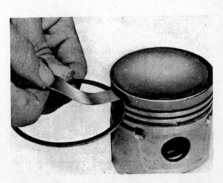

Fig. 10 Checking piston ring side clearance

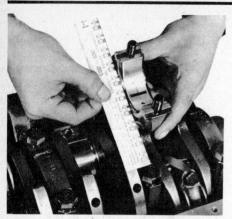

Fig. 11 Checking bearing clearance

Piston Inspection

Carefully inspect the piston and replace if it is severely scored, scratched or burned. Measure the diameter of the piston without the piston pin fitted by means of a micrometer. The standard diameter is as shown in Fig. 9. If the wear is severe, replace the piston.

Piston Clearance

Check the clearance between each piston and cylinder by measuring the diameter of the piston and cylinder. Measure the piston diameter at right angle to the piston pin and 17 mm (0.67 in) below the ring groove. The standard clearance is 0.057-0.072 mm (0.0022-0.0028 in.). If the clearance exceeds 0.15 mm (0.006 in), rebore the cylinders and use the oversize pistons and rings, referring to "Inspecting Cylinder Bore."

Piston Ring Groove Inspection

Remove the carbon from the piston ring grooves by using a ring groove cleaner or a broken piece of piston ring. With a feeler gauge, check the side clearance of the piston rings at several places, as shown in Fig. 10. If it is improper, replace the piston rings. The standard clearance are as follows:

Side clearance	
Top ring	0.035-0.070 mm (0.0014-0.0028 in)
Second ring	0.030-0.064 mm (0.0012-0.0025 in)
Oil ring	——

Checking Piston Ring End Gap

Place the piston ring in the cylinder bore below the ring travel, using a piston head to push the ring in squarely. Check the piston ring end gap with a feeler gauge. The end gap should be 0.2-0.4 mm (0.008-0.016 in) for the top and second ring, and 0.3-0.9 mm (0.012-0.035 in) for oil ring.

Checking Piston Pin Fit

Check the fit of the piston pin and the connecting rod small end bush to be 0.01-0.03 mm (0.0004-0.0012 in). Replace if they are worn heavily.

Replacing Small End Bushing

1. Press out the old bushing with a suitable mandrel.
2. Press fit the new bushing being sure to align the holes of the bushing and connecting rod.
3. Finish the bushing with a reamer or a pin hole grinder to the correct fit.

NOTE: The fit is correct when the piston pin slides through the bushing with some pressure but without any noticeable looseness.

Connecting Rod Bearing

The connecting rod bearings are of aluminum-lined and of the interchangeable type.

When properly installed, the bearings provide proper clearance without filing, scraping or shimming.

Each bearing consists of two halves and should be replaced as a set. The connecting rod bearing sets are available in the standard size and undersize of 0.25, 0.50 and 0.75 mm (0.010, 0.020 and 0.030 in).

Inspect the bearing carefully and replace if it is worn, scored or flaked.

Checking Connecting Rod Bearing Clearance

The connecting rod bearing clearance should be 0.027-0.077 mm (0.0011-0.0030 in). Check the bearing clearance by using a "Plastigauge" as follows:

1. Clean the surfaces of the bearing and crankpin.
2. Place the "Plastigauge" on the crankpin.
3. Install the bearing cap and tighten the bolts to 5.0-5.5 m-kg (36-40 ft. lbs.). That will flatten the "Plastigauge" to a width which indicates the bearing clearance.
4. Remove the cap and measure the width of the "Plastigauge," using the scale printed on the envelope, Fig. 11.

Checking Connecting Rod Side Play

Check the connecting rod side play with a feeler gauge as shown in Fig. 12. The side play should be between 0.11-0.21 mm (0.004-0.008 in).

Fig. 12 Checking crankshaft end play

Fig. 13 Checking crankshaft run-out

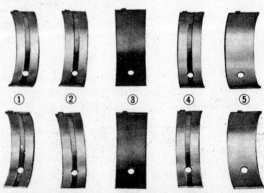

Fig. 14 Main bearing identification

Fig. 15 Checking camshaft run-out

Checking Connecting Rod Alignment

Check the connecting rod for bend or twist by using a suitable alignment fixture. Follow the instructions of the fixture manufacturer. If the bend or twist exceeds .02 mm per 50 mm (.0008 per 1.9685 inches), the connecting rod must be straightened or replaced.

Checking Main Journal & Crankpin

Clean the crankshaft thoroughly with a suitable solvent and blow out the oil passages with compressed air. Inspect the crankshaft for crack, scratch and the oil passages for clog. Measure the diameter of each crankpin and main journal with a micrometer. If the wear is more than 0.05 mm (0.0020 in), the crankshaft should be ground to the undersize of 0.25, 0.50 and 0.75 mm (0.010, 0.020 and 0.030 in). Refer to specifications for standard diameters of crankpins and main journals.

Checking Crankshaft Alignment

To check alignment, mount the crankshaft on the "V" blocks and apply a dial indicator, Fig. 13. Slowly rotate

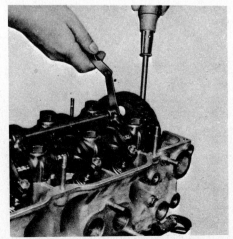

Fig. 17 Checking camshaft end play

the crankshaft and note the reading on the dial indicator. The maximum allowable run-out is 0.03 mm (0.0012 in). If necessary, correct with a press.

Main Bearing

The main bearings are of aluminum-lined and interchangeable type. They are classified into 2 types according to the shape as shown in Fig. 14. When correctly installed, it is provided proper clearance without filing, scraping or shimming. Each bearing consists of two halves and should be replaced as a set. The main bearings are available in the standard size and undersize of 0.25, 0.50 and 0.75 mm (0.010, 0.020 and 0.030 in). Inspect the bearings carefully for wear, scoring, flaking or any damage. If any of these conditions exists, replace with new bearings.

Checking Main Bearing Clearance

Check the main bearing clearance by using a "Plastigauge" in the same manner for the connecting rod bearing clearance.
Note the following differences:
1. The main bearing clearance is 0.031-0.061 mm (0.0012-0.0024 in).
2. The tightening torque of the bearing cap bolts is 8.4-9.0 m-kg (61-65 ft. lbs.).

Checking Crankshaft End Play

The end thrust of the crankshaft is taken by the thrust washers at the rear of the crankshaft.
The standard end play of the crankshaft is 0.08-0.24 mm (0.003-0.009 in).
Check the end play with a dial indicator or a feeler gauge. Correct if the end play exceeds 0.3 mm (0.012 in). The end play can be adjusted by the thrust washer. Thrust washers are available in the oversize of 0.25, 0.50 and 0.75 mm (0.010, 0.020 and 0.030 in).

Camshaft Inspection

Check to see that the cam faces and journals are smooth and are not scored or worn.
Measure the cam height with a micrometer and replace the camshaft if it is not within the specification. Measure the diameter of the camshaft journals. When they are worn more than 0.05 mm (0.0020 in), grind the journals to the undersize of 0.25, 0.50 or 0.75 mm (0.010, 0.020 or 0.030 in).

Checking Camshaft Run-Out

Check the camshaft run-out with a dial indicator, Fig. 15. The maximum permissible run-out is 0.03 mm (0.0012

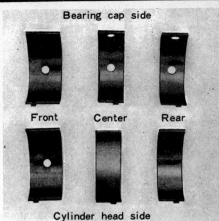

Fig. 16 Camshaft bearing identification

in). If necessary, correct the camshaft with a press.

Camshaft Bearing

The camshaft bearings are of babbitt-lined and interchangeable type. They are classified into 3 types, Fig. 16. When correctly installed, it is provided proper clearance without filing, scraping or shimming.
Each bearing consists of two halves and should be replaced as a set. The camshaft bearings are available in the standard size and undersize of 0.25, 0.50 and 0.75 mm (0.010, 0.020 and 0.030 in). Inspect the bearings carefully for wear, scoring, flaking or any damage. If any of these conditions exists, replace with new bearings.

Checking Camshaft Bearing Clearance

Check the camshaft bearing clearance by using a "Plastigauge" in the same manner for the connecting rod bearing clearance. Refer to specifications.

Checking Camshaft End Play

The end play of the camshaft is determined by the clearance between the

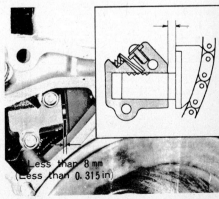

Fig. 18 Checking timing chain stretch. 1600 engine

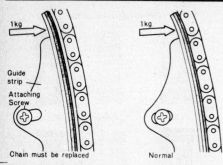

Fig. 19 Checking time chain stretch. 1800 engine

sprocket surface and the thrust plate surface. Measure this clearance with a feeler gauge as shown in Fig. 17. This clearance should be 0.02-0.18 mm (0.001-0.007 in). If the end play is excessive, replace with a new thrust plate.

Checking Timing Chain For Stretch

1600 Engine

Before disassembling the engine, check the stretch of the chain. To check the stretch of the chain, first readjust the tension of the chain, and then check the protrusion amount of the slipper head, as shown in Fig. 18. If it exceeds 8.0 mm (0.315 in), the chain must be replaced.

1800 Engine

Before disassembly, check the stretch of the timing chain, Fig. 19. To check, readjust the chain tension. If the proper adjustment can not be obtained, the chain must be replaced.

Checking Timing Chain, Oil Pump Drive Chain & Sprockets

Check each chain for broken links. Check the sprockets for cracks and worn or damaged teeth. If any defects are found, replace with new parts.

Checking Chain Adjuster

Check the slipper head on the chain

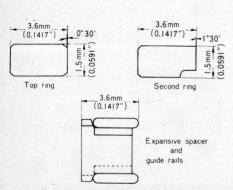

Fig. 21 Piston ring dimensions

adjuster for wear or damage and the adjuster spring for loss of tension. If they are defective, replace with a new adjuster assembly.

Checking Chain Guide Strip & Vibration Damper

Check the chain strip and chain vibration damper for wear or any damage and replace if they are defective.

ENGINE ASSEMBLY

Piston & Connecting Rod

1. Install the piston pin clip in the groove on one side of the piston.
2. Place the connecting rod in the piston and align the hole of the connecting rod with the hole of the piston.
3. Insert the piston pin with the installer (49 0223 061) until the piston pin clip can be fitted. Preheat the piston if tight.
4. Fit the piston pin clip in the groove.

NOTE: Care must be taken during the installation that relative positions of the oil hole on the connecting rod big end and the "F" mark on the piston are in accordance with Fig. 20.

Piston Ring

1. Fit the expander in the bottom ring groove and install the oil ring on it with a suitable installer.
2. Install the second ring and then the top ring.

NOTE: Be sure to install the rings with the inscription mark upward as the faces of the top and second rings are tapered as shown in Fig. 21. Do not expand the rings more than necessary to install, also be careful not to burr the piston with the end of the rings.

Fig. 22 Installing thrust washer in block

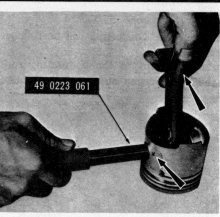

Fig. 20 Piston and connecting rod assembly

Piston & Connecting Rod Assembly

1. Place the piston rings at about 120° apart so that the gap is not located on the thrust side and the piston pin side.
2. Lubricate the entire assembly with engine oil.
3. Using a suitable piston installer, insert the piston and connecting rod assembly from the top of the cylinder block by tapping the piston lightly with a plastic hammer.

NOTE: Insert the piston to the cylinder so that "F" mark on the piston is directed to the front of the engine.

---

4. Rotate the cylinder block upside down.
5. Fit the connecting rod bearing halves into their respective locations.

Crankshaft

1. Clean the contact surfaces of the cylinder block, main bearings and crankshaft.
2. Fit the five sets of main bearings properly to the cylinder block and the bearing caps respectively.

Fig. 23 Installing rear seal

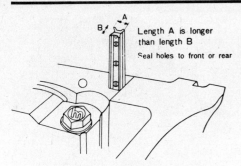

Fig. 24 Installing side seal

3. Fit the half of the thrust washers to the cylinder block with oil grooved surface facing the crankshaft thrust side, Fig. 22.
4. Lubricate the main bearing surfaces with engine oil.
5. Place the crankshaft in the cylinder block, being careful not to drop the thrust washers.
6. Fit the oil seal to the rear end of the crankshaft after applying grease to the seal lip, Fig. 23.
7. Insert the rod-shaped oil seals (side seals) into the grooves on both sides of the rear main bearing cap.

NOTE: The side seals should be installed as shown in Fig. 24.

8. Fit the half of the thrust washers to the rear main bearing cap with the grooves toward the crankshaft thrust side.
9. Install the main bearing caps.
10. Tighten the bolts to 8.4-9.0 m-kg (61-65 ft. lbs.).

NOTE: The main bearing caps are marked with a number which shows the order of their arrangement.

Connecting Rod Bearing Cap

1. Fit the connecting rod bearing

Fig. 26 Installing O-ring

halves into their respective caps.
2. Lubricate the connecting rod bearing surfaces with engine oil.
3. Install the caps to the connecting rods, ensuring that the identification numbers are matched, as shown in Fig. 25.
4. Torque the bolts 5.0-5.5 m-kg (36-40 ft. lbs.).
5. Turn the crankshaft and make sure that the rotation is light and smooth.

Oil Pump & Strainer

1. Fit the "O" ring to the outlet hole on the oil pump and install the oil pump to the cylinder block, aligning the dowel pins, Fig. 26.
2. Tighten the attaching bolts.
3. Place the "O" ring on the oil pump and install the oil strainer to the oil pump. Tighten the nuts.

Timing Chain, Oil Pump Drive Chain & Sprockets

1600 Engine
1. Place the timing chain on the crankshaft sprocket and camshaft sprocket with the timing mark and nickel-plated link aligned as shown in Fig. 27.
2. Being careful not to change the relations of timing chain, camshaft sprocket and crankshaft sprocket, fit the crankshaft sprocket onto the crankshaft.
3. Align the keyways of the crankshaft and sprocket, then install the key.
4. Fit the key on the oil pump shaft.
5. Fit the oil pump drive chain onto the oil pump sprocket and crankshaft sprocket, and install them to the crankshaft and oil pump shaft, aligning the key and keyway.
6. Check the slack of the drive chain by pressing a finger as shown in Fig. 29.
   If the slack exceeds 4.0 mm (0.157 in), install the adjusting shims between the cylinder block and the oil pump body and adjust the slack to be within 4.0 mm (0.157 in).
   The thickness of the adjusting shims are 0.15 mm (0.006 in).
7. Tighten the nut for the oil pump sprocket to 3.0-3.5 m-kg (22-25 ft. lbs.) and bend the tab of the lockwasher.

1800 Engine
1. Place the timing chain on the crankshaft sprocket and camshaft sprocket with the talley marks aligned as shown in Fig. 28.
2. Being careful not to change the relations of timing chain, camshaft sprocket and crankshaft sprocket, fit the crankshaft sprocket onto the

Fig. 25 Installing connecting rod cap. Note that identification numbers must be on same side

crankshaft so as to flush the sprocket with the end of the crankshaft.
3. Install the key on the oil pump shaft.
4. Fit the oil pump drive chain onto the oil pump sprocket and crankshaft sprocket, and then slide in the crankshaft sprocket, aligning the key on the oil pump shaft with the keyway of the pump sprocket.
5. Check the slack of the drive chain by pressing a finger as shown in Fig. 29. If the slack exceeds 4.0 mm (0.157 in), install the adjusting shims between the cylinder block, Fig. 30, and the oil pump body and adjust the slack to be within 4.0 mm (0.157 in). The thicknesses of the adjusting shims are 0.15 mm (0.006 in).
6. Tighten the nut for the oil pump sprocket to 3.0-3.5 m-kg (22-25 ft. lbs.) and bend the tab of the lockwasher.
7. Align the keyways of the crankshaft and sprocket and install the key.

Chain Adjuster

1600 Engine
1. With the snubber spring compressed fully, insert the plate in the

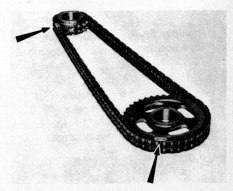

Fig. 27 Timing chain alignment marks

Fig. 28 Installing timing chain and oil pump drive chain and sprockets

Fig. 29 Checking oil pump drive chain stretch

3. Install and tighten the attaching bolts, holding the tool in place. Do not remove the plate until the timing chain is adjusted.

Chain Guide Strip & Vibration Damper

1800 Engine

1. Install the chain vibration damper to the cylinder block and tighten the attaching screws.
2. Install the chain guide strip. Do not tighten the attaching screws as the tension is adjusted by the strip, which is explained under "Adjusting Timing Chain."

Timing Chain Cover

1. Fit the oil thrower to the crankshaft with the edge turned outward.
2. Fit the oil deflector and the oil seal into the timing chain cover. Then, fill the oil seal lip with grease.
3. Place the gaskets on the cylinder block and install the chain cover, aligning the dowel pins. Tighten the bolts.
4. Cut off excess gaskets along the

adjuster release mechanism, as shown in Fig. 31.
2. Without removing the plate, install the adjuster to the cylinder block.
3. Install and tighten the attaching bolts, holding the plate in place. Do not remove the plate until the timing chain is adjusted.
4. Install the chain vibration damper to the cylinder block and tighten the attaching screws.
5. Install the chain guide strip. Do not tighten the attaching screws as the

tension is adjusted by the chain guide strip, which is explained under "Adjusting Timing Chain."

Chain Guide Strip & Vibration Damper

1800 Engine

1. With the adjuster spring compressed fully, install the chain adjuster guide (49 0660 260) to the adjuster, as shown in Fig. 32.
2. Without removing the tool, until the chain adjustment is finished.

Fig. 30 Installing oil pump drive chain adjusting shims

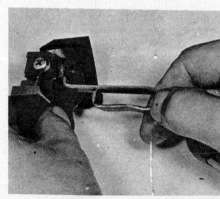

Fig. 31 Installing tool in adjuster. 1600 engine

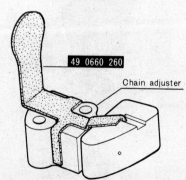

Fig. 32 Installing chain adjuster guide. 1800 engine

mounting surfaces of the oil pan and cylinder head.

Oil Pan, Flywheel & Clutch

1. Before installing the oil pan, make a final internal inspection.
2. Apply a thin coat of gasket paste on the oil pan.
3. Place a new gasket on the cylinder block.
4. Install the oil pan and tighten the bolts and nuts little by little in turn.
5. Install the flywheel and clutch.

Crankshaft Pulley

1. Lock the flywheel with the brake (49 0221 030A) or other suitable tool.
2. Install the crankshaft pulley to the crankshaft so that the key groove of the pulley aligns with the key on the crankshaft.
3. Tighten the pulley bolt to 14.0-15.0 m-kg (101-108 ft. lbs.).

Cylinder Head

1. Hold the camshaft sprocket and chain securely with a hand and rotate the cylinder block upside down.
2. Place the sprocket and the chain on the top of the chain guide strip and the vibration damper.

NOTE: Ensure that the tally marks of both the camshaft sprocket and the chain are engaged properly.

3. Place a new gasket on the cylinder block.
4. Position the cylinder head on the cylinder block, aligning the dowels.

Fig. 33 Installing camshaft

Camshaft

1. Fit the three sets of the camshaft bearings properly to the cylinder head and the bearing caps respectively.
2. Lubricate the bearing surfaces with engine oil.
3. Install the camshaft to the sprocket, Fig. 33, aligning the key and fit the camshaft journals onto the respective bearings.

Assembling Rocker Arms

Assemble the rocker arms in the formation shown in Fig. 34. Care must be taken on the following points:

1. The rocker arm shaft supporters are respectively interchangeable for the intake and the exhaust.

NOTE: The rocker arm bush and spacer were discarded and the rocker arms for inlet and exhaust are not interchangeable.

2. The rocker arm shafts for the intake and the exhaust are not interchangeable. Two shafts are installed on the intake side and one on the exhaust side. The two shafts for the intake side are interchangeable.
3. When installing the rocker arm shafts on the intake side, the ends with the longer distance between the oil hole and the tip are turned toward inside each other, as shown in Fig. 35.
4. The center bearing cap is installed with the oil hole facing toward the intake side.
5. The oil pipe is installed with the oil ejection hole facing the camshaft. In order to avoid vibration of the pipe after it has been installed, the "O" ring fitted on the pipe is pressed into the hole for the pipe on the center bearing cap.

Installing Rocker Arm Assembly

1. Aligning the dowels, position the rocker arm assembly on the cylinder head.
2. Tighten the cylinder head bolts temporarily.
3. Move the rocker arm supporters and offset each of the rocker arms 1 mm (0.04 in) from the valve stem center as shown in Fig. 36.
4. Tighten the cylinder head bolts evenly to 7.7-8.3 m-kg (56-60 ft. lbs.) in the sequence shown in Fig. 1.
5. Lock the flywheel with the brake (49 0221 030A) and tighten the camshaft sprocket lock nut to 7.0-8.0 m-kg (51-58 ft. lbs.) with the spanner (49 0164 631A). Bend the tab of the lock washer.

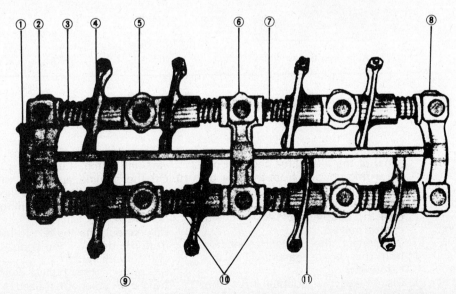

1. Thrust plate
2. Front bearing cap
3. Spring
4. Exhaust rocker arm
5. Supporter
6. Center bearing cap
7. Exhaust rocker shaft
8. Rear bearing cap
9. Oil distribution pipe
10. Inlet rocker shaft
11. Inlet rocker arm

Fig. 34 Rocker arms and shafts assembly

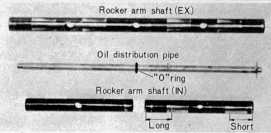

Fig. 35 Rocker arm shafts

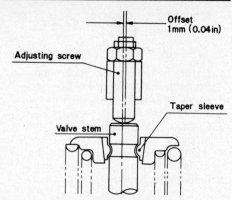

Fig. 36 Rocker arm offset

6. Aligning the key groove with the pin, install the distributor drive gear to the camshaft. Tighten the lock nut to 7.0-8.0 m-kg (51-58 ft. lbs.) and bend the tab of the lock washer.

Adjusting Timing Chain

1. Slightly rotate the crankshaft in the direction of revolution.
2. Press the top of the chain guide strip with a lever through the hole of the chain cover (do not press too hard) and tighten the guide strip attaching screws with a screwdriver inserted through two holes on the timing chain cover, Fig. 37.
3. Remove the guide which was installed to the chain adjuster. The timing chain now has the proper tension and no further manual adjustment is required.
4. Install the blind plugs and aluminum washers to the two holes on the timing chain cover.
5. Install the blind cover and gasket for the chain adjuster to the chain cover and tighten the nuts.

Manifold & Carburetor Assembly

1. Place the gasket on the cylinder head and install the inlet manifold and carburetor assembly.
2. Tighten the attaching nuts.
3. Connect the vacuum tube (distributor-carburetor) to the carburetor.
4. Connect the water hose (water pump-inlet manifold) to the inlet manifold.

5. Connect the water bypass hose (water pump-thermostat case) to the thermostat case.
6. Connect the ventilation hose to the ventilation valve at the inlet manifold.

Final Assembly

1. Install thermostat.
2. Install water pump.
3. Install fan and pulley.
4. Install oil filter.
5. Install air pump.
6. Install alternator.
7. Install distributor.

Adjusting Valve Clearance

To adjust the valve clearance, loosen

Fig. 37 Adjusting timing chain tension

the lock nut and insert the specified feeler gauge between the rocker arm and the valve stem or between the rocker arm and the cam. Then, turn the adjusting screw until the proper clearance is obtained.

After adjustment, tighten the lock nut securely and recheck the clearance.

NOTE:

a. Before adjusting make sure that the flat surface of the ball on the rocker arm is facing downward.
b. The valve clearance should be as specified under "Valve Specifications."
c. Whenever the engine is overhauled, warm up the engine and readjust the valve clearance after tightening the cylinder head bolts to the specified torque.

Rocker Arm Cover

1. Apply rubber sealer to the semicircular oil seals and fit them, with the "OUT" mark facing outward, to the front and rear of the cylinder head.
2. Place the gasket on the cylinder head.
3. Install the rocker arm cover and tighten the attaching nut to 0.15-0.2 m-kg (1.1-1.4 ft. lbs.).

Rotary Engine Service Section

ENGINE, REPLACE
Rotary Engine Models
Exc. Pick-up

1. Disconnect the negative cable at the battery.
2. Drain the cooling water by opening the drain plugs.
3. Drain the engine oil.
4. Disconnect the primary wiring couplers and the high tension cords at the ignition coils.

5. Disconnect the wire at the "B" terminal of the alternator and pull off the wiring coupler from the rear of the alternator.
6. On the California vehicle, disconnect the coupler from the vacuum control valve.
7. Disconnect the bullet connector from the choke heater lead of the carburetor.
8. Disconnect the coupler from the water temperature switch.

9. Disconnect the coupler from No. 1 vacuum switch, if used.
10. On the vehicle equipped with air conditioning, disconnect the coupler from the air conditioning solenoid valve.
11. Disconnect the bullet connectors from the deceleration control valve and air vent valve.
12. Disconnect the bullet connector from EGR solenoid, if used.
13. Disconnect the coupler to the

transmission at the rear end of the engine.

14. Disconnect the coupler from the oil thermo sensor, if used.
15. Disconnect the coupler from the oil level sensor lead.
16. Disconnect the connector from the water temperature gauge unit.
17. Disconnect the positive cable from the "B" terminal and ignition switch wire from the "S" terminal on the starting motor.
18. Remove the nuts attaching the air cleaner body and remove the air cleaner assembly.
19. Disconnect the couplers from the idle switch and air control valve.
20. Disconnect the coupler from the richer solenoid (manual transmission only).
21. Disconnect the coupler from the power solenoid valve, if used.
22. Remove the fuel pipe and fuel return pipe at the carburetor.
23. Disconnect the accelerator cable and the choke cable at the carburetor.
24. Remove the sub-zero starting assist hose at the carburetor (except California vehicles).
25. Disconnect the vacuum sensing tube from No. 2 vacuum switch, if used.
26. Disconnect the vacuum sensing tube from the vacuum pipe (automatic transmission).
27. Disconnect the vacuum sensing pipe for power brake unit from the inlet manifold.
28. Disconnect the air hose to the heat exchanger at inlet manifold.
29. Remove the air conditioning compressor, if equipped.
30. Remove the oil pump for power steering, if equipped.
31. Remove the cooling fan and fan drive assembly.
32. Remove the upper and lower radiator hoses. On the vehicle equipped with automatic transmission, disconnect the automatic transmission fluid pipes from the radiator.
33. Loosen the hose bands and disconnect the heater hoses from the radiator and rear housing.
34. Disconnect the hoses from the oil cooler.
35. Remove the expansion tank cap.
36. Remove the radiator attaching bolts and remove the radiator.
37. Remove the secondary air pipe (heat exchanger-thermal reactor).
38. Disconnect the pipe (heat exchanger-inlet manifold) at the heat exchanger.
39. Disconnect the exhaust pipe from the thermal reactor. Remove the

gasket.
40. Remove the exhaust pipe hanger from the bracket on the transmission.
41. Remove the clutch release cylinder from the clutch housing.
42. Remove the starting motor.
43. Remove the bolts supporting the transmission to the engine.
44. Support the transmission with a suitable jack.
45. Remove the nuts from the right and left engine mountings.
46. Install a suitable lifting sling on the engine hanger brackets. Attach the sling to a hoist or other lifting device and take up all slack.
47. Pull the engine forward until it clears the clutch shaft. Then, lift the engine from the vehicle.
48. Install the hanger (49 1114 005) to the engine stand (49 0107 680A or 49 0839 000) and mount the engine on the engine stand.

Pick-up

1. Disconnect the negative cable at the battery.
2. Drain the cooling water by opening the drain plugs.
3. Drain the engine oil.
4. Disconnect the primary wiring coupler and the high tension cords at the ignition coils.
5. Disconnect the wire at the "B" terminal of the alternator and pull off the wiring coupler from the rear of the alternator.
6. Disconnect the bullet connector from the choke heater lead of the carburetor.
7. Disconnect the coupler from the water temperature switch.
8. Disconnect the bullet connectors from the deceleration control valve.
9. Disconnect the coupler to the transmission at the rear end of the engine.
10. Disconnect the coupler from the oil thermo sensor, if used.
11. Disconnect the coupler from the oil level sensor lead.
12. Disconnect the connector from the water temperature gauge unit.
13. Disconnect the positive cable from the "B" terminal and ignition switch wire from the "S" terminal on the starting motor.
14. Remove the nuts attaching the air cleaner body and remove the air cleaner assembly.
15. Pull the couplers from the idle switch and air control valve, if used.
16. Disconnect the coupler from the richer solenoid, if used.
17. Disconnect the coupler from the power valve solenoid (automatic transmission only).

18. Remove the fuel pipe and fuel return pipe at the carburetor.
19. Disconnect the accelerator cable and the choke cable at the carburetor.
20. Remove the sub-zero starting assist hose at the carburetor, if used.
21. Disconnect the vacuum sensing tube from the vacuum pipe (automatic transmission).
22. Disconnect the vacuum sensing pipe for power brake unit from the inlet manifold.
23. Remove the air conditioning compressor, if equipped.
24. Remove the cooling fan and fan drive assembly.
25. Remove the upper and lower radiator hoses. On the vehicle equipped with automatic transmission, disconnect the automatic transmission fluid pipes from the radiator.
26. Loosen the hose bands and disconnect the heater hoses from the radiator and rear housing.
27. Disconnect the hoses from the oil cooler.
28. Remove the expansion tank cap.
29. Remove the radiator attaching bolts and remove the radiator.
30. Remove the exhaust pipe hanger from the bracket on the transmission.
31. Disconnect the exhaust pipe from the thermal reactor. Remove the gasket.
32. On the vehicle equipped with manual transmission, remove the clutch release cylinder from the clutch housing.
33. Remove the starting motor.
34. Remove the bolts supporting the transmission to the engine.
35. Support the transmission with a suitable jack.
36. Remove the nuts from the right and left engine mountings.
37. Install a suitable lifting sling on the engine hanger brackets. Attach the sling to a hoist or other lifting device and take up all slack.
38. Pull the engine forward until it clears the clutch shaft. Then, lift the engine from the vehicle.
39. Install the hanger (49 1114 005) to the engine stand (49 0107 680A or 49 0839 000) and mount the engine on the engine stand.

DISASSEMBLY
Preliminary Components

1. Remove deceleration control valve.
2. Remove vacuum control valve.
3. Remove EGR valve and solenoid.
4. Remove air pump.
5. Remove alternator.

Fig. 1   Removing front cover

6. Remove thermal reactor.
7. Remove distributor.
8. Remove engine mount.
9. Remove oil filter and cover.

Inlet Manifold and Carburetor

1. Disconnect the vacuum sensing tube from the vacuum control unit on the distributor.
2. Disconnect the connecting rod at the metering oil pump lever and remove the washer.
3. Disconnect the oil hoses at the metering oil pump outlets.
4. Disconnect the air outlet hose (thermal reactor-air control valve) at the air control valve.
5. Remove the bolts and nuts attaching the thermal reactor cover to the engine, and remove the reactor covers.
6. Remove the nuts attaching the inlet manifold to the engine, and remove the inlet manifold and carburetor assembly.
7. Remove the manifold gasket and "O" rings.

Fig. 3   Rear housing tension bolts removal sequence

Water Pump

1. Remove the pulley from power steering oil pump by removing the attaching bolts (if equipped).
2. Remove the nuts and bolts that attach the water pump to the front housing.
3. Remove the alternator and air pump straps, and then water pump.

Removing Oil Pan & Oil Strainer

1. Invert the engine on the engine stand.
2. Remove the bolts attaching the oil pan, and remove the oil pan.
3. Remove the bolts attaching the oil strainer, and remove the oil strainer and gasket.

Eccentric Shaft Pulley

1. Turn the engine on the engine stand so that the top of the engine is up.
2. On the engine equipped with manual transmission, attach the brake (49 1881 060) to the flywheel. On the engine equipped with automatic transmission, attach the stopper (49 1881 055) to the counter weight.
3. Remove the eccentric shaft pulley bolt and remove the pulley.

Front Cover

1. Turn the engine on the engine stand so that the front end of the engine is up.
2. Remove the front cover attaching bolts, and remove the front cover and gasket, Fig. 1.
3. Remove the "O" ring from the oil passage on the front housing.

Oil Pump Drive

1. Slide the distributor drive gear off the shaft.
2. Remove the nuts attaching the chain adjuster and remove the chain adjuster.
3. Straighten the tab of the lock washer and remove the nut and lock washer from the oil pump sprocket.
4. Slide the oil pump sprocket and eccentric shaft sprocket together with the drive chain off the eccentric shaft and oil pump shaft simultaneously, Fig. 2.

Balance Weight & Bearing Housing

1. Remove the key on the eccentric shaft.
2. Slide the balance weight, thrust washer and needle bearing off the shaft.
3. Remove the bolts attaching the bearing housing, and slide the bearing housing, needle bearing, spacer and thrust plate off the shaft.

Fig. 2   Removing oil pump drive

Oil Pump

1. Remove the key on the oil pump shaft.
2. Remove the oil pump attaching bolts, and remove the oil pump.

Clutch and Flywheel (Manual Transmission)

1. Turn the engine on the engine stand so that the top of the engine is up.
2. Attach the brake (49 1881 060) to the flywheel.
3. Remove the clutch cover attaching bolts, and remove the clutch cover assembly and clutch disc.
4. Straighten the tab of the lock washer and remove the flywheel nut, using the box wrench (49 0820 035).
5. Remove the flywheel by using the puller (49 0839 305A), turning the handle of the puller and lightly hitting the head of the puller.
6. Remove the key from the eccentric shaft.

Drive Plate & Counter Weight (Automatic Transmission)

1. Attach the stopper (49 1881 055) to the rear housing.
2. Remove the drive plate attaching

Fig. 4   Removing rear housing

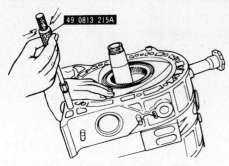

Fig. 5 Removing tubular dowel

bolts and remove the drive plate.

3. Straighten the tab of the lock washer and remove the counter weight nut using the box wrench (49 0820 035).
4. Remove the counter weight by using the puller (49 0839 305A), turning the handle of the puller and lightly hitting the head of the puller.
5. Remove the key from the eccentric shaft.

Rear Housing

1. Turn the engine on the engine stand so that the rear of the engine is up.
2. Loosen the tension bolts in the sequence shown in Fig. 3, and remove the tension bolts.

NOTE: Do not loosen the tension bolts at one time. Perform the removal in two or three procedures.

3. Lift the rear housing off the shaft, Fig. 4.
4. Remove the seals stuck on the rotor sliding surface of the rear housing and place them back into their respective original positions.

Rear Rotor Housing

1. Remove the two sealing rubbers and "O" ring from the rear side of the rear rotor housing.
2. Attach the puller (49 0813 215A), and pull the tubular dowels off the rear rotor housing while holding the rotor housing down by hand to prevent it from moving up, Fig. 5.
3. Lift the rear rotor housing away from the rotor, Fig. 6, being careful not to drop the apex seals on the rear rotor. Remove the two sealing rubbers and "O" ring from the front side of the rear rotor housing.

NOTE: Discard the used sealing rubbers and "O" ring, then use new sealing rubbers and "O" ring.

Rear Rotor

1. Remove the side pieces, each apex seal and spring from the rear rotor and place them in the seal case (49 0813 250), in accordance with the numbers near each respective groove on the face of the rotor.
2. Remove the all corner seals, corner

Fig. 6 Removing rear rotor housing

seal springs, side seals and side seal springs from the rear side of the rotor, and place them in the seal case.

3. Remove the rear rotor away from the eccentric shaft and place it internal gear side down on a clean rubber pad or cloth.
4. Remove each seal and spring on the other side of the rear rotor.
5. Place a suitable protector onto the inner oil seal lip to protect the oil seal lip and remove the outer oil seal with remover (49 0813 225). Do not exert strong pressure at only one place to prevent deformation of the oil seal.
6. Remove the inner oil seal with oil seal remover.

NOTE: Discard the used "O" rings and use new "O" rings when the engine is reassembled.

7. Remove the oil seal springs from each respective groove.
8. Remove the oil seals and springs on the other side of the rear rotor.
9. Apply identification mark onto the rear rotor, so that when reassembling the engine the rotor can be installed in its original position.

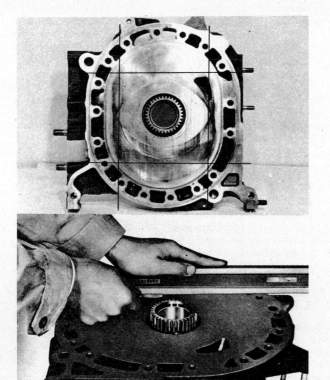

Fig. 7 Checking housing for distortion

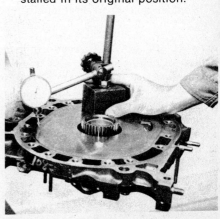

Fig. 8 Checking housing for wear

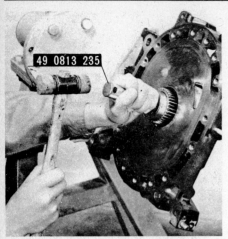

Fig. 9 Removing front stationary gear

Fig. 10 Removing and installing main bearing

Intermediate Housing

1. Holding the intermediate housing down by hand, pull the tubular dowel off the intermediate housing using the puller (49 0813 215A), Fig. 5.
2. Lift the intermediate housing off the shaft, being careful not to damage the shaft. The intermediate housing should be removed by sliding it beyond the rear rotor journal on the eccentric shaft while holding the intermediate housing up and at the same time pushing up the eccentric shaft.

Eccentric Shaft

Remove the eccentric shaft being careful not to damage the rotor bearing and main bearing.

Front Rotor Housing & Front Rotor

Remove the front housing and the front rotor assembly in the same manner as the rear rotor housing and rotor.

INSPECTION & REPAIR

Cleaning Intermediate & Rear Housings

1. Remove all carbon on the housings

Fig. 11 Installing front stationary gear

1-618

with an extra-fine emery paper. If using a carbon scraper, be careful not to damage the finished surfaces of the housings.
2. Remove the sealing agent on the housings by using a cloth or a brush soaked in a solution of ketone or thinner.

Cleaning Rotor Housing

NOTE: Before cleaning, check for traces of gas or water leakage along the inner margin of each side face of the rotor housing.

1. Remove all carbon from the inner surface of the rotor housing by wiping with cloth. Soak the cloth in a solution of ketone or thinner if it is difficult to remove the carbon.
2. Remove all deposits and rust from the cooling water passages on the housing.
3. Remove the sealing agent by wiping with a cloth or brush soaked in a solution of ketone or thinner.

Cleaning Rotor

Remove the carbon on the rotor by using a carbon remover or emery paper. Carbon in the seal grooves of the rotor should be removed with a carbon remover being careful not to damage the grooves. Wash the rotor in cleaning solution and dry by blowing with compressed air.

Cleaning Apex Seal, Side Piece & Spring

Remove all carbon from the apex seal, side piece and spring, being careful not to damage the apex seal and side piece.

Never use emery paper as it will damage the apex seal and side piece. Wash them with cleaning solution.

Cleaning Side Seal & Spring

Remove all carbon from the side seal and spring with a carbon remover.

Cleaning Corner Seal & Spring

Remove the carbon from the corner seal and spring.

Inspecting Front, Intermediate & Rear Housings

1. Check for housing distortion by placing a straight edge on the housing surface. Measure the clearance between the straight edge and the housing surface with a feeler gauge, as shown in Fig. 7. If the distortion exceeds 0.04 mm (0.0016 in), reface or replace the housing.
2. Check for wear on the rotor sliding surfaces of the housing and joint surfaces with rotor housing as shown in Fig. 8.
   If the wear exceeds 0.10 mm (0.0039 in), reface or replace the housing.

NOTE: The side housings (front housing, intermediate housing and

Fig. 12 Removing rear stationary gear

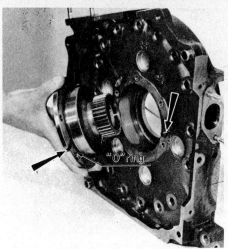

Fig. 13   Installing rear stationary gear

rear housing) can be reused by grinding them if the required finish can be maintained.

Inspecting Front Stationary Gear & Main Bearing

1. Check the stationary gear for cracked, scored, worn or chipped teeth.
2. Check the main bearing for wear, scratching, flaking or any damage.
3. Check the main bearing clearance by measuring the inner diameter of the main bearing and outer diameter of the eccentric shaft main journal.

   The standard clearance is 0.04-0.07 mm (0.0016-0.0028 in). If the bearing clearance exceeds 0.10 mm (0.0039 in), replace the main bearing.

Replacing Front Main Bearing

1. Remove the stationary gear and main bearing assembly from the front housing, using the Puller & Installer (49 0813 235), as shown in Fig. 9.
2. Using the main bearing replacer without adaptor ring, press the main bearing out of the stationary gear.
3. Using the main bearing replacer with adaptor ring, and aligning the tang of the bearing and the slot of the stationary gear, press fit the main bearing into the stationary gear until the adaptor touches the stationary gear flange, Fig. 10.
4. Press in the stationary gear to the front housing with the main bearing replacer, aligning the slot of the stationary gear flange and the dowel pin on the housing, as shown in Fig. 11.

Inspecting Rear Stationary Gear & Main Bearing

Check the rear stationary gear and main bearing according to "Front Stationary Gear & Main Bearing".

Replacing Rear Main Bearing

1. Remove the bolts attaching the stationary gear to the rear housing.
2. Using the puller & installer (49 0813 235), remove the stationary gear from the rear housing, Fig. 12.
3. Check the "O" ring on the stationary gear for damage. Replace the "O" ring if necessary.
4. Using the main bearing replacer without adaptor ring, press the main bearing out of the stationary gear.
5. Use the main bearing replacer with adaptor ring, and aligning the tang of the bearing and the slot of the stationary gear, press fit the main bearing into the stationary gear until the adaptor touches the stationary gear flange.
6. Apply a thin coat of vaseline on the "O" ring and place it in the groove of the stationary gear.
7. Apply sealing agent onto the stationary gear flange.
8. Install the stationary gear to the rear housing, being careful not to damage the "O" ring and aligning the slot of the stationary gear with the dowel pin on the rear housing, Fig. 13.
9. Tighten the bolts attaching the stationary gear.

Inspecting Rotor Housing

1. Check the chromium plated surface on the rotor housing for scoring, flaking or any damage.

   If any of these conditions exists excessively, replace the rotor housing.
2. Check the rotor housing width at points close to the trochoid surface by using a micrometer. The measurements should be taken at four points, as shown in Fig. 14.

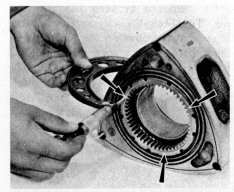

Fig. 15   Checking rotor width

Fig. 14   Checking rotor housing width points

If the difference between the value of point Ⓐ and the minimum value among the points Ⓑ, Ⓒ and Ⓓ exceeds 0.06 mm (0.0024 in), the rotor housing should be replaced with a new one.

Inspecting Rotor

1. Carefully inspect the rotor and replace if it is severely worn or damaged.
2. Check the internal gear for cracked, scored, worn or chipped teeth.
3. Check the clearance between the side housing and the rotor by measuring the rotor housing width and rotor width. The rotor width should be measured at three points, as shown in Fig. 15.

   The difference between the maximum width of the rotor and the width of the point Ⓐ of the rotor housing (see Fig. 14) should be within 0.10-0.21 mm (0.0039-0.0083 in).

   If the clearance is more than the specification, replace the rotor assembly. If the clearance is less than the specification, it indicates that the internal gear has come out, so strike the internal gear lightly with plastic hammer, being careful not to damage and recheck the clearance between the side housing and the rotor.
4. Check the corner seal bores for wear with the gauge (49 0839 165), Fig. 16.
   a. If neither end of the gauge goes into the bore, use the original corner seal.
   b. If the not-go-end of the gauge does not go into the bore while the go-end do, replace with a new corner seal.
   c. If both ends of the gauge go into the bore, replace the rotor.

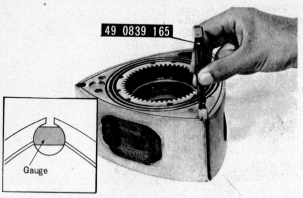

Fig. 16   Checking corner seal bore

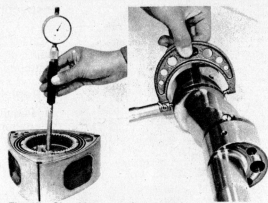

Fig. 17   Checking rotor bearing clearance

Inspecting Rotor Bearing

1. Check the rotor bearing for wear, flaking, scoring or any damage. If any of these conditions is found, replace the bearing.
2. Check the rotor bearing clearance by measuring the inner diameter of the rotor bearing and outer diameter of the eccentric shaft rotor journal, as shown in Fig. 17.
   The standard clearance is 0.04-0.08 mm (0.0016-0.0031 in). Replace the bearing if it is more than 0.10 mm (0.0039 in).

Replacing Rotor Bearing

1. Place the rotor on the support so that the internal gear is facing downward. Using the puller & installer (49 0813 240) without adaptor ring, press the bearing out of the rotor, being careful not to damage the internal gear.
2. Place the rotor on the support with internal gear faced upward, and place the new rotor bearing on the rotor so that the bearing lug is in line with the slot of the rotor bore.
3. Remove the screws attaching the adaptor ring to the replacer. Using the replacer and adaptor, press fit the new bearing until the bearing is flush with the rotor boss.

Inspecting Rotor Oil Seal and Spring

1. Check the oil seal for wear or any damage. If the lip width of the oil seal is more than 0.8 mm (0.031 in), replace the oil seal.
2. Check the free movement of the oil seal in the rotor groove by pressing with finger.
3. Check the oil seal protrusion as shown in Fig. 18 and replace the oil seal spring if the protrusion is less than 0.5 mm (0.02 in).

Inspecting Apex Seal, Side Piece and Spring

1. Check the apex seal and side piece for wear, crack or any damage. If any of these conditions is found, replace the seal. Check the spring for wear.
2. Measure the height of the apex seal with a micrometer at two positions shown in Fig. 19. Replace if the height is less than 7.0 mm (0.276 in).
3. Check the clearance between the apex seal and the groove. To check the clearance, place the apex seal in its respective groove on the rotor and measure the clearance between the apex seal and the groove with a feeler gauge. The feeler gauge should be inserted until the tip of the gauge reaches the bottom of the groove. The standard clearance is 0.05-0.090 mm (0.0020-0.0035 in). If the clearance is more than 0.15 mm (0.0006 in), replace the apex seal.
4. When the apex seal is replaced with a new one, check the clearance between the apex seal and side housing.
   To check, measure the length of the apex seal with a micrometer. Compare the measured apex seal length with the width of Ⓐ point of the rotor housing (see Fig. 14). The clearance should be 0.13-0.17 mm (0.0051-0.0067 in).
   If necessary, correct the apex seal length with emery paper.
5. Check the free height of the apex seal spring as shown in Fig. 20. It should be more than 3.8 mm (0.15 in).

Inspecting Side Seal and Spring

1. Check the free movement of the side seal in the rotor groove by pressing with finger.
2. Check the side seal protrusion from the rotor surface and replace the side seal spring if the protrusion is less than 0.5 mm (0.02 in).
3. Check the clearance between the side seal and the groove with a feeler gauge, as shown in Fig. 21. The standard clearance is 0.03-0.07 mm (0.0012-0.0028 in). If the clearance exceeds 0.10 mm (0.0040 in), replace the side seal.
4. Using a feeler gauge, check the clearance between the side seal and the corner seal with these seals installed on the rotor, as shown in Fig. 22. If the clearance exceeds 0.4 mm (0.016 in), replace the side seal.

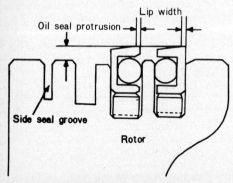

Fig. 18   Checking oil seal protrusion

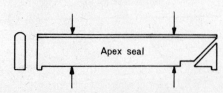

Fig. 19   Apex seal height

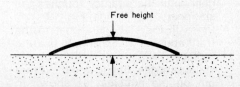

Fig. 20   Checking apex seal spring

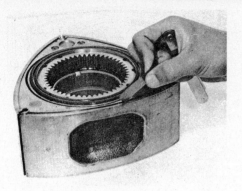

Fig. 21 Checking side seal clearance

When the side seal is replaced, adjust the clearance between the side seal and the corner seal by grinding the one end of the side seal along the round shape of the corner seal with a fine file so that the clearance will be 0.05-0.15 mm (0.002-0.006 in).

Inspecting Corner Seal & Spring

1. Check the corner seal for wear, crack or any damage. If any of these conditions is found, replace the seal. Check the spring for wear.
2. Check the free movement of the corner seal in the rotor groove by pressing with finger.
3. Check the corner seal protrusion from the rotor surface and replace the corner seal spring if the protrusion is less than 0.5 mm (0.02 in).

Inspecting Eccentric Shaft

1. Check the shaft for cracks, scratches, wear or any damage. Be sure that the oil passages are open.
2. Check the shaft for run-out. To check, mount the shaft on "V"-blocks and apply a dial indicator. Slowly rotate the shaft and note the

reading on the indicator. If the run-out is more than 0.06 mm (0.0024 in), replace the shaft with a new one.
3. Check the blind plug in the shaft end for oil leakage or looseness. If any oil leakage is found, remove the blind plug with a hexagonal Allen key and replace the "O" ring, Fig. 23.
4. The oil jets are installed in the eccentric shaft. The oil jets open when the number of engine revolutions increases and the oil pressure rises. Check for spring weakness, stick or damage of the steel ball.

Inspecting Needle Bearing

Check the needle bearing for wear or damage.
Inspect the bearing housing and thrust plate for wear or any damage.

Inspecting Eccentric Shaft Front & Rear Oil Seals

Check the front oil seal fitted into the front cover and the rear oil seal fitted into the rear stationary gear. If it is worn or damaged, replace the oil seal as follows:
1. Remove the oil seal by using a suitable tool.
2. Clean the oil seal mounting bore.
3. Position a new oil seal on its mounting bore and place a hardwood on the oil seal.
   Then, install the oil seal while tapping the hardwood with a hammer until it is firmly seated.

NOTE: Do not coat the outer surface of the oil seal with any lubricant or sealing agent. Do not tap the oil seal directly with a hammer.

Fig. 22 Checking seal clearance

Checking Oil Pump Drive Chain Sprockets

Check the oil pump drive chain for broken links. Check the eccentric shaft sprocket and oil pump sprocket for cracks and worn or damaged teeth. If any defects are found, replace with new parts.

Checking Chain Adjuster

Check the rubber pad on the chain adjuster for wear or damage and the adjuster spring for loss of tension. If they are defective, replace with a new adjuster assembly.

ENGINE ASSEMBLY

The procedures for assembling the engine when the engine is to be completely overhauled are as follows:

Oil Seal

1. Place the rotor on a rubber pad or cloth.
2. Install the oil seal springs in their respective grooves on the rotor with

On the front face of rotor

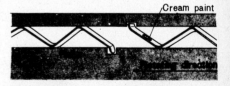

Cream paint

On the rear face of rotor

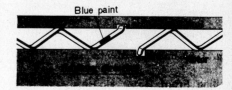

Blue paint

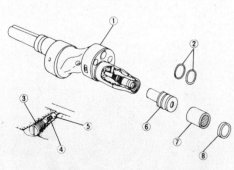

1. Eccentric shaft
2. "O" ring
3. Plug
4. Spring
5. Steel ball
6. Blind plug
7. Pilot bearing
8. Oil seal

Fig. 23 Eccentric shaft and related components

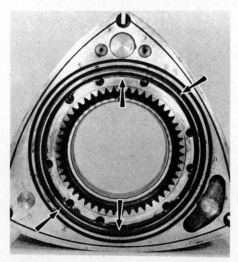

Fig. 24 Stopper hole of oil seal ring

Fig. 25 Installing oil seal rings

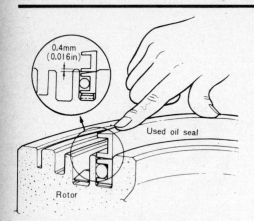

Fig. 26   Installing inner oil seal

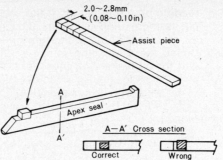

Fig. 27   Sticking assist piece

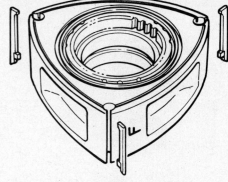

Fig. 28   Installing apex seal

each round edge of the spring fitted in the stopper hole in the oil seal grooves as shown in Fig. 24.

The oil seal springs have been painted in cream or blue color. The cream-painted springs should be fitted on the front faces of both front and rear rotors. While the blue-painted springs should be fitted on the rear faces, Fig. 25.

3. Install a new "O" ring in each oil seal.
4. Place the inner oil seal in the oil seal groove so that the square edge of the spring fits in the stopper notch of the oil seal.
5. Press the inner oil seal by using a used inner oil seal so that the lip surface of the oil seal sinks into a position approximately 0.4 mm (0.016 in) below the surface of the rotor, as shown in Fig. 26.
6. Place the outer oil seal to the oil seal groove so that the square edge of the spring fits in the stopper notch of the oil seal.
7. Push the oil seal slowly with fingers.

NOTE: When replacing the oil seal, confirm the smooth movement of the oil seal by placing the oil seal on the oil seal spring in the groove be-

fore inserting the "O" ring. Be careful not to deform the lip of the oil seal.

8. Apply sufficient engine oil onto each oil seal, and confirm the smooth movement of each oil seal by pressing the oil seal.
9. Install the oil seal springs and oil seals on the other side of the rotor.

Front Side Seals

1. On 1972-74:
   a. Place the rotor which has been fitted with the oil seals on the rubber pad or cloth.
   b. Fit the apex seals without springs and side pieces into their respective grooves so that each side piece positions on the rear side of each rotor.
2. On 1975-77:
   a. Place the front rotor on the rubber pad or cloth with the internal gear upward.
   b. Cut the assist piece with a knife so that its length becomes to 2.0-2.8 mm (0.08-0.10 in).
3. Peel the paper stuck on the assist piece and stick the assist piece on the apex seal, as shown in Fig. 27.
4. Install the apex seals without the spring and side piece into their re-

spective grooves so that the side piece positions to the rear side of the rotor, Fig. 28.
5. Place the corner seal springs and corner seals into their respective grooves.
6. Fit the side seal springs and side seals into their respective grooves, as shown in Fig. 29.
7. Apply engine oil onto each seal, and confirm the smooth movement of each seal by pressing its head.

Front Rotor

1. Mount the front housing on the engine stand.
2. Apply engine oil onto the internal gear of the rotor.
3. Place the front rotor assembly on the front housing taking care not to drop the seals into the port, Fig. 30.
4. Mesh the internal gear and stationary gear so that one of the rotor apexes is set to any one of the four places shown in Fig. 31.

Eccentric Shaft

1. Lubricate the front rotor journal and main journal on the shaft with engine oil.
2. Insert the eccentric shaft, being

Fig. 29   Installing side seal

Fig. 30   Installing front rotor

Fig. 31   Meshing internal gear

Fig. 32 Installing eccentric shaft

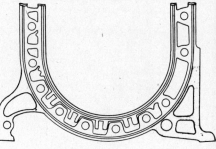

Fig. 33 Sealer application areas

Fig. 34 Front and rear rotor housing

careful not to damage the rotor bearing and main bearing, Fig. 32.

Front Rotor Housing

1. Apply sealing agent onto the front side of the front rotor housing, as shown in Fig. 33.

NOTE: The front and rear rotor housings are not interchangeable. Install the rotor housing as shown in Fig. 34.

2. Slightly apply vaseline onto new "O" ring and sealing rubbers to prevent them from coming off, and place the "O" ring and sealing rubbers on the front side of the front rotor housing.
   a. The wider line of the inner sealing rubber should face to combustion chamber and the seam of the sealing rubber should be placed at the position as shown in Fig. 35. Do not stretch the sealing rubbers.
   b. When engine overhauling, install the protector behind the inner sealing rubber, as shown in Fig. 36, to improve the durability of the sealing rubber.
3. Invert the front rotor housing and install it onto the front housing, being careful not to drop the sealing

rubbers and "O" ring out of the grooves.
4. Apply engine oil onto the tubular dowels and insert the tubular dowels through the front rotor housing holes into the front housing holes, as shown in Fig. 37.

Rear Side Seals

1. Insert the each apex seal spring confirming the spring direction as shown in Fig. 38.
2. Install the corner seal springs and corner seals into their respective grooves.
3. Install the side seal springs and side seals into their respective grooves, as shown in Fig. 39.
4. Fit each side piece to its original position, and confirm that the spring should be set correctly on the side piece.
5. Apply engine oil onto each seal, and confirm the smooth movement of each seal by pressing its head.
6. Apply the sealing agent on the rear side of the front rotor housing, as instructed under "Front Rotor Housing."
7. Place new "O" ring, sealing rubbers and protector on the rear side of the front rotor housing, as instructed under "Front Rotor Housing."
8. Apply engine oil onto the sliding surface of the front rotor housing. And make sure that the front rotor housing is free of any foreign matter.

Intermediate Housing

1. Turn the front housing so that the

top of the housing inclines to upward.
2. Pull the eccentric shaft about 25 mm (1 in), but do not pull over 35 mm (1.5 in).
3. Install the intermediate housing through the eccentric shaft on the front rotor housing.

Rear Rotor & Rear Rotor Housing

1. Turn the engine on the engine stand so that the rear of the engine is up.
2. Install the rear rotor and rear rotor housing, Figs. 40 and 41.

Rear Housing

1. Apply sufficient engine oil onto the stationary gear and main bearing.
2. Install the rear housing on the rear rotor housing.

Torquing Tensioning Bolts

1. Install a new sealing washer to each tension bolt.
2. Apply engine oil onto the thread of the bolt.
3. Fit the tension bolts and tighten the bolts in the order shown in Fig. 42. The specified torque is 3.2-3.8 m-kg (23-27 ft. lbs.). Do not tighten the tension bolts at one time.
4. Turn the eccentric shaft and make

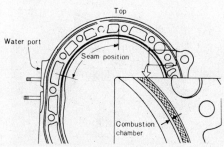

Fig. 35 Positioning inner sealing rubber

Fig. 36 Installing sealing rubber protector

Fig. 37 Installing tubular dowels

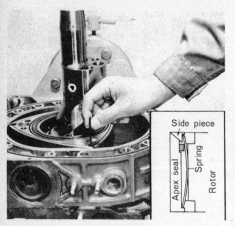

Fig. 38 Installing apex seal spring

Fig. 39 Installing side seal

Fig. 40 Installing rear rotor

sure that the rotation is light and smooth.

NOTE: Replace the sealing washer in the tension bolt when the engine is overhauled.

Flywheel (Manual Transmission)

1. Turn the engine so that the top of the engine is up.
2. Apply engine oil to the oil seal in the rear housing.
3. Fit the key into keyway on the eccentric shaft.
4. Install the flywheel to the rear end of the eccentric shaft, aligning the keyway of the flywheel with the key.
5. Apply sealing agent to both sides of the flywheel lock washer and place it in position. Install the nut.
6. Install the brake (49 1881 060) and with the box wrench (49 0820 035) tighten the nut to 40.0-50.0 m-kg (289-362 ft. lbs.).
7. Bend the tab of the lockwasher.
8. Install the clutch disc and clutch cover assembly on the flywheel.

Counter Weight (Automatic Transmission)

1. Turn the engine so that the top of the engine is up.
2. Apply engine oil to the oil seal in the rear housing.
3. Fit the key into keyway on the eccentric shaft.
4. Install counter weight to the rear end of the eccentric shaft, aligning the keyway of the counter weight with the key.
5. Apply sealing agent to both sides of the lock washer and place it in position. Install the nut.
6. Install the stopper (49 1881 055) and with the box wrench (49 0820 035) tighten the nut to 40.0-50.0 m-kg (289-362 ft. lbs.).
7. Bend the tab of the lockwasher.
8. Install the drive plate on the counter weight as shown in Fig. 43 and tighten the attaching bolts.

Checking Eccentric Shaft End Play

1. Turn the engine on the engine stand

so that the front of the engine is up.
2. Fit the thrust plate with the chamfer downward, and slide the spacer and needle bearing onto the eccentric shaft. Then apply sufficient engine oil onto them.
3. Place the bearing housing on the front housing. Tighten the attaching bolts with washers.

NOTE: If the bearing housing has not been removed from the front housing, special care should be taken, when installing the spacer, so that the center of the needle bearing in the bearing housing comes to the center of eccentric shaft, and the spacer should be seated to the thrust plate.

4. Slide the needle bearing onto the shaft, and apply engine oil onto it.
5. Slide the balance weight together with the thrust washer onto the shaft.
6. Fit the key into keyway on the oil pump shaft.
7. Fit the oil pump drive chain onto the oil pump sprocket and eccentric shaft sprocket, and install them to

Fig. 41 Installing rear housing

Fig. 42 Tension bolt tightening sequence

Fig. 43 Installing drive plate

…

Fig. 44 Installing distributor drive gear

Fig. 45 Checking eccentric shaft end play

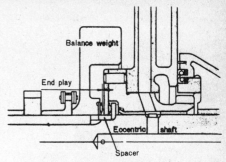

Fig. 46 Eccentric shaft end play

bolt to 10-12 m-kg (72-87 ft. lbs.).

NOTE: Use a new washer in the eccentric shaft pulley bolt when the pulley is removed.

the eccentric shaft and oil pump shaft, aligning the key and keyway, Fig. 2.

8. Aligning the keyways of the eccentric shaft sprocket and balance weight, and install the key.
9. Slide the distributor drive gear onto the eccentric shaft with "F" mark toward the front of engine, Fig. 44.
10. Install the eccentric shaft pulley onto the shaft aligning the keyway of the pulley with the key.
11. Install the pulley bolt and washer. Tighten the bolt to 10-12 m-kg (72-87 ft. lbs.).
12. Turn the engine on the engine stand so that the top of the engine is up.
13. To check the eccentric shaft end play, position a dial indicator on the rear housing so as to contact the feeler with the flywheel or the counter weight as shown in Fig. 45

Move the flywheel fore and aft, and note the reading of the indicator. The standard end play is 0.04-0.07 mm (0.0016-0.0028 in.).

If the end play is more than 0.09 mm (0.0035 in.), adjust it by grinding the spacer, Fig. 46, on the surface plate using an emery paper or by replacing the spacer with a thinner one.

If the end play is less than 0.04 mm (0.0016 in.), replace with a thicker spacer.

The spacers are available in the following thicknesses:

Identification Mark	Thickness
X	8.08 ± 0.01 mm (0.3181 ± 0.004 in.)
Y	8.04 ± 0.01 mm (0.3165 ± 0.004 in.)
V	8.02 ± 0.01 mm (0.3158 ± 0.004 in.)
Z	8.00 ± 0.01 mm (0.3150 ± 0.004 in.)

14. If the end play is 0.04-0.09 mm (0.0016-0.0035 in.), proceed as follows to install the oil pump chain adjuster.

Oil Pump Chain Adjuster

1. Turn engine on the engine stand so that the front of the engine is up.
2. Remove the eccentric shaft pulley.
3. Tighten the oil pump sprocket nut and bend the tab of the lock washer.
4. Place the chain adjuster in position and tighten the attaching nuts, then check the amount of protrusion of the chain adjuster as shown in Fig. 47. If the protrusion exceeds 12 mm (0.47 in.), replace the adjuster or chain.
5. Loosen the adjuster attaching nuts and install the guide plate. Tighten the attaching nuts securely.
6. Place a new "O" ring on the oil passage of the front housing, Fig. 48.
7. Place the gasket and front cover on the front housing, and tighten the attaching bolts.
8. Apply engine oil onto the oil seal in the front cover.
9. Install the eccentric shaft pulley onto the shaft and tighten the pulley

Oil Strainer & Oil Pan

1. Turn the engine on the engine stand so that the bottom of the engine is up.
2. Place the oil strainer gasket and strainer gasket and strainer on the front housing and tighten the attaching bolts.
3. Cut off the excess gaskets along the mounting surface of the oil pan, as shown in Fig. 49.
4. Apply the 4-6 mm (0.16-0.24 in.) diameter continuous bead of sealer (Part number 0398 77 739) on the mounting surface of the oil pan as shown in Fig. 50.

Be sure there are no gaps in the sealer bead.
5. Position the oil pan in position.
6. Install the bolts and tighten the bolts little by little in turn until the torque becomes .07-1.0 m-kg (5-7 ft. lbs.) evenly.

Manifold and Carburetor Assembly

1. Place the "O" rings and gasket in position.

Fig. 47 Checking chain adjuster protrusion

Fig. 48 Installing O-ring

Fig. 49 Cutting off excess gasket

2. Install the inlet manifold and carburetor assembly and tighten the attaching nuts.
3. Install the thermal reactor covers

and tighten the attaching bolts and nuts.
4. Connect the air outlet hose (thermal reactor—air control valve) to the air control valve.
5. Connect the oil hoses at the metering oil pump outlets.
6. Connect the metering oil pump connecting rod to the metering oil pump lever with washer and cotter pin.
7. Connect the vacuum sensing tube to the vacuum control unit of the distributor.

Final Assembly

1. Install water pump.
2. Install distributor.
3. Install thermal reactor.

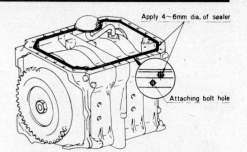

Fig. 50 Sealer application areas

4. Install alternator and belt.
5. Install air pump and belt.
6. Install oil filter and cover.
7. Install EGR valve and solenoid.
8. Install vacuum control valve.
9. Install deceleration control valve.

Carburetor Section
CARBURETOR SPECIFICATIONS

Year	Model	Carburetor	Dimension (inches)			Fast Idle Speed RPM	Fast Idle Speed Clearance	Vacuum Break Inches of Hg.	
			H	L	R @ 86°F			Operating	Testing
1972	1200	2 Barrel	.59	—	—	—	.064	—	—
	1800	—	—	—	—	—	—	—	—
	618	2 Barrel	.256	—	—	—	.063	—	—
	808	—	—	—	—	—	—	—	—
	R100	4 Barrel	.71	—	—	—	.039	—	—
	RX-2	—	—	—	—	—	—	—	—
1973	618	2 Barrel	.265	—	—	—	.063	—	—
	808	—	—	—	—	—	—	—	—
	B1600	2 Barrel	.236	—	—	—	.051	—	—
	RX-2	4 Barrel	.22①	2.2	—	—	.047	—	—
	RX-3	4 Barrel	.22①	2.2	—	—	.047	—	—
1974	808	2 Barrel	—	—	—	—	—	—	—
	B1600	2 Barrel	—	—	—	—	—	—	—
	RX-2	4 Barrel	.197	2.2	.009	—	②	—	—
	RX-3	4 Barrel	.197	2.2	.009	—	②	—	—
	RX-4	4 Barrel	.430	2.05	④	—	③	—	—
	RE-Pick-up	4 Barrel	.430	2.05	④	—	③	—	—
1975	808	2 Barrel	.256	—	.070	—	.070	5.9—7.5	9.8—12.0
	B1600	2 Barrel	.256	—	.070	—	.070	5.9—7.5	9.8—12.0
	RX-3	4 Barrel	.390	2.05	⑤	3000—3500	.078	—	—
	RX-4	4 Barrel	.390	2.05	⑥	3000—3500	.078	—	—
	RE-Pick-up	4 Barrel	.410	2.05	⑦	2800—3500	.065	—	—
1976	808 (1300)	2 Barrel	.433	.059	⑧	—	.052	—	—
	808 (1600)	2 Barrel	.236	.047	.070	—	.070	5.9—7.5	9.8—12.0
	RX-3	4 Barrel	.470	2.13	.080	3000—3500	⑨	—	—
	RX-4	4 Barrel	.340	2.05	.060	3000—3500	.073	—	—
	Cosmo	4 Barrel	.340	2.05	.060	3000—3500	.073	—	—
	RE-Pick-up	4 Barrel	.330	2.05	⑭	3000—3500	⑮	—	—
1977	GLC	2 Barrel	.433	.059	⑩	3000—4000	.054	⑪	⑫
	808 (1300)	2 Barrel	.440	.060	⑩	3000—4000	.054	⑪	⑫
	808 (1600)	2 Barrel	.236	.047	.065	2500—3500	⑬	5.9—7.5	9.8—12.0
	B1800	2 Barrel	.236	.047	⑯	2500—3500	.071	6.7—8.3	11.0—13.4
	RX-3	4 Barrel	.470	2.13	.110	3200—4000	⑰	—	—
	RX-4	4 Barrel	.100	2.05	.100	3000—3500	⑱	—	—
	Cosmo	4 Barrel	.100	2.05	.100	3000—3500	⑱	—	—

Continued

CARBURETOR SPECIFICATIONS NOTES—Continued

—Not Available
①—With gasket in place.
②—Manual trans., .0461—.0616″; Auto. trans., .0480—.0618″.
③—Manual trans., .0398—.0524″; Auto. trans., .480—.0618″.
④—Angle of choke valve; Auto. trans., 45°; Manual trans., 53°.
⑤—Manual trans., .116″; Auto. trans., .157″.
⑥—Manual trans., .116″; Auto. trans., .120″.
⑦—Manual trans., .157″; Auto. trans., .236″.
⑧—Exc. Calif., .070″; Calif., .050″.
⑨—Manual trans., .079″; Auto. trans., Exc. Calif., .079″; Calif., .087″.

⑩—Exc. Calif., .050; Calif., .070″.
⑪—Exc. Calif., 8.7″ of Hg.; Calif. 7.5″ of Hg.
⑫—Exc. Calif., 13.6″ of Hg.; Calif., 12.6″ of Hg.
⑬—Exc. Calif., .071″; Calif., .067″.
⑭—Exc. Calif., auto. trans., .225″; Manual trans., .157″; Calif., .082″.
⑮—Exc. Calif., .06″; Calif., .08″.
⑯—Exc. Calif. & High altitude .057″; Calif. & High altitude, .066″.
⑰—Exc. Calif., .035—.043; Calif., .043″—.055″.
⑱—Exc. Calif., .041″; Calif., .054″.

TWO BARREL CARBURETOR

Float Level, Adjust

Exc. GLC, 1300 & 1600

1. With the engine operating, check the fuel level in the fuel bowl sight glass.
2. If the fuel level is not to the specified mark in the sight glass, remove the carburetor from the vehicle.
3. Remove the fuel bowl sight glass.
4. Invert the carburetor on a stand and allow the float to hang by its own weight.
5. Measure the clearance "H" between the float and the bowl. If clearance is not within specifications, bend the float seat lip until the proper clearance is obtained, Fig. 1.
6. Turn the carburetor to the normal position and allow the float to hang by its own weight.
7. Measure the clearance "L" between the bottom of the float and the bowl, Fig. 2

   If the clearance is not within specifications, bend the float stopper until the proper clearance is obtained.
8. Install the fuel bowl sight glass.
9. Install the carburetor to the engine.
10. Operate the engine and make sure that the fuel level is to the specified mark in the sight glass.

GLC, 1300 & 1600

1. With the engine operating, check the fuel level in the fuel bowl sight glass.
2. If the fuel level is not to the specified mark in the sight glass, remove the air horn from the carburetor.
3. Invert the air horn on a stand and lower the float until the float seat lip just contacts the needle valve.
4. Measure the clearance "H" between the float and the air horn, Fig. 3.

   If the clearance is not within specifications, bend the float seat lip until the proper clearance is obtained.
5. Lift up the float and check the clearance "L," Fig. 4, between float seat lip and the needle valve. If the clearance is not within specifications, bend the float stopper until the proper clearance is obtained.
6. Install the carburetor to the engine.
7. Operate the engine and make sure that the fuel is at the specified mark in the sight glass.

Vacuum Break, Adjust

1. If equipped, disconnect the bullet connectors from the water thermo switch and connect a jumper wire to both connectors.

   Turn the ignition switch on.
2. Pull the choke knob and fully close the choke valve.
3. Disconnect the vacuum sensing tube from the vacuum break diaphragm and an external vacuum source to the vacuum break diaphragm.
4. Gradually apply vacuum to the vacuum break diaphragm and note reading of the gauge when the diaphragm just starts to operate.
5. Apply specified vacuum to the vacuum break diaphragm. Then, check the clearance "R" between the carburetor air horn and choke valve with wire gauge, Fig. 5. If the clearance is not within the specifications, correct the clearance by bending the connecting rod which connects the diaphragm and choke valve.

Fast Idle Speed, Adjust

1. Connect a tachometer to the engine.
2. Warm up the engine to the normal operating temperature.

   Make certain the idle speed and mixture are adjusted to specification before checking the fast idle speed.
3. Stop the engine and remove the air cleaner assembly.
4. Start the engine and run at idle.
5. Loosen the screw attaching the choke outer cable to the carburetor.
6. Hold the choke valve extension lever to wide open position and fully pull the choke cable. Note the engine speed.

Fig. 1 Checking float level. Two barrel carburetor exc. GLC, 1300 & 1600

Fig. 2 Checking float drop. Two barrel carburetor exc. GLC, 1300 & 1600

Fig. 3 Checking float level. Two barrel carburetor, GLC, 1300 & 1600

Fig. 4 Checking float level. Two barrel carburetor, GLC, 1300 & 1600

Fig. 5 Checking vacuum break. Two barrel carburetor

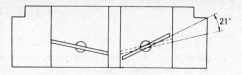

Fig. 6 Fast idle adjustment. Two & four barrel carburetor

Fig. 7 Checking float level. Four barrel carburetor

7. If it is not within the specification, adjust the fast idle as follows:
   a. Remove the carburetor from the engine.
   b. With the choke valve fully closed, measure the clearance between the primary throttle valve and the wall of the throttle bore, Fig. 6.
   c. If the clearance is not within specifications, bend the fast idle rod until the proper clearance is obtained.

FOUR BARREL CARBURETOR

Float Level, Adjust

1. With engine operating, check the fuel level in each fuel bowl sight glass.
2. If the fuel level is not within the specified mark in the sight glass, remove the air horn from the carburetor.
3. Invert the air horn on a stand and allow the float to hang.
4. Measure the clearance "H" between the float and air horn gasket, Fig. 7. If the clearance is not within specifi-

cations, bend the float seat lip until the proper clearance is obtained.
5. Turn the air horn to the normal position and allow the float to lower by its own weight.
6. Measure the distance "L" between the bottom of float and the air horn gasket, Fig. 8. If the distance is not within specifications, bend the float stopper until the proper distance is obtained.
7. Install the air horn to the carburetor.
8. Operate the engine and make sure that the fuel level is to the specified mark in each sight glass.

Choke Valve Opening, Adjust

1. Remove the air cleaner.
2. Disconnect the vacuum sensing tube from the vacuum diaphragm and connect an external vacuum source.
3. Apply the vacuum of more than 400

mm-Hg (15.7 in-Hg) to vacuum diaphragm.
4. Fully pull out the choke lever link and retain in position by wire.
5. Check the clearance between the stopper and bimetal spring lever, Fig. 9.
   If the clearance is not within specifications, adjust the adjusting screw until the proper clearance is obtained.

Bi-Metal Spring, Adjust

1. Fully pull out the choke lever link and retain in position by wire.
2. Push the diaphragm plunger in fully and position by wire.
3. Check the choke valve clearance "R," Fig. 10.
4. If the clearance "R" is not within specifications, first loosen "A" then turn "B" to adjust the clearance "R," Fig. 11.

Fig. 8 Checking float drop. Four barrel carburetor

1. Adjusting screw   3. Bimetal spring lever
2. Stopper

Fig. 9 Checking clearance between stopper & bimetal spring lever. Four barrel carburetor

Fig. 10 Checking choke valve clearance. Four barrel carburetor

Fast Idle Speed, Adjust

1. Connect a tachometer to the engine.
2. Warm up the engine to the normal operating temperature and stop the engine.
3. With the choke knob fully pulled, start the engine. If the engine speed reaches 3,000-3,500 rpm within about 10 seconds after starting, the fast idle is satisfactory.

Fig. 11 Adjusting choke valve clearance. Four barrel carburetor

4. If it is not within the specification, adjust the fast idle as follows:
   a. Remove the carburetor from the engine.
   b. With the choke valve fully closed, measure the clearance between the primary throttle valve and the wall of the throttle, Fig. 6.
   c. If the clearance is not within the specification, bend the fast idle rod until the proper clearance is obtained.

Emission Controls Section

POSITIVE CRANKCASE VENTILATION SYSTEM

Description & Operation

The positive crankcase ventilation system channels blow-by gases into the intake manifold to burn them up in the combustion chamber and helps to control air pollution caused by crankcase blow-by gas. The air and blow-by gases flow in the ventilation system as shown in Fig. 1.

System Servicing

Rotary Engine Models
1. Check to see that the air cleaner element is not clogged.
2. Install a vacuum gauge.
3. Start the engine. When the engine speed is raised to 2500-3000 rpm, the vacuum reading must be under 60 mm-Hg.

Piston Engine Models
1. Disconnect the ventilation hose from the positive crankcase ventilation valve.
2. Keep the engine idling. Close with the finger the inlet of ventilation valve, and if the clicking sound of the valve is audible or if the engine speed becomes slightly lower than the idling speed, the ventilation valve is normal.

EVAPORATIVE EMISSION CONTROL SYSTEM

Description, Fig. 2

The evaporative emission control system seals the fuel system completely and prevents emission of the fuel vapor generated by the ambient temperature around the fuel tank when the car is running or standing. The fuel vapor rising from the surface of the fuel in the fuel tank due to the high ambient temperature is channeled into the condense tank and condensed fuel is fed back to the fuel tank. The fuel vapor that has not condensed in the condense tank is led into the carbon canister. The active carbon in the canister absorbs the fuel vapors and stores them. During periods of engine operation, the fuel vapor stored in the carbon canister is purged from the active carbon by fresh air drawn from the inlet hole at the bot-

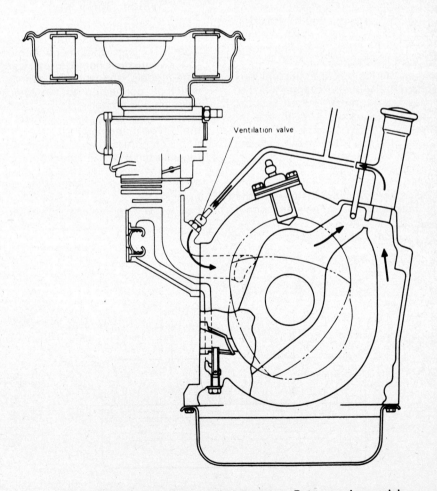

Ventilation valve

Fig. 1 Positive crankcase ventilation system. Rotary engine models

tom of the canister, and sucked into the air cleaner. Then the fuel vapor in the air cleaner is led into the combustion chamber through the intake manifold and burnt up.

Operation

Condense Tank, Fig. 3

The condense tank is installed near the fuel tank and condenses the fuel vapor coming from the fuel tank and returns it to the fuel tank.

Check Valve

The check valve located between the condense tank and the canister works appropriately when the conditions mentioned below take place, relating to the completely sealed ventilation type fuel system.

1. When the evaporative system is normal, the flow of fuel vapor and ventilation during engine operation are as shown in Fig. 4.
2. If the hose between the check valve and the canister is clogged or frozen, the ventilation of the fuel system will not work at all and as a result, the fuel supply to the engine will be cut off. Therefore, when the evaporative line is clogged, the valve, Fig. 5, is opened by the negative pressure in the fuel tank and the ventilation passage to the atmosphere is opened.
3. When the fuel vapor in the fuel tank is expanded due to intense heat, the pressure in the fuel tank will increase. In order to prevent the increase of the pressure in the fuel tank, the valve, is opened to release the pressure to the atmosphere.

Canister

The canister which is installed in the engine room on 808 models and within

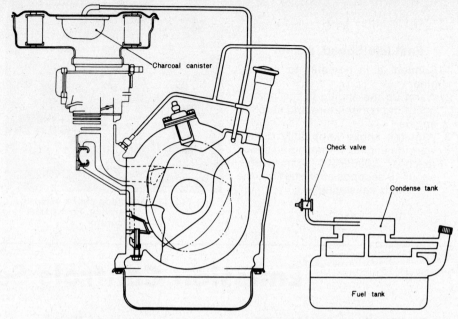

Fig. 2   Evaporative emission control system. Rotary engine models

the air cleaner housing on rotary engine models absorbs the fuel vapor generated in the fuel tank with the active carbon and stores them.

System Servicing

Checking Evaporative Line

1. Disconnect the evaporative hose from the T joint which is connected to the ventilation hose on rotary engine models, and from the canister which is connected to the check valve on 808 models.
2. Connect the disconnected hose to the U-type manometer.
3. Apply compressed air gradually into the manometer and the difference of water level should be 14.0 inches. After that, blind the inlet of the manometer.
4. Leave the manometer for five min-

utes, with the inlet blind. Then, if the difference of water level is over 13.5 inches, the evaporative line will be in good condition. If the difference is not within the specifications, inspect the following parts. If there is any defect, repair or replace as necessary.

Leaky or loose hoses.
Leaky condense tank.
Leaky fuel tank.
Leaky or loose fuel line.
Leaky filler cap.
Leaky fuel gauge unit.

Charcoal Canister Rotary Engine Models

1. Check to see that the air cleaner element is not clogged.
2. Visually check the adhering condition of oil. When the whole surface is damp with oil, measure the ventilation resistance.
3. Attach a vacuum gauge. Check to see that when the engine speed is raised to 2500-3000 rpm, the vacuum gauge reads under 60 mm-Hg.

NOTE: The charcoal canister and air

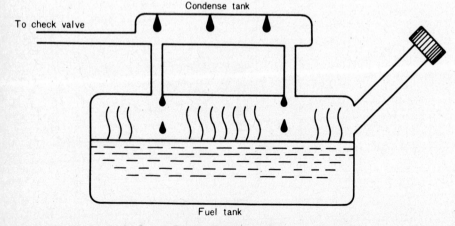

Fig. 3   Condense tank

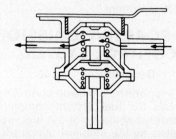

Fig. 4   Check valve operation

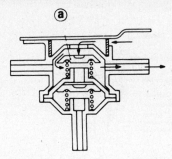

Fig. 5 Check valve operation

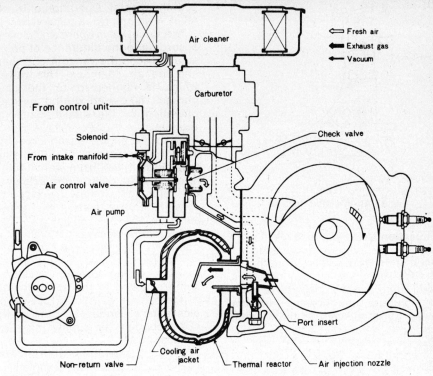

Fig. 6 Air injection system and thermal reactor. Rotary engine models

cleaner cover should be replaced as an assembly only.

Check Valve
1. Remove the check valve.
2. Cover one end of the check valve by hand, and install the pressure gauge to the other end.
3. Breathe in and out of the check valve with pressure of about 7.1 lb/in². If the valve operates it is satisfactory. If not, replace it with a new one.

AIR INJECTION SYSTEM, THERMAL REACTOR & SECONDARY AIR CONTROL SYSTEM
Rotary Engine Models, Fig. 6
Description

The air injection and thermal reactor system, consisting of a thermal reactor, an air pump, a check valve, air injection nozzles and an air control valve, injects into the exhaust ports secondary air necessary for oxidation of hydrocarbon and carbon monoxide contained in the exhaust gas.

The air sucked from the air cleaner by the air pump is sent into the air control valve. The air (secondary air) from the air control valve ordinarily flows into the exhaust ports through the check valve and the air injection nozzles. However, under the conditions mentioned below, the flow of the secondary air into the exhaust ports is stopped by the ignition and air flow control system as well as protective system (operation of air cut valve), and the air (cooling air) flows into the thermal reactor cooling air jacket to properly maintain the temperature of the reactor:
1. When the engine speed is over 4000 rpm (in case of automatic transmission, 4800 rpm when engine is cold and 3400 rpm when engine is hot). Operation of ignition and air flow control system.

2. When the engine speed is over 1200 rpm during deceleration (1400 rpm in case of automatic transmission). Operation of ignition and air flow control system.
3. When running under full load (throttle valve is nearly wide open).
4. When the floor temperature is over approximately 120°C (248°F). Operation of protective system.

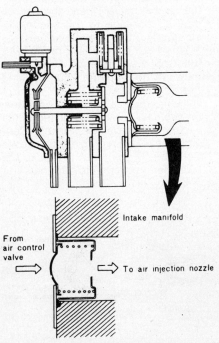

Fig. 7 Check valve operation

The timing of supplying the secondary air into the exhaust ports and the cooling air into the thermal reactor cooling air jacket is controlled in accordance with the operating conditions of the vehicle.

Operation
Air Pump

The air pump is a vane type driven by the V-belt mounted on the eccentric shaft pulley. The air pump sucks fresh filtered air from the air cleaner compresses the air and injects it through the air control valve, check valve and air injection nozzles into the exhaust ports adjacent to the thermal reactor.

Check Valve, Fig. 7

The check valve opens and closes according to the pressure difference between secondary air and exhaust gas to prevent exhaust gas from backflowing into the air injection system and scorching the air pump, hoses, etc. When the pressure of secondary air in the air injection system exceeds the exhaust gas pressure, the secondary air opens the check valve and flows through the air injection nozzles into the exhaust ports.

When the secondary air pressure drops lower than the exhaust gas pressure due to failure of the air pump belt, breaking of the secondary air hose, etc., the check valve closes to prevent the backflow of the exhaust gas into the air injection system.

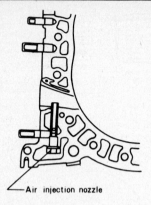

Fig. 8   Air injection nozzles

Air Injection Nozzles, Fig. 8

The air injection nozzles are attached to each of the front and rear rotor housings. The secondary air channeled via the air pump and the check valve is injected through the nozzles into the exhaust ports adjacent to the thermal reactor.

Air Control Valve, Fig. 9

The air control valve, consisting of an air cut valve, a No. 1 relief valve and a No. 2 relief valve, has the following functions:

1. When the air cut valve is not operating, it becomes the passage of the secondary air from the air pump into the exhaust ports through the check valve and air injection nozzles. Operation of air control valve.

2. When the engine speed is over 4000 rpm (in case of automatic transmission, 3400 rpm when the engine is hot and 4800 rpm when it is cold), the supply of the secondary air into the exhaust ports stops and the secondary air (cooling air) flows into the thermal reactor cooling air jacket to cool the reactor to properly maintain the temperature of the reactor. Operation of air cut valve.

3. When the engine speed is over 1200 rpm during deceleration (1400 rpm in case of automatic transmission), supply of the secondary air into the exhaust ports stops and the secondary air (cooling air) flows to the thermal reactor cooling air jacket. The secondary air cutting in this instance prevents excessive supply of the secondary air into the exhaust ports and deteriorated reaction efficiency of the exhaust gas in the reactor. Operation of air cut valve.

4. When the air pressure in the air injection system is excessive, the supply of the secondary air into the exhaust ports is adjusted properly and the excessive secondary air (cooling air) is relieved to the thermal reactor cooling air jacket to

cool the reactor. Operation of No. 1 relief valve and No. 2 relief valve.

The air cut valve opens and closes according to the difference of pressure between the vacuum chamber and the air chamber. This valve, which is connected to the diaphragm, is closed during normal operation by the intake manifold vacuum.

When the engine speed exceeds 4000 rpm (in case of automatic transmission 3400 rpm warm, 4800 rpm cold), the control unit actuates the solenoid to close the vacuum sensing. This equalizes the pressures in the two chambers. The spring force causes the valve to open and the air in the air injection system is channeled to the thermal reactor cooling air jacket before being expelled to the atmosphere. At the same time, the air cut valve closes the secondary air passage to cut secondary air supply into the exhaust ports.

During deceleration, with the accelerator pedal released completely, when the engine speed is over 1200 rpm (1400 rpm in case of automatic transmission), the solenoid of the air control valve closes the vacuum sensing between the intake manifold and the air control valve by means of the low speed switch in the control unit and the idle switch. Consequently, the spring force causes the valve to open and the air in the air injection system is channeled to the thermal reactor cooling air jacket before being expelled to the atmosphere. At the same time, the air cut valve closes the secondary air passage to cut secondary air supply into the exhaust ports.

When the engine is running with full load, the difference of pressure between the vacuum chamber and the air chamber of the air control valve diminishes because the intake manifold vacuum which is led to the vacuum chamber decreases. Consequently, the spring force causes the valve to open and the air in the air injection system is channeled to

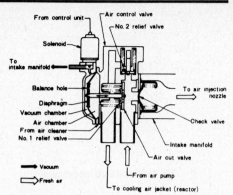

Fig. 9   Crossectional view of air control valve

the thermal reactor cooling air jacket before being expelled to the atmosphere. At the same time, the air cut valve closes the secondary air passage to cut secondary air supply into the exhaust ports. The No. 1 relief valve is opened and closed in accordance with air pressure in the air injection system and the force of the return spring. When the air pressure in the air injection system increases, the No. 1 relief valve is opened and the air is led to the thermal reactor cooling air jacket to cool it before being expelled to the atmosphere. Thus the secondary air flow rate is being controlled. When the air pressure decreases, the spring closes the valve.

The No. 2 relief valve is opened and closed in accordance with air pressure in the air injection system and the force of the return spring. When the air pressure in the air injection system exceeds the specified value, the No. 2 relief valve is opened and the air is led to the thermal reactor cooling air jacket to cool it before being expelled to the atmosphere. Thus the secondary air flow rate is controlled. When the air pressure decreases, the spring closes the valve.

Thermal Reactor

The thermal reactor is mounted just outside the exhaust ports. It oxidizes the unburned exhaust gas expelled from the engine, to reduce the noxious components such as hydrocarbon and carbon monoxide. When the engine speed is high or during deceleration or full load running, the air control valve feeds fresh air from the air pump to the thermal reactor cooling air jacket to properly maintain the temperature of the reactor. The non-return valve which prevents backflow of exhaust gas from the reactor is attached at the air inlet of the reactor.

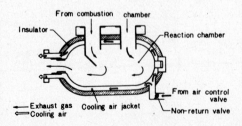

Fig. 10   Thermal reactor air flow

Manual transmission

Operating time	Parts that operate coordinately
When engine speed is over 4,000 rpm	solenoid of air control valve, air cut valve, high speed switch
During deceleration when engine speed is over 1,200 rpm	solenoid of air control valve, air cut valve, low speed switch, idle switch
When running under full load (throttle valve is nearly wide open)	air cut valve
When floor temperature is over approximately 120°C (248°F) (Protective system)	heat hazard sensor, control unit, solenoid of air control valve, air cut valve

Automatic transmission

Operating time	Parts that operate coordinately
When engine speed is over the specified value 4,800 rpm when cold 3,400 rpm when hot	solenoid of air control valve, air cut valve, high speed switch, thermosensor, thermoswitch (the last two parts when engine is hot)
During deceleration when engine speed is 1,400 rpm	solenoid of air control valve, air cut valve, low speed switch, idle switch
When running with full load (throttle valve is nearly wide open)	air cut valve
When floor temperature is over approximately 120°C (248°F) (Protective system)	heat hazard sensor, control unit, solenoid of air control valve, air cut valve

Fig. 11   Operating mode of secondary air injection system

Ignition and Air Flow Control System, Fig. 10

The ignition and air flow control system consists of a thermosensor, a thermodetector, an idle switch and a control unit including high speed switch, low speed switch, thermoswitch and trailing ignition switch. This system ignites and cuts the trailing spark plug to suit engine temperature and engine speed in order to enhance the reactivity of the thermal reactor when the engine is cold. This system has an additional function of regulating the air control valve and the deceleration control valve.

The operating time of the ignition and air flow control system is shown by the following table, Fig. 11 and 12.

Thermosensor

The thermosensor, which is placed in the cooling water passage, detects the water temperature and sends the signal to the control unit.

When the water temperature rises to the specified value, the thermoswitch and the trailing ignition switch in the control unit close by means of the thermosensor. The electric current then flows to the trailing side ignition coil and the trailing spark plug is ignited. In case of automatic transmission, the opening/closing time of the high speed switch in the control unit goes from 4800 rpm when the engine is cold to 3400 rpm when it is hot. Consequently, when the engine speed is over 3400 rpm

hot, the high speed switch closes and the electric current flows to the solenoid of the air control valve and the solenoid cuts the vacuum sensing between the intake manifold and the air chamber of the air control valve. The air cut valve of the air control valve then stops the supply of the secondary air into the exhaust ports by means of the spring force. The secondary air flows into the thermal reactor cooling air jacket to cool the reactor.

Thermodetector

The thermodetector, which detects the ambient temperature, corrects the operating temperature of the thermosensor to resume the ignition of the trailing spark plug after the minimum time required for the thermal reactor warmup.

Control Unit

In the control unit are the thermoswitch, trailing ignition switch, low speed switch and high speed switch. The functions are as follows. Refer to Fig. 13:

1. In the whole hot operating range, the thermoswitch and the trailing ignition switch close and the electric current flows to the trailing side ignition coil and the trailing spark plug is ignited. Operation of the thermoswitch and trailing ignition switch.

2. When the engine speed is over 3400 rpm hot, the thermoswitch and the high speed switch close and the electric current flows to the solenoid of the air control valve. Consequently, the solenoid cuts the vacuum sensing between the intake manifold and the vacuum chamber. This actuates the air cut valve to stop the supply of the secondary air into the exhaust ports and the air flows into the thermal reactor cooling air jacket (only in case of automatic transmission). Operation of thermoswitch and high speed switch.

3. When the engine speed is over 4000 rpm (in case of automatic transmission, 4800 rpm cold and 3400 rpm hot), the high speed switch closes and the electric current flows to the solenoid of the air control valve. The solenoid consequently cuts the vacuum sensing between the intake manifold and the vacuum chamber of the air control valve. This actuates the air cut valve to stop the supply of the secondary air into the exhaust ports and the air flows to the thermal reactor cooling air jacket. Operation of high speed switch.

Manual transmission

Operating time	Parts that operate coordinately
1. Trailing spark plug does not ignite. (Only leading spark plug ignites.)	
During cruising and acceleration (deceleration excluded) when engine speed is 1,200 ~ 4,000 rpm at cold condition	low speed switch, high speed switch, idle switch, trailing ignition switch
2. Trailing spark plug ignites. (Both leading and trailing spark plugs ignite.)	
When engine is hot	thermosensor, thermoswitch, trailing ignition switch
During cruising, acceleration and deceleration when engine speed is below 1,200 rpm or over 4,000 rpm at cold condition	low speed switch, high speed switch, trailing ignition switch, idle switch

Automatic transmission

Operating time	Parts that operate coordinately
1. Trailing spark plug does not ignite. (Only leading spark plug ignites.)	
During cruising and acceleration (deceleration excluded) when engine speed is 1,400 ~ 4,800 rpm at cold condition	low speed switch, high speed switch, idle switch, trailing ignition switch
2. Trailing spark plug ignites. (Both leading and trailing spark plugs ignite.)	
When engine is hot	thermosensor, thermoswitch, trailing ignition switch
During cruising, acceleration and deceleration when engine speed is below 1,400 rpm or over 4,800 rpm at cold condition	low speed switch, high speed switch, trailing ignition switch, idle switch

Fig. 12   Operating mode of trailing spark plug ignition

4. Whether cold or hot, when the engine speed is over 1200 rpm (1400 rpm in case of automatic transmission), point [A] of the low speed switch closes and the electric current flows to the idle switch; during deceleration when the accelerator pedal is relieved completely, point [A] of the idle switch closes, and so the electric current from the low speed switch flows to the solenoid of the air control valve. The solenoid then closes the vacuum sensing between the intake manifold and the air control valve. This actuates the air cut valve to stop the supply of the secondary air into the exhaust port and the air flows into the thermal reactor cooling air jacket. At the same time, since the electric current to the solenoid of the coasting valve stops, the solenoid opens the atmospheric pressure sensing line. This actuates the coasting valve and the fresh air from the air cleaner enters the intake manifold and prevents afterburn. Operation of low speed switch.

5. When the engine speed is below 1200 rpm (1400 rpm in case of automatic transmission), point [B] of the low speed switch closes. The electric current flows to the trailing side ignition coil through the trailing ignition switch, and ignites the trailing spark plug. Operation of low speed switch and trailing ignition switch.

Idle Switch

The idle switch detects the deceleration condition of the car. It sends the decelerating condition signal to the control unit and the coasting valve.

The functions are as follows. Refer to Fig. 13:

1. During deceleration (with the accelerator pedal released) when the engine speed is over 1200 rpm (1400 rpm in case of automatic transmission), point [A] of the idle switch closes and the electric current flows to the air control valve solenoid from the low speed switch. The solenoid consequently cuts the vacuum sensing between the intake manifold and the vacuum chamber of the air control valve. This actuates the air cut valve to stop the supply of the secondary air into the exhaust ports and the air flows to the thermal reactor cooling air jack-

2. At the same time, since the electric current to the solenoid of the coasting valve stops, the solenoid opens the atmospheric pressure sensing line. This actuates the coasting valve and the fresh air from the air

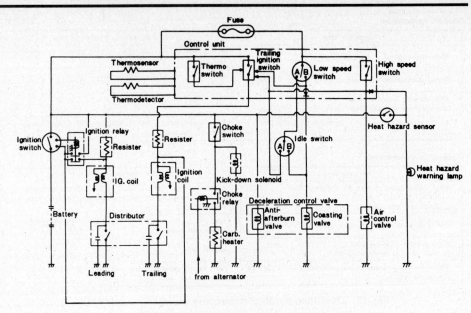

Fig. 13 Control unit wiring schematic

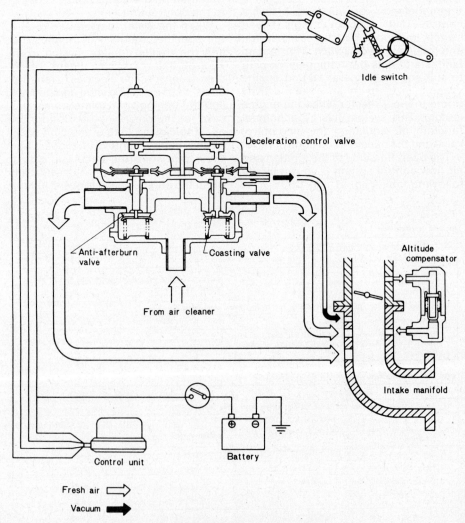

Fig. 14 Additional air control system

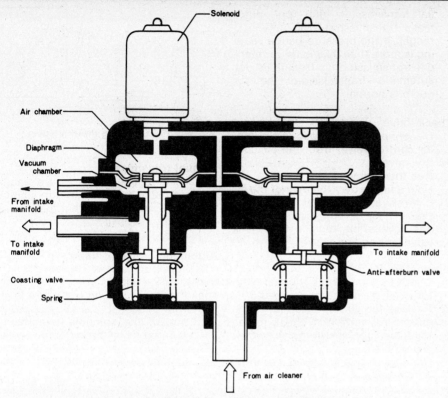

Fig. 15 Deceleration valve crossectional view

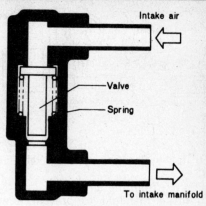

Fig. 16 Altitude compensator crossectional view

cleaner enters the intake manifold and prevents afterburn.

3. When point [B] of the low speed switch and point [A] of the idle switch are closed, the electric current flows to the trailing side ignition coil through the trailing ignition switch, and ignites the trailing spark plug.

Additional Air Control System, Fig. 14

The additional air control system consists of the deceleration control valve and the altitude compensator. During deceleration and gear shifting and immediately after turning off the ignition switch, the additional air control system sends the fresh air from the air cleaner to the intake manifold and adjusts the excessively rich fuel air mixture preventing afterburn and reducing emissions during deceleration. (Operation of deceleration control valve.) In order to adjust the excessively rich fuel air mixture in running in the highland area, the air is supplied to the intake manifold to improve the combustion.

Deceleration Control Valve, Fig. 15

The deceleration control valve consists of an anti-afterburn valve and the coasting valve. The functions are as follows:

1. When the engine speed is over 1200 rpm (1400 rpm in case of automatic transmission), and during deceleration when the accelerator pedal is

relieved completely, the deceleration control valve sends the fresh air from the air cleaner to the intake manifold. Operation of coasting valve.

2. Immediately after deceleration and during gear shifting the deceleration control valve sends the fresh air from the air cleaner to the intake manifold. Operation of anti-afterburn valve.

3. Immediately after turning off the ignition switch, the deceleration control valve sends the fresh air from the air cleaner to the intake manifold. Operation of the anti-afterburn valve and coasting valve.

The anti-afterburn valve operates by pressure difference between the vacuum chamber and the air chamber and the spring force. The balance hole in the diaphragm con-

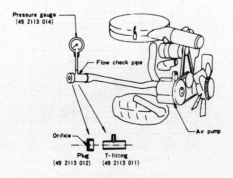

Fig. 17 Checking air pump

nects the vacuum chamber and the air chamber to control the duration of valve opening.

The intake manifold vacuum rises during deceleration and gear shifting, and the pressure difference between the two chambers opens the valve connected to the diaphragm, so that fresh air from the air cleaner is led into the intake manifold to correct overrich mixture, thus preventing afterburn. When the balance hole equalizes pressure difference, the valve is closed to shut off air. When the ignition switch is turned on, the solenoid shuts the atmospheric pressure sensing line leading to the air chamber. When the engine is switched off the solenoid opens the sensing lines, and due to the resulting pressure difference between the vacuum chamber and the air chamber, the valve connected to the diaphragm is opened. Fresh air is led from the air cleaner into the intake manifold to prevent afterburn.

The coasting valve operates by pressure difference between the vacuum chamber and the air chamber and the spring force. The rise of intake manifold vacuum during deceleration and gear shifting causes the valve to open. Air from the air cleaner is supplied into the intake manifold to prevent afterburn and to keep the thermal reactor operating.

During deceleration when the engine speed is above 1200 rpm (1400 rpm for automatic transmission), the control unit and the idle switch command solenoid to open the atmospheric pressure sensing line leading to the air chamber. Due to resulting pressure difference between the vacuum chamber and the air chamber, the valve connected to the diaphragm is opened. Fresh air

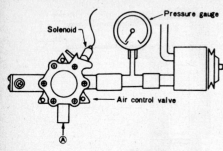

Fig. 18 Checking air control valve

is led from the air cleaner into the intake manifold to prevent afterburn. When the ignition switch is turned on, the solenoid shuts the atmospheric pressure sensing line leading to the air chamber. When the engine is switched off the solenoid opens the sensing line, and due to the resulting pressure difference between the vacuum chamber and the air chamber, the valve connected to the diaphragm is opened. Fresh air is led from the air cleaner into the intake manifold to prevent afterburn.

Altitude Compensator, Fig. 16

In order to prevent the fuel/air mixture from becoming excessively rich because of the low atmospheric pressure in high altitudes, the altitude compensator sends the air to the intake manifold and adjusts the fuel air mixture.

In high altitudes, especially during idling, part of the inhaled air is controlled by the altitude compensator and enters the intake manifold directly. This enables the overrich mixture to be properly adjusted. The hoses for altitude compensator are blue for identification.

Kickdown Control System (Auto. Trans.)

As well as the normal kickdown operation for the transmission shifting, the kickdown solenoid is energized to cause the kickdown when the choke system is in operating condition (the choke switch is closed) for semiautomatic choke system, or when the engine water temperature is cold (the water temperature switch is closed) for full-automatic choke system.

System Servicing

Air Pump
1. Check to see that the air pump V belt tension is proper.
2. Check to see that air hoses are free of air leaks.
3. Attach the air pump gauge set, Fig. 17.
4. Run the engine at idle speed (man-

ual transmission—900 rpm, automatic transmission—750 rpm in D range). If the pressure gauge reading is more than 0.68 lb/in² for manual transmission or 0.48 lb/in² for automatic transmission, the air pump is normal.

Check Valve
1. Disconnect the air hose (air pump-air control valve) from the air control valve.
2. Run the engine at idle speed.
3. Hold a finger over the inlet of the air control valve (the inlet from which the air hose is removed). If exhaust gas flow is felt, replace the check valve, spring and gasket.

Thermal Reactor
1. Check to see that the thermal reactor is not damaged or cracked.
2. Remove the air hose leading to the air control valve and check to see that the non-return valve works smoothly.
3. Start the engine and keep it running at idle speed.
4. Make sure that most exhaust gas is not released from the tail of cooling air pipe.

Air Control Valve
1. Check the air pump according to the procedures described previously.
2. Attach the connector of the solenoid terminal to the battery and check the operation of the solenoid. If the clicking sound is audible, the solenoid is normal.
3. Attach the pressure gauge as shown in Fig. 18.
4. Remove the air hose from outlet [A] of the air control valve.
5. Start the engine and keep it running at idle speed (900 rpm for manual transmission, 750 rpm in D range for automatic transmission). Check to see that there is no air leak from outlet [A] of the air control valve.

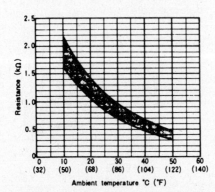

Fig. 20 Checking resistance of thermo sensor

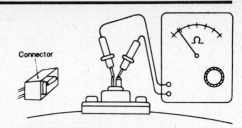

Fig. 19 Checking thermosensor

Manual transmission
Make sure that the pressure gauge reads 1.2-2.8 lb/in² when the engine speed is 3500 rpm and that there is air leak from outlet [A].

Automatic Transmission
Make sure that the pressure gauge reads 1.2-2.6 lb./in.² when the engine speed is 3000 rpm and that there is air leak from outlet [A].
6. Connect the solenoid terminal to the battery. Make sure that the pressure gauge reads 0-0.75 lb./in.² and that air flows from outlet [A] of the air control valve.
7. Simple checking of air control valve (check every valve incorporated). When the No. 1 relief valve, No. 2 relief valve or the air cut valve is faulty, the air sent from the air pump during idling flows into the air cooling pipe.

Thermosensor
1. Make sure that there is no boot breakage.
2. Connect the ohmmeter as shown in Fig. 19, and check the resistance. The readings as shown below indicate that the thermosensor is normal.

   Over 7 kilo-ohms before warmup. (When ambient and water temperatures are under 30° C (86° F).

   Under 2.3 kilo-ohms after warmup. (When temperature is over 70° C (156° F).

Thermodetector
Connect the ohmmeter to the terminals of the thermodetector and check the resistance. If the ohmmeter readings are within the range shown in Fig. 20, the thermodetector is normal.

Control Unit
1. Make sure that the fuse of the control unit is in good condition.
2. Disconnect the couplers of the thermosensor and idle switch. Check the following points:

   Connect a timing light to the high tension cord of the trailing side distributor. Check to see that the timing light does not go on when the

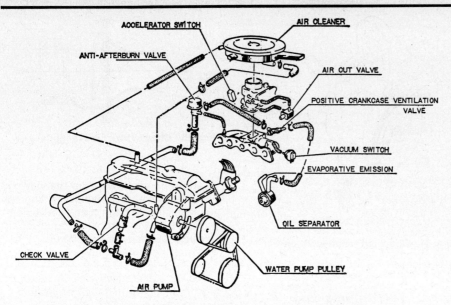

Fig. 21 Air injection system. Piston engine models

engine speed is under 3600-4400 rpm (automatic transmission: 4320-5280 rpm), and goes on when the engine speed is raised to more than 3600-4400 rpm (automatic transmission: 4320-5280 rpm).

Connect an ammeter to the air control valve solenoid. Check to see that the current does not flow to the solenoid when the engine speed is under 3600-4400 rpm (automatic transmission: 4320-5280 rpm), and

there is flow to the solenoid when the engine speed is above 3600-4400 rpm (automatic transmission: 4320-5280 rpm).
3. With the thermosensor connector terminal short-circuited, check the following points:

Connect the timing light to the high tension cord of the trailing side distributor and check to see that the timing light goes on in the whole range of revolution including under

3600-4400 rpm (automatic transmission: 4320-5280 rpm).

Only automatic transmission:

Connect an ammeter to the air control valve solenoid. Check to see that the current does not flow to the solenoid when the engine speed is under 3060-3740 rpm, and there is flow to the solenoid when the engine speed is above 3060-3740 rpm.
4. Connect the thermosensor coupler as before. With the idle switch coupler removed, check the following points:

Connect an ammeter to the coasting valve solenoid and check to see that there is current flow to the ammeter when idling.

Disconnect the hose (air cleaner-deceleration control valve) from the deceleration control valve and plug the air suction port of the deceleration control valve.

When the engine speed is gradually lowered from 2000-3000 rpm, the current begins to flow at 1100-1450 rpm (automatic transmission: 1250-1650 rpm).
5. Connect the idle switch coupler as before.
6. Connect the hose to the deceleration control valve.

Deceleration Control Valve
1. Disconnect the hose (air cleaner-deceleration control valve) from the air cleaner.
2. Run the engine at idle speed.
3. Make sure that air is not sucked in through the air suction hose of the deceleration control valve.
4. Stop the engine.
5. Disconnect the hose (coasting valve-intake manifold) from the deceleration control valve and plug the air suction port of the deceleration control valve (coasting valve).
6. Run the engine at idle speed.
7. Disconnect the solenoid terminal for the anti-afterburn valve at the quick disconnect.
8. Hold your hand over the opening of the air suction hose for the deceleration control valve. If vacuum is felt, the deceleration control valve (anti-afterburn valve) is normal.
9. Stop the engine.
10. Connect the solenoid terminal at the quick disconnect.
11. Connect the hose to the deceleration control valve (coasting valve).
12. Disconnect the hose (anti-afterburn valve-intake manifold) from the deceleration control valve and plug the air suction port of the deceleration control valve (anti-afterburn valve).

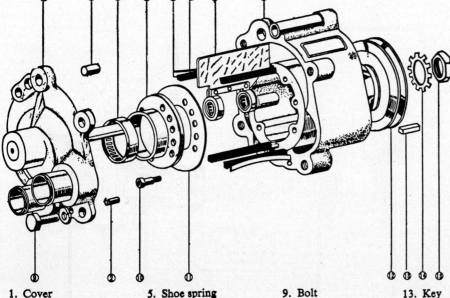

1. Cover	5. Shoe spring	9. Bolt	13. Key
2. Dowel pin	6. Carbon shoe	10. Screw	14. Washer
3. Bearing	7. Vane	11. Rear seal	15. Nut
4. Rotor ring	8. Rotor housing	12. Pulley	

Fig. 22 Air pump exploded view

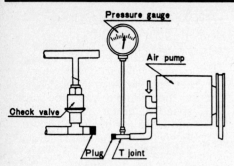

Fig. 23 Checking air pump output pressure

13. Run the engine at idle speed.
14. Disconnect the solenoid terminal for the coasting valve at the quick disconnect.
15. Hold your hand over the opening of the air suction hose for the deceleration control valve. If vacuum is felt, the deceleration control valve (coasting valve) is normal.
16. Stop the engine.
17. Connect the solenoid terminal at the quick disconnect.
18. Connect the hoses to the air cleaner and deceleration control valve (anti-afterburn valve).

Altitude Compensator

1. Disconnect the air inlet hose from the altitude compensator.
2. Run the engine at idle speed.
3. Hold a finger over the inlet of the altitude compensator (the inlet from which the air inlet hose is removed). At this moment, a decrease in the number of engine revolutions indicates the altitude compensator is in good condition. When the inspection is carried out in areas of high elevation there will be a further decrease in the number of engine revolutions.

AIR INJECTION SYSTEM

Piston Engine Models

The air injection system, as shown in Fig. 21, consists of the air pump, relief valve, anti-afterburn valve and check valve.

Air Pump

The vane-type air pump is driven by a V-belt from the crankshaft. It consists of a housing, rotor and two Bakelite vanes supported at the front by a ball bearing in the housing and at the rear by a roller bearing on the press-fitted pin in the housing cover, Fig. 22. The vanes rotate without touching the housing wall. The outlet chamber is provided with a relief valve which releases air at a preset pressure.

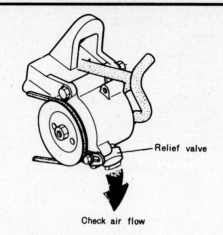

Fig. 24 Checking relief valve operation

System Servicing

Check, On-Vehicle

1. Check air supply hose and connection for leakage before checking pump, using soap solution and operating the engine.
2. Delivery pressure should be checked every 12,000 miles. Disconnect supply hose at the intake side of the check valve and plug check valve. Connect a T-joint and install a pressure gauge, Fig. 23. Run engine at 1500 rpm, at which speed the delivery pressure should be more than 2 psi. If less, the air pump or relief valve could be defective.
3. Check relief valve operation. Refer to Fig. 24. Run engine at 3000 rpm

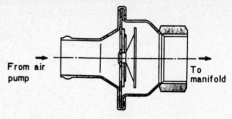

Fig. 25 Check valve crossectional view

and if no air flows from the valve, it is defective. Remove valve and replace since it cannot be overhauled.
4. Relief valve removal requires air pump service kit 49 6500 005.
5. Install new relief valve.

NOTE: Relief valve can be replaced with air pump installed on engine.

6. Air pump belt tension is adjusted in the same manner commonly employed for alternators. Use a lever and push pump away from engine until belt deflection is between .60-.70 inch at the midpoint. For a new belt, deflection should be .45-.55 inch but be sure to readjust after 500-1000 miles of run-in.

Check Valve

The purpose of the check valve, Fig. 25, between the pump and the air injection nozzle is to prevent reversal of the air flow back to the pump. This can only occur when exhaust pressure exceeds pump output due to pump failure from belt breakage, slippage, etc. The

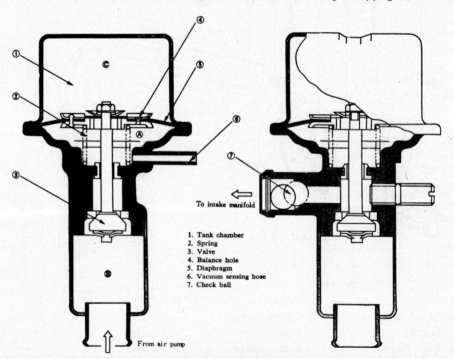

1. Tank chamber
2. Spring
3. Valve
4. Balance hole
5. Diaphragm
6. Vacuum sensing hose
7. Check ball

Fig. 26 Anti-afterburn valve

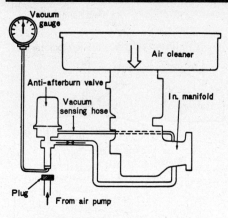

Fig. 27 Checking anti-afterburn valve

valve should be inspected every 12,000 miles.

1. Disconnect the air supply hose at the check valve on the air pump side, run engine at 1500 rpm and check for exhaust gas backflow through the valve with hand placed near the valve.

NOTE: At low engine rpm the air intake into the valve can be confused with check valve leakage due to air pulsation.

2. Check for carbon adhesion by touching the inside of the valve on the air pump side, Fig. 25.
3. Check for deterioration inside the rubber valve. Replace check valve if rubber valve is found defective since check valve cannot be overhauled.

Air Bypass Valve

An air bypass valve between the air pump and the check valve prevents exhaust system overheating during warmup when the choke is used. Whenever the choke is applied, a linkage operates the valve to bypass air from the pump away from the injection nozzles and afterburn valve and directly into the air cleaner. Inspect every 12,000 miles for freedom of operation.

Anti-Afterburn Valve

This gulp-type valve, Fig. 26, consists of an air passage, air valve, vacuum sensing hoses, tank chamber and diaphragm with metering orifices. It is designed to supply additional air to the air/fuel mixture to prevent afterburning in the exhaust manifold, when the mixture is enriched during sudden deceleration or shifting. The anti-afterburn valve is closed in normal operation and is actuated by intake manifold vacuum. It should be inspected every 12,000 miles.

1. Check all hoses for leakage and deterioration and replace if necessary.
2. Disconnect air supply hose at the valve and plug on the air pump side. Fit a vacuum gauge on the valve inlet side of the circuit, Fig. 27. Start engine and let idle. The reading on the gauge should be zero. If a vacuum is registered, the valve is not properly contacting its seat. When the throttle is rapidly opened and closed, the vacuum reading should rise suddenly and decline slowly. If a malfunction is evident, the valve assembly must be replaced as it cannot be overhauled.

Air Injection Nozzles

The air injection nozzles are made of stainless steel and press-fitted into the exhaust manifold. Anything other than complete blockage of all nozzles can only be detected by exhaust gas analysis, which should really be part of the 12,000 mile check on this or any other emission control system. The exhaust manifold must be removed to permit access to these valves.

EXHAUST GAS RECIRCULATION SYSTEM

This system is designed to reduce NO_x emissions by recirculating a limited amount of exhaust gas through intake system during partial load operation. Components of system are a vacuum controlled exhaust gas recirculation valve, solenoid, vacuum switch, delay valve and various connecting hoses.

A maintenance warning system is used to warn the driver of the vehicle to perform the necessary maintenance every 12,500 miles.

System Servicing

EGR Valve & Solenoid

1. Disconnect the connector of the EGR solenoid and connect the solenoid terminal to the battery. The solenoid valve is operating properly

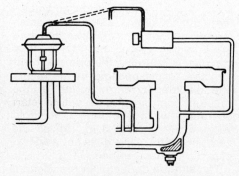

Fig. 29 Checking EGR control valve

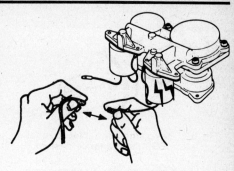

Fig. 28 Checking solenoid

if the clicking sound is audible from the solenoid, Fig. 28.

2. Warm up the engine sufficiently and stop the engine.
3. Disconnect the vacuum sensing tube (EGR solenoid-carburetor) from the carburetor.
4. Disconnect the vacuum sensing tube (No. 1 vacuum switch-inlet manifold) from the inlet manifold and connect the disconnected vacuum sensing tube in Step 3 to the inlet manifold, Fig. 29.
5. Start the engine and run it at idle. The engine should operate smoothly.
6. Connect the EGR solenoid terminal to the battery and make sure the engine stalls.
7. If the engine does not stall, remove the EGR valve from the housing. Clean the valve, valve seat and passage of the housing.
8. Apply the vacuum of 200 mm-Hg (7.9 in.-Hg) to the EGR valve and check to see the valve opens. If not, replace the valve.

Vacuum Switch & Delay Valve

1. Disconnect the bullet connector from the power valve solenoid and connect a voltmeter to the connector (from the control unit).
2. On the vehicle equipped with manual transmission, disconnect the air hose (air cleaner-deceleration control valve) from the air cleaner and blind the air hose.
3. Increase the engine speed to 3,500 rpm with throttle. Then, quickly decrease the engine speed and check to see that the current flows to power valve solenoid connector. The current should flow at 3-25 seconds. If it is not within the specification, install a new No. 1 delay valve and repeat the above test.

Maintenance Warning System

After the maintenance service has been done, disconnect the coupler and connect them oppositely for resetting the system, Fig. 30.

Fig. 30 Reversing connector to reset EGR maintenance system

CATALYTIC CONVERTER

The catalytic converter serves two purposes: it permits a faster chemical reaction to take place and although it enters into the chemical reaction, it remains unchanged, ready to repeat the process. The catalytic converter combines hydrocarbons (HC) and carbon monoxide (CO) with oxygen to form water (H_2O) and carbon dioxide (CO_2).

A hazard warning system is used to warn against an over-heating condition.

System Servicing

Heat Hazard Warning System
1. Turn the ignition switch on. The heat hazard warning lamp comes on.
2. Start the engine and the warning lamp should go off.
3. Remove the right front scarf plate and floor mat.
4. Disconnect the coupler of the heat hazard sensor and connect a jumper wire to both terminals in the coupler.
   The warning lamp comes on.

Heat Hazard Sensor
1. Remove the sensor.
2. Wrap the sensor and thermometer with aluminum foil to prevent the oil penetration and place it in oil.
3. Connect the test lamp and battery to the sensor terminals in the coupler as shown in Fig. 31.
4. Gradually heat up the oil.
   The test lamp should be ON when the temperature in aluminum foil reaches 150 ± 10°C (302 ± 18°F).
   If the sensor does not operate within the specification, replace the sensor.

NOTE: Do not heat up the oil more than 200°C (392°F).

THROTTLE OPENER SYSTEM
808 Models

The throttle opener system is composed of a servo diaphragm connected to a throttle lever, and a vacuum control valve which controls the intake manifold vacuum led to the servo diaphragm. This system reduces hydrocarbons during deceleration.

During deceleration, the air fuel mixture entering the engine is not sufficient, making normal combustion impossible and causing a large amount of hydrocarbons to be emitted into the atmosphere. The throttle opener system takes advantage of the intake manifold vacuum during deceleration to slightly open the primary throttle valve in the coasting condition (to an opening of 1400 ± 100 rpm when unloaded) so that an optimum amount of combustible mixture is fed to the engine to continue proper combustion. This arrangement brings about a large reduction of hydrocarbons during deceleration.

Vacuum Control Valve

The vacuum control valve detects the intake manifold vacuum that acts on the servo diaphragm in order to open the primary throttle valve during deceleration. A small hole fitted on the valve leads the air onto the servo diaphragm after the valve is closed to return the throttle valve back.

The vacuum control valve consists of a diaphragm, diaphragm return spring, valve attached to the diaphragm, altitude corrector, etc. and has a cross section as shown.

A high vacuum that develops in the intake manifold during deceleration is channeled to the diaphragm chamber. Vacuum in the diaphragm chamber overcomes the force of the diaphragm return spring and opens the valve. Vacuum then passes between the valve and valve seat to the servo diaphragm chamber. This causes the servo diaphragm to open the primary throttle valve to a specified opening.

As the vehicle speed falls, the intake manifold vacuum also decreases, so that the primary throttle valve linked to the servo diaphragm returns gradually to the opening of idling. The vacuum control valve is also closed by the force of the diaphragm return spring. Therefore, as soon as the vacuum ceases to act on the servo diaphragm chamber, the atmospheric pressure comes through the air passage into the servo diaphragm chamber and fills it, thus completely returning the primary throttle valve to the opening of the idling. The diaphragm return spring of the vacuum control valve is set to start operating when the intake manifold vacuum becomes 22.0 in. Hg. so the vacuum control valve does not work except during deceleration.

The altitude corrector in the vacuum control valve prevents the vacuum con-

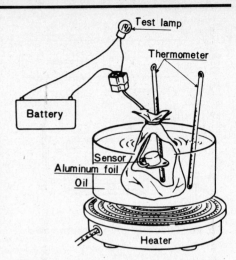

Fig. 31 Checking heat warning sensor

trol valve from showing varied responses due to difference in atmospheric pressure—altitude. The altitude corrector (bellows) contracts according to the change in atmospheric pressure, thus adjusting the diaphragm return spring to proper tension so that the vacuum control valve operates in accordance with the change in atmospheric pressure.

Servo Diaphragm

The servo diaphragm, connected to the primary throttle lever of the carburetor, responds to the intake manifold vacuum controlled by the vacuum control valve to open the primary throttle valve to a specified opening.

System Servicing

Vacuum Control Valve
1. Remove the intake manifold suction hole plug and install a vacuum gauge. The vacuum gauge tube must have 0.12 in. inner diameter and the length of the vacuum gauge tube must be within 6.6 ft.
2. Start the engine.
3. Raise the engine speed to about 3000 rpm, then drop it suddenly.
4. Read the vacuum gauge needle. When the gauge needle, after registering its highest value above 22.0 in. Hg, descends to the vicinity of 22.0 in. Hg, if it comes to a rest for a few seconds (operating depression) and then starts to fall gradually until it indicates the idle vacuum, then the vacuum control valve is normal. Adjust or replace the vacuum control valve (operating depression) if necessary.

NOTE: The operating depression is set under the atmospheric pressure of 29.92 in. Hg, so precaution should

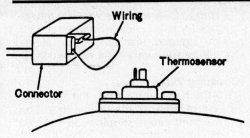

Fig. 32 Short circuiting thermosensor connector

be exercised when the atmospheric pressure is different from the above figure.

Servo Diaphragm

1. Connect the tachometer to the engine.
2. Warm up the engine sufficiently, and set the idle speed to 800-850 rpm.
3. Stop the engine.
4. Disconnect the vacuum sensing tube between the servo diaphragm and the vacuum control valve from the servo diaphragm.
5. Remove the intake manifold suction hole plug.
6. Connect the intake manifold and the servo diaphragm with a suitable test tube so that the intake manifold vacuum can be led directly to the servo diaphragm.
7. Remove the vacuum sensing tube between the carburetor and the distributor vacuum control unit.
8. Start the engine and read the engine speed. If the engine speed is 1400 ± 100 rpm, the servo diaphragm is normal. If the engine speed is not 1400 ± 100 rpm, adjust the engine speed to 1400 ± 100 rpm using the throttle opener adjusting screw. If the engine speed remains the usual idle speed (800 rpm) even after the throttle opener has been adjusted, the servo diaphragm is defective.
9. After checking the servo diaphragm, remove the test tube from the intake manifold and servo diaphragm, then connect the disconnected vacuum sensing tube to the servo diaphragm.

ACCELERATOR SWITCH & THERMOSENSOR

808 Models with Auto. Trans.

The accelerator switch attached on the accelerator linkage and the thermosensor attached on the intake manifold control the ignition timing. The accelerator switch closes the retard circuit when the accelerator pedal is depressed ¾-way, while it opens the retard circuit when the accelerator pedal is

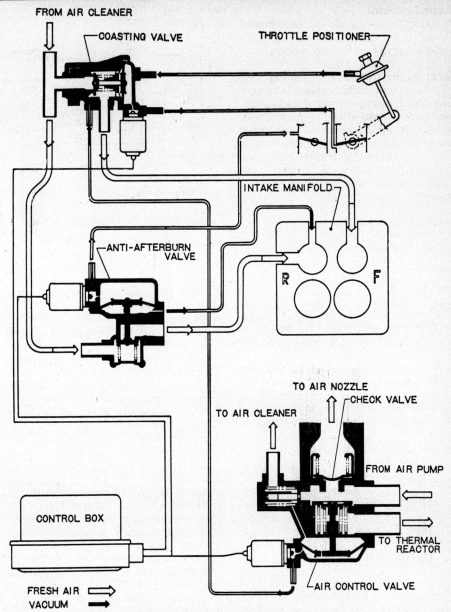

Fig. 33 Deceleration control system

depressed ¾-way. The thermosensor closes the retard circuit when the temperature of the cooling water in the engine rises above 122-140°F, while it opens the retard circuit when the temperature of the cooling water is below 122-140°F. Only at the time both the accelerator switch and the thermosensor close, the ignition timing is retarded from 8° BTDC to 4° BTDC.

IGNITION & CARBURETION CONTROLS

1972-74 R100, RX-2 & RX-3 System Servicing

Thermosensor

The purpose of the thermosensor is to monitor engine temperatures and via

the control box to regulate the firing of the trailing spark plug accordingly. It is on the coolant passage in the rotor housing.

1. With the thermosensor connector terminal short-circuited, Fig. 32, connect a timing light to the high tension circuit of the trailing distributor and check to see if the light goes on between 1900 and 4000 rpm.
2. Connect the thermosensor connector to the thermosensor. Then connect the ammeter to the coasting valve solenoid to check that there is no current flow at idle. Current should start to flow at 1250-1550 rpm, and begin to stop when speed is gradually lowered to 1300-1100 rpm.

Thermodetector

Check resistance with an ohm meter. If less than 200 k ohms, the thermodetector is functioning properly.

Deceleration Control System, Fig. 33

The purpose of this system is to prevent afterburning during deceleration, gear shifting and after engine shut-off. The deceleration system consists of the anti-afterburn valve, coasting valve, throttle positioner, air supply valve, time lag valve and control box (also used with the ignition and carburetor control system).

Anti-Afterburn Valve

1. Remove the air suction hose and idle the engine. Hold hand over hose and if strong vacuum is felt, the anti-afterburn valve should be replaced.
2. Run the engine between 3500-3800 rpm and close the throttle suddenly. Check to see, when the throttle is fully closed, if air is sucked into the hose for .2-1.0 seconds.
3. With the engine idling, remove the lead wire from the solenoid of the afterburn valve. Check to see if air continues to be sucked into the hose with the wire disconnected.

Accelerator Switch Adjustment

1. Loosen the lock nut and adjusting screw of the accelerator switch.
2. Fully depress the accelerator pedal and gradually tighten the adjusting screw until the accelerator switch clicks. Then further tighten it by 2½ turns.
3. Tighten the lock nut.

Thermosensor

To inspect the thermosensor, connect a test light to the thermosensor, and place it in water with a thermometer and gradually heat the water. Check the water temperature when the light starts to go on. If the light does not go on at the temperature of 122-140°F, replace the thermosensor.

Throttle Opener Adjustment

1. Connect a tachometer to the engine.

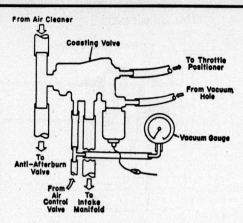

Fig. 34   Checking coasting valve

2. Start the engine and set the idle speed to 800-850 rpm.
3. Stop the engine.
4. Disconnect the vacuum sensing tube between the servo diaphragm and the vacuum control valve from the servo diaphragm.
5. Remove the intake manifold suction hole plug.
6. Attach a suitable test tube between the intake manifold and servo diaphragm to lead the intake manifold vacuum directly to the servo diaphragm.
7. Start the engine and read the engine speed. If the engine speed is above or below 1400 ± 100 rpm, adjust the engine speed to 1400 rpm using the throttle opener adjusting screw. When the engine speed is lower than the specified value, turn the adjusting screw clockwise. When it is higher, turn the adjusting screw counterclockwise.
8. Stop the engine.
9. Perform the operations of steps 4-6 in reverse sequence.
10. Attach a vacuum gauge to the intake manifold.
11. Start the engine.
12. Raise the engine speed to about 3000 rpm and drop it suddenly.
13. Operate the vacuum control valve adjusting screw so that while the engine speed descends from 3000

rpm to 1000 rpm, the vacuum gauge needle will indicate a value of 22.0 in. Hg and the gauge needle remains stationary for a few seconds.

Coasting Valve

1. Attach vacuum gauge, Fig. 34.
2. Warm up and idle the engine. The vacuum gauge should read 400 mm Hg at 800 rpm.
3. Run engine at about 2500 rpm and close the throttle suddenly. The vacuum gauge should read 0-30 mm Hg. Lower speed suddenly to 1100-1300 rpm. The vacuum reading should rise above 400 mm Hg.

Throttle Positioner

1. Remove the air hose between the air cleaner and the coasting valve air inlet, and plug the inlet.
2. Run the engine at 2000 rpm.
3. Disconnect wiring leading to the coasting valve solenoid and connect in its place wiring leading to the positive terminal of the battery. Release throttle suddenly and engine speed should stabilize at 900-1000 rpm.
4. If engine speed does not stabilize as above, adjust the adjusting nut to obtain the required speed and tighten the locknut.
5. Check again to ensure that when battery wire is disconnected, engine speed decreases to 800 rpm and when connected, it rises to 900-1000 rpm.

Air Supply Valve

Remove the air hose from the air suction pipe of the air supply valve and idle the engine. When the suction pipe of the air supply valve is blocked with the end, reduction in idle speed must be under 30 rpm. Then make sure that when the wiring to the air supply solenoid is disconnected a large amount of air is supplied to the intake manifold.

Time Lag Relay

Connect an ammeter to the positive terminal of the leading coil. Turn off the engine at idle speed. If current continues to flow for .7-1.0 seconds, the time lag relay is functioning properly.

Rear Axle & Brakes Section

AXLE SHAFT, REPLACE
Models With Pressed Bearings
Fig. 1
1. Raise and support rear of vehicle.
2. Remove the rear wheel and brake drum.
3. Remove the brake shoes assembly.
4. Remove the bolts holding the brake backing plate and bearing retainer to the axle housing.
5. Remove the axle shaft assembly with a suitable puller.
6. Remove the oil seal from the axle housing, if necessary.

Models With Bearing Housing
Fig. 2
1. Raise and support rear end of the vehicle.
2. Remove the wheel, and remove the center cap adaptor from the rear axle shaft flange.
3. Remove the rear wheel and brake drum.
4. Remove the brake shoe assembly.
5. Remove the parking brake cable retainer.
6. Disconnect the brake fluid pipes at the wheel cylinders.
7. Remove the nuts holding the backing plate and bearing housing to the axle housing.
8. Pull the axle shaft, backing plate, bearing housing assembly and shims off the axle housing.

REAR AXLE, REPLACE
1. Raise and support rear of vehicle.
2. Drain the oil by removing the drain plug.
3. Remove the rear axle shafts.
4. Mark the companion flange and propeller shaft for correct reassembly; then disconnect the propeller shaft.
5. Remove the nuts attaching the rear axle to the axle housing and the rear axle.

DISC BRAKE SERVICE
B1800, Cosmo, RX4 & Pick-up
Brake Shoes, Replace
1. Raise and support front of vehicle.
2. Remove the front wheel.
3. Remove the hair pin retainers and the stopper plates, Fig. 3.
4. Remove the caliper and anti-rattle spring and pull out the brake shoes.
5. Remove the rubber cap from the bleeder screw, and connect a drain tube onto the bleeder screw. Sub-

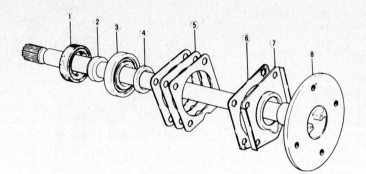

1. Oil seal
2. Bearing collar
3. Bearing
4. Spacer
5. Shim
6. Gasket
7. Bearing retainer
8. Rear axle shaft

Fig. 1   Axle shaft components. Models with pressed bearings

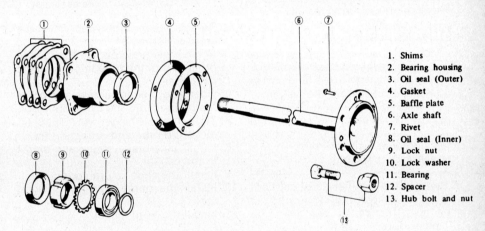

1. Shims
2. Bearing housing
3. Oil seal (Outer)
4. Gasket
5. Baffle plate
6. Axle shaft
7. Rivet
8. Oil seal (Inner)
9. Lock nut
10. Lock washer
11. Bearing
12. Spacer
13. Hub bolt and nut

Fig. 2   Axle shaft components. Models with bearing housing

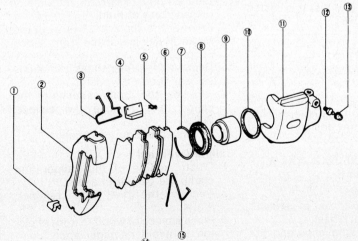

1. Anti rattle pad clip
2. Caliper bracket
3. Spring
4. Stopper plate
5. Hair pin retainer
6. Shim
7. Boot ring
8. Dust boot
9. Piston
10. Piston seal
11. Caliper body
12. Bleeder screw
13. Bleeder cap
14. Brake shoe and lining
15. Anti rattle spring

Fig. 3   Disc brake assembly. B1800, Cosmo, RX4 & Pick-up

merge the other end of the tube into a suitable container.

6. Open the bleeder screw and press the piston into the cylinder.
7. Tighten the bleeder screw and remove the tube and retracting tool.
8. Install new brake shoes and shims on the caliper.
9. Install the anti-rattle spring, caliper, stopper plates and hair pin retainers.
10. Install the front wheel and lower the vehicle.

Caliper, Replace

1. Raise the front end of the vehicle.
2. Remove the front wheel.
3. Remove the shoe and lining assembly as described previously.
4. Disconnect the brake fluid pipe from the caliper and plug the end of the fluid pipe to prevent entrance of dirt and loss of fluid.
5. Remove the caliper, Fig. 3.
6. If necessary, remove the caliper bracket by removing the two bolts.
7. Reverse procedure to install.

Caliper Overhaul

1. Clean outside of the caliper.
2. Place a piece of wood in front of piston to prevent damage to piston. Apply air pressure to the fluid port in the caliper to remove the piston.

NOTE: If the piston is seized and cannot be forced from the caliper, tap lightly around the piston while applying air pressure.

3. Remove the retainer and dust boot from the caliper, Fig. 3.
4. Remove the piston seal from the caliper bore.
5. Apply brake fluid to the piston seal and install it into the groove of the caliper bore.

NOTE: Be sure the piston does not become twisted and that it is seated fully in the groove.

6. Lubricate the piston and caliper bore.
7. Insert the piston into the caliper bore.
8. Install the dust boot by setting the flange squarely in the inner groove of the caliper bore. Install the dust boot retainer.

1200, 1300, 1600, RX2, RX3 & RX3SP

Brake Shoes, Replace

1. Raise and support front of vehicle.
2. Remove the front wheel.
3. Remove the locking clips and the guide pins, Fig. 4.
4. Remove the shoe return spring and the brake shoes and shims.

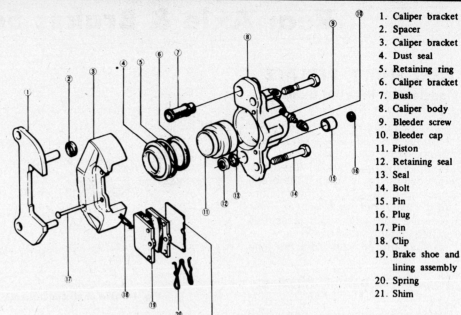

1. Caliper bracket
2. Spacer
3. Caliper bracket
4. Dust seal
5. Retaining ring
6. Caliper bracket
7. Bush
8. Caliper body
9. Bleeder screw
10. Bleeder cap
11. Piston
12. Retaining seal
13. Seal
14. Bolt
15. Pin
16. Plug
17. Pin
18. Clip
19. Brake shoe and lining assembly
20. Spring
21. Shim

Fig. 4   Disc brake assembly. 1200, 1300, 1600, RX2, RX3 & RX3SP

5. Remove the rubber cap from the bleeder screw, and connect a tube to the bleeder screw. Submerge the other end of the tube into a suitable container.
6. Open the bleeder screw and press the pistons into the cylinders.
7. Tighten the bleeder valve and remove the tube and retracting tool.
8. Install new brake shoes and shims in the caliper.
9. Install the shoe return spring.
10. Install the guide pins and locking clips.
11. Install the front wheel.

Caliper, Replace

1. Raise and support front of vehicle.
2. Remove the front wheel.
3. Disconnect the brake fluid pipes at the fender apron. Plug the end of the fluid pipe to prevent entrance of dirt and loss of fluid.
4. Remove the clip and disconnect the brake fluid pipe at the front shock absorber.
5. Remove the brake shoes and shims as described previously.
6. Remove the bolts attaching the caliper and remove the caliper, Fig. 4.
7. Reverse procedure to install.

Caliper Overhaul

1. Clean outside of the caliper and clamp the caliper in a vise.
2. Remove the dust boot retainer, Fig. 4.
3. Place a piece of wood in front of piston to avoid damage, apply compressed air to fluid pipe hole and remove the piston. Remove the dust boot from the piston.

NOTE: If the piston is seized and cannot be forced from the caliper, tap lightly around the piston while applying air pressure.

4. Remove the bolts that attach the caliper bracket to the caliper and the caliper bracket.
5. Remove the piston seal from the caliper bore.
6. Remove the bleeder screw, if necessary.
7. Apply brake fluid to the piston seal and install it into the groove of the caliper bore.

NOTE: Be sure that the piston seal does not become twisted and is seated fully in the groove.

8. Spread the dust boot over the piston as it is installed and seat the dust boot in the piston groove.
9. Lubricate the piston and caliper bore with brake fluid.
10. Install the piston and dust boot assembly to the caliper and secure the dust boot in position with the retainer.
11. Install the caliper bracket to the caliper and tighten the attaching bolts.

GLC

Brake Shoes, Replace
Refer to Fig. 5 to replace brake shoes.

Caliper, Replace
Refer to Fig. 6 to replace caliper.

Caliper Overhaul
Refer to Fig. 7 to overhaul caliper.

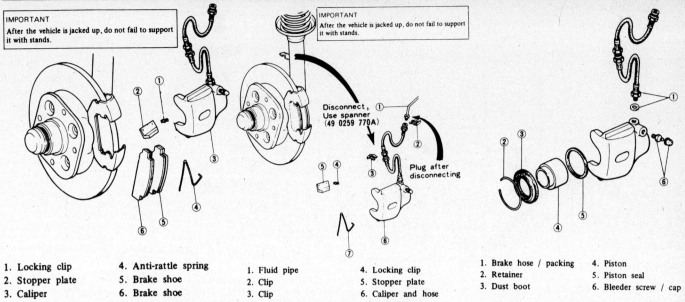

IMPORTANT
After the vehicle is jacked up, do not fail to support it with stands.

IMPORTANT
After the vehicle is jacked up, do not fail to support it with stands.

Disconnect, Use spanner (49 0259 770A)

Plug after disconnecting

1. Locking clip	4. Anti-rattle spring
2. Stopper plate	5. Brake shoe
3. Caliper	6. Brake shoe

Fig. 5 Brake shoe replacement. GLC

1. Fluid pipe	4. Locking clip
2. Clip	5. Stopper plate
3. Clip	6. Caliper and hose

Fig. 6 Caliper replacement. GLC

1. Brake hose / packing	4. Piston
2. Retainer	5. Piston seal
3. Dust boot	6. Bleeder screw / cap

Fig. 7 Caliper overhaul. GLC

Rear Suspension Section

LEAF SPRING, REPLACE

1. Raise rear end of vehicle and place a stand under frame side rail, permitting spring to hang free.
2. Support rear axle in this position with jack.
3. Remove rear wheel.
4. Disconnect rear shock absorber at lower mounting point.
5. Remove "U" bolt nuts and spring clamp, Fig. 1.
6. Remove spring pin nut and remove two bolts and nuts attaching the spring pin plate to the frame bracket.
7. Remove spring pin and remove front end of spring from vehicle. Remove rubber bushings.
8. Remove shackle pin nuts and shackle plate and remove rear end of the spring from vehicle. Remove rubber bushings.
9. Reverse procedure to install.

COIL SPRING, REPLACE

1976-77 Cosmo

1. Raise rear end of vehicle and place stands under frame side rails.
2. Remove rear wheel.
3. Place a jack under lower arm to support it.
4. Remove pivot bolt and nut that se-

cures rear end of lower arm to axle housing.
5. Carefully and slowly, lower jack to relieve spring pressure on lower arm, then remove spring.

NOTE: When replacing spring, install a suitable coil spring and adjusting plate to get equal road clearance both on the right and left. Do not use more than two adjusting plates at one side.

6. Place spring upper insulator on spring.
7. Position spring on lower arm so that lower end properly engages seat.
8. Raise lower arm carefully with a jack while guiding rear end to align with bolt hole in the axle housing.
   Insert attaching bolt in axle housing and through lower arm.
   Loosely attach nut on lower arm rear pivot bolt. Do not torque nut at this time.
9. Connect lower end of shock absorber to lower arm.
10. Place safety stands under rear axle, lower the vehicle until spring is in approximately curb load position, then torque nut on lower arm rear pivot bolt to 10-12 m-kg (72-87 ft. lbs.).
11. Install rear wheel.
12. Remove safety stands and lower vehicle.

COIL SPRING & SHOCK ABSORBER, REPLACE

1972-74 RX2, 616 & 618

1. Remove nuts attaching upper end of shock absorber from luggage compartment.
2. Remove nut from lower end of shock absorber, Fig. 3.
3. Place jack under rear axle housing and raise vehicle. Then, place a stand under frame side rail.
4. Gradually lower the jack under rear axle housing and remove rear shock absorber.
5. Apply identification mark on rear shock absorber before it is disassembled.
6. Hold shock absorber in a vise.
7. Using coil spring holder 49 0223 640A and 49 0223 641, compress coil spring.
8. Remove lock nuts.
9. Assemble rear shock absorber in reverse order of disassembly, noting following point.
   a. Adjust vehicle height by using proper combination of the coil spring and adjusting plate.
10. Install the rear shock absorber in the reverse order of removing, noting the following points.
    a. The rear shock absorber should be installed by making protector face toward the front of vehicle.
    b. Tighten rear shock absorber at-

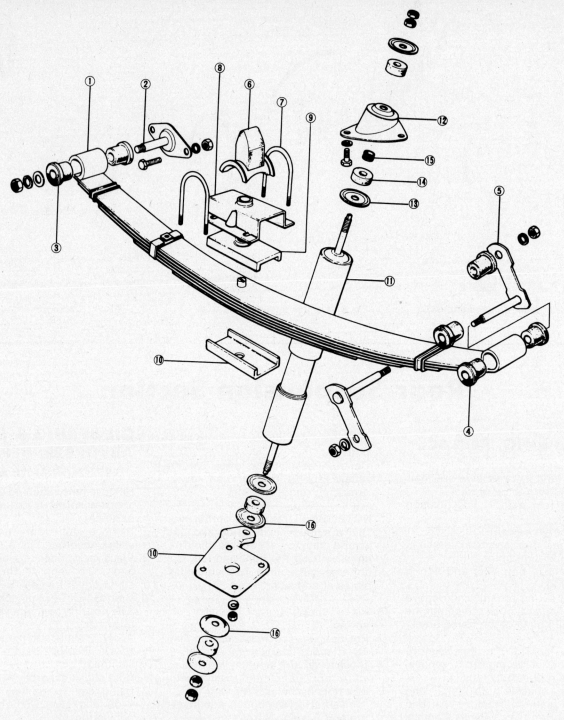

1. Rear spring	6. Bound bumper	11. Rear shock absorber	16. Centering washer
2. Spring pin	7. "U"-bolt	12. Bracket	
3. Bush (Frt.)	8. Rubber pad holder	13. Retainer	
4. Bush (Rr.)	9. Rubber pad	14. Rubber bush	
5. Shackle plate	10. Spring clamp	15. Grommet	

Fig. 1   Rear leaf spring suspension (Typical)

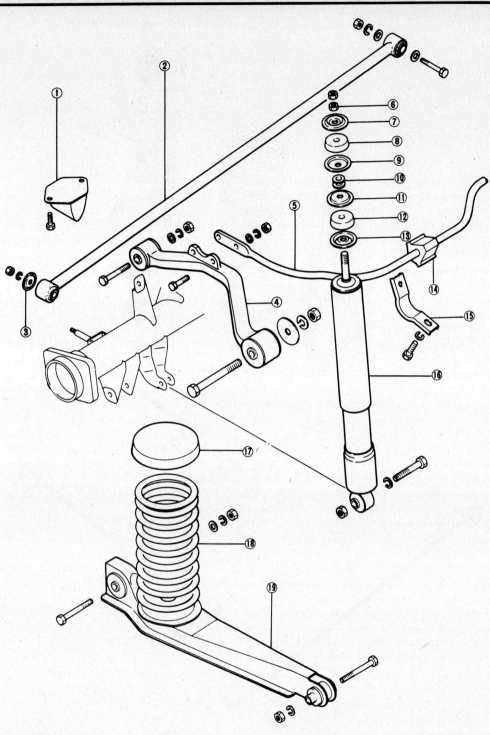

1. Bump stopper
2. Rateral rod
3. Washer
4. Upper arm
5. Rear stabilizer
6. Nut
7. Retainer
8. Rubber bush
9. Retainer
10. Grommet
11. Retainer
12. Rubber bush
13. Retainer
14. Rubber bush
15. Stabilizer plate
16. Rear shock absorber
17. Upper-rubber seat
18. Coil spring
19. Lower arm

Fig. 2   Rear coil spring suspension. 1976-77 Cosmo

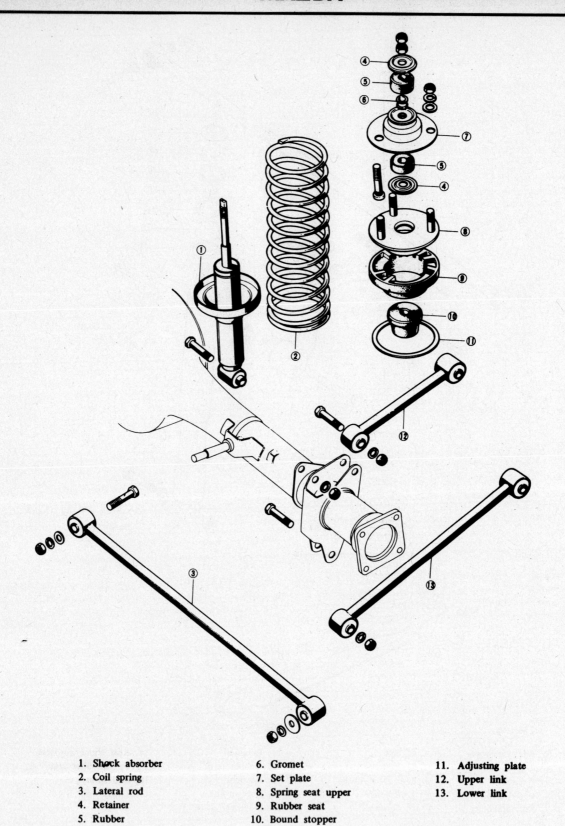

1. Shock absorber
2. Coil spring
3. Lateral rod
4. Retainer
5. Rubber
6. Gromet
7. Set plate
8. Spring seat upper
9. Rubber seat
10. Bound stopper
11. Adjusting plate
12. Upper link
13. Lower link

Fig. 3   Rear coil spring suspension. 1972-74 RX2, 616, & 618

taching nut and bolt to a torque 11 m-kg (80 ft. lbs.).

SHOCK ABSORBER, REPLACE

Models W/Leaf Spring Suspension

Except 808 Sta. Wag.
1. Open luggage compartment lid.
2. Remove nuts, washers and rubber bushings from upper end of shock absorber.
3. Remove nut and bolt attaching lower end of shock absorber to rear axle housing.
4. Compress shock absorber with lifter 49 0223 740A and remove it from vehicle.
5. Reverse procedure to install.

808 Sta. Wag.
1. Jack up rear end of vehicle and support body with safety stands.
2. Remove lock nuts, washers and rubber bushing from lower end of shock absorber.
3. Compress shock absorber with a lifter 49 0223 740A.
4. Remove bolts that attach shock absorber bracket to body and remove shock absorber together with lifter.
5. Remove lifter from shock absorber.
6. Remove nuts, washers, rubber bushing bracket and rubber bushing from shock absorber.
7. If rubber bushes appear worn, damaged or deteriorated, replace with new ones.

1976-77 Cosmo
1. Raise vehicle on a hoist.
2. Remove rear seat.
3. Remove fasteners and remove fuel tank partition board.

4. Remove nuts, washers and rubber bushes from the upper end of shock absorber.
5. Remove nut that secures lower end of shock absorber to axle bracket.
6. Compress shock absorber and remove it from vehicle.
7. Reverse procedure to install.

CONTROL ARM, REPLACE

1976-77 Cosmo

Upper Arm
1. Raise rear end of vehicle and place stands under frame side rails.
2. Remove rear wheel.
3. Remove bolts and nuts that fasten stabilizer bar to upper arm.
4. Remove upper arm pivot bolt and nut from axle bracket, then, disengage upper arm from the bracket.
5. Remove pivot bolt and nut from frame bracket and remove upper arm from vehicle.
6. Position upper arm in bracket on frame side rail. Install bolt and nut.
7. Position upper arm to axle bracket and install bolt and nut.
   Do not tighten nut at this time.
8. Install bolts and nuts, fasten stabilizer bar to upper arm. Torque to 1.8-2.7 m-kg (13-19 ft. lbs.).
9. Place safety stands under axle housing lower vehicle until spring is in approximately curb load position and then torque pivot bolts and nuts to 10-12 m-kg (72-87 ft. lbs.).
10. Install rear wheel.
11. Remove safety stands and lower the vehicle.

Lower Arm
1. Remove rear spring, as described under Coil Spring, Replace.

2. Remove pivot bolt and nut from frame bracket and remove the lower arm from vehicle.
3. Reverse procedure to install.

UPPER & LOWER LINK, REPLACE

1972-74 RX2, 616 & 618
1. Remove lower link attaching bolts and nuts and remove lower link.
2. Remove upper link attaching bolt and nuts and remove upper link.

LATERAL ROD, REPLACE

1976-77 Cosmo
1. Raise rear end of vehicle and place stands under axle housing.
2. Remove nut and washers attaching the lateral rod to the axle bracket and disengage the lateral rod from mounting stud.
3. Remove bolt and nut attaching lateral rod to the frame bracket and remove lateral rod from vehicle.
4. Position lateral rod to frame bracket and install the bolt and nut. Torque to 10-12 m-kg (72-87 ft. lbs.).
5. Position lateral rod on axle bracket mounting stud and install the washers and nut.
   Torque lateral rod attaching nut to 10-12 m-kg (72-87 ft. lbs.).
6. Remove safety stands and lower vehicle.

1972-74 RX2, 616 & 618
1. Remove lateral rod attaching nuts to rear axle housing.
2. Remove lateral rod attaching nut and bolt to body and remove lateral rod.
3. Reverse procedure to install.

Front Suspension Section
Rotary Pick-up & 72-75 B1600

DESCRIPTION

These models use the wishbone type suspension arms with the coil springs on the front and semielliptic leaf springs on the rear, Fig. 1.

The shock absorbers are of the hydraulic double action type.

SHOCK ABSORBER, REPLACE

1. Loosen the nuts that attach the upper end of the shock absorber to the cross member.
2. Remove the rubber bushes and washers.

3. Loosen the bolts that attach the lower end of the shock absorber to the lower arm.
4. Remove the shock absorber from under the lower arm, Fig. 1.
5. Worn or damaged rubber bushings should be discarded.
6. Reverse procedure to install.

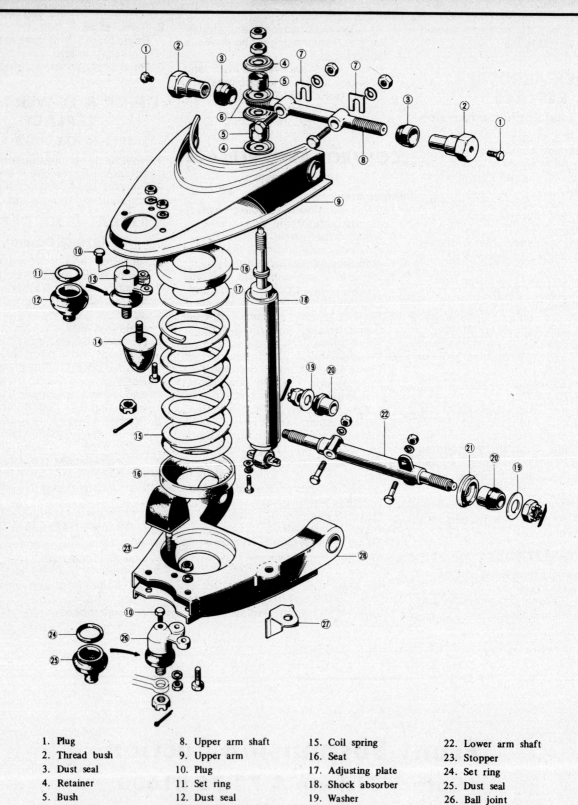

1. Plug	8. Upper arm shaft	15. Coil spring	22. Lower arm shaft
2. Thread bush	9. Upper arm	16. Seat	23. Stopper
3. Dust seal	10. Plug	17. Adjusting plate	24. Set ring
4. Retainer	11. Set ring	18. Shock absorber	25. Dust seal
5. Bush	12. Dust seal	19. Washer	26. Ball joint
6. Retainer	13. Ball joint assembly	20. Bush	27. Bracket
7. Adjusting shim	14. Stopper	21. Stopper	28. Lower arm

Fig. 1 Front suspension. Rotary Pick-Up & 1972-75 B1600

FRONT SUSPENSION, REPLACE

1. Jack up the vehicle until the front wheels are clear of the ground.
2. Remove the front wheel.
3. Remove the front shock absorber.
4. Remove the upper ball joint nut and disconnect the ball stud from the steering knuckle, using a suitable puller.
5. Remove the nuts and bolts that attach the upper arm shaft to the support bracket, noting the numbers and positions of the adjusting shims so that correct wheel alignment is obtained when reassembled.
6. Remove the upper arm assembly.
7. Disconnect the stabilizer from the lower arm.
8. With compressor, compress the coil spring.
9. Remove the lower ball joint nut and disconnect the ball stud from the steering knuckle.
10. Remove the bolts that attach the lower arm to the cross member and remove the lower arm assembly and coil spring from the vehicle, Fig. 1.
11. Reverse procedure to install.

When fitting the stabilizer, align the white line marked on the stabilizer with the outside of the support bracket. When replacing the coil spring, install a suitable coil spring and adjusting plate to get equal road clearance both on the right and left.

GLC

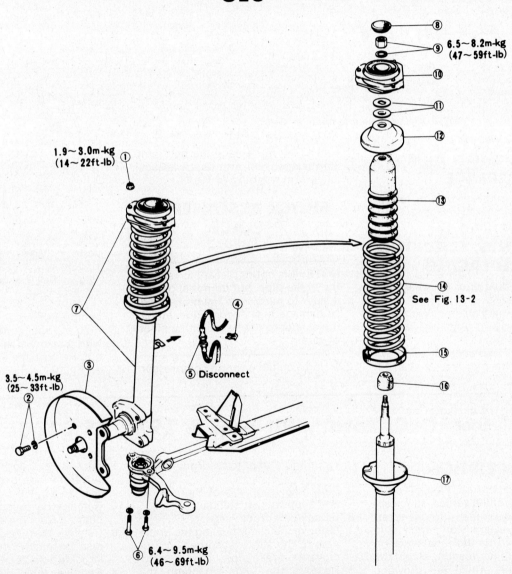

1. Nut
2. Bolt / washer
3. Caliper bracket
4. Clip
5. Brake fluid pipe
6. Bolt / washer
7. Shock absorber and spring ass'y
8. Cap
9. Nut / washer
10. Mounting block
11. Washer
12. Spring seat
13. Boot
14. Spring
15. Spring
16. Rubber stopper
17. Shock absorber

Fig. 2 Shock absorber unit. GLC

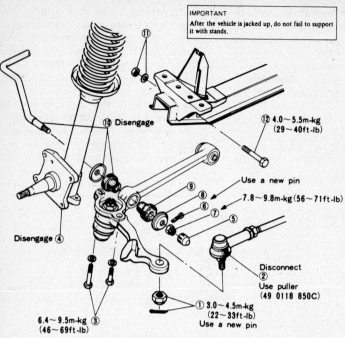

IMPORTANT
After the vehicle is jacked up, do not fail to support it with stands.

⑩ Disengage

Disengage ④

⑫ 4.0~5.5m-kg (29~40ft-lb)

Use a new pin
7.8~9.8m-kg (56~71ft-lb)

Disconnect ②
Use puller (49 0118 850C)

① 3.0~4.5m-kg (22~33ft-lb)
Use a new pin

6.4~9.5m-kg ③ (46~69ft-lb)

1. Nut / split pin
2. Tie-rod
3. Bolt / washer
4. Shock absorber
5. Stopper
6. Split pin
7. Nut
8. Washer
9. Rubber bush
10. Stabilizer bar / washer / rubber bush
11. Nut / washer
12. Bolt
13. Suspension arm and knuckle arm ass'y

Fig. 3 Suspension arm removal. GLC

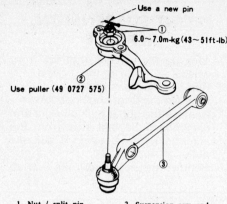

Use a new pin
6.0~7.0m-kg (43~51ft-lb) ①
Use puller (49 0727 575)

1. Nut / split pin
2. Knuckle arm
3. Suspension arm and ball joint ass'y

Fig. 4 Suspension arm installation. GLC

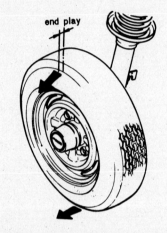

end play

Fig. 5 Ball joint inspection. GLC

SUSPENSION ARM, REPLACE

Remove the suspension arm following the order numbered in Figs. 3 and 4.

BALL JOINTS, CHECKING & REPLACING

1. Check the dust boot for wear, flaw or any damage.
2. To check the ball joint for wear, raise the vehicle until the wheels clear the ground.
3. Grip the tire and shake it as shown in Fig. 5. If the play is more than 1.0 mm (0.04 in), replace the ball joint and suspension arm as an assembled form referring to Fig. 4.

SHOCK ABSORBER, REPLACE

1. Remove the brake disc.

NOTE: It is not necessary to remove the brake pipe, but do not allow the caliper to hang from the brake pipe, as damage may occur. Thus, attach the caliper to the frame with a piece of wire.

2. Using a suitable spring compressor, compress the coil spring.
3. Hold the upper end of the piston rod with a spanner and loosen the lock nut. Remove the lock nut and washer, Fig. 2.

Exc. GLC, Rotary Pick-up & 1972-75 B1600

DESCRIPTION

The front suspension, Figs. 6 and 7, consists mainly of the vertical shock absorbers integrally made with each steering knuckle, suspension arms and stabilizer bar. This front suspension does not require lubrication, except the lower ball joints which are provided with plugs to attaching the grease fittings when required.

SHOCK ABSORBER, REPLACE

1. Open the hood and remove the four nuts attaching the shock absorber

mounting rubber to the front fender apron.
2. Raise the front end of the vehicle and support with stands.
3. Remove the front wheel.
4. Remove the clip attaching the brake pipe to the shock absorber and remove the brake pipe.
5. Remove the bolts attaching the caliper bracket and remove the caliper assembly off the brake disc.

NOTE: Never allow the caliper assembly to hang from the brake pipe, as damage may occur.

6. Remove the hub grease cap, split

pin, nut lock and bearing adjusting nut from the steering knuckle spindle.
7. Remove the thrust washer and outer bearing from the hub.
8. Remove the wheel hub and brake disc assembly from the steering knuckle spindle.
9. Remove the bolts attaching the caliper mounting adaptor to the knuckle and remove the adaptor.
10. Remove the two bolts attaching the front shock absorber to the steering knuckle arm.
11. Lower the suspension arm and remove the shock absorber and coil spring assembly.

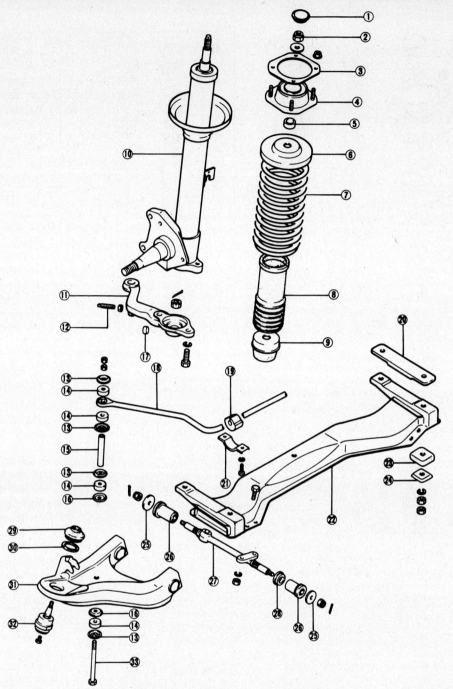

1. Cap
2. Nut
3. Adjusting plate
4. Shock absorber support
5. Spacer
6. Spring seat
7. Coil spring
8. Dust cover
9. Bound bumper

10. Front shock absorber
11. Knuckle arm
12. Stopper bolt
13. Retainer
14. Rubber bush
15. Stabitizer spacer
16. Centering washer
17. Steering stopper

18. Stabilizer
19. Rubber bush
20. Spring cushion
21. Stabilizer plate
22. Cross member
23. Lower cushion
24. Washer
25. Washer

26. Rubber bush
27. Lower arm spindle
28. Side stopper
29. Dust seal
30. Dust seal ring
31. Lower arm
32. Ball joint set
33. Stabilizer bolt

Fig. 6   Front suspension. 1976-77 Cosmo & RX4

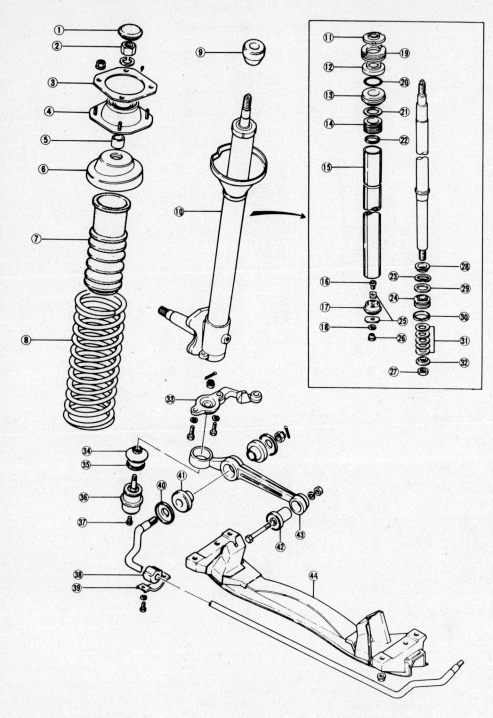

1. Cap
2. Nut
3. Road clearance adjusting plate
4. Shock absorber support
5. Spacer
6. Spring seat
7. Dust boot
8. Coil spring
9. Damper stopper
10. Front shock absorber
11. Dust cover
12. Oil seal
13. Piston rod guide
14. Stopper guide
15. Pressure tube
16. Bolt
17. Base valve casing
18. Valve seat
19. Cap nut
20. "O" ring
21. Back-up ring
22. Stopper
23. Check valve spring
24. Piston
25. Relief valve
26. Nut
27. Nut
28. Washer
29. Check valve
30. Piston ring
31. Relief valve
32. Washer
33. Knuckle arm
34. Dust seal
35. Set ring
36. Ball joint
37. Plug
38. Bush
39. Stabilizer bar bracket
40. Washer
41. Bush
42. Bush
43. Suspension arm
44. Cross member

Fig. 7   Front suspension. 1974-75 RX4

MAZDA

12. Hold the shock absorber and coil spring assembly in a vise.
13. Using a suitable spring compressor, compress the coil spring.
14. Hold the upper end of the piston rod with a spanner and loosen the lock nut. Remove the lock nut and washer.
15. Remove the shock absorber support, spring seat, coil spring, dust boot and damper stopper from the shock absorber.
16. Reverse procedure to install. When replacing the coil spring, install a suitable coil spring and adjusting plate to get equal road clearance both on the right and left. Do not use more than two adjusting plates at one side.

SUSPENSION ARM, REPLACE

1. Raise the front end of the vehicle and support with stands.
2. Remove the front wheel.
3. Disconnect the tie-rod from the knuckle arm by removing the split pin and nut and using the ball joint puller (49 0118 850C).
4. Remove the two bolts attaching the knuckle arm to the shock absorber.
5. Remove the nuts, bolt, washers and rubber bushes holding the stabilizer bar to the suspension arm, and disconnect the stabilizer bar from the suspension arm.
6. Remove the nuts and bolts supporting the suspension arm to the cross member. Remove the suspension arm, knuckle arm and suspension arm shaft.
7. Hold the suspension arm in a vise. Check the suspension arm, knuckle arm and ball joint.
8. Remove the split pin and nut, and disconnect the knuckle arm from

the suspension arm with the knuckle arm puller (49 0727 575).

NOTE: Do not remove the ball joint unless it must be replaced.

9. Reverse procedure to install. The tightening torque of the bolts attaching the knuckle arm to the shock absorber is 6.4-9.5 m-kg (46-69 ft. lbs.). The tightening torque of the nut holding suspension arm to the cross member is 4.0-5.5 m-kg (29-40 ft. lbs.). Tighten the stabilizer bar nut until the dimension between the nut and bolt end is 8 mm (0.315 in.).

CHECKING BALL JOINTS

1. Check the dust boot for wear, flaw or any damage. If the dust boot is defective, this will allow entry of water and dirt, resulting in ball joint wear.
2. Check the revolving torque of the ball stud. To check, hook the spring scale in the hole of the knuckle arm for connecting the tie-rod and pull the scale until the knuckle arm starts to turn. The reading of the spring scale should be 8-14 kg (17.6-30.8 lbs.) for Cosmo & 1976-77 RX4, or 12-18 kg (26.5-39.7 lbs.) for all other models. If it is not within the specifications, replace the ball joint in its assembled form.

BALL JOINTS, REPLACE

1. Remove the suspension arm assembly.
2. Remove the set ring and dust boot from the ball joint.
3. Using the ball joint remover and installer (49 1243 736), press the ball joint out of the suspension arm.

NOTE: Before pressing out the ball joint, clean the ball joint and suspension arm so as not to damage the mounting bore of the suspension arm.

4. Clean the mounting bore of the suspension arm and apply kerosene.
5. On all models except Cosmo and 1976-77 RX4:
   a. Using the ball joint remover and installer (49 1243 736), tighten the ball joint to the suspension arm until the ball joint flange touches the suspension arm. The tightening torque before touching to the suspension arm should be 6 to 18 m-kg (43 to 130 ft. lbs.). If the torque necessary to tighten the ball joint is less than 6 m-kg (43 ft. lbs.), the suspension arm should be replaced.
   b. Further tighten the ball joint to 25 to 40 m-kg (180-289 ft. lbs.).
   c. Install the ball joint and suspension arm to the knuckle arm.
6. On Cosmo and 1976-77 RX4 models:
   a. Clean the mounting bore of the suspension arm and apply kerosene.
   b. Press fit the ball joint to the suspension arm with the ball joint installer (49 0370 860).

NOTE: If the pressure to press in the ball joint is less than 1,500 kg (3,300 lbs.), the suspension arm should be replaced.

   c. Install the ball joint and suspension arm assembly to the knuckle arm. Tighten the nut to 6.0-7.0 m-kg (43.0-51.0 ft. lbs.) and install the cotter pin.
   d. Install the suspension arm assembly.

MERCEDES-BENZ

INDEX OF SERVICE OPERATIONS

GENERAL ENGINE SPECIFICATIONS

Year	Engine		Engine Model	Bore and Stroke In Inches (mm)	Piston Displacement, Cu. In. (cc)	Compression Ratio	Maximum Brake H.P. @ R.P.M.	Maximum Torque Ft. Lbs. @ R.P.M.	Normal Oil Pressure Pounds
1972	220	4-134	M115	3.43 x 3.7 (87 x 92.4)	134 (2197)	8.0 —	105 @ 4800 —	142 @ 3000 —	— —
	220D	4-134	OM615	3.43 x 3.7 (87 x 92.4)	134 (2197)	21.0	60 @ 4200	96 @ 2400	— —
	250,C	6-170	M130	3.4 x 3.09 (86.5 x 78.8)	170 (2778)	8.0 —	140 @ 5200	181 @ 3800	— —
	280SE	6-170	M130	3.4 x 3.09 (86.5 x 78.8)	170 (2778)	8.0	160 @ 5500 —	193 @ 4500	— —
	280SE, SEL4.5	8-275.8	M117	3.62 x 3.35 (92 x 85)	275.8 (4520)	8.0	230 @ 5000 —	279 @ 3200	—
	300SEL	8-275.8	M117	3.62 x 3.35 (92 x 85)	275.8 (4520)	8.0	230 @ 5000 —	279 @ 3200 —	—
	450SE, SEL	8-275.8	M117	3.62 x 3.35 (92 x 85)	275.8 (4520)	8.0	230 @ 5000 —	279 @ 3200 —	—
	450SL, SLC	8-275.8	M117	3.62 x 3.35 (92 x 85)	275.8 (4520)	8.0	230 @ 5000 —	279 @ 3200 —	—
1973	220	4-134	M115	3.43 x 3.7 (87 x 92.4)	134 (2197)	8.2 —	85 @ 4500 —	124 @ 2500 —	43 —
	220D	4-134	OM615	3.43 x 3.7 (87 x 92.4)	134 (2197)	21.0 —	57 @ 4200	88 @ 2400	43 —
	280,C	6-167.6	M110	3.39 x 3.10 (86 x 78.8)	167.6 (2746)	8.0 —	130 @ 5000 —	150 @ 3500 —	43
	450SE, SEL	8-275.8	M117	3.62 x 3.35 (92 x 85)	275.8 (4520)	8.0 —	190 @ 4750 —	240 @ 3000 —	43
	450SL, SLC	8-275.8	M117	3.62 x 3.35 (92 x 85)	275.8 (4520)	8.0 —	190 @ 4750 —	240 @ 3000 —	43 —
1974	230	4-140.8	M115	3.69 x 3.29 (93.75 x 83.6)	140.8 (2307)	8.0 —	99 @ 4800 —	132 @ 2500 —	43
	240D	4-146.7	OM616	3.58 x 3.64 (91 x 92.4)	146.7 (2404)	21.0 —	65 @ 4200 —	101 @ 2400 —	43
	280,C	6-167.6	M110	3.39 x 3.10 (86 x 78.8)	167.6 (2746)	8.0 —	160 @ 5500 —	167 @ 4000 —	43
	450SE, SEL	8-275.8	M117	3.62 x 3.35 (92 x 85)	275.8 (4520)	8.8 —	225 @ 5000 —	—	43
	450SL, SLC	8-275.8	M117	3.62 x 3.35 (92 x 85)	275.8 (4520)	8.8 —	225 @ 5000 —	—	43 —
1975	230	4-140.8	M115	3.69 x 3.29 (93.75 x 83.6)	140.8 (2307)	8.0 —	99 @ 4800 —	—	43
	240D	4-146.7	OM616	3.58 x 3.64 (91 x 92.4)	146.7 (2404)	21.0 —	65 @ 4200 —	—	43 —
	300D	5-183.4	OM617	3.58 x 3.64 (91 x 92.4)	183.4 (3005)	21.0 —	80 @ 4000 —	—	43
	280,C	6-167.6	M110	3.39 x 3.10 (86 x 78.8)	167.6 (2746)	9.0 —	160 @ 5500 —	—	43
	280S	6-167.6	M110	3.39 x 3.10 (86 x 78.8)	167.6 (2746)	9.0 —	160 @ 5500 —	—	43 —
	450SE, SEL	8-275.8	M117	3.62 x 3.35 (92 x 85)	275.8 (4520)	8.8 —	165 @ 5000 —	—	43
	450SL, SLC	8-275.8	M117	3.62 x 3.35 (92 x 85)	275.8 (4520)	8.8 —	165 @ 5000 —	—	43 —
1976	230	4-140.8	M115	3.69 x 3.29 (93.75 x 83.6)	140.8 (2307)	8.0	①	②	43
	240D	4-146.7	OM616	3.58 x 3.64 (91 x 92.4)	146.7 (2404)	21.0 —	62 @ 4000 —	97 @ 4000	43
	300D	5-183.4	OM617	3.58 x 3.64 (91 x 92.4)	183.4 (3005)	21.0 —	77 @ 4400 —	115 @ 2400 —	43
	280,C	6-167.6	M110	3.39 x 3.10 (86 x 78.8)	167.6 (2746)	8.0 —	120 @ 4800 —	143 @ 2800 —	43
	280S	6-107.6	M110	3.39 x 3.10 (86 x 78.8)	167.6 (2746)	8.0 —	120 @ 4800 —	143 @ 2800 —	43

GENERAL ENGINE SPECIFICATIONS—Continued

Year	Engine		Engine Model	Bore and Stroke In Inches (mm)	Piston Displacement, Cu. In. (cc)	Compression Ratio	Maximum Brake H.P. @ R.P.M.	Maximum Torque Ft. Lbs. @ R.P.M.	Normal Oil Pressure Pounds
1976	450SE, SEL	8-275.8	M117	3.62 x 3.35 (92 x 85)	275.8 (4250)	8.0 —	180 @ 4750 —	220 @ 3000 —	43 —
	450SL, SLC	8-275.8	M117	3.62 x 3.35 (92 x 85)	275.8 (4250)	8.0 —	180 @ 4750 —	220 @ 3000 —	43 —
1977	230	4-140.8	M115	3.69 x 3.29 (93.75 x 83.6)	140.8 (2307)	8.0 —	86 @ 4800 —	116 @ 3000 —	43 —
	240D	4-146.7	OM616	3.58 x 3.64 (91 x 92.4)	146.7 (2404)	21.0 —	62 @ 4000 —	97 @ 2400 —	43 —
	300D	5-183.4	OM617	3.58 x 3.64 (91 x 92.4)	183.4 (3005)	21.0 —	77 @ 4400 —	115 @ 2400 —	43 —
	280	6-167.6	M110	3.39 x 3.10 (86 x 78.8)	167.6 (2746)	8.0 —	③ —	④ —	43 —
	280S	6-167.6	M110	3.39 x 3.10 (86 x 78.8)	167.6 (2746)	8.0 —	③ —	④ —	43 —
	450SE, SEL	8-275.8	M117	3.62 x 3.35 (92 x 85)	275.8 (4520)	8.0 —	180 @ 4750 —	220 @ 3000 —	43 —
	450SL, SLC	8-275.8	M117	3.62 x 3.35 (92 x 85)	275.8 (4520)	8.0 —	180 @ 4750 —	220 @ 3000 —	43 —

—Not Available
① —Except Calif., 93 @ 4800; California, 85 @ 4500.
② —Except Calif., 125 @ 2500; California, 122 @ 2500.
③ —Except Calif., 142 @ 5750; California, 137 @ 5750.
④ —Except Calif., 149 @ 4600; California, 142 @ 4600.

GASOLINE ENGINES—TUNE UP SPECIFICATIONS

The following specifications are published from the latest information available. This data should be used only in the absence of a decal affixed in the engine compartment.

★When using a timing light, disconnect vacuum hose or tube at distributor and plug opening in hose or tube so idle speed will not be affected.

▲Before removing wires from distributor cap, determine location of the No. 1 wire in cap, as distributor position may have been altered from that shown at the end of this chart.

Year	Spark Plug		Distributor		Ignition Timing★			Carb. Adjustments					
								Hot Idle Speed		Air Fuel Ratio		Idle CO%	
	Type ①	Gap Inch	Point Gap Inch	Dwell Angle Deg.	Firing Order Fig. ▲	Timing BTDC ②	Mark	Std. Trans.	Auto. Trans.	Std. Trans.	Auto. Trans.	Std. Trans.	Auto. Trans.
1972													
220	W175T30	.024	.016	47-53	A	5°③	④	750-850	750-850	—	—	2.0-3.5	2.0-3.5
250, 250C	W175T30	.024	.016	30-36	B	4°③	④	700-850	700-850	—	—	1.0-1.5	1.0-1.5
280SE6-170	W175T30	.024	.016	30-36	—	6°③	④	700-850	700-850	—	—	1.5-3.5	1.5-3.5
280SE/SEL8-275.8	W175T30	.024	.016	30-34	C	5°③	④	700-800	700-800	—	—	.5-2.0	.5-2.0
300SEL	W175T30	.024	.016	30-34	C	5°③	④	700-800	700-800	—	—	.5-2.0	.5-2.0
450SE/SEL	W175T30	.024	.016	30-34	C	5°③	④	700-800	700-800	—	—	.5-2.0	.5-2.0
1973													
220	W175T30	.024	—	47-53	A	10°	④	750-850	750-850	—	—	1.5⑤	1.5⑤
280,C	W175T30	.024	—	34-40	D	4°③	④	750-950	750-950	—	—	1.5⑤	1.5⑤
450SE/SEL	W175T30	.024	—	30-34	C	5°③	④	700-800	700-800	—	—	.5-2.0	.5-2.0
450SL/SLC	W175T30	.024	—	30-34	C	5°③	④	700-800	700-800	—	—	.5-2.0	.5-2.0
1974													
230	W175T30	.024	—	47-53	A	10°	④	800-900	800-900	—	—	1.5⑤	1.5⑤
280,C	W175T30	.024	—	34-40	D	4°③	④	⑥	⑥	—	—	1.5⑤	1.5⑤
450SE/SEL	W175T30	.024	—	30-34	C	5°③	④	700-800	700-800	—	—	.5-2.0	.5-2.0
450SL/SLC	W175T30	.024	—	30-34	C	5°③	④	700-800	700-800	—	—	.5-2.0	.5-2.0

Continued

GASOLINE ENGINES TUNE UP SPECIFICATIONS—Continued

The following specifications are published from the latest information available. This
data should be used only in the absence of a decal affixed in the engine compartment.

★When using a timing light, disconnect vacuum hose or tube at distributor and plug opening in hose or tube so idle speed will not be affected.

▲Before removing wires from distributor cap, determine location of the No. 1 wire in cap, as distributor position may have been altered from
that shown at the end of this chart.

Year	Spark Plug		Distributor		Ignition Timing★			Carb. Adjustments					
								Hot Idle Speed		Air Fuel Ratio		Idle CO%	
	Type ①	Gap Inch	Point Gap Inch	Dwell Angle Deg.	Firing Order Fig. ▲	Timing BTDC ②	Mark	Std. Trans.	Auto. Trans.	Std. Trans.	Auto. Trans.	Std. Trans.	Auto. Trans.
1975													
230	W175T30	.024	—	47-53	A	10°	④	800-900	800-900	—	—	.4-1.5	.4-1.5
280,C,S	W175T30	.024	—	34-40	D	7°	④	800-900	800-900	—	—	1.0⑤	1.0⑤
450SE/SEL	W175T30	.024	—	30-34	C	TDC	④	700-750	700-750	—	—	.2-1.5	.2-1.5
450SL/SLC	W175T30	.024	—	30-34	C	TDC	④	700-750	700-750	—	—	.2-1.5	.2-1.5
1976													
230	W175T30	.024	—	—	A	10°	④	850	850	—	—	.4-2.0	.4-2.0
280, S	W175T30	.024	—	—	D	7°	④	800-900	800-900	—	—	1.0⑤	1.0⑤
450SE/SEL	W175T30	.024	—	—	C	TDC	④	700-800	700-800	—	—	.2-1.5	.2-1.5
450SL/SLC	W175T30	.024	—	—	C	TDC	④	700-800	700-800	—	—	.2-1.5	.2-1.5
1977													
230	W145T30	.028	—	—	A	10°	④	850	850	—	—	.4-2.0	.4-2.0
280, S	W145T30	.028	—	—	D	TDC	④	800	800	—	—	1.0⑤	1.0⑤
450SE/SEL	W145T30	.028	—	—	C	TDC	④	750	750	—	—	.2-2.0⑦	.2-2.0⑦
450SL/SLC	W145T30	.028	—	—	C	TDC	④	750	750	—	—	.2-2.0⑦	.2-2.0⑦

—Not Available.
①—Bosch.
②—BTDC: Before top dead center.
③—ATDC: After top dead center.

④—Mark located on damper or pulley.
⑤—Maximum.
⑥—Except Calif., 750-950 R.P.M.; California, 700-900 R.P.M.
⑦—High altitude models; .2-1.2.

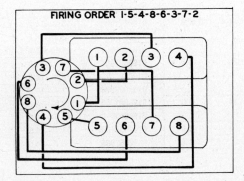

Fig. A

FIRING ORDER 1·3·4·2

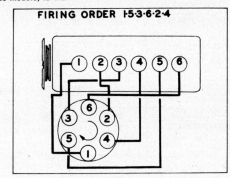

Fig. B

FIRING ORDER 1·5·3·6·2·4

FIRING ORDER 1·5·4·8·6·3·7·2

Fig. C

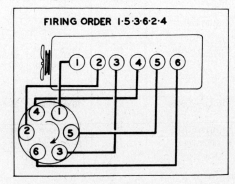

Fig. D

FIRING ORDER 1·5·3·6·2·4

DIESEL ENGINE PERFORMANCE SPECIFICATIONS

Year	Model	Firing Order	Injection Timing BTDC ①	Cranking Compression Pressure (psi.)	Injector Nozzle Pressure (psi.) New	Injector Nozzle Pressure (psi.) Used	Fuel Pump Delivery Pressure ② (psi.) @ Idle	Fuel Pump Delivery Pressure ② (psi.) @ 3000 (RPM)	Idle Speed	Max. Speed @ Zero Load or End of Control (RPM)
1972	220D	1-3-4-2	24°	313—341 ④	1635—1749	1422 ③	8.5—11.4	11.4	750—800	5100—5300
1973	220D	1-3-4-2	24°	313—341 ④	1635—1749	1422 ③	8.5—11.4	11.4	700—800	5100—5300
1974-75	240D	1-3-4-2	24°	313—341 ④	1635—1749	1422 ③	8.5—11.4	11.4	700—800	5200—5400
1975	300D	1-2-4-5-3	24°	313—341 ④	1635—1749	1422 ③	8.5—11.4	11.4	700—800	4900—5200
1976	240D	1-3-4-2	24°	313—341 ④	1635—1749	1422 ③	8.5—11.4	11.4	700—780	5200—5400
	300D	1-2-4-5-3	24°	313—341 ④	1635—1749	1422 ③	8.5—11.4	11.4	680—760	4700—5200
1977	240D	1-3-4-2	24°	313—341 ④	1635—1749	1422 ③	8.5—11.4	11.4	700	4700—5200
	300D	1-2-4-5-3	24°	313—341 ④	1635—1749	1422 ③	8.5—11.4	11.4	700	4700—5200

①—BTDC: Before top dead center.
②—Measured between injection pump and main fuel filter.
③—Minimum.
④—213 psi. minimum.

ALTERNATOR & REGULATOR SPECIFICATIONS

Year	Model ①	Alternator Rated Output	Alternator Output Test Amps @ Alt. R.P.M.			Alternator Resistance Values Stator Ohms	Alternator Resistance Values Rotor Ohms	Regulator Model	Regulator Regulated Voltage	Regulator Load Current Amps
1972	K1(RL)14V35A20	35	10 @ 1300	23 @ 2000	35 @ 6000	.26	4.0	0190601006	13.9—14.8	28—30
								0190600010	13.9—14.8	28—30
	K1(RL)14V55A20	55	10 @ 1200	36 @ 2000	55 @ 6000	.14	4.0	0190601006	13.9—14.8	44—46
								0190600010	13.9—14.8	44—46
	K1(R)14V55A20	55	10 @ 1200	36 @ 2000	55 @ 6000	.14	3.4	0192052001	13.7—14.5	5—7
1973	K1(RL)14V35A20	35	10 @ 1300	23 @ 2000	35 @ 6000	.26	4.0	0190601006	13.9—14.8	28—30
								0190600010	13.9—14.8	28—30
	K1(RL)14V55A20	55	10 @ 1200	36 @ 2000	55 @ 6000	.14	4.0	0190601006	13.9—14.8	44—46
								0190600010	13.9—14.8	44—46
	K1(R)14V55A20	55	10 @ 1200	36 @ 2000	55 @ 6000	.14	3.4	0192052001	13.7—14.5	5—7
1974	K1(RL)14V35A20	35	10 @ 1300	23 @ 2000	35 @ 6000	.26	4.0	0190601006	13.9—14.8	28—30
								0190600010	13.9—14.8	28—30
	K1(RL)14V55A20	55	10 @ 1200	36 @ 2000	55 @ 6000	.14	4.0	0190601006	13.9—14.8	44—46
								0190600010	13.9—14.8	44—46
	K1(R)14V55A20	55	10 @ 1200	36 @ 2000	55 @ 6000	.14	3.4	0192052004	13.7—14.5	5—7
1975	K1(RL)14V35A20	35	10 @ 1300	23 @ 2000	35 @ 6000	.26	4.0	0190601006	13.9—14.8	28—30
								0190600010	13.9—14.8	28—30
	K1(RL)14V55A20	55	10 @ 1200	36 @ 2000	55 @ 6000	.14	4.0	0190601006	13.9—14.8	44—46
								0190600010	13.9—14.8	44—46
	K1(R)14V55A20	55	10 @ 1200	36 @ 2000	55 @ 6000	.14	3.4	0192052001	13.7—14.5	5—7
1976-77	K1(RL)14V35A20	35	10 @ 1300	23 @ 2000	35 @ 6000	.26	4.0	0190601006	13.9—14.8	28—30
								0190600010	13.9—14.8	28—30
								0192052004	13.9—14.8	28—30
	K1(RL)14V55A20	55	10 @ 2000	36 @ 2000	55 @ 6000	.14	4.0	0190601006	13.9—14.8	44—46
								0190600010	13.9—14.8	44—46
	K1(R)14V55A20	55	10 @ 1200	36 @ 2000	55 @ 6000	.14	3.4	0192052008	13.7—14.5	5—7
	N114V75A20	75	28 @ 1500	50 @ 2000	75 @ 6000	.1	3.4	0192052008	13.7—14.5	5—7

①—Bosch designation.

Continued

DISTRIBUTOR SPECIFICATIONS

Year	Distributor Part No.	Distributor Advance @ Engine R.P.M.		
		1500 R.P.M.	3000 R.P.M.	4500 R.P.M.
1972	0231115093	−3 to −5 ①	30—36 ①	43—47 ①
	0231116068	−3 to +1 ①	36—44 ①	40—48 ①
	0231119008	11—15 ①	19—23 ①	27—31 ①
	0231142005	−1 to +7 ①	42—50 ①	46—54 ①
	0231401003	11—15 ①	18—22 ①	—
	0231402002	11—15 ①	18—22 ①	—
1973	0231176016	15—20 ②	27—32 ②	42—48 ②
	0231310002	13—17 ①	31—35 ①	37—41 ①
	0231402002	10—14 ①	18—22 ①	—
	0231402005	10—14 ①	18—22 ①	—
1974	0231170137	15—20 ②	27—32 ②	42—48 ②
	0231310002	13—17 ①	31—35 ①	37—41 ①
	0231403006	10—14 ①	18—22 ①	—
	0231403007	10—14 ①	18—22 ①	—
1975	0231170137	15—20 ②	27—32 ②	42—48 ②
	0231311001	10—16 ②	26—33 ②	29—35 ②
	0231404002	10—16 ②	18—23 ②	—
1976	0231170137	15—20 ②	27—32 ②	42—48 ②
	0231311001	10—16 ②	26—33 ②	29—35 ②
	0237405002	9—16 ②	27—33 ② ③	—
1977	0231170137	15—20 ②	27—32 ② ③	42—48 ②
	0237304001	16—20 ②	28—34 ②	—
	0237405002	9—16 ②	27—33 ② ③	—

—Not Available.
① —With vacuum.
② —Without vacuum.
③ —At 3500 R.P.M.

STARTING MOTOR SPECIFICATIONS

Year	Bosch Ident. No.	Short Circuit Test		No Load Test			Load Test	
		Amps	Volts	Amperes	Volts	R.P.M.	Amps	Volts
1972	0 001 208	235—250	6	35—45	12	6400—7900	165—200	9
1972-73	0 001 356 003	600—700	6	50—70	12	6400—8100	300—360	9
	0 001 313	600—650	6	50—70	12	9000—11000	290—330	9
	0 001 362 002	1000—1200	6	80—95	12	7500—8500	650—750	9
1974	0 001 356 003	480—600	5.5	60—90	11.5	5000—7000	—	—
1974-75	0 001 313	430—520	5.5	50—80	11.5	8000—10000	—	—
	0 001 362 029	700—880	4.5	65—95	11.5	6500—8500	—	—
1975	0 001	280—370	7.5	35—55	11.5	6000—8000	—	—
1976-77	0 001 208	280—370	7.5	35—55	11.5	6000	—	—
	0 001 208	320—410	8.5	35—55	11.5	6000	—	—
	0 001 313	430—520	5.5	50—80	11.5	8300	—	—
	0 001 313	520—610	6.5	50—80	11.5	8300	—	—
	0 001 312.1	530—720	5.0	55—85	11.0	8500	—	—
	0 001 312.1	650—730	6.0	55—85	11.0	8500	—	—
	0 001 362	530—700	3.5	65—95	11.5	6500	—	—
	0 001 362	700—880	4.5	65—95	11.5	6500	—	—

—Not Available

PISTONS, PINS, RINGS, CRANKSHAFT & BEARINGS

| Year | Engine | Piston Clearance | Ring End Gap | | Wristpin Diameter | Rod Bearings | | Main Bearing | | | |
			Comp.	Oil		Shaft Diameter	Bearing Clearance	Shaft Diameter	Bearing Clearance	Thrust on Bearing No.	Shaft End Play
1972	4-134①	.0008—.0012	.012	.010	1.024	2.0470—2.0474	.0018—.0026	2.3622—2.3626	.0014—.0022	—	—
	4-134②	.0008—.0012	.012	.010	1.024	2.0470—2.0474	.0018—.0026	2.3622—2.3626	.0014—.0022	—	—
	6-170	.0008—.0012	.012	.010	.9849	1.8894—1.8898	.0018—.0026	2.3622—2.3626	.0014—.0022	—	—
	8-275.8	.0008—.0012	.014	.010	1.024	2.0470—2.0474	.0014—.0029	2.5198—2.5202	.0014—.0026	—	—
1973	4-134①	.0008—.0012	.012	.010	—	—	.0012—.0028	—	.0004—.0020	—	—
	4-134②	.0008—.0012	.012	.010	—	—	.0012—.0028	—	.0012—.0028	—	—
	6-167.6	.0008—.0012	.012	.010	—	—	.0012—.0028	—	.0006—.0020	—	—
	8-275.8	.0008—.0012	.014	.010	—	—	.0014—.0030	—	.0014—.0026	—	—
1974	4-140.8	.0008—.0012	.012	.010	—	—	.0012—.0016	—	.0012—.0027	—	—
	4-146.7①	.0008—.0012	.012	.010	—	—	.0012—.0016	—	.0012—.0027	—	—
	6-167.6	.0008—.0012	.012	.010	—	—	.0012—.0016	—	.0006—.0020	—	—
	8-275.8	.0008—.0012	.014	.010	—	—	.0014—.0030	—	.0014—.0026	—	—
1975	4-140.8	.0010—.0013	.015	.010	—	—	.0012—.0027	—	.0012—.0027	—	—
	4-146.7①	.0007—.0015	.008	.010	—	—	.0012—.0027	—	.0012—.0027	—	—
	5-183.4①	.0007—.0015	.008	.010	—	—	.0012—.0029	—	.0012—.0029	—	—
	6-167.6	.0010—.0013	.012	.010	—	—	.0010—.0026	—	.0012—.0027	—	—
	8-275.8	.0005—.0015	.015	.010	—	—	.0009—.0027	—	.0018—.0033	—	—
1976	4-140.8	.0010—.0014	.014	.010	—	—	.0012—.0027	—	.0012—.0027	—	—
	4-146.7①	.0007—.0015	.008	.010	—	—	.0012—.0027	—	.0012—.0027	—	—
	5-183.4①	.0007—.0015	.008	.010	—	—	.0012—.0029	—	.0012—.0029	—	—
	6-167.6	.0010—.0014	.012	.010	—	—	.0005—.0026	—	.0012—.0027	—	—
	8-275.8	.0005—.0015	.014	.010	—	—	.0012—.0027	—	.0016—.0035	—	—
1977	4-140.8	.0010—.0014	.014	.010	—	—	.0012—.0027	—	.0012—.0027	—	—
	4-146.7①	.0007—.0015	.008	.010	—	—	.0012—.0027	—	.0012—.0027	—	—
	5-183.4①	.0007—.0015	.008	.010	—	—	.0012—.0029	—	.0012—.0029	—	—
	6-167.6	.0010—.0014	.012	.010	—	—	.0005—.0026	—	.0012—.0027	—	—
	8-275.8	.0005—.0015	.014	.010	—	—	.0012—.0027	—	.0016—.0035	—	—

—Not Available.
① —Diesel engine.
② —Gasoline engine.

VALVE SPECIFICATIONS

| Year | Engine | Valve Lash | | Valve Angles | | Valve Spring Installed Height | Valve Spring Pressure Lbs. @ In. | Stem Clearance | | Stem Diameter | |
		Int.	Exh.	Seat	Face			Intake	Exhaust	Intake	Exhaust
1972	4-134①	.004c	.016c	30	30	1.51	110 @ 1.18	—	—	.3903—.3908	.3908—.3916
	4-134②	.003c	.008c	45	45	③	④	—	—	.3526—.3534	.4302—.4310
	6-170	.003c	.008c	45	45	⑤	⑥	—	—	.3528—.3534	.4302—.4310
	8-275.8	.003c	.008c	45	45	⑤	⑥	—	—	.3528—.3534	.4306—.4314
1973	4-134①	.004c	.012c	30	30	—	—	—	—	.3910—.3916	.3908—.3916
	4-134②	.004c	.008c	45	45	—	—	—	—	.3526—.3534	.4302—.4310
	6-167.6	.004c	.010c	45	45	—	—	—	—	.3528—.3534	.4310—.4318
	8-275.8	.004c	.008c	45	45	—	—	—	—	.3528—.3534	.4306—.4314
1974	4-140.8	.004c	.008c	45	45	—	—	—	—	.3528—.3534	.4308—.4314
	4-146.7①	.004c	.012c	30	30	—	—	—	—	.3910—.3916	.3908—.3916
	6-167.6	.004c	.010c	45	45	—	—	—	—	.3528—.3534	.4310—.4318
	8-275.8	.004c	.008c	45	45	—	—	—	—	.3528—.3534	.4306—.4314
1975	4-140.8	.004c	.008c	45	45	—	—	—	—	.3528—.3534	.4308—.4314
	4-146.7①	.004c	.012c	30	30	—	—	—	—	.3910—.3916	.3908—.3916
	5-183.4①	.004c	.012c	30	30	—	—	—	—	.3910—.3916	.3908—.3916
	6-167.6	.004c	.010c	45	45	—	—	—	—	.3528—.3534	.4310—.4318
	8-275.8	Hydraulic		45	45	—	—	—	—	.3528—.3534	.4306—.4314

Continued

VALVE SPECIFICATIONS—Continued

Year	Engine	Valve Lash		Valve Angles		Valve Spring Installed Height	Valve Spring Pressure Lbs. @ In.	Stem Clearance		Stem Diameter	
		Int.	Exh.	Seat	Face			Intake	Exhaust	Intake	Exhaust
1976	4-140.8	.004c	.008c	45	45	—	—	—	—	.3528—.3534	.4308—.4314
	4-146.7 ①	.004c	.012c	30	30	—	—	—	—	.3910—.3916	.3908—.3916
	5-183.4 ①	.004c	.012c	30	30	—	—	—	—	.3910—.3916	.3908—.3916
	6-167.6	.004c	.010c	45	45	—	—	—	—	.3528—.3534	.4310—.4318
	8-275.8	Hydraulic		45	45	—	—	—	—	.3528—.3534	.4306—.4314
1977	4-140.8	.004c	.008c	45	45	—	—	—	—	.3528—.3534	.4308—.4314
	4-146.7 ①	.004c	.012c	30	30	—	—	—	—	.3910—.3916	.3908—.3916
	5-183.4 ①	.004c	.012c	30	30	—	—	—	—	.3910—.3916	.3908—.3916
	6-167.6	.004c	.010c	45	45	—	—	—	—	.3528—.3534	.4310—.4318
	8-275.8	Hydraulic		45	45	—	—	—	—	.3528—.3534	.4306—.4314

—Not Available.
①—Diesel engine.
②—Gasoline engine.
③—Inner spring, 1.22; outer spring, 1.54.
④—Inner spring, 53 @ .827; outer spring, 159 @ 1.18.
⑤—Inner spring, 1.30; outer spring, 1.65.
⑥—Inner spring, 55 @ .847; outer spring, 194 @ 1.20.

ENGINE TIGHTENING SPECIFICATIONS

Year	Engine	Spark Plugs or Glow Plugs Ft. Lbs.	Cylinder Head Bolts Ft. Lbs. ①	Camshaft Bearing Caps Ft. Lbs.	Rocker Arm Mount Ft. Lbs.	Cylinder Head Cover Ft. Lbs.	Connecting Rod Cap Bolts Ft. Lbs.	Main Bearing Cap Bolts Ft. Lbs.	Flywheel to Crankshaft Bolts Ft. Lbs.	Crankshaft Front Bolt Ft. Lbs.
1972	4-134 Gasoline	22	②	18	58	3.5	29—36③	65	25③	156
	4-134 Diesel	36	④	18	27	3.5	29—36③	65	25③	156
	6-170	22	②	—	58	3.5	29—36③	58	25③	223
	V8-275.8	22	⑤	36	58	3.5	29—36③	⑥	25③	188
1973	4-134 Gasoline	22	②	18	58	3.5	29—36③	65	25③	188
	4-134 Diesel	36	④	18	27	3.5	29—36③	65	25③	188
	6-167.6	22	④	—	58	3.5	29—36③	58	25③	307
	8-275.8	22	⑤	36	58	3.5	29—36③	⑥	25③	188
1974	4-140.8	22	②	18	58	3.5	29—36③	65	25③	217
	4-146.7 Diesel	36	④	18	27	3.5	29—36③	65	25③	217
	6-167.6	22	②	—	58	3.5	29—36③	58	25③	307
	8-275.8	22	⑤	36	58	3.5	29—36③	⑥	25③	217
1975	4-140.8	22	④	18	58	3.5	29—36③	65	25③	217
	4-146.7 Diesel	36	④	18	27	9	29—36③	65	25③	217
	5-183.4 Diesel	36	④	18	27	9	29—36③	65	25③	217
	6-167.6	22	②	—	58	3.5	29—36③	58	25③	307
	8-275.8	22	⑤	36	58	3.5	29—36③	⑥	25③	217
1976-77	4-140.8	22	⑦	18	59	3.5	30—37③	66	22—30③	221
	4-146.7 Diesel	36	⑧	18	27	11	30—37③	66	22—30③	221
	5-183.4 Diesel	36	⑧	18	27	11	30—37③	66	22—30③	221
	6-167.6	22	⑦	—	59	3.5	30—37③	59	22—30③	314
	8-275.8	22	5	36	59	3.5	30—37③	⑥	22—30③	221

—Not Available.
①—Coat all threads and contact area of bolts and washers with oil.
②—Initially torque bolts to 60 ft. lbs. Then start engine and run under load until engine coolant reaches normal operating temperature. After 5 minutes of operation at this temperature, retorque bolts to 65 ft. lbs.
③—After torquing bolts to specified torque, turn wrench in direction of tightening an additional 90-100°.
④—Initially torque bolts to 65 ft. lbs. Then start engine and run under load until engine coolant reaches normal operating temperature. After 5 minutes of operation at this temperature, retorque bolts to 65 ft. lbs.
⑤—Initially torque bolts to 36 ft. lbs. Then start engine and run under load until engine coolant reaches normal operating temperature. After 5 minutes of operation at this temperature, retorque bolts to 43 ft. lbs.
⑥—M10 bolts, 43 ft. lbs. M12 bolts, 72 ft. lbs.
⑦—Initially torque bolts to 74 ft. lbs. Then start engine and run under load until engine coolant reaches normal operating temperature. After 5 minutes of operation at this temperature, retorque bolts to 74 ft. lbs.
⑧—Initially torque bolts to 66 ft. lbs. Then start engine and run under load until engine coolant reaches normal operating temperature. After 5 minutes of operation at this temperature, retorque bolts to 66 ft. lbs.

Continued

COOLING SYSTEM & CAPACITY DATA

Year	Model	Cooling System Capacity Qts.	Radiator Cap Relief Pressure, Lbs.	Thermo. Opening Temp. °F	Fuel Tank, Gals.	Engine Oil Refill Qts. ①	Transmission Oil		Auto. Trans. Qts.	Rear Axle Oil, Pts.
							Manual Trans. Pts.			
							4 Speed	5 Speed		
1972	220	10.7	14	174	19.7⑤	②	3.4	—	5.8	2.4
	220D	10.9	14	174	19.7⑤	③	3.4	—	5.8	2.4
	250	11.2	14	174	19.7⑤	④	3.4	5.3	5.8	2.4
	280SE	11.4	14	174	24.6⑤	④	3.8	5.3	5.0	5.3
	280SE/SEL 4.5	14.7	14	167	24.6⑤	9	—	—	9.4	5.3
	300SEL 4.5	14.7	14	167	24.6⑤	9	—	—	9.4	5.3
	450SE/SEL	14.3	14	167	29.8⑤	9	—	—	9.4	2.8
	450SL/SLC	15.9	14	167	27.2⑤	9	—	—	9.4	3.0
1973	220	10.7	14	174	19.6⑤	②	3.4	—	5.8	⑥
	220D	10.9	14	174	19.6⑤	③	3.4	—	⑦	⑥
	280	11.6	14	188	19.6⑤	7.9	3.4	5.3	⑧	2.1
	450SE/SEL	15.9	14	167	28.8⑤	9	—	—	9.4	2.8
	450SL/SLC	15.9	14	167	27.2⑤	9	—	—	9.4	2.8
1974	230	10.6	14	174	19.6⑤	6.3	3.4	5.3	6.5	2.1
	240D	10.6	14	176	19.6⑤	6.9	3.4	5.3	6.5	2.1
	280	11.1	14	188	23.3⑤	7.4	3.4	5.3	7.0	2.1
	450SE/SEL	15.9	14	167	28.9⑤	9	—	—	9.4	2.8
	450SL/SLC	15.9	14	167	27.2⑤	9	—	—	9.4	2.8
1975	230	10.6	14	174	19.6⑤	6.3	3.4	—	6.5	2.1
	240D	10.6	14	176	19.6⑤	6.9	3.4	—	6.5	2.1
	280	11.1	14	188	⑨⑤	7.4	3.4	5.3	7.0	2.1
	300D	11.4	14	176	19.6⑤	7.4	3.4	—	6.5	2.1
	450SE/SEL	15.9	14	167	28.8⑤	9	—	—	9.4	2.8
	450SL/SLC	15.9	14	167	27.2⑤	9	—	—	9.4	2.8
1976-77	230	10.6	14	174	19.6⑤	6.3	3.4	—	6.5	2.1
	240D	10.6	14	176	19.6⑤	7.4	3.4	—	6.5	2.1
	280	11.6	14	188	⑨⑤	7.9	3.4	5.3	7.0	2.1
	300D	11.6	14	176	19.6	7.9	3.4	—	6.5	2.1
	450SE/SEL	15.9	14	167	28.8	9.5	—	—	9.4	2.8
	450SL/SLC	15.9	14	167	27.2	9.5	—	—	9.4	2.8

—Not Available.
① —Including filter.
② —First version up to chassis end No. 049764, 5.3 qts.; second version from chassis No. 049765, 5.8 qts.
③ —First version up to chassis end No. 120829, 5.8 qts.; second version from chassis end No. 120830.
④ —First version smooth oil pan bottom, 6.9 qts.; second version profiled oil pan bottom, 7.4 qts.; without oil cooler, .75 qts. less.
⑤ —Includes reserve.
⑥ —Housing with grey iron cover, 2.4 pts.; housing with light alloy cover, 2.1 pts.
⑦ —With hydr. clutch, 5.8 qts.; with torque converter, 6.5 qts.
⑧ —With hydr. clutch, 5.8 qts.; with torque converter, 7 qts.
⑨ —280 & 280C, 23.3 gals.; 280S, 28.8 gals.

Continued

MERCEDES-BENZ

BRAKE SPECIFICATIONS

Year	Model	Wheel Cylinder Bore Diameter		Master Cylinder Bore Diameter	Disc Brake Rotor Specifications					
		Front	Rear		Nominal Thickness		Minimum Thickness		Thickness Variation Parallelism	
					Front	Rear	Front	Rear	Front	Rear
1972	220,D	2.244	1.496	.9375	.4961	.3937	.4567	.3701	.0012	.0012
	250	2.244	1.496	.9375	.4961	.3937	.4567	.3701	.0012	.0012
	280	2.244	1.378	.9375	.7480	.3937	.7087	.3701	.0012	.0012
	300	2.244	1.378	.9375	.7480	.3937	.7087	.3701	.0012	.0012
	450	2.362	1.496	.9375	.8661	.3937	.8268	.3701	.0012	.0012
1973	220,D	2.244	1.496	.9375	.4961	.3937	.4567	.3701	.0008	.0008
	280	2.362	1.496	.9375	.4951	.3937	.4567	.3701	.0008	.0008
	450SE/SEL	2.362	1.496	.9375	.8661	.3937	.8268	.3701	.0004	.0004
	450SL/SLC	①	1.496	.9375	.8661	.3937	.8268	.3701	②	②
1974	230	2.244	1.496	.9375	.4961	.3937	.4567	.3701	.0008	.0008
	240	2.244	1.496	.9375	.4961	.3937	.4567	.3701	.0008	.0008
	280	2.362	1.496	.9375	.4961	.3937	.4567	.3701	.0008	.0008
	450	2.362	1.496	.9375	.8661	.3937	.8268	.3701	.0004	.0004
1975	230	2.244	1.496	.9375	.4961	.3937	.4567	.3701	.0008	.0008
	240	2.244	1.496	.9375	.4961	.3937	.4567	.3701	.0008	.0008
	280,C	2.362	1.496	.9375	.4961	.3937	.4567	.3701	.0008	.0008
	280S	2.362	1.496	③	.8661	.3937	.8268	.3701	.0004	.0004
	450SE/SEL	2.362	1.496	③	.8661	.3937	.8268	.3701	.0004	.0004
	450SL/SLC	2.362	1.496	④	.8661	.3937	.8268	.3701	.0004	.0004
1976-77	230	2.244	1.496	⑤	.4961	.3937	.4567	.3701	.0008	.0008
	240	2.244	1.496	⑤	.4961	.3937	.4567	.3701	.0008	.0008
	280,C	2.362	1.496	⑤	.4961	.3937	.4567	.3701	.0004	.0004
	280S	2.362	1.496	⑤	.8661	.3937	.8268	.3701	.0004	.0004
	300D	2.362	1.496	⑤	.4961	.3937	.4567	.3701	.0004	.0004
	450SE/SEL	2.362	1.496	③	.8661	.3937	.8268	.3701	.0004	.0004
	450SL/SLC	2.362	1.496	④	.8661	.3937	.8268	.3701	.0004	.0004

①—Version 1, 2.244"; Version 2, 2.362".
②—Version 1, .0008"; Version 2, .0004".
③—Version 1, .9375"; Version 2, stepped diameter master cylinder, front wheel brake, .9375"; rear wheel brake, .750".
④—Version 2, .9375"; Version 3, stepped diameter master cylinder, front wheel brake, .9375"; rear wheel brake, .750".
⑤—Stepped diameter master cylinder, front wheel brake, .9375"; rear wheel brake, .750".

WHEEL ALIGNMENT SPECIFICATIONS

Year	Model	Caster Angle, Degrees				Camber Angle, Degrees		Toe-In
		Measured in Straight Ahead Position		Measured Over Lock				
		Limits	Desired	Limits	Desired	Limits	Desired	Degrees
1972	220,D	①	②	③	④	−1/12 to +5/12	+1/4	5/12
	250	①	②	③	④	−1/12 to +5/12	+1/4	5/12
	280	+3¼ to +3¾	+3½	+3¼ to +3¾	+3½	+1/6 to +5/6	+½	1/3
	300	+3¾ to +4¼	+4	+3¾ to +4¼	+4	0 to +2/3	+1/3	1/3
	450SE/SEL	+9½ to +10½	+10	+9¼ to +10¼	+9¾	−1/3 to 0	−1/6	5/12
	450SL/SLC	+3⅓ to +4	+3⅔	+2¹¹/₁₂ to +3⁷/₁₂	3¼	−1/3 to +1/6	0	1/3
1973	220,D	①	②	③	④	−1/12 to +5/12	+1/4	5/12
	280	①	②	③	④	−1/12 to +5/12	+1/4	5/12
	450SE/SEL	+9½ to +10½	+10	+9¼ to +10¼	+9¾	−1/3 to 0	−1/6	5/12
	450SL/SLC	+3⅓ to +4	+3⅔	+2¹¹/₁₂ to +3⁷/₁₂	+3¼	−1/3 to +1/6	0	1/3
1974	230	①	②	③	④	−1/12 to +5/12	+1/4	5/12
	240D	①	②	③	④	−1/12 to +5/12	+1/4	5/12
	280	①	②	③	④	−1/12 to +5/12	+1/4	5/12
	450SE/SEL	+9½ to +10½	+10	+9 to +10	+9½	−1/3 to 0	−1/6	5/12
	450SL/SLC	+3⅓ to +4	+3⅔	+2¹¹/₁₂ to +3⁷/₁₂	+3¼	−1/3 to +1/6	0	1/3

WHEEL ALIGNMENT SPECIFICATIONS

Year	Model	Caster Angle, Degrees				Camber Angle, Degrees		Toe-In
		Measured in Straight Ahead Position		Measured Over Lock				
		Limits	Desired	Limits	Desired	Limits	Desired	Degrees
1975	230	①	⑤	③	⑥	$-1/12$ to $+5/12$	$-1/12$	¼
	240D	①	⑤	③	⑥	$-1/12$ to $+5/12$	$-1/12$	¼
	280,C	①	⑤	③	⑥	$-1/12$ to $+5/12$	$-1/12$	¼
	280S	$+9½$ to $+10½$	$+10$	$+9$ to $+10$	$+9½$	$-1/3$ to 0	$-1/6$	½
	300D	①	⑤	③	⑥	$-1/12$ to $+5/12$	$-1/12$	¼
	450SE/SEL	$+9½$ to $+10½$	$+10$	$+9$ to $+10$	$+9½$	$-1/3$ to 0	$-1/6$	½
	450SL/SLC	$+3^1/3$ to $+4$	$+4$	$+2^{11}/12$ to $+3^7/12$	$+3^7/12$	$-1/3$ to $+1/6$	0	⅓
1976-77	230	①	⑤	③	⑥	$-1/12$ to $+5/12$	$-1/12$	¼
	240D	①	⑤	③	⑥	$-1/12$ to $+5/12$	$-1/12$	¼
	280,C	①	⑤	③	⑥	$-1/12$ to $+5/12$	$-1/12$	¼
	280S	$+9½$ to $+10½$	$+10¼$	$+9$ to $+10$	$+9¾$	$-1/3$ to 0	$-1/6$	½
	450SE/SEL	$+9½$ to $+10½$	$+10¼$	$+9$ to $+10$	$+9¾$	$-1/3$ to 0	$-1/6$	½
	450SL/SLC	$+3^1/3$ to $+4$	$+4$	$+2^{11}/12$ to $+3^7/12$	$+3^7/12$	$-1/3$ to $+1/6$	0	⅓

①—Exc. power steering, $+2^1/3$ to $+3$; power steering, $+3^1/3$ to $+4$.
②—Exc. power steering, $+2^2/3$; power steering, $+3^2/3$.
③—Exc. power steering, $+1^{11}/12$ to $+2^7/12$; power steering, $+2^{11}/12$ to $+3^7/12$.
④—Exc. power steering, $+2¼$; power steering, $+3¼$.
⑤—Exc. power steering, $+3$; power steering, $+4$.
⑥—Exc. power steering, $+2^7/12$; power steering, $+3^7/12$.

Electrical Section

DISTRIBUTOR, REPLACE

110 & 117 Engines

1. Remove protective cover, distributor cap, cable plug connections and vacuum line.
2. Set engine to ignition TDC of the first cylinder.

NOTE: The markings on the rotor and distributor housing must be aligned. Furthermore, the pointer on the crankcase should be above the TDC mark on the vibration damper.

CAUTION: On engines having a "010" mark for BDC in addition to TDC, the TDC mark is next to the pin in the vibration damper.

3. Crank the engine with special tool SW27 (001589650900).
4. Loosen the hex socket screw holding the distributor.
5. Remove the distributor.
6. Reinstall using the reverse procedure.

115 Engines

Removal

1. Remove the protective cap, distributor cover, cable plug connections and vacuum line.
2. Set first cylinder at top dead center.

NOTE: The markings on the distributor rotor and distributor housing must be aligned, Fig. 1, and the pointer on the crankcase should be above the "010" mark of the balancing disc.

3. Crank engine using special tool combination 0015896500900.

CAUTION: Do not crank the engine at the fastening bolts of the camshaft gear. Do not rotate the engine in reverse.

4. Loosen the hex socket screw of the distributor attachment.
5. Remove the distributor.

Fig. 1 Aligning marks on distributor rotor & housing

Installation

1. Install distributor in reverse procedure, paying special attention to the ignition TDC of the first cylinder and reference marks (2 above).
2. Check dwell and timing, and adjust.

ALTERNATOR & REGULATOR ON VEHICLE TESTING

In the energized condition, the alternator may be operated only with the regulator switch and battery connected.

As long as the engine is running, neither the pole terminals of the battery, supply cable on the alternator nor plug of the regulator should be removed to avoid the risk of destroying the diodes by inductive voltage peaks.

Initial excitation is assured when the 2-watt charging lamp in the instrument cluster lights up.

Testing

1. Disconnect the battery ground cable.
2. Connect a voltmeter having a measuring range of at least up to 16 volts to terminal B+ and to the ground connection of the alternator, Fig. 2.
3. Disconnect the red cable on connection B+ of the alternator and

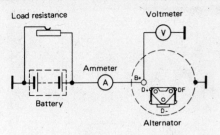

Fig. 2 Connections for alternator testing

connect an ammeter with a measuring range up to 60 amps to the charging line.

4. Connect the battery ground cable and a controllable resistance that permits a load up to 55 amps to the positive and negative connections of the battery.
5. Start the engine and increase to a speed of 2,000 to 3,000 rpm. Keep engine speed constant.
6. Adjust the current on the load resistance while simultaneously reading the regulating voltage on the voltmeter.

BRAKE LIGHT SWITCH, ADJUST

1. Measure distance "a", Fig. 3, with the brake pedal in the inoperative position. The brake pedal should have to move 15-20 mm before touching the contact button.
2. Use the two hex nuts to adjust the switch so the correct distance, "a" of Fig. 3, is obtained. The contact button of the switch should extend 6 to 8 mm from the housing.

INSTRUMENT CLUSTER, REPLACE

1. Take the cover out of the padding and remove the steering wheel, if necessary.
2. The instrument cluster is held in a recess by means of a profilated rubber section.
3. Pull the instrument cluster out as far as possible.
4. Loosen the speedometer shaft, two

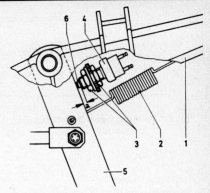

a = 6 — 8 mm

1 Brake pedal carrier   4 Brake light switch
2 Return spring   5 Brake pedal
3 Hex. nut   6 Contact button

Fig. 3 Brake light switch adjustment

electrical plug connections and oil pressure line.
5. Remove the instrument cluster.
6. Reverse procedure to install. When connecting speedometer cable, make sure that speedometer shaft is not bent.

Engine Section
110 Gasoline Engine

ENGINE, REPLACE

NOTE: The engine and transmission are removed as an assembly.

1. Remove the radiator and fan.
2. On vehicles having level control, unscrew the pressure oil pump and place it aside with its hoses connected. Do this by loosening only the screws pointed to in Fig. 1.
3. Unbolt the air conditioner compressor and move it aside. However, do not disconnect refrigerant lines.
4. Drain oil from the reservoir and disconnect the pressure lines of the power steering system on the high pressure oil pump.
5. Loosen all cooling system, vacuum, oil and electrical lines leading to the engine.
6. Remove the driveshaft.
7. Disconnect exhaust pipes on the exhaust manifold and on the exhaust strut of the transmission.
8. Attach chains and lift the engine with a hoist at an angle of about 45 deg.
9. To install, reverse this procedure.

CYLINDER HEAD, REPLACE

NOTE: Remove cylinder head only with engine cold.

Removal
1. Drain the cooling system.
2. Remove the radiator.
3. Remove the battery.
4. Remove the air conditioner com-

Fig. 1 Screw locations for removing level control oil pump

pressor and move aside. Keep refrigerant lines connected.
5. Remove the tensioning roller for the refrigerant compressor V-belt.
6. Unscrew both covers on the camshaft housing.
7. On cars with level control, remove the pressure oil pump and lay it to one side with lines connected by loosening only the screws pointed out in Fig. 1.
8. Remove the vacuum pump.
9. On engines with carburetors, disconnect hot water lines to the carburetor and intake pipe.
10. Disconnect all electrical connections, hoses, and fuel and vacuum lines connected to the cylinder head and intake pipe or carburetor.
11. Remove the longitudinal regulating shaft.
12. Unscrew the oil return pipe on the cylinder head.
13. Disconnect the water pump bypass hose.
14. Loosen the oil dipstick guide tube and bend it sideways.
15. Loosen exhaust pipes on the exhaust manifold and transmission. On carburetor engines, unscrew the

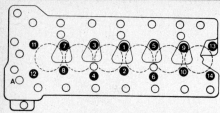

Fig. 2 Cylinder head bolt tightening sequence

preheating scoop.
16. Force out all tensioning springs with a screwdriver.
17. Remove all rocker arms using remover and installer 110589046100.
18. Crank engine with tool combination SW27, 001589650900.

CAUTION: Do not rotate the engine on the fastening screws of the camshaft gears or in reverse.

19. Set the engine to ignition TDC so that the marks on the crankshaft and camshaft are aligned.
20. Applying counter pressure to the camshaft, unscrew both fastening screws of the camshaft gears.
21. Remove the upper slide rail, knocking out bearing bolts with impact puller 115589193300.
22. Remove the chain tensioner.
23. Loosen the rear right cover on the camshaft housing and force both camshafts toward the rear by means of remover and installer 110589033300.
24. Remove camshaft gears and support.
25. Remove bearing bolt and guide wheel with impact puller 115589193300.
26. Remove the slide rail from the cylinder head by knocking out bearing bolts with impact puller 115589193300.
27. Loosen cylinder head bolts in reverse order of tightening, Fig. 2. Pull out the two M8 screws in the chain box with a magnet.

28. Pull up the timing chain and push the tensioning rail toward the center of the engine.
29. Lift off the cylinder head.

Installation
1. After cleaning the cylinder head and surfaces, mount the new cylinder head gasket.

NOTE: There are two hollow set pins in the cylinder crankcase that serve for locating the cylinder head, Fig. 3.

2. Place two strips of wood (15 x 35 x 240 mm) on the cylinder head gasket. The piece of wood at the front should be upright.
3. Lay the cylinder head on the strips of wood and install the timing chain and tensioning rail.
4. Lift the cylinder head at the front and pull out the wood strip up front. Lower the cylinder head until it seats itself in the front hollow set pin.
5. Lift the cylinder head at the rear and pull out the rear strip of wood. Lower the cylinder head until it seats itself in the rear hollow set pin.
6. Lubricate the cylinder head bolts before installing them.
7. Tighten the cylinder head bolts in sequence, Fig. 2 and in three steps as follows:

Step 1   40 Nm (4 kpm)
Step 2   60 Nm (kpm)
Step 3   90 Nm (9 kpm)

CAUTION: When the bolts have been tightened, both camshafts should rotate easily when turned manually.

8. Install the slide rail by lifting the timing chain, introducing the slide rail with pliers and knocking in bearing bolts with impact puller 115589193300.

Fig. 3 Positioning of wooden guide strips

9. Mount camshaft gears with applicable spacer ring and spacer sleeves or driver.
10. See that the adjusting marks on both camshaft gears on the camshaft housing are in alignment, Fig. 4.

CAUTION: Engines on which the vibration damper has a "010" mark in addition to a TDC mark, the TDC mark is located next to the pin in the vibration damper.

11. Install the slide rail so the timing chain cannot jump off.
12. Install the rigid chain tensioner and adjust tension.
13. Install fastening screw with washer and torque to 80 Nm (8 kpm) while applying counter pressure, Fig. 5.
14. Crank engine with tool combination SW 27, 001589650900, checking adjusting marks.
15. Check timing.
16. Install rocker arms and tensioning springs.
17. Continue reassembly.
18. Adjust valve clearance to specifications.

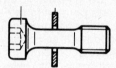

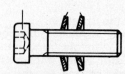

Fig. 5 Fastening screw & washer (top). Note that fastening screw & cup springs (bottom) should not be used

Fig. 4 Aligning marks on camshaft gears with marks on housing

Fig. 6 Removing rocker arm tension springs

Fig. 7 Removing rocker arm using tool No. 110589046100

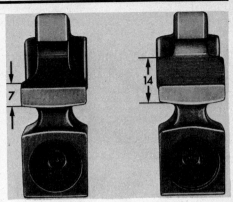

Fig. 8 Two types of rocker arms used

19. When assembly has been completed, tighten cylinder head bolts when coolant temperature is at 80°C. Tighten bolts to 90 Nm (9 kpm) in the sequence mentioned above after first loosening the bolt ¼ turn.
20. After 300-1,000 km of driving, tighten cylinder head bolts with the engine warmed up to 90 Nm (9 kpm), and readjust valve clearance.

ROCKER ARMS, REPLACE

Removal

1. Remove all rocker arm tensioning springs with a screwdriver, Fig. 6.

2. Crank engine with tool combination SW27 (001589650900) until the cam tip is facing up.

CAUTION: Do not crank the engine using the expanding screws of the camshaft gear. Do not turn the engine in reverse.

3. Remove the rocker arms using remover and installer 110589046100, Fig. 7.

Installation

NOTE: There are two rocker arm versions, Fig. 8. One has a 7 mm guide surface; the other has a 14 mm guide surface. When making repairs, exchange the rocker arms of the 7mm version for rocker arms of the 14 mm version.

CAUTION: Rocker arms and tensioning springs of engine 110 and engine 117 may not be interchanged.

1. Check to see that oil splash holes in rocker arms are unobstructed.
2. Lubricate the rocker arm supports with oil.
3. Install rocker arms.
4. Push tensioning springs into ring grooves of adjusting screws.

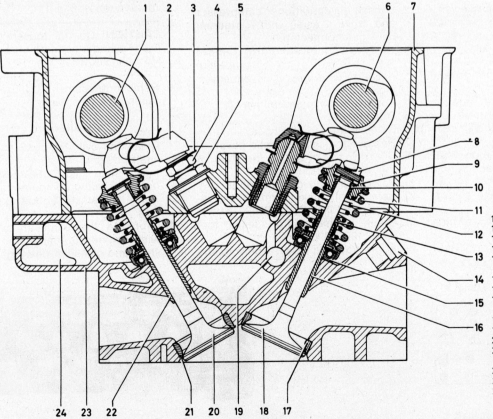

1 Exhaust camshaft
2 Rocker arm
3 Tensioning spring
4 Valve adjusting screw
5 Threaded bushing
6 Inlet camshaft
7 Camshaft housing
8 Thrust piece
9 Valve spring retainer
10 Valve cone piece
11 Outer valve spring
12 Inner valve spring
13 Valve seal
14 Bore for injection valve
15 Rotocap
16 Intake valve guide
17 Intake valve seat ring
18 Intake valve
19 Oil duct
20 Exhaust valve
21 Exhaust valve seat ring
22 Exhaust valve guide
23 Cylinder head
24 Measuring sensor box

Fig. 9 Valve train components

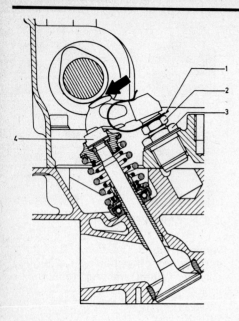

1 Tensioning spring   3 Threaded bushing
2 Valve adjusting screw 4 Thrust piece

Fig. 10 Valve adjustment

5. Adjust valve clearance.

VALVES, ADJUST

NOTE: If adjustment cannot be made, install thinner thrust pieces. Thrust pieces are available in 2.5, 3.5 and 4.5 mm thicknesses, Fig. 9. If torque valve of valve adjusting screw is below 20 Nm (2 kpm), replace the screw or threaded bushing.

1. Force off tensioning springs and remove rubber gaskets.
2. Measure valve clearance between the slide surface of the rocker arm and basic cam circle of the camshaft, Fig. 10.
3. Crank the engine with tool SW27 (001589650900) or contact handle 001589462108. Adjust valves following the firing order of the engine, Fig. 11.
4. Adjust valve clearance by turning the valve adjusting screw with valve adjusting wrench SW17

(110589000100). Valve clearance is set correctly when the feeler gauge indicates a tight fit.

VALVE GUIDES, REPLACE

1. Remove valve guide with knock-out plug (9 mm—110589021500; 11 mm—110589031500).
2. Check the basic bore in the cylinder head. If valve guides of standard dimension can be installed, knock in the valve guide with knock-in plug until the circlip is seated on the cylinder head. (9mm knock-in plug—110589001500; 11 mm knock-in plug—110589011500.)
3. If valve guides of a repair stage (oversize) must be installed, refinish the basic bore to the applicable dimension.
4. Clean the bore and heat the cylinder head in water to 80-90 deg. C. If possible, cool the valve guide with dry ice.
5. Coat the valve guides with parafin and knock them in with the knock-in plug (see above) until the circlips rest on the cylinder head.

CAMSHAFT HOUSING, REPLACE

1. Remove battery.
2. Loosen air conditioner compressor and move it aside with refrigerant lines still connected.
3. On cars with level control, remove the oil pressure pump and place it to one side with lines still connected, Fig. 1.
4. Remove the vacuum pump.
5. Drain coolant.
6. Remove the radiator hose.
7. Remove the cylinder head cover.
8. Unscrew the cover on the front of the camshaft housing.
9. Remove all tensioning springs.
10. Remove all rocker arms using remover and installer 110589046100.
11. Crank engine using special tool SW27 (001589650900).
12. Apply counterpressure only to the

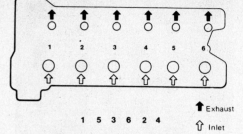

Fig. 11 Valve arrangement

⬆ Exhaust
⇧ Inlet

right-hand (exhaust) camshaft with holding wrench 116589010100 and loosen fastening screws.
13. Set piston 1 to ignition TDC and both camshafts to their marks.
14. Remove the chain tensioner.
15. Remove the slide rail in the camshaft housing. Knock out bearing bolts with impact puller 115589193300.
16. Loosen the rear right-hand cover on the camshaft housing and push the right-hand camshaft toward the rear by means of remover and installer 110589033300 while supporting the camshaft gear.
17. Remove the camshaft gear.
18. Reintroduce the camshaft into the bearing points.
19. Unscrew bolts M8 and cylinder head bolts in reverse order of the tightening sequence, Fig. 12.

CAUTION: Do not loosen the five lower cylinder head bolts or the two M8 bolts shown in Fig. 13.

20. Remove the camshaft housing containing the camshafts, Fig. 13.

Installation

1. Clean the cylinder head and camshaft housing mating surfaces.
2. Insert steel sheet 1100160480. Do not use sealing compound.
3. Place the camshaft housing in position.
4. Lubricate the camshaft bearings with engine oil. Reunite the camshaft and camshaft bearings.

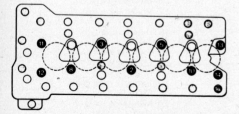

Fig. 12 Bolt pattern for camshaft housing removal

Fig. 13 Camshaft housing

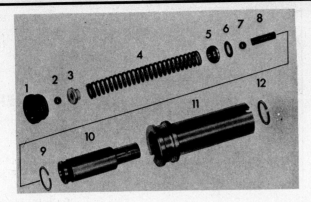

1 Ball seat ring
2 Ball
3 Ball cage
4 Compressiong spring
5 Valve disc
6 O-ring
7 Ball
8 Compression spring
9 Detent spring
10 Pressure bolt
11 Housing
12 Circlip

Fig. 14 Chain tensioner components

5. Lubricate the cylinder head bolts at threads and screw head base. Insert.
6. Tighten the cylinder head bolts in step-sequence as follows (Fig. 2):
1st step: Starting with bolt No. 2 to 40 Nm (4 kpm), Fig. 12.
2nd step: Starting with bolt No. 2 to 60 Nm (6 kpm), Fig. 12.
3rd step: Starting with bolt No. 1 to 90 Nm (9 kpm).
   For this purpose, loosen slightly the five lower cylinder head bolts individually before retightening, Fig. 12.
7. Tighten M8 bolts from inside out to 25 Nm (2.5 kpm).

CAUTION: When all bolts have been tightened, both camshafts should rotate easily when turned manually.

8. Mount the right-hand camshaft gear, observing the adjusting mark on both camshafts.

CAUTION: On engines on which the vibration damper carries on "010" mark for BDC in addition to TDC, the TDC mark is next to the pin in the vibration camper.

9. Install the slide rail. Make sure the timing chain doesn't jump across.
10. Mount the rigid chain tensioner. Apply tension manually.
11. Lubricate the spacer sleeve or driver with engine oil. Insert.

CAUTION: In doing repair jobs, install an expanding screw with washer. Do not use a fastening screw and cup springs.

12. Crank the engine with tool SW27 (001589650900). Check both adjusting marks.

CAUTION: If the camshaft housing has been face-ground, adjust timing.

13. Tighten the camshaft gear fastening screw to 80 Nm (8 kpm) while applying counterpressure to the camshaft using holding wrench 116589010100.
14. Install the chain tensioner.
15. Complete the reassembly procedure.

CAMSHAFTS, REPLACE

NOTE: Camshafts can be removed with the engine installed in the vehicle together with the camshaft housing only.

Removal

1. Remove the camshaft housing.
2. Unscrew both rear covers on the camshaft housing.
3. Unscrew the fastening screw of the lefthand camshaft while applying counterpressure with holding wrench 116589010100.
4. Push the camshaft toward the rear and remove the camshaft gear. Remove the spacer ring of the intake camshaft.
5. Remove both camshafts toward the rear.

Installation

1. Lubricate the camshaft bearings with engine oil.

2. Reinsert the intake camshaft, camshaft gear and spacer ring.
3. Lubricate the spacer sleeve with engine oil. Insert.

CAUTION: When making repairs, use fastening screws with washers. Fastening screws and cup springs should no longer be used.

4. Tighten the camshaft gear fastening screw to 80 Nm (8 kpm) while applying counterpressure to the camshaft with holding wrench 116589010100.
5. Introduce the exhaust camshaft into lubricated bearing points, but do not reassemble the gear which is slipped on after the camshaft housing has been mounted.
6. Mount both rear covers.

CAUTION: Do not tighten the right hand (exhaust end) cover. The camshaft must first be pushed back when mounting the timing chain.

7. Mount the camshaft housing and complete reassembly.

CHAIN TENSIONER
Removal

1. Remove the battery.
2. Remove the compressor and lay aside with refrigerant hoses connected.
3. Unscrew the closing plug.
4. Loosen the ball seat ring about two turns.

NOTE: The threaded ring must be tight.

5. Unscrew the threaded ring.
6. Pull out the chain tensioner by canting the wrench slightly and turning the chain tensioner to the right.

CAUTION: If the chain tensioner sticks, Fig. 16, unscrew the ball seat ring. Remove the ball, ball gauge and compression spring. Screw a M18X1.5 screw into the chain tensioner housing, which will permit a higher force for pulling out.

Installation

1. Make sure the tight side of the chain is under tension.
2. Insert the chain tensioner into the bore in the cylinder head.

CAUTION: Do not hammer the socket wrench. A jolt may cause the pressure bolt to jump forward.

3. Screw in the threaded ring. Tighten to 60 Nm (6 kpm).
4. Tighten the ball seat ring to 25 Nm (2.5 kpm). The pressure bolt should jump forward with an audible click.
5. Screw in the closing plug and sealing ring. Tighten to 50 Nm (5 kpm).
6. Complete reassembly.

TIMING CHAIN

Removal

1. Remove the cylinder head cover.
2. Remove the rocker arm of the right-hand (exhaust) camshaft.
3. Remove the chain tensioner.
4. Insert rigid chain tensioner 110589033100 and apply tension.
5. Cover the chain box with a rag and cut the timing chain with chain separating device 116589033500.

Installation

1. Attach a new timing chain and one link to the old timing chain.
2. Slowly crank the engine on the crankshaft with special tool SW17 (001589650900). Crank in the direction of rotation while simultaneously pulling up the old chain until the link comes to rest against the upper point of the right-hand camshaft gear.

CAUTION: The timing chain should always be in mesh while turning both camshaft gears.

3. Disconnect the old timing chain and connect the ends of the new timing chain with a link. Mount lockwashers.
4. Crank engine and check the adjusting marks.
5. Install the chain tensioner and complete reassembly.

OIL PAN

Removal

280 & 280C Models
1. Loosen both engine carriers at the front on the engine mounting.
2. Loosen the engine shock absorbers (front right) on the front axle carrier.
3. Suspend the engine on carrying bracket 107589026100.
4. Remove the front axle.
5. Remove automatic transmission oil lines.
6. Loosen the oil dipstick guide tube.

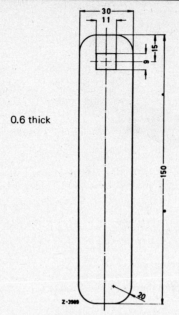

Fig. 15   Dimensions (in mm) for fabricating tool for cutting oil pan radial seal

7. Pull off the oil return line on the oil pan.
8. Drain engine oil.
9. Remove the oil pan.

280S Models
1. Remove the radiator.
2. Remove the vibration damper.
3. Disconnect the regulating linkage.
4. Attach the engine to carrying bracket 107589026100.
5. Loosen both engine carriers on the engine mounting.
6. Drain engine oil.
7. Remove the oil pan lower half and oil pump.
8. If the vehicle has a carburetor, remove the fuel pump.
9. Remove oil lines for the automatic transmission.
10. Loosen the rear engine mount and lift the engine.
11. Remove the oil pan in a forward direction.

Installation

All Models
1. Clean the mating surfaces.
2. Replace the rear oil seal, working it into place with a well oiled hammer handle.

NOTE: The seal has to be cut off about 0.6 mm above the mating surfaces. Make a gauge for this purpose, Fig. 17.

3. Coat the sealing surface with sealing compound.
4. Mount the oil pan and complete reassembly.

OIL PUMP, REPLACE

1. Remove the fuel pump if the car is equipped with a carburetor.
2. Unscrew the oil pan lower half.
3. Unscrew the fastening screw on the cylinder crankcase and on the bearing cap.
4. Pull out the oil pump.
5. Reverse procedure to reinstall, abiding by the following torque specifications:

Pressure relief valve to oil pump
    40 Nm (4.0 kpm)
Oil pump to crankcase or bearing cap
    30 Nm (3.0 kpm)
Oil pan lower half to upper half
    11 Nm (1.1 kpm)

WATER PUMP, REPLACE

1. Drain coolant.
2. Drain oil from the air:oil cooler.
3. Disconnect oil and water hoses.
4. Remove the radiator.
5. Remove fan and fan clutch.
6. Remove drive belts.
7. Unscrew the six fastening screws of the vibration damper.
8. Remove the pulley in the vibration damper.
9. Remove the water pump.
10. Reverse the procedure to reinstall, abiding by the following torque specifications:

Water pump to water pump housing
    9 Nm (0.9 kpm)
Fastening screws of vibration damper
    35 Nm (3.5 kpm)
Fan clutch to water pump
    25 Nm (2.5 kpm)
Drain plug air:oil cooler
    30-35 Nm (3-3.5 kpm)
Radiator drain plug
    6-10 Nm (0.6-1 kpm)

FUEL PUMP, REPLACE

1. Remove fuel filter.
2. Disconnect pressure and suction hoses.
3. Unscrew the electrical connecting cable and pressure connection.
4. Loosen the two fastening screws and remove the pump.

115 Gasoline Engine

ENGINE, REPLACE

NOTE: The engine and transmission are removed as an assembly.

1. Remove the radiator and shield.
2. Unscrew the air conditioner compressor with mounting bracket and lay aside.

CAUTION: Do not disconnect refrigerant lines.

3. If the car has level control, unscrew the pressure oil pump. Unscrew only the screws pointed to in Fig. 1.

CAUTION: Do not disconnect refrigerant lines.

4. Drain oil from the power steering reservoir and disconnect the pressure hoses at the pump.
5. Loosen all cooling system, vacuum, oil, fuel and electrical lines going to the engine.
6. Loosen the exhaust components from the exhaust manifold and transmission.
7. If the vehicle has an automatic transmission, unscrew the steering damper at one end and turn sideways, Fig. 2.
8. Attach engine hoist size 1.5 and lift upward at an angle of 45°.
9. To install, reverse this procedure.

CYLINDER HEAD
Removal

1. Drain coolant.
2. Remove the air conditioner air filter upper half and unscrew the compressor and bracket, moving them aside.

Fig. 2 Bolt location for disconnecting steering damper

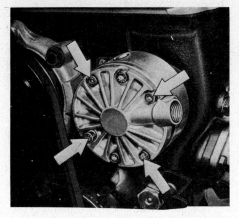

Fig. 1   Screw locations for removing level control oil pump

CAUTION: Do not disconnect refrigerant lines.

3. On vehicles since 1974, remove the distributor and vacuum pump.
4. Loosen all cylinder head connections.
5. On vehicles since 1975, loosen both supporting catalytic converter brackets and the starter cable. Unscrew the air injection lines on the cylinder head.
6. Loosen the exhaust pipe from the exhaust manifold.
7. Remove the chain tensioner.
8. Remove the inner slide rail.
9. Loosen the fastening screw of the camshaft gear while applying counterforce against the camshaft.
10. Turn the engine with special 27 mm socket wrench 0015896500900 on the crankshaft until markings on the thrust washer of the camshaft and on the camshaft bearing are aligned.
11. Remove the camshaft gear and place the timing chain in the chain box.
12. Loosen cylinder head bolts and remove the cylinder head.

Installation

1. Clean the cylinder head and cylinder crankcase joining surfaces.
2. Check the cylinder head joining

surface for roughness.
3. Install a new cylinder head gasket.
4. Mount the cylinder head and tighten cylinder head bolts as shown in Fig. 3 to specifications.

Bolt size	10	12
Step 1	20 Nm (2 kpm)	40 Nm (4 kpm)
Step 2	40 Nm (4 kpm)	60 Nm (6 kpm)
Step 3	50 Nm (5 kpm)	80 Nm (8 kpm)

5. Position camshaft gear. Tighten fastening screw to 80 Nm (8 kpm).
6. Complete assembly.

NOTE: If the cylinder head has been disassembled, adjust valve clearance to specifications.

7. After 300-1,000 km, retorque cylinder head bolts to the following specifications with engine coolant temperature at 80° C:

Bolt Size 10	Bolt Size 12
60 Nm (6 kpm)	80 Nm (8 kpm)

8. Recheck valve adjustment.

ROCKER ARMS, REPLACE

1. Take tensioning spring out of the notch on the rocker arm. Remove in an outward direction over the rocker arm, Fig. 4.

NOTE: The camshaft should be set so there is no load on the rocker arm. Rotate the engine with special 27 mm socket wrench set 001589650900 or special contact handle 001589462108. Do not rotate the engine by means of the camshaft gear.

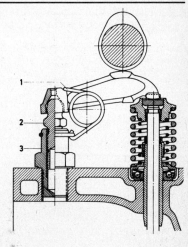

1 Tensioning spring   **3** Threaded bushing
2 Valve adjusting screw

Fig. 4   Rocker arm assembly. 115 engine

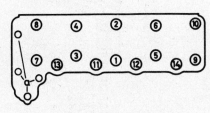

Fig. 3   Cylinder head bolt tightening sequence

Fig. 5 Removing rocker arm using tool No. 116589006100

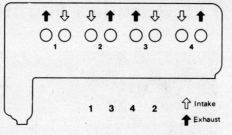

↑ Intake
↑ Exhaust

Fig. 6 Valve arrangement

2. Push down the valve spring retainer with special rocker arm and valve spring tool 116589006100, Fig. 5.
3. Remove the rocker arm.
4. Installation is done in reverse order. Check valve clearance.

VALVE CLEARANCE, ADJUST

NOTE: Checking and adjusting valve clearance may be done with the engine cold or warm.

1. Observe layout of intake and exhaust valves, Fig. 6.
2. Renew thrust piece if adjusting doesn't look possible. Thrust pieces are available in various thicknesses.
3. If the torque of the valve adjusting screw is below 20 Nm (2 kpm), renew valve adjusting screw or valve adjusting screw with threaded bushing.
4. Measure the valve clearance between the slide surface of the rocker

arm and the basic cam circle of the camshaft, Fig. 7.

NOTE: The engine may be cranked by means of special 27 mm socket wrench set 001589650900 at the hex bolt for attaching the balancing disc to the crankshaft or by connecting the special contact handle for cranking the engine (001589462108) to the battery's positive terminal and terminal 50.

CAUTION: Do not crank the engine at the fastening bolt of the camshaft gear, and don't turn the crankshaft in reverse.

5. Valve clearance is set properly when the correct feeler gauge can be tightly pulled through.
6. If adjustment is necessary, turn the valve adjusting screw with special valve adjusting wrench 110589000100 and torque wrench.

Torque Values
Nuts for cylinder head cover
15 Nm (1.5 kpm)
Valve adjusting screws
20-40 Nm (2-4 kpm)

VALVE GUIDES, REPLACE

1. Knock out valve guides. Use special 9 mm knock-out mandrel

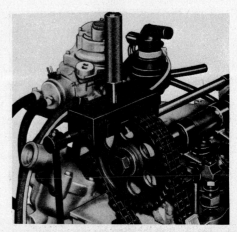

Fig. 7 Checking valve clearance

110589021500 for intake and 11 mm mandrel 110589031500 for exhaust.
2. Clean bore.
3. Ream bore, if necessary, to accept oversize guides (see important data below). Special tools are as follows:
Hand reamer for 1st repair stage, intake 115589005300.
Hand reamer for 1st repair stage, exhaust 110589005300.
Hand reamer for 2nd repair stage, intake 115589015300.
Hand reamer for 2nd repair stage, exhaust 110589015300.
4. Coat valve guides with tallow and knock in with mandrel until circlip rests against the cylinder head.
5. Check valve guides for tight fit.
6. Check ID of valve guide with plug gauges 116589082100 (9 mm, intake) or 116589092100 (11 mm, exhaust).
7. If necessary, ream the ID with a reamer 000589105300 (8.99 mm, intake) or 000589155300 (10.99 mm, exhaust).

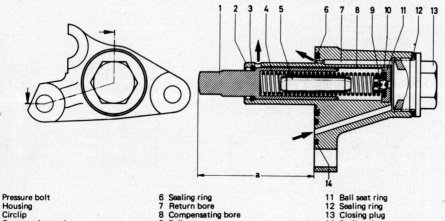

1	Pressure bolt	6	Sealing ring	11	Ball seat ring
2	Housing	7	Return bore	12	Sealing ring
3	Circlip	8	Compensating bore	13	Closing plug
4	Compression spring	9	Ball cage	14	Sealing ring
5	Bolt	10	Ball	a = 57 mm	

Fig. 8 Sectional view of chain tensioner

Fig. 9 Removing timing chain

Fig. 10 Aligning mark on timing chain gear with mark on housing

VALVE SPRINGS, REPLACE

1. Remove rocker arms.
2. Set piston to TDC by rotating engine with special 27 mm socket wrench set 001589650900.
3. Screw the compressed air hose of pressure loss tester into the spark plug bore and put the cylinder under pressure. The pressure loss tester is made by Bosch (EFAW 210A) or Sun (CLT 228).
4. Loosen the valve cone halves by means of light hammer blows against the valve spring retainer.
5. Push the valve spring retainer down with rocker arm and valve spring tool 116589006100.
6. Remove the valve cone halves with special magnet 116589066300.
7. Remove the valve spring retainer and valve springs.
8. To install, mount valve springs, inserting the outer valve spring with close coil in direction of the cylinder head. Complete reassembly, checking valve clearance.

CHAIN TENSIONER

NOTE: Always install the chain tensioner in a filled condition. Also, two chain tensioners are made for this engine. One has O-rings and one has a flat seal. Do not switch the two.

Removal

1. Drain coolant.
2. Remove the refrigerant compressor and move aside. Do not disconnect refrigerant lines.
3. Remove the thermostat housing.
4. Remove the chain tensioner, Fig. 8.
5. Replace damaged sealing rings or flat seal.

Installation

1. Fill the chain tensioner by placing it with the pressure bolt in a downward position into SAE 10 engine oil. Oil must extend above the flange.
2. Push the pressure bolt slowly seven to ten times against the stop using an upright drill press.

NOTE: Filled, the chain tensioner should allow compression only quite slowly and under high pressure.

3. Refit the chain tensioner, tightening nuts uniformly.

TIMING CHAIN

NOTE: The timing chain with connecting link is used for repairs. If only an endless chain is available, this chain can be opened using chain separating device 116589033500. Install an endless chain during engine overhaul.

Removal

1. Remove the chain tensioner.
2. Cover the chain case with a rag and cut the timing chain with chain separating device 116589033500, Fig. 9.

Installation

1. Attach the new timing chain with cut link to the old timing chain.
2. Slowly rotate the engine in the direction of rotation using special 27 mm socket wrench set 001589650900 while simultaneously pulling up the old timing chain until the cut link comes to rest against the uppermost point of the camshaft gear.

NOTE: While rotating, the timing chain should remain in mesh with the camshaft gear.

3. Disconnect the old timing chain and connect the ends of the new timing chain by means of the connecting link. Mount the lockwasher.

NOTE: Insert the new connecting link from the rear so the lockwasher can be seen from the front.

4. Rotate engine to line up adjusting marks.
5. Check timing, if necessary.
6. Install the chain tensioner and complete reassembly.

CAMSHAFT

NOTE: When renewing the camshaft,

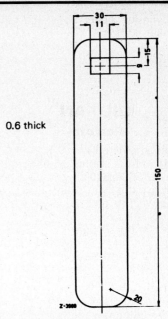

0.6 thick

Fig. 11 Dimensions (in mm) for fabricating tool for cutting oil pan radial seal

also include the rocker arms.

Removal

1. Remove the chain tensioner.
2. Remove the rocker arms.
3. Set the crankshaft to TDC and the camshaft to mark, Fig. 10. Rotate the engine using special 27 mm socket wrench set 001589650900.
4. Loosen the fastening bolt of the camshaft gear and remove the gear, applying counter force to the camshaft.
5. Loosen the camshaft bearings.
6. Remove camshaft with camshaft bearings and oil tube.

NOTE: If camshaft bearings stick, loosen with light blows with a plastic hammer.

7. Pull camshaft out of the camshaft bearings toward the rear.

Installation

1. Lubricate the camshaft bearings with engine oil.
2. Insert camshaft into camshaft bearing from the rear.
3. Install camshaft with camshaft bearings and oil tube.
4. Complete installation, checking timing and adjusting valve clearance. Torque bolts and nuts to the following specifications:
   a. Nuts for cylinder head cover
      15 Nm (1.5 kpm)
   b. Camshaft gear to camshaft
      80 Nm (8.0 kpm)

c. Cylinder head bolts (camshaft bearing bolts)

90 Nm (9.0 kpm)

OIL PAN
Removal

1. Drain engine oil.
2. Suspend the engine on engine carrier 107589026100.
3. Remove the front axle.
4. Remove the power steering pump and carrier.
5. Remove the oil pan.

Installation

1. Clean crankcase and oil pan joining surfaces.
2. Replace the rear radial sealing ring in the oil pan, working it into place with a well-oiled hammer handle.

NOTE: To obtain the required overlap, cut off the radial sealing ring about 0.6 mm above the surface. See Fig. 12 for making a gauge to measure the cut off point.

3. Coat the joining surface of the oil pan with sealing compound.
4. Install the oil pan and proceed to complete reassembly.

REAR OIL SEAL
Removal

1. Remove the engine and transmission.
2. Remove the chain tensioner.
3. Remove the camshaft gear, marking the camshaft gear and chain for reference during reassembly.
4. Remove the oil pan.
5. Remove the oil pump.
6. Remove the flywheel.

7. Remove the crankshaft.
8. Check the diameter of the expanding shaft of the connecting rod bolts which should be 8.4-0.1 mm (new); 7.2 mm (minimum).
9. Remove the old seal.

Installation

1. Clean the oil pan and crankcase joining surfaces.
2. Insert a new seal, fitting it tightly with a hammer handle. To obtain the required overlap, cut off the seal in the crankcase and oil pan about 0.6 mm above the joining surface. Use the fabricated tool pictured in Fig. 11.
3. Coat the seal with SAE 30 engine oil.
4. Install the crankshaft.
5. Rotate the crankshaft, checking for easy turning.
6. Complete reassembly.

117 Gasoline Engine

ENGINE, REPLACE

Refer to 110 Engine procedure to replace engine.

CYLINDER HEAD
Removal

NOTE: Remove the head with the engine cold only.

1. Drain the radiator and cylinder crankcase. Drain plugs located on the left and right of the crankcase, Fig. 1.
2. Remove the battery.
3. Remove the fuel ring line and injection valves.
4. Push the longitudinal regulating shaft forward and remove, Fig. 2.
5. Loosen all connections on the in-

take pipe and cylinder heads, and remove the intake pipe.
6. Unscrew the automatic transmission fluid filler tube.
7. Remove the alternator and holder.
8. Remove the distributor and power steering pump and holder.
9. Disconnect the exhaust system.
10. Remove the chain tensioner.
11. Mark the camshaft gear and chain.
12. Remove the camshaft gear.
13. Remove the upper slide rails.
14. Unscrew the cylinder head bolts *in reverse* sequence of tightening. Tightening sequence is illustrated in Fig. 3.

NOTE: Loosening and tightening of cylinder head bolts require three different types of wrenches, as follows:

Allen wrench insert 8 mm, 130 mm long—000589330700.

Allen wrench insert 8 mm, 105 mm long, offset—000589340700.

Allen wrench insert 8 mm, 175 mm long, bent—116589001300.

M8 bolts (a in Fig. 3) should be loosened with Allen wrench insert 8 mm, ⅜ inch square head—117589010700.

15. To remove the right-hand cylinder head, push the tensioning rail with timing chain toward the center of the engine to keep the tensioning rail from becoming stuck, Fig. 4.

Installation

1. Install new cylinder head gasket(s).

CAUTION: Do not mix up left and right cylinder head gaskets. The left-hand cylinder head gasket has two fastening holes in the timing

Fig. 1 Engine block drain plug location

1-676

Fig. 2 Removing longitudinal regulating shaft

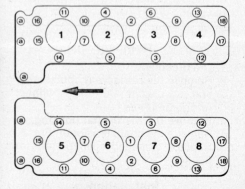

Fig. 3 Cylinder head bolt tightening sequence

Fig. 4 Tensioning rail

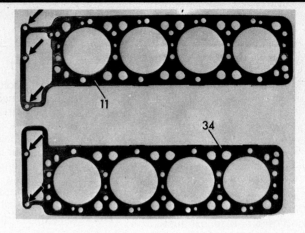

11 Righthand cylinder head gasket
34 Lefthand cylinder head gasket

Fig. 5 Cylinder head gasket identification

chain housing, Fig. 5. The right-hand cylinder head gasket has three fastening holes in the timing chain housing.

2. Position the cylinder head. Lubricate cylinder head bolts liberally on threads and bolt head contact surfaces.
3. Tighten the cylinder head bolts in the sequence shown in Fig. 3 to specifications.
4. Continue to reassemble the cylinder head in a reverse manner to that of removal.
5. Check valve clearance.
6. Retighten cylinder head bolts with the engine warmed to 80°C to 60 Nm (6 kpm).
7. Retighten cylinder head bolts once more after the car has been driven 300-1,000 km and recheck valve clearance.

ROCKER ARMS

NOTE: Install rocker arms at the same point where they are removed. If rocker arms are replaced, also replace the respective camshaft.

Fig. 6 Removing rocker arms using tool No. 116589006100

Removal

1. Remove tensioning springs.
2. Connect contact handle 001589462108 to the battery + terminal and terminal 50 and crank the engine.
3. With the respective cam facing away from the rocker arm, remove the rocker arm, Fig. 6.

Installation

1. Lubricate the bearing surface of the rocker arm.
2. Install the rocker arm.
3. Push the tensioning spring into the ring groove of the adjusting screw.
4. Adjust valve clearance.

VALVES, ADJUST

NOTE: If adjustments can no longer be made, install thinner thrust pieces. Thrust pieces are available in 2.5, 3.5 and 4.5 mm thicknesses. If the torque of the valve adjusting screw cannot be obtained at 20 Nm (2 kpm), replace the valve adjusting screw or threaded bushing. Note the layout of the intake and exhaust valves, Fig. 7.

1. Measure the valve clearance between the slide surface of the rocker arm and basic cam circle of the camshaft. Valve clearance is correct when the gauge indicates a tight fit.
2. Adjust valve clearance by turning the valve adjusting screw with valve adjusting wrench 116589020100.

CAUTION: The engine may be cranked using special tool 001589650900 applied to the

crankshaft. Do not rotate the engine in reverse.

VALVE GUIDES, REPLACE

1. Clean the valve guide and measure with check plug 116589082100 (9 mm, intake) or 116589092100 (11 mm, exhaust), Fig. 8. If "no-go" end of the check plug can be inserted, proceed to remove the valve guide with knock-out plug 110589021500 (9 mm, intake) or 110589031500 (11 mm, exhaust).
2. If oversize valve guides (pertinent repair stages) must be installed, hone the bore with one of the following applicable hand reamers:
   a. For first repair stage, intake (14.2 mm)—115589005300.
   b. For first repair stage, exhaust (15.2 mm)—110589005300.

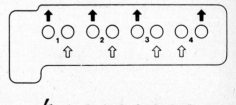

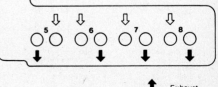

Exhaust
Intake

Fig. 7 Valve arrangement

Fig. 8 Measuring valve guide clearance

c. For second repair stage, intake (14.4 mm)—115589015300.
d. For second repair stage, exhaust (15.4 mm)—110589015300.
3. Clean the bore and heat the cylinder head in water to about 90°C.
4. If possible, undercool the valve guide with dry ice or liquid air.
5. Coat the valve guide with tallow and install the guide using a knock-in plug until the circlip rests against the cylinder head. Use 9 mm knock-in plug 110589001500 for intakes and 11 mm knock-in plug 116589081500 for exhausts.
6. Double check valve guide ID with the check plug.

CHAIN TENSIONER

NOTE: The chain tensioner is connected to the engine oil circuit. Bleeding occurs when oil pressure in the lubrication system has been established and the chain tensioner is filling with oil. A chain tensioner with venting hole for oil defoaming has been installed in models since Dec. 1974. In the event of a timing chain noise condition, this newer model chain

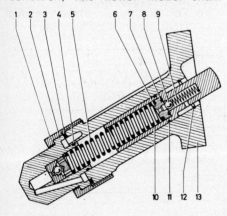

1 Closing nut	8 Ball
2 Closing cap	9 Compression spring
3 Sealing ring	10 Pressure bolt
4 Sealing ring	11 Sealing ring
5 Compression spring	12 Circlip
6 Valve disc	13 Housing
7 Sealing ring	

Fig. 10 Sectional view of chain tensioner

tensioner (white dot on closing cap) should be used.

Removal

1. Unscrew fastening bolts, Fig. 9, and remove the chain tensioner.
2. The chain tensioner in larger sedans requires these additional steps:
   a. Remove the alternator.
   b. Unscrew the upper bracket of the right-hand side engine damper. Before beginning installation, switch the bracket in such a way that it doesn't rest against the chain tensioner, Fig. 10.

Installation

1. Put the chain tensioner in a vessel filled with engine oil. Make sure the component is held vertically in a downward position in oil at least to the flange.
2. Activate the pressure bolt to fill the chain tensioner with oil. Venting will take place simultaneously.
3. After it is filled and vented, the chain tensioner should allow compression only very slowly, uniformly and with considerable effort.
4. Mount the chain tensioner using a new gasket. Tighten bolts to 25 Nm (2.5 kpm).

NOTE: The pressure bolt of the chain tensioner should rest against the lug of the tensioning rail.

TIMING CHAIN

Removal

1. Remove the rocker arm of the right bank camshaft.
2. Separate the old timing chain using chain separating device 116589033500.
3. Attach a new timing chain to the old chain by means of chain link 198.
4. Rotate the crankshaft slowly in the direction of engine rotation while simultaneously pulling up the old

Fig. 11 Correct positioning for installing compensating washer

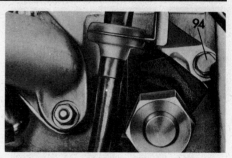

Fig. 9 Chain tensioner bolt location (94)

timing chain until the chain link comes to rest against the upper point of the right bank camshaft gear.

CAUTION: The timing chain should be in mesh as both camshaft gears are turned.

5. Disconnect the old timing chain and connect the ends of the new timing chain with a link.
6. If the adjusting marks are not aligned, check timing.

CAMSHAFT
Removal

1. Remove the rocker arms.
2. Set the piston on the first cylinder to ignition TDC using special tool 116589020100.
3. Secure the timing chain and camshaft gear with binding wire so the timing chain won't skip.
4. Remove the camshaft gear.
5. Remove the camshaft, camshaft bearing and oil line as an assembly.

Installation

1. Place the camshaft and camshaft bearing on the cylinder head and tighten progressively from the inside out.

NOTE: Concerning the camshaft in the lefthand bank, the outer fastening bolt of the rear camshaft bearing must be inserted into the camshaft

Fig. 12 Bolt locations for oil pump removal

bearing before mounting the camshaft.

---

2. Mount the oil pipe, placing connecting pieces into position and then checking the three inner connecting pieces to assure unobstructed passage through the oil line *before* knocking the camshaft bearings into place. Replace the oil pipe if the oil bores are obstructed.

CAUTION: Replace all plastic connections.

---

3. Mount the compensating washer so the keyway at the notch is in mesh with the woodruff key of the camshaft, Fig. 11.
4. Mount rocker arms and tensioning springs.
5. Adjust valve clearance.
6. If installing a new camshaft, check timing. Refer to "Valve Timing Specifications" chart found below.

OIL PAN, REPLACE
Coupes & Roadsters

1. Remove radiator shell and fan.
2. Remove front axle.
3. Remove compressor and mounting bracket.
4. Remove pulley and vibration damper.
5. Remove the supporting angle bracket on the transmission.
6. Remove the oil pan.
7. Remove the oil pump, (see Oil Pump).
8. Using grease, glue a new oil pan gasket on the oil pan and reinstall the oil pan employing a reverse procedure.

Sedans

1. Remove the compressor, mounting bracket and tensioning roller.
2. Remove the lower half of the oil pan.
3. Loosen the oil pump, remove the sprocket from the oil pump and take off the oil pump.
4. Disconnect both oil lines going to the automatic transmission.
5. Remove the supporting angle bracket on the transmission.
6. Crank the engine with special tool 001589650900 until the position of the crankshaft permits you to remove the rest of the oil pan.
7. Using grease, glue a new oil pan gasket on the oil pan and reinstall the oil pan employing a reverse procedure.

OIL PUMP

NOTE: This is a chain-driven sprocket-type oil pump. When changing the oil pump, be sure the new pump has the same number of teeth on the sprocket.

---

1. Remove the oil pan.
2. Loosen the bolt on the sprocket.
3. Unscrew the three oil pump holding bolts, Fig. 12.
4. Force the sprocket from the oil pump.
5. Lift the sprocket from the chain.
6. Install using a reverse procedure.

WATER PUMP
Removal

1. Drain the radiator and crankcase.
2. Remove the air cleaner.

3. Remove the power steering pump drive belt.
4. Disconnect the upper radiator hose.
5. Remove the fan.
6. Disconnect the lower radiator hose.
7. Remove the inlet connection from the water pump.
8. Remove the distributor.
9. Turn the vibration damper so the lower fastening bolts are accessible through the recess in the damper. Remove the bolts.
10. Remove the water pump.

Installation

1. Clean the sealing surfaces and reinstall the water pump in reverse sequence.
2. Set cylinder No. 1 to ignition TDC. Install the distributor so the distributor finger points to the notch on the distributor housing.
3. Check ignition timing.
4. Fill the system with coolant, run the engine and check for leaks.

FUEL PUMP, REPLACE

1. Unscrew the protective cover.
2. Disconnect the pressure (delivery) hoses.
3. Remove the fuel filter.
4. Remove the angle piece.
5. Disconnect the pressure and suction hose.
6. Unscrew the electrical connecting cable and pressure connection on the fuel pump.
7. Loosen both fastening screws and remove the fuel pump.
8. When installing the unit, use new sealing rings and observe correct polarity when connecting electrical cables. Terminals are identified positive (+) and negative (−).

VALVE TIMING SPECIFICATIONS①

Camshaft Code Number (left/right) ②	Intake Valve		Exhaust Valve	
	Opens (ATDC)	Closes (ABDC)	Opens (BBDC)	Closes (BTDC)
42/43 ③	4°	14°	26°	12°
46/47 ③	8°	20°	21°	7°
48/49 ③	5°	20°	23°	6°
52/53 ③	4°	14°	30°	16°
54/55 ③ & 56/57 ③	5°	21°	25°	5°

①—Timing is at a valve lift of 2 mm.
②—Camshafts having identification numbers 42, 46, 48, 52, 54 and 56 are for cylinders 5-8 left. Those with numbers 43, 47, 49, 53, 55 or 57 are for cylinders 1-4 right.
③—When the timing chain has been in use less than 20,000 km change the timing of the camshaft on the right bank to 2° in the direction of advance.

616 & 617 Diesel Engine

ENGINE, REPLACE

NOTE: The engine and transmission are removed as an assembly.

1. Remove radiator and shell.

NOTE: Remove the right-hand cooling water hose on engine 617.

2. Remove fan.
3. Remove top of the air filter.
4. On models equipped with A/C, remove A/C compressor and bracket and position aside.

CAUTION: Do not disconnect refrigerant lines.

5. On cars having level control, remove pressure oil pump and position aside. For this purpose, remove only the screws pointing out in Fig. 1.

CAUTION: Do not disconnect hoses.

6. Draw oil out of the power steering reservoir tank. Disconnect the pressure hoses on the high pressure side of power steering pump.
7. Loosen all cooling system, vacuum, oil, fuel and electrical system lines leading to the engine.
8. Loosen exhaust components.
9. On sedans with engine type 616 and automatic transmission, unscrew the steering damper at one end and turn sideways, Fig. 2.
10. On engine type 617, loosen both engine shock absorbers on the body and push them out in the direction of the engine, Fig. 3.

Fig. 1 Locations of bolts for removing pressure oil pump

11. Using a suitable engine hoist, lift out the engine at an angle of about 45 degrees.

CYLINDER HEAD, REPLACE

Removal

1. Drain cooling system.
2. On 616 engine equipped with a tensioning rail, Fig. 4, remove radiator and shroud.
3. Remove A/C compressor and bracket and position aside.

CAUTION: Do not disconnect refrigerant lines.

4. If vehicle is equipped with level control, detach level pump and driver.

CAUTION: Do not disconnect hoses.

5. Loosen all lines and hoses.
6. Disconnect exhaust pipe from exhaust manifold.
7. Remove chain tensioner.
8. Remove fuel filter, but do not loosen hoses.
9. Remove rocker arms.
10. Remove inside slide rail.
11. On 616 engine equipped with a tensioning rail, remove tensioning rail using a suitable puller for slide rail bearing bolt. The actual removal of tensioning rail is done with remover and installer 115589146100, Fig. 5.
12. Loosen attaching camshaft gear attaching bolt, using counterpressure to hold camshaft.
13. Set the ignition to TDC using special tool No. 001589650900.
14. Remove camshaft gear, placing the timing chain in the chain box.
15. Loosen cylinder head bolts and remove cylinder head.

CAUTION: If No. 4 or 5 cylinder head bolts, which are adjacent to the injection nozzles, cannot be fully removed, remove the injection nozzles.

Installation

1. Install a new cylinder head gasket.
2. Mount cylinder head and tighten the cylinder head bolts to specification in the sequence shown in Figs. 6 and 7.

CAUTION: If the cylinder head bolts have to be replaced, use bolts having the same length. If injection nozzles have been removed, insert new thrust plates into prechambers.

Fig. 2 Bolt location for removing steering damper. 616 engines

Fig. 3 Engine shock absorber (left side shown)

Fig. 4 Tensioning rail identification chart, early (A), late (B)

Fig. 5 Removing tensioning rail

3. Position camshaft gear and tighten bolt.
4. Complete installation.

ROCKER ARMS

Removal

1. Position camshaft so rocker arms have no load on them. Use tool No. 001589650900 to rotate the engine.
2. On 616 engine, mark position of bearing brackets, rocker arms and cylinder head with paint.
3. Loosen attaching bolts of rocker arm bearing brackets, Fig. 8.
4. Remove rocker arms, bearing brackets and shaft. Loosen stuck bearing brackets by striking light blows with a plastic mallet.

Installation

1. Install rocker arms with bearing brackets and shaft. The rocker arm bearing brackets are positioned with the aid of hollow set pins.
2. Complete installation and check valve clearance.

Fig. 8 Rocker arm bearing bracket bolt locations

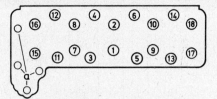

Fig. 6 Cylinder head bolt tightening sequence. 616 engines

VALVE, ADJUST

NOTE: Check the arrangement of intake and exhaust valves, Figs. 9 and 10. Crank the engine using special tool No. 001589650900 or 001589462108, but do not crank the engine at the fastening bolt of the camshaft gear and do not rotate the crankshaft in reverse direction.

1. Measure valve clearance between slide surface of rocker arm and cam base circle of the camshaft, Fig. 11. Valve clearance is correct if the gauge can be pulled through tightly.
2. Place holding wrench No. 615589000100 on the hexagon of the valve retainer.
3. Loosen cap nut while applying counterpressure to hex nut.
4. Adjust valve clearance to specifications by turning cap nut.
5. Upon making the adjustment lock the hex nut and recheck clearance.

TIMING CHAIN, REPLACE

1. Remove glow plugs.
2. Remove chain tensioner.
3. Cover chain housing and cut timing chain with chain separating device 116589033500.
4. Attach a new timing chain with cut link to the old timing chain.
5. Slowly rotate the engine in the direction of rotation with tool No. 001589650900 while pulling up the old timing chain until the cut link comes to rest against the uppermost point of the camshaft gear.

CAUTION: The timing chain must remain in mesh while the camshaft sprocket is being rotated.

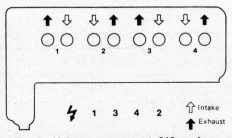

Fig. 9 Valve arrangement. 616 engine

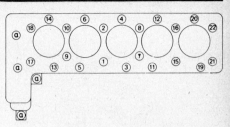

Fig. 7 Cylinder head bolt tightening sequence. 617 engines

6. Disconnect the old timing chain and connect the ends of the new timing chain with a connecting link. Mount the lockwasher.

NOTE: Insert new connecting link from rear so the lockwasher can be seen from the front.

7. Rotate engine and check adjusting marks.
8. Adjust timing, if necessary.
9. Install chain tensioner.
10. Install glow plugs.

CHAIN TENSIONER, REPLACE

NOTE: Two types of chain tensioners have been produced for these engines. Do not replace a chain tensioner having an O-ring with one having a flat seal, or vice versa.

1. Drain coolant.
2. Remove air A/C and mounting bracket, but do not disconnect refrigerant lines.
3. Remove thermostat housing.
4. Loosen and remove chain tensioner.
5. Replace damaged O-ring or flat seal, if necessary.
6. Place chain tensioner with pressure bolt in a downward position in engine oil. See that the level reaches above the flange.
7. Depress the pressure bolt using a press, seven to ten times slowly against the stop. As the chain tensioner is being filled, depressing it should be done slowly and uniformly and with considerable force.

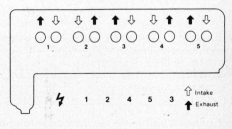

Fig. 10 Valve arrangement. 617 engine

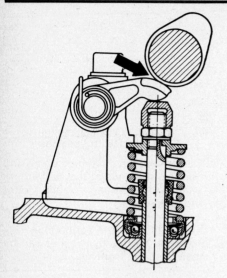

Fig. 11 Measuring valve clearance

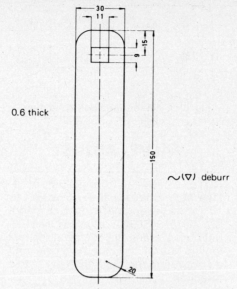

0.6 thick

~(∇) deburr

Fig. 12 Dimensions for fabricating oil pan rear radial seal gauge

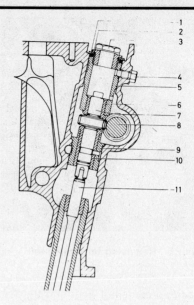

1 Rubber ring	7 Helical gear
2 Cover disc	8 Intermediate gear shaft
3 Closing plug	9 Bearing body
4 Locking screw	10 Bearing bushing
5 Thrust piece	11 Oil pump shaft
6 Bearing bushing	

Fig. 13 Oil pump drive

8. Place chain tensioner back in housing and tighten attaching bolts and nuts uniformly.

CAMSHAFT, REPLACE

Removal

1. Remove chain tensioner.
2. Remove rocker arms and rocker arm bearing brackets.
3. Remove inner slide rail on cylinder head.
4. Set crankshaft to TDC and camshaft to timing mark. Use tool No. 001589650900 to rotate engine.
5. Loosen camshaft gear attaching bolt and remove camshaft sprocket. Apply counterpressure to camshaft.
6. Loosen camshaft bearings.
7. Remove camshaft and camshaft bearings and oil line. If there is a stuck camshaft bearing, loosen it with light blows with a plastic mallet.
8. Pull camshaft from camshaft bearings from rear.

NOTE: Worn camshaft bearing journals can be reground. The required camshaft bearings are available in two oversizes.

Installation

1. Lubricate camshaft bearings with engine oil and insert camshaft into bearings from rear of engine.
2. Install camshaft assembly and oil line.
3. Complete installation.
4. Check camshaft timing. Refer to specifications chart.

OIL PAN

Removal

1. Drain engine oil.
2. Suspend engine using engine carrier 107589026100.
3. Remove front axle.
4. Remove power steering pump and carrier.
5. Remove oil pan.

Installation

1. Clean surfaces on cylinder crankcase and oil pan.
2. Renew the rear radial sealing ring in the oil pan, working in the new ring securely using the handle, well-oiled, of a hammer. To obtain the required overlap, cut off the radial sealing ring about 0.6 mm above the parting surface. Use a gauge made to plans shown in Fig. 12.
3. Coat the parting surface of the oil pan with sealing compound and install the oil pan. Torque bolts to 13 Nm (1.3 kpm).
4. Complete installation.

OIL PUMP DRIVE

Removal

1. Remove locking screw, Fig. 13.
2. Remove thrust piece with bearing

CAMSHAFT TIMING SPECIFICATIONS CHART

Camshaft Timing (Timing at 2 mm Valve Stroke)

| Engine | Camshaft Code ① | Intake | | Exhaust | |
		Opens After TDC	Closes After BDC	Opens Before BDC	Closes Before TDC
616	02②	13.5°	15.5°	19°	17°
617	00	13.5°	15.5°	19°	17°

①—Camshaft code is punched into rear of shaft
②—Valid starting August 1973

bushing and closing plug.
3. Remove helical drive gear using pliers.

Installation

1. Clean thrust piece and bearing bushing.
2. Insert helical drive gear so the lug on the oil pump shaft is seated in the slot of the helical gear shaft.
3. Insert thrust piece with bearing bushing and closing plug.

CAUTION: Make sure that the bore in the thrust piece for the locking screw is in alignment with the tapped hole in the crankcase.

---

4. Install locking screw.

REAR OIL SEAL SERVICE
Removal

1. Remove engine and transmission assembly from vehicle, then separate engine from transmission.
2. Remove chain tensioner.
3. Mark camshaft gear and chain for reference and remove the camshaft gear.
4. Remove oil pan.
5. Remove oil pump.
6. Remove flywheel.
7. Remove crankshaft.

8. Remove radial sealing ring from crankcase and oil pan.
9. Clean oil pan and crankcase mating surface.

Installation

1. Install new radial sealing ring into cylinder crankcase and oil pan, working seal into place with a well-oiled hammer handle.
2. To get the necessary overlap, cut off the radial sealing ring in the crankcase and oil pan about 0.6 mm above mating surface. Use the gauge you can fashion seen in Fig. 12.
3. Coat the radial sealing ring with SAE 30 engine oil.
4. Reverse procedure to assemble. Torque all bolts and nuts to specifications.
5. Remove the glow plugs and rotate the crankshaft to check for smooth operation.

FUEL PUMP
Removal

1. Unscrew all fuel connections.
2. Loosen the fastening nuts.
3. Remove the fuel pump.

Replacement

1. Mount the fuel pump using a new gasket.
2. On engine 616, adjust the oil level in the injection pump by unscrewing the filter on the pump and adding engine oil up to the check bore.
3. Reattach fuel connections.
4. Vent the injection system (see below).
5. Check fuel pump delivery using tester 000589492100.

VENTING THE INJECTION SYSTEM

1. Loosen the vent plug on the fuel filter. If the fuel filter doesn't have a vent plug, loosen the hollow screw.
2. On engine 616, loosen the actuating knob of the manual delivery pump.
3. Actuate the manual delivery pump until fuel immerges that is free of bubbles at the vent plug or at the hollow screw.
4. Tighten the vent screw or hollow screw and continue pumping the manual delivery pump until the overflow valve on the injection pump opens (you will hear a buzzing noise).
5. On engine 616, tighten the actuating knob of the manual delivery pump.
6. With the engine still running, make sure connections are tight.

Fuel System Section
Carburetor

110 ENGINES
Adjustment

NOTE: Do not adjust idle speed following a fast drive or after performing an output test on a dynamometer. Also, the air filter must be installed.

---

1. Check timing, and centrifugal and vacuum ignition adjustment.
2. Warm the engine to normal operating temperature (60°-80°C).
3. If the car is equipped with cruise control, check that the bowden wire rests free of tension against the control lever. If necessary, make the adjustment with the adjusting nut.
4. Adjust idle speed by means of the adjusting screw to the following specifications:

1973-74:   750-950 rpm
1975-77:   800-900 rpm

5. Check idle speed emission value. If necessary, adjust pre-1975 models by turning both mixture adjustment screws clockwise to stop; then turn both screws counterclockwise until the correct idle speed emission valve of 1.5% CO is attained.
6. Beginning with model year 1975, pull the blue/violet vacuum line for the air injection system at the connecting point so air injection is not operating (red vacuum line for California emission control system beginning 1974) and adjust as above until a maximum 1.0% CO is attained.

NOTE: Screwing adjustment screw out richens mixture. Screwing adjustment screw in leans mixture.

---

7. Adjust the vacuum governor. Run the engine at idle speed, pull off the vacuum hose at the governor and adjust by means of the adjusting screw until 1,200-1,400 rpm with vacuum line disconnected is attained, and 600-700 rpm with driving position engaged on pre-1975 models or 1,700-1,900 rpm with vacuum line disconnected is attained, and 600-700 rpm with driving position engaged on 1975-77 models.

115 ENGINES
Idle Speed, Adjust

1. Fill oil damper and piston with ATF. Capacity is approximately 60 cc.
2. Connect timing light, tachometer and CO measuring unit. Plug in oil tele-thermometer 116589272100.
3. Warm engine to operating temperature (60°-80°C oil temperature).
4. Check timing, centrifugal force and vacuum. Adjust if necessary.

Fig. 1 Idle speed adjusting screw (8). 1972-74 models

5. Check intake system for leaks.
6. Check damper oil level in storage tank by unscrewing the oil filler plug. Add oil up to the bottom edge of the threads.
7. Disconnect the regulating rod on the carburetor.
8. Check the throttle valve shaft for easy operation. Do this by increasing speed to about 2,000-2,500 rpm by means of the throttle valve lever. Release the lever, which should automatically return to the idling speed stop.

NOTE: Make sure the idling speed stop is not against the vacuum governor. Slacken the compressor spring with the adjusting nut if necessary.

9. Adjust idle speed by means of the adjusting screw, Fig. 1, to 800-900 rpm. On 1975-77 models adjust idle speed with the lower adjusting screw, Fig. 2.
10. Adjust the idle speed emission valve to 1-25% for 1972-73, 1.5% max. for 1974 or .4-1.5% on 1975-77 (CO) by loosening the hex nut and adjusting the idle speed shut-off valve outward to provide a richer mixture or inward to provide a leaner mixture.

NOTE: Following each adjustment of the idle speed shutoff valve or idle speed adjusting screw, accelerate the engine once to realign the air piston and nozzle needle.

11. For models 1975-77, to check and adjust the idling speed emission valve, pull and plug the center vacuum hose on the switch-over valve for air injection (blue vent cap).
12. Adjust the regulation valve. On cars with manual transmission, the adjustment is made so the roller in the gate lever rests free of tension in the end stop. On cars with automatic transmission, adjust the regulating rod at idle speed so the rod can be connected free of tension when in the fully extended position.
13. Adjust the vacuum governor by running the engine at idle speed, removing the vacuum hose and moving the adjusting screw until specified engine speed is attained (see below).

CAUTION: When loosening the counter nut apply counter pressure to the diaphragm rod.

14. Check if the clearance between the adjusting screw and actuating lever amounts to about 0.1 mm. If necessary, adjust vacuum governor by means of the adjusting nut to 1,200-1,400 rpm.

Choke, Adjustment

NOTE: The engine should be at operating temperature. Dwell, timing, idle speed and idle speed emission value (CO) must be adjusted to specification.

1. Check to make sure the notch on the starting device cover is aligned with the front mark. Loosen the three fastening bolts to adjust the starting device cover.
2. Check the cold start speed. Run the engine at idle. Lift the regulating rod slightly and insert a small screwdriver through the adjusting slot in the starting device housing to push the drive lever in the direction of the engine until it engages the noticeable stop of the pull-down diaphragm rod.

CAUTION: Do not apply excessive pressure against the noticeable stop. A faulty measurement will occur, because the starting valve and depth disc will be displaced.

3. Release the regulating rod, but keep the driving lever against the stop. The starter lever will be on the second notch of the stepped disc and

Fig. 2 Idle speed adjusting screw (8) & cold start speed adjusting screw (114). 1975-77 models

the starting valve will be in a pulled down position.

Read the cold starting speed on the revolution counter. Speed should be as follows:
 a. Pre-1975 models: 1,800-2,000 rpm
 b. 1975-77 models: 1,600-1,800 rpm
4. If necessary, adjust the cold starting speed by moving the connecting rod until the specified speed is attained. The rod has both left and right hand threads. Shortening the rod reduces speed; lengthening the rod increases speed.

NOTE: Moving the connecting rod one-half turn provides a change in speed of 200-300 rpm.

5. For models 1975-77, adjust cold starting speed to specified value by means of the upper adjusting screw.
6. Adjust the cold start emission valve by moving the adjusting screw within its range of travel until cold emission value of 8-9% CO for 1972-74 models, or 5-8% CO for 1975-77 models is attained.

NOTE: The allowable adjusting screw range is 8.5-9.5 mm. Moving the screw out produces a leaner mixture. Moving the screw in produces a richer mixture.

7. For models 1975-77, make the cold start emission valve adjustment without air injection by removing and plugging the center vacuum hose from the switch-over valve. Make the adjustment using the additional air adjusting screw.

Gasoline Fuel Injection System

TROUBLESHOOTING

Troubleshooting the electronically controlled gasoline injection system requires Bosch tester EFAW228 and three hose clips type 157.

IDLE SPEED, ADJUST

NOTE: Do not adjust idle speed with the engine hot.

1. Connect a tachometer and CO measuring device.
2. Turn off the air conditioner.
3. In vehicles with cruise control, see that the bowden wire rests free of tension against the control lever. If necessary, adjust the bowden wire using the adjusting nut.
4. Run the engine until the oil temperature reaches 60°-80°C.
5. Check idle speed. Adjust using the idle speed air screw, if necessary, to 700-800 rpm.
6. Check the idle speed emission valve. Adjust to the following specifications by means of the adjusting screw on the control unit. Turning the control counterclockwise provides a leaner mixture. Turning the control clockwise provides a richer mixture:
1972-74 .5-2.0% CO
1974 (Calif.) 1.0% CO (Max.)
        With Air Injection
1975-77 1.5% CO (Max.)
        Less Air Injection

Diesel Fuel Injection System

IDLE SPEED & IDLE SPEED ADJUSTER, ADJUST
616 Engine

1. Check the regulating linkage for wear and free movement.
2. Run the engine until oil temperature reaches 60-80°C. Check using oil telethermometer 116589272100.
3. Turn the idle speed adjuster completely to the right.
4. Check the distance between the adjusting ring and guide lever and make the adjustment if necessary, Fig. 1. Specification is 0.1 mm.
5. Disconnect the connecting rod, and test the throttle valve and check valve for free movement, Fig. 2.
6. Check idling speed and adjust to a specification of 700-800 rpm by means of the idle speed adjusting screw.
7. If the idle speed cannot be obtained, examine the vacuum line, sealing rings for the tickler shaft, governor housing and governor diaphragm for leaks.

617 Engine

1. Check the regulating linkage for wear and free movement.
2. Run the engine until the oil temperature reaches 60-80°C. Check using oil telethermometer 116589272100.
3. Turn the idle speed adjuster, Fig. 3, completely to the right.
4. Check the distance between the adjusting ring and shaped spring. If necessary, adjust to a dimension of about 1.0 mm.

NOTE: Make sure the shaped spring is properly installed.

5. Disconnect the connecting rod on the guide lever.
6. Set the transmission selector lever to D, turn on the air conditioner and move the power steering to full lock with the engine running at full speed. Regulate speed, if required (see below).
7. Now, adjust the idle speed adjuster by turning the knob counterclockwise. Adjust idle speed using the adjusting screw.
8. Check the idle speed. Now, if necessary, loosen the counternut and readjust idle speed using the idle speed adjusting screw to a setting of 700-800 rpm.
9. Attach the connecting rod, keeping it free of tension. Adjust the regulating linkage, if necessary, to the following specifications:
Pull rod   225 mm
Slide rod (fully extended) 158 mm
Push rod   252 mm
10. Perform the steps outlined in 5 above.
11. Now, accelerate using the accelerator pedal while turning the knob for the idle speed adjuster to the left at the same time. The idle speed should now be at 1,000-1,100 rpm. If necessary, adjust using the adjusting screw.

NOTE: The speed will not be in the idle speed adjusting range when set higher. Consequently, the engine speed may increase up to the no-load maximum speed.

Fig. 1 Checking distance (arrow) between adjusting ring and guide lever

Fig. 2 Connecting rod (4) and idle speed adjusting screw (4)

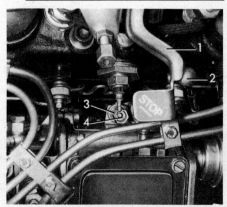

Fig. 3 Guide lever (1), connecting rod (2), counternut (3) and idle speed adjusting screw (4)

NO-LOAD MAXIMUM SPEED, ADJUST

Specification: 5,200-5,400 rpm
1. Warm the oil to a temperature of 60-80°C. Check using oil telethermometer 116589272100.
2. Accelerate slowly using the accelerator pedal and read the revolution counter (the instrument made by Gann, 7000 Stuttgart 1 or equivalent is recommended). Engine speed should be between 5,200-5,400 rpm.
3. If necessary, adjust speed at the throttle unit using the full stop screw. Moving the screw in reduces speed; moving the screw out increases speed.

ALTITUDE COMPENSATOR, ADJUST

NOTE: 1975-77 vehicles are provided with a manually adjustable altitude correction device. The correction screw may be adjusted in steps from 0 to 12,000 feet, with one step equaling 2,000 feet. Recommended adjustment steps are as follows:
a. Up to about 2,000 feet = position 0
b. From 2,000-6,000 feet = position 4,000 feet
c. From 6,000-10,000 feet = position 8,000 feet
d. Over 10,000 feet = position 12,000 feet.

Emission Controls Section

EXHAUST GAS RECIRCULATION SYSTEM, FIG. 1

Operation

Above an engine coolant temperature of approx. 40° C (104° F) in the intake manifold, a portion of exhaust gases from the exhaust manifold is recirculated to the intake manifold during acceleration, partial throttle operation and transition to coasting.

The amount of EGR is dependent on the position of the throttle valve (vacuum pick-up on throttle valve housing) and the exhaust gas back pressure in the exhaust manifold.

Depending on the position of the throttle valve, the center diaphragm chamber of the EGR, Fig. 2, valve will receive more or less vacuum via the thermo-vacuum valve 40° C/104° F (60) in the intake manifold.

In the upper diaphragm there is always atmospheric pressure present via a vent bore.

Dependent on vacuum, the shut-off diaphragm (1) with connecting pin moves downwards against spring tension and the valve can open.

The opening and closing of the EGR valve is controlled by the exhaust pressure transducer which, depending on exhaust gas back pressure in the exhaust manifold, either vents or evacuates the diaphragm chamber above the working diaphragm (3).

The exhaust pressure transducer is divided into three chambers by two springloaded diaphragms; an upper (1) and a lower (2), Fig. 3. Both diaphragms are connected with each other via a tubular shaft.

Exhaust back pressure affects the upper diaphragm chamber. The middle diaphragm chamber is continually vented via the intake air housing. The position of the two diaphragms is not influenced by this. The lower diaphragm is either vented or evacuated according to the exhaust back pressure.

Due to the various driving conditions there are three positions for the exhaust pressure transducer:

During acceleration, exhaust gas back pressure increases and pushes the upper diaphragm with the tubular shaft and the lower diaphragm downwards.

The valve disc in the tubular shaft

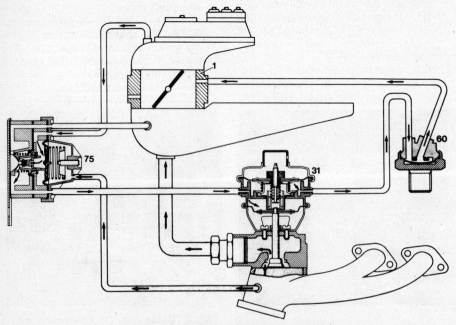

Fig. 1 Exhaust Gas Recirculation (EGR) system

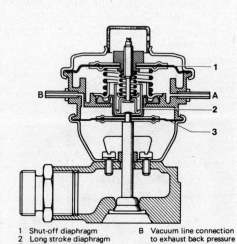

1 Shut-off diaphragm
2 Long stroke diaphragm
3 Working diaphragm
A Vacuum line connection to thermo-vacuum valve
B Vacuum line connection to exhaust back pressure transducer

Fig. 2 EGR valve

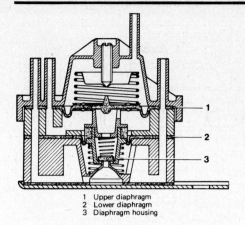

1 Upper diaphragm
2 Lower diaphragm
3 Diaphragm housing

Fig. 3 Exhaust pressure transducer

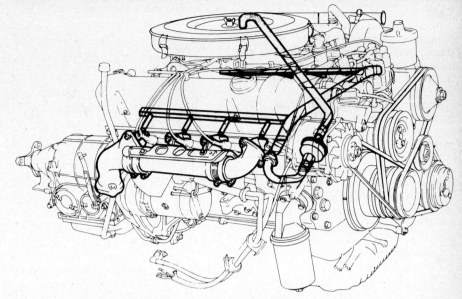

Fig. 4 Afterburning system. Except California models

closes the intake manifold vacuum line in the lower diaphragm chamber. Simultaneously, the vent bore between the middle and the lower diaphragm chamber is opened by the valve disc. The lower diaphragm chamber in the EGR valve will be vented via the vacuum control line to the lower diaphragm chamber of the exhaust pressure transducer. The spring in the EGR valve depresses the working diaphragm including the valve downwards. The valve opens completely and the maximum amount of exhaust gas enters the intake manifold.

During transition to coasting, exhaust gas back pressure decreases. The upper diaphragm (1) with the tubular shaft and the lower diaphragm in the exhaust pressure transducer slowly return to their initial position. The valve disc opens the intake manifold vacuum line and seats itself on the lower sheet metal contour of the tubular shaft. This interrupts the venting of the lower diaphragm chamber. The intake manifold vacuum now present in the lower diaphragm chamber evacuates also the lower diaphragm chamber in the EGR valve via the vacuum control line.

Depending on the amount of vacuum, the EGR valve is pulled in a closing direction against the spring force. EGR is reduced.

During steady driving operation, there is an equilibrium in the lower and upper diaphragm chambers. The EGR valve remains in its present position and the amount of EGR also remains constant.

Exhaust Gas Recirculation does not take place under the following conditions:

a. Below approx. 40° C (104° F) engine coolant temperature (thermo-vacuum valve (60) is closed).
b. While coasting.
c. At idle.
d. At full throttle.

In these cases, vacuum does not act

on the upper diaphragm chamber in the EGR valves and the shut-off diaphragm does not permit the necessary valve travel.

System Diagnosis

Remove the brown vacuum line at the EGR valve and slowly increase engine speed. Above approx. 1200 rpm, the engine should run roughly or stall. If not, check to see if vacuum lines are properly connected to the exhaust pressure transducer and the intake manifold.

Note that the connections on the exhaust pressure transducer have color-coded rings. The attached lines must have the same color code.

AFTERBURNING SYSTEM
Description

Exc. Calif.

The air injection, Fig. 4, is self-drawing: That is, with the engine run-

ning, air is continually drawn from the air filter to the exhaust valves via the air injection passages. The aspirator valve/check valve draws fresh air from the "clean" side of the air filter past a one-way diaphragm made of high-temperature material. The diaphragm opens to allow fresh air to mix with the exhaust gases during negative pressure (vacuum) pulses which occur in the exhaust ports and manifold passages. If the pressure is positive, the diaphragm closes, and no exhaust gas is allowed to flow past the valve and into the "clean" side of the air cleaner. The aspirator valve/check valve works most efficiently at idle and slightly off-idle, where the negative pulses are maximum. At higher engine speeds, the aspirator valve remains closed.

The exhaust gas and the drawn-in air are led through exhaust pipes into the catalyst. The oxygen contained in the air combines with the hot exhaust gas and this furthers catalytic action.

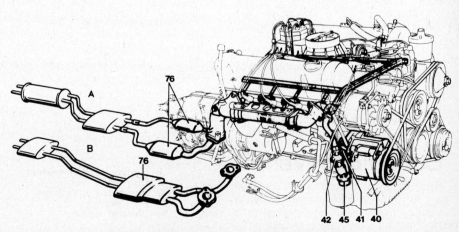

Fig. 5 Afterburning system. California models

Calif.

Above an engine coolant temperature of approximately 17° C (62° F) in the intake manifold, air is injected into the exhaust passages of the cylinder heads during idle, coasting and partial-throttle operation.

The air pump, Fig. 5, which is driven off the crank shaft, via a V-belt continually pumps air as long as the engine is running.

The air is routed to the diverter valve (41). Above approx. 17° C (62° F) engine coolant temperature, when the diverter valve diaphragm is activated by vacuum, the air is injected via the check valve (42) into the cylinder heads. Below 17° C (62° F) engine coolant temperature, when no vacuum reaches the diaphragm of the diverter valve, the air from the air pump is routed via the air filter for noise suppression (45) to the atmosphere.

The exhaust gases and the injected air are routed through the exhaust pipes into the catalysts. The oxygen-rich injected air is mixed with the hot exhaust gases and can react in the catalyst.

System Diagnosis

Exc. Calif.

1. Remove the suction hose to the aspirator/check valve at the air filter and cover with your finger.
2. Vacuum should be present (in addition suction noise is audible).
3. If no vacuum is indicated, replace the aspirator/check valve.

Calif.

1. Connect a CO tester to the exhaust gas back pressure line and read the CO-value. Remove the blue/purple vacuum hose from the vertical connection of the thermo-vacuum valve and plug the vacuum line.
2. The CO% value should increase.
3. If not, check vacuum lines.

   The blue vacuum line with the in-line check valve (35) goes from the intake manifold to the angular connection of thermo-vacuum valve (61). The blue/purple vacuum line goes from the vertical connection of thermo-vacuum valve (61) to diverter valve (41), Fig. 6.

   The check valve (35) must be attached with connection (A) towards the intake manifold, Fig. 6.

CATALYTIC CONVERTER

The catalyst consists of an oval monolith (3), a honeycomb body of ceramic material which is elastically suspended in a wire mesh structure (2). The precious metal coating on the

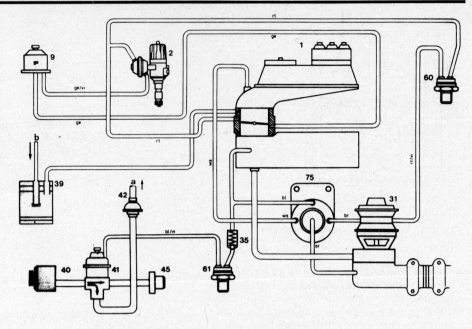

1 Mixture regulator assembly	41 Diverter valve
2 Distributor	42 Check valve
9 Switch-over valve, ignition	60 Thermo-vacuum valve 40° C/104° F
31 EGR valve	61 Thermo-vacuum valve 17° C/62° F
35 Check valve, vacuum	75 Exhaust pressure transducer
39 Charcoal canister	a Air injection line to cylinder head
40 Air pump	b Connection, fuel tank vent

Fig. 6 Emission controls component location. California models

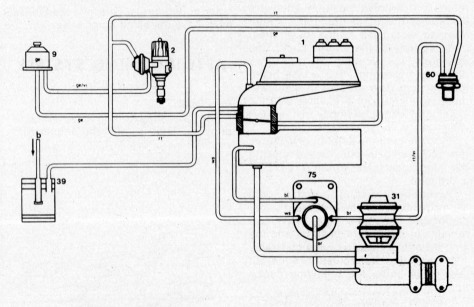

1 Mixture regulator assembly	60 Thermo-vacuum valve 40°/104° F
2 Distributor	75 Exhaust pressure transducer
9 Switch-over valve, ignition	b Connection, fuel tank vent
31 EGR valve	
39 Charcoal canister	

Fig. 7 Emission controls component location. Except California models

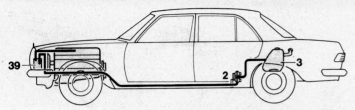

Fig. 8 Evaporative emission control system

2 Valve system
3 Fuel tank
39 Charcoal canister

nection to receive the fuel vapors from the charcoal canister.

SYSTEM DIAGNOSIS

1. Remove the black plastic line (purge line) to the throttle valve housing at the charcoal canister and cover with your finger or connect a vacuum gauge.
2. Slowly increase engine speed to approx. 2000 rpm.
3. At idle speed, no vacuum should be present (less than 15 mm Hg/0.6 in Hg).
4. With increasing engine speed, vacuum should increase.
5. If not, check purge hose. The purge hose must be attached to the throttle valve housing (arrow). Check the hose for leaks and clean the connection at the throttle valve housing with compressed air.

monolith accelerates, in conjunction with the injected fresh air, the oxidation of carbon monoxide (CO) and hydrocarbons (HC) at corresponding temperatures.

FUEL EVAPORATION CONTROL SYSTEM

The vapors from the fuel tank are routed via the valve system (2) into the charcoal canister, Fig. 8. The fuel vapors are stored in the charcoal canister when the engine is not running. When the engine is running, the vapors are purged into the throttle valve housing as of a certain position of the throttle valve.

The valve system (2) with its vacuum relief valve, pressure relief valve and safety valve remains in its construction as already known.

The throttle valve has a purge con-

Clutch & Transmission Section

CLUTCH, ADJUST

1. Loosen the adjusting screw hex nut.
2. Turn the adjusting screw so the push rod covers the clearance path ("b"), Fig. 1, to the master cylinder piston when the pedal is pressed. It is not possible to measure clearance between push rod and master cylinder piston, which should be approximately 0.2 mm. Adjustment, therefore, must be made by "feel."

CLUTCH

Removal

1. Remove transmission, as described under Transmission, Replace.
2. Loosen the pressure plate fastening bolts alternately 1 to 1½ turns each until the pressure plate is completely relieved of tension.
3. Remove the fastening bolts completely.
4. Remove the pressure plate and driven plate, Fig. 2.

Installation

1. Center the driven plate using centering mandrel 116589111500 in relation to the radial ball bearing on the crankshaft.
2. Position the pressure plate and tighten fastening bolts alternately 1 to 1½ turns each until the pressure plate is well tightened to 25 Nm.
3. Remove the centering mandrel.
4. Install the transmission.

Functional Check

Check the clutch for free, unimpeded operation by engaging reverse gear with the engine running. Notice that a perfectly operating driven plate at idle speed and with transmission fluid at operating temperature requires a little time after declutching to come to a stop. Engagement of reverse gear too soon will result in gear noise.

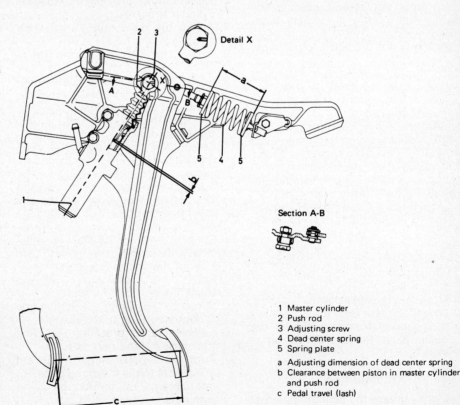

Detail X

Section A-B

1 Master cylinder
2 Push rod
3 Adjusting screw
4 Dead center spring
5 Spring plate

a Adjusting dimension of dead center spring
b Clearance between piston in master cylinder and push rod
c Pedal travel (lash)

Fig. 1 Clutch adjustment

MANUAL SHIFT TRANSMISSION

Removal

1. Disconnect the battery ground cable and support the transmission with a jack.
2. Remove the fastening screws and washers for the exhaust support on the fastening plate, and turn the exhaust support downward.
3. Unscrew the fastening nut for the rear engine rubber mounting.
4. Unscrew the screws for the crossmember on the frame floor.
5. Remove the crossmember.
6. Disconnect the shift rods on the intermediate levers of the shift bracket.
7. Pull off the speedometer (tachometer) input shaft after loosening the clamp screw on the rear transmission cover.
8. Unscrew the bracket on the rear transmission cover and remove it together with the fastening plate for the exhaust support.
9. Loosen the clamping nut of the propeller shaft.
10. Disconnect the drive shaft at the transmission and rear axle so the two companion plates remain on the shaft. To facilitate this task, raise the car on the rear axle so the wheels rotate freely.
11. Unscrew the screws holding the universal shaft intermediate bearing.
12. Unscrew the bracket on the frame floor.
13. Compress the drive shaft in the slide piece, pull it out of the centering journal, and push as far as possible toward the rear.
14. Unscrew both mountings for the pressure line going to the slave cylinder.
15. Unscrew the slave cylinder and place it out of the way without releasing the pressure line.
16. Unscrew the screws for the starter and force the starter out of its fitting.
17. Remove all screws securing the transmission to the intermediate flange. Remove the two upper screws last.
18. Move the transmission horizontally toward the rear until the drive shaft is separated from the hub of the driven plate. Remove the transmission.

Installation

1. Lightly grease the centering journal and the splines on the transmission input shaft. Use hot bearing grease.

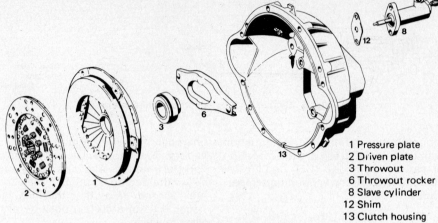

1 Pressure plate
2 Driven plate
3 Throwout
6 Throwout rocker
8 Slave cylinder
12 Shim
13 Clutch housing

Fig. 2   Clutch components

2. Engage one speed and introduce the transmission horizontally onto the clutch while rotating the transmission main shaft back and forth until the splines of the input shaft and driven plate are aligned.
3. Engage the transmission fastening bolts, starting at the top. Make sure the ground cable doesn't get caught.
4. Position the starter in its fitting and tighten screws. Screw the ground cable to the top screw.
5. Refit the slave cylinder and plastic shim into the clutch housing. Screw down.
6. Tighten both delivery line-to-slave cylinder brackets.
7. Attach the drive shaft to the rear axle.
8. Screw the bracket to the frame floor.
9. Screw in the universal shaft intermediate bearing screws for several turns, but do not tighten.
10. Engage the drive shaft to the transmission.
11. Screw the fastening plate and bracket to the rear transmission cover.
12. Connect the input shaft for the tachometer (speedometer) to the rear transmission cover. Tighten the clamp screw.
13. Connect and secure the transmission shift rods to the intermediate lever of the shift bracket.
14. Screw the crossmember to the frame floor.
15. Screw on the nut for the rear engine rubber mounting to the bracket.
16. Relieve jack pressure on the transmission and rear axle.
17. Turn the exhaust support upward and mount to the fastening plate. Do not tighten. First, tighten the clamp with nuts on the exhaust pipe. Then screw exhaust mounting bracket to the fastening plate.

18. Move the car back and forth several times and tighten the drive shaft clamping nut to a torque of 30-40 Nm (3-4 kpm).
19. Tighten the nuts of the universal shaft intermediate bearing.
20. Connect the battery ground.
21. Check transmission and clutch for perfect operation.

AUTOMATIC TRANSMISSION ADJUSTMENT

NOTE: All adjustments described here must be made with the vehicle standing on all wheels.

Control Pressure Rod

1. Remove the air filter.
2. Disconnect the control pressure linkage.
3. Push the intermediate lever against the idling speed stop on the drag lever and against the throttle valve lever of the idling speed stop on the venturi control unit.
4. Push the control pressure linkage fully toward the rear against its stop.
5. Adjust the length of the linkage in respect to the ballhead. The component should be free of stress.

NOTE: When checking the control pressure linkage for length, hold the ball socket adjacent to the ballhead.

Selector Rod

1. Disconnect the selector rod from the selector lever with the selector lever in N. See to it that about 1 mm play exists between the selector lever and N stop on the gate plate.
2. Adjust the length of the selctor rod so it can be attached free of stress.
3. Tighten the counternut.

Starter Locking & Backup Light Switch

1. Disconnect the selector rod.
2. Move the range selector lever on the transmission into N.
3. Tighten the clamping bolt.
4. Loosen the adjusting screw and insert locating pin 115589186300 through the carrier into the locating hole in the gear shift housing.
5. Tighten the adjusting screw.
6. Remove the locating pin.
7. Put the selector lever inside the car in N.
8. Attach the selector rod. It should be free of tension.
9. Check to see that the engine can be started with the selector lever in N and P.

Kickdown Switch

1. Depress the accelerator pedal fully against the kickdown position. In this position, the throttle valve lever should rest against the full-load stop of the venturi control unit.
2. To adjust, loosen the clamp bolt on the retractor lever of the accelerator pedal shaft and turn the accelerator pedal. Tighten the clamp bolt.

AUTOMATIC TRANSMISSION TROUBLESHOOTING

Preliminary

1. Check the fluid level.
2. Set engine idle speed.
3. Adjust the selector rod of the regulating linkage and kickdown switch.

   The chart in Fig. 3, outlines shifting patterns under various conditions.

AUTOMATIC TRANSMISSION

Removal

1. Drain fluid by unscrewing the oil filler pipe on the oil pan and the oil drain plug on the fluid clutch/torque converter.
2. Unscrew the lines from the oil cooler.
3. Unscrew the fastening screws and turn the lines to one side.
4. Loosen both fastening bolts of the universal shaft intermediate bearing, but don't screw them out yet.
5. Loosen the universal shaft clamping nut using wrenches 001589352100 and 000589130100.
6. Unscrew the front exhaust pipe.
7. Remove the engine carrier.

Gas Pedal Position	Shift	Upshifting km/h	Downshifting km/h
Selector Lever Position 4			
Idle throttle	1-2-1	10	7
	2-3-2	30	22
	3-4-3	50	36
Full throttle	1-2-1	29	7
	2-3-2	61	22
	3-4-3	138	60
Kickdown	1-2-1	34	20
	2-3-2	61	50
	3-4-3	138	120
Selector Lever Position 3			
Idle Throttle	1-2-1	10	7
	2-3-2	38	32
Full throttle	1-2-1	29	7
	2-3-2	82	39
Kickdown	1-2-1	34	20
	2-3-2	82	71
Selector Lever Position 2			
Idle Throttle	1-2-1	42	7
Full throttle	1-2-1	42	21
Kickdown	1-2-1	42	35

NOTE: All speed values are approximate assuming a rear axle ratio of 3.46:1 is used.

Fig. 3 Automatic transmission shift pattern chart

8. Remove the rear engine mount on the transmission.
9. Disconnect the selector rod on the range selector lever and move the selector lever to P position.
10. Disconnect the tachometer shaft on the transmission.
11. Unscrew the kickdown solenoid valve cable.
12. Remove the control pressure lever from the shaft.
13. Pull out the plug for the starter lockout and backup light switch.
14. Unscrew the drive shaft from the transmission, but leave the drive plate on the shaft.
15. Slide the shaft toward the rear as far as possible and place a wood support under the shaft at the front in the tunnel so the shaft is pushed completely upwards.
16. Unscrew the vacuum line from the modulator.
17. Remove the cover plate, and separate the torque converter from the driven plate.
18. Raise the engine and transmission slightly using remover and installer 116589066200.
19. Remove all bolts that attach the transmission to the intermediate flange. Remove the two lateral bolts last.
20. Push the transmission and torque

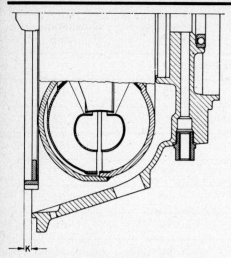

Fig. 4 Torque converter installed clearance

converter toward the rear axle until the bearing journal of the torque converter no longer touches the intermediate flange.
21. Carefully lower the transmission and torque converter and pull the assembly from the car in a forward direction.
22. Place the unit in a vertical position and screw holding plate 116589056200 on the torque converter. Pull in an upward direction.
23. Inspect the fluid clutch of the torque converter and clean inside with flushing mandrel 115589246300.

CAUTION: The torque converter itself cannot be flushed. If abrasions

are heavy or there are chips in the oil, replace the converter.

Installation

NOTE: Before installing the transmission, thoroughly flush the transmission oil cooler, plus oil lines, with syringe 112589007200 and benzine. Blow it out.

1. With the transmission in a vertical position, screw holding plate 116589056200 on the torque converter.
2. Move the claws of the drive flange into engaging position opposite the pump wheel. Grease the centering pin and drive flange of the torque converter with MolyKote.
3. Carefully insert the torque converter while turning the unit back and forth.

NOTE: If the torque converter is correctly installed, dimension "k" of Fig. 4 should be about 4 mm. Also be sure that when the torque converter is introduced the sealing lip of the radial sealing ring in the primary pump housing is not damaged.

4. Place the transmission on a lift, turning the torque converter so the two fastening bores are on the bottom.
5. Rotate the engine until the two

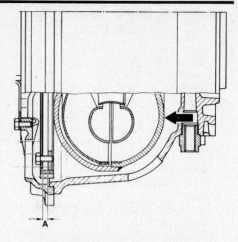

Fig. 5 Torque converter positioning

bores in the driven plate for the fastening bolts are at the bottom.
6. Insert the transmission, lifting until the lower bolt holes of the clutch housing are in alignment with the bores in the intermediate flange. Push the transmission forward until the clutch housing is well seated, but do not use force.
7. Install transmission to engine bolts.
8. Force the torque converter using a screwdriver through the cooling slots on the clutch bowl in a forward direction (in the direction of the arrow, Fig. 5) so distance "A" in Fig. 5 is cancelled out.
9. Continue the reassembly procedure in an opposite fashion to the removal procedure, above.

Rear Axle & Brakes Section

AXLE SHAFTS
Less Units W/Torque Compensation

Removal
1. Drain rear axle oil.
2. Unscrew the brake caliper and suspend it on a hook.
3. Unscrew the hex bolt for attaching the rear axle shaft to the rear axle shaft flange.
4. Force the rear axle shaft out of the rear axle shaft flange using assembly fixture 115589096100.

NOTE: If it becomes necessary, loosen the shock absorber at its upper suspension and lower the semi-trailing arm down to the deflection stop.

5. Support the rear axle housing with a vehicle jack 116589026300 for a large center housing or 115589356300 for a small center housing.
6. Unscrew the rear rubber mount from the frame floor and lower the center housing.

NOTE: The rear axle shaft is mounted floatingly and axially, sliding in the two constant velocity joints. It can be telescoped in its operating position by 15 to 20 mm. With the semi-trailing arms fully extended, it can be extended about 30 mm.

7. Clean the rear axle housing.
8. Unscrew the hex bolts for the rear axle housing cover and remove the cover.

9. Pull the locking ring between the inner constant velocity joint and the side gear with offset pliers.
10. Pull the rear axle shaft from the side gear, removing it together with the spacer ring.

Installation

CAUTION: Make sure the correct and complete rear axle shaft is mounted on the respective end of the rear axle center housing. For identification, the face of the universal spider carries a punched in "R" (right) or "L" (left).

1. If a new rear axle shaft is installed, place the previously removed spacer ring on the inner constant velocity joint.
2. Place the complete rear axle shaft into the side gear and fit a new lock-

ing ring into the groove of the inner constant velocity joint.

CAUTION: The outer constant velocity joint should not be allowed to drop down and should not be bent too much since doing so may damage the contant velocity housing and cause leaks.

3. Check the end play between the inner universal spider and differential housing. There should be no perceptible end play and it should be possible to turn the locking ring in the groove. If necessary, install a thicker or thinner spacer ring. Spacer rings are available from 2.90 to 3.40 mm in 0.1 mm steps.
4. Telescope the shaft and install it into the rear axle shaft flange using assembly fixture 115589096100.
5. Screw in the hex bolt that attaches the rear axle shaft to the rear axle shaft flange and tighten to 95 Nm (9.5 kpm).
6. Mount the end cover with sealing compound and tighten bolts to 45 Nm (4.5 kpm).
7. Lift the rear axle housing. Screw rubber mounts to the frame floor and tighten to 25 Nm (2.5 kpm).
8. Complete rassembly. Fill the rear axle housing with EP Hypoid Gear Oil SAE 90 (non-positive traction differential) or Special EP Hypoid Gear Oil (positive traction differential).

Units W/Torque Compensation

Removal

1. Drain rear axle oil.
2. Remove and plug the brake hose.
3. Remove the torsion bar.
4. Remove the shock absorber and lower the coupled semi-trailing arm to the spring stop.
5. Remove the hex bolt that attaches

1 Caliper   2 Piston   23 Holding device

Fig. 2 Positioning holding device in caliper

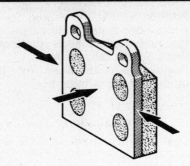

Fig. 1 Brake pad lubrication points

the rear axle shaft to the rear axle shaft flange.
6. Disconnect the brake cable control, remove the holding bracket on the wheel carrier, remove the rubber sleeve and push back the cover.
7. Force the rear axle shaft out of the rear axle shaft flange by means of assembly fixture 115589096100.

The remainder of the removing procedure and the installation procedure is the same as that for the rear axle shaft without starting torque compensation.

BRAKE PADS
Removal

1. Remove the shaft cover plate on the caliper. This instruction applies only to front wheel brakes and on calipers having a 57 mm piston diameter and solid brake discs.
2. On cars having a brake lining wear indicator, pull the cables of the clip sensors out of the plug connection on the caliper.
3. On a Teves brake caliper, use a punch to knock the holding pins out of the caliper. Remove the cross spring.
4. On a Bendix caliper, pull both eyelets out of the holding pins, and remove the holding springs and lining holding springs.
5. Pull one brake shoe out of the caliper by means of impact puller 115589143300.

NOTE: Replace clip sensors on which the insulation has been rubbed from the brake disc.

7. Using a cylindrical brush, clean the brake shoe guide in the brake caliper.
8. Check the dust cap for cracks. If the dust cap is damaged, remove the caliper for disassembly.
9. Draw off some brake fluid.
10. Force the piston back with piston resetting pliers 111589073700.

CAUTION: Always leave one brake shoe in the caliper until the other is replaced. If not, the opposite piston will be pushed forward when the other piston is forced back.

11. On vehicles with vented brake shoes, check air passages for contamination. If contamination exists, loosen with a thin wire and blow out with compressed air.

Installation

1. On cars having a brake lining wear indicator, insert the clip sensor into the lining backing plate and brake lining.
2. Coat the brake shoe lightly with lubricant at the points indicated by the arrows in Fig. 1. Use MolyKote Paste U, MolyKote Paste G Rapid, Liqui-Moly-Paste 36 or Plastilube.
3. On a Teves caliper, mount the cross spring and knock in holding pins.
4. On a Bendix caliper, mount the lining holding springs, and insert the holding pins into the caliper and eyelets into the holding pins.

NOTE: Bendix calipers having a 57 mm piston diameter up to the end of 1974 are provided with left-hand and right-hand eyelets. Make sure that the rounded off leg of the eyelet faces outward. Starting with 1975 models, the eyelets of Bendix calipers are mounted outside the brake caliper inspection shaft and are similar to calipers having a 60 mm piston diameter.

5. On cars having a brake lining wear indicator, connect the cables of the clip sensors to the plug connection of the caliper.
6. Install the cover plate.
7. Actuate the brake pedal energetically several times until solid resistance is felt. Check brake fluid level, and replenish if necessary.

Fig. 3 Piston identification, Bendex (left) & Treves (right)

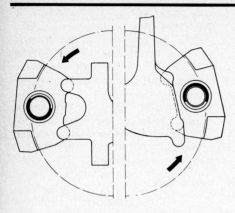

Fig. 4   Caliper location

FRONT BRAKE CALIPER
Removal

CAUTION: Do not separate the two halves of the caliper since the fastening bolts are tightened to a definite torque by the manufacturer.

1. Remove the brake shoes.
2. Force the dust cap from the housing with a screwdriver.
3. Hold one piston on the caliper with piston resetting pliers 111589073700 and force out the opposite piston with compressed air of approximately overpressure.

NOTE: A piston that is rusted to the caliper bore can't be forced out with compressed air. Remove both heat shields. Hold the piston that can be moved in the caliper with a fabricated device, Fig. 2. Release the stuck piston by energizing the master cylinder, forcing the cylinder out of the bore.

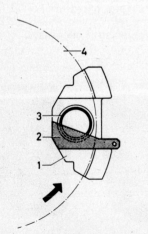

Fig. 6   Piston position. Diagonal swing rear axle

4. Position a suitable clamping device and rubber plate in the caliper so the rubber plate seals the bore. Press out the other piston.
5. Remove the piston seals from the grooves of the cylinder bores.

Installation

1. Coat new piston seals lightly with ATE-brake cylinder paste and insert the seals into the grooves of the cylinder bores.

CAUTION: When repairing a Bendix caliper, do not damage the rigid seat of the press-on ring.

2. Insert the pistons into the bores, checking the position with piston gauge 001589302100.

CAUTION: There are two piston versions, Fig. 3, Bendix and Teves. Be sure to use the correct one.

3. Move the piston into correct position with piston rotating pliers 000589363700, if needed.

NOTE: To prevent brake squeal, the caliper piston is provided with an elevation. When braking takes place, this elevation provides a one-sided contact of the brake shoes. The position of the caliper piston depends on whether the calipers are mounted before or behind the wheel center, Fig. 4.

4. On Teves calipers, position the dust cap against the flange of the caliper. Place the pressure plate on the dust cap and press the dust cap on the flange of the caliper at a pressure of about 300 Nm using an installation tool you make according to Fig. 5 and a hand press.
5. On Bendix calipers, attach the dust cap to the flange of the caliper.
6. Insert the heat shields into the piston so they fit accurately into the elevation.
7. On Teves calipers, insert seating device 000589496300 into the caliper and press the heat shield into the piston.
8. On Bendix calipers, using a suitable tool on the piston, press the heat shield into the piston.

CAUTION: The piston elevation should project at least 1 mm above the heat shield. Notice that the heat shields for inner and outer pistons differ.

9. Install brake shoes.

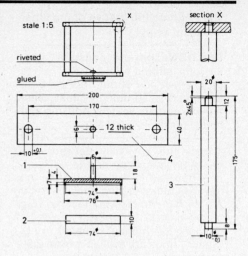

1 Pressure plate   3 Connecting bolt
2 Rubber plate   4 Clamp

Fig. 5   Dust cap installation tool. Treves caliper

Removal

The procedure for overhauling the rear brake is the same as for the front brake except as noted:

1. The elevation on the piston to stop squeal must be positioned as shown in Fig. 6 if there is a diagonal swing axle. On a caliper for a diagonal swing axle with torque compensation, the piston should be positioned according to Fig. 7.
2. To seat the dust cap on a Teves caliper, position the cap against the flange of the caliper and place a pressure plate on the dust cap. Force the dust cap on the flange with about 300 Nm pressure using an installation tool made for front caliper use.

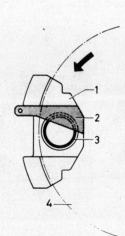

Fig. 7   Piston position. Diagonal swing rear axle with starting torque compensation

MERCEDES-BENZ

MASTER CYLINDER

NOTE: To loosen and tighten brake lines, use a 9 x 11 mm open double-box wrench only.

Removal

1. Open a front wheel and rear wheel bleed screw, and pump out fluid. Both chambers must be drained.
2. Loosen the plug connections on the contact inserts of the warning device while lifting the holding lugs with a small screwdriver.
3. Loosen all brake lines. Immediately seal all lines with rubber caps and master cylinder connections with blind plugs.
4. Loosen and remove the master cylinder and also the O-ring located in the groove of the flange of the master cylinder.

Installation

NOTE: Always replace the O-ring between the master cylinder and brake booster since the connection must be air-tight.

1. Insert the O-ring into the groove of the master cylinder.
2. Attach the mast cylinder to the brake booster and tighten hex nuts to 15 Nm.

NOTE: On vehicles manufactured beginning in the middle of 1974, brake line connections on the master cylinder are on the left. On the stepped tandem master cylinder installed beginning in the fall of 1975, brake circuits are interchanged. The front wheel brake is connected to the pushrod circuit (piston dia: 23.81 mm), and the rear wheel brake is connected to the floating circuit (piston dia: 19.05 mm).

3. Complete installation.

PARKING BRAKE, ADJUST

1. Remove a spherical flange bolt on both the left and right rear axle.
2. Jack up the car.
3. Turn one wheel so the bolt hole from which a spherical flange bolt has been removed extends about 45 degrees in an upward direction if the car has a diagonal swing axle. If the car has a diagonal swing axle with starting torque compensation, see that the flange bolt hole is in a forward direction (270 degrees from the top assuming a clockwise rotation).
4. Insert a 45 mm screwdriver through the hole and engage the adjusting wheel.
5. Turn the adjusting wheel until it can no longer be turned. Then, turn the adjusting wheel back by 2 or 3 teeth until the wheel rotates freely.

NOTE: The adjusting directions of the screwdriver to position brake shoes against discs are as follows:
a. Cars with diagonal swing axles—
   1. Left side: From bottom to top
   2. Right side: From top to bottom
b. Cars with diagonal swing axle with starting torque compensation:
   1. Left side: From the rear forward
   2. Right side: From the front rearward

6. After making the adjustment, step down on the parking brake pedal to the first detent. In this position, the brake shoes of the parking brake should rest lightly against the brake disc.

CAUTION: Do not adjust the adjusting screw on the intermediate lever when making the parking brake adjustment. The screw serves only for compensation of cable lengths.

Rear Suspension Section

SHOCK ABSORBERS

NOTE: The vehicle has to be standing on its wheels.

1. The top fasteners are reached in one of two ways:
   a. Remove rear seat, seat back and cover plate.
   b. Open the trunk and engage fasteners from within.
2. Remove the hexagonal lower suspension nuts on the semi-trailing control arm. Pull the shock down to remove it.
3. Reverse procedure to install. Torque the lower bolts to 45 Nm.

SPRINGS

CAUTION: The rear shock absorbers serve as deflection stops for the rear wheels. For this reason, only detach the shock absorber suspension when the car is on all wheels or when the control arm is supported.

Removal

1. Remove the rear shock absorber.
2. Jack up the rear of the car.
3. Insert upper and lower clamp plates (020b and 020c, respectively) of spring tensioner set 115589003100 in the spring in parallel fashion so there are five coils between them.
4. Insert clamping bolt 020a of spring tensioner set 115589003100 into the control arm opening.

CAUTION: The crosspieces on the clamping bolt and the guide sleeve must be correctly seated in the grooves in the upper and lower clamp plates.

5. Compress the spring.
6. Using a hoist and angular intermediate bracket 115589026300 lift the control arm to a horizontal position.
7. Compress the spring as much as possible and lower the hoist carefully until the control arm comes to rest on the rear axle carrier.
8. Remove the spring and its rubber mount.

Installation

1. Tension five coils.
2. Place the rubber mount in position so the coil end rests on the depression in the control arm.
3. Lift the control arm.
4. Allow the spring to expand, being careful that the rubber mount on the frame floor and the coil end on the control arm are correctly positioned.
5. Complete installation. Torque lower shock absorber bolts to 45 Nm.

Front Suspension and Steering Section

SHOCK ABSORBERS

NOTE: The front shock absorbers also serve as a deflection stop for the front wheels. For this reason, only detach the front shock absorber suspension when the vehicle is standing on its wheels or the lower control arm is supported. A safety stop is provided between the upper control arm and the front axle carrier.

Removal

1. Remove the hexagonal nuts on the upper shock absorber suspension and remove the disc and rubber ring.

NOTE: If the coolant expansion tank is in the way when removing the right side shock, remove the tank.

2. Remove the hexagonal nuts on the lower control arm to detach the lower shock absorber suspension.
3. Press in the shock absorber piston rod.
4. Attach bracket 115589116100 and remove the shock.

Disassembly

1. On Bilstein units, remove the protective tube, lower rubber ring, lower disc, and rubber spring, Fig. 1.

2. On F & S units, remove the lower rubber ring, Fig. 2.

Installation

1. Clean the lower control arm on the supporting surface of the fastening bracket of the lower shock absorber suspension.

NOTE: The fastening bracket of the lower shock absorber suspension must be tightly seated in the rubber mount, which must not be turnable within the suspension eye.

2. Reassemble units.

CAUTION: In the case of Bilstein units, be very careful not to switch the lower and upper discs.

3. Complete installation.

SPRINGS

CAUTION: Drop the lower control arm to remove the front springs. Use special cradle 115589036300 placed on the lift for support. If this tool is not available use spring tensioner BE15838 of assembly stand BE15798 to tension springs. The front shock absorbers serve as a deflection stop for the front wheels. For this reason, loosen the shock absorber suspension only when the vehicle is standing on all four wheels or when the lower control arm is supported.

Removal

1. Loosen the lower shock absorber suspension and torsion bar connecting linkage, Fig. 3.
2. Jack up the car, front and rear, and remove the wheel.
3. Mark the position of the cam bolts on the lower control arm in relation to the front axle carrier. Loosen the hex nuts.
4. Support the lower control arm with a lift and attached intermediate angle piece 115589026300 and special cradle 115589036300.
5. Knock out the cam bolts and carefully lower the lift.

CAUTION: Do not mix up the cam bolts. Know where they go. When using intermediate angle piece 115589026300, secure the lift against lateral tilting.

6. Remove special cradle 115589036300.
7. Swivel the control arm forward.
8. Remove the front spring and its rubber mounting.

Installation

1. Insert the spring and its attached rubber mount.
2. Swivel the lower control arm into

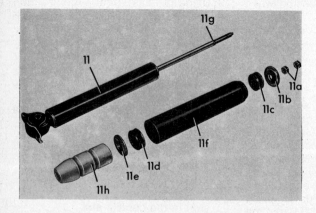

11	Shock absorber	11e	Lower plate
11a	Hex. nuts	11f	Protective sleeve
11b	Upper plate	11g	Locking ring
11c	Upper rubber ring	11h	Supplementary rubber
11d	Lower rubber ring		spring (stop buffer)

Fig. 1   Bilstein shock absorber

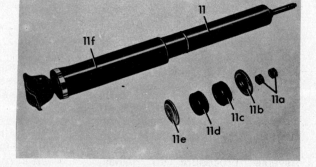

11	Shock absorber	11d	Lower rubber ring
11a	Hex. nuts	11e	Lower plate
11b	Upper plate	11f	Protective sleeve
11c	Upper rubber ring		

Fig. 2   F & S shock absorber

position, while turning the spring so the lower coil end is aligned with the indentation in the control arm.

3. Carefully raise the lower control arm, making sure the control arm rubber mounts aren't damaged by the eyes on the front axle carrier.

4. Mount the cam bolts. Torque nuts to 120 Nm.

CAUTION: Tighten cam bolt hex nuts only when the car is on all four wheels.

5. Mount the torsion bar connecting linkage.

6. Attach the shock absorber suspension to the lower control arm. Torque nuts to 25 Nm.

7. Mount the wheels and lower the car.

8. Check vehicle lever, front wheel adjustment and headlight alignment.

WHEEL BEARINGS, ADJUST

1. Jack up the car and remove the front wheel.

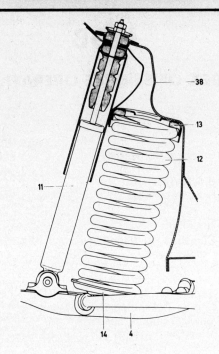

4 Lower control arm
11 Front shock absorber
12 Front spring
13 Rubber mount for front spring
14 Retainer for front spring
38 Front end

Fig. 3   Front spring & shock absorber assemblies

2. Pull off the wheel cap with tool 000589913300.

3. Remove the contact spring used for radio interference suppression.

4. Push the brake pads away from the disc.

5. Loosen the hex socket screw of the clamping nut. Then tighten the clamping nut while simultaneously rotating the hub until the wheel can be turned only with effort.

6. Tighten the clamping nut about $1/3$ turn, and loosen tension by striking the kingpin a blow.

7. Place tester and dial gauge set A1DIN878 on the front wheel hub and set the dial gauge to 2 mm pre-load.

8. Check the end play by energetically pulling and pushing on the flange.

NOTE: Rotate the wheel hub several times before measuring.

9. Tighten the hexagon socket screw of the clamping nut to a torque of 14 Nm (1.4 kpm). Check end play again. It should be 0.01-0.02 mm.

MGB

INDEX OF SERVICE OPERATIONS

GENERAL ENGINE SPECIFICATIONS

Year	Engine	Car-buretor	Bore & Stroke	Piston Displacement Cubic Inches	Compression Ratio	Maximum Brake H.P. @ R.P.M.	Maximum Torque H.P. @ R.P.M.
1972-74	4-110 (1798cc)	Twin HS4	3.16 x 3.50	110	8.8	92 @ 5400	110 @ 3000
1975-77	4-110 (1798cc)	1 Barrel	3.16 x 3.50	110	8.0	62.5 @ 5000	86 @ 2500

TUNE UP SPECIFICATIONS

Year	Spark Plug Type	Spark Plug Gap Inch	Distributor Point Gap Inch	Distributor Dwell Angle Deg.	Ignition Timing Firing Order Fig.	Ignition Timing Timing BTDC	Ignition Timing Mark Fig.	Curb Idle Speed	Idle "CO" %
1972-74	N9Y	.025	.014—.016	57—63	A	15° ①	B	900	—
1975	N9Y	.035	.014—.016	46—56	A	13° ②	B	850	4½—6½
1976 ③	N9Y	.035	.014—.016	46—56	A	13° ②	B	850	4½—6½
1976 ④	N9Y	.035	⑤	—	A	10° ②	B	850	4½—6½
1977	N9Y	.035	⑤	—	A	10° ②	B	850	4½—6½

① —With vacuum hose disconnected and plugged.
② —Set at 1500 R.P.M.
③ —Without Catalytic Converter.
④ —With Catalytic Converter.
⑤ —Pick-up air gap, .010—.017″.
— Not Available.

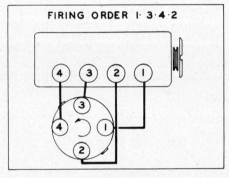

Fig. A

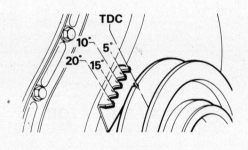

Fig. B

DISTRIBUTOR SPECIFICATIONS

Note: If unit is checked on vehicle, double the RPM and degrees to get crankshaft figures.

Year	Model	Part No.	Advance Starts	Centrifugal Advance Degrees @ RPM of Distributor Intermediate Advance		Full Advance	Vacuum Advance Inches of Vacuum to Start Plunger	Vacuum Advance Max. Advance Dist. Deg. @ Vacuum
1972-74	Lucas 25D4	41339	0 @ 450	5 @ 550	12 @ 1450	14-16 @ 2300	7	12 @ 13
1975-76	Lucas 45D4	41599	0 @ 425	8-10 @ 1000	15-17 @ 2000	17-19 @ 2500	—	—
1976-77	Lucas 45DE4	41693	0 @ 425	6.5-8.5 @ 1000	14-16 @ 1750	16.5-18.5 @ 2250	3	26 @ 11

— Not Available.

MGB

VALVE SPECIFICATIONS

Year	Valve Lash		Valve Angles		Valve Spring Pressure with Valve Closed, Lbs.	Stem Clearance		Stem Diameter	
	Int.	Exh.	Seat	Face		Intake	Exhaust	Intake	Exhaust
1972-74	.015C	.015C	45½	—	72	.0015—.0025	.0020—.0030	.3422—.3427	.3417—.3422
1975-77	.013H	.013H	45½	—	82	.0007—.0019	.0013—.0025	.3429—.3434	.3423—.3428

—Not Available.

PISTONS, PINS, RINGS, CRANKSHAFT & BEARINGS

Year	Piston Clearance		Ring End Gap ①		Wrist-Pin Diameter	Rod Bearings		Main Bearings			
	Top of Skirt	Bottom of Skirt	Comp.	Oil		Shaft Diameter	Bearing Clearance	Shaft Diameter	Bearing Clearance	Thrust on Bear. No.	Shaft End Play
1972-77	.0021—.0033	.006—.012	.012	.015	.750	1.8759—1.8764	.001—.0027	2.1262—2.127	.001—.0027	3	.004—.005

① —Minimum.

ENGINE TIGHTENING SPECIFICATIONS

Year	Cylinder Head Bolts Ft. Lbs.	Intake & Exhaust Manifolds Ft. Lbs.	Oil Pump to Crankcase Ft. Lbs.	Oil Pan Nuts Ft. Lbs.	Connecting Rod Cap Bolts Ft. Lbs	Main Bearing Cap Bolts Ft. Lbs	Flywheel to Crank-shaft Ft. Lbs	Camshaft Sprocket Nut Ft. Lbs	Rocker Arm Cover Ft. Lbs.	Crankshaft Pulley Nuts Ft. Lbs
1972-77	45—50	15	14	6	31—35	70	40	60—70	4	70

ALTERNATOR & REGULATOR SPECIFICATIONS

Year	Alternator			Regulator
	Model	Output @ 14 Volts 6000 RPM	Rotor Winding Resistance @ 68° F.	Voltage @ 5000 RPM
1972-74	Lucas 16ACR	34	4.33	14.3—14.7
1975-77	Lucas 18ACR	43	3.201	13.6—14.4

BRAKE SPECIFICATIONS

Year	Brake Drum Inside Diameter	Drum Brake Wheel Cylinder Bore Diameter	Master Cylinder Bore Diameter
1972-77	10	.80	¹³/₁₆

STARTING MOTOR SPECIFICATIONS

Year	Model	Brush Spring Tension, Ounces	Minimum Brush Length, Inches	Torque Test			
				Torque @ 1000 RPM		Lock Torque	
				Amperes	Torque, Ft. Lbs.	Amperes	Torque, Ft. Lbs.
1972-74	Lucas M418G	36	⁵/₁₆	260	7	465	17
1975-77	Lucas 2M100	36	⅜	300	7.3	463	14.4

WHEEL ALIGNMENT SPECIFICATIONS

Year	Caster Angle, Degrees		Camber Angle, Degrees		King Pin Inclination, Degrees		Toe-In, Inch
	Limits	Desired	Limits	Desired	Limits	Desired	
1972-77	+5 to +7¼	+7	−¼ to +1¼	+1	+7¼ to +9	8	¹/₁₆—³/₃₂

COOLING SYSTEM & CAPACITY DATA

Year	Cooling Capacity, Qts.	Radiator Cap Relief Pressure, Lbs.	Thermo. Opening Temp.	Fuel Tank Gals.	Engine Oil Refill, Qts. ①	Transmission Oil		Rear Axle Oil, Pints
						4 Speed, Pints	4 Speed with Overdrive, Pints	
1972-77	6	10	180	12	3.65	6	7.25	2

①—Including filter.

Electrical Section

DISTRIBUTOR, REPLACE

Electronic Ignition

1. Disconnect battery ground cable.
2. Remove distributor cap and leads.
3. Disconnect distributor wire multi-connector plug.
4. Turn the crankshaft until timing notch on the crankshaft pulley is at TDC and the rotor is in firing position for No. 1 spark plug.
5. Loosen nut and bolt to release the distributor clamp and remove the distributor.
6. Reverse procedure to install.

Conventional Ignition

1. Disconnect battery ground cable.
2. Remove distributor cap and leads.
3. Rotate crankshaft until groove in crankshaft pulley aligns with static ignition point on the timing indicator, and the rotor is in position to fire No. 1 spark plug.
4. Disconnect low tension lead from wiring harness.
5. Disconnect vacuum line from the vacuum advance and remove two screws holding the distributor clamp plate to the cylinder block, Fig. 1.
6. Remove distributor.
7. Reverse procedure to install. With the crankshaft and rotor positioned in step 3 above, rotate the distributor within the limits of the slotted holes in the flange until the

breaker points are just opening.
8. Torque flange retaining screws 8-10 ft. lbs.
9. Complete reassembly and set ignition timing.

DISTRIBUTOR SERVICE

Conventional Ignition

Refer to Fig. 1 when disassembling or assembling distributor.

Electronic Ignition

1. Disconnect the battery.
2. Remove distributor cap and leads, rotor and RF shield, Fig. 2.
3. Check air gap and adjust, if necessary. Adjust to .010-.017 in.

CAUTION: A feeler gauge must not be inserted into the pickup air gap when the ignition circuit is energized.

---

4. To adjust air gap, loosen the two screws holding the pickup and move the pickup until .010-.017 in. is obtained.
5. Tighten the two retaining screws and check the measurement.

ALTERNATOR, REPLACE

1. Remove air pump adjusting link bolt, if equipped.
2. Remove drive belt and air pump

mounting bolt, and shift the air pump aside.
3. Disconnect multi-connector plug from alternator.
4. Remove alternator adjusting link nut.
5. Loosen alternator mounting bolts, lower the alternator and remove the drive belt.
6. Remove the alternator.
7. Reverse procedure to install.

ALTERNATOR, TESTING

18 ACR Units

Battery Voltage Test
1. Remove cable connector from the alternator.
2. Connect negative side of a voltmeter to ground.
3. Switch on ignition.
4. Connect positive side of voltmeter to each of the alternator cable connectors in turn.
5. If battery voltage is not available at the IND cable connector, check the no-charge warning lamp bulb and the warning lamp circuit for continuity.
6. If battery voltage is not available at the main charging cable connector, check the circuit between battery and alternator for continuity.

Alternator Output Test
1. Reconnect cable connector to the alternator.
2. Disconnect brown cable with eyelet

from terminal on starter motor solenoid.

3. Connect an ammeter between brown cable and terminal on starter motor solenoid.

4. Connect a voltmeter across battery terminals.

5. Run the engine at 6,000 alternator rpm and wait for the ammeter reading to stabilize.

6. If a zero ammeter reading is obtained, remove the alternator end cover and disconnect the surge protection device lead. If alternator output is normal, replace the surge protection device. If the reading is still zero, replace the alternator.

7. If an ammeter reading below 10 amperes and a voltmeter reading of 13.6-14.4 volts is obtained, check alternator performance on a test bench. Alternator output should be 34 amperes at 14 volts at 6,000 rpm.

8. If an ammeter reading below 10 amperes and a voltmeter reading below 13.6 volts is obtained, replace the internal voltage regulator.

9. If an ammeter reading above 10 amperes and a voltmeter reading above 14.4 volts is obtained, replace the internal voltage regulator.

16ACR Units

Alternator Output Test

1. Disconnect both connector blocks at alternator.

2. Turn on ignition and connect a voltmeter. If battery voltage does not register, check the circuit between battery and alternator for continuity.

3. Remove the alternator end cover and install a jumper wire between the regulator green connector F and ground.

4. Replace connector blocks and connect an ammeter in series with positive lead of the connector block and the positive output terminal of the alternator.

5. Run the engine at 3,300 rpm. The ammeter should read 34 amperes and the voltmeter should read 14 volts. If conditions do not prevail, replace alternator.

Voltage Regulator Test

1. Disconnect jumper wire and connect a voltmeter across the battery terminals.

2. Run the engine at 3,300 rpm. If the ammeter reads zero, replace the regulator.

3. Adjust speed until the ammeter shows below 10 amperes. The voltmeter should indicate 14-14.4 volts. If not, the regulator is faulty or high resistance prevails.

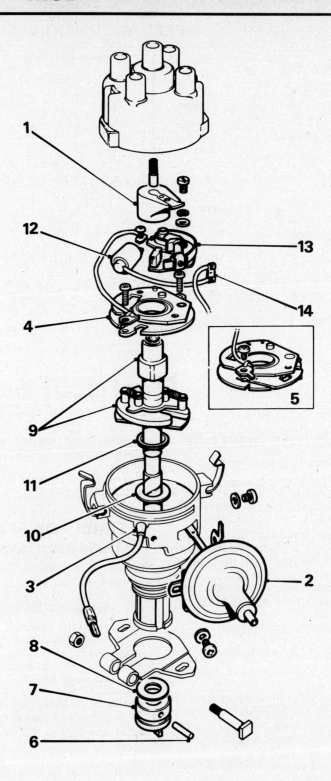

1. Rotor arm	9. Cam spindle and automatic
2. Vacuum unit	advance weights assembly
3. Low tension lead	10. Steel washer
4. Base plate	11. Spacer
5. Base plate (early cars)	12. Capacitor
6. Retaining pin – drive dog	13. Contact set
7. Drive dog	14. Low tension lead connector
8. Thrust washer	

Fig. 1 Disassembled view of conventional type distributor

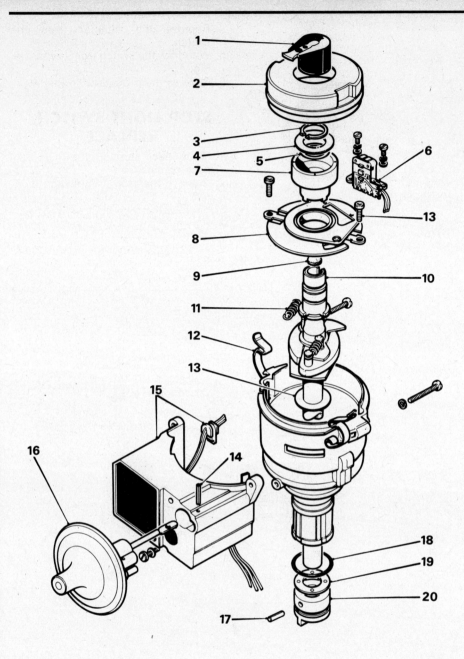

Fig. 2   Disassembled view of electronic ignition type distributor

1. Rotor
2. Anti-flash shield
3. Circlip
4. Washer
5. 'O' ring
6. Pick-up
7. Timing rotor
8. Base plate
9. Felt pad
10. Spindle
11. Return spring
12. Spring clip
13. Shim
14. Pin
15. Amplifier module
16. Vacuum unit
17. Pin for driving dog
18. 'O' ring
19. Thrust washer
20. Driving dog

STARTER MOTOR, REPLACE

1. Disconnect battery ground cable.
2. Remove starter motor plastic cover.
3. Remove starter top attaching bolt.
4. Disconnect wiring from solenoid terminals.
5. Remove the starter motor lower attaching bolt and the starter motor.
6. Reverse procedure to install.

IGNITION SWITCH, REPLACE

1977

1. Loosen steering column.
2. Remove right-hand cowl.
3. Disconnect the ignition switch multi-connector and remove tape holding the cable to column.
4. Drill out shear bolt heads from clamp plate or use a suitable extractor to remove shear bolts.
5. Remove lock assembly and clamp plate.
6. Remove the screw retaining the switch in the lock.
7. Remove the switch assembly.
8. Begin replacement by centralizing the lock body over the slot in the outer column and fitting the clamp plate.

CAUTION: Do not shear the new shear bolts.

9. Reconnect ignition switch multi-connector.
10. Check that the steering lock and ignition switch operate correctly, then tighten the shear bolts until the heads break off.
11. Replace the right hand cowl.

1972-76

1. Remove both halves of switch cowl.
2. Remove two switch retaining screws.
3. Disconnect the switch wiring at the snap connectors.
4. Remove the switch with wiring.
5. Reverse procedure to install.

LIGHT SWITCH, REPLACE

1977

1. Loosen three screws holding steering outer column to floorboard.
2. Loosen three screws holding column bracket.
3. Remove two screws securing the halves of steering column cowl.
4. Remove the securing screw and the right-hand cowl. Then remove the left-hand cowl.

5. Disconnect the light switch leads, noting position and colors as follows:

    N-Brown
    U-Blue
    RG-Red/Light Green

6. Depress retaining clips and remove the light switch, Fig. 3.
7. Reverse procedure to install.

1972-76

1. Remove the three screws holding the left-hand fascia instrument panel cover and pull the cover forward.
2. Remove the bulb holder from the switch retainer.
3. Disconnect the wiring from the switch.

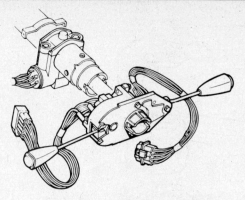

Fig. 3 Combination & light switch assembly. 1977 models

4. Remove the retainer from the switch.
5. Withdraw the switch from the fascia, Fig. 4.
6. Reverse the procedure to install.

STOP LIGHT SWITCH, REPLACE

1. Disconnect stop light switch harness connectors.
2. Remove the stop light switch locknut.
3. Remove the stop light switch.
4. Reverse procedure to install.

NOTE: The stop light switch could be screwed into the pedal to allow free movement of 1/8 inch, Fig. 5.

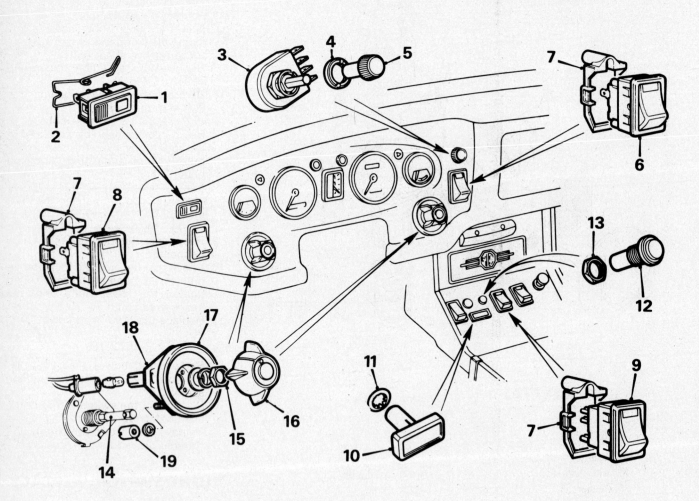

1. Brake pressure warning light test-push.	7. Retainer for rocker switch.
2. Retaining clip.	8. Lighting switch.
3. Panel lamp rheostat switch.	9. Hazard warning switch.
4. Retainer.	10. Seat belt warning lamp.
5. Knob for rheostat switch.	11. Retainer for seat belt warning lamp.
6. Heater blower switch.	12. Hazard warning lamp.
	13. Retainer for hazard warning lamp.

14. Rotary control.
15. Retaining nut.
16. Rotary control knob.
17. Dial assembly.
18. Light box.
19. Retaining nut.

Fig. 4 Control switches. 1972-76 models

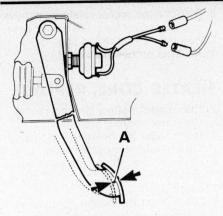

Fig. 5 Stop light switch adjustment

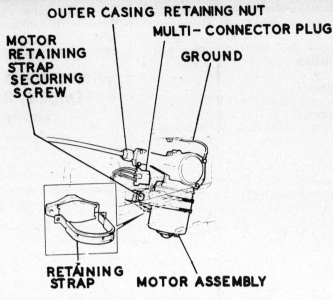

Fig. 6 W/S wiper motor. 1977 models

COMBINATION SWITCH, REPLACE

1977

1. Remove steering column cowl.
2. Remove steering wheel.
3. Disconnect switch multi-connector plugs.
4. Remove tape holding wires to steering column.
5. Loosen switch clamp screw.
6. Remove switch assembly from the steering column, Fig. 3.
7. Drill out the two rivets holding the windshield wiper/washer switch to the mounting plate.
8. Remove the screw, releasing the wiper/washer switch from the mounting plate.
9. Reverse procedure to install.

NOTE: Make certain that the lug on the inner diameter of the switch is positioned in the slot of the outer steering column.

1972-76

1. Remove left-hand and right-hand cowls.
2. Remove two retaining screws.
3. Disconnect switch wiring at snap connectors and remove switch complete with wiring.

INSTRUMENT SERVICE

1977

Speedometer, Replace
1. Remove the fascia left-hand lower panel.
2. Disconnect speedometer cable.
3. Push in and turn the speedometer clockwise 30 degrees until the three studs on the speedometer body are aligned with the cut-aways in the fascia.
4. Remove speedometer.

Oil Pressure Gauge, Replace
1. Remove the fascia left-hand lower panel.
2. Remove the two knurled nuts, washers and bridge piece from behind the gauge.
3. Disconnect the oil pressure pipe.

CAUTION: Be sure to remove the sealing washer for the oil pressure pipe.

4. Remove the gauge.

Coolant Temperature Gauge, Replace
1. Remove speedometer.
2. Pull the bulb holder from the gauge.
3. Remove the knurled nut, washer and bridge piece from behind the gauge.
4. Remove the gauge.

Fuel Gauge, Replace
1. Remove the fascia left-hand lower panel.
2. Remove the knurled nut, spring washer and bridge piece from behind the gauge.
3. Remove the gauge.

1972-76

Speedometer, Replace
1. Remove heater air control knob.
2. Remove the heater air control nut and disengage the control from bracket.
3. Remove recorder reset knob retaining nut.
4. Remove the two knurled retaining nuts and the retaining brackets.

Withdraw the speedometer from the fascia.
5. Disconnect drive cable.

Oil Pressure Gauge, Replace
1. Remove the tachometer by removing the fascia left-hand lower panel and the two knurled retaining nuts, and disconnecting wiring.
2. Remove the ignition warning light and holder.
3. Remove the two retaining nuts.
4. Withdraw the gauge.
5. Disconnect wiring.

Coolant Temperature Gauge, Replace
1. Remove heater control.
2. Remove the knurled retaining nut.
3. Withdraw the gauge.
4. Disconnect wiring.

Fuel Gauge, Replace
1. Remove the knurled retaining nut from the rear of the gauge.
2. Withdraw the gauge.
3. Disconnect wiring.

W/S WIPER MOTOR, REPLACE

1977

Removal
1. Remove wipers.
2. Remove glove box.
3. Disconnect the multi-connector plug from the windshield wiper motor.
4. Remove the outer casing retaining nut from the motor ferrule, Fig. 6.
5. Remove motor retaining strap securing screws.

6. Remove retaining strap, mounting pad and mounting plate.
7. Disconnect ground lead.
8. Remove the motor assembly and cable rack.

Installation

1. Lubricate the rack with a good quality lubricant.
2. Push the cable rack into the outer casing, ensuring the rack engages the transmission box gear teeth.
3. Position the retaining strap, mounting pad and mounting plate.
4. Complete reassembly in reverse of steps 1-5 of removal procedure.

W/S WIPER TRANSMISSION, REPLACE
1977

1. Remove the windshield wiper motor and drive rack.
2. Remove the face level ventilators.
3. Remove the retaining nut, then the spacer and gasket from each gear box.
4. Loosen nuts securing the gear box plates.

5. Release the outer casings.
6. Remove the transmission assemblies.
7. Reverse procedure to install.

WINDSHIELD WIPER ASSEMBLY, REPLACE
1972-76

NOTE: The assembly consists of the motor and transmission.

1. Remove wiper arms.
2. Remove fascia left-hand lower panel cover.
3. Disconnect wiring from the motor terminals.
4. Remove the outer cable retaining nut from the motor housing.
5. Remove two motor securing bolts.
6. Withdraw the motor and transmission assembly with the inner drive cable attached.
7. Reverse procedure to install.

BLOWER MOTOR, REPLACE

1. Disconnect wires from motor.

2. Remove the motor retaining screws and the motor from the heater case.
3. Remove fan retaining clip.
4. Reverse procedure to install.

HEATER CORE, REPLACE

1. Disconnect battery ground cable.
2. Drain the cooling system.
3. Disconnect the heater wires by pulling the multiconnector plug.
4. Release the clip holding engine breather hoses to the heater housing.
5. Disconnect the heater hoses.
6. Disconnect the washer tube and speedometer cable.
7. Remove the screws holding the heater.
8. Detach the washer motor wires from the heater housing.
9. Disconnect the temperature control cable.
10. Disconnect the ducts.
11. Remove the heater.
12. Reverse procedure to install.

NOTE: Feed the temperature control cable through the slot in the bulkhead before installing the unit.

Engine Section

ENGINE, REPLACE

NOTE: The engine and transmission are removed as a unit.

1. Remove the battery and hood. Drain engine oil, transmission lubricant and cooling system.
2. Disconnect the oil pressure gauge sending unit, and top and bottom radiator hoses.
3. Remove radiator.
4. Disconnect alternator and distributor wiring, remove the distributor cap, and disconnect the heater hose.
5. Release heater water valve and disconnect the wiring from the temperature gauge sending unit and the intake manifold heater.
6. Remove the carburetor air cleaner, disconnect the fuel line and throttle cable and the vent pipe from the top of the rocker arm cover.
7. Disconnect the charcoal canister lines, brake servo vacuum line and manifold line from the anti-dieseling control valve.
8. Remove the shift lever case and raise the rubber boot to remove the

shift lever retaining bolts.
9. Remove the shift lever.
10. Beneath the vehicle, disconnect starter motor cables and the wires from backup lights and overdrive switches.
11. Remove the clip holding the wiring harness to the transmission and starter motor flange.
12. Remove the clutch slave cylinder from the transmission case, and disconnect the speedometer cable.
13. Disconnect the exhaust pipe at the catalytic converter or from the front pipe.
14. Disconnect the exhaust pipe from hanger.

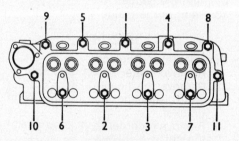

Fig. 1 Cylinder head tightening sequence

15. Remove the propeller shaft and the engine restraint rod.
16. Disconnect four bolts securing the rear mount crossmember to the chassis and lower the transmission to rest on the fixed crossmember.
17. Remove bolts securing the bottom tie bracket to the crossmember. Remove the nuts retaining the rear mounting to the crossmember.
18. Remove the crossmember.
19. Install engine lifting equipment and support transmission with a suitable jack.
20. Remove nuts securing the front engine mounting to the body and tilt the engine and transmission assembly, then remove from vehicle.
21. Reverse procedure to install.

CYLINDER HEAD, REPLACE

1. Drain coolant.
2. Remove thermostat housing and thermostat.
3. Remove carburetor, intake and exhaust manifolds.
4. Disconnect high tension cables and the spark plugs.
5. Disconnect wires from the temper-

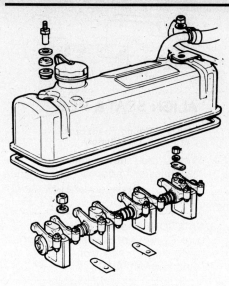

Fig. 2 Rocker arm assembly

ature sending unit and manifold induction unit.

6. Remove the air pump, if equipped.
7. Disconnect the heater water valve and position aside.
8. Remove the hot air shroud backing plate.
9. Remove the rocker assembly.
10. Remove the pushrods.
11. Remove the air manifold rail, but do not remove the check valve.
12. Remove the cylinder head nuts and washers and the special nut fitted to retain the air manifold rail.
13. Remove the cylinder head and gasket.
14. Reverse procedure to install. Use a new head gasket and tighten cylinder head nuts gradually to specification in the sequence, Fig. 1.

NOTE: Install the cylinder head gasket with the end marked "FRONT" to the water pump, and the side of the gasket marked "TOP", upwards.

ROCKER SHAFT, REPLACE

1. Drain the cooling system.
2. Disconnect the purge hose from the rocker cover.
3. Disconnect the vapor line pipe from the carburetor and remove the pipe.
4. Remove rocker cover and gasket.
5. Remove eight nuts holding the rocker shaft brackets to the cylinder head, Fig. 2.
6. Remove the lock washer from the rear rocker shaft bracket.
7. Remove the rocker shaft, and the shims beneath the two center brackets.
8. Reverse the above procedure. Torque rocker shaft bracket nuts 25

ft. lbs. Check and adjust valve clearance.

VALVES ADJUST

1. Remove the rocker cover.
2. Check clearance between valve rocker arms and valve stems, Fig. 3, in the following order:

    No. 1 valve with No. 8 valve fully open.

    No. 3 valve with No. 6 valve fully open.

    No. 5 valve with No. 4 valve fully open.

    No. 2 valve with No. 7 valve fully open.

    No. 8 valve with No. 1 valve fully open.

    No. 6 valve with No. 3 valve fully open.

    No. 4 valve with No. 5 valve fully open.

    No. 7 valve with No. 2 valve fully open.
3. Loosen the locknut.
4. Rotate the screw clockwise to decrease clearance or counterclockwise to increase clearance.
5. Tighten the locknut when correct clearance has been obtained, while holding the screw.

VALVE GUIDES, REPLACE

1. Rest the cylinder head, machined face down, on a clean surface.
2. Drive valve guides downward using a hardened steel punch that is $9/16$ in. (14 mm) in diameter and not less than 4 in. (10 cm) in length. This tool should possess a locating spigot of $5/16$ in. (7.9 mm) diameter machined on one end for a length of 1 in. (2.5 cm) to engage the bore of the guide.
3. Drive new valve guides in from the top of the cylinder head.

NOTE: Valve guides must be inserted with the end having the largest chamfer at the top.

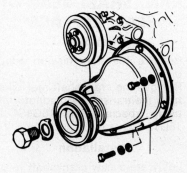

Fig. 4 Timing cover removal

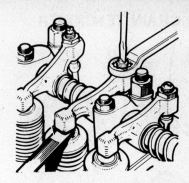

Fig. 3 Adjusting valve clearance

TIMING COVER & SEAL, REPLACE

Removal

1. Remove the radiator.
2. Remove drive belts.
3. Remove the fan and pulley.
4. Using special tool 18G98A, remove the crankshaft pulley retaining bolt.
5. Pull the pulley from the crankshaft.
6. Remove the cover and gasket, Fig. 4, and extract and discard the oil seal from the cover.

Installation

1. Dip a new oil seal in engine oil.
2. Install the new oil seal into the cover using special tools 18G134 and 18G134BD. Ensure the lips of the seal face inward.
3. Clean the cover and front plate joint faces.
4. Ensure the oil thrower is in position with the "F" marking showing.
5. Lubricate the locating faces of special tool 18G1046 with oil and install into the oil seal.
6. Install a new joint washer and position the front cover on the crankshaft.
7. Insert all screws, ensuring the seal is centered and tighten screws evenly.
8. Remove special tool 18G1046.
9. Lubricate the hub of the crankshaft pulley and slide the pulley onto the shaft, engaging the keyway.
10. Install a new lock washer, and tighten and lock the retaining bolt.
11. Complete the reassembly procedure by reversing removal steps 1-3.

TIMING CHAIN, REPLACE

Removal

1. Remove the timing gear cover.
2. Remove the oil thrower.
3. Remove the two screws holding the chain tensioner and pry the tensioner from the seat, Fig. 5.

CHAIN TENSIONER

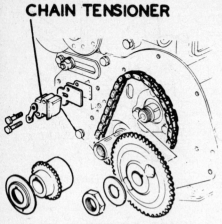

Fig. 5 Timing chain removal

CAUTION: The head is under spring tension, and components may be lost if care is not exercised.

---

4. Remove the head, spring and inner cylinder from the tensioner body.
5. Using a special tool 18G98A, remove the camshaft nut and lock washer.
6. Remove the timing chain and gears.

Installation

1. Rotate the crankshaft so keyways are at top dead center, Fig. 6.
2. Rotate the camshaft so keyway is at two o'clock, Fig. 6.
3. Reinstall the timing gears.
4. Check alignment and gap of the gears with a straight edge.
5. Remove the crankshaft drive gears, and select and fit shims as necessary.
6. Install the crankshaft drive keys.
7. Assemble the timing chain and gears.
8. Install a new camshaft gear lockwasher and a new camshaft nut. Tighten and lock the nut.
9. Reinstall the chain tensioner inner cylinder and spring into the cylinder of the tensioner head so the serrated helical seat in the inner cylinder engages the peg in the head cylinder, Fig. 7.
10. Turn the inner cylinder clockwise against spring tension until the cover serrations in the seat engage

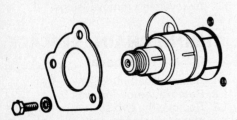

Fig. 8 Camshaft locating plate removal

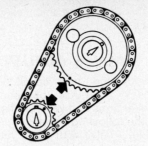

Fig. 6 Valve timing marks

the peg and retain the inner cylinder in the head cylinder.
11. Replace the timing chain tensioner.
12. Install the oil thrower with the face marked "F" towards the front of the engine and install the timing gear cover.

CAMSHAFT, REPLACE

1. Remove the radiator.
2. Remove the tappets.
3. Remove the timing chain and gears.
4. Remove the distributor drive shaft.
5. Remove the oil pump.
6. Remove the camshaft locating plate, Fig. 8.
7. Remove the camshaft.
8. Assemble the camshaft locating plate and chain wheel to the camshaft.
9. Check camshaft end play which should be 0.003 to 0.007 in.
10. Replace the camshaft locating plate if end play is excessive.
11. Remove the chain wheel and locating plate.
12. Reverse procedure to install.

PISTONS AND RINGS

Pistons and rings are available in standard size and .020 and .040 in. oversize.

Main and Rod Bearings

Main and rod bearings are available in standard size and undersizes of .010, .020, .030 and .040 in.

CRANKSHAFT REAR OIL SEAL, REPLACE

Removal

1. Remove the transmission adaptor plate.
2. Remove the crankshaft rear oil seal from the transmission adaptor plate using special tools 18G134 and 18G134CQ.

Installation

1. Lubricate a new crankshaft rear oil seal with SAE 90 Oil.

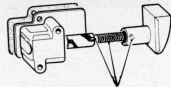

ALIGN SEAT & PEG

Fig. 7 Timing chain tensioner installation

2. Press the new seal into the transmission adaptor plate using special tools 18G134 and 18G134CQ.

CAUTION: The lips of the seal must face the front of the engine and must be flush with the front face of the transmission adaptor plate.

---

3. Replace the transmission adaptor plate.

OIL PAN, REPLACE

1. Drain the oil pan.
2. Remove bolts holding the pan.
3. Remove the pan.
4. Reverse procedure to install. Torque oil pan bolts to 6 ft. lbs.

OIL PUMP, REPLACE

1. Remove the oil pan.
2. Remove the oil strainer and gasket.
3. Remove the oil pump and gasket, Fig. 9.
4. Reverse procedure to install. Torque oil pump bolts to 14 ft. lbs.

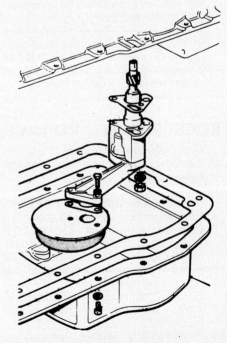

Fig. 9 Oil pump assembly

WATER PUMP, REPLACE

1. Drain the cooling system.
2. Remove the air pump adjusting link, mounting bolt and drive belt, and position the pump aside, if equipped.
3. Remove the alternator.
4. Disconnect the hose from the water pump.
5. Remove the pulleys and spacer.
6. Remove the water pump securing bolts and air pump adjusting link brackets, if equipped.
7. Remove the water pump and gasket.
8. Reverse procedure to install, but note the following:
   a. Use a new gasket.
   b. Tighten water pump securing bolts to 17 ft. lbs. (2.3 kgfm).

FUEL PUMP, REPLACE

1. Disconnect battery ground cable.
2. Open the luggage compartment door.
3. Remove the fuel pump cover. Note the capacitor.
4. Loosen the clip holding the pump in the support.
5. Disconnect the wire from the pump terminal.
6. Under the car, disconnect the intake and outlet pipe unions.
7. Disconnect the breather pipe.
8. Remove the pump.
9. Reverse procedure to install.

Carburetor Section

ADJUSTMENTS

1975-77

To obtain the correct carburetor settings, which consist of idle speed and mixture (CO) percentage, ignition timing, spark plug gap, and valve rocker clearance must be properly set. There must be adequate seals at the oil filler cap-to-valve rocker cover, valve rocker cover-to-cylinder head, side covers-to-cylinder block, oil dipstick-to-cylinder block, carburetor-to-intake manifold, intake manifold-to-cylinder head, all intake manifold taps and the carburetor spindle.

1. Ensure that the throttle control linkage functions properly.
2. Remove the air cleaner.
3. Unscrew the air valve damper, but do not remove.
4. By hand, raise the air valve slowly through full travel and release. The air valve should move freely and smoothly, and return to the carburetor bridge with a distinct "click." If the air valve doesn't move freely, the carburetor should be overhauled.
5. If necessary, add engine oil to the air valve damper to bring it to level.
6. Replace the air cleaner.
7. Warm the engine to normal operating temperature; then drive the vehicle for five minutes.
8. Disconnect and plug the air manifold hose from the air pump.
9. Disconnect the float chamber vent pipe from the carburetor.
10. Connect a tachometer and increase engine speed to 2,500 rpm for 30 seconds.

NOTE: Tuning must begin at once. If adjustment is delayed for three minutes, increase engine speed to 2,500 rpm for 30 seconds once again. As each three minute interval passes before adjustment is done, engine speed should be increased to 2,500 rpm for 30 seconds.

11. Check engine idle speed. Adjust, if necessary.
12. Using an exhaust gas analyzer, determine the CO percentage at idle. If the reading is not within prescribed limits, adjust the fine idle screw.

CAUTION: Turning the screw clockwise enriches the mixture. Turning the screw counter clockwise leans the mixture.

13. Unplug the air manifold hose and refit the hole to the air pump. Increase engine speed to 2,500 rpm for 30 seconds and reset the idle screw to provide the specified idling speed.

1972-74

1. Connect a tachometer.
2. Warm the engine to normal operating temperature.
3. Fill the damper with engine oil to correct level.
4. See that the throttle control works freely.
5. Set engine idle speed to specification as follows:
   a. Remove the air cleaner.
   b. Loosen both clamping bolts in the throttle spindle connections.
   c. Disconnect the jet control interconnection.
   d. Start the engine and adjust the throttle adjusting screws on both carburetors to attain specified idling speed.
   e. Balance the carburetors with a balancing meter by means of the throttle adjusting screws. If the carburetor cannot be balanced, inspect the intake system for air leaks.
6. Determine that the mixture control wire provides $1/16$ in. free play before it starts pulling the jet lever.
7. Pull the mixture control knob until the linkage is just about to move the carburetor jets.
8. Using the balance meter, adjust fast idle for a setting of 1,300-1,400 rpm.

Emission Controls Section

AIR PUMP SERVICE

Air Cleaner Element, Replace

1. Remove cover.
2. Remove and discard element.
3. Clean cover.
4. Reassemble using a new element.

Drive Belt, Adjust

Adjust for a total deflection of 0.5 in. (13 mm) under moderate hand pressure applied at a midway point. If the drive belt requires adjustment, proceed as follows:

1. Loosen the mounting bolt.
2. Loosen the two adjusting link bolts.
3. Shift the air pump to the required position.
4. Tighten bolts.

CAUTION: Do not overtighten.

EXHAUST GAS RECIRCULATION TEST

1. Warm the engine to normal operating temperature.
2. Disconnect the vacuum hose from the EGR valve.
2. Disconnect the vacuum hose from the gulp valve and connect to the EGR valve. Use an additional length of hose to complete the connection.
4. Start the engine, observing the valve spindle. As soon as the engine is started, and as engine speed increases, the spindle will rise, opening the valve.
5. Disconnect the vacuum hose from the valve. The spindle should fall.
6. If the above does not occur, the valve should be removed for cleaning or replacing.

GULP VALVE TEST

1. Remove the air supply hose to the gulp valve at the air pump.
2. Connect a vacuum gauge with "T" connector to the disconnected end of the gulp valve air hose.
3. Run the engine at idle.
4. Seal the open end of the "T" connector. The vacuum gauge should read zero for 15 seconds. If vacuum is registered, replace the gulp valve.
5. With the open end of the "T" connector still sealed, open and close the throttle rapidly. The gauge should register vacuum. Repeat the test several times, temporarily unsealing the connector before each operation of the throttle to destroy the vacuum. If the gauge doesn't register vacuum, replace the gulp valve.

CHECK VALVE TEST

The check valve is a one-way valve, and blowing into it orally from each end should allow passage of air through one end only. If air passes through both ends, replace the valve.

CAUTION: Do not use an air pressure supply to test the check valve.

CATALYTIC CONVERTER

On completion of each 25,000 miles, a warning light on the console will indicate that the catalytic converter should be replaced.

Clutch and Transmission Section

CLUTCH, REPLACE
Removal

1. Remove the transmission.
2. Check the position of the reassembly marks on the clutch and flywheel.
3. Remove the clutch cover securing screws.
4. Remove the clutch cover and driven plate.

Installation

1. Install the clutch driven plate to the flywheel.

CAUTION: The side marked "flywheel side" must face the flywheel.

---

2. Using special tool 18G1027, center the clutch driven plate.
3. Install the clutch cover, aligning the assembly marks on the flywheel and clutch unit.
4. Tighten securing screws.

5. Remove special tool 18G1027.
6. Install the transmission.

MANUAL TRANSMISSION, REPLACE

1. Remove the engine and transmission as an assembly from the car.
2. Remove the starter motor.
3. Remove the bolts holding the transmission to the engine.
4. Separate the transmission from the engine.

Rear Axle and Brakes Section

REAR AXLE SHAFT, BEARING & OIL SEAL, REPLACE
Removal

1. Raise rear of vehicle.
2. Place a support just forward of the rear spring front shackle.
3. Remove the wheel.
4. Remove the axle shaft collar, Fig. 1.
5. Using special tools 18G304 and 18G304A, remove the complete brake drum and driving flange from the axle shaft.
6. Remove the clevis pin to release the handbrake cable from the lever on the backing plate.
7. Disconnect the hydraulic pipe from

the rear wheel brake cylinder. Plug the end of the pipe.
8. Remove the brake backing plate assembly from the rear axle.
9. Remove the bearing cap and oil seal.
10. Remove the oil seal from the hub bearing cap.
11. Remove the axle shaft assembly. Use special tool 18G284.
12. Press the bearing, oil seal collar and bearing spacer off the axle shaft.

Installation

1. Pack the bearing with wheel bearing grease.
2. Press the bearing and spacer onto the axle shaft.
3. Using special tool 18G1067, install the axle shaft.

4. Replace the oil seal collar.
5. Complete installation by reversing removal procedure steps 1-10, bleeding the brake system and topping off the rear axle oil level.

NOTE: The axle shaft nut should be torqued to 150 ft. lbs.

BRAKE ADJUSTMENTS

If brake pedal travel is excessive, adjust rear brakes as follows:
1. Jack up each wheel in turn.
2. Turn the adjuster clockwise until the wheel locks, Fig. 2.
3. Turn the adjuster back until the wheel will rotate without linings rubbing.

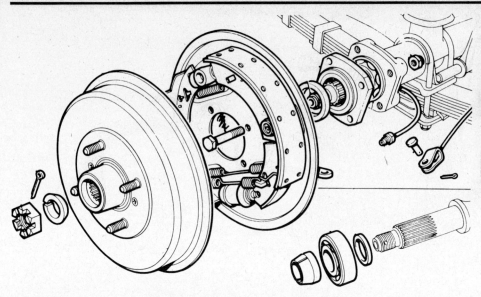

Fig. 1   Axle shaft & bearing removal

Fig. 2   Rear brake adjustment

7. Press the pistons back into bores.
8. Install pads into the caliper with lugs facing forward and the flush edge of pads on top.
9. Complete reassembly.
10. Replenish fluid level.

PARKING BRAKE, ADJUST

1. Adjust rear brakes.
2. Set the parking brake lever on the third ratchet tooth from the fully off position.
3. Check the braking effect on each rear wheel. It should be possible to just rotate the wheels.
4. Beneath the car, hold the hexagon on the parking brake cable and turn the adjuster nut until the desired tension is obtained, Fig. 3.
5. Release the parking brake and ensure the rear wheels rotate freely.

MASTER CYLINDER, REPLACE

1. Siphon the fluid from the reservoir, or attach a bleed hose to front and rear brake bleed screws. Open each screw and pump the brake pedal until the reservoir is empty.
2. Disconnect the pressure fail switch wire.
3. Disconnect primary and secondary fluid lines. Plug ports and ends of the lines.
4. Remove nuts and washers holding the master cylinder to the power assist servo.
5. Remove the master cylinder.
6. Reinstall by reversing the procedure.
7. Bleed the hydraulic system.

FRONT DISC BRAKE SERVICE

Caliper, Replace

1. Remove the wheel.

2. Disconnect the hydraulic line and plug end.
3. Knock back and lock plate tabs and remove the two retaining bolts.
4. Remove the caliper.
5. Reverse the procedure to reinstall, but install a new lock plate and torque caliper retaining bolts to 43 ft. lbs.

Brake Pads, Replace

1. Remove the wheel.
2. Open a front bleed screw and reduce fluid level in the primary reservoir 1 in. by pumping the brake pedal.
3. Tighten the bleed screw.
4. Remove the split pins.
5. Remove the retaining springs.
6. Remove the brake pads.

NOTE: Minimum pad thickness: $1/16$ in. (1.6 mm)

PARKING BRAKE ADJUSTERS

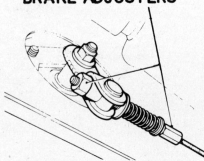

Fig. 3   Parking brake adjustment

Caliper, Disassembly

1. Remove pads, Fig. 4.
2. Release the caliper, but do not disconnect the hydraulic hose.
3. Support the caliper to prevent strain on the hose.
4. Clean the surface of the caliper.
5. Using special tool 18G590, clamp the rim-half piston in place.
6. Put a container under the caliper to catch displaced brake fluid.

NOTE: The cutaway portion of the piston is toward the mounting.

7. Depress the brake pedal to force the mounting-half piston almost from its bore.
8. Extract the piston from the bore by hand.

NOTE: If the piston seizes, replace the caliper. Do not use heavy pedal pressure in an attempt to free a seized piston.

9. Pry the wipe seal and retainer from the mouth of the bore and the fluid seal from the bore. Use a blunt instrument. Be careful not to damage the bore.

CAUTION: Do not separate the two halves of the caliper.

Caliper, Assembly

1. Coat a new fluid seal with brake fluid and install into groove in the bore, Fig. 4.
2. Coat the wiper seal with brake fluid and install into the retainer.
3. Install the retainer, seal side for-

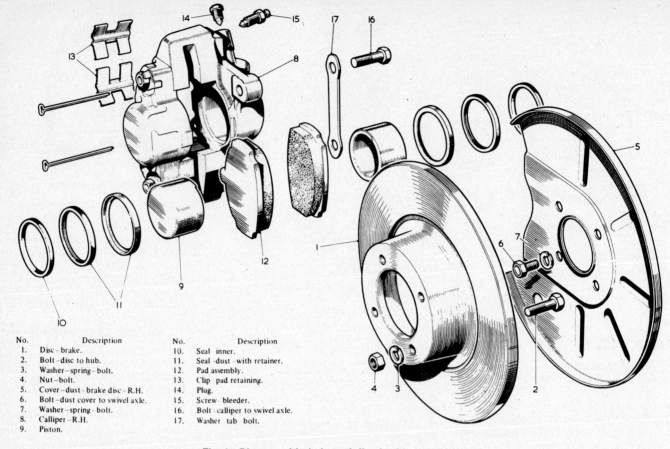

Fig. 4   Disassembled view of disc brake assembly

No.	Description	No.	Description
1.	Disc – brake.	10.	Seal inner.
2.	Bolt – disc to hub.	11.	Seal – dust – with retainer.
3.	Washer – spring – bolt.	12.	Pad assembly.
4.	Nut – bolt.	13.	Clip –pad retaining.
5.	Cover – dust – brake disc – R.H.	14.	Plug.
6.	Bolt – dust cover to swivel axle.	15.	Screw – bleeder.
7.	Washer – spring – bolt.	16.	Bolt – calliper to swivel axle.
8.	Calliper – R.H.	17.	Washer – tab – bolt.
9.	Piston.		

ward, in the bore and press into place. Use tool 18G590.
4. Loosen the bleed screw.
5. Lubricate the piston with brake fluid and insert squarely into the bore so

the cutaway part is facing toward the retaining bolt holes.
6. Clamp the mounting-half piston in place.

NOTE: At this time, service the rim-

half piston as the mounting-half piston.

7. Install the rim-half piston.
8. Replace the caliper and pads.
9. Bleed the brake system.

Rear Suspension Section

SHOCK ABSORBERS, REPLACE

1. Raise vehicle.
2. Support the body just forward of the rear spring shackle.
3. Remove the wheel.
4. Disconnect the shock absorber arm from the link assembly, Fig. 1.
5. Remove the nuts and bolts holding the shock absorber to the body.
6. Remove the shock absorber.
7. Reverse the procedure to install, but note the following:
   a. Tighten shock retaining bolts to 55-60 ft. lbs. (7.6-8.3 kgfm).
   b. Top off the shock with Armstrong Super (thin) shock absorber fluid No. 624 or equivalent.

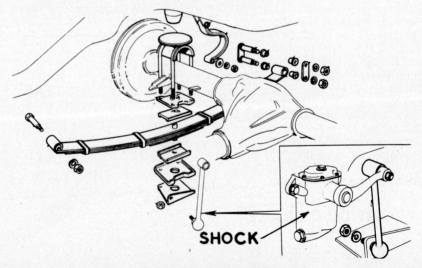

SHOCK

Fig. 1   Rear spring & shock absorber removal

SPRINGS, REPLACE

1. Raise vehicle.
2. Support the body forward of the rear spring front shackle.
3. Remove the wheel.
4. Support the rear axle.
5. Release the shock absorber link from the "U" bolt base plate, Fig. 1.
6. Release the rebound strap from the axle.
7. Remove the "U" bolt nuts and the shock absorber link bracket, lower locating plate and lower seating pad.
8. Remove "U" bolts, bump rubber pedestal assembly, upper seating pad and upper locating plate.
9. Release the shackle plate and rubber bushings.
10. Lower the rear of the spring.
11. Remove the front shackle pin and nut.
12. Remove the spring.
13. Reverse procedure to install.

CAUTION: Do not tighten the spring "U" bolts fully until the vehicle has been lowered to the ground and weight is applied to springs.

Front Suspension and Steering Section

WHEEL ALIGNMENT
Checking

1. The car must be at curb unladened weight.
2. Tires must be inflated properly and positioned straight.
3. If a basebar-type gauge is used, take a measurement in front of and behind the wheel center at the rim edge. Move the car forward half a wheel revolution. Repeat measurements at the same points.
4. If an optical gauge is used, take three readings, each at 120° of wheel rim movement. Calculate the average reading.

Adjusting

1. Loosen locknuts on both tie rods.
2. Loosen the clip holding the rubber boot to the tie rod.
3. Rotate each tie rod by an equal amount. Both tie rods have right-hand threads.

CAUTION: Tie rods must be adjusted to exactly equal lengths.

4. Tighten tie rod locknuts and boot clips.
5. Recheck wheel alignment.

WHEEL BEARINGS, ADJUST

1. After servicing bearings, assemble the hub without shims and mount on the axle.
2. Install the retaining washer and nut, tightening the nut until bearings bind.
3. Remove nut and washer.
4. Pull out roller race of the outer bearing.
5. Insert sufficient shims to produce an excessive end play. Note the thickness of the shims.
6. Install the bearing, washer and nut. Tighten the nut.
7. Using a dial indicator, measure the end play of the bearing.
8. Remove the nut, washer and outer bearing. Reduce the number of shims to produce end play of .002-.004 in.

NOTE: Shims are available in thicknesses of 0.003 in. (0.076 mm), 0.005 in. (0.127 mm) and 0.010 in. (0.254 mm).

9. Replace bearing washer and nut.
10. Torque nut to 40-70 ft. lbs.

CAUTION: The nut can be torqued within this range to align a slot in the nut with the hole in the axle so a new cotter pin can be installed.

LOWER SUSPENSION ARMS, REPLACE

1. Raise and support the vehicle.
2. Remove the wheel.
3. Remove the spring pan and spring.
4. Remove the cotter pin, castellated nut and spring washer from the swivel pin bottom link bolt and also, where the lower arms are attached to the pivot shaft, Figs. 1 and 2
5. Remove the front arm.
6. Remove the bolt and lower the rear arm.
7. Replace worn bushings.
8. Reverse procedure to install and note the following:
   a. Tighten the slotted nuts on the pivot shaft to just compress bushings, and install and tighten cotter pins with the weight of the vehicle on the suspension.
   b. Observe the following torque settings:
      1. Lower arm nuts (align to next cotter pin hole)—28 ft. lbs. (3.9 kgfm).
      2. Anti-roll bar link nut—60 ft. lbs. (8.3 kgfm).
   c. Grease the swivel pin pivot bearing.

SHOCK ABSORBERS, REPLACE
Removal

1. Raise and support vehicle.
2. Remove the wheel.
3. Jack up the spring pan and take up spring pressure until the damper arms are clear of the rebound rubbers.
4. Remove the cotter pin and slotted nut from the fulcrum pin.
5. Loosen the clamp bolt and center bolt of the damper arm, Figs. 1 and 2.
6. Remove the fulcrum pin, pull the damper arms apart and swing the trunnion aside.
7. Reverse removal procedure steps 1-6 to install, torquing fasteners to the following specifications:
   a. Swivel pin nut (align to next cotter pin hole), 60 ft. lbs.
   b. Damper to crossmember bolts, 44 ft. lbs.
8. Grease the swivel pin bearings.

Installation

1. Hold the damper vertically in a vise.
2. Remove the filler plug.
3. Work the damper arms several times through the full stroke. Travel must be firm with no free movement, and all air must be expelled.
4. Top off the fluid level.
5. Install the filler plug.
6. Check that trunnion bushings are correctly fitted.
7. Reverse removal procedure steps 1-6 to install, torquing fasteners to the following specifications:
   a. Swivel pin nut (align to next cotter pin hole), 60 ft. lbs.
   b. Damper to crossmember bolts, 44 ft. lbs.
8. Grease the swivel pin bearings.

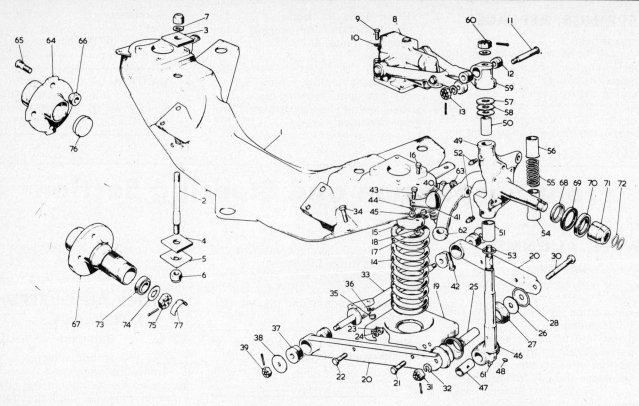

1. Cross-member.
2. Bolt—cross-member to body.
3. Pad—mounting—upper (rubber).
4. Pad—mounting—lower (rubber).
5. Plate—clamp.
6. Nut—mounting bolt.
7. Washer—plain—nut.
8. Absorber—shock.
9. Screw—shock absorber to cross-member.
10. Washer—screw—spring.
11. Pin—fulcrum—top link to shock absorber arm.
12. Bearing—link.
13. Nut fulcrum pin.
14. Spring—coil.
15. Spigot—spring.
16. Screw—spigot to cross-member.
17. Nut—screw.
18. Washer—spring—nut.
19. Pan assembly—spring.
20. Wishbone assembly—bottom.
21. Screw—spring pan to wishbone.
22. Screw—spring pan to wishbone.
23. Nut-screw.
24. Washer—spring—nut.
25. Tube—distance—link.
26. Washer—thrust—link.

27. Seal—link.
28. Support—link seal.
29. Nut—wishbone pivot.
30. Bolt—wishbone to link.
31. Nut—bolt.
32. Washer—spring—nut.
33. Pivot—wishbone.
34. Bolt—pivot to member.
35. Nut—bolt.
36. Washer—spring—nut.
37. Bush—wishbone.
38. Washer—wishbone pivot.
39. Nut—wishbone pivot.
40. Buffer—rebound.
41. Distance piece
42. Bolt—rebound buffer to cross-member.
43. Screw—rebound buffer to cross-member
44. Washer—spring.
45. Nut.
46. Pin-swivel.
47. Bush—swivel pin.
48. Screw—grub—swivel pin.
49. Axle assembly—swivel—R.H.
50. Bush—swivel—top.
51. Bush—swivel—bottom.
52. Lubricator—swivel bush.

53. Ring—swivel axle pin (cork)
54. Tube—dust excluder—bottom.
55. Spring—dust excluder.
56. Tube—dust excluder—top.
57. Washer—thrust.
58. Washer—floating thrust—.052 to .057 in. (1.32 to 1.44 mm.).
59. Trunnion—suspension link.
60. Nut—swivel axle pin.
61. Lubricator—swivel pin.
62. Lever—steering—R.H.
63. Bolt—steering lever to swivel axle.
64. Hub assembly.
65. Stud—wheel.
66. Nut—wheel stud.
67. Hub assembly — R.H.
68. Collar—oil seal.
69. Seal—oil.
70. Bearing for hub—inner.
71. Spacer—bearing.
72. Shim—.003 in. (.76mm.).
73. Bearing—hub—outer
74. Washer—bearing retaining.
75. Nut—bearing retaining.
76. Cap.
77. Cup—grease-retaining.

Fig. 1   Exploded view of front suspension. 1972-76 models

FRONT SPRINGS, REPLACE

1. Raise and support vehicle.
2. Install spring compressor tool 18G693 under the seat pan and take up spring pressure.
3. Disconnect the anti-roll bar link.
4. Remove the three screws holding the seat pan to the lower arms.

NOTE: The short screw is fitted to the outer end of the rear arm.

5. Remove the spring compressor.
6. Remove the seat pan and spring, Figs. 1 and 2
7. Reverse procedure to install.

RACK & PINION STEERING GEAR, REPLACE
Removal

1. Raise and support vehicle and remove both front wheels.

2. Remove each ball-pin locknut.
3. Disconnect ball joints from steering levers, using special tool 18G1063.
4. Remove pinch bolt holding the universal joint to the pinion.
5. Remove the bolts holding the rack to the crossmember.

NOTE: The front bolts are fitted with the nuts at the top.

6. Remove the rack assembly forward and down from the vehicle.

MGB

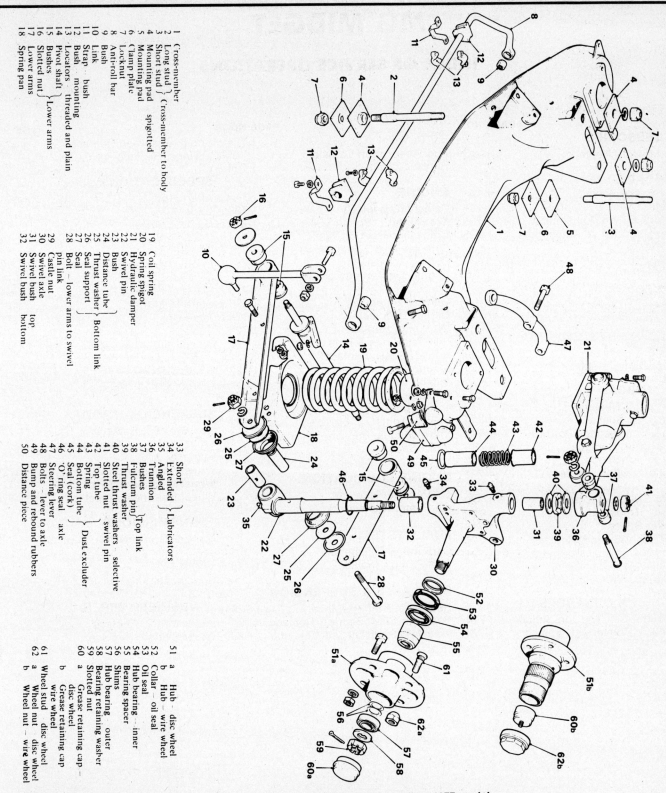

1	Cross-member
2	Long stud ⎫ Cross-member to body
3	Short stud ⎭
4	Mounting stud
5	Mounting pad spigotted
6	Clamp plate
7	Locknut
8	Anti-roll bar
9	Bush
10	Link
11	Strap — bush
12	Bush — mounting
13	Locators — threaded and plain
14	Pivot shaft
15	Bushes ⎫ Lower arms
16	Slotted nut ⎭
17	Lower arms
18	Spring pan
19	Coil spring
20	Spring spigot
21	Hydraulic damper
22	Swivel pin
23	Bush
24	Distance tube
25	Seal support ⎫ Bottom link
26	Seal ⎭
27	Thrust washer ⎭
28	Bolt — lower arms to swivel
29	Pivot link
30	Castle nut
31	Swivel axle
32	Swivel bush top
33	Short ⎫ Extended ⎫
34	Extended ⎭ Lubricators
35	Angled ⎭
36	Trunnion
37	Bushes ⎫ Top link
38	Fulcrum pin ⎭
39	Thrust washer
40	Steel thrust washers — selective
41	Slotted nut ⎫ swivel pin
42	Top tube
43	Spring
44	Bottom tube ⎭
45	Seal (cork) ⎫ Dust excluder
46	'O' ring seal ⎭
47	Steering lever axle
48	Bolts — lever to axle
49	Bump and rebound rubbers
50	Distance piece
51	a Hub — disc wheel
	b Hub — wire wheel
52	Oil seal
53	Collar — oil seal
54	Hub bearing — inner
55	Bearing spacer
56	Shims
57	Hub bearing — outer
58	Bearing retaining washer
59	Slotted nut
60	a Grease retaining cap — disc wheel
	b Grease retaining cap — wire wheel
61	Wheel stud disc wheel
62	a Wheel nut — disc wheel
	b Wheel nut — wire wheel

Fig. 2 Exploded view of front suspension. 1977 models

Installation

CAUTION: A new rack assembly must be aligned with the column using special gauges 18G1140.

1. Center the rack and set the steering wheel in a straight-ahead position.
2. Place the pinion in the universal joint.
3. Install the rack assembly.
4. Observe the following torque specifications:

a. Rack to crossmember locknuts and bolts, 30 ft. lbs.
b. Universal joint locknuts, 21 ft. lbs.
c. Ball joint locknuts, 34 ft. lbs.

5. Check and adjust front wheel alignment.

MG MIDGET

INDEX OF SERVICE OPERATIONS

GENERAL ENGINE SPECIFICATIONS

Year	Engine	Car-buretor	Bore & Stroke	Piston Displacement Cubic Inches	Com-pres-sion Ratio	Net H.P. @ R.P.M.
1972-77	4—91	Stromberg	2.90 x 3.44	91	7.5:1	—

—Not Available

TUNE UP SPECIFICATIONS

▲Before removing wires from distributor cap, determine location of the No. 1 wire in cap, as distributor position may have been altered from that shown at the end of this chart.

Year	Engine	Spark Plug		Distributor		Ignition Timing			Hot Idle Speed
		Type	Gap	Point Gap Inch	Dwell Angle Deg.	Firing order ▲	Timing B.T.D.C.	Mark Location	
1972-77	91 cu. in.	N12Y	.025	—	—	A	10	B	700—900

—Not Available

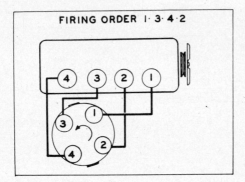

FIRING ORDER 1·3·4·2

Fig. A

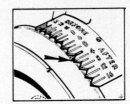

Fig. B

DISTRIBUTOR SPECIFICATIONS

★If unit is checked on vehicle, double the R.P.M. and degrees to get crankshaft figures.

Distributor Part No.	Centrifugal Advance Degrees @ R.P.M. of Distributor			Vacuum Advance	
	Advance Starts	Intermediate Advance	Full Advance	Inches of Vacuum to Start Plunger	Max. Adv. Dist. Deg. @ Vacuum
Lucas 45/DE4	½—3½ @ 600	3½—6½ @ 750 6½—8½ @ 1300	7½—9½ @ 1650	5	11 @ 10

MG MIDGET

ALTERNATOR SPECIFICATIONS

Year	Alternator		Regulator	
	Model	Output @ 14 Volts 6000 RPM Amps	Model	Control Setting Volts @ R.P.M.
1972-77	Lucas 16 ACR	34	14 TR	14—14.4 @ 2.609

STARTER MOTOR SPECIFICATIONS

Year	Model	Brush Spring Tension (ounces)	No Load Test		Torque Test	
			Amps.	R.P.M.	Amps.	Torque Ft. Lbs.
1972-77	Lucas M35J	28	260—275	1000	350—375	7

PISTON PINS, RINGS, CRANKSHAFT & BEARINGS

Year	Model	Piston Clearance Bottom of Skirt ①	Ring End Gap ①		Wristpin Diameter	Rod Bearings		Main Bearings		
			Comp.	Oil		Shaft Diameter	Bearing Clearance	Shaft Diameter	Bearing Clearance	Shaft End Play
1972-77	Midget	.002—.003	.012	.015	.8124	1.8750—1.8755	—	2.3115—2.3120	.0005—.0020	.004—.008

—Not Available
① —At right angles to the wrist pin.

ENGINE TIGHTENING SPECIFICATIONS

*Torque specifications are for clean & lightly lubricated threads only. Dry dirty threads produce increased friction which prevents accurate measurement of tightness.

Year	Engine	Spark Plug Ft. Lbs.	Cylinder Head Bolts Ft. Lbs.	Intake Manifold Ft. Lbs.	Camshaft Cap Bolts Ft. Lbs.	Camshaft Cover Bolts Ft. Lbs.	Connecting Rod Cap Bolts Ft. Lbs.	Main Bearing Cap Bolts Ft. Lbs.	Flywheel to Crank-shaft Ft. Lbs.
1972-77	4—91	—	46	25	—	2	①	65	②

—Not Available.
① —Phosphated, 50; dye colored, 46.
② —Cadmium plated, 40; Parkarised, 45.

VALVE SPECIFICATIONS

Year	Model	Valve Int.	Lash Exh.	Valve Seat	Angles Face	Valve Spring Installed Height	Stem Diameter		Stem Clearance	
							Intake	Exhaust	Intake	Exhaust
1972-77	Midget	.010c	.010c	45	—	1.342	.3107—.3113	.3100—.3105	①	①

—Not Available

① —Noncatalyst engine, .0013—.0017; Catalyst, .0297—.0303.

WHEEL ALIGNMENT SPECIFICATIONS

Year	Model	Caster Angle, Degrees	Camber Angle, Degrees	Toe-in inch
1972-77	Midget	+3	+¾	0—⅛

COOLING SYSTEM CAPACITY

Year	Cooling Capacity Qts.		Radiator Cap Relief Pressure, Lbs.		Thermo Opening Temp.	Fuel Tank Gals.	① Engine Oil Refill Pints	Transmission Oil		Axle Oil Pints
	Without Heater	With Heater	With A/C	No A/C				4 Speed Pints	Overdrive Pints	
1972-77	11.4	11.4	15	15	190	7.7	9.6	1.75	—	2.1

—Not Available

① —Filter Included

Electrical Section

CAUTION: All work should be done with the battery disconnected.

DISTRIBUTOR, REPLACE

1. Detach heater intake hose.
2. Remove distributor cap.
3. Disconnect three low tension distributor leads and vacuum advance line.
4. Turn engine until the timing notches on the crankshaft pulley are in line with the 10° BTDC point on timing indicator. The distributor rotor arm should now be in the firing position for No. 1 spark plug.
5. Release distributor clamp and remove distributor.
6. Reverse procedure to install.

ALTERNATOR, REPLACE

1. Disconnect wire connector from alternator.
2. Remove hardware holding alternator to adjusting link and air pump mounting bracket.
3. Remove drive belt.
4. Loosen bolt holding air pump bracket to engine mounting plate.
5. Loosen bolt holding air pump to air pump mounting bracket.
6. Remove alternator.
7. Reverse procedure to install.

ALTERNATOR TESTING

NOTE: To avoid misleading results, the unit should be at normal operating temperature.

1. Check drive belt adjustment and remove the multi-socket connectors.
2. Remove the molded cover and connect meters.

CAUTION: Do not reverse polarity. Keep the variable resistor connected no longer than necessary to make the test.

3. Run the engine, gradually increasing speed. At 1,500 alternator rpm (640 engine rpm), the alternator test light should be out.
4. Hold alternator speed at 6,000 rpm (engine speed of 2,560 rpm) and adjust the variable resistor so the

Fig. 1 Ignition switch removal

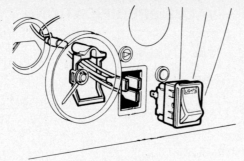

Fig. 2 Headlight switch removal

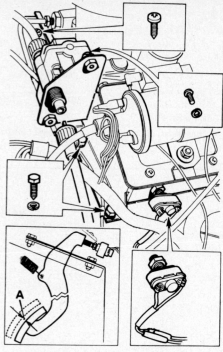

Fig. 3 Stop light switch removal

voltmeter reads 14 volts. The ammeter reading should now be about equal to a nominal output of 28 amps. If not, overhaul or replace the alternator.

Regulator Test

1. Reconnect test equipment.
2. Repeat test procedures above.
3. Holding alternator speed at 6,000 rpm, the voltmeter should be steady at 14.0-14.4 volts. If not, the regulator should be replaced.

STARTER MOTOR, REPLACE

1. Remove air vent hose and disconnect intake line from fuel pump.
2. Remove fuel pump.
3. Remove starter lead.
4. Remove starter motor.

IGNITION & WINDSHIELD WASHER/WIPER SWITCH, REPLACE

1. Remove heater air intake hose.
2. Remove steering column pinion bolt, bolts holding toe-plate fixing ring to steering column, and bolts holding column upper part to body bracket.
3. Pull steering column back enough for switch cowl to clear the fascia.
4. Remove the two cowls.
5. Detach windshield wiper/washer switch from bracket on column.
6. Disconnect wiring plug and remove ignition switch, Fig. 1.

LIGHT SWITCH, REPLACE

1. Remove bulb from switch retainer.
2. Remove retainer from switch.
3. Withdraw switch and disconnect leads, Fig. 2.

STOPLIGHT SWITCH, REPLACE

1. Disconnect transmission drive cable from maintenance service interval counter, if equipped.
2. Remove counter.
3. Loosen screws holding brake pedal cover (engine compartment).
4. Disconnect stoplight switch wire and remove switch locknut, Fig. 3.
5. Lift off pedal cover assembly and unscrew switch from cover.
6. Reverse steps 1 through 5 to install, but note following:
   a. Screw switch in until there is a brake pedal free movement of 1/8 in.
   b. Recheck this measurement after tightening the brake pedal cover holding screws.

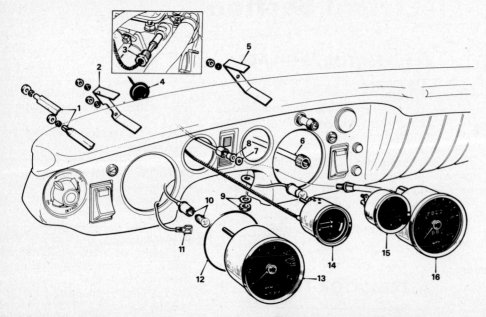

1   Tachometer and speedometer clamps.
2   Oil pressure and water temperature gauge bridge piece.
3   Temperature transmitter adaptor.
4   Grommet.
5   Fuel gauge bridge piece.
6   Speedometer cable.
7   Sealing washer for oil pressure pipe.
8   Oil pressure pipe.
9   Knurled nut and flat washer securing the speedometer remote control.
10 Bulb and bulb holder.
11 Wiring.
12 Sealing ring.
13 Tachometer.
14 Oil pressure and water temperature gauge.
15 Fuel gauge.
16 Speedometer.

Fig. 4 Instrument cluster

INSTRUMENT CLUSTER
Oil Pressure & Water Temperature Gauge, Replace

1. Drain cooling system.
2. Remove temperature sending unit from thermostat and water pump housing.
3. Release capillary tube from rocker cover.
4. Disconnect oil pressure line from oil switch connector and brake pedal cover.
5. Release center console.
6. Remove gauge retaining hardware, Fig. 4.
7. Withdraw gauge partially and unscrew oil line nut.

NOTE: Do not lose oil pressure line sealing washer.

8. Remove gauge and capillary tube.

Fuel Gauge, Replace

1. Disconnect speedometer cable from speedometer.
2. Release center console.
3. Remove gauge retaining hardware, Fig. 4.
4. Withdraw gauge partially and remove remaining retaining pieces.
5. Remove gauge.

Speedometer, Replace

1. Disconnect speedometer cable from speedometer.
2. Release center console.
3. Remove retaining hardware, Fig. 4.
4. Remove speedometer.

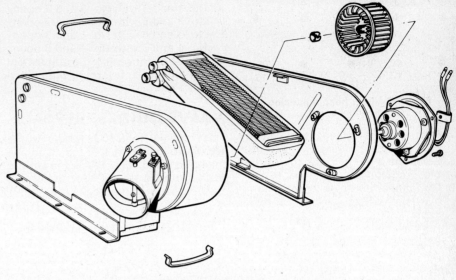

Fig. 5   Disassembled view of heater unit

Tachometer, Replace

1. Remove tachometer retaining hardware.
2. Remove tachometer, Fig. 4.

WINDSHIELD WIPER MOTOR, REPLACE

1. Remove wiper arms and blades.
2. Release drive tube at motor.
3. Disconnect wiring plug from motor.
4. Release motor clamp band.
5. Remove motor.

HEATER UNIT, REPLACE

1. Remove battery and battery tray.
2. Drain cooling system.
3. Disconnect blower motor wires.
4. Release heater control cables from bracket on heater air intake tube.
5. Disconnect air vent hose from heater air intake tube.
6. Remove heater hoses from heater.
7. Remove six screws holding heater.
8. Remove heater.
9. Separate heater unit and remove heater core and blower motor, Fig. 5.

Engine Section

ENGINE, REPLACE

The engine is removed with the transmission.
1. Disconnect the battery.
2. Remove hood.
3. Remove the radiator, air cleaner, and left and right side engine side covers.
4. Disconnect emission lines, and disconnect the exhaust pipe from the exhaust manifold if not equipped with catalytic converter. If equipped with a catalytic converter, disconnect the converter from the exhaust manifold.
5. Disconnect the heater hoses, throttle cable, mixture control cable (except for catalytic converter equipped models with automatic choke), and electrical leads to alternator, distributor, temperature sending unit and oil pressure switch.
6. Disconnect the fuel line at the pump, starter motor cable, and coil high tension lead.
7. Disconnect exhaust pipe from bracket on the transmission.
8. Disconnect the engine restraint cable and remove the transmission tunnel cover.
9. Scribe a reference mark between propeller shaft and transmission, then disconnect the shaft.
10. Disconnect speedometer cable from the transmission, and the two leads to the transmission reverse light switch or three leads to the overdrive if used.
11. Remove clutch slave cylinder and two nuts holding the transmission rubber mounting to the mounting bracket.
12. Attach lifting equipment and raise the engine sufficiently to take up the weight.
13. Remove the fasteners holding the engine to the chassis.
14. Remove the engine and transmission assembly.
15. Reverse procedure to install.

CYLINDER HEAD, REPLACE

1. Disconnect battery ground cable.
2. Drain cooling system.
3. Disconnect spark plug leads.
4. Disconnect the hose from the diverter and check valve at the check valve, and remove the vacuum line to the diverter and check valve from the manifold.
5. Disconnect vacuum line to the distributor from the manifold.
6. Loosen the alternator drive belt.

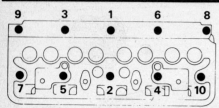

Fig. 1 Cylinder head tightening sequence

7. Remove the air cleaner and disconnect the heater hoses.
8. Disconnect the mixture control cable, if equipped.
9. Disconnect emission and evaporative control hoses, and the throttle cable.
10. Remove the rocker cover.
11. Disconnect the heater return line at the water pump housing union.
12. Remove the heat shield between the carburetor and air cleaner.
13. Disconnect the exhaust pipe or catalytic converter from the exhaust manifold.
14. Remove the three bolts holding the water pump housing to the cylinder head.
15. Remove the rocker shaft assembly.
16. Remove the push rods.
17. Loosen the cylinder head nuts in reverse sequence, Fig. 1.
18. Remove the rear lifting eye.
19. Disconnect the fuel line from the pump.
20. Lift off the cylinder head and manifolds.
21. Reverse the procedure to install, tightening cylinder head nuts in the order shown in Fig. 1.

ROCKER SHAFT, REPLACE

1. Remove rocker cover.
2. Remove cotter pin from front of shaft.
3. Slide off rockers, lifters, springs and spacers, noting the order of removal.
4. Remove the screw holding the rear lifter to the shaft.
5. Remove the rear lifter and shaft, Fig. 2.
6. Reverse this procedure to install the shaft.

VALVES, ADJUST

1. Disconnect the battery ground cable, and remove the spark plugs and rocker cover.
2. Check clearance between the rocker pad and valve tip and adjust to specifications in the following sequence:

NOTE: Count valves from the front of the engine.

No. 1 and 3 with No. 6 and 8 open
No. 2 and 5 with No. 4 and 7 open
No. 6 and 8 with No. 1 and 3 open
No. 4 and 7 with No. 2 and 5 open
3. Adjust by loosening the adjustment pin locknut and turning the adjustment pin.

VALVE GUIDES, REPLACE

Use special tool 60A. Assemble the new valve guide in the tool with the chamfered end first. Place the tool in position and drive the new guide into place while the old guide is removed.

TIMING CHAIN COVER, REPLACE

1. Remove radiator.
2. Remove air pump and alternator, then the mounting brackets.
3. Remove fan blades and crankshaft pulley.
4. Remove the timing cover fasteners.
5. Remove the timing cover and gasket.
6. Reverse procedure to install. Installation of the cover can be facilitated by using a length of welding rod bent at a right angle to hold the chain tensioner away from the chain.

TIMING CHAIN, REPLACE

1. Disconnect battery ground cable and remove the timing chain cover and oil thrower.
2. Turn the crankshaft until marks "A" are in line with scribe mark "C." Check that punch marks "B" correspond and the crankshaft keyway is at 12 o'clock.

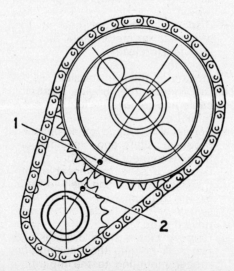

Fig. 3 Valve timing marks

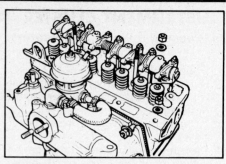

Fig. 2 Rocker arm assembly

3. Bend back the lock tab and remove the two bolts holding the camshaft sprocket to the camshaft.
4. Being careful not to move the camshaft or crankshaft, remove both sprockets with the timing chain.
5. Remove the crankshaft drive key.
6. Temporarily install the sprockets.
7. Check sprocket alignment by placing a straight edge across both sprockets. Correct misalignment by fitting shims behind the crankshaft sprocket.
8. Remove the sprockets and install the crankshaft drive key.
9. Install the chain on the sprockets, then install sprockets, ensuring that all alignment marks are aligned (1 and 2), Fig. 3.
10. Tighten the camshaft sprocket and check timing chain wear by placing a straight edge along the chain to measure slack. If movement at the midpoint is greater than ⅜ inch, replace the chain.
11. Reverse procedure to assemble.

CAMSHAFT, REPLACE

1. Disconnect battery ground cable and drain cooling system.
2. Remove the radiator, cylinder head, water pump housing and fan, alternator, air pump, crankshaft pulley timing cover, timing chain and sprockets, and camshaft keeper plate.
3. Remove the cam followers.
4. Remove the distributor driveshaft and gear, and fuel pump.
5. Remove the camshaft.
6. Reverse procedure to install.

CRANKSHAFT REAR OIL SEAL, REPLACE

Removal

1. Remove the transmission.
2. Remove the rear adaptor plate.
3. Remove the two rear center oil pan bolts.
4. Remove the oil seal housing from the crankcase, complete with the seal.

CAUTION: Do not damage the oil pan gasket.

5. Press out the seal, taking care not to distort the housing, Fig. 4.

Installation

1. Clean all mating surfaces.
2. Place the oil seal housing on a flat surface, machine side up, and lubricate the outside diameter of a new seal with grease, Fig. 4.
3. With the seal's lip side facing up, press the seal in place and wipe off excess grease.
4. Apply sealing compound to the crankcase and oil seal housing mating surfaces and install a new gasket.
5. Lubricate the oil seal inner diameter and the crankshaft with clean engine oil, and install the oil seal and housing over the crankshaft.
6. Secure the housing to the crankshaft.

NOTE: The top bolt has a copper washer under the head to prevent oil seepage.

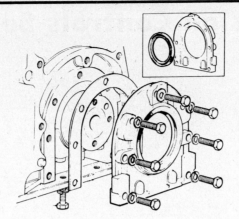

Fig. 4   Crankshaft rear oil seal removal

7. Reverse removal procedure to assemble.

OIL PAN, REPLACE

1. Drain oil.
2. Remove all bolts and washers (16) holding the pan.
3. Remove the pan.
4. Reverse procedure to install.

OIL PUMP, REPLACE

1. Drain oil.
2. Remove the oil pan.
3. Loosen the three bolts holding the pump to the crankcase.
4. Hold the pump cover and remove the pump.
5. Reverse procedure to install. Ensure the pump spindle engages firmly into the distributor drive gear shaft. Torque bolts to 7-9 ft. lbs.

WATER PUMP, REPLACE

1. Disconnect battery ground cable.
2. Remove water pump housing assembly and fan blades.
3. Remove the fasteners holding the water pump to the water pump housing.
4. Remove the water pump and viscous coupling. Separate the two.
5. Reverse procedure to install.

FUEL PUMP, REPLACE

1. Disconnect fuel lines at the pump.
2. Remove the pump from the cylinder block.
3. Remove and discard the gasket.
4. Reverse procedure to install.

Carburetor Section

CARBURETOR ADJUSTMENTS

Idle Speed

Adjust by turning the throttle adjusting screw (3), Fig. 1. Refer to "Tune-Up Specification" chart for idle speed.

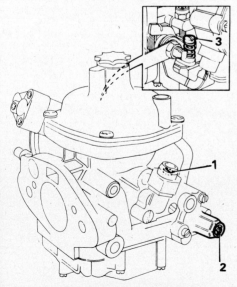

Fig. 1   Carburetor adjustments

Idle Mixture

1. A minimum adjustment can be made with the fine idle CO screw, (1) Fig. 1.
2. Remove the piston damper.
3. Insert tool S353 into the dashpot until outer tool engages in air valve and inner tool engages hexagon in needle adjuster plug, Fig. 2.
4. Turn the tool clockwise to richen the mixture or counterclockwise to lean.
5. Top off the damper and recheck the CO reading.

CAUTION: Be sure to engage the tool properly to avoid damage to the diaphragm.

Deceleration & Bypass Valve

1. Remove vacuum line from distributor and plug line.
2. The valve is operating properly if idle speed increases to about 1,500 rpm. The valve requires adjusting if idle speed increases to 2,000-2,500 rpm.
3. If adjustment is required, plug end of vacuum line.
4. Turn the bypass valve screw clockwise, (2) Fig. 1, until engine speed increases rapidly to 2,000-2,500 rpm.
5. Turn adjusting screw counterclockwise until engine speed falls to about 1,300 rpm.
6. Using the throttle, increase speed rapidly and release the throttle. Engine speed should drop back to 1,300 rpm. If not, readjust (outlined in steps 4-5).
7. When the valve has been adjusted, turn the adjustment screw counterclockwise one-half turn.

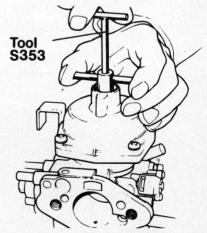

Tool S353

Fig. 2   Idle CO adjustment

Emission Controls Section

EGR VALVE

Testing

To check the operation of the EGR valve, warm up the engine, and open and close the throttle several times. Observe or feel the EGR valve, which should open and close with changes in engine speed. The EGR valve should close at once when the throttle is closed.

Service

1. Remove the EGR valve from the exhaust manifold, Fig. 1.
2. Clean valve seat with a wire brush.
3. Insert valve opening into a standard spark plug machine and lift the diaphragm.
4. Blast the valve for 30 seconds.
5. Use compressed air and a brush to remove all traces of carbon.

FUEL ABSORPTION CANISTER, REPLACE

1. Disconnect all lines at the canister, Fig. 2.

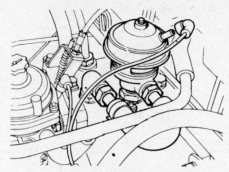

Fig. 1 Fuel evaporative emission control system

2. Remove the bracket nut and bolt.
3. Remove the canister.
4. Transfer the restrictor in the old canister to the new canister.
5. Install the new canister.

CATALYTIC CONVERTER, REPLACE

1. Remove the catalytic converter support bracket.

2. Release the catalytic converter from the tailpipe.

NOTE: It may now be necessary to remove the carburetor.

3. Remove the nuts holding the catalytic converter and front pipe to the exhaust manifold.
4. Remove the catalytic converter and front pipe, and exhaust manifold gasket.
5. Fit a new catalytic converter.
6. Reset the catalytic converter warning indicator to zero.

AIR PUMP BELT TENSION, ADJUST

1. Loosen the securing bolt and two adjusting link bolts.
2. Move the air pump to get a belt deflection of ½ in.
3. Tighten the bolts.

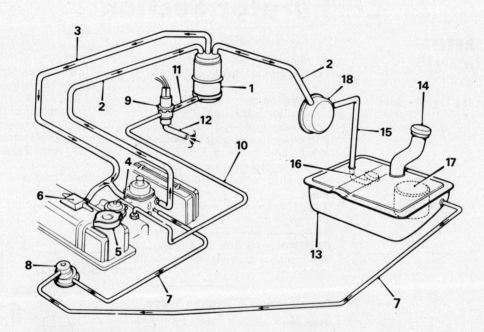

1	Charcoal adsorption canister	10	Running-on control pipe ⎤
2	Vapor lines	11	Running-on control hose ⎬ (if fitted)
3	Purge line	12	Air vent pipe ⎦
4	Restricted connection	13	Fuel tank
5	Sealed oil filter cap	14	Sealed fuel filler cap
6	Oil separator/flame trap (arrester)	15	Vapor line
7	Fuel pipe	16	Vapor tube
8	Fuel pump	17	Capacity limiting tank
9	Running-in control valve (if fitted)	18	Separation tank

Fig. 2 EGR valve

Clutch & Transmission Section

CLUTCH, REPLACE
Removal

1. Remove transmission, as described under Transmission, Replace.
2. Remove clutch cover holding screws.
3. Remove clutch cover and driven plate.

Installation

1. Install clutch driven plate to flywheel.

NOTE: The side marked "Flywheel Side" must face the flywheel.

2. Center clutch driven plate using tool No. 18G1196.
3. Install clutch cover, aligning the assembly marks on the flywheel and clutch.
4. Tighten holding screws progressively.
5. Remove tool No. 18G1196.
6. Install transmission.

TRANSMISSION, REPLACE

1. Remove engine and transmission assembly.
2. Disconnect fuel line from fuel pump.
3. Remove starter motor.
4. Remove hardware holding engine to transmission and separate the two.
5. Reverse above procedure, but note the following:
   a. The clutch driven plate should be centralized using tool No. 18G1196.
   b. The weight of the transmission must not be borne by the driven plate when replacing the transmission.
   c. Initially, all nuts and bolts are tightened finger tight.
   d. The large locating bolt is then tightened securely.
   e. Finally, all nuts and bolts are tightened with a wrench.

Rear Axle & Brakes Section

REAR AXLE SHAFT BEARING AND OIL SEAL, REPLACE
Removal

1. Support vehicle under rear axle.
2. Remove brake drum.
3. Remove half shaft.
4. Remove gasket and "O" ring seal.
5. Knock back lock tab of hub nut washer.
6. Unscrew hub nut using tool No. 18G152.

NOTE: The left-hand side has left-hand thread, and the right-hand side has a right-hand thread.

7. Use tool No. 18G304 and adapters 18G304F and 18G304H to remove hub.

8. Press bearing from hub.
9. Remove oil seal.

Installation

1. Pack bearing with lithium base grease and dip a new seal in light oil.
2. Use tool No. 18G134 and adapter 18G134Q to fit a new seal.

CAUTION: Make sure that the lip of the seal is toward the bearing.

3. Press the bearing into the hub.
4. Use tool No. 18G134 and adapter 18G134Q to drift hub into axle case.
5. Complete installation.

REAR DRUM BRAKE ADJUSTMENT

1. Jack up each wheel in turn.
2. Fully release parking brake.
3. Turn adjuster clockwise until wheel locks.
4. Turn adjuster back until the wheel turns without the linings rubbing.

PARKING BRAKE ADJUSTMENT

1. Adjust rear brakes.
2. Apply parking brake so pawl engages on third notch of ratchet.
3. If braking effect is not adequate, loosen cable rear adjusting nut.
4. Screw in front adjusting nut to attain adequate adjustment of threaded sleeve (1), Fig. 2. Adjustment is correct when wheels can just be rotated.
5. Tighten rear nut.

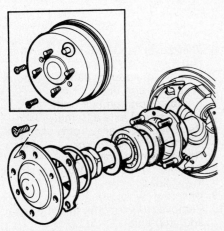

Fig. 1   Axle shaft removal

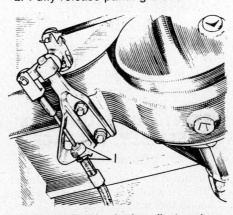

Fig. 2   Parking brake adjustment

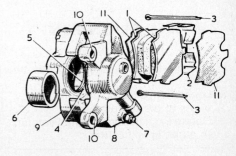

1. Friction pads.
2. Pad retaining spring.
3. Retaining pin.
4. Piston dust seal.
5. Piston fluid seal.
6. Piston.
7. Bleeder screw.
8. Calliper (mounting half).
9. Calliper (rim half).
10. Calliper mounting point.
11. Anti-squeak shims.

Fig. 3   Caliper removal

MASTER CYLINDER, REPLACE

1. Remove high tension lead from ignition coil and blue/white lead from resistor.
2. Release cover plate-ignition coil assembly.
3. Remove clevis pin.
4. Unscrew brake lines. Plug them and cylinder ports.
5. Remove master cylinder.

DISC BRAKE SERVICE
Caliper, Replace

1. Press in pad retaining spring and remove cotter pins.
2. Remove retaining spring.
3. Remove pads and anti-squeal shims.
4. Release brake line.
5. Unscrew bolts holding brake line support bracket.
6. Remove caliper.
7. Replace in reverse order to that above, but note the following:
   a. The brake line support bracket should be tightened to 48 ft. lbs.
   b. If necessary, use tool No. 18G590 to press each piston into the bore.

Rear Suspension Section

SHOCK ABSORBERS, REPLACE

1. Raise vehicle.
2. Support the body just forward of the rear spring shackle.
3. Remove the wheel.
4. Disconnect the shock absorber arm from the link assembly.
5. Remove the nuts and bolts holding the shock absorber to the body.
6. Remove the shock absorber.
7. Reverse the procedure to install, but note the following:
   a. Tighten shock retaining bolts to 55-60 ft. lbs. (7.6-8.3 kgfm).
   b. Top off the shock with Armstrong Super (thin) shock absorber fluid No 624 or equivalent.

SPRINGS, REPLACE

1. Raise vehicle.
2. Support the body forward of the rear spring front shackle.
3. Remove the wheel.

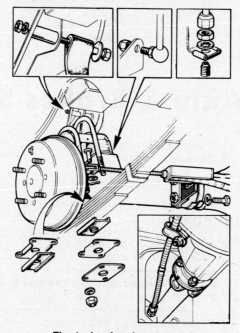

Fig. 1   Leaf spring removal

4. Support the rear axle.
5. Release the shock absorber link from the "U" bolt base plate, Fig. 1.
6. Release the rebound strap from the axle.
7. Remove the "U" bolt nuts and the shock absorber link bracket, lower locating plate and lower seating pad.
8. Remove "U" bolts, bump rubber pedestal assembly, upper seating pad and upper locating plate.
9. Release the shackle plate and rubber bushings.
10. Lower rear of the spring.
11. Remove the front shackle pin and nut.
12. Remove the spring.
13. Reverse procedure to install.

CAUTION: Do not tighten the spring "U" bolts fully until the vehicle has been lowered to the ground and weight is applied to springs.

Front Suspension & Steering Section

WHEEL ALIGNMENT
Toe-In, Adjust

1. Loosen the locknuts on both tie rods.
2. Loosen the clips holding the rubber boots to the tie rods.
3. Rotate each tie rod an equal amount to attain specification.

NOTE: Both tie rods are right-hand thread.

CAUTION: Tie rods must be adjusted exactly to equal length.

4. Tighten tie rods to 30-35 ft. lbs.

WHEEL BEARINGS, ADJUST

Wheel bearings are set properly by tightening the brake disc retaining bolts to 43 ft. lbs. and tightening the hub nut to 46 ft. lbs.

FRONT HUB STUB AXLE ASSEMBLY, REPLACE
Removal

1. Remove front spring, and release the ball joint from the steering arm using tool No. 18G1063.
2. Remove hub assembly, brake disc dust cover, and anti-sway bar link, Fig. 1.
3. Remove hydraulic damper (shock absorber) arm bolt.
4. Remove trunnion link bolt.
5. Lower swivel axle assembly.
6. Remove hardware from each inboard end of lower link.
7. Remove lower link.
8. Remove rubber bushings from lower link.
9. Unscrew swivel pin nut.
10. Remove trunnion link thrust washer and stub axle.
11. Disassemble parts of the stub axle.

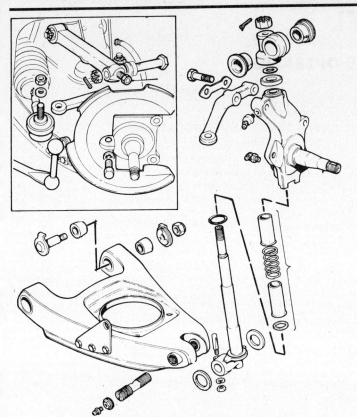

Fig. 1 Front hub stub axle assembly removal

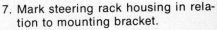

Fig. 2 Compressing coil spring

Fig. 3 Steering gear removal

Installation

1. Fit new bushings noting the following:
   a. The hole in the bushings must be aligned with the lubricating holes in swivel axle.
   b. The bottom bushing must be flush with the recessed housing and protrude about ⅛ in. above the lower housing upper face.
2. Ream bushings to the correct size using tool No. 18G1006A.
3. When fitting steering arm, tighten bolts to 39 ft. lbs.
4. Use a new sealing washer, soaked in oil, on the bottom of the swivel axle.
5. Fit .0008 in. and .012 in. shims to the swivel pin.
6. Tighten the trunnion nut to 40 ft. lbs.

COIL SPRINGS, REPLACE

1. Place a 1¼ in. thick block of wood under the hydraulic damper arm to keep it off the rebound rubber.
2. Remove the two diametrically opposed spring seat nuts and bolts.
3. Use tool No. 18G153 to compress spring, Fig. 2.
4. Remove the other spring retaining hardware and release the center screw of tool No. 18G153 to allow the spring to expand.
5. Remove tool No. 18G153 to release the spring.

6. Reverse above procedure to install, but note the following:
   a. Make sure that the guide rods of tool No. 18G153 fit into diametrically opposite holes.
   b. Make sure the wood block is removed after fitting the spring.

STEERING RACK, REPLACE
Removal

NOTE: If a seal is damaged, with a subsequent loss of lubricant, the steering rack should be disassembled and all parts inspected. If the vehicle is lifted with its front wheels off the ground, do not move wheels from lock to lock.

1. Remove radiator.
2. Steering should be straight ahead.
3. Raise and support front of vehicle.
4. Use tool No. 18G1063 to detach tie rod ends from steering rods.
5. Remove steering column pinch bolt and three toe-plate bolts.
6. Loosen upper steering column bolts and pull back column enough to disengage column sleeve from pinion.

7. Mark steering rack housing in relation to mounting bracket.
8. Remove clamps.
9. Remove steering rack assembly, Fig. 3.

Installation

1. Fit the rack into mounting brackets and fit clamps, but do not tighten bolts.
2. See that rack is in the straight-ahead position with the flat of pinch bolt on the pinion shaft facing up.
3. See that steering column is in a straight position with the slot of the clamp facing up.
4. Slide the column over the pinion shaft as far as it will go.
5. Tighten the steering column upper bolts and three toe-plate bolts.
6. Turn the steering wheel one complete turn to the left; then make a complete turn to the right; and return it to straight position.
7. See that the marks made on the steering rack housing and mounting bracket are aligned.
8. Tighten the clamp fixing bolts to 20-22 ft. lbs.
9. Tighten the steering column pinch bolt to 9-12 ft. lbs.
10. Complete installation.

OPEL

INDEX OF SERVICE OPERATIONS

OPEL

GENERAL ENGINE SPECIFICATIONS

Year	Engine	Carburetor	Bore and Stroke	Piston Displacement Cubic Inches	Compression Ratio	Maximum Brake H.P. @ R.P.M.	Maximum Torque H.P. @ R.P.M.	Normal Oil Pressure, Pounds
1972-74	4-115 (1900cc)	2 Barrel	3.66 x 2.75	115.8	7.6	90 @ 5200	111 @ 3400	—
1975	4-115 (1900cc)	Fuel Inj.	3.66 x 2.75	115.8	7.6	81 @ 5000	96 @ 2200	—
1976-77	4-110 (1800cc)	2 Barrel	3.31 x 3.23	110.8	8.5	80 @ 4000	95 @ 3000	57

—Not Available

TUNE UP SPECIFICATIONS

Year	Spark Plug		Distributor		Ignition Timing		
	Type	Gap	Point Gap Inch	Dwell Angle Deg.	Firing Order Fig.	Timing BTDC ①	Mark Fig.
1972-74	AC42FS	.030	.018	47—53	A	TDC ②	—
1975	AC426FS	.030	.016	47—53	A	—	—
1976-77	BPR6ES ③	.030	.016	50—54	B	6°	—

—Not Available
①—BTDC: Before top dead center
②—At 900 R.P.M.
③—NGK

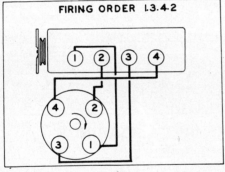

FIRING ORDER 1-3-4-2

Fig. A

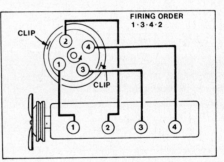

FIRING ORDER 1·3·4·2

CLIP

CLIP

Fig. B

DISTRIBUTOR SPECIFICATIONS

If unit is checked on vehicle, double RPM and degrees to get crankshaft figures.

Year	Model	Centrifugal Advance Degrees @ RPM of Distributor			Vacuum Advance	
		Advance Starts	Intermediate Advance	Full Advance	Inches of Vacuum to Start Plunger	Max. Adv. Dist. Deg. @ Vacuum
1972-74	JFU4	0 @ 500	3¾-7½ @ 700	16 @ 1800	2.9—4.1	5 @ 6.4
1975	—	0 @ 650	5-7 @ 1000	12½ @ 1700	—	—
1976-77	029100—3280	0 @ 700	7½ @ 1500	12 @ 2200	5	4.5 @ 9

—Not Available

Continued

ALTERNATOR & REGULATOR SPECIFICATIONS

Year	Alternator			Regulator	
	Model	Rated Hot Output Amps.	Output @ 14 Volts 2000 R.P.M.	Model	Volts @ 2500 Engine R.P.M.
1972-74	K114V35A20	35	23	AD1/14V	13.5—14.5
1975	K114V45A20	45	30	AD1/14V	13.9—14.8
1976-77	—	40	—		13.5—14.5

—Not Available

STARTING MOTOR SPECIFICATIONS

Year	Brush Spring Tension, Ounces	Free Speed Test			Resistance Test	
		Amps.	Volts	R.P.M.	Amps.	Volts
1972-75	40—46	30—50	10.6	7300—8500	2800—3200	6 min.
1976-77	—	—	—	—	—	—

—Not Available

VALVE SPECIFICATIONS

Year	Valve Lash		Valve Angles		Valve Spring Installed Height	Valve Spring Pressure Lbs. @ In.	Stem Clearance		Stem Diameter	
	Int.	Exh.	Seat	Face			Intake	Exhaust	Intake	Exhaust
1972-75	Hydraulic		44	44	①	②	.001—.0029	.0039	.3538—.3543	.3524—.3528
1976-77	.006C	.010C	45	45	—	③	.0029	.0098	.315	.315

—Not Available
①—Intake, 1.57"; Exhaust, 1.36".
②—1972, Intake, 153.2 @ 1.18"; Exhaust, 157 @ .96": 1973-75, Intake, 182 @ 1.18"; Exhaust 180 @ .96".
③—Inner spring, 18.7—21.5 @ 1.516"; Outer spring 32.2—37 @ 1.614

PISTONS, PINS, CRANKSHAFT & BEARINGS

Year	Piston Clearance	Ring End Gap ①		Wrist-pin Diameter	Rod Bearings		Main Bearings			
		Comp.	Oil		Shaft Diameter	Bearing Clearance	Shaft Diameter	Bearing Clearance	Thrust on Bear. No.	Shaft End Play
1972-75	.0014	.014	.015	.910	2.0461—2.0467	.0006—.0025	2.2829—2.2835	.0009—.0025	5	.0017—.0061
1976-77	.0018—.0026	.008	.008	—	1.9262—1.9268	.0007—.0030	2.2016—2.2022	.0008—.0025	3	.0024—.0094

—Not Available
①—Fit rings in tapered bore for clearance listed in tightest portion of ring travel.

ENGINE TIGHTENING SPECIFICATIONS

Torque specifications are for clean and lightly lubricated threads. Dry or dirty threads produce increased friction which prevents accurate measurement of tightness.

Year	Spark Plugs Ft. Lbs.	Cylinder Head Bolts Ft. Lbs.	Intake Manifold Ft. Lbs.	Exhaust Manifold Ft. Lbs.	Camshaft Sprocket Bolt Ft. Lbs.	Rocker Arm Shaft Ft. Lbs.	Rocker Arm Cover Ft. Lbs.	Connecting Rod Cap Bolts Ft. Lbs.	Main Bearing Cap Bolts Ft. Lbs.	Flywheel to Crankshaft Ft. Lbs.	Vibration Damper or Pulley Ft. Lbs.
1972-74	30	①	33	33	18	29②	—	36	72	43	72
1975	29	72	29	29	18	25②	—	33	73	43	72
1976-77	15—22	72	—	—	58	16	3.6	33	72	69	87

—Not Available
①—Cold, 72 Ft. Lbs.; Warm, 58 Ft. Lbs.
②—Rocker arm stud in cylinder head

Continued

OPEL

BRAKE SPECIFICATIONS

Year	Drum Brake Inside Diameter	Wheel Cylinder Bore Diameter		Master Cylinder Bore Diameter	Disc Brake Rotor			
		Disc Brakes	Drum Brakes		Nominal Thickness	Minimum Thickness	Thickness Variation Parallelism	Run out (T.I.R.)
1972	9.060	—	.625	.810	—	—	—	.004
1973-74	9.060	①	.625	.810	.430	.394	.0006	.004
1975	9.060	1.890	.625	.810	.500	.465	.0004	.004
1976-77	8.980	—	.812	—	—	.339		.006

—Not Available
① —Exc. GT, 1.890″; GT, 1.770″.

COOLING SYSTEM & CAPACITY DATA

Year	Cooling Capacity Qts.		Radiator Cap Relief Pressure, Lbs.	Thermo. Opening Temp.	Fuel Tank Gals.	Engine Oil Refill Qts. ①	Transmission Oil		Rear Axle Oil Pints
	Less A/C	With A/C					Manual Trans. Pints	Auto. Trans. Pints	
1972-75	6	6	13.2—15.2	189	②	3¼	2½	10½	2½
1976-77	6½	6½	15	180	13.7	5	2¹/₃	—	2½

—Not Available
① —With filter
② —Exc. 1900, Manta & GT, 10.6 gallons; 1900 & Manta, 11.9 gallons; GT, 13.2 gallons.

REAR AXLE SPECIFICATIONS

Year	Carrier Type	Ring Gear & Pinion Backlash		Pinion Bearing Preload			Differential Bearing Preload		
		Method	Adjustment	Method	New Bearing Inch-Lbs.	Used Bearing Inch-Lbs.	Method	New Bearing Inch-Lbs.	Used Bearing Inch-Lbs.
1972-75	Integral	Shim	.004—.008	Spacer	7—13	5—8	Shims	20—30	10—20
1976-77	Integral	Shim	.005—.007	Spacer	6—13	5—8	Shims	20—30	10—20

WHEEL ALIGNMENT SPECIFICATIONS

Year	Model	Caster Angle, Degrees		Camber Angle, Degrees		Toe-In. Inch	Toe-Out on Turns, Degrees.	
		Limits	Desired	Limits	Desired		Outer Wheel	Inner Wheel
1972-73	Opel	+1 to +3	+2	—	+1½	¹/₃₂—⅛	18½	20
	GT	+2 to +4	+3	—	+1½	¹/₃₂—⅛	18½	20
	1900	+3½ to +6½	+5	—	−1½	⅛—³/₁₆	19¼	20
1974	All	+3 to +6	+4½	−1½ to −½	−1	⅛—³/₁₆	19¼	20
1975	All	+3 to +6	+4½	−1¼ to +¼	−½	¹/₃₂—⅛	19½	20
1976-77	All	+4 to +6	+5	−½ to +½	0	⁵/₆₄—¹¹/₆₄	—	—

—Not Available

Electrical Section

DISTRIBUTOR, REPLACE

1972-75

Removal

1. On 1972-74 models, remove the fuel pump to provide clearance for removal of distributor drive gear.
2. Set No. 1 cylinder at firing point by turning engine until cutout in distributor shaft (or rotor) points to notch in distributor housing, Fig. 1.
3. Ball imbedded in flywheel should be approximately aligned with pointer in housing.
4. Remove distributor hold-down clamp and remove distributor. Cover bore in timing case to prevent foreign matter from entering the engine. To ease distributor installation, do not rotate crankshaft or oil pump.

Installation

1. Be sure oil pump slot is in proper position, Fig. 3.
2. Install new gasket on distributor housing.
3. Install distributor with vacuum units in original position and with shaft cutout (rotor tip) pointing to notch in distributor housing, Fig. 1.
4. Install distributor clamp, bolt and lockwasher finger-tight. Align marks on rotor tip and housing.
5. Install fuel pump, if removed.
6. Adjust ignition timing.

1976-77

Removal

1. Release distributor cap retaining clips and remove cap.

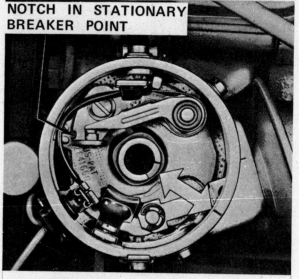

NOTCH IN STATIONARY BREAKER POINT

Fig. 1   Aligning distributor shaft cutout with notch on distributor body. 1972-75

2. Note relative position of rotor for installation.
3. Disconnect hose for vacuum advance.
4. Remove distributor clamp bolt and clamp.
5. Lift distributor assembly out of engine.

Installation

1. Rotate rotor to original position.
2. Install distributor in engine with shaft aligned with slot in oil pump drive shaft.
3. Install distributor retaining bracket with bolt finger-tight.
4. Install distributor cap.
5. Check and correct dwell and timing as necessary.
6. Tighten distributor clamp bolt and connect vacuum hose.

DISTRIBUTOR SERVICE

1972-75, Fig. 4

Disassembly

1. Remove distributor cap retaining clips and vacuum control units.
2. Push retaining ring from groove in distributor shaft.
3. Push up on distributor shaft. Remove breaker plate from distributor housing. Remove breaker points from breaker plate.
4. Disassemble breaker plate by unscrewing ball thrust spring screw. Remove spring and ball.
5. Pull distributor shaft with centrifugal advance mechanism from distributor housing. Do not disassemble advance mechanism.

6. Clean and check all parts and replace, if defective.

Assembly

1. Install new distributor points on breaker plate.
2. Install retaining ring on distributor shaft.
3. Install vacuum units, condenser and cap retaining clips.
4. Oil sliding parts of breaker plate. Oil the felt in the cam. Apply a thin layer of high-melting-point grease to the cam.
5. Grease control rod at eye.
6. Reinstall distributor cap nipples and spark plug boots

1976-77, Fig. 5

Disassembly

1. Remove rotor and dust cover.
2. Remove terminal nuts and insulator.

Fig. 3   Oil pump slot for distributor installation. 1972-75

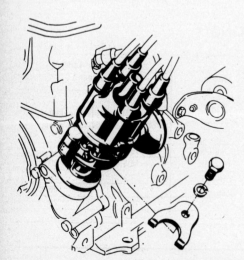

Fig. 2   Replacing distributor. 1972-75

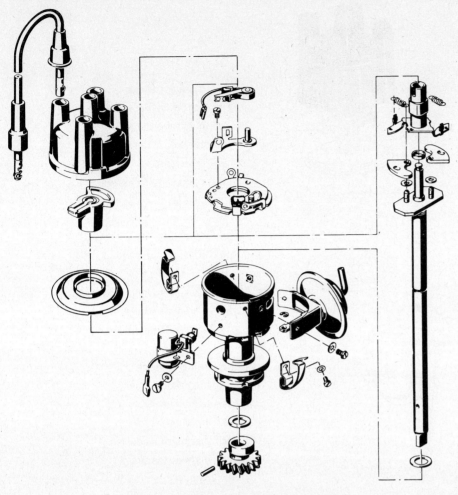

Fig. 4 Distributor disassembled. 1972-75

3. Install adjusting brace bolt, lock-washer, plain washer and nut finger-tight.
4. Place a belt tension gauge on the belt. Pull alternator outward until gauge reads 45 lbs., then tighten adjusting brace bolt.
5. Tighten the alternator pivot bolt.
6. Connect battery lead to alternator.
7. Connect three-way wiring connector into alternator and engage safety latch.
8. Connect battery ground cable.

1976-77

1. Disconnect battery ground cable.
2. Remove stone shield.
3. Remove two lower alternator attaching bolts.
4. Remove horn.
5. Disconnect wiring from alternator.
6. Remove top alternator bolt and disengage belt.
7. Remove alternator belt adjusting bracket and bolt.
8. Remove alternator.
9. Reverse procedure to install, then tighten belt.

ALTERNATOR IN-CAR TESTING
1972-75

Alternator Output Test

1. Check alternator belt condition and tension. Adjust to 45 lbs.
2. Install a battery post adapter at the positive post of the battery, Fig. 6.
3. Connect the ammeter leads to adapter with red lead toward generator and black lead toward battery positive post. Connect ground lead to battery negative post, Fig. 6.
4. Connect voltmeter across the battery; red lead at alternator side of battery post adapter and black lead to battery negative post.
5. Connect a tachometer to ignition system.
6. Be sure all electrical accessories are turned off. Start engine with battery post adapter switch closed. Open switch as soon as speed is started.
7. Adjust engine speed to 2500 RPM.
8. Turn tester control knob to "LOAD" position and adjust knob to obtain highest possible ammeter reading. Output must be 30 amperes minimum. If output is satisfactory, proceed to "Voltage Regulator Test" outlined below.
9. If output is low, defect may be in alternator or in regulator. To eliminate regulator, supply field current direct to cause full alternator output. Dis-

3. Remove condenser, circlip and vacuum advance.
4. Remove dust-proof gaskets.
5. Remove breaker points and damper spring.
6. Remove cap clamps, lead wire and breaker plate.
7. Remove centrifugal advance springs, then the screw in the end of cam assembly and cam.
8. Remove circlips and advance weights.
9. Punch out set pin, then remove collar, spacers and shaft from housing.

Assembly

1. Lubricate distributor shaft, cam, damper spring and breaker arm before installation.
2. After installing centrifugal advance weights, install the cam drive plate so the mark on the rear face is turned toward the stopper pin on the centrifugal advance weight plate. Install advance springs.
3. Install the cap clip with the projected portion turned toward the terminal side.
4. Install damper spring to maintain

.002-.004 in. clearance to flat face of cam.
5. Turn cam so the heel of breaker arm rests on high point of cam lobe.

ALTERNATOR, REPLACE
1972-75

Removal

1. Disconnect battery ground cable.
2. Disconnect wiring connector from alternator.
3. Disconnect battery lead from alternator.
4. Remove adjusting brace bolt, lockwasher, plain washer and nut.
5. Loosen pivot bolt. Push alternator inward and remove belt from pulley.
6. Lower alternator and remove pivot bolt, nut lockwasher and plain washer.
7. Remove alternator from vehicle.

Installation

1. Hold alternator in position and install pivot bolt, plain washer and nut finger-tight.
2. Install alternator belt.

1-733

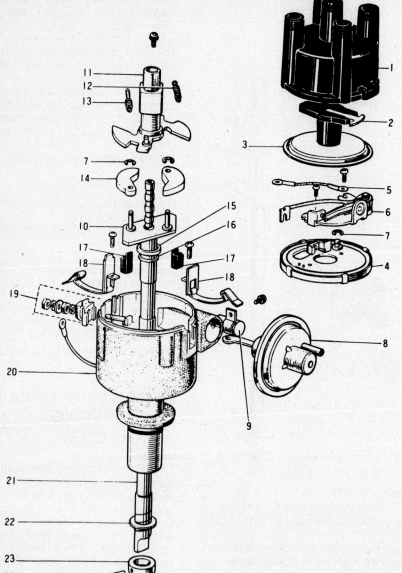

1. DISTRIBUTOR CAP
2. ROTOR ASSEMBLY
3. DUST PROOF COVER
4. BREAKER PLATE ASSEMBLY
5. LEAD WIRE
6. BREAKER POINT ASSEMBLY
7. CIRCLIP
8. VACUUM CONTROL ASSEMBLY
9. CONDENSER
10. GOVERNOR ASSEMBLY
11. CAM ASSEMBLY
12. GOVERNER SPRING (LOW-SPEED SIDE)
13. GOVERNOR SPRING (HIGH SPEED SIDE)
14. GOVERNOR WEIGHT
15. CAP WASHER
17. THRUST WASHER
17. DUST-PROOF GASKET
18. CAP CLAMP
19. TERMINAL ASSEMBLY
20. DISTRIBUTOR HOUSING
21. DISTRIBUTOR SHAFT
22. O-RING
23. COLLAR
24. PIN

Fig. 5   Distributor disassembled. 1976-77

connect three-way connector from regulator and plug in a jumper wire between the red and black leads. Retest as described in Steps 7 and 8. If output is still low, alternator is faulty and must be removed.

10. If output using field jumper is now satisfactory, defect is in the regulator or wiring harness. Check all wiring connections. If all wiring is satisfactory, replace voltage regulator and perform the "Voltage Regulator Test" outlined below.

Voltage Regulator Test & Adjustment

1. Perform alternator output test as outlined previously. Leave all test instruments connected, but be sure field jumper is removed, if used.
2. With engine speed at 2500 RPM,

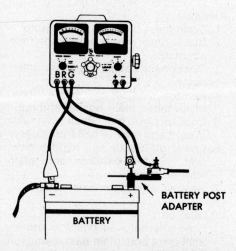

Fig. 6   Alternator test connections. 1972-75

turn tester control knob to "¼ OHM" position. Be sure all electrical accessories are turned off. After voltage reading stabilizes, a reading between 13.5 and 14.5 is satisfactory.

3. If voltage reading is not within specifications, remove regulator cover and adjust voltage regulator armature spring tension to obtain a middle reading of 14.0 volts. If voltage fluctuates, voltage contacts are dirty.

4. Replace regulator cover and recheck voltage setting. A steady voltage reading between 13.5 and 14.5 volts indicates voltage regulator is satisfactory.

5. Adjust engine speed to specified idle. Reseal voltage regulator carefully, using electrical tape.

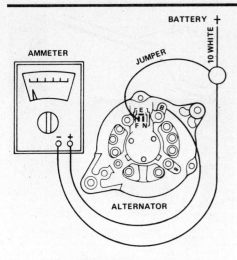

Fig. 7 Alternator output test connections. 1976-77

1976-77

Alternator Output Test

The battery must be fully charged and the drive belt properly adjusted.

1. Disconnect negative cable from battery.
2. Disconnect voltage regulator white and white-with-blue-stripe wires from "B" terminal of alternator.
3. Disconnect 3-wire connector from alternator.
4. Connect ammeter in series with "B" terminal and 10 gauge white wire, Fig. 7.
6. Connect tachometer to engine and reconnect negative cable to battery.
7. Start engine and slowly increase speed while observing alternator output. Minimum output should be 40 amps at 1200-1400 engine rpm. If minimum output cannot be obtained, remove alternator for further testing and repair.

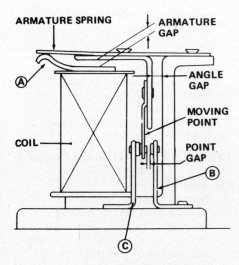

Fig. 9 Voltage relay adjustment. 1976-77

Voltage Regulator Inspection

The voltage regulator and voltage relay points are normally closed.

1. Remove regulator cover and check the parts for distortion, cracking or rusting. Replace regulator, if necessary. Closely inspect gaskets and seals, as entry of water causes permanent damage.
2. Check the points for burning or roughness and dress, if needed.
3. Using an ohmmeter, check resistance of the regulator and relay coils. The regulator coil resistance should be 102 ohms and the relay coil resistance should be 24 ohms. If an open or shorted coil is indicated, replace regulator assembly.
4. Check the resistor resistance. It should be 10.5 ohms. Replace resistor, if defective.

Voltage Regulator Operating Test

1. Connect a voltmeter between the condenser lead and ground with all electrical loads disconnected, including blower relay contacts, Fig. 8.
2. The voltage relay is working normally when the lower side points are closed while the engine is static and upper points are closed when engine is running at idle. If the points are not working normally, the relay is maybe out of adjustment or the voltage coil is open. Check the coil resistance and replace the regulator assembly, if defective. If the coil resistance is normal, adjust the voltage relay.
3. Start engine and increase engine speed gradually. Voltage should increase with engine speed up to 1400-1850 RPM. Normal condition of the regulator is indicated when the voltage is within the range of 13.5-14.5 volts. Reconnect blower relay connector.

Voltage Regulator Voltage Relay Test

Connect voltmeter between "N" terminal and ground, then increase engine speed gradually. Voltmeter reading should be 4-5.8 volts when indicator light goes out. Adjust cut-in voltage by adjusting armature core gap and point gap. Voltage should be 4-5.8 volts.

1. If cut-in voltage is too high, adjust by bending core arm "A" down, Fig. 9.
2. If adjustment of core arm does not correct cut-in voltage, proceed with point gap adjustment. Disconnect negative cable from battery. Check armature core gap with armature depressed until moving point is in contact with "B" side point. Arma-

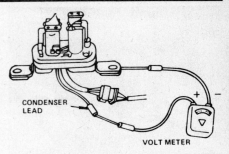

Fig. 8 Voltage regulator operating test connections. 1976-77

ture core gap should be .012 in. or more. Adjust by bending point arm "B."

3. Release the armature and adjust the gap between the "B" side point and the moving point by bending point arm "C." Point gap should be .016 to .047 in.
4. After point gap adjustment, check cut-in voltage. If not within 4-5.8 volts, repeat cut-in voltage adjustment in Step 1.

Voltage Regulator Adjustment

If no-load regulated voltage is not within the 13.5-14.5 range, adjust regulator setting.

1. If regulator voltage is too high, adjust by bending core arm "D" down. If voltage is too low, bend arm "D" up, Fig. 10.
2. If core arm adjustment will not correct regulated voltage, proceed to point gap adjustment.
3. Disconnect battery ground cable. Depress armature until the moving point contacts "E" side point. Bend point arm "E" to obtain armature gap of .012 in. or more, Fig. 10.
4. Release armature and adjust gap between "E" side point and moving point by bending point arm "F," Fig. 10. Gap should be .012-.018 in.
5. After gap adjustment is made, recheck no-load regulated voltage

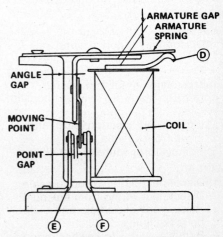

Fig. 10 Voltage regulator adjustment. 1976-77

Fig. 11 Removing ignition lock. 1972-73 Rallye GT

outlined under "Operating Test." Repeat core arm adjustment, if necessary.

STARTER, REPLACE
1972-75
Removal
1. Disconnect battery ground cable.
2. Disconnect starter wiring.
3. Remove starter support bracket.
4. Remove two starter bolts, one nut and lockwashers.
5. Remove starter.

Installation
1. Hold starter in position.
2. Install two bolts, one nut and lockwashers. Tighten securely.
3. Install support bracket. To ensure a stress-free installation, install bolts and two nuts only finger-tight. Tighten the bolt at the engine, then the two nuts at the starter end frame.
4. Connect wires to solenoid.
5. Connect battery ground cable.

1976-77
Less A/C
1. Disconnect battery ground cable.
2. Disconnect wiring from solenoid.
3. Remove starter to flywheel-housing top retaining nut and washer.
4. Remove starter to flywheel housing lower retaining bolt.
5. Lift starter, clearing stud and remove from vehicle.
6. Remove procedure to install.

With A/C
1. Disconnect battery ground cable.
2. Disconnect wiring from solenoid.
3. Raise front of vehicle and support on jack stands.
4. Remove starter to flywheel housing retaining nut and washer.

5. Remove starter to flywheel housing lower retaining bolt.
6. Lift starter, clearing stud, and remove from vehicle.
7. Reverse procedure to install.

IGNITION LOCK & SWITCH, REPLACE
1972-73 Rallye
Removal
1. Disconnect battery ground cable.
2. Turn ignition switch to "On" position.
3. Insert a suitable rod into stop pin hole on side of ignition and steering lock and remove steering and ignition lock cylinder, Fig. 11.
4. Remove two screws securing electrical switch to steering and lock housing, then the switch.

Installation
1. Install electrical switch in steering and ignition lock housing and rotate switch until the cam in lock housing recess fits into the slotted hole in the rear of the electrical switch and the projection on the electrical switch fits into recess on lock housing.
2. Install steering wheel.

1972-73 GT Sport Coupe
Ignition Lock
1. Remove steering wheel.
2. Position lock in "Run" position.
3. With a suitable piece of wire, push in lock cylinder retaining pin and remove the lock cylinder, Fig. 12.
4. Insert lock cylinder into housing.
5. Install steering wheel.

Ignition Switch
1. Remove lock cylinder as outlined

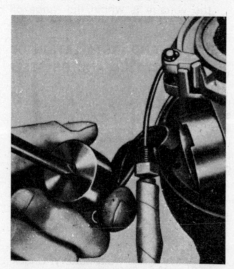

Fig. 13 Placing ignition switch in Run position. 1972-73 GT Sport Coupe

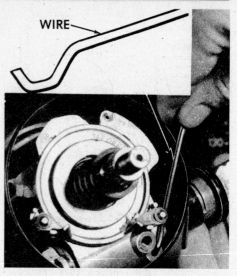

Fig. 12 Remove ignition lock. 1972-73 GT Sport Coupe

previously.
2. Disconnect ignition wire connector.
3. Remove ignition lock retaining screw.
4. Remove turn signal switch lever.
5. Remove three screws securing turn signal switch cover to housing.
6. To remove housing cover:
   a. Pull cover toward turn signal and move cover slightly toward right.
   b. Turn cover toward the left and move cover further toward the right so the left retaining screw ear is position under the left return cam.
   c. Insert turn signal lever into oblong opening in cover, push steering lock into housing and remove cover.
7. Remove ignition switch.
8. Install ignition switch.

NOTE: Before installing switch, ensure the switch is in the "Run" position. With a philips screwdriver, turn inner sleeve toward the right until a springy resistance is encountered, Fig. 13.

9. Install housing cover and secure with three retaining screws.
10. Install ignition lock retaining screw.
11. Connect ignition wire connector.
12. Install turn signal switch lever.
13. Install lock cylinder.

1972-75 All Exc. GT Sport Coupe & Rallye GT
Removal
1. Remove steering wheel.
2. Remove split signal switch housing cover and the lower half.
3. Remove lock cylinder by pushing in lock spring of the cylinder using a piece of wire, Fig. 14. Cylinder must be in the "1" position.

Installation

1. Insert lock cylinder in the "1" position into housing.
2. Install lower half of signal switch housing.
3. Install steering wheel.

1976-77

1. Disconnect battery ground cable.
2. Remove steering wheel.
3. Remove screws retaining the upper and lower steering column covers and the hazard warning button.
4. Disconnect electrical connector from ignition switch.
5. Remove screws retaining switch and the switch.
6. Reverse procedure to install.

LIGHT SWITCH, REPLACE

1972 Opel

1. Disconnect battery ground cable.
2. Disconnect speedometer cable from speedometer.
3. Reach under panel and compress the four instrument housing retaining clamps and tilt housing from panel to remove the switch retaining screws.
4. Disconnect switch wiring and remove switch retaining screws.
5. Remove switch from vehicle.
6. Reverse procedure to install.

1972-73 GT Sport Coupe

1. Disconnect battery ground cable.
2. Remove instrument cluster and position cluster aside.
3. Remove switch retaining nuts and disconnect switch wiring.
4. Remove switch from vehicle.
5. Reverse procedure to install.

1972-75 1900 & 1973-75 Manta

Removal

1. Remove instrument cluster cover panel.
2. Compress retaining springs and pull switch out.
3. Pull multiple socket off switch.

Installation

1. Plug multiple socket in switch and push switch in panel until clips lock in place.
2. Install instrument cover and secure with two screws.
3. Install 2 plugs over screws and install heater control levers and light switch knob.

1976-77

1. Loosen switch knob set screw and remove knob.
2. Remove lock nut retaining the

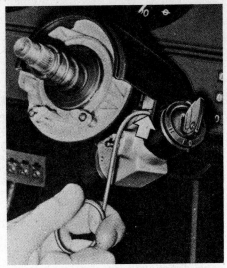

Fig. 14 Removing ignition lock. 1972-75 All exc. GT Sport Coupe & Rallye GT

switch body and the switch assembly.
3. Disconnect switch wiring connector.
4. Reverse procedure to install.

STOPLIGHT SWITCH, REPLACE

All models are equipped with mechanical stop light switches, which are activated by the rear of the brake pedal arm. To replace the switch, disconnect the wire, then remove the switch assembly. Reverse procedure to install.

NEUTRAL SAFETY SWITCH, REPLACE

1972-75

1. Remove console from floor panel by removing three attaching screws, if equipped with small console, or four screws, if equipped with large console. On large console, the ash tray must be removed to gain access to the fourth screw.
2. Unplug cigar lighter and lamps from console and remove console.
3. Remove neutral safety switch.
4. Reverse procedure to install.

1976-77

1. Remove console cover.
2. Remove neutral safety switch.
3. Reverse procedure to install.

TURN SIGNAL SWITCH, REPLACE

1972 Opel

Removal

1. Disconnect battery ground cable.
2. Pry off horn cap and disconnect wiring from cap.

3. Bend lockplate tabs downward and remove steering wheel nut, lockplate and washer.
4. With a suitable steering wheel remover, remove steering wheel.
5. Pull turn signal lever from seat. The lever is secured in place with a lock ball.
6. Remove upper attaching screws and rubber caps.
7. Remove cap nut and lower attaching screws.
8. Remove switch housing and switch housing cover from steering column.

Installation

1. Install switch housing in steering column. Insert wire set through holes in switch housing cover and steering column.
2. Slide slotted guide ring on steering shaft up to the bearing. The guide ring shoulder must face upward.
3. Install upper attaching screws and rubber cap.
4. Install cap nut and lower attaching screws.
5. Connect switch wiring.
6. Install turn signal lever.
7. Install thrust spring on steering shaft.
8. Install steering wheel.
9. Connect battery ground cable.

1972-73 GT Sport Coupe

1. Remove ignition switch and lock as outlined previously.
2. Disconnect turn signal switch wiring.
3. Remove screws and the turn signal housing and switch assembly.
4. Reverse procedure to install.

1972-75 1900 & Manta

Removal

1. Disconnect battery ground cable.
2. Pry off horn cap and remove wires from cap.
3. Bend backplate tabs down and remove steering shaft nut and lockplate.
4. Install steering wheel remover, J-21686 and remove steering wheel.
5. Remove signal switch and ignition lock wire set.
6. Pull directional signal lever from the seat. Lever is secured by a lock ball.
7. Remove lower half of signal switch housing cover.
8. Remove hex nut from steering mast jacket attachment at front of dash panel.
9. Remove slide-off base from underside of instrument panel and upper part of signal switch housing cover.
10. Place a thick block of wood on front

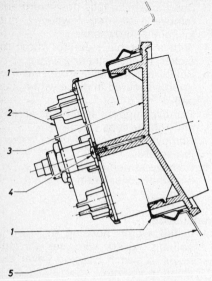

1. RETAINING CLAMP   4. SHEET METAL SCREW
2. SPEEDOMETER   5. INSTRUMENT PANEL
3. INSTRUMENT
    HOUSING

**Fig. 15   Instrument cluster retention.
1972 Opel**

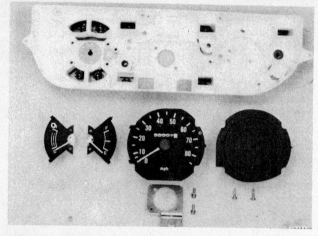

Fig. 16   Instrument cluster, disassembled. 1976-77 Opel

seat and lower the steering mast jacket assembly. Front seat must be in fully forward position.

11. Centerpunch tear-off bolt for steering and ignition lock bracket attachment. Drill a .12 in. (3mm) hole. With a bolt remover with left-hand twist, screw out the bolt.

12. Remove steering and ignition lock and the ignition switch from steering mast jacket and loosely attach slide-off base below instrument panel.

Installation

1. When installing a new directional signal switch, install new bearing and snap ring in switch assembly. The bearing must be pressed into the switch housing using Tool J-24224 with the inner nose straight edge up, or the smaller-diameter ball bearing at the top.

2. Install signal switch and the steering and ignition lock to steering mast jacket. Install steering and ignition lock bracket, using a new tear-off bolt.

3. Disconnect slide-off base, install upper half of signal switch housing cover and loosely attach slide-off base.

4. Attach steering mast jacket at front of dash panel.

5. Torque slide-off base attaching bolts to 11 ft. lbs.

6. Install lower half of signal switch housing cover and connect signal switch and the steering ignition lock wire set.

7. Before installing steering wheel, lubricate return pin and sliding area

on directional signal switch return cams and horn contact ring.

8. Be sure that clamp bolt in steering shaft flange is on top and the notch on steering shaft face is in horizontal position.

9. With the steering wheel centered, place the steering wheel on the steering shaft.

10. Install steering wheel lockplate and nut. Torque to 11 ft. lbs.

11. Bend lockplate tabs up, connect horn cap wires and install cable and cap.

12. Connect battery ground cable.

1976-77

1. Remove the two screws retaining the horn button.

2. Disconnect the horn contact.

3. Remove steering wheel hold-down nut and washer.

4. Using steering wheel puller J-21686, remove the steering wheel.

5. Remove the screws retaining the upper and lower column covers and hazard warning button.

6. Remove the combination turn signal, headlight dimmer and hazard warning switch by removing the four retaining screws.

7. Reverse procedure to install. Be sure the turn signal cancelling pin engages the hole in the back of the steering wheel when the steering wheel is installed. Torque the steering wheel washer and nut. Torque nut to 22 ft. lbs.

INSTRUMENT CLUSTER, REPLACE

1972 Opel

1. Disconnect battery ground cable.

2. Disconnect speedometer cable from speedometer.

3. From under dash, compress the four housing retaining clamps and

tilt housing out from panel, Fig. 15.

4. Disconnect electrical wiring from cluster.

5. Remove cluster from vehicle.

6. Reverse procedure to install.

1972-73 GT Sport Coupe

1. Disconnect battery ground cable.

2. Remove right access cover and screw.

3. Remove left access cover and screw.

4. Remove flasher unit.

5. Place steering wheel to position wheels in straight ahead position.

6. Remove heads from tear-bolts securing steering column using a drill, then remove bolts with a stud extractor.

7. Disconnect ignition and turn signal wiring plugs.

8. Support steering column and remove the two hex head bolts supporting steering column.

9. Lower steering column assembly to floor.

10. Disconnect speedometer cable.

11. Remove six screws from instrument cluster.

12. Pull instrument cluster from top and tilt outward.

13. Disconnect electrical wiring from radio and instrument cluster.

14. Pull cluster from panel.

15. Reverse procedure to install.

1972-75 1900 & Manta
Removal

1. Disconnect battery ground cable.

2. Remove headlight switch and rheostat switch knobs by depressing retaining clip on shaft and pulling back on switch knob.

3. Remove two plugs from instrument panel by prying out with a suitable screwdriver.

4. Remove two sheet metal screws from behind plugs.

5. Pull off heater control knobs.

15. Remove instrument panel, Fig. 16.
16. Reverse procedure to install.

W/S WIPER SWITCH, REPLACE

1972 Opel

1. Disconnect battery ground cable.
2. Disconnect speedometer cable from speedometer.
3. Reach under panel and compress the four instrument housing retaining clamps and tilt housing from panel to remove the switch retaining screws.
4. Disconnect switch wiring and remove retaining screws
5. Remove switch from vehicle.
6. Reverse procedure to install.

1972-73 GT Sport Coupe

1. Disconnect battery ground cable.
2. Remove instrument cluster and position cluster aside.
3. Remove switch retaining nuts and disconnect switch wiring.
4. Remove switch from vehicle.
5. Reverse procedure to install.

1972-75 1900 & Manta

1. Remove instrument cluster trim panel.
2. Compress retaining clips and remove switch.
3. Disconnect wiring connector.
4. Reverse procedure to install.

1976-77

1. Disconnect battery ground cable.
2. Remove steering wheel.
3. Remove steering column cover.
4. Remove screws and switch assembly.
5. Reverse procedure to install.
6. Release instrument panel harness from clips and disconnect the connectors.
7. Disconnect the heater control, control cables at the heater unit and water valve assembly in the engine compartment.
8. Pull out the heater control knobs and remove the control panel.
9. Remove screws and control lever assembly.
10. Through glove box opening, remove instrument panel attaching bracket screws and loosen bracket to cowl attaching nut.
11. Disconnect heater air duct hoses.
12. Remove three nuts retaining upper part of instrument panel.
13. Remove two bolts at each end, inside instrument panel.
14. Remove two nuts connecting steering column bracket with the instrument panel.

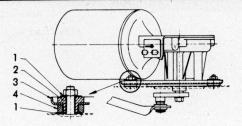

1. SLEEVE
2. DAMPER BUSHING
3. MOUNTING PLATE
4. DAMPER RING

Fig. 17 Wiper motor installation. 1972 Opel

6. Pull instrument trim panel toward steering wheel and remove panel.
7. Remove two screws from lower cluster housing.
8. Disconnect speedometer cable by turning coupling counterclockwise.
9. If equipped with heated rear window, pull switch from instrument housing and disconnect the wire connector.
10. Pull the left and right sides of the cluster out far enough to disconnect wires from cluster, then remove the cluster.

Installation

1. Place instrument cluster in position and connect wires on back of cluster.
2. If equipped with heated rear window, pull switch connector into opening and install switch.
3. Install two screws on lower housing attachment.
4. Install instrument cluster trim plate and replace two screws and plugs.
5. Connect speedometer cable by turning coupling clockwise.
6. Install light switch and rheostat switch knobs and heater control levers.
7. Connect battery ground cable.

1976-77

1. Disconnect battery ground cable.
2. Remove steering wheel.
3. Disconnect speedometer cable from speedometer end. Remove the ring nut.
4. Remove instrument panel retaining screws, rotate cluster outward and disconnect the 6- and 12-pole connectors and remove cluster assembly.
5. Remove screws, glove box door and glove box.

W/S WIPER MOTOR, REPLACE

1972 Opel

1. Disconnect battery ground cable.

2. Remove crank arm hex nut and crank arm from wiper motor drive shaft.
3. Disconnect electrical connector from motor and the ground wire from terminal plate attaching screw.
4. Remove three nuts securing motor to dash panel, Fig. 17.
5. Remove wiper motor from vehicle.
6. Reverse procedure to install.

1972-73 GT Sport Coupe

1. Disconnect battery ground cable.
2. Remove wiper transmission as outlined elsewhere in this section.
3. Disconnect electrical connector from motor.
4. Remove three bolts securing motor to left deflector panel.
5. Remove wiper motor from vehicle.
6. Reverse procedure to install.

1972-75 1900 & Manta

Removal

1. Disconnect battery ground cable.
2. Remove the wiper motor-to-crank arm attaching nut. The nut is located on inner side of cowl, above the steering column.
3. Pull crank arm from motor drive shaft.
4. Remove three wiper motor attaching screws.
5. Remove motor from cowl.
6. Remove wiper motor electrical connector from motor.

Installation

1. Connect wiper motor electrical connector to motor.
2. Place wiper motor in position on cowl and secure. Torque attaching nuts to 14-17 inch lbs.
3. Place crank arm on motor drive shaft and torque nut to 70-87 inch lbs.
4. Check the position of the windshield wiper blade after the crank arm is attached. At the point of greatest clearance, the right blade should be 1½ in. from the windshield molding, while the left blade should be 1⅛ in. from the molding.
5. Connect battery ground cable.

1976-77

1. Disconnect battery ground cable.
2. From under instrument panel, remove nut, washer and crank arm from motor.
3. Disconnect wiring connector.
4. Remove rubber boot, three screws and motor assembly.
5. Reverse procedure to install.

W/S WIPER TRANSMISSION, REPLACE

1972 Opel

1. Disconnect battery ground cable.
2. Remove wiper arms.
3. Remove clips retaining connecting rods to wiper transmission.
4. Remove screws securing transmission to dash panel.
5. Remove transmission from vehicle.
6. Reverse procedure to install.

1972-73 GT Sport Coupe

1. Disconnect battery ground cable.
2. Remove wiper arms.
3. Remove three bolts from each transmission and lower transmission from deflector panels.
4. Remove screws from left and center deflector panels.
5. Remove center deflector panel.
6. Remove left deflector panel with the wiper motor and transmission.
7. Remove nut and lockwasher from motor shaft and the transmission.
8. Reverse procedure to install.

1972-75 1900 & Manta

1. Disconnect battery ground cable.
2. Remove wiper arms.
3. Remove wiper transmission retaining nut, washer and rubber seal ring.
4. Remove instrument cluster.

NOTE: If the left transmission is being removed, no other instrument panel component need be removed. If the right transmission or both units are being removed, it is necessary to remove the instrument panel. On Rallye models, the gauge carrier should also be removed. On 1900 models, the defroster ducts are secured to the instrument panel cover by two spring clips and should not be removed from the dash cover.

5. Remove retaining clips from transmission connecting rod pins and pull the connecting rods from pins.
6. Remove screws securing wiper transmission to inner side of cowl, then the wiper transmission assemblies.
7. Reverse procedure to install.

1976-77

Left Transmission

1. Disconnect battery ground cable.
2. Remove left wiper arm retaining nut and wiper arm.
3. Remove steering wheel.
4. Remove instrument cluster.
5. Reaching through cluster opening,

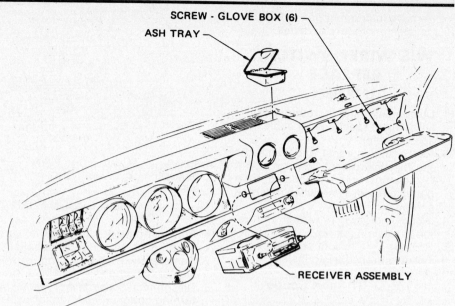

Fig. 18 Radio installation. 1972 Opel

pry linkage loose from wiper transmission. Be careful not to damage nylon bushing.
6. Remove three screws and wiper transmission from cowl.
7. Reverse procedure to install.

Right Transmission

1. Disconnect battery ground cable.
2. Remove right wiper arm retaining nut and wiper arm.
3. Remove glove box.
4. Reach through glove box opening, pry linkage from wiper transmission with a screwdriver and remove two screws and transmission from cowl.
5. Reverse procedure to install.

RADIO, REPLACE

1972 Opel

1. Disconnect battery ground cable.
2. Remove glove box and ash tray, Fig. 18.
3. On Rallye models, remove right hand defroster outlet and hose.
4. On all models, remove right hand kick panel.
5. Remove "C" clip and lower windshield wiper arm.
6. Remove fresh air vent hose.
7. Loosen right hand nut from fresh air vent bracket.
8. Remove radio cover plate.
9. Disconnect electrical wiring from radio.
10. Remove radio from vehicle.
11. Reverse procedure to install.

1972-73 GT Sport Coupe

1. Disconnect battery ground cable.
2. Remove access trim plug from right side of console and the hex head

screw through opening.
3. Remove access trim cover on left side of console and the hex head screw through opening.
4. Remove tear bolts support steering column by drilling a $3/16$ inch diameter hole and using a screw extractor.
5. Disconnect ignition and turn signal wire plugs.
6. Support steering and remove the hex head bolts, then lower steering column.
7. Disconnect speedometer cable.
8. Remove six instrument cluster retaining screws.
9. Pull instrument cluster rearward.
10. Disconnect electrical wiring from radio.
11. Remove radio knobs.
12. Remove radio and remove radio shaft retaining nuts.
13. Remove radio from vehicle.
14. Reverse procedure to install.

1972-75 1900 & Manta

1. Disconnect battery ground cable.
2. Remove control knobs and trim knobs plate.
3. Remove two hex nuts and decorative cover plate.
4. Remove support bracket from back of radio housing and air distribution housing.
5. Disconnect wiring.
6. Remove radio.
7. Reverse procedure to install.

1976-77

1. Disconnect battery ground cable.
2. Remove ash tray and ash tray support.
3. Remove radio knobs and heater control knobs.

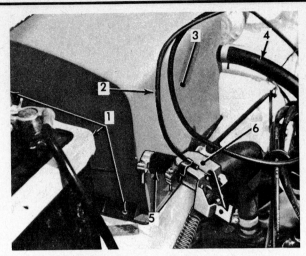

1. SHEET METAL SCREWS
2. TEMPERATURE CONTROL VALVE BOWDEN WIRE
3. HEATER HOUSING
4. HEATER HOSE, TO WATER PUMP
5. HEATER HOSE, TO TEMPERATURE CONTROL VALVE
6. TEMPERATURE CONTROL VALVE

Fig. 19 Heater housing installation. 1972 Opel

Fig. 20 Heater housing installation. 1972-75 1900 & Manta

4. Remove radio shaft nuts and trim panel.
5. Remove radio retainer screws from under dash.
6. Disconnect electrical connectors and lead-in cable and remove radio through the back of dash.
7. Reverse procedure to install.

HEATER CORE, REPLACE

1972 Opel

1. Disconnect battery ground cable and drain cooling system by removing lower radiator hose.
2. Disconnect heater hoses from core, Fig. 19.
3. Remove screws securing heater housing to dash and the housing.

4. Remove heater core from housing.
5. Reverse procedure to install.

1972-73 GT Sport Coupe

1. Disconnect battery ground cable and drain cooling system by removing lower radiator hose.
2. Disconnect heater hoses from core.
3. Remove hood lock control cable retaining clip and cable from lock bar.
4. Remove console shift cover as follows:
   a. Remove ash tray and the two screws beneath ash tray.
   b. Remove headlamp lever handle retaining screw and the handle.
   c. Unsnap retaining studs by prying

cover upward and lift cover over shift lever and rubber shift lever boot.
5. Remove left and right console access plugs and the screws through openings.
6. Remove tear bolts supporting steering column by drilling a $3/16$ inch diameter hole and using a screw extractor.
7. Disconnect ignition and turn signal wiring plugs.
8. Support steering column and remove the two hex head bolts, then lower steering column.
9. Disconnect speedometer cable.
10. Remove turn signal flasher.
11. Remove six instrument cluster retaining screws.
12. Pull instrument cluster rearward.
13. Remove heater control retaining screws and support bracket.
14. Disconnect heater and defroster hoses from instrument panel.
15. Remove all screws from instrument panel padding and the padding.
16. Remove one bolt from top of heater-blower case and two nuts from the bottom of the case.

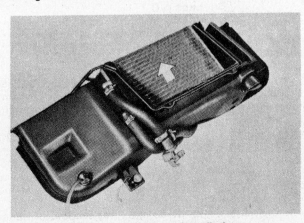

Fig. 21 Heater core installation. 1972-75 1900 & Manta

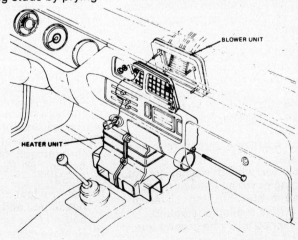

Fig. 22 Heater housing installation. 1976-77 Opel

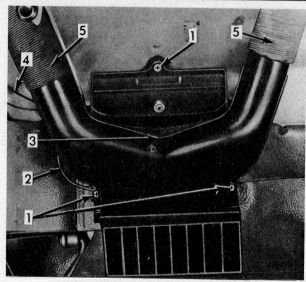

1. SHEET METAL SCREWS
2. HEATER - DEFROSTER CONTROL VALVE
3. AIR DISTRIBUTOR HOUSING
4. WIRE TO BLOWER SWITCH
5. HOSE TO DEFROSTER CONTROL OUTLET

Fig. 23 Air distributor housing installation. 1972 Opel

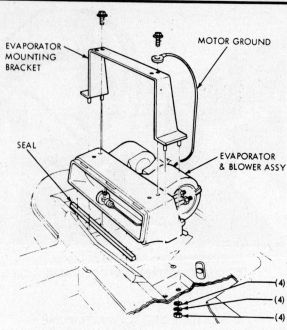

Fig. 24 Blower motor installation. 1972-73 GT Sport Coupe with A/C

17. Remove heater-blower case assembly.
18. Remove heater core or blower motor from case.
19. Reverse procedure to install.

1972-75 1900 & Manta

Removal

1. Remove hood lock with ground wire, if used.
2. Remove heater housing cover.
3. Pull hose of windshield washer from jet and remove jet from housing cover.
4. Disconnect bowden control wire from heater valve.
5. Remove heater housing from dash panel, Fig. 20.
6. Remove water hoses from heater core and pull heater core from heater housing, Fig. 21.

Installation

1. Apply sealing compound between heater housing and dash panel.
2. Install heater core into heater housing and attach water hoses, Fig. 21.
3. Install heater housing to dash panel, Fig. 22.
4. Install bowden control wire to heater valve.
5. Install windshield washer jet into housing cover and attach hose.
6. Install heater housing cover and seal with a sealing compound.
7. Install hood lock with ground wire, if used.

1976-77

1. Disconnect battery ground cable.

2. Drain cooling system.
3. Disconnect heater hoses at core and plug core tubes to prevent spillage of coolant when removing heater assembly.
4. Remove outer blower unit case cover and disconnect the fresh-air door bowden cable.
5. Disconnect the temperature cable at water valve.
6. Remove steering wheel.
7. Remove instrument cluster.
8. Disconnect wiring for console gauges and remove console retaining screws, shift lever leather and console.
9. Remove heater control and radio face plate.
10. Remove glove box.
11. Remove radio.
12. Disconnect selector mode cable from driver's side of heater unit assembly.
13. Carefully pull the temperature and fresh-air door cables through the cowl and remove control panel through the cluster opening.
14. Remove instrument panel assembly.
15. Remove heater unit assembly through bolt located at the rear and bottom of heater unit assembly, Fig. 22.
16. Remove four attaching nuts holding heater unit and blower unit together and remove heater unit assembly.
17. Remove bolts holding heater unit case halves together and the heater core.
18. Reverse procedure to install.

BLOWER MOTOR, REPLACE

1972 Opel

1. Disconnect battery ground cable.
2. Disconnect electrical wiring from blower switch, Fig. 23.
3. Disconnect control cable from air distributor door.
4. Remove screws securing air distributor housing to dash panel and partially remove housing from dash.
5. Remove air hoses from distributor housing and the housing.
6. Remove screws securing blower motor to air distributor housing and the blower motor.
7. Reverse procedure to install.

1972-73 GT Sport Coupe

Less A/C

Refer to the "Heater Core, Replace" procedure for blower motor replacement.

With A/C

1. Disconnect battery ground cable and discharge refrigerant system.
2. Remove luggage tray attaching screws and the tray.
3. Remove evaporator covers and the cover.
4. Disconnect electrical connector from resistor and the electrical connector from blower motor. Remove ground wire.
5. Disconnect two evaporator housing drain hoses.
6. Remove four nuts securing evapora-

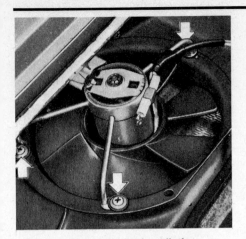

Fig. 25 Blower motor installation. 1972-75 1900 & Manta less A/C

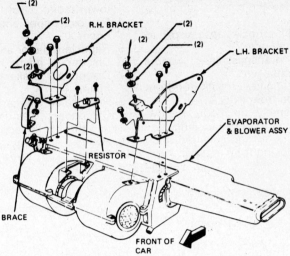

Fig. 26 Blower & evaporator assembly installation. 1973-75 1900 & Manta with A/C

tor mounting bracket to floor.
7. Disconnect evaporator inlet and outlet pipes and plug openings.
8. Remove mounting bracket, then the evaporator assembly from vehicle, Fig. 24.
9. Remove resistor assembly.
10. Remove blower case and blower motor attaching screws, then the assembly from vehicle.
11. Reverse procedure to install.

1972-75 1900 & Manta

Less A/C

1. Disconnect battery ground cable.
2. In engine compartment, remove five shroud cover attaching screws.
3. Remove cover.
4. Pull water hose from windshield wiper jet.
5. Disconnect wires to heater motor. Disconnect multiple plug connection on left side of shroud.
6. Remove three heater motor attach-

ing screws, Fig. 25.
7. Remove motor.
8. Reverse procedure to install.

With A/C

1. Disconnect battery ground cable.
2. On 1973 models, remove glove box assembly. On 1974-75 models, remove left side distributor duct and in-line fuse.
3. Discharge refrigerant system.
4. Disconnect pipe and hose from evaporator and plug openings in evaporator and hoses.
5. Disconnect delay restrictor and check valve hose assembly from vacuum cut-off switch and disconnect electrical wiring.
6. Remove evaporator attaching nuts.
8. Remove two case mounting bracket to instrument panel screws, Fig. 26.

9. Disconnect two evaporator drain hoses.
10. Remove evaporator assembly from vehicle.
11. Disconnect resistor electrical connector and remove resistor assembly.
12. Remove blower case and motor attaching screws and the assembly.
13. Reverse procedure to install.

1976-77

1. Disconnect battery ground cable.
2. Disconnect wiring at blower motor.
3. Remove heater hose bracket from cowl.
4. Remove retaining screws and pull out blower motor and squirrel cage.
5. Remove retaining clip holding squirrel cage to blower and remove cage.
6. Reverse procedure to install.

Engine Section

ENGINE, REPLACE

1972 Opel

The engine and transmission assembly is removed from beneath the vehicle.

1. Disconnect battery ground cable.
2. Remove air cleaner.
3. Drain cooling system and remove upper and lower radiator hoses.
4. Disconnect the following electrical connections: coil wire to distributor, alternator wiring, starter solenoid wiring and oil pressure switch wiring.
5. Disconnect vacuum hoses from tee on intake manifold, then remove tee from intake manifold.

6. Remove choke cable.
7. Remove heater control cable.
8. Remove throttle linkage.
9. Disconnect heater hoses from heater.
10. Disconnect water valve bracket to manifold.
11. Remove gearshift lever.
12. Raise and support vehicle.
13. Disconnect and plug fuel line from fuel pump. Detach fuel line from engine or transmission clips.
14. Disconnect speedometer cable from transmission.
15. Disconnect clutch cable.
16. Disconnect and remove propeller shaft at torque tube.
17. Disconnect exhaust pipe from mani-

fold. Do not remove the two exhaust flange bolts on the inboard side to facilitate installation.
18. Remove tailpipe and muffler hangers.
19. Remove engine to frame side rail ground strap.
20. Disconnect brake lines at brake hose.
21. Remove steering shaft clamp pinch bolt. Mark relationship between shaft and flange.
22. Remove steering mast guide sleeve stop bolt from mast jacket bracket, then pull steering column outward until column clears mast flange.
23. Support engine-transmission-front suspension assembly with a suitable

lifting device and chain assembly to the device.

24. Disconnect shock absorbers at upper mountings.
25. Remove transmission support bracket bolts.
26. Lower engine-transmission-front suspension from vehicle.
27. With assembly on floor, remove transmission from bellhousing.
28. Remove starter and solenoid, then the bellhousing from engine.
29. Support engine with a suitable stand.
30. Reverse procedure to install.

1972-73 GT Sport Coupe

The engine and transmission assembly is removed from beneath the vehicle.

1. Disconnect battery ground cable.
2. Remove air cleaner.
3. Drain cooling system by disconnecting the lower radiator hose.
4. Disconnect upper radiator hose.
5. Disconnect the following electrical connections: coil wire to distributor, alternator wiring, starter wiring and oil pressure switch.
6. Remove vacuum hoses from intake manifold tee, then the tee from manifold.
7. Remove water heated choke housing.
8. Remove throttle linkage and carburetor.
9. Disconnect heater hoses.
10. Remove gear shift lever.
11. Raise and support vehicle.
12. Using a suitable jack, raise engine slightly to relieve tension from engine mounts.
13. Disconnect and plug fuel line from fuel pump. Detach fuel line from engine or transmission retaining clips.
14. Disconnect speedometer cable from transmission.
15. Disconnect clutch cable.
16. Remove propeller shaft.
17. Disconnect exhaust pipe from exhaust manifold.
18. Remove engine to frame side rail ground strap.
19. Disconnect transmission crossmember from transmission and frame.
20. Disconnect engine crossmember from engine and frame.
21. Lower engine and transmission assembly from vehicle.
22. Reverse procedure to install.

1972-75 1900 & Manta

1. Scribe hood hinge mounting locations and remove hood.
2. Disconnect battery ground cable.
3. Drain coolant by disconnecting

lower radiator hose.
4. Remove upper and lower radiator hoses.
5. Remove radiator and fan shroud.
6. Disconnect heater hoses.
7. Disconnect brake booster vacuum hose.
8. Remove air cleaner.
9. Disconnect electrical connections and throttle linkage.
10. Remove console.
11. Remove shift lever, boot, plate and shift lever.
12. Raise and support vehicle.
13. Disconnect fuel line at pump.
14. Remove front stone shield.
15. Disconnect speedometer cable, back-up light switch and clutch cable.
16. Remove propeller shaft.
17. Disconnect exhaust pipe and bell housing support.
18. Disconnect transmission support.
19. Remove engine mount bolts.
20. Attach suitable lifting equipment to engine.
21. Remove engine and transmission assembly from vehicle.
22. Reverse procedure to install.

1976-77

1. Remove battery cables.
2. Scribe position of hinges on the engine hood, remove the four bolts attaching the hinges to the hood and the hood.
3. Remove undercover and drain cooling system by opening drain plugs at radiator and cylinder block.
4. Drain crankcase.
5. Remove air cleaner as follows:
   a. Disconnect PCV hose from cylinder head cover.
   b. Disconnect ECS hose from air cleaner body.
   c. Disconnect air hose from AIR pump.
   d. Remove bolts attaching air cleaner and loosen clamp bolt.
   e. Lift air cleaner slightly and disconnect the CCS hose (from thermostat to intake manifold), then remove air cleaner assembly.
6. Working at left side of engine, perform the following procedures:
   a. Disconnect CCS hot air hose and remove manifold cover.
   b. Disconnect alternator wiring at connector.
   c. Remove two nuts connecting exhaust pipe to exhaust manifold and disconnect exhaust manifold.
   d. Loosen the clutch control cable by turning the adjusting nut.
   e. Disconnect heater hose (from

engine to cock) at engine side.
   f. Disconnect heater hose from heater unit and joint.
   g. Disconnect control cable from the water cock and remove the cock flying screws, then the cock assembly with the heater hose.
   h. Remove engine mounting nut.
   i. Install Tool J-26555 engine hanger on the engine, using exhaust manifold stud bolts.
7. Working at right side of engine, perform the following procedures:
   a. Disconnect cable grounding the cylinder block to frame.
   b. Disconnect fuel hoses from carburetor.
   c. Disconnect high-tension cable from ignition coil.
   d. Disconnect vacuum hose from connector at rear of intake manifold.
   e. Disconnect accelerator control cable from carburetor.
   f. Disconnect starter motor electrical connections.
   g. Disconnect themo unit, oil pressure switch and distributor wiring at connector.
   h. Disconnect carburetor solenoid valve lead and automatic choke wiring at connector.
   i. Disconnect back-up light switch and top/third switch (neutral switch wiring on California vehicles) wiring at connector at rear of engine.
   j. Disconnect ECS hose from oil pan.
   k. Remove engine mounting nut and stopper plate.
   l. Install Tool No. J-26555 engine hanger on engine, using one each of engine intake manifold stud bolt and engine hanger mounting stud bolt.
   m. Raise engine slightly and remove left side engine mounting stopper plate.
8. Working at front of engine, perform the following procedures:
   a. Disconnect top water hose and lower water hose from outlet pipe and radiator.
   b. Remove four nuts holding fan shroud and the fan shroud.
   c. Remove four nuts holding radiator and the radiator assembly.
9. Remove three bolts attaching the gearshift lever and the gearshift lever assembly.
10. Working beneath the vehicle, perform the following procedures:
    a. Remove parking brake return spring and disconnect brake cable.
    b. Remove four bolts from the rear

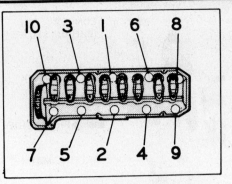

Fig. 1 Cylinder head tightening sequence. 1972-75

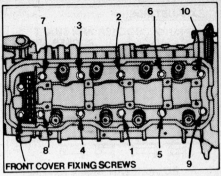

FRONT COVER FIXING SCREWS

Fig. 2 Cylinder head tightening sequence. 1976-77

extension side of the propeller shaft and disconnect the propeller shaft from the transmission.

c. Remove clutch cable heat protector.

d. Remove clutch return spring.

e. Disconnect clutch control cable from the clutch withdraw lever and remove from engine stiffener.

f. Remove front side exhaust bracket from transmission.

g. Disconnect front and rear exhaust pipes at joint and remove front side exhaust pipe.

h. Disconnect speedometer cable.

i. Remove four rear engine mounting bolts.

NOTE: The engine should be raised slightly before removing the rear mounting bolts.

11. To remove engine:

a. Check that all parts have been removed or disconnected from the engine that are fastened to the frame side.

b. Remove engine toward front of vehicle.

12. Reverse procedure to install.

CYLINDER HEAD, REPLACE
1972-75

1. Disconnect battery ground cable.
2. Drain coolant from radiator and block. Loosen drain plug on right side of engine to avoid coolant entering cylinder bores. Drain plug is located on the right rear of cylinder block above oil pressure switch.
3. Remove hoses from thermostat housing.
4. Remove six intake and exhaust manifold attaching bolts and position assembly aside.
5. Remove spark plug wires from spark plugs.
6. Remove bracket bolt holding spark plug wires away from cylinder head.
7. Remove rocker arm cover.
8. Remove 10 cylinder head bolts,

using 12 mm serrated drive, tool J-22915, and two cylinder head-to-timing-chain-cover bolts with a 6 mm hex-head wrench.

9. Remove three bolts attaching plate to front of cylinder head.

10. Remove plastic screw from end of camshaft.

11. Remove three bolts attaching camshaft sprocket to cylinder head. Slide sprocket off camshaft and remove head. Place head on bench supported at each end by a block of wood to prevent damage to valves.

12. Reverse procedure to install and note the following:

a. Clean piston tops and combustion chambers. Thoroughly clean all gasket surfaces on the cylinder block and cylinder head.

b. Lightly lubricate cylinder walls with engine oil. Install coolant passage rubber gasket ring in timing case.

c. Apply plastic sealer or equivalent to smooth sides of the cylinder head gasket where the gasket mates with the timing chain cover. Place new cylinder head gasket on cylinder block.

d. Install cylinder head. Be careful to place head squarely over guide pins. Rotate camshaft so recesses are in vertical position to allow installation of left row of bolts.

e. Install ten cylinder head bolts. Torque bolts gradually in the sequence shown in Fig. 1. Finally torque bolts to specifications in the same sequence. Use same procedure with cylinder head to timing chain cover bolts, with final torque at 17 ft. lbs.

f. Slide camshaft sprocket with assembled chain onto camshaft and guide pin and fasten with bolts. Install nylon adjusting screw. After sprocket has been attached to camshaft, recheck alignment to see that chain has not slipped. Close front access hole.

g. Check camshaft end clearance between cover and nylon screw with feeler gauge. Clearance should be .004 to .008 in. Excess clearance can be eliminated by carefully adjusting cover with a suitable drift.

1976-77

1. Disconnect battery ground cable.
2. Drain cooling system and remove air cleaner, then components from intake manifold.
3. Remove manifold cover bolts and the manifold cover.

4. Remove EGR pipe from rear of cylinder block.
5. Disconnect exhaust pipe from manifold.
6. Remove cylinder head cover and separate the timing sprocket and camshaft.
7. Disconnect air hoses from check valve and AIR Pump.
8. Remove two nuts holding the air bypass valve bracket, then the valve and bracket.
9. Remove two bolts attaching the cylinder head to the front cover.
10. Loosen cylinder head bolts, using Tool J-24239.
11. Remove cylinder head assembly with the intake and exhaust manifolds.

NOTE: When removing the cylinder head assembly, do not separate the timing sprocket and chain; keep them in position between the chain tensioner and chain guide.

12. Reverse procedure to install and note the following:

a. Wipe lower face of cylinder head and upper face of cylinder block before reassembly.

b. Apply engine oil to the threaded portion of the cylinder head bolts. Install and torque the cylinder head bolts in sequence, Fig. 2, to specifications.

c. Check valve timing.

ROCKER ARM STUDS, REPLACE
1972-75

1. Remove air cleaner, rocker arm cover and rocker arm.

NOTE: The rocker arm studs are threaded into the cylinder head. A tapered portion of the stem prevents stud from loosening.

2. Using a suitable tool, remove stud from cylinder head.

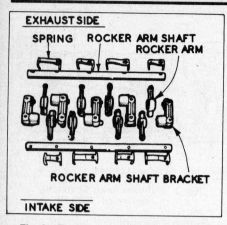

EXHAUST SIDE
SPRING   ROCKER ARM SHAFT
ROCKER ARM

ROCKER ARM SHAFT BRACKET

INTAKE SIDE

Fig. 3   Rocker arm assembly. 1976-77

3. Thread new stud into cylinder head. Seat tapered part of stud by striking stud with a rubber hammer.
4. Place two turned-down rocker arm nuts on threaded part of stud.
5. Torque stud into cylinder head to 29 ft. lbs.

ROCKER ARM ASSEMBLY SERVICE

1976-77

1. Remove the spring from the rocker arm shaft, then the rocker arm brackets and rocker arms, Fig. 3.
2. Check rocker arm shaft for run-out. Support the shaft on V-blocks at both ends and check by turning shaft slowly with plunger of a dial indicator resting on the center of the shaft. Replace the shaft if run-out exceeds .0157 inch. With a micrometer, measure shaft outside diameter at the four positions where the rocker arms are attached. Replace the shaft if diameter is less than .8012 inch.
3. Measure the inside diameter of the rocker arms. Compare this measurement with the rocker arm shaft diameter to determine clearance. If clearance exceeds .0079 in., replace the rocker arms or shaft. Check the area where the rocker arm contacts the valve stem for step wear, scores or other damage. Replace the rocker arm if the amount of wear or damage is excessive.
4. Apply engine oil to the rocker arm shaft and rocker arms. Install the longer shaft on the exhaust valve side and the shorter shaft on the intake valve side so the setting marks on the shaft are facing the top, Fig. 4. Assemble the rocker arm shaft brackets and rocker arms to the rocker arm shaft so the cylinder number mark on the upper face of the brackets is facing toward the front of the engine. Align the setting

mark on the No. 1 rocker arm shaft bracket with the mark on the intake and exhaust valve side rocker arm shafts. Check that the amount of projection of rocker arm shaft beyond the outer face of No. 1 rocker arm shaft bracket is longer on the exhaust side rocker arm shaft than on the intake side rocker arm shaft when the rocker arm shaft stud holes are aligned with rocker arm shaft bracket stud holes. Install the rocker arm spring in position between the rocker arm shaft bracket and rocker arm.

VALVE SERVICE

1972-75

1. Remove cylinder head. Place on bench and support at each end with a block of wood.
2. Using a suitable spring compressor, compress valve spring and remove cap retainers. Release tool and remove spring and cap.
3. Remove valves. Place valves in numerical order so valves can be installed in original position.
4. Remove all carbon from combustion chambers, piston heads and valves. When using scrapers or wire brushes, avoid scratching valve seats and valve faces.
5. Clean carbon and gum deposits from valve guide bores.
6. Inspect valve faces and seats for pits, burned spots or other evidence of poor seating.

NOTE: New intake valves must not be refaced or lapped with grinding compound.

7. Inspect valve guides. Worn or pitted guides can be reamed to accept valves with oversize stems. Oversized valves are used in production and are marked "1" or "2" or "A." These marks are stamped into the end of the valve stem and near the spark plug hole on the cylinder head.
8. Grind valve seats:
   a. Intake:
      With 45-degree cutter, remove burnt structure until a metallic bright seat is obtained. Lightly coat valve head with red lead, insert valve in guide and rotate valve under light pressure back and forth several times. A contact pattern is then established and the seat width can be measured. If valve does not seat perfectly, lightly recut valve seat to the specified seat width of .049-.059

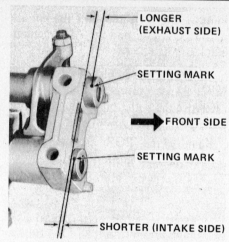

LONGER (EXHAUST SIDE)

SETTING MARK

→ FRONT SIDE

SETTING MARK

SHORTER (INTAKE SIDE)

Fig. 4   Rocker arm assembly installation. 1976-77

in. with a 30-degree correction cutter.
   b. Exhaust:
      Follow the procedure outlined for intake valves, but grind valve seat width to .063-.073 in.
9. Lubricate valves with engine oil and install valves, valve springs, caps and cap retainers, using the valve spring compressor. Install valve spring with closely wound coils toward the cylinder head.
10. Install cylinder head.

Valve Seats
1. Install valve in cylinder head and check the amount of depression from the cylinder head face using a depth gauge or a straight edge and a scale. If depression exceeds .0670 in., replace the valve seat insert.
2. Check the valve seats for poor contact, dents or damage. Correct the valve seats if the width of contact exceeds .079 in.
3. Valve seat replacement:
   a. Weld end of welding rods to several portions of the inner face of valve insert away from aluminum alloy parts.
   b. Allow the cylinder head to cool off from two to five minutes, so the contraction of inserts takes place. Apply a shock load to the welding rods and pull out the insert.
   c. Clean the valve seat insert fitting face of the cylinder head carefully, then heat the area to expand the area. Chill the valve seat insert with dry ice to contract and install in the cylinder head.
4. Grinding valve seats:
   a. Remove carbon from the valve seat face and cut the valve seat with 15-deg., 45-deg. and 75-deg. cutters. Remove just enough material to remove dents or damage. Valve seat contact width should

Fig. 5   Valve guide removal. 1976-77

be from .0472-.0630 in.

b. Apply a small amount of lapping compound to the valve seat and lap the valve seat. Lap the valve seat so the valve seat contact width is within specifications and contact is centered on the seat.

Valve Guides

1. Check the inner face of the valve guides for scuffs or abnormal wear and replace if necessary.
2. Measure the inside diameter of the valve guide and compare the measurement with the valve stem diameter to determine the clearance. If clearance exceeds .0029 in. for the intake valve or .0098 in. for the exhaust valve, check condition of valve stem wear and replace valve or valve guide as necessary.
3. Valve guide removal:
   Insert Tool J-26512 remover and installer into the valve guide and drive out the valve guide upward using a hammer, Fig. 5.
4. Valve guide installation:
   Apply engine oil to the outer circumference of the valve guide and install guide in position in the cylinder head. Hold Tool J-26512 against the valve guide and drive the valve guide into the cylinder head until the guide is the specified distance from the cylinder head, Fig. 6.

Valves

1. Replace the valve if stem diameter is less than .3102 in. for the intake valve or .3091 in. for the exhaust valve.
2. Replace any valves with heavy scores on the stems. Install a new guide when valve is replaced.
3. Measure the thickness of valve head and replace the valve if thickness is less than .0315 in. for the intake

valve or .0394 in. for the exhaust valve.
4. Grind the face of the valve head to an angle of 45 degrees. Grind the valve stem end as necessary.

Valve Springs

1. Check the valve springs visually for damage and replace if necessary.
2. Measure the free height of valve springs. Replace springs if height is less than 1.7874 in. for outer springs or 1.7244 in. for inner springs.
3. Place the valve spring on a surface plate and check for straightness using a square. Inclination should not exceed .0787 in.

VALVES, ADJUST
1972-75

Place No. 1 piston at top dead center, compression stroke. Remove distributor cap and note position of rotor. When the No. 1 piston is at top dead center, compression stroke, the rotor should be in the No. 1 firing position. Adjust the two valves for No. 1 cylinder. Adjustment is made by backing off adjusting nut at the rocker arm until clearance exists between valve stem, rocker arm and lifter. Then, slowly tighten adjusting nut until clearance is eliminated. Turn adjusting nut one full turn clockwise to position the piston of the hydraulic valve lifter at the mid-point of its travel.

Rotate engine to place the rotor in the firing position for the remaining three cylinders in the firing order and adjust the valves as previously described.

1976-77

Place No. 1 or No. 4 piston at top dead center, compression stroke by rotating the engine until the notched line on the

Fig. 7   Timing chain cover oil seal installation. 1972-75

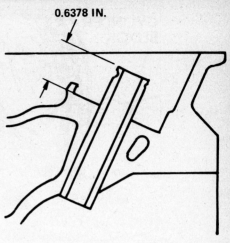

Fig. 6   Valve guide installation. 1976-77

crankshaft pulley is aligned with the "O" mark on the front cover. Check and adjust valve clearance on either No. 1 or No. 4 cylinder valves. Then, rotate engine 90 degrees. This places the next cylinder in the firing order at top dead center, compression stroke. Check and adjust the valve clearance on that cylinder. Continue to rotate the engine in 90 degree increments and adjust the remaining valves.

TIMING CHAIN COVER, REPLACE
1972-75

1. Support engine in chassis as outlined under "Oil Pan, Replace" procedure.
2. Remove radiator and shroud assembly.
3. Remove cylinder head.
4. Remove alternator belt and alternator mounting bracket.
5. On 1972-74 models, remove fuel pump.
6. On all models, remove distributor.
7. Remove chain tensioner assembly from timing cover.
8. Remove crankshaft pulley bolt.
9. Remove water pump assembly.
10. Remove oil pan.
11. Remove timing chain cover bolts.
12. Reverse procedure to install and note the following:
   a. To install new timing case oil seal, drive out the old seal from the rear, using a drift. Coat the circumference of the new seal sparingly with suitable sealer and press seal in, using Tool J-22924, Fig. 7. Be careful not to damage timing case. It is not necessary to use crankshaft bolt to install seal when cover is off engine.
   b. Inspect chain tensioner for proper operation and assembly.
   c. Install timing case rubber gaskets

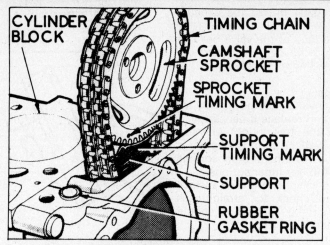

Fig. 8 Installing coolant passage sealing ring in cylinder block. 1972-75

to cylinder block, Fig. 8. Retain with grease if necessary. Gaskets will overlap with oil pan gasket.

d. Position timing cover over guide pin in upper left corner of cylinder block and insert centering bolt through timing chain cover into lower right corner of cylinder block. No sealing is required.

e. Install and tighten bolts.

f. Install cylinder head.

1976-77

Removal

1. Remove the crankshaft pulley.
2. Remove oil filter.
3. Remove distributor bracket and distributor.
4. Remove nine bolts securing front cover and the front cover assembly with the water pump and oil pump.

Installation

1. Install the gasket on the cylinder block.
2. Install water pump, oil pump and oil seal on the front cover.
3. Turn the face of the oil pump drive gear with a punch mark to the oil filter side and align the center of the dowel pin with the setting mark on the oil pump base, Fig. 9. Set the pistons in No. 1 and No. 4 cylinders

Fig. 10 Checking punch mark location. 1976-77

at top dead center.

5. Install the front cover assembly by engaging the pinion gear with the oil pump drive gear.
6. Check that the punch mark on the oil pump shaft is parallel with the front face of the cylinder block, Fig. 10.
7. Check that the slit at the end of the oil pump shaft is parallel with the front face of the cylinder block and is offset forward, Fig. 11.
8. Install the front cover assembly with the nine bolts and torque to specifications.

TIMING CHAIN, REPLACE

1972-75

Removal

1. Remove timing case cover as outlined previously.
2. Pull off sprockets with chain. Put a paint mark on front side of timing chain to permit reinstallation in original position, Fig. 12.

Installation

1. Clean all parts, check for wear and replace if necessary. Either the chain alone or the chain and two sprockets can be replaced. The sprockets should not be replaced without replacing the chain. The chain tensioner body and the complete assembly are available for replacement.
2. Turn the crankshaft so the key on the sprocket is on top and vertical. Assemble chain with camshaft sprocket, then install chain on crankshaft sprocket. Be sure paint dot on the chain is facing front, so the chain moves in the original direction of rotation, Fig. 12.
3. Be sure camshaft sprocket mark is in alignment with mark on support and that chain is parallel with damper block.

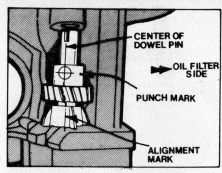

Fig. 9 Aligning oil pump shaft for front cover installation. 1976-77

4. Install timing chain cover as outlined previously.

1976-77

Removal

1. Remove timing chain cover as outlined previously.
2. Remove timing chain and camshaft sprocket, Fig. 13.

Installation

1. Turn the crankshaft so the key is turned to the cylinder head side. The pistons in No. 1 and No. 4 cylinders will now be at top dead center.
2. Install the timing chain by aligning the mark plate on the chain with the setting mark on the crankshaft sprocket so the side of the chain with the mark plate is on the front side and the side with more links between the mark plates is positioned to the chain guide side, Fig. 14. Fig. 14.
3. Install the camshaft sprocket so the setting mark is on the front side and that the triangular setting mark is aligned with the mark plate on the chain.

NOTE: Keep the timing chain engaged with the camshaft sprocket until the camshaft sprocket is installed on the camshaft.

4. Install timing chain cover as outlined previously.

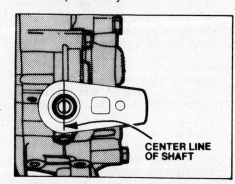

Fig. 11 Oil pump shaft installation. 1976-77

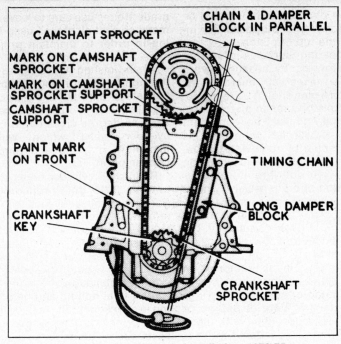

Fig. 12   Timing chain installation. 1972-75

CAMSHAFT, REPLACE

1972-75

Removal

1. Remove cylinder head as outlined previously.
2. Loosen self-locking rocker arm nuts and swing rocker arms off valve lifters.
3. Remove valve lifters. Place lifters in a suitable holding fixture so they can be installed in original position.
4. Remove cover from access hole on left side at rear of cylinder head. Remove camshaft toward front, supporting camshaft through access hole and taking care not to damage the bearings.

Installation

1. Lubricate camshaft journals and in-stall camshaft from front into cylinder head. Support shaft through access hole in left side of head to prevent damage to bearings.
2. Install valve lifters, rocker arms and self-locking rocker arm nuts.
3. Install rear and side access plates.
4. Install cylinder head as outlined previously.

1976-77

Removal

1. Lock the timing chain adjuster by depressing the automatic adjuster slide pin and turning pin 90 degrees clockwise, Fig. 15.

NOTE: When the chain adjuster is locked, check to be sure chain is slack.

2. Remove timing sprocket set bolts and remove the timing sprocket from the camshaft. Keep the sprocket on the chain damper and tensioner without removing the timing

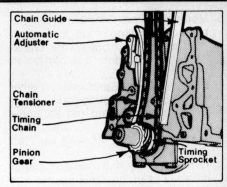

Fig. 13   Timing chain removal. 1976-77

chain from the sprocket.
3. Loosen the rocker arm shaft bracket nuts gradually in sequence, starting with the outer nuts.
4. Remove the nuts and rocker arm shaft bracket assembly.
5. Remove the camshaft.

Installation

1. Lubricate the camshaft and journals of cylinder head with engine oil.
2. Install the camshaft on the cylinder head carefully by aligning the thrust grooves, Fig. 16.
3. Check that the punch marks on the rocker arm shafts are turned upward, then install the rocker arm shaft bracket assembly on the cylinder head carefully and align the setting mark on the camshaft with the mark on the No. 1 rocker arm shaft bracket, Fig. 16.

PISTON & CONNECTING ROD SERVICE

1972-75

Piston & Rod Removal

1. Drain engine oil and cooling system.
2. Remove oil pan.
3. Remove cylinder head as outlined previously.
4. Examine the cylinder bores above the ring travel. If a ridge exists, remove with a ridge reamer to avoid damaging rings or cracking ring lands in pistons during removal.

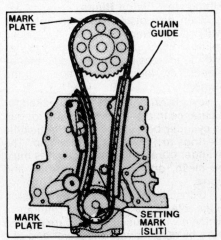

Fig. 14   Timing chain installation. 1976-77

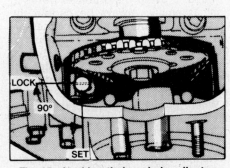

Fig. 15   Locking timing chain adjuster. 1976-77

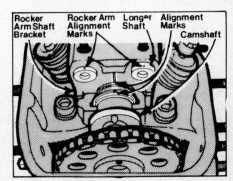

Fig. 16   Camshaft, rocker arm shafts & brackets installation. 1976-77

5. Mark the cylinder number on all pistons, connecting rods and caps. Starting at the front of the crankcase, the cylinders are numbered 1-2-3-4.
6. Remove the cap and bearing shell from No. 1 connecting rod.
7. Push the piston and rod assembly up from top of cylinder. Then reinstall cap and bearing shell on rod.
8. Remove remaining rod and piston assemblies in the same manner.
9. Remove compression rings and oil rings.
10. Remove piston pin.

Cylinder Bore Inspection

Inspect cylinder walls for scoring, roughness, or ridges which indicate excessive wear. Check cylinder bores for taper and out-of-round with an accurate cylinder gauge at top, middle and bottom of bore, both parallel and at right angles to the centerline of the engine. The diameter of the cylinder bores at any point may be measured with an inside micrometer or by setting the cylinder gauge dial at "O" and measuring across the gauge contact points with outside micrometer while the gauge is at the same "O" setting. If a cylinder bore is moderately rough or slightly scored but is not out-of-round or tapered, it is possible to repair the bore by honing to accept a standard service piston. If cylinder bore is very rough or deeply scored, it may be necessary to rebore the cylinder to fit an oversize piston in order to insure satisfactory results.

If a cylinder bore is tapered .0005" or more, or is out-of-round .0005" or more, it is advisable to hone or rebore for the smallest possible oversize piston and rings.

Piston, Ring & Pin Inspection

Clean carbon from piston surfaces and under side of piston heads. Clean carbon from ring grooves with a suitable tool and remove any gum or varnish from piston skirts with suitable solvent.

Carefully examine pistons for rough or scored bearing surfaces, cracks in skirt, head cracked or broken ring lands, and chipping or uneven wear which would cause rings to seat improperly or have excessive clearance in ring grooves. Damaged or faulty pistons should be replaced.

Fitting Pistons to Cylinders

When a piston is checked for size, it must be measured with a micrometer applied to the skirt at points 90 degrees to the piston pin. The piston should be measured for fitting purposes 2½ inches below the top of piston.

Inspect bearing surfaces of piston pins. Check for wear by measuring worn or unworn surfaces with micrometers. Rough or worn pins should be replaced. Check fit of piston pins in piston bosses. Occasionally pins will be found tight due to gum or varnish deposits. This may be corrected by removing the deposit with a suitable solvent. If piston bosses are worn out-of-round or oversize, the piston and pin assembly must be replaced. Oversize pins are not available since the pin is a press fit in the connecting rod. Piston pins must fit the piston with .0004" to .0007" clearance.

Examine all piston rings for scores, chips or cracks. Check compression rings for tension by comparing with new rings. Check gap of compression rings by placing rings in bore at bottom or ring travel. Measure gap with feeler gauge. Gap should be between .011" and .021". If gaps are excessive, it indicates the rings have worn considerably and should be replaced.

Cylinder bores may not be the same size. Standard replacement piston sizes are in the midpoint of the cylinder bore size range. Therefore, it may be necessary to hone cylinders for correct piston fit. Out-of-round on cylinder bore must not exceed .0005" maximum with a taper not to exceed .0005".

Before the honing or reboring operation is started, measure all new pistons with micrometer contacting at points exactly 90 degrees to piston pin, then select the smallest piston for the first fitting. The slight variation usually found between pistons in a set may provide for correction if the first piston has excessive clearance.

If wear of cylinder does not exceed .005", honing is recommended to true the bore. If wear or out-of-round exceeds these limits, the bore should be trued up with a fly cutter boring bar and then finish honed.

When reboring cylinders, all crankshaft bearing caps must be in place and torqued to avoid distortion of bores in final assembly. Always be certain the crankshaft is out of the way of the boring cutter when boring each cylinder. When making the final cut with boring bar, leave .001" on the diameter for finish honing to give the required clearance specified.

When honing cylinders, use clean sharp stones of proper grade for the required amount of metal to be removed, in accordance with instructions of the hone manufacturer. Dull or dirty stones cut unevenly and generate excessive heat. When using course or medium grade stones use care to leave sufficient metal so that all stones used for finishing in order to maintain proper clearance.

When finished honing, pass the hone through the entire length of cylinder at the rate of approximately 60 cycles per minute. This should produce the desired 45 degree cross hatch pattern on cylinder walls which will insure maximum ring life and minimum oil consumption.

Refinished cylinder bores should not be over .0005" out-of-round or tapered. Each bore must be final honed to remove all stone or cutter marks and provide a smooth surface. During final honing, each piston must be fitted individually to the bore in which it will be installed and should be marked to insure correct installation.

After final honing and before the piston is checked for fit, each cylinder bore must be thoroughly washed to remove all traces of abrasive, then dried. The dry bore should then be brushed clean with a power-driven fiber brush. If all traces of abrasive are not removed, rapid wear of new pistons and rings will result. Fit new pistons in the following manner:

a. Expand a telescope gauge to fit the cylinder bore at right angles to the piston pin 2½" from top.
b. Measure the piston to be installed. The piston must be measured at right angles to the piston pin 2½" below the top of piston.
c. The piston must be between .0008" and .0012" smaller than the cylinder bore.

Both block and piston must be approximately the same temperature when measurements are made or expansion errors will occur. A difference of 10 degrees F between parts is sufficient to produce a variation of .0005".

Fitting New Piston Rings

When new piston rings are installed without reboring cylinders, the glazed cylinder walls should be slightly dulled without increasing the bore diameter by means of the finest grade honing stones.

New piston rings must be checked for clearance in piston grooves and for gap in cylinder bores; however, the flexible oil rings are not checked for gap. The cylinder bores and piston grooves must be clean, dry and free of carbon and burrs.

To check the end gap of compression rings, place the ring in the cylinder in which it will be used and square it in the bore by tapping with the lower end of a piston. Measure the gap with feeler gauges. Piston ring end gap should be

.014-.022″ (top ring) and .014-.022″ (2nd ring) and the oil ring end gap should be .015-.055″.

If gap is less than specified, file the ends of rings carefully with a smooth file to obtain proper gap.

Piston Ring Installation

1. Upper ring is chrome plated and can be installed either way up. The No. two ring must be installed with the marking "top" facing upward. Oil ring can be installed either way up.
2. Install piston rings with gaps positioned as shown in Fig. 12.
3. With rings installed on piston, check clearance in grooves by inserting feeler gauges between each ring and lower land. Any wear that occurs forms a step at inner portion of the lower land. If the piston groove has worn to the extent that a relatively high step exists on the lower land, the piston should be replaced since step will interfere with the operation of new rings causing ring clearances to become excessive.
4. When fitting new rings to new pistons, the side clearance of the compression rings should be .0024-.0034″ (top ring) and .0013-.0024″ (2nd ring), and the oil ring clearance should be .0013-.0024″.

Inspect piston pin bores and piston pins for wear. Piston pin bores and piston pins must be free of varnish or scuffing when being measured. If clearance is in excess of the .001″ wear limit, the piston and piston pin assembly should be replaced.

1. Lubricate piston pin holes in piston and connecting rod to facilitate installation of pin.
2. Install piston pin.
3. Check piston for freedom of movement on piston pin.
4. Make sure cylinder bores, pistons, connecting rod bearings and crankshaft journals are clean, then coat all bearing surfaces with engine oil.
5. Before installation of a piston and rod assembly in the bore, position the crankpin straight downward.
6. Remove connecting rod cap.
7. Make sure the gap in the oil ring rails and the gaps of the compression rings are positioned correctly.
8. Lubricate the piston and rings and install in bore.
9. Select a new connecting rod bearing, if necessary. Install cap with bearing lower shell on rod and tighten bolt nuts to 36 ft. lbs. torque.
10. Install remaining piston and rod assemblies. When piston and rod assemblies are properly installed, the oil spurt holes in the connecting

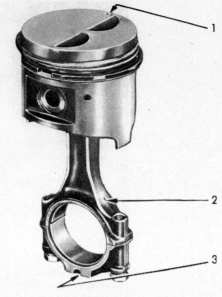

1. NOTCH IN PISTON HEAD POINTING TOWARD THE FRONT
2. OIL HOLE IN CONNECTING ROD POINTING TOWARD THE RIGHT (MANIFOLD SIDE)
3. NOTCH IN CONNECTING ROD CAP POINTING TOWARD THE REAR

Fig. 17 Piston & rod assembly. 1972-75

rods will be facing toward right, Fig. 17.
11. Check end clearance between connecting rods in each crankpin using a feeler gauge. Clearance should be between .0043″ and .0095″.
12. Install cylinder head as outlined previously.
13. Install oil pan as outlined under "Oil Pan, Replace" procedure.

1976-77

Removal

It is recommended to not remove piston from the connecting rod unless parts replacement is necessary. Note the following when piston and connecting rod assembly is disassembled.

1. Replace piston pin with a new pin.
2. Check piston pin fitting hole in the piston and connecting rod for damage and replace the parts if necessary.
3. Remove the piston rings from the piston.

NOTE: Keep the rings from each piston together to prevent interchanging.

4. Remove piston pin.

Piston Inspection

1. Check the pistons visually for scuf-

fing, cracking or wear. Replace pistons if worn or damaged.
2. Measure the diameter of the piston at a point 1.575 in. below the piston head at a right angle to the piston pin. With a cylinder bore indicator, measure the cylinder bore diameter at the lower section, where the amount of wear is least. Compare the piston diameter with the cylinder bore diameter to determine the clearance. If clearance exceeds .0026 in., replace the piston.
3. Inspect clearance between piston pin and piston. The piston pin clearance is normal when the piston pin is fitted snugly into the piston and the piston turns smoothly. Replace the piston pin and piston if excessive play is present.

Piston Ring Inspection

1. The piston rings should be replaced with new rings whenever the engine is overhauled or if rings are found to be worn or damaged.
2. Insert the piston rings into the cylinder bore and push downward to the skirt portion, where bore diameter is smallest with the piston head, so the rings are held at a right angle to the cylinder wall. Measure the end gap with a feeler gauge. Replace the rings if the gap exceeds .059 inch.
3. With a feeler gauge, measure the clearance between the piston ring and ring grooves in the piston at several points around the circumference of the piston. Replace piston rings and piston if clearance exceeds .0059 inch.

Connecting Rod Clearance

Assemble the connecting rod to the crankshaft and measure the clearance between the connecting rod big end and the side face of the crankpin, using a feeler gauge. Replace the connecting rod if clearance exceeds .0138 in.

Assembly

1. Installation of piston rings.
   a. Assemble the piston rings on the piston. Assemble the compression rings to the grooves in the piston so that the faces with the "NPR" or "TOP" mark are turned up. Neither the expander ring nor the side rail is provided with a mark. Install the oil control ring assembly in the order of expander ring, lower side rail and upper side rail.
   b. When all the piston rings are installed, apply engine oil to the entire rings, then check to see that

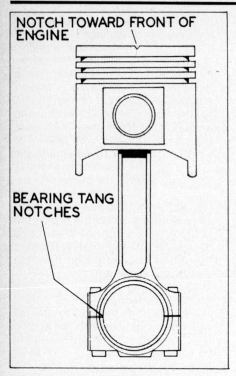

NOTCH TOWARD FRONT OF ENGINE

BEARING TANG NOTCHES

Fig. 18 Piston & rod assembly. 1976-77

they turn smoothly in the ring grooves.
2. Assemble piston to rod, Fig. 18.

REAR OIL SEAL, REPLACE

1972-75

1. Remove transmission, bell housing and clutch.
2. Remove flywheel.
3. Punch a hole in oil seal and thread a sheet metal screw. Grip the screw with pliers and pull out the seal.
4. To ensure proper sealing, lubricate the new seal with a suitable grease and install on taper ring J-22928. Turn seal to be sure lip of seal is not turned back.
5. Place tapered ring with oil seal on crankshaft flange and move lip of seal over rear of crankshaft. Be careful not to tilt seal.
6. Drive in oil seal using Tool J-22928-2, Fig. 19.
7. Install flywheel, clutch, bell housing and transmission. When replacing flywheel, use new bolts and torque to 43 ft.-lbs.

1976-77

Removal

1. Remove the clutch pressure plate assembly.
2. Flatten the flywheel bolt lock plate and remove the six bolts holding the flywheel, then the flywheel.
3. Pry off the oil seal from the seal retainer, using a screwdriver.

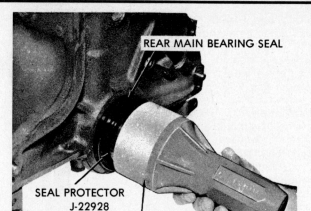

REAR MAIN BEARING SEAL

SEAL PROTECTOR J-22928

INSTALLER J-22928-2

Installation

1. Fill the clearance between lips of the oil seal with bearing grease.
2. Apply engine oil to the oil seal fitting face of the crankshaft.
3. Apply a thin coat of engine oil to the fitting face of the oil seal.
4. Install the oil seal in the oil seal retainer, using Tool J-22928-2, Fig. 20.

NOTE: When the oil seal is installed, check to be sure that flanged part of the seal is properly seated on the oil seal retainer.

5. Install remaining parts by reversing removal procedure. Discard used flywheel bolt lock plates and install new ones. Torque flywheel bolts to 69 ft. lbs.

OIL PAN, REPLACE

1972 Opel & 1972-73 GT Sport Coupe

1. Disconnect battery ground cable.
2. Support engine in chassis with suitable lifting equipment.
3. On 1972 Opel models, remove front suspension as outlined in the "Front Suspension Section."
4. On all models, drain oil pan.
5. Remove oil pan attaching bolts and the oil pan.

J 22928 - 2

Fig. 20 Rear oil seal installation. 1976-77

6. Reverse procedure to install.

1972-75 1900 & Manta

1. Disconnect battery ground cable.
2. Support engine in chassis with suitable lifting equipment.
3. Remove two motor mount bracket to motor mount retaining nuts.
4. Remove two front suspension to frame rail bolt retaining nuts.
5. Remove nut and bolt at lower end of steering shaft U-joint.
6. With a suitable jack under the center of the front suspension crossmember, raise car high enough for wheels and suspension assembly to be rolled from under car.
7. Position jack stands under both front jack brackets on underbody to support vehicle position.
8. Remove both front crossmember support to frame attaching bolts.
9. Remove brake pipe to brake hose retaining clips at frame rails and disconnect brake hose from brake pipes.
10. Lower the front suspension assembly and remove from vehicle.
11. Drain engine oil and remove the oil pan and gasket.
12. Reverse procedure to install.

1976-77

1. Remove engine from vehicle as outlined under "Engine, Replace" procedure, 1976-77 models.
2. Remove the oil pressure switch from the cylinder block. On models equipped with oil pressure gauge, remove the oil pressure unit and oil pressure switch together with the adapter.
3. Remove 14 bolts and six nuts attaching the oil pan to the cylinder block and the oil pan.
4. Reverse procedure to install. Torque oil pan bolts and nuts to 3.6 ft. lbs.

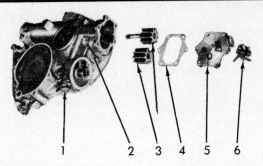

1. OLD PRESSURE RELIEF VALVE ASSEMBLY
2. TIMING CASE
3. OIL PUMP GEARS
4. COVER GASKET
5. COVER & VALVE ASSEMBLY
6. COVER ATTACHING SCREWS

Fig. 21 Oil pump. 1972-75

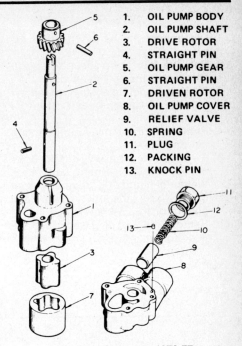

1. OIL PUMP BODY
2. OIL PUMP SHAFT
3. DRIVE ROTOR
4. STRAIGHT PIN
5. OIL PUMP GEAR
6. STRAIGHT PIN
7. DRIVEN ROTOR
8. OIL PUMP COVER
9. RELIEF VALVE
10. SPRING
11. PLUG
12. PACKING
13. KNOCK PIN

Fig. 22 Oil pump. 1976-77

OIL PUMP, REPLACE

1972-75

Removal

1. Remove screws attaching oil pump cover assembly to timing chain cover. Remove cover assembly and slide out oil pump gears, Fig. 21.

Installation

1. Liberally lubricate spindles and gear teeth. Use new cover gasket and install cover.
2. If new gears are installed, the clearance should be checked with a straight edge and a feeler gauge. The gears must not protrude more than .004 in. over pump housing.

1976-77

Removal

1. Remove engine from vehicle as outlined under "Engine, Replace," 1976-77 models.
2. Remove the PCV hose and high-tension cables with the clip, then the cylinder head cover.
3. Remove distributor.
4. Remove engine stiffener from each side of engine.
5. Remove oil pan.
6. Remove bolt securing oil pump to cylinder block and the oil pump assembly, Fig. 22.

Installation

1. Install the oil pump assembly by engaging the oil pump drive gear with the pinion gear on the crankshaft, so the setting mark on the drive gear is turned rearward and faces away from crankshaft by approximately 20 degrees in clockwise direction, Fig. 23.
2. When the oil pump is installed, check that the setting mark on the oil pump drive gear is turned to the rear side as viewed from the clearance between the front cover and cylinder block and that the slit at the end of the oil pump drive shaft is parallel with the front face of the cylinder block and is offset forward as viewed through the distributor fitting hole, Fig. 11.
3. Install the oil pump cover by the dowel pins, then secure the oil pump assembly with the four bolts.
4. Install the relief valve assembly and oil pipe rubber hose on the cover.
5. Connect oil pipe to rubber hose and attach the oil pipe assembly with the bolts.
6. Install oil pan gasket and oil pan.
7. Install cylinder head cover.
8. Install distributor.
9. Install engine in vehicle.

WATER PUMP, REPLACE

1972-74

1. Drain cooling system by disconnecting lower radiator hose. Remove radiator and shroud.
2. Remove fan belt.
3. Remove fan blade and pulley from water pump shaft.
4. Disconnect inlet hose and heater hose from water pump. Remove

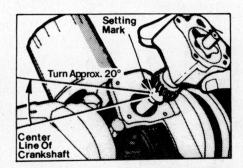

Fig. 23 Oil pump installation. 1976-77

bolts, pump assembly and gasket from timing chain cover.

Installation

1. Be sure the gasket surfaces on pump and timing chain cover are clean. Install pump assembly with new gasket.
2. Install radiator and shroud. Connect radiator hose to pump inlet and heater hose to nipple.
3. Install fan pulley and fan blade, tighten attaching bolts. Install belt and adjust for proper tension.
4. Fill cooling system and check for leaks at pump and hose joints.

1975

1. Remove radiator cap.
2. Drain radiator by disconnecting lower radiator hose. If equipped with A/C, splash shield must be removed to gain access to lower radiator hose.
3. Remove fan shroud and radiator mounting screws.
4. Disconnect upper radiator hose at radiator and radiator overflow hose.
5. Remove radiator first, then fan shroud.
6. Remove fan clutch assembly (the hold-down bolt for the fan clutch has left-hand threads).
7. Loosen fan belt.
8. Disconnect thermostat housing hose and heater hose at water pump.
9. Remove water pump (water pump and pulley are serviced as an assembly).
10. Reverse procedure to install.

1976-77

1. Disconnect the battery ground cable.
2. Remove four bolts securing splash shield and the splash shield.
3. Drain the cooling system by removing the drain plug at bottom of radiator.
4. Remove four nuts securing cooling fan and the fan.
5. Remove AIR pump mounting bolts and generator mounting bolts, then the fan belt and AIR pump drive belt by pivoting the AIR pump and generator toward the engine.
6. Remove four bolts securing the cooling fan and pulley, then remove the fan and pulley and AIR pump drive pulley.
7. Remove four bolts securing fan set plate and fan pulley, then the fan set plate and fan pulley.
8. Remove six bolts attaching the water pump and the water pump assembly.
9. Reverse procedure to install.

FUEL PUMP, REPLACE
1972-74

Removal

1. Disconnect fuel lines at pump.
2. Remove retaining bolt and fuel pump.

Installation

1. Be sure the asbestos spacer is in place, with a gasket on each side. Install the fuel pump and retaining bolt.
2. Connect fuel lines.

1975

1. Disconnect battery ground cable.
2. Disconnect wire from fuel pump, located on the bottom of the fuel tank at front of tank.
3. Remove pump.
4. Reverse procedure to install.

1976-77

1. Disconnect battery ground cable.
2. Disconnect fuel return hose from pipe and drain fuel.
3. Remove fuel tank cover.
4. Remove two screws securing the fuel pump cover and the cover.
5. Disconnect fuel hose from fuel pipe.
6. Disconnect fuel pump wiring.
7. Remove nine screws attaching the fuel pump and the fuel pump assembly from fuel tank.
8. Reverse procedure to install.

Carburetor Section

1972-74
Fast Idle Speed Adjustment

1. Remove air cleaner cover.
2. With engine static, open the throttle half-way and close the choke valve, release the throttle, then the choke.
3. Start engine without moving the throttle. Adjust to 3200 to 3300 RPM, using nuts on fast idle rod.

1976-77
Float Level Adjustment

The float level can be adjusted by adding or removing copper gaskets to or from the float valve seat. The float level increases with an increase in the total thickness of gaskets and decreases with a reduction in thickness of gaskets. The fuel level is normal when it is on the level mark provided on the float bowl glass window while the engine is running or stopped.

Choke Piston Stroke Adjustment

With the metal lever held against the stopper, check that choke piston stroke is within the range of $3/16$ to $7/32$ inch. If the piston stroke deviates from the specified range, adjust by bending piston link, Fig. 1.

Checking Relative Angles Between Primary & Secondary Throttle Valves

Gradually open the primary throttle valve until the secondary throttle arm begins to move and check the angle of the primary throttle valve using a set gauge J-26618. If the angle is incorrect, adjust by bending the throttle link, Figs. 2 and 3.

Choke Unloader Adjustment

1. Open throttle valve wide open while holding down on choke valve.
2. Choke valve will be forced open part way.
3. Using a carburetor plug gauge, measure distance from air horn wall to lower edge of choke valve. Opening must be .215 in. If not, remove choke heater coil cover and bend choke unloading tang to obtain correct setting, Fig. 4.

Choke Coil Adjustment

Align the setting mark on the ther-

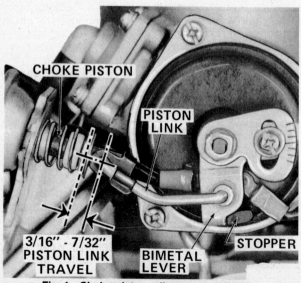

CHOKE PISTON

PISTON LINK

3/16" - 7/32" PISTON LINK TRAVEL

BIMETAL LEVER

STOPPER

Fig. 1 Choke piston adjustment. 1976-77

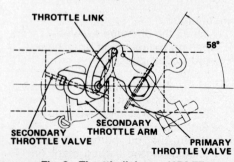

THROTTLE LINK

58°

SECONDARY THROTTLE VALVE

SECONDARY THROTTLE ARM

PRIMARY THROTTLE VALVE

Fig. 2 Throttle linkage. 1976-77

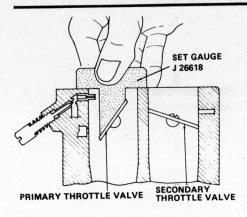

PRIMARY THROTTLE VALVE   **SECONDARY THROTTLE VALVE**

Fig. 3 Checking relative angles between primary & secondary throttle valves. 1976-77

mostat case with the setting mark on the thermostat housing, then install and tighten the three set screws.

Fast Idle Speed Adjustment

1. Disconnect and plug the vacuum advance and EGR hoses.
2. Remove air cleaner cover.
3. With engine off, open the throttle half-way and close the choke valve, release the throttle, then release the choke.
4. Start engine without moving the throttle. Using fast idle screw, set fast idle at 3000 rpm ±150 rpm on automatic transmission models and 3200 rpm ±150 rpm on standard transmission models.

FAST IDLE CAM

CHOKE UNLOADER TANG

Fuel Injection Section

DESCRIPTION

The Fuel Injection System, used on 1975 models, is a pulse time manifold injection system that injects metered fuel into the intake manifold near the intake valves by electronically controlled injection valves.

Various components of the EFI System electronically monitor a wide range of driving factors which are fed into a control unit. The control unit uses the information received from the various components to continuously compute the desired air/fuel ratio under all operating conditions. The control unit continuously calculates the proper air/fuel ratio and controls the pulse time of the fuel injectors to achieve this.

Control Unit

The control unit, Fig. 1, consists of three integrated circuits containing a certain number of electronic compo-

nents. These are to be considered as the main feature of the circuits. In addition, several semi-conductors, condensers, and resistors are used. Suppression filters are used to filter out voltage peaks so the control unit is not damaged. The control unit contains approximately 80 electronic components. Its function is to control the impulse of the injectors, to open the injectors for a definite time. The control unit, using the information received electrically from the air flow meter, throttle valve switch, coolant temperature sensor, distributor, starter solenoid, and battery, computes the proper pulse time of the injectors. The control unit then pulses the injectors by completing the electric circuit of the injectors. The electric circuit of the injectors starts at the battery and travels to the dual relay, to the preresistor unit, to the four injectors, through the coil in the injector, to the control unit which completes the circuit to ground. The period of time the circuit is energized is referred to as a pulse time. The control unit is grounded via the wiring harness of the intake manifold.

All of the injectors inject at the same time and inject twice per four stroke cycle (once per crankshaft revolution).

Air Flow Meter

The primary purpose of the air flow meter, Fig. 2, is to furnish the control unit with information concerning rate of the air flow going into the intake manifold. The air flow is measured by a baffle plate fitted in the meter. The angular position of the baffle plate is directly related to the rate of air flow. The plate is mechanically connected to a potentiometer, which converts the baffle plate position into an electric voltage signal given to the control unit. By using a compensating flap and chamber, a dampening effect is exerted on the baffle plate. This feature reduces the effect of pulsations in intake air flow and re-

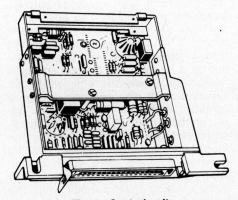

Fig. 1 Control unit

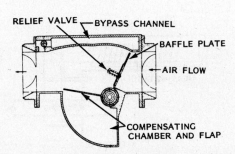

RELIEF VALVE — BYPASS CHANNEL
BAFFLE PLATE
AIR FLOW
COMPENSATING CHAMBER AND FLAP

Fig. 2 Air flow meter

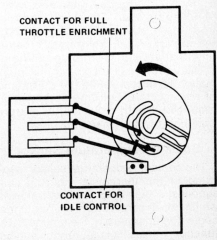

CONTACT FOR FULL THROTTLE ENRICHMENT
CONTACT FOR IDLE CONTROL

Fig. 3 Throttle valve switch

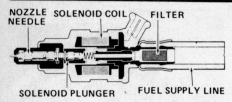

NOZZLE NEEDLE SOLENOID COIL FILTER

SOLENOID PLUNGER FUEL SUPPLY LINE

Fig. 4 Injector

sults in smoother operation of the baffle plate. To eliminate any possible damage to the air flow meter, in case of engine backfire, a one-way relief valve is built into the baffle plate.

A by-pass channel is built into the air flow meter. This "by-pass air" is not measured by the air flow meter and is used to set the fuel/air mixture at idle. An adjustment screw is provided for this purpose.

In addition to the potentiometer, an air temperature sensor is built into the air flow meter. This sensor supplies a signal to the control unit as to air temperature of the air being drawn into the intake manifold.

Also contained in the air flow meter is a set of contact points that controls the electrical supply to the electric fuel pump and auxiliary air valve. When no air flow is present, the contact points are open cutting off the electrical current to the fuel pump and auxiliary air valve. This feature prevents the fuel pump from pumping when the engine is not operating. These contacts are by-passed during cranking so that the fuel pump receives current for starting purposes.

Throttle Valve Switch

Two switch contacts are located inside the throttle valve switch, Fig. 3, which is attached to the throttle valve. The throttle valve shaft is connected to the switch contacts. One switch closes the circuit when the throttle valve is closed and the other switch closes when the throttle valve is fully opened. During part throttle operation, both switches are open. The electrical signal from these switches is transmitted to the control unit and informs the control unit what position the throttle plate is in.

The control unit then uses this information to further refine the pulse time of the injectors. Full throttle operation requires a slightly richer air/fuel mixture than part throttle operation.

Coolant Temperature Sensor

The coolant temperature sensor is located in the thermostat housing and supplies a signal to the control unit which informs the control unit as to the coolant temperature of the engine. This function takes place until engine operating temperature is normal, at

which time the temperature sensor has no effect upon the control unit. The control unit uses the information from the temperature sensor to enrich the air/fuel mixture during starting and during the warm-up period. A temperature dependent resistor is located in the housing of the temperature sensor. As temperature increases, the resistance of the resistor is reduced. This type of resistor is known as an NTC (negative temperature coefficient) resistor. Increasing the coolant temperature decreases the resistance and the enrichment of the air/fuel mixture decreases. When the engine coolant reaches 176° F, the temperature sensor has no further effect upon the control unit.

Injectors

The injectors, Fig. 4, contain a small solenoid, the core of which is a spring loaded needle. The spring holds the needle in a closed position. When current is passed through the solenoid, the needle is pulled from its seat allowing fuel to inject into the intake manifold. The length of time current is allowed to flow is in milliseconds and is regulated by the control unit. The time range is from 1.5 to 10 milliseconds depending on engine requirements. Fuel pressure at the injector is 42 ± 2 PSI when intake manifold vacuum is "O". As intake manifold vacuum increases, fuel pressure is reduced. (See Pressure Regulator section.) All of the injectors are operated simultaneously. To obtain better fuel atomization, half of the fuel quantity required for a complete working cycle is injected each crankshaft revolution.

Cold Start Injector

The cold start injector, Fig. 5, also contains an electro-magnetic valve. When energized during cranking, fuel is sprayed into the intake manifold. The position the valve is mounted in results in all cylinders getting approximately the same amount of fuel when this valve operates. Current supply is controlled by the thermo time switch. Fuel pressure is the same as applied to the injectors.

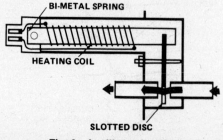

BI-METAL SPRING

HEATING COIL

SLOTTED DISC

Fig. 6 Auxiliary air valve

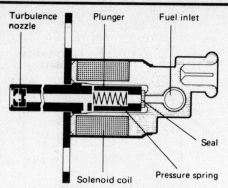

Turbulence nozzle Plunger Fuel inlet

Seal

Solenoid coil Pressure spring

Fig. 5 Cold start injector

Pre-Resistors

The purpose of the pre-resistors is mainly to reduce the response time of the injectors. The pre-resistors are connected in series between the injectors and the dual relay.

Thermo Time Switch

The thermo time switch controls the cold start injector by furnishing a ground for its solenoid. The thermo time switch has a bimetal contact surrounded by a heating coil. The heating coil receives current during cranking. The bimetal contact breaks the ground circuit of the cold start injector whenever the heating coil or water coolant heats the bimetal to a temperature of 95° Farenheit or above. In extreme cold, it requires about 8 seconds for the heating coil to heat the bimetal contact to 95° Farenheit. The warmer the outside temperature is, the less time required to heat the bimetal contact. By limiting the operation time of the cold start injector by using the thermo time switch, engine flooding is prevented during prolonged cranking.

Auxiliary Air Valve

The purpose of the auxiliary air valve, Fig. 6, is to control additional air flow through the by-pass channel in the throttle valve to the intake manifold to increase idle RPM during engine warm up. The valve contains a slotted disc that rotates to open, close, or partially close the air passage. The position of the disc is controlled by a bimetal spring. When cold, the disc is open and closes progressively as the bimetal spring is heated. The bimetal spring is heated by an electric coil, which receives current whenever the engine is running. When the valve reaches approximately 158° F, the valve closes completely. By locating the valve on the thermostat housing, engine heat is transferred to the valve which aids in keeping the valve closed or partially closed during short periods when the engine is turned off.

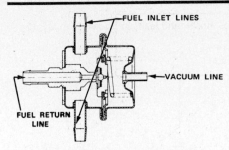

Fig. 7 Fuel pressure regulator

Fuel Pressure Regulator

Fuel enters the pressure regulator inlet connections (2) from the fuel manifold that furnishes fuel to the injectors and cold start injector. A spring loaded diaphragm maintains desired pressure and excess fuel is returned to the fuel tank. As intake manifold vacuum increases, less pressure is required by the injectors. To compensate for this, a vacuum line is connected from the intake manifold to the pressure regulator valve, Fig. 7. The vacuum pulls on the pressure regulator diaphragm with the result of lowering the fuel pressure. Depending on intake manifold vacuum, fuel pressure will vary from 31 PSI at high manifold vacuum to 44 PSI at zero or low manifold vacuum such as encountered during acceleration.

Deceleration Valve

During deceleration, the deceleration valve, Fig. 8, bypasses some air around the throttle valve. This results in more complete combustion during the coast down phase of driving. The valve is controlled by manifold vacuum. Whenever intake manifold vacuum is 12 inches of Mercury or higher, the valve is open and closed when vacuum is lower than 12 inches. The valve is closed during idle operation.

Dual Relay

The dual relay, Fig. 9, is comprised of

two relays that control the current supply for the entire electronic fuel injection system and disengages the system from the battery when the ignition switch is off.

When the ignition switch is turned on, the main relay points close providing battery voltage to the control unit and pre-resistors of the electronic fuel injection system.

The other relay within the dual relay controls current to the electric fuel pump. The points in this relay close and complete the circuit to the fuel pump during cranking and when the points close in the air flow valve. This is designed to cut off current to the fuel pump in the event the engine stops air flow valve closed.

Precautions When Servicing

1. Remove control unit from car if it will be exposed to temperature of 175° Farenheit, or higher.
2. Never start engine when battery connections are loose.
3. Never start engine when a battery fast charge is attached to the battery.
4. Always disconnect battery terminals from battery when using a booster-charger to charge the battery.
5. Never detach or attach wiring harness terminal plug to or from the control unit when the ignition switch is on.
6. Never start any diagnosis or repair of the E.F.I. system until the ignition system has been completely checked.
7. Never start any diagnosis or repair of the E.F.I. system until the circuits from the main wiring harness going to the dual relay have been completely checked.
8. Whenever using ohmmeter, make sure ignition switch is in the "OFF" position. Ohmmeter can be damaged if subjected to a live circuit.

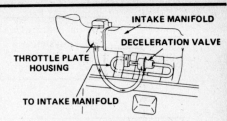

Fig. 8 Deceleration valve

TROUBLE-SHOOTING

Refer to Figs. 10 through 18 for trouble-shooting procedures.

DIAGNOSIS
Basic Checks

Ignition System

1. Hold a spark plug wire ¼" away from engine block and crank engine.
2. If a strong spark is seen, check dwell and timing. (Reset if necessary.) If dwell and timing are okay, trouble may not be the ignition system.
3. If no spark or an intermittent spark is seen, remove the coil high tension wire from the distributor cap. Hold the coil high tension wire ¼" from engine block and crank engine.
4. If strong spark is seen, check distributor cap and rotor for cracks or carbon tracking. Check lead between distributor and coil for broken or burned terminals or cracks in insulation. Replace malfunctioning parts.
5. If no spark or intermittent spark is seen, connect test lamp to ignition switch side of coil.
6. With ignition switch turned to the "ON" position, the lamp should light. If not, the problem is in the ignition switch and/or wiring harness.
7. Connect test lamp to distributor side of coil; crank engine; lamp should flicker. If lamp does not flicker, it indicates malfunctioning points, or condenser, or coil.
8. Disconnect distributor lead at coil; connect test lamp to terminal; turn on ignition switch. If test lamp does not light, malfunctioning coil is indicated.

Vacuum Leaks

A vacuum leak in the manifold system, between the air flow meter and combustion chamber, may cause or contribute to any of the following:
1. Engine misfire.
2. Poor or erratic idling.
3. Hard starting with a cold or warm engine.
4. Engine fails to keep running.

When a vacuum leak is suspected, proceed as follows:

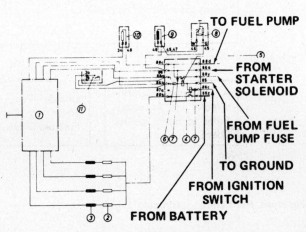

Fig. 9 Dual relay circuits

TO FUEL PUMP

FROM STARTER SOLENOID

FROM FUEL PUMP FUSE

TO GROUND

FROM IGNITION SWITCH

FROM BATTERY

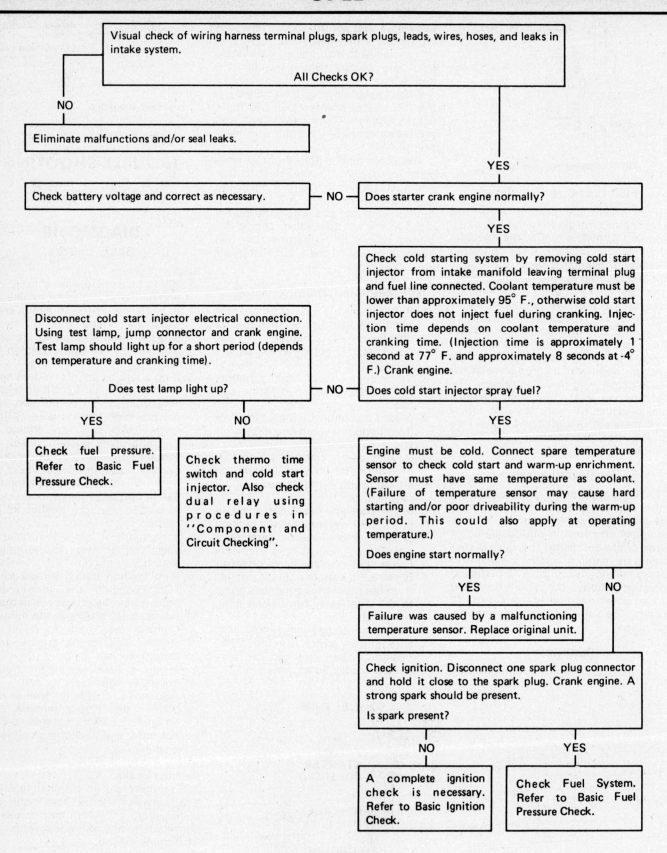

Visual check of wiring harness terminal plugs, spark plugs, leads, wires, hoses, and leaks in intake system.

All Checks OK?

NO

Eliminate malfunctions and/or seal leaks.

YES

Check battery voltage and correct as necessary. — NO — Does starter crank engine normally?

YES

Check cold starting system by removing cold start injector from intake manifold leaving terminal plug and fuel line connected. Coolant temperature must be lower than approximately 95° F., otherwise cold start injector does not inject fuel during cranking. Injection time depends on coolant temperature and cranking time. (Injection time is approximately 1 second at 77° F. and approximately 8 seconds at -4° F.) Crank engine.

Disconnect cold start injector electrical connection. Using test lamp, jump connector and crank engine. Test lamp should light up for a short period (depends on temperature and cranking time).

Does test lamp light up?

NO — Does cold start injector spray fuel?

YES

NO

Check fuel pressure. Refer to Basic Fuel Pressure Check.

Check thermo time switch and cold start injector. Also check dual relay using procedures in "Component and Circuit Checking".

YES

Engine must be cold. Connect spare temperature sensor to check cold start and warm-up enrichment. Sensor must have same temperature as coolant. (Failure of temperature sensor may cause hard starting and/or poor driveability during the warm-up period. This could also apply at operating temperature.)

Does engine start normally?

YES

NO

Failure was caused by a malfunctioning temperature sensor. Replace original unit.

Check ignition. Disconnect one spark plug connector and hold it close to the spark plug. Crank engine. A strong spark should be present.

Is spark present?

NO

YES

A complete ignition check is necessary. Refer to Basic Ignition Check.

Check Fuel System. Refer to Basic Fuel Pressure Check.

Fig. 10 Trouble-shooting chart. Hard starting with cold engine

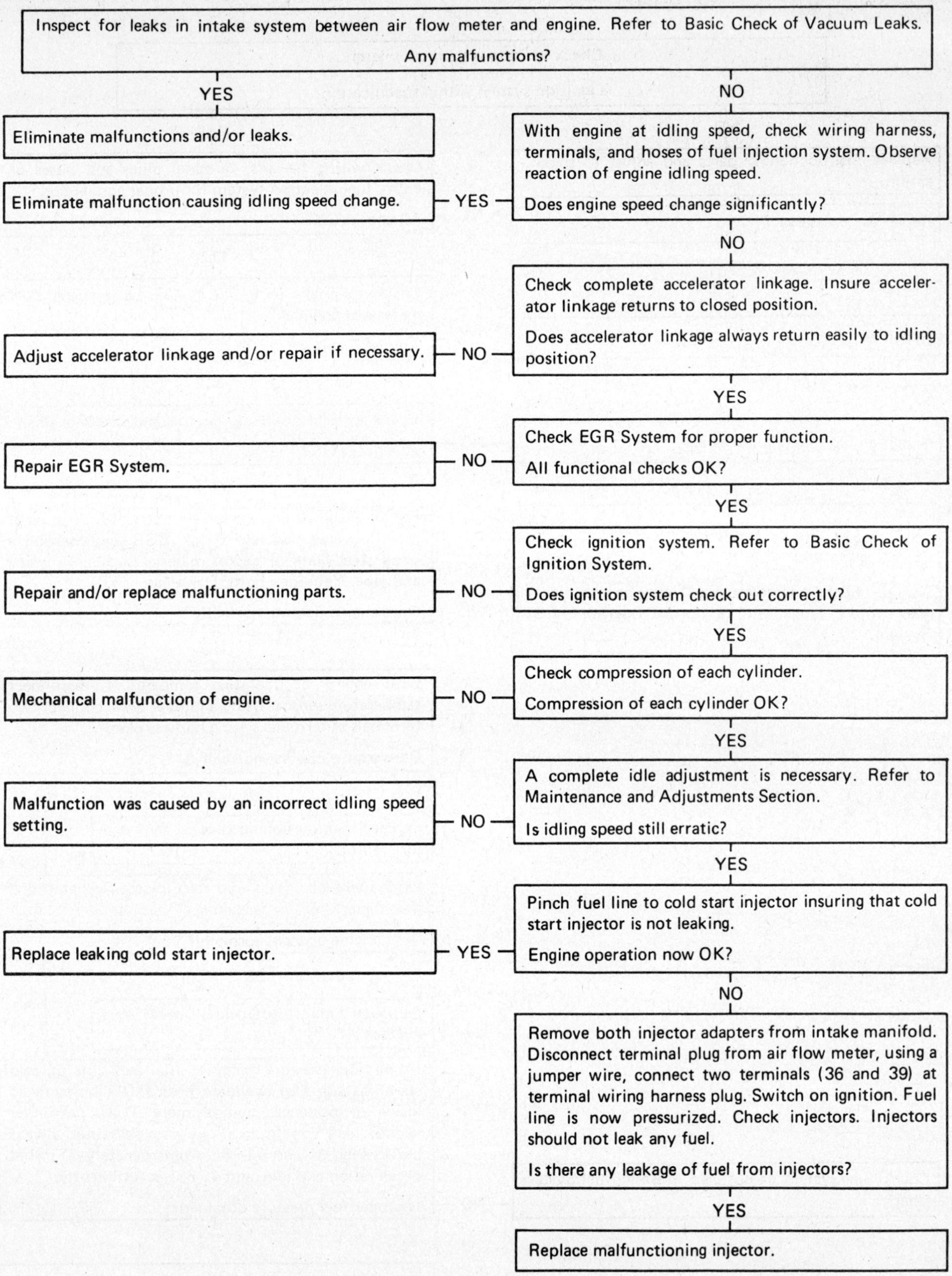
Inspect for leaks in intake system between air flow meter and engine. Refer to Basic Check of Vacuum Leaks. Any malfunctions?
YES
Eliminate malfunctions and/or leaks.
NO
With engine at idling speed, check wiring harness, terminals, and hoses of fuel injection system. Observe reaction of engine idling speed.
Does engine speed change significantly?
YES
Eliminate malfunction causing idling speed change.
NO
Check complete accelerator linkage. Insure accelerator linkage returns to closed position.
Does accelerator linkage always return easily to idling position?
NO
Adjust accelerator linkage and/or repair if necessary.
YES
Check EGR System for proper function.
All functional checks OK?
NO
Repair EGR System.
YES
Check ignition system. Refer to Basic Check of Ignition System.
Does ignition system check out correctly?
NO
Repair and/or replace malfunctioning parts.
YES
Check compression of each cylinder.
Compression of each cylinder OK?
NO
Mechanical malfunction of engine.
YES
A complete idle adjustment is necessary. Refer to Maintenance and Adjustments Section.
Is idling speed still erratic?
NO
Malfunction was caused by an incorrect idling speed setting.
YES
Pinch fuel line to cold start injector insuring that cold start injector is not leaking.
Engine operation now OK?
YES
Replace leaking cold start injector.
NO
Remove both injector adapters from intake manifold. Disconnect terminal plug from air flow meter, using a jumper wire, connect two terminals (36 and 39) at terminal wiring harness plug. Switch on ignition. Fuel line is now pressurized. Check injectors. Injectors should not leak any fuel.
Is there any leakage of fuel from injectors?
YES
Replace malfunctioning injector.

Fig. 11 Trouble-shooting chart. Poor or erratic idling

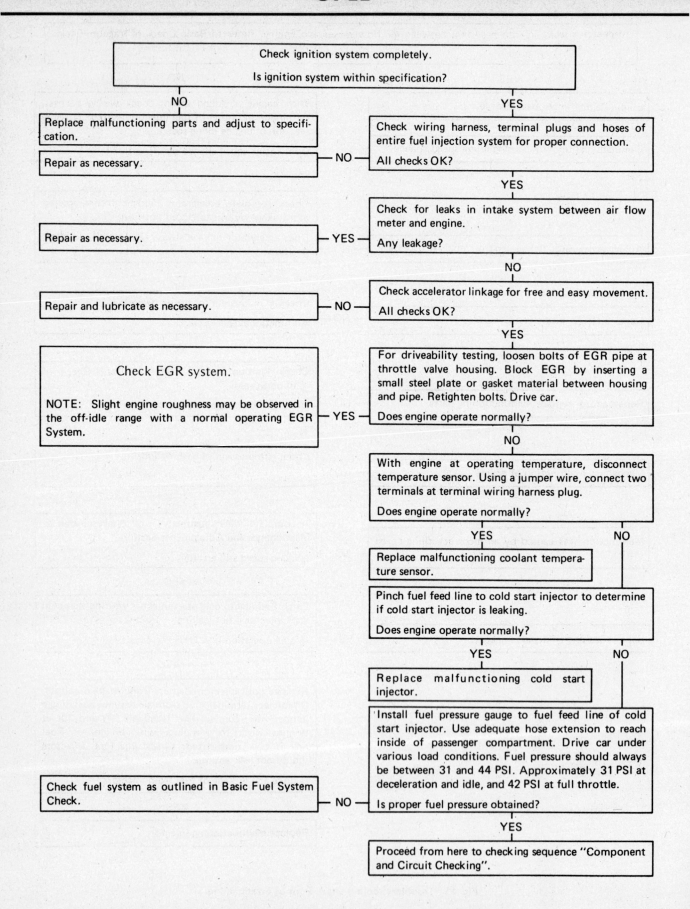

Check ignition system completely.

Is ignition system within specification?

NO

Replace malfunctioning parts and adjust to specification.

Repair as necessary.

YES

Check wiring harness, terminal plugs and hoses of entire fuel injection system for proper connection.

All checks OK?

— **NO** —

YES

Repair as necessary.

Check for leaks in intake system between air flow meter and engine.

Any leakage?

— **YES** —

NO

Repair and lubricate as necessary.

Check accelerator linkage for free and easy movement.

All checks OK?

— **NO** —

YES

Check EGR system.

NOTE: Slight engine roughness may be observed in the off-idle range with a normal operating EGR System.

For driveability testing, loosen bolts of EGR pipe at throttle valve housing. Block EGR by inserting a small steel plate or gasket material between housing and pipe. Retighten bolts. Drive car.

Does engine operate normally?

— **YES** —

NO

With engine at operating temperature, disconnect temperature sensor. Using a jumper wire, connect two terminals at terminal wiring harness plug.

Does engine operate normally?

YES   **NO**

Replace malfunctioning coolant temperature sensor.

Pinch fuel feed line to cold start injector to determine if cold start injector is leaking.

Does engine operate normally?

YES   **NO**

Replace malfunctioning cold start injector.

Check fuel system as outlined in Basic Fuel System Check.

Install fuel pressure gauge to fuel feed line of cold start injector. Use adequate hose extension to reach inside of passenger compartment. Drive car under various load conditions. Fuel pressure should always be between 31 and 44 PSI. Approximately 31 PSI at deceleration and idle, and 42 PSI at full throttle.

Is proper fuel pressure obtained?

— **NO** —

YES

Proceed from here to checking sequence "Component and Circuit Checking".

Fig. 12 Trouble-shooting chart. Poor engine operation

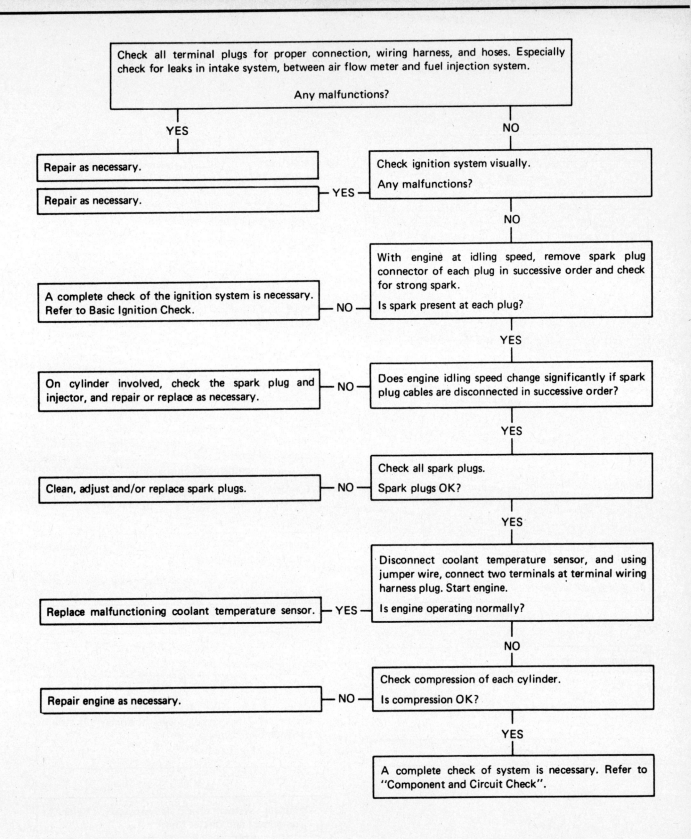

Fig. 13 Trouble-shooting chart. Engine misfires under all conditions

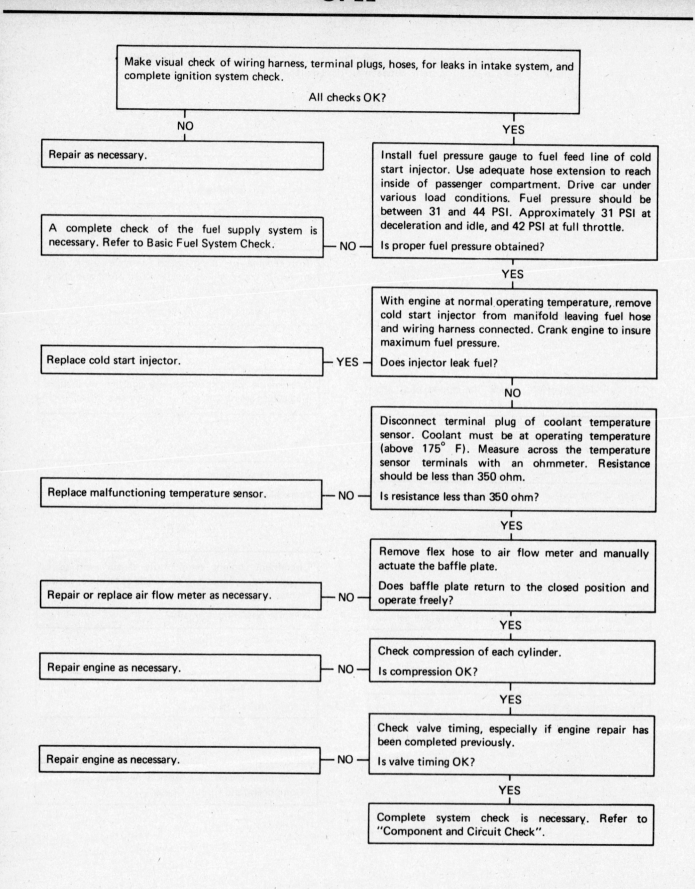

Fig. 14 Trouble-shooting chart. Excessive fuel consumption

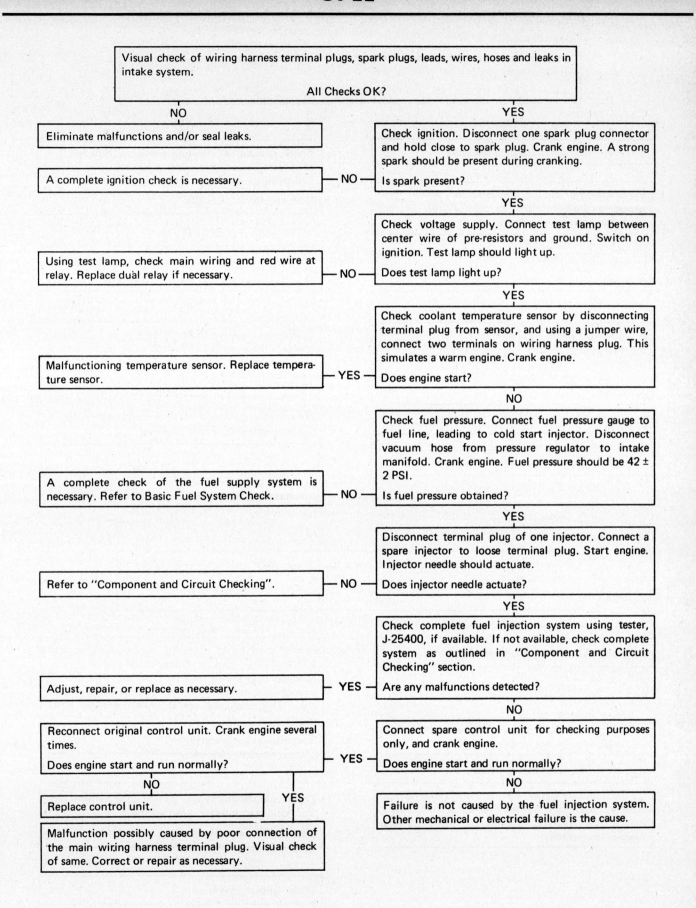

Fig. 15 Trouble-shooting chart. Engine cranks but will not start

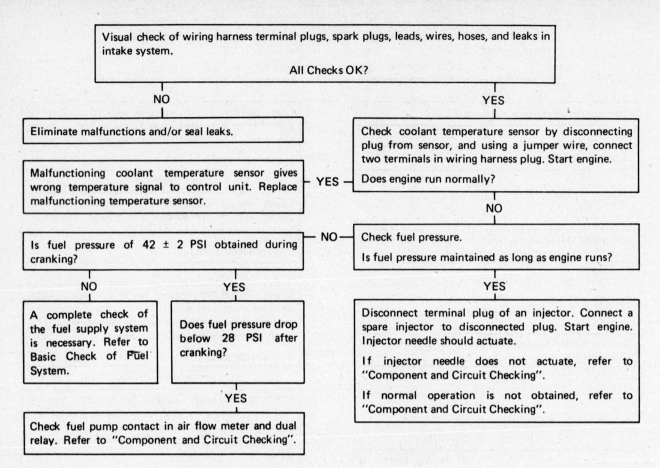

Fig. 16 Trouble-shooting chart. Engine starts but fails to run

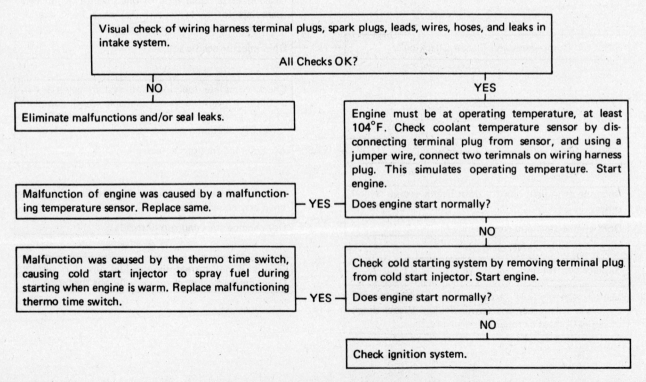

Fig. 17 Trouble-shooting chart. Hard starting with warm engine

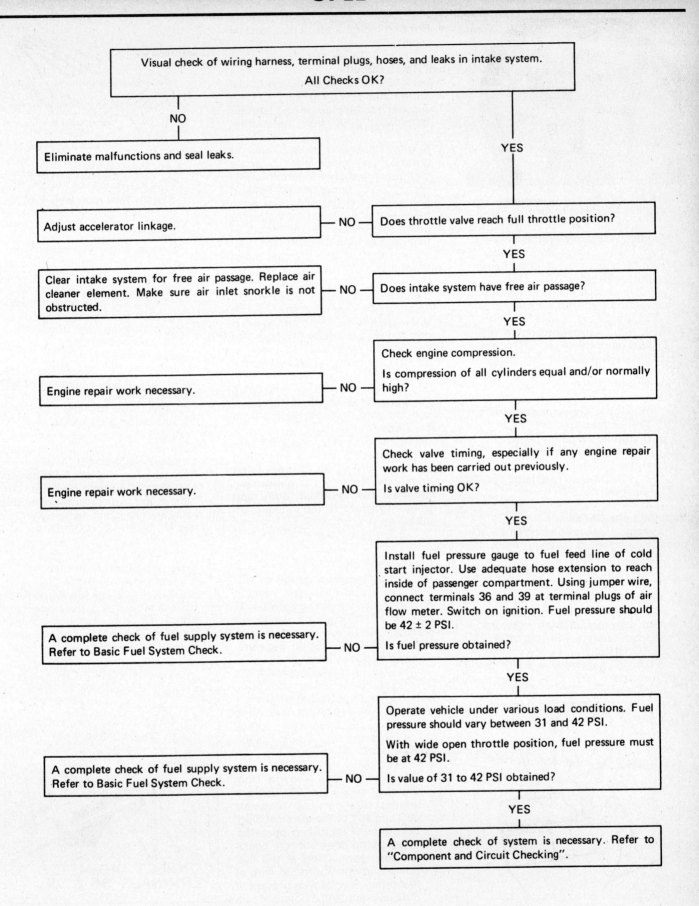

Visual check of wiring harness, terminal plugs, hoses, and leaks in intake system.

All Checks OK?

NO

Eliminate malfunctions and seal leaks.

YES

Adjust accelerator linkage. — NO — Does throttle valve reach full throttle position?

YES

Clear intake system for free air passage. Replace air cleaner element. Make sure air inlet snorkle is not obstructed. — NO — Does intake system have free air passage?

YES

Engine repair work necessary. — NO — Check engine compression.

Is compression of all cylinders equal and/or normally high?

YES

Engine repair work necessary. — NO — Check valve timing, especially if any engine repair work has been carried out previously.

Is valve timing OK?

YES

A complete check of fuel supply system is necessary. Refer to Basic Fuel System Check. — NO — Install fuel pressure gauge to fuel feed line of cold start injector. Use adequate hose extension to reach inside of passenger compartment. Using jumper wire, connect terminals 36 and 39 at terminal plugs of air flow meter. Switch on ignition. Fuel pressure should be 42 ± 2 PSI.

Is fuel pressure obtained?

YES

A complete check of fuel supply system is necessary. Refer to Basic Fuel System Check. — NO — Operate vehicle under various load conditions. Fuel pressure should vary between 31 and 42 PSI.

With wide open throttle position, fuel pressure must be at 42 PSI.

Is value of 31 to 42 PSI obtained?

YES

A complete check of system is necessary. Refer to "Component and Circuit Checking".

Fig. 18   Trouble-shooting chart. Poor acceleration

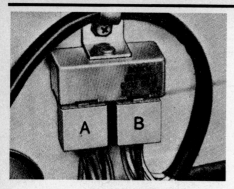

Fig. 19 Dual relay terminal identification

1. Tighten intake manifold to cylinder head bolts.
2. Visually check the following for correct installation:
   a. Hose between air flow meter and throttle plate housing, including PCV hose.
   b. Throttle valve housing to manifold connection.
   c. Pressure regulator vacuum hose.
   d. Auxiliary air valve hose.
   e. Throttle valve housing to deceleration valve hose.
   f. Automatic transmission vacuum line connections.
   g. Distributor vacuum retard line.
   h. EGR lines and hoses.
   i. Brake booster hose.
   j. Check proper installation of oil dipstick.

Vacuum Leak Check

If a vacuum leak is still suspected, the complete manifold system must be checked as follows:

1. Disconnect brake booster hose at intake manifold.
2. Install an air hose in the manifold fitting, and pressurize the intake manifold. Use regulated air pressure of approximately 5 PSI. DO NOT EXCEED 15 PSI.
3. Brush on soapy water solution to all fittings and around all gasket surfaces.

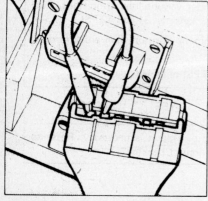

Fig. 21 Jumper wire installed on air flow meter connector plug

4. Bubbles indicate a leak that must be repaired.

Dual Relay Circuits

Check of all circuits on plug terminal "A" at the dual relay, Fig. 19.

1. Disconnect the main wiring harness terminal plug "A" from the dual relay.
2. Connect one end of test lamp to ground. Use other end to probe connector that goes to terminal 88Z, Fig. 20. Test lamp should light; if not, wire has a disconnect or open between the plug and the battery.
3. Using the test lamp, probe terminal that goes to terminal 88Y. Test lamp should light; if not, the fuel pump fuse is blown, located in its own fuse holder beside fuse box.
4. Using the test lamp, probe terminal 86C, Fig. 20. Test lamp should light when ignition switch is turned on. If not, the wire between the plug and the ignition switch has an open.
5. Using test lamp J-25401-3 in the same way, probe terminal 86A, Fig. 20. Test lamp should light when the starter is engaged; if not, black and red wire is disconnected from the starter solenoid.
6. Using an ohmmeter, check for continuity between terminal 85 in plug and ground, Fig. 20. If there is no continuity, the brown wire is broken between the terminal plug and where it fastens to the intake manifold.

Fuel Supply System

1. Install fuel pressure gauge to fuel feed line of the cold start injector. Fuel pressure should be between 31 and 44 PSI depending on intake manifold vacuum. It will vary from approximately 31 PSI on deceleration and idle to as much as 44 PSI at full throttle. Pressure between these limits should be obtained during cranking and engine running.
2. If no pressure is present, indicating fuel pump is not operating, check electrical circuit to fuel pump as follows:
   a. Check fuse.
   b. Remove "A" plug terminal from the dual relay, Fig. 20. Using a jumper wire between terminals 88D and 88Y of the terminal plug, determine if the pump operates. If fuel pump does not run, check for poor connection at the fuel pump and check ground wire at fuel pump. If voltage is present at the fuel pump and it does not run, replace the fuel pump.
   c. If pump operates with jumper

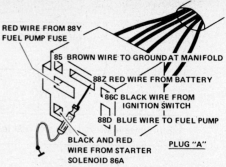

Fig. 20 Dual relay plug "A"

RED WIRE FROM 88Y FUEL PUMP FUSE
85 BROWN WIRE TO GROUND AT MANIFOLD
88Z RED WIRE FROM BATTERY
86C BLACK WIRE FROM IGNITION SWITCH
88D BLUE WIRE TO FUEL PUMP
BLACK AND RED WIRE FROM STARTER SOLENOID 86A
PLUG "A"

wire connected between terminals 88D and 88Y, and would not operate when cranking engine with terminal plug "A" connected, the dual relay may be malfunctioning. Substitute a known good relay and recheck. If problem still exists, check all circuits in plug "A" terminals of dual relay, as outlined under dual relay circuits.

3. If fuel pressure is normal during cranking but is not maintained with engine running, the circuit to the contacts in the air flow meter must be checked. Disconnect electrical connector to the air flow meter. Connect a jumper wire between terminals 36 and 39 of the wiring harness plug, Fig. 21. Turn on ignition switch; if pump operates, it indicates the wiring harness and dual relay are okay, and malfunction is in the air flow meter. Check for continuity in the air flow meter (terminals 36 and 39), Fig. 22. Disconnect hose at front of air flow meter, and manually operate baffle plate. Continuity must be made when baffle plate is moved from the closed position.

4. If fuel pump operates and no pressure is obtained, check for restric-

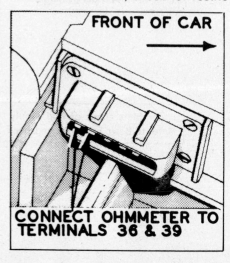

FRONT OF CAR

CONNECT OHMMETER TO TERMINALS 36 & 39

Fig. 22 Air flow meter terminals 36 & 39

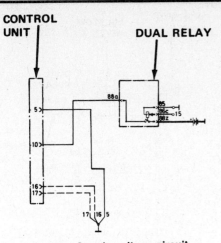

Fig. 23 Supply voltage circuit

tions in fuel lines and/or filters (filter on tank gauge unit as well as the in-line fuel filter).

5. Using the test lamp, pressure is obtained, proceed as follows:

   a. If pressure is over 44 PSI, check for restricted fuel return line from pressure regulator valve to the fuel tank. If lines are not restricted, the pressure regulator valve is malfunctioning.

   b. If pressure does not vary with intake manifold vacuum (31 to 44 PSI), it indicates no vacuum to pressure regulator valve or a malfunctioning valve.

   c. If low pressure is obtained, it indicates either a malfunctioning pressure regulator valve, or fuel pump, or restricted fuel filter and/or lines.

6. Insufficient Fuel Flow: To check fuel flow, remove fuel line from cold start injector and connect a long hose to the fuel line. Put other end of long hose into a large container. Remove "A" plug terminal from dual relay. Using a jumper wire between terminals 88D and 88Y, operate fuel pump. Pump volume should be a minimum of 1.5 qts. for one-

minute operation. If flow is inadequate, check for restricted fuel line or filters. If there are no restrictions, replace fuel pump.

Component Circuit Checks

After it has been determined that the ignition system, fuel system, all vacuum connections in the intake system, and circuits in the main wiring system to the dual relay are correct, and the system still does not operate correctly, a complete electrical check of the system must be made.

Remove right side kick panel. The control unit is now exposed; to remove the wiring harness multiple plug from the control unit, the clip, located on the forward side of the control unit, has to be pushed forward and the plug pulled upward.

NOTE: On air conditioned vehicles, access to the multiple plug and control unit can best be reached by removing the glove compartment box.

The entire system can be checked using the following chart with a 12-volt test lamp (2 Watt Bulb) and an ohmmeter. The problem could be in the component, the wiring harness or wiring harness connections. By carefully following the steps outlined in the chart, this can be determined and appropriate repairs or replacement made.

Caution must be taken to probe the correct terminals. By placing J-25401-5, Connector Overlay, over the wiring harness plug, the need for counting the terminals is eliminated. The terminals on the wiring harness plugs are not marked, and if tool J-25401-5 is not available, the terminals must be counted starting with terminal 1. Terminals 1 to 18 are located in the longest row of terminals with number 1 starting at the wiring harness end. Terminals 19 to 35 are located in the shortest row of terminals with number 19 starting at the wiring harness end. Terminals 11, 19, 21 to 31, and 35 are vacant.

Voltage Supply

Using a test lamp, connect the red probe to terminal 10 and the black probe to ground with ignition "On", Fig. 23. The test lamp should light. If not, the dual relay or terminal plugs are malfunctioning.

Ground Circuit of Injection System

Using a test lamp, connect the red probe to terminal 10 and the black probe to terminals 5, 16 and 17, in turn, Fig. 23. The test lamp should light. If not, there is no ground connection.

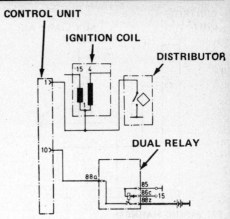

Fig. 24 Triggering impulse from distributor circuit

Check ground connection at intake manifold.

Triggering Impulse From Ignition Distributor

Using a test lamp, connect red probe to terminal 10 and the black probe to terminal 1, Fig. 24 and actuate starter for 5 seconds. The test lamp should flicker. If not, the green wire from ignition coil is open or disconnected. Check connection of green wire to EFI wiring harness approximately six inches from multiple plug inside vehicle. If satisfactory, trace green wire to coil. Also, malfunctioning ignition points may cause malfunction.

Start Signal

Using a test lamp, connect red probe to terminal 4 and the black probe to terminal 5, Fig. 25, and briefly actuate starter. The test lamp should light. If not, there may be an open in terminal 4 or a malfunctioning dual relay.

Portion of Dual Relay During Starting

Using a test lamp, connect red probe to terminal 20 and the black probe to terminal 5, Fig. 26, and briefly actuate starter. The test lamp should light. If not, the dual relay is defective.

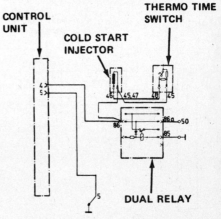

Fig. 26 Dual relay start circuit

Fig. 25 Start signal circuit

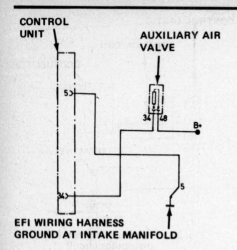

Fig. 27 Auxiliary air valve circuit

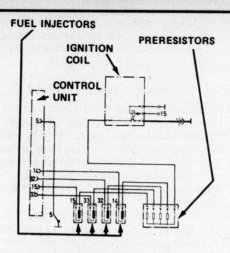

Fig. 28 Injector circuit

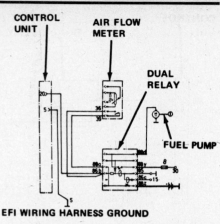

Fig. 29 Fuel pump contact in air flow meter

Auxiliary Air Valve

Using a test lamp, connect red probe to terminal 34 and the black probe to terminal 5, Fig. 27, and briefly actuate starter. The test lamp should light. If not, there may be an open in the wiring harness or a malfunctioning auxiliary air valve. To check air valve, disconnect EFI harness plug from air valve and measure resistance between air valve terminals. Resistance should be 45-55 ohms.

Injectors

Using a test lamp, connect red probe to terminals 14, 15, 32 and 33, in turn,

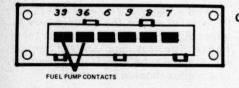

Fig. 30 Air flow meter terminals

and the black probe to terminal 5, Fig. 28, with ignition "On." The test lamp should light. If not, there may be an open in the wiring harness, a defective pre-resistor or injector.

Fuel Pump Contact In Air Flow Meter

Using a test lamp, connect red probe to terminal 20 and the black probe to terminal 5, Fig. 29. Remove air hose from air flow meter, turn ignition "On" and push baffle plate to partially open position. The test lamp should light. If not, there may be an open in the wiring harness or defective air flow meter. Disconnect terminal at air flow meter and check terminals 36 and 39 with an

ohmmeter while operating the baffle plate to check operation of contact switch, Fig. 30.

Air Flow Meter

Using an ohmmeter, connect probes between terminals 7 and 8 with ignition "Off," Fig. 31. Resistance should be 120-170 ohms. Then, place probes between terminals 6 and 9. Resistance should be 230-330 ohms. If resistance is not within specifications, there may be an open in the wiring harness or defective air flow meter. Remove terminal on air flow meter and check resistance between the same pair of terminals as outlined previously on the air flow meter, Fig. 30. Also, remove large air hose and actuate flapper valve to assure free movement.

Injectors & Pre-Resistor Resistance

Using an ohmmeter, connect probes between terminals 14 and 15, then terminals 32 and 33, Fig. 32, with ignition "Off." Resistance should be 15-19 ohms. If not, there may be an open circuit or poor contact in wiring harness or

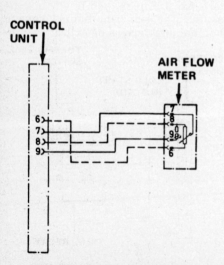

Fig. 31 Air flow meter circuit

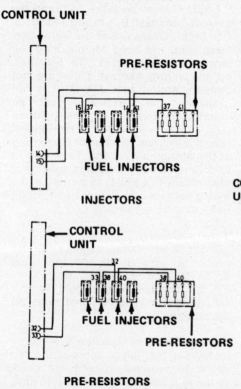

Fig. 32 Checking injectors & pre-resistors

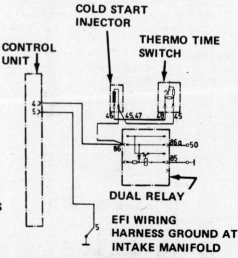

Fig. 33 Cold start injector & thermo time switch circuit

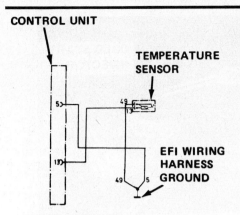

Fig. 34 Coolant temperature sensor circuit

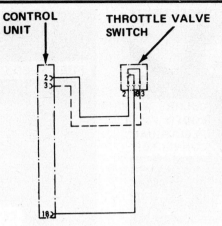

Fig. 35 Throttle valve switch circuit

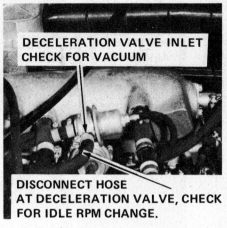

Fig. 36 Deceleration valve test

a defective injector or pre-resistor. Check resistance of injectors which should be 2-3 ohms. Check resistance of pre-resistors which should be 5.5-6.5 ohms.

Cold Start Injector & Switch

Using an ohmmeter, connect probes between terminals 4 and 5 with ignition "Off," Fig. 33. Disconnect dual relay plug "B," Fig. 19. Resistance should be 50-75 ohms above 95° F or 3-5 ohms below 95° F. If not, there may be an open in the wiring harness, a defective thermo time switch or cold start injector. Check resistance of cold start injector which should be 4 ohms at 68° F. If cold start injector is satisfactory, replace thermo time switch.

Coolant Temperature Sensor

Using an ohmmeter, connect probes between terminals 13 and 5, Fig. 34, with ignition "Off." Resistance should be 4,550-6,500 ohms at 32° F, 2,100-2,900 ohms at 68° F or 270-390 ohms at 175° F. If the engine has not been run or will not run and is at room temperature,

use resistance values for 68° F. If engine is operative, run engine until normal operating temperature is obtained and use the resistance values for 176° F. To check sensor at 32° F, immerse sensor in ice water for 10 minutes. If resistance values are not within specifications, there may be an open in the wiring harness or a defective temperature sensor.

Idle Contact In Throttle Valve Switch

Using an ohmmeter, connect probes between terminals 2 and 18, Fig. 35, with ignition "Off." Resistance should be zero ohms. Then, fully depress accelerator pedal. There should be no continuity (infinite ohmmeter reading). If resistance is not within specifications, there may be an open in the wiring harness or a defective throttle valve switch.

Full Throttle Contact In Throttle Valve Switch

Using an ohmmeter, connect probes between terminals 3 and 18, Fig. 35, with ignition "Off." There should be no continuity (infinite ohmmeter reading). Then, fully depress accelerator pedal. The resistance reading should be zero ohms. If resistance values are not within specifications, there may be an open circuit in the wiring harness, a defective throttle valve switch or the accelerator linkage may not be adjusted properly.

Deceleration Valve Functional Test

1. With engine at normal operating temperature and idling, hook up tachometer and note idle RPM.
2. Disconnect and plug vacuum hose from throttle valve to deceleration valve, Fig. 36. With a proper operating valve, the idle RPM will remain the same. If idle RPM drops significantly, the valve is malfunctioning and must be replaced.
3. To check valve for proper deceleration function, momentarily increase engine to 3500 RPM. Hold finger over valve inlet and quickly return

throttle to idle position. If operation is correct, a vacuum will be noted at valve inlet while engine is decelerating. If no vacuum is noted, valve is malfunctioning and must be replaced.
4. Connect all hoses.

Auxiliary Air Valve

If improper operation is suspected, such as high idle RPM at all times, or no high idle following cold starts in low ambient temperatures, check valve as follows:

1. Remove valve from engine.
2. Look through air passage. Rotary disc will be slightly open at room temperature. With jumper wire, connect positive terminal of 12-volt battery to one electrical contact of the auxiliary air valve and negative terminal to other electrical contact. This will heat the valve and in approximately five minutes, rotary slide should cover passage completely.

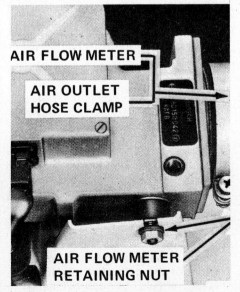

Fig. 37 Air flow meter replacement

Fig. 38 Air flow meter replacement

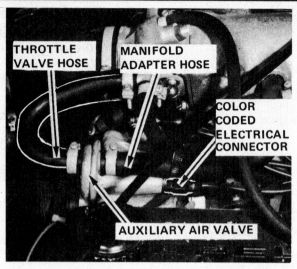

Fig. 39 Auxiliary air valve replacement

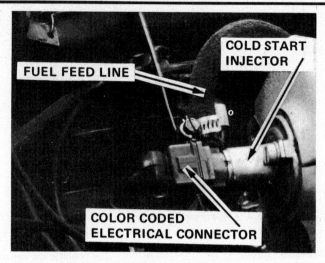

Fig. 40 Cold start injector replacement

SYSTEM SERVICE

Air Flow Meter, Replace

Removal

1. Disconnect electrical connector from air flow meter.
2. Loosen air outlet hose clamp and remove air outlet hose at the air flow meter, Fig. 37.
3. Loosen air flow meter retaining nut and air cleaner top retaining clips.
4. Remove air cleaner top and air flow meter. The air flow meter and the top of the air cleaner should be removed as an assembly.
5. Remove four air cleaner to air flow meter bolts and the gasket and air flow meter, Fig. 38.

Bench Check

Move baffle plate slowly rearward until it is completely open. The baffle plate should have an unrestricted path in which to move. Burrs, dirt, and other foreign objects should be removed if they restrict either the rearward or forward movement of the flap. After removal of foreign objects, a final cleaning of the flap and chamber should be done with a lint-free cloth. If an obstruction has been removed, the following procedure will indicate if the original air flow meter is now operable. With flapper valve in closed position, use an ohmmeter to determine if electrical circuits are operating correctly.

Using an ohmmeter, connect probes between terminals 7 and 8. Resistance should be 120-170 ohms. Then, connect ohmmeter between terminals 6 and 9. Resistance should be 230-330 ohms. If resistance values are not within specifications, the air flow meter is defective.

Use an ohmmeter between terminals 36 and 39 of the air flow meter. When baffle plate is closed, the ohmmeter should show no continuity (infinite reading). When flapper valve is moved from the closed position, ohmmeter should show zero ohms indicating continuity.

Installation

1. Install the air flow meter and gasket to the top of the air cleaner.
2. Install four air cleaner to air flow meter bolts Fig. 38.
3. Install top of air cleaner to the bottom portion of air cleaner and position the air flow meter to the air flow meter support bracket.
4. Secure top of air cleaner and tighten the air flow meter hold down nut, Fig. 37.
5. Connect outlet hose going to throttle valve.
6. Connect electrical connector to air flow meter.

Auxiliary Air Valve, Replace

Removal

1. Loosen both hose clamps; remove the throttle valve hose and the hose to the manifold adapter, Fig. 39.
2. Disconnect the auxiliary air valve color coded electrical connector.
3. Remove two hold down bolts with a 10 mm socket.
4. Remove auxiliary air valve from thermostat housing.

Installation

1. Position auxiliary air valve on the thermostat housing and torque two hold down bolts with a 10 mm socket to 2.5 ft. lbs.
2. Connect color coded electrical connector to the auxiliary air valve.

3. Secure hose from the throttle valve housing to front of auxiliary air valve and tighten hose clamp.
4. Secure hose from manifold adapter to rear of auxiliary air valve and tighten hose clamp.

Bench Check

Use an ohmmeter connected to the two prongs of the auxiliary air valve; the resistance should be between 45 to 55 ohms.

Cold Start Injector, Replace

Removal

1. Disconnect color coded electrical connector from cold start injector, Fig. 40.
2. Loosen clamp and disconnect fuel feed line.

CAUTION: Fuel is under pressure. Some fuel will be lost when fuel line is removed.

3. Remove two screws retaining injector.
4. Remove injector and gasket.

Installation

1. Install cold start injector and new gasket to intake manifold, Fig. 40.
2. Install two retaining screws. Torque screws to 2.5 ft. lbs.
3. Connect fuel feed line to cold start injector and tighten the hose clamp.
4. Connect the color coded electrical connector to the cold start injector.
5. Start engine and check for fuel leaks.

Bench Check

Connect ohmmeter to the two connectors of the cold start injector. The reading should be approximately 4 ohms at 68°F.

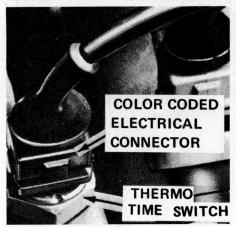

Fig. 41 Thermo time switch & coolant temperature sensor replacement

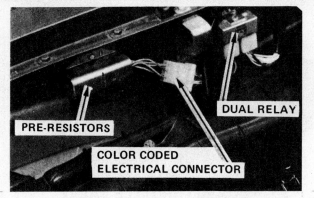

Fig. 42 Pre-resistor replacement

Thermo Time Switch, Replace

Removal

1. Release pressure at radiator cap by rotating the cap counter clockwise until the first stop is reached. Leave in this position until all pressure is released.
2. Disconnect thermo time switch color coded electrical connector, Fig. 41.
3. Remove thermo time switch using a 24 mm deep socket.

Installation

1. Install thermo time switch into thermostat housing. Torque to 21.7 ft. lbs.

NOTE: Make sure metal sealing ring is used.

2. Connect color coded electrical connector to thermo time switch.
3. Add additional coolant as necessary.
4. Tighten radiator cap.
5. Start engine and check for coolant leaks.

Bench Check

Using the ohmmeter connected to the two prongs, the resistance of the thermo time switch should be 50 to 75 ohms above 95°F., or 3 to 5 ohms below 95°F.

Dual Relay, Replace

Removal

1. Disconnect the two color coded electrical connectors from the dual relay, Fig. 19.
2. Remove the dual relay hold down screw and remove the dual relay and harness bracket.

Installation

1. Position the dual relay and harness bracket on the right inner fender and install the hold down screw.
2. Connect the two color coded electrical connectors to the dual relay.
3. Position the wiring harness going to the rear of the dual relay under the harness bracket.

Coolant Temperature Sensor, Replace

Removal

1. Release pressure at radiator cap by rotating the cap counterclockwise until first stop is reached. Leave in this position until all pressure is released.
2. Loosen clamp and remove auxiliary air valve to manifold hose.
3. Disconnect auxiliary air valve color coded electrical connector, Fig. 39.
4. Disconnect temperature sensor color coded electrical connector, Fig. 41.
5. Remove temperature sensor using a 20 mm wrench.

Installation

1. Install temperature sensor using a 20 mm wrench. Torque to 10.8 ft. lbs.
2. Connect temperature sensor color coded electrical connector.
3. Connect auxiliary air valve color coded electrical connector.
4. Secure auxiliary air valve to manifold hose and tighten clamp.
5. Add additional coolant as necessary.
6. Tighten radiator cap.
7. Start engine and check for coolant leaks.

Bench Check

Using an ohmmeter connected to the two (2) electrical prongs of the temperature sensor, the following resistance values should be obtained:

at 32°F.
4,500 to 6,500 ohms

at 68°F.
2,100 to 2,900 ohms

at 176°F.
270 to 390 ohms

NOTE: Let sensor cool to room temperature. Use 68°F values for checking. To check at 32°F submerge sensor in ice water. It is not necessary to check sensor at 176°F on the bench test; however, if desire to check sensor at that temperature, sensor must be heated using a thermostat tester or equivalent.

Control Unit, Replace

Removal

1. Loosen right door edge beading by pulling rearward.
2. Remove right kick pad by pulling the kick pad rearward and then toward inboard.
3. Remove 3 retaining screws holding control unit.
4. Disconnect control unit electrical connector; ignition switch must be off. Release clip at forward edge of the connector by pushing it forward. To detach the connector, pull up on the forward end.

Installation

1. Connect electrical connector to control unit. Insert rearward end of connector under retaining bar of control unit. Pull forward end down to secure connector to retaining clip.

NOTE: Coil input connector must be connected. This connection may become inadvertently disconnected in the removal of the control unit connector.

2. Install control unit retaining screws.
3. Install kick pad by sliding the kick pad forward and inserting kick pad retainer through slotted hole.
4. Secure door edge heading.

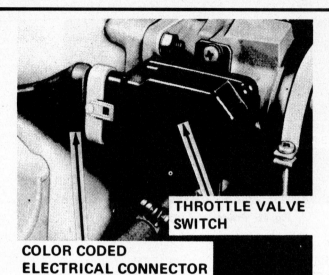

Fig. 43 Throttle valve switch replacement

Pre-resistors, Replace

Removal
1. Disconnect the pre-resistors color coded electrical connector.
2. Remove the two pre-resistors hold down screws, Fig. 42.
3. Remove pre-resistors unit.

Installation
1. Position pre-resistors and tighten the two hold down screws.
2. Connect color coded electrical connector to the pre-resistors, Fig. 42.

Bench Check
Using an ohmmeter connected from the common terminal (center prong) of the pre-resistor to individual resistors (4 outside prongs), each reading (four separate readings) should be 5.5 to 6.5 ohms.

Throttle Valve Switch, Replace

Removal
1. Disconnect the throttle valve switch color coded electrical connector, Fig. 43.
2. Remove the two throttle valve switch retaining screws.
3. Pull switch off throttle valve housing.

Installation
1. Position throttle valve switch on throttle valve housing and install the two throttle valve switch screws.
2. Connect the color coded electrical connector to the throttle valve switch, Fig. 43.

Fuel Pressure Regulator Valve, Replace

Removal
1. Remove rear injector hold down bracket bolt from the injector insulator.
2. Remove vacuum hose coming from the fuel pressure regulator valve "T."
3. Loosen the two fuel feed hose clamps and remove the fuel hoses.

CAUTION: Fuel is under pressure. Some fuel will be lost when the fuel hoses are disconnected.

---

4. Loosen the fuel return hose clamp and remove the pressure regulator valve.

Installation
1. Insert the flanged fitting on the end of the pressure regulator valve into the fuel return hose and tighten the hose clamp.
2. Insert the two flanged fittings on the side of the pressure regulator valve into the fuel feed hoses and tighten clamps.
3. Position the rear injectors to the injector insulator and install the injector hold down bracket bolt.

CAUTION: The hold down bolt is secured to a plastic insulator. Do not over-torque. Bolt torque is 2.9 ft. lbs.

---

4. Connect the vacuum line coming from the pressure regulator valve "T" to the unflanged fitting on the pressure regulator valve.
5. Start engine and check for fuel leaks.

Fuel Injectors, Replace

Removal
1. Disconnect color coded electrical

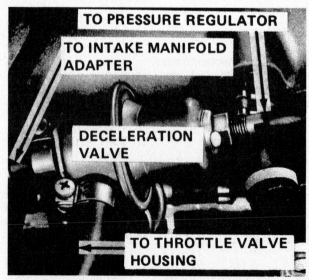

Fig. 45 Deceleration valve replacement

connectors from injectors, Fig. 44.

2. Remove injectors' center hold down bolt.
3. Loosen clamp and disconnect injector from fuel feed pipe.

CAUTION: Fuel is under pressure. Some fuel will be lost when fuel line is removed.

4. Remove injectors from hold down bracket, Fig. 44.

NOTE: When handling injectors, take care not to damage the injector needle.

Installation

1. Install injector in hold down bracket, Fig. 44.
2. Connect injector to fuel feed pipe.

3. Install injector sealing rings on injectors and install injectors into injector hold down bracket.
4. Install injectors to injector insulator.
5. Tighten center hold down bolt of injector bracket to injector insulator.

NOTE: The hold down bolt is secured to a plastic insulator. Do not over torque. Bolt torque is 2.9 ft. lbs.

6. Connect color coded electrical connectors to injectors.
7. Start car and check for fuel leaks.

Bench Check

Connect ohmmeter to the two prongs of the injector. The reading should be 2 to 3 ohms. This check determines the electrical portion. Substitute a known good injector if the injector is believed to be malfunctioning.

Deceleration Valve

Removal

1. Loosen the two hose clamps at the deceleration valve.
2. Remove the three hoses connected to the deceleration valve, Fig. 45. The hose to the pressure regulator valve does not use a hose clamp.
3. Remove deceleration valve.

Installation

1. Secure the unclamped hose coming from the pressure regulator "T" to the threaded fitting at the end of the deceleration valve.
2. Secure the clamped hose coming from the intake manifold adapter to the welded fitting at the end of the deceleration valve.
3. Secure the clamped hose coming from the throttle valve housing to the welded fitting on the side of the deceleration valve.

Emission Controls Section

HEATED AIR SYSTEM
1972-75

The heated air package consists of a heat stove, a corrugated paper heated air pipe, and an air cleaner containing a temperature controlled door operated by vacuum through a temperature sensor, Fig. 1.

The heat stove is a sheet metal cover, shaped to and bolted onto the exhaust manifold. Air drawn in along the lower edge of the stove passes across the manifold surface, picking up heat. The heated air is drawn out from the upper end of the manifold, through the heated air pipe into the snorkel of the air cleaner.

The temperature control air cleaner is designed to mix this heated air with cold air from under the hood so that carburetor inlet air temperature averages about 115 degrees on 1972-73 models and 95 degrees on 1974-75 models. This mixing is done by an air door located in the air cleaner snorkel. Most of the time, the door will be partially open, as required, to control the temperature. When the underhood temperature reaches about 135 degrees on 1972-73 models and 110 degrees on 1974-75 models, the door will close tight, not allowing any more warm air from the manifold to enter the snorkel of the air cleaner. If underhood temperatures rise above 135 degrees on 1972-73 models and 110 degrees on 1974-75 models, the air cleaner will no longer be able to control temperature and the inlet air temperature will rise with underhood temperature.

The temperature door is moved by a diaphragm type vacuum motor. When there is no vacuum present in the motor, the diaphragm spring forces the door closed. Whenever the engine is running, the amount of vacuum present in the vacuum motor depends on the temperature sensor in the air cleaner which is located in the vacuum line between the intake manifold and the vacuum motor. In the sensor, a bi-metal

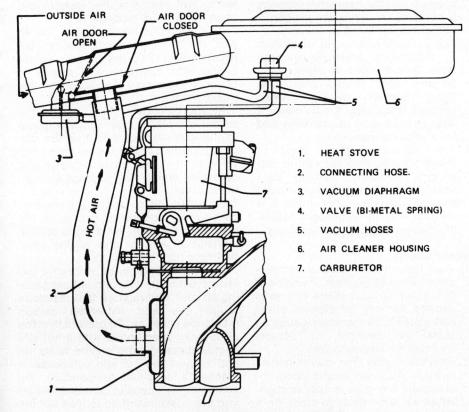

1. HEAT STOVE
2. CONNECTING HOSE.
3. VACUUM DIAPHRAGM
4. VALVE (BI-METAL SPRING)
5. VACUUM HOSES
6. AIR CLEANER HOUSING
7. CARBURETOR

Fig. 1 Heated air system. 1972-75

temperature sensing spring starts to open a valve to bleed more air into the vacuum line whenever the temperature in the air cleaner rises above about 115 degrees on 1972-73 models and 95 degrees on 1974-75 models. Whenever the temperature falls below about 115 degrees on 1972-73 models and 95 degrees on 1974-75 models, the sensing spring starts to close the air bleed into the vacuum line, allowing more manifold vacuum to reach the vacuum motor. Whenever there is nine inches or more of vacuum in the vacuum motor, the diaphragm spring is compressed, the door is opened.

When the engine is not running, the diaphragm spring will always hold the door closed. However, when the engine is running, the position of the door depends on the air temperature in the air cleaner.

When starting a cold engine (air cleaner temperature under 85 degrees), the air door will open immediately. This is because the air bleed valve in the sensor is closed so that full manifold vacuum is applied in the vacuum motor. As soon as the air cleaner starts receiving hot air from the heat stove, the sensor will cause the air door to close partially, mixing cold air with the hot air as necessary to regulate air cleaner temperature within 15-20 degrees of the desired air inlet temperature.

If underhood air temperature rises to 135 degrees on 1972-73 models and 110 degrees on 1974-75 models, the air bleed valve in the sensor will be wide open so that vacuum to the vacuum motor approaches zero. The diaphragm spring in the vacuum motor will hold the air door closed tightly. If underhood temperature rises above 135 degrees on 1972-73 models and 110 degrees on 1974-75 models, carburetor inlet air temperature will also rise.

While air cleaner temperature is being regulated, accelerating the engine hard will cause the vacuum level in the intake manifold and in the vacuum motor to drop. Whenever vacuum drops below 5 inches, the diaphragm spring will close the air door in order to get the maximum outside air flow required for maximum acceleration.

Testing

System Check

1. Start test with engine cold, air cleaner at a temperature below 85 degrees. If the engine is hot, allow to cool.
2. The air door should be closed before starting the engine.
3. Start the engine and allow it to idle. Immediately after starting the en-

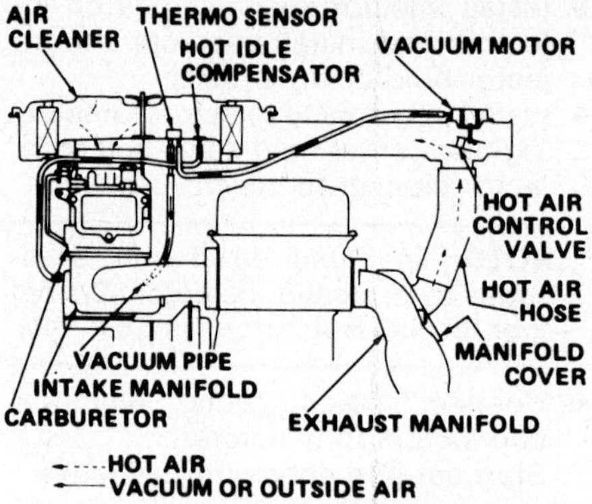

Fig. 2 Controlled combustion system. 1976-77

gine, the air door should open.
4. As the engine warms up, the air door should start to close, and the air cleaner should become warm to the hand.
5. The system is operating normally as described above. If the air cleaner fails to operate or if correct operation of the air cleaner is still in doubt, perform the "Sensor Check."

Vacuum Motor Check

1. Check all hoses for proper hookup. Check for kinked, plugged, or damaged hoses.
2. With the engine static, observe damper door position through snorkel opening. At this point damper door should be in such a position that the heat stove passage is covered, snorkel passage open. If not, check for binds in linkage.
3. Apply at least nine in. Hg. of vacuum to diaphragm assembly through hose disconnected at sensor unit. Damper door should completely close snorkel passage when vacuum is applied. If not, check if linkage is hooked up correctly and for a vacuum leak.
4. With vacuum applied, bend or clamp hose to trap vacuum in diaphragm assembly. Damper door should remain in position, closed snorkel passage. If not, there is a vacuum leak in diaphragm assembly. Replace diaphragm assembly.

Sensor Check

1. Start test with air cleaner temperature below 85 degrees. If engine is hot, allow to cool. While engine is cooling, remove air cleaner cover and install a temperature gauge as close as possible to sensor. Reinstall air cleaner cover.
2. Start the engine after approximately ½ hour. Air door should open immediately if engine is cool enough. When air door starts to close (in a few minutes), remove air cleaner

cover and read temperature gauge. It must read 115 degrees plus or minus 20 degrees.
3. If air door does not start to close at temperature specified, temperature sensor is defective and must be replaced.

CONTROLLED COMBUSTION SYSTEM
1976-77

The Controlled Combustion System consists principally of the thermo sensor, vacuum motor, hot air control valve, and hot idle compensator. These components are mounted to the air cleaner body and snorkel, Fig. 2.

When the engine is OFF, no vacuum is present at the sensor unit or at the vacuum motor. The force of the vacuum motor spring closes off the "heated air" passage from the exhaust manifold heat stove, snorkel passage open.

When the engine is started cold, the thermo sensor is cool allowing maximum vacuum to the vacuum motor. Maximum vacuum at the vacuum motor completely opens the hot air control valve, closing off the ambient air passage through the snorkel and opening the air passage from the manifold heat stove. Should the engine be heavily accelerated while in this mode, the vacuum level in the system will drop to a low enough level so that the diaphragm spring will overcome the vacuum and open the snorkel passage.

As the engine heats up and the air past the thermo sensor reaches between 100°-111°F, the thermo sensor comes into operation and begins to bleed off the supply of vacuum from the intake manifold.

At approximately 111°F, the thermo sensor completely bleeds off all vacuum to the vacuum motor so that the diaphragm spring closes the hot air control valve to the heat stove passage and opens the ambient air passage through the snorkel.

Extended idling, climbing a slope or continuous high-speed driving is immediately followed by a considerable increase in engine and engine compartment temperature.

With this heat build-up, excessive fuel vapors enter the intake manifold causing an over rich mixture that results in rough idle and increased carbon monoxide emission. To prevent this, the air cleaner is equipped with a hot idle compensator. As the engine heats up and air past the hot idle compensator reaches a specified temperature, the compensator opens to feed ambient air into the intake manifold to lean out the temporarily rich mixture.

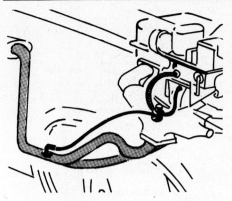

Fig. 3 EGR system. 1973 all & 1974 exc. California

EXHAUST GAS RECIRCULATION (EGR) SYSTEM
1973-74

1973 All & 1974 Exc. California Models

The E.G.R. system consists of a pipe connected to the center of the front exhaust pipe, an E.G.R. valve, a short pipe from the valve to the intake manifold and a short vacuum hose from the E.G.R. valve to the base of the carburetor, Fig. 3.

The system does not receive sufficient vacuum at idle to operate, but will operate during acceleration and part throttle providing sufficient intake manifold vacuum is present.

1974 California Models

The 1974 California EGR system is controlled by two in-line connected valves, Fig. 4.

The first valve is a control valve operating from ported vacuum which varies with throttle opening. It starts to open at a signal of 2.8 in. of vacuum and gradually opens with increasing vacuum.

The second valve is a regulating valve and is operated by manifold vacuum which varies with engine load. It is fully open between 3.5 and 9.8 in. of vacuum closing to a small flow above 11.8 in. of

vacuum. The remaining small gap insures that a limited amount of exhaust gas is returned to the intake manifold even at higher vacuum part throttle operation.

The result of having two valves is that at idle speed there is no exhaust gas recirculation, and at low partial load, a small amount of exhaust gas recirculation is present, and at higher partial load, a maximum amount of exhaust gas recirculation is obtained.

1976-77

The exhaust gas is drawn into the intake manifold through a steel pipe and EGR valve from the exhaust manifold, Fig. 5. The EGR valve vacuum diaphragm chamber is connected to a timed signal port in the carburetor flange through a thermal vacuum valve. The thermal vacuum valve, connected in series between the vacuum port in the carburetor and the EGR valve, senses coolant temperature. The system does not operate at engine idle as the mixing of exhaust gases would cause a rough engine idle.

The EGR valve is mounted under the intake - manifold and controls the exhaust gas flow drawn into the intake manifold from the exhaust manifold, Fig. 6.

The vacuum diaphragm chamber is connected to the vacuum port in the carburetor flange through the thermal vacuum valve. As the throttle valve is opened, vacuum is applied to the vacuum diaphragm. When vacuum reaches about 3.5 inches, the diaphragm moves against spring force and is in fully up position at 8 inches of vacuum.

As the diaphragm moves up, it opens the exhaust gas metering valve thus allowing exhaust gas to be pulled into the engine intake.

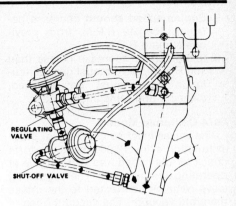

Fig. 4 EGR system. 1974 California

The thermal vacuum valve, Fig. 7, is mounted on the intake manifold and is connected in series between the vacuum port in the carburetor and the EGR valve.

While the coolant temperature is below 118°-126°F, the valve is closed. When the coolant temperature is above 118°-126°F, the valve is open.

System Testing
1973 All & 1974 California Models

The exhaust gas recirculation valve should be checked at 12,000 mile intervals as follows:

1. The fittings going into the intake manifold must be removed, cleaned and reinstalled.
2. With engine at operating temperature, connect a tachometer to engine and note R.P.M. at idle.
3. Disconnect vacuum hose at the intake manifold that goes to the air cleaner.
4. Disconnect vacuum hose for exhaust gas recirculation valve from the throttle valve and connect it to the intake manifold where vacuum hose to air cleaner was connected.

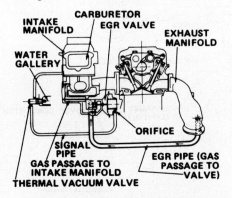

Fig. 5 EGR system. 1976-77

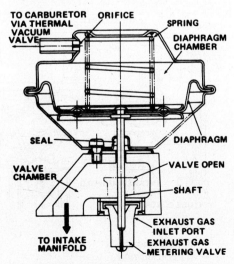

Fig. 6 EGR valve. 1976-77

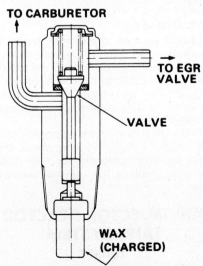

Fig. 7 Thermal vacuum valve. 1976-77 EGR system

5. Engine speed should decrease between 100-240 R.P.M. from previously noted R.P.M.

6. If the R.P.M. decrease is less than 100 R.P.M., the exhaust gas recirculation valve must be removed, cleaned, and reinstalled.

1974 California Models

The valves must be checked for proper function every 12,000 miles. Perform check at idle speed and with engine at operating temperature. The regulating valve remains connected to the intake manifold vacuum. The vacuum hose of the control valve must be temporarily attached to the fitting on the intake manifold, where normally the vacuum hose for the air cleaner is connected. This will result in a drop of engine idle speed by 270 to 300 RPM. In case the reduction of idle speed is less than 200 RPM, the valves must be cleaned.

1975 Models

With engine at normal operating temperature and engine idling, perform the following:

1. Connect a tachometer and note engine RPM.
2. Obtain a length of rubber hose the same inside diameter of the hose that hooks to the EGR valve.
3. Disconnect rubber hose at EGR valve and connect one end of spare length of rubber hose to the EGR valve and the other end to a manifold vacuum source.

Engine idle should become rough and idle RPM should drop by at least 200 RPM. If idle RPM does not drop, clean exhaust residue from the EGR valve, the EGR line, and its connection to the exhaust pipe. Recheck as outlined previously. If RPM still does not drop at least 200 RPM, replace the EGR valve.

1976-77 Models

Check vacuum diaphragm function by applying an outside vacuum source to the vacuum supply tube at the top of the vacuum diaphragm. The diaphragm should not "leak down" and should move to the fully up position at about 8 inches of vacuum.

Place the thermo sensing portion into hot water (118°-126°F) and check the valve opening by blowing air. If air does not pass, replace the thermal vacuum valve.

AIR INJECTOR REACTOR (AIR) SYSTEM

1976-77

The air injection reactor system, Figs. 8 and 9, is designed so ambient air is

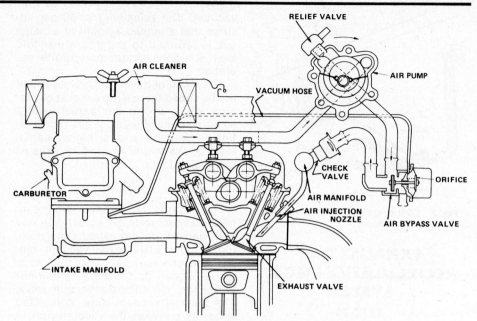

Fig. 8 AIR system. 1976-77 exc. California

pressurized by the AIR pump and is then injected, through the injection nozzles provided near each exhaust valve, into the exhaust gases. The exhaust gases are high in temperature and self-ignite when brought into contact with the oxygen of the ambient air.

AIR Pump

The AIR pump consists principally of the pump body, cover, rotor, vanes and press-fitted relief valve. The pump is belt-driven by the pulley mounted on the water pump shaft of the engine.

Air is drawn through the air cleaner and suction hose into the pump suction chamber, where it is trapped between two vanes and pump body. As the rotor turns, these vanes carry the air to the outlet chamber and then to the air manifold.

The relief valve, press-fitted into position on the outlet chamber, is held closed under normal operating conditions by means of the spring. However, when the pressure of air at the outlet overcomes the tension of the spring, the valve is pushed open and releases excess air so as not to exceed the outlet air pressure of the pump.

Check Valve

The check valve, Fig. 10, is designed to allow air to pass through in only one direction. The valve is pushed open when the pressure of air supplied from the AIR pump overcomes the valve spring tension, but closes with the counter-flow of exhaust gas from the manifold.

This protects the AIR pump and hoses against damage when air supply from the AIR pump is stopped, due to broken drivebelt or when backfiring occurs

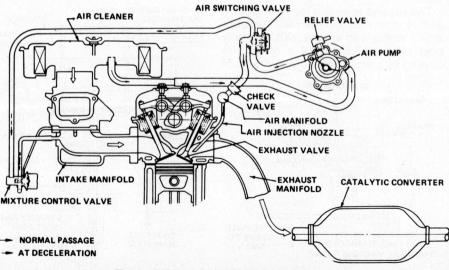

Fig. 9 AIR system. 1976-77 California

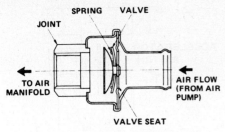

Fig. 10 Check valve. 1976-77 AIR system

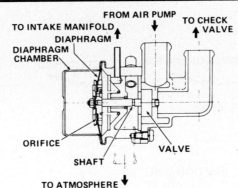

Fig. 11 Air bypass valve. 1976-77 AIR system exc. California

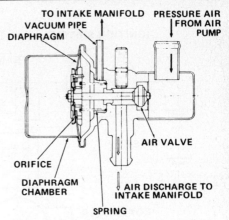

Fig. 12 Mixture control valve. 1976-77 AIR system California

within the exhaust system, causing high temperature gases to flow in reverse direction.

Air Bypass Valve, Exc. California Models

The air bypass valve is located between the AIR pump outlet and the air distribution manifold, and controls the air flow, Fig. 11. The purpose of the air bypass valve is to prevent backfiring in the exhaust system during deceleration.

Throttle closure at the beginning of a deceleration temporarily creates an air-fuel mixture too rich to burn. This mixture becomes burnable when it reaches the exhaust port and combines with secondary air. Upon receiving a high vacuum signal from the intake manifold, which occurs at the moment of a deceleration, the air bypass valve cuts off the secondary air to the air manifold, and diverts it to the atmosphere. And thus, the backfiring is prevented which would be caused by meeting the momentary rich fuel mixture with the secondary air in the exhaust port of the cylinder head, which would cause a backfire in the exhaust system.

Mixture Control Valve, California Models

The purpose of the mixture control valve is to prevent backfiring in the exhaust system during deceleration, Fig. 12. The mixture control valve is designed to supply air into the intake manifold to prevent over-enriching of air-fuel mixture, when the throttle valve in the carburetor is suddenly closed.

The mixture control valve is held closed under normal operating conditions. When the vacuum in the intake manifold increases rapidly, the valve opens, allowing the air from the AIR pump into the intake manifold.

Air Manifold & Air Injection Nozzles

Pressurized air from the AIR pump is fed through the check valve, into the air manifold, where it is distributed to the nozzles. The nozzles are installed in position near the exhaust valves and pointed toward the valve. Thus, air is continuously injected into the exhaust manifold while the engine is running.

System Testing

AIR Pump

Check the AIR pump for an abnormal noise and replace if found to be malfunctioning.

NOTE: The entire AIR pump assembly should be replaced even if minor parts replacement is necessary.

Check Valve

Remove check valve from air manifold. Test it for leakage by blowing air into the valve from the AIR pump side and from the air manifold side. If check valve is normal, air passes only from the AIR pump side. If air passes also from the air manifold side, it indicates the need for replacing check valve. A small amount of air leakage is satisfactory.

Air By-Pass Valve

If air by-pass valve is normal, the secondary air continues to blow out from the air by-pass valve for a few seconds when the accelerator pedal is depressed and released quickly. If the secondary air continues to blow out for more than 5 seconds, replace air by-pass valve.

Mixture Control Valve

Disconnect rubber hose connecting mixture control valve with intake manifold, and plug intake manifold side. If mixture control valve is normal, the secondary air continues to blow out from the mixture control valve for a few seconds when the accelerator pedal is depressed and released quickly. If secondary air continues to blow out for more than 5 seconds, replace mixture control valve.

Air Manifold & Air Injection Nozzle

Check around air manifold for air leakage with engine running at 2,000 rpm. If air is leaking from the nozzle fixing sleeve nuts, retighten them.

Hoses

Check and replace hoses if found to be fatigued or cracked. Also check hose joints and clips. Be sure that hoses are not in contact with adjacent parts.

COASTING RICHER SYSTEM
1976-77

While the engine is coasting the air fuel mixture remains lean, preventing efficient reburning of unburned gas that can only be done with the addition of secondary air and fuel. It is, therefore, necessary to enrich the air-fuel mixture while the engine is coasting to attain efficient reburning of exhaust gases.

However, enriching the air-fuel mixture with only the mixture adjusting screw will cause poor engine idle, or invite an increase in the carbon monoxide content of the exhaust gases.

The coasting richer system, Figs. 13 and 14, consists of an independent operative auxiliary air/fuel system. This system functions when the engine is coasting, to enrich the air-fuel mixture, which minimizes hydrocarbon content of the exhaust gases.

The coasting richer system consists basically of a solenoid valve connected in series to switches, described below, for detection of engine coasting conditions.

Manual transmission except California models — accelerator switch, clutch switch, transmission 4th/3rd gear switch. California manual transmission models — accelerator switch, clutch switch, transmission neutral switch, engine speed sensor. California automatic transmission models — accelerator switch, inhibitor switch, engine speed sensor.

When all of these switches activate, the solenoid valve and magnet installed on the secondary side of the carburetor become energized and cause the valve to open.

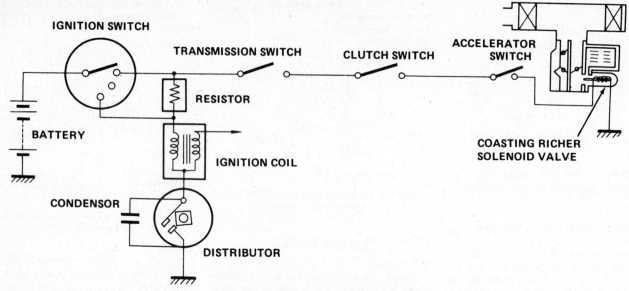

Fig. 13 Coasting richer system. 1976-77 exc. California

When the valve opens, the coasting richer fuel drawn out from the float chamber by the engine vacuum is metered via the coasting jet and mixed with air supplied through the coasting air bleed. The mixture is then supplied, via the coasting valve, into the lower part of the secondary carburetor throttle valve. As a result, the air-fuel mixture becomes temporarily enriched to facilitate effi-cient reburning of exhaust gases forced out into the engine exhaust manifold thereby reducing hydrocarbon and carbon monoxide content in the exhaust gases. When the condition of engine coasting is changed to driving, the coasting richer circuit opens and causes the coasting valve to close thereby preventing further supply of richer fuel into the exhaust manifold.

Solenoid Valve

The solenoid valve is linked to the secondary side of the carburetor and is designed to supply additional fuel into the engine when the valve is opened, Fig. 15.

Accelerator Switch

The accelerator switch is connected to the engine controlled linkage and is

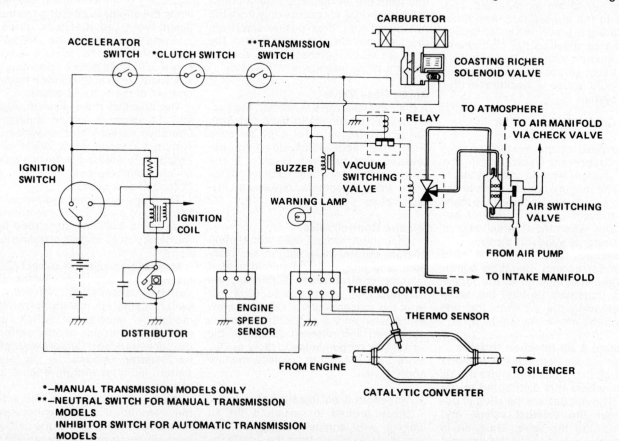

*—MANUAL TRANSMISSION MODELS ONLY
**—NEUTRAL SWITCH FOR MANUAL TRANSMISSION MODELS
INHIBITOR SWITCH FOR AUTOMATIC TRANSMISSION MODELS

Fig. 14 Coasting richer system. 1976-77 California

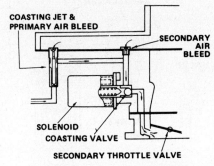

Fig. 15 Solenoid valve. 1976-77 coasting richer system

turned "On," when the accelerator pedal is not depressed. The accelerator switch is turned "Off" and opens the circuit, when the accelerator pedal is depressed, Fig. 16.

Clutch Switch

The clutch switch is installed in position near the clutch pedal and turns "Off" when the clutch pedal is depressed, Fig. 17.

When the clutch switch is turned "Off" through the operation of the clutch pedal, the coasting richer circuit is de-energized.

Transmission Switch, Manual Transmission Exc. Calif. Models

The transmission switch is installed on upper part of transmission gear box, and turns "On" when shifted into 4th or 3rd gear. When the transmission switch turns "On," the coasting richer circuit is energized. Conversely, the coasting richer circuit is de-energized when the transmission switch is turned "Off."

Transmission Neutral Switch, Calif. Manual Transmission Models

The transmission neutral switch is installed on the transmission shift quad-

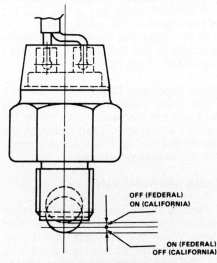

Fig. 18 Transmission or transmission neutral switch. 1976-77 coasting richer system

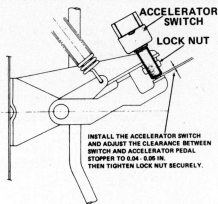

Fig. 16 Accelerator switch. 1976-77 coasting richer system

rant. It turns "On" when shifted into any gear positions and turns "Off" when shifted into neutral position. When the transmission neutral switch turns "On," the coasting richer circuit is energized. Conversely, the coasting richer circuit is de-energized when it is turned "Off."

Inhibitor Switch, Calif. Automatic Transmission Models

The inhibitor switch is installed on the automatic transmission shift lever and turns "On" when shifted into drive, low or second position. When the inhibitor switch turns "On," the coasting richer circuit is energized. Conversely, the coasting richer circuit is de-energized when it is turned "Off."

Engine Speed Sensor, Calif. Models

The engine speed sensor detects engine RPM, sensing ignition pulse from an ignition coil. When the engine speed exceeds approximately 1600 rpm, the engine speed sensor turns "On" and the coasting richer circuit becomes energized.

System Testing

Engine Speed Sensor

Disconnect the engine speed sensor wiring connector and connect "B," "BR and "BY" color-coded wiring terminals with each other with suitable cables. Then start the engine and check for the continuity between "LgB" color-coded wiring terminals. When the engine runs over 1,500-1,700 rpm, the engine speed sensor is normal, if the continuity exists.

Accelerator & Clutch Switch

1. Check setting of accelerator switch and clutch switch. These switches are normal if they are in relative position, Figs. 16 and 17. Make adjustment if necessary, Figs. 16 and 17.
2. Check function of accelerator and clutch switch by operating accelerator pedal and clutch pedal

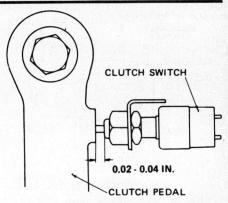

Fig. 17 Clutch switch. 1976-77 coasting richer system

with switch wiring disconnected, and a tester connected in place. Both accelerator and clutch switch are normal, if they turn "On" when the pedals are released and turn "Off" when the pedals are depressed. If switches do not work in response to the movement of the pedals, they are malfunctioning and should be replaced.

Transmission or Transmission Neutral Switch

Check operation of transmission switch by moving the gearshift lever with switch wiring disconnected and a tester connected in place, Fig. 18. The switch is normal if it turns "On" when shifted into either 4th or 3rd gear (exc. California) or any gear positions except Neutral position (California). If switch does not turn "On" through the check, it is malfunctioning and should be replaced.

OVER TEMPERATURE CONTROL SYSTEM
1976-77 California Models

This system operates as follows:
1. While the engine is coasting, the coasting richer system is operated to prevent catalyst over-temperature caused by poor combustion and the secondary air injection is operated simultaneously with the coasting richer system.
2. When the catalyst temperature reaches approximately 1350°F due

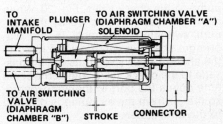

Fig. 19 Vacuum switching valve. 1976-77 over temperature control system

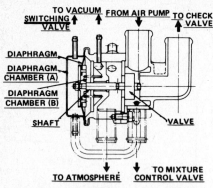

Fig. 20 Air switching valve. 1976-77 over temperature control system

to high speed and high load driving, the secondary air is diverted to the atmosphere in order to reduce chemical reaction in the catalyst.

3. When the catalyst temperature exceeds approximately 1830°F due to engine malfunctions such as ignition system failure, the warning lamp and buzzer are turned on, indicating the catalyst over-temperature.

Vacuum Switching Valve

The vacuum switching valve has 3-way ports, two of which are opened or closed by electrically controlling the solenoid plunger, Fig. 19. The solenoid plunger is energized, when the catalyst temperature is over approximately 1350°F under driving condition (not coasting condition). When energized, the vacuum switching valve connects the diaphragm chamber "B" of air switching valve to the intake manifold, permitting the manifold vacuum to be applied to the diaphragm chamber "B." When the solenoid plunger is de-energized, it plugs the port, so the diaphragm chamber "B" of air switching valve is connected to the diaphragm chamber "A."

Air Switching Valve

This valve is designed to switch air flow from the air pump, and is operated by manifold vacuum and air pump pressure which are switched by a vacuum switching valve. While air pump pressure acts in the diaphragm chamber (B) through the vacuum switching valve, this valve flows the air from the air pump to the check valve, Fig. 20. When manifold vacuum switched by the vacuum switching valve acts in the diaphragm chamber (B), the valve fitted to the shaft in this valve shuts the air passage to the check valve, and at the same time opens the port to the atmosphere, so the air from the air pump is diverted to the atmosphere.

Thermo Sensor & Thermo Controller

Thermo sensor is installed to front

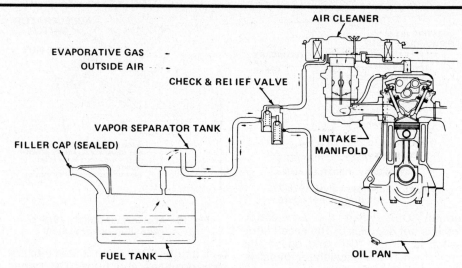

Fig. 21 Evaporative emission system (Typical)

side of the converter. The thermistor is used in this sensor, and it is covered with a stainless steel sheath.

Sensing electric resistance of the thermo sensor, the thermo controller sends "On" or "Off" signal to the vacuum switching valve, the warning lamp and buzzer. When the catalyst temperature reaches approximately 1350°F, this controller sends "On" signal to the vacuum switching valve, and when it exceeds approximately 1830°F, it sends "On" signal to the warning lamp and buzzer.

System Testing
Vacuum Switching Valve

Proper operation of the vacuum switching valve can be checked by carefully listening for noise that is accompanied by electrically operating the plunger.

The plunger can be operated electrically by connecting the connector terminals directly to the battery with suitable cables.

Air Switching Valve

Keep the vacuum switching valve in electrically operated condition and start the engine. If the air switching valve is normal, the secondary air continues to blow out from the air switching valve.

Thermo Sensor

Run the engine at idle for a few minutes, and then disconnect the thermo sensor wiring connector.

Check for thermo sensor continuity between connector terminals by using the tester. If no continuity exists, the thermo sensor is malfunctioning and should be replaced.

Thermo Controller

The thermo controller can be checked by the converter warning light

and buzzer operation. If the thermo controller is normal, the converter warning light and buzzer operate when the ignition switch is in "On" position, and then goes out automatically a few seconds later.

If the warning lamp and buzzer come on due to the catalyst temperature exceeding 1830°F., the warning lamp will remain on until it is reset. The warning lamp resetting procedure is as follows:

1. Disconnect the negative battery cable.
2. Reconnect the negative battery cable.
3. Turn on the ignition and check if the warning lamp is turned "Off."

EVAPORATIVE EMISSION SYSTEM

The evaporation emission control system, Fig. 21, is designed to lead the fuel vapor emitted from the fuel tank into the engine crankcase, where it is mixed with blow-by gases and drawn into the intake manifold for combustion. This system consists of the vapor separator tank, check and relief valve and tubes connecting these parts.

Vapor Separator Tank

The vapor separator tank separates the fuel from the vapor given off by the fuel in the fuel tank. Then it returns the fuel to the fuel tank and carries vapor into the engine crankcase.

Check and Relief Valve

When Engine is Not Running:

The fuel vapor taken up into the vapor separator is fed into the check and relief valve. When the pressure of the fuel vapor becomes as high as 0.2-0.6 in. Hg., the check valve opens, allowing the vapor into the engine crankcase. While the check valve is held open, the valve

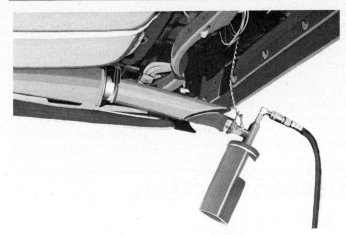

Fig. 22   Aspirator installation

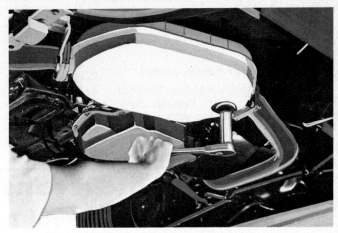

Fig. 23   Catalytic converter fill plug replacement

at the air cleaner side remains closed preventing flow of vapor into the air cleaner.

When Engine is Running:

When a vacuum is developed in the fuel tank or in the engine crankcase and the difference of pressure between the relief side and fuel tank or crankcase becomes 0.2-0.6 in. Hg., the relief valve opens, allowing ambient air from the air cleaner into the fuel tank or engine crankcase.

This ambient air replaces the vapor within the fuel tank or crankcase, bringing fuel tank or crankcase back into atmospheric pressure condition.

CATALYTIC CONVERTER SERVICE

Removal

If necessary, the catalyst in the converter can be replaced on the car with Tool J-25077.

Separate hoses should be attached to the aspirator and the vibrator with maximum available pressure. (Minimum of 60 psi in each hose.)

1. Install aspirator, Fig. 22.
2. Connect air supply line to aspirator to create a vacuum in the converter to hold beads in place when fill plug is removed.
3. Remove converter fill plug with ¾" hex wrench, Fig. 23.
4. Clamp on vibrator, Fig. 24.
5. Install empty catalyst container to vibrator (do not install fill tube extension at this time.)
6. Disconnect air supply to aspirator and connect air supply to vibrator. Catalyst will now drain from the converter into the empty container, Fig. 25.
7. When all the catalyst has been removed from the converter, disconnect air supply to vibrator and remove container from the converter.
8. Discard used catalyst.

Installation

1. Fill container with approved replacement catalyst.
2. Install fill tube extension to the fixture.
3. Connect air supply to aspirator and vibrator.
4. Attach catalyst container to the fixture.
5. After the catalyst stops flowing, disconnect air supply to the vibrator.
6. Remove vibrator and check that catalyst has filled converter flush with fill plug hole. Add catalyst if required.
7. Apply an anti-seize compound to

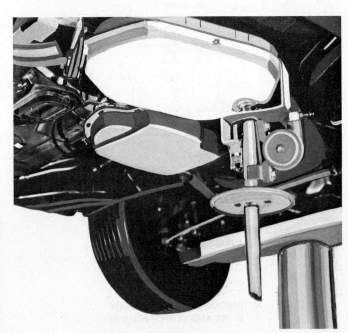

Fig. 24   Vibrator installation

Fig. 25   Draining & refilling catalytic converter

the fill plug: install and tighten to 50 ft. lbs.

8. Disconnect air supply to aspirator and remove.

Bottom Cover Replacement

If, for any reason, the bottom cover of the converter is torn or severely damaged, it can be replaced with a repair kit.

1. Remove bottom cover by cutting close to the bottom outside edge. Do not remove the fill plug. The depth of the cut must be very shallow to prevent damage to the inner shell of the converter.
2. Remove insulation.
3. Inspect inner shell of the converter for damage. If there is damage in the inner shell, the converter assembly must be replaced.
4. Place new insulation in the re-placement cover. Apply sealing compound, all around the cover after the insulation is in position. Apply extra sealer at the front and rear openings for the pipes.
5. Install replacement cover on converter.
6. Install cover retaining channels on both sides of the converter.
7. Attach 2 clamps over retaining channels at each end of the converter.

Clutch & Transmission Section
Manual Transmission

CLUTCH PEDAL, ADJUST

1972-73 GT Sport Coupe

1. Loosen lock nut on ball stud end, located at the right of the transmission on the clutch housing. Position ball stud so the outer end protrudes ¾ inch from housing and tighten lock nut finger tight, Fig. 1.
2. Adjust ball stud to obtain ¾-1¼ inch pedal lash.

1972-75 Exc. GT Sport Coupe

Clutch actuation works without clutch pedal free travel. Clutch adjustment is required only if the indicator lamp on the instrument panel lights up.

With gradual wear of the clutch linings, the clutch pedal moves from the basic adjustment position upward, toward the driver. If wear has reached the extent that the clutch pedal rests against the switch, the indicator lamp lights up. This is an indication that clutch pedal position must be corrected to ensure proper clutch operation. Adjust clutch pedal as follows:

1. If the parking brake is provided with an indicator light, the parking brake must be released. Otherwise, the same indicator lamp as for the clutch lights up.
2. Perform adjustment only with ball stud on clutch housing, whereby the distance between clutch housing contacting surface and clutch release lever must be adjusted to the rear to 4¼ inch, Fig. 2.

1976-77

1. Loosen lock and adjusting nuts on clutch cable.
2. Pull cable toward front of car to take up slack.
3. Turn adjusting nut inward until clutch pedal free travel is approximately ⅝ in.
4. Tighten lock nut.

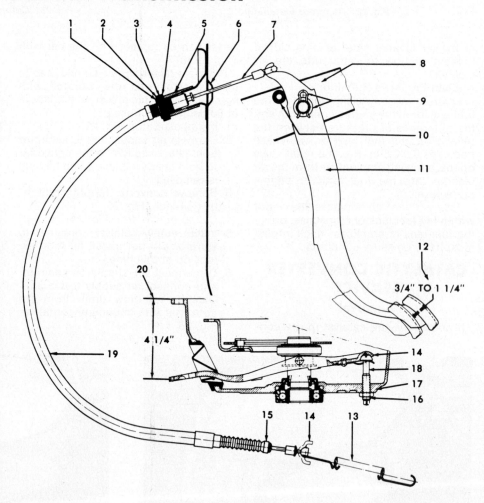

1. E-RING	12. CLUTCH PEDAL FREE TRAVEL-3/4" TO 1 1/4"
2. WASHER	13. RETURN SPRING
3. RUBBER GROMMET	14. RELEASE LEVER
4. WASHER	15. RUBBER BELLOWS
5. SLEEVE	16. BALL STUD LOCK NUT
6. DASH PANEL	17. CLUTCH HOUSING
7. BOWDEN CONTROL CABLE	18. BALL STUD
8. BRACKET	19. BOWDEN CONTROL CABLE
9. WASHER, HAIRPIN CLIP	20. DISTANCE BETWEEN RELEASE LEVER AND CLUTCH HOUSING
10. RUBBER STOP	
11. CLUTCH PEDAL	

Fig. 1 Clutch pedal adjustment. 1972-73 GT Sport Coupe

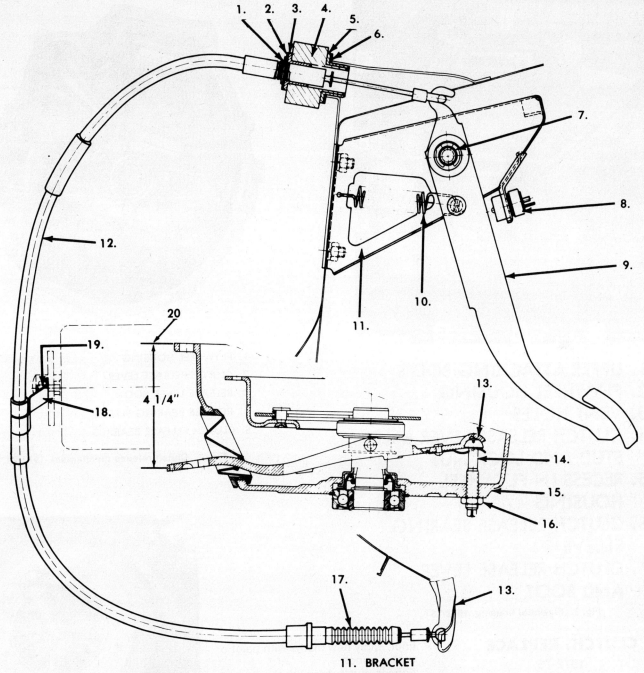

1. "E" RING
2. WASHER
3. RUBBER GROMMET
4. CLUTCH OPERATING DAMPER
5. GROMMET
6. WASHER
7. "E" RING
8. ADJUSTMENT SWITCH
9. CLUTCH PEDAL
10. RETURN SPRING
11. BRACKET
12. CABLE
13. RELEASE LEVER
14. BALL STUD
15. CLUTCH HOUSING
16. BALL STUD LOCK NUT
17. RUBBER BELLOWS
18. CABLE SUPPORT BRACKET
19. NUT, CABLE SUPPORT BRACKET
20. DISTANCE BETWEEN RELEASE LEVER AND CLUTCH HOUSING

Fig. 2   Clutch pedal adjustment. 1972-75 exc. GT Sport Coupe

1. UPPER ATTACHING BOLTS
2. FLYWHEEL HOUSING
3. VENT HOLES
4. CLUTCH RELEASE LEVER BALL STUD AND LOCK NUT
5. RECESS IN FLYWHEEL HOUSING
6. CLUTCH RELEASE BEARING SLEEVE
7. CLUTCH RELEASE LEVER AND BOOT

Fig. 3 Flywheel housing. 1972-75

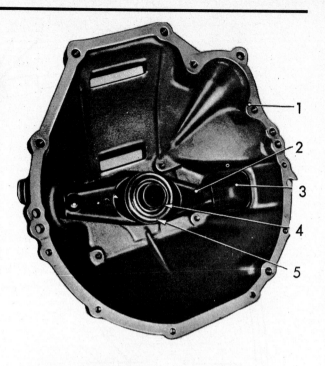

1. FLYWHEEL HOUSING
2. CLUTCH RELEASE LEVER
3. RELEASE LEVER BOOT
4. RELEASE BEARING SLEEVE
5. CLUTCH RELEASE BEARING

Fig. 4 Clutch release mechanism. 1972-75

CLUTCH, REPLACE
1972-75

Removal

1. Remove transmission as outlined elsewhere in this section.
2. Remove bolts from engine support brackets on both sides. Let brackets hang by front bolts.
3. Remove flywheel cover pin.
4. Remove bolts attaching flywell housing to engine and pry housing from locating pins, Fig. 3.
5. To remove release bearing from clevis fork, slide lever off ball stud against spring action. Remove ball, lock nut and stud from housing, Fig. 4.
6. If assembly marks on clutch assembly and flywheel have become indis-

tinct, apply new marks with paint or center punch.
7. Loosen clutch cover to flywheel attaching bolts one turn at a time to avoid bending of the clutch cover flange until spring pressure is released.
8. Support the pressure plate and cover assembly while removing last bolt, then remove pressure plate and clutch driven plate assemblies. Clutch cover, spring and pressure plate must not be disassembled. If necessary, replace complete assembly.

Installation

1. Index alignment marks on clutch assembly and flywheel. Place driven plate on pressure plate with long

1. FLYWHEEL
2. CLUTCH ASSEMBLY
3. ASSEMBLY MARKS
4. CLUTCH ALIGNING ARBOR

Fig. 5 Clutch installation. 1972-75

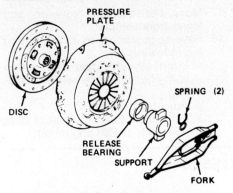

Fig. 6 Clutch assembly. 1976-77

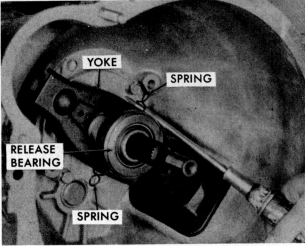

Fig. 7 Release bearing removal. 1976-77

end of splined hub facing forward toward the flywheel.

2. Insert an alignment tool through clutch cover and driven plate, Fig. 5.
3. Hold complete assembly against flywheel while inserting end of alignment tool into pilot bearing in crankshaft.
4. Index the alignment marks and install four clutch cover to flywheel bolts finger-tight. Tighten bolts alternately and evenly, one at a time.
5. Torque attaching bolts to 36 ft. lbs. and remove alignment tool.
6. Install release bearing.
7. Install flywheel housing and torque lower bolts to 36 ft. lbs.
8. Install flywheel housing lower cover.
9. Install clutch return spring and control cable.
10. Install transmission.
11. Adjust clutch cable.
   a. Adjust ball stud on clutch housing to basic dimension of approximately ¾ inch. With lower end of bowden control wire unhooked, push clutch release lever toward the front so that the clutch release bearing rests against clutch spring. Adjust ball stud so that dimension between clutch housing contacting surface and clutch release lever amounts in the rear to 4¼ inches.
   b. Pull reattached bowden cable out of dash panel so that clutch pedal rests against switch (indicator lamp lights).
   c. In this position, install lockwasher at upper control wire attachment three grooves toward the front, thereby completing control wire adjustment.

1976-77

Removal

1. Remove transmission as outlined elsewhere in this section.
2. Mark clutch assembly to flywheel for reinstallation in original position, Fig. 6.

3. Install alignment tool and remove six retaining bolts.
4. Remove release bearing to yoke retaining springs, Fig. 7, and remove release bearing with support.
5. Remove release yoke from transmission ball stud.

Installation

1. Lubricate ball stud and install release yoke.
2. Lubricate support and install release bearing and support to release yoke with retaining springs.
3. With alignment tool install clutch assembly in original position, torquing bolts evenly to 13 ft. lbs.
4. Install transmission.

MANUAL TRANSMISSION, REPLACE
1972-75

Removal

1. Remove air cleaner and throttle rod from carburetor and rear support and disconnect battery cables.
2. Remove screws from fan shroud.
3. Remove gearshift lever.
4. Raise and support vehicle.
5. Loosen front exhaust pipe to manifold flange.
6. Remove clutch cable from the fork by pushing fork to disengage the clutch and unsnap cable from slot.
7. Disconnect backup lamp switch wiring.
8. Disconnect speedometer cable from extension housing.
9. Unhook parking brake cable return spring and remove cable adjusting nut, equalizer, and spacer.
10. Disconnect drive shaft at central joint and remove as follows:
   a. Disconnect parking brake cable equalizer from rod.
   b. Mark mating parts of U-Joint and

the drive pinion extension shaft flange.
   c. Loosen bolt locks and remove bolts or nuts.
   d. Move propeller shaft slightly forward, lower rear end of shaft and slide assembly rearward. Remove thrust spring.
   e. Install a plug in the rear of the transmission to prevent loss of lubricant.
11. Remove rear engine mount bolts and lower transmission as far as possible.
12. Remove transmission case to clutch housing attaching bolts and the transmission.

Installation

1. Make certain drive gear splines are clean and dry. Also, make certain the transmission is in Neutral so the main drive gear splines may be indexed when making the installation.
2. Install transmission and support weight while installing transmission case to clutch housing bolts.
3. Install rear engine mount.
4. Install propeller shaft, align, and tighten U-Joint to pinion flange U-Bolt nuts and torque to 11 ft. lbs.
5. Attach clutch cable.
6. Perform clutch pedal adjustment.
7. Refill with 2½ pints of SAE 80 or 80-90 multi-purpose gear lubricant.

1976-77

1. Disconnect battery ground cable.
2. From inside vehicle, remove shift lever assembly.
3. Loosen clutch cable adjusting nuts at left side of engine compartment.
4. Remove upper starter mounting bolt and disconnect starter wiring.
5. Raise and support vehicle.
6. Remove propeller shaft.
7. Disconnect speedometer cable.

8. Remove clutch cable heat shield and the cable.
9. Remove starter lower bolt and the starter.
10. Disconnect exhaust pipe from manifold.
11. Remove flywheel inspection cover.
12. Remove rear transmission support mounting bolt.
13. Support transmission and remove rear transmission support from frame.
14. Lower transmission approximately 4 inches.
15. Disconnect back-up light and CRS switch wires.
16. Remove transmission housing to engine block bolts.
17. Move transmission rearward and lower from vehicle.
18. Reverse procedure to install, noting the following:
    a. Lubricate drive gear shaft with a light coat of grease before installing.
    b. Adjust clutch lash.
    c. Fill transmission to level of filler hole with SAE30 engine oil.

1972-75 Automatic Transmission

TROUBLE-SHOOTING

Low Fluid Level

1. Fluid coming out of filler tube.
2. External fluid leak.
3. Defective vacuum modulator.

Fluid Coming Out of Filler Tube

1. High fluid level.
2. Engine coolant in transmission fluid.
3. Clogged external vent.
4. Leak in pump suction circuit.

Low Fluid Pressure

1. Low fluid level.
2. Clogged screen.
3. Leak in oil pump suction or pressure circuit.
4. Stuck priming valve.
5. Faulty pressure regulator valve.
6. Missing sealing ball in valve body.

High Fluid Pressure

1. Modulator vacuum line leaking.
2. Defective vacuum modulator.
3. Leak in vacuum system.
4. Defective pressure regulator valve.

No Drive

1. Low fluid level.
2. Clogged screen.
3. Manual valve linkage or inner transmission selector lever disconnected.
4. Broken input shaft.
5. Pressure regulator valve stuck in open position.
6. Defective oil pump.

Delayed Engagement

1. Manual valve position does not coincide with valve body channels.
    a. Missing selector lever shaft retaining pin.
    b. Loose connecting rod to manual valve connection.
    c. Loose selector lever shaft nut.

No Drive When Shifting From P to D, L2 Or L1

1. Parking pawl does not disengage.

Harsh Engagement

1. Band servo piston jamming.
2. Low fluid level.
3. Defective oil pump.
4. Missing screen.
5. Missing sealing ball in valve body.

Shudder on Acceleration

1. Low fluid pressure.
2. Wrong modulator valve installed.
3. Stuck pressure regulator valve.
4. Missing sealing ball in valve body.

Drive In L1 & R But Not In D Or L2

1. Input sprag installed backwards.
2. Failed input sprag.

Drive in R But Not In D, L2 Or L1

1. Worn band, slipping.
2. Band servo piston jamming.
3. Excessive leak in band servo.
4. Parking pawl does not disengage.

Drive in D, L2 & L1 But Not In R

1. Failed reverse clutch.

Drive In Neutral Position

1. Linkage improperly adjusted.
2. Broken planetary gear set.
3. Band improperly adjusted.

No. 1-2 Upshift In D & L2

1. Stuck governor valves.
2. 1-2 shift valve stuck in first gear position.
3. Leaking seal rings in oil pump hub.
4. Excessive leak in governor pressure circuit.
5. Clogged governor screen.

No 2-3 Upshift In D

1. 2-3 shift valve stuck.
2. Excessive leak in governor pressure circuit.

Upshifts In D & L2 Only At Full Throttle

1. Faulty vacuum modulator.
2. Modulator vacuum line leaking.
3. Leak in vacuum system.
4. Stuck detent valve or cable.

Upshifts In D Or L2 Only At Part Throttle No Detent Upshift

1. Stuck detent regulator valve.
2. Detent cable broken or adjusted improperly.

Drive In 1st Gear of D Or L2

1. L1 and R control valve stuck in L1 or R position.

No Part Throttle 3-2 Downshift At Low Speeds

1. Stuck 3-2 downshift control valve.

No Forced Downshifts

1. Detent cable broken or improperly adjusted.
2. Stuck detent pressure regulator valve.

Immediate Downshift After Full Throttle Upshift & Releasing Accelerator

1. Detent valve stuck in open position.
2. Detent cable stuck.
3. Clogged or leaking vacuum modulator line.

Transmission Downshifts At High Vehicle Speeds

1. Missing selector lever shaft retaining pin.
2. Loose selector lever linkage to manual valve connection.
3. Pressure leak at governor.

Hard Disengagement From Park Position

1. Missing steel guide bushing from parking pawl actuating rod.
2. Stuck manual valve selector lever.

Slipping 1-2 Shift

1. Low fluid pressure.
2. Missing sealing ball in valve body.
3. Leaking second clutch piston seals.
4. Second clutch piston centrifugal ball stuck open.
5. Second clutch piston cracked or broken.
6. Second clutch plates worn.
7. Leaking oil pump hub sealing rings.

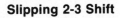

Fig. 1 Servo piston compressor tool installation

Fig. 2 Servo piston replacement

Slipping 2-3 Shift

1. Low fluid pressure.
2. Improper band adjustment.
3. Third clutch piston seals leaking.
4. Third clutch piston centrifugal ball stuck open.
5. Third clutch piston cracked or broken.
6. Worn input shaft bushing.
7. Missing sealing ball in valve body.

Harsh 1-2 Shift

1. High fluid pressure.
2. 1-2 accumulator valve stuck.
3. Second clutch spring cushion broken.
4. Second gear ball valve missing.

Harsh 2-3 Shift

1. High fluid pressure.
2. Improper band adjustment.

Harsh 3-2 Detent Downshift At High Vehicle Speeds

1. High speed downshift valve stuck open.
2. Improper band adjustment.

Harsh 3-2 Coast Downshift

1. Low speed downshift timing valve stuck open.

Engine Flare On High Speed Forced Downshift

1. Low fluid pressure.
2. Loose band adjustment.

Engine Flare On Low Speed Forced Downshift

1. Low fluid pressure.
2. Loose band adjustment.
3. High speed downshift timing valve stuck in closed position.

4. Sprag race does not engage on 3-1 downshift.

No Engine Braking In L1

1. Selector level linkage improperly adjusted.
2. Stuck low manual control valve.

No Engine Braking In L2

1. Selector lever linkage improperly adjusted.

No Park

1. Selector lever linkage improperly adjusted.
2. Parking lock actuator spring broken.
3. Parking pawl.
4. Governor hub.

Excessive Noises In All Drive Ranges

1. Excessive backlash between sun gear and planetary gears.
2. Lock plate on planetary carrier loose.
3. Defective thrust bearing.
4. Worn bearing bushings.
5. Excessive transmission axial play.
6. Unhooked parking pawl spring contacting governor hub.
7. Converter balancing weights loose.
8. Converter housing attaching bolts loose and contacting converter.

Screeching Noise On Acceleration

1. Converter failure.

Short Vibrating Hissing Noise Before 1-2 Upshift

1. Reverse clutch dampening cushion wearing into transmission case.

DETENT CABLE, ADJUST

Before performing the detent cable adjustment, the throttle control linkage should be adjusted so that full throttle opening is obtained at the carburetor.

1. Position accelerator at full throttle and loosen and tighten upper and lower adjuster nuts of detent cable except Manta and on Manta models, turn adjuster, until ball end of cable rests firmly against lever.
2. Measure length of exposed detent inner cable, Depress accelerator pedal fully and again measure inner cable. If correctly adjusted, detent cable should move approximately ⅜ inch.

IN-VEHICLE REPAIRS

Valve Body, Replace

1. Drain and remove oil pan.
2. Remove manual detent roller and spring.
3. Remove three attaching bolts strainer assembly to valve body and card gasket.
4. Remove eight bolts from transfer plate reinforcement and the reinforcement.
5. Remove four servo cover attaching bolts and the servo cover and gasket.
6. Remove remaining eight bolts attaching valve body to case. Carefully remove valve body with gasket and transfer plate.

NOTE: Care must be taken so that manual valve and manual valve link "A" are not damaged or lost during removal of valve body from the case.

7. Remove two check balls located in

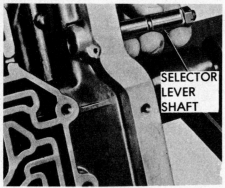

Fig. 3 Selector lever shaft replacement

the oil passages in the transmission case. Location of these check balls must be noted so that they are installed correctly.

8. Reverse procedure to install.

Servo Assembly, Replace

1. Compress servo piston using servo piston compressor tool J-23075, Fig. 1.
2. Using pliers, remove servo piston snap ring.
3. Loosen servo piston compressor tool J-23075 slowly as servo is under high spring tension. Remove tool and servo piston assembly, Fig. 2.
4. Reverse procedure to install.

Selector Lever & Shaft

NOTE: The selector lever on GT Sport Coupe models is on the opposite side from all other models, and that the selector shaft passes *through* the case. Also, one case services both models and is machined to accept selector lever on either side with unused hole being plugged.

1. Remove retaining ring from parking actuator rod to selector inner lever.
2. Remove selector inner lever locking nut from selector lever shaft.
3. Remove selector inner lever from selector lever shaft.
4. Remove selector lever shaft spring pin by pulling upwards with small pliers.
5. Remove selector lever shaft, Fig. 3.
6. Remove selector lever shaft oil seal.
7. Reverse procedure to install.

Modulator, Replace

1. Remove vacuum modulator from transmission case. Care should be taken not to lose the modulator plunger.
2. Remove modulator valve and sleeve from transmission case.
3. Reverse procedure to install.

Detent Valve, Replace

1. Remove spring pin by pulling upward with pliers.
2. Lightly tap detent valve assembly from front of case and remove detent valve, sleeve, spring, and spring seat from rear of case, Fig. 4.
3. Reverse procedure to install.

Speedometer Driven Gear & Extension Housing, Replace

1. Remove bolt holding speedometer driven gear housing retainer and carefully remove retainer and pull speedometer driven gear assembly from extension housing, Fig. 5.
2. Remove the seven attaching bolts from extension housing to case.
3. Remove extension housing and gasket.
4. Remove parking pawl actuator rod from transmission case.

TRANSMISSION, REPLACE

1972-73 GT Sport Coupe

Removal

1. Disconnect battery ground cable.
2. Remove dipstick.
3. Remove throttle control rod from ball pin.
4. Remove screws from fan shroud.
5. Raise and support vehicle.
6. Remove heat protection shield from right side.
7. Disconnect exhaust pipe from manifold flange.
8. Unhook damper rings on front muffler and tail pipe from brackets on body floor panel. Place exhaust pipe assembly onto rear axle.
9. Remove propeller shaft.
10. Disconnect rear engine support from transmission crossmember.
11. Support transmission with a suitable jack.
12. Disconnect transmission crossmember from side members.
13. Lower transmission as far as possible.

Fig. 5 Speedometer driven gear replacement

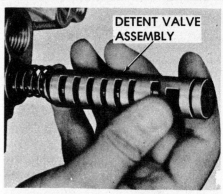

Fig. 4 Detent valve replacement

14. Drain transmission oil.
15. Disconnect selector rod from ball pin of outer transmission selector lever on right side of transmission.
16. Disconnect oil cooler pipes from transmission. Then plug oil cooler pipes.
17. Disconnect modulator line from diaphragm.
18. Disconnect detent cable retainer from transmission, pull cable from transmission and unhook from detent valve.
19. Pry detent cable and oil cooler pipes out of retainers on transmission oil pan.
20. Disconnect speedometer cable and remove from speedometer driven gear housing.
21. On both engine sides, disconnect engine support brackets from torque converter housing. Loosen front attaching bolt only.
22. Remove torque converter housing cover plate.
23. Mark flex plate and converter for reassembly.
24. Remove the three torque converter to flex plate attaching bolts.
25. Pry transmission loose from engine.
26. Move transmission rearward to provide clearance between converter and flex plate to install a suitable converter holding tool. Lower transmission from vehicle.

Installation

1. Assemble transmission to suitable jack and raise into position. Rotate converter to permit coupling with flywheel in original relationship. Remove holding fixture.
2. Install filler tube and the converter housing to engine bolts and torque to 35 ft. lbs.
3. Install and torque flywheel to converter bolts to 40 ft. lbs.
4. Install detent cable.
5. Connect oil cooler lines.
6. Install and torque lower bolt on starter to 30 ft. lbs.
7. Connect modulator line.

8. Connect speedometer cable.
9. Connect shift linkage.
10. Install transmission support.
11. Install drive shaft. Torque "U" bolts to 18 ft. lbs.
12. Install flywheel cover pan.
13. Reconnect exhaust system and heat shield.
14. Install engine support brackets.
15. Lower car.
16. Install and torque starter bolts to 40 ft. lbs.
17. Connect battery ground cable.
18. Fill transmission with fluid. Check selector lever and detent cable adjustment.

1972-75 Exc. GT Sport Coupe

Removal

1. Disconnect battery ground cable.
2. Remove dipstick.
3. Remove screws from fan shroud.
4. Remove 2 upper starter bolts.
5. Raise and support vehicle. Drain transmission.
6. Remove bolts from engine support brackets, both sides. Let brackets hang by front bolts.
7. Remove flywheel cover pan.
8. Remove exhaust pipe from manifold and unhook rubber tailpipe suspension.

9. Remove drive shaft.
10. Disconnect cooler lines at flexible hoses.
11. Detach both stabilizer supports from crossmember to body supports and loosen stabilizer bolts in lower control arms.
12. Place suitable jack under transmission and remove transmission support bolts.
13. Lower transmission enough to remove detent cable and modulator vacuum line.
14. Remove speedometer cable.
15. Remove selector lever.
16. Mark flywheel and converter for reassembly and remove converter to flywheel bolts.
17. Remove converter housing to engine bolt and filler tube.
18. Pry transmission loose from engine.
19. Keep rear of transmission lower than front to prevent converter from falling and install a suitable converter holding tool. Lower transmission from vehicle.

Installation

1. Assemble transmission to suitable jack and raise transmission into position. Rotate converter to permit coupling of fly wheel and converter

with original relationship. Remove holding tool.
2. Install filler tube and converter housing to engine block bolts and torque to 35 ft. lbs.
3. Install and torque flywheel to converter bolts to 30 ft. lbs.
4. Install detent cable to transmission.
5. Connect oil cooler lines.
6. Install and torque lower bolt on starter to 40 ft. lbs.
7. Connect shift linkage to transmission.
8. Connect modulator line.
9. Connect speedometer cable.
10. Install transmission support.
11. Install drive shaft. Torque "U" Bolts to 18 ft. lbs.
12. Install and torque flywheel cover pan to 15 ft. lbs.
13. Install engine support brackets.
14. Reconnect exhaust system.
15. Attach stabilizer supports and tighten stabilizer bolts in lower control arms.
16. Lower car.
17. Install and torque starter bolts to 40 ft. lbs.
18. Reconnect battery.
19. Fill transmission with fluid. Check selector lever and detent cable adjustment.

1976-77 Automatic Transmission (Turbo Hydra-Matic 200)

TROUBLE-SHOOTING

No Drive in Drive Range

1. Low oil level.
2. Manual linkage maladjusted.
3. Low oil pressure due to:
   a. Restricted or plugged oil screen.
   b. Oil screen gasket improperly installed.
   c. Oil pump pressure regulator.
   d. Pump drive gear tangs damaged by converter.
   e. Case porosity in intake bore.
4. Forward clutch malfunctioning due to:
   a. Foward clutch not applying due to cracked piston, damaged or missing seals, burned clutch plates, snap ring not in groove.
   b. Forward clutch seal rings damaged or missing on turbine shaft, leaking feed circuits due to damaged or mispositioned gasket.
   c. Clutch housing check ball stuck or missing.
   d. Cup plug leaking or missing from rear of turbine shaft in clutch apply passage.
   e. Incorrect forward clutch piston

assembly or incorrect number of clutch plates.
5. Roller clutch malfunctioning due to missing rollers or springs or possibly galled rollers.

Oil Pressure High Or Low

1. Throttle valve cable maladjusted, binding, disconnected or broken.
2. Throttle lever and bracket improperly installed, disconnected or binding.
3. Throttle valve shift valve, throttle valve or plunger binding.
4. Pressure regulator valve and spring malfunctioning due to:
   a. Binding valve.
   b. Incorrect spring.
   c. Oil pressure control orifice in pump cover plugged, causing high oil pressure.
   d. Pressure regulator bore plug leaking.
5. Manual valve disconnected.
6. Intermediate boost valve binding, causing oil pressures to be incorrect in 2nd and low ranges.
7. Orifice in spacer plate at end of intermediate boost valve plugged.

8. Reverse boost valve binding, causing pressure to be incorrect in reverse only.
9. Orifice in spacer plate at end of reverse boost valve plugged.

1-2 Shift At Full Throttle Only

1. Throttle valve cable maladjusted, binding, disconnected or broken.
2. Throttle lever and bracket assembly binding or disconnected.
3. Throttle valve exhaust ball lifter or number 5 check ball binding, mispositioned or disconnected.

NOTE: If number 5 ball is fully seated, it will cause full throttle valve pressure regardless of throttle valve position.

4. Throttle valve and plunger binding.
5. Valve body gaskets leaking, damaged or incorrectly installed.
6. Porous control valve assembly.

First Speed Only, No. 1-2 Shift

1. Due to governor and governor feed passages:

a. Plugged governor oil feed orifice in spacer plate.

b. Plugged orifice in spacer plate that feeds governor oil to the shift valves.

c. Balls missing in governor assembly.

d. Governor cover O-ring missing or leaking. If governor cover O-ring leaks, as external oil leak will be present and there will be no upshift.

e. Governor shaft seal missing or damaged.

f. Governor driven gear stripped.

g. Governor weights binding.

h. Governor assembly missing.

2. Control valve assembly 1-2 shift valve or 1-2 throttle valve stuck in downshift position.

3. Porosity in case channels or undrilled 2nd speed feed holes.

4. Excessive leakage between case bore and intermediate band apply ring.

5. Intermediate band anchor pin missing or disconnected from band.

6. Missing or broken intermediate band.

7. Due to intermediate servo assembly:

a. Servo to cover oil seal ring damaged or missing.

b. Porous servo cover or piston.

c. Incorrect intermediate band apply pin.

d. Incorrect cover and piston.

1st & 2nd Only, No 2-3, Shift

1. 2-3 shift valve or 2-3 throttle valve stuck in downshift position.

2. Direct clutch feed orifice in spacer plate plugged.

3. Valve body gaskets leaking, damaged or incorrectly installed.

4. Porosity between case passages.

5. Pump passages plugged or leaking.

6. Pump gasket incorrectly installed.

7. Rear seal on pump cover leaking or missing.

8. Direct clutch oil seals missing or damaged.

9. Direct clutch piston or housing cracked.

10. Direct clutch plates damaged or missing.

11. Direct clutch backing plate snap ring out of groove.

12. Intermediate servo to case oil seal broken or missing on intermediate servo piston.

13. Intermediate servo exhaust hole in case between servo piston seals plugged or undrilled.

Moves Forward In Neutral

1. Manual linkage maladjusted.

2. Forward clutch does not release.

3. Cross leakage between pump passages.

4. Cross leakage to forward clutch through clutch passages.

No Drive in Reverse or Slips in Reverse

1. Throttle valve cable binding or maladjusted.

2. Manual linkage maladjusted.

3. Throttle valve binding.

4. Reverse boost valve binding in bore.

5. Low overrun clutch valve binding in bore.

6. Reverse clutch piston cracked, broken or has missing seals.

7. Reverse clutch plates burned.

8. Reverse clutch has incorrect selective spacer ring.

9. Porosity in passages to direct clutch.

10. Pump to case gasket improperly installed or missing.

11. Pump passages cross leaking or restricted.

12. Pump cover seals damaged or missing.

13. Direct clutch piston or housing cracked.

14. Direct clutch piston seals cut or missing.

15. Direct clutch housing ball check, stuck, leaking or missing.

16. Direct clutch plates burned.

17. Incorrect direct clutch piston.

18. Direct clutch orifices plugged in spacer plate.

19. Intermediate servo to case seal cut or missing.

Slips 1-2 Shift

1. Aerated oil due to low level.

2. 2nd speed feed orifice in spacer plate partially blocked.

3. Improperly installed or missing spacer plate gasket.

4. 1-2 accumulator valve stuck, causing low 1-2 accumulator pressure.

5. Weak or missing 1-2 accumulator valve spring.

6. 1-2 accumulator piston seal leaking or spring missing or broken.

7. Leakage between 1-2 accumulator piston and pin.

8. Incorrect intermediate band apply pin.

9. Excessive leakage between intermediate band apply pin and case.

10. Porous intermediate servo piston.

11. Servo cover to servo seal damaged or missing.

12. Incorrect servo and cover.

13. Throttle valve cable improperly adjusted.

14. Shift throttle valve or throttle valve binding.

15. Intermediate band worn or burned.

16. Case porosity in 2nd clutch passages.

Rough 1-2 Shift

1. Throttle valve cable improperly adjusted or binding.

2. Throttle valve or plunger binding.

3. Shift throttle or 1-2 accumulator valve binding.

4. Incorrect intermediate servo pin.

5. Intermediate servo piston to case seal damaged or missing.

6. 1-2 accumulator oil ring damaged, piston stuck, bore damaged or spring broken or missing.

Slips 2-3 Shift

1. Low oil level.

2. Throttle valve cable improperly adjusted.

3. Throttle valve binding.

4. Direct clutch orifice in spacer plate partially blocked.

5. Spacer plate gaskets improperly installed or missing.

6. Intermediate servo to case seal damaged.

7. Porous direct clutch feed passages in case.

8. Pump to case gasket improperly installed or missing.

9. Pump passages cross feeding, leaking or restricted.

10. Pump cover oil seal rings damaged or missing.

11. Direct clutch piston or housing cracked.

12. Direct clutch piston seals cut or missing.

13. Direct clutch plates burned.

Rough 2-3 Shift

1. Throttle valve cable improperly installed or missing.

2. Throttle valve or throttle valve plunger binding.

3. Shift throttle valve binding.

4. Intermediate servo exhaust hole undrilled or plugged between intermediate servo piston seals.

5. Direct clutch exhaust valve number 4 check ball missing or improperly installed.

No Engine Braking In 2nd Speed

1. Intermediate boost valve binding in valve body.

2. Intermediate-Reverse number 3 check ball improperly installed or missing.

3. Shift throttle valve number 3 check ball improperly installed or missing.

4. Intermediate servo to cover seal missing or damaged.

5. Intermediate band off anchor pin, broken or burned.

Fig. 1   Manual linkage

No Engine Braking In 1st Speed

1. Low overrun clutch valve binding in valve body.

   NOTE: The following conditions will also cause no reverse.

2. Low-reverse clutch piston seals broken or missing.
3. Porosity in low-reverse piston or housing.
4. Low-reverse clutch housing snap ring out of case.
5. Cup plug or rubber seal missing or damaged between case and low-reverse clutch housing.

No Part Throttle Downshift

1. Throttle plunger bushing passages obstructed.
2. 2-3 throttle valve bushing passages obstructed.
3. Valve body gaskets improperly installed or damaged.
4. Spacer plate hole obstructed or undrilled.
5. Throttle valve cable maladjusted.
6. Throttle valve or shift throttle valve binding.

Low or High Shift Points

1. Throttle valve cable binding or disconnected.
2. Throttle valve or shift throttle valve binding.
3. Number 1 throttle shift check ball improperly installed or missing.
4. Throttle valve plunger, 1-2 or 2-3 throttle valves binding.
5. Valve body gaskets improperly installed or missing.
6. Pressure regulator valve binding.
7. Throttle valve exhaust number 5 check ball and lifter, improperly installed, disconnected or missing.
8. Throttle lever binding, disconnected or loose at valve body mounting bolt or not positioned at the throttle valve plunger bushing pin locator.

9. Governor shaft to cover seal broken or missing.
10. Governor cover O-rings broken or missing.

NOTE: Outer ring will leak externally and the inner ring will leak internally.

11. Case porosity.

Will Not Hold In Park

1. Manual linkage maladjusted.
2. Parking pawl binding in case.
3. Actuator rod or plunger damaged.
4. Parking pawl damaged.
5. Parking bracket loose or damaged.
6. Detent lever nut loose.
7. Detent lever hole worn or damaged.
8. Detent roller to valve body bolt loose.
9. Detent roller or pin damaged, incorrectly installed or missing.

MANUAL LINKAGE, ADJUST

1. Remove nut and lever from transmission manual shaft.
2. Place transmission in neutral position.
3. Place shift indicator in neutral position.
4. Loosen locking nut and adjust lever until it aligns with manual shaft, Fig. 1.
5. Install lever on manual shaft and retain with nut, then tighten locking nut on shift rod.
6. Check operation.

THROTTLE VALVE CABLE, ADJUST

1. Loosen cable adjusting nuts on right side of carburetor, Fig. 2.
2. Place carburetor lever in wide open position.
3. Adjust cable until play of approximately .040 in. or less is reached above the adjusting nuts.
4. Tighten adjusting nuts.

Fig. 3   Pressure regulator valve replacement

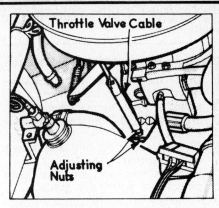

Fig. 2   Throttle valve cable adjustment

IN-VEHICLE REPAIRS

Valve Body, Replace

1. Drain transmission fluid, then remove oil pan and screen.
2. Remove detent cable retaining bolt and disconnect cable.
3. Remove throttle lever and bracket assembly. Use care to avoid bending throttle lever link.
4. Remove detent roller and spring assembly.
5. Support valve body and remove retaining bolts, then while holding manual valve, remove valve assembly, spacer plate and gaskets as an assembly to prevent dropping the five check balls.

NOTE: After removing valve body assembly, the intermediate band anchor band pin, and reverse cup plug may be removed.

6. To install control valve, reverse removal procedure and torque all valve body bolts to 8 ft. lbs.

CAUTION: Ensure that intermediate band anchor pin is located on intermediate band prior to installation of valve body, as damage will resutl.

Governor, Replace

1. Remove governor retainer ring and cover, then remove governor and washer.

NOTE: If governor to case washer falls into transmission, use a small magnet to remove it. If it cannot be easily removed, replace the washer with a new one.

2. To install governor, reverse removal procedure.

CAUTION: Do not attempt to hammer governor assembly into case, as damage to governor, case or cover may result.

Pressure Regulator Valve, Replace

1. Drain transmission fluid, then remove oil pan and screen.
2. Using a small screwdriver or tool J-24684, Fig. 3, compress regulator spring.
3. Remove retaining ring and slowly release spring tension.
4. Remove pressure regulator bore plug, valve, spring and guide.
5. To assemble, install pressure regulator spring, guide and valve with stem end first and bore plug with hole side out.
6. Using a small screwdriver or tool J-24684, Fig. 3, compress regulator spring and install retaining ring.

TRANSMISSION, REPLACE

1. Disconnect battery ground cable.
2. Disconnect throttle valve cable at right side of carburetor.
3. Remove upper starter mounting bolt and disconnect starter wiring.
4. Raise and support vehicle.
5. Disconnect exhaust pipe from manifold.
6. Remove starter lower bolt and the starter.
7. Remove flywheel inspection cover.
8. Remove flywheel to converter bolts and mark for reassembly.
9. Disconnect propeller shaft mounting pad bolts.
10. Remove rear transmission mounting pad bolts.
11. Using a suitable jack, raise transmission and remove crossmember support and mount.

12. Lower transmission leaving jack still holding full support of transmission at lowest position.
13. Disconnect shift linkage and speedometer cable.
14. Disconnect throttle valve cable and cooler lines.
15. Remove transmission to engine block mounting bolts and filler pipe.
16. Move transmission rearward and install a suitable converter holding. Lower transmission from vehicle.
17. Reverse procedure to install, noting the following:
    a. Torque transmission to engine block mounting bolts to 35 ft. lbs.
    b. Install propeller shaft in original position.
    c. Install converter and flywheel in original position and torque bolts to 30 ft. lbs.

Rear Axle & Brakes Section

AXLE SHAFT, REPLACE
1972-77

Removal

1. Raise and support rear of vehicle.
2. Remove wheel and brake drum.
3. Remove rear axle shaft retaining plate and, with a suitable puller, remove axle shaft.
4. Remove retaining ring with a chisel, Fig. 1.
5. Press bearing from axle shaft.

Installation

1. Check radial runout of axle shaft at ball bearing seat and lateral runout of axle shaft flange near largest diameter. Allowable radial runout is .002 inch and allowable lateral runout is .004 inch. An axle shaft that

exceeds these tolerances, or one that has been damaged during removal, must be replaced.
2. Press on bearing so oil seal groove on bearing faces shaft splines.
3. Press on retainer ring so shoulder faces bearing.
4. Check axle shaft end play as follows:
   a. Using a depth gauge, measure depth of rear axle bearing seat in axle housing with backing plate and gaskets in place, Fig. 2.
   b. Measure width of bearing outer race. The difference between the two measurements indicates the required thickness of the shims. The maximum permissible end play is .002 in. If necessary to reduce end play, add .004 shims behind bearing as necessary. A slight crush fit (To .006 in.) is desirable.
5. Coat rear axle shaft splines with hypoid gear lubricant prior to installation.
6. Insert axle shaft into housing. Using a mallet, drive axle shaft completely into housing.
7. Install lock washers and nuts. On 1972-75 models, torque bolts to 20 ft. lbs. or 28 ft. lbs.
8. Lower rear of vehicle.

REAR AXLE, REPLACE
1972-77

Removal

1. Raise rear of vehicle with a suitable jack under differential carrier and position jack stand under jack

bracket on each side of vehicle. Remove rear wheel assemblies and one brake drum.
2. Disconnect parking brake cable equalizer and return spring from brake rod.
3. Disconnect parking brake cable from actuator lever and backing plate at wheel with brake drum removed. Disconnect cable from lower control arm brackets and pull loose end over exhaust system.
4. Disconnect shock absorbers at lower end.
5. Disconnect track rod at left end.
6. On 1976-77 models, disconnect exhaust system bracket.
7. On vehicles equipped with a stabilizer rod, disconnect the shackles at rear axle housing.

Fig. 1 Axle bearing retainer removal

Fig. 2 Measuring axle shaft bearing depth

8. Disconnect universal joint from pinion flange and support propeller shaft aside after marking mating areas. If propeller shaft is removed, install plug in rear of transmission to prevent loss of lubricant.

9. Disconnect brake hose from brake pipe at differential and remove retaining clip.

10. Lower rear axle assembly to remove coil springs.

11. Remove central joint support bracket to underbody retaining bolts.

12. Disconnect lower control arms at rear axle assembly bracket and roll the assembly from under vehicle.

Installation

1. Roll rear axle assembly under car on floor jack and loosely attach lower control arms to rear axle housing.

2. Attach central joint support to underbody with bolts only finger tight.

3. Lower rear axle assembly, install lower damper rings in spring seats, coil springs and upper damper rings on springs. Make certain the damper rings and springs are properly positioned.

4. Install track rod on axle housing.

5. Place a load of approximately 350 lbs. in luggage compartment and raise rear axle far enough for underbody to clear jack stands.

6. Torque central joint support to underbody bolts to 36 ft. lbs.

7. Torque lower control arm to axle housing bolts to 22 ft. lbs. on 1972-75 or 50 ft. lbs. on 1976-77.

8. Torque track rod to rear axle attaching nut to 76 ft. lbs. and remove added weight.

9. Install shock absorbers and tighten nuts to 47 ft. lbs.

10. Install exhaust system bracket on 1976-77 models.

11. If vehicle is equipped with stabilizer rod, connect shackles to axle housing. Tighten to 25 ft. lbs.

12. Connect brake hose to brake pipe and install retaining clip.

13. Route parking brake cable over exhaust system and connect to lower control arm brackets, parking brake actuating lever and brake backing plate. Install brake drum.

14. Align mating marks and connect propeller shaft to pinion flange. Tighten universal joint attaching bolts to 11 ft. lbs. on 1972-75 or 18 ft. lbs. on 1976-77. Bend respective lock plate tabs to secure nuts or bolts.

15. Connect parking brake cable equalizer and return spring to brake

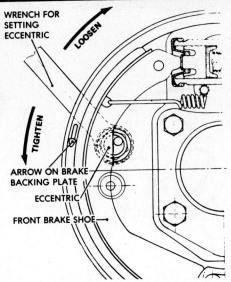

Fig. 3   Rear wheel brake adjustment. 1972-75

rod and adjust parking brake.

16. Bleed rear brake system and fill master cylinder.

17. Install wheel assemblies and torque lug nuts to 65 ft. lbs.

18. Remove jack stands and lower vehicle.

BRAKE PEDAL HEIGHT, ADJUST

1972-75

Brake pedal height can be adjusted by first removing the nut and lock tab from the brake pedal to clevis attaching bolt and then by turning the head of the bolt and rotating the eccentric until there is approximately ¼ inch play in the brake pedal. Replace lock tab and nut. If one of the tabs on lock tab breaks, replace lock tab.

1976-77

1. Adjust setting of the brake pedal by turning the pushrod as necessary, so that the distance between upper face of brake pedal and floor mat is adjusted to approximately 6¾ inch.

2. Push the brake pedal by turning the stop light switch so brake pedal free play is eliminated.

3. When the adjustment is completed, tighten the clevis lock nut and light switch lock nut.

SERVICE BRAKE, ADJUST

1972-75

At each rear wheel brake assembly there are two brake shoes, and each brake shoe has an individual adjustment eccentric, Fig. 3. Each shoe must be adjusted separately by turning adjustment eccentric which is mounted on the brake backing plate. Arrows on backing plate circumference show direction in which eccentrics should be turned to obtain brake shoe-to-drum contact.

When adjusting front brake shoe of rear brakes, turn wheel forward. When adjusting rear brake shoe of rear wheel brakes, turn wheel rearward. Adjust as follows:

1. Raise and support vehicle. Prior to adjustment, check that all brake drums rotate freely.

2. Revolve drum in forward direction and turn front brake shoe eccentric in direction of arrow until brake shoe contacts brake drum. Then turn eccentric in opposite direction until brake drum is just free to turn. Adjust rear brake shoe in the same way but revolve brake drum in rearward direction.

3. Lower vehicle and check for proper adjustment.

PARKING BRAKE, ADJUST

1972-75

1. Fully release parking brake lever and check parking brake for free movement.

2. Loosen equalizer nut or adjusting nut, depending upon whether tension is to be increased or decreased in cable.

3. Pull parking brake lever up three clicks. Adjust equalizer with adjusting and lock nuts so the rear brakes just begin to bind. The rear brake action should be equal on both rear wheels. In case of unequal brake action, apply lubricant to equalizer and brake cable.

4. After adjustment, tighten lock nut. Be certain that equalizer is in horizontal position. Check operation of parking brake.

1976-77

1. Fully release the parking brake lever; check parking brake cable for free movement.

2. Remove the cable play by turning the brake lever rod adjust nut.

3. When adjustment is completed, check that the travel of the parking brake lever is wet firmly. If the travel of the parking brake lever is more than eight clicks, readjust with the lever rod adjust nut.

1972-75 DISC BRAKE SERVICE, FIG. 4

Brake Shoe, Replace

Removal

1. Raise vehicle and remove front wheels.

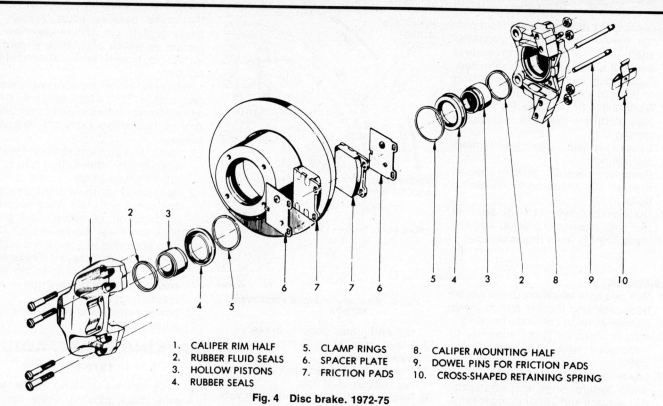

1. CALIPER RIM HALF
2. RUBBER FLUID SEALS
3. HOLLOW PISTONS
4. RUBBER SEALS
5. CLAMP RINGS
6. SPACER PLATE
7. FRICTION PADS
8. CALIPER MOUNTING HALF
9. DOWEL PINS FOR FRICTION PADS
10. CROSS-SHAPED RETAINING SPRING

Fig. 4 Disc brake. 1972-75

2. Drive dowel pins from brake caliper toward inboard side, Fig. 5. Dowel pins must be driven inward since the pins are secured by enlarged fluted inner ends.
3. Remove brake shoes from calipers, Fig. 6.

Installation

1. Install brake shoes into calipers, Fig. 6.
2. With a punch, drive one dowel pin from inboard side through caliper and brake shoes to stop. Install new cross-shaped retaining spring under installed dowel pin, then install second dowel pin. Loose-fitting dowel pins must be replaced.

Fig. 5 Dowel pin removal. 1972-75

3. Before operating vehicle, depress brake pedal several times to adjust brake shoes to brake discs. Check brake fluid level and add fluid as necessary to bring level up to "MAX" on reservoir.

Caliper, Replace

Removal

1. Remove left or right front wheel and remove brake shoes from brake caliper.
2. Loosen brake line to brake caliper union nut several turns. Remove brake caliper and brake hose bracket from steering knuckle.
3. Remove caliper attaching bolts, Fig. 7, aside. Then, disconnect brake pipe from brake hose and remove brake caliper and brake pipe. To prevent fluid loss, plug the brake hose.

Installation

1. Prior to installation, check contacting surfaces of the brake caliper and steering knuckle to be sure they are free of any burrs and dirt.
2. Install brake caliper on steering knuckle and torque attaching bolts to 72 ft. lbs., Fig. 7.
3. Attach brake pipe to brake hose.
4. Install friction pads and replace wheel.

Caliper Overhaul

1. Remove brake pipe from brake

caliper. If both calipers are being overhauled, it is advisable to mark them with "L" or "R" on removal to avoid errors when installing parts, such as pistons, etc. The brake caliper halves must not be disassembled. All work, such as pressing out pistons, replacing seals in brake caliper, is carried out with the two caliper halves bolted together.
2. Pry clamp rings from rubber seals, using a suitable screwdriver, Fig. 8, and remove rubber seals.
3. Remove piston from caliper rim half, Fig. 9, then from the caliper mounting half, Fig. 10, of the brake caliper, using mounting clamp J-22429. Force the piston out of the caliper rim half, block the piston in the caliper mounting half with mounting clamp J-22429.

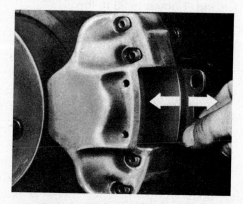

Fig. 6 Brake shoe replacement. 1972-75

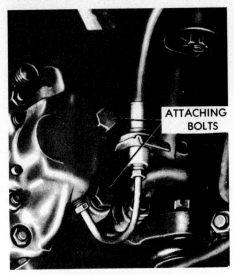

Fig. 7 Caliper attaching bolts. 1972-75

Fig. 8 Rubber seal clamp ring or dust seal replacement

Fig. 9 Caliper rim half piston removal

To force the piston out of the caliper mounting half, place the mounting clamp on caliper rim half and tighten wing nut so that the rubber plate seals off the caliper rim half bore. Then, connect compressed air hose to brake line connection in the caliper mounting half, and blow out pistons, carefully regulating air flow. When removing pistons, use extreme caution and keep the fingers holding the caliper away from piston.

4. Pry rubber fluid seals from annular grooves in the caliper half bores, Fig. 11.
5. Check all parts of the brake caliper for wear. If the caliper half bores are scored or rusted, use a new complete brake caliper and brake shoes. Small, light rust spots in the caliper half bores or on the pistons can be removed with fine emery cloth. If pistons are damaged, even though the caliper half bores are in good condition, the piston must be replaced. The rubber fluid seals and rubber seals with clamp rings for the pistons are to be replaced every time repair work is carried out on the brake caliper.
6. Thoroughly clean all reusable parts with denatured alcohol and dry with compressed air. Prior to cleaning, screw bleeder valve out of caliper.
7. Lightly coat new rubber fluid seals with brake fluid and insert fluid seals into grooves of brake caliper bores.
8. Place brake caliper into vise to install pistons. After installing one piston, change position of brake caliper in vise to install second piston. The piston to brake shoe spacer plates should be used as a gauge to locate relieved edge of piston at 20 degrees to horizontal during piston installation.
9. Place caliper mounting half in vise and coat bore and piston lightly with brake fluid. Then push piston, with hollow end towards brake disc, into the caliper bore. Turn piston so that the relieved edge faces downwards at an angle of 20 degrees and is facing in brake disc direction. The guide surface in the caliper half recess at the brake pipe connection side, will properly align the piston. Push piston into caliper bore up to the stop.
10. Change position of brake caliper and install second piston.
11. Install new rubber seals with clamp rings, Fig. 7. Make sure that the rubber seals are properly seated on the caliper half collars and the clamp rings are correctly positioned on rubber seals.

Fig. 11 Removing fluid seals from caliper

Fig. 10 Caliper mounting half piston removal

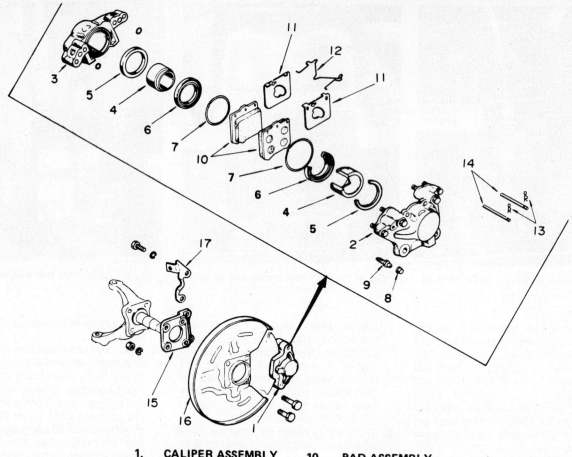

1.	CALIPER ASSEMBLY	10.	PAD ASSEMBLY
2.	INNER CALIPER	11.	PAD SHIM
3.	OUTER CALIPER	12.	M TYPE SPRING
4.	PISTON	13.	CLIP
5.	PISTON SEAL	14.	PIN
6.	DUST SEAL	15.	ADAPTER
7.	DUST SEAL RING	16.	DUST COVER
8.	BLEEDER CAP	17.	BRACKET
9.	BLEEDER		

Fig. 12   Disc brake. 1976-77

1976-77 DISC BRAKE SERVICE, FIG. 12

Brake Shoe, Replace

Removal

1. Raise and support front of car, then remove front wheels.
2. Remove clips, pins, "M" type spring, shims and brake shoes, Fig. 13.
3. Remove any dirt or foreign material from brake shoe recess of caliper.
4. Visually inspect piston seals for leakage.

Installation

1. Apply P.B.C. grease, included in shoe repair kit, to vertical edges of shoes.
2. Push pistons into bores, using Tool J-22430. While pressing pistons into bores, open bleeder valve slightly to prevent brake fluid from overflowing reservoir. Tighten bleeder valve when pistons are bottomed.
3. Assemble anti-rattle shims to brake shoes with arrow mark facing direction of normal disc rotation and install into caliper.
4. Install "M" type spring, pins and clips, Fig. 13.
5. Install wheels and lower vehicle.

Caliper, Replace

1. Raise and support front of vehicle and remove wheel.
2. Disconnect caliper brake pipe from brake hose and cap or tape or cap ends to protect against dirt.
3. Remove caliper attaching bolts, Fig. 14. This will allow the brake hose and bracket to hang fully. Remove caliper assembly. Reverse procedure to install. Bleed brakes before installing wheel. Torque caliper attaching bolts to 36.2 ft. lbs. and the brake pipe flare nut to 11.6 ft. lbs.

Caliper Overhaul

Disassembly

1. Remove dust seal ring and the dust seal from each piston, Fig. 8.
2. Install clamp J-22429 on mounting half of caliper and remove rim half piston by applying compressed air at the brake line connection, Fig. 10.
3. Install clamp J-22429 on rim half of caliper and remove mounting half piston by applying compressed air at the brake line connection, Fig. 9.
4. Remove fluid seals from annular grooves in caliper piston bores, Fig. 11.

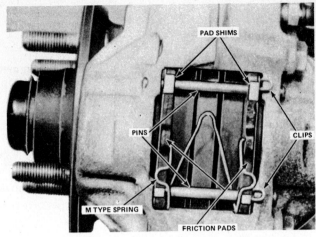

Fig. 13 Brake shoe replacement. 1976-77

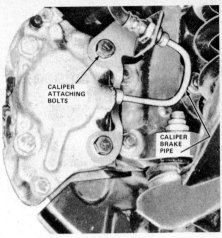

Fig. 14 Caliper attaching bolts. 1976-77

NOTE: The caliper is of an integral design and cannot be disassembled. The entire caliper assembly should be replaced if brake fluid is found to be leaking from the caliper joint. Never attempt to loosen bridge bolts, since breakage of bolts or leakage of brake fluid at the mating surface may result.

Inspection
1. Check calipers and adapter plates for distortion or cracking and replace, if necessary.
2. Inspect cylinder bores and pistons for wear, scuffing or corrosion and replace, if necessary.

Assembly
1. Apply special rubber grease (included in caliper seal repair kit) to the seal and cylinder wall, then insert new piston seal into the cylinder.

NOTE: Do not use lubricants other than those included repair kit.

2. Carefully install piston to bottom of cylinder bore using finger pressure only to avoid scratching cylinder wall, piston or seal.
3. Install dust seal and seal ring.

MASTER CYLINDER, REPLACE
1972-75
Removal
1. Remove master cylinder from brake booster by disconnecting brake pipes and removing the two self-tightening nuts securing master cylinder to brake booster. Do not loosen the front housing seal.

Installation
1. Mount master cylinder to brake booster, using a new front housing seal if old seal is damaged or distorted. Torque nuts to 12 ft. lbs.
2. Install brake pipes to master cylinder and bleed brakes.

1976-77
Removal
1. Disconnect front and rear brake pipes from master cylinder.
2. Remove nuts securing the master cylinder to brake booster and support bracket.
3. Remove bolts securing fluid reservoir bracket, then the master cylinder assembly with the fluid reservoir and rubber hoses.

Installation
1. Place master cylinder with fluid reservoir and rubber hoses in position with the fluid reservoir bracket and install bolts securing the fluid reservoir bracket.
2. Install nuts securing master cylinder to brake booster and support bracket.
3. Connect front and rear brake pipes to master cylinder.
4. Torque the master-cylinder-to-brake-booster bolt to 10 ft. lbs.
5. Torque brake line flare nut to 12 ft. lbs.
6. Bleed brake system.

POWER BRAKE UNIT, REPLACE
1972-75
Removal
1. Disconnect brake pipes from master cylinder.
2. Disconnect vacuum hose from brake booster.
3. Remove four nuts and washers at-taching brake booster to brake booster support.
4. Remove master cylinder support to fender skirt bolts.
5. Loosen thrust rod lock nut and remove the piston push rod while holding the master cylinder brake booster assembly.
6. Remove assembly from vehicle.
7. Disconnect master cylinder from brake booster.

Installation
1. Using a new seal ring, assemble master cylinder to brake booster and torque nuts to 14 ft. lbs.
2. Position assembly into brake booster bracket and thread piston push rod onto the thrust rod.
3. Install brake booster to support attaching washers and nuts and torque to 11 ft. lbs.
4. Install master cylinder support to inner fender skirt bolts.
5. Connect vacuum hose to brake booster.
6. Turning the piston push rod on the thrust rod, adjust until the brake pedal free travel is ¼ inch and tighten the lock nut.
7. Connect brake pipes to master cylinder and bleed brakes.

1976-77
1. Remove master cylinder as outlined previously.
2. Remove vacuum hose clip and hose from the check valve.
3. Pull out clevis pin and separate clevis from brake pedal arm.
4. Remove master-vac to spacer retaining nuts and the master-vac assembly.
5. Reverse procedure to install after measuring the distance between the master cylinder mounting face of the master-vac and the end of the push-rod.

Rear Suspension Section

SHOCK ABSORBER, REPLACE

1972-75

Removal

1. Remove upper attaching nut, retainer and rubber grommet, Fig. 1.
2. Remove lower attaching nut and rubber grommet retainer, compress shock absorber and remove from lower mounting pin.

Installation

1. Replace upper and lower rubber grommets, if necessary, before installing shock absorber.
2. Extend shock absorber and position in vehicle. Attach at lower end and tighten nut.
3. Install rubber grommet, retainer and self-locking nut at top of shock absorber.

1976-77

Removal

1. Raise vehicle and remove wheel.
2. Disconnect lower end of shock absorber from axle, Fig. 2.
3. Remove fuel tank cover from inside

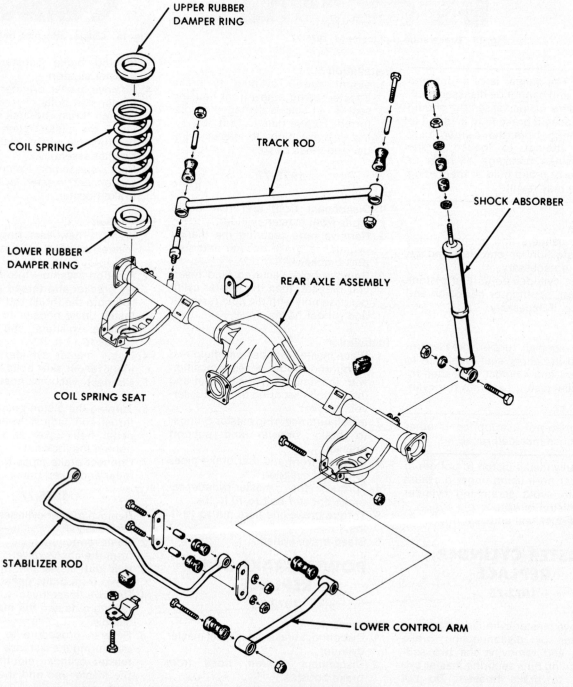

UPPER RUBBER DAMPER RING

COIL SPRING

LOWER RUBBER DAMPER RING

COIL SPRING SEAT

TRACK ROD

REAR AXLE ASSEMBLY

SHOCK ABSORBER

STABILIZER ROD

LOWER CONTROL ARM

Fig. 1 Rear suspension. 1972-75

1. CONTROL ARM ASSEMBLY
2. CONTROL ARM
3. BUSHING
4. BUSHING
5. LATERAL ROD ASSEMBLY
6. LATERAL ROD
7. BUSHING
8. SLEEVE
9. SPRING
10. INSULATOR
11. INSULATOR
12. BUSHING
13. SHOCK ABSORBER ASSEMBLY

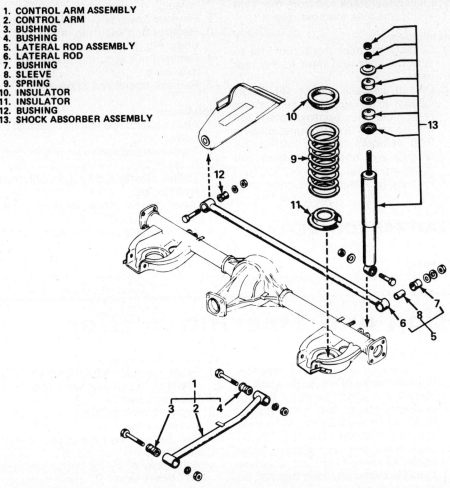

Fig. 2   Rear suspension. 1976-77

trunk and disconnect upper end of shock absorber.
4. Remove shock absorber from vehicle.

Installation
1. Attach shock absorber upper mounting.
2. Install fuel tank cover.
3. Attach lower end of shock absorber to axle. Torque nut to 29 ft. lbs.
4. Install wheel and torque nuts to 50 ft. lbs.
5. Lower vehicle.

COIL SPRING, REPLACE
1972-75
Removal
1. Raise rear of vehicle with a suitable jack and support with jackstands positioned under side jack brackets.
2. Remove rear wheels.
3. Disconnect shock absorbers from rear axle, Fig. 1.
4. Disconnect stabilizer and shackles, if equipped, from frame.
5. Lower rear axle assembly as far as possible. Do not stretch brake hoses.

6. If necessary, tilt the rear axle assembly to remove springs.
   Note the upper and lower rubber damper rings, Fig. 1

Installation
1. Make certain the lower damper rings are properly positioned in the spring seats and place the springs in proper position in the damper rings, Fig. 1.
2. Install upper damper rings on springs.
3. Raise rear axle assembly to compress springs in the seats.
4. Attach shock absorbers and torque retaining nuts to 47 ft. lbs.
5. Attach stabilizer shackles, if equipped, to axle brackets and torque bolts to 25 ft. lbs. with vehicle at curb weight.
6. Install rear wheels, torquing lug nuts to 65 ft. lbs.
7. Remove jack stands and lower vehicle.

1976-77
Removal
1. Raise vehicle and remove wheel.
2. Raise rear axle with a suitable jack.

3. Disconnect lower end of shock absorber from rear axle, Fig. 2.
4. Lower jack supporting rear axle until the coil spring can be removed.
5. Remove coil spring.

Installation
1. Install coil spring.
2. Raise rear axle with the jack.
3. Connect lower end of shock absorber to rear axle.
4. Remove jack under rear axle.
5. Install wheel and torque nuts to 50 ft. lbs.
6. Lower vehicle.

CONTROL ARM, REPLACE
1972-75
Removal
1. Disconnect parking brake cable from support bracket on control arm.
2. Loosen and remove front and rear control arm attaching bolts and remove control arm, Fig. 1.

Installation
1. On all models except GT Sport Coupe place a load of approximately 350 lbs. in luggage compartment or on GT Sport Coupe, place a load of approximately 150 lbs. on driver's seat. Torque control arm attaching nut and bolts to 18 ft. lbs. on all models except 1900 and Manta and 23 ft. lbs. on 1900 and Manta.
2. Connect parking brake cable to support bracket on control arm.

1976-77
Removal
1. Raise vehicle and remove rear wheel.
2. Remove bolt connecting the control arm to axle case, Fig. 2.
3. Remove bolt connecting the control arm to the body.
4. Remove control arm assembly.

Installation
1. Attach control arm assembly to the body and to axle case. Torque bolts to 29 ft. lbs.
2. Install wheels and torque nuts to 50 ft. lbs.

STABILIZER ROD, REPLACE
1972-75
Removal
1. Raise and support rear of vehicle.
2. Disconnect stabilizer rod to shackle bolts, Fig. 1.

3. Disconnect stabilizer rod to underbody retainers and remove stabilizer rod from vehicle.

Installation

1. Place stabilizer rod in position and loosely attach stabilizer to underbody retainers.
2. Connect stabilizer rod to shackles.
3. With the vehicle standing on its wheels or the rear axle assembly lifted, tighten stabilizer rod to underbody bracket bolts to 15 ft. lbs.
4. Remove jack stands and lower vehicle.

TRACK ROD, REPLACE
1972-75

Removal

1. Raise and support rear of vehicle.
2. Disconnect track rod from rear axle and frame side member, Fig. 1.

Installation

1. Loosely connect track rod first to side member and then to the rear axle.
2. On all models except GT Sport Coupe, load luggage compartment of vehicle with approximately 350 lbs. or on GT Sport Coupe, place a load of approximately 150 lbs. on driver's seat and tighten track rod attaching bolts.
3. Remove jack stands and lower vehicle.

LATERAL ROD, REPLACE
1976-77

Removal

1. Raise vehicle and remove rear wheels.
2. Remove lower shock absorber bolt.
3. Remove bolt securing lateral rod to body, Fig. 2.
4. Remove nut securing lateral rod to axle case.
5. Remove lateral rod assembly.

Installation

1. Attach lateral rod to axle case and to body.
2. Torque lateral rod to body bolt to 43 ft. lbs.
3. Torque lateral rod to axle case nut to 49 ft. lbs.
4. Install lower shock absorber bolt. Torque nut to 29 ft. lbs.
5. Install wheels and torque nuts to 50 ft. lbs.
6. Lower vehicle.

Front Suspension and Steering Section

CASTER, ADJUST
1972-75

1972 Opel & 1972-73 T Sport Coupe

1. Raise front of vehicle.
2. Place jack stands below front frame side members and remove front wheel on side on which caster is to be adjusted.
3. Install front spring compressor J-21689 and compress spring, Fig. 1.
4. Remove upper control arm shaft.
5. Remove upper control arm from shock absorber support, being careful not to lose toothed washers.
6. Adjust caster by installing selective toothed washers on both sides of control arm shaft, between control arm and shock absorber support. Never use more than one washer at any one location. The total thickness, front and rear washer, must equal .48 inch. There are only two possible caster changes that can be made.
7. Using a drift to align holes, replace control arm shaft in the direction as shown in Fig. 2. Torque hex nut to 33 ft. lbs. Make certain that crown of both plate washers faces outward.
8. Remove spring compressor, and install front wheel and torque wheel nuts to 72 ft. lbs.

1972-75 1900 & Manta

1. Raise vehicle and remove front wheel on the side on which caster is to be adjusted.
2. Support vehicle below both lower control arms.
3. Remove hex nut from upper control arm shaft and pull out shaft.
4. Adjust caster by replacing washers "A" (front) and "B" (rear) between upper control arm and shock absorber support, Fig. 3.
5. One .24" thick washer each is installed in production on each side. Consequently, only two adjustments are possible by adding washers of different thickness.
6. One .12 inch in front and one .36 inch in the rear (caster increase of 1

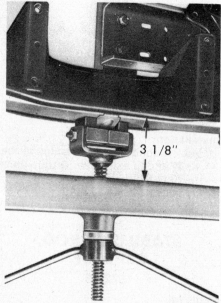

Fig. 1 Spring compressor installation. 1972 Opel & 1972-73 GT Sport Coupe

3 1/8"

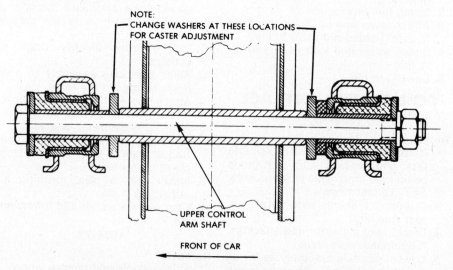

NOTE:
CHANGE WASHERS AT THESE LOCATIONS FOR CASTER ADJUSTMENT

UPPER CONTROL ARM SHAFT

FRONT OF CAR

Fig. 2 Caster adjustment. 1972 Opel & 1972-73 GT Sport Coupe

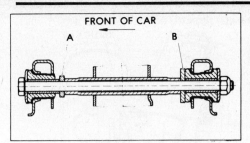

Fig. 3 Caster adjustment washer location. 1972-75 1900 & Manta

degree) or one .36 inch in front and one .12 inch in rear (caster decrease of 1 degree). Never add several washers in one place. The washers "B" installed in production have a larger outer diameter than the washer "A." For service, larger washers with an outer diameter of 1.57 inch are available.

7. Insert control arm shaft from the front into upper control arm and shock absorber support. Note that the crown of both plate washers faces inward.
8. Torque hex nut of control arm shaft to 40 ft. lbs.
9. Torque wheel nuts to 65 ft. lbs.

1976-77

Caster angle can be changed by realigning the washers located between the legs of the upper control arm, Fig. 4.

NOTE: A kit, containing 13 mm washer and one 9 mm washer, must be used for the caster adjustment.

CAMBER, ADJUST
1972-75

Camber is adjusted by turning the upper ball joint flange to 180 degrees. This means that only two possible camber adjustments can be made.

1. Raise front of vehicle using wood block on a suitable jack to prevent damage to front cross member.
2. Support vehicle below lower control arm and remove front wheel on side being adjusted.
3. Remove ball joint from upper control arm and front steering knuckle.
4. Lift upper control arm and turn the ball joint flange through 180 degrees.
5. Tighten both ball joint attaching bolts on upper control arm, then the ball stud castle nut. Torque nut to 44 ft. lbs. on all models except GT Sport Coupe or 29 ft. lbs. on GT Sport Coupe. Install new cotter pin.
6. Install front wheel and torque wheel nuts to 65 ft. lbs.
7. Recheck camber.

1976-77

Camber angle can be increased approximately 1 degree by removing the upper ball joint, rotating it ½ turn and reinstalling it with the flat of the upper flange on the inboard side of the control arm, Fig. 5.

TOE-IN, ADJUST
1972-75

1972 Opel & 1972-73 GT Sport Coupe

1. Recheck caster and camber before proceeding with toe-in adjustment. If correct, adjust toe-in.
2. Set wormshaft and ball nut to steering gear high point by turning steering wheel half way from one stop to the other, noting the following:
   a. With the steering wheel hub button removed, the "marking" on the steering shaft end should be in a horizontal position.
   b. The steering wheel spokes should also be in a centered position.
3. Remove wire clamps on left and right tie rod and push back bellows.
4. Loosen clamp bolts and tie rods.
5. Adjust toe-in to specifications.

When adjusting toe-in, never grip tie rod on inner ball stud joint. To avoid ball stud resting against inside of hole in tie rod outer end, center outer end of each tie rod to the ball stud.

6. Pull bellows over tie rods and attach with wire clamps. The bellows must not be twisted and wire ends must show towards steering gear adjusting screw opening.
7. Torque clamp bolts to 12 ft. lbs.
8. After toe-in adjustment, turn steering wheel several times completely towards the left and right to determine whether bellows are properly attached to the tie rods and steering gear housing.

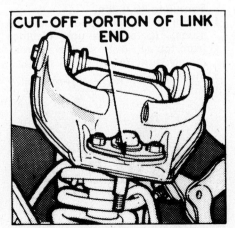

Fig. 5 Upper ball joint installation. 1976-77

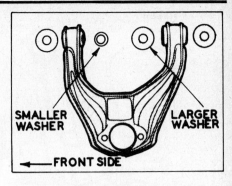

Fig. 4 Caster adjustment. 1976-77

1972-75 1900 & Manta

1. Loosen lock nut of left and right tie rod and back off nut.
2. Remove hose clamp for rubber bellows attachment from axial joint and adjust toe-in to specifications by turning axial joint. Observe that the rubber bellows, having a tight seat on the joint, is not twisted. If necessary, lubricate seat of bellows, and hold back bellows when turning.
3. Torque lock nut of left and right tie rod to 47 ft. lbs.
4. Attach respective rubber bellows with hose clamp, making sure that clamp bolt points towards the front. The rubber bellows must not be twisted, the individual grooves of bellows must be in vertical position.
5. After adjustment, turn steering wheel several times to the left and right to determine if attachment of both rubber bellows to the steering gear housing is correct.

1976-77

Toe-in is adjusted by the position of the tie-rod. To adjust the toe-in setting, loosen the nuts at the steering knuckle end of the tie-rod. Then, loosen the rubber cover at the other end. Tighten the cover and locknuts.

WHEEL BEARING, ADJUST
1972-75

1. Remove grease cap, cotter pin, and spindle nut.
2. Torque spindle nut to 18 ft. lbs. while rotating wheel to seat bearings.
3. Back off spindle nut ¼ turn. If slot and cotter pin hole are not aligned, back off nut $\frac{1}{12}$ turn until next slot in nut is in alignment with hole in spindle. Do not tighten nut. Install new cotter pin. A properly adjusted wheel bearing has a small amount of end play and a loose nut when properly adjusted.

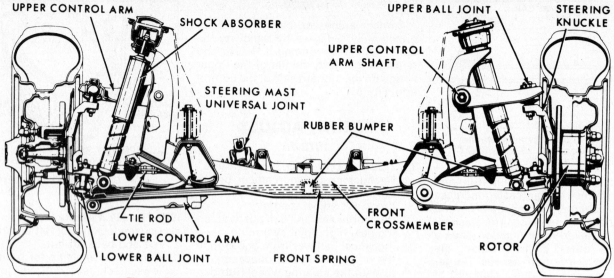

Fig. 6 Front suspension. 1972 Opel & 1972-73 GT Sport Coupe (Typical)

1976-77

1. Remove grease cap, cotter pin and spindle nut.
2. Torque spindle nut to 21 ft. lbs. while rotating wheel to seat bearings.
3. Back off spindle nut ¼ turn. If slot and cotter key hole are not aligned, back off nut until next slot in nut is in alignment with hole in spindle. Do not tighten spindle nut to bring slot in nut into alignment with hole in spindle. Install new cotter pin. A properly adjusted wheel bearing has a small amount of end play and a loose nut when properly adjusted.

SHOCK ABSORBER, REPLACE

1972-73 GT Sport Coupe

Removal

1. Remove air cleaner.
2. Remove plastic cover over shock absorber upper attachment.
3. Raise and support vehicle.
4. Remove upper attaching nuts from shock absorber, Fig. 6.
5. Remove lower attaching nut, lockwasher, and bolt.
6. Compress shock absorber and remove from vehicle.

Installation

1. Inspect shock absorber for damage and seal leaks. Always replace the upper and lower rubber grommets when replacing a shock absorber.
2. Install the lower grommet retainer and grommets on shock absorber. Compress shock absorber and place in position.
3. Install lower attaching bolt and nut. Torque to 30 ft. lbs.

4. Install nuts on upper attaching studs. Tighten nuts until distance from top of nut to stud is approximately ½ inch.
5. Install plastic cover.
6. Install air cleaner.

1972-75 Exc. GT Sport Coupe

Removal

1. Raise and support vehicle.
2. Remove upper attaching nuts from shock absorber, Figs. 6 and 7.
3. Remove lower attaching nut, lockwasher and bolt.
4. Compress shock absorber and remove from vehicle.

Installation

1. Inspect shock absorber for damage and seal leaks. Always replace the upper and lower rubber grommets when replacing a shock absorber.
2. Install the lower grommet retainer and grommets on shock absorber. Compress shock absorber and place in position.
3. Install lower attaching bolt and nut. Torque to 30 ft. lbs.
4. Install nuts on upper attaching studs. Tighten nuts until distance from top of nut to stud is approximately ½ inch.
5. Install plastic cover.

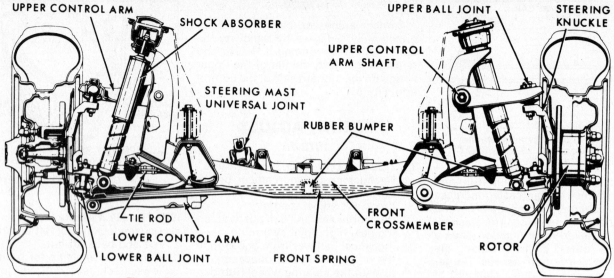

Fig. 7 Front suspension. 1972-75 1900 & Manta

1976-77

Removal

1. Raise vehicle and remove wheel.
2. Disconnect shock absorber from upper control arm, Fig. 8.
3. Remove shock absorber nuts from the engine compartment.
4. Remove shock absorber from vehicle.

Installation

1. Install shock absorber.
2. Install grommets and washers. Tighten thicker nut to the end of the threads on the rod. Install lock nut.
3. Connect shock absorber to upper control arm. Torque nut to 29 ft. lbs.
4. Install wheel and torque nuts to 50 ft. lbs.
5. Lower vehicle.

UPPER BALL JOINT, REPLACE

1972-75

Removal

1. Place a suitable jack under spring eye and raise vehicle, then remove wheel.
2. Remove cotter pin and castle nut from upper ball joint stud.
3. Press ball stud from steering knuckle, using puller J-21687, Fig. 9, and remove two bolts attaching ball joint to upper control arm.
4. Remove ball joint.

Installation

1. Install upper control arm ball joint with the off-center holes in flange facing toward the steering knuckle spindle.
2. Install two bolts attaching ball joint

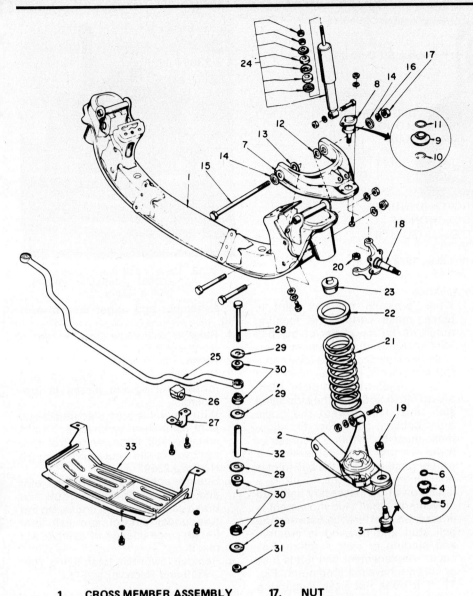

Fig. 9 Upper ball joint removal. 1972-75

1976-77

Removal
1. Raise vehicle and remove wheel.
2. Remove upper brake caliper bolt and slide hose retaining clip back approximately ¼ to ½ in.
3. Remove lower shock absorber bolt and push shock absorber upward.
4. Raise lower control arm until level and place support under outer end of control arm.
5. Loosen upper ball joint castle nut until top of nut is flush with top of ball joint. Using Tool J-26407-1, disconnect upper ball joint from the steering knuckle, Fig. 10.
6. Remove two bolts connecting upper ball joint to control arm.
7. Remove upper ball joint.

Installation
1. Install upper ball joint in control arm so the cut-off portion is facing outward, Fig. 5.
2. Install two bolts connecting upper

1.	CROSS MEMBER ASSEMBLY	17.	NUT
2.	LOWER LINK ASSEMBLY	18.	KNUCKLE
3.	LOWER LINK END ASSEMBLY	19.	NUT
4.	BOOT	20.	NUT
5.	CLAMP RING	21.	FRONT COIL SPRING
6.	CLAMP RING	22.	DAMPER RUBBER
7.	UPPER LINK ASSEMBLY	23.	BUMPER RUBBER
8.	UPPER LINK END ASSEMBLY	24.	SHOCK ABSORBER
9.	BOOT	25.	STABILIZER BAR
10.	CLAMP RING	26.	RUBBER BUSH
11.	CLAMP RING	27.	CLAMP
12.	WASHER	28.	BOLT
13.	WASHER	29.	RETAINER
14.	WASHER	30.	BUFFER
15.	BOLT	31.	NUT
16.	SPRING WASHER	32.	DISTANCE TUBE
		33.	UNDER COVER

Fig. 8 Front suspension. 1976-77

to upper control arm. Torque nuts to 29 ft. lbs.
3. Install upper ball joint stud in steering knuckle and torque castle nut to 40 ft. lbs. on all except GT Sport

Coupe and 29 ft. lbs. on GT Sport Coupe.
4. Install new cotter pin and replace wheel.

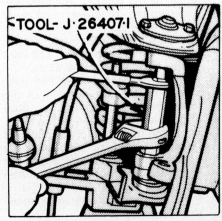

Fig. 10 Upper ball joint removal. 1976-77

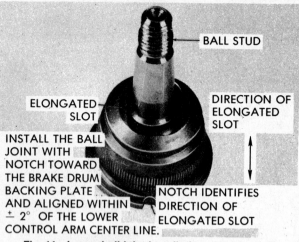

Fig. 11 Lower ball joint installation. 1972 Opel & 1972-73 GT Sport Coupe

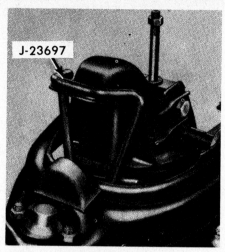

Fig. 12 Upper control arm hooks, J-23967 installation. 1972-75 1900 & Manta

ball joint to control arm. Torque nuts to 29 ft. lbs.
3. Attach upper ball joint to steering knuckle and torque castle nut to 40 ft. lbs.
4. Install lower shock absorber bolt. Torque to 29 ft. lbs.
5. Slide hose retaining clip in place and install the upper brake caliper bolt. Torque bolt to 36 ft. lbs.
6. Install wheel and torque nuts to 50 ft. lbs.

LOWER BALL JOINT, REPLACE

1972 Opel & 1972-73 GT Sport Coupe

Removal
1. Raise vehicle and support at rear of front frame rails.
2. Remove front wheel.
3. Remove cotter pin from castle nut on ball joint stud and back off castle nut two turns. Hit ball stud a sharp blow to break loose. Do not remove nut.
4. Install spring compressor, J-21689 and compress spring until a distance of 3⅛ inch is achieved between spring compressor and lower spring leaf, Fig. 1.
5. Disconnect shock absorber to lower control arm attachment bolt and position shock absorber aside.
6. Remove castle nut from ball joint stud. Prior to the removal of the lower ball joint from the control arm, note the position of the locating notch in the rim of the ball joint housing, Fig. 11. Scribe or mark the control arm to facilitate alignment of the replacement ball joint during installation.
7. Pry off dust cap retainer and remove dust cap.
8. Press ball stud from lower control arm.

Installation
1. When pressing the ball joint in place, make certain the locating notch in the lower rim of the ball joint matches the alignment reference mark placed on the lower control arm prior to removal. The notch in the ball joint bottom plate, identifying the direction of the elongated slot, must face toward the brake drum backing plate, Fig. 11. Alignment must be within 2 degrees of lower control arm center-line. If proper positioning of the ball joint is not accomplished, the result is a limitation of the necessary ball stud movement. If ball stud movement is limited, an interference between the ball stud and housing is created, and binding or even fracture may occur. Replacement ball joints may or may not have marking notch, Fig. 11. If it does not have a marking notch, the joint is completely symetrical and may be installed in any position. When pressing in ball joint do not press on bottom plate, but on ball joint housing only.
2. Install dust cap on lower ball joint and fill with chassis lubricant. Attach dust cap retainer.
3. Press ball joint into steering knuckle. Use J-9519-3 as installer and J-21690 as a supporting sleeve.
4. Install castle nut on ball joint stud and torque to 40 ft. lbs. Install new cotter pin.
5. Reconnect shock absorber to lower control arm and torque to 30 ft. lbs.
6. Remove spring compressor.
7. Install front wheel, and lower the car.

1972-75 1900 & Manta

Removal
Before raising vehicle, install Hooks J-23697 on respective vehicle side to crossmember and upper control arm, Fig. 12.
1. Raise vehicle and support at rear of front frame rails.
2. Remove front wheel.
3. Remove castle nut cotter pin and loosen nut so the thread is protected.
4. With a suitable drift, disconnect ball joint from steering knuckle. With a suitable jack, lift lower control arm, remove castle nut and remove Hooks J-23697.
5. Remove upper control arm ball joint and suspend front wheel hub and brake caliper in wheel house. Do not turn upper control arm ball joint flange since change of camber will result.
6. Remove lower ball joint, using Tool J-9519 and Receiver J-23754.

Installation
1. Drive ball joint into lower control arm, using Tools J-9519 as installer and J-23755 as a supporting sleeve. Do not strike bottom of ball joint.
2. On lower ball joint, be sure the marking groove in the housing bottom is in alignment with the axis of the lower control arm. Allowable deviation is ±2 degrees.
3. Attach steering knuckle, front wheel hub and brake caliper to lower ball joint. Torque castle nut to 54 ft. lbs.
4. Attach ball joint to lower control arm and torque to 29 ft. lbs.
5. Install wheel and tighten nuts to 65 ft. lbs.

1976-77

Removal
1. Raise vehicle and remove wheel.
2. Remove tie-rod end cotter key and castle nut. Using Tool J-21687-1, disconnect tie-rod end from steering knuckle, Fig. 13.
3. Remove stabilizer bar bolt and

Fig. 13 Disconnect tie-rod from steering knuckle. 1976-77

grommet assembly from lower control arm.

4. Remove upper brake caliper bolt and slide hose-retaining clip back approximately ¼-½ inch.
5. Remove lower shock absorber bolt and push shock absorber upward.
6. Place spring compressor over upper control arm and let hang.
7. Place support under outer extreme of lower control arm, and loosen lower ball joint castle nut until top of nut is flush with top of ball joint.
8. Using Tool J-26407-1, disconnect the lower ball joint from the steering knuckle, Fig. 14.
9. Remove hub assembly and steering knuckle from lower ball joint and secure, with a wire or equivalent, aside.
10. Install spring compressor between first exposed coil of spring and compress spring.
11. Remove support under lower control arm.
12. Remove lower ball joint from control arm, using tools J-9519 as installer and J-9519-4 as receiver, Fig. 15.

Installation

1. Install new ball joint in lower control arm using Tools J-9519 as installer and J-9519-4 as receiver. Do not strike ball joint bottom.
2. Place support under outer end of lower control arm.
3. Remove spring compressor.
4. Attach hub assembly and steering knuckle to lower ball joint. Torque castle nut to 72 ft. lbs.
5. Slide hose retaining clip in place and install upper brake caliper bolt. Torque nut to 72 ft. lbs.
6. Install stabilizer bar bolt and grommet assembly to lower control arm. Tighten the nut to the end of the threads on the bolt.
7. Attach tie-rod end to steering knuckle. Torque castle nut to 29 ft. lbs. Install new cotter key.
8. Install lower shock absorber bolt. Torque to 29 ft. lbs.
9. Install wheel and torque nuts to 50 ft. lbs.

UPPER CONTROL ARM, REPLACE

1972 Opel & 1972-73 GT Sport Coupe

Removal

1. Raise vehicle and support at rear of front frame rails.
2. Remove front wheel.
3. Install spring compressor and compress spring until there is 3⅛ inch clearance between compressor and lower spring leaf, Fig. 1.
4. Remove cotter pin and castle nut from upper ball joint stud.

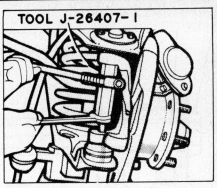

Fig. 14 Disconnecting lower ball joint from steering knuckle. 1976-77

5. Use tie rod remover J-21687, Fig. 9, remove upper ball joint from steering knuckle.
6. Support brake drum to relieve tension on brake hose.
7. Remove hex nut from upper control arm shaft, Fig. 16. Remove shaft and washers from shock absorber support. Do not damage threads on control arm shaft.
8. Remove control arm from vehicle. Do not lose inner toothed washers. Note size and location of toothed washers.

Installation

If rubber bushings on control arms are worn, the control arms must be replaced.

1. Slide rubber rings over bushings. Slide rings over inner sleeves of bushings. Place control arm in position on shock absorber support, installing toothed washers in their original positions, Fig. 16.
2. From the front, install control arm shaft. If necessary, align washers and control arm bushings with a small drift prior to installing control arm shaft, Fig. 16.
3. Tighten hex nut on control arm shaft finger tight.
4. Increase tension on spring compressor in order to relieve tension on control arm shaft. Then, torque hex nut on control arm shaft to 33 ft. lbs.
5. Press ball joint stud into steering knuckle and torque castle nut to 29 ft. lbs. Install new cotter pin.
6. Remove spring compressor and lower vehicle.

1972-75 Exc. GT Sport Coupe

Removal

1. Raise vehicle and support at rear of front frame rails.
2. Remove front wheel.
3. Remove upper control arm to crossmember self-locking attaching nut.

Fig. 15 Lower ball joint removal. 1976-77

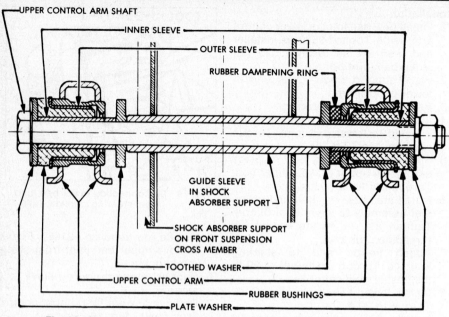

Fig. 16 Upper control arm shaft. 1972 Opel & 1972-73 GT Sport Coupe

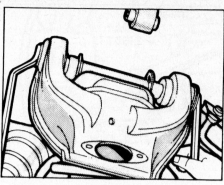

Fig. 17 Upper control arm removal. 1976-77

4. Remove ball joint from upper control arm, Fig. 9. Do not turn upper control arm ball joint flange, as this would result in a change of camber.
5. Support front wheel hub so brake hose is not stretched.
6. Remove upper control shaft to crossmember attaching bolt and the control arm. Shims must be reinstalled in their original position to maintain the proper caster setting.

Installation
1. On installation of the upper control arm, be sure that damper bushing with the rubber shoulder on both sides is located in the rear.
2. Attach upper control arm to crossmember and torque to 40 ft. lbs. The upper control arm must be tightened in horizontal position only. This applies also to all other attaching joints in connection with rubber damper bushings in the control arms of the front suspension so the rubber parts under load are in an almost twist-free position. This position exists if the Hooks J-23697 are used, Fig. 12.
3. Attach ball joint to upper control arm and torque to 29 ft. lbs.
4. Install wheel and torque nuts to 65 ft. lbs.

1976-77
Removal
1. Raise vehicle and remove wheel.
2. Remove upper brake caliper bolt and slide hose retaining clip back approximately ¼-½ inch.
3. Remove lower shock absorber bolt and push shock absorber upward.
4. Raise lower control arm until level

and place support under outer end of control arm.
5. Loosen upper ball joint castle nut until top of nut is flush with the top of the ball joint. Using Tool J-26407-1. Disconnect the upper ball joint from the steering knuckle, Fig. 10.
6. Remove through bolt connecting upper control arm to the crossmember, Fig. 17.
7. Remove upper control arm.

Installation
1. Install ball joint in upper control arm.
2. On installation of the upper control arm, make sure the smaller washer is on the inner face of the front arm and the larger washer is on the inner face of the rear arm, Fig. 4.
3. Attach upper control arm to crossmember. Do not fully tighten bolt.
4. Attach upper ball joint to steering knuckle and torque castle nut to 40 ft. lbs.
5. Torque through bolt connecting upper control arm to the crossmember to 43 ft. lbs.
6. Install lower shock absorber bolt. Torque bolt to 29 ft. lbs.
7. Slide hose retaining clip in place and install the upper brake caliper bolt. Torque bolt to 36 ft. lbs.
8. Install wheel and torque to 50 ft. lbs.

LOWER CONTROL ARM, REPLACE

1972 Opel & 1972-73 GT Sport Coupe
Removal
1. Raise vehicle and support at rear of

front frame rails.
2. Remove front wheel.
3. Remove cotter pin from castle nut on ball joint stud and back off castle nut two turns. Hit ball stud a sharp blow to break it loose. Do not remove nut.
4. Install spring compressor J-21689, and compress spring until a distance of 3⅛ inches is achieved between spring compressor and lower spring leaf, Fig. 1.
5. Disconnect and compress shock absorber.
6. Support rail of spring compressor with a jack. Remove lower control arm from frame crossmember. Nuts may have to be removed with a punch. Discard the lock nuts.
7. Remove lower ball joint stud nut. Slightly lower jack so that spring and lower control arm assembly is removed from the front crossmember and steering knuckle.
8. Lower jack, spring compressor, and front spring with control arm assembly. Remove lower control arm to spring nuts.
9. Release spring compressor and remove control arm attaching bolts and control arm.

Installation
1. Attach lower control arm to front spring eye. Torque bolts to 18 ft. lbs.
2. Install spring compressor and with a jack raise spring compressor with spring and control arm assembly into position for pressing ball joint into steering knuckle.
3. Press ball joint into steering knuckle.
4. Install castle nut on ball joint stud and torque to 54 ft. lbs. Install new cotter pin.
5. Attach lower control arm to frame crossmember.
6. Reconnect shock absorber to lower control arm and torque to 30 ft. lbs.
7. Remove spring compressor.
8. Install front wheel.

1972-75 1900 & Manta

Removal

1. Prior to raising vehicle, install upper control arm hooks, J-23697, Fig. 12.
2. Raise vehicle and support with stands. The jack should be left in raised position to maintain pressure on lower control arms.
3. Remove front wheel.
4. Disconnect both stabilizer supports from crossmember to body support.
5. In lower control arm, remove self-locking hex-head bolt from the stabilizer support and remove washer.
6. Using a suitable pry bar, pry stabilizer bar from lower control arm support.
7. Remove shock absorber.
8. At lower control arm ball joint, remove castle nut cotter pin and the nut.
9. With suitable drift, disconnect lower control arm ball joint from steering knuckle.
10. Loosen nut retaining lower control arm to front crossmember.
11. Slowly lower vehicle to release spring tension.
12. Swing lower control arm downward and remove front spring.
13. Remove nut retaining lower control arm to front crossmember and the lower control arm.

Installation

1. Loosely attach lower control arm to front crossmember.
2. Properly seat spring between lower control arm and crossmember.
3. Raise jack and place lower control arm in position.
4. Attach lower ball joint to steering knuckle and torque nut to 54 ft. lbs.
5. Tighten lower control arm to crossmember bolt to 43 ft. lbs.
6. Attach stabilizer bar to lower control arm and torque to 87 ft. lbs.
7. Attach stabilizer bar to crossmember-to-body support.
8. Install shock absorber and torque lower attaching nut and bolt to 30 ft. lbs.
9. Install nuts on upper shock absorber attaching studs. Tighten nuts until the distance from top of nut to stud is approximately ½ inch.
10. Install front wheels and tighten nuts to 65 ft. lbs.

1976-77

Removal

1. Raise vehicle and remove wheel.
2. Remove tie-rod end cotter key and castle nut. Using Tool J-21687-1, disconnect tie-rod end from steering knuckle, Fig. 13.
3. Remove lower shock absorber bolt and push shock absorber upward.
4. Remove stabilizer bar bolt and grommet assembly from lower control arm.
5. Remove upper brake caliper bolt and slide hose retaining clip back approximately ¼-½ inch.
6. Place spring compressor over upper control arm and let hang.
7. Raise lower control arm until level and place support under outer end of control arm.
8. Loosen lower ball joint castle nut until top of nut is flush with the top of the ball joint. Using Tool J-26407-1, disconnect the lower ball joint from the steering knuckle, Fig. 14.
9. Remove hub assembly and steering knuckle from lower ball joint and secure, with a wire or equivalent, to the side.
10. Install spring compressor between first exposed coil of spring.
11. Compress spring until spring clears lower spring seat.
12. Remove support under lower control arm.
13. Remove bolts connecting lower control arm to crossmember and the body.
14. Remove lower control arm.

Installation

1. Install ball joint in lower control arm.
2. Install bolts connecting front of control arm to crossmember and rear of control arm to body. Do not fully tighten bolts.
3. Raise lower control arm until level and place support under outer extreme of control arm.
4. Remove spring compressor.
5. Attach hub assembly and steering knuckle to lower ball joint. Torque castle nut to 72 ft. lbs.
6. Attach upper ball joint to steering knuckle. Torque castle nut to 40 ft. lbs.
7. Torque bolts connecting lower control arm to crossmember and body to 43 ft. lbs.
8. Install stabilizer bar bolt and grommet assembly to lower control arm. Tighten the nut to the end of the threads on the bolt.
9. Install lower shock absorber bolt. Torque bolt to 29 ft. lbs.
10. Slide hose retaining clip in place and install upper brake caliper bolt. Torque bolt to 36 ft. lbs.
11. Attach tie-rod end to steering knuckle. Torque castle nut to 29 ft. lbs. Install new cotter key.
12. Install wheel and torque nuts to 50 ft. lbs.

LEAF SPRING, REPLACE

1972 Opel & 1972-73 GT Sport Coupe

Removal

1. Raise vehicle and support at rear of front frame rails with stands.
2. Remove front wheels.
3. Remove cotter pin from castle nut on lower ball joint studs and back off castle nut two turns. Hit ball stud a sharp blow to break it loose. Do not remove nut.
4. Install J-21689 spring compressor and compress the spring until 3⅛ inch clearance is obtained between spring and compressor, Fig. 1.
5. Disconnect both shock absorbers at their lower attachment. Compress both shock absorbers.
6. Support the rail of J-21689 Spring Compressor with a jack. Remove lower control arm to crossmember attaching nuts and bolts.
7. Remove lower ball joint stud nuts. Slightly lower jack so that the spring and lower control arm assembly is removed from the front crossmember and steering knuckle.
8. Lower jack, spring compressor, and front spring and control arm assembly. Remove lower control arm to spring nuts.
9. Relieve tension on spring compressor and remove control arm attaching bolts and control arms.

Installation

1. Attach lower control arm to front spring eye. Torque bolts to 18 ft. lbs.
2. Install spring compressor on spring and compress spring to appropriate length.
3. Raise jack with spring compressor, spring and control arm assembly into position under the car.
4. Install lower ball joints and torque nuts to 54 ft. lbs. Install new cotter pin.
5. Attach lower control arms to frame crossmember, using new lock nuts.
6. Attach both shock absorbers. Torque bolts to 30 ft. lbs.
7. Remove spring compressor.
8. Install front wheels.

On replacement of the damper bushings on the front springs, only the one-part damper bushing is installed for either the two-leaf or three-leaf spring.

COIL SPRING, REPLACE

1972-75 1900 & Manta

Removal

1. Prior to raising vehicle, install upper control arm hooks J-23697, Fig. 12.

Fig. 18 Stop bolt replacement. 1972 Opel & 1972-73 GT Sport Coupe

2. Raise vehicle and support with stands. The jack should be left in the raised position to maintain pressure on lower control arm.
3. Remove front wheel.
4. Disconnect both stabilizer supports from crossmember to body support.
5. Remove shock absorber.
6. At lower control arm ball joint, remove castle nut cotter pin and remove nut.
7. With suitable drift, disconnect lower control arm ball joint from steering knuckle.
8. Loosen nut retaining lower control to front crossmember.
9. Slowly lower jack to release spring tension.
10. Swing lower control arm downward and remove front spring.

Installation

1. Properly seat spring between lower control arm and crossmember.
2. Raise jack and place lower control into position.
3. Attach lower control ball joint to steering knuckle and torque nut to 54 ft. lbs.
4. Tighten lower control arm to crossmember bolt to 43 ft. lbs.
5. Attach stabilizer bar to crossmember to body support.
6. Install shock absorber and torque lower attaching nut and bolt to 30 ft. lbs.
7. Install nuts on upper shock absorber attaching studs. Tighten nuts until a distance from top of nut to stud is approximately ½ inch.
8. Install front wheels and torque nuts to 65 ft. lbs.

1976-77

Removal

1. Raise vehicle and remove wheel.
2. Remove tie-rod end cotter key and castle nut. Using Tool J-21687-1, disconnect tie-rod end from steering knuckle, Fig. 13.
3. Remove lower shock absorber bolt and push shock absorber upward.
4. Remove stabilizer bar bolt and grommet assembly from lower control arm.
5. Remove upper brake caliper bolt and slide hose retaining clip back approximately ¼-½ inch.
6. Place spring compressor over upper control arm and let hang.
7. Raise lower control arm until level and place support under outer end of control arm.
8. Loosen lower ball joint castle nut until top of nut is flush with the top of the ball joint. Using Tool J-26407-1, disconnect the lower ball joint from the steering knuckle, Fig. 14.
9. Remove hub assembly and steering knuckle from lower ball joint and secure, with a wire or equivalent to the side.
10. Install spring compressor between first exposed coil of spring.
11. Compress spring until spring clears lower spring seat.
12. Remove support under lower control arm.
13. Loosen spring compressor while prying the lower control arm down.
14. Remove the spring.

Installation

1. Properly seat spring between lower control arm and crossmember.
2. Compress spring until lower control arm can be moved to level position.
3. Place support under outer extreme of lower control arm.
4. Remove spring compressor.
5. Attach hub assembly and steering knuckle to lower ball joint. Torque castle nut to 72 ft. lbs.
6. Attach upper ball joint to steering knuckle. Torque castle nut to 40 ft. lbs.
7. Install stabilizer bar bolt and grommet assembly to lower control arm. Tighten the nut to the end of the threads on the bolt.
8. Install lower shock absorber bolt. Torque bolt to 29 ft. lbs.
9. Slide hose retaining clip in place and install upper brake caliper bolt. Torque bolt to 36 ft. lbs.
10. Attach tie-rod end to steering knuckle. Torque castle nut to 29 ft. lbs. Install new cotter key.
11. Install wheel and torque nuts to 50 ft. lbs.

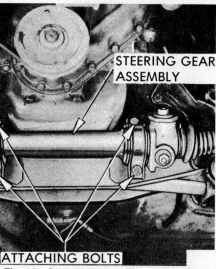

Fig. 19 Steering gear attaching bolts. 1972 Opel & 1972-73 GT Sport Coupe

STEERING GEAR, REPLACE

1972 Opel & 1972-73 GT Sport Coupe

Removal

1. Remove rubber knee protector pad.
2. Loosen clamp securing flexible coupling to steering shaft.
3. Remove stop bolt, Fig. 18, from underside of steering column securing steering shaft bushing to mast jacket, and pull steering wheel rearward approximately three inches.
4. Remove cotter pin located on left and right tie rod ends and the nut.
5. Press ball studs from steering arms.
6. Remove four bolts securing steering gear to front suspension crossmember and remove steering gear assembly and tie rods, Fig. 19.

Installation

1. Position steering gear on front suspension crossmember and torque attaching bolts to 18 ft. lbs.
2. Position tie rod ball studs in steering arms; install nuts and torque to 29 ft. lbs. Lock in position with new cotter pins.
3. Fully turn steering wheel so that flat or cutout surface on lower portion of steering shaft is parallel to flexible coupling bolt hole.
4. Install the lower end of steering shaft to the flexible coupling and adjust dimension between steering wheel hub and direction signal switch housing cover to ⅛ and ³/₃₂ inch. Maintain adjustment by tightening flexible coupling bolt and nut to 15 ft. lbs. Lock the bolt and nut in position with lock-plate tabs.
5. Reinstall stop bolt into steering column.

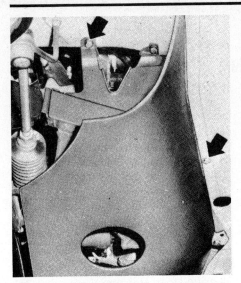

Fig. 20 Splash shield removal. 1972-75 1900 & Manta

6. Full turn steering wheel both right and left. If any resistance is noticeable, it will be necessary to remove the steering column and correct the cause.

1972-75 1900 & Manta

Removal

1. Remove splash shield from lower deflector panel and both side members, Fig. 20.
2. Remove clamp bolt securing flexible coupling to steering shaft, Fig. 21.

Fig. 22 Steering gear retaining bolts. 1976-77

3. Remove cotter pin from the left and right tie rod ends and the nuts.
4. Disconnect steering gear housing from suspension crossmember and remove steering gear and tie rods.

Installation

1. Prior to installation, set steering gear to high point. The steering wheel spokes point downward at an oblique angle. The elongated cutout of the lower steering mast must align with the clamp bolt hole of the pinion flange.
2. Position steering gear on front suspension crossmember and torque attaching bolts to 29 ft. lbs.
3. Position tie rod studs in steering arms. Install nuts and torque to 29 ft. lbs. Lock in position with new cotter pins.
4. Install the lower end of the steering shaft to flexible coupling and torque clamp bolt to 22 ft. lbs.
5. Attach guard plate to both side members and lower deflector panel.
6. Check and adjust toe-in.

1976-77

Removal

1. Raise vehicle and remove under cover.
2. Remove steering shaft coupling bolt.
3. Remove both tie-rod end cotter pins and castle nuts. Using Tool J-21687-1, disconnect tie-rod ends

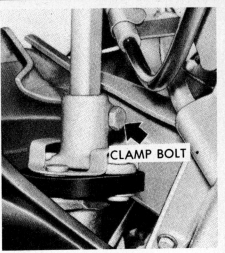

Fig. 21 Flexible coupling clamp bolt. 1972-75 1900 & Manta

from steering knuckles, Fig. 13.
4. Disconnect steering gear housing from crossmember, Fig. 22.
5. Expand steering shaft coupling and remove assembly.
6. Remove tie-rod assemblies from steering gear.

Installation

1. Attach tie-rod assemblies to steering gear.
2. Prior to installation of steering gear assembly, set steering gear to high point by positioning front wheels straight ahead with steering wheel centered.
3. Attach steering coupling to steering wheel.
4. Attach steering gear housing to crossmember. Torque bolts to 29 ft. lbs.
5. Install steering shaft coupling bolt. Torque bolt to 19 ft. lbs.
6. Attach both tie-rod ends to steering knuckles. Torque castle nuts to 29 ft. lbs. Install new cotter pins.
7. Check and adjust toe-in.
8. Install undercover.

RENAULT

INDEX OF SERVICE OPERATIONS

GENERAL ENGINE SPECIFICATIONS

Year	Engine	Carburetor	Bore x Stroke	Piston Displacement Cubic Inches (cc)	Compression Ratio	Maximum Brake H.P. @ R.P.M.	Maximum Torque Ft. Lbs. @ R.P.M.	Normal Oil Pressure Pounds
1972	4-95	2 Barrel	3.031 x 3.307 (74 x 84mm)	95 (1565)	8.6	78 @ 5000	95 @ 3000	55—70
	4-95	Fuel Inj.	3.031 x 3.307 (74 x 84mm)	95 (1565)	9.0	107 @ 6000	96 @ 5000	55—70
	4-100	2 Barrel	3.110 x 3.307 (79 x 84mm)	100.5 (1647)	7.5	65 @ 5000	88 @ 2500	55—70
1973	4-95	Fuel Inj.	3.031 x 3.307 (74 x 84mm)	95 (1565)	9.0	107 @ 6000	96 @ 5000	55—70
	4-100	2 Barrel	3.110 x 3.307 (79 x 84mm)	100.5 (1647)	7.5	65 @ 5000	88 @ 2500	55—70
	4-95	Fuel Inj.	3.031 x 3.307 (74 x 84mm)	95 (1565)	9.0	107 @ 6000	96 @ 5000	55—70
	4-100	2 Barrel	3.110 x 3.307 (79 x 84mm)	100.5 (1647)	7.5	65 @ 5000	88 @ 2500	55—70
1975	4-100	2 Barrel	3.110 x 3.307 (79 x 84mm)	100.5 (1647)	8.0	72 @ 5500	84 @ 3500	55—70
	4-100	Fuel Inj.	3.110 x 3.307 (79 x 84mm)	100.5 (1647)	8.6	90 @ 6000	86 @ 3500	55—70
1976	4-79	2 Barrel	2.874 x 3.031 (73 x 77mm)	78.66 (1289)	8.5	58 @ 6000	69.6 @ 3500	50
	4-100	2 Barrel	3.110 x 3.307 (79 x 84mm)	100.5 (1647)	8.0	72 @ 5500	84 @ 3500	55—70
	4-100	Fuel Inj.	3.110 x 3.307 (79 x 84mm)	100.5 (1647)	9.3	95 @ 5750	90 @ 3500	55—70
1977	4-79	2 Barrel	2.874 x 3.031 (73 x 77mm)	78.66 (1289)	9.5	60 @ 6000	70 @ 3500	50
	4-100	2 Barrel	3.110 x 3.307 (79 x 84mm)	100.5 (1647)	8.0	72 @ 5500	84 @ 3500	55—70
	4-100	Fuel Inj.	3.110 x 3.307 (79 x 84mm)	100.5 (1647)	9.3	95 @ 6250	90 @ 3500	55—70

TUNE UP SPECIFICATIONS

The following specifications are published from the latest information available. This data should be used only in the absence of a decal affixed in the engine compartment.

▲ Before removing wires from distributor cap, determine location of the No. 1 wire in cap, as distributor position may have been altered from that shown at the end of this chart.

Year	Engine	Spark Plug Type	Spark Plug Gap Inch	Distributor Point Gap Inch	Distributor Dwell Angle Deg.	Ignition Timing Firing Order Fig. ▲	Ignition Timing Timing BTDC ①	Ignition Timing Mark Fig.	Carb Adjustments Hot Idle Speed Std. Trans.	Carb Adjustments Hot Idle Speed Auto. Tans.	Carb Adjustments Idle "CO"% Std. Trans.	Carb Adjustments Idle "CO"% Auto. Trans.
1972	4-95 ②	N3	.025	.018	55—59	⑫	8° ③	⑬	1100	1100	—	—
	4-95 ④	N5	.025	.018	55—59	⑫	③ ⑤	⑬	850	650	—	—
	4-100	N5	.025	.018	55—59	⑫	6° ③	⑬	—	650	—	—
1973	4-95	N3	.025	.018	55—59	⑫	TDC ⑧	⑬	1000	1000	—	—
	4-100	N5	.025	.018	55—59	⑫	③ ⑨	⑬	850	650	4	4
1974	4-95	N3	.025	.018	55—59	⑫	TDC ⑧	⑬	1000	1000	—	—
	4-100	N5	.025	.018	55—59	⑫	10° ③	⑬	850	650	4	4
1975	4-100 ⑥	N3	.025	.018	55—59	⑫	12° ③	⑬	850	850	—	—
	4-100 ⑦	N9Y	.025	.018	55—59	⑫	10° ③	⑬	850	650	3	3
1976	4-79	L92Y	.025	.018	55—59	⑫	TDC ③	⑬	800	800	2.5	2.5
	4-100 ⑥	N3	.025	.018	55—59	⑫	12° ③	⑬	900	900	—	—
	4-100 ⑦	N9Y	.025	.018	55—59	⑫	③ ⑩	⑬	850	650	2.5	2.5
1977	4-79	L87Y	.025	.018	55—59	⑫	TDC ③	⑬	850	850	2.5	2.5
	4-100 ⑥	N3	.025	.018	55—59	⑫	12° ③	⑬	900	900	—	—
	4-100 ⑦	N9Y	.025	.018	55—59	⑫	③ ⑩	⑬	850	650	⑪	⑪

—Not Available.
① —BTDC: Before top dead center.
② —Model 17TS.
③ —Static timing.
④ —Model 12/15.
⑤ —Man. trans., 0°; Auto. trans., 6°.
⑥ —Model 17 Gordini.
⑦ —Model 12/15/17TL.
⑧ —With vacuum hose at distributor disconnected.
⑨ —Man. trans., 5°; Auto. trans., 3°.
⑩ —Man. trans., 10°; Auto. trans., 7°.
⑪ —Exc. Calif., 2.5°; Calif., 3°.
⑫ —Firing order, 1342: No. 1 cyl. at rear of engine.
⑬ —Mark located on flywheel or converter, timed at no. 1 cyl.

RENAULT

DISTRIBUTOR SPECIFICATIONS

If unit is checked on vehicle, double the RPM and degrees to get crankshaft figures.

Distributor Model No.	Centrifugal Advance Degrees @ RPM of Distributor			Vacuum Advance No.	Vacuum Advance		Distributor Retard
	Advance Starts	Intermediate Advance	Full Advance		Inches of Vacuum to Start Plunger	Max. Advance Dist. Deg. @ Vacuum	Max. Retard Dist. Deg. @ Vacuum
R241	0 @ 500	4 @ 750	10 @ 1500	16 @ 2250	C34	3.1	5.5 @ 13.31	—
R243	0 @ 900	—	14-20 @ 2000	28-32 @ 4000	D60	3.31	9.3 @ 15.75	—
R248	0 @ 550	7 @ 800	12.6 @ 1500	18 @ 2250	D62	4.13	—	7 @ 9.84
R258	0 @ 550	4 @ 750	8 @ 1500	13 @ 2450	D64	.94	9.2 @ 1.38	—
R269	0 @ 550	—	14 @ 1375	23 @ 2600	D73	1.1	9 @ 2.17	—
R272	2 @ 350	—	6.3 @ 1000	16 @ 2500	J-10	2.95	10 @ 9.45	—

—Not Available.

ALTERNATOR & REGULATOR SPECIFICATIONS

Year	Alternator				Regulator	
	Model	Rated Hot Output Amps.	Output @ 14 Volts		Model	Voltage @ 125° F
			1250 R.P.M. Amps.	3500 R.P.M. Amps.		
1972	A14-30	30	10	30	8369	13.4—14.4
1973-77	A13R154	50	10	45	AYB218	13.4—14.4

STARTING MOTOR SPECIFICATIONS

Year	Model	Output (Watts)	Torque Test	
			Amp.	Torque, Ft. Lbs.
1972-77	D10E54	1000	400	13
1976-77	D8E121	900	400	9

VALVE SPECIFICATIONS

Year	Model	Valve Lash		Valve Angles		Valve Spring Pressures Lbs. @ In.	Stem Diameter	
		Int.	Exh.	Seat	Face		Intake	Exhaust
1972-74	17TS	.010	.012	45	45	①	.315	.315
1972-74	12/15/17TL	.008	.010	45	45	①	.315	.315
1975-77	12/15/17TL	.008	.010	45	45	①	.315	.315
1976-77	5	.006	.008	45	45	80 @ 1.0	.276	.276

①—Outer, 99 @ 1⁵/₃₆"; Inner, 20 @ ¾".

COOLING SYSTEM & CAPACITY DATA

Year	Model or Engine	Cooling Capacity Qts.		Radiator Cap Relief Pressure Lbs.		Thermo. Opening Temp.	Fuel Tank Gals.	Engine Oil Refill Qts.	Transmission Oil		
		With Heater	With A/C	With A/C	No A/C				4 Speed Qts.	5 Speed Qts.	Auto. Trans. Qts.
1972-74	12,15,17TL	①	①	12	12	182	14.5	4.5	2	—	3.3
1972-77	17 Gordini	5.8	5.8	12	12	182	14.5	5②	2	2	—
1975-77	12,15,17TL	①	①	12	12	182	13.7	4.5②	2	—	3.3
1976	5	6.5	6.5	12	12	182	10	3.2②	2	—	—

—Not Available.
①—Exc. 12, 6 qts.; 12, 9.5 qts.
②—Includes filter.

RENAULT

PISTON, PINS, RINGS, CRANKSHAFT & BEARINGS

Year	Model & Engine	Piston Clearance	Cylinder Liner Protrusion	Ring End Gap	Wrist Pin Diameter	Rod Bearings		Main Bearings			
						Shaft Diameter	Bearing Clearance	Shaft Diameter	Bearing Clearance	Thrust On Bear. No.	Shaft End Play
1972-77	12,15,17 Hemi Head	②	.004—.0067①	③	.787	1.890	.001—.0026	2.158	.0004—.0014	3	.002—.009
1972-74	12,15,17TL Wedge Head	②	.006—.008	③	.787	1.890	.001—.0026	2.158	.0004—.0014	3	.002—.009
1976-77	5 Wedge Head	②	.0016—.005	③	.787	1.731	.001—.0026	2.158	.0004—.0014	3	.002—.009

①—Protrusion without "O" ring seal.
②—Piston clearance preset.
③—Ring gap preset.

ENGINE TIGHTENING SPECIFICATIONS

*Torque specifications are for clean and lightly lubricated threads only. Dry or dirty threads produce increased friction which prevents accurate measurement of tightness.

Engine	Cylinder Head Bolts Ft. Lbs.	Connecting Rod Cap Bolts Ft. Lbs.	Main Bearing Cap Bolts Ft. Lbs.	Intake Manifold Ft. Lbs.	Exhaust Manifold Ft. Lbs.	Camshaft Sprocket Ft. Lbs.	Camshaft Drive Pulley Ft. Lbs.	Flywheel to Crankshaft Ft. Lbs.	Vibration Damper or Pulley Ft. Lbs.
4-79	40	30	45	10	10	20	20	35	—
4-95	50-60	30	45	10	10	—	—	35	40
4-100	50-60	30	45	10	10	—	—	35	40

—Not Available.

BRAKE SPECIFICATIONS

Year	Model	Drum Brake I.D.	Wheel Cylinder Bore		Master Cylinder Bore	Disc Brake Rotor	
			Front Disc	Rear Drum		Nominal Thickness	Minimum Thickness
1972-77	12,15	7.087	1.890	.866	.748	.394	.354
1972-73	17TS	—	1.890①	—	.748	.788②	—
1974	17 Gordini	9.0	1.890	.866	.748	.788	—
1974-77	17TL	7.087	1.890	.866	.748	.394	.354
1975-77	17 Gordini	7.087	1.890	.866	.748	.394	.354
1976-77	5	7.096	1.772	.866	.811	.394	.354

—Not Available.
①—Rear, 1.417.
②—Rear, .355.

WHEEL ALIGNMENT SPECIFICATIONS

Year	Model	Caster Angle, Degrees		Camber Angle, Degrees				Toe-Out Inch
				Limits		Desired		
		Limits	Desired	Left	Right	Left	Right	
1972-77	12,15,17	0 to +4	+4	1 to 2	1 to 2	1½	1½	0 to ⅛
1976-77	5	+10 to +13	+11½	0 to 1	0 to 1	½	½	³⁄₆₄ to ³⁄₁₆

Electrical Section

DISTRIBUTOR, REPLACE

Removal

1. Disconnect distributor primary wire from coil terminal.
2. Remove distributor cap and rotor.
3. Remove vacuum line and hold down clamp.
4. Note relative position of distributor in block, then remove from engine.

Installation

1. Reinstall distributor in same relative position as removed.
2. Turn the distributor shaft so tabs on the bottom of distributor shaft engage the offset slot in distributor drive.
3. Reinstall hold down clamp, vacuum line, rotor and cap.
4. Connect distributor primary wire to coil.
5. Adjust ignition timing.

DISTRIBUTOR SERVICE

1. Remove spiral spring (1), Fig. 1.
2. Remove pin (2) with suitable punch.
3. Remove clip (3) if applicable.
4. Remove breaker plate (4) with points assembly, distributors with

vacuum advance. Mark the notched adjusting cam (C), Fig. 2, on the vacuum advance linkage to aid in reassembly.
5. Remove distributor shaft with advance weights.
6. Check counterweight operation, springs and the clearance between the shaft and the housing bearings.
7. Clean and lubricate the components.
8. Reverse procedure to assemble.
9. Check the distributor operation on a test stand, adjust centrifugal advance by altering the spring tension. Adjust the vacuum advance by turning notched cam (C), Fig. 2.

ALTERNATOR, REPLACE

1. Disconnect battery ground cable.
2. Mark and disconnect the alternator wires.
3. Loosen bolt on the alternator tensioner.
4. Remove alternator belt.
5. Remove lower securing bolt and the alternator.
6. Reverse procedure to install. Adjust the tension of the alternator belt.

ALTERNATOR IN-CAR TESTING

The alternator can be checked on the vehicle using a voltmeter. Connect a voltmeter across the battery (+) and (−) terminals.

1. At idle, the voltmeter should read approximately 14 volts.
2. On acceleration at 2,000 RPM, the voltmeter should read approximately 15 volts at no load.
3. At 2,000 RPM, turn on the headlights, heater, rear window defogger and windshield wipers. The voltmeter should read approximately 13 to 14 volts.

STARTER, REPLACE

Renault 5

1. Disconnect battery ground cable.
2. Remove air cleaner and carburetor air cleaner air intake.
3. Clamp and disconnect the carburetor heating hoses. Remove the carburetor linkage.
4. Disconnect exhaust pipe and remove intake/exhaust manifold.
5. Disconnect positive battery cable from the starter, then the solenoid feed wire.
6. Remove starter bolts. Remove upper bolt with a suitable tool.
7. Remove starter.
8. Reverse procedure to install.
9. Check the coolant level and bleed the cooling system.

Renault 12, 15 & 17

1. Disconnect battery ground cable.
2. On 1972-74 Renault 12, 15 and 17

Fig. 1 Distributor disassembled

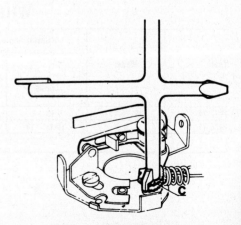

Fig. 2 Adjusting cam

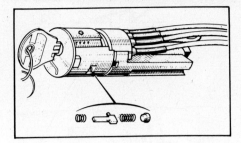

Fig. 3   Ignition switch tumbler, replace

TL, remove the air cleaner.
3. On all models, remove the positive battery cable and the solenoid feed wire from the starter.
4. On 1975-77 models, remove the starter heat shield securing bolts.
5. On all models, remove the starter securing bolts and remove the starter. Slide the starter back toward the manifold, pull out the bendix drive end of the starter and remove sideways.
6. Reverse procedure to install.

IGNITION SWITCH, REPLACE

Renault 5, 12, 15 & 17

1. Disconnect battery ground cable.
2. On Renault 12, remove steering wheel.
3. Remove the combination lighting-direction indicator switch shell. On Renault 5, remove bottom half only.
4. On all models, remove wiring junction plug.
5. Turn key to (G) "garage" position and remove.
6. Remove screw 1.
7. Push in retaining pin 2 with a punch and push the switch out from behind.

Tumbler, Replace

1. Remove ignition switch and turn the key to the (S) "stop" position.

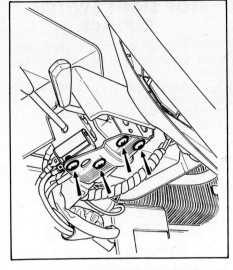

Fig. 4   Light & turn signal switch. Renault 5

2. Remove key to free locking tumbler, Fig. 3.
3. Remove two screws on the rear of the switch.
4. Pull the switch apart.

LIGHT SWITCH, REPLACE

Renault 5

Hi-Low Beam Switch
1. Disconnect battery ground cable.
2. Remove under-dash panel cover screws and the cover.
3. Remove switch retaining screws, Fig. 4.
4. Disconnect wiring plugs and remove switch.
5. Reverse procedure to install.

On-Off Switch
1. Disconnect battery ground cable.
2. Remove under-dashboard lower panel containing the switch.
3. Remove switch knob by turning to the left.
4. Remove switch retaining nut with suitable tool.

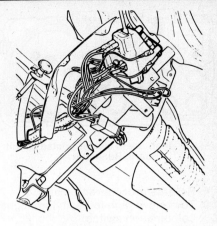

Fig. 5   Light switch location. 1972-73 Renault 12

5. Remove switch from the under-dash panel.
6. Reverse procedure to install.

Renault 12

1972-73
1. Disconnect battery ground cable.
2. Remove bottom half of the combination lighting-turn signal switch shell.
3. Disconnect wiring and wiring plugs, Fig. 5.
4. Remove the three screws holding the combination lighting switch and the switch, Fig. 6.
5. Reverse procedure to install.

1974-77
1. Disconnect battery ground cable.
2. Unscrew the switch knob by turning to the left. Remove securing nut.
3. Slide switch out the rear and disconnect the wiring.
4. Reverse procedure to install.

Renault 15 & 17

1972-76
1. Disconnect battery ground cable.
2. Pry up front edge of rocker switch and pull out of dashboard.
3. Disconnect wiring.

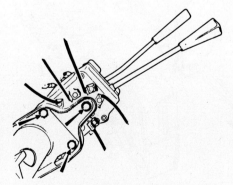

Fig. 6   Light switch retaining screws. 1972-73 Renault 12

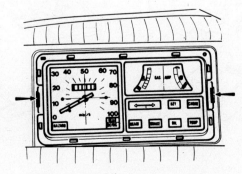

Fig. 7   Instrument cluster. Renault 5

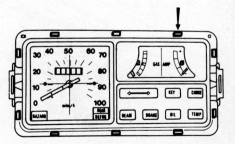

Fig. 8   Removing instrument cluster glass cover. Renault 5

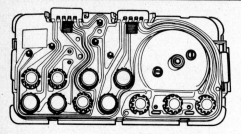

Fig. 9 Instrument cluster printed circuit board. Renault 5

4. Reverse procedure to install.
5. To remove high-lo beam/turn signal combination switch:
   a. Disconnect battery ground cable.
   b. Remove bottom half of the combination lighting-turn signal switch shell.
   c. Disconnect wiring and wiring plugs.
   d. Remove the three screws holding the switch, and the switch.
   e. Reverse procedure to install.

1977
1. Disconnect battery ground cable.
2. Lower the under-dash fuse and relay panel located to the left of the steering column.
3. Locate the metal tab securing the back of the light switch to the dash and pry it straight out.
4. Pull the plastic instrument cover straight out.
5. Remove the switch knob by turning to the left. Remove the switch securing nut and push out the switch.
6. Reverse procedure to install. Be sure to bend over the metal switch retaining tab to properly secure the switch and cluster cover.

STOP LIGHT SWITCH, REPLACE

The stop light switch is located on the brake pedal linkage under the dashboard.
1. Disconnect battery ground cable.
2. Disconnect switch wiring.
3. Remove the switch lock nut.
4. Remove the switch.
5. Reverse procedure to install.

BACK-UP LAMP & NEUTRAL SAFETY SWITCH, REPLACE
Manual Transmission

Back-Up Lamp Switch
The switch is located to the lower right of the transmission shift rail.
1. Disconnect battery ground cable.
2. Raise vehicle.
3. Disconnect switch wiring and remove switch.
4. Reinstall switch with a new copper "O" ring. Reconnect the wiring.
5. Check the transmission lubricant level.
6. Lower vehicle and reconnect battery.

Automatic Transmission

The neutral switch is located at the base of the selector lever.
1. Disconnect battery ground cable.
2. Gently pry up the plastic shift pattern plate, starting at the bottom.
3. Remove the screws securing the

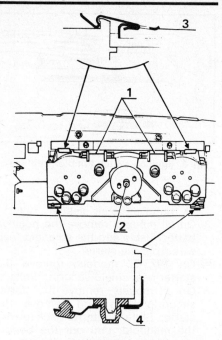

Fig. 10 Instrument cluster wiring & attachments. 1972-75 Renault 12

housing around the selector lever.
4. Remove the neutral switch (It is the switch on the left side).
5. Reverse procedure to install.

TURN SIGNAL SWITCH, REPLACE

1. Disconnect battery ground cable.
2. Remove bottom half of the combination lighting-turn signal switch shell.

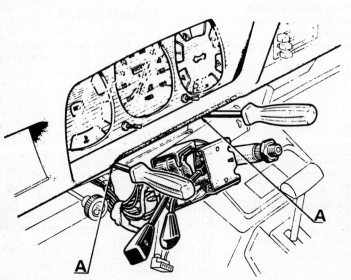

Fig. 11 Instrument cluster. 1976-77 Renault 12

Fig. 12 Instrument cluster components. 1976-77 Renault 12

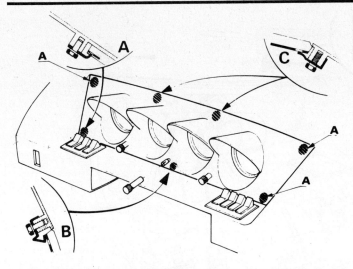

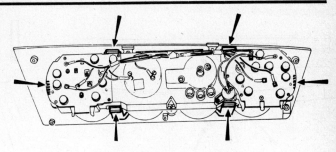

Fig. 14   Instrument cluster retaining clip locations. 1972-76 Renault 15 & 17

Fig. 13   Instrument cluster attachments. 1972-76 Renault 15 & 17

3. Remove switch retaining screws.
4. Disconnect wiring connectors.
5. Remove switch.
6. Reverse procedure to install.

INSTRUMENT CLUSTER, REPLACE

Renault 5

1. Disconnect battery ground cable.
2. Remove speedometer cable in the engine compartment from the emissions control governor. Also, disconnect the EGR mileage recorder on 1977 models.
3. Pull off the instrument panel cover.
4. Insert two small screwdrivers in the slots of the retaining clips on each side of the instrument panel, Fig. 7. Press in the clips toward the center of the panel until the clips clear the support plate. Pull the instrument panel out slightly.
5. From the engine compartment, push the speedometer cable to force the instrument panel out.
6. Disconnect the speedometer cable

and the two electrical plugs and wiring.
7. Remove the instrument cluster.
8. Reverse procedure to install.

Component Service

1. Remove the instrument cluster.
2. Remove the glass cover by bending the retaining tabs, Fig. 8.
3. Remove the various gauges by removing the securing screws on the back of the cluster.
4. To remove the printed circuit board, remove all the gauge retaining screws, remove all the light bulbs and the dowels holding the printed circuit board. Remove the printed circuit board, Fig. 9.
5. Reverse procedure to install.

Renault 12

1972-75

NOTE: It is not necessary to remove the dashboard to remove the instrument cluster.

1. Disconnect battery ground cable.
2. Disconnect the two wiring plugs (1), Fig. 10.
3. Remove the speedometer cable at (2).

4. Push up the retaining clips (3).
5. Pull the top of the instrument cluster out and free the mounting pins (4).
6. Reverse procedure to install.

1976-77

1. Disconnect battery ground cable.
2. Remove the steering wheel and the 2 half shells behind the steering wheel.
3. Remove the two instrument cluster retaining screws at (A), Fig. 11.
4. Disconnect the wiring plugs and the speedometer cable.
5. Release the cluster from the retaining clip and slide the cluster out and to the left of the steering column.
6. Reverse procedure to install.

Component Service, 1972-75

1. The instrument cluster must be removed for service.
2. To remove the speedometer, free the cover glass from the retaining notches. Remove the securing screws and pull out the speedometer.
3. To remove any one of the gauges,

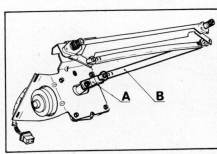

Fig. 15   W/S wiper motor removal. Renault 5

Fig. 16   W/S wiper wiper motor arm & connecting links. Renault 5

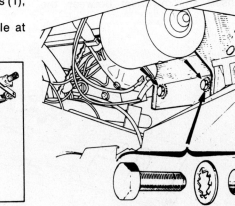

Fig. 17   W/S wiper motor mounting. Renault 12

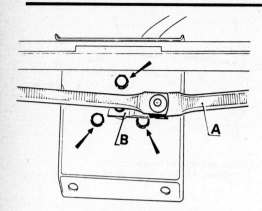

Fig. 18 W/S wiper arm positioning. Renault 12

the corresponding printed circuit must be removed.

4. Reverse procedure to install.

Component Service, 1976-77

1. The instrument cluster must be removed for service.
2. To replace the cluster lights in the cover remove screws at (B), Fig. 12, remove clips at (C) and separate the cover from the cluster.
3. To remove speedometer, separate cover from the cluster and remove the two retaining screws. Pull out the speedometer.
4. To remove the gauges, the corresponding printed circuit must be removed.
5. Reverse procedure to install.

Renault 15 & 17

1972-76

1. Disconnect battery ground cable.
2. Lower the under-dash fuse and relay panel located to the lower left of the steering column.
3. Reach up through the fuse and relay panel area and remove retaining clips, Fig. 13. To remove clips on the right hand side of the instrument cluster, remove the in-dash radio speaker grille.
4. Insert a screwdriver between the

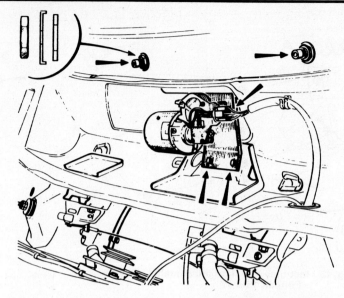

Fig. 19 W/S wiper motor mounting. Renault 15 & 17

cluster and dashboard to free up clip (B).
5. Pull on the top of the cluster to free up clips (C).

CAUTION: The printed circuit wiring connectors touch the dashboard during removal. Use caution not to damage them.

---

6. Disconnect the wiring connectors, the speedometer cable and remove the cluster.
7. Lift up the retaining clips to separate the cluster from the plastic cover, Fig. 14.
8. Reinstall clips (A) onto the plastic cover. Do not tighten the screws.
9. Reverse procedure to install. Then retighten retaining clip screws.

1977

1. Disconnect battery ground cable.
2. Lower the under-dash fuse and relay panel located to the left of the steering column.
3. Locate metal tab securing the back

of the light switch to the dash and pry it out straight.
4. Pull the plastic instrument cluster cover straight out and disconnect the cover and switch wiring.
5. Reach in behind the instrument cluster and gently push out the cluster. Release the upper securing clips behind the cluster. Disconnect the wiring and speedometer cable.
6. To service any of the gauges, the corresponding printed circuit must be removed.
7. Reverse procedure to install.

W/S WIPER SWITCH, REPLACE

1972-76 Renault 15 & 17; 1976-77 Renault 5

1. Disconnect battery ground cable.
2. Pry up the switch from the bottom

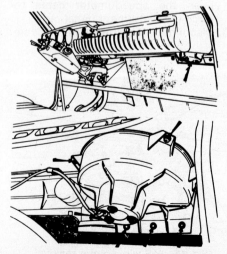

Fig. 21 Blower motor housing. Renault 12

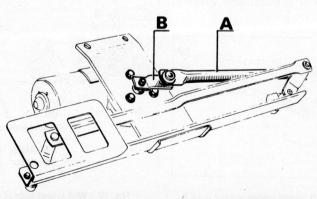

Fig. 20 W/S wiper arm positioning. Renault 15 & 17

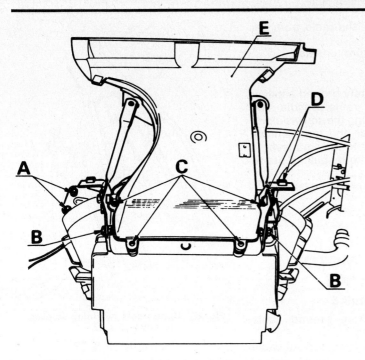

Fig. 22 **Blower motor housing attachments. Renault 15 & 17**

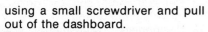

Fig. 23 **Blower motor. Renault 15 & 17**

using a small screwdriver and pull out of the dashboard.
3. Remove the wiring plug.
4. Reverse procedure to install.

1972-77 Renault 12 & 1977 Renault 17

1. Disconnect battery ground cable.
2. Loosen two securing phillips screws and remove switch.
3. Remove the wiring plug.
4. Reverse procedure to install.

W/S WIPER MOTOR, REPLACE

Renault 5

1. Disconnect battery ground cable.
2. Remove the wiper arms by lifting the base of the arm and removing the retaining nut.
3. Remove large nuts securing the arm pivots to the cowl.
4. Disconnect the wiring at the plug.
5. Remove mounting bracket securing bolts, Fig. 15.
6. Lower the motor assembly and remove by pulling out sideways.
7. Remove driving arm nut from motor shaft.
8. Remove motor mounting screws and the motor from the assembly.
9. Reverse procedure to install. Driving arm (A) and linkage (B) must be exactly in line for reassembly with the motor in the park position, Fig. 16.

Renault 12

1. Disconnect battery ground cable.
2. Remove wiper arms by lifting the base of the arm and removing the retaining nut.
3. Remove large nuts securing the arm pivots to the cowl.
4. Remove lower parcel shelf and shift console, if necessary.
5. Remove ashtray and the screws securing the heater control levers.
6. Remove air flaps.
7. Remove the mounting plate securing screws, Fig. 17.
8. Pull the motor assembly forward slightly and remove the two screws at each pivot point. Pull the assembly down and to the right of the steering column.

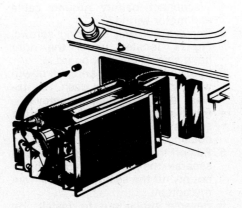

Fig. 24 **Heater core. Renault 5**

9. Remove the driving arm nut from the motor shaft.
10. Remove the mounting screws and remove the motor from the assembly.
11. Reverse procedure to install. Linkage (A) and driving arm (B) must be exactly in line for reassembly with the motor in PARK position, Fig. 18.

Renault 15 & 17

1. Disconnect battery ground cable.
2. Remove wiper blades.
3. Remove cowl section between the hood and the windshield by removing the screws on the windshield side and the hood side.
4. Remove the large nuts securing wiper arm pivots.
5. Disconnect motor wiring.
6. Remove mounting plate securing screws, Fig. 19.
7. Remove assembly by sliding out toward the right.
8. Remove nut securing the driving arm to the motor shaft, then the arm.
9. Remove the three motor securing bolts and the motor from the support plate.
10. Reverse procedure to install. When assembling the motor and the driving arm, the driving arm (B) and linkage (A) must be in line, Fig. 20.

W/S WIPER MOTOR DRIVE GEAR, REPLACE

1. Remove wiper motor from vehicle.
2. Remove wiper motor from support plate.
3. Remove cover of drive gear and pull drive gear out. Do no lose thrust washer.
4. Install new drive gear with thrust

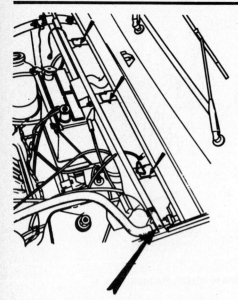

Fig. 25 Heater core retaining hooks. Renault 12

washer, lubricate thoroughly with suitable grease. Lightly grease the copper contacts on the drive gear and replace the cover.

RADIO, REPLACE

Renault 5

1. Disconnect battery ground cable.
2. Remove two phillips screws at bottom of radio console.
3. Remove radio knobs and the radio shaft securing nuts.
4. Pull out the bottom of the radio console, reach in behind the console and pull out the radio.
5. Reverse procedure to install.

Renault 12

Manual Transmission
1. Disconnect battery ground cable.
2. "Pop" off side cover at the rear of the radio console.
3. Remove radio knobs and securing nuts.
4. Pull out the radio from behind.
5. Reverse procedure to install.

Auto. Transmission
1. Disconnect battery ground cable.
2. Remove the phillips screws at the side of the radio/console cover.
3. Lift out radio/console cover unit and remove radio.
4. Reverse procedure to install.

Renault 15 & 17

1972-76
1. Disconnect battery ground cable.
2. Remove the screws at the bottom of each side of the radio/console.
3. Pull the radio/console out from the

top and remove the radio from behind.
4. Reverse procedure to install.

1977
1. Disconnect battery ground cable.
2. Remove either radio/console side cover by removing the screws along the bottom, rear and top. Remove the screws next to the shift lever.
3. Remove the radio by pulling out to the side.
4. Reverse procedure to install.

BLOWER MOTOR, REPLACE

Renault 5

1. Disconnect battery ground cable and motor wiring.
2. Remove air flap lever control cable and cable sleeve.
3. Unclip bleed hose and accelerator cable from blower motor housing.
4. Remove two housing attaching bolts located on the fender well and next to the carburetor. Lift out the blower housing assembly.
5. Separate the two halves of the housing after removing the securing clips.
6. Remove the two clips on the air intake side and then remove the flap support panel.
7. Remove the 3 motor mount screws on the top of the housing and remove the motor. Retain the rubber anti-vibration washers.
8. Pull off the fan blade locking sleeve and separate the fan from the motor. Do not pry the locking sleeve off from the bottom.
9. Reverse procedure to install. Be sure to reinstall the rubber anti-vibration washers.

Renault 12

1. Disconnect battery ground cable and motor wiring.
2. Remove housing securing screws, Fig. 21, located under the right hand side of the dashboard.
3. Loosen the housing and pull downward from under the dash. Pull toward the right for easier removal.
4. Remove the 3 motor securing screws and the motor from the housing.
5. Pull off the fan securing sleeve and separate the motor from the fan. Do not pry off the securing sleeve from the bottom.
6. Reverse procedure to install. Be sure to reseal the housing.

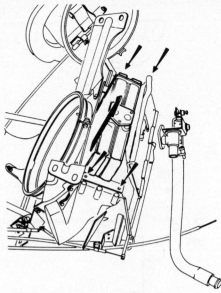

Fig. 26 Heater core retaining screws. Renault 15 & 17

Renault 15 & 17

1. Disconnect battery ground cable.
2. Clamp and disconnect the heater hoses on the engine side of the firewall.
3. Remove radio speaker grille and glove compartment.
4. Disconnect windshield washer switch wires.
5. Remove the 4 screws holding the radio console, pull up the console and move to the left side of the passenger compartment. On the 1977 Renault 17 remove the console side covers and move the center section to the left hand side of the passenger compartment.
6. Remove the screws holding the gearshift cover and turn the cover ¼ turn to the left.
7. Lower the heater control assembly and remove the four control cables by removing the clips, two on the control assembly and two on the right side of the heater assembly.
8. Remove the four bolts (A) on the firewall, the two tie bolts (B), the four housing bolts (C), the four bolts (D) under the dashboard and the two electric feed wires, Fig. 22.
9. Remove the heating unit complete with the hoses. Leave the top section (E) in position.
10. Remove the clips on the air intake shroud and the shroud. Remove the motor fan assembly, Fig. 23.
11. Remove the three motor mounting screws and the motor. Remove the fan blades from the fan. Do not lose the rubber anti-vibration mounting washers.
12. Reverse procedure to install. Be sure to install the rubber anti-vibration mounting washers.

HEATER CORE, REPLACE
Renault 5

1. Remove heater motor and housing assembly.
2. Clamp off the heater hoses leading to the heater core. Remove the bottom heater hose, the heater valve and the bleeder hose. Use Renault clamp Mot. 453 or suitable tool.
3. Remove the heater core mounting bolts and remove the heater core, Fig. 24.
4. Reverse procedure to install.
5. Check the operation of the heater valve control cable. Adjust the cable so that there is a slight clearance at lever when the heater valve is completely closed.

6. Install the motor housing assembly.
7. Adjust the air flap control lever so that there is a slight clearance at lever 2 when the air flap is completely closed.
8. Start the engine and bleed the cooling system through the heater core bleed screw.

Renault 12

1. Remove the air intake grille between the hood and the windshield.
2. Clamp and disconnect the heater hoses. Use Renault tool Mot. 453 or suitable hose clamp.
3. Pull up the three heater core retaining hooks, Fig. 25.
4. Disconnect the heater valve and the securing nut located under the left

hand side of the dashboard, Fig. 26.
5. Pull out the heater core.
6. Reverse procedure to install.
7. Check the condition of the air intake grille weatherstrips. If the weather strip located directly above the heater core is not in good condition, the fan will not circulate air properly.

Renault 15 & 17

1. Remove the heater fan assembly.
2. Remove the heater valve.
3. Remove the four heater core retaining screws, Fig. 26, and remove the heater core.
4. Reverse procedure to install. Be sure to replace the heater valve "O" rings.

Engine Section

ENGINE, REPLACE
Renault 5

The engine is removed with the transaxle attached and removed from above. The use of Renault lifting tool, MOT 498 or a chain pull with support of the engine and transaxle is recommended.

1. Raise vehicle and support the front end on jack stands.
2. Disconnect and remove battery.
3. Drain the cooling system from the radiator and the drain plug next to the timing gear cover, Fig. 1.
4. Drain transaxle oil and engine oil.
5. Remove hood, grille, two inner fender support braces and air filter.
6. Mark and disconnect the water hoses, vacuum hoses, wires and control cables.
7. Remove windshield washer bottle and position aside.
8. Remove splash pan under transaxle.

9. Remove air filter support.
10. Disconnect exhaust pipe from exhaust manifold.
11. Remove nuts holding the radiator, Fig. 2, and the radiator cooling fan assembly.
12. Remove steering column flex coupling bolts. Do not lose the rubber bushing.
13. Remove front wheels and brake calipers. Do not disconnect the brake lines.
14. Disconnect tie rods at rack end (B), Fig. 3.
15. Disconnect upper ball joints (C), Fig. 4. Use Renault tool T. Av. 476 or suitable tool. Tilt the spindles down and pull the axles out of the transmission.
16. Remove two bolts securing the steering rack and the rack.

NOTE: If the steering rack is not being changed, mark the right and

left hand shims so that the correct steering rack height can be obtained after reassembly, Fig. 5.

17. Remove air pump filter, air pump and pump bracket. If the vehicle is equipped with the notched type air pump drive belt, discard the belt. A new belt is mandatory for reassembly.
18. Remove two top bolts on bell housing.
19. Position the Renault Mot. 498 lifting hook and use two 1⅜" (35mm) long bolts to bolt the lifting hook to the transaxle bolt holes. The long bolts are used to distribute the load over a sufficient number of threads, Fig. 6.
20. Remove engine mounts from the bottom of engine, Fig. 7.
21. Remove right side reinforcement mounting bolts.
22. Remove bolts holding the shift rod support, Fig. 8. Pull shift rod down-

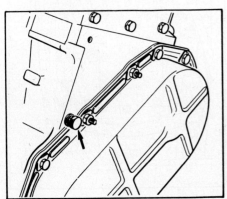

Fig. 1 Block drain plug. Renault 5

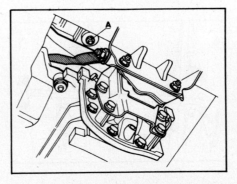

Fig. 2 Radiator attachments. Renault 5

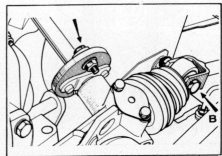

Fig. 3 Tie rod attachments. Renault 5

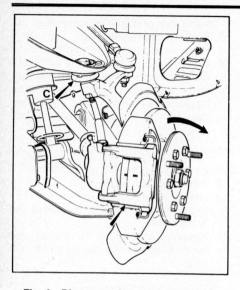

Fig. 4   Disconnecting upper ball joint. Renault 5

ward from the shift linkage.

23. Loosen clutch adjusting nuts and remove clutch cable from release fork, Fig. 9. Using a screwdriver, push back the cable sleeve retainer and push out the cable assembly from the support bracket.
24. Attach the chain fall to the lifting device to support the engine.
25. Remove the transaxle front mount shown, Fig. 10.
26. Make sure the axle shaft ends are clear of the transaxle.
27. Remove the engine and transaxle assembly.
28. Reverse procedure to install.

NOTE: Be sure to install a new air pump drive belt if vehicle is equipped with a notched type belt.

Renault 12, 15 & 17

1. Disconnect battery ground cable.
2. Remove hood, air cleaner and drain cooling system.

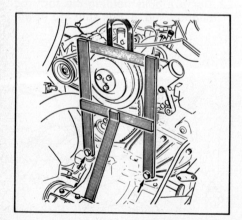

Fig. 6   Installing engine lifting device. Renault 5

3. Mark and disconnect all hoses, wiring and cables. On fuel injected vehicles, remove the fuel injection wiring harness from the injection manifold.
4. Remove radiator, starter, camshaft drive pulley and belt.
5. Remove bolts securing the top of transaxle to engine.
6. Remove exhaust pipe at the exhaust manifold and at the transaxle crossmember.
7. Remove the crankshaft drive pulley.
8. Remove the cooling fan and pulley, if equipped.
9. Remove lower clutch cover.
10. Install the engine lifting equipment and raise engine slightly.
11. Loosen and remove motor mount bolts.
12. Raise the engine until top of transaxle contacts the under side of the steering crossmember. Place jack or support under the transmission.
13. Remove the lower engine/transaxle bolts.
14. Rock the engine and pull forward. Lift the engine from vehicle.
15. Reverse procedure to install. Lightly lubricate the clutch shaft splines with white grease. Place a few drops of a suitable thread lock on the crankshaft pulley retaining bolt.

CYLINDER HEAD, REPLACE
Renault 5

Removal

1. Disconnect battery ground cable.
2. Drain cooling system.
3. Remove air cleaner and bracket assembly.
4. Mark for reassembly all hoses, wires and cables from the cylinder head.
5. Loosen the air pump and remove the drive belts. If the vehicle is equipped with a single notched drive belt discard the belt. A NEW belt is required for reassembly.
6. Disconnect exhaust pipe.
7. Remove hood latch and cable assembly.

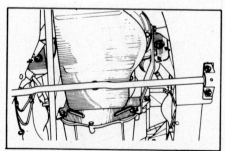

Fig. 7   Engine mount bolts. Renault 5

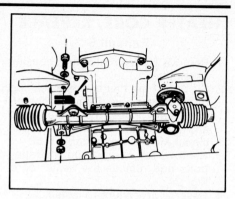

Fig. 5   Steering rack shims. Renault 5

8. Remove valve cover. Remove the head bolts, except the bolt next to the distributor. Loosen this bolt ½ a turn.
9. Using a wooden 2x4 and a hammer or a plastic hammer, break the cylinder head loose from the cylinder liners by tapping on the ends of the head. Remove the bolt and the cylinder head.
10. Remove push rods and mark for reassembly.

CAUTION: Do not turn over the engine until the cylinder liners are clamped down with Renault clamp Mot. 521 or with two head bolts and suitable spacers. If the liners are moved, the liner bottom seals may break and cause water leaks after reassembly.

11. Clean the head gasket and block surfaces with gasket remover or strong carburetor spray cleaner. Do not use any sharp steel edged tools for cleaning.

Installation

1. Install head gasket dry with the "HAUT-TOP" mark facing up.

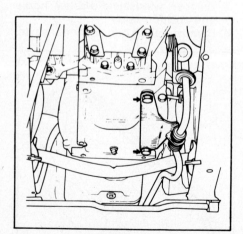

Fig. 8   Shift rod support bolts. Renault 5

Fig. 9 Disconnecting clutch cable. Renault 5

2. Reverse procedure to install cylinder head.
3. Torque the head bolts to 40 ft. lbs. (5.5 N-m). Tighten from the center out.
4. Adjust valves.

NOTE: Retorque the cylinder head after 300 miles and readjust the valves.

Renault 12, 15 & 17

Removal

1. Disconnect battery ground cable.
2. Drain cooling system and remove air cleaner.
3. Mark and disconnect all hoses, cables and wiring. Remove fuel injection wiring, if necessary.
4. Remove distributor, alternator with drive belt and water pump belt.
5. Remove valve cover.
6. Disconnect the exhaust pipe at the manifold. On Hemi Head engines, remove exhaust manifold from engine.
7. Loosen and remove rocker arm shaft and the pushrods. Keep them in correct order for replacement.
8. Loosen and remove all the head bolts except the center bolt on the distributor side of the head. Looser

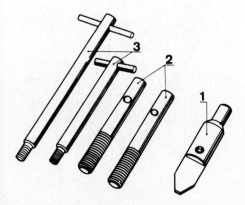

Fig. 11 Cylinder head positioning tools. Renault 12, 15 & 17

this bolt ½ turn.
9. Using a wooden 2x4 and a hammer or plastic tip hammer, break the cylinder head loose from the cylinder liners by tapping on the ends of the head. Remove the bolt.
10. Lift the cylinder head slightly and remove the lifters. Keep them in correct order.
11. Remove cylinder head.

CAUTION: Do not turn over the engine until the cylinder liners are clamped down with Renault clamp Mot. 521 or with two head bolts and suitable spacers. If the liners are moved, the liner seals may break and cause water leaks after reassembly.

12. Clean the head gasket and block surfaces with gasket remover or strong carburetor spray cleaner. Do not use any sharp steel edged tools for cleaning.

Installation

1. Remove any water from the block bolt holes.

NOTE: The cylinder head positioning is extremely important. The alignment of the distributor drive shaft gear depends on this operation. Renault positioning tools Mot. 446 (1) and Mot. 451 (2), Fig. 11, must be used for this operation.

2. Remove cylinder liner clamps. Ensure the cylinder head locating dowel between cylinders 2 and 3 are in position.
3. Install the head gasket into position. Once it is installed it should not be removed. If the head is installed in a wrong position the gasket must not be reused.
4. Screw two locating studs (2) into position at each end of the head until the ball just touches the head gasket and holds it into position.
5. Install rubber portion of the head gasket. Ensure that it fits into the slots of the head gasket and into the positioning holes in the block.
6. Install positioning tool (1) in the hole in front of the cylinder block.
7. Install the lifters in to their correct order in the cylinder head. Tap them lightly to secure into cylinder head.
8. Ensure the distributor drive gear is properly positioned.
9. Place the cylinder head into position. Do not disturb the rubber portion of the cylinder head gasket.
10. Remove locating studs with the stud remover (3). Lubricate the threads on the cylinder head bolts with heavy grease. Lubricate the washers

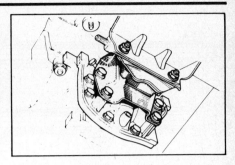

Fig. 10 Transaxle front mount. Renault 5

under the head bolts with engine oil.
11. Install the head bolts and slowly torque them to 30 ft. lbs. Install the short bolt with washer towards the timing gear and distributor end of the head.
12. Torque the head bolts to specifications in the proper sequence, Fig. 12.
13. Install the push rods, tap lightly to seat the lifters onto the camshaft.
14. Install the rocker arm shaft, align the brackets with holes to the pins on the head. Torque the securing bolts to 15 to 20 ft. lbs.
15. Adjust the rocker arm clearances.
16. Perform the additional reassembly operations in reverse order of removal.

NOTE: Retorque the cylinder head after 300 miles and readjust the valves.

ROCKER ARM SERVICE

The rocker arm shaft is not service-

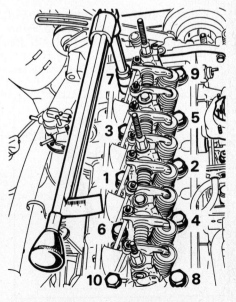

Fig. 12 Cylinder head tightening sequence. Renault 12, 15 & 17

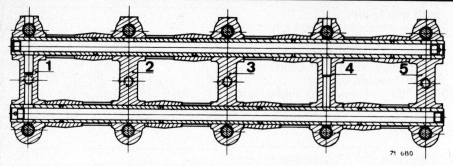

Fig. 13 Hemi head rocker shaft oil hole positions

Exh. valve fully open on cyl. no.	Adj. int. valve on cyl. no.	Adj. exh. valve on cyl. no.
1 3 4 2	3 4 2 1	4 2 1 3

Fig. 14 Valve adjusting sequence.

able except for disassembly. Remove the clips on the end of the shaft for disassembly of the rocker arm shaft from the wedge head engines 810, 821, and 841. To disassemble the rocker shaft from the hemi head engines, 807 and 841, remove the roll pins on the end of each shaft. The hemi-head rocker shafts supports 1 and 4 have lubrication holes, and supports 2, 3 and 5 have no lubrication holes, Fig. 13.

VALVE GUIDES, REPLACE

Replacing the valve guides requires pressing out the guide, reaming out the head to accept an over-size valve guide, and reaming out the valve guide bore to accept the valve. Standard valve guides have no identification marks. Replacement guides are available in the first over-size with one identification groove and in the second over-size with two identification grooves. The use of Renault reamer kits is recommended for valve guide replacement. Reamer kit Mot. 132 for the Renault 5. Reamer kit Mot. 357 for the Renault 12, 15 and 17 vehicles.

1. Press out the valve guides. The head should be held on an angle using Renault support plate Mot. 121 for the Renault 5, Mot. 355 for Renault 12, 15 and 17 wedge head engines,

to keep the valve guides vertical. Renault 12, 15 and 17 hemi-head engines should be held with blocks, the intake valve is at a 23° angle in the head and the exhaust valve at a 26° angle in the head.
2. Check the size of the guide removed. The replacement guide must be one size larger than the old guide.
3. Ream out the valve guide hole with the corresponding reamer for the new valve guide.
4. Lubricate the new valve guide with engine oil, press into place with the chamfer facing up. Press in to obtain the following dimensions between lower edge of valve seat and bottom of valve guide:

Model	Intake	Exhaust
5	1.043″ (26.5mm)	1.032″ (26.2mm)
12, 15 & 17①	1.260″ (32mm)	1.220″ (31mm)
12, 15 & 17②	1.142″ (29mm)	1.142″ (29mm)

①—Hemi-head.
②—Wedge head.

5. Ream out the valve guide bore to accept the valve using the corresponding reamer from the Renault reamer kit.
6. Regrind the valve seats to insure correct valve seating with the new guide.

VALVES, ADJUST

1. Connect a remote control starter switch between the starter solenoid and the battery.
2. Disconnect the coil ignition lead.
3. Crank over engine until the exhaust valve on cylinder 1 is fully open. (Cylinder 1 is next to the flywheel.) Adjust the intake valve on cylinder no. 3 and the exhaust valve on cylinder no. 4.
4. Repeat step 3 to adjust the remaining valves, refer to Fig. 14 for sequence.

TIMING COVER, REPLACE
Renault 5

1. Remove engine from vehicle.
2. Remove bolts securing timing cover

Fig. 15 Valve timing marks. Renault 5

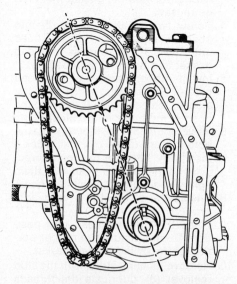

Fig. 16 Aligning valve timing marks. Renault 12, 15 & 17

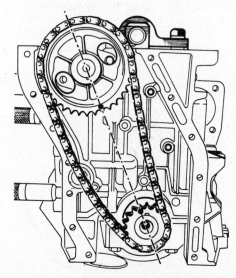

Fig. 17 Timing chain installation. Renault 12, 15 & 17

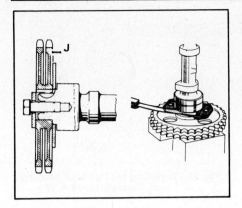

Fig. 18 Checking camshaft flange clearance

and remover.

3. Replace cover using new cork gasket and new neoprene oil pan gasket section.

Renault 12, 15 & 17

1. Remove cylinder head.
2. Remove crankshaft pulley. Use a suitable pry bar to remove pulley after removing securing bolt.
3. Remove radiator.
4. Raise engine and remove timing cover.
5. Replace crankshaft seal in the timing cover.
6. Replace the timing cover using new cork gasket.
7. Reverse procedure to install.

TIMING CHAIN, REPLACE
Renault 5

Removal

1. Remove timing cover.
2. Remove chain tensioner and retain the tensioner filter.
3. Remove the camshaft sprocket lockbolt and pull the sprocket and the chain off using a suitable puller. Do not damage the camshaft inter-

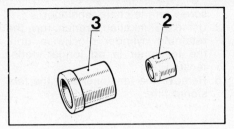

Fig. 19 Camshaft oil seal tool. Renault 5

nal bolt threads.

4. If necessary, remove the crankshaft sprocket.

Installation

1. Press crankshaft sprocket into place. Sprocket can be pressed into place using a short length of 1″ I.D. pipe. Position the pipe on the crankshaft and screw in a threaded rod into the crankshaft end. Using a thick washer and a nut, tighten up the nut and pull the sprocket into position.
2. Temporarily mount the camshaft sprocket with the timing mark facing out.
3. Align the two timing marks on the sprockets, Fig. 15.
4. Remove the camshaft sprocket.

CAUTION: Do not rotate the camshaft.

---

5. Place the timing chain over the crankshaft sprocket and over the camshaft sprocket. Remount the camshaft sprocket with the timing marks aligned, Fig. 15.
6. Torque the camshaft securing bolt to 20 ft. lbs. (3-N-m).
7. Replace the tensioner filter, the chain tensioner and thrust plate.
8. Tighten the bolts securing the tensioner and release the spring loaded thrust plate so the chain is under spring tension.

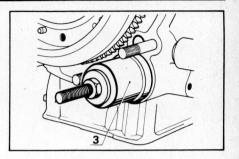

Fig. 20 Installing camshaft oil seal. Renault 5

9. Replace the timing cover with a new gasket.

Renault 12, 15 & 17
Removal

1. Remove timing chain cover.
2. Remove the chain tensioner and the chain guide shoes.
3. Loosen the camshaft securing bolts.
4. Place a bolt, with a small centering hole drilled in the center of the bolt head, in the end of the crankshaft. Remove the crankshaft pulley key.
5. Pull off the crankshaft sprocket with timing chain using a suitable puller. Push back the camshaft while pulling. Remove the timing chain.

Installation

1. Place the timing chain on the camshaft sprocket. Line up the camshaft timing mark with the centers of the camshaft and the crankshaft, Fig. 16.
2. Install the crankshaft key. Turn the crankshaft and bring the key pointing upwards.
3. Install the crankshaft pulley to the timing chain with the timing mark facing outwards and the timing mark in line with the mark on the camshaft sprocket, Fig. 17. Also, the timing marks should line up with the centers of the camshaft and the crankshaft.

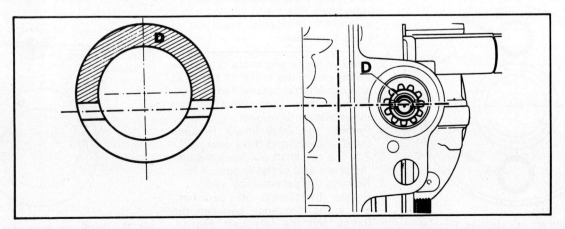

Fig. 21 Positioning distributor drive gear. Renault 5

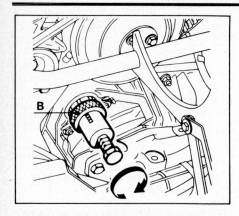

Fig. 22 Removing camshaft oil seal, in-vehicle. Renault 5

4. With the timing marks aligned, install the crankshaft pulley onto the crankshaft.
5. Tighten the camshaft securing bolts.
6. Install the chain tensioner. Install the chain guide shoes and install Renault gauge Mot. 420 against the sprockets. Push the two chain guides against the gauge and tighten the guide bolts. Remove the gauge.
7. Install the crankshaft pulley key.
8. Install the timing cover.

TIMING CHAIN TENSIONER, REPLACE

Two types of timing chain tensioners are used. The early type tensioner is manually tensioned on the engine and is used on early Renault 12, 15 and 17 models. The late type tensioner is spring loaded and is used on late production Renault 12, 15 and 17 vehicles and all Renault 5 vehicles.

Manually Adjusted Type

Removal
1. Remove the retaining cylinder

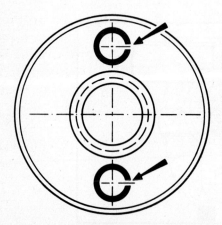

Fig. 24 Roll pin slot location. Renault 12, 15 & 17

screw on the chain tensioner.
2. Using a 3mm allen wrench, turn the retaining cylinder clockwise until the tensioner is no longer under tension.
3. Remove the tensioner and the tensioner filter.

Installation
1. Fit the tensioner with filter to the block.
2. Using a 3mm allen wrench, turn the retaining cylinder counter clockwise until the tensioner pad touches the timing chain.
3. Tighten and lock the retaining cylinder bolt.

Spring Loaded Type

Removal
1. Remove the tensioner assembly from the engine.
2. Separate the shoe from the tensioner body. Using a 3mm allen wrench, push in and turn the piston in the shoe to lock the piston.
3. Insert the shoe into the tensioner body. To prevent accidental spring release of the tensioner, place a .080″ (2mm) shim between the tensioner body and the shoe.

Installation
1. Install the tensioner assembly to the block.
2. Remove the shim. Press in the shoe until it touches the tensioner body.
3. Release the shoe and allow the spring to put the shoe under tension without assisting the spring action.

CAMSHAFT, REPLACE

Renault 5

1. Remove the engine and cylinder head.

CAUTION: Be sure to clamp the cylinder liners down with a suitable tool to prevent accidental breakage of liners base seals.

2. Remove the timing chain cover, the timing chain, the camshaft sprocket and camshaft retaining flange.
3. Remove the air pump drive belt and the camshaft drive gear.
4. Remove the valve lifters. Remove the distributor and drive gear.
5. Pull the camshaft out from the timing chain end of the engine.
6. Remove the camshaft oil seal.
7. Before installation of camshaft, check the clearance between the flange and the camshaft, Fig. 18. The clearance tolerance is J=.002″

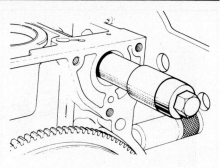

Fig. 23 Installing rear oil seal housing tool. Renault 12, 15 & 17

to .005″ (0.05 to 0.12mm). The sprocket should be bolted in place with the bolt torqued to 20 ft. lbs. Use of a new flange is required.
8. Remove sprocket and flange and install camshaft in engine.
9. Install timing chain and chain tensioner. Replace the timing chain cover.
10. Install a new camshaft oil seal. Use of Renault tool Mot. 500-01 is recommended, Fig. 19.
11. Lubricate the oil seal. Using the Mot. 500-01 tools position the sleeve 2 on the end of the camshaft.
12. Push the seal onto the sleeve and push the seal in with the inserting tool (3), Fig. 20, until the seal just touches the block. Using a threaded rod and nut or bolt, together with a washer, draw the tool and seal onto the camshaft until the tool just touches the block.
13. Install the camshaft drive pulley. Install a new water pump/air pump drive belt and tighten the air pump.
14. Turn the engine to bring the No. 1

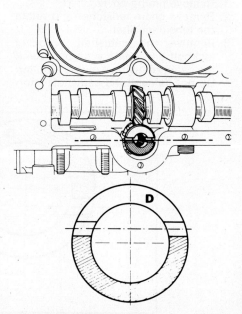

Fig. 25 Distributor drive gear installation. Renault 12, 15 & 17

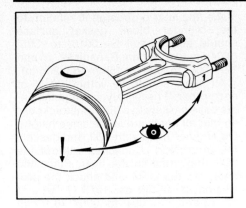

Fig. 26 Piston & rod identification marks

cylinder to firing position (No. 1 cylinder is at the flywheel end of the engine).

15. Insert distributor drive gear using a bolt (12mm diameter-175 pitch). Install with the largest offset (D) facing the clutch and the slot at right angles to the camshaft, Fig. 21.
16. Install the valve lifters and the cylinder head, then the distributor.
17. Install the engine.

SERVICE NOTE

The camshaft oil seal can be replaced without the engine or the camshaft. Changing the seal requires removal of the air filter and support bracket, the air pump and support bracket, and the camshaft drive pulley. The use of Renault Tool Mot. 500-01 is

required, Fig. 19.

1. Remove the components listed above. Cover the opening in the bell housing with a rag.
2. Put the Mot. 500-01 extracting tool in position and push it in all the way until the lip of the oil seal slips over the shoulder of the tool. Push sleeve (B) fully in, Fig. 22.
3. Extract the seal by tightening the screw on the tool.
4. To install the new oil seal, follow installation procedure outlined in the "Camshaft, Replace."

Renault 12, 15 & 17

1. Remove cylinder head.

CAUTION: Be sure to clamp the cylinder liners down with a suitable tool to prevent accidental breakage of liner's base seals.

2. Remove the timing chain cover, the timing chain, the oil pan, the grille and the radiator.
3. Remove the water pump drive pulley on the transmission end of the camshaft.
4. Remove the distributor drive gear. If necessary, thread a bolt down into the drive gear to aid in removal.
5. Remove the camshaft. If necessary, loosen the motor mounts and lower the engine.
6. Remove the camshaft rear oil seal housing.

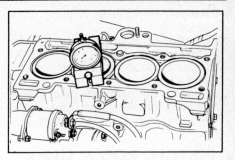

Fig. 27 Checking cylinder liner protrusion

7. Press new camshaft sprocket onto camshaft, be sure to fit retaining flange. Check the clearance between the flange and the camshaft, Fig. 18. The clearance tolerance is J=.002″ to .005″ (0.05 to 0.12mm.). Use of new flange, new sprocket and key is required.
8. Install camshaft.
9. Install new oil seal and "O" ring into rear oil seal housing.
10. Attach Renault tool Mot. 258 to the end of the camshaft, Fig. 23. This will spread the lip of the camshaft seal during installation. Secure the tool using the camshaft pulley bolt.
11. Install rear oil seal housing with new paper gasket, be sure "O" ring seal is in position. Remove the Mot. 258 tool.
12. Replace the timing chain and timing chain cover.
13. Install two new camshaft drive pulley roll pins into position. Push them partly in. When the pulley is tightened they are automatically positioned. Install the roll pin slots, Fig. 24.
14. Turn the engine to bring the No. 1 cylinder to the firing position. No. 1 cylinder is at the flywheel end of the engine.
15. Install the camshaft/distributor drive gear with the smallest off set (D) to the camshaft side and the slot parallel to the camshaft, Fig. 25. Be sure

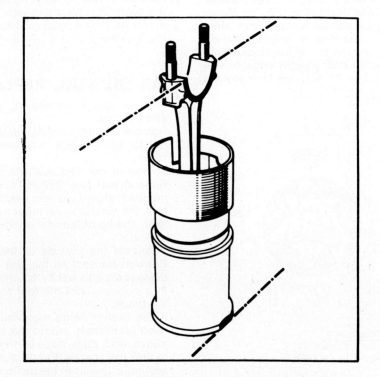

Fig. 28 Installing piston & rod assembly into cylinder liner.

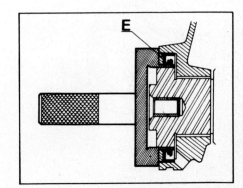

Fig. 29 Installing spacer washer

the gear engages the oil pump drive properly.

16. Fill the camshaft chamber in the block with engine oil.
17. Replace the cylinder head and the oil pan.
18. Replace the camshaft drive pulley and any other related components removed during this operation.

PISTON, ROD & LINER SERVICE

The pistons and liners are serviceable without removing the engine from the vehicle. Pistons and liners are available in standard size only and are matched sets. Do not mix the pistons or liners during assembly.

To remove the piston assemblies, remove the head and oil pan. Check the rods for numbering. If necessary, mark sides of the rods facing away from the camshaft. No. 1 cylinder is located next to the engine flywheel.

Using a press to press the piston pin, mount the pistons to the rods with the spot on the piston facing toward the flywheel and the mark on the connecting rod, made during disassembly, facing away from the camshaft, Fig. 26.

Liner protrusion must be checked prior to the final assembly of the piston and liners in the block. The liners must protrude slightly above the block to insure proper sealing by the head gasket and the head. 1976-77 Renault 5 and 1972-74 Renault 12, 15 and 17 blocks use paper gaskets on the liner bottoms. These gaskets are available in three different thicknesses so the liner protrusion can be set properly. 1975-77 Renault 12, 15 and 17 blocks are fitted with an "O" ring for sealing. Liner protrusion cannot be changed in blocks fitted with

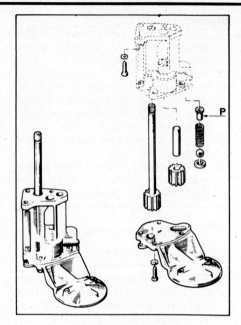

Fig. 30 Oil pump disassembled. Renault 5

"O" rings. However, the protrusion should be checked to insure proper cylinder and head sealing.

Checking Liner Protrusion

The paper base gaskets are available in the following thicknesses:

Blue spot — .003″ (0.08mm)
Red spot — .004″ (0.10mm)
Green spot — .005″ (0.12mm)

Liner protrusion is checked by fitting the liner with a paper gasket with a blue spot and placing the liner into the block. All mating surfaces must be clean. Measure the difference in height between the liner and the top of the block with a feeler gauge and straight edge or dial indicator, Fig. 27. With the liner seals in

place, the liner protrusion in relation to the cylinder block gasket surface should be: Renault 5—.0016″ to .005″ (0.04mm to 0.12mm); Renault 12, 15 and 17—.006″ to .008″ (0.15mm to 0.20mm).

All liners should be within .0016″ of each other. If necessary, change the liners base gaskets to a different thickness so that all liners are at the same height. On engines fitted with "O" ring gaskets the protrusion is checked without the "O" ring fitted to the liner. Place the liner into the block and check the protrusion. It should be: 1975-77 Renault 12, 15 and 17—.004″ to .0067″ (0.10mm to 0.17mm).

If the liner protrusion is not correct, check the protrusion with a new set of liners to determine if the liners are incorrect or the block is defective. After the liner protrusion has been checked, remove the liners from the block and assemble the piston, rod and liner assemblies.

Piston & Liner Assembly

Lubricate the pistons and rings with engine oil. Mount the piston rod assemblies and the liners with a ring compressor. The machined sides of the connecting rod bearing end must be parallel with the flat edge on the top of the liner, Fig. 28. Install the piston liner assemblies into the block with the proper base gaskets. If using an "O" ring make sure it is not twisted. Mount as follows:

a. Number 1 piston at the flywheel end.
b. Number on the connecting rod facing away from the camshaft.
c. Arrow on piston must face towards the flywheel.

REAR OIL SEAL, REPLACE

1. Remove the transmission, clutch and flywheel.
2. Remove the old oil seal. Be careful not to damage any machined surfaces.
3. To install the new seal the use of Renault tool Mot. 259-01 is recommended. Mount the new seal on the tool. Be careful when mounting the seal. The lip of the seal is extremely delicate.
4. Lubricate the outside of the seal. Position the tool on the end of the crankshaft and lightly tap the seal into position until the tool touches the block.
5. If the seal is being mounted on a used crankshaft, mount the seal as above and then remove the tool, mount the spacer (E) and push the seal in further until the tool touches the block, Fig. 29. This operation

Position 1 :

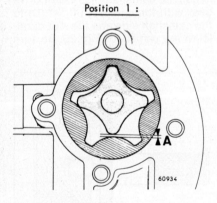

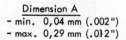

Dimension A
- min. 0,04 mm (.002″)
- max. 0,29 mm (.012″)

Position 2 :

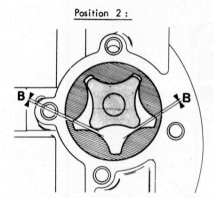

Dimension B
- min. 0,02 mm (.001″)
- max. 0,14 mm (.006″)

Fig. 31 Oil pump clearances. Renault 12, 15 & 17

will mount the seal approximately ⅛" deeper into the block.

6. Reinstall all related components.

OIL PAN, REPLACE
Renault 5

1. Drain the engine oil.
2. Remove the transaxle belly pan, loosen and lower the antisway bar and remove the two bolts securing the gear shift control rod. Remove the right reinforcement bracket. Remove the clutch cover.
3. Loosen the transaxle front support and jack up the transaxle as high as possible.
4. Remove the oil pan by tilting it down toward the back of the vehicle. If necessary turn the crankshaft so the counterweights are horizontal.
5. Remove the gaskets and clean the gasket surfaces.
6. Install new rubber gaskets on the front and rear main bearings. Use gasket cement if necessary.
7. Position new cork gaskets on the block. Make sure these gaskets overlap the ends of the bearing gaskets. Use gasket cement if necessary.
8. Install the oil pan. Be careful not to scrape the brake lines or disturb the gaskets.
9. Reinstall all other related components.
10. Fill the engine with oil.

Renault 12, 15 & 17

1. Drain the engine oil.
2. Lower the engine belly pan.
3. Loosen and lower the antisway bar.
4. Remove the frame cross brace.
5. Remove the engine vibration/counter weight assembly, if equipped.
6. Remove the oil pan.
7. Clean the gasket surfaces.
8. Position a new cork gasket on the oil pan.
9. Install the oil pan.
10. Reinstall all related components in reverse order.
11. Fill the engine with oil.

OIL PUMP SERVICE
Renault 5

1. Remove the oil pan.
2. Remove the bolts securing the pump to the block and remove the pump.
3. If the clearance between the gears and the pump body, Fig. 30, exceeds .008" (0.2mm) replace the pump.
4. Reverse procedure to install.

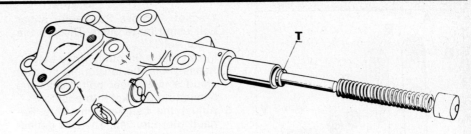

Fig. 32   Oil pump spring & guide installation. Renault 12, 15 & 17

Renault 12, 15 & 17

1. Remove the oil pan.
2. Remove the bolts securing the pump to the block and the pump. Remove the two rotors.
3. Check the clearances A & B of the rotors, Fig. 31.
   a. .002"-.012" (0.04mm-0.29mm)
   b. .001"-.006" (0.02mm-0.14mm)
   If the clearances exceed specifications replace the rotors. The inner rotor is supplied with the driving shaft.
4. When reassembling the pump make sure the spring guide has the head (T) inserted into the piston first, Fig. 32.
5. Reverse procedure to install.

WATER PUMP, REPLACE
Renault 5

1. Disconnect battery ground cable.
2. Drain the cooling system.
3. Loosen alternator, remove the drive pulley on the water pump and the alternator belt.
4. Loosen air pump and remove the air pump drive belt. If a notched type belt is used, this belt should be discarded and replaced with a new belt.
5. Disconnect radiator and heater hoses. Remove the temperature switch.
6. Loosen bolts securing the pump to the head, lightly tap the pump with a hard rubber hammer and remove the pump.
7. Clean the gasket surfaces.
   NOTE: The pump must be mounted with the gasket dry. The gasket surfaces must be clean and dry, free of any oil or dirt.
8. Reverse procedure to install.
9. A new notched type belt is required for reassembly.
10. Refill the cooling system and reconnect the battery.

Renault 12, 15 & 17

1. Disconnect battery ground cable.
2. Drain the cooling system.
3. Remove heater and radiator hoses from pump.
4. Remove alternator and water pump drive belts.
5. Remove water pump pulley and camshaft pulley.
6. Remove pump securing bolts and remove pump. Tap lightly with a hard rubber hammer if necessary.
7. Clean all gasket surfaces.

NOTE: The pump must be mounted with the gasket dry. The gasket surfaces must be clean and dry, free of any dirt or oil.

8. Reverse procedure to install.
9. Refill the cooling system and reconnect the battery.

FUEL PUMP, REPLACE
Renault 5 & 1972-74 Renault 12, 15 & 17 TL

1. Remove distributor cap.
2. Remove fuel lines at the pump, label lines for proper positioning after pump replacement.
3. Remove the securing bolts and remove the pump.
4. Reverse procedure to install. Be sure to use a new gasket.

1975-77 Renault 12, 15 & 17

1. Disconnect battery ground cable.
2. Raise the vehicle to allow for access to the fuel pump located above the right rear axle.
3. Disconnect fuel lines and remove the pump.
4. Reverse procedure to install.

WATER PUMP/AIR PUMP COG-TYPE DRIVE BELT
1976 Renault 5

The cog-type water pump/air pump drive belt used on 1976 models must not be reused or retensioned. Failure of a retensioned drive belt may result. If the drive belt is removed for any reason, a new drive belt must be used.

When the new drive belt is installed,

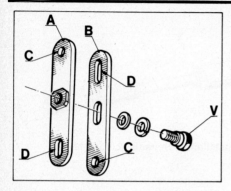

Fig. 33 Water pump/air pump drive belt tensioning bracket. 1976 Renault 5

the tensioning bracket must be re-adjusted using a new shear bolt (V), Fig. 33.

1. Remove the alternator drive belt and pulley.
2. Remove the air pump tensioning bracket. Remove the center shear bolt using large pliers. Discard the shear bolt.
3. Install a new air pump drive belt.
4. Reassemble the tensioning bracket using a new shear bolt. Install the tensioning bracket into position.
5. Adjust the belt tension using Renault tool Ele. 346. The belt deflection should be 4 to 5mm ($^5/_{32}$" to $^3/_{16}$") when measured on the section of the belt between the camshaft and water pump, Fig. 34.
6. When the tension is correct, tighten the bolts at the air pump and the transmission end of the tensioning bracket. Recheck the belt deflection.
7. If tension is correct, tighten the center shear bolt until the bolt shears off behind the hex head.
8. Reinstall the alternator drive belt and pulley. Adjust the belt tension to 2.5-3.5mm ($^7/_{64}$" to $^9/_{64}$").

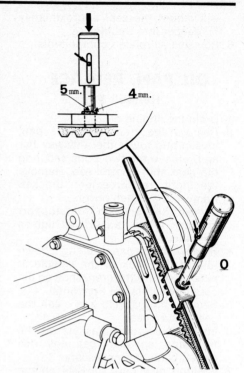

Fig. 34 Adjusting water pump/air pump drive belt tension. 1976 Renault 5

Carburetor Section

CARBURETOR SPECIFICATIONS

Year	Carb. Model	Initial Throttle Plate Opening	Choke Opening		Fast Idle Speed
			Mechanical	Vacuum	
1972	Solex 547	.047	—	—	1450
1973	Weber 4300, 4301	.047—.051	$^{15}/_{64}$	$^{23}/_{64}$	—
	Weber 4400, 4401	.051—.055	$^{15}/_{64}$	$^{25}/_{64}$	—
1974	Weber 4303	.047—.051	$^{15}/_{64}$	$^{15}/_{64}$	—
	Weber 4402	.051—.055	$^{15}/_{64}$	$^{25}/_{64}$	—
1975	Weber 5200	.047—.051	$^9/_{32}$	$^{13}/_{64}$←→$^9/_{32}$	—
	Weber 5600	.051—.055	$^9/_{32}$	$^{13}/_{64}$←→$^9/_{32}$	—
1976	Weber 6000	.047	$^{13}/_{64}$	$^1/_4$	1500
	Weber 8000	.049	$^{13}/_{64}$	$^1/_4$	1500
	Weber 8200	.047—.051	$^9/_{32}$	$^{13}/_{64}$←→$^9/_{32}$	1500
	Weber 8300	.059	$^9/_{32}$	$^{13}/_{64}$←→$^9/_{32}$	—
1977	Weber 100 ①	.049	$^9/_{32}$	$^{13}/_{64}$←→$^9/_{32}$	—
	Weber 100 ②	.059	$^9/_{32}$	$^{13}/_{64}$←→$^9/_{32}$	—
	Weber 5201	.049	$^9/_{32}$	$^{13}/_{64}$←→$^9/_{32}$	—
	Weber 5601	.059	$^9/_{32}$	$^{13}/_{64}$←→$^9/_{32}$	—
	Weber 9000	.047	.157	$^9/_{32}$	1900
	③	.049	$^{13}/_{64}$	$^9/_{32}$	1500
	④	.055	.040	.040	1500

—Not Available.
①—Man. trans.
②—Auto. trans.
③—Calif.
④—High Altitude.

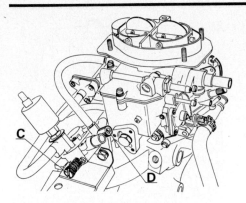

Fig. 1 Accelerated idle adjustment. Solex carburetor

SOLEX CARBURETOR
Accelerated Idle Adjustment

1. Allow engine to warm up. The engine idle speed must be set prior to this adjustment.
2. Feed battery current directly to the deceleration valve solenoid to raise the idle speed.
3. Turn AIR screw (C), Fig. 1, to obtain an engine speed of 1400 to 1500 RPM.
4. Turn MIXTURE screw (D) to obtain a CO percentage of: 2%.

Initial Throttle Plate Opening Adjustment

1. Remove carburetor from engine.
2. Close the choke flaps.
3. Check the throttle plate initial opening with a drill sized to specifications by inserting between the throttle plate and carburetor body. Bend lug (3) to change the setting, Fig. 2.

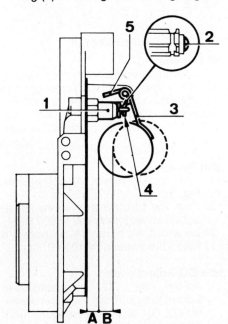

Fig. 4 Float level adjustment. Weber carburetor

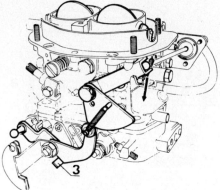

Fig. 2 Initial throttle plate opening adjustment. Solex carburetor

Accelerator Pump Travel Adjustment

1. Place throttle in IDLING position.
2. Push roller (4) in contact with cam (5), Fig. 3.
3. Screw in adjusting screw (6) in or out until it just touches plunger (7), then turn screw in ½ to 1 turn further.

WEBER CARBURETOR
Float Level Adjustment

1. Hold carburetor cover vertical, Fig. 4, so that the float closes the needle valve (1) without causing the ball (2) to enter valve.
2. Dimension (A) should be $^9/_{32}''$ (7mm), measured between the gasket face and the float. To adjust, bend arm (3). Make sure tab (4) remains perpendicular to the axis of the needle valve.
3. Check the float travel (B), it should be $^5/_{16}''$ (8mm). To adjust bend tab (5).

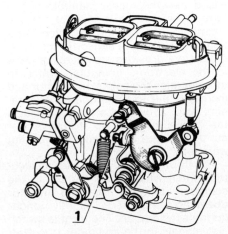

Fig. 5 Initial throttle plate opening adjustment. Weber carburetor with manual choke

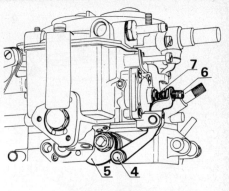

Fig. 3 Accelerator pump travel adjustment. Solex carburetor

Initial Throttle Plate Opening Adjustment

Manual Choke
1. Remove the carburetor.
2. Close the choke plates completely.
3. Measure the opening of the throttle plate against the carburetor body. Use a drill bit corresponding to the correct throttle plate opening specification.
4. To adjust, loosen the locknut and turn screw (1), Fig. 5.

Automatic Choke
1. Remove the carburetor.
2. Close the choke plates completely.
3. Measure the opening of the throttle plate against the carburetor. Use a drill bit corresponding to the correct throttle plate opening specification.
4. To adjust, turn screw (1), Fig. 6.

Initial Choke Plate Opening Adjustment

Manual Choke
Mechanical Adjustment:
1. Close the choke plates fully by moving linkage (3), Fig. 7. Press the choke plate open and bring sleeve (2) into contact with linkage (3).

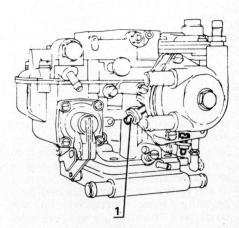

Fig. 6 Initial throttle plate opening adjustment. Weber carburetor with automatic choke

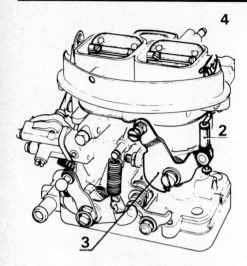

Fig. 7 Initial choke plate opening mechanical adjustment. Weber carburetor with manual choke

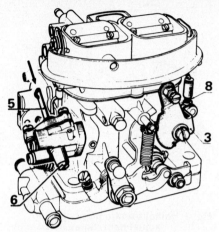

Fig. 8 Initial choke plate opening vacuum adjustment. Weber carburetor with manual choke

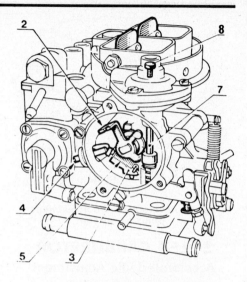

Fig. 9 Initial choke plate opening vacuum adjustment. Weber carburetor with automatic choke

2. Measure the opening of the choke plate at the bottom of the plate. Use a drill bit corresponding to the correct choke plate opening specification.
3. Adjust by bending linkage (4).

Vacuum Adjustment:
1. Push link (5) in as far as possible. Close the choke plates with arm (3), until spring (8) is slightly compressed, Fig. 8.
2. Check the choke plate opening at the bottom of the plate. Use a drill bit corresponding to the correct choke plate opening specification.

3. Adjust by removing screw (6) and turning set screw (7).

Automatic Choke
Mechanical Adjustment:
1. Open the throttle plate slightly and allow the choke plates to close under spring tension.
2. Measure the choke plate opening at the bottom of the choke plate. Use a drill bit corresponding to the correct choke plate opening specification.
3. To adjust, loosen the screws holding the choke spring housing and turn the housing.

Vacuum Adjustment:
1. Remove the carburetor.

2. Open the throttle plates slightly and allow the choke plates to close under spring tension.
3. Remove the choke spring cover.
4. Push rod (7) into the vacuum capsule as far as it will go. Hold lever (2) in contact with rod (7), Fig. 9.
5. Measure the choke plate opening at the bottom of the plate. Use a drill bit corresponding to the correct choke plate opening specification.
6. Turn set screw (8) inside the vacuum capsule cover to adjust.

Fuel Injection Section

BOSCH D-JETRONIC SYSTEM

1972-74, Fig. 1

This type of fuel injection relies on engine speed and manifold pressure for basic operation. Fuel is drawn out of the fuel tank by an electric rotary fuel pump and passes to the electro-magnetic fuel injectors. Fuel pressure is limited to 28 psi by means of a pressure regulator in the fuel line located in the engine compartment. The length of time the electro-magnetic fuel injectors are kept open is determined by the engine speed and engine load. Engine speed is determined by means of trigger points in the base of the distributor. The engine load is determined by absolute pressure in the intake manifold measured by a pressure sensor mounted on the fenderwell. The absolute manifold pressure is converted to an electrical impulse. This, along with the electrical impulses from the distributor trigger points, is sent to an electronic computer unit which determines the injector operating duration.

During warm up, additional fuel is injected into the intake manifold in the form of a cold start injector, with a slightly longer injector operating duration. A temperature sensor in the cooling system provides electrical impulses to the electronic computer, which in turn operates the cold start injector and increases the injector operating duration. Also, additional air is provided to the intake manifold to insure proper burning of the additional fuel during warm up.

The throttle is equipped with an electric switch which gives signals to the computer unit so that the injector operating duration is slightly longer during acceleration. The throttle switch also signals to the computer to cut off all injection when the throttle is released at engine speeds over 1,700 RPM.

Adjustments

Idle Speed:

Two adjustments are required: setting the idling speed with Air screw (A) and throttle stop screw (B), Fig. 2, and adjusting the CO percentage by adjusting the potentiometer (1) on the computer, Fig. 3.

Idle Speed:
1. Turn in Air screw (A) completely, Fig. 2.
2. Turn the throttle stop screw (B) to obtain an engine speed of 900 RPM.
3. Back out Air screw (A) to obtain a final idling speed of 1000 RPM.

Idle CO Adjustment:
1. Adjust the CO percentage to 2.5%-4% by turning the potentiometer (1), Fig. 3, on the computer unit. The computer is located under the right hand side of the dashboard.
2. Readjust the engine idling speed by

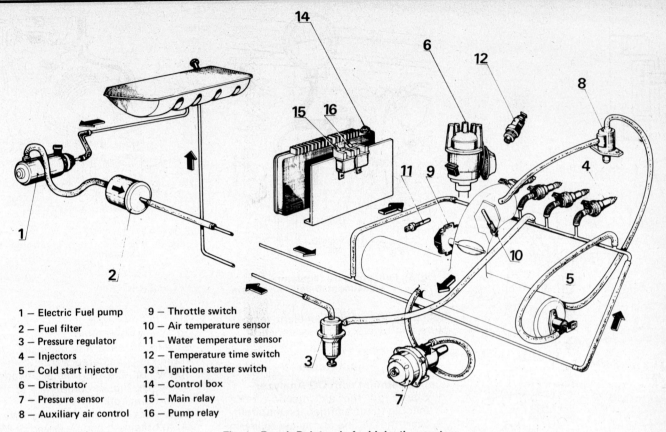

1 — Electric Fuel pump
2 — Fuel filter
3 — Pressure regulator
4 — Injectors
5 — Cold start injector
6 — Distributor
7 — Pressure sensor
8 — Auxiliary air control
9 — Throttle switch
10 — Air temperature sensor
11 — Water temperature sensor
12 — Temperature time switch
13 — Ignition starter switch
14 — Control box
15 — Main relay
16 — Pump relay

Fig. 1   Bosch D-Jetronic fuel injection system

turning the Air screw (A) to obtain an idling speed of 1000 RPM.

If the above adjustments cannot be correctly obtained, check the adjustment of the throttle switch.

Throttle Switch Adjustment

1. Remove plug from throttle switch. Connect an ohmmeter to the two terminals of the switch, Fig. 4.
2. Use a .004″ (0.10mm) and a .008″ (0.20mm) feeler gauge to adjust the switch.
3. Loosen the two securing screws on the switch slightly and turn the switch so that the contacts are closed (0 resistance) when the .004″ feeler is inserted, and the points are open (resistance) when the .008″ feeler is inserted. Tighten the screws.
4. Check the idling speed and CO %.

Fuel Pressure Regulator Adjustment

1. Connect a pressure gauge into the fuel line between the pressure regulator and the injector fuel ring using a 'T' fitting, Fig. 5.
2. Start engine and idle at 1000 RPM.
3. Adjust pressure by loosening the locknut (1) and turning screw (2). Adjust so the pressure is 28.5 to 29.5 psi (2 to 2.05 bars) at idle. Recheck at fast idle, if the pressure exceeds 31.3 psi (2.2 bars) check the fuel return line to the tank for restrictions.

BOSCH L-JETRONIC SYSTEM
1975-77

The L-Jetronic fuel injection relies on the engine speed and on the amount of air flow in the intake manifold for basic operation. Fuel is drawn out of the fuel tank by an electronic fuel pump and passes to the electro-magnetic fuel in-

jectors. Fuel pressure is limited to 35 psi (2.5 bars) by means of a pressure regulator in the fuel line and is located in the engine compartment. The duration of the injector operation is determined by the engine speed and by the air flow in the intake manifold. Engine speed is taken from the distributor in the form of RPM. The amount of air flow is determined by the measuring plate in the flow meter, which is located before the throttle.

During warm up, additional fuel is injected into the intake manifold by a cold

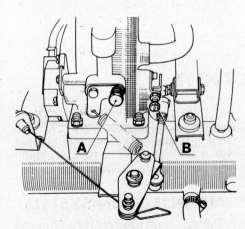

Fig. 2   Idle speed adjustment. D-Jetronic system

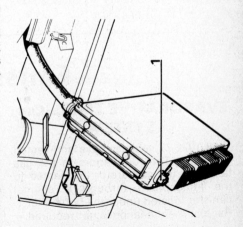

Fig. 3   Idle CO adjustment. D-Jetronic system

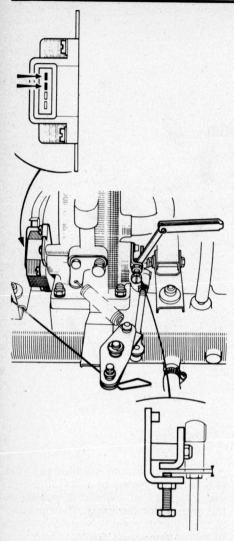

Fig. 4   Throttle switch adjustment.
D-Jetronic system

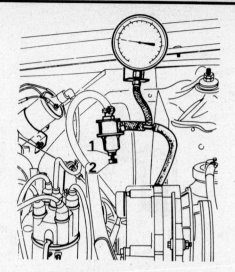

Fig. 5   Fuel pressure regulator
adjustment. D-Jetronic system

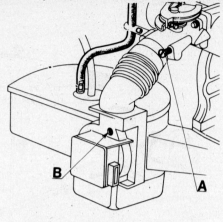

Fig. 6   Idle adjustment. L-Jetronic
system

start injector. The cold start injector is controlled by a thermal time cut out switch. Also, additional air is provided to the intake manifold to insure proper burning of the additional fuel during warm up. The auxiliary air valve is con-trolled by the engine ambient temper-ature and by electrical resistance.

Adjustments

Idle Adjustment with CO Analyzer

1. Clamp off the air injection hose leading to the air injection manifold.
2. Start the engine and allow to warm up. When the cooling fan has turned on once and off once automatically, the engine is considered warm.
3. Turn the throttle plate housing screw (A), Fig. 6, to obtain an en-gine speed of 800 RPM.
4. Adjust the Air Flow Meter bypass screw (B) to obtain a CO percentage of $2 \pm 1\%$.
5. Turn screw (A) to readjust the idle speed.
6. Remove the clamp on the air injec-tion hose. Readjust screw (A) to ob-tain correct idle speed.

Idle Adjustment without CO Analyzer

1. Clamp off the air injection hose leading to the air injection manifold.

2. Start the engine and allow to warm up. When the cooling fan has turned on and off once automatically, the engine is considered warm.
3. Screw in the flowmeter bypass screw (B), Fig. 6, completely to the closed position.
4. Adjust the throttle housing screw (A) to obtain an engine speed of 850 RPM.
5. Unscrew screw (B) to lower the idle speed by 50 RPM.
6. Remove the clamp from the air in-jection hose. Readjust the idle speed by turning screw (A) to obtain 800 to 900 RPM.

Fuel Pressure Regulator Adjustment

1. Connect a pressure gauge into the fuel line between the pressure reg-ulator and the injector fuel ring using a 'T' fitting.
2. Start the engine and allow to idle.
3. Adjust the fuel pressure by turning the lock nut on the fuel pressure regulator. Adjust so that the fuel pressure is 35 psi (2.5 bars).

Emission Control Section

EVAPORATIVE EMISSION SYSTEM

All 1972-77 vehicles have non-vented gas caps. The fuel vapors in the gas tank and the carburetor are vented to the atmosphere through a charcol canister located under the hood, Fig. 1. Regular maintenance is not required.

POSITIVE CRANKCASE VENTILATION (PCV) SYSTEM

Crankcase oil vapors are recirculated from the rocker arm cover to the intake manifold through two lines, Fig. 2. One line leads to the air cleaner side of the carburetor and the other line leads to the intake manifold side of the car-buretor. One line is fitted with flame ar-restor (B). This should be inspected and cleaned every 12,000 miles. The line leading to the intake manifold is fitted with a calibrated orifice (A) and should be cleaned every 12,000 miles.

AIR INJECTION SYSTEM

This system is used on 1973-77 model 12, 15 and 17TL; 1975-77 model 17 F.I.; 1976-77 model 5. The air injection sys-

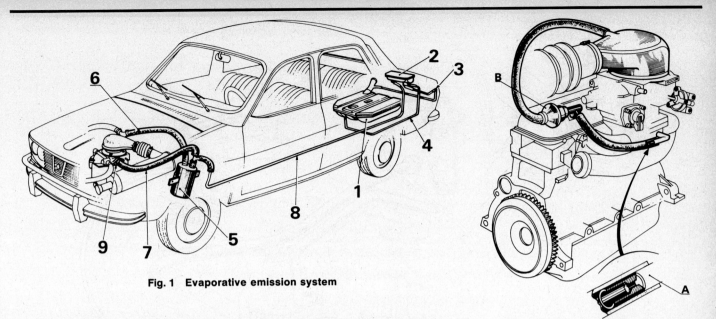

Fig. 1 Evaporative emission system

Fig. 2 Positive crankcase ventilation (PCV) system (Typical)

tem injects air under pressure into the exhaust manifold or into the head at the exhaust valves, Fig. 3. The oxygen in the air along with the heat of the exhaust gasses cause additional burning of the hydrocarbons (HC) and carbon monoxide to provide a cleaner exhaust.

The system includes a rotary air pump (2) with air intake filter (1). The air filter must be replaced every 12,000 miles. The relief valve (3) vents the injected air

to the atmosphere if air pressure exceeds 4.7 psi. The deceleration valve (4) opens and injects additional air into the intake manifold during deceleration to prevent backfire. The one way valve (5) prevents exhaust gas from entering the air injection system. To check for proper operation, remove the valve and blow air through the valve by mouth in the normal air flow direction. It should be free. Blow air through in the opposite direction. No air should go through.

EXHAUST GAS RECIRCULATION (EGR) SYSTEM

This system, Fig. 4, is used on 1974-76 model 12, 15 and 17TL with automatic transmission and all 1977 models.

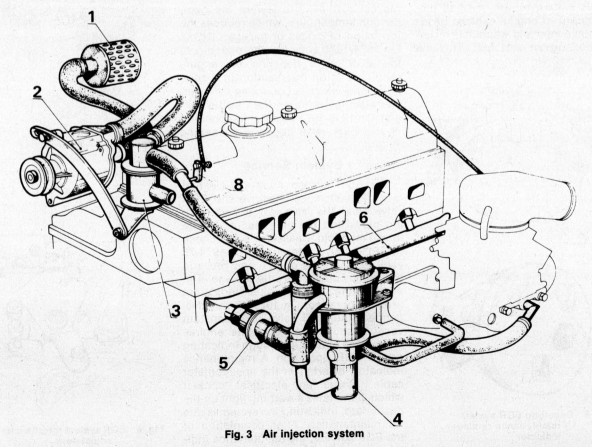

Fig. 3 Air injection system

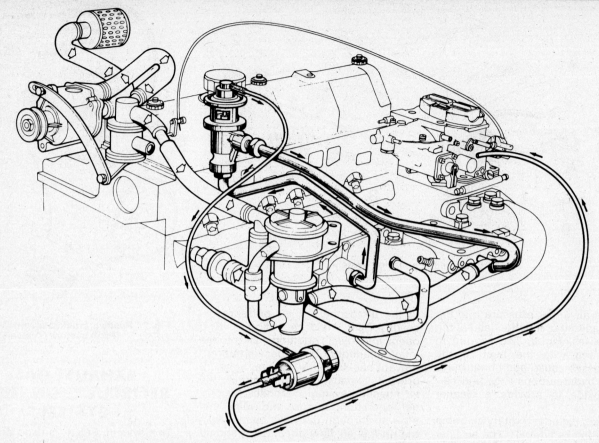

Fig. 4 Exhaust gas recirculation (EGR) system

The EGR system returns a small metered amount of engine exhaust gases to the intake manifold where it is mixed with incoming air and fuel. This air/fuel/exhaust mixture lowers the combustion temperature, which reduces the formation of oxides of nitrogen (NOx). On 1974-1975 vehicles, the opening of the EGR valve depends on engine vacuum and on the position of a solenoid valve which is controlled by a cam and electric switch on the throttle linkage. On 1976-1977 vehicles the opening of the EGR valve depends on engine vacuum.

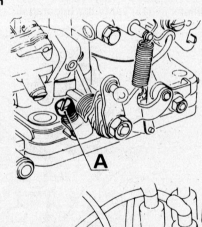

System Service

The EGR system must be cleaned every 25,000 miles. Remove the EGR valve, clean the valve seat, the connecting pipes and the pipe leading to the intake manifold. Reassemble and check the EGR valve operation. On 1974-75 vehicles, start the engine and press in the switch on the throttle linkage. The engine idle should falter indicating proper operation. On 1976-77 vehicles, connect the EGR valve to a constant vacuum source and start the engine. The engine should idle rough indicating proper EGR operation. A maintenance indicator, inserted in the speedometer cable, closes an electrical contact which illuminates a warning light on the dashboard, indicating the system is due for maintenance. After completion of the EGR service, the maintenance indi-

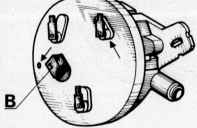

Fig. 5 Resetting EGR system maintenance reminder indicator

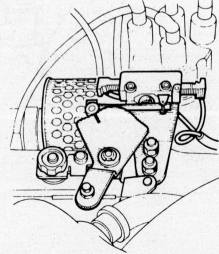

Fig. 6 EGR system throttle micro switch adjustment

cator can be reset as follows:

1. Remove the cover (C) on the maintenance indicator, Fig. 5.
2. Turn the knob (B) ¼ turn in the direction of the arrow towards mark 0. This will turn off the EGR warning light and restart the indicator for a new maintenance cycle.

EGR Throttle Micro Switch Adjustment

1. Place a .116″ (2.9mm) spacer under the throttle opening screw (A), Fig. 6, (.102″ 2.6mm Calif.).
2. Adjust the switch so the switch roller is opposite the mark on the cam.

ACCELERATED IDLE SYSTEM

This system is used on 1972 model 12 and 15, and 1976-77 model 5 and 17TL. The accelerated idle system is used during deceleration to increase fuel combustion and to reduce hydrocarbon emissions. The vehicles are equipped with a centrifugal switch which opens a vacuum valve. When the vehicle reaches 23 mph the centrifugal switch activates the vacuum valve which allows vacuum to open the accelerated idle valve on the carburetor. This raises the engine speed to approximately 1500 RPM. Below 16 mph the centrifugal switch cuts off the vacuum valve and the engine returns to idle.

Testing

The accelerated idle system can be checked by road testing the vehicle. The operation of the system can also be checked by jumping the feed wires to the centrifugal switch and observing the system.

CATALYTIC CONVERTER
1975 All & 1976-77 California Models

These vehicles are equipped with a catalytic converter in the exhaust system. The catalytic converter reduces Carbon Monoxide and Hydrocarbon emissions by converting them to CO_2 and water. The air injection system provides additional oxygen to the exhaust which helps the catalytic converter heat up to a working temperature. These vehicles require unleaded fuel to protect the catalytic converter.

Clutch & Transmission Section

CLUTCH PEDAL, ADJUST

1. Loosen lock nut (1), Fig. 1, then turn adjusting nut (2) in or out to obtain a clearance of ⅛″ to ⁵/₃₂″ (3mm to 4mm) for Renault 5 models and ⁵/₆₄″ to ⅛″ (2mm to 3mm) for Renault 12, 15 and 17 models at the end of lever.
2. After adjustment is made, tighten locknut and recheck clearance.

CLUTCH REPLACEMENT

1. Remove transaxle.
2. Loosen bolts securing pressure plate one turn at a time to avoid bending pressure plate. Remove bolts, then remove pressure plate and clutch.
3. Install clutch and pressure plate. Use Renault tool No. Emb. 319 for Renault 5 models and tool No. Emb. 257 for Renault 12, 15 and 17 models, or other suitable tooling to center clutch. Tighten pressure plate bolts one turn at a time, skipping every other bolt at first, until all bolts are tightened.
4. Lightly coat area on pressure plate which contacts throwout bearing with white grease.
5. Replace transmission.

MANUAL TRANSMISSION, REPLACE
Renault 5

1. Disconnect battery and remove transaxle ground cable.
2. Disconnect speedometer cable, then remove air cleaner and support bracket.
3. Remove water pump drive belt. If this belt is a notched type belt, discard belt. A new belt is required for reinstallation.
4. Remove camshaft pulley, air pump and mounting bracket. Check for any spacers below air pump bracket and retain these for replacement of bracket.
5. Remove two upper bolts on starter. Use of Renault tool No. Ele. 565 is recommended.
6. Remove clutch housing mounting bolts which are on engine. The use of Renault tool No. Mot. 253 is recommended to remove lower left nut of clutch housing.
7. Remove brake calipers without removing brake hoses. Caution: Do

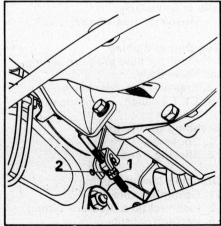

Fig. 1 Adjusting clutch pedal

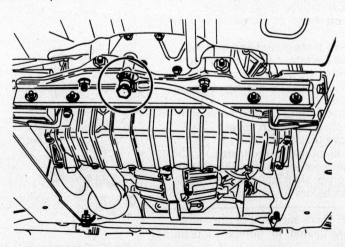

Fig. 2 Pressure gauge fitting location on transmission

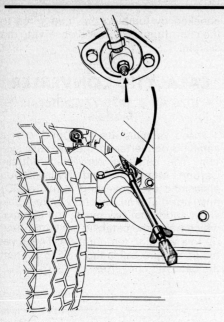

Fig. 3 Oil pressure adjusting screw. Automatic transmission

not allow calipers to hang under their own weight and stretch brake hoses.

8. Disconnect tie rods at stub axle carriers.
9. Disconnect upper ball joint stub axle carriers.
10. Remove axles from transaxle by tilting stub axle carriers down.

CAUTION: Do not damage transaxle side seals when removing drive shafts.

11. Remove two bolts securing shift linkage support. Pull shift linkage rod down and away from transaxle.
12. Disconnect clutch cable at lever. Push against cable sleeve retainer with a screwdriver to free it from supporting tab.
13. Remove tubular crossmember.
14. Support front of transaxle with a jack.
15. Remove front mount and bracket.
16. Remove starter by removing lower mounting bolt. Leave starter sitting next to engine. Do not remove from vehicle.
17. Remove side reinforcement mounting bolts and clutch cover.
18. Remove transmission.
19. Reverse procedure to install.
20. Lightly coat splines on input shaft and drive shaft splines with white grease before installation.

NOTE: Make sure end of drive shaft is fully seated in differential side gears.

Renault 12, 15 & 17

1. Disconnect and remove battery, then remove air cleaner and starter.
2. Disconect clutch cable and remove support bracket.
3. Remove camshaft and water pump pulley.
4. Loosen alternator and tilt it towards center of engine. Tighten it up in this position.
5. Fit Renault retaining tool No. T.Av. 509 or suitable supports between shock absorber lower fixing pins on upper A arm and between lower suspension hinge shafts. This support will keep springs compressed when lower suspension arms are lowered.
6. Drain transaxle.
7. Using a drift, punch out drive shaft roll pins at transaxle end of drive shaft.
8. Remove brake calipers without removing brake hoses.

CAUTION: Do not let brake calipers hang under their own weight, stretching hoses.

9. Remove tie rod ends from stub axle carrier and remove upper ball joints.
10. Tilt stub axle carriers down and pull axles out of transmission. Do not damage axle boots.
11. Disconnect speedometer cable, gear shift linkage and all switch wiring.
12. Remove exhaust pipe and tubular crossmember.
13. Support rear of transaxle with a jack and remove transaxle rear crossmember.
14. Lower jack and tilt engine transaxle assembly toward rear.
15. Remove clutch cover.
16. Remove bolts securing transaxle and remove transaxle from under vehicle. Do not damage clutch as-

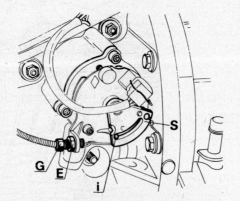

Fig. 5 Governor cable sleeve adjustment

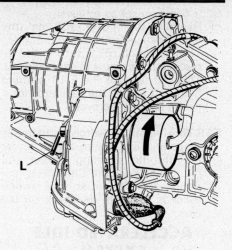

Fig. 4 Electronic computer unit replacement

sembly during removal operation.
17. Reverse procedure to install.
18. Lightly coat transaxle input shaft splines with white grease before installation.

AUTOMATIC TRANSMISSION TROUBLE SHOOTING

Renault 12, 15 & 17TL

Creep In Neutral
1. Electric computer setting.
2. E1 clutch.

Creep In Drive (Excessive)
1. Choke on.
2. Sticking throttle.
3. Torque converter.

Slip In Drive or Reverse
1. Low transmission fluid.
2. Incorrect fluid pressure setting.
3. Pressure regulator valve.
4. Torque converter.

Slip In Drive Only
1. Gear train free wheel.

Slip During Shifting
1. Incorrect fluid pressure setting.
2. Valve body.
3. Pressure regulator valve.
4. E1, E2 clutch; F1, F2 brake.

Grabbing On Starting
1. Choke on.
2. Sticking throttle

Grabbing During Shifting
1. Governor cable.
2. Incorrect fluid pressure setting.
3. Vacuum capsule.
4. Valve body.
5. Pressure regulator valve.

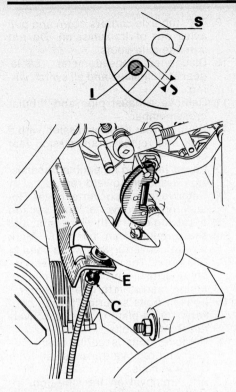

Fig. 6 Governor cable adjustment

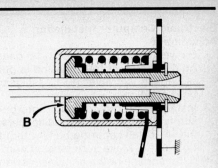

Fig. 7 Kickdown switch cable adjustment

Incorrect Shift Timing During Upshift or Downshift
1. Governor control cable.
2. Transmission electrical wiring or terminals.
3. Governor.
4. Electronic computer.
5. Solenoid ball valves.
6. Valve body.

Incorrect Shift Timing During "Kickdown"
1. Accelerator control.
2. Kickdown switch adjustment.
3. Transmission electric wiring and terminals.
4. Electronic computer.
5. Kickdown switch.

Rough Idle
1. Accelerator control.
2. Vacuum capsule.

No Drive In Drive, 1st Gear "Hold", Reverse
1. Shift control.
2. Oil pump, oil pump drive shaft.
3. Turbine shaft.
4. Axle.
5. Torque convertor drive plate.

No Drive In Drive, 1st Gear "Hold"
1. E1 clutch

No Drive In Drive or Reverse
1. Valve body.
2. E2 clutch.

No Drive In 1st Gear "Hold" or Reverse
1. Valve body.
2. F1 brake.

No 1st Gear Automatic
1. Transmission electric wiring and terminals.
2. Electronic computer.
3. Solenoid ball valves.
4. Gear train free wheel.

No 2nd Gear Automatic
1. Transmission electric wiring and terminals.
2. Electronic computer.
3. Solenoid ball valves.
4. Valve body.
5. F2 brake.

No Drive In Drive Position
1. Transmission electric wiring and terminals.
2. Governor.
3. Electronic computer.
4. Solenoid ball valves.
5. Valve body.

No 2nd Gear "Hold"
1. Electronic computer.

No 1st Gear "Hold"
1. Electronic computer.

No 1st Gear Automatic
1. Transmission electric wiring and terminals.
2. Electronic computer.
3. Solenoid ball valves.
4. Gear train free wheel.

No 2nd Gear Automatic
1. Transmission electric wiring and terminals.
2. Electronic computer.
3. Solenoid ball valves.
4. Valve body.
5. F2 brake.

No 3rd Gear (Drive)
1. Transmission electric wiring and terminals.
2. Governor.
3. Electronic computer.
4. Solenoid ball valves.
5. Valve body.

No 2nd Gear "Hold"
1. Electronic computer.

No 1st Gear "Hold"
1. Electronic computer.

Selector Lever Faulty
1. Electronic computer.
2. Linkage adjustment.
3. Selector lever defective.

Park Position Not Working
1. Linkage adjustment.
2. Parking pawl mechanism.

Starter Not Working
1. Transmission electric wiring and terminals.
2. Linkage adjustment.
3. Starter switch.
4. Selective lever.

AUTOMATIC TRANSMISSION CHECKS & ADJUSTMENTS
Renault 12, 15 & 17TL

Oil Pressure Check & Adjustment
The transmission oil pressure is checked with a pressure gauge graduated from 0 to 215 psi or Renault gauge No. B. Vi. 466.
1. Connect pressure gauge to pressure gauge fitting on lower flat cover plate of transmission, Fig. 2.
2. Engine and transmission should be at normal operating temperature, transmission fluid should be at 176°F (80°C).
3. Apply handbrake and place selector lever in park. Start engine and idle at 800 RPM.
4. The oil pressure should be 58 psi@176°F.
5. Adjust oil pressure by loosening locknut on vacuum capsule and turning adjustment screw, Fig. 3. One complete turn of adjustment screw raises or lowers pressure 1½ psi.

Vacuum Capsule Check
1. Remove vacuum hose connected from vacuum capsule to intake manifold at manifold end.
2. Connect hose to a vacuum gauge with a vacuum source. Create a vacuum of about 15 in. Hg. on capsule.
3. The needle should remain steady. If needle falls replace capsule.
4. When replacing capsule, coat gasket with suitable gasket cement.
5. Check and adjust oil pressure.

Electronic Computer Installation & Adjustment

1. Set vehicle selector lever in 1st gear hold position. If transmission is out of vehicle, set lever (L) to 1st gear hold position.
2. Install electronic computer into position with two new plastic spacers, Fig. 4. Install securing bolts without tightening. Make sure pins on computer engage notch on transmission linkage.
3. Hold lever (L) and turn computer in direction of arrow until all clearance is taken up. Do not force computer any further. Tighten securing bolts, do not squash plastic spacers.
4. Reconnect all electric wiring. Make sure terminals are clean and dry.
5. Road test vehicle, if transmission does not shift properly, recheck computer adjustment.

Governor Cable Adjustment

1. Check and adjust accelerator cable kickdown switch.
2. Adjust sleeve (G) (Governor end) to middle position, Fig. 5.
3. Press accelerator pedal or linkage completely down. Remove all cable free play by adjusting sleeve (C) (Carburetor end), Fig. 6.
4. Keep accelerator completely down and check cable clearance (J) on governor pivot (S), Fig. 6. Turn the governor pivot (S) in direction of cable to obtain clearance.
5. Tighten locknuts on adjustment screws.

Accelerator Cable Kickdown Switch Adjustment

1. Press accelerator pedal completely to floor.
2. Adjust adjustment sleeve on valve cover to obtain 1/8″ to 5/32″ (3 to 4mm) cable compression (B), Fig. 7, at kickdown switch.

AUTOMATIC TRANSMISSION, REPLACE
Renault 12, 15 & 17TL

1. Disconnect and remove battery, then remove air cleaner and starter.
2. Remove camshaft and water pump pulley.
3. Loosen alternator and tilt it towards center of engine. Tighten it up in this position.
4. Fit Renault retaining tool No. T. Av. 509 or suitable supports between shock absorber lower retaining pins on upper A arm and between lower suspension hinge shafts. This support will keep springs compressed when lower suspension arms are lowered.
5. Drain transmission.
6. Using a drift, punch out drive shaft roll pins at transmission end of drive shaft.
7. Remove brake calipers without removing brake hoses.

CAUTION: Do not let brake calipers hang under their own weight stretching hoses.

8. Remove tie rod ends from stub axle carriers and remove upper ball joints.
9. Tilt stub axle carriers down and pull axles out of transmission. Do not damage axle boots.
10. Disconnect speedometer cable, gear shift linkage and all switch wiring.
11. Remove exhaust pipe and tubular crossmember.
12. Support rear of transmission with a jack and remove transmission rear crossmember.
13. Lower jack and tilt engine transmission assembly toward rear.
14. Remove torque converter cover. Rotate torque converter until section of driving plate with white paint and sharp edges can be seen. Mark torque convertor with white paint at this point. This will aid in reassembly and insure proper alignment of timing marks on torque converter.
15. Loosen bolts securing torque converter drive plate to torque converter. Remove bolts.
16. Remove bolts securing transmission and remove transmission from under vehicle.
17. After removal on transmission, install a retaining plate to torque converter.
18. Reverse procedure to install.
19. Be sure to line up paint marks on torque converter and drive plate.
20. If a new torque converter is installed without paint marks, line up timing marks on converter with section of driving plate with sharp edges.
21. Tighten converter securing bolts in rotation to insure centering of converter. Torque bolts to 20 to 25 ft. lbs.

Rear Suspension & Brake Section

REAR TORSION BAR, REPLACE
Renault 5

1. Fabricate torsion bar removal tool, Fig. 1.
2. Raise vehicle and place on jack stands. Support on frame members.
3. Loosen adjusting cam lock nut and move cam to zero position, Fig. 2.
4. Remove shock absorber. Assemble torsion bar removal tool and put in place of the shock absorber, Fig. 3.
5. Tighten nut A, Fig. 3, tool until suspension travel is under tension. On early models, until adjusting lever lifts off cam. Length of tool "X," Fig. 4, should be approximately X=23¼″ for right side and 23⅝″ for left side.
6. Using a drift and a hammer force torsion bar outside of body. Once broken loose it will slide out easily.
7. Lubricate splines with grease and reinstall in reverse order. The torsion bar removal tool must be set to above dimensions prior to torsion bar installation. Move adjusting lever until it touches cam prior to torsion bar installation. Wiggle lower suspension arm during installation to aid in alignment of splines.

REAR SPRING, REPLACE
Renault 12, 15 & 17

Follow the same procedure outlined for the rear Shock Absorber, Replace.

SHOCK ABSORBER, REPLACE
Renault 5

1. Remove shock absorber upper nuts from inside of trunk.
2. Raise vehicle and remove lower nuts.
3. Remove shock absorber.
4. Reverse procedure to install. Attach upper mount first.
5. Lower vehicle and tighten bolts when vehicle is in normal ground position.

Renault 12, 15 & 17

1. Raise vehicle and place on jack stands. Position jack stands on a frame member.

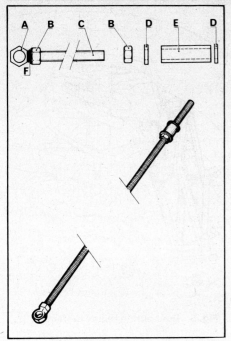

Fig. 1   Rear torsion bar removal tool. Renault 5

2. Remove shock absorber lower mounting nut and push shock absorber up.
3. Using vehicle jack, place jack between frame and rear axle and expand jack to force rear axle down. Remove rear spring, Fig. 5.
4. Remove nuts on the top of shock absorber from inside trunk. Remove shock absorber.

5. Reverse procedure to install. Make sure rubber and steel washers are installed in correct order.
6. Make sure spring is installed with correct side up (flat end to the top) and that lower end is placed against stop A, Fig. 6.

REAR WHEEL BEARING, ADJUST

1. Remove grease cover with a suitable tool.
2. Remove cotter pin, lock nut plate and loosen axle nut.
3. Torque axle nut to 25 ft. lbs. (3 N-m). Loosen axle nut ¼ turn. Assemble a dial indicator on drum to measure end play, Fig. 7. Adjust axle nut to obtain .001″ to .002″ (0.01 to 0.05mm) end play for model 5 and .001″ to .004″ (0.01 to 0.08mm) end play for models 12, 15 and 17.
4. Install lock nut plate and cotter pin. Place a small amount of grease in grease cup and install into position.

REAR WHEEL BEARING, REPLACE

1. Remove grease cover with a suitable tool.
2. Remove cotter pin, lock nut plate, axle nut and washer. Remove outer wheel bearing.
3. Pull brake drum or disc off stub

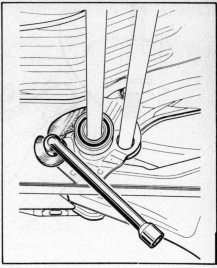

Fig. 2   Rear torsion bar cam locking nut. Renault 5

axle. On vehicles with self-adjusting rear brakes, release brake adjustment by pushing a pin punch through access hole in backing plate.
4. Remove inner bearing with a suitable puller.
5. Place locating sleeve over stub axle. Assemble two split half-shells into position over bearing. The half-shells can be placed over bearing two ways so that bearing only can be pulled or so bearing and thrust washer can be pulled. Place sleeve over half-shells.
6. Pull off bearing assembly with suitable puller.
7. Remove bearing inner seal.
8. Clean bearings and repack with suitable wheel bearing grease.
9. Reinstall bearing seal, thrust washer and inner bearing. Reinstall drum or disc outer bearing, thrust washer and stub axle nut.
10. Tighten axle nut to 25 ft. lbs. (3 N-m). Loosen axle nut ¼ turn. Assemble a dial indicator on brake drum to measure end play. Adjust axle nut to obtain .001″ to .002″ (0.01 to 0.05mm) end play on model 5 and .001″ to .004″ (0.01 to 0.08mm) on models 12, 15 and 17.
11. Install lock nut plate and cotter pin. Place a small amount of grease in grease cup and install into position.

REAR DRUM BRAKE, ADJUST

1. Adjust brakes using a suitable open end wrench.
2. Adjust leading shoe first by turning adjustment lug in an arc towards floor to tighten shoe and upwards to retract shoe.

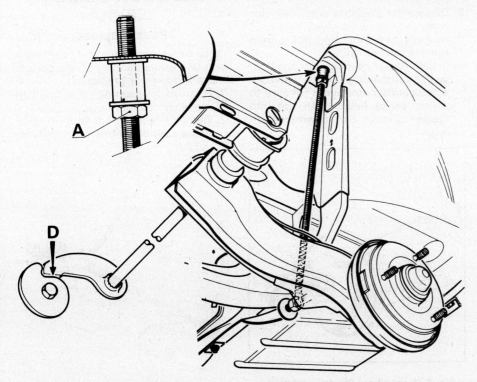

Fig. 3   Install rear torsion bar removal tool. Renault 5

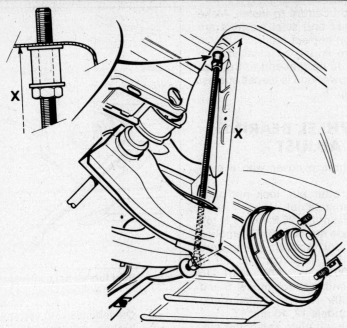

Fig. 4 Adjusting rear torsion bar removal tool. Renault

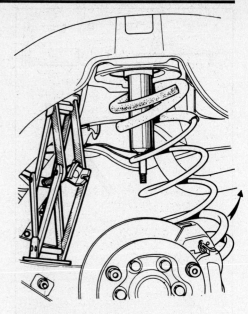

Fig. 5 Rear spring removal. Renault 12, 15 & 17

3. Rotate wheel while adjusting.
4. Adjust secondary shoe in the same manner.

NOTE: Vehicles with self adjusting rear brakes, the parking brake lever must have 12 to 14 notches of travel or rear brakes will not self-adjust.

PARKING BRAKE, ADJUST

1. Adjust rear brakes.
2. Loosen lock nut 2 on parking brake adjustment rod. Tighten or loosen nut (1) to obtain a travel of 12 to 14 notches of travel on parking brake lever, Fig. 8.
3. Tighten lock nut (2) and recheck parking brake lever travel.

NOTE: In vehicles with self adjusting

rear brakes, parking brake lever must have 12 to 14 notches of travel or rear brakes will not self-adjust.

MASTER CYLINDER, REPLACE

1. Drain brake fluid reservoir.
2. Disconnect metal brake lines. Do not loosen fittings in master cylinder.
3. Disconnect pressure drop indicator wire.
4. Remove two mounting bolts, then remove master cylinder.
5. Install master cylinder into position, seal the mounting surface with suitable sealing compound. Be sure to center brake pedal push rod into master cylinder. Secure with mounting bolts.

6. Reconnect metal brake lines. Reconnect pressure drop indicator wire.
7. Adjust rear brakes.
8. Adjust brake pedal push rod so that brake pedal has $^{13}/_{64}$" (5mm) of travel.
9. Bleed brake lines. On Renault 5, bleed rear brake pressure distribution valve by pass circuit.
10. Recheck brake pedal travel.

FRONT DISC BRAKE SERVICE
Pads, Replace

Disc brake pads must be changed in complete axle sets. Do not mix pads of different makes or grades.
1. Remove four spring clips, then remove two caliper keys.
2. Remove caliper from support plate. Place caliper on one of suspension

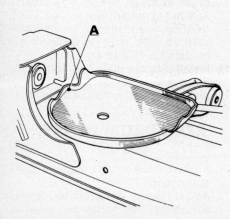

Fig. 6 Lower spring stop. Renault 12, 15 & 17

Fig. 7 Rear wheel bearing end play check

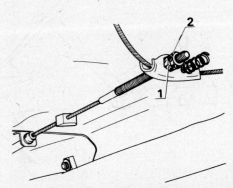

Fig. 8 Parking brake adjustment

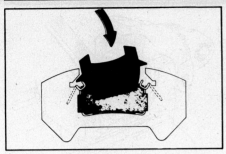

Fig. 9   Caliper installation. Front disc brake

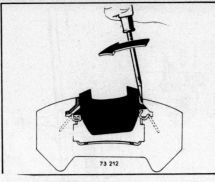

73 212

Fig. 10   Installing caliper key. Front disc brake

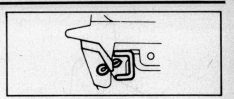

Fig. 11   Caliper spring clip. Front disc brake

components. Do not let it hang and stretch brake hose.

3. Remove pads and anti-rattle springs on caliper holder.

4. Pull dust cover back and inspect caliper for leaking brake fluid. If necessary, rebuild caliper.

5. Push piston back into caliper using a large "C" clamp or suitable tool.

6. Install two new anti-rattle springs on each backing plate, with shortest inside.

7. Install new brake pads. Place into position so that metal button on pad backing plate is at top when pad is in position.

8. Place caliper into position so that both wire springs are compressed, Fig. 9.

9. Install one key at bottom of caliper. Install second key at the top. If necessary, pry caliper down slightly so key can be slipped in, Fig. 10.

10. Install new spring clips to retain keys.

11. When installed properly, large wire spring should be behind caliper, and keys between caliper and caliper support, Fig. 11.

12. Press brake pedal several times to seat pistons against pads.

Caliper Service

1. Remove caliper and disconnect brake hose, then remove dust cover.

2. Using compressed air, push piston out of caliper. Place a block of wood or a rag between piston and caliper so that piston is not damaged when pushed out. Be careful; do not place any fingers between piston and caliper.

3. Remove piston seal with a thin bladed tool with round edges, Fig. 12.

4. Clean caliper and piston using a commercial grade disc brake cleaner. Inspect piston and caliper bore for scratches or scores. Replace if necessary.

5. Lubricate a new piston seal with clean brake fluid. Place into groove in caliper. Press firmly into place.

6. Lubricate piston with clean brake fluid. Press piston into caliper. Do not pinch or roll over piston seal.

7. Replace the dust cover.

8. Fill the caliper with brake fluid through the hole for the brake hose.

9. Install the brake hose with a new copper washer.

10. Reinstall the caliper.

11. Bleed the caliper after installation.

Caliper Cylinder & Piston, Replace

Some Renault vehicles are equipped with two piece calipers, Fig. 13. The cylinder with piston can be replaced separately from caliper bracket.

Dissassemble

1. Fabricate a wedge as shown in Fig. 14.

Wedge Dimensions

	Renault 5	Renault 12, 15 & 17
A	$2^1/_{32}$" (51.5mm)	$1^{11}/_{16}$" (43mm)
B	$5/_{16}$" (8mm)	$5/_{16}$" (8mm)
C	$2^7/_{32}$" (56mm)	$1^{15}/_{16}$" (49mm)
D	$1^3/_8$" (35mm)	$2^3/_4$" (35mm)

2. Spread legs of cast iron bracket a small amount using the wedge, Fig. 15.

3. Using a pin punch, press cylinder stop peg (A) and remove cylinder, Fig. 16. Do not remove wedge.

4. Install new cylinder, press in peg and spring assembly and slide into position. Be sure to locate peg into hole in bracket. Remove wedge.

5. Install caliper assembly.

REAR DISC BRAKE SERVICE

1972-74 Renault

Pads, Replace

Disc brake pads must be changed in complete axle sets. Do not mix pads of different makes or grades.

1. Disconnect parking brake cable from rear caliper.

2. Remove caliper and pads as described under Front Disc Brake Pads, Replace.

3. Install new pads as per front pads installation. Be sure to install new anti-rattle springs.

4. Push piston back by screwing in with a suitable tool until piston turns

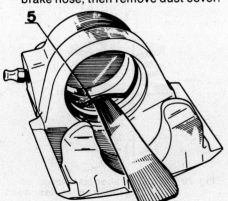

5

Fig. 12   Removing piston seal.

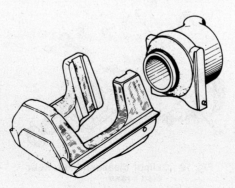

Fig. 13   Two piece caliper assembly. Front disc brake

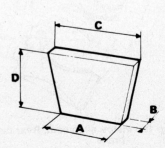

C

D

B

A

Fig. 14   Wedge dimensions. Front disc brake

1-843

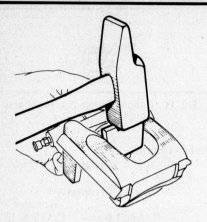

Fig. 15 Spreading cast iron bracket. Front disc brake

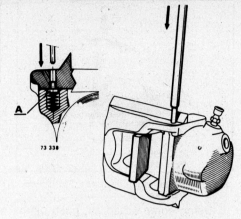

Fig. 16 Removing cylinder stop peg. Front disc brake

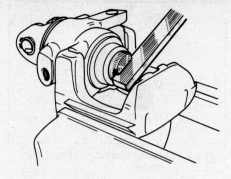

Fig. 17 Retracting piston. Rear disc brake

without moving in any further, Fig. 17.

5. Align piston so line (R) on piston face is on same side as bleed screw (P), Fig. 18.

6. Install caliper and reconnect parking brake cable. Check parking brake adjustment.

Caliper Service

1. Remove caliper and disconnect brake hose.

2. Place caliper in a vice equipped with soft jaws, then remove dust cover.

3. Remove piston by turning slot in piston face counter clockwise with a suitable tool, Fig. 17. When it turns freely, push piston fully out using compressed air. Place a rag or block of wood between piston and caliper so that piston is not damaged when pushed out. Be careful; do not place

any fingers between piston and caliper.

4. Remove piston seal with a thin bladed tool with round edges, Fig. 12.

5. Clean inside of caliper and piston with a commercial grade disc brake cleaner. Inspect piston and caliper bore for scratches or scores. Replace if necessary.

6. Remove dust cover (3) from parking brake side of caliper, Fig. 19. Remove 'C' clip (4).

7. Compress spring washers (5) with a suitable tool and release parking brake shaft (6).

8. Remove parking brake shaft (6), plunger (7) and spring (8). Remove adjusting screw (9), then washer (10) and spring washers (5).

9. Remove 'O' ring (11) on adjusting screw with a thin bladed tool with round edges.

10. Clean all parts with a commercial grade disc brake cleaner.

11. Lubricate a new adjusting screw 'O'

ring with brake fluid and install into position.

12. Reverse procedure to assemble. Assemble spring washers so parking brake remains in normal "OFF" position, Fig. 20.

13. Lubricate a new piston seal with clean brake fluid. Place into groove in caliper and press firmly into position.

14. Lubricate piston with clean brake fluid. Press piston into caliper. Do not pinch or roll over piston seal.

15. Push piston in and finish screwing in with a suitable tool until piston turns without entering any further.

16. Align piston so line (R) on piston face is on same side as bleed screw (P), Fig. 18.

17. Replace piston dust cover. Lubricate parking brake mechanism with white grease and replace mechanism dust cover.

18. Fill caliper with brake fluid through hole for brake hose.

19. Install brake hose with a new copper washer.

20. Reinstall caliper and bleed the air out of caliper.

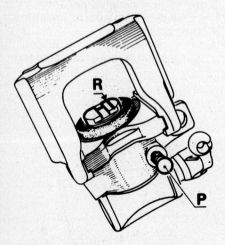

Fig. 18 Piston alignment. Rear disc brake

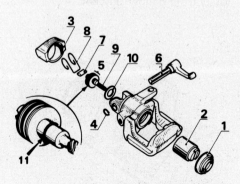

Fig. 19 Caliper disassembled. Rear disc brake

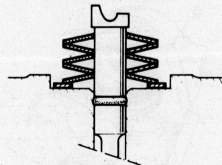

Fig. 20 Spring washer installation on parking brake cable. Rear disc brake

Front Suspension & Steering Section

WHEEL ALIGNMENT

Caster Adjustment

Renault 5

Caster is adjusted by adding shims (1) to the lower suspension arm, Fig. 1.
1. Loosen the two lower suspension arm bushing mounting bolts.
2. Add a shim to increase the caster and remove to decrease.
3. One shim changes the caster approximately 1°. Do not use more than two adjusting shims on each side of the vehicle.

Renault 12, 15 & 17

Caster is adjusted by changing the length of the tie rod bracing the upper suspension arm.
1. Loosen the lock nuts (9) and (10) on the tie rod, Fig. 2.
2. Loosen nut (8) and tighten nut (7) to reduce the caster angle.
3. Loosen nut (7) and tighten nut (8) to increase the caster angle.
4. Tighten the adjustment nuts to 40 ft. lbs. and torque the lock nuts to 50 ft. lbs. while holding the adjustment nuts.

Camber Adjustment

Camber is not adjustable. If the camber exceeds specifications, one or more of the suspension components is worn or bent.

Toe-Out Adjustment

The vehicle toe is adjusted to toe-out due to the tendency of the wheels to toe-in during acceleration and normal driving with the front wheel drive.
1. Disconnect the tie rod at the rack end.
2. Loosen lock nut (E), Fig. 3.
3. Turn the end fitting (C) in or out to change the toe. Toe-out is obtained by screwing the fitting in. Each half turn changes the toe 1/16 in. (1.5mm).

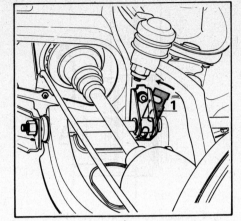

Fig. 1   Caster adjustment. Renault 5

UPPER CONTROL ARM, REPLACE

Renault 5

1. Remove the radiator expansion bottle on the right side and the ignition coil on the left side of the vehicle.
2. Raise vehicle and let wheels hang.
3. Disconnect upper ball joint.
4. Screw on and tighten a lock nut (1) on the front end of the suspension arm hinge pin, Fig. 4.
5. Hold the lock nut assembly and remove the nut on the other end of the suspension arm hinge pin.
6. Remove the lock nut hinge pin assembly by pulling out the front of the vehicle.
7. Remove the suspension arm.
8. Reverse procedure to install. Lubricate the hinge pin with suitable grease.

9. Screw the front hinge pin nut onto the end of the shaft's threads. After installation, install the nut on the end of the hinge pin which is located in the engine compartment.
10. Lower the vehicle so that the wheels are in normal position on the ground.
11. Tighten the hinge pin nuts.

Renault 12, 15 & 17

1. Disconnect caster adjustment tie rod and remove the anti-sway bar linkage.
2. Disconnect the tie rod ball joint and the upper ball joint. Support the lower arm.
3. Loosen the lock nut on the bottom of the shock absorber. Remove the suspension arm hinge pin.
4. Lower the lower suspension slightly to free the top ball joint from the stub axle carrier. Avoid pulling the drive shaft out of the transmission.
5. Remove the upper arm by unscrewing from the shock absorber.
6. Reverse procedure to install.
7. Lubricate the hinge pin before installation.
8. Install all nuts and bolts without tightening.
9. Lower the vehicle and tighten all nuts and bolts with the wheels in normal position on the ground.

UPPER CONTROL ARM BUSHING, REPLACE

Renault 5

The bushings must be replaced one at a time so that they are properly spaced

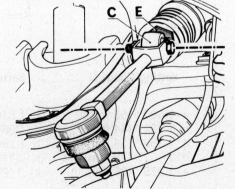

Fig. 3   Toe-out adjustment

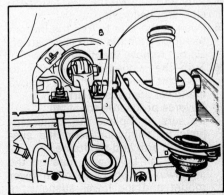

Fig. 4   Upper control arm attachment. Renault 5

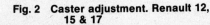

Fig. 2   Caster adjustment. Renault 12, 15 & 17

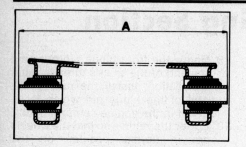

Fig. 5 Upper control arm bushing installation. Renault 5

in relation to the center line of the suspension arm.

1. Press out one of the worn bushings. Use a tube which has an outside diameter of 1 in., and another which has an inside diameter of 1¼ in. to aid in bushing removal.
2. Install one new bushing. Keep dimension (A), Fig. 5, 6¹¹/₁₆ in. (170.4mm).
3. Remove and install the second bushing in the same procedure as the first.

Renault 12, 15 & 17

1. Press out the old bushing using a tube with a diameter of 1¹/₃₂ in. (26mm).
2. Lubricate and press in the new bushing, Fig. 6. Center in the arm with dimension A = ¹⁵/₆₄ in. (6mm).

LOWER CONTROL ARM, REPLACE

Renault 5

1. Raise the vehicle and remove the torsion bar.
2. Remove the stub axle nut. Break loose the stub axle shaft end from the wheel hub.
3. Remove the anti-sway bar from the side of the vehicle being worked on. Loosen and remove the shock absorber lower mounting pin.
4. Remove the steering tie rod ball joint and remove the lower suspension arm ball joint.
5. Push in the axle to free the bottom ball joint from the stub axle carrier. Do not remove the drive shaft.
6. Turn the suspension assembly to the right or to the left and remove the lower suspension arm.
7. Reverse procedure to install.
8. Be sure to replace the caster adjustment shims between the suspension arm and the frame.
9. Tighten all bolts and nuts on the anti-sway bar, shock absorber lower mount and the lower suspension, with the front wheel in the normal "Road" position.
10. Check the front axle alignment.

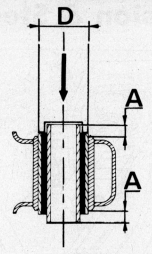

Fig. 6 Upper control arm bushing installation. Renault 12, 15 & 17

Renault 12, 15 & 17

1. Raise vehicle and let wheels hang.
2. Disconnect the lower ball joint. Remove the lower suspension arm

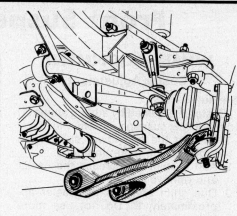

Fig. 7 Lower control arm replacement. Renault 12, 15 & 17

hinge pin by pulling out towards the front of the vehicle.

3. Remove the lower suspension arm, Fig. 7.
4. Install the lower ball joint and secure with the ball joint nut.
5. Raise the lower suspension with a

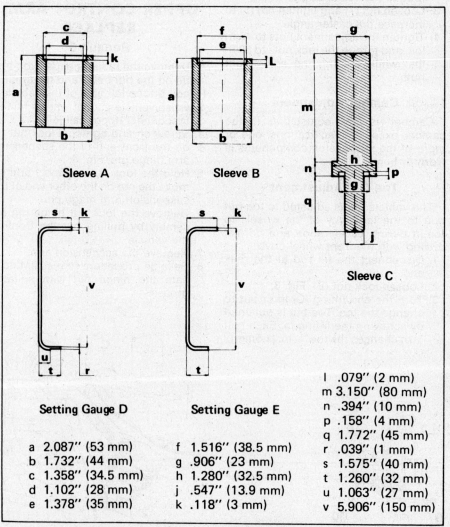

Fig. 8 Lower control arm bushing replacement tools. Renault 5

Sleeve A

Sleeve B

Sleeve C

Setting Gauge D

Setting Gauge E

Setting Gauge D

a 2.087″ (53 mm)
b 1.732″ (44 mm)
c 1.358″ (34.5 mm)
d 1.102″ (28 mm)
e 1.378″ (35 mm)

Setting Gauge E

f 1.516″ (38.5 mm)
g .906″ (23 mm)
h 1.280″ (32.5 mm)
j .547″ (13.9 mm)
k .118″ (3 mm)

l .079″ (2 mm)
m 3.150″ (80 mm)
n .394″ (10 mm)
p .158″ (4 mm)
q 1.772″ (45 mm)
r .039″ (1 mm)
s 1.575″ (40 mm)
t 1.260″ (32 mm)
u 1.063″ (27 mm)
v 5.906″ (150 mm)

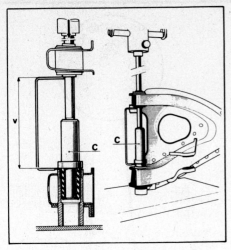

Fig. 9 Lower control arm rear bushing installation. Renault 5

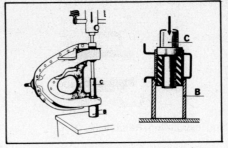

Fig. 10 Removing lower control arm front bushing. Renault 5

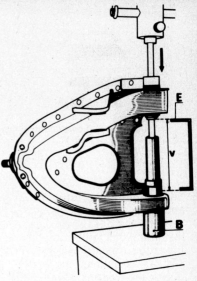

Fig. 11 Installing lower control arm front bushing. Renault 5

jack placed under the lower ball joint.

6. Lubricate the hinge pin and reassemble the lower arm.
7. Lower the vehicle and tighten the nuts and bolts with the wheels in the normal road position.

LOWER CONTROL ARM BUSHING, REPLACE

Renault 5

The bushings must be replaced one at a time so that they are properly spaced in relation to the center line of the suspension arm.

All parts removed during this operation must be replaced with new parts.

1. Fabricate the tools shown in Fig. 8.
2. Using a press and a .512″ (13mm) shaft push the hinge pin tube out of the lower suspension arm. The suspension arm must not receive any press load.
3. Using a splined portion of the torsion bar and sleeve (A) press out toe rear bushing.
4. Lubricate and install the new rear bushing. Press in until the bottom face on the flange on (C), Fig. 9, and the face on the front bushing inner sleeve are equal to a dimension, "V", of 5.906″ (150mm). Install with

centering mandrel (C) and a thrust rod with a diameter of .512″ (13mm) and a length of 7″ (180mm).
5. Use a centering mandrel (C), sleeve (B) and the thrust rod, to press out the front bushing, Fig. 10. The suspension arm must not receive any press load.
6. Lubricate and install the new front bushing. Press in place, Fig. 11, so that dimension, "V," is equal to 5.906″ (150mm). This dimension is taken between the face on the inner sleeves on both bushings.
7. Lubricate and reinstall the hinge pin tube with its bracket and spacer.
8. Line up the bracket in relation to the edge of the shock absorber mounting pin hole, Fig. 12. Measure and adjust dimension, "X," to 6½″ (165mm).
9. Use sleeve (B) with an old bushing to prevent distortion of the hinge pin tube during installation, Fig. 13.
10. When installed properly, the hinge pin tube should not have any end play.

Renault 12, 15 & 17

The bushings must be replaced one at a time so that they are replaced, properly spaced, in relation to the center line of the suspension arm.

1. Press out one of the worn bushings with a press using a piece of tube 1⁷/₃₂″ (31mm) in diameter.

2. Lubricate and install the new bushing. Install so that dimension, "A," is equal to 5¹⁵/₁₆″ (151mm), Fig. 14.
3. Install the second bushing following the same procedure as the first.

BALL JOINT, REPLACE

Upper

1. On Renault 12, 15 and 17 models, fit Renault spacer T.Av.509 or suitable tool between the lower arm hinge pin and the shock absorber lower mount. This will keep the spring compressed.
2. Raise the vehicle, or place the side being worked on, on jack stands.
3. Remove the ball joint securing nut and disengage the ball joint.
4. Remove the ball joint securing rivets and remove the ball joint.
5. Install the new ball joint into position on the suspension arm. On Renault 5 vehicles, place the shim which is supplied with the kit on top of the suspension arm.

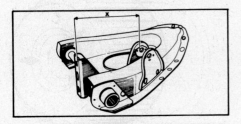

Fig. 12 Positioning hinge pin tube. Renault 5

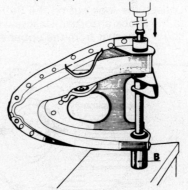

Fig. 13 Installing hinge pin tube. Renault 5

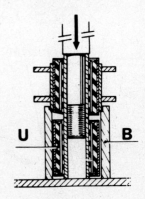

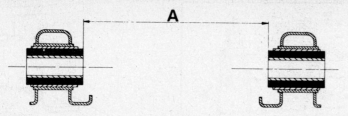

Fig. 14 Lower control arm bushing installation. Renault 12, 15 & 17

6. Secure the ball joint with the nuts and bolts supplied. Place the bolt head on the dust cover side.
7. Install the ball joint into position on the stub axle carrier.
8. Tighten all nuts and bolts.
9. Check the front axle alignment.

Lower

1. Raise the side of the vehicle and place on jack stands. Remove the wheel.
2. Chisel off the ball joint rivet heads on the ball joint side.
3. Remove the ball joint securing nut and the ball joint.

CAUTION: Do not pull on the drive shaft.

4. Install the new ball joint into the stub axle carrier; hold in place with securing nut. Do not fully tighten securing nut.
5. Raise the lower suspension arm and locate the ball joint into position.
6. Install the securing bolts with the heads of the bolts on the dust cover side.
7. Tighten all nuts and bolts.
8. Check the front axle alignment.

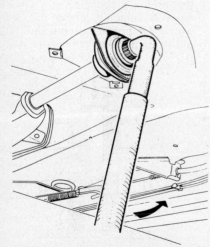

Fig. 16 Installing front torsion bar removal tool. Renault 5 early models

SHOCK ABSORBER, REPLACE

Renault 5

1. Jack up the front of the vehicle and place on jack stands. Position jack stands on the frame members.
2. Jack up the lower control arm to counter the tension of the torsion bar and the anti-sway bar.
3. Remove the nuts on top of the shock absorber. Disconnect the anti-sway bar where it attaches to the shock absorber lower bolt and where it attaches to the frame behind the shock absorber.
4. Remove the nut on the shock absorber bottom pin and remove the pin.
5. Remove the shock absorber.
6. Reverse procedure to install.
7. Lubricate the lower shock absorber pin with suitable grease.
8. Install shock absorber and hand tighten all nuts.
9. Lower the vehicle with the wheels on the ground and tighten all nuts.

Renault 12, 15 & 17

1. Jack up the front of the vehicle and place on jack stands. Position jack stands on the frame members.
2. Compress the spring with a suitable spring compressor.
3. Loosen the shock absorber top mounting.
4. Loosen the lock nut on the bottom of the shock absorber. Unscrew the shock absorber from the upper arm

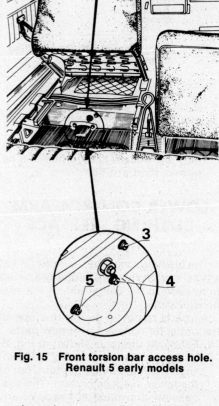

Fig. 15 Front torsion bar access hole. Renault 5 early models

by using a wrench on the flats on the bottom of the shock absorber.
5. Remove the shock absorber and compressed spring.
6. Assemble top bushings in proper order.
7. Install shock absorber and compressed spring assembly. Install the top mount first.

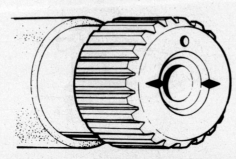

Fig. 17 Left hand torsion bar marking. Renault 5 early models

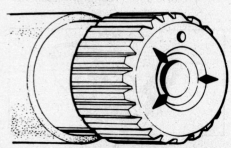

Fig. 18 Right hand torsion bar marking. Renault 5 early models

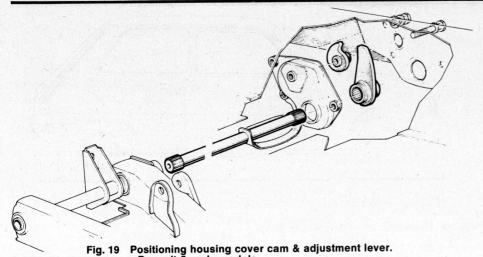

Fig. 19 Positioning housing cover cam & adjustment lever. Renault 5 early models

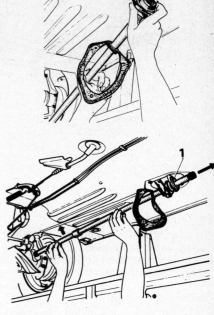

8. Screw the shock absorber into position.
9. Tighten the lock nut while holding the bottom of the shock absorber with a wrench.
10. Remove the spring compressor.

FRONT TORSION BAR, REPLACE

Renault 5

Early Models

1. Slide the seat forward and tilt it forward.
2. Loosen bolt (1) and turn cam (2), Fig. 15, to zero by turning cam toward the outside of the vehicle.
3. Raise the vehicle. Position the side of the vehicle being worked on so that the wheels hang free.
4. Remove the cover over the torsion bar adjustment lever (beneath the vehicle under the seat).
5. Insert the Renault Sus. 545 wrench in the adjustment lever on the end of the torsion bar, Fig. 16. Insert the wrench on a 45° angle towards the other side of the vehicle. Place a 3 or 4 foot extension pipe on the end of the wrench.
6. Hold the wrench/torsion bar assembly in position while an assistant removes bolts 3, 4, and 5 from the inside of the vehicle.
7. Remove the cam cover housing assembly from the end of the torsion bar and slide it toward the front of the vehicle.
8. Gently lower the wrench/torsion bar assembly to allow the torsion bar to unwind.
9. Prior to removal of the torsion bar, mark both ends of the bar with paint or chalk to indicate where the bar is located in the splines of the lower suspension arm, and where the adjusting lever is in relation to the splines on the adjustment end of the

torsion bar. Mark the position of the adjusting lever on the floor crossmember.
10. Pull the torsion bar back and pull the assembly down. Note the markings on the ends of the torsion bar. Make sure the correct bar is installed on each side of the vehicle, Figs. 17 and 18.
11. Lubricate the splines on the ends of the torsion bar.
12. Assemble the protective cover seal, the housing cover-cam assembly and the adjusting lever over the torsion bar.
13. Insert the housing cover-cam assembly and the adjusting lever up into the crossmember, Fig. 19.
14. Slide the torsion bar through the floor gusset (1) so that it can be passed up and over the anti-sway bar, Fig. 20.
15. Insert the torsion bar into the lower suspension arm. Line up the marks made during disassembly.
16. Position the adjustment lever onto the splines, line up the marks made during disassembly. It should line

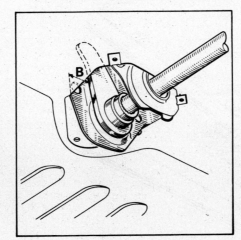

Fig. 21 Positioning adjusting lever. Renault 5 early models

Fig. 20 Positioning front torsion bar. Renault 5 early models

up with the mark made on the floor crossmember made during disassembly.
17. Position the adjusting lever 3/8" to 3/4" (10 to 20mm) as shown at B, Fig. 21.
18. Insert the Renault Sus. 545 wrench assembly into the end of the adjustment lever. Take up tension on the bar. Center the cover by resetting the cam if necessary.
19. Have an assistant bolt the cover to the floor section. Insert the cover bolts from inside the vehicle.
20. Lower the vehicle to the floor and drive at least 1/2 mile to settle the suspension.
21. Measure the under-body height, Fig. 22, and adjust tension on the cam, if necessary, by turning the adjustment cam. If correct height cannot be obtained by turning the adjustment cam, remove the cam housing cover, lower the torsion bar and offset the adjusting lever 1 spline on the end of the torsion bar. Under body height is measured by taking the height of the center line of the front wheel H1 and subtracting the height of the frame member at H2. This difference should be H1 − H2 = 2¼" ± 3/8" (58mm ± 10mm). The height variations between the right and left side of the vehicle must not exceed 3/8" (10mm).

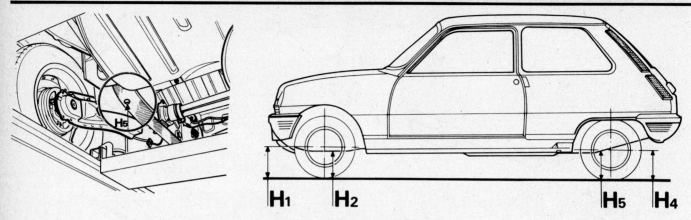

Fig. 22 Measuring car riding height. Renault 5

Late Models

1. Raise vehicle on a lift and allow the wheels to hang free.
2. At the suspension end of the torsion bar, mark the torsion bar and the suspension arm with paint or chalk to show where the torsion bar is located in the suspension arm. Mark the other end of the torsion bar and the end bearing to show the location of the end bearing to the torsion bar.
3. Loosen the two bearing mounting bolts, Fig. 23.
4. Remove the nut and washer from the vehicle outer edge of the bearing.
5. Install Renault tool Sus. 704 over the outer bolt referred to in the above step and secure with the nut.
6. Insert a 3 to 4 foot pipe on the end of the Sus. 704 wrench. Pull up on the bar slightly and remove the inner bolt, Fig. 24. Lower the tool and allow the torsion bar to unwind.
7. Remove the tool, the bearing outer bolt and the torsion bar.

8. Assemble the end bearing to the torsion bar with side A towards the top and offset B towards the front of the vehicle, Fig. 25. Rubber sleeve (C), closer to one end of the torsion bar, should be at the front of the vehicle, Fig. 26.
9. With the end bearing assembled correctly to the torsion bar, push the bearing over the splines and onto the bar.
10. Using the outer bolt only, attach the bearing and hand tighten the nut. Line up the bearing with the dimension $Y = 2^{11}/_{16}'' \pm {}^{5}/_{64}$ (68mm $\pm$ 2mm), Fig. 27.
11. Insert the torsion bar into the lower suspension arm and the end bearing. The marks made during disassembly should line up. If not, remove the bar and offset the end bearing slightly and reinstall the torsion bar.
12. Attach the Renault Sus. 704 tool the same way as for bar removal.
13. Pull up the bar with steady pressure to wind up the torsion bar. Install

the inner bearing mounting bolt.
14. Remove the tool and tighten both bolts to 90 ft. lbs. (12 N-m).
15. Lower the vehicle and drive for ½ mile to settle the suspension.
16. Check the body height as outlined for the early model vehicles. To change the body height, offset the end bearing one spline on the torsion bar.

FRONT SPRING, REPLACE

Renault 12, 15 & 17

Follow procedure given in section "Shock Absorber, Replace."

FRONT DRIVESHAFT, REPLACE

1. Raise vehicle and let the wheels hang free. On Models 12, 15 and 17, install Renault spacer bar T.Av. 509 or suitable spacer between the lower hinge pin and the lower mount of the shock absorber. Position as far forward as possible

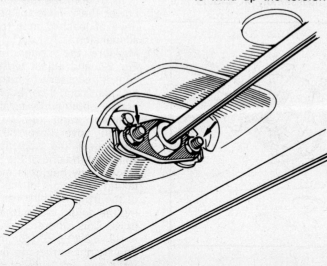

Fig. 23 Removing front torsion bar bearing mounting bolts. Renault 5 late models

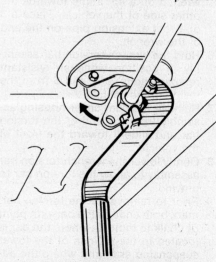

Fig. 24 Releasing torsion bar tension. Renault 5 late models

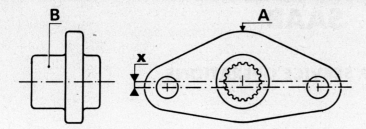

Fig. 25 Torsion bar end bearing installation. Renault 5 late models

against the upper arm so that it will not interfere with removal of the drive shaft.

2. On Models 12, 15 and 17, remove the roll pins at the transmission end of the drive shaft with a drift, Fig. 28.
3. Loosen but do not remove the tie rod and the upper ball joint on the stub axle carrier.
4. Remove the stub axle nut and washer.
5. Using suitable tool, press in the end of the drive shaft to break loose from the stub axle carrier.
6. Remove the brake caliper and place in a secure place so that it does not hang by the brake hose.
7. Remove the upper ball joint and the tie rod end from the stub axle carrier.
8. Tilt the stub axle carrier outward and back and pull the end of the axle out of the stub axle carrier.
9. Pull the axle out of the transmission.
10. Lubricate the splines and insert the drive shaft into the transmission. On Models 12, 15 and 17, be sure to line up the roll pin holes and install the roll pins. Seal the ends of the roll pins with suitable sealer.

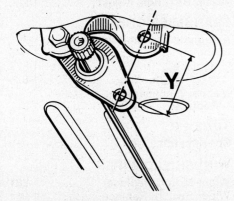

Fig. 27 Torsion bar alignment. Renault 5 late models

11. Position the outer end of the drive shaft into the stub axle carrier.
12. Reposition the stub axle carrier and pull the drive shaft through the hub. Reconnect the upper ball joint and the tie rod end.
13. Install the stub axle washer and a new stub axle nut. Torque to:
    Model 5 — 90 ft. lbs. (12 N-m)
    Models 12, 15 and 17 — 115 ft. lbs. (16 N-m)
14. Reinstall brake caliper.
15. Lower the vehicle and remove the upper suspension arm spacer on Renault 12, 15 and 17 vehicles.

STEERING GEAR, REPLACE
Renault 5

1. Disconnect the battery.
2. Remove the spare tire, air filter, support bracket and cooling fan motor relay without disconnecting.
3. Remove the air pump outlet pipe and the air pump filter.
4. Disconnect the steering shaft at the flex coupling. Retain the rubber spacer.
5. Disconnect the tie rods at the rack end.
6. Remove the rack mounting bolts. Remove and mark the adjustment shims to aid in the rack installation.
7. Remove the rack.
8. Reverse procedure to install. Be sure to install the adjustment shims in the correct position, marked during removal.

Renault 12, 15 & 17

NOTE: Early models are equipped with steering rack height adjustment eccentric cams. Do not move the eccentric adjusting cams during rack removal or installation. Late models are

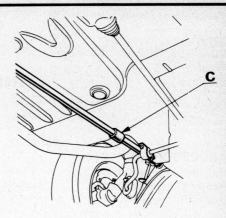

Fig. 26 Torsion bar identification. Renault 5 late models

equipped with adjustment shims. Mark these adjustment shims to aid in the rack installation.

1. Remove the battery and the battery tray.
2. Disconnect the steering shaft at the flex coupling. Retain the rubber spacer.
3. Disconnect the tie rods at the rack end.
4. Remove the rack mounting bolts, mark and remove the shims. If equipped with eccentric cams, do not move the cams. Remove the rack.
5. Reverse procedure to install. Be sure to install the adjustment shims in correct position marked during removal.

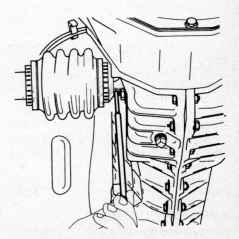

Fig. 28 Front drive shaft roll pin removal

SAAB

INDEX OF SERVICE OPERATIONS

GENERAL ENGINE SPECIFICATIONS

Year	Engine	Car- buretor	Bore x Stroke	Piston Dis- place- ment Cubic Inches (cc)	Com- pres- sion Ratio	Maximum Brake H.P. @ R.P.M.	Maximum Torque Ft. Lbs. @ R.P.M.	Normal Oil Pressure Pounds
1972	95 Horsepower .... 1.85L ①	②	3.425 x 3.07 (87 x 78mm)	113.1 (1854)	9.0	95 @ 5200	105 @ 3200	③
	88 Horsepower .... 1.85L ①	1 Barrel	3.425 x 3.07 (87 x 78mm)	113.1 (1854)	9.0	88 @ 5000	108 @ 3000	③
1972-73	65 Horsepower .... V4 ④	1 Barrel	2.54 x 2.63 (90 x 66.8mm)	104 (1698)	8.0	65 @ 4700	85 @ 2500	47-55
1973-74	110 Horsepower .... 2.0L ①	②	3.54 x 3.07 (90 x 78mm)	121.1 (1985)	8.7	110 @ 5500	123 @ 3700	57-71
	95 Horsepower .... 2.0L ①	1 Barrel	3.54 x 3.07 (90 x 78mm)	121.1 (1985)	8.7	95 @ 5200	115 @ 3500	57-71
1975-76	115 Horsepower ⑤ .... 2.0L ①	②	3.54 x 3.07 (90 x 78mm)	121.1 (1985)	8.7	115 @ 5500	123 @ 3500	57-71
	110 Horsepower ⑥ .... 2.0L ①	②	3.54 x 3.07 (90 x 78mm)	121.1 (1985)	8.7	110 @ 5500	119 @ 3500	57-71
1977	115 Horsepower ⑤ .... 2.0L ①	②	3.54 x 3.07 (90 x 78mm)	121.1 (1985)	9.25	115 @ 5500	123 @ 3500	57-71
	110 Horsepower ⑥ .... 2.0L ①	②	3.54 x 3.07 (90 x 70mm)	121.1 (1985)	8.7	110 @ 5500	119 @ 3500	57-71

① —99 models.
② —Fuel injection.
③ —Dual rotor type, 47-57 p.s.i.; rotary type, 54-60 p.s.i.
④ —95 & 96 models.
⑤ —Exc. Calif.
⑥ —California.

TUNE UP SPECIFICATIONS

The following specifications are published from the latest information available. This data should be used only in the absence of a decal affixed in the engine compartment.

★When using a timing light, disconnect vacuum hose or tube at distributor and plug opening in hose or tube so idle speed will not be affected.

▲Before removing wires from distributor cap, determine location of No. 1 wire in cap, as distributor position may have been altered from that shown at the end of this chart.

Year	Model	Spark Plug		Distributor		Ignition Timing ★			Carb. Adjustments			
		Type	Gap Inch	Point Gap Inch	Dwell Angle Deg.	Firing Order Fig. ▲	Timing BTDC ①	Mark Fig.	Hot Idle Speed		Idle "CO" %	
									Std. Trans.	Auto. Trans.	Std. Trans.	Auto. Trans.
1972	99 ②	N-11Y	.026	.015	38—42	A	9	E	825	825	3.5	3.5
	99 ③	N-11Y	.026	.014	48—52	B	5	E	825	825	3.5	3.5
1972-73	95 & 96	N-11Y	.026	.016	48—52	C	3	F	900	—	2.5	—
1973-74	99 ②	N-8Y	.026	.014	38—42	A	14	⑦	850	800	2.5	2.5
	99 ③	N-8Y	.026	.014	48—52	B	④	⑦	850	800	2.5	2.5
1975-77	99 ③	N-8Y	.026	.016	48—52	⑥	⑤	⑦	875	875	15—2	.5—2

—Not Available
① —BTDC: Before top dead center.
② —Less fuel injection.
③ —With fuel injection.
④ —1973, 5° BTDC; 1974 exc. Calif., 12° BTDC; 1974 Calif., 4° BTDC.
⑤ —Exc. Calif. 14° BTDC; Calif., 12° BTDC.
⑥ —On 1975 models, refer to Fig. B. On 1976-77 models, refer to Fig. D.
⑦ —Located on flywheel.

TUNE UP SPECIFICATIONS NOTES—Continued

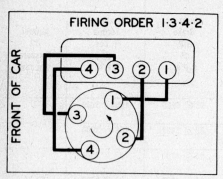

Fig. A

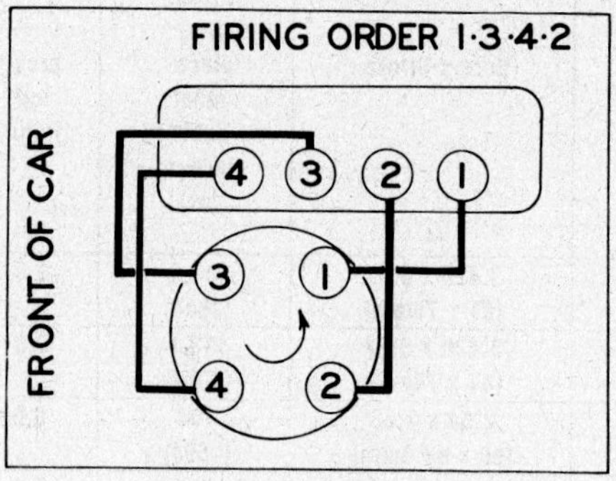

Fig. B

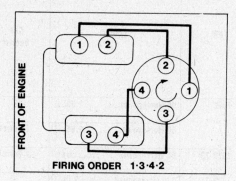

Fig. C

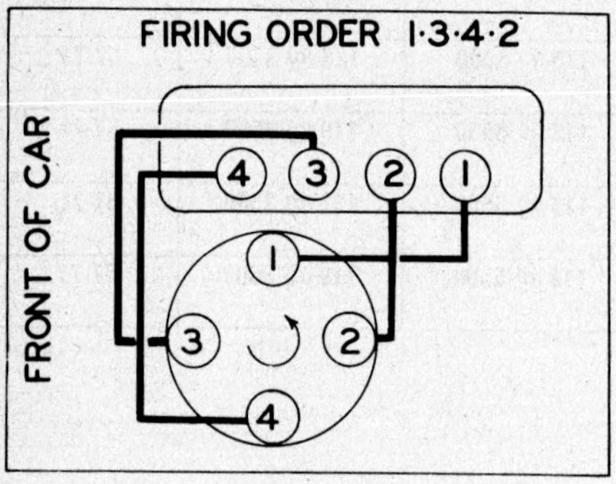

Fig. D

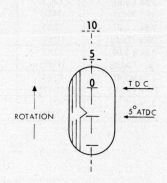

Fig. E

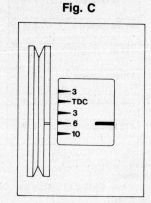

Fig. F

DISTRIBUTOR SPECIFICATIONS

★Note: If unit is checked on vehicle, double the RPM and degrees to get crankshaft figures.

Distributor Part No.	Centrifugal Advance Degrees @ RPM of Distributor				Vacuum Advance		Distributor Retard
	Advance Starts	Intermediate Advance		Full Advance	Inches of Vacuum to Start Plunger	Max. Adv. Dist. Deg. @ Vacuum	Max. Retard Dist. Deg. @ Vacuum
7953871①	0 @ 350	5 @ 1000	—	13 @ 3000	4	7 @ 16	7 @ 16
7953977①	0 @ 350	4¼ @ 1000	—	13 @ 3000	3	7 @ 15¾	—
7992142①	0 @ 400	5 @ 1000	—	13¼ @ 2525	2¾	7 @ 14⅞	—
7992196①	0 @ 400	5 @ 1000	—	13¼ @ 2525	—	—	—
0231163007②	0 @ 350	5¾ @ 1000	—	15 @ 2500	4½③	—	4 @ 9¼
0231163025②	0 @ 425	5 @ 1000	—	15 @ 2500	7½③	—	3½ @ 10¼
0231167039②	0 @ 325	8½ @ 1000	—	12½ @ 2250	6	5½ @ 15	3½ @ 11
0231170122②	0 @ 400	3 @ 1000	—	13 @ 2300	6½	5 @ 14	—
0031179001②	0 @ 400	3 @ 1000	—	14½ @ 2500	6½	5 @ 14	—

—Not Available

① —Delco.
② —Bosch.
③ —Vacuum retard.

SAAB

VALVE SPECIFICATIONS

Year	Engine Model	Valve Lash Int.	Valve Lash Exh.	Valve Angles Seat	Valve Angles Face	Valve Spring Installed Height	Valve Spring Pressure Lbs. @ in.	Stem Clearance Intake	Stem Clearance Exhaust	Stem Diameter Intake	Stem Diameter Exhaust
1972	1.85 litre	.009	.017	45	45	1.43	141 @ 1.1	.01968	.01968	.3106—.3110	.3098—.3102
1972-73	V4-1.7 litre	.014	.017	45	45	1.59	①	.0008—.0024	.0018—.0035	.3159—.3166	.3149—.3156
1973-77	2.0 litre	.009	.017	45	44.5	1.555	188 @ 1.16	.01968	.01968	.313—.3139	.313—.314

①—Exc. Monte Carlo and Model 97, 64 lbs. @ 1.59 in.; Monte Carlo and Model 97, 63 lbs. @ 1.59 in.

PISTONS, PINS, RINGS, CRANKSHAFT & BEARINGS

Year	Engine Model	Piston Clearance	Ring End Gap Comp.	Ring End Gap Oil	Wrist-pin Diameter	Rod Bearings Shaft Diameter	Rod Bearings Bearing Clearance	Main Bearing Shaft Diameter	Main Bearing Bearing Clearance	Main Bearing Thrust on Bear. No.	Main Bearing Shaft End Play
1972	1.85 litre	.0005—.0014	.012	.015	.8123	1.750—1.7505	.00078—.0020	2.125—2.126	.0009—.0025	—	.003—.0098
1972-73	V4-1.7 litre	.0011—.0024	.0098	.0149	—	①	.0004—.0016	②	.0055—.0021	2	.004—.008
1973-74	2.0 litre	.00055—.0015	③	.015	.9445	2.046—2.047	.0010—.0024	2.282—2.283	.0008—.0024	—	.003—.0110
1975-77	2.0 litre	.00055—.0015	④	.0149	.9445	2.046—2.047	.0010—.0024	2.282—2.283	.00078—.0024	—	.003—.011

—Not Available
①—Blue, 2.125—2.1255 in.; red, 2.1255—2.1259 in.
②—Blue, 2.2437—2.244 in.; red, 2.2433—2.2437 in.
③—Upper ring, .013—.021 in.; lower ring, .012—.018 in.
④—Upper ring, .013—.021 in.; lower ring, .0118—.0177 in.

ENGINE TIGHTENING SPECIFICATIONS

★Torque specifications are for clean and lightly lubricated threads only. Dry or dirty threads produce increased friction which prevents accurate measurement of tightness.

Year	Model	Spark Plug Ft. Lbs.	Cylinder Head Bolts Ft. Lbs.	Intake Manifold Ft. Lbs.	Exhaust Manifold Ft. Lbs.	Rocker Arm Shaft Bracket Ft. Lbs.	Rocker Arm Cover Ft. Lbs.	Connecting Rod Cap Bolts Ft. Lbs.	Main Bearing Cap Bolts Ft. Lbs.	Flywheel to Crankshaft Ft. Lbs.	Vibration Damper or Pulley Ft. Lbs.
1972	99	15	54	18	27	17	1.5	40	58	44	62
1972-74	95 & 96	22—29	68	15—18	—	45	4	25	72	50	36
1973-77	99	20	69	13	18	13	1.4	40	79	4.3	137

—Not Available

ALTERNATOR & REGULATOR SPECIFICATIONS

Year	Alternator Model	Rated Hot Output Amps.	Field Current 12 Volts @ 80°F	Output @ 14 Volts 2000 R.P.M. Amps.	Output @ 14 Volts 3200 R.P.M. Amps.	Regulator Model	Field Relay Air Gap In.	Field Relay Point Gap In.	Field Relay Closing Voltage	Voltage Regulator Air Gap In.	Voltage Regulator Point Gap In.	Voltage Regulator Voltage @ 125°F
1972-74	Bosch K1	35	23	—	35	Bosch AD1 ①	—	—	—	—	—	—
1975-77	Bosch K1	55	36	—	55	Bosch AD1 ①	—	—	—	—	—	—
	SEV 71212002	55	36	—	②	SEV 72717012	—	—	—	—	—	—

—Not Available
①—Not radio suppressed.
②—48A @ 3000 R.P.M.; 55A @ 5000 R.P.M.

Continued

SAAB

STARTING MOTOR SPECIFICATIONS

Year	Model	Starter Number	Brush Spring Tension Oz.	Free Speed Test			Resistance Test	
				Amps	Volts	R.P.M.	Amps.	Volts
1972-73	95, 96	0 001 311 024	41—46	35—55	11.5	6500—8500	205—235	9 ①
1972-74	99	0 001 311 039	41—46	35—55	11.5	6500—8500	205—235	9 ①
1975-77	99	0 001 311 108	41—46	35—55	11.5	6500—8500	205—235	9 ①

① —1000—1300 R.P.M.

BRAKE SPECIFICATIONS

Year	Model	Brake Drum I.D.	Wheel Cylinder Bore			Master Cylinder Bore Diameter	Disc Brake Rotor		
			Front Disc	Rear Disc	Rear Drum		Nominal Thickness	Minimum Thickness ①	Run Out (TIR)
1972-73	95, 96	8	2	—	⁵⁄₈	¹³⁄₁₆	.375	.355	.008
1972-74	99	—	1.89	1.063	—	¹¹⁄₁₆	.413	.374	.008
1975-77	99	—	2.126	1.063	—	⅞	②	③	.004

—Not Available
① —After machining
② —Front, .500; Rear, .413
③ —Front, .461; Rear, .374

COOLING SYSTEM & CAPACITY DATA

Year	Model	Cooling Capacity Qts.		Radiator Cap Relief Pressure, Lbs.		Thermo. Opening Temp.	Fuel Tank Gals.	Engine Oil Refill Qts. ①	Transmission Oil	
		Less A/C	With A/C	Less A/C	With A/C				4 Speed Pints	Auto. Trans. Qts.
1972	99	9	9	8.9	8.9	184	11.8	4.5	4.5	8.5 ②
1972-73	95, 96	7.5	7.5	8.9	8.9	181	③	3.3	3.6	—
1973-74	99	10	10	14.2	14.2	185	④	4.5	4.5	8.5 ⑤
1975-77	99	8.5	8.5	14.2	14.2	190	14.5	4	4.5	8.5 ⑤

—Not Available
① —Includes oil for filter change.
② —Final drive .8 qts. SAE 75.
③ —Model 95, 11 gals.; model 96, 10 gals.
④ —Exc. Combi Coupe, 11.8 gals.; Combi Coupe, 14.5 gals.
⑤ —Final drive, 1.3 qts. SAE 75.

WHEEL ALIGNMENT SPECIFICATIONS

Year	Model	Caster Angle, Degrees		Camber Angle, Degrees				Toe-In	Toe-Out on Turns, Deg.	
		Limits	Desired	Limits		Desired			Inner Wheel	Outer Wheel
				Left	Right	Left	Right	Inch		
1972-73	95, 96	1½ to 2½	2	½ to 1	½ to 1	¾	¾	.04—.12	22½	20
1972-74	99	½ to 1½	1	0 to 1	0 to 1	½	½	−.04 to +.04	21½	20½
1975-77	99	½ to 1½	1	0 to 1	0 to 1	½	½	①	20½	20

① —With power steering, −.04° to +.04°; without power steering, 0° to .08°.

Electrical Section

DISTRIBUTOR, REPLACE

1. Disconnect primary wire, vacuum hoses and remove distributor cap and wires.
2. On 95 and 96 models, crank engine until mark on rotor and mark on distributor housing are directly opposite each other.
3. On 99 models, crank engine until mark on flywheel is on number 1 cylinder firing position.
4. Remove distributor hold-down bolt and/or clamp and distributor.
5. Reverse procedure to install. On 95 and 96 models, make sure that marks on rotor and distributor housing are directly opposite each other. On 99 models, make sure that rotor is about 50° clockwise from mark on edge of distributor housing and that vacuum control unit is facing towards the flywheel.
6. On all models, rotate engine slightly back and forth until distributor shaft engages oil pump, then install hold-down clamp and/or bolt.

DISTRIBUTOR, SERVICE

Model 95 & 96

Bosch Distributor, Fig. 1

NOTE: On vehicles with chassis number 453130-96 and 49093-95, the distributors have been modified. The breaker plate is not removable and repair kits are not available.

1. Remove distributor.
2. Remove rotor, breaker point lead and condensor.
3. Remove snap ring from vacuum control pivot rod and remove vacuum control unit and breaker points.
4. Using a suitable punch, drive out gear retaining pin, then remove gear using a puller.
5. Reverse procedure to assemble.

1972-74 Model 99

Bosch Units (With Fuel Injection), Fig. 2

NOTE: The breaker plate, distributor shaft and mechanical advance mechanism cannot be removed on 1974 units. The distributor can only be partially disassembled.

1. Remove distributor.

2. Remove rotor, condenser and breaker point lead.
3. Remove vacuum control unit retaining snap ring, then remove vacuum control unit, spring clip screws and breaker plate.
4. Remove impulse points and holder, then drive out gear pin with a suitable punch and remove gear with a puller.
5. Remove shaft assembly and shims. Note number of shims removed.
6. Remove advance weight springs, then remove cam from centrifugal weights by prying with two screwdrivers.
7. Reverse procedure to assemble. Make sure to lubricate shaft, felt and bushing.

NOTE: Shaft end play must be between .004 to .012 inches.

Delco Units (Less Fuel Injection), Fig. 3

1. Remove distributor.
2. Remove rotor, then drive out gear pin using a suitable punch.
3. Remove distributor shaft by tapping lightly with a drift inserted through hole in drive gear.
4. Remove advance weight springs, weights and cam.
5. Disconnect breaker point lead and condenser ground lead.
6. Remove breaker plate snap ring, breaker plate and felt pad.
7. Remove vacuum advance unit, condenser and breaker points.
8. Remove rubber seal.
9. Reverse procedure to assemble. Make sure to lubricate shaft, bushing and felt pad.

NOTE: Shaft end play must be between .005 to .011 inch.

ALTERNATOR, REPLACE

1. Disconnect battery ground cable.
2. Disconnect alternator electrical connections.
3. Loosen alternator mount bolts and remove drive belt.
4. Remove alternator mount bolts and the alternator.
5. Reverse procedure to install.

ALTERNATOR IN-CAR TESTING

After checking belts, tension and

cable connections, if indicator light is still on, disconnect D, DF connector from regulator and bridge the terminal in the connector. With engine running at 2000 maximum rpm, if indicator light goes out, replace the regulator. If the indicator light flickers or does not go out, replace the alternator.

CAUTION: Do not exceed 2000 rpm while checking alternator, as excessive voltage can damage the vehicle's electrical components.

STARTER, REPLACE

1. Disconnect battery ground cable and starter solenoid wiring.
2. On models with 55 amp Bosch alternator, disconnect cooling hose if used.
3. On all except 95 and 96 models, remove flywheel cover.
4. Remove starter retaining bolts and starter.
5. Reverse procedure to install.

IGNITION SWITCH, REPLACE

Model 99

1. Disconnect battery ground cable, remove driver's seat, pull up shift lever rubber bellows and roll back carpet.
2. Remove plate between heater ducts forward of gear lever housing and remove knobs from heater controls.
3. Remove three gear lever cover screws, lift cover, disconnect electrical terminals at the switch and remove cover.
4. Disconnect wiring from ignition lock and back-up light switch.
5. Remove gear lever housing mounting screws with tool No. 8391237.
6. Raise cover and twist so cover plate screws can be removed from underneath, then remove cover plate.
7. Remove two switch mounting screws and ignition switch.
8. When replacing, insert a screwdriver in slot 4 and rotate to align mark with arrow. Ignition should be in L position.
9. Match locating lug 1 in matching recess in cover.
10. Reverse procedure to install.

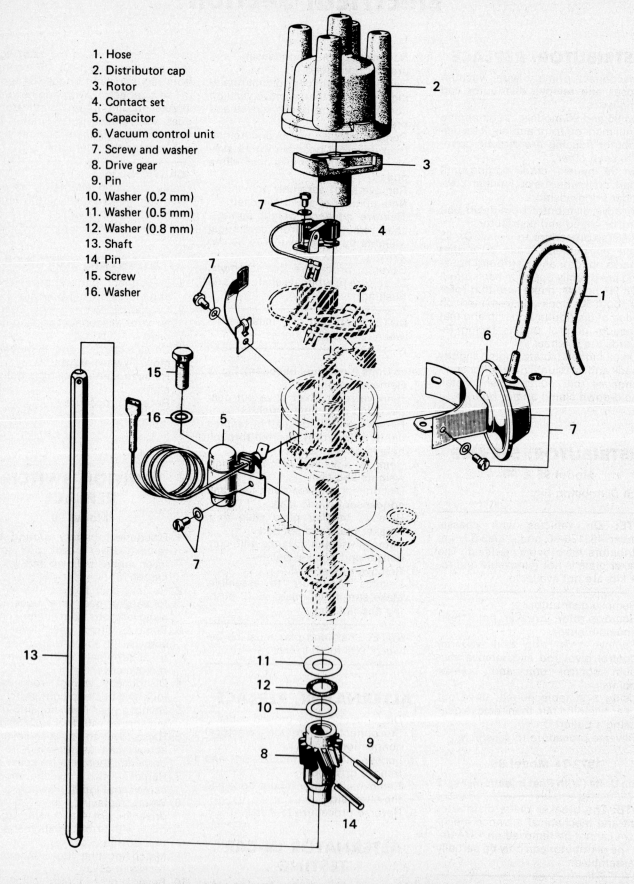

1. Hose
2. Distributor cap
3. Rotor
4. Contact set
5. Capacitor
6. Vacuum control unit
7. Screw and washer
8. Drive gear
9. Pin
10. Washer (0.2 mm)
11. Washer (0.5 mm)
12. Washer (0.8 mm)
13. Shaft
14. Pin
15. Screw
16. Washer

Fig. 1   Bosch distributor exploded view. Models without fuel injection

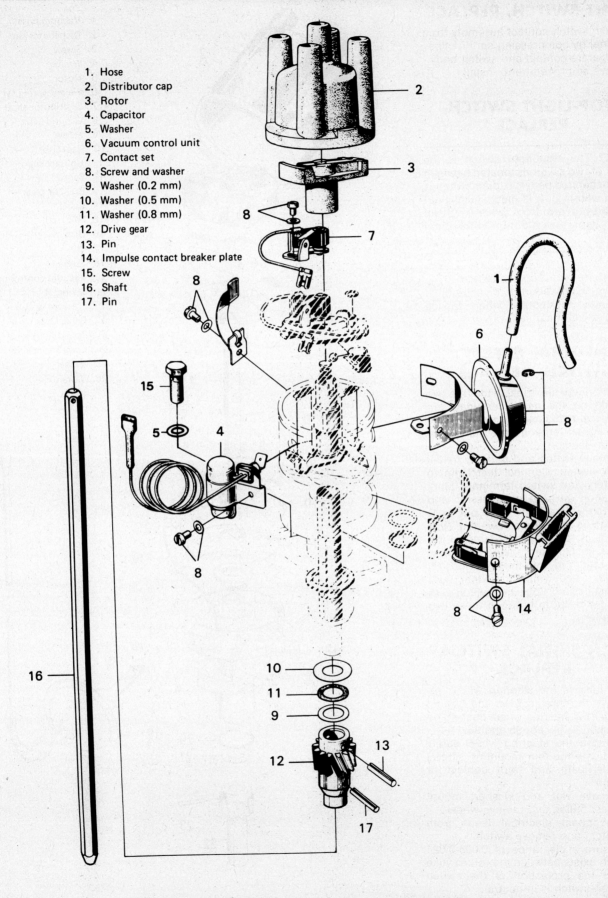

1. Hose
2. Distributor cap
3. Rotor
4. Capacitor
5. Washer
6. Vacuum control unit
7. Contact set
8. Screw and washer
9. Washer (0.2 mm)
10. Washer (0.5 mm)
11. Washer (0.8 mm)
12. Drive gear
13. Pin
14. Impulse contact breaker plate
15. Screw
16. Shaft
17. Pin

Fig. 2 Bosch distributor exploded view. Models with fuel injection

SAAB

LIGHT SWITCH, REPLACE

1. Push switch-contact assembly from panel by compressing spring clips.
2. Separate contact and switch body.
3. Reverse procedure to install.

STOP-LIGHT SWITCH, REPLACE

NOTE: The stop light switch is the lower of two switches located between the suspended pedals (Upper switch is brake warning). It is mechanically actuated by an arm from the brake pedal which depresses a button in the open position.

1. Disconnect electrical leads, loosen jamb nut, and remove switch.
2. Reverse procedure to install. Adjust plunger to depress when service brake is not applied.

NEUTRAL SAFETY SWITCH, REPLACE

1. Disconnect electrical leads (the two leads on the heavy terminals are back up lights and the two leads on the lighter terminals are the neutral safety leads.
2. Remove switch and partially install new switch. Connect test lamp to battery and switch terminals. Mark location on both transmission and switch where light goes out in D range as switch is screwed in. Now connect the same test lamp to the back-up light terminals, and screw the switch in until the light goes on again and mark switch and transmission. Lock the switch with the jamb nut in between these two positions.

TURN SIGNAL SWITCH, REPLACE

1. To remove the steering wheel, remove the three screws and bottom cover for steering wheel bearing on all models except 95 and 96.
2. Remove the steering wheel safety pad with the four mounting screws underneath and horn contact or finger.
3. Remove nut and washer, mount wheel puller, and remove wheel.
4. Disconnect electrical leads from switch, and remove switch.
5. Ensure a clearance of 0.008-0.024 inch exists between the return yoke and the projection of the switch when switch is in neutral.
6. Reverse procedure to install.

1-860

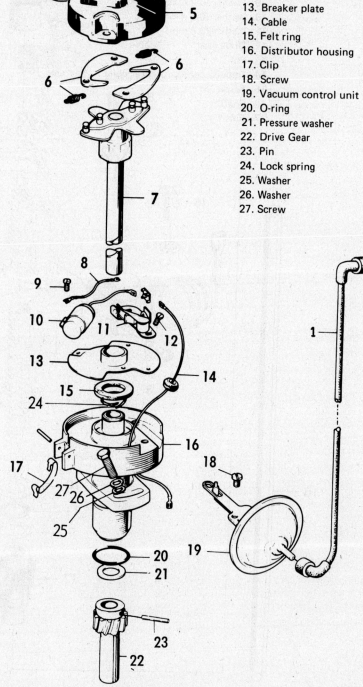

1. Vacuum hose
2. Distributor cap
3. Screw
4. Washer
5. Rotor
6. Weight spring set
7. Distributor shaft
8. Ground cable
9. Screw
10. Capacitor
11. Contact set
12. Screw
13. Breaker plate
14. Cable
15. Felt ring
16. Distributor housing
17. Clip
18. Screw
19. Vacuum control unit
20. O-ring
21. Pressure washer
22. Drive Gear
23. Pin
24. Lock spring
25. Washer
26. Washer
27. Screw

Fig. 3 Delco distributor exploded view

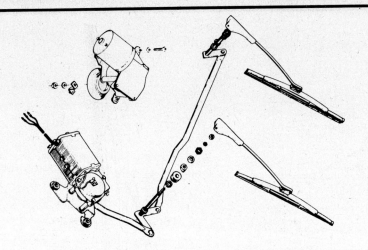

Fig. 4 Windshield wiper assembly exploded view. Model 95 & 96

W/S WIPER SWITCH, REPLACE

1. Disconnect battery ground cable.
2. Remove steering wheel as outlined previously.
3. Disconnect switch wiring and remove switch.
4. Reverse procedure to install.

INSTRUMENT CLUSTER, REPLACE

Model 95 & 96

1. Disconnect battery ground cable.
2. Disconnect speedometer cable.
3. Remove lamp holder and the knurled nuts and yokes from behind panel.
4. Remove speedometer.
5. To remove fuel gauge, temperature gauge and clock, disconnect electrical wiring and remove retaining clips.
6. Reverse procedure to install.

Model 99

1. Remove the instrument panel padding by removing three bottom screws and pulling the padding from the spring clips in front on all 1975-77 models and 99 models from chassis No. 99722011962. On 99 models prior to this chassis number, remove the screen section under the instrument panel and remove the two nuts holding the front screws of the padding. It may be necessary to remove the setting knobs for trip meter and clock.
2. Remove the four self tapping screws securing the instrument panel and disconnect speedometer, clock and combined instrument wiring, instrument light bulb holder and remove panel, Fig. 9.
3. Reverse procedure to install.

W/S WIPER MOTOR, REPLACE

1972-73 Model 95 & 96

1. Disconnect battery ground cable.
2. From under instrument panel, disconnect linkage from crank arm on wiper motor and disconnect electrical leads.
3. Remove retaining screws and remove wiper motor, Fig. 4.
4. Reverse procedure to install.

CAUTION: Before checking operation of wiper motor, make sure that crank arm on right spindle is turned upwards. If it is turned downwards, the wiper arm will go in the wrong direction and scratch the vehicle's paint.

1972-73 Model 99

1. Disconnect battery ground cable.
2. Partially drain cooling system and remove expansion tank.
3. Disconnect electrical connectors and wiper mechanism linkage from wiper motor.
4. Remove nuts and screws retaining wiper motor and remove motor, Fig. 5.
5. Reverse procedure to install. Guide flexible cable into tube while twisting cable into tube until gears on spindle mesh with cable.

NOTE: Before installing wiper arms, turn on wiper motor and note on which side spindles rest when motor is turned off, to prevent wiper arms from moving in the wrong direction when wiper motor is turned on.

1974-77 Model 99

1. Disconnect battery ground cable.
2. Disconnect electrical connectors

from wiper motor.
3. Remove nut retaining steel tube to wiper motor.
4. Disconnect wiper motor and remove motor and cable, Fig. 5.
5. Reverse procedure to install. Guide flexible cable into tube while twisting cable into tube until gears on spindle mesh with cable.

W/S WIPER TRANSMISSION, REPLACE

1972-73 Model 95 & 96

Left Side
1. Remove wiper arm, outer nut and seals.
2. Remove combination instrument.

NOTE: The speedometer should be removed for greater accessibility.

3. Pry apart ball joints between the linkages and spindle, then unscrew the spindle using the lower nut.
4. Reverse procedure to install. Make sure that rubber bushing and nut are properly installed in bracket.

CAUTION: Before checking operation of wiper motor, make sure that crank arm on right spindle is turned upwards. If it is turned downwards, the wiper arm will go in the wrong direction and damage the vehicle's paint.

Right Side
1. Remove wiper arm, outer nut and seals.
2. Remove fresh air duct located between air intake and fan.
3. Remove spindle retaining nut through fresh air intake, then pry apart ball joint and remove spindle.
4. Reverse procedure to install. If necessary, remove glove compartment for more accessibility.

CAUTION: Before checking operation of wiper motor, make sure that crank arm on right spindle is turned upwards. If it is turned downwards, the wiper arm will go in the wrong direction and damage the vehicle's paint.

1972-73 Model 99

1. Disconnect heater core unit and move it forward.
2. Remove wiper motor and rubber seal.
3. Remove wiper arms, then remove fresh air hoses from both sides of firewall.
4. Remove fan housing, motor and

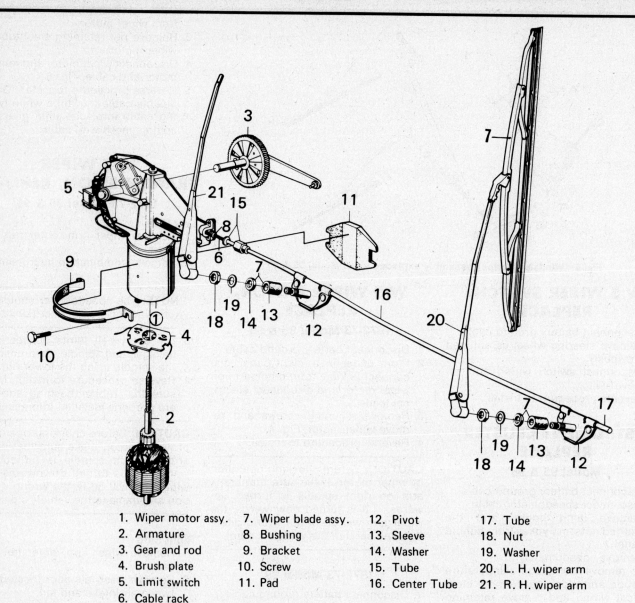

1. Wiper motor assy.
2. Armature
3. Gear and rod
4. Brush plate
5. Limit switch
6. Cable rack
7. Wiper blade assy.
8. Bushing
9. Bracket
10. Screw
11. Pad
12. Pivot
13. Sleeve
14. Washer
15. Tube
16. Center Tube
17. Tube
18. Nut
19. Washer
20. L. H. wiper arm
21. R. H. wiper arm

Fig. 5 Windshield wiper assembly exploded view. Model 99

plate assembly.
5. Remove spindle nuts, washers and rings, then push spindles through body.
6. Tie a string or wire to linkage and pull out wiper mechanism to right side, then untie string or wire.
7. Reverse procedure to install. Pull transmission mechanism using string or wire from right side to left side of vehicle.

1974-77 Model 99

1. Remove wiper arms and motor.
2. Remove base plates and disconnect tubes from spindle housing.
3. Remove spindle nuts at top of dash panel and remove spindle housings.
4. Reverse procedure to install. When installing cable, twist it until it

meshes and make sure that it operates smoothly.

NOTE: Before installing wiper arms, turn on wiper motor and note on which side spindles rest when motor is turned off, to prevent wiper arms from moving in the wrong direction when wiper motor is turned on.

RADIO, REPLACE

1972-73 Model 95 & 96

1. Disconnect battery ground cable.
2. Disconnect antenna power lead and ground wiring.
3. Remove knobs, front support plate and rear hanger, if installed.
4. Remove radio.
5. Reverse procedure to install.

1972-73 Model 99

1. Disconnect battery ground cable.
2. Disconnect antenna, power lead and ground wiring.
3. Separate speaker from radio in console beneath instrument panel.
4. Remove face plate, mounting screws, speaker and radio.
5. Reverse procedure to install.

BLOWER MOTOR, REPLACE

1972-73 All Models

1. Disconnect battery ground cable.
2. Disconnect electrical connections at motor.
3. Remove six screws mounting the fan housing cover plate to the cas-

ing, then the assembly.

4. Separate plate from motor.
5. Reverse procedure to install.

1974-77 All Models

1. Disconnect battery ground cable.
2. Remove windshield wiper motor.
3. Disconnect electrical connections and remove blower motor mounting screws.
4. Partially pull out motor and impeller, then separate the motor at the rubber coupling. Remove motor fully, then the impeller.
5. Remove fan bearing plate on opposite side.
6. Reverse procedure to install.

HEATER CORE, REPLACE

1972-73 Model 95 & 96

1. Drain coolant, remove water hoses from core and disconnect the elec-

trical connection from motor.

2. Remove the six screws holding motor and front plate, then the assembly.
3. Split the casing by removing six screws in engine compartment side and two nuts in the driver compartment side. The nuts can be reached by folding back rubber mat, removing the freewheel control handle, two trim clips and folding back insulation from the cowl plate.
4. Pull front section of fan casing and remove core.
5. Reverse procedure to install. Install the seal rings on the water outlets prior to installing core in casing.

1972-73 Model 99

1. Drain coolant and disconnect water hoses from core, fresh air hose from heater core casing and the control wire from water valve.
2. Remove fan casing.

3. Remove three piece screen beneath instrument panel, then remove the four screws securing the valve housing to heater core casing flange.
4. Move casing to the right.
5. Separate the casing and remove the heater core.
6. Reverse procedure to install. Install seal rings on the water pipes of core before assembly into casing.

1974-77 All Models

1. Drain coolant and remove alternator and coolant fan relay.
2. Remove front cover of fan casing and heater core retainer plate.
3. Remove water valve cap, control wire, valve mounting screws.
4. Disconnect and position water hoses aside.
5. Disconnect and remove thermostat coil and water valve, then the heater core.
6. Reverse procedure to install.

Engine Section

ENGINE, REPLACE

Model 95 & 96

1. Disconnect battery cables, then remove hood and grille.
2. Drain cooling system and remove radiator and expansion tank.
3. Remove air cleaner and place a cover over carburetor to prevent entry of dirt.
4. Disconnect all hoses, wires and cables from engine. Note location of each one as it is disconnected.
5. Disconnect engine side support and preheater casing.
6. Disconnect exhaust pipes from manifolds and from engine mount, then remove middle exhaust pipe center cushion and spacers from cylinder head and lower muffler as far as possible.
7. Remove the two engine mounts.
8. Remove alternator and bracket.
9. Using a suitable lifting fixture, lift engine about 2 inches, then place a wooden block under transmission and remove starter.
10. Remove clutch housing plate, then remove engine to clutch housing bolts.
11. Carefully pull engine forward until clutch shaft clears and remove engine.
12. Reverse procedure to install.

Model 99

NOTE: On these vehicles, the engine and transmission must be removed as a complete unit.

1. Remove hood, grille and battery.
2. Drain cooling system.
3. Disconnect all hoses, wires and cables from engine. Note location of each one as it is disconnected.
4. Remove air cleaner assembly and disconnect throttle linkage.
5. On vehicles with manual transmission:
   a. On 1972-75 models, remove slave cylinder.
   b. Drive out front taper pin from gear shift rod joint and pull rubber bellows from gear selector rod. Separate gear selector rod joint from selector rod.

   CAUTION: Gear selector rod joints are available in plastic or steel. If plastic gear selector rod joints are used, do not drive out taper pin.

6. On vehicles with automatic transmission, remove gear selector wire screw, then move gear selector to 1 position and pull sheath out of transmission. Place tool 879038 on

wire, then turn tool slightly and pull out wire.

7. Disconnect speedometer cable and remove engine mount bolts.
8. Remove clips from bellows on universal joints.
9. Attach a suitable lifting fixture to engine.
10. Disconnect right hand lower ball joint from control arm.
11. Turn steering wheel to left and remove left universal joint, then raise engine slightly and remove universal ball joint.
12. Disconnect starter and alternator connections.
13. Remove engine using care to avoid damaging inner drivers and rubber bellows.
14. Reverse procedure to install.

CYLINDER HEAD, REPLACE

Model 95 & 96

1. Remove engine as described under "ENGINE, REPLACE."
2. Disconnect wires, hoses and cables as necessary. Note location of each one as it is disconnected.
3. Remove carburetor, distributor, valve cover and intake manifold.
4. Remove rocker arm assembly, oil return plates and push rods.
5. Remove head bolts and cylinder head.

Fig. 1 Cylinder head tightening sequence. Model 95 & 96

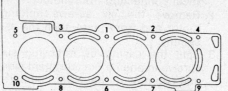

Fig. 2 Cylinder head tightening sequence. 1972-74 Model 99

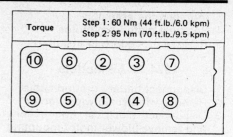

| Torque | Step 1: 60 Nm (44 ft.lb./6.0 kpm) |
| | Step 2: 95 Nm (70 ft.lb./9.5 kpm) |

Fig. 3 Cylinder head tightening sequence. 1975-77 Model 99

6. Reverse procedure to install. Torque cylinder head bolts in sequence shown in Fig. 1, and in three steps to torque listed under Engine Tightening Specifications.

Model 99
1. Disconnect battery ground cable.
2. Drain cooling system.
3. Disconnect wires, hoses and cables as necessary. Note location of each one as it is disconnected.
4. On 1975-77 models remove bellows from air flow sensor and throttle valve housing, then disconnect throttle cable from throttle valve housing.
5. On engines with fuel injection, disconnect fuel lines from fuel distributor to injection valves. Cover ends of lines to prevent entry of dirt.
6. Remove distributor cap and spark plug wires.
7. Disconnect exhaust pipe from manifold.
8. To remove camshaft sprocket, proceed as follows:
   a. On 1972-75, install a suitable nut on threaded center stud of camshaft sprocket and clamp center stud against mounting plate.
   b. On 1976-77, bolt mounting plate to center of camshaft sprocket using one of the sprocket retaining screws.

CAUTION: Tighten the nut or screw slowly to secure the center stud, otherwise the chain tensioner will tighten the chain and lock in a new position, making it impossible to install the sprocket. The engine will then have to be removed from the vehicle to reset the chain tensioner.

9. Remove camshaft sprocket retaining screws, then separate sprocket from camshaft and allow to hang in mounting plate by center stud.
10. Remove cylinder head bolts.
11. On 1975-77 models, raise engine slightly and place wooden blocks under engine, then remove engine mounting screw from cylinder head.
12. Remove transmission cover screws and remove cylinder head.
13. Reverse procedure to install. Make sure that engine reference mark is at TDC. Torque cylinder head bolts in sequence shown in Figs. 2 and 3, to torque listed under Engine Tightening Specifications.

ROCKER ARMS
Model 95 & 96
1. Remove air filter, spark plugs, wires and valve cover.

2. Remove two rocker shaft retaining bolts, loosening them alternately and remove rocker arm assembly and oil return plates, Fig. 4.
3. To disassemble rocker arm group, drive out retaining pins and remove springs, washers, brackets, shaft and rockers. Replace any worn parts and pre-lubricate.
4. When assembling make sure there is proper oil feed to this section

VALVES, ADJUST
Model 95 & 96
1. Remove rocker covers and position pulley mark at TDC of timing cover.
2. Rotate engine back and forth and observe rocker arms as the 1st or 4th cylinder will move in opposite directions.
3. If rocker arms on cylinder No. 1 move, adjust valves 3,5,7,8. If rocker arms on cylinder No. 4 move, adjust valves 1,2,4,6.
4. Now, advance the engine one revolution and adjust the other 4 valves.

Model 99
1. Remove valve cover and rotate engine until hight point of cam lobe of valve to be checked is facing upward. One other lobe will also be facing upward.
2. Check maximum and minimum clearances, refer to Valve Specifications, and if lash is beyond limit, install fixture No. 839145 and dial indicator No. 784062 for 1972-74

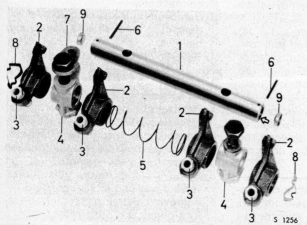

1. Rocker shaft
2. Rocker arms
3. Adjusting screws
4. Rocker shaft bracket
5. Spring
6. Clamping sleeve
7. Cover plate
8. Spring washer
9. Sealing washer

S 1256

Fig. 4 Rocker arm assembly. Model 95 & 96

Fig. 5 Reaming valve guide. Model 95 & 96

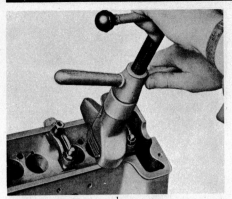

Fig. 6   Removing valve guide. Model 99

Fig. 7   Installing valve guide. Model 99

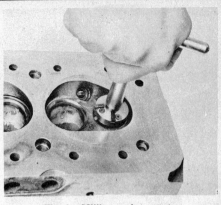

Fig. 8   Milling valve seats

models or fixture No. 8391450 and dial indicator No. 7840622 for 1975-77 models.

3. Fixture must be mounted and screwed on so that its claws grip valve depressor (follower).
4. Mount indicator so that its contact tip rests on cam tip and zero indicator.
5. Now lift depressor and note reading.
6. Remove camshaft, depressor and pallet. Measure pallet thickness in fixture No. 183963 for 1972-74 models or No. 8391633 for 1975-77 models, with indicator from step 2 installed.
7. Calculate new pallet as follows:

EXAMPLE:

	Reading from step 5	0.004 inch
+	*Reading from step 6*	*0.099 inch*
	Total distance	0.103 inch
−	*Specified Inlet Clear*	*0.009 inch*
	Required Pallet Thickness	= 0.094 inch

---

8. Repeat procedure on all valves not found within limits.

VALVE GUIDES, REAM

Model 95 & 96

The size of reamer to be used is dependent on the amount of valve guide

Fig. 9   Engine and flywheel timing marks aligned. 1972-74 Model 99

wear and the valve oversizes available. When reaming valve guides, Fig. 5, always ream from the valve seat side, starting with the smallest diameter reamer and progressing to the next larger size until the valve guide is properly reamed. Make sure to use kerosene as a cutting oil.

VALVE GUIDES, REPLACE

Model 99

Before removing valve guides, flush cylinder head with hot water. Then using tool 839043 for 1972-74 or 8390437 for 1975-77, remove valve guide, Fig. 6, from camshaft side. Before installing valve guide, flush cylinder head with hot water. Then using tool with sleeve and nut, install new valve guides through cylinder side of head, Fig. 7. On 1972-74 engines, the new valve guide must be reamed with tool 839038 after installation.

VALVE SEATS

Machine the valve seats using a 45° milling cutter, Fig. 8. After machining, if the valve seat is too wide, reduce its width with a 75° correction milling cutter from the outside and with an 11° correction milling cutter from the inside. Reduction of the valve seat width must always be performed so that the sealing surface of the valve contacts the valve seat as close as possible to the center of the seat. This can be checked with marking dye. After cutting, the valve seat width must be .059 to .070 inch (1.5 to 1.7mm) for intake and exhaust valves on 95 and 96 models, .087 to .098 inch (2.2 to 2.5mm) for both intake and exhaust on 1972-74 99 models, or .040 to .080 inch (1 to 2mm) for both intake and exhaust on 1975-77 99 models.

TIMING COVER, REPLACE

Model 95 & 96

1. Remove fan and pulley.
2. Drain cooling system and disconnect hoses from water pump.
3. Remove oil pan bolts and lower oil pan.
4. Remove balance shaft pulley and timing gear cover.
5. Reverse procedure to install.

TIMING CHAIN, REPLACE

Model 99

1. Remove timing case cover, then rotate engine until marks on camshaft, flywheel and idler sprocket are aligned as shown in Figs. 9 thru 14.
2. Remove chain tensioner, guides, mounting bracket, sprocket and chain.
3. Before assembling, make sure that marks are aligned as described in step 1.
4. Assemble sprocket and mounting plate onto timing chain, then lower chain and mounting plate past camshaft flange until center stud of sprocket is aligned with camshaft.
5. Rotate sprocket until screw holes

Fig. 10   Idler shaft gear marks aligned in a horizontal position. 1972-74 Model 99

Fig. 11 Camshaft notch aligned with bearing cap notch. 1972-74 Model 99

Fig. 12 Engine and flywheel timing marks aligned. 1975-77 Model 99

Fig. 13 Idler shaft markings aligned. The bulge in hole on sprocket should align with small hole in keeper plate. 1975-77 Model 99

align with threaded holes in camshaft, then assemble the chain over the other sprockets.

6. Make sure that sprockets are aligned as described is step 1, then guide center stud of camshaft sprocket into camshaft and install retaining screws.
7. Install chain guide and mounting plate, then install retaining screws and stretch chain slightly.
8. Make sure that marks are aligned as described in step 1, then install chain tensioner. Note that there is an early type and late type chain tensioner, Fig. 15, and the installation procedure varies as follows:
   a. On the early type, remove tensioner neck from tensioner housing, then turn ratchet sleeve clockwise while pushing it until it locks in the innermost position. Install tensioner neck and spacer so that tensioner neck will not bottom in the chain tensioner housing and release the self-

adjuster.
   b. On the late type, install lock washer with spiral rod in chain tensioner housing, then install spring with smaller diameter against lock washer. Install neck into housing by pressing it and turning it into its inner position. The tensioner neck must be held depressed until it is installed and chain has been tensioned.
   c. On both early and late type, install chain tensioner with guide plate on engine block, then press chain guide against chain to stretch it and push tensioner neck against spacer. Remove spacer while maintaining tension on chain, then adjust to maintain a clearance of .020 inch (0.5mm) between housing and tensioner neck. Tighten chain guides, then rotate engine one complete turn in normal rotation and check chain tension. Movement of tensioner neck from its seated position must be between .020 to .060 inch (.5 to 1.5 mm).
9. Remove nut or screw from camshaft

sprocket and install timing cover.

TIMING GEARS, REPLACE

Model 95 & 96

1. Remove timing cover as described previously.
2. Loosen crankshaft gear and camshaft gear screws, then turn crankshaft until timing marks align.
3. Remove retaining screws and gears. The crankshaft gear must be removed using a puller.
4. Reverse procedure to install. Make sure timing marks are aligned as shown in Fig. 16.

CAMSHAFT, REPLACE

Model 95 & 96

1. Drain cooling system, then remove air cleaner, carburetor and distributor.

Fig. 14 Camshaft notch aligned with bearing cap mark. 1975-77 Model 99

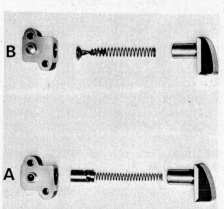

Fig. 15 Early (A) and late (B) type chain tensioner. Model 99

Fig. 16 Timing gears aligned. Model 95296

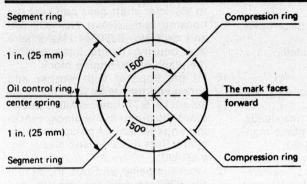

Fig. 17   Piston ring installation

2. Remove fuel pump, push rod and intake manifold.
3. Remove valve covers, rocker arm assemblies, push rods and lifters. Make sure to arrange them so that they can be reinstalled in their original locations.
4. Remove cylinder head and gasket, then remove oil pan bolts and drop oil pan.
5. Disconnect hoses from water pump and remove timing cover as described previously.
6. Remove bolt, washer and gear from camshaft, then remove thrust plate.
7. Remove camshaft using care to avoid damaging camshaft bearings.
8. Reverse procedure to install. Make sure that timing marks on gears are aligned as shown in Fig. 16.

Model 99
1. Remove camshaft cover.
2. Rotate engine until number 1 piston is at TDC firing position.
3. Install a suitable nut on camshaft sprocket center stud and tighten camshaft sprocket against retaining plate.

CAUTION: If the sprocket is not secured against the retaining plate, the chain tensioner will tighten the chain and lock in a new position, making it impossible to install the sprocket. The engine will then have to be removed from the vehicle to reset the chain tensioner.

Fig. 19   Installing crankshaft rear seal. Model 95 & 96

Fig. 18   Piston installation. Model 95 & 96

4. Remove sprocket retaining screws and separate sprocket from camshaft.
5. Remove camshaft caps and camshaft.
6. Reverse procedure to install.

PISTON & RINGS

NOTE: On 95 and 96 models, piston and connecting rod are replaced as an assembly. Do not separate piston from rod.

Pistons and rings are available in standard size and oversizes of .020 in. (.5mm) and .040 in. (1mm). When installing rings on piston, gaps must be staggered as shown in Fig. 17. On model 95 and 96, piston and rod must be installed into engine as shown in Fig. 18. On model 99, piston must be installed with notch or word "FRONT" facing front of engine.

MAIN & ROD BEARINGS

On 95 and 96 models and 99 models with 2.0 litre engine, rod and main bearings are available in standard size and under sizes of .010 in. (.25mm), .020 in. (.5mm), .030 in. (.75mm) and .040 in. (1mm). On 99 models with 1.85 litre engine, main and rod bearings are available in standard size and over sizes of .010 in. (.25 mm) and .020 in. (.5 mm).

REAR OIL SEAL, REPLACE
Model 95 & 96
1. Remove engine from vehicle.
2. Remove clutch and flywheel.
3. Remove seal with tool No. 786216.
4. Lubricate sealing lips of new seal and install with tool No. 786217 until it bottoms, Fig. 19.

Model 99
1. Remove clutch and flywheel.
2. Using a suitable screwdriver, pry old oil seal.
3. Before installing, lubricate lip of new seal with engine oil, then install seal using tool Nos. 839041, 839189 and 839192 for 1972 models, tool Nos. 839044 and 839188 for 1973-74 models and tool Nos. 8391971, 8391963 and 8391922 for 1975-77 models.
4. Seat seal by striking drift with a mallet, Fig. 20.

OIL PAN, REPLACE
Model 95 & 96
1. Remove engine from vehicle.
2. Separate engine from transmission, then drain oil.
3. Remove oil pan attaching bolts and oil pan.
4. Reverse procedure to install.

Model 99
1. On models equipped with manual transmissions, drain oil, then remove clutch cover and starter.

Fig. 20   Installing crankshaft rear seal. Model 99

2. Remove clutch shaft, then loosen and disconnect clutch lever.
3. Remove engine to transmission attaching bolts.
4. Lift engine from transmission and remove clutch release bearing guide sleeve.
5. On models equipped with automatic transmission, drain oil, then remove flywheel ring gear cover and starter.
6. Disconnect throttle valve cable at carburetor. On 1972 models, remove alternator and bracket.
7. Remove engine to transmission attaching bolts. Remove crankcase ventilation device.
8. Remove four screws joining flywheel to torque converter. These are reached through crankcase ventilation housing on 1973-74 2.0 litre engines, through starter mount on 1.85 litre engine and through the oil pump mounting on 1975-77 models.
9. Lift off engine support torque converter with tool No. 879025 on 1.7, 1.85 and 1973-74 2.0 and with tool No. 8790255 on 1975-77 models.

OIL PUMP, REPLACE

95 & 96 Models
1. With engine on work stand or fixture, drain oil and remove oil pan.
2. Remove oil pump flange mounting bolts, suction line retaining screw, pump and shaft.
3. Install shaft in block, with pointed end toward distributor.
4. Push pump onto shaft with gasket, then install attaching bolts.
5. Attach suction line.
6. Seal corner joints where timing case cover, intermediate plate and pan meet. Insert two tabs on cork gasket under recesses in rear bearing cap rubber seal.
7. Replace pan. Make sure rubber washers are properly installed at rear balance shaft bearing.

99 Models
1. Pump is mounted externally behind filter. Remove four mounting bolts, then pull out pump and sealing rubber.
2. When replacing make sure to engage distributor rotor properly.

WATER PUMP, REPLACE

95 & 96 Models
1. Drain coolant, then remove alternator and bracket.
2. Loosen bolts in timing case cover and remove pump.
3. Reverse procedure to install.

99 Models
1. Drain coolant, then disconnect battery ground cable.
2. Remove necessary electrical leads, hoses and cables from intake manifold, then remove manifold.
3. On 1973-77 models with alternator in high mount position, remove screw attaching alternator bracket to pump cover.
4. Unbolt both rear engine mounts and raise engine high enough so that screw (upper) holding alternator bracket to transmission cover can be removed. Loosen lower screw and turn bracket as far as possible away from engine.
5. On 1975-77 models remove two pump cover screws and cover. On 1975-77 model with early version pump, remove center screw from impeller, while holding impeller with water pump pliers and unscrew clockwise. Fit a slide hammer puller with adaptor No. 8392136 to pump shaft and pull pump. If bearing housing remains in block, pull it with slide hammer, nut and 1 inch O.D. flat washer. On 1975-77 Models with later version pump, place No. 8392441 tool over the pump and loosely install the screws. Rotate the tool counter-clockwise until the peg engages the impeller wings and tighten the screws. Loosen the impeller nut (L.H. thread). Then extract the pump using puller No. 8392490. If the bearing housing remains with block, remove with slide hammer puller as above.
6. On 1972-74 models, remove the three cover retaining screws from the pump and tap the lower hose from below to loosen cover. With wrench and pliers, remove center screw (L.H. thread).
7. With slide hammer puller and adaptor No. 839057 on 1.85 litre engine, or adapter 839213 on 2.0L, pull pump.
8. If housing remains in block treat as before.
9. To replace the early version pump on 1975-77 models, place the pump in the block, engage the pump gear to the idler shaft gear and seat the housing with sleeve No. 8390536 and drift No. 8390544. Make sure that housing flange butts against the plane of the engine block.
10. Fit the impeller with washer and screw and torque to 18 ft. lbs.
11. To fit 1975-77 later version pump, place the pump in the block, checking engagement of pump and idler gears. Seat housing with sleeve No. 9392490.
12. Mount impeller and nut. Place tool No. 8392441 over the impeller and rotate until peg engages impeller wing and tighten the two screws. Tighten the center nut to a torque of 10.8 ± 1.5 ft. lbs.
13. Install gasket and cover.
14. To install pumps on 1972-74 models, place pump in block, engaging pump and idler gears. Seat the housing with sleeve No. 839053.

FUEL PUMP, REPLACE

1972-74 Models

Models Less Fuel Injection
1. Disconnect fuel lines, remove mounting bolts and pump.

Models W/Fuel Injection
1. On all models except Combi coupe, pinch off the three fuel hoses at the electric pump, disconnect the electric plug, and unbolt.
2. On Combi coupe, pump is in tank mounted with a bayonet socket and sealed with an O-ring.
3. First drain and remove tank. Then with special wrench No. 839243, remove pump.

1975-77 Models
1. Pump is a sealed unit in fuel tank. To remove it, first disconnect battery ground cable, roll back carpeting, then remove circular cover over pump.
2. Disconnect electrical leads and fuel line at pump.
3. With tool No. 8392433, rotate pump counter-clockwise to nearest groove, then lift out pump, save seal and temporarily cover opening to prevent possible fire and contamination.

Carburetor Section

MODEL 95 & 96
Float Level & Float Drop

Measure float level (A) and float drop (B) as shown in Fig. 1. If float level is not 1.08 inches (27.5 mm) or float drop is not 1.34 inches (34 mm), bend stop at arrow as necessary.

Accelerator Pump Setting

To measure accelerator pump output, fill float chamber with fuel and operate throttle several times. Loosen idle ad-

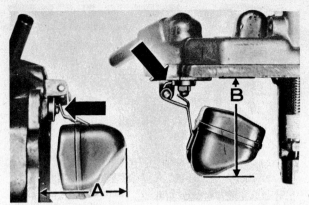

Fig. 1   Checking float level (A) & float drop (B). Model 95 & 96

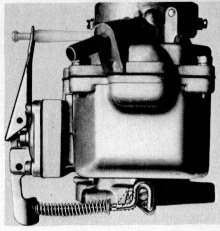

Fig. 2   Accelerator pump adjustment. Model 95 & 96

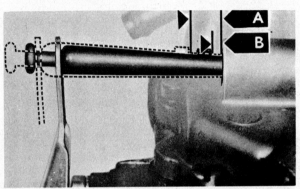

Fig. 3   Measuring float chamber dimensions. Model 95 & 96

Fig. 4   Adjusting float chamber. Model 95 & 96

justing screw and operate throttle ten full strokes while catching fuel in a graduated container. If pump output is not within 0.27 to 0.40 cubic inches (4.5 to 6 c.c.), increase by bending lever or decrease by straightening lever, Fig. 2.

Float Chamber Valve Setting

Referring to Fig. 3, dimension "A" should be .320 to .400 inch (8 to 10 mm) with throttle valve wide open, and dimension "B" should .008 to .012 inch (.2 to .3 mm) with throttle valve fully closed. If dimension "A" is not as specified, adjust by bending lower part of lever stop towards tension pin, Fig. 4. If dimension "B" is not as specified, adjust by bending lever at push rod, Fig. 4.

Choke Setting

Align mark on thermostatic spring housing with center mark of choke housing, Fig. 5. The end of the thermostatic spring should be installed in the center slot of the spring lever, Fig. 6.

Vacuum Choke Plate Setting

NOTE: Applies to engines with carburetors up to and including C8 GH-H.

1. Remove thermostatic spring housing.
2. Depress vacuum piston fully, then move choke plate towards closed position unitl tang of spring lever contacts vacuum piston lever, Fig. 7. In this position the opening of the choke plate should be .180 to .200 inch (4.5 to 5.0 mm). Use drill as gauge, Fig. 8.
3. If opening is not as specified, adjust by bending thermostatic spring lever as necessary, Fig. 9.
4. Install thermostatic spring housing, making sure spring is correctly installed.
5. Insert same drill specified in step 2 to check position of step cam. With drill inserted, Fig. 8, the mark on the 3rd step of the cam should be exactly in front of throttle valve lever stop, Fig. 10. If not, bend link rod to adjust, Fig. 11.

Fig. 5   Choke adjustment. Model 95 & 96

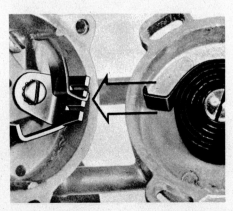

Fig. 6   Thermostatic spring installation. Model 95 & 96

Fig. 7   Positioning vacuum piston to check vacuum choke plate setting. Model 95 & 96

Fig. 8   Checking choke plate clearance. Model 95 & 96

Vaccum Choke Plate Setting

NOTE: Applies to engines with carburetors starting with 70 TW-AA

1. Remove thermostatic spring housing.
2. Insert a piece of .040 inch wire, Fig. 12, in inner slot above piston and hold vacuum piston lever to hold wire in place.
3. The clearance between choke plate and carburetor should be .080 to .100 inch (2.0 to 2.5 mm). Use drill bit as gauge, Fig. 8. If clearance is not as specified, adjust by bending spring lever, Fig. 9.
4. Insert same drill specified in step 3 to check position of step cam. With drill inserted, Fig. 8, the mark on the 3rd step of cam should be exactly in front of throttle valve lever stop, Fig. 10. Adjust by bending link rod.

Mechanical Choke Plate Setting

1. Open throttle valve fully to force choke plate opening so that arm (B) on throttle contacts stop (A) on step cam.
2. With throttle valve fully opened, the choke valve clearance should be .190 to .230 inch (4.8 to 5.8 mm). Use a drill as gauge, Fig. 8.
3. If clearance is not as specified, ad-

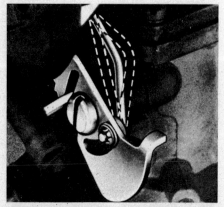

Fig. 11   Link rod adjustment. Model 95 & 96

Fig. 9   Adjusting thermostatic spring lever. Model 95 & 96

just by bending stop (A) as necessary, Fig. 10.

Fast Idle Adjustment

With engine running at normal operating temperature, hold throttle valve shaft and step cam so that contacts mark on 3rd step of cam. Engine speed should be 1800 rpm. To adjust, bend stop of throttle valve shaft.

1972 MODEL 99
Float Level Adjustment

1. Remove float housing.
2. Invert carburetor and measure distance between highest point of float and the mating surface, Fig. 13. The distance should be .67 inch.
3. Adjust by bending tongue of float valve.

Temperature Compensator Adjustment

1. Loosen the cross-recessed screw of the bi-metal screw and center the valve, Fig. 14.
2. Remove the temperature compensator from carburetor.
3. With the bi-metal at 68° F. the compensator should open .004-.012

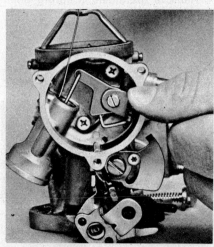

Fig. 12   Adjusting choke plate. Model 95 & 96

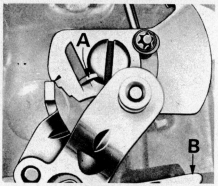

Fig. 10   Positioning cam to check vacuum choke plate setting. Model 95 & 96

inch, Fig. 15.
4. Adjust with the bi-metal spring nut.

Overflow Valve Adjustment

1. Remove rubber bellows from driver disc of throttle shaft.
2. If no hole exists in the driver disc opposite the brass washer on the overflow valve, remove the disc and drill a ¼ inch diameter hole in the disc.
3. Remove the brass washer and install the driver disc.
4. Rotate overflow valve adjusting screw fully counter-clockwise.
5. Start engine and adjust idle speed to 800-850 RPM. If this RPM cannot be obtained, check for intake leaks and also the distributor vacuum unit for leaks.
6. Rotate overflow valve adjusting screw 6 turns clockwise.
7. Start engine and run at 3000 RPM, then release driver disc. RPM should fall to 800-850 RPM. If so, the overflow valve is properly adjusted.
8. If the engine RPM does not return to

Fig. 13   Float level adjustment. Model 99

Fig. 14 Centering temperature compensator valve. 1972 Model 99

800-850 in step 7, rotate the adjusting screw one turn counter-clockwise and repeat step 7. Repeat adjustment if necessary.

1973-74 MODEL 99

Float Level Adjustment

Refer to the "Float Level Adjustment" procedure for the 1972 Model 99. However, the distance between the highest point of the float and the mating surface should be .63-.669 inch.

Choke Adjustment

Check clearance between adjustment screw on throttle shaft carrier and choke cam disc. The clearance should be .020-.039 inch. Adjust by rotating adjusting screw. Ensure that the choke control is pushed inward and the throttle is closed.

Overflow Valve Adjustment

NOTE: The engine must be at operating temperature. Also, check air preheater for proper position.

1. Run engine at idle speed and ensure that the overflow valve is closed. It may be necessary to turn adjusting screw counter-clockwise.
2. Completely open the overflow valve by rotating the adjusting screw clockwise until engine speed no longer increases.
3. Close the overflow valve by rotating the adjusting screw counter-clockwise. Engine speed should now return to normal idle speed. Then, turn the adjusting screw an additional ½-¾ turn counter-clockwise.
4. Increase engine speed to 3000 RPM and release throttle. Engine speed to drop to normal idle speed. If not,

Fig. 15 Temperature compensator adjustment. 1972 Model 99

turn the adjusting screws slightly counter-clockwise for additional adjustment.

Fuel Injection Section

DESCRIPTION

Two fuel injection systems are employed, the electronically controlled fuel system (EFI) and continuous injection system (CIS). EFI system is used on 1972-74 99 models while CIS system is used on 1975-77 99 models.

In EFI system, an electronic fuel pump takes fuel and forces it through a filter into a high pressure fuel distribution system consisting of electromagnetic injectors, cold start valve, pressure regulator (with a low pressure side for fuel tank return) and connecting piping. The electric pump has a return fuel line to fuel tank and in addition, a check valve to prevent loss of head pressure when it is switched off, and a relief valve should pressure become excessive.

Air is carried to cylinders by four individual induction pipes connected to a common air inlet duct which accommodates two controlling devices, the pressure sensor and distributor vacuum advance. The accelerator linkage operates throttle valve located at atmospheric side of duct just past air filter.

In normal driving mode, throttle valve controls air flow into duct, but at idling speed, this valve is closed and air is introduced into duct by the by-pass valve, whose cross sectional area may be varied to set idle speed. During warm-up period an auxiliary air valve provides additional air for smoother running. This valve is controlled by cooling liquid temperature which causes area of auxil-

iary air pipe to vary.

Due to nozzle shape and constant fuel pressure in high pressure fuel distribution system, quantity of injected fuel depends solely upon length of time that nozzles are electromagnetically open. This function is handled by the control unit, a computer, which receives information from various transducers (devices which convert physical information into electronic signals which control unit can read or understand). The control unit then evaluates information it receives and sends out electrical signals to various devices which translate signals into mechanical actions to assure proper air and fuel feed for varied engine demands.

Emission Controls Section

THERMOSTATICALLY CONTROLLED AIR CLEANER

95 & 96 Models

Description

The air cleaner is designed to provide the carburetor with air at a temperature of approximately 90°F under normal operating conditions. The air cleaner incorporates a valve assembly, which is fed by two air inlets, one inlet forms the cold air inlet and the other the hot air inlet, which is connected by a hose to a separate heat stove installed around the exhaust manifold. The flap valve is spring loaded and pivots to control positions of hot and cold air entering the carburetor.

Flap Valve Check

With ambient temperature at or below 85°F in engine compartment, flap valve

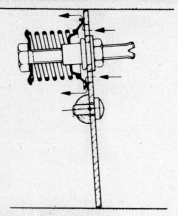

Fig. 1   Deceleration valve. 1975-76 Model 99

should be in position closing off cold air intake. Start engine and allow to run for approximately 2 to 6 minutes. If ambient temperature is 50 to 70°F, flap valve should move to mid position or to position closing off hot air intake. If valve does not function in this manner, check flap valve and linkage for wear or damage.

Flap Valve Test

1. Remove valve from air cleaner assembly and place under running water at a temperature of 82 to 85°F, while holding flap at a 15° angle. Release flap valve, it should remain in position.
2. Raise temperature of water to 87 to 90°F. Flap should move to mid position.
3. Raise temperature of water to 95 to 105°F. Flap should move to full left position.
4. If thermostat and flap does not operate as described above, replace thermostat unit.

EVAPORATIVE LOSS CONTROL UNIT

Description

This system consist of a charcoal canister and vapor lines. Fuel vapor is vented through a vapor line to charcoal canister located in engine compartment, where fuel vapor is stored until engine is started. When engine is started, fuel vapor is carried by fresh air drawn through canister to air cleaner by means of a hose, then through carburetor and into combustion chamber.

POSITIVE CRANKCASE VENTILATION (PCV) SYSTEM

Description

95 & 96 Models

Air is admitted through air cleaner to

right hand valve cover by means of hose. The air then travels through crankcase to left hand valve cover, then to an intermediate flange located beneath the carburetor. In the intermediate flange there is a valve regulating airflow through crankcase.

1972-73 99 Models

Air is drawn through air cleaner and enters oil filler tube through a flame guard and hose on 1.85 litre engines. On 2.0 litre engines, a special connection housing with a built-in flame guard allows air to enter engine block. Air flows from crankcase to valve cover, through oil traps and out through a hose to a regulator valve, which regulates vacuum in crankcase. Air then flows from regulator valve to intake manifold.

1974-77 99 Models

Pressure in crankcase is regulated by a T nipple connected to intake manifold. A hose from throttle body housing and a hose from valve cover lead to this nipple. The T nipple contains an orifice plate which supplies crankcase with proper vacuum. When crankcase pressure is too high, air flow goes from valve cover to T nipple, then to intake manifold. When crankcase pressure is too low, air is drawn from the air cleaner to T nipple, then to intake manifold.

DECELERATION VALVE

95 & 96 Models

Description

The deceleration valve is connected to the intake manifold by means of intermediate plate. The valve contains a spring loaded diaphragm which is held in place by the bottom cover. The diaphragm is subject to manifold vacuum on the top side and atmospheric on the bottom side by a bleed hole in the cover. During deceleration, manifold is sufficient for diaphragm to over come spring loading and lift deceleration valve off its' seat. The fuel air supply needed for combustion is fed to the engine through a hose which connects the deceleration valve to the deceleration section of the carburetor.

Check

1. Allow engine to reach operating temperature.
2. Check to ensure deceleration valve is not working at idle speed. Disconnect one of the hoses between carburetor and valve. If vacuum is passing valve, valve is opened and adjusting screw should be turned until valve closes.

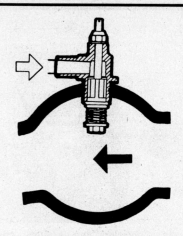

Fig. 2   Deceleration valve. 1977 Model 99

NOTE: If deceleration valve is opened at idle speed, a very fast idle will be observed, 1200-1400 rpm.

3. Connect a tachometer to engine and raise idle speed to 900 rpm.
4. Advance engine speed to 3000 rpm, then release throttle and note time required for engine to return to idle speed. Engine should return to idle speed in approximately 7 to 8 seconds, if not adjust valve.

Adjustment

1. Remove air cleaner.
2. If time required for engine to return to idle was more than 7 to 8 seconds, deceleration valve adjusting screw should be turned in until desired time is obtained.
3. If time required for engine to idle speed is less than 7 to 8 seconds, adjusting screw should be backed out until desired time is obtained.
4. Install air cleaner and recheck deceleration valve timing.

NOTE: If valve cannot be adjusted, replace diaphragm.

1975-77 99 Models

Description

A deceleration valve has been incorporated to maintain combustion during engine overrun. On 1975-76 models, the valve is located on the throttle plate, Fig. 1. On 1977 models, the valve is located on the intake manifold, Fig. 2.

Checks & Adjustment, 1975-76

1. Run engine up from idle to 3000 R.P.M. and count seconds it takes to return to idle, usually 4-5 seconds.
2. Remove bellows between air flow sensor and throttle valve housing. Open the lock nut on the deceleration valve screw.

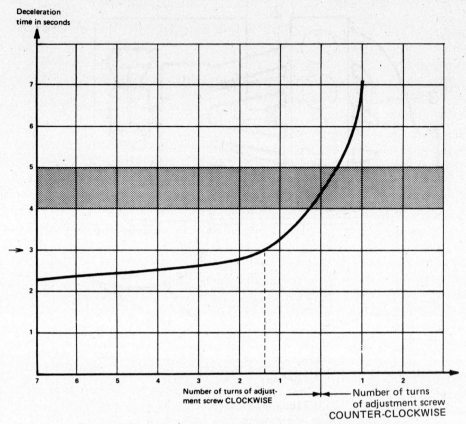

Fig. 3 Deceleration valve adjustment chart. 1975-76 Model 99

(Chart axes: vertical "Deceleration time in seconds" labeled 1–7; horizontal labeled "Number of turns of adjustment screw CLOCKWISE" 7 6 5 4 3 2 1 and "Number of turns of adjustment screw COUNTER-CLOCKWISE" 1 2)

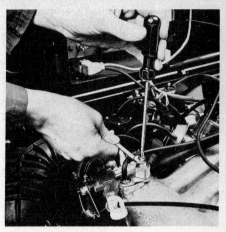

Fig. 4 Deceleration valve adjustment. 1977 Model 99

3. Using chart, Fig. 3, find time in seconds that was counted in step 1. Follow across to intersection point of curve and then down to number of turns axis. Perform these turns on screw and lock nut.
4. Replace bellows and recheck.

Checking, 1977

Increase the engine speed to 3,000 rpm. Release the throttle and note how long it takes for the engine to return to idle speed. The time should be between 4 and 6 seconds or 3-4 seconds at high altitude locations.

NOTE: This check should only be performed on warm engines.

CAUTION: If the radiator fan cuts in while the deceleration time is being measured, the readings will be faulty. This can be avoided by disconnecting the cable to the thermal switch on the fan for a few moments while the time is being recorded.

Adjustment, 1977

1. Connect the tachometer and run the engine until warm.
2. Unscrew the adjusting screw until the valve closes completely.
3. Set the specified idling speed by means of the idling adjusting screw.
4. Turn down the adjusting screw until the engine speed is at 1,600 rpm.
5. Back off the adjusting screw two turns from this position, Fig. 4.
6. Set the specified idling speed by means of the idling adjusting screw.
7. Check the deceleration time and make any necessary fine adjustments.

AIR INJECTION SYSTEM
1975-77 99 Models

Description

The air injection system consists of a belt driven air pump, an output hose, a check valve to prevent exhaust gas entering pump should belt break and an air distribution pipe with injection tubes. The injection tubes (four) enter into hottest part of the exhaust areas to facilitate afterburning in exhaust pipes and manifold, Fig. 5. There is also a relief valve in the pump in event of excessive back pressure build up in exhaust area.

Both manual and automatic transmission models for California are so equipped. Except California models are equipped with a dual branch exhaust manifold, while California models are equipped with single branch exhaust manifold which creates a back pressure differential as well as a different pulsing pattern compared to dual branch manifold. The latter helps in lowering emission levels.

Service

1. Remove air pump drive belt, pulley mounting screws, pulley.
2. Clean pulley, especially recess for centrifugal cleaner.
3. Install belt and pulley.
4. Remove air inlet hose and inspect check valve, refit hose.

EGR SYSTEM
1975-77 99 Models

Description

Two types of exhaust gas recirculation (EGR) are in use to control nitrous oxide emissions (Nox). The on-off type meets requirements, except California models, equipped with automatic transmissions while proportional type is used on both manual and automatic transmission equipped models for California.

The on-off EGR system, Fig. 6, consists of an EGR valve, PVS valve, exhaust manifold with 0.16 inch diameter metering orifice, EGR crosspipe and vacuum hoses. These components function as follows to recirculate a portion of exhaust gases to inlet side.

An EGR valve, when open, allows a quantity of exhaust gas to travel by way of metering orifice in exhaust manifold, through the EGR crosspipe, through EGR valve and into inlet manifold. A vacuum port located near throttle valve controls EGR valve, so that a vacuum signal is present during light engine loads and at engine speeds above 1800-2000. The PVS valve (a coolant temperature sensor) cuts off vacuum signal to EGR valve at temperatures lower than 109° F, providing good engine performance with a cold engine.

The proportional EGR system consists of an EGR valve, PVS valve, EGR crosspipe, venturi and venturi tap, amplifier, vacuum reservoir, vacuum signal switch and vacuum hoses.

These components operate in a proportional manner as opposed to go or no go manner of previous EGR system. The path of exhaust gases is the same in both systems but control method is more sophisticated. Some of air passing through venturi is tapped off as a proportional signal to vacuum amplifier to be increased 14 times by means of vacuum reservoir and then to PVS valve and EGR valve in turn. At engine R.P.M. less than 2400, vacuum switch cuts off vacuum signal to EGR valve. The PVS valve serves same function as in the on-off EGR system. At wide open throttle, vacuum disappears quickly closing EGR valve.

As of 1977, except California models, are equipped with proportional EGR and pulsed air (No pump) while California models uses a Lambda system and 3 way catalytic converter. Briefly three problem emissions (HC, CO, and NO_x) are difficult to remove simultaneously. The HC requires additional oxygen to become water, and carbon dioxide, CO requires oxygen to become carbon dioxide, but nitrous oxide (NO_x) must lose oxygen to become nitrogen and oxygen. These reactions can occur together in a narrow range of air-fuel ratios and temperatures, hence the lambda system which maintains a precise 14.5:1 air-fuel ratio.

The lambda system's oxygen sensor in exhaust manifold sends a continuous signal to electronic control unit which processes information and relays it to modulating valve which continually adjusts pressure in fuel distributor to keep air-fuel ratio at 14.5 to 1. The platinum and rhodium traces in three way converter then handle necessary remaining oxidation and reduction. In addition there is a full throttle enrichment switch, capable of overriding modulating valve during full throttle acceleration.

Testing

1. To check EGR valve movement, remove PVS valve end of hose between PVS and EGR valves. Apply about 4 inches Hg. suction on hose and release quickly. If you can't hear the valve close, replace.
2. To check opening pressure, connect a vacuum pump and gauge to same hose end as before. At about 2.4 inches Hg. valve should start to move (stem should be visible between diaphragm housing and valve body).
3. Check PVS valve by disconnecting

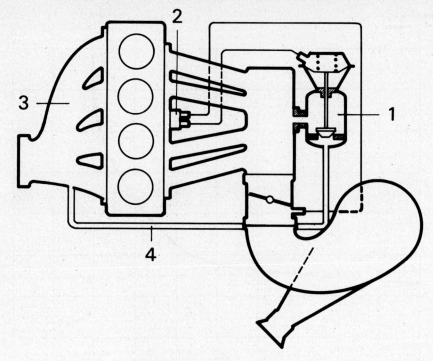

EGR, ON—OFF SYSTEM
1. EGR valve
2. PVS valve
3. Exhaust manifold
4. EGR crosspipe

Fig. 5   Air injection system. 1975-77 Model 99

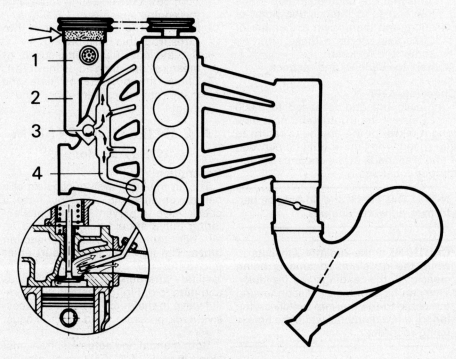

AIR INJECTION SYSTEM
1. Air pump
2. Air inlet hose
3. Check valve
4. Air distribution pipe with injection tubes

Fig. 6   EGR system. 1975-77 Model 99

and blowing through it. It should be closed when cold and open when warm.

4. If engine runs poorly at idle, check vacuum switch. Disconnect hose from blue connection on vacuum signal switch and idle engine. If idle is good, remove hose from white connection on vacuum signal switch and reconnect one you removed to blue connection. Connect a vacuum pump to white connection, applying about 12 inches Hg. If engine idles well now, replace hose between switch and throttle valve housing or in throttle valve housing outlet. You should read vacuum of 14-18 inches Hg. at outlet at 875 R.P.M. If engine still idles poorly, replace vacuum signal switch.

5. To operate properly, measurements of zero at blue outlet should be gotten up to about 2400 R.P.M. and for higher R.P.M.'s than this, you should get 1.2 inches Hg. or 2 inches Hg. for manual or automatic transmission cars respectively.

Service

1. Remove throttle valve housing, EGR crosspipe and EGR valve.
2. For on-off EGR system, clean calibrated hole in exhaust manifold with 0.16 inch diameter drill bit.
3. For proportional EGR system, clean calibrated hole with 0.39 inch diameter drill bit.
4. Clean inlet and outlet of EGR valve with rotary wire brush and drill motor.
5. Flush valve with trichloroethylene and blow out.
6. Clean inlet hole with 0.39 inch diameter bit.
7. Replace EGR valve gasket and connect hose from PVS valve.
8. Connect EGR crosspipe from exhaust manifold to EGR valve and clamp.
9. Mount throttle valve housing with new gasket and connect bellows, hoses and cable.
10. Start engine and check for leaks.
11. Remove L.H. screen under instrument panel, EGR counter cover, press button, replace cover and screen.

Clutch & Transmission Section

CLUTCH PEDAL, ADJUST

1. On all models except 95 and 96, the adjustment is made by means of a screw threaded into the transmission case, acting as a fulcrum for the clutch lever. Lash is increased when the screw is backed off. The proper clearance lash is 0.12 inch at the outer end of the lever.
2. On the 95 and 96, there is a screw in the clutch housing on the opposite side of the slave cylinder. A lash of 0.16 inch between slave cylinder push rod and clutch lever is correct. Lash is increased by turning screw clockwise.

CLUTCH, REPLACE

Model 95 & 96

1. Remove engine from vehicle.
2. Remove the six clutch cover bolts and clutch assembly.
3. Remove disc and pressure plate.
4. Install disc and pressure plate, using a centering tool.
5. Replace engine and adjust.

All Except Model 95 & 96

1. Remove hood and battery cables and drain coolant.
2. Remove wiring from radiator, fans, switch, coil, temperature and oil pressure senders.
3. Remove hoses from radiator. Then remove grilles if necessary, front sheet with radiator and air cleaner cold air hose on some models.
4. Remove return spring at slave cylinder.
5. Loosen clutch adjustment at screw and lower clutch lever.
6. Remove lock ring and sealing cap over clutch shaft.
7. Remove clutch shaft center screw with washer and O-ring or plastic propeller and O-ring.
8. Using slide hammer puller 839027, joint 839001 or 879052 on 1972-74 models, or slide hammer puller 8390270 and joint 8390015 on 1975-77 models, remove the clutch shaft.
9. Remove all cover plate screws except the two on top to prevent clutch from slipping downward.
10. Remove three retaining screws of clutch release bearing guide sleeve.
11. Install tool No. 839207 on 1972-74 models or tool No. 8392078 for 1975-77 models to clamp together the clutch and bearing.
12. Remove clutch, bearing and sleeve.
13. To install, place clutch against flywheel and clamp together with appropriate tool from step 11. Use bearing centering tool No. 879041 for 1972-74 models or No. 8790412 for 1975-77 models.
14. Place guide sleeve in bearing, tighten clutch cover screws, guide sleeve retaining screws.
15. Replace remaining parts and adjust.

MANUAL TRANSMISSION, REPLACE

Model 95 & 96

1. Perform steps 1-6, outlined under "Engine, Replace" procedure, models 95 & 96.
2. Disconnect freewheel control from transmission.
3. Disconnect slave cylinder from transmission and position aside.
4. Remove tapered pin and gearshift rod joint.
5. Disconnect speedometer cable.
6. Remove warm air channel and insulation from drivers compartment floor to expose rear engine bracket screw, then remove the screw.
7. Raise vehicle front and support on jackstands.
8. Remove transmission pin from rear bracket.
9. Attach hoist and perform steps 11 and 12, outlined under "Engine, Replace" procedure, model 99.
10. Separate engine from transmission.
11. Reverse procedure to install.

All Models Except Model 95 & 96

1. Remove engine and transmission assembly from vehicle.
2. Separate engine from transmission.
3. Reverse procedure to install.

AUTOMATIC TRANSMISSION TROUBLE-SHOOTING

Harsh Engagement in D, 1, 2, R

1. High idle speed.
2. Incorrect downshift cable adjustment.

Drive in 1 But Not in D or 2

1. Incorrect manual linkage adjustment.
2. Improper fluid level.

3. Incorrect downshift cable adjustment.
4. Dirty valve body passages.
5. Worn front clutch and seals.
6. Worn forward sun gear sealing rings.
7. Leaking or missing driven shaft cup plug.
8. Defective one-way clutch.

No Drive in D, 2 , 1, R

1. Incorrect manual linkage adjustment.
2. Improper fluid level.
3. Incorrect downshift cable adjustment.
4. Dirty valve body passages.
5. Worn front clutch and seals.
6. Worn forward sun gear sealing rings.
7. Leaking or missing driven shaft cup plug.
8. Worn or damaged front pump and drive tangs.
9. Defective one-way clutch.

Delayed or No 1-2 Shift

1. Incorrect downshift cable adjustment.
2. Dirty governor passages.
3. Dirty valve body passages.
4. Incorrect front band adjustment.
5. Leaking front servo seals or tubes.

Slips on 1-2 Shift

1. Improper fluid level.
2. Incorrect downshift cable adjustment.
3. Incorrect front band adjustment.
4. Leaking front servo seals or tubes.
5. Worn front band.
6. Dirty valve band passages.

Delayed or No 2-3 Shift

1. Incorrect downshift cable adjustment.
2. Dirty governor passages.
3. Dirty valve body passages.
4. Incorrect front band adjustment.
5. Leaking front servo seals or tubes.
6. Leaking or damaged rear clutch valve, seals or tubes.

Slips on 2-3 Shift

1. Improper fluid level.
2. Incorrect downshift cable adjustment.
3. Incorrect front band adjustment.
4. Dirty valve body passages.
5. Leaking or damaged rear clutch valve, seal or tubes.

Harsh Gear Shifts

1. Incorrect downshift cable adjustment.

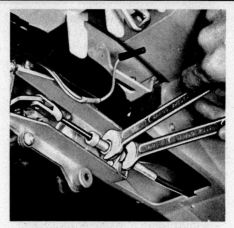

Fig. 1   Manual linkage adjustment

Drag or Binding on 2-3 Shift

1. Incorrect front band adjustment.
2. Leaking front servo seals or tubes.

Slip, Break-Away Noise or Shudder on Full Throttle Acceleration in D or 2

1. Incorrect manual linkage adjustment.
2. Improper fluid level.
3. Incorrect downshift cable adjustment.
4. Dirty valve body passages.
5. Worn front clutch and seals.
6. Worn forward sun gear sealing rings.
7. Leaking or missing driven shaft cup plug.

Loss of Performance & Overheating in D

1. Defective torque converter.

Transmission Downshifts Too Easily

1. Incorrect downshift cable adjustment.

Transmission Will Not Downshift

1. Incorrect downshift cable adjustment.
2. Dirty valve body passages.
3. Dirty governor valve passages.

No 3-2 Downshift

1. Incorrect manual linkage adjustment.
2. Incorrect front band adjustment.
3. Leaking front servo seals or tubes.
4. Worn front band.
5. Leaking or damaged rear clutch valve, seals or tubes.

No 2-1 Downshift

1. Incorrect rear band adjustment.
2. Leaking rear servo seals or tubes.
3. Worn rear band.

Slip, Break-Away Noise or Shudder on Acceleration in 1

1. Incorrect manual linkage adjustment.
2. Improper fluid level.
3. Incorrect downshift cable adjustment.
4. Dirty valve body passages.
5. Worn front clutch and seals.
6. Worn forward sun gear sealing rings.
7. Leaking or missing driven shaft cup plug.

Slip, Break-Away Noise or Shudder on Acceleration in R

1. Incorrect manual linkage adjustment.
2. Improper fluid level.
3. Incorrect downshift cable adjustment.
4. Dirty valve body passages.
5. Leaking or damaged rear clutch valve, seals or tubes.

Slips in R

1. Incorrect manual linkage adjustment.
2. Improper fluid level.
3. Incorrect downshift cable adjustment.
4. Incorrect rear band adjustment.
5. Leaking rear servo seals or tubes.
6. Worn rear band.

Drags in R

1. Incorrect front band adjustment.

No Drive in R

1. Incorrect manual linkage adjustment.
2. Improper fluid level.
3. Incorrect downshift cable adjustment.
4. Incorrect rear band adjustment.
5. Dirty valve body passages.
6. Leaking rear servo seal or tubes.
7. Worn rear band.
8. Leaking or damaged rear clutch valve, seal or tubes.

No Park

1. Incorrect manual linkage adjustment.
2. Damaged or missing parking pawl, gear or internal linkage.

AUTOMATIC TRANSMISSION ADJUSTMENTS
Manual Linkage, Adjust

1. Remove the gear selector lever cover.
2. Loosen the locking nuts and reset, Fig. 1, locking when complete.

Fig. 2   Downshift cable adjustment

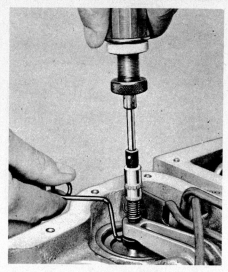

Fig. 3   Front band adjustment

Fig. 4   Rear band adjustment

3. Replace cover and check that N and D clearance are equal with respect to the gate limits.
4. Fine adjustment of the cable can be made at the transmission.

Downshift Cable, Adjust

1. Connect a tachometer to the engine and an oil pressure gauge to the transmission.
2. Start and warm up engine.
3. Apply brake and place transmission in D and observe gauge reading, Fig. 96.
4. Increase speed to 500 RPM over idle RPM and observe gauge reading.
5. At idle in D pressure reading should be 50-70 psi. At the increased en-

gine speed, the reading should be increased approximately 20-30 psi. than at idle. If the psi does not increase sufficiently, increase the outward adjustment. If increase is too high, decrease the outward adjustment.

Front Band, Adjust

1. With rear bottom cover removed, place the ¼ inch spacer tool, No. 8790073 for the 1975-77 models and No. 879007 for 1972-74 models, between piston boss and bottom of adjusting screw.
2. Torque the adjustment screw to 10 ft. lbs. and tighten lock nut, Fig. 3.

3. On transmissions with self-adjusting unit, the space between the spring and lever is 1½ to 2 threads.

Rear Band, Adjust

1. Loosen lock nut and torque the adjustment screw to 10 ft. lbs. Tighten the lock nut holding adjustment screw in position, Fig. 4.

AUTOMATIC TRANSMISSION, REPLACE

1. Remove engine and transmission assembly from vehicle.
2. Separate engine from transmission.
3. Reverse procedure to install.

Rear Axle & Brakes Section

REAR AXLE HUBS, BEARINGS & SEALS, REPLACE

Model 95 & 96

1. Raise rear of vehicle and support properly.
2. Remove wheel.
3. Remove dust cap, locking device, nut, washer and pull drum using puller No. 784002 and screw No. 784178.
4. Remove the shaft seal and snap ring from drum, Fig. 1.
5. Press out both the large and small bearing from the outer side of drum.
6. Press in the outer (small) bearing with driver No. 784033.
7. Invert drum, half fill the space with chassis grease, install spacer and

press in inner bearing with driver No. 784032.
8. Install snap ring and seal.
9. Reverse procedure to install.

All Except Model 95 & 96

1. Raise rear of vehicle and support at frame.
2. Remove wheel, caliper and disc.
3. Remove dust cap, locking device nut and washer.
4. Remove hub. A wheel puller such as No. 8995185 for 1975-77 models or No. 899518 for 1972-74 models may be required.
5. Remove seal from hub with a screwdriver, Fig. 2.
6. Remove both inner races and drive out the outer races with a brass drift inserted into the three milled recesses in hub.

7. Press in the new outer races with special drift No. 8995169 for the 1975-77 models and No. 899516 for the 1972-74 models.
8. Fill the inner bearing space with chassis grease and install inner races.
9. Seat new seal using tools from step 7.
10. Reverse procedure to assemble.

DISC BRAKE SERVICE

Brake Shoe, Replace

Model 95 & 96

1. Raise vehicle and remove wheel.
2. Remove cotter pins, spring and shoes, Fig. 3.
3. Compress piston into its bore with suitable tool.
4. Turn moveable brake parts toward

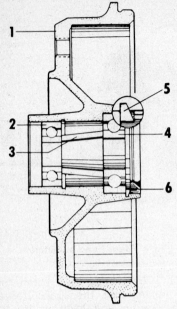

1. Brake drum
2. Outer bearing
3. Spacer sleeve
4. Inner bearing
5. Lock ring
6. Sealing ring

Fig. 1   Rear wheel bearings. Model 95 & 96

wheel and install outer shoe.

5. Turn moveable brake parts in opposite direction and install inner shoe.

NOTE: If shims are used between pads and pistons, make sure the two recesses are pointing downward and are centered on the end of the piston recess. Also make sure that the piston recess faces downward.

6. Install the small parts.

1972-74 Except Model 95 & 96

1. Raise vehicle and remove wheel.
2. Remove guard plate, locking pins with drift pin and shoe retaining spring, Fig. 4.
3. Remove brake shoes.
4. Push pistons back into the bores with suitable tool.
5. Check piston rotation direction with tool No. 899534.
6. Install brake shoes.

NOTE: Rear wheel has a washer between piston and pad to prevent piston rotation.

7. Replace small parts.

All 1975-77 Models

1. Raise vehicle and remove wheel.
2. Rotate disc so recess in disc aligns with pads.

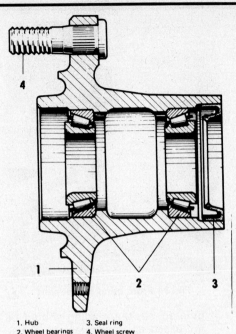

1. Hub   3. Seal ring
2. Wheel bearings   4. Wheel screw

Fig. 2   Rear wheel bearings. Exc. Model 95 & 96

3. Remove damper spring, retaining clip and pad retaining pin, Figs. 5 and 6.
4. Remove pads either by hand or with extractor No. 8995771.
5. Loosen bleeder nipple and press piston back into bore using tool No. 8996043 to rotate piston. Install pads. Close nipple. Yoke should move freely in brake housing groove.
6. Replace small parts.

Caliper, Replace and Overhaul

Model 95 & 96

1. Remove pads and calipers, then

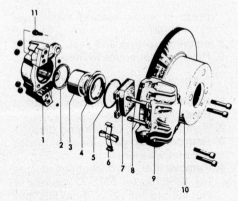

1. Brake housing half   7. Brake pad
2. Piston seal   8. Locking pins
3. Piston   9. Brake housing half
4. Gasket   10. Brake drum and disc
5. Gasket retainer   11. Bleeder screw
6. Retaining spring

Fig. 4   Disc brake. 1972-74 exc. Model 95 & 96

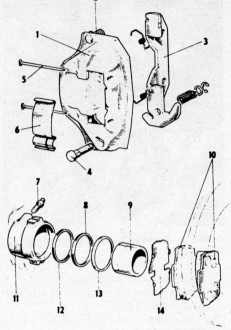

1. Brake body assembly   8. Wiper seal
2. Spring loaded   9. Piston
   steady pin   10. Friction pad
3. Support bracket   assemblies
4. Hinge pin   11. Cylinder body
5. Split pins   12. Fluid seal
6. Spring clip   13. Retainer
7. Bleed screw   14. Shim

Fig. 3   Disc brake. Model 95 & 96

suspend calipers with wire to relieve strain on brake hose.

2. Press the brake pedal enough to force out the piston so it may be removed.
3. Disconnect brake hose.
4. Remove piston retaining springs, piston and replace piston seal, Fig. 3.
5. When replacing the piston in the cylinder, coat with special lubricant and press in, making sure the recess in the piston surface facing the pad points downward on some models. Others have a ground face.
6. The piston seal should be installed either in step 4 or at this time and the retainer and seal pressed in with tool No. 786043.
7. Replace cylinder and retaining springs into body.

1972-74 Except Model 95 & 96

1. Remove brake pads and disconnect brake line.
2. Remove caliper mounting bolts and the caliper.
3. Compress one brake piston with clamp No. 786043 and force out the other piston, Fig. 4.
4. Remove the piston seal from bore with a blunt tool.
5. Replace seal and piston, repeat step 3 for opposite piston.

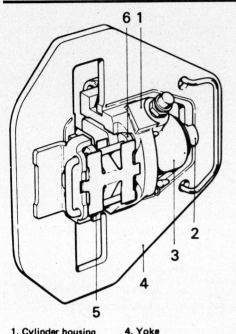

6 1

2

3

4

5

1. Cylinder housing   4. Yoke
2. Piston (indirect)   5. Brake pad (outer)
3. Piston (direct)   6. Brake pad (inner)

Fig. 5 Disc brake, Girling type. 1975-77 Model 99

NOTE: Do not hone. Also, do not separate the caliper halves.

---

6. After cleaning and pre-lubricating parts, install a piston and check for proper position with gauge No. 899534. If necessary, change the position with tool No. 899536.
7. Press the gasket, retainer and brake piston with No. 786043.
8. Repeat installation on other piston.

NOTE: Rear wheel units have a washer placed between piston and pad to prevent rotation. This washer has a special recess.

All 1975-77 Models

NOTE: The front and rear calipers are the same except the front caliper incorporates the parking brake mechanism.

---

1. Remove brake pads, disconnect parking brake cable and hydraulic line.
2. Remove two brake housing bolts and housing.
3. Remove emergency brake return spring, yoke, spring and emergency brake lever.
4. After removing dust cover, force out the indirect piston with compressed air, Fig. 5.
5. Remove the direct piston by hand pressure on the push rod.
6. Remove O-rings and seals except on handbrake lever unless damaged.
7. Replace all rubbers and seals and damaged metal parts.
8. Lubricate parts with clean brake fluid prior to assembly.
9. Reverse procedure to assemble.

PARKING BRAKE, ADJUST
Model 95 & 96

1. With parking brake lever in off position, adjust the rear brakes.
2. If necessary, adjust cable at hand-brake lever by removing right front seat and moving lever to the bottom most position.
3. Adjust left and right sides separately, checking locking of drum with parking brake applied and freedom of drum with brake off.

1972-74 Except Model 95 & 96

1. Adjust the shoes first with hand brake lever off by lining up the hole in the drum with the adjusting teeth. Tighten until the drum just moves, and then back off one or two notches.
2. Repeat this operation on the other front wheel and if necessary, adjust cable at handbrake lever nuts.

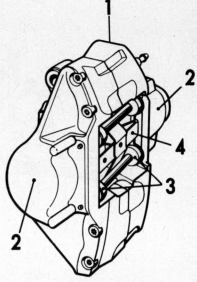

1

2

4

3

2

1. Cylinder housing   3. Brake pad
2. Piston   4. Retaining spring

Fig. 6 Disc brake, ATE type. 1975-77 Model 99

All 1975-77 Models

1. Adjust by turning adjustment nut at hand brake lever, after applying several times to make sure cable is stretched.
2. Check for proper adjustment by making sure the clearance between yoke and lever at housing is 0.019 inches as in Fig. 107.

MASTER CYLINDER, REPLACE

1. Disconnect hydraulic lines from cylinder.
2. Temporarily plug these lines to avoid loss of fluid.
3. On 1975-77 models, disconnect brake/warning switch connector.
4. Remove the two nuts connecting cylinder to servo, then the master cylinder.
5. Reverse procedure to install.

Rear Suspension Section

SHOCK ABSORBER, REPLACE
Model 95

1. Raise car and remove wheel.
2. Separate shock arm from link, Fig. 1.
3. Disconnect shock absorber body from bracket.

4. Check fluid level in body on replacement.
5. Reverse procedure to install.

All Except Model 95

1. Raise vehicle and remove wheel.
2. Remove shock mounting hardware at both ends.
3. Remove shock absorber from vehicle.
4. Reverse procedure to install.

COIL SPRING, REPLACE

1. Raise rear of vehicle and remove wheel.
2. On all models except 95 and 96, place support rear of spring link arm.

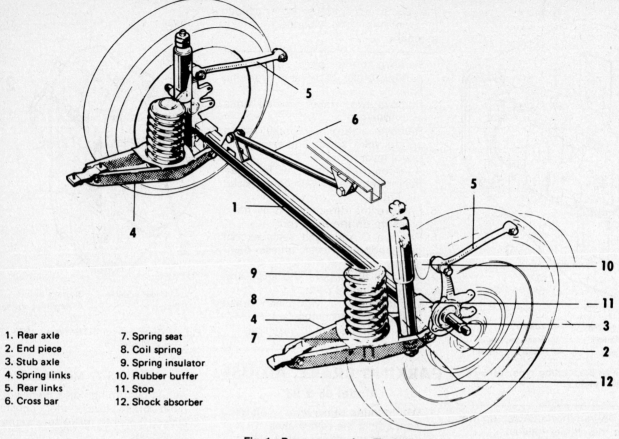

1. Rear axle
2. End piece
3. Stub axle
4. Spring links
5. Rear links
6. Cross bar
7. Spring seat
8. Coil spring
9. Spring insulator
10. Rubber buffer
11. Stop
12. Shock absorber

Fig. 1 Rear suspension (Typical)

3. On all models except 95, disconnect lower shock absorber mounting. On model 95, disconnect shock link.
4. On model 95 and 96, disconnect the rear side of the stop strap and allow the axle to lower to remove coil.

5. On all other models, disconnect the front end of the spring link arm from front mounting, Fig. 1, and lower the jack. Support axle to prevent brake line damage.
6. Remove the coil spring.

7. Reverse procedure to install.

NOTE: 1974-77 models have non-machined top coils which fit into an upper spring support.

Front Suspension & Steering Section

CASTER, ADJUST

To increase the caster, transfer shims from front upper control arm bracket to rear upper control arm bracket, Fig. 1. To decrease the caster, transfer shims from back to front.

CAMBER, ADJUST

Camber is adjusted by placing shims or spacers under the two upper control arm bearing brackets, Fig. 1. Place the same thickness under both front and rear bracket.

TOE-IN, ADJUST

1. To adjust the toe-in, loosen the lock nuts on either end of the tie rod and rotate the rod.
2. When adjusting, make sure steering wheel is centered and the free thread length on one tie rod is within 0.08 inches of the free length on the other.

NOTE: There must not be more than 1.0 inch of free thread exposed.

WHEEL BEARINGS, ADJUST

1. On 1975-77 models and on models 95, 96, no adjustment is possible and a loose condition must be corrected by parts replacement only.
2. On 1972-74 models except 95 and 96, some looseness may be corrected by changing the interbearing spacer in hub. If looseness cannot be corrected, parts must be replaced.

3. On all models, the outer stub axle is splined to the hub with castellated or lock nut and retainer.

UPPER CONTROL ARM, REPLACE

1. On all models except 95, 96, remove the engine and transmission assembly.
2. Raise vehicle, remove wheel and shock absorber, Fig. 1.
3. Compress the coil spring with tool Nos. 8995839 for 1975-77 models, 899584 on 1972-74, and 784082 on 1972-73 models 95, 96.
4. Disconnect upper ball joint from spring seat and control arm, then upper control arm bearing brackets.
5. Remove spring and control arm, Fig. 2.
6. To replace bearings and bushings,

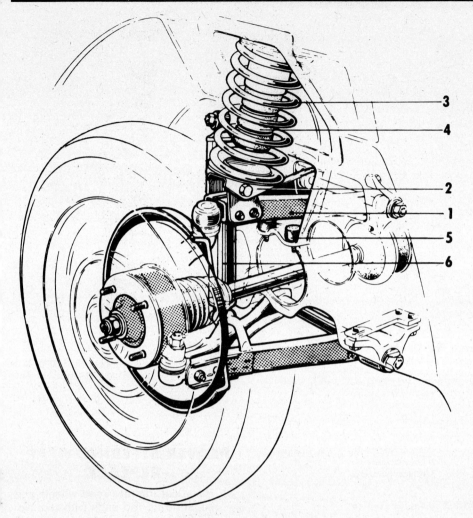

1. Upper control arm
2. Lower spring support
3. Coil spring
4. Rubber buffer
5. Rubber buffers
6. Shock absorber

Fig. 1 Front suspension (Typical)

remove bearing nuts. Rubber parts should be lubricated before installation. Use tool No. 7841331.
7. Reverse procedure to install.

LOWER CONTROL ARMS, REPLACE

1. Raise vehicle, remove wheel and disconnect lower end of shock.
2. Disconnect lower ball joint from control arm.

NOTE: On models 95, 96, this will also free the stabilizer bar bearing.

3. Disconnect lower control arm attaching screws beneath the engine compartment floor.

4. Remove lower control arm with the brackets, Fig. 2.
5. Remove control arm bearing nuts and disassemble assembly.
6. Reverse procedure to install.

BALL JOINTS, REPLACE

1. Raise vehicle and remove wheel.
2. On all models except 95 and 96, remove caliper and position aside.
3. On models 95 and 96, using spring compressor No. 784082, remove spring prior to removal of upper ball joint.
4. Remove ball joint from knuckle using tool No. 8995409 for 1975-77 models and No. 899540 for models 1972-74 except models 95 and 96.

5. Remove ball joint from control arm, Fig. 3.
6. Reverse procedure to install.

SHOCK ABSORBER, REPLACE

1. Raise vehicle and support on jackstands.
2. Disconnect shock absorber at upper and lower mountings, Fig. 1.
3. Remove shock absorber from vehicle.
4. Reverse procedure to install.

FRONT SPRINGS, REPLACE
Model 95 & 96

1. Raise vehicle and remove wheel.
2. Remove the rubber bumper inside coil.
3. Remove shock absorber.
4. Compress spring with tool No. 784082.
5. Separate upper ball joint from upper control arm.
6. Remove the spring.
7. Reverse procedure to install.

1972 Except Model 95 & 96

1. Raise vehicle and remove wheel.
2. Compress the spring with tool No. 899502 and 899506. Remove rubber buffer, then the spring.
3. Reverse procedure to install.

1973-77 Except Model 95 & 96

1. Raise vehicle and remove wheel.
2. Compress the spring with tool No. 8995839 for 1975-77 models and tool No. 899584 for 1973-74 models, engaging the upper grip of the tool on the second free coil from the top and the lower grip under the lower spring cup and compress until about 1½ inch of space appears above the top coil. Then remove spring.
3. Remove the upper cone if it remains in the housing.
4. Reverse procedure to install.

MANUAL STEERING GEAR, REPLACE
Model 95 & 96

1. Disconnect battery, remove hood, raise vehicle and remove wheels.
2. Disconnect tie rod ends with tool No. 784004 or No. 786044.
3. Remove the lower taper pin from gear shift shaft U-joint and release freewheel control from transmission.
4. Unhook the throttle control spring

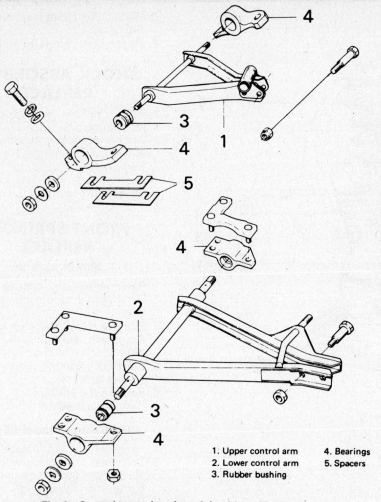

Fig. 2   Control arms, bearings & bushings (Typical)

1. Upper control arm   4. Bearings
2. Lower control arm   5. Spacers
3. Rubber bushing

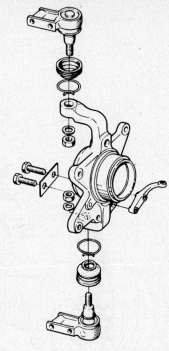

Fig. 3   Ball joint installation (Typical)

and support the gearshift shaft with the spring.

5. Disconnect speedometer cable from transmission.
6. Loosen clamping screw in steering column and lift steering wheel, separating the column from gear.
7. Remove lock nut, screw, pressure spring and piston from bottom of gear.
8. Remove pinion bearing screws, pinion bearing, shims and pinion.
9. Remove four steering gear mounting screws.
10. Remove gear through left hand wheel housing.
11. Reverse procedure to install.

1972-74 Except Model 95 & 96

1. Raise car, remove front wheels and separate tie rod end with tool No. 899540.
2. Working from the floor, roll back the carpet and slide the rubber bellows away from lower joint.
3. Loosen clamp on the pinion and

separate the joint. Remove the steering gear clamps and pull the gear out from the left.
4. Reverse procedure to install.

1975-77 All Models

1. Remove front wheels and separate tie rod ends with tool No. 8995409.
2. Working from under the instrument panel, remove screen and rubber bellows at the body opening for the intermediate shaft.
3. Loosen the steering gear pinion joint coupling and separate the column from the pinion.
4. Remove two steering gear clamps and move the rack to the right.
5. Move the gear to the right and position the tie rod downward into the opening in the engine compartment floor.
6. Pull the rack fully toward left and remove the gear through the opening.
7. Reverse procedure to install.

POWER STEERING GEAR, REPLACE

1. Raise car, remove road wheels and separate tie rod ends with tool No. 8995409 for 1975-77 and No. 899540 for 1972-74.
2. Turn wheels fully toward left and working from under instrument panel, remove left cover and slide up the rubber bellows covering the joint.
3. Loosen clamp screw on column.
4. Disconnect pressure hose on power steering pump and plug hose and port.
5. Disconnect suction hose from tube and plug both ports.
6. Disconnect speedometer cable from transmission.
7. On the vehicle, left side, remove the mounting screws and the intermediate section.
8. On the vehicle right side, remove the yoke and intermediate section. Move gear downward slightly and remove clamp and joint.
9. Move gear toward the right and position the left tie rod down through the body opening, twisting the valve housing rearwards.
10. Remove the gear to the right.
11. Reverse procedure to install. However, remove the left tie rod assembly.

SPITFIRE

INDEX OF SERVICE OPERATIONS

SPITFIRE

GENERAL ENGINE SPECIFICATIONS

Year	Engine	Carburetor	Bore & Stroke	Piston Displacement Cubic Inches	Compression Ratio	Maximum Net H.P. @ R.P.M.	Normal Oil Pressure Pounds
1972-77	4—91	Stromberg	2.90 x 3.44	91	7.5:1	—	—

—Not Available.

TUNE UP SPECIFICATIONS

▲Before removing wires from distributor cap, determine location of the No. 1 wire in cap, as distributor position may have been altered from that shown at the end of this chart.

Year	Engine	Spark Plug		Distributor		Ignition Timing			Hot Idle Speed
		Type	Gap	Point Gap Inch	Dwell Angle Deg.	Firing Order	Timing B.T.D.C.	Mark Location	
1972-77	91 cu. in.	N12Y	.025	—	—	A	10	①	700—900

—Not Available.
① —Scale on front engine cover, mark on crankshaft pulley.

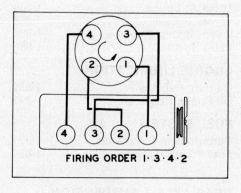

FIRING ORDER 1·3·4·2

Fig. A

DISTRIBUTOR SPECIFICATIONS

★If unit is checked on vehicle, double the R.P.M. and degrees to get crankshaft figures.

Distributor Part No.	Centrifugal Advance Degrees @ R.P.M. of Distributor				Vacuum Advance	
	Advance Starts	Intermediate Advance		Full Advance	Inches Of Vacuum to start Plunger	Max. Adv. Dist. Deg. @ Vacuum
Lucas 45/DE4	½—3½ @ 600	3½—6½ @ 750	6½—8½ @ 1300	7½—9½ @ 1650	5	11 @ 10

Continued

SPITFIRE

ALTERNATOR SPECIFICATIONS

Year	Alternator		Regulator	
	Model	Output @ 14 Volts 6000 R.P.M. Amps	Model	Control Setting Volts @ R.P.M.
1972-77	Lucas 16 ACR	34	14 TR	14—14.4 @ 2.609

STARTER MOTOR SPECIFICATIONS

Year	Model	Brush Spring Tension (ounces)	No Load Test		Torque Test	
			Amps.	R.P.M.	Amps	Torque Ft. Lbs.
1972-77	Lucas M35J	28	260—275	1000	350—375	7

VALVE SPECIFICATIONS

Year	Model	Valve Lash		Valve Angles		Valve Spring Installed Height	Stem Diameter		Stem Clearance	
		Int.	Exh.	Seat	Face		Intake	Exhaust	Intake	Exhaust
1972-77	Spitfire	.010 c	.010 c	45	—	1.342	.3107—.3113	.3100—.3105	①	①

—Not Available

① —Noncatalyst engines, .0013—.0017; Catalyst, .0297—.0303.

PISTON PINS, RINGS, CRANKSHAFT & BEARINGS

Year	Model	Piston Clearance Bottom of Skirt ①	Ring End Gap ①		Wristpin Diameter	Rod Bearings		Main Bearings		
			Comp.	Oil		Shaft Diameter	Bearing Clearance	Shaft Diameter	Bearing Clearance	Shaft End Play
1972-77	Spitfire	.002—.003	.012—.022	—	.8123—.8125	1.8750—1.8755	—	2.3115—2.3120	—	.004—.008

—Not Available

① —At right angles to the wrist pin.

ENGINE TIGHTENING SPECIFICATIONS

*Torque specifications are for clean & lightly lubricated threads only. Dry dirty threads produce increased friction which prevents accurate measurement of tightness.

Year	Engine	Spark Plug Ft. Lbs.	Cylinder Head Bolts Ft. Lbs.	Intake Manifold Ft. Lbs.	Camshaft Cap Bolts Ft. Lbs.	Camshaft Cover Bolts Ft. Lbs.	Connecting Rod Cap Bolts Ft. Lbs.	Main Bearing Cap Bolts Ft. Lbs.	Flywheel to Crank shaft Ft. Lbs.
1972-77	4—91	—	46	25	—	2	①	65	②

—Not Available.

① —Phosphated, 50; dye colored, 46.

② —Cadmium plated, 40; Parkarised, 45.

Continued

WHEEL ALIGNMENT SPECIFICATIONS

Year	Model	Caster Angle, Degrees		Camber Angle, Degrees				Toe-in Inch
		Limits	Desired	Limits		Desired		
				Front	Rear	Front	Rear	
1972-77	Spitfire	+4—+5	+4¼	+1½—+2½	+2¼—+4¼	+2	+3¼	0—¹⁄₁₆

COOLING SYSTEM CAPACITY

Year	Cooling Capacity Qts.		Radiator Cap Relief Pressure, Lbs.		Thermo Opening Temp.	Fuel Tank Gals.	① Engine Oil Refill Pints	Transmission Oil		Axle Oil
	Without Heater	With Heater	With A/C	No A/C				4 Speed Pints	Overdrive Pints	Pints
1972-77	8.4	9.6	13	13	190	8.7	9.6	1.8	3.25	1.2

①—Filter included.

Electrical Section

DISTRIBUTOR, REPLACE

1. Remove distributor cap.
2. Remove distributor primary lead from coil.
3. Remove vacuum control line.
4. Remove one bolt and washer holding the clamp bracket to the pedestal.
5. Remove the distributor.

NOTE: To facilitate re-timing, do not loosen the clamp bolt.

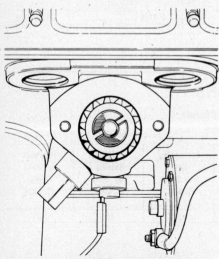

Fig. 1 Distributor drive gear slot positioned for distributor installation

6. To install the distributor, rotate the crankshaft until No. 1 piston is at TDC, compression stroke, and the offset distributor drive gear slot is in the position, Fig. 1.
7. Complete installation, adjusting ignition timing at the completion.

ALTERNATOR, REPLACE

1. Disconnect multi-socket connectors.
2. Loosen main mounting bolt and two adjustment bracket bolts.
3. Push the alternator toward the engine and remove the drive belt.
4. Remove the outer adjustment bracket bolt.
5. Support alternator and remove the main mounting bolt and spacer.
6. Reverse procedure to install.

ALTERNATOR TESTING
Alternator Output Test

NOTE: To avoid misleading results, the unit should be at normal operating temperature.

1. Check drive belt adjustment and remove the multi-socket connectors.
2. Remove the molded cover and connect test equipment, Fig. 3.

CAUTION: Do not reverse polarity. Keep the variable resistor connected no longer than necessary to make the test.

3. Run the engine, gradually increasing speed. At 1,500 alternator rpm (640 engine rpm), the alternator test light should be out.
4. Hold alternator speed at 6,000 rpm (engine speed of 2,560 rpm) and adjust the variable resistor so the voltmeter reads 14 volts. The ammeter reading should now be about equal to a nominal output of 28

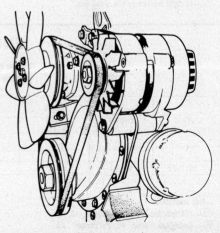

Fig. 2 Alternator mounting

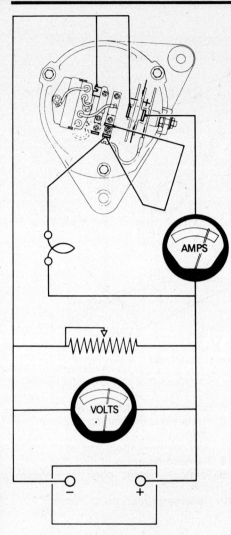

Fig. 3 Alternator output test connections

amps. If not, overhaul or replace the alternator.

Regulator Test

1. Connect test equipment, Fig. 4.
2. Repeat test procedures above.

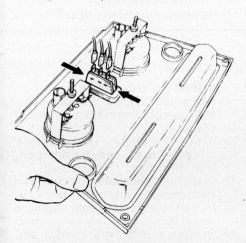

Fig. 5   Light switch installation

3. Holding alternator speed at 6,000 rpm, the voltmeter should read 14.0-14.4 volts. If not, the regulator should be replaced.

STARTER MOTOR, REPLACE

1. Disconnect the leads from the terminals.
2. Note the relationship between the starter motor, shims (if fitted), packing and clutch housing.
3. Remove lower and upper mounting bolts.
4. Working beneath vehicle, remove starter motor, complete with packing and shims (if fitted).

IGNITION SWITCH, REPLACE

1. Pull back the switch cover.
2. Withdraw the switch.
3. Disconnect the five connectors.
4. Reverse procedure to install, but when inserting the switch into the steering column lock assembly, notice the keyway and make sure that the lock shaft and switch are aligned to obtain correct engagement.
5. Connect wires as follows:
   White/red to terminal 1
   Brown to terminal 2
   White to terminal 3
   White/pink to terminal 5

LIGHT SWITCH, REPLACE

1. Lower the center panel.
2. Disconnect three connectors, Fig. 5.
3. Compress the spring and push out switch.
4. Reverse procedure to install.

STOPLIGHT SWITCH, REPLACE

1. Disconnect the two connectors.

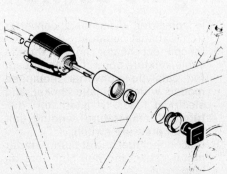

Fig. 6   W/S wiper switch installation

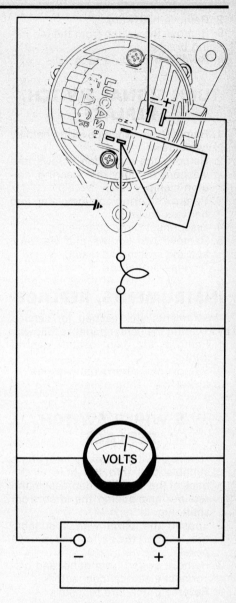

Fig. 4   Regulator test connections

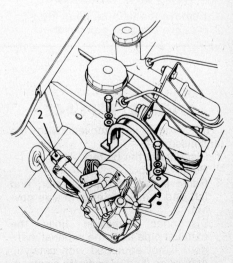

Fig. 7   W/S wiper motor installation

2. Remove hardware.
3. Remove the switch from the mounting bracket.
4. Reverse procedure to install.

TURN SIGNAL SWITCH, REPLACE

1. Remove the switch covering held by two screws.
2. Remove the two Allen screws and washers holding the steering column clamp.
3. Remove steering column clamp and harness cover.
4. Disconnect three connectors.
5. Remove two screws and washers, and the switch and leads.
6. Reverse procedure to install.

INSTRUMENTS, REPLACE

Instruments are reached for service by lowering the center panel as follows:
1. Remove the two heater control knobs.
2. Remove the screws and washers.
3. Lower the center panel.

W/S WIPER SWITCH, REPLACE

1. Remove switch knob by inserting a suitable tool into the hole in the back of the knob and depressing the retainer and pulling the knob from shaft, Fig. 6.
2. Loosen the bezel with a suitable tool, support the switch and remove bezel.
3. Remove switch from panel and disconnect electrical connectors.
4. Reverse procedure to install.

WINDSHIELD WIPER MOTOR, REPLACE

1. Remove the harness plug, Fig. 7.
2. Remove the gear box cover.

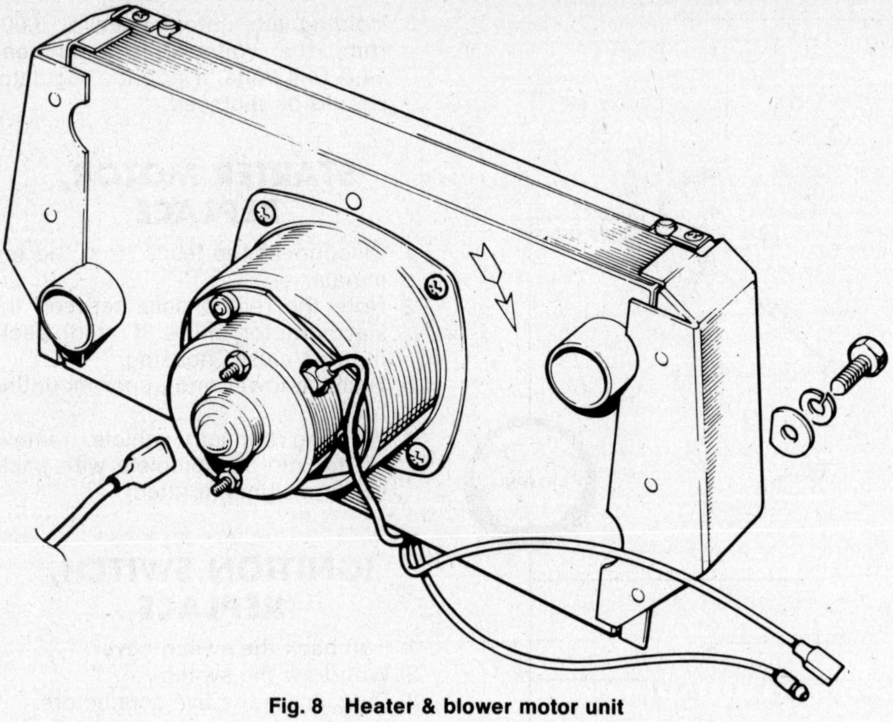

Fig. 8 Heater & blower motor unit

3. Remove the crankpin spring clip by pulling it out sideways.
4. Remove the washer.
5. Withdraw the connecting rod.
6. Remove the other washer.
7. Remove two sets of fasteners, strap and rubber sleeve.
8. Remove the motor by turning crosshead rack and tube assembly to release.
9. Reverse procedure to install. Lubricate the crankpin and crosshead end of the connecting rod and pin.

HEATER CORE, REPLACE

1. Drain cooling system.
2. Remove heater hoses.
3. Remove shelf on passenger side and lower center panel.
4. Remove air flow control and cable.
5. Disconnect connector and hoses.
6. Push screen washing tube to one side.
7. Remove mounting screws.
8. Remove heater unit, Fig. 8.
9. Remove heater core from heater unit.
10. Reverse procedure to install.

BLOWER MOTOR, REPLACE

1. Lower the center panel.
2. Disconnect electrical connectors, Fig. 8.
3. Remove the blower motor attaching screws.
4. Remove blower motor.
5. Reverse procedure to install.

Engine Section

ENGINE, REPLACE

The engine is removed with the transmission.
1. Disconnect the battery.
2. Remove hood.
3. Remove radiator, air cleaner, and left and right side engine side covers.
4. Disconnect emission lines the exhaust pipe from the exhaust manifold if not equipped with catalytic converter. If equipped with a catalyt-

ic converter, disconnect converter from exhaust manifold.
5. Disconnect heater hoses, throttle cable, mixture control cable (except for catalytic converter equipped models with automatic choke), and electrical leads to alternator, distributor, temperature sending unit and oil pressure switch.
6. Disconnect fuel line at pump, starter motor cable, and coil high tension lead.
7. Disconnect exhaust pipe from

bracket on transmission.
8. Disconnect engine restraint cable and remove transmission tunnel cover.
9. Scribe a reference mark between propeller shaft and transmission, then disconnect propeller shaft.
10. Disconnect speedometer cable from transmission, and two leads to transmission reverse light switch or three leads to overdrive unit, if used.
11. Remove clutch slave cylinder and two nuts holding transmission rub-

SPITFIRE

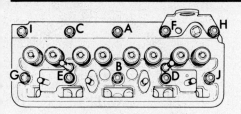

Fig. 1 Cylinder head tightening sequence

ber mounting to mounting bracket.
12. Attach lifting equipment and raise the engine sufficiently to take up the weight.
13. Remove fasteners holding engine to chassis.
14. Remove engine and transmission assembly.
15. Reverse procedure to install.

CYLINDER HEAD, REPLACE

1. Disconnect battery ground cable.
2. Drain cooling system.
3. Disconnect spark plug leads.
4. Disconnect hose from diverter and check valve at check valve and remove vacuum line to diverter and check valve from the manifold.
5. Disconnect vacuum line to distributor from manifold.
6. Loosen alternator drive belt.
7. Remove air cleaner and disconnect heater hoses.
8. Disconnect mixture control cable, if equipped.
9. Disconnect emission and evaporative control hoses, and throttle cable.
10. Remove rocker cover.
11. Disconnect heater return line at water pump housing union.
12. Remove heat shield between carburetor and air cleaner.
13. Disconnect exhaust pipe or catalytic converter from exhaust manifold.

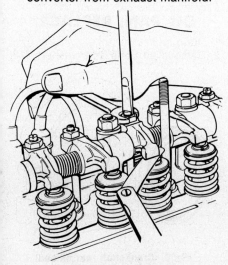

Fig. 3 Valve adjustment

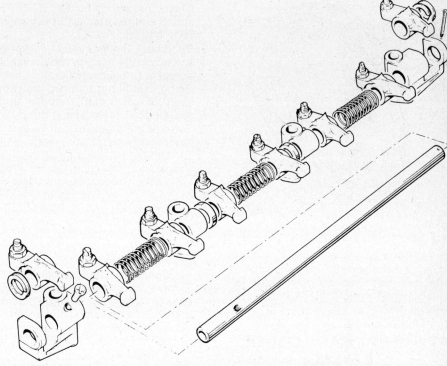

Fig. 2 Rocker shaft assembly

14. Remove three bolts holding water pump housing to cylinder head.
15. Remove rocker shaft assembly.
16. Remove push rods.
17. Loosen the cylinder head nuts in reverse sequence, Fig. 1.
18. Remove rear lifting eye.
19. Disconnect fuel line from the pump.
20. Remove cylinder head and manifolds.
21. Reverse procedure to install cylinder head nuts in sequence, Fig. 1.

ROCKER SHAFT, REPLACE

1. Remove rocker cover.
2. Remove cotter pin from front of shaft.
3. Slide off rockers, lifters, springs and spacers, noting location of components, Fig. 2.
4. Remove screw holding rear lifter to shaft.
5. Remove rear lifter and shaft.
6. Reverse procedure to install.

VALVES, ADJUST

1. Disconnect the battery ground cable, and remove the spark plugs and rocker cover.
2. Check clearance between the rocker pad and valve tip, Fig. 3, and adjust to specifications in the following sequence:

NOTE: Count valves from the front

of the engine.

No. 1 and 3 with No. 6 and 8 open
No. 2 and 5 with No. 4 and 7 open
No. 6 and 8 with No. 1 and 3 open
No. 4 and 7 with No. 2 and 5 open

3. Adjust by loosening the adjustment pin locknut and turning the adjustment pin.

VALVE GUIDES, REPLACE

Use special tool 60A. Assemble the

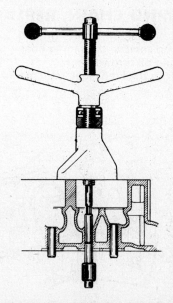

Fig. 4 Valve guide replacement

1-889

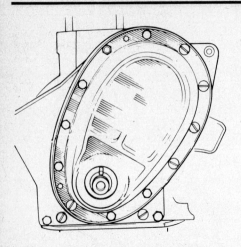

Fig. 5 Timing chain cover installation

new valve guide in the tool with the chamfered end first. Place the tool in position and drive the new guide into place while the old guide is removed, Fig. 4.

TIMING CHAIN COVER, REPLACE

1. Remove radiator.
2. Remove air pump and alternator, then the mounting brackets.
3. Remove fan blades and crankshaft pulley.
4. Remove the timing cover fasteners, Fig. 5.
5. Remove the timing cover and gasket.
6. Reverse procedure to install. Installation of the cover can be facilitated by using a length of welding rod bent at a right angle to hold the chain tensioner away from the chain.

TIMING CHAIN, REPLACE

1. Disconnect battery ground cable and remove the timing chain cover and oil thrower.
2. Turn the crankshaft until marks "A"

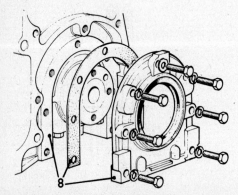

Fig. 7 Crankshaft rear oil seal housing

are in line with scribe mark "C." Check that punch marks "B" correspond and the crankshaft keyway is at 12 o'clock, Fig. 6.

3. Bend back the lock tab and remove the two bolts holding the camshaft sprocket to the camshaft.
4. Being careful not to move the camshaft or crankshaft, remove both sprockets with the timing chain.
5. Remove the crankshaft drive key.
6. Temporarily install sprockets.
7. Check sprocket alignment by placing a straight edge across both sprockets. Correct misalignment by fitting shims behind the crankshaft sprocket.
8. Remove the sprockets and install the crankshaft drive key.
9. Install the chain on the sprockets, then install sprockets, ensuring that all alignment marks are aligned.
10. Tighten the camshaft sprocket and check timing chain wear by placing a straight edge along the chain to measure slack. If movement at the midpoint is greater than ⅜ inch, replace the chain.
11. Reverse procedure to assemble.

CAMSHAFT, REPLACE

1. Disconnect battery ground cable and drain cooling system.
2. Remove the radiator, cylinder head, water pump housing and fan, alternator, air pump, crankshaft pulley timing cover, timing chain and sprockets, and camshaft keeper plate.
3. Remove the cam followers.
4. Remove the distributor driveshaft and gear, and fuel pump.
5. Remove the camshaft.
6. Reverse procedure to install.

CRANKSHAFT REAR OIL SEAL, REPLACE
Removal

1. Remove the transmission.
2. Remove the rear adaptor plate.
3. Remove the two rear center oil pan bolts.
4. Remove the oil seal housing from the crankcase, complete with the seal, Fig. 7.

CAUTION: Do not damage the oil pan gasket.

5. Press out the seal, taking care not to distort the housing, Fig. 8.

Installation

1. Clean all mating surfaces.
2. Place the oil seal housing on a flat

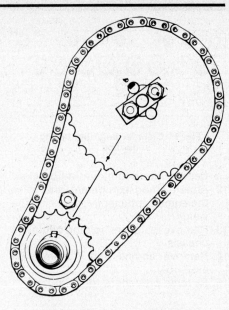

Fig. 6 Timing chain installation

surface, machined side up, and lubricate the outside diameter of a new seal with grease.

3. With the seal's lip side facing up, press the seal in place and wipe off excess grease.
4. Apply sealing compound to the crankcase and oil seal housing mating surfaces and install a new gasket.
5. Lubricate the oil seal inner diameter and the crankshaft with clean engine oil, and install the oil seal and housing over the crankshaft.
6. Secure the housing to the crankshaft.

NOTE: The top bolt has a copper washer under the head to prevent oil seepage.

7. Reverse removal procedure to assemble.

OIL PAN, REPLACE

1. Drain oil.
2. Remove all bolts and washers (16)

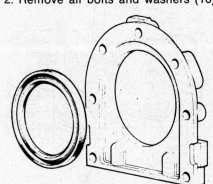

Fig. 8 Crankshaft rear oil seal installation

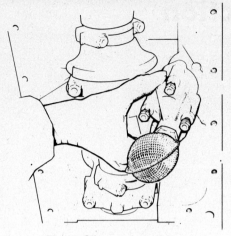

Fig. 9 Oil pump installation

OIL PUMP, REPLACE

1. Drain oil.
2. Remove the oil pan.
3. Loosen the three bolts holding the pump to the crankcase, Fig. 9.
4. Hold the pump cover and remove the pump.
5. Reverse procedure to install. Ensure the pump spindle engages firmly into the distributor drive gear shaft. Torque bolts to 7-9 ft. lbs.

WATER PUMP, REPLACE

1. Disconnect battery ground cable.
2. Remove water pump housing assembly and fan blades, Fig. 10.
3. Remove the fasteners holding the water pump to the water pump housing.
4. Remove the water pump and viscous coupling. Separate the two.
5. Reverse procedure to install.

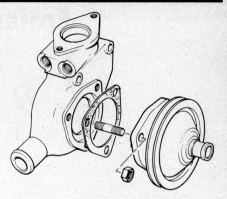

Fig. 10 Water pump installation

FUEL PUMP, REPLACE

1. Disconnect fuel lines at the fuel pump.
2. Remove fuel pump from the cylinder block.
3. Remove and discard the gasket.
4. Reverse procedure to install.

holding the pan.
3. Remove the pan.
4. Reverse procedure to install.

Carburetor Section

CARBURETOR ADJUSTMENTS

Idle Speed

Adjust by turning the throttle adjusting screw, Fig. 1. refer to "Tune-Up Specification" chart for idle speed.

Idle Mixture

1. A minimum adjustment can be made with the fine idle CO screw.
2. Remove the piston damper.
3. Insert tool S353 into the dashpot until outer tool engages in air valve and inner tool engages hexagon in needle adjuster plug, Fig. 2.
4. Turn the tool clockwise to enrich the mixture or counterclockwise to lean.

5. Top off the damper and recheck the CO reading.

CAUTION: Be sure to engage the tool properly to avoid damage to the diaphragm.

Deceleration & Bypass Valve

1. Remove vacuum line from distributor and plug line.
2. The valve is operating properly if idle speed increases to about 1,500 rpm. The valve requires adjusting if idle speed increases to 2,000-2,500 rpm.

3. If adjustment is required, plug end of vacuum line.
4. Turn the bypass valve screw clockwise, Fig. 3, until engine speed increases rapidly to 2,000-2,500 rpm.
5. Turn adjusting screw counterclockwise until engine speed falls to about 1,300 rpm.
6. Using the throttle, increase speed rapidly and release the throttle. Engine speed should drop back to 1,300 rpm. If not, readjust as outlined in steps 4-5.
7. When the valve has been adjusted, turn the adjustment screw counterclockwise one-half turn.

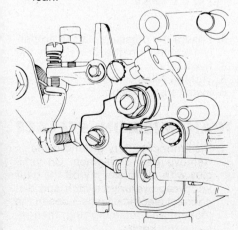

Fig. 1 Idle speed adjustment

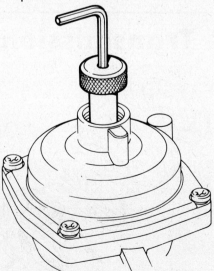

Fig. 2 Idle mixture adjustment

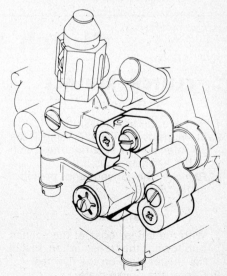

Fig. 3 Deceleration & bypass valve adjustment

Emission Controls Section

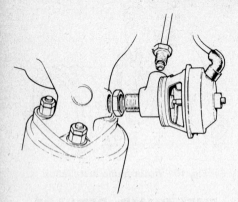

Fig. 1 EGR valve installation

EGR VALVE

To check the operation of the EGR valve, warm up the engine, and open and close the throttle several times. Observe or feel the EGR valve, which should open and close with changes in engine speed. The EGR valve should close at once when the throttle is closed.

Service the EGR valve as follows:

1. Remove the EGR valve from the exhaust manifold, Fig. 1.
2. Clean the valve seat with a wire brush.
3. Insert the valve opening into a standard spark plug machine and lift the diaphragm.
4. Blast the valve for 30 seconds.
5. Use compressed air and a brush to remove all traces of carbon.

FUEL ABSORPTION CANISTER, REPLACE

1. Disconnect lines at canister, Fig. 2.
2. Remove bracket nut and bolt.

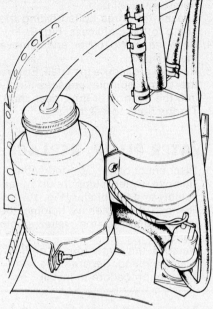

Fig. 2 Fuel absorption canister installation

3. Remove canister.
4. Transfer the restrictor in the old canister to the new canister.
5. Install new canister.

CATALYTIC CONVERTER, REPLACE

1. Remove catalytic converter support bracket.
2. Release the catalytic converter from the tailpipe, Fig. 3.

NOTE: It may be necessary to remove the carburetor.

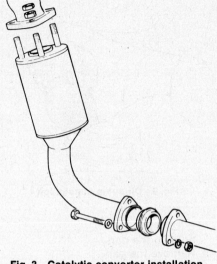

Fig. 3 Catalytic converter installation

3. Remove nuts holding catalytic converter and front pipe to exhaust manifold.
4. Remove the catalytic converter and front pipe, and exhaust manifold gasket.
5. Fit a new catalytic converter.
6. Reset the catalytic converter warning indicator to zero.

AIR PUMP BELT TENSION

1. Loosen securing bolt and two adjusting link bolts.
2. Move air pump to obtain a belt deflection of ½ inch.
3. Tighten bolts.

Clutch & Transmission Section

CLUTCH, REPLACE

Removal

1. Remove the transmission.
2. From inside the vehicle, remove the six Allen screws securing the clutch to the flywheel housing.
3. Remove the driven and pressure plates, Fig. 1.

Installation

1. With the longer boss of the splined hub toward the transmission, install the driven plate on the flywheel.
2. Center the driven plate.
3. Insert the six Allen screws securing clutch to flywheel.

Fig. 1 Clutch assembly

4. Ensure the pressure plate is properly installed on the dowels on the flywheel.
5. Tighten Allen screws.
6. Install transmission.

TRANSMISSION, REPLACE

1. Disconnect battery ground cable.
2. Remove gear shift knob. On vehicles with overdrive, pry off the gear knob cap/overdrive switch and disconnect electrical leads. Loosen the locknut and retaining ring, then remove the knob.
3. Remove transmission cover.
4. Remove driveshaft cover plate.

5. Disconnect driveshaft from transmission drive flange.
6. Disconnect speedometer cable drive.
7. Remove clutch slave cylinder.
8. Raise vehicle and drain transmission.
9. Place a suitable jack under the engine oil pan to support the engine, placing a block of wood between the jack and pan.
10. Disconnect exhaust pipe from bracket on transmission.
11. Remove transmission rear mount fasteners, engine restraining cable from the bell housing, and the bell housing bolts accessible from below.
12. Lower the vehicle.
13. Remove starter.
14. Inside the vehicle, disconnect electric harness leads for the backup lights, overdrive and seat belt warning system.
15. Detach transmission mounting assembly.
16. Remove remaining bell housing fasteners.
17. Remove transmission.
18. Reverse procedure to install.

Rear Axle & Brakes Section

REAR AXLE SHAFT BEARING & OIL SEAL, REPLACE

1. Remove inner drive shaft flange-drive shaft coupling bolts.
2. Use a suitable jack to relieve load on rear shock absorber.
3. Remove shock absorber lower fastener and swing the shock clear.
4. Remove bolt and nut holding radius rod to vertical link, Fig. 1. Remove jack.
5. Disconnect spring.
6. Remove housing plate from differential, Fig. 2.
7. Raise drive shaft clear of inner drive shaft and remove inner drive shaft.
8. Remove clip from shaft.
9. Use tools S-4221A and S-4221A-7B, press shaft from bearing.
10. Remove oil seal plate.
11. Remove oil seal.
12. Reverse procedure to install.

PARKING BRAKE, ADJUST

1. Raise and support rear of vehicle.
2. Release parking brake.
3. Turn rear brake adjusters to lock both rear wheels.
4. See that the relay lever is positioned properly, Fig. 3.
   If not, adjust front and rear cables, as necessary, to obtain proper adjustment.

Fig. 1 Radius rod & vertical link installation

Front Cable

1. Expose brake lever.
2. Loosen cable locknut at rear of cable fork. Rotate the cable clockwise to tighten or counterclockwise to loosen.
3. Tighten locknut.

NOTE: It may be necessary to release the rear brake cable.

Rear Cable

1. Disconnect cable fork ends from brake backing plate lever.
2. Adjust cable forks equally at both ends of cable until clevis pins can be inserted to hold cable forks to backing plate lever.

CAUTION: There should be slight tension on cable, but do not force the cable taut to insert the clevis pins.

MASTER CYLINDER, REPLACE

1. Raise boot to expose linkage.
2. Remove attachments and boot.
3. Disconnect brake lines, sealing all openings, Fig. 4.
4. Remove attaching parts holding master cylinder assembly and the cylinder.

DISC BRAKE SERVICE

Refer to the MGB chapter for disc brake service.

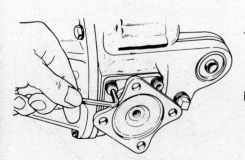

Fig. 2 Housing plate removal

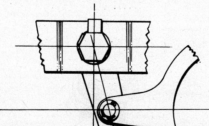

Fig. 3 Parking brake adjustment

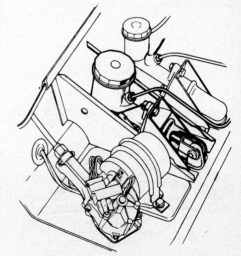

Fig. 4 Master cylinder installation

Rear Suspension Section

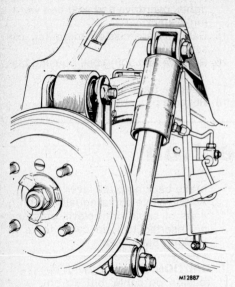

Fig. 1 Rear spring & shock absorber installation

SHOCK ABSORBERS, REPLACE

1. Raise and support vehicle and remove rear wheel.
2. Release lower bushing, Fig. 1.
3. Release upper mounting.
4. Remove shock absorber.

SPRINGS, REPLACE

1. Disconnect shock absorber lower mount, Fig. 1.
2. Remove rear panel cover, Fig. 2.
3. Remove nuts holding spring bracket to differential.
4. Remove four studs from differential.
5. Remove spring from vehicle.
6. Reverse procedure to install.

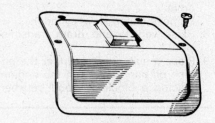

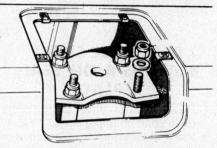

Fig. 2 Rear spring upper attachment

Front Suspension Section

WHEEL ALIGNMENT

Refer to the TR6 chapter for wheel alignment adjustment procedures. The difference is that the lower wishbone is held by two nuts in place of four nuts for camber adjustment, Fig. 1.

WHEEL BEARINGS, ADJUST

Refer to the TR6 chapter for wheel bearing adjustment. The only difference is that the end play specification is 0.002-0.005 inch.

BALL JOINTS, REPLACE

1. Raise and support vehicle.
2. Remove wheel.
3. Remove nut and plain washer holding ball joint shank to the verticle link, Fig. 2.
4. Release ball joint shank from vertical link.
5. Remove two bolts and nuts holding ball joint to upper wishbone.
6. Remove ball joint.
7. Reverse procedure to install.

LOWER TRUNNION, REPLACE

1. Raise and support vehicle.
2. Remove wheel.
3. Remove hub assembly.
4. Remove bolt securing steering arm and disc shield to vertical link.
5. Remove the disc shield.
6. Remove nut and bolt securing trunnion to lower wishbone, Fig. 3.

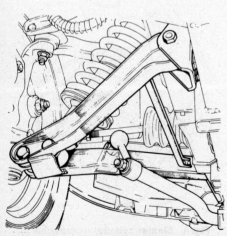

Fig. 1 Camber adjustment

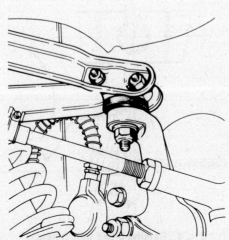

Fig. 2 Upper ball joint installation

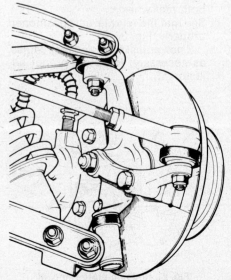

Fig. 3 Lower trunnion installation

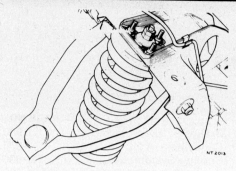

Fig. 4 Spring pad installation

7. Disconnect shock absorber from lower wishbone.
8. Disconnect trunnion from lower wishbone and remove trunnion from vehicle.
9. Reverse procedure to install.

SHOCK ABSORBER & SPRING, REPLACE

1. Raise and support vehicle and remove front wheel.
2. Loosen fastener holding steering trunnion to lower wishbone.
3. Remove fasteners holding bottom of shock absorber to lower wishbone, Fig. 3.
4. Remove three fasteners holding spring pad to bracket, Fig. 4.
5. Release shock absorber and remove shock absorber and spring assembly as a unit.
6. Using tools S4221A and S4221A-5, compress spring, Fig. 5.
7. Disconnect spring and shock and remove from vehicle.
8. Reverse procedure to install.

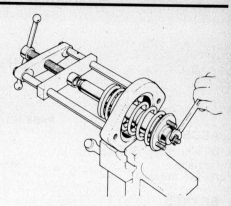

Fig. 5 Spring replacement

STEERING GEAR, REPLACE

Refer to the TR6 chapter for steering gear replacement.

SUBARU

INDEX OF SERVICE OPERATIONS

SUBARU

GENERAL ENGINE SPECIFICATIONS

Year	Engine	Car-buretor	Bore x Stroke	Piston Dis-place-ment Cubic Inches	Com-pres-sion Ratio	Maximum Brake H.P. @ R.P.M.	Maximum Torque Lbs. Ft. @ R.P.M.	Normal Oil Pressure Pounds
1972	4—1300 cc	1 Barrel	3.23 x 2.36 (82 x 60mm)	77.3 (1267 cc)	9.0	61 @ 5600	65.1 @ 4000 (88.3 joules @ 4000)	36—46
	4—1400 cc	1 Barrel	3.35 x 2.36 (85 x 60mm)	83.2 (1361 cc)	9.0	80 @ 6400	76 @ 4000 (103 joules @ 4000)	36—46
	4—1400 cc	2 Barrel	3.35 x 2.26 (85 x 60mm)	83.2 (1361 cc)	10.0	93 @ 6800	79.6 @ 4800 (108 joules @ 4800)	36—40
1973-74	4—1400 cc	2 Barrel	3.35 x 2.26 (85 x 60mm)	83.2 (1361 cc)	9.0	61 @ 5600	68.7 @ 3600 (93.8 joules @ 3600)	36—46
1975	4—1400 cc ①	2 Barrel	3.35 x 2.26 (85 x 60mm)	83.2 (1361 cc)	9.0	58 @ 5200	68 @ 2400 (92.2 joules @ 2400)	36—46
	4—1400 cc ②	2 Barrel	3.35 x 2.36 (85 x 60mm)	83.2 (1361 cc)	9.0	56 @ 5200	67 @ 2400 (90.8 joules @ 2400)	36—46
1976	4—1400 cc ①	2 Barrel	3.35 x 2.36 (85 x 60mm)	83.2 (1361 cc)	8.5	58 @ 5200	68 @ 2400 (92.2 joules @ 2400)	36—46
	4—1400 cc ②	2 Barrel	3.35 x 2.36 (85 x 60mm)	83.2 (1361 cc)	8.5	56 @ 5200	67 @ 2400 (92.2 joules @ 2400)	36—46
1976-77	4—1600 cc ①	2 Barrel	3.62 x 2.36 (92 x 60mm)	97 (1595 cc)	8.5	67 @ 5200	81 @ 2400 (109.8 joules @ 2400)	36—46
1977	4—1600 cc ②	2 Barrel	3.62 x 2.36 (92 x 60mm)	97 (1595 cc)	8.5	65 @ 5200	80 @ 2400 (108.5 joules @ 2400)	36—46

①—Front wheel drive.
②—Four wheel drive.

TUNE UP SPECIFICATIONS

★When using a timing light, disconnect vacuum hose or tube at distributor and plug opening in hose or tube so idle speed will not be affected.

●When checking compression, lowest cylinder must be within 7.2 PSI of highest.

▲Before removing wires from distributor cap, determine location of No. 1 wire in cap, as distributor position may have been altered from that shown at the end of this chart.

Year	Engine	Spark Plug		Distributor		Ignition Timing★			Carb. Adjustments			
		Type	Gap Inch	Point Gap Inch	Dwell Angle Deg.	Firing Order Fig. ▲	Timing BTDC ①	Mark Fig.	Hot Idle Speed		Idle "CO"%	
									Std. Trans.	Auto. Trans.	Std. Trans.	Auto. Trans.
1972-74	All	BP6ES	.032	.020	49—55	A	6°	B	②	800	1—3	1—3
1975	All	BP6ES	.032	.020	49—55	A	8°	B	800	900	.33—.37 ③	.33—.37 ③
1976	All	BP6ES	.032	.020	49—55	A	8°	B	900	900	.15—.55 ③	.15—.55 ③
1977	4—1600 cc ④	BP6ES	.032	.018	49—55	A	8°	B	850	850	—	—
	4—1600 cc ⑤	BP6ES	.032	—	—	A	8°	B	900	900	—	—

—Not Available
①—BTDC: Before top dead center.
②—1972, 850 RPM; 1973-74, 800 RPM.
③—With air injection connected. .5—1.5% with air injection disconnected.
④—Exc. California.
⑤—California.

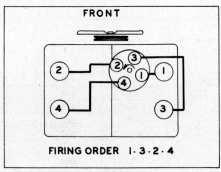

FRONT

FIRING ORDER 1·3·2·4

Fig. A

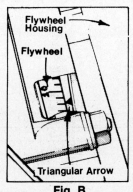

Flywheel Housing

Flywheel

Triangular Arrow

Fig. B

SUBARU

DISTRIBUTOR SPECIFICATIONS
If unit is checked on vehicle, double the RPM and degrees to get crankshaft figures.

Distributor Part No.	Centrifugal Advance Degrees @ RPM of Distributor					Vacuum Advance		Distributor Retard
	Advance Starts	Intermediate Advance			Full Advance	Inches of Vacuum to Start Plunger	Max. Adv. Dist. Deg. @ Vacuum	Max. Ret. Dist. Deg. @ Vacuum
1972-74								
D414—60 ①	0 @ 450	6—8 @ 1200	—	—	15 @ 2400	—	—	10 @ 213 (10 @ 540mm)
1975								
D414—88 ①	0 @ 500	6—8 @ 1200	—	—	15 @ 2400	—	—	11.5 @ 17.32 (11.5 @ 440mm)
1976								
029100—3710 ②	0 @ 500	2—4 @ 840	6—8 @ 1200	13—15 @ 2400	14.8 @ 3000	3.94 (100mm)	9.5 @ 11.81 (9.5 @ 300mm)	11.5 @ 13.78 (11.5 @ 350mm)
1977								
D4H6—01 ① ③	—	—	—	—	—	—	—	—
029100—3700 ②	0 @ 400	4—6 @ 1000	6—8 @ 1200	8—11 @ 2000	15 @ 2400	1 (25.4mm)	11.5 @ 11.81 (11.5 @ 300mm)	9 @ 10.8 (9 @ 275mm)
029100—4220 ② ④	—	—	—	—	—	—	—	—
029100—4270 ② ③	—	—	—	—	—	—	—	—

—Not Available
① —Hitachi.
② —Nippon denso.
③ —California.
④ —Exc. California.

ALTERNATOR & REGULATOR SPECIFICATIONS

Year	Alternator					Regulator							
	Model	Rated Hot Output Amps.	Field Current 12 Volts @ 80°F	Output @ 14 Volts		Model	Field Relay			Voltage Regulator		
				2500 R.P.M. Amps.	5000 R.P.M. Amps.		Air Gap In.	Point Gap In.	Releasing Voltage	Air Gap In.	Point Gap In.	Voltage @ 68°F
1972-73	LT135-20	35	—	23	35	TLZ-65	.035	.020	8—10	.032	①	14—15
1974	LT135-20	35	—	23	35	TLZ-74	.035	.020	8—10	.032	.014	14—15
1975	LT150-21	50	—	40	51	TLZ-74	.035	.020	8—10	.032	.014	14—15
1976	LT150-21	50	—	40	51	TLZ-90	.035	.020	8—10	.032	.014	14—15
1977	LT150-21	50	—	40	51	TLZ-94	.035	.020	8—10	.032	.014	14—15

—Not Available
① —1972, .020″; 1973, .014″.

STARTING MOTOR SPECIFICATIONS

Year	Part No.	Rotation ①	Brush Spring Tension, Ounces	No Load Test			Torque Test		
				Amperes	Volts	R.P.M.	Amperes	Volts	Torque, Ft. Lbs.
1972-75	28000-2970	cc	36—48	50	11	5000	470	7.7	9.4 (1.3 kg-m)
1975-76	028000-4210	cc	36—48	50	11	5000	470	7.7	9.4 (1.3 kg-m)
1976	028000-2970	cc	36—48	50	11	5000	470	7.7	9.4 (1.3 kg-m)
	028000-4720	cc	36—48	50	11	5000	600	7	13 (1.8 kg-m)
1977	028000-2970	cc	30—40.6	50	11	5000	600	7.7	9.4 (1.3 kg-m)
	028000-4210	cc	30—40.6	50	11	5000	600	7.7	9.4 (1.3 kg-m)
	028000-4721	cc	30—40.6	60	11	5000	600	7	13 (1.8 kg-m)

① —Viewed from drive end.

SUBARU

VALVE SPECIFICATIONS

Year	Model	Valve Lash Int.	Valve Lash Exh.	Valve Angles Seat	Valve Angles Face	Valve Spring Installed Height	Valve Spring Pressure Lbs. @ In.	Stem Clearance Intake	Stem Clearance Exhaust	Stem Diameter Intake	Stem Diameter Exhaust
1972-75	All	.012 (.30mm)	①	45	45	②	③	④	.0020—.0032 (.050—.080mm)	.3130—.3136 (7.950—7.965mm)	.3124—.3130 (7.935—7.950mm)
1976	All	.010 (.25mm)	.014 (.35mm)	45	45	⑤	⑥	.0014—.0026 (.035—.065mm)	.0020—.0032 (.050—.080mm)	.3130—.3136 (7.950—7.965mm)	.3124—.3130 (7.935—7.950mm)
1977	All	.010 (.25mm)	.014 (.35mm)	45	45	②	⑦	.0014—.0026 (.035—.065mm)	.0016—.0028 (.040—.070mm)	.3130—.3136 (7.950—7.965mm)	.3128—.3134 (7.945—7.960mm)

①—Exc. 1975, .012″ (.30mm); 1975, .014″ (.35mm).
②—Outer spring, 1.9″ (48.2mm); inner spring, 1.92″ (48.65mm).
③—Outer spring, 97.8 lbs. @ 1.22″ (44.4 kg @ 31mm); inner spring, 43.6 lbs. @ 1.14″ (19.5 kg @ 29mm).
④—Exc. 1972, .0014—.0026 (.035—.065mm); 1972, .0010—.0022 (.025—.055mm).
⑤—Outer spring, 1.9″ (48.2mm); inner spring, 1.97″ (50.05mm).
⑥—Outer spring, 94.4 lbs. @ 1.25″ (42.8 kg @ 31.8mm); inner spring, 41.8 lbs. @ 1.16″ (19 kg @ 29.5mm).
⑦—Outer spring, 97.8 lbs. @ 1.22″ (44.4 @ 31mm); inner spring, 46.3lbs. @ 1.10″ (20.7 kg @ 28mm).

PISTONS, PINS, RINGS, CRANKSHAFT & BEARINGS

Year	Model	Piston Clearance Top of Skirt	Ring End Gap Comp.	Ring End Gap Oil	Wrist-pin Diameter	Rod Bearings Shaft Diameter	Rod Bearings Bearing Clearance	Main Bearings Shaft Diameter	Main Bearings Bearing Clearance	Thrust on Bear. No.	Shaft End Play
1972	All	.0008—.0019 (.020—.049mm)	.008 (.2mm)	.008 (.2mm)	—	1.7712—1.7717 (44.989—45mm)	.0012—.0026 (.030—.067mm)	①	②	2	.0019—.0054 (.047—.137mm)
1973	All	.0008—.0020 (.020—.050mm)	.008 (.2mm)	.012 (.3mm)	—	1.7712—1.7717 (44.989—45mm)	.0012—.0026 (.030—.067mm)	③	④	2	.0016—.0054 (.040—.137mm)
1974	All	.0008—.0019 (.020—.049mm)	.012 (.3mm)	.012 (.3mm)	—	1.7711—1.7717 (44.985—45mm)	.0012—.0031 (.030—.080mm)	③	⑤	2	.0016—.0054 (.040—.137mm)
1975	All	.0008—.0019 (.020—.049mm)	.102 (.3mm)	.012 (.3mm)	—	1.7712—1.7717 (44.989—45mm)	.0012—.0031 (.030—.080mm)	①	⑤	2	.0019—.0054 (.047—.137mm)
1976	All	⑥	.012 (.3mm)	.012 (.3mm)	—	1.7711—1.7717 (44.985—45mm)	.0012-.0029 (.030—.074mm)	①	⑤	2	.0016—.0054 (.040—.137mm)
1977	All	.0004—.0016 (.010—.040mm)	.012 (.3mm)	.012 (.3mm)	.8265—.8268 (20.992—21mm)	1.7715—1.7720 (44.995—45.010mm)	⑦	⑧	⑨	2	.0016—.0054 (.040—.137mm)

—Not Available
①—Front and rear journal, 1.9667—1.9673″ (49.955—49.970mm); center journal, 1.9673—1.9677″ (49.969—49.980mm).
②—Front and rear bearings, .0004—.0023″ (.010—.058mm); center bearing, .0017″ (.044mm).
③—Front and rear journals, 1.9682—1.9688″ (49.955—49.970mm); center journal, 1.9688—1.9692″ (49.969—49.980mm).
④—Front and rear bearings, .0004—.0022″ (.010—.054mm); center bearing, 0—.0016″ (0—.040mm).
⑤—Front and rear bearings, .0004-.0020″ (.010—.050mm); center bearing, 0—.0014″ (0-.036mm).
⑥—Man. trans., .0008—.0019″ (.02—.049mm); auto. trans., .0004—.0016″ (.010—.040mm).
⑦—Bearing A17S, .0008—.0025″ (.020—.064mm); bearing F-770, .0008—.0028″ (.020—.070mm).
⑧—Front and rear journals, 1.9667—1.9673″ (49.955—49.970mm); center journal, 1.9671—1.9677″ (49.965—49.980mm).
⑨—For bearing A17S: front and rear bearings, .0004—.0016″ (.010—.040mm); center bearing, 0—.0008″ (0—.020mm); for bearing F-770: front and rear bearings, .0004—.0017″ (.010—.044mm); center bearing, 0—.0013″ (0—.034mm).

ENGINE TIGHTENING SPECIFICATIONS

★Torque specifications are for clean and lightly lubricated threads only. Dry or dirty threads produce increased friction which prevents accurate measurement of tightness.

Year	Engine	Spark Plugs Ft. Lbs.	Cylinder Head Bolts Ft. Lbs.	Intake Manifold Ft. Lbs.	Crankcase Oil Pan Ft. Lbs.	Rocker Arm Cover Ft. Lbs.	Connecting Rod Cap Bolts Ft. Lbs.	Crankcase Halves Ft. Lbs.	Flywheel to Crankshaft Ft. Lbs.	Vibration Damper or Pulley Ft. Lbs.
1972-77	All	13—17 (1.8—2.4 kg-m)	47 (6.99 kg-m)	13—16 (1.8—2.2 kg-m)	3.3—4 (.45—.55 kg-m)	2.2—2.9 (.30—.40 kg-m)	①	②	30—33 (4.2—4.6 kg-m)	39—42 (5.4—5.8 kg-m)

①—All exc. 1976 auto. trans. and all 1977 models, 36 ft. lbs. (5 kg-m); 1976 auto. trans. and all 1977, 29—31 ft. lbs. (4—4.3 kg-m).
②—10mm bolts, 29—35 ft. lbs. (4—4.8 kg-m); 8 mm bolts, 17—20 ft. lbs. (2.3—2.7 kg-m); 6mm bolts, 3.3—4 ft. lbs. (.45—.55 kg-m).

SUBARU

WHEEL ALIGNMENT SPECIFICATIONS

NOTE: See that riding height is correct before checking alignment

| Year | Model | Caster Angle, Degrees ① | | Camber Angle, Degrees ① | | | | Toe-In. Inch | Toe-Out on Turns, Deg. | |
| | | Limits | Desired | Limits | | Desired | | | Outer Wheel | Inner Wheel |
				Left	Right	Left	Right			
1972	Front Axle ②	—	¾	—	—	1½	1½	.08—.32	—	—
	Rear Axle ②	—	—	—	—	③	③	.04—.20	—	—
1973	Front Axle ②	—	¾	—	—	1½	1½	.09—.32	—	—
	Rear Axle ②	—	—	—	—	1	1	④	—	—
1974	Front Axle ②	—	¾	—	—	1½	1½	.08—.32	—	—
	Rear Axle ②	—	—	—	—	1	1	.04—.20	—	—
1975	Front Axle ②	0 to 1½	¾	1 to 2	1 to 2	1½	1½	.08—.32	—	—
	Rear Axle ②	—	—	⑥	⑥	⑦	⑦	④	—	—
1975-77	Front Axle ⑤	0 to 1½	¾	2 to 3	2 to 3	2½	2½	.24—.47	—	—
	Rear Axle ⑤	—	—	1⅓ to 2⅓	1⅓ to 2⅓	1⅚	1⅚	.08—.24	—	—
1976	Front Axle ②	0 to 1½	¾	1 to 2	1 to 2	1½	1½	.08—.32	—	—
	Rear Axle ②	—	—	¼ to 1½	¼ to 1½	1	1	④	—	—
1977	Front Axle ②	0 to 1½	¾	1⅓ to 2⅓	1⅓ to 2⅓	1⅚	1⅚	.08—.32	—	—
	Rear Axle ②	—	—	¼ to 1½	¼ to 1½	1	1	④	—	—

—Not Available
① —Non-adjustable, if not within limits, check for damaged components.
② —Front wheel drive.
③ —Exc. Station Wagon, 1°; Station Wagon, 1½°.
④ —Exc. Station Wagon, .04"—.20"; Station Wagon, .08"—.24".
⑤ —4-wheel drive.
⑥ —Exc. Station Wagon, ¼°—1½°; Station Wagon, 1°—2°.
⑦ —Exc. Station Wagon, 1°; Station Wagon, 1½°.

BRAKE SPECIFICATIONS

| Year | Model | Front Brake Drum I.D. | Rear Brake Drum I.D. | Wheel Cylinder Bore | | | Master Cylinder | | Disc Brake Rotor | |
				Front Disc	Front Drum	Rear Drum	Manual	Power	Nominal Thickness	Minimum Thickness
1972	All	8.98	7.09	2.13	15/16	①	¾	—	.39	.33
1973	All	8.98	7.09	2.13	15/16	9/16	¾	—	.39	.33
1974	All	8.98	7.09	2.13	15/16	5/8	¾	—	.39	.33
1975	All	9.00	7.09	2⅛	15/16	②	¾	¾	.39	.33
1976-77	All	—	7.09	2⅛		②	¾	¾	.39	.33

—Not Available
① —Exc. Station Wagon, 9/16"; Station Wagon, 5/8".
② —Exc. Station Wagon 5/8"; Station Wagon, 11/16".

COOLING SYSTEM & CAPACITY DATA

| Year | Model or Engine | Cooling Capacity Qts. | | Radiator Cap Relief Pressure, Lbs. | | Thermo. Opening Temp. | Fuel Tank Gals. | Engine Oil Refill Qts. | Transmission Oil | | | Axle Oil Pints |
		With Heater	With A/C	With A/C	No A/C				4 Speed	5 Speed	Auto. Trans. Qts.	
1972	All	6.2	6.2	—	—	180	①	3.4	5.2	—	—	—
1973	All	6.5	6.5	—	—	180	①	3.4	5.2	—	—	—
1974	All	6.2	6.2	—	—	180	②	3.5	5.2	5.8	6.3	—
1975	All	6.3	6.3	11.4—14.2	114.—14.2	180	②	3.8	5.2③	5.8	6.3	—
1976-77	All	6.3	6.3	④	④	190	②	3.8	5.2③	5.8	6.3	⑤

—Not Available
① —Sedan and Coupe, 13.2 gals.; Station Wagon, 9.5 gals.
② —Sedan and Coupe, 13.2 gals; Station Wagon and 4-wheel drive, 11.8 gals.
③ —4-wheel drive, 6.4 pints.
④ —1976, 11.4—14.2 psi; 1977, 13 psi.
⑤ —1977 auto. trans. 2.2 pints; 1977 4-wheel drive, 1.7 pints.

Electrical Section

DISTRIBUTOR, REPLACE

1. Disconnect vacuum line and primary wire from distributor.
2. Remove adjusting bracket lock bolt.
3. Remove distributor cap, then crank engine to line up rotor with fixed reference mark.
4. Withdraw distributor from engine.

DISTRIBUTOR, REPAIRS

1972-75

1. Remove two retaining screws, then disengage operating rod from breaker plate and remove vacuum control, Figs. 1 and 2.
2. Loosen breaker point, set screws and terminal screw, then remove breaker points with lead wire.
3. Pull upward and remove primary terminal from distributor body.
4. Remove retaining screw, then remove condenser.
5. Remove retaining screws, then remove two piece breaker plate.
6. Drive out pin that secures gear to distributor shaft, then pull distributor shaft from gear bore.
7. Remove center screw from top of cam, then remove cam.
8. Remove governor weights and springs.
9. Wash all parts except vacuum control unit and condenser in a suitable solvent.
10. Check clearance of distributor shaft in housing. If clearance exceeds 0.003-inch (0.08) mm, measure shaft diameter. Standard shaft, diameter is 0.4894 to 0.4898-inch (12.43-12.44 mm). If wear exceeds 0.0012-inch (0.03mm), replace shaft. If shaft play in housing still is excessive, replace housing.
11. Check cam surface for roughness (replace if rough) and condition of square hole in cam governor flange as shown in Fig. 5. If hole is worn, replace cam. If governor springs are deformed, replace or bend open and spring hook by about 0.02-inch (0.5mm).
12. Check two-piece breaker plate for smooth movement. If not smooth, disassemble and clean or replace steel balls.
13. If pinion gear is worn, or teeth are chipped, replace pinion gear.
14. Begin reassembly by fitting governor weights and springs, then distributor cam with screw and washers.

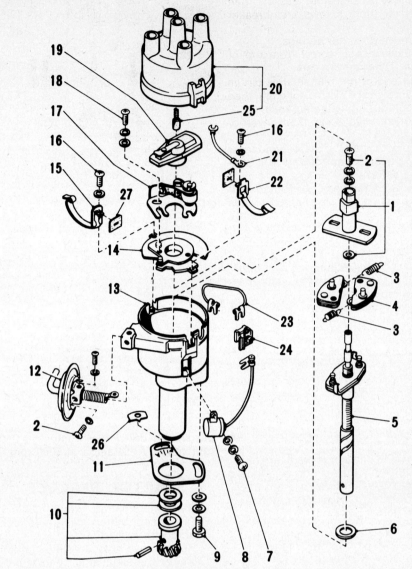

1. Cam	10. Pinion	19. Rotor head
2. Screw	11. Plate	20. Cap
3. Governor spring	12. Vacuum control	21. Ground wire
4. Governor weight	13. Housing	22. Clamp I
5. Distributor shaft	14. Contact breaker plate	23. Lead wire
6. Washer	15. Clamp II	24. Terminal
7. Screw	16. Screw	25. Carbon point
8. Condenser	17. Contact set	26. Indicator
9. Bolt	18. Contact set screw	27. Seal II

Fig. 1 Exploded view of distributor. 1972-73 models

NOTE: There are two types of governor springs, one with a round hook end, the other with a square hook, Fig. 6. The cam rotor notch should point toward round hook. Continue reassembly in reverse of disassembly.

1976-77

1. Remove dust cap and primary terminal nut, then terminal and insulator, Fig. 3.
2. Remove three set screws, then withdraw breaker points set and damper spring.
3. Remove snap ring securing vacuum

advance arm to breaker plate, then condenser and vacuum control unit.

4. Remove dust-sealing gasket, then breaker plate screws and breaker plate.
5. Remove governor springs.
6. Remove center screw from top of cam. Then remove cam.
7. Drill end of pin that secures pinion gear to end of distributor shaft, then knock out pin using a punch.
8. Remove snap rings, then governor weights.
9. Wash all parts except condenser and vacuum control unit in a suitable solvent.
10. Check clearance of distributor shaft in housing. If clearance exceeds 0.0024-inch (0.060mm), measure shaft diameter. Standard shaft diameter is 0.4894-0.4898-inch (12.43-12.44mm). If wear exceeds 0.0012-inch (0.03mm), replace shaft. If shaft play in housing is still excessive, replace housing.
11. Reverse procedure to install. Set damper spring gap to 0.002-.018-inch (0.05-0.45mm).

1977 Electronic Ignition

This distributor is basically the same as the 1976-77 breaker points type, except that breaker plate, points and condenser are replaced by pickup coil on base plated and cam is replaced by four-tooth reluctor, Fig. 4. Pickup coil resistance is measured with an ohmmeter, 130-190 ohms is normal. Models for manual transmission are not interchangeable with those for automatic transmission.

ALTERNATOR

Replace

1. Loosen mounting bolts, then remove belt.
2. Disconnect battery ground cable, then disconnect wiring from alternator.
3. Remove mounting bolts and lift off alternator.

Output Test

Make test connections as shown in Fig. 7 using a variable resistor, battery, ammeter and voltmeter. Operate engine with switch SW 1 closed, when alternator speed reaches approximatelz 800 rpm, set variable resistance to maximum and close switch SW 2. Increase alternator speed while maintaining voltage at 14 volts by adjusting resistance. Note current readings at 2500 rpm and 5000 rpm. On 1972-74 models, current reading should be 21 to 25 amps. at 2500 rpm and 33 to 37 amps. at 5000 rpm. On 1975-77 models, current read-

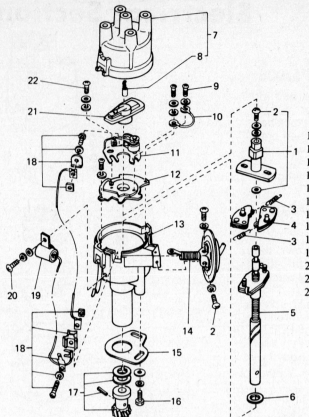

1	Cam assembly (Distributor)
2	Screw
3	Spring set (Governer)
4	Weight (Governer)
5	Shaft assembly (Distributor)
6	Thrust washer
7	Cap compl
8	Carbon point compl
9	Screw
10	Earth wire (Distributor)
11	Contact set compl
12	Plate compl (Contact breaker)
13	Housing (Distributor)
14	Vacuum controller assembly
15	Plate
16	Bolt
17	Pinion set (Distributor)
18	Terminal assembly
19	Condenser (Distributor)
20	Screw
21	Rotor (Distributor)
22	Set screw (Contact)

Fig. 2 Exploded view of distributor. 1974-75 models

ing should be 37 to 43 amps. at 2500 rpm and 48 to 54 amps. at 5000 rpm.

STARTER, REPLACE

1. Disconnect battery ground cable.
2. Disconnect battery cable and solenoid wire at starter.
3. Remove two nuts and bolts holding starter to bellhousing, then remove starter.

IGNITION SWITCH, REPLACE

1. Remove steering wheel, then remove the mast jacket plastic cover held by four screws, to expose switch mounting.
2. Drill two rounded bolt heads then remove bolts with an easy-out.
3. Remove two bolts with conventional hex heads.
4. Pull out switch with clamps.
5. Refit new switch with clamp. If clamp bolts are same as original equipment, two will have a double-head. The top portion permits tightening with a wrench, and when the necessary torque is reached, the top portion can be snapped off, leaving only the tamper-resistant lower head.

LIGHT SWITCH, REPLACE

1. Remove knob set screw, then pull off knob.
2. Remove switch to dashboard retaining nut.
3. Push switch through dashboard, then disconnect wire connector and remove switch.
4. Reverse procedure to install.

STOP LIGHT SWITCH, REPLACE

1. Switch is located on bracket under dashboard, near top of brake pedal.
2. Remove locknut on pedal side of bracket.
3. Push switch through bracket and remove wiring connector.
4. Reverse procedure to install.

NEUTRAL SAFETY SWITCH, REPLACE

1. Disconnect battery ground cable.
2. Remove wiring connector at neutral safety switch, which is on top of transmission rear cover.
3. With an open-end wrench, remove switch.

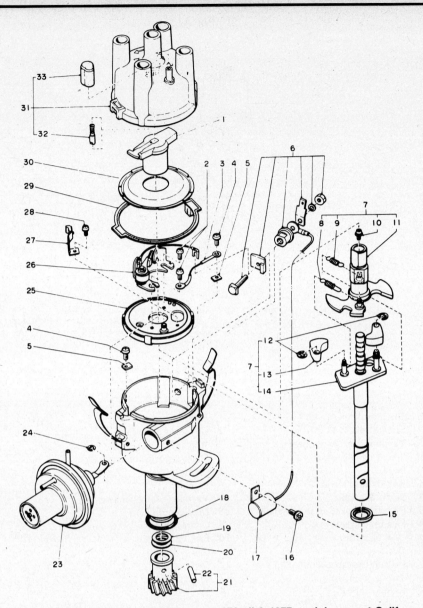

1. Distributor rotor
2. Contact breaker set screw
3. Distributor earth wire
4. Round head screw
5. Plate
6. Terminal set
7. Shaft and governor assembly
8. Governor spring B
9. Governor spring A
10. Screw & washer
11. Distributor cam assembly
12. Snap ring clip
13. Governor weight
14. Distributor shaft assembly
15. Washer
16. Screw & washer
17. Distributor condenser
18. "O" ring
19. Thrust washer (0.1)
20. Thrust washer (0.3)
21. Distributor pinion set
22. Straight pin (5 × 20)
23. Vacuum controller assembly
24. Snap ring clip
25. Contact breaker plate complete
26. Contact breaker set
27. Damper spring
28. Screw & washer
29. Dust proof packing
30. Dust proof
31. Distributor cap assembly
32. Carbon point complete
33. Rubber cap

Fig. 3 Exploded view of distributor. 1976 all & 1977 models except Calif.

COMBINATION SWITCH, REPLACE

1974-77

1. Remove steering wheel cover screws, then cover.
2. Remove steering wheel retaining nut, then steering wheel.
3. Remove hazard flasher switch knob.
4. Remove combination switch installing screws, then combination switch, Fig. 8.

TURN SIGNAL SWITCH, REPLACE

1972-73

Refer to 1974-77 COMBINATION SWITCH, REPLACE for removal procedure.

W/S WIPER SWITCH, REPLACE

1972-73

1. Remove knob set screw, then pull off knob.
2. Remove switch to dashboard retaining nut.
3. Push switch through dashboard, then disconnect wire connector and remove switch.
4. Reverse procedure to install.

W/S WIPER MOTOR, REPLACE

Front

1. Disconnect battery ground cable and wiper motor wiring harness.
2. Remove wiper arm and blade as-

semblies, then cowl panel.
3. Remove wiper link mounting nuts, Fig. 9, and wiper bracket mounting bolts.
4. Remove W/S washer tank.
5. Remove wiper motor attaching bolts and motor and linkage assembly, then disconnect linkage.
6. Reverse procedure to install.

Rear

1. Remove inner trim panel on back door.
2. Remove wiper bracket attaching bolts, then wiper motor bracket.
3. Remove wiper arm and blade assembly, then remove retaining nut.
4. Remove clip attaching linkage to motor, then remove motor.
5. Reverse procedure to install.

1) For MT   2) For AT

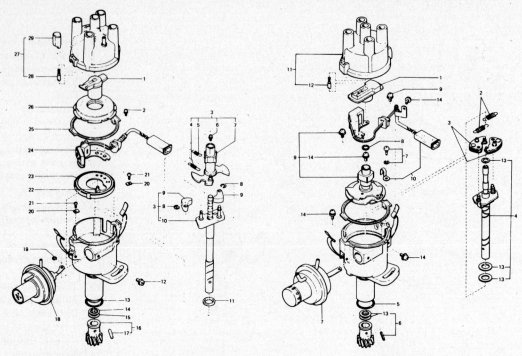

1	Distributor rotor	16	Distributor pinion set	
2	Screw & washer	17	Straight pin (5 × 20)	
3	Shaft & governor assembly	18	Vacuum controller assembly	
4	Governor spring B	19	Snap ring clip	
5	Governor spring A	20	Plate	
6	Screw & washer	21	Round head screw	
7	Signal rotor sub assembly	22	Screw & washer	
8	Snap ring clip	23	Contact breaker plate complete	
9	Governor weight	24	Pick-up coil set	
10	Distributor shaft assembly	25	Dust proof packing	
11	Washer	26	Dust proof cover	
12	Screw & washer	27	Distributor cap assembly	
13	"O" ring	28	Carbon point complete	
14	Thrust washer (0.1)	29	Rubber cap	
15	Thrust washer (0.3)			

1	Rotor
2	Governor spring set
3	Weight
4	Shaft & governor assembly
5	O-ring
6	Point set
7	Vacuum controller assembly
8	Dust proof packing
9	Contact breaker plate complete
10	Pick up coil set
11	Cap
12	Carbon point
13	Thrust washer
14	Screw kit

Fig. 4   Exploded view of breakerless distributor. 1977 California models

W/S WIPER TRANSMISSION, REPLACE

1. Remove wiper motor assembly.
2. Remove transmission cover plate and motor to transmission attaching screws, then separate parts.
3. If necessary to replace worm drive on motor armature, replace motor.

RADIO, REPLACE

1. Remove speaker grille then disconnect feed wire from speaker.
2. Remove all instrument cluster screws and pull cluster slightly forward.
3. Remove console attaching screws, then move console slightly forward.
4. Remove air outlet grille.

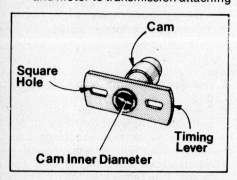

Fig. 5   Distributor cam inspection

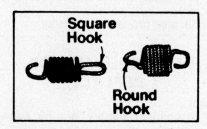

Fig. 6   Distributor governor springs

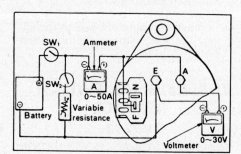

Fig. 7   Alternator output test connections

Fig. 8 Removing combination switch attaching screws

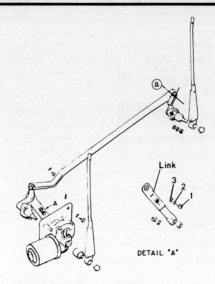

1. Flange bolt   2. Spring washer   3. Washer

Fig. 9 W/S wiper system

1. Hose
2. Heater inlet hose
3. Heater outlet hose
4. Cushion
5. Grommet
6. Spring
7. Grommet
8. Case (B)
9. Duct
10. Grommet
11. Spacer
12. Guide
13. Gasket
14. Heater core
15. Gasket
16. Gasket
17. Shutter
18. Shutter
19. Shutter
20. Gasket
21. Gasket
22. Shutter
23. Heater fan
24. Stay
25. Case (A)
26. Shutter lever
27. Speed nut
28. Return spring
29. Case (C)
30. Bracket
31. Gasket
32. Heater cock
33. Spring
34. Heater cock connecting rod
35. Washer
36. Bracket

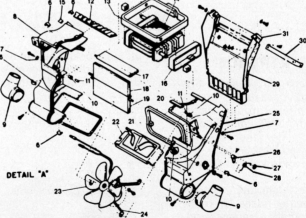

37. Heater cock rod	45. Shutter lever
38. Spacer	46. Return spring
39. Bracket	47. Shutter lever
40. Heater cock knob	48. Shutter rod
41. Shutter lever	49. Register
42. Grommet (register)	50. Clip
43. Shutter lever	51. Shutter lever
44. Return spring	52. Return spring

Fig. 10 Heater system components

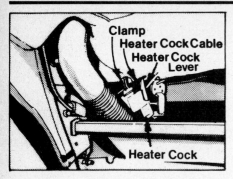

Fig. 11   Heater cable location

5. Pull off radio knobs and remove shaft nuts from dashboard.
6. Remove ashtray and heater and air outlet control knobs.
7. Remove screws that secure dashboard panel over radio and remove panel.
8. Remove radio mounting screws, then disconnect radio wiring and remove radio.
9. Reverse procedure to install.

INSTRUMENT CLUSTER, REPLACE

1. Reach up behind dashboard and disconnect speedometer cable from back of cluster, then loosen clamp and disconnect side ventilation hose duct.
2. On coupe, disconnect rear window defogger switch connector, tachometer connector and junction block connector on back of cluster.
3. On sedan and wagon, disconnect junction block connector, then remove cluster attaching screws and remove cluster from dashboard.
4. On coupe, remove trip odometer reset knob, then take out cluster screws and pull cluster forward.
5. On coupe, disconnect wiring from electric clock, brake warning light and seat belt warning lamp, then remove cluster from dashboard.
6. Cluster is separated from dashboard panel by removing screws from back of cluster. Circuit board can be removed after taking out two screws and five nuts.
7. Reverse procedure to install.

BLOWER MOTOR AND HEATER CORE, REPLACE

NOTE: Heater core and blower motor can be replaced only after removal of entire heater duct assembly, Fig. 10, as follows:

1. Disconnect battery ground cable, drain coolant from radiator and disconnect both heater hoses at engine.
2. Remove console box screws, then console.
3. Remove the small package shelf and dashboard cluster.
4. Pull out vent knob and remove center vent below radio.

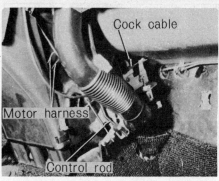

Fig. 12   Heater control rod & cable location

5. Disconnect heater cable, Fig. 11, and/or heater control rod, Fig. 12.
6. Disconnect shutter control cable (1972-73) or rod (1974-77).
7. Disconnect air inlet control rods (1972-73).
8. Disconnect wiring harnesses at fan motor.
9. Remove mounting bolts, then remove heater assembly.
10. Remove case retaining screws and springs, then remove case.
11. Remove defroster ducts.
12. Loosen hose clamps and remove hose.
13. Remove heater cock.
14. Remove link attaching screws, then link assembly.
15. Remove heater core.
16. Remove fan and motor retaining screws, then fan and motor assembly.
17. Reverse procedure to install.

Engine Section

ENGINE, REPLACE

1. Open hood and remove spare tire from engine compartment.
2. Disconnect battery ground cable from battery and intake manifold.
3. Remove air cleaner, then disconnect fuel line from carburetor.
4. Remove purge and vacuum hoses at body panel.
5. Drain cooling system, then remove radiator and heater hoses. On models with automatic transmission, disconnect oil cooler lines.
6. Disconnect wiring harness from alternator, fan motor, starter motor and engine block connector.
7. Disconnect ignition wire from coil and ignition primary wire from distributor.
8. Remove radiator. On models with four wheel drive, remove fan and pulley.
9. Remove pitching stopper front end nut, then loosen nut on body bracket side and pitching stopper rearward and out of engine hanger, Fig. 1.
10. Remove starter motor, then disconnect accelerator cable, control cables and hoses.

Fig. 1   Removing engine stopper

11. On models with automatic transmission, disconnect vacuum unit hose. On models with power brakes disconnect vacuum hose at brake unit check valve.
12. On models with automatic transmission, through timing hole in rear of engine, remove bolts attaching torque converter to drive plate. Rotate crankshaft to position bolts for removal.
13. Disconnect exhaust pipe from exhaust manifold and muffler flange.
14. Remove bolts connecting front engine mounting to engine.
15. Remove engine to transmission attaching bolts.
16. Raise engine slightly, then disconnect engine from transmission and remove engine from vehicle

NOTE: It may be necessary to raise transmission slightly when separat-

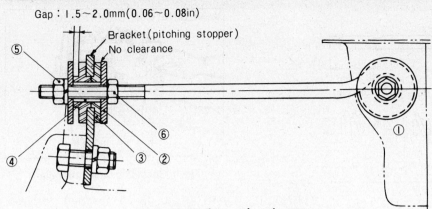

Gap : 1.5~2.0mm(0.06~0.08in)

Bracket(pitching stopper)
No clearance

Fig. 2 Adjusting engine stopper

Fig. 3 Loosening sequence of cylinder head nuts

ing engine from transmission. On models with automatic transmission, ensure torque remains with transmission when removing engine. Before removing engine, ensure all necessary wiring and lines are disconnected.

17. Reverse procedure to install. Adjust pitching stopper as shown in Fig. 2.

ENGINE MOUNT, REPLACE

Front

1. Disconnect battery ground cable, then remove pitching stopper.
2. Disconnect exhaust pipe from exhaust manifold and remove exhaust pipe bracket.
3. Remove engine mount to crossmember attaching bolts.
4. Raise engine slightly to relieve

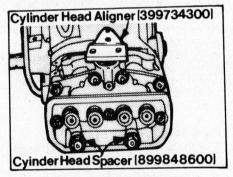

Cylinder Head Aligner (399734300)
Cyinder Head Spacer (899848600)

Fig. 4 Installing cylinder head

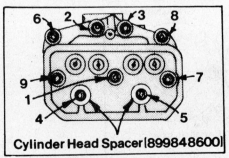

Cylinder Head Spacer (899848600)

Fig. 5 Cylinder head bolt tightening sequence

weight from mount, then remove engine mount bracket to engine attaching bolts.
5. On models with 4 wheel drive, remove mounting rubber and spacer.
6. Reverse procedure to install.

CYLINDER HEAD, REPLACE

1. Remove engine from vehicle as outlined under "Engine, Replace."
2. Remove plug from cylinder head, and allow coolant to drain.
3. Remove air cleaner assembly and emission control hoses.
4. Remove intake manifold with carburetor. Disconnect fuel line if necessary.
5. Disconnect breather hose from rocker cover and remove rocker cover.
6. If driver's side head is to be removed, remove alternator and mounting bracket.
7. Disconnect air injection manifold from cylinder head.
8. Remove rocker shaft and cylinder head retaining nuts, Fig. 3.
9. Remove cylinder head studs and lower head from engine.

10. Reverse procedure to install. To assure accurate positioning of head on block, a cylinder head aligning bracket No. 399734300 should be used to hold head in position on crankcase. Two cylinder head spacers No. 899848600, fit over long studs to permit tightening other head nuts before rocker shaft is installed, Fig. 4. After tightening all nuts, remove spacers and install rocker shaft, then install nuts and tighten to specifications. Tighten cylinder head in sequence, shown in Fig. 5, to torque listed in Engine Tightening Specifications.

ROCKER ARMS & SHAFTS

Rocker arm shafts are held to cylinder heads by head nuts and once the appropriate nuts are removed, shaft and support stands can be lifted from studs. The locations of valve rocker spring washers are different on each side of horizontally-opposed engine, therefore when disassembling be sure to keep parts in exact order and make note of which end of shaft is front, Figs. 6 and 7.

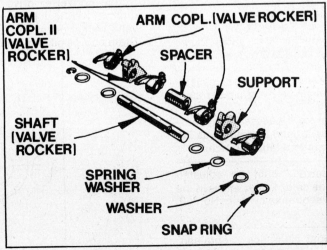

Fig. 6 Rocker arm & shaft assembly. 1972-74 1300cc & 1400cc engines

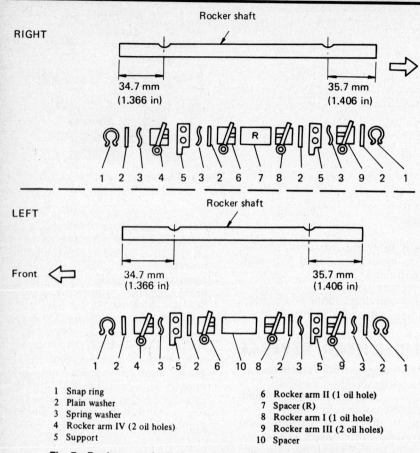

RIGHT

Rocker shaft

Front

34.7 mm
(1.366 in)   35.7 mm
(1.406 in)

1 2 3 4 5 3 2 6 7 8 2 5 3 9 2 1

LEFT

Rocker shaft

Front

34.7 mm
(1.366 in)   35.7 mm
(1.406 in)

1 2 4 3 5 2 6 10 8 2 3 5 9 3 2 1

1 Snap ring
2 Plain washer
3 Spring washer
4 Rocker arm IV (2 oil holes)
5 Support
6 Rocker arm II (1 oil hole)
7 Spacer (R)
8 Rocker arm I (1 oil hole)
9 Rocker arm III (2 oil holes)
10 Spacer

Fig. 7 Rocker arm & shaft assembly. 1975-77 1400cc & 1600cc engines

Inspect rocker arm bings and if theyeeel rough or arm is wobbly on shaft, they must be replaced.

If contact tip of rocker arm is lightly gouged, it can be resurfaced on a lathe. If badly worn or heavily gouged, it should be replaced. When reassembling rocker shaft, pay particular attention to locations of the dished or curved spring washers. If incorrectly placed, they may be broken in engine operation.

VALVES, ADJUST

1. Position piston of cylinder to be checked at T.D.C. compression stroke.
2. Using a feeler gauge measure clearance between valve stem and rocker arm.
3. Adjust valves if necessary, by loosening locknut and turning adjusting screws using suitable wrenches.

NOTE: Valve should be adjusted with engine cold. Adjust valves in the following sequence cylinder No. 1, 3, 2 and 4.

4. After proper clearance is obtained, tighten locknut and recheck clearances.

VALVE GUIDES

Valve guides are replaceable with a press. Intake guide should be pressed in so it projects 0.67-.71 inch (17-18mm) from head surface; exhaust guide should project 0.87-.91 (22-23mm) on all engine.

CAMSHAFT, REPLACE

1. Remove engine and flywheel or torque converter drive plate, then remove flywheel housing. Remove valve rocker cover and rocker shaft.
2. Drain engine oil and remove oil pan.

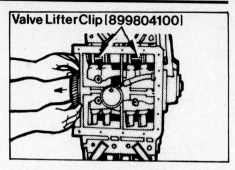

Valve Lifter Clip [899804100]

Fig. 8 Installing valve lifter clips

3. With a punch inserted through holes in camshaft gear, straighten retaining plate bolt locks, then remove bolts with a wrench.
4. Lifter bores and lifters are in crankcase, accessible when oil pan is removed. Reach in and attach valve lifter clips No. 899804100 to lifters to prevent lifters from dropping through, Fig. 8.
5. Remove crankshaft flywheel hub complete with gear. Pull camshaft straight out through back of engine, complete with gear.
6. Reverse procedure to install. Align camshaft and crankshaft gear timing marks as shown in Fig. 9.

PISTONS & RODS

The 1300 and 1400 engines are wet-sleeve, 1600 engine is not sleeved. Pistons are available in 0.25 mm and 0.5 mm oversize on wet-sleeve engines, in 0.25 mm oversize on 1600 engine. When one cylinder needs reboring, all cylinders must be rebored to same diameter. On wet-sleeve engines reboring is done after removing sleeves from engine with a sleeve puller.

Connecting rods should be checked for bend or twist in a rod aligner. Replace rod if bend or twist exceeds 0.0039-inch (0.10mm) per four inches (100mm) of length.

1300 & 1400 Engines
1. With cylinder head removed, mea-

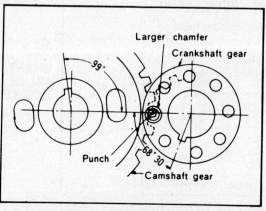

Larger chamfer
Crankshaft gear
99°
Punch
68° 30'
Camshaft gear

Fig. 9 Valve timing marks

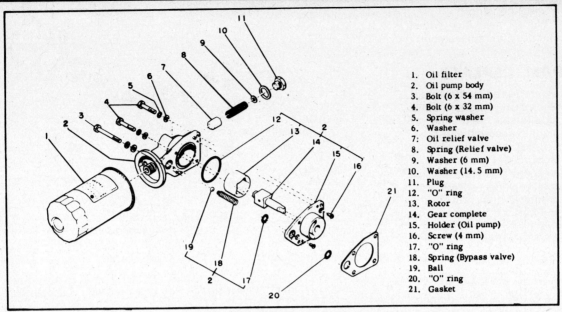

1.	Oil filter
2.	Oil pump body
3.	Bolt (6 x 54 mm)
4.	Bolt (6 x 32 mm)
5.	Spring washer
6.	Washer
7.	Oil relief valve
8.	Spring (Relief valve)
9.	Washer (6 mm)
10.	Washer (14.5 mm)
11.	Plug
12.	"O" ring
13.	Rotor
14.	Gear complete
15.	Holder (Oil pump)
16.	Screw (4 mm)
17.	"O" ring
18.	Spring (Bypass valve)
19.	Ball
20.	"O" ring
21.	Gasket

Fig. 10   Disassembled view of oil pump (Typical)

sure cylinder line protrusion above top of head; it should be .0028-.0035-inch (0.07-.09mm). If it is correct, old gasket at bottom of liner is correct thickness. Otherwise, replace with thicker or thinner gasket as required.

2. Remove plugs from front end of block with Allen wrench.
3. With sleeve puller No. 899704100, pull out cylinder sleeves (liners). Also remove liner gaskets at bottom and keep sleeves and gaskets together. As you remove sleeves, mark them to a reference point on block for exact reinstallation.
4. With special pliers No. 898968600 remove spring clips holding piston pins, then insert piston pin remover No. 899094100 through engine block plug hole and withdraw pins. Also mark pistons so they can be installed in the same direction.
5. If rods are to be removed for inspection and service, crankcase must be split apart and crankshaft and rods removed.
6. Compression piston rings are stamped with the letter "R" or "N" on end. This letter should face upward.
7. To install pistons, insert into bottom of sleeve only far enough to cover area of rings. This will leave piston pin area exposed, permitting installation in reverse manner of removal. Rear end spring clips should be installed before refitting piston, and then pin and front spring clips can be installed working through crankcase plug hole. Rear pistons and cylinders must be installed first.

1600 Engine

Service procedure is similar except that there are no sleeves to be removed no sleeve height to measure and no sleeve gasket to replace. There are front and rear crankcase plugs with an Allen slot on each side of block for removal of spring clips and piston pins. For installation, a rod and piston aligning tool No. 399284300, is recommended. Spring clips can be removed and installed with needle-nose pliers instead of special tool required for 1300 and 1400 engines, but piston pin removal also is necessary for this engine.

Piston rings may have letter "R" or "N" on face that is installed upward.

MAIN & ROD BEARINGS

Main and rod bearings are available in standard size and undersizes of .05mm and .25mm.

CRANKSHAFT REAR OIL SEAL, REPLACE

1. Remove engine and flywheel or torque converter drive plate, then

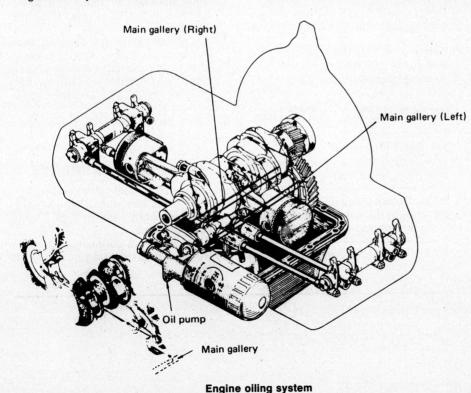

Main gallery (Right)

Main gallery (Left)

Oil pump

Main gallery

Engine oiling system

remove flywheel housing.
2. Drive out old oil seal in flywheel housing and drive in replacement.

OIL PAN, REPLACE

The oil pan can be removed without raising engine or disturbing any other parts. The side-to-side rear line of screws has limited accessibility, however, all oil pan screws have hex heads and Phillips screwdriver slots, permitting a choice of tools. There are slots in the crossmember, which covers rear line of oil pan screws, that provide the limited access. Once all screws are removed, oil pan can be lowered and pulled out through front.

OIL PUMP, REPLACE

The oil pump is externally mounted, bolted to front of engine, a self-contained component that includes pressure and relief valves and a flange onto which spin-on oil filter is installed. The pump can be removed from engine without disturbing any other parts.

OIL PUMP, REPLACE

Remove oil pump attaching bolts and lift pump from engine. When installing pump align rotor shaft with groove in camshaft end.

OIL PUMP INSPECTION & REPAIRS

1. Remove oil filter from pump body, Fig. 10.
2. Remove two bolts attaching oil pump holder to pump case, then remove rotor.
3. Remove relief valve plug, spring valve and washer.
4. Inspect oil pump drive gear and shaft and replace if worn or damaged.
5. Using a feeler gauge, check clearance between drive gear and rotor. Clearance should be .0008-.0047 in. (.02-.12mm). If clearance is in excess of .0079 in. (.2mm), replace gear and rotor.
6. Using a straight edge and feeler gauge, measure clearance between pump rotor and gear to pump case.

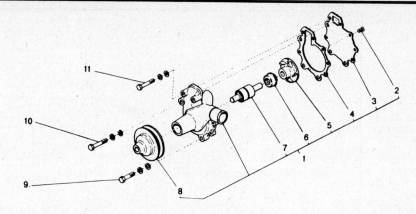

1. Water pump
2. Screw
3. Plate (water pump)
4. Gasket (water pump)
5. Impeller (water pump)
6. Mechanical oil seal
7. Shaft (water pump)
8. Pulley (water pump)
9. Bolt (8 x 35 mm)
10. Bolt (8 x 45 mm)
11. Bolt (6 x 44 mm)

Fig. 11   Disassembled view of water pump (Typical)

Clearance should be .0020-.0047 (.05-.12mm). If clearance is in excess of .0079 in. (.2mm), replace rotor or case as necessary.
7. Using a feeler gauge measure radial clearance between pump rotor and case. Clearance should be .0059-.0083 in. (.15-.21mm). If clearance exceeds .0098 in (.25mm), replace rotor or case.
8. Check condition of relief valve and spring.
9. Reverse procedure to assemble.

WATER PUMP, REPLACE

1. Drain cooling system, then disconnect radiator and by-pass hose from pump.
2. Remove fan belt, then remove pump attaching bolts and pump.
3. Reverse procedure to install.

WATER PUMP, REPAIRS

1. Remove water pump plate and gasket, Fig. 11.
2. Press pump shaft with impeller and seal from pump body.

NOTE: Do not press on shaft or bearing, otherwise damage may result. Press on bearing outer race.

3. Remove impeller and seal from shaft.

4. Inspect impeller shaft, seal washer and impeller for wear and damage and replace if necessary.
5. Inspect plate for flatness.
6. Press water pump shaft into pump body. Before pressing heat pump body to 176-212 F, press on bearing outer race.
7. Apply liquid gasket to outer surface of seal, then press seal into pump body with carbon washer of seal facing impeller.
8. Apply a thin coat of silicone grease to shaft surface, then press impeller onto shaft. Check to ensure clearance between impeller and pump body is .020-.028 in. (.5-.7mm) and correct if necessary.
9. Support impeller side of pump, then press pulley onto shaft. Check to ensure clearance between pump body and center of pulley belt groove is 2.34-2.37 in. (59.5-60.1mm).
10. Apply sealer to plate gasket, then install plate.

FUEL PUMP, REPLACE

1. Disconnect inlet and outlet fuel lines from fuel pump, which is located at right rear side of engine compartment.
2. Remove wiring connector.
3. Remove two retaining nuts and lift pump off.

Carburetor Section

CARBURETOR SERVICE

Refer to Figs. 1 and 2 when servicing carburetor.

FLOAT LEVEL, ADJUST

There is a sight glass in the float bowl and if fuel level is within 0.006-inch (1.5mm) of the mark, float level is correct. If not, remove cover and adjust float tab to obtain H dimension as shown. See specifications section, and refer to Fig. 3. Check clearance between float seat and valve stem. If necessary adjust by bending float stopper to obtain .051 to .067 in. (1.3 to 1.7mm) clearance, dimension L, Fig. 3.

THROTTLE & CHOKE INTERLOCK ADJUSTMENT

Set adjusting lever on third step of cam. Clearance between choke valve and air horn wall should be 0.026-.037 inch (0.65-.95mm). If necessary to adjust, slightly bend pawl at top of fast idle cam (bending to right will increase clearance).

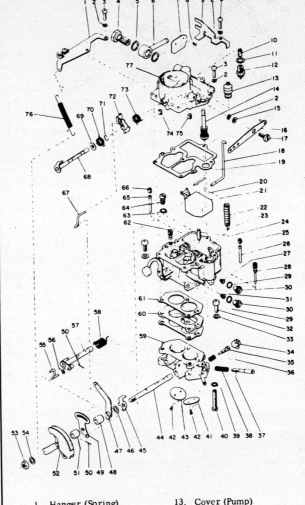

25.	Air bleed
26.	Emulsion tube (P)
27.	Main jet
28.	Slow jet
29.	Washer
30.	Plug (Float chamber drain)
31.	Main jet (S)
32.	Screw (Pan head)
33.	Spring washer
34.	Cap (Idle limiter)
35.	Screw (Idle adjusting)
36.	Spring (Idle adjusting screw)
37.	Screw (Throttle adjust)
38.	Spring (Idle adjust screw)
39.	Washer
40.	Screw
41.	Valve (Throttle) (P)
42.	Screw
43.	Valve (Throttle) (S)
44.	Shaft (Throttle) (P)
45.	Plate (Adjust)
46.	Washer
47.	Lever (Connecting)
48.	Sleeve
49.	Connecting lever
50.	Cotter pin
51.	Sleeve (Throttle)
52.	Lever (Throttle)
53.	Nut
54.	Spring washer
55.	Connecting rod
56.	Washer
57.	Shaft S (Throttle)
58.	Spring (Throttle)
59.	Throttle chamber
60.	Insulator
61.	Gasket (Throttle chamber)
62.	Slow jet (S)
63.	Washer
64.	Power valve
65.	Emulsion tube
66.	Air bleed
67.	Connecting rod (Choke)
68.	Shaft (Choke)
69.	Sleeve (A)
70.	Spring (Adjust screw)
71.	Clip
72.	Lever (Choke)
73.	Spring (Choke)
74.	Air bleed
75.	Slow air bleed (P)
76.	Spring (Throttle return)
77.	Choke chamber

1.	Hanger (Spring)	13.	Cover (Pump)
2.	Spring washer	14.	Piston
3.	Screw (Pan head)	15.	Washer
4.	Bolt (Filter)	16.	Lever (Pump)
5.	Washer	17.	Shaft (Pump lever)
6.	Nipple	18.	Connecting rod (Pump)
7.	Valve (Choke)	19.	Gasket (Float chamber)
8.	Screw	20.	Shaft (Float)
9.	Nipple guide	21.	Float (Carburetor)
10.	Filter	22.	Spring (Piston return)
11.	Washer	23.	Ball
12.	Needle valve	24.	Weight (Injector)

Fig. 1   Exploded view of carburetor. 1972-73 models

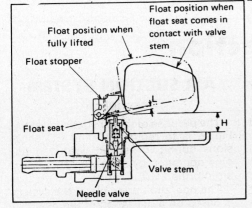

Float position when fully lifted

Float position when float seat comes in contact with valve stem

Float stopper

Float seat

L

H

Needle valve

Valve stem

Fig. 3   Float level adjustment

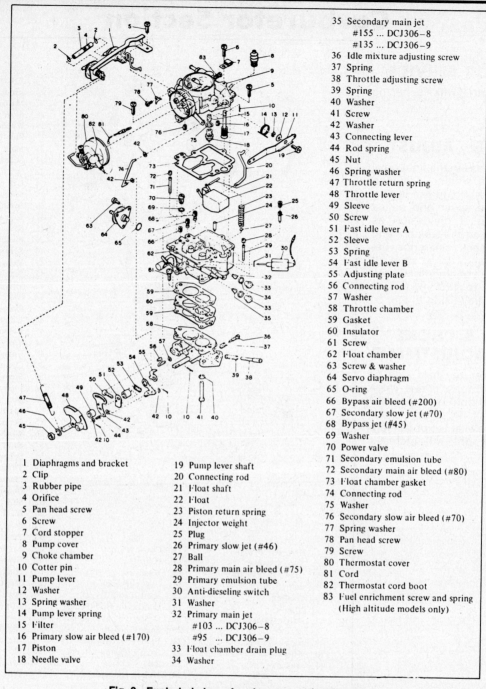

35 Secondary main jet
   #155 ... DCJ306-8
   #135 ... DCJ306-9
36 Idle mixture adjusting screw
37 Spring
38 Throttle adjusting screw
39 Spring
40 Washer
41 Screw
42 Washer
43 Connecting lever
44 Rod spring
45 Nut
46 Spring washer
47 Throttle return spring
48 Throttle lever
49 Sleeve
50 Screw
51 Fast idle lever A
52 Sleeve
53 Spring
54 Fast idle lever B
55 Adjusting plate
56 Connecting rod
57 Washer
58 Throttle chamber
59 Gasket
60 Insulator
61 Screw
62 Float chamber
63 Screw & washer
64 Servo diaphragm
65 O-ring
66 Bypass air bleed (#200)
67 Secondary slow jet (#70)
68 Bypass jet (#45)
69 Washer
70 Power valve
71 Secondary emulsion tube
72 Secondary main air bleed (#80)
73 Float chamber gasket
74 Connecting rod
75 Washer
76 Secondary slow air bleed (#70)
77 Spring washer
78 Pan head screw
79 Screw
80 Thermostat cover
81 Cord
82 Thermostat cord boot
83 Fuel enrichment screw and spring
   (High altitude models only)

1 Diaphragms and bracket
2 Clip
3 Rubber pipe
4 Orifice
5 Pan head screw
6 Screw
7 Cord stopper
8 Pump cover
9 Choke chamber
10 Cotter pin
11 Pump lever
12 Washer
13 Spring washer
14 Pump lever spring
15 Filter
16 Primary slow air bleed (#170)
17 Piston
18 Needle valve

19 Pump lever shaft
20 Connecting rod
21 Float shaft
22 Float
23 Piston return spring
24 Injector weight
25 Plug
26 Primary slow jet (#46)
27 Ball
28 Primary main air bleed (#75)
29 Primary emulsion tube
30 Anti-dieseling switch
31 Washer
32 Primary main jet
   #103 ... DCJ306-8
   #95 ... DCJ306-9
33 Float chamber drain plug
34 Washer

Fig. 2   Exploded view of carburetor. 1974-77 models

Emission Controls Section

POSITIVE CRANKCASE VENTILATION (PCV) SYSTEM
Description

The crankcase emission control system, Fig. 1, is employed to prevent air pollution which will be caused by blow-by gas being emitted from the crankcase. In this system the blow-by gases are routed into the intake manifold through the air cleaner for recombustion. The system consists of a sealed oil filler cap, rocker covers with an emission outlet, connecting hoses and air cleaner. Blow-by gas in crankcase is drawn through the rocker covers and the connecting hoses into the air cleaner, and drawn into the intake manifold through the carburetor.

AIR SUCTION SYSTEM
Description

The purpose of the air suction system, Fig. 2, is to reduce HC and CO emissions during low-speed light-load engine operation by supplying secondary air into the exhaust ports.

The operation principle of the system is based on a utilization of the negative pressure caused by exhaust gas pulsation and intake manifold pressure during valve overlap period.

The gas pressure in each exhaust port is transmitted to the air suction valve through the air suction hole and air suction pipe. When pressure transmitted is negative, the reed of the air suction valve is opened towards the valve stopper and simultaneously fresh air is drawn from the air cleaner through the air suction hose and silencer into the exhaust port. When positive pressure reaches the air suction valve, the reed is closed in an instant to prevent the flow of exhaust gas.

COASTING BY-PASS SYSTEM

The purpose of the coasting by-pass system, Fig. 3, is to control HC emissions while the vehicle is coasting, or decelerating, by supplying an appropriate amount of air-fuel mixture through the coasting by-pass passage in the carburetor for improved combustion in the cylinders.

During coasting, vacuum develops in the intake manifold because the primary throttle valve is closed. When this vacuum is transmitted to the chamber A of the vacuum control valve through the vacuum hose, the diaphragm is attracted toward the chamber and consequently the poppet valve is opened, Fig. 4.

The vacuum that reaches the servo diaphragm of the carburetor forces the by-pass valve in the carburetor to open. The by-pass passage connects the air horn of the carburetor with the secondary throttle bore at a portion slightly below the secondary throttle valve.

With the by-pass valve opened, air is admitted into the by-pass valve from the air horn, and meanwhile, through the by-pass jet and the by-pass air bleed, fuel and air are metered respectively to obtain an appropriate air-fuel mixture in the by-pass passage. The formed mixture is fed from the by-pass port into the secondary throttle bore.

When the vehicle changes its operation from coasting to acceleration, the poppet valve in the vacuum control valve closes and the vacuum that remained between chamber B and servo diaphragm is released through the orifice in the vacuum control valve, Fig. 4.

EXHAUST PORT LINER

An exhaust port-liner fabricated of stainless steel plate is integrated with the cylinder head as one-unit.

The port-liner has an air layer sealed by itself in order to decrease heat trans-

fer to the cylinder head and keep the exhaust port at a higher temperature. The exhaust port insulated by this port-liner facilitates oxidation of residual HC and CO with the help of remaining air contained in exhaust gas.

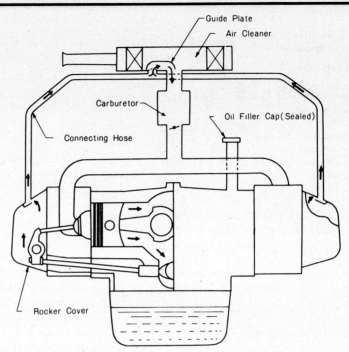

Fig. 1   Positive crankcase ventillation (PCV) system (Typical)

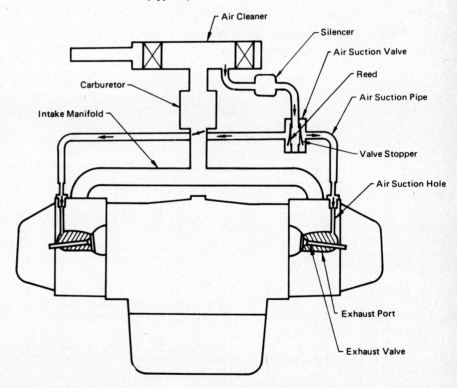

Fig. 2   Air suction system (Typical)

EXHAUST GAS RECIRCULATION (EGR) SYSTEM

Description

The exhaust gas recirculation system,

SUBARU

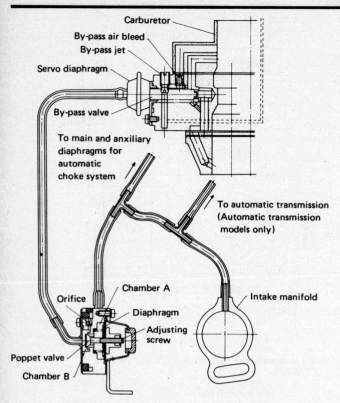

Fig. 3 Coasting by-pass system (Typical)

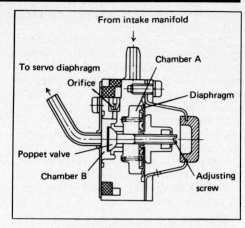

Fig. 4 Sectional view of vacuum control valve

Fig. 5, is to control NOx formation by recirculating part of exhaust gas into the intake manifold and depressing the combustion temperature in the cylinder. The system is designed to circulate part of exhaust gas from the exhaust port into the intake manifold through the EGR valve. The amount of exhaust gas recirculated is regulated by the EGR valve, which is actuated by the vacuum signals according to engine operating conditions.

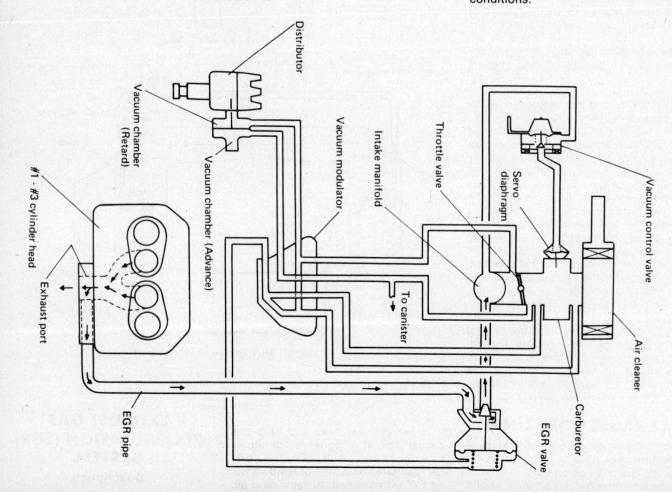

Fig. 5 Exhaust gas recirculation system (Typical)

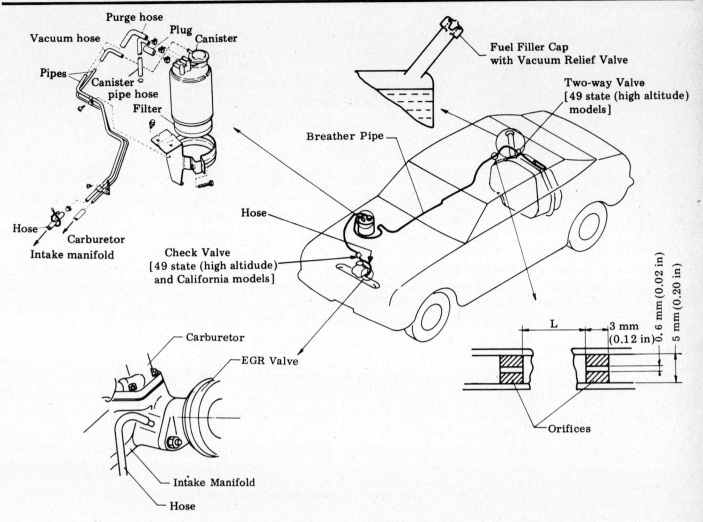

Fig. 6 Evaporative emission control system (Typical). All models except station wagon

Inspection

1. Viewing through an opening in the EGR valve body, check that the valve shaft moves when the engine speed is 3000 to 3500 rpm under no-load condition.
2. If the shaft does not move as specified, remove the EGR valve and press the diaphragm with finger to check the movement.
3. If no failure is found in the EGR valve, check the fittings of the vacuum lines.
4. If any failure is found in the EGR valve, it would be due to the damaged diaphragm or the sticking valve. In the former case, replace the EGR valve; in the latter case, clean the EGR valve.
5. If cleaning does not work, replace the EGR valve with a new one.
6. Check the EGR pipe and gas passages for clogging and leaks. Clean or replace if necessary.

EVAPORATIVE EMISSION CONTROL SYSTEM

Description

The evaporative emission control system, Figs. 6 and 7, is employed to prevent evaporative fuel in the fuel tank from being discharged into the atmosphere. This system includes a charcoal canister, a check valve, a two-way valve on all models except California, two orifices, and two reserve tanks on station wagons with 4-wheel drive.

Fuel vapor evaporated from the fuel tank is routed into the canister located in the engine compartment. When the engine is idling, this vapor is stored in the canister because the purge valve on the canister is closed by the force of high intake manifold vacuum. During this time, the vapor is absorbed in the activated charcoal particles.

As the engine speed is increased, the purge valve opens because the vacuum in the carburetor above the throttle valve becomes as high as the vacuum in the intake manifold and the return spring overcomes the vacuum force to raise the purge valve. The absorbed vapor is drawn from the canister into the intake manifold through the open purge valve and purge hose. While the purge valve is open, fresh air is drawn into the canister through the bottom filter, purging the absorbed vapor from the activated charcoal.

When the engine is not running, the purge valve is opened by the return spring but the vapor remains in the canister because there is no vacuum to draw the vapor out of the canister at this time.

THERMOSTATICALLY CONTROLLED AIR CLEANER

Description

This system includes the air cleaner,

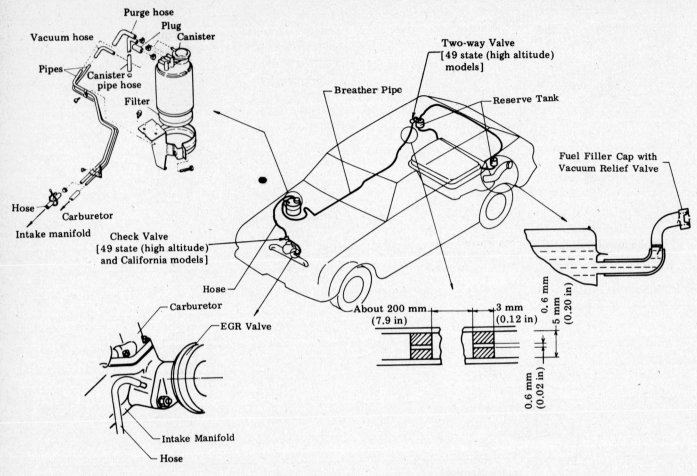

Fig. 7 Evaporative emission control system (Typical). Station wagon including 4 wheel drive

the air stove on the exhaust manifold, and the air intake hose connecting the air cleaner and air stove. The air cleaner is equipped with an air control valve which maintains the temperature of the air being drawn into the carburetor at 100° to 127° F to reduce HC emission when the under hood temperature is below 100°F.

In addition to that, the air control valve also serves to prevent carburetor icing and improve the warm-up characteristics of the engine. The temperature sensor detects the intake air temperature and opens or closes the vacuum passage between the intake manifold and vacuum motor.

The flame arrester prevents flame from entering the crankcase through the crankcase ventilation hoses in case back fire occurs. The air stove is mounted at the front end of the exhaust pipe. Fresh air is warmed up in this air stove and then introduced into the air cleaner through the air intake hose.

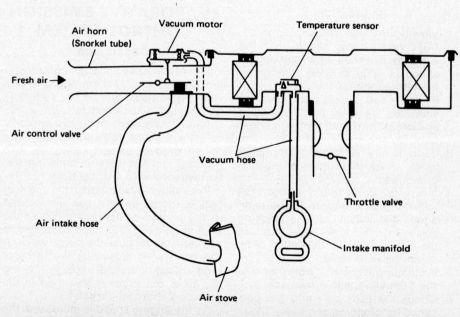

Fig. 8 Thermostatically controlled air cleaner system (Typical)

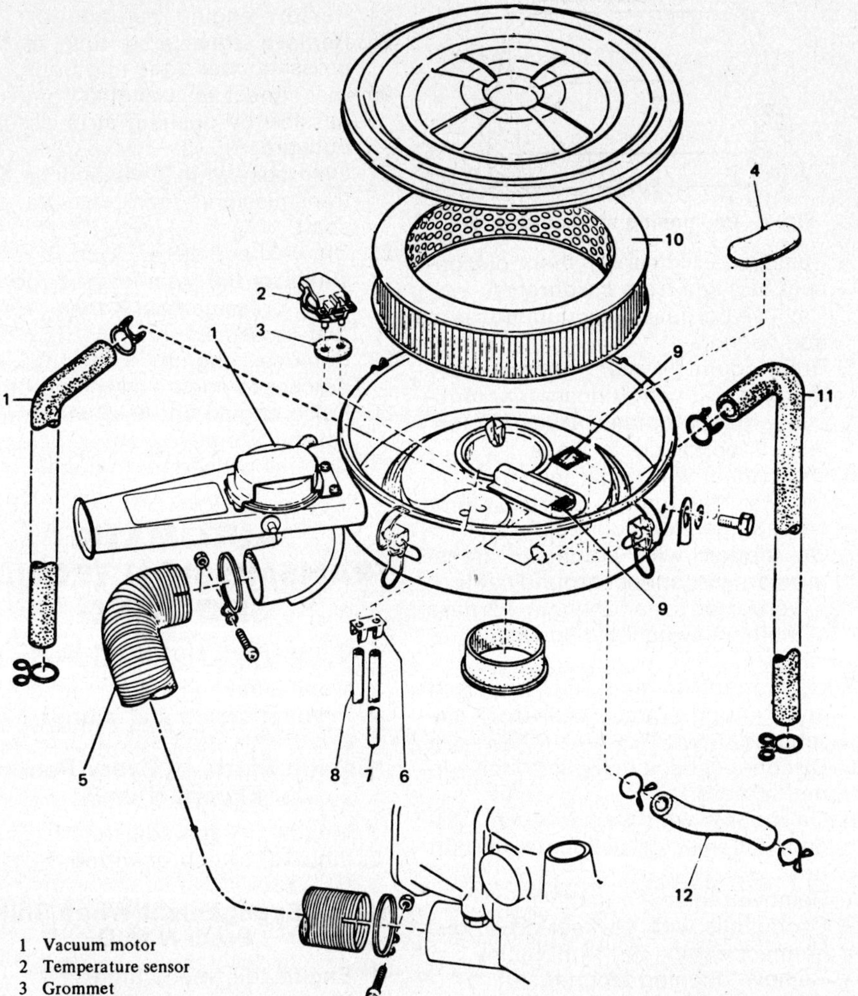

Operation

The air control valve is controlled by the inlet air temperature and the engine operating condition. The temperature sensor detects the inlet air temperature and controls the flow of vacuum to the vacuum motor.

When the under hood temperature is low and the intake manifold vacuum is high, the sensor valve remains closed and establishes vacuum passage from the intake manifold to the vacuum motor diaphragm. In this condition, the vacuum actuates the diaphragm which opens the air control valve to introduce hot air into the air cleaner through the air intake hose from the air stove.

When the under hood temperature is low but the intake manifold vacuum is too weak to actuate the diaphragm, the sensor valve remains closed and the air control valve closes the hot air passage, allowing only under-hood air (cool air) into the air cleaner through its snorkel tube. When the under-hood air temperature is high, the sensor valve opens fully to break the vacuum passage between the intake manifold and the vacuum motor diaphragm. In this condition, the diaphragm return spring presses the air control valve to close the hot air passage and the under-hood air (cool air) is admitted into the air cleaner through its snorkel tube.

When the under-hood air temperature is around 100°F, the sensor valve is partially opened and the opening of the air control valve varies with the vacuum from the intake manifold.

With the air control valve partially opened, cool air and hot air are drawn together and mixed, controlling the temperature of the air to be introduced to the air cleaner.

1 Vacuum motor
2 Temperature sensor
3 Grommet
4 Rubber plate
5 Air intake hose
6 Clip
7 Vacuum hose
8 Vacuum hose
9 Flame arrester
10 Air cleaner element
11 Crankcase ventilation hose
12 Air suction hose

Fig. 9   Thermostatically controlled air cleaner system components (Typical)

Clutch & Transmission Section

CLUTCH PEDAL, ADJUST

1. Remove clutch release for spring, then loosen lock nut.
2. Turn adjusting nut until there is an end play of .14-.18 in. (3.6-4.6 mm) at fork, Fig. 1.
3. On 1972-76 models, clutch pedal play should be 1.18-1.46 in. (30-37 mm). On 1977 models, clutch pedal play should be .94-1.18 in. (24-30 mm).

CLUTCH, REPLACE

1. Remove transmission as described

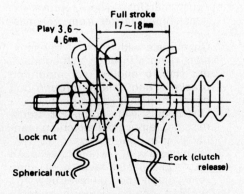

Fig. 1   Clutch adjustment

under "Transmission, Replace."
2. Remove six attaching bolts from pressure plate, then remove pressure plate and clutch disc.
3. When installing, apply light coat of grease to transmission main drive shaft spline.
4. Install clutch disc guide into clutch disc. Then install on flywheel by inserting end of guide into needle bearing.
5. Install pressure plate and tighten attaching bolts.

NOTE: Clutch pressure plate should be installed so there is a gap of 120 degrees or more between "O" marks on flywheel and pressure plate, to insure best balance.

6. Remove clutch disc guide and reinstall transmission.

TRANSMISSION, REPLACE

1972-73 Models

1. Disconnect battery ground cable and remove air cleaner.
2. Remove pitching stopper.
3. Disconnect wiring harness from starter and back-up lamp switch.
4. Remove starter mounting nuts and starter.
5. Remove clutch return spring, then clutch release fork, adjusting nut and clutch cable from lever.
6. Disconnect speedometer cable from transmission.
7. Remove shift lever knob, console, shift lever boot cover and shift lever.
8. Raise front of vehicle and support properly.
9. On sedan models, disconnect exhaust pipe from exhaust manifold. On coupe models, remove exhaust manifold from engine.
10. Remove nuts and bolts securing engine to transmission.
11. Remove gear shift rod clamp nuts and move gear shift assembly rearward, then drive out pin.
12. Remove gear shift assembly from transmission leaving it connected to body.
13. Drive out axle shaft spring pin.
14. Remove self-locking nut securing stabilizer to transverse link, then washer and bushing from stabilizer.
15. Support transmission using a suitable jack.
16. Remove parking cable mounting bracket to rear crossmember.
17. Remove bolts attaching stabilizer bracket to rear crossmember. Then remove stabilizer from transverse link.
18. Remove self locking nut securing transverse link to crossmember. Then, using a pry bar, pull transverse link out of crossmember.
19. Push struts outward and remove axle shafts from transmission, Fig. 2.
20. Pull transmission rearward and lower from vehicle.
21. Reverse procedure to install.

1974-77 Models

1. Open hood and remove spare tire from engine compartment.
2. Disconnect battery ground cable from battery and intake manifold.

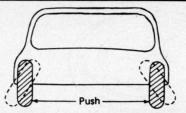

Fig. 2 Positioning struts outward

3. Remove air cleaner, then disconnect fuel line from carburetor.
4. Remove purge and vacuum hoses at body panel.
5. Drain cooling system, then remove radiator and heater hoses. On models with automatic transmission, disconnect oil cooler lines.
6. Disconnect wiring harness from alternator, fan motor, starter motor and engine block connector.
7. On models with automatic transmission, disconnect ground cable at governor cover and wiring harness at inhibitor switch and downshift solenoid.
8. Disconnect ignition wire from coil and ignition primary wire from distributor.
9. Disconnect back-up light switch wiring harness.
10. On models with 4-wheel drive, disconnect selector switch wiring harness.
11. Remove radiator assembly.
12. On models with 4-wheel drive, disconnect engine fan from pulley.
13. Remove pitching stopper.
14. Disconnect accelerator cable at carburetor.
15. On models with manual transmission, disconnect clutch cable at release lever.
16. Disconnect speedometer cable from transmission.
17. Disconnect power brake unit vacuum hose from check valve.
18. On models with automatic transmission, drain fluid from transmission. Then disconnect oil cooler hoses connected to transmission from tubes attached to body.
19. Disconnect exhaust pipe from exhaust manifold. Then remove exhaust pipe bracket from transmission.
20. On models with manual transmission, remove through bolt connecting stay to engine rear mounting bracket. Then remove through bolt connecting shift rod to joint.
21. On models with automatic transmission, remove pin attaching manual lever to control rod.
22. On models with 4-wheel drive, push up drive selector lever boot, then remove bolt and pull lever upward.
23. Support engine using a suitable hoist.

24. Remove engine rear mount.
25. Remove transverse link to front crossmember attaching bolts.
26. Disconnect axle shafts from transmission by pushing strut assembly outward, Fig. 2.
27. On models with 4-wheel drive, drain transmission, then remove drive shaft.
28. On 4-wheel drive models, remove stabilizer bar from leading rods and rear crossmember, then remove rear crossmember.
29. Remove engine front mounting bracket to engine attaching bolts.
30. Raise engine and transmission and carefully remove from vehicle.
31. Reverse procedure to install.

AUTOMATIC TRANSMISSION TROUBLE SHOOTING

Engine Does Not Start In N or P

1. Manual linkage adjustment.
2. Inhibitor switch and wiring.

Engine Starts In Every Position Except N or P

1. Manual linkage adjustment.
2. Inhibitor switch or wiring.

Harsh Engagement When Shifted From N to D

1. Engine idle speed high.
2. Vacuum diaphragm or line.
3. Check control pressure.
4. Valve body.
5. Forward clutch.

No Drive In D Only

1. Manual linkage adjustment.
2. Check control pressure.
3. Valve body.
4. One-way clutch.

No Drive In D, 1, 2; Slips Easily or Is Difficult to Accelerate

1. Manual linkage adjustment.
2. Check control pressure.
3. Valve body.
4. Defective gasket between transmission case and differential and reduction case or between differential and reduction case and converter housing.
5. Forward clutch.
6. Leakage in hydraulic system.
7. Reverse clutch.

No Drive In R; Slips Easily or Is Hard to Accelerate

1. Manual linkage adjustment.
2. Check control pressure.
3. Valve body.

4. Reverse clutch.
5. Forward clutch.
6. Leakage in hydraulic system.
7. Reverse clutch check ball.

No Drive In Any Selector Position

1. Check fluid level.
2. Manual linkage adjustment.
3. Check control pressure.
4. Valve body.
5. Oil pump.
6. Leakage in hydraulic system.
7. Parking linkage.

Vehicle Moves Sluggishly

1. Check fluid level.
2. Manual linkage adjustment.
3. Check control pressure.
4. Valve body.
5. Oil pump.
6. Leakage in hydraulic system.
7. One-way clutch.

Vehicle Moves In N

1. Manual linkage adjustment.
2. Valve body.
3. Forward clutch.

Maximum Speed to Low or Insufficient Acceleration

1. Check fluid level.
2. Manual linkage adjustment.
3. Check control pressure.
4. Check stall speed.
5. Band adjustment.
6. Valve body.
7. Defective band.
8. Low-reverse brake.
9. Forward clutch.
10. Reverse clutch.
11. Oil pump.

Drags When Shifted to R

1. Band adjustment.
2. Forward clutch.
3. Defective band.
4. Parking linkage

Excessive Creeping

1. Engine idle speed high.

Total Absence of Creeping

1. Check fluid level.
2. Manual linkage adjustment.
3. Incorrect engine idle speed.
4. Valve body.
5. Oil pump.
6. Leakage in hydraulic system.
7. Forward clutch.
8. Reverse clutch.

No 1-2 Shift In D

1. Manual linkage adjustment.
2. Vacuum diaphragm or line.

3. Valve body.
4. Governor valve.
5. Band adjustment.
6. Servo pipe.
7. Defective band.
8. Leakage in hydraulic system.

No 2-3 Shift In D

1. Manual linkage adjustment.
2. Vacuum diaphragm or line.
3. Valve body.
4. Governor valve.
5. Band adjustment.
6. Servo pipe.
7. Reverse clutch.
8. Leakage in hydraulic system.
9. Reverse clutch check ball.

1-2 or 2-3 Shift Speed Too High

1. Vacuum diaphragm or line.
2. Downshift solenoid, kickdown switch and wiring.
3. Check control pressure.
4. Valve body.
5. Governor valve.
6. Leakage in hydraulic system.

Shifts From 1-3

1. Valve body.
2. Governor valve.
3. Defective band.
4. Leakage in hydraulic system.

Harsh 1-2 Shift

1. Vacuum diaphragm or line.
2. Check stall speed.
3. Valve body.
4. Band adjustment.
5. Defective band.

Harsh 2-3 Shift

1. Vacuum diaphragm or line.
2. Check control pressure.
3. Valve body.
4. Band adjustment.
5. Reverse clutch.

1-2 Slips

1. Check fluid level.
2. Manual linkage adjustment.
3. Vacuum diaphragm or line.
4. Check control pressure.
5. Valve body.
6. Band adjustment.
7. Servo pipe.

2-3 Slips

1. Check fluid level.
2. Manual linkage adjustment.
3. Vacuum diaphragm or line.
4. Check control pressure.
5. Valve body.
6. Band adjustment.
7. Servo pipe.
8. Reverse clutch.

9. Leakage in hydraulic system.
10. Reverse clutch check ball.

Drags When Shifted From 1-2

1. Valve body.
2. Low and reverse band.
3. Reverse clutch.
4. One-way clutch.

No 3-2 Shift

1. Vacuum diaphragm or line.
2. Valve body.
3. Governor valve.
4. Band adjustment.
5. Servo pipe.
6. Reverse clutch.
7. Defective band.
8. Leakage in hydraulic system.

No 2-1 or 3-1 Shift

1. Vacuum diaphragm or line.
2. Valve body.
3. Governor valve.
4. Band adjustment.
5. Defective band.
6. One-way clutch.

Shock Due to Speed Shifting Felt When Accelerator Pedal Is Released

1. Manual linkage adjustment.
2. Vacuum diaphragm or line.
3. Downshift solenoid, kickdown switch and wiring.
4. Check control pressure.
5. Valve body.
6. Governor valve.
7. Leakage in hydraulic system.

3-2 or 2-1 Shift Speed Too High

1. Manual linkage adjustment.
2. Vacuum diaphragm or line.
3. Downshift solenoid, kickdown switch and wiring.
4. Check control pressure.
5. Valve body.
6. Governor valve.
7. Leakage in hydraulic system.

No 3-2 Downshift Within Kickdown Limits

1. Downshift solenoid, kickdown switch and wiring.
2. Vacuum diaphragm or line.
3. Valve body.
4. Governor valve.
5. Servo pipe.
6. Defective band.
7. Forward clutch.

Downshift At Speed Above Kickdown Limit

1. Manual linkage adjustment.
2. Vacuum diaphragm or line.

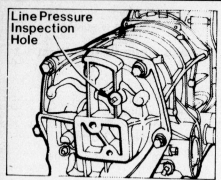

Fig. 3 Line pressure gauge tap location. 1974-76 models

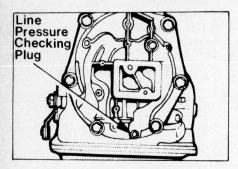

Fig. 4 Line pressure gauge tap location. 1977 models

3. Check control pressure.
4. Valve body.
5. Governor valve.
6. Reverse clutch.
7. Leakage in hydraulic system.

Slips 3-2 Downshift

1. Vacuum diaphragm or line.
2. Check control pressure.
3. Valve body.
4. Band adjustment.
5. Servo pipe.
6. Reverse clutch.
7. Defective band.
8. Leakage in hydraulic system.
9. Reverse clutch check ball.

No 3-2 Forced Downshift

1. Manual linkage adjustment.
2. Check control pressure.
3. Valve body.
4. Band adjustment.
5. Defective band.
6. Leakage in hydraulic system.

Downshifting 2-1 or Upshifting 2-3 When Selector Lever Is Placed In 2

1. Manual linkage adjustment.
2. Check control pressure.
3. Valve body.

No 3-2 Downshift When Selector Lever is Placed In 1

1. Manual linkage adjustment.
2. Check control pressure.

Stalling speed	Diagnosis	Cause of abnormality	Remarks
Higher than 2,100 rpm.	Slippage of clutches and bands in the automatic transmission can be assumed. Further testing is not required.	o When excessive stalling speeds are noted in all speed ranges... ...due to lowering of line pressure. o When noted only in D, 2 and 1 ranges... ...due to slippage of the forward clutch. o When noted only in D range (with normal stalling speed being noted at 1 and 2 speed ranges)........ due to slippage of the one-way clutch. o When noted only in 2 range......(*1) due to slippage of the bands. o When noted only in R range......(*2) due to slippage of the reverse clutch or low and reverse brake.	*1 The existence of a condition of band slippage cannot be determined by stalling test alone, but can be concluded from the increase of engine speed during 2 range-speed running. *2 To ascertain that slippage exists either on the reverse clutch or the low and reverse brake, a road test should be performed. Slippage of the reverse clutch can be assumed when the engine brake comes into effect during 1 speed range running. Conversely, slippage of the low and reverse brake will render the engine brake ineffective.
In the standard speed range. (1,800 to 2,100 rpm)	o All of the pertinent parts are functioning normally throughout D, 2, 1 and R speed ranges. o Engine exhibits normal performance.		The one-way clutch of the torque converter should be checked by means of a road test.
Lower than 1,800 rpm	Either some sort of engine troubles or a slippery one-way clutch in the torque converter may be assumed.		

Fig. 5 Stall speed diagnosis chart

3. Valve body.
4. Governor valve.
5. Band adjustment.
6. Reverse clutch.
7. Defective band.
8. Leakage in hydraulic system.

No Engine Braking In 1

1. Manual linkage adjustment.
2. Check control pressure.
3. Valve body.
4. Low and reverse band.
5. Leakage in hydraulic system.

Vacuum (in. Hg.)	Line Pressure (psi.)
11	74-85
12	69-80
13	63.5-74.5
14	58-69
15	52.5-63.5
16	47-58
17	45-52.5
18	45-47

Fig. 6 Line pressure test chart

Range	Throttle Position					
	Full Throttle Pressure (psi.)		Half Throttle Pressure (psi.)		Minimum Throttle Pressure (psi.)	
	Before Cut Down	After Cut Down	Before Cut Down	After Cut Down	Before Cut Down	After Cut Down
D	135-157	78-92.5	94-108	63-77	43-57	—
2	145-168	84-98	145-168	84-98	145-168	84-98
R	200-227		140-162		67-81	

Fig. 7 Line pressure at throttle position

Upshifting From 1-2 or 2-3 When Selector Lever Is Placed In 1

1. Manual linkage adjustment.
2. Valve body.
3. Leakage in hydraulic system.

No 2-1 Shift When Selector Lever Is Placed In 1

1. Check fluid level.
2. Manual linkage adjustment.
3. Valve body.
4. Governor valve.
5. Band adjustment.
6. Low and reverse band.
7. Leakage in hydraulic system.

Harsh 2-1 Downshift When Selector Is Placed In 1

1. Vacuum diaphragm or line.
2. Check stall speed.
3. Valve body.
4. Low and reverse band.

Transmission Overheated

1. Check fluid level.
2. Check control pressure.
3. Check stall speed.
4. Valve body.
5. Band adjustment.
6. Reverse clutch.
7. Defective band.
8. Low and reverse band.
9. Oil pump.
10. Leakage in hydraulic system.
11. Planetary gear.

Excessive Chatter In N or P

1. Check fluid level.
2. Check control pressure.
3. Valve body.

AUTOMATIC TRANSMISSION DIAGNOSIS & TESTING
Stall Test

NOTE: Before performing stall test, ensure engine oil, cooling system and transmission fluid are at proper levels.

With engine and transmission at operating temperature, connect a tachometer to engine and a pressure gauge to transmission pressure gauge port, Figs. 3 and 4. Position gauges so they can be viewed from driver's seat.

Perform the following test in each of the driving positions. With service and parking brake applied, slowly depress accelerator pedal to wide open position and note tachometer and pressure gauge readings. Stall speed should be 1800 to 2100 rpm. Do not hold accelerator in wide open position for more than 5 seconds. Also operate engine at 1200 rpm in N or P for 1 minute or more to allow converter to cool after each test. If a relatively high stall speed is noted, release accelerator pedal immediately to prevent damage to transmission.

If stall speed is below 1800 rpm or above 2100 rpm, refer to Fig. 5.

Control Pressure Check

With transmission and engine at operating temperature, connect pressure gauge to transmission pressure

	Result	Cause of abnormality
At idling speed	Low pressure in all speed ranges	Faulty pressure feeding line or low oil pump discharge pressure may be assumed, due to the following: o Worn oil pump or improperly adjusted internal clearances. o Oil leakage from the oil pump, valve body, governor or transmission case. o Sticky pressure regulator valve.
	Low pressure in only one certain range	Oil leakage from the pertinent parts or circuits such as: o Forward clutch or governor .... causes low pressure at D, 2 and 1 ranges. o Low and reverse brake circuit ...... causes low pressure at R and P ranges.
	Excessive pressure	o Leaky vacuum tube or vacuum diaphragm, or excessive length of vacuum rod. o Sticky pressure regulator valve.
At full or half-throttle	Pressure does not rise.	If pressure does not rise in spite of considerable lowering of vacuum, misassembly of the vacuum rod may be assumed.
	Pressure rises, but does not come into the standard range.	Sticky vacuum throttle valve, pressure regulator valve and pressure regulator plug may be assumed.

Fig. 8 Line pressure diagnosis chart

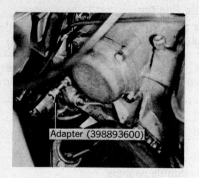

Fig. 9 Pressure gauge tap location for governor pressure check

Throttle Position	Range	Shift Speed (m.p.h.)
Kickdown	D1-D2 D2-D3 D3-D2 D2-D1	28-34 52-58 47-53 25-31
Half Throttle	D1-D2 D2-D3 D3-D2 D3-D1 D2-D1	11-16 28-34 12-19 12-19 11-16
Full Throttle	1₂-1₁ ①	22-28
Minimum Throttle	1₂-1₁ ①	22-28

①—Shift selector lever from D to 1 when vehicle is running at 31 m.p.h.

Fig. 14 Shift point test chart. 1974 models

Speed (m.p.h.)	Governor Pressure (psi.)
Below 5	0
Below 30	23-28
Below 60	63-75

Fig. 10 Governor pressure chart. 1974 models

Speed (m.p.h.)	Governor Pressure (psi.)
Below 6	0-3
Below 28	23-27
Below 48	57-62.5

Fig. 11 Governor pressure chart. 1975 models

Throttle Position	Range	Shift Speed (m.p.h.)
Kickdown	D3-D2 D2-D1	46-53 21-27
Half Throttle	D1-D2 D2-D3 D3-D2 D3-D1 D2-D1	10.5-14.5 24-30 12-17.5 12-17.5 5.5-12
Full Throttle	1₂-1₁ ① D1-D2 D2-D3	20.5-26 26-32 50-56
Minimum Throttle	1₂-1₁ ①	20.5-26

①—Shift selector lever from D to 1 when vehicle is running at 31 m.p.h.

Fig. 15 Shift point test chart. 1975 models

Speed (m.p.h.)	Governor Pressure (psi.)
Below 6	0-2.8
Below 25	23-27
Below 50	60-65

Fig. 12 Governor pressure chart. 1976 models

Throttle Position	Range	Shift Speed (m.p.h.)
Kickdown	D1-D2 D2-D3 D3-D2 D2-D1	29-35 54-60 49-55 24-30
Half Throttle	D1-D2 D2-D3 D3-D2 D3-D1 D2-D1	11-16 25-32 12-19 12-19 6-12
Full Throttle	1₂-1₁ ①	22-29
Minimum Throttle	1₂-1₁ ①	22-29

①—Shift selector lever from D to 1 when vehicle is running at 31 m.p.h.

Speed (m.p.h.)	Governor Pressure (psi.)
Below 6	0-2.8
Below 25	23-27
Below 50	57-63

Fig. 13 Governor pressure chart. 1977 models

Fig. 16 Shift point test chart. 1976 models

gauge tap, Figs. 3 and 4. Position gauge so that it can be viewed from driver's seat. When checking line pressure, start with engine idling and slowly increase engine speed. Changes of line pressure at neutral or drive range against throttle valve opening and intake manifold vacuum are shown in Fig. 6. Line pressure in D, 2 and R ranges will change at certain points, when pressure modifier valve functions. This point is known as cut down point. Before cut-down point as stated in Fig. 7, implies slow driving condition, less than 9.5 mph. After cut down point implies vehicle speed of more than 22 mph. Line pressure during idling of engine corresponds to oil pressure before cut down operation with minimum throttle. If pressures are not within limits, refer to diagnosis chart, Fig. 8.

Governor Pressure Check

With transmission at operating temperature, connect pressure gauge to gauge tap located on right hand side of differential and reduction case, Fig. 9. Position gauge so that it can be viewed from driver's seat. Position selector lever in 2 position and start checking governor pressure, Figs. 10 through 13.

Shift Point Check

Refering to Figs. 14 through 17, check shift speeds. The feeling of speed shifting should be checked when testing shift speeds. If shifting is not smooth and is accompanied by considerable shock or if shifting is not sharp and is accompanied by dragging, this indicates the presence of inaccurate negative throttle pressure or other related defects. If shift speeds are not within limits, refer to diagnosis chart, Fig. 18.

AUTOMATIC TRANSMISSION ADJUSTMENTS

Manual Linkage

1. Move selector lever from P to 1 and lever should come to a set position with a click, which indicates manual valve has gone into its detent position. If lever is not in alignment with proper mark on dial when lever is released, an adjustment is necessary.

2. Move lever to N, loosen locknuts on linkage arm at transmission lever and turn as necessary for transmission lever to click into detent position when selector lever is in N.
3. If necessary for selector lever alignment with console marks, loosen four screws holding the indicator and reposition as necessary.

Throttle Position	Range	Shift Speed (m.p.h.)
Kickdown	D1-D2 D2-D3 D3-D2 D2-D1	28-34 54-60 48-54 16-22
Half Throttle	D1-D2 D2-D3 D3-D2 D3-D1 D2-D1	12-16 16-22 12-18 12-18 6-12
Full Throttle	1_2-1_1 ①	21-27
Minimum Throttle	1_2-1_1 ①	21-27

①—Shift selector lever from D to 1 when vehicle is running at 31 m.p.h.

Fig. 17   Shift point test chart. 1977 models

Stalling speed	Diagnosis	Cause of abnormality	Remarks
Road test	o Insufficient acceleration during road test of the car at speeds below 50 km/h (31 MPH).	Due to the slippery one-way clutch of the torque converter.	
	o Max. speed is limited to 80 km/h (50 MPH) during road test.	(*3) Due to seizing of the one-way clutch of the torque converter.	*3 Be careful to prevent damage to the torque converter resulting from overheating.
	o Improper running of the car throughout all speed ranges.	Due to improper engine performance.	

Fig. 18   Shift point test diagnosis chart

Band Adjustment

1. Band should be adjusted if 1-2 shift is not smooth, or if there is a delay of greater than 0.7 second on 3-2 kickdown downshift.
2. Loosen locknut and turn adjusting screw 90 degrees, then tighten locknut, Fig. 1.

Driving Axle & Brake Section

FRONT AXLE SHAFT, SEALS & BEARINGS, REPLACE

Refer to Fig. 1, which shows components for drum brakes and Fig. 2, which shows disc brake arrangement.

Drum Brakes

1. Raise front of vehicle and remove wheels.
2. Remove lock plates and nuts securing brake drum to spindle. Do this with parking brake applied.
3. Using a suitable puller, remove brake drum, then remove backing plate.
4. Remove bolts holding strut to knuckle arm and disconnect tie-rod end from arm with a puller.
5. Carefully pull knuckle arm downward to separate it from strut.
6. Remove castle nut and disengage ball joint from the knuckle arm.
7. Using a suitable puller, remove knuckle arm housing.
8. If only oil seals are being replaced, they can be pried out and new ones driven in. If bearings also are to be removed, reach inside hub, Fig. 3, and push spacer up or down to expose an edge on bearing inner race. With a brass drift against bearing inner race edge, drive out old bearing and seal.
9. Press in new bearings, then oil seals. Apply grease to seal inner lip before installing.
10. Reverse procedure to install. Torque ball joint castle nut to 25-29 ft. lbs. (3.5-4 kgm), tie-rod and castle nut to 18-22 ft. lbs. (2.5-3 kgm) and axle nut to 160-188 ft. lbs. (22-26 kgm).

Disc Brakes

1. Raise front of vehicle and remove wheels.
2. Remove pins and stoppers that secure caliper to bracket, Fig. 4 and refer to disc brake service.
3. Take out two bolts that hold caliper bracket and remove from hub.
4. Remove bolts that hold strut to knuckle arm housing, remove brake hanger on tie-rod end and remove parking cable bracket from knuckle arm housing.
5. Separate tie-rod end from knuckle arm housing with a puller, then carefully pull knuckle arm down to separate strut from it.

6. Remove castle nut and separate ball joint from knuckle and pull disc and hub out of axle shaft with a puller. Inner bearing and oil seal in some case may remain on axle shaft, in which case they should be removed with a puller. Otherwise, proceed as in steps 8 through 10 for drum brakes, observing the following

torque value: caliper and bracket to hub 36-51 ft. lbs. (5-7 kgm).

MASTER CYLINDER, REPLACE

1. Disconnect brake tubes from master cylinder and plug ends.

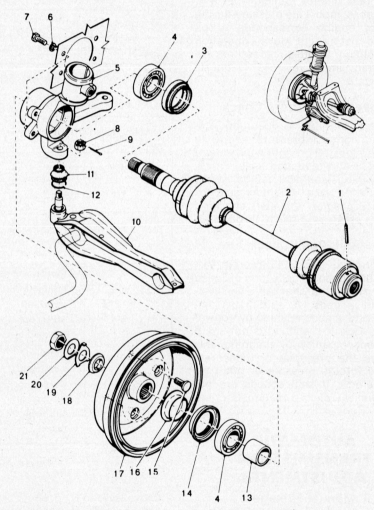

1. Spring pin	12. Circlip
2. Axle shaft	13. Spacer
3. Oil seal (in.)	14. Oil seal (out)
4. Bearing	15. Hub bolt
5. Housing	16. Sleeve
6. Spring washer	17. Brake drum
7. Bolt	18. Center piece
8. Castle nut	19. Lock washer
9. Cotter pin	20. Lock plate
10. Transverse link	21. Nut
11. Dust seal (Ball joint)	

Fig. 1 Front axle components. Models with drum brakes

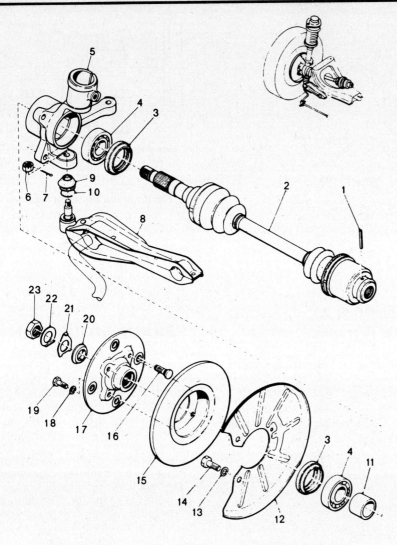

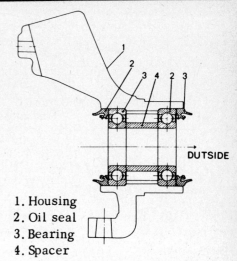

1. Housing
2. Oil seal
3. Bearing
4. Spacer

Fig. 3   Bearing & oil seal installation

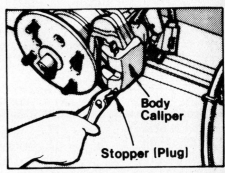

Fig. 4   Removing stopper plug from caliper body

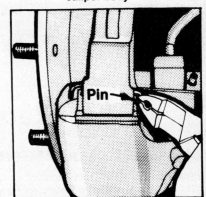

Fig. 5   Removing pins from caliper

1. Spring pin	13. Spring washer
2. Axle shaft	14. Bolt
3. Oil seal	15. Disc
4. Bearing	16. Hub bolt
5. Housing	17. Disc hub
6. Castle nut	18. Spring washer
7. Cotter pin	19. Bolt
8. Transverse link	20. Center piece
9. Dust seal (Ball joint)	21. Lock washer
10. Circlip	22. Lock plate
11. Spacer	23. Nut
12. Disc cover	

Fig. 2   Front axle components. Models with disc brakes

2. Remove two or three nuts retaining master cylinder and pull off studs.
3. Reverse procedure to install.

BRAKE PADS, REPLACE

1. Raise front of vehicle, remove wheel and outer parking brake cable clip, then take out cable.
2. Remove four pins from caliper stoppers, Fig. 5.

3. Tap stoppers out or tap partly out and pull with pliers, Fig. 6.
4. Hold caliper body, push upper part in and pull lower part out to disengage from bracket.
5. Replace brake shoes if lining is worn to .06-inch (1.6 mm).
6. Check disc thickness at contact surface. Standard thickness is .39 inch (10 mm). The minimum thickness acceptable is .33 inch (8.5 mm). If

Fig. 6   Removing stoppers from caliper assembly

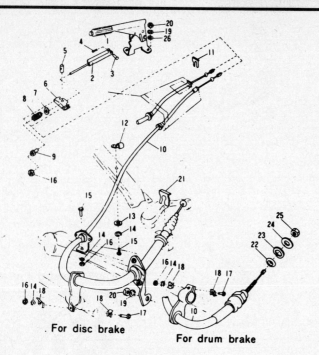

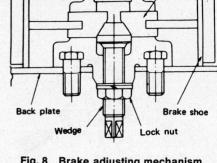

Fig. 8 Brake adjusting mechanism

disc is scored and must be machined or replaced, remove as explained in Front Axle Shaft & Bearing, Replace.

BRAKE ADJUSTMENTS

The parking brake is adjusted at the equalizer, Fig. 7. Front disc brakes are inherently self-adjusting. Front drum brakes are of the self-adjusting type, with cable, adjusting lever and star wheel. Rear drum brakes require periodic, manual adjustment as follows:
1. Jack up rear of car and slacken adjuster locknut on backing plate.
2. Turn wedge adjuster clockwise until wheel locks up, Fig. 8.
3. Back off adjuster 180 degrees, to provide approximately .004-.006 inch shoe clearance, then tighten the locknut.

For disc brake

For drum brake

1. Lever assembly (hand brake)	10. Hand brake cable assembly	19. Spring washer
2. Rod complete (hand brake)	11. Clamp	20. Nut
3. Clevis pin	12. Clamp	21. Clamp
4. Cotter pin	13. Washer	22. O ring
5. Pin	14. Spring washer	23. Spring washer
6. Equalizer	15. Bolt	24. Washer
7. Washer	16. Nut	25. Nut
8. Spring	17. Bolt	26. Washer
9. Adjuster (hand brake)	18. Washer (hand brake)	

Fig. 7 Parking brake components

Rear Suspension Section

REAR WHEEL ALIGNMENT

Except Four Wheel Drive Models

On rear suspension, camber and toe-in are adjustable at torsion bar mountings on center of underbody. To reduce camber, insert shim as shown in Fig. 1. To reduce, remove shim. Each shim changes camber ¼°, and car normally is built with two shims inserted. To adjust toe, move mounting cap forward to increase, rearward to reduce, in its elongated holes, as shown in Fig. 2.

REAR WHEEL BEARING, ADJUST

1972-73 Models Except Four Wheel Drive

1. Remove rear wheel and attach dial indicator as shown in Figs. 3 and 4, then measure in-and-out and up-and-down free play.
2. If free play at center is more than .012-inch (0.3 mm) or more than .016-inch (0.4 mm) at point 3.5 inches (90 mm) from center, wheel bearing adjustment is required.

1974-77 Models Except Four Wheel Drive

1. Tighten axle nut to approximately 36 ft. lbs. (5kgm).
2. Loosen nut 1/8 to 1/10 turn. Using a

Fig. 1 Inserting camber adjusting shim

Fig. 2 Adjusting toe-in

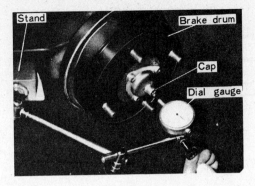

Fig. 3 Checking end play at center

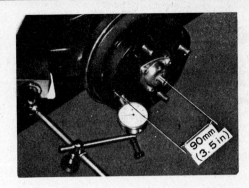

Fig. 4 Checking end play 3.5 in. from center

suitable spring scale measure starting force, Fig. 5. Starting force should be 2.2 to 3.1 lbs. (1-1.4 kg.).

3. Bend lock plate to lock nut in position, then install bearing cap and gasket.

SHOCK ABSORBER, REPLACE

1. On sedans and coupes, lift up on rear seat back and pull it forward from top to gain access to upper shock mountings. On station wagons, remove plastic access cover over fender walls inside cargo area.
2. Disconnect upper and lower shock mountings, remove old shock, install new one and tighten upper and lower mountings.
3. Remove rear seat cushion on sedans and coupes, reinstall seat back over clips, then refit cushion.

TORSION BAR, REPLACE & ADJUST

Rear springs are torsion bar type, Fig. 6. Right and left side torsion bars must not be interchanged, or premature failure will result. Each torsion bar is

splined at each end, and fits into a splined retaining arrangement. There may be an alignment marking on the edges of bars and retainers, Fig. 7, particularly on torsion bar. If no alignment markings exist, mark torsion bar and retainer prior to removal or adjustment.

If problem is riding height, this can be corrected without removing torsion bar. Take measurements at each side as shown in Fig. 8. Distance from level ground to point A should be 11.29-11.89 inches for 6.15-13-4PT tires, and 11.06-11.66 inches for 145-SR-13 tires.

1. Raise and support rear of car, then remove rear wheel(s) and brake drum(s).
2. Disconnect shock from trailing arm, then push up on trailing arm and move shock out of way.
3. Remove torsion bar outer bushing lock bolt, Fig. 9.
4. If springs are to removed, remove bushing lockbolts at inside end of

torsion bar (center rear of car), then tap torsion bar out of its outer bushing with a hammer and brass drift.

5. If torsion bars are merely to be adjusted to correct riding height, tap inner end of torsion bar toward wheel far enough to disengage splines at both ends from bushings. Each spline-tooth change alters riding height about .2-inch (5 mm) at point shown in Fig. 8. To increase riding height, torsion bar should be turned in the direction opposite to arrow mark on outer end surface of bar. Turning in direction of the arrow will reduce riding height.
6. First, set inner end of torsion bar in desired position, tapping it in far enough for splines to engage bushing but not so far as to engage outer bushing splines (inner splines are longer).
7. Raise (to reduce riding height) or lower (to raise height) trailing arm

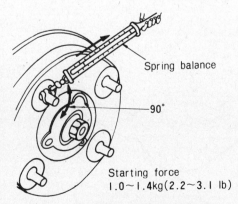

Fig. 5 Checking rear wheel bearing adjustment

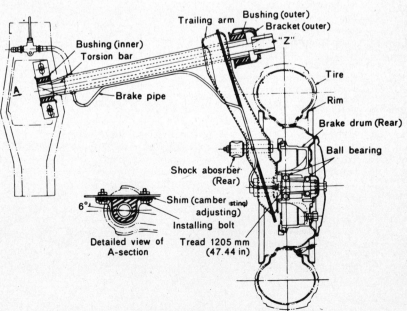

Fig. 6 Rear Suspension components

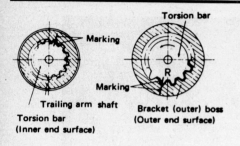

Fig. 7 Torsion bar markings

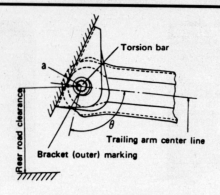

Fig. 8 Measuring riding height

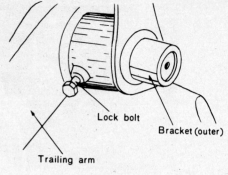

Fig. 9 Outer bushing lock bolt

and when alignment marks have been shifted same number of teeth as at inside bushing, tap in torsion bar to engage outside bushing, then install lockbolt and shock absorber.

NOTE: It may be helpful to place a small jack under trailing arm to sup-

port it and torsion bar while making adjustment and engaging torsion bar in inner bushing splines.

Front Suspension & Steering Section

1. Nut
2. Spring washer
3. Washer
4. Cap (strut mount)
5. Self locking nut
6. Washer
7. Strut mount
8. Oil seal (strut mount)
9. Washer (thrust bearing)
10. Thrust washer
11. Spring retainer (upper)
12. Rubber seat (coil spring)
13. Helper
14. Coil spring
15. Shock absorber complete
16. Washer
17. Spring washer
18. Bolt
19. Bracket compl. (brake hose: RH)
20. Bracket compl. (brake hose: LH)
21. Spring washer
22. Bolt
23. Self locking nut
24. Washer (transverse link inner)
25. Bushing (link outer)
26. Bushing (link outer)
27. Washer (transverse link outer)
28. Bushing (stabilizer)
29. Stabilizer
30. Bolt
31. Washer
32. Bolt (10 x 40)
33. Washer
34. Lock plate
35. Bracket (stabilizer)
36. Nut
37. Spring washer
38. Washer
39. Crossmember compl. (F)
40. Washer (transverse link inner)
41. Bushing (inner pivot)
42. Washer (transverse link outer)
43. Self locking nut

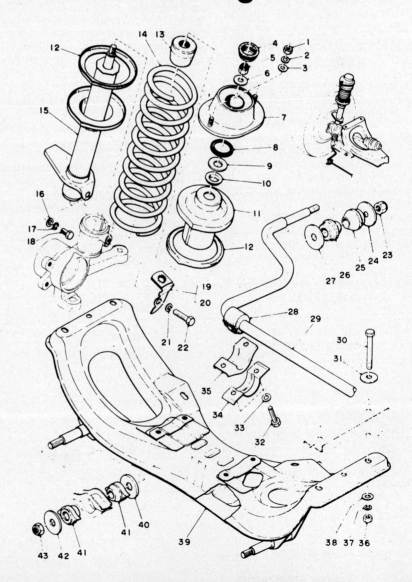

Fig. 1 Front suspension components. 1972-74 models

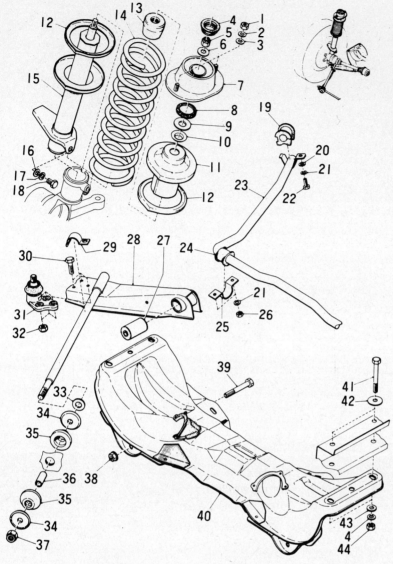

Fig. 3 Removing spring upper retaining nut

Fig. 2 Front suspension components. 1975-77 models

1. Nut
2. Spring washer
3. Washer
4. Cap(strut mounting)
5. Self-locking nut
6. Washer
7. Strut mounting
8. Oil seal(strut mounting)
9. Washer(thrust bearing)
10. Thrust washer
11. Sqring retainer (upper)
12. Rubber seat(coil spring)
13. Helper
14. Coil spring
15. Shock absorber
16. Washer
17. Spring washer
18. Bolt
19. Bushing(stabilizer F)
20. Washer
21. Spring washer
22. Bolt
23. Stabilizer
24. Bushing(stabilizer R)
25. Bracket(stabilizer R)
26. Nut
27. Rubber busing(IN)
28. Transverse link
29. Bracket(stabilizer F)
30. Bolt
31. Ball joint
32. Self-locking nut
33. Washer
34. Plate(leading rod)
35. Bushing(leading rod)
36. Pipe(leading rod)
37. Self-locking nut
38. Self-locking nut
39. Bolt
40. Crossmember(F)
41. Bolt
42. Washer
43. Washer
44. Nut

WHEEL ALIGNMENT

Although caster and camber can be measured, the strut front suspension does not require or provide for readjustment Figs. 1 and 2. If adjustment is necessary, it is because of damaged parts, which should be replaced. Toe adjustment is by threaded sleeve on tie-rod.

SUSPENSION STRUT, REPLACE

1. Raise front of vehicle and remove wheel and tire assembly.
2. Remove bolts clamping strut to steering knuckle.
3. Disconnect tie-rod end from knuckle, so knuckle can be lowered

without damage to ball joint.
4. Lower knuckle and ease strut out.
5. Remove nuts at strut upper mounting then remove strut from body.
6. Reverse procedure to install.

COIL SPRING, REPLACE

1. Remove suspension strut as described above.
2. Compress spring using a suitable compressor.
3. Remove upper retainer nut, Fig. 3, retainer and coil spring.
4. Reverse procedure to install. Torque retainer nut to 43-54 ft. lbs. (6-7.5kgm).

CONTROL ARM (TRANSVERSE LINK) SERVICE

1. Raise and support front of vehicle and remove wheels and tire assembly.
2. Remove parking brake cable bracket from control arm.
3. Remove self-locking nut attaching control arm to crossmember.
4. Remove self-locking nut connecting stabilizer rod to control arm.
5. Pry control arm rearward to free from crossmember, then forward to free from stabilizer.
6. Remove castle nut from ball joint and separate ball joint stud from knuckle.
7. If ball joint play exceeds .012-inch (0.3 mm) on bench test, chisel out rivet and replace ball joint. Inspect ball joint boot and if cut, replace.
8. Check control arm for cracks or bends. Replace if necessary.
9. Begin reinstallation of arm by tightening ball joint castle nut to knuckle, to 35-40 ft. lbs. (4.8 to 5.5 kgm).
10. If stabilizer and/or control arm bushings are worn or deteriorated, replace. Obtain new self-locking nuts for control arm and stabilizer.

11. Insert stabilizer into control arm, fit bushing and nut Figs. 1 and 2.

12. Fit inner washer and bushing onto pivot of crossmember, install control arm, then fit bushing and outer washer.

NOTE: Washers have holes of different diameters, the inner washer has hold diameter larger than that of the outer washer.

13. Thread on self-locking nut and tighten moderately.

14. Attach parking brake cable bracket, install wheels and lower vehicle, then tighten stabilizer and control arm self-locking nuts to 72-87 ft. lbs. (10-12 kgm). Check wheel alignment and adjust toe if necessary.

STEERING GEAR, REPLACE

Except 4 Wheel Drive Models

1. Raise and support front of vehicle and remove wheels and tire assembly.
2. Remove cotter pin and castle nut, then using a puller, remove tie-rod end from knuckle arm.
3. Remove parking brake cable hanger from tie-rod end.
4. Disconnect pinion from steering shaft at rubber coupling by pulling out cotter pins and removing coupling bolts, Fig. 4.
5. Straighten lockplate and remove bolts holding gearbox bracket to crossmember.
6. Loosen front engine mounts and raise engine about 0.2-inch (5 mm) to provide clearance.
7. Pull gearbox from crossmember toward left side of vehicle, being careful not to damage gearbox boot.
8. Reverse procedure to install.

4 Wheel Drive Models

Follow procedure for Front Wheel Drive Models with the following additional steps.

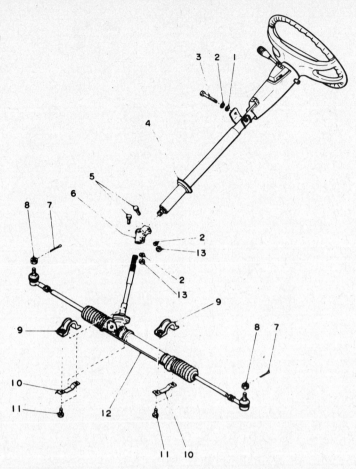

1. Washer
2. Spring washer
3. Bolt
4. Bushing (steering column)
5. Bolt
6. Universal joint
7. Cotter pin
8. Castle nut
9. Gear box bracket
10. Lock plate
11. Bolt
12. Steering gear box
13. Nut

Fig. 4 Steering system components

1. Remove fan protector on top of radiator.
2. Remove pitching stopper.
3. Loosen engine front mounts, but do not remove nuts and bolts.
4. Raise engine using a hoist until it is stopped by contact with engine mount nut. Do not remove nuts and attempt to raise engine any further, or you may damage inner universal joint boot can clip.
5. After installing steering gear, lower engine and tighten mounting nuts, then install pitching stopper.

TOYOTA

INDEX OF SERVICE OPERATIONS

TOYOTA

VEHICLE IDENTIFICATION

Model	Year	Engine Code	Displacement (cc)
Celica	1972-74	18R-C	1968
	1975-77	20R	2189
Corolla	1972-74	3K-C	1166
	1972-76	2T-C	1588
Corona	1972-74	18R-C	1968
	1975-77	20R	2189
Hi Lux	1972-74	18R-C	1968
	1975-77	20R	2189
Mark II	1972 (Early)	18R-C	1968
	1972 (Late)	2M	2253
	1973-76	4M	2563

ENGINE IDENTIFICATION

Engine	Model
2M	1972 (Late) Mark II
3K-C	1972-74 Corolla
4M	1973-76 Mark II
18R-C	1972-74 Celica
	1972-74 Corona
	1972-74 Hi Lux
	1972 (Early) Mark II
20R	1975-77 Celica
	1975-77 Corona
	1975-77 Hi Lux

GENERAL ENGINE SPECIFICATIONS

Year	Engine	Carburetor	Bore & Stroke	Piston Displacement Cubic Inches	Compression Ratio	Maximum Brake H.P. @ R.P.M.	Maximum Torque Ft. Lbs. @ R.P.M.
1972	4-1166cc	2 Barrel	2.95 x 2.60	71.2	9.0	65 @ 6000	67 @ 3800
	4-1588cc	2 Barrel	3.35 x 2.76	96.9	8.5	88 @ 6000	91.3 @ 3800
	4-1968cc	2 Barrel	3.48 x 3.15	120.0	8.5	97 @ 5500	106 @ 3600
	6-2253cc	2 Barrel	2.95 x 3.35	137.4	8.5	109 @ 5200	120 @ 3600
1973	4-1166cc	2 Barrel	2.95 x 2.60	71.2	9.0	65 @ 6000	67 @ 3800
	4-1588cc	2 Barrel	3.35 x 2.76	96.9	8.5	88 @ 6000	91.3 @ 3800
	4-1968cc	2 Barrel	3.48 x 3.15	120.0	8.5	97 @ 5500	106 @ 3600
	6-2563cc	2 Barrel	3.15 x 3.35	156.4	8.5	122 @ 5200	141 @ 3600
1974	4-1166cc	2 Barrel	2.95 x 2.60	71.2	9.0	65 @ 6000	67 @ 3800
	4-1588cc	2 Barrel	3.35 x 2.76	96.9	①	88 @ 6000	91.3 @ 3800
	4-1968cc	2 Barrel	3.48 x 3.15	120.0	8.5	97 @ 5500	106 @ 3600
	6-2563cc	2 Barrel	3.15 x 3.35	156.4	8.5	②	③
1975	4-1588cc	2 Barrel	3.35 x 2.76	96.9	9.0	⑤	83 @ 3800
	4-2189cc	2 Barrel	3.48 x 3.50	133.6	8.4	④	120 @ 2800
	6-2563cc	2 Barrel	3.15 x 3.35	156.4	8.5	108 @ 5000	130 @ 2800
1976	4-1588cc	2 Barrel	3.35 x 2.76	96.9	9.0	⑤	83 @ 3800
	4-2189cc	2 Barrel	3.48 x 3.50	133.6	8.4	④	120 @ 2800
	6-2563cc	2 Barrel	3.15 x 3.35	156.4	8.5	108 @ 5000	130 @ 2800
1977	4-1166cc	2 Barrel	2.95 x 2.60	71.2	9.0	58 @ 5800	63 @ 3800
	4-1588cc	2 Barrel	3.35 x 2.76	96.9	8.5	⑤	83 @ 3800
	4-2189cc	2 Barrel	3.48 x 3.50	133.6	8.4	⑥	122 @ 2400

①—Exc. Calif. 8.5; Calif. 9.0.
②—Exc. Calif., 122 @ 5200; Calif. 117 @ 5200.
③—Exc. Calif. 141 @ 3600; Calif. 138 @ 3600.
④—Exc. Calif. 96 @ 4800; Calif. 90 @ 4800.
⑤—Exc. Calif. 75 @ 5800; Calif. 73 @ 5800.
⑥—Exc. Calif. 95 @ 4800; Calif. & High Alt. 90 @ 4800.

TUNE UP SPECIFICATIONS

▲Before removing wires from distributor cap, determine location of the No. 1 wire in cap, as distributor position may have been altered from that shown at the end of this chart.

Year	Spark Plug Type	Spark Plug Gap Inches	Point Gap Inch	Dwell Angle Deg.	Firing Order ▲	Timing BTDC	Mark Fig.	Hot Idle Speed Std. Trans.	Hot Idle Speed Auto. Trans.	Idle CO% Std. Trans.	Idle CO% Auto. Trans.
1972											
4-1166cc	BP5ES-L	.030	.018	52	A	5	B	650	—	2—3%	—
4-1588cc	BP5ES-L	.030	.018	52	A	5	C	750	650D	2—3%	—
4-1968cc	①	.029	.018	52	A	7	D	650	650D	2—3%	2—3%
6-2253cc	BP6ES	.030	.018	41	E	7	F	700	600	—	—

Continued

TUNE UP SPECIFICATIONS—Continued

▲Before removing wires from distributor cap, determine location of the No. 1 wire in cap, as distributor position may have been altered from that shown at the end of this chart.

| Year | Spark Plug | | Distributor | | Ignition Timing | | | Carburetor Adjustment | | | |
| | Type | Gap Inches | Point Gap Inch | Dwell Angle Deg. | Firing Order ▲ | Timing BTDC | Mark Fig. | Hot Idle Speed | | Idle CO% | |
								Std. Trans.	Auto. Trans.	Std. Trans.	Auto. Trans.
1973											
4-1166cc	BP5ES-L	.030	.018	52	A	5	B	650	—	1—4%	—
4-1588cc	BP5ES-L	.030	.018	52	A	5	C	750	650D	1—4%	1—4%
4-1968cc	①	.029	.018	52	A	7	D	650	650D	1—4%	1—4%
6-2563cc	BP5ES	.030	.018	41	E	5	F	700	650D	1—3%	1—3%
1974											
4-1166cc	BP5ES-L	.030	.018	52	A	5	B	750	—	1—4%	—
4-1588cc	BP5ES-L	.030	.018	52	A	③	C	④	④	⑤	⑤
4-1968cc	①	.029	.018	52	A	7	D	650	800N	1—4%	1—4%
6-2563cc	BP5ES-L	.030	.018	41	E	5	F	700	750N	⑥	⑥
1975											
4-1588cc	BP5ES-L	.030	.018	⑦	A	⑧	C	850N	850N	—	—
4-2189cc	BP5ES-L	.030	.018	52	G	8	H	850	850	—	—
6-2563cc	BP5ES-L	.030	.018	41	E	③	F	800	750	—	—
1976											
4-1588cc	BP5ES-L	.030	.018	52	A	10	C	850	850N	—	—
4-2189cc	BP5ES-L	.030	.018	52	G	8	H	850	850N	—	—
6-2563cc	BP5ES-L	.030	.018	41	E	③	F	800	750	—	—
1977											
4-1166cc	⑨	.031	.018	52	A	8	B	750	—	—	—
4-1588cc	⑨	.031	.018	52	A	10	C	850	850N	—	—
4-2189cc	⑨	.031	.018	52	G	8	H	800	850N	—	—

—Not Available
① —Calif. BP5ES-L; Exc. Calif. BP6ES.
② —Man. Trans. 7°; Auto. trans. 5°.
③ —Exc. Calif. 5°; Calif. 10°.
④ —Calif. 850; Exc. Calif. M/T, 750; Exc. Calif. A/T, 800N.
⑤ —Exc. Calif. 1—4%; Calif. .5—3%.

⑥ —Exc. Calif. 1—3%; Calif. 1—2%.
⑦ —Single Pts. 52°; Dual Pts. 57.
⑧ —Single Pts. 10°; Dual Pts. 12° main points, 19° to 25° sub points.
⑨ —BP5ES-L or BP5EA-L.

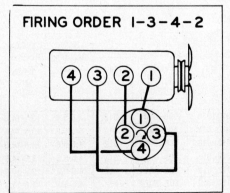

FIRING ORDER 1-3-4-2

Fig. A

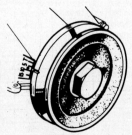

Fig. B

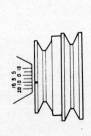

Fig. C

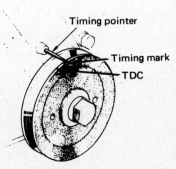

Timing pointer
Timing mark
TDC

Fig. D

TUNE UP SPECIFICATIONS NOTES—Continued

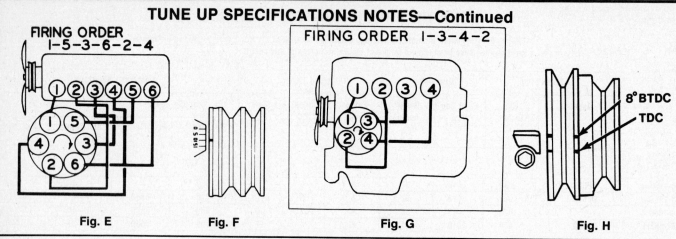

Fig. E   Fig. F   Fig. G   Fig. H

DISTRIBUTOR SPECIFICATIONS

★If unit is checked on vehicle, double the RPM and degrees to get crankshaft figures.

Distributor Part No.	Advance Starts	Centrifugal Advance Degrees @ R.P.M. of Distributor			Full Advance	Vacuum Advance	
		Intermediate Advance				Inches of Vac. to Start Plunger	Max. Adv. Dist. Deg. @ Vacuum
19100-24013	0 @ 575	4 @ 1100	8 @ 1500	10 @ 1700	13 @ 2100	4.33	10 @ 9.84
19100-26030	0 @ 500	8.5 @ 1000	16.5 @ 2300	—	—	3.15	—
19100-26050	0 @ 500	11 @ 1500	16.5 @ 2300	—	—	3.15	—
19100-26051	0 @ 500	11 @ 1500	16.5 @ 2300	—	—	3.15	—
19100-26071	0 @ 650	—	13 @ 2600	—	—	3.54	—
19100-34170	0 @ 555	5.5 @ 1030/1070	13 @ 2600	—	—	3.47/5.98	—
19100-34053	0 @ 850	11 @ 1850	13 @ 2600	—	—	2.28/4.02	—
19100-38010	0 @ 550	8.5 @ 1350	12.5 @ 2500	12.2 @ 3000	—	3.39/4.49	—
19100-33013	0 @ 500	10 @ 1600	15 @ 2800	—	—	2.28/4.02	—
2M & 4M ①	0 @ 500	5 @ 925	8 @ 1275	12 @ 1775	15 @ 2000	3.15	8 @ 8
2 M ②	0 @ 400	5 @ 900	8 @ 1150	12 @ 1600	15 @ 2000	.80	10 @ 11.5
4 M ②	0 @ 775	5 @ 1150	8 @ 1350	12 @ 1650	15 @ 1775	3.00	10 @ 8.6
19100-26110-A	0 @ 500	8 @ 1300	—	13 @ 2800	—	3.54	—
19100-26120-A	0 @ 500	7 @ 1500	—	13 @ 2700	—	3.54	—
Dual Points	0 @ 750	7 @ 1300	—	9 @ 1800	—	3.54	—
19100-61010	0 @ 490	7 @ 900	15 @ 1800	14.3 @ 3000	—	3.15	—
1910-61030	0 @ 490	7 @ 900	15 @ 1800	14.3 @ 3000	—	3.15	—

—Not Available.
①—Without air injection.
②—With air injection.

ALTERNATOR & REGULATOR SPECIFICATIONS

Year	Model	Alternator			Regulator									Relay Operating Voltage	Voltage Regulator Voltage
		Model	Maximum Output, Amps	Rotor Coil Resistance Ohms	Voltage Relay				Voltage Regulator						
					Angle Gap	Point Gap	Contact Spring Deflection	Armature Gap	Angle Gap	Point Gap	Contact Spring Deflection	Armature Gap			
1972-77	3K-C	27020-12011	30	4.1-4.3	—	.016-.047	.008-.018	—	.008	.010-.018	.008-.024	.012		4.5-5.8	13.8-14.8
1972-77	2T-C		40	4.2	.020	.016-.047	.008-.024	0	.008	.012-.018	.008-.024	.012		4.0-5.8	13.8-14.8
1972-74	18R-C	27020-36021	40	4.2	—	.016-.047	.008-.024	—	.008	.012-.018	.008-.0024	.012		4.5-5.8	13.8-14.8
		27020-36041	45	4.2	—	.016-.047	.008-.024	—	.008	.012-.018	.008-.0024	.012		4.5-5.8	13.8-14.8
1972-74	2M, 4M	—	45	4.2	—	.016-.047	.008-.018	—	.008	.012-.018	.008-.0024	.012		4.5-5.8	13.8-14.8
		—	55	4.2	—	.016-.047	.008-.018	—	.008	.012-.018	.008-.0024	.012		4.5-5.8	13.8-14.8
1975-76	4M	—	45	4.2	.020	.016-.024	.008-.024	0	.008	.012-.018	.008-.024	.012		4.0-5.8	13.8-14.8
1975-77	20R-C	27020-38010	40	—	—	—	—	—	—	—	—	—		4.0-5.8	13.8-14.8
		27020-34030	45	—	—	—	—	—	—	—	—	—		4.0-5.8	13.8-14.8

—Not Available

Continued

TOYOTA

STARTING MOTOR SPECIFICATIONS

Year	Engine	Starter No.	Brush Spring Tension, Ounces	No Load Test			Torque Test		
				Amperes	Volts	R.P.M.	Amperes	Volts	Torque, Ft. Lbs.
1972-77	3K-C	28100—24030	37—47.6	55	11	3500	450	8.5	8.0
		28100—24012	37—47.6	55	11	3500	450	8.5	8.0
		28100—24022	30—40.6	50	11	5000	470	7.7	9.4
1972-77	2T-C	28100—26040	54—66	90	11.5	3500	—	—	—
		28100—26050	54—66	90	11.5	4000	—	—	—
1972-74	18R-C	28100—36030	44—55	50	11	5000	470	7.7	9.4
		28100—40041	44—55	45	11	6000	550	7.0	10.1
		28100—36020	44—55	50	11	5000	600	7.0	13.0
		28100—33020	44—55	50	11	5000	600	7.0	13.0
1972-74	2M, 4M	—	37—47	45	11	6000	—	—	—
1974-76	4M	28100—45022	54—66	90	11.5	4000	—	—	—
		28100—41020	38—48	50	11.5	5000	—	—	—
1975-77	20R-C	28100—33020	—	50	11	5000	—	—	—
		28100—36050	—	50	11	5000	—	—	—
		28100—34041	—	80	11.5	3500	—	—	—

—Not Available

VALVE SPECIFICATIONS

Year	Model	Valve Lash		Valve Angles		Valve Spring Installed Height	Valve Spring Pressure Lbs. @ In.	Stem Clearance		Stem Diameter	
		Int.	Exh.	Seat	Face			Intake	Exhaust	Intake	Exhaust
1972-77	3KC	.008 H	.012 H	45	45	1.512	70.1 @ 1.512	.0014—.0026	.0014—.0028	.3136—.3140	.3134—.3140
1972-74	2T-C	.008 H	.013 H	45	45	1.484	58 @ 1.484	.0010—.0024	.0012—.0026	.3138—.3146	.3138—.3142
1975-77	2T-C	.008 H	.013 H	45	45	1.484	58 @ 1.484	.0010—.0024	.0012—.0026	.3137—.3143	.3135—.3141
1972-74	18R-C	.007 C	.013 C	45	45	①	②	.0098—.00236	.00137—.00276	.31376—.31454	.3134—.3142
1975-77	20R	.008 H	.012 H	45	45	1.594	60 @ 1.594	.0006—.0024	.0012—.0026	.3138—.3144	.3136—.3142
1972	2M	.007 H	.010 H	45	45	③	④	.0006—.0018	.0014—.0030	—	—
1972-76	4M	.007 H	.010 H	45	45	⑤	⑥	.0006—.0018	.0010—.0024	.3144—.3148	.3138—.3144

—Not Available
①—Inner 1.445; Outer 1.607.
②—Inner 16.8 @ 1.445; Outer 57.8 @ 1.607.
③—Intake Inner 1.535; Intake Outer 1.654; Exhaust Inner 1.535; Exhaust Outer 1.661.
④—Intake Inner 11.9 @ 1.535; Intake Outer 68 @ 1.654; Exhaust Inner 11.5 @ 1.535; Exhaust Outer 66.6 @ 1.661.
⑤—Intake Inner 1.504; Intake Outer 1.642; Exhaust Inner 1.520; Exhaust Outer 1.657.
⑥—Intake Inner 25.7 @ 1.504; Intake Outer 63.1 @ 1.642; Exhaust Inner 24.6 @ 1.520; Exhaust Outer 59.4 @ 1.657.

PISTONS, PINS, RINGS, CRANKSHAFT & BEARINGS

Year	Model	Piston Clearance Bottom of Skirt	Ring End Gap		Wrist Pin Dia.	Rod Bearings			Main Bearings			Shaft End Play
			Comp. ①	Oil ①		Shaft Dia.	Bearing Clearance	Shaft Dia.	Bearing Clearance	Thrust on Bear. No.		
1972-77	3K-C	.0012—.0020	.0039	.0079	—	1.6526—1.6535	.0009—.0019	1.9676—1.9685	.0006—.0016	3	.0016—.0087	
	2T-C	.0020—.0024	②	.008	—	1.8888—1.8898	.0009—.0019	2.2825—2.2835	.0013—.0022	3	.003—.007	
	18R-C	.0020—.0028	.0039	—	.86655	2.0856—2.0870	.00094—.00189	2.3612—2.3622	.00063—.00157	3	.0008—.008	
	20R	.0012—.0020	.004	—	—	2.0862—2.0866	.0010—.0022	2.3614—2.3622	.0010—.0022	3	.0008—.0079	
	2M, 4M	.0010—.0020	.006	.008	.86625	2.0463—2.0472	.0008—.0021	2.3617—2.3627	.0012—.0021	4	.002—.010	

—Not Available
①—Tightest fit.
②—No. 1 compression ring, .008″, No. 2 compression ring, .004″.

Continued

ENGINE TIGHTENING SPECIFICATIONS★

★Torque specifications are for clean and lightly lubricated threads only. Dry or dirty threads produce increased friction which prevents accurate measurement of tightness.

Year	Engine Model	Spark Plugs Ft. Lbs.	Cylinder Head Bolts Ft. Lbs.	Intake Manifold Ft. Lbs.	Rocker Arm Shaft Bracket Ft. Lbs.	Rocker Arm Cover Ft. Lbs.	Connecting Rod Cap Bolts Ft. Lbs.	Main Bearing Cap Bolts Ft. Lbs.	Flywheel to Crankshaft Ft. Lbs.	Vibration Damper or Pulley Ft. Lbs.
1972-77	3K-C	10.9—15.2	39.1—47.7	14.5—21.7	13.0—17.4	1.4—2.2	28.9—37.6	39.1—47.7	39.1—47.7	32.5—39.8
1972-77	2T-C	10.9—15.2	52.1—63.7	7.2—11.6	52.1—63.7	2.9—5.1	28.9—36.2	52.1—63.7	42.0—47.7	28.9—43.4
1972-74	18R-C	—	72.3—86.8	30.4—34.7	12.3—16.6	—	39.1—47.7	68.7—83.2	50.6—57.9	65.1—79.6
1975-77	20R	—	52.1—63.7	—	—	—	39.1—47.7	68.7—83.2	61.5—68.7	79.6—94.0
1972-77	2M, 4M	10—14	①	17—21	22—33	3—5	30—35	72—78	41—46	69—76

—Not Available
①—8 mm, 11—16. 12 mm, 54—61.

BRAKE SPECIFICATIONS

Year	Model	Brake Drum Inside Diameter	Wheel Cylinder Bore Diameter — Disc Brake	Wheel Cylinder Bore Diameter — Drum Brake	Master Cylinder Bore Diameter	Disc Brake Rotor — Nominal Thickness	Disc Brake Rotor — Minimum Thickness	Disc Brake Rotor — Lateral Run-out (T.I.R.)
1972-74	Corolla	①	—	②	②	—	0.350	.006
1975-77	Corolla③	7.874	1.894	.750	—	0.390	0.350	.006
	Corolla④	9.000	2.000	.811	—	0.390	0.350	.006
1972-75	Celica	9.000	1.874	.750	.8126—.8146	0.394	0.354	.006
1976-77	Celica	8.980	1.874	.750	.8126—.8146	0.492	0.453	.006
1972-73	Corona	9.0068	2.0025	.8132—.8153	.8175—.8755	0.394	0.355	.006
1974-77	Corona	9.000	—	—	—	0.492	0.453	.006
1972	Mark II RT	9.000	—	.688—.689	.8748—.8768	0.3934	0.3740	.006
1972-77	Mark II⑤	9.000	—	.7500—.7520	.9373—.9374	0.3930	0.354	.006
	Mark II⑥	9.000	—	.8748—.8768	.7500—.7520	0.492	0.453	.006
1972	Hi-Lux	9.055	—	⑦	1.0000—1.0200	—	—	.006
1972-77	Hi-Lux	10.000	—	⑧	⑨	—	—	—

—Not Available
①—Wear limit; 7.95 inch.
②—Maximum clearance between cylinder & piston; .006 inch.
③—With 3K-C engine.
④—With 2T-C engine.
⑤—Hardtop & Sedan.
⑥—Wagon.
⑦—Front drum; 1.2524 & Rear drum; .8136.
⑧—Front drum; 1.12480—1.12685 & Rear drum; 0.87480—0.87685.
⑨—With booster; 1.0000—1.0020 & without booster; 0.8126—0.8146.

WHEEL ALIGNMENT SPECIFICATIONS

★The specifications listed below are for unloaded vehicles

Year	Model	Caster Angle, Degrees — Limits	Caster Angle, Degrees — Desired	Camber Angles Degrees — Limits	Camber Angles Degrees — Desired	Toe-in, Inch.	Toe-Out on Turns, Deg. — Outer Wheel	Toe-Out on Turns, Deg. — Inner Wheel
1972-74	Corolla①	+1 2/3—+2 1/3	+2	+1/3—+1 1/3	+2/3	.04—.20	—	—
1972-74	Corolla②	+1 7/12—+2 1/4	+1 10/12	+1/2—+1 1/2	+1	.04—.20	—	—
1975-76	Corolla③	+1 1/2—+2 1/6	+1 5/6	+1/4—+1 1/4	+3/4	.04	29 5/12—33 5/12	37—39
	Corolla④	+3/4—+1 5/12	+11/12	+1/12—+1 1/12	+7/12	.04	29 5/12—33 5/12	37—39
	Corolla⑤	+1 1/2—+2 1/6	+1 5/6	+1/3—+1 1/3	+5/6	.04	29 5/12—33 5/12	37—39
	Corolla⑥	+1 1/2—2 1/6	+1 5/6	+1/4—+1 1/4	+3/4	.04	29 5/12—33 5/12	37—39
	Corolla⑦	+3/4—+1 5/12	+1 1/12	+1/6—+1 1/6	+2/3	.04	29 5/12—33 5/12	37—39
1977	Corolla③	+1 1/2—+2 1/6	+1 5/6	+2/3—+1 2/3	+1 1/6	⑧	29 5/12—33 5/12	37—39
	Corolla④	+3/4—1 5/12	+11/12	+1/12—+1 1/12	+7/12	⑧	29 5/12—33 5/12	37—39
	Corolla⑨	+1 1/3—+2 1/3	+1 5/6	+1/2—+1 1/2	+1	⑧	29 5/12—33 5/12	37—39
1972-73	Celica	+1/2—+1 1/2	+1	+1/2—+1 1/2	+1	.20—.28	28—34	38—40
1976-77	Celica	1 1/4—2 1/4	+1 3/4	+1/2—+1 1/2	+1	⑧	28 1/4—32 1/4	36 1/6—38 1/6
1976-77	Celica GT	1 1/3—2 1/3	+1 5/6	+1/3—+1 1/3	+5/6	⑧	28 1/4—32 1/4	36 1/6—38 1/6
1972-73	Corona⑩	−1/6—+5/6	+1/3	—	+1 1/3	.16—.24	31	38 1/2
1972-73	Corona⑪	−5/12—+7/12	+1/12	+5/6—+1 5/6	+1 1/3	.16—.24	31	38 1/2

Continued

TOYOTA

WHEEL ALIGNMENT SPECIFICATIONS—Continued
★The specifications listed below are for unloaded vehicles

| Year | Model | Caster Angle, Degrees | | Camber Angles Degrees | | Toe-in, Inch. | Toe-Out on Turns, Deg. | |
		Limits	Desired	Limits	Desired		Outer Wheel	Inner Wheel
1974-77	Corona	$+\frac{1}{3}$—$+1\frac{1}{3}$	$+\frac{5}{6}$	$+\frac{1}{12}$—$+1\frac{1}{12}$	$+\frac{7}{12}$	.04—.12	31	$36\frac{1}{2}$—$38\frac{1}{2}$
1972-76	Corona Mark II	⑫	⑫	$+\frac{7}{12}$—$+1\frac{7}{12}$	+1	.16—.24	$31\frac{1}{3}$—$32\frac{1}{3}$	$36\frac{1}{2}$—$38\frac{1}{2}$
1972	Hi-Lux	—	$-\frac{1}{3}$	—	+1	.24	$31\frac{1}{2}$	39
1972-77	Hi-Lux	$-1\frac{1}{4}$—$+\frac{1}{4}$	$-\frac{1}{2}$	$+\frac{1}{4}$—$+1\frac{3}{4}$	+1	.08—.28	$27\frac{1}{2}$—$31\frac{1}{2}$	36—39

—Not Available
①—3K-C Engine.
②—2T-C Engine.
③—KE 30R & KE 35R.
④—KE 36R.
⑤—TE 31L-A.
⑥—TE 37L-A TE 47R.
⑦—TE 38L-A.
⑧—Radial tires; .04, Bias tires; .12.
⑨—KE 30L-A, KE 35L-A & TE series.
⑩—RT80 & 83L.
⑪—RT 86.
⑫—RX Sedan & Hardtop; Limits $-\frac{1}{4}$—$+\frac{3}{4}$, Desired $+\frac{1}{4}$, RX & MX Wagon; Limits $+\frac{1}{6}$—$+1\frac{1}{6}$, Desired $+\frac{7}{12}$ & MX Sedan & Hardtop; Limits $-\frac{1}{12}$—$+\frac{11}{12}$, Desired $+\frac{5}{12}$.

REAR AXLE SPECIFICATIONS

| Year | Model | Carrier Type | Ring Gear & Pinion | | Pinion Bearing Preload | | | Differential Bearing Preload | | |
			Backlash Method	Adjustment	Method	New Bearing Lbs.	Used Bearings Lbs.	Method	New Bearings Lbs.	Used Bearings Lbs.
1972-74	Corolla KE	Removable	Threaded adj.	.004—.006	Spacer & Shims	2.6—4.9	.8—2.9	—	3.6—6.6	1.3—4.2
1972-74	Corolla TE	Removable	Threaded adj.	.0052—.0072	Spacer & Shims	4.4—7.0	.8—2.9	—	5.3—8.8	1.3—3.8
1972-77	Celica	Removable	Threaded adj.	.005—.007	Spacer & Shims	4.8—6.2	.9—2.6	—	5.7—8.0	1.3—3.5
1972-73	Corona RT80-83	Removable	Threaded adj.	.004—.006	Spacer & Shims	4.4—6.2	.9—2.6	—	5.3—8.8	1.3—3.5
	Corona RT82S-86V	Removable	Threaded adj.	.004—.006	Spacer & Shims	7.0—9.7	.9—2.6	—	7.9—11.4	1.3—3.5
1972-77	MK II Sta. Wag.	Removable	Threaded adj.	.0051—.0071	Spacer & Shims	7.1—9.7	1.5—4.4	—	8.9—12.3	1.9—5.3
	MK II Exc. Sta. Wag.	Removable	Threaded adj.	.0051—.0071	Spacer & Shims	5.3—9.7	1.2—4.4	—	6.6—11.9	1.6—5.3
1974-77	Corona 6.7	Removable	Threaded adj.	.0051—.0071	Spacer & Shims	10.4—19.1①	2.3—8.7①	—	13.0—23.4①	3.6—11.3①
	Corona 7.1	Removable	Threaded adj.	.0051—.0071	Spacer & Shims	13.9—19.1①	3.0—8.7①	—	17.4—24.3①	4.3—11.3①
1972④	Hi-Lux	Removable	Threaded adj.	.006—.008	Spacer & Shims	—	—	—	—	—
1972⑤	Hi-Lux	Removable	Threaded adj.	.0051—.0071	Spacer & Shims	8.4—11.5	2.2—6.6	—	②	③
1973-77	Hi-Lux	Removable	Threaded adj.	.0051—.0071	Shims	8.4—11.5	2.2—6.6	Threaded adj.	9.7—14.1	3.5—10.6

①—Ft. lbs. ②—9.7—14.1; Flange 19.1—27.8. ③—3.5—10.6; Flange 6.9—20.8. ④—Early. ⑤—Late. —Not Available

COOLING SYSTEM & CAPACITY DATA

| Year | Model | Cooling Capacity Qts. | | Radiator Cap Relief Pressure, Lbs. | Thermo. Opening Temp. | Fuel Tank Gals. | Engine Oil Refill Qts. | Transmission Oil | | | Rear Axle Oil Pints |
		Less A/C	With A/C					4 Speed Pints	5 Speed Pints	Auto. Trans. Qts.	
1972-77	Corolla①	5.1	5.1	12.8	180	⑤	3.7	1.8	—	—	2.6
1972-77	Corolla②	6.9	6.9	12.8	180	⑤	3.9	1.6	1.6	③	2.6
1972-74	Corona	④	④	12.8	180	14.5	5.3	2.1	—	③	2.6
1975-77	Corona	8.5	8.5	12.8	180	14.5	5.3	2.9	2.7	6.1	2.6
1972-76	Mark II	12	12	12.8	180	15.9	5.5	1.8	—	6.8	2.6
1972-74	Celica	8.3	8.3	12.8	180	13.2	5.3	1.6	—	③	2.2
1975-77	Celica	8.5	8.5	12.8	180	13.2	4.8	1.6	1.6	7.4	2.2
1972-74	Pick-up	9.0	9.0	12.8	180	12.1	5.2	2.1	—	6.8	3.2
1975-77	Pick-up	8.5	8.5	12.8	180	12.1	4.8	2.1	—	6.8	3.2

—Not Available
①—With 3K-C engine.
②—With 2T-C engine.
③—2 speed Auto. trans., 5 qts.; 3 speed Auto. trans., 7.4 qts.
④—Models RT 104, 114 & 118, 8.7 qts.; All others, 8.4 qts.
⑤—Exc. Wagon, 11.9 gals.; wagon 10.6 gals.

Electrical Section

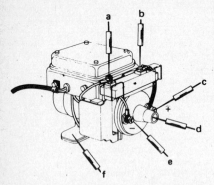

Fig. 1 Checking ignition coil resistance

DISTRIBUTOR, REPLACE

1. Disconnect wires from spark plugs.
2. Disconnect electrical leads and vacuum hose from distributor.
3. Remove distributor hold-down bolt and distributor.
4. Reverse procedure to install. Make sure to set engine to No. 1 TDC compression stroke and distributor rotor pointing towards No. 1 tower of distributor cap.

ELECTRONIC IGNITION
On Vehicle Test

1. Disconnect wire from center of distributor and hold its end close to ground while cranking the engine to check for spark.
2. Check all wiring and connectors.
3. Check ignition coil resistance, Fig. 1. Primary coil resistance (terminals C and E) should be 1.35-1.65 ohms. Secondary coil resistance (terminals C and D) should be 12.8-15.2 kilo-ohms. Resistor resistance (terminals A and B) should be 1.3-1.7 ohms. Insulation resistance (terminals C and F) should be infinite.
4. Using a non-magnetic feeler gauge, check air gap between timing rotor and pickup, Fig. 2. Air gap should be .008-.016 inch (.2-.4 mm).

5. Using an ohmmeter, check resistance of signal generator, Fig. 3. Resistance should be 130-190 ohms.
6. Using a voltmeter, check voltage between negative (−) terminal of ignition coil and resistor, Fig. 4. Voltage should be 12 volts.
7. Check the igniter as follows, Fig. 5:
   a. Disconnect wiring connector from distributor.
   b. Select either the 1 ohm or 10 ohm range on the ohmmeter, then connect the ohmmeter between the two terminals as shown, to provide resistance between the terminals.

CAUTION: Make sure not to reverse polarity of ohmmeter.

   c. Turn ignition switch on.
   d. Using a voltmeter, check voltage between ignition coil negative (−) terminal and resistor terminal. Voltage reading should be nearly zero.

DISTRIBUTOR OVERHAUL

Exc. Electronic Ignition, Figs. 6 thru 8
1. Remove the distributor cap together with the high tension wires.
2. Remove the rotor and the metal dust proof cover and gasket.
3. Loosen the distributor primary wire terminal nut. Remove the snap ring from the breaker arm pivot, and remove the contact point breaker plate retaining screw.
4. Take out the contact point plate with the breaker arm assembly.
5. Remove the vacuum advancer retainer, and slide the advancer out of the distributor.
6. Remove the distributor stationary plate from the distributor housing.
7. Remove the distributor cam retaining screw and remove the distributor cam.

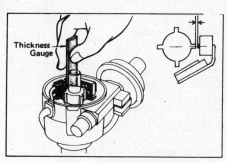

Fig. 2 Checking air gap

8. Carefully unhook and remove the governor springs.
9. Remove E-rings and then the governor weights from the pivot pins.
10. Remove the gear roll pin, and remove the spiral gear. To remove the pin, drill or file the riveted pin end.
11. Remove the shaft and governor plate. Keep track of the shim washers installed on the distributor shaft.
12. Wash all the parts with the exception of the vacuum advancer and the condenser in cleaning solvent.
13. Check the distributor shaft for wear, and check the fit with the housing.
14. Check the fitting portions of the governor weights with the support pins for binding. Check the governor spring fitting surfaces for wear. The governor weight and pin clearance limit is .2mm (.008″).
15. Install the distributor shaft, washers, spiral gear and the pin onto the distributor housing, measure the thrust clearance with a feeler gauge. The clearance should be .15-.50mm (.006-.020″). Adjust the clearance with the steel shim washers.

NOTE: The washers must be installed between the housing and the governor plate with the bakelite washer sandwiched between the steel washers.

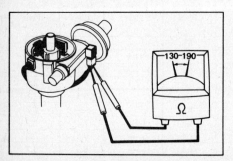

Fig. 3 Checking signal generator resistance

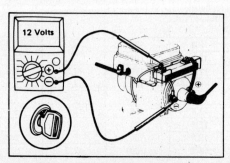

Fig. 4 Checking voltage between ignition coil and resistor

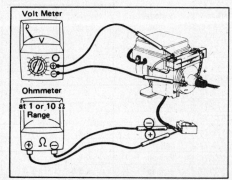

Fig. 5 Checking voltage at igniter

cracks, carbon tracks, and burned or corroded terminals, and also the wear of the center carbon piece. Carbon protrusion is 9mm (.35"), and limit is 7mm (.27").

21. Reverse disassembly procedure to assemble.

Electronic Ignition, Fig. 9

1. Remove cap and rotor.
2. Remove dust cover and gasket.
3. Remove signal generator and connector.
4. Remove vacuum advance unit and breaker plate.
5. Using a suitable punch, drive out drive gear retaining pin and remove drive gear.
6. Remove the two retaining screws from bottom of distributor, then using a plastic hammer, drive out distributor shaft.
7. Remove washer, spring and thrust washer from shaft.
8. Remove governor springs and grease stopper from end of governor shaft.
9. Remove signal rotor.
10. Remove governor weight snap rings and governor weights.
11. Reverse procedure to assemble. Make sure to adjust air gap between timing rotor and pickup to .008-.016 inch (.2-.4 mm) using a non-magnetic feeler gauge.

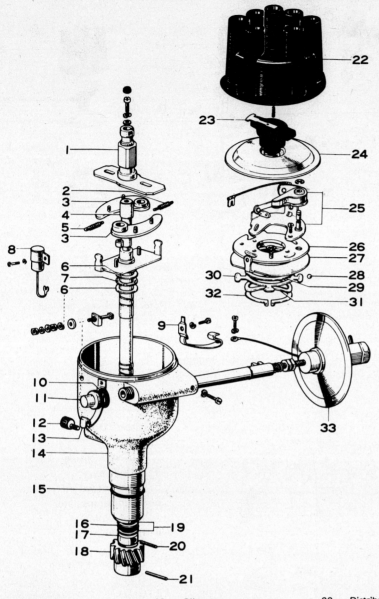

1.	Distributor cam	12.	Oil cup	23.	Distributor rotor
2.	Governor spring "B"	13.	Cap spring "A"	24.	Dust proof cover
3.	Governor weight	14.	Distributor housing	25.	Breaker point kit
4.	Distributor shaft	15.	"O" ring	26.	Breaker plate
5.	Governor spring "A"	16.	Bakelite washer	27.	Stationary plate
6.	Steel washer	17.	Space collar	28.	Ball
7.	Bakelite washer	18.	Spiral gear	29.	Adjusting washer
8.	Condenser	19.	Adjusting washer	30.	Set spring
9.	Cap spring "B"	20.	Space collar pin	31.	Wave washer
10.	Adjuster cap washer	21.	Spiral gear pin	32.	Snap ring
11.	Adjuster cap	22.	Distributor cap	33.	Vacuum advancer

Fig. 6 Distributor exploded view. 2M, 4M, 3K-H engines

16. Insert two screwdrivers between the breaker plate and the stationary plate. Pry the breaker plate carefully with the screwdrivers.
17. Coat distributor grease onto the sliding surface of the stationary plate with the breaker plate after washing, and assemble the disassembled parts.
18. Check sliding resistance of breaker plate. Sliding resistance should be less than 19 ounces on 2M and 4M engines, 17.6 ounces on 3K-H engines, or 2.2 lbs. on T and 2T engines.
19. Inspect the distributor cam lobes for scoring and signs of wear. If any lobe is scored or worn, replace the cam.
20. Check the distributor cap for

ALTERNATOR, REPLACE

1. Disconnect battery ground cable.
2. Remove fan belt and disconnect wiring from alternator.
3. Remove alternator retaining bolts and alternator.
4. Reverse procedure to install.

ALTERNATOR, TESTING

The following tests must be conducted with an alternator volt-amp tester, connected in accordance with manufacturer's instructions.

Voltage & Ampere Output

With battery in a good state of charge, the terminal voltage reading should be between 13.8 to 14.8 volts. Ampere reading should be no more than 10 amperes.

High Voltmeter Readings

If voltage reading is high, check the following:
a. Voltage regulator.
b. Generator regulator ground is defective.
c. Lead wires to regulator N and B terminals are broken.

1. Clamp, distributoe
2. Terminal subassembly, distributor
3. Condenser, distributor
4. Spring subassembly, housing cap, B
5. Spring, governor, B
6. Washer, snap
7. Weight, governor
8. Cap, adjuster
9. Washer, rubber
10. Pin
11. Gear, spiral
12. Ring, "O"
13. Housing subassembly, distributor
14. Washer, steel
15. Shaft and plate, governor
16. Spring, governor, B
17. Weight, governor
18. Cam subassembly, distributor
19. Advancer subassembly, distributor
20. Plate subassembly, breaker
21. Kit, distributor
22. Wire, earth
23. Spring subassembly, housing cap A

24. Spring, damping
25. Cover, dustproof

26. Rotor subassembly, distributor
27. Cap subassembly, distributor

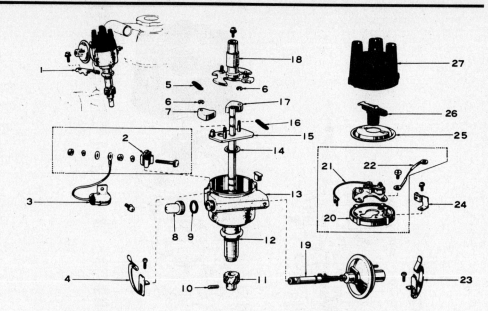

Fig. 7 Distributor exploded view. T, 2T, 16R, 18R engines

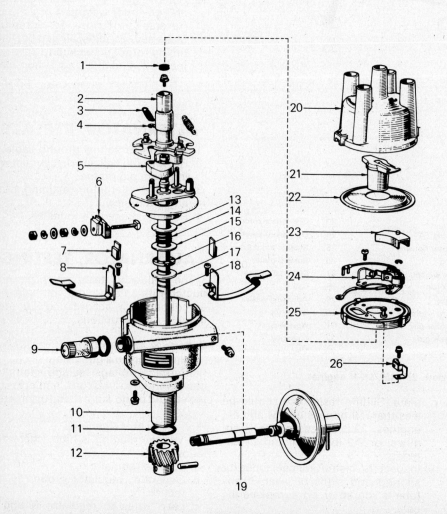

1. Grease stopper
2. Cam
3. Governor spring
4. E ring
5. Governor weight
6. Terminal insulator
7. Rubber plate
8. Hold-down clip
9. Cap
10. Distributor housing
11. O ring
12. Gear
13. Washer
14. Spring
15. Washer
16. Bearing
17. Washer
18. Governor shaft
19. Vacuum advancer
20. Distributor cap
21. Rotor
22. Dustproof cover
23. Point cover
24. Breaker points
25. Breaker plate
26. Damping spring

Fig. 8 Distributor exploded view. 20R engine

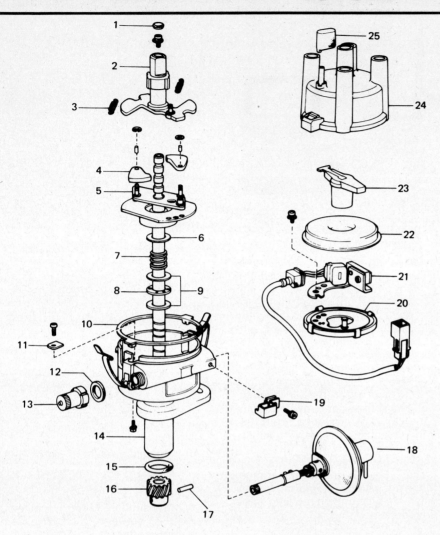

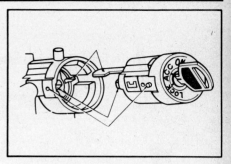

Fig. 10   Ignition switch removal

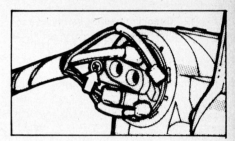

Fig. 11   Ignition switch attaching screw location

1	Cam Grease Stopper	14	Housing
2	Signal Rotor	15	O Ring
3	Governor Spring	16	Spiral Gear
4	Governor Weight	17	Pin
5	Governor Shaft	18	Vacuum Advancer
6	Plate Washer	19	Cord Clamp
7	Compression Coil Spring	20	Breaker Plate
8	Thrust Bearing	21	Signal Generator
9	Washer	22	Dustproof Cover
10	Dustproof Packing	23	Distributor Rotor
11	Steel Plate Washer	24	Distributor Cap
12	Rubber Washer	25	Rubber Cap
13	Octane Selector Cap		

Fig. 9   Electronic ignition distributor exploded view

IGNITION LOCK, REPLACE

1. Disconnect battery ground cable.
2. Turn ignition switch to "ACC" position.
3. Insert a small diameter rod into hole located on side of lock cylinder, then while holding down pin, remove lock cylinder, Fig. 10.
4. Reverse procedure to install. Ensure lock cylinder is in "ACC" position.

IGNITION SWITCH, REPLACE

1972 Corona Mark II RT Series

1. Disconnect battery ground cable.
2. Remove instrument panel under tray, then remove fuse box and bracket.
3. Disconnect ignition switch wire connector.
4. Remove steering wheel, turn signal switch and wiper switch housing.
5. Remove screw attaching ignition switch to steering column, then pull switch out from column, Fig. 11.
6. Reverse procedure to install.

1972-73 Corona, 1972-76 Corona Mark II MX & RX Series, & 1972-77 Celica & Hi Lux

1. Disconnect battery ground cable.
2. Remove steering column cover.
3. Disconnect ignition switch wire connector.
4. Remove switch mounting screws, then remove switch, Fig. 11.
5. Reverse procedure to install.

Unstable Voltmeter Readings

If voltmeter readings are unstable, check the following:
  a. Generator regulator points are dirty or slightly fused.
  b. Defective contact at F terminal.

Ammeter Reading Too High

If ammeter readings are too high, check the following:

  a. Discharged battery.
  b. Internal short in battery.

STARTER, REPLACE

1. Disconnect battery ground cable.
2. Disconnect starter wires.
3. Remove starter retaining nuts and starter.
4. Reverse procedure to install.

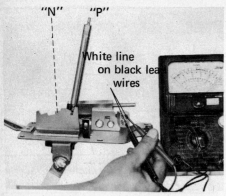

Fig. 12 Checking neutral safety switch in Park and Neutral positions. Exc. models with RT engine

1972-74 Corolla

1. Remove steering column upper cover.
2. Disconnect ignition switch wire connector.
3. Remove screw securing switch to steering column mounting, then remove switch, Fig. 11.
4. Reverse procedure to install.

1974-77 Corona & 1975-77 Corolla

1. Remove steering wheel and upper and lower steering column covers.
2. Disconnect ignition switch wire connector.
3. Remove screw securing switch to steering column mounting, then remove switch, Fig. 11.
4. Reverse procedure to install.

STOP LIGHT SWITCH, REPLACE

1. Remove brake pedal tension spring.
2. Disconnect switch wire connector.
3. Remove switch mounting nut, then slide switch from mounting bracket.
4. Reverse procedure to install.

NEUTRAL SAFETY SWITCH, ADJUST

2 Speed Toyoglide

Except RT Engine

1. Check operation of switch. The en-

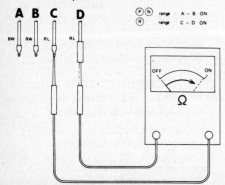

Fig. 15 Neutral safety switch continuity test. RT series

Fig. 13 Checking neutral safety switch in Reverse position. Exc. models with RT engine

gine should start only when transmission selector lever is in Neutral or Park positions.
2. To adjust switch, install switch so that shaft of switch contacts slightly with push plate of shift lever with transmission selector lever in Reverse range.
3. Make sure that back-up light glows with selector lever in Reverse range.
4. Check switch for proper contact. Connect a tester onto switch terminal. With transmission in Neutral or Park position, the tester needle should move only when the white line on black lead wires are connected, Fig. 12. In Reverse range, the tester needle should move only when the blue line on red lead wires are connected, Fig. 13.

RT Engine

1. Connect tester probes to switch terminals and check the "ON" and "OFF" points between Drive and Neutral ranges, and compare with Fig. 14.
2. If adjustment is required, adjust setting position of switch body and tighten bolts.
3. After adjusting, make sure that starter operates only when shift control lever is in Park or Neutral positions, and that back up lights go on only when shift control lever is in Reverse.

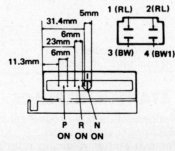

Fig. 16 Checking neutral safety switch. Floor shift models

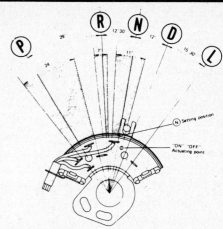

Fig. 14 Checking neutral safety switch. RT series

A-30 3 Speed Toyoglide

Floor Shift

1. Using a suitable tester, check continuity between terminals of switch, Fig. 16. There should be continuity between terminals 3 and 4 when in Neutral and Park, and between terminals 1 and 2 when in Reverse.
2. When installing switch, set shift lever to neutral position and place switch so that its mating mark will align, Fig. 17.
3. After installing switch, check continuity as in step 1.

Column Switch, Fig. 18

1. Using a suitable tester, locate the ON-OFF between the Drive and Neutral ranges.
2. Adjust screw (1) so that lever will stop at 7° (13 mm at lever tip) from this point, then tighten lock nut (2).

HEADLIGHT SWITCH, REPLACE

NOTE: For procedures for column mounted switches, refer to Turn Signal/Combination Switch, Replace.

1972 Corona Mark II RT Series

1. Disconnect battery ground cable.

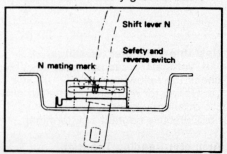

Fig. 17 Installing neutral safety switch. Floor shift models

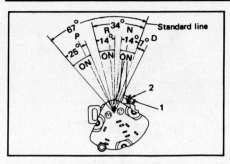

Fig. 18   Adjusting neutral safety switch. Column shift models

2. Remove fuse block and bracket.
3. Remove switch knob, then using a suitable tool remove nut attaching switch to front of instrument panel.
4. Pull switch out from rear of instrument panel, then disconnect switch wire connector and remove switch.
5. Reverse procedure to install.

1972-73 Corona & 1972-74 Corolla

1. Disconnect battery ground cable.
2. Loosen switch knob lock screw and remove switch knob.
3. Using a suitable tool remove nut attaching switch to instrument panel.
4. Pull switch out from rear of instrument panel, then disconnect wire connector and remove switch.
5. Reverse procedure to install.

1972-75 Celica

1. Disconnect battery ground cable.
2. Remove headlight switch knob.
3. Pull instrument cluster rearward as described under Instrument Cluster, Replace.
4. Remove switch to instrument cluster attaching nut, then remove switch.
5. Reverse procedure to install.

1972-76 Corona Mark II MX & RX Series & 1972-77 Hi Lux

1. Remove instrument panel lower cover.
2. Remove fuse block and mounting bracket.
3. Loosen switch knob attaching screw, then remove knob by turning counter clockwise.
4. Using a suitable tool, remove switch lock nut.
5. Disconnect switch wire connector, then remove switch.
6. Reverse procedure to install.

TURN SIGNAL/COMBINATION SWITCH, REPLACE

1. Disconnect battery ground cable.
2. On 1972 Corona Mark II RT series,

Fig. 19   Instrument cluster. 1972 Corona Mark II RT Series

1. Water temperature receiving gauge
2. Fuel receiving gauge
3. Turn-signal indicator light
4. Speedometer
5. Parking brake indicator light
6. High-beam indicator light
7. Odometer
8. Trip meter
9. Charge warning light
10. Oil pressure warning light

remove instrument panel under tray and fuse block and bracket.
3. On all models, remove steering wheel and steering column cover.
4. On 1972 Corona Mark II RT series, loosen steering column clamp bolts.
5. On all models, disconnect switch wire connect from wiring harness.
6. Remove switch mounting screws and wire clamp attaching screws, then remove switch.
7. Reverse procedure to install.

STEERING WHEEL, REPLACE

1. Remove steering wheel pad. On models with 4 spoke wheel, remove trim cover from center of steering wheel.
2. Remove nut attaching steering wheel to steering shaft.
3. Using a suitable puller, remove steering wheel.

INSTRUMENT CLUSTER, REPLACE

1972 Corona Mark II RT Series

1. Disconnect battery ground cable.
2. Remove instrument panel under tray, then remove fuse box and bracket.
3. On RT-60-S and 72-S models, remove side ventilator and console, then remove headlight switch.
4. On all models except RT-60-S and 72-S, remove instrument panel moulding and lower side pad.

1. Parking brake indicator light
2. High-beam indicator light
3. Turn-signal indicator light
4. Oil pressure receiving gauge
5. Speedometer
6. Engine tachometer
7. Water temperature receiving gauge
8. Charge warning light
9. Fuel receiving gauge
10. Trip meter
11. Odometer

Fig. 20   Instrument cluster. 1972 Corona Mark II RT Series Models RT-60-s & RT-72-S

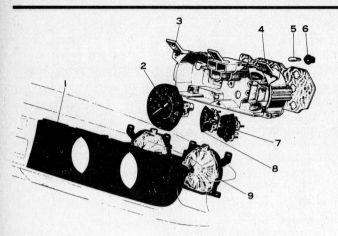

1. Meter panel
2. Speedometer assembly
3. Meter case
4. Meter circuit plate sub-assy.
5. Bulb (3.5W)
6. Meter bulb socket sub-assy.
7. Fuel receiver gauge assy.
8. Water temperature receiver gauge assembly
9. Meter lens body

Fig. 21 Instrument cluster. 1972-74 Corolla standard cluster

1. Meter panel
2. Meter lens body
3. Speedometer assembly
4. Meter case
5. Meter circuit plate sub-assy.
6. Bulb (3.5W)
7. Meter bulb socket sub-assy.
8. Water temperature receiver gauge assy.
9. Fuel receiver gauge assy.
10. Engine tachometer assy.

Fig. 22 Instrument cluster. 1972-74 Corolla Model S

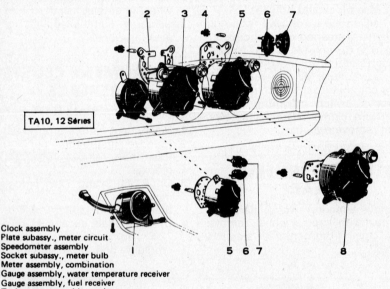

1. Clock assembly
2. Plate subassy., meter circuit
3. Speedometer assembly
4. Socket subassy., meter bulb
5. Meter assembly, combination
6. Gauge assembly, water temperature receiver
7. Gauge assembly, fuel receiver
8. Tachometer assembly, engine
9. Lamp assembly, oil pressure warning
10. Lamp assembly, brake warning indicator
11. Lamp assembly, turn signal indicator
12. Gauge assembly, ampere and oil pressure receiver

Fig. 23 Instrument cluster. 1972-75 Celica

5. Disconnect speedometer cable and wire connector from instrument cluster.
6. Remove instrument cluster attaching bolts and instrument cluster, Figs. 19 and 20.

1972-73 Corona

1. Disconnect battery ground cable.
2. Remove ash tray, glove box and radio.
3. Remove fuse box and mounting bracket, then remove lower side pad.
4. Remove heater control lamp, then remove steering column clamp nut.

NOTE: Place a cloth over steering column cover to prevent damage.

5. Remove three heater control cable clamps, then disconnect control cable from heater.
6. Disconnect speedometer cable.
7. Remove six upper and eight lower cluster housing attaching bolts and pull cluster housing outward.
8. Disconnect wire connector from instrument cluster, then remove instrument cluster.

1972-74 Corolla

1. Disconnect battery ground cable.
2. Disconnect speedometer cable, then remove instrument panel center and right mouldings.
3. Remove screw attaching cluster assembly and instrument panel moulding retainer.
4. From rear of instrument panel, remove two cluster assembly attaching nuts.
5. Pull cluster assembly outward and disconnect wire connectors, then

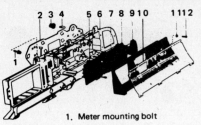

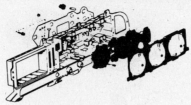

1. Meter mounting bolt
2. Circuit plate
3. Meter light bulb socket
4. Meter light bulb
5. Autoclock
6. Meter case
7. Speedometer
8. Water temperature gauge
9. Fuel gauge
10. Meter lens
11. Washer
12. Meter lens mounting screw

Fig. 24 Instrument cluster. 1972-76 Corona Mark II MX Series

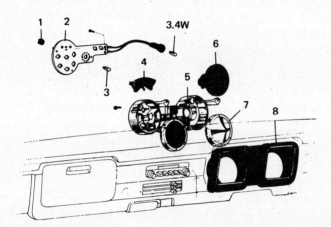

1	Meter bulb socket sub-assembly	5	Combination meter body
2	Meter circuit plate sub-assembly	6	Speedometer assembly
3	Bulb (3.4W)	7	Combination meter lens
4	Fuel receiver gauge assembly	8	Meter front hood

Fig. 25 Instrument cluster. 1972-77 Hi Lux

Fig. 26 Instrument cluster. 1974-77 Corona

remove cluster assembly, Figs. 21 and 22.

NOTE: When removing cluster assembly, use care not to scratch steering column upper cover.

1972-75 Celica

1. Disconnect battery ground cable.
2. Disconnect choke cable at carburetor.
3. Disconnect heater control cable at heater.
4. Loosen steering column clamp nuts and lower steering column.

NOTE: Cover steering column cover to prevent damage.

5. Remove instrument cluster housing attaching screws, then draw instrument cluster to rear.
6. Disconnect speedometer cable and wire connectors, then remove cluster housing.
7. Reverse procedure to install, Fig. 23.

1972-76 Corona Mark II MX & RX Series

1. Disconnect battery ground cable.
2. Remove knobs from heater and radio.
3. Remove heater control indicator light attaching screws.
4. Remove nine cluster bezel attaching screws, then push up on safety pad and pull cluster bezel out slightly.
5. Remove heater control indicator light from cluster bezel.
6. Remove cluster bezel.
7. Remove right and left garnish panels.
8. Remove ash tray then remove heater control panel.
9. Remove mounting screw from right side of ventilator outlet.
10. Remove radio. On models with stereo tape player, remove ash tray bracket, then remove lower radio mounting bolts with an off set screwdriver.
11. Remove heater control cable mounting bracket attaching bolts.
12. Pull instrument cluster outward and disconnect speedometer cable and wire connectors, then remove instrument cluster, Fig. 24.

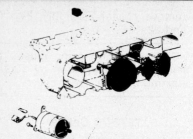

Fig. 27   Instrument cluster. 1975-77 Corolla sedan

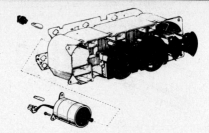

Fig. 28   Instrument cluster. 1975-77 Corolla hardtop

Fig. 29   Instrument cluster. 1975-77 Corolla Trueno

Fig. 30   Gauge assembly. 1975-77 Corolla

1972-77 Hi Lux

1. Disconnect battery ground cable.
2. Loosen steering column clamp bolts.
3. Remove instrument cluster bezel, then pull instrument cluster forward.
4. Disconnect speedometer cable and wire connectors, then remove instrument cluster, Fig. 25.

GAUGES, REPLACE

1974-77 Corona

Speedometer, Tachometer & Fuel Gauge

1. Disconnect battery ground cable.
2. Remove instrument cluster finish panel.
3. Remove side ventilator outlet knob.
4. Remove knob from clock stem.
5. Remove cluster housing attaching screws and pull cluster forward.
6. Disconnect speedometer cable and wire connectors, then remove instrument cluster, Fig. 26.

Ammeter, Oil & Temperature Gauges

1. Disconnect battery ground cable.
2. Remove gauge assembly finish panel.
3. Remove heater control indicator lens.
4. Remove instrument center panel.
5. Remove heater control indicator light.
6. Remove gauge assembly attaching screws, then pull gauge unit forward.
7. Disconnect wire connector and remove gauge assembly, Fig. 26.

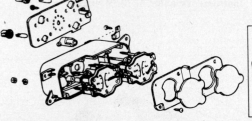

1	Battery Terminal (Ground)	5	Combination Meter
2	Ash Receptacle	6	Clock
3	Heater Control Indicator Panel	7	Combination Gauge
4	Instrument Cluster Finish Panel		

Fig. 31   Instrument cluster. 1976-77 Celica

1975-77 Corolla

Speedometer & Combination Gauge

1. Disconnect battery ground cable.
2. Remove instrument finish panel, then disconnect speedometer cable.
3. Remove instrument cluster attaching screws and pull cluster forward.
4. Disconnect wire connector and remove cluster assembly, Figs. 27, 28 and 29.

Ammeter, Oil & Temperature Gauges

1. Disconnect battery ground cable.
2. Remove instrument center finish panel.
3. Remove two gauge assembly attaching screws and pull gauge assembly forward.

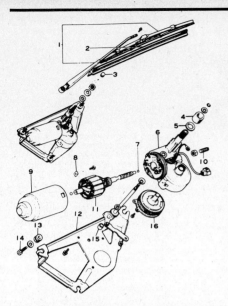

1. Windshield Wiper Arm And Blade
2. Windshield Wiper Blade
3. Cap Nut
4. Wiper Link Packing
5. Wiper Link Washer
6. Gear Housing
7. Boll
8. Nut
9. Wiper Motor Stator
10. Stop Screw
11. Wiper Motor Armature
12. Wiper Bracket
13. Bush
14. Bolt
15. Stopper
16. Wiper Motor Gear

Fig. 32 Rear w/s wiper motor assembly. 1976-77 Corolla Lift Back

W/S WIPER MOTOR, REPLACE

1972 Corona Mark II RT Series

1. Disconnect battery ground cable.
2. Remove w/s wiper arms, then remove cowl grille and service cover.
3. Remove shield cap, then disconnect wiper link from wiper motor crank arm.
4. Remove wiper motor attaching bolts, then disconnect wire connector and remove wiper motor.
5. Reverse procedure to install.

1972-74 Corolla

1. Disconnect battery ground cable.
2. Disconnect wire connector from wiper motor.
3. Remove instrument panel under tray.
4. Disconnect w/s wiper linkage from wiper motor crank arm.
5. Remove three wiper motor attaching bolts, then pull wiper motor out from right hand side of steering column.

1972-76 Corona Mark II MX & RX Series

1. Remove service cover, then position wiper motor crank 180° from stop position.
2. Using a screwdriver separate wiper link from wiper motor crank.
3. Disconnect wiper motor wire connector, then remove wiper motor attaching bolts and wiper motor.
4. Reverse procedure to install.

4. Disconnect wire connectors and remove gauge assembly, Fig. 30.

1976-77 Celica

1. Disconnect battery ground cable.
2. Remove ash tray, then remove heater control knobs and heater control panel.
3. Remove instrument cluster finish panel.
4. Remove speedometer and tachometer housing attaching screws. Pull housing outward and disconnect speedometer cable and tachometer wire connector, then remove cluster.
5. Remove ammeter, fuel, oil and temp. gauge housing attaching screws. Pull housing outward and disconnect wire connectors, then remove cluster, Fig. 31.
6. Reverse procedure to install.

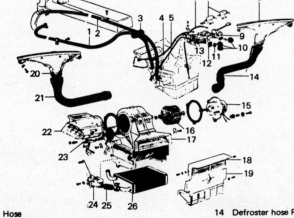

1	Hose	14	Defroster hose RH
2	Hose	15	Blower motor
3	Grommet	16	Blower fan
4	Heater air inlet butterfly cable	17	Heater case
5	Heater control cable	18	Ventilator louver
6	Defroster control cable	19	Cover
7	Heater control indicator lamp	20	Defroster nozzle LH
8	Defroster nozzle RH	21	Defroster hose LH
9	Heater blower switch	22	Air damper
10	Heater control lever knob	23	Blower resister
11	Heater control lever retainer	24	Water valve
12	Lever guide	25	Hose
13	Heater control	26	Radiator unit

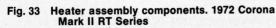

Fig. 33 Heater assembly components. 1972 Corona Mark II RT Series

1.	Screw w/washer	10.	Resistor
2.	Bushing	11.	Blower casing complete
3.	Bushing	12.	Bolt w/washer
4.	Blower motor	13.	Clamp
5.	Adapter	14.	Radiator unit
6.	Blower fan	15.	Cover (for water cover)
7.	Tooth washer	16.	Water valve
8.	Nut	17.	Clamp
9.	Screw w/washer	18.	Hose

Fig. 34 Heater assembly components. 1972-74 Corolla

1972-77 Celica, Corona & Hi Lux & 1975-77 Corolla

1. Disconnect battery ground cable.
2. Disconnect wiper motor wire connector, then remove wiper motor service cover.
3. Remove wiper motor attaching bolts.
4. Using a screwdriver disconnect wiper link from wiper motor and remove wiper motor.
5. Reverse procedure to install.

REAR W/S WIPER MOTOR, REPLACE

1976-77 Corolla Lift Back

1. Disconnect battery ground cable.
2. Remove wiper arm and rear door trim cover.
3. Disconnect wiper motor wire connector.
4. Remove wiper motor bracket attaching bolts and wiper motor and bracket, Fig. 32.

W/S WIPER TRANSMISSION

1972-74 Corolla

1. Disconnect battery ground cable.
2. Remove wiper arms and pivot caps.
3. Remove instrument cluster as described under, Instrument Cluster, Replace.
4. Remove defroster hose and right defroster nozzle.
5. Using a screwdriver disconnect wiper link from wiper motor crank arm.
6. Remove pivot attaching bolts and pivots.
7. Remove wiper link assemblies.

1972-76 Corona Mark II

1. Remove wiper arms, then remove cowl grille and cowl service cover.
2. Remove wiper link mounting screws.
3. Remove service cover at wiper motor mounting.
4. Disconnect wiper motor crank from link.
5. Remove wiper motor linkage through service hole.
6. Reverse procedure to install.

Except 1972-74 Corolla & 1972-76 Corona Mark II

1. Disconnect battery ground cable.
2. Remove nut and wiper arms.
3. Remove w/s wiper motor as described under W/S Wiper Motor, Replace.

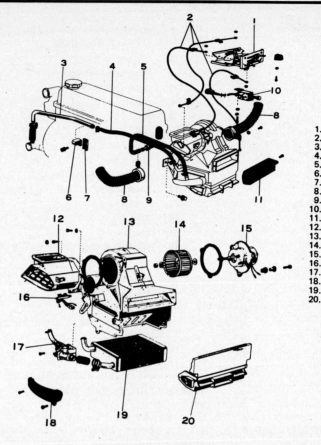

1.	Control, heater
2.	Cable subassy., control
3.	Pipe, water, No. 2
4.	Hose, water, No. 2
5.	Hose, water, No. 1
6.	Retainer, water hose
7.	Bracket, water hose
8.	Hose, defroster
9.	Joint, water hose through
10.	Switch assembly, heater blower
11.	Louver, ventilation
12.	Damper assembly, air
13.	Case subassy., heater
14.	Fan subassy., blower
15.	Motor subassy., blower
16.	Register, blower
17.	Valve assembly, water
18.	Cover, water valve
19.	Unit subassy., radiator
20.	Cover, heater

Fig. 35   Heater assembly components. 1972-75 Celica

4. Remove nut attaching w/s wiper transmission pivots to cowl grille.
5. Remove w/s wiper transmission through opening where wiper motor was mounted.
6. Reverse procedure to install.

W/S WIPER SWITCH, REPLACE

NOTE: On models with column mounted switch, refer to Turn Signal/

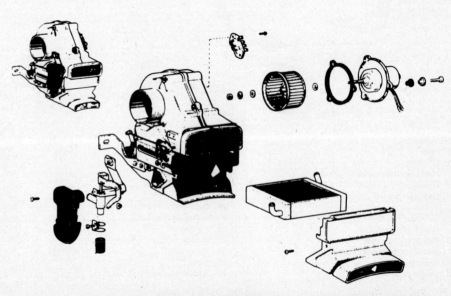

Fig. 36   Heater assembly components. 1972-76 Corona Mark II MX Series

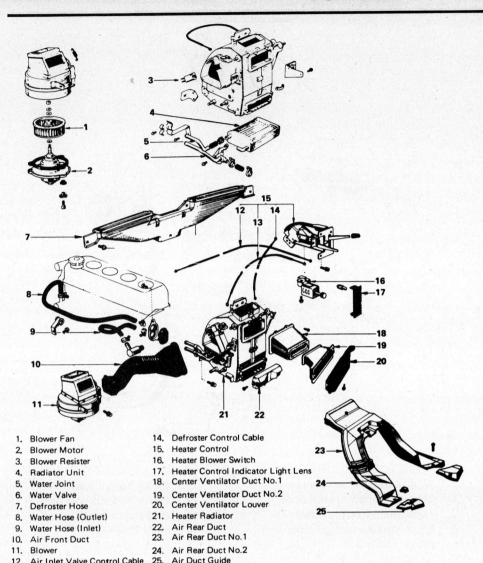

1. Blower Fan
2. Blower Motor
3. Blower Resister
4. Radiator Unit
5. Water Joint
6. Water Valve
7. Defroster Hose
8. Water Hose (Outlet)
9. Water Hose (Inlet)
10. Air Front Duct
11. Blower
12. Air Inlet Valve Control Cable
13. Heater Control Cable
14. Defroster Control Cable
15. Heater Control
16. Heater Blower Switch
17. Heater Control Indicator Light Lens
18. Center Ventilator Duct No.1
19. Center Ventilator Duct No.2
20. Center Ventilator Louver
21. Heater Radiator
22. Air Rear Duct
23. Air Rear Duct No.1
24. Air Rear Duct No.2
25. Air Duct Guide

Fig. 37 Heater assembly components. 1974-77 Corona

Combination Switch, Replace for service procedure.

1972 Corona Mark II RT Series

1. Disconnect battery ground cable.
2. Remove steering wheel and turn signal switch.
3. Remove screw from underneath switch, then lift switch from column.

1972-73 Corona, 1972-74 Corolla, 1972-75 Celica & 1972-77 Hi Lux

1. Disconnect battery ground cable.
2. Loosen switch knob lock screw and remove switch knob.
3. Using a suitable tool remove nut securing switch to instrument panel.
4. Pull switch out from rear of instrument panel, then disconnect switch wire connector and remove switch.
5. Reverse procedure to install.

1972-76 Corona Mark II MX & RX Series

1. Remove instrument panel lower cover.
2. Remove fuse box and mounting bracket.
3. Loosen W/S wiper switch mounting screw, then remove knob by turning counter clockwise.
4. Remove switch lock nut using tool No. SST-09810-25010.

---

5. Disconnect wire connector from switch and remove switch.
6. Reverse procedure to install.

RADIO, REPLACE

1972 Corona Mark II RT Series

1. Disconnect battery ground cable.
2. Remove left and right instrument panel mouldings.
3. Remove heater control knobs, control panel and blower switch.
4. Remove five lower center instrument panel pad attaching screws, then remove pad.
5. Disconnect antenna lead and wire connectors from radio and clock.
6. Remove radio knobs and spacers.
7. Remove three screws attaching radio and clock to front of instrument panel.
8. Remove one screw attaching radio bracket to heater support.
9. Remove radio and clock from instrument panel, then remove radio from trim panel.

1972-73 Corona

1. Disconnect battery ground cable.
2. Remove ash tray and glove box.
3. Remove tuning knobs and nuts from radio control shaft.
4. Disconnect antenna lead and wire connector.
5. Remove two bolts attaching radio to rear of instrument panel and remove radio.
6. Reverse procedure to install.

1972-74 Corolla

1. Disconnect battery ground cable.
2. Remove knobs and retaining nuts from radio control shafts.
3. Disconnect antenna lead and radio wire connectors.
4. Remove cowl vent duct.
5. Remove nuts and screws attaching radio to mounting bracket, then remove radio.

1972-75 Celica

1. Disconnect battery ground cable.
2. Remove radio knobs and mounting nuts.
3. Disconnect wire connector and lower radio from instrument panel.
4. Reverse procedure to install.

1972-76 Corona Mark II MX & RX Series

1. Remove instrument cluster housing.
2. Remove heater control panel.
3. Remove two radio mounting bolts.
4. Disconnect wire connector and antenna lead from radio, then remove radio.
5. Reverse procedure to install.

1974-77 Corona

Instrument Panel Mounted
1. Disconnect battery ground cable.
2. Remove instrument panel finish panel and center panel.
3. Remove radio tuner bracket, then disconnect antenna lead and radio wire connector.
4. Remove radio from instrument panel.
5. Reverse procedure to install.

Console Mounted
1. Disconnect battery ground cable.
2. Remove console box, then disconnect antenna lead and radio wire connector.
3. Remove tuner bracket, then remove radio.
4. Reverse procedure to install.

1976-77 Celica

1. Disconnect battery ground cable.
2. Remove console upper front panel.
3. Remove console upper front retainer from console box.
4. Disconnect antenna lead and wire connector, then remove radio.
5. Reverse procedure to install.

HEATER CORE, REPLACE

1972 Corona Mark II RT Series

1. Disconnect battery ground cable.
2. Drain cooling system, then disconnect heater hose from heater core.
3. Remove instrument panel under tray.
4. Disconnect defroster hoses, heater control cable and blower motor wire connector.
5. Remove cigar lighter and ash tray.
6. Remove bolt attaching radio bracket to heater support.
7. Remove two heater unit attaching bolts and lower heater unit from under dash board.
8. Remove coolant valve assembly with hose and clamp.
9. Remove heater case covers and slide heater core from case, Fig. 33.

1972-74 Corolla

1. Perform steps 1 through 6 as described under Blower Motor, Replace.
2. Disassemble heater case and remove heater core, Fig. 34

1972-75 Celica

1. Disconnect battery ground cable and drain cooling system.
2. Remove console box and carpet.

3. Remove ash tray and vent outlet grille.
4. Disconnect defroster hose, heater hoses, control cables and wire connector.
5. Remove heater mounting bolts, then draw heater unit out from right side.
6. Remove heater cover and water valve assembly, then remove heater core, Fig. 35.
7. Reverse procedure to install.

1972-76 Corona Mark II MX & RX Series

1. Drain cooling system, then disconnect heater hoses from heater core.
2. Remove console box.
3. Remove heater duct and heater cover.
4. Remove water valve protector and water valve.
5. Remove heater core from heater case, Fig. 36.
6. Reverse procedure to install.

1974-77 Corona

1. Disconnect battery ground cable.
2. Drain cooling system, then remove heater hoses.
3. Remove console box, instrument

1	Air inlet damper control cable	11	Blower fan subassy.
2	Defroster damper control cable	12	Heater motor blower packing
3	Temp. damper control cable	13	Blower motor subassy.
4	Boost ventilator control cable	14	Water hose
5	Heater control assy.	15	Protector
6	Air damper case assy.	16	Water valve assy.
7	Air duct	17	Radiator unit subassy.
8	Defroster hose	18	Heater cover
9	Control resistor	19	Heater rear air duct
10	Heater assy.		

Fig. 38 Heater assembly components. 1975-77 Corolla

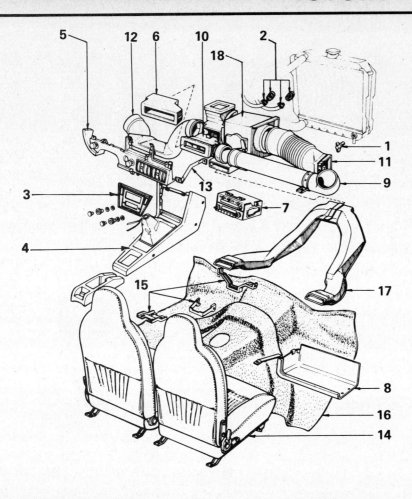

1 Radiator Drain Cock
2 Water Hoses & Grommets
3 Console Upper Front Panel
4 Console Box
5 Instrument Panel Finish Lower Panel LH
6 Interior Air Center Duct No. 2
7 Radio & Tape Player
8 Under Tray
9 Air Duct No. 3

10 Interior Air Center Duct No. 1
11 Heater Air Supply Duct
12 Air Duct No. 2
13 Instrument Panel To Cowl Brace
14 Front Seat RH & LH
15 Console Box Support Braket
16 Front Floor Carpet
17 Heater Air Rear Duct
18 Heater Unit

Fig. 39   Heater assembly components. 1976-77 Celica

panel under tray and glove box.
4. Remove heater air duct and heater rear duct.
5. Remove ventilator duct.
6. Remove instrument cluster as described under Instrument Cluster, Replace.
7. Remove radio as described under Radio, Replace.
8. Remove heater control assembly and defroster nozzle.
9. Tilt heater unit toward left and draw out through under tray side.
10. Remove water valve and outlet hose.
11. Remove clip band and bolt, then remove heater core, Fig. 37.
12. Reverse procedure to install.

1975-77 Corolla

1. Disconnect battery ground cable.
2. Drain cooling system, then disconnect heater hoses from engine compartment side of dash panel.
3. Remove defroster hose and air duct.
4. Remove control lever knob and blower switch, then remove heater control panel.
5. Remove heater control assembly with cables attached.
6. Disconnect wire connector and control cables from heater case.
7. Remove heater assembly attaching bolts and heater assembly, Fig. 38.
8. Disassemble heater housing and remove heater core.

1976-77 Celica

1. Disconnect battery ground cable and drain cooling system.
2. Remove instrument panel lower finish panel.
3. Remove fuse block cover, instrument panel lower finish sub panel.
4. Remove rear ash tray and rear console.
5. Remove radio finish panel, then remove heater control knobs and heater control panel.
6. Remove finish panel from gauge cluster, then disconnect wire connector and remove gauge assembly.
7. Remove glove box and glove box door.
8. Remove side air duct attaching screws and side air duct.
9. Remove instrument cluster as described under Instrument Cluster, Replace.
10. Remove instrument lower finish panel and separate panel from heater control.
11. Disconnect heater control cables and wire connectors from heater unit.
12. Remove three heater unit mounting bolts and heater unit, Fig. 39.
13. Disassemble heater unit and remove heater core.

BLOWER MOTOR, REPLACE

1972 Corona Mark II RT Series

1. Perform steps 1 through 7 as described under Heater Core, Replace.
2. Remove blower motor to heater case attaching screws, then remove blower motor.

1972-74

1. Disconnect battery ground cable.
2. Drain cooling system.
3. Remove instrument panel under tray.
4. Disconnect heater hoses from heater unit.
5. Disconnect heater control cables, then remove cowl vent duct.
6. Disconnect wire connects, remove four bolts attaching heater unit to dash panel and remove heater assembly.
7. Remove blower motor to heater case attaching bolts and remove blower motor, Fig. 34.

1972-75 Celica

1. Disconnect battery ground cable.
2. Remove defroster hoses and disconnect wire connectors.
3. Remove blower motor attaching bolts and blower motor, Fig. 35.
4. Reverse procedure to install.

1972-76 Corona Mark II MX & RX Series

1. Remove parking brake plunger attaching bolt.
2. Disconnect blower motor wire connector, then remove blower motor mounting bolts.
3. Remove blower motor and fan as an assembly, Fig. 36.
4. Reverse procedure to install.

1974-77 Corona

1. Remove instrument panel under tray and trim board.
2. Disconnect blower motor wire connector.
3. Remove three blower motor attaching screws, then remove blower motor, Fig. 37.
4. Reverse procedure to install.

1975-77 Corolla

1. Disconnect battery ground cable.
2. Disconnect blower motor wire connector.
3. Remove right hand defroster hose.
4. Remove three bolts attaching blower motor to heater case and remove blower motor, Fig. 38.

1976-77 Celica

1. Disconnect battery ground cable.
2. Remove heater air supply duct from heater unit.
3. Remove heater air inlet control cable.
4. Remove blower motor attaching bolts.
5. Disconnect wire connector and remove blower motor, Fig. 40.
6. Reverse procedure to install.

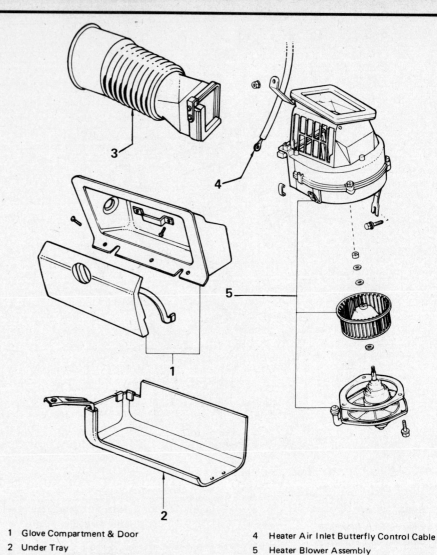

1 Glove Compartment & Door
2 Under Tray
3 Heater Air Supply Duct
4 Heater Air Inlet Butterfly Control Cable
5 Heater Blower Assembly

Fig. 40 Blower motor removal. 1976-77 Celica

Engine Section

ENGINE, REPLACE
T & 2T Engine

1. Disconnect battery cables and drain cooling system.
2. Remove hood. Make scribe marks around hinge areas to assure correct alignment upon installation.
3. On Sedan models, remove headlamp doors, radiator grille, grille lower moulding, hood lock base and brace.
4. On Coupe models, remove radiator grille, radiator upper baffle, hood lock base and brace.
5. Remove radiator and disconnect heater hoses from engine.
6. Disconnect all hoses, wires, lines and linkages from engine.
7. Remove air cleaner and disconnect exhaust pipe from manifold.
8. Disconnect the right and left engine mounts.
9. Raise vehicle and support on jack stands.
10. Disconnect exhaust pipe from support bracket and remove propeller shaft.
11. Disconnect speedometer cable and shift linkage from transmission.
12. Using a suitable jack, support transmission and remove rear support.
13. Remove engine using a suitable hoist.
14. Reverse procedure to install.

CYLINDER HEAD, REPLACE
2M, 4M Engine

1. Disconnect battery ground cable.
2. Drain cooling system and disconnect top radiator hose.
3. Remove camshaft cover, rocker arm and shaft assemblies and camshaft.
4. Remove cylinder head bolts in sequence shown in Fig. 1, then remove cylinder head assembly.
5. Reverse procedure to install. Torque cylinder head bolts to specifications and in sequence shown in Fig. 2.

2T-C Engine
Removal

1. Disconnect battery ground cable

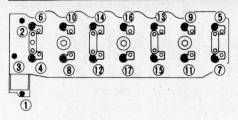

Fig. 1 Cylinder head bolt removal sequence. 2M, 4M engine

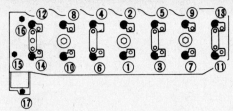

Fig. 2 Cylinder head torquing sequence. 2M, 4M engine

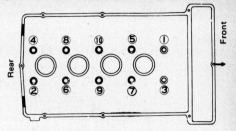

Fig. 3 Cylinder head bolt removal sequence. 2-TG engine

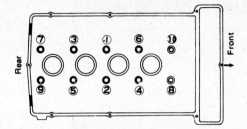

Fig. 4 Cylinder head bolt torquing sequence. 2-TG engine

Fig. 5 Setting exhaust camshaft. 2-TG engine

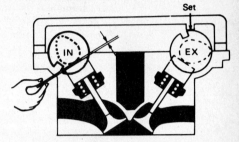

Fig. 6 Setting intake camshaft. 2-TG engine

and drain cooling system.
2. Remove camshaft cover.
3. Disconnect or remove any components which will interfere with cylinder head removal.
4. Remove distributor, water pump by-pass hose and heater hoses.
5. Remove camshaft tensioner No. 2 and camshaft timing gears.
6. Disconnect exhaust pipe from exhaust manifold.
7. Remove cylinder head bolts by loosening them evenly in sequence shown in Fig. 3.
8. Remove cylinder head.

Installation
1. Before installing cylinder head, make sure that timing check slits in camshaft flanges are positioned vertically and that piston No. 1 is at TDC compression stroke.
2. Install cylinder head while keeping timing chain pulled upward to remove slack. Install cylinder head bolts and torque in sequence shown in Fig. 4 to specifications.
3. Remove spark plugs, then while keeping timing chain pulled upward, rotate crankshaft and set piston No. 1 90° clockwise from TDC compression stroke.

4. Using tool 09248-27010, set exhaust camshaft to position shown in Fig. 5 so that slit will be inward from vertical position by the amount equal to slit width.
5. Measure clearance of intake valves and record results. Refer to specifications.
6. Using tool 09248-27010, set intake camshaft to position shown in Fig. 6 so that slit will be inward from vertical position by the amount equal to slit width.
7. Measure clearance of exhaust valves and record results. Refer to specifications.

NOTE: If valve clearance is not within specifications, refer to "VALVES, ADJUST" to select the correct adjusting pads to obtain the desired clearance.

---

8. Install adjusting pads, lifters and camshafts onto cylinder head.
9. Recheck valve clearance and readjust if necessary.
10. Using tool 09248-27010, set intake and exhaust camshaft slits vertically, Fig. 7.

11. Set No. 1 piston at TDC compression stroke.
12. Install vibration damper on cylinder head, then install oil nozzle with slot positioned horizontally. Do not overtighten.
13. Install timing chain and gears so that alignment marks made during disassembly are aligned.
14. Fill chain tensioner with oil and install onto cylinder head.
15. Install pins, washers and bolts. Do not tighten bolts.
16. Rotate crankshaft slightly until all slack has been removed from camshafts, gears and pins, then tighten bolts.
17. Rotate engine until No. 4 piston is at TDC compression stroke and adjust chain tensioner as follows:
   a. Using a screwdriver, apply 6.6-11 pounds (3-5 kg) force until plunger is bottomed.
   b. Tighten adjusting nut until it is tight against plunger, then back off adjusting nut ⅓-⅔ turn and tighten locknut.

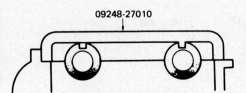

Fig. 7 Aligning intake and exhaust camshafts. 2-TG engine

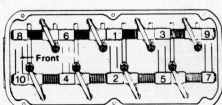

Fig. 8 Cylinder head bolt torquing sequence. T & 2T engine

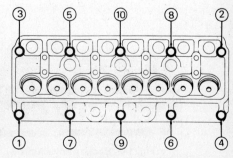

Fig. 9 Cylinder head bolt removal sequence. 3K-H engine

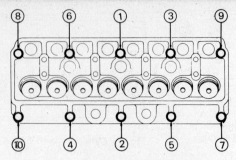

Fig. 10 Cylinder head bolt torquing sequence. 3K-H engine

Fig. 11 Rocker arm shafts bolts removal sequence. 16R, 18R engine

Fig. 12 Cylinder head bolts removal sequence. 16R, 18R engine

Fig. 13 Cylinder head bolts torquing sequence. 16R, 18R engine

18. Turn engine in normal direction of rotation until No. 1 piston is at TDC compression stroke and check positions of camshaft slits using tool 09248-27010. If valve timing is incorrect, adjust as described under "VALVE TIMING, ADJUST."
19. Reverse procedure to install the remaining components.

T & 2T Engine

1. Disconnect battery ground cable and drain cooling system.
2. Remove air cleaner and disconnect accelerator linkage and fuel line from carburetor.
3. Disconnect all wiring and hoses from cylinder head as necessary.
4. Disconnect exhaust pipe from manifold and remove valve cover.
5. Remove rocker arm assembly and push rods.

6. Remove cylinder head retaining bolts and cylinder head.
7. Reverse procedure to install. Torque bolts evenly to specifications and in order shown in Fig. 8.

3K-C Engine

1. Disconnect battery ground cable and drain cooling system.
2. Disconnect all cables, wires and hoses which will interfere with head removal.
3. Remove intake and exhaust manifold from engine.
4. Remove valve cover and gasket.
5. Remove rocker shaft assembly and push rods.

NOTE: Identify pushrods so that they can be reinstalled in their original locations.

6. Loosen and remove cylinder head bolts in sequence shown in Fig. 9.
7. Remove cylinder head.
8. Reverse procedure to install. Torque cylinder head bolts to specifications and in sequence shown in Fig. 10.

16R & 18R Engine

1. Drain cooling system.
2. Remove rocker arm shafts by loosening the bolts gradually and in sequence shown in Fig. 11.
3. Remove oil pipe.
4. Remove camshaft timing gear, bearing caps and camshaft.
5. Loosen and remove the cylinder head bolts gradually and in sequence shown in Fig. 12, then remove cylinder head.

Fig. 14 Rocker arm shafts bolts torquing sequence. 16R, 18R engine

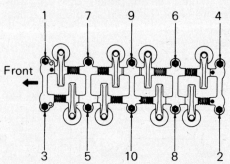

Fig. 15 Cylinder head bolts removal sequence. 20R engine

Fig. 16 Cylinder head bolts torquing sequence. 20R engine

Fig. 17 Rocker arms and shafts bolt removal sequence. 2M, 4M, engine

6. Reverse procedure to install. Torque cylinder head bolts, camshaft bearing cap bolts and rocker arm shaft bolts to specifications and in sequence shown in Figs. 13 and 14.

20R Engine

1. Disconnect battery ground cable, drain cooling system and remove air cleaner.
2. Disconnect exhaust pipe from manifold.
3. Disconnect all hoses, linkages and wires from intake manifold, carburetor and cylinder head.
4. Remove distributor and valve cover.
5. Crank engine to bring No. 1 cylinder to TDC compression, then make alignment marks on sprocket and timing chain and remove sprocket bolt and distributor drive gear. Allow cam sprocket and chain to remain in position.
6. Remove the chain cover bolt located in front of the cylinder head.

NOTE: This must be done before any of the cylinder head bolts are removed.

7. Remove cylinder head bolts gradually and in sequence shown in Fig. 15.
8. Remove rocker arm assembly by prying up on front and rear of assembly evenly.
9. Remove cylinder head.

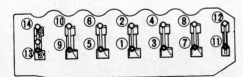

Tightening Torque 3.0~4.5 m-kg (22~29 ft-lb)

Fig. 18 Rocker arms and shafts bolt torquing sequence. 2M, 4M engine

10. Reverse procedure to install. Make sure that alignment marks made on camshaft sprocket and timing chain are aligned. Torque cylinder head bolts gradually to specifications and in sequence shown in Fig. 16.

ROCKER ARMS & SHAFTS
2M, 4M Engine

When removing rocker arms and shaft assemblies, make sure to remove bolts evenly as shown in Fig. 17. Upon installation, torque bolts to specifications and in sequence shown in Fig. 18. To disassemble rocker arms and shafts, remove spring retainer and retaining screw. Identify all parts so that they can be installed in their original locations. When assembling, make sure that the rocker shaft with the retainer groove is on the exhaust side. Also, make sure the rocker shafts are marked with either S or E. The S mark is for the intake and the E mark is for the exhaust.

VALVES, ADJUST
2M, 4M Engine

1. Check cylinder head bolts rocker arm support bolts and make sure that they are properly torqued.
2. Rotate engine until No. 1 cylinder is at TDC compression and adjust the following valves:
   Intake   No. 1, 2, 4
   Exhaust   No. 1, 3, 5
3. Rotate engine one complete revolution and adjust the following valves:
   Intake   No. 3, 5, 6
   Exhaust   No. 2, 4, 6

2T-C Engine

1. Rotate engine until camshaft lobe is facing away from the valve to be checked.
2. Using a feeler gauge, check valve clearance. Refer to specifications.
3. If adjustment is required, remove camshaft, valve lifter and adjusting pad.

4. Using a micrometer, measure thickness of adjusting pad. Select a new adjusting pad that will bring the valve clearance within specifications.

NOTE: The adjusting pads are available in 41 sizes, ranging in thicknesses from .039-.118 inch (1-3 mm) in increments of .002 inch (.05 mm).

5. Install the new adjusting pad, then install lifter and camshaft.
6. Recheck clearance and readjust if necessary.

T & 2T Engine

1. Rotate engine to No. 1 TDC firing position, and adjust the following valves to specifications:
   No. 1 and 2 intake
   No. 1 and 3 exhaust
2. Rotate engine one complete revolution clockwise, and adjust the following valves to specifications:
   No. 3 and 4 intake
   No. 2 and 4 exhaust

3K-C Engine

1. Crank engine until No. 1 cylinder is at TDC compression stroke and adjust valves indicated by numbers 1, 2, 3 and 5 shown in Fig. 19.
2. Crank engine one complete revolution and adjust valves indicated by numbers 4, 6, 7 and 8 shown in Fig. 19.

16R & 18R Engine

1. Crank engine until No. 1 cylinder is at TDC compression stroke and ad-

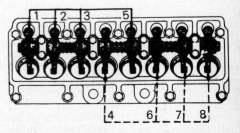

Fig. 19 Valve adjustment. 3K-H engine

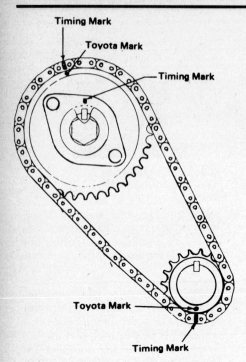

Fig. 20 Timing marks aligned. T & 2T engine

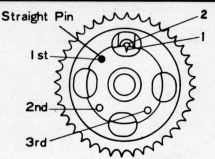

Fig. 21 Checking timing chain adjustment. 2M, 4M engine

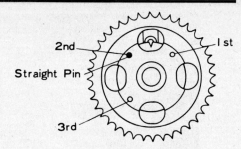

Fig. 22 Altering camshaft timing to compensate for 3-9 degrees of retard. 2M, 4M, engine

just the following valves to specifications:

Intake No. 1, 2
Exhaust No. 1, 3

2. Rotate engine one complete revolution clockwise and adjust the following valves to specifications:

Intake No. 3, 4
Exhaust No. 2, 4

VALVE TIMING, ADJUST
2T-C Engine

1. Rotate engine in normal direction of rotation until No. 1 piston is at TDC compression stroke.
2. Remove camshaft cover and check timing using tool 09248-27010. Valve timing is correct if slits on camshafts align with protrusions on tool, Fig. 7.
3. If timing is incorrect, loosen cam-

shaft mounting bolt, then shift washer and remove pin.
4. Turn camshaft so that slit will align with adjustment gauge then reinstall pin and tighten bolt.
5. Adjust tensioner as described under "TIMING CHAIN, ADJUST."
6. Rotate engine again as specified in step 1, and recheck timing. If timing requires readjustment, repeat steps 1 thru 5.

VALVE GUIDE, REPLACE
Exc. 20R Engine

1. Using a brass rod and hammer, strike bushing to break it off at the snap ring portion.
2. Heat cylinder head to 176-212°F (80-100°C).
3. Using tool 09201-60010, drive out bushing from the outside towards the combustion chamber side.
4. Install snap ring on new valve guide, then apply sealer to valve guide and install new valve guide using tool as above and driving from the outside towards the combustion chamber side.
5. Ream new valve guide to bring valve guide to stem clearance within specifications, if necessary.

VALVE LIFTERS, REPLACE
T & 2T Engine

To remove valve lifters, the cylinder

head must be removed first as described previously.

CAMSHAFT, REPLACE
2M, 4M Engine

1. Remove camshaft cover.
2. Remove chain tensioner, then remove timing gear and chain from camshaft.
3. Remove rocker arm shafts and arm assemblies.
4. Remove camshaft bearing caps and camshaft.
5. Reverse procedure to install.

3K-C Engine

1. Remove oil pan, then remove crankshaft pulley bolt and pulley.
2. Remove timing chain cover, chain tensioner and vibration damper.
3. Remove timing sprocket bolts, sprocket and timing chain.
4. Remove camshaft thrust plate, front end plate and gasket.
5. Remove camshaft. Use care to avoid damaging bearings.
6. Reverse procedure to install.

T & 2T Engine

1. Disconnect battery ground cable, then raise vehicle and support on jackstands.
2. On TE, Coupe and Sprinter models, remove radiator grille, upper baffle, hood lock base and brace.
3. Drain cooling system and remove radiator.

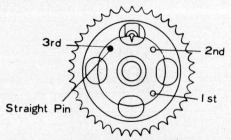

Fig. 23 Altering camshaft timing to compensate for 9-15 degrees of retard. 2M, 4M engine

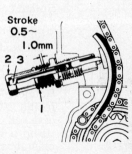

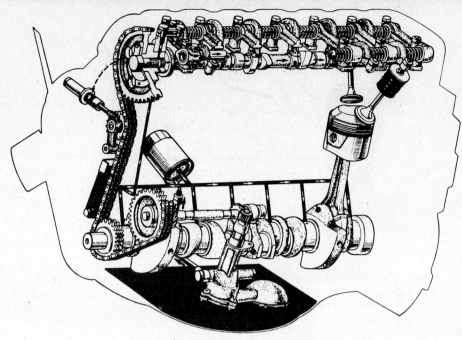

Engine lubrication system. 2M & 4M engines

4. Remove water pump and crankshaft pulley.
5. Remove engine undercover, stiffener plate and oil pan.
6. Remove timing chain cover, tensioner, timing gear bolt, timing chain and gears.
7. Remove cylinder head, distributor and fuel pump.
8. Using a suitable jack, support transmission and remove rear support.
9. Remove shaft lever and thrust plate.

10. Remove camshaft, using care to avoid damaging the bearings with the camshaft lobes.
11. Reverse procedure to install. Make sure that timing marks are as shown in Fig. 20.

20R Engine

1. Remove valve cover.
2. Crank engine to bring No. 1 cylinder to TDC compression stroke, then make alignment marks on sprocket and timing chain and remove sprocket and distributor drive gear. Allow camshaft sprocket and chain to remain in position.
3. Remove chain cover bolt located in front of cylinder head.

NOTE: This must be done before any of the cylinder head bolts are removed.

4. Remove cylinder head/rocker arm assembly retaining bolts in sequence shown in Fig. 15.
5. Remove rocker arm assembly by lifting up on front and rear of assembly.
6. Remove camshaft bearing cap bolts and caps, then remove camshaft.
7. Reverse procedure to install. Make sure that alignment marks made on camshaft sprocket and timing chain are aligned. Torque cylinder head/rocker arm assembly retaining bolts in sequence shown in Fig. 16.

TIMING CHAIN, ADJUST
2M, 4M Engine

1. Rotate engine to No. 1 TDC compression stroke and align crankshaft damper "V" groove with timing chain cover "O" mark.
2. If "V" groove in camshaft flange is near center of the 4 mm hole in No. 1 camshaft bearing cap, the chain is adjusted properly, Fig. 21.
3. If chain needs adjustment, rotate crankshaft to align center of 4 mm hole of No. 1 camshaft bearing cap with "V" groove of camshaft flange.
4. Determine amount of timing retard by means of alignment of "V" groove at top of crankshaft damper and casting marks on timing chain cover.
5. If "V" groove on crankshaft damper is retarded 3-9°, remove camshaft timing gear retaining bolt (left-hand thread) and change meshing of gear with chain so that camshaft slotted pin can be inserted into second hole of camshaft timing gear, Fig. 22.
6. If retard is 9-15°, align third hole with pin, Fig. 23.
7. If retard exceeds 15°, replace timing chain, camshaft timing gear and crankshaft gear.

NOTE: When changing position of gear, install gear after aligning crankshaft damper "V" groove with "O" mark on timing cover. Also, each of the three holes in camshaft gear advances valve timing by 6°, and the width of the 4 mm hole in the camshaft bearing cap is equal to 12° of crankshaft.

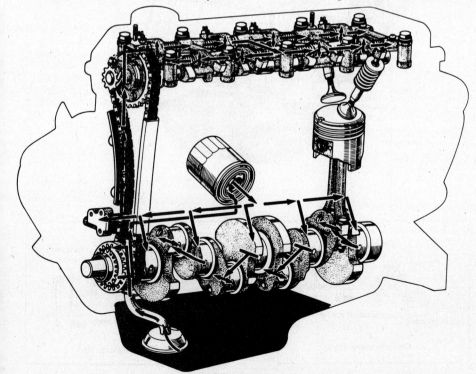

Engine lubrication system. 3K-C engine

2T-C Engine

1. To check adjustment, press down on plunger with 6.6-11 pounds (3-5 kg) of force, Fig. 24. If plunger movement is not within .02-.04 inch (.5-1.0 mm), the chain requires adjustment.
2. To adjust, loosen plunger lock nut, then with 6.6-11 pounds (3-5 kg) of force applied to plunger, turn in adjusting nut until it rests on plunger.
3. Back off adjusting nut ⅓ to ⅔ turn and tighten lock nut.
4. Recheck adjustment and adjust if necessary.

TIMING CHAIN COVER, REPLACE

2M, 4M Engine

1. Drain cooling system.
2. Remove water pump and crankshaft damper.
3. Remove oil pan.
4. Remove cover retaining bolts and cover.
5. Reverse procedure to install.

T & 2T Engine

To replace timing chain cover, refer to "CAMSHAFT, REPLACE" procedure, then follow steps 1 thru 5 and remove timing chain cover. Reverse procedure to install.

TIMING CHAIN COVER, CHAIN & GEARS

2T-C Engine

Removal

1. Raise and support vehicle.
2. Remove radiator grille and radiator.
3. Remove alternator bracket and water pump.
4. Remove camshafts cover and cylinder head.
5. Remove crankshaft pulley.
6. Remove oil pan protector, engine undercover and right hand stiffener plate.
7. Drain engine oil, then remove oil pan retaining bolts and lower oil pan onto crossmember. If oil pan is to be removed, raise lower portion of clutch housing, then remove oil pump retaining bolt and remove oil pan and pump.
8. Remove timing chain cover.
9. Remove No. 2 chain and pump drive gear.
10. Remove No. 1 chain tensioner damper and chain tensioner.
11. Remove pump drive gear, No. 1 timing chain and crankshaft timing gear.
12. Remove fuel pump, then remove

Engine lubrication system. 20R engine

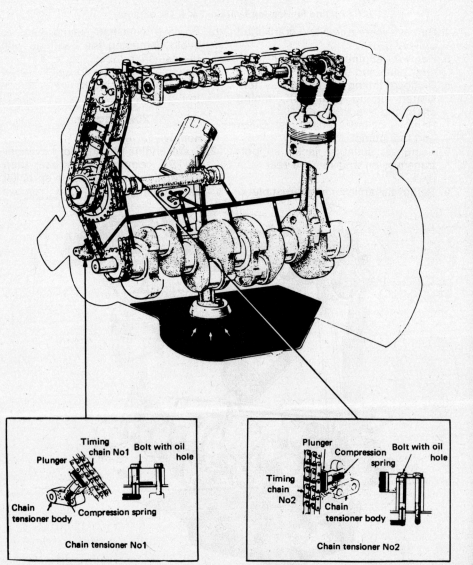

Engine lubrication system. 16R & 18R engines

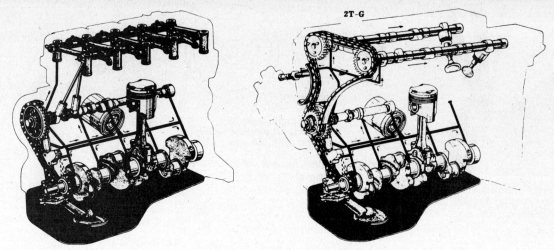

Engine lubrication system. T & 2T engines

drive shaft thrust plate and remove drive shaft.

Installation

1. Insert pump drive shaft and bolt on thrust plate, then install chain vibration damper No. 1. Do not tighten bolt.
2. Rotate engine until No. 1 piston is at TDC compression stroke. Key must be pointing vertically upward. Then set pump drive shaft so that its key is tilted 1° 34' to the left from upper side of vertical axis.
3. Assemble No. 1 chain on crankshaft timing gear and pump drive gear with timing marks aligned, then install gears. Make sure marks are still aligned. Torque bolt to 39.8-47 ft. lbs. (550-650 kg-cm).
4. Install No. 1 chain tensioner and bolt. Do not tighten bolt.

CAUTION: After installing, push plunger to make sure that it moves freely.

5. Make sure that there is a clearance of .020 inch (.5 mm) between No. 1 chain vibration and chain, then tighten retaining bolt.
6. Install No. 2 chain with camshaft gear alignment mark properly aligned.
7. Install chain tensioner slipper on timing chain cover and install timing chain cover and gasket.

NOTE: Using a sharp knife, remove portion of gasket which protrudes out toward cylinder head.

8. Install crankshaft pulley and bolt.
9. Using tool shown in Fig. 7, make sure that timing check slits in camshaft flanges are positioned vertically upward.

10. Install No. 3 vibration damper, then make sure that oil nozzle is positioned horizontally.
11. Pass No. 2 chain between No. 3 vibration damper and chain slipper.
12. Install cylinder head.
13. Assemble No. 2 chain on camshaft timing gears after aligning marks.
14. Install No. 2 chain tensioner. Do not tighten bolt.
15. Insert pins with dowel holes in camshafts and timing gears aligned. If holes are not aligned, turn camshaft not more than 45° to align the next nearest hole.
16. Install but do not tighten camshaft bolts and lock.
17. Adjust No. 2 chain tensioner.
18. Rotate engine in normal direction of rotation two complete turns and bring No. 1 piston to TDC compression stroke.
19. Check camshaft timing as described in step 9.
20. Torque camshaft bolts to 50.6-57.8 ft. lbs. (700-800 kg-cm), then install No. 2 vibration damper.
21. Reverse procedure to install the remaining components.

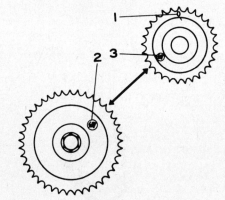

Fig. 25 Crankshaft gear and pump driveshaft gear timing marks. X, 2M, 4M engine

CHAIN TENSIONER (2), CAMSHAFT GEARS, CAMSHAFTS, VALVE LIFTERS
2T-C Engine

1. Remove camshaft cover, then place No. 1 piston at TDC compression stroke and disconnect battery ground cable.
2. Make alignment marks between chain, gears and pin holes.

NOTE: Make sure that the marks are permanent, to prevent erasure by oil, grease, etc.

3. Remove chain tensioner and timing gears.
4. Remove camshaft bearing caps in sequence shown in Fig. 3.
5. Remove camshafts, valve lifters and adjusting pads.

NOTE: Make sure to keep all parts in order so that they can be reinstalled in their original locations.

6. Reverse procedure to install.

TIMING CHAIN, REPLACE
2M, 4M Engine

Removal

1. Remove camshaft cover.
2. Remove timing chain tensioner.
3. Remove timing gear bolt and timing gear.

NOTE: Timing gear bolt threads are left-hand.

4. Remove oil pan, timing chain cover, tension gear and arm, vibration damper and guide, oil slinger and timing chain.

Fig. 26 Securing timing chain to No. 2 chain vibration damper. 2M, 4M engine

Installation

1. Position crankshaft timing gear O-mark (1) towards oil pan and align pump drive shaft gear mark (2) with the other mark (3) of crankshaft timing gear, Fig. 25.
2. Install tension gear assembly.

NOTE: The installation position of straight pin is 1.5 inches (38 mm) from block surface.

3. Install timing chain onto gears while holding chain tight.
4. Install No. 2 vibration damper, timing chain guide and chain damper assembly. Tighten chain damper assembly bolt.
5. Install oil slinger, chain cover and crankshaft damper.
6. Pull chain to apply tension on chain and tie chain to No. 2 chain vibration damper, Fig. 26.

CAUTION: Do not rotate crankshaft

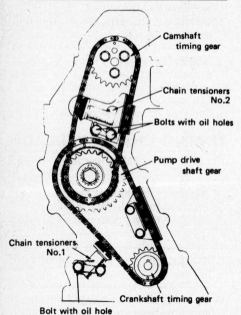

Fig. 29 Timing chain installation. 16R, 18R engine

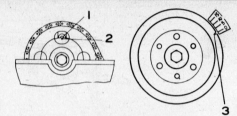

Fig. 27 Timing chain gear and crankshaft damper timing marks. 2M, 4M engine

7. Align valve timing mark (4 mm diameter hole) (1) on camshaft bearing No. 1 with camshaft "V" flange groove (2), Fig. 27. Make sure that "V" groove on crankshaft damper is aligned with timing chain cover "O" mark.
8. Install camshaft timing gear with chain to camshaft while aligning flange straight pin with gear hole.
9. Tighten timing gear bolt (left-hand thread) and secure bolt with lockplate.
10. Install chain tensioner and bolt.
11. Rotate crankshaft two complete revolutions and check to make sure that valve timing marks are aligned. If marks are not aligned, repeat procedure.
12. Install the remaining components in reverse order of removal.

TIMING CHAIN, REPLACE
16R, 18R Engine

Removal

1. Rotate engine until No. 1 piston is at TDC compression stroke.
2. Remove timing gear cover and the two chain tensioners.
3. Remove camshaft drive gear, crankshaft timing gear, pump drive gear and timing chain.

Installation

1. Make sure that No. 1 piston is at

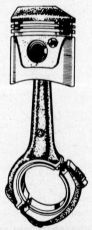

Fig. 30 Piston and connecting rod assembly. 2M, 4M engine

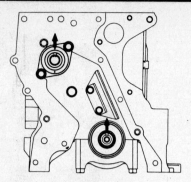

Fig. 28 Crankshaft and pump driveshaft timing marks. 16R, 18R engine

TDC compression stroke. The crankshaft keyway and pump drive shaft keyway should both be pointing vertically upward, Fig. 28.
2. Install pump drive shaft gear and chain dampers.
3. Assemble crankshaft timing gear and pump drive shaft gear onto No. 1 timing chain, then install these gears simultaneously onto their shafts, Fig. 28.
4. Install timing chain cover gasket and install the two chain tensioners.

CAUTION: Three of the chain tensioner bolts have oil holes, therefore make sure that they are installed in the correct locations. Make sure that plungers for chain tensioners are installed in their original locations. Also, if oil remains in the No. 2 tensioner body, it will be difficult to install the camshaft timing gear. If plunger will not go in when pressed, loosen the vibration damper bolts and drain out oil. Make sure to use liquid sealer on bolt threads and gasket.

5. Install camshaft drive gear, camshaft gear and pump drive shaft gear and assemble the No. 2 timing chain onto the gears.

NOTE: Before installing chain onto camshaft timing gear, make sure

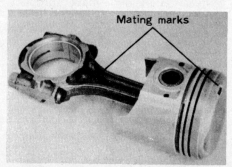

Fig. 31 Piston and connecting rod assembly. T, 2T engine

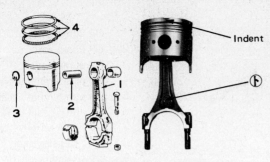

Fig. 32 Piston and connecting rod assembly. 16R, 18R engine

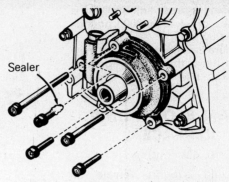

Fig. 33 Location of sealed bolt. 20R engine

that the punch mark and knock pin is vertically upward, Fig. 29.

6. Reverse the remainder of the disassembly procedure to install the remaining components.

PISTON & CONNECTING RODS

Pistons are available in standard and oversizes of .25, .50, .75 and 1.00 millimeters. When assembling piston onto connecting rod, make sure that mark on top of piston and mark on connecting rod are on the same side, Figs. 30, 31 and 32. When installing piston and connecting rod assembly, make sure that mark on top of piston is facing towards front of engine.

MAIN & CONNECTING ROD BEARINGS

These bearings are available in standard sizes and undersizes of .05, .25, .50, and .75 millimeter.

CAMSHAFT BEARINGS

These bearings are available in standard sizes and undersizes of .125 and .250 millimeter.

LINER, REPLACE
2M Engine

NOTE: If cylinders are worn and the 1.50 millimeter oversize piston cannot be used, insert new liners and use standard size pistons.

1. Remove old liner. If removal is difficult, bore liner thin to ease removal.
2. When installing liners, bore cylinders so that the press fit will be .0016-.0024 inch (.04-.06 mm).
3. Press in new liner until liner top surface is flush with top surface of

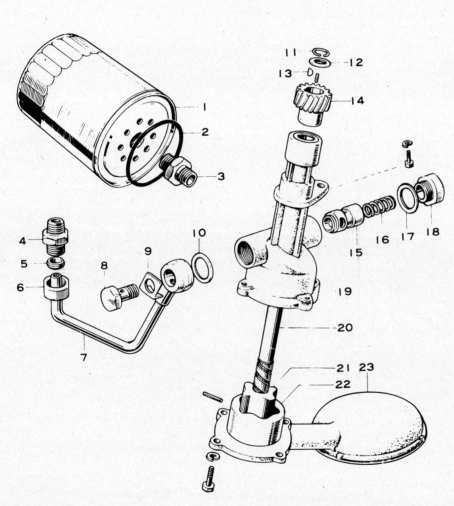

1.	Oil filter	13.	Woodruff key
2.	Filter gasket	14.	Oil pump drive shaft gear
3.	Union	15.	Oil pump relief valve
4.	Olive straight connector	16.	Oil pump relief valve spring
5.	Olive	17.	Oil pump relief valve gasket
6.	Olive "E" nut	18.	Oil pump relief valve plug
7.	Oil pump outlet pipe	19.	Oil pump body
8.	Union bolt	20.	Oil pump shaft
9.	Lock plate	21.	Oil pump drive rotor
10.	Gasket	22.	Oil pump driven rotor
11.	Shaft snap ring	23.	Oil pump cover
12.	Spacer		

Fig. 34 Oil pump exploded view. 2M, 4M engine

block using a press and applying a pressure of 4,400-6,600 pounds (2,000-3,000 kg).

4. If pressure required to install new liner is less than 4,400 pounds (2,000 kg), use the next oversize liner.

OIL PAN & OIL PUMP, REPLACE

2M, 4M Engine

1. Raise and support vehicle on jackstands and drain oil.
2. Disconnect steering relay rod from idler arm and pitman arm.
3. Remove exhaust pipe support bracket, flywheel housing cover, and rear cover underneath engine.
4. Remove oil pan retaining bolts and oil pan.
5. Remove oil pump outlet pipe and oil pump.
6. Reverse procedure to install.

2T-C Engine

1. Raise and support vehicle, then drain engine oil.
2. Remove oil pan retaining bolts and lower oil pan to crossmember.
3. Remove oil pump retaining bolt, then remove oil pump and pan together.
4. Reverse procedure to install.

2M, 4M, 3K-C, 16R, 18R, T & 2T Engines

To remove oil pump, remove oil pan, then remove attaching bolts and oil pump.

20R Engine

1. Remove oil pan and oil strainer.
2. Remove crankshaft bolt and pulley.
3. Remove oil pump assembly.
4. Reverse procedure to install. Make sure to apply sealer to bolt shown in Fig. 33.

OIL PUMP, SERVICE

Exc. 20R Engine Figs. 34, 35 & 36

1. Remove oil strainer sub-assembly and oil pump cover.

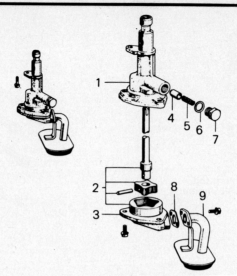

1. Oil pump body
2. Oil pump rotor set
3. Oil pump cover
4. Oil pump relief valve
5. Oil pump relief valve spring
6. Oil pump relief valve gasket
7. Oil pump relief valve plug
8. Oil strainer gasket
9. Oil strainer subassy.

Fig. 35 Oil pump exploded view. 3K-H engine

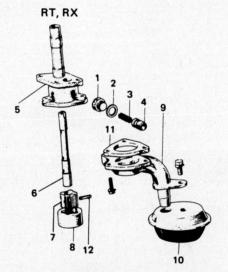
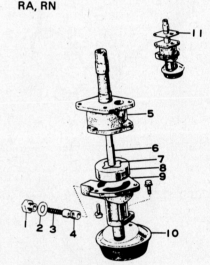

1. Oil pump relief valve plug
2. Oil pump relief valve gasket
3. Oil pump relief valve spring
4. Oil pump relief valve
5. Oil pump body
6. Oil pump shaft
7. Oil pump drive rotor
8. Oil pump driven rotor
9. Oil pump cover
10. Oil strainer
11. Oil pump gasket

Fig. 36 Oil pump exploded view. 16R, 18R engine

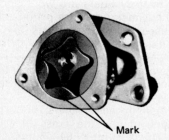

Fig. 37 Oil pump gear installation. Except 20R engine

Fig. 38 Checking clearance between rotors. Except 20R engine

Fig. 39 Checking side clearance. Except 20R engine

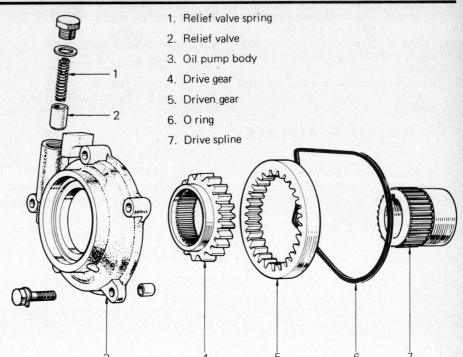

1. Relief valve spring
2. Relief valve
3. Oil pump body
4. Drive gear
5. Driven gear
6. O ring
7. Drive spline

Fig. 41 Oil pump exploded view. 20R engine

Fig. 42 Checking driven gear to housing clearance. 20R engine

2. Remove rotors, relief valve plug, spring and valve.
3. Reverse procedure to assemble. Make sure to install rotors with punch marks facing in the same direction, Fig. 37.

Inspection

1. Inspect oil pump shaft side and top end, and replace if worn or damaged.
2. Measure clearance between drive rotor and driven rotor tooth tips, Fig. 38. If clearance is greater than .008 inch (.2 mm) on all except T and 2T engine and .010 (.25 mm) on T and 2T engine, replace both rotors.
3. Place a straight edge across rotors and housing, then using a feeler gauge, measure side clearance between rotors and straight edge, Fig. 39. If clearance is greater than .006 inch (.15 mm), replace both rotors.
4. Measure clearance between driven rotor and housing, Fig. 40. If clearance is greater than .008 inch (.2 mm), replace, on all except T and 2T engine and .010 inch (.25 mm) on T and 2T engine.
5. Inspect relief valve for correct fit. Check oil passages and sliding surfaces for damage, and replace if defective.
6. Inspect valve spring, and replace if damaged or weak.
7. Inspect oil strainer, and replace if damaged.

20R Engine, Fig. 41

1. To disassemble pump, remove oil pump drive spline and O-ring, then remove relief valve plug, spring, relief valve piston and gears.
2. Inspect drive spline, drive and driven gears, pump body and timing chain cover for excessive wear or damage.
3. Measure driven gear to body clearance, Fig. 42. Maximum clearance is .008 inch (.2 mm).
4. Measure clearances between drive gear and crescent and driven gear and crescent, Fig. 43. Maximum clearance is .012 inch.
5. Measure side clearance using a straight edge placed across the housing and gears and using a feel-

Fig. 43 Checking drive and driven gears to crescent clearances. 20R engine

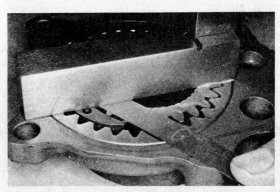

Fig. 44 Checking side clearance. 20R engine

er gauge, Fig. 44. Maximum clearance is .0059 inch (.15 mm).
6. Check relief valve piston, oil passages and sliding surfaces for burrs or scoring.
7. Inspect crankshaft front oil seal and replace if worn, damaged or cracked.

WATER PUMP, REPLACE

20R Engine

1. Drain cooling system and remove fan belt.
2. Loosen the four pulley flange nuts and remove clutch fan and pulley.
3. Remove the eight retaining bolts and water pump.
4. Reverse procedure to install.

2M & 4M Engine

1. Drain cooling system.
2. Remove fan shroud and fan belt.
3. Remove retaining bolts and water pump.
4. Reverse procedure to install.

T & 2T Engine

1. Drain cooling system.
2. Disconnect radiator hoses, by-pass hose and heater hose from water pump.
3. Remove fan belt, then remove the retaining bolts and water pump.

NOTE: Remove water pump together with fan toward battery side.

4. Reverse procedure to install.

FUEL PUMP, REPLACE

1. Disconnect fuel lines from pump.
2. Remove fuel pump retaining bolts or nuts and fuel pump.
3. Reverse procedure to install.

Carburetor Section

CARBURETOR SPECIFICATIONS

Engine	Float Level	Float Drop	Idle Mix Screw Turns Open	Unloader	Accelerator Pump Stroke	Throttle Valve Opening	Kick up	Fast Idle (Bench)	Choke Setting
2M, 4M	.37	.91	1½	—	.22	①	.008—.016	—	Index
3K-C	.26	.035	②	—	③	④	—	⑤	—
2T & T	.138	.047	3	47°	⑦	⑧	.008	⑥	Index
2T-C	⑨	—	½	—	—	—	—	—	—
16R-18R	.20	.04	⑩	47°	.177	90	.0079	.04	Index
20R	.20	.04	1¾	50°	.177	⑧	.008	.047	Index

①—Starting angle; 62°. Fully opened angle; 77°.
②—Except 3K-B engine; 2 turns. 3K-B engine; 3 turns.
③—2K and 3K engines; .24 inch. 3K-H engine; .138 inch. 3K-B engine; .138 inch. 3K-C engine; .191 inch.
④—Vertical position.
⑤—Except 3K-B engine; .051 inch. 3K-B engine; .020 inch.
⑥—T engine; .035 inch. 2T engine; .031 inch. 2T-B engine; .014 inch. 2T-C engine; .043 inch.
⑦—Except 2T-B engine; .20 inch. 2T-B engine; .12 inch.
⑧—Perpendicular to flange face.
⑨—From center of bore; .945 inch. From carburetor body upper surface; .67-.75 inch.
⑩—Except carburetor numbers 21100-34039 and 21100-34235; 2½ turns. Carburetor numbers 21100-34039 and 21100-34235; 2 turns.

NOTE: Refer to Figs. 1 thru 10 for exploded view of carburetors.

FLOAT LEVEL, ADJUST

Float Level, Fig. 11

1. Invert air horn and allow float to hang by its own weight.
2. Measure clearance between float tip and air horn.
3. If clearance is not within specifications, adjust by bending float arm at point "A."

Float Drop, Fig. 12

1. Raise float and check clearance between needle valve push pin and float lip.
2. If clearance is not within specifications, adjust by bending float arm at point "B."

THROTTLE VALVE OPENING, ADJUST

1. Open the throttle valves separately and check if throttle valves are perpendicular to flange surface when fully opened.
2. If not, adjust by bending the respective throttle lever stoppers at the first side (1) and second side (2), Fig. 13.

NOTE: After adjustment, make sure that linkage operates smoothly.

KICK UP, ADJUST

With primary throttle valve (1) set to between 64° and full open position, adjust clearance to specifications between secondary throttle valve (2) and body by bending secondary throttle lever (3), Fig. 14.

FAST IDLE, ADJUST

Except 3K-C, 2M, 4M Engines

With throttle fully closed, check clearance between bore and primary throttle valve. Adjust by turning screw (1), Fig. 15.

3K-C Engines

Check fast idle lever "O" point mark is aligned with center of roller. If not aligned, correct with fast idle connector (1), Fig. 16. To adjust, turn screw (2), Fig. 16.

2M, 4M Engines

1. Check that when choke valve is fully closed, the top step of idle cam (1) will be contacting fast idle lever (2), Fig. 17.

NOTE: If not contacting, adjust by bending choke lever link (3), Fig. 7.

2. Adjust by turning fast idle screw (4) so that first throttle valve will be set at the specified angle when the choke valve is fully closed:

2M, 4M	14°
2M W/AIS	24°
4M W/AIS	16°

3. Adjust by bending fast idle lever (1) so that choke valve opening will be 20° when first throttle valve is fully opened.

SECONDARY THROTTLE VALVE OPENING ANGLE, ADJUST

2M, 4M Engines

Adjust by bending first kick lever (1) so that second throttle valve will start to open when first throttle valve opening is at 62°, first kick arm (1) touches first kick lever (2), Fig. 18.

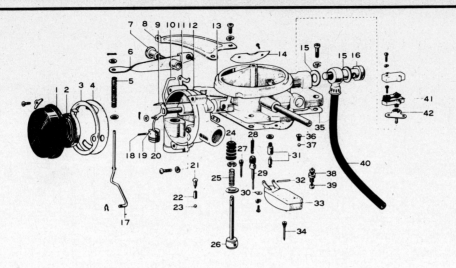

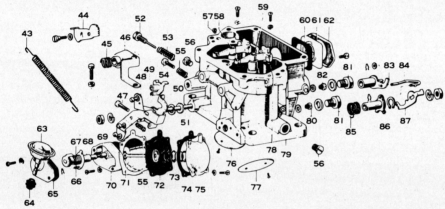

1.	Coil housing	30.	Power piston stopper	59.	Secondary small venturi
2.	Thermostatic bimetal coil	31.	Needle valve	60.	Level gauge gasket
3.	Coil housing gasket	32.	Float lever pin	61.	Level gauge glass
4.	Coil housing plate	33.	Float	62.	Level gauge clamp
5.	Pump damping spring	34.	Secondary slow jet	63.	Dash pot
6.	Pump lever	35.	Air horn gasket	64.	Boot
7.	Pump lever set screw	36.	Nut plug	65.	Diaphragm housing cap gasket
8.	Back spring support	37.	Steel ball	66.	Diaphragm relief lever
9.	Choke shaft	38.	Power valve	67.	Diaphragm relief spring
10.	Choke lever link	39.	Power jet	68.	Collar
11.	Fast idle cam lever	40.	Fuel hose	69.	Secondary throttle shaft
12.	Thermostat case	41.	Thermostatic valve	70.	Diaphragm housing
13.	Air horn	42.	Bracket	71.	Diaphragm housing gasket
14.	Choke valve	43.	Primary throttle return spring	72.	Diaphragm rod
15.	Union fitting gasket	44.	Fast idle cam	73.	Diaphragm spring
16.	Union fitting w/strainer	45.	Lever return spring	74.	Diaphragm cap gasket
17.	Pump connecting link	46.	Dash pot lever	75.	Diaphragm housing cap
18.	Piston pin	47.	Fast idle adjusting screw	76.	Primary throttle valve
19.	Piston connector	48.	Primary throttle lever	77.	Secondary throttle valve
20.	Vacuum piston	49.	Fast idle adjusting lever	78.	Venturi gasket
21.	Discharge weight stopper	50.	Throttle valve adjusting shim	79.	Carburetor body
22.	Pump dishcarge weight	51.	Primary throttle shaft	80.	Secondary main jet
23.	Steel ball	52.	Idle mixture adjusting screw	81.	Main passage plug
24.	Boot	53.	Adjusting screw spring	82.	Primary main jet
25.	Plunger return spring	54.	Idle speed adjusting screw	83.	First kick lever
26.	Pump plunger	55.	Adjusting screw spring	84.	Throttle shaft link
27.	Primary slow jet	56.	Nut plug	85.	Secondary throttle return spring
28.	Power piston spring	57.	Pump jet plug	86.	Second kick lever
29.	Power piston	58.	Primary small venturi	87.	Second kick arm

Fig. 1 Carburetor exploded view. 2M, 4M engine

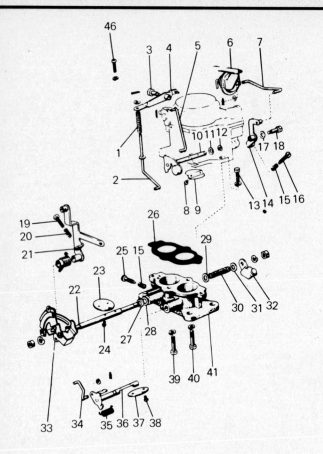

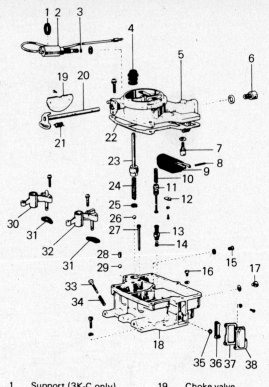

1	Pump arm spring	21	Fast idle adjusting lever
2	Connecting link	22	First throttle shaft
3	Pump arm set screw	23	First throttle valve
4	Pump lever subassy.	24	Valve set screw
5	Fast idle connector	25	Idle adjusitng screw
6	Pisitioner (3K-C only)	26	Body flange gasket
7	Connector (3K-C only)	27	Collar
8	Valve set screw	28	Shim
9	High speed valve	29	Shim
10	High speed valve shaft	30	Spring
11	Shim	31	Shim
12	Retainer ring	32	Throttle lever
13	Screw	33	First throttle shaft arm
14	Stop lever (3K-C only)	34	Throttle shaft link
15	Idle adjusting screw	35	Second throttle back spring
	spring (3K-C only)	36	Second throttle shaft
16	Screw (3K-C only)	37	Second throttle valve
17	Shim (3K-C only)	38	Valve set screw
18	Screw (3K-C only	39	Set Screw
19	Fast idle adjusting screw	40	Set screw
20	Fast idle spring	41	Flange

Fig. 2   Carburetor exploded view. 3K-H engine (part 1 of 2)

1	Support (3K-C only)	19	Choke valve
2	Solenoid valve subassy.	20	Choke shaft subassy.
	(3K-C only)	21	Choke valve relief spring
3	O ring (3K-C only)	22	Air horn gasket
4	Boot	23	Pump plunger subassy.
5	Air horn	24	Pump damping spring
6	Union nipple	25	Choke ball retainer
7	Needle valve subassy.	26	Steel ball
8	Float lever pin	27	Slow jet subassy.
9	Float subassy.	28	Pump discharge weight
10	Power piston spring	29	Steel ball
11	Power piston	30	First small venturi
12	Power piston stopper	31	Venturi gasket
13	Power valve	32	Second small venturi
14	Power jet	33	Throttle adjusting screw
15	First main jet	34	Spring
16	Second main jet	35	O ring
17	Main passage plug	36	Thermostatic valve
18	Carburetor body	37	Gasket
		38	Cover

Fig. 3   Carburetor exploded view. 3K-H engine (part 2 of 2)

3K-C Engines

With the first throttle valve completely opened, check the second throttle valve to see if it had opened to position vertical with the flange surface. Make the adjustment by bending the throttle shaft link (1), Fig. 19.

SECONDARY THROTTLE VALVE FULLY OPENING ANGLE, ADJUST
2M, 4M Engines

Adjust by bending second kick arm (1) so that second throttle valve when fully opened will be 77°, Fig. 20.

HIGH SPEED VALVE, ADJUST
3K-H Engines

Fully open high speed valve and check for .008-.016 inch clearance between valve and bore. To adjust, loosen valve set screws and shift high speed valve, Fig. 21.

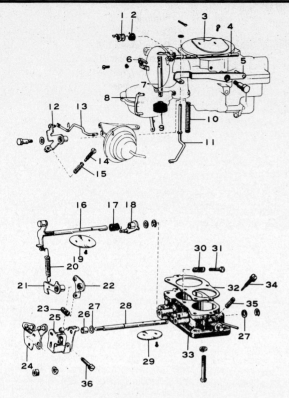

1	Fast idle cam
2	Fast idle cam spring
3	Choke valve
4	Choke shaft
5	Pump lever
6	Fast idle cam follower
7	Sliding rod
8	Connecting link
9	Boot
10	Pump spring
11	Pump connecting link
12	Lever
13	Connector
14	Screw (for T.P.)
15	Spring
16	Second throttle shaft
17	Diaphragm relief spring
18	Diaphragm relief lever
19	Second throttle valve
20	Back spring
21	Second kick lever
22	Fast idle adjusting lever
23	Fast idle adjust spring
24	First throttle lever
25	First throttle shaft arm
26	Collar
27	First throttle shaft shim
28	First throttle shaft
29	First throttle valve
30	Spring
31	Screw
32	Body flange gasket
33	Flange
34	Idle adjusting screw
35	Idle adjusting spring
36	Fast idle adjusting screw

Fig. 4   Carburetor exploded view. 16R, 18R engine

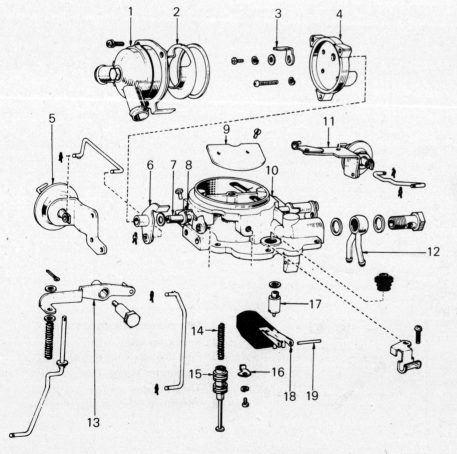

1. Water and coil housing
2. Coil housing plate
3. Choke lever
4. Coil housing body
5. Choke breaker
6. Relief lever
7. Choke shaft
8. Connecting lever
9. Choke valve
10. Air horn
11. Choke opener
12. Union
13. Pump arm
14. Spring
15. Power piston
16. Piston retainer
17. Needle valve set
18. Float
19. Float pivot pin

Fig. 5   Carburetor exploded view. 20R engine (part 1 of 3)

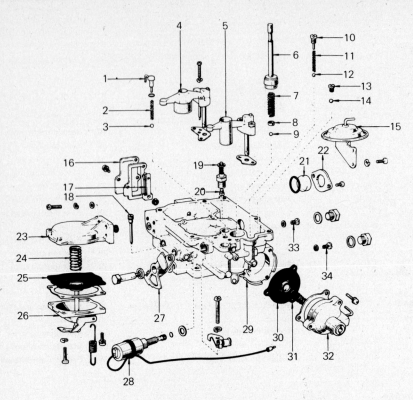

1. Pump jet
2. Spring
3. Outlet check ball
4. Secondary small venturi
5. Primary small venturi
6. Pump plunger
7. Spring
8. Ball retainer
9. Inlet check ball
10. Plug
11. Spring
12. AAP outlet check ball
13. Plug
14. AAP inlet check ball
15. Throttle positioner
16. Thermostatic valve cover
17. Thermostatic valve
18. Primary slow jet
19. Power valve
20. Power jet
21. Sight glass
22. Glass retainer
23. Diaphragm housing cap
24. Spring
25. Diaphragm
26. Housing
27. Fast idle cam
28. Solenoid valve
29. Carburetor body
30. Diaphragm
31. Spring
32. AAP housing
33. Secondary main jet
34. Primary main jet

Fig. 6   Carburetor exploded view. 20R engine (part 2 of 3)

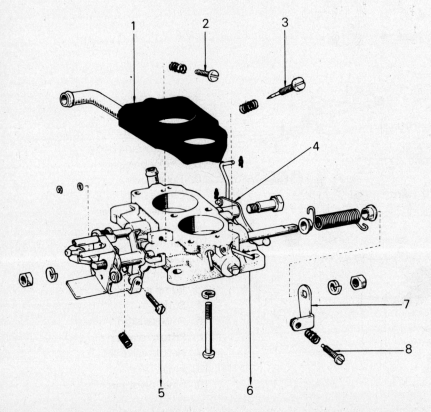

1. Insulator
2. Idle speed adjusting screw
3. Idle mixture adjusting screw
4. Positioner lever
5. Fast idle adjusting screw
6. Carburetor flange
7. Throttle lever
8. Throttle positioner adjusting screw

Fig. 7   Carburetor exploded view. 20R engine (part 3 of 3)

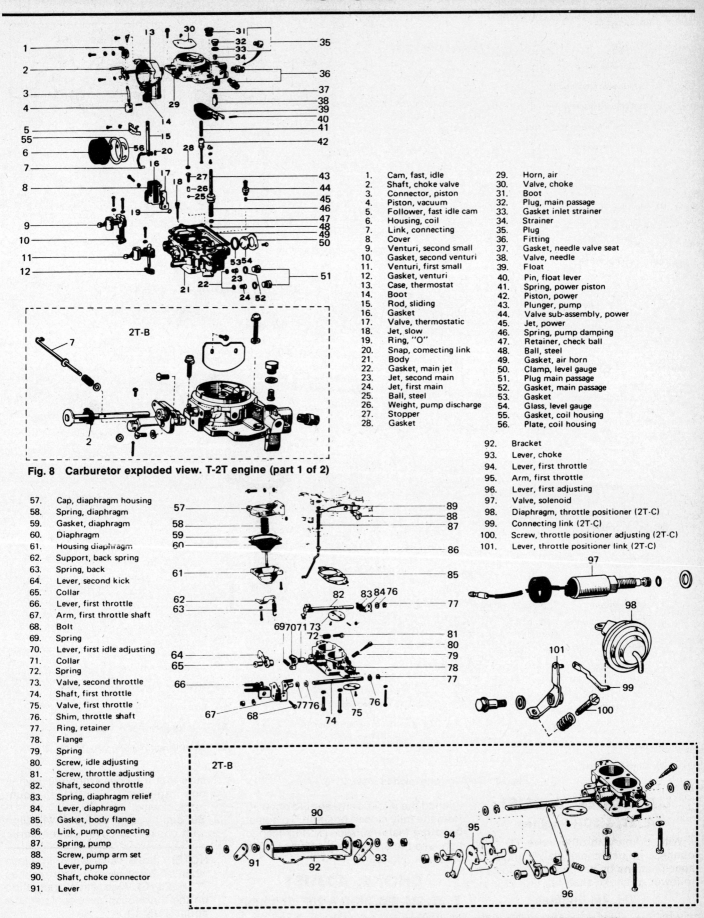

Fig. 8 Carburetor exploded view. T-2T engine (part 1 of 2)

1. Cam, fast, idle
2. Shaft, choke valve
3. Connector, piston
4. Piston, vacuum
5. Follower, fast idle cam
6. Housing, coil
7. Link, connecting
8. Cover
9. Venturi, second small
10. Gasket, second venturi
11. Venturi, first small
12. Gasket, venturi
13. Case, thermostat
14. Boot
15. Rod, sliding
16. Gasket
17. Valve, thermostatic
18. Jet, slow
19. Ring, "O"
20. Snap, connecting link
21. Body
22. Gasket, main jet
23. Jet, second main
24. Jet, first main
25. Ball, steel
26. Weight, pump discharge
27. Stopper
28. Gasket

29. Horn, air
30. Valve, choke
31. Boot
32. Plug, main passage
33. Gasket inlet strainer
34. Strainer
35. Plug
36. Fitting
37. Gasket, needle valve seat
38. Valve, needle
39. Float
40. Pin, float lever
41. Spring, power piston
42. Piston, power
43. Plunger, pump
44. Valve sub-assembly, power
45. Jet, power
46. Spring, pump damping
47. Retainer, check ball
48. Ball, steel
49. Gasket, air horn
50. Clamp, level gauge
51. Plug main passage
52. Gasket, main passage
53. Gasket
54. Glass, level gauge
55. Gasket, coil housing
56. Plate, coil housing

92. Bracket
93. Lever, choke
94. Lever, first throttle
95. Arm, first throttle
96. Lever, first adjusting
97. Valve, solenoid
98. Diaphragm, throttle positioner (2T-C)
99. Connecting link (2T-C)
100. Screw, throttle positioner adjusting (2T-C)
101. Lever, throttle positioner link (2T-C)

57. Cap, diaphragm housing
58. Spring, diaphragm
59. Gasket, diaphragm
60. Diaphragm
61. Housing diaphragm
62. Support, back spring
63. Spring, back
64. Lever, second kick
65. Collar
66. Lever, first throttle
67. Arm, first throttle shaft
68. Bolt
69. Spring
70. Lever, first idle adjusting
71. Collar
72. Spring
73. Valve, second throttle
74. Shaft, first throttle
75. Valve, first throttle
76. Shim, throttle shaft
77. Ring, retainer
78. Flange
79. Spring
80. Screw, idle adjusting
81. Screw, throttle adjusting
82. Shaft, second throttle
83. Spring, diaphragm relief
84. Lever, diaphragm
85. Gasket, body flange
86. Link, pump connecting
87. Spring, pump
88. Screw, pump arm set
89. Lever, pump
90. Shaft, choke connector
91. Lever

Fig. 9 Carburetor exploded view. T-2T engine (part 2 of 2)

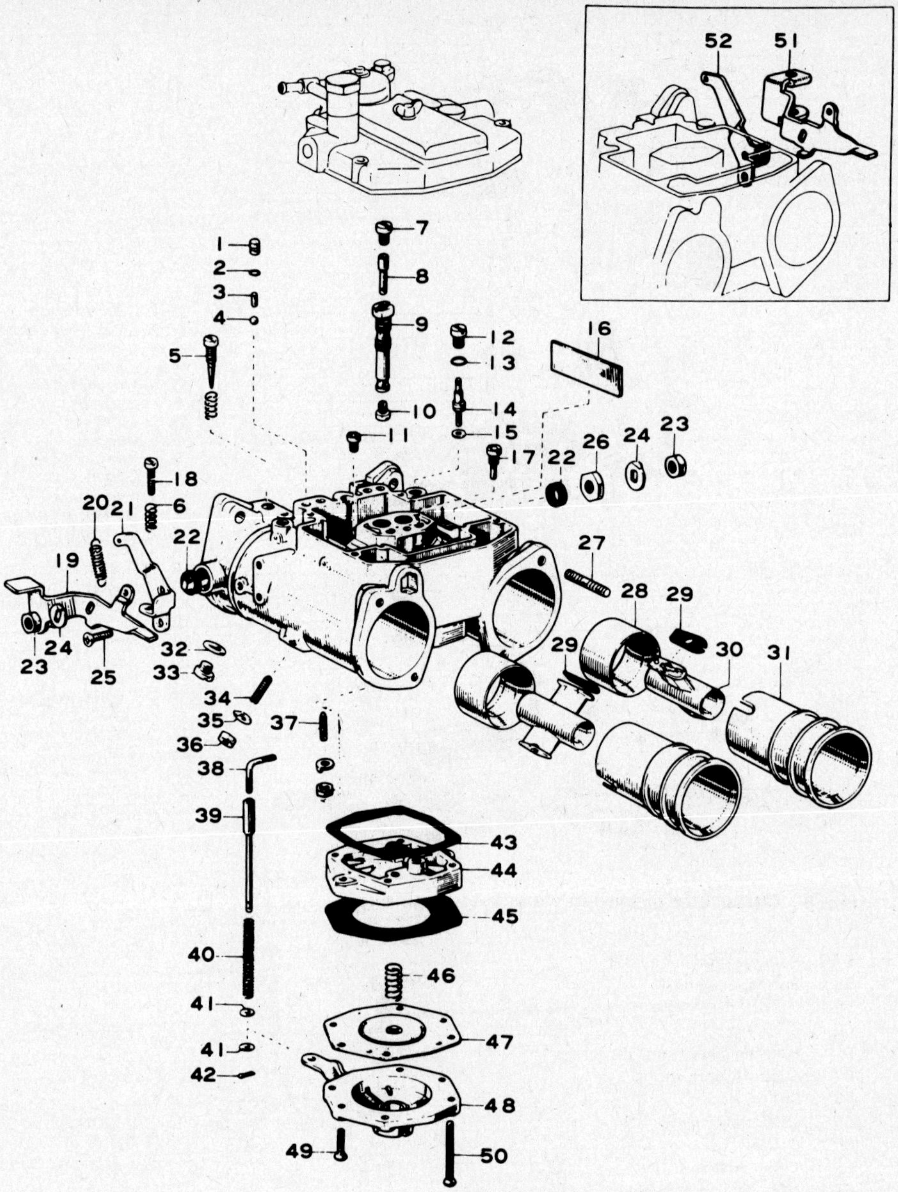

1. Pump passage plug No. 1
2. "O" ring
3. Pump valve weight
4. Pump valve check ball
5. Idle adjusting screw
6. Throttle adjusting screw spring
7. Main air bleed jet
8. Main air bleed tube
9. Main jet holder
10. Main jet
11. Starter jet
12. Screw plug
13. "O" ring
14. Pump nozzle
15. Pump jet screw gasket
16. Float chamber plate
17. Slow jet
18. Throttle adjusting screw
19. Throttle lever subassembly (for No. 1)
20. Throttle lever return spring
21. Throttle return spring stop (for No. 1)
22. Seal
23. Set nut
24. Lock washer No. 1
25. Screw
26. Set nut collar
27. Stud bolt
28. Large venturi
29. Small venturi gasket
30. Small venturi
31. Sleeve
32. Gasket
33. Slow passage plug No. 1
34. Set screw
35. Lock washer No. 2
36. Nut
37. Set bolt
38. Connecting rod

39. Pump rod
40. Pump spring
41. Washer
42. Cotter pin
43. Diaphragm housing gasket
44. Diaphragm housing sub-assembly
45. Pump cylinder gasket

46. Diaphragm spring
47. Diaphragm rod sub-assembly
48. Pump lever sub-assembly
49. Screw
50. Screw
51. Throttle lever (for No. 2)
52. Throttle return spring stop (for No. 2)

Fig. 10 Carburetor exploded view. 2T-G engine

UNLOADER, AJDUST
T, 2T, & 20R Engines

With primary throttle valve (1) fully opened, adjust choke valve angle to specifications by bending fast idle cam follower or choke shaft lip, Fig. 22.

2M, 4M Engines

With the primary throttle valve fully opened the choke valve should open 20° from the fully closed position. To adjust, bend the fast idle lever (1). For inspection, use the angle gauge stamped with 35° mark, Fig. 22.

CHOKE, ADJUST
T, 2T, 2M, 4M, 3K-C & 20R Engines

1. With choke valve fully opened, make sure that it closes completely when coil housing is rotated counterclockwise.
2. Set coil housing so that it will align with choke coil cover center mark.

NOTE: Choke valve will fully close when ambient temperature reaches 77° F (25° C). Also, each graduation on the thermostat case scale equals about 9° (5° C).

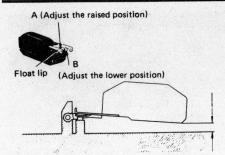

Fig. 11   Float level adjustment

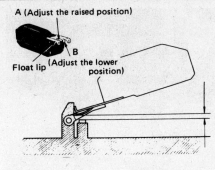

Fig. 12   Float drop adjustment

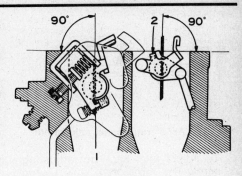

Fig. 13   Throttle valve opening adjustment

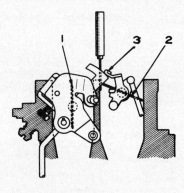

Fig. 14   Kick up adjustment

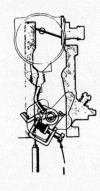

Fig. 15   Fast idle adjustment. Except 3 KB, 2M, 4M engine

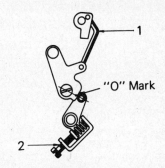

Fig. 16   Fast idle adjustment. 3 KB engine

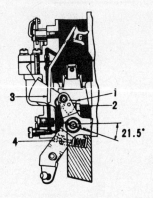

Fig. 17   Fast idle adjustment. 2M, 4M engine

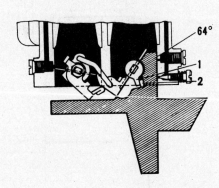

Fig. 18   Secondary throttle valve opening angle adjustment. 2M, 4M engine

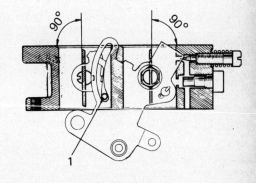

Fig. 19   Secondary throttle valve opening angle adjustment. 3K-H engine

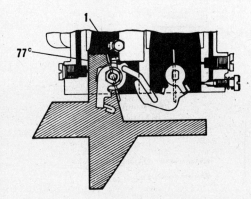

Fig. 20   Secondary throttle valve fully opening angle adjustment. 2M, 4M engine

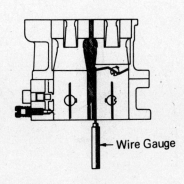

Fig. 21   High speed valve adjustment

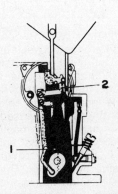

Fig. 22   Unloader adjustment

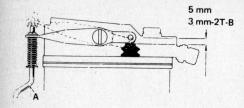

Fig. 23 Accelerator pump adjustment

3. To adjust idle, back out adjusting screw 2½ turns from fully closed position.

ACCELERATOR PUMP, ADJUST

T, 2T, 2M, 4M, 3K-C & 20R Engines

Adjust pump stroke by bending rod at point "A," Fig. 23.

Fig. 24 Choke opener adjustment

CHOKE OPENER, ADJUST
20R Engines

Push in choke opener rod (1) to open choke valve and check choke valve for a 55° angle. To adjust, bend choke opener link (2), Fig. 24.

Fig. 25 Choke breaker adjustment

CHOKE BREAKER, ADJUST
20R Engines

Push in choke breaker rod (1) to open choke valve and check choke valve for a 40° angle. Adjust by bending relief lever (2), Fig. 25.

Emission Controls Section

POSITIVE CRANKCASE VENTILATION (PCV) SYSTEM

This system, Figs. 1 and 2, leads the blow-by gases collected in the crankcase to the intake manifold, where they are then drawn into the combustion chamber and burned with the normal air fuel mixture. It consists of a hose connecting the air cleaner to the crankcase, and a hose connecting the crankcase to the intake manifold with a ventilation valve connected to it.

Air enters the system from the air cleaner to the cylinder head cover. Fresh air mixes with crankcase fumes and enters ventilation tube into ventilation valve. Ventilation valve regulates the amount of air flow to meet the change in operating conditions. The air is then drawn into the intake manifold, through a connecting hose, where it enters the combustion system and is burned.

The ventilation valve is operated by pressure difference between crankcase and intake manifold. When there is no pressure difference (engine not running) or when the pressure of the intake manifold is greater than that of the crankcase, the valve is closed. During engine idle, high intake manifold vacuum overcomes the valve spring and the valve is pulled toward the intake manifold side by vacuum. This causes air to pass through the restricted passage between the valve and the housing. During normal engine operation,

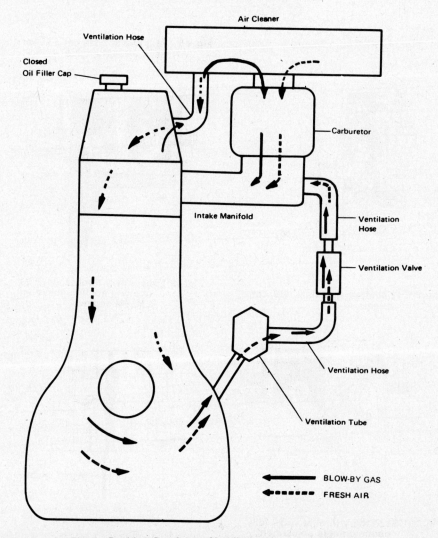

Fig. 1 Positive Crankcase Ventilation System. 1972 models

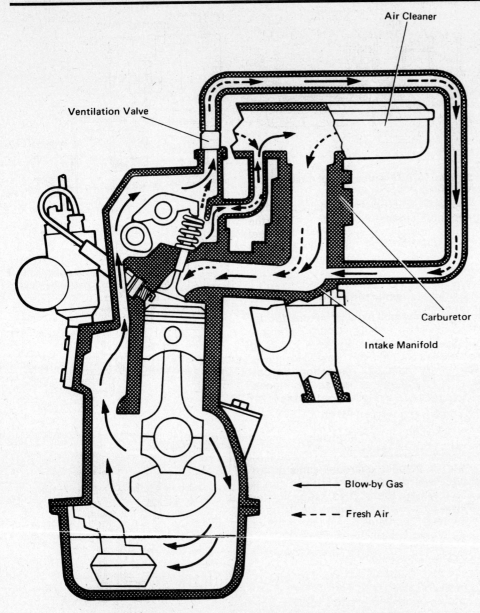

Fig. 2 Positive Crankcase Ventilation System. 1973-77 models

the valve remains in a position where spring pressure and intake manifold vacuum balance. The amount of air flow then depends on the position of valve.

Maintenance

To check ventilation valve, remove it from engine and alternately apply air to both sides of valve. Air should flow freely when applied from the crankcase end of valve. Air should not flow when applied from the intake manifold side.

Check all hoses for deterioration, obstructions, wear or damage. Replace hoses as necessary. Also make sure that hoses fit tight.

EVAPORATIVE EMISSION CONTROL SYSTEM

This system, Figs. 3 thru 7, is designed to prevent raw fuel vapors from escaping into the atmosphere by the use of one or more of the following components—a fuel tank with a sealed filler cap, fuel and vapor separator, check valves, charcoal canister, vacuum switching valve speed sensor, computer, purge valve and a connection at either the intake manifold or carburetor.

The sealed filler cap incorporates a check valve which opens to allow outside air into the tank, when the pressure within the tank drops below a predetermined value. A defective filler can cause severe deformation of the fuel tank.

Operation

1972-73 All

When the vehicle is stopped or run-

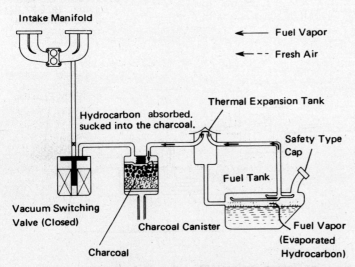

Fig. 3 Evaporative Emission Control System. 1972-73 models

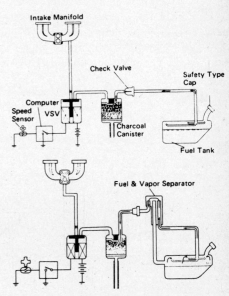

Fig. 4 Evaporative Emission Control System. 1974-75 models

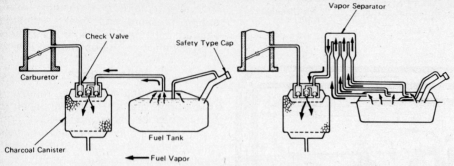

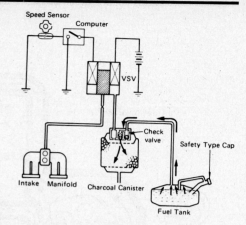

Fig. 5 Evaporative Emission Control System. 1976 TE series except Calif. and 1977 TE & KE series except Calif. and high altitude

ning at low speeds, the vacuum switching valve is closed, and all the fuel vapors are absorbed by and stored in the charcoal canister. When the vehicle is running at speeds above 15 mph, the vacuum switching valve opens. Fresh air and fuel vapors from the tank and charcoal canister are then drawn into the combustion chamber where they are burned.

1974-77 Exc. MX & 1977 TE Calif. & Hi Alt

When the vehicle is stopped or running at low speeds, the speed sensor transmits a signal to the computer which will not permit the vacuum switching valve (VSV) to open until the vehicle has reached a predetermined speed. At this time, any fuel vapors will be absorbed by and stored in the charcoal canister. When the vehicle has reached the predetermined speed, the speed sensor sends a signal to the computer, which in turns activates the VSV to allow the fuel vapors to be drawn from the charcoal canister and into the intake manifold.

1975-76 MX, 1977 KE & TE Exc. Calif. & Hi Alt

When the vehicle is stopped or idling, and the fuel tank pressure reaches a specified value, the fuel vapors are absorbed by the charcoal canister. When

the vehicle is under normal operation, the intake manifold vacuum causes the purge control valve to open. The fuel vapors in the tank, lines and charcoal canister are then drawn into the carburetor.

Maintenance

Check thermal expansion tank for deformities or cracks. Check charcoal canister for clogging and clean if necessary. Check all hoses for deterioration, damage, restriction or collapse and repair or replace as necessary. Also check hoses for tightness on fittings.

System Diagnosis

NOTE: Inspect charcoal canister for cracks or damage, and replace canister if any are found. Also, keep canister away from open flames, as a used canister contains gasoline vapors which are extremely flammable.

1974 Exc. Calif. 4M & 1975 Exc. MX, Fig. 8

Cover port "B" and apply compressed air to port "A." Air should flow freely through port "C" and should not contain any charcoal. If charcoal flows out of port "C" or if canister is obstruct-

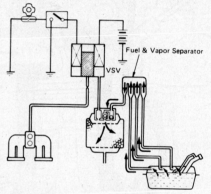

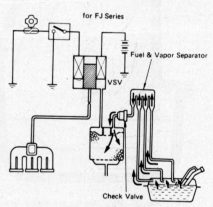

Fig. 6 Evaporative Emission Control System. 1976-77 RA, RT, RN and FJ series Calif.

Fig. 7 Evaporative Emission Control System. 1976 MX series

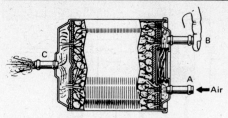

Fig. 8 Charcoal canister test. 1975 except Calif. 4M engine and 1975 except MX series

ed, it should be replaced. Do not attempt to wash canister.

1974 4M & 1975 MX, Fig. 9

Apply compressed air to port "A." Air should flow freely through ports "B" and "C" and should not contain any charcoal. Apply compressed air to port "B." Air should not flow out of ports "A" and "C." If air flow is not described previously or if charcoal flows out of the ports, the canister should be replaced. Do not attempt to wash canister.

1976 Exc. Calif. TE & 1977 KE, TE Exc. Calif. & Hi Alt., Fig. 10

Apply compressed air to port "A." Air should flow freely through ports "B" and "C" and should not contain any charcoal. Apply compressed air to port "B." Air should not flow out of ports "A" and "C." If air flow is not as described previously or if charcoal flows out of ports, then canister should be replaced. These canisters can be cleaned by applying 40 psi (3 kg/cm²) of compressed air to port "A" while closing port "B."

1976-77 TE Calif & Hi Alt & 1976-77 RA, RN, RT, Fig. 11

Apply compressed air to port "A." Air should flow freely through ports "B" and "C" and should not contain any charcoal. Apply compressed air to port "B." There should be no air flow through ports "A" and "C." If air flow is not as described previously, or if charcoal flows out of ports, the canister

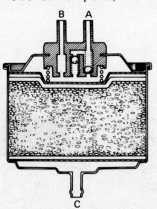

Fig. 11 Charcoal canister test. 1976-77 TE series Calif. and high altitude and 1976-77 RA, RN and RT series

Fig. 9 Charcoal canister test. 1976-77 TE series Calif. & High altitude and 1976-77 RA, RN and RT series

should be replaced. Do not attempt to wash canister.

Vacuum Switch Valve

1972-73 Models

1. Disconnect hose between VSV and canister, then connect a vacuum gauge to VSV. Place vacuum gauge where it can be observed while the vehicle is being driven.
2. Road test vehicle while observing reading on vacuum gauge. When vehicle reaches 15 mph, there should be a reading on the gauge. If not, check vacuum switching valve, speed marker relay, computer and speed sensor. Replace any component found to be defective.

Speed Sensor & Vacuum Switch Valve

1974 Models

1. Disconnect speedometer cable at transmission.
2. Disconnect computer connector

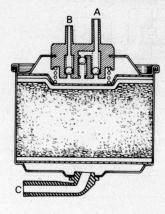

Fig. 10 Charcoal canister test. 1976 except Calif. TE series and 1977 KE, and TE series except Calif. & high altitude

and connect an ohmmeter as shown in Fig. 12.
3. Turn speedometer cable once and check number of cycles indicated on ohmmeter. If ohmmeter indicates 4 cycles, the sensor is operating properly.
4. To check vacuum switch valve, disconnect connector from VSV and check continuity as shown in Fig. 13. If there is no continuity between any of the terminals, the VSV is operating properly.
5. Check resistance between positive (+) terminal and the other terminals as shown in Fig. 14. If resistance is as shown in Fig. 15, the VSV is operating properly.

1975-77 Models

1. Inspect all vacuum hoses and wiring connectors and make sure they are all securely connected. Check fuses to make sure they are not burned.

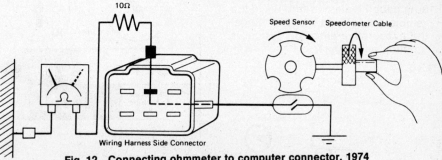

Fig. 12 Connecting ohmmeter to computer connector. 1974

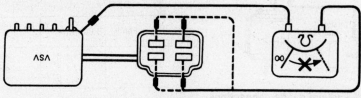

Fig. 13 Checking vacuum switch for short circuiting. 1974

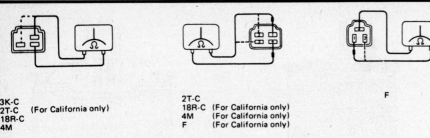

3K-C (For California only)
2T-C
18R-C
4M

2T-C
18R-C (For California only)
4M (For California only)
F (For California only)

F

Fig. 14   Check vacuum switch resistance. 1974

Engine Family	+ to 1	+ to 2	+ to 3
3K-C	56	56	—
2T-C	56	56	56
2T-C (For California only)	56	—	56
18R-C	56	56	—
18R-C (For California only)	56	56	56
4M	56	56	—
4M (For California only)	56	56	56
F	56	56	—
F (For California only)	56	56	56

Fig. 15   Resistance chart. 1974

2. On 1975 models disconnect hose between canister and vacuum switch valve, then connect a vacuum gauge to vacuum switch valve port where hose was disconnected, Fig. 16. On 1976-77 models, connect vacuum gauge to hose between VSV and canister using a tee which has an orifice of not more than .040 inch (1 mm) at the canister side, Figs. 17 and 18. Place vacuum gauge where it can be observed while the vehicle is being driven.

3. Perform road test while observing speedometer and vacuum gauge readings.

4. Referring to Figs. 19 thru 21, if vacuum gauge indicates zero while the vehicle speed is in the OFF range, the evaporative emission system is functioning properly.

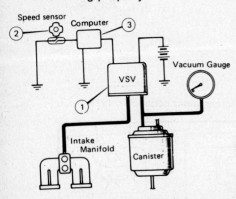

Fig. 18   Vacuum gauge connections. 1977

5. If vacuum gauge indications are not as specified in step 4, check vacuum switch valve as follows:
a. Disconnect vacuum switch wiring connector and check continuity between each terminal as shown in Figs. 22, 23 and 24. If there is no continuity between any of the terminals and the VSV body, the VSV is operating properly.
b. Disconnect vacuum switch wiring connector and check resistance between terminals as

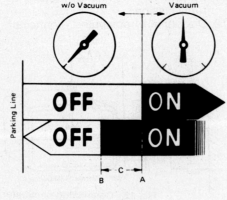

Engine Family	B Point (mph)	Hysteresis C = A − B (mph)
2T-C	11 ± 3	4 ± 2
20R	17 ± 3	4 ± 2
2F	9 ± 2	3 ± 2

Fig. 19   Vehicle speed range chart. 1975

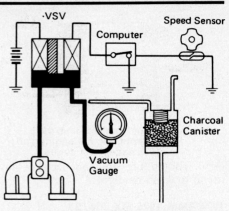

Fig. 16   Vacuum gauge connections. 1975

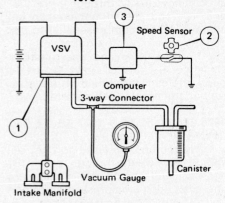

Fig. 17   Vacuum gauge connections. 1976

shown in Figs. 25, 26 and 27. If resistance values are as specified, the VSV is operating properly.
c. Replace vacuum switch valve if not operating properly.

6. If VSV is operating properly, check the speed sensor for all models except California TE, as follows:
a. Make sure that speed sensor terminals behind speedometer are properly connected.
b. Raise one of the rear wheels, then release parking brake and place transmission in Neutral.

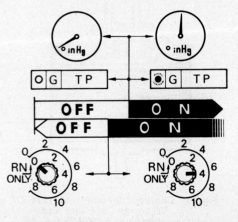

Fig. 20   Vehicle speed range chart. 1976

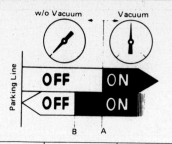

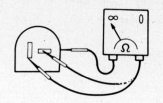

Fig. 22 Short circuit test. 1975

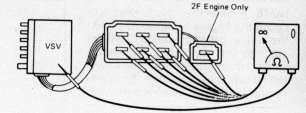

Engine	B Point	A Point
2T–C 20R 2F	7–11 mph (11–18 km/h)	8–16 mph (13–26 km/h)
2F for Calif.	14–20 mph (22–32 km/h)	15–25 mph (24–40 km/h)

Fig. 21 Vehicle speed range chart. 1977

c. Connect positive (+) terminal of ohmmeter on inspection terminal and negative (−) to ground, Figs. 28, 29 and 30.
d. Turn rear wheel slowly while observing needle on ohmmeter.
e. If ohmmeter needle deflects while rear wheel is being turned, the speed sensor is operating properly. If not, the speed sensor is malfunctioning, and the speedometer must be replaced.

NOTE: Check all connections carefully and make sure that all wiring is in good condition.

7. To check VSV on TE except California models, proceed as follows:
a. Disconnect computer connector.
b. Raise one of the rear wheels, then release parking brake and place transmission in Neutral.
c. Connect positive (+) terminal of ohmmeter to disconnected connector outer terminal, and negative (−) terminal of ohmmeter to ground, Fig. 31.
d. Turn rear wheel slowly while observing needle on ohmmeter.
e. If ohmmeter needle deflects, the VSV is operating properly. If not, the speed sensor is malfunctioning and the speedometer must be replaced.

NOTE: Check all connections carefully and make sure that all wiring is in good condition.

8. If speed sensor is operating properly, replace computer.

Check Valve

1. Inspect check valve for cracks or other damage. Replace if necessary.
2. When air is blown through fuel tank side, or canister side, the valve should open after showing slight resistance.

NOTE: Do not inhale fumes from the valve, as they can be hazardous to health. Also, when installing valve, make sure that it is not installed backwards.

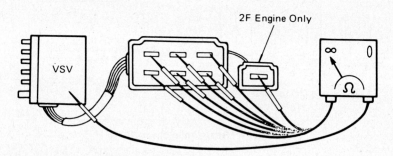

Fig. 23 Short circuit test. 1976

Caution : The ohmmeter probe should be inserted from the rear side of the connector.

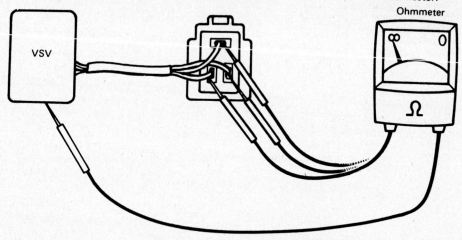

Fig. 24 Short circuit test. 1977

Engine Family		⊕ to 1	⊕ to 2	⊕ to 3	⊕ to 4	⊕ to 5	⊕ to 6
2T-C		56	—	—	—	—	—
2T-C	(California)	56	—	56	53	53	—
20R		56	56	—	56	56	—
20R	(California)	56	56	—	56	56	—
4M		56	56	—	56	28	—
4M	(California)	56	56	—	56	28	—
2F		56	56			56	53

Fig. 25 Resistance chart. 1975

NOTE: A defective check valve can cause the engine to run rough when the fuel tank is filled due to fuel flowing into the vapor line. To check, clamp hose between VSV and canister. If engine operation becomes normal, the check valve is defective.

Engine Family		⊕ to 1	⊕ to 2	⊕ to 3	⊕ to 4	⊕ to 5	⊕ to 6
2T-C	(California)	56	–	56	–	53	–
20R		56	56	–	56	56	
20R	(California)	56	56	–	56	56	
4M		56	56		56	28	
4M	(California)	56	56		56	28	
2F		56	56	–		56	53

Fig. 26 Resistance chart. 1976

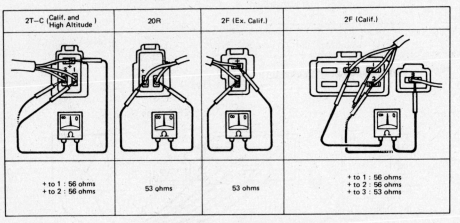

Fig. 27 Resistance chart. 1977

AIR INJECTION SYSTEM
Description

This system, Figs. 32 thru 47, injects compressed air into the exhaust gases in the exhaust manifold to extend the combustion process into the exhaust system. The addition of this secondary air helps to further burn the hydrocarbon (HC) and carbon monoxide (CO) content of the exhaust gases to minimize these pollutants. On vehicles equipped with catalytic converters, this secondary air is also used as the oxygen source for the oxidation process.

Operation
1972-74

Air under pressure from the air pump flows through a check valve to the air distribution manifold where it enters the exhaust manifold through air injection nozzles. A check valve is used to prevent a back flow of exhaust gas from entering the air pump when exhaust pressure exceeds air pump delivery pressure. During periods of engine deceleration, air is diverted to the atmosphere through a by-pass valve to prevent engine popping.

1975-77 2T-C Engine Exc. Calif.

The air is drawn from the air cleaner, then compressed by the pump and routed through the air by-pass valve (ABV), air switching valve (ASV) air man-

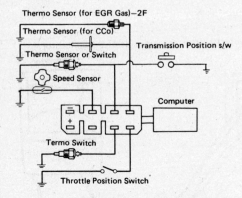

Fig. 28 Speed sensor system wiring diagram

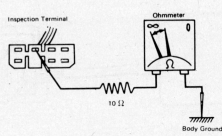

Fig. 29 Speed sensor test connections. 1975-76

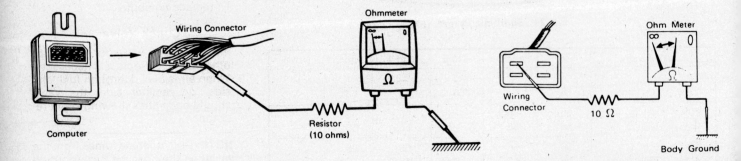

Fig. 30 Speed sensor test connections. 1977

Fig. 31 Vacuum switching valve connections. TE series except Calif.

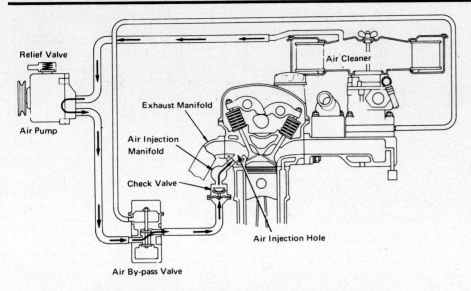

Fig. 32   Manifold air injection system. 1972 4M engine

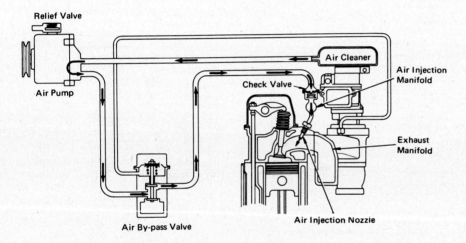

Fig. 33   Manifold air injection system. 1973-74 F engine except Calif.

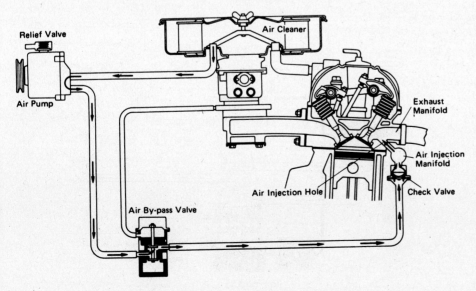

Fig. 34   Manifold air injection system. 1974 2T-C engine Calif.

ifolds, check valve and into the discharge ports.

When the air pump discharge pressure rises above a certain amount, the ASV relief valve opens and relieves the excess pressure back to the air cleaner.

During sudden deceleration, the intake manifold vacuum acts on the ABV valve and lowers the valve. The air from the pump is temporarily relieved from the ABV and into the air cleaner to prevent afterburning in the exhaust system.

During heavy loads, the decrease in the intake manifold causes the ASV to close the passage at the air injection manifold, thereby relieving the air to the air cleaner. This action is delayed by the vacuum transmitting valve (VTV).

1975 2T-C Calif. & 20 R

The operation of this system is basically the same as that described previously for 1975-77 2T-C except California engines. However when the vehicle speed, coolant temperature and catalytic converter temperature all reach the "ON" range, the computer turns the VSV "ON", causing the intake manifold vacuum to act on the ASV and inject the air. If any one of the "ON" conditions changes to the "OFF" range, the computer turns the VSV "OFF" allowing atmospheric pressure to act on the ASV to close it. The air injection is then relieved into the air cleaner.

1976-77 2T-C Calif. & 1977 2T-C High Altitude

On 1976 models, when coolant temperature is between 43-221° F, the thermo switch turns the VSV "OFF." On 1977 models, when coolant temperature is below 55-221° F, or the catalytic converter temperature is below 1380° F, the VSV is "OFF".

When the VSV is turned "OFF", the intake manifold vacuum acts on the ASV and the air is injected to the exhaust manifold.

When the air pump discharge pressure rises above the specified value, the ASV relief valve opens to relieve the air back to the air cleaner.

Under sudden deceleration, the intake manifold vacuum acts on the ABV and lowers the valve. The air from the air pump is temporarily diverted through the ABV into the air cleaner to prevent after-burning.

Under heavy load, the decrease in the intake manifold vacuum causes the ASV to close the passage at the air injection manifold side. The air is then relieved into the air cleaner. This action is delayed by the vacuum transmitting valve (VTV).

On 1976 models, when engine coolant temperature is below 43° F, or above 221° F, the thermo switch turns the VSV "ON". On 1977 models, when engine coolant temperature is below 55° F, or above 221° F, or the catalytic converter temperature is above 1380° F, the VSV is turned "ON".

When the VSV is turned "ON", atmospheric pressure is allowed to act on the ASV and causes the ASV to close the spring action. Air is then bypassed to the air cleaner.

1975-76 4M Engine

When vehicle speed, coolant temperature and catalytic converter all reach the "ON" range, the VSV (attached to the AVS) closes off the vacuum passage between the chambers "A" and "B" in the ASV, causing the ASV to close by spring tension. The compressed air is then injected to the exhaust ports.

When the air pump discharge pressure rises above a specified value, the relief valve in the ASV opens and causes the air from the pump to be relieved to the air cleaner.

During sudden deceleration, the intake manifold vacuum acts on the ASV and lowers the valve. The air from the pump is then temporarily relieved to the air cleaner.

If any one of the "ON" conditions changes to the "OFF" range, the VSV opens the passage between the chambers "A" and "B" in the ASV. The air pump pressure acts on chamber "B" to lower the valve. The air from the pump is bypassed by the VSB into the air cleaner.

1975-77 2F Engine

Compressed air from the air pump flows through the ABV, check valve, air injection manifold and then into the injection nozzle.

When the air pump discharge pressure rises above the specified value, the air pump relief valve opens to discharge the excess pressure into the atmosphere.

The "A" and "B" chambers in the ABV are normally under the same intake manifold pressure due to continuity provided by the balancing hole. Under this condition, the diaphragm will be pushed up by spring tension. Under sudden deceleration, the balance between chambers "A" and "B" will become unbalanced due to manifold vacuum acting suddenly on chamber "B". The diaphragm will then drop temporarily until the balance in vacuum between chambers "A" and "B" is restored. The air from the pump will then be bypassed into the atmosphere dur-

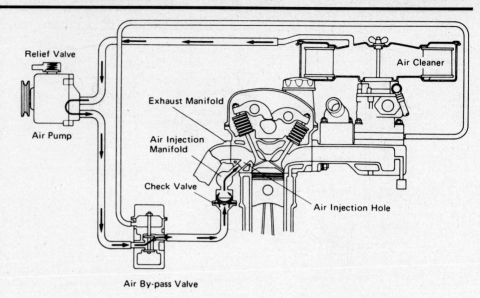

Fig. 35 Manifold air injection system. 1973-74 4M engine.

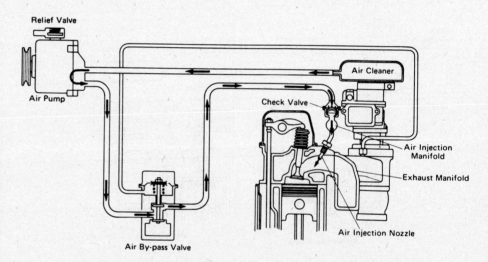

Fig. 36 Manifold air injection system. 1973 F engine and 1974 F engine except Calif.

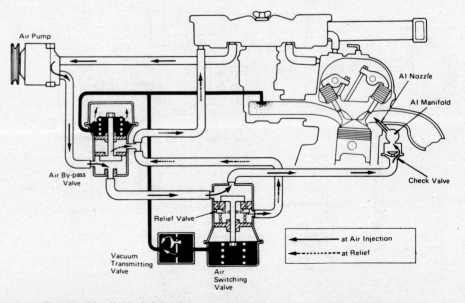

Fig. 37 Manifold air injection system. 1975-76 2T-C engine except Calif.

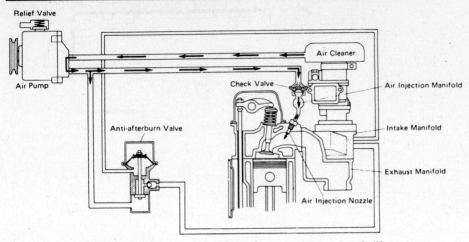

Fig. 38   Manifold air injection system. 1974 F engine Calif.

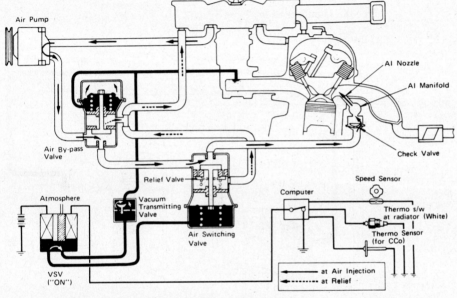

Fig. 39   Manifold air injection system. 1975 2T-C engine Calif.

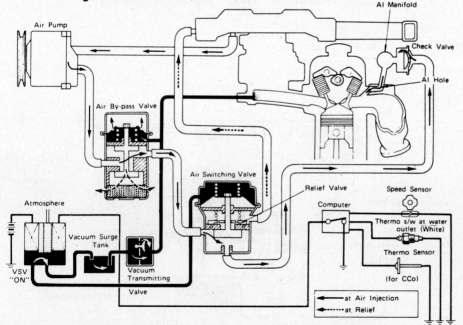

Fig. 40   Manifold air injection system. 1975 20R engine

ing the time the diaphragm is in its lowest position.

1976 20R Engine

When vehicle speed and coolant temperature reach the "ON" range, the computer turns on the VSV. This causes the intake manifold vacuum to act on the ASV and air is injected into the exhaust manifold. When air pump discharge pressure rises above a specified value, the ASV relief valve opens to relieve the air back to the air cleaner.

During sudden deceleration, the intake manifold vacuum acts on the ABV and lowers the valve. The air from the pump is then temporarily relieved from the ABV to the atmosphere to prevent after-burning.

Under heavy load, the decrease in intake manifold vacuum causes the ASV to close the passage to the air injection manifold. The air is then relieved into the air cleaner.

If any one of the "ON" conditions changes to the "OFF" range, the computer turns the VSV "OFF". This allows atmospheric pressure to act on the ASV and causes it to close by spring tension. The air is then relieved to the air cleaner.

1977 20R Engine

When engine coolant temperature is below 55° F, the TVSV closes the vacuum passage between the ASV and intake manifold. This causes the ASV to close the air injection passage and diverts the compressed air from the pump to the air cleaner.

When engine coolant temperature is above 55° F and the vehicle is operating at low speeds, the TVSV opens the passage between the ASV and intake manifold. Under this condition, as the intake manifold vacuum acts on the ASV "A" chamber and atmospheric pressure from the air injection out port acts on the ASV "B" chamber, the ASV opens. The compressed air from the pump passes through the ASV, check valve, air injection manifold and into the exhaust ports.

When the air pump discharge pressure rises above a specified value, the ASV relief valve opens to relieve the air.

When engine is at normal operating temperature and vehicle is operating at high speeds, the vacuum from the air injection out port acts on the ASV "B" port chamber and the intake manifold vacuum acts on the ASA "A" chamber. Since the same vacuum acts on the ASV diaphragm, the diaphragm is pushed down by spring tension and the valve closes the air injection passage, and the air from the pump is bypassed into the air cleaner. This action is delayed by the vacuum transmitting valve (VTV).

Under sudden deceleration, the balance between chambers "A" and "B" will be disrupted due to intake manifold vacuum pressure acting suddenly on chamber "B" of the VCV. The diaphragm will then drop temporarily until the balance in vacuum between chambers "A" and "B" is restored. Since chambers "A" and "B" in the ASV are connected by the VCV, the diaphragm in the ASV is pushed down by spring tension. The ASV temporarily closes the air injection passage.

Under heavy engine load, the decrease in intake manifold pressure causes the ASV to close the passage on the air injection side. The air is then bypassed to the air cleaner. This action is delayed by the vacuum transmitting valve (VTV).

If engine coolant temperature rises above 212° F, the BVSV opens the vacuum passage between chambers "A" and "B" in the ASV. Since vacuum chambers "A" and "B" are the same, the diaphragm in the ASV is pushed down by spring tension. The air from the air pump is then bypassed into the air cleaner to prevent the engine from overheating.

Maintenance

1. Check drive belt for cracks or damage and replace if necessary.
2. Check drive belt deflection. Belt should deflect about ¾-⅞ inch when a force of about 22 lbs. is applied to belt at its midway position between the two pulleys. Adjust if necessary.
3. Inspect all hoses and tubes for deterioration and cracking. Replace if necessary.
4. Check all hoses and tubes for proper connections. Correct as necessary.
5. Check air injection manifold for leaks. Correct as necessary.

Component Functional Check

Air Pump

1. Check air pump for abnormal noise.
2. Check air pump discharge pressure as follows:
   a. Connect tester, Fig. 48, to engine.
   b. Start engine and raise speed as specified:
      1975-77 2F .... 1450 RPM
      1975-77 2T-C .... 1800 RPM
      1975-76 4M .... 1750 RPM
      1975-76 20R .... 1750 RPM
      1977 20R .... 1800 RPM
   c. With engine running at the

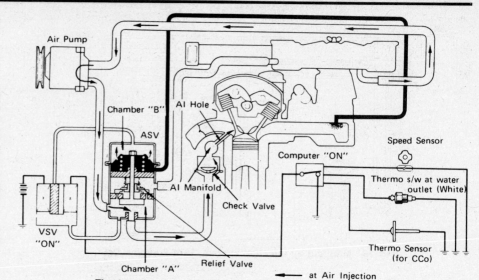
Fig. 41   Manifold air injection system. 1975-76 4M engine

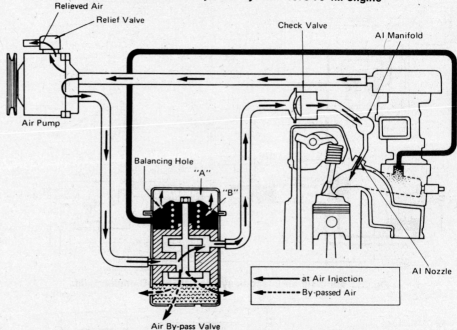
Fig. 42   Manifold air injection system. 1975-77 2F engine

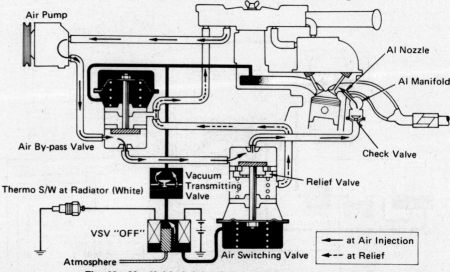
Fig. 43   Manifold air injection system. 1976 2T-C engine

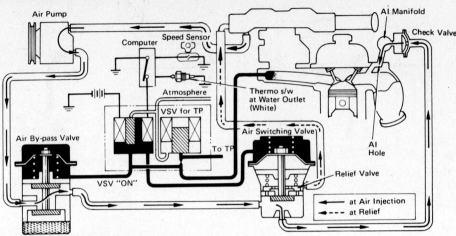

Fig. 44 Manifold air injection system. 1976 20R engine

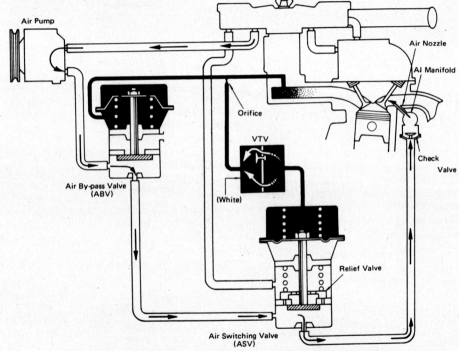

Fig. 45 Manifold air injection system. 1977 2T-C engine except Calif. and high altitude

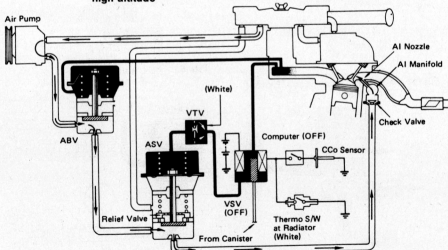

Fig. 46 Manifold air injection system.1977 2T-C engine Calif. and high altitude

specified speed, the tester should indicate in the green zone.

d. On all except 1975-76 2F engines, if tester indicates in the red zone, the pump assembly is defective.

e. On 1975-76 2F engines, if tester indicates in the red zone close relief valve outlet with hand and recheck. If tester indicates in the green zone, the relief valve is defective. If tester still indicates in the red zone, the air pump assembly is defective.

Air By-pass Valve (ABV)

1. With engine idling, air pump air should pass out toward the check valve (2F engine) or ASV (2T-C and 20R engines), Fig. 49.
2. Raise engine speed and then suddenly close throttle. The air from the pump should be momentarily discharged into the atmosphere (20R and 2F engine) or to air cleaner (2T-C engine), Fig. 50.

Air Switching Valve (ASV)
Except 4M Engine

1. With engine idling, air from the ABV should be discharged toward the check valve, Fig. 51.
2. When the ASV vacuum hose is disconnected, the air from the ABV should be discharged out toward the air cleaner, Fig. 52.
3. On 4M engine:
   a. With engine idling, air from the pump should be discharged out toward the check valve, Fig. 53.
   b. Raise engine speed, then suddenly close the throttle valve. Air from the pump should be discharged out toward the air cleaner, Fig. 54.

ASV Relief Valve Opening Pressure Check

1. Referring to Fig. 55, disconnect hose between ASV and check valve at check valve end and connect tool.
2. Raise engine speed gradually and measure relief valve opening pressure which should be 2.7 to 6.5 psi (.19 to .46 kg/cm²) for all except 4M engines, or 3.7 to 7.7 psi (.26 to .54 kg/cm²) on 4M engines.

Check Valve

1. Make air passage test from ASV or ABV side. There should be air passage toward the air injection manifold side, Fig. 56.
2. There should be no passage of air from the air injection manifold side toward the ASV or ABV side, Fig. 56.

Vacuum Transmitting Valve (VTV)

Check that air flows more freely when applied from the ASV side than from the intake manifold side, Fig. 57.

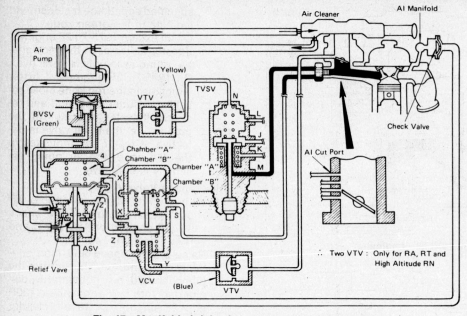

Fig. 47   Manifold air injection system. 1977 20R engine

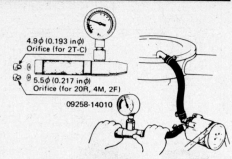

Fig. 48   Air pump discharge pressure test

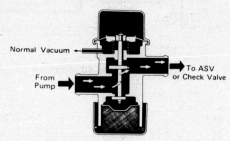

Fig. 49   ABV functional check

Vacuum Surge Tank

Inspect vacuum surge tank to make sure it is free of cracks or deformation.

Vacuum Switching Valve (VSV)

1. Disconnect wiring connector from VSV, Fig. 58, and check for passage of air through the VSV upper and lower pipes.
2. Connect a battery to VSV connector as shown in Fig. 59, or have engine warm and turned off and ignition switch on. Check that there is no passage of air through VSV upper and lower pipes.

AIR SUCTION (AS) SYSTEM

1977 3K-C

This system, Fig. 60, is used to direct air into the exhaust port to extend the combustion of unburned hydrocarbons (HC) and carbon monoxide (CO) into the exhaust system. This air is also used as the oxygen source for the catalytic converter.

System Operation

This system draws fresh air from the air suction valve into the exhaust port by using negative pressure created by the overlap of the valves and pulsation in the exhaust port. When the vacuum acts on the valve, the valve opens and fresh air is drawn in from the exhaust ports of Nos. 1 and 4 cylinders.

System Inspection

1. Check all tubes to make sure they are not cracked, loose or deteriorated. Repair or replace as necessary.
2. Start engine, then place a thin piece of paper to the inlet port of the air

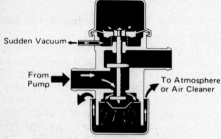

Fig. 50   ABV functional check

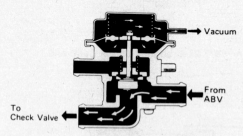

Fig. 51   ASV functional check. Except 4M engine

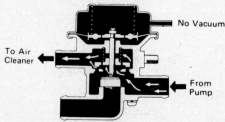

Fig. 52   ASV functional check. Except 4M engine

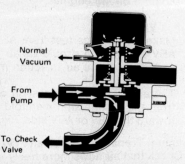

Fig. 53   ASV functional check. 4M engine

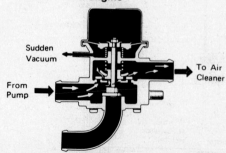

Fig. 54   ASV functional check. 4M engine

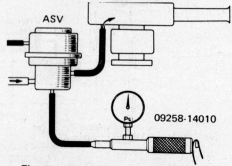

Fig. 55   Relief valve opening pressure test

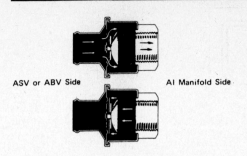

Fig. 56 Check valve functional check

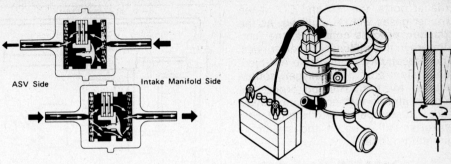

Fig. 57 VTV functional check

Fig. 58 VSV functional check

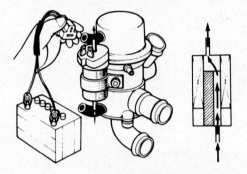

Fig. 59 VSV functional check

suction filter. If the paper is drawn in, the system is normal. If not, remove filter and recheck in same manner. If paper is drawn in, replace filter. If not, replace air suction valve.

CATALYTIC CONVERTER (CCo) SYSTEM
1975-77

The catalytic converter system, Figs. 61 and 62, consists of a granular alumina carrier, coated with a catalyst (activated material) such as platinum or palladium and is enclosed in a heat resistant steel case.

When the mixture of the exhaust gases and secondary air is passed through the catalytic converter, the hydrocarbon (HC) and carbon monoxide (CO) content of the exhaust gases is oxidized and converted into water (H_2O) and carbon dioxide (CO_2).

The secondary air supplied by the Air Injection System is also used as the oxygen source for the oxidizing reaction.

Since large amounts of unburned fuel gases will cause the temperature of the catalytic converter to rise, a high temperature warning light is provided to warn of an overheating condition.

Operation

When secondary air from the Air Injection System is injected into the

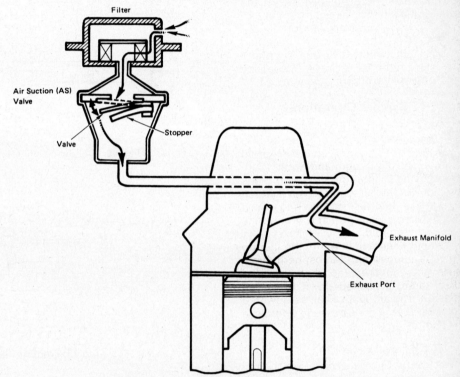

Fig. 60 Air Suction (AS) system. 1977 3K-C engine

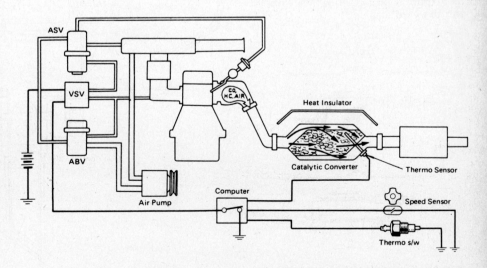

Fig. 61 Catalytic Converter (CCo) System. 1975-76 models

exhaust ports, the HC and CO in the exhaust gases will be oxidized. As the oxidation process continues, the temperature in the catalytic converter rises. When secondary air from the Air Injection System stops, the oxygen source required for the oxidation process is stopped and no further oxidation takes place. The temperature of the catalytic converter will drop, if the system is operating normally.

AUTOMATIC HOT AIR INTAKE (HAI) SYSTEM

This system is used to maintain the temperature of the air entering the carburetor at a constant and predetermined temperature. In cold weather, this system directs a hot air supply to the carburetor to improve driveability and prevent carburetor icing.

System Operation

20R & 2T-C Engine, Fig. 63

When the engine is cold, the thermo valve is closed and the intake manifold acts on the diaphragm and draws it up. Raising the diaphragm causes the link to pull up the air control valve which closes the cold air passage and opens the hot air passage which is around the exhaust manifold.

When the engine is warm, the thermo valve is opened and atmospheric pressure acts on the diaphragm and the diaphragm is pushed down by spring tension. The air control valve is lowered to open the cold air passage and close the hot air passage.

2F Engine, Fig. 64

When the engine is cold, the thermo wax contracts and the link draws in to close the cold air inlet.

When the engine is hot, the thermo wax expands and pushes the link to open the cold air inlet.

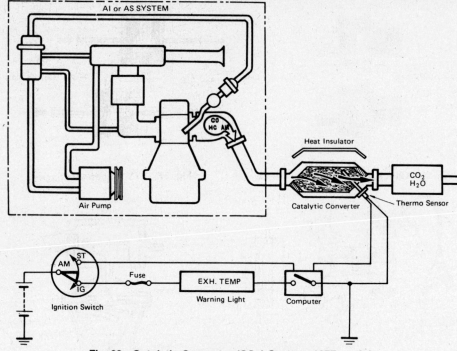

Fig. 62   Catalytic Converter (CCo) System. 1977 models

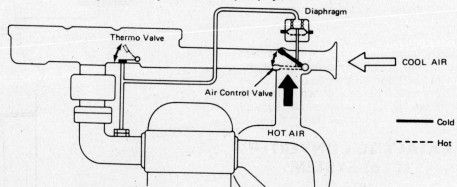

Fig. 63   Automatic Hot Air Intake (HAI) System. 20R engine

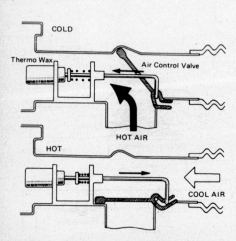

Fig. 64   Automatic Hot Air Intake (HAI) System. 2F engine

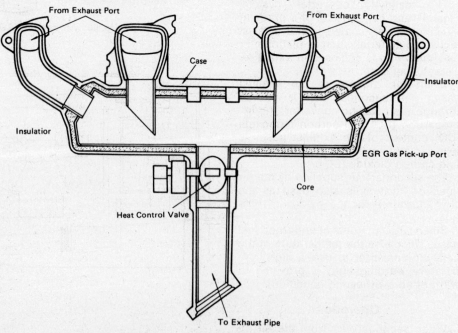

Fig. 65   Thermal Reactor System

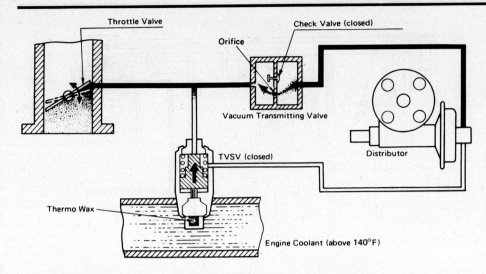

Fig. 66   Spark delay System. 1976 2T-C engine

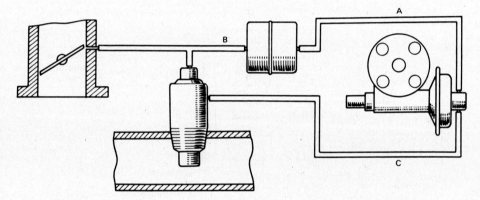

Fig. 67   Spark delay system vacuum hose connections. 1976 2T-C engine

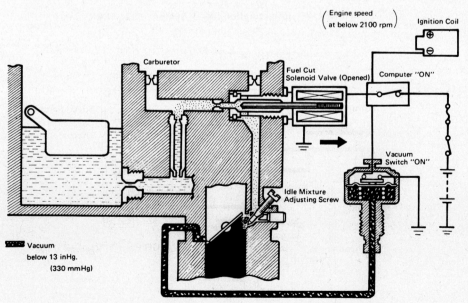

Fig. 68   Deceleration Fuel Cut System. 1977 3K-C engine

System Diagnosis

To check operation of the diaphragm, connect the diaphragm hose directly to the intake manifold. With engine idling, the cold air inlet should close.

THERMAL REACTOR SYSTEM

1977 2F Calif. Engine

This system, Fig. 65, is installed on the engine in place of exhaust manifold and is designed to maintain the exhaust gases at a higher temperature for a greater amount of time to further increase the efficiency of exhaust gases and secondary air. This system operates in conjunction with the Air Injection System to minimize unburned hydrocarbons (HC) and carbon monoxide (CO).

SPARK DELAY SYSTEM

1976 2T-C Calif.

This system, Figs. 66 and 67, reduces nitrogen oxides (NOx) and hydrocarbon (HC) emissions by delaying the vacuum advance for a predetermined amount of time.

Operation

When engine coolant temperature is about 140° F, the thermostatic vacuum switching valve (TVSV) is closed so that opening the throttle valve and having the vacuum act on the advancer port will cause the check valve inside the vacuum transmitting valve (VTV) to close. Since vacuum can only act on the distributor diaphragm through the orifice in the VTV, vacuum will be delayed.

On throttle closure, the vacuum will no longer act on the advancer port and the check inside the VTV will open. The low vacuum from the advancer port will then be acting on the distributor diaphragm so that the diaphragm will quickly return to the position corresponding to the vacuum.

When the engine is cold, the TVSV is open. The advancer port vacuum will act directly on the distributor diaphragm so that the vacuum will not be delayed.

DECELERATION FUEL CUT SYSTEM

1977 3K-C Engine

This system, Fig. 68, is used to prevent overheating and/or afterburning in the exhaust system when the vehicle is decelerating by momentarily cutting off the fuel supply in the system.

System Operation

While the vehicle is operating with engine speed below 2100 rpm and/or carburetor vacuum is below 13 inches Hg, the computer is turned on by the signal from the ignition switch and/or vacuum switch. Under this condition, the battery current energizes the fuel cut solenoid and opens the slow circuit of the carburetor.

When decelerating, if engine speed is above 2100 rpm and carburetor vacuum is above 13 inches Hg, the computer deactivates the fuel cut solenoid and closes the slow circuit in the carburetor. Under this condition, the fuel from the float chamber does not flow into the slow circuit. This action is delayed for 1½ seconds by the delay circuit of the computer.

HIGH ALTITUDE COMPENSATION (HAC) SYSTEM

1977 2F, 2T-C & 20R Engines

This system, Fig. 69, is used to minimize hydrocarbon (HC) and carbon monoxide (CO) content of the exhaust gases by maintaining the proper air fuel mixture at high altitudes. At altitudes above 4000 feet, additional air is supplied to the low and/or high speed circuits of the carburetor. On 2T-C and 20R engines, this system also advances the ignition timing at the higher altitudes.

Operation

At altitudes above 4000 feet, the low atmospheric pressure allows the bellows in the HAC to expand and close port "A". The intake manifold vacuum then acts on the HAC valve diaphragm through the check valve and passages between the carburetor and atmosphere are opened. Air from the HAC valve flows into the low and/or high speed circuits of the carburetor resulting in leaner air fuel mixtures.

On 2T-C and 20R engines, intake manifold also acts on the sub-diaphragm of the distributor to advance the timing to the maximum advanced position of the sub-diaphragm. If the distributor port vacuum rises above 6.8 inches on 2T-C engines or 5 inches on 20R engines, the vacuum advance will correspond to the main diaphragm characteristics.

At low altitudes, the bellows in the HAC valve contracts by the higher atmospheric pressure and opens port

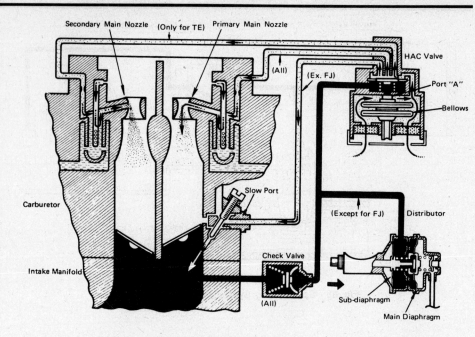

Fig. 69 High Altitude Compensation (HAC) System. 1977 2F, 2T-C and 20R engine

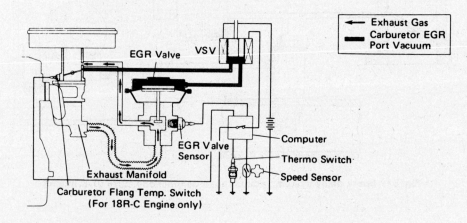

Fig. 70 Exhaust Gas Recirculation (EGR) System. 1974 18R-C and F engine

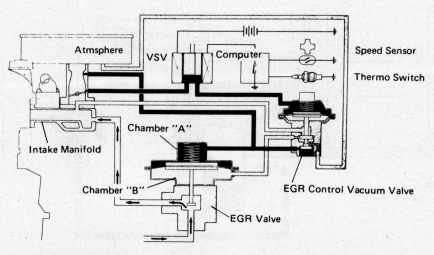

Fig. 71 Exhaust Gas Recirculation (EGR) System. 1974 4M engine

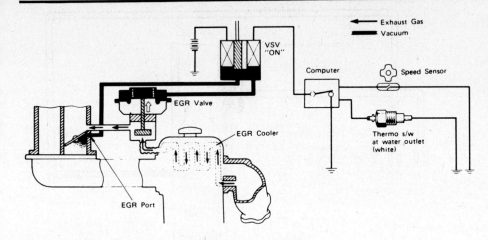

Fig. 72   Exhaust Gas Recirculation (EGR) System. 1975-76 20R engine

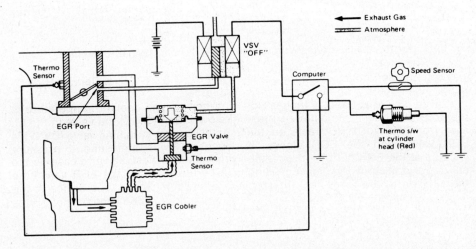

Fig. 73   Exhaust Gas Recirculation (EGR) System. 1975-76 2F engine

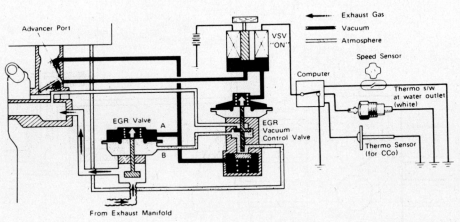

Fig. 74   Exhaust Gas Recirculation (EGR) System. 1975-76 4M engine

"A". Since intake manifold vacuum does not act on the HAC valve diaphragm, the air passage from the carburetor to the atmosphere is closed by the diaphragm. Since intake manifold vacuum also does not act on the distributor sub-diaphragm, vacuum advance will only correspond to the main diaphragm characteristics.

EXHAUST GAS RECIRCULATION (EGR) SYSTEM

This system, Figs. 70 thru 79 is used to dilute the incoming air fuel mixture with recirculated exhaust gases. Dilution of the incoming mixture lowers the peak flame temperatures and thus limits the formation of nitrous oxides (NOx).

System Operation

1974 F & 18R-C Engines

When vehicle speed is above 13± 3 mph for F engines, or above 16± 3 mph on 18R-C engines, engine coolant temperature is above 113° F for F engines, or 140° F for 18R-C engines and exhaust gas recirculation valve temperature is above 248° F for F engines, or 194° F for 18R-C engines, the computer closes the vacuum switching ground circuit. The valve in the vacuum switching valve (VSV) closes the passage from the EGR valve to atmosphere and opens the passage from the EGR port to the EGR valve. The EGR valve opens and exhaust gas recirculation is started.

When either or all of the vehicle speed and temperatures are at their "OFF" range, that is vehicle speed above 65 mph, engine coolant temperature above 217° F, and exhaust gas recirculation valve temperature above 320° F for F engines, or 260° F for 18R-C engines, the computer opens the vacuum switching valve ground circuit. The valve in the vacuum switching valve returns to its original position and opens the passage from atmosphere to the EGR valve. The exhaust gas passage closes and stops exhaust gas recirculation.

1974-76 4M Engine

When vehicle speed, coolant temperature and catalytic converter temperature (1975-76 only) all reach their "ON" range, the computer closes the VSV ground.

The valve in the VSV opens the vacuum passage from the carburetor advancer port to the EGR control vacuum valve, causing advancer port vacuum to act on the valve diaphragm. Carburetor venturi vacuum acts on the EGR valve "A" chamber, while atmospheric pressure from the EGR control valve acts on the "B" chamber. As a result, the exhaust gas passage opens in accordance with venturi vacuum and exhaust gas recirculation starts.

When either one or all of the vehicle speed and temperatures are in their "OFF" range, the computer opens the VSV ground.

The valve in the VSV returns to its original position and closes the vacuum passage from the carburetor advancer port to the EGR control vacuum valve. Atmospheric pressure from the EGR control vacuum valve acts on the "A" chamber, while vacuum from the intake manifold acts on the "B" chamber. Thus, exhaust gas recirculation is stopped.

1976 2F & 20R Engine

When vehicle speed, coolant temperature, EGR gas temperature (2F only) and carburetor flange temperature (2F only) all reach their "ON" range, the computer turns the vacuum switching valve (VSV) "ON".

When the VSV is turned "ON", the vacuum passage between the EGR port and EGR valve opens, thus exhaust gas recirculation starts. Part of the exhaust gases pass through the EGR cooler, EGR valve and into the upper side of the carburetor throttle valve.

When either or all of the vehicle speed and temperatures are at their "OFF" range, the computer turns the VSV "OFF".

When the VSV is turned "OFF", the vacuum passage between the EGR port and EGR valve is closed and exhaust gas recirculation is stopped.

1977 2F Engine

When engine coolant temperature is below 122° F (50° C), the bi-metal vacuum switching valve closes the vacuum passage. The EGR port vacuum does not affect the EGR valve, regardless of whether the VCV is opened or closed. Therefore, the EGR valve closes the exhaust gas recirculation passage.

When engine coolant temperature is above 122° F (50° C), and the vacuum in the surge tank is below 3.15 inches Hg, the BVSV opens the vacuum passage. Since the EGR cut port vacuum is delayed by the VTV and the vacuum surge tank, the VCV No. 1 does not open until the vacuum in the surge tank reaches 3.15 inches Hg. The EGR port vacuum then opens the EGR valve. Part of the exhaust gases from the exhaust manifold passes through the EGR cooler, EGR valve and into the upper side of the carburetor throttle valve.

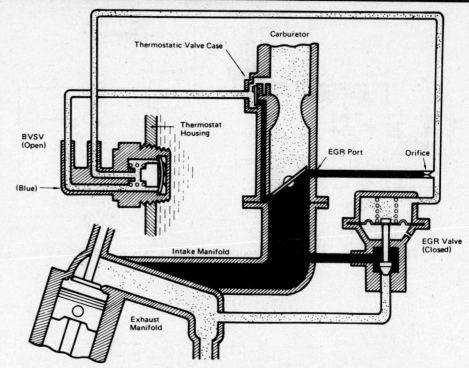

Fig. 75   Exhaust Gas Recirculation (EGR) System. 1977 3K-C engine

When engine coolant temperature is above 122° F (50° C), and the vacuum in the surge tank is above 3.15 inches Hg, the No. 1 VCV opens, atmospheric pressure from the No. 1 VCV acts on the EGR valve, and the EGR closes. If vacuum at the EGR cut port drops, the check valve in the VTV opens, causing the vacuum in the surge tank to drop quickly for engine acceleration.

1977 3K-C & 2T-C Exc. Calif. & High Altitude

When engine coolant temperature is below 122° F (50° C) the valve in the bi-metal vacuum switching valve (BVSV) is opened. Since atmospheric pressure from the thermostatic valve case on the carburetor acts on the EGR valve, the EGR valve is closed. The orifice in the 3-way fitting on 3K-C engines, or orifice

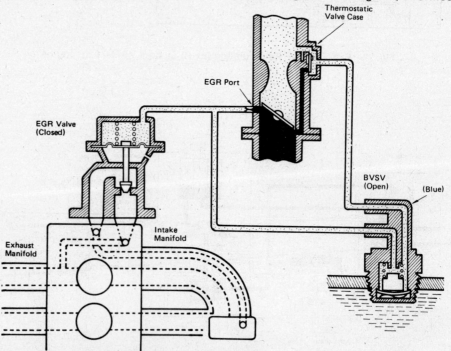

Fig. 76   Exhaust Gas Recirculation (EGR) System. 1977 2T-C engine except Calif. and high altitude

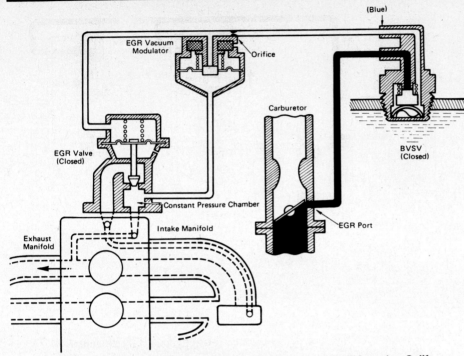

Fig. 77 Exhaust Gas Recirculation (EGR) System. 1977 2T-C engine Calif. and high altitude

in EGR port in pipe on 2T-C engine keeps the EGR port vacuum high.

When engine coolant temperature is above 122° F (50° C), the BVSV is closed. Since atmospheric pressure from the thermostatic valve case is cut by the BVSV, the vacuum from the EGR port lifts the EGR valve diaphragm and opens the EGR valve. Part of the exhaust gas from the exhaust manifold passes through the EGR valve and is routed into the intake manifold.

1977 2T-C Calif. & High Altitude

When engine coolant temperature is below 122° F (50° C), the valve in the bi-metal vacuum switching valve (BVSV) is closed. Since vacuum the EGR port does not act on the EGR valve, the EGR valve closes.

When engine coolant temperature is above 122° F (50° C), the BVSV is open. Since pressure from the constant pressure chamber acts on the EGR vacuum modulator, the valve in the EGR modulator is closed. The vacuum from the EGR port then lifts the EGR valve diaphragm and opens the EGR valve. Part of the exhaust gases from the pick-up port passes through the EGR valve and is routed into the intake manifold.

The open EGR valve causes the pressure in the constant pressure chamber to drop and the EGR vacuum modulator to open. Atmospheric pressure from the air filter in the EGR vacuum modulator acts on the EGR valve and closes it. This causes the pressure in the constant pressure chamber to increase and the EGR valve to open again.

To increase the amount of exhaust gas recirculation under high engine loads, the EGR valve jet diameter is larger and the opening timing is carefully controlled by the EGR vacuum modulator.

1977 20R Engine

When engine coolant temperature is below 50° F (10°C), the thermo vacuum switching valve (TVSV) closes the vacuum passage between the EGR port and EGR valve. Since vacuum does not act on the EGR valve, the EGR valve closes the exhaust gas recirculation passage.

When engine coolant temperature is above 50° F (10° C), the valve in the TVSV is open. Since vacuum from the EGR port acts on the EGR valve, the EGR valve opens. Part of the exhaust gases from the exhaust manifold passes through the EGR cooler, the EGR valve and into the upper side of the carburetor throttle valve.

EGR Valve Functional Check

1974 18R-C Engine
1. Bring engine up to normal operating temperature, then remove air cleaner top.
2. Disconnect EGR valve sensing hose from EGR valve.
3. Disconnect red hose to intake manifold from VSV valve and connect it to EGR valve.
4. When red hose is connected to EGR valve, a hollow sound should be heard from carburetor, and should disappear when hose is disconnected.
5. If operation is not as specified, replace the EGR valve and recheck.

4M Engine
1. Disconnect vacuum sensing hose from EGR valve chamber "A."
2. Disconnect sensing hose from EGR valve chamber "B" which leads to EGR control vacuum valve.
3. Reconnect vacuum sensing hose disconnected from "B" chamber to "A" chamber. When this connection is made, the engine should idle rough or should stall.
4. If operation is not as specified, replace EGR valve and recheck.

1974 F Engine
With engine idling, connect manifold vacuum directly to EGR valve using a hose. Engine speed should drop be-

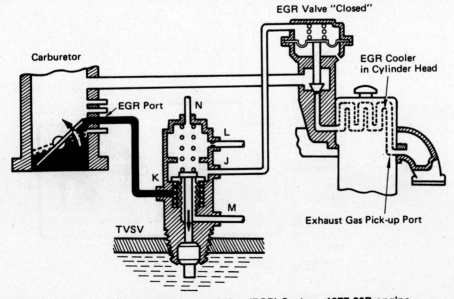

Fig. 78 Exhaust Gas Recirculation (EGR) System. 1977 20R engine

tween 50-100 rpm. If operation is not as specified, replace EGR valve and recheck.

1975-76 20R & 2F Engine
1. Bring engine up to normal operating temperature, then remove air cleaner top.
2. With engine idling, connect the EGR valve and intake manifold together using a length of vacuum hose. This should cause the carburetor to produce a bubbling sound.
3. This sound should disappear when vacuum hose is disconnected from EGR valve.
4. If operation is not as specified, replace the EGR valve and recheck.

1975-76 4M Engine
With engine idling at normal operating temperature, interchange the EGR valve upper and lower hoses. This should cause the engine to idle rough or stall. If operation is not as specified, replace EGR valve and recheck.

EGR Vacuum Control Valve Functional Check
1975-76 4M Engine
1. Connect carburetor advancer port and EGR vacuum control valve directly to each other.
2. Disconnect hoses from EGR valve and connect a vacuum gauge to each hose.
3. Accelerate the engine and observe the following:
   a. EGR "A" chamber should indicate venturi vacuum.
   b. EGR "B" chamber should indicate atmospheric pressure.
4. With engine idling, disconnect the hose from carburetor advancer port and observe the following:
   a. EGR "A" chamber should indicate approximately atmospheric pressure.
   b. EGR "B" chamber should indicate manifold vacuum.
5. If operation is not as specified, replace control valve and recheck.

Thermo Sensor Functional Check
1974 18R-C Engine
If the resistance between center electrode and case of sensor is 2.55 kilo ohms when sensor is heated to 260° F, the sensor is operating normally.

1974 F Engine
If the resistance between center electrode and case of sensor is 2.0 kilo ohms when sensor is heated to 320° F, the sensor is operating normally.

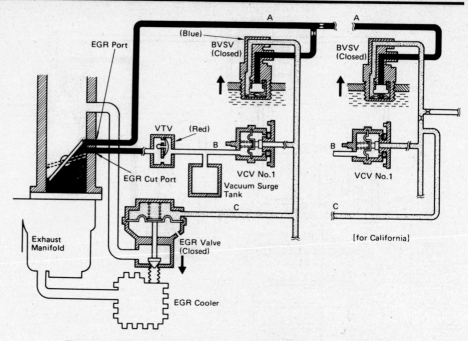
Fig. 79 Exhaust Gas Recirculation (EGR) System. 1977 2F engine

EGR Functional Check
20R & 2F Engine
1. Warm engine to normal operating temperature, then remove air cleaner top.
2. With engine idling, connect the EGR valve and intake manifold together using a length of vacuum hose. This should cause carburetor to produce a bubbling sound.
3. This sound should disappear when vacuum hose is disconnected from EGR valve.

4M Engine
With engine idling at normal operating temperature, interchange the EGR valve upper and lower hoses. This should cause the engine to idle rough or stall.

DOUBLE VACUUM ADVANCE DISTRIBUTOR
1976 Calif. 2T-C & 1977 All 2T-C
This system, Figs. 80 and 81, is used to improve cold engine performance by advancing the ignition timing. The dis-

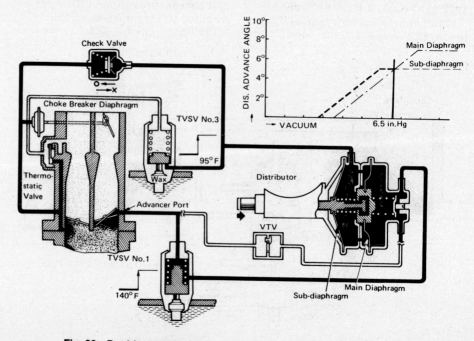
Fig. 80 Double vacuum advance distributor. 1976 2T-C engine Calif.

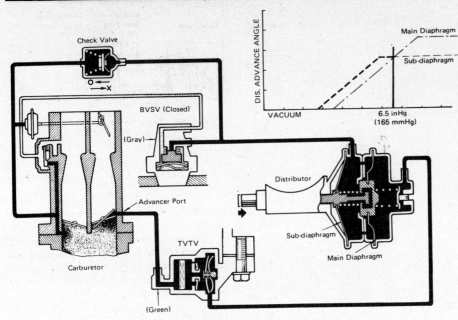

Fig. 81 Double vacuum advance distributor. 1977 2T-C engine

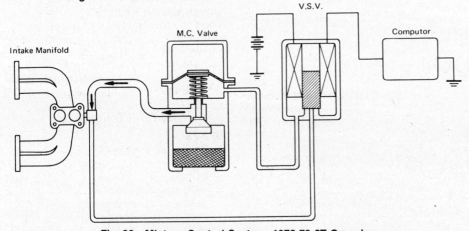

Fig. 82 Mixture Control System. 1972-73 2T-C engine

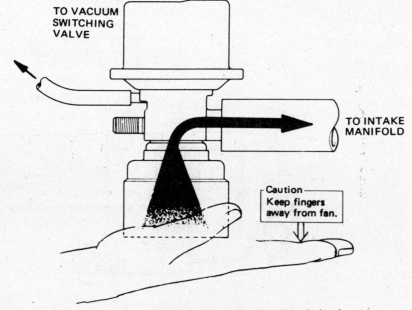

Fig. 83 Mixture control valve functional check

tributor in this system has two vacuum diaphragms which have different advance characteristics.

Operation

1976

When engine coolant temperature is below 95° F and intake manifold vacuum is under 6.5 inches Hg, the No. 3 thermo switch closes the passage and intake manifold vacuum acts on the sub-diaphragm through the check valve. The No. 1 thermo switch opens the passage and vacuum from the advancer port acts on the main diaphragm through the No. 1 TVSV. When the vacuum acting on both diaphragm chambers is equal, the main diaphragm is returned by spring tension. The vacuum advance timing will correspond to the advance characteristics of the sub-diaphragm. The vacuum in the subdiaphragm will be maintained by the check valve even if intake manifold vacuum decreases, so that ignition timing will remain fixed. If vacuum in the sub-diaphragm rises above 6.0 inches Hg, the diaphragm shaft strikes against the main diaphragm rear side. Since the main diaphragm will not move until the vacuum rises above 6.5 inches Hg, the sub-diaphragm will not move.

When engine coolant temperature is below 95° F and advancer port vacuum is above 6.5 inches Hg, the diaphragms shift to the right as a unit and vacuum advance timing will correspond to the main diaphragm characteristics. The sub-diaphragm vacuum is maintained by the check valve so that even if the vacuum fluctuates, the ignition timing will not drop below the sub-diaphragms greatest advance characteristic. When the engine is idling, there is no vacuum at the advancer port, but the ignition timing will be advanced to stabilize the idling when engine is cold. Also, under acceleration, the advancer port vacuum drops, but due to the advanced timing acceleration is also improved with a cold engine.

When engine coolant is between 95° F and 140° F, the No. 3 thermo switch opens the passage, allowing atmospheric pressure to act on the sub-diaphragm to cause it to not affect the timing. The No. 1 thermo switch remains contracted so that the TVSV keeps the vacuum passage open. The vacuum from the advancer port acts on the main diaphragm through the No. TVSV. The distributor operates in the spark delay system OFF condition.

When engine coolant temperature is above 140° F, the No. 3 thermo switch opens the passage and the No. 1 thermo switch closes the passage. The distributor then operates in the spark delay system "ON" condition.

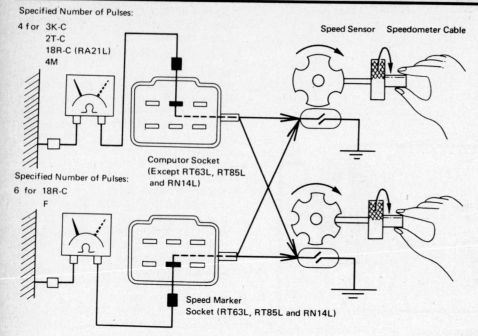

Specified Number of Pulses:

4 f or 3K-C
2T-C
18R-C (RA21L)
4M

Computor Socket
(Except RT63L, RT85L
and RN14L)

Specified Number of Pulses:

6 for 18R-C
F

Speed Marker
Socket (RT63L, RT85L and RN14L)

Fig. 84 Speed sensor functional check

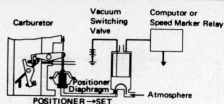

Fig. 85 Throttle Positioner System. 1972-73

1977

When engine coolant temperature is below 68° F (20° C) and intake manifold vacuum is under 6.5 inches Hg, the BVSV is closed. Intake manifold vacuum acts on the sub-diaphragm through the check valve and vacuum from the advancer port acts on the main diaphragm through the TVTV. When the vacuum acting on both diaphragm chambers is equal, the main diaphragm is returned by spring tension and the vacuum advance will correspond to the sub-diaphragm advance characteristics. The vacuum in the sub-diaphragm is maintained by the check valve so that even if intake vacuum is decreased, the ignition timing will remain fixed.

When vacuum at the advancer port rises above 6.5 inches Hg when engine coolant temperature is below 68° F (20° C), the main and sub-diaphragms shift to the right as a single unit and the advance timing will correspond to the main diaphragm characteristics. The vacuum at the sub-diaphragm is retained by the check valve so that even if the vacuum does fluctuate, the vacuum advance timing will not drop below the sub-diaphragm greatest advance characteristics. While the engine is idling, there is no vacuum at the advancer port, but the ignition timing will already be advanced, causing a more stable idle due to the higher engine speed. Under acceleration, the advance port vacuum drops but due to the advanced timing, performance is improved.

When engine coolant temperature is above 68°, the BVSV is open. Atmospheric pressure acts on the sub-diaphragm and the timing advance operates in the spark control system "ON" condition.

MIXTURE CONTROL SYSTEM

This system, Fig. 82, consists of a mixture control valve connected to intake manifold and to vacuum switching valve. The unit is controlled by vacuum switching valve, computer and speed sensor. The mixture control valve allows fresh air to pass into the intake manifold during deceleration from high or intermediate speeds. The valve serves to control air/fuel ratio during these periods.

Operation

When idling or at low speed, the speed sensor signals the computer to cut off vacuum to switching valve and no vacuum is allowed to the mixture control valve. During normal running at intermediate and high speed, the vacuum switching valve receives signals from the speed sensor which allows vacuum to reach the mixture control diaphragm. This vacuum is not high enough to activate the valve at this time. When the throttle is released suddenly, additional vacuum is created. This causes the control valve to open momentarily and allows fresh air to be drawn through the mixture control valve and into the intake manifold.

System Diagnosis

1972-73

1. Raise rear axle housing and support it on stands. Block both front wheels with chocks.
2. With engine running, check if vacuum can be felt when hand is placed over mixture control valve, Fig. 83. If vacuum can be felt, replace mixture control valve.
3. Place transmission into gear and check if vacuum can be felt at the mixture control valve when engine is decelerated from 41 mph. If no vacuum is felt, the system is not operating properly. Refer to step 5.
4. Place transmission into gear and

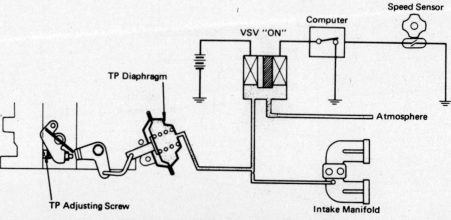

Fig. 86 Throttle Positioner System. 1974-75

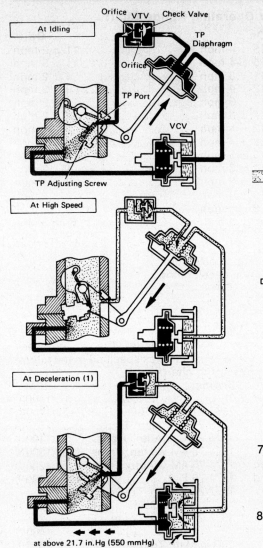

At Idling

Orifice VTV   Check Valve

TP Diaphragm

Orifice

TP Port

VCV

TP Adjusting Screw

At High Speed

At Deceleration (1)

at above 21.7 in. Hg (550 mmHg)

Fig. 87 Throttle Positioner System. 1976-77

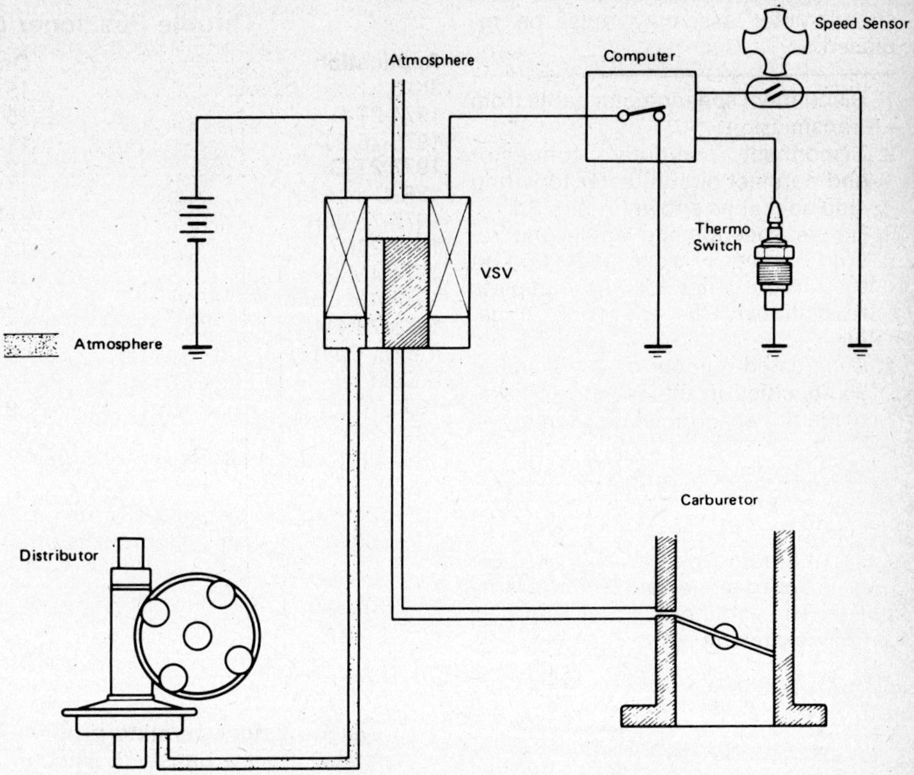

check if vacuum can be felt momentarily at the mixture control valve when engine is decelerated from below 28 mph. If vacuum can be felt, the system is not operating properly. Refer to step 5. If no vacuum can be felt, the system is operating normally.

5. Run engine at 1000 rpm and disconnect sensing hose from vacuum switching valve. Apply vacuum to sensing line and check if mixture control valve turns "ON" momentarily. If not, replace mixture control valve. If it does, proceed to step 6.

6. Disconnect vacuum switch valve electrical connector, then using a circuit tester, check for shorting between the various terminals and the vacuum switching valve body. If any shorting exists, replace the vacuum switching valve.

Fig. 88 Transmission Controlled Spark System. 1974 2T-C, 3K-C and 18R engines

Atmosphere

Computer

Speed Sensor

VSV

Thermo Switch

Atmosphere

Distributor

Carburetor

7. Refer to "Speed Sensor, Testing" and check speed sensor for proper operation. Replace speedometer assembly if speed sensor is not operating properly.

8. Replace computer assembly with a good known unit. If problem still exists, replace speedometer assembly.

1974

1. To check mixture control valve:
   a. Disconnect sensing hose mixture control valve and vacuum switching valve, then start engine and check if vacuum can be felt when hand is placed over the mixture control valve. No vacuum should be felt.
   b. Under the same conditions as above, apply vacuum to the sensing hose. Suction should be felt momentarily.

2. To check speed sensor:
   a. Disconnect vacuum sensing hose between mixture control valve and vacuum switching valve, then connect a vacuum gauge to vacuum switching valve. Place vacuum gauge where it can be observed while the vehicle is being road tested.
   b. With vehicle speed at 41±2 mph,

vacuum should be indicated on the gauge.
   c. With vehicle speed at 31±5 mph, vacuum should not be indicated on the gauge.

3. To check overall performance of system:
   a. Check all wiring and hoses for proper and tight connections. Correct as necessary.
   b. Under the conditions listed in step 1a, if vacuum can be felt, the mixture control valve is defective, and should be replaced.
   c. Under the conditions listed in step 2, if vacuum is not indicated while vehicle is being driven at 41±2 mph, or if vacuum is felt when vehicle is driven at 31±5 mph, check vacuum switching valve operation and replace if defective. If vacuum switching valve is not defective, check speed sensor operation and replace speedometer assembly if speed sensor is defective. If speed sensor is not defective, replace computer.

Speed Sensor, Testing

NOTE: The speedometer sensor is an integral part of the speedometer assembly. Therefore, if the speed sensor is found to be defective, the entire speedometer assembly must be replaced.

1. Disconnect speedometer cable from transmission.
2. Disconnect computer connector and connect circuit tester to wiring side socket as shown in Fig. 84.
3. Rotate speedometer cable and record number of cycles indicated on the circuit tester for one complete revolution of the speedometer cable.
4. If indicated number of cycles is not as specified in the chart below, replace the speedometer assembly.

THROTTLE POSITIONER

This system, Figs. 85 thru 87, consists of a diaphragm-type vacuum actuator which is linked to the carburetor throttle linkage. The actuator is controlled by a vacuum switching valve and prevents complete throttle closing under certain deceleration conditions.

Operation

The positioner is controlled through the speed sensor by vacuum switching valve. At low speeds the valve allows atmospheric air to the diaphragm of throttle positioner. This sets the throttle positioner so that when the throttle is released, the throttle valve contacts the positioner and holds the throttle in a slightly opened position. Refer to Throttle Positioner Operating Range Chart for operating speeds.

When the vehicle speed decreases to about 10 mph (for specific engine speeds see Throttle Positioner Operating Range table), the vacuum switching valve, because of signals from the speed sensor, allows vacuum to the diaphragm of the throttle positioner. This releases the throttle positioner lever from its set position and allows the throttle valve to return to normal idling position.

System Diagnosis

1972-74

1. Disconnect positioner diaphragm hose from vacuum switching valve and connect a vacuum gauge to vacuum switching valve and place vacuum gauge where it can be observed while the vehicle is being road tested.
2. Road test vehicle while observing vacuum gauge readings at various vehicle speeds. Refer to "Throttle Positioner Operating Range" chart for speeds at which system turns on and off. When gauge indicates vacuum, the system is off. When the

Throttle Positioner Operating Range Chart

Application	On ①	Off ②
3K-C	15 ± 4 mph	11 ± 2 mph
1974 2T-C	15 ± 4 mph	11 ± 3 mph
1975-76 2T-C	11 ± 3 mph	4 ± 2 mph
1977 2T-C	12 ± 4 mph	9 ± 2 mph
18R-C	14 ± 5 mph	11 ± 2 mph
1975-76 20R	17 ± 3 mph	4 ± 2 mph
1977 20R	12 ± 4 mph	9 ± 2 mph
1974 4M Exc. Calif.	15 ± 4 mph	11 ± 2 mph
1974 4M Calif.	15 ± 5 mph	11 ± 3 mph
1975-76 4M	11 ± 3 mph	4 ± 2 mph
F Exc. Calif.	13 ± 2 mph	9 ± 4 mph
F Calif.	13 ± 3 mph	9 ± 4 mph
1975-76 2F	9 ± 3 mph	3 ± 2 mph
1977 2F Calif.	20 ± 5 mph	17 ± 3 mph
1977 2F Exc. Calif.	12 ± 3 mph	9 ± 2 mph

①—Speed at which system turns on upon acceleration.
②—Speed at which system turns off upon deceleration.

gauge indicates no vacuum, the system is on.
3. If system is not operating properly, refer to "Speed Sensor & Vacuum Switch Valve" diagnosis under "Evaporative Emissions Control System" to check the system.

1975-77

1. Disconnect vacuum hose between throttle positioner diaphragm and vacuum switching valve.
2. On 1975 models, connect a vacuum gauge to vacuum switching valve and place gauge where it can be observed while driving the vehicle.
3. On 1976-77 models, connect a vacuum gauge between throttle positioner and vacuum switching valve, then place gauge where it can be observed while driving the vehicle.
4. Road test vehicle while observing the vacuum gauge readings at various vehicle speeds. Refer to "Throttle Positioner Operating Range" chart for speeds at which system turns on and off. When gauge indicates vacuum, the system is off. When gauge indicates near zero vacuum, the system is on.
5. If system is not operating properly, refer to "Speed Sensor & Vacuum Switch Valve" diagnosis under "Evaporative Emission Control System" to check system.

Throttle Positioner, Adjust

1. Warm engine and make sure that idling speed is to specifications.
2. Disconnect vacuum hose from throttle positioner.
3. Race engine and then release ac-

celerator pedal. The engine speed should be as specified in the following chart:

Engine	RPM
3K-C	1500
1974 2T-C & 18R-C	1400①
1975 2T-C w/Man. Trans.	1500①
1975 2T-C w/Auto. Trans.	1400①
1974-76 4M w/Man. Trans.	1300①
1974-76 4M w/Auto. Trans.	1200①
1974-76 F	1200①
1977 2F w/Man. Trans. Exc. Calif.	1200①
1977 2F w/Man. Trans. Calif.	1400①
20R w/Man. Trans.	1400①
20R w/Auto. Trans.	1200①

①—Plus or minus 100 rpm.

4. If speed is not within specifications, adjust by turning throttle positioner screw.

TRANSMISSION CONTROLLED SPARK

This system, Figs. 88 thru 96, controls the formation of oxides of nitrogen (NO_x) by regulating the engine's timing according to engine temperature, vehicle speed and transmission gear. To accomplish this, this system consists of a computer, vacuum switching valve, speed sensor and thermo sensor.

System Diagnosis

1972-73

1. Disconnect vacuum hose from vacuum advance unit and connect hose to a vacuum gauge. Place vacuum gauge where it can be observed while the vehicle is being driven.

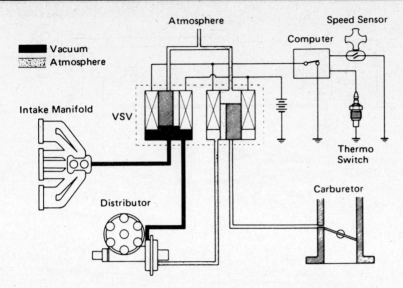

Fig. 89 Transmission Controlled Spark System. 1974 4M engine

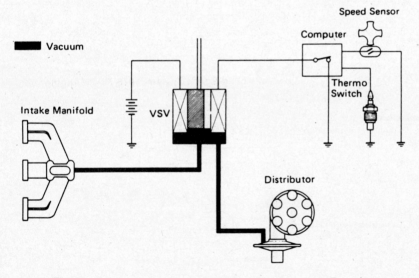

Fig. 90 Transmission Controlled Spark System. 1974 F engine

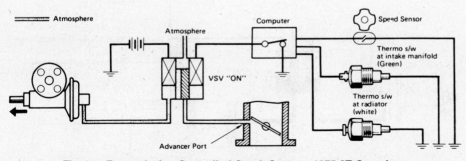

Fig. 91 Transmission Controlled Spark System. 1975 2T-C engine

2. With engine at normal operating temperature check the system. The system is operating normally if vacuum gauge readings vary as the vehicle is being driven at various speeds.

1974 Exc. F Engine
1. Check all hoses for tight and proper connections. Replace any hoses which are damaged or loose on the fitting.
2. Check thermo switch and vacuum advance unit for proper operation. Replace if defective.
3. With engine in the "ON" range of the thermo switch, Fig. 97, operating temperature and running at 2000 rpm, check that system turns ON. If system does not turn ON, check vacuum switch valve and replace if defective. If vacuum switch valve is normal, replace computer.
4. With engine coolant temperature in the "ON" range of the thermo switch, Fig. 97, and vehicle accelerated to point "A," Fig. 98, check that system turns OFF. If system does not turn off, disconnect vacuum switch valve and again check if system turns OFF. If system does not turn OFF, replace vacuum switch valve. If system does turn OFF, check speed sensor and replace if defective. If speed sensor is normal, replace computer.
5. With engine coolant temperature in the ON range, Fig. 97, and the vehicle decelerated to point "B," check that system turns ON. If system turns ON, the system is normal. If system does not turn ON, check speed sensor and replace if defective. If speed sensor is normal, replace computer.

1974 F Engine
1. Check all hoses for tight and proper connections. Replace any hoses which are damaged or loose on the fitting. Check all electrical connections.
2. Check thermo switch and vacuum advance unit for proper operation. Replace if defective.
3. With engine coolant temperature in the "ON" range, Fig. 97, and the vehicle speed at the "OFF" range, Fig. 98, the TCS system should turn OFF. If not, disconnect connector from vacuum switch valve, then again check if system goes OFF. If system does not go OFF, replace vacuum switch valve. If system goes OFF, replace computer.
4. With engine coolant temperature in the "ON" range, Fig. 97, and vehicle

speed in the "ON" range, Fig. 98, check that system goes ON. If system goes ON, the system is normal. If system does not go ON, check vacuum switch valve and replace if defective. If vacuum switch valve is normal, check speed sensor and replace if defective.

1975 2T-C Engine

1. Check all hoses and wiring for tightness and correct connections. Replace any hoses which are damaged or loose on their fittings. Repair or replace any defective wiring.

2. With engine cold, start engine and check if octane selector moves when throttle valve is opened and closed.

3. If octane selector does not move under the conditions described in step 2, check distributor vacuum advance unit and replace if defective. If distributor vacuum advance unit is not defective, disconnect and ground the thermo switch connector, and again check if octane selector moves. If it does move, replace thermo switch. If it does not move, disconnect VSV electrical connector, and again check if octane selector moves. If it does move, replace computer. If it does not move, replace VSV.

4. With engine running at normal operating temperature, check if octane selector moves when throttle valve is opened and closed.

5. If octane selector moves under the conditions described in step 4, disconnect electrical connector from thermo switch and check if octane selector still moves. If it does not move, replace thermo switch. If it does move, check power source at VSV wiring. If there is no power, repair or replace fuse or wiring. If there is power, check VSV and replace if defective. If VSV is not defective, replace computer.

6. Disconnect hose between VSV and distributor, then connect a vacuum gauge to VSV hose and place gauge where it can be observed while the vehicle is driven. While the vehicle is being driven, gradually increase and decrease the speed and check if vacuum reading goes up at 38-44 mph and down at 17-23 mph.

7. If the vacuum readings do not go up and down as specified under the conditions described in step 6, check the speed sensor and replace speedometer if defective. If speed sensor is not defective, replace computer.

8. Under the conditions described in step 6, if the vacuum readings go up

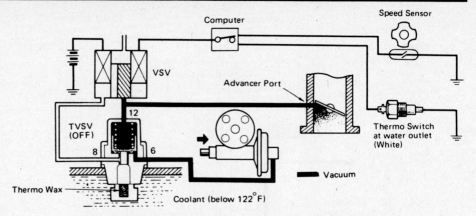

Fig. 92 Transmission Controlled Spark System. 1975 20R engine

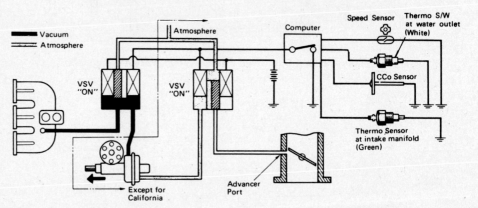

Fig. 93 Transmission Controlled Spark System. 1975-76 4M engine

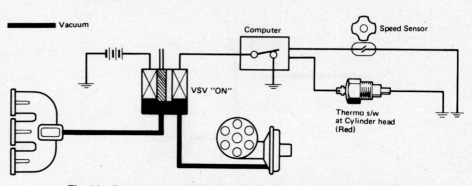

Fig. 94 Transmission Controlled Spark System. 1975-76 2F engine

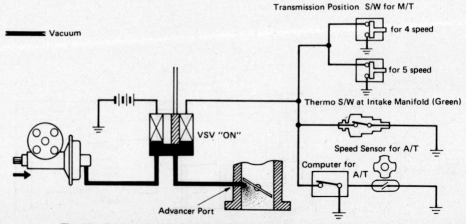

Fig. 95 Transmission Controlled Spark System. 1976 2T-C engine

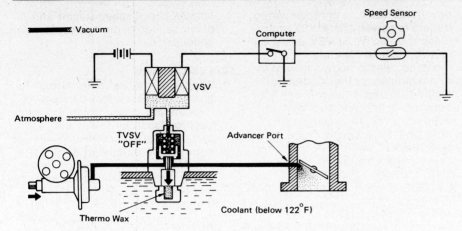

Engine	A (ON)	B (OFF)	C (ON)	D (OFF)
3K–C	140°F	212°F	C is lower than B by 3.6-12.6°F	D is lower than A by 3.6-12.6°F
2T-C, 4M	140°F	221°F		
18R-C	140°F	217°F		
F	140°F	208°F		
F (For California only)	113°F	217°F		

Fig. 97 Thermo switch temperature operating range chart

Fig. 96 Transmission Controlled Spark System. 1976 20R engine

and down as specified according to vehicle speed, the TCS system is operating normally.

1975 20R Engine

1. Check all hoses and wiring for tightness and correct connections. Replace any hoses which are damaged or loose on their fittings. Repair or replace any defective wiring.
2. With engine cold (coolant temperature below 40° F), start engine and check if octane selector moves when throttle valve is opened and closed.
3. If octane selector does not move under the conditions described in step 2, check distributor vacuum advance unit and replace if defective. If distributor vacuum advance unit is not defective, disconnect thermostatic vacuum switching valve (TVSV) #8 hose from Vacuum Switch Valve (VSV), and check if octane selector moves when vacuum is applied to hose. If octane selector moves, replace TVSV. If it does not move, replace VSV.
4. With engine temperature below 40° F, interchange the two hoses on the TVSV which come from the VSV.

Then start engine and check if octane selector moves when throttle valve is quickly opened and closed. If it does not move, proceed to step 5. If it does move, replace TVSV.
5. With engine at normal operating temperature and running, connect #8 hose on TVSV directly to distributor vacuum advance unit, then check if octane selector moves when throttle valve is quickly opened and closed.
6. If octane selector does move under the conditions described under step 5, check if octane selector still moves when thermo switch connector is disconnected. If it does not move, replace the thermo switch. If it does move, check power source at VSV wiring. If there is no power, replace fuse or repair wiring. If there is power, check if air will flow from port #8 to port #6 on TVSV. If air does not flow, replace TVSV. If air does flow, check VSV and replace if defective. If VSV is not defective, replace computer.
7. If octane selector does not move under the conditions described under step 5, connect the #8 hose from the VSV to the TVSV directly to

a vacuum gauge, then place gauge where it can be observed while the vehicle is being driven. While the vehicle is being driven, gradually increase and decrease the speed and check if vacuum reading goes up at 38-44 mph and goes down at 17-33 mph.
8. If vacuum readings do not go up and down as specified under the conditions described in step 7, check the speed sensor and replace speedometer if defective. If speed sensor is not defective, replace computer.
9. Under the conditions described in step 7, if the vacuum readings go up and down as specified according to vehicle speed, the TCS system is operating normally.

1976 20R Engine

1. Check all hoses and wiring for tightness and correct connections. Replace any hoses which are damaged or loose on their fittings. Repair or replace any defective wiring.
2. Disconnect hoses between thermostatic vacuum switching valve (TVSV) and vacuum switching valve (VSV), then with engine temperature below 77° F and running, check if octane selector moves when throttle valve is opened and closed.
3. If octane selector does not move under the conditions described in step 2, check distributor vacuum advance unit and replace if defective. If vacuum advance unit is not defective, replace TVSV.
4. If octane selector does move under the conditions described in step 2, allow engine to reach normal operating temperature, then check if octane selector moves when throttle valve is opened and closed. If it does move, replace TVSV. If it does not move, proceed to step 5.

NOTE: Even if TVSV is operating normally, a small amount of vacuum will be acting on the diaphragm so that a small amount of movement of the octane selector will be noticed.

5. If octane selector does not move under the conditions described in step 4, reconnect the hoses between the TVSV and VSV, then con-

Engine Family	A point (mph)	B point (mph)
3K–C	36±2	11±5
2T–C	41±2	31±5
2T–C M/T (For California only)	41±3	16±3
2T–C A/T (For California only)	65±3	24±3
18R–C	62$^{+6}_{0}$	16±3
18R–C (For California only)	41±2	11±3
4M	62$^{+6}_{0}$	16±3
4M (For California only)	65±3	16±3

Engine Family	A point (mph)	B point (mph)	C point (mph)	D point (mph)
F	13±2	41±2	31±3	9±4
F (For California only)	13±3	41±3	26±8	9±4

Fig. 98 Transmission Controlled Spark System operating range chart

nect a vacuum gauge using a T-fitting between the TVSV and VSV and place gauge where it can be observed while the vehicle is being driven. While the vehicle is being driven, gradually increase and decrease the speed and check if vacuum reading goes up at 38-44 mph and goes down at 17-33 mph.

6. If vacuum readings do not go up and down as specified under the conditions described in step 5, check the power supply at the VSV wiring side. If there is no power supply, replace fuse or repair wiring. If there is power, check the VSV and replace if defective. If VSV is not defective, check the speed sensor and replace speedometer if sensor is defective. If speed sensor is not defective, replace computer.

7. Under the conditions described in step 5, if the vacuum readings go up and down as specified according to vehicle speed, the TCS system is operating normally.

1975-76 4M Engine

1. Check all hoses and wiring for tightness and correct connections. Replace any hoses which are damaged or loose on their fittings. Repair or replace any defective wiring.

2. With engine cold (engine coolant temperature below 40° F), start engine then check if octane selector moves towards advance side when throttle valve is opened and closed.

3. If octane selector does not move under the conditions described in step 2, check distributor vacuum advance unit and replace if defective. If vacuum advance unti is not defective, disconnect connector from thermo sensor and check if octane selector moves toward advance side. If it does, replace thermo sensor. If it still does not move, disconnect VSV connector and again check if octane selector moves towards advance side. If it does not move, replace VSV. If it does move, replace computer.

4. With engine running at normal operating temperature, check if octane selector moves toward retard side when engine is accelerated. If it does, proceed to step 5. If it does not, disconnect thermo sensor connector and check if octane selector moves toward retard side. If it does, replace thermo sensor switch. If it does not move, ground thermo sensor connector and check if octane selector moves toward retard side. If it does, replace thermo sensor. If it does not move, check power source at VSV wiring side. If there is not

power, replace fuse or repair wiring. If there is power, check VSV and replace if defective. If VSV is not defective, replace computer.

5. If octane selector moves toward the retard side under the conditions described in step 4, disconnect hose between distributor and VSV, then connect a vacuum gauge to VSV hose and place gauge where it can be observed while the vehicle is being driven. While driving the vehicle, gradually increase and decrease the speed and check if vacuum reading goes up at 62-68 mph and goes down at 6-10 mph.

6. If vacuum readings do not go up and down as specified under the conditions described in step 5, check the speed sensor and replace speedometer if sensor is defective.

7. Under the conditions described in step 5, if the vacuum readings go up and down as specified according to vehicle speed, the TCS system is operating normally.

1975-76 2F Engine

1. Check all hoses and wiring for tightness and correct connections. Replace any hoses which are damaged or loose on their fittings. Repair or replace any defective wiring.

2. Using an ohmmeter, check thermo switch resistance. Resistance should be zero when engine is cold and infinity when engine is warm. If not, replace thermo switch.

3. Remove distributor cap, then apply vacuum to distributor vacuum advance unit and check if breaker plate moves clockwise. If not, replace distributor vacuum advance unit.

4. Disconnect hose between distributor vacuum advance unit and vacuum switch valve (VSV), then connect a vacuum gauge to VSV and place vacuum gauge where it can be observed while the vehicle is being driven. While driving the vehicle, gradually increase the speed and check if vacuum reading goes up at about 5 mph and goes off at about 38-44 mph. Gradually decrease the speed and check if the vacuum goes on at 17-23 mph and goes off at 7-11 mph.

5. If vacuum readings do go up and down under the conditions described in step 4, the TCS system is operating normally. If vacuum readings do not go up and down as described in step 4, check power source at VSV wiring. If there is no power replace fuse or repair wiring. If there is power, check VSV and replace if defective. If VSV is not de-

fective, check speed sensor and replace speedometer if speed sensor is defective.

1976 2T-C Engine

1. Check all hoses and wiring for tightness and correct connections. Replace any hoses which are damaged or loose on their fittings. Repair or replace any defective wiring.

2. With engine cold, start engine and check if octane selector moves when throttle valve is closed and opened.

3. If octane selector does not move under the conditions described in step 2, check distributor vacuum advance unit and replace if defective. If distributor advance unit is not defective, disconnect and ground the thermo switch connector, and again check if octane selector moves. If it does move, replace thermo switch. If it does not move, check power supply at VSV wiring. If there is no power, replace fuse or repair wiring. On vehicles with manual transmission, if there is power, replace VSV. On vehicles with automatic transmission, if there is power, check VSV and replace if defective. If VSV is not defective, replace computer.

4. With engine running at normal operating temperature, check if octane selector moves when throttle valve is opened and closed.

5. If octane selector does move under the conditions described in step 4, check if octane selector still moves when thermo switch connector is disconnected. If not, replace thermo switch. If it does, check if octane selector still moves when VSV connector is disconnected. If it does, replace VSV. If not, on automatic transmission vehicles, replace computer. If not, on manual transmission vehicles, replace transmission position switch.

6. On manual transmission vehicles, with engine running at normal operating temperature, check if octane selector moves while the throttle is being opened and closed and transmission is shifted in 4th and 5th speed with clutch pedal depressed. If it does, TCS system is operating properly. If it does not, replace transmission position switch.

7. On automatic transmission vehicles, disconnect hose between VSV and distributor, then connect a vacuum gauge to VSV hose and place gauge where it can be observed while the vehicle is being driven. While vehicle is being driven, gradually in-

crease and decrease speed and check if vacuum reading goes up at 62-68 mph and down at 6-10 mph.
8. If vacuum readings do not go up and down as specified under the

conditions described in step 7, check speed sensor and replace speedometer if defective. If speed sensor is not defective, replace computer.

9. Under the conditions described in step 7, if vacuum readings go up and down as specified according to vehicle speed, the TCS system is operating normally.

Clutch & Transmission Section
Clutch & Manual Transmission

CLUTCH PEDAL, ADJUST
Except Corolla KE Series

Clutch Pedal Height
1. Adjust distance from clutch pedal pad to floor board to dimension shown in Fig. 1, by adjusting stopper bolt (3), Fig. 2.

Clutch Pedal Play
1. Adjust clutch pedal play by loosening lock nut (2) and adjusting push rod (1), Fig. 2. Push rod end play should be as shown in Fig. 3.
2. Adjust release fork end play by loosening lock nut (4) and rotating end of push rod (6) while holding push rod (5) nut with a wrench, Fig. 4. Release fork end play should be as shown in Fig. 5.
3. After completing the above adjustment, end play at clutch pedal, Fig. 2, should be as shown in Fig. 6.

Corolla KE Series

Clutch Pedal Height
1. Adjust distance from pedal pad to floor board to 6.65 in. by means of the pedal support bolt and nut, Fig. 7.

Clutch Pedal Free Play
1. From engine compartment side of dash panel, pull upper end of release cable until release bearing contacts clutch diaphragm.
2. Count the number of grooves and crests on clutch cable outer cap between cable inner retainer and E

Model	Year	Height In Inches
Corolla①	1972-74 1975-76 1977	5.5-5.9 6.46 6.65
Celica	1972-77	6.34
Corona	1972-73 1974-77	5.7-6.1 6.34-6.73
Corona Mark II	1972② 1972-76③	6-6.2 6.2-6.6
Hi Lux	Early 1972 Late 1972-77	6.024 6.3

①—TE series.
②—RT series.
③—Mx & RX series.

Fig. 1 Clutch pedal height adjustment chart. Except Corolla KE series

Model	Year	End Play In Inches
Corolla①	1972-74 1975-77	— .020-.197②
Celica	1972-77	.02-.20②
Corona	1972-73 1974-77	.02-.12② .004-.028②
Corona Mark II	1972③ 1972-76④	— .004-.028②
Hi Lux	Early 1972 Late 1972-77	— .02-.12②

①—TE series.
②—Measure at clutch pedal.
③—RT series.
④—MX & RX series.

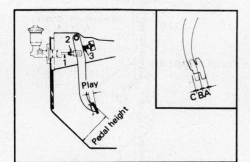

Fig. 2 Clutch pedal height adjustment. Except Corolla KE series

Fig. 3 Clutch pedal free play adjustment chart. Except Corolla KE series

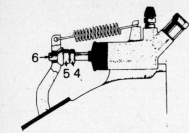

Fig. 4 Clutch release cylinder adjustment. Except Corolla KE series

ring, Fig. 8. E ring should be inserted in groove 5 to 6 grooves and crests away from inner cable retainer.

3. Operate clutch pedal several times, then check to ensure clutch pedal free play is .79 to 1.38 in.

CLUTCH, REPLACE

1. Remove transmission as described under Transmission, Replace.
2. Mark clutch cover and flywheel so they can be installed in the same position.
3. Loosen clutch cover to flywheel attaching bolts one turn at a time until spring tension is relieved, then remove bolts.
4. Remove clutch cover and disc.
5. Remove clutch release bearing and fork from transmission.
6. Reverse procedure to install making sure to index alignment marks.

MANUAL TRANSMISSION, REPLACE

1972 Corona Mark II RT Series

1. Disconnect battery ground cable.
2. Disconnect exhaust pipe from

Model	Year	End Play In Inches
Corolla①	1972-74	—
	1975-77	.079-.138
Celica	1972-77	.08-.12
Corona	1972-73②	.118-.197
	1972-73③	.079-.138
	1974-77	.079-.118
Corona Mark II	1972④⑤	.08-.14
	1972④⑥	.14-.20
	1972-76⑦	.08-.12
Hi Lux	Early 1972	.15
	Late 1972-77	.14-.20

①—TE series.
②—2R engine.
③—8R engine.
④—RT Series.
⑤—Except 2R engine.
⑥—2R engine.
⑦—MX & RX series.

Fig. 5 Clutch release fork end play. Except Corolla KE series

exhaust manifold, then remove exhaust pipe bracket.
3. Remove parking brake equalizer support bracket.
4. Disconnect speedometer cable and backup light switch.
5. Remove shift lever retainer attaching bolts, then pull out shift lever.
6. Remove clutch release cylinder.
7. Mark drive shaft and pinion flanges for reassembly, then remove drive shaft.

NOTE: After removing drive shaft install seal replacer tool in extension housing to prevent leakage.

8. Support transmission using a suitable jack, then remove rear crossmember.

9. Remove clutch housing to engine block attaching bolts, then pull transmission rearward and remove from vehicle.
10. Reverse procedure to install.

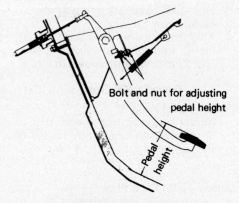

Fig. 7 Clutch pedal height adjustment. Corolla KE series

Models	Year	End Play In Inches
Corolla①	1972-74	.8-1.4
	1975-77	.079-1.58
Celica	1972-77	—
Corona	1972-73	1-1.75
	1974-77	—
Corona Mark II	1972②	.79-1.58
	1972-76③	1.4-2
Hi Lux	Early 1972	1.3
	Late 1972-77	1-2

①—TE series.
②—RT series.
③—MX & RX series.

Fig. 6 Final clutch pedal end play chart. Except Corolla KE series

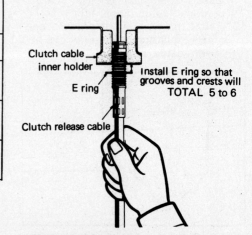

Fig. 8 Clutch release cable adjustment. Corolla KE series

TOYOTA

1972-76 Corona Mark II MX & RX Series

1. Disconnect battery ground cable.
2. Remove air cleaner.
3. Loosen connecting rod from accelerator link rod, then remove link rod.
4. Remove starter, rear cover and clutch release cylinder.
5. Disconnect exhaust pipe from exhaust manifold.
6. Remove flywheel housing under cover and stiffener plates.
7. Remove console, then remove four shift lever retainer attaching screws and pull out shift lever.
8. Disconnect speedometer cable and backup light switch wire connector.
9. Mark drive shaft and pinion flanges for reassembly, then remove drive shaft.

NOTE: After removing drive shaft, install seal replacer tool in extension housing to prevent leakage.

10. Support transmission using a suitable jack, then remove rear crossmember.
11. Lower jack, then position a suitable jack and wooden block under engine and raise front of engine. Place shop towels on rear of valve cover to prevent damage to dash panel.
12. Remove clutch housing to engine attaching bolts, then pull transmission rearward and lower from vehicle.
13. Reverse procedure to install.

1972-77 Corolla

1. Position shift lever in neutral, then remove shift lever boot.
2. Remove shift lever cover attaching screws.
3. Remove snap ring and lift shift lever from housing.
4. Disconnect battery positive cable and backup light switch wire connector.
5. Drain cooling system, then disconnect upper radiator hose.
6. Disconnect bond cable at rear of engine, if equipped.
7. On all except models with 3K-N engine, remove air cleaner.
8. On all models except KC series, remove starter.
9. On all models, position cooling fan horizontally.
10. Disconnect exhaust pipe at exhaust manifold, then remove exhaust pipe clamp bolt from clutch housing.
11. On TE series, remove clutch release cylinder body.
12. On KE series, disconnect clutch cable from release fork and bracket.

13. On all models, disconnect speedometer cable from extension housing.
14. Mark drive shaft and pinion flanges, then remove drive shaft.

NOTE: Insert seal replacer tool into extension housing after removing drive shaft.

15. Support transmission using a suitable jack, then remove engine rear support.
16. On KE series, remove starter mounting bolts.
17. On all models, remove clutch housing to engine mounting bolts, then slide transmission rearward and lower vehicle.
18. Reverse procedure to install.

1972-77 Celica

1. Remove shift boot and shift lever retainer attaching bolts, then lift out shift lever.
2. Disconnect battery ground cable.
3. Drain cooling system, then disconnect upper radiator hose.
4. Remove air cleaner and starter.
5. Disconnect backup light switch wire connector.
6. Disconnect exhaust pipe from exhaust manifold, then remove exhaust pipe clamp.
7. Remove release cylinder and cable.
8. Mark drive shaft and pinion flanges for reassembly, then remove drive shaft.

NOTE: After removing drive shaft install seal replacer tool in extension housing to prevent leakage.

9. Support transmission using a suitable jack, then remove rear crossmember.
10. Lower jack slightly and remove clutch housing attaching bolts.
11. Pull transmission rearward and lower from vehicle.
12. Reverse procedure to install.

1972-77 Corona

1. Disconnect battery ground cable.
2. Drain cooling system, then disconnect upper radiator hose.
3. Disconnect accelerator rod and link rod from engine side of dash panel.
4. Remove clutch release cylinder.
5. Disconnect speedometer cable and backup light switch wire connector.
6. Mark drive shaft and pinion flanges for reassembly, then remove drive shaft.

NOTE: After removing drive shaft,

install seal replacer tool in extension housing to prevent leakage.

7. Disconnect exhaust pipe bracket.
8. Support transmission using a suitable jack, then remove rear crossmember.
9. Lower jack, then remove shift lever retainer bolts and lift out shift lever.

NOTE: Before lowering jack place shop towel on rear of cylinder head cover to prevent damage to firewall.

10. Remove starter.
11. Remove clutch housing to engine block attaching bolts, then pull transmission rearward and lower from vehicle.
12. Reverse procedure to install.

1972-77 Hi Lux

1. Remove shift lever boot retainer and boot.
2. Remove shift lever using tool No. SST-09305-20011.
3. Disconnect battery ground cable.
4. Drain cooling system, then disconnect upper radiator hose.
5. Remove clutch release cylinder hose bracket.
6. Remove accelerator torque rod.
7. Remove starter motor, then remove clutch release cylinder.
8. Disconnect exhaust pipe from exhaust manifold, then remove exhaust pipe bracket and heat insulator, if equipped.
9. Release parking brake, then disconnect parking brake cable from intermediate lever.
10. On models with 18R engine, disconnect control link coupling.
11. Mark drive shaft and pinion flanges for reassembly, then remove drive shaft.

NOTE: After removing drive shaft, install seal replacer tool in extension housing to prevent leakage.

12. Support transmission using a suitable jack, then remove rear crossmember.
13. Lower jack and remove clutch housing to engine block attaching bolts.

NOTE: To prevent oil pan from striking suspension member or EGR valve from striking dash panel, position wooden block and suitable jack under oil pan for support.

14. Pull transmission rearward and lower from vehicle.
15. Reverse procedure to install.

2 Speed Toyoglide Automatic Transmission

TROUBLE SHOOTING GUIDE

Vehicle Does Not Move In Any Range

1. Low oil pressure in low servo and in reverse piston due to worn front oil pump, stuck regulator valve, pump cavitation (low oil level), oil leakage at pump discharge side.
2. Incorrect operation of shift lever due to incorrectly assembled control rod or manual valve lever.
3. Deformed transmission mechanism.

Vehicle Does Not Move In "L" & "D" Ranges

1. Inoperative low servo piston due to worn low servo cylinder or broken piston ring.
2. Inoperative low brake band due to broken low band and/or strut, or abnormal wear of band.

Vehicle Does Not Move In "R" Range

1. Inoperative reverse clutch due to worn clutch disc, damaged reverse piston O-ring or inoperative reverse clutch piston.

Shock During Upshift

1. High forward clutch operating pressure due to stuck regulator valve, incorrectly adjusted regulator valve shim, or stuck throttle relay valve.
2. Stuck throttle valve.
3. Improper operation of orifice control valve.
4. Worn or burned forward clutch disc.
5. Throttle connecting rod too long.

Shock During Downshift

1. High oil pressure in low servo.
2. Seized low band due to incorrectly adjusted low band.
3. Incorrect operation of orifice control valve.
4. Throttle connecting rod to short.

Shock During Shifting Into Gear At Standstill

1. Engine idle speed too high.
2. Excessive backlash in planetary gear unit.
3. Worn universal joint.
4. High oil pressure in low servo and in reverse piston.

Chatter When Starting In "L" & "D" Range

1. Improper operation of low band due to incorrect adjustment of low band, abnormal wear of low servo cylinder.
2. Low oil pressure in low servo.

Chatter When Starting In "R" Range

1. Improper operation of reverse clutch due to worn or burned reverse clutch disc, or improper operation of reverse piston.
2. Low reverse clutch operating pressure.

Slips When Starting In "L" & "D" Range

1. Low oil pressure in low servo.
2. Inproper operation of low servo piston.

Slips When Starting In "R" Range

1. Low reverse clutch operating pressure due to worn front oil pump, improper operation of check valve, or damage reverse piston O-ring.
2. Improper operation reverse clutch.

Slips When Transmission Shifts Into High Range

1. Low forward clutch operating pressure due to worn front and rear pumps, damaged forward clutch outer ring and O-ring, incorrect operation of clutch piston oil check ball.
2. Improper operation of forward multiple disc clutch due to worn clutch disc.

Slips During Down-Shift

1. Low oil pressure in low servo due to worn front oil pump.
1. Improper operation of brake band.
3. Improper operation of throttle relay valve.
4. Improper operation of shift valve.
5. Throttle connecting rod too long.
6. Forward clutch does not release due to seized clutch disc.

Slips During Upshift

1. Low forward clutch operating pressure.
2. Improper operation of forward clutch due to worn clutch disc.

Transmission Does Not Upshift

1. Low forward clutch operating pressure.
2. Forward clutch does not operate due to worn clutch disc.
3. Low governor oil pressure.

4. Improper operation of shift valve.
5. Throttle connecting rod too short.

Transmission Does Not Downshift

1. Low oil pressure in low servo.
2. Improper operation of brake band.
3. Improper operation of shift valve.
4. High oil pressure due to governor valve weight stuck or seized.

Incorrect Shift Points

1. Throttle link connecting rod improperly adjusted.
2. Improper governor oil pressure.
3. Improper operation of shift valve, or throttle valve.
4. Improper operation of throttle relay valve.

Mechanical Noise In Transmission

1. Excessively worn planetary gears.
2. Contact between oil pump gear and crescent.
3. Sliding thrust washer.
4. Sliding oil seal ring.

Oil Pressure System Noise

1. Pump cavitation (air being drawn in and mixed with the oil).
2. Pressure regulator valve vibrating and causing resonance.
3. Oil flow causing noise.

Parking Lock Fails To Engage

1. Improperly adjusted shift lever.
2. Broken parking pawl or lock pawl.

Excessive Fuel Consumption Due To Transmission

1. Improper operation of one-way clutch or stator.
2. Abnormal friction within the transmissin

Oil Leakage

1. Front oil pump body O-ring damaged.
2. Type "T" oil seal damaged.
3. Oil Leaking from oil filler tube due to foaming of oil caused by overfilling, or clogged breather plug.

TRANSMISSION DIAGNOSIS

Road Test

1. Before road testing vehicle, make sure that engine idle speed is set to specifications and that transmission fluid level is correct.

Fig. 1 Oil pressure test ports

2. Start engine and allow transmission oil to reach normal operating temperature of 180-250° F (80 to 120° C).
3. Check shift point variation in comparison with accelerator valve opening as follows:
   a. With selector lever in "D" range drive vehicle with a steady acceleration and record shift points from low to high gear.
   b. Repeat above step with increase acceleration and record shift points.
   c. Repeat above test several times. If shift points vary gradually, transmission is operating satisfactorily.
   d. If shift points fail to vary, check throttle valve, shift valve and throttle relay valve for proper operation. Also check that throttle connecting rod is not adjusted too short.
4. With vehicle speed at 28-31 mph (45-50 kph) and in "D" range, check kickdown operation by depressing accelerator pedal fully. If transmission does not downshift, the throttle connecting rod may be adjusted too long. If transmission downshifts before accelerator pedal is fully depressed, the throttle connecting rod may be adjusted too short.
5. Slow down vehicle to a stop while observing for downshift into first gear. If no downshift is felt, the transmission is operating in low gear. This could be caused by improper operation of governor valve, shift valve or throttle valve.

Oil Pressure Test

1. Make sure the transmission oil level is correct.
2. Chock front wheels and apply parking brake.
3. Raise and support rear of vehicle if necessary to rotate rear wheels.
4. Start engine and allow transmission oil to reach normal operating temperature of 180-250° F (80-120° C).

5. Remove oil plugs and connect a pressure gauge to each port as shown in Fig. 1. The following designations indicate the pressure which each gauge tests:

P_D : Forward Clutch Pressure (low servo piston releasing pressure)

P_L : Low Servo Pressure

P_{GO} : Governor Pressure

P_R : Reverse Multiple Clutch Pressure.

6. Check operation of pressure regulator valve and throttle relay valve by measuring low servo piston operating pressure, and reverse clutch operating pressure at various engine speeds.
7. Measure low servo piston operating pressure with engine idling and transmission in "L" range. Pressure should be greater than 107 psi (7.5 kg/cm²).
8. Measure low servo piston operating pressure with engine idling and transmission in "D" range, then measure reverse clutch operating pressure with engine idling and transmission in "R" range. Both pressure readings should exceed 57 psi (4 kg/cm²).
9. As engine speed is increased gradually, pressure should increase, and when accelerator pedal is fully depressed, the low servo piston and reverse clutch operating pressure should be 121-156 psi (11 kg/cm²).
10. If control pressures are too low in all ranges with engine idling, check the following:
    a. Excessively worn front oil pump.
    b. Weak pressure regulator spring.
    c. Improper operation of pressure regulator valve.
    d. Front oil pump cavitation (drawing air).
    e. Improper operation of throttle pressure check valve or relay valve.
    f. Oil leakage in vacuum line and pressure line.
11. If control pressures are too low with throttle valve fully opened, check the following.
    a. Improper operation of pressure regulator valve or relay valve.
    b. Oil leakage in vacuum line and pressure line.
12. If control pressures are slightly too high or too low with throttle valve fully opened, adjust by using pressure regulator valve shims. One .039 inch (1mm) additional shim will lower control pressure about 7 psi

Output Shaft rpm	Vehicle Speed Km/h (mph)	Governor Pressure kg/cm² (Psi)	
		RT, TE	KE
1000	Approx. 25 (16)	1.7~2.5 (24.2~35.6)	1.8~2.6 (25.6~37.0)
1800	Approx. 45 (28)	2.9~3.7 (41.2~52.6)	2.8~3.6 (39.8~51.2)
3500	Approx. 90 (56)	4.8~5.6 (68.3~79.6)	5.2~6.0 (73.9~85.3)

Fig. 2 Governor pressure chart

(.5 kg/cm²). Shims are available in thicknesses of .039 inch (1mm) and .012 inch (.3 mm).
13. Check operation of governor valve and weights by measuring governor pressure at various vehicle speeds as follows:
    a. Raise and support vehicle so that the rear wheels are free to rotate freely.
    b. Shift selector lever to "D" range, then depress accelerator pedal and note governor pressure. Governor pressure should be as shown in chart in Fig. 2.
    c. If governor pressure is too low at all speeds, check for weak governor valve springs, improper operation of governor weights, or excessively worn rear oil pump.
14. If governor pressure does not rise at all, check for defective E-ring on governor, or stick governor weights.

Stall Test

NOTE: This test is performed in "L," "D" and "R" ranges at full throttle to check engine performance, converter clutch operation and holding capabilities of the forward clutch, reverse clutch and low band. When performing this test, do not hold throttle completely opened for more than 5 seconds at a time.

1. Chock all wheels and apply parking brake.
2. Connect tachometer and start engine.
3. Shift selector lever through all the ranges, and at each range accelerate engine speed gradually while observing engine speed. When the engine speed becomes constant, it has reached its stall point. This speed should be the same in all ranges, and should be 1800-2100 for TE and 1900-2100 for RT and KE.
4. If stall speed is the same in each range, but is below 1950 rpm, check the following:
    a. Engine is not operating properly. Also make sure that carburetor throttle valve is opening com-

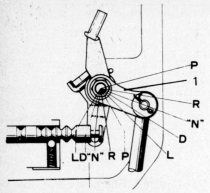

Fig. 3 Manual valve and rod outer lever

Fig. 4 Floor shift lever adjustment

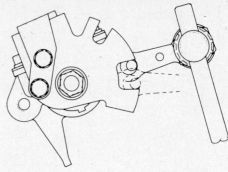

Fig. 5 Column shift lever adjustment

pletely in relation with accelerator pedal.

b. Torque converter stator one-way clutch is slipping.

5. If stall speed exceeds specifications, band or clutch slippage is indicated. Excessive engine speeds in "L" and "D" range indicate low band slippage. Excessive engine speed in "R" indicates reverse clutch slippage.

6. If stall speeds are the same in each range, but are above 1800 rpm and discharge pressure from front oil pump is normal, and there is no slippage indicated, check the following:

a. Oil circulation to converter has stopped.

b. Aeration of oil has occurred, due to overheating.

IN VEHICLE ADJUSTMENTS

Manual Linkage, Adjust

Shift Lever

1. Place manual valve control rod outer lever (1) to "N" position, Fig. 3.

2. Position shift lever pin to "N" position stop of detent plate by loosening lock nut on control rod swivel (2), Fig. 4, and adjust length of control rod.

3. To check adjustment, operate lever through all positions to make cer-

tain that manual lever on transmission is fully in detent in all ranges. Readjust if necessary.

Control Rod (RT)

1. Place manual valve control outer lever to N position, then set selector lever pointer to "N" position by loosening lock nut on connecting rod swivel and adjusting length of control rod.

2. The relationship between the control rod shaft lever and retainer should be set properly so that clearance between lever pin and upper stopper in "N" range is equal to clearance between lever pin and lower stopper in "L" range, Fig. 5. To adjust, loosen lock nut on control shaft lever stop pin and rotate stop pin.

Throttle Linkage, Adjust

1. Place carburetor throttle valve in wide open position.

2. Loosen turnbuckle nuts, at each end of throttle linkage, Fig. 5.

3. Adjust length of connecting rod so that throttle link indicator aligns with mark on side of transmission case, Fig. 7.

4. Tighten turnbuckle locknuts, then make sure that link indicator aligns with mark on side of transmission case when throttle valve is completely opened.

5. Road test vehicle, and readjust if necessary.

Low Servo Brake Band, Adjust

1. Lower rear end of transmission.

2. Loosen lock nut, then tighten anchor bolt firmly and loosen it exactly 3½ turns.

3. While holding anchor bolt, tighten lock nut to 17-22 ft. lbs. (2.3-3.1 m-kg).

IN VEHICLE REPAIRS

Valve Body & Low Servo Piston

1. Raise and support vehicle.

2. Drain transmission fluid and remove oil pan.

3. Remove detent spring seat, spring and ball. Use care to avoid losing ball.

4. Remove valve body and strainer retaining bolts. If valve body is difficult to remove, move manual valve lever to its extreme outward end and disconnect if from manual valve, then using a mallet tap valve body lightly and remove.

5. Remove throttle pressure check ball and low servo piston.

6. Reverse procedure to install, while observing the following precautions. Make sure to align groove of low servo piston rod with end of low brake band apply strut, then install low servo piston. Use a feeler gauge to prevent piston from falling. Also secure pressure check ball to case using multi-purpose grease. Before installing valve body, remove transmission dust cover and move manual valve lever towards its outer extreme so that valve body does not contact manual valve lever. Torque valve body bolts and oil pan bolts to 3-5 ft. lbs. (.4-.7 m-kg).

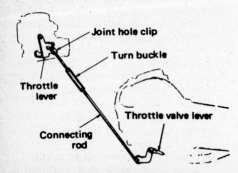

Fig. 6 Throttle linkage adjustment

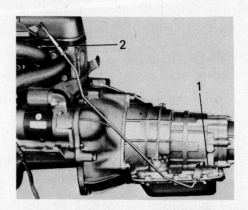

Fig. 7 Throttle linkage adjustment

Governor Valve & Rear Oil Pump

1. Lower rear end of transmission.
2. Remove extension housing retaining bolts and extension housing.
3. Remove shaft snap ring, speedometer drive gear and woodruff key.
4. Loosen lock nut and remove governor body retaining screw, then lock output shaft by shifting manual valve control lever to "P" range and remove governor valve shaft retaining E-ring.
5. Remove governor valve shaft and valve, then remove governor body.
6. Remove oil pump retaining bolts, then remove oil pump body, gears, pin and rear oil pump plate.
7. Reverse procedure to install. Torque pump attaching bolts to 8-11 ft. lbs. (1-1.6 m-kg and lock nut to 6-9 ft. lbs. (.8-1.2 m-kg).

TRANSMISSION, REPLACE

1. Drain engine coolant, then disconnect radiator inlet hose.
2. Remove air cleaner and heater hose clamp from engine.
3. Disconnect throttle link connecting rod from accelerator bellcrank.
4. Loosen exhaust pipe flange retaining nuts.
5. Disconnect oil cooler lines from retaining clamps.
6. Raise and support vehicle.
7. Drain transmission fluid and remove propeller shaft.
8. Disconnect exhaust pipe from support bracket at transmission, then disconnect front exhaust pipe from center exhaust pipe.
9. Disconnect transmission control rod throttle link connecting rod and speedometer cable from transmission.
10. Using a suitable jack, and a wooden block, support transmission lightly, then remove the crossmember retaining bolts and crossmember.
11. Disconnect oil cooler lines. Make sure to use a back-up wrench to avoid twisting lines.
12. Remove transmission-to-converter housing attaching bolts, then move transmission rearward to remove.

NOTE: Place a suitable container under converter housing to catch the oil which will flow out of the converter as the transmission is removed. Also, use care to avoid damaging the front oil pump seal.

13. Remove the six converter retaining bolts through hole provided in rear end plate, then remove torque converter.
14. Remove converter housing, if necessary.
15. Reverse procedure to install. Make sure to align pump drive keys of pump impeller with key holes of pump drive gear. Torque converter-to-flexplate bolts to 8-11 ft. lbs. (1-1.6 m-kg), transmission housing-to-engine bolts to 37-50 ft. lbs. (5-7 m-kg) and transmission-to-housing bolts to 14-22 ft. lbs. (1.9-3.1 m-kg).

3 Speed (A30) Toyoglide Automatic Transmission

TROUBLE SHOOTING GUIDE

Vehicle Does Not Move In Any Forward Range

1. Extremely low oil discharge pressure from front oil pump.
2. Pressure regulator valve frozen.
3. Improper operation of manual shift linkage.
4. Locked by parking lock pawl.
5. Fluid insufficient.
6. Front clutch does not operate.

Vehicle Does Not Move In "R" Range

1. Rear clutch does not operate.
2. Rear band does not operate.

Transmission Does Not Shift From First To Second

1. 1-2 shift valve does not operate.
2. Governor valve does not operate.
3. Throttle valve does not operate.
4. Front band does not operate.

Transmission Does Not Shift From Second To Third

1. 2-3 shift valve does not operate.
2. Governor valve does not operate.
3. Throttle valve does not operate.
4. Extremely high throttle modulator pressure.
5. Rear clutch does not operate.

Transmission Does Not Shift From Third To Second

1. Extremely high governor pressure.
2. 2-3 shift valve does not operate.
3. Governor valve does not operate.
4. Throttle valve does not operate.
5. Front band does not operate.
6. Extremely low throttle modulator pressure.

Transmission Does Not Shift From Second To First

1. Extremely high governor pressure.
2. 1-2 shift valve does not operate.
3. Governor valve does not operate.
4. Throttle valve does not operate.

Incorrect Shift Points

1. Fluid insufficient
2. 1-2 shift valve does not operate.
3. 2-3 shift valve does not operate.
4. Throttle modulator valve does not operate.
5. Maladjustment of throttle connecting rod.
6. Governor pressure is abnormal.
7. Throttle pressure is abnormal.
8. Throttle modulator pressure is abnormal.
9. Line pressure is abnormal.
10. Improper operation of throttle check ball.

Shock During Upshifts & Downshifts In All Ranges

1. High engine idling
2. High line pressure.
3. Power train excessive backlash.

Shock During Upshift Or Downshift to Second Gear In "D" or "2" Range

1. High line pressure.
2. Excessive wear of front band.
3. Improper operation of orifice control valve.

Shock During Upshift From Second To Third

1. High line pressure.
2. Improper operation of orifice control valve.

Shock During Downshift To First Gear

1. Improper operation of one-way clutch.

Slips When Starting In Any Forward Range

1. Fluid insufficient
2. Improper operation of front oil pump.
3. Improper operation of pressure regulator valve.
4. Improper operation of front clutch.
5. Improper operation of one-way clutch. ("D" or "2" range).

Slips When Starting Or Driving In "R" Range

1. Fluid insufficient.

TOYOTA

Fig. 1 Front oil pump and rear oil pump pressure test ports

2. Improper operation of front oil pump.
3. Improper operation of rear clutch.
4. Improper operation of rear band.

Slips In "D" Or Second Speed Range

1. Improper operation of front clutch.
2. Improper operation of front band.

Slips In Third Speed

1. Improper operation of front clutch.
2. Improper operation of rear clutch.

Slips During Engine Braking

1. Improper operation of rear band. (at Low range shift).
2. Improper operation of front band. (at second range shift)

Slips During Hard Acceleration

1. Fluid insufficient.
2. Low throttle pressure.
3. Improper operation of throttle relay valve.
4. Maladjustment of shift control rod.

Metallic Noise

1. Excessive play due to worn planetary gears.
2. Excessive wear of oil pump gears and other related parts.
3. Turbine runner of torque converter hits the case.
4. Maladjusting of parking rod.

Noisy Oil Pressure System

1. Air sucked in oil pump suction side and is mixed with oil.
2. Pressure regulator valve vibrates and causes resonance.
3. Oil leakage in line pressure passage.

Poor Acceleration

1. Engine misses.
2. Maladjusting of throttle connecting rod.
3. Improper operation of one-way clutch.
4. Improper grade Automatic Transmission fluid.

Oil Leakage From Front Of Transmission

1. Front oil pump body "O" ring damaged.
2. Front oil pump body Type "T" oil seal or bushing damaged.
3. Improper installation of front oil pump body.
4. Engine rear oil seal damaged.
5. Torque converter damaged.

Leakage From Transmission Housing

1. Loose bolts and nuts.
2. Damaged gasket.
3. Improper installation of union bolts and test plugs.
4. Damaged oil seal.
5. Excessive fluid.

TRANSMISSION DIAGNOSIS
Preliminary

Make sure that front wheels are chocked securely. Make sure that transmission is filled to the specified level with the recommended transmission fluid, and that transmission fluid is up to operating temperature 176-248° F (80°-120° C).

Oil Pressure Test

1. Check front oil pump pressures with transmission in each range.
2. Block front and rear wheels and apply parking brake.
3. Check that transmission throttle lever will set against stamped mark on transmission case when carburetor throttle is fully opened.
4. Connect a 300-400 psi pressure gauge to front oil pump pressure hole Fig. 1.
6. Start engine. Shift transmission in Drive range and read pressure when throttle valve is fully opened. Repeat this for 2nd and Low ranges. Oil pump pressures should be 128-156 psi (9-11 kg/cm²).

NOTE: Do not perform test for more than 5 seconds at any one time. Also, do not shift transmission when throttle valve is wide open.

7. If oil pressures are high in all ranges, check the following:
   a. Pressure regulator out of adjustment or not operating.
   b. Throttle valve improperly adjusted.
8. If oil pressures are lower than specified, check the following:
   a. Defective front oil pump.

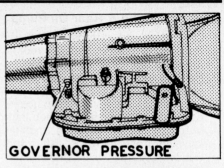

Fig. 2 Governor pressure test port

   b. Pressure regulator out of adjustment or not operating.
   c. Throttle valve improperly adjusted.
9. If low pressures are obtained in only certain ranges, it indicates a large fluid leak in the hydraulic circuit of the range concerned.
10. If low pressures are obtained in Drive and 2nd ranges, it indicates an overstroke of front clutch piston due to burnt or worn out front clutch.
11. Start engine, then while maintaining speed at 1800-2000 rpm, shift successively into Reverse, Neutral and Park ranges and note oil pressure readings.

NOTE: Do not test transmission in Reverse range for more than 5 seconds.

12. If low oil pressures are obtained in Reverse, Neutral and Park ranges, it indicates an overstroke of rear servo piston due to burnt or worn rear brake band.
13. If low oil pressures are obtained in Reverse range only, it indicates an overstroke of rear clutch piston.
14. Raise rear wheels of ground and support vehicle on stands.
15. Connect a pressure gauge to rear oil pump pressure test port, Fig. 1.
16. Shift transmission into Drive, while maintaining engine speed at 2000-2200 rpm. Rear oil pump pressure should be 71-89.6 psi (5-6.3 kg/cm²).
17. Low rear oil pump pressures indicate a defective rear oil pump or overstroke of rear clutch piston.
18. Connect pressure gauge to governor test pressure port, Fig. 2, and measure governor pressures at output shaft speeds or vehicle speeds specified in chart in Fig. 3.

Stall Test

1. Make sure that front wheels are chocked and that parking brake is applied securely. Make sure that transmission is filled to the specified level with the recom-

Velocity	Velocity (km/h) [mph]							Governor Pressures (kg/cm²) (psi)
Output (rpm) \ Series Ratio	MS · RS		RT			TA		
	4.111	4.375	3.700	3.900	4.111	4.111	4.375	
1000	28 [18]	27 [17]	29 [18]	27 [17]	26 [16]	26 [16]	25 [16]	1.6 ∿2.1 (23 ∿30)
1800	51 [32]	48 [30]	52 [33]	50 [31]	47 [29]	48 [30]	45 [28]	2.4 ∿3.0 (34 ∿43)
3500	100 [63]	94 [59]	103 [64]	97 [61]	93 [58]	94 [59]	88 [55]	5.8 ∿7.0 (83 ∿100)

Fig. 3 Governor pressure chart

mended fluid, and that transmission fluid is up to operating temperatures of 176-248° F (80-120° C).

2. Check movement of accelerator and throttle linkage and adjust if necessary.

3. Shift selector lever through all ranges, and at each range accelerate engine speed gradually while observing engine speed. When the engine speed becomes constant, it has reached its stall speed. Refer to chart in Fig. 4, for stall speeds according to engine and converter application.

4. If stall speeds are the same in all ranges but are lower than specifications, check the following:
   a. Engine lacks power.
   b. Stator weight clutch not operating properly.

5. If stall speeds are higher than specifications in the forward ranges, check the following:
   a. Worn or burnt front clutch disc.
   b. Low line pressure.
   c. Defective transmission one-way clutch.

6. If stall speeds are higher than specified in Reverse range, check the following:
   a. Worn or burned rear clutch disc.
   b. Worn or burned rear brake band.
   c. Line pressure too low.

Road Test

1. Start moving vehicle with accelerator pedal opened ¼ of total opening, and record road speed at which the upshift takes place as the vehicle speed increases. Repeat this test several times, and each time start moving vehicle with accelerator pedal depressed ¼ as

great as the previous time. Check upshift speed with chart in Fig. 5.

2. If upshift points fail to vary in ratio to vehicle speed, then throttle link connecting rod is out of adjustment or the throttle valve 2-3 shift valve, 1-2 shift valve or govenor valve is defective.

3. Refering to chart in Fig. 6, check that when vehicle speed reaches A and B points with throttle valve opened about ²/₄, kickdown will occur and transmission will downshift to second or first gear.

4. Drive vehicle in D or 2 range at speed above the C point, then shift to Low range and check that after entering into the 2nd range, the downshift to L range will occur when C point is reached.

5. If vehicle shift points are not within specifications, check the following:
   a. Adjust throttle valve lever pointer so that it sets against the stamped mark on the transmission, using care not to deform pointer.
   b. If shift speeds are too high, adjust to pull back throttle lever.
   c. If shift speeds are too low, adjust to push throttle lever.
   d. If shift speeds do not vary according to throttle opening, check for improper operation of governor valve, throttle valve, 1-2 shift valve or 2-3 shift valve.

IN VEHICLE ADJUSTMENTS
Manual Linkage, Adjust
Floor Shift, Fig. 7
1. Check control rod bushings and

shafts and replace if damaged or worn.

2. Loosen control rod to shaft swivel.

3. Place transmission manual lever in Neutral and shift control lever in Neutral.

4. Tighten swivel nut with detent plate hitting against pin.

5. Check shift lever for proper operation. Make sure that it moves freely and that each range is properly indicated.

6. Adjust parking lock rod, Fig. 8, as follows:
   a. Shift manual lever shaft to Park position.
   b. Loosen the two nuts at parking lock rod swivel.
   c. Turn parking lock shaft, and when parking lock roller is pressed against parking lock pawl and parking lock pawl is striking against bottom of governor body support gear, tighten parking lock rod swivel nuts.

NOTE: Turn output shaft in both directions to make sure parking pawl locks governor support.

   d. Shift transmission to Reverse and turn output shaft to make sure that parking lock pawl does not interfere with the governor support.
   e. Shift transmission to Park, then attempt to rotate output shaft to make sure that lock pawl will not disengage from governor support.

Column Shift
1. Check control rod bushrings and

Engine Model	Torque converter classifi	Stall (rpm)
2M	248ϕ2	2,100 ± 100
4M	248ϕ1	2,000 ± 100
M	248ϕ1	2,050 ± 100
5R	248ϕ2	2,050 ± 100
18R	248ϕ2	2,050 ± 100
8R	248ϕ2	2,000 ± 150
6R	248ϕ2	1,850 ± 150
2T	248ϕ3	2,050 ± 150

Fig. 4 Stall test chart

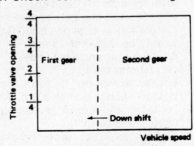

Fig. 5 Upshift graph

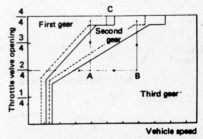

Fig. 6 Upshift graph

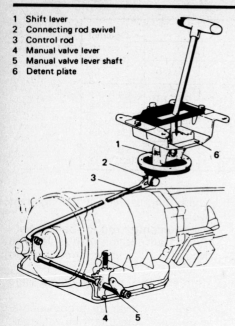

1 Shift lever
2 Connecting rod swivel
3 Control rod
4 Manual valve lever
5 Manual valve lever shaft
6 Detent plate

7 Control shaft lever LH
8 Parking rock rod
9 Parking rock rod swivel
10 Nut

Fig. 7 Floor shift lever adjust

shafts and replace if worn or damaged.

2. Loosen connecting rod swivel locknut and move shift lever to make sure that position indicator shows the ranges corresponding to shift lever movement. Also, make sure that position indicator is pointing to Neutral range when control shaft lever is at Neutral position.

3. Place transmission manual lever to Neutral and adjust length of control first rod so that control position indicator will be pointing to Neutral position, then tighten lock nut at connecting rod swivel.

4. Adjust parking lock rod as described for Floor Shift models.

IN VEHICLE REPAIRS
Valve Body

1. Drain transmission fluid and remove oil pan.
2. Remove the line pressure tubes, front oil strainer and rear oil strainer.
3. Remove valve body bolts and valve body, gasket and spacer plate.

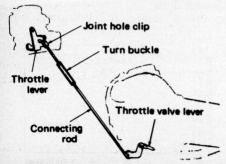

Fig. 10 Throttle linkage adjustment

Joint hole clip
Turn buckle
Throttle lever
Throttle valve lever
Connecting rod

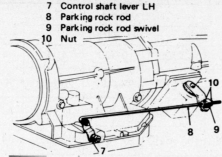

Fig. 8 Parking rod adjust

NOTE: Use care to avoid losing the oil check valves, compression springs and shift restrict ball.

4. Reverse procedure to install.

Throttle Linkage, Adjust, Figs. 9 & 10

With throttle valve wide open, the lever pointer should be aligned with stamped marking on case, Fig. 11. If not aligned, adjust as follows:

1. Loosen turnbuckle nuts and disconnect throttle link connecting second rod from carburetor.

NOTE: T engines have a throttle link connecting rod instead of a turnbuckle.

2. Adjust turnbuckle so that throttle link connecting rod first (throttle link connecting rod end on T engines) will be aligned with hole at carburetor when throttle valve lever pointer is set against stamped mark on case.
3. Fully open throttle valve and check that throttle valve lever pointer sets against the stamped mark on the case, Fig. 11.
4. Road test vehicle and check for proper shift points.

Front & Rear Bands, Adjust

1. To adjust front band:
   a. Drain transmission fluid and remove oil pan.
   b. Using a screwdriver, pry apply lever towards the band apply side and measure gap between end of piston rod and apply bolt. Gap should be .118 inch (3 mm).
   c. Adjust by turning apply bolt.
2. To adjust rear band:
   a. Loosen anchor bolt lock nut, then tighten anchor bolt to 3.6 ft. lbs. (.5 kg/cm and loosen anchor bolt exactly one turn.
   b. Tighten lock nut while holding anchor bolt from turning.

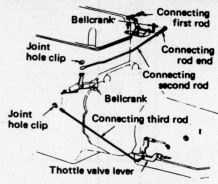

Bellcrank
Connecting first rod
Joint hole clip
Connecting rod end
Connecting second rod
Bellcrank
Joint hole clip
Connecting third rod
Thottle valve lever

Fig. 9 Throttle linkage adjustment

Front & Rear Servos

1. Drain transmission fluid and remove oil pan.
2. Remove oil pressure tube (s).
3. Remove servo retaining bolts, then remove servo and apply strut.

NOTE: Do not intermix the front servo apply strut with rear servo apply strut as they differ. Also, one of the rear servo apply bolts is also the center support bolt.

4. Reverse procedure to install.

TRANSMISSION, REPLACE

1. Disconnect battery ground cable, then drain cooling system and disconnect radiator upper hose.
2. Remove air cleaner and accelerator torque rod with torque rod support attached.
3. Raise entire vehicle and support on jackstands.
4. Disconnect exhaust pipe from manifold and remove flywheel cover.
5. Drain transmission fluid, then disconnect oil cooler tube clamps and tubes from transmission.
6. Disconnect shift control rods, throttle link connecting rods and speedometer from transmission.
7. Disconnect parking brake pull rod from intermediate lever, then remove return spring and lever from support bracket. Remove parking brake cable from crossmember.
8. Remove propeller shaft.
9. Support transmission with a suit-

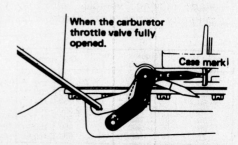

When the carburetor throttle valve fully opened.

Case mark

Fig. 11 Throttle valve lever and pointer

able jack and wooden block placed between transmission and jack, then remove engine mounting rear support.

10. Remove torque converter to drive plate bolts, then slowly lower the jack and remove the oil filler tube and transmission to engine bolts.

11. Carefully lower transmission and remove it using care not to drop converter.

12. Reverse procedure to install.

3 Speed (A40) Automatic Transmission

TROUBLE SHOOTING GUIDE

Vehicle Does Not Move In Any Forward Range

1. Incorrect shift linkage adjustment.
2. Valve body malfunction.
3. Defect in front clutch piston or front clutch.
4. Defect in No. 2 one-way clutch.

Vehicle Does Not Move in Reverse Range

1. Incorrect shift linkage adjustment.
2. Defect in valve body and/or primary regulator.
3. Defect in oil pump.
4. Defect in rear clutch components.
5. Brake No. 3 pistons.

Vehicle Does Not Move In Any Range

1. Incorrect shift linkage adjustment.
2. Parking lock pawl not disengaging.
3. Defective torque converter.
4. Defect in clutches, brake bands or planetary gear.
5. Defect in valve body.
6. Defective oil pump.
7. Internal leakage in transmission.

Vehicle Moves Either Forward Or Rearward With Shift Lever In Neutral

1. Incorrect shift linkage adjustment.
2. Defect in manual valve in valve body.
3. Defect in front clutch (vehicles which move forward).
4. Defect in rear clutch (vehicles which move rearward).

Harsh Engagement Into Any Range

1. Improper throttle cable adjustment.
2. Defective accumulator pistons, seals and/or springs.
3. Defect in valve body primary valve.
4. Defect in valve body pressure relief valve.

Screeching Or Whining Sound Which Increases With Engine Speed

1. Broken converter drive plate.
2. Defect in oil pump.

3. Internal transmission damage.

CAUTION: Do not operate engine when transmission is making noise, as additional serious damage can result to transmission.

Knocking, Metallic Or Grinding Noises

CAUTION: Do not operate engine when transmission is making noises, as additional serious damage can result.

1. Broken converter drive plate.
2. Defective torque converter.
3. Defective one-way clutches.
4. Defective planetary gears.
5. Worn bushings.
6. Defective oil pump.

Intermittent Squawk

CAUTION: Do not operate engine when transmission is making noises, as additional serious damage can result.

1. Broken converter drive plate.
2. Defective clutch plates and brake discs.

Delayed Upshifts, Downshifts From 3rd To 2nd & Then Shifts Back To Third

1. Incorrect throttle cable adjustments.
2. Throttle cam and cable not operating smoothly.
3. Defective governor, or obstructed governor oil passages.
4. Primary regulator and pressure relief valve.
5. Secondary regulator and throttle valve.

Slips During 1-2 Upshift

1. Manual linkage incorrectly adjusted.
2. Incorrectly adjusted throttle cable.
3. Defective primary regulator.
4. Internal transmission damage.
5. Defective one-way clutch.
6. Defective No. 2 brake piston O-ring.

Slips On 2-3 Upshift

1. Manual linkage incorrectly adjusted.
2. Throttle cable incorrectly adjusted.
3. Defective primary regulator and pressure relief valve.
4. Defective oil pump oil seals.
5. Defective rear clutch.
6. Defective center support oil seal rings.
7. Defective valve body.

Drag, Binding Or Tie-Up On 1-2 Shift

1. Manual linkage incorrectly adjusted.
2. Defective primary regulator and pressure relief valve.
3. Defective oil pump.
4. Defective brake No. 3 components.
5. Internal transmission failure.
6. Valve body leakage past seals or gaskets, or sticking valves.
7. Defective No. 2 one-way clutch.
8. Accumulator pistons, seals and/or springs.

Drag, Binding Or Tie-Up On 2-3 Shift

1. Manual linkage incorrectly adjusted.
2. Primary regulator and pressure relief valve.
3. Defective oil pump.
4. Defective rear clutch.
5. Valve body leakage past seals, or sticking valves.
6. Defective one-way No. 1 clutch.
7. Brake No. 2 defective.

Slip, Squawk Or Shudder On Full Throttle Acceleration In Forward Gears

1. Manual linkage incorrectly adjusted.
2. Throttle cable incorrectly adjusted.
3. Defect in primary regulator and throttle valve.
4. Defective oil pump.
5. Internal transmission pressure leakage.
6. Defective front clutch assembly.
7. Defective valve body.
8. Defective one-way clutch No. 2.

Slip, Squawk Or Shudder On Acceleration In Reverse

1. Manual linkage incorrectly adjusted.
2. Defective rear clutch.
3. Defective brake No. 3.
4. Sticking valve body valves.
5. Defective primary regulator and pressure relief valve.
6. Defective oil pump.
7. Rear clutch piston leakage.

Harsh Upshift

1. Throttle cable incorrectly adjusted.
2. Defective throttle cam and/or cable.
3. Defective accumulator pistons, seals or springs.
4. Defective clutch and/or brakes.
5. Defective sequence valves.
6. Primary regulator and throttle valve.

No Coast Downshift

1. Defective governor.
2. Defective downshift plug.
3. Defective detent regulator valve.

No Kickdown From Any Gear Or Kickdown Occurs Above Specified Speed

1. Incorrect throttle cable adjustment.
2. Defective governor.
3. Defective downshift plug.
4. Defective detent regulator valve.

No Engine Braking In 2nd Range

1. Defective intermediate modulator valve.
2. Defective brake No. 1.

Coast Downshift Occurs Too Early Or Too Late

1. Defective throttle cable, or throttle cable is incorrectly adjusted.
2. Defective governor.
3. Defective low coast shift valve.
4. Defective clutch and brake pistons.
5. Defective primary regulator and throttle valve.
6. Defective pressure relief valve.
7. Defective oil pump or leaking seals.
8. Internal transmission pressure leakage.

Vehicle Does Not Hold In Park

1. Manual linkage incorrectly adjusted.
2. Defective parking lock pawl, cam and/or spring.

Stall Speed Higher Than Specified With Clutch Or Brake Squawk In Drive Range

1. Incorrect throttle cable adjustment.

(continued)

2. Defective primary regulator and pressure relief valve.
3. Defective oil pump.
4. Defective front clutch piston.

Stall Speed Higher Than Specified With Clutch Or Brake Squawk In Reverse Range

1. Incorrect throttle cable adjustment.
2. Primary regulator and throttle valve.
3. Defective oil pump.
4. Defective rear clutch.
5. Defective brake No. 3.

Time Lag Between Neutral To Drive Is Excessive

1. Incorrect manual linkage adjustment.
2. Defective primary regulator valve.
3. Defective oil pump and/or seals.
4. Defective front clutch piston.
5. Defective valve body.

Time Lag Between Neutral To Reverse Is Excessive

1. Incorrect manual linkage adjustment.
2. Incorrect line pressure.
3. Defective primary valve.
4. Defective brake No. 3 pistons.
5. Defective rear clutch pistons.
6. Defective oil pump and/or seals.
7. Defective rear clutch.
8. Defective valve body.

Incorrect Governor Pressure

1. Defective governor.
2. Defective governor valve in valve body.
3. Defective primary regulator and/or pressure relief valve.
4. Defective oil pump and/or seals.
5. Defective oil seal rings on output shaft.

Line Pressure Higher Than Normal In All Ranges

1. Incorrect throttle cable adjustment.
2. Defective throttle cable or cam.
3. Defective primary regulator valve and throttle valve.

Line Pressure Lower Than Normal In All Ranges

1. Defective throttle and primary regulator valve.
2. Defective oil pump.

Line Pressure Lower Than Normal In Drive

1. Defective front clutch.
2. Obstruction in front clutch circuit of valve body.

3. Obstruction in lower valve body ports.

Line Pressure Lower Than Normal In Reverse

1. Defective rear clutch.
2. Defective brake No. 3.
3. Defective center support seal rings.
4. Defective oil pump.
5. Defective rear clutch sequence valve in valve body.
6. Defective brake No. 3 sequence valve.

IN-VEHICLE ADJUSTMENTS

Throttle Cable, Adjust

1. Remove air cleaner, then push connecting rod to check if throttle valve opens completely. If not, correct by the adjusting link.
2. To adjust throttle cable, loosen the adjustment nuts enough so that cable housing can be adjusted.
3. Fully depress accelerator pedal to open throttle valve, then adjust cable housing so that distance between end of housing and stopper collar is 2.05 inches (52 mm).
4. Tighten the adjustment nuts and recheck adjustment.

Shift Linkage, Adjust

1. Check linkage for freedom of operation.
2. Loosen adjustment nut on linkage, then push manual valve lever fully toward front of vehicle.
3. Return manual valve lever three detent positions which is Neutral.
4. While an assistant holds the selector lever inside vehicle in Neutral, tighten the nut securely.
5. Check transmission operation in all ranges.

ROAD TEST

NOTE: Before road testing vehicle, make sure that transmission is at normal operating temperature, and that oil level is up to specifications. Also make sure that throttle linkage and shift linkage are properly adjusted.

1. Place shift lever in DRIVE position and drive vehicle at full throttle from a standing start and observe road speeds at which transmission shifts. Refer to chart in Fig. 1, for correct shift points according to differential gear ratio.
2. Place shift lever in DRIVE position and drive vehicle at approximately half throttle and observe road

DIFF GEAR RATIO	"D" RANGE THROTTLE FULL OPEN	
	1 - 2	2 - 3
4.111	30-39 mph 48-62 kph	54-63 mph 86-101 kph
3.900	32-41 mph 51-65 kph	56-66 mph 90-106 kph
3.700	33-43 mph 53-68 kph	59-69 mph 95-111 kph

Fig. 1   Upshift chart

DIFF GEAR RATIO	"D" RANGE HALF THROTTLE (NOMINAL SPEEDS)	
	1 - 2	2 - 3
4.111	23 mph 38 kph	47 mph 75 kph
3.900	24 mph 40 kph	48 mph 78 kph
3.700	36 mph 57 kph	52 mph 83 kph

Fig. 2   Upshift chart

DIFF GEAR RATIO	3 — 1 DOWNSHIFT
4.111	6 to 8 mph 8 to 12 kph
3.900	7 to 9 mph 9 to 14 kph
3.700	8 to 10 mph 11 to 16 kph

Fig. 3   Downshift chart

DIFF GEAR RATIO	"D" RANGE KICKDOWN SPEEDS	
	3 - 2	2 - 1
4.111	49 to 59 mph 79 to 95 kph	25 to 34 mph 40 to 55 kph
3.900	52 to 63 mph 84 to 100 kph	26 to 36 mph 41 to 57 kph
3.700	55 to 72 mph 88 to 115 kph	27 to 38 mph 43 to 60 kph

Fig. 4   Kickdown chart

DIFF GEAR RATIO	MANUAL DOWNSHIFT 2 — 1
4.111	25 to 34 mph 40 to 55 kph
3.900	26 to 36 mph 41 to 57 kph
3.700	27 to 38 mph 43 to 60 kph

Fig. 5   Manual downshift chart

DIFF GEAR RATIO	"2" RANGE FULL THROTTLE UPSHIFT AND KICKDOWN	
	1 - 2 UPSHIFT	2 - 1 KICKDOWN
4.111	31 to 39 mph 50 to 63 kph	25 to 34 mph 40 to 55 kph
3.900	33 to 41 mph 52 to 65 kph	26 to 36 mph 41 to 57 kph
3.700	34 to 43 mph 55 to 69 kph	27 to 38 mph 43 to 60 kph

Fig. 6   Upshift and kickdown chart

speeds at which transmission shifts. Refer to chart in Fig. 2, for correct shift points according to differential gear ratio.

3. With vehicle running in 3rd speed, release accelerator and allow speed to decrease. Engine speed should decrease in direct relation to vehicle speed, and a downshift from 3rd to 2nd should occur. Refer to chart in Fig. 3, for correct shifting points according to differential gear ratio.

4. With vehicle decelerating from high speed in 3rd speed, attempt to kickdown transmission (depress accelerator pedal to full throttle) at 5 mph (8 kph) intervals. Record highest speed at which kickdown from 3rd speed to second speed occurs, then repeat for kickdown from second speed to first speed. Refer to chart in Fig. 4, for correct kickdown points according to differential ratio.

DIFF GEAR RATIO	"2" RANGE HALF THROTTLE UPSHIFT (NOMINAL)
4.111	23 mph 38 kph
3.900	24 mph 40 kph
3.700	36 mph 57 kph

Fig. 7   Upshift chart

CAUTION: In the following test, do not attempt to manually downshift transmission while vehicle speed is in excess of 65 mph (104 kph) as this may cause damage to transmission.

5. With vehicle running in 3rd speed, manually shift into 2nd range. A 3rd to 2nd downshift should occur immediately, and engine braking should decelerate vehicle. Manually shift into Low range, a 2nd to 1st downshift should occur after vehicle has decelerated to the speed specified in chart in Fig. 5.

6. With range selector lever in 2nd, drive vehicle at full throttle from a standing start, while observing road speed at which upshift occurs. Release accelerator pedal and attempt a kickdown while observing highest speed at which kickdown occurs. Refer to chart in Fig. 6, for correct upshift and kickdown speeds according to differential ratio.

7. With range selector lever in 2nd, drive vehicle at about half throttle while observing road speeds at which the 1st to 2nd upshifts occurs. Refer to chart in Fig. 7, for correct speeds according to differential ratio.

8. With range selector lever in Low, drive and accelerate vehicle to about 40 mph (65 kph). Transmission should remain in 1st. Release

accelerator pedal and check for engine braking.

9. With range selector lever in Reverse, drive vehicle and check for slipping.

STALL TEST & PRESSURE TEST

1. Connect a tachometer to engine and connect a 0-300 psi pressure gauge to pressure line fitting on transmission.

2. Place wheel chocks behind and in front of all four wheels.

CAUTION: Do not maintain stall speed longer than five seconds.

3. Start engine and place range selector lever in Drive. Firmly apply foot brake and depress accelerator to full throttle position. Immediately read highest line pressure and engine rpm obtained. Refer to chart in

RANGE SELECTED	STALL RPM	LINE PRESSURE
D Range	1900 – 2150	135 – 171 PSI (9.5 – 12.0 kg/cm²)
R Range	1900 – 2150	182 – 242 PSI (13.5 – 17.0 kg/cm²)

Fig. 8   Stall pressure chart

DIFF GEAR RATIO	VEHICLE SPEED			GOVERNOR PRESSURE
	4.111	3.900	3.700	
	16 mph 26 km/h	17 mph 27 km/h	18 mph 29 km/h	12.8 to 21.3 psi 0.9 to 1.5 kg/cm²
	29 mph 47 km/h	31 mph 50 km/h	32 mph 52 km/h	22.8 to 31.3 psi 1.6 to 2.2 kg/cm²
	58 mph 93 km/h	60 mph 97 km/h	64 mph 103 km/h	58.3 to 75.4 psi 4.1 to 5.3 kg/cm²

Fig. 9 Governor pressure chart

RANGE SELECTED	RPM RPM	LINE PRESSURE
D Range	1000	57 – 64 PSI (4.0 – 4.5 kg/cm²)
R Range	1000	82 – 97 PSI (5.8 – 6.8 kg/cm²)

Fig. 10 Line pressure chart

Fig. 8 for correct line pressure and stall speed.

4. Set range selector lever in Reverse, then firmly apply foot brake and depress accelerator to full throttle position. Immediately read highest line pressure and engine rpm obtained. Refer to chart in Fig. 8 for correct line pressure and stall speed.
5. Check time lag when transmission is shifted into Drive and Reverse from Neutral position. Time lag when shifting into Drive should be less than 1.2 seconds. Time lag when shifting into Reverse should be less than 1.5 seconds.
6. Raise rear of vehicle and support on stands so that rear wheels are free to rotate. Place chocks in front of and behind front wheels and make sure that emergency brake is released.

7. Connect a 0-100 psi pressure gauge to governor test port, and connect a 0-300 psi pressure gauge to line pressure test port.
8. Start engine and set range selector lever in Drive. Operate vehicle to obtain speeds indicated in chart in Fig. 9. Governor pressure gauge readings should be as specified in chart.
9. Apply parking brake and place range selector lever in Drive. Apply foot brake and accelerate engine to 1000 rpm. Line pressure reading on test gauge should be as specified in chart in Fig. 10.

Rear Axle & Brakes Section

AXLE SHAFT, BEARING & OIL SEAL, REPLACE

Except Hi Lux

Removal

1. Raise and support rear of vehicle, then remove wheel and tire assembly and brake drum, Fig. 1.
2. Through holes in axle shaft flange remove axle shaft outer bearing retainer attaching bolts, Fig. 2.
3. Using a suitable puller, remove axle shaft from axle housing. Use care not to damage oil seal, Fig. 3.
4. To replace axle shaft bearing, grind a groove on one side of inner bearing retainer, then using a chisle, split retainer and remove from axle shaft, Fig. 4. Using tool No. SST-09527-20011 or SST-09527-21011, press bearing from axle shaft and remove spacer and outer bearing retainer, Fig. 5.
5. Remove oil seal from axle housing.

Installation

1. Coat contact surfaces of oil seal with grease, then install oil seal in axle housing using a suitable mandrel.
2. Position outer bearing retainer and spacer on axle shaft, then press bearing onto axle shaft using tool

No. SST-09527-20011 or SST-09527-21011, Fig. 6.
3. Heat inner bearing retainer to approximately 284° to 320°F (140° to 160°C), then press inner bearing retainer onto axle shaft with cham-

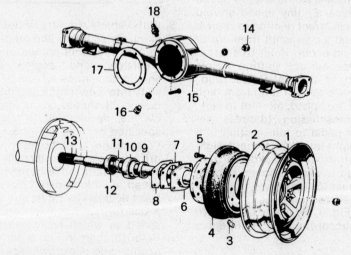

1	Balance weight	10	Rear axle bearing
2	Disc wheel subassy	11	Rear axle bearing inner retainer
3	Balance piece	12	Type T oil seal
4	Brake durm subassy	13	Rear axle shaft
5	Hub bolt	14	Filler plug
6	Rear axle bearing outer retianer	15	Rear axle housing
7	Rear axle bearing retainer gasket	16	Drain plug
8	Rear axle housing end gasket	17	Differential carrier gasket
9	Spacer	18	Bleeder plug

Fig. 1 Axle shaft, bearing & oil seal assembly. Except Hi Lux

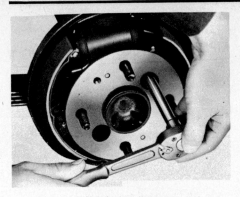

Fig. 2 Removing axle shaft bearing retainer attaching bolts. Except Hi Lux

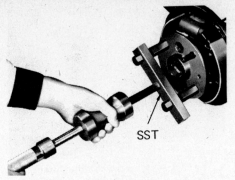

Fig. 3 Removing axle shaft from axle housing. Except Hi Lux

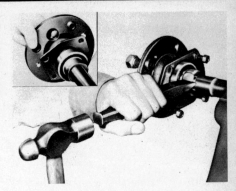

Fig. 4 Removing inner bearing retainer. Except Hi Lux

Fig. 5 Pressing bearing from axle shaft. Except Hi Lux

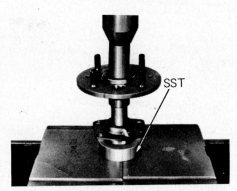

Fig. 6 Pressing bearing onto axle shaft. Except Hi Lux

Fig. 7 Installing inner bearing retainer. Except Hi Lux

fered side facing toward bearing using tool No. SST-09527-20011 or SST-09527-21011, Fig. 7.

NOTE: When retainer is heated to 302°F (150°C), its surface will show a faint yellow color, do not heat retainer above this point.

4. On Corolla and Corona Mark II models, measure thickness of brake backing plate and select correct axle housing end gasket, Fig. 8. Place gasket on axle shaft.
5. Install axle shaft in axle housing.

Hi Lux

Removal

1. Raise and support front of vehicle, then remove wheel and brake drum, Fig. 9.

2. Remove brake shoes from backing plate.
3. Disconnect parking brake cable from backing plate.
4. Disconnect brake line from wheel cylinder.
5. Remove four nuts retaining brake backing plate to axle housing.
6. Using tool No. SST-09905-00010, remove shaft snap ring.
7. Install tool No. SST-09521-25010 to rear axle bearing case and tighten nuts firmly. Press axle shaft out of bearing case.

8. Remove rear axle shaft puller from bearing case.
9. Remove axle shaft bearing from bearing case.
10. Using a brass drift, drive out bolts and separate bearing case from backing plate.
11. If necessary, press out hub bolts and brake drum oil deflector.

Installation

1. Coat oil seal lip with grease, then install oil seal in axle housing using a suitable tool.

Gasket Thickness In In. (mm)	Backing plate Thickness In In. (mm)	
	Corolla (KE) & Corona MkII	Corolla (TE)
.012 (.3)	.1047-.1087 (2.66-2.76)	.0929-.0976 (2.36-2.48)
.024 (.6)	.0961-.1047 (2.44-2.66)	.0835-.0929 (2.12-2.36)

Fig. 8 Axle housing end gasket identification chart. Corolla & Corona Mark II

1. Rear axle shaft
2. Type "S" oil seal
3. Shaft snap ring
4. Rear axle bearing retainer
5. Bearing
6. "O" ring
7. Rear axle bearing case
8. Type "K" oil seal
9. Hub bolt
10. Brake drum oil deflector
11. Brake drum oil deflector gasket
12. Brake drum gasket
13. Brake drum
14. Disc wheel sub-assembly

Fig. 9 Axle shaft, bearing & oil seal assembly. Hi Lux

Fig. 10 Measuring brake shoe to brake drum clearance. 1972-73 Corona, 1972-76 Corona Mark II & 1972-77 Hi Lux

2. Position brake backing plate onto bearing case, align holes of backing plate and bearing case, then press bolts in firmly.
3. Using a suitable tool, install oil seal into bearing case.
4. Position brake drum oil deflector on flange of axle shaft, then press hub bolts into axle shaft and secure oil deflector.
5. Position axle shaft into bearing case. Hold bearing inner race with tool No. SST-09515-30010 and press axle shaft into bearing case.
6. Slide bearing onto axle shaft, then install shaft snap ring and secure bearing retainer.
7. Position O-ring on axle housing, then install axle shaft with brake backing plate. Use care not to damage oil seal. Tighten brake backing plate attaching nuts.
8. Install brake shoes, connect parking brake cables and connect brake line to wheel cylinder. Bleed brake system and adjust service brake and parking brake.

BRAKE ADJUSTMENTS

1972-77 Celica & Corolla & 1974-77 Corona

1. Check brake pedal reserve travel.
2. Operate parking brake lever while pressing down on lever knob.
3. Recheck brake pedal travel.
4. Check to ensure wheels rotate freely.

Fig. 13 Parking brake adjustment. 1974-75 Corona

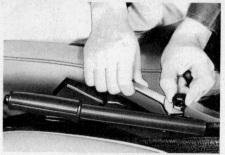

Fig. 11 Parking brake adjustment. 1972-77 Celica & Corolla

1972-73 Corona, 1972-76 Corona Mark II & 1972-77 Hi Lux

Measure brake drum inside diameter and maximum diameter of brake shoes using brake shoe clearance gauge, Fig. 10. Turn adjuster so that brake shoe diameter will be .012-.024 in. (.3-.6 mm) for Corona, 1972 Corona Mark II (RT series) and Hi Lux smaller than brake drum inner diameter. Turn adjuster so that brake shoe diameter will be .008-.020 in. (.2-.5 mm) smaller than brake drum inner diameter for 1972-76 Corona Mark II (MX & RX Series).

PARKING BRAKE ADJUST

1972-77 Celica & Corolla

1. Apply parking brake and count the number of notches on parking brake sector. The specified number of notches should be 5-8 notches for 1972-74 Corolla TE series, 7-8 notches for 1972-74 Corolla KE series, 3-7 notches for 1972-77 Celica and 2-6 notches for 1975-77 Corolla.
2. If adjustment is required, loosen adjusting cap and turn nut until required number of notches is obtained, Fig. 11.
3. Check to ensure rear wheels rotate freely, then tighten adjusting cap.

1972-73 Corona, 1972-76 Corona Mark II & 1972-77 Hi Lux

1. Release parking brake and check to ensure warning light switch is off at this point. If adjustment is required, loosen parking brake warning light switch bracket and reposition switch.
2. Adjust nut at parking brake cable equalizer so that there is no looseness at No. 2 and No. 3 parking brake cables, Fig. 12. Check to ensure that both rear wheels rotate freely.
3. After adjusting, apply parking brake lever and count the number of notches on brake lever. The specified number of notches should be 6-9 notches on Early 1972 Hi Lux, 8-13 notches on 1972 Corona Mark II (RT series, within 13 notches on

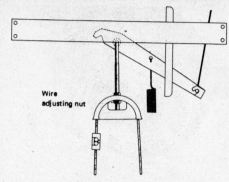

Wire adjusting nut

Fig. 12 Parking brake adjustment. 1972-73 Corona, 1972-76 Corona Mark II & 1972-77 Hi Lux

1972-73 Corona, 8-10 notches on 1972-76 Corona Mark II (MX & RX series) and 8-12 notches on Late 1972-77 Hi Lux.

1974-75 Corona

Adjust parking brake lever travel by rotating turn buckle at parking brake equalizer, Fig. 13. Parking brake lever travel should be 3-6 notches for center floor type lever and 8-15 notches for under dashboard type lever.

1976-77 Corona

1. Check parking brake pedal lock release rod free play. Free play should be .2-.4 in. (5-10 mm).
2. Adjust parking brake travel through turn buckle or equalizer, Fig. 13. Check to ensure rear wheels rotate freely.
3. Check parking brake pedal travel, Fig. 14. Before checking pedal travel, apply and release parking brake several times. Parking brake pedal travel should be 2-4 clicks.

DISC BRAKE SERVICE

1972-77 Celica, Corolla & Corona F Type Disc Brake

Brake Pads, Replace

1. Raise and support front of vehicle, then remove wheel and tire assembly.
2. Remove four clips, then lift out guides, Fig. 15.

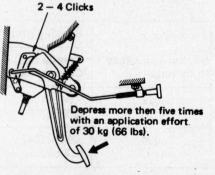

2 — 4 Clicks

Depress more then five times with an application effort of 30 kg (66 lbs)

Fig. 14 Parking brake adjustment. 1976-77 Corona

Disc brake cylinder

1. Plate, pad support, No. 1
2. Plate, pad support, No. 2
3. Pad, disc brake
4. Mounting, disc brake cylinder
5. Guide, disc brake
6. Spring, cylinder support
7. Clip
8. Cylinder assembly, disc brake
9. Piston
10. Ring
11. Boot, cylinder
12. Ring, set

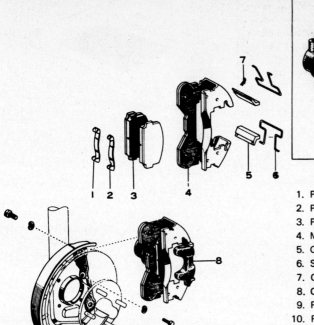

Fig. 15   F type disc brake assembly. 1972-77 Celica, Corolla & Corona

3. Remove caliper assembly as described under Caliper, Replace.
4. Remove brake pads from caliper.
5. Reverse procedure to install.

Caliper, Replace
1. Raise and support front of vehicle, then remove wheel and tire assembly.
2. Disconnect brake hose from caliper. Cap brake line and caliper fitting.
3. Remove four clips, then lift out cylinder guides, Fig. 15.
4. Remove mounting bolts and caliper assembly.
5. Reverse procedure to install. Bleed brake system.

Disc, Replace
1. Remove caliper assembly as described under Caliper, Replace, then remove caliper mounting.
2. Remove hub grease cap, cotter pin and castellated nut, then remove disc and hub assembly from spindle.
3. Reverse procedure to install. Adjust wheel bearing and bleed brake system.

Caliper Overhaul
1. Carefully remove cylinder boot, Fig. 15.
2. To remove piston, apply air pressure

to caliper brake line connection hole.

NOTE: Use care not to damage piston.

3. Remove ring from cylinder.
4. Clean all parts in clean brake fluid before assembling.
5. Lubricate cylinder and ring with clean brake fluid before assembling.
6. Install ring and piston in cylinder. Carefully press piston into cylinder to prevent damage to piston.

1972-76 Corona Mark II
Brake Pads, Replace
1. Raise and support front of vehicle, then remove wheel and tire assembly.
2. Remove clips and pins, then remove pads and shims, Fig. 16.
3. Install pads and shims, then install springs, pins and clips.

NOTE: Shims must be installed with arrow facing upward.

4. Apply brakes several times to position brake pads.
5. Install wheel and tire assembly, then lower vehicle.

Caliper, Replace
1. Raise and support front of vehicle, then remove wheel and tire assembly.
2. Disconnect brake hose from caliper. Cap brake hose and caliper fitting.
3. Remove caliper mounting bolts and caliper assembly, Fig. 16.

NOTE: Shims are installed between steering knuckle and caliper body to adjust disc and caliper centerline position. Do not intermix shims installed at upper and lower parts.

4. Measure distance from brake disc to steering knuckle, (A) Fig. 17. Select shims from Figs. 18 and 19 to match disc center line with caliper center.

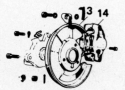

1	Ring	8	Shim, anti-squeal
2	Piston, disc plate	9	Pad, disc brake
3	Spacer	10	Spring, anti-rattle
4	Ring, "O"	11	Pin, with hole
5	Insert, disc brake piston	12	Clip
6	Boot, cylinder	13	Cover sub-assy., disc brake dust
7	Ring, set	14	Caliper assembly, disc brake

Fig. 16   Disc brake assembly. 1972-76 Corona Mark II

Fig. 17   Measuring distance from rotor to steering knuckle. 1972-76 Corona Mark II

Dimension of A part	Shims Required
Less than 19.15 mm (0.754'')	0.8 mm (0.031'') 2 pcs.
19.15 ~ 19.55 mm (0.754~0.770'')	0.8 mm & 0.4 mm 1 of each
19.55 ~ 19.95 mm (0.770 ~0.785'')	0.8 mm 1 pc.
19.55 ~ 20.35 mm (0.785 ~0.801'')	0.4 mm (0.016'') 1 pc.
More than 20.35 mm (0.801'')	None required

Fig. 18   Shim identification chart. 1972-76 Corona Mark II MX series

Dimension of "A" part	Shims Required
Less than 18.15 (0.714'')	0.8 mm (0.031'')-2 Pcs.
18.15 ~18.55 mm (0.714 ~0.730'')	0.8 mm (0.031'') & 0.4 mm (0.016'') -one of each
18.55 ~18.95 mm (0.730 ~0.746'')	0.8 mm (0.031'')—2 Pcs.
18.95 ~19.35 mm (0.746 ~0.762'')	0.4 mm (0.016'')-1 Pc.
More than 19.35 mm (0.762'')	None required

Fig. 19   Shim identification chart. 1972-76 Corona Mark II RX series

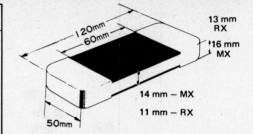

Fig. 20   Dimension for fabricating tool for caliper piston removal. 1972-76 Corona Mark II

5. After selecting shims, install caliper assembly on steering knuckle. On all models except station wagon, torque caliper mounting bolts to 36-47 ft. lbs. On station wagons, torque caliper mounting bolts to 67-87 ft. lbs. Lock mounting bolts with wire.
6. Connect brake line and bleed brake system. Install wheel and tire assembly then lower vehicle.

Disc, Replace

1. Remove caliper assembly, as described under Caliper, Replace.
2. Remove hub grease cap, cotter pin and castellated nut.
3. Remove disc and hub assembly from spindle.
4. Reverse procedure to install. Adjust wheel bearing and bleed brake system.

Caliper Overhaul

1. Remove clips, pins, spring, pads and anti squeal shims, Fig. 16.
2. Remove set ring and cylinder boot.
3. Fabricate tool from block of wood, Fig. 20, then apply compressed air to brake line fitting on caliper.
4. Remove rings from inside cyliner.

NOTE: Do not loosen bridge bolts clamping caliper halves together.

5. Disassemble piston by applying air pressure to hole at center of piston insert.

NOTE: Spacer is oil impregnated type, so that it must not be placed on any material with oil absorbing qualities.

6. Coat cylinder wall and ring with grease supplied with cylinder repair kit, then insert ring into cylinder.
7. Install O-ring on piston insert, then assemble them to piston with spacer.
8. Place cylinder boot on piston, then carefully push piston into cylinder

9. Fit cylinder boot on cylinder and clamp with set ring.
10. Position anti-squeal shim with arrow facing upward and install into caliper with brake pads.
11. Install spring, pins and clips. Position springs so they will return pads.

1974-77 Corona & 1975-77 Hi Lux Girling Type Disc Brake

Brake Pads, Replace

1. Raise and support front of vehicle, then remove wheel and tire assembly.
2. Remove clips, pins, and springs, then remove brake pads and anti-squeal shims, Fig. 21.

NOTE: On Corona models with ESP, disconnect wiring harness from steering knuckle harness clamp. Remove pad and separate connection between pad and wear sensor.

3. Install pads and anti squeal shims. Install shims so that folded portion will be facing pad and arrow mark will be facing upward. Lightly coat both sides of antisqueal shim with anti squeal lubricant. On Corona models with ESP, mount wear sensor in the inner side pad before installing the pad.
4. Install springs, pins and clips.
5. On Corona models with ESP, insert wiring harness into clamp on steering knuckle.

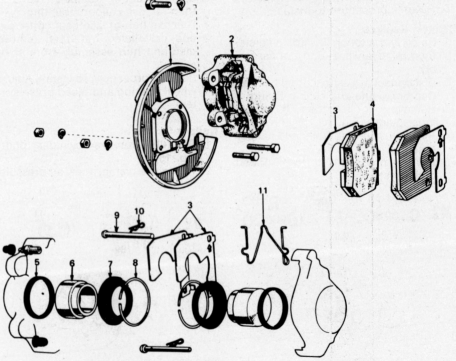

1. **Disc brake dust cover**	7. **Cylinder boot**	
2. **Disc brake caliper assembly**	8. **Set ring**	
3. **Anti-squeal shim**	9. **With hole pin**	
4. **Disc brake pad**	10. **Clip**	
5. **Piston cup**	11. **Anti-rattle spring**	

Fig. 21   Girling type disc brake assembly. 1974-77 Corona & 1975-77 Hi Lux

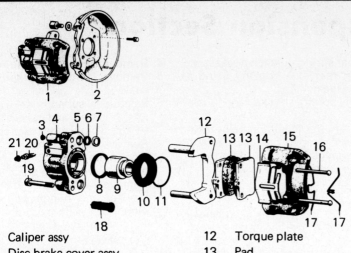

1 Caliper assy
2 Disc brake cover assy
3 Hole plug
4 Torque plate pin cap
5 Cylinder body
6 Dust seal
7 Dust seal retainer
8 Piston seal
9 Piston
10 Cylinder boot
11 Ring

12 Torque plate
13 Pad
14 Pad protector
15 Outer body
16 Pin with hole
17 Anti-rattle spring
18 Torque plate pin bushing
19 Bridge bolt
20 Bleeder plug
21 Bleeder plug cap

Fig. 22 PS type disc brake assembly. 1975-77 Corolla

6. Install wheel and tire assembly, then lower vehicle.

Caliper, Replace
1. Remove brake pads as described under Brake Pads, Replace.
2. Disconnect brake line from caliper, then remove caliper mounting bolts and caliper, Fig. 21.
3. Reverse procedure to install. Bleed brake system.

Disc, Replace
1. Remove caliper assembly as described under Caliper, Replace.
2. Remove hub grease cap, then remove cotter pin and castellated nut.
3. Slide disc and hub assembly off spindle.
4. Reverse procedure to install. Adjust wheel bearing and bleed brake system.

Caliper Overhaul
1. Remove set ring and cylinder boot from caliper assembly, Fig. 21.
2. Place a suitable wooden block between pistons, then apply compressed air to brake line fitting caliper to remove pistons.
3. Remove seal rings from inside cylinder. Do not loosen bridge bolts.

4. Coat cylinder wall and seal with brake fluid, then insert seal rings into cylinder grooves.
5. Carefully push pistons into cylinders, then install cylinder boots and engage set rings.

1975-77 Corolla PS Type Disc Brake

Pads, Replace
1. Raise an support front of vehicle, then remove wheel and tire assembly.
2. Remove pad protectors and anti rattle springs, Fig. 22.
3. Remove pins, then lift out brake pads.
4. Reverse procedure to install.

Caliper, Replace
1. Remove brake pads as described under Brake Pads, Replace.
2. Disconnect brake line from caliper, cap line and caliper fitting.
3. Remove caliper mounting bolts and caliper assembly, Fig. 22.
4. Reverse procedure to install. Bleed brake system.

Disc, Replace
1. Remove caliper assembly as de-

scribed under Caliper, Replace.
2. Remove hub grease cap, cotter pin and castellated nut.
3. Reverse procedure to install. Bleed brake system and adjust wheel bearings.

Caliper Overhaul
1. Loosen two bridge bolts, then separate cylinder body from outer body, then pull torque plate, Fig. 22.
2. Remove ring and dust boot. Apply compressed air to caliper brake line fitting to remove piston.
3. Remove piston seal, bushings, hole plugs, retainers and dust seals from cylinder.
4. Install dust seals, retainer and bushings into cylinder body.
5. Coat cylinder bore and piston seal with clean brake fluid, then install piston seal in cylinder and carefully push piston in by hand.
6. Install dust boot and ring.
7. Insert torque plate pins into cylinder body. Torque plate can be inserted smoothly if pin cap hole plug is removed before hand. After inserting, check to ensure that torque plate slides smoothly.
8. Apply castor oil or alcohol to bridge bolts and bolt on outer body. Install and torque bolts to 57.9-68.7 ft. lbs. (8-9.5 kg-cm).

MASTER CYLINDER, REPLACE
1. Disconnect brake lines from master cylinder.
2. Disconnect wire connector from brake pressure switch.
3. Remove master cylinder to brake unit attaching nuts, then remove master cylinder.
4. Reverse procedure to install. Bleed brake system.

POWER BRAKE UNIT, REPLACE
1. Disconnect brake lines from master cylinder and wire connectors from brake warning switches.
2. Disconnect vacuum hose from power brake unit.
3. Remove brake unit to dash panel attaching nuts, then remove brake unit and master cylinder as an assembly.
4. Remove master cylinder from brake unit.

Rear Suspension Section

COIL SPRING, REPLACE

1. Raise rear of vehicle and support rear axle housing on stands.
2. Disconnect shock absorber from lower mounting, Figs. 1 and 2.
3. Lower jack until spring tension is relieved, then remove coil spring with insulator.
4. Reverse procedure to install.

LEAF SPRING, REPLACE

Except Hi Lux

1. Raise rear of vehicle and support body on stands.
2. Disconnect shock absorbers from lower mounting, Fig. 3.
3. Remove two U-bolts at spring center.
4. Disconnect parking brake cable from rear spring guide, if necessary.
5. Support rear axle housing using a suitable jack.
6. Remove spring shackle and bushing.
7. Remove two bolts attaching bracket pin, then remove bracket pin and two bushings from rear of spring.
8. Reverse procedure to install.

Hi Lux

1. Raise rear of vehicle and place stands under frame and rear axle housing.
2. Disconnect shock absorber from upper and lower mountings and remove shock absorber from vehicle, Fig. 4.
3. Disconnect parking brake equalizer from parking brake intermediate lever.
4. Remove three way securing bolt.
5. Remove U-bolts and spring U-bolt seats.
6. Position a suitable jack under rear axle housing and raise housing to relieve weight from rear springs.
7. Remove spring shackle nuts and inner plate, then using a suitable pry bar, remove spring shackle.
8. Remove two bolts retaining spring bracket and hanger pin nut, then drive out spring hanger pin.
9. Remove spring assembly from vehicle.
10. Reverse procedure to install.

SHOCK ABSORBER, REPLACE

1. Raise rear of vehicle and support rear axle housing on stands.

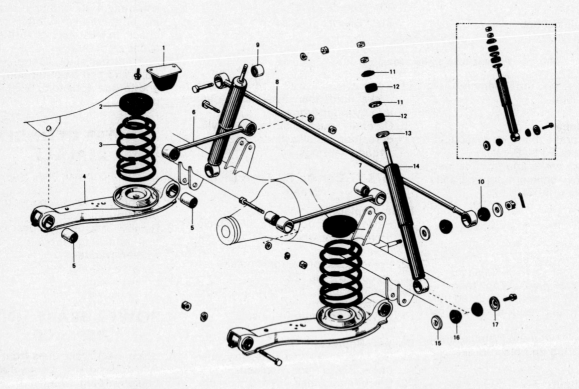

1	Bumper, rear spring	10	Busing
2	Insulator, coil spring	11	Retainer, cushion
3	Spring, coil	12	Cushion, shock absorber
4	Arm, lower control	13	Retainer, cushion
5	Bushing, control arm	14	Absorber, rear shock
6	Arm, upper control	15	Washer
7	Bushing, control arm	16	Bushing
8	Bushing, lateral control arm	17	Washer
9	Rod, lateral control		

Fig. 1 Coil spring rear suspension. 1972-76 Corona Mark II (RX series) except sta. wag.

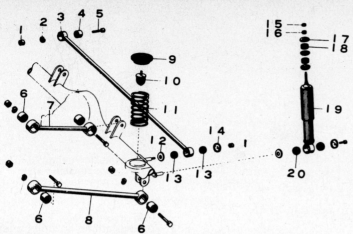

2. Disconnect shock absorber from lower mounting.
3. Disconnect shock absorber from upper mounting and remove from vehicle.

CONTROL ARMS, REPLACE

1972-76 Corona Mark II (RX Series) Except Sta. Wag.

Upper

1. Raise rear of vehicle and support rear axle housing on stands.
2. Remove bolts attaching upper control arm to axle housing and frame, then remove control arm, Fig. 1.
3. Use tool No. SST- 09716-30010 to replace bushings, if necessary.
4. Reverse procedure to install.

Lower

1. Raise rear of vehicle and support axle housing on stands, then remove wheel and tire assembly.
2. If control arm on right hand side of vehicle is to be removed, remove exhaust pipe supports. If control

1. Nut
2. Washer, spring
3. Rod, lateral control
4. Bushing, lateral control rod
5. Bolt, hexagon
6. Bushing, control arm
7. Arm, upper control
8. Arm, lower control
9. Insulator, rear coil spring
10. Bumper, rear spring
11. Spring, coil rear
12. Washer, shock absorber cushion
13. Bushing
14. Washer, shock absorber cushion
15. Nut
16. Nut
17. Washer, shock absorber cushion
18. Bushing
19. Absorber, shock rear
20. Bushing

Fig. 2   Coil spring rear suspension. 1972-77 Celica

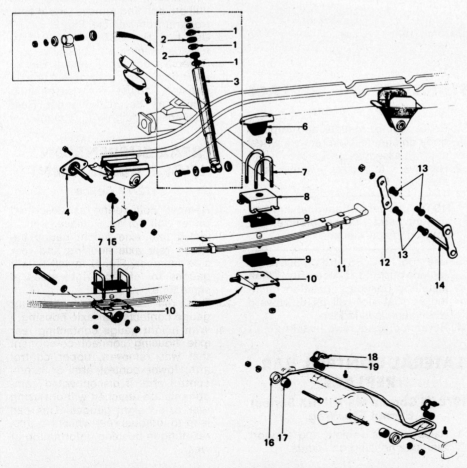

1. Cushion retainer
2. Cushion
3. Shock absorber
4. Bracket pin
5. Bushing
6. Spring bumper
7. U bolt
8. Pad retainer
9. Pad
10. Spring U bolt seat
11. Leaf spring assembly
12. Shackle plate
13. Bushing
14. Shackle pin
15. U bolt retainer
16. Stabilizer bar
17. Bushing
18. Bracket cover
19. Bushing

Fig. 3   Leaf spring rear suspension (Typical). Except Hi Lux

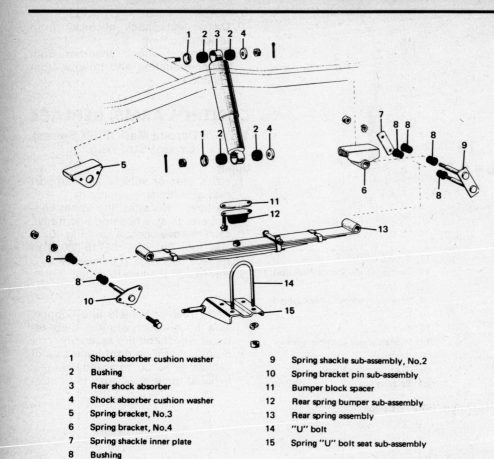

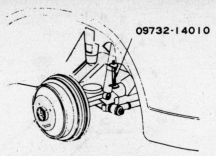

Fig. 5 Installing gauge for rear suspension height adjustment. 1972-77 Celica

1	Shock absorber cushion washer
2	Bushing
3	Rear shock absorber
4	Shock absorber cushion washer
5	Spring bracket, No.3
6	Spring bracket, No.4
7	Spring shackle inner plate
8	Bushing
9	Spring shackle sub-assembly, No.2
10	Spring bracket pin sub-assembly
11	Bumper block spacer
12	Rear spring bumper sub-assembly
13	Rear spring assembly
14	"U" bolt
15	Spring "U" bolt seat sub-assembly

Fig. 4 Leaf spring rear suspension. 1972-77 Hi Lux

arm on left hand side of vehicle is to be removed, remove parking brake cable clamp.

3. Remove bolts attaching lower control arm to axle housing and frame, then remove control arm from vehicle, Fig. 1.
4. Use tool No. SST-09716-30010 to replace bushings, if necessary.
5. Reverse procedure to install.

1972-77 Celica

1. Remove coil springs as described under Coil Spring, Replace.
2. Remove bolts attaching control arm to rear axle housing, Fig. 2.
3. Raise rear axle housing.
4. Remove bolt attaching control arm to frame, then remove control arm from vehicle.
5. Use tool No. SST-09710-14010 to replace bushings, if necessary.
6. Reverse procedure to install. Before attaching control arm to rear axle housing, adjust rear suspension height as described under Rear Suspension Height Adjustment.

STABILIZER BAR, REPLACE
1974-77 Corona

1. Raise rear of vehicle and support body on stands, then remove wheel and tire assembly.
2. Remove attaching bolts and stabilizer, Fig. 3.

NOTE: Use care when removing bolt at right hand side of stabilizer bar not to damage fuel line.

3. Use tool No. SST-09716-30010 to replace bushing, if necessary. When installing bushings, position bushing so that slot will be downward when vehicle is ladden.
4. Reverse procedure to install.

LATERAL CONTROL BAR, REPLACE
1972-76 Corona Mark II (RX Series) Except Sta. Wag.

1. Raise rear of vehicle and support rear axle housing on stands.

2. Disconnect shock absorber from lower mounting.
3. Remove attaching bolts and lateral control arm, Fig. 1.
4. Use tool No. SST-09716-30020 to replace bushings, if necessary.
5. Reverse procedure to install.

1972-77 Celica

1. Remove coil spring as described under Coil Spring, Replace.
2. Remove cotter pin, nut, washer and outer bushing from lateral control arm rear axle housing mounting.
3. Raise rear axle housing using a suitable jack.
4. Remove nut and washer from lateral control arm frame mounting, then pull out bolt and remove lateral control arm from vehicle, Fig. 2.
5. Use tool No. SST-09710-14010 to replace bushing, if necessary.
6. Reverse procedure to install. Before attaching lateral control arm to axle housing, adjust rear suspension height as described under Rear Suspension Height Adjustment.

REAR SUSPENSION HEIGHT ADJUSTMENT
1972-77 Celica

1. Remove coil spring as described under Coil Spring, Replace.
2. Install rear axle height gauge between rear axle housing and rear side member, Fig. 5. Install height gauges to left and right sides at same time.
3. Raise rear axle housing until height gauge contacts rear axle housing.
4. With height gauge contacting rear axle housing connect component that was removed, upper control arm, lower control arm or lateral control arm. If disconnected components are attached without using rear axle height gauges. This can lead to unequal rear wheel heights, resulting in bushing deformation or wear.

Front Suspension & Steering Section

WHEEL ALIGNMENT
Caster & Camber

1972-77 Celica & Corolla
Caster and camber are not adjustable on the strut type front suspension. If caster and camber are not within limits, check for worn or damaged parts.

1972-73 Corona, 1972-76 Corona Mark II & 1972-77 Hi Lux
Caster and camber are adjusted by increasing or decreasing the number of shims between upper arm shaft and frame mounting surface. The thickness between front and rear shim packs should not exceed .16 in. (4 mm) on all models except 1972 Corona Mark II (RT series). On 1972 Corona Mark II (RT series), the thickness should not exceed .20 in. (5 mm).

1974-77 Corona
Caster and camber are adjusted by rotating front and rear cams located on the lower control arm, Fig. 1. Measure camber and adjust rear cam as necessary. Measure caster and adjust front cam as necessary. Check caster and camber to see that they are within limits. Torque lower control arm mounting bolts to 94-130.2 ft. lbs. (13-18 kg-m).

NOTE: The setting of front and rear cams should not exceed more than 6 graduations. If 6 graduations are exceeded, check suspension components for damage.

Toe In, Adjust
Measure length of tie rod on each side and adjust to be equal. Adjust toe-in by turning adjusting tubes equal amounts. Clamp adjusting tubes after aligning clamps with tube slots. Lock tie rod ends so that inner and outer ends are at right angles to each other.

WHEEL BEARINGS, ADJUST
Exept Hi Lux

1. Remove wheel and tire assembly, then remove hub grease cap and cotter pin.
2. Loosen castellated nut.
3. Tighten castellated nut to 18.8-23.2 ft. lbs. (260-320 kg-cm), then rotate hub and disc assembly several times to ensure bearings are seated.
4. Loosen nut until it can be turned with fingers, then retighten nut finger tight.
5. Using a spring scale measure preload, Fig. 2. Preload should be 10.6-24.7 oz. (.3-.7 kg).
6. Install cotter pin, grease cap and wheel and tire assembly.

NOTE: If cotter pin holes do not line up, tighten nut by the least amount possible until holes are aligned.

Hi Lux

1. Raise and support front of vehicle, then remove wheel and tire assembly.
2. Remove hub grease cap and cotter pin, then loosen castellated nut.
3. Tighten castellated nut to 36.1 ft. lbs. (500 kg-cm) and rotate hub several times to seat bearings.
4. Loosen nut to finger tightness, then retighten nut to 36.1 ft. lbs. (500 kg-cm.) Tighten nut 1/6 to 1/3 turn further and install cotter pin.
5. After rotating hub several times, measure preload using a spring scale, Fig. 2. The starting torque when measured at drum rim should be 3.5-13 in. lbs. (4-15 kg-cm) or 10.6-38.8 oz. (300-1100 g). If reading is not within limits, readjust bearing.

SHOCK ABSORBER UNIT & COIL SPRING, REPLACE
1972-77 Celica & Corolla

Removal
1. Raise and support front of vehicle, then remove wheel and tire assembly.
2. Disconnect brake line and hose from clamp.
3. Remove three suspension unit attaching nuts from top of fender apron.
4. Remove three bolts attaching shock absorber to steering knuckle.

NOTE: Bolt holes in steering knuckle are provided with positioning collars that extend about 3/16 in. from arm surface and fit into bolt holes in shock absorber lower end, therefore the lower suspension arm must be pressed downward to remove shock absorber.

5. Attach shock absorber stand to lower end of shock absorber, then position holder in a vise.
6. Using a suitable spring compressor, compress coil spring, Fig. 3.
7. Remove bearing dust cover.
8. Using a suitable tool to hold upper seat, remove nut at upper end of shock absorber, Fig. 4.
9. Remove front suspension support and coil spring from shock absorber unit, Figs. 5, 6 and 7.
10. Remove caliper and disc from spindle.

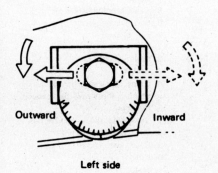

Outward   Inward

Left side

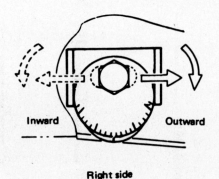

Inward   Outward

Right side

As seen from rear

Fig. 1 Caster & camber adjustment. 1974-77 Corona

Fig. 2 Measuring wheel bearing preload

Fig. 3 Compressing coil spring. 1972-77 Celica & Corolla

Installation

Reverse procedure to install. Torque piston rod to suspension support nut to 28.9-39.8 ft. lbs. (400-550 kg-cm). Torque suspension support unit to fender apron attaching nuts to 13.7-22.4 ft. lbs. (190-310 kg-cm). Torque shock absorber shell to steering knuckle arm bolts to 57.9-86.8 ft. lbs. for Celica and 50.6-65.1 ft. lbs. for Corolla. Adjust front wheel bearings and bleed brake system. Pack grease into bearing part at suspension support.

SHOCK ABSORBER UNIT SERVICE

1972-77 Celica & Corolla

Disassemble, Figs. 5, 6 & 7

1. Mount shock absorber unit on tool No. SST-09741-14010, then clamp tool in a vise.
2. Using ring nut wrench SST-09728-14010 for Celica models or SST-09728-14011 for Corolla models, remove ring nut from shell using care not to damage oil seal, Fig. 8.
3. Using a needle, remove gasket installed around upper part of piston rod guide, Fig. 9.
4. Carefully pull piston with rod guide from shell.
5. Remove cylinder from shell.
6. Remove shell from vise and drain fluid.
7. From inside cylinder, drive out base valve.
8. Insert screwdrivers into slots at base valve side and pry base valve from base valve case.
9. Remove piston valve from piston rod, by clamping flat part of piston rod in a soft jawed vise and removing piston nut, then remove piston valve, spring, piston, cylinder valve and other components.
10. Remove piston ring from piston.

Assemble Figs. 5, 6 & 7

1. Repair staked portions of piston rod, then lubricate components with light oil prior to assembling.
2. Clamp flat end of piston rod in a soft jawed vise and position cylinder valve, piston, spring, piston valve and other components on piston rod, then install piston rod nut. On Corolla KE series, piston valve must gradually be threaded on piston rod using tool No. SST-09720-12012 until tool becomes hard to turn, from this point back piston valve out 1½ turns, Fig. 10. Torque piston rod nut to 13.7-22.4 ft. lbs. On Celica and Corolla TE series and to 43.4-54.3 ft. lbs. on Corolla KE series. On Celica and Corolla TE series stake nut at four places. On Corolla KE series stake nut at two places.

NOTE: On all models, set non-return valve properly into center of non-return valve stopper before tightening piston rod nut. On Corolla KE series, if piston valve is not backed out 1½ turns, the specified shock dampening force will not be obtained.

3. Install piston ring on piston.
4. Press base valve into base valve case, then using a plastic mallet, drive base valve into cylinder.
5. Carefully install piston into cylinder, then install cylinder into shell.
6. Fill shell with shock absorber fluid. Capacity for Celica is 10.5 fl. oz. (315 cc). Capacity on Corolla is 16.78-17.39 cu. in. (275-285 cc) for 1972-74

Fig. 4 Removing upper seat retaining nut. 1972-77 Celica & Corolla

models, 17.1-17.7 cu. in. (280-290 cc) for 1975-77 KE series and 19.2 cu. in. (315 cc) for 1975-77 TE series.

7. Install rod guide into shell, then install gasket.
8. Install ring nut as follows:
   a. Apply grease to lip of oil seal inside ring nut.
   b. Insert ring nut from upper end of piston rod using care not to damage oil seal.
   c. Piston rod must be raised 3-3½ in. above shell on Celica models before tightening nut. On Corolla piston rod must be raised 3.15-3.54 in. before tightening nut.
   d. Tighten nut using tool No. SST-09728-14010 or SST-09728-14011. Torque nut to 75-100 ft. lbs. on 1972-74 Corolla, and 72.3-108.5 ft. lbs. on 1972-77 Celica and 1975-77 Corolla.

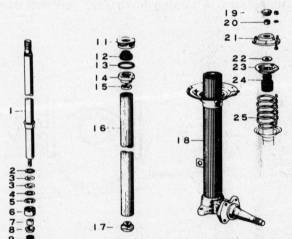

1. Rod, shock absorber piston
2. Stopper, non-return valve No. 1
3. Spring, non-return valve
4. Valve, non-return
5. Ring, piston
6. Piston, non-return
7. Collar
8. Valve, shock absorber main
9. Spring, compression
10. Nut, piston
11. Nut, shock absorber ring
12. Seal, type "D" oil
13. Gasket
14. Guide, shock absorber rod
15. Stopper, shock absorber rebound
16. Cylinder
17. Valve assy., shock absorber base
18. Shell, with steering knuckle
19. Cover, bearing dust
20. Nut
21. Support, front suspension
22. Seal, dust
23. Seat, front spring
24. Bumper, front spring
25. Spring, front coil

Fig. 5 Shock absorber unit & coil spring. 1972-77 Celica

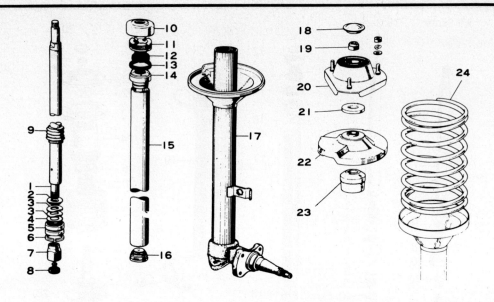

1	Shock absorber piston rod	13	Gasket
2	Non-return valve stopper	14	Piston rod guide
3	Non-return valve spring	15	Cylinder
4	Non-return valve	16	Base valve
5	Non-return piston	17	W/steering knuckle shell
6	Piston ring	18	Bearing dust cover
7	Piston nut	19	Nut
8	Piston valve	20	Front suspension support
9	Rebound stopper	21	Dust seal
10	Shock absorber upper cap	22	Front spring seat
11	Ring nut	23	Front spring bumper
12	Type "D" oil seal	24	Front coil spring

Fig. 6 Shock absorber unit & coil spring. 1972-74 Corolla

LOWER SUSPENSION ARM, REPLACE

1972-77 Celica & Corolla

1. Raise and support front of vehicle, then remove wheel and tire assembly.

NOTE: Do not support suspension arm on stand otherwise damage may result.

2. Remove stabilizer mounting bolts, Figs. 11 and 12.
3. Remove strut bar mounting bolts.
4. Remove lower suspension arm mounting bolts, then disconnect lower suspension arm from suspension member.

5. Using a suitable puller, separate steering knuckle from lower suspension arm.
6. Reverse procedure to install.

STABILIZER BAR, REPLACE

1972-77 Celica & Corolla

1. Raise and support front of vehicle.
2. Remove engine under cover, if equipped.
3. Remove bolts attaching stabilizer bar to lower suspension arms, Figs. 11 and 12.
4. Remove stabilizer bar brackets and bushings.
5. Remove stabilizer bar from vehicle.
6. Reverse procedure to install.

STRUT BAR, REPLACE

1972-77 Celica & Corolla

1. Raise and support front of vehicle.
2. Remove nut and washers from strut bar, Figs. 11 and 12.
3. Remove strut bar to lower suspension arm attaching bolts.
4. Reverse procedure to install. Adjust strut bar to 82 mm for Celica models, 62.4 mm for 1972-74 Corolla and 87.2 mm for 1975-77 Corolla, Fig. 13.

LOWER CONTROL ARM & COIL SPRING, REPLACE

1972-73 Corona

Removal

1. Raise and support front of vehicle,

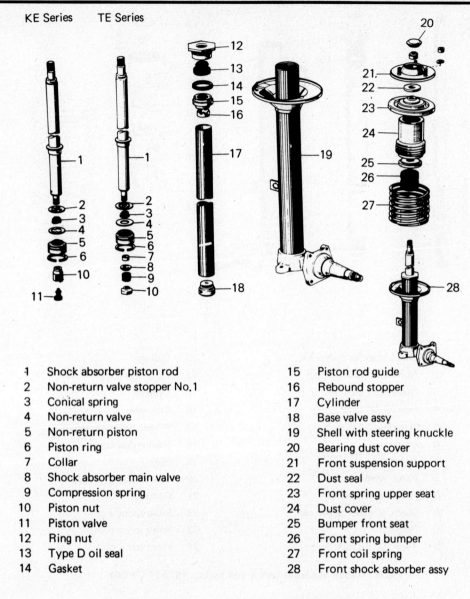

KE Series   TE Series

1	Shock absorber piston rod	15	Piston rod guide
2	Non-return valve stopper No.1	16	Rebound stopper
3	Conical spring	17	Cylinder
4	Non-return valve	18	Base valve assy
5	Non-return piston	19	Shell with steering knuckle
6	Piston ring	20	Bearing dust cover
7	Collar	21	Front suspension support
8	Shock absorber main valve	22	Dust seal
9	Compression spring	23	Front spring upper seat
10	Piston nut	24	Dust cover
11	Piston valve	25	Bumper front seat
12	Ring nut	26	Front spring bumper
13	Type D oil seal	27	Front coil spring
14	Gasket	28	Front shock absorber assy

Fig. 7 Shock absorber unit & coil spring. 1975-77 Corolla

then remove wheel and tire assembly.
2. Remove shock absorber, and dust cover, then disconnect stabilizer bar from control arm, Fig. 14.
3. Compress coil spring using a suitable spring compressor.
4. Position a suitable jack under lower control arm, then remove ball joint mounting bolts and detach lower ball joint with steering knuckle attached from lower control arm.
5. Carefully loosen spring compressor until all spring tension is relieved, then remove coil spring.

6. Remove lower control arm from crossmember.
7. Remove bushings from each end of lower arm shaft.

Installation
1. Reverse procedure to install. Torque pivot bushing to 86.8 ft. lbs. (1200 kg-cm). When installing pivot bushing, thread in bushing by the same amount at each end of lower arm shaft. Torque lower control arm to crossmember attaching bolts to 32.6-43.4 ft. lbs. (450-600 kg-cm)

Torque lower ball joint to control arm bolts to 57.9-83.2 ft. lbs. (800-1150 kg-cm) for 12 mm bolts and 10.9-15.9 ft. lbs. (150-220 kg-cm) for 8 mm bolts. Check to ensure coil spring is properly positioned in seat at lower control arm. Adjust front wheel alignment as necessary.

1974-77 Corona
Removal
1. Raise and support front of vehicle, then remove wheel and tire assembly.

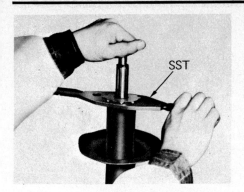

Fig. 8   Removing ring nut from shock absorber unit. 1972-77 Celica & Corolla

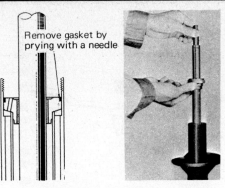

Fig. 9   Removing upper piston rod guide gasket

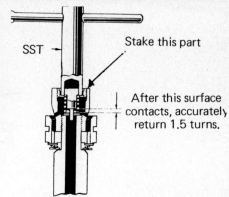

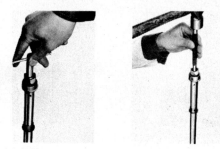

Fig. 10   Installing piston valve. 1972-77 Corolla KE series

2. Remove shock absorber, then disconnect stabilizer bar from lower control arm, Fig. 15.
3. Using a suitable spring compressor, compress coil spring.
4. Position a suitable jack under lower control arm seat.
5. Disconnect lower ball joint from steering knuckle, then lower jack.
6. Remove ball joint from lower control arm.
7. Remove cam plates and bolts, then remove lower control arm.

NOTE: Mark position of each cam plate before removing.

8. Loosen spring compressor and remove coil spring.

Installation

1. Install lower ball joint on lower control arm.

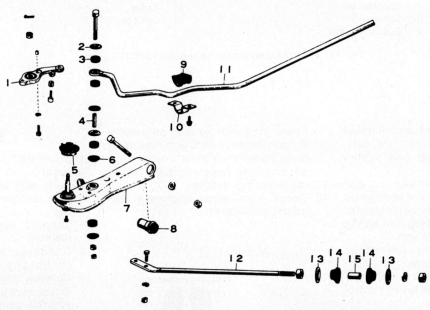

1. Arm, steering knuckle
2. Retainer, cushion
3. Cushion, stabilizer
4. Collar
5. Cover, lower ball joint dust
6. Retainer, cushion
7. Arm subassy., suspension lower
8. Bushing, suspension lower arm
9. Bushing, stabilizer
10. Bracket, stabilizer
11. Bar, stabilizer
12. Bar, strut
13. Retainer, strut bar cushion
14. Cushion, strut bar
15. Collar

Fig. 11   Front suspension components. 1972-77 Celica

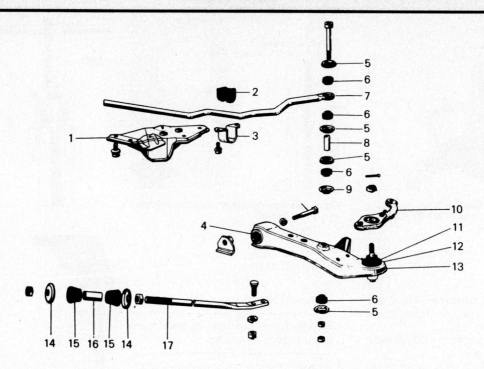

1	Strut bar bracket	10	Steering knuckle arm
2	Stabilizer bushing	11	Lower ball joint dust cover
3	Stabilizer bracket	12	Set ring
4	Suspension lower arm bushing	13	Suspension lower arm subassy
5	Cushion retainer	14	Strut bar cushion retainer
6	Stabilizer cushion	15	Strut bar cushion
7	Stabilizer bar	16	Collar
8	Collar	17	Strut bar
9	Cushion retainer		

Fig. 12   Front suspension components. 1972-77 Corolla

2. Position lower control arm on frame and insert bolts from rear side. Place cams on bolts and tighten nuts finger tight.
3. Install spring compressor on coil spring, then position coil spring into shock absorber tower over insulator and lower end of spring into spring seat on lower control arm.
4. Completely compress coil spring with spring compressor.
5. Position a suitable jack under lower control arm and raise lower control arm.

NOTE: Pry spring into lower control arm seat using a wooden bar.

6. Attach ball joint to steering knuckle.
7. Install stabilizer bar. Ensure bushings and retainer are properly positioned.
8. Remove spring compressor and install shock absorber.
9. Lower vehicle and rock several

times, then with no load on vehicle tighten lower control arm mounting nuts. Install cam plate inside stopper on frame. Align cam plate marks made during removal.
10. Check front wheel alignment and adjust as necessary.

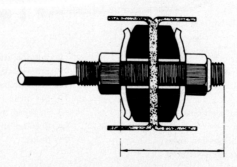

Fig. 13   Strut bar adjustment. 1972-77 Celica & Corolla

Hi Lux

COIL SPRING
Removal

1. Raise and support front of vehicle, then remove wheel and tire assembly.
2. Support front suspension crossmember.
3. Disconnect stabilizer bar from lower control arm, Fig. 16.
4. Remove cotter pin and nut, then disconnect tie rod end from steering knuckle using tool No. SST-09611-20014.
5. Remove shock absorber and disconnect flexible hose.
6. Raise lower control arm using a suitable jack.
7. Loosen lower ball joint attaching nut and disconnect lower control arm from steering knuckle using tool No. SST-09628-62010.
8. Carefully lower jack positioned under lower control arm until all

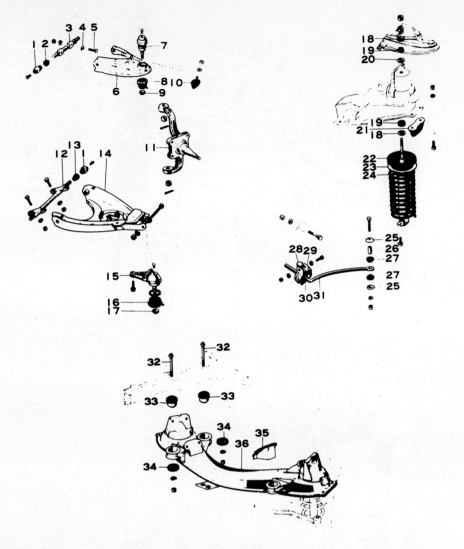

1.	Bush, arm pivot	13.	Seal, arm pivot dust	25.	Retainer, cushion
2.	Seal, arm pivot	14.	Arm, lower suspension	26.	Collar
3.	Arm, upper suspension, inner	15.	Joint assembly, lower ball	27.	Cushion, stabilizer
4.	Shim, camber adjust	16.	Cover, lower ball joint dust	28.	Link, stabilizer
5.	Bolt, upper shaft, set	17.	Plate, dust cover	29.	Cover, stabilizer link
6.	Arm, upper suspension	18.	Retainer, cushion	30.	Bush, stabilizer
7.	Joint assembly, upper ball	19.	Cushion, shock absorber	31.	Bar, stabilizer
8.	Cover, upper ball joint dust	20.	Retainer, cushion	32.	Bolt, hexagon
9.	Plate, dust cover	21.	Bumper, front spring	33.	Cushion, front body support
10.	Bumper, front spring	22.	Insulator, coil spring	34.	Cushion, body rebound stopper
11.	Knuckle, steering	23.	Spacer, coil spring	35.	Bracket, engine mounting
12.	Arm, lower suspension, inner	24.	Spring, coil	36.	Crossmember, front suspension

Fig. 14 Front suspension. 1972-73 Corona

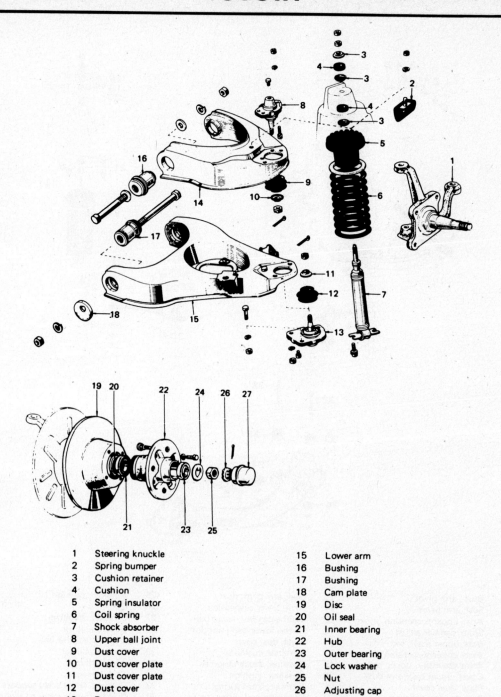

1	Steering knuckle	15	Lower arm
2	Spring bumper	16	Bushing
3	Cushion retainer	17	Bushing
4	Cushion	18	Cam plate
5	Spring insulator	19	Disc
6	Coil spring	20	Oil seal
7	Shock absorber	21	Inner bearing
8	Upper ball joint	22	Hub
9	Dust cover	23	Outer bearing
10	Dust cover plate	24	Lock washer
11	Dust cover plate	25	Nut
12	Dust cover	26	Adjusting cap
13	Dust cover	27	Grease cap
14	Upper arm		

Fig. 15 Front suspension. 1974-77 Corona

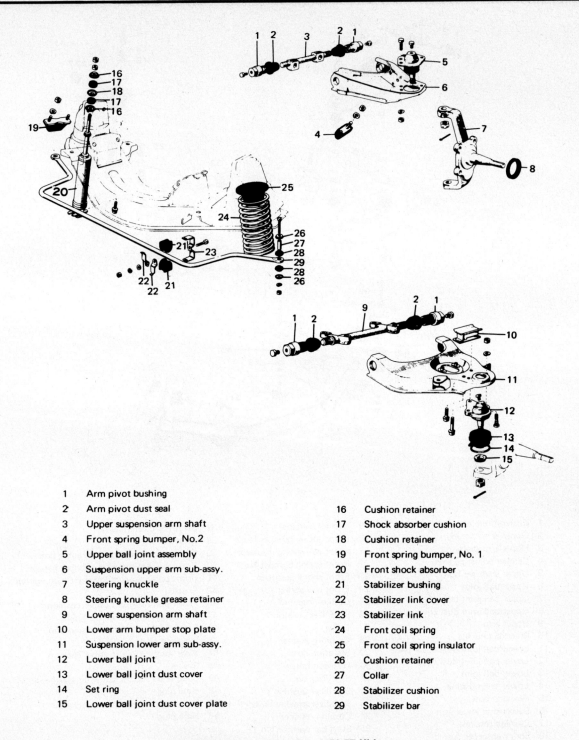

1	Arm pivot bushing	16	Cushion retainer
2	Arm pivot dust seal	17	Shock absorber cushion
3	Upper suspension arm shaft	18	Cushion retainer
4	Front spring bumper, No.2	19	Front spring bumper, No. 1
5	Upper ball joint assembly	20	Front shock absorber
6	Suspension upper arm sub-assy.	21	Stabilizer bushing
7	Steering knuckle	22	Stabilizer link cover
8	Steering knuckle grease retainer	23	Stabilizer link
9	Lower suspension arm shaft	24	Front coil spring
10	Lower arm bumper stop plate	25	Front coil spring insulator
11	Suspension lower arm sub-assy.	26	Cushion retainer
12	Lower ball joint	27	Collar
13	Lower ball joint dust cover	28	Stabilizer cushion
14	Set ring	29	Stabilizer bar
15	Lower ball joint dust cover plate		

Fig. 16   Front suspension. 1972-77 Hi Lux

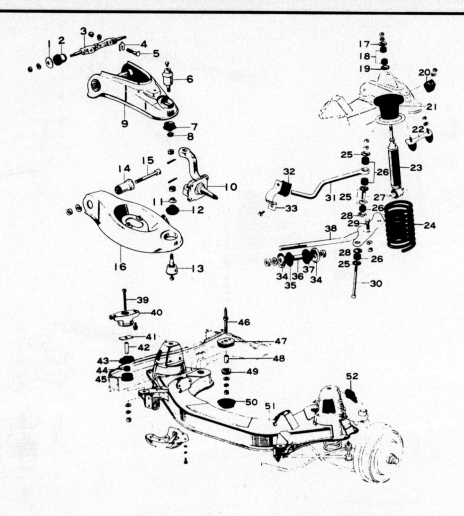

1 Cushion retainer	19 Cushion retainer	37 Strut bar cushion No.2
2 Upper arm bushing	20 Front spring bumper No.2	38 Strut bar
3 Upper arm shaft	21 Front coil spring insulator	39 Front suspension member guide bolt
4 Camber adjusting shim	22 Front spring bumper No.1	40 Front suspension cross-member hanger
5 Upper shaft set bolt	23 Front shock absorber	41 Front body support lower cushion washer
6 Upper ball joint	24 Front coil spring	42 Spacer
7 Upper ball joint dust cover	25 Cushion retainer	43 Front body support upper cushion
8 Upper ball joint dust cover plate	26 Stabilizer cushion	44 Cowl body mount spacer holder
9 Upper arm	27 Collar	45 Front body support lower cushion
10 Steering knuckle	28 Cushion retainer	46 Hexagon bolt
11 Lower ball joint dust cover plate	29 Serration bolt	47 Rear body support upper cushion
12 Lower ball joint dust cover	30 Hexagon bolt	48 Spacer
13 Lower ball joint	31 Stabilizer bar	49 Cowl body mount spacer holder
14 Lower arm bushing	32 Stabilizer bushing	50 Hole plug
15 Hexagon bolt	33 Stabilizer bracket cover	51 Front suspension cross-member
16 Suspension lower arm	34 Cushion retainer	52 Hole plug
17 Cushion retainer	35 Strut bar cushion No.1	
18 Shock absorber cushion	36 Collar	

Fig. 17 Front suspension. 1972 Corona Mark II RT series

spring tension is relieved, then remove coil spring and insulator.

Installation

1. Position coil spring insulator into coil spring housing on front suspension crossmember.
2. Install spring compressor on coil spring, then install coil spring with compressor into coil spring housing.

NOTE: Position spring compressor onto the No. 3 coil from spring base.

---

3. Compress coil spring with spring compressor, then raise and support lower control arm using a suitable jack.
4. Install lower ball joint to steering knuckle, then install nut and cotter pin. Torque nut to 86.8-123 ft. lbs. (12-17 kg-m).
5. Lower jack and remove spring compressor, then install shock absorber.
6. Connect tie rod end to steering knuckle. Torque nut to 54.2-79.6 ft. lbs. (7.5-11 kg-m).
7. Connect stabilizer bar to lower control arm.
8. Install wheel and tire assembly and lower vehicle.
9. Adjust wheel alignment as necessary.

LOWER CONTROL ARM
Removal & Disassembly

1. Remove coil spring as described above.
2. Remove four bolts attaching lower control arm inner shaft to front suspension crossmember, then remove lower control arm with inner shaft, Fig. 16.
3. Position control arm inner shaft in a vise and remove ball joint.
4. Loosen and remove control arm pivot bushings at both ends of control arm inner shaft.
5. Remove inner shaft and dust seals from control arm.

Assembly & Installation

1. Install arm pivot dust seals onto both ends of inner shaft, then position inner shaft into lower control arm.
2. Apply grease to pivot bushing threads, then install pivot bushing to each side of inner shaft. Tighten pivot bushings alternately an equal amount. Torque bushings to 160-181 ft. lbs. (22-25 kg-m).
3. Install ball joint on lower control arm.

4. Install lower control arm on crossmember and tighten inner shaft attaching bolts. Torque bolts to 32.5-43.3 ft. lbs. (4.5-6 kg-m).
5. Install coil spring as described above.
6. Apply grease to control arm pivot bushings, then lower vehicle and adjust wheel alignment as necessary.

LOWER CONTROL ARM, STRUT BAR & COIL SPRING, REPLACE

1972-76 Corona Mark II
Removal

1. Raise and support front of vehicle, then remove wheel and tire assembly.
2. Detach stabilizer bar from lower control arm, Figs. 17 and 18.
3. Measure length of strut bar from center of serration bolt holes at front end to strut bar attaching nut at cushion retainer contact surface and note measurement for installation. The standard length for the strut bar is 348 mm for 1972 RT series and 359.7 mm for 1972-76 MX & RX series.
4. Remove strut bar.
5. Remove shock absorber, then compress coil spring using a suitable spring compressor.

NOTE: Install spring compressor onto third coil from bottom of spring.

---

6. Disconnect lower ball joint from steering knuckle.
7. Remove lower control arm to frame attaching nuts, then remove control arm.
8. Loosen spring compressor until all spring tension is relieved, then remove coil spring.
9. Remove lower control arm bushing using tool No. SST-09710-22020, if necessary.

Installation

1. Press bushing into lower control arm using tool No. SST-09710-22020, if removed.
2. Install lower control arm on frame, then compress coil spring using spring compressor. Install spring compressor on third coil from bottom of spring.
3. Install lower ball joint to steering knuckle. Torque attaching nut to 50.6-65 ft. lbs. (700-900 kg-cm).

4. Install strut bar as follows:
   a. Install strut bar to lower control arm and temporarily install to frame.
   b. Install strut bar in accordance with measurement taken during disassembly. If a new lower control arm or strut bar is to be installed, strut bar length should be adjusted to 348 mm for 1972 RT series and 359.7 mm for 1972-76 MX & RX series. Torque rear strut bar nut to 50.6-65 ft. lbs. (700-900 kg-cm).
5. Loosen spring compressor until spring tension is relieved, then remove spring compressor and install shock absorber.
6. Install stabilizer to lower control arm.
7. Tighten lower control arm and strut bar attaching bolts with weight of vehicle on front suspension. Torque lower control arm to 65-86.8 ft. lbs. (900-1200 kg-cm) and strut bar front end attaching bolts to 43.4-54.2 ft. lbs. (600-750 kg-cm).

SHOCK ABSORBER, REPLACE

Except 1972-77 Celica & Corolla

1. Raise and support front of vehicle.
2. Disconnect shock absorber from upper and lower mountings.
3. Remove shock absorber from vehicle.
4. Reverse procedure to install.

UPPER CONTROL ARM, REPLACE

1972-73 Corona
Removal

1. Raise and support front of vehicle, then remove wheel and tire assembly.
2. Separate upper ball joint from steering knuckle using puller SST-09628-10010.
3. Remove nuts attaching upper control arm shaft to crossmember, then remove upper control arm, Fig. 14.

NOTE: Record number and thickness of shims removed for installation.

---

4. Remove pivot bushings from end of upper control arm shaft.

Installation

1. Install pivot bushings to upper control arm shaft ends. Torque bush-

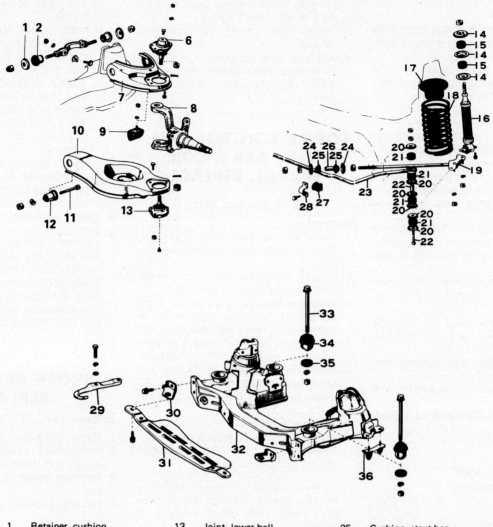

1	Retainer, cushion	13	Joint, lower ball	25	Cushion, strut bar
2	Bushing, upper arm	14	Retainer, cushion	26	Collar
3	Shaft, upper arm	15	Cushion	27	Bushing, stabilizer
4	Shim, camber adjusting	16	Absorber, shock, front	28	Bracket, stabilizer
5	Bolt, upper shaft setting	17	Insulator, coil spring	29	Hook, front
6	Joint, assembly, upper ball	18	Spring, coil	30	Bracket, engine under cover
7	Arm, upper	19	Bar, strut	31	Cover, engine under
8	Knuckle, steering	20	Retainer, cushion	32	Crossmember
9	Bumper, spring, No.2	21	Cushion, stabilizer	33	Bolt
10.	Arm, lower	22	Collar	34	Cushion
11	Bolt	23	Bar, stabilizer	35	Cushion
12	Bushing, lower arm	24	Retainer, cushion	36	Bumper, spring, No.1

Fig. 18   Front suspension. 1972-76 Corona Mark II MX & RX series

ings to 86.8 ft. lbs. (1200 kg-cm). Tighten bushing to each end of shaft by equal amount.
2. Install upper control arm to crossmember. Torque nuts to 32.6-43.4 ft. lbs. (450-600 kg-cm).
3. Attach upper ball joint to steering knuckle. Torque nut to 28.9-39.8 ft. lbs. (400-550 kg-cm).

1974-77 Corona

Removal

1. From inside engine compartment, remove nuts from upper control arm bolts.

NOTE: Do not remove upper control arm bolts.

---

2. Raise and support front of vehicle, then remove wheel and tire assembly.
3. On models equipped with ESP, disconnect wiring harness clamp from upper control arm.
4. Remove upper ball joint from upper control arm.

NOTE: Do not subject brake hose to stress.

---

5. Remove upper control arm mounting bolts, Fig. 15.
6. Remove upper control arm using a suitable pry bar.

Installation

1. Install upper ball joint on upper control arm.
2. Install upper control arm, then insert bolts and tighten nuts finger tight.
3. Connect ball joint to steering knuckle.
4. Install wheel and tire assembly, then lower vehicle and tighten upper control arm mounting bolts. Torque bolts to 94-130.2 ft. lbs. (13-18 kg-m).
5. Check adjust front wheel alignment as necessary.

1972-76 Corona Mark II

Removal

1. Raise and support front of vehicle, then remove wheel and tire assembly.
2. Remove brake hose from dust cover.
3. Raise lower control arm using a suitable jack, then separate upper ball joint from steering knuckle using tool No. SST-09628-10011.
4. Remove upper control arm, Figs. 17 and 18, using tool No. SST-09647-22010.

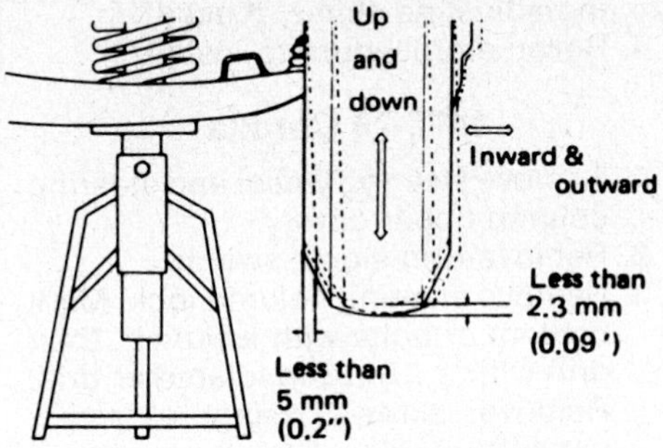

Fig. 19 Lower ball joint inspection. Except 1972-77 Celica & Corolla

---

NOTE: When removing, record amount and thickness of shims for installation.

---

5. Remove ball joint from upper control arm.
6. Remove bolts attaching bushing to each end of upper control arm, if necessary.
7. Press bushings from control arm using tool No. SST-09710-22020, if necessary.

Installation

1. Install upper control arm shaft and bushings tool No. SST-09710-22010, if removed.
2. Install cushion retainer and temporarily secure with nut.
3. Install upper control arm in vehicle using tool No. SST-09647-22010. Install same thickness and quantity of shims as removed. Torque upper control arm shaft nuts to 50.6-65 ft. lbs. (700-900 kg-cm).
4. Install upper ball joint on steering knuckle. Torque attaching nut to 39.8-50.6 ft. lbs. (550-700 kg-cm).
5. Install wheel and tire assembly, then lower vehicle and tighten nuts securing bushing on both sides of upper control arm. Torque nuts to 32.5-43.4 ft. lbs. (450-600 kg-cm).
6. Check front wheel alignment and adjust as necessary.

1972-77 Hi Lux

Removal

1. Raise front of vehicle and support front suspension crossmember, then remove wheel and tire assembly.
2. Raise lower control arm using a suitable jack.
3. Remove cotter pin and nut retaining upper ball joint to steering knuckle.
4. Using tool No. SST-09628-62010, separate upper ball joint from steering knuckle.
5. Remove two bolts attaching upper control arm shaft to crossmember,

then remove upper control arm and inner shaft, Fig. 16.

NOTE: Record number and thickness of shims for installation.

---

6. Mount control arm shaft in a vise and remove arm pivot bushings, if necessary. Remove dust seals from control arm.

Installation

1. If removed, install control arm dust seal on each end of control arm inner shaft. Position inner shaft into upper control arm. Apply grease to pivot bushing threads. Assemble pivot bushings to each side of inner shaft, tighten pivot bushings alternately an equal amount. Torque bushings to 160-181 ft. lbs. (22-25 kg-m).

NOTE: When installing inner shaft on control arm, position side with offset bolt hole toward front.

---

2. Install ball joint on upper control arm.
3. Install control arm on crossmember. Install same amount and thickness of shim as removed. Torque control arm mounting nuts to 95-153 ft. lbs. (13-21 kg-m).
4. Connect upper ball joint to steering knuckle. Torque attaching nut to 65.1-94 ft. lbs. (9-13 kg-m), then install cotter pin.
5. Install wheel and tie assembly then lower vehicle and check and adjust front wheel alignment as necessary.

BALL JOINT INSPECTION

Except 1972-77 Celica & Corolla

Upper Ball Joint

1. Disconnect upper control arm from steering knuckle.
2. Rotate ball stud with fingers and check for looseness in vertical and lateral directions. If looseness is noticeable, replace ball joint.
3. Attach upper ball joint to steering knuckle and install attaching nut and cotter pin.

Lower Ball Joint

1. Raise vehicle and support lower control arm.
2. With brakes applied, move wheel vertically and horizontally to check for looseness, Fig. 19. If tire bottom end movement exceeds .24 in for 1972-73 Corona, .08 in. for 1972-76 Corona Mark II, .2 in. for 1972-77 Hi Lux and .08 in. for 1974-77 Corona.

when wheel is moved inward and outward, replace ball joint. Ball joint movement should not exceed .10 in. for 1972-73 Corona, .04 in. for 1972-76 Corona Mark II and 1974-77 Corona and .09 in. for 1972-77 Hi Lux when wheel is moved upward and downward.

STEERING GEAR, REPLACE

Except 1972-74 Corolla

1. Remove pitman arm retaining nut, then disconnect pitman arm using a suitable puller.
2. Remove pinch bolt from flexible coupling.
3. Remove nuts attaching gear housing to frame, then remove steering gear assembly from vehicle. Note number and position of gear housing adjusting shims, if used.
4. Reverse procedure to install.

1972-74 Corolla

1. Remove steering wheel and steering column upper cover.
2. Remove turn signal switch.
3. Remove steering column lock. Mark centers of bolts with a punch, then drill with a .16-.20 in. diameter drill. Remove screws using a screw extractor.
4. Remove steering column upper housing.

NOTE: Use care not to apply excessive pressure to steering column.

5. Remove instrument panel under tray.
6. Remove steering column cover plate.
7. Remove clutch pedal.
8. Remove nut, then disconnect pitman arm using a suitable puller.
9. Remove steering gear to frame attaching bolts.
10. Remove steering column clamp bolts, then remove steering gear from vehicle.
11. Reverse procedure to install. When installing steering gear housing, temporarily tighten housing to frame attaching bolts, after aligning steering column tighten bolts. Align main shaft in center of steering column tube. Adjust clearance between steering wheel and column tube to .1 in. When installing steering column clamp bolts, be sure to insert wedge between instrument panel and clamp. Tighten bolts to 22-32 ft. lbs. When installing steering column lock, tighten bolts evenly until they break away.

TRIUMPH TR-6

INDEX OF SERVICE OPERATIONS

TRIUMPH TR6

GENERAL ENGINE SPECIFICATIONS

Year	Car-buretor	Bore & Stroke	Piston Displacement Cubic Inches	Com-press-ion Ratio	Maximum Brake H.P. @ R.P.M.	Minimum Torque Ft. Lbs. @ R.P.M.	Normal Oil Pressure Pounds
1972-76	①	2.94 x 3.74 (74.7 x 95mm)	152	7.5:1	—	—	—

—Not Available
① —Two Stromberg 175.

TUNE UP SPECIFICATIONS

The following specifications are published from the latest information available. This data should be used only in the absence of a decal affixed in the engine compartment.

▲Before removing wires from distributor cap, determine location of the No. 1 wire in cap, as distributor position may have been altered from that shown at the end of this chart.

Year	Spark Plug		Distributor		Ignition Timing			Hot Idle Speed
	Type	Gap	Point Gap Inch	Dwell Angle Deg.	Firing Order	Timing ATDC	Mark Location	
1972-74	N9Y	.025	.015	34—37	A	4°	①	700—900
1974-76	N9Y	.025	.015	34—48	A	4°	①	700—900

① —Mark located on pulley.

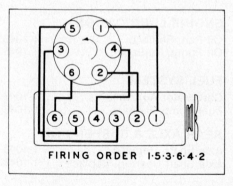

FIRING ORDER 1·5·3·6·4·2

Fig A

DISTRIBUTOR SPECIFICATIONS

If unit is checked on vehicle, double the R.P.M. and degrees to get crankshaft figures.

Distributor Part No.	Centrifugal Advance Degrees @ R.P.M. of Distributor				Vacuum Retard	
	Advance Starts	Intermediate Advance		Full Advance	Inches of Vacuum to Start Plunger	Maximum Retard Dist. Deg. @ Vacuum
41558①	0—1 @ 480	.5 @ 600 4 @ 900	7 @ 1400	9 @ 1900	2	8 @ 14

① —Lucas.

Continued

TRIUMPH TR6

ALTERNATOR & REGULATOR SPECIFICATIONS

Year	Alternator				Regulator	
	Make	Model	Field Winding Resistance ohms (68°F)	Output @ 14 Volts 6000 R.P.M. Amps	Model	Voltage Setting
1972-76	Lucas	18 ACR	3.2	43	—	13.6—14.4

—Not Available.

STARTING MOTOR SPECIFICATIONS

Year	Part No.	Brush Spring Tension (Ounces)	No Load Test			Torque Test	
			Amperes	Ft. Lbs.	R.P.M.	Amperes	Ft. Lbs.
1972-76	①	36	300	7.3	1,000	463	14.4

① —Lucas 2M100 pre-engaged.

VALVE SPECIFICATIONS

Year	Valve Lash		Valve Angles		Valve Spring Pressure Lbs. @ In.	Stem Clearance		Stem Diameter	
	Intake	Exhaust	Seat	Face		Intake	Exhaust	Intake	Exhaust
1972-76	.010	.010	45°	—	—	.0017—.0027	.0020—.0036	.3107—.3113	.3100—.3106

—Not Available.

PISTONS, PINS, RINGS, CRANKSHAFT & BEARINGS

Year	Piston Clearance Top of Skirt	Ring End Gap		Wrist-pin Diameter	Rod Bearings		Main Bearings			
		Comp.	Oil		Shaft Diameter	Bearing Clearance	Shaft Diameter	Bearing Clearance	Thrust on Bear. No.	Shaft End Play
1972-76	—	.012①	.015②	.8124	—	—	—	—	—	.006—.008

—Not Available.
① —Second Compression Rings .008.
② —Oil control, expander rail ring: END to BUT.

ENGINE TIGHTENING SPECIFICATIONS

*Torque specifications are for clean lightly lubricated threads only.

Dry dirty threads produce increased friction which prevents accurate measurement of tightness.

Year	Spark Plugs Ft. Lbs.	Cylinder Head Bolts Ft. Lbs.	Intake Manifold Ft. Lbs.	Camshaft Sprocket Bolts Ft. Lbs.	Rocker Cover Bolts Ft. Lbs.	Connecting Rod Cap Bolts Ft. Lbs.	Main Bearing Cap Bolts Ft. Lbs.	Flywheel to Crank-shaft Ft. Lbs.
1972-76	14—20	80	20	18—24	—2	①	65	95

① —Phosphated, 46 & Dye Colored, 50.

Continued

WHEEL ALIGNMENT SPECIFICATIONS

Year	Front & Rear Wheel Alignment	Caster Angle, Degrees		Camber Angle, Degrees				Toe-In Inch	Toe-Out on Turns Deg.	
		Limits	Desired	Limits		Desired			Outer Wheel	Inner Wheel
				Left	Right	Left	Right			
1972-76	Front	+2¼ to +3¼	+2¾	−¾ to +¼	−¾ to +¼	−¼	−¼	0—¹/₁₆	—	—
	Rear	—	—	−1½ to −½	−1½ to −½	−½	−½	—	—	—

—Not Available

COOLING SYSTEM CAPACITY DATA

Year	Cooling Capacity Qts.		Radiator Cap Relief Pressure, Lbs.		Thermo Opening Temp.	Fuel Tank Gals.	Engine Oil Refill Pints ①	Transmission Oil			Axle Oil Pints
	Without Heater	With A/C	With A/C	No A/C				4 Speed Pints	Overdrive Pints	Auto. Trans. Qts.	
1972-76	12	13.2	13	13	180	11.4	9.6	2.4	3.2	—	2.7

—Not Available

① —With filter change, 10.8 pts.

Electrical Section

DISTRIBUTOR, REPLACE

1. Remove secondary wires and distributor cap.
2. Disconnect primary wire.
3. Disconnect the vacuum advance line.
4. Disconnect the tachometer drive cable.
5. Loosen the bolt holding the distributor clamp plate.
6. Remove the distributor.
7. When installing the distributor, make sure the coupling offset key is positioned properly in the drive gear slot.
8. Reverse procedure to install.
9. Adjust ignition timing.

ALTERNATOR, REPLACE

Removal

1. Disconnect connector at temperature sending unit.
2. Disconnect two multi-socket connectors and remove adjustment bolt lock nut.
3. Loosen link bolt.
4. Remove adjustment bolt and washers.
5. Remove the main mounting bolt while supporting the alternator.
6. Remove the alternator from the mounting bracket and drive belt.

Installation

1. Tap the bushing in the alternator's rear mounting lug slightly rearward.

2. Assemble the main mounting bolt, washer, alternator and large spacer. Position assembly on mounting bracket and drive belt.
3. Insert main mounting bolt in mounting bracket.
4. Position small spacer and insert the main mounting bolt and nut.
5. Install the adjustment bolt with two washers positioned on either side of the link.
6. Adjust the drive belt and connect the connectors.

ALTERNATOR TESTING
Output Test

NOTE: To avoid misleading results, the unit should be at normal operating temperature.

1. Check drive belt adjustment and remove the multi-socket connectors.

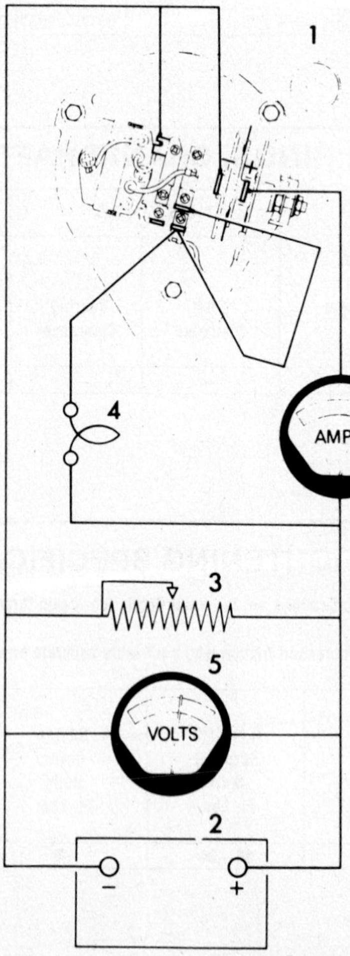

1. Alternator
2. Battery . . . 12 volt
3. Variable resistor . 0-15 ohm — 35 amp
4. Light . . 12 volt — 2·2 watt
5. Voltmeter . . 0-20 volt
6. Ammeter . . 0-40 amp

Fig. 1 Alternator output test connections

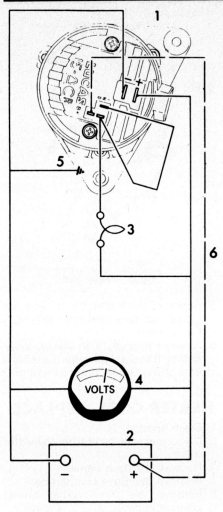

1. Alternator
2. Battery . . . 12 volt
3. Light . . . 12 volt — 2·2 watt
4. Voltmeter . . 0-20 volt
5. Earth connection to alternator body
6. This wire is only necessary for Lucas battery-sensed ACR alternators. It is not required for Lucas machine-sensed ACR alternators.

Fig. 2 Regulator tests connections

2. Remove the molded cover and connect test equipment, Fig. 1.

CAUTION: Do not reverse polarity. Keep the variable resistor connected no longer than necessary to make the test.

3. Run the engine, gradually increasing speed. At 1,500 alternator rpm (640 Engine rpm), the alternator test light should be out.
4. Hold alternator speed at 6,000 rpm (engine speed of 2,560 rpm) and ad-

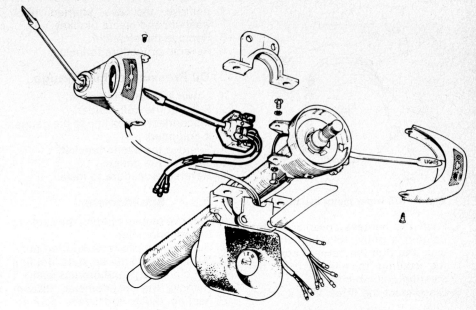

Fig. 3 Ignition switch & turn signal switch installation

just the variable resistor so the voltmeter reads 14 volts. The ammeter reading should now be about equal to a nominal output of 43 amps. If not, overhaul or replace the alternator.

Regulator Test

1. Connect test equipment, Fig. 2.
2. Repeat test procedures above.
3. Holding alternator speed at 6,000 rpm, the voltmeter should be steady at 14.0-14.4 volts. If not, the regulator should be replaced.

STARTER MOTOR, REPLACE

1. Remove air cleaner.
2. Disconnect the single connector.
3. Disconnect all cables.
4. Remove mounting bolts.
5. Remove the starter from engine.
6. Reverse procedure to install. Place star washers for grounding purposes under both bolt heads.

IGNITION SWITCH, REPLACE

1. Disconnect switch harness at the five-pin harness plug, Fig. 3.
2. Remove the small screw holding the switch to the steering column lock.
3. Remove the switch.
4. Reverse procedure to install.

CAUTION: When inserting the switch into the steering column lock assembly, note the keyway and make

sure the lock shaft and switch are aligned.

LIGHT SWITCH, REPLACE

1. Remove the speedometer.
2. Depress the two plastic clips on the switch and remove the switch.
3. Disconnect the three connectors.
4. Reverse procedure to install.

STOPLIGHT SWITCH, REPLACE

NOTE: The switch is located adjacent to the brake pedal arm.

1. Disconnect the two connectors.
2. Loosen the large hex nut and unscrew the switch from the nut.
3. Install by assembling the switch, two washers and the nut to the bracket. A washer should be positioned on either side of the bracket.

CAUTION: Do not overtighten the nut on the plastic threads since the switch could be damaged.

TURN SIGNAL SWITCH, REPLACE

1. Remove the adjacent speedometer or tachometer.
2. Pry off the two cap bolts, Fig. 3.
3. Remove the upper half of the steering column clamp.

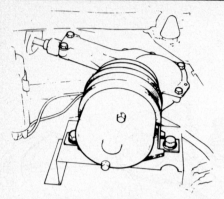

Fig. 4 W/S wiper motor installation

4. Push the harness cover down the column slightly, releasing the top clip, and pull the harness cover up the column to release from the steering column clamp.
5. Disconnect the three snap connectors.
6. Remove the two screws and the escutcheon plate.
7. Remove the switch and harness.
8. Thread the switch harness into place. This may be facilitated by taping the ends of the wires together. Secure with screws and washers.
9. Reverse procedure to install. Connect connectors as follows:
   a. Light green/brown switch wire to light green/brown main harness wire.
   b. Green/red switch wire to green/red main harness wire.
   c. Green/white switch wire to green/white main harness wire.

INSTRUMENTS, REPLACE

Ammeter or Temperature Gauge

1. Reach over the transmission cover side trim panel to gain access to the ammeter.
2. Pull the panel light bulb holder.
3. Disconnect the three connectors.

4. Remove the two knurled nuts, washers and clamp bracket.
5. Remove the ammeter.
6. Reverse procedure to install.

Oil Pressure or Fuel Gauge

1. Lower the veneered panel.
2. Pull out the bulb holder.
3. Disconnect the oil line to the gauge, if equipped.
4. Remove the clamp bracket.
5. Remove the gauge.
6. Reverse procedure to install.

Speedometer

1. Remove the nut holding the cable to the speedometer.
2. Remove the trip reset knurled nut.
3. Remove the knurled nuts holding the clamp legs and ground lead.
4. Remove the speedometer, disconnecting bulbs and spade connectors.
5. Reverse procedure to install.

W/S WIPER SWITCH, REPLACE

1. From behind panel, push switch and escutcheon assembly from panel.
2. Disconnect electrical connectors.
3. Push the spring clips inward to remove switch from escutcheon.
4. Reverse procedure to install.

WINDSHIELD WIPER MOTOR, REPLACE

1. Remove the harness plug.
2. Remove the gear box cover, Fig. 4.
3. Remove the crankpin spring clip by pulling clip out sideways.
4. Remove the washer.
5. Remove the connecting rod.
6. Remove the second washer.
7. Remove two sets of fasteners, strap and rubber sleeve.

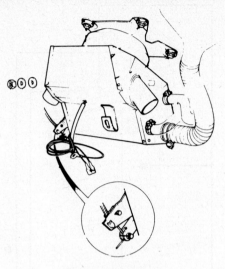

Fig. 5 Heater unit

8. Position the motor by turning the crosshead rack and tube assembly for removal.
9. Reverse procedure to install, lubricating the crankpin and crosshead end of the connecting rod and pin.

HEATER CORE, REPLACE

1. Drain coolant.
2. Disconnect the hose from the water valve.
3. Remove the dash panel.
4. Remove the glove compartment.
5. Remove the transmission tunnel cover trim pads.
6. Disconnect the four ventilation hoses from the heater, Fig. 5.
7. Disconnect the two water hoses from the heater.
8. Disconnect the flow control cable.
9. Pull the connectors from the blower switch.
10. Disconnect the blower ground lead from the steering column.
11. Remove the heater unit.
12. Reverse procedure to install.

Engine Section

ENGINE, REPLACE

1. Disconnect battery cables.
2. Remove hood.
3. Drain cooling system.
4. Disconnect hoses from the fuel evaporation charcoal canister.
5. Remove radiator and hoses, then carburetor air cleaner.
6. Remove chassis crossmember.
7. Disconnect the alternator, coil, oil warning light and gauge, main fuel line, ground strap from the rear lifting eye, water temperature gauge

lead, tachometer drive, throttle cable, brake servo line, heater hoses and control cable, and starter leads.
8. Raise and support the vehicle.
9. Disconnect the clutch slave cylinder and bracket, and exhaust pipe.
10. Lower vehicle.
11. Remove the transmission tunnel cover and transmission lever.
12. Disconnect the transmission switch leads and propeller shaft.
13. Remove the engine and transmission rear mounting bolts.
14. Attach a lifting sling to the engine

lifting eyes and release the weight of the engine from front mountings.
15. Disconnect the engine mountings on both sides.
16. Raise the engine and pull forward to clear the bulkhead, and raise the assembly from the car.
17. Reverse procedure to install.

CYLINDER HEAD, REPLACE

1. Disconnect the battery ground cable.
2. Drain cooling system.

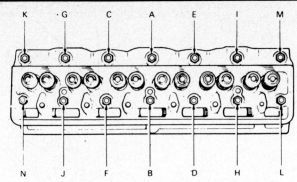

Fig. 1 Cylinder head tightening sequence

Fig. 3 Valve adjustment

3. Disconnect the hose at the intake manifold, rocker cover breather pipe, spark plug leads, water temperature sensor, water hoses at the thermostat housing and water pump, hose to the heater control valve, throttle linkage at the bulkhead cross shaft, mixture control cable and heater control cable at the heater valve.
4. Remove the air pump, and loosen the alternator and position aside.
5. Remove the water pump, rocker cover, rocker shaft and push rods.
6. Disconnect the exhaust manifold.
7. Remove the intake manifold and carburetor assembly.
8. Position the exhaust manifold away from the cylinder head studs.
9. Remove the cylinder head nuts in reverse sequence, Fig. 1.
10. Remove cylinder head and gasket.
11. Clean the cylinder block and head mating surfaces.
12. Install a new gasket.
13. Install cylinder head and nuts. Torque nuts in sequence, Fig. 1, to specifications.
14. Reverse procedure to assemble.
15. After 1,000 miles of operation, recheck cylinder head nut torque with engine hot. Working in sequence, Fig. 1, loosen each nut in turn one flat and retorque to specification.

ROCKER SHAFT, REPLACE

1. Remove the rocker cover.
2. Remove the six nuts and washers securing the rocker shaft to the cylinder head.
3. Remove the rocker shaft, Fig. 2.
4. Reverse procedure to install. Ensure that the rocker adjustment screw bolt ends are located properly in the push rod caps. Torque securing nuts to 26-34 ft. lbs.
5. Adjust valve clearance.

VALVES, ADJUST

1. Disconnect the battery ground cable, and remove the spark plugs and rocker cover.
2. Check clearance between the rocker pad and valve tip, Fig. 3, and adjust to specifications in the following sequence:

NOTE: Count valves from the front of the engine.

a. No. 1 and 3 with No. 10 and 12 open.
b. No. 8 and 11 with No. 2 and 5 open.
c. No. 4 and 6 with No. 7 and 9 open.

Fig. 2 Rocker shaft assembly

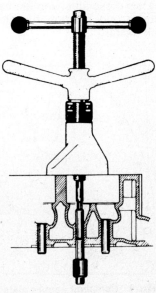

Fig. 4 Valve guide replacement

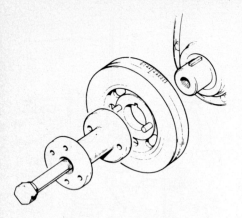

Fig. 5   Crankshaft pulley removal

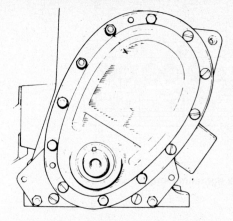

Fig. 6   Timing chain cover installation

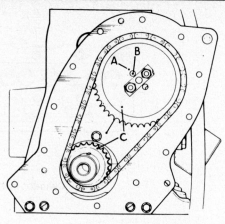

Fig. 7   Timing chain installation

d. No. 10 and 12 with No. 1 and 3 open.

e. No. 2 and 5 with No. 8 and 11 open.

f. No. 7 and 9 with No. 4 and 6 open.

3. Adjust by loosening the adjustment pin locknut and turning the adjustment pin.

VALVE GUIDES, REPLACE

Use special tool 60A. Assemble the new valve guide in the tool with the chamfered end first. Place the tool in position and drive the new guide into place while the old guide is removed, Fig. 4.

TIMING CHAIN COVER, REPLACE

1. Disconnect battery ground cable.
2. Drain cooling system.
3. Remove the radiator, fan blades, chassis cross tube, and fan belt.
4. Loosen and position the steering rack forward.

5. Remove the center bolt holding the fan extension and crankshaft pulley, then the extension by tapping with a hammer.
6. Remove the crankshaft pulley, Fig. 5.
7. Remove the set screws, bolts, nuts and spring washers holding the timing chain cover, Fig. 6.
8. Pry the timing chain cover from the engine.

CAUTION: Do not damage or distort the cover.

9. Remove the oil seal sleeve.
10. Remove the cover.
11. Clean all surfaces and install gasket cover.
12. Install the timing cover into place, positioning it over the studs and dowels. Replace fasteners and tighten evenly.

CAUTION: To ease cover installation, compress the timing chain tensioner with a length of wire, being careful not to tear the gasket when withdrawing the wire.

13. Lubricate the timing cover oil seal and sleeve with oil. With the cham-

fered end first, press the sleeve on the crankshaft and through the timing cover oil seal.
14. Reverse procedure to assemble.

NOTE: Use special tool S341 to replace the steering rack.

TIMING CHAIN, REPLACE
Removal

1. Disconnect battery ground cable and remove timing chain cover.
2. Remove the oil seal sleeve and oil thrower.
3. Crank the engine until No. 1 and 6 pistons are at TDC.
4. Check to see that timing marks A and B are visible and that marks C on the camshaft and crankshaft sprockets are aligned, Fig. 7.
5. Straighten the lock tabs on the camshaft sprocket and remove the bolts.
6. Remove the timing chain with the camshaft and crankshaft sprockets.

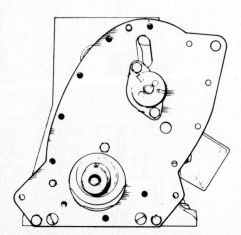

Fig. 8   Camshaft keeper plate installation

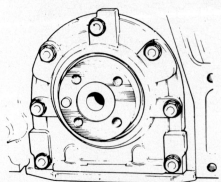

Fig. 9   Crankshaft rear oil seal housing installation

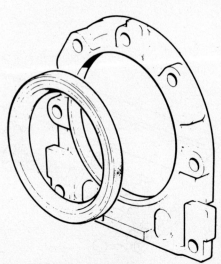

Fig. 10   Crankshaft rear oil seal

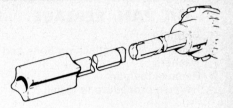

Fig. 12 Oil pump spindle

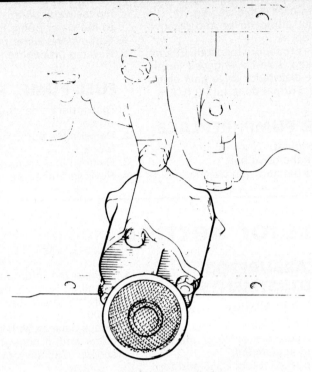

Fig. 11 Oil pump installation

15. Check camshaft and crankshaft sprocket alignment.
16. Ensure numbers 1 and 6 pistons are at TDC.
17. Reverse procedure to assemble.

PISTONS AND RINGS

Pistons are available in standard size and 0.020 inch oversize. Rings are available in standard size and 0.010, 0.020 and 0.030 inch oversize.

CRANKSHAFT REAR OIL SEAL, REPLACE
Removal

1. Remove the transmission.
2. Remove the rear adaptor plate.
3. Remove the two rear center oil pan bolts.
4. Remove the oil seal housing from the crankcase with the seal, Fig. 9.

CAUTION: Do not damage the oil pan gasket.

5. Press out the seal, taking care not to distort the housing.

Installation

1. Clean all mating surfaces.
2. Place the oil seal housing on a flat surface, machined side up, and lubricate the outside diameter of a new seal with grease.
3. With the seal lip facing up, press the seal in place and wipe off excess grease, Fig. 10.
4. Apply sealing compound to the crankcase and oil seal housing mating surfaces and install a new gasket.
5. Lubricate the oil seal inner diameter and the crankshaft with clean engine oil, and install the oil seal and housing over the crankshaft.
6. Secure the housing to the crankshaft, Fig. 9.

NOTE: The top bolt has a copper washer under the head to prevent oil seepage.

7. Reverse removal procedure to assemble.

Installation

1. Install the sprockets in position.
2. Check alignment by placing a straight edge across the sprocket.
3. If the sprockets are not aligned, adjust by removing the drive key and fitting shims behind the crankshaft sprocket. Refit the key.

NOTE: Shim thickness available: 0.004 in. and 0.006 in.

4. Remove the sprockets and place the timing chain on the sprockets.
5. Install the sprockets and chain, keeping the chain taut.
6. If the original sprockets are being used, make sure punch marks A, B and C line up correctly, Fig. 7. If new sprockets are being installed, check alignment, fit and secure them, and make punch marks in the appropriate spots.
7. Reverse procedure to assemble.

CAUTION: The oil thrower must be installed with the dished face toward the timing cover.

CAMSHAFT, REPLACE

1. Remove the grille.
2. Remove the cylinder head.
3. Remove the cam followers.
4. Remove the fuel pump.

5. Disconnect tachometer drive.
6. Remove distributor and plate assembly.
7. Ensure the distributor drive slot is positioned to ease assembly and remove the distributor drive gear.
8. Remove timing chain and sprockets.
9. Remove camshaft keeper plate, Fig. 8.
10. Disconnect the left-hand engine mounting from the chassis bracket, and raise the engine to remove the camshaft.

CAUTION: Before raising the engine, position the speedometer cable so it won't be trapped between the bell housing and bulkhead.

11. With the flat end first, insert the camshaft into the engine.

NOTE: Do not damage the bearing surfaces.

12. Secure the shaft with the keeper plate, and tighten retaining bolts.
13. Lower the engine and connect the left-hand mounting.
14. Check camshaft end play by pulling the shaft out against the keeper plate and measuring the gap between the shaft and plate. The gap should be .004-.008 inch. Replace the keeper plate if the gap is not within specifications.

OIL PAN, REPLACE

1. Drain oil.
2. Remove oil pan attaching bolts and washers.
3. Remove the pan.
4. Reverse procedure to install.

OIL PUMP, REPLACE

1. Drain oil.
2. Remove oil pan.
3. Loosen three bolts holding the pump to the crankcase, Fig. 11.
4. Hold the pump cover and remove the pump.
5. Reverse procedure to install. Ensure the pump spindle engages firmly into the distributor drive gear shaft, Fig. 12. Torque bolts to 7-9 ft. lbs.

WATER PUMP, REPLACE

1. Drain coolant.
2. Remove the drive belt.
3. Remove the nuts and washers holding the water pump mounting flange to the water pump housing.
4. Remove the water pump.
5. Reverse procedure to install.

FUEL PUMP, REPLACE

1. Disconnect the fuel lines at the pump.
2. Remove the pump from the cylinder block.
3. Remove and discard the gasket.
4. Reverse procedure to install.

Carburetor Section

CARBURETOR ADJUSTMENTS

Idle Mixture

1. Remove the piston dampers from both carburetors or from the one requiring adjustment.
2. Insert special jet tool S353 and turn it clockwise to enrich the mixture or counterclockwise to lean out the mixture, Fig. 1.

Idle Speed

1. Using a synchrocheck meter against both carburetor intakes in turn, adjust the idle screws to give 800-850 rpm while maintaining an identical air flow reading from both carburetors.
2. Shut off the engine, checking that the relay lever is against the stop, Fig. 2.
3. Insert a 3/32 inch drill shank between the tongue and slot of the interconnection lever.

4. Tighten the interconnection spring coupling. Remove the drill.
5. Start the engine and increase rpm to 1,500.
6. Check balance with a synchrocheck meter and, if necessary, adjust idle screws to achieve an equal reading.

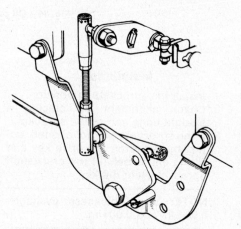

Fig. 1   Idle mixture adjustment

Fig. 2   Idle speed adjustment

Emission Controls Section

EGR VALVE

To check the operation of the EGR valve, warm up the engine, and open and close the throttle several times. Observe or feel the EGR valve, which should open and close with changes in engine speed. The EGR valve should close at once when the throttle is closed.

Service the EGR valve as follows:
1. Remove the EGR valve from the cylinder head.
2. Clean the valve seat with a wire brush.
3. Insert the valve opening into a standard spark plug machine and lift the diaphragm.

4. Blast the valve for 30 seconds.
5. Use compressed air and a brush to remove all traces of carbon.

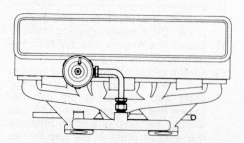

Fig. 1   EGR valve installation

FUEL ABSORPTION CANISTER, REPLACE

1. Disconnect all lines at the canister, Fig. 2.
2. Remove the bracket nut and bolt.
3. Remove the canister.
4. Transfer the restrictor in the old canister to the new canister.
5. Install the new canister.

CATALYTIC CONVERTER, REPLACE

1. Remove the catalytic converter support bracket.

2. Release the catalytic converter from the tailpipe.

NOTE: It may be necessary to remove the carburetor.

3. Remove the nuts holding the catalytic converter and front pipe to the exhaust manifold.
4. Remove the catalytic converter and front pipe, and exhaust manifold gasket.

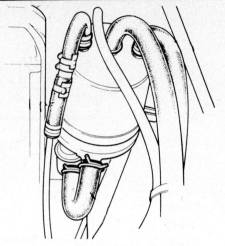

Fig. 2   Fuel absorption canister

5. Fit a new catalytic converter.
6. Reset the catalytic converter warning indicator to zero.

AIR PUMP BELT TENSION

1. Loosen the securing bolt and two adjusting link bolts.
2. Move the air pump to obtain a belt deflection of ½ inch.
3. Tighten the bolts.

Clutch & Transmission Section

CLUTCH, REPLACE
Removal

1. Remove the transmission.
2. Progressively loosen and remove the six bolts and washers holding the clutch to the flywheel, Fig. 1.
3. Remove the clutch and driven plate, Fig. 1.

Installation

1. Install the driven plate up to the flywheel using a dummy input shaft.

CAUTION: The longer boss of the driven plate hub must be fitted away from the flywheel.

2. Engage the clutch assembly in the three flywheel locating dowels.
3. Install and evenly torque the six securing bolts and washers to 16-20 ft. lbs.

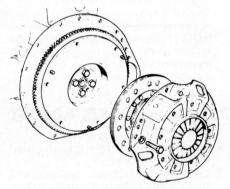

Fig. 1   Clutch assembly

4. Remove the dummy input shaft.
5. Reverse removal procedure to complete installation.

TRANSMISSION, REPLACE

1. Remove both front seats.
2. Remove transmission side trim panels and the panel support bracket.
3. Remove gear shift lever.
4. Remove carpet and transmission cover panel.
5. Disconnect driveshaft.
6. Disconnect speedometer drive cable.
7. Remove mounting bolts and nuts.
8. Remove exhaust support bracket.
9. Remove mounting plate bolts.
10. Remove the nine upper engine-bell housing fasteners.
11. Raise and support vehicle.
12. Disconnect clutch slave cylinder pushrod from cross shaft lever.
13. Place a suitable jack under the engine and raise the engine and transmission slightly to remove the mounting plate assembly.
14. Remove remaining seven engine-bell housing fasteners.
15. Remove transmission from vehicle.
16. Reverse procedure to install.

Rear Axle & Brakes Section

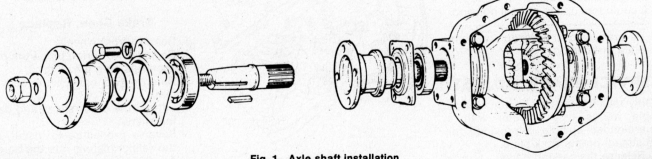

Fig. 1   Axle shaft installation

Fig. 2   Parking brake cable attachment

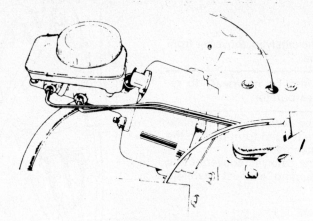

Fig. 3   Master cylinder installation

AXLE SHAFT, BEARING & OIL SEAL, REPLACE

Removal

1. On right side of vehicle, remove exhaust components.
2. Disconnect the inner drive shaft from the flange.
3. Remove four bolts and washers holding the shaft oil seal housing to the case.
4. Remove the shaft with drive flange, oil seal housing and ball race.
5. Remove the holding nut and plain washer from the shaft, and the drive flange, key and oil seal.
6. Remove ball race from the shaft.
7. Remove the oil seal from the housing.

Installation

1. Install the ball race to the shaft until the race's outer face is approximately aligned with the end of the shaft taper.
2. Lay the oil seal housing flat on a bench with the smaller diameter facing upward.
3. Insert the oil seal, lip first, into the housing until the plain face of the seal is flush with the housing.
4. Lubricate the lip and slide the seal over the drive flange.

CAUTION: Make sure the drive flange deflector seal is not damaged. It could foul up the oil seal housing.

5. Reverse removal procedure to complete installation.

SERVICE BRAKE, ADJUST

Only rear brakes can be adjusted. A single wedge type adjuster with a square-ended spindle is provided for adjustment on the back plate.

1. Release the parking brake.

2. Rotate the adjuster spindle clockwise, viewed from the rear of the back plate, until the wheel is locked.
3. Rotate the adjuster spindle counterclockwise until the wheel can be turned freely.

NOTE: Failure of an adjuster spindle to lock a rear wheel indicates excessively worn brake linings.

PARKING BRAKE, ADJUST

1. Release the parking brake.
2. Tighten the rear brake adjuster until both wheels lock.
3. Loosen the locknuts holding the brake cable forks to the brake cable.
4. Remove the clevis pins holding the brake cable forks to the back plate levers, Fig. 2.
5. Adjust the cable forks until the clevis pins can be engaged in the

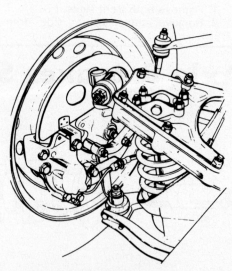

Fig. 4   Caliper attachment

forks and back plate levers without force.
6. Tighten the locknuts.

NOTE: The adjustment should be made equally to the forks so the compensator is kept in a central position.

7. Install the clevis pins to the cable forks and back plate levers, and secure with new cotter pins.
8. Loosen the rear brake adjusters until the wheels rotate freely.

MASTER CYLINDER, REPLACE

1. Disconnect brake lines, sealing the ends, Fig. 3.
2. Remove the two mounting nuts and washers.
3. Remove the master cylinder.

DISC BRAKE SERVICE

Caliper, Replace

1. Remove front wheel.
2. Disconnect front caliper brake line at the flex hose.
3. Remove bolts and washers holding the caliper to the mounting disc, Fig. 4.
4. Remove the caliper.
5. Reverse procedure to install.

Brake Shoe, Replace

1. Remove front wheels.
2. Remove two spring pins from brake shoe retaining pins, Fig. 5.
3. Remove two brake shoe retaining pins.
4. Lift out the brake shoes and damping shims.
5. Reverse procedure to install, ease the caliper pistons into the bores to provide clearance by applying pres-

has moved the necessary amount and repeat the procedure on the opposite piston in the caliper.

a. Clean dust and clean off the pad seats.
b. Install pads and damping shims to the caliper.

NOTE: Make sure the arrows on the damping shims point in the direction of forward disc rotation.

Caliper, Overhaul

1. Remove the caliper, and remove brake pads and shims.
2. Remove the clip holding the piston dust covers.
3. Remove the dust covers.
4. Remove the pistons using low pressure air.

NOTE: Pistons must be installed in

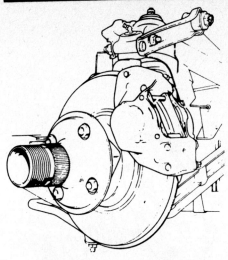

Fig. 5   Brake shoe replacement

sure to the piston and simultaneously opening the bleed nipple. Close the nipple when the piston

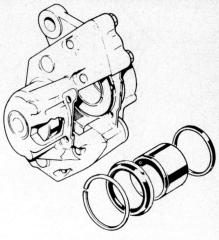

Fig. 6   Caliper disassembled

original bores.

5. Pry out the cylinder seals, Fig. 6.
6. Reverse procedure to assemble.

Rear Suspension Section

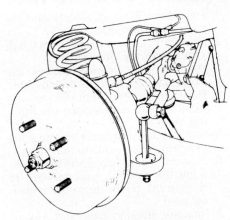

Fig. 1   Shock absorber installation

SHOCK ABSORBER, REPLACE

1. Raise and support vehicle and remove rear wheels.

2. Place a jack under the trailing arm and raise until the spring is slightly compressed.
3. Remove shock absorber link to the trailing arm attachments, Fig. 1.
4. Remove the shock absorber complete with link. Separate link from shock absorber.
5. Reverse procedure to install.

SPRING, REPLACE

1. Raise and support vehicle, remove the wheel and release the parking brake.
2. Support the trailing arm with a suitable jack.
3. Remove shock absorber link to the trailing arm attachments.
4. Lower the jack under the trailing arm until the spring tension is removed.

Fig. 2   Spring installation

5. Remove the spring, and the upper and lower rubber insulating rings, Fig. 2.
6. Reverse procedure to install.

Front Suspension Section

WHEEL ALIGNMENT, ADJUST

NOTE: Only two adjustments are possible: toe-in and camber.

Toe-in

1. Loosen the outer clips on the steering rack.
2. Loosen the tie rod end locknuts.
3. Shorten or extend both tie rods equally to adjust toe-in.

CAUTION: Tie rods must be equally adjusted. Differences in lengths will result in incorrect toe-out on turns.

Camber

1. Raise and support vehicle.
2. Loosen the four nuts holding the lower wishbone brackets to the chassis, Fig. 1.
3. Remove or add shims equally to both wishbone brackets as required. Adding shims increases

negative camber while removing shims increases positive camber.

WHEEL BEARINGS, ADJUST

1. Remove the disc brake pads and hub cap.
2. Remove the cotter pin from the slotted adjusting nut.
3. Loosen or tighten the slotted adjusting nut, Fig. 2, to obtain .003-.005 inch end play.

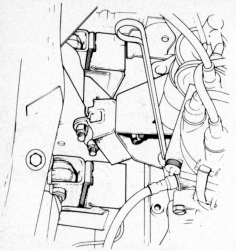

Fig. 1 Camber adjustment

4. Reassemble the unit using a new cotter pin.

BALL JOINTS, REPLACE

1. Raise and support vehicle and re-move wheels.
2. Place a suitable jack under the spring pad on the lower wishbone and raise the jack to remove tension from upper ball joint.
3. Remove ball joint to the vertical link attachments, Fig. 3.
4. With tool S166, remove the ball joint from the vertical link.
5. Remove ball joint housing to the upper wishbone attachments, Fig. 4.

NOTE: The outer bolt enters from the rear side of the wishbone. The inner bolt enters from the forward side of the wishbone.

6. Remove the ball joint and housing from the upper wishbone.

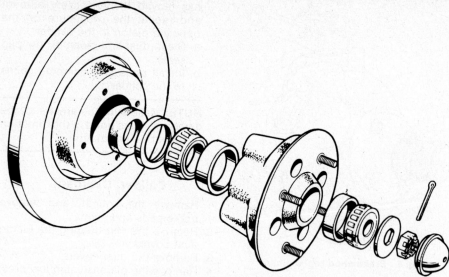

Fig. 2 Wheel bearing adjustment

7. Reverse procedure to install. Torque bolts securing ball joint housing to upper wishbone—24-32 ft. lbs. Torque nut securing ball joint to vertical link to 35-50 ft. lbs.

SHOCK ABSORBER, REPLACE

1. Raise and support vehicle and re-move the wheel.
2. Remove the four nuts and washers holding the shock absorber lower mounting brackets to the underside of the lower wishbone, Fig. 5.
3. Remove the hardware and upper rubber mounting from the top of the shock absorber, Fig. 6.
4. Remove the shock from the lower wishbone and remove the rubber mounting.
5. Remove the bolt and nut holding the lower bracket to the shock ab-sorber. Remove shock absorber from vehicle.
6. Reverse procedure to install.

STEERING GEAR, REPLACE

1. Raise and support vehicle and re-move front wheels.
2. Disconnect the tie rod outer ball joints from the steering arms.
3. Remove the hardware holding the universal joint to the steering gear.
4. Remove the plug from the steering rack damper and release the hold-ing strap.
5. Remove the hardware holding the steering rack U bolts to the chassis.
6. Remove the "U" bolts and brackets.
7. Slide the steering gear forward to release the pinion from the univer-sal joint.
8. Remove steering gear and mount-ing bushings.
9. Reverse procedure to install.

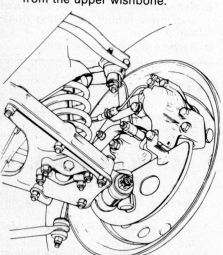

Fig. 3 Ball joint attachment

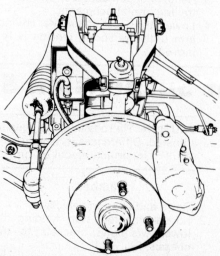

Fig. 4 Ball joint attachment & shock absorber upper attachment

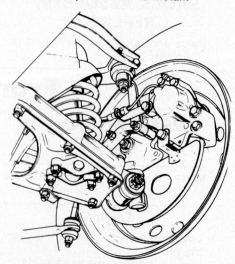

Fig. 5 Shock absorber lower attachment

TRIUMPH TR7

INDEX OF SERVICE OPERATIONS

GENERAL ENGINE SPECIFICATIONS

Year	Engine	Car-buretor	Bore and Stroke	Piston Displace-ment Cubic Inches	Com-pression Ratio	Maximum Brake H.P. @ RPM	Maximum Torque Lbs. Ft. @ RPM	Normal Oil Pressure
1976-77	4-122	①	3.56 x 3.07	122	8.0	—	—	—

—Not Available

①—Two Zenith Strombergs.

TUNE UP SPECIFICATIONS

Year	Spark Plug		Ignition Timing			Hot Idle Speed
	Type	Gap Inch	Firing Order Fig.	Timing BTDC ①	Mark Fig.	
1976-77	N12Y	.025	A	2	B	800

①—BTDC: Before top dead center.

②—Exc. Calif., 10° BTDC, Calif., 2° ATDC.

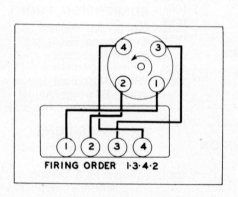

FIRING ORDER 1·3·4·2

Fig. A

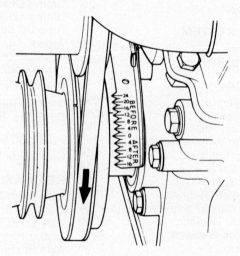

Fig. B

DISTRIBUTOR SPECIFICATIONS

If unit is checked on vehicle, double the RPM and degrees to get crankshaft figures.

Year	Advance Starts	Centrifugal Advance Degrees @ RPM of Distributor				Distributor Retard	
		Intermediate Advance			Full Advance	Inches of Vacuum to Start Plunger	Max. Retard Dist. Deg. @ Vacuum
1976-77①	0 @ 400	1-4 @ 650	4-6 @ 950	6½-8½ @ 1400	7-9 @ 2500	—	—
1976-77②	0 @ 400	1-4 @ 650	4-6 @ 950	6½-8½ @ 1400	7-9 @ 2500	3	5-7 @ 15

—Not Available

①—Exc. Calif.

②—Calif.

Continued

TRIUMPH TR7

ALTERNATOR & REGULATOR SPECIFICATIONS

Year	Make	Model	Alternator — Rated Hot Output			Regulator Model No.
			Amps	Volts	Engine RPM	
1976-77 ①	Lucas	17 ACR	36	14	2540	14TR
1976-77 ②	Lucas	20 ACR	66	14	2540	14TR

①—Exc. Air conditioning.
②—With Air conditioning.

BRAKE SPECIFICATIONS

Year	Brake Drum Inside Diameter	Disc Brake Rotor Thickness
1976-77	8.0	.375

STARTER MOTOR SPECIFICATIONS

Year	Make	Model	Brush Spring Tension Ounces	No Load Test		Lock Torque Test	
				Amps	RPM	Amps	Torque Ft. Lbs.
1976-77	Lucas	2M100 PE	36	40	6000	463	14.4

PISTONS, PINS, RINGS, CRANKSHAFT & BEARINGS

Year	Piston Clearance Bottom of Skirt	Ring End Gap ① Comp.	Ring End Gap ① Oil	Wristpin Diameter	Rod Bearings Shaft Diameter	Rod Bearings Bearing Clearance	Main Bearings Shaft Diameter	Main Bearings Bearing Clearance	Thrust on Bear. No.	Shaft End Play
1976-77	.0005-.0015	.015	.015	.9375	1.7500—1.7505	.0008—.0023	2.1260—2.1265	.0012—.0022	3	.003—.011

①—Fit rings in tapered bore for clearance listed in tightest portion of ring travel.

VALVE SPECIFICATIONS

Year	Valve Lash Int.	Valve Lash Exh.	Valve Angles Seat	Valve Angles Face	Valve Spring Installed Height	Stem Clearance Intake	Stem Clearance Exhaust	Stem Diameter Intake	Stem Diameter Exhaust
1976-77	.008C	.018C	44½	45	1²/₅	.00—.0023	.0014—.0030	.3107—.3113	.3100—.3106

ENGINE TIGHTENING SPECIFICATIONS

Torque specifications are for clean and lightly lubricated threads only. Dry or dirty threads produce increased friction which prevents accurate measurement of tightness.

Year	Cylinder Head Bolts Ft. Lbs.	Intake & Exhaust Manifold Ft. Lbs.	Connecting Rod Cap Bolt Ft. Lbs.	Main Bearing Cap Bolt Ft. Lbs.	Flywheel to Crankshaft Ft. Lbs.	Vibration Damper or Pulley Ft. Lbs.
1976-77	55	20	45	65	45	120

WHEEL ALIGNMENT SPECIFICATIONS

Year	Caster Angle, Degrees		Camber Angle, Degrees		Toe-In Inch	King Pin Inclination	
	Limits	Desired	Limits	Desired		Limits	Desired
1976-77	+2½ to +4½	+3½	−1¼ to +¾	−¼	0—¹/₁₆	10¼ to 12¼	11¼

REAR AXLE SPECIFICATIONS

Year	Carrier Type	Ring Gear & Pinion Backlash		Pinion Bearing Preload		Differential Bearing Preload	
		Method	Adjustment Inch	Method	Adjustment Inch-Lbs.	Method	Adjustment Inch
1976-77	Removable	Shims	.005	Spacer	13—20	Shims	.004
1976-77	Integral	Shims	.004—.006	Spacer	13—20	Shims	.002—.004

COOLING SYSTEM & CAPACITY DATA

Year	Cooling Capacity Qts.	Radiator Cap Relief Pressure, Lbs.	Thermostat Opening Temp.	Fuel Tank Gals.	Engine Oil Refill Qts. ①	Transmission Oil			Rear Axle Oil Pints
						4 Speed Pints	5 Speed Pints	Auto Trans. Qts.	
1976-77	6½	15	190°	12	4	2	2.7	4¾	②

①—With filter
②—With four speed, 2.25 pts.; with five speed, 1.6 pts.

Electrical Section

DISTRIBUTOR, REPLACE

Removal

1. Remove fresh air duct.
2. Remove distributor cover.
3. Pull off retard unit line on California models only.
4. Remove two distributor mounting bolts and washers.
5. Maneuver distributor out of engine block.

Installation

1. Rotate crankshaft to bring No. 1 piston to TDC.
2. Align index on the pulley with 0° mark on timing cover.
3. Insert distributor with the vacuum unit facing toward the rear, and engage drive gear so the rotor points toward the rear manifold mounting bolt, Fig. 1.
4. Complete installation.

DISTRIBUTOR SERVICE

Disassemble

1. Remove distributor cap and rotor, Fig. 2.
2. Remove cover and felt pad.

Fig. 1 Aligning distributor rotor with rear manifold mounting bolt

3. Carefully remove two screws, lock washers and washers to release pick-up.
4. Remove two long screws and lock washers.
5. Hold amplifier module in position and remove on short screw, lock washer and washer.
6. Hold distributor body in one hand and amplifier module in the other, then carefully unhook retard unit link from moving plate pin.
7. Hold distributor body and amplifier module slightly apart, then withdraw two clips.
8. Pull out wire grommet, then remove amplifier module and pick-up.
9. Tap out retard unit pin, then remove retard unit.
10. Using a suitable pair of snap ring pliers, remove snap ring.
11. Remove plain washer and O-ring.
12. Carefully withdraw timing rotor.
13. Remove two attaching screws and lift out base plate.

14. Tap out drive gear pin, then remove drive gear and thrust washer.
15. Remove metal spacer.
16. Remove control springs, using care not to distort springs.

NOTE: Do not attempt to further disassemble shaft and mechanism.

Assemble

1. Lubricate weight assembly working surfaces.
2. Install control springs, using care not to distort springs, Fig. 2.
3. Install metal spacer.
4. Lubricate shaft, then insert shaft into body. Install thrust washer and drive gear and secure with drive gear pin.
5. Lubricate moving plate pin, then position base plate so that moving plate pin is correctly positioned for retard unit link. Secure with two attaching screws.
6. Carefully insert timing rotor. Ensure master projection locates correctly in master slot.
7. Install O-ring, washer and snap ring.
8. Install retard unit and secure with retard unit pin.
9. Hold distributor body and amplifier unit slightly apart, then push in wire grommet.
10. Install two clips.
11. Hold distributor body in one hand and amplifier module in the other hand, then slightly rotate moving plate to hook retard unit to moving plate pin.
12. Hold amplifier module in position, then install one short screw, lock washer and washer finger tight.
13. Install two long screws and lock washers finger tight.
14. Ensure that amplifier module and two wire grommets are correctly seated, then tighten three attaching screws evenly.
15. Position pick-up and carefully install two attaching screws, lock washers and washers finger tight.
16. Adjust pick-up air gap to .014 to .016 in.
17. Install felt pad, then install cover with two recess positioned adjacent to clips.
18. Install rotor and distributor cap.

ALTERNATOR, REPLACE

1. Slide harness plug in and down to disconnect harness.
2. Loosen adjustment bolt, support bracket bolt and main mounting bolt.
3. Push alternator toward engine to remove drive belt.

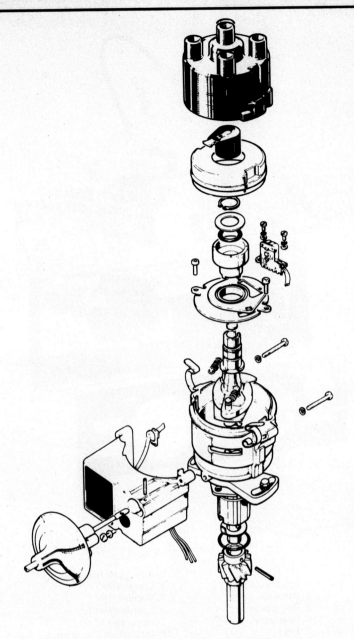

Fig. 2   Disassembled view of distributor

4. Remove adjustment bolt and washer.
5. Remove main mounting bolt and lift alternator out.
6. Reverse procedure to install.

STARTER MOTOR, REPLACE

1. Raise vehicle.
2. Disconnect and lower complete exhaust system.

NOTE: It is not necessary to remove system.

3. Remove heat shield from the starter solenoid.
4. Swing front of exhaust pipe under engine and secure it temporarily.
5. Disconnect wire connection.
6. Disconnect battery lead.
7. Loosen bell housing exhaust bracket bolt.
8. Remove mounting bolts in this order: lower, middle, upper.
9. Maneuver starter motor from vehicle.
10. Reverse procedure to install.

IGNITION SWITCH, REPLACE

1. Remove two long screws and remove steering column covers.
2. Disconnect switch harness plug.
3. Remove two small screws, which hold switch and harness.

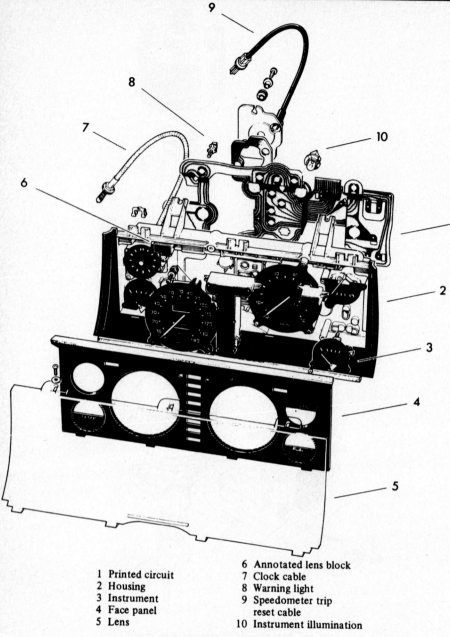

1 Printed circuit	6 Annotated lens block
2 Housing	7 Clock cable
3 Instrument	8 Warning light
4 Face panel	9 Speedometer trip
5 Lens	reset cable
	10 Instrument illumination

Fig. 3 Instrument cluster

squeezing the projection.

4. Unhook two harness plugs.
5. Loosen switch clamp screw.
6. Remove switch and harness.

INSTRUMENT CLUSTER, REPLACE

NOTE: All instruments, except the speedometer, are removed in the same way, as follows:

1. Remove the lens, Fig. 3.
2. Lift away the face panel.
3. Remove the holding screws, which release the gauge.

Speedometer
1. Remove the lens.
2. Lift away the face panel.
3. Depress the lever to release catch from annular groove in boss.
4. Pull speedometer cable free.
5. Remove three screws, holding instrument.

WINDSHIELD WIPER MOTOR & DRIVE

1. Remove wiper arms.
2. Remove fresh air duct.
3. Disconnect two 35 amp connectors from battery lead connector.
4. Remove windshield washer reservoir tank.
5. Remove battery.
6. Disconnect harness plug.
7. Remove clamp strap from vehicle body slot.
8. Remove plate adjacent to brake master cylinder servo.
9. At wiper arms, remove spindle nut and all other hardware.
10. Remove motor-drive assembly from vehicle.

LIGHT SWITCH, REPLACE

1. Remove dash switch panel.
2. Pry off the two clips.
3. Remove face panel and switch identification strip assembly.
4. Push in plastic clip holding switch, and remove the switch.

STOP LIGHT SWITCH, REPLACE

1. Find the switch, which is adjacent to the brake pedal arm attachment to the brake servo.
2. Disconnect the two connectors.
3. Push brake pedal forward, and remove nut and washers.

NOTE: Do not rotate switch in bracket.

4. Remove switch from bracket.

COMBINATION SWITCH, REPLACE

1. Unscrew the two long screws, which release the upper and lower steering column covers.
2. Remove steering wheel.
3. Remove harness clip holding the harness to rail support strut.

NOTE: The clip is released by

HEATER CORE, REPLACE

1. Drain coolant.
2. Remove fresh air duct.
3. Disconnect heater hoses from heater core.
4. Remove dash.
5. Remove two air hoses from heater.
6. Remove console assembly.
7. Remove control cowl.
8. Remove two distribution ducts from heater.
9. Remove bolt holding heater air intake to bulkhead.
10. Remove control cowl support bracket.
11. Loosen two bolts holding heater to front of the heater support bracket on transmission tunnel.

12. Remove two heater support brackets.
13. Remove hardware holding support rails to support bracket on transmission tunnel.
14. Disconnect black and green leads from blower motor.
15. Remove hardware holding water line bracket to bulkhead.
16. Remove hardware holding rear of heater to bulkhead.
17. Remove heater assembly from vehicle.
18. Disassemble heater case and remove heater core.

BLOWER MOTOR, REPLACE

1. Remove heater assembly as outlined under Heater Core, Replace.
2. Loosen trunnion and disconnect air intake control rod.
3. Disconnect air intake from heater.
4. Drill out four rivets.
5. Release clip and detach resistor from heater.
6. Disconnect two connectors from blower motor.
7. Detach 14 clips and lift off upper part of the case.
8. Lift out blower motor.

Engine Section

ENGINE, REPLACE

1. Drain cooling system and disconnect battery.
2. Remove hood, radiator, fresh air duct and air hose.
3. Disconnect heater hoses, brake servo hoses, adsorption canister hoses, cooling system overflow hose, vacuum hoses, electrical leads, fuel line, choke cable and throttle cable.
4. Remove gear shift lever assembly.
5. Raise front and rear of the car and support on chassis stands.
6. Disconnect drive shaft.
7. Remove exhaust pipe, engine stabilizer bar and lefthand engine mounting rubber.
8. Disconnect speedometer cable and starter leads.
9. Release harness for bell housing clips.
10. Disconnect clutch hydraulic line and main ground lead.
11. Discharge air conditioner system.
12. Attach a sling with a 23 inch reach to rear lifting eye and an 18 inch reach to front lifting eye. Raise hoist to take up weight.
13. Disconnect right-hand engine mounting rubber.
14. Release rear engine mounting crossmember.
15. Raise rear of vehicle.
16. Lift engine out of vehicle.

CYLINDER HEAD, REPLACE

1. With vehicle on a lift (lowered), disconnect battery, drain cooling system and remove air duct, air cleaner, intake manifold and carburetors, camshaft cover and distributor cap.
2. Turn engine so camshaft sprocket bottom bolt is accessible. Remove bolt and anchor camshaft sprocket to support bracket.
3. Turn engine so timing mark on camshaft flange is in line with groove in camshaft front bearing cap, and distributor rotor arm points to manifold rear attachment hole in cylinder head.
4. Remove camshaft sprocket top retaining bolt.
5. Disconnect pipes to check valve and from water transfer housing.
6. Raise vehicle and disconnect exhaust front pipe from manifold flange.
7. Lower vehicle and remove two cylinder head bolts at timing cover.
8. Loosen cylinder head retaining nuts and bolts in reverse order shown in Fig. 1. Remove five cylinder head studs and bolts.
9. Remove cylinder head complete with exhaust manifolds and cylinder head gasket.
10. Reverse procedure to install, noting following:
    a. To facilitate fitting cylinder head and gasket, insert two guide studs in cylinder block bolt holes shown in Fig. 2. Guide studs may be fabricated as seen in Fig. 3.
    b. When fitting the assembly, number 1 and 4 pistons should be at TDC and rotor arm should be positioned as noted in step 3 above.
    c. Remove guide studs after fitting five cylinder head studs.
    d. Finger tighten all fasteners. Then tighten nuts and bolts in sequence shown in Fig. 1.

VALVES, ADJUST

1. Remove camshaft cover.
2. Loosen camshaft bearing cap nuts and retighten to 14 ft. lbs.
3. Rotate engine and check the maximum clearance of each valve with a feeler gauge between cam heel and tappet, Fig. 4. Maximum clearance exists when cam is vertical to cylinder head. If an adjustment is needed, proceed.
4. Remove camshaft.
5. Remove each tappet and shim where clearance requires adjust-

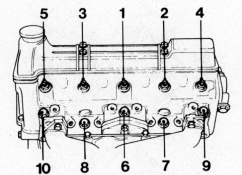

Fig. 1 Cylinder head tightening sequence

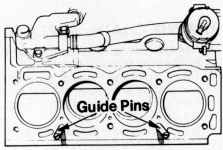

Fig. 2 Guide pins installed on cylinder block

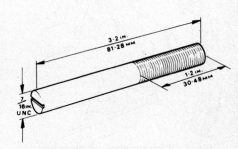

Fig. 3 Dimensions for fabricating guide pins

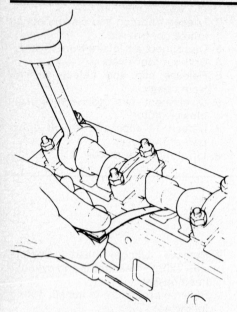

Fig. 4   Checking valve clearance

ment, keeping them in their numbered sequence, Fig. 5.

6. Measure thickness of each shim.
7. The following calculations are examples which, if followed as a guide, will allow selection of a new shim of correct thickness to provide correct valve clearance:
8. Excessive clearance (exhaust valve used as an example):

Valve clearance recorded	0.023 in.
Valve clearance required	20.018 in.
Valve clearance excess	+0.005 in.
Plus shim thickness recorded	*0.090 in.*
Shim thickness required	0.095 in.

9. Insufficient clearance (intake valve used as an example):

Valve clearance recorded	*0.005 in.*
Valve clearance required	*0.008 in.*
Insufficient clearance	−0.003 in.
Shim thickness recorded	*0.100 in.*
Shim thickness required	
	0.097 in.

Alignment Marks

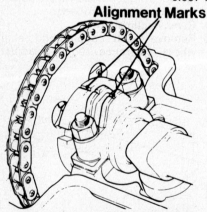

Fig. 6   Aligning mark on camshaft flange with mark on front bearing cap

VALVE GUIDES

1. Remove cylinder head, exhaust manifold, camshaft, tappets and shims; keep in correct order. Compress each valve spring in turn with special tool No. S352 to extract valve assembly.
2. Check valve guides for wear by inserting a new valve in each guide and tilting it. If movement across valve seat exceeds 0.20 inch, replace valve guide.
3. Position tool No. S60A on top of cylinder head. Using adaptor S60A-2, remove worn valve guide.
4. Apply graphite grease to new valve guide. Assemble tool No. S60A and adaptors S60A-2 and S60A-8 and cylinder head and insert new valve guide.
5. Ream out newly fitted valve guide with a 0.3125 in. reamer, and cut valve seats and grind-in valves.

TIMING CHAIN COVER, REPLACE

1. With vehicle on a lift, remove hood and disconnect battery.
2. Remove crankshaft pulleys, alternator and mounting bracket, alternator adjusting link, air pump, diverter and relief valve with attaching bracket, air pump bracket and lifting eye and compressor stabilizing bracket.
3. Remove two bolts and nuts holding timing cover to cylinder head.
4. Loosen four bolts holding compressor carrying bracket to engine.
5. Remove three compressor adjusting bolts and adjusting bracket.
6. Remove two front oil pan bolts and one bolt on each side.
7. Remove timing cover center attaching bolt and bottom left-hand bolt, viewing the engine from the front.
8. Remove fan and torquatrol assembly.
9. Remove timing cover and gaskets.
10. Place a rag over the access hole to pan to prevent objects from falling in.
11. Reverse procedure to install.

TIMING CHAIN, REPLACE

1. Remove timing chain cover, camshaft cover and distributor cap.
2. Turn engine so timing mark on camshaft is at bottom, 180 degrees from groove in camshaft front bearing cap.
3. Unlock and remove exposed camshaft retaining bolt.
4. Turn the engine until the mark on the camshaft flange is in line with

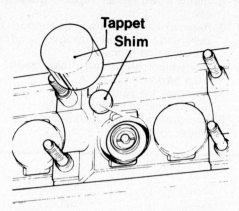

Fig. 5   Valve tappet & shim installation

groove on camshaft front bearing cap, Fig. 6.

5. See that distributor rotor arm points to head of rear bolt holding intake manifold, Fig. 7. This puts number 1 cylinder at TDC.
6. Secure camshaft sprocket to support bracket with a slave nut.
7. Remove remaining bolt holding camshaft sprocket.
8. Remove hydraulic timing chain tensioner and guide plate.
9. Remove locking bolt from adjustable chain guide.
10. Remove bolt holding the adjustable guide and camshaft sprocket support bracket.
11. Remove adjustable guide.
12. Remove bolt holding camshaft support bracket and fixed guide as you hold camshaft sprocket.
13. Remove fixed guide.
14. Release chain and remove along with the camshaft sprocket and bracket.
15. Reverse procedure to install, noting the following:
   a. After fitting chain, fixed guide and bracket, and adjustable guide, fit a slave bolt to timing cover center retaining bolt hole.
   b. Secure camshaft sprocket.

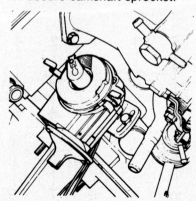

Fig. 7   Aligning distributor rotor with rear manifold bolt

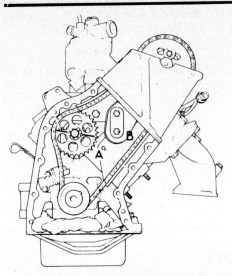

Fig. 8 Rocker shaft alignment marks

c. Turn rocker shaft sprocket so scribed line across this sprocket is equal in distance between slave bolt (B) and bottom bolt (A) on adjustable guide, Fig. 8.

d. Proceed to fit hydraulic timing chain tensioner.

e. Now, remove the slave nut.

NOTE: Support camshaft sprocket and make sure that threaded end does not get caught in support bracket hole.

f. Complete installation.

CAMSHAFT, REPLACE

1. Disconnect battery and remove fresh air duct and camshaft cover.
2. Turn engine so timing mark on camshaft flange is 180 degrees from groove in camshaft front bearing cap.
3. Anchor camshaft sprocket to support bracket with a slave nut.
4. Remove exposed camshaft sprocket lower retaining bolt.
5. Turn engine so timing mark on camshaft flange is aligned with groove in camshaft front bearing cap, Fig. 6.

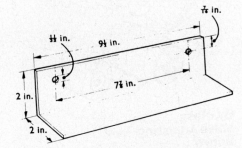

Fig. 10   Dimensions for fabricating support bracket

6. Remove remaining sprocket retaining bolt and lock washer.
7. Loosen evenly 10 camshaft bearing cap nuts, then remove nuts and washers.
8. Check that bearing caps are numbered for identification. Starting at front of engine, No. 1 is recognized by timing grooves. The remainder are numbered 2 to 4.
9. Remove caps and camshaft.
10. Reverse procedure to install, noting the following:
    a. Fit bearing caps in correct order.
    b. Make sure timing mark on camshaft flange is in line with groove in front bearing cap before fitting and tightening bearing cap nuts to avoid damage, Fig. 6.
    c. If you check valve clearances after fitting and tightening bearing caps, turn crankshaft 90 degrees so pistons are not at TDC and will not be damaged by valve heads.

PISTONS & RINGS

Two grades of standard pistons designated F and G are fitted in production. The cylinder block is stamped on the left-hand side to indicate the bore grade. The grade of the corresponding piston is stamped on the crown.

While these pistons are not supplied for service purposes, a single standard piston 0.001 inch oversize is available. If it becomes necessary to fit a new piston to a standard bore, the bore will have to be honed.

Piston rings are available in 0.010 and 0.020 inch oversize.

CRANKSHAFT REAR OIL SEAL, REPLACE

1. Disconnect battery.
2. Remove transmission, clutch, flywheel and two rear oil pan bolts.
3. Loosen two rear most right-hand and left-hand side oil pan bolts.
4. Remove six bolts holding crankcase oil seal housing to crankcase, Fig. 9.
5. Press oil seal from housing.

OIL PAN, REPLACE

1. Disconnect battery.
2. Remove fresh air duct and fan guard.
3. Drain oil.
4. Remove coupling plate bolts and engine stabilizer.
5. Fabricate a support bracket from angle iron to dimensions seen in Fig. 10.

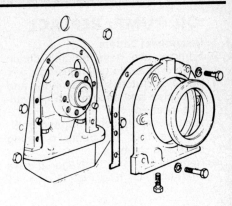

Fig. 9   Crankshaft rear oil seal installation

6. Remove alternator support strap bolt and move link out of way.
7. Remove opposite timing cover lower bolt.
8. Using two bolt holes, attach support bracket and support engine under bracket with a jack.
9. Remove two engine right-hand mounting bolts and the left-hand mounting to subframe nut.
10. Remove the oil pan nuts and bolts.
11. Raise engine enough to remove oil pan along with left-hand engine mounting and crossmember.

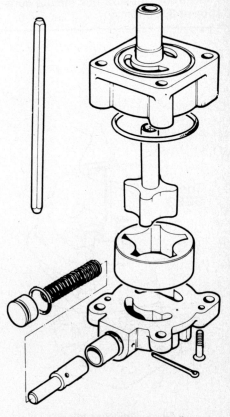

Fig. 11   Disassembled view of oil pump

OIL PUMP, REPLACE

1. Disconnect battery.
2. Remove two bolts holding clutch slave cylinder to bell housing.
3. Remove clutch slave cylinder and fluid pipe and secure in a convenient location.
4. Remove bell housing nut and bolt.
5. Remove four oil pump retaining bolts and washers.
6. Remove pump and hexagonal drive shaft and "O" ring, Fig. 11.

WATER PUMP, REPLACE
Removal

1. With engine cold, disconnect battery and remove intake manifold and carburetors.
2. Remove bottom hose and connecting tube from water pump cover.
3. Remove three bolts that hold pump cover to cylinder block and lift off the cover and gaskets.
4. Using a spanner wrench on impeller center bolt, turn bolt clockwise until water pump is released or center bolt comes off. If the latter, fit impact tool, No. S4235A/10 and adapter 4235A and remove pump.

Installation

1. Fit water pump into cylinder block housing, making sure that pump and gears mesh. Check by turning impeller center bolt counterclockwise.
2. Temporarily fit pump cover, leaving bolts finger tight.
3. Using feeler gauges, check and note that the gap between the pump cover and cylinder block is equal. Equalize gap by adjusting bolts.

Carburetor Section

NOTE: The following must not be changed or modified, to assure compliance with emission control laws: fuel jet assembly, piston assembly, depression cover. The following must not be adjusted, but should be replaced with factory-set units: temperature compensator, piston assembly return spring, starter assembly.

CAUTION: When making adjustments, do not allow the engine to idle for longer than three minutes without a "clear-out" burst of one minute duration at 2,000 rpm.

Idle Speed & Air Flow

1. Remove fresh air duct.
2. Warm engine to operating temperature.
3. Remove air cleaner.
4. See that fast idle screw is clear of fast idle cam.
5. Using an air flow meter, check that air flow through both carburetors is the same, if not proceed as follows:
   a. Adjust spring-loaded screws equally until adjusting bar is in center of both forks.
   b. Unscrew throttle adjusting screws on both carburetors to permit throttles to close fully.
   c. Rotate throttle adjusting screws so they just touch throttle levers. Give an additional one-half turn.
   d. Continue to rotate screws by equal amounts while holding an air flow meter to each carburetor intake in turn until a balanced air flow is achieved at an engine speed of 800 rpm.

CO Level

1. Disconnect and plug outlet hose from air pump.
2. Check and, if necessary, adjust ignition timing, idle speed and air flow.
3. Insert a gas analyzer probe.
4. If necessary, adjust mixture as follows with outlet hose reconnected to air pump and engine shut off:
   a. Remove piston dampers from both carburetors.
   b. Insert special tool No. S353 into dashpot until outer tool engages in air valve and inner tool engages in hexagon in the needle adjuster plug, Fig. 1.
   d. Hold outer tool and turn the inner tool clockwise to enrich the mixture or counterclockwise to lean the mixture.

Deceleration Bypass Valve
Except Calif. Models

1. Slowly turn bypass valve adjusting screw located at rear of carburetor clockwise from fully loaded position until engine speed starts to increase, Fig. 2.
2. Turn bypass valve adjusting screw counterclockwise three full revolutions.
3. Repeat operation number 1 on front carburetor bypass valve adjusting screw.
4. Turn front carburetor adjusting screw counterclockwise two full revolutions.
5. Turn rear carburetor adjusting screw counterclockwise one full revolution.

California Models

1. With engine idling and at operating temperature, disconnect vacuum line from distributor and place finger over end of line.

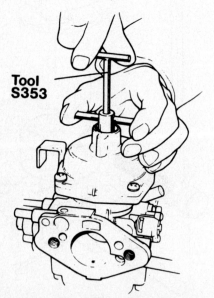

Tool S353

Fig. 1 Adjusting idle CO

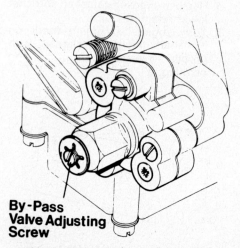

By-Pass Valve Adjusting Screw

Fig. 2 By-pass valve adjusting screw

2. If valves are correctly adjusted, engine idle speed should increase to approximately 1300 rpm.

3. Should one or both valves be out of adjustment, engine speed will increase to approximately 2000 to 2500 rpm. If throttle is momentarily opened the resulting increase in rpm will be slow to fall.

4. Without removing spring clip, turn bypass valve adjusting screw counterclockwise fully on to seat on carburetor not being adjusted, Fig. 2.

NOTE: This procedure will prevent one bypass valve from working while valve on other carburetor is being adjusted. It is not necessary to repeat this procedure when adjusting valve on second carburetor.

5. Remove and plug distributor vacuum line.

6. With engine running, turn bypass valve clockwise until engine speed increases to approximately 2000 to 2500 rpm, causing valve to float on seat.

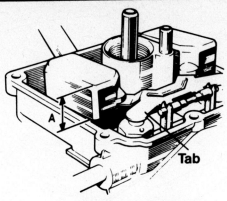

Fig. 3   Float level adjustment

7. Turn adjusting screw counterclockwise until engine speed drops to approximately 1300 rpm.

8. Use throttle to momentarily increase engine speed, then immediately release throttle. If valve is correctly adjusted, engine speed should drop to approximately 1300 rpm. If not, the valve is still floating and the above adjustment procedure must be repeated.

9. When the correct adjustment has been obtained on both carburetors, turn bypass adjusting screw on both carburetors one half turn counterclockwise to seat valves.

10. Remove plug from vacuum line and connect to distributor.

Float Level Check

1. Remove carburetors from intake manifold.
2. Remove six screws attaching float chamber to carburetor.
3. Remove float chamber and gasket.
4. With carburetor in the inverted position, check distance between gasket surface on carburetor and highest point of each float, dimension A Fig. 3.

NOTE: The height of both floats must be the same, .625 to .627 in. (16 to 17 mm).

Float Level Adjust

Bend tab that contacts needle valve, but ensure that it sits at right angles to the valve to prevent the possibility of sticking, Fig. 3.

Emission Controls Section

EGR VALVE

Testing

To check the operation of the EGR valve, Fig. 1, warm up the engine, and open and close the throttle several times. Observe or feel the EGR valve, which should open and close with changes in engine speed. The EGR valve should close when the throttle is closed.

Service

1. Remove the EGR valve from the exhaust manifold.
2. Clean valve seat with a wire brush.
3. Insert valve opening into a standard spark plug machine and lift the diaphragm.
4. Blast the valve for 30 seconds.
5. Use compressed air and a brush to remove all traces of carbon.

FUEL ABSORPTION CANISTER, REPLACE

1. Disconnect all lines at the canister, Fig. 2.
2. Remove the bracket nut and bolt.
3. Remove the canister.

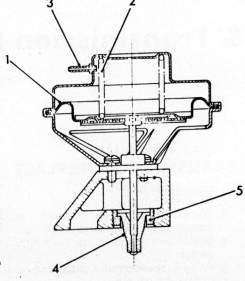

1 Diaphragm.
2 Spring.
3 To vacuum source.
4 Metering pintle.
5 Valve seat adjustable for production setting and sealed.

Fig. 1   Sectional view of EGR valve

4. Transfer the restrictor in the old canister to the new canister.
5. Install the new canister.

CATALYTIC CONVERTER, REPLACE

1. Remove the catalytic converter support bracket.
2. Release the catalytic converter from the tailpipe.

NOTE: It may now be necessary to remove the carburetor.

3. Remove the nuts holding the catalytic converter and front pipe to the exhaust manifold.
4. Remove the catalytic converter and front pipe, and exhaust manifold gasket.
5. Fit a new catalytic converter.
6. Reset the catalytic converter warning indicator to zero.

AIR PUMP BELT TENSION

1. Loosen the securing bolt and two adjusting link bolts.
2. Move the air pump to get a belt deflection of ½ in.
3. Tighten the bolts.

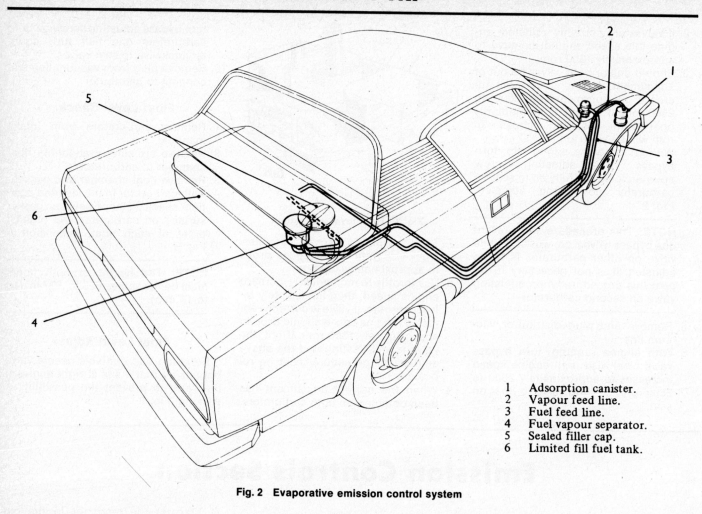

1 Adsorption canister.
2 Vapour feed line.
3 Fuel feed line.
4 Fuel vapour separator.
5 Sealed filler cap.
6 Limited fill fuel tank.

Fig. 2 Evaporative emission control system

Clutch & Transmission Section

CLUTCH, REPLACE

Removal

1. Remove transmission as described under Transmission, Replace.
2. Evenly loosen and remove the six bolts and washers holding the clutch to the flywheel.
3. Remove clutch assembly and drive plate.

Installation

1. Using a substitute first gear shaft, engage drive plate to flywheel.

NOTE: The longer boss of flywheel must be adjacent to transmission.

2. Engage clutch assembly on flywheel dowels.
3. Fit six bolts and washers and torque evenly.

4. Remove substitute shaft.
5. Install the transmission.

MANUAL TRANSMISSION, REPLACE

1. Disconnect battery.
2. Remove shift lever.
3. Disconnect propeller shaft at transmission flange and wire it up.
4. Disconnect leads at back-up light switch.
5. Release speedometer cable and remove exhaust pipe.
6. Remove starter motor heat shield.
7. Support engine with a jack under oil pan.
8. Remove bolts holding clutch slave cylinder.
9. Remove bolts holding oil pan support.
10. Remove bolts holding transmission

rear crossmember.
11. Remove jack holding oil pan.
12. Remove starter motor.
13. Remove bolts holding clutch housing to engine.
14. Carefully remove transmission and clutch housing.
15. Reverse procedure to install.

AUTOMATIC TRANSMISSION TROUBLESHOOTING

Road test vehicle, being observant of an engagement problem, a defect in take-off, and shifting trouble. The fault diagnosis chart, Fig. 1, will lead you to the cause.

NOTE: The numbers on the chart indicate the recommended sequence of diagnosis.

Symptom	Engagement: Bumpy	Engagement: Delayed	Engagement: None	Take off: None forward	Take off: None reverse	Take off: Seizure reverse	Take off: No neutral	Take off: Slip	Take off: Squawk	Upshifts: No 1-2	Upshifts: No 2-3	Upshifts: Above normal speed	Upshifts: Below normal speed	Upshift Quality: Slip 1-2	Upshift Quality: Slip 2-3	Upshift Quality: Rough 1-2	Upshift Quality: Rough 2-3	Upshift Quality: Siezure 1-2	Upshift Quality: Siezure 2-3	Downshifts: No 3-2	Downshifts: No 2-1	Downshifts: Involuntary 3-2	Downshifts: Above normal speed	Downshifts: Below normal speed	Downshift Quality: Slip 3-2	Downshift Quality: Slip 2-1	Downshift Quality: Rough 3-2	Downshift Quality: Rough 2-1
ADJUSTMENT FAULTS																												
Fluid level insufficient		1	1					1						1	1							1						
Downshift cable incorrectly assembled or adjusted	2						2					1	1	2	2	1	1			1	1		1	1				
Manual linkage incorrectly assembled or adjusted		2	2	1	1		1	3	1	1	1					3	3											
Incorrect engine idling speed	1	3								2				4	4	2	2	1									1	1
Incorrect front band adjustment							1																					
Incorrect rear band adjustment						2																						
HYDRAULIC CONTROL FAULTS																												
Oil tubes incorrectly installed, missing or leaking		4	3	7				7		8	8			8	9				2	2					6			
Sealing ring missing or broken		7	4	3	6				5	9	9	8	5	9	10			5	3				5	5	8	5	7	3
Valve block screws missing or loose	5	6	5	2	5		3			10	10	9	6	10	11	10	6	6	4				6	6				
Primary regulator valve sticking	3	5	6									10		6	7	3	3								5	4	4	3
Throttle valve sticking	4									6	6	2	2	7	8	4	4						4	4	5		4	
Modulator valve sticking										7	7	7				5												
Governor valve sticking, leaking or incorrectly assembled										3	3	2	3					6		3	3	2	2		3		2	
Orifice control valve sticking										4		4								2	2							
1-2 shift valve sticking				3									4											7				
2-3 shift valve sticking				4							3	5												8				
2-3 shift valve plunger sticking											4	6	4										3	3				
Converter 'out' check valve sticking or missing			13																									
Check valve sticking or missing			8																									
MECHANICAL FAULTS																												
Front clutch slipping		9		4		4												9									2	
Front clutch seized or plates distorted	6				2	2																						
Rear clutch slipping		10		9		6												5		3					9			6
Rear clutch seized or plates distorted	7																	5	2				4					7
Front band slipping due to faulty servo or worn band										5				5	6								5		2			8
Rear band slipping due to faulty servo or worn band		11		8																		4						
Uni-directional clutch slipping or incorrectly installed				5														7	3						1	1		
Uni-directional clutch seized																		8	4									
Input shaft broken			7																									
Front pump drive tangs on converter hub broken			8																									
Front pump worn	12		9																									
Converter blading and/or uni-directional clutch failed			10																									

Fig. 1 Automatic transmission trouble shooting chart

AUTOMATIC TRANSMISSION DIAGNOSIS & TESTING

Control Pressure Check

1. Start and run engine until transmission reaches operating temperature.
2. Remove plug from pressure tap and connect a pressure gauge, Fig. 2.
3. Check wheels and apply parking and service brakes.
4. Start engine and place selector lever in Drive.
5. With engine idling at 750 rpm, note pressure gauge reading which should be 60 to 75 psi.
6. Increase engine speed to 1000 rpm and note pressure increase, which should be 15 to 20 psi.
7. Stop engine.
8. If pressure increase is less than 15 psi., increase effective length of outer cable. If increase is more than 20 psi., decrease effective length of outer cable.
9. Repeat steps 4 through 8 until pressure increase is within limits.
10. Disconnect pressure gauge and install pressure tap plug.

Stall Test

1. Check condition of engine. If engine is not developing full power, the stall test reading will be affected.
2. Allow engine and transmission to reach operating temperature.
3. Check wheels and apply parking and service brakes.
4. Place selector lever in "1" or "R" and depress accelerator pedal to kickdown position. Note reading on tachometer which should be 2200 rpm. If reading is below 1400 rpm, check converter for stator slip. If reading is in excess of 2400 rpm, check for band or clutch slippage.

NOTE: Do not perform test for more than ten seconds, otherwise transmission may become overheated.

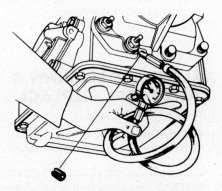

Fig. 2 Pressure gauge installation for control pressure check

AUTOMATIC TRANSMISSION ADJUSTMENTS

Downshift Cable, Adjust

1. Start engine and place transmission in "D," then adjust idle speed to 750 rpm, and stop engine.
2. Loosen adjusting locknut.
3. Adjust outer cable to 1/16 inch from stop, Fig. 3.
4. Remove transmission oil pan.
5. See that downshift cam is in idle position.
6. Fully open throttle and check that downshift cam is in kickdown position.
7. Adjust outer cable until idling and kickdown positions can be correctly achieved in downshift cam.

Manual Linkage, Adjust

1. Place selector lever in "N" and apply parking brake.
2. Loosen locknut, then push clip off hand lever.
3. Disconnect selector rod and ensure transmission lever is in the neutral position.
4. Adjust length of selector rod by adjusting turnbuckle until end of rod

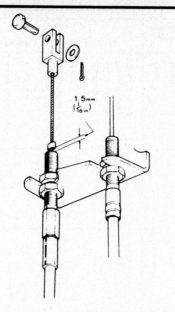

Fig. 3 Downshift cable initial setting

can be located in hand lever.
5. Tighten locknut, then push clip onto lever and secure rod.

Front & Rear Brake Bands, Adjust

1. Loosen locknut (front or rear brake adjuster).
2. Tighten adjusting screw to 36 in. lbs. and back off ¾ of a turn.
3. Torque locknut to 22 ft. lbs.

AUTOMATIC TRANSMISSION, REPLACE

1. Place selector lever in N.
2. Release downshift cable from throttle linkage.
3. Remove front exhaust pipe.
4. Disconnect dipstick tube from transmission oil pan and drain transmission fluid.
5. Disconnect selector lever, breather pipe, neutral safety and backup light switch, cooler lines, speedometer cable and propeller shaft.
6. Remove bolts holding torque converter to flywheel.
7. Support engine and transmission using a suitable jack.
8. Remove center bolt and plate from rear mount, sway bar, rear crossmember, heat shield, radiator lower mounting and exhaust support bracket.
9. Lower transmission and detach all hardware holding bell housing and starter motor.
10. Lower unit from rear.
11. Reverse procedure to install.

Rear Axle & Brakes Section

REAR AXLE, REPLACE

1. Position a suitable jack under rear axle housing, then raise vehicle and place support stands under body.
2. Remove rear wheels, then disconnect propeller shaft at rear axle.
3. Disconnect forward end of rear brake hose.
4. Disconnect parking brake cables at brake backing plates.
5. Remove nut and bolt attaching parking brake compensator to rear axle housing, then position parking brake cables clear of rear axle housing brackets.
6. Disconnect shock absorbers from rear axle housing.
7. Carefully lower rear axle housing until spring tension is relieved, then remove rear coil springs.
8. Remove nuts and bolts attaching radius rods to rear axle housing, then remove parking brake cable bracket from left hand side.
9. Remove two nuts and bolts attaching rear axle housing to rear control arms.

10. Lower jack and release radius rods from axle brackets.
11. Lift axle assembly clear of rear control arms and roll bar and remove from vehicle.

AXLE SHAFT, REPLACE

1. Remove rear wheel.
2. Remove brake drum, Fig. 1.
3. Remove hardware holding shaft assembly to axle tube flange.
4. Using tool Nos. 18G284-1 and 284, withdraw shaft.

AXLE SHAFT BEARING & OUTER SEAL, REPLACE

Removal

1. Remove axle shaft.
2. With a drill, bore out retaining collar.

NOTE: Do not allow drill to penetrate collar and damage shaft.

3. With a hammer and chisel, remove collar, Fig. 2.
4. Press out bearing, outer seal and retaining plate.
5. With tool Nos. 18G284AR and 284, remove outer bearing race.

Installation

1. Fit outer bearing race to axle casing.
2. Fit retaining plate to shaft, with welded member adjacent to shaft flange, Fig. 3.
3. Lubricate lip of new oil seal.
4. Slide seal on shaft.
5. Fit bearing.

NOTE: Install with tapered face toward shaft splines.

6. Wipe shaft in front of bearing clean.
7. Smear shaft with Loctite 602 compound and also bore of the new retaining collar.
8. Fit new retaining collar and pressing on until it butts against the bearing.

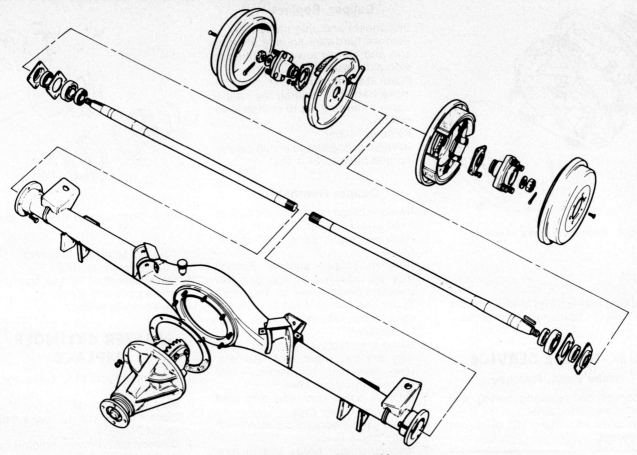

Fig. 1   Rear axle assembly

NOTE: A force of not less than three tons should be required to slide the retaining collar into position over the last 0.125 inch. If less force is needed, refit another collar.

9. Smear bearing oil seal and axle tube with lithium base grease and fit the shaft.

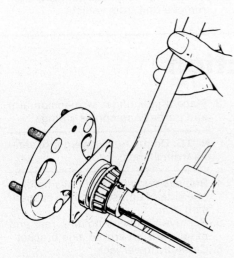

Fig. 2   Splitting inner bearing retainer for removal

AXLE SHAFT INNER SEAL, REPLACE

1. Remove shaft.
2. Remove inner seal using tool No. 18G1271.
3. Evenly install new seal with the lip of the seal facing toward the differential.

BRAKE ADJUSTMENTS

The self adjusting rear brakes, Fig. 4, incorporate a self adjusting mechanism in the brake shoe parking brake linkage, which maintains a fixed brake lining to drum clearance. Self adjustment occurs when the parking brake is applied.

PARKING BRAKE, ADJUST

1. Release parking brake.
2. Disconnect parking brake cables from rear brake backing plate levers.
3. Using finger pressure, push brake operating levers in to make sure that levers are in contact with brake shoe webs.
4. Maintaining compensator in vertical

position, adjust cable forks so clevis pin can be entered through them and operating levers without straining cables. Ensure that rear wheels do not drag.
5. Insert and fix clevis pins.
6. Screw in each fork and adjuster 3½ complete revolutions and tighten locknuts.
7. Apply parking and foot brakes alternately several times.
8. Exerting about 25 lbs. of effort to

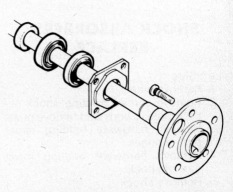

Fig. 3   Installing bearing & oil seal

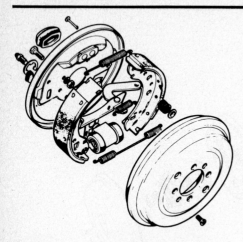

Fig. 4   Rear drum brake assembly

parking brake, travel of lever should be between four and seven notches.

DISC BRAKE SERVICE

Brake Pads, Replace

1. Depress pad-retaining spring and withdraw cotter pins.
2. Lift pads and shims out of caliper recesses.

NOTE: Shims do not have to be replaced if they are in good condition.

---

3. Ease pistons into bores.

NOTE: During operation, open caliper bleed screw to prevent brake fluid from being displaced. Close screw when piston has moved enough to allow installation of pads.

---

4. Insert new pads and shims.
5. Fit pad-retaining spring and cotter pins.

Caliper, Replace

1. Disconnect and plug brake line.
2. Remove hardware holding steering arm and caliper lower mounting to stub axle assembly.
3. Push steering arm clear, then remove hardware holding the caliper upper mounting lug to stub axle assembly.
4. Remove caliper.
5. Reverse procedure to install caliper. Torque bolts to 74 ft. lbs.

Caliper Overhaul

1. Remove caliper from vehicle as outlined under Caliper, Replace.
2. Remove brake pads and shims, Fig. 5.
3. Remove caliper pistons. Pistons may be removed by applying low pressure compressed air to caliper brake line fitting. If either piston is seized, the caliper assembly must be replaced.
4. Using a suitable screwdriver, carefully pry out wiper seal retainers. Use care not to damage seal grooves in caliper bore.
5. Remove wiper dust seal and fluid seal from caliper bore.
6. Clean caliper bores and pistons with clean brake fluid.
7. Inspect caliper bores and pistons for corrosion, damage and wear and replace as necessary.
8. Install fluid seals into grooves in caliper bores. Ensure seals are properly located.
9. Lubricate caliper bores with clean brake fluid, then insert pistons. Leave approximately $5/16$ in. of each piston projecting from caliper bore.
10. Insert a wiper seal into each seal retainer, slide assemblies, seal first, into each caliper bore using the pistons as a guide.
11. Carefully press seal into bore, using

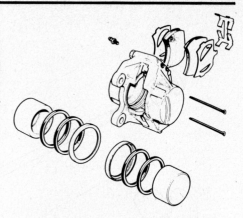

Fig. 5   Disassembled view of caliper

care not to distort retainers.
12. Push pistons into bore.
13. Install caliper on vehicle, then install brake pads and shims.
14. Bleed brake system.

MASTER CYLINDER, REPLACE

1. Disconnect and plug brake lines at cylinder.
2. Plug cylinder ports.
3. Disconnect wires to brake failure switch.
4. Disconnect hardware holding cylinder to booster and remove cylinder.

POWER BRAKE UNIT, REPLACE

1. Remove master cylinder as outlined under Master Cylinder, Replace.
2. Disconnect vacuum line from check valve.
3. Remove clevis pin attaching push rod to brake pedal.
4. Remove nuts and bolts attaching brake unit to pedal support, then remove unit from vehicle.

Rear Suspension Section

SHOCK ABSORBERS, REPLACE

Left Side
1. Remove wheel.
2. Remove screws holding shock access plate to body and remove plate.
3. Remove hardware holding upper part of shock.
4. Remove hardware holding lower part of shock.
5. Remove shock.
6. Reverse procedure to install.

Right Side
1. Remove wheel.
2. Remove fuel filler cap and filler assembly.
3. Remove hardware securing upper and lower ends of shock.
4. Remove shock.
5. Reverse procedure to install.

COIL SPRINGS, REPLACE

1. Support vehicle on stands.
2. Remove wheel and tire assembly.

3. Place a jack under suspension arm and partially compress spring.

NOTE: Do not relieve weight of vehicle from stands.

---

4. Remove two nuts and bolts holding one side of anti-sway bar to suspension arm.
5. Remove hardware holding rear end of suspension arm to axle bracket.
6. Carefully lower jack.
7. Remove spring.
8. Reverse procedure to install.

TRIUMPH TR7

CONTROL ARM, REPLACE

1. Raise rear of vehicle and support body on stands.
2. Remove wheel and tire assembly.
3. Using a suitable jack to support control arm, partially compress spring, using care not to relieve weight on stands.
4. Remove two nuts and bolts securing roll bar to control arm.
5. Remove nut and bolt securing control arm to axle bracket.
6. Carefully lower jack, then remove spring after spring tension is relieved.
7. Remove nut and bolt attaching control arm to body bracket.
8. Detach control arm from bracket and remove from vehicle.

ROLL BAR, REPLACE

1. Raise and support rear of vehicle.
2. Remove four nuts and bolts attaching roll bar to rear control arms.
3. Remove roll bar and shims.

RADIUS ROD, REPLACE

1. Raise rear of vehicle and support body on stands.
2. Remove nut and bolt attaching radius rod to rear axle bracket.
3. Remove nut and bolt attaching radius rod to body bracket.
4. Remove radius rod.

Front Suspension & Steering Section

FRONT WHEEL ALIGNMENT

1. Park vehicle level with all wheels in straight ahead position.
2. Using wheel alignment equipment, check front wheels for toe-in. Four requirements should be met:
   a. Centralized steering wheel.
   b. Centralized steering rack.
   c. Front wheels parallel to 1/16 inch toe-in.
   d. Ball centers of both tie-rods equal.

Toe-In, Adjust

1. Loosen outer clips on rack.
2. Loosen locknut at tie-rod outer ball joints.
3. Shorten or extend both tie-rods by an equal amount to get required setting of 0 to 1/16 inch.
4. Tighten locknuts and clips.

WHEEL BEARINGS, ADJUST

1. Remove wheel, hub cap and cotter pin.
2. Tighten slotted nut to eliminate play and back off one flat.

NOTE: A torque of 5 ft. lbs. must not be exceeded or the bearing may be damaged.

---

3. Refit cotter pin, hubcap and wheel.

WHEEL BEARING, REPLACE

1. Raise front of vehicle and support body on stands.
2. Remove front wheel.
3. Slacken locknut securing brake hose to bracket on shock absorber.
4. Remove two bolts securing steering arm to steering knuckle assembly.
5. Remove bolt securing brake caliper to steering knuckle assembly.
6. Withdraw caliper clear of brake disc, ensuring that strain is not imposed on brake hose and support caliper.
7. Pry off hub cap and wipe grease from end of spindle.
8. Remove cotter pin, nut retaining cap, nut and washer from the spindle, Fig. 1.
9. Withdraw hub complete with disc, bearings and oil seal.
10. Remove outer bearing, inner oil seal and inner bearing.
11. Thoroughly clean the hub.
12. Drive bearing races out of hub using a suitable drift.
13. Reverse procedure to install. Adjust wheel bearing as described under Wheel Bearings, Adjust.

BALL JOINTS, REPLACE

Removal

1. Remove bottom link.
2. Remove plastic boot from ball joint, Fig. 2.
3. Remove locking clip.
4. Press out ball joint.

Installation

1. Using a short length of suitable bore steel tubing, press a new ball joint squarely into bottom link.

NOTE: Do not apply pressure to cen-

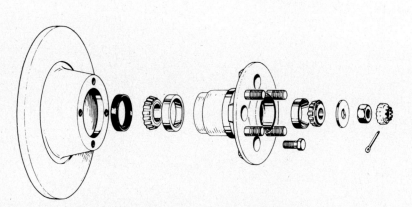

Fig. 1   Inner & outer bearing installation

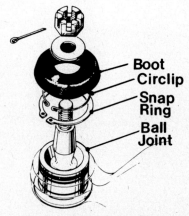

Boot
Circlip
Snap Ring
Ball Joint

Fig. 2   Ball joint installation

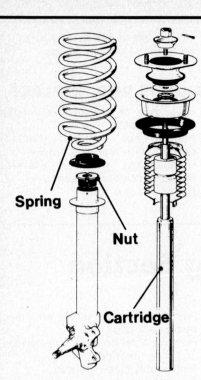

Fig. 3   Front suspension unit disassembled

ter of housing end cap.

2. Install clip, plastic boot and bottom link, Fig. 2.

SHOCK ABSORBER, REPLACE

Removal

1. Remove springs as described under Coil Spring, Replace.

2. Using special tool No. RTR359, remove locking cap.
3. Remove shock cartridge, Fig. 3.

Installation

1. Fit a new shock cartridge.
2. Fit locking cap. Torque to 59 ft. lbs.
3. Fit spring.

COIL SPRINGS, REPLACE

1. Support vehicle on stands.
2. Remove wheel.
3. Detach steering arm from stub axle assembly.
4. Loosen locknut holding brake hose to bracket on shock absorber tube.
5. Release and support brake caliper.
6. Release ball joint.
7. Remove three nuts holding shock and spring to valence.
8. Pull strut clear of vehicle.
9. Fit two clamps tool No. P5045Z to spring and compress coils evenly, Fig. 4.
10. Remove nut from shock piston rod.
11. Lift off spring pan with top mounting and swivel assembly.
12. Remove spring from shock strut and progressively loosen clamps.
13. Reverse procedure to install, with the only deviation being to use special tool No. RTR360 to fit rubber mounting to shock piston rod and securing it.

STEERING GEAR, REPLACE

1. Set front wheels in straight ahead position.
2. Scribe a line across pinion shaft and lower steering coupling.
3. Disconnect rack tie-rod outer ball

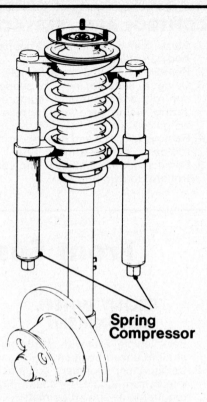

Fig. 4   Compressing coil spring

joints from steering arms.
4. Remove bolt holding steering coupling to rack pinion.
5. Remove hardware holding pinion end of rack to frame.
6. Remove hardware holding rack to frame.
7. Disconnect lower coupling from pinion shaft.
8. Remove rack.
9. Reverse procedure to install.

VOLVO

INDEX OF SERVICE OPERATIONS

VOLVO

GENERAL ENGINE SPECIFICATIONS

Year	Engine	Carburetor	Bore & Stroke	Piston Displacement Cubic Inches (Litres)	Compression Ratio	Maximum Brake H.P. @ R.P.M.	Maximum Torque Lbs. Ft. @ R.P.M.	Normal Oil Pressure Pounds
1972	B20B	Dual SU	3.500 x 3.150 (88.91 x 80 mm)	121 (1.99)	9.3	118 @ 5800	123 @ 3500	36—85
	B30A	Dual ZS	3.501 x 3.150 (88.92 x 80 mm)	181 (2.98)	9.3	145 @ 5500	163 @ 3000	36—85
1973	B20F	Fuel Inj.	3.501 x 3.150 (88.92 x 80 mm)	121 (1.99)	8.7	112 @ 6000	115 @ 3500	36—85
	B30F	Fuel Inj.	3.501 x 3.150 (88.92 x 80 mm)	181 (2.98)	8.7	138 @ 5500	155 @ 3500	36—85
1974	B20F	Fuel Inj.	3.501 x 3.150 (88.92 x 80 mm)	121 (1.99)	8.7	98 @ 6000	110 @ 3500	36—85
	B30F	Fuel Inj.	3.501 x 3.150 (88.92 x 80 mm)	181 (2.98)	8.7	160 @ 5800	167 @ 2500	36—85
1975	B20F	Fuel Inj.	3.501 x 3.150 (88.92 x 80 mm)	121 (1.99)	8.7	98 @ 6000	110 @ 3500	36—85
	B30F	Fuel Inj.	3.501 x 3.150 (88.92 x 80 mm)	181 (2.98)	8.7	160 @ 5800	167 @ 2500	36—85
1976-77	B21F	Fuel Inj.	3.623 x 3.150 (92 x 80 mm)	130 (2.1)	8.5	①	114 @ 2500	35—85
	B27F	Fuel Inj.	3.46 x 2.87 (88 x 73 mm)	162 (2.7)	8.2	②	③	26—58

①—Exc. Calif., 102 @ 5200; Calif., 99 @ 5200.
②—Exc. Calif., 125 @ 5500; Calif., 121 @ 5500.
③—Exc. Calif., 150 @ 2750; Calif., 148 @ 2750.

TUNE UP SPECIFICATIONS

The following specifications are published from the latest information available. This data should be used only in the absence of a decal affixed in the engine compartment.

When using a timing light, disconnect vacuum hose or tube at distributor and plug opening in hose or tube so idle speed will not be affected.

Before removing wires from distributor cap, determine location of the No. 1 wire in cap, as distributor position may have been altered from that shown at the end of this chart.

Year	Engine	Spark Plug Type	Spark Plug Gap Inch	Distributor Point Gap Inch	Distributor Dwell Angle Deg.	Ignition Timing Firing Order Fig.	Ignition Timing Timing BTDC ①	Ignition Timing Mark Fig.	Carb. Adjustments Hot Idle Speed Std. Trans.	Carb. Adjustments Hot Idle Speed Auto. Trans.	Carb. Adjustments Idle "CO"% Std. Trans.	Carb. Adjustments Idle "CO"% Auto. Trans.
1972	B20B	W200 T35	.028	.014	59—65	A	10	B	800	700	2.5	2.5
	B20F	W200 T35	.028	.014	59—65	A	10	B	800	700	.5—1.5	.5—1.5
	B30A	W200 T35	.028	.010	41	C	10	D	800	700	2.5	2.5
	B30F	W200 T35	.028	.010	41	C	10	B	800	700	.5—1.5	.5—1.5
1973	B20F	W200 T35	.028	.014	59—65	A	10	B	800	700	.7—1.3	.7—1.3
	B30F	W200 T35	.028	.010	59—65	C	10	D	800	700	.7—1.3	.7—1.3
1974	B20F	W200 T35	.028	.014	59—65	A	10	B	800	700	1.2—1.8	1.2—1.8
	B30F	W200 T35	.028	.010	41	C	10	D	800	700	.7—1.3	.7—1.3
1975	B20F	W200 T35	.028	—	—	A	10	B	800	700	1.2—1.8	1.2—1.8
	B30F	W200 T35	.028	—	—	C	10	D	800	700	.7—1.3	.7—1.3
1976-77	B21F	W175 T30	.028	—	—	E	15	F	900	800	1.2—1.8	1.2—1.8
	B27F	WA200 T30	.028	—	—	G	10	H	900	900	1.4—2.0	1.4—2.0

—Not Available
①—BTDC: Before top dead center.

Continued

TUNE UP SPECIFICATIONS—Continued

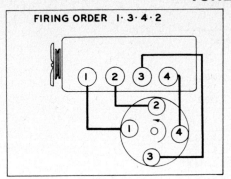

Fig. A

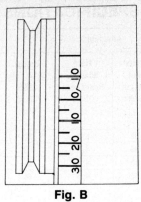

Fig. B

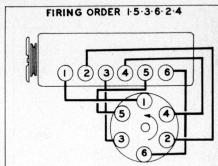

Fig. C

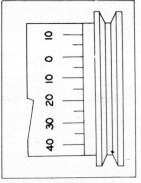

Fig. D

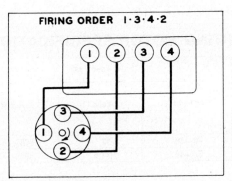

Fig. E

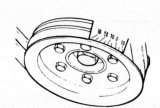

Fig. F

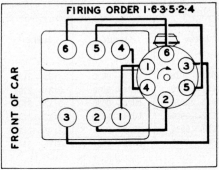

Fig. G

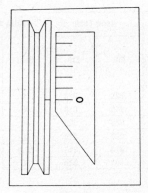

Fig. H

DISTRIBUTOR SPECIFICATIONS

If unit is checked on vehicle, double the R.P.M. and degrees to get crankshaft figures.

| Distributor Part No. | Advance Starts | Centrifugal Advance Degrees @ R.P.M. of Distributor | | | Full Advance | Vacuum Retard | |
		Intermediate Advance				Inches of Vacuum to Start Plunger	Max. Adv. Dist. Deg. @ Vacuum
JFUR4	0 @ 500	5 @ 750-950	10 @ 1220-1750	—	13 @ 2400	—	2.5-3.5 @ 11
JFURX4	0 @ 375	5 @ 610-800	7 @ 970-1140	11 @ 1300-1450	12 @ 1500	1.18—4.33	5 @ 5
JFUR6	0 @ 425	5 @ 625-725	10 @ 1150-1650	—	12 @ 1850	—	3 @ 11
JFURX6	0 @ 400	5 @ 885-1080	9 @ 1275-1500	—	10.5 @ 1600	—	3 @ 11
PFUX6	0 @ 500	5 @ 750-900	9 @ 1200-1500	—	10.5 @ 1600	—	5 @ 5
0237-002-007	0 @ 400	5 @ 910-1100	9 @ 1400-2070	—	11 @ 2400	—	5 @ 6
0237-402-004	0 @ 450	5 @ 760-910	10 @ 1100-1560	—	14 @ 2250	—	5 @ 6

—Not Available

VOLVO

ALTERNATOR & REGULATOR SPECIFICATIONS

| Year | Alternator | | | | Regulator | |
	Model	Rated Hot Output Amps	Field Winding Resistance Ohms	Output @ 14 Volts 3000 R.P.M. Amps	Model	Voltage @ 125°F
1972	SEV 35A	35	5.2	30	33525	13.8—14.2
	SEV 55A	55	3.7	48	33544	13.8—14.2
	BOSCH K1	55	4.0	48	Bosch AD	13.9—14.8
1973-77	All	55	4.0	48	All	13.8—14.2

STARTING MOTOR SPECIFICATIONS

| Year | Part No. | Brush Spring Tension, Ounces | No Load Test | | | Torque Test | |
			Amperes	Volts	R.P.M.	Amperes	Volts
1972-74	All	1.15	40—50	12	6900—8100	185—200	9
1975-77	All	3.1—3.5	30—50	11.5	5800—7800	180—220	9

VALVE SPECIFICATIONS

| Year | Model | Valve Lash | | Valve Angles | | Valve Spring Pressure Lbs. @ In. | Stem Clearance | | Stem Diameter | |
		Int.	Exh.	Seat	Face		Intake	Exhaust	Intake	Exhaust
1972-75	B30B	.020	.020	45	44.5	181.5 @ 1.18	.0012—.0026	.0024—.0038	.3132—.3138	.3120—.3126
	B20F	.016	.016	45	44.5	181.5 @ 1.18	.0012—.0026	.0024—.0038	.3132—.3138	.3120—.3126
	B30A	.020	.020	45	44.5	145 @ 1.20	.0012—.0026	.0024—.0038	.3132—.3138	.3120—.3126
	B30F	.020	.020	45	44.5	181.5 @ 1.18	.0012—.0026	.0024—.0038	.3132—.3138	.3120—.3126
1976-77	B21F	.014	.016	45.5	44.7	168.6 @ 1.06	.0012—.0024	.0024—.0035	.3132—.3135	.3126—.3128
	B27F	.004	.006	30	30	125 @ 1.27	.0020—.0037	.0020—.0037	.3136—.3142	.3128—.3134

PISTONS, PINS, RINGS, CRANKSHAFT & BEARINGS

| Year | Model | Piston Clearance Top of Skirt | Ring End Gap | | Wrist-pin Diameter | Rod Bearings | | Main Bearings | | | |
			Comp.	Oil		Shaft Diameter	Bearing Clearance	Shaft Diameter	Bearing Clearance	Thrust on Bear. No.	Shaft End Play
1972-73	B20B	.0014—.0020	.016	.016	.866	2.1299—2.1304	.0012—.0028	2.4981—2.4986	.0011—.0033	5	.0018—.0054
	B20F	.0016—.0024	.016	.016	.866	2.1299—2.1304	.0012—.0028	2.4981—2.4986	.0011—.0033	5	.0018—.0054
	B30	.0016—.0024	.016	.016	.866	2.1299—2.1304	.0012—.0028	2.4981—2.4986	.0011—.0033	7	.0018—.0054
1974-75	B20F	.0004—.0012	.016	.016	.945	2.1255—2.1260	.0012—.0028	2.4981—2.4986	.0011—.0033	5	.0018—.0054
	B30F	.0004—.0012	.016	.016	.945	2.1255—2.1260	.0012—.0028	2.4981—2.4986	.0011—.0033	7	.0018—.0054
1976-77	B21F	.0004—.0012	.014	.014	.945	2.1255—2.1260	.0012—.0028	2.4981—2.4986	.0011—.0033	5	.0018—.0054
	B27F	.0035—.0043	.016	.016	①	2.0580—2.0590	.0012—.0031	2.7576—2.7580	.0015—.0035	4	.0028—.0106

① —Selective.

Continued

VOLVO

ENGINE TIGHTENING SPECIFICATIONS

★Torque specifications are for clean and lightly lubricated threads only. Dry or dirty threads produce increased friction which prevents accurate measurement of tightness.

Year	Engine	Spark Plugs Ft. Lbs.	Cylinder Head Bolts Ft. Lbs.	Intake Manifold Ft. Lbs.	Camshaft Sprocket Bolt Ft. Lbs.	Camshaft Carrier Bolts Ft. Lbs.	Connecting Rod Cap Bolts Ft. Lbs.	Main Bearing Cap Bolts Ft. Lbs.	Flywheel to Crankshaft Ft. Lbs.	Vibration Damper or Pulley Ft. Lbs.
1972-75	B20	25—30	72	—	94—108	—	38—42	87—94	36—40	50—58
	B30	25—30	65	—	94—108	—	38—42	87—94	36—40	51—58
1976-77	B21	20	81	15	37	15	43	92	52	—
	B27	15	①	11	55	—	35	①	35	120

—Not Available
① —See text.

BRAKE SPECIFICATIONS

Year	Model	Wheel Cyl. Bore Front	Wheel Cyl. Bore Rear	Nominal Thickness Front	Nominal Thickness Rear	Minimum Thickness Front	Minimum Thickness Rear	Thickness Variation (Parallelism) Front	Thickness Variation (Parallelism) Rear	Run Out (TIR) Front	Run Out (TIR) Rear	Finish (Micro In.) Front	Finish (Micro In.) Rear	Master Cyl. I.D.
1972-77	140	—	—	①	.378	②	.331	—	—	.004	.006	—	—	.875
	164	—	—	1.0	.378	.90	.331	—	—	.004	.006	—	—	③
	240	—	—	.563	.378	.518	.331	—	—	.004	.004	—	—	④
	260	—	—	.945	.378	.898	.331	—	—	.004	.004	—	—	④

—Not Available
① —Exc. with B20E engine, .500"—.504"; With B20E engine, .562"—.567".
② —Exc. with B20E engine, .457"; with B20E engine, .557".
③ —1972-73, .940"; 1974, .875".
④ —Primary bore, .877"; Secondary bore, .620".

REAR AXLE SPECIFICATIONS

Year	Model	Carrier Type	Ring Gear & Pinion Backlash Method	Ring Gear & Pinion Backlash Adjustment	Pinion Bearing Preload Method	Pinion Bearing Preload New Bearings Inch Lbs.	Pinion Bearing Preload Used Bearings Inch Lbs.	Differential Bearing Preload Method	Differential Bearing Preload New Bearings Inch Lbs.	Differential Bearing Preload Used Bearings Inch Lbs.
1972-77	140	Integral	Shims	.003—.008	Shims	9.55—20	5.21—9.55	Shims	—	—
	164	Integral	Shims	.005—.008	Shims	9.55—20	5.21—9.55	Shims	—	—
	240,260	Integral	Shims	.005—.008	Shims	9.55—20	5.21—9.55	Shims	—	—

—Not Available

COOLING SYSTEM & CAPACITY DATA

Year	Model or Engine	Cooling Capacity Qts. With Heater	Cooling Capacity Qts. With A/C	Radiator Cap Relief Pressure Lbs. With A/C	Radiator Cap Relief Pressure Lbs. No A/C	Thermo. Opening Temp.	Fuel Tank Gals.	Engine Oil Refill Qts. ①	Transmission Oil 4 Speed Pints	Transmission Oil Overdrive Pints	Transmission Oil Auto. Trans. Qts. ②	Axle Oil Pints
1972-77	140	10.5	10.5	10	10	180	15	3.5	1.6	3.4	6.7	2.7
	164	9	9	10	10	180	15	3.5	—	3.4	6.7	2.7
	240	10	10	12	12	200	15	3.5	1.6	4.8	6.9	2.7
	260	12	12	12	12	200	15	6.8	—	4.8	6.9	2.7

—Not Available
① —Add ½ qt. with filter change.
② —Approximate, make final check with dipstick.

VOLVO

WHEEL ALIGNMENT SPECIFICATIONS

NOTE: See that riding height is correct before checking alignment.

| Year | Model | Caster Angle, Degrees ① | | Camber Angle, Degrees ① | | | | Toe-In, Inch | Toe-Out on Turns, Deg. | |
| | | Limits | Desired | Limits | | Desired | | | Outer Wheel | Inner Wheel |
				Left	Right	Left	Right			
1972	140	0 to +1	+½	0 to +½	0 to +½	+½	+½	⁵⁄₆₄—¹³⁄₆₄	20	21.5—23.5
	164	0 to +1	+½	0 to +½	0 to +½	+½	+½	⁵⁄₆₄—¹³⁄₆₄	20	21.5—23.5
1973	140	+1 to +2	+1½	0 to +½	0 to +½	+½	+½	⁵⁄₆₄—¹³⁄₆₄	20	21.5—23.5
	164	+1½ to +2½	+2	0 to +½	0 to +½	+½	+½	⁵⁄₆₄—¹³⁄₆₄	20	21.5—23.5
1974-77	140	+1 to +2	+2	0 to +½	0 to +½	+½	+½	⁵⁄₆₄—¹³⁄₆₄	20	21.5—23.5
	164	+½ to +1½	+1	−¾ to −1¼	−¾ to −1¼	−1	−1	¹⁄₁₆—³⁄₁₆	20	21.5—23.5
	240, 260	①	①	+1 to +1½	+1 to +1½	+1¼	+1¼	②	20	20.8

①—Non Adjustable.
②—Exc. Power steering, ³⁄₁₆; Power steering, ⅛.

Electrical Section

DISTRIBUTOR, REPLACE

B-20 & B-30 Engines

1. Release retaining clips for distributor cap and remove cap.
2. Disconnect primary lead and vacuum hose from distributor. When removing vacuum hose from bakelite connector on the distributor, use care so as not to damage connector.
3. On engines equipped with electronic fuel injection, disconnect contact plug for triggering contacts.
4. Loosen pinch bolt which holds distributor and pull out the distributor.

NOTE: Because the distributor is driven by an off-set key, the distributor can only be installed with the rotor in the correct position.

B-21 Engine

1. Rotate crankshaft until #1 piston is at TDC on compression. To determine this position, remove oil filler cap and watch both cam lobes for #1 cylinder. When both cam lobes are pointing up and crankshaft pulley mark is on O°, #1 cylinder is at TDC.
2. Remove distributor cap, then disconnect primary wire and vacuum hose.
3. Remove attaching bolt and lift out distributor.
4. When reinstalling distributor, turn

rotor so the mark on the rotor is 60° from the mark on the distributor housing.
5. Push distributor into the engine block. As the distributor goes into position, the rotor will turn 60° until the mark on the rotor aligns with mark on the distributor housing.
6. Install retaining bolt, primary lead, vacuum hose and cap. Set ignition timing.

B-27 Engine

1. Rotate crankshaft until #1 piston is at TDC on compression. To determine this, remove #1 spark plug and hold finger over the spark plug hole. Rotate crankshaft until gas pressure pushes up finger. At the same time, watch the crankshaft pulley. Mark should be at O°.
2. Remove distributor cap and rotor. Disconnect vacuum hose and primary wire from distributor.
3. Remove distributor retaining nut and remove distributor.

NOTE: As the distributor is withdrawn from the engine, the rotor will rotate clockwise until it aligns with one of the distributor cap retaining clips. When reinstalling the distributor, be sure the rotor is in this position. As the distributor is installed, the rotor will rotate counterclockwise until it aligns with the reference mark on the distributor housing.

DISTRIBUTOR REPAIR

1972-74 B-20 & B-30 Engines

Disassembly
1. Remove rotor, Figs. 1 through 4.
2. Remove snap ring from pull rod of vacuum regulator.
3. Remove two mounting screws and remove vacuum regulator.
4. Mark location of distributor cap lock clasps, then remove clasps.
5. Remove primary lead connection from housing, then lift out breaker plate.
6. Disconnect centrifugal advance springs and mark the position of the breaker cam on the shaft.
7. Secure the breaker cam in a vise with soft jaws and tap distributor housing with a plastic mallet, until snap ring has released, then remove breaker cam.
8. On Electronic Fuel Injection engines, remove mounting screws for trigger contact set and remove trigger contacts.
9. Remove retaining ring at lower end of distributor shaft and drive out the drive collar retaining pin.

NOTE: The drive collar teeth are offset to properly index the distributor shaft in the camshaft drive. Therefore, it is important to mark the drive collar in relation to the distributor shaft before removing the collar so it can be reinstalled properly.

10. Remove the drive collar. Use care to be certain that no washers are lost.

1-1074

11. Remove lock springs for centrifugal weights and remove weights.

Inspection
1. Wash all parts.
2. Check to be sure breaker plate is not loose, worn or damaged.
3. Play between distributor shaft and breaker cam must not exceed .004".
4. Breaker cam surfaces must not be scored or worn.
5. Holes in advance weights must not be oval or otherwise deformed.
6. Advance weight springs must not be deformed in any way.
7. Play between distributor shaft and housing must not exceed .008".

Assembly
To assemble, reverse disassembly procedure, being sure to index the drive collar correctly to the shaft. Check also that axial adjusting washers are installed so that fiber washer contacts distributor housing. Check to be sure axial clearance on shaft is .004-.010". Any adjustments are done by changing the number of washers on the shaft.

1975 B-20 & B-30, 1976-77 B-21 & B-27 Engines

1. Remove cap, rotor and dust cover, Figs. 5 and 6.
2. Remove vacuum unit and cap retaining clips.

NOTE: The retaining screws have different lengths and if improperly installed can damage moving parts.

3. Remove screws securing primary wires. Remove primary wire retainer by pulling it straight out.
4. Remove impulse sender retaining screws.
5. Remove snap ring and shims.
6. Lift off armature and small lock pin.
7. Remove second snap ring and lift off impulse sender and plate.
8. Remove three screws and remove impulse sender from plate.
9. Reverse procedure to assemble.

ALTERNATOR, REPLACE

1. Disconnect battery ground cable.
2. Disconnect alternator leads.
3. Remove bolt from adjusting arm and mounting bolt securing alternator to engine.
4. Remove fan belt and lift out alternator.

ALTERNATOR IN CAR TESTS

NOTE: When testing an alternator, it is

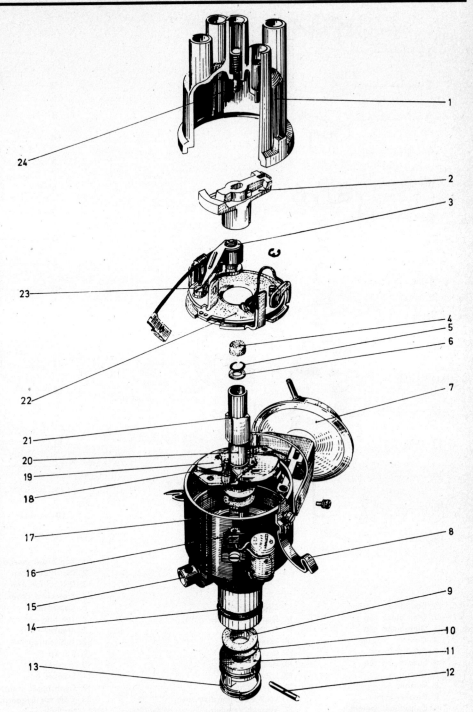

1. Distributor cap	7. Vacuum regulator	13. Resilient ring	19. Centrifugal weight
2. Distributor arm	8. Cap clasp	14. Rubber seal	20. Breaker camshaft
3. Contact breaker	9. Fiber washer	15. Lubricator	21. Breaker cam
4. Lubricating felt	10. Steel washer	16. Primary connection	22. Breaker plate
5. Circlip	11. Driving collar	17. Distributor housing	23. Lock screw for breaker contacts
6. Washer	12. Lock pin	18. Centrifugal governor spring	24. Rod brush (carbon)

Fig. 1   Disassembled view of distributor. 1972 B-20B

important that a fully charged battery be used.

Voltage Drop
1. With headlights on, engine running and alternator supplying 10 amps, connect a voltmeter between battery positive terminal and B+ terminal of alternator. A voltage reading of 0.3 volt or more indicates that cable or terminal connections are faulty and must be repaired before testing further.
2. With the same load as above, mea-

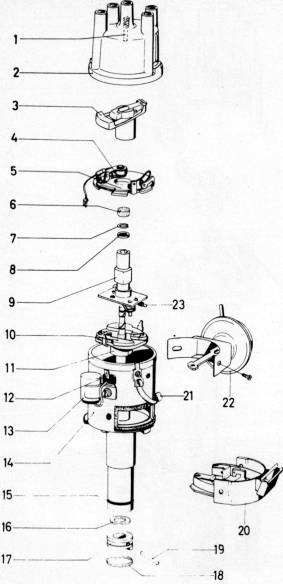

1. Rod brush (carbon)
2. Distributor cap
3. Distributor arm
4. Contact breaker
5. Breaker plate
6. Lubricating felt
7. Circlip
8. Washer
9. Breaker cam
10. Centrifugal weight
11. Cam for triggering contacts
12. Primary terminal
13. Capacitor
14. Distributor body
15. Rubber real
16. Washers
17. Driving collar
18. Resilient ring
19. Lock pin
20. Contact device
21. Lock clasp for distr. cap
22. Vacuum regulator
23. Centrifugal governor spring

Fig. 2 Disassembled view of distributor. 1972-74 B-20F

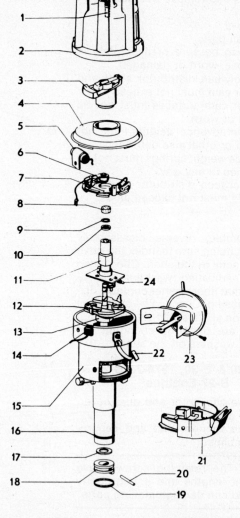

1. Rod brush (carbon)
2. Distributor cap
3. Distributor arm
4. Protective cover
5. Capacitor
6. Ignition contact breaker
7. Breaker plate
8. Lubricating felt
9. Circlip
10. Washer
11. Breaker cam
12. Centrifugal weight
13. Cam for triggering contacts
14. Primary terminal
15. Distributor body
16. Rubber seal
17. Washers
18. Driving collar
19. Resilient ring
20. Lock pin
21. Contact device
22. Lock clamp for distr. cap
23. Vacuum regulator
24. Centrifugal governor spring

Fig. 3 Disassembled view of distributor. 1972-74 B-30F

sure voltage drop between battery negative terminal and D– terminal of alternator. If voltage drop here exceeds 0.2 volt, check battery ground, alternator contact with engine and engine-to-chassis ground connection.

Bosch Alternator
1. Complete test connections as shown in Fig. 7.
2. With alternator warm, approx. 140°F, run engine at approx. 3000 rpm. Alternator should produce 55 amps at 14 volts.

NOTE: Regulate voltage by means of variable load resistance.

3. Check that warning lamp is not lighted. If alternator does not meet the above specifications, check brush holders and diodes.

Bosch Voltage Regulator
1. Complete test connections as shown in Fig. 8.
2. With engine running at 2000 rpm, load the alternator with 44-46 amps.
3. Cycle the charging system by allow-

ing the engine to return to idle then again increase speed to 2000 rpm and adjust the load to 44-46 amps. Voltage should read 13.9-14.8.

4. The regulator should be adjusted on the lower left contact, 1 on Fig. 9. Reading should be taken within 30 seconds after test has begun. If stop clamp is bent downwards, voltage should drop. If bent upwards, voltage should increase.

5. If voltage in the upper regulating range is not within proper relation to lower range, (same value to 0.3 volt lower) adjust by bending the holder for the left contact while at the same time, correcting the distance between the right contact and the movable contact as shown in Fig. 9. If the holder is bent towards the right contact, voltage is reduced in the upper range.

6. In order to avoid faulty adjustments due to residual magnetism in the iron parts of the regulator, it is necessary to cycle the charging system after each adjustment by allowing engine speed to return to idle then increase speed to make a new adjustment.

Motorola Alternator

1. Complete test connections as shown in Fig. 10.

2. Check that current through the field winding with ammeter C, is 3-3.5 amps. If not, check brushes and field winding.

3. Run engine at approx. 1500 rpm. Alternator should deliver at least 48 amps at 14 volts.

NOTE: An extra load may have to be cut into the circuit to hold voltage at 14 volts.

4. Check voltage at B+ and 61 with alternator charging. Voltage should be 0.8-0.9 volt higher at 61 than at B+. If not, the isolation diode is damaged and should be replaced.

Motorola Voltage Regulator

1. Complete test connections as shown in Fig. 11.

2. Run engine at approx. 2500 rpm for 15 seconds. With no load on the alternator, voltmeter should read 13.1-14.4 volts with alternator temperature of 77°F.

3. Load alternator with 10-15 amps by switching on high beams. Voltage should remain at previous reading.

4. If adjustment is required, remove regulator cover and carefully bend the spring bracket to achieve proper setting. If no setting can be made, regulator must be replaced.

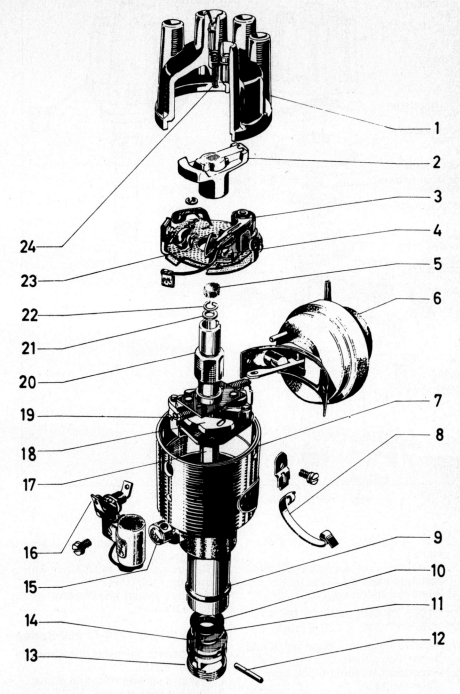

1. Distributor cap	7. Distributor housing	13. Spring ring	19. Centrifugal governor spring
2. Distributor arm	8. Cap clamp	14. Flange	20. Breaker cam
3. Contact breaker	9. Rubber seal	15. Lubricator	21. Washer
4. Lock screw for breaker contacts	10. Fiber washer	16. Primary connection	22. Snap ring
5. Lubricating felt	11. Steel washer	17. Distributor shaft	23. Breaker plate
6. Vacuum regulator	12. Lock pin	18. Centrifugal weight	24. Rod brush (carbon)

Fig. 4   Disassembled view of distributor. 1972 B-30A

STARTER, REPLACE

1. Disconnect battery cable.
2. Disconnect starter leads.
3. Remove two starter mounting bolts and remove starter.

IGNITION SWITCH, REPLACE

1972 140 & 160 Series

1. Disconnect battery ground cable.

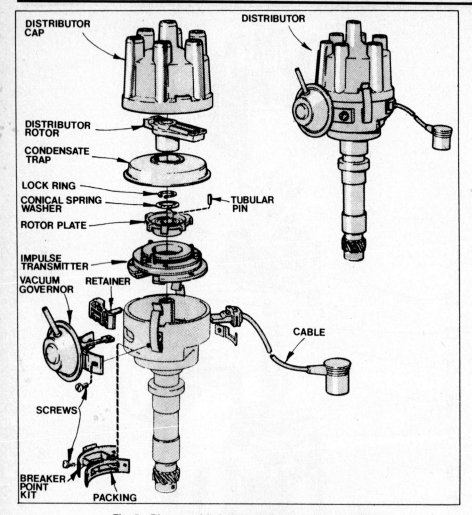

DISTRIBUTOR CAP

DISTRIBUTOR

DISTRIBUTOR ROTOR

CONDENSATE TRAP

LOCK RING

CONICAL SPRING WASHER

TUBULAR PIN

ROTOR PLATE

IMPULSE TRANSMITTER

VACUUM GOVERNOR

RETAINER

CABLE

SCREWS

BREAKER POINT KIT

PACKING

Fig. 5 Disassembled view of distributor. 1975 B-30F

2. Remove plastic covers around switch.
3. Remove two screws holding ignition switch to steering wheel lock.
4. Remove ignition switch.

1973-74 140, 1973-75 164, 1975-77 240 & 260 Series

1. Remove noise insulation panel and center side panel.
2. Disconnect terminal block from ignition switch.
3. Remove ignition switch.

LIGHT SWITCH, REPLACE

1972 140 & 160 Series

1. Disconnect battery ground cable.
2. Unscrew the switch knob. The knob is threaded onto the switch rod.
3. Using a suitably modified screwdriver, loosen the switch retaining nut.
4. Remove switch.

1973-74 140, 1973-75 164 Series

1. Remove switch knob.

2. Remove impact guard by pulling it straight back.
3. Remove nut for the switch with a suitable tool.
4. Remove switch and transfer wiring to new switch.

1975-77 240 & 1976-77 260 Series

1. Disconnect defroster hose from defroster outlet.
2. Remove screws retaining outlet.
3. Pull out switch knob.
4. Lift out defroster outlet.
5. Remove nut and lift out switch.

STOP LIGHT SWITCH, REPLACE

1. Disconnect battery ground cable.
2. Disconnect switch wires.
3. Remove switch retaining nut. Remove switch.
4. When installing switch, be sure that distance between brake pedal when fully released, and thread bronze hub on switch is 4 mm (.008"). If

necessary, adjust by loosening bracket attaching screw and moving bracket.

NEUTRAL SAFETY SWITCH, REPLACE

1972-75 140, 164, & 240 Series

The safety switch is screwed into the right side of the transmission. Latest switches are pre-set and adjust as they are installed. Do not depress the stem of the switch manually before installing it or the calibration will be upset.

Early 1976 Units

The switch is located on the right front of the outside of the transmission case.

Late 1976 & 1977 Units

The switch is located inside the passenger compartment and is mounted directly beneath the gear shift selector. Remove the selector cover and loosen the two retaining bolts to adjust or replace the switch.

TURN SIGNAL SWITCH, REPLACE

140, 164, 240 & 260 Series

1. Remove screws holding upper and lower switch covers and remove covers.
2. Where necessary, remove overdrive switch bracket.
3. Remove turn signal switch mounting screws and remove switch.

INSTRUMENT CLUSTER, REPLACE

1972 140 & 164 Series

1. Disconnect battery ground cable.
2. Remove both screws holding instrument cluster in place.
3. Remove trim panel below dashboard.
4. Pull upper section of cluster rearward (toward rear seat) so it loosens from clips in dashboard.
5. Loosen the panel from hood release cable.
6. Move the cluster, short side first, through opening in dashboard.
7. Disconnect speedometer cable and flange nuts on instruments.
8. Turn cluster ¼ turn so reverse side of cluster faces upwards.
9. Detach electrical connections from cluster and lift cluster through the opening in the dashboard.

VOLVO

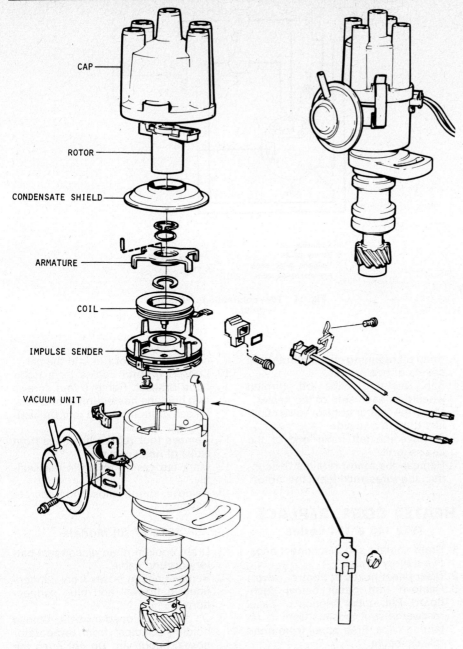

Fig. 6 Disassembled view of distributor. 1975 B-20F & 1976-77 B-21 & B-27

- CAP
- ROTOR
- CONDENSATE SHIELD
- ARMATURE
- COIL
- IMPULSE SENDER
- VACUUM UNIT

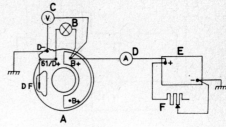

A. Alternator
B. Control lamp 12 volts 2 watts
C. Voltmeter 0—20 volts
D. Ammeter 0—50 amps
E. Battery 60 amperehours
F. Load resistance

Fig. 7 Test connections. Bosch Alternator

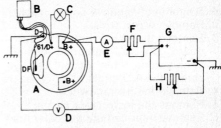

A. Alternator
B. Voltage regulator
C. Control lamp 12 volts 2 watts
D. Voltmeter 0—20 volts
E. Ammeter 0—50 amps
F. Control resistance
G. Battery 60 amperehours
H. Load resistance

Fig. 8 Test connections. Bosch regulator

1973-77 All Models

1. Remove covers over the steering column.
2. Remove attaching screws for the bracket and allow it to drop down towards the steering column. Remove the cluster attaching screws.
3. Disconnect speedometer cable.
4. Take hold of back side of the speedometer unit and press upwards and out until the snap lock in the upper edge releases.
5. Lift out the cluster and disconnect the electrical leads.

W/S WIPER SWITCH, REPLACE

1972 140 & 164 Series

Follow the same procedure as that for replacing the light switch.

1973-77 All Models

1. Remove covers over steering column.
2. Remove switch retaining screws.
3. Transfer wires to new switch and install retaining screws and covers.

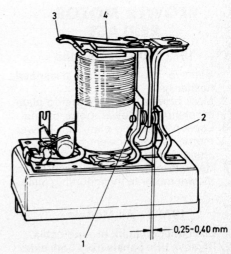

0,25-0,40 mm

1. Regulator contact for lower control range (lower contact)
2. Regulator contact for upper control range (upper contact)
3. Stop clamp
4. Spring upper section: Steel spring
   lower section: Bimetal spring

Fig. 9 Voltage regulator adjustment. Bosch regulator

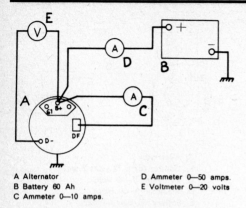

A Alternator
B Battery 60 Ah
C Ammeter 0—10 amps.
D Ammeter 0—50 amps.
E Voltmeter 0—20 volts

Fig. 10 Test connections. Motorola alternator

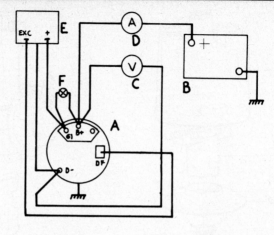

A Alternator
B Battery 60 Ah
C Voltmeter 0—20 amps.
D Ammeter 0—50 amps.
E Voltage regulator
F Warning lamp 12 volts.
  2 watts

Fig. 11 Test connections. Motorola regulator

W/S WIPER MOTOR, REPLACE

140 & 164 Series

1. Disconnect negative battery cable.
2. Remove wiper arms.
3. Remove the panel under the dashboard. On cars equipped with air conditioning, this panel also includes the A/C ducts.
4. Remove the heater switch.
5. Remove the instrument cluster.
6. Remove intermediate defroster nozzle and its hoses.
7. Remove wiper motor.

240 & 260 Series

1. Disconnect battery ground cable. Remove side panel.
2. Remove glove box.
3. Disconnect the linkage-to-motor retaining nut and remove retaining bolts. Lift motor off of firewall.

BLOWER MOTOR, REPLACE

1972 140 & 164 Series

1. Remove heater unit as described further on.
2. Mark blower motor mounting plate in relation to blower motor casing.
3. Loosen mounting plate and blower motor from blower housing by straightening tabs.
4. Remove screws which secure the blower motor to the mounting plate.

1973-77 All Models

1. Disconnect battery ground cable.
2. Remove trim panels from both sides of center console.

3. Snap off retaining clips for both side covers of heater unit.
4. Slip retaining clips off turbine wheels on each side of the heater.
5. Move the heater control valve capillary tube to one side.
6. Remove the left inner end of the central unit.
7. Remove the motor retainer, disconnect the wires and lift out the motor.

HEATER CORE, REPLACE

1972 140 & 164 Series

1. Drain coolant and disconnect negative battery cable.
2. Disconnect hoses at control valve.
3. Remove trim panel below dashboard. Pull upper section of panel rearwards so it loosens from its retaining clips. Free panel from hood release cable.
4. Remove carpet from transmission tunnel.
5. Loosen and remove the defroster hoses and control wires.
6. Remove fan switch and disconnect wires from blower fan motor.
7. Remove two screws holding fusebox to heater.
8. Remove control valve and loosen upper hose from heater unit. Care must be taken with control valve and copper tube between valve and heater.
9. Plug heater outlets so the remaining

coolant does not run into the car.
10. Loosen ground cables from right-hand bracket. Remove four screws that hold the heater unit to brackets, loosen drain hose and remove heater unit.
11. Remove four rubber bushings from sides of heater unit.
12. Mark fan casing to aid in reassembly.
13. Remove spring clips and separate housing.

1973-77 All Models

1. Drain coolant, then disconnect battery ground cable.
2. Remove heater hoses from connections at firewall and plug connections.
3. On air conditioned models, remove holding clamps from evaporator hoses. Important: Do not open the air conditioning system, simply loosen the retaining clamps to allow removal of the firewall door.
4. Remove instrument cluster.
5. Disconnect air ducts and vacuum hoses.
6. Remove unit mounting bolts.
7. Carry out Steps 2-6 under Blower Motor, Replace.
8. Remove evaporator from central unit without disconnecting evaporator hoses.
9. Disconnect heater valve hoses and remove the heater core.

Engine Section

ENGINE, REPLACE
1972 140 & 164 Series
Except Fuel Injection

1. Remove gear lever.
2. Remove hood. On A/C models, remove A/C compressor mounting bolts and position compressor to one side.
3. Drain coolant by removing lower radiator hose. Remove upper radiator hose. On auto. trans. models, disconnect cooler lines. Remove radiator and shroud.
4. Disconnect positive battery cable. Remove distributor cap and disconnect cables from spark plugs. Disconnect distributor primary wire. Remove ignition coil and place it to one side.
5. Disconnect inlet fuel line from pump. Remove wires from starter motor.
6. Remove air cleaner and its hoses. Disconnect wiring from alternator, temperature unit and oil pressure unit.
7. Remove preheating plate and nuts from exhaust manifold. Disconnect back-up light wires at quick disconnect plug. On Overdrive models, disconnect overdrive wire.
8. Remove throttle control shaft from pedal shaft, link rods and bracket. Remove choke wire from carburetor and vacuum hose from brake booster and manifold. Disconnect water hoses for heater element from engine.
9. Attach a suitable lifting fixture.
10. Raise vehicle and drain engine oil. Remove lower nuts from front engine mounts.
11. Adjust lifting fixture so rear of engine begins to rise.
12. Where necessary, remove return spring and clutch cable from lever and cable sleeve from clutch casing.
13. Disconnect lower ground strap from engine.
14. Remove exhaust pipe clamp from its bracket. Remove rear crossmember.
15. Disconnect speedometer cable. Disconnect front universal joint flange from gearbox.
16. Lift and remove engine, adjusting lifting fixture as necessary to allow engine to clear.
17. Reverse procedure to install.

NOTE: When reinstalling the engine, be sure the exhaust manifold does not contact the oil filter.

1972-73 140 & 1972-75 164 Series With Fuel Injection

1. Remove gear lever.
2. Remove hood. On A/C models, remove A/C compressor mounting bolts and position compressor to one side.
3. Remove positive battery cable.
4. Drain coolant by removing lower radiator hose. Remove cap from expansion tank.
5. Remove pressure sensor vacuum hose from inlet manifold, fuel hose for cold start valve from fuel distribution pipe and fuel hoses from fuel pipes at firewall.
6. Remove electrical contact plugs for temperature sensors, cold start valve and throttle switch. Remove induction air hose.
7. Disconnect back-up light wires at quick disconnect plug. On Overdrive models, disconnect overdrive wires. Remove ground leads from inlet manifold.
8. Remove bolts for pressure regulator bracket.
9. Remove fuel injectors from cylinder head by rotating their locking collars and pulling injectors from head. Position injectors, distribution pipe and pressure regulator on windshield washer fluid container.
10. Remove throttle cable bracket from inlet manifold and throttle cable from throttle switch.
11. Disconnect electrical leads from oil pressure sensor and alternator. Remove heater hoses from engine. Remove brake booster hose.
12. Remove leads from spark plugs. Remove distributor cap. Disconnect distributor primary connection and leads from starter motor. Remove wires from thermal timer.
13. Continue steps 9-17 under Engine, Replace, 1972 140 & 164 Except Fuel Injection.

1974 140 & 1975 240 Series

1. On manual transmission units, remove gearshift lever.
2. Remove hood.
3. Disconnect battery ground cable.
4. Remove splash shield from under vehicle.
5. Drain coolant. Disconnect lower radiator hose and open drain cock on right side of engine.
6. Disconnect PCV hose. Disconnect brake vacuum hoses from intake manifold.

7. Disconnect high tension lead at ignition coil. Unplug distributor wires.
8. Disconnect wires from starter. Remove battery ground cable from engine block.
9. Disconnect air bellows connecting CI unit and intake manifold.
10. Disconnect fuel hoses from: fuel filter to engine (two hoses) control pressure regulator, cold start injector and four hoses at injectors.
11. Disconnect fuel filter from firewall and put it aside.
12. Disconnect wires at: control pressure regulator including ground, cold start injector, auxiliary air valve, thermal timer, oil pressure switch and temperature sender.
13. Remove air injection reaction pipe.
14. Disconnect two vacuum hoses for charcoal cannister at intake manifold.
15. Disconnect throttle cable.
16. Disconnect alternator wire connector.
17. Remove EGR valve from intake manifold.
18. Remove thermal time switch complete with extension.
19. Disconnect expansion tank hose at radiator. On auto. trans. models, disconnect transmission oil cooler lines from radiator.
20. Remove fan shroud retaining screws and push it to the rear.
21. Disconnect upper radiator hose and remove radiator.
22. Disconnect heater hoses at firewall.
23. Remove windshield washer container.
24. Loosen power steering pump drive belt and remove pump pulley. Disconnect power pump from engine bracket and lay it aside.
25. Remove idler roller for air pump drive belt.
26. On auto. trans. models, remove transmission filler pipe.
27. Raise vehicle and place it on stands.
28. Remove exhaust pipe flange nuts from manifold.
29. Remove front and rear engine mount retaining nuts.
30. Install a suitable lifting fixture and adjust it so weight is off rear of the engine.
31. Disconnect transmission ground cable. On manual trans. models, disconnect clutch cable. On auto. trans. models, disconnect gear shift control from transmission.
32. Remove front exhaust pipe clamp and rear crossmember.

33. Disconnect speedometer cable and electrical leads from transmission.
34. Disconnect drive shaft from transmission flange.
35. On auto. trans. models, remove front heat shield. Remove oil pipes between engine and transmission.
36. Lift engine out of chassis.

1976-77 240 Series

1. On manual trans. models, remove gearshift lever.
2. Disconnect battery cables.
3. Remove hood.
4. Remove expansion tank cap.
5. Drain coolant by disconnecting lower radiator hose. Open drain cock at right rear of engine.
6. Disconnect crankcase ventilation hose at cylinder head. Disconnect upper radiator hose at engine.
7. Disconnect expansion tank hoses at radiator.
8. On auto trans. models, disconnect oil cooler pipes at radiator.
9. Remove fan shroud attaching screws and push shroud to the rear. Disconnect radiator retaining bolts. Lift out radiator and shroud.
10. Remove air cleaner.
11. Loosen air pump tensioner nut and remove drive belt. Disconnect hoses at air pump. Remove pump retaining bolts and remove pump.
12. Remove vacuum pump.
13. Loosen power steering pump, remove drive belt. Remove pump retaining bolts. Remove power steering pump and tie it to the wheel housing. It is not necessary to disconnect power steering hoses.
14. On cars equipped with air conditioning, disconnect electrical connector from compressor. Remove front half of crankshaft pulley and lift off A/C belt. Temporarily attach front half of the pulley with two bolts. Remove A/C compressor and tie it to the wheel housing. It is not necessary to disconnect hoses.
15. Mark and disconnect four vacuum hoses at engine. Mark and disconnect two hoses for carbon cannister at engine.
16. Disconnect wire connector at distributor, high tension lead at coil, starter wires and clutch cable at starter motor.
17. Disconnect wiring harness at voltage regulator and two wire clips.
18. Disconnect throttle cable at pulley. Remove wire from A/C solenoid.
19. Remove gas cap to eliminate fuel system pressure and disconnect fuel hose at filter and fuel return hose at return pipe.

20. Disconnect remaining wire connectors.
21. Disconnect heater hoses at firewall.
22. Raise vehicle. Drain engine oil.
23. Remove exhaust pipe flange nuts at manifold.
24. Remove front engine mount bolts.
25. Remove front exhaust pipe bracket.
26. On auto trans. models, disconnect gearshift control rod.
27. On manual trans. models, disconnect clutch cable.
28. Disconnect speedometer cable and drive shaft from transmission. Disconnect gearshift selector from control rod. On models equipped with overdrive, disconnect OD wire.
29. Attach a suitable lifting fixture and adjust it so the weight of the transmission is taken up. Remove rear crossmember.
30. Hoist engine out of chassis.

1976-77 260 Series

1. On manual transmission models, remove gearshift lever. On auto trans. models, place shift lever in Park position.
2. Disconnect battery cables.
3. Remove hood and air cleaner.
4. Remove splash shield under front of engine.
5. Drain coolant by removing lower radiator hose from radiator. Remove expansion tank cap. Open both petcocks on engine, one on each side. Petcocks are easily accessible from below. Hoses can be attached to petcocks to channel coolant into a container. Remove expansion tank hoses at radiator. Disconnect upper radiator hose.
6. On auto trans. models, disconnect transmission oil cooler lines at radiator.
7. Remove fan shroud attaching bolts and push shroud to rear. Disconnect radiator retaining bolts. Lift out radiator and shroud.
8. Disconnect heater hose at intake pipe, power brake hose at intake manifold and vacuum pump hose at pump.
9. Remove vacuum pump.
10. Disconnect fuel hoses at fuel filter and return pipe, wire connectors, high tension lead at distributor and heater hoses at firewall.
11. Disconnect carbon filter hose connections at filter and EGR hose at EGR valve.
12. Disconnect wire connector at voltage regulator. Disconnect wire connector from distributor.
13. Disconnect throttle cable and kickdown cable. Disconnect vacuum

amplifier hose at Tee fitting on California models and hoses at wax thermostat. Pull up hose to battery shelf.
14. Remove hose from air pump to backfire valve.
15. Disconnect wire at solenoid valve. On California models, disconnect wire at micro switch. Pull up wires for ignition coil.
16. Remove exhaust pipe flange nuts from exhaust manifolds.
17. Remove air conditioning compressor mounting bolts, then remove drive belt. Place compressor to one side and secure it to hood hinge. It is not necessary to disconnect hoses.
18. Drain engine oil.
19. Remove power steering pump drive belt. Remove pump mounting bolts and allow pump to hang by the hoses.
20. Remove front engine mount retaining nuts.
21. On cars equipped with catalytic converter, remove front exhaust pipe. Without catalytic converter, remove exhaust pipe clamps.
22. On auto trans. models, disconnect shift control lever at transmission.
23. On manual trans. models, remove clutch slave cylinder retaining bolts and allow cylinder to hang by its hose.
24. Disconnect speedometer cable and drive shaft flange from transmission.
25. Raise car and place it on stands.
26. Install a suitable lifting fixture and adjust it so the weight of the transmission is taken up. Remove crossmember. Be sure transmission is supported before removing crossmember.
27. Hoist engine out of chassis.

CYLINDER HEAD, REPLACE
B-20 & B-30 Engines
Except Fuel Injection

1. Drain coolant and remove rocker arm cover. Disconnect spark plug wires. Remove air cleaner.
2. Disassemble throttle control. Disconnect choke wire from carburetor. Disconnect fuel line at carburetor.
3. Remove exhaust manifold flange-to-pipe nuts. Disconnect upper radiator hose and heater hose at rear of the cylinder head. Disconnect wire from temperature gauge sanding unit.
4. On A/C equipped models, remove A/C compressor retaining bolts and position compressor to one side.

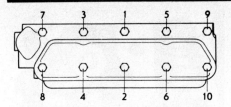

Fig. 1 Cylinder head tightening sequence. B-20 engines

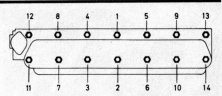

Fig. 2 Cylinder head tightening sequence. B-30 engines

5. Remove rocker arm shaft and push rods.
6. Loosen alternator tensioner arm. Remove cylinder head bolts and lift off head.
7. Reverse procedure to install, taking care to use proper torque and tightening sequence, Figs. 1 and 2.

1972-73 B-20F, 1972-75 B-30F Fuel Injection

1. Drain coolant and remove rocker arm cover.
2. Disconnect spark plug wires. Remove air cleaner.
3. Disconnect positive battery cable. Remove ground connections from inlet manifold on B20F.
4. Disconnect hoses for pressure sensor, brake booster, crankcase ventilation and ignition distributor. Place upper hoses on left wheel housing.
5. Disconnect wires from throttle switch, cold start valve, coolant temperature sensor and injectors.
6. Remove induction air hose.
7. Remove lock pin and bracket for throttle cable.
8. Remove fuel injectors by rotating their locking collars and pulling injectors from head. Position injectors, distribution pipe and pressure regulator to one side.
9. Remove heater hose and upper radiator hose.
10. On A/C equipped cars, remove A/C compressor mounting bolts and position compressor to one side.
11. Remove alternator tension bar from

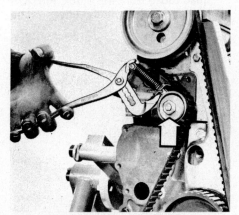

Fig. 3 Locking timing belt roller in retracted position. B-21 engine

cylinder head. Remove bolts for inlet duct stay.
12. Remove clamp for water pipe.
13. Remove rocker arm shaft and push rods.
14. Remove cylinder head bolts and lift off head. Remove gasket and rubber O rings for water pump.
15. Reverse procedure to install, taking care to use proper torque and tightening sequence, Figs. 1 and 2.

1974-75 B-20F Engine

1. Remove splash guard under engine. Drain coolant by disconnecting lower radiator hose from radiator.
2. Disconnect battery ground cable.
3. Disconnect upper radiator hose from engine.
4. Disconnect air bellows between air cleaner and CI unit.
5. Remove positive crankcase ventilation from intake manifold and oil trap on block. Disconnect vacuum pump hose at intake manifold.
6. Disconnect hoses at diverter valve.
7. Remove air pump and bracket.
8. Disconnect fuel hoses from filter, two distributor pipes at engine, hose at control pressure regulator, hose at cold start injector and four hoses at injectors.
9. Disconnect: wire at the control pressure regulator (including the ground wire), wire at the cold start injector, wire at the auxiliary air regulator, wire at the temperature sender.
10. Disconnect throttle cable and kick down cable (on auto. trans.).
11. Disconnect two hoses for the charcoal canister and one hose for the EGR valve from the intake manifold.
12. With auto. trans., disconnect the oil filter pipe from the flywheel housing.
13. Remove water pipe rear clamp from manifold.
14. Remove retaining bolts for intake manifold brace.
15. Remove exhaust pipe flange nuts at manifold.
16. Disconnect spark plug leads.
17. Disconnect upper heater hose at firewall.
18. Remove valve cover, rocker arm shaft and push rods.
19. Remove cylinder head bolts. Remove cylinder head.
20. Reverse procedure to install, taking care to use proper torque and tightening sequence, Fig. 1.

1976-77 B-21 Engine

1. Remove splash guard under engine. Drain coolant by disconnecting lower radiator hose from radiator.

2. Disconnect battery ground cable.
3. Disconnect upper radiator hose from engine.
4. Disconnect vacuum hoses from intake manifold.
5. Disconnect hoses from diverter valve.
6. Remove air injection reactor pump retaining bolts and position pump to one side.
7. Remove rubber bellows from between CI unit and intake manifold.
8. Remove bolts from intake manifold brace.
9. Remove intake manifold retaining nuts. Slide manifold off its studs and lay it to one side.
10. On some air conditioned models, it may be necessary to discharge system and disconnect suction hose from compressor in order to gain sufficient clearance.
11. Remove exhaust pipe flange nuts from manifold.
12. Remove injectors from cylinder head.
13. Disconnect spark plug leads from plugs.
14. Disconnect vacuum hoses from wax thermostat, wires from temperature sensor and thermal time switch.
15. Disconnect heater hose from rear of cylinder head.
16. Remove timing belt cover retaining bolts and remove cover.
17. Loosen nut for belt tensioner and press idler roller back. Lock roller by inserting a 3 mm drill through the pusher rod, Fig. 3. Remove belt.
18. Remove the uppermost bolt from the timing belt guard plate.
19. Remove vacuum pump.
20. Remove valve cover retaining nuts. Remove valve cover.
21. Remove cylinder head retaining bolts (10mm Allen) and remove head.
22. When installing head, follow sequence in Fig. 4 and torque in two

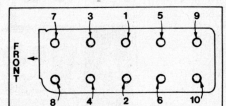

Fig. 4 Cylinder head tightening sequence. B-21 engines

Fig. 5 Positioning camshaft sprocket for camshaft removal. B-27 engine

stages, stage 1: 60 Nm (44 ft. lbs.); stage 2: 110 Nm (81 ft. lbs.). Follow instructions given under Timing Belt, Replace to install and correctly time the timing belt.

1976-77 B-27 Engine

1. Disconnect battery ground cable.
2. Remove air cleaner.
3. Disconnect throttle cable from its bracket and pulley. On auto trans. models, disconnect kickdown cable.
4. Disconnect wiring connector from cold start injector and control pressure regulator.
5. Disconnect fuel lines from control pressure regulator.
6. Disconnect wiring connector and ground connection from auxiliary air regulator.
7. Disconnect wiring connector from fuel distributor.
8. Disconnect spark plug leads from both banks.
9. Loosen injector retaining clips and pull all injectors out of both banks.
10. Disconnect vacuum hoses from intake manifold.
11. On models equipped with EGR vac-

uum amplifier, disconnect wires at micro switch and solenoid valve.
12. Disconnect fuel lines from filter and return pipe.
13. Remove four intake manifold retaining bolts and lift off manifold.

NOTE: Clearances are very close between manifold and ignition distributor and water pump. Use care to avoid interference with these parts.

14. Remove splash shield under engine.
15. Drain engine block coolant. Open both drain cocks on engine block. Hoses can be attached to drain cocks to channel coolant into a container.
16. On left cylinder head, remove air pump and vacuum pump.
17. On right cylinder head, remove upper radiator hose. Remove air conditioner compressor retaining bolts and place compressor to one side. It is not necessary to disconnect A/C hoses. Remove ignition distributor. Remove EGR valve with bracket and pipe. Remove A/C compressor bracket.
18. Disconnect wiring connectors at relays.
19. Remove hose from water pump to head. On left side, disconnect lower radiator hose at water pump.
20. At rear of head, disconnect coolant hose, then separate air injection reactor air manifold. Remove diverter valve and air hose.
21. Remove valve cover retaining bolts and remove cover.
22. Remove uppermost four bolts from timing cover.
23. On left side, remove 8mm Allen bolt from the timing cover. On right side, remove cover plate from timing cover.
24. Raise car and remove exhaust pipe clamp at crossmember.
25. On right side, remove dipstick pipe.
26. Remove exhaust pipe retaining nuts from manifold.

Fig. 6 Camshaft locking fork installed. B-27 engine

27. Remove cover plate from rear of cylinder head.
28. Rotate engine until camshaft sprocket is in position with large hole in sprocket and opposite the rocker arm shaft, Fig. 5.
29. Loosen lock retaining bolt and push camshaft locking fork to one side, Fig. 6.
30. Install tool 5104. Tool is tightened in position with two bolts in timing cover. Locate bolt in camshaft sprocket hole and tighten tool by hand. The tool holds tension on the camshaft chain when the camshaft is removed. If chain loosens, the tensioner will take up any slack. If this occurs, the timing cover will have to be removed.
31. Remove rocker arm and shaft assembly. Bolts must be removed in the proper sequence, Fig. 7.
32. Remove camshaft sprocket center bolt. Push camshaft to the rear. The camshaft stud should be free from sprocket before cylinder head is lifted up.
33. Insert two cylinder head bolts into cylinder head. Do not thread bolts into block. Use bolts to lever the head loose from the block, Fig. 8. It is vital that the cylinder liners not be

Fig. 7 Cylinder head tightening sequence. B-27 engine

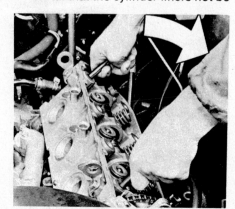

Fig. 8 Removing cylinder head. B-27 engines

Fig. 9 Cylinder liner retainers installed. B-27 engines

disturbed or removal and complete disassembly of the engine will be necessary. Be sure not to pull head straight up during removal or liners may be disturbed.

34. As soon as head is removed, install cylinder liner retainers, Fig. 9. Push down two guide sleeves and remove gasket. When cleaning gasket surfaces on block and head, do not use a carbon scraper as this will damage the aluminum. Saturate the gasket surfaces with paint remover then use a wooden paint scraper to remove old gasket.

CAUTION: Use extreme care to prevent paint remover from coming in contact with bodywork. The slightest contact of paint remover will damage the vehicle's finish.

35. When installing cylinder head gasket, be sure the narrow metal edge of the gasket faces upward.
36. Position cylinder head, install rocker arm shaft assembly, oil threads of head bolts and install head bolts.
37. Tighten head bolts in the stages, according to Fig. 7. Stage 1: 10 Nm (7 ft. lbs.); stage 2: 30 Nm (22 ft. lbs.); stage 3: 60 Nm (44 ft. lbs.). Allow head to stabilize for 15 min.
38. While head is stabilizing, install camshaft into timing chain sprocket and install retaining bolt and camshaft lock.

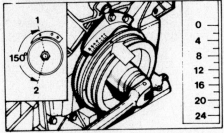

Fig. 11 Crankshaft pully timing marks. B-27 engine

39. Using sequence shown in Fig. 7, loosen each bolt in turn then tighten to 15-20 Nm (11-14 ft. lbs.). Install special tool 5098 onto the socket. Using protractor, tighten bolts 116-120°.

VALVE GUIDES

1. Press out the old guides using tool SVO 2818.
2. Press in new guides using tool SVO 2819. Press guide down until the tool bottoms.

NOTE: For B20F engines, place a .016" (.40 mm) thick washer between the tool and the head.

VALVE ADJUSTMENT
B-20 Engines

1. Remove rocker arm cover.
2. Turn the engine until valves of #4 cylinder are "rocking." That is, exhaust valve will be closing and intake valve will just begin to open. With valves of #4 cylinder in this position, #1 piston will be at TDC and both valves on #1 cylinder can be adjusted.
3. Rotate crankshaft clockwise until rocker arms for #2 cylinder are rocking. Both valves of #3 cylinder can now be adjusted.
4. Rotate crankshaft clockwise until rocker arms for #1 cylinder are rocking. Adjust both valves for #4 cylinder.
5. Rotate crankshaft clockwise until #3 cylinder is rocking. Adjust both valves on #2 cylinder.

B-30 Engines

1. Remove rocker arm cover.
2. Turn engine until valves of #6 cylinder are "rocking." That is, exhaust valve will be closing and intake valve will just begin to open. Both valves of #1 cylinder can now be adjusted.
3. Rotate crankshaft clockwise until #2 cylinder is in rocking position. Adjust both valves of #5 cylinder.
4. Rotate crankshaft clockwise until #4 cylinder is rocking. Adjust both valves of #3 cylinder.
5. Rotate crankshaft clockwise until #1 cylinder is rocking. Adjust both valves of #6 cylinder.
6. Rotate crankshaft clockwise until #5 cylinder is rocking. Adjust both valves of #2 cylinder.
7. Rotate crankshaft clockwise until #3 cylinder is rocking. Adjust both valves of #4 cylinder.
8. Reinstall rocker arm cover.

Fig. 10 Valve adjustment. B-21 engines

B-21 Engines

1. Remove valve cover.
2. Rotate engine until both valves for #1 cylinder are on the heel of cam lobes.
3. Insert feeler gauge between cam lobe and valve shim to check clearance. If clearance is incorrect, line up valve depressors so notches are at right angles to engine center line, arrows in Fig. 10.
4. Attach tool 5022. Screw down tool spindle until depressor groove is just above edge of head and accessible with pliers, Fig. 10.
5. Use special pliers 5026 to remove valve shim.
6. Use a micrometer to measure shim thickness. Calculate shim thickness necessary to obtain correct clearance.
7. Coat new shim with oil and install it in valve depressor.
8. Repeat adjustment procedure for cylinders 3, 4 and 2.

B-27 Engine

1. Remove valve covers.
2. Rotate crankshaft until #1 cylinder is in firing position.

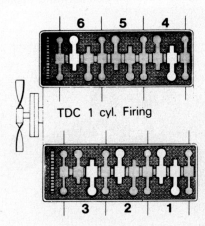

Fig. 12 Valve adjustment No. 1 cylinder firing. B-27 engine

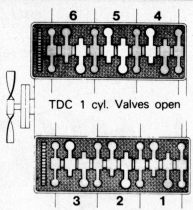

Fig. 13 Valve adjustment No. 1 cylinder on exhaust stroke. B-27 engine

NOTE: The crankshaft pulley has two timing marks on it, Fig. 11. Mark #1 is the only one to be used on valve adjustment.

3. Adjust valves indicated in Fig. 12.
4. Rotate engine one full revolution clockwise to bring #1 timing mark back in line with the O on the timing plate.
5. Adjust remaining valves, Fig. 13.
6. Replace valve covers.

TIMING COVER, REPLACE

B20 Engines

1. Remove fan and water pump pulley. Disconnect stabilizer bar from frame.
2. Remove crankshaft pulley retaining bolt and remove pulley.
3. Remove timing gear cover retaining bolts. Be sure to remove oil pan to timing cover bolts and loosen a few oil pan retaining bolts and use caution not to damage oil pan gasket. Remove timing gear cover.
4. Remove snap ring, washer and felt ring from cover.
5. When reinstalling cover, be sure drain holes are clear.
6. Place cover in position and install

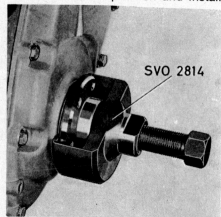

Fig. 15 Crankshaft hub removal. B-30 engines

retaining bolts without tightening them.
7. Center cover with tool SVO 2438, Fig. 14. Turn tool while tightening cover bolts and adjust cover so tool does not bind.
8. Fit a new felt ring, washer and snap ring.
9. Replace pulleys and belt(s).

B30 Engines

1. Drain coolant and remove radiator. Remove fan and fan belt.
2. Remove harmonic balancer from pulley.
3. Remove polygon hub by hand if possible. If hub is too tight to be removed by hand, use tool SVO 2814, Fig. 15.

NOTE: If only front crankshaft seal is to be replaced, carry out steps 4-6. If timing cover is to be replaced complete (as for timing gears) skip to Step 7.

4. Remove oil seal. Lubricate sealing lip on new seal and install with tool SVO 2816.
5. Install polygon hub using tool SVO 2815. Note the marking of the hub and crankshaft end. Center punch marks on each should correspond. Torque bolt to 50-57 ft. lbs.
6. Install harmonic balancer and pulley.
7. Remove timing gear cover retaining bolts. Be sure to remove timing gear cover to oil pan bolts and loosen a few oil pan retaining bolts. Use caution not to damage oil pan gasket. Remove timing cover.

B-21 Engines

Timing belt cover is retained by four 10 mm bolts. Remove bolts and remove cover.

B-27 Engines

1. Remove both valve covers. When dismounting air conditioner compressor, it is not necessary to discharge the unit.

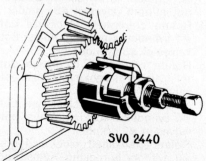

Fig. 16 Crankshaft hub removal. B-20 engine

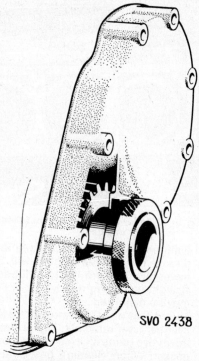

Fig. 14 Centering timing gear cover. B-20 engines

2. Remove fan and pulley.
3. Remove lower crankshaft pulley nut. Rotate engine so woodruff key points to 12 o'clock and remove pulley.
4. Remove timing cover retaining bolts and remove timing cover.

TIMING GEARS, REPLACE

B20 & B30 Engines

1. Drain coolant and remove radiator.
2. Remove timing cover as outlined above.
3. On B20 engines, remove crankshaft hub using tool SVO 2440, Fig. 16.
4. Remove camshaft gear retaining nut and, using tool SVO 2250, or similar puller, remove camshaft gear, Fig. 17.

Fig. 17 Camshaft gear removal. B-20 & B-30 engines

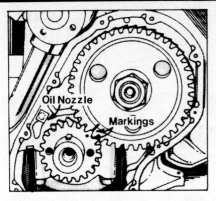

Fig. 18   Valve timing marks. B-20 & B-30 engines

5. Using a suitable puller, remove crankshaft gear. Screw out oil nozzle and blow it clean then reinstall it.
6. Press crankshaft gear on using tool SVO 2407 and press on camshaft gear with SVO 2408.

CAUTION: Do not attempt to drive either gear on by striking it. Do not push the camshaft backwards as this could loosen the camshaft welsh plug.

---

7. On B20 engines, install crankshaft hub.
8. Check to be sure the gears are in the correct position, Fig. 18.

TIMING BELT, REPLACE
B-21 Engines

1. Remove timing belt cover.
2. Loosen tensioner nut. Push tensioner roller back against spring. Lock roller by inserting a 3 mm drill into the roller shaft.
3. Remove timing belt.
4. Align timing marks as per Fig. 19. Stretch on tension side and fit drive

Fig. 20   Positioning left camshaft for sprocket installation. B-27 engine

belt on camshaft sprocket.
5. Slip belt over tensioner roller.

CAUTION: Prying with tools will damage the belt.

---

6. Loosen tensioner nut to let spring tension act on roller and tension belt. Tighten tensioner nut.
7. Check timing marks as per Fig. 19 to be sure belt has not slipped.

TIMING CHAINS, INSTALL
B-27 Engines

1. Position crankshaft so the crankshaft woodruff key points to the left camshaft (one o'clock). Position left camshaft so its keyway points to twelve o'clock, Fig. 20.
2. Slip chain over camshaft sprocket, being sure that timing mark on camshaft sprocket is between two painted timing marks on the chain.
3. Holding chain on camshaft sprocket, slip the other end of the chain over the crankshaft inner sprocket. Be sure that timing mark on gear aligns with painted link on the chain.
4. Install sprocket onto camshaft. Pin in sprocket must go into slot in camshaft.
5. Install Allen bolt. Insert a screwdriver through sprocket to prevent engine from turning and torque retaining bolt to 70-80 Nm (51-59 ft. lbs.).
6. Rotate engine clockwise to position crankshaft woodruff key at six o'clock. Position right camshaft so its groove is at seven o'clock.
7. Install chain on camshaft sprocket, being sure timing mark on sprocket is between two painted marks on chain.
8. Holding chain on camshaft sprocket, slip other end of chain over crankshaft intermediate sprocket. Be sure that timing mark on gear aligns with painted link on chain.
9. Install sprocket on camshaft. Pin in sprocket must go into slot in sprocket.
10. Install Allen bolt. Insert a screw driver through sprocket to prevent engine from turning and torque retaining bolt to 70-80 Nm (51-59 ft. lbs.).
11. Turn lock screw on each chain tensioner ¼ turn clockwise to release tensioner shoes.
12. Install oil pump and pump drive chain. Be sure to center pump while installing to prevent binding of the gears against aluminum housing.
13. Install timing gear cover and torque retaining bolts to 10-15 Nm (7-11 ft. lbs.).

Fig. 19   Valve timing marks. B-21 engine

CAMSHAFT, REPLACE
B-20 & B30 Engines

1. Remove cylinder head as outlined under Cylinder Head, Replace.
2. Remove valve lifters using tool 2424, Fig. 21.
3. Remove camshaft timing gear as outlined under Timing Gears, Replace.
4. Remove ignition distributor and oil pump drive.
5. Remove camshaft retaining bolts and remove camshaft.
6. Be sure to lubricate all lobes and bearing surfaces of the new camshaft before installing.
7. Reinstall timing gears as outlined in that section.

NOTE: When timing marks on timing gears are aligned, number four cylinder is in firing position. In order to install oil pump and distributor drive,

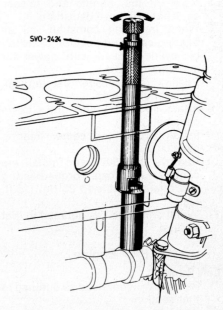

Fig. 21   Removing lifters. B-20 & B-30 engines

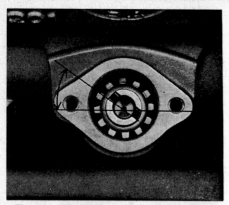

Fig. 22 Distributor drive position. B-20 & B-30 engines

engine must be positioned with number one cylinder in firing position. This position can be found by turning engine until valves for number four cylinder are in the "rock" position.

8. With number one cylinder in firing position, install distributor drive with its offset groove as per Fig. 22.

B-21 Engines

1. Remove valve cover. Remove timing belt.
2. Remove center camshaft bearing cap.

NOTE: The camshaft bearing caps are matched to bores and must not be interchanged.

3. Attach tool 5021, Fig. 23, and tighten handle to hold camshaft in place while removing other bearing caps.
4. Remove four remaining caps.
5. Back off tool handle and release camshaft. Remove camshaft.
6. When installing camshaft, oil all bearing caps and position camshaft on cylinder head with dowel for sprocket upward.
7. Position rear camshaft bearing cap. Do not tighten cap.
8. Attach tool 5021 and press down camshaft.
9. Install all but the center bearing caps.
10. Remove tool 5021 and install the center bearing cap. Torque bearing cap retaining nuts to 20 Nm (15 ft. lbs.).
11. Install timing belt as outlined in that section.

B-27 Engine

Left Bank
1. Remove cylinder head as outlined in that section.
2. Slide camshaft out rear of cylinder head.

3. Reinstall camshaft and install cylinder head as outlined.

Right Bank

NOTE: The camshaft can be removed from right bank without removing cylinder head.

1. Remove valve cover.
2. Attach tool 5104 as outlined under Cylinder Head, Replace.
3. Remove timing sprocket retaining bolt, camshaft lock and access cover at rear of cylinder head.
4. Remove cap from coolant expansion tank.
5. Remove cylinder head retaining bolts and rocker arm assembly.

NOTE: Do not disturb cylinder head.

6. Remove access cover from firewall. Slide camshaft rearward and through firewall into passenger compartment.

PISTON & ROD ASSEMBLY
B20 & B30 Engines

Assemble connecting rods to pistons so pistons can be installed with notch on piston top facing forward while number marking on connecting rod faces away from the camshaft side of the engine.

To install pistons, use tool SVO 2823 or other suitable ring compressor.

B-21 Engines

Assemble connecting rods to pistons so pistons can be installed with notch on piston top facing forward. Mark on connecting rod should also face forward, Fig. 24.

To install pistons, use tool 5031 or other suitable ring compressor.

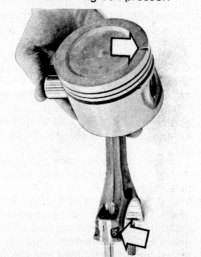

Fig. 24 Piston & rod assembly. B-21 engine

Fig. 23 Camshaft tensioning tool. B-21 engine

B-27 Engines

Two makes of pistons are used in the B-27 engine, the Demolin which has a height of 68.45 mm and the Mahle, 62.85 mm high. Pistons are available only as a piston/cylinder liner set. Piston pins are press fit in piston and connecting rod. Pins are removed by pressing them out with the aid of special tool 5092. To install a new piston pin, the piston end of the connecting rod is heated on an electric heater. To gauge the correct heat, place a small piece of solder on the connecting rod. The solder will melt when the rod reaches the proper temperature. When the rod is sufficiently heated, place it and the piston in the tool fixture. Arrow on the piston should face upward.

NOTE: The tool fixture has a side for rods 1, 2 & 3 and the opposite side for rods 4, 5 & 6. It is important that the rods face in the proper direction. With the piston and rod correctly set in the tool, install the piston pin in the mandrill, dip the pin in oil and quickly push the mandrill/pin assembly into the piston until it is stopped by the tool.

PISTON PINS
B-20, B-21 & B-30

Piston pins are available in .002″ oversize. If pin hole in piston is so worn as to require an oversize pin, the hole should first be reamed until the pin can be pushed through by hand with only a light pressure.

PISTONS & RINGS
Piston Fit

B20 & B30 Engines
1. Install piston into cylinder bore without rings installed.

2. Insert a feeler gauge between the piston and cylinder wall to determine clearance. Piston clearance is measured at right angles to the wrist pin hole. See specification table in the front of this chapter for the correct clearance.
3. Attach a spring scale to the feeler gauge and check force necessary to move feeler gauge. Scale should read 2.2 lbs. with proper clearance.

NOTE: Bore sizes are marked with a letter stamped on the cylinder block deck surface adjacent to each cylinder bore. Each piston is marked with a letter code on the top of the piston. Code numbers should coincide.

Piston Ring End Gap

1. Using a piston turned upside-down, push each ring down into the cylinder in which it is to be installed.
2. Measure the gap between ends of the ring with a feeler gauge.
3. Ring gap should be .016-.022 in. for B20 & B30 units. If necessary, gap can be increased by filing ring ends. B-21 engines should have a ring end gap of .014-.022 in. for compression rings and .010-.016 in. for oil scrape rings.
4. After installing rings on pistons, check to be sure rings are not binding in their grooves.

CRANKSHAFT REAR OIL SEAL, REPLACE
1972-73 B20 Engines

1. Remove transmission, clutch and flywheel.
2. Remove sealing flange, taking care not to damage oil pan gasket. Remove seal.
3. Make sure flange is clean. The drain hole must not be plugged and the sealing ring must not be fitted in flange.
4. Install sealing flange but do not tighten bolts.
5. Center flange with tool SVO 2439, Fig. 25 and tighten bolts. Rotate tool while tightening flange retaining bolts to be sure flange is not binding on sleeve.
6. Fit new felt ring and place on the washer and snap ring. Press snap ring on with centering sleeve. Check that snap ring engages its groove.

NOTE: Early B20 rear oil seals can be replaced with later type described below. If later seal is to be installed, sealing flange must also be replaced with later type.

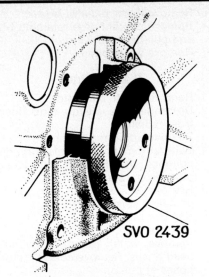

Fig. 25 Centering rear sealing flange. 1972-73 B-20 engine

1974-75 B20 & All B21 & B30 Engines

1. Remove transmission, clutch and flywheel.
2. Remove sealing flange, taking care not to damage oil pan gasket.
3. Press out seal with drift from tool SVO 2817. Use suitable cushion for flange to prevent it from being damaged.
4. Press in seal with tool SVO 2817.

NOTE: Inspect seal surface of the crankshaft. The seal can be installed to different depths.

5. Coat seal lightly with engine oil then install flange using a new gasket.

1976-77 B-27 Engines

1. Remove transmission, clutch and flywheel.
2. Remove rear seal housing (6 mm Allen bolts). The lower crankcase half does not have a gasket. After removing rear housing, clean away sealant from lower crankcase half.
3. Press in new seal using tools 1801 and 5107. Coat mating surfaces of rear seal housing and lower crankcase half with sealing compound, Volvo part number 1128088. Torque attaching bolts to 7-11 ft. lbs. (10-11 Nm).

OIL PAN, REPLACE
140 & 164 Series

1. Install a suitable lifting tool on engine. Raise front end of engine until there is no weight on engine mountings.
2. Raise car and support it on jack stands. Drain the oil and remove dipstick.
3. Remove lower nuts from front engine mounts.
4. Disconnect steering rods from pitman arm.
5. Place a floor jack under front crossmember and support crossmember. Remove two rear crossmember bolts and install two bolts of same thread but of sufficiently greater length as to allow crossmember to be lowered enough to allow removal of oil pan.
6. Remove front crossmember and lower crossmember. Remove floor jack.
7. Remove oil temperature gauge plug if used. Remove reinforcing bracket at flywheel housing.
8. Remove oil pan bolts and oil pan.

240 Series

1. Remove front engine mount bolts.
2. Attach a suitable lifting fixture to forward lifting eye of the engine and lift the engine slightly.
3. Remove splash guard.
4. On B-21 engines, remove left front engine mount.
5. Remove lower reinforcement bracket and oil pan retaining bolts.
6. Tap oil pan loose from its gasket and remove it. On B-21 engines, it is necessary to turn oil pan so the front of pan is to left side before removing.

260 Series

1. Remove splash shield and oil pan.

OIL PUMP, REPLACE
B-20, B-21 & B-30 Engines

1. Remove oil pan as outlined in that section.
2. Remove oil pump retaining bolts and remove pump and its pickup pipe.

B-27 Engine

1. Remove timing cover as outlined in that section.
2. Remove three oil pump sprocket attaching bolts and remove sprocket and chain.
3. Remove four oil pump attaching bolts and remove pump.
4. When reinstalling pump, use extreme caution to prevent binding of pump gears against aluminum bore. Be sure to rotate pump as pump retaining bolts are torqued (7-11 ft. lbs.). Any binding will then be evident.

VOLVO

WATER PUMP, REPLACE

B20 & B30 Engines

1. Drain cooling system and remove radiator.
2. Remove fan assembly and pulley.
3. Remove water pump retaining bolts and remove water pump.
4. When installing pump, be sure gasket and seal surfaces are clean. Be sure sealing rings on upper side of pump locate correctly by pressing pump upward against cylinder head of extension.

B-21 Engine

1. Drain cooling system and remove radiator shroud retaining screws and move shroud to rear. Remove fan and fan clutch.
2. Loosen and remove drive belts for alternator and air pump.
3. Remove fan pulley.
4. Remove timing gear cover.

5. Remove lower radiator hose.
6. Remove coolant pipe retaining bolt and pull pipe rearward.
7. Remove water pump.

B-27 Engine

1. Remove intake manifold.
2. Disconnect expansion tank hoses from radiator.
3. Remove upper radiator hose.
4. With automatic transmission, disconnect transmission oil cooler pipes from radiator.
5. Remove screws from fan shroud and slide shroud to the rear.
6. Remove radiator.
7. Remove fan.
8. Remove water pump to cylinder head hoses. Remove coolant return hoses at pump.
9. Remove fan belts and water pump pulley.
10. Disconnect thermal timer and temperature sender wires.

11. Remove water pump from engine block.

FUEL PUMP, REPLACE

B-20B & B-30B Engines

1. Disconnect fuel lines at the pump. Plug tank to pump hose.
2. Remove pump retaining bolts and remove fuel pump.

B-20E, B-20F, B-30F, B-21F & B-27F

NOTE: The fuel pump is located on the left side of the fuel tank.

1. Clamp off the tank-to-pump hose with suitable pliers. Disconnect fuel lines from pump.
2. Disconnect wire connector from pump.
3. Remove pump retaining bolts and remove the pump.

Carburetor Section

SU HIF6 CARBURETORS

1972 B-20B Engines

Float Level

With float bowl cover removed and carburetor inverted, dimension should be as shown in Fig. 1.

Mixture & Idle Speed Adjustment

1. Remove air cleaner.
2. Make basic jet adjustment for each carburetor as follows: Lift air valve and, with jet adjusting screw, raise jet so upper edge of jet just comes level with bridge. Lower jet by turning adjusting screw 2½ turns clockwise.

NOTE: This basic setting applies to a carb. temp. of approx. 70 degrees F.

3. Fill damper cylinders to ¼" from its

upper edge with type A automatic trans. oil.
4. Connect a tachometer and, if available, a CO meter. Run engine at 1500 rpm until thermostat opens.
5. With throttle stop screws, adjust idle speed to 800 rpm with manual trans. and 700 rpm with auto. trans. Be sure both air valves have the same amount of lift above the bridge. This is easily checked by simply looking into the carburetor throats. A more accurate synchronization is not necessary.
6. If a CO meter is not available, adjust jets to obtain maximum idle speed, then turn jet adjusting screws equally counter-clockwise until engine speed starts to falter. This is the proper setting.
   If a CO meter is to be used, adjust jet screws to obtain a CO value of 2.0-3.0%.
   Reinstall plastic plugs over adjusting screws.
7. Adjust link rods so that with the control against its stop bracket on the manifold, there is a clearance of .004" between the lever and flange of the throttle spindle on each carburetor.
8. Adjust hot start valves so that with carburetor throttles closed, and hot start valve spindle fully bottomed, there is a clearance of .040" between the hot start valve spindle and the carburetor lever.

Fast Idle Adjustment

With choke control on instrument

panel pulled out approx. 1", adjust fast idle screw to obtain engine speed of 1400-1500 rpm.

ZENITH-STROMBERG ADJUSTMENTS

1972 B-30A Engines

Float Level

With float bowl removed and carburetor inverted, dimension should be as shown in Fig. 2

NOTE: When removing float bowl, always remove the brass float chamber plug before removing the float bowl retaining screws.

Adjust float level by bending tang at float needle and seat.

Mixture & Idle Speed Adjustment

NOTE: The fuel jet is pressed into the carburetor body. Jet adjustment must

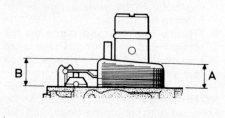

A = 9—13 mm (1/2")
B = 15—17 mm (5/8")

Fig. 2   Float level adjustment. Zenith-Stromberg carburetor

A = 0.5—1.5 mm (0.02—0.06")

Fig. 1   Float level adjustment. SU HIF6 carburetor

be done with a set of special tools, Fig. 3.

1. Remove the air cleaner cover.
2. Screw the idle trim screw for each carburetor to its bottom position.
3. Remove float chamber plug from each carburetor. Screw out spindle (approx. to rubber ring) on tool SVO 2895 and fit tool into hole for float chamber plug of each carburetor.
4. Insert spacer SVO 2896 between air valve and carburetor body.

NOTE: Be sure to insert end of spacer marked B-20B regardless of whether carburetors are on a B20 or B30 engine.

5. If there is clearance between shoulder of spacer and carburetor body bridge, remove damper piston and install tool SVO 2897.
6. Press down jet by screwing in spindle on SVO 2897 so spacer shoulder bottoms on bridge. The carburetor is now adjusted to a rich setting.

CAUTION: Before screwing in spindle on SVO 97, be sure spindle of SVO 2895 is backed off sufficiently

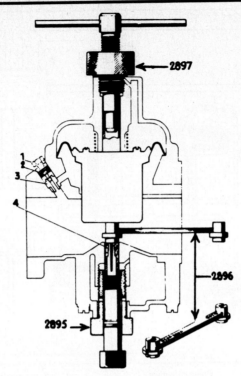

**Fig. 3   Float jet adjustment.
Zenith-Stromberg carburetor**

to avoid contact with jet.

7. Remove SVO 2897 and spacer and reinstall damper piston.
8. Connect a tachometer and CO meter.
9. Run engine until thermostat opens. The adjustment must be completed within 8 minutes after the thermostat opens.
10. Adjust idle speed to 800 rpm (700 rpm with auto. trans.). Check that the air valves have the same lift as speed is being adjusted.
11. Press up the jets on each carburetor equally by tightening the spindles of tools SVO 2895 until the CO meter registers 2.5%. Race the engine briefly each time an adjustment is made.
12. Remove tools and reinstall float chamber plugs.
13. Adjust link rods.
14. Reinstall air cleaner cover.

Fast Idle Adjustment

With choke control on the instrument panel pulled out approx. 1", the index mark on the fast idle cam should be in line with the centerline of the fast idle screw. In this position, adjust fast idle screw to give a speed of 1100-1300 rpm.

Fuel Injection Section
Electronic Fuel Injection

1972-73 B20E & 1972-74 B30E & B30F ENGINES
Description

This system, Figs. 1 and 2, consists of a fuel filter, electric fuel pump, pressure regulator, injectors, cold start valve, inlet duct, throttle valve switch, auxillary air regulator, induction air temperature sensor, coolant temperature sensor, pressure sensor, triggering contacts in ignition distributor and electronic control unit. Fuel is drawn from the tank by the fuel pump, through the fuel filter into the fuel pressure line to the injectors. The pressure regulator limits fuel pressure in fuel line to 28 psi. on 140 and 30 psi on 164. From the pressure regulator excessive fuel flows back to the tank through the return line. Fuel injectors are mounted in inlet ducts on cylinder head. Injection by the injector is governed by engine speed and engine load. The pressure sensor senses pressure in the inlet duct and converts this to an electrical impulse which is sent to the control unit. The control unit re-

ceives information on engine load in this manner. Contacts in the distributor provide the control unit with information on engine speed. The control unit processes this information to determine how long the injectors should remain open to provide the proper amount of fuel.

The cold start valve provides extra fuel to the engine at cold start. The opening interval of the cold start valve is controlled by the thermal timer. During warm engine operation, the control unit receives information from the coolant temperature sensor, which allows injector to remain open for a longer period. Increased air flow is provided by the auxillary air regulator which gradually closes as engine temperature rises. When the accelerator pedal is depressed the control unit receives impulses for extra fuel from the throttle valve switch, which will cause injectors to inject a number of times between ordinary injections. If accelerator pedal is quickly depressed, duration of injection will be longer than the normal injection cycle.

Fuel Pump Test

On 1972-73 B20E engines, fuel pump should deliver 26.5 gals. per hour at 28 psi. On 1972-74 B30E and B30F engines, fuel pump should deliver 24.6 gals. per hour at 30 psi. At this load, current reading should be 5 amps.

Injector Test

Measure resistance between terminal pins, resistance should be 2.4 ohms at 68°F. On 1972-73 B20E engines, maximum leakage should be five drops per minute at 28 psi. On 1972-74 B30E and B30F engines, maximum leakage should be two drops per minute at 30 psi.

NOTE: When checking injections, never use a voltage source higher than three volt, otherwise injector may become damaged.

Induction Air Temperature Sensor

Measure resistance between terminal

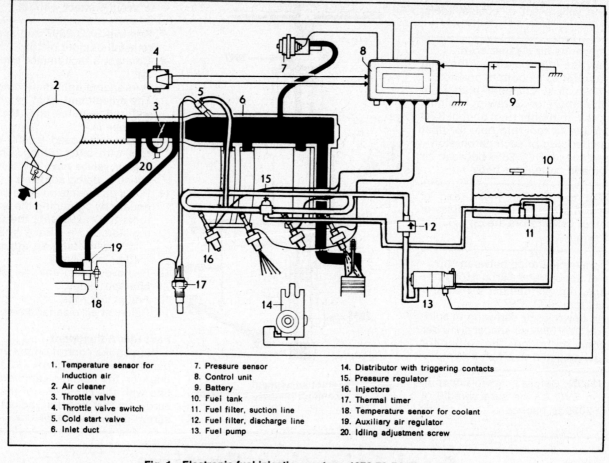

1. Temperature sensor for induction air
2. Air cleaner
3. Throttle valve
4. Throttle valve switch
5. Cold start valve
6. Inlet duct
7. Pressure sensor
8. Control unit
9. Battery
10. Fuel tank
11. Fuel filter, suction line
12. Fuel filter, discharge line
13. Fuel pump
14. Distributor with triggering contacts
15. Pressure regulator
16. Injectors
17. Thermal timer
18. Temperature sensor for coolant
19. Auxiliary air regulator
20. Idling adjustment screw

Fig. 1 Electronic fuel injection system. 1972-73 B20E engine

pins. Resistance should be as shown in Fig. 3.

Coolant Temperature Sensor Test

Measure resistance between terminal pins. Resistance should be as shown in Fig. 4.

Throttle Valve Switch Test

Place ignition switch in on position. Open and close throttle slowly. A clicking noise should come from the injectors indicating extra fuel for acceleration has been injected.

Pressure Sensor Test

Measure resistance between terminal pins. Resistance should be approximately 90 ohms between terminals 7 and 15, primary winding. Resistance should be 350 ohms between terminals 8 and 10, secondary winding. All other connections should read infinite.

Pressure Regulator, Adjust

1. Loosen hose clamps and remove hoses from header pipe.
2. Connect pressure gauge as shown in Fig. 5.
3. Start engine, then loosen lock nut

and adjust pressure to 28 psi. for 1972-73 B20E engines and 30 psi. for 1972-74 B30E and B30F engines. If pressure cannot be adjusted to specification, replace regulator.
4. Disconnect pressure regulator and connect fuel hose to distributor pipe. Check to ensure there is no leakage.

Throttle Valve, Adjust

1. Loosen lock nut for stop screw on throttle valve, then loosen screw a couple of turns so it does not rest on throttle valve spindle.
2. On 1972-73 B20E engines, turn screw in until it contacts stop on throttle valve spindle, then turn screw in an additional ¼ to ⅓ turn and tighten lock nut.
3. On 1972-74 B30E and B30F engines, turn screw in until it contacts stop on throttle valve spindle, then turn screw in an additional turn and tighten lock nut.
4. On all models, check to ensure throttle valve is not jammed or sticking in the closed position.
5. Adjust throttle valve switch as described under Throttle Valve Switch, Adjust.

Throttle Valve Switch, Adjust

1. Connect Bosch tester EFAW 228.
2. Place switch A to position measuring and switch B to position throttle valve switch III.
3. Loosen screws so that throttle valve switch can be turned. Mark inlet duct at upper screws.
4. Rotate throttle valve switch clockwise as far as possible, then slowly rotate switch counter clockwise until pointer on tester moves from infinite reading to 0. Turn switch one degree on tester scale further and tighten switch attaching screws.
5. Check to ensure tester moves to an infinite reading when throttle valve opens one degree. Place a .020 in. (.5 mm) feeler gauge between throttle valve spindle stop and stop screw. Change to a .012 in. (.3 mm) feeler gauge. Pointer should not move to an infinite reading on tester.

Idle Mixture (CO), Adjust

Control units incorporate a CO adjusting screw. This is a large, gray plastic screw which can be found on the end of the control unit, Fig. 6. Before attempt-

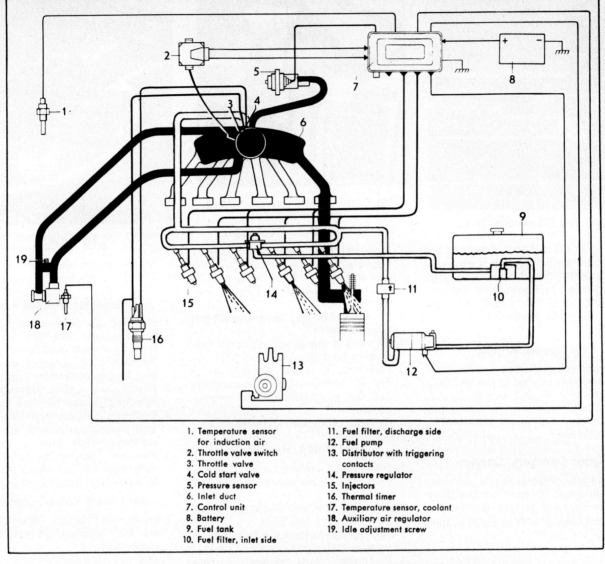

1. Temperature sensor for induction air
2. Throttle valve switch
3. Throttle valve
4. Cold start valve
5. Pressure sensor
6. Inlet duct
7. Control unit
8. Battery
9. Fuel tank
10. Fuel filter, inlet side
11. Fuel filter, discharge side
12. Fuel pump
13. Distributor with triggering contacts
14. Pressure regulator
15. Injectors
16. Thermal timer
17. Temperature sensor, coolant
18. Auxiliary air regulator
19. Idle adjustment screw

Fig. 2   Electronic fuel injection system. 1972-74 B30E & B30F engines

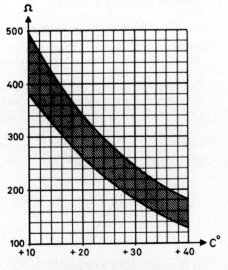

Fig. 3   Induction air temperature sensor resistance chart

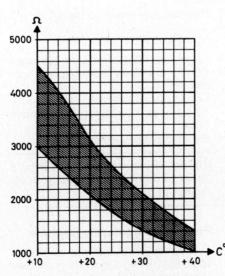

Fig. 4   Coolant temperature sensor resistance chart

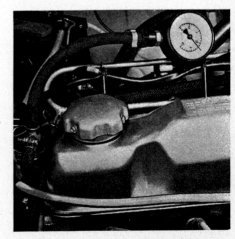

Fig. 5   Connecting pressure gauge

1-1093

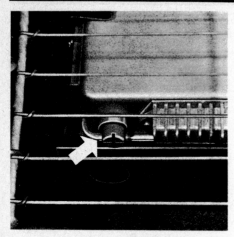

Fig. 6   Idle CO adjusting screw

ing to adjust CO content of system, be sure throttle switch has been properly adjusted. CO is then adjusted by turning adjusting screw on control unit. To correctly carry out this adjustment, an infra-red CO meter is necessary.

Idle Speed, Adjust

Idle speed is adjusted by means of the idle speed screw placed in the auxiliary air by-pass line, Figs. 7 and 8. Do not use the throttle stop screw to adjust idle speed as this will upset the throttle switch adjustment.

Trigger Contacts, Service

The trigger contacts, Fig. 9, are non-adjustable but it is important that they be cleaned at each service. Use electrical contact cleaner only to clean trigger contacts.

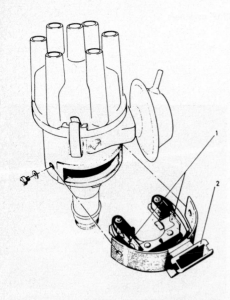

1. Triggering contacts   2. Electrical connection

Fig. 9   Triggering contacts

Fig. 7   Idle adjusting screw. 1972-73 B20E engine

Control Unit, Replace

1. Move rear seat to rear stop position.
2. Remove bolt between tubular bend and link screw, then move seat to front stop position and fold backwards.
3. Remove attaching bolts and lift out control unit.
4. Remove screw attaching cable harness to control unit.
5. Fabricate a puller as shown in Fig. 10, then using puller, carefully pull out plug contact and remove control unit.
6. Reverse procedure to install.

Fuel Pump, Replace

1. Disconnect battery ground cable, then clean hose connection at fuel pump.
2. Pinch suction and discharge hoses using tool No. 999 2901.
3. Remove hoses from fuel pump, then remove fuel pump from fuel tank.
4. Disconnect wire connectors from fuel pump and remove fuel pump.
5. Remove rubber pads from fuel pump.
6. Reverse procedure to install.

Fuel Filter, Replace

1. Clean fuel filter hose connections.
2. Punch fuel filter hoses using tool No. 2901.
3. Loosen hose clamps, then disconnect hoses from filter and remove filter.
4. Reverse procedure to install.

NOTE: When installing, ensure arrow on filter body is facing in direction of fuel flow.

Pressure Regulator, Replace

1. Disconnect three hose connections to pressure regulator, then remove pressure regulator.
2. Install replacement regulator, then

Fig. 8   Idle adjusting screw. 1972-74 B30E & B30F engines

install hoses and tighten clamps. Check connection for leaks.

Injector, Replace

1. Remove air cleaner, then disconnect vacuum line from servo and hose from inlet duct to oil trap.
2. Remove plug contacts from injectors and throttle valve switch.
3. Disconnect cable harness from header pipe and position aside.
4. Disconnect hoses from header pipe and pressure regulator, also hoses between header pipe.
5. Remove injector by turning lock ring counter clockwise so that it loosens from bayonet fitting.

Cold Start Valve, Replace

1. Remove air cleaner, then install tool No. 2901 to pinch off hose for cold start valve.
2. Remove plug contact and fuel hose from valve.
3. Remove cold start valve attaching screws and cold start valve.
4. Reverse procedure to install.

Throttle Valve Switch, Replace

1. Remove air cleaner, then disconnect plug contact from throttle valve switch.
2. Remove two screws attaching throttle valve switch to air inlet duct and remove switch.

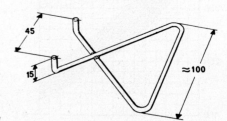

Fig. 10   Fabricating puller for plug contact from 5/64 in. welding rod

3. Reverse procedure to install. Adjust switch as outlined under Throttle Valve Switch, Adjust.

Induction Air Temperature Sensor, Replace

1. Remove right drip protection.
2. Remove air hose from right side plate, then disconnect plug contact from temperature sensor.
3. Remove temperature sensor.
4. Reverse procedure to install.

Coolant Temperature Sensor, Replace

1. Disconnect plug contact from sensor, then remove sensor.
2. Install replacement sensor and con-

nect plug contact.

Auxillary Air Regulator, Replace

1. Drain cooling system and engine block.
2. Disconnect hoses from auxillary air regulator, then remove regulator.
3. Place packing in position, then install pressure regulator.

Distributor Triggering Contacts, Replace

1. Remove distributor and clean outside housing.
2. Remove two attaching screws and remove insert, Fig. 9.
3. Lubricate fiber tabs of new insert

with Bosch Ft-1v4 or equivalent.
4. Ensure packing is not damaged, then install contact insert.

Thermal Timer, Replace

1. Drain cooling system, then disconnect wire connector from thermal timer.
2. Remove thermal timer.
3. Reverse procedure to install.

Pressure Sensor, Replace

1. Disconnect wire connector and hose from pressure sensor.
2. Remove three screws attaching pressure sensor to wheel housing.
3. Reverse procedure to install.

Continuous Fuel Injection

TROUBLE SHOOTING

NOTE: Before checking the fuel injection system, be sure the ignition system is operating properly and the engine is in mechanically good condition.

1. Check fuel pump operation. On 1974-77 models disconnect the electrical plug at the air flow sensor housing. If the fuel pump runs after the air sensor electrical plug is disconnected, check the adjustment of the air sensor plate. If the fuel pump does not operate:
   a. Check fuel pump fuse.
   b. Check for voltage at the electrical connector of the auxiliary air regulator.
2. If voltage is available at the auxiliary air valve terminal but the fuel pump does not operate, check for voltage at terminal 87 (yellow wire) of the fuel pump relay.
3. If voltage is available at terminal 87

of the pump relay but the pump does not run, a bad fuel pump, pump ground or pump connection is indicated. If voltage is not available at terminal 87 of the fuel pump relay, check terminal 86 of the fuel pump relay.
4. If voltage is available at terminal 86 of the fuel pump relay but not terminal 87, a bad relay is indicated.
5. If voltage is not available at terminal 86 of the fuel pump relay, check the main relay as follows:
   a. Bridge terminals in the air sensor plate electrical connector and operate the starter motor. Check for voltage at terminal 30/51 of the main relay while the starter motor is operating. If voltage exists, be sure the engine is cold then remove the cold start valve from the intake manifold and operate the starter. The cold start valve should spray. If not, check for voltage at the cold start valve terminals, while the starter is being operated. Voltage indicates a bad cold start valve. No voltage indicates defective thermal time switch or wiring. No voltage at terminal 87 indicates that the wire from the starter motor to the main relay terminal 87 is open. Voltage indicates a defective main relay.

System Pressure Test

NOTE: Be sure engine is cold.

1. Connect fuel pressure gauge. On 1974 B20 engines, disconnect the fuel distributor-to-control pressure regulator fuel line from the center

tower of the fuel distributor. Connect one hose of fuel pressure gauge 5011 to the fuel distributor. Connect the other gauge hose to the fuel line previously removed from the fuel distributor.

On 1975 B20, 1976-77 B21 and B27 engines, disconnect the fuel distributor-to-control pressure regulator line from the control pressure regulator and using special tools 5116 and 5032, connect fuel pressure gauge 5011 between the line and the control pressure regulator, Figs. 1 and 2.
2. Disconnect electrical connectors from the auxiliary air valve and the control pressure regulator.
3. Operate the fuel pump. Disconnect primary coil wire from coil terminal 15. Switch on ignition.

On 1974-77 engines, disconnect the electrical connector from the air flow sensor.

NOTE: It is important that fuel pressure tests be performed only in the above manner. Movement of the air

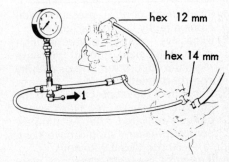

Fig. 2 Fuel pressure gauge connections. B27F engine

hex 12 mm

hex 14 mm

Fig. 1 Fuel pressure gauge connections. B21F engine

5032

5116

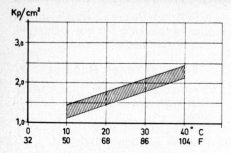

Fig. 3 Control pressure ranges

sensor plate will cause fuel to be injected, flooding the cylinders.

Line Pressure Test

1. Turn the gauge lever toward the fuel distributor. Correct line pressure is 64-75 psi. (4.5-5.3 kp/cm²). Insufficient line pressure can be caused by:
   a. Leaking fuel line.
   b. Insufficient fuel pump capacity. To check fuel pump, disconnect fuel delivery line at fuel distributor. Run the pump for 30 seconds and check delivered fuel quantity. Minimum quantity is 23.3 oz. (750cc).
   c. Line pressure regulator incorrectly adjusted.

NOTE: If pump operates but there is no line pressure, check for clogged fuel lines, filter or fuel distributor. Excessive line pressure can be caused by fuel return line clogged or the line pressure regulator incorrectly adjusted.

Control Pressure Test

NOTE: Be sure control pressure regulator is at ambient temperature, with electrical plug disconnected. Place gauge lever in the center position (position 2) at right angles to the hoses. Operate fuel pump as outlined above. Check that the control pressure agrees with Fig. 3.

1. Insufficient control pressure indicates a faulty control regulator.
2. Excessive control pressure indicates a blocked control pressure regulator fuel return line or a faulty control regulator.
3. Reconnect the electrical plug to the control pressure regulator while pump is activated. After 3-5 minutes, control pressure should have risen to 44-50 psi. (3.5-3.9 kp/cm²).
4. If control pressure does not meet specifications check for voltage at

the electrical plug while the fuel pump is running.
5. If voltage is present, the control pressure regulator should be replaced.
6. If no voltage is present, check the electrical circuit and relays as outlined under Trouble Shooting.

Auxiliary Air Valve Test

The valve should be partially open at room temperature. This can be checked by disconnecting the air by-pass hoses and, with the aid of a light and a small mirror, observe the valve.
1. Reconnect the electrical plug at the auxiliary air valve. The valve should be fully closed after 5 minutes. If the valve does not close:
   a. Tap the valve lightly. Engine vibrations contribute to the closing of the valve. If valve still does not close, check for voltage at the electrical plug. Voltage indicates a faulty valve. If no voltage is available, check the electrical circuit as outlined under Trouble Shooting.

Rest Pressure Test

1. With the fuel pump activated, turn the gauge lever to position 2 (right angles to the gauge hoses).
2. Stop pump.
3. Pressure must not drop noticeably within one minute.
4. In case of hot start problems, repeat the rest pressure test for an extended period. A rest pressure of 14.2 psi. (1 kp/cm²) should remain for 20 minutes.
5. In case of a drop in rest pressure, the following tests will isolate the trouble.

Control Pressure Regulator

1. Momentarily activate the fuel pump to build up pressure.
2. Set gauge lever to number 3 position (lever pointing towards the control pressure regulator).
3. Stop the pump. If pressure still drops, either the control pressure regulator or its return line is leaking.

Fuel Pump Check Valve

1. Momentarily activate fuel pump to build up pressure.
2. Set gauge lever in position 2 (right angles to the gauge hoses).
3. Clamp off the suction hose from the tank to the pump.
4. Stop pump. If pressure drop stops, a leaking fuel pump check valve is indicated.

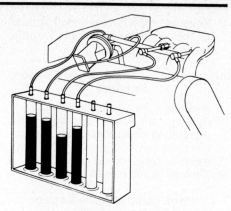

Fig. 4 Fuel injector volume test

Line Pressure Regulator

1. Momentarily activate fuel pump to build up pressure.
2. Set gauge lever to position 2 (right angles to gauge hoses).
3. Block the fuel distributor-to-tank return line.
4. Stop the pump. If pressure drop stops, a leaking line pressure regulator is indicated.

Fuel Injectors & Fuel Distributor Tests

1. Remove injectors from cylinder head. On B20 engines, unscrew retaining bolts and injector clamps then pull injectors out. On B21 and B27 engines, snap retaining clips off and pull injectors out.

NOTE: Do not disconnect fuel lines.

2. Connect tool 5014. This fixture contains a set of calibrated measuring tubes to record the flow of each injector, Fig. 4.
   On B20 engines, the injector lines are long enough to reach the tool. On B21 and B27 engines, an extension hose must be slipped over the end of each injector in order to make the hook-up.
3. Install fuel pressure gauge as outlined under "System Pressure Tests."
4. On B20 and B21 engines, remove the bellows from the air sensor so the sensor plate can be reached. On B27 engines, remove the air cleaner.
5. Switch on the ignition.
6. Disconnect the electrical connector at the air flow sensor to start the fuel pump.
7. Set gauge lever in position 1 (toward fuel distributor).
8. Lift (on B20 and B21) or depress (B27) the air sensor plate fully and hold it there for approximately 4 seconds. Line pressure may drop no more than 4.2 psi. (.3kp/cm²). If

pressure drops excessively, the following reasons are indicated:
a. Low fuel level in tank.
b. Clogged fuel lines or filters.
c. Fuel line leakage or insufficient fuel pump capacity.
9. To check fuel pump capacity, disconnect the fuel delivery line at the fuel distributor; run the pump for 30 seconds into a calibrated measuring container. Minimum quantity is 25 oz. (750cc).

Injector Deviation

NOTE: This test is necessary only in the case of a definite engine malfunction.

1. Perform steps 1 through 5 in Fuel Injectors & Fuel Distributor above.
2. Lift (on B20 and B21) or depress (B27) the air sensor plate half way until one of the measuring tubes has been filled to 3.4 oz. (100cc).
3. Read the remaining tubes. Maximum deviation is 20%.

NOTE: To obtain correct readings, all hoses must be either empty or full at the start of the test.

4. If readings are incorrect, repeat the test to confirm the results.
5. If test results are incorrect, swap two injector hoses at the fuel distributor (exchange hoses of one correct and one incorrect operating injector).
6. Repeat test.
7. If the same injector still performs improperly, the injector or its fuel line is faulty.
8. If fault changes to the other injector, the fault is in the fuel distributor.

Injector Leakage Test

1. Remove injectors from cylinder head as outlined under Fuel Injectors and Fuel Distributor Tests.
2. On 1974-77 models, disconnect the electrical plug at the air flow sensor housing.
3. Examine the tip of each injector while the pump is running. A slight seepage may be observed at the injector tips but no drops should be formed. If drops form at the injector tips, check for:
a. Maladjusted air flow sensor.
b. Fuel distributor plunger seized.
c. Leaking fuel distributor "O" ring.
d. Internal fuel distributor leaks at the steel diaphragm.
4. Lift (on B20 and B21) or depress (B27) the air flow sensor plate to cause the injectors to spray.

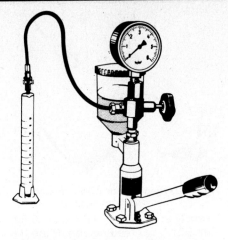

Fig. 5 Fuel injector testing tool

5. Release the sensor plate. Injectors must not seep more than one drop in 15 seconds.
6. If one injector leaks, see "Testing & Cleaning Injectors." If all injectors leak, check the line and rest pressures.

Testing Injectors

1. Remove injector from the engine. Disconnect injector fuel line.
2. Connect injector to special tool 9934, Fig. 5. Before tightening the tester fitting onto the injector, tightly pump the tester to bleed out any air from the tester and the injector.
3. Open tester valve (handwheel). Pump up pressure slowly until the injector opens. Correct opening pressure is 37-51 psi. (2.6-3.6 kp/cm²).

NOTE: Never exceed a pressure of 85 psi. (6 kp/cm²).

4. Lower pressure to 34 psi. (2.4 kp/cm²) by screwing out the handwheel. Check that injector leak does not exceed one drop per 15 seconds.

ADJUSTMENTS
Idle, Speed & CO

Preliminary Connections:
1. Connect tachometer and timing light.
2. Connect CO meter. On vehicles without catalytic converter, insert the CO sensor in the tailpipe a minimum of 18 inches (48 cm). On B20 and B21 units equipped with catalytic converter, raise the car on a lift, remove the 17 mm plug from the exhaust pipe just in front of the converter. Install special tool 5151. On B27 engines, each exhaust pipe has a 17 mm plug on its top side

immediately behind each cylinder head. Install one pipe from tool 5151 in each exhaust pipe.
3. Disconnect AIR pump hose if so equipped and plug hose.
4. Disconnect and plug the vacuum hose at the EGR valve if so equipped.
5. On Lambda-Sond equipped engines, disconnect the green wire for the oxygen sensor.

Basic Throttle Setting
1. Disconnect the link and cable at the throttle control pulley.
2. Loosen throttle stop screw lock nut. Back out throttle stop screw until it is off its stop.
3. Turn the throttle stop screw in until it contacts its stop. Then turn the stop screw one full turn. Tighten the lock nut.
4. Adjust the throttle link until it just fits onto the pulley and throttle lever without changing the position of the throttle.
5. Attach the throttle cable to the pulley. Adjust the cable sheath. The cable should have no free play but should not influence the position of the pulley.
6. Depress the accelerator pedal completely and check that the pulley touches the throttle boss.
7. On automatic transmission models, adjust transmission kickdown cable.
8. On units equipped with a micro switch (amplified EGR system) connect a test lamp to the micro switch.
a. Switch on ignition.
b. Place a .060" (1.5 mm) feeler gauge between the throttle screw and its boss. The light should stay on.
c. Remove the .060" (1.5 mm) gauge and insert a .080" (2 mm). The light should go out. If not, proceed as follows.
d. Place the .060" (1.5 mm) feeler gauge between the throttle screw and its boss.
e. Loosen the lock nut and screw out the micro switch adjusting screw until the test light goes out.
f. Screw in the adjusting screw until a click is heard from the micro switch and the light comes on.
g. Tighten the lock nut, remove the feeler gauge and test lamp.

Idle Speed & CO Adjustment, B20 & B21 Engines
1. Carry out all operations under preliminary connections and basic throttle settings.
2. Set ignition timing.

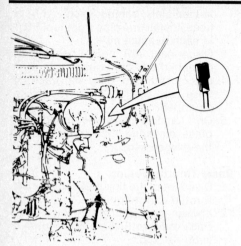

Fig. 6 Frequency valve test pickup. Lambda-Sond system

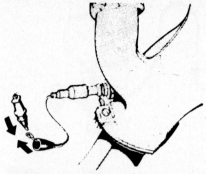

Fig. 7 Oxygen sensor wire connection. Lambda-Sond system

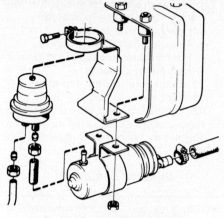

Fig. 8 Fuel pump assembly

3. Set idle speed with the air by-pass screw.
4. Remove the small plug from the air sensor housing and using a 3 mm Allen wrench, turn the CO adjusting screw until correct reading is obtained.

NOTE: Be sure to remove the Allen wrench and allow the engine to stabilize after every adjustment.

Lambda-Sond Function Test

1. Connect CO meter as outlined under Preliminary Connections.
2. Connect the red lead of a dwell meter to the vacant red wire located near the brake master cylinder, Fig. 6. Connect dwell meter black lead to ground.
3. Start engine. Frequency valve should buzz. If not, check dwell meter reading. No reading indicates a bad connection at the control unit (located behind the passenger side kick panel) a faulty sensor or a bad ground.

    A reading at the dwell meter but no buzzing at the frequency valve indicates bad electrical connections at the valve or a bad valve.

4. Separate the wire connection for the oxygen sensor, Fig. 7. Engine will run rough for approx. 10 secs., then smooth out.

    Dwell meter reading should be

steady at 40-50° on B27F and 50-60° on B21F. CO reading should be the same as a non-Lambda-Sond Continuous Injected Engine.

5. Hold the green sensor wire on a good ground. Dwell meter reading should rise to 70-80°. CO reading should be 6-8%.

    If not:

    a. High dwell, low CO indicates faulty frequency valve, blocked return line or clogged fuel distributor.

    b. No change in dwell indicates bad connection at control unit or valve, or bad control unit.

6. Remove green wire from ground. Engine will run rough for approx. 10 secs. Before 10 secs. elapse, momentarily touch the green wire to ground. This intermittent ground sends a "rich" signal to the control unit. The system should respond by leaning out the engine.

    Dwell reading will shorten to approx. 30° and CO will be very lean.

7. Reconnect sensor lead. CO should be .6-.9%.

NOTE: The Lambda-Sond system does not operate until the sensor reaches 300° C. temperature. It is possible, during periods of storage or operation below this temperature, for the sensor to become coated with fuel and be made inoperative. In such a case, do not attempt to clean the sensor. Drive the vehicle for approx. 20 minutes to allow the fuel to be burned off the sensor.

FUEL DISTRIBUTOR, REPLACE

1. Disconnect fuel lines to injectors at fuel distributor.
2. Disconnect fuel feed lines and fuel return lines.
3. Remove fuel distributor retaining screws and lift off fuel distributor.

CAUTION: When lifting off fuel distributor, do not allow the plunger to fall out. As the distributor is raised from the air sensor plate, hold a hand under it in case the plunger falls out.

FUEL PUMP, REPLACE

1. Using pliers 2901, or other suitable pinch pliers, close off the flexible tank-to-pump fuel line.
2. Clean all connections carefully. Remove pump and pressure accumulator as a unit, Fig. 8.
3. Disconnect fuel lines, electrical connector and remove pump.

FUEL INJECTORS, REPLACE

1. On 1974, remove injector retaining screws and retainers. On 1975-77, unsnap injector retaining clips.
2. Slip injectors out of cylinder head.
3. Disconnect fuel lines from injectors.

Emission Controls Section

POSITIVE CRANKCASE VENTILATION (PCV) SYSTEM

Description

This system prevents crankcase gases from being released into the at-

mosphere, Figs. 1 and 2. The gases are drawn into the engine through the intake manifold and take part in the combustion process.

Between the oil trap and the intake manifold there is a hose. It is connected to the intake manifold by means of a calibrated nipple. Between the rocker

arm casing and air cleaner there is a hose connected for the fresh-air supply. At the connection to the rocker arm casing there is a flame arrester, which consists of a metal filter. The partial vacuum which arises in the intake manifold when the engine is driven, brings about a partial vacuum in the crankcase

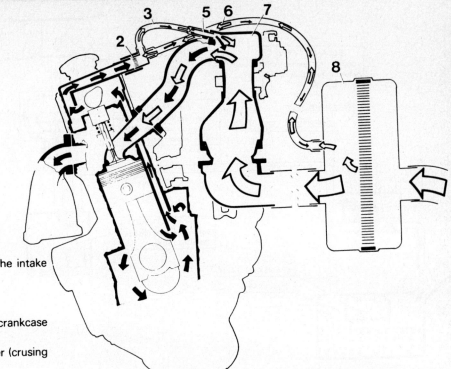

2. Flame guard.
3. Hose, channeling crankcase fumes to the intake manifold.
5. Nipple with orifice.
6. Hose, channeling:
   - fresh air from the air cleaner to the crankcase (idle)
   - or crankcase fumes to the air cleaner (crusing speeds)
7. Intake manifold.
8. Air cleaner.

Fig. 1   Positive crankcase ventilation system. B21F engine

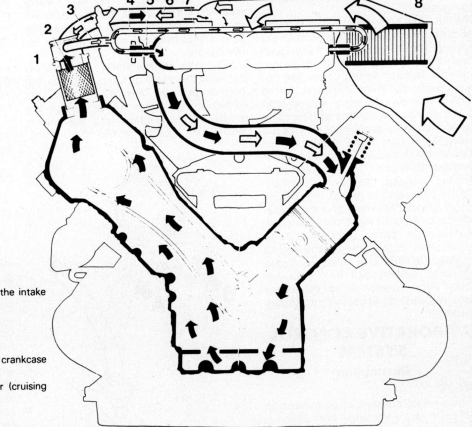

1. Oil trap.
2. Flame guard.
3. Hose, channeling crankcase fumes to the intake manifold.
4. Distributor pipe.
5. Nipple with orificie.
6. Hose, channeling:
   - fresh air from the air cleaner to the crankcase (idle)
   - crankcase fumes to the air cleaner (cruising speeds)
7. Intake manifold.
8. Air cleaner.

Fig. 2   Positive crankcase ventilation system. B27F engine

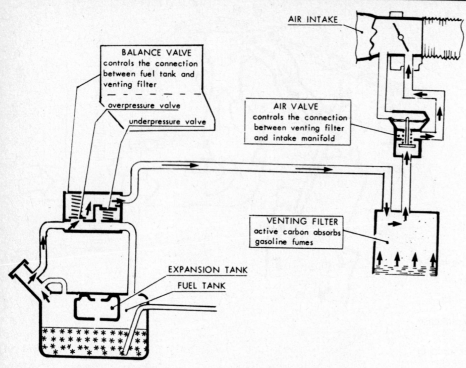

Fig. 3 Evaporative emissions control system (Typical)

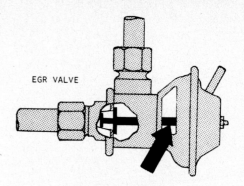

Fig. 4 Observing EGR valve rod movement

through the hose.

Fresh air is supplied to the rocker arm casing through the air cleaner and hose. A plate in the rocker arm casing ensures that the fresh air circulates sufficiently in order to mix with the crankcase gases.

As the fresh air supply passes through the carburetor air cleaner, inpurities are prevented from getting into the engine. Where there is a high or medium degree of partial vacuum in the crankcase (intake manifold), which happens during idling and when operating under a light load, the system functions as described above. When the partial vacuum in the crankcase is less than that in the air cleaner, which occurs at full load and/or with large flow quantities, no fresh air is supplied. Instead, the flow in the connection between the rocker arm casing and air cleaner reverses and the crankcase gases go both ways, partly through the hose an partly through the air cleaner and carburetor to the intake manifold. In this way, the crankcase ventilation system can deal with relatively large quantities of crankcase gases without any escaping into the atmosphere.

EVAPORATIVE CONTROL SYSTEM
Description

1972-73

This system consists of an expansion container and a venting filter, which is filled with active carbon, Fig. 3. Also included are the connection hoses be-

tween the various components. The venting filter is located in the engine compartment.

Gas fumes forming in the sealed container, particularly during warm weather, are conveyed to the expansion container and from there to the venting filter where they are mixed with the active carbon.

When the engine starts, air is drawn through the venting filter and into the engine through the inlet duct. Gas fumes stored in the active carbon are drawn by the air flow into the engine where they take part in the combustion.

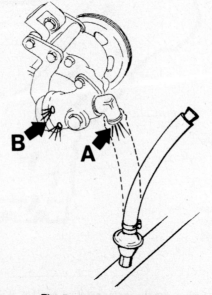

Fig. 5 A.I.R. system check

1974

The system consists of a charcoal canister, equalizing valve and hose connections, Fig. 3.

The expansion tank is also part of the gas evaporative emission control system as it absorbs the fuel expansion caused by raising temperature, at full tank.

The equalizing valve consists of the overpressure valve and the underpressure valve. The overpressure valve opens when the pressure exceeds .7-3 psi. and the fuel fumes are directed to the venting filter where they are absorbed by the active carbon.

The equalizing valve prevents fuel, when driving in curves, from being pressed up in the hose and to the venting filter. The underpressure valve opens when the underpressure exceeds 1.4-3 psi. and directs air to the fuel tank through the venting filter. When the engine starts, air is drawn through the venting filter and into the engine. Gas fumes stored in the active carbon are drawn by the air flow into the engine where they take part in the combustion.

1975-77

Refer to Fig. 3 for components and operation of system.

EGR SYSTEM
Testing & Adjustments

The EGR valve operates on a vacuum signal from the throttle plate. With the engine idling, the valve must be closed (check by observing the rod movement through the observation window in the valve housing, Fig. 4). If the valve is open at idle, rough idle will result. Adjust the throttle stop screw to position the throttle butterfly so that the valve will be closed at idle. This can be checked by connecting a vacuum gauge to the vacuum line from the intake manifold to the EGR valve. With the throttle plate properly adjusted, there should be no vacuum gauge reading at idle.

1976-77 systems incorporate a thermostatic valve on certain models. This valve cuts off the vacuum signal to the EGR valve when the engine is cold.

Maintenance

The EGR valve should be checked and cleaned every 12,000 miles and replaced at 24,000 miles on 1974-75 models.

The EGR valve should be checked and cleaned every 15,000 miles and replaced at 30,000 miles on 1976-77 models.

After servicing the EGR valve, the EGR indicator light switch must be reset. To do this, remove the rear cover on the special odometer and depress the white button. The special odometer is located under the dashboard at the rear of the instrument panel.

A.I.R. SYSTEM CHECKS

1. Air Pump; check the air pump for: air leak, pump touching other components, loose pump or no air flow from the pump.
2. Check backfire valve for the following:
   a. Disconnect the hose from the diverter valve.
   b. Apply a vacuum to the hose.
   c. Valve should not leak vacuum.
3. Diverter Valve:
   a. Disconnect and plug hose at air pump.
   b. Run the engine at idle. Air should blow only from the diverter valve outlet A in Fig. 5.
   c. Increase engine speed to 3000-3500 rpm and quickly release the throttle. Air should blow out of the valve vent holes, B in Fig. 5.

CATALYTIC CONVERTER

Engines equipped with catalytic converters must be kept in proper tune. Certain engine malfunctions, particularly involving the electrical, fuel or ignition systems, may cause unusually high converter temperatures.

Testing

Upstream of the catalytic converter is a plug for connecting a CO meter. The efficiency of the converter can be measured by comparing readings obtained upstream (plug connection) and downstream (inserting a probe in the tailpipe).

Clutch & Transmission Section
Clutch & Manual Transmission

CLUTCH, ADJUST
140, 164 & 240 Series

Adjustment is carried out at point at which cable attaches to fork, or by turning adjusting nuts on clutch actuating cable where cable attaches to side of clutch housing. Clutch lever play should be .16 to .20 in. (4 to 5 mm) on 164 models and ⅛ in. (3 to 5 mm) on 140 and 240 models.

260 Series

The clutch on 260 models is hydraulically operated. The system is designed so clutch fork and throw-out bearing touch lightly on pressure plate.

CLUTCH, REPLACE

1. Remove transmission as described under Manual Transmission, Replace.
2. Remove upper bolt from starter motor.
3. Remove release bearing. Unhook cable from release fork. Remove cable sleeve from bracket.
4. Remove flywheel housing.
5. Remove bolt holding release fork ball joint. Remove ball joint and fork.
6. Remove clutch retaining bolts and remove clutch.

TRANSMISSION, REPLACE
140 Series

1. Install lifting fixture, and take up slack.

2. Remove rubber protector and gear lever.
3. Raise vehicle and support, then drain transmission.
4. Remove rear crossmember. Disconnect front universal joint from transmission flange.
5. Disconnect speedometer cable.
6. Lower rear of engine approximately .8 inch and disconnect back up light wires and overdrive wires, if so equipped.
7. Remove transmission retaining bolts and the transmission.

164 Series

1. Install engine lifting fixture, and take up slack.
2. Raise vehicle and support, then drain transmission.
3. Remove gear lever and disconnect upper radiator mounting bolts, exhaust manifold flange nuts, battery cable, throttle shaft and clutch cable from flywheel housing.
4. Remove rear crossmember, exhaust pipe bracket, speedometer cable and drive shaft.
5. Lower rear of engine approximately 1.8 in. and remove back up light wires and overdrive leads, if so equipped.
6. Support transmission with a suitable jack, remove transmission retaining bolts and remove transmission.

1975 240 Series

1. Remove gearshift lever.
2. Raise vehicle and place it on stands.

Drain transmission oil.
3. Use a jack to support transmission. Loosen and remove rear crossmember. Disconnect front universal joint from transmission flange.
4. Disconnect speedometer cable, rear engine mount and exhaust pipe bracket.
5. Install a piece of wood between engine and firewall and lower jack supporting transmission. Disconnect wires at transmission.
6. Remove transmission retaining bolts and remove transmission.

1976-77 240 & 260 Series

1. Disconnect battery ground cable.
2. Disconnect back-up light wire harness connector at firewall.
3. From underneath vehicle, disconnect gearshift lever from gearshift rod.
4. From inside vehicle, remove rubber bellows. Remove fork for reverse gear detent. Remove lock ring and gearshift lever.
5. Disconnect clutch cable and return spring on 240 models. On 260 models, disconnect slave cylinder linkage. It is not necessary to open any hydraulic lines.
6. Remove front exhaust pipe bracket.
7. Place a jack under transmission to support it and remove rear transmission mounting bolts. Remove crossmember.
8. Disconnect front universal joint from transmission flange. Disconnect speedometer cable.
9. Lower transmission jack and re-

move bell housing-to-engine retaining bolts. Remove all of these bolts except one at top right.

10. Remove starter motor front bracket bolts and pull starter out until it is free of bell housing.

11. Remove bell housing bolt at top right and remove transmission.

Automatic Transmission

TROUBLE SHOOTING

BW 35 Units

Harsh Engagement Of R, D Or L
1. Incorrect fluid level.
2. Improperly adjusted downshift valve cable.
3. Primary regulator valve sticking.
4. Throttle valve sticking.
5. Valve body assembly improperly installed.
6. Front clutch seized or plates distorted.
7. Rear clutch seized or plates distorted.

Delayed Engagement Of R, D Or L
1. Incorrect fluid level.
2. Manual linkage improperly adjusted.
3. Incorrect engine idle speed.
4. Oil tubes incorrectly installed.
5. Primary regulator valve sticking.
6. Valve body improperly installed.
7. Sealing rings damaged.
8. Pump check valve sticking.
9. Front clutch slipping due to worn plate or defective parts.
10. Rear clutch slipping due to worn plates or defective check valve in piston.
11. Rear band slipping due to defective servo or damaged band.
12. Defective oil pump.

No Engagement Of D, R Or L
1. Incorrect fluid level.
2. Manual linkage improperly adjusted.
3. Oil tubes improperly installed.
4. Sealing rings damaged.
5. Valve body improperly installed.
6. Primary regulator valve sticking.

No Drive In Forward Ranges
1. Manual linkage improperly adjusted.
2. Valve body improperly installed.
3. Front clutch slipping due to worn plate or defective parts.
4. Sealing rings damaged.
5. One-way clutch slipping.

No Drive In Reverse
1. Manual linkage improperly adjusted.
2. Incorrect rear band adjustment.
3. 1-2 shift valve sticking.
4. 2-3 shift valve sticking.
5. Valve body improperly installed.
6. Sealing rings damaged.

7. Oil tubes improperly installed.
8. Rear band slipping due to defective servo or damaged or worn band.
9. Rear clutch slipping due to worn plates or defective check valve in piston.

Seizure In Reverse
1. Incorrect front band adjustment.
2. Front clutch seized or plates distorted.

No Neutral
1. Manual linkage improperly adjusted.
2. Front clutch seized or plates distorted.
3. Valve body improperly installed.

No 1-2 Upshift
1. Manual linkage improperly adjusted.
2. Incorrect front band adjustment.
3. Governor valve sticking or leaking.
4. 1-2 shift valve sticking.
5. Front band slipping due to defective servo or damaged or worn band.
6. Throttle valve sticking.
7. Modulator valve sticking.
8. Oil tubes improperly installed
9. Sealing rings damaged.
10. Valve body improperly installed.

No 2-3 Upshift
1. Manual linkage improperly adjusted.
2. Governor valve sticking or leaking.
3. 2-3 shift valve sticking.
4. 2-3 shift valve plunger sticking.
5. Rear clutch slipping due to worn plates or defective check valve in piston.
6. Throttle valve sticking.
7. Modulator valve sticking.
8. Oil tubes improperly installed.
9. Sealing rings damaged.
10. Valve body improperly installed.

Above Normal Shift Speed
1. Downshift valve cable improperly adjusted.
2. Throttle valve sticking.
3. Governor valve sticking or leaking.
4. 1-2 shift valve sticking.
5. 2-3 shift valve sticking.
6. 2-3 shift valve plunger sticking.
7. Modulator valve sticking.
8. Sealing rings damaged.
9. Valve body improperly installed.
10. Primary regulator valve sticking.

Below Normal Shift Speeds
1. Manual linkage improperly adjusted.
2. Throttle valve sticking.
3. Sealing rings damaged.
4. 2-3 shift valve plunger sticking.
5. Sealing rings damaged.
6. Valve body improperly installed.

Slips On 1-2 Shift
1. Incorrect fluid level.
2. Down shift valve cable improperly adjusted.
3. Manual linkage improperly adjusted.
4. Incorrect front band adjustment.
5. Front band slipping due to defective servo or damaged or worn band.
6. Primary regulator valve sticking.
7. Throttle valve sticking.
8. Oil tubes improperly installed.
9. Sealing rings damaged.
10. Valve body improperly installed.

Slip On 3-2 Shift
1. Incorrect fluid level.
2. Down shift valve cable improperly adjusted.
3. Manual linkage improperly adjusted.
4. Incorrect front band adjustment.
5. Rear clutch slipping due to worn plates or defective check valve in piston.
6. Front band slipping due to defective servo or damaged or worn band.
7. Primary regulator valve sticking.
8. Throttle valve sticking.
9. Oil tubes improperly installed.
10. Sealing rings damaged.
11. Valve body improperly installed.

Harsh 1-2 Shift
1. Down shift valve cable improperly adjusted.
2. Incorrect front band adjustment.
3. Primary regulator valve sticking.
4. Throttle valve sticking.
5. Modulator valve sticking.
6. Governor valve sticking or leaking.
7. One-way clutch seized.
8. Input shaft broken.
9. Front clutch slipping due to worn plates or defective parts.
10. Valve body improperly installed.

Harsh 2-3 Shift
1. Downshift valve cable improperly adjusted.
2. Incorrect front band adjustment.
3. Primary regulator valve sticking.

4. Throttle valve sticking.
5. Rear clutch seized or plates distorted.
6. Valve body improperly installed.

Seizure On 1-2 Shift
1. Incorrect rear band adjustment.
2. Rear clutch seized or plates distorted.
3. One-way clutch slipping.
4. One-way clutch seized.
5. Sealing rings damaged.
6. Valve body improperly installed.

Seizure On 2-3 Shift
1. Incorrect front band adjustment.
2. Oil tubes improperly installed.
3. Sealing rings damaged.
4. Valve body improperly installed.

No 2-1 Downshift
1. Downshift valve cable improperly adjusted.
2. 1-2 shift valve sticking.
3. Governor valve sticking or leaking.
4. Rear brake band slipping due to defective servo or broken or worn band.

No 3-2 Downshift
1. Downshift valve cable improperly adjusted.
2. 2-3 shift valve sticking.
3. Governor valve sticking or leaking.
4. Rear clutch seized or plates distorted.
5. Front band slipping due to faulty servo or damaged or worn band.

Involuntary High Speed 3-2 Shift
1. Incorrect fluid level.
2. Oil tubes improperly installed.
3. Rear clutch slipping due to worn plates or defective check valve in piston.

Above Normal Downshift Speed
1. Downshift valve cable improperly adjusted.
2. Governor valve sticking or leaking.
3. 2-3 shift valve plunger sticking.
4. Throttle valve sticking.
5. Sealing rings damaged.
5. Valve body improperly installed.

Below Normal Downshift Speed
1. Downshift valve cable improperly adjusted.
2. Governor valve sticking or leaking.
3. 2-3 shift valve plunger sticking.
4. Throttle valve sticking.
5. Sealing rings damaged.
6. Valve body improperly installed.
7. 1-2 shift valve sticking.
8. 2-3 shift valve sticking.

Slips On 2-1 Downshift
1. One-way clutch slipping.

Slips On 3-2 Downshift
1. Incorrect front band adjustment.
2. Front band slipping due to defective servo or defective or worn band.
3. Primary regulator valve sticking.
4. Throttle valve sticking.
5. Valve body improperly installed.
6. Rear clutch slipping due to worn plates or defective check valve in piston.
7. Rear clutch seized or plates distorted.
8. Rear band slipping due to defective servo or damaged or worn band.

Overheating
1. Incorrect fluid level.
2. Incorrect front band adjustment.
3. Incorrect rear band adjustment.
4. Converter blading and/or one-way clutch defective.

AW 55 / BW 55 Units

No Drive Or Slips In D
1. Check for proper operation in R.
   a. If proper operation is obtained in R, this indicates that rear clutch and brake B3 (rear most brake) are operating properly.
   b. If vehicle fails to operate in R, this would indicate that either rear clutch or its oil circuit or brake B3 or its oil circuit is defective.
2. Check for proper operation in 1 position.
   a. If vehicle operates properly in R and 1, but slips in "D", this would indicate a defective one-way clutch in planetary gear assembly.
   b. If vehicle operates properly in R, but not in I or D, this would indicate a defective front clutch or its oil circuit. Perform stall test.
   c. If vehicle does not operate in R, 1, or D, proceed to No Drive In Any Selector Lever Position.
3. Check for a defective torque converter, defective spline connections and defective shaft; also listen for noise.

No Drive Or Slips In R
1. Check for proper operation in high gear, also check for engine braking in 1.
2. Normal operation in high indicates proper operation of rear clutch. Perform stall test. If transmission does not brake in 1 position, this would indicate a defect in brake B3 (rear most brake) or its oil circuit. If transmission operates properly in high gear and 1, make stall speed test. Correct pressure and slipping indicates a defective control system (check reverse clutch sequence

valve) or a defective rear clutch or its oil circuit.
3. Check for a defective torque converter, or defective splines; also listen for noise.

No Drive In Any Selector Lever Position
1. Check to ensure that parking pawl is not jammed by pushing vehicle in position D. Vehicle should move freely.
2. Check for a defective torque converter or splines, also listen for noise.
3. Fault may also be a combination of No Drive Or Slips In D and No Drive Or Slips In R.

Harsh Engagement
1. Harsh shifting from N to D and N to R.
   a. Accumulator piston for front or rear clutch leaking or seized.
2. Harsh shifting 1 to 2 and 2 to 1.
   a. Brake B2 accumulator piston leaking or seized.
   b. Intermediate coast shift valve seized.
3. Harsh shifting 2 to 3 and 3 to 2.
   a. Rear clutch accumulator piston leaking or seized.
   b. Defective control system for rear clutch (check intermediate coast modulator valve).

Slips On 1-2 Shift
1. BW 55.
   a. Intermediate coast shift valve, which controls engagement of brake B1 seized. A further indication on this is that there is no engine braking effect in 2.
2. AW 55 and BW 55.
   a. Brakes B1 or B2 or their oil circuits may be defective.
   b. One-way clutch in center support assembly may be defective.

NOTE: On AW 55 units, brake B1 is engaged only in 2. That means there is no engine braking in 2 if gear selector is in D.

Slip On 2-3 Shift
1. Rear clutch or its oil circuit defective.
2. Control system defective (check for seized 2-3 shift valve).
3. Check stall speed.

No Engine Braking In 1
1. Check operation in R.
   a. Normal operation in R, indicates that brake B3 is operating properly.
2. Check for seized low coast modulator valve or seized low coast shift valve.

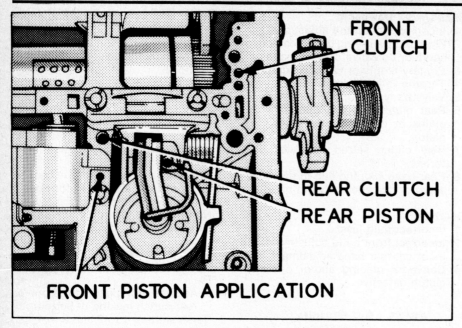

Fig. 1 Air pressure test passages. BW 35 Units

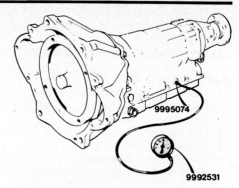

Fig. 2 Pressure gauge connection for line pressure check & stall speed test. AW 55/ BW 55 Units

No Manual 2-1 Shift
1. If vehicle operates properly in R, this indicates that brake B3 is operating properly.
2. Check for seized low coast modulator valve or low coast shift valve.

No Engine Braking In 2
1. Indicates defective brake B1 or its oil circuit.
2. Check for slipping at 1-2 shifts.
3. Check for seized intermediate coast modulator valve.

Vehicle Starts In 2
1. Check that governor pressure is zero when vehicle is standing still.
2. Check for seized 1-2 shift valve.

Transmission Noisy
1. Check transmission oil level.
2. Test drive vehicle and listen for abnormal noises. Ensure noise originates from transmission. Establish conditions and selector positions when noise occurs.
3. Growling noise that appears or is intensified at stall or acceleration.
   a. Check torque converter.
4. Gear noise, buzzing noise or knocking noise.
   a. Check bolts retaining torque converter to flywheel.
   b. Check couplings for one-way clutches.
   c. Check planetary gear assembly.
   d. Check thrust needle bearings.
   e. Check bushings.
5. Whining or humming noise.
   a. Check torque converter.
   b. Check oil pump.

AIR PRESSURE CHECKS
BW 35 Units

Air pressure checks can be made to the transmission assembly to determine whether clutches and bands are operating. Drain fluid from transmission, then remove oil pan and valve body with oil tubes. If clutch and bands operate satisfactorily with air pressure, check hydraulic system of transmission for defects.

To check front clutch, apply air pressure to passage A Fig. 1. A thump sound should be heard, indicating that clutch is functioning.

To check rear clutch, apply air pressure to passage B Fig. 1. Apply air pressure for several seconds to check for leaks. A thump sound should be heard indicating that clutch is releasing when air pressure is removed.

To check front piston, apply air pressure to passage C Fig. 1. Observe movement of piston pin.

To check rear piston, apply air pressure to passage D Fig. 1. Observe movement of piston lever.

LINE PRESSURE CHECK
AW 55 / BW 55 Units
1. Remove plug from pressure tap, then install fitting 9995074 and a suitable pressure gauge, Fig. 2.
2. Position selector lever in N and operate engine at 900 rpm.
3. Depress brake pedal, then place selector lever to D and note pressure gauge reading. Pressure gauge reading should be 57 to 64 psi. for AW 55 units and 75 to 90 psi. for BW 55 units.
4. Place selector in R and note reading. Pressure gauge reading should be 82 to 97 psi. for AW 55 units and 104 to 129 psi, for BW 55 units.

Diagnosis
If excessive pressure is indicated, this is usually caused by a seized valve, providing the throttle valve is properly adjusted. Increase engine speed; if primary regulator valve is seized, normal control of pressure will fail. Pressure will vary directly in proportion to oil pump speed, engine rpm.

To check throttle valve, which influences line pressure, place selector lever in N with engine at idle speed. Pull transmission cable by hand, not influencing throttle opening (engine speed). Pressure should increase; if not, the throttle valve is seized.

If low pressure is obtained, primary regulator valve or throttle valve may be seized. Check primary regulator valve and throttle valve as outlined above. If pressure regulator valve and throttle are found not to be defective, check for a defective pressure relief valve (on early units) or a defective oil pump. A defective oil pump will usually make noise.

STALL TEST
AW 55 / BW 55 Units

The stall test is performed to check the condition of torque converter and transmission clutches. Ensure engine output is correct before performing the stall test. Line pressure must also be correct before performing stall test. A low line pressure could cause damage to transmission.

1. Remove plug from pressure tap and install fitting 9995074 and a suitable pressure gauge, Fig. 2. Position pressure gauge so that it can be read from driver's seat.

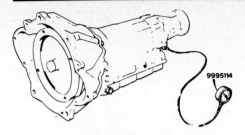

Fig. 3 Pressure gauge connection for governor pressure check. AW 55/ BW 55 Units.

2. Connect a tachometer to engine, then start engine and allow to reach operating temperature.
3. With parking brake and service brakes applied, place selector lever D, then depress accelerator pedal completely and note tachometer and pressure gauge readings.

NOTE: Do not perform test for longer than 5 seconds, otherwise damage to transmission may result.

4. Let engine idle in N for a period of time to allow transmission to cool, then repeat test in R.
5. On AW 55 units, stall speed should be 2400 to 2650 rpm. Line pressure at stall speed should be 135 to 170 psi. (9.5 to 12 kp/cm²) in D position and 192 to 241 psi. (13.5 to 17 kp/cm²) in R position.
6. On BW 55 units, stall speed on models with B21F engines should be 2150 to 2400 rpm. On models with B27F engines, stall speed should be 2400 to 2650. Line pressure at stall speed should be 159 to 195 psi. (11.2 to 13.7 kp/cm²) in D position and 220 to 280 psi. (15.4 to 19.6 kp/cm²) in R position.

Diagnosis

1. If stall speed is approximately 600 rpm lower than specified, torque converter is defective.
2. If acceleration is insufficient from start, but normal above 45 mph, replace torque converter.
3. If converter one-way clutch binds and locks stator, this will result in low top speed and inadequate acceleration above approximately 30 mph and overheating. This fault does not alter the stall speed. Replace torque converter.
4. If stall speed is approximately 300 rpm lower than specified, check engine output.
5. If stall speed is more than 300 rpm above normal and in R position, a clutch or brake is slipping, then transmission must be disassembled. Check rear clutch and brake B3 (rear most brake). If brake B3 slips, symption is insufficient or no engine braking in 1 position.

Engine	Transmission Model	Rear Axle Ratio	Speed In M.p.h.	Governor Pressure In Psi.
B21F	AW 55	3.91	19	13-21
			35	23-31
			67	58-75
B21F	AW 55	4.10	17	13-21
			31	23-31
			60	58-75
B21F	BW 55	3.91	19	14-18
			35	23-28
			67	53-62
B21F	BW 55	4.10	17	14-18
			31	23-28
			60	53-62
B27F	BW 55	3.54	20	14-18
			35	21-27
			68	51-65

Fig. 4 Governor pressure test chart. AW 55 / BW 55 Units

6. If stall speed is more than 300 rpm above specified and in position 1, 2 or D, a clutch is slipping. Transmission must be disassembled. Check front clutch.
7. If stall speed is more than 300 rpm above normal and no clutches or brake are slipping, check transmission fluid level. Also check for clogged oil strainer.

GOVERNOR PRESSURE CHECK
AW 55 / BW 55 Units

NOTE: Perform line pressure check before performing governor pressure check.

1. Connect a suitable pressure gauge to governor pressure tap on transmission case, Fig. 3.
2. Test drive vehicle in D and note readings. Refer to Fig. 4, for correct pressure readings.

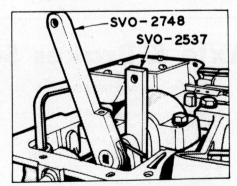

Fig. 5 Front band adjustment. BW 35 Units

NOTE: Pressure should be zero when vehicle is standing still or in R position.

Diagnosis

1. If excessive governor pressure is observed, governor jams and should be removed and inspected.
2. If low governor pressure is indicated, governor jams or is leaking. Also check for oil leak at cover for governor oil ducts and governor oil seals on output shaft.

BANDS, ADJUST
BW 35 Units

Front Band
1. Remove oil pan.
2. Place spacer block 2537 between adjusting screw and servo, Fig. 5.
3. Tighten adjusting bolt with wrench 2748 until the handle clicks out 10 inch lbs.
4. If a lock nut is used, tighten the lock nut. If a self adjusting spring is used, adjust the spring on the screw. It should be 1-2 threads from the lever. Remove tools and install the cam. Insert the long end of the spring in the cam.
5. Install oil pan.

Rear Band
1. Loosen lock nut on adjusting screw.
2. Torque adjusting screw to 14 Nm (10 ft. lbs.) then back off adjusting screw one full turn, Fig. 6.
3. Tighten the lock nut.

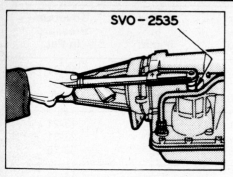

Fig. 6 Rear band adjustment. BW 35 Units

GEARSHIFT LINKAGE, ADJUST

BW 35 Units

Adjust shift rod so there is equal clearance between gear lever and its stop when lever is in D position and in 2 position, Fig. 7.

AW 55 / BW 55 Units

Adjust shift rod so there is equal clearance between gear lever and its stop when lever is in D and in 2 position, Fig. 8.

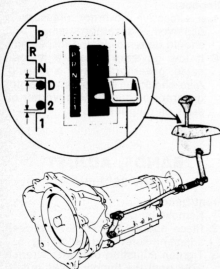

Fig. 8 Gearshift linkage adjustment. AW 55 / BW 55 Units

THROTTLE CABLE, ADJUST

BW 35 Units

Throttle cable should be adjusted so there is a slight slack in the inner cable when the throttle is closed.

AW 55 / BW 55 Units

Adjust kick-down cable so that at idle there is 1 mm (.04 in.) clearance between cable sheath and the crimped stop on the inner cable. With throttle depressed completely, there should be 52 mm (2 in.) clearance between the cable sheath and the inner cable, Fig. 9.

TRANSMISSION, REPLACE

1. Remove oil dipstick and filler pipe clamp. Remove bracket and throttle cable from dashboard and throttle control. Disconnect exhaust pipe at flange. Disconnect battery ground cable.
2. Raise car and support it on stands.
3. Drain transmission oil.
4. Disconnect front universal joint from transmission flange.
5. Disconnect selector shaft lever and reinforcing bracket under oil pan.
6. Remove converter attaching bolts.

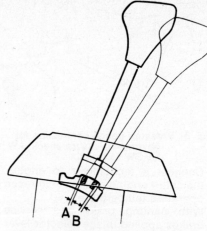

Fig. 7 Gearshift linkage adjustment. BW 35 Units

7. Place a jack under transmission and take up weight of transmission. Remove rear crossmember.
8. Disconnect exhaust pipe bracket, speedometer cable and lower transmission.
9. Disconnect starter inhibitor switch wires. Remove starter mounting bolts.
10. Remove bell housing to engine bolts and lever transmission rearwards. Lower and remove transmission from vehicle.

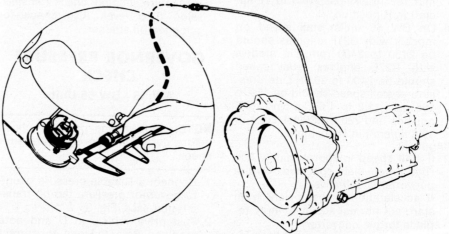

Fig. 9 Throttle cable adjustment. AW 55/ BW 55 Units

Rear Axle & Brakes Section

REAR AXLE ASSEMBLY, REPLACE

140 & 164 Series

1. Raise rear of vehicle and position jack stands under front of rear jack attachments, then remove rear wheels.
2. Position lifting fixture 2714 on a suitable jack and raise rear axle assembly slightly.
3. Remove upper shock absorber attaching bolts, then disconnect parking brake cables from levers and brackets at brake backing plates.
4. Disconnect propeller shaft at pinion flange, then remove brake line union from rear axle casing.
5. Loosen support arm front attaching

bolts approximately 1 turn.
6. Remove torque rod rear attaching bolts.
7. Disconnect track bar from bracket on rear axle casing, then remove lower spring attaching bolts.
8. Lower rear axle assembly until support arms release from springs, then remove bolts attaching rear axle casing to support arms. Lower axle

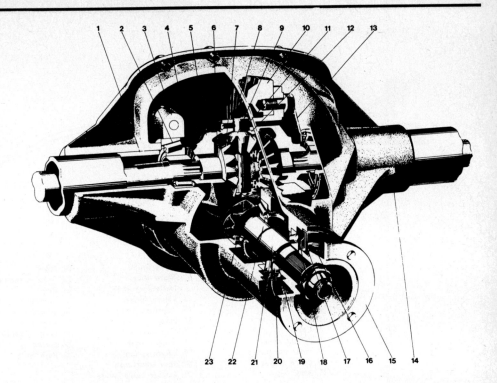

1. Tubular shaft
2. Differential carrier bearing
3. Bearing cap
4. Shims
5. Differential carrier
6. Thrust washer
7. Differential side gear
8. Lock pin
9. Differential pinion
10. Crown wheel
11. Shaft
12. Thrust washer
13. Lock plate
14. Rear axle casing
15. Flange
16. Dust cover plate
17. Oilseal
18. Oilslinger
19. Shims
20. Front pinion bearing
21. Pinion
22. Rear pinion bearing
23. Shims

Fig. 1 Rear axle assembly (Typical)

assembly and remove from vehicle, Fig. 1.

240 & 260 Series

1. Position fixture No. 2714 on a suitable jack, then position jack and fixture under rear axle assembly and raise rear of vehicle.
2. Place jack stands in front of rear jack supports, then slightly lower rear of vehicle and remove rear wheels.
3. Disconnect shock absorbers from upper mountings.
4. Disconnect brake lines from rear axle, then remove caliper retaining screws.
5. Use wire to hook calipers to top shock absorber supports to prevent brake lines from becoming damaged.
6. Remove brake drums, then remove brake shoes.
7. Press out pins attaching parking brake cables to levers.
8. Remove screws and pull out cable and hose with seals, then remove springs retaining parking brake cable to rear axle.
9. Disconnect propeller shaft at pinion flange.
10. Disconnect track rod from body bracket.
11. Disconnect springs from trailing arms, then lower rear axle and remove springs.
12. Remove screws retaining rear axle and remove rear axle assembly from vehicle, Fig. 1.

AXLE SHAFT, BEARING & SEAL, REPLACE

1. Raise rear of vehicle and support on jack stands.
2. Remove brake disc.
3. Working through holes in axle shaft flange, remove axle shaft retaining nuts. Using tool 2709 or other suitable puller, pull out axle shaft.
4. Pull out inner seal ring with a screwdriver.
5. Remove and reinstall bearing using tool Nos. 2838 & 5010, Fig. 2.
6. Install inner seal in axle housing using tool Nos. 5009 & 1801.

PARKING BRAKE ADJUSTMENT

1972-74 140-164 Series

1. Adjust wheel units before adjusting

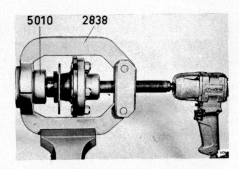

Fig. 2 Axle shaft bearing installation

cable. Raise vehicle and remove rear wheels, Fig. 3.
2. Check to be sure that brake pads are pushed back in their bores slightly to be sure they do not drag on discs.
3. Remove cable tension from wheel units by installing tool No. 2742 at cable lever of wheel units or by disconnecting cable from each wheel lever.
4. Turn each wheel so adjusting hole is at 12 o'clock and working through adjusting hole, tighten parking brake shoes until drum can no longer be rotated easily, then back off adjuster 4-5 serrations. Be sure parking brake shoes do not drag. The shoes are tightened by moving handle of adjusting tool upward. If shoes drag, back off adjuster until wheel is free.
5. Apply parking brake and check to see that wheels lock (without road wheels installed) on 3rd-4th notch of handle. If necessary, cable is adjusted at cable block under car where cables from each rear wheel join.
6. Reinstall road wheels.

1975-77 164, 240 & 260 Series

1. Remove rear ash tray.
2. Working through ash tray hole, tighten adjusting nut at rear of parking lever so that brake is fully applied after 2-3 notches, Fig. 4.

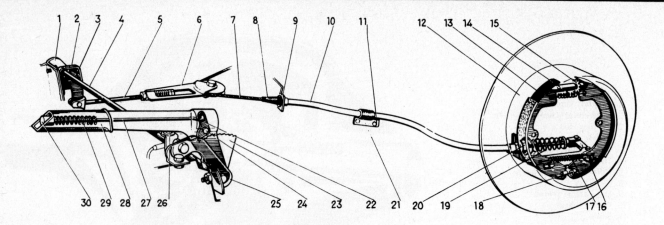

1. Inside support attachment	12. Brake drum	22. Pawl
2. Rubber cover	13. Brake shoe	23. Ratchet segment
3. Lever	(secondary shoe)	24. Rivet
4. Shaft	14. Return spring	25. Outside support attachment
5. Pull rod	15. Adjusting device	26. Warning valve switch
6. Pulley	16. Lever	27. Push rod
7. Cable	17. Movable rod	28. Parking brake
8. Rubber cover	18. Anchor bolt	29. Spring
9. Front attachment	19. Return spring	30. Push button
10. Cable sleeve	20. Rear attachment	
11. Attachment	21. Rubber cable guide	

Fig. 3 Parking brake components. 140 & 164 Series

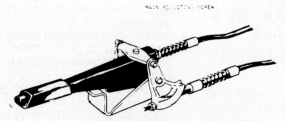

Fig. 4 Parking brake adjustment. 240 & 264 Series

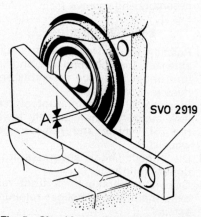

Fig. 5 Checking caliper piston position

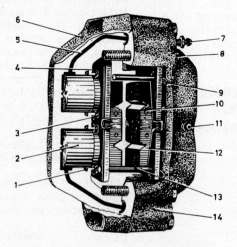

1. Seal	8. Bolt
2. Piston	10. Brake pad
3. Rubber dust cover	11. Lower bleeder nipple
4. Retaining ring	12. Damping spring
5. Channel	13. Retaining pin
6. Outer half	14. Inner half
7. Upper bleeder nipple	

Fig. 6 Front caliper assembly. 140 Series

BRAKE PADS, REPLACE

1. Raise car and remove wheels.
2. On Girling units, remove hairpin shaped locking clips for guide pins. Tap out one of guide pins while holding damper springs in place. Remove springs and other guide pin.
3. On ATE units, tap out upper guide pin with a drift. Remove tensioning spring. Tap out lower guide pin.
4. Pull out pads using tool No. 2917.
5. Carefully clean out cavity in which pads are located. Replace any dust covers that are damaged. If dirt has penetrated into cylinder due to a damaged cover, recondition brake caliper. Check brake disc and resurface if necessary.

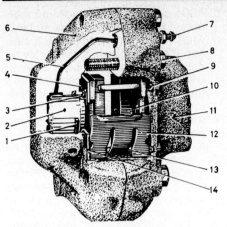

1. Seal
2. Piston
3. Rubber dust cover
4. Retaining ring
5. Channel
6. Outer half
7. Bleeder nipple
8. Bolt
9. Retaining clip
10. Brake pad
11. Inner half
12. Damping spring (alt. 1)
13. Retaining pin
14. Washer

Fig. 7   Rear caliper assembly. 140 Series

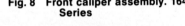

1. Sealing ring
2. Piston
3. Rubber dust cover
4. Channel
5. Upper bleeder nipple
6. Outer half
7. Inner half
8. Bolt
9. Guide pin
10. Inner bleeder nipple
11. Damping spring
12. Brake pad

Fig. 8   Front caliper assembly. 164 Series

1. Bolt
2. Outer half
3. Rubber dust cover
4. Piston
5. Sealing ring
6. Channel
7. Bleeder nipple
8. Inner half
9. Brake pad
10. Damping spring
11. Guide pin

Fig. 9   Rear caliper assembly. 164 Series

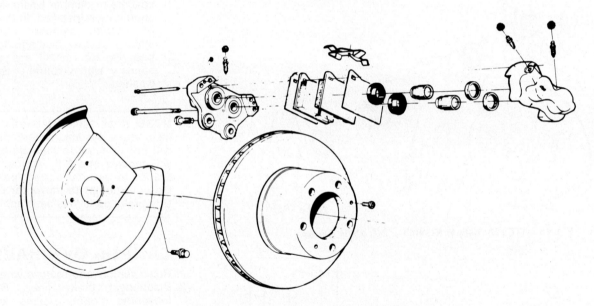

Fig. 10   ATE front caliper assembly. 240 & 264 Series

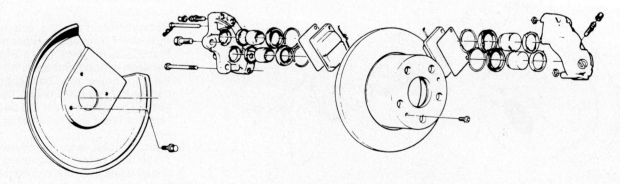

Fig. 11   Girling front caliper assembly. 240 & 264 Series

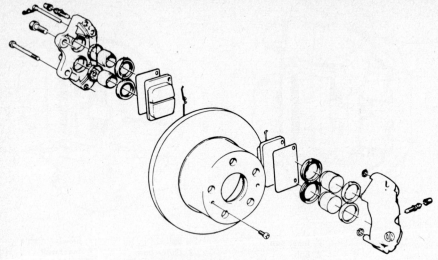

Fig. 12 Girling front caliper assembly. 240 & 264 Series

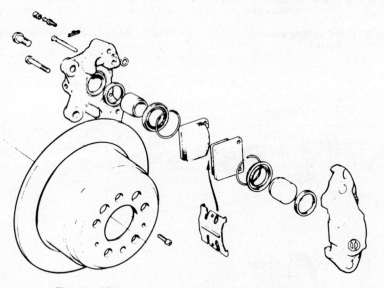

Fig. 13 ATE rear caliper assembly. 240 & 264 Series

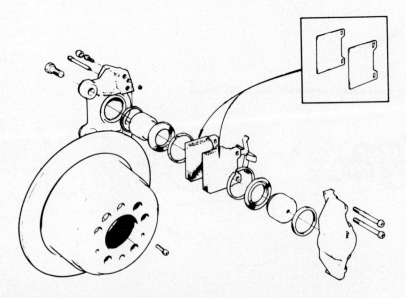

Fig. 14 Girling rear caliper assembly. 240 & 264 Series

6. Press caliper pistons back into their bores with tool 2809 or a suitable wide bladed screwdriver. Use caution if a screwdriver is used to avoid damage to rubber dust covers. When pistons are pressed back into their bores, brake fluid in master cylinder can overflow.
7. Install new pads using the following notes:
   a. For ATE rear pads, check to be sure caliper pistons are in proper position to avoid squeal. Piston recess should incline 20° in relation to lower guide area of caliper. Check with tool No. 2919, Fig. 5. If necessary, rotate piston with tool No. 2918.
   b. On ATE units, when installing guide pins, tap them in with a hammer without use of a drift. Do not use a drift because tensioning sleeve can be sheared off.
   c. On Girling units, if caliper has previously been equipped with intermediate shims, rubber coated spacers or damper washers, they should be reinstalled. In the case of round damper washers, smaller contact face should face pad. Do not install spacers or shims with round damper washers.

NOTE: After replacing pads on any disc brake system, caliper pistons will be retracted in their bores and will require one full application of brakes to assume correct position. Do not attempt to move car until a firm brake pedal has been achieved.

CALIPER, OVERHAUL

1. Raise vehicle and remove wheels.
2. Disconnect brake lines. Before loosening mounting bolts, loosen all bleeder screws, Figs. 6 through 14.
3. Remove caliper mounting bolts and remove caliper. Do not loosen bridge bolts.
4. Remove retaining ring and rubber dust cover from each caliper piston. Place a ⅝ in. thick piece of wood between pistons and apply air pressure to brake line connection of caliper to blow pistons out. Remove seals. The caliper must not be separated or leaks may result after reassembly.
5. Coat pistons and cylinders with brake fluid before assembling.
6. Install seals in cylinders, install pistons, dust covers and lock rings.
7. Reinstall calipers and bleed system.

Torque caliper retaining bolts to 90-100 Nm (65-70 ft. lbs.) for front and 52-64 Nm for rear.

MASTER CYLINDER, REPLACE

1. Place a cover over the fender to protect paint from brake fluid.
2. Disconnect brake lines and install plastic plugs.
3. Remove retaining nuts and remove cylinder.
4. Before installing, be sure to "bench bleed" cylinder.

POWER BRAKE UNIT, REPLACE

1. Remove master cylinder, then disconnect vacuum hose from power brake unit.
2. Disconnect link arm from brake pedal, then remove bracket with clutch pedal stop.
3. Remove nuts attaching power brake unit to dash panel.
4. Pull power brake unit forward, then disconnect fork from link arm and remove brake unit.

Rear Suspension Section

SHOCK ABSORBER, REPLACE

1. Raise car and place stands under the jacking points of body.
2. Remove the wheel. Unload axle by jacking up the axle.
3. Remove upper and lower retaining bolts and remove shock absorber.
4. Install upper screw, washer and rubber spacer inside spring and firmly secure spring to upper attachment.
5. Raise jack and secure spring to the lower attachment with washer and screw.
6. Install shock absorber and wheel.

REAR SPRINGS, REPLACE

1. Raise car and place stands under jacking points of body.
2. Remove wheel, then raise rear axle so spring compresses. Loosen upper and lower spring attachments.
3. Remove upper attachment for shock absorber. Lower jack carefully and remove spring, Fig. 1.

CONTROL ARM, REPLACE

1. Raise and support rear of vehicle.
2. Position a suitable jack under rear axle housing, then raise rear axle housing to compress springs.
3. Disconnect lower shock absorber at lower mounting, then remove lower spring attaching screw.
4. Slowly lower jack until spring releases from control arm, then move spring backwards so that it is free from control arm.
5. Raise jack until axle housing is in a level position.
6. Disconnect control arm from axle and frame mounting brackets and remove control arm.
7. Reverse procedure to install.

ROLL BAR, REPLACE

1. Raise rear of vehicle, then position jack stands in front of rear shock absorber mountings.
2. Disconnect roll bar at axle and frame mounting brackets, then remove roll bar.
3. Reverse procedure to install.

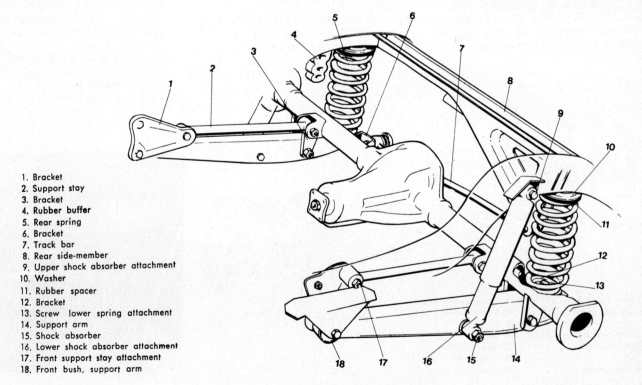

1. Bracket
2. Support stay
3. Bracket
4. Rubber buffer
5. Rear spring
6. Bracket
7. Track bar
8. Rear side-member
9. Upper shock absorber attachment
10. Washer
11. Rubber spacer
12. Bracket
13. Screw lower spring attachment
14. Support arm
15. Shock absorber
16. Lower shock absorber attachment
17. Front support stay attachment
18. Front bush, support arm

Fig. 1 Rear suspension (Typical)

Front Suspension & Steering Section

WHEEL ALIGNMENT
140 & 164 Series

Caster and camber are adjusted by adding or removing shims at upper control arm shaft, Figs. 1 & 2. The lock bolts can be loosened with tool 2713.

Positive caster is obtained by either adding shims to rear bolt or removing shims at the front bolt.

Positive camber is obtained by removing an equal number of shims at upper control arm shaft.

Negative camber is obtained by adding an equal number of shims at upper control arm shaft.

To adjust toe-in, loosen lock nuts on each end of center adjusting sleeve, then turn sleeve until correct toe-in is achieved.

240 & 260 Series

NOTE: Caster is not adjustable.

Camber
1. Loosen upper strut attaching nuts, Fig. 3.
2. Adjust camber using tool 5038, Fig. 4.
3. Tighten lock nuts.

Toe-In
1. Loosen lock nut on each tie rod.
2. Turn each tie rod to obtain proper toe-in. Length of tie rods may not differ more than 2mm (.080″).

3. If after toe-in adjustment, steering wheel is not properly centered, remove steering wheel and reinstall in correct alignment.

WHEEL BEARINGS, ADJUST

Adjust front wheel bearings by first tightening nut with a torque wrench to 70 Nm (50 ft. lbs.). Then loosen nut $1/3$ of a turn. If slot in nut does not coincide with cotter pin hole in spindle, loosen it further to enable cotter pin to be installed. Be sure to rotate wheel while tightening nut to be sure wheel bearings are properly seated.

BALL JOINTS, REPLACE
140 & 164 Series

Upper Ball Joint
1. Raise vehicle and remove wheel.
2. Loosen but do not remove upper ball joint retaining nut. Knock on steering knuckle around ball joint pin until it loosens from knuckle. Remove nut and suspend end of knuckle with a wire to avoid straining brake hose.
3. Loosen upper control arm nuts ½ turn. Lift up control arm slightly and press out ball joint with tools 2699 and 2701.
4. Press new ball joint into arm using tools 2699, 2704 and 2701.
5. Reinstall control arm and wheel.

Lower Ball Joint
1. Raise car and remove wheel.
2. Disconnect steering rod from steering arm and disconnect brake lines from stabilizer bolt.
3. Loosen nuts from upper and lower ball joints but do not remove them. Knock with a hammer until both ball joints loosen from knuckle. Raise lower control arm with a jack and remove nuts.
4. Remove steering knuckle with hub and front wheel brake unit and place them on a stand or similar support.
5. Using tools 2699 and 2700, press out ball joint. Reinstall ball joint using tools 2699, 270l and 2703.
6. Reinstall control arm nuts and wheel.

CONTROL ARM & BUSHING, REPLACE
140 & 164 Series

Upper Control Arm
1. Carry out operations 1 and 2 under Upper Ball Joints, Replace.
2. Remove control arm retaining bolts. Be sure to retain shims.
3. Remove control arm shaft nuts and washers. Place the control arm securely in a vise. Carefully bend out the control arm ends so that tool 2729 can be fitted. Support the arm with tool 2702 and drive out control arm shaft with a plastic mallet, Fig. 5. Turn control arm, then move tool 2729 to other side and drive other bushing out.
4. Hold tool 2699 firmly in a vise. Press in one of the bushings using tool 2702 and 2706.

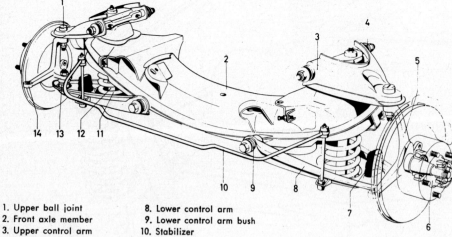

1. Upper ball joint
2. Front axle member
3. Upper control arm
4. Upper control arm bush
5. Steering knuckle
6. Hub
7. Rubber buffer
8. Lower control arm
9. Lower control arm bush
10. Stabilizer
11. Spring
12. Shock absorber
13. Lower ball joint
14. Steering arm

Fig. 1   Front suspension. 140 & 164 Series

SVO 2713

Fig. 2   Adjusting caster & camber (A = shims). 140 & 164 Series

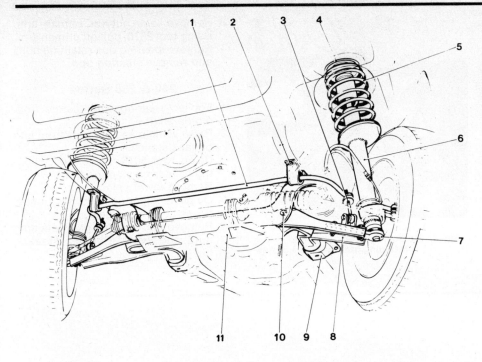

1. Stabilizer bar
2. Bracket
3. Link
4. Strut upper pivot point
5. Spring
6. Strut assembly
7. Ball joint
8. Control arm
9. Rear bracket for control arm
10. Front bracket for control arm
11. Front axle member

Fig. 3   Front suspension. 240 & 264 Series

5. Fit control arm shaft and press in other bushing.
6. Install washers and nuts.
7. Install control arm.

Lower Control Arm

1. Raise vehicle and remove wheel.
2. Remove shock absorber.
3. Disconnect steering rod from steering arm. Loosen clamp for brake hoses. Remove screw for stabilizer.
4. Place a jack under control arm.

Loosen ball joint nuts and knock with a hammer until ball joints loosen from knuckle. Remove nuts and lower jack enough to release steering knuckle.

5. Remove steering knuckle with brake caliper and support them to keep any strain off brake hose.
6. Fully lower jack and remove spring.
7. Remove control arm.
8. Clamp tool 2699 in a vise, then remove washer, rubber ring and spacer ring.
9. Using tool 2701, press out bushings.
10. Install bushings using tool 2904 if vehicle is equipped with bias tires and 2905 for radial tires. Both bushings should be installed with flange toward rear of car. If radial tires are used, bushings must be installed as shown in Fig. 6.

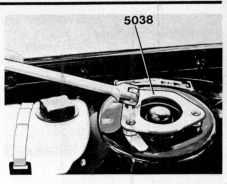

Fig. 4   Adjusting camber. 240 & 264 Series

SHOCK ABSORBER, REPLACE
140 & 164 Series

1. Remove upper nut, washer and rubber bushing.
2. Raise vehicle and remove lower retaining bolts. Remove shock absorber.

240 & 260 Series

1. Install two 5040 spring compressors. Be sure compressor spans five coils or spring will not be sufficiently compressed. Tighten compressors.
2. Raise vehicle and place stands under jacking points.
3. Disconnect steering rod from steering arm using tool 5043.
4. Disconnect stabilizer bar from link attachment.
5. Disconnect brake line bracket.
6. Remove cover for spring and strut assembly upper attachment.
7. Using tool 5036 and 5037, remove center nut, Fig. 7.
8. Lower jack, support strut assembly when lowering jack so that brake lines and hoses do not become damaged. Hook tool No. 5045 to strut assembly and stabilizer bar.
9. Remove spring seat, rubber bumper and shock absorber protector.

Fig. 5   Driving out control arm shaft. 140 & 164 Series

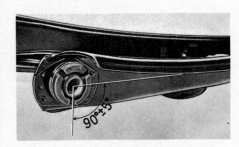

Fig. 6   Positioning control arm bushing for models with radial tires. 140 & 164 Series

Fig. 7   Removing strut center nut. 240 & 264 Series

10. Loosen spring compressors and remove coil spring.
11. Using tool 5039, loosen shock absorber retaining nut. Use a pipe wrench to hold the outer housing. Be sure to place the pipe wrench on the weld of the housing, Fig. 8.
12. Pull shock absorber out of housing.
13. Reverse procedure to install.

STEERING GEAR, REPLACE
140 & 164 Series

1. Raise front of vehicle.
2. Loosen pinch bolt at lower flange. Remove steering column-to-lower flange nuts. Push flange as far down steering box flange as possible. On power steering units, disconnect oil lines.

Fig. 8   Removing shock absorber retaining nut. 240 & 264 Series

3. Remove lock nut for pitman arm. Using tool 2370, pull off pitman arm.
4. Remove steering box retaining bolts and remove steering box.

240 & 260 Series

1. Loosen steering shaft flange from pinion shaft.
2. Raise vehicle and support front end on jack stands.
3. Using tool 5043, disconnect steering rods from steering arms.
4. Remove lower splash pan.
5. On power steering units, disconnect hoses at steering gear.
6. Remove four steering gear retaining nuts and bolts. Remove steering gear.

VOLKSWAGEN • AUDI FOX
INDEX OF SERVICE OPERATIONS

VOLKSWAGEN • AUDI FOX

GENERAL ENGINE SPECIFICATIONS

Year	Engine	Car-buretor	Bore and Stroke	Piston Displacement Cubic Inches	Compression Ratio	Maximum Brake H.P. @ R.P.M.	Maximum Torque Ft. Lbs. @ R.P.M.	Normal Oil Pressure Pounds
1972-74	4-1600cc ①	1 Barrel	3.366 x 2.717 (85.5 x 69mm)	97.6 (1600cc)	7.3	46 @ 4000	72 @ 2000	42
1972-73	4-1700cc ②	1 Barrel	3.543 x 2.598 (90 x 66mm)	103.7 (1700cc)	7.3	63 @ 4800	81 @ 3200	42
1974	4-1800cc ②	1 Barrel	3.661 x 2.598 (93 x 66mm)	109.8 (1800cc)	7.3	65 @ 4200	92 @ 3000	42
1974	4-1500cc ③	2 Barrel	3.01 x 3.15 (76.5 x 80mm)	91.5 (1500cc)	8.1	75 @ 5800	—	40
1975-77	4-1600cc ①	Fuel Inj.	3.366 x 2.717 (85.5 x 69mm)	97.6 (1600cc)	7.3	48 @ 4200	73 @ 2800	42
1975	4-1800cc ②	Fuel Inj.	3.661 x 2.598 (93 x 66mm)	109.8 (1800cc)	7.3	67 @ 4400	90 @ 2400	42
1975	4-1500cc ③ ④	2 Barrel	3.01 x 3.15 (76.5 x 80mm)	91.5 (1500cc)	8.1	70 @ 5800	80 @ 3500	40
1976-77	4-2000cc ②	Fuel Inj.	3.70 x 2.795 (94 x 71mm)	122 (2000cc)	7.3	67 @ 4200	101 @ 3000	42
1976	4-1600cc ③ ④	2 Barrel	3.13 x 3.15 (79.5 x 80mm)	97.6 (1600cc)	8.1	71 @ 5600	86 @ 3000	40
1977	4-1600cc ③ ④	Fuel Inj.	3.13 x 3.15 (79.5 x 80mm)	97.6 (1600cc)	8.1	78 @ 5500	84 @ 3200	40
1977	4-1500cc ⑤	Fuel Inj.	3.01 x 3.15 (76.5 x 80mm)	91.5 (1500cc)	23.5	48 @ 5000	—	—

—Not Available
① —Beetle
② —Bus
③ —Dasher
④ —Rabbit & Scirocco
⑤ —Diesel

TUNE UP SPECIFICATIONS

The following specifications are published from the latest information available. This data should be used only in the absence of a decal affixed in the engine compartment.

Before removing wires from distributor cap, determine location of the No. 1 wire in cap, as distributor position may have been altered from that shown at the end of this chart.

Year	Model	Spark Plug Type	Gap	Point Gap Inch	Dwell Angle Degrees	Firing Order Fig.	Ignition Timing Timing ATDC ①	Mark Fig.	Hot Idle Speed Std. Trans.	Hot Idle Speed Auto. Trans.	Idle CO% Std. Trans.	Idle CO% Auto. Trans.
1972-74	Beetle	L88A	.024	.018	44—50	A	②	②	850	950	—	—
1972-73	Bus	N88	.024	.018	44—50	A	5°	E	850	950	2.0	2.0
1974	Bus	N88	.024	.018	44—50	A	③	③	850	950	1.0	1.0
	Dasher	N8Y	.028	.016	⑩	F	3°	G	925	925	2.0	2.0
	Audi Fox	N12Y	.028	.015	44—50	F	3°	G	950	950	⑥	⑥
1975	Beetle	L288	.024	.018	44—50	A	⑤	⑤	875	925	0.2—2.0	0.2—2.0
	Bus	N288	.024	.018	44—50	A	5°	E	900	950	0.2—2.0	0.2—2.0
	Dasher	N8Y	.026	.016	44—50	F	3°	G	925	925	1.5—2.5	1.5—2.5
	Audi Fox	N12Y	.028	.015	44—50	F	3°	G	950	950	⑥	⑥
	Rabbit	N8Y	.026	.016	44—50	F	3°	H	950	950	2.0	2.0
	Scirocco	N8Y	.026	.016	44—50	F	3°	H	950	950	2.0	2.0
1976	Beetle	L288	.024	.018	44—50	A	④	④	875	925	0.2—2.0 ⑨	0.2—2.0 ⑨
	Bus	N-288	.028	.018	44—50	A	7½° ⑤	C	900	950	0.2—2.0 ⑨	0.2—2.0 ⑨
	Dasher	N7Y	.026	.016	44—50	F	3°	G	925	925	1.5—⑦⑧	1.0—⑦⑧
	Audi Fox	—	.028	.016	44—50	F	3°	G	—	—	—	—
	Rabbit	N8Y	.026	.016	44—50	F	3°	H	950	950	0.8—2.2 ⑨	0.3—1.7 ⑨
	Scirocco	N8Y	.026	.016	44—50	F	3°	H	950	950	0.8—2.2 ⑨	0.3—1.7 ⑨

Continued

The following specifications are published from the latest information available. This data should be used only in the absence of a decal affixed in the engine compartment.

Before removing wires from distributor cap, determine location of the No. 1 wire in cap, as distributor position may have been altered from that shown at the end of this chart.

Year	Model	Spark Plug		Distributor		Ignition Timing			Carburetor Adjustments			
									Hot Idle Speed		Idle CO%	
		Type	Gap	Point Gap Inch	Dwell Angle Degrees	Firing Order Fig.	Timing ATDC ①	Mark Fig.	Std. Trans.	Auto. Trans.	Std. Trans.	Auto. Trans.
1977	Beetle	L-288	.028	.016	44—50	A	5°	B	925	925	2.0⑨	2.0⑨
	Bus	N-288	.028	.016	44—50	A	7½°⑤	C	875	925	2.0⑨	2.0⑨
	Dasher	N7Y	.026	.016	44—50	F	3°	G	925	925	1.5⑦⑧	1.0⑦⑧
	Audi Fox	—	—	—	—	F	3°	H	—	—	—	—
	Rabbit	N7Y	.026	.016	44—50	F	3°	H	950	950	1.5⑦⑧	1.0⑦⑧
	Scirocco	N7Y	.026	.016	44—50	F	3°	H	950	950	1.5⑦⑧	1.0⑦⑧

—Not Available

① —ATDC: After top dead center
② —1972 to spring 1973, 5° ATDC, Fig. B: From spring 1973, 7½° BTDC, Fig. B.
③ —Manual trans., 10° ATDC, Fig. D: Auto. trans., 5° ATDC, Fig. E
④ —Manual trans., 5° ATDC, Fig. B: Auto. trans., TDC, Fig. B.
⑤ —Before top dead center.
⑥ —Vehicles without air pump; 1.3±.7%. On vehicles with air pump, disconnect hose at pump and plug hose with suitable plug. Adjust CO valve to 1.5%. After reconnecting hose, CO valve must drop to below 1%.
⑦ —Max.; Calif., all, 0.5% max.
⑧ —Measured at tailpipe.
⑨ —Measured ahead of converter.
⑩ —Except Calif., 44—50. Calif., 47—53.

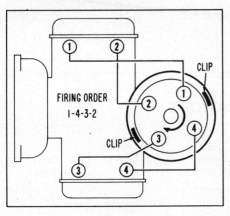

Fig. A

Fig. D

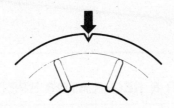

Fig. B

Fig. E

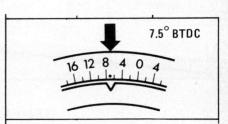

Fig. C

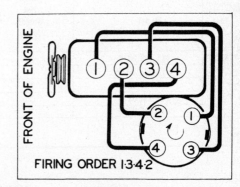

Fig. F

Fig. G

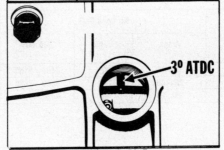

Fig. H

DISTRIBUTOR SPECIFICATIONS

If unit is checked on vehicle, double the RPM and degrees to get crankshaft figures.

| Year | Distributor Number | Centrifugal Advance Degrees @ RPM of Distributor | | | | Vacuum Advance | | Vacuum Retard | |
		Advance Starts	Intermediate Advance		Full Advance	Inches of Vacuum to Start Plunger	Max. Adv. Dist. Deg. @ Vacuum	Inches of Vacuum to Start Plunger	Max. Retard Dist. Deg. @ Vacuum
1972-73	021905205E	0 @ 525	6½—8 @ 1000	—	13 @ 1800	3—4	6 @ 8	3—4	7½ @ 7
	021905205F	0 @ 500	7—8½ @ 850	—	12½ @ 1700	3—4	6 @ 8	3—4	7 @ 7
1972-74	043905205	0 @ 525	3—6 @ 750	—	12½ @ 1900	2—4	6 @ 8	—	—
	043905205A	0 @ 500	6—7½ @ 800	—	12½ @ 1900	2—4	6 @ 8	—	—
	113905205AN	0 @ 500	3—6 @ 750	—	12½ @ 1900	4—6	4 @ 8	3—6	6½ @ 9
	113905205AH	0 @ 500	6—7½ @ 800	—	12½ @ 1900	4—6	2½ @ 7	3—5	6½ @ 9
1974	021905205S	0 @ 500	4½—7 @ 800	—	12½ @ 1700	4—5	6 @ 8	2—5	6½ @ 8
	021905205N	0 @ 500	4½—7 @ 800	—	12½ @ 1700	4—6	6 @ 7	3—5	9 @ 8
1974-75	055905205C	0 @ 525	8—10 @ 1125	9½—11½ @ 1500	15 @ 2500	8—9½	7 @ 13¾	6¼—8½	4½ @ 11½
	056905205C	0 @ 550	7½—10 @ 1075	9½—11½ @ 1500	15 @ 2500	8—9½	7½ @ 13¾	6—8½	4½ @ 12
1975	022905205AB	0 @ 500	5½—8½ @ 1000	—	12½ @ 1800	3—5	5½ @ 8	2—5	6½ @ 8
	021905205AB	0 @ 500	5½—8½ @ 1000	—	12½ @ 1800	3—5	5½ @ 8	2—5	6½ @ 8
	022905205AC	0 @ 500	5½—8½ @ 1000	—	12½ @ 1800	3—5	3½ @ 7	2—5	6½ @ 8
	021905205AC	0 @ 500	5½—8½ @ 1000	—	12½ @ 1800	3—5	3½ @ 7	2—5	6½ @ 8
	055905205B	0 @ 550	7½—9½ @ 1075	—	15 @ 2500	—	7½ @ 14	—	4½ @ 12
1975-77	043905205H	0 @ 500	3—6 @ 750	—	11½ @ 1750	6—8	4 @ 8	2—6	6½ @ 9
	043905209J	0 @ 512	3—5½ @ 750	—	11½ @ 1750	4—6	6 @ 9	2—6	4 @ 8
1976	055905205F	0 @ 550	9—11½ @ 1500	—	15 @ 2500	—	7½ @ 14	—	4½ @ 12
1976-77	021905205P	0 @ 500	5½—8½ @ 1000	—	12½ @ 1800	3—5	5½ @ 8	—	—
	022905205S	0 @ 500	4—6½ @ 800	—	12½ @ 1700	3—5	5½ @ 8	—	—
1977	049905205A	0 @ 560	5½—9 @ 1000	12½—14½ @ 2400	15 @ 2600	—	4 @ 12	—	5 @ 11

—Not Available

GENERATOR & REGULATOR SPECIFICATIONS

Year	Model	Rated Hot Output Amps	Cut-in Voltage	No Load Regulating Voltage	Load Regulating Voltage	Load Amps	Return Amps
1972-76	113 903 031K	30	12.4—13.1	13.5—14.5	12.8—13.8	45	2—7.5
	113 903 031P	30	12.4—13.1	13.5—14.5	12.8—13.8	45	2—7.5
	113 903 031Q	30	12.4—13.1	13.5—14.5	12.8—13.8	45	2—7.5
	211 903 031A	30	12.4—13.1	13.5—14.5	12.8—13.8	45	2—7.5
	211 903 031D	38	12.5—13.2	13.5—14.2	12.9—13.6	35	5—11.5

STARTING MOTOR SPECIFICATIONS

| Year | Model | No Load Test | | | Load Test | | | Stall Torque Test | |
		Amps	Volts	Speed	Amps	Volts	Speed	Amps	Volts
1972-76	311 911 023B	35—45	12	7400—9100	170—205	9	900—1300	220—260	6
	111 911 023A	25—40	12	6200—7800	170—195	9	1050—1350	270—290	6
	003 911 023A	35—50	12	6400—7900	160—200	9	1100—1400	250—300	6

VOLKSWAGEN • AUDI FOX

VALVE SPECIFICATIONS

Year	Model	Valve Lash		Valve Angles		Valve Spring Installed Height	Valve Spring Pressure Lbs. @ In.	Stem Clearance		Stem Diameter	
		Int.	Exh.	Int.	Exh.			Intake	Exhaust	Intake	Exhaust
1972-77	Beetle	.006	.006①	45°	45°	1.220	126 @ 1.22	.009—.031	.009—.031	.311—.313	.310—.312
	Bus	.006	.006①	30°	45°	1.142	177 @ 1.15	.018—.035	.014—.470	.311—.313	.349—.351
1974-77	Dasher, Audi Fox	.010②	.018②	45°	45°	—	—	.016	.031	.314	.313
1975-77	Rabbit, Scirocco	.010②	.018②	45°	45°	—	—	.039	.051	.314	.313

—Not Available
①—Sodium filled exhaust valve; .008 in.
②—Warm (95°F)

PISTONS, PINS, RINGS, CRANKSHAFT & BEARINGS

Year	Model	Piston Clearance	Ring End Gap		Wrist-Pin Diameter	Rod Bearings		Main Bearing			Shaft End Play
			Comp.	Oil		Shaft Diameter	Bearing Clearance	Shaft Diameter	Bearing Clearance	Thrust on Bear. No.	
1972-77	Beetle	.001—.008	.012—.035	.010—.037	—	2.165	.001—.006	①	.001—.007	—	.003—.005
	Bus	.001—.008	.012—.035	.010—.037	—	③	.001—.006	②	.001—.007	—	.003—.005
1974-77	Dasher, Audi Fox	.001—.003	.012—.040	.010—.040	—	1.800	.001—.005	2.126	.001—.007	—	.003—.015
1975-77	Rabbit, Scirocco	.001—.003	.012—.040	.010—.040	—	1.800	.001—.005	2.126	.001—.007	—	.003—.015

—Not Available
①—Bearing 1,2 & 3; 2.164—2.165, Bearing 4; 1.5740—1.5748.
②—Bearing 1,2 & 3; 2.3610—2.3618, Bearing 4; 1.5740—1.5748
③—1972-75; 2.1645—2.1653, 1976-77; 1.9677—1.9685

ENGINE TIGHTENING SPECIFICATIONS

Beetle & Bus

Torque specifications are for clean and lightly lubricated threads only. Dry or dirty threads produce increased friction which prevents accurate measurement of tightness.

Year	Model	Spark Plugs Ft. Lbs.	Cylinder Head Bolts Ft. Lbs.	Crank-Case Halves Ft. Lbs.	Rocker Arm Shaft Ft. Lbs.	Connecting Rods Ft. Lbs.	Drive Plate to Crankshaft Ft. Lbs.	Flywheel to Crankshaft Ft. Lbs.	Vibration Damper or Pulley Ft. Lbs.
1972-77	Beetle	25	①	②	16	24	—	253	32
	Bus	22	23	③	10	24	65	80	23

—Not Available
①—M8 nut, 18 ft. lbs.; M10 nut, 23 ft. lbs.
②—Exc. sealing nut, 14 ft. lbs.; sealing nut, 18 ft. lbs.
③—Exc. sealing nut, 14 ft. lbs.; sealing nut, 25 ft. lbs.

Dasher, Rabbit, Scirocco & Audi Fox

Year	Model	Sprk plug Ft. Lbs.	Cylinder Head Bolts Ft. Lbs.	Intake & Exhaust Manifold Ft. Lbs.	Camshaft Bearing Cap Bolts Ft. Lbs.	Connecting Rod Cap Bolts Ft. Lbs.	Main Bearing Cap Bolts Ft. Lbs.	Flywheel to Crankshaft Ft. Lbs.	Vibration Damper or Pulley Ft. Lbs.
1974-77	Exc. Rabbit Diesel	—	54①	18	14	33	47	54	58
	Rabbit Diesel			18	—	33	47	54	56

BRAKE SPECIFICATIONS

Year	Model	Brake Drum Inside Dia. (Inches)		Wheel Cylinder Bore Dia. (Inches)			Master Cylinder Bore Dia. (Inches)
		Front	Rear	Disc Brake	Front Drum Brake	Rear Drum Brake	
1972-77	Beetle	9.768	9.055	—	.937	.687	.75
	Bus	—	9.98	2.126	—	.937	.937

—Not Available

DIFFERENTIAL SPECIFICATIONS

Year	Model	Pinion Bearing Preload			Differential Bearing Preload			Ring Gear	
		New Bearings Inch-Lbs.	Used Bearings Inch-Lbs.	Method	New Bearings Inch-Lbs.	Used Bearings Inch-Lbs.	Method	Backlash Inches	Method
1972-77	Beetle	●	2.5—6	①	26—30	2.5—6	Shim	.006—.010	Shim
	Bus ②	5—15	2.5—6	①	26—30	2.5—6	Shim	.006—.010	Shim
	Bus ③	12—18	1	④	⑤	⑤	Shim	.006—.010	④
1975-77	Rabbit & Scirocco ⑥	4—13	⑦	Shim	10—22	⑦	Sihim	—	—
	Rabbit & Scirocco ③	4—11	⑦	Shim	⑧	⑧	④	—	—

—Not Available
①—Not adjustable. If preload is incorrect, replace bearing.
②—With Auto-Stickshift.
③—With automatic transmission.
④—Threaded bearing carrier.
⑤—Measure pinion shaft turning torque, then add an additional 3 inch lbs. for new bearings, or 1-2.5 inch lbs. for used bearings.
⑥—With manual transmission.
⑦—Use existing shim.
⑧—For intermediate gear, measure pinion turning torque, then add an additional 13 inch lbs. For differential bearings (both measured from pinion) measure pinion shaft and intermediate gear combined turning torque, then add an additional 6 inch lbs.

FRONT WHEEL ALIGNMENT SPECIFICATIONS

Year	Model	Caster Angle, Degrees		Camber Angle, Degrees		Toe, Degrees
		Limits	Desired	Limits	Desired	
1972-77	Beetle	$+2^{1}/_3$ to $+4^{1}/_3$	$+3^{1}/_3$	$^{1}/_6$—$^{5}/_6$	½	¼ to ¾
	Bus	$+2^{1}/_3$ to $+3^{2}/_3$	+3	$^{1}/_3$ to 1	$^{2}/_3$	0 to ½
1972-75	Super Beetle	$+1^{5}/_{12}$ to $+2^{7}/_{12}$	+2	1	1	¼ to ¾
1975-76	Rabbit, Scirocco	$+1½$ to $+2½$	+2	0 to +1	$^{1}/_3$	$+½$ to $-^{5}/_{12}$
1977	Rabbit, Scirocco	$+1^{1}/_3$ to $2^{1}/_3$	$+1^{2}/_3$	$-^{1}/_6$ to $+^{5}/_6$	½	$-¼$ to $-^{5}/_{12}$

REAR WHEEL ALIGNMENT SPECIFICATIONS

| Year | Model | Camber Angle, Degrees | | Toe, Degrees | Track Deviation, Degrees |
		Limits	Desired		
1972-76	Beetle	$-1^2/_3$ to $-1/_3$	$-5/_{12}$	$-3/_{12}$ to $+3/_{12}$	$1/_6$ Maximum
1972-76	Bus	$-1^1/_3$ to $-1/_3$	-1	$-1/_6$ to $+1/_2$	$1/_6$ Maximum
1975-76	Rabbit, Scirocco	$-1/_2$ to $-1^1/_2$	-1	$-3/_{12}$ to $+3/_{12}$	$3/_{12}$ Maximum
1977	Rabbit, Scirocco	$-2/_3$ to $-1^5/_6$	$-1^1/_{12}$	$-1/_6$ to $+1/_2$	$3/_{12}$ Maximum

COOLING SYSTEM & CAPACITY DATA

| Year | Model or Engine | Cooling Capacity, Qts. | | | Radiator Cap Relief Pressure, Lbs. | Thermo Opening Temp. | Fuel Tank Gals. | Engine Oil Refill Pints | Transmission Oil | | Final Drive quts. |
		No Heat	With Heat	With A/C					Manual Trans. Qts.	Auto. Trans. Qts.	
1972-77	Beetle	—	—	—	—	—	①	5.3	1.3	—	—
	Bus	—	—	—	—	—	14.8	②	3.7	6.4	1.5
1974-76	Dasher, Audi Fox	—	6.4	—	13—15	198	—	7.4	1.7	6.4	1.5
1975-77	Rabbit, Scirocco	—	6.8	—	13—15	176	—	7.4	1.3	6.4	0.8
1977	Dasher, Audi Fox	—	6.3	—	13—15	198	—	6.4	1.7	6.2	0.8

—Not available
① —Beetle; 10.6 gal., Super Beetle, 11.1 gals.
② —Fuel injection & Dual Carb; 7.4 pints, Single Carb.; 5.3 pints.

Electrical Section

Beetle & Bus

DISTRIBUTOR, REPLACE

1. Remove distributor cap.
2. Rotate engine until rotor tip aligns with notch on distributor housing.
3. Disconnect vacuum advance line and electrical lead from coil.
4. Loosen distributor retainer bolt and remove distributor, Fig. 1.
5. Reverse procedure to install. Make sure that rotor tip is aligned with distributor housing notch.

STARTER, REPLACE

1. Disconnect battery ground cable.
2. Disconnect wires from starter solenoid.
3. While an assistant holds nut inside engine compartment, remove upper starter mounting bolt, then remove the lower nut and remove starter.

NOTE: On vehicles with Bosch starters, inspect bushing in transmission case. If bushing is worn or damaged, it should be replaced.

4. Reverse procedure to install.

ALTERNATOR, REPLACE

1. Remove air cleaner, carburetor, and paper hoses for heater.
2. Remove right side lower push rod tube shield, then remove thermostat.
3. Remove four bolts on fan cover and two screws on side of fan housing.
4. Remove large nut holding fan to alternator shaft (front of fan housing) and V-belt pulley nut, also remove rear half of pulley and V-belt, hold armature shaft with screwdriver in V-belt pulley notches.
5. Lift up fan housing until fan cover clears intake manifold.
6. Remove alternator with fan cover.

NOTE: When installing alternator on fan cover, make sure cooling slots face downward.

7. Reverse procedure to install.

IGNITION SWITCH, REPLACE

1. Remove turn signal/wiper switch assembly as outlined previously.
2. Remove multi-connector plug from back of ignition switch.
3. Loosen set screw on steering lock housing and remove ignition switch.
4. Align "tab" on new switch with set screw and tighten.
5. Reinstall multi-connector plugs, turn signal/wiper switch assembly, and steering wheel.
6. Torque steering wheel nut to 31-38 ft./lbs. and reconnect horn wires when reinstalling center cap.
7. Reconnect battery ground strap and check switch operation.

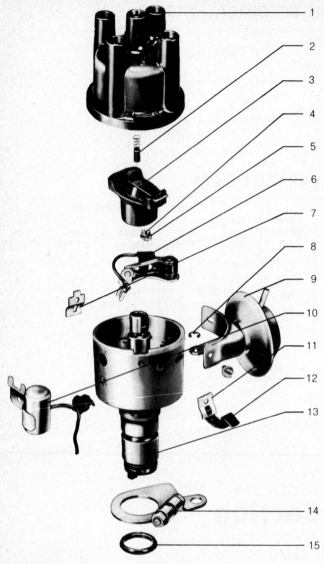

1. Distributor cap
2. Carbon brush and spring
3. Distributor rotor
4. Screw (2)
5. Washer (1)
6. Breaker point assembly
7. Retaining clip mount with
8. E-clip for pull rod
9. Vacuum chamber unit
10. Condenser
11. Retaining clip mount
12. Retaining clip (2)
13. Distributor body assembly
14. Distributor clamp

Fig. 1   Distributor disassembled (Typical)

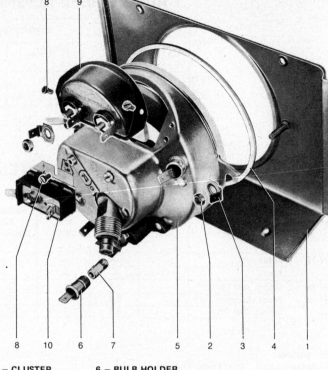

1 — CLUSTER	6 — BULB HOLDER
2 — NUT	7 — BULB
3 — GROUND TAB	8 — SCREW
4 — SEAL	9 — FUEL GAUGE
5 — SPEEDOMETER	10 — VIBRATOR

Fig. 3   Speedometer assembly. Beetle & Bus

IGNITION LOCK
Removal

1. Remove turn signal/wiper switch assembly and ignition switch as outlined previously.
2. Remove retaining plate on steering lock assembly.
3. Turn ignition key to "on" position and pull out steering lock assembly.
4. To remove lock cylinder from steering lock housing, turn key to "off" position and insert piece of wire into hole in steering lock housing.

NOTE: On some switch assemblies

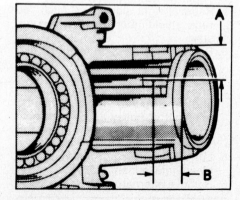

Fig. 2   Drilling hole in steering lock housing

the hole in the steering lock housing is missing, drill a 1/8-inch hole in side of housing about 11 mm (.43 inch) down from top of housing, Fig. 2.

5. Now depress retaining spring on lock cylinder with wire and turn key slightly toward "on" position until lock cylinder can be removed easily.

Installation

1. Insert key into lock cylinder and push bottom of cylinder toward key.
2. Turn key to "locked steering" position and remove from lock cylinder.
3. Now slide lock cylinder into steering lock housing without force.
4. Insert key again and turn to "on" position.
5. Slide steering lock assembly into column and install retaining plate.
6. Reinstall all switches, multiconnector plugs and steering wheel.
7. Torque steering wheel nut to 31-38 ft. lbs. and reconnect horn wires before installing center cap.
8. Reconnect battery ground strap and

4. Remove five attaching screws.
5. Pull left side of switch panel out far enough to depress two "snap-lock" tabs and release switch.
6. Pull out switch body far enough to reach connections easily.
7. Transfer wire connectors from old to new switch one at a time.
8. Snap new switch into switch panel. Operate rocker lever several times before installing panel to make sure switch is installed correctly.
9. Install switch panel five attaching screws, cover strips and cap.
10. Connect battery ground strap and check switch operation.

Standard Beetle and Bus

1. Remove battery ground strap.
2. Remove switch knob.
3. Remove special slotted nut using special tool VW 674/1 or homemade tool (grind two driving "tangs" on end of piece of tubing to fit slots in special nut).
4. On Bus models, reach up under instrument panel and remove switch body. On standard Beetle models, open trunk lid and remove cardboard cover on back of instrument panel, now remove "fresh air box" (be careful not to damage the paper connecting hoses).
5. Pull out switch body far enough to reach connections easily.
6. Transfer wire connectors from old switch to new switch one at a time.
7. Hold new switch in place while someone else tightens special slotted nut (no helper required on Bus). Make sure connectors do not touch other components.
8. Reinstall battery ground strap and check switch operation.

STOP LIGHT SWITCH, REPLACE

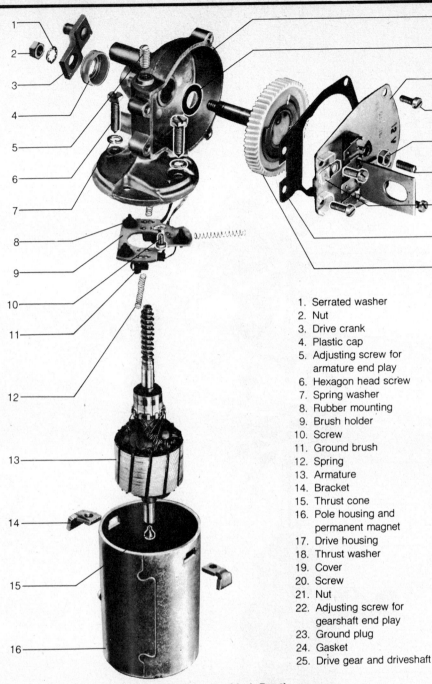

1. Serrated washer
2. Nut
3. Drive crank
4. Plastic cap
5. Adjusting screw for armature end play
6. Hexagon head screw
7. Spring washer
8. Rubber mounting
9. Brush holder
10. Screw
11. Ground brush
12. Spring
13. Armature
14. Bracket
15. Thrust cone
16. Pole housing and permanent magnet
17. Drive housing
18. Thrust washer
19. Cover
20. Screw
21. Nut
22. Adjusting screw for gearshaft end play
23. Ground plug
24. Gasket
25. Drive gear and driveshaft

Fig. 4 Wiper motor disassembled. Beetle

check operation of steering lock and switches.

NOTE: Ignition switches on late buses are practically the same as on the Beetle. Some earlier buses had switch assemblies in which the steering column housing, steering lock, ignition switch and lock cylinder were replaced as a unit.

HEADLIGHT SWITCH, REPLACE

NOTE: On Super Beetle models the switch can be removed from the passenger compartment after removing a small panel. On "standard" Beetle models part of the procedure must be done from the front trunk after removing the fresh air box.

Super Beetle

1. Disconnect battery ground strap.
2. Pop out plastic cover strips carefully with small screwdriver: one on left of headlight switch, the other on right of four-way flasher switch.
3. Also pop out small plastic cap immediately over steering column.

NOTE: The switch is accessible from the front left underside of all Beetles. The front splash shield must be removed first on all Buses.

1. Make sure ignition key is "off."
2. Peel back rubber boot and remove wire connectors from switch: If multi-connector plug is not used, be sure to note position of each connector.
3. Remove old switch, hold new switch nearby.
4. Install new switch, if master cylinder is "open" *less* than three seconds, bleeding affected brake circuit is *not* necessary.

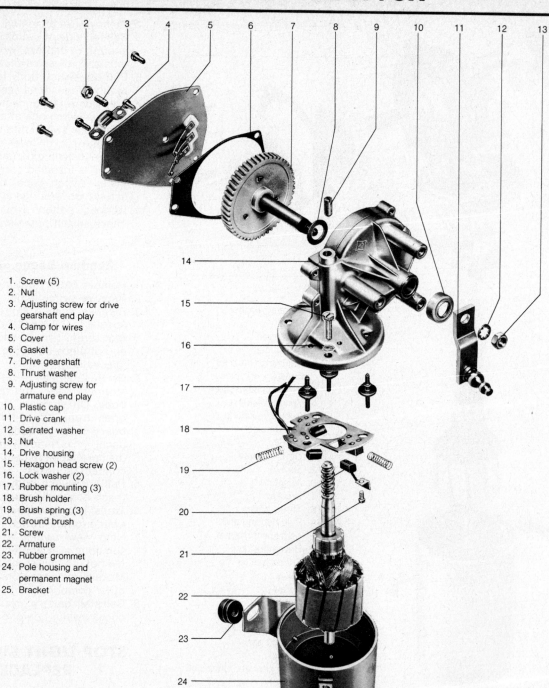

1. Screw (5)
2. Nut
3. Adjusting screw for drive gearshaft end play
4. Clamp for wires
5. Cover
6. Gasket
7. Drive gearshaft
8. Thrust washer
9. Adjusting screw for armature end play
10. Plastic cap
11. Drive crank
12. Serrated washer
13. Nut
14. Drive housing
15. Hexagon head screw (2)
16. Lock washer (2)
17. Rubber mounting (3)
18. Brush holder
19. Brush spring (3)
20. Ground brush
21. Screw
22. Armature
23. Rubber grommet
24. Pole housing and permanent magnet
25. Bracket

Fig. 5 Wiper motor disassembed. Bus

5. Install wire connectors and rubber boot correctly.
6. Turn on ignition and check operation of brake warning light and stop lights.

NEUTRAL SAFETY SWITCH, REPLACE

Neutral safety switches are used only in Beetles with "automatic stickshift" transmission and Buses with fully automatic transmission.

Beetle

The neutral safety switch is located on the front left side of the transmission housing and is not adjustable. If switch is replaced, use a new sealing washer and torque the switch body to 18 ft. lbs.

Bus

NOTE: The neutral safety switch is located under the housing at the base of the shift lever.

1. Check that starter operates only in "N" and "P" shift lever positions.
2. If "neutral safety" function does not work properly, lift up housing and check switch visually.
3. Loosen two screws and move switch body in slotted holes to adjust.

TURN SIGNAL & WINDSHIELD WASHER SWITCH, REPLACE

NOTE: The windshield wiper/washer switch is incorporated into the steering column with an operating lever like the turn signal switch. The three switches are removed as a unit but can be replaced individually.

1. Release pressure from windshield washer reservoir tank.
2. Disconnect battery ground strap.
3. Remove lower steering column cover.
4. Disconnect multi-connector plugs for turn signal and wiper switches.
5. Remove two hoses for windshield washer circuit.
6. Pull off steering wheel center cover and disconnect horn wires.
7. Remove steering wheel nut and washer.
8. Turn steering wheel to center position and remove.
9. Remove four screws from switch assembly.
10. Remove switch assembly from steering column carefully.
11. Replace defective switch, and install four spacer pins between switches.
12. Install switch assembly and electrical plugs and washer hoses.
13. Install steering wheel in center position.
14. Torque steering wheel nut to 31-38 ft./lbs.
15. Install center cover and connect horn wires.
16. Install battery ground strap and check operation of horn, wipers washer, and turn signals, also make sure turn signal cancellation mechanism works properly.

SPEEDOMETER & INSTRUMENT CLUSTER, REPLACE

NOTE: The fuel gauge and many of the indicator lights are incorporated in the speedometer face. in the Bus and Standard Beetle most operations can be done with the speedometer installed. Although the speedometer must be removed for most of this work on the Super Beetle, it is held in only by a ridged rubber ring.

Bus & Standard Beetle

1. Remove battery ground strap.
2. On Beetle, open trunk lid and remove cardboard cover on back of panel. Bus: reach up under instrument panel.
3. Unscrew knurled nut to disconnect speedometer cable.
4. Loosen two "Phillips head" screws several turns, but do not remove them, Fig. 3.
5. Turn speedometer head slightly to release slotted "tabs" from screws.
6. Pull out speedometer far enough to reach connections without removing wires.
7. Transfer bulb sockets and fuel gauge assembly from old to new gauge.
8. Install speedometer, make sure tabs and screws are seated correctly (a mirror is helpful on the Bus).
9. Install speedometer cable, the knurled nut should be hand-tight.
10. Install battery ground strap and check operation of indicator lights and fuel gauge.
11. Road test vehicle to check operation of speedometer.

Super Beetle

1. Disconnect battery ground strap.
2. Remove cardboard panel under dashboard.
3. Reach up under dashboard and unscrew knurled nut to disconnect speedometer cable.
4. Push speedometer assembly out toward back of car, if rubber ring is tight, remove headlight switch panel and reach up behind speedometer from switch panel opening, Fig. 7.
5. Replace assembly components as necessary.
6. Push speedometer back in place until firmly seated.
7. Install speedometer cable, tighten knurled nut handtight before installing cardboard panel and/or switch panel.
8. Install battery ground strap and check operation of indicator lights and fuel gauge.
9. Road test vehicle to check operation of speedometer.

WIPER MOTOR, REPLACE

Beetle

1. Remove battery ground strap.
2. Remove wiper arms (small nut on shaft).
3. Remove wiper shaft nuts.
4. From inside trunk compartment, remove "fresh air" box. Use care not to damage paper connecting hoses. On Super Beetle, remove cover without damaging water seal.
5. Disconnect wire connector at wiper motor.
6. Remove wiper motor and frame carefully.

NOTE: Wiper shafts or operating rods with bushings can be replaced at this time.

7. Remove operating rod from motor crank and loosen large nut under motor crank.
8. Remove small nut on frame and slide motor out of frame, Fig. 4.

NOTE: When installing motor assembly, check operation of wipers, including park position.

Bus

1. Remove battery ground strap.
2. Remove wiper arms.
3. Remove wiper shaft nuts.
4. Remove heater hoses under instrument panel.
5. Remove wiper motor wires from switch.
6. Remove mounting bolt and slide frame and motor down and out to right.
7. Pry operating rods off ball joints on crank using a screwdriver.
8. Remove motor from frame, Fig. 5.

Dasher

DISTRIBUTOR, REPLACE

1. Remove distributor cap.
2. Rotate engine until rotor tip aligns with notch on distributor housing.
3. Disconnect vacuum advance line and electrical lead from coil.
4. Remove distributor hold-down bolt and retainer, then remove distributor, Fig. 1.
5. Reverse procedure to install. Make sure that rotor tip is aligned with notch on distributor housing.

STARTER, REPLACE

1. Disconnect battery ground cable.
2. Disconnect wires from starter solenoid.
3. Remove starter bracket retaining

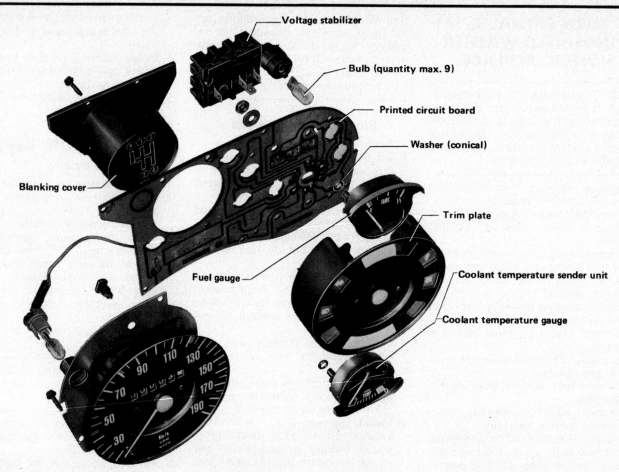

Fig. 6 Instrument cluster. Dasher

Labels in figure: Voltage stabilizer, Bulb (quantity max. 9), Printed circuit board, Washer (conical), Trim plate, Coolant temperature sender unit, Coolant temperature gauge, Fuel gauge, Blanking cover

nuts, or clamp, then remove starter retaining nuts and remove starter.

4. Reverse procedure to install.

ALTERNATOR, REPLACE

1. Disconnect battery ground cable.
2. Disconnect electrical connectors from alternator.
3. Loosen alternator adjusting bolt and remove belt from alternator pulley.
4. Remove alternator bolts, and then the alternator.
5. Reverse procedure to install. Make sure to reconnect ground strap to stud on back of alternator, as rubber mounts will prevent alternator from charging.

ALTERNATOR ON VEHICLE TESTING

Most alternator charging systems use a voltage regulator incorporated into the alternator housing which simplifies trouble-shooting:

1. Check battery voltage with ignition off: hould be 11-12 volts (too low: re-charge battery, too high: leave highbeams on)

2. Turn ignition on: charging indicator must light up.

NOTE: System will not charge without a working bulb circuit: replace bulb or check connections before proceeding!

---

3. Run engine at 2000 RPM for two minutes and check that charging voltage is 12.5-14.8 volts.
  *voltage too high: replace voltage regulator
  *voltage too low: replace voltage regulator and re-check charging voltage
  *voltage too low with good regulator: replace alternator

TURN SIGNAL/WIPER WASHER SWITCH, REPLACE

NOTE: Make sure turn signal switch is in neutral position before reinstallation, to prevent damaging the cancelling lug.

---

1. Disconnect battery ground cable.
2. Pull off steering wheel center cover and remove horn wires.

3. Remove large nut and washer and slide off steering wheel.
4. Remove four Phillips screws on perimeter of horn contact ring and lift switch assembly off steering column.
5. Pull off multi-connector plugs and lever out small plate around switch handle.
6. Remove two Phillips screws in switch handle opening and remove switch from housing.
7. Reverse procedure to install.

IGNITION SWITCH

1. Disconnect battery ground strap.
2. Remove left side glove box and panel over pedals (three Phillips screws).
3. Pull off multi-connector plug from back of switch body.
4. Loosen set screw in side of steering lock housing and remove switch body.

STEERING LOCK

1. Remove steering wheel and column switches as described previously.
2. Remove left side glove box and panel over pedals (three Phillips screws).

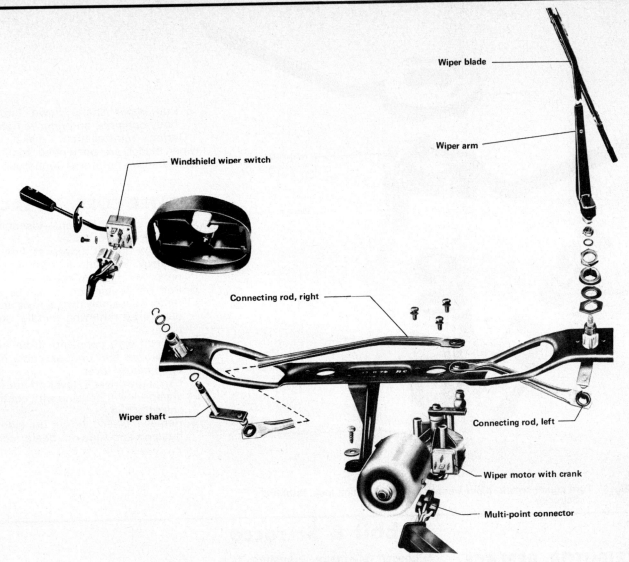

Windshield wiper switch

Wiper blade

Wiper arm

Connecting rod, right

Wiper shaft

Connecting rod, left

Wiper motor with crank

Multi-point connector

Fig. 7 Wiper motor & linkage. Dasher

3. Remove multi-connector plug from back of ignition switch, insert key, and turn switch to the ON position.
4. Drill out the special bolt heads holding the steering lock housing to the column (center-punch and use 5/16 inch drill bit) and remove housing.

NOTE: Make sure that housing "lug" fits into recess on column during reassembly. Use new shear bolts—tighten until heads break off.

LIGHT SWITCHES, REPLACE
Late Models

1. Disconnect battery ground strap.
2. Remove left side glove box and panel over pedals (three Phillips head screws).
3. Reach up behind switch and compress retaining tabs—remove switch from underneath and pull off electrical connectors.

Early Models

1. Disconnect battery ground strap.
2. Grip switch button on sides carefully and pull switch body out of opening.
3. Pull multi-connector plug off switch body.

NOTE: Indicator bulb inside switch can be replaced without removing switch body—just grip switch button on top and bottom and pop out: pull bulb straight out without twisting.

INSTRUMENT CLUSTER

1. Disconnect battery ground strap.
2. Remove left side glove box and panel over pedals (three Phillips screws).
3. Reach up behind instrument cluster and unscrew knurled nut on speedometer cable.
4. Unhook two securing springs on sides of instrument cluster (use

long, needle-nosed pliers or screwdriver with notch cut in side).
5. Push cluster out toward steering wheel then disconnect multiconnector plug, and remove cluster, Fig. 6.

SPEEDOMETER

1. Remove instrument cluster as described previously.
2. Remove small screws on back of speedometer housing and lift out speedometer.

WIPER MOTOR, REPLACE

1. Lift up hinged cap at base of wiper arms and remove retaining nuts.
2. Remove wiper arm assemblies and wiper shaft nuts and washers, Fig. 7.
3. Open engine compartment lid and remove battery ground strap.
4. Pull off multi-connector electrical plug on wiper motor and remove bolt on wiper frame bracket.

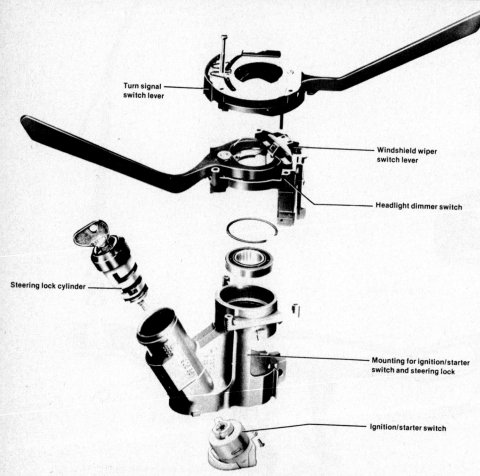

Turn signal switch lever

Windshield wiper switch lever

Headlight dimmer switch

Steering lock cylinder

Mounting for ignition/starter switch and steering lock

Ignition/starter switch

Fig. 8 Turn signal switch, wiper-washer switch & ignition lock. Rabbit & Scirocco

5. Pull wiper shafts down through body openings and remove frame. During reinstallation, make sure wiper blades are positioned about 1½ inches above bottom of windshield.

HEATER CORE, REPLACE

1. Drain engine coolant—disconnect bottom radiator hose.
2. Remove heater hoses at firewall: remove windshield washer container and ignition coil first.
3. Pull off heater control knobs and remove assembly (two screws under dash after removing middle "kick-panel").
4. Pull off wire connector from fresh air blower and unhook cable from temperature lever.
5. Use screwdriver to lever off housing clamp—lower housing with controls still attached.
6. Remove plastic cover on side of housing and slide out heater core.

Rabbit & Scirocco

DISTRIBUTOR, REPLACE

1. Remove distributor cap.
2. Rotate engine until rotor tip aligns with notch on distributor housing.
3. Disconnect vacuum advance line and electrical lead from coil.
4. Remove distributor hold-down bolt and retainer, then remove distributor.
5. Reverse procedure to install. Make sure that rotor tip is aligned with notch on distributor housing.

STARTER, REPLACE

1. Disconnect battery ground cable.
2. Disconnect wires from starter solenoid.
3. Remove starter bracket retaining nuts, or clamp, then remove starter retaining nuts and remove starter.
4. Reverse procedure to install.

ALTERNATOR, REPLACE

1. Disconnect battery ground cable.
2. Disconnect electrical connectors from alternator.

3. Loosen alternator adjusting bolt and remove belt from alternator pulley.
4. Remove alternator bolts, and then the alternator.
5. Reverse procedure to install.

ALTERNATOR ON VEHICLE TESTING

Test system with a tester connected according to specifications of the manufacturer. With engine running and a load resistance of 35 amps, the alternator output should be 12.5-14.5 volts.

TURN SIGNAL, WIPER-WASHER SWITCH, REPLACE

The switches for turn signals, high-low beams, windshield wiper, and electric washer are integrated in one unit on the steering column, Fig. 8.
1. Disconnect battery ground strap.
2. Pull off steering wheel center cover and remove steering wheel nut.

3. Remove steering wheel after centering.
4. Remove steering column lower cover and pull off multi-connector plugs.
5. Remove four screws and pull out turn signal/wiper switch assembly carefully.
6. Slide in new switch without force.
7. Install mounting screws and multi-connector plugs.
8. Install steering wheel in center position with cancelling lug on left.
9. Torque steering wheel nut to 5 mkg (36 ft. lbs.).
10. Install center cover and lower column cover.
11. Reconnect battery ground strap.
12. Check operation of horn and all column switches, including turn signal cancelling function.

NEUTRAL SAFETY SWITCH, REPLACE

1. Hold ignition key in "start" position and move shift lever to check that

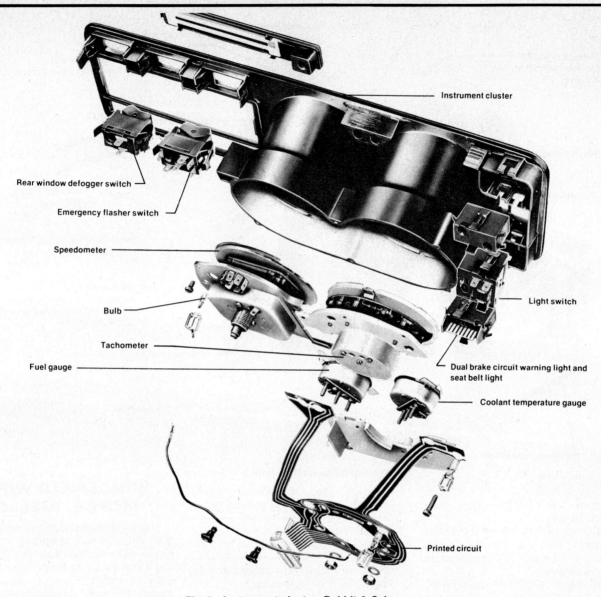

Instrument cluster

Rear window defogger switch

Emergency flasher switch

Speedometer

Bulb

Tachometer

Fuel gauge

Light switch

Dual brake circuit warning light and seat belt light

Coolant temperature gauge

Printed circuit

Fig. 9 Instrument cluster. Rabbit & Scirocco

starter operates only in "neutral" and "park."
2. If neutral safety function does not work properly, loosen set screw and remove shift lever handle.
3. Pop out lettered cover and inspect contact plate; replace if worn.
4. Adjust position of contact plate with mounting screws loose.
5. Tighten screws to re-check neutral safety function.

STOP LIGHT SWITCH, REPLACE

NOTE: These switches are easily accessible since the master cylinder is located in the left/rear of the engine compartment.

1. Remove electrical plug from switch.

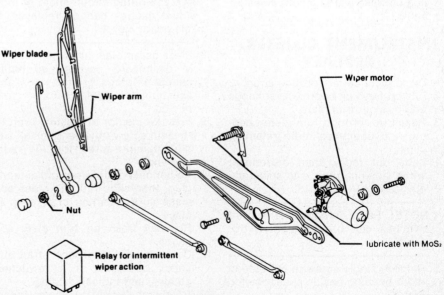

Wiper blade

Wiper arm

Wiper motor

Nut

Relay for intermittent wiper action

lubricate with MoS₂

Fig. 10 Wiper assembly. Rabbit & Scirocco

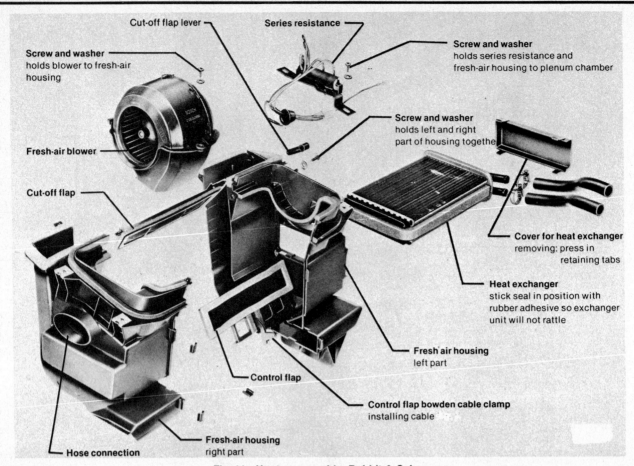

Cut-off flap lever

Series resistance

Screw and washer
holds blower to fresh-air housing

Screw and washer
holds series resistance and fresh-air housing to plenum chamber

Fresh-air blower

Screw and washer
holds left and right part of housing together

Cut-off flap

Cover for heat exchanger
removing: press in retaining tabs

Heat exchanger
stick seal in position with rubber adhesive so exchanger unit will not rattle

Fresh air housing
left part

Control flap

Control flap bowden cable clamp
installing cable

Fresh-air housing
right part

Hose connection

Fig. 11 Heater assembly. Rabbit & Scirocco

2. Unscrew old switch—hold new switch nearby.
3. Install new switch, if master cylinder is "open" less than three seconds, bleeding affected brake circuit is not necessary.
4. Install electrical plug on new switch.
5. Turn on ignition and check operation of brake warning light and stop lights.

INSTRUMENT CLUSTER, REPLACE

1. Disconnect battery ground strap.
2. Pull off fresh air control lever knobs and pop out trim plate.
3. Reach up through trim plate opening and compress radio retaining clips.
4. Slide out radio, then disconnect wires, antenna plug, and speedometer cable.

NOTE: Rear defogger or hazard switches can be replaced at this point.

5. Remove single screw in left side of radio opening beside speedometer, Fig. 1.
6. Pull out instrument cluster far

enough to disconnect multi-connector plugs and ground wires.

NOTE: Headlight switch can be replaced at this point.

7. Remove instrument cluster and lay face down on soft cloth.

NOTE: Printed circuit sheet or individual gauges can be replaced at this point, Fig. 9.

8. Place assembled instrument cluster in dashboard opening so multi-connector plugs, ground wires, and speedometer cable can be connected.
9. Press on center of cluster carefully to align screw holes and install single retaining screw through radio opening.
10. Re-connect radio wires and antenna plug, then slide radio in place and make sure retaining clips snap in place.
11. Reinstall fresh air trim plate and knobs.
12. Connect battery ground strap and check operation of all switches, gauges, and indicator lights.
13. Road-test vehicle to check speedometer.

WINDSHIELD WIPER MOTOR, REPLACE

The wiper motor can be removed with the wiper arms, operating rods, and frame still installed. If all four bolts holding wiper motor to frame are not accessible, operate ignition switch with wiper switch ON until linkage stops with all four bolts are accessible.

1. Remove multi-connector plug from motor located in "well" of rear of engine compartment.
2. Remove connecting rods from motor crank, leaving crank connected.
3. Remove four mounting bolts and remove wiper motor, Fig. 10.

When installing motor, check operation of wipers, including "park" position.

HEATER CORE, REPLACE

1. From in engine compartment, drain engine coolant by removing lower thermostat housing.
2. Disconnect two hoses behind heater control valve (by double grommet on rear firewall).
3. Remove heater cover and cut-off flap in center of "well" (rear of engine compartment).

4. Disconnect wiring and remove fan motor.
5. From inside passenger compartment, remove felt or cardboard panels under instrument panel.
6. Release retaining clips from sides of air housing located at underside of instrument panel.

7. Carefully remove air housing assembly, make sure heater core pipes come free without disturbing double grommet, Fig. 11.
8. Place assembly on floor with cables still attached.
9. Remove cover on left side of air housing and slide out heater core.

NOTE: When installing air housing assembly, make sure cables are routed correctly and hoses are connected securely. Refill system with clean coolant and recheck coolant level after engine is warm.

Gasoline Engine Section

ENGINE, REPLACE
Beetle & Bus

1. Disconnect battery ground cable, then remove air cleaner.
2. Disconnect all electrical wires from engine.
3. Disconnect cable from accelerator throttle linkage.
4. Remove hoses from fan housing and rear cover plate.
5. On Bus models, remove rear body panel.
6. On models with Automatic Stickshift, remove wires and hoses from shift control valve and oil pump.
7. Raise and support vehicle.
8. From underneath vehicle, disconnect fuel line from engine, then plug hose to prevent spillage of fuel.
9. On models with fuel injection, remove injectors from intake manifold. Leave lines connected.
10. Pull accelerator cable free of engine.
11. Disconnect heater cables from levers on engine heater boxes, then pull off heater hoses from front of engine heater boxes.
12. On models with Automatic Stickshift, remove the four bolts retaining torque converter to engine drive plate. Turn crankshaft to position each bolt in the transmission bell housing opening, Fig. 1.
13. Remove the two nuts from the lower engine mounting studs (manual transmission) or bolts (Automatic Stickshift), Fig. 2.
14. Remove the top engine bolt located behind clutch cable lever.
15. Slightly lower the vehicle and place floor jack under engine with jack pad contacting the oil strainer plate.
16. From inside engine compartment, remove the other top bolt located on right side in front of fan housing.
17. Pull engine to rearward until it clears the transmission mainshaft, while at the same time using the jack to lower the engine and remove it from vehicle.
18. Reverse procedure to install.

Volkswagen Dasher & Audi Fox

1. Disconnect battery ground cable and drain cooling system.
2. Remove air cleaner assembly and disconnect accelerator cable.
3. Disconnect clutch cable and then fuel hose. Plug hose to prevent spillage of fuel.
4. On 1974 models, detach relay/plate fuse box and bend harness clip open after loosening screws.

5. Disconnect heater control cable by pulling off clip.
6. Remove front engine mounting and support.
7. Disconnect all electrical wires from engine.
8. Loosen air duct attachments, mounting bolt and nut on side of support.
9. Loosen radiator grille mounting bracket bolt.
10. Remove starter.
11. Remove the engine mount nuts.
12. Remove the lower and loosen the upper transmission to engine bolts.
13. On vehicles with automatic transmission, remove the torque converter bolts.
14. Support transmission with tool 785/1 or other suitable device.
15. Using a chain hoist attached to engine, lift engine until transmission housing contacts steering drive.
16. Raise transmission support to this height, then remove engine to transmission upper bolts.
17. Pry engine/transmission mounting apart at joint and remove intermediate plate from engine.
18. Lift engine and carefully guide it out of engine compartment. Engine must be turned and lifted at same time to prevent damaging main drive shaft, clutch and body.
19. Reverse procedure to install.

Fig. 1   Converter bolt access hole location. Beetle & Bus

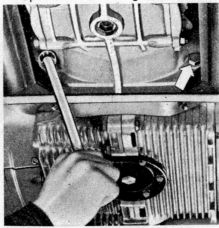

Fig. 2   Removing transmission to engine lower attachments. Beetle & Bus

Fig. 3   Removing push rod tube retaining clips. Beetle & Bus

1. Cam follower (8)
2. Exhaust valve (4)
3. Intake valve (4)
4. Pushrod tube (8)
5. Exhaust valve guide (4)
6. Intake valve guide (4)
7. Cylinder head (2)

8. Washer (16)
9. M 10 nut (16)
10. Oil deflector ring (8)
11. Valve spring (8)
12. Spring retainer (8)
13. Valve keeper (16)
14. Spring washer (8)

15. M 7 nut (8)
16. Black sealing ring (8)
17. Pushrod (8)
18. White sealing ring (8)
19. Deflector plate (2)
20. Washer (4)
21. M 6 fillister head screw
22. Washer (2)
23. M 5 fillister head screw
24. Support (8)
25. Exhaust rocker arm (4)

26. Thrust washer (discontinued in early 1974) (8)
27. Spacer spring (4)
28. Rocker shaft (4)
29. Intake rocker arm (4)
30. Adjusting screw (8)
31. M 8 nut (8)
32. Pushrod tube retaining wire (2)
33. Cylinder head cover gasket (2)
34. Cylinder head cover (2)

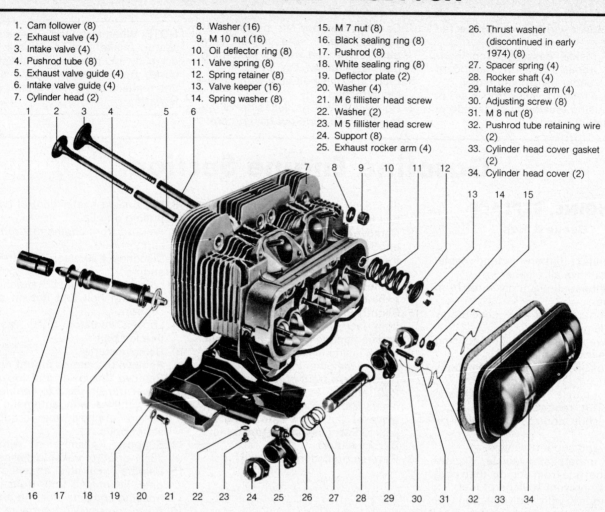

Fig. 4   Cylinder head disassembled. Beetle & Bus

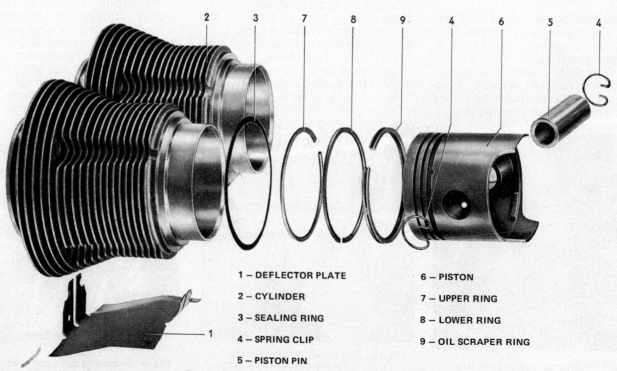

1 – DEFLECTOR PLATE

2 – CYLINDER

3 – SEALING RING

4 – SPRING CLIP

5 – PISTON PIN

6 – PISTON

7 – UPPER RING

8 – LOWER RING

9 – OIL SCRAPER RING

Fig. 5   Piston & cylinder assembly. Beetle & Bus

1. Oil filter mounting flange
2. M 8 nut (2)
3. Spring washer (2)
4. Oil cooler seal (2)
5. Oil pressure switch
6. Breather seal
7. Oil breather
8. Oil pressure control valve plunger*

* Discontinued after November 1975.

9. Oil pressure control valve spring*
10. Sealing ring*
11. Control valve plug*
12. Rubber bellows
13. Oil pump bearing plate
14. Oil pump driven gear
15. Oil pump drive gearshaft
16. Oil filler pipe

17. Oil dipstick
18. Oil filler clamp
19. Oil filler with cover
20. Oil cooler
21. Washer (3)
22. Spring washer (3)
23. M 6 nut (3)
24. Sealing ring
25. Plug
26. Oil filter
27. Oil strainer gasket (2)
28. Oil strainer
29. Oil strainer cover
30. Drain plug seal
31. Oil drain plug
32. Relief valve plug

33. Sealing ring
34. Oil pressure relief valve spring
35. Oil pressure relief valve plunger
36. Filter flange gasket
37. Oil filler pipe gasket
38. Oil pump gasket
39. Spring washer (2)
40. M 8 nut (2)
41. Oil pump O-ring
42. M 6 self-locking nut
43. Spring washer (4)
44. Oil pump housing
45. Spring washer (4)
46. M 8 nut (4)

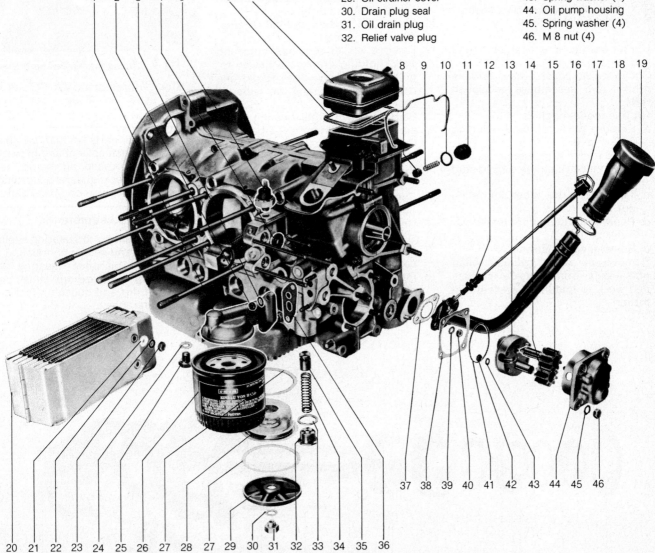

Fig. 6 Engine crankcase. Beetle equipped with fuel injection & Bus

Rabbit & Scirocco

1. Disconnect battery ground cable, then drain cooling system by removing bottom radiator hose flange.
2. Remove radiator and air cleaner assembly. On models with fuel injection, remove mixture control unit with injectors.
3. Disconnect all wires, hoses, lines and cables from engine.
4. Remove transmission assembly, then disconnect exhaust pipe from manifold.
5. Remove left-side engine mount bolts.
6. Using a suitable hoist, remove engine.
7. Reverse procedure to install.

BEETLE & BUS ENGINE SERVICE
Disassemble

1. Remove all remaining external parts from engine.
2. Unbolt clutch and flywheel assembly.

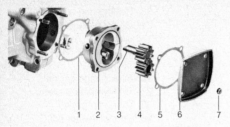

1. Housing gasket
2. Oil pump housing
3. Oil pump drive gearshaft
4. Oil pump driven gear
5. Cover gasket
6. Oil pump cover
7. Sealing nut

Fig. 7 Oil pump disassembled. Beetle less fuel injection

3. Unbolt muffler and heat exchange boxes.
4. Unclip valve covers then, remove rocker arm assemblies and push rods.
5. On Bus model engines:
   a. Remove push rod tube retaining wire, Fig. 3.
   b. Store rocker arm assemblies with homemade retaining pins in stud holes.
   c. Twist push rod tubes and slide out.
   d. Remove air deflectors under cylinder barrels.
   e. Remove cam followers.
6. Remove all eight cylinder head nuts—start from outside corners and work to middle to prevent distortion.

7. Lift off cylinder heads, Fig. 4. (Beetle only: remove push rod tubes and air deflector plates at this point also.)
8. Mark cylinder number on each barrel, then slide off cylinder barrels, Fig. 5.
9. Remove all eight piston pin circlips. If ridge has formed on outside of circlip groove, scrape clean before removing pins.
10. Tap out piston pins carefully and remove pistons—warm piston slightly if pin is tight.
11. Unbolt oil cooler and oil strainer plate with screen.
12. Remove all 13 mm hex nuts and bolts holding crankcase halves together. (Bus only: don't forget one behind flywheel and on side of case.)
13. Remove six large sealing nuts around cylinder openings. (Through-bolts on Bus engine: hold other end also.)
14. Now remove oil pump housing nuts and slide out housing, Figs. 6 and 7.
15. Separate crankcase halves, then lift out camshaft and crankshaft, Fig. 8.
16. Unscrew oil control valve plugs: slide out pistons and springs.
17. Remove connecting rod nuts and separate caps.
18. Remove crankshaft circlip and press off gears with bearing "splitter" or suitable pieces of "flat

Fig. 9 Timing marks. Beetle & Bus

stock." (press plate VW 402 can also be used on Beetle crankshaft), Fig. 8.

NOTE: All parts should be rinsed clean in fresh solvent and blown dry with compressed air before reassembly. Check all parts according to dimensions given on specs chart.

Assemble

1. Dip connecting rod bearing shells in clean oil and seat in connecting rod "halves"—oil under bearing shell will help "squeeze out" small particles of dirt and doesn't affect bearing clearance.

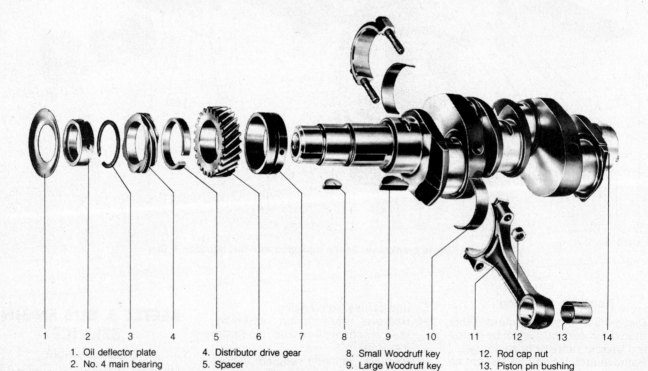

1. Oil deflector plate
2. No. 4 main bearing
3. Circlip
4. Distributor drive gear
5. Spacer
6. Crankshaft gear
7. No. 3 main bearing
8. Small Woodruff key
9. Large Woodruff key
10. Rod bearing shell
11. Connecting rod
12. Rod cap nut
13. Piston pin bushing
14. Crankshaft

Fig. 8 Crankshaft, exploded view. Beetle & Bus

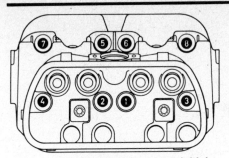

Fig. 10 Cylinder head stud nut initial tightening sequence. Beetle less fuel injection

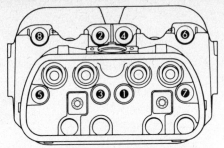

Fig. 11 Cylinder head stud nut final tightening sequence. Beetle less fuel injection

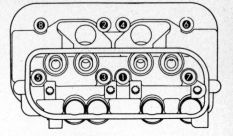

Fig. 12 Cylinder head stud nut tightening sequence. Beetle with fuel injection & Bus

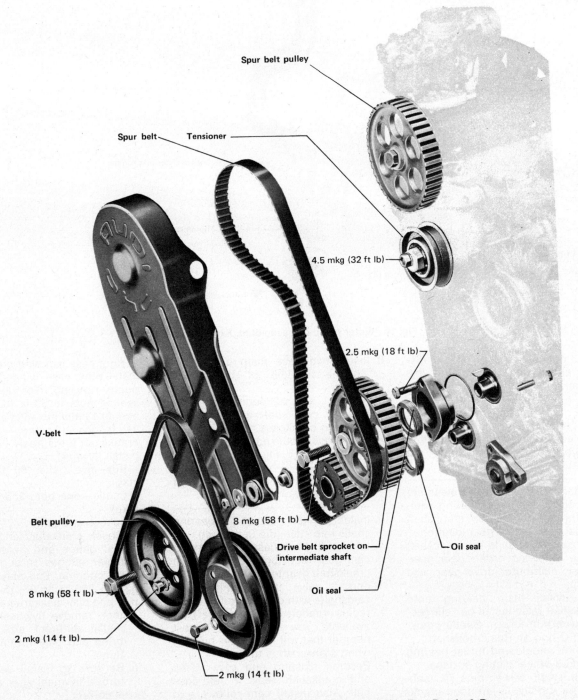

Spur belt pulley

Spur belt   Tensioner

4.5 mkg (32 ft lb)

V-belt

2.5 mkg (18 ft lb)

8 mkg (58 ft lb)

Belt pulley

Drive belt sprocket on intermediate shaft

Oil seal

Oil seal

8 mkg (58 ft lb)

2 mkg (14 ft lb)

2 mkg (14 ft lb)

Fig. 13   Engine front cover, timing belt, sprockets pulleys & belts. Exc. Beetle & Bus

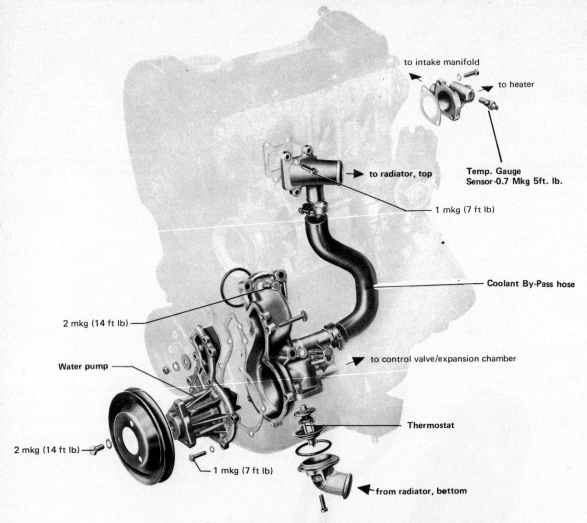

to intake manifold

to heater

to radiator, top

Temp. Gauge
Sensor-0.7 Mkg 5ft. lb.

1 mkg (7 ft lb)

Coolant By-Pass hose

2 mkg (14 ft lb)

to control valve/expansion chamber

Water pump

Thermostat

2 mkg (14 ft lb)

1 mkg (7 ft lb)

from radiator, bottom

Fig. 14   Water pump disassembled. Exc. Beetle & Bus

2. Install connecting rods onto crankshaft and torque nuts to 25 ft. lbs. (3½ mkg).

NOTE: Connecting rod casting "lug" should face up on fully assembled Beetle engine. Installation direction on the Bus engine is not critical.

3. Dip new main bearings in clean engine oil. Install large bearing without thrust shoulder on crankshaft journal beside cam gear location.

4. Heat gears and slide on crankshaft in the following order: cam gear, spacer, distributor drive gear, and circlip.

5. Slide small main bearing onto crankshaft (also install oil "slinger" and woodruff key on Beetle crankshaft; O-ring on Bus crankshaft.)

6. Slide on shouldered thrust bearing behind flywheel mating surface.

7. Install small dowel pins in main bearing saddles in left-hand crankcase half.

8. Install two-piece main bearing in "middle" saddle of both case halves.

9. Hold #1 and #2 connecting rods and lay crankshaft assembly into left-hand crankcase half. Number 3 and 4 rods should hang through cylinder openings, Fig. 9.

NOTE: Rotate bearings to seat dowel pins before continuing.

10. Install all six camshaft bearing shells into case (dip in oil first).

11. Lay camshaft in case with mark on cam gear tooth between marks on crankshaft gear teeth (marks ensure correct valve timing), Fig. 9. *If camshafts with different pitch circle radius numbers (on side of gear) are available, use shaft with largest number that will fit without binding when crankshaft is turned.

12. Position existing end play shims and crankshaft seals in left case half. Also install cam followers in Beetle engine case. Hold followers

in right case half with grease.

13. Install other case half and slide in oil pump housing: Torque six large sealing nuts to 23 ft. lb. (3.2 mkg) and all 13 mm hex nuts and bolts to 14 ft. lbs. (2 mkg)—check that crankshaft turns freely.

14. Install flywheel:
    Bus—five bolts: 80 ft. lbs. (11 mkg)
    Beetle—one bolt: 253 ft. lbs. (35 mkg)

15. To check end play:
    a. Check crankshaft end play with dial gauge and holder or with feeler gauges through cylinder #3 opening. End play should be .003-.006 inch (.07-.15 mm).
    b. If end play measurement is incorrect, remove flywheel and seal. Install different size shims to bring end play within specifications.
    c. Be sure to install seal and retorque flywheel after adjustment is correct.

16. Use ring expander to install rings on

pistons—manufacturer's markings should face toward combustion chamber.

17. Install pistons on connecting rods: arrows on piston crown should face toward flywheel (do not forget all eight piston pin circlips).
18. Use piston ring compressor to install cylinder barrels—seat barrels against crankcase without sealing gasket (gaskets are still provided in some overhaul kits, but have been discontinued to *improve* sealing).
19. Install cylinder heads (On Beetle engine, install air deflector plates and push rod tubes first.)
20. Torque cylinder head nuts to 23 ft. lbs. (3 mkg) in sequence shown in Figs. 10, 11 and 12. Beetle with 8 mm cylinder studs—18 ft. lbs. (2½ mkg).

NOTE: Over-torquing cylinder head nuts causes cylinder head leakage; thermal expansion of aluminum head increases torque and can pull out studs or "dig in" barrel.

21. On Bus models, install air deflector shields, cam followers, and push rod tubes.
22. Install push rods and rocker arm assemblies. Adjust valve clearance between adjuster and valve stem end to specifications at TDC position.
23. Install distributor drive gear with shims so that distance from top of drive gear to case surface is 1.76 in. (44.6 mm), Fig. 13. Refer to Fig. 14 for installation angle direction of distributor drive gear slot.

NOTE: Hold shim to bottom of distributor drive gear with grease before installation on Bus. Shim(s) must be installed before distributor drive on Beetle: place shim on long screwdriver, place screwdriver in bore, and drop shim in bore carefully—this prevents losing shim inside case.

24. With crankshaft still at TDC, insert distributor and turn rotor until drive is seated—now turn distributor body counterclockwise until ignition points just begin to open and tighten clamp bolt.
25. Install cooling air ducts and heat exchange boxes.
26. Fit fan housing (with alternator).
27. Install fan hub: 23 ft. lbs. (3 mkg) and fan: 14 ft. lbs. (2 mkg)—Bus. Install crankshaft pulley: 36 ft. lbs. (5 mkg)—Beetle.
28. Install fan belt—adjust belt tension. (½ inch deflection).
29. Bolt on muffler.

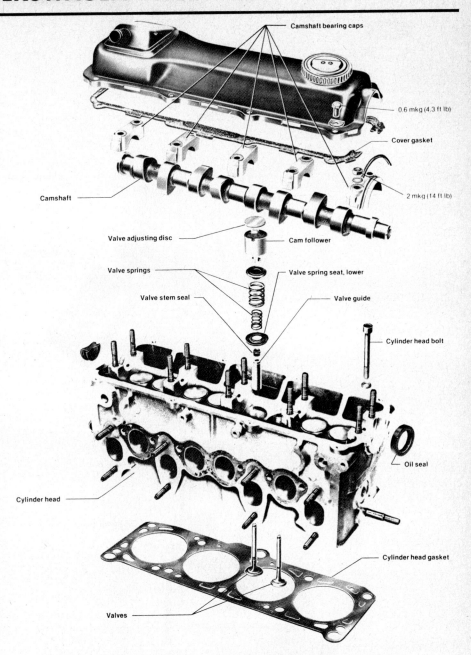

Fig. 15 Cylinder head disassembled (Typical of diesel). Exc. Beetle & Bus

Cylinder Head Service

1. Remove cylinder heads from engine as previously described, Fig. 4.
2. Compress valve springs with suitable valve spring compressor and remove keepers with small magnet.
3. Remove retainers, springs, and valves.
4. Insert good valve (stem lightly oiled) in guide until stem end is flush with rocker arm end of guide. Cap end of guide with finger and pull out valve quickly. If "popping" sound is heard, valve guide is good. If valve does not "pop," guide should be extracted and replaced (valves can be checked with a dial gauge according to specifications, but "quick-check" will produce same results.)
5. To remove worn guides, cut thread in rocker arm end of guide about ½ inch deep using ⅜ inch or 10 mm tap: now install soft threaded rod in guide and place old piston pin around rod; place flat washer on wrist pin and screw on nut until valve guide has been extracted into pin.

CAUTION: Do not hammer out guides from combustion chamber side as guide end can "mushroom" and enlarge hole in cylinder head so

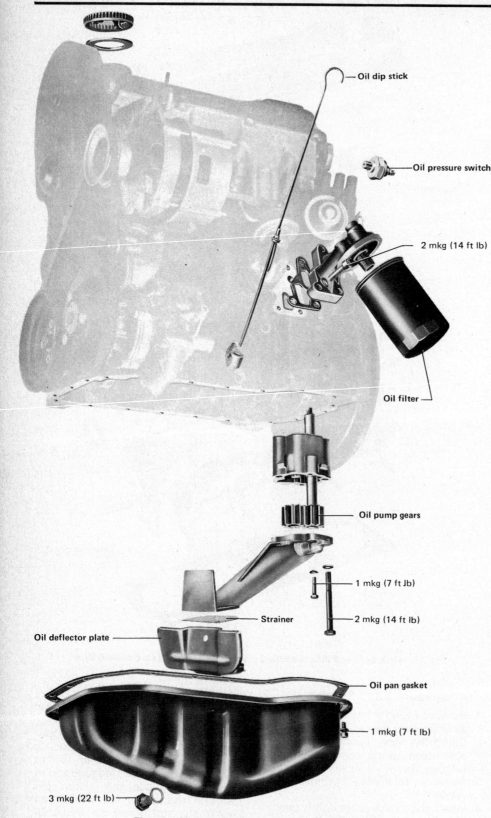

Fig. 16 Oil pump, pan & filter. Exc. Beetle & Bus

Oil dip stick

Oil pressure switch

2 mkg (14 ft lb)

Oil filter

Oil pump gears

1 mkg (7 ft lb)

2 mkg (14 ft lb)

Strainer

Oil deflector plate

Oil pan gasket

1 mkg (7 ft lb)

3 mkg (22 ft lb)

that new guide does not fit tightly.

6. Press in new guides using angle plate. Press should register at least one ton force.

NOTE: Oversize guides are available but require special machine work for proper fit.

7. Check inside diameter of installed guide with reamer (standard size guides usually do not require reaming).
8. Now install seat re-facing pilot in valve guide.
9. Re-face valve seat to 45° angle and check with seat run-out gauge if possible (30° angle on Bus intake seats)
10. Correct seat width to 1½-2½ mm (.060-.100″) if necessary with 15° cutter.
11. Reface valve contact angle to 45° (30° for Bus intake valves) and reface stem end.
12. Valve "margin" should be at least .020 in. (.5 mm)
13. Check spark plug threads and install helicoil inserts if threads are damaged (use bushing inserts only for emergency repairs with engine in car).
14. Make sure heads and parts are rinsed clean in fresh solvent. Oil valve stems and place in guides (although valve seals are included in some repair kits, do *not* use them on horizontally-opposed air-cooled engines).
15. Install valve springs (if spring is progressively wound, place closely wound coils next to head).
16. Install retainers, compress springs, and install valve keepers.

DASHER, AUDI-FOX, RABBIT & SCIROCCO ENGINE SERVICE
Disassemble

1. Remove engine from car as previously described and drain oil and coolant.
2. Mount engine in engine stand.
3. Loosen alternator mounting bolt and remove V-belt, Fig. 13.
4. Unbolt spur belt cover and valve cover.
5. Remove belt tensioner and spur belt.
6. Unbolt both intake and exhaust manifolds.
7. Remove coolant by-pass hose and spark plug wires, Fig. 14.
8. Remove cylinder head bolts—start from outside and work toward center (ten 10 mm socket head bolts)—set cylinder head aside, Fig. 15.
9. Remove alternator mounting bolts, ground strap, and alternator.
10. Remove both V-belt pulleys (use flywheel lock for crankshaft pulley and screwdriver to lock water pump shaft,) Fig. 13.
11. Remove water pump housing (13 mm hex bolts) Fig. 14.

12. Unscrew oil filter element and re-move flange, Fig. 16.
13. Unbolt distributor clamp and re-move distributor.
14. Turn engine over and remove oil pan, Fig. 16.
15. Unbolt oil pump housing and slide out assembly.
16. Unbolt connecting rod caps and remove by tapping on bolts with brass drift or hammer handle, Fig. 17.
17. Push connecting rod and piston as-semblies out of block.
18. Lock flywheel and loosen spur belt pulley nut on crankshaft.
19. Slide off spur belt pulley and re-move crankshaft seal holder, Fig. 18.
20. Unbolt flywheel and clutch assem-bly—remove flywheel seal holder.
21. Unbolt main bearing caps and lift out crankshaft.
22. Lock intermediate shaft pulley with screwdriver and loosen bolt.
23. Slide off pulley and unbolt inter-mediate shaft seal holder.
24. Slide out intermediate shaft—reach inside engine block and support shaft so distributor drive gear does not damage bearing.

Engine block and all parts must be rinsed clean in fresh solvent before reassembly. Check all parts for wear marks and check clearances according to specs chart.

Assemble

1. Slide in intermediate shaft carefully and install seal cover (torque to 2 mkg—14 ft. lbs.): check for slight in-termediate shaft end play, Fig. 18.
2. Seat grooved main bearing shells in "saddles" in engine block (shoul-dered bearing in center)—coat with oil, Fig. 18.
3. Lay crankshaft in bearings, Fig. 18.
4. Seat ungrooved main bearing shells in main caps and install caps in block—numbers on caps should face *away* from oil pump: #1 on spur belt side to #5 on clutch side.
5. Screw in main bearing cap bolts finger tight and shake crankshaft back and forth to center shouldered thrust bearing.
6. Torque main bearing cap bolts to 47 ft. lbs. (6.5 mkg).
7. Check with feeler gauge for .03-.17 mm (.001-.007 in.) crankshaft end play—also turn crankshaft to check for free movement.
8. Use ring expander to install piston rings on pistons, chromed ring nearest cylinder head and manufac-turer's markings on all rings facing cylinder head, Fig. 17.

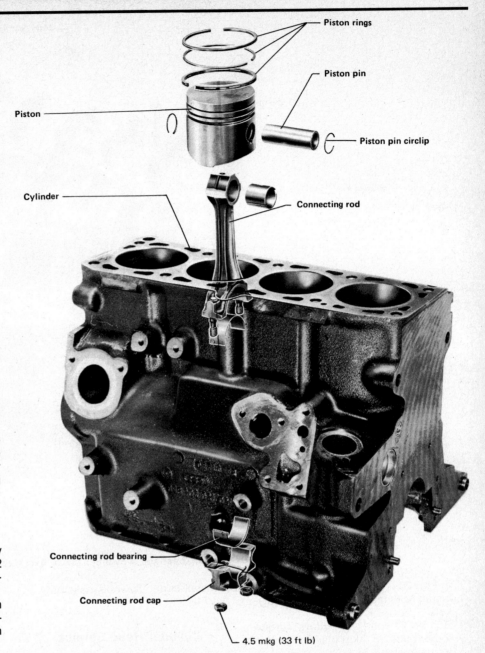

Fig. 17   Piston, connector rod & cylinder block. Exc. Beetle & Bus

9. Install pistons on connecting rods—warm piston carefully if pis-ton pin is tight—don't forget both piston pin circlips.
10. Install rod bearing shell in each connecting rod with protective piece of rubber hose over each rod bolt.
11. Position engine block on side: use ring compressor to install piston and rod assembly in block—make sure arrow marking on each piston crown faces toward spur belt.
12. Check that rods seat on crankshaft journals—remove protective pieces of rubber hose and install rod caps with remaining bearing shells.
13. Torque connecting rod nuts to 33 ft.

lbs. (4.5 mkg) and check that crank-shaft still turns freely.
14. Assemble oil pump gears and hous-ing and install on block—(torque 13 mm hex bolts to 14 ft. lbs. (2 mkg), Fig. 16.
15. Install "flywheel" seal holder and oil pan: torque pan bolts to 14 ft. lbs. (2 mkg).
16. Place engine block in upright position—lay head gasket on block: make sure camshaft oil supply hole in gasket and block are realigned.
17. Lay assembled cylinder head on gasket—cylinder head bolts act as locating pins—torque head bolts to 54 ft. lbs. (7.5 mkg) 1 mkg higher on diesel models, in sequence shown

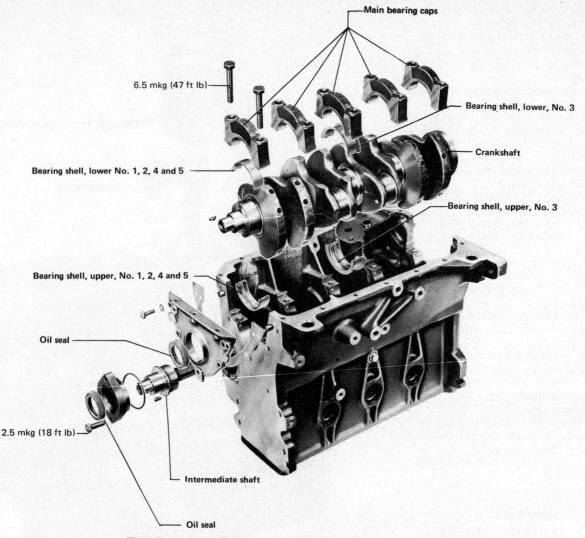

Fig. 18 Crankshaft, bearings & cylinder block. Exc. Beetle & Bus

Labels in figure:
- Main bearing caps
- 6.5 mkg (47 ft lb)
- Bearing shell, lower, No. 3
- Bearing shell, lower No. 1, 2, 4 and 5
- Crankshaft
- Bearing shell, upper, No. 3
- Bearing shell, upper, No. 1, 2, 4 and 5
- Oil seal
- 2.5 mkg (18 ft lb)
- Intermediate shaft
- Oil seal

in Fig. 20.

18. Install both manifolds with new gaskets.

19. Bolt on all spur belt pulleys: torque to 58 ft. lbs. (8 mkg) diesel injection pump pulley—33 ft. lbs. (4.5 mkg), Fig. 13.

20. Position camshaft at cylinder #1 TDC and crankshaft at TDC mark: install spur belt carefully and set tensioner (torque tensioner to 4.5 mkg)—install spur belt cover.

21. Install water pump, alternator, V-belt pulleys, and V-belt—set V-belt tension and tighten alternator mounting bolt (don't forget alternator ground strap)

22. With engine still positioned at cylinder #1 TDC, install distributor so that rotor is aligned with mark on distributor body: rotate distributor body until ignition points just open, then tighten hold-down clamp.

23. Install coolant by-pass hose, thermostat with housing, and oil filter flange with element. Fig. 14.

24. Install clutch/flywheel assembly.

Cylinder Head Service

1. Remove cylinder head from engine as previously described, Fig. 15.

2. Turn camshaft to cylinder #1 "TDC."

3. Remove cam bearing caps 1, 3, and 5, Fig. 19.

4. Loosen cam bearing caps 2 and 4, Fig. 19, carefully until valve spring tension is released—remove caps, camshaft, and cam followers, Fig. 15.

5. Depress spring retainers with valve spring compressor. Be careful not to damage cam follower bores.

6. Remove spring retainers, springs, and spring seats.

7. Check valve "rock" with dial indicator gauge. Valve stem should be flush with top of guide during checking.

8. If valve rock is more than .040 in.

(1 mm) press out worn valve guides from combustion chamber side of head using stepped drift tool (VW 10-206)

9. Press in new guides from camshaft side of head until guide shoulder "bottoms" on cylinder head.

10. Hand-ream guides with tool 10-215. Use cutting oil.

11. Install valve seat refacing pilot properly.

12. Reface seats to 45°—check with seat run-out gauge if possible.

13. Use 30° cutter to "narrow" valve seat to proper width: intake—2 mm (.080 in.), exhaust—2.4 mm (.094 in.)

14. Replace valves if stem bearing surface is visibly worn or if valve head is "burned."

15. Reface valve contact angle to 45°— valve margin must be at least .5 mm (.020 in.)

16. Oil valve stem and install valves in cylinder head without "lapping." If refacing is done properly, lapping is not necessary. If refacing is not

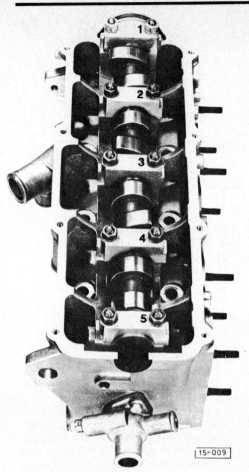

Fig. 19 Camshaft & bearing caps. Exc. Beetle & Bus

Fig. 20 Cylinder head bolt tightening sequence. Exc. Beetle & Bus

done properly, lapping valves and seats will not correct the problem.

NOTE: Because of the critical compression ratio on diesel engines, check distance between head gasket surface and valve face at this point. Distance must be no more than 1.5 mm (.060 in.) If dimension is too great with new valve installed, cylinder head must be replaced.

17. Install spring seats, new valve seats, springs, retainers, and keepers.
18. Insert cam followers with valve adjustment shims in place.
19. Lay camshaft in position and bolt down cam caps 2 and 4 carefully and evenly.
20. Install remaining cam caps and torque all cap nuts to 14 ft. lbs. (2 mkg).
21. Check valve clearance between each lobe and adjustment shim with feeler gauges. Turn camshaft to "TDC" position to check each pair of valves. Adjust to specifications,

Thickness	Part Number	Thickness	Part Number
3.00	056 109 555	3.65	056 109 568
3.05	056 109 556	3.70	056 109 569
3.10	056 109 557	3.75	056 109 570
3.15	056 109 558	3.80	056 109 571
3.20	056 109 559	3.85	056 109 572
3.25	056 109 560	3.90	056 109 573
3.30	056 109 561	3.95	056 109 594
3.35	056 109 562	4.00	056 109 575
3.40	056 109 563	4.05	056 109 576
3.45	056 109 564	4.10	056 109 577
3.50	056 109 565	4.15	056 109 578
3.55	056 109 566	4.20	056 109 579
3.60	056 109 567	4.25	056 109 580

Thickness of valve adjusting disc is etched on underside.
When installing make sure that etching faces toward cam follower.

Fig. 21 Valve adjusting shim chart. Exc. Beetle & Bus

by selecting the correct shim, Fig. 21.

If clearance is too small, use thinner shim; if clearance is too large, use thicker shim.

NOTE: If clearance is too small with smallest shim (3 mm) and new valves, special valves which are .5 mm shorter must be installed (do not shorten standard valve since stem end is specially hardened).

Diesel Engine Section

ENGINE, REPLACE

1. Disconnect battery ground cable.
2. Open heater valve, then drain cooling system.
3. Remove radiator, fan and alternator.
4. Disconnect fuel filter from body of vehicle, then disconnect fuel supply line and return line from injection pump.
5. Disconnect accelerator cable from pump lever and remove injection pump with bracket.
6. Disconnect wires from stop control, glow plugs, oil pressure switch, coolant sensor, starter and back-up light switch.
7. Remove front transmission mount and disconnect clutch cable.
8. Remove relay lever, then disconnect connecting rod from transmission and turn relay shaft rearward.
9. Disconnect selector rod and remove support.
10. Disconnect exhaust pipe from manifold and remove rear transmission mount.
11. Attach a suitable hoist to engine and raise engine slightly, then remove left transmission mount and right engine mount.
12. Carefully guide engine and remove from vehicle.
13. To separate engine from transmission, remove plug from transmission, then turn flywheel to align recess in flywheel with hole in transmission housing. Remove cover plate over driveshaft flange, then remove engine to transmission bolts and separate the assemblies.
14. Reverse procedure to install while noting the following:
    a. When attaching engine to transmission, turn flywheel so that recess in flywheel is level with drive shaft flange.
    b. Torque engine to transmission bolts to 40 ft. lbs., and drive shaft flange bolts to 33 ft. lbs.

DIESEL FUEL SYSTEM

Fuel is drawn through the filter from the tank by the injection pump, Fig. 1. The injection pump meters and distributes fuel under pressure to the injectors in the correct firing order.

Excess fuel from the pump and injectors returns to the tank via a separate line.

The fuel circulation cools and lubricates the injection pump and injectors and also warms the fuel in the tank slightly to help prevent wax formation during cold weather.

Injectors

Diesel injectors spray fuel directly into the combustion chamber near the end of each compression stroke, Fig. 2. The injectors are threaded into the cylinder head and are subject to the direct heat of combustion like a gasoline engine spark plug. Each injector is protected by a heat shield between the cylinder head and injector body. The heat shield acts as an insulating and sealing washer.

Fuel pressure from the injection

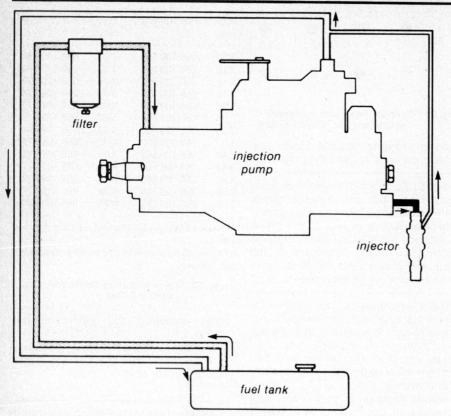

Fig. 1   Fuel system

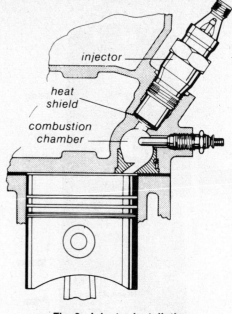

Fig. 2   Injector installation

pump forces the needle up against spring pressure so that the injector sprays a cone-shaped mist of diesel fuel at the proper time. A small quantity of fuel leaks around the injector needle to lubricate and cool the injector: this fuel returns to the tank via a separate fuel line, Fig. 3.

Removal & Testing

Always keep hands away from the nozzle end of the injector when it is mounted in the "pop" tester: the high-pressure spray can penetrate skin and cause blood poisoning.

1. Clean fuel connections and area around injectors with compressed air.
2. Remove injector lines as a unit (use 17 mm open end wrench).
3. Remove injectors with 27 mm deep-well socket.
4. Install injector on "pop" tester (use US 1322 or equivalent) and make sure knob is closed, Fig. 4.

5. Operate gauge lever with rapid strokes to prime tester and injector: check that injector sprays with compact, even cone pattern.
6. Operate lever with slow strokes: injector should make "creaking" sound if nozzle is in good condition.
7. Turn knob out to open gauge and operate lever slowly: note gauge reading when injector begins to spray which should be 1706-1849 psi.
8. Operate lever carefully to hold 1563 psi. The injector should not drip in 15 seconds.

Installation

1. Install new injector heat shields with larger diameter sealing surface facing injector, Fig. 5.
2. Install injectors in cylinder head and torque to 51 ft. lbs.

Repair

1. Invert injector and hold in vise: grip upper body along flats.
2. Remove lower body carefully with 27 deep-well socket.
3. Check visually that needle and nozzle are in good condition; clean in solvent or replace needle-nozzle unit.

NOTE: Brass scrapers and brushes could be used to remove hardened "coke" deposits on high-mileage vehicles, but must be done very

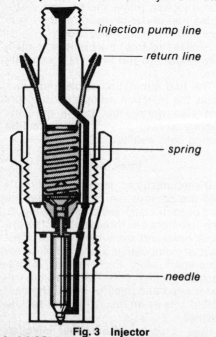

Fig. 3   Injector

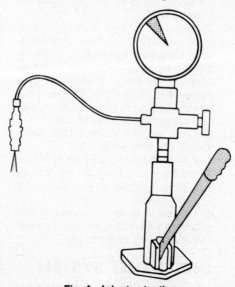

Fig. 4   Injector testing

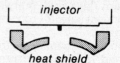

Fig. 5   Heat shield installation

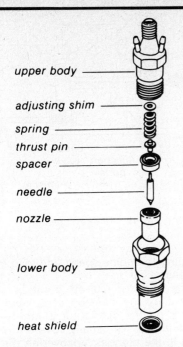

Fig. 6 Injector disassembled

carefully to avoid damaging the needle or nozzle.

4. Correct opening pressure if necessary: check shim thickness with micrometer and substitute different shim—each .5 mm shim thickness changes opening pressure about 71 psi.
5. Install all six internal parts in upper body as shown in Fig. 6.
6. Install and torque lower body to 51 ft. lbs. Recheck injector on tester.

NOTE: Always use new heat shields when reinstalling injectors, compression leaks can occur if heat shields are reused, or if injectors are torqued improperly.

CHECKING ENGINE COMPRESSION

1. Remove fuel shut-off solenoid wire

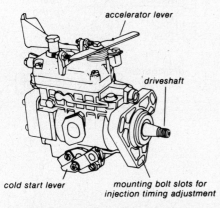

Fig. 9 Injection pump, rear view

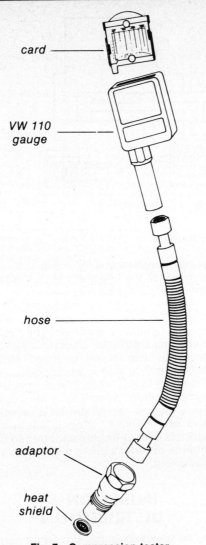

Fig. 7 Compression tester

on injection pump and insulate end.

NOTE: This prevents mechanical fuel pump from spraying fuel during cranking. Be sure that wire connector does not touch any conductor in engine compartment.

2. Remove three heat shields so that compression force during cranking does not blow them out.
3. Installed threaded adapter into injector opening with remaining heat shield and install VW1110 gauge assembly into adapter, Fig. 7.
4. Crank engine until gauge reaches highest reading: note reading, then release pressure.
5. Repeat procedure on remaining cylinders, making sure recording card advances for each reading.

NOTE: Be sure to use old heat shield to seal gauge and don't forget to remove loose heat shield after each check.

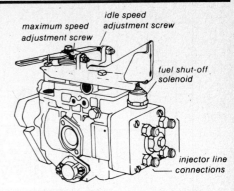

Fig. 8 Injection pump, front view

6. Readings should all be between 400-500 psi. Readings should also be within 71 psi.
   a. Low readings on adjacent cylinders can mean head gasket leakage between cylinders.
   b. Low readings on one cylinder usually mean valve leakage.
   c. Low readings on all cylinders could mean worn piston rings.
7. A low cylinder can be checked again after squirting about a tablespoon of engine oil onto the piston through the injector opening:
   a. If the compression reading remains low during the 2nd check, the cause is probably burnt or improperly seated valves.
   b. If the second reading increases, piston rings are probably worn.

INJECTION PUMP

The injection pump is a single-plunger mechanical pump, Figs. 8 and 9, which meters and distributes fuel to the injectors in the correct firing order. The pump is driven by the camshaft spur belt at one-half engine speed. All moving parts inside the pump are lubricated by diesel fuel so the pump is maintenance-free; diesel pumps operate reliably for a long time if clean fuel is

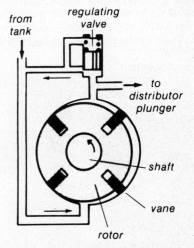

Fig. 10 Vane pump

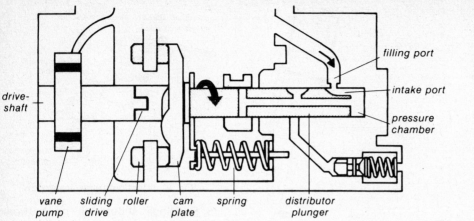

drive-shaft

filling port

intake port

pressure chamber

vane pump · sliding drive · roller · cam plate · spring · distributor plunger

Fig. 11 Plunger & rollers

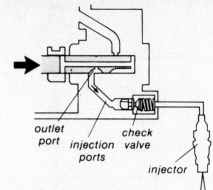

outlet port

injection ports

check valve

injector

Fig. 12 Plunger injection

used. Idle speed, maximum speed, and injection timing can be adjusted with workshop equipment; the fuel shut-off solenoid can be replaced separately, but any internal problem means replacement of the pump. Since diesel pumps should not be disassembled, normal shopwork consists only of trouble-shooting to determine whether a pump might need replacement.

Vane Pump

The rotary-vane pump inside the injection pump draws fuel through the filter from the tank and supplies it to the distributor plunger, Fig. 10. The vane pump is driven by the engine camshaft spur belt. As the rotor spins, centrifugal force holds the vanes against the walls of the pressure chamber—the off-center layout of the rotor and pressure chamber "squeezes" fuel trapped between the vanes and forces it out the delivery port.

Vane pump delivery pressure varies from 3-7 bar depending on engine speed and is controlled by the regulating valve. The relief port is actually a series of small holes which open progressively to allow vane pump pressure to vary with engine speed. Vane pump pressure: lubricates moving parts in the

pump; supplies fuel to the distributor plunger for the injector; controls injection timing advance mechanism.

Injection pump manufacturers use a special test "bench" to set and check internal pump pressures. The vane pump and distributor plunger injection pressures cannot be checked easily with normal workshop equipment.

If clean fuel is used, diesel injection pumps operate reliably for a long time. Diesel pumps should not be disassembled or "adjusted." Normal shopwork consists only of trouble-shooting to determine whether a pump might need replacement.

INJECTION & DISTRIBUTION

The injection pump driveshaft turns the vane pump, distributor plunger, and cam plate as a unit. Springs hold the cam plate against stationary rollers—in this way, the plunger also moves back and forth as it turns.

Whenever an intake port in the plunger is in line with the filling port in the pump body, fuel from the vane pump fills the pressure chamber, Fig. 11. As the plunger turns, the intake port is covered up so that fuel is trapped in the pressure chamber, now the cam plate and rollers push the plunger and pressurize the fuel to about 1800 psi.

As the plunger continues to turn, the outlet port in the plunger lines up with the injection passage in the pump body, opening the check valve and supplying high-pressure fuel to the injector, Fig. 12.

The pump and plunger are designed with ports to supply each injector with fuel in the proper firing order, Fig. 13.

Fuel Metering

The amount of fuel is controlled by changing the injection cut-off point ac-

cording to engine speed and load conditions.

The injection cut-off point is controlled by the position of a metering sleeve on the distributor plunger—the metering sleeve usually covers a relief port in the plunger: uncovering the relief port stops injection. The position of the metering sleeve is controlled by linkage connected to a centrifugal governor and also to the accelerator pedal.

STARTING—When the engine is not running, the leaf spring presses the starting lever to the left so that the metering sleeve moves to the right. The distributor plunger must move farther before the relief port is exposed; injection lasts longer so that more fuel is supplied during starting, Fig. 14.

IDLE—At idle speed, the weights in the centrifugal governor are partly expanded so the governor sleeve moves to the right. The starting lever is pushed against the control lever so the metering sleeve moves to the left. The distributor plunger now moves a short distance before the relief port is uncovered—injection lasts a short time

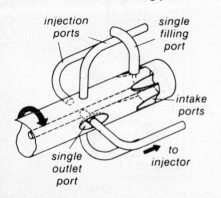

injection ports

single filling port

intake ports

single outlet port

to injector

Fig. 13 Plunger & ports

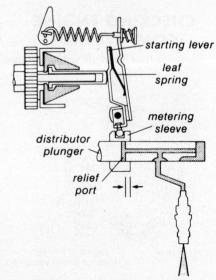

starting lever

leaf spring

metering sleeve

distributor plunger

relief port

Fig. 14 Starting fuel metering

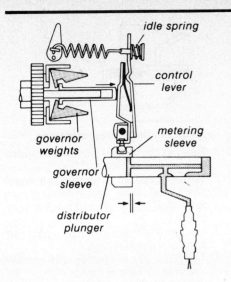

Fig. 15   Idling fuel metering

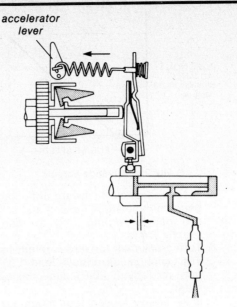

Fig. 16   Acceleration fuel metering

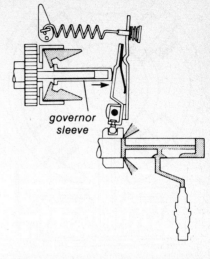

Fig. 17   Maximum speed fuel metering

so that a small amount of fuel is supplied at idle, Fig. 15.

The injection pump automatically compensates for effects of temperature and load changes at idle; when idle speed begins to drop, the governor weights and the governor sleeve retract; the idle spring then pushes the metering sleeve to the right, increasing the amount of fuel to correct the idle speed.

ACCELERATION—During acceleration, the control lever is pulled to the left by linkage from the accelerator pedal. The metering sleeve is moved to the right so more fuel is injected before the relief port is uncovered—engine speed increases until the movement of the governor "neutralizes" the effect of the pedal linkage, Fig. 16.

MAXIMUM SPEED—With pedal linkage at "full load," engine speed increases to about 5400 RPM—at this point, the governor is spinning with enough force for the governor sleeve to stretch the pedal linkage spring and

force the control lever to the right, Fig. 17.

The metering sleeve moves far enough to the left to uncover the relief port at the beginning of the distributor plunger stroke—there is no pressure for injection until engine speed drops and the metering sleeve moves to the right again. This provision acts as a speed limiter and is designed to react slowly enough so that engine performance simply "flattens out" at the top limit.

Injection Timing Advance

Near the end of each compression stroke, diesel fuel is injected directly into the combustion chamber—injection must continue well beyond piston TDC in order to burn the necessary amount of fuel to provide engine power. As engine speed increases, stroke time becomes shorter and injec-

tion time becomes longer: burning must begin sooner to ensure the peak combustion pressures still occur at the most efficient point after TDC.

Diesel injection timing is advanced by a hydraulic piston in the injection pump. As engine speed increases, fuel pressure from the vane pump also increases. Vane pump pressure pushes the injection advance piston to the left against the spring so that the roller housing turns slightly. Since the cam plate is turning in the opposite direction, the "ramps" on the cam plate engage the rollers sooner whenever the injection advance piston moves to the left; this means that the distributor plunger begins injection sooner, Fig. 18. The injection timing advance piston is located in the bottom of the injection pump body, Fig. 19.

The only cold start and warm-up device necessary for the diesel fuel system is a manual control which advances injection timing at idle and during low speed running. A cable-operated lever

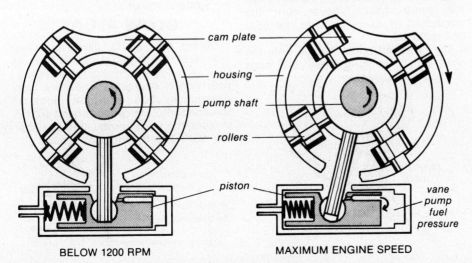

BELOW 1200 RPM   MAXIMUM ENGINE SPEED

Fig. 18   Injection timing advance

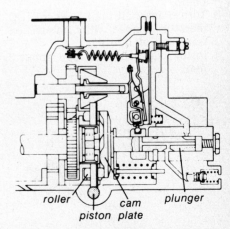

Fig. 19   Advance piston location

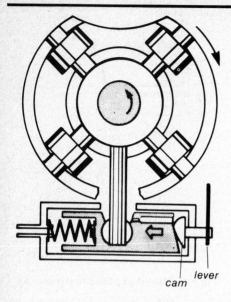

Fig. 20 Cold start advance

turns a cam which pushes the piston to the left. This advances injection timing about 5°.

This injection advance provides more time for fuel to burn, which improves performance and prevents smoking during cold starts and warm-up, Fig. 20. The cold start cam does not advance the complete range of injection timing: above 2200 RPM the piston operates normally and does not contact the cam, Fig. 21.

CHECKING INJECTION TIMING

Injection timing is checked by determining injection pump plunger movement at engine TDC with a dial gauge, Fig. 22:

1. Check that cold start lever is in the "off" position: reading will be incorrect if cold start cam is "on"—adjust cable if necessary.
2. Remove 12 hex bolt from end of pump and mount adaptor 2006 in pump.
3. Turn crankshaft until flywheel TDC mark is aligned with pointer on transmission housing.
4. Install dial gauge to read about 3 mm.

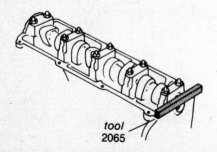

Fig. 23 Valve timing tool

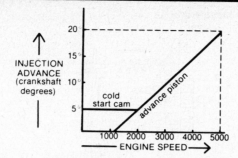

Fig. 21 Advance curve

5. Turn crankshaft backward until dial gauge needle stops moving and set dial gauge zeroing ring to read exactly 1 mm.
6. Turn crankshaft forward carefully to TDC: dial gauge should read 1.83 mm movement (0.83 mm movement).
7. If necessary loosen four mounting bolts on pump and turn pump body until dial gauge reads 1.83 mm.
8. Re-tighten bolts and recheck injection timing (don't forget the 4th bolt on left underside of pump body).

Incorrect injection timing can cause hard starting, exhaust smoking, lack of power, high fuel consumption, abnormal noise and eventual engine damage.

VALVE TIMING & SPUR BELT TENSION

A toothed rubber belt reinforced with synthetic cords turns both the camshaft and diesel injection pump from the crankshaft at ½ engine speed; the oil pump is driven by the back of the spur belt via the intermediate shaft.

The condition and tension of the spur belt is especially important with the diesel engine: if the belt breaks or "jumps time," the engine will be damaged because the valves will hit the pistons; for this same reason, never turn the crankshaft or camshaft with the spur belt removed.

The camshaft pulley is held onto the shaft with a "locking taper" and does not use a locating key:

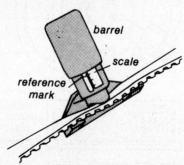

Fig. 24 Belt tension tool installation

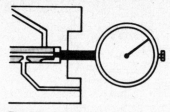

Fig. 22 Dial gauge installation

1. Remove spur belt cover and valve cover.
2. Turn crankshaft to align slot in camshaft with valve cover sealing surface and lock camshaft with tool 2065, Fig. 23.
3. Loosen belt tensioner locknut and cam drive pulley bolt.
4. Tap back of cam pulley with rubber hammer until it is loose.
5. Lock injection pump pulley with pin 2064; check that marks on pulley, bracket, and pump body are aligned (engine at TDC).
6. Install measuring tool VW 210 on belt between cam and pump pulleys.

NOTE: Be sure belt is not cracked or frayed—replace if necessary.

7. Set tool to 12 mm (align edge of barrel with scale line).
8. Turn belt tensioner until reference mark on tool is aligned with edge of barrel and tighten locknut, Fig. 24.
9. Now tighten cam drive pulley bolt to 33 ft. lbs.
10. Remove both locking tools and turn crankshaft 2 turns.
11. Use locking tool to recheck valve timing: tool should fit in camshaft slot when TDC mark on flywheel is aligned correctly.
12. Strike belt between cam and pump pulleys with rubber hammer and recheck belt tension.
13. Reinstall both covers and check injection timing.

GLOW PLUGS

During cold starts, diesel compression heat is dissipated rapidly through the cold engine so that a "pre-heating" provision is necessary to ensure compression ignition. The glow plugs are threaded into the cylinder head so they project into each combustion chamber, Fig. 25. A heating element in each plug

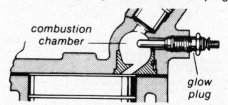

Fig. 25 Glow plug installation

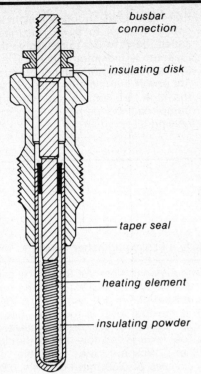

Fig. 26 Glow plug

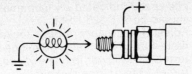

Fig. 27 Glow plug current check

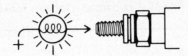

Fig. 28 Glow plug continuity check

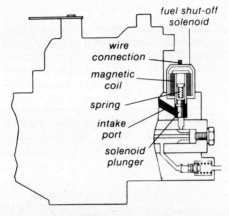

Fig. 29 Fuel shut-off solenoid

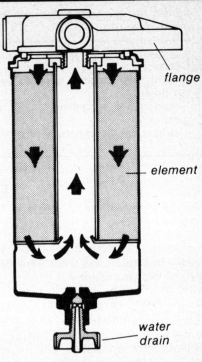

Fig. 30 Fuel filter

gets red hot whenever current is applied to the plug terminals.

Current is supplied to the glow plugs directly from the battery by a relay which is controlled by the ignition switch. A temperature sensor connected to a time circuit in the relay controls pre-heating time; the colder the temperature, the longer the pre-heating time. The glow plug light is on when the plugs are being heated and goes off when the engine is ready to start, Fig. 26.

Testing

Defective glow plugs cause hard starting and rough running during warm-up. Most problems in the pre-heat system can be found with a test light:

1. Connect test light clip to ground and touch test light probe to any glow plug connection with key in "glow" position; test light should light up if key switch and relay are working properly, Fig. 27.
2. Remove busbar from glow plug connections.
3. Connect test light clip to battery positive post and probe to each glow plug connection; test light should light up each time if heating elements are OK, Fig. 28.

Glow plugs can also be checked with an ohmmeter: the resistance value is about .25 ohms. Carbon deposits can insulate the heating element: if the system seems OK, but the engine is hard to start, the glow plugs can be removed for cleaning.

FUEL SHUT-OFF SOLENOID

Since diesels do not use spark ignition systems, the engine is switched off by a fuel shut-off solenoid on the injection pump.

Current is supplied to the fuel shut-off solenoid whenever the ignition key is "on." The magnetic coil pulls the solenoid plunger up against the spring, opening the injection port for injection, Fig. 29.

Whenever the ignition key is turned off, the solenoid closes the intake port, cutting off the supply of fuel for injection from the vane pump.

The engine will not run if the fuel shut-off solenoid sticks closed; if it sticks open, the engine will continue to run after the ignition key is turned off.

FUEL FILTER

Diesel fuel systems operate reliably as long as the fuel is free from dirt and water—moving parts inside the injection pump and injectors can be damaged by a small amount of dirt or corrosion.

The diesel fuel filter is designed to allow unrestricted flow of fuel from the tank but stops any dirt or water before it reaches the pump.

The replaceable element is similar to an oil filter—it threads onto a removable flange in the engine compartment, Fig. 30.

Some filter elements have a water drain in the bottom—if poor quality fuel is used, water separated by the filter can be drained to prevent freezing and blocking of the filter in cold weather.

Replace

The filter element should be replaced at normal maintenance intervals to ensure reliable operation of the pump and injectors:

1. Remove filter flange with element from body panel and invert the assembly on the mounting studs.
2. Remove element from flange with 22 wrench.
3. Fill new element with clean diesel fuel (no further priming should be necessary when filter is full of fuel).
4. Coat rubber seal with diesel fuel and install new element on flange hand-tight.
5. Remount flange to body.
6. Start engine and check for fuel leaks at flange.

CHECKING IDLE & MAXIMUM SPEED

1. Run engine until radiator is warm.
2. Mount sensor US 1324 on valve cover (magnetic end).

NOTE: Since diesel engines do not need spark ignition systems, RPM signals are generated through this vibration sensor.

---

3. Connect:

tachometer positive cable to sensor post

tachometer negative cable to ground

sensor cables to battery posts

4. Idle speed indicated on tachometer should be 775-825 RPM
5. Adjust if necessary: loosen locknut first—turn IN to raise idle speed, turn OUT to lower idle speed; don't forget to re-tighten locknut.
6. Now accelerate engine briefly to "full load" position: engine speed should be 5400-5450 RPM.
7. Adjust if necessary: loosen locknut

first—turn OUT to raise maximum speed, turn IN to lower maximum speed; don't forget to re-tighten the locknut. If maximum speed is set too low, the engine will not produce full power. If maximum speed is set too high, the engine and injection pump can be damaged by over-revving.

Carburetor Section

SOLEX

Refer to Figs. 1 and 2 for exploded views of this carburetor.

Float Level, Adjust

Either the carburetor must be level, or the car positioned on a level surface. If the carburetor is installed, idle the engine briefly to ensure the the float bowl

is full. If the carburetor is not installed, fill the float bowl using a piece of hose attached to the fuel inlet pipe. Then remove the carburetor upper part and the gasket so that the fuel level can be measured as shown in Fig. 3.

CAUTION: Disconnect the battery ground strap. Do not smoke or work near heaters or other fire hazards.

Have a fire extinguisher handy.

The distance from the top of the carburetor body to the surface of the fuel should be 19.5 ± 1.0 mm ($.767 \pm .040$ in.). If the fuel level is too high, use a thicker washer under the float valve. If the fuel level is too low, use a thinner washer. Washers are available in thicknesses of 0.50 mm (.020 in.), 0.80

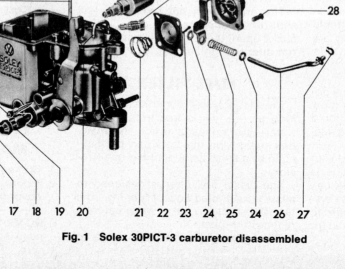

1. Fillister head screw
2. Spring washer
3. Carburetor upper part
4. Float valve washer
5. Float valve
6. Gasket
7. Float pin retainer
8. Float with pivot pin
9. Air correction jet with emulsion tube
10. Carburetor body
11. Volume control screw
12. Nut
13. Lockwasher
14. Throttle return spring
15. Spring washer
16. Main jet cover plug
17. Main jet cover plug seal
18. Main jet
19. Bypass screw
20. Accelerator pump injector
21. Pump diaphragm spring
22. Pump diaphragm
23. Cotter pin
24. 1-mm (.040 in.) thick washer
25. Connecting rod spring
26. Connecting link
27. Clip
28. Screw
29. Pump cover
30. Pilot jet
31. Electromagnetic cutoff valve
32. Vacuum diaphragm
33. Oval head screw
34. Vacuum diaphragm cover
35. Vacuum diaphragm spring
36. Plastic cap
37. Choke heating element
38. Cover retaining ring
39. Retaining ring spacer
40. Small fillister head screw

Fig. 1 Solex 30PICT-3 carburetor disassembled

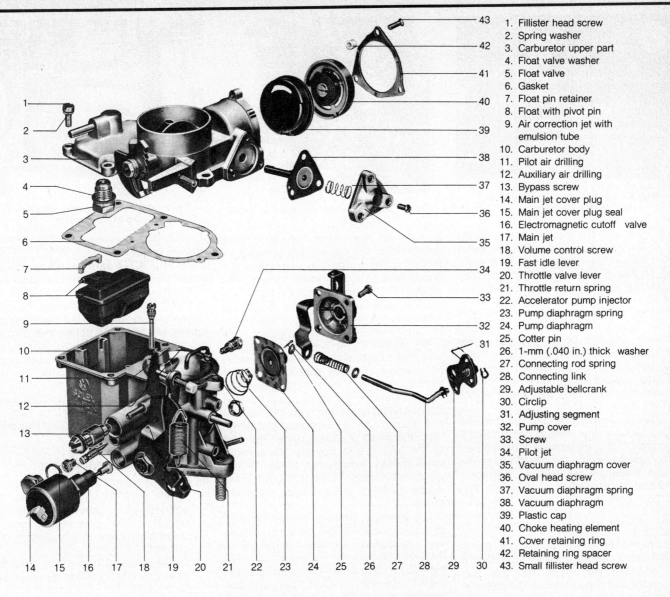

1. Fillister head screw
2. Spring washer
3. Carburetor upper part
4. Float valve washer
5. Float valve
6. Gasket
7. Float pin retainer
8. Float with pivot pin
9. Air correction jet with emulsion tube
10. Carburetor body
11. Pilot air drilling
12. Auxiliary air drilling
13. Bypass screw
14. Main jet cover plug
15. Main jet cover plug seal
16. Electromagnetic cutoff valve
17. Main jet
18. Volume control screw
19. Fast idle lever
20. Throttle valve lever
21. Throttle return spring
22. Accelerator pump injector
23. Pump diaphragm spring
24. Pump diaphragm
25. Cotter pin
26. 1-mm (.040 in.) thick washer
27. Connecting rod spring
28. Connecting link
29. Adjustable bellcrank
30. Circlip
31. Adjusting segment
32. Pump cover
33. Screw
34. Pilot jet
35. Vacuum diaphragm cover
36. Oval head screw
37. Vacuum diaphragm spring
38. Vacuum diaphragm
39. Plastic cap
40. Choke heating element
41. Cover retaining ring
42. Retaining ring spacer
43. Small fillister head screw

Fig. 2   Solex 34PICT-3 carburetor disassembled

Fig. 3   Float level adjustment. Solex carburetor

mm (.031 in.), 1.00 mm (.040 in.), and 1.50 mm (.059 in.).

Throttle Valve Positioner, Adjust

A tachometer with a range of at least 0 to 3000 rpm must be installed to adjust the throttle valve positioner. Start the engine. Then check the fast idle speed by pulling the fast idle lever back against the adjusting screw in the fast idle lever stop as shown in Fig. 4.

The fast idle should be 1550 rpm ± 100 rpm. If it is not, turn the adjusting screw in the fast idle lever stop to bring it within this range. After a warmup drive, the fast idle should not exceed 1700 rpm.

Fig. 4   Throttle valve positioner adjustment. Solex carburetor

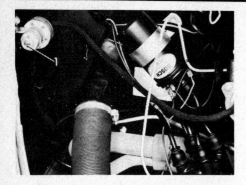

Fig. 5   Adjusting altitude corrector. Solex carburetor

Fig. 6   Throttle valve adjustment. Solex carburetor

Fig. 7   Accelerator pump adjustment. Solex carburetor

Next, check the throttle valve closing time. To do this, pull the throttle valve lever away from the fast idle lever until the engine is running at 3000 rpm. Release the lever. It should take 3.5 seconds ± 1 second for the engine to return to its normal idle. If the throttle valve closing time is not within specifications, adjust it by turning the screw on the altitude corrector, Fig. 5. Turning the screw clockwise will increase throttle valve closing time. Turning it counterclockwise will decrease throttle valve closing time.

After a warmup drive, the throttle valve closing time should not exceed 6 seconds. If the adjustment produces erratic results, check the condition of the hoses between the altitude corrector and the throttle valve positioner's diaphragm unit.

Dashpot, Adjust

Late-model cars with manual transmissions are equipped with a dashpot. It is adjusted by loosening the two locknuts and repositioning the dashpot in its mounting bracket. Dimension a in Fig. 6 should be adjusted to 1.00 mm (.040 in.) with the dashpot's plunger fully in and the throttle fully closed on the warm running position of the fast idle cam.

Accelerator Pump, Adjust

The accelerator pump's injection quantity is adjustable. On 30 PICT-3 carburetors, the adjustment is made by installing the cotter pin through a different hole in the connecting link. The 34 PICT-3 carburetors have a bellcrank with an adjusting segment. A spring-loaded screw is used to adjust the quantity on 34 PICT-4 carburetors.

To measure the injection quantity, first make certain that the float bowl is filled with fuel. Then attach a length of hose or tubing to the discharge end of the accelerator pump injector so that the expelled gasoline can be caught and measured in a 25-cc glass graduate. Hold the glass graduate under the end of the tubing and operate the throttle valve rapidly exactly ten times. Divide the amount caught by ten to get the average quantity of a single injection pulse.

The average quantity should be 1.20 to 1.35 cc for 30 PICT-3 carburetors; the average should be 1.45 to 1.75 cc for 34 PICT-3 carburetors installed on 1972 vehicles with manual transmissions, except those sold in California; and the average should be 1.3 to 1.6 cc on all other models with 34 PICT-3 carburetors. At temperatures above 23° to 24°C (73° to 75°F), the average injection quantity should be approximately 1.1 cc per stroke for the 34 PICT-4 carburetor installed on 1974 cars sold in California.

At lower temperatures, the average should be 1.7 cc.

On 30 PICT-3 carburetors, move the cotter pin to the outer hole to decrease injection quantity. Move the cotter pin to the inner hole to increase injection quantity. On 34 PICT-3 carburetors, loosen the retaining screw and turn the adjusting segment clockwise to decrease injection quantity or counterclockwise to increase the injection quantity. Then tighten the retaining screw and recheck the injection quantity. On 34 PICT-4 carburetors, turn the spring-loaded screw to adjust the injection quantity.

Idle Speed, Adjust

30 PICT, 34 PDSIT-2, -3 Models
1. Clean and regap or replace the spark plugs as necessary. Make certain the valve clearances, ignition dwell angle, and ignition timing are correct.
2. On vehicles with dual carburetors, check synchronization as described further on.
3. Connect a dwell meter/tachometer to the ignition system. Replace the

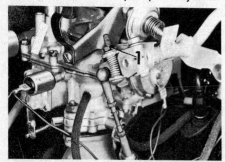

Fig. 8   Synchronization screw of left hand carburetor. Solex installations

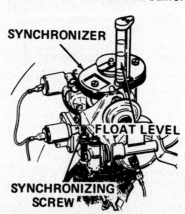

Fig. 9   Synchronization tool installed on carburetor. Solex installations

Fig. 10   Adjusting throttle rod on right hand carburetor. Solex installations

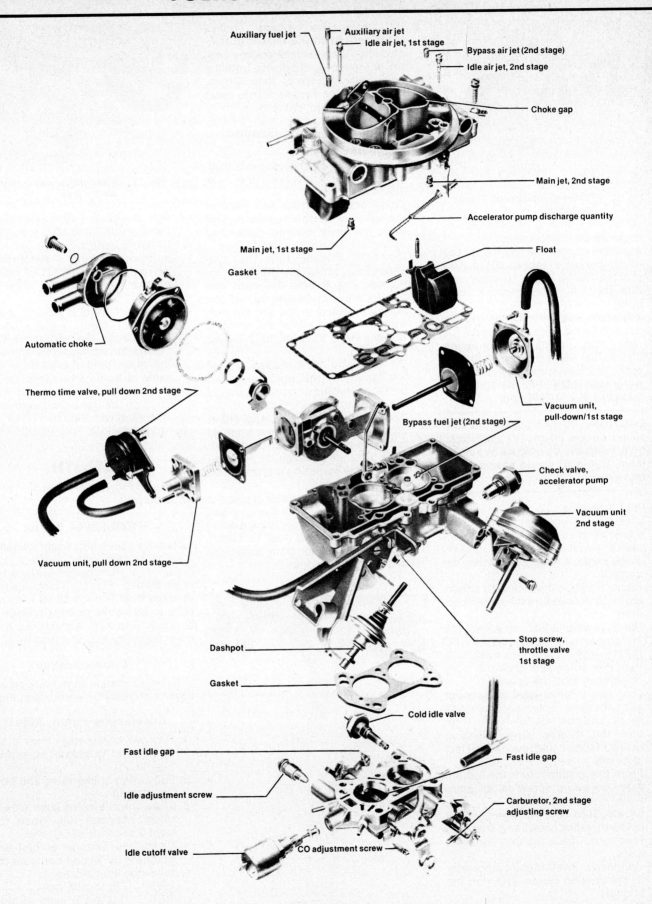

Fig. 11   Zenith carburetor disassembled

Auxiliary fuel jet
Auxiliary air jet
Idle air jet, 1st stage
Bypass air jet (2nd stage)
Idle air jet, 2nd stage
Choke gap
Main jet, 2nd stage
Accelerator pump discharge quantity
Main jet, 1st stage
Float
Gasket
Automatic choke
Thermo time valve, pull down 2nd stage
Vacuum unit, pull-down/1st stage
Bypass fuel jet (2nd stage)
Check valve, accelerator pump
Vacuum unit 2nd stage
Vacuum unit, pull down 2nd stage
Stop screw, throttle valve 1st stage
Dashpot
Gasket
Cold idle valve
Fast idle gap
Fast idle gap
Idle adjustment screw
Carburetor, 2nd stage adjusting screw
Idle cutoff valve
CO adjustment screw

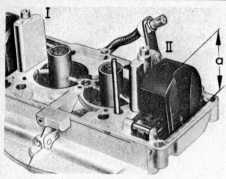

Fig. 12 Flat level adjustment. Zenith carburetor

oil dipstick with a thermometer to measure the oil temperature.

4. Start the engine and run it until the oil temperature reaches 50° to 70°C (122° to 158°F). Check to make sure that the automatic choke is fully open.

5. Adjust the idle speed by turning the bypass screw. The idle speed for cars with manual transmissions should be adjusted to 800 to 900 rpm. The idle speed for cars with Automatic Stick Shift should be adjusted to 900 to 1000 rpm.

CAUTION: Do not adjust the idle speed on the 30 PICT-3 carburetor by turning the throttle valve adjustment. Doing so would adversely affect exhaust emissions.

34 PICT-3 Models

1. Clean and regap or replace the spark plugs as necessary. Make certain that valve clearances, ignition dwell angle, and ignition timing are correct.

2. Replace the oil dipstick with a thermometer to measure the oil temperature.

3. Start the engine and run it until the oil temperature reaches 50° to 70°C (122° to 158°F). Check to make sure that the automatic choke is fully open, then stop the engine.

4. Turn the throttle valve adjustment out until there is clearance between its tip and the fast idle cam. Then turn the throttle valve adjusting screw in until it just touches the fast idle cam.

5. From this position, turn the throttle valve adjusting screw in an additional one-quarter turn.

6. Slowly turn the volume control screw in until it comes to a stop, and then turn it back 2½ to 3 complete turns.

7. Connect a dwell meter/tachometer to the ignition system and start the engine.

8. By turning the bypass screw, adjust the idle speed to 800 to 900 rpm.

9. By turning the volume control screw, adjust to the fastest obtainable idle. Then turn the volume control screw slowly clockwise until the engine speed drops by 20 to 30 rpm.

10. By turning the bypass screw, reset the idle to 800 to 900 rpm.

Carburetor Synchronization

Dual Carburetor Models

1. Dismount the air cleaner ducts from both carburetors, leaving the hose attached.

2. Disconnect the lower ball joint of the right-hand throttle operating rod from the lever on the right-hand carburetor's throttle valve switch.

3. On 1972 models, turn the synchronizing screw on the left carburetor, Fig. 8, until the right carburetor's throttle operating rod can be reconnected to the throttle arm without moving either carburetor's throttle valve from its fully closed position.

4. On 1973 and 1974 models, adjust the length of the right-hand carburetor's throttle operating rod until the rod can be reconnected to the throttle arm without moving either carburetor's throttle valve from its fully closed position. The approximate distance between the two ball joints of the operating rod should be 107 mm (4$^{7}/_{32}$ in.).

5. Insert an oil thermometer in place of the oil dipstick. Start the engine and run it until the oil temperature reaches 50° to 70°C (122° to 158°F). Check to see that both automatic chokes are fully open.

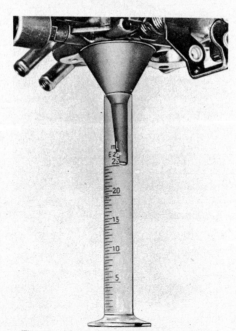

Fig. 14 Measuring accelerator pump discharge. Zenith carburetor

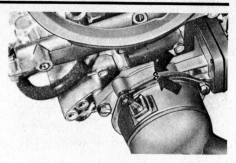

Fig. 13 Choke adjustment. Zenith carburetor

6. Run the engine at a steady speed between 2000 and 3000 rpm. Place a Unisyn®, Auto-Syn®, or other airflow-measuring synchronizing device over the throat of one carburetor and then the other. See Fig. 9.

7. If one carburetor is passing more air than the other, adjust the synchronization. On 1972 models, turn the synchronizing screw one way or the other until the air flow is the same at both carburetors. On 1973 and 1974 models, turn the adjustment on the right-hand carburetor's operating rod, Fig. 10.

8. Adjust the idle.

ZENITH

Refer to Fig. 11 for an exploded view of carburetor.

Float Level, Adjust

Remove air horn from carburetor, then with carburetor inverted, check distance (a) from gasket surface to top of carburetor, Fig. 12. If distance for 1st (I) stage float is not 1.08 to 1.12 inches (27.5 to 28.5 mm), or 2nd (II) stage float is not 1.16 to 1.20 inches (29.5 to 30.5 mm), adjust by bending bracket.

Choke, Adjust

To adjust choke, align mark on choke cover with mark on carburetor, Fig. 13.

Accelerator Pump, Adjust

1. Remove carburetor, then place a funnel and graduate as shown in Fig. 14.

2. Fully open choke valve and hold in this position.

3. Move throttle valve lever slowly 10 times. Maintain fully open for at least 3 seconds per stroke.

4. Divide the amount of fuel in the graduate by 10 and compare to the following specifications:

1975	.75 to 1.05 cm³
1976	1.3 to 1.7 cm³ (Cold)
	.6 to .9 cm³ (Warm)

5. To adjust on 1975 models:

Fig. 15 Accelerator pump discharge quantity adjustment. 1975 Zenith carburetor

Fig. 16 Temperature valve. Zenith carburetor

Fig. 17 Check valve. Zenith carburetor

Fig. 18 Throttle valve adjustment. Zenith carburetor

Fig. 19 Fast idle gap adjustment. 1975 Zenith carburetor

Fig. 20 Fast idle gap adjustment. 1976 Zenith carburetor

a. Turn adjusting nut as necessary to adjust the discharge quantity, Fig. 15.
b. Lock adjusting nut with locking compound after adjustment.
c. If discharge quantity cannot be adjusted to specifications, check fuel pump piston, pump diaphragm and injection tube for blockage.
6. To adjust on 1976 models:
a. Make sure that hose (arrow) from temperature valve, Fig. 16 is connected to check valve, Fig. 17.
b. Check temperature valve by applying air to temperature valve. Air must flow when coolant temperature is 113° F (45° C), and must not flow when engine coolant temperature is above about 141° F (61° C).
c. Turn adjusting nut as necessary to adjust the discharge quantity.
d. Recheck discharge quantity by applying vacuum to check valve. If discharge quantity cannot be adjusted to specifications, replace check valve.

Throttle Valve, Adjust

NOTE: The throttle valve screw, Fig. 18, is factory preset and should not be tampered with. However, if screw has been tampered with, the basic adjustment can be adjusted as follows:

1. Open choke valve and close throttle valve.
2. Remove plastic cap from screw.
3. Turn screw (a), Fig. 18, out until there is a gap between fast idle cam and screw, then turn screw (a) until it just touches cam.
4. Turn screw ¼ turn in from there.
5. Adjust idle speed and CO.

Fast Idle Gap, Adjust

1975
1. Remove carburetor.
2. Using a drill bit, check fast idle gap (a), Fig. 19. Gap must be .45 to .50 mm.

3. If not within specifications, adjust by turning screw (b), Fig. 19.

1976

NOTE: Position of fast idle gap must be determined by engine speed with engine at normal operating temperature.

1. Adjust ignition timing to specifications.
2. Disconnect vacuum hose from choke pulldown unit (second stage small unit) and plug hose.
3. Open throttle valve slightly and fully close choke valve.
4. Close throttle valve. Choke valve must now be fully open and stop screw for fast idle cam must rest on highest step of cam.
5. Start engine and check that the following speeds are attained:
   Manual Trans.   3150-3250 rpm
   Auto. Trans.   3350-3450 rpm
6. If speeds are not as specified, adjust screw, Fig. 20.

Gasoline Fuel Injection Section

CIS FUEL INJECTION SYSTEM

Air flow through the intake manifold is measured by the air sensor which controls the fuel distributor.

Fuel from the tank is delivered to the fuel distributor by the electric fuel pump via an accumulator and filter, Fig. 1.

The fuel distributor controls the quantity of fuel delivered through the injectors to each cylinder.

The control pressure regulator provides fuel enrichment during engine warmup by changing fuel pressure on top of the control plunger inside the fuel distributor.

The cold start valve provides additional fuel during cold starting.

The auxiliary air regulator supplies additional air during engine warm-up as a fast-idle provision.

Mixture Control Unit

The mixture control unit is located between the air filter and the throttle plate assembly and consists of the air sensor

and the Fuel Distributor.

The air sensor measures the amount of air entering the intake manifold and controls the amount of fuel injected by the fuel distributor, Fig. 2.

The slightest flow of air through the air cone lifts the sensor plate causing the plate lever to lift the control plunger inside the fuel distributor.

As the control plunger rises, it allows more fuel to be supplied to the injectors.

The movement of the plate, lever, and plunger is also controlled and dampened by a balance weight and the fuel "counter-pressure" on top of the control plunger.

The more air an engine uses, the more fuel it needs to run efficiently—since the air sensor is constantly measuring air flow and controlling fuel quantity by raising and lowering the control plunger, the air-fuel mixture should always be correct.

The air sensor operation is based on the "floating body principle" which states that a floating body suspended in a cone moves in a line according to the rate of air flow through the cone.

The CIS "floating body" is the circular plate bolted to a lever which moves freely around a pivot point. The weight of the sensor plate and lever is countered by the balance weight, Fig. 3.

As "1" slight air flow at idle lifts the plate only enough to raise the control plunger slightly. The metering slit in the fuel distributor is opened to allow enough fuel for idle.

As air flow increases, more of the metering slit is uncovered until at full throttle (3), fuel flow is at the mixture, Fig. 3.

This graph, Fig. 4, shows an engine's basic air-fuel requirement. Notice that with CIS, the fuel flow is automatically correct for any volume of air flow from idle to full load.

In actual use, the air-fuel requirements of an engine are not usually a straight line on a graph: this graph shows an engine's actual air-fuel requirement as a broken line. The basic requirement of fuel and air is still shown as a solid straight line, Fig. 5.

At idle the engine runs slightly rich.

At part load the engine can run leaner for best fuel economy.

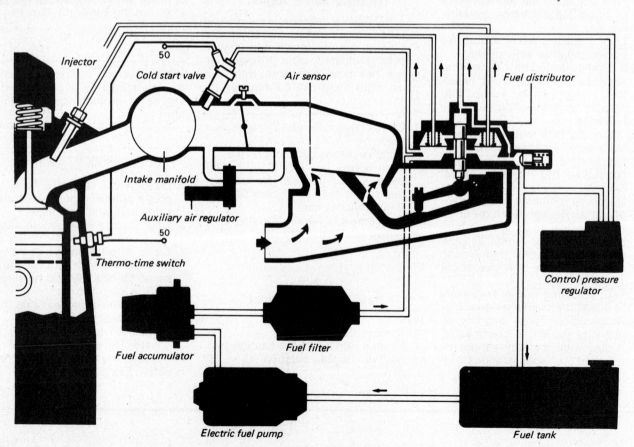

Fig. 1 Fuel injection system

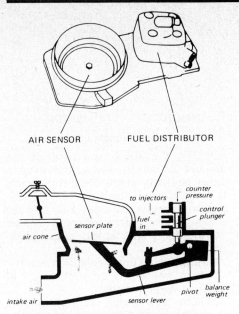

AIR SENSOR   FUEL DISTRIBUTOR

to injectors
counter pressure
control plunger
sensor plate
fuel in
air cone
balance weight
intake air   sensor lever   pivot

Fig. 2   Air sensor & fuel distributor

At full load a richer mixture is needed for maximum power.

Correction stages are built into the air cone to tailor the air-fuel ratio for an engine's actual requirements.

The corrected cone shown with broken lines, causes the sensor plate to float higher with the same air flow that it would in a simple cone at idle. This raises the control plunger slightly and richens the air-fuel mixture slightly, Fig. 6.

At part load the sensor plate and control plunger float lower than in a simple cone so that the air-fuel mixture is leaner.

When the engine is not running, the sensor plate and lever rest on a spring-loaded stop. The control plunger com-

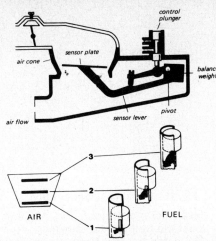

control plunger
sensor plate
air cone
balance weight
air flow
sensor lever   pivot

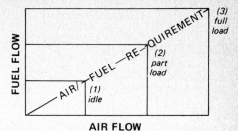

AIR   FUEL

Fig. 3   Air sensor

pletely closes the metering ports so that fuel cannot reach the injectors. If a backfire occurs in the intake manifold, the sensor plate is forced down against the springloaded stop—this creates a larger opening around the sensor plate to reduce pressure and prevent damage to the air sensor assembly, Fig. 7.

The metering slits can only control the amount of fuel to the injectors if the fuel pressure difference on either side of the metering slit is kept constant. A stainless steel diaphragm separates the two chambers of each regulating valve. About .1 bar (1½ psi) of fuel pressure is "used up" to deflect the diaphragm and open the spring-loaded disk valve; for this reason, pressure on the injector side of the metering slit is always .1 bar lower than on the inlet side—in this manner the control plunger can accurately control fuel volume without being affected by pressure changes.

System pressure in the lower half of the fuel distributor is controlled by a

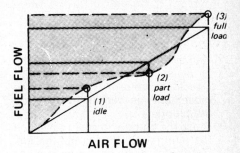

Fig. 4   Theoretical air flow graph

Fig. 5   Actual air flow graph

pressure relief valve in the body of the fuel distributor, Fig. 8.

The delivery pump near the fuel tank supplies fuel to the fuel distributor. The relief piston controls system pressure by allowing excess fuel to flow back to the tank through the return line, Fig. 9.

Checking Mixture Control Unit

Both the sensor plate and the control plunger must move freely to ensure accurate control of the fuel-air mixture. Checking for free movement is one of the most important checks in the CIS system, and it is also one of the quickest and easiest:

1. Run the engine for a few seconds. This ensures that control pressure keeps the control plunger pushed against the sensor lever.
2. Turn off ignition.
3. Remove rubber connecting boot.
4. Lift sensor plate with a strong magnet or small pliers: the plate should move in both directions without "hanging up," Fig. 10.

If the plate hangs up only on upward movement:

Idle slightly rich

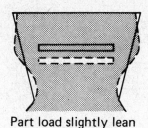

Part load slightly lean

Fig. 6   Air cone

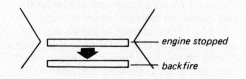

engine stopped
backfire

Fig. 7   Backfire cone

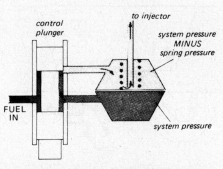

control plunger
to injector
system pressure MINUS spring pressure
FUEL IN
system pressure

Fig. 8   Pressure regulating valve

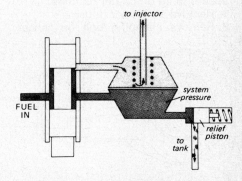

to injector
system pressure
FUEL IN
relief piston
to tank

Fig. 9   Pressure relief valve

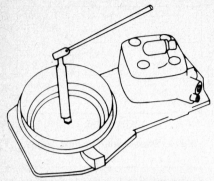

Fig. 10   Free movement check

1. Remove the fuel distributor from the air sensor housing.
2. Check the control plunger for free movement (be careful not to drop the plunger)
3. Rinse the plunger in clean solvent. If the plunger still hangs up, the fuel distributor must be replaced since the plunger cannot be repaired or replaced separately. Never use emery cloth.
4. Be sure to install the plunger into the fuel distributor with small shoulder first, Fig. 11.

If the plate hangs up in both directions, the problem can usually be corrected by centering the sensor plate or lever:

1. Remove the bolt from the center of the plate.
2. Coat the bolt with Loctite.
3. Re-install the bolt fingertight.
4. Lay centering tool US1109 on top of the sensor plate: "feeler-tips on tool should be inserted into air gap around plate with rivets touching the air cone (plate should also be contacting bottom of tool).
5. Torque bolt to 46 ft. lbs.

NOTE: If centering tool is not available, run a .10 mm (.004″) feeler gauge carefully in air gap around plate before torquing bolt (re-check centering to make sure plate has not moved during torquing), Fig. 12.

If plate cannot be centered and lever appears to be off-center on cone:
1. Remove air sensor housing.
2. Remove clamping bolt on sensor

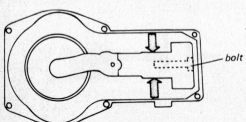

Fig. 13   Air sensor lever

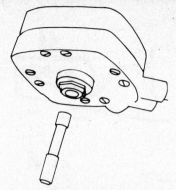

Fig. 11   Control plunger position

lever counter-weight, Fig. 13, and coat the bolt with Loctite.
3. Re-install the bolt finger-tight.
4. Slide lever to center position and re-tighten clamping bolt.

The sensor plate should be even with the bottom rim of the air cone (at the edge nearest the fuel distributor) to ensure correct fuel-air mixture during starting:

1. Loosen line to fuel distributor at control pressure regulator and wrap clean rag around connection to catch fuel.
2. Remove rubber connecting boot and check level of plate.
3. If necessary bend clip up or down to adjust; lift the plate to the fully open position and use small pliers. Be careful not to scratch the plate or air cone with the tool, Fig. 14.

Idle Adjustments, Fig. 15

Correct CO adjustment in the CIS system is especially important since it affects not only the air-fuel mixture at idle but throughout the entire operating range.

The relationship of the control plunger to the sensor plate can be changed by an adjustment screw on the two-piece air sensor lever: turning the CO adjustment screw in raises the control plunger in the fuel distributor, supplying more fuel to the injectors and raising CO. CIS idle speed adjustment is just like other fuel injection equipped

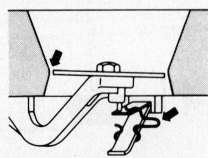

Fig. 14   Sensor plate height adjustment

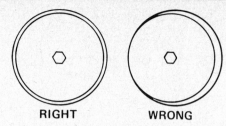

Fig. 12   Sensor plate adjustment

vehicles: the adjustment controls the amount of air bypassing the throttle valve. Normally at idle the throttle valve is fully closed: "backingout" the adjustment screw enlarges the by-pass drilling and simulates opening throttle valve slightly so that idle speed is increased.

1. Run engine until radiator is warm.
2. Turn headlights on high beam to load engine slightly.
3. Turn idle speed screw until idle speed is 925 RPM (850-1000 RPM).
4. Remove wire handle with rubber plug on air sensor.
5. Insert long, 4 mm allen wrench.

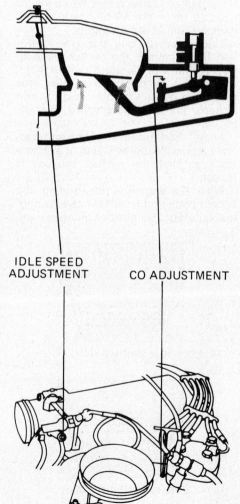

Fig. 15   Mixture control unit

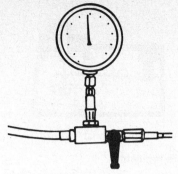

Fig. 16 Pressure gauge with closed lever

6. Turn CO adjustment screw: in to raise CO, out to lower CO.
7. Remove tool after each adjustment attempt.
8. Accelerate engine briefly before reading CO gauge.

Always check the sticker in the engine compartment for exact CO setting; various models require different settings even though the procedure is the same for all CIS-equipped vehicles.

Fuel Distributor Checks & Adjustment

System pressure is established during manufacture with shims behind the pressure relief valve spring. There are three types of CIS fuel pressure checking gauges, but they all operate similarly, Fig. 16:

1. Connect gauge in line between fuel distributor and control pressure regulator. Make sure all connections are clean first.
2. Run pump with gauge lever in closed position, check gauge connections for leaks. Gauge should read 4.5-5.2 bar (65-75 psi).

The pressure relief valve may be removed for cleaning, replacing rubber seal rings, or correcting system pressure. Make sure fuel pump delivery is adequate, filter is not clogged, and fuel lines are not restricted before adjusting system pressure, Figs. 17 and 18.

1. Remove carrier or plug with shims.
2. Check piston for free movement: use wood dowel or coffee stick. Be careful of piston since it is fitted to the fuel distributor and cannot be replaced separately.
3. Check condition of rubber seal rings and replace if necessary; wash metal parts in clean solvent.

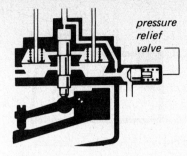

Fig. 17 Pressure relief valve

4. Change shims if necessary:
   thicker shims—higher pressure
   thinner shims—lower pressure
5. Install parts with new copper seal rings and recheck system pressure. On some 1977 models, the control pressure regulator return circuit is routed back through the fuel distributor. A needle valve inside the system pressure relief valve helps maintain some control pressure when the engine is not running, Fig. 19. The small end plug and needle valve do not need to be removed from the carrier unless the control pressure regulator leakage check reads low: this would indicate a leaking rubber seal ring on the needle valve.

Although the new shims are different system pressure can be adjusted like earlier models after removing the carrier with the small end plug still installed. The carrier has a special hex which can only be loosened with a 16 mm six point socket.

The fuel distributor and injectors should supply the same amount of fuel to each engine cylinder; unequal volume is one reason for poor idle and part-throttle performance problems. To check supply volume:

1. Pull injectors out of cylinder head bushings and place them in tool US 4480 or other appropriate measuring glasses, Fig. 20.
2. Run fuel pump and lift sensor plate slightly until at least one glass measures 50 cc.

NOTE: Also check injectors for even, cone-shaped spray as sensor plate is lifted.

3. Close sensor plate: no fuel droplets

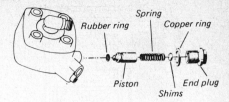

Fig. 18 Pressure relief valve exploded view

should form on injectors in 15 seconds.
4. Fuel quantities in all measuring glasses should be within 7 cc.
5. If quantities vary by more than 7 cc, swap injectors with the widest variation and repeat test.
6. If the same injector shows low volume on the second test, that injector is defective; if the same fuel line shows low volume on the second test, the fuel distributor is defective.

Control Pressure Regulator

The control pressure regulator determines the fuel pressure on top of the control plunger to help regulate the air-fuel mixture, primarily during engine warm-up.

Control pressure on top of the control plunger is supplied through a small hole in the fuel distributor separator plate, Fig. 21. This enables control pressure to be regulated without affecting system pressure. Another restriction dampens control plunger movement so that it changes position smoothly.

When the engine is cold, the bi-metallic strip presses on the spring causing the fuel line to open, reducing control pressure, Fig. 22.

Heat from the engine and the heating coil which is connected to the fuel pump circuit straightens out the bi-

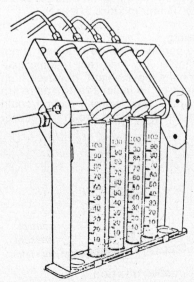

Fig. 20 Fuel volume tester

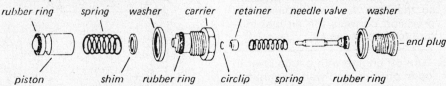

Fig. 19 New relief valve exploded view

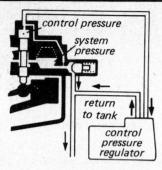

Fig. 21   Control pressure diagram

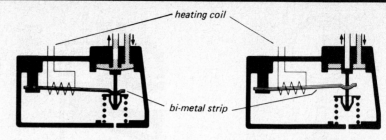

Cold engine—low control pressure.

Warm engine—normal control pressure.

Fig. 22   Control pressure regulator

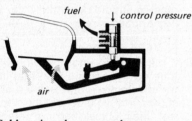

Cold engine—low control pressure

Warm engine—normal control pressure

Fig. 23   Control pressure effects

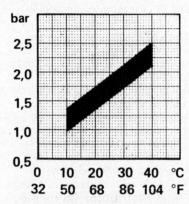

Fig. 24   Control pressure graph

metallic strip. The spring closes the return line so that control pressure gradually increases as the engine warms up, Fig. 23.

Cold Engine—Low Control Pressure

Reduced control pressure allows the sensor plate to open further with the same air flow. The control plunger supplies more fuel for the same amount of air so the air-fuel mixture is richer during engine warm-up.

Warm Engine—Normal Control Pressure

Control pressure increases as the engine warms up. With the same air flow acting on the sensor plate, control pressure keeps the plunger lower. Less fuel is supplied for the same amount of air, so the fuel-air mixture is leaner.

Checking

The control pressure regulator is not adjustable. Any incorrect reading usually means replacement: however, high readings could mean a restricted return line, and a low "warm" reading could mean a break in the ground circuit or

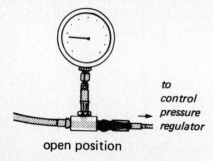

open position

Fig. 25   Pressure gauge with lever open

1-1158

current supply (should be a minimum of 11½ volts whenever the pump is running).

1. Make sure engine is cold, room temperature, and unplug connector on control pressure regulator.
2. Install pressure gauge in line between fuel distributor and control pressure regulator and set gauge lever to open position.
3. Run engine at idle (maximum of one minute) or "hotwire" fuel pump and check gauge reading: should read within range band on air temperature graph, Fig. 24, about 1.3-1.7 bar at normal room temperature.
4. Re-install electrical connector on control pressure regulator: gauge reading should increase and stabilize after several minutes at 49-57 psi.

NOTE: If control pressure regulator has vacuum hose, additional check should be performed—pull off and plug hose: reading should drop to about 2.7-3.1 bar.

NOTE: All readings may be higher on control pressure regulators with open vacuum connection for high altitude compensation. At high altitudes the compensation diaphragm increases control pressure so that less fuel is supplied—this provision corrects the air-fuel mixture for less dense air.

5. Turn off engine with gauge lever in open position and wait 20 minutes: gauge should read 1.6 bar or above, Fig. 25.

6. If gauge reads below 1.6 bar (and there are no external leaks) run the engine with gauge lever in closed position, Fig. 16.
7. If gauge reads 1.6 bar or above with lever in closed position (but was below 1.6 bar in open position), control pressure regulator is leaking and should be replaced.

NOTE: On models with the control pressure regulator fuel return line routed back through the fuel distributor, rubber seal rings on needle valve may be leaking.

8. If gauge reads below 1.6 bar in both lever positions (and there are no external leaks) the fuel pump check valve or rubber seal ring on the pressure relief valve may be leaking internally.

Fuel Pump

The roller-cell fuel pump is driven by a permanent magnet electric motor and is usually located near the fuel tank, Fig. 26. Steel rollers are held loosely in

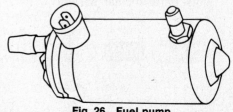

Fig. 26   Fuel pump

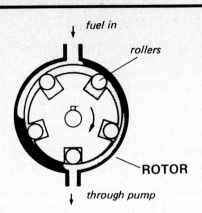

Fig. 27   Rotor & rollers

cut-outs on the shaft-mounted rotor, Fig. 27, so that centrifugal force seals the rollers against the walls of the pressure chamber as the rotor spins; the off-center lay-out of the rotor and pressure chamber "squeezes" fuel trapped between the rollers and forces it out the delivery port, Fig. 28.

The pump is designed to be cooled and lubricated by the fuel flowing through the motor; there is no possibility of fire because there is never a combustible mixture inside the pump: the pump is subject to damage if it is ever allowed to run "dry"—even for a few minutes. For this reason, the CIS fuel filter is located on the pressure side of the pump.

A non-serviceable relief valve is designed to vent fuel back to the intake side of the pump if pressure ever exceeds system pressure range. A replaceable check valve holds about 2 bars of residual pressure and works in conjunction with the accumulator and the piston seal in the fuel distributor to ensure good hot starting.

The pump delivers several times the amount of fuel required at any time; the excess fuel is diverted back to the tank by the pressure relief valve in the fuel distributor.

Checking

1. Disconnect return line at fuel distributor, Fig. 29.
2. Place return line in measuring con-

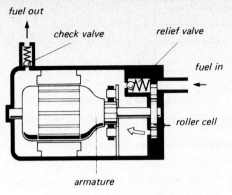

Fig. 28   Fuel pump

tainer, minimum of one quart capacity.
3. Operate pump for exactly 40 seconds. Delivery quantity should be at least one quart.

If delivery quantity is low, check that filter is not partially clogged and at least 11.5 volts is available to pump before replacing.

Pump can also be checked for proper current draw, Fig. 30.
1. Connect ammeter in series with pump and current supply plug. (Jumper wire must be used on pumps with multi-connector plugs.)
2. Operate pump at correct system pressure: ammeter should read 7.5-8.5 amp.

Pump check valve can be checked separately:
1. Install CIS pressure gauge in line between fuel distributor and control pressure regulator with gauge lever in closed position, Fig. 16.

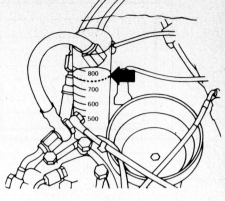

Fig. 29   Checking fuel volume

2. Run engine for a few seconds to activate pump; then turn off engine and wait 20 minutes: gauge should still read at least 1.6 bar.
3. If gauge reads below 1.6 bar and there are no external leaks, replace check valve at pump inlet connection.

NOTE: If leakage check reading is still low after replacement of pump check valve, check condition of rubber seal ring on fuel distributor pressure relief piston.

Fuel Pump Relay

1975 Audi Fox

With ignition on, and the air sensor contact closed, the pull-in coil of the control relay is energized, completing the circuit from terminal z50 to the

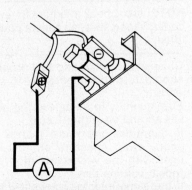

Fig. 30   Checking current draw

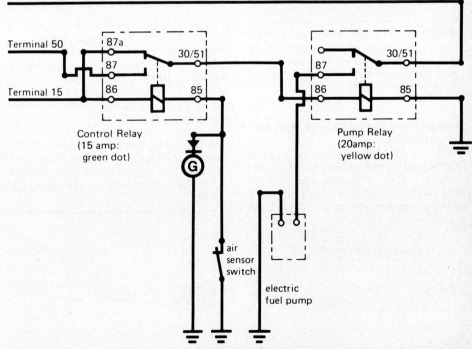

Fig. 31   Wiring diagram. 1975 Audi

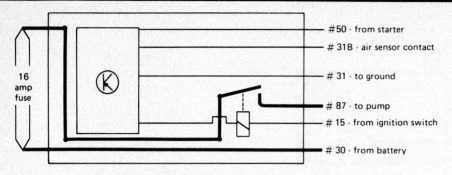

Fig. 32 Relay diagram. 1976 Audi & VW

- #50 - from starter
- #31B - air sensor contact
- #31 - to ground
- #87 - to pump
- #15 - from ignition switch
- #30 - from battery

16 amp fuse

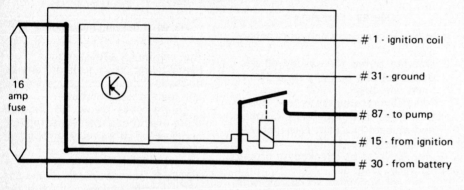

Fig. 33 Relay diagram. Late Audi & VW

- #1 - ignition coil
- #31 - ground
- #87 - to pump
- #15 - from ignition
- #30 - from battery

16 amp fuse

pull-in coil of the pump relay so that the pump runs only during starting.

With the air sensor contact open during normal running, the control relay is in the de-energized position, completing the circuit directly from terminal $z15$ to the pull-in coil of the pump relay. The alternator connection provides an additional anti-flooding circuit by ensuring that the pump does not run in the event that the sensor plate sticks open with the engine not running, Fig. 31.

NOTE: To run pump with engine off for testing purposes, turn on ignition remove air sensor electrical connector, and remove electrical connector on back of alternator.

1976 VW & Audi Fox Models With Air Sensor Wiring

With ignition on, current is supplied to the pull-in coil which is grounded through the transisterized circuit whenever the starter is operating ($z50$) or the air sensor contact ($z31B$) is open

during normal running. The pull-in coil completes the circuit between battery terminal $z30$ and the fuel pump via the 16 amp fuse on top of the pump relay, Fig. 32.

NOTE: To run pump with engine off for testing purposes, remove air sensor electrical connector with ignition on.

Models Without Air Sensor Wiring

With ignition on, current is supplied to the pull-in coil which is grounded through the transisterized circuit whenever impulses are received from the ignition coil during starting or normal running, Fig. 33.

NOTE: To run pump with engine off for testing purposes, remove relay and bridge relay board terminals L13 and L14 with jumper wire or accessory US 4480.

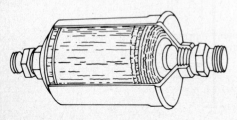

Fig. 34 Fuel filter

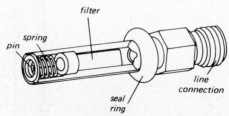

filter
spring
pin
seal ring
line connection

Fig. 35 Injector

Fuel Filter

The fuel filter removes particles from the fuel that might clog the fuel distributor or injectors; it is located on the pressure side of the pump so that a possible clogged filter will not damage the pump by causing it to run dry, Fig. 34.

The nylon-paper element inside the filter housing is designed to work best with fuel flow in one direction, Fig. 34, an arrow on the housing denotes the proper installation direction.

The fuel filter is automatically checked during the fuel pump delivery volume test. If delivery volume is sufficient, the fuel filter can be assumed to be in good condition.

Injectors

CIS injectors open at a pre-set pressure and continually spray atomized fuel into the intake ports near each intake valve. The injectors are a push-fit into plastic bushings in the cylinder head, and the rubber seal ring also acts as a retainer.

A vibrator pin inside the injector helps to break up and atomize the fuel droplets, Fig. 35. Each injector also has its own fuel filter to catch any particles which might enter the system after the main filter. The pin and spring seal about 3 bar of residual pressure in the line between the injector and the fuel distributor to help ensure quick starting.

Checking

The injectors and fuel distributor should supply the same amount of fuel to each engine cylinder; unequal volume is one reason for poor idle and part-throttle performance problems. To check supply volume:

1. Pull injectors out of cylinder head bushings and place them in tool US 4480 or other appropriate measuring glasses, Fig. 20.
2. Run fuel pump and lift sensor plate slightly until at least one glass measures 50 cc.

NOTE: Also check injectors for even, cone-shaped spray as sensor plate is lifted.

3. Close sensor plate: no fuel droplets should form on injector in 15 seconds.
4. Fuel quantity in all measuring glasses should be within 7 ccs.
5. If quantities are more than 7 cc apart, swap injectors on the fuel lines with the widest variation and repeat volume test.
6. If the same injector shows low volume on the second test, the injector

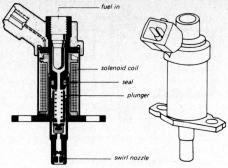

Fig. 36 Cold start valve

is defective; if the same fuel line shows low volume on the second test, the fuel distributor is defective.

NOTE: If injector pressure-testing equipment is available, make sure that opening pressures are at least 2.6 bar; opening pressures within a set should not vary by more than 0.6 bar.

Cold Start Valve

The cold start valve, Fig. 36, is located in the intake manifold to provide necessary fuel enrichment to all cylinders during starting. The solenoid coil of the cold start valve receives current from the starter and is grounded by the thermo-time switch so that it operates only for a short time while starting a cold engine.

Checking

1. Remove cold start valve from intake manifold and hold in container. Leave fuel line connected.
2. Connect jumper wire from one terminal of cold start valve to ignition coil terminal #15, Fig. 37.
3. Connect second jumper wire from other cold start valve terminal to ground.
4. Run pump and turn ignition on to check valve nozzle for steady, cone-shaped spray pattern.
5. Turn ignition off, pump still running.

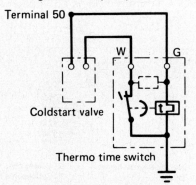

Fig. 39 Cold start valve & thermo-time switch wiring diagram

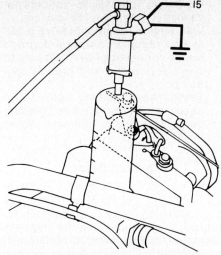

Fig. 37 Checking cold start valve

6. Wipe nozzle dry with clean rag to check for leakage. No drops should form within one minute.

Thermo-Time Switch

The thermo-time switch, Fig. 38, controls opening time of the cold start valve; it is affected by starter current and coolant temperature.

The thermo-time switch consists of a bi-metallic strip, heating coil, and contacts which are connected to an external plug.

Depending on coolant temperature conducted through the switch housing, the heater coil takes from 3 to 10 seconds to deflect the bi-metallic strip and open the contact points during starting. Opening the points interrupts the ground circuit of the cold start valve.

The bi-metallic strip and contacts within the switch are connected to the ground side of the cold start valve, and the heating cable is connected to terminal 50 of the starter circuit, Fig. 39. This ensures that the cold start valve operates only for a short time during starting.

Checking

1. Remove electrical connector from cold start valve and bridge harness

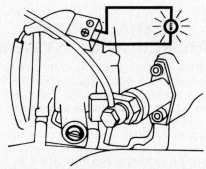

Fig. 40 Checking thermo-time switch

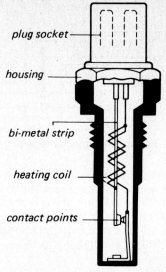

Fig. 38 Thermo-Time switch

connection with a test light, Fig. 40.
2. Connect jumper wire between ignition coil terminal $z1$ and ground to prevent starting.
3. Operate starter: test light should light up for several seconds and then go out if thermo-time switch is OK.

NOTE: Since the thermo-time switch contact points are designed to open at 95° F. This check can only be done with coolant temperature below 95°.

Auxiliary Air Regulator

The auxiliary air regulator prevents stalling at idle during engine warm-up by supplying additional air to the engine, Fig. 41.

Since any engine is less efficient when cold, some provisions like a carburetor "fast-idle" are necessary. The auxiliary air regulator controls the amount of air by-passing the closed throttle valve—on CIS equipped cars, it is calibrated so there is little difference in the idle speed of a cold or warm engine.

When the engine is cold, the gate valve is open. The heating coil is connected to the fuel pump and the control

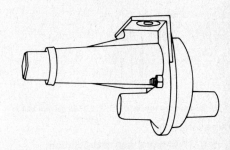

Fig. 41 Auxiliary air regulator

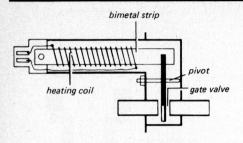

Fig. 42   Auxiliary air regulator

pressure regulator circuit so that as the engine warms up, the bi-metallic strip is heated. The deflection of the bi-metallic strip rotates the gate valve, gradually cutting off the passage for additional air as the engine warms up, Fig. 42.

Checking

1. Cold engine: Remove connecting hoses and check visually that air passage is open (use a flashlight and mirror if necessary).
2. Warm engine: Pinch either connect-

ing hose; idle speed should not change if gate valve has closed.
3. With engine running, remove auxiliary air regulator harness plug and bridge connections with test light to check for current and ground continuity.
4. Resistance of heating coil can be checked with an ohmmeter: reading between regulator contacts should be 20-30 ohms.

Accumulator

The accumulator is located between the fuel pump and the filter. It improves hot starting by helping to maintain residual fuel pressure when the engine is turned off. It also helps to reduce fuel pump noise by its damping action and protects the metal diaphragms in the fuel distributor from rapid pressure build-up when the pump begins running, Fig. 43.

When the fuel pump begins running, the fuel chamber inside the ac-

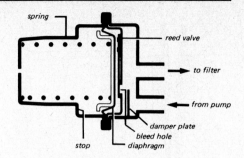

Fig. 43   Accumulator

cumulator is filled through the one-way reed valve, and the diaphragm is forced to the left against the spring until it reaches the stop. Only after the diaphragm reaches the stop does system pressure reach its operating limit.

After the engine is turned off, the spring slowly pushes the diaphragm to the right, forcing about 40 ccs of fuel through a small hole in the reed valve to help maintain residual fuel pressure and avoid vaporization.

Emission Controls Section

EVAPORATIVE EMISSION CONTROL SYSTEM

The evaporative emission control system prevents gasoline fumes from escaping into the atmosphere. The fuel tank is vented into a system that traps and contains fuel vapors until they can be burned by the engine.

The ventilation hose from the tank is connected to an expansion chamber located under the cowl panel. Liquid fuel, expelled from a full tank by expansion, is stored in this chamber and then returned to the tank as the fuel level falls. Evaporated fuel escapes from the expansion chamber into a ventilation line that carries it to an activated charcoal

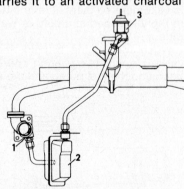

1. Exhaust flange of Number 4 cylinder
2. Element-type filter
3. Exhaust gas recirculation valve

Fig. 1   Exhaust gas recirculation system. Beetle exc. California Models

canister located at the rear of the car. The activated charcoal absorbs the vapor, preventing it from entering the atmosphere. When the engine is started, air from the engine's cooling fan is directed into the canister, blowing trapped fumes from the activated charcoal into the air cleaner. The filtered vapors are drawn through the carburetor and into the cylinders of the engine.

System Servicing

The activated charcoal filter canister must be replaced after every 30,000 miles (48,000 km).

To replace the canister, remove the hoses which are connected to it, then remove the mounting bracket retaining screw. Note the hose installation positions so that the hoses may be reconnected in correct positions on the new canister.

EXHAUST GAS RECIRCULATION SYSTEM

This system, Figs. 1 thru 4, diverts a portion of the exhaust gases into the intake manifold below the carburetor, modifying the density and content of the incoming air fuel mixture. The recirculated exhaust gases lower the flame peaks in the combustion process, thereby reducing the formation of nitrous oxides (NOx).

System Servicing

To check the 1973 exhaust gas recirculation valves, remove them from the intake manifolds and make sure that they are clean. Hand-press the valve pin to make sure that it moves freely. Then connect the valve to a vacuum hose on an engine other than that of the vehicle you are servicing. Start the engine. At 1500 to 2000 rpm the valve pin should pull in and then return to its original position when you slow down the engine. To check the 1974 valve, simply run the engine and observe whether the visible pin moves in and out proportional to rpm.

THROTTLE POSITIONER

A throttle positioner is installed on 1972, California models equipped with

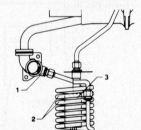

1. Exhaust flange of Number 4 cylinder
2. Cooling coil
3. Cyclone-type filter

Fig. 2   Exhaust gas recirculation filtering system. Beetle, California models

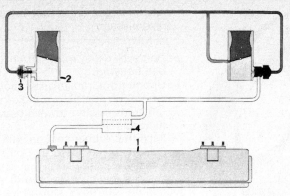

1. Muffler
2. Carburetor and intake manifold (2)
3. Exhaust gas recirculation valve (2)
4. Element type filter

Fig. 3 Exhaust gas recirculation system. Bus with manual transmission

manual transmissions. The positioner automatically adjusts the throttle closing rate for minimum exhaust emissions and prevents the carburetor throttle valve from closing suddenly when the accelerator pedal is released—again to reduce emissions.

System Servicing

To adjust the throttle positioner, refer to Carburetor Section.

EXHAUST AFTERBURNING SYSTEM

This system, Fig. 5, is used to inject a controlled amount of air into the exhaust gases to extend the combustion process into the exhaust system, thereby reducing the hydrocarbon and carbon monoxide content of the exhaust gases.

System Diagnosis

If the engine backfires, especially during deceleration, check for leakage in the exhaust system, insufficient valve clearance, and incorrect ignition timing. If these faults are not present, check for leakage in the hoses attached to the

1. Muffler
2. Carburetor and intake manifold (2)
3. Exhaust gas recirculation valve (2)
4. Element type filter
5. Solenoid-operated vacuum valve
6. Temperature-controlled switch
7. Off/on switch on throttle valve shaft
8. Vacuum hose connected to the vacuum powered brake servo system.

Fig. 4 Exhaust gas recirculation system. Bus with automatic transmission

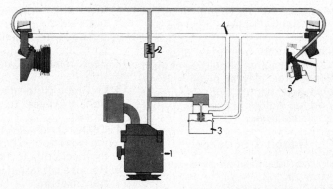

1. Air pump
2. Check valve
3. Anti-backfire idle mixture valve
4. Vacuum connection to central idling system
5. Exhaust port in cylinder head

Fig. 5 Exhaust afterburning system

anti-backfire idle mixture valve. The valve itself is seldom faulty. However, if no other cause for the backfiring can be found, check to see that the valve diaphragm is not leaking. Faulty valves must be replaced.

Clutch & Transmission Section

CLUTCH, REPLACE
Beetle & Bus

1. Remove engine as previously described.
2. Carefully unbolt clutch pressure plate from flywheel, keep plate parallel to flywheel until spring tension is released.
3. Remove clutch disk and replace if worn or oil-soaked.
4. Check friction surface on flywheel and replace if scored or blue.
5. Check pilot needle bearing in crankshaft (in "gland nut" on Beetle engines) and replace if needles are missing or feel rough.
6. Place a dab of wheel bearing grease in pilot needle bearing.
7. Seat clutch disk against flywheel friction surface, using an old mainshaft to center the clutch disk. If

disk is not centered properly, engine will not bolt up to transmission housing.
8. Place pressure plate on flywheel and install bolts finger-tight. Keep plate parallel to flywheel while tightening bolts and torque to 18 ft. lbs. (2½ mkg).
9. Remove clutch "pilot" and re-install engine. If replacement pressure plate has tensioning clips, be sure

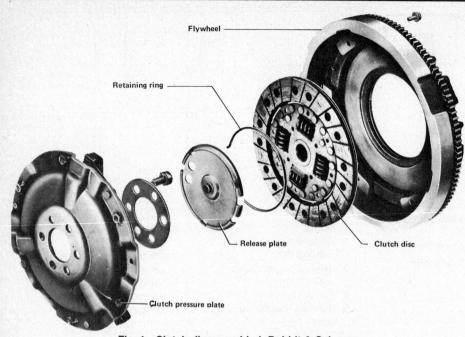

Flywheel

Retaining ring

Release plate

Clutch disc

Clutch pressure plate

Fig. 1 Clutch disassembled. Rabbit & Scirocco

to remove the clips with a screwdriver before re-installing the engine.

10. Check clutch free play after re-installing engine; should be at least ½ inch free play at pedal and reverse gear should engage without grinding. Adjust at cable wing nut on release lever.

Rabbit & Scirocco

1. Remove transmission as described further on.
2. Lock flywheel with suitable tool.
3. Remove flywheel bolts, keeping flywheel parallel, Fig. 1.
4. Remove flywheel and clutch disk, Fig. 1.
5. Remove retaining clip and release plate, Fig. 1.
6. Lock pressure plate with VW558 and flywheel bolt.
7. Remove pressure plate bolts and pressure plate, Fig. 1.
8. If clutch disk is oily, replace clutch operating rod seal inside mainshaft: remove transmission end cover, cross-shaft, and throw-out bearing—use 10 mm rod (old automatic transmission pump drive shaft or Beetle crankcase stud) to tap out operating rod bushing with seal.
9. Tap in bushing and new operating rod seal with hammer handle. Also re-install operating rod, throw-out bearing, cross-shaft, lever and end cover before re-installing transmission.
10. Replace pressure plate, disk, and/or flywheel if worn or "blue."
11. Install pressure plate on crankshaft:

lock with VW558 and flywheel bolt—coat pressure plate bolt threads with "Loctite" and torque to 54 ft. lbs. (7½ mkg).
12. Seat release plate and retaining ring.
13. Lay good clutch disk in flywheel and bolt flywheel to pressure plate loosely.
14. Center clutch disk in flywheel opening with tool VW547. Now torque flywheel bolts to 14 ft. lbs. (2 mkg).
15. Remove centering tool and re-install transmission.
16. Check clutch free play after re-installing transmission. It should be at least ½ inch at pedal and reverse should engage without grinding.

TRANSMISSION, REPLACE
Beetle & Bus

1. Remove engine as described previously.
2. Disconnect battery ground strap and starter connections.
3. Lift up rear seat, then remove "trap door" and disconnect shift rod coupling; on Bus, from underside of vehicle.
4. Disconnect both driveshafts at transmission drive flanges (12-point socket bolts).

NOTE: On Automatic Stickshift models, disconnect two ATF banjo fittings (seal connections), thermo-switch plug, selector switch plug, neutral safety switch plug and clutch servo vacuum hose. On manual shift models, remove clutch cable wing-

nut and unbolt cable tube bracket on transmission.

5. Remove bolts from mount under bell housing.
6. Unbolt front transmission mount, be careful of chassis ground strap.
7. Lift transmission toward rear of vehicle to remove.
Check that rubber seal on shift housing is in place before re-installing transmission. Make sure that clutch is re-adjusted and chassis ground strap is connected correctly during re-installation.

Rabbit & Scirocco

NOTE: On this transversely-mounted drive unit, the right-side driveshaft flange is very close to the engine flywheel: the transmission cannot be removed without first aligning one of the recesses on the flywheel with the driveshaft flange. Also, since the engine and transmission "hang" as a unit, the engine should be supported during transmission removal.

1. Remove battery ground strap.
2. Install engine support 10-222 or homemade support (use pipe or wood beam with chain and turnbuckle).
3. Remove four bolts on left transmission mount.
4. Disconnect speedometer cable (plug hole so oil does not leak out), back-up light wires, starter wires, clutch cable (selector cable and throttle/shift control cables on automatic transmission), top two engine-transmission mounting bolts (near opening for timing mark), front two engine-transmission mounting bolts (also for front mount) and two transverse shift linkage rods (manual transmission only).
5. From underside of car, remove rear transmission mount, including brackets to body, final drive housing, and exhaust system.
6. Disconnect both driveshafts at transmission flanges—tie up left-side driveshaft with wire.
7. Remove bolts for large cover plate on bottom of bell housing (cover plate stays with engine). On automatic transmission also remove three bolts connecting engine drive plate to torque converter.
8. Unbolt small cover plate beside right-side driveflange, and also remove large nut from nearby engine-transmission mounting stud.
9. Turn crankshaft clockwise until

flywheel recess is aligned with driveshaft flange.
10. Use support to lower engine-transmission unit until transmission clears left side inner fender panel.
11. Rock transmission case carefully until case is free of locating dowels.
12. Lower transmission out of car carefully.

NOTE: When re-installing the transmission, torque engine-transmission mounting bolts to 47 ft. lbs. (5.5 mkg) and socket head bolts for driveshafts to 32 ft. lbs. (4.5 mkg).

Axle Shafts & Brakes

CONSTANT VELOCITY JOINT, REPLACE

Beetle & Bus

1. Remove 12-point socket head bolts holding joints to transmission drive flange and stub axle, Fig. 1.
2. Remove driveshaft assemblies from vehicle.
3. Loosen clamps on boots. Late models have no clamps, large end is crimped into sheet metal caps.
4. Use drift to tap off caps.
5. Remove circlip on shaft and press shaft out of ball hub, Fig. 2.
6. Remove concave washer from driveshaft.
7. Repack or replace joints. When repacking joints, use only MoS2 grease.

NOTE: Don't mix up outer rings and hubs since they are matched.

8. Turn ball hub and cage then push out of outer ring, Fig. 3.
9. Push balls out of cage.
10. Align ball grooves in hub with edge of cage and slide hub out, Fig. 4.
11. Check all parts for wear.
12. Re-assemble hub, cage, balls, and outer ring, Fig. 5. Make sure chamfer on inside splines of ball hub, Fig. 6, and the larger diameter end on the outer ring face in the same direction.
13. Ball hub can be moved back and forth if joint is assembled properly, but there should be little or no radial play.
14. Place concave washer against step on driveshaft and press inner hub onto shaft—make sure chamfer on inner splines of hub faces toward concave washer.
15. Install new circlip on shaft and squeeze with pliers until fully seated.
16. Install shafts into vehicle and torque 12-point socket head bolts to 25 ft. lbs. (3½ mkg).

Audi Fox, Dasher, Rabbit & Scirocco

NOTE: Constant velocity joint procedures for front-wheel drive vehicles are much like VW rear drive designs except for a few additional steps on the outer joints.

1. Remove front axle nuts with vehicle on ground.
2. Unbolt inner joint from transmission driveshaft flange, Fig. 7.
3. Tap on axle until driveshaft assembly with joints is free.
4. Grip driveshaft in vise, then pull back boot on outer joint and spread "ears" of circlip inside hub, Fig. 8.
5. Tap on hub and remove outer joint with splined shaft.
6. Mark position of hub, cage, and outer housing—then pivot cage at two larger ball openings and slide out.
7. Pivot hub so "segment" can be pushed into large opening in cage—then swing hub out of cage, Fig. 9.
8. Check for pitting or other major wear—shiny ball track is OK.
9. Reassemble outer joint following position marks.
10. Install concave washer and thrust washer against step on shaft: place new circlip in hub and drive onto shaft until circlip seats in groove on shaft.

REAR WHEEL BEARINGS & BRAKES, ADJUST

1. Adjust wheel bearing clearance with large nut so that washer still "slides" without force.
2. Install new cotter pin and tap on grease cap.
3. Lever brake adjuster with screwdriver through backing plate hole until drum is "locked."
4. Back off brake adjuster until drum turns freely.

PARKING BRAKE, ADJUST

1. Adjust rear brakes as described previously.

Fig. 1 Removing velocity joint to transmission drive flange bolts. Beetle & Bus

Fig. 2 Pressing driveshaft from ball hub. Beetle & Bus

Fig. 3 Removing hub & ball cage. Beetle & Bus

Fig. 4 Removing ball hub from cage. Beetle & Bus

Fig. 5 Assembling hub, cage, balls & outer rings. Beetle & Bus

Fig. 6 Aligning chamfer, ball hub splines & large diameter end with outer ring face. Beetle & Bus

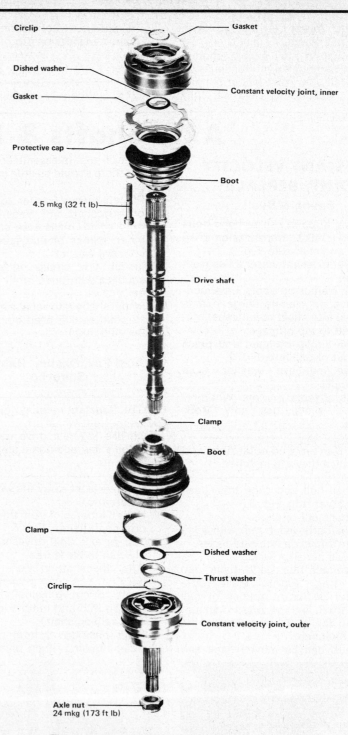

Circlip

Gasket

Dished washer

Gasket

Constant velocity joint, inner

Protective cap

Boot

4.5 mkg (32 ft lb)

Drive shaft

Clamp

Boot

Clamp

Dished washer

Thrust washer

Circlip

Constant velocity joint, outer

Axle nut
24 mkg (173 ft lb)

Fig. 7 Axle shaft & velocity joint assembly. Dasher, Rabbit, Scirocco & Audi Fox

2. Pull up hand brake lever two "notches."
3. Loosen lock nuts and tighten adjusting nuts until wheels are locked.
4. Back off adjusting nuts until wheels turn freely. Tighten lock nuts.

FRONT DISC BRAKE PADS, REPLACE

1. Look through wheel slots: if at least 6 mm (¼ inch) of pad material remains, caliper is not leaking, and rotor is not excessively scored, brakes are OK.
2. If pads are worn, remove wheel and drive out pad retaining pins, Fig. 10.
3. Pull out inner pads (use US 1023/3 or water-pump pliers).
4. Push floating frame outward to free positioning tab—slide out outer pad.

Fig. 8   Removing circlip. Dasher, Rabbit, Scirocco & Audi Fox

NOTE: After re-installation of pads, depress pedal firmly several times to position pistons.

5. Install new outer pads first and push floating frame inward so positioning tab engages pad.
6. Now slide in inner pads—also install spreader spring, pins, and clip.
7. If worn, remove wheels and unbolt caliper.

NOTE: Hang calipers on frame without disconnecting brake hoses during rotor work.

8. Remove single screw on rotor and remove rotor.
9. Rotors can be reground, but if thickness is less than 10.5 mm (.472 in.) after grinding, rotor must be replaced.

NOTE: If caliper sticks or is leaking, replace caliper cylinder.

10. Torque caliper bolts without washers to 43 ft. lbs.

MASTER CYLINDER, REPLACE

NOTE: If brake warning light comes on and pedal is low, check wheel cylinders and brake lines for leakage: if no leaks are evident, master cylinder probably needs to be repaired or replaced.

1. Disconnect all four brake lines and two mounting nuts on master cylinder—also remove electrical connections.

2. Remove master cylinder from brake booster (or firewall) and pull off reservoir (catch fluid in clean container).
3. Remove circlip in end of cylinder and empty all springs and pistons.
4. Check for pitting on master cylinder walls: if bore is pitted, replace cylinder assembly; if surface is only dirty or discolored, hone bore and install new parts. (Don't forget to coat parts with brake cylinder paste; do not interchange conical and cylindrical springs.)
5. Install brake lines handtight on cylinder.
6. Now install cylinder on brake booster (or firewall).
7. Tighten brake lines and install electrical connections.
8. Install reservoir and fill with clean brake fluid.
9. Bleed brakes.

Brake Booster

If excessive pedal pressure indicates no booster assistance, check vacuum connections to booster and "one-way" valve in vacuum line: blow through valve should be open in direction of arrow and closed in other direction. If valve and connections seem OK, replace booster.

1. Remove "clevis" pin and rod from top of brake pedal.

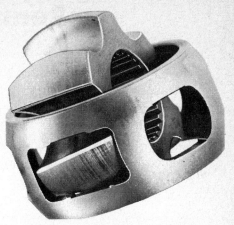

Fig. 9   Disassembling velocity joints. Dasher, Rabbit, Scirocco & Audi Fox

2. Remove master cylinder as previously described.
3. Disconnect vacuum line and three mounting nuts.

During re-installation, check that brake pedal is even with clutch pedal. If pedal is not level, turn push rod to adjust and re-tighten locknut.

NOTE: On models without brake boosters, turn pedal stop until brake pedal is even with clutch pedal; then adjust pedal push rod until pedal has about 4 mm (⅛ inch) free play.

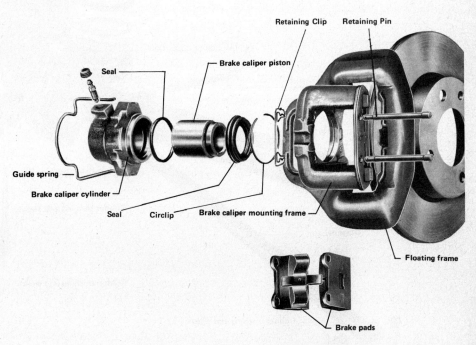

Fig. 10   Front disc brake assembly

Rear Suspension Section

REAR AXLE, REPLACE

Dasher & Audi Fox

1. Remove attaching nuts from brake equalizer bar, Fig. 1.
2. Press out parking brake cable plastic bushing.
3. Disconnect exhaust pipe from front of muffler.
4. Disconnect brake cables from body attachments.
5. Disconnect and plug brake hoses.
6. Raise axle slightly with a suitable jack.
7. Disconnect diagonal arm from axle.
8. Disconnect shock absorber from axle.
9. Remove rear axle assembly from vehicle.
10. Reverse procedure to install.

Rabbit & Scirocco

1. Disconnect parking brake cable "A", Fig. 2, from parking brake lever inside vehicle.

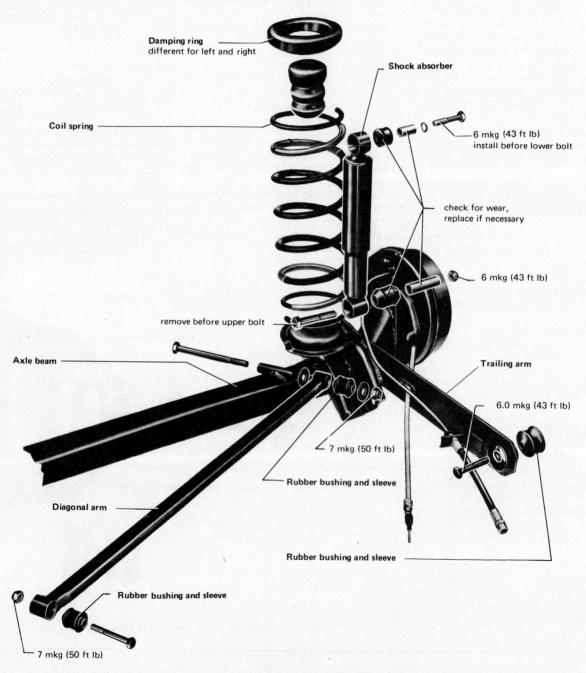

Damping ring different for left and right

Shock absorber

Coil spring

6 mkg (43 ft lb) install before lower bolt

check for wear, replace if necessary

6 mkg (43 ft lb)

remove before upper bolt

Axle beam

Trailing arm

6.0 mkg (43 ft lb)

7 mkg (50 ft lb)

Rubber bushing and sleeve

Diagonal arm

Rubber bushing and sleeve

Rubber bushing and sleeve

7 mkg (50 ft lb)

Fig. 1   Rear axle & suspension. Dasher & Audi Fox

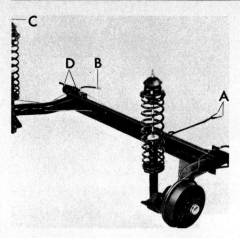

Fig. 2 Rear axle attachments. Rabbit & Scirocco

2. Disconnect brake hose "B", Fig. 2.
3. Remove suspension strut from body at "C", Fig. 2.
4. Disconnect rear axle from body at "D", Fig. 2.
5. Remove rear axle assembly from vehicle.
6. Reverse procedure to install.

REAR SUSPENSION SERVICE

Refer to Figs. 1 and 3 for rear suspension service.

> **CAUTION**
>
> If rear axle beam is removed, always bleed brake system and readjust brakes.

> **CAUTION**
>
> Do not attempt to straighten or weld rear axle beam or stub axles.

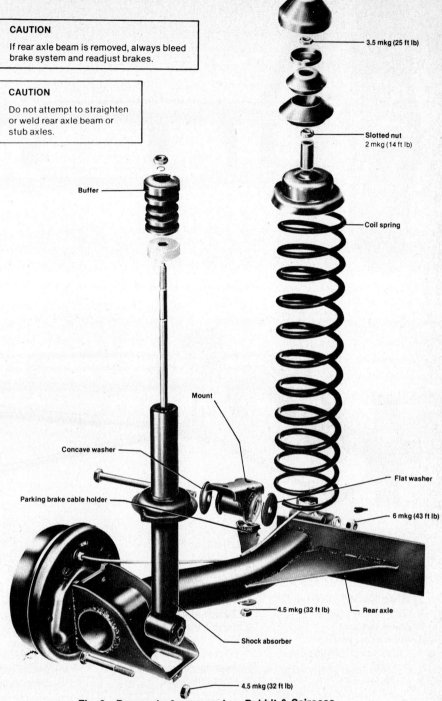

Fig. 3 Rear axle & suspension. Rabbit & Scirocco

Front Suspension & Steering Section

Figs. 1 thru 4 show cross sectional views of the front suspension system on these vehicles.

WHEELBEARING, ADJUST
Beetle & Bus

1. Raise the wheel, then pry off the dust cap.

2. If the bearings have just been installed, torque the clamp nut to about 1.0 mkg (7 ft. lb.) while you hand-turn the brake disc or drum.

CAUTION: Never torque the clamp nut to more than 1.3 mkg (9.5 ft. lb.). Doing so will damage the bearing races.

3. To measure the bearing axial play, install a dial indicator on one of the wheel lugs (or use a dial indicator with a magnetic base).
4. Position the dial indicator pin against the end of the stub axle.
5. Move the brake disc or drum in and out by hand. Turn the clamp nut one way or the other until the axial play

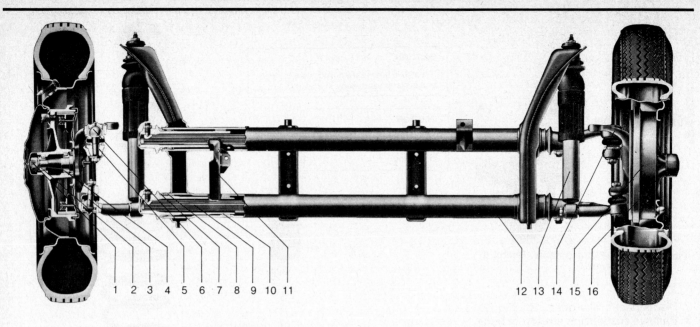

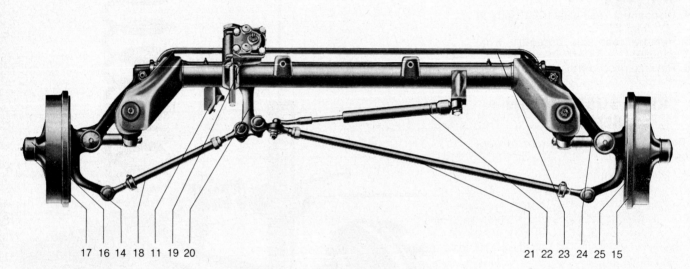

1.	Wheel bearing clamp nut	7.	Torsion arm seal	13.	Shock absorber	20.	Drop arm
2.	Outer wheel bearing	8.	Torsion arm needle bearing	14.	Steering knuckle	21.	Right tie rod
3.	Lower ball joint	9.	Torsion bar	15.	Brake drum	22.	Steering damper
4.	Inner wheel bearing	10.	Plastic seat and metal	16.	Dust cap	23.	Stabilizer bar
5.	Eccentric camber adjusting		bushing	17.	Speedometer cable	24.	Torsion arm
	bushing	11.	Steering lock stop	18.	Left tie rod	25.	Brake backing plate
6.	Upper ball joint	12.	Front axle beam	19.	Steering gearbox		

Fig. 1 Front suspension. Beetle exc. Super Beetle

is between 0.03 and 0.12 mm (.001 and .005 in.).

6. Torque the socket head screw to 1.0 to 1.3 mkg (7.0 to 9.5 ft. lb.).

7. Install the dust cap and lower the wheel to the ground.

BALL JOINTS, REPLACE
Beetle & Bus

1. Remove torsion bar, Figs. 1 and 3, then press the old ball joint out of the torsion arm.

2. If necessary, press the eccentric camber adjusting bushing off the ball joint for an upper torsion arm.

3. Align the installation-position groove with the notch in the torsion arm.

CAUTION: Never reinstall used ball joints. They will not fit tightly and could come out of the torsion arm while the car is being driven.

---

4. Being careful to keep the groove

and the notch aligned, press the new ball joint into the torsion arm.

BALL JOINTS, REPLACE
1972-73 Super Beetle

1. Remove the self-locking nut from the ball joint stud where it passes through the track control arm.

2. Press the ball joint stud out of the track control arm.

3. Bend down the lockplates, then re- move the three M 10 bolts that hold

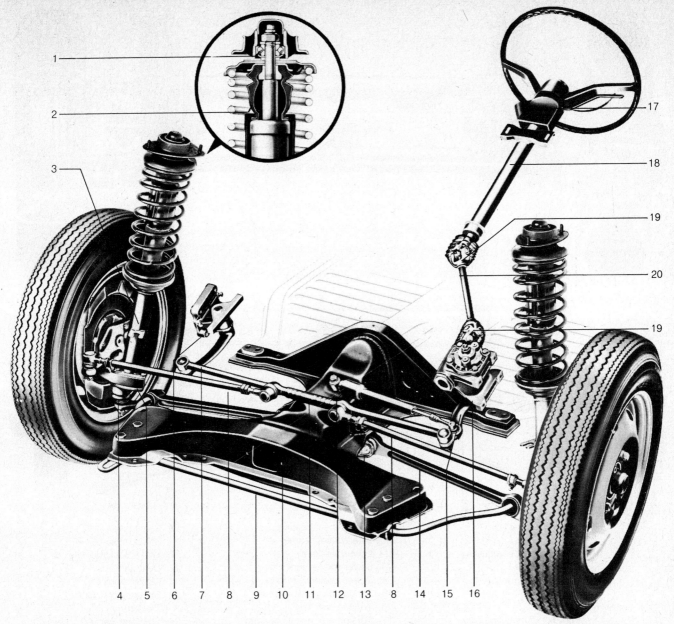

1. Ball thrust bearing
2. Hollow rubber buffer
3. Suspension strut
4. Ball joint
5. Steering knuckle
6. Idler arm bracket
7. Idler arm
8. Side tie rod
9. Stabilizer bar
10. Frame head
11. Center tie rod
12. Steering damper
13. Eccentric camber adjusting bolt
14. Track control arm
15. Drop arm
16. Steering gearbox
17. Column switch housing
18. Column tube
19. Universal joint
20. Universal joint shaft

Fig. 2   Front suspension. Super Beetle

the ball joint and steering knuckle on the strut.

4. Using a loop of wire, suspend the steering knuckle and brake assembly from the brake hose bracket or the strut. Doing so will make it unnecessary to dismount the brake hose.

5. Remove the ball joint from the steering knuckle.

Installation is the reverse of removal. Use new lockplates under the M 10 bolts and a new self-locking nut on the ball joint stud. The ball joint stud must be grease-free when it is inserted into the track control arm. If necessary, grip the flat sides on the lower end of the ball joint stud with an open wrench while tightening the self-locking nut. Torque the M 10 bolts and the self-locking nut to 4.0 mkg (29 ft. lb.). Check the camber and toe following installation of the ball joint and correct them if necessary.

1974-75 Super Beetle

1. Remove the track control arm, Fig. 2.

2. Using a press tool that can be threaded onto or slipped over the ball joint stud, press the ball joint downward out of the track control arm.

3. Using press tools that will apply pressure only to the track control arm eye and the outer housing of the ball joint, press in the new ball joint from the deeper section (bottom) of the control arm.

CAUTION: Never reinstall used ball joints. They will not fit tightly and

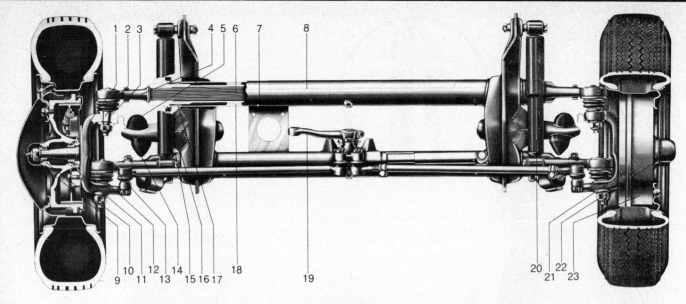

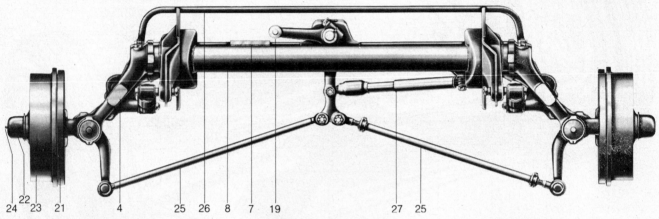

1. Steering knuckle
2. Upper ball joint
3. Eccentric camber adjusting bushing
4. Upper torsion arm
5. Upper torsion arm stop
6. Torsion bar
7. Brake servo mounting plate
8. Front axle beam
9. Wheel bearing clamp nut

10. Outer wheel bearing
11. Inner wheel bearing
12. Lower ball joint
13. Lower torsion arm
14. Lower torsion arm stop
15. Torsion arm seal retainer
16. Torsion arm seal
17. Torsion arm needle bearing
18. Plastic seat and metal bushing

19. Relay lever
20. Shock absorber
21. Brake backing plate
22. Dust cap
23. Brake drum
24. Speedometer cable
25. Tie rods
26. Stabilizer bar
27. Steering damper

Fig. 3 Front suspension. Bus

could come out of the track arm while the car is being driven.

Rabbit & Scirocco

1. Drill out rivets using a ¼ inch drill bit.
2. Chisel off rivet heads.
3. Attach new ball joint with the bolts supplied. Torque retaining bolts to 18 ft. lbs.

SHOCK ABSORBER, REPLACE
Beetle & Bus

1. Raise the car and remove the front wheel.

2. Remove the M 10 nut from the top of the buffer pin. If necessary, slide the buffer and outer tube down and hold the buffer pin.
3. Reverse procedure to install. The rubber bushings, buffer pin, and buffer should be replaced or reused depending on their condition. Clean the corrosion from the pin on the torsion arm. If the old pins are damaged, press in new ones. The rubber bushing goes on the buffer pin with the shoulder upward, as shown in Fig. 3. Torque the nut on the torsion arm pin to 3.0 to 3.5 mkg (22 to 25 ft. lb.) and the nut atop the buffer pin to 2.0 mkg (14 ft. lb.).

SPRINGS & SHOCK ABSORBER, REPLACE
Rabbit & Scirocco

The strut assembly must be removed from the vehicle and disassembled in order to replace either springs or shocks, Fig. 4.

1. Remove 13 mm hex nuts at top of strut in engine compartment.
2. Unclip brake hose from strut tube without disconnecting line.
3. Remove bolts holding strut tube to wheel bearing housing.
4. Lower strut assembly out of car.
5. Compress spring with US4475 or

suitable spring compressor.

6. Hold shock plunger with 7 mm hex key and loosen large nut with offset box wrench.
7. Loosen spring compressor carefully: disassemble spring and retainer parts.

NOTE: Shock absorber inserts can be replaced without replacing strut tube (unscrew large nut at top of tube and slide out inserts). Springs or shocks must always be replaced "in pairs." Note color stripe ID on springs.

8. Compress spring again to reassemble strut and install retaining parts.
9. Now hold large nut at top with box wrench and torque shock plunger (7 mm hex key) counterclockwise so that *nut* is torqued to 58 ft. lbs. (8 mkg).
10. Re-install strut assembly into car. Be sure to re-adjust front camber and toe.

STABILIZER BAR, REPLACE
Super Beetle

1. Remove the cotter pins from the two castellated nuts, then take the castellated nuts off the stabilizer bar.
2. Remove the four grooved bolts that hold the two mounting clamps to the frame head.
3. Take the mounting clamps off the rubber stabilizer mountings.
4. Pull the stabilizer bar out of the bonded rubber bushings in the track control arms, Fig. 2.

Installation is the reverse of removal. If the rubber stabilizer mountings are worn, cut them off the stabilizer bar. Clean the stabilizer bar with a wire brush, then lubricate the new rubber stabilizer mountings with silicone spray and slide them into position on the stabilizer bar.

Torque the castellated nuts to 3.0 mkg (22 ft. lb.). If necessary, advance them to uncover the cotter pin holes, then install new cotter pins. On 1972 through 1973 models, torque the grooved bolts for the mounting clamps to 2.0 mkg (14 ft. lb.); on 1974 models, torque the bolts to 4.0 mkg (29 ft. lb.).

STRUTS, REPLACE
Super Beetle

1. From the left wheel only, pry off the speedometer cable circlip. Then pull the speedometer cable out of the back of the steering knuckle.
2. Pry off the retaining plate.
3. On 1972-73 models, bend down the

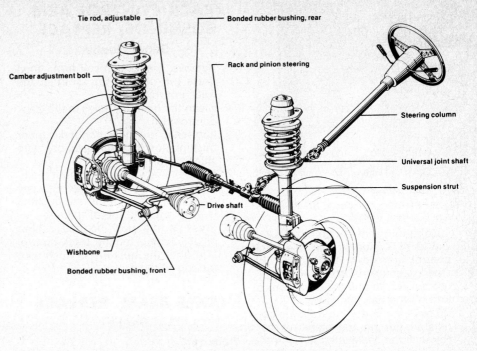

Fig. 4   Front suspension. Dasher, Rabbit, Scirocco & Audi Fox

lockplates, then remove the three M 10 bolts that hold the ball joint and steering knuckle on the strut. On 1974 and later models, remove the two bolts and nuts that mount the steering knuckle on the strut.
4. Pull the strut off the steering knuckle. Then, on 1972-73 models, install one bolt to support the knuckle.
5. Working inside the front luggage compartment, remove two of the three nuts.
6. Reach under the fender and support the strut while removing the third nut. Take the strut out downward when the last nut is off.
7. Reverse procedure to install. Torque the three nuts for the upper mount to 2.0 mkg (14 ft. lb.). On 1972-73 models, install new lockplates under the M 10 bolts at the lower end of the strut, then torque the bolts to 4.0 mkg (29 ft. lb.). On 1974-77 models, torque the two knuckle mounting bolts to 8.5 mkg (61 ft. lb.) and the clamp bolt for the ball joint stud to 3.5 mkg (25 ft. lb.). Check the camber and toe following installation of the strut and correct them if necessary.

TORSION BAR, REPLACE
Beetle & Bus

NOTE: Each torsion arm is held on its torsion bar by a socket head setscrew and locknut.

1. Remove the steering knuckle complete with brake assembly.
2. If the lower torsion arm is to be removed, disconnect the stabilizer bar by driving the retainers off the two stabilizer bar rubber mounting clamps.

NOTE: It is necessary to bend down the locking tabs on the retainers before driving them off. Obtain new retainers for use during assembly.

3. Loosen the locknut on the socket head setscrew that holds the torsion arm on the torsion bar. Then remove the setscrew.
4. Remove the torsion arm from the end of the torsion bar.
5. Reverse procedure to install.

CONTROL ARM, REPLACE
Rabbit & Scirocco

1. Remove front left engine mounting.
2. Remove rear mounting nut.
3. Remove engine mounting support.
4. Raise engine using a suitable hoist until control arm bolts can be removed, then remove bolts and control arm.
5. Reverse procedure to install.

TRACK CONTROL ARM
Super Beetle
Removal

1. On 1974-75 models, loosen the clamp bolt for the ball joint stud. On earlier models, remove the self-

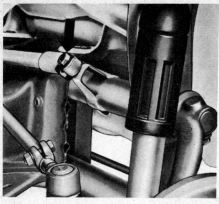

Fig. 5 Steering damper to bracket arm bolt. Beetle

locking nut from the ball joint stud.

2. On 1974-77 models, pull the track control arm down and out of the steering knuckle. On earlier models, use a puller to pull the track control arm off the ball joint stud.

3. Remove the cotter pin from the castellated nut on the stabilizer bar. Remove the castellated nut and the self-locking nut at the frame head.

4. Pull the track control arm downward and off, Fig. 2.

Installation

1. Check the track control arm for cracks and bends.

2. Inspect the bonded rubber bushings for wear. If necessary, replace them.

3. Insert the stabilizer bar into the track control arm, then install the castellated nut finger-tight.

NOTE: The rubber lugs on the end of the bonded rubber bushing for the stabilizer bar must be positioned horizontally.

---

4. Make sure that the ball joint stud and its hole are grease-free. Then install the ball joint stud.

5. Install the track control arm on the frame head using the eccentric bolt, the eccentric washer, and a new self-locking nut.

6. Torque the castellated nut to 3.0 mkg (22 ft. lb.), advancing it, if necessary, to uncover the cotter pin hole. Then install a new cotter pin.

7. On 1974-77 models, torque the clamp bolt to 3.5 mkg (25 ft. lb.). On earlier cars, install a new self-locking nut on the ball joint stud and torque it to 4.0 mkg (29 ft. lb.). If necessary, hold the flat sides on the ball joint stud with an open end wrench to keep the stud from turning as the nut is tightened.

8. Adjust the camber, then torque the self-locking nut on the eccentric bolt to 4.0 mkg (29 ft. lb.).

9. Adjust toe to specifications.

TRACK CONTROL ARM BUSHINGS, REPLACE
Super Beetle

1. Remove track control arm, then press the old bushings out of the track control arm.

2. Clean the bushing holes in the track control arm.

3. Lubricate the new bonded rubber bushing for the stabilizer bar with silicone spray.

4. Press the new bonded rubber bushing for the stabilizer bar into the track control arm until the bushing is flush with the top of the arm.

5. Press in the new bonded rubber pivot bushing for the track control arm until the bushing is flush with the top of the arm.

AXLE BEAM, REPLACE
Beetle

Removal

1. Raise the car and remove the front road wheels.

2. Working through the left front wheel opening, pull the fuel hose off the tube in the frame head and plug the hose.

CAUTION: Disconnect the battery ground strap. Do not smoke or work near heaters or other fire hazards. Have a fire extinguisher handy.

---

3. Remove the fuel tank.

4. Loosen the clamp on the steering column, and disconnect the horn wire at the flexible coupling.

5. Remove the bolt, Fig. 5, then detach the steering damper from the bracket on the upper axle beam tube.

6. Remove the E-clip from the speed-

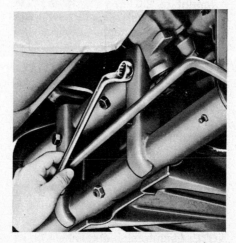

Fig. 7 Removing axle beam mounting bolts. Beetle exc. Super Beetle

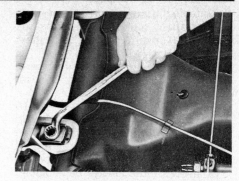

Fig. 6 Removing axle beam to body mounting bolt. Beetle exc. Super Beetle

ometer cable where it passes through the dust cap on the left front wheel hub. Then, working behind the brake assembly, pull the speedometer cable out of the steering knuckle.

7. Unscrew the brake hoses from the front brake assemblies and plug them with the dust covers from the brake bleeder valves.

8. Remove the cotter pins from both tie rod end studs on the long (right-hand) tie rod. Then remove the castellated nuts.

9. Using a tie rod removal tool, press the tie rod ends out of the drop arm and the right-hand steering knuckle. Then remove the long tie rod together with the steering damper.

CAUTION: Do not hammer out the tie rod ends. Doing so will ruin the threads and make reinstallation impossible.

---

10. Working in the front luggage compartment through the fuel tank opening, remove the two body mounting bolts, Fig. 6.

11. Position a floor jack with the VW 610 front axle supporting adapter under the front axle.

12. Raise the jack until the adapter is in firm contact with the axle beam.

CAUTION: If you do not have a suitable jack and adapter, have at least two helpers support the front axle while you are unbolting it. Trying to handle this job by yourself could lead to serious injury owning to the weight of the axle.

---

13. Remove the four axle beam mounting bolts as shown in Fig. 7.

14. While carefully guiding the steering coupling out of the steering column, lower the axle beam with the floor jack.

Installation

1. Place the axle in the floor jack front axle adapter VW 610. Adjust the axle